THE COLLINS
PAPERBACK
ENGLISH
DICTIONARY

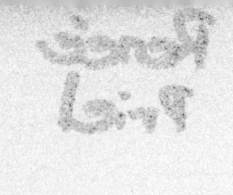

THE COLLINS
PAPERBACK
ENGLISH
DICTIONARY

HarperCollins*Publishers*

First Edition 1986
New Edition 1990
Latest Reprint 1993
© HarperCollins Publishers 1990
ISBN 0 00 433245-8

British Library Cataloguing in Publication Data
The Collins paperback English dictionary. – 2nd. ed.
1. English language. Dictionaries
423

Computer typeset by Barbers Ltd.,
Wrotham, England

Printed and bound in Great Britain
by HarperCollins Manufacturing
P.O. Box, Glasgow G4 0NB

FOREWORD

This new edition of THE COLLINS PAPERBACK ENGLISH DICTIONARY is derived from the best-selling COLLINS POCKET ENGLISH DICTIONARY. It is designed to be practical, up to date, easy to use, and easy to understand. Every word defined is given as a main entry in a single alphabetical sequence. Every definition is presented in clear concise straightforward English. Where a word has more than one sense, the one given first is the normal everyday meaning in today's language. Other senses of a word — for example historical and technical senses — are explained after the main present-day meaning. Each sense is separately numbered, so that it is easy to see how many different senses a word has and to find the one required.

The entries contain not only the spelling and meaning of each word, but also a guide to its pronunciation and its grammatical class. Guidance is also given on appropriate levels of usage: for example, some uses are appropriate only in informal contexts, others in extremely formal contexts. These are clearly marked as such. Words and meanings that have gone out of use are marked as obsolete or archaic; they are included in the dictionary if they are common in the literature of the past. Help is given on disputed or problematic points of usage, which are discussed in usage notes at the end of the relevant entries.

Although this is only a small dictionary, the compilers have been able to draw on an unprecedented range of data as raw material. In the first place, the dictionary is based on the Collins English Dictionary databank, which has been painstakingly constructed over the years by Collins lexicographers and their expert advisers in many different fields of knowledge.

Computer technology has, in addition, provided other kinds of evidence, not previously available. The compilers were able to consult the Cobuild corpus of 20 million words of contemporary English, a collection of texts assembled and studied using computers at the English Department of the University of Birmingham. In many cases, the examples of use given in this dictionary are based on an examination of the uses recorded in the Cobuild corpus.

The new edition of THE COLLINS PAPERBACK ENGLISH DICTIONARY has thus used the latest techniques to provide a practical and clear guide to today's language for today's users.

EDITORIAL STAFF

ABBREVIATIONS AND SYMBOLS USED IN THE DICTIONARY

adj.	adjective	N	North(ern)
adv.	adverb(ial)	n.	noun
Anat.	Anatomy	Naut.	Nautical
Archaeol.	Archaeology	NE	Northeast(ern)
Archit.	Architecture	NW	Northwest(ern)
Astrol.	Astrology	N.Z.	New Zealand
Astron.	Astronomy		
Austral.	Australian		
		Obs.	Obsolete
		orig.	originally
Biol.	Biology		
Bot.	Botany		
Brit.	Britain; British		
		Photog.	Photography
		pl.	plural
°C	degrees Celsius	p.p.	past participle
Canad.	Canadian	prep.	preposition(al)
cap.	capital	pron.	pronoun
Chem.	Chemistry	Psychol.	Psychology
comp.	comparative	p.t.	past tense
conj.	conjunction		
E	east(ern)	S	south(ern)
Econ.	Economics	S. African	South African
esp.	especially	Scot.	Scottish; Scots
		SE	southeast(ern)
		sing.	singular
fem.	feminine	sup.	superlative
foll.	followed	SW	southwest(ern)
Geog.	Geography	Theol.	Theology
Geol.	Geology		
Geom.	Geometry		
		U.S.	United States
imit.	imitative		
interj.	interjection		
		var.	variant
		vb.	verb
lit.	literally		
masc.	masculine	W	west(ern)
Maths.	Mathematics		
Med.	Medicine		
Mil.	Military		
Myth.	Mythology	Zool.	Zoology

PRONUNCIATION KEY

The following consonant symbols have their usual English values: *b, d, f, h, k, l, m, n, p, r, s, t, v, w, z*. The remaining symbols and their interpretations are listed below.

ɑː	as in *father* ('fɑːðə), *heart* (hɑːt)
æ	as in *act* (ækt)
aɪ	as in *dive* (daɪv)
aɪə	as in *fire* ('faɪə)
aʊ	as in *out* (aʊt)
aʊə	as in *flour* ('flaʊə)
ɛ	as in *bet* (bɛt)
eɪ	as in *paid* (peɪd)
ɛə	as in *bear* (bɛə)
g	as in *get* (gɛt)
ɪ	as in *give* (gɪv)
iː	as in *see* (siː)
ɪə	as in *fear* (fɪə)
j	as in *yes* (jɛs)
ɒ	as in *pot* (pɒt)
əʊ	as in *note* (nəʊt)
ɔː	as in *thaw* (θɔː), *organ* ('ɔːgən)
ɔɪ	as in *void* (vɔɪd)
ʊ	as in *pull* (pʊl)
uː	as in *zoo* (zuː)
ʊə	as in *poor* (pʊə)
ə	as in *potter* ('pɒtə), *alone* (ə'ləʊn)
ɜː	as in *fern* (fɜːn), *burn* (bɜːn)
ʌ	as in *cut* (kʌt)
ʃ	as in *ship* (ʃɪp)
ʒ	as in *treasure* ('trɛʒə)
tʃ	as in *chew* (tʃuː)
dʒ	as in *jaw* (dʒɔː)
θ	as in *thin* (θɪn)
ð	as in *these* (ðiːz)
ŋ	as in *sing* (sɪŋ), *finger* ('fɪŋgə)
̩	as in *bundle* ('bʌndᵊl), *button* ('bʌtᵊn)
x	as in *loch* (lɒx)

Stress marks are placed immediately *before* the affected syllable. Primary or strong stress is shown by ', while secondary or weak stress is shown by ˌ. Unstressed syllables are not marked. In *photographic* (ˌfəʊtə'græfɪk), for example, the first syllable carries secondary stress and the third primary stress, while the second and fourth are unstressed.

Length
The symbol : denotes length and is shown together with certain vowel symbols when the vowels are typically long.

A

a *or* **A** (eɪ) *n., pl.* **a's, A's,** *or* **As.** **1.** the first letter of the English alphabet. **2.** the first in a series. **3. from A to Z.** from start to finish.

a (ə; *emphatic* eɪ) *det.* (*indefinite article*; used before an initial consonant. Compare **an**) **1.** used preceding a singular countable noun that has not been mentioned before: *a dog; a great pity.* **2.** used preceding a noun or determiner of quantity: *a dozen eggs; a great many; to read a lot.* **3.** (preceded by *once, twice, several times,* etc.) each or every; per: *once a day.*

A **1.** *Music.* the sixth note of the scale of C major. **2.** ampere(s). **3.** atomic: *an A-bomb.*

Å angstrom unit.

A. answer.

a- *or before a vowel* **an-** *prefix.* not; without: *atonal; asocial; anaphrodisiac.*

A1, A-1, *or* **A-one** ('eɪ'wʌn) *adj. Informal.* first-class; excellent.

A4 *n.* a standard paper size, 297 × 210 mm.

AA **1.** Alcoholics Anonymous. **2.** (in Britain) Automobile Association.

AAA ('θriː'eɪz) *Brit.* Amateur Athletic Association.

A & R artists and repertoire.

aardvark ('ɑːd,vɑːk) *n.* an African mammal which has long ears and snout and which feeds on termites.

AB able-bodied seaman.

ab- *prefix.* away from; opposite to: *abnormal.*

aback (ə'bæk) *adv.* **taken aback.** startled or disconcerted.

abacus ('æbəkəs) *n.* **1.** a counting device consisting of a frame holding rods on which beads are moved backwards and forwards by the person doing the counting. **2.** *Archit.* the flat upper part of the capital of a column.

abaft (ə'bɑːft) *adv., adj. Naut.* closer to the stern of a ship.

abalone (,æbə'ləʊnɪ) *n.* an edible sea creature with an ear-shaped shell lined with mother-of-pearl.

abandon (ə'bændən) *vb.* **1.** to leave (someone or something): *he abandoned his wife.* **2.** to give up completely: *abandon hope.* **3.** to surrender (oneself) to emotion without restraint. ~*n.* **4.** freedom from inhibitions or restraint. —**a'bandonment** *n.*

abandoned (ə'bændənd) *adj.* **1.** deserted: *an abandoned windmill.* **2.** uninhibited: *abandoned behaviour.*

abase (ə'beɪs) *vb.* **abase oneself.** to degrade oneself. —**a'basement** *n.*

abashed (ə'bæʃt) *adj.* embarrassed and ashamed.

abate (ə'beɪt) *vb.* to make or become less strong: *the storm abated.* —**a'batement** *n.*

abattoir ('æbə,twɑː) *n.* a slaughterhouse.

abbacy ('æbəsɪ) *n., pl.* **-cies.** the office or jurisdiction of an abbot or abbess.

abbé ('æbeɪ) *n.* a French abbot or other clergyman.

abbess ('æbɪs) *n.* the female superior of a convent.

abbey ('æbɪ) *n.* **1.** a building inhabited by monks or nuns. **2.** a church associated with such a building. **3.** a community of monks or nuns.

abbot ('æbət) *n.* the superior of an abbey of monks.

abbreviate (ə'briːvɪ,eɪt) *vb.* **1.** to shorten (a word) by omission of some letters. **2.** to cut short. —**abbreviation** (ə,briːvɪ'eɪʃən) *n.*

ABC *n.* **1.** the alphabet. **2.** an alphabetical guide.

abdicate ('æbdɪ,keɪt) *vb.* **1.** to give up the throne formally. **2.** to give up (one's responsibilities). —**,abdi'cation** *n.*

abdomen ('æbdəmən) *n.* the part of the body that contains the stomach and intestines; belly. —**abdominal** (æb'dɒmɪn°l) *adj.*

abduct (æb'dʌkt) *vb.* to remove (a person) by force; kidnap. —**ab'duction** *n.* —**ab'ductor** *n.*

abeam (ə'biːm) *adv., adj.* at right angles to the length of a vessel or aircraft.

Aberdeen Angus ('æbədiːn 'æŋgəs) *n.* a black hornless breed of beef cattle originating in Scotland.

aberrant (ə'bɛrənt) *adj.* deviating from what is right, true, or normal.

aberration (,æbə'reɪʃən) *n.* **1.** deviation from what is right, true, or normal. **2.** a lapse: *a mental aberration.*

abet (ə'bɛt) *vb.* **abetting, abetted.** to assist or encourage (someone) in wrongdoing.

abeyance (ə'beɪəns) *n.* (usually preceded by *in* or *into*) a state of being put aside temporarily.

abhor (əb'hɔː) *vb.* **-horring, -horred.** to detest (something) vehemently.

abhorrent (əb'hɒrənt) *adj.* hateful; loathsome. —**ab'horrence** *n.*

abide (ə'baɪd) *vb.* **1.** to tolerate: *I can't*

abide liars. **2. abide by. a.** to comply with: *to abide by the decision.* **b.** to remain faithful to: *to abide by your promise.* **3.** *Archaic.* to dwell.

abiding (ə'baɪdɪŋ) *adj.* permanent; enduring.

ability (ə'bɪlɪtɪ) *n., pl.* **-ties. 1.** possession of the necessary skill or power to do something. **2.** great skill or competence: *a man of ability.* **3.** (*pl.*) special talents.

abject ('æbdʒɛkt) *adj.* **1.** utterly miserable: *abject poverty.* **2.** contemptible; servile. —**'abjectly** *adv.*

abjure (əb'dʒʊə) *vb.* to renounce or retract (something) under oath. —**ˌabjuˈration** *n.*

ablation (æb'leɪʃən) *n.* **1.** the surgical removal of an organ or part. **2.** the melting of a part, such as the heat shield of a space reentry vehicle. **3.** the wearing away of a rock or glacier.

ablative ('æblətɪv) *Grammar.* ~*adj.* **1.** (in Latin) denoting a case of nouns indicating the agent, instrument, or place of the action. ~*n.* **2.** the ablative case.

ablaze (ə'bleɪz) *adj.* **1.** on fire. **2.** brightly illuminated: *ablaze with lights.* **3.** emotionally aroused: *ablaze with anger.*

able ('eɪb'l) *adj.* **1.** having the necessary power, skill, or opportunity to do something. **2.** capable; talented.

-able *suffix forming adjectives.* **1.** capable of: *washable.* **2.** inclined to: *variable.* —**-ably** *suffix forming adverbs.* —**-ability** *suffix forming nouns.*

able-bodied *adj.* strong and healthy.

able-bodied seaman *or* **able seaman** *n.* a seaman who is trained in certain skills.

able rating *n.* a seaman of the lowest rank in a navy.

ablutions (ə'bluːʃənz) *pl. n.* **1.** the act of washing: *perform one's ablutions.* **2.** *Mil. informal.* a washing place.

ably ('eɪblɪ) *adv.* competently or skilfully.

ABM antiballistic missile.

abnegation (ˌæbnɪ'geɪʃən) *n.* the act of giving something up.

abnormal (æb'nɔːməl) *adj.* not normal; deviating from the usual or typical. —**abnormality** (ˌæbnɔː'mælɪtɪ) *n.* —**ab'normally** *adv.*

aboard (ə'bɔːd) *adv., adj., prep.* on, in, onto, or into (a ship, plane, or train).

abode (ə'bəʊd) *n.* one's home.

abolish (ə'bɒlɪʃ) *vb.* to do away with (laws, regulations, or customs).

abolition (ˌæbə'lɪʃən) *n.* **1.** the act of abolishing or the state of being abolished. **2.** (*cap.*) the ending of slavery. —**ˌabo'litionist** *n., adj.*

A-bomb *n.* short for **atom bomb.**

abominable (ə'bɒmɪnəb'l) *adj.* detestable; very bad: *an abominable waste of money.* —**a'bominably** *adv.*

abominable snowman *n.* a large manlike or apelike creature alleged to inhabit the Himalayas.

abominate (ə'bɒmɪˌneɪt) *vb.* to dislike intensely; detest. —**abomination** (əˌbɒmɪ'neɪʃən) *n.*

aboriginal (ˌæbə'rɪdʒɪn'l) *adj.* existing in a place from the earliest known period.

Aboriginal (ˌæbə'rɪdʒɪn'l) *adj.* **1.** of the Aborigines of Australia. ~*n.* **2.** an Aborigine.

aborigine (ˌæbə'rɪdʒɪnɪ) *n.* an original inhabitant of a country or region.

Aborigine (ˌæbə'rɪdʒɪnɪ) *n.* a member of a dark-skinned people who were already living in Australia when European settlers arrived.

abort (ə'bɔːt) *vb.* **1.** (of a woman) to end a pregnancy before the fetus is viable; miscarry. **2** to perform an abortion on (a pregnant woman). **3.** to terminate (a mission or project) prematurely or (of a mission or project) to be terminated prematurely.

abortion (ə'bɔːʃən) *n.* **1.** an operation to terminate pregnancy. **2.** the premature termination of pregnancy by expulsion of a nonviable fetus from the womb. **3.** the failure of a mission or project. **4.** *Informal.* something that is grotesque. —**a'bortionist** *n.*

abortive (ə'bɔːtɪv) *adj.* failing to achieve a purpose.

abound (ə'baʊnd) *vb.* **1.** to exist in large numbers. **2. abound in.** to have a large number of.

about (ə'baʊt) *prep.* **1.** relating to; concerning. **2.** near to. **3.** carried on: *I haven't any money about me.* **4.** on every side of. ~*adv.* **5.** near in number, time, or degree; approximately. **6.** nearby. **7.** here and there: *walk about to keep warm.* **8.** all around; on every side. **9.** in or to the opposite direction. **10.** in rotation: *turn and turn about.* **11.** used to indicate understatement: *it's about time you stopped.* **12. about to.** on the point of; intending to: *she was about to jump.* **13. not about to.** determined not to: *I'm not about to miss the game.* ~*adj.* **14.** active: *up and about.*

about turn *or U.S.* **about face** *interj.* **1.** a military command to reverse the direction in which one is facing. ~*n.* **about-turn** *or U.S.* **about-face. 2.** reversal of the direction in which one is facing. **3.** a complete change of opinion or direction.

above (ə'bʌv) *prep.* **1.** higher than; over. **2.** greater than in quantity or degree: *above average.* **3.** superior to or higher than in quality, rank, or ability. **4.** too high-minded for: *above petty gossiping.* **5.** too respected for; beyond: *above suspicion.* **6.** too difficult to be understood by: *the talk was above me.* **7.** louder or higher than (other noise). **8.** in preference to. **9. above**

all. most of all; especially. ~*adv.* **10.** in or to a higher place: *the sky above.* **11.** in a previous place (in something written or printed). **12.** higher in rank or position. ~*n.* **13. the above.** something previously mentioned. ~*adj.* **14.** appearing in a previous place (in something written or printed).

above board *adj.* in the open; without dishonesty.

abracadabra (ˌæbrəkəˈdæbrə) *n.* a word used in magic spells, which is supposed to possess magic powers.

abrasion (əˈbreɪʒən) *n.* **1.** a scraped area on the skin; graze. **2.** *Geog.* the erosion of rock by rock fragments scratching and scraping it.

abrasive (əˈbreɪsɪv) *adj.* **1.** irritating in manner. **2.** causing abrasion; rough. ~*n.* **3.** a substance used for cleaning, smoothing, or polishing.

abreast (əˈbrɛst) *adj.* **1.** alongside each other and facing in the same direction: *two abreast.* **2. abreast of.** up to date with.

abridge (əˈbrɪdʒ) *vb.* to reduce the length of (a written work) by condensing it. —a'**bridgment** *or* a'**bridgement** *n.*

abroad (əˈbrɔːd) *adv.* **1.** to or in a foreign country or countries. **2.** (of rumours) in general circulation.

abrogate (ˈæbrəʊˌgeɪt) *vb.* to cancel (a law or an agreement) formally. —ˌabro'**gation** *n.*

abrupt (əˈbrʌpt) *adj.* **1.** sudden; unexpected. **2.** rather rude in speech or manner. —ab'**ruptly** *adv.* —ab'**ruptness** *n.*

abscess (ˈæbsɛs) *n.* **1.** a swelling containing pus as a result of inflammation. ~*vb.* **2.** to form a swelling containing pus. —'**abscessed** *adj.*

abscissa (æbˈsɪsə) *n., pl.* -**scissas** *or* -**scissae** (-ˈsɪsiː). *Maths.* (in a two-dimensional system of Cartesian coordinates) the distance from the vertical axis measured parallel to the horizontal axis.

abscond (əbˈskɒnd) *vb.* to run away secretly, usually to avoid prosecution.

abseil (ˈæbseɪl) *Mountaineering.* ~*vb.* **1.** to descend a steep drop by a rope secured from above and coiled around one's body. ~*n.* **2.** an instance of abseiling.

absence (ˈæbsəns) *n.* **1.** the state of being away. **2.** the time during which a person or thing is away. **3.** the fact of being without something; lack.

absent *adj.* (ˈæbsənt). **1.** not present. **2.** lacking. **3.** inattentive. ~*vb.* (æbˈsɛnt). **4. absent oneself.** to stay away. —'**absently** *adv.*

absentee (ˌæbsənˈtiː) *n.* **a.** a person who is absent. **b.** (*as modifier*): *an absentee landlord.*

absenteeism (ˌæbsənˈtiːɪzəm) *n.* persistent absence from work or school.

absent-minded *adj.* preoccupied; forgetful. —ˌabsent-'**mindedly** *adv.*

absinthe *or* **absinth** (ˈæbsɪnθ) *n.* a potent green alcoholic drink, originally containing wormwood.

absolute (ˈæbsəˌluːt) *adj.* **1.** complete; perfect. **2.** free from restrictions or exceptions: *an absolute ruler.* **3.** undoubted; certain: *the absolute truth.* **4.** not dependent on or relative to anything else. **5.** pure; unmixed: *absolute alcohol.* ~*n.* **6.** something that is absolute. **7. the Absolute.** *Philosophy.* that which is totally unconditioned, perfect, or complete.

absolutely (ˌæbsəˈluːtlɪ) *adv.* **1.** completely or perfectly. ~*interj.* **2.** yes indeed, certainly.

absolute majority *n.* a number of votes totalling over 50 per cent, such as the total number of votes that beats the combined opposition.

absolute pitch *n.* the ability to identify exactly the pitch of a note without comparing it with another.

absolute zero *n. Physics.* the lowest temperature theoretically attainable, at which the particles that make up matter would be at rest: equivalent to $-273.15°C$ or $-459.67°F$.

absolution (ˌæbsəˈluːʃən) *n. Christianity.* a formal forgiveness of sin pronounced by a priest.

absolutism (ˈæbsəluːˌtɪzəm) *n.* the principle of a political system in which a monarch or dictator has unrestricted power.

absolve (əbˈzɒlv) *vb.* to clear (someone) of all blame.

absorb (əbˈsɔːb) *vb.* **1.** to soak up (a liquid). **2.** to engage the interest of (someone). **3.** to receive the force of (an impact). **4.** *Physics.* to take in (radiant energy) and retain it. **5.** to take in; incorporate: *the refugees were absorbed into the community.* —ab'**sorbent** *adj.* —ab'**sorbing** *adj.*

absorption (əbˈsɔːpʃən) *n.* **1.** the process of absorbing something or the state of being absorbed. **2.** *Physiol.* the process by which nutrients enter the tissues of an animal or a plant. —ab'**sorptive** *adj.*

abstain (əbˈsteɪn) *vb.* **1.** to choose to refrain: *he abstained from drinking alcohol.* **2.** to refrain from voting. —ab'**stainer** *n.*

abstemious (əbˈstiːmɪəs) *adj.* sparing in the consumption of alcohol or food. —ab'**stemiously** *adv.* —ab'**stemiousness** *n.*

abstention (əbˈstɛnʃən) *n.* **1.** the act of abstaining from something, such as drinking alcohol. **2.** the act of withholding one's vote.

abstinence (ˈæbstɪnəns) *n.* the act or practice of refraining from some action, such as drinking alcohol. —'**abstinent** *adj.*

abstract *adj.* (ˈæbstrækt). **1.** referring to

ideas or qualities rather than material objects: *an abstract noun*. **2.** not applied or practical; theoretical: *abstract science*. **3.** denoting art in which the subject is represented by shapes and patterns rather than by a realistic likeness. ~*n*. (ˈæbstrækt). **4.** a summary. **5.** an abstract word or idea. **6.** an abstract painting or sculpture. **7. in the abstract.** without referring to specific circumstances. ~*vb*. (æbˈstrækt). **8.** to remove oneself or an object. **9.** to summarize.

abstracted (æbˈstræktɪd) *adj*. lost in thought; preoccupied. —**abˈstractedly** *adv*.

abstraction (æbˈstrækʃən) *n*. **1.** preoccupation. **2.** a generalized concept formulated by extracting common qualities from specific examples: *good and evil are abstractions*.

abstruse (əbˈstruːs) *adj*. not easy to understand.

absurd (əbˈsɜːd) *adj*. incongruous; ridiculous. —**abˈsurdity** *n*. —**abˈsurdly** *adv*.

abundance (əˈbʌndəns) *n*. **1.** a great amount. **2.** degree of plentifulness. —**aˈbundant** *adj*.

abundantly (əˈbʌndəntlɪ) *adv*. **1.** very: *he made it abundantly plain*. **2.** plentifully; in abundance.

abuse *vb*. (əˈbjuːz). **1.** to use incorrectly: *he abuses his position*. **2.** to mistreat: *the child had been physically abused*. **3.** to speak insultingly or cruelly to. ~*n*. (əˈbjuːs). **4.** improper use. **5.** mistreatment; injury. **6.** insulting comments. —**aˈbuser** *n*.

abusive (əˈbjuːsɪv) *adj*. rude or insulting: *abusive language*. —**aˈbusively** *adv*.

abut (əˈbʌt) *vb*. **abutting, abutted.** (foll. by *on*) to adjoin, touch, or border on (something) at one end.

abutment (əˈbʌtmənt) *n*. a construction that supports the end of a bridge.

abysmal (əˈbɪzməl) *adj*. *Informal*. extremely bad. —**aˈbysmally** *adv*.

abyss (əˈbɪs) *n*. a very deep hole in the ground.

Ac *Chem*. actinium.

AC 1. alternating current. **2.** athletic club.

a/c 1. account. **2.** account current.

acacia (əˈkeɪʃə) *n*. a shrub or tree with small yellow or white flowers.

academic (ˌækəˈdɛmɪk) *adj*. **1.** relating to a college or university. **2.** of theoretical interest only: *the question is academic as a decision has already been reached*. **3.** (of pupils) having an aptitude for study. **4.** relating to studies such as languages and pure science rather than technical or professional studies. ~*n*. **5.** a member of the teaching or research staff of a college or university. —ˌacaˈdemically *adv*.

academy (əˈkædəmɪ) *n., pl*. **-mies. 1.** a society for the advancement of literature,

art, or science. **2.** a school for training in a particular skill: *a military academy*. **3.** (in Scotland) a secondary school. —ˌacaˈdemical *adj*.

acanthus (əˈkænθəs) *n*. **1.** a plant with large spiny leaves and spikes of white or purplish flowers. **2.** a carved ornament based on the leaves of the acanthus plant.

ACAS (ˈeɪkæs) (in Britain) Advisory Conciliation and Arbitration Service.

acc. *Grammar*. accusative.

accede (ækˈsiːd) *vb*. (foll. by *to*) **1.** to give one's consent to. **2.** to take up (an office or position): *the prince acceded to the throne*.

accelerando (ækˌsɛləˈrændəʊ) *adv*. *Music*. with increasing speed.

accelerate (ækˈsɛləˌreɪt) *vb*. **1.** to move or cause (something) to move more quickly; speed up. **2.** to cause (something) to happen sooner than expected. —**acceleration** (ækˌsɛləˈreɪʃən) *n*.

accelerator (ækˈsɛləˌreɪtə) *n*. **1.** a pedal in a motor vehicle that is pressed to increase speed. **2.** *Physics*. a machine for increasing the speed and energy of charged particles.

accent *n*. (ˈæksənt). **1.** the distinctive style of pronunciation of a person or group from a particular area, country, or social background. **2.** the relative prominence of a spoken or sung syllable. **3.** a mark used in writing to indicate the prominence of a syllable or the way a vowel is pronounced. **4.** *Music*. stress placed on certain notes. **5.** a distinctive characteristic of anything: *a wine bar with a nautical accent*. **6.** particular emphasis: *an accent on learning*. ~*vb*. (ækˈsɛnt). **7.** to mark with an accent. **8.** to lay particular emphasis on.

accentuate (ækˈsɛntʃʊˌeɪt) *vb*. to stress or emphasize. —**acˌcentuˈation** *n*.

accept (əkˈsɛpt) *vb*. **1.** to take or receive (something offered). **2.** to agree to. **3.** to take on the responsibilities of: *he accepted office*. **4.** to consider (something) as true. **5.** to receive (someone) into a community or group. **6.** to receive (something) as adequate or valid.

acceptable (əkˈsɛptəbəl) *adj*. **1.** satisfactory; adequate. **2.** tolerable. —**acˌceptaˈbility** *n*. —**acˈceptably** *adv*.

acceptance (əkˈsɛptəns) *n*. **1.** the act of accepting something. **2.** favourable reception. **3.** belief or assent.

accepted (əkˈsɛptɪd) *adj*. commonly approved or recognized; established.

access (ˈæksɛs) *n*. **1.** a means of approaching or entering a place. **2.** the condition of allowing entry, for example entry to a building by wheelchairs or prams. **3.** the right to approach, enter, or make use of something. ~*vb*. **4.** to obtain (information) from a computer.

accessible (əkˈsɛsəbəl) *adj*. **1.** easy to approach, enter, or use. **2. accessible to. a.**

obtainable by; available to. **b.** understandable by. —**ac,cessi'bility** n.

accession (ək'sɛʃən) n. the act of taking up
an office or position: *accession to the
throne.*

accessory (ək'sɛsərɪ) n., pl. -ries. **1.** a
supplementary part or object. **2.** a small
accompanying item of dress, such as a belt.
3. a person involved in a crime although
absent during its commission.

access road n. a road providing a way to
a particular place or on to a motorway.

access time n. the time required to retrieve a piece of stored information from a
computer.

accident ('æksɪdənt) n. **1.** a mishap, usually one causing injury or death. **2.** an unforeseen event or one without apparent
cause: *I met him by accident.*

accidental (,æksɪ'dɛnt²l) adj. **1.** occurring
by chance or unintentionally. ~n. **2.** *Music.* a symbol denoting that the following
note is a sharp, flat, or natural that is not a
part of the key signature. —**,acci'dentally** adv.

accident-prone adj. (of a person) often
involved in accidents.

acclaim (ə'kleɪm) vb. **1.** to acknowledge
publicly the excellence of (a person or act).
2. to acknowledge publicly: *they acclaimed
him king.* ~n. **3.** an enthusiastic expression of approval.

acclamation (,æklə'meɪʃən) n. **1.** an enthusiastic reception or exhibition of approval. **2.** *Canad.* an instance of being
elected without opposition.

acclimatize or -tise (ə'klaɪmə,taɪz) vb. to
adapt to a new climate or environment.
—**ac,climati'zation** or -ti'sation n.

accolade ('ækə,leɪd) n. **1.** an award,
praise, or honour. **2.** a touch on the shoulder with a sword conferring knighthood.

accommodate (ə'kɒmə,deɪt) vb. **1.** to
supply or provide (someone) with lodgings.
2. to oblige or do a favour for (someone). **3.**
to adapt. **4.** to have room for (someone or
something).

accommodating (ə'kɒmə,deɪtɪŋ) adj. willing to help; obliging.

accommodation (ə,kɒmə'deɪʃən) n. **1.**
lodgings. **2.** willingness to oblige.

accommodation address n. an address
on letters to a person who cannot or does
not wish to receive mail at a permanent
address.

accompaniment (ə'kʌmpənɪmənt) n. **1.**
something that accompanies something
else. **2.** *Music.* a supporting part for an
instrument, a band, or an orchestra.

accompanist (ə'kʌmpənɪst) n. a person
who plays a musical accompaniment.

accompany (ə'kʌmpənɪ) vb. -nying, -nied.
1. to go along with. **2.** to occur or be

associated with. **3.** to provide a musical
accompaniment for.

accomplice (ə'kʌmplɪs) n. a person who
helps another commit a crime.

accomplish (ə'kʌmplɪʃ) vb. **1.** to manage to
do; achieve. **2.** to complete.

accomplished (ə'kʌmplɪʃt) adj. **1.** expert;
proficient. **2.** successfully completed.

accomplishment (ə'kʌmplɪʃmənt) n. **1.**
the act of successfully completing something. **2.** something successfully completed. **3.** (pl.) social or other skills.

accord (ə'kɔːd) n. **1.** agreement; accordance. **2.** a settlement, for example between
nations. **3. of one's own accord.** voluntarily. **4. with one accord.** unanimously.
~vb. **5.** (foll. by *with*) to fit in with or be
consistent with. **6.** to grant; give: *he appre-
ciated the courtesy accorded him.*

accordance (ə'kɔːdəns) n. **in accordance
with.** in conformity with.

according (ə'kɔːdɪŋ) adj. **1. according to.
a.** as stated by. **b.** in conformity with. **2.
according as.** depending on whether.

accordingly (ə'kɔːdɪŋlɪ) adv. **1.** in an appropriate manner. **2.** consequently.

accordion (ə'kɔːdɪən) n. a box-shaped musical instrument consisting of metallic
reeds, a set of bellows controlled by the
player's hands, and studs or keys by which
notes are produced. —**ac'cordionist** n.

accost (ə'kɒst) vb. to approach, stop, and
speak to (a person), for example to ask a
question or solicit sex.

account (ə'kaʊnt) n. **1.** a report or description. **2.** an explanation of conduct. **3.**
importance or value: *it's of no account.* **4.**
profit or advantage: *to good account.* **5.**
part or behalf: *don't bother on my account.*
6. *Finance.* a business relationship between
a bank or other institution and a customer
permitting the latter certain banking or
credit services. **7.** a statement of financial
transactions with the resulting balance. **8.
call someone to account. a.** to insist that
someone explains himself. **b.** to reprimand
someone. **9. give a good account of oneself.** to perform well. **10. on account. a.** on
credit. **b.** as partial payment. **11. on account of.** because of. **12. take account of**
or **take into account.** to take into consideration; allow for. ~vb. **13.** to consider as:
he accounts himself poor.

accountable (ə'kaʊntəb²l) adj. responsible
to someone or for some action. —**ac,count-
a'bility** n.

accountant (ə'kaʊntənt) n. a person concerned with the maintenance and auditing
of business accounts. —**ac'countancy** n.

account for vb. **1.** to give reasons for.
2. to make or provide a reckoning of (expenditure).

accounting (ə'kaʊntɪŋ) n. the skill or practice of maintaining and auditing business accounts.

accoutrements (ə'ku:trəmənts) *or U.S.* **accouterments** (ə'ku:tərmənts) *pl. n.* clothing and equipment for a particular activity.

accredit (ə'krɛdɪt) *vb.* **1.** to give official recognition to. **2.** to certify as meeting required standards. **3.** to send (a diplomat) with official credentials to a particular country. **4.** to attribute (a quality or an action) to (a person). **5.** *N.Z.* to pass (a candidate for university entrance) on school recommendation, without external examination. —**ac,credi'tation** *n.*

accretion (ə'kri:ʃən) *n.* **1.** a gradual increase in size, through growth or addition. **2.** something added, such as an extra layer.

accrue (ə'kru:) *vb.* **-cruing, -crued.** **1.** (of money or interest) to increase gradually over a period of time. **2.** (foll. by *to*) to fall naturally to.

accumulate (ə'kju:mjʊˌleɪt) *vb.* to gather together in an increasing quantity; collect. —**ac'cumulative** *adj.*

accumulation (əˌkju:mjʊ'leɪʃən) *n.* **1.** the act or process of collecting together or becoming collected. **2.** something that has been collected.

accumulator (ə'kju:mjʊˌleɪtə) *n.* **1.** a rechargeable device for storing electrical energy. **2.** *Horse racing, Brit.* a collective bet on successive races, with both stake and winnings being carried forward to accumulate progressively.

accuracy ('ækjʊrəsɪ) *n.* faithful representation of the truth; precision.

accurate ('ækjərɪt) *adj.* faithfully representing the truth; precise. —**'accurately** *adv.*

accursed (ə'kɜːsɪd) *adj.* **1.** hateful; detestable. **2.** under a curse.

accusation (ˌækjʊ'zeɪʃən) *n.* **1.** an allegation that a person is guilty of some wrongdoing. **2.** a formal charge brought against a person.

accusative (ə'kju:zətɪv) *Grammar.* ~*adj.* **1.** denoting the object case in some languages. ~*n.* **2.** the accusative case.

accuse (ə'kju:z) *vb.* to charge (a person or persons) with wrongdoing. —**ac'cuser** *n.* —**ac'cusing** *adj.* —**ac'cusingly** *adv.*

accused (ə'kju:zd) *n.* **the.** *Law.* the defendant appearing on a criminal charge.

accustom (ə'kʌstəm) *vb.* (foll. by *to*) to make (oneself) familiar with or used to.

accustomed (ə'kʌstəmd) *adj.* **1.** usual; customary. **2. accustomed to. a.** used to. **b.** in the habit of.

ace (eɪs) *n.* **1.** a playing card with one symbol on it. **2.** *Tennis.* a winning serve that the opponent fails to reach. **3.** a fighter pilot who has destroyed several enemy aircraft. **4.** *Informal.* an expert. **5. within**

an ace of. very close to. ~*adj.* **6.** *Informal.* superb; excellent.

acerbic (ə'sɜːbɪk) *adj.* harsh or bitter.

acerbity (ə'sɜːbɪtɪ) *n., pl.* **-ties.** **1.** embittered speech or temper. **2.** bitterness of taste.

acetaldehyde (ˌæsɪ'tældɪˌhaɪd) *n. Chem.* a colourless volatile liquid, used as a solvent.

acetate ('æsɪˌteɪt) *n.* **1.** *Chem.* any salt or ester of acetic acid. **2.** Also: **acetate rayon.** a synthetic textile fibre made from cellulose acetate. **3.** an audio disc with an acetate lacquer coating.

acetic (ə'si:tɪk) *adj. Chem.* of, containing, producing, or from acetic acid or vinegar.

acetic acid *n. Chem.* a strong-smelling colourless liquid used to make vinegar.

acetone ('æsɪˌtəʊn) *n. Chem.* a strong-smelling colourless liquid used as a solvent for paints and lacquers.

acetylene (ə'sɛtɪˌli:n) *n. Chem.* a colourless soluble flammable gas used in welding metals.

ache (eɪk) *vb.* **1.** to feel or be the source of a continuous dull pain. **2.** to suffer mental anguish. ~*n.* **3.** a continuous dull pain.

achieve (ə'tʃi:v) *vb.* to gain (something) by hard work or effort. —**a'chiever** *n.*

achievement (ə'tʃi:vmənt) *n.* **1.** something that has been accomplished by hard work, ability, or heroism. **2.** the condition of having been accomplished.

Achilles heel (ə'kɪli:z) *n.* a small but fatal weakness.

Achilles tendon *n.* the fibrous cord that connects the muscles of the calf to the heelbone.

achromatic (ˌeɪkrə'mætɪk) *adj.* **1.** without colour. **2.** refracting light without breaking it up into its component colours. **3.** *Music.* involving no sharps or flats. —ˌ**achro-'matically** *adv.*

acid ('æsɪd) *n.* **1.** any substance that when dissolved in water yields a sour corrosive solution, turning litmus red. **2.** a sour-tasting substance. **3.** *Slang.* LSD. ~*adj.* **4.** *Chem.* of, from, or containing acid. **5.** sharp or sour in taste. **6.** sharp in speech or manner. —**'acidly** *adv.*

Acid House *or* **Acid** *n.* a type of funk-based, electronically edited disco music of the late 1980s, which has hypnotic sound effects and which is associated with hippie culture and the use of the drug ecstasy.

acidic (ə'sɪdɪk) *adj.* containing acid.

acidify (ə'sɪdɪˌfaɪ) *vb.* **-fying, -fied.** to convert into acid.

acidity (ə'sɪdɪtɪ) *n.* **1.** the quality of being acid. **2.** the amount of acid in a solution.

acid rain *n.* rain containing pollutants released into the atmosphere by burning coal or oil.

acid test *n.* a rigorous and conclusive test of worth or value.

acidulous (ə'sɪdjʊləs) *adj.* **1.** rather sour. **2.** sharp in speech or manner.

ack-ack ('æk,æk) *n. Mil.* anti-aircraft fire.

acknowledge (ək'nɒlɪdʒ) *vb.* **1.** to recognize or admit the truth of (a statement). **2.** to indicate recognition of (a person) by a greeting or glance. **3.** to express gratitude for (a favour or compliment). **4.** to make known the receipt of (a letter or message).

acknowledgment *or* **acknowledgement** (ək'nɒlɪdʒmənt) *n.* **1.** the act of acknowledging something or someone. **2.** something done or given as an expression of gratitude.

acme ('ækmɪ) *n.* the highest point of achievement or excellence.

acne ('æknɪ) *n.* a skin disease in which pus-filled spots form on the face.

acolyte ('ækə,laɪt) *n.* **1.** a follower or attendant. **2.** *Christianity.* a person who assists a priest.

aconite ('ækə,naɪt) *n.* **1.** a poisonous plant with hoodlike flowers. **2.** dried aconite root, used as a narcotic.

acorn ('eɪkɔːn) *n.* the fruit of the oak tree, consisting of a smooth nut in a scaly cuplike base.

acoustic (ə'kuːstɪk) *adj.* **1.** of sound, hearing, or acoustics. **2.** designed to absorb sound: *an acoustic hood.* **3.** (of a musical instrument) without electronic amplification. **—a'coustically** *adv.*

acoustics (ə'kuːstɪks) *n.* **1.** (*functioning as sing.*) the scientific study of sound. **2.** (*functioning as pl.*) the characteristics of a room or theatre that determine how well sound can be heard within it.

acquaintance (ə'kweɪntəns) *n.* **1.** a person whom one knows slightly. **2.** slight knowledge of a person or subject. **3. make the acquaintance of.** to come into social contact with. **4.** those persons collectively whom one knows: *a lawyer of my acquaintance.*

acquainted (ə'kweɪntɪd) *adj.* **1.** on terms of familiarity but not intimacy. **2.** (foll. by *with*) familiar with: *acquainted with the facts.*

acquiesce (,ækwɪ'ɛs) *vb.* to assent to someone's wishes without protest. **—,acqui'escence** *n.* **—,acqui'escent** *adj.*

acquire (ə'kwaɪə) *vb.* to get or develop (something such as an object, trait, or ability). **—ac'quirement** *n.*

acquired taste *n.* **1.** a liking for something at first considered unpleasant. **2.** the thing liked.

acquisition (,ækwɪ'zɪʃən) *n.* **1.** the act of acquiring something. **2.** something acquired, often to add to a collection.

acquisitive (ə'kwɪzɪtɪv) *adj.* eager to acquire material possessions. **—ac'quisitively** *adv.* **—ac'quisitiveness** *n.*

acquit (ə'kwɪt) *vb.* **-quitting, -quitted.** **1.** to pronounce (someone) not guilty: *he was acquitted of arson.* **2.** to conduct (oneself): *she acquitted herself well in the exams.* **—ac'quittal** *n.*

acre ('eɪkə) *n.* **1.** a unit of area equal to 4840 square yards or 4046.86 square metres. **2.** (*pl.*) **a.** a large area of land. **b.** *Informal.* a large amount: *acres of flesh.*

acreage ('eɪkərɪdʒ) *n.* land area in acres.

acrid ('ækrɪd) *adj.* **1.** unpleasantly strong-smelling. **2.** sharp in speech or manner. **—acridity** (ə'krɪdɪtɪ) *n.* **—'acridly** *adv.*

acrimony ('ækrɪmənɪ) *n.* bitterness or sharpness of speech or manner. **—acrimonious** (,ækrɪ'məʊnɪəs) *adj.*

acrobat ('ækrə,bæt) *n.* an entertainer who performs acts that require skill, agility, and coordination, such as swinging from a trapeze. **—,acro'batic** *adj.* **—,acro'batically** *adv.*

acrobatics (,ækrə'bætɪks) *pl. n.* the skills or feats of an acrobat.

acronym ('ækrənɪm) *n.* a word made from a series of initial letters or parts of words, for example *UNESCO* for the *United Nations Educational, Scientific, and Cultural Organization.*

acrophobia (,ækrə'fəʊbɪə) *n.* abnormal fear of being at a great height.

acropolis (ə'krɒpəlɪs) *n.* the citadel of an ancient Greek city.

across (ə'krɒs) *prep.* **1.** from one side to the other side of. **2.** on or at the other side of. *~adv.* **3.** from one side to the other. **4.** on or to the other side.

across-the-board *adj.* affecting everyone in a particular group or place equally: *an across-the-board pay rise.*

acrostic (ə'krɒstɪk) *n.* a number of lines of writing, such as a poem, in which the first or last letters form a word or proverb.

acrylic (ə'krɪlɪk) *adj.* **1.** made of acrylic fibre or acrylic resin. *~n.* **2.** short for **acrylic fibre** *or* **acrylic resin.**

acrylic acid *n. Chem.* a strong-smelling colourless corrosive liquid, used in the manufacture of acrylic resins.

acrylic fibre *n.* a man-made fibre used for clothes and blankets.

acrylic resin *n. Chem.* any of a group of polymers of acrylic acid, used as synthetic rubbers, in paints, and as plastics.

act (ækt) *n.* **1.** something done. **2.** a formal decision reached or law passed by a lawmaking body: *an act of parliament.* **3.** a major division of a play. **4.** a short performance, such as a sketch or dance. **5.** a pretended attitude. **6. get in on the act.** *Informal.* to become involved in something in order to share the benefit. **7. get one's act together.** *Informal.* to organize oneself.

~*vb.* **8.** to do something. **9.** to perform (a part or role) in a play, film, or broadcast. **10.** to present (a play) on stage. **11.** (foll. by *for*) to be a substitute for: *I'm acting for the headmaster.* **12.** (foll. by *as*) to serve the function of. **13.** to conduct oneself: *she acts like a lady.* **14.** to behave in an unnatural way. ~See also **act up.**

acting (ˈæktɪŋ) *adj.* **1.** taking on duties temporarily: *the acting headmaster.* ~*n.* **2.** the art of an actor.

actinide series (ˈæktɪˌnaɪd) *n. Chem.* a series of 15 radioactive elements with increasing atomic numbers from actinium to lawrencium.

actinium (ækˈtɪnɪəm) *n. Chem.* a radioactive element of the actinide series, occurring as a decay product of uranium. Symbol: Ac

action (ˈækʃən) *n.* **1.** the process of doing something. **2.** something done. **3.** movement during some physical activity. **4.** activity, force, or energy. **5.** (*pl.*) behaviour. **6.** a lawsuit. **7.** the operating mechanism in a gun or machine. **8.** the way in which something operates or works. **9. out of action.** not functioning. **10. the action. a.** the events that form the plot of a story or play. **b.** *Slang.* the main activity in a place. **11.** *Mil.* **a.** a minor engagement. **b.** fighting.

actionable (ˈækʃənəbᵊl) *adj. Law.* giving grounds for legal action.

action painting *n.* an art form in which paint is thrown, smeared, dripped, or spattered on the canvas.

action replay *n.* the rerunning of a small section of a television tape, for example of a sporting event, usually in slow motion.

action stations *pl. n.* the positions taken up by individuals in preparation for battle or for some other activity.

activate (ˈæktɪˌveɪt) *vb.* **1.** to make (something) active. **2.** *Physics.* to make (something) radioactive. **3.** *Chem.* to increase the rate of (a reaction).

active (ˈæktɪv) *adj.* **1.** moving, working, or doing something. **2.** busy and energetic. **3.** effective: *an active ingredient.* **4.** *Grammar.* denoting a form of a verb used to indicate that the subject is performing the action, for example *kicked* in *The boy kicked the football.* **5.** fully engaged in military service. **6.** (of a volcano) erupting periodically. ~*n.* **7.** *Grammar.* the active form of a verb. —ˈ**actively** *adv.*

active list *n. Mil.* a list of officers available for full duty.

activism (ˈæktɪˌvɪzəm) *n.* a policy of taking direct action to achieve a political or social goal. —ˈ**activist** *n.*

activity (ækˈtɪvɪtɪ) *n.* **1.** the state of being active. **2.** lively movement. **3.** (*pl.* -**ties**) any specific action or pursuit: *recreational activities.*

act of God *n. Law.* a sudden occurrence caused by natural forces, such as a flood.

actor (ˈæktə) *or* (*fem.*) **actress** (ˈæktrɪs) *n.* a person who acts in a play, film, or broadcast.

actual (ˈæktʃʊəl) *adj.* existing in reality or as a matter of fact.

actuality (ˌæktʃʊˈælɪtɪ) *n., pl.* -**ties.** reality.

actually (ˈæktʃʊəlɪ) *adv.* as an actual fact; really.

actuary (ˈæktʃʊərɪ) *n., pl.* -**aries.** a statistician who calculates insurance risks, policy premiums, and dividends. —**actuarial** (ˌæktʃʊˈɛərɪəl) *adj.*

actuate (ˈæktʃʊˌeɪt) *vb.* **1.** to start up (a mechanical device). **2.** to motivate (someone).

act up *vb. Informal.* to behave in a troublesome way.

acuity (əˈkjuːɪtɪ) *n.* acuteness of vision or thought.

acumen (ˈækjʊˌmɛn) *n.* the ability to judge well; insight.

acupuncture (ˈækjʊˌpʌŋktʃə) *n.* the practice of inserting needles into someone's skin at specific points to treat various disorders by stimulating nerve impulses. —ˈ**acu-ˌpuncturist** *n.*

acute (əˈkjuːt) *adj.* **1.** penetrating in perception or insight. **2.** sensitive; keen: *an acute sense of smell.* **3.** of extreme importance; crucial. **4.** severe or intense: *acute embarrassment.* **5.** *Maths.* (of an angle) less than 90°. **6.** (of a disease) sudden and severe. ~*n.* **7.** an acute accent. —**aˈcutely** *adv.* —**aˈcuteness** *n.*

acute accent *n.* the mark (´), used in some languages to indicate that the vowel over which it is placed is pronounced in a certain way.

ad (æd) *n. Informal.* an advertisement.

A.D. *or* **AD** (indicating years numbered from the supposed year of the birth of Christ) in the year of the Lord.
Usage. A.D. is only used to refer to a particular year: *he died in 1621 A.D.,* but *he died in the 17th century.* It is not strictly necessary to use "in" when A.D. is used, because the Latin *anno Domini* means "in the year of Our Lord". But in practice "in" is generally used, as in the example above. B.C. is used with both specific dates and indications of the period: *Julius Caesar was born in 100 B.C.; the battle took place in the 4th century B.C.*

ad- *prefix.* **1.** to; towards: *adverb.* **2.** near; next to: *adrenal.*

adage (ˈædɪdʒ) *n.* a traditional saying that is generally accepted as being true.

adagio (əˈdɑːdʒɪˌəʊ) *Music.* ~*adv.* **1.** slowly. ~*n., pl.* -**gios.** **2.** a movement or piece to be performed slowly.

Adam (ˈædəm) *n.* **1.** *Bible.* the first man

(Genesis 2–3). **2. not know someone from Adam.** to have no knowledge of someone.

adamant ('ædəmənt) *adj.* unshakable in determination or purpose; inflexible. —'**adamantly** *adv.*

Adam's apple *n.* the lump of thyroid cartilage at the front of a person's neck.

adapt (ə'dæpt) *vb.* **1.** (often foll. by *to*) to adjust (something or oneself) to different conditions. **2.** to modify (something) to suit a new purpose. —**a**'**daptable** *adj.* —**a**,**dapta**'**bility** *n.*

adaptation (,ædəp'teɪʃən) *n.* **1.** the act of adapting. **2.** something that is produced by adapting something else.

adaptor *or* **adapter** (ə'dæptə) *n.* **1.** a device used to connect several electrical appliances to a single socket. **2.** any device for connecting two parts of different sizes or types.

add (æd) *vb.* **1.** to combine (numbers or quantities) so as to make a larger number or quantity. **2.** to join (something) to something else so as to increase its size, effect, or scope: *to add insult to injury.* **3.** to say or write (something) further. **4. add in.** to include. ~See also **add up.**

addendum (ə'dɛndəm) *n.*, *pl.* **-da** (-də). **1.** an addition. **2.** an appendix to a book or magazine.

adder ('ædə) *n.* **1.** a common viper, found in Britain, which has a black zigzag pattern along the back. **2.** any of various similar snakes.

addict ('ædɪkt) *n.* **1.** a person who is addicted to narcotic drugs. **2.** *Informal.* a person who is devoted to something: *a TV addict.* —**ad**'**dictive** *adj.*

addicted (ə'dɪktɪd) *adj.* **1.** dependent on a narcotic drug. **2.** *Informal.* devoted to something: *addicted to chocolate.* —**ad**'**diction** *n.*

addition (ə'dɪʃən) *n.* **1.** the act of adding. **2.** a person or thing that is added. **3.** a mathematical operation in which the sum of two or more numbers or quantities is calculated. **4. in addition to.** besides; as well as. —**ad**'**ditional** *adj.*

additive ('ædɪtɪv) *n.* any substance added to something, such as food, to improve it or prevent deterioration.

addle ('æd³l) *vb.* **1.** to make (someone's mind or brain) confused. **2.** to make rotten: *addled eggs.* ~*adj.* **3.** indicating a confused state: *addle-brained.*

address (ə'drɛs) *n.* **1.** the conventional form by which the location of a building is described. **2.** the place at which someone lives. **3.** a formal speech. **4.** *Computers.* a number giving the location of a piece of stored information. ~*vb.* **5.** to mark (a letter or parcel) with an address. **6.** to speak to (someone). **7. address oneself to. a.** to speak or write to. **b.** to apply oneself

to: *he addressed himself to the task.* **8.** to direct (a message or warning) to someone. **9.** to direct one's attention to (a problem or an issue).

addressee (,ædrɛ'siː) *n.* a person to whom a letter or parcel is addressed.

adduce (ə'djuːs) *vb.* to cite (something) as evidence.

add up *vb.* **1.** to calculate the sum of (two or more numbers or quantities). **2.** *Informal.* to make sense. **3.** (foll. by *to*) to amount to.

adenoidal (,ædɪ'nɔɪd³l) *adj.* having a nasal voice or impaired breathing because of enlarged adenoids.

adenoids ('ædɪ,nɔɪdz) *pl. n.* a mass of tissue at the back of the throat.

adept *adj.* (ə'dɛpt). **1.** proficient in something requiring skill. ~*n.* ('ædɛpt). **2.** a person skilled in something. —**a**'**deptness** *n.*

adequate ('ædɪkwɪt) *adj.* sufficient without being abundant or outstanding. —**adequacy** ('ædɪkwəsɪ) *n.* —'**adequately** *adv.*

à deux (ɑː 'dɜː) *adj., adv.* of or for two persons.

adhere (əd'hɪə) *vb.* (foll. by *to*) **1.** to stick to. **2.** to be devoted to (a political party or religion). **3.** to follow (a rule) exactly.

adherent (əd'hɪərənt) *n.* **1.** a supporter or follower. ~*adj.* **2.** sticking or attached. —**ad**'**herence** *n.*

adhesion (əd'hiːʒən) *n.* **1.** the quality or condition of sticking together. **2.** attachment, for example to a political party or religion. **3.** *Pathol.* the joining together of two structures or parts of the body that are normally separate, for example after surgery.

adhesive (əd'hiːsɪv) *adj.* **1.** able or designed to stick to things. ~*n.* **2.** a substance used for sticking things together.

ad hoc (æd 'hɒk) *adj., adv.* for a particular purpose only.

adieu (ə'djuː) *interj., n., pl.* **adieus** *or* **adieux** (ə'djuːz). goodbye.

ad infinitum (æd ,ɪnfɪ'naɪtəm) *adv.* endlessly: *and so on ad infinitum.*

adipose ('ædɪ,pəʊs) *adj.* of or containing fat; fatty: *adipose tissue.*

adj. adjective.

adjacent (ə'dʒeɪs³nt) *adj.* next: *the adjacent room; the house adjacent to ours.*

adjective ('ædʒɪktɪv) *n.* a word that describes a noun or pronoun. —**adjectival** (,ædʒɪk'taɪv³l) *adj.*

adjoin (ə'dʒɔɪn) *vb.* to be next to and joined onto. —**ad**'**joining** *adj.*

adjourn (ə'dʒɜːn) *vb.* **1.** (of a court) to close at the end of a session. **2.** to postpone or be postponed. **3.** *Informal.* to go else-

where: *shall we adjourn to the pub?*
—**ad'journment** *n.*

adjudge (ə'dʒʌdʒ) *vb.* to declare (someone) to be something specified: *he was adjudged guilty.*

adjudicate (ə'dʒuːdɪ,keɪt) *vb.* **1.** to give a formal decision on (a dispute). **2.** to serve as a judge, for example in a competition. —**ad,judi'cation** *n.* —**ad'judi,cator** *n.*

adjunct ('ædʒʌŋkt) *n.* **1.** something added that is not essential. **2.** a person who is subordinate to another.

adjure (ə'dʒʊə) *vb.* **1.** to command (someone) to do something. **2.** to appeal earnestly to (someone). —**adjuration** (,ædʒʊə-'reɪʃən) *n.*

adjust (ə'dʒʌst) *vb.* **1.** to alter (something) slightly, so as to achieve accuracy. **2.** to adapt to a new environment. **3.** to arrange (one's clothing). **4.** *Insurance.* to determine the amount payable in settlement of (a claim). —**ad'justable** *adj.* —**ad'juster** *n.*

adjustment (ə'dʒʌstmənt) *n.* **1.** the act of adjusting. **2.** a slight alteration.

adjutant ('ædʒətənt) *n.* an officer in an army who acts as administrative assistant to a superior.

ad-lib (æd'lɪb) *vb.* **-libbing, -libbed. 1.** to improvise while speaking. *~adj.* **2.** improvised: *an ad-lib remark. ~n.* **3.** an improvised remark. *~adv.* **ad lib. 4.** spontaneously; freely.

Adm. Admiral.

adman ('æd,mæn) *n., pl.* **-men.** *Informal.* a man who works in advertising.

admin ('ædmɪn) *n. Informal.* administration.

administer (əd'mɪnɪstə) *vb.* **1.** to manage (an organization or estate). **2.** to dispense: *administer justice.* **3.** to give (medicine) to someone. **4.** to supervise the taking of (an oath).

administrate (əd'mɪnɪ,streɪt) *vb.* to manage (an organization).

administration (əd,mɪnɪ'streɪʃən) *n.* **1.** management of the affairs of an organization. **2.** the duties of an administrator. **3.** the people who administer an organization. **4.** a government: *the Reagan administration.* **5.** the act of administering something, such as medicine or an oath. —**ad'ministrative** *adj.*

administrator (əd'mɪnɪ,streɪtə) *n.* a person who administers an organization or estate.

admirable ('ædmərəb'l) *adj.* deserving or inspiring admiration; excellent. —**'admirably** *adv.*

admiral ('ædmərəl) *n.* **1.** Also called: **admiral of the fleet.** a naval officer of the highest rank. **2.** any of various brightly coloured butterflies.

Admiralty ('ædmərəltɪ) *n.* the government department in charge of naval affairs.

admire (əd'maɪə) *vb.* to regard (someone or

something) with esteem or approval. —**admiration** (,ædmə'reɪʃən) *n.* —**ad'mirer** *n.* —**ad'miring** *adj.* —**ad'miringly** *adv.*

admissible (əd'mɪsəb'l) *adj. Law.* (of evidence) capable of being admitted in a court of law.

admission (əd'mɪʃən) *n.* **1.** permission or the right to enter. **2.** the price charged for entrance. **3.** acceptance for a position or as a member of an institution. **4.** a confession: *he was, by his own admission, a compulsive gambler.*

admit (əd'mɪt) *vb.* **-mitting, -mitted. 1.** to confess or acknowledge (a crime or mistake). **2.** to concede (the truth of something). **3.** to allow to enter. **4.** (foll. by *to*) to allow (someone) to participate in something. **5. admit of.** to allow for: *his plan does not admit of defeat.*

admittance (əd'mɪt'ns) *n.* **1.** the right to enter. **2.** the act of giving entrance.

admittedly (əd'mɪtɪdlɪ) *adv.* willingly conceded: *admittedly I am afraid.*

admixture (əd'mɪkstʃə) *n.* **1.** a mixture. **2.** an ingredient.

admonish (əd'mɒnɪʃ) *vb.* to reprove (someone) firmly but not harshly. —**admonition** (,ædmə'nɪʃən) *n.* —**ad'monitory** *adj.*

ad nauseam (æd 'nɔːzɪ,æm) *adv.* to a disgusting extent: *she went on and on ad nauseam about her new job.*

ado (ə'duː) *n.* bustling activity; fuss: *without more ado.*

adobe (ə'dəʊbɪ) *n.* **1.** a sun-dried brick. **2.** a building constructed of such bricks. **3.** the clayey material from which such bricks are made.

adolescence (,ædə'lesəns) *n.* the period between puberty and adulthood.

adolescent (,ædə'les°nt) *adj.* **1.** of or relating to adolescence. **2.** *Informal.* (of behaviour) immature. *~n.* **3.** an adolescent person.

Adonis (ə'dəʊnɪs) *n.* a handsome young man.

adopt (ə'dɒpt) *vb.* **1.** *Law.* to take (someone else's child) as one's own. **2.** to choose (a plan or method). **3.** to choose (a country or name) to be one's own. —**a'doption** *n.*

adoptive (ə'dɒptɪv) *adj.* due to adoption: *an adoptive parent.*

adorable (ə'dɔːrəb'l) *adj.* very attractive; lovable.

adore (ə'dɔː) *vb.* **1.** to love (someone) intensely or deeply. **2.** to worship (a god) with religious rites. **3.** *Informal.* to like very much: *I adore chocolate.* —**adoration** (,ædə'reɪʃən) *n.* —**a'doring** *adj.* —**a'doringly** *adv.*

adorn (ə'dɔːn) *vb.* to decorate; increase the beauty or distinction of. —**a'dornment** *n.*

ADP automatic data processing.

adrenal (ə'driːn'l) *adj. Anat.* **1.** on or near

the kidneys. **2.** of or relating to the adrenal glands.

adrenal glands *pl. n. Anat.* two endocrine glands covering the upper surface of the kidneys.

adrenaline *or* **adrenalin** (ə'drɛnəlɪn) *n. Biochem.* a hormone secreted by the adrenal gland in response to stress. It increases heart rate, pulse rate, and blood pressure.

adrift (ə'drɪft) *adj., adv.* **1.** drifting. **2.** without purpose. **3.** *Informal.* off course.

adroit (ə'drɔɪt) *adj.* **1.** skilful or dexterous. **2.** quick: *mentally adroit.* **—a'droitly** *adv.* **—a'droitness** *n.*

adsorb (əd'sɔːb) *vb.* (of a substance such as a gas) to accumulate on the surface of a solid, forming a thin film. **—ad'sorbent** *adj.* **—adsorption** (əd'sɔːpʃən) *n.*

ADT Atlantic Daylight Time.

adulation (ˌædjʊ'leɪʃən) *n.* uncritical admiration.

adult ('ædʌlt, ə'dʌlt) *n.* **1.** a mature fully grown person, animal, or plant. *~adj.* **2.** having reached maturity; fully developed. **3.** of or intended for mature people. **—'adulthood** *n.*

adulterant (ə'dʌltərənt) *n.* **1.** a substance that adulterates. *~adj.* **2.** adulterating.

adulterate (ə'dʌltə,reɪt) *vb.* to debase (something) by adding inferior material. **—a,dulter'ation** *n.*

adulterer (ə'dʌltərə) *or (fem.)* **adulteress** *n.* a person who has committed adultery.

adultery (ə'dʌltərɪ) *n., pl.* **-teries.** sexual intercourse between a married person and someone other than his or her spouse. **—a'dulterous** *adj.*

adumbrate ('ædʌm,breɪt) *vb.* **1.** to give a faint indication of. **2.** to obscure. **—,adum'bration** *n.*

adv. adverb.

ad valorem (æd və'lɔːrəm) *adj., adv.* (of taxes) in proportion to the estimated value of the goods taxed.

advance (əd'vɑːns) *vb.* **1.** to go or bring forward. **2.** (foll. by *on*) to move towards (someone) in a threatening manner. **3.** to present (an idea) for consideration. **4.** to further (a cause). **5.** to lend (someone a sum of money). *~n.* **6.** a forward movement. **7.** improvement. **8.** a payment made before it is legally due. **9.** a loan of money. **10.** an increase in price: *any advance on fifty pounds?* **11. in advance. a.** beforehand. **b.** (foll. by *of*) ahead of in time or development. **12.** (*modifier*) previous: *advance booking.* —See also **advances.**

advanced (əd'vɑːnst) *adj.* **1.** ahead in development, knowledge, or progress. **2.** in a comparatively late stage: *a man of advanced age.*

Advanced level *n.* a formal name for A level.

advancement (əd'vɑːnsmənt) *n.* promotion in rank or status.

advances (əd'vɑːnsɪz) *pl. n.* overtures made in an attempt to start a romantic or sexual relationship with someone.

advantage (əd'vɑːntɪdʒ) *n.* **1.** a more favourable position; superiority. **2.** benefit or profit: *to my advantage.* **3.** *Tennis.* the point scored after deuce. **4. take advantage of. a.** to make good use of. **b.** to impose upon the weakness or good nature of. **c.** to seduce. **5. to advantage.** to good effect.

advantaged (əd'vɑːntɪdʒd) *adj.* in a superior social or financial position.

advantageous (ˌædvən'teɪdʒəs) *adj.* producing advantage. **—,advan'tageously** *adv.*

advection (əd'vɛkʃən) *n.* the transference of heat in a horizontal stream of gas.

advent ('ædvənt) *n.* an arrival: *before the advent of television.*

Advent ('ædvənt) *n.* the season that includes the four Sundays preceding Christmas.

Adventist ('ædvəntɪst) *n.* a member of a Christian group that believes that the Second Coming of Christ is imminent.

adventitious (ˌædvɛn'tɪʃəs) *adj.* added or appearing accidentally.

adventure (əd'vɛntʃə) *n.* **1.** a risky undertaking of unknown outcome. **2.** exciting or unexpected events.

adventure playground *n. Brit.* a playground for children that contains building materials and other equipment to build with or climb on.

adventurer (əd'vɛntʃərə) *or (fem.)* **adventuress** *n.* **1.** a person who seeks adventure. **2.** a person who seeks money or power by unscrupulous means.

adventurism (əd'vɛntʃə,rɪzəm) *n.* recklessness in politics or finance.

adventurous (əd'vɛntʃərəs) *adj.* daring or enterprising.

adverb ('ædvɜːb) *n.* a word that modifies a sentence, verb, adverb, or adjective, for example *easily, very,* and *happily* in *They could easily envy the very happily married couple.* **—ad'verbial** *adj.*

adversary ('ædvəsərɪ) *n., pl.* **-saries.** an opponent in a fight, disagreement, or sporting contest.

adverse ('ædvɜːs) *adj.* **1.** antagonistic; hostile. **2.** unfavourable to one's interests: *adverse circumstances.* **—'adversely** *adv.*

adversity (əd'vɜːsɪtɪ) *n., pl.* **-ties.** affliction; hardship.

advert ('ædvɜːt) *n. Informal.* an advertisement.

advertise ('ædvə,taɪz) *vb.* **1.** to present or praise (goods or a service) to the public, in order to encourage sales. **2.** to make (a vacancy, an event, or an article for sale) publicly known. —**'adver,tiser** n. —**'adver,tising** n.

advertisement (əd'vɜːtɪsmənt) n. any public announcement designed to sell goods or publicize an event.

advice (əd'vaɪs) n. **1.** recommendation as to appropriate choice of action. **2.** formal notification of facts.

advisable (əd'vaɪzəb'l) adj. worthy of recommendation; prudent. —**ad,visa'bility** n.

advise (əd'vaɪz) vb. **1.** to offer advice to (someone). **2.** to inform or notify (someone). —**ad'viser** or **ad'visor** n.

advisedly (əd'vaɪzɪdlɪ) adv. deliberately; after careful consideration: I use the word advisedly.

advisory (əd'vaɪzərɪ) adj. empowered to make recommendations.

advocaat ('ædvəʊ,kɑː) n. a liqueur with a raw egg base.

advocacy ('ædvəkəsɪ) n. active support of a cause or course of action.

advocate vb. ('ædvə,keɪt). **1.** to recommend (a course of action) publicly. ~n. ('ædvəkɪt). **2.** a person who upholds or defends a cause or course of action. **3.** a person who speaks on behalf of another in a court of law. **4.** Scots Law. a barrister.

adze or U.S. **adz** (ædz) n. a tool with a blade at right angles to the handle, used for shaping timber.

AEA Atomic Energy Authority.

AEC U.S. Atomic Energy Commission.

aegis ('iːdʒɪs) n. **under the aegis of.** with the sponsorship or protection of.

aeolian harp (iː'əʊlɪən) n. a musical instrument that produces sounds when the wind passes over its strings.

aeon or U.S. **eon** ('iːən) n. **1.** an immeasurably long period of time. **2.** the longest division of geological time; two or more eras.

aerate ('ɛəreɪt) vb. to put gas into (a liquid), for example when making fizzy drinks. —**aer'ation** n.

aerial ('ɛərɪəl) adj. **1.** existing, moving, or operating in the air. **2.** extending high into the air. **3.** of or relating to aircraft. ~n. **4.** the part of a radio or television system which transmits or receives radio waves.

aero ('ɛərəʊ) n. (modifier) of or relating to aircraft or aeronautics.

aero-, aeri-, or **aer-** combining form. **1.** denoting air, atmosphere, or gas. **2.** denoting aircraft.

aerobatics (,ɛərəʊ'bætɪks) n. (functioning as sing. or pl.) spectacular manoeuvres, such as loops or rolls, performed by aircraft.

aerobic (ɛə'rəʊbɪk) adj. designed for or relating to aerobics: aerobic shoes; aerobic dances.

aerobics (ɛə'rəʊbɪks) n. (functioning as sing.) exercises to increase the amount of oxygen in the blood and strengthen the heart and lungs.

aerodrome ('ɛərə,drəʊm) n. a small airport.

aerodynamics (,ɛərəʊdaɪ'næmɪks) n. (functioning as sing.) the study of the dynamics of air and gases and of bodies passing through air. —**,aerody'namic** adj.

aero engine n. an engine for an aircraft.

aerofoil ('ɛərəʊ,fɔɪl) n. a cross section of the wing, fin, or rotor blade of an aircraft.

aerogram ('ɛərə,græm) n. an air-mail letter on a single sheet of light paper that folds and is sealed to form an envelope.

aerolite ('ɛərə,laɪt) n. a stony meteorite.

aeronautics (,ɛərə'nɔːtɪks) n. (functioning as sing.) the study or practice of flight through the air. —**,aero'nautical** adj.

aeroplane ('ɛərə,pleɪn) or U.S. & Canad. **airplane** n. a heavier-than-air powered flying vehicle with fixed wings.

aerosol ('ɛərə,sɒl) n. a small metal pressurized container from which a substance can be dispensed in a fine spray.

aerospace ('ɛərə,speɪs) n. **1.** the earth's atmosphere and space beyond. **2.** (modifier) of rockets or space vehicles: the aerospace industry.

aerostatics (,ɛərə'stætɪks) n. (functioning as sing.) the study of gases in equilibrium and bodies held in equilibrium in gases.

aesthete or U.S. **esthete** ('iːsθiːt) n. a person who has or who affects a highly developed appreciation of beauty.

aesthetic or U.S. **esthetic** (ɪs'θɛtɪk) adj. relating to the appreciation of art and beauty. —**aes'thetically** or U.S. **es'thetically** adv. —**aestheticism** or U.S. **estheticism** (ɪs'θɛtɪ,sɪzəm) n.

aesthetics or U.S. **esthetics** (ɪs'θɛtɪks) n. (functioning as sing.) **1.** the branch of philosophy concerned with the study of the concepts of beauty and taste. **2.** the study of the rules and principles of art.

aether ('iːθə) n. same as **ether** (senses 2, 3).

a.f. audio frequency.

afar (ə'fɑː) n. **from afar.** from a great distance.

affable ('æfəb'l) adj. showing warmth and friendliness; easy to talk to. —**,affa'bility** n. —**'affably** adv.

affair (ə'fɛə) n. **1.** a thing to be done or attended to: it's not my affair. **2.** an event or happening: the Profumo affair. **3.** something previously specified: our house is a tumbledown affair. **4.** a sexual relationship outside marriage.

affairs (ə'fɛəz) pl. n. **1.** personal or business interests. **2.** matters of public interest: current affairs.

affect[1] (ə'fɛkt) vb. **1.** to influence (someone or something): *the postal strike will affect us all.* **2.** to move (someone) emotionally: *I was deeply affected by that film.* **3.** (of pain or disease) to attack: *measles affects mainly children.*

affect² (ə'fɛkt) *vb.* **1.** to put on a show of: *to affect ignorance.* **2.** to wear or use by preference: *he affects a white straw hat.*

affectation (ˌæfɛk'teɪʃən) *n.* an attitude or manner put on to impress others.

affected (ə'fɛktɪd) *adj.* **1.** behaving or speaking in a manner put on to impress others. **2.** pretended: *affected indifference.*

affecting (ə'fɛktɪŋ) *adj.* arousing feelings of pity; moving.

affection (ə'fɛkʃən) *n.* **1.** fondness or tenderness for a person or thing. **2.** (*pl.*) emotions: *to play on his affections.*

affectionate (ə'fɛkʃənɪt) *adj.* having or displaying tenderness, affection, or warmth. —**af'fectionately** *adv.*

affianced (ə'faɪənst) *adj. Old-fashioned.* engaged to be married.

affidavit (ˌæfɪ'deɪvɪt) *n. Law.* a declaration in writing made upon oath.

affiliate *vb.* (ə'fɪlɪˌeɪt). **1.** (foll. by *to* or *with*) to bring (someone) into close connection or association with a larger body or group. ~*n.* (ə'fɪlɪt). **2.** a person or organization that is affiliated with another. —**af₁fili'ation** *n.*

affiliation order *n. Law.* an order that the father of an illegitimate child shall contribute towards the child's maintenance.

affinity (ə'fɪnɪtɪ) *n., pl.* **-ties. 1.** a feeling of closeness to and understanding of a person. **2.** a close similarity in appearance, structure, or quality.

affirm (ə'fɜːm) *vb.* **1.** to declare (something) to be true. **2.** to uphold or confirm (an idea or a belief). —**affirmation** (ˌæfə-'meɪʃən) *n.*

affirmative (ə'fɜːmətɪv) *adj.* **1.** indicating agreement: *an affirmative reply.* ~*n.* **2.** a word or phrase indicating agreement, such as *yes.*

affix *vb.* (ə'fɪks). **1.** to attach or fasten. ~*n.* ('æfɪks). **2.** a word or syllable added to a word to produce a derived or inflected form, as *-ment* in *establishment.*

afflict (ə'flɪkt) *vb.* to cause (someone) suffering or unhappiness.

affliction (ə'flɪkʃən) *n.* **1.** a condition of great distress or suffering. **2.** something that causes physical or mental suffering.

affluent ('æfluənt) *adj.* rich; wealthy. —**'affluence** *n.*

affluent society *n.* a society in which the material benefits of prosperity are widely available.

afford (ə'fɔːd) *vb.* **1.** (preceded by *can* or *could*) to be able to do or spare something without risking financial difficulties or undesirable consequences. **2.** to give or sup-

ply: *the union affords us some protection.* —**af'fordable** *adj.*

afforest (ə'fɒrɪst) *vb.* to plant trees on. —**af₁forest'ation** *n.*

affray (ə'freɪ) *n.* a noisy fight in a public place.

affront (ə'frʌnt) *n.* **1.** a deliberate insult. ~*vb.* **2.** to insult; offend the pride or dignity of.

Afghan ('æfgæn) *n.* **1.** a person from Afghanistan. ~*adj.* **2.** of Afghanistan or its people.

Afghan hound *n.* a large slim dog with long silky hair.

aficionado (ə,fɪʃjə'nɑːdəʊ) *n., pl.* **-dos.** a devotee of some sport or pastime.

afield (ə'fiːld) *adv.* **far afield.** far away.

aflame (ə'fleɪm) *adv., adj.* **1.** in flames. **2.** deeply aroused: *aflame with desire.*

afloat (ə'fləʊt) *adj., adv.* **1.** floating. **2.** aboard ship; at sea. **3.** free of debt: *to keep the business afloat.*

afoot (ə'fʊt) *adj., adv.* in operation; astir: *there's trouble afoot.*

afore (ə'fɔː) *adv., prep., conj. Archaic* or *dialect.* before.

aforementioned (ə'fɔːˌmɛnʃənd) *adj.* mentioned before.

aforesaid (ə'fɔːˌsɛd) *adj.* referred to previously.

aforethought (ə'fɔːˌθɔːt) *adj.* premeditated: *malice aforethought.*

a fortiori (eɪ ˌfɔːtɪ'ɔːraɪ) *adv.* for similar but more convincing reasons.

Afr. Africa(n).

afraid (ə'freɪd) *adj.* **1.** feeling fear or apprehension. **2.** regretful: *I'm afraid I can't help you.*

afresh (ə'frɛʃ) *adv.* once more; anew.

African ('æfrɪkən) *adj.* **1.** of Africa or its peoples or languages. ~*n.* **2.** a person from Africa.

Africana (ˌæfrɪ'kɑːnə) *n.* objects of cultural or historical interest from Africa.

Africander (ˌæfrɪ'kændə) *n.* a breed of humpbacked cattle originally from southern Africa.

African lily *n.* a S African plant with blue or white funnel-shaped flowers.

African time *n. S. African slang.* unpunctuality.

African violet *n.* a flowering house plant with hairy leaves.

Afrikaans (ˌæfrɪ'kɑːns, -'kɑːnz) *n.* an official language of South Africa, closely related to Dutch and Flemish.

Afrikaner (ˌæfrɪ'kɑːnə) *n.* a White native of South Africa whose native language is Afrikaans.

Afro ('æfrəʊ) *n., pl.* **-ros.** a wide frizzy bushy hairstyle.

Afro- *combining form.* indicating Africa or African: *Afro-Asiatic.*

Afro-American *n.* **1.** an American Black. ~*adj.* **2.** of American Blacks, their history, or their culture.

aft (ɑːft) *adv., adj. Chiefly naut.* towards or at the rear.

after (ˈɑːftə) *prep.* **1.** following in time or place. **2.** in pursuit of: *he's only after your money.* **3.** concerning: *to inquire after someone's health.* **4.** considering: *after what you have done, you shouldn't complain.* **5.** next in excellence or importance to. **6.** in imitation of; in the manner of. **7.** in accordance with: *a man after my own heart.* **8.** the same name as: *I'm called after my grandmother.* **9.** *U.S.* past (the hour of): *twenty after three.* **10. after all. a.** in spite of everything: *it's only a game after all.* **b.** in spite of expectations or efforts. **11. after you.** please go before me. ~*adv.* **12.** at a later time; afterwards. ~*conj.* **13.** at a time later than the time when: *after they left, the party really livened up.* ~*adj.* **14.** *Naut.* further aft: *the after cabin.*

afterbirth (ˈɑːftəˌbɜːθ) *n.* the placenta and fetal membranes expelled from the mother's womb after the birth of a baby or young animal.

aftercare (ˈɑːftəˌkɛə) *n.* the help and support given to a person discharged from a hospital or prison.

afterdamp (ˈɑːftəˌdæmp) *n.* a poisonous gas formed after the explosion of firedamp in a coal mine.

aftereffect (ˈɑːftərɪˌfɛkt) *n.* any result occurring some time after its cause.

afterglow (ˈɑːftəˌgləʊ) *n.* **1.** the glow left after the source of a light has disappeared, for example after sunset. **2.** a pleasant feeling remaining after an enjoyable experience.

afterlife (ˈɑːftəˌlaɪf) *n.* life after death or at a later time in a person's lifetime.

aftermath (ˈɑːftəˌmæθ) *n.* signs or results of an event considered collectively: *the aftermath of war.*

aftermost (ˈɑːftəˌməʊst) *adj.* closest to the rear; last.

afternoon (ˌɑːftəˈnuːn) *n.* the period between noon and evening.

afterpains (ˈɑːftəˌpeɪnz) *pl. n.* pains caused by contraction of a woman's womb after childbirth.

afters (ˈɑːftəz) *n. Brit. informal.* dessert; sweet.

aftershave (ˈɑːftəˌʃeɪv) *n.* a scented lotion applied to a man's face after shaving.

aftershock (ˈɑːftəˌʃɒk) *n.* one of a series of minor tremors occurring after the main shock of an earthquake.

aftertaste (ˈɑːftəˌteɪst) *n.* a taste that lingers on after eating or drinking.

afterthought (ˈɑːftəˌθɔːt) *n.* **1.** something

thought of after the opportunity to use it has passed. **2.** an addition to something already completed.

afterwards (ˈɑːftəwədz) *or* **afterward** *adv.* after an earlier event or time.

Ag *Chem.* silver.

again (əˈgɛn, əˈgeɪn) *adv.* **1.** another or a second time: *do it again.* **2.** once more in a previously experienced state or condition: *here we are again.* **3.** in addition to the original amount: *half as much again.* **4.** on the other hand. **5.** moreover; furthermore. **6. again and again.** continually; repeatedly.

against (əˈgɛnst, əˈgeɪnst) *prep.* **1.** standing or leaning beside: *a ladder against the wall.* **2.** coming in contact with: *he bumped against me.* **3.** in contrast to: *silhouettes are outlines against a light background.* **4.** opposed to; in disagreement with. **5.** having an unfavourable effect on: *the system works against small companies.* **6.** as a protection from: *a safeguard against contaminated water.* **7.** in exchange for. **8. as against.** as opposed to; as compared with.

agape (əˈgeɪp) *adj.* **1.** (of the mouth) wide open. **2.** (of a person) very surprised.

agar (ˈeɪgə) *or* **agar-agar** *n.* a jelly-like substance obtained from certain seaweeds and used as a culture medium for bacteria and for thickening food.

agaric (ˈægərɪk) *n.* any fungus with gills on the underside of the cap, for example the edible mushroom.

agate (ˈægɪt) *n.* a hard semiprecious form of quartz with striped colouring.

agave (əˈgeɪvɪ) *n.* a tropical Amercian plant with tall flower stalks rising from thick fleshy leaves.

age (eɪdʒ) *n.* **1.** the period of time that a person, animal, or plant has lived. **2.** the period of time that something, such as an object or group, has existed. **3.** a period or state of human life. **4.** the latter part of human life. **5.** a period of history marked by some feature. **6.** (*pl.*) *Informal.* a long time. **7. come of age.** to become legally responsible for one's actions (usually at 18 years). ~*vb.* **ageing** *or* **aging, aged. 7.** to become old. **9.** to begin to seem older or cause (someone) to seem older: *she has aged a lot in the past year; that hairstyle ages her.*

-age *suffix forming nouns.* indicating: **1.** a collection or set: *baggage.* **2.** an action or its result: *breakage.* **3.** a state or relationship: *bondage.* **4.** a house or place: *orphanage.* **5.** a charge or rate: *postage.*

aged *adj.* **1.** (ˈeɪdʒɪd). advanced in years; old. **2.** (eɪdʒd). having the age of: *a woman aged twenty.*

ageing *or* **aging** (ˈeɪdʒɪŋ) *n.* **1.** the fact or process of growing old. ~*adj.* **2.** becoming or appearing older.

ageless (ˈeɪdʒlɪs) *adj.* **1.** apparently never growing old. **2.** timeless; eternal.

agency (ˈeɪdʒənsɪ) *n., pl.* **-cies. 1.** an organization providing a specific service: *an employment agency.* **2.** the business or functions of an agent. **3.** *Old-fashioned.* action or power: *we met through the agency of fate.*

agenda (əˈdʒɛndə) *n.* a schedule or list of items to be attended to, for example at a meeting.

agent (ˈeɪdʒənt) *n.* **1.** a person who acts on behalf of another person or organization. **2.** a person or thing that is the means or cause of something happening. **3.** a substance or organism that exerts some force or effect: *a chemical agent.* **4.** a travelling salesman.

agent provocateur (ˈæʒɒn prəˌvɒkəˈtɜː) *n., pl agents provocateurs* (ˈæʒɒn prəˌvɒkəˈtɜː). a secret agent who provokes people to commit illegal acts and so be discredited or liable to punishment.

age-old *adj.* very old; ancient.

agglomerate *vb.* (əˈglɒməˌreɪt). **1.** to form or be formed into a mass. ~*n.* (əˈglɒmərɪt). **2.** a confused mass. **3.** a volcanic rock consisting of fused angular fragments of rock. ~*adj.* (əˈglɒmərɪt). **4.** formed into a mass. —**agˌglomerˈation** *n.*

agglutinate (əˈgluːtɪˌneɪt) *vb.* to stick with or as if with glue. —**agglutination** (əˌgluːtɪˈneɪʃən) *n.*

aggrandize *or* **-dise** (əˈgrændaɪz) *vb.* to increase the power, wealth, prestige, or scope of. —**aggrandizement** *or* **-disement** (əˈgrændɪzmənt) *n.*

aggravate (ˈægrəˌveɪt) *vb.* **1.** to make (a disease, situation or problem) worse. **2.** *Informal.* to annoy. —**ˈaggraˌvating** *adj.* —ˌaggraˈvation *n.*

aggregate *n.* (ˈægrɪgɪt). **1.** an amount or total formed from separate units. **2.** *Geol.* a rock, such as granite, consisting of a mixture of minerals. **3.** the sand and stone mixed with cement and water to make concrete. **4. in the aggregate.** taken as a whole. ~*adj.* (ˈægrɪgɪt). **5.** formed of separate units collected into a whole. ~*vb.* (ˈægrɪˌgeɪt). **6.** to combine or be combined into a whole. **7.** to amount to (a particular number). —ˌaggreˈgation *n.*

aggression (əˈgrɛʃən) *n.* a tendency to make unprovoked attacks or an instance of unprovoked attack. —**agˈgressor** *n.*

aggressive (əˈgrɛsɪv) *adj.* **1.** quarrelsome or belligerent. **2.** assertive; vigorous. —**agˈgressively** *adv.*

aggrieved (əˈgriːvd) *adj.* upset and angry.

aggro (ˈægrəʊ) *n. Brit. slang.* aggressive behaviour.

aghast (əˈgɑːst) *adj.* overcome with amazement or horror.

agile (ˈædʒaɪl) *adj.* **1.** quick in movement; nimble. **2.** mentally quick or acute. —**agility** (əˈdʒɪlɪtɪ) *n.*

agin (əˈgɪn) *prep. Informal or dialect.* against: *I'm agin capital punishment.*

agitate (ˈædʒɪˌteɪt) *vb.* **1.** to excite, disturb, or trouble (someone). **2.** to shake, stir, or disturb (a liquid). **3.** to attempt to stir up public opinion for or against something. —**ˈagiˌtated** *adj.* —**ˈagiˌtatedly** *adv.* —**agitation** (ˌædʒɪˈteɪʃən) *n.* —**ˈagiˌtator** *n.*

agitprop (ˈædʒɪtˌprɒp) *n.* any promotion of political propaganda.

agley (əˈglaɪ) *adv. Scot.* awry; askew.

aglitter (əˈglɪtə) *adj.* sparkling; glittering.

aglow *or* (əˈgləʊ) *adj.* glowing.

aglu *or* **agloo** (ˈægluː) *n. Canad.* a breathing hole made in ice by a seal.

AGM annual general meeting.

agnostic (ægˈnɒstɪk) *n.* **1.** a person who believes that it is impossible to know whether God exists. **2.** a person who claims that the answer to some specific question cannot be known with certainty. ~*adj.* **3.** of or relating to agnostics. —**agnosticism** (ægˈnɒstɪˌsɪzəm) *n.*

ago (əˈgəʊ) *adv.* in the past: *years ago.*
Usage. Ago should not be followed by *since* (*It's ten years ago since she wrote the novel*) because both words mean the same. It is correct either to use *since*: *it's ten years since she wrote the novel* or to use *ago* followed by *that*: *it's ten years ago that she wrote the novel.*

agog (əˈgɒg) *adj.* eager or curious.

agonize *or* **-nise** (ˈægəˌnaɪz) *vb.* **1.** to suffer or cause (someone) to suffer agony. **2.** to struggle; strive. —**ˈagoˌnizing** *or* **-ˌnising** *adj.* —**ˈagoˌnizingly** *or* **-ˌnisingly** *adv.*

agony (ˈægənɪ) *n., pl.* **-nies.** acute physical or mental pain.

agony aunt *n.* a person who replies to readers' letters in an agony column.

agony column *n.* a newspaper or magazine feature offering advice on readers' personal problems.

agoraphobia (ˌægərəˈfəʊbɪə) *n.* an illogical fear of open spaces. —ˌagoraˈphobic *adj., n.*

AGR advanced gas-cooled reactor.

agrarian (əˈgrɛərɪən) *adj.* of or relating to land or agriculture. —**aˈgrarianism** *n.*

agree (əˈgriː) *vb.* **agreeing, agreed. 1.** (often foll. by *with*) to be of the same opinion (as). **2.** to give assent; consent. **3.** to reach a joint decision: *we agreed on a price for the car.* **4.** (foll. by *with*) to be consistent with. **5.** (foll. by *with*) to be agreeable or suitable to (one's health or appearance): *prawns don't agree with me.* **6.** to concede: *they agreed that the price was too high.* **7.** *Grammar.* to be the same in number, gender, and case as a connected word.

agreeable (ə'griːəb'l) *adj.* **1.** pleasing; pleasant. **2.** prepared to consent: *we would like to move in right away if you are agreeable.* —a'**greeably** *adv.*

agreement (ə'griːmənt) *n.* **1.** the act or state of agreeing. **2.** a settlement, esp. one that is legally enforceable, or the document containing it.

agriculture ('ægrɪ,kʌltʃə) *n.* the rearing of crops and livestock; farming. —,**agri'cultural** *adj.* —,**agri'culturalist** *n.*

agrimony ('ægrɪmənɪ) *n.* a plant with long spikes of small yellow flowers and bristly burlike fruits.

agronomy (ə'grɒnəmɪ) *n.* the science of land cultivation, soil management, and crop production. —a'**gronomist** *n.*

aground (ə'graʊnd) *adv.* onto the ground: *the ship ran aground.*

ague ('eɪgjuː) *n.* **1.** malarial fever with successive stages of fever and chills. **2.** a fit of shivering.

ah (ɑː) *interj.* an exclamation expressing pleasure, pain, sympathy, etc., according to the intonation of the speaker.

aha (ɑː'hɑː) *interj.* an exclamation expressing triumph, surprise, etc., according to the intonation of the speaker.

ahead (ə'hɛd) *adv.* **1.** at or in the front; before. **2.** forwards: *go straight ahead.* **3. get ahead.** to achieve success. ~*adj.* **4.** in a leading position: *Cram is ahead with one lap to go.*

ahem (ə'hɛm) *interj.* a clearing of the throat, used to attract attention or express doubt.

ahoy (ə'hɔɪ) *interj. Naut.* a hail used to call a ship or to attract attention.

AI 1. artificial insemination. **2.** artificial intelligence.

aid (eɪd) *vb.* **1.** to help financially or in other ways. ~*n.* **2.** assistance; help; support. **3.** a person or device that helps or assists.

Aid *or* **-aid** *n. combining form.* denoting a charitable organization that raises money for a particular cause: *Band Aid; Ferryaid.*

AID artificial insemination by donor.

aide (eɪd) *n.* an assistant: *the President's aides.*

aide-de-camp ('eɪd də 'kɒŋ) *n., pl.* **aides-de-camp.** a military officer serving as personal assistant to a senior.

AIDS (eɪdz) acquired immunodeficiency syndrome: a viral disease that destroys the body's ability to fight infection.

AIH artificial insemination by husband.

ail (eɪl) *vb. Literary.* **1.** to trouble; afflict. **2.** to feel unwell.

aileron ('eɪlərɒn) *n.* a hinged flap on the back of an aircraft wing which controls rolling.

ailing ('eɪlɪŋ) *adj.* unwell over a long period.

ailment ('eɪlmənt) *n.* a slight illness.

aim (eɪm) *vb.* **1.** to point (a weapon or missile) or direct (a blow or remark) at a particular person or object. **2.** to propose or intend: *I aim to finish by Friday.* ~*n.* **3.** the action of directing something at an object. **4. take aim.** to point a weapon or missile at a person or object. **5.** intention; purpose.

aimless ('eɪmlɪs) *adj.* having no purpose or direction. —'**aimlessly** *adv.*

ain't (eɪnt) *Not standard.* am not, is not, are not, have not, *or* has not: *I ain't seen it.*

air (ɛə) *n.* **1.** the mixture of gases that forms the earth's atmosphere. It consists chiefly of nitrogen, oxygen, argon, and carbon dioxide. **2.** the space above and around the earth; sky. **3.** a breeze; slight wind. **4.** a distinctive quality, appearance, or manner: *an air of authority.* **5.** a simple tune. **6.** transportation in aircraft: *we're going by air.* **7. in the air.** in circulation; current: *there's a rumour in the air.* **8. into thin air.** leaving no trace behind. **9. on the air.** in the act of broadcasting on radio or television. **10. up in the air.** uncertain. ~*vb.* **11.** to let fresh air into (a room) so as to cool or freshen it. **12.** to expose or be exposed to warm or heated air so as to dry: *to air linen.* **13.** to make known publicly: *to air one's opinions.* ~See also **airs.**

air base *n.* a centre from which military aircraft operate.

airborne ('ɛə,bɔːn) *adj.* **1.** carried by air. **2.** (of aircraft) flying; in the air.

air brake *n.* a brake in heavy vehicles that is operated by compressed air.

airbrick ('ɛə,brɪk) *n. Chiefly Brit.* a brick with holes in it, put into the wall of a building for ventilation.

airbus ('ɛə,bʌs) *n.* a short-distance airliner.

air chief marshal *n.* a very senior officer in an air force.

air commodore *n.* a senior officer in an air force.

air conditioning *n.* a system for controlling the temperature and humidity of the air in a building. —'**air-con,ditioned** *adj.* —**air conditioner** *n.*

aircraft ('ɛə,krɑːft) *n., pl.* -**craft.** any machine capable of flying, such as a glider or aeroplane.

aircraft carrier *n.* a warship with a long flat deck for the launching and landing of aircraft.

aircraftman ('ɛə,krɑːftmən) *n., pl.* -**men.** a serviceman of the most junior rank in an air force. —'**aircraft,woman** *fem. n.*

air cushion *n.* **1.** an inflatable cushion. **2.** the pocket of air that supports a hovercraft.

Airedale ('ɛə,deɪl) *n.* a large rough-haired tan-coloured terrier with a black back.

airfield ('ɛə,fiːld) *n.* a landing and taking-off area for aircraft.

air force *n.* the branch of a nation's armed services that is responsible for air warfare.

air gun *n.* a gun fired by means of compressed air.

air hostess *n.* a stewardess on an airliner.

airily ('ɛərɪlɪ) *adv.* 1. in a jaunty or high-spirited manner. 2. in a light or delicate manner.

airing ('ɛərɪŋ) *n.* 1. exposure to air or warmth for drying or ventilation. 2. exposure to public debate: *I shall give my proposal an airing at tomorrow's meeting.*

airing cupboard *n.* a heated cupboard in which laundry is aired and kept dry.

airless ('ɛəlɪs) *adj.* lacking fresh air; stuffy.

air letter *n.* same as **aerogram.**

airlift ('ɛə,lɪft) *n.* 1. the transportation by air of troops or cargo when other routes are blocked. ~*vb.* 2. to transport by an airlift.

airline ('ɛə,laɪn) *n.* an organization that provides scheduled flights for passengers or cargo.

airliner ('ɛə,laɪnə) *n.* a large passenger aircraft.

airlock ('ɛə,lɒk) *n.* 1. a bubble in a pipe causing an obstruction. 2. an airtight chamber used to gain access to a space that has air under pressure in it.

air mail *n.* 1. the system of conveying mail by aircraft. 2. mail conveyed by aircraft.

airman ('ɛəmən) *n., pl.* **-men.** a man serving in an air force.

air marshal *n.* 1. a senior Royal Air Force officer of equivalent rank to a vice admiral in the Royal Navy. 2. a Royal New Zealand Air Force officer of the highest rank when chief of defence forces.

airplane ('ɛə,pleɪn) *n. U.S. & Canad.* an aeroplane.

airplay ('ɛə,pleɪ) *n.* (of a gramophone record) the fact of being played on radio.

air pocket *n.* a small descending air current that causes an aircraft to lose height suddenly.

airport ('ɛə,pɔːt) *n.* a landing and taking-off area for civil aircraft, with facilities for aircraft maintenance and passenger arrival and departure.

air pump *n.* a device for pumping air into or out of something.

air raid *n.* an attack by enemy aircraft.

air rifle *n.* a rifle fired by means of compressed air.

airs (ɛəz) *pl. n.* manners put on to impress people: *to put on airs.*

airship ('ɛə,ʃɪp) *n.* a lighter-than-air self-propelled aircraft.

airsick ('ɛə,sɪk) *adj.* nauseated from travelling in an aircraft.

airspace ('ɛə,speɪs) *n.* the atmosphere above a particular country.

airspeed ('ɛə,spiːd) *n.* the speed of an aircraft relative to the air in which it moves.

airstrip ('ɛə,strɪp) *n.* a cleared area for the landing and taking-off of aircraft.

air terminal *n.* a building in a city from which air passengers are transported to an airport.

airtight ('ɛə,taɪt) *adj.* 1. sealed so that air cannot enter. 2. having no weak points: *an airtight argument.*

air vice-marshal *n.* a senior officer in an air force.

airwaves ('ɛə,weɪvz) *pl. n. Informal.* radio waves used in radio and television broadcasting.

airy ('ɛərɪ) *adj.* **airier, airiest.** 1. (of a room or building) spacious and well ventilated. 2. jaunty; nonchalant. 3. fanciful; insubstantial: *airy promises.*

aisle (aɪl) *n.* a passageway separating seating areas in a church, theatre, or cinema, or separating rows of shelves in a supermarket.

aitch (eɪtʃ) *n.* the letter *h.*

aitchbone ('eɪtʃ,bəʊn) *n.* a cut of beef from the rump bone.

ajar (ə'dʒɑː) *adj., adv.* (of a door) slightly open.

AK Alaska.

akimbo (ə'kɪmbəʊ) *adv.* (**with**) **arms akimbo.** with hands on hips and elbows turned out.

akin (ə'kɪn) *adj.* **akin to.** similar to; very close to: *that is akin to murder.*

Al *Chem.* aluminium.

AL *or* **Ala.** Alabama.

à la (ɑː lɑː) *prep.* 1. in the manner or style of. 2. as prepared in, by, or for.

alabaster ('ælə,bɑːstə) *n.* a kind of white stone used for making statues and vases.

à la carte (ɑː lɑː 'kɑːt) *adj., adv.* (of a menu) having dishes individually priced.

alacrity (ə'lækrɪtɪ) *n.* speed; eagerness: *we accepted with alacrity.*

à la mode (ɑː lɑː 'məʊd) *adj.* fashionable.

alarm (ə'lɑːm) *n.* 1. fear aroused by awareness of danger. 2. a noise warning of danger: *sound the alarm.* 3. a device that transmits a warning, such as the bell or buzzer in an alarm clock. 4. short for **alarm clock.** ~*vb.* 5. to fill (someone) with fear. 6. to warn (someone) about danger. —a'**larming** *adj.*

alarm clock *n.* a clock that sounds at a set time to wake a person up.

alarmist (ə'lɑːmɪst) *n.* 1. a person who alarms others needlessly. ~*adj.* 2. alarming others needlessly.

alas (ə'læs) *adv.* 1. unfortunately; regret-

tably: *there were, alas, none left.* ~*interj.*
2. *Archaic.* an exclamation of grief or alarm.

Alas. Alaska.

alb (ælb) *n.* a long white linen robe worn by a Christian priest.

albacore ('ælbə,kɔː) *n.* a sea fish with very long pectoral fins that is a valued food fish.

albatross ('ælbə,trɒs) *n.* a large bird of cool southern oceans that has very long wings.

albeit (ɔːl'biːt) *conj.* even though.

albino (æl'biːnəʊ) *n., pl.* **-nos.** a person or animal with white or almost white hair and skin and pinkish eyes. —**albinism** ('ælbɪ,nɪzəm) *n.*

Albion ('ælbɪən) *n. Archaic or poetic.* Britain or England.

album ('ælbəm) *n.* **1.** a book with blank pages, for keeping photographs or stamps in. **2.** a long-playing record.

albumen ('ælbjʊmɪn) *n.* **1.** egg white. **2.** *Biochem.* same as **albumin.**

albumin *or* **albumen** ('ælbjʊmɪn) *n. Biochem.* a water-soluble protein found in blood plasma, egg white, milk, and muscle.

alchemy ('ælkəmɪ) *n.* a medieval form of chemistry concerned with trying to change base metals into gold and to find an elixir to prolong life indefinitely. —'**alchemist** *n.*

alcohol ('ælkə,hɒl) *n.* **1.** a colourless flammable liquid, the active principle of intoxicating drinks. **2.** intoxicating drinks generally.

alcoholic (,ælkə'hɒlɪk) *n.* **1.** a person who is addicted to alcohol. ~*adj.* **2.** of or relating to alcohol.

alcoholism ('ælkəhɒ,lɪzəm) *n.* a condition in which dependence on alcohol harms a person's health and everyday life.

alcove ('ælkəʊv) *n.* a recess in the wall of a room.

aldehyde ('ældɪ,haɪd) *n. Chem.* any organic compound containing the group -CHO, derived from alcohol by oxidation.

alder ('ɔːldə) *n.* a tree with toothed leaves and conelike fruits, which grows in damp places.

alderman ('ɔːldəmən) *n., pl.* **-men.** **1.** (in England and Wales until 1974) a senior member of a local council, elected by other councillors. **2.** (in the U.S. and Canada) a member of the governing body of a city.

ale (eɪl) *n.* **1.** an alcoholic drink made by fermenting a cereal such as barley, originally without hops. **2.** *Chiefly Brit.* beer.

aleatory ('eɪlɪətrɪ) *adj.* dependent on chance.

alehouse ('eɪl,haʊs) *n. Archaic.* a public house.

alembic (ə'lɛmbɪk) *n.* **1.** an obsolete type of container used for distillation. **2.** anything that distils or purifies things.

alert (ə'lɜːt) *adj.* **1.** watchful and attentive.

2. alert to. aware of. ~*n.* **3.** a warning or the period during which a warning remains in effect. **4. on the alert.** watchful. ~*vb.* **5.** to warn (someone) of danger. **6.** (foll. by *to*) to make (someone) aware of (a fact).

A level *n. Brit.* **1.** the advanced level of a subject taken for the General Certificate of Education. **2.** a pass in a subject at A level.

alfalfa (æl'fælfə) *n.* a plant widely used for feeding farm animals.

alfresco (æl'frɛskəʊ) *adj., adv.* in the open air.

algae ('ældʒiː) *pl. n., sing.* **alga** ('ælgə). plants which grow in water or moist ground, and which have no true stems, roots, or leaves.

algebra ('ældʒɪbrə) *n.* a branch of mathematics in which arithmetical operations are generalized by using symbols to represent numbers. —**algebraic** (,ældʒɪ'breɪk) *adj.*

ALGOL ('ælgɒl) *n.* a computer programming language designed for mathematical and scientific purposes.

algorism ('ælgə,rɪzəm) *n.* the Arabic or decimal system of counting.

algorithm ('ælgə,rɪðəm) *n.* a logical arithmetical or computational procedure for solving problems.

alias ('eɪlɪəs) *adv.* **1.** also known as: *William Bonney, alias Billy the Kid.* ~*n., pl.* **-ases.** **2.** a false name.

alibi ('ælɪ,baɪ) *n., pl.* **-bis.** **1.** *Law.* a plea of being elsewhere at the time a crime was committed. **2.** *Informal.* an excuse. ~*vb.* **3.** to provide (someone) with an alibi.

alien ('eɪlɪən) *n.* **1.** a person who is a citizen of a country other than the one in which he lives. **2.** a person who does not seem to fit in with his environment. **3.** a being from another world. ~*adj.* **4.** foreign. **5.** (foll. by *to*) repugnant or opposed to: *deceit is alien to her nature.* **6.** from another world.

alienable ('eɪlɪənəbˈl) *adj. Law.* transferable to another owner.

alienate ('eɪlɪə,neɪt) *vb.* **1.** to cause (a friend) to become unfriendly or hostile. **2.** *Law.* to transfer the ownership of (property) to another person. —,**alien'ation** *n.*

alight[1] (ə'laɪt) *vb.* **alighting, alighted** *or* **alit.** **1.** (foll. by *from*) to step out of (a vehicle). **2.** to land: *birds alighting on the lawn.*

alight[2] (ə'laɪt) *adj., adv.* **1.** on fire. **2.** illuminated.

align (ə'laɪn) *vb.* **1.** to place in a line. **2.** to bring (parts) into proper coordination. **3.** to bring (a person or country) into agreement with the policy of another. —**a'lignment** *n.*

alike (ə'laɪk) *adj.* **1.** similar: *the two brothers are very alike.* ~*adv.* **2.** in a similar manner: *we think alike.* **3.** considered together: *men and women alike.*

alimentary (ˌælɪˈmɛntrɪ) *adj.* of or relating to nutrition.

alimentary canal *n.* the tubular passage in the body through which food is passed and digested.

alimony (ˈælɪmənɪ) *n. Law.* (formerly) an allowance paid under a court order by one spouse to another after separation.

A-line (ˈeɪˌlaɪn) *adj.* (of a skirt) slightly flared.

aliphatic (ˌælɪˈfætɪk) *adj. Chem.* (of an organic compound) having an open chain structure.

aliquant (ˈælɪkwənt) *adj. Maths.* denoting or belonging to a number that is not an exact divisor of a given number.

aliquot (ˈælɪˌkwɒt) *adj. Maths.* denoting or belonging to an exact divisor of a number.

alive (əˈlaɪv) *adj.* **1.** living; having life. **2.** in existence: *the way to keep your marriage alive.* **3.** lively. **4. alive to.** aware of; sensitive to. **5. alive with.** teeming with.

alkali (ˈælkəˌlaɪ) *n.* **1.** *Chem.* a soluble base or a solution of a base. **2.** a soluble mineral salt that occurs in arid soils.

alkaline (ˈælkəˌlaɪn) *adj. Chem.* having the properties of or containing an alkali. —**alkalinity** (ˌælkəˈlɪnɪtɪ) *n.*

alkaloid (ˈælkəˌlɔɪd) *n. Chem.* any of a group of nitrogenous compounds found in plants. Many are poisonous and some are used as drugs.

all (ɔːl) *det.* **1.** the whole quantity or number (of): *all the rice; all are welcome.* **2.** every one of a class: *all men are mortal.* **3.** the greatest possible: *in all earnestness.* **4.** any whatever: *beyond all doubt.* **5. all along.** since the beginning. **6. all but.** nearly. **7. all in all.** everything considered. **8. all over. a.** finished. **b.** everywhere in or on: *all over the world.* **c.** *Informal.* typically: *that's him all over.* **9. all the.** so much (more or less) than otherwise: *we must work all the faster now.* **10. at all.** used for emphasis: *nothing at all; I'm surprised you came at all.* **11. be all for.** *Informal.* to be strongly in favour of. **12. for all.** in spite of: *for all my pushing, I still couldn't move it.* **13. in all.** altogether: *there were five in all.* ~*adv.* **14.** (in scores of games) each: *the score was three all.* ~*n.* **15. give one's all.** to make the greatest possible effort.

Allah (ˈælə) *n.* the name of God in Islam.

allay (əˈleɪ) *vb.* to relieve (pain or grief) or reduce (fear or anger).

all clear *n.* a signal indicating that danger is over.

allegation (ˌælɪˈgeɪʃən) *n.* an unproved assertion or accusation.

allege (əˈlɛdʒ) *vb.* to state (something) without proof.

alleged (əˈlɛdʒd) *adj.* stated to be such: *the alleged rape.* —**allegedly** (əˈlɛdʒɪdlɪ) *adv.*

allegiance (əˈliːdʒəns) *n.* loyalty or dedication to a person, cause, or belief.

allegory (ˈælɪgərɪ) *n., pl.* -**ries.** a poem, play, or story in which the characters and events have a moral or spiritual meaning. —ˌalle**'gorical** *adj.* —**'allego,rize** *or* -ˌ**rise** *vb.*

allegretto (ˌælɪˈgrɛtəʊ) *Music.* ~*adv.* **1.** fairly quickly or briskly. ~*n., pl.* -**tos.** **2.** a piece or passage to be performed fairly quickly or briskly.

allegro (əˈlɛgrəʊ) *Music.* ~*adv.* **1.** in a brisk lively manner. ~*n., pl.* -**gros.** **2.** a piece or passage to be performed in a brisk lively manner.

alleluia (ˌælɪˈluːjə) *interj.* praise the Lord!

allergen (ˈæləˌdʒɛn) *n.* a substance capable of causing an allergy. —ˌaller**'genic** *adj.*

allergic (əˈlɜːdʒɪk) *adj.* **1.** having or caused by an allergy. **2.** (foll. by *to*) *Informal.* having an aversion to: *allergic to work.*

allergy (ˈælədʒɪ) *n., pl.* -**gies.** **1.** extreme sensitivity to a substance such as a food or pollen, which causes the body to react to any contact with it. **2.** *Informal.* an aversion.

alleviate (əˈliːvɪˌeɪt) *vb.* to lessen (pain or suffering). —al,levi**'ation** *n.*

alley[1] (ˈælɪ) *n.* **1.** a narrow passage between or behind buildings. **2. a.** a building containing lanes for tenpin bowling. **b.** a long narrow wooden lane down which the ball is rolled in tenpin bowling. **3.** a path in a garden, often lined with trees.

alley[2] (ˈælɪ) *n.* a large playing marble.

alleyway (ˈælɪˌweɪ) *n.* a narrow passage; alley.

all found *adj.* (of charges for accommodation) inclusive of meals, heating, and other living expenses.

Allhallows (ˌɔːlˈhæləʊz) *n.* same as **All Saints' Day.**

alliance (əˈlaɪəns) *n.* **1.** the state of being allied. **2.** a formal agreement between two or more countries or political parties to work together. **3.** the countries or parties involved.

allied (ˈælaɪd) *adj.* united by a common aim or common characteristics.

alligator (ˈælɪˌgeɪtə) *n.* a large reptile of the southern U.S. and China, similar to the crocodile but with a shorter broader snout.

all in *adj.* **1.** *Informal.* exhausted. **2.** (of wrestling) freestyle. ~*adv.* **3.** with all expenses included.

alliteration (əˌlɪtəˈreɪʃən) *n.* the use of the same letter at the beginning of each word or each stressed word in a phrase or line of verse, as in *round the rock the ragged rascal ran.* —al**'literative** *adj.*

allocate (ˈæləˌkeɪt) *vb.* to assign (something) to someone or for a particular purpose. —ˌallo**'cation** *n.*

allopathy (ə'lɒpəθɪ) n. Med. a method of treating a disease by using remedies that will produce effects that are opposed to the symptoms of the disease. —**allopathic** (ˌæləˈpæθɪk) adj.

allot (ə'lɒt) vb. **-lotting, -lotted.** to assign (something) to someone or for a particular purpose.

allotment (ə'lɒtmənt) n. **1.** a portion allotted. **2.** Brit. a small piece of land rented by a person to grow vegetables on.

allotrope ('ælə,trəʊp) n. Chem. any of two or more physical forms in which an element can exist.

allotropy (ə'lɒtrəpɪ) n. Chem. the existence of an element in two or more physical forms. —**allotropic** (ˌælə'trɒpɪk) adj.

all-out adj. Informal. using one's maximum powers.

allow (ə'laʊ) vb. **1.** to permit (someone) to do something. **2.** to set aside: five hours were allowed to do the job. **3.** to acknowledge (a point or claim). **4. allow for.** to take into account. —**al'lowable** adj.

allowance (ə'laʊəns) n. **1.** an amount of money or food given at regular intervals. **2.** (in Britain) an amount of a person's income that is not subject to income tax. **3. make allowances for. a.** to treat or judge (someone) less severely because he has special problems. **b.** to take (something) into account in one's plans.

allowedly (ə'laʊɪdlɪ) adv. by general admission; admittedly.

alloy ('ælɔɪ) n. **1.** a mixture of two or more metals. ~vb. **2.** to mix (metals) in order to obtain a substance with a desired property.

all-purpose adj. useful for many purposes.

all right adj. **1.** adequate; satisfactory. **2.** unharmed; safe. ~interj. **3.** an expression of approval or agreement. ~adv. **4.** satisfactorily. **5.** safely. **6.** without doubt.

all-round adj. **1.** having many skills; versatile: an all-round player. **2.** comprehensive: an all-round education.

all-rounder n. a person with many skills, for example a cricketer who is good at both batting and bowling.

All Saints' Day n. a Christian festival celebrated on Nov. 1 to honour all the saints.

All Souls' Day n. R.C. Church. a day of prayer (Nov. 2) for the dead in purgatory.

allspice ('ɔːl,spaɪs) n. a spice used in cooking, which comes from the berries of a tropical American tree.

all-time adj. Informal. unsurpassed: he's one of the all-time greats.

allude (ə'luːd) vb. (foll. by to) to refer indirectly to.

allure (ə'lʊə) vb. **1.** to entice or attract (someone). ~n. **2.** attractiveness; appeal. —**al'luring** adj.

allusion (ə'luːʒən) n. an indirect reference.

alluvial (ə'luːvɪəl) adj. **1.** of or relating to alluvium. ~n. **2.** same as **alluvium.**

alluvium (ə'luːvɪəm) n., pl. **-via** (-vɪə). a fertile soil consisting of mud, silt, and sand deposited by flowing water.

ally n. ('ælaɪ), pl. **-lies. 1.** a country, person, or group having an agreement to support another. ~vb. (ə'laɪ), **-lying, -lied. 2. ally oneself with.** to agree to support another country, person, or group.

alma mater ('ælmə 'mɑːtə) n. the school, college, or university that one attended.

almanac ('ɔːlmə,næk) n. a yearly calendar with information about matters such as the phases of the moon and anniversaries.

almighty (ɔːl'maɪtɪ) adj. **1.** having power over everything. **2.** Informal. very great: an almighty row. ~n. **3. the Almighty.** God.

almond ('ɑːmənd) n. an edible nut with a yellowish-brown shell, which grows on a small tree.

almoner ('ɑːmənə) n. Brit. a former name for a trained hospital social worker.

almost ('ɔːlməʊst) adv. very nearly.

alms (ɑːmz) pl. n. Old-fashioned. donations of money or goods to the poor.

almshouse ('ɑːmz,haʊs) n. Brit. (formerly) a house, financed by charity, which offered accommodation to the poor.

aloe ('æləʊ) n. **1.** a plant with fleshy spiny-toothed leaves. **2.** (pl.) a bitter drug made from aloe leaves.

aloft (ə'lɒft) adv. **1.** in the air. **2.** Naut. in the rigging of a ship.

alone (ə'ləʊn) adj., adv. **1.** without anyone or anything else. **2. leave someone** or **something alone.** to refrain from annoying someone or interfering with something. **3. let alone.** not to mention: he can't afford beer, let alone whisky.

along (ə'lɒŋ) prep. **1.** over part or all of the length of: running along the road. ~adv. **2.** moving in a particular direction: running along. **3.** in company with another or others: come along for the ride. **4. along with.** together with: consider the advantages along with the disadvantages. Usage. see **plus.**

alongside (ə,lɒŋ'saɪd) prep. **1.** close beside. ~adv. **2.** near the side of something.

aloof (ə'luːf) adj. distant or haughty in manner.

alopecia (ˌælə'piːʃə) n. loss of hair, usually due to illness.

aloud (ə'laʊd) adv. **1.** in a normal voice. **2.** in a spoken voice; not silently.

alp (ælp) n. **1.** a high mountain. **2. the Alps.** a high mountain range in S central Europe.

alpaca (æl'pækə) n. **1.** a South American mammal related to the llama, with dark shaggy hair. **2.** wool or cloth obtained from this hair.

alpenstock ('ælpən,stɒk) *n.* a stout stick with an iron tip used by hikers and mountain climbers.

alpha ('ælfə) *n.* **1.** the first letter in the Greek alphabet (Α, α). **2.** *Brit.* the highest grade in an examination or for a piece of academic work. **3. alpha and omega.** the first and last.

alphabet ('ælfə,bɛt) *n.* a set of letters in fixed conventional order, used in a writing system.

alphabetical (,ælfə'bɛtɪk^əl) *adj.* in the conventional order of the letters of an alphabet. —,**alpha'betically** *adv.*

alphabetize *or* **-ise** ('ælfəbə,taɪz) *vb.* to arrange in conventional alphabetical order. —,**alphabeti'zation** *or* **-i'sation** *n.*

alphanumeric (,ælfənjuː'mɛrɪk) *adj.* consisting of alphabetical and numerical symbols.

alpha particle *n. Physics.* a positively charged particle, emitted during some radioactive transformations.

alpha ray *n. Physics.* a stream of alpha particles.

alpine ('ælpaɪn) *adj.* **1.** of high mountains. **2.** (*cap.*) of the Alps. ~*n.* **3.** a plant grown in or native to high altitudes.

already (ɔːl'rɛdɪ) *adv.* before the present time or an implied or expected time.

alright (ɔːl'raɪt) *adj., interj., adv. Not universally accepted.* same as **all right.**

Alsatian (æl'seɪʃən) *n.* a large wolflike dog.

also ('ɔːlsəʊ) *adv.* in addition; too.
Usage. Because *also* is not a conjunction, it should not be used on its own as a connector in sentences like *he bought pens, paper, ink, also notebooks.* In such sentences, *and* or *and also* would be the appropriate words: *he bought pens, paper, ink, and notebooks* or *he bought pens, paper, ink, and also notebooks.*

also-ran *n.* a loser in a race, competition, or election.

Alta. Alberta.

altar ('ɔːltə) *n.* **1.** (in Christian churches) the communion table. **2.** a raised structure where sacrifices are offered and religious rites performed.

altarpiece ('ɔːltə,piːs) *n.* a work of art set above and behind the altar in a Christian church.

alter ('ɔːltə) *vb.* to make or become different; change.

alteration (,ɔːltə'reɪʃən) *n.* a change or modification.

altercation (,ɔːltə'keɪʃən) *n.* a heated argument.

alter ego ('ɔːltər 'iːgəʊ) *n.* **1.** a second self. **2.** a very close friend.

alternate *vb.* ('ɔːltə,neɪt). **1.** to occur or

cause to occur by turns. **2.** to interchange regularly or in succession. ~*adj.* (ɔːl'tɜːnɪt). **3.** occurring by turns. **4.** every second (one) of a series: *alternate Fridays.* **5.** being a second choice; alternative. —**al'ternately** *adv.* —**alternation** (,ɔːltə'neɪʃən) *n.*

alternate angles *pl. n. Geom.* two angles at opposite ends and on opposite sides of a line intersecting two other lines.

alternating current *n.* an electric current that reverses direction at frequent regular intervals.

alternative (ɔːl'tɜːnətɪv) *n.* **1.** a possibility of choice between two or more things. **2.** either or any of such choices. ~*adj.* **3.** presenting a choice between two or more possibilities. **4.** denoting a lifestyle, culture, etc., that is less conventional, materialistic, or institutionalized than that of contemporary society. —**al'ternatively** *adv.*

alternative medicine *n.* the treatment of disease by osteopathy, homeopathy, or other nonconventional means.

alternator ('ɔːltə,neɪtə) *n.* an electrical machine that generates an alternating current.

although (ɔːl'ðəʊ) *conj.* in spite of the fact that.

altimeter ('æltɪ,miːtə) *n.* an instrument that indicates altitude.

altitude ('æltɪ,tjuːd) *n.* height above sea level.

alto ('æltəʊ) *n., pl.* **-tos. 1.** short for **contralto. 2.** the highest adult male voice. **3.** a singer with an alto voice. **4.** a musical instrument that is the second or third highest in its group. ~*adj.* **5.** denoting such an instrument.

altogether (,ɔːltə'gɛðə) *adv.* **1.** completely. **2.** with everything included. **3.** on the whole. ~*n.* **4. in the altogether.** *Informal.* naked.

altruism ('æltruː,ɪzəm) *n.* unselfish concern for the welfare of others. —**'altruist** *n.* —,**altru'istic** *adj.*

alum ('æləm) *n. Chem.* a double sulphate of aluminium and potassium, used in manufacturing and in medicine.

aluminium (,æljʊ'mɪnɪəm) *or U.S. & Canad.* **aluminum** (ə'luːmɪnəm) *n. Chem.* a lightweight malleable silvery-white metallic element that resists corrosion. Symbol: Al

aluminize *or* **-ise** (ə'luːmɪ,naɪz) *vb.* to cover with aluminium.

alumnus (ə'lʌmnəs) *or* (*fem.*) **alumna** (ə'lʌmnə) *n., pl.* **-ni** (-naɪ) *or* **-nae** (-niː). *Chiefly U.S. & Canad.* a graduate of a school or college.

always ('ɔːlweɪz) *adv.* **1.** without exception: *he always arrives on time.* **2.** continually: *he is always moaning.* **3.** in any case: *you could always take a day off work.*

alyssum ('ælɪsəm) *n.* a garden plant with clusters of small yellow or white flowers.

am (æm) *vb.* (used with *I*) a form of the present tense of **be**.

Am *Chem.* americium.

AM amplitude modulation.

Am. America(n).

a.m. before noon.

amadoda (ˌæmæˈdɒdə) *pl. n. S. African.* men.

amah (ˈɑːmə) *n.* (in the East, formerly) a nurse or maidservant.

amalgam (əˈmælgəm) *n.* **1.** a blend or combination. **2.** an alloy of mercury with another metal: *dental amalgam.*

amalgamate (əˈmælgəˌmeɪt) *vb.* **1.** to combine or unite. **2.** to alloy (a metal) with mercury. —**amalgamation** (əˌmælgəˈmeɪʃən) *n.*

amanuensis (əˌmænjʊˈɛnsɪs) *n., pl.* -ses (-siːz). a person employed to take dictation.

amaranth (ˈæməˌrænθ) *n.* **1.** *Poetic.* an imaginary flower that never fades. **2.** a plant with small green, red, or purple flowers.

amaryllis (ˌæməˈrɪlɪs) *n.* a plant native to southern Africa with large lily-like reddish or white flowers.

amass (əˈmæs) *vb.* to accumulate or collect (riches or information).

amateur (ˈæmətə) *n.* **1.** a person who engages in a sport or other activity as a pastime rather than for gain. **2.** a person unskilled in a subject or activity. ~*adj.* **3.** not professional. —ˈ**amateurish** *adj.* —ˈ**amateurism** *n.*

amatory (ˈæmətrɪ) *adj.* of or relating to romantic or sexual love.

amaze (əˈmeɪz) *vb.* to fill (someone) with surprise; astonish. —aˈ**mazement** *n.* —aˈ**mazing** *adj.*

Amazon (ˈæməzˀn) *n.* **1.** *Greek myth.* one of a race of women warriors of Scythia near the Black Sea. **2.** any tall, strong, or aggressive woman. —**Amazonian** (ˌæməˈzəʊnɪən) *adj.*

ambassador (æmˈbæsədə) *n.* **1.** a diplomat of the highest rank, sent to another country as permanent representative of his own country. **2.** a representative or messenger. —**ambassadorial** (æmˌbæsəˈdɔːrɪəl) *adj.*

amber (ˈæmbə) *n.* **1.** a yellow translucent fossil resin, used in jewellery. ~*adj.* **2.** brownish-yellow.

ambergris (ˈæmbəˌgriːs) *n.* a waxy substance secreted by the intestinal tract of the sperm whale, which is used in the manufacture of perfumes.

ambidextrous (ˌæmbɪˈdɛkstrəs) *adj.* equally expert with each hand.

ambience *or* **ambiance** (ˈæmbɪəns) *n.* the atmosphere of a place.

ambient (ˈæmbɪənt) *adj.* surrounding.

ambiguity (ˌæmbɪˈgjuːɪtɪ) *n., pl.* -ties. the possibility of interpreting an expression in more than one way.

ambiguous (æmˈbɪgjʊəs) *adj.* having more than one possible interpretation. —amˈ**biguously** *adv.*

ambit (ˈæmbɪt) *n.* limits or boundary.

ambition (æmˈbɪʃən) *n.* **1.** strong desire for success. **2.** something so desired; a goal.

ambitious (æmˈbɪʃəs) *adj.* **1.** having a strong desire for success. **2.** requiring great effort or ability: *an ambitious plan.*

ambivalence (æmˈbɪvələns) *n.* the state of feeling two conflicting emotions at the same time. —amˈ**bivalent** *adj.*

amble (ˈæmbˀl) *vb.* **1.** to walk at a leisurely pace. ~*n.* **2.** a leisurely motion in walking.

ambrosia (æmˈbrəʊzɪə) *n.* **1.** *Classical myth.* the food of the gods, said to bestow immortality. **2.** anything delightful to taste or smell.

ambulance (ˈæmbjʊləns) *n.* a motor vehicle designed to carry sick or injured people.

ambush (ˈæmbʊʃ) *n.* **1.** the act of waiting in a concealed position to make a surprise attack. **2.** an attack from such a position. ~*vb.* **3.** to attack (people) suddenly from a concealed position. ~Also: **ambuscade** (ˌæmbəˈskeɪd).

ameliorate (əˈmiːljəˌreɪt) *vb.* to make (something) better. —aˌmelioˈ**ration** *n.*

amen (ˌeɪˈmɛn, ˌɑːˈmɛn) *interj.* so be it: used at the end of a prayer.

amenable (əˈmiːnəbˀl) *adj.* likely or willing to cooperate.

amend (əˈmɛnd) *vb.* to improve or correct (something).
Usage. *Amend* is sometimes confused with *emend. Amend* means to improve, and can be used of a situation, character, etc., as well as of making improvements to written or spoken material: *we will amend our lifestyle; they all participate in amending or adding to the text. Emend* should be used only of correcting errors in a manuscript or text.

amendment (əˈmɛndmənt) *n.* an improvement or correction.

amends (əˈmɛndz) *pl. n.* **make amends for.** to compensate for some injury or insult.

amenity (əˈmiːnɪtɪ) *n., pl.* -ties. a useful or enjoyable facility.

amenorrhoea *or esp. U.S.* **amenorrhea** (eɪˌmɛnəˈrɪə) *n.* abnormal absence of menstruation.

American (əˈmɛrɪkən) *adj.* **1.** of the United States of America or the American continent. ~*n.* **2.** a person from the United States of America or the American continent.

American Indian *n.* **1.** a member of any of the original peoples of America. ~*adj.* **2.** of any of these peoples, their languages, or their cultures.

Americanism (əˈmɛrɪkəˌnɪzəm) *n.* an expression or custom that is peculiar to or characteristic of the people of the United States.

americium (ˌæməˈrɪsɪəm) n. Chem. a white metallic element artificially produced from plutonium. Symbol: Am

amethyst (ˈæmɪθɪst) n. 1. a purple or violet variety of quartz used as a gemstone. ~adj. 2. purple or violet.

Amharic (æmˈhærɪk) n. the official language of Ethiopia.

amiable (ˈeɪmɪəbʰl) adj. having a pleasant nature; friendly. —ˌamiaˈbility n. —ˈamiably adv.

amicable (ˈæmɪkəbʰl) adj. characterized by friendliness: an amicable agreement. —ˌamicaˈbility n. —ˈamicably adv.

amice (ˈæmɪs) n. a rectangular piece of white linen worn by Christian priests around the neck and shoulders.

amid (əˈmɪd) or **amidst** prep. in the middle of; among.

amide (ˈæmaɪd) n. Chem. 1. any organic compound containing the group -CONH₂. 2. an inorganic compound having the general formula $M(NH_2)_x$, where M is a metal atom.

amidships (əˈmɪdʃɪps) adv. Naut. at, near, or towards the centre of a ship.

amine (əˈmiːn) n. Chem. an organic base formed by replacing one or more of the hydrogen atoms of ammonia by organic groups.

amino acid (əˈmiːnəʊ) n. Chem. any of a group of organic compounds containing the amino group, -NH₂, and one or more carboxyl groups, -COOH, esp. one that is a component of protein.

amir (əˈmɪə) n. same as **emir**.

amiss (əˈmɪs) adv. 1. in an incorrect or defective manner. 2. **take something amiss**. to be offended by something. ~adj. 3. wrong or faulty.

amity (ˈæmɪtɪ) n. friendship; cordiality.

ammeter (ˈæmˌmiːtə) n. an instrument for measuring an electric current in amperes.

ammo (ˈæməʊ) n. Informal. ammunition.

ammonia (əˈməʊnɪə) n. a colourless strong-smelling gas used in fertilizers and as a refrigerant and solvent.

ammonite (ˈæməˌnaɪt) n. the coil-shaped fossilized shell of an extinct sea creature.

ammonium (əˈməʊnɪəm) n. (modifier) Chem. of or containing the chemical group NH₄⁻ or the ion NH_4^+.

ammunition (ˌæmjʊˈnɪʃən) n. 1. bullets, bombs, and shells that can be fired from or as a weapon. 2. any means of defence or attack in an argument.

amnesia (æmˈniːzɪə) n. a partial or total loss of memory. —**amnesiac** (æmˈniːzɪˌæk) adj., n.

amnesty (ˈæmnɪstɪ) n., pl. -ties. 1. a general pardon for offences against a govern-

ment. 2. a period during which a law is suspended, to allow people to confess to crime or give up weapons without fear of prosecution.

amniocentesis (ˌæmnɪəʊsɛnˈtiːsɪs) n., pl. -ses (-siːz). removal of amniotic fluid from the womb of a pregnant woman in order to detect possible abnormalities in the fetus.

amnion (ˈæmnɪən) n., pl. -nia (-nɪə). the innermost of two membranes enclosing an embryo. —**amniotic** (ˌæmnɪˈɒtɪk) adj.

amniotic fluid n. the fluid surrounding the fetus in the womb.

amoeba or U.S. **ameba** (əˈmiːbə) n., pl. -bae (-biː) or -bas. a microscopic single-cell creature that lives in fresh water or soil or as a parasite in other animals.

amok (əˈmʌk, əˈmɒk) or **amuck** adv. **run amok**. to run about in a violent frenzy.

among (əˈmʌŋ) or **amongst** prep. 1. in the midst of: he lived among the Indians. 2. to each of: divide it among yourselves. 3. in the group, class, or number of: among the greatest writers. 4. with one another within a group: decide it among yourselves.

amontillado (əˌmɒntɪˈlɑːdəʊ) n. a medium-dry sherry.

amoral (ˌeɪˈmɒrəl) adj without moral standards or principles. —**amorality** (ˌeɪmɒˈrælɪtɪ) n.
Usage. Amoral is sometimes confused with immoral. Immoral is used to describe behaviour or actions which offend against accepted ideas of what is right or decent, especially in sexual matters: the cruel and immoral use of animals in medical research; an immoral seducer of young girls. Amoral also implies disapproval, but it is used to describe people who behave with an apparent disregard of all principles of right and wrong: using their power to subvert other nations to their will in an amoral fashion.

amorous (ˈæmərəs) adj. feeling, displaying, or relating to sexual love or desire.

amorphous (əˈmɔːfəs) adj. 1. lacking a definite shape. 2. of no recognizable character or type.

amortize or **-tise** (əˈmɔːtaɪz) vb. Finance. to liquidate (a debt or mortgage) by payments or by periodic transfers to a sinking fund.

amount (əˈmaʊnt) n. 1. extent; quantity. ~vb. 2. (foll. by to) to be equal or add up to.

amour (əˈmʊə) n. a secret love affair.

amp (æmp) n. 1. an ampere. 2. Informal. an amplifier.

amperage (ˈæmpərɪdʒ) n. the strength of an electric current measured in amperes.

ampere (ˈæmpɛə) n. the basic unit of electric current. Symbol: A

ampersand (ˈæmpəˌsænd) n. the character &, meaning and.

amphetamine (æm'fɛtə,miːn) *n.* a drug used for its stimulant action.

amphibian (æm'fɪbɪən) *n.* **1.** a vertebrate, such as a newt, frog, or toad, that lives on land but breeds in water. **2.** a vehicle that can travel on both water and land.

amphibious (æm'fɪbɪəs) *adj.* **1.** able to live or operate both on land and in or on water. **2.** relating to military forces launching an attack from the sea against a shore.

amphitheatre *or U.S.* **amphitheater** ('æmfɪ,θɪətə) *n.* a circular or oval building without a roof, in which tiers of seats rise from a central open arena.

amphora ('æmfərə) *n., pl.* **-phorae** (-fə,riː). a Greek or Roman two-handled narrow-necked jar.

ample ('æmpˀl) *adj.* **1.** more than sufficient: *an ample helping.* **2.** large: *of ample proportions.*

amplifier ('æmplɪ,faɪə) *n.* an electronic device used to increase the strength of a current or sound signal.

amplify ('æmplɪ,faɪ) *vb.* **-fying, -fied. 1.** *Electronics.* to increase the strength of (a current or sound signal). **2.** to expand (a speech or story). **3.** to increase the size, extent, or effect of. **—amplification** (,æmplɪfɪ'keɪʃən) *n.*

amplitude ('æmplɪ,tjuːd) *n.* **1.** greatness of extent; breadth or scope. **2.** *Physics.* the maximum displacement from the zero or mean position of a wave or oscillation.

amplitude modulation *n. Electronics.* a method of transmitting information using radio waves in which the amplitude of the carrier wave is varied in accordance with the amplitude of the input signal.

amply ('æmplɪ) *adv.* fully; generously.

ampoule ('æmpuːl) *or U.S.* **ampule** *n. Med.* a small glass container in which liquids for injection are sealed.

ampulla (æm'pʊlə) *n., pl.* **-pullae** (-'pʊliː). **1.** *Christianity.* a container for the wine and water, or the oil, used in church. **2.** a Roman two-handled bottle for oil, wine, or perfume.

amputate ('æmpjʊ,teɪt) *vb.* to remove (all or part of a limb). **—amputation** (,æmpjʊ-'teɪʃən) *n.*

amuck (ə'mʌk) *adv.* same as **amok.**

amulet ('æmjʊlɪt) *n.* a trinket or jewel worn as a protection against evil; charm.

amuse (ə'mjuːz) *vb.* **1.** to entertain or divert (someone). **2.** to cause (someone) to laugh or smile. **—a'musing** *adj.*

amusement (ə'mjuːzmənt) *n.* **1.** something that amuses someone. **2.** the state of being amused.

an (æn) *det.* (*indefinite article*) a form of **a,** used before an initial vowel sound: *an old car; an hour.*

an- *prefix.* See **a-.**

Anabaptist (,ænə'bæptɪst) *n.* **1.** a member of a 16th-century Protestant movement that believed in adult baptism. *~adj.* **2.** of this movement.

anabolic steroid (,ænə'bɒlɪk) *n.* a synthetic steroid hormone used to stimulate muscle and bone growth.

anabolism (ə'næbə,lɪzəm) *n. Biol.* a metabolic process in which body tissues are synthesized from food.

anachronism (ə'nækrə,nɪzəm) *n.* **1.** the representation of something in a historical context in which it could not have occurred or existed. **2.** a person or thing that seems to belong to another time. **—a,nachro-'nistic** *adj.*

anaconda (,ænə'kɒndə) *n.* a very large S American snake.

anaemia *or U.S.* **anemia** (ə'niːmɪə) *n.* a deficiency of red blood cells or their haemoglobin content, resulting in paleness and lack of energy.

anaemic *or U.S.* **anemic** (ə'niːmɪk) *adj.* **1.** having anaemia. **2.** pale and sickly-looking; lacking vitality.

anaerobe (æ'nɛərəʊb) *n. Biol.* an organism that does not require oxygen. **—,anae'ro-bic** *adj.*

anaesthesia *or U.S.* **anesthesia** (,ænɪs-'θiːzɪə) *n.* loss of bodily sensation caused by disease or accident or by drugs such as ether: called **general anaesthesia** when consciousness is lost and **local anaesthesia** when only a specific area of the body is involved.

anaesthetic *or U.S.* **anesthetic** (,ænɪs-'θɛtɪk) *n.* **1.** a substance that causes anaesthesia. *~adj.* **2.** causing anaesthesia.

anaesthetist (ə'niːsθətɪst) *n. Brit.* a doctor who administers anaesthetics.

anaesthetize, anaesthetise, *or U.S.* **anesthetize** (ə'niːsθə,taɪz) *vb.* to cause (someone) to feel no pain by administering an anaesthetic.

Anaglypta (,ænə'glɪptə) *n. Trademark.* a thick embossed wallpaper, designed to be painted.

anagram ('ænə,græm) *n.* a word or phrase the letters of which can be rearranged into another word or phrase.

anal ('eɪnˀl) *adj.* of or relating to the anus.

analgesic (,ænˀl'dʒiːzɪk) *n.* **1.** a drug that relieves pain. *~adj.* **2.** pain-relieving.

analog ('ænə,lɒg) *n. U.S. & computers.* same as **analogue.**

analogize *or* **-gise** (ə'nælə,dʒaɪz) *vb.* **1.** to use analogy in argument. **2.** to reveal analogy between (one thing and another).

analogous (ə'næləgəs) *adj.* similar in some respect.

analogue *or U.S.* **analog** ('ænə,lɒg) *n.* **1. a.** a physical object or quantity used to measure or represent another quantity. **b.**

(*as modifier*): *an analogue watch.* **2.** something that is analogous to something else.

analogy (ə'nælədʒɪ) *n., pl.* **-gies. 1.** a similarity, usually in a limited number of features. **2.** a comparison made to show such a similarity. **—analogical** (ˌænə'lɒdʒɪk^əl) *adj.*

analyse *or U.S.* **-lyze** ('æn^əˌlaɪz) *vb.* **1.** to examine (something) in detail in order to discover its meaning or essential features. **2.** to break (something) down into its components. **3.** to psychoanalyse (someone).

analysis (ə'nælɪsɪs) *n., pl.* **-ses** (-ˌsiːz). **1.** the division of a whole into its constituent parts to examine or determine their relationship. **2.** a statement of the results of this. **3.** short for **psychoanalysis.**

analyst ('ænəlɪst) *n.* **1.** a person who is skilled in analysis. **2.** short for **psychoanalyst.**

analytic (ˌænə'lɪtɪk) *or* **analytical** *adj.* relating to or using analysis.

anarchism ('ænəˌkɪzəm) *n.* a doctrine advocating the abolition of government and its replacement by a social system based on voluntary cooperation.

anarchist ('ænəkɪst) *n.* **1.** a person who advocates anarchism. **2.** a person who causes disorder or upheaval. **—ˌanar'chistic** *adj.*

anarchy ('ænəkɪ) *n.* **1.** general lawlessness and disorder. **2.** the absence of government. **—anarchic** (æn'ɑːkɪk) *adj.*

anathema (ə'næθəmə) *n.* a detested person or thing.

anathematize *or* **-tise** (ə'næθɪməˌtaɪz) *vb.* to curse (someone or something).

anatomy (ə'nætəmɪ) *n., pl.* **-mies. 1.** the science of the physical structure of animals and plants. **2.** the structure of an animal or plant. **3.** *Informal.* a person's body: *a delicate part of his anatomy.* **4.** any detailed analysis: *the anatomy of a murder.* **—anatomical** (ˌænə'tɒmɪk^əl) *adj.*

ancestor ('ænsɛstə) *n.* **1.** a person in former times from whom one is descended; forefather. **2.** a forerunner: *the ancestor of the modern camera.*

ancestral (æn'sɛstrəl) *adj.* of or inherited from ancestors.

ancestry ('ænsɛstrɪ) *n., pl.* **-tries. 1.** lineage or descent: *of Italian ancestry.* **2.** forerunners collectively.

anchor ('æŋkə) *n.* **1.** a hooked device attached to a boat by a cable and dropped overboard so as to grip the sea bottom and restrict movement. **2.** a source of stability or security. ~*vb.* **3.** to use an anchor to hold (a boat) in one place. **4.** to fasten (something) securely.

anchorage ('æŋkərɪdʒ) *n.* a place to anchor boats.

anchorite ('æŋkəˌraɪt) *n.* a religious recluse.

anchor man *n.* **1.** a broadcaster in a central studio, who links up and presents items from outside camera units and reporters in other studios. **2.** the last person to compete in a relay team.

anchovy ('æntʃəvɪ) *n., pl.* **-vies.** a small marine food fish with a salty taste.

ancien régime ('ɒnsjɑːn reɪ'ʒiːm) *n.* **1.** the political and social system of France before the 1789 Revolution. **2.** a former system.

ancient ('eɪnʃənt) *adj.* **1.** dating from very long ago. **2.** very old. **3.** of the far past, esp. before the collapse of the Western Roman Empire (476 A.D.). ~*n.* **4.** (*pl.*) people who lived in the ancient world, esp. Greeks or Romans.

ancillary (æn'sɪlərɪ) *adj.* **1.** auxiliary; supplementary: *hospital ancillary workers.* **2.** subsidiary.

and (ænd; *unstressed* ənd) *conj.* **1.** in addition to: *boys and girls.* **2.** as a consequence: *he fell and cut his knee.* **3.** afterwards: *we pay and go in.* **4.** used for emphasis or to indicate repetition or continuity: *it rained and rained.* **5.** used to express a contrast between instances of something: *there are jobs and jobs.* **6.** *Informal.* used in place of *to* in infinitives after verbs such as *try, go,* and *come: try and see it my way.*
Usage. *And/or* is considered acceptable in legal and commercial contexts, but should not be used in general written English when *or* is meant: *he must bring his car or his motorbike* (not *his car and/or his motorbike*).

andante (æn'dæntɪ) *Music.* ~*adv.* **1.** moderately slowly. ~*n.* **2.** a passage or piece to be performed in this manner.

andantino (ˌændæn'tiːnəʊ) *Music.* ~*adv.* **1.** slightly faster than andante. ~*n., pl.* **-nos. 2.** a passage or piece to be performed in this manner.

andiron ('ændˌaɪən) *n.* either of a pair of metal stands for supporting logs in a hearth.

and/or *conj. Not universally accepted.* either one or the other or both.

androgynous (æn'drɒdʒɪnəs) *adj.* (of a person, animal, or plant) having both male and female characteristics.

android ('ændrɔɪd) *n.* a robot resembling a human being.

anecdote ('ænɪkˌdəʊt) *n.* a short amusing account of an incident. **—ˌanec'dotal** *adj.*

anemia (ə'niːmɪə) *n. U.S.* anaemia.

anemometer (ˌænɪ'mɒmɪtə) *n.* an instrument for recording the speed of wind.

anemone (ə'nɛmənɪ) *n.* a flowering plant related to the buttercup, which has white or coloured flowers.

aneroid barometer ('ænəˌrɔɪd) *n.* a device for measuring atmospheric pressure, consisting of a partially evacuated chamber, in which variations in pressure cause a pointer on the lid to move.

anesthesia (ˌænɪsˈθiːzɪə) n. U.S. anaesthesia.

aneurysm or **aneurism** (ˈænjəˌrɪzəm) n. Med. a permanent swelling of a blood vessel.

anew (əˈnjuː) adv. 1. once more. 2. in a different way.

angel (ˈeɪndʒəl) n. 1. a spiritual being believed to be an attendant or messenger of God. 2. a conventional representation of an angel as a human being with wings. 3. Informal. a person who is kind, pure, or beautiful. 4. Informal. an investor in a theatrical production.

angel cake or esp. U.S. **angel food cake** n. a very light sponge cake.

angelfish (ˈeɪndʒəlˌfɪʃ) n., pl. **-fish** or **-fishes.** a South American aquarium fish with large fins.

angelic (ænˈdʒɛlɪk) adj. 1. very kind, pure, or beautiful. 2. of or relating to angels. —**anˈgelically** adv.

angelica (ænˈdʒɛlɪkə) n. 1. an aromatic plant used in medicine and cookery. 2. the candied stems of this plant, used in sweet dishes.

Angelus (ˈændʒɪləs) n. R.C. Church. 1. prayers recited in the morning, at midday, and in the evening. 2. the bell signalling the times of these prayers.

anger (ˈæŋgə) n. 1. a feeling of annoyance or antagonism; rage; wrath. ~vb. 2. to make (someone) angry; enrage.

angina (ænˈdʒaɪnə) or **angina pectoris** (ˈpɛktərɪs) n. a sudden intense chest pain caused by momentary lack of adequate blood supply to the heart muscle.

angle[1] (ˈæŋgˀl) n. 1. the space between or shape formed by two straight lines or surfaces that extend from a common point. 2. the divergence between two such lines or surfaces, measured in degrees. 3. a recess; corner. 4. point of view. ~vb. 5. to move in or place (something) at an angle. 6. to produce (something, such as an article) from a particular point of view.

angle[2] (ˈæŋgˀl) vb. 1. to fish with a hook and line. 2. (foll. by for) to attempt to get: he was angling for a compliment.

angler (ˈæŋglə) n. a person who fishes with a hook and line.

Angles (ˈæŋgˀlz) pl. n. a people from N Germany who settled in E and N England in the 5th and 6th centuries A.D.

Anglican (ˈæŋglɪkən) adj. 1. of or relating to the Church of England. ~n. 2. a member of the Anglican Church. —**ˈAnglicanˌism** n.

Anglicism (ˈæŋglɪˌsɪzəm) n. an expression or custom that is peculiar to or characteristic of the English.

anglicize or **-cise** (ˈæŋglɪˌsaɪz) vb.

-**cizing, -cized** or **-cising, -cised.** to make or become English in outlook, form, etc.

angling (ˈæŋglɪŋ) n. the art or sport of fishing with a hook and line.

Anglo (ˈæŋgləʊ) n., pl. **-glos.** 1. U.S. a White inhabitant of the U.S. who is not of Latin extraction. 2. Canad. an English-speaking Canadian of Anglo-Celtic origin.

Anglo- combining form. denoting English or England: Anglo-Saxon.

Anglo-French adj. 1. of England and France. 2. of the Anglo-French language. ~n. 3. the Norman-French language of medieval England.

Anglo-Indian adj. 1. of England and India. 2. denoting or relating to Anglo-Indians. ~n. 3. a person of mixed English and Indian descent. 4. an English person who has lived for a long time in India.

Anglo-Norman adj. 1. of or relating to the Norman conquerors of England or their language. ~n. 2. a Norman inhabitant of England after 1066. 3. the Anglo-French language.

Anglophile (ˈæŋgləʊˌfaɪl) n. a person who admires England or the English.

Anglo-Saxon n. 1. a member of any of the West Germanic tribes that settled in Britain from the 5th century A.D. 2. any White person whose native language is English. 3. same as **Old English.** 4. Informal. plain, blunt, and often rude English. ~adj. 5. of the Anglo-Saxons or the Old English language. 6. of the White Protestant culture of Britain and the U.S.

angora (æŋˈgɔːrə) n. 1. a variety of goat, cat, or rabbit with long silky hair. 2. the hair of the angora goat or rabbit. 3. cloth made from the hair of the angora goat or rabbit.

Angostura Bitters (ˌæŋgəˈstjʊərə) pl. n. Trademark. a bitter aromatic tonic, used to flavour alcoholic drinks.

angry (ˈæŋgrɪ) adj. **-grier, -griest.** 1. feeling or expressing annoyance or antagonism. 2. dark and stormy: angry clouds. 3. severely inflamed: an angry wound. —**ˈangrily** adv.

angst (æŋst) n. acute but nonspecific anxiety.

angstrom (ˈæŋstrəm) n. a unit of length equal to 10^{-10} metre, used to measure wavelengths.

anguish (ˈæŋgwɪʃ) n. extreme pain or misery; agony.

anguished (ˈæŋgwɪʃt) adj. feeling or showing extreme pain or misery.

angular (ˈæŋgjʊlə) adj. 1. lean and bony. 2. having an angle or angles. 3. measured by an angle: angular momentum. —**angularity** (ˌæŋgjʊˈlærɪtɪ) n.

anhydrous (ænˈhaɪdrəs) adj. Chem. containing no water.

anil ('ænıl) *n.* a West Indian shrub which is a source of indigo.

aniline ('ænɪ,liːn) *n. Chem.* a colourless oily poisonous liquid, obtained from coal tar and used for making dyes, plastics, and explosives.

animadversion (,ænɪmæd'vɜːʃən) *n.* criticism or censure.

animal ('ænɪməl) *n.* **1.** *Zool.* any living being that is capable of voluntary movement and possesses specialized sense organs. **2.** any living being other than a human being. **3.** any living being with four legs. **4.** a brutish person. **5.** *Facetious.* a person or thing: *there is no such animal.* ~*adj.* **6.** of or from animals. **7.** of or relating to physical needs or desires; carnal.

animalcule (,ænɪ'mælkjuːl) *n.* a microscopic animal.

animal husbandry *n.* the science of breeding, rearing, and caring for farm animals.

animalism ('ænɪmə,lɪzəm) *n.* **1.** preoccupation with physical matters; sensuality. **2.** the doctrine that human beings lack a spiritual nature.

animality (,ænɪ'mælɪtɪ) *n.* **1.** the animal side of human beings. **2.** the state of being an animal.

animalize *or* **-ise** ('ænɪmə,laɪz) *vb.* to make (a person) brutal or sensual.

animal magnetism *n.* the quality of being sexually attractive.

animal spirits *pl. n.* boisterous exuberance.

animate *vb.* ('ænɪ,meɪt). **1.** to give life to. **2.** to make lively. **3.** to produce (a story) as an animated cartoon. ~*adj.* ('ænɪmɪt). **4.** having life. —'**ani,mated** *adj.* —'**ani,matedly** *adv.*

animated cartoon *n.* a film produced by photographing a series of gradually changing drawings, which give the illusion of movement when the series is projected rapidly.

animation (,ænɪ'meɪʃən) *n.* **1.** the techniques used in the production of animated cartoons. **2.** vivacity.

animism ('ænɪ,mɪzəm) *n.* the belief that natural objects possess souls. —,**ani'mistic** *adj.*

animosity (,ænɪ'mɒsɪtɪ) *n., pl.* **-ties.** a powerful dislike or hostility.

animus ('ænɪməs) *n.* intense dislike; hatred; animosity.

anion ('æn,aɪən) *n.* a negatively charged ion. —**anionic** (,ænaɪ'ɒnɪk) *adj.*

anise ('ænɪs) *n.* a Mediterranean plant with liquorice-flavoured seeds.

aniseed ('ænɪ,siːd) *n.* the liquorice-flavoured seeds of the anise plant, used for flavouring.

ankh (æŋk) *n.* a T-shaped cross with a loop on the top, which symbolized eternal life in ancient Egypt.

ankle ('æŋkᵊl) *n.* **1.** the joint connecting the leg and the foot. **2.** the part of the leg just above the foot.

anklet ('æŋklɪt) *n.* an ornamental chain worn around the ankle.

ankylosis (,æŋkɪ'ləʊsɪs) *n.* abnormal immobility of a joint, caused by a fibrous growth within the joint.

anna ('ænə) *n.* a former Indian coin.

annals ('ænᵊlz) *pl. n.* **1.** yearly records of events. **2.** regular reports of the work of a society or other organization. —'**annalist** *n.*

anneal (ə'niːl) *vb.* to toughen (glass or metal) by heat treatment.

annelid ('ænəlɪd) *n.* a worm with a segmented body, for example the earthworm.

annex ('ænɛks) *vb.* **1.** to seize (territory) by conquest or occupation. **2.** to take (something) without permission. **3.** to join or add (something) to something larger. —,**annex'ation** *n.*

annexe *or esp. U.S.* **annex** ('ænɛks) *n.* **a.** an extension to a main building. **b.** a building used as an addition to a main one nearby.

annihilate (ə'naɪə,leɪt) *vb.* **1.** to destroy (a place or a group of people) completely. **2.** *Informal.* to defeat (someone) totally in an argument or a contest. —**annihilation** (ə,naɪə'leɪʃən) *n.*

anniversary (,ænɪ'vɜːsərɪ) *n., pl.* **-ries.** **1.** the date on which an event, such as a wedding, occurred in some previous year. **2.** the celebration of this.

annotate ('ænə,teɪt) *vb.* to supply (a written work) with critical or explanatory notes. —**annotation** (,ænə'teɪʃən) *n.*

announce (ə'naʊns) *vb.* **1.** to make (something) known publicly. **2.** to declare the arrival of (a person). **3.** to be a sign of: *the dark clouds announced rain.* —**an'nouncement** *n.*

announcer (ə'naʊnsə) *n.* a person who introduces programmes on radio or television.

annoy (ə'nɔɪ) *vb.* **1.** to irritate or displease. **2.** to harass (someone) sexually. —**an'noyance** *n.* —**an'noying** *adj.*

annual ('ænjʊəl) *adj.* **1.** occurring or done once a year: *my annual holiday.* **2.** lasting for a year: *an annual subscription.* ~*n.* **3.** a plant that completes its life cycle in one year. **4.** a book published once every year. —'**annually** *adv.*

annualize *or* **-ise** ('ænjʊə,laɪz) *vb.* to calculate (a rate) for or as if for a year.

annuity (ə'njuːɪtɪ) *n., pl.* **-ties.** a fixed sum payable at specified intervals over a period.

annul (ə'nʌl) *vb.* **-nulling, -nulled.** to declare (something, such as a marriage) invalid.

annular ('ænjʊlə) *adj.* ring-shaped.

annular eclipse *n.* an eclipse of the sun in which a ring of sunlight can be seen surrounding the shadow of the moon.

annulate ('ænjʊlɪt) *adj.* having, composed of, or marked with rings.·

annulment (ə'nʌlmənt) *n.* the formal invalidation of something such as a marriage.

Annunciation (ə,nʌnsɪ'eɪʃən) *n.* **1. the.** the announcement by the angel Gabriel to the Virgin Mary of her conception of Christ. **2.** the festival commemorating this, on March 25 (Lady Day).

anode ('ænəʊd) *n. Electronics.* the positive electrode in an electrolytic cell or in an electronic valve or tube.

anodize *or* **-dise** ('ænə,daɪz) *vb. Chem.* to coat (a metal) with a protective oxide film by electrolysis.

anodyne ('ænə,daɪn) *n.* **1.** something that relieves pain or distress. ~*adj.* **2.** capable of relieving pain or distress.

anoint (ə'nɔɪnt) *vb.* to apply oil to (someone) as a sign of consecration.

anomalous (ə'nɒmələs) *adj.* deviating from the normal or usual order or type.

anomaly (ə'nɒməlɪ) *n., pl.* **-lies.** something that deviates from the normal; an irregularity.

anomie *or* **anomy** ('ænəmɪ) *n.* lack of social or moral standards.

anon (ə'nɒn) *adv. Archaic or informal.* soon: *see you anon.*

anon. anonymous.

anonymous (ə'nɒnɪməs) *adj.* **1.** (of an action or thing) by someone whose name is unknown or withheld: *an anonymous letter.* **2.** having no known name: *an anonymous donor.* **3.** lacking distinguishing characteristics. —**anonymity** (,ænə'nɪmɪtɪ) *n.*

anorak ('ænə,ræk) *n.* a waterproof hip-length jacket, usually with a hood.

anorexia (,ænə'rɛksɪə) *or* **anorexia nervosa** (nɜː'vəʊsə) *n.* a disorder characterized by the fear of becoming fat and the consequent refusal of food. —**,ano'rexic** *adj., n.*

another (ə'nʌðə) *det.* **1.** one more: *another chance; help yourself to another.* **2.** a different one: *another country; try one, then another.*

anserine ('ænsə,raɪn) *adj.* of or resembling a goose.

answer ('ɑːnsə) *n.* **1.** a reply to a question, request, letter, or article. **2.** a reaction or response. **3.** a solution to a mathematical problem. ~*vb.* **4.** to reply or respond (to) by word or act. **5.** to reply correctly to a question. **6.** to respond or react: *the steering answers to the slightest touch.* **7.** to meet the requirements of. **8.** to be responsible (to a person). **9.** to give a defence of (a charge).

answerable ('ɑːnsərəb'l) *adj.* (foll. by *for* or *to*) responsible for or accountable to.

answer back *vb.* to reply rudely to (someone).

ant (ænt) *n.* a small often wingless insect, typically living in highly organized colonies.

antacid (ænt'æsɪd) *Chem.* ~*n.* **1.** a substance used to treat acidity. ~*adj.* **2.** having the properties of this substance.

antagonism (æn'tægə,nɪzəm) *n.* openly expressed opposition.

antagonist (æn'tægənɪst) *n.* an opponent or adversary. —**an,tago'nistic** *adj.*

antagonize *or* **-nise** (æn'tægə,naɪz) *vb.* to make (someone) hostile; annoy or irritate.

antalkali (ænt'ælkə,laɪ) *n. Chem.* a substance that neutralizes alkalis.

Antarctic (ænt'ɑːktɪk) *n.* **the.** the area around the South Pole.

Antarctic Circle *n.* the imaginary circle around the earth at latitude 66° 32′ S.

ante ('æntɪ) *n.* **1.** the stake put up before the deal in poker by the players. **2.** *Informal.* a sum of money representing a person's share. ~*vb.* **-teing, -ted** *or* **-teed. 3.** to place (one's stake) in poker. **4.** (foll. by *up*) *Informal.* to pay.

ante- *prefix.* before in time or position: *antedate; antechamber.*

anteater ('ænt,iːtə) *n.* a mammal with a long snout used for eating termites.

antecedent (,æntɪ'siːd³nt) *n.* **1.** an event or circumstance that happens or exists before another. **2.** *Grammar.* a word or phrase to which a relative pronoun, such as *who,* refers. **3.** (*pl.*) a person's ancestors and past history. ~*adj.* **4.** preceding in time or order; prior.

antechamber ('æntɪ,tʃeɪmbə) *n.* an anteroom.

antedate (,æntɪ'deɪt) *vb* **1.** to be or occur at an earlier date than. **2.** to give (something) a date that is earlier than the actual date.

antediluvian (,æntɪdɪ'luːvɪən) *adj.* **1.** belonging to the ages before the biblical Flood. **2.** old-fashioned.

antelope ('æntɪ,ləʊp) *n., pl.* **-lopes** *or* **-lope.** any of a group of graceful deerlike mammals of Africa and Asia, which have long legs and horns.

antenatal (,æntɪ'neɪt³l) *adj.* before birth; during pregnancy.

antenna (æn'tɛnə) *n.* **1.** (*pl.* **-nae** (-niː)) one of a pair of mobile feelers on the heads of insects, lobsters, and certain other creatures. **2.** (*pl.* **-nas**) an aerial.

antepenult (,æntɪpɪ'nʌlt) *n.* the third last syllable in a word.

antepenultimate (,æntɪpɪ'nʌltɪmɪt) *adj.* **1.** third from last. ~*n.* **2.** anything that is third from last.

anterior (æn'tɪərɪə) *adj.* **1.** at or towards the front. **2.** earlier.

anteroom ('æntɪˌruːm) *n.* a small room giving entrance to a larger room, often used as a waiting room.

anthem ('ænθəm) *n.* **1.** a song of loyalty or devotion: *a national anthem.* **2.** a musical composition for a choir, usually set to words from the Bible.

anther ('ænθə) *n. Bot.* the part of the stamen of a flower in which the pollen matures.

ant hill *n.* a mound of soil built by ants around the entrance to their nest.

anthology (æn'θɒlədʒɪ) *n., pl.* **-gies.** a collection of poems or other literary pieces by various authors. **—an'thologist** *n.*

anthracite ('ænθrəˌsaɪt) *n.* a hard coal that burns slowly with little smoke or flame but intense heat.

anthrax ('ænθræks) *n.* a dangerous infectious disease of cattle and sheep, which can be transmitted to man.

anthropocentric (ˌænθrəpəʊ'sɛntrɪk) *adj.* regarding the human being as the central factor in the universe.

anthropoid ('ænθrəˌpɔɪd) *adj.* **1.** resembling a human being. **~***n.* **2.** an ape, such as the chimpanzee, that resembles a human being.

anthropology (ˌænθrə'pɒlədʒɪ) *n.* the study of human origins, institutions, and beliefs. **—anthropological** (ˌænθrəpə'lɒdʒɪkˀl) *adj.* **—ˌanthro'pologist** *n.*

anthropomorphism (ˌænθrəpə'mɔːfɪzəm) *n.* the attribution of human form or behaviour to a god, animal, or object. **—ˌanthropo'morphic** *adj.*

anthropomorphous (ˌænθrəpə'mɔːfəs) *adj.* shaped like a human being.

anti ('æntɪ) *Informal.* **~***adj.* **1.** opposed to a party, policy, or attitude. **~***n.* **2.** an opponent of a party, policy, or attitude.

anti- *prefix.* **1.** against; opposed to: *antiwar.* **2.** opposite to: *anticlimax.* **3.** counteracting or neutralizing: *antifreeze.*

anti-aircraft (ˌæntɪ'ɛəkrɑːft) *n. (modifier)* for defence against aircraft attack.

antiballistic missile (ˌæntɪbə'lɪstɪk) *n.* a missile designed to destroy a ballistic missile in flight.

antibiotic (ˌæntɪbaɪ'ɒtɪk) *n.* **1.** a chemical substance capable of destroying bacteria. **~***adj.* **2.** of or relating to antibiotics.

antibody ('æntɪˌbɒdɪ) *n., pl.* **-bodies.** a protein produced in the blood, which destroys bacteria.

Antichrist ('æntɪˌkraɪst) *n.* **1.** *New Testament.* the principle antagonist of Christ. **2.** an enemy of Christ or Christianity.

anticipate (æn'tɪsɪˌpeɪt) *vb.* **1.** to foresee and act in advance of: *I had anticipated his question.* **2.** to look forward to (something). **3.** to make use of (something, such as one's salary) before receiving it. **4.** to mention (part of a story) before its proper time. **—an'tici,patory** *adj.*

anticipation (ænˌtɪsɪ'peɪʃən) *n.* the act of anticipating; expectation, premonition, or foresight.

anticlerical (ˌæntɪ'klɛrɪkˀl) *adj.* opposed to the power and influence of the clergy in politics.

anticlimax (ˌæntɪ'klaɪmæks) *n.* a disappointing conclusion to a series of events. **—anticlimactic** (ˌæntɪklaɪ'mæktɪk) *adj.*

anticline ('æntɪˌklaɪn) *n. Geol.* a fold of rock raised up into a broad arch so that the strata slope down on both sides.

anticlockwise (ˌæntɪ'klɒkˌwaɪz) *adv., adj.* in the opposite direction to the rotation of the hands of a clock.

anticoagulant (ˌæntɪkəʊ'ægjʊlənt) *n.* a substance that prevents the clotting of blood.

antics ('æntɪks) *pl. n.* absurd acts or postures.

anticyclone (ˌæntɪ'saɪkləʊn) *n. Meteorol.* an area of moving air of high pressure in which the winds rotate outwards.

antidepressant (ˌæntɪdɪ'prɛsˀnt) *n.* **1.** a drug used to treat depression. **~***adj.* **2.** denoting such a drug.

antidote ('æntɪˌdəʊt) *n.* **1.** *Med.* a substance that counteracts a poison. **2.** anything that counteracts a harmful condition.

antifreeze ('æntɪˌfriːz) *n.* a liquid added to water to lower its freezing point, used in the radiator of a motor vehicle to prevent freezing.

antigen ('æntɪdʒən) *n.* a substance, usually a toxin, that causes the body to produce antibodies.

antihero ('æntɪˌhɪərəʊ) *n., pl.* **-roes.** a central character in a novel, play, or film, who lacks the traditional heroic virtues.

antihistamine (ˌæntɪ'hɪstəˌmiːn) *n.* a drug that neutralizes the effects of histamine, used in the treatment of allergies.

antiknock (ˌæntɪ'nɒk) *n.* a substance added to motor fuel to reduce knocking in the engine caused by too rapid combustion.

antilogarithm (ˌæntɪ'lɒgəˌrɪðəm) *n. Maths.* a number corresponding to a given logarithm.

antimacassar (ˌæntɪmə'kæsə) *n.* a cloth put over the back of a chair to prevent soiling.

antimatter ('æntɪˌmætə) *n. Physics.* a hypothetical form of matter composed of antiparticles.

antimony ('æntɪmənɪ) *n. Chem.* a silvery-white metallic element that is added to alloys to increase their strength. Symbol: Sb

antinomian (ˌæntɪ'nəʊmɪən) *adj.* **1.** holding the view that by faith a Christian is released from the obligation of observing moral law. ~*n.* **2.** a member of a Christian sect holding this view.

antinomy (æn'tɪnəmɪ) *n., pl.* **-mies.** contradiction between two laws or principles that are reasonable in themselves.

antinovel ('æntɪˌnɒvˀl) *n.* a type of prose fiction in which conventional elements of the novel are rejected.

antinuclear (ˌæntɪ'njuːklɪə) *adj.* opposed to nuclear weapons or nuclear power.

antiparticle ('æntɪˌpɑːtɪkˀl) *n. Nuclear physics.* an elementary particle that has the same mass as its corresponding particle, but opposite charge and opposite magnetism.

antipasto (ˌæntɪ'pæstəʊ) *n., pl.* **-tos.** an appetizer in an Italian meal.

antipathy (æn'tɪpəθɪ) *n.* a feeling of dislike or hostility. —**antipathetic** (ˌæntɪpə'θɛtɪk) *adj.*

antipersonnel (ˌæntɪˌpɜːsə'nɛl) *adj.* (of weapons or bombs) designed to be used against people rather than equipment.

antiperspirant (ˌæntɪ'pɜːspərənt) *n.* a substance applied to the skin to reduce or prevent perspiration.

antiphon ('æntɪfən) *n.* a hymn sung in alternate parts by two groups of singers.

antipodes (æn'tɪpəˌdiːz) *pl. n.* **1.** any two places that are situated diametrically opposite one another on the earth's surface. **2. the Antipodes.** Australia and New Zealand. —**antipodean** (æn'tɪpə'diːən) *adj.*

antipope ('æntɪˌpəʊp) *n.* a pope set up in opposition to the one chosen by church laws.

antipyretic (ˌæntɪpaɪ'rɛtɪk) *adj.* **1.** reducing fever. ~*n.* **2.** a drug that reduces fever.

antiquarian (ˌæntɪ'kwɛərɪən) *adj.* **1.** collecting or dealing with antiquities or rare books. ~*n.* **2.** an antiquary.

antiquary ('æntɪkwərɪ) *n., pl.* **-quaries.** a person who collects, deals in, or studies antiques or ancient works of art.

antiquated ('æntɪˌkweɪtɪd) *adj.* obsolete or old-fashioned.

antique (æn'tiːk) *n.* **1.** a decorative object or piece of furniture, of an earlier period, that is valued for its beauty, workmanship, and age. ~*adj.* **2.** made in an earlier period. **3.** *Informal.* old-fashioned.

antiquity (æn'tɪkwɪtɪ) *n., pl.* **-ties. 1.** great age. **2.** the far distant past, esp. before the Middle Ages. **3.** (*pl.*) remains that date from ancient times.

antirrhinum (ˌæntɪ'raɪnəm) *n.* a two-lipped flower of various colours.

antiscorbutic (ˌæntɪskɔː'bjuːtɪk) *adj.* preventing or curing scurvy.

anti-Semitic (ˌæntɪsɪ'mɪtɪk) *adj.* discriminating against Jews. —**anti-Semite** (ˌæntɪ'siːmaɪt) *n.* —**anti-Semitism** (ˌæntɪ'sɛmɪˌtɪzəm) *n.*

antiseptic (ˌæntɪ'sɛptɪk) *adj.* **1.** preventing infection by killing germs. ~*n.* **2.** an antiseptic substance.

antiserum (ˌæntɪ'sɪərəm) *n.* blood serum containing antibodies used to treat or provide immunity to a disease.

antisocial (ˌæntɪ'səʊʃəl) *adj.* **1.** avoiding the company of other people. **2.** (of behaviour) annoying to other people.

antistatic (ˌæntɪ'stætɪk) *adj.* reducing the effects of static electricity.

antitank (ˌæntɪ'tæŋk) *adj.* (of weapons) designed to destroy military tanks.

antithesis (æn'tɪθɪsɪs) *n., pl.* **-ses** (-ˌsiːz). **1.** the exact opposite. **2.** *Rhetoric.* the placing together of contrasting ideas or words to produce an effect of balance, such as *where gods command, mere mortals must obey.* —**antithetical** (ˌæntɪ'θɛtɪkˀl) *adj.*

antitoxin (ˌæntɪ'tɒksɪn) *n.* an antibody that acts against a toxin. —ˌanti'toxic *adj.*

antitrades ('æntɪˌtreɪdz) *pl. n.* winds blowing in the opposite direction from and above the trade winds.

antitrust (ˌæntɪ'trʌst) *adj. Chiefly U.S.* (of laws) opposing business monopolies.

antler ('æntlə) *n.* one of a pair of branched horns on the heads of male deer.

antonym ('æntənɪm) *n.* a word that means the opposite of another.

antrum ('æntrəm) *n., pl.* **-tra** (-trə). *Anat.* a natural cavity, esp. in a bone.

anus ('eɪnəs) *n.* the opening at the end of the alimentary canal, through which faeces are discharged.

anvil ('ænvɪl) *n.* a heavy iron block on which metals are hammered into particular shapes.

anxiety (æŋ'zaɪtɪ) *n., pl.* **-ties. 1.** a state of uneasiness about what may happen. **2.** eagerness: *her anxiety to please.*

anxious ('æŋkʃəs, 'æŋʃəs) *adj.* **1.** worried and tense. **2.** causing anxiety: *an anxious time.* **3.** intensely desiring: *anxious to succeed.* —'**anxiously** *adv.*

any ('ɛnɪ) *det.* **1.** one, some, or several, no matter how much or what kind: *you may take any clothes you like; take any you like.* **2.** (*used with a negative or question*) even the smallest amount or even one: *I can't stand any noise; don't give her any.* **3.** whatever or whichever: *any dictionary will do.* **4.** an indefinite or unlimited: *any number of friends.* ~*adv.* **5.** (*used with a negative or question*) to even the smallest extent: *it isn't any worse.*

anybody ('ɛnɪˌbɒdɪ) *pron.* same as **anyone.** Usage. see **everyone.**

anyhow ('ɛnɪˌhaʊ) *adv.* same as **anyway.**

anyone ('ɛnɪˌwʌn) *pron.* **1.** any person; anybody. **2.** (*used with a negative or question*) a person of any importance: *is he anyone?* Usage. see **everyone.**

anything (ˈɛnɪˌθɪŋ) pron. **1.** any object, event, or action whatever: *anything might happen.* ~adv. **2.** in any way: *he wasn't anything like his father.* **3. anything but.** not at all: *she was anything but happy.*

anyway (ˈɛnɪˌweɪ) adv. **1.** at any rate; nevertheless. **2.** carelessly. **3.** in any manner.

anywhere (ˈɛnɪˌwɛə) adv. **1.** in, at, or to any place. **2. get anywhere.** to be successful: *you'll never get anywhere with that attitude.*

Anzac (ˈænzæk) n. (in World War I) a soldier serving with the Australian and New Zealand Army Corps.

AOB (on the agenda for a meeting) any other business.

aorta (eɪˈɔːtə) n., pl. **-tas** or **-tae** (-tiː). the main artery of the body, which carries oxygen-rich blood from the heart.

apace (əˈpeɪs) adv. *Literary.* quickly.

Apache (əˈpætʃɪ) n., pl. **Apaches** or **Apache.** a North American Indian of the southwestern U.S. and N Mexico.

apache dance (əˈpæʃ) n. a fast violent dance in French vaudeville, supposedly between a Parisian gangster and his girl.

apart (əˈpɑːt) adj., adv. **1.** to or in pieces: *he took the television apart.* **2.** separate in time, place, or position: *he stood apart from the group.* **3.** not being taken into account: *these difficulties apart, the project ran smoothly.* **4.** individual; distinct: *a race apart.* **5. apart from.** other than: *all sports apart from athletics.*

apartheid (əˈpɑːthaɪt) n. the official government policy of racial segregation in South Africa.

apartment (əˈpɑːtmənt) n. **1.** any room in a building, usually one of several forming a suite, used as living accommodation. **2.** *Chiefly U.S. & Canad.* a flat.

apathy (ˈæpəθɪ) n. lack of interest or enthusiasm. —**apathetic** (ˌæpəˈθɛtɪk) adj.

ape (eɪp) n. **1.** an animal, such as a chimpanzee or gorilla, which is closely related to human beings and the monkeys, and which has no tail. **2.** a stupid, clumsy, or ugly man. ~vb. **3.** to imitate. —ˈape-ˌlike adj.

apeman (ˈeɪpˌmæn) n., pl. **-men.** an extinct primate thought to have been the forerunner of true humans.

aperient (əˈpɪərɪənt) *Med.* ~adj. **1.** having a mild laxative effect. ~n. **2.** a mild laxative.

apéritif (əˌpɛrɪˈtiːf) n. an alcoholic drink taken before a meal.

aperture (ˈæpətʃə) n. **1.** a hole or opening. **2.** an opening in a camera or telescope that controls the amount of light entering it.

apex (ˈeɪpɛks) n. the highest point.

APEX (ˈeɪpɛks) Advance Purchase Excursion: a reduced fare for journeys booked a specified period in advance.

aphasia (əˈfeɪzɪə) n. a disorder of the central nervous system that affects the ability to use and understand words.

aphelion (æˈfiːlɪən) n., pl. **-lia** (-lɪə). *Astron.* the point in the orbit of a planet or comet when it is farthest from the sun.

aphid (ˈeɪfɪd) or **aphis** (ˈeɪfɪs) n., pl. **aphids** or **aphides** (ˈeɪfɪˌdiːz). a small insect which feeds by sucking the juices from plants.

aphorism (ˈæfəˌrɪzəm) n. a short clever saying expressing a general truth.

aphrodisiac (ˌæfrəˈdɪzɪæk) n. **1.** a substance that arouses sexual desire. ~adj. **2.** arousing sexual desire.

apiary (ˈeɪpɪərɪ) n., pl. **-aries.** a place where bees are kept. —ˈapiarist n.

apical (ˈeɪpɪkˀl) adj. of, at, or being an apex.

apiculture (ˈeɪpɪˌkʌltʃə) n. the breeding and care of bees. —ˌapiˈculturist n.

apiece (əˈpiːs) adv. each: *they were given two apples apiece.*

apish (ˈeɪpɪʃ) adj. **1.** stupid; foolish. **2.** resembling an ape.

aplomb (əˈplɒm) n. stylish self-possession.

apocalypse (əˈpɒkəlɪps) n. the end of the world or some other event of great destructive violence. —aˌpocaˈlyptic adj.

Apocalypse (əˈpɒkəlɪps) n. **the.** *Bible.* the Book of Revelation.

Apocrypha (əˈpɒkrɪfə) n. (*functioning as sing. or pl.*) **the.** the 14 books included as an appendix to the Old Testament, which are not in the Hebrew canon.

apocryphal (əˈpɒkrɪfəl) adj. of questionable authenticity.

apogee (ˈæpəˌdʒiː) n. **1.** *Astron.* the point in its orbit around the earth when the moon or an artificial satellite is farthest from the earth. **2.** the highest point.

apolitical (ˌeɪpəˈlɪtɪkˀl) adj. not concerned with political matters.

apologetic (əˌpɒləˈdʒɛtɪk) adj. showing or expressing regret. —aˌpoloˈgetically adv.

apologetics (əˌpɒləˈdʒɛtɪks) n. (*functioning as sing.*) the branch of theology concerned with the reasoned defence of Christianity.

apologia (ˌæpəˈləʊdʒɪə) n. a formal written defence of a cause.

apologist (əˈpɒlədʒɪst) n. a person who offers a formal defence of a cause.

apologize or **-gise** (əˈpɒləˌdʒaɪz) vb. to say that one is sorry for some wrongdoing.

apology (əˈpɒlədʒɪ) n., pl. **-gies. 1.** an expression of regret for some wrongdoing. **2.** (foll. by *for*) a poor example of: *an apology for a man.* **3.** same as **apologia.**

apophthegm (ˈæpəˌθɛm) n. a short clever saying expressing a general truth.

apoplectic (ˌæpəˈplɛktɪk) adj. **1.** of apoplexy. **2.** *Informal.* furious.

apoplexy (ˈæpəˌplɛksɪ) n. *Med.* a stroke.

apostasy (ə'pɒstəsɪ) n., pl. **-sies.** abandonment of one's religious faith, political party, or cause.

apostate (ə'pɒstɪt) n. **1.** a person who has abandoned his religion, political party, or cause. ~adj. **2.** guilty of apostasy.

a posteriori (eɪ pɒsˌterɪ'ɔːraɪ) adj. Logic. involving reasoning from effect to cause.

apostle (ə'pɒs²l) n. **1.** (cap.) one of the 12 disciples chosen by Christ to preach his gospel. **2.** an ardent supporter of a cause or movement.

apostolic (ˌæpə'stɒlɪk) adj. **1.** of or relating to the Apostles or their teachings. **2.** of or relating to the pope.

Apostolic See n. the see of the pope, at Rome.

apostrophe[1] (ə'pɒstrəfɪ) n. the punctuation mark ' used to indicate the omission of a letter or letters, such as *he's* for *he has* or *he is*, and to form the possessive, as in *John's father*.

apostrophe[2] (ə'pɒstrəfɪ) n. Rhetoric. a digression from a speech to address an imaginary or absent person or thing.

apostrophize or **-phise** (ə'pɒstrəˌfaɪz) vb. Rhetoric. to address an apostrophe to.

apothecary (ə'pɒθɪkərɪ) n., pl. **-caries.** Archaic. a chemist.

apotheosis (əˌpɒθɪ'əʊsɪs) n., pl. **-ses** (-siːz). **1.** elevation to the rank of a god. **2.** a perfect example: *the apotheosis of generosity*.

appal or U.S. **appall** (ə'pɔːl) vb. **-palling, -palled.** to fill (someone) with horror.

appalling (ə'pɔːlɪŋ) adj. **1.** causing dismay, horror, or revulsion. **2.** very bad. —**ap'pallingly** adv.

apparatus (ˌæpə'reɪtəs, -'rɑːtəs) n. **1.** a collection of equipment used for a particular purpose. **2.** any complicated device, system, or organization.

apparel (ə'pærəl) n. Archaic. clothing.

apparent (ə'pærənt) adj. **1.** readily seen or understood; obvious. **2.** seeming, as opposed to real: *his apparent innocence*. —**ap'parently** adv.

apparition (ˌæpə'rɪʃən) n. a ghost or ghost-like figure.

appeal (ə'piːl) n. **1.** an earnest request for money or help. **2.** the power to attract, please, or interest people. **3.** an application to a higher authority to change a decision that has been made. **4.** Law. a request for a review by a superior court of the decision of a lower tribunal. ~vb. **5.** to make an earnest request. **6.** (foll. by *to*) to attract, please, or interest (someone). **7.** to resort to a higher authority to change a decision. **8.** to call on in support of an earnest request: *I appealed to his sense of reason*. **9.** Law. to apply to a superior court to review (a case or issue decided by a lower tribu-

nal). **10.** *Cricket.* to request the umpire to declare a batsman out. —**ap'pealing** adj.

appear (ə'pɪə) vb. **1.** to come into sight. **2.** to seem: *the evidence appears to support you*. **3.** to develop; occur: *faults appeared during testing*. **4.** to be published or become available: *his biography appeared last month*. **5.** to perform: *he has appeared in many London productions*. **6.** to be present in court before a magistrate or judge: *he appeared on two charges of theft*.

appearance (ə'pɪərəns) n. **1.** the act or an instance of appearing. **2.** the outward aspect of a person or thing. **3. keep up appearances.** to maintain the public impression of wellbeing or normality. **4. put in an appearance.** to attend an event briefly. **5. to all appearances.** apparently.

appease (ə'piːz) vb. **1.** to pacify (someone) by yielding to his demands. **2.** to satisfy or relieve (a feeling). —**ap'peasement** n.

appellant (ə'pɛlənt) Law. ~n. **1.** a person who appeals to a higher court to review the decision of a lower tribunal. ~adj. **2.** same as **appellate.**

appellate (ə'pɛlɪt) adj. Law. **1.** of appeals. **2.** (of a tribunal) having the power to review appeals.

appellation (ˌæpɪ'leɪʃən) n. a name or title.

append (ə'pɛnd) vb. to add as a supplement: *to append a footnote*.

appendage (ə'pɛndɪdʒ) n. a secondary part attached to a main part.

appendicectomy (əˌpɛndɪ'sɛktəmɪ) or esp. U.S. & Canad. **appendectomy** (ˌæpən-'dɛktəmɪ) n., pl. **-mies.** surgical removal of the appendix.

appendicitis (əˌpɛndɪ'saɪtɪs) n. inflammation of the appendix.

appendix (ə'pɛndɪks) n., pl. **-dixes** or **-dices** (-dɪˌsiːz). **1.** separate additional material at the end of a book. **2.** Anat. a short thin tube, closed at one end and attached to the large intestine at the other end.

appertain (ˌæpə'teɪn) vb. (foll. by *to*) to belong to, relate to, or be connected with.

appetence ('æpɪtəns) or **appetency** n., pl. **-tences** or **-tencies.** a craving or desire.

appetite ('æpɪˌtaɪt) n. **1.** a desire for food or drink. **2.** (foll. by *for*) a liking or willingness: *a great appetite for work*.

appetizer or **-iser** ('æpɪˌtaɪzə) n. a small amount of food or drink taken at the start of a meal to stimulate the appetite.

appetizing or **-ising** ('æpɪˌtaɪzɪŋ) adj. stimulating the appetite; looking or smelling delicious.

applaud (ə'plɔːd) vb. **1.** to show approval of (a performance, an entertainer, or a speaker) by clapping one's hands. **2.** to express approval of: *I applaud your decision*.

applause (ə'plɔːz) n. appreciation shown by clapping one's hands.

apple ('æp³l) n. **1.** a round firm fruit with red, yellow, or green skin and crisp whitish flesh, that grows on trees. **2. apple of one's eye.** a person that one loves very much.

apple-pie bed n. a bed made with the sheets folded so as to prevent the person from entering it.

apple-pie order n. **in apple-pie order.** Informal. very tidy.

appliance (ə'plaɪəns) n. a machine or device that has a specific function.

applicable ('æplɪkəb³l) adj. appropriate or relevant.

applicant ('æplɪkənt) n. a person who applies for something, such as a job or grant.

application (,æplɪ'keɪʃən) n. **1.** a formal request, for example for a job. **2.** the act of applying something to a particular use. **3.** diligent effort: a job requiring application. **4.** the act of putting something, such as a lotion or paint, on to a surface.

applicator ('æplɪ,keɪtə) n. a device for applying cosmetics, medication, or some other substance.

applied (ə'plaɪd) adj. put to practical use: applied mathematics.

appliqué (æ'pliːkeɪ) n. a kind of decoration in which one material is cut out and sewn or fixed onto another.

apply (ə'plaɪ) vb. **-plying, -plied. 1.** (foll. by for) to make a formal request for (something, such as a job or grant). **2.** to put (a rule or theory) to practical use. **3.** to be relevant or appropriate. **4.** to put (something, such as a lotion or paint) on to a surface. **5. apply oneself.** to concentrate one's efforts or faculties.

appoint (ə'pɔɪnt) vb. **1.** to assign (someone) officially, to a job or position. **2.** to establish (a time or place for an event). **3.** to equip or furnish: a well-appointed hotel. **—appoin'tee** n.

appointment (ə'pɔɪntmənt) n. **1.** an arrangement to meet a person. **2.** the act of placing someone in a job or position. **3.** the person appointed. **4.** the job or position to which a person is appointed. **5.** (pl.) fixtures or fittings.

apportion (ə'pɔːʃən) vb. to divide, distribute, or assign shares of.

apposite ('æpəzɪt) adj. appropriate; apt.

apposition (,æpə'zɪʃən) n. a grammatical construction in which a noun or group of words is placed after another to modify its meaning, for example my friend the mayor.

appraisal (ə'preɪz³l) n. an assessment of the worth or quality of a person or thing; valuation.

appraise (ə'preɪz) vb. to assess the worth, value, or quality of.

appreciable (ə'priːʃəb³l) adj. enough to be noticed; significant. **—ap'preciably** adv.

appreciate (ə'priːʃɪ,eɪt) vb. **1.** to feel grateful for: I appreciate your kindness. **2.** to be aware of and understand: I appreciate your problem. **3.** to value highly: he doesn't appreciate good music. **4.** to increase in value.

appreciation (ə,priːʃɪ'eɪʃən) n. **1.** gratitude. **2.** awareness and understanding of a problem or difficulty. **3.** sensitive recognition of good qualities, as in art. **4.** an increase in value.

appreciative (ə'priːʃɪətɪv) or **appreciatory** adj. feeling or expressing appreciation.

apprehend (,æprɪ'hɛnd) vb. **1.** to arrest (someone) and take him into custody. **2.** to grasp (something) mentally; understand.

apprehension (,æprɪ'hɛnʃən) n. **1.** anxiety or dread. **2.** the act of arresting. **3.** understanding.

apprehensive (,æprɪ'hɛnsɪv) adj. fearful or anxious about the future.

apprentice (ə'prɛntɪs) n. **1.** someone who works for a skilled person for a fixed period in order to learn his trade. ~vb. **2.** to take or place (someone) as an apprentice. **—ap'prentice,ship** n.

apprise or **-ize** (ə'praɪz) vb. (foll. by of) to make (someone) aware: let me apprise you of the facts.

appro ('æprəʊ) n. **on appro.** Informal. on approval.

approach (ə'prəʊtʃ) vb. **1.** to come close or closer to (someone or something). **2.** to make a proposal or suggestion to (someone). **3.** to begin to deal with (a matter). ~n. **4.** the act of coming close or closer. **5.** the way or means of reaching a place; access. **6.** a proposal or suggestion made to a person. **7.** a way of dealing with a matter. **8.** the course followed by an aircraft preparing for landing. **9.** an approximation. **—ap'proachable** adj.

approbation (,æprə'beɪʃən) n. approval or permission.

appropriate adj. (ə'prəʊprɪɪt). **1.** right or suitable. ~vb. (ə'prəʊprɪ,eɪt). **2.** to take (something) for one's own use without permission. **3.** to put (money) aside for a particular purpose. **—ap'propriately** adv.

appropriation (ə,prəʊprɪ'eɪʃən) n. **1.** the act of putting money aside for a particular purpose. **2.** money put aside for a particular purpose.

approval (ə'pruːv³l) n. **1.** consent. **2.** a favourable opinion. **3. on approval.** (of articles for sale) with an option to return them to the shop if not suitable: I got this hat on approval.

approve (ə'pruːv) vb. **1.** (foll. by of) to consider fair, good, or right. **2.** to authorize or sanction.

approx. approximate.

approximate *adj.* (ə'prɒksɪmɪt). **1.** almost exact. ~*vb.* (ə'prɒksɪˌmeɪt). **2.** (foll. by *to*) to come close to; be almost the same as. —**ap'proximately** *adv.* —**approximation** (əˌprɒksɪ'meɪʃən) *n.*

appurtenances (ə'pɜːtɪnənsɪz) *pl. n.* minor or additional features or possessions.

Apr. April.

après-ski (ˌæpreɪ'skiː) *n.* social activity following a day's skiing.

apricot ('eɪprɪˌkɒt) *n.* **1.** a yellowish-orange juicy fruit which resembles a small peach and which grows on a tree. ~*adj.* **2.** yellowish-orange.

April ('eɪprəl) *n.* the fourth month of the year.

April fool *n.* a victim of a practical joke played on the first of April (**April Fools' Day** or **All Fools' Day**).

a priori (eɪ praɪ'ɔːraɪ) *adj. Logic.* involving reasoning from cause to effect.

apron ('eɪprən) *n.* **1.** a garment worn over the front of the body to protect one's clothes. **2.** the part of a stage extending in front of the curtain. **3.** a hard-surfaced area at an airport or hangar for manoeuvring and loading aircraft. **4. tied to one's mother's** or **wife's apron strings.** dominated by one's mother or wife.

apropos (ˌæprə'pəʊ) *adj.* **1.** appropriate. ~*adv.* **2.** by the way; incidentally. **3. apropos of.** with regard to.

apse (æps) *n.* a domed or vaulted semicircular recess at the east end of a church.

apsis ('æpsɪs) *n., pl.* **apsides** ('æpsɪˌdiːz). *Astron.* either of two points lying at the extremities of the elliptical orbit of a planet or satellite.

apt (æpt) *adj.* **1.** suitable; appropriate. **2.** having a tendency (to behave as specified): *I am apt to forget my keys.* **3.** quick to learn: *an apt pupil.* —**'aptly** *adv.* —**'aptness** *n.*

apteryx ('æptərɪks) *n.* same as **kiwi.**

aptitude ('æptɪˌtjuːd) *n.* natural tendency or ability.

aqua ('ækwə) *adj.* bluish-green.

aqua fortis ('fɔːtɪs) *n. Obs.* nitric acid.

aqualung ('ækwəˌlʌŋ) *n.* a self-contained underwater breathing apparatus consisting of a mouthpiece attached to air cylinders strapped to one's back.

aquamarine (ˌækwəmə'riːn) *n.* **1.** a clear greenish-blue stone used in jewellery. ~*adj.* **2.** greenish-blue.

aquaplane ('ækwəˌpleɪn) *n.* **1.** a board on which a person stands to be towed by a motorboat for sport. ~*vb.* **2.** to ride on an aquaplane. **3.** (of a motor vehicle) to skim uncontrollably on a thin film of water.

aqua regia ('riːdʒɪə) *n.* a mixture of nitric acid and hydrochloric acid.

aquarium (ə'kwɛərɪəm) *n., pl.* **aquariums** or **aquaria** (ə'kwɛərɪə). **1.** a tank in which fish and other underwater creatures are kept. **2.** a building in a zoo in which fish and other underwater creatures are kept.

Aquarius (ə'kwɛərɪəs) *n. Astrol.* the eleventh sign of the zodiac: the water carrier.

aquatic (ə'kwætɪk) *adj.* **1.** growing or living in water. **2.** *Sport.* performed in or on water. ~*n.* **3.** an aquatic animal or plant. **4.** (*pl.*) water sports.

aquatint ('ækwəˌtɪnt) *n.* a print resembling watercolour, produced by etching copper with acid.

aqua vitae ('viːtaɪ) *n. Archaic.* brandy.

aqueduct ('ækwɪˌdʌkt) *n.* a structure, often a bridge, that carries water across a valley or river.

aqueous ('eɪkwɪəs) *adj.* **1.** of, like, or containing water. **2.** produced by the action of water.

aqueous humour *n. Physiol.* the watery fluid in the eyeball, between the cornea and the lens.

aquifer ('ækwɪfə) *n.* a deposit of rock, such as sandstone, containing water that can be used to supply wells.

aquiline ('ækwɪˌlaɪn) *adj.* **1.** (of a nose) curved like an eagle's beak. **2.** of or like an eagle.

Ar *Chem.* argon.

AR Arkansas.

Arab ('ærəb) *n.* **1.** a member of a Semitic people originally from Arabia. **2.** a small horse, used for riding. ~*adj.* **3.** of or relating to the Arabs.

arabesque (ˌærə'bɛsk) *n.* **1.** a ballet position in which the dancer has one leg raised behind and the arms extended. **2.** an ornate piece of music. **3.** *Arts.* an elaborate design of intertwined leaves, flowers, and scrolls.

Arabian (ə'reɪbɪən) *adj.* **1.** of Arabia or the Arabs. ~*n.* **2.** same as **Arab.**

Arabic ('ærəbɪk) *n.* **1.** the language of the Arabs. ~*adj.* **2.** of this language, the Arabs, or Arabia.

Arabic numeral *n.* one of the numbers 1,2,3,4,5,6,7,8,9,0.

arable ('ærəb'l) *adj.* (of land) suitable for growing crops on.

arachnid (ə'ræknɪd) *n.* an eight-legged insect-like creature, such as a spider, scorpion, or tick.

arak ('ærək) *n.* same as **arrack.**

Aramaic (ˌærə'meɪɪk) *n.* a branch of the Semitic group of languages, spoken in parts of Syria and the Lebanon.

arbiter ('ɑːbɪtə) *n.* **1.** a person empowered to judge in a dispute; referee. **2.** a person having influence over something: *the arbiter of good taste.*

arbitrary ('ɑːbɪtrərɪ) *adj.* **1.** based on one's

personal choice or whims. **2.** dictatorial. —**'arbitrarily** *adv.*

arbitrate ('ɑːbɪ,treɪt) *vb.* to settle (a dispute) by arbitration. —**'arbi,trator** *n.*

arbitration (,ɑːbɪ'treɪʃən) *n.* the hearing and settlement of a dispute by an impartial referee chosen by both sides.

arbor[1] ('ɑːbə) *n. U.S.* same as **arbour**.

arbor[2] ('ɑːbə) *n.* a revolving shaft or axle in a machine.

arboreal (ɑː'bɔːrɪəl) *adj.* **1.** of or resembling a tree. **2.** living in or among trees.

arboretum (,ɑːbə'riːtəm) *n., pl.* **-ta** (-tə). a botanical garden where rare trees or shrubs are cultivated.

arboriculture ('ɑːbərɪ,kʌltʃə) *n.* the cultivation of trees or shrubs.

arbor vitae ('ɑːbə 'viːtaɪ) *n.* an evergreen tree.

arbour *or U.S.* **arbor** ('ɑːbə) *n.* a shelter in a garden shaded by trees or climbing plants.

arbutus (ɑː'bjuːtəs) *n.* an evergreen shrub with berries like strawberries.

arc (ɑːk) *n.* **1.** something curved in shape. **2.** *Maths.* a section of a circle or other curve. **3.** *Electricity.* a stream of very bright light that forms when an electric current flows between two electrodes separated by a small gap. ~*vb.* **4.** to form an arc.

ARC AIDS-related complex: relatively mild symptoms suffered in the early stages of infection with the AIDS virus.

arcade (ɑː'keɪd) *n.* **1.** a covered passageway, usually lined with shops. **2.** a set of arches and their supporting columns.

Arcadian (ɑː'keɪdɪən) *adj.* **1.** ideally rustic. ~*n.* **2.** a person who leads a quiet simple country life.

arcane (ɑː'keɪn) *adj.* very mysterious.

arch[1] (ɑːtʃ) *n.* **1.** a curved structure that spans an opening or supports a bridge or roof. **2.** something curved like an arch. **3.** the curved lower part of the foot. ~*vb.* **4.** to form an arch or cause (something) to form an arch.

arch[2] (ɑːtʃ) *adj.* knowing or superior; coyly playful: *an arch look.* —**'archly** *adv.*

arch- *or* **archi-** *combining form.* chief; principal: *archbishop.*

Archaean *or esp. U.S.* **Archean** (ɑː'kiːən) *adj.* of the earliest geological period.

archaeology *or* **archeology** (,ɑːkɪ'ɒlədʒɪ) *n.* the study of ancient cultures by the scientific analysis of physical remains. —**archaeological** *or* **archeological** (,ɑːkɪə'lɒdʒɪk°l) *adj.* —**archae'ologist** *or* **,arche'ologist** *n.*

archaeopteryx (,ɑːkɪ'ɒptərɪks) *n.* an extinct primitive bird with teeth, a long tail, and well-developed wings.

archaic (ɑː'keɪɪk) *adj.* **1.** ancient; of a much earlier period. **2.** out of date; old-

fashioned. **3.** (of a word or phrase) no longer in everyday use; found only in literature of an earlier period. —**ar'chaically** *adv.*

archaism ('ɑːkeɪ,ɪzəm) *n.* **1.** the use or imitation of archaic words or style. **2.** an archaic word or style. —**,archa'istic** *adj.*

archangel ('ɑːk,eɪndʒəl) *n.* an angel of the highest rank.

archbishop ('ɑːtʃ'bɪʃəp) *n.* a bishop of the highest rank.

archbishopric ('ɑːtʃ'bɪʃəprɪk) *n.* the rank, office, or diocese of an archbishop.

archdeacon ('ɑːtʃ'diːkən) *n.* a church official ranking just below a bishop. —**'arch'deaconry** *n.*

archdiocese (,ɑːtʃ'daɪə,siːs) *n.* the diocese of an archbishop.

archduchess ('ɑːtʃ'dʌtʃɪs) *n.* the wife of an archduke.

archduchy ('ɑːtʃ'dʌtʃɪ) *n., pl.* **-duchies.** the territory ruled by an archduke or archduchess.

archduke ('ɑːtʃ'djuːk) *n.* a chief duke, esp. a prince of the former Austrian imperial dynasty.

Archean (ɑː'kiːən) *adj. U.S.* same as **Archaean.**

archenemy ('ɑːtʃ'ɛnɪmɪ) *n., pl.* **-mies.** a chief enemy.

archeology (,ɑːkɪ'ɒlədʒɪ) *n.* same as **archaeology.**

archer ('ɑːtʃə) *n.* a person who shoots with a bow and arrow.

archery ('ɑːtʃərɪ) *n.* the art or sport of shooting with a bow and arrow.

archetype ('ɑːkɪ,taɪp) *n.* **1.** a perfect or typical specimen. **2.** an original model; prototype. —**,arche'typal** *adj.*

archfiend (,ɑːtʃ'fiːnd) *n.* **the.** the Devil.

archidiaconal (,ɑːkɪdaɪ'ækən°l) *adj.* of an archdeacon or his office.

archiepiscopal (,ɑːkɪɪ'pɪskəp°l) *adj.* of an archbishop or his office.

archipelago (,ɑːkɪ'pɛlə,gəʊ) *n., pl.* **-gos. 1.** a group of islands. **2.** a sea studded with islands.

architect ('ɑːkɪ,tɛkt) *n.* **1.** a person qualified to design buildings or other structures and to supervise their construction. **2.** any planner or creator.

architecture ('ɑːkɪ,tɛktʃə) *n.* **1.** the science of designing and superintending the construction of buildings or other structures. **2.** a style of building. **3.** the structure or design of anything. —**,archi'tectural** *adj.*

architrave ('ɑːkɪ,treɪv) *n. Archit.* **1.** a beam that rests on top of columns. **2.** a moulding around a doorway or window opening.

archive ('ɑːkaɪv) *n.* **1.** a place where records or documents are kept. **2.** (*pl.*) a collection of records or documents.

archivist ('ɑːkɪvɪst) *n.* a person in charge of archives.

archway ('ɑːtʃˌweɪ) *n.* a passageway under an arch.

arctic ('ɑːktɪk) *adj. Informal.* cold; freezing.

Arctic ('ɑːktɪk) *n.* **the.** the area around the North Pole.

Arctic Circle *n.* the imaginary circle around the earth at latitude 66° 32′ N.

arctic hare *n.* a large hare of the Canadian Arctic whose fur turns white in winter.

arctic willow *n.* a low-growing shrub of the Canadian Arctic.

arc welding *n.* a technique in which metal is welded by heat generated by an electric arc.

ardent ('ɑːdʰnt) *adj.* **1.** passionate. **2.** intensely enthusiastic; eager. —**'ardently** *adv.*

ardour *or U.S.* **ardor** ('ɑːdə) *n.* **1.** emotional warmth; passion. **2.** intense enthusiasm.

arduous ('ɑːdjuːəs) *adj.* difficult to accomplish; strenuous.

are[1] (ɑː) *vb.* the plural form of the present tense of **be** and the singular form used with *you.*

are[2] (ɑː) *n.* a unit of area equal to 100 square metres.

area ('ɛərɪə) *n.* **1.** a section, part, or region. **2.** a part having a specified function: *reception area.* **3.** any flat, curved, or irregular expanse of a surface. **4.** the size of a two-dimensional surface. **5.** range or scope. **6.** a subject field. **7.** a sunken area giving access to a basement.

arena (əˈriːnə) *n.* **1. a.** an area surrounded by seats, where sports events take place. **b.** a building housing an arena. **2.** the area of an ancient Roman amphitheatre where gladiators fought. **3.** a sphere of intense activity: *the political arena.*

aren't (ɑːnt) are not.

areola (əˈrɪələ) *n., pl.* **-lae** (-ˌliː) *or* **-las.** a small circular area, such as the coloured ring around the human nipple.

arête (əˈreɪt, əˈrɛt) *n.* a sharp ridge separating valleys.

argon ('ɑːgɒn) *n.* an unreactive odourless element of the rare gas series, forming almost 1 per cent of the atmosphere. Symbol: Ar

argosy ('ɑːgəsɪ) *n., pl.* **-sies.** *Archaic or poetic.* a large merchant ship, or a fleet of such ships.

argot ('ɑːgəʊ) *n.* slang or jargon peculiar to a particular group.

argue ('ɑːgjuː) *vb.* **-guing, -gued. 1.** to quarrel. **2.** to try to prove by presenting reasons. **3.** to debate. **4.** to persuade: *we argued her out of going.* **5.** to suggest: *her looks argue despair.* —**'arguable** *adj.* —**'arguably** *adv.*

argument ('ɑːgjʊmənt) *n.* **1.** a quarrel. **2.** a discussion. **3.** a point presented to support or oppose a proposition.

argumentation (ˌɑːgjʊmɛnˈteɪʃən) *n.* the process of reasoning methodically.

argumentative (ˌɑːgjʊˈmɛntətɪv) *adj.* given to arguing.

argy-bargy *or* **argie-bargie** ('ɑːdʒɪˈbɑːdʒɪ) *n., pl.* **-bargies.** *Brit. informal.* a wrangling argument.

aria ('ɑːrɪə) *n.* an elaborate song for solo voice, esp. from an opera.

Arianism ('ɛərɪəˌnɪzəm) *n.* the doctrine of Arius, 3rd-century A.D. Greek, who asserted that Christ was not of one substance with God. —**'Arian** *adj., n.*

arid ('ærɪd) *adj.* **1.** having little or no rain. **2.** devoid of interest. —**aridity** (əˈrɪdɪtɪ) *n.*

Aries ('ɛəriːz) *n. Astrol.* the first sign of the zodiac: the Ram.

aright (əˈraɪt) *adv.* correctly; properly.

arise (əˈraɪz) *vb.* **arising, arose, arisen** (əˈrɪzʰn). **1.** to come into being. **2.** to get or stand up. **3.** to come into notice. **4. arise from.** to proceed as a consequence of.

aristocracy (ˌærɪˈstɒkrəsɪ) *n., pl.* **-cies. 1.** a class of people of high social rank. **2.** a group of people considered to be outstanding in a particular sphere of activity.

aristocratic (ˌærɪstəˈkrætɪk) *adj.* **1.** of the aristocracy. **2.** grand or elegant. —**'aristoˌcrat** *n.*

Aristotelian (ˌærɪstəˈtiːlɪən) *adj.* of or relating to Aristotle, 4th-century B.C. Greek philosopher, or to his philosophy.

arithmetic *n.* (əˈrɪθmətɪk). **1.** the branch of mathematics concerned with numerical calculations, such as addition, subtraction, multiplication, and division. **2.** calculations involving numerical operations. **3.** knowledge of or skill in arithmetic: *my arithmetic is rotten.* ~*adj.* (ˌærɪθˈmɛtɪk), *also* **arithmetical. 4.** of or using arithmetic. —ˌarithˈmetically *adv.* —aˌrithmeˈtician *n.*

arithmetic mean *n.* the average value of a set of terms, expressed as their sum divided by their number: *the arithmetic mean of 3, 4, and 8 is 5.*

arithmetic progression *n.* a sequence, each term of which differs from the preceding term by a constant amount, such as 3,6,9,12.

Ariz. Arizona.

ark (ɑːk) *n. Bible.* the vessel that Noah built, which survived the Flood.

Ark (ɑːk) *n. Judaism.* **1.** Also called: **Holy Ark.** the cupboard in a synagogue in which the Torah scrolls are kept. **2.** Also called: **Ark of the Covenant.** a chest containing the laws of the Jewish religion, regarded as the most sacred symbol of God's presence among the Hebrew people.

Ark. Arkansas.

arm[1] (ɑːm) *n.* **1.** (in humans, apes and monkeys) either of the upper limbs from the shoulder to the wrist. **2.** an object that covers or supports the arm, such as a sleeve or the side of a chair. **3.** anything resembling an arm in appearance or function: *the arm of a record player*. **4.** an administrative subdivision of an organization: *an arm of the government*. **5.** authority: *the arm of the law*. **6. arm in arm.** with arms linked. **7. at arm's length.** at a distance. **8. with open arms.** with warmth and hospitality.

arm² (ɑːm) *vb*. **1.** to equip with weapons. **2.** to provide (a person or thing) with something that strengthens, or protects. **3.** to prepare (an explosive device) for use. ~See also **arms**. —**armed** *adj*.

armada (ɑːˈmɑːdə) *n*. **1.** a large number of ships. **2. the Armada.** the great fleet sent by Spain against England in 1588.

armadillo (ˌɑːməˈdɪləʊ) *n., pl*. **-los.** a burrowing mammal of Central and South America with a covering of strong horny plates.

Armageddon (ˌɑːməˈgɛdᵊn) *n*. **1.** *New Testament*. the final battle between good and evil at the end of the world. **2.** a catastrophic and extremely destructive conflict.

armament (ˈɑːməmənt) *n*. **1.** the weapon equipment of a military vehicle, ship, or aircraft. **2.** preparation for war.

armature (ˈɑːmətjʊə) *n*. **1.** a revolving structure in an electric motor or generator, wound with the coils that carry the current. **2.** a soft iron or steel bar placed across the poles of a magnet to close the magnetic circuit. **3.** *Sculpture*. a framework to support the clay or other material used in modelling.

armchair (ˈɑːmˌtʃɛə) *n*. **1.** an upholstered chair with side supports for the arms. **2.** (*modifier*) taking no active part: *an armchair revolutionary*.

armed forces *pl. n*. all the military forces of a nation or nations.

armhole (ˈɑːmˌhəʊl) *n*. the opening in an article of clothing through which the arm passes.

armistice (ˈɑːmɪstɪs) *n*. an agreement between opposing armies to stop fighting.

Armistice Day (ˈɑːmɪstɪs) *n*. the anniversary of the signing of the armistice that ended World War I, on Nov. 11, 1918.

armlet (ˈɑːmlɪt) *n*. a band or bracelet worn around the arm.

armorial (ɑːˈmɔːrɪəl) *adj*. of or relating to heraldry or heraldic arms.

armour or *U.S.* **armor** (ˈɑːmə) *n*. **1.** clothing of plate metal or chain mail worn by medieval warriors for protection in battle. **2.** the protective metal plates on a tank or warship. **3.** *Mil*. armoured fighting vehicles in general. **4.** any protective covering, such as the shell of certain animals. **5.** a

quality or attitude that gives protection. ~*vb*. **6.** to equip or cover with armour.

armoured or *U.S.* **armored** (ˈɑːməd) *adj*. **1.** having a protective covering. **2.** comprising armoured vehicles: *an armoured brigade*.

armourer or *U.S.* **armorer** (ˈɑːmərə) *n*. **1.** a person who makes or mends arms and armour. **2.** a person in charge of small arms in a military unit.

armour plate *n*. a tough heavy steel for protecting warships and vehicles. —**armour-ˈplated** *adj*.

armoury or *U.S.* **armory** (ˈɑːmərɪ) *n., pl*. **-mouries** or **-mories. 1.** a secure place for the storage of weapons. **2.** military supplies. **3.** resources on which to draw: *a few choice terms from her armoury of invective*.

armpit (ˈɑːmˌpɪt) *n*. the depression beneath the arm where it joins the shoulder.

armrest (ˈɑːmˌrɛst) *n*. the part of a chair or sofa, that supports the arm.

arms (ɑːmz) *pl. n*. **1.** weapons collectively. **2.** military exploits: *prowess in arms*. **3.** the heraldic symbols of a family, state, etc. **4. take up arms.** to prepare to fight. **5. under arms.** armed and prepared for war. **6. up in arms.** indignant; prepared to protest strongly.

army (ˈɑːmɪ) *n., pl*. **-mies. 1.** the military land forces of a nation. **2.** a large number of people or animals.

aroha (ˈɑːrohə) *n. N.Z*. love, compassion, or affectionate regard.

aroma (əˈrəʊmə) *n*. **1.** a distinctive, usually pleasant smell. **2.** a subtle pervasive quality or atmosphere.

aromatherapy (əˌrəʊməˈθɛrəpɪ) *n*. massage with fragrant oils to relieve tension.

aromatic (ˌærəˈmætɪk) *adj*. **1.** having a distinctive, usually fragrant smell. **2.** (of an organic compound) having an unsaturated ring of atoms, usually six carbon atoms. ~*n*. **3.** something, such as a plant or drug, giving off a fragrant smell.

arose (əˈrəʊz) *vb*. the past tense of **arise.**

around (əˈraʊnd) *prep*. **1.** situated at various points in: *a lot of shelves around the house*. **2.** from place to place in: *driving around Ireland*. **3.** somewhere in or near. **4.** approximately in: *around 1957*. ~*adv*. **5.** in all directions from a point of reference: *he owns the land for ten miles around*. **6.** in the vicinity, esp. restlessly but idly: *to stand around*. **7.** in no particular place or direction: *dotted around*. **8.** *Informal*. present in some unknown or unspecified place. **9.** *Informal*. available: *that type of phone has been around for years*. **10. have been around.** *Informal*. to have gained considerable experience of a worldly or social nature.

arouse (əˈraʊz) *vb*. **1.** to produce (a reaction, emotion, or response). **2.** to awaken from sleep. **—a'rousal** n.

arpeggio (ɑːˈpedʒɪəʊ) n., pl. **-gios.** a chord whose notes are played or sung in rapid succession.

arquebus (ˈɑːkwɪbəs) n. a portable long-barrelled gun dating from the 15th century.

arr. 1. arranged (by). **2.** arrival. **3.** arrive(d).

arrack or **arak** (ˈærək) n. a coarse spirit distilled in Eastern countries from grain or rice.

arraign (əˈreɪn) vb. **1.** to bring (a prisoner) before a court to answer a charge. **2.** to accuse. **—ar'raignment** n.

arrange (əˈreɪndʒ) vb. **1.** to put into a proper or systematic order. **2.** to agree. **3.** to plan in advance: *we arranged for her to be met.* **4.** to adapt (a musical composition) for performance in a different way, esp. on different instruments.

arrangement (əˈreɪndʒmənt) n. **1.** (often pl.) a preparation. **2.** an understanding. **3.** a thing composed of various ordered parts: *a flower arrangement.* **4.** the form in which things are arranged. **5.** an adaptation of a piece of music for performance in a different way.

arrant (ˈærənt) adj. utter; out-and-out: *an arrant fool.*

arras (ˈærəs) n. a wall hanging, esp. of tapestry.

array (əˈreɪ) n. **1.** an impressive display or collection. **2.** an orderly arrangement, as of troops in battle order. **3.** *Poetic.* rich clothing. **4.** *Computers.* a data structure in which elements may be located by index numbers. ~vb. **5.** to arrange in order. **6.** to dress in rich attire.

arrears (əˈrɪəz) pl. n. **1.** something outstanding or owed. **2. in arrears.** late in paying a debt or meeting an obligation.

arrest (əˈrest) vb. **1.** to take (a person) into custody. **2.** to slow or stop the development of (a disease or growth). **3.** to catch and hold (one's attention). ~n. **4.** the act of taking a person into custody. **5. under arrest.** being held in custody by the police. **6.** the slowing or stopping of something: *a cardiac arrest.*

arresting (əˈrestɪŋ) adj. attracting attention; striking.

arrival (əˈraɪvᵊl) n. **1.** the act of arriving. **2.** a person or thing that has just arrived. **3.** *Informal.* a recently born baby.

arrive (əˈraɪv) vb. **1.** to reach a place or destination. **2.** to come to a conclusion, idea, or decision. **3.** to occur eventually: *the moment arrived when pretence was useless.* **4.** *Informal.* to be born. **5.** *Informal.* to attain success.

arrogant (ˈærəgənt) adj. having or showing an exaggerated opinion of one's own impor-

tance or ability. **—'arrogance** n. **—'arrogantly** adv.

arrogate (ˈærəˌgeɪt) vb. to claim, for oneself or another, without justification. **—,arro'gation** n.

arrow (ˈærəʊ) n. **1.** a long slender pointed weapon, usually having feathers at one end, that is shot from a bow. **2.** an arrow-shaped sign or symbol, such as one used to show the direction to a place.

arrowhead (ˈærəʊˌhed) n. the pointed tip of an arrow.

arrowroot (ˈærəʊˌruːt) n. an easily digestible starch obtained from the rhizomes of a West Indian plant.

arse (ɑːs) or U.S. & Canad. **ass** n. Taboo. the buttocks or anus.

arsehole (ˈɑːsˌhəʊl) or U.S. & Canad. **asshole** n. Taboo. **1.** the anus. **2.** a stupid person; fool.

arsenal (ˈɑːsənᵊl) n. **1.** a building for storing and making arms and ammunition. **2.** a store of anything regarded as weapons.

arsenic n. (ˈɑːsnɪk). **1.** a toxic metalloid element. Symbol: As **2.** a nontechnical name for **arsenic trioxide**, used as rat poison and an insecticide. ~adj. (ɑːˈsenɪk), also **arsenical. 3.** of or containing arsenic.

arson (ˈɑːsᵊn) n. the crime of intentionally setting fire to property. **—'arsonist** n.

art¹ (ɑːt) n. **1.** the creation of works of beauty or other special significance. **2.** human creativity as distinguished from nature. **3.** works of art collectively. **4.** any branch of the visual arts, esp. painting. **5.** skill: *the art of government.* **6. get something down to a fine art.** to become proficient at something through practice.

art² (ɑːt) vb. Archaic. (used with thou) a singular form of the present tense of **be.**

Art Deco (ˈdekəʊ) n. a style of design, at its height in the 1930s, characterized by geometrical shapes.

artefact or **artifact** (ˈɑːtɪˌfækt) n. something made by man, such as a tool or a work of art.

arterial (ɑːˈtɪərɪəl) adj. **1.** of or affecting an artery or the blood that circulates in the arteries. **2.** being a major route.

arteriosclerosis (ɑːˌtɪərɪəʊsklɪəˈrəʊsɪs) n., pl. **-ses** (-siːz). thickening and loss of elasticity of the walls of the arteries. Nontechnical name: **hardening of the arteries.**

artery (ˈɑːtərɪ) n., pl. **-teries. 1.** any of the tubular vessels that convey oxygenated blood from the heart to various parts of the body. **2.** a major road or means of communication.

artesian well (ɑːˈtiːzɪən) n. a well receiving water from a higher altitude, so the water is forced to flow upwards.

art form n. a recognized mode or medium of artistic expression.

artful ('ɑːtfʊl) *adj.* **1.** cunning. **2.** skilful in achieving a desired end. —'**artfully** *adv.*

arthritis (ɑː'θraɪtɪs) *n.* inflammation of a joint or joints characterized by pain and stiffness. —**arthritic** (ɑː'θrɪtɪk) *adj., n.*

arthropod ('ɑːθrə,pɒd) *n.* a creature, such as an insect or a spider, which has jointed legs and a hard case on its body.

artic (ɑː'tɪk) *n. Informal.* an articulated lorry.

artichoke ('ɑːtɪ,tʃəʊk) *n.* **1.** Also called: **globe artichoke.** the flower head of a thistle-like plant, edible when cooked. **2.** same as **Jerusalem artichoke.**

article ('ɑːtɪk*ə*l) *n.* **1.** an item or object. **2.** a written composition in a magazine or newspaper. **3.** *Grammar.* any of the words *a, an,* or *the.* **4.** a clause in a written document.

articled ('ɑːtɪk*ə*ld) *adj.* bound by a written contract, such as one that governs a period of training: *an articled clerk.*

articular (ɑː'tɪkjʊlə) *adj.* of or relating to joints.

articulate *adj.* (ɑː'tɪkjʊlɪt). **1.** able to express oneself fluently and coherently. **2.** distinct, clear, or definite: *an articulate document.* **3.** *Zool.* possessing joints. ~*vb.* (ɑː'tɪkjʊ,leɪt). **4.** to speak clearly and distinctly. **5.** to express coherently in words. —**ar'ticulately** *adv.*

articulated lorry *n.* a large lorry in two separate sections connected by a pivoted bar.

articulation (ɑː,tɪkjʊ'leɪʃən) *n.* **1.** the expressing of an idea in words. **2.** the process of articulating a speech sound or the sound so produced. **3.** a being jointed together. **4.** *Zool.* a joint between bones or arthropod segments.

artifact ('ɑːtɪ,fækt) *n.* same as **artefact.**

artifice ('ɑːtɪfɪs) *n.* **1.** a clever expedient. **2.** subtle deception. **3.** skill; cleverness.

artificer (ɑː'tɪfɪsə) *n.* a skilled craftsman.

artificial (,ɑːtɪ'fɪʃəl) *adj.* **1.** produced by man; not occurring naturally. **2.** made in imitation of a natural product: *artificial cream.* **3.** pretended or affected. —**artificiality** (,ɑːtɪ,fɪʃɪ'ælɪtɪ) *n.* —,**arti'ficially** *adv.*

artificial insemination *n.* introduction of semen into the womb by means other than sexual union.

artificial respiration *n.* any method of restarting breathing after it has stopped.

artillery (ɑː'tɪlərɪ) *n.* **1.** large-calibre guns. **2.** military units specializing in using such guns.

artisan ('ɑːtɪ,zæn, ,ɑːtɪ'zæn) *n.* a skilled workman; craftsman.

artist ('ɑːtɪst) *n.* **1.** a person who practises or is skilled in painting, drawing, or sculpture. **2.** a person skilled in some task or occupation. **3.** same as **artiste.** —**ar'tistic** *adj.* —**ar'tistically** *adv.*

artiste (ɑː'tiːst) *n.* an entertainer, such as a singer or dancer.

artistry ('ɑːtɪstrɪ) *n.* **1.** artistic ability. **2.** great skill.

artless ('ɑːtlɪs) *adj.* **1.** free from deceit; ingenuous: *an artless remark.* **2.** natural; unpretentious. —'**artlessly** *adv.*

Art Nouveau (ɑː nuː'vəʊ) *n.* a style of art and architecture of the 1890s, characterized by sinuous outlines and stylized natural forms.

arts (ɑːts) *pl. n.* **1. the.** the nonscientific branches of knowledge. **2.** See **fine art. 3.** cunning schemes.

arty ('ɑːtɪ) *adj.* **artier, artiest.** *Informal.* having an affected interest in art. —'**artiness** *n.*

arum ('ɛərəm) *n.* a plant with arrow-shaped leaves and a white sheath-like leaf surrounding a spike of flowers.

arum lily *n.* a plant with a white funnel-shaped leaf surrounding a yellow spike of flowers.

Aryan ('ɛərɪən) *n.* **1.** (in Nazi ideology) a non-Jewish person of the Nordic type. **2.** a person supposedly descended from the Indo-Europeans. ~*adj.* **3.** of Aryans.

as (æz) *conj.* **1.** (often preceded by *just*) while; when: *he caught me as I was leaving.* **2.** in the way that: *dancing as only she can.* **3.** that which; what: *I did as I was told.* **4.** (of) which fact or event (referring to the previous statement): *to become wise, as we all know, is not easy.* **5. as it were.** in a way; in a manner of speaking: *they are, as it were, being used as human guinea pigs.* **6.** since; seeing that. **7.** for instance. ~*adv., conj.* **8.** used to indicate extent, amount, etc.: *she is as heavy as her sister; the same height as her sister.* ~*prep.* **9.** in the role of; being: *as his friend, my opinions are probably biased.* **10. as for** *or* **to.** with reference to. **11. as if** *or* **though.** as it would be if: *he talked as if he knew all about it.* **12. as** (**it**) **is.** in the existing state of affairs.

As *Chem.* arsenic.

ASA Amateur Swimming Association.

asafoetida (,æsə'fɛtɪdə) *n.* a plant resin with an unpleasant smell, formerly used to treat flatulence.

a.s.a.p. as soon as possible.

asbestos (æs'bɛstɒs) *n.* a fibrous mineral which does not burn, formerly widely used as a heat-resistant material.

asbestosis (,æsbɛs'təʊsɪs) *n.* inflammation of the lungs resulting from chronic inhalation of asbestos particles.

ascend (ə'sɛnd) *vb.* **1.** to go or move up (a ladder, hill, or slope). **2.** to slope upwards. **3. ascend the throne.** to become king or queen.

ascendancy, ascendency (ə'sɛndənsı) *or* **ascendance, ascendence** *n.* the condition of being dominant.

ascendant *or* **ascendent** (ə'sɛndənt) *adj.* 1. dominant or influential. ~*n.* 2. *Astrol.* the sign of the zodiac that is rising on the eastern horizon at a particular moment. 3. **in the ascendant.** having or increasing in influence.

ascension (ə'sɛnʃən) *n.* the act of ascending.

Ascension (ə'sɛnʃən) *n. Christianity.* the passing of Jesus Christ from earth into heaven.

ascent (ə'sɛnt) *n.* 1. the act of ascending; upward movement. 2. an upward slope.

ascertain (ˌæsə'teɪn) *vb.* to find out definitely. —ˌascer'tainment *n.*

ascetic (ə'sɛtɪk) *n.* 1. a person who abstains from worldly comforts and pleasures. ~*adj.* 2. rigidly abstinent and self-denying.

ascorbic acid (ə'skɔːbɪk) *n.* same as **vitamin C.**

ascribe (ə'skraɪb) *vb.* 1. to credit or assign, as to a particular origin. 2. to consider that (a particular quality) is possessed by something or someone: *ascribing virtue to hypocrisy.* —**ascription** (ə'skrɪpʃən) *n.*

aseptic (eɪ'sɛptɪk) *adj.* free from harmful bacteria. —**a'sepsis** *n.*

asexual (eɪ'sɛksjʊəl) *adj.* 1. having no apparent sex or sex organs. 2. (of reproduction) not involving sexual activity. —**a'sexually** *adv.*

ash¹ (æʃ) *n.* 1. the powdery substance formed when something is burnt. 2. fine particles of lava thrown out by an erupting volcano.

ash² (æʃ) *n.* a tree with grey bark and winged seeds.

ashamed (ə'ʃeɪmd) *adj.* 1. overcome with shame or remorse. 2. (foll. by *to*) unwilling through fear of humiliation or shame.

ash can *n. U.S.* dustbin.

ashen ('æʃən) *adj.* drained of colour through shock.

ashes ('æʃɪz) *pl. n.* 1. remains, as after burning. 2. the remains of a human body after cremation.

Ashes ('æʃɪz) *pl. n.* **the.** a cricket trophy competed for by England and Australia since 1882.

ashlar *or* **ashler** ('æʃlə) *n.* 1. a square block of hewn stone for use in building. 2. a thin dressed stone used to face a wall.

ashore (ə'ʃɔː) *adv.* towards or on land.

ashram ('æʃrəm) *n.* a religious retreat where a Hindu holy man lives.

ashtray ('æʃ,treɪ) *n.* a receptacle for tobacco ash and cigarette butts.

Ash Wednesday *n.* the first day of Lent,

named from the former Christian custom of sprinkling ashes on penitents' heads.

ashy ('æʃɪ) *adj.* **ashier, ashiest.** 1. pale greyish. 2. covered with ash.

Asian ('eɪʃən, 'eɪʒən) *adj.* 1. of or from Asia, the largest of the continents, or any of its peoples or languages. ~*n.* 2. a person from Asia or a descendant of one. **Usage.** *Asian* is the correct noun to use meaning "a person from Asia". The use of *Asiatic* in this sense should be avoided, because some people consider it offensive.

Asiatic (eɪzɪ'ætɪk) *adj.* Asian.

aside (ə'saɪd) *adv.* 1. to one side. 2. out of other people's hearing: *she took me aside to tell me her fears.* 3. out of mind: *he put aside all fears.* 4. into reserve: *to put aside money for one's old age.* ~*n.* 5. an actor's words supposedly heard only by the audience and not by the other characters. 6. a confidential statement in undertones. 7. an incidental remark.

asinine ('æsɪ,naɪn) *adj.* obstinate or stupid.

ask (ɑːsk) *vb.* 1. to say or write (something) in a form that requires an answer: *she asked me the time; "When is the next bus?" Jim asked.* 2. to inquire about: *she asked the way.* 3. to make a request or demand: *they asked for a deposit.* 4. to expect: *to ask too much of someone.*

ask after *vb.* to make polite inquiries about the health of: *he asked after her mother.*

askance (ə'skæns) *adv.* 1. with an oblique glance. 2. with doubt or mistrust.

askew (ə'skjuː) *adv., adj.* towards one side.

ask for *vb.* 1. to request (of). 2. *Informal.* to behave in a provocative manner that is regarded as inviting (trouble, etc.): *you're asking for it.*

asking price *n.* the price suggested by a seller.

asleep (ə'sliːp) *adj.* 1. in or into a state of sleep. 2. *Informal.* not listening or paying attention. 3. (of limbs) numb.

asp (æsp) *n.* a viper of S Europe, similar to but smaller than the adder.

asparagus (ə'spærəgəs) *n.* the young shoots of a plant of the lily family, which can be cooked and eaten.

aspartame (ə'spɑː,teɪm) *n.* an artificial sweetener.

aspect ('æspɛkt) *n.* 1. a distinct feature or element in a problem or situation. 2. the way in which a problem or idea may be considered. 3. appearance: *a severe aspect.* 4. a position facing a particular direction: *the southern aspect of a house.*

aspen ('æspən) *n.* a poplar tree whose leaves quiver in the wind.

asperity (æ'spɛrɪtɪ) *n., pl.* **-ties.** roughness or sharpness of temper.

aspersion (ə'spɜːʃən) *n.* **cast aspersions**

on someone. to make disparaging or malicious remarks about someone.

asphalt ('æsfælt) n. 1. a black tarlike substance used in road-surfacing and roofing materials. ~vb. 2. to cover with asphalt.

asphyxia (æs'fɪksɪə) n. unconsciousness or death caused by lack of oxygen.

asphyxiate (æs'fɪksɪˌeɪt) vb. to smother or suffocate. —**as,phyxi'ation** n.

aspic ('æspɪk) n. a savoury jelly based on meat or fish stock, used as a mould for meat or vegetables.

aspidistra (ˌæspɪ'dɪstrə) n. a house plant with long tough evergreen leaves.

aspirant ('æspɪrənt) n. a person who aspires, as to a powerful position.

aspirate Phonetics. ~vb. ('æspɪˌreɪt). 1. to pronounce (a word or syllable) with an initial h. ~n. ('æspɪrɪt). 2. the sound represented in English and several other languages as h.

aspiration (ˌæspɪ'reɪʃən) n. 1. strong desire to achieve something. 2. the aim of such desire. 3. Phonetics. the pronunciation of an aspirated consonant. —,**aspi'rational** adj.

aspirator ('æspɪˌreɪtə) n. a device for removing fluids from a body cavity by suction.

aspire (ə'spaɪə) vb. (usually foll. by to) to yearn for, or hope (to do or be): to aspire to be a great leader. —**as'piring** adj.

aspirin ('æsprɪn) n., pl. -**rin** or -**rins.** 1. a white crystalline compound widely used to relieve pain and fever. 2. a tablet of aspirin.

ass¹ (æs) n. 1. a mammal resembling the horse but with longer ears. 2. a foolish person.

ass² (æs) n. U.S. and Canad. taboo. same as **arse.**

assail (ə'seɪl) vb. 1. to attack violently. 2. to criticize vehemently. 3. to disturb: his mind was assailed by doubts. —**as'sailant** n.

assassin (ə'sæsɪn) n. a murderer of a prominent political figure.

assassinate (ə'sæsɪˌneɪt) vb. 1. to murder (a political figure). 2. to ruin or harm (a person's reputation or character) by slander. —**as,sassi'nation** n.

assault (ə'sɔːlt) n. 1. a violent attack, either physical or verbal. ~vb. 2. to make an assault upon.

assault and battery n. Criminal law. a threat of attack to another person followed by actual attack.

assault course n. an obstacle course designed to give soldiers practice in negotiating hazards.

assay vb. (ə'seɪ). 1. to analyse (a substance, such as gold) to find out how pure it is. ~n. (ə'seɪ, 'æseɪ). 2. an analysis of the purity of an ore or precious metal.

assegai or **assagai** ('æsəˌgaɪ) n., pl. -**gais.** a sharp light spear used in southern Africa.

assemblage (ə'sɛmblɪdʒ) n. 1. a number of things or persons assembled together. 2. the act of assembling.

assemble (ə'sɛmb°l) vb. 1. to collect or congregate. 2. to fit together the parts of (something, such as a machine).

assembler (ə'sɛmblə) n. 1. a person or thing that assembles. 2. a computer program that converts a set of low-level symbolic data into machine language.

assembly (ə'sɛmblɪ) n., pl. -**blies.** 1. a number of people gathered together, esp. for a formal meeting held at regular intervals. 2. the act of assembling.

assembly line n. a sequence of machines and workers in a factory, arranged so that at each stage a further process is carried out.

assemblyman (ə'sɛmblɪmən) n., pl. -**men.** a member of a legislative assembly, esp. that of Northern Ireland.

assent (ə'sɛnt) n. 1. agreement, consent. ~vb. 2. to agree.

assert (ə'sɜːt) vb. 1. to insist upon (one's rights, etc.). 2. to state or declare. 3. **assert oneself.** to put oneself forward in an insistent manner.

assertion (ə'sɜːʃən) n. 1. a positive statement, usually made without evidence. 2. the act of asserting.

assertive (ə'sɜːtɪv) adj. dogmatic or aggressive. —**as'sertively** adv. —**as'sertiveness** n.

assess (ə'sɛs) vb. 1. to judge the worth or importance of. 2. to estimate the value of (income or property), as for taxation purposes. —**as'sessment** n.

assessor (ə'sɛsə) n. 1. a person who values property for taxation or insurance purposes. 2. a person with technical expertise called in to advise a court. 3. a person who evaluates the merits of something.

asset ('æsɛt) n. 1. a thing or person that is valuable or useful. 2. (pl.) any property owned by a person or firm.

asset-stripping n. Commerce. the practice of taking over a failing company at a low price and then selling the assets piecemeal. —'**asset-,stripper** n.

asseverate (ə'sɛvəˌreɪt) vb. to declare solemnly. —**as,sever'ation** n.

assiduous (ə'sɪdjʊəs) adj. 1. hardworking; persevering. 2. undertaken with perseverance and care. —**assiduity** (ˌæsɪ'djuːɪtɪ) n. —**as'siduously** adv.

assign (ə'saɪn) vb. 1. to select (someone) for a post or task. 2. to allot (a task). 3. to set apart (a place or time) for a particular function or event: to assign a day for the meeting. 4. to attribute to a specified cause. 5. to transfer (one's right, interest, or title to property) to someone else.

assignation (ˌæsɪgˈneɪʃən) n. a secret arrangement to meet, esp. one between lovers.

assignment (əˈsaɪnmənt) n. **1.** something that has been assigned, such as a task. **2.** the act of assigning. **3.** Law. the transfer to another of a right, interest, or title to property.

assimilate (əˈsɪmɪˌleɪt) vb. **1.** to learn (information) and understand it thoroughly. **2.** to absorb (food). **3.** to become absorbed, incorporated, or learned and understood. **4.** to adjust or become adjusted: the new immigrants assimilated easily. —asˈsimilable adj. —as,simiˈlation n.

assist (əˈsɪst) vb. to give help or support (to).

assistance (əˈsɪstəns) n. help; support.

assistant (əˈsɪstənt) n. **1.** a helper or subordinate. **2.** same as **shop assistant.** ~adj. **3.** junior or deputy: assistant manager.

assizes (əˈsaɪzɪz) pl. n. (formerly in England and Wales) the sessions of the principal court in each county.

assoc. 1. associate(d). **2.** association.

associate vb. (əˈsəʊʃɪˌeɪt, -sɪ-). (usually foll. by with) **1.** to connect in the mind. **2.** to mix socially: to associate with writers. **3. be associated** or **associate oneself with.** to be involved with (a group or an organization), esp. because of shared views: she had long been associated with the far right. ~n. (əˈsəʊʃɪɪt, -sɪ-). **4.** a person joined with another or others in an enterprise or business. **5.** a companion or friend. ~adj. (əˈsəʊʃɪɪt, -sɪ-). **6.** joined with another or others in an enterprise or business: an associate director. **7.** having partial rights or subordinate status: an associate member.

association (əˌsəʊsɪˈeɪʃən, -ʃɪ-) n. **1.** a group of people having a common interest; a society or club. **2.** the act of associating or the state of being associated. **3.** friendship: their association will not last. **4.** a mental connection of ideas or feelings.

association football n. same as **soccer.**

associative (əˈsəʊʃɪətɪv, -sɪ-) adj. Maths. (of an operation such as multiplication or addition) producing the same answer regardless of the way the elements are grouped: $(2 \times 3) \times 4 = 2 \times (3 \times 4)$.

assonance (ˈæsənəns) n. the use of the same vowel sound with different consonants, as in verse, e.g. time and light.

assorted (əˈsɔːtɪd) adj. **1.** consisting of various kinds mixed together. **2.** classified: assorted categories. **3.** matched: an ill-assorted couple.

assortment (əˈsɔːtmənt) n. a collection of various things or sorts.

assuage (əˈsweɪdʒ) vb. to relieve (grief, pain, or thirst).

assume (əˈsjuːm) vb. **1.** to take for granted; suppose. **2.** to undertake or take on or over: to assume office. **3.** to make a pre-

tence of: he assumed indifference. **4.** to take or put on; adopt: the problem assumed gigantic proportions.

assuming (əˈsjuːmɪŋ) conj. (often foll. by that) if it is assumed or taken for granted: assuming for the moment that it was Davis.

assumption (əˈsʌmpʃən) n. **1.** the act of taking something for granted or something that is taken for granted. **2.** the act of assuming power or possession.

Assumption (əˈsʌmpʃən) n. Christianity. the taking up of the Virgin Mary into heaven when her earthly life was ended.

assurance (əˈʃʊərəns) n. **1.** a statement or assertion intended to inspire confidence. **2.** freedom from doubt; certainty. **3.** Chiefly Brit. insurance providing for certainties such as death as contrasted with fire.

assure (əˈʃʊə) vb. **1.** to convince: he assured her of his love. **2.** to promise; guarantee. **3.** to make (an event) certain. **4.** Chiefly Brit. to insure against loss of life.

assured (əˈʃʊəd) adj. **1.** sure; guaranteed. **2.** self-assured. **3.** Chiefly Brit. insured. —**assuredly** (əˈʃʊərɪdlɪ) adv.

Assyrian (əˈsɪrɪən) n. an inhabitant of ancient Assyria, a kingdom of Mesopotamia.

AST Atlantic Standard Time.

astatine (ˈæstəˌtiːn) n. a radioactive element occurring naturally in minute amounts or artificially produced by bombarding bismuth with alpha particles. Symbol: At

aster (ˈæstə) n. a plant having white, blue, purple, or pink daisy-like flowers.

asterisk (ˈæstərɪsk) n. **1.** a star-shaped character (*) used in printing or writing to indicate a cross-reference, omission, etc. ~vb. **2.** to mark with an asterisk.

astern (əˈstɜːn) adv., adj. Naut. **1.** at or towards the stern. **2.** backwards. **3.** behind a vessel.

asteroid (ˈæstəˌrɔɪd) n. any of the small celestial bodies that move around the sun mainly between Mars and Jupiter.

asthma (ˈæsmə) n. a respiratory disorder characterized by difficulty in breathing. —**asthˈmatic** adj., n.

astigmatic (ˌæstɪgˈmætɪk) adj. of, having, or correcting astigmatism.

astigmatism (əˈstɪgməˌtɪzəm) n. a defect of a lens, esp. of the eye, resulting in the formation of distorted images, caused by light rays not meeting at a single focal point.

astir (əˈstɜː) adj. **1.** out of bed. **2.** in motion.

astonish (əˈstɒnɪʃ) vb. to surprise greatly. —**aˈstonishing** adj. —**aˈstonishment** n.

astound (əˈstaʊnd) vb. to overwhelm with amazement. —**aˈstounding** adj.

astraddle (əˈstrædˀl) prep. astride.

astrakhan (ˌæstrəˈkæn) n. **1.** a fur made of

the closely curled dark wool of lambs from Astrakhan in the U.S.S.R. **2.** a cloth resembling this.

astral (ˈæstrəl) *adj.* relating to or resembling the stars.

astray (əˈstreɪ) *adj., adv.* out of the right or expected way.

astride (əˈstraɪd) *adj.* **1.** with a leg on either side. **2.** with legs far apart. *~prep.* **3.** with a leg on either side of. **4.** spanning.

astringent (əˈstrɪndʒənt) *adj.* **1.** severe; harsh. **2.** causing contraction of body tissues, checking blood flow. *~n.* **3.** an astringent drug or lotion. **—asˈtringency** *n.*

astro- *combining form.* indicating a star or stars: *astrology.*

astrolabe (ˈæstrəˌleɪb) *n.* an instrument formerly used to measure the altitude of stars and planets.

astrology (əˈstrɒlədʒɪ) *n.* the study of the alleged influence of the planets, sun, and moon on human affairs. **—asˈtrologer** *or* **asˈtrologist** *n.* **—astrological** (ˌæstrəˈlɒdʒɪkəl) *adj.*

astronaut (ˈæstrəˌnɔːt) *n.* a person trained for travelling in space.

astronautics (ˌæstrəˈnɔːtɪks) *n.* (*functioning as sing.*) the science and technology of space flight. **—ˌastroˈnautical** *adj.*

astronomical (ˌæstrəˈnɒmɪkəl) *or* **astronomic** *adj.* **1.** enormously large. **2.** of astronomy. **—ˌastroˈnomically** *adv.*

astronomy (əˈstrɒnəmɪ) *n.* the scientific study of celestial bodies. **—asˈtronomer** *n.*

astrophysics (ˌæstrəʊˈfɪzɪks) *n.* (*functioning as sing.*) the study of the physical and chemical properties of celestial bodies. **—ˌastroˈphysical** *adj.* **—ˌastroˈphysicist** *n.*

astute (əˈstjuːt) *adj.* having insight; shrewd. **—asˈtutely** *adv.* **—asˈtuteness** *n.*

asunder (əˈsʌndə) *adv., adj.* into parts or pieces; apart.

asylum (əˈsaɪləm) *n.* **1.** shelter; refuge; sanctuary. **2.** refuge afforded to a political refugee from a foreign country. **3.** (formerly) a mental hospital.

asymmetry (æˈsɪmɪtrɪ, eɪ-) *n.* lack of symmetry. **—asymmetric** (ˌæsɪˈmɛtrɪk, eɪ-) *or* **ˌasymˈmetrical** *adj.*

asymptote (ˈæsɪmˌtəʊt) *n.* a straight line that is closely approached but never met by a curve. **—asymptotic** (ˌæsɪmˈtɒtɪk) *adj.*

at (æt) *prep.* **1.** indicating location or position: *are they at the table?* **2.** towards; in the direction of: *looking at television.* **3.** indicating position in time: *come at three o'clock.* **4.** engaged in: *children at play.* **5.** during the passing of: *he used to work at night.* **6.** for; in exchange for: *it's selling at four pounds.* **7.** indicating the object of an emotion: *shocked at his behaviour.*

At *Chem.* astatine.

at. **1.** atmosphere. **2.** atomic.

atavism (ˈætəˌvɪzəm) *n.* **1.** the recurrence of primitive characteristics that were present in distant ancestors but not in more recent ones. **2.** reversion to a former type. **—ˌataˈvistic** *adj.*

ataxia (əˈtæksɪə) *n. Pathol.* lack of muscular coordination. **—aˈtaxic** *adj.*

ate (ɛt, eɪt) *vb.* the past tense of **eat.**

atheism (ˈeɪθɪˌɪzəm) *n.* the belief that there is no God. **—ˈatheist** *n.*

atherosclerosis (ˌæθərəʊsklɪəˈrəʊsɪs) *n., pl.* **-ses** (-siːz). a disease characterized by thickening of the walls of the arteries by deposits of fat. **—atherosclerotic** (ˌæθərəʊsklɪəˈrɒtɪk) *adj.*

athirst (əˈθɜːst) *adj.* (often foll. by *for*) longing: *athirst for knowledge.*

athlete (ˈæθliːt) *n.* **1.** a person trained to compete in sports or exercises. **2.** *Chiefly Brit.* a competitor in track-and-field events.

athlete's foot *n.* a fungal infection of the skin of the foot.

athletic (æθˈlɛtɪk) *adj.* **1.** physically fit or strong. **2.** of or for an athlete or athletics. **—athˈletically** *adv.* **—athˈleticism** *n.*

athletics (æθˈlɛtɪks) *n.* (*functioning as pl. or sing.*) *Chiefly Brit.* track-and-field events.

athwart (əˈθwɔːt) *adv.* transversely; from one side to another.

Atlantic (ətˈlæntɪk) *n.* **the.** short for the **Atlantic Ocean,** the world's second largest ocean.

Atlantis (ətˈlæntɪs) *n.* (in ancient legend) a continent said to have sunk beneath the Atlantic west of Gibraltar.

atlas (ˈætləs) *n.* a collection of maps, usually in book form.

atmosphere (ˈætməsˌfɪə) *n.* **1.** the gaseous envelope surrounding the earth or any other celestial body. **2.** the air in a particular place. **3.** a pervasive feeling or mood: *the atmosphere was tense.* **4.** a unit of pressure equal to the normal pressure of the air at sea level. **—atmospheric** (ˌætməsˈfɛrɪk) *adj.* **—ˌatmosˈpherically** *adv.*

atmospherics (ˌætməsˈfɛrɪks) *pl. n.* radio interference; static.

at. no. atomic number.

atoll (ˈætɒl) *n.* a circular coral reef surrounding a lagoon.

atom (ˈætəm) *n.* **1. a.** the smallest quantity of an element that can take part in a chemical reaction. **b.** this entity as a source of nuclear energy. **2.** a very small amount.

atom bomb *or* **atomic bomb** *n.* a type of bomb in which the energy is provided by nuclear fission.

atomic (əˈtɒmɪk) *adj.* **1.** of or using atom bombs or atomic energy. **2.** of atoms. **—aˈtomically** *adv.*

atomic energy *n.* same as **nuclear energy.**

atomic mass unit *n.* a unit of mass that is equal to one twelfth of the mass of an atom of carbon-12.

atomic number *n.* the number of protons in the nucleus of an atom of an element.

atomic theory *n.* any theory in which matter is regarded as consisting of atoms.

atomic weight *n.* the ratio of the average mass per atom of an element to one twelfth of the mass of the atom of carbon-12.

atomize *or* **-ise** ('ætə,maɪz) *vb.* **1.** to separate into free atoms. **2.** to reduce or be reduced to fine particles or spray. **3.** to destroy by nuclear weapons.

atomizer *or* **-iser** ('ætə,maɪzə) *n.* a device for reducing a liquid to a fine spray.

atonality (,eɪtəʊ'nælɪtɪ) *n.* absence of an established musical key in a composition. —a**'tonal** *adj.*

atone (ə'təʊn) *vb.* to make amends (for sin or wrongdoing).

atonement (ə'təʊnmənt) *n.* **1.** satisfaction or expiation given for a wrong. **2.** *Christian theol.* the reconciliation of man with God through the sacrificial death of Christ.

atop (ə'tɒp) *prep.* on top of.

atrium ('eɪtrɪəm) *n., pl.* **atria** ('eɪtrɪə). **1.** the open main court of a Roman house. **2.** a central hall that extends through several storeys in a modern building. **3.** *Anat.* the upper chamber of each half of the heart. —'**atrial** *adj.*

atrocious (ə'trəʊʃəs) *adj.* **1.** extremely cruel or wicked. **2.** horrifying or shocking. **3.** *Informal.* very bad. —a**'trociously** *adv.*

atrocity (ə'trɒsɪtɪ) *n., pl.* **-ties.** **1.** behaviour or action that is wicked or cruel. **2.** (*pl.*) acts of extreme cruelty.

atrophy ('ætrəfɪ) *n., pl.* **-phies.** **1.** a wasting away of an organ or part, or a failure to grow. ~*vb.* **-phying, -phied.** **2.** to waste away or cause to waste away.

atropine ('ætrə,piːn) *n.* a poisonous alkaloid obtained from deadly nightshade.

attach (ə'tætʃ) *vb.* **1.** to join, fasten, or connect. **2. attach oneself** or **be attached to.** to become associated with or join. **3.** (foll. by *to*) to be connected (with): *responsibility attaches to the job.* **4.** to ascribe: *he attaches great importance to the way he looks.* **5.** *Law.* to arrest or take (a person or property) with lawful authority.

attaché (ə'tæʃeɪ) *n.* a specialist attached to a diplomatic mission.

attaché case *n.* a flat rectangular briefcase for carrying documents and papers.

attached (ə'tætʃt) *adj.* (foll. by *to*) **1.** fond (of). **2.** married, engaged, or in an exclusive sexual relationship.

attachment (ə'tætʃmənt) *n.* **1.** a fastening. **2.** (often foll. by *to*) affection or regard

(for). **3.** an accessory that can be fitted to a device to change what it can do. **4.** the lawful seizure of property.

attack (ə'tæk) *vb.* **1.** to launch a physical assault (against). **2.** to take the initiative in a game or sport. **3.** to criticize vehemently. **4.** to turn one's energies to (a job or problem). **5.** to begin to affect adversely: *a car attacked by rust.* ~*n.* **6.** the act of attacking. **7.** any sudden appearance of a disease or symptoms: *a bad attack of mumps.* —**at'tacker** *n.*

attain (ə'teɪn) *vb.* **1.** to achieve or accomplish (a task or aim). **2.** to reach. —**at'tainable** *adj.*

attainment (ə'teɪnmənt) *n.* an achievement or the act of achieving; accomplishment.

attar ('ætə) *n.* a perfume made from damask roses.

attempt (ə'tɛmpt) *vb.* **1.** to make an effort (to do or achieve something); try. **2.** to try to climb or surmount (an obstacle). ~*n.* **3.** an endeavour to achieve something; effort. **4. attempt on someone's life.** an attack on someone with the intention to kill.

attend (ə'tɛnd) *vb.* **1.** to be present at (an event). **2.** to give care (to); look after. **3.** to pay attention. **4.** to accompany. **5.** (foll. by *on* or *upon*) to follow as a consequence (of). **6.** (foll. by *to*) to apply oneself: *I must attend to the weeding.*

attendance (ə'tɛndəns) *n.* **1.** the act of attending. **2.** the number of persons present. **3.** regularity in attending.

attendant (ə'tɛndənt) *n.* **1.** a person employed to assist, guide, or provide a service. ~*adj.* **2.** being in attendance. **3.** associated.

attention (ə'tɛnʃən) *n.* **1.** concentrated direction of the mind. **2.** consideration, notice, or observation. **3.** detailed care or treatment. **4.** (*pl.*) an act of courtesy. **5.** the upright motionless position of formal military alertness.

attentive (ə'tɛntɪv) *adj.* **1.** paying attention. **2.** (often foll. by *to*) careful to fulfil the needs (of). —**at'tentively** *adv.* —**at'tentiveness** *n.*

attenuate (ə'tɛnjʊ,eɪt) *vb.* **1.** to weaken. **2.** to make or become thin; extend. —**at,tenu'ation** *n.*

attest (ə'tɛst) *vb.* **1.** to affirm the truth of. **2.** to witness or bear witness to (an act or event). **3.** to provide evidence for something being true. —**attestation** (,ætɛ'steɪʃən) *n.*

attested (ə'tɛstɪd) *adj. Brit.* (of cattle) certified to be free from a disease, such as tuberculosis.

attic ('ætɪk) *n.* **1.** a space or room within the roof of a house. **2.** *Archit.* a storey above the cornice of a classical façade.

Attic ('ætɪk) *adj.* **1.** of or relating to Attica, the area around Athens, or the dialect of

Greek spoken there. **2.** (*often not cap.*) classically elegant. *~n.* **3.** the dialect of Ancient Greek in Athens.

attire (əˈtaɪə) *n.* fine or formal clothes.

attired (əˈtaɪəd) *adj.* dressed in a specified way.

attitude (ˈætɪˌtjuːd) *n.* **1.** the way a person views something. **2. strike an attitude.** to pose for effect. **3.** a position of the body. **4.** the orientation of an aircraft or spacecraft in relation to some plane or direction.

attitudinize *or* **-nise** (ˌætɪˈtjuːdɪˌnaɪz) *vb.* to adopt a pose or opinion for effect.

attorney (əˈtɜːnɪ) *n.* **1.** a person legally appointed to act for another. **2.** *U.S.* a lawyer.

attorney general *n.*, *pl.* **attorneys general** *or* **attorney generals.** a chief law officer of some governments.

attract (əˈtrækt) *vb.* **1.** to exert a pleasing or fascinating influence (upon). **2.** to draw to oneself (esp. in **attract attention**). **3.** to exert a force on (a body) that tends to oppose a separation.

attraction (əˈtrækʃən) *n.* **1.** the act or quality of attracting. **2.** a person or thing that attracts. **3.** a force by which one object attracts another.

attractive (əˈtræktɪv) *adj.* appealing to the senses or mind. —**atˈtractively** *adv.* —**atˈtractiveness** *n.*

attribute *vb.* (əˈtrɪbjuːt). **1.** (usually foll. by *to*) to regard as belonging (to): *to attribute a painting to Picasso.* *~n.* (ˈætrɪˌbjuːt). **2.** a quality or feature representative of a person or thing. —**atˈtributable** *adj.* —**attribution** (ˌætrɪˈbjuːʃən) *n.*

attributive (əˈtrɪbjutɪv) *adj.* **1.** relating to an attribute. **2.** *Grammar.* (of an adjective) preceding the noun modified.

attrition (əˈtrɪʃən) *n.* **1.** the act of wearing away, as by friction. **2.** constant wearing down to weaken or destroy (often in **war of attrition**).

attune (əˈtjuːn) *vb.* to adjust or accustom (a person or thing); acclimatize.

atypical (eɪˈtɪpɪkəl) *adj.* not typical. —**aˈtypically** *adv.*

Au *Chem.* gold.

aubergine (ˈəʊbəˌʒiːn) *n.* the dark purple fruit of a tropical plant, cooked and eaten as a vegetable.

aubrietia (ɔːˈbriːʃə) *n.* a trailing purple-flowered rock plant.

auburn (ˈɔːbən) *adj.* (esp. of hair) reddish-brown.

auction (ˈɔːkʃən) *n.* **1.** a public sale at which the highest bidder secures each item. *~vb.* **2.** to sell by auction.

auctioneer (ˌɔːkʃəˈnɪə) *n.* a person who conducts an auction.

audacious (ɔːˈdeɪʃəs) *adj.* **1.** recklessly bold or daring. **2.** impudent or presumptuous. —**audacity** (ɔːˈdæsɪtɪ) *n.*

audible (ˈɔːdɪbəl) *adj.* loud enough to be heard. —,**audiˈbility** *n.* —ˈ**audibly** *adv.*

audience (ˈɔːdɪəns) *n.* **1.** a group of spectators or listeners at a concert or play. **2.** the people reached by a book, film, or radio or television programme. **3.** a formal interview.

audio (ˈɔːdɪəʊ) *n.* (*modifier*) **1.** of or relating to sound or hearing. **2.** of or for the transmission or reproduction of sound.

audio frequency *n.* a frequency in the range 20 hertz to 20 000 hertz, audible to the human ear.

audiometer (ˌɔːdɪˈɒmɪtə) *n.* an instrument for testing hearing.

audiotypist (ˈɔːdɪəʊˌtaɪpɪst) *n.* a typist trained to type from a dictating machine. —ˈ**audio**,**typing** *n.*

audiovisual (ˌɔːdɪəʊˈvɪʒʊəl) *adj.* (esp. of teaching aids) involving both hearing and sight.

audit (ˈɔːdɪt) *n.* **1.** an inspection and verification of business accounts by a qualified accountant. **2.** any thoroughgoing examination or check. *~vb.* **3.** to inspect, correct, and certify (accounts).

audition (ɔːˈdɪʃən) *n.* **1.** a test of a performer's or musician's ability for a particular role. *~vb.* **2.** to judge by or be tested in an audition.

auditor (ˈɔːdɪtə) *n.* a person qualified to audit accounts.

auditorium (ˌɔːdɪˈtɔːrɪəm) *n.*, *pl.* -**toriums** *or* -**toria** (-ˈtɔːrɪə). **1.** the area of a concert hall or theatre in which the audience sits. **2.** *U.S. & Canad.* a building for public meetings.

auditory (ˈɔːdɪtrɪ) *adj.* of or relating to hearing.

au fait (ˌəʊ ˈfeɪ) *adj.* fully informed; expert.

Aug. August.

Augean (ɔːˈdʒiːən) *adj.* extremely dirty or corrupt.

auger (ˈɔːgə) *n.* a hand tool with a corkscrew-like point for boring holes in wood.

aught (ɔːt) *pron. Archaic or literary.* anything whatever (esp. in **for aught I know**).

augment (ɔːgˈmɛnt) *vb.* to make or become greater in number or strength. —,**augmenˈtation** *n.*

augmentative (ɔːgˈmɛntətɪv) *adj.* tending to augment.

au gratin (ˌəʊ ˈgrætæn) *adj.* covered and cooked with breadcrumbs and sometimes cheese.

augur (ˈɔːgə) *vb.* to foreshadow future events: *this augurs well for us.*

augury (ˈɔːgjʊrɪ) *n.*, *pl.* -**ries.** an omen.

august (ɔːˈgʌst) *adj.* dignified or imposing.

August ('ɔːgəst) *n.* the eighth month of the year.

Augustan (ɔː'gʌstən) *adj.* **1.** of the Roman emperor Augustus Caesar or the poets writing during his reign. **2.** of any literary period noted for refinement and classicism.

auk (ɔːk) *n.* a diving bird of northern oceans with a heavy body, narrow wings, and a black-and-white plumage.

auld lang syne ('ɔːld læŋ 'saɪn) *n.* times past.

aunt (ɑːnt) *n.* **1.** a sister of one's father or mother. **2.** the wife of one's uncle. **3.** a child's term of address for a female friend of the parents.

auntie *or* **aunty** ('ɑːntɪ) *n., pl.* **-ies.** *Informal.* an aunt.

Aunt Sally ('sælɪ) *n., pl.* **-lies.** *Brit.* **1.** a figure used in fairgrounds as a target. **2.** any target for insults or criticism.

au pair (əʊ 'pɛə) *n.* a young foreign woman who undertakes housework in exchange for board and lodging.

aura ('ɔːrə) *n., pl.* **auras** *or* **aurae** ('ɔːriː). **1.** a distinctive air or quality associated with a person or thing. **2.** any invisible emanation.

aural ('ɔːrəl) *adj.* of or using the ears or hearing. —'**aurally** *adv.*

aureate ('ɔːrɪɪt) *adj.* **1.** covered with gold. **2.** excessively elaborate.

aureole ('ɔːrɪ,əʊl) *or* **aureola** (ɔː'riːələ) *n.* **1.** a border of light enveloping the head of a figure represented as holy. **2.** the sun's corona, visible as a faint halo during eclipses.

au revoir (,əʊ rə'vwɑː) *interj.* goodbye.

auric ('ɔːrɪk) *adj.* of or containing gold, esp. in the trivalent state.

auricle ('ɔːrɪk²l) *n.* **1.** the upper chamber of the heart. **2.** the external part of the ear. —**au'ricular** *adj.*

auricula (ɔː'rɪkjʊlə) *n., pl.* **-lae** (-,liː) *or* **-las.** an alpine primrose with leaves shaped like a bear's ear.

auriferous (ɔː'rɪfərəs) *adj.* containing gold.

aurochs ('ɔːrɒks) *n., pl.* **-rochs.** a recently extinct European wild ox.

aurora (ɔː'rɔːrə) *n., pl.* **-ras** *or* **-rae** (-riː). **1.** an atmospheric phenomenon of bands, curtains, or streamers of light, sometimes seen in polar regions. **2.** *Poetic.* the dawn.

aurora australis (ɒ'streɪlɪs) *n.* the aurora seen around the South Pole.

aurora borealis (,bɔːrɪ'eɪlɪs) *n.* the aurora seen around the North Pole.

auscultation (,ɔːskəl'teɪʃən) *n.* the listening to of the internal sounds made by the body, usually with a stethoscope, to help with medical diagnosis.

auspices ('ɔːspɪsɪz) *pl. n.* **under the auspices of.** with the support and approval of.

auspicious (ɔː'spɪʃəs) *adj.* favourable or propitious.

Aussie ('ɒzɪ) *n., adj. Informal.* Australian.

austere (ɒ'stɪə) *adj.* **1.** stern or severe. **2.** self-disciplined or ascetic. **3.** severely simple or plain.

austerity (ɒ'stɛrɪtɪ) *n., pl.* **-ties.** **1.** the state of being austere. **2.** reduced availability of luxuries and consumer goods.

austral ('ɔːstrəl) *adj.* of or from the south.

Austral. **1.** Australasia. **2.** Australia(n).

Australasian (,ɒstrə'leɪʒən) *adj.* of or from Australia, New Zealand, and neighbouring islands.

Australian (ɒ'streɪlɪən) *n.* **1.** a person from Australia. ~*adj.* **2.** of Australia or the Australians.

autarchy ('ɔːtɑːkɪ) *n., pl.* **-chies.** unlimited rule; autocracy.

autarky ('ɔːtɑːkɪ) *n., pl.* **-kies.** a policy of economic self-sufficiency.

authentic (ɔː'θɛntɪk) *adj.* **1.** of undisputed origin or authorship; genuine. **2.** trustworthy; reliable. —**au'thentically** *adv.* —**authenticity** (,ɔːθɛn'tɪsɪtɪ) *n.*

authenticate (ɔː'θɛntɪ,keɪt) *vb.* to establish as genuine. —**au,thenti'cation** *n.*

author ('ɔːθə) *n.* **1.** a person who writes a book, article, or other written work. **2.** an originator or creator.

authoritarian (ɔː,θɒrɪ'tɛərɪən) *adj.* **1.** favouring or characterized by strict obedience to authority. ~*n.* **2.** a person who favours or practises authoritarian policies.

authoritative (ɔː'θɒrɪtətɪv) *adj.* **1.** recognized as being reliable. **2.** possessing authority; official.

authority (ɔː'θɒrɪtɪ) *n., pl.* **-ties.** **1.** the power or ability to influence, control, or judge others. **2.** (*often pl.*) a person or group of people having this power. **3.** a position that commands such a power or right (often in **in authority**). **4.** official permission: *you have no authority to do that.* **5.** an expert or authoritative work in a particular field. **6.** evidence or testimony. **7.** confidence resulting from expertise.

authorize *or* **-rise** ('ɔːθə,raɪz) *vb.* **1.** to confer authority upon (someone to do something). **2.** to give official permission. —,**authori'zation** *or* **-ri'sation** *n.*

Authorized Version *n.* **the.** an English translation of the Bible published in 1611.

authorship ('ɔːθə,ʃɪp) *n.* **1.** the origin or originator of a written work or plan. **2.** the profession of writing.

autism ('ɔːtɪzəm) *n. Psychiatry.* abnormal self-absorption, usually affecting children, characterized by lack of response to people and limited ability to communicate. —**au'tistic** *adj.*

auto ('ɔːtəʊ) *n., pl.* **-tos.** *U.S. & Canad. informal.* short for **automobile.**

auto- *or sometimes before a vowel* **aut-** *combining form.* **1.** self; of or by the same one: *autobiography.* **2.** self-propelling: *automobile.*

autobahn (ˈɔːtəˌbɑːn) *n.* a German or Austrian motorway.

autobiography (ˌɔːtəʊbaɪˈɒɡrəfɪ) *n., pl.* **-phies.** an account of a person's life written by that person. —ˌautobiˈographer *n.* —**autobiographical** (ˌɔːtəˌbaɪəˈɡræfɪkᵊl) *adj.*

autoclave (ˈɔːtəˌkleɪv) *n.* an apparatus for sterilizing objects by steam under pressure.

autocracy (ɔːˈtɒkrəsɪ) *n., pl.* **-cies.** government by an individual with unrestricted authority.

autocrat (ˈɔːtəˌkræt) *n.* **1.** a ruler with absolute authority. **2.** a dictatorial person. —ˌautoˈcratic *adj.* —ˌautoˈcratically *adv.*

autocross (ˈɔːtəʊˌkrɒs) *n.* a sport in which cars race over a circuit of rough grass.

Autocue (ˈɔːtəʊˌkjuː) *n. Trademark.* an electronic television device displaying a speaker's script, unseen by the audience.

auto-da-fé (ˌɔːtəʊdəˈfeɪ) *n., pl.* **autos-da-fé.** **1.** *History.* the ceremonial passing of sentence on heretics by the Spanish Inquisition. **2.** the burning to death of heretics.

autogiro *or* **autogyro** (ˌɔːtəʊˈdʒaɪrəʊ) *n., pl.* **-ros.** a self-propelled aircraft supported mainly by unpowered rotating horizontal blades.

autograph (ˈɔːtəˌɡrɑːf) *n.* **1.** a handwritten signature of a famous person. ~*vb.* **2.** to write one's signature on or in.

automat (ˈɔːtəˌmæt) *n. U.S.* a vending machine.

automate (ˈɔːtəˌmeɪt) *vb.* to make (a manufacturing process) automatic.

automatic (ˌɔːtəˈmætɪk) *adj.* **1. a.** (of a device or mechanism) able to activate or regulate itself. **b.** (of a process) performed by such automatic equipment. **2.** performed without conscious thought. **3.** occurring as a necessary consequence: *promotion is automatic.* **4.** (of a firearm) utilizing some of the force of each explosion to reload and fire continuously. ~*n.* **5.** an automatic firearm. **6.** a motor vehicle having automatic transmission. —ˌautoˈmatically *adv.*

automatic pilot *n.* **1.** a device that automatically maintains an aircraft on a preset course. **2. on automatic pilot.** repeating an action or process without thought.

automatic transmission *n.* a transmission system in a motor vehicle in which the gears change automatically.

automation (ˌɔːtəˈmeɪʃən) *n.* the use of automatic, often electronic, methods to control industrial processes.

automaton (ɔːˈtɒmətᵊn) *n., pl.* **-tons** *or* **-ta.** **1.** a mechanical device operating under its own power. **2.** a person who acts mechanically.

automobile (ˈɔːtəməˌbiːl) *n. U.S.* a motorcar.

automotive (ˌɔːtəˈməʊtɪv) *adj.* **1.** relating to motor vehicles. **2.** self-propelling.

autonomous (ɔːˈtɒnəməs) *adj.* **1.** having self-government. **2.** independent of others.

autonomy (ɔːˈtɒnəmɪ) *n., pl.* **-mies.** **1.** the right or state of self-government. **2.** freedom to determine one's own actions and behaviour.

autopilot (ˌɔːtəˈpaɪlət) *n.* an automatic pilot.

autopsy (ˈɔːtəpsɪ, ɔːˈtɒp-) *n., pl.* **-sies.** examination of a dead body to determine the cause of death.

autoroute (ˈɔːtəʊˌruːt) *n.* a French motorway.

autostrada (ˈɔːtəʊˌstrɑːdə) *n.* an Italian motorway.

autosuggestion (ˌɔːtəʊsəˈdʒɛstʃən) *n.* a process in which a person unconsciously supplies the means of influencing his own behaviour or beliefs.

autumn (ˈɔːtəm) *n.* **1.** the season of the year between summer and winter. **2.** a period of late maturity, esp. followed by a decline. —**autumnal** (ɔːˈtʌmnᵊl) *adj.*

aux. auxiliary.

auxiliaries (ɔːɡˈzɪljərɪz, -ˈzɪlə-) *pl. n.* foreign troops serving another nation.

auxiliary (ɔːɡˈzɪljərɪ, -ˈzɪlə-) *adj.* **1.** secondary or supplementary. **2.** supporting. ~*n., pl.* **-ries.** **3.** a person or thing that supports or supplements.

auxiliary verb *n.* a verb used to indicate the tense, voice, or mood of another verb, such as *will* in *he will go.*

AV Authorized Version.

av. **1.** average. **2.** avoirdupois.

avail (əˈveɪl) *vb.* **1.** to be of use, advantage, or assistance (to). **2. avail oneself of** (something). to make use of (something) to one's advantage. ~*n.* **3.** use or advantage (esp. in **of no avail**).

available (əˈveɪləbᵊl) *adj.* obtainable or accessible; capable of being made use of. —aˌvailaˈbility *n.* —aˈvailably *adv.*

avalanche (ˈævəˌlɑːntʃ) *n.* **1.** a fall of large masses of snow and ice down a mountain. **2.** a sudden or overwhelming appearance of a large quantity of things.

avant-garde (ˌævɒŋˈɡɑːd) *n.* **1.** those artists, writers or musicians, whose techniques and ideas are in advance of those generally accepted. ~*adj.* **2.** (of a work of art) using ideas or techniques in advance of those generally accepted.

avarice (ˈævərɪs) *n.* extreme greed for riches. —**avaricious** (ˌævəˈrɪʃəs) *adj.*

avast (əˈvɑːst) *interj. Naut.* stop! cease!

avatar ('ævə,tɑː) *n. Hinduism.* the manifestation of a god in human or animal form.

avdp. avoirdupois.

Ave ('ɑːvɪ) *or* **Ave Maria** (mə'riːə) *n.* same as **Hail Mary.**

Ave. avenue.

avenge (ə'vɛndʒ) *vb.* to inflict a punishment in retaliation for (harm done) or on behalf of (the person harmed). —a'**venger** *n.*

avenue ('ævɪnjuː) *n.* 1. a street. 2. an approach road, as to a country house. 3. a road bordered by two rows of trees. 4. a line of approach: *try all avenues before giving up.*

aver (ə'vɜː) *vb.* **averring, averred.** to state to be true. —a'**verment** *n.*

average ('ævərɪdʒ, 'ævrɪdʒ) *n.* 1. the typical or normal amount or quality. 2. the result obtained by adding the numbers or quantities in a set and dividing the total by the number of members in the set. 3. **on (the** *or* **an) average.** usually; typically. ~*adj.* 4. usual or typical. 5. mediocre or inferior. 6. constituting a numerical average. ~*vb.* 7. to obtain or estimate a numerical average of. 8. to assess the general quality of. 9. to amount to or be on average.

averse (ə'vɜːs) *adj.* (usually foll. by *to*) opposed, disinclined, or loath.

Usage. *To* is the preposition now normally used with *averse* (*he was averse to giving any assistance*), although *from* is often used with *averse* and *aversion* and was at one time considered to be grammatically correct.

aversion (ə'vɜːʃən) *n.* 1. (usually foll. by *to* or *for*) extreme dislike or disinclination. 2. a person or thing that arouses this.

avert (ə'vɜːt) *vb.* 1. to turn away: *to avert one's gaze.* 2. to ward off: *to avert danger.*

Avesta (ə'vɛstə) *n.* a collection of sacred writings of Zoroastrianism.

avian ('eɪvɪən) *adj.* of or like a bird.

aviary ('eɪvjərɪ) *n., pl.* **aviaries.** a large enclosure in which birds are kept.

aviation (,eɪvɪ'eɪʃən) *n.* the art or science of flying aircraft.

aviator ('eɪvɪ,eɪtə) *n. Old-fashioned.* the pilot of an aircraft. —'**avi,atrix** *fem. n.*

avid ('ævɪd) *adj.* 1. very keen; enthusiastic: *an avid reader.* 2. (often foll. by *for* or *of*) eager: *avid for revenge.* —**avidity** (ə'vɪdɪtɪ) *n.* —'**avidly** *adv.*

avocado (,ævə'kɑːdəʊ) *n., pl.* -**dos.** a pear-shaped fruit with a leathery green skin and greenish-yellow edible pulp.

avocation (,ævə'keɪʃən) *n. Archaic.* 1. a minor occupation undertaken as a diversion. 2. a person's regular job.

avocet ('ævə,sɛt) *n.* a long-legged shore bird having a long slender upward-curving bill.

avoid (ə'vɔɪd) *vb.* 1. to keep out of the way of. 2. to refrain from doing. 3. to prevent from happening. —a'**voidable** *adj.* —a'**voidably** *adv.* —a'**voidance** *n.*

avoirdupois *or* **avoirdupois weight** (,ævədə'pɔɪz) *n.* a system of weights based on the pound, which contains 16 ounces or 7000 grains.

avow (ə'vaʊ) *vb.* 1. to state or affirm. 2. to admit openly. —a'**vowal** *n.* —a'**vowed** *adj.* —**avowedly** (ə'vaʊɪdlɪ) *adv.*

avuncular (ə'vʌŋkjʊlə) *adj.* friendly, helpful or caring.

await (ə'weɪt) *vb.* 1. to wait for. 2. to be in store for.

awake (ə'weɪk) *vb.* **awaking; awoke** *or* **awaked; awoken** *or* **awaked.** 1. to emerge or rouse from sleep. 2. to become or cause to become alert. ~*adj.* 3. not sleeping. 4. (sometimes foll. by *to*) alert or aware: *awake to the danger.* **Usage.** see **wake¹.**

award (ə'wɔːd) *vb.* 1. to give (something, as for merit). 2. *Law.* to declare to be entitled, as by decision of a court. ~*n.* 3. something awarded, such as a prize. 4. *Law.* the decision of an arbitrator or court.

aware (ə'wɛə) *adj.* 1. (foll. by *of*) having knowledge: *aware of his error.* 2. informed: *politically aware.* —a'**wareness** *n.*

awash (ə'wɒʃ) *adv., adj.* 1. at a level with the surface of the sea. 2. washed over by the waves.

away (ə'weɪ) *adv.* 1. from a particular place: *swim away.* 2. in or to another, a usual, or a proper place: *to put toys away.* 3. at a distance: *keep away from strangers.* 4. out of existence: *fade away.* 5. indicating motion or distance from a normal or proper place: *to turn one's head away.* 6. continuously: *laughing away.* ~*adj.* 7. not present: *away from school.* 8. distant: *a good way away.* 9. *Sport.* played on an opponent's ground.

awayday (ə'weɪ,deɪ) *n.* a day trip taken for pleasure.

awe (ɔː) *n.* 1. overwhelming wonder, respect, or dread. ~*vb.* 2. to inspire with reverence or dread.

aweigh (ə'weɪ) *adj. Naut.* (of an anchor) no longer hooked into the bottom.

awesome ('ɔːsəm) *adj.* inspiring or displaying awe.

awful ('ɔːfʊl) *adj.* 1. very bad; unpleasant. 2. *Archaic.* inspiring reverence or dread. 3. *Informal.* large or great: *an awful pity.* ~*adv.* 4. *Not standard.* very: *an awful cold day.*

awfully ('ɔːfəlɪ) *adv.* 1. in an unpleasant, bad, or reprehensible manner. 2. *Informal.* very: *I'm awfully keen to come.*

awhile (ə'waɪl) *adv.* for a brief period.

awkward ('ɔːkwəd) *adj.* 1. clumsy or ungainly. **2.** unwieldy: *this keyboard is awkward to use.* **3.** embarrassing: *an awkward moment.* **4.** embarrassed: *he felt awkward about leaving.* **5.** difficult to deal with. —'**awkwardly** *adv.* —'**awkwardness** *n.*

awl (ɔːl) *n.* a pointed hand tool for piercing wood, leather, etc.

awn (ɔːn) *n.* any of the bristles growing from the flowering parts of certain grasses and cereals.

awning ('ɔːnɪŋ) *n.* a roof of canvas supported by a frame to provide protection from the weather.

awoke (ə'wəʊk) *vb.* a past tense and (now rare or dialectal) past participle of **awake.**

AWOL ('eɪwɒl) *Mil.* absent without leave but without intending to desert.

awry (ə'raɪ) *adv., adj.* **1.** with a twist to one side; askew. **2.** amiss.

axe *or U.S.* **ax** (æks) *n., pl.* **axes. 1.** a hand tool with one side of its head sharpened to a cutting edge, used for felling trees and splitting timber. **2. an axe to grind.** an ulterior motive. **3.** *Informal.* a severe cut in spending or in the number of staff employed. ~*vb.* **4.** to chop with an axe. **5.** *Informal.* to dismiss (employees), restrict (expenditure), or terminate (a project).

axes¹ ('æksiːz) *n.* the plural of **axis.**

axes² ('æksɪz) *n.* the plural of **axe.**

axial ('æksɪəl) *adj.* **1.** forming or of an axis. **2.** in, on, or along an axis. —'**axially** *adv.*

axil ('æksɪl) *n.* the upper angle between a leafstalk and the stem from which it grows.

axiom ('æksɪəm) *n.* **1.** a generally accepted proposition or principle. **2.** a self-evident statement.

axiomatic (ˌæksɪə'mætɪk) *adj.* **1.** self-evident. **2.** containing axioms. —ˌ**axio-'matically** *adv.*

axis ('æksɪs) *n., pl.* **axes. 1.** a real or imaginary line about which a body can rotate or about which an object or geometrical construction is symmetrical. **2.** one of two or three reference lines used in coordinate geometry to locate a point in a plane or in space.

axle ('æksəl) *n.* a shaft on which a wheel or pair of wheels revolves.

axolotl (ˌæksə'lɒtʲl) *n.* an aquatic salamander of N America.

ayah ('aɪə) *n.* (in parts of the former British Empire) a native maidservant or nursemaid.

ayatollah (ˌaɪə'tɒlə) *n.* one of a class of Islamic religious leaders in Iran.

aye *or* **ay** (aɪ) *interj.* **1.** yes. ~*n.* **2.** an affirmative vote or voter.

Ayrshire ('ɛəʃə) *n.* one of a breed of brown-and-white dairy cattle.

AZ Arizona.

azalea (ə'zeɪljə) *n.* a shrub allied to the rhododendron cultivated for its showy flowers.

azimuth ('æzɪməθ) *n.* **1.** *Astron., navigation.* the angle between the north or south point of the horizon and the intersection with the horizon of a vertical circle passing through a celestial body. **2.** *Surveying.* the horizontal angle of a bearing measured clockwise from north.

Aztec ('æztɛk) *n.* **1.** a member of a Mexican Indian people who established a great empire, overthrown by the Spanish in the early 16th century. **2.** the language of the Aztecs. ~*adj.* **3.** of the Aztecs or their language.

azure ('æʒə, 'eɪ-) *n.* **1.** the deep blue colour of a clear blue sky. **2.** *Poetic.* a clear blue sky.

B

b or **B** (biː) n., pl. **b's**, **B's**, or **Bs**. **1.** the second letter of the English alphabet. **2.** the second in a series, class, or rank.

B 1. *Music.* the seventh note of the scale of C major. **2.** the less important of two things. **3.** *Chem.* boron. **4.** *Chess.* bishop.

b. 1. born. **2.** *Cricket.* **a.** bowled. **b.** bye.

Ba *Chem.* barium.

BA 1. Bachelor of Arts. **2.** British Airways.

baa (bɑː) vb. **baaing, baaed. 1.** to make the cry of a sheep. ~n. **2.** the cry made by a sheep.

baas (bɑːs) n. *S. African.* a boss.

baasskap (ˈbɑːsˌkæp) n. (in South Africa) control by Whites of non-Whites.

babbalas (ˈbæbəˌlæs) n. *S. African.* a hangover.

babble (ˈbæbᵊl) vb. **1.** to utter (words or sounds) in an incoherent jumble. **2.** to talk foolishly or irrelevantly. **3.** to disclose (secrets) carelessly. **4.** (of streams or birds) to make a low murmuring sound. ~n. **5.** incoherent or foolish speech. **6.** a murmuring sound. —ˈ**babbler** n.

babe (beɪb) n. **1.** a baby. **2.** *Informal.* a naive or gullible person. **3.** *Slang, chiefly U.S.* a girl.

babel (ˈbeɪbᵊl) n. **1.** a confusion of noises or voices. **2.** a scene of noise and confusion.

baboon (bəˈbuːn) n. a medium-sized monkey with a long face, large teeth, and a fairly long tail.

baby (ˈbeɪbɪ) n., pl. **-bies. 1.** a newborn child. **2.** the youngest or smallest of a family or group. **3.** a recently born animal. **4.** an immature person. **5.** *Slang.* a sweetheart. **6.** a project of personal concern. **7. be left holding the baby.** to be left with a responsibility. ~adj. **8.** comparatively small of its type: *a baby car.* ~vb. **-bying, -bied. 9.** to treat (someone) like a baby; pamper. —ˈ**babyhood** n. —ˈ**babyish** adj.

baby bonus n. *Canad. informal.* Family Allowance.

baby-sit vb. **-sitting, -sat.** to act or work as a baby-sitter. —ˈ**baby-ˌsitting** n., adj.

baby-sitter n. a person who takes care of a child while the parents are out.

baccalaureate (ˌbækəˈlɔːrɪt) n. the university degree of Bachelor of Arts.

baccarat (ˈbækəˌrɑː, ˌbækəˈrɑː) n. a card game in which the punters gamble against the banker.

bacchanal (ˈbækənᵊl) n. **1.** a follower of Bacchus, Greek god of wine. **2.** a drunken celebration.

bacchanalia (ˌbækəˈneɪlɪə) pl. n. **1.** an ancient Roman festival in honour of Bacchus. **2.** any drunken revelry.

bacchant (ˈbækənt) or (*fem.*) **bacchante** (bəˈkæntɪ) n., pl. **bacchants** or **bacchantes** (bəˈkæntɪz). **1.** a priest, priestess, or worshipper of Bacchus. **2.** a drunken reveller.

Bacchic (ˈbækɪk) adj. of Bacchus.

baccy (ˈbækɪ) n. *Brit. informal.* tobacco.

bachelor (ˈbætʃələ) n. **1.** an unmarried man. **2.** a person who holds the lowest university degree. —ˈ**bachelorhood** n.

bachelor girl n. a young unmarried woman.

Bachelor of Arts n. a person with a first degree from a university or college, usually in the arts.

bacillary (bəˈsɪlərɪ) adj. of or caused by bacilli.

bacillus (bəˈsɪləs) n., pl. **-cilli** (-ˈsɪlaɪ). a rod-shaped bacterium, esp. one causing disease.

back (bæk) n. **1.** the rear part of the human body, from the neck to the pelvis. **2.** the spinal column. **3.** the part or side of an object opposite the front. **4.** the part of anything less often seen or used. **5.** *Ball games.* a defensive player or position. **6. at the back of one's mind.** not in one's conscious thoughts. **7. behind someone's back.** secretly or deceitfully. **8. put** or **get someone's back up.** to annoy someone. **9. turn one's back on someone.** to refuse to help someone. ~vb. **10.** to move or cause to move backwards. **11.** to provide money for (a person or enterprise). **12.** to bet on the success of: *to back a horse.* **13.** to provide (a singer) with a musical accompaniment. **14.** (foll. by *on* or *onto*) to have the back facing (towards): *the house backs onto a river.* **15.** (of the wind) to change direction anticlockwise. ~adj. **16.** situated behind. **17.** owing from an earlier date: *back rent.* **18.** remote: *a back road.* ~adv. **19.** at, to, or towards the rear. **20.** to or towards the original starting point or condition: *I went back home.* **21.** in reply or retaliation: *to hit someone back.* **22.** in concealment or reserve: *to keep something back.* **23. back and forth.** to and fro. **24. back to front. a.** in reverse. **b.** in disorder. ~See also **back down, back out, back up.**

backbencher (ˈbækˈbentʃə) n. *Brit., Austral., N.Z., etc.* a Member of Parliament who does not hold office in the government or opposition.

backbite ('bæk,baɪt) *vb.* **-biting, -bit; -bitten** *or* **-bit.** to talk spitefully about (an absent person). —'**back,biter** *n.*

back boiler *n.* a tank at the back of a fireplace for heating water.

backbone ('bæk,bəʊn) *n.* **1.** the spinal column. **2.** strength of character; courage.

backbreaking ('bæk,breɪkɪŋ) *adj.* (of work) exhausting.

backburn ('bæk,bɜːn) *Austral. & N.Z.* ~*vb.* **1.** to clear (an area of bush) by creating a new fire that burns in the opposite direction from the line of advancing fire. ~*n.* **2.** the act or result of backburning.

backchat ('bæk,tʃæt) *n. Informal.* the act of answering back, esp. impudently.

backcloth ('bæk,klɒθ) *n.* a painted curtain at the back of a stage set. Also called: **backdrop.**

backcomb ('bæk,kəʊm) *vb.* to comb (the hair) towards the roots to give more bulk to a hairstyle.

back country *n. Austral. & N.Z.* land remote from settled areas.

backdate (,bæk'deɪt) *vb.* to make (a document) effective from an earlier date.

back door *n.* a means of entry to a job or position that is secret or obtained through influence.

back down *vb.* to withdraw an earlier claim.

backer ('bækə) *n.* a person who gives financial or other support.

backfire (,bæk'faɪə) *vb.* **1.** (of an internal-combustion engine) to make a loud noise as a result of an explosion of unburnt gases in the exhaust system. **2.** (of a plan or scheme) to fail to have the desired effect.

backgammon ('bæk,gæmən) *n.* a game for two people played on a board with pieces moved according to throws of the dice.

background ('bæk,graʊnd) *n.* **1.** the part of a scene furthest from the viewer. **2.** an inconspicuous position: *in the background.* **3.** the space behind the chief figures or objects in a picture. **4.** a person's social class, education, or experience. **5.** the events or circumstances that help to explain something.

backhand ('bæk,hænd) *n.* **1.** *Tennis, etc.* a stroke made across the body with the back of the hand facing the direction of the stroke. **2.** the side on which backhand strokes are made.

backhanded (,bæk'hændɪd) *adj.* **1.** (of a blow or shot) performed with the arm moving across the body. **2.** ambiguous or sarcastic: *a backhanded compliment.*

backhander ('bæk,hændə) *n.* **1.** *Slang.* a bribe. **2.** a backhanded stroke or blow.

backing ('bækɪŋ) *n.* **1.** support. **2.** something that forms or strengthens the back of something. **3.** musical accompaniment for a pop singer.

backing dog *n. N.Z.* a dog that moves a flock of sheep by jumping on their backs.

backlash ('bæk,læʃ) *n.* **1.** a sudden and adverse reaction. **2.** a recoil between interacting badly fitting parts in machinery.

backlog ('bæk,lɒg) *n.* an accumulation of uncompleted things to be dealt with.

back number *n.* **1.** an old issue of a newspaper or magazine. **2.** *Informal.* a person or thing considered to be old-fashioned.

back out *vb.* (often foll. by *of*) to withdraw (from an agreement).

backpack ('bæk,pæk) *n.* **1.** a rucksack. ~*vb.* **2.** to go hiking with a backpack.

back passage *n.* the rectum.

back-pedal *vb.* **-pedalling, -pedalled** *or* *U.S.* **-pedaling, -pedaled.** to retract or modify a previous opinion or principle.

back room *n.* **a.** a place where secret research or planning is done. **b.** (*as modifier*): *back-room boys.*

back seat *n. Informal.* a subordinate or inconspicuous position: *I prefer to take a back seat.*

back-seat driver *n. Informal.* a person, for example a passenger in a car, who offers unwanted advice.

backside (,bæk'saɪd) *n. Informal.* the buttocks.

backslide (,bæk'slaɪd) *vb.* **-sliding, -slid.** to relapse into former bad habits or vices. —,**back'slider** *n.*

backspace ('bæk,speɪs) *vb.* to move (a typewriter carriage or computer cursor) backwards.

backspin ('bæk,spɪn) *n. Sport.* a backward spin imparted to a ball to reduce its speed at impact.

backstage (,bæk'steɪdʒ) *adv.* **1.** behind the stage in a theatre. ~*adj.* **2.** situated backstage.

backstairs (,bæk'stɛəz) *or* **backstair** *adj.* underhand: *backstairs gossip.*

backstreet ('bæk,striːt) *n.* **1.** a street in a town remote from the main roads. **2.** (*modifier*) denoting secret or illegal activities: *a backstreet abortion.*

backstroke ('bæk,strəʊk) *n. Swimming.* a stroke performed on the back, using backward circular strokes of each arm.

backtrack ('bæk,træk) *vb.* **1.** to return by the same route by which one has come. **2.** to retract or reverse one's opinion or policy.

back up *vb.* **1.** to support. **2.** *Computers.* to make a copy of (a data file), esp. as a security copy. ~*n.* **backup. 3.** a support or reinforcement. **4. a.** a reserve or substitute. **b.** (*as modifier*): *a backup copy.*

backveld ('bæk,felt, -,vɛlt) *n. S. African informal.* a remote sparsely populated rural area.

backward ('bækwəd) *adj.* **1.** directed towards the rear. **2.** retarded in physical, material, or intellectual development. **3.** reluctant or bashful. *~adv.* **4.** same as **backwards.** —'**backwardness** *n.*

backwards ('bækwədz) *or* **backward** *adv.* **1.** towards the rear. **2.** with the back foremost. **3.** in the reverse of the usual direction. **4.** into a worse state. **5.** towards the point of origin. **6. bend over backwards.** *Informal.* to make a special effort to please someone.

backwash ('bæk,wɒʃ) *n.* **1.** water washed backwards by the motion of oars or a ship. **2.** a repercussion.

backwater ('bæk,wɔːtə) *n.* **1.** a body of stagnant water connected to a river. **2.** an isolated or backward place or condition.

backwoods ('bæk,wʊdz) *pl. n.* **1.** partially cleared, sparsely populated forests. **2.** any remote sparsely populated place. —'**back,woodsman** *n.*

back yard *n.* **1.** a yard at the back of a house, etc. **2. in one's own back yard. a.** close at hand. **b.** involving or implicating one.

bacon ('beikən) *n.* **1.** meat from the back and sides of a pig, dried, salted, and usually smoked. **2. bring home the bacon.** *Informal.* **a.** to achieve success. **b.** to provide material support.

bacteria (bæk'tɪərɪə) *pl. n., sing.* -**rium.** a large group of microorganisms, many of which cause disease. —**bac'terial** *adj.*

bacteriology (bæk,tɪərɪ'ɒlədʒɪ) *n.* the study of bacteria. —**bac,teri'ologist** *n.*

Bactrian camel ('bæktrɪən) *n.* a two-humped camel.

bad (bæd) *adj.* **worse, worst. 1.** not good; of poor quality. **2.** lacking skill or talent: *bad at maths.* **3.** harmful: *smoking is bad for you.* **4.** immoral; evil. **5.** naughty; mischievous. **6.** rotten; decayed: *a bad egg.* **7.** severe: *a bad headache.* **8.** incorrect; faulty: *bad grammar.* **9.** sorry or upset: *I feel bad about saying no.* **10.** unfavourable; distressing: *bad news.* **11.** offensive; unpleasant: *bad language.* **12.** not valid: *a bad cheque.* **13.** not recoverable: *a bad debt.* **14.** (**badder, baddest**) *Slang.* good; excellent. **15. not bad** *or* **not so bad.** *Informal.* fairly good. **16. too bad.** *Informal.* (often used dismissively) regrettable. *~n.* **17.** unfortunate or unpleasant events: *you've got to take the bad with the good.* *~adv.* **18.** *Not standard.* badly: *to want something bad.* —'**badness** *n.*

bad blood *n.* a feeling of intense hatred or hostility; enmity.

bade (bæd, beid) *or* **bad** *vb.* a past tense of **bid.**

badge (bædʒ) *n.* **1.** a distinguishing emblem or mark worn to signify membership or achievement. **2.** any revealing feature or mark.

badger ('bædʒə) *n.* **1.** a stocky burrowing mammal with a thick coat striped black and white on the head. *~vb.* **2.** to pester or harass.

badinage ('bædɪ,nɑːʒ) *n.* playful and witty conversation.

badly ('bædlɪ) *adv.* **worse, worst. 1.** poorly; inadequately. **2.** unfavourably: *our scheme worked out badly.* **3.** severely: *badly hurt.* **4.** very much: *need badly.* **5. badly off.** poor.

badminton ('bædmɪntən) *n.* a game played with rackets and a shuttlecock which is hit back and forth across a high net.

baffle ('bæfᵊl) *vb.* **1.** to perplex; puzzle. **2.** to frustrate (someone's plans or efforts). *~n.* **3.** a mechanical device to limit or regulate the flow of fluid, light, or sound. —'**bafflement** *n.* —'**baffling** *adj.*

bag (bæg) *n.* **1.** a flexible container with an opening at one end. **2.** the contents of such a container. **3.** a piece of luggage. **4.** a handbag. **5.** anything that sags, such as a loose fold of skin under the eyes. **6.** any sac in the body of an animal. **7.** the amount of game taken by a hunter. **8.** *Offensive slang.* an ugly or bad-tempered woman: *an old bag.* **9. in the bag.** *Slang.* almost assured of succeeding. *~vb.* **bagging, bagged. 10.** to put into a bag. **11.** to bulge or cause to bulge. **12.** to capture or kill, as in hunting. **13.** *Brit. informal.* to secure the right to do or to have: *he bagged the best chair.* ~See also **bags.**

bagatelle (,bægə'tɛl) *n.* **1.** something of little value. **2.** a board game in which balls are struck into holes. **3.** a short piece of music.

bagel ('beigᵊl) *n.* a hard ring-shaped bread roll.

baggage ('bægɪdʒ) *n.* **1.** suitcases packed for a journey; luggage. **2.** an army's portable equipment.

baggy ('bægɪ) *adj.* -**gier,** -**giest.** (of clothes) hanging loosely. —'**bagginess** *n.*

bag lady *n.* a homeless woman who wanders the streets with all her possessions in shopping bags.

bagpipes ('bæg,paɪps) *pl. n.* a musical wind instrument in which sounds are produced in reed pipes by air from an inflated bag.

bags (bægz) *pl. n.* **1.** *Informal.* a lot. *~interj.* **2.** Also: **bags I.** *Children's slang, Brit.* an indication of the desire to do, be, or have something.

bah (bɑː, bæ) *interj.* an expression of contempt or disgust.

bail¹ (beil) *Law.* *~n.* **1.** a sum of money deposited with the court as security for a person's reappearance in court. **2.** the person giving such security. **3. jump bail.** to fail to appear in court to answer to a charge. **4. stand** *or* **go bail.** to act as surety for someone. ~*vb.* **5.** (foll. by *out*) to obtain the release of (a person) from custody, security having been made.

bail² *or* **bale** (beɪl) *vb.* (foll. by *out*) to remove (water) from (a boat). See also **bale out.**

bail³ (beɪl) *n.* **1.** *Cricket.* either of two small wooden bars across the tops of the stumps. **2.** a partition between stalls in a stable or barn. **3.** *Austral. & N.Z.* a framework in a cowshed used to secure the head of a cow during milking. **4.** a movable bar on a typewriter that holds the paper against the platen.

bailey (ˈbeɪlɪ) *n.* the outermost wall or court of a castle.

Bailey bridge (ˈbeɪlɪ) *n.* a temporary bridge that can be rapidly assembled.

bailiff (ˈbeɪlɪf) *n.* **1.** *Brit.* the agent of a landlord or landowner. **2.** a sheriff's officer who serves writs and summonses.

bailiwick (ˈbeɪlɪwɪk) *n.* **1.** *Law.* the area over which a bailiff has jurisdiction. **2.** a person's special field of interest.

bail up *vb. Austral. & N.Z.* to confine (a cow) or (of a cow) to be confined by the head in a bail.

bain-marie (ˌbænmæˈriː) *n., pl.* **bains-marie** (ˌbænmæˈriː). a vessel for holding hot water, in which sauces and other dishes are gently cooked or kept warm.

bairn (bɛən) *n. Scot. & N English.* a child.

bait (beɪt) *n.* **1.** something edible fixed to a hook or in a trap to attract fish or animals. **2.** an enticement; temptation. ~*vb.* **3.** to put a piece of food on or in (a hook or trap). **4.** to persecute or tease. **5.** to set dogs upon (a bear or badger).

baize (beɪz) *n.* a woollen fabric resembling felt, used for the tops of billiard or card tables.

bake (beɪk) *vb.* **1.** to cook by dry heat as in an oven. **2.** to cook bread, pastry, or cakes. **3.** to make or become hardened by heat. **4.** *Informal.* to be extremely hot.

baked beans *pl. n.* haricot beans, baked and tinned in tomato sauce.

baker (ˈbeɪkə) *n.* a person whose business is to make or sell bread, cakes, etc.

baker's dozen *n.* thirteen.

bakery (ˈbeɪkərɪ) *n., pl.* **-eries.** a place where bread, cakes, etc., are baked or sold.

baking powder *n.* a powdered mixture that contains sodium bicarbonate and cream of tartar: used in baking as a substitute for yeast.

baksheesh (ˈbækʃiːʃ) *n.* (in some Eastern countries) money given as a tip or present.

Balaclava (ˌbæləˈklævə) *or* **Balaclava helmet** *n.* a close-fitting woollen hood that covers the ears and neck.

balalaika (ˌbæləˈlaɪkə) *n.* a Russian musical instrument with a triangular body and three strings.

balance (ˈbæləns) *n.* **1.** a weighing device, with a horizontal beam pivoted at its centre, from the ends of which two pans are suspended. **2.** a state of equilibrium. **3.** stability of mind or body: *lose one's balance.* **4.** harmony in the parts of a whole. **5.** the power to influence or control: *the balance of power.* **6.** something that remains: *the balance of what you owe.* **7.** *Accounting.* **a.** the matching of debit and credit totals in an account. **b.** a difference between such totals. **8. in the balance.** in an undecided condition. **9. on balance.** after weighing up all the factors. ~*vb.* **10.** to weigh in or as if in a balance. **11.** to be or come into equilibrium. **12.** to bring into or hold in equilibrium. **13.** to compare the relative weight or importance of. **14.** to arrange so as to create a state of harmony. **15.** *Accounting.* to compare or equalize the credit and debit totals of (an account).

balance of power *n.* the equal distribution of military and economic power among countries.

balance of trade *n.* the difference in value between exports and imports of goods.

balance sheet *n.* a statement that shows the financial position of a business.

balcony (ˈbælkənɪ) *n., pl.* **-nies. 1.** a platform projecting from a building with a balustrade along its outer edge, often with access from a door. **2.** an upper tier of seats in a theatre or cinema.

bald (bɔːld) *adj.* **1.** having no hair or fur, esp. (of a man) having no hair on the scalp. **2.** lacking natural covering. **3.** plain or blunt: *a bald statement.* **4.** (of a tyre) having a worn tread. —**ˈbaldly** *adv.* —**ˈbaldness** *n.*

balderdash (ˈbɔːldəˌdæʃ) *n.* stupid or illogical talk.

balding (ˈbɔːldɪŋ) *adj.* becoming bald.

bale¹ (beɪl) *n.* **1.** a large bundle of hay or goods bound by ropes or wires for storage or transportation. ~*vb.* **2.** to make (hay) or put (goods) into a bale or bales.

bale² (beɪl) *vb.* same as **bail².**

baleen (bəˈliːn) *n.* whalebone.

baleen whale *n.* same as **whalebone whale.**

baleful (ˈbeɪlful) *adj.* harmful, menacing, or vindictive. —**ˈbalefully** *adv.*

bale out *or* **bail out** *vb.* **1.** to make an emergency parachute jump from an aircraft. **2.** *Informal.* to help (a person or organization) out of a predicament.

balk *or* **baulk** (bɔːk, bɔːlk) *vb.* **1.** to stop short: *the horse balked at the jump.* **2.** to recoil: *he balked at the idea of murder.* **3.** to thwart, check, or foil: *he was balked in* *his plans.* ~*n.* **4.** a roughly squared timber beam. **5.** an obstacle; hindrance.

Balkan (ˈbɔːlkən) *adj.* of a peninsula in SE Europe, between the Adriatic and Aegean Seas.

ball¹ (bɔːl) *n.* **1.** a spherical or nearly spherical object. **2.** a round or roundish object of a size suitable for use in various games. **3.** a single delivery of the ball in a game. **4.** a solid nonexplosive projectile for a firearm or cannon. **5.** any more or less rounded part: *the ball of the foot.* **6. have the ball at one's feet.** to have the chance of doing something. **7. on the ball.** *Informal.* alert; informed. **8. play ball.** *Informal.* to cooperate. **9. start** or **keep the ball rolling.** to initiate or maintain the progress of an action, discussion, or project. ~*vb.* **10.** to form into a ball. ~See also **balls, balls-up.**

ball² (bɔːl) *n.* **1.** a lavish or formal social function for dancing. **2. have a ball.** *Informal.* to have a very enjoyable time.

ballad (ˈbæləd) *n.* **1.** a narrative song with a recurrent refrain. **2.** a narrative poem in short stanzas of popular origin. **3.** a slow sentimental song.

ballade (bæˈlɑːd) *n.* **1.** *Prosody.* a verse form consisting of three stanzas and an envoy, all ending with the same line. **2.** *Music.* a romantic instrumental composition.

ball-and-socket joint *n.* *Anat.* a joint in which a rounded head fits into a rounded cavity, allowing a wide range of movement.

ballast (ˈbæləst) *n.* **1.** a substance, such as sand, used to stabilize a ship when it is not carrying cargo. **2.** crushed rock used for the foundation of a road or railway track. ~*vb.* **3.** to give stability or weight to.

ball bearing *n.* **1.** a bearing consisting of steel balls placed between moving parts of a machine in order to reduce friction. **2.** a metal ball used in such a bearing.

ball boy or (*fem.*) **ball girl** *n.* (in tennis) a person who retrieves balls that go out of play.

ball cock *n.* a device consisting of a floating ball and valve for regulating the flow of liquid into a tank or cistern.

ballerina (ˌbæləˈriːnə) *n.* a female ballet dancer.

ballet (ˈbæleɪ, bæˈleɪ) *n.* **1.** a classical style of expressive dancing based on precise conventional steps. **2.** a theatrical representation of a story performed by ballet dancers. —**balletic** (bæˈlɛtɪk) *adj.*

ball game *n.* **1.** *U.S. & Canad.* a game of baseball. **2.** *Informal.* a state of affairs: *a whole new ball game.*

ballista (bəˈlɪstə) *n.*, *pl.* **-tae** (-tiː). an ancient catapult for hurling stones.

ballistic missile *n.* a missile guided automatically in flight but which falls freely at its target.

ballistics (bəˈlɪstɪks) *n.* (*functioning as sing.*) the study of the flight of projectiles and the effects of firing on firearms. —**ballistic** *adj.*

ballocks (ˈbɒləks) *pl. n., interj.* same as **bollocks.**

balloon (bəˈluːn) *n.* **1.** an inflatable rubber bag used as a plaything or party decoration. **2.** a large bag inflated with a lighter-than-air gas, designed to rise and float in the atmosphere with a basket for carrying passengers. **3.** an outline containing the words or thoughts of a character in a cartoon. ~*vb.* **4.** to fly in a balloon. **5.** to inflate or be inflated. —**balloonist** *n.*

ballot (ˈbælət) *n.* **1.** the practice of selecting a representative or course of action by voting secretly. **2.** the number of votes cast in an election. **3.** the actual vote or paper indicating a person's choice. ~*vb.* **-loting, -loted.** **4.** to vote or ask for a vote from: *we balloted the members on this issue.* **5.** to vote for or decide on something by ballot.

ballot box *n.* a box into which ballot papers are dropped after voting.

ballot paper *n.* a paper used for voting.

ballpark (ˈbɔːlˌpɑːk) *n.* **1.** *U.S. & Canad.* a stadium used for baseball games. **2.** *Informal.* approximate range: *in the right ballpark.*

ballpoint or **ballpoint pen** (ˈbɔːlˌpɔɪnt) *n.* a pen having a small ball bearing as a writing point.

ballroom (ˈbɔːlˌruːm, -ˌrʊm) *n.* a large hall for dancing.

ballroom dancing *n.* social dancing in couples to music in conventional rhythms, such as the waltz.

balls (bɔːlz) *pl. n.* *Taboo slang.* **1.** the testicles. **2.** nonsense.

balls-up *Taboo slang.* ~*n.* **1.** something botched or muddled. ~*vb.* **balls up.** **2.** to muddle or botch.

bally (ˈbælɪ) *adj., adv.* *Brit. slang, euphemistic.* bloody.

ballyhoo (ˌbælɪˈhuː) *n.* *Informal.* **1.** a noisy or confused situation. **2.** sensational advertising.

balm (bɑːm) *n.* **1.** an aromatic substance obtained from certain tropical trees and used for healing and soothing. **2.** something comforting or soothing. **3.** an aromatic herb, lemon balm.

balmy (ˈbɑːmɪ) *adj.* **balmier, balmiest.** **1.** (of weather) mild and pleasant. **2.** same as **barmy.**

baloney or **boloney** (bəˈləʊnɪ) *n.* *Informal.* nonsense.

balsa (ˈbɔːlsə) *n.* **1.** a tree of tropical America that yields light wood used for making rafts, models, etc. **2.** a light raft.

balsam (ˈbɔːlsəm) *n.* **1.** an aromatic resin

obtained from various trees and shrubs and used in medicines and perfumes. **2.** any plant yielding balsam. **3.** a flowering plant, such as busy lizzie.

Baltic ('bɔːltɪk) *adj.* denoting or relating to the Baltic Sea in N Europe, or the states bordering it.

baluster ('bæləstə) *n.* any of a set of posts supporting a rail.

balustrade ('bælə,streɪd) *n.* an ornamental rail supported by balusters.

bamboo (bæm'buː) *n.* a tall treelike tropical grass with hollow stems which are used to make canes, furniture, etc.

bamboozle (bæm'buːz'l) *vb. Informal.* **1.** to cheat; mislead. **2.** to confuse. —**bam'boozlement** *n.*

ban (bæn) *vb.* **banning, banned. 1.** to prohibit or forbid, esp. officially. ~*n.* **2.** an official prohibition.

banal (bə'nɑːl) *adj.* lacking force or originality. —**banality** (bə'nælɪtɪ) *n.*

banana (bə'nɑːnə) *n.* a crescent-shaped fruit that grows on a tropical or subtropical treelike plant.

banana republic *n. Informal.* a small politically unstable country whose economy is dominated by foreign interests.

band¹ (bænd) *n.* **1.** a group of musicians playing together, esp. on brass or percussion instruments. **2.** a group of people having a common purpose: *a band of revolutionaries.* ~*vb.* **3.** (foll. by *together*) to unite.

band² (bænd) *n.* **1.** a strip of some material, used to hold objects together: *a rubber band.* **2.** a strip of fabric used as an ornament or to reinforce clothing. **3.** a stripe of contrasting colour or texture. **4.** a driving belt in machinery. **5.** *Physics.* a range of frequencies or wavelengths between two limits. **6.** a section of a gramophone record. ~*vb.* **7.** to fasten or mark with a band.

bandage ('bændɪdʒ) *n.* **1.** a piece of material used to dress a wound or bind a broken limb. ~*vb.* **2.** to cover or bind with a bandage.

bandanna *or* **bandana** (bæn'dænə) *n.* a large brightly-coloured handkerchief or neckerchief.

b. and b. *or* **B & B** bed and breakfast.

bandbox ('bænd,bɒks) *n.* a lightweight usually cylindrical box for hats.

bandeau ('bændəʊ) *n., pl.* **-deaux** (-dəʊz). a narrow ribbon worn round the head.

banderole ('bændə,rəʊl) *n.* **1.** a narrow flag usually with forked ends. **2.** a ribbonlike scroll bearing an inscription.

bandicoot ('bændɪ,kuːt) *n.* **1.** a ratlike marsupial of Australia with a long pointed muzzle and a long tail. **2. bandicoot rat.** any of three burrowing rats of S and SE Asia.

bandit ('bændɪt) *n.* a robber, esp. a member of an armed gang. —**'banditry** *n.*

bandmaster ('bænd,mɑːstə) *n.* the conductor of a band.

bandoleer *or* **bandolier** (,bændə'lɪə) *n.* a shoulder belt with small pockets for cartridges.

band saw *n.* a power-operated saw consisting of an endless toothed metal band running over two wheels.

bandsman ('bændzmən) *n., pl.* **-men.** a player in a musical band.

bandstand ('bænd,stænd) *n.* a roofed outdoor platform for a band.

bandwagon ('bænd,wægən) *n.* **climb** *or* **jump on the bandwagon.** to join a party or movement that seems assured of success.

bandy ('bændɪ) *adj.* **-dier, -diest. 1.** Also: **bandy-legged.** having legs curved outwards at the knees. **2.** (of legs) curved thus. ~*vb.* **-dying, -died. 3.** to exchange (words) in a heated manner. **4.** (foll. by *about*) to circulate (a name, rumour, etc.).

bane (beɪn) *n.* **1.** a person or thing that causes misery or distress: *the bane of my life.* **2.** a fatal poison: *ratsbane.* —**'baneful** *adj.*

bang (bæŋ) *n.* **1.** a short loud explosive noise, as of the report of a gun. **2.** a hard blow or loud knock. **3.** *Taboo slang.* an act of sexual intercourse. **4. with a bang.** successfully: *the party went with a bang.* ~*vb.* **5.** to hit or knock, esp. with a loud noise. **6.** to close (a door) noisily; slam. **7.** to make or cause to make a loud noise, as of an explosion. **8.** *Taboo slang.* to have sexual intercourse (with). ~*adv.* **9.** with a sudden impact: *the car drove bang into a lamppost.* **10.** precisely: *bang in the middle.*

banger ('bæŋə) *n. Brit.* **1.** *Slang.* a sausage. **2.** *Informal.* an old decrepit car. **3.** a firework that explodes loudly.

bangle ('bæŋg'l) *n.* a bracelet worn round the arm or sometimes round the ankle.

banian ('bænjən) *n.* same as **banyan.**

banish ('bænɪʃ) *vb.* **1.** to send (someone) into exile. **2.** to drive away: *to banish gloom.* —**'banishment** *n.*

banisters *or* **bannisters** ('bænɪstəz) *pl. n.* the railing and supporting balusters on a staircase.

banjo ('bændʒəʊ) *n., pl.* **-jos** *or* **-joes.** a stringed musical instrument with a long neck and a circular drumlike body. —**'banjoist** *n.*

bank¹ (bæŋk) *n.* **1.** an institution offering services, such as the safekeeping of money and lending of money at interest. **2.** the building used by such an institution. **3.** the funds held by a banker or dealer in some gambling games. **4.** any supply, store, or reserve: *a data bank.* ~*vb.* **5.** to deposit (cash or cheques) in a bank. **6.** to transact business with a bank. ~See also **bank on.**

bank² (bæŋk) n. **1.** a long raised mass, esp. of earth; ridge. **2.** a slope, as of a hill. **3.** the sloping side and ground on either side of a river. ~vb. **4.** to form into a bank or mound. **5.** to cover (a fire) with ashes and fuel so that it will burn slowly. **6.** to cause (an aircraft) or (of an aircraft) to tip to one side in turning.

bank³ (bæŋk) n. **1.** an arrangement of similar objects in a row or in tiers. ~vb. **2.** to arrange in a bank.

bank account n. an account created by the deposit of money at a bank by a customer.

bank or **banker's card** n. same as **cheque card.**

banker¹ (ˈbæŋkə) n. **1.** a person who owns or manages a bank. **2.** the keeper of the bank in various gambling games.

banker² (ˈbæŋkə) n. Austral. & N.Z. informal. a stream almost overflowing its banks: the creek was running a banker.

banker's order n. same as **standing order** (sense 1).

bank holiday n. (in Britain) a public holiday when banks are closed by law.

banking (ˈbæŋkɪŋ) n. the business engaged in by a bank.

banknote (ˈbæŋkˌnəʊt) n. a promissory note issued by a central bank, serving as money.

bank on vb. to rely on.

bankrupt (ˈbæŋkrʌpt, -rəpt) n. **1.** a person, declared by a court to be unable to pay his debts, whose property is sold and the proceeds distributed among his creditors. **2.** a person whose resources in a certain field are exhausted: a spiritual bankrupt. ~adj. **3.** declared insolvent. **4.** financially ruined. **5.** depleted in resources: spiritually bankrupt. ~vb. **6.** to make bankrupt. —ˈbankruptcy n.

banner (ˈbænə) n. **1.** a long strip of material displaying a slogan, advertisement, etc. **2.** a placard carried in a demonstration. **3.** Also called: **banner headline.** a large headline in a newspaper extending across the page.

bannock (ˈbænək) n. a round flat cake made from oatmeal or barley.

banns (bænz) pl. n. the public declaration of an intended marriage.

banquet (ˈbæŋkwɪt) n. **1.** an elaborate formal dinner often followed by speeches. ~vb. **-queting, -queted. 2.** to hold or take part in a banquet.

banshee (ˈbænʃiː, bænˈʃiː) n. (in Irish folklore) a female spirit whose wailing warns of impending death.

bantam (ˈbæntəm) n. **1.** a small breed of domestic fowl. **2.** a small but aggressive person.

bantamweight (ˈbæntəmˌweɪt) n. **1.** a professional boxer weighing up to 118 pounds or an amateur weighing up to 54 kg. **2.** an amateur wrestler weighing usually up to 57 kg.

banter (ˈbæntə) vb. **1.** to tease jokingly. ~n. **2.** teasing or joking conversation.

Bantu (ˈbɑːntuː) n. **1.** a group of languages of Africa. **2.** (pl. **-tu** or **-tus**) Offensive. a Black speaker of a Bantu language. ~adj. **3.** of the Bantu languages or the peoples who speak them.

Bantustan (ˈbɑːntʊˌstɑːn) n. Offensive. an area reserved for occupation by a Black African people.

banyan or **banian** (ˈbænjən) n. an Indian tree whose branches grow down into the soil forming additional trunks.

baobab (ˈbeɪəʊˌbæb) n. an African tree that has a very thick trunk, angular branches, and a gourdlike fruit.

bap (bæp) n. Brit. a large soft bread roll.

baptism (ˈbæpˌtɪzəm) n. a Christian religious rite in which a person is immersed in or sprinkled with water as a sign of being cleansed from sin and accepted as a member of the Church. —**bapˈtismal** adj.

baptism of fire n. **1.** a soldier's first experience of battle. **2.** any initiating ordeal.

Baptist (ˈbæptɪst) n. **1.** a member of a Protestant denomination that believes in the necessity of baptism by immersion. **2. the Baptist.** John the Baptist.

baptize or **-ise** (bæpˈtaɪz) vb. **1.** Christianity. to immerse (a person) in water or sprinkle water on (a person) as part of the rite of baptism. **2.** to give a name to; christen.

bar¹ (bɑː) n. **1.** a rigid usually straight length of metal, wood, etc., used as a barrier or structural part. **2.** a solid usually rectangular block of any material: a bar of soap. **3.** anything that obstructs or prevents. **4.** a counter or room where alcoholic drinks are served. **5.** a narrow band or stripe, as of colour or light. **6.** a heating element in an electric fire. **7.** See **Bar. 8.** the place in a court of law where the accused stands during trial. **9.** Music. a group of beats that is repeated with a consistent rhythm throughout a piece of music. **10.** Football, etc. same as **crossbar. 11.** Heraldry. a narrow horizontal line across a shield. **12. behind bars.** in prison. ~vb. **barring, barred. 13.** to secure with a bar: to bar the door. **14.** to obstruct: the fallen tree barred the road. **15.** to exclude: to bar a person from membership. **16.** to mark with a bar or bars. ~prep. **17.** except for.

bar² (bɑː) n. a cgs unit of pressure equal to 10^6 dynes per square centimetre.

Bar (bɑː) n. **1. the.** barristers collectively. **2. be called to the Bar.** Brit. to become a barrister.

barathea (ˌbærəˈθɪə) n. a fabric made of silk and wool.

barb (bɑːb) n. 1. a point facing in the opposite direction to the main point of a fish-hook, harpoon, etc. 2. a cutting remark. 3. a beardlike growth, hair, or projection. ~vb. 4. to provide with a barb or barbs. —**barbed** adj.

barbarian (bɑːˈbɛərɪən) n. 1. a member of a primitive or uncivilized people. 2. a coarse or vicious person. ~adj. 3. uncivilized. 4. uncultured or brutal.

barbaric (bɑːˈbærɪk) adj. 1. of barbarians. 2. primitive; unrestrained. 3. brutal.

barbarism (ˈbɑːbəˌrɪzəm) n. 1. a brutal, coarse, or ignorant act. 2. the condition of being backward, coarse, or ignorant. 3. a substandard word or expression.

barbarity (bɑːˈbærɪtɪ) n., pl. **-ties.** 1. the state of being barbaric or barbarous. 2. a vicious act.

barbarous (ˈbɑːbərəs) adj. 1. uncivilized. 2. brutal or cruel. 3. lacking refinement.

barbecue (ˈbɑːbɪˌkjuː) n. 1. a grill on which meat, fish, etc., is cooked over hot charcoal, usually out of doors. 2. the food so cooked. 3. a party or picnic at which barbecued food is served. ~vb. **-cuing,** **-cued.** 4. to cook (meat, fish, etc.) on a grill, usually over charcoal.

barbed wire n. strong wire with sharply pointed barbs at close intervals.

barbel (ˈbɑːbʔl) n. 1. a long thin growth that hangs from the jaws of certain fishes, such as the carp. 2. a freshwater fish with such a growth.

barbell (ˈbɑːˌbɛl) n. a metal rod to which heavy discs are attached at each end for weightlifting.

barber (ˈbɑːbə) n. a person whose business is cutting men's hair and shaving beards.

barberry (ˈbɑːbərɪ) n., pl. **-ries.** a shrub with orange or red berries.

barbershop (ˈbɑːbəˌʃɒp) n. (modifier) denoting a type of close four-part harmony for male voices: a barbershop quartet.

barber's pole n. a barber's sign consisting of a pole painted with red-and-white spiral stripes.

barbican (ˈbɑːbɪkən) n. a walled defence to protect a gate or drawbridge of a fortification.

barbiturate (bɑːˈbɪtjʊrɪt, -ˌreɪt) n. a derivative of barbituric acid used in medicine as a sedative or hypnotic.

barbituric acid (ˌbɑːbɪˈtjʊərɪk) n. a crystalline solid used in the preparation of barbiturate drugs.

barcarole or **barcarolle** (ˈbɑːkəˌrəʊl) n. 1. a Venetian boat song. 2. an instrumental composition resembling this.

bar code n. an arrangement of numbers and parallel lines on a package, which can be electronically scanned at a checkout to give the price of the goods.

bard (bɑːd) n. 1. **a.** (formerly) an ancient Celtic poet. **b.** a poet who wins a verse competition at a Welsh eisteddfod. 2. Archaic or literary. any poet.

bare (bɛə) adj. 1. unclothed: used esp. of a part of the body. 2. without the natural, conventional, or usual covering. 3. lacking appropriate furnishings, etc. 4. simple: the bare facts. 5. just sufficient: the bare minimum. ~vb. 6. to uncover. —**bareness** n.

bareback (ˈbɛəˌbæk) adj., adv. (of horseriding) without a saddle.

barefaced (ˈbɛəˌfeɪst) adj. obvious or shameless: a barefaced lie.

barefoot (ˈbɛəˌfʊt) or **barefooted** adj., adv. with the feet uncovered.

bareheaded (ˌbɛəˈhɛdɪd) adj., adv. with the head uncovered.

barely (ˈbɛəlɪ) adv. 1. only just: barely enough. 2. scantily: barely furnished. Usage. see hardly.

bargain (ˈbɑːgɪn) n. 1. an agreement establishing what each party will give, receive, or perform in a transaction. 2. something acquired or received in such an agreement. 3. something bought or offered at a low price. 4. **into the bargain.** in excess; besides. ~vb. 5. to negotiate the terms of an agreement or transaction.

bargain for vb. to expect; anticipate.

bargain on vb. to rely or depend on.

barge (bɑːdʒ) n. 1. a flat-bottomed boat, used for transporting freight, esp. on canals. 2. a boat, often decorated, used in pageants, etc. ~vb. Informal. 3. (foll. by into) to bump into. 4. to push (someone or one's way) violently. 5. (foll. by into or in) to interrupt rudely: to barge into a conversation.

bargee (bɑːˈdʒiː) n. a person in charge of a barge.

bargepole (ˈbɑːdʒˌpəʊl) n. 1. a long pole used to propel a barge. 2. **not touch with a bargepole.** Informal. to refuse to have anything to do with.

bar graph n. a graph consisting of vertical or horizontal bars whose lengths are proportional to amounts or quantities.

baritone (ˈbærɪˌtəʊn) n. 1. the second lowest adult male voice. 2. a singer with such a voice.

barium (ˈbɛərɪəm) n. a soft silvery-white metallic chemical element. Symbol: Ba

barium meal n. a preparation of barium sulphate, which is opaque to x-rays, used in x-ray examination of the alimentary canal.

bark[1] (bɑːk) n. 1. the loud harsh cry of a dog or certain other animals. 2. a similar sound, such as one made by a person or gun. ~vb. 3. (of a dog or other animal) to make its typical cry. 4. to shout in an angry tone: he barked an order. 5. **bark up the wrong**

tree. *Informal.* to misdirect one's attention or efforts.

bark[2] (bɑːk) *n.* **1.** a protective layer of dead corklike cells on the outside of the stems of woody plants. ~*vb.* **2.** to scrape or rub off skin, as in an injury. **3.** to remove the bark from (a tree).

barker ('bɑːkə) *n.* a person at a fairground who loudly addresses passers-by to attract customers.

barley ('bɑːlɪ) *n.* **1.** a tall grasslike plant with dense bristly flower spikes, widely cultivated for grain and forage. **2.** the grain of this grass used in making beer and whisky and for soups.

barleycorn ('bɑːlɪˌkɔːn) *n.* a grain of barley, or barley itself.

barley sugar *n.* a brittle clear amber-coloured sweet.

barley water *n.* a drink made from an infusion of barley.

barm (bɑːm) *n.* the yeasty froth on fermenting malt liquors.

barmaid ('bɑːˌmeɪd) *n.* a woman who serves in a pub.

barman ('bɑːmən) *n., pl.* **-men.** a man who serves in a pub.

bar mitzvah (bɑː 'mɪtsvə) *Judaism.* ~*adj.* **1.** (of a Jewish boy) having assumed full religious obligations, being at least thirteen years old. ~*n.* **2.** the occasion or celebration of this.

barmy ('bɑːmɪ) *adj.* **-mier, -miest.** *Slang.* insane.

barn (bɑːn) *n.* a large farm outbuilding, chiefly for storing grain, but also for livestock.

barnacle ('bɑːnək²l) *n.* **1.** a marine shellfish that lives attached to rocks, ship bottoms, etc. **2.** a person or thing that is difficult to get rid of. —**barnacled** *adj.*

barnacle goose *n.* a goose with a black-and-white head and body.

barn dance *n.* **1.** *Brit.* a progressive round country dance. **2.** *U.S. & Canad.* a party with square-dancing.

barney ('bɑːnɪ) *n. Informal.* a noisy fight or argument.

barn owl *n.* an owl with a pale brown-and-white plumage and a heart-shaped face.

barnstorm ('bɑːnˌstɔːm) *vb.* **1.** to tour rural districts putting on shows. **2.** *Chiefly U.S. & Canad.* to tour rural districts making speeches in a political campaign. —'**barn-ˌstorming** *n., adj.*

barnyard ('bɑːnˌjɑːd) *n.* a yard adjoining a barn.

barograph ('bærəˌgrɑːf) *n. Meteorol.* a barometer that automatically keeps a record of changes in atmospheric pressure.

barometer (bə'rɒmɪtə) *n.* an instrument for measuring atmospheric pressure, used to determine altitude or weather changes. —**barometric** (ˌbærə'mɛtrɪk) *adj.*

baron ('bærən) *n.* **1.** a member of the lowest rank of nobility in the British Isles. **2.** a powerful businessman or financier: *a press baron.* —**baronial** (bə'rəʊnɪəl) *adj.*

baroness ('bærənɪs) *n.* **1.** the wife or widow of a baron. **2.** a woman holding the rank of baron.

baronet ('bærənɪt, -ˌnɛt) *n.* a commoner who holds the lowest hereditary British title. —'**baronetcy** *n.*

baron of beef *n.* a cut of beef consisting of a double sirloin joined at the backbone.

barony ('bærənɪ) *n., pl.* **-nies.** the domain or rank of a baron.

baroque (bə'rɒk, bə'rəʊk) *n.* **1.** a highly ornamented European style of architecture and art from the late 16th to the early 18th century. **2.** a highly ornamented 17th-century style of music. ~*adj.* **3.** denoting, in, or relating to the baroque.

baroscope ('bærəˌskəʊp) *n.* any instrument for measuring atmospheric pressure.

barouche (bə'ruːʃ) *n.* a four-wheeled horse-drawn carriage with a retractable hood over the rear half.

barque (bɑːk) *n.* **1.** a sailing ship, esp. with three masts. **2.** *Poetic.* any boat.

barrack[1] ('bærək) *vb.* to house (soldiers) in barracks.

barrack[2] ('bærək) *vb. Informal.* to criticize loudly or shout against (a team or speaker); jeer.

barracks ('bærəks) *pl. n. (sometimes functioning as sing.)* **1.** a building or group of buildings used to accommodate military personnel. **2.** a large and bleak building.

barracuda (ˌbærə'kjuːdə) *n., pl.* **-da** *or* **-das.** a predatory marine mostly tropical fish, which attacks man.

barrage ('bærɑːʒ) *n.* **1.** *Mil.* the firing of artillery continuously over an area. **2.** a continuous delivery of something, as questions. **3.** a construction across a watercourse.

barrage balloon *n.* a tethered balloon with cables or net suspended from it, used to deter low-flying air attack.

barratry ('bærətrɪ) *n.* a fraudulent act by the master or crew of a ship that causes loss to the owner.

barre (bɑː) *n.* a rail at hip height used for ballet practice.

barrel ('bærəl) *n.* **1.** a cylindrical container usually bulging outwards in the middle and held together by metal hoops. **2.** a unit of capacity of varying amount in different industries. **3.** the tube through which the projectile of a firearm is discharged. **4.** **over a barrel.** *Informal.* powerless. ~*vb.* **-relling, -relled** *or U.S.* **-reling, -reled.** **5.** to put into a barrel or barrels.

barrel organ *n.* an instrument consisting

of a cylinder turned by a handle and having pins on it that interrupt the air flow to certain pipes or pluck strings, thereby playing tunes.

barren ('bærən) adj. 1. incapable of producing offspring; sterile. 2. unable to support the growth of crops, fruit, etc.: barren land. 3. dull. 4. unprofitable: a barren period. —'barrenness n.

barricade (ˌbærɪ'keɪd, 'bærɪˌkeɪd) n. 1. a barrier, esp. one erected hastily for defence. ~vb. 2. to erect a barricade across (an entrance).

barrier ('bærɪə) n. 1. anything that blocks a way or makes a separation, such as a gate. 2. anything that prevents progress. 3. anything that separates or hinders union: a language barrier.

barrier cream n. a cream used to protect the skin, esp. of the hands.

barrier reef n. a long narrow coral reef near the shore, separated from it by deep water.

barring ('bɑːrɪŋ) prep. unless (something) occurs; except for.

barrister ('bærɪstə) n. a lawyer who is qualified to plead in the higher courts.

barrow[1] ('bærəʊ) n. 1. same as **wheelbarrow**. 2. a handcart, used esp. by street vendors.

barrow[2] ('bærəʊ) n. a heap of earth placed over a prehistoric tomb.

barrow boy n. Brit. a man who sells his wares from a barrow.

bar sinister n. same as **bend sinister**.

Bart. Baronet.

barter ('bɑːtə) vb. 1. to trade (goods or services) in exchange for other goods or services, rather than for money. ~n. 2. trade by the exchange of goods.

baryon ('bærɪˌɒn) n. an elementary particle that has a mass greater than or equal to that of the proton.

baryta (bə'raɪtə) n. a compound of barium, such as barium oxide.

barytes (bə'raɪtiːz) n. a colourless or white mineral: a source of barium.

basal ('beɪs°l) adj. 1. at, of, or constituting a base. 2. basic; fundamental.

basalt ('bæsɔːlt) n. a dark volcanic rock. —ba'saltic adj.

bascule ('bæskjuːl) n. a drawbridge that operates by a counterbalanced weight.

base[1] (beɪs) n. 1. the bottom or supporting part of anything. 2. the fundamental principle or part. 3. a centre of operations, organization, or supply. 4. a starting point: the new discovery became the base for further research. 5. the main ingredient of a mixture: to use rice as a base in cookery. 6. a chemical compound that combines with an acid to form a salt. 7. the lower side or face of a geometric construction. 8. Maths. the number of units in a counting system that is

equivalent to one in the next higher counting place: 10 is the base of the decimal system. 9. a starting or finishing point in any of various games. ~vb. 10. (foll. by on or upon) to use as a basis for; found on.

base[2] (beɪs) adj. 1. dishonourable or immoral: base motives. 2. of inferior quality or value: base metal. 3. debased; counterfeit: base currency.

baseball ('beɪsˌbɔːl) n. a team game in which the object is to score runs by batting the ball and running round all four bases.

baseless ('beɪslɪs) adj. not based on fact; unfounded.

baseline ('beɪsˌlaɪn) n. 1. a value or starting point on an imaginary scale with which other things are compared. 2. a line at each end of a tennis court that marks the limit of play.

basement ('beɪsmənt) n. a partly or wholly underground storey of a building.

base metal n. a common metal such as copper or lead, as distinct from a precious metal.

bases[1] ('beɪsiːz) n. the plural of **basis**.

bases[2] ('beɪsɪz) n. the plural of **base**.

bash (bæʃ) Informal. ~vb. 1. to strike violently or crushingly. 2. (foll. by into) to crash into. ~n. 3. a heavy blow. 4. **have a bash**. Informal. to make an attempt.

bashful ('bæʃful) adj. shy or modest. —'bashfully adv.

-bashing n. and adj. combining form. Informal or slang. a. indicating a malicious attack on members of a group: unionbashing. b. indicating various other activities: Bible-bashing. —**basher** n. combining form.

basic ('beɪsɪk) adj. 1. of or forming a base or basis; fundamental. 2. elementary or simple. 3. excluding additions or extras: basic pay. 4. Chem. of or containing a base. ~n. 5. (pl.) fundamental principles, facts, etc. —'basically adv.

BASIC ('beɪsɪk) n. a computer programming language that uses common English terms.

basic slag n. a slag produced in steelmaking, containing calcium phosphate.

basil ('bæz°l) n. an aromatic herb used for seasoning food.

basilica (bə'zɪlɪkə) n. 1. a Roman building, used for public administration, which has a rectangular nave with an aisle on each side and a rounded end. 2. a Christian church of similar design.

basilisk ('bæzɪˌlɪsk) n. 1. (in classical legend) a serpent that could kill by its breath or glance. 2. a lizard of tropical America with an inflatable head crest.

basin ('beɪs°n) n. 1. a round container open and wide at the top. 2. the amount a basin will hold. 3. a washbasin or sink. 4. any partially enclosed area of water where ships or boats may be moored. 5. the catchment area of a particular river. **6.** a depression in the earth's surface.

basis ('beɪsɪs) *n., pl.* **-ses** (-siːz). **1.** something that underlies, supports, or is essential to something else, esp. an idea. **2.** a principle on which something depends.

bask (bɑːsk) *vb.* (foll. by *in*) **1.** to lie in or be exposed to (pleasant warmth, esp. that of the sun). **2.** to feel secure under (some kindly influence or favourable conditions).

basket ('bɑːskɪt) *n.* **1.** a container made of interwoven strips of wood or cane. **2.** the amount a basket will hold. **3.** *Basketball.* **a.** the high fixed hoop through which a player must throw the ball to score points. **b.** a point scored in this way. —'**basketry** *n.*

basketball ('bɑːskɪt,bɔːl) *n.* a team game in which points are scored by throwing the ball through a high horizontal hoop.

basket weave *n.* a weave of yarns, resembling that of a basket.

basketwork ('bɑːskɪt,wɜːk) *n.* same as **wickerwork**.

basking shark *n.* a very large plankton-eating shark, often floating at the sea surface.

basque (bæsk) *n.* a type of tight-fitting bodice for women.

Basque (bæsk, bɑːsk) *n.* **1.** a member of a people living in the W Pyrenees in France and Spain. **2.** the unique language of this people. ~*adj.* **3.** of this people or their language.

bas-relief (,bɑːrɪ'liːf, 'bæsrɪ,liːf) *n.* sculpture in which the forms project slightly from the background.

bass[1] (beɪs) *n.* **1.** the lowest adult male voice. **2.** a singer with such a voice. **3.** *Informal.* same as **bass guitar, double bass.** ~*adj.* **4.** relating to or denoting the lowest range of musical notes.

bass[2] (bæs) *n.* **1.** any of various sea perches. **2.** a European spiny-finned freshwater fish.

bass clef (beɪs) *n.* the clef that establishes F a fifth below middle C on the fourth line of the staff.

bass drum (beɪs) *n.* a large drum of low pitch.

basset hound ('bæsɪt) *n.* a smooth-haired hound with short legs and long ears.

bass guitar (beɪs) *n.* an electrically amplified guitar with the same pitch and tuning as a double bass.

bassinet (,bæsɪ'nɛt) *n.* a wickerwork or wooden cradle or pram, usually hooded.

basso ('bæsəʊ) *n., pl.* **-sos** *or* **-si** (-sɪ). a singer with a bass voice.

bassoon (bə'suːn) *n.* a woodwind instrument, the tenor of the oboe family. —**bas'soonist** *n.*

bast (bæst) *n.* fibrous material obtained from the inner tissue of jute and flax, used for making rope, matting, etc.

bastard ('bɑːstəd, 'bæs-) *n.* **1.** a person born of parents not married to each other. **2.** *Informal, offensive.* an obnoxious or despicable person. **3.** *Informal.* something extremely difficult or unpleasant. ~*adj.* **4.** illegitimate by birth. **5.** counterfeit; spurious. —'**bastardy** *n.*

bastardize *or* **-ise** ('bɑːstə,daɪz, 'bæs-) *vb.* **1.** to debase. **2.** to declare illegitimate.

baste[1] (beɪst) *vb.* to sew with loose temporary stitches.

baste[2] (beɪst) *vb.* to moisten (meat) during cooking with hot fat.

baste[3] (beɪst) *vb.* to beat; thrash.

bastinado (,bæstɪ'neɪdəʊ) *n., pl.* **-does. 1.** a beating on the soles of the feet with a stick. ~*vb.* **-doing, -doed. 2.** to beat (a person) thus.

bastion ('bæstɪən) *n.* **1.** a projecting part of a fortification. **2.** a thing or person regarded as defending a principle, etc.: *the last bastion of opposition.*

bat[1] (bæt) *n.* **1.** any of various types of club used to hit the ball in certain sports, such as cricket. **2.** *Cricket.* a batsman. **3.** **off one's own bat. a.** of one's own accord. **b.** by one's own unaided efforts. ~*vb.* **batting, batted. 4.** to strike with or as if with a bat. **5.** *Cricket, etc.* to take a turn at batting.

bat[2] (bæt) *n.* **1.** a nocturnal mouselike animal flying with a pair of leathery wings. **2.** **blind as a bat.** having extremely poor eyesight.

bat[3] (bæt) *vb.* **batting, batted. 1.** to wink or flutter (one's eyelids). **2. not bat an eyelid.** *Informal.* to show no surprise.

batch (bætʃ) *n.* **1.** a group of similar objects or people, esp. if sent off, handled, or arriving at the same time. **2.** the bread, cakes, etc., produced at one baking. ~*vb.* **3.** to group (items) for efficient processing.

batch processing *n.* a system by which the computer programs of a number of users are submitted as a single batch.

bated ('beɪtɪd) *adj.* **with bated breath.** in suspense or fear.

bath (bɑːθ) *n., pl.* **baths** (bɑːðz). **1.** a large container in which to wash the body. **2.** the act of washing in such a container. **3.** the amount of liquid in a bath. **4.** (*pl.*) a public swimming pool. **5. a.** a liquid solution for maintaining a constant temperature, developing photographs, etc. **b.** the vessel containing such a solution. ~*vb.* **6.** *Brit.* to wash in a bath.

Bath chair *n.* a wheelchair for invalids.

bath cube *n.* a cube of soluble scented material for use in a bath.

bathe (beɪð) *vb.* **1.** to swim in open water, esp. for pleasure. **2.** to apply liquid to (the skin or a wound) in order to cleanse or soothe. **3.** to immerse or be immersed in a liquid. **4.** *Chiefly U.S. & Canad.* to wash in a bath. **5.** to suffuse: *bathed in sunlight.*

~*n.* **6.** *Brit.* a swim in open water. —**'bather** *n.*

bathos ('beɪθɒs) *n.* a sudden ludicrous descent from exalted to ordinary matters or style in speech or writing. —**bathetic** (bə'θetɪk) *adj.*

bathrobe ('bɑːθ,rəʊb) *n.* **1.** a loose-fitting garment for wear before or after a bath or swimming. **2.** *U.S. & Canad.* a dressing gown.

bathroom ('bɑːθ,ruːm, -,rʊm) *n.* **1.** a room with a bath or shower, washbasin, and toilet. **2.** *U.S. & Canad.* a toilet.

bathyscaph ('bæθɪ,skæf) *or* **bathyscaphe** ('bæθɪ,skeɪf, -,skæf) *n.* a deep-sea diving vessel for observation.

bathysphere ('bæθɪ,sfɪə) *n.* a strong steel deep-sea diving sphere, lowered by cable.

batik ('bætɪk) *n.* **a.** a process of printing fabric in which parts not to be dyed are covered by wax. **b.** fabric printed in this way.

batiste (bæ'tiːst) *n.* a fine plain-weave cotton.

batman ('bætmən) *n., pl.* **-men.** an officer's servant in the armed forces.

baton ('bætən) *n.* **1.** a thin stick used by the conductor of an orchestra or choir. **2.** *Athletics.* a short bar transferred from one runner to another in a relay race. **3.** a police truncheon.

baton round *n.* same as **plastic bullet.**

batrachian (bə'treɪkɪən) *n.* **1.** any amphibian, esp. a frog or toad. ~*adj.* **2.** of or relating to frogs and toads.

bats (bæts) *adj. Informal.* mad or eccentric.

batsman ('bætsmən) *n., pl.* **-men.** *Cricket, etc.* a person who bats or specializes in batting.

battalion (bə'tæljən) *n.* a military unit comprised of three or more companies.

batten[1] ('bæt²n) *n.* **1.** a sawn strip of wood used to cover joints, support lathing, etc. **2.** a lath used for holding a tarpaulin along the side of a hatch on a ship. ~*vb.* **3.** to strengthen or fasten with battens.

batten[2] ('bæt²n) *vb.* (foll. by *on*) to thrive, esp. at the expense of (someone else).

batter[1] ('bætə) *vb.* **1.** to hit (someone or something) repeatedly. **2.** to damage or injure, as by blows, heavy wear, etc. **3.** to subject (a person, esp. a close relative) to repeated physical violence. —**'batterer** *n.* —**'battering** *n.*

batter[2] ('bætə) *n.* a mixture of flour, eggs, and milk, used in cooking.

batter[3] ('bætə) *n. Baseball, etc.* a player who bats.

battering ram *n.* (esp. formerly) a large beam used to break down fortifications.

battery ('bætərɪ) *n., pl.* **-teries. 1.** two or more primary cells connected, usually in series, to provide a source of electric current. **2.** a number of similar things occurring together: *a battery of questions.* **3.** *Criminal law.* unlawful beating or wounding of a person. **4.** a fortified structure on which artillery is mounted. **5.** *Chiefly Brit.* **a.** a series of cages for intensive rearing of poultry and other farm animals. **b.** (*as modifier*): *battery hens.*

battle ('bæt²l) *n.* **1.** a fight between large armed forces. **2.** conflict; struggle. ~*vb.* **3.** to fight in or as if in military combat. **4.** to struggle: *he battled through the crowd.*

battle-axe *n.* **1.** *Informal.* a domineering woman. **2.** (formerly) a large broad-headed axe.

battle cruiser *n.* a high-speed warship of battleship size but with lighter armour.

battle cry *n.* **1.** a slogan used to rally the supporters of a campaign, movement, etc. **2.** a shout uttered by soldiers going into battle.

battledore ('bæt²l,dɔː) *n.* **1.** Also called: **battledore and shuttlecock.** an ancient racket game. **2.** a light racket used in this game.

battledress ('bæt²l,drɛs) *n.* the ordinary uniform of a soldier.

battlefield ('bæt²l,fiːld) *or* **battleground** *n.* the place where a battle is fought.

battlement ('bæt²lmənt) *n.* a wall with indentations, originally for shooting through.

battle royal *n.* **1.** a fight involving many combatants. **2.** a long violent argument.

battleship ('bæt²l,ʃɪp) *n.* a heavily armoured warship of the largest type.

batty ('bætɪ) *adj.* **-tier, -tiest.** *Slang.* **1.** insane; crazy. **2.** odd; eccentric.

bauble ('bɔːb²l) *n.* a trinket of little value.

baulk (bɔːk, bɔːlk) *vb., n.* same as **balk.**

bauxite ('bɔːksaɪt) *n.* a claylike substance that is the chief source of aluminium.

bawdy ('bɔːdɪ) *adj.* **bawdier, bawdiest.** (of language, writing, etc.) containing humorous references to sex. —**'bawdily** *adv.* —**'bawdiness** *n.*

bawdyhouse ('bɔːdɪ,haʊs) *n. Archaic.* a brothel.

bawl (bɔːl) *vb.* **1.** to utter long loud cries, as from pain. **2.** to shout loudly, as in anger. ~*n.* **3.** a loud shout or cry. —**'bawling** *n.*

bay[1] (beɪ) *n.* a wide semicircular indentation of a shoreline.

bay[2] (beɪ) *n.* **1.** a recess in a wall. **2.** any partly enclosed compartment. **3.** same as **bay window. 4.** an area off a road in which vehicles may park or unload. **5.** a compartment in an aircraft: *the bomb bay.*

bay[3] (beɪ) *n.* **1.** a deep howl, esp. of a hound on the scent. **2. at bay. a.** forced to turn and face attackers: *the dogs held the deer at bay.* **b.** at a distance: *keeping poverty at bay.* **3. bring to bay.** to force into a position from which retreat is impossible. ~*vb.* **4.** to howl in deep prolonged tones.

bay[4] (beı) *n.* **1.** a Mediterranean laurel tree with glossy aromatic leaves. **2.** (*pl.*) a wreath of bay leaves.

bay[5] (beı) *adj.* **1.** reddish-brown. ~*n.* **2.** a reddish-brown horse.

bayberry ('beıbərı) *or* **bay** *n., pl.* **-ries.** a tropical American tree that yields an oil used in making bay rum.

bay leaf *n.* the dried leaf of a laurel, used in cooking to flavour soups and stews.

bayonet ('beıənıt) *n.* **1.** a blade that can be attached to the muzzle of a firearm and used as a weapon. ~*vb.* **-neting, -neted** *or* **-netting, -netted.** **2.** to stab or kill with a bayonet.

bay rum *n.* an aromatic liquid, used in medicines, etc., and originally obtained by distilling bayberry leaves with rum.

bay window *n.* a window projecting from a wall and forming an alcove of a room.

bazaar (bə'zɑ:) *n.* **1.** (esp. in the Orient) a market area, esp. a street of small stalls. **2.** a sale in aid of charity.

bazooka (bə'zu:kə) *n.* an antitank rocket launcher.

BB Boys' Brigade.

BBC British Broadcasting Corporation.

BC **1.** (indicating years numbered back from the supposed year of the birth of Christ) before Christ. **2.** British Columbia. **Usage.** see **A.D.**

BCG Bacillus Calmette-Guérin (antituberculosis vaccine).

BCNZ Broadcasting Corporation of New Zealand.

B complex *n.* short for **vitamin B complex.**

BD Bachelor of Divinity.

bdellium ('dɛlıəm) *n.* an aromatic gum resin produced by an African or W Asian tree.

BDS Bachelor of Dental Surgery.

be (bi:; *unstressed* bı) *vb. present sing. 1st person* **am;** *2nd person* **are;** *3rd person* **is.** *present pl.* **are.** *past sing. 1st person* **was;** *2nd person* **were;** *3rd person* **was.** *past pl.* **were.** *present participle* **being.** *past participle* **been.** **1.** to have presence in perceived reality; exist; live: *I think, therefore I am.* **2.** to pay a visit; go: *have you been to Spain?* **3.** to take place: *my birthday was last Thursday.* **4.** used as a linking verb between the subject of a sentence and its complement: *John is a musician; honey is sweet; the dance is on Saturday.* **5.** forms the progressive present tense: *the man is running.* **6.** forms the passive voice of all transitive verbs: *a good film is being shown on television tonight.* **7.** expresses intention, expectation, or obligation: *the president is to arrive at 9.30.*

Be *Chem.* beryllium.

BE Bachelor of Engineering.

be- *prefix forming verbs mainly from*

nouns. **1.** to surround or cover: *befog.* **2.** to affect completely: *bedazzle.* **3.** to consider as or cause to be: *befriend.* **4.** to provide or cover with: *bejewel.* **5.** (*from verbs*) at, for, against, on, or over: *bewail.*

beach (bi:tʃ) *n.* **1.** an area of sand or pebbles, esp. between the high- and low-water marks on a seashore. ~*vb.* **2.** to run or haul (a boat) onto a beach.

beachcomber ('bi:tʃˌkəʊmə) *n.* a person who searches shore debris for anything of worth.

beachhead ('bi:tʃˌhɛd) *n.* *Mil.* a beach captured from the enemy, on which troops and equipment are landed.

beacon ('bi:kən) *n.* **1.** a signal fire or light on a hill or tower, esp. formerly as a warning of invasion. **2.** a lighthouse. **3.** a radio or other signal marking a flight course in air navigation. **4.** same as **Belisha beacon.**

bead (bi:d) *n.* **1.** a small pierced usually spherical piece of glass, wood, plastic, etc., which may be strung with others to form a necklace, rosary, etc. **2.** a small drop of moisture. **3.** a small metallic knob acting as the sight of a firearm. **4. draw a bead on.** to aim a rifle or pistol at. ~*vb.* **5.** to decorate with beads. —**beaded** *adj.*

beading ('bi:dıŋ) *n.* a narrow rounded strip of moulding used for edging or ornamentation on furniture.

beadle ('bi:d²l) *n.* **1.** *Brit.* (formerly) a minor parish official who acted as an usher. **2.** *Scot.* a church official who attends the minister.

beady ('bi:dı) *adj.* **beadier, beadiest.** small, round, and glittering: *beady eyes.*

beagle ('bi:g²l) *n.* a small hound with a smooth coat, short legs, and drooping ears.

beak[1] (bi:k) *n.* **1.** the projecting horny jaws of a bird. **2.** *Slang.* a person's nose. **3.** the pouring lip of a bucket, jug, etc. —**beaky** *adj.*

beak[2] (bi:k) *n. Brit. slang.* a judge, magistrate, or headmaster.

beaker ('bi:kə) *n.* **1.** a tallish drinking cup. **2.** a lipped glass container used in laboratories.

beam (bi:m) *n.* **1.** a long thick piece of wood, metal, etc., used in building. **2.** the breadth of a ship at its widest part. **3.** a ray of light. **4.** a broad smile. **5.** the central shaft of a plough to which all the main parts are attached. **6.** a narrow flow of electromagnetic radiation or particles: *an electron beam.* **7.** the crossbar of a balance. **8. off (the) beam.** *Informal.* mistaken or irrelevant. **9. on the beam.** *Informal.* correct, relevant, or appropriate. ~*vb.* **10.** to send out or radiate. **11.** to divert or aim (a radio signal, light, etc.) in a certain direction: *to beam a programme to Tokyo.* **12.** to smile broadly.

beam-ends *pl. n.* **on one's beam-ends.** out of money.

bean (biːn) *n.* **1.** the edible seed or pod of various leguminous plants. **2.** any of various beanlike seeds, as coffee. **3. full of beans.** *Informal.* full of energy and vitality. **4. not have a bean.** *Slang.* to be without money.

beanbag ('biːn,bæg) *n.* **1.** a small cloth bag filled with dried beans and thrown in games. **2.** a very large cushion filled with polystyrene granules and used as a seat.

beanfeast ('biːn,fiːst) *n. Brit. informal.* **1.** an annual dinner for employees. **2.** any festive or merry occasion.

beano ('biːnəʊ) *n., pl.* **beanos.** *Brit. slang.* a celebration or party.

beanpole ('biːn,pəʊl) *n.* **1.** a tall stick used to support bean plants. **2.** *Slang.* a tall thin person.

bean sprout *n.* the sprout of a bean seed, eaten esp. in Chinese dishes.

bear[1] (bɛə) *vb.* **bearing, bore, borne. 1.** to support or hold up. **2.** to bring: *to bear gifts.* **3.** to accept the responsibility of: *to bear an expense.* **4.** (**born** in passive use except when foll. by *by*) to give birth to. **5.** to produce as by natural growth: *to bear fruit.* **6.** to tolerate or endure. **7.** to stand up to; sustain: *his story does not bear scrutiny.* **8.** to hold in the mind: *to bear a grudge.* **9.** to show or be marked with: *he still bears the scars.* **10.** to have, be, or stand in (relation or comparison): *his account bears no relation to the facts.* **11.** to move in a specified direction: *bear left.* **12. bring to bear.** to bring into effect. ~See also **bear down on, bear on,** etc.

bear[2] (bɛə) *n., pl.* **bears** *or* **bear. 1.** a large heavily-built mammal with a long shaggy coat. **2.** a bearlike animal, such as the koala. **3.** an ill-mannered person. **4.** *Stock Exchange.* a speculator who sells in anticipation of falling prices to make a profit on repurchase. **5. like a bear with a sore head.** *Informal.* bad-tempered; irritable.

bearable ('bɛərəbᵊl) *adj.* endurable; tolerable.

bear-baiting *n. Hist.* an entertainment in which dogs attacked a chained bear.

beard (bɪəd) *n.* **1.** the hair growing on the lower parts of a man's face. **2.** any similar growth in animals. ~*vb.* **3.** to oppose boldly. —'**bearded** *adj.*

bear down on *vb.* **1.** to press down on (something). **2.** to approach (someone) in a determined manner.

bearer ('bɛərə) *n.* **1.** a person or thing that bears, presents, or upholds. **2.** a person who presents a note or bill for payment.

bear garden *n.* a scene of tumult.

bear hug *n.* a rough tight embrace.

bearing ('bɛərɪŋ) *n.* **1.** a part of a machine that supports another part, esp. one that

reduces friction. **2.** (foll. by *on* or *upon*) relevance (to): *it has no bearing on this problem.* **3.** a person's general social conduct. **4.** the act of producing fruit or young. **5.** the angular direction of a point measured from a known position. **6.** the position, as of a ship, fixed with reference to two or more known points. **7.** (*pl.*) a sense of one's relative position: *I lost my bearings in the dark.* **8.** *Heraldry.* a device on a heraldic shield.

bear on *vb.* to be relevant to.

bear out *vb.* to show to be truthful: *the witness will bear me out.*

bearskin ('bɛə,skɪn) *n.* **1.** the pelt of a bear, esp. when used as a rug. **2.** a tall fur helmet worn by certain British Army regiments.

bear up *vb.* to endure cheerfully: *is she bearing up under the strain?*

bear with *vb.* to be patient with.

beast (biːst) *n.* **1.** a large wild animal. **2.** savage nature or characteristics: *the beast in man.* **3.** a brutal or uncivilized person.

beastly ('biːstlɪ) *Informal.* ~*adj.* **-lier, -liest. 1.** unpleasant; disagreeable. ~*adv.* **2.** extremely: *the weather is so beastly hot.*

beat (biːt) *vb.* **beating, beat; beaten** *or* **beat. 1.** to strike with a series of violent blows. **2.** to punish by striking; flog. **3.** to move (wings) up and down. **4.** to throb rhythmically; pulsate. **5.** *Cookery.* to stir or whisk vigorously. **6.** to shape (metal) by repeated blows. **7.** *Music.* to indicate (time) by one's hand or a baton. **8.** to produce (a sound) by striking a drum. **9.** to overcome; defeat. **10.** to form (a path or track) by repeated use. **11.** to arrive, achieve, or finish before (someone or something). **12.** (foll. by *back, down, off,* etc.) to drive, push, or thrust. **13.** to scour (woodlands or undergrowth) so as to rouse game for shooting. **14.** *Slang.* to puzzle or baffle: *it beats me.* ~*n.* **15.** a stroke or blow. **16.** the sound made by a stroke or blow. **17.** a regular throb. **18.** an assigned route, as of a policeman. **19.** the basic rhythmic unit in a piece of music. **20.** pop or rock music characterized by a heavy rhythmic beat. ~*adj.* **21.** *Slang.* totally exhausted. ~See also **beat down, beat up.**

beatbox ('biːt,bɒks) *n.* same as **drum machine.**

beat down *vb.* **1.** *Informal.* to force or persuade (a seller) to accept a lower price. **2.** (of the sun) to shine intensely.

beater ('biːtə) *n.* **1.** a device used for beating: *a carpet beater.* **2.** a person who rouses wild game.

beatific (,biːə'tɪfɪk) *adj.* **1.** displaying great happiness. **2.** conferring a state of celestial happiness.

beatify (bɪ'ætɪ,faɪ) *vb.* **-fying, -fied. 1.** *R.C. Church.* to declare (a deceased person) to be among the blessed in heaven: the first step towards canonization. **2.** to make extremely happy. —**beatification** (bɪˌætɪfɪˈkeɪʃən) n.

beatitude (bɪˈætɪˌtjuːd) n. supreme blessedness or happiness.

Beatitude (bɪˈætɪˌtjuːd) n. *Christianity.* any of the blessings on the poor, meek, etc., in the Sermon on the Mount.

beatnik (ˈbiːtnɪk) n. a type of young person in the late 1950s who rebelled against conventional attitudes, dress, etc.

beat up *Informal.* ~vb. **1.** to strike or kick (someone) repeatedly, so as to inflict severe physical damage. ~adj. **beat-up. 2.** worn-out; dilapidated.

beau (bəʊ) n., pl. **beaus** (bəʊz) or **beaux. 1.** a man who is greatly concerned with his appearance. **2.** *Chiefly U.S.* a boyfriend.

Beaufort scale (ˈbəʊfət) n. *Meteorol.* a scale of wind velocities from 0 (calm) to 12 (hurricane).

Beaujolais (ˈbəʊʒəˌleɪ) n. a red or white wine from southern Burgundy in France.

beauteous (ˈbjuːtɪəs) adj. *Poetic.* beautiful.

beautician (bjuːˈtɪʃən) n. a person who works in a beauty salon.

beautiful (ˈbjuːtɪfʊl) adj. **1.** possessing beauty. **2.** highly enjoyable; very pleasant. —ˈbeautifully adv.

beautify (ˈbjuːtɪˌfaɪ) vb. -fying, -fied. to make or become beautiful. —**beautification** (ˌbjuːtɪfɪˈkeɪʃən) n.

beauty (ˈbjuːtɪ) n., pl. -ties. **1.** the combination of all the qualities of a person or thing that delight the senses and mind. **2.** a very attractive woman. **3.** *Informal.* an outstanding example of its kind. **4.** *Informal.* an advantageous feature: *one beauty of the job is the short hours.*

beauty queen n. a woman who has won a beauty contest.

beauty salon or **parlour** n. an establishment that provides services such as hairdressing, facial treatment, and massage.

beauty spot n. **1.** a place of outstanding beauty. **2.** a small dark-coloured spot formerly worn on a lady's face as an adornment.

beaver[1] (ˈbiːvə) n. **1.** a large amphibious rodent with soft brown fur, a broad flat tail, and webbed hind feet. **2.** its fur. **3.** a tall hat made of this fur. ~vb. **4. beaver away.** to work industriously or steadily.

beaver[2] (ˈbiːvə) n. a movable piece on a medieval helmet used to protect the lower face.

bebop (ˈbiːbɒp) n. same as **bop.**

becalmed (bɪˈkɑːmd) adj. (of a sailing ship) motionless through lack of wind.

became (bɪˈkeɪm) vb. the past tense of **become.**

because (bɪˈkɒz, -ˈkəz) conj. **1.** on account

of the fact that; since: *because it's so cold we'll go home.* **2. because of.** on account of: *I lost my job because of her.*

béchamel sauce (ˌbeɪʃəˈmɛl) n. a thick white sauce flavoured with onion and seasonings.

beck[1] (bɛk) n. **at someone's beck and call.** subject to someone's slightest whim.

beck[2] (bɛk) n. (in N England) a stream.

beckon (ˈbɛkən) vb. **1.** to summon with a gesture. **2.** to lure: *fame beckoned.*

become (bɪˈkʌm) vb. -coming, -came, -come. **1.** to come to be; develop or grow into: *he became a monster.* **2.** (foll. by *of*) to happen to: *what became of him?* **3.** to suit: *that dress becomes you.*

becoming (bɪˈkʌmɪŋ) adj. suitable; appropriate.

becquerel (ˌbɛkəˈrɛl) n. the SI unit of activity of a radioactive source.

bed (bɛd) n. **1.** a piece of furniture on which to sleep. **2.** *Informal.* sexual intercourse. **3.** a plot of ground in which plants are grown. **4.** the bottom of a river, lake, or sea. **5.** any underlying structure or part. **6.** a layer of rock, esp. sedimentary rock. **7. get out of bed on the wrong side.** *Informal.* to begin the day in a bad mood. **8. go to bed with.** to have sexual intercourse with. ~vb. **bedding, bedded. 9.** (foll. by *down*) to go to or put into a place to sleep or rest. **10.** to have sexual intercourse with. **11.** to place firmly into position; embed. **12.** *Geol.* to form or be arranged in a distinct layer. **13.** to plant in a bed of soil.

BEd Bachelor of Education.

bed and breakfast n. *Chiefly Brit.* overnight accommodation and breakfast.

bedaub (bɪˈdɔːb) vb. to smear over with something sticky or dirty.

bedbug (ˈbɛdˌbʌg) n. a small bloodsucking wingless insect that infests dirty houses.

bedclothes (ˈbɛdˌkləʊðz) pl. n. sheets, blankets, and other coverings for a bed.

bedding (ˈbɛdɪŋ) n. **1.** bedclothes, sometimes with a mattress. **2.** litter, such as straw, for animals. **3.** the stratification of rocks.

bedeck (bɪˈdɛk) vb. to cover with decorations.

bedevil (bɪˈdɛvˀl) vb. -illing, -illed or U.S. -iling, -iled. **1.** to harass or torment. **2.** to throw into confusion. —be'devilment n.

bedew (bɪˈdjuː) vb. to wet as with dew.

bedfellow (ˈbɛdˌfɛləʊ) n. **1.** a person with whom one shares a bed. **2.** a temporary associate.

bedizen (bɪˈdaɪzˀn, -ˈdɪzˀn) vb. *Archaic.* to dress gaudily or tastelessly.

bedlam (ˈbɛdləm) n. a noisy confused situation.

bed linen n. sheets and pillowcases for a bed.

Bedouin ('bɛduɪn) n. 1. (pl. -ins or -in) a nomadic Arab tribesman of the deserts of Arabia, Jordan, and Syria. 2. a wanderer.

bedpan ('bɛd,pæn) n. a shallow vessel used as a toilet by bedridden people.

bedraggled (bɪ'dræg²ld) adj. having hair or clothing that is untidy or dirty, as with rain or mud.

bedridden ('bɛd,rɪd²n) adj. confined to bed because of illness, esp. for a long period.

bedrock ('bɛd,rɒk) n. 1. the solid rock beneath the surface soil. 2. basic principles or facts.

bedroom ('bɛd,ruːm, -,rʊm) n. 1. a room used for sleeping. 2. (modifier) containing references to sex: a bedroom comedy.

Beds (bɛdz) Bedfordshire.

bedside ('bɛd,saɪd) n. the space beside a bed, esp. a sickbed.

bedsitter ('bɛd,sɪtə) or **bedsit** n. a furnished sitting room with a bed.

bedsore ('bɛd,sɔː) n. a chronic ulcer on the skin of a bedridden person, caused by prolonged pressure.

bedspread ('bɛd,sprɛd) n. a top cover on a bed.

bedstead ('bɛd,stɛd) n. the framework of a bed.

bedstraw ('bɛd,strɔː) n. a plant with small white or yellow flowers.

bed-wetting n. involuntarily urinating in bed.

bee¹ (biː) n. 1. a four-winged insect that collects nectar and pollen to make honey and wax. 2. **have a bee in one's bonnet.** to be obsessed with an idea.

bee² (biː) n. Chiefly U.S. a social gathering to carry out a communal task: quilting bee.

Beeb (biːb) n. **the.** Informal. the BBC.

beebread ('biː,brɛd) n. a mixture of pollen and nectar prepared and eaten by some bees.

beech (biːtʃ) n. 1. a European tree with smooth greyish bark. 2. the hard wood of this tree. 3. See **copper beech.**

beechnut ('biːtʃ,nʌt) n. the small brown triangular edible nut of the beech tree.

beef (biːf) n. 1. the flesh of a cow, bull, or ox when killed for eating. 2. Informal. human flesh, esp. when muscular. 3. Slang. a complaint. ~vb. 4. Slang. to complain. ~See also **beef up.**

beefburger ('biːf,bɜːgə) n. a flat fried cake of minced beef; hamburger.

beefcake ('biːf,keɪk) n. Slang. musclemen as displayed in photographs.

beefeater ('biːf,iːtə) n. a yeoman warder of the Tower of London.

beef tea n. a drink made by boiling pieces of lean beef.

beef up vb. Informal. to strengthen; reinforce.

beefy ('biːfɪ) adj. **beefier, beefiest.** 1. like

beef. 2. Informal. muscular; brawny. —'**beefiness** n.

beehive ('biː,haɪv) n. 1. a man-made receptacle used to house bees. 2. a place where busy people are assembled.

beekeeper ('biː,kiːpə) n. a person who keeps bees for their honey. —'**bee-keeping** n.

beeline ('biː,laɪn) n. **make a beeline for.** to take the most direct route to.

Beelzebub (bɪ'ɛlzɪ,bʌb) n. Satan or any devil.

been (biːn, bɪn) vb. the past participle of **be.**

beep (biːp) n. 1. a high-pitched sound, as made by a car horn. ~vb. 2. to make or cause to make such a noise.

beer (bɪə) n. 1. an alcoholic drink brewed from malt, sugar, hops, and water. 2. a glass, can, or bottle containing this drink.

beer and skittles n. (functioning as sing.) Informal. enjoyment or pleasure.

beer parlour n. Canad. a licensed place in which beer is sold and drunk.

beery ('bɪərɪ) adj. **beerier, beeriest.** smelling or tasting of beer.

beeswax ('biːz,wæks) n. 1. a wax secreted by honeybees for constructing honeycombs. 2. this wax after refining, used in polishes, etc.

beeswing ('biːz,wɪŋ) n. a filmy crust that forms in some wines after long storage.

beet (biːt) n. a plant widely cultivated in such varieties as the sugar beet and beetroot.

beetle¹ ('biːt²l) n. 1. an insect with a hard wing-case closed over the back for protection. ~vb. 2. (foll. by along, off, etc.) Informal. to scuttle or scurry; hurry.

beetle² ('biːt²l) vb. 1. to overhang; jut. ~adj. 2. overhanging; prominent. —'**beetling** adj.

beetle-browed adj. having bushy or overhanging eyebrows.

beetroot ('biːt,ruːt) n. a variety of the beet plant with a dark red root that may be eaten as a vegetable, in salads, or pickled.

beet sugar n. the sucrose obtained from sugar beet.

befall (bɪ'fɔːl) vb. -**falling, -fell, -fallen.** Archaic or literary. to happen to (someone).

befit (bɪ'fɪt) vb. -**fitting, -fitted.** to be appropriate to or suitable for. —be'**fitting** adj.

before (bɪ'fɔː) conj. 1. earlier than the time when. 2. rather than: he'll resign before he agrees to it. ~prep. 3. preceding in space or time; in front of; ahead of: standing before the altar. 4. in the presence of: to be brought before a judge. 5. in preference to: to put friendship before money. ~adv. 6. previously. 7. in front.

beforehand (bɪ'fɔː,hænd) adj., adv. early; in advance; in anticipation.

befriend (bɪ'frɛnd) vb. to be a friend to; assist.

befuddle (bɪ'fʌdªl) vb. to stupefy or confuse, as with alcoholic drink.

beg (bɛg) vb. **begging, begged. 1.** to solicit (for money or food), esp. in the street. **2.** to ask formally, humbly, or earnestly: *I beg forgiveness; I beg to differ*. **3. beg the question**. to assume the thing under examination as proved. **4. go begging**. to be unwanted or unused.

began (bɪ'gæn) vb. the past tense of **begin**.

beget (bɪ'gɛt) vb. **-getting, -got** or **-gat; -gotten** or **-got. 1.** to father. **2.** to cause or create.

beggar ('bɛgə) n. **1.** a person who begs, esp. one who lives by begging. **2.** *Chiefly Brit.* a fellow: *lucky beggar!* ~vb. **3. beggar description**. to be impossible to describe. —'**beggarly** adj.

begin (bɪ'gɪn) vb. **-ginning, -gan, -gun. 1.** to start or cause to start (something or to do something). **2.** to bring or come into being; arise or originate. **3.** to start to say or speak. **4.** to have the least capacity (to do something): *he couldn't begin to compete*. —be'**ginner** n.

beginner's luck n. exceptional luck supposed to attend a beginner.

beginning (bɪ'gɪnɪŋ) n. **1.** a start. **2.** (pl.) an early part or stage. **3.** the place where or time when something starts. **4.** an origin; source.

begone (bɪ'gɒn) interj. go away!

begonia (bɪ'gəʊnjə) n. a plant of warm and tropical regions, with ornamental leaves and waxy flowers.

begot (bɪ'gɒt) vb. a past tense and past participle of **beget**.

begotten (bɪ'gɒtªn) vb. a past participle of **beget**.

begrudge (bɪ'grʌdʒ) vb. **1.** to give, admit, or allow unwillingly. **2.** to envy (someone) the possession of (something).

beguile (bɪ'gaɪl) vb. **1.** to charm; fascinate. **2.** to delude, cheat, or mislead. —be'**guiling** adj.

beguine (bɪ'giːn) n. **1.** a dance of South American origin. **2.** music for this dance.

begum ('beɪgəm) n. (in certain Muslim countries) a woman of high rank.

begun (bɪ'gʌn) vb. the past participle of **begin**.

behalf (bɪ'hɑːf) n. **on** or *U.S. & Canad.* **in behalf of**. in the interest of or for the benefit of.

behave (bɪ'heɪv) vb. **1.** to act or function in a specified or usual way. **2.** to conduct (oneself) in a specified way: *he behaved badly*. **3.** to conduct (oneself) properly.

behaviour or *U.S.* **behavior** (bɪ'heɪvjə) n.

1. manner of behaving. **2.** *Psychol.* the response of an organism to a stimulus. —be'**havioural** or *U.S.* be'**havioral** adj.

behavioural science n. the scientific study of the behaviour of organisms.

behaviourism or *U.S.* **behaviorism** (bɪ'heɪvjə,rɪzəm) n. a school of psychology that regards objective observation of the behaviour of organisms as the only valid subject for study. —be'**haviourist** or *U.S.* be'**haviorist** adj., n.

behead (bɪ'hɛd) vb. to remove the head from.

beheld (bɪ'hɛld) vb. past of **behold**.

behemoth (bɪ'hiːmɒθ) n. **1.** *Bible*. a gigantic beast described in Job 40:15. **2.** a huge person or thing.

behest (bɪ'hɛst) n. an order or earnest request.

behind (bɪ'haɪnd) prep. **1.** in or to a position further back than. **2.** in the past in relation to: *I've got the exams behind me now*. **3.** late according to: *running behind schedule*. **4.** concerning the circumstances surrounding: *the reasons behind his departure*. **5.** supporting: *I'm right behind you in your application*. ~adv. **6.** in or to a position further back. **7.** remaining after someone's departure: *he left his books behind*. **8.** in arrears: *to fall behind with payments*. ~adj. **9.** in a position further back. ~n. **10.** *Informal.* the buttocks.

behindhand (bɪ'haɪnd,hænd) adj., adv. **1.** in arrears. **2.** backward. **3.** late.

behold (bɪ'həʊld) vb. **-holding, -held.** *Archaic or literary*. to look (at); observe. —be'**holder** n.

beholden (bɪ'həʊldªn) adj. indebted; obliged.

behove (bɪ'həʊv) vb. *Archaic*. to be necessary or fitting for: *it behoves me to warn you*.

beige (beɪʒ) adj. **1.** very light brown, sometimes with a yellowish tinge. ~n. **2.** a fabric made of undyed wool.

being ('biːɪŋ) n. **1.** the state or fact of existing. **2.** essential nature; self. **3.** something that exists or is thought to exist: *a being from outer space*. **4.** a human being.

bejewelled or *U.S.* **bejeweled** (bɪ'dʒuː-əld) adj. decorated with jewels.

bel (bɛl) n. a measure for comparing two power levels, equal to 10 decibels.

belabour or *U.S.* **belabor** (bɪ'leɪbə) vb. to attack verbally or physically.

belated (bɪ'leɪtɪd) adj. late or too late: *belated greetings*. —be'**latedly** adv.

belay (bɪ'leɪ) vb. **-laying, -layed. 1.** *Naut.* to secure (a line) to a pin or cleat. **2.** *Naut.* to stop. **3.** ('biː,leɪ). *Mountaineering.* to secure (a climber) by fixing a rope round a rock or piton.

belch (bɛltʃ) vb. **1.** to expel wind from the stomach noisily through the mouth. **2.** to expel or be expelled forcefully: *smoke belching from factory chimneys.* ~*n.* **3.** an act of belching.

beleaguer (bɪˈliːɡə) *vb.* **1.** to lay siege to. **2.** to harass.

belfry (ˈbɛlfrɪ) *n., pl.* **-fries. 1.** the part of a tower or steeple in which bells are hung. **2.** a tower or steeple.

Belial (ˈbiːlɪəl) *n.* the devil or Satan.

belie (bɪˈlaɪ) *vb.* **-lying, -lied. 1.** to show to be untrue: *the facts belied the theory.* **2.** to misrepresent: *her looks belied her age.* **3.** to fail to justify: *the promises were soon belied.*

belief (bɪˈliːf) *n.* **1.** a principle, etc., accepted as true, esp. without proof. **2.** opinion; conviction: *it's my firm belief.* **3.** religious faith. **4.** trust or confidence: *belief in progress.*

believe (bɪˈliːv) *vb.* **1.** to accept as true or real: *I believe God exists.* **2.** to accept the statement or opinion of (a person) as true. **3.** (foll. by *in*) to be convinced of the truth or existence of: *to believe in fairies.* **4.** to have religious faith. **5.** to think, assume, or suppose: *I believe you know my mother.* —**beˈlievable** *adj.* —**beˈliever** *n.*

Belisha beacon (bəˈliːʃə) *n. Brit.* a flashing orange globe mounted on a post, indicating a pedestrian crossing.

belittle (bɪˈlɪtʳl) *vb.* to treat (something or someone) as having little value or importance.

bell¹ (bɛl) *n.* **1.** a hollow, usually metal, cup-shaped instrument that emits a ringing sound when struck. **2.** the sound made by such an instrument. **3.** an electrical device that rings or buzzes as a signal. **4.** something shaped like a bell. **5.** *Brit. slang.* a telephone call. **6. ring a bell.** to sound familiar; recall something previously experienced.

bell² (bɛl) *n.* **1.** a bellowing or baying cry. ~*vb.* **2.** to utter (such a cry).

belladonna (ˌbɛləˈdɒnə) *n.* **1.** a drug obtained from deadly nightshade. **2.** same as **deadly nightshade.**

bell-bottoms *pl. n.* trousers that flare from the knee. —**ˈbell-ˌbottomed** *adj.*

belle (bɛl) *n.* a beautiful woman, esp. the most attractive woman at a function: *the belle of the ball.*

belles-lettres (ˌbɛlˈlɛtrə) *n.* (functioning as sing.) literary works, esp. essays and poetry.

bellicose (ˈbɛlɪˌkəʊs, -ˌkəʊz) *adj.* warlike; aggressive.

belligerence (bɪˈlɪdʒərəns) *n.* the act or quality of being belligerent or warlike.

belligerent (bɪˈlɪdʒərənt) *adj.* **1.** marked by readiness to fight; aggressive. **2.** relating to or engaged in a war. ~*n.* **3.** a person or country engaged in war.

bell jar *n.* a bell-shaped glass cover used to protect flower arrangements or cover apparatus to confine gases in experiments.

bellow (ˈbɛləʊ) *vb.* **1.** to make a loud deep cry like that of a bull; roar. **2.** to shout (something), as in anger. ~*n.* **3.** the characteristic noise of a bull. **4.** a loud deep sound, as of pain or anger.

bellows (ˈbɛləʊz) *n.* (functioning as sing. or pl.) **1.** an instrument consisting of an air chamber with flexible sides that is used to create a stream of air, as for producing a draught for a fire or for sounding organ pipes. **2.** a flexible corrugated part, as that connecting the lens system of some cameras to the body.

bell pull *n.* a handle or cord pulled to operate a bell.

bell push *n.* a button pressed to operate an electric bell.

bell-ringer *n.* a person who rings church bells or musical handbells. —**ˈbell-ˌringing** *n.*

bellwether (ˈbɛlˌwɛðə) *n.* a sheep that leads the flock, often bearing a bell.

belly (ˈbɛlɪ) *n., pl.* **-lies. 1.** the part of the body of a vertebrate containing the intestines and other organs; abdomen. **2.** the stomach. **3.** the front, lower, or inner part of something. ~*vb.* **-lying, -lied. 4.** to swell out or cause to swell out; bulge.

bellyache (ˈbɛlɪˌeɪk) *n.* **1.** *Informal.* a pain in the abdomen. ~*vb.* **2.** *Slang.* to complain repeatedly.

bellybutton (ˈbɛlɪˌbʌtʳn) *n. Informal.* the navel.

belly dance *n.* **1.** a sensuous dance performed by women, with undulating movements of the abdomen. ~*vb.* **belly-dance. 2.** to dance thus. —**belly dancer** *n.*

belly flop *n.* **1.** a dive into water in which the body lands horizontally. ~*vb.* **bellyflop, -flopping, -flopped. 2.** to perform a belly flop.

bellyful (ˈbɛlɪˌfʊl) *n.* **1.** *Slang.* more than one can tolerate. **2.** as much as one wants or can eat.

belly laugh *n.* a loud deep hearty laugh.

belong (bɪˈlɒŋ) *vb.* **1.** (foll. by *to*) to be the property of. **2.** (foll. by *to*) to be bound to by ties of affection, etc. **3.** (foll. by *to, under, with,* etc.) to be classified with: *this plant belongs to the daisy family.* **4.** (foll. by *to*) to be a part of: *this lid belongs to that tin.* **5.** to have a proper or usual place. **6.** *Informal.* to be acceptable, esp. socially.

belonging (bɪˈlɒŋɪŋ) *n.* secure relationship: *they have a strong sense of belonging.*

belongings (bɪˈlɒŋɪŋz) *pl. n.* the things that a person owns or has with him.

beloved (bɪˈlʌvɪd, -ˈlʌvd) *adj.* **1.** dearly loved. ~*n.* **2.** a person who is dearly loved.

below (bɪˈləʊ) *prep.* **1.** at or to a position lower than; under. **2.** less than. **3.** unworthy of; beneath. ~*adv.* **4.** at or to a lower position. **5.** at a later place (in something written). **6.** *Archaic.* on earth or in hell.

belt (belt) *n.* **1.** a band of cloth, leather, etc., worn around the waist. **2.** an area where a specific thing is found; zone: *a belt of high pressure.* **3.** same as **seat belt. 4.** a band of flexible material between rotating shafts or pulleys to transfer motion or transmit goods: *a fan belt; a conveyer belt.* **5.** *Informal.* a sharp blow. **6. below the belt.** *Informal.* unscrupulous or cowardly. **7. tighten one's belt.** to reduce expenditure. **8. under one's belt.** as part of one's experience: *he had a degree under his belt.* ~*vb.* **9.** to fasten with or as if with a belt. **10.** to hit with a belt. **11.** *Slang.* to give (someone) a sharp blow. **12.** (foll. by *along*) *Slang.* to move very fast.

belt out *vb. Informal.* to sing (a song) loudly.

belt up *vb.* **1.** *Slang.* to stop talking. **2.** to fasten something with a belt.

beluga (bɪˈluːɡə) *n.* **1.** a large white sturgeon of the Black and Caspian Seas: a source of caviar and isinglass. **2.** same as **white whale.**

belvedere (ˈbɛlvɪˌdɪə, ˌbɛlvɪˈdɪə) *n.* a building, such as a summerhouse, sited to command a fine view.

bemoan (bɪˈməʊn) *vb.* to lament: *he's always bemoaning his fate.*

bemused (bɪˈmjuːzd) *adj.* preoccupied; lost in thought.

ben (bɛn) *n. Scot., Irish.* a mountain peak: *Ben Lomond.*

bench (bɛntʃ) *n.* **1.** a long seat for more than one person. **2.** a plain stout work-table. **3. the bench. a.** a judge or magistrate sitting in court. **b.** judges or magistrates collectively. **4.** (in a gymnasium) a low table, which may be inclined, used for various exercises.

bench mark *n.* **1.** a mark on a fixed object, used as a reference point in surveying. **2.** a criterion by which to measure something.

bend[1] (bɛnd) *vb.* **bending, bent. 1.** to form or cause to form a curve. **2.** to turn or cause to turn from a particular direction: *the road bends left.* **3.** (often foll. by *down*, etc.) to incline the body; stoop. **4.** to submit or cause to submit: *to bend before superior force.* **5.** to turn or direct (one's eyes, steps, or attention). **6. bend the rules.** *Informal.* to ignore or change rules to suit oneself. ~*n.* **7.** a curved part. **8.** the act of bending. **9. round the bend.** *Brit. slang.* mad. —ˈ**bendy** *adj.*

bend[2] (bɛnd) *n. Heraldry.* a diagonal line across a shield.

bender (ˈbɛndə) *n. Informal.* a drinking bout.

bends (bɛndz) *pl. n.* (*functioning as sing. or pl.*) **the.** *Informal.* decompression sickness.

bend sinister *n. Heraldry.* a diagonal line across a shield, indicating a bastard line.

beneath (bɪˈniːθ) *prep.* **1.** below, esp. if covered or obscured by. **2.** not as good as would be demanded by: *beneath his dignity.* ~*adv.* **3.** below; underneath.

Benedictine *n.* **1.** (ˌbɛnɪˈdɪktɪn, -taɪn). a monk or nun of the order of Saint Benedict. **2.** (ˌbɛnɪˈdɪktiːn). a liqueur first made by Benedictine monks. ~*adj.* (ˌbɛnɪˈdɪktɪn,-taɪn). **3.** of Saint Benedict or his order.

benediction (ˌbɛnɪˈdɪkʃən) *n.* **1.** a prayer for divine blessing. **2.** a Roman Catholic service in which the congregation is blessed with the sacrament. —ˌbeneˈdictory *adj.*

benefaction (ˌbɛnɪˈfækʃən) *n.* **1.** the act of doing good, esp. by giving a donation to charity. **2.** the donation or help given.

benefactor (ˈbɛnɪˌfæktə, ˌbɛnɪˈfæk-) *n.* a person who supports a person or institution, esp. by giving money. —ˈbeneˌfactress *fem. n.*

benefice (ˈbɛnɪfɪs) *n. Christianity.* an endowed Church office yielding an income to its holder.

beneficent (bɪˈnɛfɪsənt) *adj.* charitable; generous. —beˈneficence *n.*

beneficial (ˌbɛnɪˈfɪʃəl) *adj.* advantageous.

beneficiary (ˌbɛnɪˈfɪʃərɪ) *n., pl.* -ciaries. **1.** a person who gains or benefits. **2.** *Law.* a person entitled to receive funds or property under a trust, will, etc.

benefit (ˈbɛnɪfɪt) *n.* **1.** something that improves or promotes. **2.** advantage or sake: *I'm doing this for your benefit.* **3.** a payment made by an institution or government to a person who is ill, unemployed, etc. **4.** a theatrical performance or sports event to raise money for a charity. ~*vb.* -fiting, -fited *or U.S.* -fitting, -fitted. **5.** to do or receive good; profit.

benefit society *n. U.S.* same as **friendly society.**

benevolence (bɪˈnɛvələns) *n.* **1.** inclination to do good; charity. **2.** an act of kindness. —beˈnevolent *adj.*

Bengali (bɛŋˈɡɔːlɪ, bɛŋ-) *n.* **1.** a member of a people living chiefly in Bangladesh and West Bengal (in NE India). **2.** their language. ~*adj.* **3.** of Bengal, the Bengalis, or their language.

benighted (bɪˈnaɪtɪd) *adj.* lacking cultural, moral, or intellectual enlightenment.

benign (bɪˈnaɪn) *adj.* **1.** showing kindliness. **2.** favourable; propitious. **3.** *Pathol.* (of a tumour, etc.) not malignant. —beˈnignly *adv.*

benignant (bɪˈnɪɡnənt) *adj.* **1.** kind; gracious. **2.** same as **benign** (senses 2, 3). —beˈnignancy *n.*

benignity (bɪ'nɪgnɪtɪ) *n., pl.* **-ties.** kindliness.

bent¹ (bɛnt) *adj.* **1.** not straight; curved. **2.** *Slang.* **a.** dishonest; corrupt. **b.** sexually deviant. **3. bent on.** determined to pursue (a course of action). ~*n.* **4.** personal inclination or aptitude.

bent² (bɛnt) *n.* **1.** a grass with irregularly branched flowers. **2.** *Archaic.* any stiff grass or sedge.

Benthamism ('bɛnθəmɪzəm) *n.* the utilitarian philosophy of Jeremy Bentham, which holds that the ultimate goal of society should be to promote the greatest happiness of the greatest number. —'**Benthamite** *n., adj.*

bentwood ('bɛnt,wʊd) *n.* **a.** wood bent in moulds, used mainly for furniture. **b.** (*as modifier*): *a bentwood chair.*

benumb (bɪ'nʌm) *vb.* **1.** to make numb or powerless. **2.** to stupefy (the mind, senses, will, etc.).

benzene ('bɛnziːn) *n.* a flammable poisonous liquid used as a solvent, insecticide, etc.

benzine ('bɛnziːn, bɛn'ziːn) *n.* a volatile liquid obtained from coal tar and used as a solvent.

bequeath (bɪ'kwiːð, -'kwiːθ) *vb.* **1.** *Law.* to dispose of (property) by will. **2.** to hand down.

bequest (bɪ'kwɛst) *n.* **1.** the act of bequeathing. **2.** something that is bequeathed.

berate (bɪ'reɪt) *vb.* to scold harshly.

Berber ('bɜːbə) *n.* **1.** a member of a Muslim people of N Africa. **2.** the language of this people. ~*adj.* **3.** of this people or their language.

berberis ('bɜːbərɪs) *n.* any of a genus of mainly N temperate shrubs.

berceuse (bɛə'sɜːz) *n.* **1.** a lullaby. **2.** an instrumental piece suggestive of this.

bereaved (bɪ'riːvd) *adj.* having recently lost a close relative or friend through death. —be'**reavement** *n.*

bereft (bɪ'rɛft) *adj.* (foll. by *of*) deprived: *bereft of hope.*

beret ('bɛreɪ) *n.* a round close-fitting brimless cap.

berg (bɜːg) *n.* short for **iceberg.**

bergamot ('bɜːgə,mɒt) *n.* **1.** a small Asian tree with sour pear-shaped fruit. **2. essence of bergamot.** a fragrant essential oil from the fruit rind of this plant, used in perfumery.

beriberi (,bɛrɪ'bɛrɪ) *n.* a disease, endemic in E and S Asia, caused by dietary deficiency of thiamine (vitamin B₁).

berk (bɜːk) *n. Brit. slang.* same as **burk.**

berkelium (bɜː'kiːlɪəm, 'bɜːklɪəm) *n.* a radioactive element produced by bombardment of americium. Symbol: Bk

Berks (bɑːks) Berkshire.

Bermuda shorts (bə'mjuːdə) *pl. n.* close-fitting shorts that come down to the knees.

berry ('bɛrɪ) *n., pl.* **-ries.** **1.** any of various small edible fruit such as the strawberry. **2.** *Bot.* a fruit with seeds and a fleshy pulp, such as the grape.

berserk (bə'zɜːk, -'sɜːk) *adj.* **go berserk** to become violent or destructive.

berth (bɜːθ) *n.* **1.** a bunk in a ship or train. **2.** *Naut.* a place assigned to a ship at a mooring. **3.** *Naut.* sufficient room for a ship to manoeuvre. **4. give a wide berth to.** to keep clear of. **5.** *Informal.* a job, esp. as a member of a ship's crew. ~*vb.* **6.** *Naut.* to dock (a vessel). **7.** to provide with a sleeping place. **8.** *Naut.* to pick up a mooring in an anchorage.

beryl ('bɛrɪl) *n.* a green, blue, yellow, pink, or white hard mineral, used as a source of beryllium and as a gemstone.

beryllium (bɛ'rɪlɪəm) *n.* a toxic silvery-white metallic element. Symbol: Be

beseech (bɪ'siːtʃ) *vb.* **-seeching, -sought** *or* **-seeched.** to ask (someone) earnestly (to do something or for something); beg.

beset (bɪ'sɛt) *vb.* **-setting, -set.** **1.** to trouble or harass constantly. **2.** to surround or attack from all sides.

beside (bɪ'saɪd) *prep.* **1.** next to; at, by, or to the side of. **2.** as compared with. **3.** away from; wide of: *beside the point.* **4. beside oneself.** overwhelmed; overwrought: *beside oneself with grief.* ~*adv.* **5.** at, by, to, or along the side of something or someone.

besides (bɪ'saɪdz) *prep.* **1.** apart from; even considering. ~*adv.* **2.** as well. **3.** anyway; moreover.

besiege (bɪ'siːdʒ) *vb.* **1.** to surround (a fortified area) with military forces to bring about its surrender. **2.** to hem in. **3.** to overwhelm, as with requests.

besmirch (bɪ'smɜːtʃ) *vb.* to sully (someone's name or reputation).

besom ('biːzəm) *n.* a broom made of a bundle of twigs tied to a handle.

besotted (bɪ'sɒtɪd) *adj.* **1.** stupefied with alcohol. **2.** infatuated. **3.** foolish; muddled.

besought (bɪ'sɔːt) *vb.* past of **beseech.**

bespangle (bɪ'spæŋg'l) *vb.* to cover with or as if with spangles.

bespatter (bɪ'spætə) *vb.* **1.** to splash, as with dirty water. **2.** to defile; besmirch.

bespeak (bɪ'spiːk) *vb.* **-speaking, -spoke; -spoken** *or* **-spoke.** **1.** to engage or ask for in advance. **2.** to indicate or suggest.

bespectacled (bɪ'spɛktək'ld) *adj.* wearing spectacles.

bespoke (bɪ'spəuk) *adj. Chiefly Brit.* **1.** (esp. of a suit) made to the customer's specifications. **2.** making or selling such suits: *a bespoke tailor.*

best (bɛst) *adj.* **1.** the superlative of **good**. **2.** most excellent of a particular group, category, etc. **3.** most suitable, desirable, etc. ~*adv.* **4.** the superlative of **well**. **5** in a manner surpassing all others; most attractively, etc. ~*n.* **6. the best.** the most outstanding or excellent person, thing, or group in a category. **7.** the utmost effort: *I did my best.* **8.** a person's finest clothes. **9. at best. a.** in the most favourable interpretation. **b.** under the most favourable conditions. **10. for the best. a.** for an ultimately good outcome. **b.** with good intentions. **11. get the best of.** to defeat or outwit. **12. make the best of.** to cope as well as possible with. ~*vb.* **13.** to defeat.

bestial ('bɛstɪəl) *adj.* **1.** brutal or savage. **2.** of or relating to a beast.

bestiality (,bɛstɪ'ælɪtɪ) *n., pl.* **-ties. 1.** bestial behaviour, character, or action. **2.** sexual activity between a person and an animal.

bestiary ('bɛstɪərɪ) *n., pl.* **-aries.** a medieval collection of descriptions of animals.

bestir (bɪ'stɜː) *vb.* **-stirring, -stirred.** to cause (oneself) to become active.

best man *n.* the male attendant of the bridegroom at a wedding.

bestow (bɪ'stəʊ) *vb.* to present (a gift) or confer (an honour). —**be'stowal** *n.*

bestrew (bɪ'struː) *vb.* **-strewing, -strewed; -strewn** *or* **-strewed.** to scatter or lie scattered over (a surface).

bestride (bɪ'straɪd) *vb.* **-striding, -strode.** to have or put a leg on either side of.

best seller *n.* a book or other product that has sold in great numbers. —,**best-'selling** *adj.*

bet (bɛt) *n.* **1.** an agreement between two people that a sum of money or other stake will be paid by the loser to the one who correctly predicts the outcome of an event. **2.** the stake risked. **3.** a course of action: *your best bet is to go to the local library.* **4.** *Informal.* an opinion: *my bet is that you've been up to no good.* ~*vb.* **betting, bet** *or* **betted. 5.** to make or place a bet with (a person or persons). **6.** to stake (money, etc.) in a bet. **7.** *Informal.* to predict (a certain outcome): *I bet he doesn't turn up.* **8. you bet.** *Informal.* of course.

beta ('biːtə) *n.* **1.** the second letter in the Greek alphabet (B or β). **2.** the second in a group or series.

beta-blocker *n.* a drug that increases the activity of the heart: used in the treatment of high blood pressure and angina pectoris.

betake (bɪ'teɪk) *vb.* **-taking, -took, -taken. betake oneself.** to go; move.

beta particle *n.* a high-speed electron or positron emitted by a nucleus during radioactive decay or nuclear fission.

betatron ('biːtə,trɒn) *n.* a type of particle accelerator for producing high-energy beams of electrons.

betel ('biːt'l) *n.* an Asian climbing plant, the leaves and nuts of which are chewed by some Asians.

bête noire (,beɪt 'nwɑː) *n., pl.* **bêtes noires** (,beɪt 'nwɑː). a person or thing that one particularly dislikes or dreads.

betide (bɪ'taɪd) *vb.* to happen or happen to: *woe betide us if we're not ready on time.*

betimes (bɪ'taɪmz) *adv. Archaic.* in good time; early.

betoken (bɪ'təʊkən) *vb.* to indicate; signify.

betray (bɪ'treɪ) *vb.* **1.** to hand over or expose (one's nation, friend, etc.) treacherously to an enemy. **2.** to disclose (a secret or confidence) treacherously. **3.** to break (a promise) or be disloyal to (a person's trust). **4.** to reveal unintentionally: *his grin betrayed his satisfaction.* —**be'trayal** *n.* —**be'trayer** *n.*

betroth (bɪ'trəʊð) *vb. Archaic.* to promise to marry or to give in marriage. —**be'trothal** *n.*

betrothed (bɪ'trəʊðd) *adj.* **1.** engaged to be married. ~*n.* **2.** the person to whom one is engaged.

better ('bɛtə) *adj.* **1.** the comparative of **good. 2.** more excellent than others. **3.** more suitable, attractive, etc. **4.** improved or fully recovered in health. **5. better off.** in more favourable circumstances, esp. financially. **6. the better part of.** a large part of. ~*adv.* **7.** the comparative of **well. 8.** in a more excellent manner. **9.** in or to a greater degree. **10. had better.** would be sensible, etc., to: *I had better be off.* ~*n.* **11. the better.** something that is the more excellent, useful, etc., of two such things. **12.** (*pl.*) people who are one's superiors, esp. in social standing. **13. get the better of.** to defeat or outwit. ~*vb.* **14.** to improve upon; surpass.

better half *n. Humorous.* one's spouse.

betterment ('bɛtəmənt) *n.* improvement.

better-off *adj.* comparatively affluent: *suburbs were originally built for the better-off workers who could afford to travel.*

betting shop *n.* (in Britain) a licensed bookmaker's premises not on a racecourse.

between (bɪ'twiːn) *prep.* **1.** at a point intermediate to two other points in space, time, etc. **2.** in combination; together: *between them, they saved enough money to buy a car.* **3.** confined to: *between you and me.* **4.** indicating a linking relation or comparison. **5.** indicating alternatives, strictly only two alternatives. ~*adv. also* **in between. 6.** between one specified thing and another.
Usage. *Between* should be used when only two people, objects, possibilities, etc., are concerned. Grammatically, *between you*

and I is incorrect. The proper construction is *between you and me*.

betwixt (bɪ'twɪkst) *prep., adv.* **1.** *Archaic.* between. **2. betwixt and between.** in an intermediate or indecisive position.

bevel ('bɛv°l) *n.* **1.** a surface that meets another at an angle other than a right angle. ~*vb.* **-elling, -elled** *or U.S.* **-eling, -eled. 2.** to be inclined; slope. **3.** to cut a bevel on (a piece of timber, etc.).

bevel gear *n.* a toothed gear meshed with another at an angle to it.

beverage ('bɛvərɪdʒ, 'bɛvrɪdʒ) *n.* any drink other than water.

beverage room *n. Canad.* same as **beer parlour.**

bevvy ('bɛvɪ) *n., pl.* **-vies.** *Dialect.* **1.** an alcoholic drink. **2.** a night of drinking.

bevy ('bɛvɪ) *n., pl.* **bevies. 1.** a flock of quails. **2.** a group, esp. of girls.

bewail (bɪ'weɪl) *vb.* to express great sorrow over (a person or thing); lament.

beware (bɪ'wɛə) *vb.* (often foll. by *of*) to be wary (of); be on one's guard (against).

bewilder (bɪ'wɪldə) *vb.* to confuse utterly; puzzle. —**be'wildering** *adj.* —**be'wilderment** *n.*

bewitch (bɪ'wɪtʃ) *vb.* **1.** to attract and fascinate. **2.** to cast a spell over. —**be'witching** *adj.*

bey (beɪ) *n.* **1.** (in modern Turkey) a title of address, corresponding to *Mr.* **2.** (in the Ottoman Empire) a title given to provincial governors.

beyond (bɪ'jɒnd) *prep.* **1.** at or to a point on the other side of; at or to the further side of: *beyond those hills.* **2.** outside the limits or scope of. ~*adv.* **3.** at or to the other or far side of something. **4.** outside the limits of something. ~*n.* **5. the beyond.** the unknown, esp. life after death.

bezel ('bɛz°l) *n.* **1.** the sloping edge of a cutting tool. **2.** the slanting face of a cut gem. **3.** a groove holding a gem, watch crystal, etc.

bezique (bɪ'ziːk) *n.* a card game for two or more players.

B/F *or* **b/f** *Book-keeping.* brought forward.

BFPO British Forces Post Office.

bhang (bæŋ) *n.* a preparation of the leaves and flower tops of Indian hemp, which when chewed or smoked acts as a narcotic and intoxicant.

bhangra ('bæŋɡrə) *n.* a type of traditional Indian folk music of the Punjab, now sometimes combined with elements of Western pop music.

bhp brake horsepower.

Bi *Chem.* bismuth.

bi- *combining form.* **1.** having two: *bifocal.* **2.** occurring or lasting for two: *biennial.* **3.** on both sides, directions, etc.: *bilateral.* **4.**

occurring twice during: *biweekly.* **5.** *Chem.* **a.** denoting a compound containing two identical cyclic hydrocarbon systems: *biphenyl.* **b.** indicating an acid salt of a dibasic acid: *sodium bicarbonate.*

Usage. Care should be taken to observe the distinction between *bi-* and *semi-* in *biweekly, bimonthly, biyearly* (once in two weeks, months, years) and *semiweekly, semimonthly, semiyearly* (twice during one week, month, year). In strict usage, *biennial* (lasting or occurring once in two years) is distinguished from *biannual* (occurring twice in one year).

biannual (baɪ'ænjʊəl) *adj.* occurring twice a year. —**bi'annually** *adv.*

bias ('baɪəs) *n.* **1.** mental tendency, esp. prejudice. **2.** a diagonal cut across the weave of a fabric. **3.** *Bowls.* a bulge or weight inside one side of a bowl that causes it to roll in a curve. ~*adv.* **4.** diagonally. ~*vb.* **-asing, -ased** *or* **-assing, -assed. 5.** to cause to have a bias; prejudice. —**'biased** *or* **'biassed** *adj.*

bias binding *n.* a strip of material cut on the bias, used for binding hems.

biaxial (baɪ'æksɪəl) *adj.* (esp. of a crystal) having two axes.

bib (bɪb) *n.* **1.** a piece of cloth or plastic worn to protect a child's clothes while eating. **2.** the upper front part of some aprons, dungarees, etc.

bibcock ('bɪb,kɒk) *n.* a tap with a nozzle bent downwards.

bibelot ('bɪbləʊ) *n.* an attractive or curious trinket.

bibl. 1. bibliographical. **2.** bibliography.

Bible ('baɪb°l) *n.* **1. the.** the sacred writings of the Christian religion, comprising the Old and New Testaments. **2.** (*usually not cap.*) a book regarded as authoritative. —**biblical** ('bɪblɪk°l) *adj.*

Usage. The *Bible* is written with a capital initial but should not be put in inverted commas. The adjective *biblical* is written without a capital initial: *a new translation of the Bible; life in biblical times.*

bibliography (,bɪblɪ'ɒɡrəfɪ) *n., pl.* **-phies. 1.** a list of books on a subject or by a particular author. **2.** a list of sources used in a book, etc. **3.** the study of the history, etc., of literary material. —**,bibli'ographer** *n.*

bibliophile ('bɪblɪə,faɪl) *n.* a person who collects or is fond of books.

bibulous ('bɪbjʊləs) *adj.* addicted to alcohol.

bicameral (baɪ'kæmərəl) *adj.* (of a legislature) consisting of two chambers.

bicarb ('baɪkɑːb) *n.* short for **bicarbonate of soda.**

bicarbonate (baɪ'kɑːbənɪt, -,neɪt) *n.* a salt of carbonic acid.

bicarbonate of soda *n.* sodium bicarbonate, esp. as medicine or a raising agent in baking.

bicentenary (ˌbaɪsɛnˈtiːnərɪ) *or U.S.* **bicentennial** (ˌbaɪsɛnˈtɛnɪəl) *adj.* **1.** marking a 200th anniversary. ~*n., pl.* **-naries.** **2.** a 200th anniversary.

biceps ('baɪsɛps) *n., pl.* **-ceps.** *Anat.* a muscle with two origins, esp. the muscle that flexes the forearm.

bicker ('bɪkə) *vb.* to argue over petty matters; squabble.

bicolour ('baɪˌkʌlə), **bicoloured** *or U.S.* **bicolor, bicolored** *adj.* two-coloured.

bicuspid (baɪˈkʌspɪd) *adj.* **1.** having two points. ~*n.* **2.** a bicuspid tooth; premolar.

bicycle ('baɪsɪkᵊl) *n.* **1.** a vehicle with a metal frame and two wheels, one behind the other. The rider propels the vehicle by means of pedals. ~*vb.* **2.** to ride a bicycle.

bid (bɪd) *vb.* **bidding; bad, bade,** *or* (esp. for senses 1, 3, 4) **bid; bidden** *or* (esp. for senses 1, 3, 4) **bid.** **1.** to offer (an amount) in attempting to buy something. **2.** to say (a greeting, etc.): *to bid farewell.* **3.** to order; command: *do as you are bid!* **4.** *Bridge, etc.* to declare how many tricks one expects to make. ~*n.* **5. a.** an offer of a specified amount. **b.** the price offered. **6. a.** the quoting by a seller of a price. **b.** the price quoted. **7.** an attempt, esp. to attain power. **8.** *Bridge, etc.* the number of tricks a player undertakes to make. —'**bidder** *n.*

biddable ('bɪdəbᵊl) *adj.* docile; obedient.

bidding ('bɪdɪŋ) *n.* **1.** an order; command. **2.** an invitation; summons. **3.** the bids in an auction, card game, etc.

biddy ('bɪdɪ) *n., pl.* **-dies.** *Informal.* a woman, esp. an old gossipy one.

bide (baɪd) *vb.* **biding, bided** *or* **bode, bided.** **1.** *Archaic or dialect.* to continue in a certain place or state; stay. **2. bide one's time.** to wait patiently for an opportunity.

bidet ('biːdeɪ) *n.* a small low basin for washing the genital area.

biennial (baɪˈɛnɪəl) *adj.* **1.** occurring every two years. ~*n.* **2.** a plant that completes its life cycle in two years.

bier (bɪə) *n.* a stand on which a corpse or a coffin rests before burial.

biff (bɪf) *Slang.* ~*n.* **1.** a blow with the fist. ~*vb.* **2.** to give (someone) such a blow.

bifid ('baɪfɪd) *adj.* divided into two by a cleft in the middle.

bifocal (baɪˈfəʊkᵊl) *adj.* having two different focuses, esp. (of a lens) permitting near and distant vision.

bifocals (baɪˈfəʊkᵊlz) *pl. n.* a pair of spectacles with bifocal lenses.

bifurcate *vb.* ('baɪfəˌkeɪt). **1.** to fork into two branches. ~*adj.* ('baɪfəˌkeɪt, -kɪt). **2.** forked into two branches. —ˌbifur-'**cation** *n.*

big (bɪg) *adj.* **bigger, biggest.** **1.** of great or considerable size, weight, number, or capacity. **2.** having great significance; important. **3.** important through having power, wealth, etc. **4. a.** elder: *my big brother.* **b.** grown-up. **5.** generous: *that's very big of you.* **6.** extravagant; boastful: *big talk.* **7. too big for one's boots.** conceited; unduly self-confident. **8.** in an advanced stage of pregnancy: *big with child.* **9. in a big way.** in a very grand or enthusiastic way. ~*adv. Informal.* **10.** boastfully; pretentiously: *he talks big.* **11.** on a grand scale: *think big.*

bigamy ('bɪgəmɪ) *n.* the crime of marrying a person while still legally married to someone else. —'**bigamist** *n.* —'**bigamous** *adj.*

big-bang theory *n.* a cosmological theory that suggests that the universe was created as the result of a massive explosion.

Big Brother *n.* a person or organization that exercises total dictatorial control.

big business *n.* large commercial organizations collectively.

big end *n. Brit.* the larger end of a connecting rod in an internal-combustion engine.

big game *n.* large animals that are hunted or fished for sport.

bighead ('bɪgˌhɛd) *n. Informal.* a conceited person. —ˌbig-'**headed** *adj.*

bight (baɪt) *n.* **1.** a long curved shoreline. **2.** the slack part or a loop in a rope.

bigot ('bɪgət) *n.* a person who is intolerant, esp. regarding religion, politics, or race. —'**bigoted** *adj.* —'**bigotry** *n.*

big shot *n. Informal.* an important person.

big stick *n. Informal.* force or the threat of force.

big time *n.* **the.** *Informal.* the highest level of a profession, esp. entertainment. —'**big-'timer** *n.*

big top *n. Informal.* the main tent of a circus.

bigwig ('bɪgˌwɪg) *n. Informal.* an important person.

bijou ('biːʒuː) *n., pl.* **-joux** (-ʒuːz). **1.** something small and delicately worked. **2.** (*modifier*) small but tasteful: *a bijou residence.*

bike (baɪk) *n. Informal.* a bicycle or motorcycle.

bikini (bɪˈkiːnɪ) *n.* a brief two-piece swimming costume worn by women.

bilateral (baɪˈlætərəl) *adj.* affecting or undertaken by two parties; mutual.

bilberry ('bɪlbərɪ) *n., pl.* **-ries.** a blue or blackish edible berry that grows on a shrub such as the whortleberry.

bile (baɪl) *n.* **1.** a greenish fluid secreted by the liver to aid digestion of fats. **2.** irritability or peevishness.

bilge (bɪldʒ) *n.* **1.** *Naut.* the bottom of a

ship's hull. **2.** the dirty water that collects in a ship's bilge. **3.** *Informal.* nonsense.

bilharzia (bɪlˈhɑːtsɪə) *n.* a disease caused by infestation of the body with blood flukes.

biliary (ˈbɪlɪərɪ) *adj.* of bile, the ducts that convey bile, or the gall bladder.

bilingual (baɪˈlɪŋgwəl) *adj.* **1.** able to speak two languages. **2.** expressed in two languages. ~*n.* **3.** a bilingual person. —**bi-ˈlingual‚ism** *n.*

bilious (ˈbɪlɪəs) *adj.* **1.** denoting any disorder related to secretion of bile. **2.** *Informal.* bad-tempered; irritable.

bilk (bɪlk) *vb.* to cheat or deceive, esp. to avoid making payment to. —**ˈbilker** *n.*

bill[1] (bɪl) *n.* **1.** a statement of money owed for goods or services supplied. **2.** any list of items, events, etc., such as a theatre programme. **3.** a draft of a proposed new law presented to a law-making body. **4.** a printed notice or advertisement. **5.** *U.S. & Canad.* a piece of paper money; note. ~*vb.* **6.** to send or present an account for payment to (a person). **7.** to advertise by posters. **8.** to schedule as a future programme.

bill[2] (bɪl) *n.* **1.** the projecting jaws of a bird; beak. ~*vb.* **2. bill and coo.** (of lovers) to kiss and whisper amorously.

bill[3] (bɪl) *n.* **1.** a weapon with a narrow hooked blade. **2.** same as **billhook.**

billabong (ˈbɪləˌbɒŋ) *n. Austral.* a stagnant pool in the bed of an intermittent stream.

billboard (ˈbɪlˌbɔːd) *n. Chiefly U.S. & Canad.* a hoarding.

billet[1] (ˈbɪlɪt) *n.* **1.** accommodation, esp. for a soldier, in civilian lodgings. **2.** the official requisition for such lodgings. ~*vb.* **3.** to assign a lodging to (a soldier).

billet[2] (ˈbɪlɪt) *n.* **1.** a chunk of wood, esp. for fuel. **2.** a small bar of iron or steel.

billet-doux (ˌbɪlɪˈduː) *n., pl.* **billets-doux** (ˌbɪlɪˈduːz). *Old-fashioned or jocular.* a love letter.

billhook (ˈbɪlˌhʊk) *n.* a tool with a hooked blade, used for chopping, etc.

billiards (ˈbɪljədz) *n.* (*functioning as sing.*) a game in which a long cue is used to drive balls on a rectangular table covered with a smooth cloth and having raised cushioned edges.

billion (ˈbɪljən) *n., pl.* **-lions** *or* **-lion.** **1.** (in Britain, originally) one million million: 1 000 000 000 000; 10^{12}. **2.** (in the U.S., Canada, and increasingly in Britain and elsewhere) one thousand million: 1 000 000 000; 10^9. **3.** (*often pl.*) any exceptionally large number. —**ˈbillionth** *adj., n.*

billionaire (ˌbɪljəˈnɛə) *n.* a person whose wealth exceeds a billion monetary units of his country.

bill of exchange *n.* a document in-structing a third party to pay a stated sum at a designated date or on demand.

bill of fare *n.* a menu.

bill of health *n.* **1.** a certificate that confirms the health of a ship's company. **2. clean bill of health.** *Informal.* **a.** a good report of one's physical condition. **b.** a favourable account of a person's or a company's financial position.

bill of lading *n.* a document containing full particulars of goods shipped.

billow (ˈbɪləʊ) *n.* **1.** a large sea wave. **2.** a swelling or surging mass, as of smoke or sound. ~*vb.* **3.** to rise up or swell out. —**ˈbillowing** *adj., n.* —**ˈbillowy** *adj.*

billy (ˈbɪlɪ) *or* **billycan** (ˈbɪlɪˌkæn) *n., pl.* **-lies** *or* **-lycans.** a metal can or pot for boiling water, etc., over a campfire.

billy goat *n.* a male goat.

biltong (ˈbɪlˌtɒŋ) *n. S. African.* strips of meat dried and cured in the sun.

bimbo (ˈbɪmbəʊ) *n., pl.* **-bos.** *Slang.* an attractive but empty-headed young woman.

bimetallism (baɪˈmɛtəˌlɪzəm) *n.* the use of two metals, esp. gold and silver, in fixed relative values as the standard of value and currency. —**biˈmetallist** *n.*

bin (bɪn) *n.* **1.** a large container for storing something in bulk, such as coal, grain, or bottled wine. **2.** a container for rubbish, etc.

binary (ˈbaɪnərɪ) *adj.* **1.** composed of two parts. **2.** *Maths, computers.* of or expressed in a system with two as its base. **3.** containing atoms of two different elements. ~*n., pl.* **-ries. 4.** something composed of two parts.

binary star *n.* a system of two stars revolving around a common centre of gravity.

bind (baɪnd) *vb.* **binding, bound. 1.** to make or become fast or secure with or as if with a rope. **2.** to encircle with a band. **3.** to place (someone) under obligation. **4.** to impose legal obligations or duties upon (a person). **5.** to make (a bargain or agreement) irrevocable; seal. **6.** to restrain or confine with or as if with ties, as of responsibility or loyalty. **7.** to place under certain constraints: *bound by the rules.* **8.** (foll. by *up*) to bandage. **9.** to stick together or cause to stick: *egg binds fat and flour.* **10.** to enclose and fasten (the pages of a book) between covers. **11.** to provide (a garment) with an edging. ~*n.* **12.** *Informal.* a difficult or annoying situation. ~See also **bind over.**

binder (ˈbaɪndə) *n.* **1.** a firm cover for holding loose sheets of paper together. **2.** a person who binds books. **3.** something used to fasten or tie, such as rope or twine. **4.** *Obs.* a machine for cutting and binding grain into sheaves.

bindery (ˈbaɪndərɪ) *n., pl.* **-eries.** a place in which books are bound.

binding ('baɪndɪŋ) n. **1.** anything that binds or fastens. **2.** the covering within which the pages of a book are bound. ~adj. **3.** imposing an obligation or duty.

bind over vb. to place (a person) under a legal obligation, esp. to keep the peace.

bindweed ('baɪnd,wiːd) n. a plant that twines around a support.

binge (bɪndʒ) n. Informal. **1.** a bout of excessive drinking. **2.** excessive indulgence in anything.

bingo ('bɪŋgəʊ) n. a gambling game in which random numbers are called out and the players cover them on their individual cards. The first to cover a given arrangement is the winner.

binnacle ('bɪnək³l) n. a housing for a ship's compass.

binocular (bɪ'nɒkjʊlə, baɪ-) adj. involving or intended for both eyes: binocular vision.

binoculars (bɪ'nɒkjʊləz, baɪ-) pl. n. an optical instrument for use with both eyes, consisting of two small telescopes joined together.

binomial (baɪ'nəʊmɪəl) n. **1.** a mathematical expression consisting of two terms, such as $3x + 2y$. ~adj. **2.** referring to two names or terms.

binomial theorem n. a general mathematical formula that expresses any power of a binomial without multiplying out, as in $(a+b)^2 = a^2 + 2ab + b^2$.

bio- combining form. indicating: **1.** life or living organisms: biogenesis. **2.** a human life or career: biography.

bioastronautics (,baɪəʊ,æstrə'nɔːtɪks) n. (functioning as sing.) the study of the effects of space flight on living organisms.

biochemistry (,baɪəʊ'kɛmɪstrɪ) n. the study of the chemical compounds, reactions, etc., occurring in living organisms. —**biochemical** (,baɪəʊ'kɛmɪk³l) adj. —**bio'chemist** n.

biocoenosis or U.S. **biocenosis** (,baɪəʊsiː'nəʊsɪs) n. the relationships between animals and plants subsisting together.

biodegradable (,baɪəʊdɪ'greɪdəb³l) adj. (of sewage, etc.) capable of being decomposed by natural means.

bioengineering (,baɪəʊ,ɛndʒɪ'nɪərɪŋ) n. the design and manufacture of aids, such as artificial limbs, to help people with disabilities.

biogenesis (,baɪəʊ'dʒɛnɪsɪs) n. the principle that a living organism must originate from a parent organism similar to itself.

biography (baɪ'ɒgrəfɪ) n., pl. **-phies. 1.** an account of a person's life by another. **2.** such accounts collectively. —**bi'ographer** n. —**biographical** (,baɪə'græfɪk³l) adj.

biol. 1. biological. **2.** biology.

biological (,baɪə'lɒdʒɪk³l) adj. of or relating to biology. —,**bio'logically** adv.

biological clock n. an inherent timing mechanism that controls the rhythmic repetition of processes in living organisms.

biological control n. the control of destructive organisms, esp. by nonchemical means, such as introducing a natural predator of the pest.

biological warfare n. the use of living organisms or their toxic products to induce death or incapacity in humans.

biology (baɪ'ɒlədʒɪ) n. the study of living organisms. —**bi'ologist** n.

biomedicine (,baɪəʊ'mɛdɪsɪn) n. the medical and biological study of the effects of unusual environmental stress.

bionic (baɪ'ɒnɪk) adj. **1.** of or relating to bionics. **2.** (in science fiction) having physical functions augmented by electronic equipment.

bionics (baɪ'ɒnɪks) n. (functioning as sing.) **1.** the study of biological functions in order to develop electronic equipment that operates similarly. **2.** the replacement of limbs or body parts by artificial electronically powered parts.

biophysics (,baɪəʊ'fɪzɪks) n. (functioning as sing.) the physics of biological processes and the application of methods used in physics to biology. —,**bio'physical** adj. —**biophysicist** (,baɪəʊ'fɪzɪsɪst) n.

biopic ('baɪəʊ,pɪk) n. Informal. a film based on the life of a famous person.

biopsy ('baɪɒpsɪ) n., pl. **-sies.** examination of tissue from a living body to determine the cause or extent of a disease.

biorhythm ('baɪəʊ,rɪðəm) n. a complex recurring pattern of physiological states, believed to affect physical, emotional, and mental states.

bioscope ('baɪə,skəʊp) n. **1.** a kind of early film projector. **2.** S. African. a cinema.

biosphere ('baɪə,sfɪə) n. the part of the earth's surface and atmosphere inhabited by living things.

biosynthesis (,baɪəʊ'sɪnθɪsɪs) n. the formation of complex compounds by living organisms. —**biosynthetic** (,baɪəʊsɪn'θɛtɪk) adj.

biotin ('baɪətɪn) n. a vitamin of the B complex, abundant in egg yolk and liver.

bipartisan (,baɪpɑːtɪ'zæn, baɪ'pɑːtɪ,zæn) adj. consisting of or supported by two political parties.

bipartite (baɪ'pɑːtaɪt) adj. **1.** consisting of or having two parts. **2.** affecting or made by two parties: a bipartite agreement.

biped ('baɪpɛd) n. **1.** any animal with two feet. ~adj. also **bipedal** (baɪ'piːd³l, -'pɛd³l). **2.** having two feet.

biplane ('baɪ,pleɪn) n. an aeroplane with two sets of wings, one above the other.

bipolar (baɪ'pəʊlə) adj. **1.** having two poles. **2.** having two extremes. —,**bipo'larity** n.

birch (bɜːtʃ) *n.* **1.** a tree with thin peeling bark and hard close-grained wood. **2. the birch.** a bundle of birch twigs or a birch rod used, esp. formerly, for flogging offenders. ~*vb.* **3.** to flog with a birch.

bird (bɜːd) *n.* **1.** an egg-laying vertebrate with feathers and wings. **2.** *Informal.* a person: *he's a rare bird.* **3.** *Slang, chiefly Brit.* a girl or young woman. **4. a bird in the hand.** something definite or certain. **5. birds of a feather.** people with the same ideas or interests. **6. kill two birds with one stone.** to accomplish two things with one action.

birdie (ˈbɜːdɪ) *n.* **1.** *Informal.* a bird. **2.** *Golf.* a score of one stroke under par for a hole.

birdlime (ˈbɜːd,laɪm) *n.* a sticky substance smeared on twigs to catch small birds.

bird of paradise *n.* a songbird of New Guinea, the male of which has brilliantly coloured plumage.

bird of passage *n.* **1.** a bird that migrates seasonally. **2.** a person who travels about constantly.

bird of prey *n.* a bird, such as a hawk or owl, that hunts other animals for food.

birdseed (ˈbɜːd,siːd) *n.* a mixture of various kinds of seeds for feeding caged birds.

bird's-eye view *n.* **1.** a view seen from above. **2.** a general or overall impression of something.

bird-watcher *n.* a person who studies wild birds in their natural surroundings.

biretta (bɪˈrɛtə) *n.* *R.C. Church.* a stiff square clerical cap.

Biro (ˈbaɪrəʊ) *n., pl.* **-ros.** *Trademark, Brit.* a kind of ballpoint pen.

birth (bɜːθ) *n.* **1.** the process of bearing young; childbirth. **2.** the act of being born. **3.** the beginning of something; origin. **4.** ancestry: *of high birth.* **5. give birth to. a.** to bear (offspring). **b.** to produce or originate (an idea, plan, etc.).

birth certificate *n.* an official form stating the time and place of a person's birth.

birth control *n.* limitation of childbearing by means of contraception.

birthday (ˈbɜːθ,deɪ) *n.* **1.** an anniversary of the day of one's birth. **2.** the day on which a person was born.

birthmark (ˈbɜːθ,mɑːk) *n.* a blemish on the skin formed before birth.

birthplace (ˈbɜːθ,pleɪs) *n.* the place where someone was born or where something originated.

birth rate *n.* the ratio of live births to population, usually expressed per 1000 population per year.

birthright (ˈbɜːθ,raɪt) *n.* privileges or possessions that a person has or is believed to be entitled to as soon as he is born.

biscuit (ˈbɪskɪt) *n.* **1.** *Brit.* a small flat dry sweet or plain cake of many varieties. **2.** porcelain that has been fired but not glazed. ~*adj.* **3.** pale brown or yellowish-grey.

bisect (baɪˈsɛkt) *vb.* **1.** *Maths.* to divide into two equal parts. **2.** to cut or split into two. —**bisection** (baɪˈsɛkʃən) *n.*

bisexual (baɪˈsɛksjʊəl) *adj.* **1.** sexually attracted by both men and women. **2.** showing characteristics of both sexes. ~*n.* **3.** a bisexual person. —**bisexuality** (baɪˌsɛksjʊˈælɪtɪ) *n.*

bishop (ˈbɪʃəp) *n.* **1.** a clergyman having spiritual and administrative powers over a diocese. **2.** a chesspiece capable of moving diagonally.

bishopric (ˈbɪʃəprɪk) *n.* the see, diocese, or office of a bishop.

bismuth (ˈbɪzməθ) *n.* a brittle pinkish-white metallic element. Some compounds are used in alloys and in medicine. Symbol: Bi

bison (ˈbaɪsᵊn) *n., pl.* **-son.** an animal of the cattle family with a massive head, shaggy forequarters, and a humped back, formerly very common in North America and Europe.

bisque[1] (bɪsk) *n.* a thick rich soup made from shellfish.

bisque[2] (bɪsk) *adj.* **1.** pink-to-yellowish-tan. ~*n.* **2.** *Ceramics.* same as **biscuit** (sense 2).

bistre *or U.S.* **bister** (ˈbɪstə) *n.* a brownish-yellow pigment made by boiling the soot of wood.

bistro (ˈbiːstrəʊ) *n., pl.* **-tros.** a small restaurant.

bit[1] (bɪt) *n.* **1.** a small piece, portion, or quantity. **2.** a short time or distance. **3.** a small coin. **4.** same as **bit part.** **5. a bit.** rather; somewhat: *a bit dreary.* **6. a bit of.** rather: *a bit of a dope.* **7. bit by bit.** gradually. **8. do one's bit.** to make one's expected contribution.

bit[2] (bɪt) *n.* **1.** a metal mouthpiece on a bridle for controlling a horse. **2.** a cutting or drilling tool, part, or head in a brace, drill, etc.

bit[3] (bɪt) *vb.* the past tense of **bite.**

bit[4] (bɪt) *n.* *Maths, computers.* **1.** a single digit of binary notation, represented either by 0 or by 1. **2.** the smallest unit of information, indicating the presence or absence of a single feature.

bitch (bɪtʃ) *n.* **1.** a female dog, fox, or wolf. **2.** *Slang, offensive.* a malicious or spiteful woman. **3.** *Informal.* a difficult situation or problem. ~*vb.* **4.** *Informal.* to complain; grumble.

bitchy (ˈbɪtʃɪ) *adj.* **bitchier, bitchiest.** *Informal.* spiteful or malicious. —**ˈbitchiness** *n.*

bite (baɪt) *vb.* **biting, bit, bitten.** **1.** to grip, cut off, or tear as with the teeth or jaws. **2.** (of animals, insects, etc.) to injure by puncturing (the skin) with the teeth, fangs, etc. **3.** (of corrosive material) to eat away or into. **4.** to smart or cause to smart; sting. **5.** *Angling.* (of a fish) to take or attempt to take the bait or lure. **6.** to take firm hold of or act effectively upon: *turn the screw till it bites the wood.* **7.** *Slang.* to annoy or worry: *what's biting her?* ~*n.* **8.** the act of biting. **9.** a thing or amount bitten off. **10.** a wound or sting inflicted by biting. **11.** *Angling.* an attempt by a fish to take the bait or lure. **12.** a snack. **13.** a stinging or smarting sensation. —'**biter** *n.*

biting ('baɪtɪŋ) *adj.* **1.** piercing; keen: *a biting wind.* **2.** sarcastic; incisive.

bit part *n.* a very small acting role with few lines to speak.

bitten ('bɪt²n) *vb.* the past participle of **bite.**

bitter ('bɪtə) *adj.* **1.** having an unpalatable harsh taste, as the peel of an orange. **2.** showing or caused by hostility or resentment. **3.** difficult to accept: *a bitter blow.* **4.** sarcastic: *bitter words.* **5.** bitingly cold: *a bitter night.* ~*n.* **6.** *Brit.* draught beer with a slightly bitter taste. —'**bitterly** *adv.* —'**bitterness** *n.*

bittern ('bɪtən) *n.* a large wading marsh bird with a booming call.

bitters ('bɪtəz) *pl. n.* bitter-tasting spirits flavoured with plant extracts.

bittersweet ('bɪtə,swiːt) *n.* **1.** same as **woody nightshade.** ~*adj.* **2.** tasting of or being a mixture of bitterness and sweetness. **3.** pleasant but tinged with sadness.

bitty ('bɪtɪ) *adj.* **-tier, -tiest.** lacking unity; disjointed.

bitumen ('bɪtjʊmɪn) *n.* a sticky or solid impure mixture of hydrocarbons that occurs naturally in asphalt and tar and is used in road surfacing. —**bituminous** (bɪ'tjuːmɪnəs) *adj.*

bituminous coal *n.* a soft black coal that burns with a smoky yellow flame.

bivalent (baɪ'veɪlənt, 'bɪvə-) *adj. Chem.* same as **divalent.** —**bi'valency** *n.*

bivalve ('baɪ,vælv) *n.* **1.** a marine mollusc, such as the oyster or mussel, with a shell consisting of two hinged valves, and gills for respiration. ~*adj.* **2.** of these molluscs.

bivouac ('bɪvʊ,æk, 'bɪvwæk) *n.* **1.** a temporary encampment, as used by soldiers, mountaineers, etc. ~*vb.* **-acking, -acked. 2.** to make such an encampment.

biz (bɪz) *n. Informal.* business.

bizarre (bɪ'zɑː) *adj.* odd or unusual, esp. in an interesting or amusing way.

bk 1. bank. **2.** book.

Bk *Chem.* berkelium.

BL 1. Bachelor of Law. **2.** Bachelor of Letters. **3.** Barrister-at-Law.

blab (blæb) *vb.* **blabbing, blabbed. 1.** to divulge (secrets, etc.) indiscreetly. **2.** to chatter thoughtlessly; prattle.

blabber ('blæbə) *n.* **1.** a person who blabs. ~*vb.* **2.** to talk without thinking; chatter.

black (blæk) *adj.* **1.** of the colour of jet or carbon black. **2.** without light. **3.** without hope; gloomy: *the future looked black.* **4.** dirty or soiled. **5.** angry or resentful: *black looks.* **6.** unpleasant in a cynical or macabre manner: *black comedy.* **7.** (of coffee or tea) without milk or cream. **8.** wicked or harmful: *a black lie.* **9.** *Brit.* (of goods, works, etc.) being subject to boycott by trade unionists. ~*n.* **10.** a black colour. **11.** a dye or pigment producing this colour. **12.** black clothing, worn esp. in mourning. **13.** complete darkness: *the black of the night.* **14. in the black.** in credit or without debt. ~*vb.* **15.** same as **blacken. 16.** to polish (shoes, etc.) with blacking. **17.** *Brit., Austral., & N.Z.* (of trade unionists) to organize a boycott of (specified goods, work, etc.). ~See also **blackout.** —'**blackness** *n.*

Black (blæk) *n.* **1.** a member of a dark-skinned race, esp. a Negro. ~*adj.* **2.** of or relating to a Black or Blacks.

blackamoor ('blækə,mʊə, -,mɔː) *n. Archaic.* a Negro or other person with dark skin.

black-and-blue *adj.* (of the skin) bruised, as from a beating.

black-and-white *n.* **1.** a photograph, film, etc. in black, white, and shades of grey, rather than in colour. **2. in black and white. a.** in print or writing. **b.** in extremes: *she tends to see things in black and white.*

black art *n.* **the.** same as **black magic.**

black-backed gull *n.* a large common black-and-white European coastal gull.

blackball ('blæk,bɔːl) *n.* **1.** a negative vote or veto. ~*vb.* **2.** to vote against. **3.** to exclude (someone) from a group, etc.

black bear *n.* **1.** a bear inhabiting forests of North America. **2.** a bear of central and E Asia.

black belt *n. Judo, karate, etc.* **a.** a black belt worn by an instructor or expert. **b.** a person entitled to wear this.

blackberry ('blækbərɪ) *n., pl.* **-ries.** a small blackish edible fruit that grows on a woody bush with thorny stems. Also called: **bramble.**

blackbird ('blæk,bɜːd) *n.* a common European thrush the male of which has black plumage and a yellow bill.

blackboard ('blæk,bɔːd) *n.* a hard black or dark-coloured surface used for writing or drawing on with chalk, esp. in teaching.

black box *n. Informal.* a flight recorder.

blackcap ('blæk,kæp) *n.* a brownish-grey warbler, the male of which has a black crown.

blackcock ('blæk,kɒk) *n.* the male of the black grouse.

Black Country *n.* **the.** the heavily industrialized West Midlands of England.

blackcurrant (,blæk'kʌrənt) *n.* a small

blackish edible fruit that grows in bunches on a bush.

blackdamp ('blæk,dæmp) n. air that is low in oxygen content and high in carbon dioxide as a result of an explosion in a mine.

Black Death n. **the.** a form of bubonic plague in Europe and Asia during the 14th century.

black economy n. that portion of the income of a nation that remains illegally undeclared.

blacken ('blækən) vb. **1.** to make or become black or dirty. **2.** to defame; slander.

black eye n. bruising round the eye.

black flag n. same as **Jolly Roger.**

Black Friar n. a Dominican friar.

blackguard ('blægɑːd, -gəd) n. an unprincipled contemptible person.

blackhead ('blæk,hɛd) n. **1.** a black-tipped plug of fatty matter clogging a pore of the skin. **2.** a bird with black plumage on the head.

black hole n. Astron. a hypothetical region of space resulting from the collapse of a star and surrounded by a gravitational field from which neither matter nor radiation can escape.

black ice n. a thin transparent layer of new ice on a road.

blacking ('blækɪŋ) n. any preparation for giving a black finish to shoes, metals, etc.

blackjack[1] ('blæk,dʒæk) n. Chiefly U.S. & Canad. a truncheon of leather-covered lead with a flexible shaft.

blackjack[2] ('blæk,dʒæk) n. pontoon or a similar card game.

black lead (lɛd) n. same as **graphite.**

blackleg ('blæklɛg) n. **1.** Brit. a person who continues to work or does another's job during a strike. ~vb. **-legging, -legged. 2.** Brit. to refuse to join a strike.

blacklist ('blæk,lɪst) n. **1.** a list of persons or organizations considered untrustworthy, disloyal, etc. ~vb. **2.** to put (someone) on a blacklist.

black magic n. magic used for evil purposes.

blackmail ('blæk,meɪl) n. **1.** the act of attempting to obtain money by threatening to disclose discreditable information. **2.** the exertion of unfair pressure in an attempt to influence someone. ~vb. **3.** to obtain or attempt to obtain money from (a person) by intimidation. **4.** to attempt to influence (a person) by unfair pressure. —'**black,mailer** n.

Black Maria (mə'raɪə) n. a police van for transporting prisoners.

black mark n. an indication of disapproval, failure, etc.

black market n. a place or a system for buying or selling goods or currencies illegal-

ly, esp. in violation of controls or rationing. —**black marketeer** n.

black mass n. a blasphemous travesty of the Christian Mass, used in black magic.

blackout ('blæk,aʊt) n. **1.** the extinguishing or hiding of all artificial light as a precaution against a night air attack. **2.** a momentary loss of consciousness, vision, or memory. **3.** a temporary electrical power failure. **4.** the suspension of the broadcasting of information: a news blackout. ~vb. **black out. 5.** to extinguish (lights). **6.** to lose vision, consciousness, or memory temporarily. **7.** to stop (news, a television programme, etc.) from being broadcast.

black pepper n. a hot seasoning made by grinding the dried berries and husks of the pepper plant.

Black Power n. a movement of Black people to obtain equality with Whites.

black pudding n. a black sausage made from pig's blood, suet, etc.

Black Rod n. (in Britain) the chief usher of the House of Lords and of the Order of the Garter.

black sheep n. a person who is regarded as a disgrace or failure by his family or peer group.

Blackshirt ('blæk,ʃɜːt) n. a member of the Italian Fascist party before and during World War II.

blacksmith ('blæk,smɪθ) n. a smith who works iron with a furnace, anvil, hammer, etc.

black spot n. **1.** a place on a road where accidents frequently occur. **2.** an area where a particular situation is exceptionally bad: an unemployment black spot.

black tea n. tea made from fermented tea leaves.

blackthorn ('blæk,θɔːn) n. a thorny shrub with black twigs, white flowers, and small sour plumlike fruits.

black tie n. **1.** a black bow tie worn with a dinner jacket. **2.** (modifier) denoting an occasion when a dinner jacket should be worn.

black velvet n. a mixture of stout and champagne in equal proportions.

Black Watch n. **the.** the Royal Highland Regiment in the British Army.

black widow n. an American spider the female of which is highly venomous and commonly eats its mate.

bladder ('blædə) n. **1.** Anat. a membranous sac, usually containing liquid, esp. the urinary bladder. **2.** a hollow bag made of leather, etc., which becomes round when filled with air or liquid. **3.** a hollow saclike part in certain plants, such as seaweed. —'**bladdery** adj.

blade (bleɪd) n. **1.** the part of a sharp weapon, tool, etc., that forms the cutting edge. **2.** the thin flattish part of a propeller, oar, etc. **3.** the flattened part of a leaf, sepal, or petal. **4.** the long narrow leaf of a grass or related plant.

blaeberry ('bleɪbərɪ) *n.*, *pl.* **-ries.** *Brit.* same as **whortleberry.**

blain (bleɪn) *n.* a blister, blotch, or sore on the skin.

blame (bleɪm) *n.* **1.** responsibility for something that is wrong. **2.** an expression of condemnation. ~*vb.* **3.** to consider (someone) responsible for: *I blame him for the failure.* **4.** (foll. by *on*) to put responsibility for (something) on (someone): *I blame the failure on him.* **5.** to find fault with. **6. be to blame.** to be at fault. —**blamable** *or* **blameable** *adj.* —**blameless** *adj.*

blameworthy ('bleɪm,wɜːðɪ) *adj.* deserving censure. —**blame,worthiness** *n.*

blanch (blɑːntʃ) *vb.* **1.** to whiten. **2.** to become pale, as with sickness or fear. **3.** to prepare (meat, vegetables, etc.) by plunging them in boiling water. **4.** to cause (celery, chicory, etc.) to grow white from lack of light.

blancmange (blə'mɒnʒ) *n.* a jelly-like dessert of milk, stiffened usually with cornflour.

bland (blænd) *adj.* **1.** dull and uninteresting. **2.** gentle and agreeable; suave. —**blandly** *adv.*

blandish ('blændɪʃ) *vb.* to persuade by mild flattery; coax.

blandishments ('blændɪʃmənts) *pl. n.* flattery intended to coax or cajole.

blank (blæŋk) *adj.* **1.** (of a writing surface) not written on. **2.** (of a form, etc.) with spaces left for details to be filled in. **3.** without ornament or break: *a blank wall.* **4.** not filled in; empty. **5.** showing no interest or expression: *a blank look.* **6.** devoid of ideas or inspiration: *his mind went blank.* ~*n.* **7.** an empty space. **8.** an empty space for writing in. **9.** a printed form containing such empty spaces. **10.** something characterized by incomprehension: *my mind went a complete blank.* **11.** a mark, often a dash, in place of a word. **12.** same as **blank cartridge. 13. draw a blank.** to get no results from something. ~*vb.* **14.** (foll. by *out*) to cross out, blot, or obscure. —**blankly** *adv.*

blank cartridge *n.* a cartridge containing powder but no bullet.

blank cheque *n.* **1.** a signed cheque on which the amount payable has not been specified. **2.** complete freedom of action.

blanket ('blæŋkɪt) *n.* **1.** a large piece of thick cloth for use as a bed covering. **2.** a concealing cover, as of smoke, leaves, or snow. **3.** (*modifier*) applying to or covering a wide group or variety of people, conditions, situations, etc.: *blanket insurance against loss, injury, and theft.* ~*vb.* **4.** to cover as with a blanket. **5.** to cover a wide area; give blanket coverage to.

blanket stitch *n.* a strong reinforcing stitch for the edges of blankets.

blank verse *n.* unrhymed verse.

blare (blɛə) *vb.* **1.** to sound loudly and harshly. **2.** to proclaim loudly. ~*n.* **3.** a loud harsh noise.

blarney ('blɑːnɪ) *n.* **1.** flattering talk. ~*vb.* **2.** to cajole with flattery; wheedle.

blasé ('blɑːzeɪ) *adj.* indifferent or bored, esp. through familiarity.

blaspheme (blæs'fiːm) *vb.* **1.** to speak disrespectfully of (God or sacred things). **2.** to utter curses. —**blas'phemer** *n.*

blasphemy ('blæsfɪmɪ) *n.*, *pl.* **-mies.** behaviour or language that shows disrespect for God or sacred things. —**blasphemous** *adj.*

blast (blɑːst) *n.* **1.** an explosion, as of dynamite. **2.** the charge used in a single explosion. **3.** a sudden strong gust of wind or air. **4.** a sudden loud sound, as of a trumpet. **5.** a violent verbal outburst, as of criticism. **6.** (**at**) **full blast.** at maximum speed, volume, etc. ~*interj.* **7.** *Slang.* an exclamation of annoyance. ~*vb.* **8.** to blow up (a rock, tunnel, etc.) with explosives. **9.** to make or cause to make a loud harsh noise. **10.** to criticize severely.

blasted ('blɑːstɪd) *adj.*, *adv. Slang.* extreme or extremely: *a blasted idiot.*

blast furnace *n.* a furnace for smelting into which a blast of preheated air is forced.

blastoff ('blɑːst,ɒf) *n.* **1.** the launching of a rocket under its own power. ~*vb.* **blast off. 2.** to be launched.

blatant ('bleɪtᵊnt) *adj.* **1.** glaringly conspicuous or obvious: *a blatant lie.* **2.** offensively noticeable; obtrusive. —**blatantly** *adv.*

blather ('blæðə) *vb.*, *n.* same as **blether.**

blaze[1] (bleɪz) *n.* **1.** a strong fire or flame. **2.** a very bright light or glare. **3.** an outburst (of passion, patriotism, etc.). ~*vb.* **4.** to burn fiercely. **5.** to shine brightly. **6.** to become stirred, as with anger or excitement. **7. blaze away.** to shoot continuously. ~See also **blazes.**

blaze[2] (bleɪz) *n.* **1.** a mark, usually indicating a path, made on a tree. **2.** a light-coloured marking on the face of an animal. ~*vb.* **3.** to mark (a tree, path, etc.) with a blaze. **4. blaze a trail.** to explore new territories, areas of knowledge, etc.

blaze[3] (bleɪz) *vb.* **blaze something abroad.** to make something widely known.

blazer ('bleɪzə) *n.* a fairly lightweight jacket, often in the colours of a sports club, school, etc.

blazes ('bleɪzɪz) *pl. n. Slang, euphemistic.* hell.

blazon ('bleɪzᵊn) *vb.* **1.** to proclaim publicly. **2.** *Heraldry.* to describe or colour (heraldic arms) conventionally. ~*n.* **3.** *Heraldry.* a coat of arms.

bleach (bliːtʃ) *vb.* **1.** to make or become white or colourless, as by exposure to sunlight, by the action of chemical agents, etc. ~*n.* **2.** a bleaching agent.

bleaching powder *n.* a white powder consisting of chlorinated calcium hydroxide.

bleak (bliːk) *adj.* **1.** exposed and barren. **2.** cold and raw. **3.** offering little hope; dismal: *a bleak future.*

bleary (ˈblɪərɪ) *adj.* **blearier, bleariest. 1.** with eyes dimmed, as by tears or tiredness. **2.** indistinct or unclear. —ˈ**blearily** *adv.*

bleary-eyed *or* **blear-eyed** *adj.* with eyes blurred, as with old age or after waking.

bleat (bliːt) *vb.* **1.** (of a sheep, goat, or calf) to utter its plaintive cry. **2.** to whine. ~*n.* **3.** the characteristic cry of sheep, goats, and calves. **4.** a weak complaint or whine.

bleed (bliːd) *vb.* **bleeding, bled** (blɛd). **1.** to lose or emit blood. **2.** to remove or draw blood from (a person or animal). **3.** (of plants) to exude (sap or resin), esp. from a cut. **4.** *Informal.* to obtain money, etc., from (someone), esp. by extortion. **5.** to draw liquid or gas from (a container or enclosed system). **6. my heart bleeds for you.** I am sorry for you: often used ironically.

bleeding (ˈbliːdɪŋ) *adj., adv. Brit. slang.* extreme or extremely: *a bleeding fool.*

bleep (bliːp) *n.* **1.** a short high-pitched signal made by an electronic apparatus. **2.** same as **bleeper.** ~*vb.* **3.** to make a bleeping signal. **4.** to call (somebody) by means of a bleeper.

bleeper (ˈbliːpə) *n.* a small portable radio receiver that makes a bleeping signal.

blemish (ˈblɛmɪʃ) *n.* **1.** a defect; flaw; stain. ~*vb.* **2.** to spoil or tarnish.

blench (blɛntʃ) *vb.* to shy away, as in fear; quail.

blend (blɛnd) *vb.* **1.** to mix or mingle (components). **2.** to mix (different varieties of tea, whisky, etc.). **3.** to look good together; harmonize. **4.** (esp. of colours) to shade gradually into each other. ~*n.* **5.** a mixture produced by blending.

blende (blɛnd) *n.* a mineral consisting mainly of zinc sulphide: the chief source of zinc.

blender (ˈblɛndə) *n.* an electrical kitchen appliance for puréeing vegetables, etc.

blenny (ˈblɛnɪ) *n., pl.* **-nies.** a small fish of coastal waters with a tapering scaleless body and long fins.

blesbok *or* **blesbuck** (ˈblɛsˌbʌk) *n., pl.* **-boks, -bok** *or* **-bucks, -buck.** an antelope of southern Africa with a reddish-brown coat and lyre-shaped horns.

bless (blɛs) *vb.* **blessing, blessed** *or* **blest. 1.** to make holy by means of a religious rite. **2.** to give honour or glory to (a person or thing) as holy. **3.** to call upon God to protect. **4.** to worship or adore (God). **5.** (*usually passive*) to endow with health, happiness, a talent, beauty, etc.: *blessed with immense energy.* **6. bless me!** an exclamation of surprise. **7. bless you!** said to a person who has just sneezed.

blessed (ˈblɛsɪd, blɛst) *adj.* **1.** made holy. **2.** *R.C. Church.* (of a person) beatified by the pope. **3.** bringing great happiness or good fortune. **4.** (blɛst). *Euphemistic.* damned: *I'm blessed if I know.*

blessing (ˈblɛsɪŋ) *n.* **1.** the act of invoking divine protection or aid. **2.** a short prayer before or after a meal. **3.** approval; good wishes. **4.** a happy event.

blest (blɛst) *vb.* a past of **bless.**

blether (ˈblɛðə) *Scot.* ~*vb.* **1.** to speak foolishly. ~*n.* **2.** foolish talk; nonsense.

blew (bluː) *vb.* the past tense of **blow.**

blight (blaɪt) *n.* **1.** any plant disease characterized by withering and shrivelling without rotting. **2.** a fungus, insect, etc., that causes blight in plants. **3.** a person or thing that spoils or prevents growth. **4.** an ugly urban district. ~*vb.* **5.** to cause to suffer a blight. **6.** to frustrate or disappoint. **7.** to destroy.

blighter (ˈblaɪtə) *n. Brit. informal.* a despicable or irritating person or thing.

Blighty (ˈblaɪtɪ) *n. Brit. slang.* (used esp. by troops serving abroad) **1.** Britain; home. **2.** (*pl.* **Blighties**) (esp. in World War I) a wound that causes the recipient to be sent home to Britain.

blimey (ˈblaɪmɪ) *interj. Brit. slang.* an exclamation of surprise or annoyance.

blimp[1] (blɪmp) *n.* **1.** a small nonrigid airship. **2.** *Films.* a soundproof cover fixed over a camera during shooting.

blimp[2] (blɪmp) *n. Chiefly Brit.* a person who is stupidly complacent and reactionary. Also called: **Colonel Blimp.**

blind (blaɪnd) *adj.* **1.** unable to see. **2.** unable or unwilling to understand: *he is blind to her faults.* **3.** not determined by reason: *blind hatred.* **4.** acting or performed without control or preparation. **5.** done without being able to see, relying on instruments for information. **6.** hidden from sight: *a blind corner.* **7.** closed at one end: *a blind alley.* **8.** completely lacking awareness or consciousness: *a blind stupor.* **9.** having no openings: *a blind wall.* ~*adv.* **10.** without being able to see ahead or using only instruments: *flying blind.* **11.** without adequate information: *to buy a house blind.* **12. blind drunk.** *Informal.* very drunk. ~*vb.* **13.** to deprive of sight permanently or temporarily. **14.** to deprive of good sense, reason, or judgment. **15.** to darken;

conceal. **16.** to overwhelm by showing detailed knowledge: *to blind somebody with science.* ~*n.* **17.** a shade for a window, sometimes on a roller. **18.** any obstruction or hindrance to sight, light, or air. **19.** a person, action, or thing that serves to deceive or conceal the truth. —'**blinding** *adj.* —'**blindly** *adv.* —'**blindness** *n.*

blind alley *n.* **1.** an alley open at one end only. **2.** *Informal.* a situation in which no further progress can be made.

blind date *n. Informal.* a date, arranged by a third person, between two people who have not met before.

blindfold ('blaɪnd,fəʊld) *vb.* **1.** to prevent (a person or animal) from seeing by covering the eyes. ~*n.* **2.** a piece of cloth used to cover the eyes. ~*adj., adv.* **3.** having the eyes covered with a cloth.

blind man's buff *n.* a game in which a blindfolded person tries to catch and identify the other players.

blind spot *n.* **1.** a small oval-shaped area of the retina in which vision is not experienced. **2.** a place where vision is obscured. **3.** a subject about which a person is ignorant or prejudiced.

blindworm ('blaɪnd,wɜːm) *n.* same as **slowworm.**

blink (blɪŋk) *vb.* **1.** to close and immediately reopen (the eyes or an eye), usually involuntarily. **2.** to shine intermittently or unsteadily. ~*n.* **3.** the act or an instance of blinking. **4.** a glance; glimpse. **5. on the blink.** *Slang.* not working properly.

blinker ('blɪŋkə) *vb.* **1.** to provide (a horse) with blinkers. **2.** to obscure or be obscured with or as with blinkers. —'**blinkered** *adj.*

blinkers ('blɪŋkəz) *pl. n. Chiefly Brit.* leather sidepieces attached to a horse's bridle to prevent sideways vision.

blinking ('blɪŋkɪŋ) *adj., adv. Informal.* extreme or extremely: *a blinking idiot.*

blip (blɪp) *n.* **1.** a repetitive sound, such as that produced by an electronic device. **2.** the spot of light on a radar screen indicating the position of an object.

bliss (blɪs) *n.* **1.** perfect happiness; serene joy. **2.** the joy of heaven. —'**blissful** *adj.* —'**blissfully** *adv.*

blister ('blɪstə) *n.* **1.** a small bubble on the skin filled with a watery fluid, caused by a burn, mechanical irritation, etc. **2.** a swelling containing air or liquid, as on a painted surface. ~*vb.* **3.** to have or cause to have blisters. **4.** to attack verbally with great scorn. —'**blistering** *adj.*

blithe (blaɪð) *adj.* **1.** heedless; casual and indifferent. **2.** very happy or cheerful. —'**blithely** *adv.*

blithering ('blɪðərɪŋ) *adj. Informal.* stupid; foolish: *you blithering idiot.*

BLitt Bachelor of Letters.

blitz (blɪts) *n.* **1.** a violent and sustained

attack by enemy aircraft. **2.** any intensive attack or concerted effort. ~*vb.* **3.** to attack suddenly and intensively.

Blitz (blɪts) *n.* **the.** the systematic bombing of Britain in 1940–41 by the German Air Force.

blitzkrieg ('blɪts,kriːg) *n.* a swift intensive military attack designed to defeat the opposition quickly.

blizzard ('blɪzəd) *n.* a strong wind accompanied by heavy snowfall.

bloat (bləʊt) *vb.* **1.** to cause to swell, as with a liquid or air. **2.** to cause to be puffed up, as with conceit. **3.** to cure (fish, esp. herring) by half drying in smoke. —'**bloated** *adj.*

bloater ('bləʊtə) *n.* a herring that has been salted in brine, smoked, and cured.

blob (blɒb) *n.* **1.** a soft mass or drop. **2.** a spot of colour, ink, etc. **3.** an indistinct or shapeless form or object.

bloc (blɒk) *n.* a group of people or countries combined by a common interest.

block (blɒk) *n.* **1.** a large solid piece of wood, stone, etc. **2.** such a piece on which particular tasks may be done, as chopping, cutting, etc. **3.** one of a set of wooden or plastic cubes as a child's toy. **4.** *Slang.* a person's head. **5.** a large building of offices, flats, etc. **6.** a group of buildings in a city bounded by intersecting streets on each side. **7.** *N.Z.* an area of bush reserved by licence for a trapper or hunter. **8.** a piece of wood, metal, etc., engraved for printing. **9.** a casing housing one or more freely rotating pulleys. See also **block and tackle.** **10.** an obstruction or hindrance. **11. a.** a quantity considered as a single unit **b.** (*as modifier*): *a block booking.* ~*vb.* **12.** to obstruct or impede by introducing an obstacle: *to block the traffic; to block up a pipe.* **13.** to impede, retard, or prevent (an action, procedure, etc.). **14.** to stamp (a title, design, etc.) on (a book cover, etc.). **15.** *Cricket.* to play (a ball) defensively. ~See also **block out.** —'**blockage** *n.*

blockade (blɒ'keɪd) *n.* **1.** *Mil.* the closing off of a port or region by enemy ships or other forces to prevent the passage of goods. ~*vb.* **2.** to impose a blockade on.

block and tackle *n.* a hoisting device in which a rope or chain is passed around a pair of blocks containing one or more pulleys.

blockbuster ('blɒk,bʌstə) *n. Informal.* **1.** a film, novel, etc., that has been or is expected to be highly successful. **2.** a large bomb used to demolish extensive areas.

blockhead ('blɒk,hed) *n.* a stupid person. —'**block,headed** *adj.*

blockhouse ('blɒk,haʊs) *n.* **1.** a concrete structure for defence or observation. **2.** (formerly) a wooden fortification with openings for defensive fire, observation, etc.

block letter *n.* a plain capital letter. Also called: **block capital.**

block out *vb.* **1.** to plan or describe (something) in a general fashion. **2.** to prevent the entry or consideration of (something).

bloke (bləʊk) *n. Brit. informal.* a man.

blonde *or (masc.)* **blond** (blɒnd) *adj.* **1.** (of hair) fair. **2.** (of a person) having fair hair and a light complexion. ~*n,* **3.** a person having light-coloured hair and skin. —'**blondeness** *or* '**blondness** *n.*

blood (blʌd) *n.* **1.** a reddish fluid in vertebrates that is pumped by the heart through the arteries and veins. **2.** bloodshed, esp. when resulting in murder. **3.** life itself; lifeblood. **4.** relationship through being of the same family, race, or kind; kinship. **5.** **flesh and blood. a.** near kindred or kinship, esp. that between a parent and child. **b.** human nature: *it's more than flesh and blood can stand.* **6. in one's blood.** as a natural or inherited characteristic or talent. **7. the blood.** royal or noble descent: *a prince of the blood.* **8.** people viewed as members of a group, esp. as an invigorating force: *new blood.* **9. in cold blood.** showing no passion; ruthlessly. **10. make one's blood boil.** to cause to be angry or indignant. **11. make one's blood run cold.** to fill with horror. ~*vb.* **12.** *Hunting.* to cause (young hounds) to taste the blood of a freshly killed quarry. **13.** to initiate (a person) to war or hunting.

blood-and-thunder *adj.* relating to a melodramatic adventure story.

blood bank *n.* a place where blood is stored until required for transfusion.

blood bath *n.* a massacre.

blood brother *n.* a man or boy who has sworn to treat another as his brother, often in a ceremony in which their blood is mingled.

blood count *n.* determination of the number of red and white blood corpuscles in a specific sample of blood.

bloodcurdling ('blʌd,kɜːdlɪŋ) *adj.* terrifying.

blood donor *n.* a person who gives blood to be used for transfusion.

blood group *n.* any one of the various groups into which human blood is classified.

blood heat *n.* the normal temperature of the human body, 98.4°F or 37°C.

bloodhound ('blʌd,haʊnd) *n.* a large hound, formerly used in tracking and police work.

bloodless ('blʌdlɪs) *adj.* **1.** without blood. **2.** conducted without violence: *a bloodless revolution.* **3.** anaemic-looking; pale. **4.** lacking vitality; lifeless.

blood-letting *n.* **1.** the therapeutic removal of blood. **2.** bloodshed, esp. in a feud.

blood money *n.* **1.** compensation paid to the relatives of a murdered person. **2.** money paid to a hired murderer.

blood orange *n.* a variety of orange the pulp of which is dark red when ripe.

blood poisoning *n.* same as **septicaemia.**

blood pressure *n.* the pressure exerted by the blood on the inner walls of the blood vessels.

blood relation *or* **relative** *n.* a person related to another by birth.

bloodshed ('blʌd,ʃɛd) *n.* slaughter; killing.

bloodshot ('blʌd,ʃɒt) *adj.* (of an eye) inflamed.

blood sport *n.* any sport involving the killing of an animal, esp. hunting.

bloodstained ('blʌd,steɪnd) *adj.* discoloured with blood.

bloodstock ('blʌd,stɒk) *n.* thoroughbred horses.

bloodstream ('blʌd,striːm) *n.* the flow of blood through the vessels of a living body.

bloodsucker ('blʌd,sʌkə) *n.* **1.** an animal that sucks blood, esp. a leech. **2.** *Informal.* a person who preys upon another person, esp. by extorting money.

bloodthirsty ('blʌd,θɜːstɪ) *adj.* **-thirstier, -thirstiest.** taking pleasure in bloodshed or violence.

blood vessel *n.* an artery, capillary, or vein.

bloody ('blʌdɪ) *adj.* **bloodier, bloodiest. 1.** covered with blood. **2.** marked by much killing and bloodshed: *a bloody war.* **3.** cruel or murderous: *a bloody tyrant.* ~*adv., adj.* **4.** *Slang.* extreme or extremely: *a bloody fool.* ~*vb.* **bloodying, bloodied. 5.** to stain with blood.

Bloody Mary ('mɛərɪ) *n.* a drink consisting of tomato juice and vodka.

bloody-minded *adj. Brit. informal.* deliberately obstructive and unhelpful.

bloom (bluːm) *n.* **1.** a blossom on a flowering plant. **2.** the state or period when flowers open. **3.** a healthy or flourishing condition; prime. **4.** a youthful or healthy glow. **5.** a fine whitish coating on the surface of fruits, leaves, etc. ~*vb.* **6.** (of flowers) to open. **7.** to bear flowers. **8.** to flourish or grow. **9.** to be in a healthy, glowing condition.

bloomer¹ ('bluːmə) *n. Brit. informal.* a stupid mistake; blunder.

bloomer² ('bluːmə) *n.* a medium-sized loaf with diagonal marks on top.

bloomers ('bluːməz) *pl. n.* **1.** *Informal.* women's baggy knickers. **2.** (formerly) loose trousers gathered at the knee worn by women.

blooming ('bluːmɪŋ) *adv., adj. Brit. informal.* extreme or extremely: *blooming painful.*

blossom ('blɒsəm) *n.* **1.** the flower or flowers of a plant, esp. producing edible fruit. **2.** the period of flowering. ~*vb.* **3.** (of plants) to flower. **4.** to come to a promising stage.

blot (blɒt) *n.* **1.** a stain or spot, esp. of ink. **2.** something that spoils. **3.** a stain on one's character. ~*vb.* **blotting, blotted.** **4.** to stain or spot. **5.** to cause a blemish in or on: *you've blotted your copybook by getting into a fight.* **6.** to soak up (excess ink, etc.) by using blotting paper. **7.** **blot out.** to darken or hide completely; obscure; obliterate.

blotch (blɒtʃ) *n.* **1.** an irregular spot or discoloration. ~*vb.* **2.** to become or cause to become marked by such discoloration. —'**blotchy** *adj.*

blotter ('blɒtə) *n.* a sheet of blotting paper.

blotting paper *n.* a soft absorbent unsized paper, used for soaking up surplus ink.

blotto ('blɒtəʊ) *adj. Slang.* unconscious, esp. through drunkenness.

blouse (blaʊz) *n.* **1.** a woman's shirtlike garment. **2.** a waist-length belted jacket worn by soldiers. ~*vb.* **3.** to hang or make so as to hang in full loose folds.

blouson ('bluːzɒn) *n.* a tight-waisted jacket or top that blouses out.

blow[1] (bləʊ) *vb.* **blowing, blew, blown.** **1.** (of a current of air, the wind, etc.) to be or cause to be in motion. **2.** to move or be carried by or as if by wind. **3.** to expel (cigarette smoke, etc.) through the mouth or nose. **4.** to force or cause (air, dust, etc.) to move something into, in, over, etc., by using an instrument or by expelling breath. **5.** to breathe hard; pant. **6.** to inflate with air or the breath. **7.** (of wind, etc.) to make a roaring sound. **8.** to cause (a wind instrument, whistle, etc.) to sound by forcing air into it or (of a wind instrument, whistle, etc.) to sound thus. **9.** (often foll. by *up, down, in,* etc.) to explode, break, or disintegrate completely. **10.** *Electronics.* to burn out (a fuse or valve) because of excessive current or (of a fuse or valve) to burn out. **11.** to shape (glass, etc.) by forcing air or gas through the material when molten. **12.** *Slang.* to spend (money) freely. **13.** *Slang.* to use (an opportunity) ineffectively. **14.** *Slang.* to go suddenly away (from): *it was time to blow town.* **15.** *Slang.* to expose or betray (a secret). **16.** (*past participle* **blowed**). *Informal.* same as **damn.** **17.** **blow hot and cold.** *Informal.* to keep changing one's attitude towards someone or something. **18.** **blow one's top.** *Informal.* to lose one's temper. ~*n.* **19.** the act or an instance of blowing. **20.** the sound produced by blowing. **21.** a blast of air or

wind. ~See also **blow out, blow over,** etc.

blow[2] (bləʊ) *n.* **1.** a powerful or heavy stroke with the fist, a weapon, etc. **2.** a sudden setback. **3.** **come to blows. a.** to fight. **b.** to result in a fight. **4.** an attacking action: *a blow for freedom.*

blow-by-blow *adj.* explained in great detail: *a blow-by-blow account.*

blow-dry *vb.* **-drying, -dried.** **1.** to style (the hair) while drying it with a hand-held hair dryer. ~*n.* **2.** this method of styling hair.

blower ('bləʊə) *n.* **1.** a mechanical device, such as a fan, that blows. **2.** *Informal.* a telephone.

blowfly ('bləʊ,flaɪ) *n., pl.* **-flies.** a fly that lays its eggs in meat.

blowhole ('bləʊ,həʊl) *n.* **1.** the nostril of a whale. **2.** a hole in ice through which seals, etc., breathe. **3.** a vent for air or gas.

blowlamp ('bləʊ,læmp) *n.* a small burner that produces a very hot flame, used to remove old paint, melt soft metal, etc.

blown (bləʊn) *vb.* a past participle of **blow.**

blow out *vb.* **1.** to extinguish (a flame, etc.) or (of a flame, etc.) to become extinguished. **2.** (of a tyre) to puncture suddenly. **3.** (of an oil or gas well) to lose oil or gas in an uncontrolled manner. ~*n.* **blowout.** **4.** a sudden burst in a tyre. **5.** the uncontrolled escape of oil or gas from a well. **6.** *Slang.* a large filling meal.

blow over *vb.* **1.** to be forgotten. **2.** to cease or be finished: *the storm blew over.*

blowpipe ('bləʊ,paɪp) *n.* **1.** a long tube from which pellets, poisoned darts, etc., are shot by blowing. **2.** a tube for blowing air into a flame to intensify its heat. **3.** an iron pipe used to blow glass into shape.

blow up *vb.* **1.** to explode or cause to explode. **2.** to inflate with air. **3.** to increase the importance of (something): *they blew the whole affair up.* **4.** *Informal.* to lose one's temper. **5.** *Informal.* to reprimand (someone). **6.** *Informal.* to enlarge (a photograph). **7.** to come into existence with sudden force: *a storm had blown up.* ~*n.* **blow-up.** **8.** an explosion. **9.** *Informal.* an enlarged photograph.

blowy ('bləʊɪ) *adj.* **blowier, blowiest.** windy.

blowzy *or* **blowsy** ('blaʊzɪ) *adj.* **blowzier, blowziest** *or* **blowsier, blowsiest.** (of a woman) **1.** slovenly or sluttish. **2.** ruddy in complexion.

blubber ('blʌbə) *vb.* **1.** to sob without restraint. **2.** to utter while sobbing. ~*n.* **3.** the fatty tissue of aquatic mammals such as the whale. **4.** *Informal.* flabby body fat.

bludge (blʌdʒ) *Austral. & N.Z. informal.* ~*vb.* **1.** (foll. by *on*) to scrounge (from). **2.** to evade work. ~*n.* **3.** a very easy task.

bludgeon ('blʌdʒən) *n.* **1.** a stout heavy club, typically thicker at one end. ~*vb.* **2.**

to hit as with a bludgeon. **3.** to force; bully; coerce.

blue (bluː) *n.* **1.** a colour, such as that of a clear unclouded sky or the deep sea. **2.** a dye or pigment of this colour. **3.** blue cloth or clothing: *dressed in blue.* **4.** a sportsman who represents or has represented Oxford or Cambridge University. **5.** *Brit. informal.* a Tory. **6.** *Austral. & N.Z. slang.* an argument or fight. **7.** Also: **bluey.** *Austral. & N.Z. informal.* a court summons. **8.** *Austral. & N.Z. informal.* a mistake; error. **9. out of the blue.** unexpectedly. ~*adj.* **bluer, bluest.** **10.** of the colour blue. **11.** (of the flesh) having a purple tinge, as from cold. **12.** depressed or unhappy. **13.** pornographic: *blue movies.* ~*vb.* **blueing** *or* **bluing, blued.** **14.** to make, dye, or become blue. **15.** *Slang.* to spend extravagantly or wastefully. ~See also **blues.** —**'blueness** *n.*

blue baby *n.* a baby born with a bluish tinge to the skin because of lack of oxygen in the blood.

bluebell ('bluːˌbɛl) *n.* a woodland plant with blue bell-shaped flowers.

blueberry ('bluːbərɪ, -brɪ) *n., pl.* **-ries.** a blackish edible berry that grows on a North American shrub.

bluebird ('bluːˌbɜːd) *n.* a North American songbird with a blue plumage.

blue blood *n.* royal or aristocratic descent.

bluebook ('bluːˌbʊk) *n.* **1.** (in Britain) a government publication, usually the report of a commission. **2.** (in Canada) an annual statement of government accounts.

bluebottle ('bluːˌbɒt³l) *n.* **1.** a large fly with a blue body; blowfly. **2.** *Austral. & N.Z. informal.* a Portuguese man-of-war.

blue cheese *n.* cheese containing a blue mould, esp. Stilton, Roquefort, or Danish blue.

blue chip *n.* **1.** *Finance.* a stock considered reliable. **2.** (*modifier*) denoting something considered to be a valuable asset.

blue-collar *adj.* of or designating manual industrial workers.

blue-eyed boy *n. Informal, chiefly Brit.* a favourite.

blue funk *n. Slang.* a state of great terror.

blue pencil *n.* **1.** deletion or alteration of the contents of a book or other work. ~*vb.* **blue-pencil, -cilling, -cilled** *or* *U.S.* **-ciling, -ciled.** **2.** to alter or delete parts of (a book, film, etc.).

blue peter *n.* a signal flag of blue with a white square at the centre, displayed by a vessel about to leave port.

blueprint ('bluːˌprɪnt) *n.* **1.** an original description of a plan or idea that explains how something is expected to work. **2.** a photographic print of plans, technical drawings, etc., consisting of white lines on a blue background.

blue ribbon *n.* **1.** (in Britain) a badge of blue silk worn by members of the Order of the Garter. **2.** a badge awarded as the first prize in a competition.

blues (bluːz) *pl. n.* (*sometimes functioning as sing.*) **the.** **1.** a feeling of depression or deep unhappiness. **2.** a type of folk song originating among Black Americans.

bluestocking ('bluːˌstɒkɪŋ) *n. Usually disparaging.* a scholarly or intellectual woman.

bluetit ('bluːˌtɪt) *n.* a European tit with a blue crown, wings, and tail and yellow underparts.

blue whale *n.* a very large bluish-grey whalebone whale.

bluff¹ (blʌf) *vb.* **1.** to pretend to be confident about an uncertain issue in order to influence (someone). ~*n.* **2.** deliberate deception to create the impression of a strong position. **3. call someone's bluff.** to challenge someone to give proof of his claims.

bluff² (blʌf) *n.* **1.** a steep promontory, bank, or cliff. **2.** *Canad.* a clump of trees on the prairie; copse. ~*adj.* **3.** good-naturedly frank and hearty.

bluish *or* **blueish** ('bluːɪʃ) *adj.* somewhat blue.

blunder ('blʌndə) *n.* **1.** a stupid or clumsy mistake. ~*vb.* **2.** to make stupid or clumsy mistakes. **3.** to act clumsily; stumble. —**'blundering** *n., adj.*

blunderbuss ('blʌndəˌbʌs) *n.* an obsolete short musket with large bore and flared muzzle.

blunt (blʌnt) *adj.* **1.** (esp. of a knife) lacking sharpness. **2.** not having a sharp edge or point: *a blunt instrument.* **3.** (of people, manner of speaking, etc.) straightforward and uncomplicated. ~*vb.* **4.** to make less sharp. **5.** to diminish the sensitivity or perception of. —**'bluntly** *adv.*

blur (blɜː) *vb.* **blurring, blurred.** **1.** to make or become vague or less distinct. **2.** to smear or smudge. **3.** to make (the judgment, memory, or perception) less clear; dim. ~*n.* **4.** something vague, hazy, or indistinct. **5.** a smear or smudge. —**blurred** *adj.* —**'blurry** *adj.*

blurb (blɜːb) *n.* a promotional description, as on the jackets of books.

blurt (blɜːt) *vb.* (foll. by *out*) to utter suddenly and involuntarily.

blush (blʌʃ) *vb.* **1.** to become suddenly red in the face, esp. from embarrassment or shame. ~*n.* **2.** a sudden reddening of the face, esp. from embarrassment or shame. **3.** a rosy glow.

blusher ('blʌʃə) *n.* a cosmetic applied to the cheeks to give a rosy colour.

bluster ('blʌstə) *vb.* **1.** to speak or say loudly or in a bullying way. **2.** (of the wind) to be gusty. ~*n*. **3.** empty threats or protests. —**'blustery** *adj*.

BM 1. Bachelor of Medicine. **2.** British Museum.

BMA British Medical Association.

B-movie *n*. a film originally made as a supporting film, now considered a genre in its own right.

BMus Bachelor of Music.

BMX *n*. **1.** bicycle motocross: stunt riding over an obstacle course on a bicycle. **2.** a bicycle designed for bicycle motocross.

BO 1. *Informal*. body odour. **2.** box office.

boa ('bəʊə) *n*. **1.** a large nonvenomous snake of Central and South America that kills its prey by constriction. **2.** a woman's long thin scarf, usually of feathers or fur.

boa constrictor *n*. a very large snake of tropical America and the West Indies that kills its prey by constriction.

boar (bɔː) *n*. **1.** an uncastrated male pig. **2.** a wild pig.

board (bɔːd) *n*. **1.** a long wide flat piece of sawn timber. **2.** a smaller flat piece of rigid material for a specific purpose: *ironing board*. **3.** a person's meals, provided regularly for money. **4. a.** a group of people who officially administer a company, trust, etc. **b.** any other official group, as of examiners or interviewers. **5.** stiff cardboard or similar material, used for the outside covers of a book. **6.** a flat thin rectangular sheet of composite material, such as chipboard. **7.** *Naut*. the side of a ship. **8.** a portable surface for indoor games such as chess or backgammon. **9. go by the board.** *Informal*. to be in disuse, neglected, or lost. **10. on board.** on or in a ship, aeroplane, etc. **11. the boards.** the stage. ~*vb*. **12.** to go aboard (a train or other vehicle). **13.** to attack (a ship) by forcing one's way aboard. **14.** (foll. by *up, in,* etc.) to cover with boards. **15.** to receive meals and lodging in return for money. **16. board out.** to arrange for (someone, esp. a child) to receive food and lodging away from home. **17.** (in ice hockey and box lacrosse) to bodycheck an opponent against the boards.

boarder ('bɔːdə) *n*. a pupil who lives at school during term time.

boarding ('bɔːdɪŋ) *n*. **1.** a structure of boards. **2.** timber boards collectively. **3.** the act of embarking on an aircraft, train, ship, etc. **4.** (in ice hockey and box lacrosse) an act of bodychecking an opponent against the boards.

boarding house *n*. a private house in which accommodation and meals are provided for paying guests.

boarding school *n*. a school providing living accommodation for pupils.

boardroom ('bɔːd,ruːm, -,rum) *n*. a room where the board of directors of a company meets.

boards (bɔːdz) *pl. n*. a wooden wall forming the enclosure in which ice hockey or box lacrosse is played.

boast (bəʊst) *vb*. **1.** to speak in excessively proud terms of one's possessions, superior qualities, etc. **2.** to possess (something to be proud of): *the city boasts a fine cathedral*. ~*n*. **3.** a bragging statement. **4.** something that is bragged about.

boastful ('bəʊstfʊl) *adj*. tending to boast.

boat (bəʊt) *n*. **1.** a small vessel propelled by oars, paddle, sails, or motor. **2.** *Informal*. a ship. **3.** See **gravy boat, sauce boat. 4. in the same boat.** sharing the same problems. **5. miss the boat.** to lose an opportunity. **6. rock the boat.** *Informal*. to cause a disturbance in the existing situation. ~*vb*. **7.** to travel or go in a boat, esp. as recreation.

boater ('bəʊtə) *n*. a stiff straw hat with a straight brim and flat crown.

boathouse ('bəʊt,haʊs) *n*. a shelter by the edge of a river, lake, etc., for housing boats.

boating ('bəʊtɪŋ) *n*. rowing, sailing, or cruising in boats as a form of recreation.

boatman ('bəʊtmən) *n., pl.* **-men.** a man who works on, hires out, or repairs boats.

boatswain, bo's'n, *or* **bosun** ('bəʊs°n) *n*. an officer who is responsible for the maintenance of a ship and its equipment.

boat train *n*. a train scheduled to take passengers to or from a particular ship.

bob¹ (bɒb) *vb*. **bobbing, bobbed. 1.** to move or cause to move up and down repeatedly, as while floating in water. **2.** to move or cause to move with a short abrupt movement, as of the head. **3. bob up.** to appear or emerge suddenly. ~*n*. **4.** a short abrupt movement, as of the head.

bob² (bɒb) *n*. **1.** a hairstyle in which the hair is cut short evenly all round the head. **2.** a dangling weight on a pendulum or plumb line. ~*vb*. **bobbing, bobbed. 3.** to cut (the hair) in a bob.

bob³ (bɒb) *n., pl.* **bob.** *Brit. informal.* (formerly) a shilling.

bobbejaan ('bɒbə,jɑːn) *n. S. African.* a baboon.

bobbejaan spanner *n. S. African.* a monkey wrench.

bobbin ('bɒbɪn) *n*. a reel on which thread or yarn is wound.

bobble ('bɒb°l) *n*. a tufted ball, usually for ornament, as on a knitted hat.

bobby ('bɒbɪ) *n., pl.* **-bies.** *Informal.* a British policeman.

bobby calf *n*. an unweaned calf culled for slaughter.

bobby pin *n. U.S., Canad., Austral., & N.Z.* a metal hairpin.

bobsleigh ('bɒb,sleɪ) *n*. **1.** a sledge for racing down a steeply banked ice-covered run. ~*vb*. **2.** to ride on a bobsleigh.

bobtail ('bɒb,teɪl) *n.* **1.** a docked tail. **2.** an animal with such a tail. ~*adj. also* **bobtailed. 3.** having the tail cut short.

Boche (bɒʃ) *n. Offensive slang.* a German, esp. a German soldier.

bod (bɒd) *n. Informal.* a fellow; chap: *he's a queer bod.*

bode¹ (bəʊd) *vb.* to be an omen of (good or ill, esp. ill); portend.

bode² (bəʊd) *vb.* a past tense of **bide.**

bodega (bəʊ'diːgə) *n.* a shop in a Spanish-speaking country that sells wine.

bodge (bɒdʒ) *vb. Informal.* to make a mess of; botch.

bodice ('bɒdɪs) *n.* **1.** the upper part of a woman's dress, from the shoulder to the waist. **2.** a tight-fitting corset worn laced over a blouse, or (formerly) as a woman's undergarment.

bodily ('bɒdɪlɪ) *adj.* **1.** relating to the human body. ~*adv.* **2.** by taking hold of the body: *he threw him bodily from the platform.* **3.** in person; in the flesh.

bodkin ('bɒdkɪn) *n.* a blunt large-eyed needle.

body ('bɒdɪ) *n., pl.* **bodies. 1.** the entire physical structure of an animal or human. **2.** the trunk or torso. **3.** a corpse. **4.** the flesh as opposed to the spirit. **5.** the main part of anything: *the body of a vehicle.* **6.** a separate mass of water or land. **7.** a group regarded as a single entity: *a local voluntary body.* **8.** the characteristic full quality of certain wines. **9.** a person. **10. keep body and soul together.** to manage to survive.

body building *n.* regular exercising designed to enlarge the muscles.

bodycheck ('bɒdɪ,tʃɛk) *Ice hockey, etc.* ~*n.* **1.** obstruction of another player. ~*vb.* **2.** to deliver a bodycheck to (an opponent).

bodyguard ('bɒdɪ,gɑːd) *n.* a man or group of men who escort and protect someone.

body politic *n.* **the.** the people of a nation or the nation itself considered as a political entity.

body popping *n.* a dance of the 1980s characterized by schematic rhythmic movements. —**body popper** *n.*

body shop *n.* a repair yard for vehicle bodywork.

body snatcher *n.* (formerly) a person who robbed graves and sold the corpses for dissection.

body stocking *n.* **1.** a one-piece undergarment for women, covering the torso. **2.** a tightly-fitting garment covering the whole of the body, worn esp. for dancing or exercising.

body warmer *n.* a sleeveless quilted jerkin, worn as an outer garment.

bodywork ('bɒdɪ,wɜːk) *n.* the external shell of a motor vehicle.

Boer (bʊə) *n.* a descendant of any of the Dutch or Huguenot colonists who settled in South Africa.

boerbul ('bʊəbəl) *n. S. African.* a crossbred mastiff, often used as a watchdog.

boer goat *n. S. African.* a hardy native goat.

boerperd ('bʊə,pɜːt) *n.* a rugged S African horse, often palomino.

boffin ('bɒfɪn) *n. Brit. informal.* a scientist.

bog (bɒg) *n.* **1.** a wet spongy area of land. **2.** *Slang.* a toilet. —'**boggy** *adj.* —'**bogginess** *n.*

bog down *vb.* **bogging, bogged.** to impede physically or mentally.

bogey *or* **bogy** ('bəʊgɪ) *n.* **1.** an evil or mischievous spirit. **2.** something that worries or annoys. **3.** *Golf.* **a.** a standard score for a hole or course that a good player should make. **b.** *U.S.* a score of one stroke over par on a hole. **4.** *Slang.* a piece of dried mucus from the nose.

bogeyman ('bəʊgɪ,mæn) *n., pl.* -**men.** a person, real or imaginary, used as a threat, esp. to children.

boggle ('bɒg³l) *vb.* **1.** to be surprised, confused, or alarmed: *the mind boggles.* **2.** to hesitate or be evasive when confronted with a problem.

bogie *or* **bogy** ('bəʊgɪ) *n.* an assembly of wheels forming a pivoted support at either end of a railway coach.

bog oak *n.* oak found preserved in peat bogs.

bogus ('bəʊgəs) *adj.* not genuine.

bogy ('bəʊgɪ) *n., pl.* -**gies.** same as **bogey** or **bogie.**

Bohemian (bəʊ'hiːmɪən) *n.* **1.** a person from Bohemia; Czech. **2.** a person, esp. an artist or writer, who lives an unconventional life. ~*adj.* **3.** of or relating to Bohemia or its people. **4.** unconventional in appearance, behaviour, etc. —**Bo'hemian,ism** *n.*

boil¹ (bɔɪl) *vb.* **1.** to change or cause to change from a liquid to a vapour so rapidly that bubbles of vapour are formed in the liquid. **2.** to reach or cause to reach boiling point. **3.** to cook or be cooked by the process of boiling. **4.** to bubble and be agitated like something boiling; seethe: *the ocean was boiling.* **5.** to be extremely angry. ~*n.* **6.** the state or action of boiling. ~See also **boil away, boil down, boil over.**

boil² (bɔɪl) *n.* a red painful swelling with a hard pus-filled core caused by infection of the skin.

boil away *vb.* to cause (liquid) to evaporate completely by boiling or (of liquid) to evaporate completely.

boil down *vb.* **1.** to reduce or be reduced in quantity by boiling. **2. boil down to.** to be the essential element in.

boiler ('bɔɪlə) *n.* **1.** a closed vessel in which water is heated to provide heat. **2.** a domestic device to provide hot water, esp. for central heating. **3.** a large tub for boiling laundry.

boilermaker ('bɔɪlə,meɪkə) *n.* a person who works with metal in heavy industry.

boiler suit *n. Brit.* a one-piece overall.

boiling point *n.* **1.** the temperature at which a liquid boils. **2.** *Informal.* the condition of being angered or highly excited.

boil over *vb.* **1.** to overflow or cause to overflow while boiling. **2.** to burst out in anger or excitement.

boisterous ('bɔɪstərəs, -strəs) *adj.* **1.** noisy and lively; unruly. **2.** (of the sea, etc.) turbulent or stormy.

bold (bəʊld) *adj.* **1.** courageous, confident, and fearless. **2.** immodest or impudent: *she gave him a bold look.* **3.** standing out distinctly; conspicuous: *a figure carved in bold relief.* —'**boldly** *adv.* —'**boldness** *n.*

bole (bəʊl) *n.* the trunk of a tree.

bolero (bə'lɛərəʊ) *n., pl.* **-ros. 1.** a Spanish dance, usually in triple time. **2.** music for this dance. **3.** (*also* 'bɒlərəʊ). a short open bodice-like jacket not reaching the waist.

boll (bəʊl) *n.* the fruit of such plants as flax and cotton, consisting of a rounded capsule containing the seeds.

bollard ('bɒlɑːd, 'bɒləd) *n.* **1.** a strong wooden or metal post on a wharf, quay, etc., used for securing mooring lines. **2.** *Brit.* a small post marking a kerb or traffic island or barring cars from entering.

bollocks ('bɒləks) *or* **ballocks** *Taboo slang.* ~*pl. n.* **1.** the testicles. ~*interj.* **2.** an exclamation of annoyance, disbelief, etc.

Bolshevik ('bɒlʃɪvɪk) *n.* **1.** (formerly) a Russian Communist. **2.** any Communist. **3.** *Informal, offensive.* any political radical, esp. a revolutionary. —'**Bolshe,vism** *n.* —'**Bolshevist** *adj., n.*

bolshie *or* **bolshy** ('bɒlʃɪ) *Brit. informal.* ~*adj.* **1.** difficult to manage; rebellious. **2.** politically radical or left-wing. ~*n., pl.* **-shies. 3.** any political radical.

bolster ('bəʊlstə) *vb.* **1.** to support or strengthen: *to bolster morale.* ~*n.* **2.** a long narrow pillow. **3.** any pad or support.

bolt[1] (bəʊlt) *n.* **1.** a bar that can be slid into a socket to lock a door, gate, etc. **2.** a metal rod or pin that has a head and a screw thread to take a nut. **3.** a flash (of lightning). **4. a bolt from the blue.** a sudden, unexpected, and usually unwelcome event. **5.** a sudden movement, esp. in order to escape. **6.** an arrow, esp. for a crossbow. **7. shoot one's bolt.** to exhaust one's efforts. ~*vb.* **8.** to secure or lock with or as with a bolt. **9.** to eat hurriedly: *don't bolt your food.* **10.** to run away suddenly. **11.** (of a horse) to run away without control. **12.** (of cultivated plants) to produce flow-

ers and seeds prematurely. ~*adv.* **13. bolt upright.** stiff and rigid.

bolt[2] *or* **boult** (bəʊlt) *vb.* **1.** to pass (flour, a powder, etc.) through a sieve. **2.** to examine and separate.

bolt hole *n.* a place of escape from danger.

bomb (bɒm) *n.* **1.** a hollow projectile containing explosive, incendiary, or other destructive substance. **2.** an object in which an explosive device has been planted: *a car bomb.* **3.** *Brit. slang.* a large sum of money: *it cost a bomb.* **4.** *U.S. & Canad. slang.* a disastrous failure: *the new play was a total bomb.* **5. like a bomb.** *Brit. & N.Z. informal.* with great speed or success. **6. the bomb.** a hydrogen or an atom bomb considered as the ultimate destructive weapon. ~*vb.* **7.** to attack with or as if with a bomb or bombs; drop bombs (on). **8.** (foll. by *along*) *Informal.* to move or drive very quickly. **9.** *U.S. & Canad. slang.* to fail disastrously. —'**bombing** *n.*

bombard (bɒm'bɑːd) *vb.* **1.** to attack with concentrated artillery fire or bombs. **2.** to attack persistently. **3.** to attack verbally, esp. with questions. **4.** *Physics.* to direct high-energy particles or photons against (atoms, nuclei, etc.). —**bom'bardment** *n.*

bombardier (,bɒmbə'dɪə) *n.* **1.** *Brit.* a non-commissioned rank in the Royal Artillery. **2.** *U.S.* the member of a bomber aircrew who releases the bombs. **3.** *Canad. trademark.* a snow tractor, usually having caterpillar tracks at the rear and skis at the front.

bombast ('bɒmbæst) *n.* pompous and grandiloquent language. —**bom'bastic** *adj.*

Bombay duck (bɒm'beɪ) *n.* a fish that is eaten dried with curry dishes as a savoury.

bombazine (,bɒmbə'ziːn, 'bɒmbə,ziːn) *n.* a twilled fabric, esp. one of silk and worsted.

bomber ('bɒmə) *n.* **1.** a military aircraft designed to carry out bombing missions. **2.** a person who plants bombs.

bombshell ('bɒm,ʃel) *n.* a shocking or unwelcome surprise.

bona fide ('bəʊnə 'faɪdɪ) *adj.* **1.** genuine: *a bona fide manuscript.* **2.** undertaken in good faith: *a bona fide agreement.*

bonanza (bə'nænzə) *n.* **1.** a source, usually sudden and unexpected, of luck or wealth. **2.** *U.S. & Canad.* a mine or vein rich in ore.

bonbon ('bɒnbɒn) *n.* a sweet.

bond (bɒnd) *n.* **1.** something that binds, fastens, or holds together, such as a chain or rope. **2.** something that brings or holds people together; tie: *a bond of friendship.* **3.** (*pl.*) something that restrains or imprisons. **4.** a written or spoken agreement, esp. a promise. **5.** *Finance.* a certificate of debt issued in order to raise funds. **6.** *Law.* a written acknowledgment of an obligation to pay a sum or to perform a contract. **7.**

Chem. a means by which atoms are combined in a molecule. **8. in bond.** *Commerce.* securely stored until duty is paid. ~*vb.* **9.** to hold or be held together, as by a rope or an adhesive; bind. **10.** to put or hold (goods) in bond.

bondage ('bɒndɪdʒ) *n.* **1.** slavery or serfdom; servitude. **2.** subjection to some influence or duty. **3.** a sexual practice in which one partner is tied or chained up.

bonded ('bɒndɪd) *adj.* **1.** *Finance.* consisting of, secured by, or operating under a bond or bonds. **2.** *Commerce.* in bond.

bond paper *n.* superior quality writing paper.

bondservant ('bɒnd,sɜːvənt) *n.* a serf or slave.

bone (bəʊn) *n.* **1.** any of the various structures that make up the skeleton in most vertebrates. **2.** the porous rigid tissue of which these parts are made. **3.** something consisting of bone or a bonelike substance. **4.** (*pl.*) the human skeleton. **5.** a thin strip of plastic, etc., used to stiffen corsets and brassieres. **6. have a bone to pick.** to have grounds for a quarrel. **7. make no bones about. a.** to be direct and candid about. **b.** to have no scruples about. **8. near** or **close to the bone.** risqué or indecent. **9. the bare bones.** the essentials. ~*vb.* **10.** to remove the bones from (meat for cooking, etc.). **11.** to stiffen (a corset, etc.) by inserting bones. ~See also **bone up on.** —'**boneless** *adj.*

bone china *n.* porcelain containing powdered bone.

bone-dry *adj. Informal.* completely dry.

bone-idle *adj.* very idle; extremely lazy.

bone meal *n.* dried and ground animal bones, used as a fertilizer or in stock feeds.

boneshaker ('bəʊn,ʃeɪkə) *n. Slang.* a decrepit or rickety vehicle.

bone up on *vb. Informal.* to study intensively.

bonfire ('bɒn,faɪə) *n.* a large outdoor fire.

bongo ('bɒŋgəʊ) *n., pl.* **-gos** or **-goes.** a small bucket-shaped drum, usually one of a pair, played by beating with the fingers.

bonhomie ('bɒnəmiː) *n.* exuberant friendliness.

bonk (bɒŋk) *vb. Informal.* **1.** to have sexual intercourse. **2.** to hit. —'**bonking** *n.*

bonkers ('bɒŋkəz) *adj. Slang, chiefly Brit.* mad; crazy.

bon mot (,bɒn 'məʊ) *n., pl.* **bons mots** (,bɒn 'məʊ). a clever and fitting remark.

bonnet ('bɒnɪt) *n.* **1.** *Brit., Austral., N.Z., & S. African.* the hinged metal part of a motor vehicle body that provides access to the engine. **2.** any of various hats worn, esp. formerly, by women and babies and tied with ribbons under the chin. **3.** (in Scotland) a soft cloth cap.

bonny ('bɒnɪ) *adj.* **-nier, -niest. 1.** *Scot. &*

N English dialect. beautiful: *a bonny lass.* **2.** good or fine.

bonsai ('bɒnsaɪ) *n., pl.* **-sai.** an ornamental tree or shrub grown in a small shallow pot in order to stunt its growth.

bontebok ('bɒntɪ,bʌk) *n., pl.* **-boks** or **-bok.** an antelope of southern Africa having a deep reddish-brown coat with a white blaze, tail, and rump patch.

bonus ('bəʊnəs) *n.* something given, paid, or received above what is due or expected.

bon voyage (,bɒn vɔɪ'ɑːʒ) *interj.* a phrase used to wish a traveller a pleasant journey.

bony ('bəʊnɪ) *adj.* **bonier, boniest. 1.** resembling or consisting of bone. **2.** having many bones. **3.** thin or emaciated.

bonze (bɒnz) *n.* a Chinese or Japanese Buddhist priest or monk.

boo (buː) *interj.* **1.** an exclamation uttered to startle someone. **2.** a shout uttered to express dissatisfaction or contempt. ~*vb.* **booing, booed. 3.** to shout "boo" at (someone or something) as an expression of disapproval.

boob (buːb) *Slang.* ~*n.* **1.** *Brit.* an embarrassing mistake; blunder. **2.** a female breast. ~*vb.* **3.** *Brit.* to make a blunder.

booby ('buːbɪ) *n., pl.* **-bies. 1.** an ignorant or foolish person. **2.** a tropical marine bird related to the gannet.

booby prize *n.* a mock prize given to the person with the lowest score in a competition.

booby trap *n.* **1.** a hidden explosive device primed so as to be set off by an unsuspecting victim. **2.** a trap for an unsuspecting person, esp. one intended as a practical joke.

boodle ('buːdᵊl) *n. Slang.* money or valuables, esp. when stolen, counterfeit, or used as a bribe.

boogie ('buːgɪ) *vb.* **-gieing, -gied.** *Slang.* to dance to pop music.

boogie-woogie ('bʊgɪ'wʊgɪ, 'buːgɪ'wuːgɪ) *n.* a style of piano jazz using a dotted bass pattern and blues harmonies.

boohai (buː'haɪ) *n.* **up the boohai.** *N.Z. informal.* thoroughly lost.

boohoo (,buː'huː) *vb.* **-hooing, -hooed. 1.** to sob or pretend to sob noisily. ~*n., pl.* **-hoos. 2.** distressed or pretended sobbing.

book (bʊk) *n.* **1.** a number of printed or written pages bound together along one edge and usually protected by covers. **2.** a written work or composition, such as a novel. **3.** a number of sheets of paper bound together: *an account book.* **4.** (*pl.*) a record of the transactions of a business or society. **5.** the libretto of an opera, musical, etc. **6.** a major division of a written composition, as of a long novel or of the Bible. **7.** a number of tickets, stamps, etc., fastened together along one edge. **8.** a record of betting transactions. **9. a closed**

book. a subject that is beyond comprehension: *chemistry is a closed book to him.* **10. bring to book.** to reprimand or require (someone) to give an explanation of his conduct. **11. by the book.** according to the rules. **12. in someone's good** (*or* **bad**) **books.** regarded by someone with favour (*or* disfavour). **13. throw the book at someone. a.** to charge someone with every relevant offence. **b.** to inflict the most severe punishment on someone. ~*vb.* **14.** to reserve (a place, passage, etc.) or engage the services of (a performer, driver, etc.) in advance. **15.** (of a police officer) to take the name and address of (a person) for an alleged offence with a view to prosecution. **16.** (of a football referee) to take the name of (a player) who has broken the rules seriously. ~See also **book in.**

bookcase ('bʊk,keɪs) *n.* a piece of furniture containing shelves for books.

book club *n.* a club that sells books at low prices to members, usually by mail order.

book end *n.* one of a pair of supports for holding a row of books upright.

bookie ('bʊkɪ) *n. Informal.* short for **bookmaker.**

book in *vb. Chiefly Brit.* to register one's arrival at a hotel.

booking ('bʊkɪŋ) *n.* **1.** *Chiefly Brit.* a reservation, as of a table or seat. **2.** *Theatre.* an engagement of a performer.

bookish ('bʊkɪʃ) *adj.* **1.** fond of reading; studious. **2.** forming opinions through reading rather than experience.

book-keeping *n.* the skill or occupation of systematically recording business transactions. —'**book-,keeper** *n.*

booklet ('bʊklɪt) *n.* a thin book with paper covers.

bookmaker ('bʊk,meɪkə) *n.* a person who as an occupation accepts bets, esp. on horseraces. —'**book,making** *n.*

bookmark ('bʊk,mɑːk) *n.* a strip of some material put between the pages of a book to mark a place.

bookplate ('bʊk,pleɪt) *n.* a label bearing the owner's name and a design, pasted into a book.

bookstall ('bʊk,stɔːl) *n.* a stall or stand where periodicals, newspapers, or books are sold.

bookworm ('bʊk,wɜːm) *n.* **1.** a person devoted to reading. **2.** a small insect that feeds on the binding paste of books.

Boolean algebra ('buːlɪən) *n.* a system of symbolic logic devised to codify nonmathematical logical operations: used in computers.

boom¹ (buːm) *vb.* **1.** to make a deep prolonged resonant sound. **2.** to prosper vigorously and rapidly: *business boomed.* ~*n.* **3.** a deep prolonged resonant sound. **4.** a period of high economic growth.

boom² (buːm) *n.* **1.** *Naut.* a spar to which the foot of a sail is fastened to control its position. **2.** a pole carrying an overhead microphone and projected over a film or television set. **3.** a barrier across a waterway.

boomerang ('buːmə,ræŋ) *n.* **1.** a curved wooden missile of Australian Aborigines which can be made to return to the thrower. **2.** an action or statement that recoils on its originator. ~*vb.* **3.** (of a plan) to recoil unexpectedly, harming its originator.

boomslang ('buːm,slæŋ) *n.* a large greenish venomous tree-living snake of southern Africa.

boon¹ (buːn) *n.* something extremely useful, helpful, or beneficial.

boon² (buːn) *adj.* close or intimate: *boon companion.*

boor (bʊə) *n.* an ill-mannered, clumsy, or insensitive person. —'**boorish** *adj.*

boost (buːst) *n.* **1.** encouragement or help: *a boost to morale.* **2.** an upward thrust or push. **3.** an increase or rise. ~*vb.* **4.** to encourage or improve: *to boost morale.* **5.** to cause to rise; increase: *to boost sales.* **6.** to advertise on a big scale.

booster ('buːstə) *n.* **1.** a supplementary injection of a vaccine given to ensure that the first injection will remain effective. **2.** a radio-frequency amplifier to strengthen signals. **3.** the first stage of a multistage rocket.

boot¹ (buːt) *n.* **1.** an outer covering for the foot that extends above the ankle. **2.** *Brit., Austral., N.Z., & S. African.* an enclosed compartment of a car for holding luggage. **3.** *Informal.* a kick: *he gave the door a boot.* **4. lick someone's boots.** to behave flatteringly towards someone. **5. put the boot in.** *Slang.* **a.** to kick a person, esp. when he is already down. **b.** to finish something off with unnecessary brutality. **6. the boot.** *Slang.* dismissal from employment. ~*vb.* **7.** to kick. **8. boot out.** *Informal.* **a.** to eject forcibly. **b.** to dismiss from employment.

boot² (buːt) *n.* **to boot.** as well; in addition.

bootee ('buːtiː, buː'tiː) *n.* a soft shoe for a baby, esp. a knitted one.

booth (buːð, buːθ) *n., pl.* **booths** (buːðz). **1.** a small partially enclosed cubicle, such as one for telephoning (**telephone booth**) or for voting (**polling booth**). **2.** a stall, esp. a temporary one at a fair or market.

bootleg ('buːt,lɛg) *vb.* **-legging, -legged. 1.** to make, carry, or sell (illicit goods, esp. alcohol). ~*adj.* **2.** produced, distributed, or sold illicitly. —'**boot,legger** *n.*

bootless ('buːtlɪs) *adj.* of little or no use; vain; fruitless.

bootlicker ('buːt,lɪkə) *n. Informal.* one who seeks favour by grovelling to someone in authority.

boot sale *n*. a sale of goods from car boots in a car park hired for the occasion.

booty ('buːtɪ) *n., pl.* **-ties.** any valuable article or articles, esp. when obtained as plunder.

booze (buːz) *Informal.* ~*n*. **1.** alcoholic drink. ~*vb*. **2.** to drink alcohol, esp. in excess. —'**boozy** *adj*.

boozer ('buːzə) *n. Informal.* **1.** a person who is fond of drinking. **2.** *Brit., Austral., & N.Z.* a bar or pub.

booze-up *n. Brit., Austral., & N.Z. slang.* a drinking spree.

bop (bɒp) *n*. **1.** a form of jazz with complex rhythms and harmonies. ~*vb*. **bopping, bopped. 2.** *Informal.* to dance to pop music. —'**bopper** *n*.

boracic (bə'ræsɪk) *adj*. same as **boric.**

borage ('bɒrɪdʒ, 'bʌrɪdʒ) *n*. a Mediterranean plant with star-shaped blue flowers. The young leaves are sometimes used in salads.

borax ('bɔːræks) *n*. a white mineral in crystalline form used in making glass, soap, etc.

Bordeaux (bɔː'dəʊ) *n*. a red or white wine produced around Bordeaux in SW France.

border ('bɔːdə) *n*. **1.** a band or margin around or along the edge of something. **2.** the dividing line between political or geographic regions. **3.** a region straddling such a boundary. **4.** a design around the edge of something. **5.** a narrow strip of ground planted with flowers or shrubs: *a herbaceous border.* ~*vb*. **6.** to provide with a border. **7. a.** to be adjacent to; lie along the boundary of. **b.** to be nearly the same as; verge on: *his stupidity borders on madness.*

borderland ('bɔːdə,lænd) *n*. **1.** land located on or near a boundary. **2.** an indeterminate state or condition.

borderline ('bɔːdə,laɪn) *n*. **1.** a dividing line. **2.** an indeterminate position between two conditions: *the borderline between friendship and love.* ~*adj*. **3.** on the edge of one category and verging on another: *a borderline failure.*

Borders ('bɔːdəz) *pl. n.* **the.** the area straddling the border between England and Scotland.

bore¹ (bɔː) *vb*. **1.** to produce (a hole) in (a material) with a drill, etc. **2.** to produce (a tunnel, mine shaft, etc.) as by drilling. ~*n*. **3.** a hole or tunnel in the ground, esp. one drilled in search of minerals, oil, etc. **4. a.** the hollow of a gun barrel. **b.** the diameter of this hollow; calibre.

bore² (bɔː) *vb*. **1.** to tire or make weary by being dull, repetitious, or uninteresting. ~*n*. **2.** a dull or repetitious person, activity, or state. —**bored** *adj*. —'**boring** *adj*.

bore³ (bɔː) *n*. a high wave moving up a narrow estuary, caused by the tide.

bore⁴ (bɔː) *vb*. the past tense of **bear¹**

boreal forest ('bɔːrɪəl) *n*. the forest of northern latitudes, esp. in Scandinavia, Canada, and Siberia, consisting mainly of spruce and pine.

boredom ('bɔːdəm) *n*. the state of being bored.

boric ('bɔːrɪk) *adj*. of or containing boron.

boric acid *n*. a white soluble weakly acid crystalline solid used as a mild antiseptic.

born (bɔːn) *vb*. **1.** the past participle of **bear¹** (sense 4). **2. not have been born yesterday.** not to be gullible or foolish. ~*adj*. **3.** possessing certain qualities from birth: *a born musician.* **4.** being at birth in a particular social status: *ignobly born.*

born-again *adj*. **1.** having experienced conversion, esp. to evangelical Christianity. **2.** showing the enthusiasm of someone newly converted to any cause: *a born-again jogger.*

borne (bɔːn) *vb*. a past participle of **bear¹**.

boron ('bɔːrɒn) *n*. a hard almost colourless crystalline metalloid element that occurs principally in borax and is used in hardening steel. Symbol: B

borough ('bʌrə) *n*. **1.** a town, esp. (in Britain) one that forms the constituency of an MP or that was originally incorporated by royal charter. **2.** any of the constituent divisions of Greater London or New York City.

borrow ('bɒrəʊ) *vb*. **1.** to obtain (something, such as money) on the understanding that it will be returned to the lender. **2.** to adopt (ideas, words, etc.) from another source. —'**borrower** *n*. —'**borrowing** *n*.

borsch (bɔːʃ) *or* **borscht** (bɔːʃt) *n*. a Russian soup based on beetroot.

borstal ('bɔːstəl) *n*. (in Britain) an establishment in which offenders aged 15 to 21 may be detained for corrective training.

borzoi ('bɔːzɔɪ) *n*. a tall dog with a narrow head and a long coat.

bosh (bɒʃ) *n. Informal.* meaningless talk or opinions; nonsense.

bosom ('buzəm) *n*. **1.** the chest or breast of a person, esp. the female breasts. **2.** a protective centre or part: *the bosom of the family.* **3.** the breast considered as the seat of emotions. **4.** (*modifier*) very dear; intimate: *a bosom friend.*

boss¹ (bɒs) *Informal.* ~*n*. **1.** a person in charge of or employing others. ~*vb*. **2.** to employ, supervise, or be in charge of. **3. boss around** *or* **about.** to be domineering or overbearing towards.

boss² (bɒs) *n*. a raised knob or stud, esp. an ornamental one on a vault, shield, etc.

bossa nova ('bɒsə 'nəʊvə) *n*. **1.** a dance similar to the samba, originating in Brazil. **2.** music for this dance.

bossy ('bɒsɪ) *adj*. **bossier, bossiest.** *Informal.* domineering, overbearing, or authoritarian. —'**bossiness** *n*.

bosun ('bəʊsᵊn) n. Naut. same as **boat-swain**.

bot. 1. botanical. **2.** botany.

botany ('bɒtənɪ) n., pl. **-nies.** the study of plants, including their classification, structure, etc. —**botanical** (bə'tænɪkᵊl) or **botanic** adj. —'**botanist** n.

botch (bɒtʃ) vb. **1.** to spoil through clumsiness or ineptitude. **2.** to repair badly or clumsily. ~n. also **botch-up. 3.** a badly done piece of work or repair.

both (bəʊθ) det. **1.** the two; two considered together: both dogs were dirty; both are to blame. ~conj. **2.** used preceding words, phrases, or clauses joined by and: both Ellen and Keith enjoyed the play.

bother ('bɒðə) vb. **1.** to give annoyance, pain, or trouble to. **2.** to trouble (a person) by repeatedly disturbing; pester. **3.** to take the time or trouble: don't bother to come with me. ~n. **4.** a state of worry, trouble, or confusion. **5.** a person or thing that causes fuss, trouble, or annoyance. **6.** Informal. a disturbance or fight: a spot of bother. ~interj. **7.** Chiefly Brit. an exclamation of slight annoyance.

botheration (,bɒðə'reɪʃən) interj. Informal. same as **bother**.

bothersome ('bɒðəsəm) adj. causing bother.

bothy ('bɒθɪ) n., pl. **bothies.** Chiefly Scot. **1.** a hut used for temporary shelter. **2.** formerly, a farmworker's quarters.

bottle ('bɒtᵊl) n. **1.** a vessel, often of glass and typically cylindrical with a narrow neck, for containing liquids. **2.** the amount such a vessel will hold. **3.** Brit. slang. courage; nerve; initiative. **4. the bottle.** Informal. drinking of alcohol, esp. to excess. ~vb. **5.** to put or place in a bottle or bottles. ~See also **bottle up**.

bottle-feed vb. **-feeding, -fed.** to feed (a baby) with milk from a bottle.

bottle-green adj. dark green.

bottleneck ('bɒtᵊl,nɛk) n. **1.** a narrow stretch of road or a junction at which traffic is or may be held up. **2.** something that holds up progress.

bottlenose dolphin ('bɒtᵊl,nəʊz) n. a grey or greenish dolphin with a bottle-shaped snout.

bottle party n. a party to which guests bring drink.

bottler ('bɒtlə) n. Austral. & N.Z. informal. an exceptional person or thing.

bottle store n. S. African & N.Z. an off-licence.

bottle up vb. to restrain (powerful emotion).

bottom ('bɒtəm) n. **1.** the lowest, deepest, or farthest removed part of a thing: the bottom of a hill. **2.** the least important or successful position: the bottom of a class. **3.** the ground underneath a sea, lake, or river. **4.** the underneath part of a thing. **5.** Naut. the parts of a vessel's hull that are under water. **6.** (in literary or commercial contexts) a ship. **7.** the buttocks. **8. at bottom.** in reality; basically. **9. be at the bottom of.** to be the ultimate cause of. **10. get to the bottom of.** to discover the real truth about. ~adj. **11.** lowest or last.

bottom drawer n. Brit. a woman's collection of linen, cutlery, etc., made in anticipation of marriage.

bottomless ('bɒtəmlɪs) adj. **1.** having no bottom. **2.** unlimited; inexhaustible. **3.** very deep.

bottom line n. **1.** the conclusion or main point of a process, discussion, etc. **2.** the last line of a financial statement that shows the net profit or loss of a company or organization.

bottom out vb. to reach the lowest point and level out.

botulism ('bɒtjʊ,lɪzəm) n. severe food poisoning resulting from the toxin, **botulin**, produced in imperfectly preserved food.

bouclé ('buːkleɪ) n. a curled or looped yarn or fabric giving a thick knobbly effect.

boudoir ('buːdwɑː, -dwɔː) n. a woman's bedroom or private sitting room.

bouffant ('buːfɔːŋ) adj. (of a hairstyle) having extra height and width through backcombing.

bougainvillea (,buːgən'vɪlɪə) n. a tropical climbing plant with flowers surrounded by showy red or purple bracts.

bough (baʊ) n. any of the main branches of a tree.

bought (bɔːt) vb. past of **buy**.

bouillon ('buːjɒn) n. a thin clear broth or stock.

boulder ('bəʊldə) n. a smooth rounded mass of rock shaped by erosion.

boulder clay n. an unstratified glacial deposit of clay, boulders, and pebbles.

boules (buːl) n. (functioning as sing.) a game, popular in France, played on rough surfaces with metal bowls.

boulevard ('buːlvɑː, -vɑːd) n. a wide usually tree-lined road in a city.

boult (bəʊlt) vb. same as **bolt**².

bounce (baʊns) vb. **1.** (of a ball, etc.) to rebound from an impact. **2.** to cause (a ball, etc.) to hit a solid surface and spring back. **3.** to move or cause to move suddenly; spring: she bounced up from her chair. **4.** Slang. (of a bank) to send (a cheque) back or (of a cheque) to be sent back unredeemed because of lack of funds in the account. ~n. **5.** the action of rebounding from an impact. **6.** a leap or jump. **7.** springiness. **8.** Informal. vitality; vigour; resilience. **9.** Brit. swagger or impudence. —'**bouncy** adj.

bounce back vb. to recover one's health, good spirits, confidence, etc., easily.

bouncer ('baʊnsə) *n. Slang.* a person employed at a club, disco, etc., to prevent unwanted people from entering and to eject drunks or troublemakers.

bouncing ('baʊnsɪŋ) *adj.* vigorous and robust: *a bouncing baby.*

bound[1] (baʊnd) *vb.* **1.** past of **bind.** ~*adj.* **2.** tied as with a rope. **3.** restricted; confined: *housebound.* **4.** certain: *it's bound to happen.* **5.** compelled or obliged. **6.** (of a book) secured within a cover or binding. **7. bound up with.** closely or inextricably linked with.

bound[2] (baʊnd) *vb.* **1.** to move forwards by leaps or jumps. **2.** to bounce; spring away from an impact. ~*n.* **3.** a jump upwards or forwards. **4.** a bounce, as of a ball.

bound[3] (baʊnd) *vb.* **1.** to place restrictions on; limit. **2.** to form a boundary of. ~*n.* **3.** See **bounds.** —**'boundless** *adj.*

bound[4] (baʊnd) *adj.* going or intending to go towards: *homeward bound.*

boundary ('baʊndərɪ, -drɪ) *n., pl.* **-ries.** **1.** something that indicates the farthest limit, as of an area. **2.** *Cricket.* **a.** the marked limit of the playing area. **b.** a stroke that hits the ball beyond this limit, scoring four or six runs.

bounden ('baʊndən) *adj.* morally obligatory: *bounden duty.*

bounder ('baʊndə) *n. Old-fashioned Brit. slang.* a morally reprehensible person; cad.

bounds (baʊndz) *pl. n.* **1.** a limit; boundary: *his ignorance knows no bounds.* **2.** something that restrains or confines, esp. the standards of a society: *within the bounds of modesty.*

bountiful ('baʊntɪfʊl) *or* **bounteous** ('baʊntɪəs) *adj.* **1.** plentiful; ample: *a bountiful supply.* **2.** giving freely; generous.

bounty ('baʊntɪ) *n., pl.* **-ties.** **1.** generosity; liberality. **2.** a generous gift. **3.** a reward or premium by a government.

bouquet (buː'keɪ) *n.* **1.** a bunch of flowers, esp. a large carefully arranged one. **2.** the aroma of wine.

bouquet garni ('buːkeɪ gɑː'niː) *n., pl.* **bouquets garnis** ('buːkeɪz gɑː'niː). a bunch of herbs tied together and used for flavouring soups, stews, etc.

bourbon ('bɜːb'n) *n.* a whiskey distilled, chiefly in the U.S., from maize.

bourgeois ('bʊəʒwɑː) *Often disparaging.* ~*n., pl.* **-geois.** **1.** a member of the middle class, esp. one regarded as being conservative and materialistic. ~*adj.* **2.** characteristic of or comprising the middle class. **3.** conservative or materialistic in outlook. **4.** (in Marxist thought) dominated by capitalism.

bourgeoisie (ˌbʊəʒwɑː'ziː) *n.* **the. 1.** the middle classes. **2.** (in Marxist thought) the capitalist ruling class.

bourn (bɔːn) *n. Chiefly S Brit.* a stream.

bourrée ('bʊəreɪ) *n.* **1.** a traditional French dance in fast duple time. **2.** music for this dance.

Bourse (bʊəs) *n.* a stock exchange, esp. of Paris.

bout (baʊt) *n.* **1. a.** a period of time spent doing something, such as drinking. **b.** a period of illness. **2.** a boxing or wrestling match.

boutique (buː'tiːk) *n.* a shop, esp. a small one selling fashionable clothes.

bouzouki (buː'zuːkɪ) *n.* a Greek long-necked stringed musical instrument related to the mandolin.

bovine ('bəʊvaɪn) *adj.* **1.** of or relating to cattle. **2.** (of people) dull, sluggish, or ugly.

bow[1] (baʊ) *vb.* **1.** to lower (one's head) or bend (one's knee or body) as a sign of respect, greeting, agreement, or shame. **2.** to bend or cause to bend. **3.** to comply or accept: *bow to the inevitable.* **4. bow and scrape.** to behave in a slavish manner. ~*n.* **5.** a lowering or bending of the head or body as a mark of respect, etc. **6. take a bow.** to acknowledge applause. ~See also **bow out.**

bow[2] (bəʊ) *n.* **1.** a weapon for shooting arrows, consisting of an arch of flexible wood, plastic, etc., bent by a string fastened at each end. **2.** a long stick across which are stretched strands of horsehair, used for playing a violin, viola, cello, etc. **3.** a decorative knot usually having two loops and two loose ends. **4.** something that is curved, bent, or arched. ~*vb.* **5.** to form or cause to form a curve or curves. **6.** to make strokes of a bow across (violin strings).

bow[3] (baʊ) *n.* **1.** *Chiefly Naut.* the front end or part of a vessel. **2.** *Rowing.* the oarsman at the bow.

bowdlerize *or* **-ise** ('baʊdlə,raɪz) *vb.* to remove passages or words regarded as indecent from (a play, novel, etc.). —ˌbowdleri'zation *or* -i'sation *n.*

bowel ('baʊəl) *n.* **1.** an intestine, esp. the large intestine in man. **2.** (*pl.*) entrails. **3.** (*pl.*) the innermost part: *the bowels of the earth.*

bower ('baʊə) *n.* a shady leafy shelter in a wood or garden.

bowerbird ('baʊə,bɜːd) *n.* a brightly-coloured songbird of Australia and New Guinea.

bowie knife ('bəʊɪ) *n.* a stout hunting knife.

bowl[1] (bəʊl) *n.* **1.** a round container open at the top, used for holding liquid or serving food. **2.** the amount a bowl will hold. **3.** the hollow part of an object, esp. of a spoon or tobacco pipe.

bowl[2] (bəʊl) *n.* **1.** a wooden ball used in the game of bowls. ~*vb.* **2.** to roll smoothly or cause to roll smoothly along the ground. **3.** *Cricket.* **a.** to send (a ball) from one's hand towards the batsman. **b.** Also: **bowl out.** to dismiss (a batsman) by delivering a ball that breaks his wicket. **4.** to play bowls. **5. bowl along.** to move easily and rapidly, as in a car. ~See also **bowl over, bowls.**

bow-legged (ˌbəʊˈlɛgɪd, ˌbəʊˈlɛgd) adj. having legs that curve outwards at the knees.

bowler[1] (ˈbəʊlə) n. **1.** one who bowls in cricket. **2.** a player at the game of bowls.

bowler[2] (ˈbəʊlə) n. a stiff felt hat with a rounded crown and narrow curved brim.

bowline (ˈbəʊlɪn) n. Naut. **1.** a line used to keep the sail taut against the wind. **2.** a knot used for securing a loop that will not slip at the end of a piece of rope.

bowling (ˈbəʊlɪŋ) n. **1.** a game in which a heavy ball is rolled down a long narrow alley at a group of wooden pins. **2.** Cricket. the act of delivering the ball to the batsman.

bowl over vb. **1.** Informal. to surprise (a person) greatly, esp. in a pleasant way; astound; amaze. **2.** to knock down.

bowls (bəʊlz) n. (functioning as sing.) a game played on a very smooth area of grass in which two opponents take turns to roll biased wooden bowls as near a small bowl (the jack) as possible.

bow out (baʊ) vb. to retire or withdraw gracefully.

bowsprit (ˈbəʊsprɪt) n. Naut. a spar projecting from the bow of a sailing ship.

bowstring (ˈbəʊˌstrɪŋ) n. the string of an archer's bow.

bow tie (bəʊ) n. a man's tie tied in a bow.

bow window (bəʊ) n. a bay window in the shape of a curve.

bow-wow n. **1.** (ˈbaʊˌwaʊ). a child's word for **dog**. **2.** (ˈbaʊˈwaʊ). an imitation of the bark of a dog.

box[1] (bɒks) n. **1.** a container made of wood, cardboard, etc., usually rectangular and having a removable or hinged lid. **2.** the contents of such a container. **3.** a separate compartment for a small group of people, as in a theatre. **4.** a compartment for a horse in a stable or a vehicle. **5.** a section of printed matter on a page, enclosed by lines or a border. **6.** a central agency to which mail is addressed and from which it is collected or redistributed: a post-office box. **7.** same as **penalty box. 8.** the raised seat on which the driver sits in a horse-drawn coach. **9. the box.** Brit. informal. television. ~vb. **10.** to put into a box. ~See also **box in.** —ˈbox,like adj.

box[2] (bɒks) vb. **1.** to fight (an opponent) in a boxing match. **2.** to engage in boxing. **3.** to hit (a person or his ears) with the fist. ~n. **4.** a punch with the fist, esp. on the ear.

box[3] (bɒks) n. a slow-growing evergreen tree or shrub with small shiny leaves.

boxer (ˈbɒksə) n. **1.** a man who boxes. **2.** a medium-sized smooth-haired breed of dog with a short nose.

boxer shorts pl. n. men's underpants shaped like shorts but with a front opening.

box girder n. a girder that is hollow and square or rectangular in shape.

box in vb. to prevent from moving freely; confine.

boxing (ˈbɒksɪŋ) n. the act, art, or profession of fighting with the fists.

Boxing Day n. Brit. the first weekday after Christmas, observed as a holiday.

box junction n. (in Britain) a road junction marked with yellow crisscross lines. Vehicles may only enter it when their exit is clear.

box lacrosse n. Canad. lacrosse played indoors.

box office n. **1.** an office at a theatre, cinema, etc., where tickets are sold. **2. a.** the public appeal of an actor or production. **b.** (as modifier): a box-office success.

box pleat n. a flat double pleat made by folding under the fabric on either side of it.

boxroom (ˈbɒksˌruːm, -ˌrʊm) n. a small room in which boxes, cases, etc., may be stored.

box spring n. a coiled spring contained in a boxlike frame, used for mattresses, chairs, etc.

boxwood (ˈbɒksˌwʊd) n. the hard close-grained yellow wood of the box tree, used to make tool handles, etc. See **box**[3].

boy (bɔɪ) n. **1.** a male child. **2.** a man regarded as immature or inexperienced. **3.** S. African offensive. a Black male servant. —ˈboyhood n. —ˈboyish adj.

boycott (ˈbɔɪkɒt) vb. **1.** to refuse to have dealings with (a person or organization) or refuse to buy (a product) as a protest or means of coercion. ~n. **2.** an instance or the use of boycotting.

boyfriend (ˈbɔɪˌfrɛnd) n. a male friend with whom a person is romantically or sexually involved.

Boyle's law (bɔɪlz) n. the principle that the pressure of a gas varies inversely with its volume at constant temperature.

boy scout n. See **Scout**.

BP 1. blood pressure. **2.** British Pharmacopoeia.

bpi bits per inch (used of a computer tape).

Bq Physics. becquerel.

Br Chem. bromine.

br. 1. branch. **2.** bronze.

Br. 1. Breton. **2.** Britain. **3.** British.

bra (brɑː) n. a woman's undergarment for covering and supporting the breasts.

braaivleis (ˈbraɪˌfleɪs) n. S. African. a barbecue.

brace (breɪs) n. **1.** a hand tool for drilling holes. **2.** something that steadies, binds, or holds up another thing. **3.** a beam or prop, used to stiffen a framework. **4.** a pair, esp. of game birds. **5.** either of a pair of characters, { }, used for connecting lines of printing or writing. **6.** an appliance of metal bands and wires for correcting unevenness of teeth. **7.** See **braces**. ~*vb.* **8.** to provide, strengthen, or fit with a brace. **9.** to steady or prepare (oneself) before an impact.

brace and bit *n.* a hand tool for boring holes, consisting of a cranked handle into which a drilling bit is inserted.

bracelet ('breɪslɪt) *n.* an ornamental chain worn around the arm or wrist.

bracelets ('breɪslɪts) *pl. n. Slang.* handcuffs.

braces ('breɪsɪz) *pl. n. Brit.* a pair of straps worn over the shoulders for holding up the trousers.

brachiopod ('breɪkɪəˌpɒd, 'bræk-) *n.* an invertebrate sea animal with a coiled feeding organ and a shell consisting of two valves.

brachium ('breɪkɪəm, 'bræk-) *n., pl.* **-chia** (-kɪə). *Anat.* the arm, esp. the upper part.

bracing ('breɪsɪŋ) *adj.* refreshing; stimulating; invigorating.

bracken ('brækən) *n.* **1.** a fern with large fronds. **2.** a clump of these ferns.

bracket ('brækɪt) *n.* **1.** a pair of characters, [ ], ( ), or { }, used to enclose a section of writing or printing. **2.** a group or category falling within certain defined limits: *the lower income bracket.* **3.** an L-shaped or other support fixed to a wall to hold a shelf, etc. ~*vb.* **4.** to put (written or printed matter) in brackets. **5.** to group or class together.

brackish ('brækɪʃ) *adj.* (of water) slightly salty.

bract (brækt) *n.* a leaf, usually small and scaly, growing at the base of a flower.

brad (bræd) *n.* a small tapered nail with a small head.

bradawl ('brædˌɔːl) *n.* a hand tool for making holes in wood, leather, etc.

brae (breɪ) *n. Scot.* a hill or hillside.

brag (bræg) *vb.* **bragging, bragged. 1.** to speak arrogantly and boastfully. ~*n.* **2.** boastful talk or behaviour. **3.** a card game: an old form of poker.

braggart ('brægət) *n.* **1.** a person who boasts loudly or exaggeratedly. ~*adj.* **2.** boastful.

Brahma ('brɑːmə) *n.* **1.** a Hindu god, the Creator. **2.** same as **Brahman** (sense 2).

Brahman ('brɑːmən) *n., pl.* **-mans. 1.** Also: **Brahmin.** a member of the highest or priestly caste in the Hindu caste system. **2.** *Hinduism.* the ultimate and impersonal divine reality of the universe. —**Brahmanic** (brɑːˈmænɪk) *adj.*

braid (breɪd) *vb.* **1.** to interweave (hair, thread, etc.); plait. **2.** to decorate with an ornamental trim or border. ~*n.* **3.** a length of hair that has been braided. **4.** narrow ornamental tape of woven silk, wool, etc. —**'braiding** *n.*

Braille (breɪl) *n.* a system of writing for the blind consisting of raised dots interpreted by touch.

brain (breɪn) *n.* **1.** the soft mass of nervous tissue within the skull of vertebrates that controls and coordinates the nervous system. **2.** (*often pl.*) *Informal.* intellectual ability: *he's got brains.* **3.** *Informal.* an intelligent person. **4. on the brain.** *Informal.* constantly in mind: *I had that song on the brain.* **5. the brains.** *Informal.* a person who plans and organizes something: *who is the brains behind this scheme?* ~*vb.* **6.** *Slang.* to hit (someone) hard on the head.

brainchild ('breɪnˌtʃaɪld) *n. Informal.* an idea or plan produced by creative thought.

brain death *n.* complete stoppage of breathing due to irreparable brain damage.

brain drain *n. Informal.* the emigration of scientists, technologists, academics, etc.

brainless ('breɪnlɪs) *adj.* stupid or foolish.

brainstorm ('breɪnˌstɔːm) *n.* **1.** a sudden and violent attack of insanity. **2.** *Brit. informal.* a sudden mental aberration. **3.** *U.S. & Canad. informal.* same as **brain wave** (sense 1).

brains trust *n.* a group of knowledgeable people who discuss topics in public or on radio or television.

brain-teaser *n. Informal.* a difficult problem.

brainwash ('breɪnˌwɒʃ) *vb.* to effect a radical change in the beliefs of (a person), esp. by isolation, sleeplessness, etc. —**'brain-ˌwashing** *n.*

brain wave *n.* **1.** *Informal.* a sudden idea or inspiration. **2.** a fluctuation of electrical potential in the brain.

brainy ('breɪnɪ) *adj.* **brainier, brainiest.** *Informal.* clever; intelligent.

braise (breɪz) *vb.* to cook (meat, vegetables, etc.) by cooking slowly in a closed pan with a small amount of liquid.

brak (bræk) *n. S. African.* a crossbred dog; mongrel.

brake[1] (breɪk) *n.* **1.** a device for slowing or stopping a vehicle. **2.** a machine or tool for crushing flax or hemp. **3.** a heavy harrow for breaking up clods. ~*vb.* **4.** to slow down or cause to slow down, by or as if by using a brake. **5.** to break up (clods) using a brake.

brake[2] (breɪk) *n.* an area of dense undergrowth, brushwood, etc.

brake[3] (breɪk) *n.* same as **bracken.**

brake horsepower *n.* the rate at which an engine does work, measured by the resistance of an applied brake.

brake light *n.* a red light at the rear of a

motor vehicle that lights up when the brakes are applied.

brake lining *n.* a renewable strip of asbestos riveted to a brake shoe to increase friction.

brake shoe *n.* a curved metal casting that acts as a brake on a wheel.

bramble ('bræmbʳl) *n.* **1.** a prickly plant or shrub such as the blackberry. **2.** *Scot. & N English.* a blackberry. —'brambly *adj.*

brambling ('bræmblɪŋ) *n.* a finch with a speckled head and back.

bran (bræn) *n.* husks of cereal grain separated from the flour.

branch (brɑːntʃ) *n.* **1.** a secondary woody stem extending from the trunk or main branch of a tree. **2.** an offshoot or secondary part: *a branch of a deer's antlers.* **3.** a subdivision or subsidiary section of something larger or more complex: *branches of learning.* ~*vb.* **4.** (of a tree or other plant) to produce or possess branches. **5.** (of stems, roots, etc.) to grow and diverge (from another part). **6.** to divide or be divided into subsidiaries or offshoots. —'branch,like *adj.*

branch off *vb.* to diverge from the main way, road, topic, etc.

branch out *vb.* to expand or extend one's interests.

brand (brænd) *n.* **1.** a particular product or a characteristic that identifies a particular producer. **2.** a particular kind or variety. **3.** an identifying mark made, usually by burning, on the skin of animals as a proof of ownership. **4.** an iron used for branding animals. **5.** a mark of disgrace. **6.** a burning or burnt piece of wood. **7.** *Archaic or poetic.* a flaming torch. ~*vb.* **8.** to label, burn, or mark with or as with a brand. **9.** to denounce; stigmatize: *they branded him a traitor.*

brandish ('brændɪʃ) *vb.* to wave (a weapon, etc.) in a triumphant or threatening way.

brand-new *adj.* absolutely new.

brandy ('brændɪ) *n., pl.* **-dies.** an alcoholic spirit distilled from wine.

brandy snap *n.* a crisp sweet biscuit, rolled into a cylinder and filled with whipped cream.

bran tub *n. Brit.* a tub containing bran in which small wrapped gifts are hidden.

brash (bræʃ) *adj.* **1.** tastelessly or offensively loud, showy, or bold. **2.** impudent. —'brashness *n.*

brass (brɑːs) *n.* **1.** an alloy of copper and zinc. **2.** an object, ornament, or utensil made of brass. **3. a.** the large family of wind instruments including the trumpet, trombone, etc., made of brass. **b.** instruments of this family forming a section in an orchestra. **4.** same as **top brass.** **5.** *N English dialect.* money. **6.** *Brit.* an en-

graved brass memorial tablet in a church. **7.** *Informal.* bold self-confidence; nerve.

brass band *n.* a group of musicians playing brass and percussion instruments.

brass hat *n. Brit. informal.* a top-ranking official, esp. a military officer.

brassica ('bræsɪkə) *n.* any plant of the cabbage and turnip family.

brassiere ('bræsɪə, 'bræz-) *n.* same as **bra.**

brass rubbing *n.* an impression of an engraved brass tablet made by rubbing a paper placed over it with heelball or chalk.

brass tacks *pl. n.* **get down to brass tacks.** *Informal.* to discuss the realities of a situation.

brassy ('brɑːsɪ) *adj.* **brassier, brassiest. 1.** insolent; brazen. **2.** flashy; showy. **3.** (of sound) harsh and strident. **4.** like brass, esp. in colour.

brat (bræt) *n.* a child, esp. one who is unruly.

bravado (brə'vɑːdəʊ) *n.* an outward display of self-confidence; swagger.

brave (breɪv) *adj.* **1.** having or displaying courage, resolution, or daring. **2.** fine; splendid: *a brave sight.* ~*n.* **3.** a warrior of a North American Indian tribe. ~*vb.* **4.** to confront with resolution or courage: *to brave the storm.* —'bravery *n.*

bravo *interj.* **1.** (brɑː'vəʊ). well done! ~*n.* **2.** (brɑː'vəʊ). (*pl.* **-vos**) a cry of "bravo." **3.** ('brɑːvəʊ). (*pl.* **-voes** *or* **-vos**) a hired killer or assassin.

bravura (brə'vjʊərə, -'vʊərə) *n.* **1.** a display of boldness or daring. **2.** *Music.* brilliance of execution.

brawl (brɔːl) *n.* **1.** a loud disagreement or fight. ~*vb.* **2.** to quarrel or fight noisily; squabble.

brawn (brɔːn) *n.* **1.** strong well-developed muscles. **2.** physical strength. **3.** *Brit.* a seasoned jellied loaf made from the head of a pig. —'brawny *adj.*

bray (breɪ) *vb.* **1.** (of a donkey) to utter its characteristic loud harsh sound; heehaw. **2.** to utter something with a loud harsh sound. ~*n.* **3.** the loud harsh sound uttered by a donkey. **4.** a similar loud sound.

braze (breɪz) *vb.* to join (two metal surfaces) by fusing brass between them.

brazen ('breɪzʳn) *adj.* **1.** shameless and bold. **2.** made of or resembling brass. **3.** having a ringing metallic sound. ~*vb.* **4. brazen it out.** to face and overcome a difficult or embarrassing situation boldly or shamelessly. —'brazenly *adv.*

brazier[1] ('breɪzɪə) *n.* a worker in brass.

brazier[2] ('breɪzɪə) *n.* a portable metal container for burning charcoal or coal.

brazil (brə'zɪl) *n.* **1.** the red wood of various tropical trees of America. **2.** same as **brazil nut.**

brazil nut *n.* a large three-sided nut of a

tropical American tree, with a woody shell and an oily edible kernel.

breach (briːtʃ) n. 1. a breaking or violation of a promise, obligation, etc. 2. any serious disagreement or separation. 3. a crack, break, or gap. ~vb. 4. to break (a promise, law, etc). 5. to break through or make an opening or hole in.

breach of promise n. Law. (formerly) failure to carry out one's promise to marry.

breach of the peace n. Law. an offence against public order causing an unnecessary disturbance of the peace.

bread (brɛd) n. 1. a food made from a dough of flour or meal mixed with water or milk, usually raised with yeast and then baked. 2. necessary food; nourishment. 3. Slang. money. ~vb. 4. to cover (food) with breadcrumbs before cooking.

bread and butter n. Informal. a means of support; livelihood.

breadboard ('brɛdˌbɔːd) n. 1. a wooden board on which bread is sliced. 2. an experimental arrangement of electronic circuits.

breadfruit ('brɛdˌfruːt) n., pl. -fruits or -fruit. a tree of the Pacific Islands, the edible round fruit of which is eaten baked or roasted and has a texture like bread.

breadline ('brɛdˌlaɪn) n. **on the breadline.** impoverished; living at subsistence level.

breadth (brɛdθ) n. 1. the extent or measurement of something from side to side; width. 2. openness and lack of restriction, esp. of viewpoint or interest; liberality.

breadwinner ('brɛdˌwɪnə) n. a person supporting a family with his or her earnings.

break (breɪk) vb. **breaking, broke, broken.** 1. to separate or become separated into two or more pieces. 2. to damage or become damaged so as to be inoperative. 3. to burst or cut the surface of (skin). 4. to discontinue (a journey). 5. to fail to observe (an agreement, promise, or law): to break one's word. 6. (foll. by with) to discontinue an association with. 7. to disclose or be disclosed: he broke the news gently. 8. to fracture (a bone) in (a limb, etc.). 9. to bring or come to an end: the summer weather broke at last. 10. to weaken or overwhelm or be weakened or overwhelmed, as in spirit. 11. to cut through or penetrate: a cry broke the silence. 12. to improve on or surpass: to break a record. 13. (often foll. by in) to accustom (a horse) to the bridle and saddle, to being ridden, etc. 14. (foll. by of) to cause (a person) to give up (a habit): this cure will break you of smoking. 15. to weaken the impact or force of: this net will break his fall. 16. to decipher: to break a code. 17. to lose the order of: to break ranks. 18. to reduce to poverty or the state of bankruptcy. 19. to come into being: light broke over the mountains. 20. (foll. by into) a. to burst into (song, laughter, etc.). b. to change to (a faster pace). 21. to open with explosives: to break a safe. 22. (of waves) a. to strike violently. b. to collapse into foam or surf. 23. Billiards. to scatter the balls at the start of a game. 24. Boxing, wrestling. (of two fighters) to separate from a clinch. 25. (of the male voice) to undergo a change in register, quality, and range at puberty. 26. to interrupt the flow of current in (an electrical circuit). 27. **break camp.** to pack up and leave a camp. 28. **break even.** to make neither a profit nor a loss. ~n. 29. the act or result of breaking; fracture. 30. a brief respite. 31. a sudden rush, esp. to escape: to make a break for freedom. 32. any sudden interruption in a continuous action. 33. Brit. a short period between classes at school. 34. Informal. a fortunate opportunity, esp. to prove oneself. 35. Informal. a piece of good or bad luck. 36. Billiards, snooker. a series of successful shots during one turn. 37. Billiards, snooker. the opening shot that scatters the placed balls. 38. a discontinuity in an electrical circuit. 39. **break of day.** the dawn. ~See also **breakaway, break down,** etc. —'**breakable** adj.

breakage ('breɪkɪdʒ) n. 1. the act or result of breaking. 2. compensation or allowance for goods damaged while in use, transit, etc.

breakaway ('breɪkəˌweɪ) n. 1. **a.** loss or withdrawal of a group of members from an association, club, etc. **b.** (as modifier): a breakaway faction. ~vb. **break away.** 2. to leave hastily or escape. 3. to withdraw or secede.

break dance n. 1. an acrobatic dance style of the 1980s. ~vb. **break-dance.** 2. to perform a break dance. —'**break dancing** n.

break down vb. 1. to cease to function; become ineffective. 2. to yield to strong emotion or tears. 3. to crush or destroy. 4. to have a nervous breakdown. 5. to analyse or be subjected to analysis. ~n. **breakdown.** 6. an act or instance of breaking down; collapse. 7. same as **nervous breakdown.** 8. an analysis of something into its parts.

breaker ('breɪkə) n. 1. a large wave with a white crest on the open sea or one that breaks into foam on the shore. 2. a citizens' band radio operator.

breakfast ('brɛkfəst) n. 1. the first meal of the day. ~vb. 2. to eat or supply with breakfast.

break in vb. 1. to enter a house, etc., illegally, esp. by force. 2. to interrupt. 3. to accustom (a person or animal) to normal duties or practice. 4. to use or wear (new shoes or new equipment) until comfortable or running smoothly. ~n. **break-in.** 5. the act of illegally entering a building, esp. by thieves.

breaking and entering *n.* (formerly) the act of gaining unauthorized access to a building with intent to commit a crime.

breaking point *n.* the point at which something or someone gives way under strain.

breakneck ('breɪk,nɛk) *adj.* (of speed or pace) excessively fast and dangerous.

break off *vb.* **1.** to sever or detach. **2.** to end (a relationship or association). **3.** to stop abruptly.

break out *vb.* **1.** to begin or arise suddenly: *a riot broke out during the concert.* **2.** to make an escape, esp. from prison. **3.** (foll. by *in*) (of the skin) to erupt (in a rash or spots). ~*n.* **break-out. 4.** an escape, esp. from prison.

break through *vb.* **1.** to penetrate. **2.** to achieve success after lengthy efforts. ~*n.* **breakthrough. 3.** a significant development or discovery, esp. in science.

break up *vb.* **1.** to separate or cause to separate. **2.** to put an end to (a relationship) or (of a relationship) to come to an end. **3.** to dissolve or cause to dissolve; disrupt or be disrupted: *the meeting broke up at noon.* **4.** *Brit.* (of a school) to close for the holidays. ~*n.* **break-up. 5.** a separation or disintegration.

breakwater ('breɪk,wɔːtə) *n.* a massive wall built out into the sea to protect a shore or harbour from the force of waves.

bream (briːm) *n., pl.* **bream. 1.** a freshwater fish with a deep compressed body covered with silvery scales. **2.** a food fish of European seas.

breast (brɛst) *n.* **1.** either of the two soft fleshy milk-secreting glands on the chest in sexually mature human females. **2.** the front part of the body from the neck to the abdomen; chest. **3.** the corresponding part in certain other mammals. **4.** a source of nourishment. **5.** the source of human emotions. **6.** the part of a garment that covers the breast. **7. make a clean breast of something.** to confess to something. ~*vb.* **8.** to confront boldly; face: *breast the storm.* **9.** to reach the summit of: *breasting the mountain top.*

breastbone ('brɛst,bəʊn) *n.* same as **sternum.**

breast-feed *vb.* **-feeding, -fed.** to feed (a baby) with milk from the breast; suckle.

breastplate ('brɛst,pleɪt) *n.* a piece of armour covering the chest.

breaststroke ('brɛst,strəʊk) *n.* a swimming stroke in which the arms are extended in front of the head and swept back on either side.

breastwork ('brɛst,wɜːk) *n. Fortifications.* a temporary defensive work, usually breast-high.

breath (brɛθ) *n.* **1.** the taking in and letting out of air during breathing. **2.** a single

instance of this. **3.** the air taken in or let out during breathing. **4.** the vapour, heat, or odour of air breathed out. **5.** a slight gust of air. **6.** a short pause or rest. **7.** a suggestion or slight evidence; suspicion: *a breath of scandal.* **8.** a whisper or soft sound. **9. catch one's breath. a.** to rest until breathing is normal. **b.** to stop breathing momentarily from excitement, fear, etc. **10. out of breath.** gasping for air after exertion. **11. save one's breath.** to refrain from useless talk. **12. take someone's breath away.** to overwhelm someone with surprise, etc. **13. under one's breath.** in a quiet voice or whisper.

Breathalyser *or* **-lyzer** ('brɛθə,laɪzə) *n. Brit., trademark.* a device for estimating the amount of alcohol in the breath. —**'breatha,lyse** *or* **-,lyze** *vb.*

breathe (briːð) *vb.* **1.** to take in oxygen and give out carbon dioxide; respire. **2.** to exist; be alive. **3.** to rest to regain breath or composure. **4.** (esp. of air) to blow lightly. **5.** to exhale or emit: *the dragon breathed fire.* **6.** to impart; instil: *to breathe confidence into the actors.* **7.** to speak softly; whisper. **8. breathe again, freely,** *or* **easily.** to feel relief. **9. breathe one's last.** to die.

breather ('briːðə) *n. Informal.* a short pause for rest.

breathing ('briːðɪŋ) *n.* **1.** the passage of air into and out of the lungs to supply the body with oxygen. **2.** the sound this makes.

breathless ('brɛθlɪs) *adj.* **1.** out of breath; gasping, etc. **2.** holding one's breath or having it taken away by excitement, etc. **3.** (esp. of the atmosphere) motionless and stifling.

breathtaking ('brɛθ,teɪkɪŋ) *adj.* causing awe or excitement.

breath test *n. Brit.* a chemical test of a driver's breath to determine the amount of alcohol he has consumed.

bred (brɛd) *vb.* past of **breed.**

breech (briːtʃ) *n.* **1.** the buttocks. **2.** the part of a firearm behind the barrel or bore.

breech delivery *n.* birth of a baby with the feet or buttocks appearing first.

breeches ('brɪtʃɪz, 'briː-) *pl. n.* trousers extending to the knee or just below, worn for riding, etc.

breeches buoy *n.* a life buoy with a support of a pair of short breeches, in which a person is suspended for safe transfer from a ship.

breed (briːd) *vb.* **breeding, bred. 1.** to bear (offspring). **2.** to bring up; raise. **3.** to produce or cause to produce by mating. **4.** to produce new or improved strains of (domestic animals and plants). **5.** to produce or be produced: *to breed trouble.* ~*n.* **6.** a group of animals, esp. domestic animals, within a species, that have certain clearly defined characteristics. **7.** a lineage or race. **8.** a kind, sort, or group. —ˈ**breeder** n.

breeder reactor n. a nuclear reactor that produces more fissionable material than it uses.

breeding (ˈbriːdɪŋ) n. **1.** the process of bearing offspring. **2.** the process of producing plants or animals by controlled methods of reproduction. **3.** the result of good upbringing or training.

breeze[1] (briːz) n. **1.** a gentle or light wind. **2.** U.S. & Canad. informal. an easy task. ~vb. **3.** to move quickly or casually: he breezed into the room.

breeze[2] (briːz) n. ashes of coal, coke, or charcoal.

breeze block n. a light building brick made from the ashes of coal, coke, etc., bonded together by cement.

breezy (ˈbriːzɪ) adj. **breezier, breeziest. 1.** fresh; windy. **2.** casual or carefree.

Bren gun (brɛn) n. an air-cooled gas-operated light machine gun used by the British in World War II.

brent (brɛnt) or esp. U.S. **brant** (brænt) n. a small goose with a dark grey plumage.

brethren (ˈbrɛðrɪn) pl. n. Archaic except when referring to fellow members of a religion, society, etc. a plural of **brother.**

Breton (ˈbrɛtˀn) adj. **1.** of Brittany, its people, or their language. ~n. **2.** a person from Brittany. **3.** the Celtic language of Brittany.

breve (briːv) n. an accent, ˘, placed over a vowel to indicate that it is short or is pronounced in a specified way.

breviary (ˈbriːvjərɪ) n., pl. **-ries.** R.C. Church. a book of psalms, hymns, prayers, etc., to be recited daily.

brevity (ˈbrɛvɪtɪ) n. **1.** a short duration; brief time. **2.** lack of verbosity.

brew (bruː) vb. **1.** to make (beer, ale, etc.) from malt and other ingredients by steeping, boiling, and fermentation. **2.** to prepare (a drink, such as tea) by infusing. **3.** to devise or plan: to brew a plot. **4.** to be in the process of being brewed. **5.** to be impending or forming: there's a storm brewing. ~n. **6.** a beverage produced by brewing, esp. tea or beer. **7.** an instance of brewing: last year's brew. —ˈ**brewer** n.

brewery (ˈbruərɪ) n., pl. **-eries.** a place where beer, ale, etc., is brewed.

briar[1] or **brier** (ˈbraɪə) n. **1.** a shrub of S Europe, with a hard woody root (briarroot). **2.** a tobacco pipe made from this root.

briar[2] (ˈbraɪə) n. same as **brier**[1].

bribe (braɪb) vb. **1.** to promise, offer, or give something, often illegally, to (a person) to procure services or gain influence. ~n. **2.** a reward, such as money or favour, given or offered for this purpose. —ˈ**bribery** n.

bric-a-brac (ˈbrɪkəˌbræk) n. miscellaneous small ornamental objects.

brick (brɪk) n. **1.** a rectangular block of baked or dried clay, used in building construction. **2.** the material used to make such blocks. **3.** any rectangular block: a brick of ice. **4.** bricks collectively. **5.** Informal. a reliable, trustworthy, or helpful person. **6. drop a brick.** Brit. informal. to make a tactless or indiscreet remark. ~vb. **7.** (foll. by in, up, or over) to construct, line, pave, fill, or wall up with bricks: to brick up a window.

brickbat (ˈbrɪkˌbæt) n. **1.** blunt criticism. **2.** a piece of brick used as a weapon.

bricklayer (ˈbrɪkˌleɪə) n. a person who builds with bricks.

brick-red adj. reddish-brown.

bridal (ˈbraɪdˀl) adj. of a bride or a wedding.

bride (braɪd) n. a woman who has just been or is about to be married.

bridegroom (ˈbraɪdˌgruːm, -ˌgrʊm) n. a man who has just been or is about to be married.

bridesmaid (ˈbraɪdzˌmeɪd) n. a girl or young woman who attends a bride at her wedding.

bridge[1] (brɪdʒ) n. **1.** a structure that provides a passage over a railway, river, etc. **2.** the hard ridge at the upper part of the nose. **3.** a dental plate containing artificial teeth that is secured to natural teeth. **4.** a platform from which a ship is piloted and navigated. **5.** a piece of wood supporting the strings of a violin, guitar, etc. ~vb. **6.** to build or provide a bridge over (something). **7.** to connect or reduce the distance between: let us bridge our differences.

bridge[2] (brɪdʒ) n. a card game for four players, based on whist, in which the trump suit is decided by bidding between the players.

bridgehead (ˈbrɪdʒˌhɛd) n. Mil. a fortified or defensive position at the end of a bridge nearest to the enemy.

bridgework (ˈbrɪdʒˌwɜːk) n. a partial denture attached to the surrounding teeth.

bridging loan n. a loan made to cover the period between two transactions, such as the buying of another house before the sale of the first is completed.

bridle (ˈbraɪdˀl) n. **1.** headgear for a horse, consisting of a series of buckled straps and a metal mouthpiece (bit) by which the animal is controlled through the reins. **2.** something that curbs or restrains. ~vb. **3.** to put a bridle on (a horse). **4.** to restrain; curb: he bridled his rage.

bridle path n. a path suitable for riding or leading horses.

Brie (briː) n. a soft creamy white cheese.

brief (briːf) adj. **1.** short in duration. **2.** short in length or extent; scanty: a brief bikini. **3.** terse or concise. ~n. **4.** a condensed statement or written synopsis. **5.** *Law.* a document containing all the facts and points of law of a case by which a solicitor instructs a barrister to represent a client. **6.** *R.C. Church.* a papal letter that is less formal than a bull. **7.** Also called: **briefing.** instructions. **8. hold a brief for.** to argue for; champion. **9. in brief.** in short; to sum up. ~*vb.* **10.** to prepare or instruct (someone) by giving him a summary of relevant facts. **11.** *English law.* **a.** to instruct (a barrister) by brief. **b.** to retain (a barrister) as counsel. —'**briefly** *adv.*

briefcase ('briːfˌkeɪs) *n.* a flat portable case for carrying papers, books, etc.

briefs (briːfs) *pl. n.* men's or women's underpants without legs.

brier[1] *or* **briar** ('braɪə) *n.* any of various thorny shrubs or other plants, such as the sweetbrier.

brier[2] ('braɪə) *n.* same as **briar**[1].

brig[1] (brɪg) *n. Naut.* a two-masted square-rigger.

brig[2] (brɪg) *n. Scot. & N English.* a bridge.

Brig. Brigadier.

brigade (brɪ'geɪd) *n.* **1.** a military formation smaller than a division and usually commanded by a brigadier. **2.** a group of people organized for a certain task: *a rescue brigade.*

brigadier (ˌbrɪgə'dɪə) *n.* a senior officer in an army, usually commanding a brigade.

brigand ('brɪgənd) *n.* a bandit, esp. a member of a gang operating in mountainous areas.

brigantine ('brɪgənˌtiːn, -ˌtaɪn) *n.* a two-masted sailing ship, rigged square on the foremast and fore-and-aft on the mainmast.

bright (braɪt) *adj.* **1.** emitting or reflecting much light; shining. **2.** (of colours) intense or vivid. **3.** full of promise: *a bright future.* **4.** lively or cheerful. **5.** *Informal.* quick-witted or clever. ~*adv.* **6.** brightly: *the fire was burning bright.* —'**brightly** *adv.* —'**brightness** *n.*

brighten ('braɪt°n) *vb.* **1.** to make or become bright or brighter. **2.** to make or become cheerful.

brill (brɪl) *n., pl.* **brill** *or* **brills.** a European flatfish similar to the turbot.

brilliance ('brɪljəns) *or* **brilliancy** *n.* **1.** great brightness. **2.** excellence in physical or mental ability. **3.** splendour.

brilliant ('brɪljənt) *adj.* **1.** shining with light; sparkling. **2.** (of a colour) vivid. **3.** splendid; magnificent: *a brilliant show.* **4.** of outstanding intelligence or intellect. ~*n.* **5.** a diamond cut with many facets to increase its sparkle.

brilliantine ('brɪljənˌtiːn) *n.* a perfumed oil used to make the hair smooth and shiny.

brim (brɪm) *n.* **1.** the upper rim of a cup, bowl, etc. **2.** a projecting edge of a hat.

~*vb.* **brimming, brimmed. 3.** to be full to the brim: *eyes brimming with tears.* —'**brimless** *adj.*

brimful (ˌbrɪm'fʊl) *adj.* (foll. by *of*) filled up to the brim with.

brimstone ('brɪmˌstəʊn) *n. Obs.* sulphur.

brindled ('brɪnd°ld) *adj.* brown or grey streaked with a darker colour: *a brindled dog.*

brine (braɪn) *n.* **1.** a strong solution of salt and water, used for pickling. **2.** the sea or its water.

bring (brɪŋ) *vb.* **bringing, brought. 1.** to carry, convey, or take (something or someone) to a designated place or person. **2.** to cause to happen: *responsibility brings maturity.* **3.** to cause to come to mind: *it brought back memories.* **4.** to cause to be in a certain state, position, etc.: *the punch brought him to his knees.* **5.** to make (oneself): *I couldn't bring myself to do it.* **6.** to sell for: *the painting brought £20.* **7.** *Law.* **a.** to institute (proceedings, charges, etc.). **b.** to put (evidence, etc.) before a tribunal. **8. bring forth.** to give birth to. ~See also **bring about, bring down,** etc.

bring about *vb.* to cause to happen: *they brought about a peaceful settlement.*

bring-and-buy sale *n. Brit. & N.Z.* an informal sale, often for charity, to which people bring items for sale and buy those that others have brought.

bring down *vb.* to cause to fall.

bring forward *vb.* **1.** to move (a meeting, lecture, etc.) to an earlier date or time. **2.** to present or introduce (a subject) for discussion. **3.** *Book-keeping.* to transfer (a sum) to the top of the next page or column.

bring in *vb.* **1.** to yield (income, profit, or cash). **2.** to introduce (a legislative bill, etc.). **3.** to produce or return (a verdict).

bring off *vb.* to succeed in achieving (something difficult).

bring out *vb.* **1.** to produce, publish, or have (a book) published. **2.** to expose, reveal, or cause to be seen: *she brought out the best in me.* **3.** (foll. by *in*) to cause (a person) to become covered with (a rash, spots, etc.).

bring over *vb.* to cause (a person) to change allegiances.

bring round *vb.* **1.** to restore (a person) to consciousness after a faint. **2.** to convince (another person) of an opinion or point of view.

bring to *vb.* to restore (a person) to consciousness: *the smelling salts brought her to.*

bring up *vb.* **1.** to care for and train (a child); rear. **2.** to raise (a subject) for discussion; mention. **3.** to vomit (food).

brinjal ('brɪndʒəl) *n.* (in India and Africa) same as **aubergine.**

brink (brɪŋk) *n.* **1.** the edge, border, or

verge of a steep place. **2.** the land at the edge of a body of water. **3. on the brink of.** very near, on the point of: *on the brink of disaster.*

brinkmanship ('brɪŋkmən‚ʃɪp) *n.* the practice of pressing a dangerous situation to the limit of safety in order to win an advantage.

briny ('braɪnɪ) *adj.* **brinier, briniest. 1.** of or like brine; salty. ~*n.* **2. the.** *Informal.* the sea.

briquette (brɪ'kɛt) *n.* a small brick made of compressed coal dust, used for fuel.

brisk (brɪsk) *adj.* **1.** lively and quick; vigorous: *a brisk walk.* **2.** invigorating or sharp: *brisk weather.* ~*vb.* **3.** (foll. by *up*) to enliven; make brisk.

brisket ('brɪskɪt) *n.* beef from the breast of a cow.

brisling ('brɪslɪŋ) *n.* same as **sprat.**

bristle ('brɪs³l) *n.* **1.** any short stiff hair, such as on a pig's back. **2.** something resembling these hairs: *toothbrush bristle.* ~*vb.* **3.** to stand up or cause to stand up like bristles. **4.** to show anger or indignation: *she bristled at the suggestion.* **5.** to be thickly covered or set: *the target bristled with arrows.* —'**bristly** *adj.*

Brit (brɪt) *n. Informal.* a British person.

Brit. 1. Britain. **2.** British.

Britannia (brɪ'tænɪə) *n.* a female warrior carrying a trident and wearing a helmet, personifying Great Britain.

Britannia metal *n.* an alloy of tin with antimony and copper.

Britannic (brɪ'tænɪk) *adj.* of Britain; British: *Her Britannic Majesty.*

britches ('brɪtʃɪz) *pl. n.* same as **breeches.**

British ('brɪtɪʃ) *adj.* **1.** of Great Britain or the British Commonwealth. **2.** relating to or denoting the English language as spoken and written in Britain. ~*n.* **3. the British.** (*functioning as pl.*) the people of Great Britain.

Briton ('brɪt³n) *n.* **1.** a person from Britain. **2.** *History.* any of the early Celtic inhabitants of S Britain.

brittle ('brɪt³l) *adj.* **1.** easily cracked or broken; fragile. **2.** curt or irritable: *a brittle reply.* **3.** hard or sharp in quality: *a brittle laugh.* —'**brittlely** or '**brittly** *adv.*

broach (brəʊtʃ) *vb.* **1.** to initiate (a topic) for discussion. **2.** to tap or pierce (a container) to draw off (a liquid). **3.** to open in order to begin to use. ~*n.* **4.** a tapered tool for enlarging holes. **5.** a spit for roasting meat.

broad (brɔːd) *adj.* **1.** having great breadth or width. **2.** spacious. **3.** not detailed; general. **4.** clear and open: *broad daylight.* **5.** obvious: *broad hints.* **6.** tolerant: *a broad view.* **7.** extensive: *broad support.* **8.** vulgar or coarse. **9.** strongly marked: *a broad Yorkshire accent.* ~*n.* **10.** the broad part of something. **11.** *Slang, chiefly U.S. &*

Canad. a woman. **12. the Broads.** in East Anglia, a group of shallow lakes connected by a network of rivers. —'**broadly** *adv.*

B-road *n.* a secondary road in Britain.

broad bean *n.* the large edible flattened seed of a Eurasian bean plant.

broadcast ('brɔːd‚kɑːst) *vb.* **-casting, -cast** or **-casted. 1.** to transmit (announcements or programmes) on radio or television. **2.** to take part in a radio or television programme. **3.** to make widely known throughout an area: *to broadcast news.* **4.** to scatter (seed, etc.). ~*n.* **5.** a transmission or programme on radio or television. —'**broad‚caster** *n.* —'**broad‚casting** *n.*

broadcloth ('brɔːd‚klɒθ) *n.* a closely woven fabric of wool, worsted, cotton, or rayon with a lustrous finish, used for clothing.

broaden ('brɔːd³n) *vb.* to make or become broad or broader; widen.

broad gauge *n.* a railway track with a greater distance between the lines than the standard gauge of 56½ in.

broad-leaved *adj.* denoting trees other than conifers; having broad rather than needle-shaped leaves.

broadloom ('brɔːd‚luːm) *n.* (*modifier*) of or designating carpets woven on a wide loom.

broad-minded *adj.* **1.** tolerant of opposing viewpoints; liberal. **2.** not easily shocked.

broadsheet ('brɔːd‚ʃiːt) *n.* a newspaper in a large format.

broadside ('brɔːd‚saɪd) *n.* **1.** a strong or abusive verbal or written attack. **2.** *Naval.* the simultaneous firing of all the guns on one side of a ship. **3.** *Naut.* the entire side of a ship. ~*adv.* **4.** with a broader side facing an object.

broadsword ('brɔːd‚sɔːd) *n.* a broad-bladed sword used for cutting rather than stabbing.

brocade (brəʊ'keɪd) *n.* **1.** a rich fabric woven with a raised design. ~*vb.* **2.** to weave with such a design.

broccoli ('brɒkəlɪ) *n.* a variety of cabbage with greenish flower heads eaten as a vegetable before the buds have opened.

brochette (brɒ'ʃɛt) *n.* a skewer used for holding pieces of meat or vegetables while grilling.

brochure ('brəʊʃjʊə, -ʃə) *n.* a pamphlet or booklet, esp. one containing introductory information or advertising.

broderie anglaise ('brəʊdəriː ɑːŋ'glɛz) *n.* open embroidery on white cotton, fine linen, etc.

brogue[1] (brəʊg) *n.* a broad gentle-sounding dialectal accent, esp. that used by the Irish in speaking English.

brogue[2] (brəʊg) *n.* a sturdy walking shoe, often with ornamental perforations.

broil (brɔɪl) *vb. U.S. & Canad.* same as **grill** (sense 1).

broiler ('brɔɪlə) n. a young tender chicken suitable for roasting.

broke (brəʊk) vb. 1. the past tense of **break**. ~adj. 2. Informal. having no money.

broken ('brəʊkən) vb. 1. the past participle of **break**. ~adj. 2. fractured, smashed, or splintered. 3. interrupted; disturbed: broken sleep. 4. not functioning. 5. (of a promise or contract) violated; infringed. 6. (of the speech of a foreigner) imperfectly spoken: broken English. 7. Also: **broken-in**. made tame by training. 8. exhausted or weakened, as through ill-health or misfortune.

broken chord n. same as **arpeggio**.

broken-down adj. 1. worn out, as by age or long use; dilapidated. 2. not in working order.

brokenhearted (ˌbrəʊkən'hɑːtɪd) adj. overwhelmed by grief or disappointment.

broken home n. a family which does not live together because the parents are separated or divorced.

broker ('brəʊkə) n. 1. an agent who buys or sells goods, securities, etc.: insurance broker. 2. same as **stockbroker**. 3. a person who deals in second-hand goods.

brokerage ('brəʊkərɪdʒ) n. commission charged by a broker.

brolly ('brɒlɪ) n., pl. -lies. Brit. informal. an umbrella.

bromide ('brəʊmaɪd) n. 1. any compound of bromine with another element or radical. 2. a dose of sodium or potassium bromide given as a sedative. 3. a boring, meaningless, or obvious remark.

bromide paper n. a type of photographic paper coated with an emulsion of silver bromide.

bromine ('brəʊmiːn, -mɪn) n. a dark red liquid chemical element that gives off an irritating vapour. Symbol: Br

bronchial ('brɒŋkɪəl) adj. of or relating to the bronchi or the smaller tubes into which they divide.

bronchitis (brɒŋ'kaɪtɪs) n. inflammation of the bronchial tubes, characterized by coughing, difficulty in breathing, etc.

bronchus ('brɒŋkəs) n., pl. -chi (-kaɪ). either of the two main branches of the windpipe.

bronco ('brɒŋkəʊ) n., pl. -cos. (in the U.S. and Canada) a wild or partially tamed pony of the western plains.

brontosaurus (ˌbrɒntə'sɔːrəs) n. a very large plant-eating four-footed dinosaur that had a long neck and long tail.

bronze (brɒnz) n. 1. an alloy of copper and smaller proportions of tin. 2. a statue, medal, or other object made of bronze. ~adj. 3. made of or resembling bronze. 4. yellowish-brown. ~vb. 5. (esp. of the skin) to make or become brown; tan.

Bronze Age n. a phase of human culture, lasting in Britain from about 2000 to 500 B.C., during which weapons and tools were made of bronze.

bronze medal n. a medal awarded as third prize.

brooch (brəʊtʃ) n. an ornament with a hinged pin and catch, worn fastened to clothing.

brood (bruːd) n. 1. a number of young animals, esp. birds, produced at one hatching. 2. all the children in a family: often used jokingly. ~vb. 3. (of a bird) to sit on or hatch eggs. 4. (sometimes foll. by on or over) to ponder morbidly or persistently. —'brooding n., adj.

broody ('bruːdɪ) adj. broodier, broodiest. 1. moody; introspective. 2. (of poultry) wishing to sit on or hatch eggs. 3. Informal. (of a woman) wishing to have a baby.

brook[1] (brʊk) n. a natural freshwater stream smaller than a river.

brook[2] (brʊk) vb. to bear; tolerate: she will brook no nonsense.

broom (bruːm, brʊm) n. 1. a type of long-handled sweeping brush. 2. a yellow-flowered shrub. 3. **a new broom**. a newly appointed official, etc., eager to make radical changes.

broomstick ('bruːmˌstɪk, 'brʊm-) n. the long handle of a broom.

bros. or **Bros.** brothers.

broth (brɒθ) n. a soup made by boiling meat, fish, vegetables, etc., in water.

brothel ('brɒθəl) n. a house where men pay to have sexual intercourse with prostitutes.

brother ('brʌðə) n. 1. a man or boy with the same parents as another person. 2. a man belonging to the same group, trade union, etc., as another or others; fellow member. 3. comrade; friend. 4. Christianity. a member of a male religious order.

brotherhood ('brʌðəˌhʊd) n. 1. the state of being a brother. 2. an association, such as a trade union. 3. fellowship.

brother-in-law n., pl. **brothers-in-law**. 1. the brother of one's wife or husband. 2. the husband of one's sister.

brotherly ('brʌðəlɪ) adj. of or like a brother, esp. in showing loyalty and affection.

brougham ('bruːəm, bruːm) n. a four-wheeled horse-drawn closed carriage with a raised open driver's seat in front.

brought (brɔːt) vb. past of **bring**.

brouhaha ('bruːhɑːˌhɑː) n. a loud confused noise; commotion; uproar.

brow (braʊ) n. 1. the part of the face from the eyes to the hairline; forehead. 2. same as **eyebrow**. 3. the jutting top of a hill.

browbeat ('braʊˌbiːt) vb. -beating, -beat, -beaten. to frighten (someone) with threats.

brown (braʊn) n. 1. any of various dark

colours, such as those of wood or earth. **2.** a dye or pigment producing these colours. ~*adj.* **3.** of the colour brown. **4.** (of bread) made from wheatmeal or wholemeal flour. **5.** deeply tanned. ~*vb.* **6.** to make (food) brown or (of food) to become brown as a result of cooking. —'**brownish** *or* '**browny** *adj.*

brown bear *n.* a large ferocious brownish bear inhabiting temperate forests of North America, Europe, and Asia.

brown coal *n.* same as **lignite.**

browned-off *adj. Informal, chiefly Brit.* thoroughly discouraged or disheartened; fed up.

brownie ('braʊnɪ) *n.* **1.** (in folklore) an elf said to do helpful work, esp. household chores, at night. **2.** a small square nutty chocolate cake.

Brownie Guide *or* **Brownie** ('braʊnɪ) *n.* a member of the junior branch of the Guides.

Brownie point *n.* a notional mark to one's credit for being seen to do the right thing.

browning ('braʊnɪŋ) *n. Brit.* a substance used to darken gravies.

brown paper *n.* a kind of coarse unbleached paper used for wrapping.

brown rice *n.* unpolished rice, in which the grains retain the outer yellowish-brown layer (bran).

Brown Shirt *n.* **1.** (in Nazi Germany) a storm trooper. **2.** a member of any fascist party or group.

brown sugar *n.* sugar that is unrefined or only partially refined.

brown trout *n.* a common brownish trout that occurs in the rivers of N Europe.

browse (braʊz) *vb.* **1.** to look through (a book or articles for sale) in a casual leisurely manner. **2.** (of deer, goats, etc.) to feed upon vegetation by continual nibbling. ~*n.* **3.** an instance of browsing.

brucellosis (ˌbruːsɪ'ləʊsɪs) *n.* an infectious disease of cattle, goats, and pigs, caused by bacteria and transmittable to humans.

bruise (bruːz) *vb.* **1.** to injure (body tissue) without breaking the skin, usually with discoloration, or (of body tissue) to be injured in this way. **2.** to hurt (someone's feelings). **3.** to damage (fruit). ~*n.* **4.** a bodily injury without a break in the skin, usually with discoloration.

bruiser ('bruːzə) *n.* a strong tough person, esp. a boxer or a bully.

bruit (bruːt) *vb.* **be bruited about.** to be reported or rumoured.

brunch (brʌntʃ) *n.* a meal eaten late in the morning, combining breakfast with lunch.

brunette (bruː'nɛt) *n.* a girl or woman with dark brown hair.

brunt (brʌnt) *n.* the main force or shock of a blow, attack, etc.: *I had to bear the brunt of his anger.*

brush[1] (brʌʃ) *n.* **1.** a device made of bristles, hairs, wires, etc., set into a firm back or handle: used to apply paint, groom the hair, etc. **2.** the act of brushing. **3.** a brief encounter, esp. an unfriendly one. **4.** the bushy tail of a fox. **5.** an electric conductor, esp. one made of carbon, that conveys current between stationary and rotating parts of a generator, motor, etc. ~*vb.* **6.** to clean, scrub, paint, etc., with a brush. **7.** to apply or remove with a brush or brushing movement. **8.** to touch lightly and briefly. ~See also **brush aside, brush off, brush up.**

brush[2] (brʌʃ) *n.* a thick growth of shrubs and small trees; scrub.

brush aside *or* **away** *vb.* to dismiss (a suggestion or an idea) without consideration; disregard.

brushed (brʌʃt) *adj. Textiles.* treated with a brushing process to raise the nap and give a softer and warmer finish: *brushed nylon.*

brush off *Slang.* ~*vb.* **1.** to dismiss and ignore (a person), esp. curtly. ~*n.* **brush-off. 2. give someone the brushoff.** to reject someone.

brush up *vb.* **1.** (often foll. by *on*) to refresh one's knowledge or memory of (a subject). ~*n.* **brush-up. 2.** *Brit.* the act of tidying one's appearance: *have a wash and brush-up.*

brushwood ('brʌʃˌwʊd) *n.* **1.** cut or broken-off tree branches, twigs, etc. **2.** same as **brush**[2].

brushwork ('brʌʃˌwɜːk) *n.* a characteristic manner of applying paint with a brush: *Rembrandt's brushwork.*

brusque (bruːsk, brʊsk) *adj.* blunt or curt in manner or speech. —'**brusquely** *adv.* —'**brusqueness** *n.*

Brussels sprout ('brʌsᵊlz) *n.* a vegetable like a tiny cabbage.

brutal ('bruːtᵊl) *adj.* **1.** cruel; vicious; savage. **2.** extremely honest or coarse in speech or manner. —**bru'tality** *n.* —'**brutally** *adv.*

brutalize *or* **-ise** ('bruːtəˌlaɪz) *vb.* **1.** to make or become brutal. **2.** to treat (someone) brutally. —ˌ**brutali'zation** *or* **-i'sation** *n.*

brute (bruːt) *n.* **1.** any animal except man; beast; lower animal. **2.** a brutal person. ~*adj.* **3.** wholly instinctive or physical, like that of an animal: *we will never yield to brute force.* **4.** without reason or intelligence. **5.** coarse and grossly sensual.

brutish ('bruːtɪʃ) *adj.* **1.** of or resembling a brute; animal. **2.** coarse; cruel; stupid.

bryony ('braɪənɪ) *n., pl.* **-nies.** a climbing plant with greenish flowers and red or black berries.

Brythonic (brɪ'θɒnɪk) *n.* **1.** the S group of Celtic languages, consisting of Welsh, Cornish, and Breton. ~*adj.* **2.** of this group of languages.

BS 1. Bachelor of Surgery. **2.** British Standard(s).

BSc Bachelor of Science.

BSI British Standards Institution.

B-side *n.* the less important side of a gramophone record.

BST 1. British Standard Time. **2.** British Summer Time.

Bt Baronet.

BT British Telecom.

btu *or* **BThU** British thermal unit.

bubble ('bʌbˀl) *n.* **1.** a thin film of liquid forming a ball around air or a gas: *a soap bubble.* **2.** a small globule of air or a gas in a liquid or a solid. **3.** an unreliable scheme or enterprise. **4.** a dome, esp. a transparent glass or plastic one. ~*vb.* **5.** to form bubbles. **6.** to move or flow with a gurgling sound. **7. bubble over.** to express an emotion freely: *she was bubbling over with excitement.*

bubble and squeak *n. Brit.* a dish of boiled cabbage and potatoes fried together.

bubble bath *n.* **1.** a substance used to scent, soften, and foam in bath water. **2.** a bath with such a substance.

bubble car *n. Brit.* a small car with a transparent bubble-shaped top.

bubble gum *n.* a type of chewing gum that can be blown into large bubbles.

bubbly ('bʌblɪ) *adj.* **-blier, -bliest. 1.** full of or resembling bubbles. **2.** lively; animated; excited. ~*n.* **3.** *Informal.* champagne.

bubo ('bjuːbəʊ) *n., pl.* **-boes.** *Pathol.* inflammation and swelling of a lymph node, esp. in the armpit or groin. —**bubonic** (bjuː'bɒnɪk) *adj.*

bubonic plague *n.* an acute infectious disease characterized by the formation of buboes.

buccaneer (ˌbʌkə'nɪə) *n.* a pirate, esp. in the Caribbean in the 17th and 18th centuries.

buck¹ (bʌk) *n.* **1.** the male of the goat, hare, kangaroo, rabbit, and reindeer. **2.** *Archaic.* a spirited young man. **3.** the act of bucking. ~*vb.* **4.** (of a horse or other animal) to jump vertically, with legs stiff and back arched. **5.** (of a horse, etc.) to throw (its rider) by bucking. **6.** *Chiefly U.S., Canad., & Austral. informal.* to resist or oppose obstinately. ~See also **buck up.**

buck² (bʌk) *n. U.S., Canad., & Austral. slang.* a dollar.

buck³ (bʌk) *n.* **pass the buck.** *Informal.* to shift blame or responsibility onto another.

bucket ('bʌkɪt) *n.* **1.** an open-topped cylindrical container. **2.** the amount a bucket will hold. **3.** a bucket-like part of a machine, such as the scoop on a mechanical shovel. **4. kick the bucket.** *Slang.* to die.

bucket down *vb.* (of rain) to fall very heavily.

bucket shop *n.* **1.** *Chiefly Brit.* a travel agency specializing in cheap airline tickets. **2.** an unregistered firm of stockbrokers that engages in fraudulent speculation.

buckle ('bʌkˀl) *n.* **1.** a clasp for fastening together two loose ends, esp. of a belt or strap. ~*vb.* **2.** to fasten or be fastened with a buckle. **3.** to bend or cause to bend out of shape, esp. as a result of pressure or heat.

buckle down *vb. Informal.* to apply oneself with determination.

buckler ('bʌklə) *n.* a small round shield worn on the forearm.

buckram ('bʌkrəm) *n.* stiffened cotton or linen used in lining or stiffening clothes, bookbinding, etc.

Bucks (bʌks) Buckinghamshire.

buckshee (ˌbʌk'ʃiː) *adj. Brit. slang.* without charge; free.

buckshot ('bʌkˌʃɒt) *n.* large lead shot used for hunting game.

buckskin ('bʌkˌskɪn) *n.* **1.** a strong greyish-yellow suede leather, originally made from deerskin. **2.** (*pl.*) trousers made of buckskin.

buckteeth (ˌbʌk'tiːθ) *pl. n.* projecting upper front teeth. —**buck-toothed** (ˌbʌk-'tuːθt) *adj.*

buckthorn ('bʌkˌθɔːn) *n.* a thorny shrub whose berries were formerly used as a purgative.

buck up *vb. Informal.* **1.** to make or become more cheerful, confident, etc. **2.** to make haste.

buckwheat ('bʌkˌwiːt) *n.* **1.** a type of small black seed used as animal fodder and in making flour. **2.** the flour obtained from such seeds.

bucolic (bjuː'kɒlɪk) *adj.* **1.** of the countryside or country life; rustic. **2.** of or relating to shepherds; pastoral. ~*n.* **3.** a pastoral poem.

bud (bʌd) *n.* **1.** a swelling on the stem of a plant that develops into a flower or leaf. **2.** a partially opened flower: *rosebud.* **3.** any small budlike outgrowth: *taste buds.* **4. nip something in the bud.** to put an end to something in its initial stages. ~*vb.* **budding, budded. 5.** (of plants and some animals) to produce buds. **6.** to begin to develop or grow: *a budding actor.* **7.** *Horticulture.* to graft (a bud) from one plant onto another.

Buddhism ('bʊdɪzəm) *n.* a religion founded by the Buddha that teaches that all suffering can be brought to an end by overcoming greed, hatred, and delusion. —'**Buddhist** *n., adj.*

buddleia ('bʌdlɪə) *n.* an ornamental shrub which has long spikes of typically purple flowers.

buddy ('bʌdɪ) n., pl. **-dies. 1.** Chiefly U.S. & Canad. informal. a friend. **2.** a volunteer who helps and supports a person suffering from AIDS. ~vb. **-dying, -died. 3.** to act as a buddy to a person suffering from AIDS.

budge (bʌdʒ) vb. **1.** to move slightly: she refuses to budge off that chair. **2.** to change or cause to change opinions: she will not budge on any of the important issues.

budgerigar ('bʌdʒərɪˌgɑː) n. a small caged bird bred in many different-coloured varieties.

budget ('bʌdʒɪt) n. **1.** a plan of expected income and expenditure over a specified period. **2.** (modifier) inexpensive: budget meals for a family. **3.** the total amount of money allocated for a specific purpose during a specified period. ~vb. **4.** to enter or provide for in a budget. **5.** to plan the expenditure of (money or time). —**'budgetary** adj.

Budget ('bʌdʒɪt) n. **the.** an annual estimate of British government expenditures and revenues and the financial plans for the following financial year.

budgie ('bʌdʒɪ) n. Informal. same as **budgerigar.**

buff[1] (bʌf) n. **1.** a soft thick flexible undyed leather. **2.** a cloth or pad of material used for polishing. **3. in the buff.** Informal. completely naked. ~adj. **4.** dull yellowish-brown. ~vb. **5.** to clean or polish (a metal, floor, shoes, etc.) with a buff.

buff[2] (bʌf) n. Informal. an expert on or devotee of a given subject: an opera buff.

buffalo ('bʌfəˌləʊ) n., pl. **-loes** or **-lo. 1.** a type of cattle with upward-curving horns. **2.** same as **water buffalo. 3.** U.S. & Canad. a bison.

buffer[1] ('bʌfə) n. **1.** one of a pair of spring-loaded steel pads attached at both ends of railway vehicles and at the end of a railway track to reduce shock due to contact. **2.** a person or thing that lessens shock or protects from damaging impact, circumstances, etc. **3.** Chem. **a.** a substance added to a solution to resist changes in its acidity or alkalinity. **b.** Also called: **buffer solution.** a solution containing such a substance. **4.** Computers. a device for temporarily storing data.

buffer[2] ('bʌfə) n. Brit. informal. a stupid or bumbling person, esp. a man: an old buffer.

buffer state n. a small and usually neutral state between two rival powers.

buffet[1] ('bʊfeɪ) n. **1.** a counter where light refreshments are served. **2.** a meal at which guests help themselves from a number of dishes.

buffet[2] ('bʌfɪt) vb. **-feting, -feted. 1.** to knock against or about; batter: the ship was buffeted by huge waves. **2.** to hit, esp. with the fist. ~n. **3.** a blow, esp. with a hand.

buffet car ('bʊfeɪ) n. Brit. a railway coach where light refreshments are served.

buffoon (bə'fuːn) n. a person who amuses others by silly behaviour. —**buf'foonery** n.

bug (bʌg) n. **1.** any of various insects having piercing and sucking mouthparts. **2.** Chiefly U.S. & Canad. any insect. **3.** Informal. a minor illness such as a stomach infection caused by a germ or virus. **4.** Informal. an obsessive idea or hobby; craze. **5.** Informal. a concealed microphone used for recording conversations, as in spying. ~vb. **bugging, bugged.** Informal. **6.** to irritate or upset (someone). **7.** to conceal a microphone in (a room or telephone).

bugbear ('bʌgˌbɛə) n. a thing that causes obsessive anxiety.

bugger ('bʌgə) n. **1.** Taboo slang. a person or thing considered to be unpleasant or difficult. **2.** Slang. a humorous or affectionate term for a man or child: a friendly little bugger. **3.** a person who practises buggery. ~vb. **4.** Slang. to tire; weary. **5.** to practise buggery with. ~interj. **6.** Taboo slang. an exclamation of annoyance or disappointment.

bugger about or **around** vb. Slang. **1.** to fool about and waste time. **2.** to create difficulties for: they really buggered me about when I tried to get my money back.

bugger off vb. Taboo slang. to go away; depart.

bugger up vb. Slang. to spoil or ruin (something).

buggery ('bʌgərɪ) n. anal intercourse.

buggy ('bʌgɪ) n., pl. **-gies. 1.** a light horse-drawn carriage having two or four wheels. **2.** a lightweight folding pram for babies or young children.

bugle ('bjuːg°l) Music. ~n. **1.** a brass instrument used chiefly for military calls. ~vb. **2.** to play or sound (on) a bugle. —**'bugler** n.

build (bɪld) vb. **building, built. 1.** to make, construct, or form by joining parts or materials: to build a house. **2.** to establish and develop: it took ten years to build a business. **3.** to make in a particular way or for a particular purpose: the car was not built for speed. **4.** (often foll. by up) to increase in intensity. ~n. **5.** physical form, figure, or proportions: a man with an athletic build.

builder ('bɪldə) n. a person who contracts for and supervises the construction of buildings.

building ('bɪldɪŋ) n. **1.** a structure, such as a house, with a roof and walls. **2.** the business of building houses, etc.

building society n. a cooperative banking enterprise financed by deposits on which interest is paid and from which mortgage loans are advanced on homes and real property.

build up vb. 1. to construct (something) gradually, systematically, and in stages. 2. to increase, accumulate, or strengthen, esp. by degrees: *the murmur built up to a roar.* 3. to prepare for or gradually approach a climax. ~n. **build-up.** 4. a progressive increase in number or size: *the build-up of industry.* 5. a gradual approach to a climax. 6. extravagant publicity or praise, esp. in the form of a campaign.

built (bɪlt) vb. past of **build.**

built-in adj. 1. incorporated as an integral part: *a built-in cupboard.* 2. essential; inherent.

built-up adj. 1. having many buildings: *a built-up area.* 2. increased by the addition of parts: *built-up heels.*

bulb (bʌlb) n. 1. the onion-shaped base of the stem of some plants, which sends down roots. 2. a plant, such as a daffodil, which grows from a bulb. 3. same as **light bulb.** 4. any bulb-shaped thing. —'**bulbous** adj.

bulge (bʌldʒ) n. 1. a swelling or an outward curve on a normally flat surface. 2. a sudden increase in number, esp. of population. ~vb. 3. to swell outwards. —'**bulging** adj.

bulimia (bʊ'lɪmɪə) n. a disorder characterized by compulsive overeating followed by vomiting.

bulk (bʌlk) n. 1. volume, size, or magnitude, esp. when great. 2. the main part: *the bulk of the work is repetitious.* 3. a large body, esp. of a person. 4. the part of food which passes unabsorbed through the digestive system. ~vb. 5. **bulk large.** to be or seem important or prominent.

bulk buying n. the purchase of goods in large amounts, often at reduced prices.

bulkhead ('bʌlk,hed) n. any upright wall-like partition in a ship or aeroplane.

bulky ('bʌlkɪ) adj. **bulkier, bulkiest.** very large and massive, esp. so as to be unwieldy. —'**bulkiness** n.

bull[1] (bʊl) n. 1. a male of domestic cattle, esp. one that is sexually mature. 2. the male of various other animals including the elephant and whale. 3. a very large, strong, or aggressive person. 4. *Stock Exchange.* a speculator who buys in anticipation of rising prices in order to make a profit on resale. 5. *Chiefly Brit.* same as **bull's-eye** (senses 1, 2). 6. **like a bull in a china shop.** clumsy. 7. **take the bull by the horns.** to face and tackle a difficulty without shirking.

bull[2] (bʊl) n. a ludicrously self-contradictory or inconsistent statement.

bull[3] (bʊl) n. a formal document issued by the pope.

bulldog ('bʊl,dɒg) n. a sturdy thickset dog with a broad head and a muscular body.

bulldog clip n. a clip for holding papers together, consisting of two metal clamps and a spring.

bulldoze ('bʊl,dəʊz) vb. 1. to move, demolish, or flatten with a bulldozer. 2. *Informal.* to coerce (someone) into doing something by intimidation.

bulldozer ('bʊl,dəʊzə) n. a powerful tractor fitted with caterpillar tracks and a blade at the front, used for moving earth.

bullet ('bʊlɪt) n. a small metallic missile used as the projectile of a gun or rifle.

bulletin ('bʊlɪtɪn) n. 1. a broadcast summary of the news 2. an official statement on a matter of public interest. 3. a periodical published by an organization for its members.

bullfight ('bʊl,faɪt) n. a public show, popular in Spain, in which a matador baits and usually kills a bull in an arena. —'**bull,fighter** n. —'**bull,fighting** n.

bullfinch ('bʊl,fɪntʃ) n. a common European songbird with a black head and, in the male, a pinkish breast.

bullfrog ('bʊl,frɒg) n. a large American frog with a loud deep croak.

bullion ('bʊljən) n. gold or silver in the form of bars and ingots.

bull-necked adj. having a short thick neck.

bullock ('bʊlək) n. a gelded bull; steer.

bullring ('bʊl,rɪŋ) n. an arena for bull-fighting.

bull's-eye n. 1. the small central disc of a target or a dartboard. 2. a shot hitting this. 3. *Informal.* something that exactly achieves its aim. 4. a peppermint-flavoured boiled sweet. 5. a small circular window. 6. a thick disc of glass set into a ship's deck, etc., to admit light. 7. the glass boss at the centre of a sheet of blown glass. 8. **a.** a convex lens used as a condenser. **b.** a lamp or lantern containing such a lens.

bullshit ('bʊl,ʃɪt) *Taboo slang.* ~n. 1. exaggerated or foolish talk; nonsense. ~vb. -**shitting, -shitted.** 2. to talk bullshit to: *don't bullshit me.*

bull terrier n. a terrier with a muscular body and a short smooth coat.

bully ('bʊlɪ) n., pl. -**lies.** 1. a person who hurts, persecutes, or intimidates weaker people. ~vb. -**lying, -lied.** 2. to hurt, intimidate, or persecute (a weaker or smaller person), esp. to make him do something. ~interj. 3. **bully for you, him,** etc. *Informal.* well done! bravo!: now usually used sarcastically.

bully beef n. canned corned beef.

bully-off *Hockey.* ~n. 1. the method of starting play in which two opposing players stand with the ball between them and strike their sticks together three times before trying to hit the ball. ~vb. **bully off.** 2. to start play with a bully-off.

bulrush ('bʊl,rʌʃ) *n.* **1.** a tall reedlike marsh plant with brown spiky flowers. **2.** *Bible.* same as **papyrus** (the plant).

bulwark ('bʊlwək) *n.* **1.** a wall or similar structure used as a fortification; rampart. **2.** a person or thing acting as a defence. ~*vb.* **3.** to defend or fortify with or as if with a bulwark.

bum[1] (bʌm) *n. Brit. slang.* the buttocks or anus.

bum[2] (bʌm) *Informal, chiefly U.S. & Canad.* ~*n.* **1.** a disreputable loafer or idler. **2.** a tramp; hobo. ~*vb.* **bumming, bummed. 3.** to get by begging; cadge: *to bum a lift.* **4. bum around.** to spend time to no good purpose; loaf. ~*adj.* **5.** of poor quality; useless: *he hit a bum note.*

bumble ('bʌmb²l) *vb.* **1.** to speak or do in a clumsy, muddled, or inefficient way. **2.** to move in a clumsy or unsteady way. —'**bumbling** *adj., n.*

bumblebee ('bʌmb²l,biː) *n.* a large hairy social bee.

bumf (bʌmf) *n.* same as **bumph.**

bump (bʌmp) *vb.* **1.** to knock or strike (someone or something) with a jolt. **2.** to travel or proceed in jerks and jolts. **3.** to hurt by knocking. ~*n.* **4.** an impact; knock; jolt; collision. **5.** a dull thud from an impact or collision. **6.** a lump on the body caused by a blow. **7.** a raised uneven part, as on a road surface. ~See also **bump into, bump off, bump up.** —'**bumpy** *adj.*

bumper[1] ('bʌmpə) *n.* a horizontal bar attached to the front or rear of a vehicle to protect against damage from impact.

bumper[2] ('bʌmpə) *n.* **1.** a glass or tankard, filled to the brim, esp. as a toast. **2.** an unusually large or fine example of something. ~*adj.* **3.** unusually large, fine, or abundant: *a bumper crop.*

bumph *or* **bumf** (bʌmf) *n. Brit.* **1.** *Informal.* official documents or forms. **2.** *Slang.* toilet paper.

bump into *vb. Informal.* to meet (someone) by chance; encounter (someone) unexpectedly.

bumpkin ('bʌmpkın) *n.* an awkward simple rustic person: *a country bumpkin.*

bump off *vb. Slang.* to murder (someone).

bumptious ('bʌmpʃəs) *adj.* offensively self-assertive or conceited.

bump up *vb. Informal.* to increase (prices) by a large amount.

bun (bʌn) *n.* **1.** a small sweetened roll, similar to bread but often containing currants or spices. **2.** *Chiefly Scot. & N English.* a small round cake. **3.** a hairstyle in which long hair is gathered into a bun shape at the back of the head.

bunch (bʌntʃ) *n.* **1.** a number of things growing, fastened, or grouped together: *a bunch of grapes; a bunch of keys.* **2.** a collection; group: *a bunch of queries.* **3.**

Informal. a group or company: *a bunch of boys.* ~*vb.* **4.** to group or be grouped into a bunch.

bundle ('bʌnd²l) *n.* **1.** a number of things or a quantity of material gathered or loosely bound together: *a bundle of sticks.* **2.** something wrapped or tied for carrying; package. **3.** *Biol.* a collection of strands of specialized tissue such as nerve fibres. **4.** *Bot.* a strand of conducting tissue within plants. ~*vb.* **5.** (foll. by *out, off, into,* etc.) to cause to go, esp. roughly or unceremoniously. **6.** to push (someone) or throw (something), esp. in a quick untidy way.

bundle up *vb.* to make (something) into a bundle or bundles, esp. by tying.

bun fight *n. Brit. slang.* **1.** a tea party. **2.** an official function.

bung (bʌŋ) *n.* **1.** a stopper, esp. of cork or rubber, used to close something such as a cask or flask. **2.** same as **bunghole.** ~*vb.* **3.** (foll. by *up*) *Informal.* to close or seal (something) with or as if with a bung. **4.** *Brit. slang.* to throw (something) somewhere in a careless manner; sling.

bungalow ('bʌŋgə,ləʊ) *n.* a one-storey house.

bunghole ('bʌŋ,həʊl) *n.* a hole in a cask or barrel through which liquid can be drained.

bungle ('bʌŋg²l) *vb.* **1.** to spoil (an operation) through clumsiness or incompetence; botch. ~*n.* **2.** a clumsy or unsuccessful performance; mistake; botch. —'**bungler** *n.* —'**bungling** *adj., n.*

bunion ('bʌnjən) *n.* an inflamed swelling of the first joint of the big toe.

bunk[1] (bʌŋk) *n.* **1.** a narrow shelflike bed fixed along a wall, esp. in a caravan or ship. **2.** same as **bunk bed.**

bunk[2] (bʌŋk) *n. Informal.* same as **bunkum.**

bunk[3] (bʌŋk) *n.* **do a bunk.** *Brit. slang.* to make a hurried departure, usually under suspicious circumstances.

bunk bed *n.* one of a pair of beds constructed one above the other to save space.

bunker ('bʌŋkə) *n.* **1.** a large storage container or tank, as for coal. **2.** an obstacle on a golf course, usually a sand-filled hollow bordered by a ridge. **3.** an underground shelter.

bunkum ('bʌŋkəm) *n.* empty talk; nonsense.

bunny ('bʌnı) *n., pl.* **-nies.** a child's word for **rabbit.**

bunny girl *n.* a night-club hostess whose costume includes a rabbit-like tail and ears.

Bunsen burner ('bʌns²n) *n.* a gas burner consisting of a metal tube with an adjustable air valve at the base.

bunting[1] ('bʌntıŋ) *n.* **1.** a loosely woven cotton fabric used for flags. **2.** decorative flags, pennants, and streamers.

bunting[2] ('bʌntıŋ) *n.* a songbird with a short stout bill.

buoy (bɔı; *U.S.* 'buːı) *n.* **1.** a brightly-coloured floating object anchored to the seabed for designating moorings, navigable channels, or obstructions in the water. ~*vb.* **2.** (foll. by *up*) to prevent from sinking: *the life belt buoyed him up.* **3.** to raise the spirits of; hearten: *the news really buoyed him up.* **4.** *Naut.* to mark (a channel or obstruction) with a buoy or buoys.

buoyant (ˈbɔɪənt) *adj.* **1.** able to float in or rise to the surface of a liquid. **2.** (of a liquid or gas) able to keep a body afloat. **3.** cheerful or resilient. —ˈ**buoyancy** *n.*

BUPA (ˈbjuːpə, ˈbuːpə) British United Provident Association: a private medical insurance scheme.

bur *or* **burr** (bɜː) *n.* **1.** a seed case or flower head with hooks or prickles. **2.** any plant that produces burs.

burble (ˈbɜːbᵊl) *vb.* **1.** to make or utter with a bubbling sound; gurgle. **2.** to talk quickly and excitedly.

burbot (ˈbɜːbət) *n., pl.* **-bots** *or* **-bot.** a freshwater fish of the cod family that has barbels around its mouth.

burden[1] (ˈbɜːdᵊn) *n.* **1.** something that is carried; load. **2.** something that is exacting, oppressive, or difficult to bear. ~*vb.* **3.** to put or impose a burden on; load. **4.** to weigh down; oppress. —ˈ**burdensome** *adj.*

burden[2] (ˈbɜːdᵊn) *n.* **1.** a line of words recurring at the end of each verse of a song. **2.** the theme of a speech, book, etc.

burdock (ˈbɜːˌdɒk) *n.* a weed with large heart-shaped leaves, and burlike fruits.

bureau (ˈbjuərəʊ) *n., pl.* **-reaus** *or* **-reaux** (-rəʊz). **1.** *Chiefly Brit.* a writing desk with pigeonholes and drawers against which the writing surface can be closed when not in use. **2.** *U.S.* a chest of drawers. **3.** an office or agency, esp. one providing services for the public. **4.** *U.S.* a government department.

bureaucracy (bjuəˈrɒkrəsɪ) *n., pl.* **-cies.** **1.** a system of administration based upon organization into bureaus, division of labour, a hierarchy of authority, etc. **2.** government by such a system. **3.** government officials collectively. **4.** any administration in which action is impeded by unnecessary official procedures.

bureaucrat (ˈbjuərəˌkræt) *n.* **1.** an official in a bureaucracy. **2.** an official who adheres rigidly to bureaucracy. —ˌ**bureauˈcratic** *adj.*

burette *or U.S.* **buret** (bjuˈrɛt) *n.* a graduated glass tube with a stopcock on one end for dispensing known volumes of fluids.

burgeon (ˈbɜːdʒən) *vb.* to develop or grow rapidly; flourish.

burger (ˈbɜːgə) *n. Informal.* same as **hamburger.**

burgess (ˈbɜːdʒɪs) *n.* **1.** (in England) a citizen, freeman, or inhabitant of a borough. **2.** *English history.* a Member of Parliament from a borough, corporate town, or university.

burgh (ˈbʌrə) *n.* **1.** (in Scotland until 1975) a town with a degree of self-government. **2.** *Archaic.* a borough.

burgher (ˈbɜːgə) *n. Archaic.* a person from a corporate town, esp. on the Continent.

burglar (ˈbɜːglə) *n.* a person who commits burglary.

burglary (ˈbɜːglərɪ) *n., pl.* **-ries.** the crime of entering a building as a trespasser to commit theft or another offence.

burgle (ˈbɜːgᵊl) *vb.* to break into (a house, shop, etc.).

burgomaster (ˈbɜːgəˌmɑːstə) *n.* the chief magistrate of a town in Austria, Belgium, Germany, or the Netherlands.

burial (ˈbɛrɪəl) *n.* the burying of a dead body.

burin (ˈbjuərɪn) *n.* a steel chisel used for engraving metal, wood, or marble.

burk *or* **berk** (bɜːk) *n. Brit. slang.* a stupid person; fool.

burl *or* **birl** (bɜːl) *n. Informal.* **1.** *Scot., Austral., & N.Z.* an attempt; try: *give it a burl.* **2.** *Austral. & N.Z.* a ride in a car.

burlesque (bɜːˈlɛsk) *n.* **1.** an artistic work, esp. literary or dramatic, satirizing a subject by caricaturing it. **2.** *U.S. & Canad. theatre.* a bawdy comedy show of the late 19th and early 20th centuries. ~*adj.* **3.** of or characteristic of a burlesque.

burly (ˈbɜːlɪ) *adj.* **-lier, -liest.** large and thick of build; sturdy.

burn[1] (bɜːn) *vb.* **burning, burnt** *or* **burned.** **1.** to be or set on fire. **2.** to destroy or be destroyed by fire. **3.** to damage, injure, or mark by heat: *he burnt his hand.* **4.** to die or put to death by fire. **5.** to be or feel hot: *my forehead is burning.* **6.** to smart or cause to smart: *brandy burns your throat.* **7.** to feel strong emotion, esp. anger or passion. **8.** to use for the purposes of light, heat, or power: *to burn coal.* **9.** to form by or as if by fire: *to burn a hole.* **10.** to char or become charred: *the potatoes are burning.* **11. burn one's boats** *or* **bridges.** to commit oneself to a particular course of action with no possibility of turning back. **12. burn one's fingers.** to suffer from having meddled or interfered. ~*n.* **13.** an injury caused by exposure to heat, electrical, chemical, or radioactive agents. **14.** a mark caused by burning. ~See also **burn out.**

burn[2] (bɜːn) *n. Scot.* a small stream; brook.

burner (ˈbɜːnə) *n.* the part of a stove or lamp that produces flame or heat.

burning (ˈbɜːnɪŋ) *adj.* **1.** intense; passionate. **2.** urgent; crucial: *a burning problem.*

burning glass *n.* a convex lens for concentrating the sun's rays to produce fire.

burnish (ˈbɜːnɪʃ) *vb.* to make or become shiny or smooth by friction; polish.

burnous (bɜːˈnuːs) *n.* a long circular cloak with a hood, worn esp. by Arabs.

burn out *vb.* **1.** to become or cause to become inoperative as a result of heat or friction: *the clutch burnt out.* ~*n.* **burn-out. 2.** total exhaustion and inability to work effectively as a result of excessive demands or overwork.

burnt (bɜːnt) *vb.* **1.** a past tense and past participle of **burn**¹. ~*adj.* **2.** affected by or as if by burning; charred.

burnt sienna *n.* **1.** a reddish-brown pigment obtained by roasting raw sienna. ~*adj.* **2.** reddish-brown.

burp (bɜːp) *n.* **1.** *Informal.* a belch. ~*vb.* **2.** *Informal.* to belch. **3.** to cause (a baby) to belch.

burr (bɜː) *n.* **1.** a whirring or humming sound. **2.** the soft trilling sound given to the letter (r) in some English dialects. **3.** a rough edge left on metal or paper after cutting. **4.** a small hand-operated drill.

burrow (ˈbʌrəʊ) *n.* **1.** a hole dug in the ground by a rabbit or other small animal. ~*vb.* **2.** to dig (a tunnel or hole) in, through, or under ground. **3.** to move through a place by or as by digging. **4.** to delve deeply: *he burrowed into his pockets.* **5.** to live in a burrow.

bursar (ˈbɜːsə) *n.* a treasurer of a school, college, or university.

bursary (ˈbɜːsərɪ) *n., pl.* -**ries.** a scholarship awarded esp. in Scottish and New Zealand schools and universities.

burst (bɜːst) *vb.* **bursting, burst. 1.** to break or cause to break open or apart suddenly and noisily; explode. **2.** to come or go suddenly and forcibly: *he burst into the room.* **3.** to be full to the point of breaking open: *bursting at the seams.* **4.** (foll. by *into*) to give vent to (something) suddenly or loudly: *to burst into song.* ~*n.* **5.** an instance of breaking open suddenly; explosion. **6.** a break; breach; rupture. **7.** a sudden increase of effort; spurt: *a burst of speed.* **8.** a sudden and violent occurrence or outbreak: *a burst of applause.*

burton (ˈbɜːt²n) *n.* **go for a burton.** *Brit. slang.* **a.** to be broken, useless, or lost. **b.** to die.

bury (ˈbɛrɪ) *vb.* **burying, buried. 1.** to place (a corpse) in a grave. **2.** to place (something) in the earth and cover it with soil. **3.** to cover (something) from sight; hide. **4.** to occupy (oneself) with deep concentration: *to be buried in a book.* **5.** to dismiss (a feeling) from the mind: *to bury old hatreds.*

bus (bʌs) *n.* **1.** a large motor vehicle designed to carry passengers between stopping places along a regular route. **2.** *Informal.* a car or aircraft that is old and shaky. **3.** *Electronics, computers.* an electrical conductor used to make a common connection between several circuits. ~*vb.* **busing, bused** *or* **bussing, bussed. 4.** to travel or transport by bus. **5.** *Chiefly U.S. & Canad.* to transport (children) by bus from one area to another in order to create racially integrated schools.

busby (ˈbʌzbɪ) *n., pl.* -**bies.** a tall fur helmet worn by certain British soldiers.

bush¹ (bʊʃ) *n.* **1.** a dense woody plant, smaller than a tree, with many branches; shrub. **2.** a dense cluster of such shrubs; thicket. **3.** something resembling a bush, esp. in density: *a bush of hair.* **4. the.** uncultivated area covered with trees or shrubs in Australia, Africa, New Zealand, and Canada. **5.** *Canad.* an area on a farm on which timber is grown and cut. **6. beat about the bush.** to avoid the point at issue.

bush² (bʊʃ) *n.* **1.** a thin metal sleeve or tubular lining serving as a bearing. ~*vb.* **2.** to fit a bush to (a casing or bearing).

bushbaby (ˈbʊʃˌbeɪbɪ) *n., pl.* -**babies.** a small agile tree-living mammal with large eyes and a long tail.

bushed (bʊʃt) *adj. Informal.* extremely tired; exhausted.

bushel (ˈbʊʃəl) *n.* a British unit of dry or liquid measure equal to 8 imperial gallons.

bush jacket *n.* a casual jacket with four patch pockets and a belt.

bush line *n.* an airline operating in the bush country of Canada's northern regions.

bush lot *n. Canad.* same as **bush**¹ (sense 5).

bushman (ˈbʊʃmən) *n., pl.* -**men.** *Austral. & N.Z.* a person who lives or travels in the bush.

Bushman (ˈbʊʃmən) *n., pl.* -**men.** a member of a hunting and gathering people of southern Africa.

bush pilot *n. Canad.* a pilot who operates in the bush country.

bush sickness *n. N.Z.* a disease of animals caused by mineral deficiency in old bush country. —ˈbush-ˌsick *adj.*

bush tea *n.* a beverage prepared from the dried leaves of a shrub of southern Africa.

bush telegraph *n.* a means of spreading rumour or gossip.

bushveld (ˈbʊʃˌfɛlt, -vɛlt) *n. S. African.* bushy countryside.

bushy (ˈbʊʃɪ) *adj.* **bushier, bushiest. 1.** (of hair) thick and shaggy. **2.** covered or overgrown with bushes.

business (ˈbɪznɪs) *n.* **1.** a trade or profession. **2.** the purchase and sale of goods and services. **3.** a commercial or industrial establishment. **4.** commercial activity; dealings: *firms that do business with Britain.* **5.** proper or rightful concern or responsibility: *mind your own business.* **6.** an affair; matter: *it's a dreadful business.* **7.** serious work or activity: *get down to business.* **8.** a difficult or complicated matter. **9. mean business.** to be in earnest.

businesslike ('bɪznɪs,laɪk) *adj.* efficient and methodical.

businessman ('bɪznɪs,mæn, -mən) *or (fem.)* **businesswoman** *n., pl.* **-men** *or* **-women.** a person engaged in commercial or industrial business, usually an owner or executive.

business park *n.* an area specially designated to accommodate business offices, light industry, etc.

business school *n.* an institution that offers courses to managers in aspects of business, such as marketing, finance, and law.

busker ('bʌskə) *n.* a person who entertains for money in streets or stations. —**busk** *vb.*

busman's holiday ('bʌsmənz) *n. Informal.* a holiday spent doing the same as one does at work.

bust[1] (bʌst) *n.* **1.** a woman's bosom. **2.** a sculpture of the head, shoulders, and upper chest of a person.

bust[2] (bʌst) *Informal.* ~*vb.* **busting, busted** *or* **bust.** **1.** to burst or break. **2.** (of the police) to raid or search (a place) or arrest (someone). **3.** *U.S. & Canad.* to demote in military rank. ~*adj.* **4.** broken. **5. go bust.** to become bankrupt.

bustle[1] ('bʌsəl) *vb.* **1.** (often foll. by *about*) to hurry with a great show of energy or activity. ~*n.* **2.** energetic and noisy activity. —'**bustling** *adj.*

bustle[2] ('bʌsəl) *n.* a cushion or framework worn by women in the late 19th century at the back in order to expand the skirt.

bust-up *Informal.* ~*n.* **1.** a serious quarrel, esp. one ending a relationship. **2.** *Brit.* a disturbance or brawl. ~*vb.* **bust up. 3.** to quarrel and part. **4.** to disrupt (a meeting), esp. violently.

busy ('bɪzɪ) *adj.* **busier, busiest. 1.** actively or fully engaged; occupied. **2.** crowded with or characterized by activity. **3.** *Chiefly U.S. & Canad.* (of a telephone line) in use; engaged. ~*vb.* **busying, busied. 4.** to make or keep (someone, esp. oneself) busy; occupy. —'**busily** *adv.*

busybody ('bɪzɪ,bɒdɪ) *n., pl.* **-bodies.** a meddlesome, prying, or officious person.

but (bʌt; *unstressed* bət) *conj.* **1.** contrary to expectation: *he cut his knee but didn't cry.* **2.** in contrast; on the contrary: *I like opera but my husband doesn't.* **3.** other than: *we can't do anything but wait.* **4.** without it happening: *we never go out but it rains.* ~*prep.* **5.** except: *they saved all but one.* **6. but for.** were it not for: *but for you, we couldn't have managed.* ~*adv.* **7.** only: *I can but try; he was but a child.* ~*n.* **8.** an objection: *ifs and buts.*

but and ben *n. Scot.* a two-roomed cottage consisting of an outer room (**but**) and an inner room (**ben**).

butane ('bju:teɪn, bju:'teɪn) *n.* a colourless gas used in the manufacture of rubber and fuels.

butch (bʊtʃ) *adj. Slang.* (of a woman or man) markedly or aggressively masculine.

butcher ('bʊtʃə) *n.* **1.** a retailer of meat. **2.** a person who slaughters animals for meat. **3.** an indiscriminate or brutal murderer. ~*vb.* **4.** to slaughter (animals) for meat. **5.** to kill (people) indiscriminately or brutally. **6.** to make a mess of; botch.

butchery ('bʊtʃərɪ) *n., pl.* **-eries. 1.** senseless slaughter. **2.** the business of a butcher.

butler ('bʌtlə) *n.* the head manservant of a household, in charge of the wines, table, etc.

butt[1] (bʌt) *n.* **1.** the thicker or blunt end of something, such as the stock of a rifle. **2.** the unused end of something, esp. a cigarette; stub. **3.** *U.S. & Canad. slang.* the buttocks.

butt[2] (bʌt) *n.* **1.** a person or thing that is the target of ridicule or teasing. **2.** *Shooting, archery.* **a.** a mound of earth behind the target. **b.** (*pl.*) the target range.

butt[3] (bʌt) *vb.* **1.** to strike (something or someone) with the head or horns. **2.** (foll. by *in* or *into*) to intrude, esp. into a conversation; interfere. ~*n.* **3.** a blow with the head or horns.

butt[4] (bʌt) *n.* a large cask for collecting or storing liquids.

butte (bju:t) *n. U.S. & Canad.* an isolated steep flat-topped hill.

butter ('bʌtə) *n.* **1.** an edible fatty yellow solid made from cream by churning. **2.** any substance with a butter-like consistency, such as peanut butter. ~*vb.* **3.** to put butter on or in (something). ~See also **butter up.** —'**buttery** *adj.*

butter bean *n.* a large pale flat edible bean.

buttercup ('bʌtə,kʌp) *n.* a small yellow flower.

butterfingers ('bʌtə,fɪŋgəz) *n.* (*functioning as sing.*) *Informal.* a person who drops things by mistake or fails to catch things.

butterflies ('bʌtə,flaɪz) *pl. n. Informal.* a nervous feeling in the stomach.

butterfly ('bʌtə,flaɪ) *n., pl.* **-flies. 1.** an insect with a slender body and brightly coloured wings. **2.** a person who never settles with one interest or occupation for long. **3.** a swimming stroke in which the arms are plunged forward together in large circular movements.

butterfly nut *n.* same as **wing nut.**

buttermilk ('bʌtə,mɪlk) *n.* the sourish liquid remaining after the butter has been separated from milk.

butter muslin *n.* a fine loosely woven cotton material originally used for wrapping butter.

butterscotch (ˈbʌtəˌskɒtʃ) *n.* a hard brittle toffee made with butter, brown sugar, etc.

butter up *vb.* to flatter.

buttery (ˈbʌtərɪ) *n., pl.* **-teries.** *Brit.* (in some universities) a room in which food and drink are sold to students.

buttock (ˈbʌtək) *n.* **1.** either of the two large fleshy masses that form the human rump. **2.** the corresponding part in some mammals.

button (ˈbʌtᵊn) *n.* **1.** a disc or knob of plastic, wood, etc., attached to a garment, for fastening two surfaces together by passing it through a buttonhole. **2.** a small round object, such as a sweet or badge. **3.** a small disc that operates a doorbell or machine when pressed. **4. not worth a button.** *Brit.* of no value; useless. ~*vb.* **5.** to fasten (a garment) with a button or buttons.

buttonhole (ˈbʌtᵊnˌhəʊl) *n.* **1.** a slit in a garment through which a button is passed to fasten two surfaces together. **2.** a flower worn pinned to the lapel or in the buttonhole. ~*vb.* **3.** to detain (a person) in conversation.

button mushroom *n.* an unripe mushroom.

button up *vb.* **1.** to fasten (a garment) with a button or buttons. **2.** *Informal.* to conclude (business) satisfactorily: *she's got it all buttoned up.*

buttress (ˈbʌtrɪs) *n.* **1.** a construction, usually of brick or stone, built to support a wall. **2.** any support or prop. ~*vb.* **3.** to support (a wall) with a buttress. **4.** to support or sustain (an argument).

butty (ˈbʌtɪ) *n., pl.* **-ties.** *Chiefly N English dialect.* a sandwich: *a jam butty.*

butyl (ˈbjuːˌtaɪl, -tɪl) *n.* (*modifier*) of or containing any of four isomeric forms of the group C_4H_9–: *butyl rubber.*

buxom (ˈbʌksəm) *adj.* (of a woman) healthily plump, attractive, and full-bosomed.

buy (baɪ) *vb.* **buying, bought.** **1.** to acquire (something) by paying a sum of money for it; purchase. **2.** to be capable of purchasing: *money can't buy love.* **3.** to acquire by any exchange or sacrifice: *to buy time by equivocation.* **4.** to bribe (someone). **5.** *Slang.* to accept (something) as true. **6.** (foll. by *into*) to purchase shares of (a company). ~*n.* **7.** a purchase: *a good buy.*

buyer (ˈbaɪə) *n.* **1.** a person who buys; customer. **2.** a person employed to buy merchandise, as for a shop or factory.

buy in *vb.* to purchase (goods) in large quantities.

buy off *vb.* to pay (someone) to drop a charge or end opposition.

buy out *vb.* **1.** to purchase the ownership of a company or property from (someone). ~*n.* **buy-out.** **2.** the purchase of a company, often by its former employees.

buy up *vb.* **1.** to purchase all that is available of (something). **2.** to purchase a controlling interest in (a company).

buzz (bʌz) *n.* **1.** a rapidly vibrating humming sound, as of a bee. **2.** a low sound, as of many voices in conversation. **3.** *Informal.* a telephone call. **4.** *Informal.* a sense of excitement. ~*vb.* **5.** to make a vibrating sound like that of a prolonged *z.* **6.** (of a place) to be filled with an air of excitement: *the town buzzed with the news.* **7.** to summon (someone) with a buzzer. **8.** *Informal.* to fly an aircraft very low over (people, buildings, or another aircraft). **9. buzz about** *or* **around.** to move around quickly and busily.

buzzard (ˈbʌzəd) *n.* a bird of prey with broad wings and tail and a soaring flight.

buzzer (ˈbʌzə) *n.* an electronic device that produces a buzzing sound as a signal.

buzz off *vb. Informal, chiefly Brit.* to go away; depart.

buzz word *n. Informal.* a word, originally from a particular jargon, which becomes a popular vogue word.

bwana (ˈbwɑːnə) *n.* (in E Africa) a master, often used as a form of address corresponding to *sir.*

by (baɪ) *prep.* **1.** used to indicate the performer of the action of a passive verb: *seeds eaten by the birds.* **2.** used to indicate the person responsible for a creative work: *this song is by Schubert.* **3.** via; through: *enter by the back door.* **4.** used to indicate a means used: *he frightened her by hiding behind the door.* **5.** beside; next to; near: *a tree by the house.* **6.** passing the position of; past: *he drove by the old cottage.* **7.** not later than; before: *return the books by Tuesday.* **8.** used to indicate extent: *it is hotter by five degrees.* **9.** multiplied by: *four by three equals twelve.* **10.** during the passing of: *by night.* **11.** placed between measurements of the various dimensions of something: *a plank fourteen inches by seven.* ~*adv.* **12.** near: *the house is close by.* **13.** away; aside: *he put some money by each week.* **14.** passing a point near something; past: *he drove by.* ~*n., pl.* **byes.** **15.** same as **bye**[1].

by and by *adv.* presently or eventually.

by and large *adv.* in general; on the whole.

bye[1] (baɪ) *n.* **1.** *Sport.* status of a player or team who wins a preliminary round by virtue of having no opponent. **2.** *Cricket.* a run scored off a ball not struck by the batsman. **3. by the bye.** incidentally; by the way.

bye[2] (baɪ) *or* **bye-bye** *interj. Brit. informal.* goodbye.

by-election *or* **bye-election** *n.* an election held during the life of a parliament to fill a vacant seat.

bygone (ˈbaɪˌgɒn) *adj.* **1.** past; former: *a*

bygone age. ~*n.* **2.** an artefact, implement, etc., of former domestic or industrial use.

bygones ('baɪˌgɒnz) *pl. n.* **let bygones be bygones.** to agree to forget past quarrels.

bylaw *or* **bye-law** ('baɪˌlɔː) *n.* a rule made by a local authority.

by-line *n.* **1.** a line under the title of a newspaper or magazine article giving the author's name. **2.** same as **touchline.**

BYO(G) *n. Austral. & N.Z.* an unlicensed restaurant at which diners may bring their own alcoholic drink.

bypass ('baɪˌpɑːs) *n.* **1.** a main road built to avoid a city. **2.** a secondary pipe, channel, or appliance through which the flow of a substance, such as gas or electricity, is redirected. **3.** a surgical operation in which the blood flow is redirected away from a diseased or blocked part of the heart. ~*vb.* **4.** to go around or avoid (a city, obstruction, problem, etc.). **5.** to proceed without reference to (regulations or a superior); get round; avoid.

by-play *n.* secondary action in a play, carried on apart while the main action proceeds.

by-product *n.* **1.** a secondary or incidental product of a manufacturing process. **2.** a side effect.

byre ('baɪə) *n. Brit.* a shelter for cows.

byroad ('baɪˌrəʊd) *n.* a secondary or side road.

bystander ('baɪˌstændə) *n.* a person present but not involved; onlooker; spectator.

byte (baɪt) *n. Computers.* a group of bits processed as one unit of data.

byway ('baɪˌweɪ) *n.* a secondary or side road, esp. in the country.

byword ('baɪˌwɜːd) *n.* **1.** a person or thing regarded as a perfect example of something: *their name is a byword for good service.* **2.** a common saying; proverb.

Byzantine (bɪˈzænˌtaɪn, -ˌtiːn, baɪ-; 'bɪzənˌtiːn, -ˌtaɪn) *adj.* **1.** of Byzantium, an ancient Greek city on the Bosphorus. **2.** of the Byzantine Empire, the continuation of the Roman Empire in the East. **3.** of the style of architecture developed in the Byzantine Empire, with massive domes, rounded arches, and mosaics. **4.** (of attitudes, methods, etc.) inflexible or complicated. ~*n.* **5.** an inhabitant of Byzantium.

C

c *or* **C** (siː) *n., pl.* **c's, C's,** *or* **Cs. 1.** the third letter of the English alphabet. **2.** the third in a series.

c 1. centi-. **2.** cubic. **3.** the speed of light in free space.

C 1. *Music.* the first note of a major scale containing no sharps or flats (**C major**). **2.** *Chem.* carbon. **3.** capacitance. **4.** Celsius. **5.** centigrade. **6.** century: *C20.* **7.** coulomb. **8.** the Roman numeral for 100.

c. 1. carat. **2.** cent(s). **3.** century *or* centuries. **4.** (*pl.* **cc.**) chapter. **5.** (used esp. preceding a date) about: *c. 1800.* **6.** copyright.

Ca *Chem.* calcium.

ca. about.

CA 1. California. **2.** Chartered Accountant.

cab (kæb) *n.* **1.** a taxi. **2.** the enclosed driver's compartment of a lorry, crane, or other vehicle. **3.** (formerly) a horse-drawn vehicle for public hire.

cabal (kəˈbæl) *n.* **1.** a small group of political intriguers. **2.** a secret plot; conspiracy.

cabaret (ˈkæbəˌreɪ) *n.* **1.** a floor show of dancing and singing at a nightclub or restaurant. **2.** a place providing such entertainment.

cabbage (ˈkæbɪdʒ) *n.* **1.** a vegetable with a short thick stalk and a large head of green or reddish edible leaves. **2.** *Informal.* a person who has no mental faculties and is dependent on others.

cabbage white *n.* a large white butterfly, the larvae of which feed on the leaves of cabbages and related vegetables.

cabby *or* **cabbie** (ˈkæbɪ) *n., pl.* **-bies.** *Informal.* a cab driver.

caber (ˈkeɪbə) *n. Scot.* a heavy section of trimmed tree trunk tossed in competition at Highland games.

cabin (ˈkæbɪn) *n.* **1.** a small simple dwelling. **2.** a room used as living quarters in a ship. **3.** a covered section in a small boat. **4.** the enclosed part of an aircraft in which the passengers or crew sit.

cabin boy *n.* a boy who waits on the officers and passengers of a ship.

cabin cruiser *n.* a motorboat with a cabin.

cabinet (ˈkæbɪnɪt) *n.* **1.** a piece of furniture containing shelves, cupboards, or drawers for storage or display. **2.** the outer case of a television or radio. **3.** (*often cap.*) a committee of senior government ministers or advisers to a president.

cabinet-maker *n.* a craftsman who makes fine furniture. —ˈcabinet-ˌmaking *n.*

cabin fever *n. Canad.* acute depression resulting from being isolated or sharing cramped quarters in the wilderness.

cable (ˈkeɪbʔl) *n.* **1.** a strong thick rope of twisted hemp or wire. **2.** a ship's anchor chain. **3.** a bundle of wires that conducts electricity: *a submarine cable.* **4.** a telegram sent abroad by submarine cable or telephone line. **5.** Also: **cable stitch.** a knitting pattern resembling a twisted rope. ~*vb.* **6.** to send (a message) to (someone) by cable.

cable car *n.* a vehicle which is pulled up a steep slope by a moving cable.

cablegram (ˈkeɪbʔlˌgræm) *n.* a more formal name for **cable** (sense 4).

cable television *n.* a television service in which the subscriber's television is connected to a central receiver by cable.

caboodle (kəˈbuːdʔl) *n.* **the whole caboodle.** *Informal.* the whole lot.

caboose (kəˈbuːs) *n.* **1.** *Railways, U.S. & Canad.* a guard's van. **2.** *Naut.* a galley aboard ship. **3.** *Canad.* a mobile bunkhouse used by lumbermen.

cabriolet (ˌkæbrɪəʊˈleɪ) *n.* a small two-wheeled horse-drawn carriage with a folding hood.

cacao (kəˈkɑːəʊ, -ˈkeɪəʊ) *n.* **1.** a tropical American tree with seed pods from which cocoa and chocolate are prepared. **2. cacao bean.** the seed pod; cocoa bean.

cachalot (ˈkæʃəˌlɒt) *n.* the sperm whale.

cache (kæʃ) *n.* **1.** a hidden store of provisions, weapons, or treasure. **2.** the place where such a store is hidden. ~*vb.* **3.** to store in a cache.

cachet (ˈkæʃeɪ) *n.* **1.** prestige; distinction. **2.** an official seal on a document or letter. **3.** a distinguishing mark.

cachou (ˈkæʃuː, -ˈʃuː) *n.* a lozenge eaten to sweeten the breath.

cack-handed (ˌkækˈhændɪd) *adj. Informal.* **1.** clumsy. **2.** left-handed.

cackle (ˈkækʔl) *vb.* **1.** (of a hen) to squawk with shrill broken notes. **2.** to laugh or chatter shrilly. **3.** to utter with a cackle. ~*n.* **4.** the noise or act of cackling. **5. cut the cackle.** *Informal.* to be quiet. —ˈcackling *n., adj.*

cacophony (kəˈkɒfənɪ) *n., pl.* **-nies.** harsh discordant sound. —caˈcophonous *adj.*

cactus (ˈkæktəs) *n., pl.* **-tuses** *or* **-ti** (-taɪ).

a thick fleshy desert plant with spines but no leaves.

cad (kæd) *n. Brit. informal, old-fashioned.* a man who behaves dishonourably. —**'caddish** *adj.*

cadaver (kə'deɪvə, -'dɑːv-) *n. Med.* a corpse.

cadaverous (kə'dævərəs) *adj.* **1.** deathly pale, like a corpse. **2.** thin and haggard.

caddie ('kædɪ) *Golf.* ~*n., pl.* **-dies. 1.** an attendant who carries clubs and other equipment for a player. ~*vb.* **-dying, -died. 2.** to act as a caddie.

caddis worm *or* **caddis** ('kædɪs) *n.* the aquatic larva of the **caddis fly,** which constructs a protective case around itself made of silk, sand, and stones.

caddy¹ ('kædɪ) *n., pl.* **-dies.** *Chiefly Brit.* a small container for tea.

caddy² ('kædɪ) *n., pl.* **-dies,** *vb.* **-dying, -died.** same as **caddie.**

cadence ('keɪd²ns) *n.* **1.** the beat or measure of something rhythmic. **2.** a fall in the pitch of the voice. **3.** intonation. **4.** the close of a musical phrase.

cadenza (kə'dɛnzə) *n.* a virtuoso solo passage during a piece of music.

cadet (kə'dɛt) *n.* a young person training for the military services or police. —**ca-'detship** *n.*

cadge (kædʒ) *vb.* to get (food, money, or help) by sponging or begging. —**'cadger** *n.*

cadi ('kɑːdɪ, 'keɪdɪ) *n., pl.* **-dis.** a judge in a Muslim community.

cadmium ('kædmɪəm) *n.* a bluish-white metallic element found in zinc ores and used in electroplating and alloys. Symbol: Cd

cadre ('kɑːdə) *n.* **1.** the nucleus of trained servicemen forming the basis of a military unit. **2.** a group of activists, esp. in the Communist Party.

caduceus (kə'djuːsɪəs) *n., pl.* **-cei** (-sɪ,aɪ). an emblem of the medical profession, showing a winged staff with two serpents twined round it.

caecum *or U.S.* **cecum** ('siːkəm) *n., pl.* **-ca** (-kə). the pouch at the beginning of the large intestine.

Caenozoic (,siːnə'zəʊɪk) *adj.* same as **Cenozoic.**

Caerphilly (kɛə'fɪlɪ) *n.* a creamy white mild-flavoured cheese.

Caesar ('siːzə) *n.* **1.** a Roman emperor. **2.** any emperor, autocrat, or dictator.

Caesarean, Caesarian, *or U.S.* **Cesarean, Cesarian** (sɪ'zɛərɪən) *n.* a Caesarean section.

Caesarean section *n.* surgical incision into the womb in order to deliver a baby.

caesium *or U.S.* **cesium** ('siːzɪəm) *n.* a silvery-white metallic element used in photocells. Symbol: Cs

caesura (sɪ'zjʊərə) *n., pl.* **-ras** *or* **-rae** (-riː). a pause in a line of verse.

café ('kæfeɪ, 'kæfɪ) *n.* a small or inexpensive restaurant serving refreshments and, sometimes, meals.

cafeteria (,kæfɪ'tɪərɪə) *n.* a self-service restaurant.

caff (kæf) *n. Slang.* a café.

caffeine ('kæfiːn) *n.* a stimulant in tea, coffee, and cocoa.

caftan ('kæf,tæn, -,tɑːn) *n.* same as **kaftan.**

cage (keɪdʒ) *n.* **1.** an enclosure of bars or wires, for keeping birds or animals. **2.** the enclosed platform of a lift in a mine. ~*vb.* **3.** to confine in or as in a cage.

cagey *or* **cagy** ('keɪdʒɪ) *adj.* **cagier, cagiest.** *Informal.* not frank; wary. —**'caginess** *n.*

cagoule (kə'guːl) *n.* a lightweight usually knee-length type of anorak.

cahoots (kə'huːts) *pl. n.* **in cahoots.** *Informal.* in league.

caiman ('keɪmən) *n., pl.* **-mans.** same as **cayman.**

Cainozoic (,kaɪnəʊ'zəʊɪk, ,keɪ-) *adj.* same as **Cenozoic.**

cairn (kɛən) *n.* **1.** a mound of stones erected as a memorial or marker. **2.** Also: **cairn terrier.** a small rough-haired breed of terrier.

cairngorm (,kɛən'gɔːm) *n.* a smoky yellow or brown quartz gemstone.

caisson (kə'suːn, 'keɪs²n) *n.* a watertight chamber used to carry out construction work under water.

cajole (kə'dʒəʊl) *vb.* to persuade by flattery; wheedle; coax. —**ca'jolery** *n.*

cake (keɪk) *n.* **1.** a baked mixture of flour, sugar, and eggs. **2.** other food in a flat round shape: *a fish cake.* **3.** a flat, compact mass: *a cake of soap.* **4. go** *or* **sell like hot cakes.** *Informal.* to be sold very quickly. **5. have one's cake and eat it.** to enjoy both of two incompatible alternatives. **6. piece of cake.** *Informal.* something that is easily accomplished. ~*vb.* **7.** to form into a hardened mass or crust.

cakewalk ('keɪk,wɔːk) *n.* **1.** an old-fashioned Black American dance. **2.** *Informal.* an easy task.

cal. 1. calendar. **2.** calibre. **3.** calorie (small).

Cal. Calorie (large).

calabash ('kælə,bæʃ) *n.* **1.** a tropical American tree that produces large round gourds. **2.** the gourd. **3.** the dried hollow shell of the gourd used as a pipe or bowl.

calabrese (,kælə'breɪzɪ) *n.* a kind of green sprouting broccoli.

calamine ('kælə,maɪn) *n.* a pink powder consisting chiefly of zinc oxide, used in skin lotions or ointments.

calamitous (kə'læmɪtəs) *adj.* involving or resulting in a calamity; disastrous.

calamity (kə'læmɪtɪ) *n., pl.* **-ties. 1.** a disaster or misfortune. **2.** deep distress or misery.

calcareous (kælˈkɛərɪəs) *adj.* of or containing calcium carbonate.

calces (ˈkælsiːz) *n.* a plural of **calx.**

calciferol (kælˈsɪfərɒl) *n.* a substance found in fish-liver oils and used in the treatment of rickets. Also called: **vitamin D₂.**

calciferous (kælˈsɪfərəs) *adj.* producing salts of calcium, esp. calcium carbonate.

calcify (ˈkælsɪˌfaɪ) *vb.* **-fying, -fied. 1.** to convert or be converted into lime. **2.** to harden by the depositing of calcium salts. —ˌcalcifiˈcation *n.*

calcine (ˈkælsaɪn, -sɪn) *vb.* to oxidize (a substance) by heating or (of a substance) to be oxidized by heating. —**calcination** (ˌkælsɪˈneɪʃən) *n.*

calcite (ˈkælsaɪt) *n.* a colourless or white form of calcium carbonate.

calcium (ˈkælsɪəm) *n.* a soft silvery-white metallic element found in bones, teeth, limestone, and chalk. Symbol: Ca

calcium carbonate *n.* a white crystalline salt found in limestone, chalk, and pearl.

calcium hydroxide *n.* a white crystalline alkali used in cement, water softening, and the neutralization of acid soils.

calcium oxide *n.* same as **quicklime.**

calculable (ˈkælkjʊləbˀl) *adj.* that may be computed or estimated.

calculate (ˈkælkjʊˌleɪt) *vb.* **1.** to solve (a problem) by a mathematical procedure. **2.** to determine by judgment or reasoning; estimate. **3.** (*usually passive*) to aim: *calculated to annoy me.* **4.** (foll. by *on*) to rely. **5.** *U.S. dialect.* to suppose.

calculated (ˈkælkjʊˌleɪtɪd) *adj.* **1.** undertaken after considering the likelihood of success. **2.** premeditated: *a calculated insult.*

calculating (ˈkælkjʊˌleɪtɪŋ) *adj.* **1.** selfishly scheming. **2.** shrewd.

calculation (ˌkælkjʊˈleɪʃən) *n.* **1.** the act or result of calculating. **2.** selfish scheming.

calculator (ˈkælkjʊˌleɪtə) *n.* a small electronic device for doing mathematical calculations.

calculus (ˈkælkjʊləs) *n.* **1.** (*pl.* **-luses**). the branch of mathematics concerned with the effect on a function of an infinitesimal change in the independent variable. **2.** (*pl.* **-li** (-ˌlaɪ)). *Pathol.* same as **stone.**

caldron (ˈkɔːldrən) *n.* same as **cauldron.**

Caledonian (ˌkælɪˈdəʊnɪən) *adj.* **1.** Scottish. ~*n.* **2.** *Literary.* a person from Scotland.

calendar (ˈkælɪndə) *n.* **1.** a system for determining the beginning, length, and divisions of years. **2.** a table showing such an arrangement. **3.** a schedule of events or

appointments. ~*vb.* **4.** to enter in a calendar; schedule.

calender (ˈkælɪndə) *n.* **1.** a machine in which paper or cloth is smoothed by passing it between rollers. ~*vb.* **2.** to smooth in such a machine.

calends *or* **kalends** (ˈkælɪndz) *pl. n.* (in the ancient Roman calendar) the first day of each month.

calendula (kæˈlɛndjʊlə) *n.* a plant having orange-and-yellow rayed flowers.

calf¹ (kɑːf) *n., pl.* **calves. 1.** the young of cattle. **2.** a young elephant, giraffe, buffalo, whale, or seal. **3.** same as **calfskin** (sense 2).

calf² (kɑːf) *n., pl.* **calves.** the back of the leg between the ankle and the knee.

calf love *n.* temporary infatuation of an adolescent for another person.

calfskin (ˈkɑːfˌskɪn) *n.* **1.** the skin or hide of a calf. **2.** fine leather made from this.

calibrate (ˈkælɪˌbreɪt) *vb.* **1.** to measure the calibre of (something). **2.** to mark the scale or check the accuracy of (a measuring instrument). —ˌcaliˈbration *n.* —ˈcaliˌbrator *n.*

calibre *or U.S.* **caliber** (ˈkælɪbə) *n.* **1.** the diameter of the bore of a firearm or of a shell or bullet. **2.** ability; personal worth.

calices (ˈkælɪˌsiːz) *n.* the plural of **calix.**

calico (ˈkælɪˌkəʊ) *n., pl.* **-coes** *or* **-cos. 1.** a white or unbleached cotton fabric. **2.** *Chiefly U.S.* a coarse printed cotton fabric.

Calif. California.

californium (ˌkælɪˈfɔːnɪəm) *n.* an artificial radioactive element. Symbol: Cf

caliper (ˈkælɪpə) *n. U.S.* same as **calliper.**

caliph (ˈkeɪlɪf, ˈkæl-) *n. Islam.* the title of the successors of Mohammed as rulers of the Islamic world.

caliphate (ˈkeɪlɪˌfeɪt) *n.* the office, jurisdiction, or reign of a caliph.

calisthenics (ˌkælɪsˈθɛnɪks) *n.* same as **callisthenics.**

calix (ˈkeɪlɪks, ˈkæ-) *n., pl.* **calices.** a cup; chalice.

calk (kɔːk) *vb.* same as **caulk.**

call (kɔːl) *vb.* **1.** (often foll. by *out*) to speak loudly so as to attract attention. **2.** to summon: *to call a policeman.* **3.** to visit. **4.** (often foll. by *up*) to telephone (a person). **5.** to summon to a specific office or profession. **6.** (of animals or birds) to utter (a characteristic cry). **7.** to name: *he's called Bob.* **8.** to regard as being (something specified): *I call it a waste of time; she called him a liar.* **9.** to read (a list) aloud to check for omissions or absentees. **10.** to give an order for: *to call a strike.* **11.** to try to predict the result of tossing a coin. **12.** to awaken: *I was called early this morning.* **13.** to cause to assemble: *to call a meeting.* **14.** *Sport.* (of an umpire or referee) to judge (a ball) to be in or out of play. **15.** *Cards.* to bid. **16.** (foll. by *for*) **a.** to require: *this problem calls for study.* **b.** to come and fetch. **17.** (foll. by *on* or *upon*) to make an appeal or request to: *they called upon him to reply.* **18. call someone's bluff.** See **bluff¹**. **19. call to mind.** to remember or cause to be remembered. ~*n.* **20.** a cry or shout. **21.** the characteristic cry of a bird or animal. **22.** a summons or invitation. **23.** a short visit: *the doctor made six calls this morning.* **24.** an inner urge to some task or profession; vocation. **25.** allure or fascination: *the call of the forest.* **26.** need, demand, or occasion: *there is no call to shout.* **27.** demand or claim: *the call of duty.* **28.** a conversation or a request for a connection by telephone. **29.** a bid or a player's turn to bid. **30.** *Sport.* a decision of an umpire or referee as to whether a ball is in or out of play. **31.** Also called: **call option.** *Stock Exchange.* an option to buy stock during a specified period. **32. on call.** available at short notice. **33. within call.** within shouting distance. ~See also **call in, call off,** etc. —**'caller** *n.*

call box *n.* a soundproof enclosure for a public telephone.

call girl *n.* a prostitute with whom appointments are made by telephone.

calligraphy (kə'lɪgrəfɪ) *n.* handwriting, esp. beautiful handwriting. —**cal'ligrapher** or **cal'ligraphist** *n.* —**calligraphic** (ˌkælɪ-'græfɪk) *adj.*

call in *vb.* **1.** to pay a brief visit. **2.** to demand payment of: *to call in a loan.* **3.** to take (something) out of circulation, because it is faulty. **4.** to summon to one's assistance: *to call in a specialist.*

calling ('kɔːlɪŋ) *n.* **1.** a strong inner urge to follow a profession or trade; vocation. **2.** an occupation, profession, or trade.

calliper or *U.S.* **caliper** ('kælɪpə) *n.* **1.** (*often pl.*) a measuring instrument consisting of two steel legs hinged together. **2.** a metal splint for supporting the leg.

callisthenics or **calisthenics** (ˌkælɪs-'θɛnɪks) *n.* light exercises designed to promote general fitness. —ˌ**callis'thenic** or ˌ**calis'thenic** *adj.*

call off *vb.* **1.** to cancel or abandon: *the game was called off.* **2.** to order to desist: *the man called off his dog.*

callosity (kə'lɒsɪtɪ) *n., pl.* **-ties.** a callus.

callous ('kæləs) *adj.* **1.** insensitive. **2.** (of skin) hardened and thickened. ~*vb.* **3.** *Pathol.* to make or become callous. —**'callously** *adv.* —**'callousness** *n.*

call out *vb.* **1.** to utter loudly. **2.** to summon: *call out the troops.* **3.** to order (workers) to strike. **4.** to challenge to a duel.

callow ('kæləʊ) *adj.* young and inexperienced; immature. —**'callowness** *n.*

call up *vb.* **1.** to summon for active mili-

tary service. **2.** to evoke. **3.** to summon (people) to action. ~*n.* **call-up.** **4.** a general order to report for military service.

callus ('kæləs) *n., pl.* **-luses.** **1.** a hard or thick area of skin. **2.** an area of bony tissue formed during the healing of a broken bone.

calm (kɑːm) *adj.* **1.** still: *a calm sea.* **2.** windless. **3.** tranquil; serene. ~*n.* **4.** an absence of disturbance or rough motion. **5.** absence of wind. **6.** tranquillity. ~*vb.* **7.** (often foll. by *down*) to make or become calm. —**'calmly** *adv.* —**'calmness** *n.*

calomel ('kæləˌmɛl, -məl) *n.* a colourless tasteless powder used as a cathartic.

Calor Gas ('kælə) *n. Trademark.* butane gas liquefied under pressure in containers for domestic use.

caloric (kə'lɒrɪk) *adj.* of heat or calories.

calorie or **calory** ('kælərɪ) *n., pl.* **-ries.** the quantity of heat required to raise the temperature of 1 gram of water by 1°C. Also: **small calorie.**

Calorie ('kælərɪ) *n.* **1.** Also: **large calorie.** a unit of heat, equal to one thousand calories. **2.** the amount of a food capable of producing one calorie of energy.

calorific (ˌkælə'rɪfɪk) *adj.* of or generating heat.

calorimeter (ˌkælə'rɪmɪtə) *n.* a device for measuring amounts of heat.

calumniate (kə'lʌmnɪˌeɪt) *vb.* to slander. —**caˌlumni'ation** *n.*

calumny ('kæləmnɪ) *n., pl.* **-nies.** a false or malicious statement; slander. —**calumnious** (kə'lʌmnɪəs) *adj.*

Calvary ('kælvərɪ) *n.* the place just outside the walls of Jerusalem where Jesus was crucified.

calve (kɑːv) *vb.* to give birth to (a calf).

calves (kɑːvz) *n.* the plural of **calf.**

Calvinism ('kælvɪˌnɪzəm) *n.* the theological system of Calvin, 16th-century French theologian, and his followers, stressing predestination and salvation solely by God's grace. —**'Calvinist** *n., adj.* —ˌ**Calvin'istic** or ˌ**Calvin'istical** *adj.*

calx (kælks) *n., pl.* **calxes** or **calces.** the powdery metallic oxide left when an ore or mineral is roasted.

calypso (kə'lɪpsəʊ) *n., pl.* **-sos.** a West Indian song with improvised topical lyrics and a syncopated rhythm.

calyx ('keɪlɪks, 'kælɪks) *n., pl.* **calyxes** or **calyces** ('kælɪˌsiːz, 'keɪlɪ-). the sepals of a flower that protect the developing bud.

cam (kæm) *n.* a rotating cylinder attached to a revolving shaft to give a back-and-forward motion to a part in contact with it.

camaraderie (ˌkæmə'rɑːdərɪ) *n.* familiarity and trust between friends.

camber ('kæmbə) *n.* **1.** a slight upward curve to the centre of a surface. ~*vb.* **2.** to form or be formed with a camber.

Cambrian ('kæmbrɪən) *adj. Geol.* of a period of geological time about 600 million years ago.

cambric ('keɪmbrɪk) *n.* a fine white linen fabric.

Cambs (kæmbz) Cambridgeshire.

came (keɪm) *vb.* the past tense of **come.**

camel ('kæməl) *n.* **1.** either of two humped mammals (see **dromedary, Bactrian camel**) that can survive long periods without food or water in desert regions. ~*adj.* **2.** fawn.

camellia (kə'miːlɪə) *n.* an ornamental shrub with glossy evergreen leaves and showy white, pink, or red flowers.

camel's hair *or* **camelhair** ('kæməl,hɛə) *n.* **1.** the fine soft hair of a camel. **2.** soft, usually tan cloth made of this hair. **3.** (*modifier*) (of a painter's brush) made from the tail hairs of squirrels.

Camembert ('kæməm,bɛə) *n.* a soft creamy cheese.

cameo ('kæmɪ,əʊ) *n., pl.* **cameos. 1.** a brooch or ring with a profile head carved in relief. **2.** an engraving upon a gem or stone with the background a different colour from the raised design. **3.** a stone with such an engraving. **4.** a brief but creative part in a film or play played by a well-known actor or actress. **5.** a short descriptive literary work.

camera ('kæmərə) *n.* **1.** a photographic device in which light is allowed through a lens to form an image on light-sensitive film. **2.** *Television.* the equipment used to convert an optical image into electrical signals. **3. in camera.** in private.

camera obscura (ɒb'skjʊərə) *n.* a darkened room with an aperture through which images of outside objects are projected onto a flat surface.

camiknickers ('kæmɪ,nɪkəz) *pl. n.* women's knickers attached to a camisole top.

camisole ('kæmɪ,səʊl) *n.* a woman's underbodice with shoulder straps.

camomile *or* **chamomile** ('kæmə,maɪl) *n.* **1.** an aromatic plant whose leaves and flowers are used medicinally. **2. camomile tea.** a medicinal beverage made from the leaves and flowers of this plant.

camouflage ('kæmə,flɑːʒ) *n.* **1.** the use of natural surroundings or artificial aids to conceal or disguise something. **2.** something designed to conceal or deceive. ~*vb.* **3.** to conceal by camouflage.

camp[1] (kæmp) *n.* **1.** a place where tents, huts, or cabins are erected. **2.** temporary lodgings composed of tents, huts, or cabins. **3.** a group supporting a given doctrine. **4.** (*modifier*) suitable for use in temporary lodgings: *camp bed.* **5.** to set up a camp. **6.** (often foll. by *out*) to live temporarily in or as if in a tent. —'**camper** *n.* —'**camping** *n.*

camp[2] (kæmp) *Informal.* ~*adj.* **1.** effeminate or homosexual. **2.** consciously artificial, vulgar, or affected. ~*vb.* **3.** to behave or do in a camp way. **4. camp it up.** to overact. —'**campy** *adj.*

campaign (kæm'peɪn) *n.* **1.** a series of coordinated activities designed to achieve a goal. **2.** *Mil.* a number of operations aimed at achieving a single objective. ~*vb.* **3.** (often foll. by *for*) to conduct or take part in a campaign. —**cam'paigner** *n.*

campanile (,kæmpə'niːlɪ) *n.* a bell tower, not usually attached to another building.

campanology (,kæmpə'nɒlədʒɪ) *n.* the art of ringing bells. —,**campa'nologist** *n.*

campanula (kæm'pænjʊlə) *n.* a plant having blue or white bell-shaped flowers.

camp follower *n.* **1.** a civilian who unofficially provides services to military personnel. **2.** a nonmember who supports a particular group or cause.

camphor ('kæmfə) *n.* an aromatic crystalline substance obtained from the wood of an Asian or Australian laurel (**camphor tree**): used medicinally and in mothballs.

camphorate ('kæmfə,reɪt) *vb.* to treat or impregnate with camphor.

campion ('kæmpɪən) *n.* a plant related to the pink, having red, pink, or white flowers.

camp oven *n. Austral. & N.Z.* a metal pot or box with a heavy lid, used for baking over an open fire.

camp site *n.* a place for camping.

campus ('kæmpəs) *n., pl.* **-puses.** the grounds and buildings of a university or college.

camshaft ('kæm,ʃɑːft) *n.* a shaft having one or more cams attached to it.

can[1] (kæn; *unstressed* kən) *vb. past* **could.** used to indicate: **1.** ability, skill, or fitness to perform a task: *I can run.* **2.** *Informal.* permission or the right to something: *can I have a drink?* **3.** knowledge of how to do something: *he can speak three languages.* **4.** possibility, opportunity, or likelihood: *my trainer says I can win the race.* Usage. see **may**[1].

can[2] (kæn) *n.* **1.** a metal container, esp. for liquids. **2.** Also: **canful.** the contents of a can or the amount a can will hold. **3.** *Slang.* prison. **4.** *U.S. & Canad. slang.* a toilet. **5. in the can.** finished; finalized. ~*vb.* **canning, canned. 6.** to put (something) into a can or cans.

Can. 1. Canada. **2.** Canadian.

Canada Day *n.* (in Canada) July 1, a public holiday marking the anniversary of the day in 1867 when Canada became a dominion.

Canada goose *n.* a greyish-brown North American goose with a black neck and head and a white throat patch.

Canada jay *n.* a grey jay of northern N America, notorious for its stealing.

Canadian (kə'neɪdɪən) *adj.* **1.** of Canada or its people. ~*n.* **2.** a person from Canada.

Canadiana (kə,neɪdɪ'ɑːnə; *Canad.* -'ænə) *n.* objects relating to Canadian history and culture.

Canadian football *n.* a game like American football played on a grass pitch between teams of 12 players.

Canadianism (kə'neɪdɪə,nɪzəm) *n.* **1.** the Canadian national character or spirit. **2.** a linguistic feature peculiar to Canada or Canadians.

Canadianize *or* **-ise** (kə'neɪdɪə,naɪz) *vb.* to make or become Canadian.

Canadien *or* (*fem.*) **Canadienne** (kə,næ-dɪ'ɛn) *n.* a French Canadian.

canaille (kæ'naɪ) *n.* the masses; rabble.

canal (kə'næl) *n.* **1.** an artificial waterway constructed for navigation or irrigation. **2.** a passage or duct in an animal or plant body: *the alimentary canal.*

canalize *or* **-lise** ('kænə,laɪz) *vb.* **1.** to provide with or convert into a canal or canals. **2.** to give direction to or provide an outlet for. —,**canali'zation** *or* **-li'sation** *n.*

canapé ('kænəpɪ, -,peɪ) *n.* a small piece of bread or toast spread with a savoury topping.

canard (kæ'nɑːd) *n.* a false report; rumour or hoax.

canary (kə'neərɪ) *n., pl.* **-naries. 1.** a small yellow songbird often kept as a pet. ~*adj.* **2.** Also: **canary-yellow.** light yellow.

canasta (kə'næstə) *n.* a card game like rummy, using two packs of cards.

cancan ('kæn,kæn) *n.* a high-kicking dance performed by a female chorus.

cancel ('kæns²l) *vb.* **-celling, -celled** *or U.S.* **-celing, -celed. 1.** to postpone (something) indefinitely; call off. **2.** to revoke or annul. **3.** to delete; cross out. **4.** to mark (a cheque or stamp) with an official stamp to prevent further use. **5.** (usually foll. by *out*) to counterbalance: *his generosity cancelled out his past unkindness.* **6.** *Maths.* to eliminate (common factors) from both the numerator and denominator of a fraction or equal terms from opposite sides of an equation.

cancellation (,kænsɪ'leɪʃən) *n.* **1.** the act or an instance of cancelling. **2.** something that has been cancelled: *we have a cancellation in the balcony.* **3.** the marks made by cancelling.

cancer ('kænsə) *n.* **1.** a malignant growth or tumour, caused by abnormal and uncontrolled cell division. **2.** the disease resulting from this. **3.** an evil influence that spreads dangerously. —'**cancerous** *adj.* —**cancroid** ('kæŋkrɔɪd) *adj.*

Cancer ('kænsə) *n.* **1.** *Astrol.* the fourth sign of the zodiac; the crab. **2. tropic of Cancer.** See **tropic** (sense 1).

candela (kæn'diːlə, -'deɪlə) *n.* the basic SI unit of luminous intensity.

candelabrum (,kændɪ'lɑːbrəm) *or* **candelabra** *n., pl.* **-bra** (-brə), **-brums,** *or* **-bras.** a large, branched candleholder.

candid ('kændɪd) *adj.* **1.** frank and outspoken. **2.** (of a photograph) unposed or informal. —'**candidly** *adv.* —'**candidness** *n.*

candidate ('kændɪ,deɪt) *n.* **1.** a person seeking a job or position. **2.** a person taking an examination. **3.** a person or thing regarded as suitable or likely for a particular fate or position. —**candidacy** ('kændɪdəsɪ) *or* **candidature** ('kændɪdətʃə) *n.*

candied ('kændɪd) *adj.* impregnated or coated with sugar.

candle ('kænd²l) *n.* **1.** a stick or block of wax or tallow surrounding a wick, which is burned to produce light. **2. burn the candle at both ends.** to exhaust oneself by doing too much. **3. not hold a candle to.** *Informal.* to be inferior in comparison with. **4. not worth the candle.** *Informal.* not worth doing.

candlelight ('kænd²l,laɪt) *n.* the light from a candle or candles. —'**candle,lit** *adj.*

Candlemas ('kænd²lməs) *n. Christianity.* Feb. 2, the Feast of the Purification of the Virgin Mary.

candlepower ('kænd²l,paʊə) *n.* the luminous intensity of a source of light: now expressed in candelas.

candlestick ('kænd²l,stɪk) *or* **candleholder** ('kænd²l,həʊldə) *n.* a holder for a candle.

candlewick ('kænd²l,wɪk) *adj.* made of cotton or muslin with a tufted pattern.

candour *or U.S.* **candor** ('kændə) *n.* openness; frankness.

candy ('kændɪ) *n., pl.* **-dies. 1.** *Chiefly U.S. & Canad.* a sweet or sweets. ~*vb.* **-dying, -died. 2.** (of sugar) to become or cause to become crystalline. **3.** to preserve by boiling in sugar: *candied peel.*

candyfloss ('kændɪ,flɒs) *n. Brit.* a light fluffy mass of spun sugar, held on a stick.

candy-striped *adj.* having narrow coloured stripes on a white background. —**candy stripe** *n.*

cane (keɪn) *n.* **1. a.** the long flexible stem of the bamboo or any similar plant. **b.** a plant having such a stem. **2.** strips of such stems, woven to make wickerwork. **3.** the woody stem of a reed, blackberry, or loganberry. **4.** a flexible rod used to beat someone. **5.** a slender walking stick. ~*vb.* **6.** to beat with a cane. **7.** to make or repair with cane.

cane sugar *n.* sucrose obtained from sugar cane.

canine ('keɪnaɪn, 'kæn-) *adj.* **1.** of or like a dog. **2.** of the family of mammals including dogs, wolves, and foxes. ~*n.* **3.** an animal of the dog family. **4.** a sharp-pointed tooth between the incisors and the premolars.

canister ('kænɪstə) *n.* a container, usually made of metal, in which dry food is stored.

canker ('kæŋkə) *n.* **1.** an ulceration or ulcerous disease. **2.** something evil that spreads and corrupts. ~*vb.* **3.** to infect or become infected with canker. —**'cankerous** *adj.*

cankerworm ('kæŋkə,wɜm) *n.* a moth larva harmful to fruit trees.

cannabis ('kænəbɪs) *n.* **1.** the hemp plant. **2.** the drug obtained from the dried leaves and flowers of the hemp plant.

canned (kænd) *adj.* **1.** preserved in tins. **2.** *Informal.* recorded in advance. **3.** *Slang.* drunk.

cannelloni *or* **canneloni** (,kænɪ'ləʊnɪ) *pl. n.* tubular pieces of pasta filled with meat or cheese.

cannery ('kænərɪ) *n., pl.* **-neries.** a place where foods are canned.

cannibal ('kænɪb³l) *n.* **1.** a person who eats human flesh. **2.** an animal that feeds on the flesh of others of its kind. —**'canniba,lism** *n.*

cannibalize *or* **-lise** ('kænɪbə,laɪz) *vb.* to use parts from (one machine) to repair another. —,**cannibali'zation** *or* **-li'sation** *n.*

canning ('kænɪŋ) *n.* the process of sealing food in cans to preserve it.

cannon ('kænən) *n., pl.* **-nons** *or* **-non.** **1.** an automatic aircraft gun. **2.** *History.* a gun consisting of a metal tube mounted on a carriage. **3.** *Billiards.* a shot in which the cue ball strikes two balls successively. ~*vb.* **4.** to rebound; collide. **5.** *Billiards.* to make a cannon.

cannonade (,kænə'neɪd) *n.* **1.** continuous heavy gunfire. ~*vb.* **2.** to attack (a target) with cannon.

cannonball ('kænən,bɔl) *n.* a heavy metal ball fired from a cannon.

cannon fodder *n.* men regarded as expendable in war.

cannot ('kænɒt, kæ'nɒt) can not.

canny ('kænɪ) *adj.* **-nier, -niest.** **1.** shrewd, esp. in business. **2.** *Scot. & NE English dialect.* good or nice. —**'cannily** *adv.* —**'canniness** *n.*

canoe (kə'nuː) *n.* **1.** a light narrow open boat, propelled by one or more paddles. ~*vb.* **-noeing, -noed.** **2.** to go in or transport by canoe. —**ca'noeist** *n.*

canon¹ ('kænən) *n.* **1.** *Christianity.* a Church decree regulating morals or religious practices. **2.** (*often pl.*) a general rule or standard. **3.** *R.C. Church.* the list of the canonized saints. **4.** *R.C. Church.* the prayer in the Mass in which the Host is consecrated. **5.** a list of sacred writings recognized as genuine. **6.** a piece of music in which a melody in one part is taken up in one or more other parts successively. **7.** a

list of the works of an author that are accepted as authentic.

canon² ('kænən) *n.* a priest serving in a cathedral.

canonical (kə'nɒnɪk³l) *or* **canonic** *adj.* **1.** included in a canon of writings. **2.** conforming with canon law. **3.** accepted; authoritative. **4.** of a canon (clergyman).

canonical hour *n. R.C. Church.* one of the seven prayer times appointed for each day.

canonicals (kə'nɒnɪk³lz) *pl. n.* the official clothes worn by clergy when taking services.

canonist ('kænənɪst) *n.* a specialist in canon law.

canonize *or* **-ise** ('kænə,naɪz) *vb.* **1.** *R.C. Church.* to declare (a person) to be a saint. **2.** to regard as a saint. **3.** to sanction by canon law. —,**canoni'zation** *or* **-i'sation** *n.*

canon law *n.* the codified body of laws of a Christian Church.

canoodle (kə'nuːd³l) *vb. Slang.* to kiss and cuddle.

canopy ('kænəpɪ) *n., pl.* **-pies.** **1.** an ornamental awning above a bed, person, or throne. **2.** a rooflike covering over an altar, niche, or door. **3.** any large or wide covering: *the sky was a grey canopy.* **4.** the part of a parachute that opens out. **5.** the transparent hood of an aircraft cockpit. ~*vb.* **-pying, -pied.** **6.** to cover with a canopy.

canst (kænst) *vb. Archaic.* the form of **can¹** used with the pronoun *thou.*

cant¹ (kænt) *n.* **1.** insincere talk, esp. concerning religion or morals. **2.** specialized vocabulary of a particular group, such as thieves or lawyers. ~*vb.* **3.** to use cant.

cant² (kænt) *n.* **1.** a tilted position. **2.** a sudden movement that tilts or turns something. **3.** the angle or tilt thus caused. **4.** a corner or outer angle. **5.** a slanting surface. ~*vb.* **6.** to tilt or overturn.

can't (kænt) *vb.* can not.

cantabile (kæn'tɑːbɪlɪ) *Music.* ~*adv.* **1.** flowingly and melodiously. ~*n.* **2.** a piece or passage performed in this way.

cantaloupe *or* **cantaloup** ('kæntə,luːp) *n.* a kind of melon with ribbed warty rind and orange flesh.

cantankerous (kæn'tæŋkərəs) *adj.* quarrelsome; bad-tempered. —**can'tankerously** *adv.* —**can'tankerousness** *n.*

cantata (kæn'tɑːtə) *n.* a musical setting of a text, consisting of arias, duets, and choruses.

canteen (kæn'tiːn) *n.* **1.** a restaurant attached to a workplace or school. **2.** a small shop that provides a limited range of items to a military unit. **3. a.** a box containing cutlery. **b.** the cutlery itself. **4.** a flask for carrying water.

canter ('kæntə) *n.* **1.** a gait of horses between a trot and a gallop in speed. ~*vb.* **2.** to move or cause to move at a canter.

canticle ('kæntɪkˀl) *n.* a nonmetrical hymn with a Biblical text.

cantilever ('kæntɪˌliːvə) *n.* **1.** a beam or structural framework fixed at one end only. **2.** a part of a beam or a structure projecting outwards beyond its support.

cantilever bridge *n.* a bridge made of two cantilevers which meet in the middle.

canto ('kæntəʊ) *n., pl.* **-tos.** a main division of a long poem.

canton *n.* **1.** ('kænton, kæn'ton). a political division of a country, esp. Switzerland. ~*vb.* **2.** (kæn'ton). to divide into cantons.

Cantonese (ˌkæntə'niːz) *n.* **1.** the Chinese dialect of Canton. **2.** (*pl.* **-ese**) a person from Canton. ~*adj.* **3.** of Canton or its dialect.

cantonment (kən'tuːnmənt) *n. History.* a permanent military camp in British India.

cantor ('kæntɔː) *n.* **1.** *Judaism.* a man employed to lead synagogue services. **2.** *Christianity.* a church choir leader.

Canuck (kə'nʌk) *n., adj. U.S. & Canad. informal.* Canadian.

canvas ('kænvəs) *n.* **1.** a heavy cloth of cotton, hemp, or jute, used for sails and tents. **2. a.** a piece of cloth on which an oil painting is done. **b.** an oil painting. **3.** a tent or tents collectively. **4.** a sail or sails collectively. **5. under canvas. a.** in tents. **b.** *Naut.* with sails unfurled.

canvass ('kænvəs) *vb.* **1.** to try to get votes or support (from). **2.** to determine the opinions of (people) by conducting a survey. **3.** to investigate or discuss (something) thoroughly. ~*n.* **4.** an attempt to get opinions or votes. —'**canvasser** *n.*

canyon *or* **cañon** ('kænjən) *n.* a gorge or ravine.

caoutchouc ('kaʊtʃʊk) *n.* same as **rubber**[1] (sense 1).

cap (kæp) *n.* **1.** a soft close-fitting covering for the head. **2.** such a covering worn to identify the wearer's rank or occupation: *a nurse's cap.* **3.** a cover: *lens cap.* **4.** a top part: *the cap of a wave.* **5. a.** See **percussion cap. b.** a small amount of explosive enclosed in paper and used in a toy gun. **6.** *Sport, chiefly Brit.* **a.** a cap given to someone chosen for a representative team. **b.** a player chosen for such a team. **7.** an artificial protective top for a tooth. **8.** a contraceptive device placed over the mouth of the womb. **9.** a mortarboard. **10. cap in hand.** humbly. ~*vb.* **capping, capped. 11.** to cover with or as if with a cap: *snow capped the mountain.* **12.** to impose an upper level on (a tax): *rate-capping.* **13.** *Informal.* to outdo; excel. **14. to cap it all.** to provide the finishing touch. **15.** *Sport, Brit.* to select (a player) for a representative team.

CAP (in the EC) Common Agricultural Policy.

cap. 1. capacity. **2.** capital. **3.** capital letter.

capability (ˌkeɪpə'bɪlɪtɪ) *n., pl.* **-ties. 1.** the quality of being capable; ability. **2.** (*usually pl.*) potential aptitude.

capable ('keɪpəbˀl) *adj.* **1.** having ability; competent. **2.** (foll. by *of*) able or having the skill (to do something): *she is capable of hard work.* **3.** (foll. by *of*) able or ready (to do something): *he seemed capable of murder.* —'**capably** *adv.*

capacious (kə'peɪʃəs) *adj.* spacious; roomy. —**ca'paciousness** *n.*

capacitance (kə'pæsɪtəns) *n.* **1.** the ability of a system to store electric charge. **2.** a measure of this.

capacitor (kə'pæsɪtə) *n.* a device for storing electric charge.

capacity (kə'pæsɪtɪ) *n., pl.* **-ties. 1.** the ability to contain, absorb, or hold. **2.** the maximum amount something can contain or absorb. **3.** mental ability. **4.** the maximum output of which an installation or producer is capable: *the factory must expand its capacity.* **5.** a position or function. **6.** *Computers.* **a.** the number of words or characters that can be stored in a storage device. **b.** the range of numbers that can be processed in a register. **7.** legal competence: *the capacity to make a will.* ~*modifier.* **8.** of the maximum amount or number possible: *a capacity crowd.*

caparison (kə'pærɪsˀn) *n.* **1.** a decorated covering for a horse. **2.** rich clothing or equipment. ~*vb.* **3.** to put a caparison on.

cape[1] (keɪp) *n.* a short sleeveless cloak.

cape[2] (keɪp) *n.* a headland or promontory.

Cape (keɪp) *n.* **the. 1.** the Cape of Good Hope. **2.** the SW region of South Africa's Cape Province.

cape pigeon *n.* a S African petrel.

caper[1] ('keɪpə) *n.* **1.** a playful skip or leap. **2.** a high-spirited prank. **3. cut a caper** *or* **capers.** to skip, leap, or frolic. ~*vb.* **4.** to skip or leap about light-heartedly.

caper[2] ('keɪpə) *n.* **1.** a spiny trailing Mediterranean shrub with edible flower buds. **2.** (*pl.*) its pickled flower buds, used in sauces.

capercaillie *or* **capercailzie** (ˌkæpə'keɪljɪ) *n.* a large black European woodland grouse.

Cape sparrow *n.* a S African sparrow.

capillarity (ˌkæpɪ'lærɪtɪ) *n.* a phenomenon caused by surface tension and resulting in the attraction or repulsion of the surface of a liquid in contact with a solid.

capillary (kə'pɪlərɪ) *adj.* **1.** like a hair; slender. **2.** (of tubes) having a fine bore. **3.** *Anat.* of the capillaries. ~*n., pl.* **-laries. 4.** *Anat.* one of the very fine blood vessels linking the arteries and the veins.

capital[1] (ˈkæpɪt²l) n. 1. the seat of government of a country. 2. the total wealth owned or used in business by an individual or group. 3. wealth used to produce more wealth. 4. **make capital (out) of.** to get advantage from. 5. (*sometimes cap.*) capitalists collectively. 6. a capital letter. ~adj. 7. *Law.* involving or punishable by death: *a capital offence.* 8. chief or principal: *our capital concern.* 9. designating the large letter used as the initial letter in a sentence, personal name, or place name. 10. *Chiefly Brit.* excellent; first-rate: *a capital idea.*

capital[2] (ˈkæpɪt²l) n. the top part of a column or pillar.

capital gain n. profit from the sale of an asset.

capital goods pl. n. *Econ.* goods that are themselves utilized in the production of other goods.

capitalism (ˈkæpɪtəˌlɪzəm) n. an economic system based on the private ownership of the means of production and distribution.

capitalist (ˈkæpɪtəlɪst) n. 1. a person who owns capital. 2. *Politics.* a supporter of capitalism. ~adj. 3. relating to capitalists or capitalism. —ˌcapitalˈistic adj.

capitalize or **-ise** (ˈkæpɪtəˌlaɪz) vb. 1. (foll. by *on*) to take advantage of. 2. to write or print (text) in capital letters. 3. to convert (debt or earnings) into capital stock. 4. to provide with capital. —ˌcapitaliˈzation or -iˈsation n.

capital levy n. a tax on capital or property as contrasted with a tax on income.

capitally (ˈkæpɪtəlɪ) adv. *Chiefly Brit.* in an excellent manner; admirably.

capital punishment n. the punishment of death for a crime; death penalty.

capital stock n. 1. the value of the total shares that a company can issue. 2. the total capital existing in an economy at a given time.

capital transfer tax n. (in Britain) a tax payable on the transfer of money or property as a gift or bequest.

capitation (ˌkæpɪˈteɪʃən) n. a tax of so much per person.

capitulate (kəˈpɪtjʊˌleɪt) vb. to surrender under agreed conditions.

capitulation (kəˌpɪtjʊˈleɪʃən) n. 1. the act of capitulating. 2. a document containing terms of surrender.

capo (ˈkæpəʊ) n., pl. **-pos.** a device fitted across the strings of a guitar or similar instrument so as to raise the pitch.

capon (ˈkeɪpən) n. a castrated cock fowl fattened for eating.

cappuccino (ˌkæpʊˈtʃiːnəʊ) n., pl. **-nos.** coffee with steamed milk, usually sprinkled with powdered chocolate.

caprice (kəˈpriːs) n. 1. a sudden change of

attitude or behaviour. 2. a tendency to such changes.

capricious (kəˈprɪʃəs) adj. given to sudden unpredictable changes; erratic.

Capricorn (ˈkæprɪˌkɔːn) n. 1. *Astrol.* the tenth sign of the zodiac; the Goat. 2. **tropic of Capricorn.** See **tropic** (sense 1).

capriole (ˈkæprɪˌəʊl) n. 1. an upward but not forward leap made by a horse. ~vb. 2. to perform a capriole.

caps. 1. capital letters. 2. capsule.

capsicum (ˈkæpsɪkəm) n. a kind of pepper used as a vegetable or ground to produce a spice.

capsize (kæpˈsaɪz) vb. to overturn accidentally; upset.

capstan (ˈkæpstən) n. 1. a rotating cylinder round which a ship's rope or cable is wound. 2. the rotating shaft in a tape recorder that pulls the tape past the head.

capstone (ˈkæpˌstəʊn) n. same as **copestone** (sense 2).

capsule (ˈkæpsjuːl) n. 1. a soluble case of gelatin enclosing a dose of medicine. 2. *Bot.* a plant's seed case that opens when ripe. 3. *Anat.* a membrane or sac surrounding an organ or part. 4. See **space capsule.** 5. (*modifier*) in a highly concise form: *a capsule summary.* —ˈcapsular adj.

capsulize or **-ise** (ˈkæpsjuˌlaɪz) vb. 1. to state (information) in a highly condensed form. 2. to enclose in a capsule.

Capt. Captain.

captain (ˈkæptɪn) n. 1. the person in charge of a vessel. 2. a middle-ranking naval officer. 3. a junior officer of the armed forces. 4. the officer in command of a civil aircraft. 5. the leader of a team in games. 6. a person in command over a group or organization: *a captain of industry.* 7. *U.S.* a policeman in charge of a precinct. ~vb. 8. to be captain of. —ˈcaptaincy n.

caption (ˈkæpʃən) n. 1. a title, brief explanation, or comment accompanying an illustration. 2. a heading or title of a chapter or article. 3. graphic material used in television presentation. ~vb. 4. to provide with a caption or captions.

captious (ˈkæpʃəs) adj. tending to make trivial criticisms. —ˈcaptiousness n.

captivate (ˈkæptɪˌveɪt) vb. to hold the attention of by fascinating; enchant. —ˈcaptiˌvating adj. —ˌcaptiˈvation n.

captive (ˈkæptɪv) n. 1. a person or animal that is confined or restrained. ~adj. 2. held as prisoner. 3. restrained: *a captive balloon.* 4. forced to listen or act in a particular way: *a captive audience.*

captivity (kæpˈtɪvɪtɪ) n., pl. **-ties.** imprisonment.

captor (ˈkæptə) n. a person who holds another captive.

capture (ˈkæptʃə) vb. 1. to take prisoner or

gain control over: *to capture a town*. **2.** to succeed in representing (something elusive): *the artist captured her likeness*. **3.** *Physics*. (of an atomic nucleus) to acquire an additional particle. ~*n*. **4.** a capturing. **5.** the person or thing captured.

capuchin ('kæpjʊtʃɪn, -jʊʃɪn) *n.* a S American monkey with a cowl of thick hair on the top of its head.

Capuchin ('kæpjʊtʃɪn, -jʊʃɪn) *n.* **1.** a friar belonging to a branch of the Franciscan Order founded in 1525. ~*adj.* **2.** of this order.

car (kɑː) *n.* **1.** a motorized road vehicle designed to carry a small number of people. **2.** the passenger compartment of a cable car, airship, lift, or balloon. **3.** *Chiefly U.S. & Canad.* a railway carriage or van.

caracal ('kærə,kæl) *n.* a lynx with reddish fur, which inhabits deserts of N Africa and S Asia.

carafe (kə'ræf, -'rɑːf) *n.* **1.** a wide-mouthed bottle for water or wine. **2.** the amount held by a carafe.

carambola (,kærəm'bəʊlə) *n.* the yellow edible star-shaped fruit of a Brazilian tree.

caramel ('kærəməl) *n.* **1.** burnt sugar, used for colouring and flavouring food. **2.** a chewy sweet made from sugar and milk.

caramelize *or* **-ise** ('kærəmə,laɪz) *vb.* to turn into or be turned into caramel.

carapace ('kærə,peɪs) *n.* the thick hard upper shell of tortoises and crustaceans.

carat ('kærət) *n.* **1.** a unit of weight of precious stones, equal to 0.20 grams. **2.** a measure of the purity of gold in an alloy, expressed as the number of parts of gold in 24 parts of the alloy.

caravan ('kærə,væn) *n.* **1.** a large enclosed vehicle designed to be pulled by a car or horse and equipped to be lived in. **2.** (in some Eastern countries) a company of traders or other travellers journeying together. ~*vb.* **-vanning, -vanned. 3.** *Brit.* to travel or have a holiday in a caravan.

caravanserai (,kærə'vænsə,raɪ) *n.* (in some Eastern countries) a large inn enclosing a courtyard, providing accommodation for caravans.

caraway ('kærə,weɪ) *n.* **1.** a Eurasian plant with small whitish flowers. **2. caraway seed.** the pungent aromatic fruit of this plant, used in cooking.

carbide ('kɑːbaɪd) *n.* a binary compound of carbon with a metal.

carbine ('kɑːbaɪn) *n.* a type of light rifle.

carbohydrate (,kɑːbəʊ'haɪdreɪt) *n.* any of a large group of energy-producing compounds, including sugars and starches, that contain carbon, hydrogen, and oxygen.

carbolic acid (kɑː'bɒlɪk) *n.* same as **phenol.**

carbon ('kɑːb°n) *n.* **1.** a nonmetallic element occurring in three forms, charcoal,

graphite, and diamond, and present in all organic compounds. The isotope **carbon-12** is the standard for atomic weight; **carbon-14** is used in carbon dating. Symbol: C **2.** short for **carbon paper** or **carbon copy.**

carbonaceous (,kɑːbə'neɪʃəs) *adj.* of, resembling, or containing carbon.

carbonate *n.* ('kɑːbə,neɪt, -nɪt). **1.** a salt or ester of carbonic acid. ~*vb.* ('kɑːbə,neɪt). **2.** to fill (a drink) with carbon dioxide.

carbon black *n.* powdered carbon produced by partial burning of natural gas or petroleum: used in pigments and ink.

carbon copy *n.* **1.** a duplicate obtained by using carbon paper. **2.** *Informal.* a person or thing that is identical to another.

carbon dating *n.* a technique for finding the age of organic materials, such as wood, based on their content of the radioisotope carbon-14.

carbon dioxide *n.* a colourless odourless incombustible gas formed during breathing, and used in fire extinguishers.

carbonic (kɑː'bɒnɪk) *adj.* containing carbon.

carbonic acid *n.* a weak acid formed when carbon dioxide combines with water.

carboniferous (,kɑːbə'nɪfərəs) *adj.* yielding coal or carbon.

Carboniferous (,kɑːbə'nɪfərəs) *adj. Geol.* of a period of geological time about 330 million years ago, during which coal seams were formed.

carbonize *or* **-ise** ('kɑːbə,naɪz) *vb.* **1.** to turn into carbon as a result of partial burning. **2.** to coat (a substance) with carbon. —**,carboni'zation** *or* **-i'sation** *n.*

carbon monoxide *n.* a colourless odourless poisonous gas formed by the incomplete burning of carbon compounds.

carbon paper *n.* a thin sheet of paper coated on the underside with a dark waxy pigment, containing carbon, placed between two sheets of paper so that what is written or typed on the top sheet is transferred on to the bottom sheet.

carbon tetrachloride (,tɛtrə'klɔːraɪd) *n.* a colourless nonflammable liquid used as a solvent, cleaning fluid, and insecticide.

Carborundum (,kɑːbə'rʌndəm) *n. Trademark.* an abrasive material, esp. one consisting of silicon carbide.

carboxyl group *or* **radical** (kɑː'bɒksaɪl) *n.* the chemical group -COOH: the functional group in organic acids.

carboy ('kɑː,bɔɪ) *n.* a large bottle protected by a basket or box.

carbuncle ('kɑː,bʌŋk°l) *n.* **1.** a large skin eruption like a boil. **2.** a rounded garnet cut without facets. —**carbuncular** (kɑː'bʌŋkjʊlə) *adj.*

carburettor (,kɑːbjʊ'rɛtə, 'kɑːbjʊ,rɛtə) *or* *U.S.* **carburetor** ('kɑːbjʊ,reɪtə) *n.* a device in engines which mixes petrol with air and regulates the intake of the mixture into the engine.

carcass *or* **carcase** (ˈkɑːkəs) *n.* **1.** the dead body of an animal. **2.** *Informal.* a person's body. **3.** the skeleton or framework of something. **4.** the worthless remains of something.

carcinogen (kɑːˈsɪnədʒən) *n.* any substance that produces cancer. —ˌ**carcinoˈgenic** *adj.*

carcinoma (ˌkɑːsɪˈnəʊmə) *n., pl.* **-mas** *or* **-mata** (-mətə). a malignant tumour or cancer.

card[1] (kɑːd) *n.* **1.** a piece of stiff paper or thin cardboard used for identification, reference, proof of membership, or sending greetings or messages: *a birthday card.* **2.** one of a set of small pieces of cardboard, marked with figures or symbols, used for playing games or for fortune-telling. **3.** a small rectangle of stiff plastic with identifying numbers for use as a credit card or banker's card. **4.** *Informal.* a witty or eccentric person. **5.** Also called: **racecard.** *Horse racing.* a daily programme of all the races at a meeting. **6. a card up one's sleeve.** something advantageous kept in reserve until needed. **7.** *Computers.* See **punched card.** ~See also **cards.**

card[2] (kɑːd) *n.* **1.** a machine or tool, typically a leather-covered board with wire points sticking through it, for combing fibres of cotton or wool to disentangle them before spinning. **2.** a comblike tool for raising the nap on cloth. ~*vb.* **3.** to process with such a machine or tool. —ˈ**carder** *n.*

cardamom (ˈkɑːdəməm) *or* **cardamon** *n.* the seeds of a tropical plant, used as a spice.

cardboard (ˈkɑːdˌbɔːd) *n.* a thin stiff board made from paper pulp.

card-carrying *adj.* being an official member of an organization: *a card-carrying Communist.*

cardiac (ˈkɑːdɪˌæk) *adj.* of or relating to the heart.

cardigan (ˈkɑːdɪgən) *n.* a knitted jacket or sweater with buttons up the front.

cardinal (ˈkɑːdɪnᵊl) *n.* **1.** *R.C. Church.* any of the high-ranking clergymen who elect the pope and act as his chief counsellors. **2.** a cardinal number. **3.** a bright red crested North American songbird. ~*adj.* **4.** fundamentally important; principal. **5.** deep red.

cardinal number *or* **numeral** *n.* a number denoting quantity but not order in a group.

cardinal points *pl. n.* the four main points of the compass: north, south, east, and west.

cardinal virtues *pl. n.* the most important moral qualities, traditionally justice, prudence, temperance, and fortitude.

card index *or* **file** *n.* an index in which each item is separately listed on systematically arranged cards.

cardiogram (ˈkɑːdɪəʊˌgræm) *n.* an electrocardiogram. See **electrocardiograph.**

cardiograph (ˈkɑːdɪəʊˌgrɑːf) *n.* **1.** an instrument for recording heart movements. **2.** same as **electrocardiograph.** —ˌ**cardiˈographer** *n.* —ˌ**cardiˈography** *n.*

cardiology (ˌkɑːdɪˈɒlədʒɪ) *n.* the branch of medicine dealing with the heart and its diseases. —ˌ**cardiˈologist** *n.*

cardiovascular (ˌkɑːdɪəʊˈvæskjʊlə) *adj.* of or relating to the heart and the blood vessels.

card reader *n.* a device for reading information on a punched card and transferring it to a computer storage device.

cards (kɑːdz) *n.* **1. a.** any game played with cards. **b.** the playing of such a game. **2.** an employee's tax and national insurance documents, held by his employer. **3. get one's cards.** to be sacked from one's job. **4. on the cards.** likely. **5. play one's cards (right).** to handle a situation (cleverly). **6. put** *or* **lay one's cards on the table.** to declare one's intentions.

cardsharp (ˈkɑːdˌʃɑːp) *or* **cardsharper** *n.* a professional card player who cheats.

card vote *n. Brit.* a vote by delegates in which each delegate's vote counts as a vote by all his constituents.

care (kɛə) *vb.* **1.** to be worried or concerned: *he is dying, and she doesn't care.* **2.** (foll. by *for* or *about*) to have regard or consideration for: *he cares more for his hobby than his job.* **3.** (foll. by *for*) to have a desire for: *would you care for tea?* **4.** (foll. by *for*) to look after or provide for. **5.** to like (to do something): *would you care to sit down?* **6. for all I care** *or* **I couldn't care less.** I am completely indifferent. ~*n.* **7.** careful or serious attention: *he does his work with care.* **8.** protection or charge: *in the care of a doctor.* **9.** (*often pl.*) trouble; worry. **10.** an object of or cause for concern. **11.** caution: *handle with care.* **12. care of.** at the address of: written on envelopes. **13. in** *or* **into care.** *Brit.* made the legal responsibility of a local authority by order of a court. —ˈ**carer** *n.*

careen (kəˈriːn) *vb.* **1.** to tilt over to one side. **2.** *Naut.* to tilt (a ship) over to one side for cleaning or repairs.

career (kəˈrɪə) *n.* **1.** a path through life or history. **2.** a profession or occupation. **3.** a headlong course or path. ~*vb.* **4.** to rush in an uncontrolled way.

careerist (kəˈrɪərɪst) *n.* a person who seeks to advance his career by any possible means. —**caˈreerism** *n.*

carefree ('kɛə,friː) adj. without worry or responsibility. —'care,freeness n.

careful ('kɛəful) adj. 1. cautious in attitude or action. 2. painstaking; exact and thorough. 3. (foll. by of, in, or about) solicitous; protective. —'carefully adv. —'carefulness n.

careless ('kɛəlɪs) adj. 1. done or acting with insufficient attention. 2. unconcerned in attitude or action. 3. carefree. —'carelessly adv. —'carelessness n.

caress (kə'rɛs) n. 1. a gentle affectionate touch or embrace. ~vb. 2. to touch gently and affectionately.

caret ('kærɪt) n. a symbol (ʌ) indicating the place in written or printed matter at which something is to be inserted.

caretaker ('kɛə,teɪkə) n. 1. a person employed to look after a place or thing. 2. (modifier) interim: a caretaker government.

careworn ('kɛə,wɔːn) adj. showing signs of care, stress, or worry: a careworn face.

cargo ('kɑːgəʊ) n., pl. -goes or esp. U.S. -gos. goods carried by a ship, aircraft, or other vehicle; freight.

Carib ('kærɪb) n. 1. (pl. -ibs or -ib) a member of a group of peoples of NE South America and the S West Indies. 2. their languages.

Caribbean (,kærɪ'biːən) adj. 1. of the Caribbean Sea and its islands. 2. of the Caribs or any of their languages. ~n. 3. the Caribbean Sea. 4. a Carib.

caribou ('kærɪ,buː) n., pl. -bous or -bou. a large North American reindeer.

caricature ('kærɪkə,tjʊə) n. 1. a representation of a person which exaggerates his characteristic features for comic effect. 2. a ridiculously poor imitation. ~vb. 3. to make or give a caricature of. —'cari-ca,turist n.

caries ('kɛəriːz) n., pl. -ies. progressive decay of a bone or a tooth.

carillon (kə'rɪljən) n. 1. a set of bells usually hung in a tower and played either on a keyboard or mechanically. 2. a tune played on such bells.

carinate ('kærɪ,neɪt) adj. Biol. having a keel or ridge.

Carlovingian (,kɑːləʊ'vɪndʒɪən) adj., n. same as **Carolingian.**

Carmelite ('kɑːmə,laɪt) R.C. Church. ~n. 1. a friar or nun belonging to the order of Our Lady of Carmel. ~adj. 2. of this order.

carminative ('kɑːmɪnətɪv) adj. 1. able to relieve flatulence. ~n. 2. a carminative drug.

carmine ('kɑːmaɪn) adj. 1. vivid red. ~n. 2. a pigment of this colour obtained from cochineal.

carnage ('kɑːnɪdʒ) n. extensive slaughter.

carnal ('kɑːn³l) adj. relating to the appetites and passions of the body. —car'nality n.

carnation (kɑː'neɪʃən) n. 1. a plant with clove-scented white, pink, or red flowers. ~adj. 2. rosy pink.

carnelian (kɑː'niːljən) n. a reddish-yellow variety of chalcedony, used as a gemstone.

carnet ('kɑːneɪ) n. a customs licence permitting motorists to take their cars across certain frontiers.

carnival ('kɑːnɪv³l) n. 1. a festive period marked by merrymaking. 2. a travelling funfair.

carnivore ('kɑːnɪ,vɔː) n. 1. any of an order of mammals with teeth specialized for eating flesh, such as cats, dogs, and weasels. 2. any animal or plant that feeds on animals.

carnivorous (kɑː'nɪvərəs) adj. feeding on flesh.

carob ('kærəb) n. the long brown pod of an evergreen Mediterranean tree, used as animal fodder and sometimes for human food.

carol ('kærəl) n. 1. a joyful religious song, esp. one celebrating the birth of Christ. ~vb. -olling, -olled or U.S. -oling, -oled. 2. to sing carols. 3. to sing joyfully.

Carolingian (,kærə'lɪndʒɪən) adj. 1. of the Frankish dynasty founded in 751 A.D. by Charlemagne. ~n. 2. a member of this dynasty.

carotid (kə'rɒtɪd) n. 1. either of the two arteries that supply blood to the head and neck. ~adj. 2. of either of these arteries.

carousal (kə'raʊz³l) n. a merry drinking party.

carouse (kə'raʊz) vb. 1. to have a merry drinking party. ~n. 2. a carousal.

carousel (,kærə'sɛl, -'zɛl) n. 1. a revolving conveyor, esp. for luggage at an airport or slides for a projector. 2. U.S. & Canad. a merry-go-round.

carp¹ (kɑːp) n., pl. carp or carps. a freshwater food fish having one long dorsal fin, and two barbels on each side of the mouth.

carp² (kɑːp) vb. (often foll. by at) to complain or find fault. —'carper n. —'carping adj., n.

carpal ('kɑːp³l) n. a wrist bone.

car park n. an area or building reserved for parking cars.

carpel ('kɑːp³l) n. the female reproductive organ of flowering plants.

carpenter ('kɑːpɪntə) n. 1. a person skilled in woodwork, esp. in buildings. ~vb. 2. to do the work of a carpenter. 3. to make or fit together by carpentry.

carpentry ('kɑːpɪntrɪ) n. 1. the art or technique of working wood. 2. the work produced by a carpenter; woodwork.

carpet ('kɑːpɪt) n. 1. a heavy fabric for covering floors. 2. a covering like a carpet: a carpet of leaves. 3. on the carpet. Informal. a. being reprimanded. b. under consideration. ~*vb*. **4.** to cover with or as if with a carpet.

carpetbag ('kɑːpɪtˌbæg) *n*. a travelling bag originally made of carpeting.

carpetbagger ('kɑːpɪtˌbægə) *n*. a politician who seeks office in a place where he has no connections.

carpeting ('kɑːpɪtɪŋ) *n*. carpet material or carpets in general.

car phone *n*. a telephone that operates by cellular radio for use in a car.

carport ('kɑːˌpɔːt) *n*. a shelter for a car, consisting of a roof supported by posts.

carpus ('kɑːpəs) *n., pl*. **-pi** (-paɪ). **1.** *Anat*. the wrist. **2.** the set of eight bones of the human wrist.

carrageen *or* **carragheen** ('kærəˌgiːn) *n*. an edible red seaweed of rocky shores of North America and N Europe.

carriage ('kærɪdʒ) *n*. **1.** *Brit*. a railway coach for passengers. **2.** the way a person holds and moves his head and body. **3.** a four-wheeled horse-drawn passenger vehicle. **4.** the moving part of a machine that supports and shifts another part: *a typewriter carriage*. **5.** ('kærɪdʒ, 'kærɪdʒ). **a.** the act of conveying goods. **b.** the charge made for conveying goods.

carriage clock *n*. a style of portable clock, originally used by travellers.

carriageway ('kærɪdʒˌweɪ) *n. Brit*. the part of a road along which traffic passes in one direction: *a dual carriageway*.

carrier ('kærɪə) *n*. **1.** a person, thing, or organization employed to carry goods or passengers. **2.** a person or animal that, without suffering from a disease, is capable of transmitting it to others. **3.** same as **aircraft carrier**.

carrier bag *n. Brit*. a large paper or plastic bag for carrying shopping.

carrier pigeon *n*. a homing pigeon used for carrying messages.

carrion ('kærɪən) *n*. **1.** dead and rotting flesh. **2.** something filthy or vile.

carrion crow *n*. a scavenging European crow like the rook but having a black bill.

carrot ('kærət) *n*. **1.** a long tapering orange root vegetable. **2.** something offered as an incentive.

carroty ('kærətɪ) *adj*. of a reddish or yellowish-orange colour.

carry ('kærɪ) *vb*. **-rying, -ried. 1.** to take (something) from one place to another. **2.** to have on one's person: *he carries a watch*. **3.** to be transmitted or be a medium for transmitting: *sound carries over water*. **4.** to bear the weight, pressure, or responsibility of: *her efforts carry the whole production*. **5.** to have as a quality or result: *it carries a two-year guarantee; this crime carries a heavy penalty*. **6.** to be pregnant with (young). **7.** to bear (the head or body) in a specified manner: *she carried her head

high*. **8.** to conduct (oneself) in a specified manner: *she carried herself well*. **9.** to win over, esp. by emotional appeal: *his words carried the crowd*. **10.** to secure the passage of (a bill or motion). **11.** to capture: *our troops carried the town*. **12.** (of communications media) to include in the contents: *this newspaper carries no book reviews*. **13.** *Maths*. to transfer (a number) from one column of figures to the next. **14.** (of a shop or trader) to keep in stock. **15.** (of a ball or projectile) to travel through the air or reach a specified point: *his first drive carried to the green*. **16. carry the can for**. *Informal*. to take all the blame for something on behalf of. ~*n., pl*. **-ries. 17.** the act of carrying. **18.** the range or distance covered by a ball or projectile. ~See also **carry away, carry forward**, etc.

carry away *vb*. **1.** to remove forcefully. **2.** (*usually passive*) to cause (a person) to lose self-control. **3.** (*usually passive*) to delight: *he was carried away by the music*.

carrycot ('kærɪˌkɒt) *n*. a light portable cot for a baby.

carry forward *vb*. to transfer (an amount) to the next column, page, or accounting period.

carry off *vb*. **1.** to remove forcefully. **2.** to win. **3.** to handle (a situation) successfully: *he carried off the introductions well*. **4.** to cause to die: *he was carried off by pneumonia*.

carry on *vb*. **1.** to continue or persevere. **2.** to conduct: *to carry on a business*. **3.** (often foll. by *with*) *Informal*. to have an affair. **4.** *Informal*. to cause a fuss. ~*n*. **carry-on. 5.** *Informal, chiefly Brit*. a fuss.

carry out *vb*. **1.** to put (something) into practice. **2.** to accomplish. ~*n*. **carry-out.** *Chiefly Scot*. **3.** alcohol bought for consumption elsewhere. **4.** a shop which sells hot cooked food for consumption away from the premises.

carry over *vb*. **1.** to postpone or defer. **2.** same as **carry forward**.

carry through *vb*. **1.** to accomplish. **2.** to enable to endure (hardship or trouble); support.

carsick ('kɑːˌsɪk) *adj*. nauseated from riding in a car or other vehicle. —'**car,sickness** *n*.

cart (kɑːt) *n*. **1.** an open horse-drawn vehicle, usually having two wheels, used to carry goods or passengers. **2.** any small vehicle drawn or pushed by hand. **3. put the cart before the horse**. to reverse the usual order of things. ~*vb*. **4.** to carry (something) in a cart. **5.** to carry with effort: *to cart wood home*. —'**carter** *n*.

carte blanche ('kɑːt 'blɑːntʃ) *n., pl*. **cartes blanches** ('kɑːts 'blɑːntʃ). complete authority: *the government gave their negotiator carte blanche*.

cartel (kɑːˈtɛl) n. an association of competing firms formed in order to fix prices.

Cartesian (kɑːˈtiːzɪən) adj. of Descartes, 17th-century French philosopher and mathematician, or his works. —**Carˈtesianˌism** n.

Cartesian coordinates pl. n. a system of coordinates that defines the location of a point by its perpendicular distance from each of a set of axes intersecting at right angles.

carthorse (ˈkɑːtˌhɔːs) n. a large heavily built horse kept for pulling carts or for farmwork.

Carthusian (kɑːˈθjuːzɪən) n. 1. a member of a strict monastic order founded in 1084. ~adj. 2. of this order.

cartilage (ˈkɑːtɪlɪdʒ) n. a strong flexible tissue forming part of the skeleton. —**cartilaginous** (ˌkɑːtɪˈlædʒɪnəs) adj.

cartography (kɑːˈtɒɡrəfɪ) n. the skill or practice of making maps or charts. —**carˈtographer** n. —**cartographic** (ˌkɑːtəˈɡræfɪk) adj.

carton (ˈkɑːtᵊn) n. 1. a cardboard box or container. 2. a container of waxed paper in which liquids are sold.

cartoon (kɑːˈtuːn) n. 1. a humorous or satirical drawing, usually in a newspaper or magazine. 2. same as **comic strip**. 3. same as **animated cartoon**. 4. a full-size sketch for a fresco, tapestry, or mosaic. —**carˈtoonist** n.

cartouche or **cartouch** (kɑːˈtuːʃ) n. 1. an ornamental tablet or panel in the form of a scroll. 2. (in ancient Egypt) an oblong or oval figure containing royal or divine names.

cartridge (ˈkɑːtrɪdʒ) n. 1. a metal casing containing an explosive charge, and often the bullet, for a firearm. 2. a unit in the pick-up of a record player, which converts the movements of the stylus into electrical signals. 3. an enclosed container of material for insertion into a device.

cartridge belt n. a belt with loops or pockets for holding cartridges.

cartridge clip n. a metallic container holding cartridges for an automatic firearm.

cartridge paper n. a type of heavy rough drawing paper.

cartwheel (ˈkɑːtˌwiːl) n. 1. the wheel of a cart, usually having wooden spokes. 2. a sideways somersault supported by the hands with legs outstretched.

carve (kɑːv) vb. 1. to cut in order to form something: to carve wood. 2. to form (something) by cutting: to carve statues. 3. to slice (meat) into pieces. ~See also **carve out**, **carve up**. —**ˈcarver** n.

carve out vb. Informal. to make or create (a career): he carved out his own future.

carvery (ˈkɑːvərɪ) n., pl. -veries. a restaurant where customers pay a set price for unrestricted helpings of meat and other food.

carve up vb. 1. to cut (something) up. 2. to divide or share out (something). ~n. **carve-up**. 3. Slang. the sharing-out of something.

carving (ˈkɑːvɪŋ) n. a figure or design produced by carving stone or wood.

carving knife n. a long-bladed knife for carving cooked meat.

carwash (ˈkɑːˌwɒʃ) n. a place fitted with equipment for automatically washing cars.

caryatid (ˌkærɪˈætɪd) n., pl. -ids or -ides (-ɪˌdiːz). a statue of a draped female figure used as a supporting column.

Casanova (ˌkæsəˈnəʊvə) n. a womanizer; philanderer.

casbah (ˈkæzbɑː) n. same as **kasbah**.

cascade (kæsˈkeɪd) n. 1. a waterfall or series of waterfalls over rocks. 2. something flowing or falling like this. ~vb. 3. to flow or fall in a cascade.

cascara (kæsˈkɑːrə) n. 1. the bark of a N American buckthorn, used as a laxative. 2. the shrub it is prepared from.

case¹ (keɪs) n. 1. a single instance or example of something. 2. a matter for discussion. 3. a specific condition or state of affairs; situation. 4. a set of arguments supporting an action or cause. 5. a person attended or served by a doctor, social worker, or solicitor. 6. a. an action or lawsuit: he has a good case. b. the evidence offered in court to support a claim. 7. Grammar. any of a set of grammatical categories of nouns, pronouns, and adjectives showing the relation of that particular word to other words in the sentence: the nominative case. 8. Informal. an eccentric. 9. in any case. no matter what. 10. in case. a. so as to allow for eventualities. b. so as to allow for the possibility that: take your coat in case it rains. 11. in case of. in the event of.

case² (keɪs) n. 1. a container, such as a box or chest. 2. a protective outer cover. 3. a container and its contents: a case of ammunition. 4. Printing. a tray in which a compositor keeps individual metal types of a particular size and style. ~vb. 5. to put into or enclose in a case. 6. Slang. to inspect carefully (a place to be robbed).

case-harden vb. 1. Metallurgy. to form a hard surface layer on (an iron alloy). 2. to make callous: a case-hardened judge.

case history n. a record of a person's background or medical history.

casein (ˈkeɪsɪɪn, -siːn) n. a protein found in milk, which forms the basis of cheese.

case law n. law established by following judicial decisions made in earlier cases.

casement (ˈkeɪsmənt) n. 1. a window frame hinged on one side. 2. a window with frames hinged at the side.

casework ('keɪs,wɜːk) *n.* social work based on close study of an individual's personal history and family background. —'**case-,worker** *n.*

cash (kæʃ) *n.* **1.** banknotes and coins, esp. in hand or readily available. **2.** immediate payment for goods or services. **3.** (*modifier*) of, for, or paid by cash: *a cash transaction.* ~*vb.* **4.** to obtain or pay ready money for. ~See also **cash in.**

cash-and-carry *adj., adv.* sold or operated on a basis of cash payment for goods that are taken away by the purchaser.

cash-book *n. Book-keeping.* a journal in which all money transactions are recorded.

cash crop *n.* a crop produced for sale rather than for subsistence.

cash desk *n.* a counter or till in a shop where purchases are paid for.

cash discount *n.* a discount granted to a purchaser who pays within a specified period.

cash dispenser *n.* a computerized device outside a bank which supplies cash when a special card is inserted and the user's code number keyed in.

cashew ('kæʃuː, kæ'ʃuː) *n.* the edible kidney-shaped nut of a tropical American evergreen tree.

cash flow *n.* the movement of money into and out of a business.

cashier[1] (kæ'ʃɪə) *n.* a person responsible for handling cash in a bank, shop, or other business.

cashier[2] (kæ'ʃɪə) *vb.* to dismiss with dishonour from the armed forces.

cash in *vb.* **1.** to exchange for cash. **2.** (often foll. by *on*) *Informal.* to gain a profit or advantage (from).

cashmere ('kæʃmɪə) *n.* **1.** a fine soft wool from goats of Kashmir. **2.** cloth made from this or similar wool.

cash on delivery *n.* a system involving cash payment to the carrier on delivery of merchandise.

cash register *n.* a till that has a mechanism for displaying and adding the prices of the goods sold.

casing ('keɪsɪŋ) *n.* a protective case or covering.

casino (kə'siːnəʊ) *n., pl.* **-nos.** a public building or room in which gaming takes place.

cask (kɑːsk) *n.* **1.** a strong barrel, esp. one used to hold alcoholic drink. **2.** the amount held in a cask.

casket ('kɑːskɪt) *n.* **1.** a small box for valuables. **2.** *Chiefly U.S.* a coffin.

casque (kæsk) *n. Zool.* a helmet-like structure, as on the bill of most hornbills.

Cassandra (kə'sændrə) *n.* anyone whose prophecies of doom are unheeded.

cassava (kə'sɑːvə) *n.* a starch obtained from the root of a tropical American plant: used to make tapioca.

casserole ('kæsə,rəʊl) *n.* **1.** a covered dish in which food is cooked and served. **2.** any food cooked and served in such a dish: *chicken casserole.* ~*vb.* **3.** to cook or be cooked in a casserole.

cassette (kæ'sɛt) *n.* **1.** a plastic container for magnetic tape, inserted into a tape deck to be played. **2.** *Photog.* a sealed case with film in it, which can be loaded quickly into a camera.

cassia ('kæsɪə) *n.* **1.** a tropical plant whose pods yield **cassia pulp**, a mild laxative. **2.** **cassia bark.** the cinnamon-like bark of a tropical Asian tree, used as a spice.

cassock ('kæsək) *n.* an ankle-length garment, usually black, worn by Christian priests.

cassowary ('kæsə,wɛərɪ) *n., pl.* **-waries.** a large flightless bird of Australia and New Guinea, with a horny head crest, black plumage, and brightly coloured neck.

cast (kɑːst) *vb.* **casting, cast. 1.** to throw with force. **2.** to reject: *he cast the idea from his mind.* **3.** to shed: *the horse cast a shoe.* **4.** to cause to appear: *to cast a shadow.* **5.** to express (doubts or aspersions). **6.** to direct (a glance): *cast your eye over this.* **7.** *Angling.* to throw (a line) into the water. **8.** to draw or choose (lots). **9.** to roll or throw (a dice). **10.** to give or deposit (a vote). **11.** to select (actors) to play parts in (a play or film). **12. a.** to shape (molten material) by pouring it into a mould. **b.** to make (an object) by such a process. **13.** to draw up (a horoscope). **14. cast a spell.** to perform magic. **15.** to formulate: *he cast his work in the form of a chart.* **16.** to twist or cause to twist. ~*n.* **17.** the act of throwing. **18.** something that is shed, such as the coil of earth left by an earthworm. **19. a.** a throw at dice. **b.** the resulting number shown. **20.** *Angling.* the casting of a line. **21.** the actors in a play collectively. **22. a.** an object made of material that has been shaped, while molten, by a mould. **b.** the mould used to shape such an object. **23.** form or appearance. **24.** a sort, kind, or style. **25.** a slight squint in the eye. **26.** *Surgery.* a rigid casing, often made of plaster of Paris, for immobilizing broken bones while they heal. **27.** a slight tinge or shade. ~See also **cast about, castaway,** etc.

cast about *vb.* to make a mental or visual search: *to cast about for a plot.*

castanets (,kæstə'nɛts) *pl. n.* a musical instrument consisting of curved pieces of hollow wood, held between the fingers and thumb and clicked together: used esp. by Spanish dancers.

castaway ('kɑːstə,weɪ) *n.* **1.** a person who has been shipwrecked. ~*adj.* **2.** shipwrecked.

cast back vb. to turn (the mind) to the past.

cast down vb. to make (a person) discouraged or dejected.

caste (kɑːst) n. 1. any of the four major hereditary classes into which Hindu society is divided. 2. a social class or system based on distinctions of heredity, rank, or wealth. 3. **lose caste.** Informal. to lose one's social position.

castellated (ˈkæstɪˌleɪtɪd) adj. having turrets and battlements, like a castle. —ˌcastelˈlation n.

caster (ˈkɑːstə) n. 1. a bottle with a perforated top for sprinkling sugar, salt, or flour. 2. a small swivelled wheel fixed to a leg of a piece of furniture to enable it to be moved easily.

caster sugar (ˈkɑːstə) n. finely ground white sugar.

castigate (ˈkæstɪˌgeɪt) vb. to rebuke or criticize severely. —ˌcastiˈgation n. —ˈcastiˌgator n.

casting (ˈkɑːstɪŋ) n. an object that has been cast in metal from a mould.

casting vote n. the deciding vote used by the chairman of a meeting when an equal number of votes are cast on each side.

cast iron n. 1. iron containing so much carbon that it is brittle and must be cast into shape rather than wrought. ~adj. **cast-iron.** 2. made of cast iron. 3. rigid or unchallengeable: a cast-iron decision.

castle (ˈkɑːsˀl) n. 1. a fortified building or set of buildings as in medieval Europe. 2. Chess. same as **rook**². ~vb. 3. Chess. to move (the king) two squares sideways and place the nearer rook on the square passed over by the king.

castle in the air or **in Spain** n. a hope or desire unlikely to be realized; daydream.

cast-off adj. 1. abandoned or discarded: cast-off shoes. ~n. **castoff.** 2. a person or thing that has been abandoned or discarded. ~vb. **cast off.** 3. to abandon or discard. 4. to untie (a ship) from a dock. 5. to knot and remove (a row of stitches, esp. the final row) from the needle in knitting.

castor (ˈkɑːstə) n. same as **caster**.

castor oil n. an oil obtained from the seeds of a tall Indian plant (**castor-oil plant**) and used as a lubricant and purgative.

castrate (kæˈstreɪt) vb. 1. to remove the testicles of. 2. to deprive of vigour or masculinity. —casˈtration n.

cast steel n. steel containing varying amounts of carbon and manganese, that is cast into shape rather than wrought.

casual (ˈkæʒjʊəl) adj. 1. happening by chance. 2. offhand: a casual remark. 3. shallow or superficial: a casual affair. 4. being or seeming careless or nonchalant: he assumed a casual attitude. 5. for informal wear: a casual coat. 6. occasional or irregular: a casual labourer. ~n. 7. (usually pl.) informal clothing or footwear. 8. an occasional worker. 9. (usually pl.) a young man wearing expensive casual clothes who goes to football matches in order to start fights. —ˈcasually adv. —ˈcasualness n.

casualty (ˈkæʒjʊəltɪ) n., pl. -ties. 1. a person who is killed or injured in an accident or war. 2. the hospital department treating victims of accidents. 3. anything that is lost, damaged, or destroyed as the result of an accident or happening.

casuistry (ˈkæzjʊɪstrɪ) n., pl. -ries. reasoning that is misleading or oversubtle. —ˈcasuist n.

cat (kæt) n. 1. a small domesticated feline mammal, having thick soft fur and whiskers. 2. any wild feline mammal, such as the lynx, lion, or tiger. 3. Informal. a spiteful woman. 4. Slang. a person. 5. short for **catamaran**. 6. short for **cat-o'-nine-tails.** 7. **let the cat out of the bag.** to disclose a secret, often by mistake. 8. **like a cat on a hot tin roof** or **on hot bricks.** uneasy or agitated. 9. **put** or **set the cat among the pigeons.** to stir up trouble. 10. **rain cats and dogs.** to rain very heavily. 11. **the cat's pyjamas** or **whiskers.** an excellent person or thing. —ˈcatˌlike adj.

cat. catalogue.

catabolism (kəˈtæbəˌlɪzəm) n. a metabolic process in which complex molecules are broken down into simple ones with the release of energy. —**catabolic** (ˌkætəˈbɒlɪk) adj.

cataclysm (ˈkætəˌklɪzəm) n. 1. a violent upheaval. 2. a disastrous flood. —ˌcataˈclysmic adj.

catacomb (ˈkætəˌkəʊm) n. (usually pl.) an underground burial place consisting of tunnels with side recesses for tombs.

catafalque (ˈkætəˌfælk) n. a raised platform on which a body lies in state before or during a funeral.

Catalan (ˈkætəˌlæn) n. 1. a language of Catalonia in NE Spain, closely related to Spanish and Provençal. 2. a person from Catalonia. ~adj. 3. of Catalonia, its inhabitants, or their language.

catalepsy (ˈkætəˌlɛpsɪ) n. a trancelike state in which the body is rigid. —ˌcataˈleptic adj.

catalogue or U.S. **catalog** (ˈkætəˌlɒg) n. 1. a complete, usually alphabetical, list of items. 2. a book containing details of items for sale. 3. a list of all the books of a library. 4. a list of events, qualities, or things considered as a group: a catalogue of crimes. ~vb. 5. to compile a catalogue of (items). 6. to enter (an item) in a catalogue. 7. to list a series of (events, qualities, or things). —ˈcataˌloguer n.

catalpa (kəˈtælpə) n. tree of N America and

Asia, having bell-shaped whitish flowers, and long slender pods.

catalyse or U.S. **-lyze** (ˈkætəˌlaɪz) vb. to influence (a chemical reaction) by catalysis.

catalysis (kəˈtælɪsɪs) n., pl. **-ses** (-ˌsiːz). acceleration of a chemical reaction by the action of a catalyst. **—catalytic** (ˌkætəˈlɪtɪk) adj.

catalyst (ˈkætəlɪst) n. **1.** a substance that speeds up a chemical reaction without itself undergoing any permanent chemical change. **2.** a person or thing that causes a change.

catalytic cracker n. a unit in an oil refinery in which mineral oils are converted into fuels by a catalytic process.

catamaran (ˌkætəməˈræn) n. **1.** a boat with twin parallel hulls. **2.** a primitive raft made of logs lashed together.

catamite (ˈkætəˌmaɪt) n. a boy kept as a homosexual partner.

catapult (ˈkætəˌpʌlt) n. **1.** a Y-shaped device with a loop of elastic fastened to the ends of the prongs, used mainly by children for firing stones. **2.** an ancient weapon for hurling large rocks. **3.** a device installed in warships to launch aircraft. ~vb. **4.** to shoot forth from or as if from a catapult.

cataract (ˈkætəˌrækt) n. **1.** a large waterfall. **2.** a downpour. **3.** Pathol. **a.** a condition in which the lens of the eye becomes partially or totally opaque. **b.** the opaque area.

catarrh (kəˈtɑː) n. inflammation of a mucous membrane with increased production of mucus, esp. affecting the nose and throat. **—caˈtarrhal** adj.

catastrophe (kəˈtæstrəfɪ) n. **1.** a great and sudden disaster. **2.** the denouement of a play. **3.** a disastrous end. **—catastrophic** (ˌkætəˈstrɒfɪk) adj.

catatonia (ˌkætəˈtəʊnɪə) n. a form of schizophrenia characterized by stupor, with outbreaks of excitement. **—catatonic** (ˌkætəˈtɒnɪk) adj., n.

cat burglar n. a burglar who enters buildings by climbing through upper windows.

catcall (ˈkætˌkɔːl) n. **1.** a shrill whistle or cry expressing disapproval or derision. ~vb. **2.** to utter such a call (at).

catch (kætʃ) vb. **catching, caught. 1.** to seize and hold. **2.** to capture. **3.** to ensnare or deceive. **4.** to surprise in an act: I caught him stealing. **5.** to strike: the stone caught him on the side of the head. **6.** to reach in time to board: catch a train. **7.** to see or hear; attend: did you catch the film last night? **8.** to be infected with: to catch a cold. **9.** to entangle or become entangled. **10.** to fasten or be fastened. **11.** to attract: she tried to catch his eye. **12.** to comprehend or make out: I couldn't catch what he said. **13.** to captivate. **14.** to reproduce accurately: the painter managed to catch

his model's beauty. **15.** to check suddenly: he caught his breath in surprise. **16.** to become alight: the fire won't catch. **17.** Cricket. to dismiss (a batsman) by catching a ball struck by him before it touches the ground. **18.** (often foll. by at) **a.** to grasp or attempt to grasp. **b.** to take advantage (of): he caught at the chance. **19. catch it.** Informal. to be punished. ~n. **20.** a catching or grasping. **21.** a device that catches and fastens. **22.** anything that is caught. **23.** the amount caught. **24.** Informal. a person worth having as a husband or wife. **25.** an emotional break in the voice. **26.** Informal. a concealed or unforeseen drawback. **27.** Cricket. the catching of a ball struck by a batsman before it touches the ground, resulting in him being out. **28.** Music. a type of round with a humorous text. ~See also **catch on, catch out, catch up.**

catching (ˈkætʃɪŋ) adj. **1.** infectious. **2.** catchy.

catchment (ˈkætʃmənt) n. **1.** the act of catching or collecting water. **2.** the water so collected. **3.** Brit. all those served by a school or hospital in a particular catchment area.

catchment area n. **1.** the area of land draining into a river, basin, or reservoir. **2.** the area served by a particular school or hospital.

catch on vb. Informal. **1.** to become popular or fashionable. **2.** to understand.

catch out vb. Informal, chiefly Brit. to trap (a person) in an error.

catchpenny (ˈkætʃˌpɛnɪ) adj. designed to have instant appeal in order to sell quickly: catchpenny ornaments.

catch phrase n. a well-known frequently used phrase or slogan.

catch-22 n. a situation in which a person is frustrated by a set of circumstances that prevent any attempt to escape from them.

catch up vb. **1.** to pick up (something) quickly. **2.** to reach or pass (someone or something): he caught up with him. **3.** (usually foll. by on or with) to make up for lost ground or deal with a backlog. **4.** (often passive) to absorb or involve: she was caught up in her reading.

catchword (ˈkætʃˌwɜːd) n. **1.** same as **catch phrase. 2.** a word positioned so as to draw attention.

catchy (ˈkætʃɪ) adj. **catchier, catchiest.** (of a tune) easily remembered.

catechism (ˈkætɪˌkɪzəm) n. instruction on the doctrine of a Christian Church by a series of questions and answers, esp. a book containing such instruction.

catechize or **-ise** (ˈkætɪˌkaɪz) vb. **1.** to instruct in Christianity by using a catechism. **2.** to question (someone) thoroughly. **—ˈcatechist** n.

categorical (ˌkætɪˈgɒrɪkᵊl) *or* **categoric** *adj.* unqualified; unconditional: *a categorical statement.* —ˌ**cateˈgorically** *adv.*

categorize *or* **-ise** (ˈkætɪgəˌraɪz) *vb.* to place in a category. —ˌ**categoriˈzation** *or* **-iˈsation** *n.*

category (ˈkætɪgərɪ) *n., pl.* **-ries.** a class or group of things or people possessing some quality or qualities in common.

cater (ˈkeɪtə) *vb.* **1.** (foll. by *for* or *to*) to provide what is needed or wanted for. **2.** to provide food or services: *we cater for parties.* —ˈ**catering** *n.*

caterer (ˈkeɪtərə) *n.* someone who makes a living by providing food for social events such as parties or weddings.

caterpillar (ˈkætəˌpɪlə) *n.* **1.** the wormlike larva of a butterfly or moth, having numerous pairs of legs. **2.** *Trademark.* Also: **caterpillar track.** an endless track, driven by cogged wheels, used to propel a heavy vehicle. **3.** *Trademark.* a vehicle driven by such tracks.

caterwaul (ˈkætəˌwɔːl) *vb.* **1.** to make a yowling noise like a cat. *~n.* **2.** such a noise.

catfish (ˈkætˌfɪʃ) *n., pl.* **-fish** *or* **-fishes.** a freshwater fish having whisker-like barbels around the mouth.

catgut (ˈkætˌgʌt) *n.* a strong cord made from the dried intestines of sheep or other animals, used to string musical instruments and sports rackets.

Cath. **1.** Cathedral. **2.** Catholic.

catharsis (kəˈθɑːsɪs) *n., pl.* **-ses.** **1.** the relief of strong suppressed emotions, esp. through drama or psychoanalysis. **2.** purgation of the bowels.

cathartic (kəˈθɑːtɪk) *adj.* **1.** purgative. **2.** causing catharsis. *~n.* **3.** a purgative drug.

Cathay (kæˈθeɪ) *n.* a literary or archaic name for China.

cathedral (kəˈθiːdrəl) *n.* the principal church of a diocese, containing the bishop's throne.

Catherine wheel (ˈkæθrɪn) *n.* a firework which rotates, producing sparks and coloured flame.

catheter (ˈkæθɪtə) *n.* a slender flexible tube inserted into a body cavity to drain fluid.

cathode (ˈkæθəʊd) *n.* **1.** the negative electrode in an electrolytic cell. **2.** the positive terminal of a battery. —**cathodic** (kæˈθɒdɪk, -ˈθəʊ-) *adj.*

cathode rays *pl. n.* a stream of electrons emitted from the surface of a cathode in a vacuum tube.

cathode-ray tube *n.* a vacuum tube in which a beam of electrons is focused onto a fluorescent screen to produce a visible image: used in television receivers and visual display units.

catholic (ˈkæθəlɪk, ˈkæθlɪk) *adj.* **1.** universal; relating to all men. **2.** broad-minded; liberal. —**catholicity** (ˌkæθəˈlɪsɪtɪ) *n.*

Catholic (ˈkæθəlɪk, ˈkæθlɪk) *Christianity.* *~adj.* **1.** of the Roman Catholic Church. *~n.* **2.** a member of the Roman Catholic Church.

Catholicism (kəˈθɒlɪˌsɪzəm) *n.* short for **Roman Catholicism.**

cation (ˈkætaɪən) *n.* a positively charged ion. —**cationic** (ˌkætaɪˈɒnɪk) *adj.*

catkin (ˈkætkɪn) *n.* a hanging spike of very small flowers found on trees such as the birch, hazel, and willow.

catmint (ˈkætˌmɪnt) *n.* a Eurasian plant with purple-spotted white flowers and scented leaves of which cats are fond. Also: **catnip.**

catnap (ˈkætˌnæp) *n.* **1.** a short sleep or doze. *~vb.* **-napping, -napped.** **2.** to sleep or doze for a short time or intermittently.

cat-o'-nine-tails *n., pl.* **-tails.** a rope whip consisting of nine knotted thongs attached to a handle.

cat's cradle *n.* a game played by making patterns with a loop of string between the fingers.

Catseyes (ˈkætsaɪz) *pl. n. Trademark, Brit.* glass reflectors set into the road at intervals to indicate traffic lanes by reflecting light from headlights.

cat's paw *n.* a person used by another as a tool; dupe.

cattle (ˈkætᵊl) *n.* (*functioning as pl.*) domesticated cows, bulls, or oxen.

cattle-cake *n.* concentrated food for cattle in the form of cakelike blocks.

cattle-grid *or N.Z.* **cattle-stop** *n.* a grid covering a hole dug in a roadway, intended to prevent livestock crossing while allowing vehicles to pass unhindered.

catty (ˈkætɪ) *adj.* **-tier, -tiest.** *Informal.* spiteful: *a catty remark.* —ˈ**cattiness** *n.*

catwalk (ˈkætˌwɔːk) *n.* a narrow pathway such as one over the stage of a theatre or along a bridge.

Caucasian (kɔːˈkeɪzɪən) *adj.* **1.** of the Caucasus in the SW Soviet Union. *~n.* **2.** a person from the Caucasus. *~adj., n.* **3.** same as **Caucasoid.**

Caucasoid (ˈkɔːkəˌzɔɪd) *adj.* **1.** of the predominantly light-skinned racial group of mankind, which includes the native peoples of Europe, N Africa, SW Asia, and the Indian subcontinent. *~n.* **2.** a member of this group.

caucus (ˈkɔːkəs) *n., pl.* **-cuses.** **1.** *Chiefly U.S.* a local meeting of party members. **2.** *Brit.* a faction within a political party, who discuss tactics or choose candidates. **3.** *Chiefly U.S., Canad., & N.Z.* a meeting of the members of one party in a legislative body. **4.** *Austral.* a group of MPs from one party who meet to discuss tactics.

caudal (ˈkɔːdᵊl) *adj.* **1.** *Anat.* of the posterior part of the body. **2.** *Zool.* like or in the position of the tail. —**ˈcaudate** *adj.*

caught (kɔːt) *vb.* past of **catch.**

caul (kɔːl) *n. Anat.* a membrane sometimes covering a child's head at birth.

cauldron *or* **caldron** (ˈkɔːldrən) *n.* a large pot used for boiling.

cauliflower (ˈkɒlɪˌflaʊə) *n.* a variety of cabbage having a large head of crowded white flower buds, which is eaten as a vegetable.

cauliflower ear *n.* permanent swelling and distortion of the ear, caused by repeated blows usually received in boxing.

caulk (kɔːk) *vb.* to stop up (cracks, esp. the seams in the hull of a ship) with a filler.

causal (ˈkɔːzᵊl) *adj.* **1.** of or being a cause. **2.** relating to cause and effect. —**ˈcausally** *adv.*

causality (kɔːˈzælɪtɪ) *n., pl.* **-ties. 1. a.** the relationship of cause and effect. **b.** the principle that everything has a cause. **2.** causal agency or quality.

causation (kɔːˈzeɪʃən) *n.* **1.** the production of an effect by a cause. **2.** the relationship of cause and effect.

causative (ˈkɔːzətɪv) *adj.* **1.** *Grammar.* (of a verb such as *persuade*) expressing cause. **2.** producing an effect. *~n.* **3.** a causative verb.

cause (kɔːz) *n.* **1.** a person or thing that produces an effect. **2.** grounds for action; justification: *she had good cause to shout like that.* **3.** an aim or principle which an individual or group is interested in and supports: *the Communist cause.* **4. a.** a matter giving rise to a lawsuit. **b.** the lawsuit itself. *~vb.* **5.** to be the cause of. —**ˈcauseless** *adj.*

cause célèbre (ˈkɔːz səˈlɛbrə) *n., pl.* **causes célèbres** (ˈkɔːz səˈlɛbrəz). a controversial legal case, issue, or person.

causerie (ˈkəʊzərɪ) *n.* an informal talk or piece of writing.

causeway (ˈkɔːzˌweɪ) *n.* **1.** a raised path across water or marshland. **2.** a paved footpath.

caustic (ˈkɔːstɪk) *adj.* **1.** capable of burning or corroding by chemical action: *caustic soda.* **2.** sarcastic; cutting: *a caustic reply.* *~n.* **3.** *Chem.* a caustic substance. —**ˈcaustically** *adv.* —**causticity** (kɔːˈstɪsɪtɪ) *n.*

caustic soda *n.* See **sodium hydroxide.**

cauterize *or* **-ise** (ˈkɔːtəˌraɪz) *vb.* to burn (tissue) with a hot iron or caustic agent in order to treat a wound. —**ˌcauteriˈzation** *or* **-iˈsation** *n.*

caution (ˈkɔːʃən) *n.* **1.** care or prudence, esp. in the face of danger. **2.** a warning. **3.** *Law, chiefly Brit.* a formal warning given to a person suspected of an offence. **4.** *Informal.* an amusing or surprising person or thing. *~vb.* **5.** to warn or advise: *he cautioned against optimism.* **6.** *Law, chiefly Brit.* to give a caution to (a person). —**ˈcautionary** *adj.*

cautious (ˈkɔːʃəs) *adj.* showing or having caution. —**ˈcautiously** *adv.*

cavalcade (ˌkævəlˈkeɪd) *n.* a procession of people on horseback or in cars.

cavalier (ˌkævəˈlɪə) *adj.* **1.** supercilious; offhand. *~n.* **2.** a courtly gentleman. **3.** *Archaic.* an armed horseman.

Cavalier (ˌkævəˈlɪə) *n.* a supporter of Charles I during the English Civil War.

cavalry (ˈkævəlrɪ) *n., pl.* **-ries.** the part of an army originally mounted on horseback, but now often using fast armoured vehicles. —**ˈcavalryman** *n.*

cave (keɪv) *n.* a hollow in the side of a hill or cliff, or underground.

caveat (ˈkeɪvɪˌæt, ˈkæv-) *n.* **1.** *Law.* a formal notice requesting the court not to take a certain action without warning the person lodging the caveat. **2.** a caution.

cave in *vb.* **1.** to collapse inwards. **2.** *Informal.* to yield completely under pressure. *~n.* **cave-in. 3.** the sudden collapse of a roof or piece of ground.

cavel (ˈkeɪvᵊl) *n. N.Z.* a drawing of lots among miners for a good place at the coalface.

caveman (ˈkeɪvˌmæn) *n., pl.* **-men. 1.** a Stone Age man; cave dweller. **2.** *Informal.* a man who is primitive or brutal in behaviour.

cavern (ˈkævᵊn) *n.* a large cave.

cavernous (ˈkævənəs) *adj.* **1.** like a cavern in vastness, depth, or hollowness: *cavernous eyes.* **2.** (of rocks) containing caverns.

caviar *or* **caviare** (ˈkævɪˌɑː, ˌkævɪˈɑː) *n.* the salted roe of sturgeon, usually eaten as an appetizer.

cavil (ˈkævɪl) *vb.* **-illing, -illed** *or U.S.* **-iling, -iled. 1.** (foll. by *at* or *about*) to raise annoying petty objections. *~n.* **2.** a trivial objection. —**ˈcaviller** *or U.S.* **-iler** *n.*

caving (ˈkeɪvɪŋ) *n.* the sport of climbing in and exploring caves. —**ˈcaver** *n.*

cavity (ˈkævɪtɪ) *n., pl.* **-ties. 1.** a hollow space. **2.** *Dentistry.* a decayed area on a tooth.

cavort (kəˈvɔːt) *vb.* to prance; caper.

caw (kɔː) *n.* **1.** the cry of a crow, rook, or raven. *~vb.* **2.** to make this cry.

cay (keɪ, kiː) *n.* a small low island or bank of sand and coral fragments.

cayenne pepper *or* **cayenne** (keɪˈɛn) *n.* a very hot red spice made from the dried seeds of capsicums.

cayman *or* **caiman** (ˈkeɪmən) *n., pl.* **-mans.** a tropical American reptile similar to an alligator.

CB Citizens' Band.

CBC Canadian Broadcasting Corporation.

CBE Commander of the Order of the British Empire.

CBI Confederation of British Industry.

cc *or* **c.c.** **1.** carbon copy *or* copies. **2.** cubic centimetre(s).

CC **1.** County Council. **2.** Cricket Club.

cc. chapters.

CCTV closed-circuit television.

cd candela.

Cd *Chem.* cadmium.

CD **1.** Civil Defence (Corps). **2.** compact disc. **3.** Diplomatic Corps.

Cdn. Canadian.

CDT Central Daylight Time.

Ce *Chem.* cerium.

CE **1.** Church of England. **2.** civil engineer.

cease (siːs) *vb.* **1.** to bring or come to an end. ~*n.* **2. without cease.** without stopping.

cease-fire *n.* **1.** a temporary period of truce. **2.** the order to stop firing.

ceaseless ('siːslıs) *adj.* without pause; incessant. —'**ceaselessly** *adv.*

cedar ('siːdə) *n.* **1.** a coniferous tree having needle-like evergreen leaves, and erect barrel-shaped cones. **2.** the wood of this tree. ~*adj.* **3.** made of cedar.

cede (siːd) *vb.* **1.** (often foll. by *to*) to transfer or surrender (territory or legal rights). **2.** to concede (a point in an argument).

cedilla (sı'dılə) *n.* a character (¸) placed underneath a *c*, esp. in French or Portuguese, denoting that it is to be pronounced (s), not (k).

Ceefax ('siːfæks) *n. Trademark.* the BBC teletext service.

ceilidh ('keılı) *n.* an informal social gathering with singing, dancing, and storytelling.

ceiling ('siːlıŋ) *n.* **1.** the inner upper surface of a room. **2.** an upper limit set on something. **3.** the upper altitude to which an aircraft can climb.

celandine ('sɛlən,daın) *n.* a plant with yellow flowers.

celebrant ('sɛlıbrənt) *n.* a person participating in a religious ceremony.

celebrate ('sɛlı,breıt) *vb.* **1.** to hold festivities to mark (a happy event, birthday, or anniversary). **2.** to perform (a solemn or religious ceremony). **3.** to praise publicly. —,**cele'bration** *n.* —'**cele,brator** *n.* —'**cele,bratory** *adj.*

celebrated ('sɛlı,breıtıd) *adj.* famous: *a celebrated pianist.*

celebrity (sı'lɛbrıtı) *n., pl.* -**ties.** **1.** a famous person. **2.** fame.

celeriac (sı'lɛrı,æk) *n.* a variety of celery with a large turnip-like root, eaten as a vegetable.

celerity (sı'lɛrıtı) *n.* swiftness.

celery ('sɛlərı) *n.* a Eurasian plant whose stalks are used in salads or cooked as a vegetable.

celesta (sı'lɛstə) *n.* an instrument resembling a small piano in which key-operated hammers strike metal plates.

celestial (sı'lɛstıəl) *adj.* **1.** heavenly; divine: *celestial peace.* **2.** of or relating to the sky: *celestial bodies.*

celestial equator *n.* an imaginary circle lying on the celestial sphere in a plane perpendicular to the earth's axis.

celestial sphere *n.* an imaginary sphere of infinitely large radius enclosing the universe.

celibate ('sɛlıbıt) *n.* **1.** a person who does not marry or have sex because he or she has taken a religious vow of chastity. **2.** a person who has gone without sex for a considerable period. ~*adj.* **3.** unmarried or abstaining from sex because of a religious vow of chastity. **4.** having gone without sex for a considerable period. —'**celibacy** *n.*

cell (sɛl) *n.* **1.** a small simple room in a prison or convent. **2.** any small compartment: *the cells of a honeycomb.* **3.** *Biol.* the smallest unit of an organism that is able to function independently, consisting of a nucleus surrounded by cytoplasm. **4.** a device which uses energy from a chemical action to produce electrical energy, usually consisting of a container with two electrodes immersed in an electrolyte. **5.** a small group of persons operating as a nucleus of a larger organization: *Communist cell.*

cellar ('sɛlə) *n.* **1.** an underground room, usually used for storage. **2.** a place where wine is stored. **3.** a stock of bottled wines.

cellarage ('sɛlərıdʒ) *n.* **1.** an area of a cellar. **2.** a charge for storing goods in a cellar.

cello ('tʃɛləu) *n., pl.* -**los.** a low-pitched musical instrument of the violin family, held between the knees and played by bowing the four strings. —'**cellist** *n.*

cellophane ('sɛlə,feın) *n.* a flexible thin transparent sheeting made from cellulose and used as a moisture-proof wrapping.

cellular ('sɛljulə) *adj.* **1.** of, consisting of, or resembling a cell or cells. **2.** woven with an open texture: *a cellular blanket.* **3.** designed for or using cellular radio: *a cellular phone.*

cellular radio *n.* radio communication based on a network of transmitters each serving a small area known as a "cell": used esp. in car phones.

cellule ('sɛljuːl) *n.* a very small cell.

cellulite ('sɛlju,laıt) *n.* fat deposits under the skin alleged to resist dieting.

celluloid ('sɛlju,lɔıd) *n.* a flammable plastic made from cellulose nitrate and camphor.

cellulose ('sɛlju,ləuz, -,ləus) *n.* the main

constituent of plant cell walls, used in making paper, rayon, and film.

cellulose acetate *n.* nonflammable material used in the manufacture of film, lacquers, and artificial fibres.

cellulose nitrate *n.* a compound used in plastics, lacquers, and explosives.

Celsius ('sɛlsɪəs) *adj.* denoting a measurement on the Celsius scale.

Usage. see **centigrade.**

Celsius scale *n.* a scale of temperature in which 0° represents the melting point of ice and 100° represents the boiling point of water.

Celt (kɛlt, sɛlt) *n.* 1. a person who speaks a Celtic language. 2. a member of a people inhabiting Britain, Gaul, and Spain in pre-Roman times.

Celtic ('kɛltɪk, 'sɛl-) *n.* 1. a group of Indo-European languages that includes Gaelic, Welsh, and Breton. ~*adj.* 2. of the Celts or the Celtic languages. —**Celticism** ('kɛltɪˌsɪzəm, 'sɛl-) *n.*

cement (sɪ'mɛnt) *n.* 1. a fine grey powder made of limestone and clay, mixed with water and sand to make mortar or concrete. 2. something that unites, binds, or joins. 3. *Dentistry.* a material used in filling teeth. ~*vb.* 4. to join or bind with or as if with cement. 5. to cover with cement.

cemetery ('sɛmɪtrɪ) *n., pl.* **-teries.** a place where the dead are buried, usually one not attached to a church.

cenobite ('siːnəʊˌbaɪt) *n.* same as **coenobite.**

cenotaph ('sɛnəˌtɑːf) *n.* a monument honouring a dead person or people buried elsewhere.

Cenozoic *or* **Caenozoic** (ˌsiːnəʊ'zəʊɪk) *adj. Geol.* of the most recent geological era, characterized by the development and increase of the mammals.

censer ('sɛnsə) *n.* a container for burning incense.

censor ('sɛnsə) *n.* 1. a person authorized to examine films, letters, or publications, in order to ban or cut anything considered obscene or objectionable. ~*vb.* 2. to ban or cut portions of (a film, letter, or publication). —**censorial** (sɛn'sɔːrɪəl) *adj.*

censorious (sɛn'sɔːrɪəs) *adj.* harshly critical. —**cen'soriously** *adv.*

censorship ('sɛnsəˌʃɪp) *n.* a practice or policy of censoring.

censure ('sɛnʃə) *n.* 1. severe disapproval. ~*vb.* 2. to criticize (someone or something) severely. —**'censurable** *adj.*

census ('sɛnsəs) *n., pl.* **-suses.** an official periodic count of a population including such information as sex, age, and occupation.

cent (sɛnt) *n.* a monetary unit worth one hundredth of the standard unit of many countries, such as the United States.

cent. 1. centigrade. 2. central. 3. century.

centaur ('sɛntɔː) *n. Greek myth.* a creature with the head, arms, and torso of a man, and the lower body and legs of a horse.

centenarian (ˌsɛntɪ'nɛərɪən) *n.* 1. a person who is at least 100 years old. ~*adj.* 2. at least 100 years old. 3. of a centenarian.

centenary (sɛn'tiːnərɪ) *adj.* 1. of a period of 100 years. 2. occurring every 100 years. ~*n., pl.* **-naries.** 3. a 100th anniversary or its celebration.

centennial (sɛn'tɛnɪəl) *adj.* 1. of a period of 100 years. 2. occurring every 100 years. ~*n.* 3. *U.S. & Canad.* same as **centenary.**

center ('sɛntə) *n., vb. U.S.* same as **centre.**

centesimal (sɛn'tɛsɪməl) *n.* 1. one hundredth. ~*adj.* 2. of or divided into hundredths.

centi- *or before a vowel* **cent-** *prefix.* denoting: 1. one hundredth: *centimetre.* 2. a hundred: *centipede.*

centigrade ('sɛntɪˌɡreɪd) *adj.* 1. same as **Celsius.** ~*n.* 2. a unit of angle equal to one hundredth of a grade.

Usage. *Celsius,* rather than *centigrade,* is now the usual term by which to indicate the Celsius scale of temperature. *Celsius* is preferred because, in scientific terminology, *centigrade* can also mean one-hundredth part of a grade, a grade being a unit of angle.

centigram *or* **centigramme** ('sɛntɪˌɡræm) *n.* one hundredth of a gram.

centilitre *or U.S.* **centiliter** ('sɛntɪˌliːtə) *n.* one hundredth of a litre.

centime ('sɒnˌtiːm) *n.* a monetary unit worth one hundredth of the standard unit of many countries, such as France.

centimetre *or U.S.* **centimeter** ('sɛntɪˌmiːtə) *n.* one hundredth of a metre.

centipede ('sɛntɪˌpiːd) *n.* an arthropod having a body of many segments, each bearing one pair of legs.

central ('sɛntrəl) *adj.* 1. in, at, of, or forming the centre of something: *the central street in a city.* 2. main or principal: *the central cause of the problem.* —**centrality** (sɛn'trælɪtɪ) *n.* —**'centrally** *adv.*

central bank *n.* a national bank that acts as the government's banker, controls credit, and issues currency.

central heating *n.* a system for heating a building by means of radiators or air vents connected to a central source of heat. —**centrally heated** *adj.*

centralism ('sɛntrəˌlɪzəm) *n.* the principle or act of bringing something under central control. —**'centralist** *n., adj.*

centralize *or* **-lise** ('sɛntrəˌlaɪz) *vb.* 1. to draw or move (something) towards a centre. 2. to bring or come under central control. —**ˌcentrali'zation** *or* **-li'sation** *n.*

central locking *n.* a system by which all

the doors of a motor vehicle are locked automatically when the driver's door is locked manually.

central nervous system *n.* the mass of nerve tissue that controls the activities of an animal. In vertebrates it consists of the brain and spinal cord.

central processing unit *n.* the part of a computer that performs logical and arithmetical operations on the data.

central reservation *n. Brit.* the strip that separates the two sides of a motorway or dual carriageway.

centre *or U.S.* **center** ('sɛntə) *n.* **1.** a point, area, or part in the middle of a larger area or volume, esp. the point within a circle or sphere that is equidistant from any point on the circumference or surface. **2.** the point, axis, or pivot about which a body rotates. **3.** a place at which some specified activity is concentrated: *a shopping centre.* **4.** a person or thing that is a focus of interest. **5.** a place of activity or influence: *a centre of power.* **6.** (*usually cap.*) *Politics.* a political party or group favouring moderation. **7.** *Sport.* a player who plays in the middle of the field rather than on a wing. ~*vb.* **8.** to move towards or mark, put, or be at a centre. **9.** to focus or bring together: *to centre one's thoughts.* **10.** (foll. by *on*) to have as a centre or main theme.
Usage. Many people consider that *to centre round* is illogical; the use of the more precise phrase *to centre on* is preferable.

centreboard ('sɛntə,bɔːd) *n.* a supplementary keel for a sailing vessel.

centrefold *or U.S.* **centerfold** ('sɛntə,fəʊld) *n.* a large coloured illustration folded to form the central spread of a magazine.

centre forward *n. Sport.* the middle player in the forward line of a team.

centre half *or* **centre back** *n. Soccer.* a defender who plays in the middle of the defence.

centre of gravity *n.* the point in a body around which its mass is evenly distributed.

centrepiece ('sɛntə,piːs) *n.* **1.** the most important item of a group. **2.** an ornament for the centre of a table.

centric ('sɛntrɪk) *or* **centrical** *adj.* **1.** being central or having a centre. **2.** relating to a nerve centre. —**centricity** (sɛn'trɪsɪtɪ) *n.*

centrifugal (sɛn'trɪfjʊgʔl, ˌsɛntrɪ,fjuːgʔl) *adj.* **1.** moving or tending to move away from a centre. **2.** of or operated by centrifugal force: *centrifugal pump.*

centrifugal force *n.* a force that acts outwards on any body that rotates or moves along a curved path.

centrifuge ('sɛntrɪ,fjuːdʒ) *n.* **1.** a machine which separates substances by the action of

centrifugal force. **2.** a rotating device for subjecting human beings or animals to varying accelerations.

centring ('sɛntrɪŋ) *or U.S.* **centering** ('sɛntərɪŋ) *n.* a temporary structure used to support an arch during construction.

centripetal (sɛn'trɪpɪtʔl, ˌsɛntrɪ,piːtʔl) *adj.* **1.** moving or tending to move towards a centre. **2.** of or operated by centripetal force.

centripetal force *n.* a force that acts inwards on any body that rotates or moves along a curved path.

centrist ('sɛntrɪst) *n.* a person holding moderate political views. —**centrism** *n.*

centurion (sɛn'tjʊərɪən) *n.* the officer commanding a Roman century.

century ('sɛntʃərɪ) *n., pl.* **-ries. 1.** a period of 100 years. **2.** one of the successive periods of 100 years dated before or after an epoch or event, esp. the birth of Christ. **3.** a score or grouping of 100: *to score a century in cricket.* **4.** (in ancient Rome) a unit of foot soldiers, originally consisting of 100 men.
Usage. In strict usage, the dating of any century begins with a year ending -01 and ends with a year ending -00: *the nineteenth century covers the years 1801 to 1900.* This is because the system of dating by *A.D.* is based on the supposed year in which Christ was born, so that it begins with A.D. 1. In popular practice, however, the dating of a century is often moved back by one year so that it includes all the years starting with the same number: *the nineteenth century covers the years 1800 to 1899.*

cephalic (sɪ'fælɪk) *adj.* **1.** of the head. **2.** situated in, on, or near the head.

cephalopod ('sɛfələ,pɒd) *n.* a marine mollusc with a well-developed head and eyes and a ring of sucker-bearing tentacles, such as the octopus, squid, or cuttlefish.

ceramic (sɪ'ræmɪk) *n.* **1.** a hard brittle material made by firing clay and similar substances. **2.** an object made from such a material. ~*adj.* **3.** of or made from a ceramic: *a ceramic hob.* **4.** of ceramics: *ceramic arts.*

ceramics (sɪ'ræmɪks) *n.* (*functioning as sing.*) the art of producing articles of clay or porcelain. —**ceramist** ('sɛrəmɪst) *n.*

cere (sɪə) *n.* a soft waxy swelling, containing the nostrils, at the base of the upper beak in some birds, such as the parrot.

cereal ('sɪərɪəl) *n.* **1.** any grass that produces an edible grain, such as oat, wheat, or rice. **2.** the grain produced by such a plant. **3.** a breakfast food made from this grain.

cerebellum (ˌsɛrɪ'bɛləm) *n., pl.* **-lums** *or* **-la** (-lə). the rear part of the brain which coordinates voluntary movements.

cerebral ('sɛrɪbrəl; *U.S. also* sə'riːbrəl) *adj.*

1. of the brain. **2.** involving intelligence rather than emotions or instinct.

cerebral palsy *n.* impaired muscular function and weakness of the limbs, caused by damage to the brain before or during birth.

cerebrate ('sɛrɪˌbreɪt) *vb. Usually facetious.* to use the mind; think. —ˌcere'bration *n.*

cerebrospinal (ˌsɛrɪbrəʊ'spaɪn³l) *adj.* of the brain and spinal cord: *cerebrospinal fluid.*

cerebrovascular (ˌsɛrɪbrəʊ'væskjʊlə) *adj.* of the blood vessels and blood supply of the brain.

cerebrum ('sɛrɪbrəm) *n., pl.* -brums *or* -bra (-brə). **1.** the main part of the human brain, consisting of two hemispheres: associated with thought, emotion, and personality. **2.** the brain considered as a whole.

cerecloth ('sɪəˌklɒθ) *n.* waxed waterproof cloth of a kind formerly used as a shroud.

ceremonial (ˌsɛrɪ'məʊnɪəl) *adj.* **1.** of ceremony or ritual. ~*n.* **2.** a system of formal rites; ritual. —ˌcere'monially *adv.*

ceremonious (ˌsɛrɪ'məʊnɪəs) *adj.* **1.** excessively polite or formal. **2.** involving formalities. —ˌcere'moniously *adv.*

ceremony ('sɛrɪmənɪ) *n., pl.* -nies. **1.** a formal act or ritual performed for a special occasion: *a wedding ceremony.* **2.** a religious rite or series of rites. **3.** an action of formal politeness. **4.** ceremonial observances or gestures collectively. **5. stand on ceremony.** to insist on or act with excessive formality.

cerise (sə'riːz, -'riːs) *adj.* cherry-red.

cerium ('sɪərɪəm) *n.* a steel-grey metallic element of the lanthanide series. Symbol: Ce

CERN (sɜːn) Conseil Européen pour la Recherche Nucléaire; a European organization for research in high-energy particle physics.

cert (sɜːt) *n. Informal.* a certainty: *a dead cert.*

cert. 1. certificate. **2.** certified.

certain ('sɜːt³n) *adj.* **1.** positive and confident about the truth of something: *I am certain that he wrote a book.* **2.** definitely known: *it is certain that they were on the bus.* **3.** sure; bound: *he was certain to fail.* **4.** reliable or unerring. **5.** some but not much: *to a certain extent.* **6. for certain.** without doubt. ~*det.* **7.** known but not named: *certain people.* **8.** named but not known: *he had written to a certain Mrs Smith.*

certainly ('sɜːt³nlɪ) *adv.* without doubt: *he certainly rides very well.*

certainty ('sɜːt³ntɪ) *n., pl.* -ties. **1.** the condition of being certain. **2.** something established as inevitable. **3. for a certainty.** without doubt.

certificate *n.* (sə'tɪfɪkɪt). **1.** an official document setting out the details of something such as birth, death, completion of an academic course, or ownership of something. ~*vb.* (sə'tɪfɪˌkeɪt). **2.** to authorize by or present with an official document. —**cer'tificatory** *adj.*

Certificate of Secondary Education *n.* See CSE.

certified ('sɜːtɪˌfaɪd) *adj.* **1.** holding or guaranteed by a certificate. **2.** endorsed or guaranteed: *a certified cheque.* **3.** (of a person) declared legally insane.

certify ('sɜːtɪˌfaɪ) *vb.* -fying, -fied. **1.** to confirm or attest (to). **2.** to guarantee (that certain required standards have been met). **3.** to declare legally insane. —'**certiˌfiable** *adj.* —ˌcertifi'cation *n.*

certitude ('sɜːtɪˌtjuːd) *n.* confidence; certainty.

cerulean (sɪ'ruːlɪən) *adj.* of a deep blue colour.

cervical smear *n. Med.* a smear taken from the neck (cervix) of the womb for detection of cancer symptoms.

cervix ('sɜːvɪks) *n., pl.* **cervixes** *or* **cervices** (sə'vaɪsiːz). **1.** *Anat.* the neck. **2.** the lower part of the womb that extends into the vagina. —**cervical** (sə'vaɪk³l, 'sɜːvɪk³l) *adj.*

cesium ('siːzɪəm) *n. U.S.* same as **caesium.**

cessation (sɛ'seɪʃən) *n.* a ceasing; pause: *cessation of hostilities.*

cession ('sɛʃən) *n.* **1.** a ceding of territory or legal rights. **2.** something that is ceded.

cesspool ('sɛsˌpuːl) *or* **cesspit** ('sɛsˌpɪt) *n.* a covered tank or pit for collecting and storing sewage or waste water.

cesura (sɪ'zjʊərə) *n., pl.* -ras *or* -rae (-riː). same as **caesura.**

cetacean (sɪ'teɪʃən) *n.* **1.** a member of an order of aquatic mammals having no hind limbs, front limbs modified into paddles, and a blowhole for breathing: includes whales, dolphins, and porpoises. ~*adj.* **2.** of cetaceans.

cetane ('siːteɪn) *n.* a colourless insoluble liquid hydrocarbon present in diesel fuel.

cetane number *n.* a measure of the quality of a diesel fuel expressed as the percentage of cetane in it.

Cf *Chem.* californium.

CF Canadian Forces.

cf. compare.

CFB Canadian Forces Base.

CFC chlorofluorocarbon.

CFL Canadian Football League.

cg centigram.

CH Companion of Honour (a Brit. title).

ch. 1. chapter. **2.** *Chess.* check. **3.** church.

Chablis ('ʃæblɪ) *n.* a dry white wine made around Chablis, France.

cha-cha-cha (ˌtʃɑːtʃɑː'tʃɑː) *or* **cha-cha** *n.*

1. a modern ballroom dance from Latin America. **2.** music for this dance.

chaconne (ʃəˈkɒn) n. *Music.* a set of continuous variations on a ground bass.

chafe (tʃeɪf) vb. **1.** to make or become sore or worn by rubbing. **2.** to warm by rubbing. **3.** to annoy or be annoyed or impatient. **4.** (often foll. by *on* or *against*) to rub. ~n. **5.** a soreness caused by rubbing.

chafer (ˈtʃeɪfə) n. a large slow-moving beetle.

chaff[1] (tʃɑːf) n. **1.** grain husks separated from the seeds during threshing. **2.** finely cut straw and hay used to feed cattle. **3.** something of little worth; rubbish: *separate the wheat from the chaff.*

chaff[2] (tʃɑːf) n. **1.** light-hearted teasing or joking. ~vb. **2.** to tease good-naturedly.

chaffinch (ˈtʃæfɪntʃ) n. a common European finch with black-and-white wings and, in the male, a reddish body and blue-grey head.

chafing dish n. a dish with a heating apparatus beneath it, for cooking or keeping food warm at the table.

chagrin (ˈʃægrɪn) n. **1.** a feeling of annoyance and embarrassment. ~vb. **2.** to annoy and embarrass.

chain (tʃeɪn) n. **1.** a flexible length of metal links, used for confining or connecting, or in jewellery. **2.** (*usually pl.*) anything that confines or restrains: *the chains of poverty.* **3.** a series of connected facts or events. **4.** a number of establishments, such as hotels or shops, having the same owner or management. **5.** a unit of length equal to 22 yards. **6.** *Chem.* two or more atoms or groups bonded together so that the resulting molecule, ion, or radical resembles a chain. **7.** *Geog.* a series of natural features, esp. mountain ranges. ~vb. **8.** (often foll. by *up*) to confine, tie, or fasten with or as if with a chain.

chain gang n. *U.S.* a group of convicted prisoners chained together.

chain letter n. a letter, often with a request for and promise of money, that is sent to many people who are asked to add to or recopy it and send it on.

chain mail n. same as **mail**[2].

chain reaction n. **1.** a chemical or nuclear reaction in which the product of one step triggers the following step. **2.** a series of events, each of which causes the next. —ˌchain-reˈact vb.

chain saw n. a motor-driven saw in which the cutting teeth form links in a continuous chain.

chain-smoke vb. to smoke (cigarettes) continuously, esp. lighting one from the preceding one. —**chain smoker** n.

chair (tʃɛə) n. **1.** a seat with a back on which one person sits, usually having four legs. **2.** an official position of authority or

the person holding it: *questions are to be addressed to the chair.* **3.** a professorship. **4.** short for **sedan chair**. **5. take the chair.** to preside over a meeting. **6. the chair.** *Informal.* the electric chair. ~vb. **7.** to preside over (a meeting). **8.** *Brit.* to carry (a person) aloft in a sitting position after a triumph. **9.** to install in a chair of authority.

chair lift n. a series of chairs suspended from a power-driven cable for carrying people, esp. skiers, up a slope.

chairman (ˈtʃɛəmən) n., pl. **-men.** a person who presides over a company's board of directors, a committee, or a debate. Also: **chairperson** or (*fem.*) **chairwoman.**

chaise (ʃeɪz) n. a light open horse-drawn carriage, usually with two wheels.

chaise longue (ˈʃeɪz ˈlɒŋ) n., pl. **chaise longues** or **chaises longues** (ˈʃeɪz ˈlɒŋ). a long low chair with a back and single armrest.

chalcedony (kælˈsɛdənɪ) n., pl. **-nies.** a form of quartz composed of very fine crystals: a gemstone.

chalet (ˈʃæleɪ) n. **1.** a type of Swiss wooden house with wide projecting eaves. **2.** a similar house used as a ski lodge or holiday home.

chalice (ˈtʃælɪs) n. **1.** *Poetic.* a drinking cup; goblet. **2.** *Christianity.* a gold or silver goblet containing the wine at Mass.

chalk (tʃɔːk) n. **1.** a soft fine-grained white rock consisting of calcium carbonate. **2.** a piece of chalk or similar substance, often coloured, used for writing and drawing on blackboards. **3. as different as chalk and cheese.** *Informal.* totally different. **4. by a long chalk.** *Brit. informal.* by far. **5. not by a long chalk.** *Brit. informal.* by no means. ~vb. **6.** to draw or mark (something) with chalk. —**chalky** adj. —ˈchalkiness n.

chalk up vb. *Informal.* **1.** to score or register (something). **2.** to charge or credit (money) to an account.

challenge (ˈtʃælɪndʒ) vb. **1.** to invite or call (someone) to take part in a contest, fight, or argument. **2.** to call (something) into question. **3.** to make demands on; stimulate: *the job challenges his ingenuity.* **4.** to order (a person) to halt and be identified. **5.** *Law.* to make formal objection to (a juror or jury). ~n. **6.** a call to engage in a contest, fight, or argument. **7.** a questioning of a statement or fact. **8.** a demanding or stimulating situation. **9.** a demand by a sentry for identification or a password. **10.** *Law.* a formal objection to a juror or jury. —ˈchallenger n. —ˈchallenging adj.

chalybeate (kəˈlɪbɪɪt) adj. containing or impregnated with iron salts.

chamber (ˈtʃeɪmbə) n. **1.** a meeting hall, usually one used for a legislative or judicial assembly. **2.** *Archaic or poetic.* a room in a house, esp. a bedroom. **3.** a room equipped for a particular purpose: *decompression chamber.* **4.** a legislative or judicial assembly. **5.** a compartment; cavity. **6.** a compartment for a cartridge or shell in a gun. **7.** (*modifier*) of or suitable for chamber music: *a chamber concert.* ~See also **chambers.**

chamberlain ('tʃeɪmbəlɪn) *n. History.* **1.** an officer who manages the household of a king or nobleman. **2.** the treasurer of a municipal corporation.

chambermaid ('tʃeɪmbə,meɪd) *n.* a woman employed to clean bedrooms in hotels.

chamber music *n.* music for performance by a small group of players.

chamber of commerce *n.* (*sometimes cap.*) an organization of local businessmen to promote, regulate, and protect their interests.

chamber pot *n.* a receptacle for urine, formerly used in bedrooms.

chambers ('tʃeɪmbəz) *pl. n.* **1.** a judge's room for hearing private cases not taken in open court. **2.** (in England) the set of rooms used as offices by a barrister.

chameleon (kə'miːlɪən) *n.* **1.** a small lizard having the ability to change colour according to its surroundings. **2.** a changeable or fickle person.

chamfer ('tʃæmfə) *n.* **1.** a bevelled surface at an edge or corner. ~*vb.* **2.** to cut such a surface on (an edge or corner).

chamois ('ʃæmɪ; *for sense 1* 'ʃæmwɑː) *n., pl.* **-ois.** **1.** a small mountain antelope of Europe and SW Asia. **2.** a soft suede leather formerly made from this animal, now obtained from sheep and goats. **3.** *Also:* **chamois leather, shammy, chammy.** a piece of such leather or similar material, used for cleaning and polishing. ~*vb.* **4.** to polish with a chamois.

champ¹ (tʃæmp) *vb.* **1.** to chew noisily. **2.** **champ at the bit.** *Informal.* to be restless or impatient to do something. ~*n.* **3.** the act or noise of champing.

champ² (tʃæmp) *n. Informal.* short for **champion** (sense 1).

champagne (ʃæm'peɪn) *n.* **1.** (*sometimes cap.*) a white sparkling wine produced around Reims and Epernay, France. **2.** (loosely) any similar wine. ~*adj.* **3.** pale straw-coloured.

champers ('ʃæmpəz) *n.* (*functioning as sing.*) *Slang.* champagne.

champion ('tʃæmpɪən) *n.* **1.** a person, plant, or animal that has defeated all others in a competition: *a chess champion.* **2.** someone who defends a person or cause: *champion of the underprivileged.* ~*adj.* **3.** *N English dialect.* excellent. ~*adv.* **4.** *N English dialect.* very well. ~*vb.* **5.** to support: *to champion a cause.* —'**championship** *n.*

chance (tʃɑːns) *n.* **1.** the unknown and unpredictable element that causes something to happen in one way rather than another. **2.** fortune; luck; fate. **3.** an opportunity or occasion. **4.** a risk; gamble. **5.** the extent to which something is likely to happen; probability. **6.** an unpredicted event. **7. by chance.** accidentally: *we met by chance.* **8. on the (off) chance.** acting on the (remote) possibility. ~*vb.* **9.** to risk; hazard. **10.** to happen by chance: *I chanced to catch sight of her.* **11. chance on *or* upon.** to come upon by accident. **12. chance one's arm.** to attempt to do something although the chance of success may be slight.

chancel ('tʃɑːnsəl) *n.* the part of a church containing the altar and choir.

chancellery *or* **chancellory** ('tʃɑːnsələrɪ) *n., pl.* **-leries** *or* **-lories.** **1.** the residence or office of a chancellor. **2.** the rank of a chancellor. **3.** *U.S.* the office of an embassy or consulate.

chancellor ('tʃɑːnsələ) *n.* **1.** the head of the government in several European countries. **2.** *U.S.* the president of a university. **3.** *Brit. & Canad.* the honorary head of a university. —'**chancellor,ship** *n.*

Chancellor of the Exchequer *n. Brit.* the cabinet minister responsible for finance.

chancery ('tʃɑːnsərɪ) *n., pl.* **-ceries.** (*usually cap.*) **1.** (in England) the Lord Chancellor's court, a division of the High Court of Justice. **2.** same as **chancellery.** **3.** a court of public records. **4. in chancery. a.** *Law.* (of a suit) awaiting litigation in court. **b.** in an awkward situation.

chancre ('ʃæŋkə) *n. Pathol.* a small hard growth, which is the first sign of syphilis. —'**chancrous** *adj.*

chancy *or* **chancey** ('tʃɑːnsɪ) *adj.* **chancier, chanciest.** *Informal.* uncertain; risky.

chandelier (,ʃændɪ'lɪə) *n.* an ornamental branched hanging light with several candles or bulbs.

chandler ('tʃɑːndlə) *n.* **1.** a dealer in a specified trade or merchandise: *ship's chandler.* **2.** a maker or seller of candles. —'**chandlery** *n.*

change (tʃeɪndʒ) *vb.* **1.** to make or become different; transform or be transformed. **2.** to replace with or exchange for another: *to change one's name.* **3.** to give and receive (something) in return: *to change places.* **4.** to give or receive (money) in exchange for its equivalent sum in a smaller denomination or different currency. **5.** to remove or replace the coverings of: *to change a baby; change the bed.* **6.** to put on other clothes. **7.** to alight from (one bus or train) and board another. ~*n.* **8.** a changing or being changed. **9.** a variation or modification. **10.** anything that is or may be substituted for something else. **11.** variety or novelty: *for a change.* **12.** a different set, esp. of clothes. **13.** money exchanged for its equivalent in a larger denomination or in a different currency. **14.** the balance of money when the amount paid is larger than the amount due. **15.** coins of a small denomination. **16.** the order in which a peal of bells may be rung. **17. get no change out of someone.** *Slang.* not to be successful in attempts to exploit someone. **18. ring the changes.** to vary the way of doing something. ~See also **change down, changeover, change up.** —'**changeful** *adj.* —'**changeless** *adj.*

changeable ('tʃeɪndʒəb'l) *adj.* **1.** able to change or be changed: *changeable weather.* **2.** varying in colour when viewed from different angles. —,**changea'bility** *n.*

change down *vb.* to select a lower gear when driving.

changeling ('tʃeɪndʒlɪŋ) *n.* a child believed to have been exchanged by fairies for the parents' true child.

change of life *n.* the menopause.

changeover ('tʃeɪndʒ,əʊvə) *n.* **1.** a complete change from one system, attitude, or product to another. ~*vb.* **change over. 2.** to adopt (a different position or attitude): *the driver and navigator changed over.*

change up *vb.* to select a higher gear when driving.

channel ('tʃæn'l) *n.* **1.** a broad strait connecting two areas of sea. **2.** the bed or course of a river, stream, or canal. **3.** a navigable course through a body of water. **4.** (*often pl.*) a means of access or communication: *through official channels.* **5.** a course along which something can be directed or moved. **6.** a band of radio frequencies assigned for the broadcasting of a radio or television signal. **7.** a path for an electrical signal or computer data: *a stereo set has two channels.* **8.** a groove. ~*vb.* **-nelling, -nelled** or *U.S.* **-neling, -neled. 9.** to make channels in (something). **10.** to direct or convey through a channel or channels: *information was channelled through to them.*

Channel ('tʃæn'l) *n.* **the.** the English Channel.

channelize or **-ise** ('tʃæn'laɪz) *vb.* to make the channel of (a river) deeper or straighter, so that water flow is improved. —,**channeli'zation** or **-i'sation** *n.*

chant (tʃɑːnt) *n.* **1.** a short simple melody in which several words or syllables are sung on one note. **2.** a religious song with such a melody. **3.** a rhythmic or repetitious slogan spoken or sung, usually by more than one person. ~*vb.* **4.** to sing or recite (a psalm) as a chant. **5.** to intone (a slogan). —'**chanting** *n.*, *adj.*

chanter ('tʃɑːntə) *n.* the pipe on a set of bagpipes on which the melody is played.

chanticleer (,tʃæntɪ'klɪə) *n.* a name for a cock, used in fables.

chanty ('ʃæntɪ, 'tʃæn-) *n.*, *pl.* **-ties.** same as **shanty²**.

Chanukah or **Hanukkah** ('hɑːnəkə, -nʊkɑː) *n.* a Jewish festival commemorating the rededication of the temple by Judas Maccabeus.

chaos ('keɪɒs) *n.* **1.** (*usually cap.*) the disordered formless matter supposed to have existed before the ordered universe. **2.** complete disorder or confusion. —**cha'otic** *adj.* —**cha'otically** *adv.*

chap¹ (tʃæp) *vb.* **chapping, chapped. 1.** (of the skin) to make or become raw and cracked, by exposure to cold. ~*n.* **2.** (*usually pl.*) a cracked patch on the skin.

chap² (tʃæp) *n.* *Informal.* a man or boy; fellow.

chapatti or **chapati** (tʃə'pætɪ, -'pɑːtɪ) *n.*, *pl.* **-ti, -tis,** or **-ties.** (in Indian cookery) a flat thin unleavened bread.

chapel ('tʃæp'l) *n.* **1.** a place of worship with its own altar, in a church or cathedral. **2.** a similar place of worship in a large house or institution. **3.** (in Britain) a Nonconformist place of worship. **4.** the members of a trade union in a newspaper office, printing house, or publishing firm.

chaperon or **chaperone** ('ʃæpə,rəʊn) *n.* **1.** an older woman who supervises a young unmarried woman on social occasions. ~*vb.* **2.** to act as a chaperon to. —**chaperonage** ('ʃæpərənɪdʒ) *n.*

chaplain ('tʃæplɪn) *n.* a clergyman attached to a chapel or serving a military body or institution. —'**chaplaincy** *n.*

chaplet ('tʃæplɪt) *n.* **1.** a garland worn on the head. **2.** a string of beads. **3.** *R.C. Church.* a string of prayer beads constituting one third of the rosary.

chapman ('tʃæpmən) *n.*, *pl.* **-men.** *Archaic.* a travelling pedlar.

chappie ('tʃæpɪ) *n.* *Informal.* a chap or fellow.

chaps (tʃæps, ʃæps) *pl.* *n.* leather leggings without a seat, worn by cowboys.

chapter ('tʃæptə) *n.* **1.** a division of a written work. **2.** a sequence of events: *a chapter of disasters.* **3.** a period in a life or history. **4.** a branch of some societies or clubs. **5.** the body of or a meeting of the canons of a cathedral or the members of a monastic order. **6. chapter and verse.** exact authority for an action or statement.

char¹ (tʃɑː) *vb.* **charring, charred. 1.** to scorch. **2.** to reduce (wood) to charcoal by partial burning.

char² or **charr** (tʃɑː) *n.*, *pl.* **char, chars** or **charr, charrs.** a troutlike fish of cold lakes and northern seas.

char³ (tʃɑː) *n.* **1.** *Informal.* short for **charwoman.** ~*vb.* **charring, charred. 2.** *Brit. informal.* to do cleaning as a job.

char⁴ (tʃɑː) *n.* *Brit. slang.* tea.

charabanc (ˈʃærəˌbæŋ) n. Brit. a coach for sightseeing.

character (ˈkærɪktə) n. 1. the combination of qualities distinguishing an individual person or thing. 2. a distinguishing quality; characteristic. 3. moral strength: a man of character. 4. reputation, esp. good reputation. 5. a person represented in a play, film, or story. 6. an outstanding person: one of the great characters of the century. 7. Informal. an odd or eccentric person: he's quite a character. 8. Informal. a person: a shady character. 9. Printing. a single letter, numeral, or symbol used in writing or printing. 10. Computers. any letter or numeral which can be represented uniquely by a binary pattern. 11. Genetics. a structure, function, or attribute in an organism that is determined by a gene or genes. 12. in (or out of) character. typical (or not typical) of the apparent character of a person. —ˈcharacterless adj.

characteristic (ˌkærɪktəˈrɪstɪk) n. 1. a distinguishing feature or quality. 2. Maths. the integral part of a logarithm: the characteristic of 2.4771 is 2. ~adj. 3. distinctive; typical. —ˌcharacterˈistically adv.

characterize or **-ise** (ˈkærɪktəˌraɪz) vb. 1. to be a characteristic of. 2. to distinguish as a characteristic. 3. to describe the character of. —ˌcharacteriˈzation or -iˈsation n.

charade (ʃəˈrɑːd) n. Chiefly Brit. a farce; travesty.

charades (ʃəˈrɑːdz) n. (functioning as sing.) a game in which one team acts out each syllable of a word, which the other team has to guess.

charcoal (ˈtʃɑːˌkəʊl) n. 1. a black form of carbon made by partially burning wood or other organic matter. 2. a stick of this for drawing. 3. a drawing done in charcoal. ~adj. 4. Also: **charcoal-grey**. dark grey.

charge (tʃɑːdʒ) vb. 1. to set or ask (a price). 2. to enter a debit against (a person or his account). 3. to accuse (someone) formally, as of a crime in a court of law. 4. to command; assign responsibility to: I was charged to take the message to headquarters. 5. to make a rush at or sudden attack upon (a person or thing). 6. to fill (a receptacle) with the required quantity. 7. (often foll. by up) to cause (an accumulator or capacitor) to take and store electricity. 8. to saturate with liquid or gas: to charge water with carbon dioxide. 9. to fill with a feeling or mood: the atmosphere was charged with excitement. 10. to load (a firearm). ~n. 11. a price charged for something; cost. 12. a formal accusation, as of a crime in a court of law. 13. a. an onrush or attack. b. the call to such an attack in battle. 14. custody or guardianship. 15. a person or thing committed to someone's care. 16. a. a cartridge or shell.

b. the explosive required to discharge a firearm. 17. the quantity of anything that a receptacle is intended to hold. 18. Physics. a. the attribute of matter responsible for all electrical phenomena, existing in two forms, positive and negative. b. the total amount of electricity stored in a capacitor or an accumulator. 19. a burden or responsibility. 20. a command or injunction. 21. Heraldry. a design depicted on heraldic arms. 22. in charge. in command. 23. in charge of. a. responsible for. b. U.S. under the care of.

chargeable (ˈtʃɑːdʒəbᵊl) adj. 1. liable to be charged: chargeable expenses. 2. liable to result in a legal charge.

chargé d'affaires (ˈʃɑːʒeɪ dæˈfɛə) n., pl. **chargés d'affaires** (ˈʃɑːʒeɪ, -ʒeɪz). 1. the temporary head of a diplomatic mission in the absence of the ambassador or minister. 2. the head of a small or unimportant diplomatic mission.

charge hand n. Brit. a workman whose grade of responsibility is just below that of a foreman.

charge nurse n. the male equivalent of a hospital sister.

charger (ˈtʃɑːdʒə) n. 1. a warhorse. 2. a device for charging an accumulator.

chariot (ˈtʃærɪət) n. a two-wheeled horse-drawn vehicle used in ancient times for wars and races.

charioteer (ˌtʃærɪəˈtɪə) n. a chariot driver.

charisma (kəˈrɪzmə) or **charism** (ˈkærɪzəm) n. 1. the quality or power of an individual to attract, influence, or inspire people. 2. Christianity. a divinely bestowed gift. —**charismatic** (ˌkærɪzˈmætɪk) adj.

charismatic movement n. Christianity. a group, within an existing denomination, emphasizing divine gifts such as instantaneous healing and uttering unintelligible sounds while in a religious ecstasy.

charitable (ˈtʃærɪtəbᵊl) adj. 1. generous in giving to the needy. 2. kind or lenient in one's attitude towards others. 3. of or for charity. —**charitably** adv.

charity (ˈtʃærɪtɪ) n., pl. **-ties**. 1. the giving of help, such as money or food, to those in need. 2. an organization set up to provide help to those in need. 3. help given to the needy; alms. 4. a kindly attitude towards people. 5. love of one's fellow human beings.

charlatan (ˈʃɑːlətᵊn) n. someone who claims expertise that he does not have. —ˈcharlatanˌism n.

charleston (ˈtʃɑːlstən) n. a lively dance of the 1920s, characterized by twisting kicks from the knee.

charlie (ˈtʃɑːlɪ) n. Brit. informal. a fool.

charlock (ˈtʃɑːlɒk) n. a weed with hairy leaves and yellow flowers.

charlotte (ˈʃɑːlət) *n.* a dessert made with fruit and bread or cake crumbs: *apple charlotte.*

charm (tʃɑːm) *n.* **1.** the quality of attracting, fascinating, or delighting people. **2.** a small object worn for supposed magical powers; amulet. **3.** a trinket worn on a bracelet. **4.** a magic spell. **5. like a charm.** perfectly; successfully. ~*vb.* **6.** to attract or fascinate; delight. **7.** to protect, influence, or heal, as if by magic. **8.** to influence or obtain by personal charm. —ˈ**charmer** *n.* —ˈ**charmless** *adj.*

charming (ˈtʃɑːmɪŋ) *adj.* delightful; attractive. —ˈ**charmingly** *adv.*

charnel house (ˈtʃɑːnəl) *n.* (formerly) a building or vault where corpses or bones are deposited.

Charon (ˈkɛərən) *n. Greek myth.* the ferryman who brought the dead across the river Styx to Hades.

chart (tʃɑːt) *n.* **1.** a map designed to aid navigation by sea or air. **2.** an outline map on which weather information is plotted. **3.** a graph, table, or sheet of information in the form of a diagram. **4. the charts.** *Informal.* the weekly lists of the best-selling pop records. ~*vb.* **5.** to make a chart of. **6.** to plot the course of. **7.** to appear in the pop charts.

charter (ˈtʃɑːtə) *n.* **1.** (*sometimes cap.*) a formal document granting or demanding certain rights or liberties. **2.** (*often cap.*) the fundamental principles of an organization; constitution. **3.** the hire or lease of transportation for private use. ~*vb.* **4.** to lease or hire by charter. **5.** to grant a charter to.

chartered accountant *n.* (in Britain) an accountant who has passed the examinations of the Institute of Chartered Accountants.

Chartism (ˈtʃɑːtɪzəm) *n. English history.* a movement (1838-48) for social and political reforms, such as votes for all men and secret ballots, demand for which was presented to Parliament in charters. —ˈ**Chartist** *n., adj.*

chartreuse (ʃɑːˈtrɜːz) *n.* a green or yellow liqueur made from herbs.

charwoman (ˈtʃɑːˌwʊmən) *n., pl.* -**women.** *Brit.* a woman employed to clean a house.

chary (ˈtʃɛərɪ) *adj.* **charier, chariest. 1.** wary; careful. **2.** sparing; mean. —ˈ**chariness** *n.*

Charybdis (kəˈrɪbdɪs) *n.* a ship-devouring monster in classical mythology, identified with a whirlpool off the coast of Sicily.

chase[1] (tʃeɪs) *vb.* **1.** to pursue (a person, animal, or goal) persistently or quickly. **2.** (often foll. by *out, away,* or *off*) to force to run (away); drive (out). **3.** *Informal.* to court (someone) in an unsubtle manner. **4.** (often foll. by *up*) *Informal.* to pursue energetically in order to obtain results or information. **5.** *Informal.* to hurry; rush. ~*n.* **6.** a chasing; pursuit. **7.** *Brit.* an unenclosed area of land, originally one where wild animals were kept to be hunted. **8. the chase.** the act or sport of hunting. **9. give chase.** to set off in pursuit of (a person or animal).

chase[2] (tʃeɪs) *n.* **1.** a rectangular metal frame into which type is locked for printing. **2.** a groove.

chase[3] (tʃeɪs) *vb.* to engrave or emboss (metal).

chaser (ˈtʃeɪsə) *n.* a drink drunk after another of a different kind, as beer after spirits.

chasm (ˈkæzəm) *n.* **1.** a deep crack in the ground; abyss. **2.** a wide difference in interests or feelings.

chassis (ˈʃæsɪ) *n., pl.* -**sis** (-sɪz). **1.** the steel frame, wheels, and mechanical parts of a motor vehicle. **2.** a mounting for the components of an electronic device, such as a radio or television. **3.** the landing gear of an aircraft.

chaste (tʃeɪst) *adj.* **1.** abstaining from sex outside marriage or from all sexual intercourse. **2.** (of conduct or speech) pure; decent; modest. **3.** (of style) simple. —ˈ**chastely** *adv.* —ˈ**chasteness** *n.*

chasten (ˈtʃeɪsən) *vb.* **1.** to correct by punishment. **2.** to subdue; restrain.

chastise (tʃæsˈtaɪz) *vb.* **1.** to punish, esp. by beating. **2.** to scold severely. —**chastisement** (ˈtʃæstɪzmənt) *n.*

chastity (ˈtʃæstɪtɪ) *n.* **1.** the state of being chaste; purity. **2.** abstention from sexual intercourse.

chasuble (ˈtʃæzjʊbəl) *n. Christianity.* a long sleeveless outer vestment worn by a priest when celebrating Mass.

chat (tʃæt) *n.* **1.** informal conversation in an easy familiar manner. **2.** a songbird with a harsh chattering cry. ~*vb.* **chatting, chatted. 3.** to talk in an easy familiar way. ~See also **chat up.**

chateau or **château** (ˈʃætəʊ) *n., pl.* -**teaux** (-təʊ, -təʊz) or -**teaus. 1.** a French country house or castle. **2.** (in the name of a wine) estate or vineyard.

chatelaine (ˈʃætəˌleɪn) *n.* **1.** (esp. formerly) the mistress of a large house or castle. **2.** *History.* a chain with keys attached worn at the waist by women.

chat show *n. Brit.* a television or radio show in which guests are interviewed informally.

chattel (ˈtʃætəl) *n.* (*often pl.*) *Property law.* a movable personal possession.

chatter (ˈtʃætə) *vb.* **1.** to speak about trivial matters rapidly and incessantly. **2.** (of birds or monkeys) to make rapid repetitive high-pitched noises. **3.** (of the teeth) to click together rapidly through cold or fear. ~*n.* **4.** idle talk; gossip. **5.** the high-pitched repetitive noise made by a bird or monkey.

chatterbox ('tʃætə,bɒks) n. Informal. a person who talks constantly about trivial matters.

chatty ('tʃætɪ) adj. **-tier, -tiest. 1.** full of trivial conversation; talkative. **2.** informal and friendly; gossipy. —'**chattiness** n.

chat up vb. Brit. informal. **1.** to chat to (a person), usually with an ulterior motive. **2.** to talk flirtatiously to (someone).

chauffeur ('ʃəʊfə, ʃəʊ'fɜː) n. **1.** a person employed to drive a car. ~vb. **2.** to act as driver for (someone). —**chauffeuse** (ʃəʊ-'fɜːz) fem. n.

chauvinism ('ʃəʊvɪ,nɪzəm) n. **1.** aggressive or fanatical patriotism; jingoism. **2.** smug irrational belief that one's own race, group, or sex is superior: male chauvinism. —'**chauvinist** n., adj. —,**chauvin'istic** adj.

cheap (tʃiːp) adj. **1.** costing relatively little; inexpensive. **2.** charging low prices: a cheap hairdresser. **3.** of poor quality; shoddy: cheap furniture. **4.** easily got or made; of little value: talk is cheap. **5.** Informal. mean; despicable: a cheap liar. ~n. **6. on the cheap.** Brit. informal. at a low cost. ~adv. **7.** at a low cost. —'**cheaply** adv. —'**cheapness** n.

cheapen ('tʃiːpᵊn) vb. **1.** to make or become lower in reputation or quality. **2.** to make or become cheap or cheaper.

cheap-jack Informal. ~n. **1.** a seller of cheap and shoddy goods. ~adj. **2.** shoddy or inferior.

cheapskate ('tʃiːp,skeɪt) n. Informal. a miserly person.

cheat (tʃiːt) vb. **1.** to deceive for gain; trick or swindle (someone). **2.** to obtain unfair advantage by trickery: he cheats at cards. **3.** to escape (something unpleasant) by luck or cunning: to cheat death. **4.** (often foll. by on) Informal. to be unfaithful to (one's spouse or lover). ~n. **5.** a person who cheats. **6.** a fraud; deception. —'**cheater** n.

check (tʃɛk) vb. **1.** to examine, investigate, or make an inquiry into (something). **2.** to slow the growth or progress of. **3.** to rebuke or rebuff. **4.** to stop abruptly. **5.** Chiefly U.S. & Canad. to tick so as to indicate approval, correctness, or preference. **6.** (often foll. by with) Chiefly U.S. & Canad. to correspond or agree: this report checks with the other. **7.** Chiefly U.S., Canad., & N.Z. to leave in or accept for temporary custody. ~n. **8.** a test to ensure accuracy or progress. **9.** a means to ensure against fraud or error. **10.** a break in progress; stoppage. **11.** a rebuke or rebuff. **12.** a person or thing that restrains or halts. **13.** U.S. same as **tick**¹. **14.** U.S. a cheque. **15.** U.S. & Canad. the bill in a restaurant. **16.** Chiefly U.S. & Canad. a tag used to identify property left in custody. **17.** a pattern of squares or crossed lines. **18.** a single square in such a pattern. **19.** fabric with such a pattern. **20.** Chess. the state or position of a king under direct attack. **21. in check.** under control or restraint. ~interj. **22.** Chiefly U.S. & Canad. an expression of agreement. ~See also **check in, check out, checkup.**

checked (tʃɛkt) adj. having a pattern of squares.

checker¹ ('tʃɛkə) U.S. & Canad. ~n., vb. **1.** same as **chequer.** ~n. **2.** same as **draughtsman** (sense 3).

checker² ('tʃɛkə) n. Chiefly U.S. **1.** a cashier. **2.** an attendant in a cloakroom or left-luggage office.

checkers ('tʃɛkəz) n. (functioning as sing.) U.S. & Canad. draughts.

check in vb. **1.** to register one's arrival; sign in. **2.** to register the arrival of (passengers or staff). ~n. **check-in. 3.** the formal registration of arrival at an airport or hotel. **4.** the place where one registers one's arrival.

check list n. a list to be referred to for identification or verification.

checkmate ('tʃɛk,meɪt) n. **1.** Chess. the winning position in which an opponent's king is under attack and unable to escape. **2.** utter defeat. ~vb. **3.** Chess. to place (an opponent's king) in checkmate. **4.** to thwart or defeat.

check out vb. **1.** to pay the bill and depart from a hotel. **2.** to depart or register one's departure from a place. **3.** to investigate, examine, or look at: the police checked out all the statements. **4.** Informal. to have a look at; inspect: check out the wally in the pink shirt. ~n. **checkout. 5.** a counter in a supermarket, where customers pay.

checkpoint ('tʃɛk,pɔɪnt) n. a place where vehicles or travellers are stopped for identification or inspection.

checkup ('tʃɛk,ʌp) n. **1.** a thorough examination to see if a person or thing is in good condition. ~vb. **check up. 2.** (sometimes foll. by on) to investigate (something, such as a person's background).

Cheddar ('tʃɛdə) n. a firm orange or yellowy-white cheese.

cheek (tʃiːk) n. **1.** either side of the face below the eye. **2.** Informal. impudence; effrontery. **3.** (often pl.) Informal. a buttock. **4. cheek by jowl.** close together; intimate. **5. turn the other cheek.** to refuse to retaliate. ~vb. **6.** Informal. to speak or behave disrespectfully to.

cheekbone ('tʃiːk,bəʊn) n. the bone at the top of the cheek, just below the eye.

cheeky ('tʃiːkɪ) adj. **cheekier, cheekiest.** disrespectful; impudent. —'**cheekily** adv. —'**cheekiness** n.

cheep (tʃiːp) n. 1. the short weak high-pitched cry of a young bird; chirp. ~vb. 2. to utter such sounds.

cheer (tʃɪə) vb. 1. (usually foll. by up) to make or become happy or hopeful; comfort or be comforted. 2. to applaud or encourage with shouts. ~n. 3. a shout of applause or encouragement. 4. state of mind; spirits (archaic, except in **be of good cheer**).

cheerful ('tʃɪəful) adj. 1. having a happy disposition; in good spirits. 2. pleasantly bright: a cheerful room. 3. ungrudging: cheerful help. —'**cheerfully** adv. —'**cheerfulness** n.

cheerio (ˌtʃɪərɪ'əʊ) interj. Informal, chiefly Brit. a farewell greeting.

cheerleader ('tʃɪəˌliːdə) n. U.S. & Canad. a person who leads a crowd in cheers, usually at sports events.

cheerless ('tʃɪəlɪs) adj. dreary or gloomy.

cheers (tʃɪəz) interj. Informal, chiefly Brit. 1. a drinking toast. 2. goodbye! 3. thanks!

cheery ('tʃɪərɪ) adj. **cheerier, cheeriest.** cheerful. —'**cheerily** adv. —'**cheeriness** n.

cheese[1] (tʃiːz) n. 1. a food made from coagulated milk curd. 2. a block of this. 3. a substance of similar consistency: lemon cheese. —'**cheesy** adj.

cheese[2] (tʃiːz) n. **big cheese.** an important person.

cheeseburger ('tʃiːzˌbɜːgə) n. a hamburger cooked with a slice of cheese on top of it.

cheesecake ('tʃiːzˌkeɪk) n. 1. a rich tart with a filling or topping which contains cream cheese. 2. Slang. women, usually scantily clad, displayed for their sex appeal.

cheesecloth ('tʃiːzˌklɒθ) n. a loosely woven cotton cloth.

cheesed off adj. Brit. slang. bored, disgusted, or angry.

cheeseparing ('tʃiːzˌpeərɪŋ) adj. 1. stingy. ~n. 2. stinginess.

cheetah ('tʃiːtə) n. a large feline of Africa and SW Asia: the swiftest mammal, having very long legs, and a black-spotted coat.

chef (ʃef) n. a cook, usually the principal cook in a restaurant.

chef-d'oeuvre (ˌʃeɪ'dɜːvrə) n., pl. **chefs-d'oeuvre** (ˌʃeɪ'dɜːvrə). a masterpiece.

Chelsea Pensioner ('tʃelsɪ) n. an inhabitant of the Chelsea Royal Hospital in SW London, a home for old and infirm soldiers.

chem. 1. chemical. 2. chemist. 3. chemistry.

chemical ('kemɪk'l) n. 1. any substance used in or resulting from a reaction involving changes to atoms or molecules. ~adj. 2. of or used in chemistry. 3. of, made from, or using chemicals: chemical fertilizer. —'**chemically** adv.

chemical engineering n. the applica-

tions of chemistry in industrial processes. —**chemical engineer** n.

chemical warfare n. warfare using weapons such as gases, poisons, and defoliants.

chemin de fer (ʃə'mæn də 'fɛə) n. a gambling game, a variation of baccarat.

chemise (ʃə'miːz) n. a woman's old-fashioned loose-fitting undergarment or dress.

chemist ('kemɪst) n. 1. Brit. a shop selling medicines and cosmetics. 2. Brit. a qualified dispenser of prescribed medicines. 3. a specialist in chemistry.

chemistry ('kemɪstrɪ) n. the branch of science concerned with the composition, properties, and reactions of substances.

chemotherapy (ˌkiːməʊ'θerəpɪ) n. treatment of disease by means of chemical agents.

chemurgy ('kemɜːdʒɪ) n. the branch of chemistry concerned with the industrial use of organic raw materials, usually from farms.

chenille (ʃə'niːl) n. 1. a thick soft tufty yarn. 2. a fabric made of this.

cheque or U.S. **check** (tʃek) n. a written order to someone's bank to pay money from their account to the person to whom the cheque is made out.

cheque book ('tʃekˌbʊk) n. a book of detachable blank cheques issued by a bank.

cheque card n. a plastic card issued by a bank guaranteeing payment of a customer's cheques up to a specified value.

chequer or U.S. **checker** ('tʃekə) n. 1. a piece used in Chinese chequers. 2. **a.** a pattern of squares. **b.** one of the squares in such a pattern. ~vb. 3. to make irregular in colour or character; variegate. 4. to mark with alternating squares of colour. ~See also **chequers.**

chequered or U.S. **checkered** ('tʃekəd) adj. marked by varied fortunes: a chequered career.

chequers or U.S. **checkers** ('tʃekəz) n. (functioning as sing.) the game of draughts.

cherish ('tʃerɪʃ) vb. 1. to hold dear; care for. 2. to cling to (an idea or feeling): to cherish a hope.

cheroot (ʃə'ruːt) n. a cigar with both ends cut off squarely.

cherry ('tʃerɪ) n., pl. **-ries.** 1. a small round fleshy fruit containing a hard stone. 2. the wood of the tree bearing this fruit. ~adj. 3. cold red.

cherub ('tʃerəb) n., pl. **cherubs** or (for sense 1) **cherubim** ('tʃerəbɪm, -ʊbɪm). 1. Christianity. an angel, often represented as a winged child. 2. an innocent or sweet child. —**cherubic** (tʃə'ruːbɪk) adj.

chervil ('tʃɜːvɪl) n. a Eurasian plant with aniseed-flavoured leaves used a herb.

chess (tʃes) n. a game of skill for two

players using a chessboard on which chessmen are moved. The object is to checkmate the opponent's king.

chessboard ('tʃɛsˌbɔːd) *n.* a square board divided into 64 squares of two alternating colours, used for playing chess or draughts.

chessman ('tʃɛsˌmæn, -mən) *n., pl.* **-men.** a piece used in chess.

chest (tʃɛst) *n.* **1.** the front of the body, from the neck to the belly. **2. get (something) off one's chest.** *Informal.* to unburden oneself of (worries or secrets) by talking about them. **3.** a heavy box for storage or shipping: *a tea chest.*

chesterfield ('tʃɛstəˌfiːld) *n.* a large sofa with straight arms of the same height as the back.

chestnut ('tʃɛsˌnʌt) *n.* **1.** the edible nut of a N temperate tree. **2.** the hard wood of this tree. **3.** a horse of a reddish-brown colour. **4.** *Informal.* an old or stale joke. ~*adj.* **5.** reddish-brown.

chest of drawers *n.* a piece of furniture consisting of a set of drawers in a frame.

chesty ('tʃɛstɪ) *adj.* **chestier, chestiest.** *Brit. informal.* suffering from or symptomatic of chest disease: *a chesty cough.* —'**chestiness** *n.*

cheval glass (ʃə'væl) *n.* a full-length mirror mounted so as to swivel within a frame.

chevalier (ˌʃɛvə'lɪə) *n.* **1.** a member of the French Legion of Honour. **2.** a chivalrous man.

Cheviot ('tʃiːvɪət, 'tʃɛv-) *n.* **1.** a large British breed of sheep reared for its wool. **2.** (*often not cap.*) a rough woollen fabric.

chevron ('ʃɛvrən) *n.* a V-shaped pattern or device, usually one on a military uniform to indicate rank.

chew (tʃuː) *vb.* **1.** to work the jaws and teeth in order to grind (food). **2.** to bite repeatedly: *she chewed her nails anxiously.* **3. chew the fat** *or* **rag.** *Slang.* **a.** to discuss a point. **b.** to talk idly; gossip. ~*n.* **4.** the act of chewing. **5.** something that is chewed.

chewing gum *n.* a flavoured gum used for chewing.

chew over *vb.* to consider carefully.

chewy ('tʃuːɪ) *adj.* **chewier, chewiest.** of a consistency requiring a lot of chewing.

chez (ʃeɪ) *prep.* at the home of.

chianti (kɪ'æntɪ) *n.* (*sometimes cap.*) a dry red wine produced in Tuscany, Italy.

chiaroscuro (kɪˌɑːrə'skjʊərəʊ) *n., pl.* **-ros.** the distribution of light and shade in a picture.

chic (ʃiːk) *adj.* **1.** stylish or elegant. ~*n.* **2.** stylishness; fashionable good taste.

chicane (ʃɪ'keɪn) *n.* **1.** an obstacle placed on a motor-racing circuit to slow the cars down. **2.** a less common word for **chicanery.** ~*vb.* **3.** to trick by chicanery. **4.** to use chicanery.

chicanery (ʃɪ'keɪnərɪ) *n., pl.* **-eries.** **1.** clever but deceptive talk. **2.** a trick or deception.

chick (tʃɪk) *n.* **1.** the young of a domestic fowl or other bird. **2.** *Slang.* a girl or young woman.

chicken ('tʃɪkɪn) *n.* **1.** a domestic fowl bred for its flesh or eggs. **2.** the flesh of this bird used for food. **3.** *Slang.* a coward. **4.** *Slang.* a young person: *she's no chicken.* **5. count one's chickens before they are hatched.** to be overoptimistic in acting on expectations which are not yet fulfilled. ~*adj.* **6.** *Slang.* cowardly; timid.

chicken feed *n.* *Slang.* a trifling amount of money.

chicken-hearted *or* **chicken-livered** *adj.* easily frightened; cowardly.

chicken out *vb.* *Informal.* to fail to do something through cowardice.

chickenpox ('tʃɪkɪnˌpɒks) *n.* an infectious viral disease usually affecting children, characterized by an itchy rash.

chicken wire *n.* wire netting.

chickpea ('tʃɪkˌpiː) *n.* the edible pealike seed of a Mediterranean and Asian plant.

chickweed ('tʃɪkˌwiːd) *n.* a common garden weed with small white flowers.

chicle ('tʃɪk'l) *n.* a gumlike substance used to make chewing gum.

chicory ('tʃɪkərɪ) *n., pl.* **-ries.** **1.** a plant cultivated for its leaves, which are used in salads, and for its roots. **2.** the root of this plant, roasted, dried, and used as a coffee substitute.

chide (tʃaɪd) *vb.* **chiding, chided** *or* **chid** (tʃɪd); **chided, chid** *or* **chidden** ('tʃɪd'n). to rebuke or scold.

chief (tʃiːf) *n.* **1.** the head of a group or body of people. **2. in chief.** primarily; especially. ~*adj.* **3.** most important; principal. **4.** highest in rank.

chiefly ('tʃiːflɪ) *adv.* **1.** especially or essentially. **2.** mainly; mostly.

chief petty officer *n.* a senior noncommissioned officer in a navy.

chieftain ('tʃiːftən, -tɪn) *n.* the leader of a tribe or clan. —'**chieftaincy** *or* '**chieftain-** ˌship *n.*

chief technician *n.* a noncommissioned officer in the Royal Air Force.

chiffchaff ('tʃɪfˌtʃæf) *n.* a European warbler with a yellowish-brown plumage.

chiffon (ʃɪ'fon, 'ʃɪfon) *n.* **1.** a fine almost transparent fabric of silk or nylon. ~*adj.* **2.** made of chiffon. **3.** *Cooking.* having a very light fluffy texture.

chiffonier *or* **chiffonnier** (ˌʃɪfə'nɪə) *n.* **1.** a tall elegant chest of drawers. **2.** a wide low open-fronted cabinet.

chignon ('ʃiːnjɒn) *n.* a roll or knot of long hair arranged at the back of the head.

chigoe ('tʃɪɡəʊ) *n.* a tropical flea which

burrows into the skin. Also: **chigger** ('tʃɪgə).

Chihuahua (tʃɪ'wɑːwɑː, -wə) n. a tiny short-haired dog, originally from Mexico.

chilblain ('tʃɪl,bleɪn) n. an inflammation of the fingers or toes, caused by exposure to cold.

child (tʃaɪld) n., pl. **children. 1.** a boy or girl between birth and puberty. **2.** a baby or infant. **3.** an unborn baby. **4.** with **child**. Old-fashioned. pregnant. **5.** a son or daughter. **6.** a childish or immature person. **7.** a descendant: a child of Israel. **8.** the product of an influence or environment: a child of nature. —'**childless** adj. —'**childlessness** n.

childbearing ('tʃaɪld,bɛərɪŋ) n. **a.** the process of giving birth to a child. **b.** (as modifier): of childbearing age.

child benefit n. Brit. a regular government payment to parents of children up to a certain age.

childbirth ('tʃaɪld,bɜːθ) n. the act of giving birth to a child.

childhood ('tʃaɪldhʊd) n. the time or condition of being a child.

childish ('tʃaɪldɪʃ) adj. **1.** of or like a child. **2.** immature; silly: childish fears.

childlike ('tʃaɪld,laɪk) adj. like or befitting a child, as in being innocent or trustful.

child minder n. a person who looks after children whose parents are working.

children ('tʃɪldrən) n. the plural of **child**.

child's play n. Informal. something easy to do.

chill (tʃɪl) n. **1.** a moderate coldness. **2.** a feeling of coldness resulting from a cold or damp environment or from sudden fear. **3.** a feverish cold. **4.** a depressing influence. ~adj. **5.** chilly. ~vb. **6.** to make or become cold. **7.** to cool (something). **8.** to depress. —'**chilling** adj. —'**chillingly** adv. —'**chillness** n.

chiller ('tʃɪlə) n. **1.** short for **spine-chiller**. **2.** N.Z. a refrigerated storage area for meat.

chilli or **chili** ('tʃɪlɪ) n., pl. **chillies** or **chilies**. the small red or green hot-tasting pod of a type of capsicum, used in cookery, often in powdered form.

chilli con carne (kɒn 'kɑːnɪ) n. a highly seasoned Mexican dish of meat, onions, beans, and chilli powder.

chilly ('tʃɪlɪ) adj. **-lier, -liest. 1.** causing or feeling moderately cold. **2.** without warmth; unfriendly. —'**chilliness** n.

chilly bin n. N.Z. informal. a portable insulated container with provision for packing food and drink in ice.

Chiltern Hundreds ('tʃɪltən) pl. n. (in Britain) short for **Stewardship of the Chiltern Hundreds**; a nominal office that an MP applies for in order to resign his seat.

chime (tʃaɪm) n. **1.** a bell or the sound it makes when struck. **2.** Also called: **bell**. a percussion instrument consisting of a set of hanging metal tubes which are struck with a hammer. ~vb. **3. a.** to ring (a bell) or (of a bell) to be rung. **b.** to produce (music or sounds) by chiming. **4.** to indicate (time) by chiming. **5.** (foll. by with) to agree or harmonize.

chimera or **chimaera** (kaɪ'mɪərə, kɪ-) n. **1.** (often cap.) Greek myth. a fire-breathing monster with the head of a lion, body of a goat, and tail of a serpent. **2.** a grotesque product of the imagination.

chimerical (kaɪ'mɛrɪkᵊl, kɪ-) or **chimeric** adj. **1.** wildly fanciful; imaginary. **2.** indulging in fantasies.

chimney ('tʃɪmnɪ) n. **1.** a hollow vertical structure that carries smoke or steam away from a fire or engine. **2.** same as **flue. 3.** a glass tube protecting the flame of an oil or gas lamp. **4.** the vent of a volcano. **5.** a vertical fissure in a rock face.

chimney breast n. the walls surrounding the base of a chimney or fireplace.

chimneypot ('tʃɪmnɪ,pɒt) n. a short pipe on the top of a chimney.

chimney stack n. the part of a chimney projecting above a roof.

chimney sweep or **sweeper** n. a person who cleans soot from chimneys.

chimp (tʃɪmp) n. Informal. short for **chimpanzee**.

chimpanzee (,tʃɪmpæn'ziː) n. an intelligent anthropoid ape of central W Africa.

chin (tʃɪn) n. **1.** the front part of the face below the lips. **2. keep one's chin up**. Informal. to keep cheerful under difficult circumstances. **3. take it on the chin**. Informal. to face squarely up to a defeat or difficulty.

Chin. 1. China. **2.** Chinese.

china ('tʃaɪnə) n. **1.** ceramic ware of a type originally from China. **2.** crockery. **3.** (modifier) made of china.

china clay n. same as **kaolin**.

Chinaman ('tʃaɪnəmən) n., pl. **-men**. Archaic or offensive. a man from China.

Chinatown ('tʃaɪnə,taʊn) n. any town outside China with a mainly Chinese population.

chinchilla (tʃɪn'tʃɪlə) n. **1.** a small S American rodent bred in captivity for its soft silvery grey fur. **2.** the fur of this animal.

chine (tʃaɪn) n. **1.** the backbone. **2.** a cut of meat including part of the backbone. **3.** a ridge of land. ~vb. **4.** to cut (meat) along the backbone.

Chinese (tʃaɪ'niːz) adj. **1.** of China, its people, or their languages. ~n. **2.** (pl. **-nese**) a person from China or a descendant of one. **3.** any of the languages of China.

Chinese chequers n. (functioning as sing.) a game played with marbles or pegs on a six-pointed star-shaped board.

Chinese lantern n. a collapsible lantern made of thin paper.

Chinese leaves *pl. n.* the edible leaves of a Chinese plant of the cabbage family.

Chinese puzzle *n.* a complicated puzzle or problem.

chink[1] (tʃɪŋk) *n.* a fissure or crack.

chink[2] (tʃɪŋk) *vb.* **1.** to make or cause to make a light ringing sound, as by the striking of glasses or coins. *~n.* **2.** such a sound.

chinless wonder (ˈtʃɪnlɪs) *n. Brit. informal.* a person, usually upper-class, lacking strength of character.

chinoiserie (ʃiːnˌwɑːzəˈriː, -ˈwɑːzərɪ) *n.* **1.** a style of decorative art based on imitations of Chinese motifs. **2.** an object or objects in this style.

Chinook (tʃɪˈnuːk, -ˈnʊk) *n.* **1.** (*pl.* **-nook** *or* **-nooks**) a N American Indian people of the Pacific coast. **2.** the language of this people.

Chinook salmon *n.* a Pacific salmon valued as a food fish.

chinos (ˈtʃiːnəʊz) *pl. n.* trousers made of a durable cotton twill cloth.

chintz (tʃɪnts) *n.* a printed, patterned cotton fabric with a glazed finish.

chintzy (ˈtʃɪntsɪ) *adj.* **chintzier, chintziest. 1.** of, like, or covered with chintz. **2.** *Brit. informal.* typical of the decor associated with the use of chintz soft furnishings.

chinwag (ˈtʃɪnˌwæg) *n. Brit. informal.* a chat.

chip (tʃɪp) *n.* **1.** a small piece removed by chopping, cutting, or breaking. **2.** a mark left after a small piece has been broken off something. **3.** (in gambling) a counter used to represent money. **4.** a thin strip of potato fried in deep fat. **5.** *U.S. & Canad.* a potato crisp. **6.** *Electronics.* a tiny wafer of semiconductor material, such as silicon, processed to form an integrated circuit. **7.** a thin strip of wood or straw used for weaving hats and baskets. **8. chip off the old block.** *Informal.* a person who resembles one of his or her parents in behaviour. **9. have a chip on one's shoulder.** *Informal.* to be resentful or bear a grudge. **10. have had one's chips.** *Brit. informal.* to be defeated, doomed, or killed. **11. when the chips are down.** *Informal.* at a time of crisis. *~vb.* **chipping, chipped. 12.** to break small pieces from or be broken off in small pieces: *will the paint chip?* **13.** to break or cut into small pieces: *to chip ice.* **14.** to shape by chipping.

chip-based *adj.* using microchips.

chipboard (ˈtʃɪpˌbɔːd) *n.* a thin rigid board made of compressed wood particles.

chip heater *n. Austral. & N.Z.* a domestic water heater that burns chips of wood.

chip in *vb. Informal.* **1.** to contribute (money) to a cause or fund. **2.** to interrupt with a remark.

chipmunk (ˈtʃɪpˌmʌŋk) *n.* a squirrel-like

striped burrowing rodent of North America and Asia.

chipolata (ˌtʃɪpəˈlɑːtə) *n. Chiefly Brit.* a small sausage.

Chippendale (ˈtʃɪpⁿˌdeɪl) *adj.* (of furniture) by or in the style of Thomas Chippendale (?1718-79): having Chinese and Gothic motifs, curved legs, and massive carving.

chirography (kaɪˈrɒgrəfɪ) *n.* same as **calligraphy.**

chiromancy (ˈkaɪrəˌmænsɪ) *n.* same as **palmistry.**

chiropody (kɪˈrɒpədɪ) *n.* the treatment of minor foot complaints like corns. **—chiropodist** *n.*

chiropractic (ˌkaɪrəˈpræktɪk) *n.* a system of treating bodily disorders by manipulation of the spine and other parts. **—ˈchiroˌpractor** *n.*

chirp (tʃɜːp) *vb.* **1.** (of some birds and insects) to make a short high-pitched sound. **2.** to speak in a lively fashion. *~n.* **3.** a chirping sound.

chirpy (ˈtʃɜːpɪ) *adj.* **chirpier, chirpiest.** *Informal.* cheerful; lively. **—ˈchirpiness** *n.*

chirrup (ˈtʃɪrəp) *vb.* **1.** (of some birds) to chirp repeatedly. *~n.* **2.** such a sound.

chisel (ˈtʃɪzⁿl) *n.* **1.** a hand tool for working wood, stone, or metal, consisting of a flat steel blade sharpened at one end. *~vb.* **-elling, -elled** *or U.S.* **-eling, -eled. 2.** to carve (a material) or form (something) with or as if with a chisel. **3.** *Slang.* to cheat or get by cheating. **—ˈchiseller** *or U.S.* **-eler** *n.*

chit[1] (tʃɪt) *n.* **1.** a voucher for a small sum of money owed. **2.** Also called: **chitty.** *Chiefly Brit.* **a.** a note or memorandum. **b.** a requisition or receipt.

chit[2] (tʃɪt) *n. Facetious.* a pert, impudent, or self-confident girl.

chitchat (ˈtʃɪtˌtʃæt) *n.* gossip.

chitin (ˈkaɪtɪn) *n.* the tough substance forming the outer layer of the bodies of arthropods.

chitterlings (ˈtʃɪtəlɪŋz) *pl. n.* (*sometimes sing.*) the intestines of a pig or other animal prepared as a dish.

chivalrous (ˈʃɪvəlrəs) *adj.* **1.** gallant; courteous. **2.** of chivalry. **—ˈchivalrously** *adv.*

chivalry (ˈʃɪvəlrɪ) *n., pl.* **-ries. 1.** the qualities expected of a medieval knight, such as courage, honour, and a readiness to help the weak. **2.** courteous behaviour, esp. towards women. **3.** the medieval system and principles of knighthood. **—ˈchivalric** *adj.*

chive (tʃaɪv) *n.* a small Eurasian plant, whose long slender hollow leaves are used in cooking for their onion-like flavour.

chivy *or* **chivvy** (ˈtʃɪvɪ) *vb.* **chivying, chivied** *or* **chivvying, chivvied.** *Brit.* to harass or nag.

chloral (ˈklɔːrəl) *n.* **1.** a colourless pungent

oily liquid used to make chloral hydrate and DDT. **2.** short for **chloral hydrate.**

chloral hydrate *n.* a colourless crystalline solid produced by the reaction of chloral with water and used as a sedative.

chlorate ('klɔːreɪt, -rɪt) *n.* any salt containing the ion ClO₃⁻.

chloric ('klɔːrɪk) *adj.* of or containing chlorine in the pentavalent state.

chloride ('klɔːraɪd) *n.* **1.** any salt of hydrochloric acid, containing the chloride ion Cl⁻. **2.** any compound containing a chlorine atom.

chlorinate ('klɔːrɪˌneɪt) *vb.* **1.** to combine or treat (a substance) with chlorine. **2.** to disinfect (water) with chlorine. —ˌchlori'nation *n.*

chlorine ('klɔːriːn) *n.* an element, a toxic pungent greenish-yellow gas, used in water purification, and as a disinfectant and bleaching agent. Symbol: Cl

chloro- *combining form.* green.

chlorofluorocarbon (ˌklɔːrəˌflʊərəʊ'kɑːbʰn) *n. Chem.* any of various gaseous compounds of carbon, hydrogen, chlorine, and fluorine, used as refrigerants and aerosol propellants: some break down the ozone in the atmosphere.

chloroform ('klɔːrəˌfɔːm) *n.* a liquid with a sweet odour, used as a solvent and cleansing agent, and formerly as an inhalation anaesthetic.

chlorophyll *or U.S.* **chlorophyl** ('klɔːrəfɪl) *n.* the green pigment of plants that traps the energy of sunlight for photosynthesis: used as a colouring agent (**E140**) in medicines and food.

chloroplast ('klɔːrəʊˌplæst) *n.* one of the parts of a plant cell that contains chlorophyll.

chock (tʃɒk) *n.* **1.** a block or wedge of wood used to prevent the sliding or rolling of a heavy object. ~*vb.* **2.** to fit with or secure by a chock.

chock-a-block *adj., adv.* filled to capacity.

chock-full *adj.* completely full.

chocolate ('tʃɒkəlɪt, 'tʃɒklɪt, -lət) *n.* **1.** a food made from roasted ground cacao seeds, usually sweetened and flavoured. **2.** a drink or sweet made from this. ~*adj.* **3.** deep brown. —'**chocolaty** *adj.*

choice (tʃɔɪs) *n.* **1.** a choosing or selecting. **2.** the opportunity or power of choosing. **3.** a person or thing chosen or that may be chosen: *he was a possible choice.* **4.** an alternative action or possibility: *what choice did I have?* **5.** a range from which to select. ~*adj.* **6.** of superior quality: *choice wine.* —'**choiceness** *n.*

choir ('kwaɪə) *n.* **1.** an organized group of singers, usually for singing in church. **2.** the part of a church, in front of the altar, occupied by the choir.

choirboy ('kwaɪəˌbɔɪ) *n.* a young boy who sings the treble part in a church choir.

choke (tʃəʊk) *vb.* **1.** to hinder or stop the breathing of (a person or animal) by strangling or asphyxiation. **2.** to have trouble in breathing, swallowing, or speaking. **3.** to block or clog (something) up. **4.** to retard the growth or action of: *the weeds are choking my plants.* ~*n.* **5.** a device in the carburettor of a petrol engine that enriches the petrol-air mixture by reducing the air supply. **6.** *Electronics.* a device used to prevent the passage of high frequencies or to smooth the output of a rectifier. —'**choky** *or* '**chokey** *adj.*

choke back *or* **down** *vb.* to suppress (anger, tears, or other emotions).

choker ('tʃəʊkə) *n.* **1.** a woman's high collar. **2.** a tightly-fitting necklace.

choke up *vb.* **1.** to block (something) completely. **2.** (*usually passive*) *Informal.* to overcome (a person) with emotion.

choko ('tʃəʊkəʊ) *n., pl.* **-kos.** *Austral. & N.Z.* the cucumber-like fruit of a tropical American vine.

choler ('kɒlə) *n.* anger or ill humour.

cholera ('kɒlərə) *n.* a dangerous intestinal infection characterized by severe diarrhoea and cramp: caused by ingestion of contaminated water or food. —**choleraic** (ˌkɒlə'reɪɪk) *adj.*

choleric ('kɒlərɪk) *adj.* bad-tempered.

cholesterol (kə'lɛstəˌrɒl) *n.* a fatty alcohol found in all animal fats, tissues, and fluids: thought to contribute to atherosclerosis.

chomp (tʃɒmp) *vb.* **1.** to chew (food) noisily. ~*n.* **2.** the act or sound of chewing in this manner.

chook (tʃʊk) *n. Informal, chiefly Austral. & N.Z.* a hen or chicken.

choose (tʃuːz) *vb.* **choosing, chose, chosen.** **1.** to select (a person, thing, or course of action) from a number of alternatives. **2.** to consider it desirable or proper: *I don't choose to read that book.* **3.** to like; please: *you may stand if you choose.*

choosy ('tʃuːzɪ) *adj.* **choosier, choosiest.** *Informal.* particular; fussy; hard to please.

chop¹ (tʃɒp) *vb.* **chopping, chopped.** **1.** (*often foll. by down or off*) to cut (something) with a blow from an axe or other sharp tool. **2.** (*often foll. by up*) to cut into pieces. **3.** *Brit. informal.* to dispense with or reduce. **4.** *Sport.* to hit (a ball) sharply downwards. **5.** *Boxing, karate.* to hit (an opponent) with a short sharp blow. ~*n.* **6.** a cutting blow. **7.** a slice of mutton, lamb, or pork, usually including a rib. **8.** *Sport.* a sharp downward blow or stroke. **9. the chop.** *Slang, chiefly Brit.* dismissal from employment.

chop² (tʃɒp) *vb.* **chopping, chopped.** **1. chop and change.** to change one's ideas or plans repeatedly; vacillate. **2. chop logic.**

to use excessively subtle or involved argument.

chop chop *adv. Pidgin English.* quickly.

chophouse ('tʃɒpˌhaʊs) *n.* a restaurant specializing in steaks, grills, and chops.

chopper ('tʃɒpə) *n.* **1.** *Chiefly Brit.* a small hand axe. **2.** a butcher's cleaver. **3.** *Informal.* a helicopter. **4.** a type of bicycle or motorcycle with very high handlebars. **5.** *N.Z.* a child's bicycle.

choppy ('tʃɒpɪ) *adj.* -**pier**, -**piest.** (of the sea) fairly rough. —'**choppiness** *n.*

chops (tʃɒps) *pl. n.* **1.** the jaws; jowls. **2.** the mouth. **3. lick one's chops.** *Informal.* to anticipate something with pleasure.

chopsticks ('tʃɒpstɪks) *pl. n.* a pair of thin sticks of ivory, wood, or plastic, used as eating utensils by the Chinese and Japanese.

chop suey ('suːɪ) *n.* a Chinese-style dish consisting of chopped meat, bean sprouts, and other vegetables, fried in soy sauce and served with rice.

choral ('kɔːrəl) *adj.* of or for a chorus or choir.

chorale *or* **choral** (kɒ'rɑːl) *n.* **1.** a slow stately hymn tune. **2.** *Chiefly U.S.* a choir or chorus.

chord[1] (kɔːd) *n.* **1.** *Maths.* a straight line connecting two points on a curve or curved surface. **2.** *Anat.* same as **cord. 3.** an emotional response, usually of sympathy: *the story struck the right chord.*

chord[2] (kɔːd) *n.* the simultaneous sounding of three or more musical notes.

chore (tʃɔː) *n.* **1.** a small routine task. **2.** an unpleasant task.

chorea (kɒ'rɪə) *n.* a disorder of the nervous system characterized by uncontrollable brief jerky movements.

choreography (ˌkɒrɪ'ɒɡrəfɪ) *n.* **1.** the composition of dance steps and movements for ballet and other dancing. **2.** the steps and movements of a ballet or dance. **3.** the art of dancing. —ˌ**chore**'**ographer** *n.* —**choreographic** (ˌkɒrɪə'ɡræfɪk) *adj.*

chorister ('kɒrɪstə) *n.* a singer in a choir, usually a choirboy.

chortle ('tʃɔːtə̩l) *vb.* **1.** to chuckle gleefully. ~*n.* **2.** a gleeful chuckle.

chorus ('kɔːrəs) *n., pl.* -**ruses. 1.** a large choir of singers or a piece of music composed for such a choir. **2.** a body of singers or dancers who perform together. **3.** the refrain of a song. **4.** (in ancient Greece) a group of actors who commented on the action of a play. **5.** (in Elizabethan drama) **a.** the actor who spoke the prologue and epilogue. **b.** the part spoken by this actor. **6. a.** a group of people or animals producing words or sounds in unison. **b.** the words or sounds produced by such a group: *the dawn chorus.* **7. in chorus.** in unison. ~*vb.* **8.** to sing or utter (words or sounds) in unison.

chorus girl *n.* a girl who dances or sings in the chorus of a show or film.

chose (tʃəʊz) *vb.* the past tense of **choose.**

chosen ('tʃəʊzə̩n) *vb.* **1.** the past participle of **choose.** ~*adj.* **2.** selected for some special quality.

chough (tʃʌf) *n.* a large black bird of the crow family, found in parts of Europe, Asia, and Africa.

choux pastry (ʃuː) *n.* a very light pastry made with eggs.

chow (tʃaʊ) *n.* **1.** *Informal.* food. **2.** a thick-coated dog with a curled tail, originally from China.

chowder ('tʃaʊdə) *n. Chiefly U.S. & Canad.* a thick soup or stew containing clams or fish.

chow mein (meɪn) *n.* a Chinese-American dish, consisting of chopped meat or vegetables, fried with noodles.

Chr. 1. Christ. **2.** Christian.

chrism ('krɪzəm) *n.* consecrated oil used for sacramental anointing in the Greek Orthodox and Roman Catholic Churches.

Christ (kraɪst) *n.* **1.** Jesus of Nazareth (Jesus Christ), regarded by Christians as the Messiah of Old Testament prophecies. **2.** the Messiah of Old Testament prophecies. **3.** an image or picture of Christ. ~*interj.* **4.** *Taboo slang.* an oath expressing annoyance or surprise.

christen ('krɪsə̩n) *vb.* **1.** same as **baptize. 2.** to give a name to (a person or thing). **3.** *Informal.* to use for the first time. —'**christening** *n.*

Christendom ('krɪsə̩ndəm) *n.* the collective body of Christians throughout the world.

Christian ('krɪstʃən) *n.* **1.** a person who believes in and follows Jesus Christ. **2.** *Informal.* a person who possesses Christian virtues. ~*adj.* **3.** of Jesus Christ, Christians, or Christianity. **4.** (*sometimes not cap.*) exhibiting kindness or goodness.

Christian Era *n.* the period beginning with the year of Christ's birth.

Christianity (ˌkrɪstɪ'ænɪtɪ) *n.* **1.** the Christian religion. **2.** Christian beliefs or practices. **3.** same as **Christendom.**

Christianize *or* -**ise** ('krɪstʃəˌnaɪz) *vb.* **1.** to convert to Christianity. **2.** to imbue with Christian principles, spirit, or outlook. —ˌ**Christiani**'**zation** *or* -**i**'**sation** *n.*

Christian name *n. Brit.* a personal name formally given to Christians at baptism: loosely used to mean any person's first name.

Christian Science *n.* the religious system founded by Mary Baker Eddy (1866), which emphasizes spiritual healing. —**Christian Scientist** *n.*

Christmas ('krɪsməs) *n.* **a.** the annual commemoration by Christians of the birth of Christ, held by most Churches to have occurred on Dec. 25. **b.** Also: **Christmas Day.**

Dec. 25, as a day of secular celebrations when gifts and greetings are exchanged. —'**Christmassy** adj.

Christmas box n. a tip or present given at Christmas, esp. to postmen or tradesmen.

Christmas Eve n. the evening or the whole day before Christmas Day.

Christmas pudding n. Brit. a rich steamed pudding containing suet, dried fruit, and spices.

Christmas rose n. an evergreen plant of S Europe and W Asia with white or pinkish winter-blooming flowers.

Christmas tree n. an evergreen tree or an imitation of one, decorated as part of Christmas celebrations.

chromate ('krəʊmeɪt) n. any salt or ester of chromic acid.

chromatic (krə'mætɪk) adj. 1. of or in colour or colours. 2. Music. a. involving the sharpening or flattening of notes or the use of such notes. b. of the chromatic scale. —**chro'matically** adv.

chromatics (krəʊ'mætɪks) n. (functioning as sing.) the science of colour.

chromatic scale n. a twelve-note scale including all the semitones of the octave.

chromatin ('krəʊmətɪn) n. the part of the nucleus that forms the chromosomes and stains easily.

chromatography (,krəʊmə'tɒgrəfɪ) n. the technique of separating and analysing the components of a mixture of liquids or gases by selective adsorption.

chrome (krəʊm) n. 1. another word for **chromium**. 2. anything plated with chromium. ~vb. 3. to plate or be plated with chromium.

chromite ('krəʊmaɪt) n. a brownish-black mineral which is the only commercial source of chromium.

chromium ('krəʊmɪəm) n. a hard grey metallic element, used in steel alloys and electroplating to increase hardness and corrosion resistance. Symbol: Cr

chromosome ('krəʊmə,səʊm) n. any of the microscopic rod-shaped structures that appear in a cell nucleus during cell division, consisting of units (genes) that are responsible for the transmission of hereditary characteristics.

chromosphere ('krəʊmə,sfɪə) n. a gaseous layer of the sun's atmosphere extending from the photosphere to the corona.

chronic ('krɒnɪk) adj. 1. continuing for a long time; constantly recurring. 2. (of a disease) developing slowly or lasting for a long time. 3. hardened; habitual: a chronic smoker. 4. Informal. a. very bad: the play was chronic. b. very serious: he left her in a chronic condition. —'**chronically** adv. —**chronicity** (krɒ'nɪsɪtɪ) n.

chronicle ('krɒnɪk'l) n. 1. a record of events in chronological order. ~vb. 2. to record in or as if in a chronicle. —'**chronicler** n.

chronological (,krɒnə'lɒdʒɪk'l) adj. 1. (esp. of a sequence of events) arranged in order of occurrence. 2. relating to or in accordance with chronology. —,**chrono- 'logically** adv.

chronology (krə'nɒlədʒɪ) n., pl. -**gies**. 1. the determination of the proper sequence of past events. 2. the arrangement of dates or events in order of occurrence. 3. a table of events arranged in order of occurrence. —**chro'nologist** n.

chronometer (krə'nɒmɪtə) n. a timepiece designed to be accurate in all conditions: used esp. at sea.

chrysalis ('krɪsəlɪs) n. the pupa of a moth or butterfly, in a case or cocoon.

chrysanthemum (krɪ'sænθəməm) n. a garden plant with brightly coloured showy flower heads in autumn.

chrysoberyl ('krɪsə,berɪl) n. a rare very hard greenish-yellow mineral used as a gemstone.

chrysolite ('krɪsə,laɪt) n. a brown or yellowish-green olivine: used as a gemstone.

chrysoprase ('krɪsə,preɪz) n. an apple-green variety of chalcedony: used as a gemstone.

chub (tʃʌb) n., pl. **chub** or **chubs**. a common European freshwater game fish of the carp family with a cylindrical dark greenish body.

chubby ('tʃʌbɪ) adj. -**bier**, -**biest**. (esp. of the human form) plump and round. —'**chubbiness** n.

chuck[1] (tʃʌk) vb. 1. Informal. to throw. 2. to pat (someone) affectionately under the chin. 3. Informal. (sometimes foll. by in or up) to give up; reject: he chucked up his job. ~n. 4. a throw or toss. 5. a pat under the chin. ~See also **chuck off, chuck out**.

chuck[2] (tʃʌk) n. 1. Also: **chuck steak**. a cut of beef from the neck to the shoulder blade. 2. a device that holds a workpiece in a lathe or a tool in a drill.

chuck[3] (tʃʌk) n. W Canada. 1. a large body of water. 2. Also: **saltchuck**. the sea.

chuckle ('tʃʌk'l) vb. 1. to laugh softly or to oneself. ~n. 2. a partly suppressed laugh.

chuck off vb. (often foll. by at) Austral. & N.Z. informal. to sneer.

chuck out vb. Informal. to throw out.

chuddy ('tʃʌdɪ) n. Austral. & N.Z. informal. chewing gum.

chuff (tʃʌf) n. 1. a puffing sound, as of a steam engine. ~vb. 2. to move while emitting such sounds.

chuffed (tʃʌft) adj. Brit. slang. pleased or delighted: he was chuffed by his pay rise.

chug (tʃʌg) n. 1. a short dull sound, as of an engine. ~vb. **chugging, chugged**. 2. (esp. of an engine) to operate while making such sounds.

chukker *or* **chukka** (ˈtʃʌkə) *n. Polo.* a period of continuous play, usually 7½ minutes.

chum (tʃʌm) *n.* **1.** *Informal.* a close friend. ~*vb.* **chumming, chummed.** **2.** (usually foll. by *up with*) to be or become a close friend (of).

chummy (ˈtʃʌmɪ) *adj.* **-mier, -miest.** *Informal.* friendly. —ˈchummily *adv.* —ˈchumminess *n.*

chump (tʃʌmp) *n.* **1.** *Informal.* a stupid person. **2.** a thick heavy block of wood. **3.** the thick blunt end of anything, esp. of a piece of meat. **4. off one's chump.** *Brit. slang.* crazy.

chunk (tʃʌŋk) *n.* **1.** a thick solid piece, such as one of meat or wood. **2.** a considerable amount.

chunky (ˈtʃʌŋkɪ) *adj.* **chunkier, chunkiest.** **1.** thick and short. **2.** containing thick pieces. **3.** *Chiefly Brit.* (of clothes, esp. knitwear) made of thick bulky material. —ˈchunkiness *n.*

church (tʃɜːtʃ) *n.* **1.** a building for public Christian worship. **2.** public worship. **3.** the clergy as distinguished from the laity. **4.** (*usually cap.*) institutional religion as a political or social force: *conflict between Church and State.* **5.** (*usually cap.*) the collective body of all Christians. **6.** (*often cap.*) a particular Christian denomination or group.

churchgoer (ˈtʃɜːtʃˌɡəʊə) *n.* a person who attends church regularly.

Church of England *n.* the reformed established state Church in England, with the sovereign as its temporal head.

Church of Scotland *n.* the established Presbyterian church in Scotland.

churchwarden (ˌtʃɜːtʃˈwɔːdən) *n.* **1.** *Church of England, Episcopal Church.* one of two assistants of a parish priest who administer the secular affairs of the church. **2.** a long-stemmed tobacco pipe made of clay.

churchyard (ˈtʃɜːtʃˌjɑːd) *n.* the grounds round a church, used as a graveyard.

churl (tʃɜːl) *n.* **1.** a surly ill-bred person. **2.** *Archaic.* a farm labourer. —ˈchurlish *adj.*

churn (tʃɜːn) *n.* **1.** *Brit.* a large container for milk. **2.** a vessel or machine in which cream or whole milk is vigorously agitated to produce butter. ~*vb.* **3. a.** to agitate (milk or cream) to make butter. **b.** to make (butter) by this process. **4.** (sometimes foll. by *up*) to move with agitation.

churn out *vb. Informal.* to produce (something) rapidly and in large numbers.

chute[1] (ʃuːt) *n.* an inclined channel or vertical passage down which water, parcels, coal, etc., may be dropped.

chute[2] (ʃuːt) *n., vb. Informal.* short for **parachute.**

chutney (ˈtʃʌtnɪ) *n.* a pickle of Indian origin, made from fruit, vinegar, spices, and sugar: *mango chutney.*

chutzpah (ˈxʊtspə) *n. U.S. & Canad. informal.* shameless audacity; impudence.

chyle (kaɪl) *n.* a milky fluid formed in the small intestine during digestion.

chyme (kaɪm) *n.* the thick fluid mass of partially digested food that leaves the stomach.

chypre (ˈʃiːprə) *n.* a perfume made from sandalwood.

Ci curie.

CI Channel Islands.

CIA Central Intelligence Agency; a U.S. bureau that conducts espionage and intelligence activities.

cicada (sɪˈkɑːdə) *n.* a large broad insect, most common in warm regions: the males produce a high-pitched drone.

cicatrix (ˈsɪkətrɪks) *n., pl.* **cicatrices** (ˌsɪkəˈtraɪsiːz). the tissue that forms in a wound during healing; scar.

cicerone (ˌsɪsəˈrəʊnɪ, ˌtʃɪtʃ-) *n., pl.* **-nes** *or* **-ni** (-nɪ). a person who guides and informs sightseers.

CID (in Britain) Criminal Investigation Department; the detective division of a police force.

cider (ˈsaɪdə) *n.* an alcoholic drink made from the fermented juice of apples.

CIF cost, insurance, and freight (included in the price quoted).

cigar (sɪˈɡɑː) *n.* a cylindrical roll of cured tobacco leaves, for smoking.

cigarette (ˌsɪɡəˈrɛt) *n.* a short tightly rolled cylinder of tobacco, wrapped in thin paper for smoking.

cilium (ˈsɪlɪəm) *n., pl.* **cilia** (ˈsɪlɪə). **1.** any of the short threads projecting from a cell or organism, whose rhythmic beating causes movement. **2.** an eyelash. —ˈciliary *adj.*

C in C *Mil.* Commander in Chief.

cinch (sɪntʃ) *n.* **1.** *Slang.* an easy task. **2.** *Slang.* a certainty. **3.** *U.S. & Canad.* same as **girth** (sense 2).

cinchona (sɪŋˈkəʊnə) *n.* **1.** a South American tree or shrub with medicinal bark. **2.** its dried bark which yields quinine. **3.** a drug made from cinchona bark.

cincture (ˈsɪŋktʃə) *n.* something that encircles, esp. a belt or girdle.

cinder (ˈsɪndə) *n.* **1.** a piece of material that will not burn, left after burning coal or wood. **2.** (*pl.*) ashes.

Cinderella (ˌsɪndəˈrɛlə) *n.* **1.** a girl who achieves fame after being obscure. **2.** a poor, neglected, or unsuccessful person or thing.

cine- *combining form.* indicating motion pictures or cinema: *cine camera.*

cinema (ˈsɪnɪmə) *n.* **1.** *Chiefly Brit.* a place designed for showing films. **2. the cinema. a.** the art or business of making films. **b.**

films collectively. —**cinematic** (ˌsɪnɪ-ˈmætɪk) *adj.*

cinematograph (ˌsɪnɪˈmætəˌgrɑːf) *Chiefly Brit.* ~*n.* **1.** a combined camera, printer, and projector. ~*vb.* **2.** to take (pictures) with a film camera. —**cinematographer** (ˌsɪnɪməˈtɒgrəfə) *n.* —**cinematographic** (ˌsɪnɪˌmætəˈgræfɪk) *adj.* —ˌcinemaˈtography *n.*

cineraria (ˌsɪnəˈrɛərɪə) *n.* a plant grown for its blue, purple, red, or variegated daisy-like flowers.

cinerarium (ˌsɪnəˈrɛərɪəm) *n., pl.* -**raria** (-ˈrɛərɪə). a place for keeping the ashes of the dead after cremation. —**cinerary** (ˈsɪnərərɪ) *adj.*

cinnabar (ˈsɪnəˌbɑː) *n.* **1.** a heavy red mineral: the chief ore of mercury. **2.** a large red-and-black European moth. ~*adj.* **3.** bright red; vermilion.

cinnamon (ˈsɪnəmən) *n.* **1.** the spice obtained from the aromatic bark of a tropical Asian tree, used for flavouring food and drink. ~*adj.* **2.** light yellowish-brown.

cinque (sɪŋk) *n.* the number five in cards or dice.

cinquefoil (ˈsɪŋkˌfɔɪl) *n.* **1.** a plant with five-lobed compound leaves. **2.** an ornamental carving in the form of five arcs arranged in a circle.

Cinque Ports *pl. n.* an association of ports on the SE coast of England, with certain ancient duties and privileges.

cipher *or* **cypher** (ˈsaɪfə) *n.* **1.** a method of secret writing using substitution of letters according to a key. **2.** a secret message. **3.** the key to a secret message. **4.** *Obs.* the numeral zero. **5.** a person or thing of no importance; nonentity. ~*vb.* **6.** to put (a message) into secret writing.

circa (ˈsɜːkə) *prep.* (used with a date) approximately; about: *circa 1182 B.C.*

circadian (sɜːˈkeɪdɪən) *adj.* of biological processes that occur regularly at 24-hour intervals.

circle (ˈsɜːkᵊl) *n.* **1.** a closed plane curve every point of which is equidistant from a given fixed point, the centre. **2.** the figure enclosed by such a curve. **3.** *Theatre.* the section of seats above the main level of the auditorium. **4.** something formed or arranged in the shape of a circle. **5.** a group of people sharing an interest, activity, or upbringing: *golf circles; a family circle.* **6.** a process or chain of events or parts that forms a connected whole; cycle. **7. come full circle.** to arrive back at one's starting point. ~*vb.* **8.** to move in a circle (around). **9.** to enclose in a circle; encircle.

circlet (ˈsɜːklɪt) *n.* a small circle or ring, esp. a circular ornament worn on the head.

circuit (ˈsɜːkɪt) *n.* **1.** a complete route or course, esp. one that is circular or that lies around an object. **2.** a complete path

through which an electric current can flow. **3. a.** a periodical journey around an area, as made by judges or salesmen. **b.** the places visited on such a journey. **4.** a number of theatres or cinemas under one management. **5.** *Sport.* a series of tournaments in which the same players regularly take part: *the international tennis circuit.* **6.** *Chiefly Brit.* a motor-racing track.

circuit breaker *n.* a device that stops the flow of current in an electrical circuit if there is a fault.

circuitous (səˈkjuːɪtəs) *adj.* indirect and lengthy; roundabout: *a circuitous route.*

circuitry (ˈsɜːkɪtrɪ) *n.* **1.** the design of an electrical circuit. **2.** the system of circuits used in an electronic device.

circular (ˈsɜːkjʊlə) *adj.* **1.** of or like a circle. **2.** circuitous. **3.** (of arguments) not valid because a statement is used to prove the conclusion and the conclusion to prove the statement. **4.** travelling or occurring in a cycle. **5.** (of letters or announcements) intended for general distribution. ~*n.* **6.** a printed advertisement or notice for mass distribution. —**circularity** (ˌsɜːkjʊˈlærɪtɪ) *n.*

circularize *or* -**ise** (ˈsɜːkjʊləˌraɪz) *vb.* to distribute circulars to.

circular saw *n.* a power-driven saw in which a circular disc with a toothed edge is rotated at high speed.

circulate (ˈsɜːkjʊˌleɪt) *vb.* **1.** to send, go, or pass from place to place or person to person: *don't circulate the news.* **2.** to distribute or be distributed over a wide area. **3.** to move or cause to move through a circuit or system, returning to the starting point: *blood circulates through the body.* —ˈcirculatory *adj.*

circulating library *n. Chiefly U.S.* a library that lends out books.

circulation (ˌsɜːkjʊˈleɪʃən) *n.* **1.** the flow of blood from the heart through the arteries, and then back through the veins to the heart, where the cycle is renewed. **2.** the spreading of something to a wider group of people or area. **3.** (of air and water) free movement within an area or volume. **4. a.** the distribution of newspapers or magazines. **b.** the number of copies of an issue that are distributed. **5. in circulation. a.** (of currency) serving as a medium of exchange. **b.** (of people) active in a social or business context.

circum- *prefix.* around; surrounding; on all sides: *circumlocution.*

circumambient (ˌsɜːkəmˈæmbɪənt) *adj.* surrounding.

circumcise (ˈsɜːkəmˌsaɪz) *vb.* **1.** to remove the foreskin of (a male). **2.** to incise the skin over, or remove, the clitoris of (a female). **3.** to perform such an operation as a religious rite on (someone). —**circumcision** (ˌsɜːkəmˈsɪʒən) *n.*

circumference (sə'kʌmfərəns) n. 1. the boundary of a specific area or figure, esp. of a circle. 2. the length of a closed geometric curve, esp. of a circle. —**circumferential** (sə,kʌmfə'rɛnʃəl) adj.

circumflex ('sɜːkəm,flɛks) n. a mark (ˆ) placed over a vowel to show that it is pronounced in a particular way, for instance as a long vowel in French.

circumlocution (,sɜːkəmlə'kjuːʃən) n. 1. an indirect way of expressing something. 2. an indirect expression. —**circumlocutory** (,sɜːkəm'lɒkjətrɪ) adj.

circumnavigate (,sɜːkəm'nævɪ,geɪt) vb. to sail or fly completely around. —,**circum-,navi'gation** n.

circumscribe ('sɜːkəm,skraɪb) vb. 1. to restrict within limits. 2. to mark or set the bounds of. 3. to draw a geometric construction around (another construction) so that the two are in contact but do not intersect. —**circumscription** (,sɜːkəm-'skrɪpʃən) n.

circumspect ('sɜːkəm,spɛkt) adj. cautious, prudent, or discreet. —,**circum'spection** n. —'**circum,spectly** adv.

circumstance ('sɜːkəmstəns) n. 1. (usually pl.) a condition that accompanies or influences an event or condition. 2. an incident or occurrence, esp. a chance one. 3. **pomp and circumstance.** formal display or ceremony. 4. **under** or **in no circumstances.** in no case; never. 5. **under the circumstances.** because of conditions; this being the case.

circumstantial (,sɜːkəm'stænʃəl) adj. 1. of or dependent on circumstances. 2. fully detailed.

circumstantial evidence n. indirect evidence that tends to establish a conclusion by inference.

circumstantiate (,sɜːkəm'stænʃɪ,eɪt) vb. to support by giving particulars.

circumvent (,sɜːkəm'vɛnt) vb. 1. to avoid or get round (a rule, restriction etc.). 2. to outwit (a person). —,**circum'vention** n.

circus ('sɜːkəs) n., pl. **-cuses.** 1. a travelling company of entertainers such as acrobats, clowns, trapeze artists, and trained animals. 2. a public performance given by such a company. 3. a travelling group of professional sportsmen: a cricket circus. 4. (in ancient Rome) an open-air stadium for chariot races or public games. 5. Brit. an open place in a town where several streets converge. 6. Informal. noisy or rowdy behaviour.

cirrhosis (sɪ'rəusɪs) n. a chronic progressive disease of the liver, often caused by drinking too much alcohol.

cirrocumulus (,sɪrəu'kjuːmjuləs) n., pl. **-li** (-,laɪ). a high cloud of ice crystals grouped into small separate globular masses.

cirrostratus (,sɪrəu'strɑːtəs) n., pl. **-ti** (-taɪ). a uniform layer of cloud above about 6000 metres.

cirrus ('sɪrəs) n., pl. **-ri** (-raɪ). 1. a thin wispy fibrous cloud at high altitudes, composed of ice particles. 2. a plant tendril. 3. a slender tentacle in certain sea creatures.

cisalpine (sɪs'ælpaɪn) adj. on this (the southern) side of the Alps, as viewed from Rome.

cisco ('sɪskəu) n., pl. **-coes** or **-cos.** a whitefish, esp. the lake herring of cold deep lakes of North America.

cissy ('sɪsɪ) n., pl. **-sies,** adj. same as **sissy.**

Cistercian (sɪ'stɜːʃən) n. 1. a monk or nun who follows an especially strict form of the Benedictine rule. ~adj. 2. of or relating to this order.

cistern ('sɪstən) n. 1. a tank for the storage of water, esp. on or within the roof of a house or connected to a WC. 2. an underground reservoir.

citadel ('sɪtəd'l, -,dɛl) n. a stronghold within or close to a city.

citation (saɪ'teɪʃən) n. 1. the quoting of a book or author. 2. a passage or source cited. 3. an official commendation or award, esp. for bravery.

cite (saɪt) vb. 1. to quote or refer to (a passage, book, or author). 2. to mention or commend (someone) for outstanding bravery. 3. to summon to appear before a court of law. 4. to enumerate: he cited the king's virtues.

citified ('sɪtɪ,faɪd) adj. Often disparaging. having the customs, manners, or dress of city people.

citizen ('sɪtɪz'n) n. 1. a native or naturalized member of a state or nation. 2. an inhabitant of a city or town.

citizenry ('sɪtɪzənrɪ) n. citizens collectively.

Citizens' Band n. a range of radio frequencies assigned officially for use by the public for private communication.

citizenship ('sɪtɪzən,ʃɪp) n. the condition or status of a citizen, with its rights and duties.

citrate ('sɪtreɪt, -rɪt; 'saɪtreɪt) n. any salt or ester of citric acid.

citric ('sɪtrɪk) adj. of or derived from citrus fruits or citric acid.

citric acid n. a weak acid found in many fruits, esp. citrus fruits, and used in pharmaceuticals and as a flavouring (**E330**).

citron ('sɪtrən) n. 1. a lemon-like fruit with a thick aromatic rind, which grows on a small Asian tree. 2. the candied rind of this fruit.

citronella (,sɪtrə'nɛlə) n. 1. a tropical Asian grass with bluish-green lemon-scented leaves. 2. the yellow aromatic oil obtained from this grass, used in insect repellents, soaps, and perfumes.

citrus ('sɪtrəs) n., pl. **-ruses.** 1. any tree or

shrub of a tropical and subtropical genus which includes the orange, lemon, and lime. ~*adj. also* **citrous**. **2.** of or relating to the plants of this genus or their fruits.

city (ˈsɪtɪ) *n., pl.* **cities**. **1.** any large town. **2.** (in Britain) a town that has received this title from the Crown: usually the seat of a bishop. **3.** (in the U.S. and Canada) a large town with its own government established by charter from the state or provincial government. **4.** the people of a city collectively.

City (ˈsɪtɪ) *n.* **the. 1.** the area in central London in which the United Kingdom's major financial business is transacted. **2.** the various financial institutions in this area.

city editor *n.* (on a newspaper) **1.** *Brit.* the editor in charge of business news. **2.** *U.S. & Canad.* the editor in charge of local news.

city-state *n. Ancient history.* a state consisting of a sovereign city and its dependencies.

civet (ˈsɪvɪt) *n.* **1.** a spotted catlike mammal of Africa and S Asia, which secretes a powerful-smelling fluid. **2.** this fluid, used in the manufacture of perfumes.

civic (ˈsɪvɪk) *adj.* of or relating to a city, citizens, or citizenship. —ˈ**civically** *adv.*

civic centre *n. Brit.* a complex of public buildings, including recreational facilities and offices of local administration.

civics (ˈsɪvɪks) *n.* (*functioning as sing.*) the study of the rights and responsibilities of citizenship.

civil (ˈsɪvˀl) *adj.* **1.** of the ordinary life of citizens, as distinguished from military, legal, or ecclesiastical affairs. **2.** of or relating to the citizen as an individual: *civil rights.* **3.** of or occurring within the state or between citizens: *civil strife.* **4.** polite or courteous: *a civil manner.* —ˈ**civilly** *adv.*

civil defence *n.* the organizing of civilians to deal with enemy attacks.

civil disobedience *n.* a nonviolent protest, such as a refusal to obey laws or pay taxes.

civil engineer *n.* a person qualified to design and construct public works, such as roads or harbours. —**civil engineering** *n.*

civilian (sɪˈvɪljən) *n.* **a.** a person who is not a member of the armed forces or police. **b.** (*as modifier*): *civilian life.*

civility (sɪˈvɪlɪtɪ) *n., pl.* -**ties. 1.** politeness or courtesy. **2.** (*often pl.*) an act of politeness.

civilization *or* -**isation** (ˌsɪvɪlaɪˈzeɪʃən) *n.* **1.** a human society that has a complex cultural, political, and legal organization. **2.** the peoples or nations collectively who have achieved such a state. **3.** the total culture and way of life of a particular people, nation, region, or period. **4.** intellectual, cultural, and moral refinement. **5.**

cities or populated areas, as contrasted with sparsely inhabited areas.

civilize *or* -**ise** (ˈsɪvɪˌlaɪz) *vb.* **1.** to bring out of savagery or barbarism into a state of civilization. **2.** to refine, educate, or enlighten. —ˈ**civi,lized** *or* -**ised** *adj.*

civil law *n.* **1.** the law of a state, relating to private and civilian affairs. **2.** a system of law based on that of ancient Rome.

civil list *n.* (in Britain) the annual amount given by Parliament to the royal household and the royal family.

civil marriage *n. Law.* a marriage performed by an official other than a clergyman.

civil rights *pl. n.* **1.** the personal rights of the individual citizen. **2.** (*modifier*) of, relating to, or promoting equality in social, economic, and political rights.

civil servant *n.* a member of the civil service.

civil service *n.* the service responsible for the public administration of the government of a country. It excludes the legislative, judicial, and military branches.

civil war *n.* war between parties or factions within the same nation.

civvies (ˈsɪvɪz) *pl. n. Slang.* civilian clothes as opposed to uniform.

civvy street (ˈsɪvɪ) *n. Slang.* civilian life.

Cl *Chem.* chlorine.

clack (klæk) *vb.* **1.** to make a sound like that of two pieces of wood hitting each other. ~*n.* **2.** a short sharp sound.

clad[1] (klæd) *vb.* past of **clothe.**

clad[2] (klæd) *vb.* **cladding, clad.** to bond a metal to (another metal), esp. to form a protective coating.

cladding (ˈklædɪŋ) *n.* **1.** a protective metal coating bonded to another metal. **2.** the material used for the outside facing of a building, etc.

cladistics (kləˈdɪstɪks) *n.* (*functioning as sing.*) a method of grouping animals by measurable likenesses.

claim (kleɪm) *vb.* **1.** to demand as being due or as one's property: *he claimed the record.* **2.** to assert as a fact: *he claimed to be telling the truth.* **3.** to call for or need; deserve: *this problem claims our attention.* **4.** to take: *the accident claimed four lives.* ~*n.* **5.** an assertion of a right; a demand for something as due. **6.** an assertion of something as true, real, or factual. **7.** a right or just title to something: *a claim to fame.* **8.** anything that is claimed, such as a piece of land staked out by a miner. **9. a.** a demand for payment in connection with an insurance policy. **b.** the sum of money demanded. —ˈ**claimant** *n.*

clairvoyance (kleəˈvɔɪəns) *n.* **1.** the alleged power of perceiving things beyond the natural range of the senses. **2.** keen intuitive understanding.

clairvoyant (klɛə'vɔɪənt) *adj.* **1.** of or possessing clairvoyance. ~*n.* **2.** a person claiming to have the power to foretell future events.

clam (klæm) *n.* a sea creature with a soft edible body and a shell in two parts that closes tightly. See also **clam up.**

clamber ('klæmbə) *vb.* **1.** to climb (something) awkwardly, using hands and feet. ~*n.* **2.** a climb performed in this manner.

clammy ('klæmɪ) *adj.* **-mier, -miest. 1.** unpleasantly sticky; moist. **2.** (of the weather) close; humid. —'**clammily** *adv.* —'**clamminess** *n.*

clamour *or U.S.* **clamor** ('klæmə) *n.* **1.** a loud persistent outcry. **2.** a strong expression of collective feeling or outrage. **3.** a loud and persistent noise. ~*vb.* **4.** (often foll. by *for* or *against*) to make a loud noise or outcry; make a public demand. —'**clamorous** *adj.*

clamp[1] (klæmp) *n.* **1.** a mechanical device with movable jaws with which an object can be secured to something else. **2.** See **wheel clamp.** ~*vb.* **3.** to fix or fasten with a clamp. **4.** to immobilize (a car) by means of a wheel clamp.

clamp[2] (klæmp) *n.* a mound of a harvested root crop, covered with straw and earth to protect it from winter weather.

clamp down *vb.* **1.** (often foll. by *on*) to suppress (something regarded as undesirable). ~*n.* **clampdown. 2.** a sudden restrictive measure.

clam up *vb.* **clamming, clammed.** *Informal.* to keep or become silent.

clan (klæn) *n.* **1.** a group of people interrelated by ancestry or marriage. **2.** a group of families with a common surname and a common ancestor, esp. among the Scots. **3.** a group of people united by common characteristics, aims, or interests. —'**clansman** *n.*

clandestine (klæn'dɛstɪn) *adj.* secret and concealed; furtive. —**clan'destinely** *adv.*

clang (klæŋ) *vb.* **1.** to make a loud resounding noise, as metal when struck. ~*n.* **2.** a resounding metallic noise.

clanger ('klæŋə) *n.* **drop a clanger.** *Informal.* to make a conspicuous mistake.

clangour *or U.S.* **clangor** ('klæŋgə, 'klæŋə) *n.* **1.** a loud resonant often-repeated noise. ~*vb.* **2.** to make or produce a loud resonant noise. —'**clangorous** *adj.*

clank (klæŋk) *n.* **1.** an abrupt harsh metallic sound. ~*vb.* **2.** to make such a sound.

clannish ('klænɪʃ) *adj.* **1.** of or characteristic of a clan. **2.** tending to associate closely within a group to the exclusion of outsiders; cliquish.

clap[1] (klæp) *vb.* **clapping, clapped. 1.** to make a sharp abrupt sound, as of two objects struck together. **2.** to applaud (someone or something) by striking the palms of one's hands together sharply. **3.** to strike (a person) lightly with an open hand as in greeting. **4.** to place or put quickly or forcibly: *they clapped him in jail.* **5. clap eyes on.** *Informal.* to catch sight of. ~*n.* **6.** the sharp abrupt sound produced by striking one's hands together. **7.** the act of clapping, esp. in applause. **8.** a sudden sharp sound, esp. of thunder. **9.** a light blow.

clap[2] (klæp) *n.* (usually preceded by *the*) *Slang.* gonorrhoea.

clapped out *adj. Informal.* **1.** *Brit., Austral., & N.Z.* worn out; dilapidated. **2.** *Austral. & N.Z.* extremely tired; exhausted.

clapper ('klæpə) *n.* **1.** a small piece of metal hanging inside a bell, which causes it to sound when struck against its side. **2. go, run,** *or* **move like the clappers.** *Brit. informal.* to move extremely fast.

clapperboard ('klæpə,bɔːd) *n.* a pair of hinged boards clapped together during film shooting to aid in synchronizing sound and picture prints.

claptrap ('klæp,træp) *n. Informal.* foolish or pretentious talk: *politicians' claptrap.*

claque (klæk) *n.* **1.** a group of people hired to applaud. **2.** a group of fawning admirers.

claret ('klærət) *n.* **1.** a red wine, esp. a Bordeaux. ~*adj.* **2.** purplish-red.

clarify ('klærɪ,faɪ) *vb.* **-fying, -fied. 1.** to make or become clear or easy to understand. **2.** to make or become free of impurities, esp. by heating: *clarified butter.* —,**clarifi'cation** *n.*

clarinet (,klærɪ'nɛt) *n.* a keyed woodwind instrument with a single reed. —,**clari'nettist** *n.*

clarion ('klærɪən) *n.* **1.** an obsolete high-pitched small-bore trumpet. **2.** the sound of such an instrument or any similar sound. ~*adj.* **3.** clear and ringing; inspiring: *a clarion call to action.*

clarity ('klærɪtɪ) *n.* clearness.

clash (klæʃ) *vb.* **1.** to make a loud harsh sound, esp. by striking together. **2.** to be incompatible. **3.** to engage together in conflict. **4.** (of dates or events) to coincide. **5.** (of colours) to look inharmonious together. ~*n.* **6.** a loud harsh noise. **7.** a collision or conflict.

clasp (klɑːsp) *n.* **1.** a fastening, such as a catch or hook, for holding things together. **2.** a firm grasp or embrace. ~*vb.* **3.** to hold in a firm grasp. **4.** to grasp tightly in one's hands or arms. **5.** to fasten together with a clasp.

clasp knife *n.* a large knife with blades which fold into the handle.

class (klɑːs) *n.* **1.** a group of people or things sharing a common characteristic. **2.** a group of persons sharing a similar social and economic position. **3.** the pattern of divisions that exist within a society on the basis of social or economic status. **4. a.** a group of pupils or students who are taught together. **b.** a meeting of a group of students for tuition. **5.** one of several grades, of accommodation, quality, or attainment: *second class.* **6.** *Informal.* excellence or elegance, esp. in dress, design, or behaviour. **7.** *Biol.* any of the groups into which a phylum is divided. **8. in a class by oneself** *or* **in a class of its own.** unequalled; unparalleled. ~*vb.* **9.** to assign a place within a group, grade, or class.

class. 1. classic(al). 2. classification. 3. classified.

class-conscious *adj.* aware of belonging to a particular social rank.

classic ('klæsɪk) *adj.* **1.** of the highest class, esp. in art or literature. **2.** serving as a standard or model of its kind. **3.** characterized by simplicity, balance, regularity, and purity of form; classical. **4.** of lasting interest or significance. ~*n.* **5.** an author, artist, or work of art of the highest excellence. **6.** a creation or work considered as definitive.

Usage. The adjectives *classic* and *classical* can often be treated as synonyms, but there are two contexts in which they are not interchangeable. *Classic* is applied to things which are of the first rank, esp. in art and literature, as in: *Lewis Carroll's classic works for children. Classical* is used to refer to ancient Greek and Roman culture.

classical ('klæsɪk³l) *adj.* **1.** of or influenced by the ancient Greeks and Romans or their civilization. **2.** *Music.* **a.** in a style or from a period marked by stability of form, intellectualism, and restraint. **b.** denoting serious art music in general. **3.** of or in a restrained conservative style: *a classical style of painting.* **4.** (of an education) based on the humanities and the study of Latin and Greek. **5.** of the form of a language historically used for formal and literary purposes: *classical Arabic.* —'**classically** *adv.*

Usage. see **classic.**

classicism ('klæsɪ,sɪzəm) *n.* **1.** a style based on Greek and Roman models, showing emotional restraint and regularity of form. **2.** knowledge of the culture of ancient Greece and Rome. **3.** a Greek or Latin expression. —'**classicist** *n.*

classics ('klæsɪks) *pl. n.* **1. the.** a body of literature regarded as great or lasting. **2. the.** the ancient Greek and Latin languages. **3.** (*functioning as sing.*) ancient Greek and Roman culture as a subject for academic study.

classification (,klæsɪfɪ'keɪʃən) *n.* **1.** systematic placement in categories. **2.** one of the divisions in a system of classifying. —,**classifi'catory** *adj.*

classify ('klæsɪ,faɪ) *vb.* **-fying, -fied. 1.** to arrange or order by classes; categorize. **2.** *Government.* to declare (information) to be of possible aid to an enemy and therefore to be kept secret. —'**classi,fiable** *adj.*

classmate ('klɑːs,meɪt) *n.* a friend or contemporary of the same class in a school.

classroom ('klɑːs,ruːm, -,rʊm) *n.* a room in which classes are conducted, esp. in a school.

classy ('klɑːsɪ) *adj.* **classier, classiest.** *Slang.* elegant; stylish. —'**classiness** *n.*

clatter ('klætə) *vb.* **1.** to make a rattling noise, esp. as a result of movement. ~*n.* **2.** a rattling sound or noise.

clause (klɔːz) *n.* **1.** *Grammar.* a group of words, consisting of a subject and a predicate including a finite verb, that does not necessarily constitute a sentence. **2.** a section of a legal document such as a contract, will, or draft statute. —'**clausal** *adj.*

claustrophobia (,klɔːstrə'fəʊbɪə, ,klɒs-) *n.* an abnormal fear of being in a confined space. —,**claustro'phobic** *adj.*

clavichord ('klævɪ,kɔːd) *n.* an early keyboard instrument with a very soft tone.

clavicle ('klævɪk³l) *n.* either of the two bones connecting the shoulder blades with the upper part of the breastbone; the collarbone.

claw (klɔː) *n.* **1.** a curved pointed nail on the foot of birds, some reptiles, and certain mammals. **2.** a corresponding structure in some invertebrates, such as the pincer of a crab. ~*vb.* **3.** to scrape, tear, or dig (something or someone) with claws. **4.** to create by scratching as with claws: *to claw an opening.*

claw back *vb.* **1.** to get back (something) with difficulty. **2.** to recover (a part of a grant or allowance) in the form of a tax or financial penalty.

clay (kleɪ) *n.* **1.** a very fine-grained material that occurs as rock or soil. It becomes plastic when moist but hardens on heating and is used in the manufacture of bricks, ceramics, etc. **2.** earth or mud. **3.** *Poetic.* the material of the human body. —'**clayey,** '**clayish,** *or* '**clay,like** *adj.*

claymore ('kleɪ,mɔː) *n.* a large two-edged broadsword used formerly by Scottish Highlanders.

clay pigeon *n.* a disc of baked clay hurled into the air from a machine as a target to be shot at.

CLC Canadian Labour Congress.

clean (kliːn) *adj.* **1.** without dirt or other impurities; unsoiled. **2.** without anything in it or on it: *a clean page.* **3.** recently washed; fresh. **4.** free of radioactive contamination. **5.** pure; morally sound: *clean living.* **6.** without objectionable language or obscenity: *good clean fun.* **7.** thorough or complete: *a clean break.* **8.** dexterous or adroit: *a clean throw.* **9.** *Sport.* played fairly and without fouls. **10.** simple and streamlined in design: *a ship's clean lines.* **11.** habitually hygienic and neat. **12.** (esp. of a driving licence) showing or having no record of offences. **13.** *Slang.* **a.** innocent; not guilty. **b.** not carrying illegal drugs, weapons, etc. ~*vb.* **14.** to make or become free of dirt: *remember to clean your teeth; the stove cleans easily.* ~*adv.* **15.** in a clean way; cleanly. **16.** *Not standard.* completely: *clean forgotten.* **17. come clean.** *Informal.* to make a revelation or confession. ~*n.* **18.** the act or an instance of cleaning: *he gave his shoes a clean.* ~See also **clean up.**

clean-cut *adj.* **1.** clearly outlined; neat: *clean-cut lines of a ship.* **2.** definite.

cleaner ('kliːnə) *n.* **1.** a person, device, or substance that removes dirt, as from clothes or carpets. **2.** (*usually pl.*) a shop or firm that provides a dry-cleaning service. **3. take a person to the cleaners.** *Informal.* to rob or defraud a person.

cleanly *adv.* ('kliːnlɪ). **1.** in a fair manner. **2.** easily or smoothly. ~*adj.* ('klɛnlɪ), **-lier, -liest. 3.** habitually clean or neat. —**cleanliness** ('klɛnlɪnɪs) *n.*

cleanse (klɛnz) *vb.* **1.** to remove dirt, filth, etc., from. **2.** to remove guilt from. —**cleanser** *n.*

clean-shaven *adj.* (of men) having the facial hair shaved off.

clean up *vb.* **1.** to rid (something) of dirt, filth, or other impurities. **2.** to make (someone or something) orderly or presentable. **3.** to rid (a place) of undesirable people or conditions. **4.** *Informal.* to make a great profit. ~*n.* **cleanup. 5.** the process of cleaning up.

clear (klɪə) *adj.* **1.** free from darkness or obscurity; bright. **2.** (of weather) free from dullness or clouds. **3.** transparent: *clear water.* **4.** even and pure in tone or colour. **5.** without blemish or defect: *a clear skin.* **6.** easy to see or hear; distinct. **7.** free from doubt or confusion. **8.** certain in the mind; sure: *are you clear?* **9.** perceptive, alert: *clear-headed.* **10.** evident or obvious: *it is clear that he won't come now.* **11.** (of sounds or the voice) not harsh or hoarse. **12.** without qualification or limitation; complete: *a clear victory.* **13.** free of suspicion, guilt, or blame: *a clear conscience.* **14.** free of obstruction; open: *a clear passage.* **15.** free from debt or obligation. **16.** (of money) without deduction; net. ~*adv.* **17.** in a clear or distinct manner. **18.** (often foll. by *of*) not in contact (with); free: *stand clear of the gates.* ~*n.* **19.** a clear space. **20. in the clear.** free of suspicion, guilt, or blame. ~*vb.* **21.** to make or become free from darkness or obscurity. **22. a.** (of the weather) to become free from dullness, fog, or rain. **b.** (of mist or fog) to disappear. **23.** to free from impurity or blemish. **24.** to

free from doubt or confusion. **25.** to rid of objects or obstructions. **26.** to make or form (a path) by removing obstructions. **27.** to free or remove (a person or thing) from something, as of suspicion, blame, or guilt. **28.** to move or pass by or over without contact: *he cleared the wall easily.* **29.** to rid (one's throat) of phlegm. **30.** to make or gain (money) as profit. **31.** to discharge or settle (a debt). **32.** (of a cheque) to pass through one's bank and be charged against one's account. **33.** to obtain or give (clearance). **34.** to permit (someone) to see or handle classified information. **35. clear the air.** to dispel tension or confusion by settling misunderstandings. ~See also **clear away, clear off,** etc. —'**clearly** *adv.*

clearance ('klɪərəns) *n.* **1.** the process or an instance of clearing: *slum clearance.* **2.** space between two parts in motion or in relative motion. **3.** permission for a vehicle or passengers to proceed. **4.** official permission to have access to secret information or areas. **5. a.** the selling of goods at reduced prices. **b.** (*as modifier*): *a clearance sale.*

clear away *vb.* to remove (dishes, etc.) from (the table) after a meal.

clear-cut *adj.* **1.** definite; not vague: *a clear-cut proposal.* **2.** clearly outlined.

clearing ('klɪərɪŋ) *n.* an area with few or no trees or shrubs in wooded or overgrown land.

clearing bank *n.* (in Britain) any bank that makes use of the central clearing house in London.

clearing house *n.* **1.** *Banking.* an institution where cheques and other commercial papers drawn on member banks are cancelled against each other so that only net balances are payable. **2.** a central agency for the collection and distribution of information or materials.

clear off *vb.* *Informal.* to go away: often used imperatively.

clear out *vb.* **1.** *Informal.* to go away: often used imperatively. **2.** to remove and sort the contents of (a room or container).

clear up *vb.* **1.** to explain or solve (a mystery or misunderstanding). **2.** to put (a place or thing that is disordered) in order. **3.** (of the weather) to become brighter.

clearway ('klɪə,weɪ) *n.* *Brit.* a stretch of road on which motorists may stop only in an emergency.

cleat (kliːt) *n.* **1.** a wedge-shaped block attached to a structure to act as a support. **2.** a device consisting of two prongs projecting in opposite directions from a central base, used for tying ropes or lines to.

cleavage ('kliːvɪdʒ) *n.* **1.** *Informal.* the separation between a woman's breasts, esp. as revealed by a low-cut dress. **2.** a division or split. **3.** (of crystals) the act of splitting or the tendency to split along definite planes so as to yield smooth surfaces.

cleave[1] (kliːv) *vb.* **cleaving; cleft, cleaved,** *or* **clove; cleft, cleaved,** *or* **cloven.** **1.** to split, esp. along a natural weakness. **2.** to make by or as if by cutting: *to cleave a path.*

cleave[2] (kliːv) *vb.* to cling or adhere.

cleaver ('kliːvə) *n.* a heavy knife or long-bladed hatchet, esp. one used by butchers.

cleavers ('kliːvəz) *n.* (*functioning as sing.*) a Eurasian plant with small white flowers and fruits which stick to clothing.

clef (klɛf) *n.* a symbol placed at the beginning of each stave indicating the pitch of the music written after it.

cleft (klɛft) *vb.* **1.** past of **cleave**[1]. ~*n.* **2.** a fissure or crevice. **3.** an indentation or split in something, such as the chin, palate, etc. ~*adj.* **4.** split; divided.

cleft palate *n.* a congenital crack in the midline of the hard palate.

clematis ('klɛmətɪs, klə'meɪtɪs) *n.* a N temperate climbing plant cultivated for its large colourful flowers.

clement ('klɛmənt) *adj.* **1.** merciful. **2.** (of the weather) mild. —'**clemency** *n.*

clementine ('klɛmən,tiːn, -,taɪn) *n.* a citrus fruit resembling a tangerine.

clench (klɛntʃ) *vb.* **1.** to close or squeeze together (the teeth or a fist) tightly. **2.** to grasp or grip firmly. ~*n.* **3.** a firm grasp or grip.

clerestory ('klɪə,stɔːrɪ) *n.*, *pl.* **-ries.** a row of windows in the upper part of the wall of the nave of a church above the roof of the aisle.

clergy ('klɜːdʒɪ) *n.*, *pl.* **-gies.** the collective body of ordained ministers of the Christian Church.

clergyman ('klɜːdʒɪmən) *n.*, *pl.* **-men.** a member of the clergy.

cleric ('klɛrɪk) *n.* a member of the clergy.

clerical ('klɛrɪkᵊl) *adj.* **1.** relating to or associated with the clergy: *clerical dress.* **2.** of or relating to office clerks or their work: *a clerical error.*

clerical collar *n.* a stiff white collar with no opening at the front, which buttons at the back of the neck; worn by the clergy in certain Churches.

clerihew ('klɛrɪ,hjuː) *n.* a form of comic or satiric verse, consisting of two couplets and containing the name of a well-known person.

clerk (klɑːk; *U.S.* klɜːrk) *n.* **1.** an employee in an office, bank, or court who keeps records, files, and accounts. **2.** *U.S. & Canad.* a hotel receptionist. **3.** *Archaic.* a scholar. ~*vb.* **4.** to serve as a clerk. —'**clerkship** *n.*

clerk of the works *n.* an employee who oversees building work.

clever ('klɛvə) *adj.* **1.** displaying sharp intelligence or mental alertness. **2.** skilful with one's hands. **3.** smart in a superficial way. **4.** *Brit. informal.* sly; cunning. —'**cleverly** *adv.* —'**cleverness** *n.*

clianthus (klɪ'ænθəs) *n.* a plant of Australia and New Zealand with ornamental clusters of slender flowers.

cliché ('kliːʃeɪ) *n.* an expression, idea, action, or habit that has become trite from overuse. —'**clichéd** *or* '**cliché'd** *adj.*

click (klɪk) *n.* **1.** a short light often metallic sound. **2.** the locking member of a ratchet mechanism. ~*vb.* **3.** to make a clicking sound: *to click one's heels.* **4.** *Slang.* to be a great success: *that idea really clicked.* **5.** *Informal.* to become suddenly clear: *it finally clicked when her name was mentioned.* **6.** *Slang.* (of two people) to get on well together: *they clicked from their first meeting.*

client ('klaɪənt) *n.* **1.** someone who seeks the advice of a professional person or organization. **2.** a customer.

clientele (,kliːɒn'tɛl) *n.* customers or clients collectively.

cliff (klɪf) *n.* a steep high rock face, esp. along the seashore.

cliffhanger ('klɪf,hæŋə) *n.* a situation of imminent disaster usually occurring at the end of each episode of a serialized film. —'**cliff,hanging** *adj.*

climacteric (klaɪ'mæktərɪk, ,klaɪmæk'tɛrɪk) *n.* **1.** same as **menopause.** **2.** the period in the life of a man corresponding to the menopause, during which sexual drive and fertility diminish.

climate ('klaɪmɪt) *n.* **1.** the long-term prevalent weather conditions of an area. **2.** an area having a particular kind of climate. **3.** a prevailing trend: *the political climate.* —**climatic** (klaɪ'mætɪk) *adj.* —**cli'matically** *adv.*

climax ('klaɪmæks) *n.* **1.** the most intense or highest point of an experience or of a series of events: *the party was the climax of the week.* **2.** a decisive moment in a dramatic or other work. **3.** an orgasm. ~*vb.* **4.** *Not universally accepted.* to reach or bring to a climax. —**cli'mactic** *adj.*

climb (klaɪm) *vb.* **1.** (often foll. by *up*) to go up or ascend (stairs, a mountain, etc.). **2.** (often foll. by *along*) to progress with difficulty: *to climb along a ledge.* **3.** to rise to a higher point or intensity: *the temperature climbed.* **4.** to incline or slope upwards: *the road began to climb.* **5.** to ascend in social position. **6.** (of plants) to grow upwards by twining, using tendrils or suckers. **7.** *Informal.* (foll. by *into*) to put on or get into. ~*n.* **8.** the act or an instance of climbing. **9.** a place or thing to be climbed, esp. a route in mountaineering. —'**climbable** *adj.* —'**climber** *n.* —'**climbing** *n.*, *adj.*

climb down vb. 1. (often foll. by *from*) to retreat (from an opinion or position). ~n. **climb-down.** 2. a retreat from an opinion or position.

clime (klaim) n. *Poetic.* a region or its climate.

clinch (klintʃ) vb. 1. to secure (a driven nail) by bending the protruding point over. 2. to settle (something, such as an argument or bargain) in a definite way. 3. to engage in a clinch, as in boxing or wrestling. ~n. 4. the act of clinching. 5. *Boxing, wrestling.* an act or an instance in which one or both competitors hold on to the other to avoid punches or regain wind. 6. *Slang.* a lovers' embrace.

clincher ('klintʃə) n. *Informal.* something decisive, such as a fact, argument, or point scored.

cling (kliŋ) vb. **clinging, clung.** 1. (often foll. by *to*) to hold fast or adhere closely to (something), as by gripping or sticking. 2. (foll. by *together*) to remain in contact with each other. 3. to be or remain physically or emotionally close. —'**clinging** or '**clingy** adj.

clingfilm ('kliŋ,film) n. a thin polythene material having the power to seal closely: used for wrapping food.

clinic ('klinik) n. 1. a place in which outpatients are given medical treatment or advice. 2. a similar place staffed by specialist physicians or surgeons: *eye clinic.* 3. *Brit.* a private hospital or nursing home. 4. the teaching of medicine to students at the bedside.

clinical ('klinikᵊl) adj. 1. of or relating to a clinic. 2. of or relating to the observation and treatment of patients directly: *clinical medicine.* 3. scientifically detached; strictly objective: *a clinical attitude to life.* 4. (of buildings, decoration, or furniture) plain, simple, and usually unattractive. —'**clinically** adv.

clinical thermometer n. a thermometer for determining the temperature of the body.

clink¹ (kliŋk) vb. 1. to make a light and sharply ringing sound. ~n. 2. such a sound.

clink² (kliŋk) n. *Slang.* prison.

clinker ('kliŋkə) n. the ash and partially fused residues from a coal-fired furnace or fire.

clinker-built adj. (of a boat or ship) having a hull constructed with each plank overlapping the one below.

clip¹ (klip) vb. **clipping, clipped.** 1. to cut, snip, or trim with or as if with scissors or shears, esp. in order to shorten or remove a part. 2. *Brit.* to punch a hole in (something, esp. a ticket). 3. to remove a short section from (a film or newspaper). 4. to shorten (a word). 5. *Informal.* to strike with a

sharp, often slanting, blow. 6. *Slang.* to swindle, esp. by overcharging. ~n. 7. the act or process of clipping. 8. something clipped off. 9. a short extract from a film or newspaper. 10. *Informal.* a sharp, often slanting, blow. 11. *Informal.* speed: *a rapid clip.* 12. *Austral. & N.Z.* the total quantity of wool shorn, as in one place or season.

clip² (klip) n. 1. any of various small implements used to hold loose articles together or to attach one article to another. 2. an article of jewellery that can be clipped onto a dress or hat. 3. short for **paperclip** or **cartridge clip.** ~vb. **clipping, clipped.** 4. to hold together tightly, as with a clip.

clipboard ('klip,bɔːd) n. a portable writing board with a clip at the top for holding paper.

clip joint n. *Slang.* a place, such as a nightclub or restaurant, in which customers are overcharged.

clipper ('klipə) n. a fast sailing ship.

clippers ('klipəz) pl. n. 1. a hand tool for clipping fingernails, etc. 2. a hairdresser's tool for cutting short hair.

clippie ('klipi) n. *Brit. informal.* a bus conductress.

clipping ('klipiŋ) n. something cut out, esp. an article from a newspaper; cutting.

clique (kliːk) n. a small exclusive group of friends or associates. —'**cliquey, 'cliquy,** or **cliquish** adj.

clitoris ('klitəris, 'klai-) n. a small sexually sensitive erectile organ at the upper end of the vulva. —'**clitoral** adj.

Cllr councillor.

cloaca (kləʊ'eikə) n., pl. **-cae** (-siː). a cavity in most animals, except higher mammals, into which the alimentary canal and the genital and urinary ducts open.

cloak (kləʊk) n. 1. a loose sleeveless outer garment, fastened at the throat and falling straight from the shoulders. 2. something that covers or conceals. ~vb. 3. to cover with or as if with a cloak. 4. to hide or disguise.

cloak-and-dagger n. (*modifier*) of or involving intrigue and espionage.

cloakroom ('kləʊk,ruːm, -rʊm) n. 1. a room in which hats or coats may be temporarily left. 2. *Brit., euphemistic.* a toilet.

clobber¹ ('klɒbə) vb. *Slang.* 1. to batter. 2. to defeat utterly. 3. to criticize severely.

clobber² ('klɒbə) n. *Brit. slang.* personal belongings, such as clothes.

cloche (klɒʃ) n. 1. a small glass or plastic structure used to protect young plants. 2. a woman's close-fitting hat.

clock¹ (klɒk) n. 1. a device for showing the time, either through pointers that revolve over a numbered dial, or through a display of figures. 2. any clocklike device for recording or measuring something. 3. the downy head of a dandelion that has gone to seed. **4.** short for **time clock. 5.** *Informal.* same as **speedometer** or **mileometer. 6.** *Brit. slang.* the face. **7. round the clock.** all day and all night. ~*vb.* **8.** *Brit., Austral., & N.Z. slang.* to strike, esp. on the face or head. **9.** to record (time) as with a stopwatch, esp. in the calculation of speed. **10.** *Informal.* to turn back the mileometer on (a car) illegally so that its mileage appears less.

clock² (klɒk) *n.* an ornamental design on the side of a sock.

clock off *or* **out** *vb.* to depart from work, esp. when it involves registering the time of departure on a card.

clock on *or* **in** *vb.* to arrive at work, esp. when it involves registering the time of arrival on a card.

clock up *vb.* to record or register: *this car has clocked up 80 000 miles.*

clockwise (ˈklɒkˌwaɪz) *adv., adj.* in the direction in which the hands of a clock rotate.

clockwork (ˈklɒkˌwɜːk) *n.* **1.** the mechanism of a spring-driven clock. **2.** any similar mechanism, as in a wind-up toy. **3. like clockwork.** with complete regularity and precision; smoothly.

clod (klɒd) *n.* **1.** a lump of earth or clay. **2.** a dull or stupid person. —ˈ**cloddish** *adj.*

clodhopper (ˈklɒdˌhɒpə) *n. Informal.* **1.** a clumsy person; lout. **2.** (*usually pl.*) a large heavy shoe.

clog (klɒg) *vb.* **clogging, clogged. 1.** to obstruct or become obstructed with thick or sticky matter. **2.** to encumber; hinder. **3.** to stick in a mass. ~*n.* **4.** any of various wooden or wooden-soled shoes. **5.** something that impedes motion or action; hindrance.

cloisonné (klwɑːˈzɒneɪ) *n.* a design made by filling in a wire outline with coloured enamel.

cloister (ˈklɔɪstə) *n.* **1.** a covered walk, usually around a quadrangle in a religious institution, with an open colonnade on the inside. **2.** (*sometimes pl.*) a place of religious seclusion, such as a monastery. ~*vb.* **3.** to confine or seclude in or as if in a monastery. —ˈ**cloistered** *adj.* —ˈ**cloistral** *adj.*

clomp (klɒmp) *n., vb.* same as **clump** (senses 2, 3).

clone (kləʊn) *n.* **1.** a group of organisms or cells of the same genetic constitution that are descended from a common ancestor by asexual reproduction. **2.** *Informal.* a person or thing that closely resembles another. ~*vb.* **3.** to produce or cause to produce a clone. **4.** *Informal.* to produce near copies of (a person or thing). —ˈ**cloning** *n.*

clonk (klɒŋk) *vb.* **1.** to make a loud dull thud. **2.** *Informal.* to hit. ~*n.* **3.** a loud thud.

close¹ (kləʊs) *adj.* **1.** near in space or time; in proximity. **2.** having the parts near together; dense: *a close formation.* **3.** near to the surface; short: *a close haircut.* **4.** near in relationship: *a close relative.* **5.** intimate: *a close friend.* **6.** almost equal: *a close contest.* **7.** not deviating or varying greatly from something: *a close resemblance.* **8.** careful, strict, or searching: *a close study.* **9.** confined or enclosed. **10.** shut or shut tight. **11.** oppressive, heavy, or airless: *a close atmosphere.* **12.** strictly guarded: *close custody.* **13.** secretive or reticent. **14.** miserly; not generous. **15.** restricted as to public admission or membership. **16.** hidden or secluded. ~*adv.* **17.** closely; tightly. **18.** near or in proximity. —ˈ**closely** *adv.* —ˈ**closeness** *n.*

close² (kləʊz) *vb.* **1.** to shut: *the door closed behind him.* **2.** to bar, obstruct, or fill up (an entrance, a hole, etc.): *to close a road.* **3.** to bring the parts or edges of (something, such as a wound or circuit) together or (of a wound or circuit) to be brought together. **4.** to take hold: *his hand closed over the money.* **5.** to end; terminate. **6.** (of agreements or deals) to complete or be completed successfully. **7.** to cease or cause to cease giving service: *the shop closed at six.* **8.** *Stock Exchange.* to have a value at the end of a day's trading, as specified: *steels closed two points down.* ~*n.* **9.** the act of closing. **10.** the end or conclusion: *the close of the day.* **11.** (kləʊs). *Brit.* a courtyard or quadrangle enclosed by buildings. **12.** (kləʊs). *Scot.* the entry from the street to a tenement building. ~See also **close down, close in,** etc.

closed (kləʊzd) *adj.* **1.** blocked against entry; shut. **2.** restricted; exclusive. **3.** not open to question or debate. **4.** *Maths.* **a.** (of a curve or surface) completely enclosing an area or volume. **b.** (of a set) made up of members on which a specific operation, such as addition, gives as its result another existing member of the set. **5.** not open to public entry or membership: *a closed society.*

closed circuit *n.* a complete electrical circuit through which current can flow.

closed-circuit television *n.* a television system in which signals are transmitted from the camera to the receivers by cables or telephone links.

close down (kləʊz) *vb.* **1.** to cease or cause to cease operations. ~*n.* **close-down. 2.** *Brit. radio, television.* the end of a period of broadcasting, esp. late at night.

closed shop *n.* a contract between a trade union and an employer permitting the employment of the union's members only.

close harmony (kləʊs) *n.* a type of singing in which all parts except the bass lie close together.

close in (kləʊz) *vb.* **1.** (of days) to become

shorter with the approach of winter. **2.** (foll. by *on* or *upon*) to advance on so as to encircle or surround.

close quarters (kləʊs) *pl. n.* **at close quarters. 1.** engaged in hand-to-hand combat. **2.** in close proximity; very near together.

close season (kləʊs) *n.* the period of the year when it is prohibited to kill certain game or fish.

close shave (kləʊs) *n. Informal.* a narrow escape.

closet (ˈklɒzɪt) *n.* **1.** a small cupboard. **2.** a small private room. **3.** short for **water closet. 4.** (*modifier*) private or secret. ~*vb.* **5.** to shut away in private, esp. for conference or meditation.

close-up (ˈkləʊsˌʌp) *n.* **1.** a photograph or film or television shot taken at close range. **2.** a detailed or intimate view or examination. ~*vb.* **close up** (kləʊz). **3.** to shut entirely. **4.** to draw together: *the ranks closed up.* **5.** (of wounds) to heal completely.

close with (kləʊz) *vb.* to engage in battle with (an enemy).

closure (ˈkləʊʒə) *n.* **1.** the act of closing or the state of being closed. **2.** something that closes or shuts. **3.** (in a deliberative body) a procedure by which debate may be halted and an immediate vote taken. ~*vb.* **4.** (in a deliberative body) to end (debate) by closure.

clot (klɒt) *n.* **1.** a soft thick lump or mass. **2.** *Brit. informal.* a stupid person; fool. ~*vb.* **clotting, clotted. 3.** to form or cause to form into a soft thick lump or lumps.

cloth (klɒθ) *n., pl.* **cloths** (klɒθs, klɒðz). **1.** a fabric formed by weaving, felting, or knitting fibres. **2.** a piece of such fabric used for a particular purpose, as for a dishcloth. **3.** (usually preceded by *the*) the clergy.

clothe (kləʊð) *vb.* **clothing, clothed** *or* **clad. 1.** to dress (a person). **2.** to provide with clothing. **3.** to conceal or disguise.

clothes (kləʊðz) *pl. n.* **1.** articles of dress. **2.** *Chiefly Brit.* short for **bedclothes.**

clotheshorse (ˈkləʊðzˌhɔːs) *n.* a frame on which to hang laundry for drying or airing.

clothesline (ˈkləʊðzˌlaɪn) *n.* a piece of rope from which clean washing is hung to dry.

clothes peg *n.* a small wooden or plastic clip for attaching washing to a clothesline.

clothier (ˈkləʊðɪə) *n.* a person who makes, sells, or deals in clothes or cloth.

clothing (ˈkləʊðɪŋ) *n.* **1.** garments collectively. **2.** something that covers or clothes.

clotted cream *n. Brit.* a thick cream made from scalded milk, esp. in SW England.

cloud (klaʊd) *n.* **1.** a mass of water or ice particles visible in the sky. **2.** any collection of particles visible in the air, esp. of smoke or dust. **3.** a large number of insects or other small animals in flight. **4.** something that darkens, threatens, or carries gloom. **5. in the clouds.** not in contact with reality. **6. on cloud nine.** *Informal.* elated; very happy. **7. under a cloud. a.** under reproach or suspicion. **b.** in a state of gloom or bad temper. ~*vb.* **8.** to make or become cloudy, overcast, or indistinct. **9.** to confuse or impair: *anxiety clouded his judgment.* **10.** to make or become gloomy or depressed. **11.** to render (liquids) milky or (of liquids) to become milky. —ˈcloudless *adj.*

cloudburst (ˈklaʊdˌbɜːst) *n.* a heavy downpour.

cloud chamber *n. Physics.* an apparatus for detecting high-energy particles by observing their tracks through a chamber containing a supersaturated vapour.

cloud-cuckoo-land *n.* a realm of fantasy or impractical notions.

cloudy (ˈklaʊdɪ) *adj.* **cloudier, cloudiest. 1.** covered with cloud or clouds. **2.** opaque or muddy. **3.** confused or unclear. —ˈcloudily *adv.* —ˈcloudiness *n.*

clough (klʌf) *n. Dialect.* a ravine.

clout (klaʊt) *n.* **1.** *Informal.* a blow, esp. with the hand. **2.** power or influence. ~*vb.* **3.** *Informal.* to give a hard blow to, esp. with the hand.

clove[1] (kləʊv) *n.* a dried unopened flower bud of a tropical tree of the myrtle family, used as a pungent fragrant spice.

clove[2] (kləʊv) *n.* any of the segments of a compound bulb, esp. of a garlic bulb.

clove[3] (kləʊv) *vb.* a past tense of **cleave**[1].

clove hitch *n.* a knot used for securing a rope to a spar, post, or larger rope.

cloven (ˈkləʊvˈn) *vb.* **1.** a past participle of **cleave**[1]. ~*adj.* **2.** split; cleft; divided.

cloven hoof *or* **foot** *n.* the divided hoof of a pig, goat, cow, or deer.

clover (ˈkləʊvə) *n.* **1.** a plant with three-lobed leaves and dense flower heads. **2. in clover.** *Informal.* in ease or luxury.

clown (klaʊn) *n.* **1.** a comic entertainer, usually grotesquely costumed and made up, appearing in the circus. **2.** a person who acts in a buffoon-like manner. **3.** a clumsy rude person; boor. ~*vb.* **4.** to perform as a clown. **5.** to play jokes or tricks. **6.** to act foolishly. —ˈclownish *adj.*

cloy (klɔɪ) *vb.* to nauseate or satiate through an excess of something initially pleasurable or sweet. —ˈcloying *adj.*

club (klʌb) *n.* **1.** a stout stick used as a weapon. **2.** a stick or bat used to strike the ball in various sports, esp. golf. **3.** short for **Indian club. 4.** a group or association of people with common aims or interests. **5.** the room, building, or facilities used by such a group. **6.** a building in which members go to meet, dine, read, etc. **7.** *Chiefly Brit.* an organization, esp. in a shop, set up as a means of saving. **8.** a playing card marked with one or more black trefoil symbols. ~*vb.* **clubbing, clubbed. 9.** to beat with or as if with a club. **10.** (foll. by *together*) to unite or combine (resources or efforts) for a common purpose.

club foot *n.* a congenital deformity of the foot.

clubhouse ('klʌb,haʊs) *n.* the premises of a sports or other club, esp. a golf club.

club root *n.* a fungal disease of cabbages and related plants, in which the roots become thickened and distorted.

cluck (klʌk) *n.* **1.** the low clicking sound made by a hen or any similar sound. ~*vb.* **2.** (of a hen) to make a clicking sound. **3.** to express (a feeling) by making a similar sound.

clue (kluː) *n.* **1.** something that helps to solve a problem or unravel a mystery. **2. not have a clue. a.** to be completely baffled. **b.** to be ignorant or incompetent. ~*vb.* **cluing, clued. 3.** (usually foll. by *in* or *up*) to provide with helpful information.

clueless ('kluːlɪs) *adj. Slang.* helpless; stupid.

clump (klʌmp) *n.* **1.** a cluster, as of trees or plants. **2.** a dull heavy tread or any similar sound. ~*vb.* **3.** to walk or tread heavily. **4.** to gather or be gathered into clumps, clusters, or clots. —'**clumpy** *adj.*

clumsy ('klʌmzɪ) *adj.* **-sier, -siest. 1.** lacking in skill or physical coordination. **2.** awkwardly constructed or contrived. —'**clumsily** *adv.* —'**clumsiness** *n.*

clung (klʌŋ) *vb.* past of **cling.**

clunk (klʌŋk) *n.* **1.** a dull metallic sound. ~*vb.* **2.** to make such a sound.

cluster ('klʌstə) *n.* **1.** a number of things growing, fastened, or occurring close together. **2.** a number of people or things grouped together. ~*vb.* **3.** to gather or be gathered in clusters.

clutch[1] (klʌtʃ) *vb.* **1.** to seize with or as if with hands or claws. **2.** to grasp or hold firmly. **3.** (usually foll. by *at*) to attempt to get hold or possession of. ~*n.* **4.** a device that enables two revolving shafts to be joined or disconnected, esp. one that transmits the drive from the engine to the gearbox in a vehicle. **5.** the pedal which operates the clutch in a car. **6.** a firm grasp. **7.** a hand or claw in the act of clutching: *in the clutches of a bear.* **8.** (*often pl.*) power or control: *in the clutches of the Mafia.* **9.** Also: **clutch bag.** a handbag without handles.

clutch[2] (klʌtʃ) *n.* **1.** a nest of eggs laid at the same time. **2.** a brood of chickens.

clutter ('klʌtə) *vb.* **1.** (often foll. by *up*) to strew objects about (a place) in a disorderly manner. ~*n.* **2.** a disordered heap or mass of objects. **3.** a state of disorder.

Clydesdale ('klaɪdz,deɪl) *n.* a heavy powerful carthorse, originally from Scotland.

cm centimetre.

Cm *Chem.* curium.

CMG Companion of St Michael and St George (a Brit. title).

CND Campaign for Nuclear Disarmament.

Co *Chem.* cobalt.

CO **1.** Colorado. **2.** Commanding Officer.

Co. *or* **co. 1.** Company. **2. and co.** (kəʊ). *Informal.* and the rest of them: *Harold and co.*

Co. County.

co- *prefix.* **1.** together; joint or jointly: *coproduction.* **2.** indicating partnership or equality: *costar; copilot.* **3.** to the same or a similar degree: *coextend.* **4.** (in mathematics and astronomy) of the complement of an angle: *cosecant.*

c/o 1. care of. **2.** *Book-keeping.* carried over.

coach (kəʊtʃ) *n.* **1.** a large comfortable single-decker bus used for sightseeing or long-distance travel. **2.** a large four-wheeled enclosed carriage, usually horse-drawn. **3.** a railway carriage. **4.** a trainer or instructor: *a drama coach.* **5.** a tutor who prepares students for examinations. ~*vb.* **6.** to give tuition or instruction to (a pupil). —'**coaching** *n.*

coachman ('kəʊtʃmən) *n., pl.* **-men.** the driver of a coach or carriage.

coachwork ('kəʊtʃ,wɜːk) *n.* the body of a car.

coagulate (kəʊ'ægjʊ,leɪt) *vb.* to change from a fluid state into a soft semisolid mass; clot; curdle. —**co'agulant** *n.* —**co,agu'lation** *n.*

coal (kəʊl) *n.* **1.** a compact black or dark brown rock consisting largely of carbon formed from partially decomposed vegetation: a fuel and a source of coke, coal gas, and coal tar. **2.** one or more lumps of coal. **3. coals to Newcastle.** something supplied to a place where it is already plentiful.

coalesce (,kəʊə'lɛs) *vb.* to unite or come together in one body or mass; fuse. —,**coa'lescence** *n.* —,**coa'lescent** *adj.*

coalface ('kəʊl,feɪs) *n.* the exposed seam of coal in a mine.

coalfield ('kəʊl,fiːld) *n.* an area rich in deposits of coal.

coal gas *n.* a mixture of gases produced by the distillation of bituminous coal and used for heating and lighting.

coalition (,kəʊə'lɪʃən) *n.* a temporary alliance between groups or parties, esp. for some specific reason.

coal scuttle *n.* a container to supply coal to a domestic fire.

coal tar *n.* a black tar, produced by the distillation of bituminous coal, used for making drugs and chemical products.

coal tit *n.* a small European songbird having a black head with a white patch on the nape.

coaming ('kəʊmɪŋ) n. a raised frame round a ship's hatchway for keeping out water.

coarse (kɔːs) adj. **1.** rough in texture or structure; not fine. **2.** lacking refinement or taste; indelicate; vulgar: coarse jokes. **3.** of inferior quality. —'coarsely adv. —'coarseness n.

coarse fish n. any freshwater fish that is not of the salmon family. —coarse fishing n.

coarsen ('kɔːs²n) vb. to make or become coarse.

coast (kəʊst) n. **1.** the place where the land meets the sea; seaside. **2. the coast is clear.** Informal. the obstacles or dangers are gone. ~vb. **3.** to move by momentum or force of gravity, without the use of power. **4.** to proceed without great effort: to coast to victory. —'coastal adj.

coaster ('kəʊstə) n. **1.** Brit. a ship used for coastal trade. **2.** a small mat placed under a bottle or glass to protect a table.

coastguard ('kəʊst,gɑːd) n. **1.** an organization which aids shipping, saves lives at sea, and prevents smuggling. **2.** a member of such an organization.

coastline ('kəʊst,laɪn) n. the outline of a coast.

coat (kəʊt) n. **1.** an outer garment with sleeves, covering the body from the shoulders to below the waist. **2.** the hair, wool, or fur of an animal. **3.** any layer that covers a surface. ~vb. **4.** (often foll. by with) to cover with a layer of (something).

coat hanger n. a curved piece of wood, wire, or plastic, fitted with a hook and used to hang up clothes.

coating ('kəʊtɪŋ) n. a layer or film spread over a surface.

coat of arms n. the heraldic arrangement of emblems of a person, family, or corporation.

coat of mail n. a protective garment made of linked metal rings or plates.

coax (kəʊks) vb. **1.** to persuade (someone) by tenderness, flattery, or pleading. **2.** to obtain (something) by persistent coaxing. **3.** to work on (something) carefully and patiently so as to make it function as desired: he coaxed the engine into starting.

coaxial (kəʊˈæksɪəl) adj. **1.** having a common axis. **2.** Electronics. (of a cable) transmitting by means of two concentric conductors separated by an insulator.

cob (kɒb) n. **1.** a male swan. **2.** a thickset type of horse. **3.** short for a **corncob**. **4.** Brit. a hazel tree or hazelnut. **5.** Brit. a round loaf of bread.

cobalt ('kəʊbɔːlt) n. a brittle hard silvery-white metallic element used in alloys. Symbol: Co

cobalt-blue adj. deep blue.

cobber ('kɒbə) n. Austral. archaic. & N.Z. informal. friend; mate: used as a term of address to males.

cobble[1] ('kɒb²l) n. a cobblestone.

cobble[2] ('kɒb²l) vb. **1.** to make or mend (shoes). **2.** to put together clumsily.

cobbled ('kɒb²ld) adj. (of a street or road) paved with cobblestones.

cobbler ('kɒb²l) n. a person who makes or mends shoes.

cobblers ('kɒbləz) pl. n. Brit. taboo slang. rubbish; nonsense.

cobblestone ('kɒb²l,stəʊn) n. a rounded stone used for paving.

COBOL ('kəʊ,bɒl) n. a high-level computer programming language designed for general commercial use.

cobra ('kəʊbrə) n. a highly venomous snake of tropical Africa and Asia. When alarmed it spreads the skin of its neck into a hood.

cobweb ('kɒb,wɛb) n. **1.** a web spun by certain spiders. **2.** a single thread of such a web. —'cob,webbed adj. —'cob,webby adj.

cobwebs ('kɒb,wɛbz) pl. n. mustiness, confusion, or obscurity.

coca ('kəʊkə) n. the dried leaves of a S American shrub, which contain cocaine and are chewed for their stimulating effects.

cocaine (kəˈkeɪn) n. an addictive drug derived from coca leaves, used as a narcotic and local anaesthetic.

coccus ('kɒkəs) n., pl. **cocci** ('kɒkaɪ, 'kɒksaɪ). any spherical bacterium.

coccyx ('kɒksɪks) n., pl. **coccyges** (kɒkˈsaɪdʒiːz). a small triangular bone at the foot of the spine in human beings and some apes.

cochineal (,kɒtʃɪˈniːl, 'kɒtʃɪ,niːl) n. **1.** a crimson substance obtained from a Mexican insect, used for colouring food and for dyeing. **2.** the insect from which the dye is obtained.

cochlea ('kɒklɪə) n., pl. **-leae** (-lɪ,iː). the spiral tube in the internal ear, which converts sound vibrations into nerve impulses.

cock (kɒk) n. **1.** a male bird, esp. the male of the domestic fowl. **2.** a stopcock. **3.** Taboo slang. a penis. **4.** the hammer of a gun. **5.** Brit. informal. friend; mate: used as a term of address. ~vb. **6.** to set the hammer of (a gun) so that it is ready to fire. **7.** (sometimes foll. by up) to lift and turn (part of the body) in a particular direction. ~See also **cockup**.

cockabully (,kɒkəˈbʊlɪ) n. a small freshwater fish of New Zealand.

cockade (kɒˈkeɪd) n. a feather or rosette worn on the hat as a badge.

cock-a-hoop adj. in very high spirits.

cock-a-leekie (,kɒkəˈliːkɪ) n. a Scottish soup of chicken boiled with leeks.

cock-and-bull story n. Informal. an obviously improbable story, esp. one used as an excuse.

cockatoo (ˌkɒkəˈtuː, ˈkɒkəˌtuː) *n., pl.* **-toos.** **1.** a light-coloured crested parrot of Australia and the East Indies. **2.** *Austral. & N.Z.* a small farmer or settler.

cockchafer (ˈkɒkˌtʃeɪfə) *n.* a large European beetle.

cocked hat *n.* **1.** a hat with three corners and a turned-up brim. **2. knock into a cocked hat.** *Slang.* to outdo or defeat.

cockerel (ˈkɒkərəl, ˈkɒkrəl) *n.* a young domestic cock, less than a year old.

cocker spaniel (ˈkɒkə) *n.* a small breed of spaniel.

cockeyed (ˈkɒkˌaɪd) *adj. Informal.* **1.** crooked; askew. **2.** foolish or absurd. **3.** cross-eyed.

cockfight (ˈkɒkˌfaɪt) *n.* a fight between two gamecocks fitted with sharp metal spurs.

cockle (ˈkɒkʲl) *n.* **1.** an edible bivalve shellfish that has a rounded shell with radiating ribs. **2.** its shell. **3. warm the cockles of one's heart.** to make one feel happy.

cockleshell (ˈkɒkʲlˌʃel) *n.* **1.** the shell of the cockle. **2.** a small light boat.

cockney (ˈkɒknɪ) *n.* **1.** a native of London, esp. of its East End. **2.** the urban dialect of London or its East End. *~adj.* **3.** characteristic of cockneys or their dialect.

cockpit (ˈkɒkˌpɪt) *n.* **1.** the compartment in an aircraft for the pilot and crew. **2.** the driver's compartment in a racing car. **3.** *Naut.* a space in a small vessel containing the wheel and tiller. **4.** the site of numerous battles or conflicts. **5.** an enclosure used for cockfights.

cockroach (ˈkɒkˌrəʊtʃ) *n.* an insect having an oval flattened body and long antennae: a household pest.

cockscomb *or* **coxcomb** (ˈkɒksˌkəʊm) *n.* **1.** the comb of a domestic cock. **2.** *Informal.* a conceited dandy.

cocksure (ˌkɒkˈʃʊə, -ˈʃɔː) *adj.* overconfident; arrogant.

cocktail (ˈkɒkˌteɪl) *n.* **1.** any mixed drink with a spirit base. **2.** an appetizer of seafood or mixed fruits. **3.** any combination of diverse elements.

cockup (ˈkɒkˌʌp) *Brit. slang. ~n.* **1.** something done badly. *~vb.* **cock up.** **2.** to botch.

cocky[1] (ˈkɒkɪ) *adj.* **cockier, cockiest.** excessively proud of oneself. —ˈ**cockily** *adv.* —ˈ**cockiness** *n.*

cocky[2] (ˈkɒkɪ) *n., pl* **cockies.** *Austral. & N.Z. informal.* short for **cockatoo** (sense 2).

coco (ˈkəʊkəʊ) *n., pl.* **-cos.** the coconut palm.

cocoa (ˈkəʊkəʊ) *or* **cacao** *n.* **1.** a powder made by roasting and grinding cocoa beans. **2.** a hot or cold drink made from cocoa powder and milk or water.

cocoa bean *n.* a cacao seed.

cocoa butter *n.* a fatty solid obtained from cocoa beans and used for confectionery and toiletries.

coconut *or* **cocoanut** (ˈkəʊkəˌnʌt) *n.* **1.** the fruit of a type of palm tree (**coconut palm**), which has a thick fibrous oval husk and a thin hard shell enclosing edible white flesh. The hollow centre is filled with a milky fluid (**coconut milk**). **2.** the flesh of the coconut.

coconut matting *n.* coarse matting made from the fibrous husk of the coconut.

cocoon (kəˈkuːn) *n.* **1.** a silky protective envelope produced by a silkworm or other insect larva, in which the pupa develops. **2.** a protective covering. *~vb.* **3.** to wrap in or protect as if in a cocoon.

cocotte (kəʊˈkɒt) *n.* a small fireproof dish in which individual portions of food are cooked and served.

cod[1] (kɒd) *n., pl.* **cod** *or* **cods.** a food fish found in the North Atlantic.

cod[2] (kɒd) *Brit. slang. ~vb.* **codding, codded.** **1.** to make fun of. **2.** to play a trick on; hoax. *~n.* **3.** a hoax or trick.

COD cash (in the U.S. collect) on delivery.

coda (ˈkəʊdə) *n. Music.* the final part of a musical structure.

coddle (ˈkɒdʲl) *vb.* **1.** to pamper or overprotect. **2.** to cook (something, esp. eggs) in water just below boiling point.

code (kəʊd) *n.* **1.** a system of letters, symbols, or prearranged signals, by which information can be communicated secretly or briefly. **2.** a conventionalized set of principles or rules: *a code of behaviour.* **3.** a system of letters or digits used for identification purposes. *~vb.* **4.** to translate or arrange into a code.

codeine (ˈkəʊdiːn) *n.* an alkaloid prepared mainly from morphine, used as a painkiller and sedative.

codex (ˈkəʊdɛks) *n., pl.* **codices** (ˈkəʊdɪˌsiːz, ˈkɒdɪ-). a volume of manuscripts of an ancient text.

codfish (ˈkɒdˌfɪʃ) *n., pl.* **-fish** *or* **-fishes.** a cod.

codger (ˈkɒdʒə) *n. Informal.* a man, esp. an old or eccentric one.

codicil (ˈkɒdɪsɪl) *n. Law.* a supplement altering a will.

codify (ˈkəʊdɪˌfaɪ, ˈkɒ-) *vb.* **-fying, -fied.** to organize or collect together (rules or procedures) systematically. —ˌ**codifiˈcation** *n.*

codling (ˈkɒdlɪŋ) *n.* a young cod.

cod-liver oil *n.* an oil extracted from the livers of cod and related fish, rich in vitamins A and D.

codpiece (ˈkɒdˌpiːs) *n. Hist.* a bag covering the male genitals, attached to breeches.

codswallop ('kɒdz,wɒləp) *n. Brit. slang.* nonsense.

coeducation (,kəʊɛdjʊ'keɪʃən) *n.* an educational system in which classes are attended by both sexes. —,**coedu'cational** *adj.*

coefficient (,kəʊɪ'fɪʃənt) *n.* **1.** *Maths.* a number or constant placed before and multiplying another quantity: *the coefficient of the term 3xyz is 3.* **2.** *Physics.* a number or constant used to calculate the behaviour of a given substance under specified conditions.

coelacanth ('siːlə,kænθ) *n.* a primitive marine bony fish, thought to be extinct until a living specimen was discovered in 1938.

coelenterate (sɪ'lɛntə,reɪt, -rɪt) *n.* any invertebrate having a saclike body with a single opening, such as jellyfishes, sea anemones, and corals.

coeliac *or U.S.* **celiac** ('siːlɪ,æk) *adj.* of the abdomen.

coenobite ('siːnəʊ,baɪt) *n.* a member of a religious order in a monastic community.

coequal (kəʊ'iːkwəl) *adj., n.* equal.

coerce (kəʊ'ɜːs) *vb.* to compel or restrain by force. —**co'ercible** *adj.* —**co'ercion** *n.*

coeval (kəʊ'iːvʰl) *adj., n.* contemporary. —**co'evally** *adv.*

coexist (,kəʊɪg'zɪst) *vb.* **1.** to exist together at the same time or in the same place. **2.** to exist together in peace despite differences. —,**coex'istence** *n.* —,**coex'istent** *adj.*

coextend (,kəʊɪk'stɛnd) *vb.* to extend or cause to extend equally in space or time. —,**coex'tension** *n.* —,**coex'tensive** *adj.*

C of E Church of England.

coffee ('kɒfɪ) *n.* **1.** a drink made from the roasted and ground seeds of a tall tropical shrub and water. **2.** Also called: **coffee beans.** the beanlike seeds of this shrub. **3.** the shrub yielding these seeds. ~*adj.* **4.** light brown.

coffee bar *n.* a café; snack bar.

coffee house *n.* a place where coffee is served, esp. one that was a fashionable meeting place in 18th-century London.

coffee mill *n.* a machine for grinding roasted coffee beans.

coffee table *n.* a small low table.

coffee-table book *n.* a large, expensive, illustrated book.

coffer ('kɒfə) *n.* **1.** a chest for storing valuables. **2.** (*pl.*) a store of money. **3.** an ornamental sunken panel in a ceiling or dome.

cofferdam ('kɒfə,dæm) *n.* a watertight enclosure pumped dry to enable construction work or ship repairs to be carried out.

coffin ('kɒfɪn) *n.* a box in which a corpse is buried or cremated.

cog (kɒg) *n.* **1.** one of the teeth on the rim of a gearwheel. **2.** a gearwheel, esp. a small one. **3.** an unimportant member of a large organization or process.

cogent ('kəʊdʒənt) *adj.* forcefully convincing. —'**cogency** *n.*

cogitate ('kɒdʒɪ,teɪt) *vb.* to think deeply about (something); ponder. —,**cogi'tation** *n.* —'**cogitative** *adj.*

cognac ('kɒnjæk) *n.* high-quality brandy distilled near Cognac in SW France.

cognate ('kɒgneɪt) *adj.* **1.** derived from a common original form: *cognate languages.* **2.** related to or descended from a common ancestor. ~*n.* **3.** a cognate word or language. **4.** a relative. —**cog'nation** *n.*

cognition (kɒg'nɪʃən) *n.* **1.** the processes of acquiring knowledge, including perception, intuition, and reasoning. **2.** the results of such a process. —**cognitive** ('kɒgnɪtɪv) *adj.*

cognizance *or* **cognisance** ('kɒgnɪzəns, 'kɒnɪ-) *n.* **1.** knowledge; perception. **2. take cognizance of.** to take notice of; acknowledge. **3.** the range or scope of knowledge or perception. —'**cognizant** *or* '**cognisant** *adj.*

cognomen (kɒg'nəʊmɛn) *n., pl.* -**nomens** *or* -**nomina** (-'nɒmɪnə, -'nəʊ-). **1.** a nickname. **2.** a surname. **3.** an ancient Roman's third name or nickname.

cognoscenti (,kɒnjəʊ'ʃɛntɪ, ,kɒgnəʊ-) *pl. n., sing.* -**te** (-tiː). (*sometimes sing.*) connoisseurs.

cogwheel ('kɒg,wiːl) *n.* same as **gearwheel.**

cohabit (kəʊ'hæbɪt) *vb.* to live together as husband and wife, esp. without being married. —**co,habi'tation** *n.*

cohere (kəʊ'hɪə) *vb.* **1.** to hold or stick firmly together. **2.** to be connected logically; be consistent.

coherent (kəʊ'hɪərənt) *adj.* **1.** capable of intelligible speech. **2.** logical and consistent. **3.** cohering or sticking together. **4.** *Physics.* (of two or more waves) having the same frequency and a constant fixed phase difference. —**co'herence** *n.*

cohesion (kəʊ'hiːʒən) *n.* **1.** the act or state of cohering; tendency to unite. **2.** *Physics.* the force that holds together the atoms or molecules in a solid or liquid. —**co'hesive** *adj.*

cohort ('kəʊhɔːt) *n.* **1.** a band of warriors or associates. **2.** a tenth part of an ancient Roman Legion.

coif *n.* **1.** (kɔɪf). a close-fitting cap worn in the Middle Ages. **2.** (kwɑːf). a hairstyle. ~*vb.* (kwɑːf), **coiffing, coiffed. 3.** to arrange (the hair).

coiffeur (kwɑː'fɜː) *n.* a hairdresser. —**coiffeuse** (kwɑː'fɜːz) *fem. n.*

coiffure (kwɑː'fjʊə) *n.* a hairstyle.

coil¹ (kɔɪl) *vb.* **1.** to wind or be wound into loops. **2.** to move in a winding course. ~*n.* **3.** something wound in a connected series of loops. **4.** a single loop of such a series. **5.** an electrical conductor wound into a spiral, to provide inductance. **6.** a contraceptive device in the shape of a coil, inserted in the womb.

coil[2] (kɔɪl) *n.* **mortal coil.** the troubles of the world.

coin (kɔɪn) *n.* **1.** a metal disc or piece used as money. **2.** metal currency, coins collectively. ~*vb.* **3.** to make or stamp (coins). **4.** to make into a coin. **5.** to invent (a new word or phrase). **6. coin it in** *or* **coin money.** *Informal.* to make money rapidly.

coinage (ˈkɔɪnɪdʒ) *n.* **1.** the act of coining. **2.** coins collectively. **3.** the currency of a country. **4.** a newly invented word or phrase.

coincide (ˌkəʊɪnˈsaɪd) *vb.* **1.** to occur at the same time. **2.** occupy the same place in space. **3.** to agree or correspond exactly.

coincidence (kəʊˈɪnsɪdəns) *n.* **1.** a chance occurrence of events remarkable either for being simultaneous or for apparently being connected. **2.** a coinciding.

coincident (kəʊˈɪnsɪdənt) *adj.* **1.** having the same position in space or time. **2.** (usually foll. by *with*) in exact agreement; identical. —**co,inci'dental** *adj.* —**co,inci-'dentally** *adv.*

coir (ˈkɔɪə) *n.* coconut fibre, used in making rope and matting.

coitus (ˈkəʊɪtəs) *or* **coition** (kəʊˈɪʃən) *n.* sexual intercourse. —**'coital** *adj.*

coke[1] (kəʊk) *n.* **1.** a solid fuel left after the gases have been extracted from coal: used as a smokeless fuel and for smelting pig iron out of iron ore. ~*vb.* **2.** to become or convert into coke.

coke[2] (kəʊk) *n. Slang.* cocaine.

col (kɒl) *n.* the lowest point of a ridge connecting two mountain peaks.

Col. 1. Colonel. **2.** Colorado.

cola *or* **kola** (ˈkəʊlə) *n.* **1.** a W African tree whose nuts yield an extract used as a tonic and in soft drinks. **2.** a sweet carbonated drink flavoured with this extract.

colander (ˈkɒləndə, ˈkʌl-) *n.* a bowl with a perforated bottom for straining or rinsing foods.

cold (kəʊld) *adj.* **1.** low in temperature: *cold weather; cold hands.* **2.** not hot enough: *this meal is cold.* **3.** lacking in affection or enthusiasm. **4.** not affected by emotion: *cold logic.* **5.** dead. **6.** (of a trail or scent in hunting) faint. **7.** (of a colour) having violet, blue, or green predominating; giving no sensation of warmth. **8.** *Slang.* unconscious. **9.** *Informal.* (of a seeker) far from the object of a search. **10. cold comfort.** little or no comfort. **11. have** *or* **get cold feet.** to be or become fearful or reluctant. **12. in cold blood.** deliberately and without mercy. **13. leave (someone) cold.** *Informal.* to fail to excite or impress (some-

one). **14. throw cold water on.** *Informal.* to discourage. ~*n.* **15.** the absence of heat. **16.** the sensation caused by loss or lack of heat. **17. (out) in the cold.** *Informal.* neglected; ignored. **18.** a viral infection of the nose and throat characterized by catarrh and sneezing. ~*adv.* **19.** *Informal.* unrehearsed; unprepared: *he played his part cold.* —**'coldly** *adv.* —**'coldness** *n.*

cold-blooded *adj.* **1.** callous or cruel. **2.** (of all animals except birds and mammals) having a body temperature that varies with that of the surroundings. —**,cold-'blooded-ness** *n.*

cold chisel *n.* a toughened steel chisel.

cold cream *n.* a creamy preparation used for softening and cleansing the skin.

cold frame *n.* an unheated wooden frame with a glass top, used to protect young plants.

cold front *n. Meteorol.* the boundary line between a warm air mass and the cold air pushing it from beneath and behind.

cold-hearted *adj.* lacking in feeling or warmth; unkind. —**,cold-'heartedness** *n.*

cold shoulder *Informal.* ~*n.* **1. give someone the cold shoulder.** to snub someone. ~*vb.* **cold-shoulder. 2.** to treat with indifference.

cold sore *n.* a cluster of blisters at the margin of the lips, caused by a virus.

cold storage *n.* **1.** the storage of things in a refrigerated place. **2.** *Informal.* a state of temporary disuse; postponement: *to put an idea into cold storage.*

cold sweat *n. Informal.* coldness and sweating as a bodily reaction to fear or nervousness.

cold turkey *n. Slang.* a method of curing drug addiction by abrupt withdrawal of all doses.

cold war *n.* a state of political hostility between two countries without actual warfare.

cole (kəʊl) *n.* any of various plants such as the cabbage and rape.

coleslaw (ˈkəʊlˌslɔː) *n.* a dressed salad of shredded raw cabbage with carrots and onions.

coley (ˈkəʊlɪ, ˈkɒlɪ) *n. Brit.* an edible fish with white or grey flesh.

colic (ˈkɒlɪk) *n.* severe spasmodic pain in the stomach and bowels. —**'colicky** *adj.*

colitis (kɒˈlaɪtɪs) *n.* inflammation of the colon.

collaborate (kəˈlæbəˌreɪt) *vb.* **1.** to work with another or others on a joint project. **2.** to cooperate with an enemy invader. —**col,labo'ration** *n.* —**col'laborative** *adj.* —**col'labo,rator** *n.*

collage (kəˈlɑːʒ, kɒ-) *n.* **1.** an art form in which compositions are made out of pieces of paper, cloth, photographs, or other materials. **2.** a composition made in this way. —**col'lagist** *n.*

collagen ('kɒlədʒən) *n.* a fibrous protein found in cartilage and bone that yields gelatin on boiling.

collapse (kə'læps) *vb.* **1.** to fall down or cave in suddenly. **2.** to fail completely. **3.** to break down or fall down from lack of strength. **4.** to fold compactly, esp. for storage. ~*n.* **5.** the act or instance of falling down or falling to pieces. **6.** a sudden failure or breakdown. —**col'lapsible** *adj.*

collar ('kɒlə) *n.* **1.** the part of a garment around the neck. **2.** a band of leather, rope, or metal placed around an animal's neck. **3.** *Biol.* a ringlike marking around the neck of a bird or animal. **4.** a cut of meat, esp. bacon, from the neck of an animal. **5.** a ring or band around a pipe, rod or shaft. ~*vb.* **6.** to seize by the collar. **7.** *Informal.* to seize; arrest; detain. **8.** to take for oneself.

collarbone ('kɒlə,bəʊn) *n.* same as **clavicle.**

collate (kɒ'leɪt, kə-) *vb.* **1.** to examine and compare (texts or data) in order to note differences. **2.** to check the number and order of (the pages of a book). —**col'lator** *n.*

collateral (kɒ'lætərəl, kə-) *n.* **1.** security pledged for the repayment of a loan. **2.** a person, animal, or plant descended from the same ancestor as another but through a different line. ~*adj.* **3.** situated or running side by side. **4.** descended from a common ancestor but through different lines. **5.** additional but subordinate.

collation (kɒ'leɪʃən, kə-) *n.* **1.** the act or result of collating. **2.** a light meal.

colleague ('kɒliːg) *n.* a fellow worker, esp. in a profession.

collect[1] (kə'lɛkt) *vb.* **1.** to gather together or be gathered together. **2.** to gather (stamps, books, or other articles) as a hobby or for study. **3.** to call for or receive payment of (taxes, dues, or contributions). **4.** to regain control of (oneself or one's emotions). **5.** to fetch.

collect[2] ('kɒlɛkt) *n. Christianity.* a short prayer said during certain church services.

collected (kə'lɛktɪd) *adj.* **1.** calm and self-controlled. **2.** brought together into one book or set of books: *the collected works of Dickens.*

collection (kə'lɛkʃən) *n.* **1.** the act or process of collecting. **2.** things collected or accumulated. **3.** a sum of money collected, as in church. **4.** regular removal of letters from a postbox.

collective (kə'lɛktɪv) *adj.* **1.** formed or assembled by collection. **2.** assembled as a group; combined. **3.** done by or characteristic of individuals acting in cooperation.

~*n.* **4.** a group of people working together on an enterprise and sharing the benefits from it. —**col'lectively** *adv.*

collective bargaining *n.* negotiation between a trade union and an employer on the wages and working conditions of the employees.

collective noun *n.* a noun that is singular in form but that refers to a group of people or things, as *crowd* or *army.*

Usage. Collective nouns are usually used with singular verbs: *the family is on holiday; General Motors is mounting a big sales campaign.* Plural verbs are, however, used when a collective noun is being thought of as a collection of individuals, rather than as a group: *the family are all on holiday; the sales force have all received a copy of the figures.*

collectivism (kə'lɛktɪ,vɪzəm) *n.* the principle of ownership of the means of production by the state or the people.

collectivize *or* **-vise** (kə'lɛktɪ,vaɪz) *vb.* to organize according to the principles of collectivism. —**col,lectivi'zation** *or* **-vi'sation** *n.*

collector (kə'lɛktə) *n.* **1.** a person who collects objects as a hobby. **2.** a person employed to collect debts, rents, or tickets.

colleen ('kɒliːn, kɒ'liːn) *n. Irish.* a girl.

college ('kɒlɪdʒ) *n.* **1.** an institution of higher or further education that is not a university. **2.** a self-governing section of certain universities. **3.** the staff and students of a college. **4.** an organized body of persons with specific rights and duties: *an electoral college.* **5.** a body organized within a particular profession, concerned with regulating standards. **6.** *Brit.* a name given to some secondary schools.

collegian (kə'liːdʒɪən) *n.* a member of a college.

collegiate (kə'liːdʒɪt) *adj.* **1.** of a college or college students. **2.** (of a university) composed of various colleges.

collide (kə'laɪd) *vb.* **1.** to crash together with a violent impact. **2.** to conflict; clash; disagree.

collie ('kɒlɪ) *n.* a silky-coated breed of dog used for herding sheep and cattle.

collier ('kɒlɪə) *n. Chiefly Brit.* **1.** a coal miner. **2.** a ship designed to transport coal.

colliery ('kɒljərɪ) *n., pl.* **-lieries.** *Chiefly Brit.* a coal mine and its buildings.

collision (kə'lɪʒən) *n.* **1.** a violent impact of moving objects; crash. **2.** the conflict of opposed ideas or wishes.

collocation (,kɒlə'keɪʃən) *n.* a grouping together of things in a certain order, as of the words in a sentence. —**'collo,cate** *vb.*

colloid ('kɒlɔɪd) *n.* a mixture having particles of one substance suspended in a different substance. —**col'loidal** *adj.*

collop ('kɒləp) *n.* a small slice of meat.

colloquial (kə'ləʊkwɪəl) *adj.* informal; used in conversation rather than formal writing. —**col'loquially** *adv.*

colloquialism (kə'ləʊkwɪə,lɪzəm) *n.* **1.** a colloquial word or phrase. **2.** the use of colloquial words and phrases.

colloquium (kə'ləʊkwɪəm) *n., pl.* -**quiums** *or* -**quia** (-kwɪə). an academic conference or seminar.

colloquy ('kɒləkwɪ) *n., pl.* -**quies.** a conversation or conference. —**'colloquist** *n.*

collusion (kə'luːʒən) *n.* secret or illegal agreement or cooperation; conspiracy. —**col'lusive** *adj.*

collywobbles ('kɒlɪ,wɒbªlz) *pl. n. Slang.* **1.** an upset stomach. **2.** an intense feeling of nervousness.

cologne (kə'ləʊn) *n.* a perfumed toilet water.

colon[1] ('kəʊlən) *n., pl.* -**lons.** the punctuation mark : used before an explanation or an example, a list, or an extended quotation.

colon[2] ('kəʊlən) *n., pl.* -**lons** *or* -**la** (-lə). the part of the large intestine connected to the rectum. —**colonic** (kə'lɒnɪk) *adj.*

colonel ('kɜːnªl) *n.* a senior commissioned officer of land or air forces. —**'colonelcy** *n.*

colonial (kə'ləʊnɪəl) *adj.* **1.** of or inhabiting a colony or colonies. ~*n.* **2.** an inhabitant of a colony.

colonial goose *n. N.Z.* an old-fashioned name for stuffed roast mutton.

colonialism (kə'ləʊnɪə,lɪzəm) *n.* the policy of acquiring and maintaining colonies, esp. for exploitation. —**co'lonialist** *n., adj.*

colonist ('kɒlənɪst) *n.* a settler in or inhabitant of a colony.

colonize *or* -**ise** ('kɒlə,naɪz) *vb.* **1.** to send colonists to or establish a colony in (an area). **2.** to settle in (an area) as colonists. —**,coloni'zation** *or* -**i'sation** *n.*

colonnade (,kɒlə'neɪd) *n.* a set of evenly spaced columns, usually supporting a roof. —**,colon'naded** *adj.*

colony ('kɒlənɪ) *n., pl.* -**nies.** **1.** a body of people who settle in a country distant from their homeland but still under its control. **2.** the territory occupied by such a settlement. **3.** a group of people with the same nationality or interests, forming a community in a particular place: *an artists' colony.* **4.** *Zool.* a group of the same type of animal or plant living or growing together. **5.** *Bacteriol.* a group of microorganisms when grown on a culture medium.

colophon ('kɒlə,fɒn, -fən) *n.* a publisher's emblem on a book.

color ('kʌlə) *n., vb. U.S.* same as **colour.**

Colorado beetle (,kɒlə'rɑːdəʊ) *n.* a black-and-yellow beetle that is a serious pest of potatoes.

coloration *or* **colouration** (,kʌlə'reɪʃən) *n.* colouring; arrangement of colours.

coloratura (,kɒlərə'tʊərə) *n. Music.* **1.** an elaborate and complicated vocal passage. **2.** a soprano who specializes in such music.

colossal (kə'lɒsªl) *adj.* **1.** of immense size; huge. **2.** *Informal.* remarkable; splendid.

colossus (kə'lɒsəs) *n., pl.* -**si** (-saɪ) *or* -**suses.** **1.** a very large statue. **2.** any huge or important person or thing.

colostomy (kə'lɒstəmɪ) *n., pl.* -**mies.** an operation to form an opening from the colon onto the surface of the body, for emptying the bowel.

colour *or* *U.S.* **color** ('kʌlə) *n.* **1.** a property of things that results from the particular wavelengths of light which they reflect or give out, producing a sensation in the eye. **2.** a colour, such as red or green, that possesses hue, as opposed to black, white, or grey. **3.** a substance, such as a dye, that gives colour. **4.** the skin complexion of a person, esp. as determined by his race. **5.** the use of all the colours in painting, drawing, or photography. **6.** the distinctive tone of a musical sound. **7.** vividness or authenticity: *period colour.* **8.** semblance or pretext: *under colour of.* ~*vb.* **9.** to apply colour to (something). **10.** to give a convincing appearance to: *to colour an alibi.* **11.** to influence or distort: *anger coloured her judgment.* **12.** to become red in the face, esp. when embarrassed or annoyed. ~See also **colours.**

colour bar *n.* racial discrimination by whites against non-whites.

colour-blind *adj.* unable to distinguish between certain colours, esp. red and green. —**colour blindness** *n.*

coloured *or* *U.S.* **colored** ('kʌləd) *adj.* **1.** possessing colour. **2.** having a strong element of fiction or fantasy; distorted (esp. in **highly coloured**).

Coloured *or* *U.S.* **Colored** ('kʌləd) *n.* **1.** an individual who is not a White. **2.** in South Africa, a person of racially mixed parentage or descent. ~*adj.* **3.** of mixed White and non-White parentage.

colourful *or* *U.S.* **colorful** ('kʌləful) *adj.* **1.** having intense or richly varied colours. **2.** vivid, rich, or distinctive in character.

colouring *or* *U.S.* **coloring** ('kʌlərɪŋ) *n.* **1.** the process or art of applying colour. **2.** anything used to give colour, such as paint. **3.** appearance with regard to shade and colour. **4.** the colour of a person's complexion.

colourless *or* *U.S.* **colorless** ('kʌləlɪs) *adj.* **1.** without colour. **2.** dull and uninteresting: *a colourless individual.* **3.** grey or pallid in tone or hue.

colours *or* *U.S.* **colors** ('kʌləz) *pl. n.* **1.** the flag of a country, regiment, or ship. **2.** *Sport, Brit.* a badge or other symbol denoting membership of a team, esp. at a school or college. **3. nail one's colours to the mast.** to commit oneself publicly and irrevocably to a course of action. **4. show one's true colours.** to display one's true nature or character.

colour sergeant *n.* a sergeant who carries the regimental, battalion, or national colours.

colour supplement *n. Brit.* an illustrated magazine accompanying a newspaper.

colt (kəʊlt) *n.* **1.** a young male horse or pony. **2.** *Sport.* a young and inexperienced player; a member of a junior team.

coltsfoot (ˈkəʊltsˌfʊt) *n., pl.* **-foots.** a European plant with yellow daisy-like flowers and heart-shaped leaves: a common weed.

columbine (ˈkɒləmˌbaɪn) *n.* a plant that has brightly coloured flowers with five spurred petals.

column (ˈkɒləm) *n.* **1.** an upright pillar usually having a cylindrical shaft, a base, and a capital. **2.** a form or structure in the shape of a column: *a column of air.* **3.** *Mil.* a narrow formation in which individuals or units follow one behind the other. **4. a. a** single row of type on a newspaper. **b.** a regular feature in a paper: *the fashion column.* **5.** a vertical arrangement of numbers. —**columnar** (kəˈlʌmnə) *adj.*

columnist (ˈkɒləmnɪst, -əmɪst) *n.* a journalist who writes a regular feature in a newspaper.

com- *or* **con-** *prefix.* used with a main word to mean: together; with; jointly: *commingle.*

coma (ˈkəʊmə) *n.* a state of unconsciousness from which a person cannot be aroused, caused by injury, disease, or drugs.

comatose (ˈkəʊməˌtəʊs) *adj.* **1.** in a state of coma. **2.** drowsy; lethargic.

comb (kəʊm) *n.* **1.** a toothed strip of rigid material for disentangling or arranging hair. **2.** a tool or machine that cleans and straightens wool or cotton. **3.** a fleshy serrated crest on the head of a domestic fowl. **4.** a honeycomb. ~*vb.* **5.** to use a comb on. **6.** to search with great care: *the police combed the woods.*

combat *n.* (ˈkɒmbæt, -bət, ˈkʌm-). **1.** a fight, conflict, or struggle. ~*vb.* (kəmˈbæt; ˈkɒmbæt, ˈkʌm-). **2.** to fight: *to combat disease.* —ˈ**combative** *adj.*

combatant (ˈkɒmbətᵊnt, ˈkʌm-) *n.* **1.** a person taking part in a combat. ~*adj.* **2.** engaged in or ready for combat.

combe *or* **comb** (kuːm) *n.* same as **coomb.**

comber (ˈkəʊmə) *n.* **1.** a person, tool, or machine that combs wool or flax. **2.** a long curling wave; roller.

combination (ˌkɒmbɪˈneɪʃən) *n.* **1.** the act of combining or state of being combined. **2.**

a union of separate parts or qualities. **3.** an alliance of people or parties. **4.** the set of numbers or letters that opens a combination lock. **5.** *Maths.* an arrangement of the members of a set into specified groups without regard to order in the group.

combination lock *n.* a lock that can only be opened when a set of dials is turned to show a specific sequence of numbers or letters.

combinations (ˌkɒmbɪˈneɪʃənz) *pl. n. Brit.* a one-piece undergarment with long sleeves and legs.

combine *vb.* (kəmˈbaɪn). **1.** to join together. **2.** to unite or cause to unite to form a chemical compound. ~*n.* (ˈkɒmbaɪn). **3.** short for **combine harvester. 4.** an association of persons, or firms for a common purpose.

combine harvester (ˈkɒmbaɪn) *n.* a machine used to reap and thresh grain in one process.

combings (ˈkəʊmɪŋz) *pl. n.* the loose hair or fibres removed by combing.

combining form *n.* a part of a word that occurs only as part of a compound word, such as *anthropo-* in *anthropology.*

combo (ˈkɒmbəʊ) *n., pl.* **-bos.** a small group of jazz musicians.

combustible (kəmˈbʌstɪbᵊl) *adj.* capable of igniting and burning easily.

combustion (kəmˈbʌstʃən) *n.* **1.** the process of burning. **2.** a chemical reaction in which a substance combines with oxygen to produce heat and light.

come (kʌm) *vb.* **coming, came, come. 1.** to move towards a place considered near to the speaker or hearer: *I'll come to see you soon.* **2.** to arrive or reach: *we soon came to a pub.* **3.** to occur: *Christmas comes but once a year.* **4.** to happen as a result: *no good will come of this.* **5.** to occur to the mind: *the truth suddenly came to me.* **6.** to reach a specified point, state, or situation: *she comes up to my shoulder; to come to grief.* **7.** to be produced: *that dress comes in red.* **8.** (foll. by *from*) to be or have been a resident or native (of): *I come from London.* **9.** to become: *your wishes will come true.* **10.** *Slang.* to have an orgasm. **11.** *Brit. informal.* to play the part of: *don't come the innocent with me.* **12.** (*subjunctive use*) when a specified time arrives: *come next August.* **13. as ... as they come.** the most characteristic example of a type. **14. come again?** *Informal.* what did you say? **15. come to light.** to be revealed. ~*interj.* **16.** an exclamation expressing annoyance or impatience: *come now!* ~See also **come about, come across,** etc.

come about *vb.* to take place; happen.

come across *vb.* **1.** to meet or find by accident. **2.** to communicate the intended meaning or impression. **3.** to give a certain impression.

come at vb. to attack: he came at me with an axe.

comeback ('kʌm,bæk) n. Informal. 1. a return to a former position or status. 2. a response or retaliation. ~vb. **come back.** 3. to return, esp. to the memory. 4. to become fashionable again.

come between vb. to cause the estrangement or separation of (two people).

come by vb. to find or obtain, esp. accidentally: do you ever come by any old books?

Comecon ('kɒmɪ,kɒn) n. an economic league of Soviet-oriented Communist nations.

comedian (kə'miːdɪən) n. 1. an entertainer who specializes in jokes or comic skits. 2. an actor in comedy.

comedown ('kʌm,daʊn) n. 1. a decline in status or prosperity. 2. Informal. a disappointment. ~vb. **come down.** 3. (of prices) to become lower. 4. to reach a decision: the report came down in favour of a pay increase. 5. (often foll. by to) to be handed down by tradition or inheritance. 6. (foll. by with) to begin to suffer from (illness). 7. (foll. by on) to rebuke harshly. 8. (foll. by to) to amount (to): it comes down to two choices. 9. **come down in the world.** to lose status or prosperity.

comedy ('kɒmɪdɪ) n., pl. -dies. 1. a humorous film, play, or broadcast. 2. such works as a genre. 3. (in classical literature) a play in which the main characters triumph over adversity. 4. the humorous aspect of life or of events.

come forward vb. 1. to offer one's services; volunteer. 2. to present oneself.

come-hither adj. Informal. flirtatious; seductive: a come-hither look.

come in vb. 1. to prove to be: it came in useful. 2. to become fashionable or seasonable. 3. to finish a race (in a certain position). 4. to be received: news is coming in of a fire in Hull. 5. (of money) to be received as income. 6. to be involved in a situation: where do I come in? 7. (foll. by for) to be the object of: she came in for a lot of criticism.

come into vb. 1. to enter. 2. to inherit.

comely ('kʌmlɪ) adj. -lier, -liest. good-looking; attractive. —'**comeliness** n.

come of vb. to result from: nothing came of it.

come off vb. 1. to emerge from a situation in a certain position: they came off badly. 2. Informal. to take place. 3. Informal. to have the intended effect: his jokes did not come off.

come-on n. 1. Informal. a lure or enticement. ~vb. **come on.** 2. (of power or water) to start running or functioning. 3. to make progress: my plants are coming on

nicely. 4. to begin: I feel a cold coming on. 5. to make an entrance on stage.

come out vb. 1. to be made public or revealed: the news of her death came out last week. 2. to be published: the paper comes out on Fridays. 3. Also: **come out of the closet.** to reveal something formerly concealed, esp. that one is a homosexual. 4. Chiefly Brit. to go on strike. 5. to declare oneself: the council came out in favour of the project. 6. to end up or turn out: he came out on top; the figures came out exactly right. 7. (foll. by in) to become covered with (a rash or spots). 8. (foll. by with) to say or disclose: you can rely on him to come out with the facts. 9. to enter society formally.

come over vb. 1. to influence or affect: I don't know what came over me lately. 2. to communicate the intended meaning or impression. 3. to give a certain impression. 4. to change sides or opinions. 5. Informal. to feel a particular sensation: I came over faint.

come round vb. 1. to recover consciousness. 2. to change one's opinion.

comestibles (kə'mɛstɪb²lz) pl. n. food.

comet ('kɒmɪt) n. an object that travels around the sun, with a frozen nucleus and a long luminous tail.

come through vb. to survive or endure (an illness or difficult situation) successfully.

come to vb. 1. to regain consciousness. 2. to amount to (a total figure).

come up vb. 1. to be mentioned or arise: that question will come up again. 2. to be about to happen: there's a big concert coming up. 3. **come up against.** to come into conflict with. 4. **come up in the world.** to rise in status. 5. **come up to.** to meet a standard. 6. **come up with.** to produce or propose.

come upon vb. to meet or encounter unexpectedly.

comeuppance (,kʌm'ʌpəns) n. Informal. deserved punishment.

comfit ('kʌmfɪt, 'kɒm-) n. a sugar-coated sweet.

comfort ('kʌmfət) n. 1. a state of physical ease or wellbeing. 2. relief from suffering or grief. 3. a person or thing that brings ease. ~vb. 4. to soothe or console. 5. to bring physical ease. —'**comforting** adj.

comfortable ('kʌmftəb²l) adj. 1. giving comfort; relaxing. 2. at ease; free from trouble or pain. 3. Informal. having or being a fairly large income. —'**comfortably** adv.

comforter ('kʌmfətə) n. 1. Chiefly Brit. a woollen scarf. 2. a baby's dummy.

comfrey ('kʌmfrɪ) n. a tall plant with bell-shaped blue, purplish, or white flowers.

comfy ('kʌmfɪ) *adj.* **-fier, -fiest.** *Informal.* comfortable.

comic ('kɒmɪk) *adj.* **1.** of or relating to comedy. **2.** humorous; funny. ~*n.* **3.** a comedian. **4.** a magazine, esp. for children, containing comic strips.

comical ('kɒmɪk²l) *adj.* **1.** causing laughter. **2.** ludicrous; laughable. —**'comically** *adv.*

comic opera *n.* a play largely set to music, with comic effects or situations.

comic strip *n.* a sequence of drawings in a newspaper or magazine, telling a humorous story or an adventure.

coming ('kʌmɪŋ) *adj.* **1.** (of time or events) approaching or next. **2.** likely to be important in the future: *the coming thing.* **3. have it coming to one.** *Informal.* to deserve what one is about to suffer. ~*n.* **4.** arrival or approach.

comity ('kɒmɪtɪ) *n., pl.* **-ties.** friendly politeness; courtesy, esp. between nations.

comma ('kɒmə) *n.* the punctuation mark , indicating a slight pause and used where there is a list of items or to separate the parts of a sentence.

command (kə'mɑːnd) *vb.* **1.** to order or compel. **2.** to have or be in control or authority over. **3.** to deserve and get: *his nature commands respect.* **4.** to be able to see clearly as from a height. ~*n.* **5.** an order. **6.** the authority to command. **7.** knowledge; control: *a command of French.* **8.** a military or naval unit with a specific function. **9.** *Computers.* a part of a program consisting of a coded instruction to the computer to perform a specified function.

commandant ('kɒmən,dænt, -,dɑːnt) *n.* an officer commanding a military group or establishment.

commandeer (,kɒmən'dɪə) *vb.* **1.** to seize for public or military use. **2.** to take arbitrarily.

commander (kə'mɑːndə) *n.* **1.** an officer in command of a particular military formation or operation. **2.** a naval commissioned rank. **3.** a high-ranking member of some knightly orders.

commander in chief *n., pl.* **commanders in chief.** the officer holding supreme command of a nation's armed forces.

commanding (kə'mɑːndɪŋ) *adj.* **1.** being in charge. **2.** having the air of authority: *a commanding voice.* **3.** having a wide view.

commandment (kə'mɑːndmənt) *n.* a divine command, esp. one of the Ten Commandments of the Old Testament.

commando (kə'mɑːndəʊ) *n., pl.* **-dos** *or* **-does. a.** a military unit trained for swift, destructive raiding in enemy territory. **b.** a member of such a unit.

commedia dell'arte (kɒ'meɪdɪə dɛl'ɑːtɪ) *n.* a form of improvised comedy popular in Italy in the 16th century, with stock characters and a stereotyped plot.

commemorate (kə'mɛmə,reɪt) *vb.* to honour or keep alive the memory of. —**com,memo'ration** *n.* —**com'memorative** *adj.*

commence (kə'mɛns) *vb.* to begin.

commencement (kə'mɛnsmənt) *n.* **1.** the beginning; start. **2.** *U.S. & Canad.* a graduation ceremony.

commend (kə'mɛnd) *vb.* **1.** to recommend. **2.** to give in charge; entrust. **3.** to praise. —**com'mendable** *adj.* —,**commen'dation** *n.*

commensurable (kə'mɛnsərəbəl) *adj.* **1.** *Maths.* **a.** having a common factor. **b.** having units of the same dimensions and being related by whole numbers. **2.** measurable by the same standards. —**com,mensura'bility** *n.*

commensurate (kə'mɛnʃərɪt) *adj.* **1.** corresponding in degree, amount, or value. **2.** commensurable.

comment ('kɒmɛnt) *n.* **1.** a remark, criticism, or observation. **2.** talk or gossip. **3.** a note explaining or criticizing a passage in a text. ~*vb.* **4.** (often foll. by *on*) to remark or express an opinion. **5. no comment.** I decline to say anything about the matter.

commentary ('kɒməntrɪ) *n., pl.* **-taries. 1.** a spoken accompaniment to an event, broadcast, or film. **2.** an explanatory series of notes on a text or other subject.

commentate ('kɒmən,teɪt) *vb.* to act as a commentator.

commentator ('kɒmən,teɪtə) *n.* **1.** a person who provides a spoken commentary for a broadcast or film, esp. of a sporting event. **2.** an expert who reports on and analyses a particular subject.

commerce ('kɒmɜːs) *n.* **1.** the purchase and sale of goods and services; trade. **2.** social relations.

commercial (kə'mɜːʃəl) *adj.* **1.** of or engaged in commerce. **2.** sponsored or paid for by an advertiser: *commercial television.* **3.** having profit as the main aim: *commercial music.* ~*n.* **4.** a radio or television advertisement.

commercialism (kə'mɜːʃə,lɪzəm) *n.* **1.** the principles and practices of commerce. **2.** exclusive or inappropriate emphasis on profit.

commercialize *or* **-lise** (kə'mɜːʃə,laɪz) *vb.* **1.** to make commercial. **2.** to exploit for profit, esp. at the expense of quality. —**com,merciali'zation** *or* **-li'sation** *n.*

commercial traveller *n.* same as **travelling salesman.**

commie *or* **commy** ('kɒmɪ) *n., pl.* **-mies,** *adj. Informal & offensive.* short for **communist.**

commination (,kɒmɪ'neɪʃən) *n.* the act of

threatening divine punishment or vengeance.

commingle (kɒˈmɪŋgᵊl) vb. to mix or be mixed.

commis (ˈkɒmɪs, ˈkɒmɪ) n., pl. -mis. an apprentice waiter or chef.

commiserate (kəˈmɪzəˌreɪt) vb. (usually foll. by with) to feel or express sympathy or pity (for). —com‚miser'ation n.

commissar (ˈkɒmɪˌsɑː, ˌkɒmɪˈsɑː) n. (in the Soviet Union) an official of the Communist Party responsible for political education.

commissariat (ˌkɒmɪˈsɛərɪət) n. a military department in charge of food supplies.

commissary (ˈkɒmɪsərɪ) n., pl. -saries. 1. U.S. a shop supplying food or equipment, as in a military camp. 2. a representative or deputy.

commission (kəˈmɪʃən) n. 1. a duty given to a person or group to perform. 2. authority to perform certain duties. 3. Mil. a. a document conferring a rank on an officer. b. the rank granted. 4. a body or board appointed to perform certain duties: a commission of inquiry. 5. the fee or percentage paid to an agent, esp. a salesman, for services rendered. 6. the act of committing a sin or crime. 7. in (or out of) commission. in good (or bad) working order. ~vb. 8. to grant authority to. 9. Mil. to confer a rank on. 10. to prepare (a ship) for active service. 11. to place an order for (something): to commission a portrait.

commissionaire (kəˌmɪʃəˈnɛə) n. Chiefly Brit. a uniformed doorman at a hotel, theatre, or cinema.

commissioned officer n. a military officer holding rank by a commission.

commissioner (kəˈmɪʃənə) n. 1. an appointed official in a government department or other organization. 2. a member of a commission.

commit (kəˈmɪt) vb. -mitting, -mitted. 1. to hand over, as for safekeeping; entrust. 2. **commit to memory.** to memorize. 3. **commit to paper** or **writing.** to write down. 4. to send (someone) to prison or hospital against their will. 5. (usually passive) to pledge or bind (oneself), as to a particular cause: a committed radical. 6. to perform (a crime or error).

commitment (kəˈmɪtmənt) n. 1. the act of committing or state of being committed. 2. an obligation, responsibility, or promise that restricts freedom of action. 3. dedication to a cause or principle.

committee (kəˈmɪtɪ) n. a group of people appointed to perform a specified service or function.

commode (kəˈməʊd) n. 1. a chair with a hinged flap concealing a chamber pot. 2. a chest of drawers.

commodious (kəˈməʊdɪəs) adj. roomy; spacious.

commodity (kəˈmɒdɪtɪ) n., pl. -ties. something of use or profit, esp. something that can be bought or sold.

commodore (ˈkɒməˌdɔː) n. 1. Brit. a senior commissioned officer in the navy. 2. the president of a yacht club.

common (ˈkɒmən) adj. 1. belonging to two or more people: common property. 2. belonging to the whole community; public: a common culture. 3. widespread among people in general: common decency; common knowledge. 4. frequently encountered: a common brand of soap. 5. lowclass, vulgar, or coarse. 6. not belonging to the upper classes: the common man. 7. Maths. belonging to two or more: common denominator. 8. **common or garden.** Informal. ordinary; usual. ~n. 9. a piece of open land belonging to all the members of a community. 10. **in common.** shared, in joint use. ~See also **commons.** —'**commonly** adv.

commonality (ˌkɒməˈnælɪtɪ) n., pl. -ties. 1. the sharing of common attributes. 2. the ordinary people.

commonalty (ˈkɒmənəltɪ) n., pl. -ties. 1. the ordinary people. 2. the members of an incorporated society.

commoner (ˈkɒmənə) n. a person who does not belong to the nobility.

common fraction n. same as **simple fraction.**

common law n. law based on judges' decisions and custom, as distinct from written laws.

common-law marriage n. a relationship regarded as a marriage, between a man and a woman who have lived together for a number of years.

Common Market n. **the.** an economic association of European countries, who make decisions on trade and agriculture. Also called: **European Community, European Economic Community.**

commonplace (ˈkɒmənˌpleɪs) adj. 1. ordinary; everyday. 2. dull; trite: commonplace prose. ~n. 3. a cliché; trite remark. 4. an ordinary thing.

common room n. Chiefly Brit. a sitting room for students or staff in schools or colleges.

commons (ˈkɒmənz) pl. n. 1. Brit. shared food or rations. 2. **short commons.** reduced rations.

Commons (ˈkɒmənz) n. **the.** same as **House of Commons.**

common sense n. 1. good practical sense. ~adj. **common-sense.** 2. inspired by or displaying this.

common time n. Music. a time signature with four crotchet beats to the bar; fourfour time.

commonwealth (ˈkɒmənˌwɛlθ) n. the people of a state or nation viewed politically.

Commonwealth ('kɒmən,wɛlθ) *n.* **the. 1.** Official name: **the Commonwealth of Nations.** an association of sovereign states that are or at some time have been ruled by Britain. **2.** the official title of the federated states of Australia.

commotion (kə'məʊʃən) *n.* **1.** violent disturbance; upheaval. **2.** a confused noise; din.

communal ('kɒmjʊn³l) *adj.* **1.** belonging to or used by a community as a whole. **2.** of a commune. —**'communally** *adv.*

commune[1] (kə'mjuːn) *vb.* (usually foll. by *with*) **1.** to talk intimately. **2.** to experience strong emotion (for): *to commune with nature.*

commune[2] ('kɒmjuːn) *n.* **1.** a group of families or individuals living together and sharing possessions and responsibilities. **2.** the smallest district of local government in Belgium, France, Italy, and Switzerland.

communicable (kə'mjuːnɪkəb³l) *adj.* **1.** capable of being communicated. **2.** (of a disease) capable of being passed on readily.

communicant (kə'mjuːnɪkənt) *n. Christianity.* a person who receives Communion.

communicate (kə'mjuːnɪ,keɪt) *vb.* **1.** to exchange (thoughts) or make known (information or feelings) by speech, writing, or other means. **2.** (usually foll. by *to*) to transmit (to): *the dog communicated his fear to the other animals.* **3.** to have a sympathetic mutual understanding. **4.** (usually foll. by *with*) to connect: *the kitchen communicates with the dining room.* **5.** *Christianity.* to receive Communion. —**com'muni,cator** *n.* —**com'municative** *adj.*

communication (kə,mjuːnɪ'keɪʃən) *n.* **1.** the imparting or exchange of information, ideas, or feelings. **2.** something communicated, such as a message.

communication cord *n. Brit.* a cord or chain in a train which may be pulled by a passenger to stop the train in an emergency.

communion (kə'mjuːnjən) *n.* **1.** a sharing of thoughts, emotions, or beliefs. **2.** (foll. by *with*) strong feelings (for): *communion with nature.* **3.** a religious group having common beliefs and practices.

Communion (kə'mjuːnjən) *n. Christianity.* **1.** a ritual commemorating Christ's Last Supper by the consecration of bread and wine. **2.** the consecrated bread and wine. ~Also called: **Holy Communion.**

communiqué (kə'mjuːnɪ,keɪ) *n.* an official communication or announcement.

communism ('kɒmjʊ,nɪzəm) *n.* **1.** the belief that private ownership should be abolished and all work and property should be shared by the community. **2.** (*cap.*) a political movement based upon the writings of Marx that advocates communism. **3.** (*cap.*) the political and social system established

in countries with a ruling Communist Party, esp. in the Soviet Union.

communist ('kɒmjʊnɪst) *n.* **1.** a supporter of communism. **2.** (*cap.*) a member of a Communist party. ~*adj.* **3.** of or favouring communism. —**,commu'nistic** *adj.*

community (kə'mjuːnɪtɪ) *n., pl.* **-ties. 1.** the people living in one locality. **2.** a group of people having cultural or other characteristics in common: *the Chinese community.* **3.** a group of nations having certain interests in common. **4.** the public; society. **5.** a group of interdependent plants and animals inhabiting the same region.

community centre *n.* a building used by a community for social gatherings or activities.

community charge *n.* the formal name for **poll tax.**

commutative (kə'mjuːtətɪv, 'kɒmjʊ,teɪtɪv) *adj. Maths.* giving the same result irrespective of the order of the numbers or symbols; thus addition is commutative but subtraction is not.

commutator ('kɒmjʊ,teɪtə) *n.* a device used to reverse the direction of flow of an electric current.

commute (kə'mjuːt) *vb.* **1.** to travel some distance regularly between one's home and one's place of work. **2.** to substitute. **3.** *Law.* to reduce (a sentence) to one less severe. **4.** to pay (an annuity or pension) at one time, instead of in instalments. —**com'mutable** *adj.* —**commutation** (,kɒmjʊ'teɪʃən) *n.*

commuter (kə'mjuːtə) *n.* a person who travels a considerable distance to work, usually from the suburbs to the centre of a city.

compact[1] *adj.* (kəm'pækt). **1.** closely packed together. **2.** neatly fitted into a restricted space. **3.** concise; brief. ~*vb.* (kəm'pækt). **4.** to pack closely together; compress. ~*n.* ('kɒmpækt). **5.** a small flat case containing a mirror and face powder. —**com'pactly** *adv.* —**com'pactness** *n.*

compact[2] ('kɒmpækt) *n.* a contract or agreement.

compact disc ('kɒmpækt) *n.* a small digital audio disc on which the sound is read by an optical laser system.

companion (kəm'pænjən) *n.* **1.** a person who associates with or accompanies another. **2.** (esp. formerly) a woman paid to live or travel with another. **3.** one of a pair. **4.** a guidebook or handbook. —**com'panion,ship** *n.*

companionable (kəm'pænjənəb³l) *adj.* sociable; friendly. —**com'panionably** *adv.*

companionway (kəm'pænjən,weɪ) *n.* a ladder from one deck to another in a ship.

company ('kʌmpənɪ) *n., pl.* **-nies. 1.** a number of people gathered together; assembly. **2.** the fact of being with someone;

companionship: *I enjoy her company.* **3.** a guest or guests. **4.** a person's associates. **5.** a business organization. **6.** a group of actors. **7.** a small unit of troops. **8.** the officers and crew of a ship. **9. keep someone company.** to accompany someone. **10. part company** to disagree or separate.

company sergeant-major *n. Mil.* the senior noncommissioned officer in a company.

comparable ('kɒmpərəb³l) *adj.* **1.** worthy of comparison. **2.** able to be compared (with). —,**compara'bility** *n.*

comparative (kəm'pærətɪv) *adj.* **1.** involving comparison: *comparative literature.* **2.** relative: *comparative peace.* **3.** *Grammar.* the form of an adjective or adverb that indicates that the quality denoted is possessed to a greater extent. In English the comparative is marked by the suffix *-er* or the word *more.* ~*n.* **4.** the comparative form of an adjective or adverb. —**com'paratively** *adv.*

compare (kəm'pɛə) *vb.* **1.** (foll. by *to*) to regard as similar; liken: *the general has been compared to Napoleon.* **2.** to examine in order to observe resemblances or differences: *to compare rum and gin.* **3.** (usually foll. by *with*) to resemble: *gin compares with rum in strength.* **4.** to bear a specified relation when examined: *this car compares badly with the other.* **5. compare notes.** to exchange opinions. ~*n.* **6. beyond compare.** without equal.
Usage. *Compare* is followed by *to* when it is used in the sense of "liken, point out a resemblance": *I don't know how to describe it — I haven't anything to compare it to;* and by *with* when points of resemblance are being made: *in my next lecture I shall compare seventeenth-century French drama with classical Greek theatre.*

comparison (kəm'pærɪs³n) *n.* **1.** a comparing or being compared. **2.** likeness: *there was no comparison between them.* **3.** *Grammar.* the positive, comparative, and superlative forms of an adjective or adverb. **4. in comparison to** *or* **with.** compared to. **5. bear** *or* **stand comparison with.** to be able to be compared with (something else), esp. favourably.

compartment (kəm'pɑːtmənt) *n.* **1.** (esp. formerly) one of the sections into which a railway carriage is divided. **2.** any separate section: *a compartment of the mind.* **3.** a small storage space.

compartmentalize *or* **-lise** (,kɒmpɑːt-'mɛnt³,laɪz) *vb.* to put into categories, esp. to an excessive degree.

compass ('kʌmpəs) *n.* **1.** an instrument for finding direction, having a magnetized needle which points to magnetic north. **2.** (*often pl.*) an instrument used for drawing circles or measuring distances, that consists

of two arms, joined at one end. **3.** limits or range: *within the compass of education.*

compassion (kəm'pæʃən) *n.* a feeling of distress and pity for the suffering or misfortune of another.

compassionate (kəm'pæʃənɪt) *adj.* showing or having compassion. —**com'passionately** *adv.*

compatible (kəm'pætɪb³l) *adj.* **1.** (usually foll. by *with*) able to exist together harmoniously. **2.** (usually foll. by *with*) consistent: *her deeds were not compatible with her ideology.* **3.** (of pieces of equipment) capable of being used together. —**com,pati'bility** *n.*

compatriot (kəm'pætrɪət) *n.* a fellow countryman.

compel (kəm'pɛl) *vb.* **-pelling, -pelled. 1.** to force (someone) (to be or do something). **2.** to obtain by force; exact: *to compel obedience.*

compelling (kəm'pɛlɪŋ) *adj.* forceful; arousing strong interest.

compendious (kəm'pɛndɪəs) *adj.* brief but comprehensive.

compendium (kəm'pɛndɪəm) *n., pl.* **-diums** *or* **-dia** (-dɪə). **1.** *Brit.* a selection of different table games in one container. **2.** a concise but comprehensive summary.

compensate ('kɒmpɛn,seɪt) *vb.* **1.** to make amends to (someone), esp. for loss or injury. **2.** to serve as compensation for (injury or loss). **3.** to cancel out the effects of (something). —**compensatory** ('kɒmpɛn,seɪtrɪ, kɒm'pɛnsətrɪ) *adj.*

compensation (,kɒmpɛn'seɪʃən) *n.* **1.** the act of making amends for something. **2.** something given as reparation for loss or injury.

compere ('kɒmpɛə) *Brit.* ~*n.* **1.** a person who introduces a radio or television show, esp. a variety show. ~*vb.* **2.** to act as a compere (for).

compete (kəm'piːt) *vb.* (often foll. by *with*) to take part in a contest or competition (against).

competence ('kɒmpɪtəns) *or* **competency** *n.* **1.** the condition of being capable; ability. **2.** a sufficient income to live on. **3.** the state of being legally competent or qualified.

competent ('kɒmpɪtənt) *adj.* **1.** having sufficient skill or knowledge; capable. **2.** suitable or sufficient for the purpose: *a competent answer.*

competition (,kɒmpɪ'tɪʃən) *n.* **1.** the act of competing; rivalry. **2.** an event in which people compete. **3.** a series of games or sports events. **4.** the opposition offered by competitors. **5.** competitors offering opposition.

competitive (kəm'pɛtɪtɪv) *adj.* **1.** involving rivalry: *competitive sports.* **2.** of sufficiently good value to be successful against commercial rivals. **3.** characterized by an urge to compete: *a competitive personality.* —**com'petitiveness** n.

competitor (kəm'pɛtɪtə) n. a person, team, or firm, that vies or competes; rival.

compile (kəm'paɪl) vb. **1.** to collect and arrange (information) from various sources, esp. to form a book. **2.** *Computers.* to create (a set of machine instructions) from a high-level programming language, using a compiler. —**compilation** (ˌkɒmpɪ-'leɪʃən) n.

compiler (kəm'paɪlə) n. **1.** a person who compiles information, esp. to form a book. **2.** a computer program which converts a high-level programming language into the machine language used by a computer.

complacency (kəm'pleɪsənsɪ) n. extreme self-satisfaction; smugness. —**com'placent** adj.

complain (kəm'pleɪn) vb. **1.** to express resentment or displeasure. **2.** (foll. by *of*) to state the presence of pain or illness: *she complained of a headache.* **3.** to make a formal protest: *she complained to the police about the noise.*

complainant (kəm'pleɪnənt) n. *Law.* a plaintiff.

complaint (kəm'pleɪnt) n. **1.** the act of complaining. **2.** a cause for complaining; grievance. **3.** a mild ailment. **4.** a formal protest.

complaisant (kəm'pleɪz²nt) adj. willing to please or oblige. —**com'plaisance** n.

complement n. ('kɒmplɪmənt). **1.** a person or thing that completes something. **2.** a complete amount or number: *the full complement.* **3.** the officers and crew needed to man a ship. **4.** *Grammar.* a word or words added to the verb to complete the meaning of the predicate in a sentence, as *a fool* in *He is a fool* or *that he would come* in *I hoped that he would come.* **5.** *Maths.* the angle that when added to a specified angle produces a right angle. ~vb. ('kɒmplɪ-ˌmɛnt). **6.** to complete or form a complement to.

complementary (ˌkɒmplɪ'mɛntrɪ) adj. **1.** forming a complement. **2.** forming a complete or balanced whole.

complementary medicine n. same as **alternative medicine.**

complete (kəm'pliːt) adj. **1.** having every necessary part; entire. **2.** finished. **3.** thorough; absolute: *he is a complete rogue.* **4.** perfect in quality or kind: *he is a complete scholar.* **5. complete with.** having as an extra feature or part: *a mansion complete with swimming pool.* ~vb. **6.** to make whole or perfect. **7.** to finish. —**com'pletely** adv. —**com'pletion** n.

complex ('kɒmplɛks) adj. **1.** made up of interconnected parts. **2.** intricate or complicated. **3.** *Maths.* of or involving complex numbers. ~n. **4.** a whole made up of related parts: *a sports complex.* **5.** *Psychoanal.* a group of emotional impulses that have been banished from the conscious mind but continue to influence a person's behaviour. **6.** *Informal.* an obsession or phobia: *he's got a complex about cats.*

complex fraction n. *Maths.* a fraction in which the numerator or denominator or both contain fractions.

complexion (kəm'plɛkʃən) n. **1.** the colour and general appearance of a person's skin, esp. of the face. **2.** aspect, character, or nature: *the general complexion of a nation's finances.*

complexity (kəm'plɛksɪtɪ) n., pl. -ties. **1.** the state or quality of being intricate or complex. **2.** something intricate; complication.

complex number n. any number of the form $a + bi$, where a and b are real numbers and $i = \sqrt{-1}$.

compliance (kəm'plaɪəns) n. **1.** acquiescence. **2.** a tendency to yield to others. —**com'pliant** adj.

complicate ('kɒmplɪˌkeɪt) vb. to make or become complex or difficult.

complicated ('kɒmplɪˌkeɪtɪd) adj. difficult to understand or deal with.

complication (ˌkɒmplɪ'keɪʃən) n. **1.** a complicated or confused state of affairs. **2.** a complicating factor: *her coming was a serious complication.* **3.** a medical condition arising as a consequence of another.

complicity (kəm'plɪsɪtɪ) n., pl. -ties. the fact of being an accomplice, esp. in a criminal act.

compliment n. ('kɒmplɪmənt). **1.** a remark or praise expressing respect. **2.** (pl.) a greeting of respect or regard. ~vb. ('kɒmplɪˌmɛnt). **3.** to express admiration for; congratulate.

complimentary (ˌkɒmplɪ'mɛntrɪ) adj. **1.** expressing a compliment. **2.** given free, esp. as a courtesy or for publicity purposes.

comply (kəm'plaɪ) vb. -plying, -plied. (usually foll. by *with*) to act in accordance with a rule, order or request.

component (kəm'pəʊnənt) n. **1.** a constituent part or feature of a whole. **2.** *Maths.* one of a set of two or more vectors whose resultant is a given vector. ~adj. **3.** forming or functioning as a part or feature; constituent.

comport (kəm'pɔːt) vb. **1.** to conduct or behave (oneself) in a specified way. **2.** (foll. by *with*) to suit or befit. —**com'portment** n.

compose (kəm'pəʊz) vb. **1.** to put together or make up. **2.** to be the component elements of. **3.** to create (a musical or literary work). **4.** to calm (oneself). **5.** to arrange artistically; design. **6.** *Printing.* to set up (type). —**com'poser** n.

composed (kəm'pəʊzd) *adj.* (of people) calm; tranquil.

composite ('kɒmpəzɪt) *adj.* **1.** composed of separate parts. **2.** (of a plant) having flower heads made up of many small flowers, as the dandelion or daisy. **3.** *Maths.* capable of being factorized: *a composite function.* ~*n.* **4.** something composed of separate parts. **5.** a composite plant.

composite school *n. Canad.* a secondary school which offers both academic and nonacademic courses.

composition (,kɒmpə'zɪʃən) *n.* **1.** the act of putting together or composing. **2.** something composed. **3.** the things or parts which make up a whole. **4.** a work of music, art, or literature. **5.** the harmonious arrangement of the parts of a work of art. **6.** a written exercise; an essay. **7.** *Printing.* the act or technique of setting up type.

compositor (kəm'pɒzɪtə) *n. Printing.* a person who sets and corrects type.

compos mentis Latin. ('kɒmpəs 'mɛntɪs) *adj.* of sound mind; sane.

compost ('kɒmpɒst) *n.* **1.** a mixture of decaying plants and manure, used as a fertilizer. **2.** soil mixed with fertilizer, used for growing plants. ~*vb.* **3.** to make (vegetable matter) into compost.

composure (kəm'pəʊʒə) *n.* calmness; tranquillity; serenity.

compote ('kɒmpəʊt) *n.* fruit stewed with sugar or in a syrup.

compound[1] *n.* ('kɒmpaʊnd). **1.** a substance that contains atoms of two or more chemical elements held together by chemical bonds. **2.** any combination of two or more parts, features, or qualities. **3.** a word formed from two existing words or combining forms. ~*vb.* (kəm'paʊnd). **4.** to combine so as to create a compound. **5.** to make by combining parts or features: *to compound a new plastic.* **6.** to intensify by an added element: *his anxiety was compounded by her crying.* **7.** *Law.* to agree not to prosecute in return for payment: *to compound a crime.* ~*adj.* ('kɒmpaʊnd). **8.** composed of two or more parts or elements. **9.** *Music.* with a time in which the number of beats per bar is a multiple of three: *six-four is an example of compound time.* —**com'poundable** *adj.*

compound[2] ('kɒmpaʊnd) *n.* a fenced enclosure containing buildings, such as a camp for prisoners of war.

compound fracture *n.* a fracture in which the broken bone pierces the skin.

compound interest *n.* interest paid on both the sum invested and its accumulated interest.

compound sentence *n.* a sentence containing at least two clauses linked by *and*, *or*, or *but*.

comprehend (,kɒmprɪ'hɛnd) *vb.* **1.** to understand. **2.** to comprise; include. —**compre'hensible** *adj.*

comprehension (,kɒmprɪ'hɛnʃən) *n.* **1.** understanding. **2.** inclusion.

comprehensive (,kɒmprɪ'hɛnsɪv) *adj.* **1.** of broad scope or content; fully inclusive. **2.** (of car insurance) providing protection against most risks, including third-party liability, fire, theft, and damage. **3.** of the comprehensive school system. ~*n.* **4.** a comprehensive school.

comprehensive school *n. Chiefly Brit.* a secondary school for children of all abilities from the same district.

compress *vb.* (kəm'prɛs). **1.** to squeeze together; condense. ~*n.* ('kɒmprɛs). **2.** a cloth or pad applied firmly to some part of the body to relieve discomfort or reduce fever.

compression (kəm'prɛʃən) *n.* **1.** the act of compressing or state of being compressed. **2.** the reduction in volume and increase in pressure of the fuel mixture in an internal-combustion engine before ignition.

compressor (kəm'prɛsə) *n.* any device that compresses a gas.

comprise (kəm'praɪz) *vb.* **1.** to be made up of: *the Council comprised 28 members.* **2.** to constitute the whole: *her singing comprised the entertainment.*
Usage. Comprise when it means "to consist of, be made up of" is not itself followed by *of: the work comprises the following duties.* It differs from *include* in being comprehensive; the above example means that all the duties are about to be mentioned, whereas *the work includes the following duties* implies that there may be others in addition to those about to be mentioned.

compromise ('kɒmprə,maɪz) *n.* **1.** settlement of a dispute by concessions on each side. **2.** the terms of such a settlement. **3.** something midway between different things. ~*vb.* **4.** to settle (a dispute) by making concessions. **5.** to expose (oneself or another) to disrepute. —**'compro,mising** *adj.*

Comptometer (kɒmp'tɒmɪtə) *n. Trademark.* a high-speed calculating machine.

comptroller (kən'trəʊlə) *n.* a financial controller.

compulsion (kəm'pʌlʃən) *n.* **1.** the act of compelling or the state of being compelled. **2.** something that compels. **3.** an irresistible urge to perform some action.

compulsive (kəm'pʌlsɪv) *adj.* **1.** resulting from or acting from a compulsion. **2.** irresistible or absorbing. —**com'pulsively** *adv.*

compulsory (kəm'pʌlsərɪ) *adj.* required by regulations or laws; obligatory.

compulsory purchase *n.* the enforced purchase of a property by a local authority or government department.

compunction (kəmˈpʌŋkʃən) *n.* a feeling of remorse, guilt, or regret.

computation (ˌkɒmpjuˈteɪʃən) *n.* a calculation involving numbers or quantities. —ˌcompuˈtational *adj.*

compute (kəmˈpjuːt) *vb.* to calculate (an answer or result), often with the aid of a computer.

computer (kəmˈpjuːtə) *n.* a device, usually electronic, that processes data according to a set of instructions. See **digital computer.**

computerize *or* **-ise** (kəmˈpjuːtəˌraɪz) *vb.* **1.** to equip with a computer. **2.** to control or perform (operations) by means of a computer. —comˌputeriˈzation *or* -iˈsation *n.*

comrade (ˈkɒmreɪd, -rɪd) *n.* **1.** a companion. **2.** a fellow member of a political party, esp. a fellow Communist. —ˈcomradely *adj.* —ˈcomradeˌship *n.*

con[1] (kɒn) *Informal.* ~*n.* **1.** same as **confidence trick.** ~*vb.* **conning, conned. 2.** to swindle or defraud.

con[2] (kɒn) *n.* See **pros and cons.**

con[3] (kɒn) *n. Slang.* a convict.

Con *Politics.* Conservative.

con- See **com-.**

concatenation (ˌkɒnkætɪˈneɪʃən) *n.* a series of linked events.

concave (ˈkɒnkeɪv, kɒnˈkeɪv) *adj.* curving inwards like the inside surface of a ball. —**concavity** (kɒnˈkævɪtɪ) *n.*

conceal (kənˈsiːl) *vb.* to keep hidden or secret. —**conˈcealment** *n.*

concede (kənˈsiːd) *vb.* **1.** to admit (something) as true or correct. **2.** to give up or grant (something, such as a right). **3.** to acknowledge defeat in (a contest or argument).

conceit (kənˈsiːt) *n.* **1.** an excessively high opinion of oneself or one's merits. **2.** *Literary.* a far-fetched or clever comparison.

conceited (kənˈsiːtɪd) *adj.* having an excessively high opinion of oneself or one's merits. —**conˈceitedness** *n.*

conceivable (kənˈsiːvəb³l) *adj.* capable of being understood, believed, or imagined; possible. —**conˈceivably** *adv.*

conceive (kənˈsiːv) *vb.* **1.** to form in the mind; imagine; think (of). **2.** to consider in a certain way; believe: *we must do what we conceive to be right.* **3.** to become pregnant with (a child).

concentrate (ˈkɒnsənˌtreɪt) *vb.* **1.** to focus all one's attention, thoughts, or efforts (on): *stop talking and concentrate on your work.* **2.** to make a liquid stronger by the removal of water from it. **3.** to bring or come together in large numbers or amounts, in one place: *power is concentrated in the hands of the rich.* ~*n.* **4.** a concentrated substance. —ˈconcenˌtrated *adj.*

concentration (ˌkɒnsənˈtreɪʃən) *n.* **1.** intense mental application. **2.** the act of concentrating. **3.** something that is concentrated. **4.** the amount or proportion of a substance in a mixture or solution.

concentration camp *n.* a prison camp for nonmilitary prisoners, as in Nazi Germany.

concentric (kənˈsɛntrɪk) *adj.* having a common centre: *concentric circles.*

concept (ˈkɒnsɛpt) *n.* an idea, esp. an abstract or generalized one: *the concepts of biology.*

conception (kənˈsɛpʃən) *n.* **1.** a notion, idea, or plan. **2.** the fertilization of an egg by a sperm in the womb. **3.** origin or beginning.

conceptual (kənˈsɛptjʊəl) *adj.* of or characterized by concepts.

conceptualize *or* **-lise** (kənˈsɛptjʊəˌlaɪz) *vb.* to form a concept or idea of (something). —conˌceptualiˈzation *or* -liˈsation *n.*

concern (kənˈsɜːn) *vb.* **1.** to be relevant or important to. **2.** (usually foll. by *with* or *in*) to involve or interest (oneself): *he concerns himself with other people's affairs.* **3.** to worry or make anxious. ~*n.* **4.** something that is of interest or importance to a person. **5.** regard or interest: *he felt a strong concern for her.* **6.** anxiety or worry. **7.** a business or firm.

concerned (kənˈsɜːnd) *adj.* **1.** interested or involved: *I shall find the boy concerned and punish him.* **2.** worried or anxious.

concerning (kənˈsɜːnɪŋ) *prep.* about; regarding.

concert (ˈkɒnsɜːt) *n.* **1.** a performance of music by players or singers in front of an audience. **2. in concert. a.** acting with a common purpose. **b.** (of musicians or singers) performing live.

concerted (kənˈsɜːtɪd) *adj.* decided or planned by mutual agreement; done in co-operation: *a concerted effort.*

concertina (ˌkɒnsəˈtiːnə) *n.* **1.** a small musical instrument similar to the accordion, in which two flat end pieces, joined by folds of material, are pressed together and pulled apart to force air through reeds. ~*vb.* **-naing, -naed. 2.** to collapse or fold up like a concertina.

concerto (kənˈtʃɛətəʊ) *n., pl.* **-tos** *or* **-ti** (-tɪ). a large-scale composition for an orchestra and one or more soloists.

concert pitch *n.* the internationally agreed pitch to which concert instruments are tuned for performance.

concession (kənˈsɛʃən) *n.* **1.** the act of yielding or conceding. **2.** something conceded. **3.** any grant of rights, land, or property by a government, local authority, or company. **4.** a reduction in price for a certain category of person: *there is a special concession for students.* **5.** *Canad.* **a.** a land subdivision in a township survey. **b.** same as **concession road.** —**con'cessionary** *adj.*

concessionaire (kənˌsɛʃə'nɛə) *n.* someone who holds a concession.

concession road *n. Canad.* one of a series of roads separating concessions in a township.

conch (kɒŋk, kɒntʃ) *n., pl.* **conchs** (kɒŋks) *or* **conches** ('kɒntʃɪz). **1.** a marine mollusc with a large brightly coloured spiral shell. **2.** the shell of such a mollusc.

concierge (ˌkɒnsɪ'ɛəʒ) *n.* (in France) a porter or door-keeper, esp. of a block of flats.

conciliate (kən'sɪlɪˌeɪt) *vb.* to overcome the hostility of; win over. —**con,cili'ation** *n.* —**con'cili,ator** *n.*

conciliatory (kən'sɪljətrɪ) *adj.* intended to placate or reconcile.

concise (kən'saɪs) *adj.* brief and to the point. —**con'cisely** *adv.* —**con'ciseness** *or* **concision** (kən'sɪʒən) *n.*

conclave ('kɒnkleɪv) *n.* **1.** a secret meeting. **2.** *R.C. Church.* a private meeting of cardinals to elect a new pope.

conclude (kən'kluːd) *vb.* **1.** to come or bring to an end. **2.** to decide by reasoning; deduce: *the judge concluded that the witness had told the truth.* **3.** to arrange or settle finally: *to conclude a treaty.*

conclusion (kən'kluːʒən) *n.* **1.** end or ending. **2.** outcome or result: *a foregone conclusion.* **3.** a final decision, opinion or judgment based on reasoning: *to come to a conclusion.* **4. in conclusion.** lastly; to sum up. **5. jump to conclusions.** to come to a conclusion too quickly, without sufficient thought or evidence.

conclusive (kən'kluːsɪv) *adj.* putting an end to doubt; decisive; final. —**con'clusively** *adv.*

concoct (kən'kɒkt) *vb.* **1.** to make by combining different ingredients. **2.** to invent or make up (a story or plan). —**con'coction** *n.*

concomitant (kən'kɒmɪtənt) *adj.* **1.** existing or along with (something else). ~*n.* **2.** something which is concomitant.

concord ('kɒnkɔːd) *n.* **1.** agreement or harmony. **2.** peaceful relations between nations. **3.** *Music.* a harmonious combination of musical notes. —**con'cordant** *adj.*

concordance (kən'kɔːd²ns) *n.* **1.** a state of harmony or agreement. **2.** an alphabetical list of the principal words in a literary work, with the context and often an account of the meaning.

concordat (kɒn'kɔːdæt) *n.* a pact or treaty, such as one between the Vatican and another state concerning church affairs.

concourse ('kɒnkɔːs) *n.* **1.** a large open space in a public place, where people can meet: *the station concourse.* **2.** a crowd; throng.

concrete ('kɒnkriːt) *n.* **1.** a building material made of cement, sand, stone and water that hardens to a stonelike mass. ~*adj.* **2.** specific as opposed to general. **3.** relating to things that can be perceived by the senses, as opposed to abstractions. ~*vb.* **4.** to make from or cover with concrete.

concretion (kən'kriːʃən) *n.* **1.** the act of solidifying; coalescence. **2.** a solidified mass.

concubine ('kɒŋkjuˌbaɪn, 'kɒn-) *n.* **1.** a woman who cohabits with a man to whom she is not married. **2.** a secondary wife in polygamous societies. —**concubinage** (kɒn'kjuːbɪnɪdʒ) *n.*

concupiscence (kən'kjuːpɪsəns) *n.* strong sexual desire. —**con'cupiscent** *adj.*

concur (kən'kɜː) *vb.* **-curring, -curred.** to agree; be in accord.

concurrence (kən'kʌrəns) *n.* **1.** agreement; accord. **2.** simultaneous occurrence.

concurrent (kən'kʌrənt) *adj.* **1.** taking place at the same time or place. **2.** meeting at, approaching, or having a common point: *concurrent lines.* **3.** in agreement; harmonious.

concuss (kən'kʌs) *vb.* to subject to concussion.

concussion (kən'kʌʃən) *n.* **1.** a jarring of the brain, caused by a blow or a fall, usually resulting in loss of consciousness. **2.** violent shaking; shock, as from impact.

condemn (kən'dɛm) *vb.* **1.** to express strong disapproval of. **2.** to pronounce sentence on in a court of law. **3.** to indicate the guilt of: *his secretive behaviour condemned him.* **4.** to judge or declare (something) unfit for use. **5.** to force into a particular state: *his disposition condemned him to boredom.* —**,condem'nation** *n.* —**,condem'natory** *adj.*

condensation (ˌkɒndɛn'seɪʃən) *n.* **1.** the act of condensing, or the state of being condensed. **2.** anything that has condensed from a vapour, esp. on a window.

condense (kən'dɛns) *vb.* **1.** to increase the density of; compress. **2.** to express in fewer words. **3.** to change from a gas to a liquid or solid.

condensed milk *n.* milk thickened by evaporation, with sugar added.

condenser (kən'dɛnsə) *n.* **1.** an apparatus for reducing gases to their liquid or solid form by the removal of heat. **2.** a lens that concentrates light. **3.** same as **capacitor.**

condescend (ˌkɒndɪ'sɛnd) *vb.* **1.** to behave patronizingly towards one's supposed inferiors. **2.** to do something in a way that suggests one believes it to be beneath one's own level. —**,conde'scending** *adj.* —**,conde'scension** *n.*

condiment ('kɒndɪmənt) *n.* any seasoning for food, such as salt, pepper, or sauces.

condition (kən'dɪʃən) *n.* **1.** a particular state of being: *the human condition.* **2.**

something that limits or restricts; a qualification. **3.** (*pl.*) circumstances: *conditions were right for a takeover.* **4.** state of physical fitness, esp. good health: *out of condition.* **5.** an ailment: *a heart condition.* **6.** an indispensable requirement: *food is a necessary condition for survival.* **7.** a term of an agreement: *the conditions of the lease are set out.* **8. on condition that.** provided that. ~*vb.* **9.** to accustom or alter the reaction of (a person or animal) to a particular stimulus or situation. **10.** to put into a fit condition. **11.** to improve the condition of (one's hair) by use of special cosmetics. **12.** to subject to a condition. —**con'ditioner** *n.* —**con'ditioning** *n., adj.*

conditional (kən'dɪʃən²l) *adj.* **1.** depending on other factors. **2.** *Grammar.* expressing a condition on which something else depends: "*If he comes*" *is a conditional clause in the sentence* "*If he comes I shall go*".

condo ('kɒndəʊ) *n., pl.* **-dos.** *U.S. & Canad. informal.* a condominium building or apartment.

condole (kən'dəʊl) *vb.* (foll. by *with*) to express sympathy with someone in grief or pain. —**con'dolence** *n.*

condom ('kɒndəm) *n.* a rubber sheath worn on the penis during sexual intercourse to prevent conception or infection.

condominium (ˌkɒndə'mɪnɪəm) *n., pl.* **-ums.** **1.** joint rule or sovereignty of a state by two or more other states. **2.** *U.S. & Canad.* **a.** an apartment building in which each apartment is individually owned. **b.** an apartment in such a building.

condone (kən'dəʊn) *vb.* to overlook or forgive (an offence or wrongdoing).

condor ('kɒndɔː) *n.* a very large rare New World vulture.

conducive (kən'djuːsɪv) *adj.* (often foll. by *to*) likely to lead to or produce (a result).

conduct *n.* ('kɒndʌkt). **1.** behaviour. **2.** the management or handling of an activity or business. ~*vb.* (kən'dʌkt). **3.** to accompany and guide (people or a party): *a conducted tour.* **4.** to carry out; organize: *conduct a survey.* **5.** to behave (oneself). **6.** to control (an orchestra or choir) by the movements of the hands or a baton. **7.** to transmit (heat or electricity).

conductance (kən'dʌktəns) *n.* the ability of a specified body to conduct electricity.

conduction (kən'dʌkʃən) *n.* the transmission of something, esp. heat or electricity, through a medium.

conductivity (ˌkɒndʌk'tɪvɪtɪ) *n., pl.* **-ties.** the property of transmitting heat, electricity, or sound.

conductor (kən'dʌktə) *n.* **1.** a person who conducts an orchestra or choir. **2.** an official on a bus who collects fares. **3.** *U.S. & Canad.* a railway official in charge of a

train. **4.** something that conducts electricity or heat. —**con'ductress** *fem. n.*

conduit ('kɒndɪt, -djʊɪt) *n.* a channel or tube for carrying a fluid or electrical cables.

cone (kəʊn) *n.* **1.** a geometric solid consisting of a circular or oval base and curved sides narrowing evenly to a point. **2.** a cone-shaped wafer shell used to contain ice cream. **3.** the reproductive fruit of conifers, made up of overlapping woody scales. **4.** a plastic cone used as a temporary traffic marker on roads.

confab ('kɒnfæb) *n. Informal.* a conversation.

confabulation (kənˌfæbjʊ'leɪʃən) *n.* a chat or conversation.

confection (kən'fɛkʃən) *n.* **1.** any sweet food, such as a cake or a sweet. **2.** *Old-fashioned.* an elaborate article of clothing.

confectioner (kən'fɛkʃənə) *n.* a person who makes or sells sweets or confections.

confectionery (kən'fɛkʃənərɪ) *n., pl.* **-eries.** **1.** sweets and other confections collectively. **2.** the art or business of a confectioner.

confederacy (kən'fɛdərəsɪ) *n., pl.* **-cies.** a union of states or people joined for a common purpose.

confederate *n.* (kən'fɛdərɪt). **1.** a state or individual that is part of a confederacy. **2.** an accomplice or conspirator. ~*adj.* (kən'fɛdərɪt). **3.** united; allied. ~*vb.* (kən'fɛdəˌreɪt). **4.** to unite in a confederacy.

Confederate (kən'fɛdərɪt) *adj.* of or supporting those American states which withdrew from the U.S.A. in 1860-61, leading to the U.S. Civil War.

confederation (kənˌfɛdə'reɪʃən) *n.* **1.** the act of confederating or the state of being confederated. **2.** a union or alliance of states. **3.** a federation.

confer (kən'fɜː) *vb.* **-ferring, -ferred.** **1.** (foll. by *on* or *upon*) to grant or bestow (an honour, gift or status). **2.** to consult together. —**con'ferment** *n.* —**con'ferrable** *adj.*

conference ('kɒnfərəns) *n.* a meeting for consultation or discussion, esp. one with a formal agenda.

confess (kən'fɛs) *vb.* **1.** (often foll. by *to*) to admit (a fault or crimes). **2.** to admit to be true, esp. reluctantly. **3.** *Christianity.* to declare (one's sins) to God or to a priest, so as to obtain forgiveness.

confession (kən'fɛʃən) *n.* **1.** something confessed. **2.** an admission of one's faults, sins, or crimes. **3. confession of faith.** a formal public statement of religious beliefs.

confessional (kən'fɛʃən²l) *n.* **1.** *Christianity.* a small stall where a priest hears confessions. ~*adj.* **2.** of or suited to a confession.

confessor (kən'fɛsə) *n.* **1.** *Christianity.* a priest who hears confessions and gives spiritual counsel. **2.** *History.* a person who demonstrates his Christian religious faith by the holiness of his life: *Edward The Confessor*.

confetti (kən'fɛtɪ) *n.* small pieces of coloured paper thrown at weddings.

confidant or (*fem.*) **confidante** (ˌkɒnfɪ'dænt, 'kɒnfɪˌdænt) *n.* a person to whom private matters are confided.

confide (kən'faɪd) *vb.* **1.** (usually foll. by *in*) to disclose (secret or personal matters) in confidence (to). **2.** to entrust into another's keeping.

confidence ('kɒnfɪdəns) *n.* **1.** trust in a person or thing. **2.** belief in one's own abilities; self-assurance. **3.** trust or a trustful relationship: *take me into your confidence.* **4.** something confided; secret. **5. in confidence.** as a secret.

confidence trick or *U.S. & Canad.* **confidence game** *n.* a swindle in which the victim's trust is won by the swindler.

confident ('kɒnfɪdənt) *adj.* **1.** having or showing certainty; sure: *confident of success.* **2.** sure of oneself. —'**confidently** *adv.*

confidential (ˌkɒnfɪ'dɛnʃəl) *adj.* **1.** spoken or given in confidence; private. **2.** entrusted with another's secret affairs: *a confidential secretary.* **3.** suggestive of intimacy: *a confidential approach.* —ˌconfiˌdenti'ality *n.* —ˌconfi'dentially *adv.*

confiding (kən'faɪdɪŋ) *adj.* unsuspicious; trustful. —con'fidingly *adv.*

configuration (kənˌfɪgjʊ'reɪʃən) *n.* **1.** the arrangement of the parts of something. **2.** the form or outline of such an arrangement.

confine *vb.* (kən'faɪn). **1.** to keep within bounds; restrict. **2.** to restrict the free movement of: *arthritis confined him to bed.* ~*n.* ('kɒnfaɪn). **3.** (*often pl.*) a limit; boundary.

confinement (kən'faɪnmənt) *n.* **1.** a confining or being confined. **2.** the period of childbirth.

confirm (kən'fɜːm) *vb.* **1.** to prove to be true or valid; corroborate. **2.** to reaffirm (something), so as to make (it) more definite, or finalize (it): *he confirmed that he would appear in court.* **3.** to strengthen: *his story confirmed my doubts.* **4.** to formally make valid; ratify. **5.** to administer the rite of confirmation to.

confirmation (ˌkɒnfə'meɪʃən) *n.* **1.** the act of confirming. **2.** something that confirms. **3.** a rite in several Christian churches that admits a baptized person to full church membership.

confirmed (kən'fɜːmd) *adj.* longestablished in a habit or condition: *a confirmed bachelor.*

confiscate ('kɒnfɪˌskeɪt) *vb.* to seize (property) as a penalty. —ˌconfis'cation *n.*

conflagration (ˌkɒnflə'greɪʃən) *n.* a large destructive fire.

conflate (kən'fleɪt) *vb.* to combine or blend (two or more accounts or pieces of writing) so as to form a whole. —con'flation *n.*

conflict *n.* ('kɒnflɪkt). **1.** a struggle or battle. **2.** opposition between ideas or interests; controversy. ~*vb.* (kən'flɪkt). **3.** to be incompatible; clash. —con'flicting *adj.*

confluence ('kɒnflʊəns) *n.* **1.** a place where rivers flow into one another. **2.** a gathering. —'confluent *adj.*

conform (kən'fɔːm) *vb.* **1.** (usually foll. by *to*) to comply with accepted standards, rules, or customs. **2.** (usually foll. by *with*) to be like or in accordance with: *he conforms with my idea of a teacher.* —con'formist *n., adj.*

conformation (ˌkɒnfɔː'meɪʃən) *n.* **1.** the general shape of an object; configuration. **2.** the arrangement of the parts of an object.

conformity (kən'fɔːmɪtɪ) *n., pl.* -**ities**. **1.** compliance in actions or behaviour with certain accepted rules, customs, or standards. **2.** likeness; agreement.

confound (kən'faʊnd) *vb.* **1.** to astound; bewilder. **2.** to confuse; to fail to distinguish between. **3.** ('kɒn'faʊnd). **confound it!** damn it!

confounded (kən'faʊndɪd) *adj.* **1.** bewildered; confused. **2.** *Informal.* damned.

confrère ('kɒnfrɛə) *n.* a colleague; fellow worker.

confront (kən'frʌnt) *vb.* **1.** (usually foll. by *with*) to present (with something), esp. in order to accuse or criticize. **2.** to meet face to face in hostility or defiance. **3.** (of a problem or task) to present itself to. —**confrontation** (ˌkɒnfrʌn'teɪʃən) *n.*

Confucianism (kən'fjuːʃəˌnɪzəm) *n.* the ethical system of Confucius (551–479 B.C.), the ancient Chinese philosopher, emphasizing moral order. —**Con'fucian** *n., adj.* —**Con'fucianist** *n.*

confuse (kən'fjuːz) *vb.* **1.** to perplex or disconcert. **2.** to mix up; throw into disorder. **3.** to make unclear; complicate: *he confused his talk with irrelevant details.* **4.** to fail to distinguish between one thing and another. —con'fusing *adj.* —con'fusingly *adv.*

confusion (kən'fjuːʒən) *n.* **1.** bewilderment; perplexity. **2.** disorder. **3.** lack of clarity.

confute (kən'fjuːt) *vb.* to prove (a person or thing) to be incorrect or false. —**confutation** (ˌkɒnfjʊ'teɪʃən) *n.*

conga ('kɒŋgə) *n.* **1.** a Latin American dance performed by a number of people in single file. **2.** a large single-headed drum played with the hands. ~*vb.* -**gaing**, -**gaed**. **3.** to dance the conga.

congeal (kən'dʒiːl) *vb.* to change from a liquid to a semisolid state or a coagulated mass.

congenial (kən'dʒiːnjəl) *adj.* **1.** friendly, pleasant, or agreeable: *a congenial atmosphere to work in.* **2.** having a similar disposition or tastes; compatible. —**congeniality** (kən,dʒiːnɪ'ælɪtɪ) *n.*

congenital (kən'dʒenɪt³l) *adj.* (of an abnormal condition) nonhereditary but existing at birth: *congenital blindness.* —**con'genitally** *adv.*

conger ('kɒŋgə) *n.* a large sea eel.

congested (kən'dʒestɪd) *adj.* **1.** crowded to excess; overfilled. **2.** (of an organ) clogged with blood. **3.** (of the nose) blocked with mucus. —**con'gestion** *n.*

conglomerate *n.* (kən'glɒmərɪt). **1.** a thing composed of several different elements. **2.** a rock consisting of rounded pebbles or fragments held together by silica or clay. **3.** a large corporation formed by the merging of many diverse firms. ~*vb.* (kən'glɒmə,reɪt). **4.** to form into a mass. ~*adj.* (kən'glɒmərɪt). **5.** made up of several different elements. **6.** (of rock) consisting of rounded pebbles or fragments held together by silica or clay. —**con,glomer'ation** *n.*

congratulate (kən'grætjʊ,leɪt) *vb.* **1.** (usually foll. by *on*) to express one's pleasure to (a person) at his success or good fortune. **2. congratulate oneself.** (often foll. by *on*) to consider oneself clever or fortunate (as a result of): *she congratulated herself on her tact.* —**con'gratulatory** *adj.*

congratulations (kən,grætjʊ'leɪʃənz) *pl. n.,* *interj.* expressions of pleasure or joy on another's success or good fortune.

congregate ('kɒŋgrɪ,geɪt) *vb.* to collect together in a body or crowd; assemble.

congregation (,kɒŋgrɪ'geɪʃən) *n.* a group of worshippers. —**congre'gational** *adj.*

Congregationalism (,kɒŋgrɪ'geɪʃənə,lɪzəm) *n.* a system of Protestant church government in which each church is self-governing. —**Congre'gationalist** *adj., n.*

congress ('kɒŋgres) *n.* a formal meeting of representatives of an organization, held for discussion. —**congressional** (kən'greʃən³l) *adj.*

Congress ('kɒŋgres) *n.* the federal legislature of the U.S., consisting of the House of Representatives and the Senate. —**Congressional** (kən'greʃən³l) *adj.*

congruent ('kɒŋgrʊənt) *adj.* **1.** agreeing; corresponding. **2.** *Geom.* identical in shape and size: *congruent triangles.* —**'congruence** *n.*

congruous ('kɒŋgrʊəs) *adj.* **1.** corresponding or agreeing. **2.** appropriate. —**congruity** (kən'gruːɪtɪ) *n.*

conical ('kɒnɪk³l) *adj.* of or in the shape of a cone.

conic section ('kɒnɪk) *n.* a figure, either a circle, ellipse, parabola, or hyperbola,

formed by the intersection of a plane and a cone.

conifer ('kəʊnɪfə, 'kɒn-) *n.* a tree or shrub bearing cones and evergreen leaves, such as the pine, spruce, fir, or larch. —**co'niferous** *adj.*

conjecture (kən'dʒektʃə) *n.* **1.** the formation of conclusions from incomplete evidence; guessing. **2.** a guess. ~*vb.* **3.** to form (an opinion or conclusion) from incomplete evidence. —**con'jectural** *adj.*

conjugal ('kɒndʒʊg³l) *adj.* of marriage or the relationship between husband and wife: *conjugal rights.*

conjugate *vb.* ('kɒndʒʊ,geɪt). **1.** *Grammar.* to give the conjugation of (a verb). **2.** (of a verb) to undergo inflection according to a specific set of rules. ~*adj.* ('kɒndʒʊgɪt). **3.** joined together in pairs; fused. **4.** (of words) cognate; related in origin. ~*n.* ('kɒndʒʊgɪt). **5.** one of a pair of conjugate words or things.

conjugation (,kɒndʒʊ'geɪʃən) *n.* **1.** *Grammar.* **a.** inflection of a verb for person, number, tense, voice and mood. **b.** the complete set of the inflections of a given verb. **2.** a joining.

conjunction (kən'dʒʌŋkʃən) *n.* **1.** joining together; union; combination. **2.** simultaneous occurrence of events; coincidence. **3.** a word or group of words that connects words, phrases, or clauses; for example *and*, *if*, and *but*. **4.** *Astron.* the apparent proximity of two heavenly bodies to each other. —**con'junctional** *adj.*

conjunctiva (,kɒndʒʌŋk'taɪvə) *n., pl.* **-vas** or **-vae** (-viː). the delicate mucous membrane that covers the eyeball and inner eyelid. —**,conjunc'tival** *adj.*

conjunctive (kən'dʒʌŋktɪv) *adj.* **1.** joining; connective. **2.** joined. **3.** used as a conjunction. ~*n.* **4.** a word or words used as a conjunction.

conjunctivitis (kən,dʒʌŋktɪ'vaɪtɪs) *n.* inflammation of the conjunctiva.

conjuncture (kən'dʒʌŋktʃə) *n.* a combination of events, esp. a critical one.

conjure ('kʌndʒə) *vb.* **1.** to practise conjuring. **2.** to summon (a spirit or demon) by magic. **3.** (kən'dʒʊə). to appeal earnestly to: *I conjure you to help me.*

conjurer *or* **conjuror** ('kʌndʒərə) *n.* **1.** a person who practises conjuring, esp. for people's entertainment. **2.** a magician.

conjure up *vb.* **1.** to call to mind; evoke or imagine: *he conjured up a picture of his childhood.* **2.** to produce as if from nowhere.

conjuring ('kʌndʒərɪŋ) *n.* the performance of tricks that appear to defy natural laws.

conk (kɒŋk) *Slang.* ~*vb.* **1.** to strike (someone) on the head or nose. ~*n.* **2.** the head or nose.

conker (ˈkɒŋkə) n. same as **horse chestnut** (the nut).

conkers (ˈkɒŋkəz) n. (functioning as sing.) Brit. a game in which a player swings a horse chestnut (conker), threaded onto a string, against that of another player to try to break it.

conk out vb. Informal. 1. (of a machine or car) to fail suddenly. 2. to tire suddenly or collapse.

con man n. Informal. a person who swindles another by means of a confidence trick.

Conn. Connecticut.

connect (kəˈnɛkt) vb. 1. to link or be linked. 2. to associate: I connect him with my childhood. 3. to put into telephone communication with. 4. to relate by birth or marriage: she was distantly connected with the Wedgwood family. 5. (of two public vehicles) to have the arrival of one timed to occur just before the departure of the other, for the convenient transfer of passengers. —**conˈnective** adj.

connection or **connexion** (kəˈnɛkʃən) n. 1. the act of connecting; union. 2. a link or bond. 3. a relationship or association. 4. logical sequence in thought or expression; coherence. 5. (often pl.) an influential acquaintance. 6. a relative. 7. a. an opportunity to transfer from one public vehicle to another. b. the vehicle scheduled to provide such an opportunity. 8. a link between two components in an electric circuit. 9. a telephone link. 10. Slang. a supplier of illegal drugs, such as heroin. 11. **in connection with.** with reference to; concerning: the police want to interview him in connection with the murder.

connective tissue n. body tissue that supports organs, fills the spaces between them, and forms tendons and ligaments.

conning tower (ˈkɒnɪŋ) n. the superstructure of a submarine containing the periscope and serving as an entrance when the vessel is on the surface.

connivance (kəˈnaɪvəns) n. tacit encouragement of or assent to another's wrongdoing.

connive (kəˈnaɪv) vb. 1. (foll. by at) to give assent or encouragement to (another's wrongdoing) by pretending not to notice it. 2. to conspire. —**conˈniver** n.

connoisseur (ˌkɒnɪˈsɜː) n. a person with special knowledge or appreciation of the arts, food, or drink.

connote (kɒˈnəʊt) vb. (of a word or phrase) to imply or suggest (associations or ideas other than the literal meaning): the word "maiden" connotes modesty. —ˌconnoˈtation n.

connubial (kəˈnjuːbɪəl) adj. of marriage: connubial bliss.

conquer (ˈkɒŋkə) vb. 1. to defeat (an opponent or opponents). 2. to overcome (a difficulty or feeling). 3. to gain possession or control of by force or war. —ˈconquering adj. —ˈconqueror n.

conquest (ˈkɒnkwɛst) n. 1. the act of conquering or the state of having been conquered. 2. a person or thing that has been conquered. 3. a person whose compliance or love has been won.

conquistador (kɒnˈkwɪstəˌdɔː) n., pl. -dors or **conquistadores** (kɒnˌkwɪstəˈdɔːrɛs). one of the Spanish conquerors of Mexico and Peru in the 16th century.

Cons. Conservative.

consanguineous (ˌkɒnsæŋˈgwɪnɪəs) adj. having the same ancestor; closely related. —ˌconsanˈguinity n.

conscience (ˈkɒnʃəns) n. 1. the sense of right and wrong that governs a person's thoughts and actions. 2. a feeling of guilt: he has a conscience about his unkind action. 3. **in (all) conscience.** in fairness; justifiably. 4. **on one's conscience.** causing feelings of guilt.

conscience money n. money paid voluntarily to relieve one's conscience.

conscience-stricken adj. feeling guilty because of having done something wrong.

conscientious (ˌkɒnʃɪˈɛnʃəs) adj. 1. scrupulous; painstaking. 2. governed by conscience. —ˌconsciˈentiously adv. —ˌconsciˈentiousness n.

conscientious objector n. a person who refuses to serve in the armed forces on the grounds of conscience.

conscious (ˈkɒnʃəs) adj. 1. alert and awake. 2. aware of one's surroundings and of oneself. 3. aware (of something): I am conscious of your great kindness to me. 4. deliberate or intentional: a conscious effort. 5. denoting a part of the human mind that is aware of a person's self, surroundings, and thoughts, and that to a certain extent determines his choices of action. ~n. 6. the conscious part of the mind. —ˈconsciously adv. —ˈconsciousness n.

conscript n. (ˈkɒnskrɪpt). 1. a person who is enrolled for compulsory military service. ~vb. (kənˈskrɪpt). 2. to enrol (someone) for compulsory military service.

conscription (kənˈskrɪpʃən) n. compulsory military service.

consecrate (ˈkɒnsɪˌkreɪt) vb. 1. to make or declare sacred or for religious use. 2. to devote or dedicate (something) to a specific purpose. 3. Christianity. to sanctify (bread and wine) to be received as the body and blood of Christ. —ˌconseˈcration n.

consecutive (kənˈsɛkjʊtɪv) adj. 1. following in order without interruption; successive. 2. in logical order. —conˈsecutively adv.

consensus (kənˈsɛnsəs) n. general or widespread agreement (esp. in **consensus of opinion**).

consent (kən'sɛnt) *vb.* **1.** to give assent or permission; agree. ~*n.* **2.** agreement, permission, or approval. **3. age of consent.** the age at which sexual intercourse is permitted by law. —**con'senting** *adj.*

consequence ('kɒnsɪkwəns) *n.* **1.** a logical result or effect. **2.** significance or importance: *it's of no consequence; a man of consequence.* **3. in consequence.** as a result. **4. take the consequences.** to accept whatever results from one's action.

consequent ('kɒnsɪkwənt) *adj.* **1.** following as an effect. **2.** following as a logical conclusion.

Usage. see **consequential.**

consequential (,kɒnsɪ'kwɛnʃəl) *adj.* **1.** important or significant. **2.** following as a result.

Usage. Although both *consequential* and *consequent* can refer to something that follows as a result, *consequent* is more frequently used in this sense in general contexts, while *consequential* is often used in commercial or legal contexts.

consequently ('kɒnsɪkwəntlɪ) *adv.* as a result; therefore.

conservancy (kən'sɜːvənsɪ) *n.* environmental conservation.

conservation (,kɒnsə'veɪʃən) *n.* **1.** protection from change, loss, or injury. **2.** protection, preservation, and careful management of the environment and natural resources. **3.** *Physics.* the principle that the quantity of a specified aspect of a system, such as momentum or charge, remains constant. —,**conser'vationist** *n.*

conservative (kən'sɜːvətɪv) *adj.* **1.** favouring the preservation of established customs and values, and opposing change. **2.** moderate or cautious: *a conservative estimate.* **3.** conventional in style: *a conservative suit.* ~*n.* **4.** a conservative person; conformist. —**con'servatism** *n.*

Conservative (kən'sɜːvətɪv) *adj.* **1.** of or supporting the Conservative Party, the major right-wing political party in Britain, which believes in private enterprise and capitalism. **2.** of or supporting a similar right-wing party in other countries. ~*n.* **3.** a supporter or member of a Conservative Party.

conservatoire (kən'sɜːvə,twɑː) *n.* a school or college of music.

conservatory (kən'sɜːvətrɪ) *n., pl.* -**tories.** **1.** a greenhouse attached to a house. **2.** a conservatoire.

conserve *vb.* (kən'sɜːv). **1.** to protect from harm, decay, or loss. **2.** to preserve (fruit or other food) with sugar. ~*n.* ('kɒnsɜːv, kən'sɜːv). **3.** a preparation like jam but containing a higher proportion of fruit.

consider (kən'sɪdə) *vb.* **1.** to think carefully about (a problem or decision). **2.** to

believe to be: *I consider him a fool.* **3.** to have regard for or care about: *consider your mother's feelings.* **4.** to look at: *he considered her face.* **5.** to bear in mind: *when buying a car consider this make.* **6.** to discuss (something) in order to make a decision.

considerable (kən'sɪdərəb'l) *adj.* **1.** large enough to reckon with; important: *a considerable quantity.* **2.** a lot of; much: *he had considerable courage.* —**con'siderably** *adv.*

considerate (kən'sɪdərɪt) *adj.* thoughtful towards other people; kind.

consideration (kən,sɪdə'reɪʃən) *n.* **1.** deliberation; contemplation. **2. take into consideration.** to bear in mind; consider. **3. under consideration.** being currently discussed. **4.** a fact to be taken into account when making a decision. **5.** thoughtfulness for other people; kindness. **6.** payment for a service.

considered (kən'sɪdəd) *adj.* **1.** presented or thought out with care: *a considered opinion.* **2.** (*with a preceding adverb*) thought of in a specified way: *highly considered.*

considering (kən'sɪdərɪŋ) *conj., prep.* **1.** in view of (a specified fact): *he's very fit, considering his age.* ~*adv.* **2.** *Informal.* taking into account the circumstances: *it's not bad considering.*

consign (kən'saɪn) *vb.* **1.** to give into the care or charge of; entrust. **2.** to put irrevocably: *he consigned the papers to the flames.* **3.** to put (in a specified place or situation): *to consign someone to jail.* **4.** to address or deliver (goods): *it was consigned to his London address.* —,**consign'ee** *n.* —**con'signor** *n.*

consignment (kən'saɪnmənt) *n.* **1.** a consigning or commitment. **2.** a shipment of goods.

consist (kən'sɪst) *vb.* **1.** (foll. by *of* or *in*) to be composed of. **2.** (foll. by *in* or *of*) to have as its main or only part: *his religion consists only in going to church.*

consistency (kən'sɪstənsɪ) *n., pl.* -**encies.** **1.** degree of thickness, smoothness, or firmness. **2.** conformity with previous behaviour or practice.

consistent (kən'sɪstənt) *adj.* **1.** (usually foll. by *with*) showing consistency, harmony, or compatibility. **2.** holding to the same principles; constant. —**con'sistently** *adv.*

consolation (,kɒnsə'leɪʃən) *n.* **1.** a consoling or being consoled. **2.** a person or thing that is a comfort in a time of sadness or distress.

console[1] (kən'səʊl) *vb.* to comfort (someone) in sadness or distress. —**con'solable** *adj.*

console[2] ('kɒnsəʊl) *n.* **1.** an ornamental bracket used to support a wall fixture. **2.** the desklike case of an organ, containing the pedals, stops, and keys. **3.** a desk or table on which the controls of an electronic system are mounted. **4.** a cabinet for a television or audio equipment, designed to stand on the floor.

consolidate (kənˈsɒlɪˌdeɪt) vb. **1.** to combine into a whole. **2.** to make or become stronger or more stable. —**conˌsoliˈdation** n. —**conˈsoliˌdator** n.

consommé (kənˈsɒmeɪ) n. a thin clear soup made from meat juices.

consonance (ˈkɒnsənəns) n. agreement or harmony, esp. of musical tones.

consonant (ˈkɒnsənənt) n. **1. a.** a speech sound made by partially or completely blocking the breath streams, as b, l, f. **b.** a letter representing this. ~adj. **2.** (foll. by with or to) consistent; in agreement. **3.** harmonious.

consort vb. (kənˈsɔːt). **1.** (usually foll. by with) to associate (with undesirable people). ~n. (ˈkɒnsɔːt). **2.** (esp. formerly) a small group of voices or instruments. **3.** a husband or wife of a reigning monarch.

consortium (kənˈsɔːtɪəm) n., pl. **-tia** (-tɪə). an association of financiers or business firms.

conspectus (kənˈspɛktəs) n. **1.** an overall view; survey. **2.** a summary; résumé.

conspicuous (kənˈspɪkjʊəs) adj. **1.** clearly visible. **2.** noteworthy or striking: *conspicuous stupidity*. —**conˈspicuously** adv.

conspiracy (kənˈspɪrəsɪ) n., pl. **-cies. 1.** a secret plan to carry out an illegal or harmful act. **2.** the act of making such plans.

conspire (kənˈspaɪə) vb. **1.** to plan (a crime) together in secret. **2.** to act together as if by design: *the elements conspired to spoil our picnic.* —**conspirator** (kənˈspɪrətə) n. —**conspiratorial** (kənˌspɪrəˈtɔːrɪəl) adj.

constable (ˈkʌnstəbⁱl) n. a police officer of the lowest rank.

constabulary (kənˈstæbjʊlərɪ) n., pl. **-laries.** *Chiefly Brit.* the police force of a district or town.

constant (ˈkɒnstənt) adj. **1.** unchanging. **2.** continuous: *constant interruptions.* **3.** resolute; loyal. ~n. **4.** something that is unchanging. **5.** *Maths, physics.* a quantity or number which remains invariable: *the velocity of light is a constant.* —**ˈconstancy** n. —**ˈconstantly** adv.

constellation (ˌkɒnstɪˈleɪʃən) n. **1.** a group of stars which form a pattern as seen from the earth and are given a name. **2.** a group of people or things.

consternation (ˌkɒnstəˈneɪʃən) n. a feeling of anxiety, dismay, or confusion.

constipate (ˈkɒnstɪˌpeɪt) vb. to cause constipation in. —**ˈconstiˌpated** adj.

constipation (ˌkɒnstɪˈpeɪʃən) n. a condition in which the faeces are hardened making the emptying of the bowels difficult.

constituency (kənˈstɪtjʊənsɪ) n., pl. **-cies.**

1. the whole body of voters who elect someone to represent them in parliament. **2.** the district that sends one representative to parliament.

constituent (kənˈstɪtjʊənt) adj. **1.** forming part of a whole; component. **2.** having the power to make or change a constitution or to elect a government: *constituent assembly.* ~n. **3.** a component part; ingredient. **4.** a resident of a constituency, esp. one entitled to vote.

constitute (ˈkɒnstɪˌtjuːt) vb. **1.** to form; compose: *the people who constitute a jury.* **2.** to set up (an institution) formally; found.

constitution (ˌkɒnstɪˈtjuːʃən) n. **1.** physical make-up; structure. **2.** the fundamental principles on which a state is governed. **3. the Constitution.** (in certain countries) the statute embodying such principles. **4.** a person's state of health.

constitutional (ˌkɒnstɪˈtjuːʃən⁰l) adj. **1.** involving or related to a constitution. **2.** authorized by or in accordance with the Constitution of a nation or state: *constitutional monarchy.* **3.** inherent in the nature of a person or thing: *a constitutional weakness.* ~n. **4.** a regular walk taken for the benefit of one's health. —**ˌconstiˈtutionally** adv.

constitutive (ˈkɒnstɪˌtjuːtɪv) adj. **1.** having power to appoint, enact, or establish. **2.** forming a part of something.

constrain (kənˈstreɪn) vb. **1.** to compel or force. **2.** to restrain or confine.

constrained (kənˈstreɪnd) adj. embarrassed, unnatural, or forced: *a constrained smile.*

constraint (kənˈstreɪnt) n. **1.** compulsion or restraint. **2.** repression of natural feelings. **3.** a forced unnatural manner. **4.** something that constrains; a restrictive condition.

constrict (kənˈstrɪkt) vb. **1.** to make smaller or narrower, esp. by compressing at one place. **2.** to hold in or inhibit; limit. —**conˈstrictive** adj.

constriction (kənˈstrɪkʃən) n. **1.** a feeling of tightness in some part of the body, such as the chest. **2.** a narrowing. **3.** something that constricts.

constrictor (kənˈstrɪktə) n. **1.** a snake that coils around and squeezes its prey to kill it. **2.** a muscle that contracts an opening.

construct vb. (kənˈstrʌkt). **1.** to build or assemble by putting together parts systematically. **2.** to frame (an argument or sentence) mentally. **3.** *Geom.* to draw (a figure) to specified requirements. ~n. (ˈkɒnstrʌkt). **4.** something formulated or built systematically. **5.** a complex idea resulting from the combination of simpler ideas. —**conˈstructor** n.

construction (kənˈstrʌkʃən) n. **1.** the act of constructing or manner in which a thing is constructed. **2.** something that has been constructed. **3.** the business or work of building dwellings or other structures. **4.** an interpretation: *they put a sympathetic construction on her behaviour.* **5.** *Grammar.* the way in which words are arranged in a sentence, clause, or phrase. —**con-'structional** *adj.*

constructive (kən'strʌktɪv) *adj.* **1.** serving to improve; positive: *constructive criticism.* **2.** *Law.* deduced by inference; not expressed. —**con'structively** *adv.*

construe (kən'struː) *vb.* **-struing, -strued.** **1.** to interpret the meaning of (something): *you can construe that in different ways.* **2.** to analyse the grammatical structure of. **3.** to combine (words) grammatically. **4.** *Old-fashioned.* to translate literally.

consul ('kɒns'l) *n.* **1.** an official appointed by a state to protect its business interests and help its citizens in a foreign city. **2.** either of two annually elected chief magistrates in ancient Rome. —**consular** ('kɒnsjʊlə) *adj.* —**'consul,ship** *n.*

consulate ('kɒnsjʊlɪt) *n.* **1.** the offices and official home of a consul. **2.** the office or period of office of a consul.

consult (kən'sʌlt) *vb.* **1.** (often foll. by *with*) to ask advice from or discuss matters with (someone). **2.** to refer to for information: *to consult a map.*

consultant (kən'sʌlt'nt) *n.* **1.** a specialist doctor with a senior position in a hospital. **2.** a specialist who gives expert professional advice. —**con'sultancy** *n.*

consultation (,kɒns'l'teɪʃən) *n.* **1.** the act of consulting. **2.** a meeting for discussion or the seeking of advice. —**consultative** (kən'sʌltətɪv) *adj.*

consulting (kən'sʌltɪŋ) *adj.* acting as an adviser on professional matters: *a consulting engineer.*

consulting room *n.* a room in which a doctor sees his patients.

consume (kən'sjuːm) *vb.* **1.** to eat or drink. **2.** to obsess. **3.** to use up; waste. **4.** to destroy: *fire consumed the forest.* —**con'sumable** *adj.* —**con'suming** *adj.*

consumer (kən'sjuːmə) *n.* a person who buys things for his own personal needs.

consumer goods *pl. n.* goods bought for personal needs rather than those required for the production of other goods or services.

consumerism (kən'sjuːmə,rɪzəm) *n.* protection of the interests of consumers.

consummate *vb.* ('kɒnsə,meɪt). **1.** to bring to completion; fulfil. **2.** to make (a marriage) legal by sexual intercourse. ~*adj.* ('kɒnsəmɪt). **3.** supremely skilled: *a consummate artist.* **4.** complete or extreme: *a consummate fool.* —,**consum'mation** *n.*

consumption (kən'sʌmpʃən) *n.* **1.** a con-

suming or being consumed. **2.** *Econ.* purchase of goods and services for personal use. **3.** the quantity consumed. **4.** *Old-fashioned.* tuberculosis of the lungs.

consumptive (kən'sʌmptɪv) *adj.* **1.** wasteful; destructive. **2.** of or having tuberculosis of the lungs. ~*n.* **3.** a person with tuberculosis of the lungs.

cont. 1. contents. **2.** continued.

contact ('kɒntækt) *n.* **1.** the act or state of touching. **2.** the state or act of communication: *in contact; make contact.* **3.** a connection between two electrical conductors in a circuit. **4.** an acquaintance, esp. one who might be useful in business. **5.** any person who has been exposed to a contagious disease. ~*vb.* **6.** to come or be in touch or communication with.

contact lens *n.* a small lens placed directly on the surface of the eye to correct defects of vision.

contagion (kən'teɪdʒən) *n.* **1.** the spreading of disease from one person to another by contact. **2.** a contagious disease. **3.** a corrupting influence that tends to spread.

contagious (kən'teɪdʒəs) *adj.* **1.** (of a disease) capable of being passed on by contact. **2.** (of a person) capable of passing on a transmissible disease. **3.** spreading from person to person: *her laughter was contagious.*

contain (kən'teɪn) *vb.* **1.** to hold or be capable of holding: *this contains five pints.* **2.** to check or restrain (feelings or behaviour). **3.** to consist of: *the book contains three sections.* **4.** to prevent from spreading beyond fixed limits. —**con'tainable** *adj.*

container (kən'teɪnə) *n.* **1.** an object used to hold, carry, or store things in. **2.** a large standard-sized box designed for the transport of cargo by lorry or ship.

containerize *or* **-ise** (kən'teɪnə,raɪz) *vb.* **1.** to pack (cargo) in large standard-sized containers. **2.** to equip (a port or transportation system) to carry goods in standard-sized containers. —**con,taineri'zation** *or* **-i'sation** *n.*

containment (kən'teɪnmənt) *n.* the prevention of the expansion of a hostile country or its influence.

contaminate (kən'tæmɪ,neɪt) *vb.* **1.** to make impure; pollute. **2.** to make radioactive. —**con'taminant** *n.* —**con,tami'nation** *n.*

contemn (kən'tɛm) *vb. Formal.* to regard with contempt; scorn.

contemplate ('kɒntɛm,pleɪt) *vb.* **1.** to think about intently and at length. **2.** to meditate. **3.** to look at thoughtfully. **4.** to consider as a possibility. —,**contem'plation** *n.*

contemplative ('kɒntɛm,pleɪtɪv, -təm-; kən'tɛmplə-) *adj.* **1.** of or given to contemplation; meditative. ~*n.* **2.** a person dedicated to religious contemplation.

contemporaneous (kən͵tɛmpə'reɪnɪəs) *adj.* existing or occurring at the same time. —**contemporaneity** (kən͵tɛmpərə'niːɪtɪ) *n.*

contemporary (kən'tɛmprərɪ) *adj.* **1.** living or occurring in the same period. **2.** existing or occurring at the present time. **3.** modern in style or fashion. **4.** of approximately the same age. ~*n., pl.* -**raries.** **5.** a person or thing living at the same time or of approximately the same age as another.

Usage. Contemporary is most acceptable when used to mean of the same period, in a sentence like *it is useful to compare Shakespeare's plays with those of contemporary* (that is, other Elizabethan) *playwrights.* The word is, however, often used to mean modern or up-to-date in contexts such as *the furniture was of a contemporary design.* The second use should be avoided where ambiguity is likely to arise, as in *a production of* Othello *in contemporary dress.*

contempt (kən'tɛmpt) *n.* **1.** scorn. **2. hold in contempt.** to scorn or despise. **3.** deliberate disrespect for the authority of a court of law: *contempt of court.*

contemptible (kən'tɛmptɪb°l) *adj.* deserving or worthy of contempt.

contemptuous (kən'tɛmptjʊəs) *adj.* showing or feeling contempt; disdainful. —**con-'temptuously** *adv.*

contend (kən'tɛnd) *vb.* **1.** (often foll. by *with*) to compete or fight; vie. **2.** to argue earnestly. **3.** to assert. —**con'tender** *n.*

content[1] ('kɒntɛnt) *n.* **1.** (*pl.*) everything inside a container. **2.** (*pl.*) a list of chapters or divisions printed at the front of a book. **3.** the meaning or substance of a piece of writing, speech, or other work, often as distinguished from its style or form. **4.** the amount of a substance contained in a mixture: *the lead content of petrol.*

content[2] (kən'tɛnt) *adj.* **1.** satisfied with things as they are. **2.** willing to accept a situation or a proposed course of action. ~*vb.* **3.** to satisfy (oneself or another person). ~*n.* **4.** peace of mind. —**con'tentment** *n.*

contented (kən'tɛntɪd) *adj.* satisfied with one's situation or life. —**con'tentedly** *adv.* —**con'tentedness** *n.*

contention (kən'tɛnʃən) *n.* **1.** disagreement or dispute. **2.** a point asserted in argument. **3. bone of contention.** a point of dispute.

contentious (kən'tɛnʃəs) *adj.* **1.** tending to quarrel. **2.** causing disagreement; controversial. —**con'tentiousness** *n.*

contest *n.* ('kɒntɛst). **1.** a game or match in which people or teams compete. **2.** a struggle for power or control. ~*vb.* (kən-'tɛst). **3.** to dispute; call into question: *he*

decided to contest the will. **4.** to take part in (a contest or struggle for power): *to contest an election.* —**con'testable** *adj.*

contestant (kən'tɛstənt) *n.* a person who takes part in a contest; competitor.

context ('kɒntɛkst) *n.* **1.** the parts of a piece of writing or speech that come before and after a word or passage and contribute to its full meaning: *it is unfair to quote out of context.* **2.** the circumstances relevant to an event or fact. —**con'textual** *adj.*

contiguous (kən'tɪgjʊəs) *adj.* **1.** touching; in contact. **2.** near or adjacent.

continent[1] ('kɒntɪnənt) *n.* one of the earth's large landmasses (Asia, Australia, Africa, Europe, North and South America, and Antarctica). —**continental** (͵kɒntɪ'nɛnt°l) *adj.*

continent[2] ('kɒntɪnənt) *adj.* **1.** able to control urination and defecation. **2.** sexually restrained; chaste. —'**continence** *n.*

Continent ('kɒntɪnənt) *n.* **the.** the mainland of Europe as distinct from the British Isles. —**Continental** (͵kɒntɪ'nɛnt°l) *adj.*

continental breakfast *n.* a light breakfast of coffee and rolls.

continental climate *n.* a climate with hot summers, cold winters, and little rainfall, typical of the interior of a continent.

continental drift *n. Geol.* the theory that the earth's continents drift gradually over the surface of the planet, due to currents in its mantle.

continental quilt *n. Brit.* a large quilt used as a bed cover in place of the top sheet and blankets.

continental shelf *n.* the gently sloping shallow sea bed surrounding a continent.

contingency (kən'tɪndʒənsɪ) *n., pl.* -**cies.** **1.** an unknown or unforeseen future event or condition. **2.** something dependent on a possible future event.

contingent (kən'tɪndʒənt) *adj.* **1.** (often foll. by *on* or *upon*) dependent (on events or conditions not yet known); conditional. **2.** happening by chance; accidental. ~*n.* **3.** a military group that is part of a larger force. **4.** a group of people with a common interest, that represents a larger group.

continual (kən'tɪnjʊəl) *adj.* **1.** recurring frequently. **2.** occurring without interruption; constant. —**con'tinually** *adv.*

continuance (kən'tɪnjʊəns) *n.* **1.** the act of continuing; continuation. **2.** duration.

continuation (kən͵tɪnjʊ'eɪʃən) *n.* **1.** a part or thing added, such as a sequel. **2.** a renewal of an interrupted action or process; resumption. **3.** the act of continuing.

continue (kən'tɪnjuː) *vb.* -**tinuing, -tinued.** **1.** to remain or cause to remain in a particular condition. **2.** to carry on (a course of action) uninterruptedly: *he continued running.* **3.** to resume after an interruption: *we'll continue after lunch.* **4.** to prolong or be prolonged: *continue the chord until it meets the tangent.*

continuity (ˌkɒntɪˈnjuːɪtɪ) *n., pl.* **-ties.** **1.** the state of being continuous or in a logical sequence. **2.** a continuous or connected whole. **3.** the smooth arrangement of scenes in a film or broadcast so that they follow each other without breaks or inconsistencies.

continuo (kənˈtɪnjʊəʊ) *n., pl.* **-tinuos.** *Music.* a continuous bass accompaniment played usually on a keyboard instrument.

continuous (kənˈtɪnjʊəs) *adj.* **1.** unceasing: *a continuous noise.* **2.** in an unbroken series. **—conˈtinuously** *adv.*

continuum (kənˈtɪnjʊəm) *n., pl.* **-tinua** (-ˈtɪnjʊə) *or* **-tinuums.** a continuous series or whole ranging between two extremes: *the left-right political continuum.*

contort (kənˈtɔːt) *vb.* to twist or bend out of shape. **—conˈtortion** *n.*

contortionist (kənˈtɔːʃənɪst) *n.* a performer who contorts his body to entertain others.

contour (ˈkɒntʊə) *n.* **1.** the outline of a mass of land, figure, or body; a defining line. **2.** same as **contour line.** ~*vb.* **3.** to shape so as to form or follow the contour of something. **4.** to mark contour lines on.

contour line *n.* a line on a map or chart joining points of equal height or depth.

contra- *prefix.* **1.** against; opposing: *contraceptive.* **2.** (in music) lower in pitch: *contrabass.*

contraband (ˈkɒntrəˌbænd) *n.* **1.** goods that are prohibited by law from being exported or imported; smuggled goods. ~*adj.* **2.** (of goods) forbidden by law from being imported or exported; smuggled.

contraception (ˌkɒntrəˈsɛpʃən) *n.* the intentional prevention of pregnancy by artificial or natural means. **—ˌcontraˈceptive** *adj., n.*

contract *vb.* (kənˈtrækt). **1.** to make or become smaller, narrower, or shorter. **2.** (ˈkɒntrækt). to make a formal agreement with (a person or company) to do or deliver (something). **3.** to draw (the brow or muscles) together or (of the brow or muscles) to be drawn together. **4.** to become affected by (an illness). **5.** to shorten (a word or phrase) by omitting letters or syllables, usually indicated in writing by an apostrophe. ~*n.* (ˈkɒntrækt). **6.** a formal agreement between two or more parties. **7.** marriage considered as a formal agreement. **—conˈtractible** *adj.*

contract bridge (ˈkɒntrækt) *n.* the most common variety of bridge, in which only tricks bid and won count towards the game.

contraction (kənˈtrækʃən) *n.* **1.** a contracting or being contracted. **2.** a shortening of a word or group of words, often marked by an apostrophe, for example *I've* come for *I have come.*

contractor (kənˈtræktə) *n.* a person or firm that contracts to supply materials or labour.

contract out (ˈkɒntrækt) *vb. Brit.* to agree not to take part in a scheme.

contractual (kənˈtræktjʊəl) *adj.* of or in the nature of a contract.

contradict (ˌkɒntrəˈdɪkt) *vb.* **1.** to declare the opposite of (a statement) to be true. **2.** (of a fact or statement) to be at variance with or in contradiction to (another). **—ˌcontraˈdiction** *n.*

contradictory (ˌkɒntrəˈdɪktrɪ) *adj.* (of facts or statements) inconsistent or incompatible.

contradistinction (ˌkɒntrədɪˈstɪŋkʃən) *n.* a distinction made by contrasting different qualities. **—ˌcontradisˈtinctive** *adj.*

contraflow (ˈkɒntrəˌfləʊ) *n.* a flow, esp. of road traffic, going alongside but in an opposite direction to the usual flow.

contralto (kənˈtræltəʊ) *n., pl.* **-tos** *or* **-ti** (-tɪ). **1.** the lowest female voice. **2.** a singer with such a voice.

contraption (kənˈtræpʃən) *n. Informal, often facetious.* a device or gadget, esp. one considered strange, elaborate, or badly made.

contrapuntal (ˌkɒntrəˈpʌntəl) *adj. Music.* of or in counterpoint.

contrariwise (ˈkɒntrərɪˌwaɪz) *adv.* **1.** from a contrasting point of view. **2.** in the opposite way. **3.** (kənˈtrɛərɪˌwaɪz). perversely.

contrary (ˈkɒntrərɪ) *adj.* **1.** opposed; completely different: *contrary ideas.* **2.** (kənˈtrɛərɪ). perverse; obstinate. **3.** (of the wind) unfavourable. ~*n., pl.* **-ries.** **4. on** *or* **to the contrary.** in opposition to what has just been said or implied. ~*adv.* (usually foll. by *to*) **5.** in opposition or contrast (to): *contrary to popular belief.* **6.** in conflict (with): *contrary to nature.* **—conˈtrariness** *n.*

contrast *vb.* (kənˈtrɑːst). **1.** (often foll. by *with*) to compare or be compared in order to show the differences between (things). ~*n.* (ˈkɒntrɑːst). **2.** a difference which is clearly seen when two things are compared: *by contrast; in contrast to.* **3.** a person or thing showing differences when compared with another. **4.** the degree of difference between the colours or tones in a photograph or television picture. **—conˈtrasting** *adj.*

contravene (ˌkɒntrəˈviːn) *vb.* to break (a rule or law). **—contravention** (ˌkɒntrəˈvɛnʃən) *n.*

contretemps (ˈkɒntrəˌtɑːn) *n., pl.* **-temps** (-ˌtɑːnz). an awkward or embarrassing situation or mishap.

contribute (kənˈtrɪbjuːt) *vb.* (often foll. by *to*) **1.** to give (support or money) for a common purpose or fund. **2.** to supply (ideas or opinions). **3.** to be partly responsible (for): *drink contributed to the accident.* **4.** to write (an article) for a publication. —**contribution** *n.* —**contributory** *adj.* —**contributor** *n.*

contrite (kən'traɪt, 'kɒntraɪt) *adj.* full of guilt or regret. —**contritely** *adv.* —**contrition** (kən'trɪʃən) *n.*

contrivance (kən'traɪvəns) *n.* **1.** an ingenious device. **2.** an elaborate or deceitful plan. **3.** the act or power of contriving.

contrive (kən'traɪv) *vb.* **1.** to manage (something), esp. by a trick: *he contrived to make them meet.* **2.** to invent and construct ingeniously: *he contrived a new mast for the boat.*

control (kən'trəʊl) *vb.* **-trolling, -trolled.** **1.** to command or direct. **2.** to limit, curb, or restrain: *to control one's emotions.* **3.** to regulate or operate (a machine). ~*n.* **4.** power to direct: *under control.* **5.** a curb; check: *a frontier control.* **6.** (*pl.*) a device or apparatus used to operate a machine. **7.** a standard of comparison used in an experiment. **8.** an experiment used to verify another by having all aspects identical except for the one which is which is being tested. —**controllable** *adj.*

controller (kən'trəʊlə) *n.* **1.** a person who directs. **2.** a person in charge of the financial side of a business or department.

control tower *n.* a tall building at an airport from which air traffic is controlled.

controversy ('kɒntrə,vɜːsɪ, kən'trɒvəsɪ) *n.,* *pl.* **-sies.** argument or debate concerning a matter about which there is strong disagreement. —**controversial** (,kɒntrə'vɜːʃəl) *adj.*

contumacy ('kɒntjuməsɪ) *n.,* *pl.* **-cies.** obstinate and wilful resistance to authority. —**contumacious** (,kɒntjʊ'meɪʃəs) *adj.*

contumely ('kɒntjumɪlɪ) *n.,* *pl.* **-lies.** **1.** scornful or insulting treatment. **2.** a humiliating insult.

contuse (kən'tjuːz) *vb.* to bruise. —**contusion** *n.*

conundrum (kə'nʌndrəm) *n.* **1.** a riddle whose answer contains a pun. **2.** a puzzling question or problem.

conurbation (,kɒnɜː'beɪʃən) *n.* a large densely populated urban area formed by the growth and merging of individual towns or cities.

convalesce (,kɒnvə'lɛs) *vb.* to recover from illness, injury, or an operation.

convalescence (,kɒnvə'lɛsəns) *n.* **1.** gradual return to health after illness, injury, or an operation. **2.** the period during which such recovery occurs. —**convalescent** *n., adj.*

convection (kən'vɛkʃən) *n.* the transmission of heat caused by movement of molecules from cool regions to warmer regions of lower density.

convector (kən'vɛktə) *n.* a heating device from which heat is transferred to the surrounding air by convection.

convene (kən'viːn) *vb.* to gather or summon for a formal meeting.

convener *or* **convenor** (kən'viːnə) *n.* a person who convenes or chairs a meeting or committee: *a convener of shop stewards.*

convenience (kən'viːnɪəns) *n.* **1.** the quality of being suitable or convenient. **2. at your convenience.** at a time suitable to you. **3.** an object that is useful, esp. a labour-saving device. **4.** *Euphemistic, chiefly Brit.* a toilet, esp. a public one.

convenient (kən'viːnɪənt) *adj.* **1.** suitable; opportune. **2.** easy to use. **3.** close by; handy.

convent ('kɒnvənt) *n.* **1.** a building inhabited by a group of nuns. **2.** the nuns inhabiting such a building. **3.** a school in which the teachers are nuns.

conventicle (kən'vɛntɪkʰl) *n.* a secret or unauthorized religious meeting.

convention (kən'vɛnʃən) *n.* **1.** a large formal assembly of a group with common interests. **2.** a formal agreement or contract between persons and nations. **3.** the established view of what is thought to be proper behaviour. **4.** an accepted rule or method: *a convention used by printers.*

conventional (kən'vɛnʃənʰl) *adj.* **1.** following the accepted customs and lacking originality. **2.** established by accepted usage or general agreement. **3.** (of weapons or warfare) not nuclear. —**conventionally** *adv.*

conventionality (kən,vɛnʃə'nælɪtɪ) *n.,* *pl.* **-ties.** **1.** the quality of being conventional. **2.** something conventional.

converge (kən'vɜːdʒ) *vb.* **1.** to move towards or meet at the same point. **2.** (of opinions or effects) to tend towards a common conclusion or result. —**convergence** *n.* —**convergent** *adj.*

conversant (kən'vɜːsʰnt) *adj.* (usually foll. by *with*) experienced (in) or familiar (with).

conversation (,kɒnvə'seɪʃən) *n.* informal talk between two or more people.

conversational (,kɒnvə'seɪʃənʰl) *adj.* **1.** of or used in conversation: *conversational French.* **2.** inclined to conversation. —**conversationalist** *n.*

conversation piece *n.* something, esp. an unusual object, that provokes conversation.

converse¹ (kən'vɜːs) *vb.* (often foll. by *with*) to have a conversation.

converse² ('kɒnvɜːs) *adj.* **1.** reversed; opposite; contrary. ~*n.* **2.** a statement or idea that is the opposite of another. —**conversely** *adv.*

conversion (kən'vɜːʃən) *n.* **1.** a change or adaptation in form, character, or function.

2. a change to another belief or religion. **3.** *Maths.* a calculation in which a weight, volume, or distance is worked out in a different system of measurement: *the conversion of miles to kilometres.* **4.** *Rugby.* a score made after a try by kicking the ball over the crossbar from a place kick.

convert *vb.* (kən'vɜːt) **1.** to change or adapt in form, character, or function. **2.** to cause (someone) to change in opinion or belief. **3.** *Rugby.* to make a conversion after (a try). **4.** to change (a measurement) from one system of units to another. **5.** to change (money) into a different currency. ~*n.* ('kɒnvɜːt). **6.** a person who has been converted to another belief or religion. —**con'verter** *or* **con'vertor** *n.*

convertible (kən'vɜːtɪbᵊl) *adj.* **1.** capable of being converted. **2.** *Finance.* (of a currency) freely exchangeable into other currencies. ~*n.* **3.** a car with a folding or removable roof.

convex ('kɒnvɛks, kɒn'vɛks) *adj.* curving outwards like the outside surface of a ball. —**con'vexity** *n.*

convey (kən'veɪ) *vb.* **1.** to carry or transport from one place to another. **2.** to communicate (a message, idea, or information). **3.** (of a channel or path) to conduct, transfer, or transmit. **4.** *Law.* to transfer (the title to property). —**con'veyable** *adj.*

conveyance (kən'veɪəns) *n.* **1.** the act of conveying. **2.** a means of transport. **3.** *Law.* **a.** a transfer of the legal title to property. **b.** the document effecting such a transfer. —**con'veyancer** *n.* —**con'veyancing** *n.*

conveyor (kən'veɪə) *or* **conveyor belt** *n.* an endless moving belt driven by rollers and used to transport objects, esp. in a factory.

convict *vb.* (kən'vɪkt) **1.** to pronounce (someone) guilty of an offence. ~*n.* ('kɒnvɪkt). **2.** a person serving a prison sentence.

conviction (kən'vɪkʃən) *n.* **1.** a convincing or being convinced. **2.** a firmly held belief or opinion. **3.** an instance of being found guilty of a crime: *he had two previous convictions for assault.* **4. carry conviction.** to be convincing.

convince (kən'vɪns) *vb.* to persuade by argument or evidence. —**con'vinced** *adj.* —**con'vincible** *adj.* —**con'vincing** *adj.*

convivial (kən'vɪvɪəl) *adj.* sociable; lively or festive: *a convivial atmosphere.* —**conviviality** (kən,vɪvɪ'ælɪtɪ) *n.*

convocation (,kɒnvə'keɪʃən) *n.* a large formal meeting.

convoke (kən'vəʊk) *vb.* to call (a meeting); summon.

convoluted ('kɒnvə,luːtɪd) *adj.* **1.** (of an argument or sentence) difficult to understand because of its complexity. **2.** coiled.

convolution (,kɒnvə'luːʃən) *n.* **1.** a turn, twist, or coil. **2.** an intricate or confused matter or condition. **3.** a convex fold in the surface of the brain.

convolvulus (kən'vɒlvjʊləs) *n., pl.* **-luses** *or* **-li** (-,laɪ). a twining plant with funnel-shaped flowers and triangular leaves.

convoy ('kɒnvɔɪ) *n.* a group of vehicles or ships travelling together.

convulse (kən'vʌls) *vb.* **1.** to shake or agitate violently. **2.** (of muscles) to undergo violent spasms. **3.** (often foll. by *with*) *Informal.* to be overcome (with laughter or rage). —**con'vulsive** *adj.*

convulsion (kən'vʌlʃən) *n.* **1.** a violent involuntary muscular contraction. **2.** a violent upheaval. **3.** (*pl.*) *Informal.* uncontrollable laughter: *I was in convulsions.*

cony *or* **coney** ('kəʊnɪ) *n., pl.* **-nies** *or* **-neys.** a rabbit; rabbit fur.

coo (kuː) *vb.* **cooing, cooed. 1.** (of doves or pigeons) to make a characteristic soft throaty call. **2. bill and coo.** to murmur softly or lovingly. ~*n.* **3.** a cooing sound. ~*interj.* **4.** *Brit. slang.* an exclamation of surprise or amazement. —**'cooing** *adj., n.*

cooee ('kuːiː) *interj.* a call used to attract attention.

cook (kʊk) *vb.* **1.** to prepare (food) by the action of heat or (of food) to be prepared in this way. **2.** *Slang.* to alter or falsify (figures or accounts): *to cook the books.* ~*n.* **3.** a person who prepares food for eating. ~See also **cook up.**

cooker ('kʊkə) *n.* **1.** an apparatus, heated by gas or electricity, for cooking food. **2.** *Brit.* an apple suitable for cooking but not for eating raw.

cookery ('kʊkərɪ) *n.* the art or practice of cooking.

cookery book *or* **cookbook** ('kʊk,bʊk) *n.* a book containing recipes.

cookie ('kʊkɪ) *n., pl.* **cookies. 1.** *U.S. & Canad.* a biscuit. **2. that's the way the cookie crumbles.** *Informal, chiefly U.S. & Canad.* that is how things inevitably are.

cook up *vb. Informal.* to devise or invent (a story, alibi, or scheme).

cool (kuːl) *adj.* **1.** moderately cold: *a cool day.* **2.** comfortably free of heat: *a cool room.* **3.** calm and unemotional: *a cool head.* **4.** indifferent or unfriendly: *a cool welcome.* **5.** calmly impudent. **6.** *Informal.* (of a large sum of money) without exaggeration: *a cool ten thousand.* **7.** (of a colour) having violet, blue, or green predominating. **8.** *Informal.* sophisticated or elegant; unruffled. **9.** *Informal, chiefly U.S. & Canad.* marvellous. ~*n.* **10.** coolness: *the cool of the evening.* **11.** *Slang.* calmness; composure: *don't lose your cool.* ~*vb.* (usually foll. by *down* or *off*) **12.** to make or become cooler. **13.** to calm down.

coolant ('kuːlənt) *n.* a fluid used to remove

heat from a machine or system while it is working.

cooler ('ku:lə) n. a container for making or keeping things cool.

coolie ('ku:lɪ) n. an unskilled Oriental labourer.

cooling tower n. a tall hollow structure in a factory or power station, inside which hot water trickles down, becoming cool as it does so.

coomb or **coombe** (ku:m) n. Chiefly southeastern English. a short valley or deep hollow.

coon (ku:n) n. **1.** Informal. short for **raccoon**. **2.** Offensive slang. a Negro or Australian Aborigine.

coop[1] (ku:p) n. **1.** a cage or pen for poultry or small animals. ~vb. **2.** (often foll. by up or in) to confine in a restricted area.

coop[2] or **co-op** ('kəʊˌɒp) n. a cooperative society or a shop run by a cooperative society.

cooper ('ku:pə) n. a person who makes or repairs barrels or casks.

cooperate or **co-operate** (kəʊˈɒpəˌreɪt) vb. **1.** to work or act together. **2.** to assist or be willing to assist. —**coˌoperˈation** or **co-ˌoperˈation** n.

cooperative or **co-operative** (kəʊˈɒpərətɪv, -ˈɒprə-) adj. **1.** cooperating or willing to cooperate. **2.** (of an enterprise or farm) owned collectively and managed for joint economic benefit. ~n. **3.** a cooperative organization.

cooperative society n. a commercial enterprise owned and run by customers or workers, in which the profits are shared among the members.

coopt or **co-opt** (kəʊˈɒpt) vb. to add (someone) to a group by the agreement of the existing members.

coordinate or **co-ordinate** vb. (kəʊˈɔːdɪˌneɪt). **1.** to bring together and organize (diverse elements) into a harmonious order or relation. ~n. (kəʊˈɔːdɪnɪt). **2.** Maths. any of a set of numbers that defines the location of a point with reference to a system of axes. ~adj. (kəʊˈɔːdɪnɪt). **3.** of or involving coordination. **4.** of or involving the use of coordinates: coordinate geometry. —**coˌordiˈnation** or **co-ˌordiˈnation** n. —**coˈordiˌnator** or **co-ˈordiˌnator** n.

coordinates or **co-ordinates** (kəʊˈɔːdɪnɪts) pl. n. matching items of clothing.

coot (ku:t) n. **1.** an aquatic bird like a duck, with black feathers and a white bill and forehead. **2.** a foolish person.

cop (kɒp) Slang. ~n. **1.** a policeman. **2.** **not much cop.** of little value or worth. ~vb. **copping, copped. 3.** to take or seize. **4.** to suffer (a punishment): you'll cop a clout if you do that! **5. cop it.** to get into trouble or be punished. ~See also **cop out.**

copartner (kəʊˈpɑːtnə) n. a partner or associate. —**coˈpartnership** n.

cope[1] (kəʊp) vb. (foll. by with) **1.** to contend against. **2.** to deal successfully (with); manage: she coped well with the problem.

cope[2] (kəʊp) n. **1.** a large ceremonial cloak worn by some Christian priests. **2.** any covering shaped like a cope. ~vb. **3.** to cover with a cope.

cope[3] (kəʊp) vb. to provide (a wall) with a coping.

copeck ('kəʊpek) n. same as **kopeck.**

Copernican (kəˈpɜːnɪkən) adj. of the theory that the earth and the planets rotate round the sun.

copestone ('kəʊpˌstəʊn) n. **1.** Also called: **coping stone.** a stone used to form a coping. **2.** the stone at the top of a building or wall.

copier ('kɒpɪə) n. a person or machine that copies.

copilot ('kəʊˌpaɪlət) n. the second pilot of an aircraft.

coping ('kəʊpɪŋ) n. the sloping top row of a wall, usually made of masonry or brick.

coping saw n. a handsaw with a U-shaped frame, used for cutting curves in wood.

copious ('kəʊpɪəs) adj. abundant; plentiful. —**ˈcopiously** adv.

cop out Slang. ~vb. **1.** to fail to assume responsibility or commit oneself. ~n. **copout. 2.** a way or an instance of avoiding responsibility or commitment.

copper[1] ('kɒpə) n. **1.** a soft reddish metallic element, used in such alloys as brass and bronze. Symbol: Cu **2.** Informal. any copper or bronze coin. **3.** Chiefly Brit. a large metal container used to boil water. ~adj. **4.** reddish-brown.

copper[2] ('kɒpə) n. Slang. a policeman.

copper beech n. a cultivated European beech with reddish leaves.

copper-bottomed adj. financially reliable.

copperplate ('kɒpəˌpleɪt) n. **1.** a polished copper plate etched or engraved for printing. **2.** a print taken from such a plate. **3.** a fine handwriting based upon that used on copperplate engravings.

copper sulphate n. a blue crystalline copper salt used in electroplating and in plant sprays.

coppice ('kɒpɪs) n. a dense growth of small trees, bushes, and undergrowth.

copra ('kɒprə) n. the dried oil-yielding kernel of the coconut.

copse (kɒps) n. same as **coppice.**

Copt (kɒpt) n. **1.** a member of the Coptic Church, a part of the Christian Church which was founded in Egypt. **2.** an Egyptian descended from the ancient Egyptians.

Coptic ('kɒptɪk) n. **1.** the language of the

Copts, descended from Ancient Egyptian and surviving only in the Coptic Church. ~*adj.* **2.** of the Copts or their language.

copula ('kɒpjʊlə) *n., pl.* **-las** *or* **-lae** (-ˌliː). a verb, such as *be or seem*, that is used to link the subject with the complement of a sentence, as in *he became king; you seem tired.*

copulate ('kɒpjʊˌleɪt) *vb.* to perform sexual intercourse. —ˌcopu'**lation** *n.*

copy ('kɒpɪ) *n., pl.* **copies. 1.** an imitation or reproduction of an original. **2.** a single specimen of a book, magazine, or record of which there are many others exactly the same. **3.** written matter or text as distinct from graphic material in books. **4.** the text of an advertisement. **5.** *Journalism, informal.* suitable material for an article: *disasters are always good copy.* ~*vb.* **copying, copied. 6.** to make a copy (of). **7.** to imitate.

copybook ('kɒpɪˌbʊk) *n.* **1.** a book of specimens of handwriting for imitation. **2. blot one's copybook.** *Informal.* to spoil one's reputation by a mistake or indiscretion. ~(*modifier*) **3.** done exactly according to the rules. **4.** trite or unoriginal.

copycat ('kɒpɪˌkæt) *n. Informal.* a person who imitates or copies another.

copyist ('kɒpɪɪst) *n.* **1.** a person who makes written copies. **2.** an imitator.

copyright ('kɒpɪˌraɪt) *n.* **1.** the exclusive legal right to reproduce and control an original literary, musical, or artistic work. ~*adj.* **2.** protected by copyright. ~*vb.* **3.** to take out a copyright on.

copy typist *n.* a typist whose job is to type from written or typed drafts rather than dictation.

copywriter ('kɒpɪˌraɪtə) *n.* a person employed to write advertising copy.

coquette (kəʊ'kɛt) *n.* a woman who flirts. —**coquetry** ('kɒkɪtrɪ) *n.* —co'**quettish** *adj.*

coracle ('kɒrək²l) *n.* a small roundish boat made of waterproof material stretched over a wicker frame.

coral ('kɒrəl) *n.* **1.** the stony substance formed by the skeletons of marine animals called polyps, often forming an island or reef. **2.** any of the polyps whose skeletons form coral. ~*adj.* **3.** yellowish-pink.

cor anglais ('kɔːr 'ɑːŋgleɪ) *n., pl.* **cors anglais** ('kɔːz 'ɑːŋgleɪ). *Music.* an alto woodwind instrument of the oboe family.

corbel ('kɔːb²l) *n. Archit.* a supporting bracket projecting from a wall, usually of stone or brick.

corbie ('kɔːbɪ) *n. Scot.* a raven or crow.

cord (kɔːd) *n.* **1.** string or thin rope made of twisted strands. **2.** a ribbed fabric, esp. corduroy. **3.** *U.S. & Canad.* an electrical flex. **4.** *Anat.* a structure in the body resembling a rope: *the spinal cord.* **5.** a unit for measuring cut wood, equal to 128 cubic feet. ~*vb.* **6.** to bind with a cord or cords. ~See also **cords.**

corded ('kɔːdɪd) *adj.* **1.** bound or fastened with cord. **2.** (of a fabric) ribbed. **3.** (of muscles) standing out like cords.

cordial ('kɔːdɪəl) *adj.* **1.** warm and friendly: *a cordial greeting.* **2.** heartfelt or sincere: *cordial dislike.* ~*n.* **3.** a drink with a fruit base: *lime cordial.* —'**cordially** *adv.*

cordiality (ˌkɔːdɪ'ælɪtɪ) *n.* warmth of feeling.

cordite ('kɔːdaɪt) *n.* a smokeless explosive used in guns and bombs.

cordon ('kɔːd²n) *n.* **1.** a chain of police, soldiers, or ships stationed around an area to guard it. **2.** a ribbon, cord, or braid worn as insignia of honour or as an ornament. **3.** *Horticulture.* a fruit tree trained to grow as a single stem bearing fruit. ~*vb.* **4.** (often foll. by *off*) to put or form a cordon (around); close (off).

cordon bleu (ˌkɔːdɒn 'blɜː) *adj.* (of cookery or cooks) of the highest standard: *a cordon bleu chef.*

cordon sanitaire (ˌkɔːdɒn ˌsænɪ'tɛə) *n.* **1.** a guarded line isolating an infected area. **2.** a line of buffer states shielding a country.

cords (kɔːdz) *pl. n.* trousers made of corduroy.

corduroy ('kɔːdəˌrɔɪ, ˌkɔːdə'rɔɪ) *n.* a heavy cotton pile fabric with lengthways ribs

corduroys (ˌkɔːdə'rɔɪz, 'kɔːdəˌrɔɪz) *pl. n.* trousers of corduroy.

core (kɔː) *n.* **1.** the central part of certain fleshy fruits, containing the seeds. **2.** the central or essential part of something: *the core of the argument.* **3.** a piece of magnetic soft iron inside an electromagnet or transformer. **4.** *Geol.* the central part of the earth. **5.** a cylindrical sample of rock or soil, obtained by the use of a hollow drill. **6.** *Physics.* the region of a nuclear reactor containing the fissionable material. **7.** *Computers.* **a.** a ferrite ring used in a computer memory to store one bit of information. **b.** the whole memory of a computer when made up of such rings. ~*vb.* **8.** to remove the core from (fruit).

co-respondent (ˌkəʊrɪ'spɒndənt) *n. Law.* a person alleged to have committed adultery with the person an action for divorce is being brought against (the **respondent**).

corf (kɔːf) *n., pl.* **corves** (cɔːrvz) *Brit.* a wagon or basket formerly used in mines.

corgi ('kɔːgɪ) *n.* a short-legged sturdy dog.

coriander (ˌkɒrɪ'ændə) *n.* **1.** a European plant, cultivated for its aromatic seeds. **2.** the dried seeds of this plant used as a flavouring.

Corinthian (kə'rɪnθɪən) *adj.* **1.** of Corinth in Greece. **2.** of one of the five classical orders of architecture, characterized by a bell-shaped capital with carved leaf-shaped ornaments. ~*n.* **3.** a person from Corinth.

cork (kɔːk) *n.* **1.** the thick light porous outer bark of a Mediterranean oak. **2.** a piece of cork used as a stopper. **3.** *Bot.* the outer bark of a woody plant. ~*vb.* **4.** to stop up (a bottle) with a cork. **5.** (often foll. by *up*) to restrain.

corkage (ˈkɔːkɪdʒ) *n.* a charge made at a restaurant for serving wine bought elsewhere.

corked (kɔːkt) *adj.* (of wine) tainted through having a decayed cork.

corker (ˈkɔːkə) *n. Old-fashioned slang.* a splendid or outstanding person or thing.

corkscrew (ˈkɔːkˌskruː) *n.* **1.** a device for drawing corks from bottles, usually consisting of a pointed metal spiral attached to a handle. **2.** (*modifier*) resembling a corkscrew in shape. ~*vb.* **3.** to move or cause to move in a spiral or zigzag course.

corm (kɔːm) *n.* the scaly bulblike underground stem of certain plants.

cormorant (ˈkɔːmərənt) *n.* a fish-eating aquatic bird with a long neck and body and a slender hooked beak.

corn[1] (kɔːn) *n.* **1.** *Brit.* **a.** a cereal plant such as wheat, oats, or barley. **b.** the seeds of such plants; grain. **2.** *U.S., Canad., & N.Z.* maize. **3.** *Slang.* anything, such as a song, regarded as banal or sentimental.

corn[2] (kɔːn) *n.* a painful hardening of the skin of the toes, caused by pressure.

corncob (ˈkɔːnˌkɒb) *n.* the core of an ear of maize, to which the kernels are attached.

corncrake (ˈkɔːnˌkreɪk) *n.* a brown bird with a harsh grating cry.

cornea (ˈkɔːnɪə) *n., pl.* **-neas** *or* **-neae** (-nɪ-ˌiː). the transparent membrane that forms the outer covering of the eyeball. —ˈ**corneal** *adj.*

corned (kɔːnd) *adj.* cooked and then preserved in salt or brine: *corned beef.*

cornelian (kɔːˈniːljən) *n.* same as **carnelian.**

corner (ˈkɔːnə) *n.* **1.** the place or angle formed by the meeting of two converging lines or surfaces. **2.** the space within the angle formed, as in a room. **3.** a remote place: *far-off corners of the globe.* **4.** any secluded or private place. **5.** the place where two streets meet. **6.** *Sports.* a free kick or shot taken from the corner of the field. **7. cut corners.** to take the shortest or easiest way at the expense of high standards. **8. turn the corner.** to pass the critical point of an illness or a difficult time. **9.** (*modifier*) on a corner: *a corner shop.* ~*vb.* **10.** to force (a person or animal) into a difficult or inescapable position. **11. a.** to acquire enough of (a commodity) to attain control of the market. **b.** to attain control of (a market) in such a manner. **12.** (of a vehicle or its driver) to turn a corner.

cornerstone (ˈkɔːnəˌstəʊn) *n.* **1.** a stone at the corner of a wall, uniting two intersect-ing walls. **2.** a stone placed at the bottom corner of a building during a ceremony to mark the start of construction. **3.** an indispensable part or basis: *the cornerstone of the whole argument.*

cornet (ˈkɔːnɪt) *n.* **1.** a brass instrument of the trumpet family. **2.** *Brit.* a cone-shaped wafer container for ice cream. —**cornetist** (kɔːˈnetɪst) *n.*

corn exchange *n.* a building where corn is bought and sold.

cornflakes (ˈkɔːnˌfleɪks) *pl. n.* a breakfast cereal made from toasted maize.

cornflour (ˈkɔːnˌflaʊə) *n.* a fine maize flour, used for thickening sauces.

cornflower (ˈkɔːnˌflaʊə) *n.* a small plant, usually with blue flowers, formerly a common weed in corn fields.

cornice (ˈkɔːnɪs) *n.* **1.** *Archit.* the projecting mouldings at the top of a column. **2.** a continuous horizontal moulding around the top of a wall or building.

Cornish (ˈkɔːnɪʃ) *adj.* **1.** of Cornwall or its inhabitants. ~*n.* **2.** a Celtic language of Cornwall, extinct by 1800. **3. the Cornish.** (*functioning as pl.*) the people of Cornwall.

Cornish pasty (ˈpæstɪ) *n.* a pastry case with a filling of meat and vegetables.

cornucopia (ˌkɔːnjʊˈkəʊpɪə) *n.* **1.** a symbol of plenty, consisting of a horn overflowing with fruit, flowers, and corn. **2.** a great abundance.

corny (ˈkɔːnɪ) *adj.* **cornier, corniest.** *Slang.* **1.** trite or banal. **2.** sickly sentimental.

corolla (kəˈrɒlə) *n.* the petals of a flower collectively, forming an inner envelope.

corollary (kəˈrɒlərɪ) *n., pl.* **-laries. 1.** a proposition that follows directly from another that has been proved. **2.** a natural consequence.

corona (kəˈrəʊnə) *n., pl.* **-nas** *or* **-nae** (-niː). **1.** a circle of light around a luminous body, usually the moon. **2.** the outermost part of the sun's atmosphere, visible as a faint halo during a total eclipse. **3.** *Bot.* a crownlike part of some flowers on top of the seed or on the inner side of the corolla. **4.** a long cigar with blunt ends. **5.** *Physics.* an electrical glow appearing around the surface of a charged conductor.

coronary (ˈkɒrənərɪ) *adj.* **1.** *Anat.* of the arteries that supply blood to the heart. ~*n., pl.* **-naries. 2.** a coronary thrombosis.

coronary thrombosis *n.* a condition where the blood flow to the heart is blocked by a clot in a coronary artery.

coronation (ˌkɒrəˈneɪʃən) *n.* the act or ceremony of crowning a monarch.

coroner (ˈkɒrənə) *n.* a public official responsible for the investigation of violent, sudden, or suspicious deaths.

coronet (ˈkɒrənɪt) *n.* **1.** a small crown

worn by princes or peers. **2.** a band of jewels worn as a headdress.

corporal[1] ('kɔːpərəl) *n.* a noncommissioned officer in an army.

corporal[2] ('kɔːpərəl, 'kɔːprəl) *adj.* of the body.

corporal punishment *n.* punishment of a physical nature, such as caning.

corporate ('kɔːpərɪt) *adj.* **1.** forming a corporation; incorporated. **2.** of a business corporation or corporations: *corporate finance.* **3.** of or shared by a united group; joint.

corporation (,kɔːpə'reɪʃən) *n.* **1.** a large business or company. **2.** a city or town council. **3.** *Brit. informal.* a large paunch. —'**corporative** *adj.*

corporatism ('kɔːpərətɪzəm) *n.* organization of a state on the lines of a business enterprise, with substantial government management of the economy.

corporeal (kɔː'pɔːrɪəl) *adj.* of the nature of the physical body; material; not spiritual.

corps (kɔː) *n., pl.* **corps** (kɔːz). **1.** a military body with a specific function: *medical corps.* **2.** a body of people associated together in a particular activity: *the diplomatic corps.*

corps de ballet ('kɔː də 'bæleɪ) *n.* the members of a ballet company.

corpse (kɔːps) *n.* a dead body, esp. of a human being.

corpulent ('kɔːpjulənt) *adj.* physically bulky; fat. —'**corpulence** *n.*

corpus ('kɔːpəs) *n., pl.* **-pora** (-pərə). a body of writings, such as one by a single author or on a specific topic: *the corpus of Dickens' works.*

corpuscle ('kɔːpʌsˀl) *n.* **1.** a red blood cell (see **erythrocyte**) or white blood cell (see **leucocyte**). **2.** any minute particle. —**corpuscular** (kɔː'pʌskjulə) *adj.*

corral (kɒ'rɑːl) *n.* **1.** *Chiefly U.S. & Canad.* an enclosure for cattle or horses. ~*vb.* **-ralling, -ralled. 2.** *U.S. & Canad.* to drive into a corral.

correct (kə'rɛkt) *vb.* **1.** to make free from or put right errors. **2.** to indicate the errors in (something). **3.** to rebuke or punish in order to improve: *to stand corrected.* **4.** to adjust or make conform to a standard. ~*adj.* **5.** true; accurate: *the correct version.* **6.** in conformity with accepted standards: *correct behaviour.* —**cor'rective** *adj.* —**cor'rectly** *adv.* —**cor'rectness** *n.*

correction (kə'rɛkʃən) *n.* **1.** an act or instance of correcting. **2.** something substituted for an error; an improvement. **3.** a reproof or punishment. —**cor'rectional** *adj.*

correlate ('kɒrɪ,leɪt) *vb.* **1.** to place or be placed in a complementary or mutual relationship: *poverty can be correlated with*

poor health. ~*n.* **2.** either of two things mutually related. —,**corr'elation** *n.*

correlative (kɒ'rɛlətɪv) *adj.* **1.** having a mutual relationship; corresponding. **2.** *Grammar.* (of words, usually conjunctions) corresponding to each other and occurring regularly together, for example *neither* and *nor.*

correspond (,kɒrɪ'spɒnd) *vb.* **1.** (usually foll. by *with* or *to*) to be consistent or compatible (with); tally (with). **2.** (usually foll. by *to*) to be similar (to). **3.** (usually foll. by *with*) to communicate (with) by letter. —,**corre'sponding** *adj.* —,**corre'spondingly** *adv.*

correspondence (,kɒrɪ'spɒndəns) *n.* **1.** similarity. **2.** agreement or conformity. **3. a.** communication by letters. **b.** the letters so exchanged.

correspondence course *n.* a course of study conducted by post.

correspondent (,kɒrɪ'spɒndənt) *n.* **1.** a person who communicates by letter. **2.** a person employed by a newspaper to report on a special subject or from a foreign country.

corridor ('kɒrɪ,dɔː) *n.* **1.** a passage connecting parts of a building. **2.** a strip of land or airspace that provides access through the territory of a foreign country. **3.** a passageway connecting the compartments of a railway coach. **4. corridors of power.** the higher levels of government or the Civil Service.

corrie ('kɒrɪ) *n.* (in Scotland) a circular hollow on a hillside.

corrigendum (,kɒrɪ'dʒɛndəm) *n., pl.* **-da** (-də). **1.** an error to be corrected. **2.** (*sometimes pl.*) a slip of paper inserted into a book after printing, listing corrections.

corroborate (kə'rɒbə,reɪt) *vb.* to confirm or support (facts or opinions), esp. by providing fresh evidence. —**cor,robo'ration** *n.* —**corroborative** (kə'rɒbərətɪv) *adj.*

corrode (kə'rəud) *vb.* **1.** to eat away or be eaten away by chemical action or rusting. **2.** to destroy gradually: *jealousy corroded his happiness.*

corrosion (kə'rəuʒən) *n.* **1.** the process by which something, esp. a metal, is corroded. **2.** the result of corrosion. —**cor'rosive** *adj.*

corrugate ('kɒru,geɪt) *vb.* to fold into alternate grooves and ridges. —,**corru'gation** *n.*

corrugated iron *n.* a thin sheet of iron or steel, formed with alternating ridges and troughs.

corrupt (kə'rʌpt) *adj.* **1.** open to or involving bribery or other dishonest practices: *a corrupt official; corrupt practices.* **2.** morally depraved. **3.** (of a text or manuscript) made unreliable or suspect by scribal errors or alterations. ~*vb.* **4.** to become or cause to become corrupt. —**cor'ruptive** *adj.*

corruptible (kə'rʌptɪb°l) *adj.* capable of being corrupted, esp. morally.

corruption (kə'rʌpʃən) *n.* **1.** a making or being corrupt. **2.** depravity. **3.** dishonesty, esp. bribery. **4.** decay. **5.** alteration, as of a manuscript. **6.** an altered form of a word.

corsage (kɔː'sɑːʒ) *n.* a small bouquet worn pinned to the shoulder or bosom of a dress.

corsair ('kɔːsɛə) *n.* **1.** a pirate. **2.** a privateer. **3.** a pirate ship.

corselet ('kɔːslɪt) *n.* a woman's one-piece undergarment, combining corset and bra.

corset ('kɔːsɪt) *n.* **1.** a stiffened close-fitting garment, worn by women to support or shape the torso. **2.** a similar garment worn because of injury or weakness, by either sex. —**'corsetry** *n.*

cortege *or* **cortège** (kɔː'teɪʒ) *n.* a funeral procession.

cortex ('kɔːtɛks) *n., pl.* **-tices** (-tɪˌsiːz). *Anat.* the outer layer of the brain or some other internal organ. —**cortical** ('kɔːtɪk°l) *adj.*

cortisone ('kɔːtɪˌzəʊn) *n.* a steroid hormone used in treating rheumatoid arthritis, allergies, and skin diseases.

corundum (kə'rʌndəm) *n.* a hard mineral consisting of aluminium oxide, used as an abrasive. The ruby and sapphire are precious forms of it.

coruscate ('kɒrəˌskeɪt) *vb.* to emit flashes of light; sparkle. —**ˌcorus'cation** *n.*

corvette (kɔː'vɛt) *n.* a lightly armed escort warship.

corymb ('kɒrɪmb, -rɪm) *n.* a flat-topped flower cluster with the stems growing progressively shorter towards the centre.

cos[1] *or* **cos lettuce** (kɒs) *n.* a lettuce with a long slender head and crisp leaves.

cos[2] (kɒz) cosine.

cosec ('kəʊsɛk) cosecant.

cosecant (kəʊ'siːkənt) *n.* (in trigonometry) the ratio of the length of the hypotenuse to that of the opposite side in a right-angled triangle.

cosh (kɒʃ) *Brit.* ~*n.* **1.** a heavy blunt weapon, often made of hard rubber. ~*vb.* **2.** to hit on the head with a cosh.

cosignatory (kəʊ'sɪgnətrɪ) *n., pl.* **-ries.** a person or country that signs a document jointly with others.

cosine ('kəʊˌsaɪn) *n.* (in trigonometry) the ratio of the length of the adjacent side to that of the hypotenuse in a right-angled triangle.

cosmetic (kɒz'mɛtɪk) *n.* **1.** anything applied to the face or body with the intention of beautifying it. ~*adj.* **2.** used to improve the appearance of the face or body. **3.** only superficially improving: *it was a purely cosmetic measure.*

cosmic ('kɒzmɪk) *adj.* **1.** of or relating to the whole universe: *cosmic laws.* **2.** occurring in or coming from outer space: *cosmic rays.*

cosmogony (kɒz'mɒgənɪ) *n., pl.* **-nies.** the study of the origin of the universe.

cosmology (kɒz'mɒlədʒɪ) *n.* the study of the origin and nature of the universe. —**cosmological** (ˌkɒzmə'lɒdʒɪk°l) *adj.* —**cos'mologist** *n.*

cosmonaut ('kɒzməˌnɔːt) *n.* a Soviet astronaut.

cosmopolitan (ˌkɒzmə'pɒlɪt°n) *adj.* **1.** having lived and travelled in many countries; free of national prejudices. **2.** composed of people or elements from many different countries or cultures. ~*n.* **3.** a cosmopolitan person. —**ˌcosmo'politanism** *n.*

cosmos ('kɒzmɒs) *n.* the universe considered as an ordered system.

Cossack ('kɒsæk) *n.* **1.** a member of a S Russian people, famous as horsemen and dancers. ~*adj.* **2.** of the Cossacks: *a Cossack dance.*

cosset ('kɒsɪt) *vb.* to pamper or pet.

cost (kɒst) *n.* **1.** the amount of money, time, or energy required to obtain or produce something. **2.** suffering or sacrifice: *I know to my cost.* **3.** the amount paid for a commodity by its seller: *to sell at cost.* **4.** (*pl.*) *Law.* the expenses of a lawsuit. **5. at all costs.** regardless of any cost, effort, or risk involved. **6. at the cost of.** at the expense of losing. ~*vb.* **costing, cost.** **7.** to be obtained or obtainable in exchange for: *the ride cost one pound.* **8.** to cause (someone) a loss or sacrifice: *the accident cost him dearly.* **9.** to estimate the cost of producing something.

cost accounting *n.* the recording and controlling of all the costs involved in running a business. —**cost accountant** *n.*

costermonger ('kɒstəˌmʌŋgə) *n. Brit., rare.* a person who sells fruit and vegetables from a barrow.

costive ('kɒstɪv) *adj.* constipated or constipating.

costly ('kɒstlɪ) *adj.* **-lier, -liest. 1.** expensive. **2.** involving great loss or sacrifice: *a costly victory.* **3.** splendid; lavish. —**'costliness** *n.*

cost of living *n.* the average cost of the basic necessities of life, such as food, housing, and clothing.

costume ('kɒstjuːm) *n.* **1.** a style of dressing, including all the clothes and accessories, typical of a particular country or period. **2.** the clothes worn by an actor or performer: *a jester's costume.* **3.** short for **swimming costume.** ~*vb.* **4.** to provide with a costume.

costume jewellery *n.* inexpensive but attractive jewellery.

costumier (kɒˈstjuːmɪə) n. a person who makes or supplies theatrical or fancy costumes.

cosy or U.S. **cozy** ('kəʊzɪ) adj. -sier, -siest or U.S. -zier, -ziest. **1.** warm and snug. **2.** intimate; friendly. ~n., pl. -sies or U.S. -zies. **3.** a cover for keeping things warm: tea cosy. —'**cosiness** or U.S. '**coziness** n.

cot[1] (kɒt) n. **1.** a bed with high sides for a baby or very young child. **2.** a small portable bed.

cot[2] (kɒt) n. **1.** Literary or archaic. a small cottage. **2.** a cote.

cot[3] (kɒt) cotangent.

cotangent (kəʊˈtændʒənt) n. (in trigonometry) the ratio of the length of the adjacent side to that of the opposite side in a right-angled triangle.

cot death n. the unexplained sudden death of an infant during sleep.

cote (kəʊt) or **cot** n. a small shelter for birds or animals.

coterie ('kəʊtərɪ) n. a small exclusive group of friends or people with common interests; clique.

cottage ('kɒtɪdʒ) n. a small simple house, usually one in the country. —'**cottager** n.

cottage cheese n. a mild soft white cheese made from skimmed milk curds.

cottage industry n. a craft industry in which employees work at home.

cotter[1] ('kɒtə) n. Machinery. a bolt or wedge that is used to secure parts of machinery.

cotter[2] ('kɒtə) n. Hist. & Scot. a farm labourer occupying a cottage and land rent-free.

cotter pin n. Machinery. a split pin used to hold parts together and fastened by having the ends spread apart after it is inserted.

cotton ('kɒt²n) n. **1.** the soft white downy fibre surrounding the seeds of a plant grown in warm climates, used to make cloth and thread. **2.** cloth or thread made from cotton fibres. —'**cottony** adj.

cotton on vb. (often foll. by to) Informal. to understand or realize the meaning (of).

cotton wool n. Chiefly Brit. absorbent fluffy cotton, used for surgical dressings and to apply liquids or creams to the skin.

cotyledon (ˌkɒtɪˈliːd²n) n. the first leaf produced by a plant embryo.

couch (kaʊtʃ) n. **1.** a piece of upholstered furniture for seating more than one person; sofa. **2.** a bed on which patients of a doctor or a psychoanalyst lie during examination or treatment. ~vb. **3.** to express in a particular style of language: couched in an archaic style. **4.** Archaic. (of an animal) to crouch, as when preparing to leap.

couchette (kuːˈʃɛt) n. a bed converted from seats in a railway carriage or ship.

couch grass (kaʊtʃ, kuːtʃ) n. a grassy weed with a creeping underground stem by which it spreads quickly.

cougar ('kuːgə) n. same as **puma.**

cough (kɒf) vb. **1.** to expel air abruptly and noisily from the lungs. **2.** (of an engine or other machine) to make a sound similar to this. ~n. **3.** an act or sound of coughing. **4.** a condition of the lungs or throat which causes frequent coughing.

cough up vb. **1.** Informal. to give up (money or information). **2.** to bring into the mouth or eject (phlegm, food, or blood) by coughing.

could (kʊd) vb. used: **1.** to make the past tense of **can**[1]. **2.** to make the subjunctive mood of **can**[1], esp. in polite requests or conditional sentences: could I see you tonight? **3.** to indicate the suggestion of a course of action: you could take the car if it's raining. **4.** (often foll. by well) to indicate a possibility: he could well be a spy.

couldn't ('kʊd²nt) could not.

coulomb ('kuːlɒm) n. the SI unit of electric charge.

coulter ('kəʊltə) n. a vertical blade on a plough in front of the ploughshare.

council ('kaʊnsəl) n. **1.** an assembly of people meeting for discussion or consultation. **2.** an administrative, legislative, or advisory body: a student council. **3.** Brit. the local governing authority of a town or county. **4.** (modifier) of, used, or provided by a local council: council offices; a council house.

councillor or U.S. **councilor** ('kaʊnsələ) n. a member of a council.

counsel ('kaʊnsəl) n. **1.** advice or guidance. **2.** discussion; consultation: to take counsel with a friend. **3.** a barrister or group of barristers who conduct cases in court and advise on legal matters. ~vb. -selling, -selled or U.S. -seling, -seled. **4.** to give advice or guidance to. **5.** to recommend; urge. —'**counselling** or U.S. '**counseling** n.

counsellor or U.S. **counselor** ('kaʊnsələ) n. **1.** an adviser. **2.** U.S. a lawyer who conducts cases in court.

count[1] (kaʊnt) vb. **1.** to add up or check (each thing in a group) in order to find the total: count your change. **2.** to recite numbers in ascending order up to and including: I'm going to count to ten. **3.** (often foll. by in) to take into account or include: we must count him in. **4.** **not counting.** excluding. **5.** to consider: count yourself lucky. **6.** to be important: only winning counts nowadays. **7.** Music. to keep time by counting beats. ~n. **8.** the act of counting. **9.** the number reached by counting: a blood count. **10.** Law. any of the separate charges in an indictment. **11.** **keep** or **lose count.** to keep or fail to keep an accurate record of items or events. **12. out for the count.** unconscious. ~See also **count against, countdown,** etc. —'**countable** adj.

count[2] (kaʊnt) n. a middle-ranking European nobleman.

count against vb. to have influence to the disadvantage of.

countdown ('kaʊnt͵daʊn) n. the act of counting backwards to zero to time exactly an operation such as the launching of a rocket.

countenance ('kaʊntɪnəns) n. **1.** the face or facial expression. ~vb. **2.** to support or approve. **3.** to tolerate; endure.

counter[1] ('kaʊntə) n. **1.** a long narrow flat surface in a shop, cafeteria, or bank, where food is sold, goods are displayed, or business is done. **2.** a small flat disc used in various board games. **3.** a disc or token used as an imitation coin. **4. under the counter.** (of the sale of goods) illegal.

counter[2] ('kaʊntə) n. an apparatus that records the number of occurrences of events.

counter[3] ('kaʊntə) adv. **1.** in an opposite or opposing direction or manner. **2. run counter to.** to be in direct contrast with. ~adj. **3.** opposing; opposite; contrary. ~n. **4.** something that is contrary or opposite to something else. **5.** an opposing action. **6.** a return attack, such as a blow in boxing or a parry in fencing. ~vb. **7.** to say or do (something) in retaliation or response. **8.** to oppose or act against (a person or thing). **9.** to return the attack of (an opponent).

counter- prefix. **1.** against; opposite; contrary: counterattack. **2.** complementary; corresponding: counterpart.

counteract (͵kaʊntər'ækt) vb. to act against or neutralize by contrary action. —͵**counter**'**action** n. —͵**counter**'**active** adj.

counterattack ('kaʊntərə͵tæk) n. **1.** an attack in response to an attack. ~vb. **2.** to make a counterattack (against).

counterbalance n. ('kaʊntə͵bæləns). **1.** a weight or influence that balances or offsets another. ~vb. (͵kaʊntə'bæləns). **2.** to act as a counterbalance to.

counterblast ('kaʊntə͵blɑːst) n. an aggressive response to a verbal attack.

counterclockwise (͵kaʊntə'klɒk͵waɪz) adv., adj. U.S. & Canad. same as **anticlockwise.**

counterespionage (͵kaʊntər'ɛspɪə͵nɑːʒ) n. activities to counteract enemy espionage.

counterfeit ('kaʊntəfɪt) adj. **1.** made in imitation of something genuine with the intent to deceive or defraud; forged: counterfeit money. **2.** pretended; sham: counterfeit affection. ~n. **3.** an imitation designed to deceive or defraud. ~vb. **4.** to make a fraudulent imitation of. **5.** to make counterfeits. **6.** to feign.

counterfoil ('kaʊntə͵fɔɪl) n. Brit. the part of a cheque or receipt retained as a record.

counterintelligence (͵kaʊntərɪn'tɛlɪdʒəns) n. activities designed to frustrate enemy espionage.

countermand (͵kaʊntə'mɑːnd) vb. to revoke or cancel (an order).

countermeasure ('kaʊntə͵mɛʒə) n. action taken to counteract or retaliate against some other action.

counterpane ('kaʊntə͵peɪn) n. a bedspread.

counterpart ('kaʊntə͵pɑːt) n. **1.** a person or thing that closely resembles another. **2.** one of two parts that complement or correspond to each other. **3.** a duplicate of a legal document.

counterpoint ('kaʊntə͵pɔɪnt) n. **1.** the harmonious combining of two or more parts or melodies. **2.** a melody or part combined with another melody or part. ~vb. **3.** to set in contrast.

counterpoise ('kaʊntə͵pɔɪz) vb. to oppose with something of equal effect, weight, or force; offset.

counterproductive (͵kaʊntəprə'dʌktɪv) adj. having an effect contrary to the one intended.

countersign vb. ('kaʊntə͵saɪn, ͵kaʊntə-'saɪn). **1.** to add a confirming signature to (a document already signed by another). ~n. ('kaʊntə͵saɪn). **2.** the signature so written.

countersink ('kaʊntə͵sɪŋk) vb. -**sinking,** -**sank, -sunk. 1.** to enlarge the upper part of (a hole) in timber or metal, so that the head of a bolt or screw can be sunk below the surface. **2.** to drive (a screw) or sink (a bolt) into such a hole.

countertenor (͵kaʊntə'tɛnə) n. **1.** an adult male voice with an alto range. **2.** a singer with such a voice.

countess ('kaʊntɪs) n. **1.** the wife or widow of a count or earl. **2.** a woman of the rank of count or earl.

countless ('kaʊntlɪs) adj. too many to count.

count noun n. a noun that may be preceded by an indefinite article and can be used in the plural, as telephone and thing but not airs and graces or bravery.

count on vb. to rely or depend on.

count out vb. **1.** Informal. to leave out; exclude. **2.** (of a boxing referee) to declare (a floored boxer) defeated when he has failed to recover within a count of ten seconds.

countrified or **countryfied** ('kʌntrɪ͵faɪd) adj. rustic in appearance or manner; rural.

country ('kʌntrɪ) n., pl. **-tries. 1.** an area distinguished by its people, culture, language, or government. **2.** the territory of a nation or state. **3.** the people of a nation or state. **4.** the part of the land that is away from cities or industrial areas; rural districts. **5.** same as **country and western. 6. across country.** not keeping to roads. **7. go to the country.** *Chiefly Brit.* to dissolve Parliament and hold a general election. **8.** one's native land or nation of citizenship.

country and western *n.* popular music in the style of White folk music of the Southern United States.

country club *n.* a club in the country, which has sporting and social facilities.

country dance *n.* a type of British folk dance in which couples face one another in a line.

countryman ('kʌntrɪmən) *n., pl.* -**men. 1.** a person who lives in the country. **2.** a person from one's own country. —'**country,woman** *fem. n.*

countryside ('kʌntrɪ,saɪd) *n.* land away from the cities; rural areas.

county ('kaʊntɪ) *n., pl.* -**ties. 1.** an administrative, political, or judicial subdivision in Britain, Ireland, or the U.S.A. ~*adj.* **2.** *Brit. informal.* upper-class; of or like the landed gentry.

coup (kuː) *n.* **1.** a brilliant and successful stroke or action. **2.** a coup d'état.

coup de grâce (,kuː də 'grɑːs) *n.* a final or decisive stroke.

coup d'état (,kuː deɪ'tɑː) *n., pl.* **coups d'état** (,kuːz deɪ'tɑː). a sudden violent or illegal overthrow of government.

coupé ('kuːpeɪ) *n.* a four-seater car with a sloping back and usually two doors.

couple ('kʌp°l) *n.* **1.** two people who are married or involved in a romantic relationship. **2.** two people considered as a pair, as for dancing or games. **3. a couple of. a.** a combination of two; a pair of: *a couple of men.* **b.** *Informal.* a small number of; a few: *a couple of days.* ~*pron.* **4.** (usually preceded by *a*) **a.** two. **b.** *Informal.* a few: *give him a couple.* ~*vb.* **5.** to connect. **6.** to have sexual intercourse.

couplet ('kʌplɪt) *n.* two successive lines of verse, usually rhymed and of the same metre.

coupling ('kʌplɪŋ) *n.* a device for connecting things, such as railway cars or trucks.

coupon ('kuːpɒn) *n.* **1.** a small, often detachable piece of paper entitling the holder to a discount or free gift. **2.** a detachable slip that can be used as a commercial order form. **3.** *Brit.* a football pools entry form.

courage ('kʌrɪdʒ) *n.* **1.** the ability to face danger, pain, or difficulty without fear. **2. the courage of one's convictions.** the confidence to act in accordance with one's beliefs.

courageous (kə'reɪdʒəs) *adj.* brave; showing courage. —**cou'rageously** *adv.*

courgette (kʊə'ʒɛt) *n.* a small variety of vegetable marrow.

courier ('kʊərɪə) *n.* **1.** a person who makes arrangements for or accompanies a group of travellers or tourists. **2.** a messenger who carries urgent or important correspondence.

course (kɔːs) *n.* **1.** an onward movement in time or space. **2.** a route or direction taken. **3.** the path or channel along which a river moves. **4.** an area on which a sport is played or a race is held: *a golf course.* **5.** a period of time; duration: *in the course of the next hour.* **6.** the natural development of a sequence of events: *the illness ran its course.* **7.** a mode of conduct or action: *if you follow that course, you will fail.* **8.** a complete series of lessons or lectures in an educational curriculum. **9.** a sequence of medical treatment prescribed for a specific period of time: *a course of injections.* **10.** any of the successive parts of a meal. **11.** a continuous, usually horizontal layer of building material, such as bricks or tiles, at one level in a building. **12. as a matter of course.** as a natural or normal consequence or event. **13. in the course of.** in the process of. **14. in due course.** at the natural or appropriate time. **15. of course. a.** (*adv.*) as expected; naturally. **b.** (*interj.*) certainly; definitely. ~*vb.* **16.** to run, race, or flow. **17.** to cause (hounds) to hunt by sight rather than scent or (of hounds) to hunt (a quarry) thus.

coursebook ('kɔːs,bʊk) *n.* a book that is used as part of an educational course.

courser[1] ('kɔːsə) *n.* **1.** a person who courses hounds. **2.** a hound trained for coursing.

courser[2] ('kɔːsə) *n. Literary.* a swift horse; steed.

coursework ('kɔːs,wɜːk) *n.* work done by a student and assessed as part of an educational course.

coursing ('kɔːsɪŋ) *n.* hunting with hounds trained to hunt game by sight.

court (kɔːt) *n.* **1.** *Law.* **a.** a judicial body which hears and makes decisions on legal cases. **b.** the room or building in which such an assembly takes place. **2.** a marked area used for any of various ball games, such as tennis or squash. **3.** an area of ground wholly or partly surrounded by walls or buildings. **4.** a block of flats. **5.** a mansion or country house. **6.** a short street, sometimes closed at one end. **7.** the residence, household, or retinue of a sovereign. **8.** any formal assembly held by a sovereign. **9.** flattering attention (esp. in **pay court to someone**). **10. go to court.** to take legal action. **11. hold court.** to preside over a group of admirers. **12. out of court.** without a trial or legal case. ~*vb.* **13.** to attempt to gain the love of; woo. **14.** to pay attention to (someone) in order to gain favour. **15.** to try to obtain (something): *to court favour.* **16.** to make oneself open or vulnerable to; risk: *court disaster.*

court card n. (in a pack of playing cards) a king, queen, or jack.

courteous ('kɜːtɪəs) adj. polite and considerate in manner. —'**courteously** adv. —'**courteousness** n.

courtesan (ˌkɔːtɪ'zæn) n. (esp. formerly) a prostitute with clients of high rank.

courtesy ('kɜːtɪsɪ) n., pl. -**sies. 1.** politeness; good manners. **2.** a courteous act or remark. **3. by courtesy of.** with the consent of.

courthouse ('kɔːt,haʊs) n. a public building in which courts of law are held.

courtier ('kɔːtɪə) n. an attendant at a royal court.

courtly ('kɔːtlɪ) adj. -**lier**, -**liest. 1.** of or suitable for a royal court. **2.** refined in manner; gracious. —'**courtliness** n.

court martial n., pl. **court martials** or **courts martial. 1.** the trial of a member of the armed forces charged with breaking military law. ~vb. **court-martial, -tialling, -tialled** or U.S. -**tialing, -tialed. 2.** to try by court martial.

courtship ('kɔːtʃɪp) n. the courting of an intended spouse or mate.

court shoe n. a low-cut shoe for women, without laces or straps.

courtyard ('kɔːt,jɑːd) n. an open area of ground surrounded by walls or buildings; court.

couscous ('kuːskuːs) n. a spicy North African dish, consisting of steamed semolina served with a meat stew.

cousin ('kʌz²n) n. the child of one's aunt or uncle. Also called: **first cousin.**

couture (kuː'tʊə) n. high-fashion designing and dressmaking.

couturier (kuː'tʊərɪˌeɪ) n. a person who designs, makes, and sells fashion clothes for women.

covalency (kəʊ'veɪlənsɪ) or U.S. **covalence** n. **1.** the ability to form a bond in which two atoms share a pair of electrons. **2.** the number of covalent bonds which a particular atom can make with others. —co'**valent** adj.

cove[1] (kəʊv) n. a small bay or inlet.

cove[2] (kəʊv) n. Brit. old-fashioned & Austral. slang. a fellow; chap.

coven ('kʌv²n) n. a meeting of witches.

covenant ('kʌvənənt) n. **1.** a binding agreement; contract. **2.** Law. a formal sealed agreement. **3.** Bible. God's promise to the Israelites and their commitment to worship him alone. ~vb. **4.** to agree by a legal covenant. —'**covenanter** n.

Covenanter ('kʌvənəntə, ˌkʌvə'næntə) n. Scot. history. a person upholding either of two 17th-century covenants to establish and defend Presbyterianism.

Coventry ('kɒvəntrɪ) n. **send someone to Coventry.** to punish someone for something he has done by refusing to speak to him.

cover ('kʌvə) vb. **1.** to place something over so as to protect or conceal. **2.** to put a garment on; clothe. **3.** to extend over or lie thickly on the surface of: snow covered the fields. **4.** (sometimes foll. by up) to screen or conceal; hide from view. **5.** to protect (an individual or group) by taking up a position from which fire may be returned if those being protected are fired upon. **6.** (foll. by for) to deputize for (a person). **7.** (foll. by for or up for) to provide an alibi (for). **8.** to travel over. **9.** to keep a gun aimed at. **10.** to include or deal with: the course covers a variety of topics. **11.** (of a sum of money) to be enough to pay for (something). **12. a.** to insure against loss or risk. **b.** to provide for (loss or risk) by insurance. **13.** to act as reporter or photographer on (a news event) for a newspaper or magazine: to cover sports events. **14.** Music. to record a cover version of. **15.** Sport. to guard or obstruct (an opponent, team-mate, or area). ~n. **16.** anything that covers, protects, or conceals. **17.** a blanket or bedspread. **18.** a pretext, disguise, or false identity: the thief sold brushes as a cover. **19.** an envelope or other postal wrapping: under plain cover. **20.** an individual table setting, esp. in a restaurant. **21.** a cover version. **22. break cover.** to come out from a shelter or hiding place. **23. take cover.** to make for a place of safety or shelter. **24. under cover.** protected, concealed, or in secret. ~See also **cover-up.** —'**covering** adj., n.

coverage ('kʌvərɪdʒ) n. Journalism. the amount of reporting given to a subject or event.

cover charge n. a fixed service charge added to the cost of the food or drink in a nightclub or restaurant.

cover girl n. a young woman whose picture appears on the cover of a magazine.

covering letter n. an accompanying letter sent as an explanation.

coverlet ('kʌvəlɪt) n. same as **bedspread.**

cover note n. Brit. a temporary certificate from an insurance company giving proof of a current policy.

covert ('kʌvət) adj. **1.** concealed or secret. ~n. **2.** a thicket or woodland providing shelter for game. **3.** Ornithol. any of the small feathers on the wings and tail of a bird that surround the bases of the larger feathers. —'**covertly** adv.

cover-up n. **1.** concealment or attempted concealment of a mistake or crime. ~vb. **cover up. 2.** to cover completely. **3.** to attempt to conceal (a mistake or crime).

cover version n. a version by a different artist of a previously recorded musical item.

covet (ˈkʌvɪt) *vb.* to long to possess (something belonging to another person).

covetous (ˈkʌvɪtəs) *adj.* (usually foll. by *of*) jealously longing to possess something. —ˈ**covetously** *adv.* —ˈ**covetousness** *n.*

covey (ˈkʌvɪ) *n.* **1.** a small flock of grouse or partridge. **2.** a small group of people.

cow¹ (kaʊ) *n.* **1.** the mature female of any species of cattle. **2.** the mature female of various other mammals, including the elephant, whale, and seal. **3.** (not in technical use) any domestic species of cattle. **4.** *Informal, offensive.* a disagreeable woman.

cow² (kaʊ) *vb.* to frighten or subdue, as with threats.

coward (ˈkaʊəd) *n.* a person who is easily frightened and avoids dangerous or difficult situations. —ˈ**cowardly** *adj.*

cowardice (ˈkaʊədɪs) *n.* lack of courage; cowardly behaviour.

cowbell (ˈkaʊˌbɛl) *n.* a bell hung around a cow's neck.

cowboy (ˈkaʊˌbɔɪ) *n.* **1.** (in the U.S. and Canada) a ranch worker who herds and tends cattle, usually on horseback. **2.** a conventional character of Wild West folklore or films. **3.** *Informal.* an irresponsible or unscrupulous worker or businessman. —ˈ**cow**ˌ**girl** *fem. n.*

cowcatcher (ˈkaʊˌkætʃə) *n. U.S. & Canad.* a fender on the front of a locomotive to clear the track of animals or other obstructions.

cow cocky *n. Austral. & N.Z.* a one-man dairy farmer.

cower (ˈkaʊə) *vb.* to crouch or cringe, as in fear.

cowl (kaʊl) *n.* **1.** a loose hood. **2.** the hooded garment of a monk. **3.** a cover fitted to a chimney to increase ventilation and prevent draughts. ~*vb.* **4.** to cover or provide with a cowl.

cowlick (ˈkaʊˌlɪk) *n.* a tuft of hair which stands up over the forehead.

cowling (ˈkaʊlɪŋ) *n.* a streamlined detachable metal covering around an engine.

co-worker *n.* a fellow worker; associate.

cow parsley *n.* a hedgerow plant with umbrella-shaped clusters of white flowers.

cowpat (ˈkaʊˌpæt) *n.* a pool of cow dung.

cowpox (ˈkaʊˌpɒks) *n.* a contagious disease of cows, the virus of which is used to make smallpox vaccine.

cowrie *or* **cowry** (ˈkaʊrɪ) *n., pl.* -ries. the glossy, brightly marked shell of a marine mollusc, formerly used as money in Africa and S Asia.

cowslip (ˈkaʊˌslɪp) *n.* a European wild plant with yellow flowers.

cox (kɒks) *n.* **1.** a coxswain. ~*vb.* **2.** to act as coxswain of (a boat).

coxcomb (ˈkɒksˌkəʊm) *n.* **1.** same as **cockscomb**. **2.** *Obs.* a medieval jester's cap, resembling a cock's comb.

coxswain (ˈkɒksən, -ˌsweɪn) *n.* the person who steers a lifeboat or rowing boat.

coy (kɔɪ) *adj.* **1.** affectedly shy and modest. **2.** evasive, esp. in an annoying way. —ˈ**coyly** *adv.* —ˈ**coyness** *n.*

coyote (kɔɪˈəʊtɪ) *n., pl.* -otes *or* -ote. a small wolf of the deserts and prairies of North America.

coypu (ˈkɔɪpuː) *n., pl.* -pus *or* -pu. an aquatic rodent, originally from South America, which resembles a small beaver and is bred for its fur.

cozen (ˈkʌzªn) *vb.* to cheat or trick (someone). —ˈ**cozenage** *n.*

Cr 1. Councillor. **2.** *Chem.* chromium.

crab (kræb) *n.* **1.** a crustacean with a broad flattened shell and five pairs of legs, the first pair modified into pincers. **2.** short for **crab louse**. **3. catch a crab.** *Rowing.* to make a stroke in which the oar misses the water or digs too deeply, causing the rower to fall backwards.

crab apple *n.* a kind of small sour apple.

crabbed (ˈkræbɪd) *adj.* **1.** irritable; peevish. **2.** (of handwriting) cramped and hard to read.

crabby (ˈkræbɪ) *adj.* -bier, -biest. bad-tempered.

crab louse *n.* a parasitic louse that infests the pubic region in humans.

crack (kræk) *vb.* **1.** to break or split without complete separation of the parts. **2.** to break with a sudden sharp sound; snap. **3.** to make or cause to make a sudden sharp sound: *to crack a whip.* **4.** (of the voice) to become harsh or change pitch suddenly; break. **5.** *Informal.* to fail or break down. **6.** to yield or cease to resist: *he cracked under torture.* **7.** to hit with a forceful or resounding blow. **8.** to break into or force open: *to crack a safe.* **9.** to solve or decipher (a code or problem). **10.** *Informal.* to tell (a joke). **11.** to break (a molecule) into smaller molecules or radicals by heat or catalysis as in the distillation of petroleum. **12.** to open (a bottle) for drinking. **13.** *Informal.* to achieve (esp. in **crack it**). ~*n.* **14.** a sudden sharp noise. **15.** a break or fracture without complete separation of the two parts. **16.** a narrow opening or fissure. **17.** *Informal.* a resounding blow. **18. crack of dawn** *or* **day.** daybreak. **19.** a broken or cracked tone of voice. **20.** (often foll. by *at*) *Informal.* an attempt. **21.** *Slang.* a gibe or joke. **22.** *Slang.* a highly addictive form of cocaine. **23. a fair crack of the whip.** *Informal.* a fair chance or opportunity. ~*adj.* **24.** *Slang.* first-class; excellent: *a crack shot.* ~See also **crack down, crack up.**

crackbrained (ˈkrækˌbreɪnd) *adj.* idiotic or crazy: *a crackbrained scheme.*

crack down *vb.* (often foll. by *on*) **1.** to take severe measures (against); become stricter (with). ~*n.* **crackdown. 2.** severe or repressive measures.

cracked (krækt) *adj.* **1.** damaged by cracking. **2.** harsh-sounding. **3.** *Informal.* crazy.

cracker ('krækə) *n.* **1.** a decorated cardboard tube that emits a bang when pulled apart, releasing a toy, a joke, or a paper hat. **2.** short for **firecracker. 3.** a thin crisp biscuit, usually unsweetened. **4.** *Brit. slang.* an excellent or notable thing or person.

crackers ('krækəz) *adj. Brit. slang.* insane.

cracking ('krækɪŋ) *adj.* **1. a cracking pace.** *Informal.* a high speed. **2. get cracking.** *Informal.* to start doing something immediately. ~*adv., adj.* **3.** *Brit. informal.* first-class; excellent. ~*n.* **4.** the oil-refining process in which heavy oils are broken down into smaller molecules by heat or catalysis.

crackle ('kræk°l) *vb.* **1.** to make a series of slight sharp popping noises. ~*n.* **2.** the act or sound of crackling. —'**crackly** *adj.*

crackling ('kræklɪŋ) *n.* **1.** a rapid series of slight, sharp popping noises. **2.** the crisp browned skin of roast pork.

crackpot ('kræk,pɒt) *Informal.* ~*n.* **1.** an eccentric person; crank. ~*adj.* **2.** eccentric; crazy.

crack up *vb.* **1.** to break into pieces. **2.** *Informal.* to suffer a physical or mental breakdown. **3. not all it is cracked up to be.** *Informal.* not as good as its favourable reputation would make one believe. ~*n.* **crackup. 4.** *Informal.* a physical or mental breakdown.

cradle ('kreɪd°l) *n.* **1.** a baby's bed on rockers. **2.** a place where something originates: *the cradle of civilization.* **3.** a supporting framework or structure. **4.** a platform or trolley in which workmen are suspended on the side of a building or ship. ~*vb.* **5.** to rock or place in or as if in a cradle; hold tenderly.

cradle-snatcher *n.* a person who marries or has a sexual relationship with someone much younger than himself or herself.

craft (krɑːft) *n.* **1.** skill or ability. **2.** cunning or guile. **3.** an occupation requiring skill or manual dexterity. **4.** (*pl.* **craft**) a boat, ship, aircraft, or spacecraft. ~*vb.* **5.** to make skilfully.

craftsman ('krɑːftsmən) *n., pl.* **-men. 1.** a skilled workman; artisan. **2.** a skilled artist. —'**craftsman,ship** *n.*

crafty ('krɑːftɪ) *adj.* **-tier, -tiest.** sly; shrewd; cunning. —'**craftily** *adv.* —'**craftiness** *n.*

crag (kræg) *n.* a steep rugged rock or peak. —'**craggy** *adj.*

crake (kreɪk) *n. Zool.* a bird of the rail family, such as the corncrake.

cram (kræm) *vb.* **cramming, crammed. 1.**

to force (more people or things) into (a place) than it can hold; stuff. **2.** to eat or feed to excess. **3.** *Informal.* to study intensively for an examination by hastily learning facts.

crammer ('kræmə) *n.* a person or school that prepares pupils for an examination.

cramp[1] (kræmp) *n.* **1.** a sudden painful involuntary contraction of a muscle. **2.** temporary stiffness of a muscle group from overexertion: *writer's cramp.* **3.** severe stomach pain. ~*vb.* **4.** to affect with a cramp.

cramp[2] (kræmp) *vb.* **1.** to confine or restrict. **2. cramp someone's style.** *Informal.* to prevent someone from using his abilities or acting freely.

cramped (kræmpt) *adj.* **1.** closed in; restricted. **2.** (of handwriting) small and irregular.

crampon ('kræmpɒn) *n.* one of a pair of spiked iron plates strapped to boots for climbing or walking on ice or snow.

cranberry ('krænbərɪ, -brɪ) *n., pl.* **-ries.** a sour edible red berry that grows on a trailing shrub.

crane (kreɪn) *n.* **1.** a large long-necked long-legged wading bird. **2.** a machine for lifting and moving heavy objects, usually by suspending them from a movable projecting arm or beam. ~*vb.* **3.** to stretch out (the neck) in order to see something.

crane fly *n.* a fly having long legs, slender wings, and a narrow body.

cranial ('kreɪnɪəl) *adj.* of or relating to the skull.

craniology (,kreɪnɪ'ɒlədʒɪ) *n.* the scientific study of the human skull.

cranium ('kreɪnɪəm) *n., pl.* **-niums** or **-nia** (-nɪə). **1.** the skull. **2.** the part of the skull that encloses the brain.

crank (kræŋk) *n.* **1.** a device for transmitting or converting motion, consisting of an arm projecting at right angles from a shaft. **2.** a handle incorporating a crank, used to start an engine or motor. **3.** *Informal.* **a.** an eccentric or odd person. **b.** *U.S. & Canad.* a bad-tempered person. ~*vb.* **4.** to cause to move by means of a crank. **5.** (sometimes foll. by *up*) to start (an engine or motor) by means of a crank handle.

crankcase ('kræŋk,keɪs) *n.* the metal case that encloses the crankshaft in an internal-combustion engine.

crankpin ('kræŋk,pɪn) *n.* a short cylindrical pin in a crankshaft, to which the connecting rod is attached.

crankshaft ('kræŋk,ʃɑːft) *n.* a shaft having one or more cranks, to which the connecting rods are attached.

cranky ('kræŋkɪ) *adj.* **crankier, crankiest.** *Informal.* **1.** eccentric. **2.** *U.S., Canad., & Irish.* fussy and bad-tempered. —'**crankiness** *n.*

cranny (ˈkrænɪ) *n.*, *pl.* **-nies.** a narrow opening; crevice.

crap¹ (kræp) *n.* same as **craps.**

crap² (kræp) *Slang.* ~*n.* **1.** nonsense. **2.** rubbish; junk. **3.** *Taboo.* faeces. ~*vb.* **crapping, crapped.** **4.** *Taboo.* to defecate. —ˈ**crappy** *adj.*

crape (kreɪp) *n.* same as **crepe.**

craps (kræps) *n.* (*functioning as sing.*) **1.** a gambling game using two dice. **2.** **shoot craps.** to play this game.

crapulent (ˈkræpjʊlənt) *or* **crapulous** (ˈkræpjʊləs) *adj.* given to, suffering from, or resulting from intemperance. —ˈ**crapulence** *n.*

crash (kræʃ) *vb.* **1.** to make or cause to make a loud smashing noise. **2.** to drop with force and break into pieces with a loud noise. **3.** to break or smash into pieces with a loud noise. **4.** (of a business or stock exchange) to collapse or fail suddenly. **5.** to cause (a vehicle or aircraft) to collide with another vehicle, the ground, or some other object or (of vehicles or aircraft) to be involved in a collision. **6.** to move violently or noisily. **7.** (of a computer system or program) to fail suddenly because of a malfunction. **8.** *Brit. informal.* to gate-crash. ~*n.* **9.** a breaking and falling to pieces. **10.** a sudden loud noise. **11.** a collision involving a vehicle or vehicles. **12.** a sudden descent of an aircraft as a result of which it crashes. **13.** the sudden collapse of a business or stock exchange. **14.** (*modifier*) requiring or using intensive effort and all possible resources in order to accomplish something quickly: *a crash course.*

crash barrier *n.* a barrier erected along the centre of a motorway, around a racetrack, or at the side of a dangerous road, for safety purposes.

crash dive *n.* **1.** a sudden steep emergency dive by a submarine. ~*vb.* **crash-dive.** **2.** to perform a crash dive.

crash helmet *n.* a helmet worn by motorcyclists to protect the head in case of a crash.

crashing (ˈkræʃɪŋ) *adj. Informal.* extreme: *a crashing bore.*

crash-land *vb.* to perform an emergency landing of (an aircraft), causing some damage, or (of an aircraft) to land in this way. —ˈ**crash-ˌlanding** *n.*

crass (kræs) *adj.* stupid; gross. —ˈ**crassly** *adv.* —ˈ**crassness** *n.*

crate (kreɪt) *n.* **1.** a large container made of wooden slats, used for packing, storing, or transporting goods. **2.** *Slang.* an old car or aeroplane. ~*vb.* **3.** to pack or place in a crate. —ˈ**crateful** *n.*

crater (ˈkreɪtə) *n.* **1.** the bowl-shaped opening in a volcano or a geyser. **2.** a cavity formed by the impact of a meteorite or exploding bomb. **3.** a roughly circular cavity on the surface of the moon and some other planets. ~*vb.* **4.** to make or form craters in (a surface, such as the ground).

cravat (krəˈvæt) *n.* a scarf worn round the neck instead of a tie.

crave (kreɪv) *vb.* **1.** (foll. by *for* or *after*) to desire intensely; long for. **2.** to beg or plead for. —ˈ**craving** *n.*

craven (ˈkreɪvᵊn) *adj.* **1.** cowardly. ~*n.* **2.** a coward.

craw (krɔː) *n.* **1.** the crop of a bird. **2.** the stomach of an animal. **3.** **stick in one's craw.** *Informal.* to be unacceptable.

crawl (krɔːl) *vb.* **1.** to move on one's hands and knees. **2.** to proceed very slowly. **3.** to act in a servile manner; fawn. **4.** to be or feel as if overrun by crawling creatures: *the pile of refuse crawled with insects; his threats made my skin crawl.* **5.** (of insects, worms or snakes) to creep slowly. ~*n.* **6.** a slow creeping pace or motion. **7.** *Swimming.* a stroke in which the feet are kicked like paddles while each arm in turn reaches forward and pulls back through the water.

crayfish (ˈkreɪˌfɪʃ) *or esp. U.S.* **crawfish** *n.*, *pl.* **-fish** *or* **-fishes.** a freshwater crustacean resembling a small lobster.

crayon (ˈkreɪən, -ɒn) *n.* **1.** a small stick or pencil of coloured wax, clay, or chalk. ~*vb.* **2.** to draw or colour with crayons.

craze (kreɪz) *n.* **1.** a short-lived fashion or enthusiasm. ~*vb.* **2.** to make mad. **3.** *Ceramics, metallurgy.* to develop or cause to develop fine cracks. —**crazed** *adj.*

crazy (ˈkreɪzɪ) *adj.* **-zier, -ziest.** **1.** *Informal.* insane. **2.** fantastic; ridiculous. **3.** (foll. by *about* or *over*) *Informal.* extremely fond of. —ˈ**craziness** *n.*

crazy paving *n. Brit.* a form of paving on a path, made of irregular slabs of stone.

creak (kriːk) *vb.* **1.** to make or move with a harsh squeaking sound. ~*n.* **2.** a harsh squeaking sound. —ˈ**creaky** *adj.* —ˈ**creakiness** *n.*

cream (kriːm) *n.* **1.** the fatty part of milk, which rises to the top. **2.** anything, such as a cosmetic, resembling cream in consistency. **3.** the best part of something; pick. **4.** any of various foods resembling or containing cream. ~*adj.* **5.** yellowish-white. ~*vb.* **6.** to remove the cream from (milk). **7.** to beat (foodstuffs) to a light creamy consistency. **8.** (sometimes foll. by *off*) to take away the best part of. **9.** to prepare or cook (foodstuffs) with cream or milk. —ˈ**creamy** *adj.*

cream cheese *n.* a rich soft white cheese made from soured cream and skimmed milk.

creamer (ˈkriːmə) *n.* a powdered substitute for cream, used in coffee.

creamery (ˈkriːmərɪ) *n.*, *pl.* **-eries.** a place where dairy products are made or sold.

cream of tartar *n.* purified tartar, the main ingredient in baking powder.

crease (kriːs) n. **1.** a line or mark produced by folding, pressing, or wrinkling. **2.** a wrinkle or furrow, esp. on the face. **3.** *Cricket.* any of three lines near each wicket marking positions for the bowler or batsman. ~*vb.* **4.** to make or become wrinkled or furrowed. —'**creasy** *adj.*

create (kriː'eɪt) *vb.* **1.** to cause to come into existence. **2.** to appoint to a new rank or position. **3.** to be the cause of. **4.** *Brit. slang.* to make a fuss or uproar.

creation (kriː'eɪʃən) n. **1.** a creating or being created. **2.** something brought into existence or created.

Creation (kriː'eɪʃən) n. *Christianity.* **the. 1.** God's act of bringing the universe into being. **2.** the universe as thus brought into being by God.

creative (kriː'eɪtɪv) *adj.* **1.** having the ability to create. **2.** imaginative or inventive. —ˌcrea'tivity n.

creator (kriː'eɪtə) n. a person who creates; originator.

Creator (kriː'eɪtə) n. **the.** God.

creature ('kriːtʃə) n. **1.** an animal, bird, or fish. **2.** a person: usually used as a term of contempt or pity. **3.** a person or thing controlled by another.

crèche (krɛʃ, kreɪʃ) n. *Chiefly Brit.* a day nursery for very young children.

credence ('kriːdəns) n. belief in the accuracy or trustworthiness of a statement: *I don't give much credence to that theory.*

credential (krɪ'dɛnʃəl) n. **1.** something that entitles a person to credit or confidence. **2.** (*pl.*) a letter or certificate giving evidence of the bearer's identity or qualifications.

credibility gap n. the difference between claims or statements made and the true facts.

credible ('krɛdɪbªl) *adj.* **1.** capable of being believed. **2.** trustworthy. —ˌcredi'bility n.

credit ('krɛdɪt) n. **1.** praise or approval, as for an achievement or quality. **2.** a person or thing who is a source of praise or approval. **3.** influence or reputation coming from the good opinion of others. **4.** belief or confidence in someone or something. **5.** a sum of money or equivalent purchasing power, available for a person's use. **6. a.** the positive balance in a person's bank account. **b.** the sum of money that a bank makes available to a client in excess of any deposit. **7. a.** the practice of allowing a buyer to receive goods or services before payment. **b.** the time allowed for paying for such goods or services. **8.** reputation for trustworthiness in paying debts, inducing confidence among creditors. **9.** *Accounting.* **a.** acknowledgment of a sum of money by entry on the right-hand side of an account. **b.** an entry or total of entries on

this side. **10.** *Education.* **a.** distinction awarded to an examination candidate obtaining good marks. **b.** certification that a section of an examination syllabus has been satisfactorily completed. **11. on credit.** with payment to be made at a future date. ~*vb.* **12.** (foll. by *with*) to attribute to; give credit for. **13.** to believe. **14.** *Accounting.* **a.** to enter (an item) as a credit in an account. **b.** to acknowledge (a payer) by making such an entry. ~See also **credits.**

creditable ('krɛdɪtəbªl) *adj.* deserving credit or honour; praiseworthy. —'**creditably** *adv.*

credit card n. a card issued by banks or shops, allowing the holder to obtain goods and services on credit.

creditor ('krɛdɪtə) n. a person or company to whom money is owed.

credit rating n. an evaluation of the creditworthiness of a person or a business.

credits ('krɛdɪts) *pl. n.* a list of those responsible for the production of a record, film, or television programme.

creditworthy ('krɛdɪtˌwɜːðɪ) *adj.* (of a person or a business) regarded as meriting credit on the basis of earning power and previous record of debt repayment. —'**creditˌworthiness** n.

credo ('kriːdəʊ, 'kreɪ-) n., *pl.* -dos. a creed.

credulity (krɪ'djuːlɪtɪ) n. tendency to believe something on little evidence; gullibility.

credulous ('krɛdjʊləs) *adj.* **1.** tending to believe something on little evidence. **2.** arising from or showing credulity: *credulous beliefs.*

creed (kriːd) n. **1.** a concise formal statement of the essential articles of Christian belief. **2.** any statement or system of beliefs or principles.

creek (kriːk) n. **1.** *Chiefly Brit.* a narrow inlet or bay. **2.** *U.S., Canad., Austral., & N.Z.* a small stream or tributary. **3. up the creek.** *Slang.* in trouble; in a difficult position.

creel (kriːl) n. a wickerwork basket used by fishermen.

creep (kriːp) *vb.* **creeping, crept. 1.** to crawl with the body near to or touching the ground. **2.** to move slowly, quietly, or cautiously. **3.** (of plants) to grow along the ground or over rocks. **4.** to have the sensation of something crawling over the skin, as from fear or disgust: *he makes my flesh creep.* ~*n.* **5.** the act of creeping or a creeping movement. **6.** *Slang.* an obnoxious or servile person.

creeper ('kriːpə) n. **1.** a plant, such as ivy, that grows by creeping. **2.** *U.S. & Canad.* same as **tree creeper. 3.** *Informal.* a shoe with a soft sole.

creeps (kriːps) *pl. n.* **the creeps.** *Informal.* a feeling of fear, repulsion, or disgust.

creepy ('kriːpɪ) *adj.* **creepier, creepiest.** *Informal.* having or causing a sensation of repulsion or fear. —**'creepiness** *n.*

creepy-crawly *n., pl.* **-crawlies.** *Brit. informal.* a small crawling creature.

cremate (krɪ'meɪt) *vb.* to burn (a corpse) to ash. —**cre'mation** *n.*

crematorium (ˌkrɛmə'tɔːrɪəm) *n., pl.* **-riums** *or* **-ria** (-rɪə). *Brit.* a building in which corpses are cremated.

crème (krɛm) *n.* **1.** cream. **2.** a thick sweet liqueur: *crème de moka.*

crème de menthe ('krɛm də 'mɛnθ) *n.* a liqueur flavoured with peppermint.

crenellate *or U.S.* **crenelate** ('krɛnɪ,leɪt) *vb.* to supply with battlements. —**'crenel,lated** *or U.S.* **'crene,lated** *adj.* —**ˌcrenel'lation** *or U.S.* **ˌcrene'lation** *n.*

creole ('kriːəʊl) *n.* **1.** a language that has developed from a mixture of different languages and has become the main language in a particular place. ~*adj.* **2.** of or relating to a creole.

Creole ('kriːəʊl) *n.* **1.** (in the West Indies and Latin America) a native-born person of mixed European and Negro ancestry who speaks a creole. **2.** (in the Gulf States of the U.S.) a native-born person of French ancestry. **3.** the French creole spoken in the Gulf States.

creosote ('krɪə,səʊt) *n.* **1.** a thick dark liquid mixture prepared from coal tar and used as a preservative for wood. **2.** a colourless liquid distilled from wood tar and used as an antiseptic. ~*vb.* **3.** to treat (wood) with creosote.

crepe (kreɪp) *n.* **1.** a thin light fabric with a fine ridged or crinkled surface. **2.** a black mourning armband originally made of this. **3.** a very thin pancake, often folded around a filling. **4.** a type of sheet rubber with a wrinkled surface, used for the soles of shoes.

crepe paper *n.* thin crinkled paper, resembling crepe and used for decorations.

crept (krɛpt) *vb.* past of **creep.**

crepuscular (krɪ'pʌskjʊlə) *adj.* **1.** of or like twilight; dim. **2.** (of certain creatures) active at twilight.

Cres. Crescent.

crescendo (krɪ'ʃɛndəʊ) *n., pl.* **-dos** *or* **-di** (-dɪ). **1.** a gradual increase in loudness. **2.** a musical passage that gradually gets louder. ~*adv.* **3.** gradually getting louder.

crescent ('krɛs³nt) *n.* **1.** the curved shape of the moon when in its first or last quarter. **2.** *Chiefly Brit.* a crescent-shaped street. ~*adj.* **3.** crescent-shaped.

cress (krɛs) *n.* a plant with pungent-tasting leaves, often used in salads and as a garnish.

crest (krɛst) *n.* **1.** a tuft or growth of feathers, fur, or skin along the top of a bird's or animal's head. **2.** the top or highest point of something. **3.** an ornamental plume or emblem on top of a helmet. **4.** a heraldic device used on a coat of arms, notepaper, or elsewhere. ~*vb.* **5.** to come or rise to a high point. **6.** to lie at the top of; *cap.* **7.** to reach the top of (a hill or wave). —**'crested** *adj.*

crestfallen ('krɛst,fɔːlən) *adj.* dejected or disheartened.

Cretaceous (krɪ'teɪʃəs) *adj. Geol.* of a period of geological time about 135 million years ago, at the end of which the dinosaurs died out.

cretin ('krɛtɪn) *n.* **1.** a person afflicted with cretinism. **2.** a very stupid person. —**'cretinous** *adj.*

cretinism ('krɛtɪ,nɪzəm) *n.* dwarfism and mental retardation caused by a thyroid deficiency.

cretonne (krɛ'tɒn, 'krɛtɒn) *n.* a heavy printed cotton or linen fabric, used for furnishing.

crevasse (krɪ'væs) *n.* a deep open crack, as in the ice of a glacier.

crevice ('krɛvɪs) *n.* a narrow fissure or crack; cleft.

crew¹ (kruː) *n.* **1.** the people who man a ship or aircraft. **2.** a group of people working together: *a film crew.* **3.** *Informal.* any group of people. ~*vb.* **4.** to serve on (a ship) as a crew member.

crew² (kruː) *vb. Archaic.* a past tense of **crow².**

crew cut *n.* a closely cropped haircut for men.

crewel ('kruːɪl) *n.* a loosely twisted worsted yarn, used in fancy work and embroidery. —**'crewel,work** *n.*

crew neck *n.* a plain round neckline. —**'crew-,neck** *or* **'crew-,necked** *adj.*

crib (krɪb) *n.* **1.** a baby's cradle; cot. **2.** a fodder rack or manger. **3.** a model of the manger scene at Bethlehem. **4.** *Informal, chiefly Brit.* a translation of a foreign text or a list of answers used by students, often illicitly, as an aid in lessons or examinations. **5.** short for **cribbage.** ~*vb.* **crib-bing, cribbed.** **6.** to confine in a small space. **7.** *Informal.* to plagiarize (another's writings or thoughts). **8.** *Informal.* to copy either from a crib or from someone else during a lesson or examination.

cribbage ('krɪbɪdʒ) *n.* a card game for two to four, in which players try to win a set number of points before their opponents.

crick (krɪk) *Informal.* ~*n.* **1.** a painful muscle spasm or cramp, esp. in the neck or back. ~*vb.* **2.** to cause a crick in.

cricket¹ ('krɪkɪt) *n.* a jumping insect like a grasshopper, which produces a chirping sound by rubbing together its forewings.

cricket² ('krɪkɪt) *n.* **1.** a game played by two teams of eleven players using a ball, bats, and wickets. **2. not cricket.** *Informal.* not fair play. —**'cricketer** *n.*

crier ('kraɪə) *n.* formerly, an official who made public announcements in a town or court.

crime (kraɪm) *n.* **1.** an act prohibited and punished by law. **2.** unlawful acts collectively. **3.** *Informal.* a senseless or deplorable act: *destroying the rainforests is a crime against nature.*

criminal ('krɪmɪnᵊl) *n.* **1.** a person guilty of a crime or crimes. ~*adj.* **2.** of or relating to crime or its punishment. **3.** *Informal.* senseless or deplorable. —**criminality** (,krɪmɪ'nælɪtɪ) *n.*

criminology (,krɪmɪ'nɒlədʒɪ) *n.* the scientific study of crime. —,crimi'nologist *n.*

crimp (krɪmp) *vb.* **1.** to fold or press into ridges. **2.** to fold and pinch together (something, such as two pieces of metal). **3.** to curl or wave (the hair) tightly with curling tongs. ~*n.* **4.** the act or result of crimping.

Crimplene ('krɪmpliːn) *n. Trademark.* a crease-resistant synthetic fabric.

crimson ('krɪmzən) *adj.* deep vivid red.

cringe (krɪndʒ) *vb.* **1.** to shrink or flinch in fear or servility. **2.** to behave in a servile or timid way. **3.** *Informal.* to have a sudden feeling of embarrassment or distaste. ~*n.* **4.** the act of cringing.

crinkle ('krɪŋkᵊl) *vb.* **1.** to wrinkle, twist, or fold. ~*n.* **2.** a wrinkle, twist, or fold. —**'crinkly** *adj.*

crinoline ('krɪnᵊlɪn) *n.* a petticoat stiffened with a framework of steel hoops, worn to make skirts stand out.

cripple ('krɪpᵊl) *n.* **1.** a person who is lame. **2.** a person who is disabled or deficient in some way: *a mental cripple.* ~*vb.* **3.** to make a cripple of; disable.

crisis ('kraɪsɪs) *n., pl.* -ses (-siːz). **1.** a crucial stage or turning point in the course of anything. **2.** a time of extreme trouble or danger.

crisp (krɪsp) *adj.* **1.** dry and brittle: *crisp bacon.* **2.** fresh and firm: *crisp lettuce.* **3.** invigorating or bracing: *a crisp breeze.* **4.** clear; sharp: *crisp reasoning.* **5.** lively or brisk. **6.** clean and neat. ~*vb.* **7.** to make or become crisp. ~*n.* **8.** *Brit.* a very thin slice of potato fried till crunchy, eaten cold as a snack. —**'crisply** *adv.* —**'crispness** *n.*

crispbread ('krɪsp,brɛd) *n.* a thin dry biscuit made of wheat or rye.

crispy ('krɪspɪ) *adj.* **crispier, crispiest.** crisp. —**'crispiness** *n.*

crisscross ('krɪs,krɒs) *vb.* **1.** to move in, mark with, or consist of a crosswise pattern. ~*adj.* **2.** (of lines) crossing one another in different directions.

criterion (kraɪ'tɪərɪən) *n., pl.* -ria (-rɪə) or -rions. a standard by which something can be judged or decided.

Usage. *Criteria,* the plural of *criterion,* is not acceptable as a singular noun in careful English.

critic ('krɪtɪk) *n.* **1.** a professional judge of art, music, or literature. **2.** a person who finds fault and criticizes.

critical ('krɪtɪkᵊl) *adj.* **1.** fault-finding or disparaging. **2.** containing analytical evaluations. **3.** of a critic or criticism. **4.** of or forming a crisis; crucial. **5.** *Physics.* denoting a constant value at which the properties of a system undergo an abrupt change: *the critical temperature at which water turns to ice.* **6.** (of a nuclear power station or reactor) having reached a state in which a nuclear chain reaction becomes self-sustaining. —**'critically** *adv.*

criticism ('krɪtɪ,sɪzəm) *n.* **1.** fault-finding or censure. **2.** an analysis or evaluation of a work of art or literature. **3.** the occupation of a critic. **4.** a work that sets out to evaluate or analyse.

criticize *or* **-ise** ('krɪtɪ,saɪz) *vb.* **1.** to find fault with; censure. **2.** to evaluate or analyse (something).

critique (krɪ'tiːk) *n.* **1.** a critical essay or commentary. **2.** the act or art of criticizing.

croak (krəʊk) *vb.* **1.** (of frogs or crows) to make a low hoarse cry. **2.** to utter (something) in this manner. **3.** *Slang.* to die. ~*n.* **4.** a low hoarse utterance or sound. —**'croaky** *adj.*

Croatian (krəʊ'eɪʃən) *adj.* **1.** of Croatia in Yugoslavia, its people, or their dialect of Serbo-Croatian. ~*n.* **2.** the dialect of Croatia. **3.** a person from Croatia.

crochet ('krəʊʃeɪ, -ʃɪ) *vb.* -cheting (-ʃeɪɪŋ, -ʃɪŋ), -cheted (-ʃeɪd, -ʃɪd). **1.** to make (a piece of needlework) by looping and intertwining thread with a hooked needle. ~*n.* **2.** work made by crocheting.

crock¹ (krɒk) *n.* an earthenware pot or jar.

crock² (krɒk) *n.* **old crock.** *Slang, chiefly Brit.* a person or thing that is old or broken-down.

crockery ('krɒkərɪ) *n.* china dishes or earthenware vessels collectively.

crocodile ('krɒkə,daɪl) *n.* **1.** a large tropical reptile with a broad head, tapering snout, huge jaws, and thick scales. **2.** *Brit. informal.* a line of schoolchildren walking two by two.

crocodile tears *pl. n.* an insincere show of grief; false tears.

crocus ('krəʊkəs) *n., pl.* -cuses. a plant with white, yellow, or purple flowers.

croft (krɒft) *n. Brit.* a small enclosed plot of land, adjoining a house, worked by the tenant and his family, as in N Scotland. —**'crofter** *n.* —**'crofting** *adj., n.*

croissant ('krwʌsɒŋ) *n.* a flaky crescent-shaped bread roll.

cromlech ('krɒmlɛk) *n.* **1.** a circle of prehistoric standing stones. **2.** (no longer in technical usage) same as **dolmen.**

crone (krəʊn) *n.* a witchlike old woman.

crony ('krəʊnɪ) *n., pl.* **-nies.** a friend or companion.

crook (krʊk) *n.* **1.** a curved or hooked thing or place: *she held the puppy in the crook of her arm.* **2.** a bishop's or shepherd's staff with a hooked end. **3.** *Informal.* a dishonest person such as a swindler or thief. ~*vb.* **4.** to bend or curve.

crooked ('krʊkɪd) *adj.* **1.** bent, winding, or twisted. **2.** set at an angle; not straight or level. **3.** *Informal.* dishonest or illegal. —'**crookedly** *adv.* —'**crookedness** *n.*

croon (kruːn) *vb.* **1.** to sing, hum, or speak in a soft low tone. ~*n.* **2.** a soft low singing or humming. —'**crooner** *n.*

crop (krɒp) *n.* **1.** a cultivated plant, such as a cereal, vegetable, or fruit plant. **2.** the season's total yield of farm produce. **3.** any group of things appearing at one time: *the current crop of school leavers.* **4.** the handle of a thonged whip. **5.** short for **riding crop.** **6.** a pouchlike part of the gullet of a bird, in which food is stored or prepared for digestion. **7.** a short cropped hairstyle. ~*vb.* **cropping, cropped. 8.** to cut (something) very short. **9.** to grow, bear or harvest (produce) as a crop. **10.** to clip part of (the ear or ears) of (an animal), esp. for identification. **11.** (of herbivorous animals) to feed by grazing. ~also see **crop up.**

cropper ('krɒpə) *n.* **come a cropper.** *Informal.* **a.** to fall heavily. **b.** to fail completely.

crop up *vb. Informal.* to occur or appear unexpectedly.

croquet ('krəʊkeɪ, -kɪ) *n.* a game played on a lawn in which the players hit a wooden ball through iron hoops with mallets in order to hit a peg.

croquette (krəʊ'kɛt, krɒ-) *n.* a savoury cake of mashed potato, meat, or fish, fried in breadcrumbs.

crosier *or* **crozier** ('krəʊʒə) *n.* a hooked staff carried by bishops as a symbol of office.

cross (krɒs) *n.* **1.** any structure, symbol, or mark consisting of two intersecting lines. **2.** an upright post with a bar across it, used in ancient times as a means of execution. **3.** a representation of the Cross on which Jesus Christ was executed as an emblem of Christianity. **4.** a symbol (×) used as a signature or error mark. **5. the sign of the cross.** a sign made with the hand by some Christians to represent the Cross. **6.** a medal in the shape of a cross. **7.** a monument in the shape of a cross. **8.** the place in a town or village where a cross has been set up. **9.** *Biol.* **a.** the process of crossing; hybridization. **b.** a hybrid. **10.** a mixture of two things. **11.** a hindrance or misfortune; affliction. **12.** *Football.* a pass of the ball from a wing to the middle of the field.

~*vb.* **13.** (sometimes foll. by *over*) to move or go across (something): *she crossed the street to avoid him; this street crosses the main road a little further on.* **14. a.** to meet and pass. **b.** (of each of two letters in the post) to be dispatched before receipt of the other. **15.** (usually foll. by *out, off,* or *through*) to cancel with a cross or with lines; delete. **16.** to place across or crosswise: *to cross one's legs.* **17.** to mark with a cross or crosses. **18.** *Brit.* to draw two parallel lines across (a cheque) and so make it payable only into a bank account. **19.** to make the sign of the cross upon (someone or something) as a blessing. **20.** (of telephone lines) to interfere with each other so that several callers are connected together at one time. **21.** to interbreed or cross-fertilize. **22.** to thwart or oppose. **23.** *Football.* to pass (the ball) from a wing to the middle of the field. **24. cross one's fingers.** to fold one finger across another in the hope of bringing good luck. **25. cross one's heart.** to promise, esp. by making the sign of a cross over one's heart. **26. cross one's mind.** to occur to one briefly or suddenly. ~*adj.* **27.** angry; in a bad mood. **28.** lying or placed across; transverse: *a cross timber.* —'**crossly** *adv.* —'**crossness** *n.*

Cross (krɒs) *n.* **the. 1.** the cross on which Jesus Christ was crucified. **2.** Christianity.

cross- *combining form.* **1.** indicating action from one individual or group to another: *cross-cultural; cross-refer.* **2.** indicating movement or position across something: *crosscurrent; crosstalk.* **3.** indicating a crosslike figure or intersection: *crossbones.*

crossbar ('krɒs,bɑː) *n.* **1.** a horizontal beam across a pair of goal posts. **2.** the horizontal bar on a man's bicycle.

cross-bench *n.* (usually *pl.*) *Brit.* a seat in Parliament occupied by members belonging to neither the government nor the opposition. —'**cross-,bencher** *n.*

crossbill ('krɒs,bɪl) *n.* a finch that has a bill with crossed tips.

crossbow ('krɒs,bəʊ) *n.* a weapon consisting of a bow fixed across a wooden stock, which releases an arrow when the trigger is pulled.

crossbreed ('krɒs,briːd) *vb.* **-breeding, -bred. 1.** to produce (a hybrid animal or plant) by crossing two different species. ~*n.* **2.** a hybrid animal or plant.

crosscheck (,krɒs'tʃɛk) *vb.* **1.** to check the accuracy of (something) by using a different method of verification from the one originally used. ~*n.* **2.** a crosschecking.

cross-country *adj., adv.* **1.** by way of open country or fields, as opposed to roads. ~*n.* **2.** a long race held over open ground.

crosscut ('krɒs,kʌt) *adj.* **1.** cut across. ~*n.* **2.** a transverse cut or course. ~*vb.* **-cutting, -cut. 3.** to cut across.

cross-examine *vb.* **1.** *Law.* to question

(a witness for the opposing side), in order to check or discredit his testimony. **2.** to question closely or relentlessly. —**'cross-ex,ami'nation** n. —,**cross-ex'aminer** n.

cross-eyed adj. having one or both eyes turning inwards towards the nose.

cross-fertilize vb. to fertilize (an animal or plant) by fusion of male and female reproductive cells from different individuals of the same species. —**'cross-,fertili'zation** n.

crossfire ('krɒs,faɪə) n. **1.** Mil. converging fire from one or more positions. **2.** a lively exchange of ideas or opinions.

crosshatch ('krɒs,hætʃ) vb. Drawing. to shade with two or more sets of parallel lines that cross one another.

crossing ('krɒsɪŋ) n. **1.** the place where one thing crosses another. **2.** a place where a street, railway, or river may be crossed. **3.** a journey across the sea.

cross-legged ('krɒs'lɛgɪd, -'lɛgd) adj. sitting with one leg crossed over the other.

crosspatch ('krɒs,pætʃ) n. Informal. a bad-tempered person.

cross-ply adj. (of a motor tyre) having the fabric cords in the outer casing running diagonally to stiffen the sidewalls.

cross-purpose n. **at cross-purposes.** disagreeing due to a misunderstanding about the subject of the discussion.

cross-question vb. to cross-examine.

cross-refer vb. -**referring, -referred.** to refer from one part of something esp. a book, to another.

cross-reference n. **1.** a reference within a text to another part of the text. ~vb. **2.** to cross-refer.

crossroads ('krɒs,rəʊdz) n. (functioning as sing.) **1.** the point at which roads cross one another. **2. at the crossroads.** at the point at which an important choice has to be made.

cross section n. **1.** Maths. a surface formed by cutting across a solid, usually at right angles to its longest axis. **2.** a random sample regarded as representative. —,**cross-'sectional** adj.

cross-stitch n. an embroidery stitch made from two crossing stitches.

crosstalk ('krɒs,tɔːk) n. **1.** unwanted signals transferred between communication channels. **2.** Brit. rapid or witty talk.

crosswise ('krɒs,waɪz) or **crossways** ('krɒs,weɪz) adj., adv. **1.** across; transversely. **2.** in the shape of a cross.

crossword puzzle or **crossword** ('krɒs,wɜːd) n. a puzzle in which vertically and horizontally crossing words suggested by numbered clues are written into a grid of squares.

crotch (krɒtʃ) n. **1. a.** the forked part of the human body between the legs. **b.** the corresponding part of a pair of trousers or pants. **2.** any forked part formed by the joining of two things. —**crotched** adj.

crotchet ('krɒtʃɪt) n. Music. a note having the time value of a quarter of a semibreve.

crotchety ('krɒtʃɪtɪ) adj. Informal. irritable; contrary.

crouch (kraʊtʃ) vb. **1.** to bend low with the limbs pulled up close together. ~n. **2.** the act of crouching.

croup[1] (kruːp) n. inflammation of the breathing passage, usually in children, causing a hoarse cough and laboured breathing.

croup[2] (kruːp) n. the hindquarters of a horse.

croupier ('kruːpɪə) n. a person in charge of a gaming table, who collects bets and pays out winnings.

crouton ('kruːtɒn) n. a small piece of fried or toasted bread, served in soup.

crow[1] (krəʊ) n. **1.** a large bird such as the raven, rook, or jackdaw, which has glossy black plumage, and a harsh call. **2. as the crow flies.** in a straight line.

crow[2] (krəʊ) vb. **1.** (past tense **crowed** or **crew**) to utter a shrill squawking sound, as a cock. **2.** (often foll. by over) to boast one's superiority. **3.** (esp. of babies) to utter cries of pleasure. ~n. **4.** a crowing sound.

crowbar ('krəʊ,bɑː) n. a heavy iron lever with one end forged into a wedge shape.

crowd (kraʊd) n. **1.** a large number of things or people gathered together. **2.** a particular group of people, esp. considered as a set: the crowd from the office. **3.** (preceded by the) the common people; the masses. ~vb. **4.** to gather together in large numbers; throng. **5.** to press together into a confined space. **6.** to fill to excess; fill by pushing into. **7.** Informal. to make (someone) uncomfortable by coming too close. —**'crowded** adj.

crown (kraʊn) n. **1.** a monarch's ornamental headdress, usually made of gold and jewels. **2.** an award or honour given for merit or victory, such as a wreath for the head. **3.** (formerly) a British coin worth 25 pence. **4.** the highest or central point of anything arched or curved: crown of a road. **5.** the outstanding quality or achievement: the crown of his career. **6. a.** the enamel-covered part of a tooth projecting beyond the gum. **b.** a substitute crown, usually of gold or porcelain, fitted over a decayed or broken tooth. ~vb. **7.** to put a crown on the head of (someone), to give them royal authority. **8.** to place something on or over the top of. **9.** to reward. **10.** to form the summit or topmost part of. **11.** to cap or put the finishing touch to (a series of events): to crown it all, it rained too. **12.** Draughts. to promote (a draught) to a king by placing another draught on top of it. **13.**

to attach a crown to (a tooth). **14.** *Slang.* to hit over the head.

Crown (kraʊn) *n.* **the.** the power or institution of the monarchy.

crown colony *n.* a British colony whose administration is controlled by the Crown.

crown court *n. English law.* a court of criminal jurisdiction holding sessions in towns throughout England and Wales.

Crown Derby *n.* a type of fine porcelain made at Derby.

crown jewels *pl. n.* the jewellery used by a sovereign on ceremonial occasions.

crown prince *n.* the male heir to a sovereign throne. —**crown princess** *n.*

crow's feet *pl. n.* wrinkles at the outer corners of the eye.

crow's nest *n.* a lookout platform fixed at the top of a ship's mast.

crucial (ˈkruːʃəl) *adj.* **1.** of exceptional importance; critical. **2.** *Slang.* very good. —**ˈcrucially** *adv.*

crucible (ˈkruːsɪbʰl) *n.* a pot in which metals or other substances are melted or heated to very high temperatures.

crucifix (ˈkruːsɪfɪks) *n.* a model cross with a figure of Christ upon it.

crucifixion (ˌkruːsɪˈfɪkʃən) *n.* a method of execution by fastening to a cross, normally by the hands and feet.

Crucifixion (ˌkruːsɪˈfɪkʃən) *n.* **1. the.** the crucifying of Christ. **2.** a representation of this.

cruciform (ˈkruːsɪˌfɔːm) *adj.* shaped like a cross.

crucify (ˈkruːsɪˌfaɪ) *vb.* **-fying, -fied. 1.** to put to death by crucifixion. **2.** *Slang.* to defeat or ridicule totally. **3.** to persecute or torment.

crud (krʌd) *n. Slang.* a sticky or encrusted substance or residue. —**ˈcruddy** *adj.*

crude (kruːd) *adj.* **1.** tasteless or vulgar. **2.** in a natural or unrefined state. **3.** lacking polish or skill. **4.** stark; blunt. ~*n.* **5.** short for **crude oil.** —**ˈcrudely** *adv.* —**ˈcrudity** *or* **ˈcrudeness** *n.*

crude oil *n.* unrefined petroleum.

cruel (ˈkruːəl) *adj.* **1.** deliberately causing pain without pity. **2.** causing pain or suffering. —**ˈcruelly** *adv.* —**ˈcruelty** *n.*

cruet (ˈkruːɪt) *n.* **1.** a small container for holding pepper, salt, vinegar, or oil at table. **2.** a set of such containers on a stand.

cruise (kruːz) *vb.* **1.** to sail about from place to place for pleasure. **2.** (of a vehicle, aircraft, or vessel) to travel at a moderate and efficient speed. ~*n.* **3.** a cruising voyage.

cruise missile *n.* a low-flying subsonic missile that is guided throughout its flight.

cruiser (ˈkruːzə) *n.* **1.** a large, fast warship armed with medium-calibre weapons. **2.**

Also called: **cabin cruiser.** a motorboat with a cabin.

cruiserweight (ˈkruːzəˌweɪt) *n. Boxing.* same as **light heavyweight.**

crumb (krʌm) *n.* **1.** a small fragment of bread, cake, or other dry foods. **2.** a small bit or scrap: *a crumb of comfort.*

crumble (ˈkrʌmbʰl) *vb.* **1.** to break into crumbs or fragments. **2.** to fall apart or decay. ~*n.* **3.** *Brit.* a baked pudding consisting of a crumbly topping over stewed fruit: *apple crumble.* —**ˈcrumbly** *adj.* —**ˈcrumbliness** *n.*

crumby (ˈkrʌmɪ) *adj.* **crumbier, crumbiest. 1.** full of crumbs. **2.** same as **crummy.**

crummy (ˈkrʌmɪ) *adj.* **-mier, -miest.** *Slang.* **1.** of very bad quality; worthless. **2.** unwell or out of sorts: *I feel crummy.*

crumpet (ˈkrʌmpɪt) *n. Chiefly Brit.* **1.** a light soft yeast cake, eaten toasted and buttered. **2.** *Slang.* sexually attractive women collectively.

crumple (ˈkrʌmpʰl) *vb.* (often foll. by *up*) **1.** to collapse or cause to collapse. **2.** to crush or become crushed into untidy wrinkles or creases. ~*n.* **3.** an untidy crease or wrinkle. —**ˈcrumply** *adj.*

crunch (krʌntʃ) *vb.* **1.** to bite or chew with a noisy crushing sound. **2.** to make or cause to make a crisp or brittle sound. ~*n.* **3.** the sound or act of crunching. **4. the crunch.** *Informal.* the critical moment or situation. —**ˈcrunchy** *adj.* —**ˈcrunchiness** *n.*

crupper (ˈkrʌpə) *n.* **1.** a strap from the back of a saddle that passes under a horse's tail. **2.** the horse's rump.

crusade (kruːˈseɪd) *n.* **1.** any of the medieval military expeditions undertaken by the Christian powers of Europe to recapture the Holy Land from the Muslims. **2.** a vigorous campaign in favour of a cause. ~*vb.* **3.** to engage in a crusade. —**cruˈsader** *n.*

cruse (kruːz) *n.* a small earthenware container for liquids.

crush (krʌʃ) *vb.* **1.** to press or squeeze so as to injure, break, or put out of shape. **2.** to break or grind into small particles. **3.** to oppress or subdue by force. **4.** to extract (liquid) by pressing. **5.** to defeat or humiliate utterly, as in argument or by a cruel remark. **6.** to crowd; throng. ~*n.* **7.** a dense crowd. **8.** the act of crushing; pressure. **9.** a drink made by crushing fruit: *orange crush.* **10.** *Informal.* an infatuation: *she had a crush on him.* —**ˈcrusher** *n.*

crush barrier *n.* a barrier put up to separate sections of large crowds and prevent crushing.

crust (krʌst) *n.* **1. a.** the hard outer part of bread. **b.** a piece of bread consisting mainly of this. **2.** the baked shell of a pie or tart. **3.** any hard outer layer: *a crust of ice.*

4. the solid outer shell of the earth. *~vb.*
5. to cover with, form, or acquire a crust.

crustacean (krʌˈsteɪʃən) *n.* **1.** a usually
aquatic arthropod with a hard outer shell
and several pairs of legs, such as the lobster, crab, or shrimp. *~adj.* **2.** of crustaceans.

crusty (ˈkrʌstɪ) *adj.* **crustier, crustiest. 1.**
having a crust. **2.** rude or irritable; harsh.
—ˈ**crustiness** *n.*

crutch (krʌtʃ) *n.* **1.** a long staff with a rest
for the armpit, used by a lame person to
support the weight of the body. **2.** something that supports, helps, or sustains. **3.**
Brit. same as **crotch** (of the body).

crux (krʌks) *n., pl.* **cruxes** *or* **cruces**
(ˈkruːsiːz). a crucial or decisive point.

cry (kraɪ) *vb.* **crying, cried. 1.** (often foll.
by *out*) to make a loud vocal sound, usually
to express pain or fear or to appeal for help.
2. to shed tears; weep or sob. **3.** (often foll.
by *out*) to utter loudly or shout (words of
appeal, exclamation, or fear). **4.** (often
foll. by *out*) (of an animal or bird) to utter
loud characteristic sounds. **5.** (foll. by *for*)
to clamour or beg. *~n., pl.* **cries. 6.** the act
or sound of crying; a shout, scream, or wail.
7. the characteristic utterance of an animal
or bird. **8.** a fit of weeping. **9.** an urgent
appeal. **10.** a public demand. **11. a far
cry. a.** a long way. **b.** something very
different. **12. in full cry.** in eager pursuit.
~See also **cry off.**

crying (ˈkraɪɪŋ) *adj.* **a crying shame.** something that demands immediate attention; an
injustice.

cry off *vb. Informal.* to withdraw from or
cancel (an agreement or arrangement).

cryogenics (ˌkraɪəˈdʒɛnɪks) *n.* (*with sing.
vb.*) the branch of physics concerned with
very low temperatures and their effects.
—ˌ**cryoˈgenic** *adj.*

crypt (krɪpt) *n.* a vault or underground
chamber, such as one beneath a church,
used as a burial place.

cryptic (ˈkrɪptɪk) *adj.* **1.** hidden; secret. **2.**
obscure in meaning. —ˈ**cryptically** *adv.*

cryptogam (ˈkrɪptəʊˌgæm) *n.* a plant that
does not produce flowers or seeds but reproduces by spores, such as algae, mosses,
and ferns.

cryptography (krɪpˈtɒgrəfɪ) *n.* the art of
writing in and deciphering codes.
—ˈ**cryptographer** *n.* —**cryptographic**
(ˌkrɪptəˈgræfɪk) *adj.*

crystal (ˈkrɪstˀl) *n.* **1.** a solid with a regular
shape in which the sides intersect in a
regular and symmetrical arrangement. **2.** a
single grain of a crystalline substance. **3.** a
highly transparent and brilliant type of
glass. **4.** something made of or resembling
crystal. **5.** crystal glass articles collectively. **6.** *Electronics.* a crystalline element
used in certain electronic devices, such as a

detector or oscillator. *~adj.* **7.** like crystal; transparent: *crystal water.*

crystal ball *n.* the glass globe used in
crystal gazing.

crystal gazing *n.* **1.** the act of staring
into a crystal ball supposedly in order to see
future events. **2.** the act of trying to foresee or predict. —**crystal gazer** *n.*

crystalline (ˈkrɪstəˌlaɪn) *adj.* **1.** having the
characteristics or structure of crystals. **2.**
made of or containing crystals. **3.** made of
or like crystal; transparent; clear.

crystallize, -ise, *or* **crystalize, -ise**
(ˈkrɪstəˌlaɪz) *vb.* **1.** to form or cause to form
crystals. **2.** to coat with sugar. **3.** to give a
definite form or expression to (an idea) or
(of an idea) to assume a definite form.
—ˌ**crystalliˈzation, -iˈsation,** *or* ˌ**crystali-
ˈzation, -iˈsation** *n.*

crystallography (ˌkrɪstəˈlɒgrəfɪ) *n.* the science of crystal structure.

crystalloid (ˈkrɪstəˌlɔɪd) *n.* a substance that
in solution can pass through a membrane.

Cs *Chem.* caesium.

CSE (in Britain) Certificate of Secondary
Education: an examination the first grade
pass of which is an equivalent to a GCE O
level.

CS gas *n.* a gas causing tears and painful
breathing, used in civil disturbances.

CST (in the U.S. and Canada) Central
Standard Time.

CT Connecticut.

CTV Canadian Television (Network Limited).

Cu *Chem.* copper.

cu. cubic.

cub (kʌb) *n.* **1.** the young of certain mammals, such as the lion or bear. **2.** a young or
inexperienced person. *~vb.* **cubbing,
cubbed. 3.** to give birth to (cubs).

Cub (kʌb) *n.* short for **Cub scout.**

cubbyhole (ˈkʌbɪˌhəʊl) *n.* a small enclosed
space or room.

cube (kjuːb) *n.* **1.** an object with six equal
square faces. **2.** the product of a number
multiplied by its square: *the cube of 2 is 8.*
~vb. **3.** to find the cube of (a number). **4.**
to shape or cut into cubes.

cube root *n.* the number or quantity
whose cube is a given number or quantity: *2
is the cube root of 8.*

cubic (ˈkjuːbɪk) *adj.* **1.** having the shape of
a cube. **2. a.** having three dimensions. **b.**
having the same volume as a cube with
length, width, and depth each measuring
the given unit: *a cubic metre.* **3.** *Maths.*
involving or relating to the cubes of numbers.

cubicle (ˈkjuːbɪkˀl) *n.* an enclosed compartment screened for privacy, as in a dormitory.

cubic measure *n.* a system of units for the measurement of volumes.

cubism ('kju:bɪzəm) *n.* a style of art, begun in the early 20th century, in which objects are represented by geometrical shapes. —'**cubist** *adj., n.*

cubit ('kju:bɪt) *n.* an ancient measure of length based on the length of the forearm.

cuboid ('kju:bɔɪd) *adj.* **1.** shaped like a cube. ~*n.* **2.** *Maths.* a geometric solid whose six faces are rectangles.

Cub Scout *or* **Cub** *n.* a member of the junior branch of the Scout Association.

cuckold ('kʌkəld) *n.* **1.** a man whose wife has been unfaithful to him. ~*vb.* **2.** to make a cuckold of.

cuckoo ('koku:) *n., pl.* **cuckoos. 1.** a migratory bird with a characteristic two-note call, noted for laying its eggs in the nests of other birds. ~*adj.* **2.** *Informal.* insane or foolish.

cuckoopint ('koku:,paɪnt) *n.* a plant with arrow-shaped leaves, a pale purple spike of flowers, and scarlet berries.

cuckoo spit *n.* a white frothy mass produced on plants by the larvae of some insects.

cucumber ('kju:,kʌmbə) *n.* **1.** a long fruit with thin green rind and crisp white flesh, used in salads. **2. as cool as a cucumber.** calm and self-possessed.

cud (kʌd) *n.* **1.** partially digested food brought back from the first stomach of ruminants to the mouth for a second chewing. **2. chew the cud.** to reflect or ponder something.

cuddle ('kʌd²l) *vb.* **1.** to hug or embrace fondly. **2.** (foll. by *up*) to lie close and snug; nestle. ~*n.* **3.** a fond hug, esp. when prolonged. —'**cuddly** *adj.*

cudgel ('kʌdʒəl) *n.* a short stout stick used as a weapon.

cue[1] (kju:) *n.* **1.** a signal to an actor or musician to begin speaking, playing, or doing something. **2.** any signal, hint, or reminder. **3. on cue.** at the right moment. ~*vb.* **cueing, cued. 4.** to give a cue to (an actor or musician).

cue[2] (kju:) *n.* **1.** a long tapering stick used to drive the balls in billiards, snooker, or pool. ~*vb.* **cueing, cued. 2.** to drive (a ball) with a cue.

cuff[1] (kʌf) *n.* **1.** the end of a sleeve. **2.** *U.S., Canad., & Austral.* a turn-up on trousers. **3. off the cuff.** *Informal.* improvised; impromptu.

cuff[2] (kʌf) *vb.* **1.** to strike with an open hand. ~*n.* **2.** a blow of this kind.

cuff link *n.* either of a pair of decorative fastenings for shirt cuffs.

cuisine (kwɪ'zi:n) *n.* **1.** a style or manner of cooking: *French cuisine.* **2.** the range of food served in a restaurant or household.

cul-de-sac ('kʌldə,sæk, 'kʊl-) *n., pl.* **culs-**

de-sac *or* **cul-de-sacs.** a road with one end blocked off.

culinary ('kʌlɪnərɪ) *adj.* of the kitchen or cookery.

cull (kʌl) *vb.* **1.** to choose or gather; pick out. **2.** to remove or kill (the inferior or surplus) animals from (a herd). ~*n.* **3.** the act of culling.

culminate ('kʌlmɪ,neɪt) *vb.* (usually foll. by *in*) to reach the highest point or climax. —,**culmi'nation** *n.*

culottes (kju:'lɒts) *pl. n.* women's flared trousers cut to look like a skirt.

culpable ('kʌlpəb²l) *adj.* deserving censure; blameworthy. —,**culpa'bility** *n.*

culprit ('kʌlprɪt) *n.* the person responsible for a particular offence or misdeed.

cult (kʌlt) *n.* **1.** a specific system of religious worship. **2.** a sect devoted to the beliefs of a cult. **3.** devoted attachment to a person, idea, or activity. **4.** any popular fashion; craze.

cultivate ('kʌltɪ,veɪt) *vb.* **1.** to prepare (land) for the growth of crops. **2.** to grow (plants). **3.** to develop or improve (something) by giving special attention to it: *try to cultivate a sense of humour.* **4.** to try to develop a friendship with (a person). —'**culti,vated** *adj.*

cultivation (,kʌltɪ'veɪʃən) *n.* **1.** the act of cultivating. **2.** culture or refinement.

cultivator ('kʌltɪ,veɪtə) *n.* a farm implement used to break up soil and remove weeds.

culture ('kʌltʃə) *n.* **1.** the ideas, customs, and art produced or shared by a particular society. **2.** a particular civilization at a particular period. **3.** activity or an interest in the arts in general. **4.** knowledge or refinement resulting from an interest in the arts. **5.** development or improvement by special attention or training: *physical culture.* **6.** the cultivation and rearing of plants or animals. **7.** a growth of microorganisms in a specially prepared substance. ~ *vb.* **8.** to grow (microorganisms) in a special medium. —'**cultural** *adj.*

cultured ('kʌltʃəd) *adj.* **1.** showing or having good taste, manners, and education. **2.** artificially grown or synthesized: *cultured pearls.*

cultured pearl *n.* a pearl made to grow in the shell of an oyster, by the insertion of a foreign body.

culvert ('kʌlvət) *n.* a drain or covered channel that crosses under a road or railway.

cum (kʌm) *prep.* used between nouns to indicate something with a combined nature: *a kitchen-cum-dining room.*

cumbersome ('kʌmbəsəm) *or* **cumbrous** ('kʌmbrəs) *adj.* **1.** awkward because of size, weight, or shape. **2.** difficult because of extent or complexity: *a cumbersome system.*

cumin *or* **cummin** (ˈkʌmɪn) *n.* **1.** the sweet-smelling seeds of a Mediterranean herb, used in Indian cooking. **2.** the plant from which these seeds are obtained.

cummerbund (ˈkʌməˌbʌnd) *n.* a wide sash, worn with a dinner jacket.

cumulative (ˈkjuːmjʊlətɪv) *adj.* growing in amount, strength, or effect by successive additions.

cumulus (ˈkjuːmjʊləs) *n.*, *pl.* **-li** (-ˌlaɪ). a thick or billowing white or dark grey cloud.

cuneiform (ˈkjuːnɪˌfɔːm) *adj.* **1.** of or using a system of writing with wedge-shaped characters, as in several ancient languages of Mesopotamia and Persia. ~*n.* **2.** cuneiform characters.

cunnilingus (ˌkʌnɪˈlɪŋɡəs) *n.* the kissing and licking of a woman's genitals by her partner.

cunning (ˈkʌnɪŋ) *adj.* **1.** crafty and sly. **2.** made with skill; ingenious. ~*n.* **3.** craftiness; slyness. **4.** skill or ingenuity.

cunt (kʌnt) *n. Taboo.* **1.** the female genitals. **2.** *Offensive slang.* a stupid or obnoxious person.

cup (kʌp) *n.* **1.** a small bowl-shaped container, usually having one handle, used for drinking from. **2.** the contents of a cup. **3.** something shaped like a cup: *the cups of a bra.* **4.** a cup-shaped trophy awarded as a prize. **5.** *Brit.* a sporting contest in which a cup is awarded to the winner. **6.** a mixed drink with one ingredient as a base: *claret cup.* **7.** one's lot in life. **8. one's cup of tea.** *Informal.* one's chosen or preferred thing. ~*vb.* **cupping, cupped.** **9.** to form (something, esp. the hands) into the shape of a cup. **10.** to put into or hold as if in a cup.

cupboard (ˈkʌbəd) *n.* a piece of furniture or a recessed area of a room, with a door concealing storage space.

cupboard love *n.* a show of love inspired only by some selfish motive.

Cup Final *n.* **1.** the annual final of the FA or Scottish Cup soccer competition. **2.** (*often not cap.*) the final of any cup competition.

Cupid (ˈkjuːpɪd) *n.* **1.** the Roman god of love, represented as a winged boy with a bow and arrow. **2. cupid.** a picture or statue of Cupid.

cupidity (kjuːˈpɪdɪtɪ) *n.* strong desire for wealth or possessions.

cupola (ˈkjuːpələ) *n.* **1.** a domed roof or ceiling. **2.** a small dome on the top of a roof. **3.** an armoured revolving gun turret on a warship.

cupreous (ˈkjuːprɪəs) *adj.* of, containing, or resembling copper.

cupric (ˈkjuːprɪk) *adj.* of or containing copper in the divalent state.

cupriferous (kjuːˈprɪfərəs) *adj.* containing or yielding copper.

cupronickel (ˌkjuːprəʊˈnɪk°l) *n.* a copper alloy containing up to 40 per cent nickel.

cuprous (ˈkjuːprəs) *adj.* of or containing copper in the monovalent state.

cup tie *n. Sport.* an eliminating match or round between two teams in a cup competition.

cur (kɜː) *n.* **1.** a vicious mongrel dog. **2.** a despicable or cowardly person.

curable (ˈkjʊərəb°l) *adj.* capable of being cured. —ˌcura'bility *n.*

curaçao (ˌkjʊərəˈsəʊ) *n.* an orange-flavoured liqueur originally made in Curaçao, a Caribbean island.

curacy (ˈkjʊərəsɪ) *n.*, *pl.* **-cies.** the work or position of a curate.

curare (kjʊˈrɑːrɪ) *n.* a black resin obtained from certain South American plants, used medicinally as a muscle relaxant and by some Indians as an arrow poison.

curate (ˈkjʊərɪt) *n.* a clergyman appointed to assist a vicar or parish priest.

curative (ˈkjʊərətɪv) *adj.* **1.** curing or able to cure. ~*n.* **2.** anything able to cure.

curator (kjʊəˈreɪtə) *n.* the administrative head of a museum or art gallery. —**curatorial** (ˌkjʊərəˈtɔːrɪəl) *adj.* —**cu'ratorˌship** *n.*

curb (kɜːb) *n.* **1.** something that restrains or holds back. **2.** a raised edge that strengthens or encloses. **3.** a horse's bit with an attached chain or strap, used to check the horse. ~*vb.* **4.** to control or restrain with or as if with a curb. ~See also **kerb.**

curd (kɜːd) *n.* **1.** (*often pl.*) a substance formed when milk coagulates, used in making cheese or as a food. **2.** any similar substance: *bean curd.*

curdle (ˈkɜːd°l) *vb.* **1.** to turn into curd; coagulate. **2. make someone's blood curdle.** to fill someone with horror.

cure (kjʊə) *vb.* **1.** to get rid of (an ailment or problem); heal. **2.** to restore to health. **3.** to preserve (meat or fish) by salting or smoking. **4.** to preserve (leather or tobacco) by drying. **5.** to vulcanize (rubber). ~*n.* **6.** a restoration to health. **7.** a course of medicinal or medical treatment that restores health. **8.** a means of restoring health or improving a situation. **9.** a curacy.

curet *or* **curette** (kjʊəˈret) *n.* **1.** a surgical instrument for removing dead tissue or growths from the walls of body cavities. ~*vb.* **-retting, -retted.** **2.** to scrape or clean with a curet. —**curettage** (ˌkjʊərɪˈtɑːʒ) *n.*

curfew (ˈkɜːfjuː) *n.* **1.** an official rule or law which states that people must stay inside their houses after a specific time at night. **2.** the time set as a deadline by such a law. **3.** *Hist.* the ringing of a bell at a fixed time, as a signal to people to extinguish fires and lights.

Curia ('kjʊərɪə) *n., pl.* **-riae** (-rɪ,iː). the papal court and government of the Roman Catholic Church. —**'curial** *adj.*

curie ('kjʊərɪ, -riː) *n.* the metric unit of radioactivity.

curio ('kjʊərɪ,əʊ) *n., pl.* **-rios.** a rare or unusual article valued as a collector's item.

curiosity (,kjʊərɪ'ɒsɪtɪ) *n., pl.* **-ties.** **1.** an eager desire to know; inquisitiveness. **2.** something strange, rare, or fascinating.

curious ('kjʊərɪəs) *adj.* **1.** eager to learn or know. **2.** prying; nosy. **3.** interesting because of oddness or novelty. —**'curiously** *adv.*

curium ('kjʊərɪəm) *n.* a silvery-white metallic radioactive element artificially produced from plutonium. Symbol: Cm

curl (kɜːl) *vb.* **1.** to twist or roll (hair) or (of hair) to grow in coils or ringlets. **2.** to form into or move in a spiral or curve. **3.** to play the game of curling. **4. curl one's lip.** to show contempt by raising a corner of the lip. ~*n.* **5.** a curve or coil of hair. **6.** a curved or spiral shape or mark. ~See also **curl up.** —**'curly** *adj.*

curler ('kɜːlə) *n.* **1.** a pin or roller used to curl hair. **2.** a person who plays curling.

curlew ('kɜːljuː) *n.* a large shore bird with a long downward-curving bill and long legs.

curlicue ('kɜːlɪ,kjuː) *n.* an intricate ornamental curl or twist.

curling ('kɜːlɪŋ) *n.* a game played on ice, in which heavy stones with handles are slid towards a target circle.

curl up *vb.* **1.** to lie or sit with legs drawn up. **2.** to be embarrassed or horrified.

curmudgeon (kɜː'mʌdʒən) *n.* an irritable or miserly person. —**cur'mudgeonly** *adj.*

currant ('kʌrənt) *n.* **1.** a small dried seedless raisin. **2.** a small round acid berry which grows on shrubs, such as the redcurrant.

currency ('kʌrənsɪ) *n., pl.* **-cies.** **1.** the system of money or the actual coins and banknotes in use in a particular country. **2.** general acceptance or use: *these theories have yet to gain much currency.*

current ('kʌrənt) *adj.* **1.** of the immediate present; happening now: *current affairs.* **2.** most recent; up-to-date. **3.** commonly accepted: *current opinion.* **4.** circulating and valid at present: *current coins.* ~*n.* **5.** a steady flow or rate of flow of water or air in a particular direction. **6.** *Physics.* a flow or rate of flow of electric charge through a conductor. **7.** a general trend or drift: *currents of opinion.* —**'currently** *adv.*

current account *n.* a bank account from which money may be drawn at any time using a chequebook or computerized card.

curriculum (kə'rɪkjʊləm) *n., pl.* **-la** (-lə) *or* **-lums.** **1.** a course of study in one subject at a school or college. **2.** all the courses of study offered by a school or college. —**cur'ricular** *adj.*

curriculum vitae ('viːtaɪ, 'vaɪtiː) *n., pl.* **curricula vitae.** an outline of someone's personal, educational, and professional history, usually prepared for job applications.

curry[1] ('kʌrɪ) *n., pl.* **-ries.** **1.** a dish of Indian origin consisting of meat or vegetables in a hot spicy sauce. **2.** curry seasoning or sauce. **3. curry powder.** a mixture of spices used for making curry. ~*vb.* **-rying, -ried.** **4.** to prepare (food) with curry powder or sauce.

curry[2] ('kʌrɪ) *vb.* **-rying, -ried.** **1.** to groom (a horse). **2.** to dress and finish (leather) after it has been tanned. **3. curry favour.** to ingratiate oneself, esp. with superiors.

currycomb ('kʌrɪ,kəʊm) *n.* a ridged comb used for grooming horses.

curse (kɜːs) *n.* **1.** a profane or obscene expression, usually of anger; oath. **2.** an appeal to a supernatural power for harm to come to a person. **3.** harm resulting from a curse. **4.** something that causes great trouble or harm. **5. the curse.** *Informal.* menstruation or a menstrual period. ~*vb.* **cursing, cursed.** **6.** to swear or swear at (someone). **7.** to call on supernatural powers to bring harm to (someone or something). **8.** to bring harm upon by a curse.

cursed ('kɜːsɪd, kɜːst) *adj.* **1.** under a curse. **2.** deserving to be cursed; hateful.

cursive ('kɜːsɪv) *adj.* **1.** of handwriting or print in which letters are joined in a flowing style. ~*n.* **2.** a cursive letter or printing type.

cursor ('kɜːsə) *n.* **1.** the sliding part of a slide rule or other measuring instrument. **2.** a movable point of light that shows a specific position on a visual display unit.

cursory ('kɜːsərɪ) *adj.* hasty and usually superficial; brief. —**'cursoriness** *n.*

curt (kɜːt) *adj.* so blunt and brief as to be rude. —**'curtly** *adv.* —**'curtness** *n.*

curtail (kɜː'teɪl) *vb.* to cut short; abridge. —**cur'tailment** *n.*

curtain ('kɜːtᵊn) *n.* **1.** a piece of material hung at an opening or window to shut out light or to provide privacy. **2.** something that conceals or shuts off: *a dense curtain of vegetation.* **3.** a hanging cloth that conceals all or part of a theatre stage from the audience. **4.** the end of a scene of a performance, marked by the fall or closing of the curtain. **5.** the rise or opening of the curtain at the start of a performance. ~*vb.* **6.** (sometimes foll. by *off*) to shut off or conceal as with a curtain. **7.** to provide with curtains.

curtain call *n.* *Theatre.* the audience's summons to an actor or actors to come to the front of the stage after a performance to receive applause.

curtains (ˈkɜːtˀnz) pl. n. Informal. death or ruin; the end.

curtsy or **curtsey** (ˈkɜːtsɪ) n., pl. **-sies** or **-seys**. 1. a woman's formal gesture of greeting and respect, in which the knees are bent and the head slightly bowed. ~vb. **-sying, -sied** or **-seying, -seyed**. 2. to make a curtsy.

curvaceous (kɜːˈveɪʃəs) adj. Informal. (of a woman) having a curved shapely body.

curvature (ˈkɜːvətʃə) n. the state or degree of being curved or bent.

curve (kɜːv) n. 1. a continuously bending line with no straight parts. 2. something that curves or is curved. 3. curvature. 4. Maths. a system of points whose coordinates satisfy a given equation. 5. a line representing data on a graph. ~vb. 6. to form into or move in a curve; bend. —ˈcurvy adj.

curvet (kɜːˈvɛt) n. 1. a horse's low leap with all four feet off the ground. ~vb. **-vetting, -vetted** or **-veting, -veted**. 2. to make such a leap.

curvilinear (ˌkɜːvɪˈlɪnɪə) adj. consisting of or bounded by a curved line.

cushion (ˈkʊʃən) n. 1. a bag filled with a soft material, used to make a seat more comfortable. 2. anything that relieves distress, provides comfort, or absorbs shock. 3. the resilient felt-covered rim of a billiard table. ~vb. 4. to provide with cushions. 5. to protect from injury or shock; relieve from distress. 6. to lessen or suppress the effects of. —ˈcushiony adj.

cushy (ˈkʊʃɪ) adj. **cushier, cushiest.** Informal. easy; comfortable.

cusp (kʌsp) n. 1. a small point on the grinding or chewing surface of a tooth. 2. a point or pointed end, such as one where two curves meet. 3. Astron. either of the points of a crescent moon. 4. Astrol. any division between houses or signs of the zodiac.

cuss (kʌs) Informal. ~n. 1. a curse; an oath. 2. a person or animal, esp. an annoying one. ~vb. 3. to swear or swear at (someone).

cussed (ˈkʌsɪd) adj. Informal. 1. same as **cursed**. 2. obstinate or annoying. —ˈcussedness n.

custard (ˈkʌstəd) n. 1. a sauce made of milk and sugar thickened with cornflour. 2. a baked sweetened mixture of eggs and milk.

custodian (kʌˈstəʊdɪən) n. the person in charge of something, such as a public building. —cusˈtodian,ship n.

custody (ˈkʌstədɪ) n., pl. **-dies**. 1. the act of keeping safe or guarding. 2. the state of being held by the police; arrest. —**custodial** (kʌˈstəʊdɪəl) adj.

custom (ˈkʌstəm) n. 1. a usual practice or habit. 2. the long-established habits or traditions of a society; convention. 3. a. a practice which by long-established usage has come to have the force of law. b. such practices collectively: custom and practice. 4. regular use of a shop or business. ~adj. 5. made to the specifications of an individual customer. ~See also **customs**.

customary (ˈkʌstəmərɪ) adj. in accordance with custom. —ˈcustomarily adv. —ˈcustomariness n.

custom-built adj. made according to the specifications of an individual customer.

customer (ˈkʌstəmə) n. 1. a person who buys. 2. Informal. a person with whom one has to deal: a rough customer.

custom house n. a government office where customs are levied.

customs (ˈkʌstəmz) n. (functioning as sing. or pl.) 1. duty charged on imports or exports. 2. the government department responsible for the collection of these duties. 3. the part of a port, airport, or border, where baggage and freight are examined for dutiable goods.

cut (kʌt) vb. **cutting, cut.** 1. to open up or penetrate (a person or thing) with.a sharp-edged instrument. 2. (of a sharp instrument) to penetrate or open up (a person or thing). 3. to divide or be divided with or as if with a sharp instrument. 4. to trim. 5. to reap or mow. 6. (sometimes foll. by out) to form or shape by cutting. 7. Sports. to hit (the ball) so that it spins and swerves. 8. to hurt the feelings of (a person): her rudeness cut me to the core. 9. Informal. to pretend not to recognize; snub. 10. Informal. to absent oneself from without permission: to cut a class. 11. to stop (doing something): cut the nonsense. 12. to abridge or shorten. 13. (often foll. by down) to reduce or curtail. 14. to dilute or adulterate: to cut whisky with water. 15. (foll. by across or through) to cross or traverse; intersect. 16. to make a sharp or sudden change in direction; veer. 17. to grow (teeth) through the gums. 18. Films. a. to call a halt to a shooting sequence. b. (foll. by to) to move quickly to (another scene). 19. Films. to edit (film). 20. to switch off (a light or engine). 21. to make (a gramophone record). 22. Cards. a. to divide (the pack) at random into two parts after shuffling. b. to pick cards from a spread pack to decide the dealer, partners, or who plays first. 23. **cut a dash.** to make a stylish impression. 24. **cut a person dead.** Informal. to ignore a person completely. 25. **cut and run.** Informal. to make a rapid escape. 26. **cut both ways. a.** to have both good and bad effects. **b.** to serve both sides of an argument. 27. **cut it fine.** Informal. to allow little margin of time or space. 28. **cut no ice.** Informal. to fail to make an impression. 29. **cut one's teeth on.** Informal. to acquire experience from. ~adj. 30. made, detached, or shaped by cutting. **31.** reduced by cutting: *cut prices.* **32.** adulterated or diluted. **33. cut and dried.** *Informal.* settled or arranged in advance. ~*n.* **34.** the act of cutting. **35.** a stroke or incision made by cutting. **36.** a piece or part cut off: *a cut of meat.* **37.** a passage, channel, or path cut or hollowed out. **38.** an omission or deletion in a text, film, or play. **39.** a reduction, as in prices or government spending. **40.** *Informal.* a portion or share. **41.** the style in which hair or a garment is cut. **42.** a direct route; short cut. **43.** *Sports.* a stroke which makes the ball spin and swerve. **44.** *Films.* an immediate transition from one shot to the next. **45.** a refusal to recognize someone; snub. **46.** *Brit.* a canal. **47. a cut above.** *Informal.* superior to; better than. ~See also **cut across, cutback,** etc.

cut across *vb.* **1.** to be contrary to (ordinary procedure or limitations); transcend. **2.** to cross or traverse, making a shorter route.

cutaneous (kjuːˈteɪnɪəs) *adj.* of the skin.

cutaway (ˈkʌtəˌweɪ) *adj.* (of a drawing or model of something) having part of the exterior omitted to reveal the interior.

cutback (ˈkʌtˌbæk) *n.* **1.** a decrease or reduction. ~*vb.* **cut back.** **2.** to shorten by cutting off the end; prune. **3.** (often foll. by *on*) to decrease or make a reduction (in).

cut down *vb.* **1.** to fell. **2.** (often foll. by *on*) to decrease or make a reduction (in). **3.** to kill. **4. cut a person down to size.** to cause a person to feel less important or to be less conceited.

cute (kjuːt) *adj.* **1.** appealing or attractive, esp. in a pretty way. **2.** *Informal, chiefly U.S. & Canad.* affecting cleverness or prettiness. **3.** clever; shrewd. —**'cuteness** *n.*

cut glass *n.* **1.** glass decorated by facet-cutting or grinding. **2.** (*modifier*) upper-class; refined: *a cut-glass accent.*

cuticle (ˈkjuːtɪkˀl) *n.* **1.** hardened skin round the base of a fingernail or toenail. **2.** same as **epidermis.**

cut in *vb.* **1.** to interrupt. **2.** to move in front of another vehicle, leaving too little space.

cutlass (ˈkʌtləs) *n.* a curved, one-edged sword formerly used by sailors.

cutler (ˈkʌtlə) *n.* a person who makes or sells cutlery.

cutlery (ˈkʌtlərɪ) *n.* knives, forks, and spoons, used for eating.

cutlet (ˈkʌtlɪt) *n.* **1.** a small piece of meat taken from the neck or ribs. **2.** a flat croquette of chopped meat or fish.

cut off *vb.* **1.** to remove or separate by cutting. **2.** to interrupt (a person who is speaking), esp. during a telephone conversation. **3.** to stop the supply of. **4.** to bring to an end. **5.** to disinherit: *cut off without a penny.* **6.** to intercept so as to prevent

retreat or escape; isolate. ~*n.* **cutoff.** **7.** the point at which something is cut off; limit. **8.** *Chiefly U.S.* a short cut. **9.** a device to stop the flow of a fluid in a pipe or duct.

cut out *vb.* **1.** to delete or remove. **2.** to shape or form by cutting. **3. be cut out for.** to be suited or equipped for: *you're not cut out for this job.* **4.** (of an engine) to cease to operate suddenly. **5.** (of an electrical device) to switch off, usually automatically. **6. cut it out.** *Informal.* to stop doing something. **7. have one's work cut out.** to have as much work as one can manage. ~*n.* **cutout.** **8.** something that has been or is intended to be cut out from something else. **9.** a device that automatically switches off an electric circuit or engine, esp. as a safety device.

cut-price *or esp. U.S.* **cut-rate** *adj.* **1.** available at prices below the standard price. **2.** offering goods or services at prices below the standard price.

cutter (ˈkʌtə) *n.* **1.** a person or tool that cuts, esp. a person who cuts cloth for clothing. **2.** any of various small fast boats, such as a lightly-armed one used by customs officers.

cutthroat (ˈkʌtˌθrəʊt) *n.* **1.** a person who cuts throats; murderer. **2.** *Brit.* a razor with a long blade that folds into its handle. ~*adj.* **3.** fierce or relentless in competition: *cutthroat prices.* **4.** (of a card game) played by three people: *cutthroat poker.*

cutting (ˈkʌtɪŋ) *n.* **1.** a piece cut from a plant for rooting or grafting. **2.** an article or photograph cut from a newspaper or magazine. **3.** the editing process of a film. **4.** an excavation for a road or railway through high ground. ~*adj.* **5.** designed for cutting; sharp: *a cutting tool.* **6.** keen; piercing: *a cutting wind.* **7.** likely to hurt the feelings: *a cutting remark.*

cuttlefish (ˈkʌtˀlˌfɪʃ) *n., pl.* **-fish** *or* **-fishes.** a flat squidlike mollusc which squirts an inky fluid when in danger.

cut up *vb.* **1.** to cut into pieces. **2. be cut up.** to be very upset. **3. cut up rough.** *Brit. informal.* to become angry or bad-tempered.

CV curriculum vitae.

cwm (kuːm) *n.* (in Wales) a valley.

cwt hundredweight.

cyanic (saɪˈænɪk) *adj.* **1.** of or containing cyanogen. **2.** blue.

cyanic acid *n.* a colourless poisonous volatile liquid acid.

cyanide (ˈsaɪəˌnaɪd) *n.* a highly poisonous salt of hydrocyanic acid.

cyanogen (saɪˈænədʒɪn) *n.* a poisonous colourless flammable gas.

cyanosis (ˌsaɪəˈnəʊsɪs) *n. Pathol.* a blue discoloration of the skin, caused by a deficiency of oxygen in the blood.

cybernetics (ˌsaɪbəˈnɛtɪks) *n.* (*functioning*

as sing.) the branch of science in which the control systems and methods of communication of electronic and mechanical devices are studied and compared to biological systems. —,**cyber'netic** *adj.*

cyclamen ('sıkləmən, -,mɛn) *n.* a plant having white, pink, or red flowers, with turned-back petals.

cycle ('saɪk²l) *n.* **1.** a complete series of recurring events or phenomena. **2.** the time taken or needed for one such series. **3.** a very long period of time. **4.** a group of poems, plays, or songs about a central figure or event: *the Arthurian cycle.* **5.** short for **bicycle, motorcycle. 6.** a single complete movement in an electrical, electronic, or mechanical process consisting of a continuous repetition of such movements. ~*vb.* **7.** to occur in cycles. **8.** to travel by or ride a bicycle or motorcycle.

cyclic ('saɪklık, 'sıklık) *or* **cyclical** *adj.* **1.** recurring in cycles. **2.** (of an organic compound) containing a closed ring of atoms.

cyclist ('saɪklıst) *or U.S.* **cycler** *n.* a person who rides a bicycle or motorcycle.

cyclometer (saɪ'klɒmɪtə) *n.* a device that records the number of revolutions made by a wheel and hence the distance travelled.

cyclone ('saɪkləʊn) *n.* **1.** a body of moving air below normal atmospheric pressure, which often brings rain; depression. **2.** a violent tropical storm; hurricane. —**cyclonic** (saɪ'klɒnık) *adj.*

cyclopedia *or* **cyclopaedia** (,saɪkləʊ-'piːdɪə) *n.* same as **encyclopedia.**

Cyclops ('saɪklɒps) *n., pl.* **Cyclopes** (saɪ-'kləʊpiːz) *or* **Cyclopses.** *Classical myth.* one of a race of giants having a single eye in the middle of the forehead.

cyclotron ('saɪklə,trɒn) *n.* an apparatus, used in atomic research, which accelerates charged particles by means of a strong vertical magnetic field.

cygnet ('sıgnıt) *n.* a young swan.

cylinder ('sılındə) *n.* **1.** a solid or hollow body with circular equal ends and straight parallel sides. **2.** any object shaped like a cylinder. **3.** the chamber in an internal-combustion engine within which the piston moves. **4.** the rotating mechanism of a revolver, containing cartridge chambers. —**cy'lindrical** *adj.*

cymbal ('sımb²l) *n.* a percussion instrument consisting of a thin circular piece of brass, which is clashed together with another cymbal or struck with a stick. —'**cymbalist** *n.*

cyme (saɪm) *n.* a flower cluster which has a single flower on the end of each stem and of

which the central flower blooms first. —'**cymose** *adj.*

Cymric ('kımrık) *n.* **1.** the Welsh language. ~*adj.* **2.** of Wales, the Welsh, or their language.

cynic ('sınık) *n.* a person who believes that people always act selfishly.

Cynic ('sınık) *n.* a member of an ancient Greek philosophical school that scorned worldly things. —**Cynicism** ('sını,sızəm) *n.*

cynical ('sınık²l) *adj.* **1.** believing that people always act selfishly. **2.** sarcastic; sneering. —'**cynically** *adv.*

cynicism ('sını,sızəm) *n.* **1.** the attitude or beliefs of a cynic. **2.** a cynical action or idea.

cynosure ('sınə,zjʊə, -ʃʊə) *n.* a centre of interest or attention

cypress ('saɪprəs) *n.* **1.** an evergreen tree with dark green scalelike leaves and rounded cones. **2.** the wood of this tree. **3.** cypress branches used as a symbol of mourning.

Cypriot ('sıprɪət) *n.* **1.** a person from Cyprus, an island in the E Mediterranean. **2.** the dialect of Greek spoken in Cyprus. ~*adj.* **3.** of Cyprus, its inhabitants, or dialect.

Cyrillic (sı'rılık) *adj.* of the Slavic alphabet devised supposedly by Saint Cyril, now used primarily for Russian and Bulgarian.

cyst (sıst) *n.* **1.** *Pathol.* any abnormal membranous sac containing fluid or diseased matter. **2.** *Anat.* any normal sac in the body.

cystic fibrosis ('sıstık) *n.* a congenital disease, usually affecting young children, which causes breathing disorders and malfunctioning of the pancreas.

cystitis (sı'staɪtıs) *n.* inflammation of the bladder.

cytology (saɪ'tɒlədʒɪ) *n.* the study of plant and animal cells. —**cytological** (,saɪtə-'lɒdʒık²l) *adj.* —**cy'tologist** *n.*

cytoplasm ('saɪtəʊ,plæzəm) *n.* the protoplasm of a cell excluding the nucleus. —,**cyto'plasmic** *adj.*

czar (zɑː) *n. Chiefly U.S.* same as **tsar.**

Czech (tʃɛk) *adj.* **1.** of Bohemia, Moravia, and, loosely, of Czechoslovakia, their people, or language. ~*n.* **2.** one of the two closely related official languages of Czechoslovakia (Czech and Slovak). **3.** a person from Bohemia, Moravia, or loosely, from Czechoslovakia.

Czechoslovak (,tʃɛkəʊ'sləʊvæk) *or* **Czechoslovakian** (,tʃɛkəʊsləʊ'vækɪən) *adj.* **1.** of Czechoslovakia, its peoples, or languages. ~*n.* **2.** a person from Czechoslovakia.

D

d or **D** (diː) *n., pl.* **d's, D's,** or **Ds.** the fourth letter of the modern English alphabet.

d *Physics.* density.

D **1.** *Music.* the second note of the scale of C major. **2.** *Chem.* deuterium. **3.** the Roman numeral for 500.

d. **1.** daughter. **2.** *Brit.* (before decimalization) penny *or* pennies. **3.** died.

dab¹ (dæb) *vb.* **dabbing, dabbed.** **1.** to pat lightly and quickly. **2.** to daub with short tapping strokes: *to dab the wall with paint.* **3.** to apply (a substance) with short tapping strokes. *~n.* **4.** a small amount of something soft or moist. **5.** a light stroke or tap. **6.** (*pl.*) *Slang, chiefly Brit.* fingerprints.

dab² (dæb) *n.* a small flatfish covered with rough toothed scales.

dabble (ˈdæbᵊl) *vb.* **1.** (usually foll. by *in*) to deal with or work at (something) frivolously or superficially. **2.** to dip or splash (the fingers or feet) in a liquid. —ˈdabbler *n.*

dab hand *n. Brit. informal.* a person who is particularly skilled at something: *a dab hand at chess.*

da capo (dɑː ˈkɑːpəʊ) *adv. Music.* to be repeated from the beginning.

dace (deɪs) *n., pl.* **dace** *or* **daces.** a freshwater fish of the carp family.

dachshund (ˈdæksˌhʊnd) *n.* a long-bodied short-legged dog.

dactyl (ˈdæktɪl) *n. Prosody.* a metrical foot of three syllables, one long followed by two short (–᷄᷄). —**dacˈtylic** *adj.*

dad (dæd) *or* **daddy** *n. Informal.* father.

Dada (ˈdɑːdɑː) *or* **Dadaism** (ˈdɑːdɑːˌɪzəm) *n.* an art movement of the early 20th century that systematically used arbitrary and absurb concepts. —**ˈDadaist** *n., adj.*

daddy-longlegs *n. Brit. informal.* a crane fly.

dado (ˈdeɪdəʊ) *n., pl.* **-does** *or* **-dos.** **1.** the lower part of an interior wall that is decorated differently from the upper part. **2.** *Archit.* the part of a pedestal between the base and the cornice.

daemon (ˈdiːmən) *n.* **1.** a demigod. **2.** the guardian spirit of a place or person.

daffodil (ˈdæfədɪl) *n.* **1.** a widely cultivated Eurasian plant with spring-blooming yellow flowers. *~adj.* **2.** brilliant yellow.

daft (dɑːft) *adj. Informal, chiefly Brit.* foolish or frivolous.

dag (dæg) *n. N.Z. informal.* a person with a good sense of humour.

dagger (ˈdægə) *n.* **1.** a short stabbing weapon with a pointed blade. **2.** a character (†) used to indicate a cross-reference. **3. at daggers drawn.** in a state of open hostility. **4. look daggers.** to glare with hostility.

daguerreotype (dəˈgɛrəʊˌtaɪp) *n.* a type of early photograph produced on chemically treated silver.

dahlia (ˈdeɪljə) *n.* a herbaceous plant with showy flowers.

Dáil Eireann (ˌdɔɪl ˈɛərən) *or* **Dáil** *n.* (in the Republic of Ireland) the lower chamber of parliament.

daily (ˈdeɪlɪ) *adj.* **1.** occurring every day or every weekday. *~n., pl.* **-lies. 2.** a daily newspaper. **3.** *Brit.* a charwoman. *~adv.* **4.** every day.

dainty (ˈdeɪntɪ) *adj.* **-tier, -tiest. 1.** delicate or elegant. **2.** choice: *a dainty morsel. ~n., pl.* **-ties. 3.** a delicacy. —**ˈdaintily** *adv.*

daiquiri (ˈdaɪkɪrɪ, ˈdæk-) *n., pl.* **-ris.** an iced drink containing rum, lime juice, and sugar.

dairy (ˈdɛərɪ) *n., pl.* **dairies. 1.** a company or shop that sells milk and milk products. **2.** a place where milk and cream are stored or made into butter and cheese. **3.** (*modifier*) of milk or milk products: *dairy butter.*

dais (ˈdeɪɪs, deɪs) *n.* a raised platform in a hall, used by speakers.

daisy (ˈdeɪzɪ) *n., pl.* **-sies. 1.** a small low-growing flower with a yellow centre and pinkish-white outer rays. **2.** any of various similar flowers.

daisywheel (ˈdeɪzɪˌwiːl) *n.* a disc-shaped part of the printer of a word processor with many radiating spokes, each with a character on the end.

dal (dɑːl) *n.* same as **dhal.**

Dalai Lama (ˈdælaɪ ˈlɑːmə) *n.* the chief lama and (until 1959) ruler of Tibet.

dale (deɪl) *n.* an open valley.

dally (ˈdælɪ) *vb.* **-lying, -lied. 1.** to dawdle. **2. dally with.** to amuse oneself with; trifle with. —**ˈdalliance** *n.*

Dalmatian (dælˈmeɪʃən) *n.* a large dog with a smooth white coat and black spots.

dal segno (ˈdæl ˈsɛnjəʊ) *adv. Music.* repeat from the point marked.

dam¹ (dæm) *n.* **1.** a barrier built across a river to create a body of water. **2.** a reservoir of water created by such a barrier. *~vb.* **damming, dammed. 3.** (often foll. by *up*) to restrict by a dam.

dam² (dæm) *n.* the female parent of an animal, esp. a sheep or horse.

damage (ˈdæmɪdʒ) *n.* **1.** injury or harm to

a person or thing. **2.** *Informal.* cost: *what's the damage?* ~*vb.* **3.** to cause damage to. —**'damaging** *adj.*

damages ('dæmɪdʒɪz) *pl. n. Law.* money to be paid as compensation for injury or loss.

damask ('dæməsk) *n.* **1.** a fabric with a pattern woven into it, used for table linen, curtains, etc. ~*adj.* **2.** greyish-pink.

dame (deɪm) *n.* **1.** *Slang, chiefly Scot., U.S., & Canad.* a woman. **2.** *Brit.* the role of a comic old woman in a pantomime, usually played by a man. **3.** (formerly) a woman of rank or dignity; lady.

Dame (deɪm) *n.* (in Britain) the title of a woman who has been awarded the Order of the British Empire or another order of chivalry.

damn (dæm) *interj.* **1.** *Slang.* an exclamation of annoyance. ~*adv., adj.* **2.** *Slang.* extreme or extremely: *a damn good pianist.* ~*vb.* **3.** to condemn as bad or worthless. **4.** to curse. **5.** to condemn to hell or eternal punishment. **6.** to prove (someone) guilty: *damning evidence.* **7. damn with faint praise.** to praise so unenthusiastically that the effect is condemnation. ~*n.* **8. not give a damn.** *Informal.* not care.

damnable ('dæmnəb'l) *adj.* hateful; detestable. —**'damnably** *adv.*

damnation (dæm'neɪʃən) *interj.* **1.** an exclamation of anger. ~*n.* **2.** *Theol.* eternal punishment.

damned (dæmd) *adj.* **1.** condemned to hell. ~*adv., adj. Slang.* **2.** extreme or extremely: *a damned good try.* **3.** used to indicate amazement or refusal: *damned if I care.*

damnedest ('dæmdɪst) *n.* **do one's damnedest.** *Informal.* to do one's utmost.

damp (dæmp) *adj.* **1.** slightly wet. ~*n.* **2.** slight wetness; moisture. ~*vb.* **3.** to make slightly wet. **4.** (often foll. by *down*) to stifle or deaden: *to damp one's ardour.* **5.** (often foll. by *down*) to reduce the flow of air to (a fire) to make it burn more slowly. —**'damply** *adv.* —**'dampness** *n.*

dampcourse ('dæmp,kɔːs) *n.* a layer of impervious material in a wall, to stop moisture rising.

dampen ('dæmpən) *vb.* **1.** to stifle; deaden. **2.** to make damp.

damper ('dæmpə) *n.* **1. put a damper on.** to produce a depressing or stultifying effect on. **2.** a movable plate to regulate the draught in a stove or furnace. **3.** the pad in a piano or harpsichord that deadens the vibration of each string as its key is released.

damsel ('dæmz'l) *n. Archaic or poetic.* a young woman.

damson ('dæmzən) *n.* a small blue-black edible plumlike fruit that grows on a tree.

dan (dæn) *n. Judo, karate.* **1.** any of the 10 black-belt grades of proficiency. **2.** a competitor entitled to dan grading.

dance (dɑːns) *vb.* **1.** to move the feet and body rhythmically in time to music. **2.** to perform (a particular dance): *to dance a jig.* **3.** to skip or leap. **4.** to move in a rhythmical way: *the fairy lights danced in the breeze.* **5. dance attendance on someone.** to attend someone solicitously. ~*n.* **6.** a social meeting arranged for dancing. **7.** a series of rhythmical steps and movements in time to music. **8.** a piece of music in the rhythm of a particular dance. —**'dancer** *n.* —**'dancing** *n., adj.*

D and C *n. Med.* dilatation of the cervix and curettage of the uterus: a minor operation to clear the womb or remove tissue for diagnosis.

dandelion ('dændɪ,laɪən) *n.* a plant with yellow rayed flowers and deeply notched leaves.

dander ('dændə) *n.* **get one's dander up.** *Informal.* to become annoyed or angry.

dandified ('dændɪ,faɪd) *adj.* dressed like or resembling a dandy.

dandle ('dænd'l) *vb.* to move (a young child) up and down on one's knee or in one's arms.

dandruff ('dændrəf) *n.* loose scales of dry dead skin shed from the scalp.

dandy ('dændɪ) *n., pl.* **-dies. 1.** a man who is greatly concerned with the elegance of his appearance. ~*adj.* **-dier, -diest. 2.** *Informal.* very good or fine.

dandy-brush *n.* a stiff brush used for grooming a horse.

Dane (deɪn) *n.* a person from Denmark.

danger ('deɪndʒə) *n.* **1.** the state of being vulnerable to injury or loss; risk. **2.** a person or thing that may cause injury or pain. **3.** a likelihood that something unpleasant will happen.

danger money *n.* extra money paid to compensate for the risks involved in dangerous jobs.

dangerous ('deɪndʒərəs) *adj.* causing danger; perilous. —**'dangerously** *adv.*

dangle ('dæŋg'l) *vb.* **1.** to hang or cause to hang freely. **2.** to display (something attractive) as an enticement.

Danish ('deɪnɪʃ) *adj.* **1.** of Denmark, its people, or their language. ~*n.* **2.** the official language of Denmark.

Danish blue *n.* a white cheese with blue veins.

Danish pastry *n.* a rich puff pastry filled with apple, almond paste, icing, etc.

dank (dæŋk) *adj.* (esp. of cellars or caves) unpleasantly damp and chilly.

daphne ('dæfnɪ) *n.* a shrub with small bell-shaped flowers.

dapper ('dæpə) *adj.* neat in dress and bearing.

dappled ('dæp'ld) *adj.* marked with spots of a different colour; mottled.

dapple-grey *n.* a horse with a grey coat having spots of a darker colour.

Darby and Joan ('dɑːbɪ; dʒəʊn) *n.* an elderly happily married couple.

dare (dɛə) *vb.* 1. to be courageous enough to try (to do something). 2. to challenge (a person to do something) as proof of courage. 3. **I dare say. a.** it is quite possible (that). **b.** probably. ~*n.* 4. a challenge to do something as proof of courage.

daredevil ('dɛə,dɛv'l) *n.* 1. a recklessly bold person. ~*adj.* 2. reckless; daring; bold.

daring ('dɛərɪŋ) *adj.* 1. bold or adventurous. ~*n.* 2. courage in taking risks; boldness. —'**daringly** *adv.*

dark (dɑːk) *adj.* 1. having little or no light. 2. (of a colour) reflecting or transmitting little light: *dark brown.* 3. (of the complexion or hair) not fair; swarthy; brunette. 4. gloomy. 5. sinister; evil: *a dark purpose.* 6. unenlightened: *a dark period in our history.* 7. secret or mysterious. ~*n.* 8. absence of light; darkness. 9. night or nightfall. 10. **in the dark.** in ignorance. —'**darkly** *adv.* —'**darkness** *n.*

Dark Continent *n.* **the.** a term for Africa when it was relatively unexplored by Europeans.

darken ('dɑːkən) *vb.* 1. to make or become dark or darker. 2. to make angry or sad.

dark horse *n.* a person who reveals unexpected talents.

darkroom ('dɑːk,ruːm, -,rʊm) *n.* a room in which photographs are processed in darkness or safe light.

darling ('dɑːlɪŋ) *n.* 1. a person very much loved. 2. a favourite. ~*adj.* 3. beloved. 4. pleasing: *a darling hat.*

darn[1] (dɑːn) *vb.* 1. to mend (a hole or a garment) with a series of interwoven stitches. ~*n.* 2. a patch of darned work on a garment.

darn[2] (dɑːn) *interj., adj., adv., vb., n. Euphemistic.* same as **damn.**

darnel ('dɑːn'l) *n.* a weed that grows in grain fields.

dart (dɑːt) *n.* 1. a small narrow pointed missile that is thrown or shot, as in the game of darts. 2. a sudden quick movement. 3. a tapered tuck made in dressmaking. ~*vb.* 4. to move or throw swiftly and suddenly. —'**darting** *adj.*

dartboard ('dɑːt,bɔːd) *n.* a circular board used as the target in the game of darts.

darts (dɑːts) *n.* (*functioning as sing.*) a game in which darts are thrown at a dartboard.

Darwinism ('dɑːwɪn,ɪzəm) *or* **Darwinian theory** *n.* the theory of the origin of animal and plant species by evolution. —**Dar'winian** *adj., n.* —'**Darwinist** *n., adj.*

dash (dæʃ) *vb.* 1. to move hastily; rush. 2.

to hurl; crash: *he dashed the cup to the floor.* 3. to frustrate: *his hopes were dashed.* ~*n.* 4. a sudden quick movement. 5. a small admixture: *a dash of cream.* 6. panache; style: *he rides with dash.* 7. the punctuation mark —, used to indicate a change of subject or to enclose a parenthetical remark. 8. the symbol (—), used in combination with the symbol *dot* (·) in Morse code. 9. *Athletics, chiefly U.S. & Canad.* the sprint. ~See also **dash off.**

dashboard ('dæʃ,bɔːd) *n.* the instrument panel in a car, boat, or aircraft.

dasher ('dæʃə) *n. Canad.* the ledge along the top of the boards of an ice hockey rink.

dashing ('dæʃɪŋ) *adj.* 1. spirited; lively: *a dashing young man.* 2. stylish; showy.

dash off *vb.* to write down or finish off hastily.

dassie ('dæsɪ) *n.* a hyrax, esp. a rock hyrax.

dastardly ('dæstədlɪ) *adj.* mean and cowardly.

dat. dative.

data ('deɪtə, 'dɑːtə) *n.* 1. a series of observations, measurements, or facts; information. 2. *Computers.* the numbers, digits, characters, and symbols operated on by a computer.
Usage. Although *data* is, strictly, a plural noun, it is now generally accepted as singular.

data base *n.* a store of information in a form that can be easily handled by a computer.

data capture *n.* a process for converting information into a form that can be handled by a computer.

data processing *n.* a sequence of operations performed on data, esp. by a computer, in order to extract or interpret information.

date[1] (deɪt) *n.* 1. a specified day of the month. 2. the particular day or year when an event happened. 3. **a.** an appointment, esp. with a person of the opposite sex. **b.** the person with whom the appointment is made. 4. **to date.** up to now. ~*vb* 5. to mark (a letter, cheque, etc.) with the date. 6. to assign a date of occurrence or creation to. 7. (foll. by *from* or *back to*) to have originated (at a specified time). 8. to reveal the age of: *that dress dates her.* 9. to make or become old-fashioned: *good films hardly date at all.* 10. *Informal, chiefly U.S. & Canad.* to be a boyfriend or girlfriend of. —'**dated** *adj.*

date[2] (deɪt) *n.* the dark-brown, sweet tasting fruit of the date palm.

dateless ('deɪtlɪs) *adj.* likely to remain fashionable or interesting regardless of age.

date line *n.* the line approximately following the 180° meridian from Greenwich, on the east side of which the date is one day earlier than on the west.

date palm *n.* a tall palm grown in tropical regions for its fruit.

date stamp *n.* a rubber stamp with movable figures for recording the date.

dative ('deɪtɪv) *n.* in certain languages, including Latin and German, the form of the noun that expresses the indirect object.

datum ('deɪtəm, 'dɑːtəm) *n., pl.* **-ta.** a single piece of information; fact.

daub (dɔːb) *vb.* **1.** to smear or spread (paint, mud, etc.), esp. carelessly. **2.** to paint (a picture) clumsily or badly. ~*n.* **3.** an unskilful or crude painting. **4.** something daubed on.

daughter ('dɔːtə) *n.* **1.** a female child. **2.** a girl or woman who comes from a certain place or is connected with a certain thing: *a daughter of the church.* ~(*modifier*) **3.** *Biol.* denoting a cell, chromosome, etc. produced by the division of one of its own kind. **4.** *Physics.* (of a nuclide) formed from another nuclide by radioactive decay. —'**daughterly** *adj.*

daughter-in-law *n., pl.* **daughters-in-law.** the wife of one's son.

daunt (dɔːnt) *vb.* to frighten or dishearten. —'**daunting** *adj.*

dauntless ('dɔːntlɪs) *adj.* fearless; not discouraged.

dauphin ('dɔːfɪn) *n.* (from 1349–1830) the eldest son of the king of France.

davenport ('dævən,pɔːt) *n.* **1.** *Chiefly Brit.* a writing desk with drawers at the side. **2.** *U.S. & Canad.* a large sofa, esp. one convertible into a bed.

davit ('dævɪt, 'deɪ-) *n.* a cranelike device on a ship, usually one of a pair, for suspending or lowering a lifeboat.

Davy Jones's locker ('deɪvɪ 'dʒəʊnzɪz) *n.* the ocean's bottom, regarded as the grave of those lost or buried at sea.

Davy lamp *n.* same as **safety lamp.**

dawdle ('dɔːd²l) *vb.* **1.** to be slow or lag behind. **2.** to waste time.

dawn (dɔːn) *n.* **1.** daybreak. **2.** the beginning of something. ~*vb.* **3.** to begin to grow light after the night. **4.** to begin to develop or appear. **5.** (usually foll. by *on* or *upon*) to become apparent (to).

dawn chorus *n.* the singing of birds at dawn.

day (deɪ) *n.* **1.** the period of 24 hours from one midnight to the next. **2.** the period of light between sunrise and sunset. **3.** the part of a day occupied with regular activity, esp. work. **4.** a period or point in time: *in days gone by; in Shakespeare's day.* **5.** (*often cap.*) a day of special observance: *Christmas Day.* **6.** a time of success or recognition: *his day will come.* **7.** a struggle or issue: *the day is lost.* **8.** **all in a day's work.** part of one's normal activity. **9. at the end of the day.** in the final reckoning. **10. call it a day.** to stop work

or other activity. **11. day in, day out.** every day without changing. **12. that'll be the day. a.** that is most unlikely to happen. **b.** I look forward to that.

Usage. Numerals are used for the day of the month. In written English, either cardinal numbers: *June 15, 1989* or ordinal numbers: *June 15th, 1989* may be used. It is equally acceptable to put the numeral before or after the month.

day bed *n.* a narrow couchlike bed.

daybreak ('deɪ,breɪk) *n.* the time in the morning when light first appears.

daydream ('deɪ,driːm) *n.* **1.** a pleasant fantasy indulged in while awake. ~*vb.* **2.** to indulge in idle fantasy. —'**day,dreamer** *n.*

daylight ('deɪ,laɪt) *n.* **1.** light from the sun. **2.** daytime. **3.** daybreak. **4. see daylight.** to realize that the end of a difficult task is approaching. ~See also **daylights.**

daylight robbery *n. Informal.* blatant overcharging.

daylights ('deɪ,laɪts) *pl. n.* **1. beat the living daylights out of someone.** to beat someone soundly. **2. scare the living daylights out of someone.** to frighten someone greatly.

daylight-saving time *n.* time set one hour ahead of the local standard time, to provide extra daylight in the evening in summer.

day release *n. Brit.* a system whereby workers go to college one day a week for vocational training.

day return *n.* a reduced fare for a train or bus journey travelling both ways in one day.

day room *n.* a communal living room in a residential institution, such as a hospital.

day-to-day *adj.* routine; everyday.

daze (deɪz) *vb.* **1.** to stun, esp. by a blow or shock. ~*n.* **2.** a state of confusion or shock: *in a daze.*

dazzle ('dæz²l) *vb.* **1.** to blind temporarily by sudden excessive light. **2.** to amaze, as with brilliance. ~*n.* **3.** bright light that dazzles. —'**dazzling** *adj.* —'**dazzlingly** *adv.*

dB *or* **db** decibel(s).

DBE Dame Commander of the Order of the British Empire.

DC 1. *Music.* da capo. **2.** direct current. **3.** District of Columbia.

DCB Dame Commander of the Order of the Bath.

DCM *Brit. mil.* Distinguished Conduct Medal.

DD Doctor of Divinity.

D-day *n.* the day selected for the start of some operation.

DDR Deutsche Demokratische Republik (East Germany; GDR).

DDS *or* **DDSc** Doctor of Dental Surgery *or* Science.

DDT *n.* dichlorodiphenyltrichloroethane; an insecticide.

DE Delaware.

de- *prefix.* indicating: **1.** removal: *deforest; dethrone.* **2.** reversal: *decode; desegregate.* **3.** departure from: *decamp.*

deacon (ˈdiːkən) *n. Christianity.* **1.** (in episcopal churches) an ordained minister ranking immediately below a priest. **2.** (in some Protestant churches) a lay official who assists the minister.

deaconess (ˈdiːkənɪs) *n. Christianity.* a female member of the laity with duties similar to those of a deacon.

deactivate (diːˈæktɪˌveɪt) *vb.* **1.** to make (an explosive device) inoperative. **2.** to become less radioactive.

dead (dɛd) *adj.* **1.** no longer alive. **2.** inanimate. **3.** no longer in use or relevant: *a dead issue; a dead language.* **4.** unresponsive. **5.** (of a limb) numb. **6.** no longer burning: *dead coals.* **7.** complete: *a dead stop.* **8.** *Informal.* very tired. **9.** (of a place) lacking activity. **10.** *Electronics.* **a.** drained of electric charge. **b.** not connected to a source of electric charge. **11.** *Sport.* (of a ball) out of play. **12. dead from the neck up.** *Informal.* stupid. **13. dead to the world.** *Informal.* fast asleep; in a drunken stupor. ~*n.* **14.** a period during which coldness or darkness is most intense: *the dead of winter.* ~*adv.* **15.** extremely: *dead easy.* **16.** suddenly: *stop dead.* **17. dead on.** exactly right.

deadbeat (ˈdɛdˌbiːt) *n. Informal, chiefly U.S. & Canad.* a lazy or socially undesirable person.

dead beat *adj. Informal.* exhausted.

dead duck *n. Slang.* something that is doomed to failure.

deaden (ˈdɛdᵊn) *vb.* **1.** to make less sensitive, intense, or lively. **2.** to make less resonant. —ˈ**deadening** *adj.*

dead end *n.* **1.** a cul-de-sac. **2.** a situation in which further progress is impossible.

deadhead (ˈdɛdˌhɛd) *U.S. & Canad.* ~*n.* **1.** *Informal.* a person who uses a free ticket, as for the theatre. **2.** *Informal.* a commercial vehicle travelling empty. **3.** *Slang.* a dull person. **4.** a log sticking out of the water. ~*vb.* **5.** *Informal.* to drive (an empty commercial vehicle). **6.** to remove dead flower heads from plants.

dead heat *n.* a tie for first place between two or more participants in a race or contest.

dead letter *n.* a law or rule that is no longer enforced.

deadline (ˈdɛdˌlaɪn) *n.* a time limit.

deadlock (ˈdɛdˌlɒk) *n.* **1.** a state of affairs in which further action between two opposing forces is impossible. ~*vb.* **2.** to bring to a deadlock.

dead loss *n. Informal.* a useless person or thing.

deadly (ˈdɛdlɪ) *adj.* **-lier, -liest. 1.** likely to cause death. **2.** *Informal.* extremely boring. ~*adv., adj.* **3.** like or suggestive of death. **4.** extremely.

deadly nightshade *n.* a poisonous plant with purple bell-shaped flowers and black berries.

dead man's handle *or* **pedal** *n.* a safety switch on a piece of machinery that allows operation only while depressed by the operator.

dead march *n.* solemn funeral music played to accompany a procession.

dead marine *n. Austral. & N.Z. informal.* an empty beer bottle.

dead-nettle *n.* a plant with leaves resembling nettles but lacking stinging hairs.

deadpan (ˈdɛdˌpæn) *adj., adv.* with a deliberately emotionless face or manner.

dead reckoning *n.* a method of establishing one's position using the distance and direction travelled.

dead set *adv.* **1.** absolutely: *he is dead set against going to Spain.* ~*n.* **2.** a serious attempt or effort.

dead weight *n.* **1.** a heavy weight or load. **2.** the difference between the loaded and the unloaded weights of a ship.

dead wood *n. Informal.* a useless person or persons.

deaf (dɛf) *adj.* **1.** unable to hear. **2. deaf to.** refusing to listen or take notice of. —ˈ**deafness** *n.*

deaf-and-dumb *adj. Offensive.* unable to hear or speak.

deafen (ˈdɛfᵊn) *vb.* to make deaf, esp. momentarily by a loud noise. —ˈ**deafeningly** *adv.*

deaf-mute *n.* a person who is unable to hear or speak.

deal[1] (diːl) *vb.* **dealing, dealt. 1.** (often foll. by *out*) to apportion or distribute. **2.** to inflict (a blow) on. **3.** *Slang.* to sell any illegal drug. **4. deal in.** to engage in commercially. ~*n.* **5.** a transaction or agreement. **6.** a particular type of treatment received: *a fair deal.* **7.** a large amount (esp. in **a good** *or* **great deal**). **8.** *Cards.* a player's turn to distribute the cards. **9. big deal.** *Slang.* an important matter: often used sarcastically. ~See also **deal with.** —ˈ**dealer** *n.*

deal[2] (diːl) *n.* **1.** a plank of softwood timber. **2.** the sawn wood of various coniferous trees.

dealignment (ˈdiːəˌlaɪnmənt) *n.* the process by which voters abandon traditional loyalties to a political party or social class.

dealings (ˈdiːlɪŋz) *pl. n.* transactions or business relations.

dealt (dɛlt) *vb.* past of **deal**[1].

deal with *vb.* **1.** to take action on: *to deal with each problem in turn.* **2.** to be concerned with: *the book deals with architecture.* **3.** to do business with.

dean (diːn) *n.* **1.** the chief administrative official of a college or university faculty. **2.** *Chiefly Church of England.* the chief administrator of a cathedral or collegiate church.

deanery ('diːnərɪ) *n., pl.* **-eries. 1.** the office or residence of a dean. **2.** the parishes presided over by a rural dean.

dear (dɪə) *adj.* **1.** beloved; precious. **2.** used in conventional forms of address, as in *Dear Sir.* **3. a.** highly priced. **b.** charging high prices. **4. dear to.** important or close to. *~interj.* **5.** used in exclamations of surprise or dismay, such as *Oh dear! ~n.* **6.** (*often used in direct address*) someone regarded with affection. *~adv.* **7.** dearly. **—'dearly** *adv.*

dearth (dɜːθ) *n.* an inadequate amount; scarcity.

death (dɛθ) *n.* **1.** the permanent end of all functions of life in an organism. **2.** an instance of this: *his death ended an era.* **3.** ending or destruction. **4.** (*usually cap.*) a personification of death, usually a skeleton holding a scythe. **5. at death's door.** likely to die soon. **6. catch one's death (of cold).** *Informal.* to contract a severe cold. **7. like death warmed up.** *Informal.* very ill. **8. put to death.** to execute. **9. to death. a.** until dead. **b.** very much.

deathbed ('dɛθ,bɛd) *n.* the bed in which a person dies or is about to die.

deathblow ('dɛθ,bləʊ) *n.* a thing or event that destroys hope, esp. suddenly.

death certificate *n.* a document issued by a medical practitioner certifying the death of a person and stating the cause if known.

death duty *n.* a tax on property inheritances, in Britain replaced by capital transfer tax since 1975.

deathless ('dɛθlɪs) *adj.* immortal, esp. because of greatness.

deathly ('dɛθlɪ) *adj.* **1.** resembling death: *a deathly quiet.* **2.** deadly.

death rate *n.* the ratio of deaths in an area or group to the population of that area or group.

death's-head *n.* a human skull or a representation of one.

deathtrap ('dɛθ,træp) *n.* a place or vehicle considered very unsafe.

death warrant *n.* **1.** the official authorization for carrying out a sentence of death. **2. sign one's (own) death warrant.** to cause one's own destruction.

deathwatch beetle ('dɛθ,wɒtʃ) *n.* a beetle that bores into wood and produces a tapping sound.

deb (dɛb) *n.* *Informal.* a debutante.

debacle (deɪ'bɑːk²l, dɪ-) *n.* a disastrous collapse or defeat; rout.

debag (diː'bæg) *vb.* **-bagging, -bagged.** *Brit. slang.* to remove the trousers from (someone) by force.

debar (dɪ'bɑː) *vb.* **-barring, -barred.** to exclude; bar. **—de'barment** *n.*

debase (dɪ'beɪs) *vb.* to lower in quality, character, or value; adulterate. **—de'basement** *n.*

debate (dɪ'beɪt) *n.* **1.** a formal discussion, as in a legislative body, in which opposing arguments are put forward. **2.** discussion. *~vb.* **3.** to discuss (a motion), esp. in a formal assembly. **4.** to deliberate upon (a course of action). **—de'batable** *adj.*

debauch (dɪ'bɔːtʃ) *n.* an instance of extreme dissipation. **—de'bauchery** *n.*

debauched (dɪ'bɔːtʃt) *adj.* leading a life of depraved self-indulgence.

debenture (dɪ'bɛntʃə) *n.* a long-term bond, bearing fixed interest and usually unsecured, issued by a company or governmental agency. **—de'bentured** *adj.*

debenture stock *n.* shares issued by a company, guaranteeing a fixed return at regular intervals.

debilitate (dɪ'bɪlɪ,teɪt) *vb.* to make feeble; weaken. **—de,bili'tation** *n.*

debility (dɪ'bɪlɪtɪ) *n., pl.* **-ties.** weakness or infirmity.

debit ('dɛbɪt) *n.* **1.** acknowledgment of a sum owing by entry on the left side of an account. *~vb.* **2. a.** to record (an item) as a debit in an account. **b.** to charge (an account) with a debt.

debonair *or* **debonnaire** (,dɛbə'nɛə) *adj.* **1.** suave and refined. **2.** carefree and cheerful.

debouch (dɪ'baʊtʃ) *vb.* **1.** (esp. of troops) to move into a more open space. **2.** (of a river, glacier, etc.) to flow into a larger area or body. **—de'bouchment** *n.*

debrief (diː'briːf) *vb.* to elicit a report from (a soldier, diplomat, etc.) after a mission or event. **—de'briefing** *n.*

debris *or* **débris** ('deɪbrɪ, 'dɛbrɪ) *n.* **1.** fragments of something destroyed; rubble. **2.** a collection of loose material derived from rocks.

debt (dɛt) *n.* **1.** something owed, esp. money. **2. bad debt.** a debt that has little prospect of being paid. **3.** the state of owing something (esp. in **in debt, in someone's debt**).

debt of honour *n.* a debt that is morally but not legally binding.

debtor ('dɛtə) *n.* a person who owes a financial obligation.

debug (diː'bʌg) *vb.* **-bugging, -bugged.** *Informal.* **1.** to remove concealed microphones from (a room). **2.** to locate and remove defects in (a device or system). **3.** to remove insects from.

debunk (diːˈbʌŋk) vb. *Informal.* to expose the pretensions or falseness of. —**deˈbunker** n.

debut (ˈdeɪbjuː, ˈdɛbjuː) n. the first public appearance of a performer.

debutante (ˈdɛbjuːˌtɑːnt, -ˌtænt) n. a young upper-class woman who is formally presented to society.

Dec. December.

decade (ˈdɛkeɪd) n. **1.** a period of ten years. **2.** a group of ten.
Usage. Specific decades are referred to as follows: *the 1660s; the 1980s.* In contexts where it is clear which century is being referred to, contractions are allowable though it is preferable to write out the contracted forms in words rather than numerals: *the sixties* rather than *the 60s* or *the '60s.*

decadence (ˈdɛkədəns) n. a state of deterioration of morality or culture. —**ˈdecadent** adj., n.

decaffeinated (dɪˈkæfɪˌneɪtɪd) adj. (of coffee, etc.) with caffeine removed.

decagon (ˈdɛkəˌgɒn) n. a polygon with ten sides. —**decagonal** (dɪˈkægənˀl) adj.

decahedron (ˌdɛkəˈhiːdrən) n. a solid figure with ten plane faces. —**ˌdecaˈhedral** adj.

decalitre or U.S. **decaliter** (ˈdɛkəˌliːtə) n. a measure of volume equivalent to 10 litres.

Decalogue (ˈdɛkəˌlɒg) n. same as **Ten Commandments.**

decametre or U.S. **decameter** (ˈdɛkəˌmiːtə) n. a measure of length equivalent to 10 metres.

decamp (dɪˈkæmp) vb. **1.** to depart secretly or suddenly. **2.** to leave a camp; break camp.

decant (dɪˈkænt) vb. **1.** to pour (a liquid, esp. wine) from one container to another. **2.** to rehouse (people) while their homes are being refurbished.

decanter (dɪˈkæntə) n. a stoppered bottle into which a drink is poured for serving.

decapitate (dɪˈkæpɪˌteɪt) vb. to behead. —**deˌcapiˈtation** n.

decapod (ˈdɛkəˌpɒd) n. **1.** a creature such as a crab or lobster, which has five pairs of walking limbs. **2.** a creature such as a squid or cuttlefish, which has eight short tentacles and two longer ones.

decarbonize or **-ise** (diːˈkɑːbəˌnaɪz) vb. to remove carbon from (an internal-combustion engine). —**deˌcarboniˈzation** or **-iˈsation** n.

decathlon (dɪˈkæθlɒn) n. an athletic contest in which each athlete competes in ten different events: 100m sprint, long jump, shot put, high jump, 400m, 110m hurdles, discus, pole vault, javelin, and 1500m. —**deˈcathlete** n.

decay (dɪˈkeɪ) vb. **1.** to decline gradually in health, prosperity, or excellence; deteriorate. **2.** to rot or cause to rot. **3.** *Physics.* (of an atomic nucleus) to undergo radioactive disintegration. ~n. **4.** the process of decline, as in health or mentality. **5.** the state brought about by this process. **6.** *Physics.* disintegration of a nucleus, occurring spontaneously or as a result of electron capture.

decease (dɪˈsiːs) n. *Formal.* death.

deceased (dɪˈsiːst) adj. **a.** *Formal.* dead. **b.** (*as n.*): *the deceased.*

deceit (dɪˈsiːt) n. behaviour intended to deceive.

deceitful (dɪˈsiːtfʊl) adj. full of deceit.

deceive (dɪˈsiːv) vb. **1.** to mislead by lying. **2. deceive oneself.** to delude oneself. **3.** to be unfaithful to (one's sexual partner).

decelerate (diːˈsɛləˌreɪt) vb. to slow down. —**deˌcelerˈation** n.

December (dɪˈsɛmbə) n. the twelfth month of the year.

decencies (ˈdiːsˀnsɪz) pl. n. generally accepted standards of good behaviour.

decency (ˈdiːsˀnsɪ) n. conformity to the prevailing standards of what is right.

decennial (dɪˈsɛnɪəl) adj. **1.** lasting for ten years. **2.** occurring every ten years.

decent (ˈdiːsˀnt) adj. **1.** polite or respectable. **2.** proper; fitting. **3.** conforming to conventions of sexual behaviour. **4.** good or adequate: *a decent wage.* **5.** *Informal.* kind; generous. —**ˈdecently** adv.

decentralize or **-ise** (diːˈsɛntrəˌlaɪz) vb. to reorganize into smaller more autonomous units. —**deˌcentraliˈzation** or **-iˈsation** n.

deception (dɪˈsɛpʃən) n. **1.** the act of deceiving someone or the state of being deceived. **2.** something that deceives; trick.

deceptive (dɪˈsɛptɪv) adj. likely or designed to deceive. —**deˈceptively** adv. —**deˈceptiveness** n.

deci- *prefix.* one tenth: *decimetre.*

decibel (ˈdɛsɪˌbɛl) n. a unit for measuring the intensity of a sound.

decide (dɪˈsaɪd) vb. **1.** (foll. by *on* or *about*) to reach a decision: *decide what you want; he decided to go.* **2.** to cause to reach a decision. **3.** to settle (a contest or question). **4.** (foll. by *for* or *against*) to pronounce a formal verdict.

decided (dɪˈsaɪdɪd) adj. **1.** unmistakable. **2.** determined; resolute. —**deˈcidedly** adv.

deciduous (dɪˈsɪdjʊəs) adj. **1.** (of a tree) shedding all leaves annually. **2.** (of antlers or teeth) being shed at the end of a period of growth.

decilitre or U.S. **deciliter** (ˈdɛsɪˌliːtə) n. a measure of volume equivalent to one-tenth of a litre.

decimal (ˈdɛsɪməl) n. **1.** a fraction with an unwritten denominator of a power of ten.

It is indicated by a decimal point before the numerator: ·2 = ²⁄₁₀. ~*adj.* **2.** relating to or using powers of ten. **3.** expressed as a decimal.

decimal currency *n.* a system of currency in which the units are parts or powers of ten.

decimalize *or* **-ise** (ˈdɛsɪməˌlaɪz) *vb.* to change (a system or number) to the decimal system. —ˌdecimaliˈzation *or* -iˈsation *n.*

decimal point *n.* the dot between the unit and the fraction of a number in the decimal system.

Usage. Conventions relating to the use of the decimal point are confused. The IX General Conference on Weights and Measures resolved in 1948 that the decimal point should be a point on the line or a comma, but not a centre dot. It also resolved that figures could be grouped in threes about the decimal point, but that no point or comma should be used for this purpose. These conventions are adopted in this dictionary. However, the Decimal Currency Board recommended that for sums of money the centre dot should be used as the decimal point and that the comma should be used as the thousand marker. Moreover, in some countries the position is reversed, the comma being used as the decimal point and the dot as the thousand marker.

decimal system *n.* a number system in general use with a base of ten, in which numbers are expressed by combinations of the digits 0 to 9.

decimate (ˈdɛsɪˌmeɪt) *vb.* to destroy or kill a large proportion of. —ˌdeciˈmation *n.*

decimetre *or U.S.* **decimeter** (ˈdɛsɪˌmiːtə) *n.* one tenth of a metre.

decipher (dɪˈsaɪfə) *vb.* **1.** to make out the meaning of (something obscure or illegible). **2.** to convert from code into plain text. —deˈcipherable *adj.*

decision (dɪˈsɪʒən) *n.* **1.** a judgment, conclusion, or resolution. **2.** the act of making up one's mind. **3.** firmness of purpose or character.

decisive (dɪˈsaɪsɪv) *adj.* **1.** influential; conclusive. **2.** having the ability to make decisions, esp. quickly. —deˈcisively *adv.* —deˈcisiveness *n.*

deck (dɛk) *n.* **1.** an area of a ship that forms a floor, at any level. **2.** a similar area in a bus. **3. a.** the platform that supports the turntable and pick-up of a record player. **b.** same as **tape deck. 4.** *Chiefly U.S.* a pack (of playing cards). **5.** *Computers.* a collection of punched cards relevant to a particular program. **6. clear the decks.** *Informal.* to prepare for action, as by removing obstacles. ~*vb.* **7.** (often foll. by *out*) to dress or decorate.

deck chair *n.* a folding chair consisting of a wooden frame suspending a length of canvas.

deck hand *n.* a seaman assigned duties on the deck of a ship.

deckle edge (ˈdɛkʰl) *n.* a rough edge on paper, often left as ornamentation. —ˈdeckle-ˈedged *adj.*

declaim (dɪˈkleɪm) *vb.* **1.** to make (a speech) loudly and dramatically. **2. declaim against.** to protest against loudly and publicly. —declamation (ˌdɛkləˈmeɪʃən) *n.* —declamatory (dɪˈklæmətrɪ) *adj.*

declaration (ˌdɛkləˈreɪʃən) *n.* **1.** an emphatic statement. **2.** a formal announcement. —declaratory (dɪˈklærətrɪ) *adj.*

declare (dɪˈklɛə) *vb.* **1.** to announce publicly or officially: *war was declared.* **2.** to state officially that (a person, fact, etc.) is as specified: *he declared him fit.* **3.** to state emphatically. **4.** (often foll. by *for* or *against*) to make known one's opinion. **5.** to acknowledge (dutiable goods or income) for tax purposes. **6.** *Cards.* to decide (the trump suit) by making the winning bid. **7.** *Cricket.* to close an innings voluntarily before all ten wickets have fallen.

declassify (diːˈklæsɪˌfaɪ) *vb.* **-fying, -fied.** to release (a document or information) from the security list. —deˌclassifiˈcation *n.*

declension (dɪˈklɛnʃən) *n.* *Grammar.* changes in the form of nouns, pronouns, or adjectives to show case, number, and gender.

declination (ˌdɛklɪˈneɪʃən) *n.* **1.** *Astron.* the angular distance of a star or planet north or south from the celestial equator. **2.** the angle made by a compass needle with the direction of the geographical north pole.

decline (dɪˈklaɪn) *vb.* **1.** to refuse, esp. politely. **2.** to grow smaller; diminish. **3.** *Grammar.* to list the inflections of (a noun, pronoun, or adjective). ~*n.* **4.** gradual deterioration or loss. **5.** a movement downward; diminution. **6.** *Archaic.* a slowly progressive disease, such as tuberculosis.

declivity (dɪˈklɪvɪtɪ) *n., pl.* **-ties.** a downward slope. —deˈclivitous *adj.*

declutch (dɪˈklʌtʃ) *vb.* to disengage the clutch of a motor vehicle.

decoct (dɪˈkɒkt) *vb.* to extract the essence from (a substance) by boiling. —deˈcoction *n.*

decode (diːˈkəʊd) *vb.* to convert from code into ordinary language. —deˈcoder *n.*

decoke (diːˈkəʊk) *vb.* same as **decarbonize.**

décolletage (ˌdeɪkɒlˈtɑːʒ) *n.* a low-cut dress or neckline.

décolleté (deɪˈkɒlteɪ) *adj.* (of a woman's garment) low-cut.

decompose (ˌdiːkəmˈpəʊz) *vb.* **1.** to rot. **2.** to break up constituent parts. —decomposition (ˌdiːkɒmpəˈzɪʃən) *n.*

decompress (ˌdiːkəmˈprɛs) *vb.* **1.** to relieve of pressure. **2.** to return (a diver) to normal atmospheric pressure. —**decom-pression** n.

decompression sickness n. a condition of severe pain and difficulty in breathing caused by a sudden change in atmospheric pressure.

decongestant (ˌdiːkənˈdʒɛstənt) n. a drug that relieves nasal congestion.

decontaminate (ˌdiːkənˈtæmɪˌneɪt) vb. to render harmless by the removal of poisons, radioactivity, etc. —**deconˌtamiˈnation** n.

décor or **decor** (ˈdeɪkɔː) n. a style or scheme of interior decoration and furnishings in a room or house.

decorate (ˈdɛkəˌreɪt) vb. 1. to ornament; adorn. 2. to paint or wallpaper. 3. to confer a mark of distinction, esp. a medal, upon. —**ˈdecorative** adj. —**ˈdecoˌrator** n.

Decorated style n. a 14th-century style of English architecture characterized by geometrical tracery and floral decoration.

decoration (ˌdɛkəˈreɪʃən) n. 1. an addition that makes something more attractive or ornate. 2. the way in which a room or building is decorated. 3. something, esp. a medal, conferred as a mark of honour.

decorous (ˈdɛkərəs) adj. polite, calm, and sensible in behaviour. —**ˈdecorously** adv. —**ˈdecorousness** n.

decorum (dɪˈkɔːrəm) n. decorous behaviour.

decoy n. (ˈdiːkɔɪ, dɪˈkɔɪ). 1. a person or thing used to lure someone into danger. 2. an image of a bird or animal, used to lure game into a trap or within shooting range. ~vb. (dɪˈkɔɪ). 3. to lure by or as if by means of a decoy.

decrease vb. (dɪˈkriːs). 1. to diminish or cause to diminish in size, strength, or quantity. ~n. (ˈdiːkriːs, dɪˈkriːs). 2. a diminution; reduction. 3. the amount by which something has been diminished. —**deˈcreasingly** adv.

decree (dɪˈkriː) n. 1. a law made by someone in authority. 2. a judgment of a court. ~vb. **decreeing, decreed.** 3. to order by decree.

decree absolute n. the final decree in divorce proceedings, which leaves the parties free to remarry.

decree nisi (ˈnaɪsaɪ) n. a provisional decree in divorce proceedings, which will later be made absolute unless cause is shown why it should not.

decrepit (dɪˈkrɛpɪt) adj. weakened or worn out by age or long use. —**deˈcrepiˌtude** n.

decrescendo (ˌdiːkrɪˈʃɛndəʊ) n., adv. same as **diminuendo.**

decretal (dɪˈkriːtˀl) n. R.C. Church. a papal decree.

decry (dɪˈkraɪ) vb. **-crying, -cried.** to express open disapproval of.

dedicate (ˈdɛdɪˌkeɪt) vb. 1. (often foll. by to) to devote (oneself, one's time, etc.) wholly to a special purpose or cause. 2. (foll. by to) to address a book, etc., to a person as a token of affection or respect. 3. (foll. by to) to play (a record) on radio for someone as a greeting. 4. to set apart for sacred uses.

dedicated (ˈdɛdɪˌkeɪtɪd) adj. 1. devoted to a particular purpose or cause. 2. Computers. designed to fulfil one function.

dedication (ˌdɛdɪˈkeɪʃən) n. 1. wholehearted devotion. 2. an inscription in a book dedicating it to a person.

deduce (dɪˈdjuːs) vb. to work out; infer. —**deˈducible** adj.

deduct (dɪˈdʌkt) vb. to subtract (a number, quantity, or part).

deductible (dɪˈdʌktɪbˀl) adj. 1. capable of being deducted. 2. U.S. tax-deductible.

deduction (dɪˈdʌkʃən) n. 1. the act or process of deducting or subtracting. 2. something that is deducted. 3. Logic. a. a process of reasoning by which a conclusion necessarily follows from a set of general premises. b. a conclusion reached by this process. —**deˈductive** adj.

deed (diːd) n. 1. something that is done or performed; act. 2. a notable achievement. 3. action as opposed to words. 4. Law. a legal document, esp. to effect a conveyance or transfer of property.

deed box n. a strong box in which deeds and other documents are kept.

deed poll n. Law. a deed made by one party only, esp. to change one's name.

deejay (ˈdiːˌdʒeɪ) n. Informal. a disc jockey.

deem (diːm) vb. to judge or consider: take whatever measures are deemed necessary.

deemster (ˈdiːmstə) n. either of the two justices in the Isle of Man.

deep (diːp) adj. 1. extending or situated far down from a surface: a deep pool. 2. extending or situated far inwards, backwards, or sideways. 3. of a specified dimension downwards, inwards, or backwards: six feet deep. 4. coming from or penetrating to a great depth. 5. difficult to understand. 6. of great intensity: deep trouble. 7. **deep in.** immersed in: deep in study. 8. (of a colour) intense or dark. 9. low in pitch: a deep voice. 10. **go off the deep end.** Informal. to lose one's temper. 11. **in deep water.** Informal. in a tricky position or in trouble. ~n. 12. any deep place on land or under water. 13. **the deep. a.** Poetic. the ocean. **b.** Cricket. the area of the field relatively far from the pitch. 14. the most profound, intense, or central part: the deep of winter. ~adv. 15. late: deep into the night. 16. profoundly or intensely. —**ˈdeeply** adv.

deepen (ˈdiːpˀn) vb. to make or become deeper or more intense.

deep-freeze n. 1. same as **freezer**. ~vb. **-freezing, -froze, -frozen**. 2. to freeze or keep in a deep-freeze.

deep-laid adj. (of a plan) carefully worked out and kept secret.

deep-rooted or **deep-seated** adj. (of ideas, beliefs, etc.) firmly fixed or held.

deer (dɪə) n., pl. **deer** or **deers**. a hoofed ruminant mammal with antlers in the male.

deerstalker ('dɪəˌstɔːkə) n. a hat, peaked in front and behind, with earflaps.

de-escalate (diːˈɛskəˌleɪt) vb. to reduce the intensity of (a problem or situation). —**de-ˌescaˈlation** n.

def (dɛf) adj. **deffer, deffest**. Slang. very good.

deface (dɪˈfeɪs) vb. to spoil the surface or appearance of; disfigure. —**deˈfacement** n.

de facto (deɪ ˈfæktəʊ) adv. 1. in fact. ~adj. 2. existing in fact, whether legally recognized or not.

defalcate ('diːfælˌkeɪt) vb. Law. to misappropriate funds entrusted to one. —ˌde-falˈcation n.

defame (dɪˈfeɪm) vb. to attack the good reputation of. —**defamation** (ˌdɛfə-ˈmeɪʃən) n. —**defamatory** (dɪˈfæmətrɪ) adj.

default (dɪˈfɔːlt) n. 1. a failure to do something, esp. to meet a financial obligation or to appear in court. 2. **by default**. because of lack of prevention or opposition. 3. **in default of**. in the absence of. ~vb. 4. (often foll. by on or in) to fail to fulfil an obligation, esp. to make payment when due.

defeat (dɪˈfiːt) vb. 1. to overcome; win a victory over. 2. to thwart or frustrate. ~n. 3. the act of defeating or state of being defeated.

defeatism (dɪˈfiːtɪzəm) n. a ready acceptance or expectation of defeat. —**deˈfeatist** n., adj.

defecate ('dɛfɪˌkeɪt) vb. to discharge waste from the body through the anus. —ˌdefeˈcation n.

defect n. ('diːfɛkt). 1. an imperfection or blemish. ~vb. (dɪˈfɛkt). 2. to desert one's country or cause to join the opposing forces. —**deˈfection** n. —**deˈfector** n.

defective (dɪˈfɛktɪv) adj. having a flaw; imperfect.

defence or U.S. **defense** (dɪˈfɛns) n. 1. resistance against attack. 2. something that provides such resistance. 3. a plea, essay, etc., in support of something. 4. a country's military resources. 5. Law. a defendant's denial of the truth of a charge. 6. Law. the defendant and his legal advisers collectively. 7. Sport. (usually preceded by the) the players in a team whose function is to prevent the opposing team from scoring. 8. (pl.) fortifications. —**deˈfenceless** or U.S. **deˈfenseless** adj.

defend (dɪˈfɛnd) vb. 1. to protect from harm or danger. 2. to support in the face of

criticism, esp. by argument. 3. to represent (a defendant) in court. 4. to protect (a title or championship) against a challenge. —**deˈfender** n.

defendant (dɪˈfɛndənt) n. a person against whom an action is brought in a court of law.

defensible (dɪˈfɛnsɪbˀl) adj. capable of being defended because believed to be right.

defensive (dɪˈfɛnsɪv) adj. 1. intended for defence. 2. rejecting criticisms of oneself. ~n. 3. **on the defensive**. in a position of defence, as in being ready to reject criticism. —**deˈfensively** adv.

defer[1] (dɪˈfɜː) vb. **-ferring, -ferred**. to delay (something) until a future time; postpone. —**deˈferment** or **deˈferral** n.

defer[2] (dɪˈfɜː) vb. **-ferring, -ferred**. (foll. by to) to yield (to) or comply with the wishes (of).

deference ('dɛfərəns) n. 1. compliance with the wishes of another. 2. courteous regard; respect.

deferential (ˌdɛfəˈrɛnʃəl) adj. showing respect. —**deferˈentially** adv.

defiance (dɪˈfaɪəns) n. open resistance to authority or opposition. —**deˈfiant** adj.

deficiency (dɪˈfɪʃənsɪ) n., pl. **-cies**. 1. the state of being deficient. 2. a lack or shortage.

deficiency disease n. any condition, such as scurvy, produced by a lack of vitamins or other essential substances.

deficient (dɪˈfɪʃənt) adj. 1. lacking some essential. 2. inadequate in quantity or quality.

deficit ('dɛfɪsɪt, dɪˈfɪsɪt) n. the amount by which a sum is lower than that expected or required.

defile[1] (dɪˈfaɪl) vb. 1. to make (something) filthy or polluted. 2. to violate or damage (something holy or respected). —**deˈfilement** n.

defile[2] ('diːfaɪl, dɪˈfaɪl) n. 1. a narrow pass or gorge. ~vb. 2. to march in single file.

define (dɪˈfaɪn) vb. 1. to state precisely the meaning of. 2. to describe the nature of. 3. (often passive) to show clearly the outline of. 4. to fix with precision; specify. —**deˈfinable** adj.

definite ('dɛfɪnɪt) adj. 1. clear and exact in meaning. 2. having precise limits. 3. known for certain. —**ˈdefinitely** adv.

Usage. Definite and definitive should be carefully distinguished. Definite indicates precision and firmness, as in a definite decision. Definitive includes these senses but also indicates conclusiveness. A definite answer indicates a clear and firm answer to a particular question; a definitive answer implies an authoritative resolution of a complex question.

definite article n. Grammar. the word "the".

definition (ˌdɛfɪˈnɪʃən) n. 1. a statement of

the meaning of a word or phrase. **2.** a description of the essential qualities of something. **3.** the quality of being clear and distinct. **4.** sharpness of outline.

definitive (dɪ'fɪnɪtɪv) *adj.* **1.** serving to decide finally. **2.** most reliable or authoritative. **Usage.** see **definite.**

deflate (diː'fleɪt) *vb.* **1.** to collapse or cause to collapse through the release of gas. **2.** to take away the self-esteem or conceit from. **3.** *Econ.* to cause deflation of (an economy).

deflation (diː'fleɪʃən) *n.* **1.** *Econ.* a reduction in economic activity resulting in lower levels of output and investment. **2.** a feeling of sadness following excitement. —**de'flationary** *adj.*

deflect (dɪ'flɛkt) *vb.* to turn or cause to turn aside from a course. —**de'flection** *n.* —**de'flector** *n.*

deflower (diː'flaʊə) *vb. Literary.* to deprive (a woman) of virginity.

defoliate (diː'fəʊlɪˌeɪt) *vb.* to deprive (a plant) of leaves. —**de'foliant** *n.* —**de,foli'ation** *n.*

deform (dɪ'fɔːm) *vb.* **1.** to make misshapen or distorted. **2.** to make ugly; disfigure.

deformed (dɪ'fɔːmd) *adj.* disfigured or misshapen.

deformity (dɪ'fɔːmɪtɪ) *n., pl.* **-ties.** **1.** *Pathol.* a distortion of an organ or part. **2.** a deformed condition.

defraud (dɪ'frɔːd) *vb.* to take away or withhold money, rights, etc., from (a person) by fraud.

defray (dɪ'freɪ) *vb.* to provide money for (costs or expenses). —**de'frayal** *n.*

defrock (diː'frɒk) *vb.* to deprive (a priest) of ecclesiastical status.

defrost (diː'frɒst) *vb.* **1.** to make or become free of frost or ice. **2.** to thaw, esp. through removal from a deep-freeze.

deft (dɛft) *adj.* quick and neat in movement; dexterous. —**'deftly** *adv.* —**'deftness** *n.*

defunct (dɪ'fʌŋkt) *adj.* no longer existing or operative.

defuse *or U.S. (sometimes)* **defuze** (diː'fjuːz) *vb.* **1.** to remove the triggering device of (an explosive device). **2.** to remove the cause of tension from (a crisis, etc.).

defy (dɪ'faɪ) *vb.* **-fying, -fied.** **1.** to resist openly and boldly. **2.** to elude, esp. in a baffling way. **3.** *Formal.* to challenge (someone to do something).

degenerate *adj.* (dɪ'dʒɛnərɪt). **1.** having deteriorated to a lower mental, moral, or physical level; degraded. ~*n.* (dɪ'dʒɛnərɪt). **2.** a degenerate person. ~*vb.* (dɪ'dʒɛnəˌreɪt). **3.** to become degenerate. —**de'generacy** *n.*

degeneration (dɪˌdʒɛnə'reɪʃən) *n.* **1.** the process of degenerating. **2.** *Biol.* the loss of specialization or function by organisms.

degrade (dɪ'greɪd) *vb.* **1.** to reduce to dishonour or disgrace. **2.** to reduce in status or quality. **3.** *Chem.* to decompose into atoms or smaller molecules. —**degradation** (ˌdɛgrə'deɪʃən) *n.* —**de'grading** *adj.*

degree (dɪ'griː) *n.* **1.** a stage in a scale of relative amount or intensity: *a high degree of competence.* **2.** an academic award conferred by a university or college on successful completion of a course. **3.** any of three categories of seriousness of a burn. **4.** (in the U.S.) any of the categories into which a crime is divided according to seriousness. **5.** *Grammar.* any of the forms of an adjective used to indicate relative amount or intensity. **6.** a unit of temperature. Symbol: ° **7.** a measure of angle equal to one three-hundred-and-sixtieth of the circumference of a circle. Symbol: ° **8.** a unit of latitude or longitude. Symbol: ° **9. by degrees.** little by little; gradually.

dehisce (dɪ'hɪs) *vb.* (of fruits, anthers, etc.) to burst open spontaneously. —**de'hiscence** *n.* —**de'hiscent** *adj.*

dehumanize *or* **-ise** (diː'hjuːməˌnaɪz) *vb.* **1.** to deprive of human qualities. **2.** to render mechanical or routine. —**de,humani'zation** *or* **-i'sation** *n.*

dehydrate (diː'haɪdreɪt) *vb.* **1.** to cause to lose water. **2.** to deprive (the body) of water. —**,dehy'dration** *n.*

de-ice (diː'aɪs) *vb.* to free of ice. —**de-'icer** *n.*

deify ('diːɪˌfaɪ, 'deɪɪ-) *vb.* **-fying, -fied.** **1.** to exalt to the position of a god. **2.** to accord divine honour or worship to. —**,deifi'cation** *n.*

deign (deɪn) *vb.* to think it worthy of oneself (to do something); condescend.

deism ('diːɪzəm, 'deɪɪ-) *n.* belief in the existence of God based on natural reason, rather than revelation. —**'deist** *n., adj.* —**de'istic** *adj.*

deity ('diːɪtɪ, 'deɪɪ-) *n., pl.* **-ties.** **1.** a god or goddess. **2.** the state of being divine.

Deity ('diːɪtɪ, 'deɪɪ-) *n.* **the.** God.

déjà vu ('deɪʒæ 'vuː) *n.* a feeling of having experienced before something that is actually happening now.

dejected (dɪ'dʒɛktɪd) *adj.* miserable; despondent; downhearted. —**de'jectedly** *adv.* —**de'jection** *n.*

de jure (deɪ 'dʒʊəreɪ) *adv.* according to law.

deke (diːk) *Canad. slang.* ~*vb.* **1.** (in ice hockey or box lacrosse) to draw (a defending player) out of position by faking a shot or movement. ~*n.* **2.** such a shot or movement.

dekko ('dɛkəʊ) *n., pl.* **-kos.** *Brit. slang.* a look (esp. in **have a dekko**).

Del. Delaware.

delay (dɪ'leɪ) *vb.* **1.** to put (something) off to a later time. **2.** to slow up or cause to be late. **3.** to be irresolute in doing something.

4. to linger; dawdle. ~*n.* **5.** the act of delaying. **6.** a period of inactivity or waiting before something happens or continues.

delectable (dɪˈlɛktəb²l) *adj.* delightful.

delectation (ˌdiːlɛkˈteɪʃən) *n. Formal.* great pleasure and enjoyment.

delegate *n.* (ˈdɛlɪgɪt). **1.** a person chosen to act for others, esp. at a conference or meeting. ~*vb.* (ˈdɛlɪˌgeɪt). **2.** to entrust (duties or powers) to another person. **3.** to authorize (a person) as representative.

delegation (ˌdɛlɪˈgeɪʃən) *n.* **1.** a group chosen to represent others. **2.** the act of delegating.

delete (dɪˈliːt) *vb.* to remove or cross out (something printed or written). —**deˈletion** *n.*

deleterious (ˌdɛlɪˈtɪərɪəs) *adj.* harmful; injurious.

Delft (dɛlft) *n.* tin-glazed earthenware which originated in Delft in the Netherlands typically with blue decoration on a white ground.

deliberate *adj.* (dɪˈlɪbərɪt). **1.** carefully thought out in advance; intentional. **2.** careful and unhurried: *a deliberate pace.* ~*vb.* (dɪˈlɪbəˌreɪt). **3.** to consider (something) deeply; think over.

deliberation (dɪˌlɪbəˈreɪʃən) *n.* **1.** careful consideration. **2.** (*pl.*) formal discussions. **3.** calmness and absence of hurry.

delicacy (ˈdɛlɪkəsɪ) *n., pl.* **-cies.** **1.** fine or subtle quality or workmanship. **2.** fragile, graceful beauty. **3.** something that is considered particularly nice to eat. **4.** frail health. **5.** refinement of feeling, manner, or appreciation. **6.** need for tactful or sensitive handling.

delicate (ˈdɛlɪkɪt) *adj.* **1.** fine or subtle in quality or workmanship. **2.** having a fragile beauty. **3.** (of colour, smell, or taste) pleasantly subtle. **4.** easily damaged; fragile. **5.** precise or sensitive in action: *a delicate mechanism.* **6.** requiring tact: *a delicate situation.* **7.** showing regard for the feelings of others. —**ˈdelicately** *adv.*

delicatessen (ˌdɛlɪkəˈtɛsᵊn) *n.* a shop selling unusual or imported foods, already cooked or prepared.

delicious (dɪˈlɪʃəs) *adj.* **1.** very appealing, esp. to taste or smell. **2.** extremely enjoyable. —**deˈliciously** *adv.*

delight (dɪˈlaɪt) *vb.* **1.** to please greatly. **2. delight in.** to take great pleasure in. ~*n.* **3.** extreme pleasure. **4.** something or someone that causes this. —**deˈlightful** *adj.* —**deˈlightfully** *adv.*

delimit (diːˈlɪmɪt) *vb.* to mark or prescribe the limits of. —**deˌlimiˈtation** *n.*

delineate (dɪˈlɪnɪˌeɪt) *vb.* **1.** to show by drawing. **2.** to describe in words. —**deˌlineˈation** *n.*

delinquent (dɪˈlɪŋkwənt) *n.* **1.** someone, esp. a young person, guilty of an offence.

~*adj.* **2.** guilty of an offence. —**deˈlinquency** *n.*

deliquesce (ˌdɛlɪˈkwɛs) *vb.* (esp. of certain salts) to dissolve in water absorbed from the air. —ˌ**deliˈquescence** *n.* —ˌ**deliˈquescent** *adj.*

delirious (dɪˈlɪrɪəs) *adj.* **1.** suffering from delirium. **2.** wildly excited, esp. with joy. —**deˈliriously** *adv.*

delirium (dɪˈlɪrɪəm) *n.* **1.** a state of excitement and mental confusion, often with hallucinations. **2.** violent excitement.

delirium tremens (ˈtrɛmɛnz, ˈtriː-) *n.* a condition caused by chronic alcoholism, characterized by delirium, trembling, and vivid hallucinations.

deliver (dɪˈlɪvə) *vb.* **1.** to carry (goods or mail) to a destination. **2.** (often foll. by *over* or *up*) to hand over. **3.** (often foll. by *from*) to release or rescue (from captivity or danger). **4.** to aid in the birth of (offspring). **5.** to present (a speech, etc.). **6.** to strike (a blow) suddenly. **7.** *Informal.* Also: **deliver the goods.** to produce something promised. —**deˈliverance** *n.*

delivery (dɪˈlɪvərɪ) *n., pl.* **-eries.** **1. a.** the act of delivering goods or mail. **b.** something that is delivered. **2.** the act of giving birth to a child. **3.** manner or style, esp. in public speaking.

dell (dɛl) *n.* a small wooded hollow.

delouse (diːˈlaʊs, -ˈlaʊz) *vb.* to rid (a person or animal) of lice.

Delphic (ˈdɛlfɪk) *adj.* obscure or ambiguous, like the ancient Greek oracle at Delphi.

delphinium (dɛlˈfɪnɪəm) *n., pl.* **-iums** or **-ia** (-ɪə). a plant with spikes of blue flowers.

delta (ˈdɛltə) *n.* **1.** the fourth letter in the Greek alphabet (Δ or δ). **2.** the flat area at the mouth of some rivers where the main stream splits up into several tributaries.

delta wing *n.* a triangular aircraft wing.

delude (dɪˈluːd) *vb.* to deceive.

deluge (ˈdɛljuːdʒ) *n.* **1.** a great flood of water. **2.** torrential rain. **3.** an overwhelming number. ~*vb.* **4.** to flood. **5.** to overwhelm.

Deluge (ˈdɛljuːdʒ) *n.* **the.** same as the **Flood.**

delusion (dɪˈluːʒən) *n.* **1.** a mistaken idea or belief. **2.** *Psychiatry.* a belief held in the face of evidence to the contrary, that is resistant to all reason. **3.** the state of being deluded. —**deˈlusive** *adj.* —**delusory** (dɪˈluːsərɪ) *adj.*

de luxe (də ˈlʌks, ˈlʊks) *adj.* rich or sumptuous; superior in quality: *the de luxe model of a car.*

delve (dɛlv) *vb.* **1.** to research deeply or intensively (for information). **2.** *Archaic.* to dig.

demagnetize *or* **-ise** (diːˈmægnəˌtaɪz) *vb.* to remove magnetic properties. —**deˌmagnetiˈzation** *or* **-iˈsation** *n.*

demagogue *or U.S.* (*sometimes*) **demagog** ('dɛmə‚gɒg) *n.* a political agitator who appeals to the prejudice and passions of the mob. —‚dema'gogic *adj.* —'dema‚gogy *n.*

demand (dɪ'mɑːnd) *vb.* **1.** to request peremptorily. **2.** to require as just, urgent, etc.: *the situation demands attention.* **3.** to claim as a right. ~*n.* **4.** a peremptory request. **5.** something that requires special effort or sacrifice. **6.** *Econ.* willingness and ability to purchase goods and services. **7. in demand.** sought after. **8. on demand.** as soon as requested.

demanding (dɪ'mɑːndɪŋ) *adj.* requiring great patience, skill, etc.: *a demanding job.*

demarcation (‚diːmɑː'keɪʃən) *n.* the act of establishing limits or boundaries, esp. between the kinds of work performed by members of different trade unions.

demean (dɪ'miːn) *vb.* to lower (someone, esp. oneself) in dignity, status, or character; debase.

demeanour *or U.S.* **demeanor** (dɪ'miːnə) *n.* the way a person behaves.

demented (dɪ'mɛntɪd) *adj.* mad; insane. —de'mentedly *adv.*

dementia (dɪ'mɛnʃə, -ʃɪə) *n.* a state of serious mental deterioration.

demerara sugar (‚dɛmə'rɛərə) *n.* brown crystallized cane sugar from the West Indies.

demerit (diː'mɛrɪt) *n.* **1.** a fault. **2.** *U.S. & Canad.* a mark given against a student for failure or misconduct.

demesne (dɪ'meɪn, -'miːn) *n.* **1.** land surrounding a house or manor. **2.** *Property law.* the possession of one's own property or land. **3.** domain; region.

demi- *prefix.* **1.** half: *demirelief.* **2.** of less than full size, status, or rank: *demigod.*

demigod ('dɛmɪ‚gɒd) *n.* **1. a.** a being who is part mortal, part god. **b.** a lesser deity. **2.** a godlike person.

demijohn ('dɛmɪ‚dʒɒn) *n.* a large bottle with a short narrow neck, often encased in wickerwork.

demilitarize *or* **-ise** (diː'mɪlɪtə‚raɪz) *vb.* to remove any military presence from: *demilitarized zone.* —de‚militari'zation *or* -i'sation *n.*

demimonde (‚dɛmɪ'mɒnd) *n.* **1.** (esp. in the 19th century) women considered to be outside respectable society, esp. on account of sexual promiscuity. **2.** any group considered not wholly respectable.

demise (dɪ'maɪz) *n.* **1.** *Euphemistic, formal.* death. **2.** *Property law.* a transfer of an estate by lease. ~*vb.* **3.** *Property law.* to transfer for a limited period; lease.

demisemiquaver ('dɛmɪ‚sɛmɪ‚kweɪvə) *n. Music.* a note having the time value of one thirty-second of a semibreve.

demo ('dɛməʊ) *n., pl.* **-os.** *Informal.* **1.**

short for **demonstration** (sense 1). **2.** a demonstration record or tape.

demob (diː'mɒb) *vb.* **-mobbing, -mobbed.** *Brit. informal.* to demobilize.

demobilize *or* **-ise** (diː'məʊbɪ‚laɪz) *vb.* to release from the armed forces. —de‚mobili-'zation *or* -i'sation *n.*

democracy (dɪ'mɒkrəsɪ) *n., pl.* **-cies.** **1.** government by the people or their elected representatives. **2.** a political or social unit governed ultimately by all its members. **3.** social equality.

democrat ('dɛmə‚kræt) *n.* **1.** an advocate of democracy. **2.** a member or supporter of a democratic party or movement.

Democrat ('dɛmə‚kræt) *n. U.S. politics.* a member or supporter of the Democratic Party. —‚Demo'cratic *adj.*

democratic (‚dɛmə'krætɪk) *adj.* **1.** of or relating to the principles of democracy. **2.** upholding democracy or the interests of the common people. —‚demo'cratically *adv.*

demodulation (‚diːmɒdjʊ'leɪʃən) *n. Electronics.* the process by which an output wave or signal is obtained having the characteristics of the original modulating wave or signal.

demography (dɪ'mɒgrəfɪ) *n.* the study of human populations. —**demographic** (‚diːmə'græfɪk, ‚dɛmə-) *adj.*

demolish (dɪ'mɒlɪʃ) *vb.* **1.** to tear down or break up (buildings). **2.** to put an end to (an argument, etc.). **3.** *Facetious.* to eat up. —de'molisher *n.* —**demolition** (‚dɛmə-'lɪʃən) *n.*

demon ('diːmən) *n.* **1.** an evil spirit. **2.** a person, obsession, etc., thought of as evil. **3.** a person extremely skilful in or devoted to a given activity: *a demon at cycling.* **4.** same as **daemon** (sense 1). —**demonic** (dɪ-'mɒnɪk) *adj.*

demonetize *or* **-ise** (diː'mʌnɪ‚taɪz) *vb.* to withdraw (a coin, etc.) from use as currency. —de‚moneti'zation *or* -i'sation *n.*

demoniac (dɪ'məʊnɪ‚æk) *or* **demoniacal** (‚diːmə'naɪəkᵊl) *adj.* **1.** suggesting inner possession: *the demoniac fire of genius.* **2.** frantic; frenzied. —‚demo'niacally *adv.*

demonolatry (‚diːmə'nɒlətrɪ) *n.* the worship of demons.

demonology (‚diːmə'nɒlədʒɪ) *n.* the study of demons or demonic beliefs.

demonstrable ('dɛmənstrəbᵊl, dɪ'mɒn-) *adj.* able to be proved. —'demonstrably *adv.*

demonstrate ('dɛmən‚streɪt) *vb.* **1.** to show or prove by reasoning or evidence. **2.** to reveal the existence of: *the plan later demonstrated a serious flaw.* **3.** to display and explain the workings of (a machine, product, etc.). **4.** to show support or protest by public parades or rallies.

demonstration (‚dɛmən'streɪʃən) *n.* **1.** a manifestation of support or protest by public parades or rallies. **2.** proof. **3.** an explanation, illustration, or experiment showing how something works. **4.** a show of emotion.

demonstrative (dɪ'mɒnstrətɪv) *adj.* **1.** tending to express one's feelings unreservedly. **2. demonstrative of.** giving proof of. **3.** *Grammar.* denoting a word used to point out the person or thing referred to, such as *this* and *those*. —**de'monstratively** *adv.*

demonstrator ('dɛmənˌstreɪtə) *n.* **1.** a person who demonstrates machines, products, etc. **2.** a person who takes part in a public demonstration.

demoralize *or* **-ise** (dɪ'mɒrəˌlaɪz) *vb.* to undermine the morale of; dishearten. —**deˌmoraliˈzation** *or* **-iˈsation** *n.*

demote (dɪ'məʊt) *vb.* to lower in rank or position; relegate. —**de'motion** *n.*

demotic (dɪ'mɒtɪk) *adj.* of or relating to the common people.

demur (dɪ'mɜː) *vb.* **-murring, -murred.** **1.** to show reluctance; object. ~*n.* **2. without demur.** without objecting.

demure (dɪ'mjʊə) *adj.* quiet, reserved, and rather shy. —**de'murely** *adv.* —**de'mureness** *n.*

demurrer (dɪ'mʌrə) *n.* *Law.* a pleading that admits an opponent's point but denies its relevance.

demystify (diː'mɪstɪˌfaɪ) *vb.* **-fying, -fied.** to remove the mystery from; make clear. —**deˌmystifiˈcation** *n.*

den (dɛn) *n.* **1.** the home of a wild animal; lair. **2.** a small secluded room in a home, often used for a hobby. **3.** a site or haunt: *a den of vice.*

denarius (dɪ'nɛərɪəs) *n., pl.* **-narii** (-'nɛərɪˌaɪ). a silver coin of ancient Rome, often called a penny in translation.

denary ('diːnərɪ) *adj.* calculated by tens; decimal.

denationalize *or* **-ise** (diː'næʃən²ˌlaɪz) *vb.* to transfer (an industry or a service) from public to private ownership. —**deˌnationaliˈzation** *or* **-iˈsation** *n.*

denature (diː'neɪtʃə) *vb.* **1.** to change the nature of. **2.** to make (alcohol) unfit to drink by adding nauseous substances.

dendrology (dɛn'drɒlədʒɪ) *n.* the study of trees.

Dene ('dɛnɪ) *pl. n.* the North American Indian peoples of the Northwest Territories in Canada.

dengue ('dɛŋgɪ) *n.* a viral disease transmitted by mosquitoes, characterized by headache, fever, pains in the joints, and rash.

denial (dɪ'naɪəl) *n.* **1.** a statement that something is not true. **2.** a rejection of a request. **3.** a refusal to acknowledge; disowning.

denier ('dɛnɪˌeɪ, 'dɛnjə) *n.* a unit of weight used to measure the fineness of silk and man-made fibres.

denigrate ('dɛnɪˌgreɪt) *vb.* to criticize unfairly; belittle. —**ˌdeniˈgration** *n.* —**'deniˌgrator** *n.*

denim ('dɛnɪm) *n.* **1.** a hard-wearing cotton fabric used for trousers, work clothes, etc. **2.** (*pl.*) jeans made of denim.

denizen ('dɛnɪzən) *n.* **1.** an inhabitant; resident. **2.** a plant or animal established in a place to which it is not native.

denominate (dɪ'nɒmɪˌneɪt) *vb.* to give a specific name to; designate.

denomination (dɪˌnɒmɪ'neɪʃən) *n.* **1.** a group having a distinctive interpretation of a religious faith. **2.** a grade or unit of value, weight, measure, etc. **3.** a name. —**deˌnomiˈnational** *adj.*

denominator (dɪ'nɒmɪˌneɪtə) *n.* the divisor of a fraction, as 8 in ⅞.

denote (dɪ'nəʊt) *vb.* **1.** to be a sign of; designate. **2.** (of a word or phrase) to have as a literal or obvious meaning. —**ˌdenoˈtation** *n.*

denouement *or* **dénouement** (deɪ'nuːmɒn) *n.* the final outcome or solution, esp. in a play or book.

denounce (dɪ'naʊns) *vb.* **1.** to condemn openly or vehemently. **2.** to give information against.

dense (dɛns) *adj.* **1.** thickly crowded or closely packed. **2.** impenetrable: *dense smoke.* **3.** stupid; dull. —**'densely** *adv.*

density ('dɛnsɪtɪ) *n., pl.* **-ties.** **1.** the degree to which something is filled or occupied: *a high population density.* **2.** a measure of the compactness of a substance, expressed as its mass per unit volume. **3.** a measure of a physical quantity per unit of length, area, or volume.

dent (dɛnt) *n.* **1.** a hollow in a surface, as made by a blow. ~*vb.* **2.** to make a dent in.

dental ('dɛnt²l) *adj.* of or relating to the teeth or dentistry.

dental floss *n.* a waxed thread used to remove food particles from between the teeth.

dental surgeon *n.* same as **dentist.**

dentate ('dɛnteɪt) *adj.* having teeth or toothlike processes.

dentifrice ('dɛntɪfrɪs) *n.* paste or powder for cleaning the teeth.

dentine ('dɛntiːn) *n.* the calcified tissue comprising the bulk of a tooth.

dentist ('dɛntɪst) *n.* a person qualified to practise dentistry.

dentistry ('dɛntɪstrɪ) *n.* the branch of medicine concerned with the teeth and gums.

dentition (dɛn'tɪʃən) *n.* the arrangement, type, and number of teeth in a species.

denture ('dɛntʃə) *n.* (*often pl.*) a partial or full set of artificial teeth.

denude (dɪ'njuːd) *vb.* to make bare; strip. —**ˌdenuˈdation** *n.*

denumerable (dɪˈnjuːmərəbᵊl) *adj. Maths.* countable.

denunciation (dɪˌnʌnsɪˈeɪʃən) *n.* open condemnation; denouncing.

deny (dɪˈnaɪ) *vb.* **-nying, -nied.** **1.** to declare (a statement) to be untrue. **2.** to refuse to give or allow: *we were denied access to the information.* **3.** to refuse to acknowledge; disown.

deodar (ˈdiːəʊˌdɑː) *n.* a Himalayan cedar with drooping branches.

deodorant (diːˈəʊdərənt) *n.* a substance applied to the body to suppress or mask the odour of perspiration.

deodorize *or* **-ise** (diːˈəʊdəˌraɪz) *vb.* to remove or disguise the odour of. **—deˌodoriˈzation** *or* **-iˈsation** *n.*

dep. **1.** department. **2.** departure.

depart (dɪˈpɑːt) *vb.* **1.** to leave. **2.** to differ; vary: *to depart from normal procedure.*

departed (dɪˈpɑːtɪd) *adj. Euphemistic.* dead.

department (dɪˈpɑːtmənt) *n.* **1.** a specialized division of a large organization, such as a business, store, or university. **2.** a major subdivision of the administration of a government. **3.** an administrative division in several countries, such as France. **4.** *Informal.* a specialized sphere of activity: *winemaking is my wife's department.* **—departmental** (ˌdiːpɑːtˈmentᵊl) *adj.*

department store *n.* a large shop divided into departments selling many kinds of goods.

departure (dɪˈpɑːtʃə) *n.* **1.** the act of departing. **2.** a variation from previous custom. **3.** a course of action or venture: *selling is a new departure for him.*

depend (dɪˈpɛnd) *vb.* **1.** (foll. by *on* or *upon*) to put trust (in); rely (on). **2.** (usually foll. by *on* or *upon*) to be influenced or determined (by): *it all depends on you.* **3.** (foll. by *on* or *upon*) to rely (on) for income or support.

dependable (dɪˈpɛndəbᵊl) *adj.* able to be depended on; reliable. **—deˌpendaˈbility** *n.* **—deˈpendably** *adv.*

dependant (dɪˈpɛndənt) *n.* a person who depends on another for financial support.

dependence (dɪˈpɛndəns) *n.* **1.** the state or fact of being dependent, esp. for support or help. **2.** reliance.

dependency (dɪˈpɛndənsɪ) *n., pl.* **-cies.** **1.** a territory subject to a state on which it does not border. **2.** *Psychol.* overreliance on another person or on a drug.

dependent (dɪˈpɛndənt) *adj.* **1.** depending on a person or thing for aid or support. **2.** **dependent on** *or* **upon.** influenced or conditioned by.

depict (dɪˈpɪkt) *vb.* **1.** to represent by drawing, painting, etc. **2.** to describe in words. **—deˈpiction** *n.*

depilatory (dɪˈpɪlətrɪ) *adj.* **1.** able or serving to remove hair. ~*n., pl.* **-ries.** **2.** a chemical used to remove hair.

deplete (dɪˈpliːt) *vb.* **1.** to use up (supplies or money). **2.** to reduce in number. **—deˈpletion** *n.*

deplorable (dɪˈplɔːrəbᵊl) *adj.* very bad. **—deˈplorably** *adv.*

deplore (dɪˈplɔː) *vb.* to express or feel strong disapproval of.

deploy (dɪˈplɔɪ) *vb.* to organize (troops or resources) into a position ready for immediate and effective action. **—deˈployment** *n.*

deponent (dɪˈpəʊnənt) *n. Law.* a person who makes an affidavit or a deposition.

depopulate (diːˈpɒpjʊˌleɪt) *vb.* to cause to be reduced in population. **—deˌpopuˈlation** *n.*

deport (dɪˈpɔːt) *vb.* **1.** to remove forcibly from a country. **2. deport oneself.** to behave oneself in a specified manner.

deportation (ˌdiːpɔːˈteɪʃən) *n.* the act of expelling someone from a country.

deportee (ˌdiːpɔːˈtiː) *n.* a deported person.

deportment (dɪˈpɔːtmənt) *n.* the manner in which a person behaves, esp. in physical bearing: *military deportment.*

depose (dɪˈpəʊz) *vb.* **1.** to remove from an office or position of power. **2.** *Law.* to testify on oath.

deposit (dɪˈpɒzɪt) *vb.* **1.** to put down. **2.** to entrust for safekeeping. **3.** to place (money) in a bank or similar institution to earn interest or for safekeeping. **4.** to lay down naturally: *the river deposits silt.* ~*n.* **5. a.** the entrusting of money to a bank or similar institution. **b.** the money so entrusted. **6.** money given in part payment or as security. **7.** an accumulation of sediments, minerals, ore.

deposit account *n. Brit.* a bank account that earns interest.

depositary (dɪˈpɒzɪtrɪ) *n., pl.* **-taries.** a person or group to whom something is entrusted for safety.

deposition (ˌdɛpəˈzɪʃən) *n.* **1.** *Law.* the sworn statement of a witness used in court in his absence. **2.** the act of deposing. **3.** the act of depositing. **4.** something deposited.

depositor (dɪˈpɒzɪtə) *n.* a person who places or has money on deposit, esp. in a bank.

depository (dɪˈpɒzɪtrɪ) *n., pl.* **-ries.** **1.** a store for furniture, valuables, etc. **2.** same as **depositary.**

depot (ˈdɛpəʊ) *n.* **1.** a storehouse or warehouse. **2.** *Chiefly Brit.* a building used for the storage and servicing of buses or railway engines. **3.** *Chiefly U.S. & Canad.* a bus or railway station.

deprave (dɪˈpreɪv) *vb.* to make morally bad; corrupt. **—deˈpraved** *adj.*

depravity (dɪˈprævɪtɪ) n., pl. -ties. moral corruption.

deprecate (ˈdɛprɪˌkeɪt) vb. to express disapproval of; protest against. —ˌdepreˈcation n. —ˈdeprecatory adj.

depreciate (dɪˈpriːʃɪˌeɪt) vb. 1. to decline in value or price. 2. to deride or criticize. —depreciatory (dɪˈpriːʃiətrɪ) adj.

depreciation (dɪˌpriːʃɪˈeɪʃən) n. 1. Accounting. the reduction in value of a fixed asset through use, obsolescence, etc. 2. the act or an instance of belittling. 3. a decrease in the exchange value of a currency.

depredation (ˌdɛprɪˈdeɪʃən) n. plundering; pillage.

depress (dɪˈprɛs) vb. 1. to lower (someone's) spirits; make gloomy. 2. to lower (prices). 3. to push down. —deˈpressing adj. —deˈpressingly adv.

depressant (dɪˈprɛsᵊnt) adj. 1. Med. able to reduce nervous or functional activity. ~n. 2. a depressant drug.

depressed (dɪˈprɛst) adj. 1. low in spirits; downcast. 2. pressed down or flattened. 3. characterized by economic hardship, such as unemployment: a depressed area.

depression (dɪˈprɛʃən) n. 1. a mental state characterized by feelings of gloom and inadequacy. 2. an economic condition characterized by substantial unemployment, low output and investment; slump. 3. Meteorol. a body of moving air below normal atmospheric pressure, which often brings rain. 4. a sunken place.

Depression (dɪˈprɛʃən) n. the. the worldwide economic depression of the early 1930s.

deprive (dɪˈpraɪv) vb. (foll. by of) to prevent from possessing or enjoying. —deprivation (ˌdɛprɪˈveɪʃən) n.

deprived (dɪˈpraɪvd) adj. lacking adequate living conditions, education, etc.: deprived inner-city areas.

depth (dɛpθ) n. 1. the distance downwards, backwards, or inwards. 2. intensity of emotion. 3. profundity of character or thought. 4. intensity of colour. 5. lowness of pitch. 6. (pl.) a. a remote inaccessible region: the depths of the country. b. the most severe part: the depths of winter. c. a low moral state. 7. out of one's depth. a. in water deeper than one is tall. b. beyond the range of one's competence or understanding.

depth charge n. a bomb used to attack submarines that explodes at a preset depth of water.

deputation (ˌdɛpjʊˈteɪʃən) n. a body of people appointed to represent others.

depute (dɪˈpjuːt) vb. to appoint (someone) to act on one's behalf.

deputize or **-ise** (ˈdɛpjʊˌtaɪz) vb. to act as deputy.

deputy (ˈdɛpjʊtɪ) n., pl. -ties. a. a person

appointed to act on behalf of another. b. (as modifier): the deputy chairman.

derail (dɪˈreɪl) vb. to cause (a train) to go off the rails. —deˈrailment n.

derange (dɪˈreɪndʒ) vb. 1. to make insane. 2. to throw into disorder. —deˈrangement n.

derby (ˈdɜːbɪ) n., pl. -bies. U.S. & Canad. a bowler hat.

Derby (ˈdɑːbɪ; U.S. ˈdɜːbɪ) n., pl. -bies. 1. the. an annual horse race run at Epsom Downs, Surrey. 2. local derby. a sporting event between teams from the same area.

Derby. Derbyshire.

deregulate (diːˈrɛgjʊlɛt) vb. to remove regulations or controls from. —deˌreguˈlation n.

derelict (ˈdɛrɪlɪkt) adj. 1. deserted or abandoned, as by an owner or occupant. 2. falling into ruins. ~n. 3. a social outcast or vagrant.

dereliction (ˌdɛrɪˈlɪkʃən) n. 1. dereliction of duty. wilful neglect of one's duty. 2. the state of being abandoned.

derestrict (ˌdiːrɪˈstrɪkt) vb. to make (a road) free from speed limits. —ˌdereˈstriction n.

deride (dɪˈraɪd) vb. to speak of or treat with contempt or ridicule. —derision (dɪˈrɪʒən) n.

de rigueur (də rɪˈgɜː) adj. required by fashion.

derisive (dɪˈraɪsɪv) adj. mocking; scornful. —deˈrisively adv.

derisory (dɪˈraɪsərɪ) adj. so small or inadeqate that it is not worth serious consideration.

derivation (ˌdɛrɪˈveɪʃən) n. the origin or descent of something, such as a word.

derivative (dɪˈrɪvətɪv) adj. 1. based on other sources; not original. ~n. 2. a word, idea, etc., that is derived from another. 3. Maths. the rate of change of one quantity with respect to another.

derive (dɪˈraɪv) vb. (usually foll. by from) to draw or be drawn (from) in source or origin.

dermatitis (ˌdɜːməˈtaɪtɪs) n. inflammation of the skin.

dermatology (ˌdɜːməˈtɒlədʒɪ) n. the branch of medicine concerned with the skin. —ˌdermaˈtologist n.

derogate (ˈdɛrəˌgeɪt) vb. (foll. by from) to cause to seem inferior; detract from. —ˌderoˈgation n.

derogatory (dɪˈrɒgətrɪ) adj. intentionally offensive.

derrick (ˈdɛrɪk) n. 1. a simple crane that has lifting tackle slung from a boom. 2. the framework erected over an oil well to enable drill tubes to be raised and lowered.

derring-do (ˈdɛrɪŋˈduː) n. Archaic or literary. boldness or bold action.

derv (dɜːv) *n. Brit.* diesel oil, when used for road transport.

dervish ('dɜːvɪʃ) *n.* a member of a Muslim religious order noted for a frenzied, ecstatic, whirling dance.

desalination (diːˌsælɪ'neɪʃən) *n.* the process of removing salt, esp. from sea water.

descant ('dɛskænt) *n.* **1.** a decorative counterpart added above a basic melody. ~*adj.* **2.** of the highest member in a family of musical instruments: *a descant recorder.*

descend (dɪ'sɛnd) *vb.* **1.** to move down (a slope, staircase, etc.). **2.** to move to a lower level, pitch, etc.; fall. **3. be descended from.** to be connected by a blood relationship to (a dead person). **4.** to sink to (a shameful action). **5. descend on.** to visit unexpectedly.

descendant (dɪ'sɛndənt) *n.* a person or animal when described as descended from an individual, race, or species.

descendent (dɪ'sɛndənt) *adj.* descending.

descent (dɪ'sɛnt) *n.* **1.** the act of descending. **2.** a downward slope. **3.** a path or way leading downwards. **4.** derivation from an ancestor; lineage. **5.** a degeneration. **6.** (often foll. by *on*) a sudden arrival or attack.

describe (dɪ'skraɪb) *vb.* **1.** to give an account of (something or someone) in words. **2.** to trace the outline of (a circle, etc.).

description (dɪ'skrɪpʃən) *n.* **1.** a statement or account that describes. **2.** the act of describing. **3.** sort: *reptiles of every description.*

descriptive (dɪ'skrɪptɪv) *adj.* characterized by or containing description. —**de'scriptively** *adv.*

descry (dɪ'skraɪ) *vb.* **-scrying, -scried. 1.** to catch sight of. **2.** to discover by looking carefully.

desecrate ('dɛsɪˌkreɪt) *vb.* to violate the sacred character of (an object or place). —ˌ**dese'cration** *n.*

desegregate (diː'sɛgrɪˌgeɪt) *vb.* to end racial segregation in (a public institution). —ˌ**desegre'gation** *n.*

deselect (ˌdiːsɪ'lɛkt) *vb. Brit. politics.* (of a constituency organization) to refuse to select (an MP) for re-election. —ˌ**dese'lection** *n.*

desert[1] ('dɛzət) *n.* a region that has little or no vegetation because of low rainfall.

desert[2] (dɪ'zɜːt) *vb.* **1.** to abandon (a person or place) without intending to return. **2.** *Chiefly mil.* to abscond from (a post or duty) with no intention of returning. —**de'serter** *n.* —**de'sertion** *n.*

desertification (ˌdɛzətɪfɪ'keɪʃən) *n.* a process by which fertile land turns into desert.

deserts (dɪ'zɜːts) *pl. n.* just rewards or punishment.

deserve (dɪ'zɜːv) *vb.* to be entitled to or worthy of; merit.

deserved (dɪ'zɜːvd) *adj.* rightfully earned; warranted. —**deservedly** (dɪ'zɜːvɪdlɪ) *adv.*

deserving (dɪ'zɜːvɪŋ) *adj.* (often foll. by *of*) worthy, esp. of praise or help.

deshabille (ˌdeɪzæ'biːl) *n.* same as **dishabille.**

desiccate ('dɛsɪˌkeɪt) *vb.* to remove most of the water from; dry. —**'desic,cated** *adj.* —ˌ**desic'cation** *n.*

design (dɪ'zaɪn) *vb.* **1.** to work out the structure or form of (something), as by making a sketch or plans. **2.** to plan and make (something) artistically. **3.** to intend (something) for a specific purpose; plan. ~*n.* **4.** a preliminary drawing. **5.** the arrangement or features of an artistic or decorative work: *the design of the desk is Chippendale.* **6.** a finished artistic or decorative creation. **7.** the art of designing. **8.** an intention; purpose. **9. have designs on.** to plot to gain possession of.

designate *vb.* ('dɛzɪgˌneɪt). **1.** to give a name to; entitle. **2.** to select (someone) for an office or duty; appoint. ~*adj.* ('dɛzɪgnɪt). **3.** appointed, but not yet in office: *a minister designate.*

designation (ˌdɛzɪg'neɪʃən) *n.* **1.** something that designates, such as a name. **2.** the act of designating.

designedly (dɪ'zaɪnɪdlɪ) *adv.* by intention.

designer (dɪ'zaɪnə) *n.* **1.** a person who draws up original sketches or plans from which things are made. **2.** (*modifier*) designed by a well-known fashion designer: *designer jeans.*

designing (dɪ'zaɪnɪŋ) *adj.* scheming.

desirable (dɪ'zaɪərəb'l) *adj.* **1.** worthy of desire: *a desirable residence.* **2.** arousing sexual desire. —**de,sira'bility** *n.* —**de'sirably** *adv.*

desire (dɪ'zaɪə) *vb.* **1.** to long for; crave. **2.** to request. ~*n.* **3.** a wish or longing. **4.** a request. **5.** sexual appetite. **6.** a person or thing that is desired.

desirous (dɪ'zaɪərəs) *adj.* (foll. by *of*) having a desire (for).

desist (dɪ'zɪst) *vb.* (often foll. by *from*) to stop or abstain.

desk (dɛsk) *n.* **1.** a piece of furniture with a writing surface and usually drawers. **2.** a service counter in a public building, such as a hotel. **3.** the section of a newspaper or television station responsible for a particular subject: *the news desk.*

desktop ('dɛskˌtɒp) *n.* (*modifier*) denoting a computer system small enough to use at a desk but sophisticated enough to produce print-quality documents: *desktop publishing.*

desolate *adj.* ('dɛsəlɪt). **1.** uninhabited; deserted. **2.** laid waste. **3.** without hope. **4.** dismal; depressing. ~*vb.* ('dɛsəˌleɪt). **5.** to deprive (a place) of inhabitants. **6.** to lay waste. **7.** to make (someone) wretched or forlorn. —**'desolately** adv. —**'desolateness** n.

desolation (ˌdɛsə'leɪʃən) n. **1.** ruin or devastation. **2.** solitary misery; wretchedness.

despair (dɪ'spɛə) vb. **1.** to lose or give up hope: *I despair of his coming.* ~n. **2.** total loss of hope.

despatch (dɪ'spætʃ) vb., n. same as **dispatch.**

desperado (ˌdɛspə'rɑːdəʊ) n., pl. **-does** or **-dos.** a reckless person ready to commit any violent illegal act.

desperate ('dɛsprɪt) adj. **1.** careless of danger, as from despair. **2.** (of an action) undertaken as a last resort. **3.** very grave: *in desperate need.* **4.** (often foll. by *for*) having a great need or desire. —**'desperately** adv.

desperation (ˌdɛspə'reɪʃən) n. **1.** desperate recklessness. **2.** the state of being desperate.

despicable ('dɛspɪkəb'l, dɪ'spɪk-) adj. worthy of being despised; contemptible. —**'despicably** adv.

despise (dɪ'spaɪz) vb. to look down on with contempt.

despite (dɪ'spaɪt) prep. in spite of.

despoil (dɪ'spɔɪl) vb. *Formal.* to plunder. —**despoliation** (dɪˌspəʊlɪ'eɪʃən) n.

despondent (dɪ'spɒndənt) adj. downcast or disheartened. —**de'spondency** n. —**de'spondently** adv.

despot ('dɛspɒt) n. any person in power, esp. a ruler, who acts tyrannically. —**des'potic** adj. —**des'potically** adv.

despotism ('dɛspəˌtɪzəm) n. **1.** absolute or tyrannical government. **2.** tyrannical behaviour.

dessert (dɪ'zɜːt) n. the sweet, usually last course of a meal.

dessertspoon (dɪ'zɜːtˌspuːn) n. a spoon between a tablespoon and a teaspoon in size.

destination (ˌdɛstɪ'neɪʃən) n. the place to which something or someone is going.

destine ('dɛstɪn) vb. to set apart (for a certain purpose); intend.

destiny ('dɛstɪnɪ) n., pl. **-nies.** **1.** the future destined for a person or thing. **2.** the predetermined course of events. **3.** the power that predetermines the course of events.

destitute ('dɛstɪˌtjuːt) adj. lacking the means to live; totally impoverished. —ˌdesti'tution n.

destroy (dɪ'strɔɪ) vb. **1.** to ruin; demolish. **2.** to put an end to. **3.** to kill (an animal). **4.** to crush or defeat.

destroyer (dɪ'strɔɪə) n. **1.** a small heavily armed warship. **2.** a person or thing that destroys.

destruct (dɪ'strʌkt) vb. **1.** to destroy (one's own equipment) for safety. **2.** (of equipment) to be destroyed, for safety, by

those in control. ~adj. **3.** capable of destroying itself or the object containing it: *destruct mechanism.*

destructible (dɪ'strʌktɪb'l) adj. capable of being destroyed.

destruction (dɪ'strʌkʃən) n. **1.** the act of destroying something or state of being destroyed. **2.** a cause of ruin.

destructive (dɪ'strʌktɪv) adj. **1.** causing or tending to cause destruction. **2.** intended to discredit, without positive suggestions: *destructive criticism.* —**de'structively** adv.

desuetude (dɪ'sjuːɪˌtjuːd) n. the condition of not being in use.

desultory ('dɛsəltrɪ) adj. **1.** passing from one thing to another in a fitful way. **2.** random: *a desultory thought.* —**'desultorily** adv.

detach (dɪ'tætʃ) vb. **1.** to disengage and separate. **2.** *Mil.* to separate (a small unit) from a larger. —**de'tachable** adj.

detached (dɪ'tætʃt) adj. **1.** standing apart; not attached: *a detached house.* **2.** showing no emotional involvement.

detachment (dɪ'tætʃmənt) n. **1.** indifference; aloofness. **2.** *Mil.* a small unit separated from its main body.

detail ('diːteɪl) n. **1.** an item that is considered separately; particular. **2.** an item that is unimportant: *passengers' comfort was regarded as a detail.* **3.** treatment of particulars: *this essay includes too much detail.* **4.** a small section of a work of art, when considered in isolation. **5.** *Chiefly mil.* **a.** personnel assigned a specific duty. **b.** the duty. **6. in detail.** including all the important particulars. ~vb. **7.** to list fully. **8.** *Chiefly mil.* to select (personnel) for a specific duty.

detailed ('diːteɪld) adj. having many details.

detain (dɪ'teɪn) vb. **1.** to delay (someone). **2.** to confine or hold (someone) in custody. —**detainee** (ˌdiːteɪ'niː) n. —**de'tainment** n.

detect (dɪ'tɛkt) vb. **1.** to perceive or notice. **2.** to discover the existence or presence of (something likely to elude observation). —**de'tectable** adj. —**de'tector** n.

detection (dɪ'tɛkʃən) n. **1.** the act of discovering or the fact of being discovered. **2.** the act or process of extracting information.

detective (dɪ'tɛktɪv) n. **a.** a police officer who investigates crimes. **b.** same as **private detective.**

détente (deɪ'tɑːnt) n. the easing of tension between nations.

detention (dɪ'tɛnʃən) n. **1.** imprisonment, esp. of a suspect awaiting trial. **2.** a form of punishment in which a pupil is detained after school.

detention centre n. a place where young people may be detained for short periods by order of a court.

deter (dɪˈtɜː) vb. **-terring, -terred.** to discourage (someone) from doing something or prevent (something) from occurring, by instilling fear, doubt, or anxiety.

detergent (dɪˈtɜːdʒənt) n. **1.** a chemical cleansing agent, widely used in industry, laundering, etc. ~adj. **2.** having cleansing power.

deteriorate (dɪˈtɪərɪəˌreɪt) vb. to become worse. —**deˌterioˈration** n.

determinant (dɪˈtɜːmɪnənt) adj. **1.** serving to determine. ~n. **2.** a factor that influences or determines. **3.** Maths. a square array of elements that represents the sum of certain products of these elements.

determinate (dɪˈtɜːmɪnɪt) adj. **1.** definitely limited or fixed. **2.** determined.

determination (dɪˌtɜːmɪˈneɪʃən) n. **1.** the condition of being determined; resoluteness. **2.** the act of making a decision. **3.** the act of fixing the quality, limit, or position of something.

determine (dɪˈtɜːmɪn) vb. **1.** to settle (an argument or a question) conclusively. **2.** to conclude, esp. after observation or consideration. **3.** to fix in scope, variety, etc.: *the river determined the edge of the property.* **4.** to make a decision.

determined (dɪˈtɜːmɪnd) adj. of unwavering mind; resolute; firm. —**deˈterminedly** adv.

determiner (dɪˈtɜːmɪnə) n. Grammar. a word, such as *the* or *all*, that determines the object to which a noun phrase refers.

determinism (dɪˈtɜːmɪˌnɪzəm) n. the philosophical doctrine that all events are determined by preceding events, and so freedom of choice is illusory. —**deˈterminist** n., adj.

deterrent (dɪˈtɛrənt) n. **1.** something that deters. **2.** a weapon, esp. nuclear, held by one state to deter attack by another. ~adj. **3.** tending to deter. —**deˈterrence** n.

detest (dɪˈtɛst) vb. to dislike intensely. —**deˈtestable** adj.

detestation (ˌdiːtɛsˈteɪʃən) n. intense hatred.

dethrone (dɪˈθrəʊn) vb. to remove from a throne or deprive of any high position. —**deˈthronement** n.

detonate (ˈdɛtəˌneɪt) vb. to cause (an explosive device) to explode or (of an explosive device) to explode. —**ˌdetoˈnation** n.

detonator (ˈdɛtəˌneɪtə) n. a small amount of explosive, or a device, such as an electrical generator, used to set off an explosion.

detour (ˈdiːtʊə) n. a deviation from a direct route or course of action.

detoxify (diːˈtɒksɪˌfaɪ) vb. **-fying, -fied.** to remove poison from. —**deˌtoxifiˈcation** n.

detract (dɪˈtrækt) vb. (foll. by *from*) to diminish: *her anger detracts from her beauty.* —**deˈtractor** n. —**deˈtraction** n.

detriment (ˈdɛtrɪmənt) n. disadvantage or damage. —**ˌdetriˈmental** adj.

detritus (dɪˈtraɪtəs) n. **1.** a loose mass of stones and silt worn away from rocks. **2.** debris. —**deˈtrital** adj.

de trop (də ˈtrəʊ) adj. not wanted; in the way.

detumescence (ˌdiːtjʊˈmɛsəns) n. the subsidence of a swelling.

deuce¹ (djuːs) n. **1.** a playing card or dice with two spots. **2.** Tennis. a tied score that requires one player to gain two successive points to win the game.

deuce² (djuːs) Informal. ~interj. **1.** an expression of annoyance or frustration. ~n. **2. the deuce.** used for emphasis in such phrases as **what the deuce, where the deuce.**

deuterium (djuːˈtɪərɪəm) n. a stable isotope of hydrogen. Symbol: D or ²H

deuterium oxide n. same as **heavy water.**

Deutschmark (ˈdɔɪtʃˌmɑːk) or **Deutsche Mark** (ˈdɔɪtʃə) n. the standard monetary unit of West Germany.

devalue (diːˈvæljuː) vb. **-valuing, -valued.** **1.** to reduce the exchange value of (a currency). **2.** to reduce the value of (something or someone). —**deˌvaluˈation** n.

devastate (ˈdɛvəˌsteɪt) vb. **1.** to lay waste; destroy. **2.** to shock or upset greatly. —**ˌdevasˈtation** n.

develop (dɪˈvɛləp) vb. **1.** to grow or bring to a later, more elaborate, or more advanced stage. **2.** to make or become gradually clearer or more widely known. **3.** to come or bring into existence: *he developed a new faith in God.* **4.** to follow as a result of something: *a row developed after her remarks.* **5.** to contract (an illness). **6.** to improve the value or change the use of (land). **7.** to exploit the natural resources of (a country or region). **8.** Photog. to treat (exposed film) with chemical solutions in order to produce a visible image.

developer (dɪˈvɛləpə) n. **1.** a person who develops property. **2.** Photog. a chemical used to develop photographs or films.

developing country n. a poor or nonindustrial country that is seeking to develop its resources by industrialization.

development (dɪˈvɛləpmənt) n. **1.** the process of growing or developing. **2.** the product of developing. **3.** a fact or event that changes a situation. **4.** an area of land that has been developed. —**deˌvelopˈmental** adj.

development area n. (in Britain) an area which has experienced economic depression and which is given government assistance to establish new industry.

deviant (ˈdiːvɪənt) adj. **1.** deviating from what is considered acceptable behaviour. ~n. **2.** a person whose behaviour deviates from what is considered to be acceptable. —'**deviance** n.

deviate ('di:vɪ,eɪt) vb. **1.** to differ (from others) in belief or thought. **2.** to turn aside (from a course of action). —,**devi'ation** n.

device (dɪ'vaɪs) n. **1.** a machine or tool used for a specific task. **2.** Euphemistic. a bomb. **3.** a scheme or trick. **4.** a design or emblem. **5. leave someone to his own devices.** to leave someone alone to do as he wishes.

devil ('dɛv³l) n. **1. the Devil.** Theol. the chief spirit of evil and enemy of God. **2.** any evil spirit. **3.** a person regarded as wicked or ill-natured. **4.** a person: poor devil. **5.** a person regarded as daring: be a devil! **6.** Informal. something difficult or annoying. **7. between the devil and the deep blue sea.** between equally undesirable alternatives. **8. give the devil his due.** to acknowledge the talent or success of an unpleasant person. **9. talk of the devil!** used when an absent person who has been the subject of conversation appears. **10. the devil.** used for emphasis in such phrases as **what the devil, where the devil.** ~vb. -**illing, -illed** or U.S. -**iling, -iled. 11.** to prepare (food) by coating with a highly flavoured spiced mixture. **12.** Chiefly Brit. to do routine literary work, esp. for a lawyer or author.

devilish ('dɛvəlɪʃ) adj. **1.** diabolic; fiendish. ~adv., adj. **2.** Informal. extreme or extremely: devilish good food. —'**devilishly** adv.

devil-may-care adj. reckless; happy-go-lucky.

devilment ('dɛv³lmənt) n. devilish or mischievous conduct.

devilry ('dɛv³lrɪ) n. **1.** reckless fun or mischief. **2.** wickedness.

devil's advocate n. a person who advocates an opposing or unpopular view for the sake of argument.

devious ('di:vɪəs) adj. **1.** not sincere or straightforward. **2.** (of a route or course of action) indirect. —'**deviously** adv.

devise (dɪ'vaɪz) vb. **1.** to work out (something) in one's mind. **2.** Law. to dispose of (real property) by will.

devoid (dɪ'vɔɪd) adj. (foll. by of) destitute (of); free (from).

devolution (,di:və'lu:ʃən) n. a transfer of authority from a central government or organization to regional governments or administration. —,**devo'lutionist** n., adj.

devolve (dɪ'vɒlv) vb. (foll. by on, upon or to) to pass or cause to pass to a successor or substitute, as duties or power.

Devonian (də'vəʊnɪən) adj. **1.** Geol. of a period of geological time about 405 million years ago. **2.** of or relating to Devon.

devote (dɪ'vəʊt) vb. to apply or dedicate (oneself, money, etc.) to some pursuit or cause.

devoted (dɪ'vəʊtɪd) adj. **1.** feeling or demonstrating loyalty or devotion. **2.** (foll. by to) dedicated or consecrated. —**de'votedly** adv.

devotee (,dɛvə'ti:) n. **1.** a person ardently enthusiastic about something, such as a sport. **2.** a zealous follower of a religion.

devotion (dɪ'vəʊʃən) n. **1.** strong attachment to or affection for a cause or person. **2.** religious zeal; piety. **3.** (pl.) religious observance or prayers. —**de'votional** adj.

devour (dɪ'vaʊə) vb. **1.** to eat up greedily. **2.** to engulf and destroy. **3.** to read avidly. —**de'vouring** adj.

devout (dɪ'vaʊt) adj. **1.** deeply religious. **2.** sincere. —**de'voutly** adv.

dew (dju:) n. drops of water condensed on a cool surface at night from vapour in the air. —'**dewy** adj.

dewclaw ('dju:,klɔː) n. a nonfunctional claw on a dog's leg.

Dewey Decimal System ('dju:ɪ) n. a system of library book classification with ten main subject classes.

dewlap ('dju:,læp) n. a loose fold of skin hanging under the throat in cattle, dogs, etc.

dew-worm n. a large earthworm used as fishing bait.

dexter ('dɛkstə) adj. of or on the right side of a shield, etc., from the bearer's point of view.

dexterity (dɛk'stɛrɪtɪ) n. **1.** skill in using one's hands. **2.** mental quickness.

dexterous ('dɛkstrəs) adj. possessing or done with dexterity. —'**dexterously** adv.

dextrin ('dɛkstrɪn) or **dextrine** ('dɛkstrɪn, -triːn) n. a sticky substance obtained from starch: used as a thickening agent in food.

dextrose ('dɛkstrəʊz, -trəʊs) n. a glucose occurring in fruit, honey, and in the blood of animals.

DF Defender of the Faith.

DFC Distinguished Flying Cross.

DFM Distinguished Flying Medal.

dg decigram.

dhal or **dal** (dɑːl) n. the nutritious pealike seed of a tropical shrub.

dharma ('dɑːmə) n. **1.** Hinduism. moral law or behaviour. **2.** Buddhism. ideal truth.

dhoti ('dəʊtɪ) n., pl. -**tis.** a long loincloth worn by men in India.

DHSS (in Britain) Department of Health and Social Security.

di- prefix. **1.** twice; two; double: dicotyledon. **2.** containing two specified atoms or groups of atoms: carbon dioxide.

diabetes (,daɪə'biːtiːz) n. an illness characterized by excretion of an abnormal amount of urine containing an excess of sugar, caused by a deficiency of insulin.

diabetic (ˌdaɪəˈbɛtɪk) adj. 1. of or having diabetes. ~n. 2. a person who has diabetes.

diabolic (ˌdaɪəˈbɒlɪk) adj. 1. of the devil; satanic. 2. extremely cruel or wicked.

diabolical (ˌdaɪəˈbɒlɪkʲl) adj. Informal. 1. excruciatingly bad. 2. extreme: a diabolical liberty. —**diaˈbolically** adv.

diabolism (daɪˈæbəˌlɪzəm) n. a. witchcraft or sorcery. b. worship of devils. —**diˈabolist** n.

diaconate (daɪˈækənɪt, -ˌneɪt) n. the position or period of office of a deacon. —**diˈaconal** adj.

diacritic (ˌdaɪəˈkrɪtɪk) n. a sign placed above or below a character or letter to indicate phonetic value or stress.

diadem (ˈdaɪəˌdɛm) n. a royal crown, esp. a light jewelled circlet.

diaeresis or esp. U.S. **dieresis** (daɪˈɛrɪsɪs) n., pl. **-ses** (-ˌsiːz). the mark ¨ placed over the second of two adjacent vowels to indicate that it is to be pronounced separately, as in naïve.

diagnose (ˈdaɪəgˌnəʊz) vb. to determine by diagnosis.

diagnosis (ˌdaɪəgˈnəʊsɪs) n., pl. **-ses** (-siːz). the discovery and identification of diseases from the examination of symptoms. —**diagnostic** (ˌdaɪəgˈnɒstɪk) adj.

diagonal (daɪˈægənʲl) adj. 1. Maths. connecting any two vertices in a polygon that are not adjacent. 2. slanting. ~n. 3. a diagonal line, plane, or pattern. —**diˈagonally** adv.

diagram (ˈdaɪəˌgræm) n. a sketch or plan demonstrating the form or workings of something. —**diagrammatic** (ˌdaɪəgrəˈmætɪk) adj.

dial (ˈdaɪəl) n. 1. the face of a clock or watch, marked with divisions representing units of time. 2. the graduated disc on a measuring instrument. 3. the control on a radio or television set used to change the station. 4. a numbered disc on a telephone that is rotated a set distance for each digit of a number. ~vb. **dialling, dialled** or U.S. **dialing, dialed.** 5. to try to establish a telephone connection with (someone) by indicating (his number) on the dial.

dialect (ˈdaɪəˌlɛkt) n. a form of a language spoken in a particular area, distinguished by its vocabulary, grammar, and pronunciation. —**diaˈlectal** adj.

dialectic (ˌdaɪəˈlɛktɪk) n. 1. logical debate by question and answer to resolve differences between two views. 2. the art of logical argument. —**diaˈlectical** adj.

dialling tone or U.S. & Canad. **dial tone** n. a continuous sound heard over a telephone, indicating that a number can be dialled.

dialogue or U.S. (often) **dialog** (ˈdaɪəˌlɒg) n. 1. conversation between two people. 2. a conversation in a literary or dramatic work. 3. a discussion between representatives of two nations or groups.

dialysis (daɪˈælɪsɪs) n., pl. **-ses** (-ˌsiːz). 1. Med. the filtering of blood through a semipermeable membrane to remove waste products. 2. the separation of the particles in a solution by filtering through a semipermeable membrane. —**ˈdiaˌlyser** or **-ˌlyzer** n. —**dialytic** (ˌdaɪəˈlɪtɪk) adj.

diamagnetism (ˌdaɪəˈmægnɪˌtɪzəm) n. the phenomenon exhibited by substances that are repelled by both poles of a magnet.

diamanté (ˌdaɪəˈmæntɪ) adj. decorated with glittering bits of material, such as sequins.

diameter (daɪˈæmɪtə) n. a. a straight line through the centre of a circle or sphere. b. the length of such a line.

diametric (ˌdaɪəˈmɛtrɪk) or **diametrical** adj. 1. of or relating to a diameter. 2. completely opposed. —**ˌdiaˈmetrically** adv.

diamond (ˈdaɪəmənd) n. 1. a usually colourless exceptionally hard precious stone of crystallized carbon. 2. Geom. a figure with four sides of equal length forming two acute and two obtuse angles. 3. a playing card marked with one or more red lozenge-shaped symbols. 4. Baseball. the playing field.

diamond wedding n. the 60th anniversary of a marriage.

diapason (ˌdaɪəˈpeɪzʲn) n. Music. 1. either of two stops found throughout the range of a pipe organ. 2. the range of an instrument or voice.

diaper (ˈdaɪəpə) n. U.S. & Canad. a nappy.

diaphanous (daɪˈæfənəs) adj. (of fabrics) fine and translucent.

diaphragm (ˈdaɪəˌfræm) n. 1. Anat. the muscular partition that separates the abdominal cavity and chest cavity. 2. same as **cap** (sense 8). 3. a device to control the amount of light entering an optical instrument. 4. a vibrating disc to convert sound signals to electrical signals or vice versa, as in telephones.

diapositive (ˌdaɪəˈpɒzɪtɪv) n. a positive transparency; slide.

diarist (ˈdaɪərɪst) n. a person who writes a diary, esp. one that is published.

diarrhoea or esp. U.S. **diarrhea** (ˌdaɪəˈrɪə) n. frequent and copious discharge of abnormally liquid faeces.

diary (ˈdaɪərɪ) n., pl. **-ries.** 1. a record of daily events, appointments, or observations. 2. a book for this.

Diaspora (daɪˈæspərə) n. 1. the dispersion of the Jews after the Babylonian conquest of Palestine. 2. a dispersion of people originally belonging to one nation.

diastase (ˈdaɪəˌsteɪs, -ˌsteɪz) n. an enzyme that hydrolyses starch to maltose.

diatom (ˈdaɪətəm) n. a microscopic unicellular alga.

diatomic (ˌdaɪəˈtɒmɪk) adj. **a.** containing two atoms. **b.** containing two characteristic groups or atoms.

diatonic (ˌdaɪəˈtɒnɪk) adj. of or relating to any scale of five tones and two semitones produced by playing the white keys of a keyboard instrument.

diatribe (ˈdaɪəˌtraɪb) n. a bitter critical attack.

dibble (ˈdɪbᵊl) n. a small hand tool used to make holes in the ground for bulbs, seeds, or roots.

dice (daɪs) n., pl. **dice.** **1.** a small cube, each of whose sides has a different number of spots (1 to 6), used in games of chance. ~vb. **2.** to cut (food) into small cubes. **3. dice with death.** to take a risk.

dicey (ˈdaɪsɪ) adj. **dicier, diciest.** Informal, chiefly Brit. dangerous; tricky.

dichotomy (daɪˈkɒtəmɪ) n., pl. **-mies.** division into two parts or classifications, esp. when they are opposed. —**diˈchotomous** adj.

dichromatic (ˌdaɪkrəʊˈmætɪk) adj. having two colours.

dick (dɪk) n. Slang. **1.** Taboo. a penis. **2. clever dick.** Brit. an opinionated person.

dickens (ˈdɪkɪnz) n. Informal, euphemistic. used for emphasis in such phrases as **what the dickens.**

Dickensian (dɪˈkɛnzɪən) adj. **1.** of Charles Dickens (1812–70), English novelist. **2.** denoting poverty, distress, and exploitation, as depicted in the novels of Dickens.

dicky[1] (ˈdɪkɪ) n., pl. **dickies.** **1.** a false shirt front. **2.** Also called: **dicky bow.** Brit. a bow tie. **3.** Also called: **dicky-bird.** a child's word for a bird.

dicky[2] (ˈdɪkɪ) adj. **dickier, dickiest.** Brit. informal. shaky or weak: a dicky heart.

dicotyledon (ˌdaɪkɒtɪˈliːdᵊn) n. a flowering plant with two seed leaves.

Dictaphone (ˈdɪktəˌfəʊn) n. Trademark. a tape recorder for recording dictation for subsequent typing.

dictate vb. (dɪkˈteɪt). **1.** to say (letters, speeches, etc.) aloud for transcription by another person. **2.** to give (commands) authoritatively. **3.** to seek to impose one's will on others. ~n. (ˈdɪkteɪt). **4.** an authoritative command. **5.** a guiding principle: the dictates of reason.

dictation (dɪkˈteɪʃən) n. **1.** the act of dictating material to be taken down in writing. **2.** the material dictated. **3.** the act of giving authoritative commands.

dictator (dɪkˈteɪtə) n. **1.** a ruler who is not bound by a constitution or laws. **2.** a person who behaves in a tyrannical manner. —**dicˈtatorship** n.

dictatorial (ˌdɪktəˈtɔːrɪəl) adj. **1.** of or characteristic of a dictator. **2.** tyrannical; overbearing. —ˌ**dictaˈtorially** adv.

diction (ˈdɪkʃən) n. the manner of enunciating words and sounds.

dictionary (ˈdɪkʃənərɪ) n., pl. **-aries.** **1. a.** a book that consists of an alphabetical list of words with their meanings. **b.** a similar book giving equivalent words in two languages. **2.** a reference book listing terms and giving information about a particular subject.

dictum (ˈdɪktəm) n., pl. **-tums** or **-ta** (-tə). **1.** a formal statement; pronouncement. **2.** a popular saying or maxim.

did (dɪd) vb. the past tense of **do**[1].

didactic (dɪˈdæktɪk) adj. **1.** intended to instruct, esp. excessively. **2.** morally instructive. —**diˈdactically** adv. —**diˈdacticism** n.

diddle (ˈdɪdᵊl) vb. Informal. to swindle. —ˈ**diddler** n.

didgeridoo (ˌdɪdʒərɪˈduː) n. Music. a native deep-toned Australian wind instrument.

didn't (ˈdɪdᵊnt) did not.

die[1] (daɪ) vb. **dying, died.** **1.** (of an organism) to cease all biological activity permanently. **2.** (of something inanimate) to cease to exist. **3.** (often foll. by away, down, or out) to lose strength, power, or energy by degrees. **4.** to stop working: the engine died. **5. be dying.** to be eager (for something or to do something). **6. be dying of.** Informal. to be nearly overcome with (laughter, boredom, etc.). **7. die hard.** to change or disappear only slowly: old habits die hard. ~See also **die down, die out.**

die[2] (daɪ) n. **1.** a shaped block used to cut or form metal. **2.** a casting mould. **3. the die is cast.** an irrevocable decision has been taken.

die down vb. **1.** to lose strength or power by degrees. **2.** to become calm.

die-hard n. a person who resists change.

dielectric (ˌdaɪɪˈlɛktrɪk) n. **1.** a substance of very low electrical conductivity; insulator. ~adj. **2.** having the properties of a dielectric.

die out or **off** vb. to become extinct or disappear after a gradual decline.

diesel (ˈdiːzᵊl) n. **1.** same as **diesel engine.** **2.** a vehicle driven by a diesel engine. **3.** Informal. diesel oil.

diesel-electric n. a locomotive with a diesel engine driving an electric generator.

diesel engine n. an internal-combustion engine in which atomized fuel oil is ignited by compression.

diesel oil or **fuel** n. a fuel obtained from petroleum distillation, used in diesel engines.

diet[1] (ˈdaɪət) n. **1.** the food that a person or animal regularly eats. **2.** a specific allowance or selection of food, to control weight

or for health reasons: *a salt-free diet.* ~*vb.*
3. to follow a special diet so as to lose
weight. —**'dietary** *adj.* —**'dieter** *n.*

diet² ('daɪət) *n.* a legislative assembly in
various countries.

dietary fibre *n.* fibrous substances in
fruits and vegetables that aid digestion.

dietetic (,daɪɪ'tɛtɪk) *adj.* prepared for special dietary requirements.

dietetics (,daɪɪ'tɛtɪks) *n.* (*functioning as
sing.*) the study of food intake and preparation.

dietician (,daɪɪ'tɪʃən) *n.* a person who specializes in dietetics.

differ ('dɪfə) *vb.* **1.** to be dissimilar in
quality, nature, or degree. **2.** to disagree.

difference ('dɪfərəns) *n.* **1.** the state or
quality of being unlike. **2.** a specific instance of being unlike. **3.** a disagreement
or argument. **4.** the result of the subtraction of one number or quantity from another. **5. make a difference.** to have an effect. **6. split the difference. a.** to compromise. **b.** to divide a remainder equally.

different ('dɪfərənt) *adj.* **1.** partly or completely unlike. **2.** new or unusual. —**'differently** *adv.*

differential (,dɪfə'rɛnʃəl) *adj.* **1.** of, relating to, or using a difference. **2.** *Maths.*
involving differentials. ~*n.* **3.** a factor
that differentiates between two comparable
things. **4.** *Maths.* a minute difference between values in a scale. **5.** *Chiefly Brit.* the
difference between rates of pay for different types of labour, esp. within an industry.

differential calculus *n.* the branch of
calculus concerned with the study, evaluation, and use of derivatives and differentials.

differential gear *n.* the gear in the driving axle of a road vehicle that permits one
driving wheel to rotate faster than the other, when cornering.

differentiate (,dɪfə'rɛnʃɪ,eɪt) *vb.* **1.** to
serve to distinguish (one thing from another). **2.** (often foll. by *between*) to perceive
or make a difference (in or between); discriminate. **3.** *Maths.* to determine the derivative of a function or variable. —**,dif-
fer,enti'ation** *n.*

difficult ('dɪfɪk°lt) *adj.* **1.** not easy to do,
understand, or solve. **2.** troublesome; not
easily pleased or satisfied: *a difficult child.*
3. full of hardships or trials.

difficulty ('dɪfɪk°ltɪ) *n., pl.* -**ties. 1.** the
quality of being difficult. **2.** a problem that
is hard to deal with. **3.** (*often pl.*) a troublesome or embarrassing situation, esp. a
financial one. **4.** (*often pl.*) an objection or
obstacle. **5.** lack of ease; awkwardness.

diffident ('dɪfɪdənt) *adj.* lacking self-
confidence; shy. —**'diffidence** *n.* —**'diffi-
dently** *adv.*

diffract (dɪ'frækt) *vb.* to cause to undergo
diffraction. —**dif'fractive** *adj.*

diffraction (dɪ'frækʃən) *n.* **1.** *Physics.* a
deviation in the direction of a wave at the
edge of an obstacle in its path. **2.** the
formation of light and dark fringes by the
passage of light through a small aperture.

diffuse *vb.* (dɪ'fjuːz). **1.** to spread in all
directions. **2.** to cause to undergo diffusion. ~*adj.* (dɪ'fjuːs). **3.** spread out over a
wide area. **4.** lacking conciseness.
—**diffusible** (dɪ'fjuːzɪb°l) *adj.*

diffusion (dɪ'fjuːʒən) *n.* **1.** the act of dif-
fusing or the fact of being diffused; dispersion. **2.** *Physics.* the random thermal motion of atoms and molecules in gases, liquids, and some solids. **3.** *Physics.* the
transmission or reflection of light, in which
the radiation is scattered in many directions.

dig (dɪg) *vb.* **digging, dug. 1.** (often foll. by
up) to cut into, break up, and turn over or
remove (earth, etc.), esp. with a spade. **2.**
to excavate (a hole or tunnel) by digging,
usually with an implement or (of animals)
with claws. **3.** (foll. by *out* or *up*) to obtain
by digging. **4.** (foll. by *out* or *up*) to find by
effort or searching: *to dig out facts.* **5.**
(foll. by *in* or *into*) to thrust or jab. **6.**
Informal. to like or understand. ~*n.* **7.** the
act of digging. **8.** a thrust or poke. **9.** a
cutting remark. **10.** an archaeological excavation. ~See also **dig in.**

digest *vb.* (dɪ'dʒɛst, daɪ-). **1.** to subject
(food) to a process of digestion. **2.** to assimilate mentally. ~*n.* ('daɪdʒɛst). **3.** a
comprehensive and systematic compilation
of information, often condensed.
—**di'gestible** *adj.*

digestion (dɪ'dʒɛstʃən, daɪ-) *n.* **1.** the process of breaking down food into easily absorbed substances. **2.** the body's system
for doing this.

digestive (dɪ'dʒɛstɪv, daɪ-) *adj.* relating to
digestion.

digestive biscuit *n.* a biscuit made from
wholemeal flour.

digger ('dɪgə) *n.* **1.** a machine used for
excavation. **2.** *Austral. & N.Z. informal.* an
Australian or New Zealander: often used as
a friendly term of address.

dig in *vb.* **1.** to mix (compost or fertilizer)
into the soil by digging. **2.** *Informal.* to
begin to eat vigorously. **3. dig oneself in.**
Informal. to entrench oneself. **4. dig one's
heels in.** *Informal.* to refuse to move or be
persuaded.

digit ('dɪdʒɪt) *n.* **1.** a finger or toe. **2.** any
numeral from 0 to 9.

digital ('dɪdʒɪt°l) *adj.* **1.** representing data
as a series of numerical values. **2.** displaying information as numbers rather than
with a dial. **3.** of or possessing digits.
—**'digitally** *adv.*

digital audio tape *n.* magnetic tape on which sound is recorded digitally, giving high-fidelity reproduction.

digital clock *or* **watch** *n.* a clock or watch in which the time is indicated by digits rather than by hands on a dial.

digital computer *n.* a computer in which the input consists of numbers, letters, etc., that are represented internally in binary notation.

digitalis (‚dɪdʒɪ'teɪlɪs) *n.* a drug prepared from foxglove leaves: used as a heart stimulant.

digital recording *n.* a sound recording process that converts audio or analogue signals into a series of pulses.

digitate ('dɪdʒɪ‚teɪt) *adj.* **1.** (of leaves) having leaflets in the form of a spread hand. **2.** (of animals) having digits.

digitize *or* **-ise** ('dɪdʒɪ‚taɪz) *vb.* to transcribe (data) into a digital form for processing by a computer. —'**digi‚tizer** *or* **-iser** *n.*

dignified ('dɪgnɪ‚faɪd) *adj.* characterized by dignity of manner; noble.

dignify ('dɪgnɪ‚faɪ) *vb.* **-fying, -fied. 1.** to add distinction to. **2.** to add a semblance of dignity to (something or someone) by the use of a pretentious name or title.

dignitary ('dɪgnɪtrɪ) *n., pl.* **-taries.** a person of high official position or rank.

dignity ('dɪgnɪtɪ) *n., pl.* **-ties. 1.** serious, calm, and controlled behaviour or manner. **2.** the quality of being worthy of honour. **3.** sense of self-importance: *he considered the job beneath his dignity.* **4.** high rank, esp. in government or the church.

digraph ('daɪgrɑːf) *n.* two letters used to represent a single sound, such as *gh* in *tough.*

digress (daɪ'grɛs) *vb.* to depart from the main subject in speech or writing. —**di'gression** *n.*

digs (dɪgz) *pl. n. Brit. informal.* lodgings.

dihedral (daɪ'hiːdrəl) *adj.* having or formed by two intersecting planes.

dike (daɪk) *n., vb.* same as **dyke.**

dilapidated (dɪ'læpɪ‚deɪtɪd) *adj.* (of a building) having fallen into ruin. —**di‚lapi'dation** *n.*

dilate (daɪ'leɪt, dɪ-) *vb.* **1.** to make or become wider or larger. **2.** to speak or write at length. —**di'lation** *or* **dilatation** (‚daɪlə'teɪʃən) *n.*

dilatory ('dɪlətrɪ) *adj.* **1.** (of a person) tending to delay or waste time. **2.** (of an action) intended to waste time or defer action. —'**dilatorily** *adv.* —'**dilatoriness** *n.*

dildo ('dɪldəʊ) *n., pl.* **-dos.** an object used as a substitute for an erect penis.

dilemma (dɪ'lɛmə, daɪ-) *n.* a situation necessitating a choice between two equally undesirable alternatives.

dilettante (‚dɪlɪ'tɑːntɪ) *n., pl.* **-tantes** *or* **-tanti** (-'tɑːntɪ). a person whose interest in a subject, esp. art, is superficial rather than serious. —‚**dilet'tantism** *n.*

diligent ('dɪlɪdʒənt) *adj.* **1.** careful and persevering in carrying out tasks or duties. **2.** carried out with care and perseverance: *diligent work.* —'**diligence** *n.* —'**diligently** *adv.*

dill (dɪl) *n.* an aromatic herb used for flavouring.

dilly-dally (‚dɪlɪ'dælɪ) *vb.* **-lying, -lied.** *Informal.* to loiter or vacillate.

dilute (daɪ'luːt) *vb.* **1.** to make (a liquid) less concentrated, esp. by adding water. **2.** to make (a quality, etc.) weaker in force or effect. ~*adj.* **3.** *Chem.* (of a solution) having a low concentration. —**di'lution** *n.*

diluvial (daɪ'luːvɪəl, dɪ-) *or* **diluvian** *adj.* of a flood, esp. the great Flood described in Genesis.

dim (dɪm) *adj.* **dimmer, dimmest. 1.** badly illuminated. **2.** not clearly seen; faint. **3.** not seeing clearly. **4.** mentally dull. **5.** not clear in the mind; obscure: *a dim memory.* **6.** lacking in brightness. **7. take a dim view of.** to disapprove of. ~*vb.* **dimming, dimmed. 8.** to become or cause to become dim. **9.** to cause to seem less bright. **10.** *U.S. & Canad.* same as **dip** (sense 4). —'**dimly** *adv.* —'**dimness** *n.*

dime (daɪm) *n.* a coin of the U.S. and Canada worth ten cents.

dimension (dɪ'mɛnʃən) *n.* **1.** (*often pl.*) a measurement of the size of something in a particular direction, such as the length, width, height, or diameter. **2.** (*pl.*) scope; extent. **3.** aspect: *a new dimension to politics.* —**di'mensional** *adj.*

dimer ('daɪmə) *n. Chem.* a molecule made up of two identical molecules bonded together.

diminish (dɪ'mɪnɪʃ) *vb.* **1.** to make or become smaller, fewer, or less. **2.** *Music.* to decrease (a minor interval) by a semitone. **3.** to reduce in authority or status.

diminuendo (dɪ‚mɪnjʊ'ɛndəʊ) *Music.* ~*n., pl.* **-dos. 1. a.** a gradual decrease in loudness. **b.** a passage affected by a diminuendo. ~*adv.* **2.** gradually decreasing in loudness.

diminution (‚dɪmɪ'njuːʃən) *n.* reduction; decrease.

diminutive (dɪ'mɪnjʊtɪv) *adj.* **1.** very small; tiny. **2.** *Grammar.* **a.** denoting an affix added to a word to convey the meaning *small* or *unimportant* or to express affection. **b.** denoting a word formed by the addition of a diminutive affix. ~*n.* **3.** *Grammar.* a diminutive word or affix. —**di'minutiveness** *n.*

dimmer ('dɪmə) *n.* **1.** a device for dimming

an electric light. **2.** *U.S.* **a.** a dipped headlight on a road vehicle. **b.** a parking light on a car.

dimple ('dimp²l) *n.* **1.** a small natural dent, esp. on the cheeks or chin. ~*vb.* **2.** to produce dimples by smiling.

dimwit ('dim,wit) *n. Informal.* a stupid person. —,**dim-'witted** *adj.*

din (din) *n.* **1.** a loud discordant confused noise. ~*vb.* **dinning, dinned.** **2. din something into someone.** to instil something into someone by constant repetition.

dinar ('di:nɑ:) *n.* a monetary unit of Yugoslavia and various Middle Eastern and North African countries.

Dincs *or* **DINKS** (diŋks) double income no children (*or* kids): used of couples.

dine (dain) *vb.* **1.** to eat dinner. **2.** (foll. by *on, off,* or *upon*) to make one's meal (of): *the guests dined upon roast beef.*

diner ('dainə) *n.* **1.** a person eating a meal, esp. in a restaurant. **2.** *Chiefly U.S. & Canad.* a small cheap restaurant. **3.** short for **dining car.**

dinette (dai'nɛt) *n.* an alcove or small area for use as a dining room.

ding (diŋ) *vb.* **1.** to ring, esp. with tedious repetition. ~*n.* **2.** an imitation of the sound of a bell.

ding-dong *n.* **1.** (,diŋ'dɒŋ). the sound of a bell. **2.** ('diŋdɒŋ). a violent exchange of blows or words.

dinges ('diŋəs) *n. S. African informal.* a jocular word for something whose name is unknown or forgotten; thingumabob.

dinghy ('diŋi) *n., pl.* **-ghies.** a small boat, powered by sail, oars, or outboard motor.

dingle ('diŋg²l) *n.* a small wooded dell.

dingo ('diŋgəʊ) *n., pl.* **-goes.** a wild dog of Australia.

dingy ('dindʒi) *adj.* **-gier, -giest.** **1.** dull, neglected, and drab. **2.** dirty; discoloured. —'**dinginess** *n.*

dining car *n.* a railway coach in which meals are served.

dining room *n.* a room where meals are eaten.

dinkum ('diŋkəm) *adj. Austral. & N.Z. informal.* **1.** genuine or right: *a fair dinkum offer.* **2. dinkum oil.** the truth.

dinky ('diŋki) *adj.* **dinkier, dinkiest.** *Brit. informal.* small and neat; dainty.

dinner ('dinə) *n.* **1.** a meal taken in the evening. **2.** a meal taken at midday, esp. when it is the main meal of the day. **3.** a formal social occasion at which an evening meal is served.

dinner jacket *n.* a man's semiformal evening jacket without tails, usually black.

dinner service *n.* a set of matching dishes suitable for serving a meal.

dinosaur ('dainə,sɔ:) *n.* any of a large order

of extinct prehistoric reptiles many of which were gigantic.

dint (dint) *n.* **by dint of.** by means of: *by dint of hard work.*

diocesan (dai'ɒsis²n) *adj.* of or relating to a diocese.

diocese ('daiəsis) *n.* the district under the jurisdiction of a bishop.

diode ('daiəʊd) *n.* **1.** a semiconductor device for converting alternating current to direct current. **2.** an electronic valve with two electrodes between which a current can flow only in one direction.

dioecious (dai'i:ʃəs) *adj.* (of plants) having the male and female reproductive organs on separate plants.

Dionysian (,daiə'niziən) *adj.* wild or orgiastic.

dioptre *or U.S.* **diopter** (dai'ɒptə) *n.* a unit for measuring the refractive power of a lens.

diorama (,daiə'rɑːmə) *n.* **1.** a miniature three-dimensional scene, in which models of figures are seen against a background. **2.** a picture made up of illuminated translucent curtains, viewed through an aperture.

dioxide (dai'ɒksaid) *n.* an oxide containing two oxygen atoms per molecule.

dip (dip) *vb.* **dipping, dipped.** **1.** to plunge or be plunged quickly or briefly into a liquid. **2.** to undergo a slight decline, esp. temporarily: *sales dipped in November.* **3.** to slope downwards. **4.** to switch (car headlights) from the main to the lower beam. **5.** to immerse (farm animals) briefly in a chemical to rid them of insects. **6.** to lower or be lowered briefly. **7.** to plunge a container or one's hands into something, esp. to obtain an object. ~*n.* **8.** the act of dipping. **9.** a brief swim. **10.** a liquid chemical in which farm animals are dipped. **11.** a depression, esp. in a landscape. **12.** a momentary sinking down. **13.** a creamy mixture into which pieces of food are dipped before being eaten. **14.** a candle made by plunging a wick into wax. ~See also **dip into.**

Dip Ed (in Britain) Diploma in Education.

diphtheria (dip'θiəriə) *n.* a contagious disease producing fever and difficulty in breathing and swallowing.

diphthong ('difθɒŋ) *n.* a vowel sound, occupying a single syllable, in which the speaker's tongue moves continuously from one position to another, as in the pronunciation of *a* in *late.*

dip into *vb.* **1.** to draw upon: *he dipped into his savings.* **2.** to read passages at random from (a book or journal).

diploma (di'pləʊmə) *n.* a document conferring a qualification or recording successful completion of a course of study.

diplomacy (di'pləʊməsi) *n.* **1.** the conduct of the relations of one state with another by peaceful means. **2.** skill in the management of international relations. **3.** tact or skill in dealing with people.

diplomat ('dɪplə,mæt) *n.* an official, such as an ambassador, engaged in diplomacy.

diplomatic (,dɪplə'mætɪk) *adj.* **1.** of or relating to diplomacy. **2.** skilled in negotiating between states. **3.** tactful in dealing with people. —,**diplo'matically** *adv.*

diplomatic immunity *n.* the freedom from legal action and exemption from taxation which diplomats have in the country where they are working.

dipole ('daɪ,pəʊl) *n.* **1.** two equal but opposite electric charges or magnetic poles separated by a small distance. **2.** a molecule that has two such charges or poles. —**di'polar** *adj.*

dipper ('dɪpə) *n.* **1.** a ladle used for dipping. **2.** a songbird that inhabits fast-flowing streams.

dipsomania (,dɪpsəʊ'meɪnɪə) *n.* a compulsive desire to drink alcoholic beverages. —,**dipso'maniac** *n., adj.*

dipstick ('dɪp,stɪk) *n.* a rod with notches on it dipped into a container to indicate the fluid level.

dip switch *n.* a device for dipping car headlights.

dipterous ('dɪptərəs) *adj.* having two wings or winglike parts.

diptych ('dɪptɪk) *n.* a painting on two hinged panels.

dire ('daɪə) *adj.* **1.** desperate; urgent: *dire need.* **2.** likely to bring disaster; ominous.

direct (dɪ'rɛkt) *vb.* **1.** to conduct or control the affairs of. **2.** to give orders with authority to (a person or group). **3.** to tell (someone) the way to a place. **4.** to address (a letter, package, remarks, etc.). **5.** to provide guidance to (actors, cameramen, etc.) in (a play or film). ~*adj.* **6.** without evasion; straightforward. **7.** shortest; straight: *a direct route.* **8.** without intervening persons or agencies: *a direct link.* **9.** honest; frank. **10.** precise; exact: *a direct quotation.* **11.** diametrical: *the direct opposite.* **12.** in an unbroken line of descent: *a direct descendant.* ~*adv.* **13.** directly; straight. —**di'rectness** *n.*

direct access *n.* a method of reading data from a computer file without reading through the file from the beginning.

direct current *n.* an electric current that flows in one direction only.

direction (dɪ'rɛkʃən) *n.* **1.** the course or line along which a person or thing moves, points, or lies. **2.** management or guidance. **3.** the work of a stage or film director.

directional (dɪ'rɛkʃən²l) *adj.* **1.** of or showing direction. **2.** *Electronics.* (of an aerial) transmitting or receiving radio waves more effectively in some directions than in others.

directions (dɪ'rɛkʃənz) *pl. n.* instructions for doing something or for reaching a place.

directive (dɪ'rɛktɪv) *n.* an instruction; order.

directly (dɪ'rɛktlɪ) *adv.* **1.** in a direct manner. **2.** at once; without delay. **3.** (often foll. by *before* or *after*) immediately; just. ~*conj.* **4.** as soon as.

direct object *n. Grammar.* a noun, pronoun, or noun phrase denoting the person or thing receiving the direct action of a verb. For example, *a book* in *They bought Anne a book.*

director (dɪ'rɛktə) *n.* **1.** a person or thing that directs or controls. **2.** a member of the governing board of a business or an institution, trust, etc. **3.** the person responsible for the artistic and technical aspects of the making of a film or television programme. —,**direc'torial** *adj.* —**di'rector,ship** *n.*

directorate (dɪ'rɛktərɪt) *n.* **1.** a board of directors. **2.** the position of director.

directory (dɪ'rɛktrɪ) *n., pl.* **-ries.** a book listing names, addresses, and telephone numbers of individuals or firms.

direct speech *n.* the reporting of what someone has said by quoting the exact words.

direct tax *n.* a tax paid by the person or organization on which it is levied.

dirge (dɜːdʒ) *n.* **1.** a chant of lamentation for the dead. **2.** any mournful song.

dirigible ('dɪrɪdʒɪb²l) *adj.* **1.** able to be steered. ~*n.* **2.** same as **airship.**

dirk (dɜːk) *n.* a dagger, formerly worn by Scottish Highlanders.

dirndl ('dɜːnd²l) *n.* **1.** a woman's dress with a full gathered skirt and fitted bodice. **2.** a gathered skirt of this kind.

dirt (dɜːt) *n.* **1.** any unclean substance, such as mud; filth. **2.** loose earth; soil. **3. a.** packed earth, cinders, etc., used to make a racetrack. **b.** (*as modifier*): *a dirt track.* **4.** obscene speech or writing.

dirt-cheap *adj., adv. Informal.* at an extremely low price.

dirty ('dɜːtɪ) *adj.* **dirtier, dirtiest. 1.** covered or marked with dirt; filthy. **2. a.** obscene: *dirty books.* **b.** sexually clandestine: *a dirty weekend.* **3.** causing one to become grimy: *a dirty job.* **4.** (of a colour) not clear and bright. **5.** unfair, dishonest, or unkind. **6.** revealing dislike or anger: *a dirty look.* **7.** (of weather) rainy or stormy. **8. dirty work.** unpleasant or illicit activity. ~*n.* **9. do the dirty on.** *Informal.* to behave meanly towards. ~*vb.* **dirtying, dirtied. 10.** to make dirty; soil. —'**dirtiness** *n.*

dis- *prefix.* indicating: **1.** reversal: *disconnect.* **2.** negation or lack: *dissimilar; disgrace.* **3.** removal or release: *disembowel.*

disability (,dɪsə'bɪlɪtɪ) *n., pl.* **-ties. 1.** the condition of being physically or mentally impaired. **2.** something that disables; handicap.

disable (dɪsˈeɪbᵊl) *vb.* to make ineffective, unfit, or incapable, as by crippling. —**dis-ˈabled** *adj.* —**disˈablement** *n.*

disabuse (ˌdɪsəˈbjuːz) *vb.* (foll. by *of*) to rid (someone) of a mistaken idea.

disadvantage (ˌdɪsədˈvɑːntɪdʒ) *n.* **1.** an unfavourable circumstance, thing, or situation: *at a disadvantage.* **2.** injury, loss, or detriment. —ˌdisadvanˈtageous *adj.*

disadvantaged (ˌdɪsədˈvɑːntɪdʒd) *adj.* socially or economically deprived.

disaffected (ˌdɪsəˈfɛktɪd) *adj.* having lost loyalty to or affection for someone or something; alienated. —ˌdisafˈfection *n.*

disagree (ˌdɪsəˈgriː) *vb.* **-greeing, -greed.** (often foll. by *with*) **1.** to dissent in opinion or dispute (about an idea or fact). **2.** to fail to correspond; conflict. **3.** to cause physical discomfort to: *curry disagrees with me.*

disagreeable (ˌdɪsəˈgrɪəbᵊl) *adj.* **1.** (of a person) not likable; bad-tempered or disobliging. **2.** (of an incident or situation) not to one's liking; unpleasant. —ˌdisaˈgreeably *adv.*

disagreement (ˌdɪsəˈgriːmənt) *n.* **1.** refusal or failure to agree. **2.** a failure to correspond. **3.** an argument or dispute.

disallow (ˌdɪsəˈlaʊ) *vb.* to reject as untrue or invalid; cancel.

disappear (ˌdɪsəˈpɪə) *vb.* **1.** to cease to be visible; vanish. **2.** to go away or become lost, esp. without explanation. **3.** to cease to exist. —ˌdisapˈpearance *n.*

disappoint (ˌdɪsəˈpɔɪnt) *vb.* **1.** to fail to meet the expectations or hopes of; let down. **2.** to prevent the fulfilment of (a plan, etc.); frustrate. —ˌdisapˈpointed *adj.* —ˌdisapˈpointing *adj.*

disappointment (ˌdɪsəˈpɔɪntmənt) *n.* **1.** the feeling of being disappointed. **2.** a person or thing that disappoints.

disapprobation (ˌdɪsæprəʊˈbeɪʃən) *n.* disapproval.

disapprove (ˌdɪsəˈpruːv) *vb.* (often foll. by *of*) to consider wrong or bad. —ˌdisapˈproval *n.* —ˌdisapˈproving *adj.*

disarm (dɪsˈɑːm) *vb.* **1.** to deprive of weapons. **2.** to win the confidence or affection of. **3.** (of a nation) to decrease the size and capability of one's armed forces.

disarmament (dɪsˈɑːməmənt) *n.* the reduction of fighting capability by a nation.

disarming (dɪsˈɑːmɪŋ) *adj.* tending to neutralize hostility or suspicion. —disˈarmingly *adv.*

disarrange (ˌdɪsəˈreɪndʒ) *vb.* to throw into disorder. —ˌdisarˈrangement *n.*

disarray (ˌdɪsəˈreɪ) *n.* **1.** confusion and lack of discipline. **2.** extreme untidiness. ~*vb.* **3.** to throw into confusion.

disassociate (ˌdɪsəˈsəʊʃɪˌeɪt, -sɪ-) *vb.* same as **dissociate.** —ˌdisasˌsociˈation *n.*

disaster (dɪˈzɑːstə) *n.* **1.** an occurrence that causes great distress or destruction. **2.** a thing, project, etc., that fails or has been ruined. —disˈastrous *adj.* —disˈastrously *adv.*

disavow (ˌdɪsəˈvaʊ) *vb.* to deny connection with or responsibility for (something). —ˌdisaˈvowal *n.*

disband (dɪsˈbænd) *vb.* to cease to function or cause to stop functioning as a unit or group. —disˈbandment *n.*

disbelieve (ˌdɪsbɪˈliːv) *vb.* **1.** to reject as false or lying. **2.** (foll. by *in*) to have no faith (in). —ˌdisbeˈlief *n.*

disburse (dɪsˈbɜːs) *vb.* to pay out. —disˈbursement *n.*

disc (dɪsk) *n.* **1.** a flat circular object. **2.** a gramophone record. **3.** *Anat.* a circular flat structure in the body, esp. between the vertebrae. **4.** *Computers.* same as **disk.**

discard (dɪsˈkɑːd) *vb.* **1.** to get rid of (something or someone) as useless or undesirable. **2.** *Cards.* to play (a card of little value) when unable to follow suit.

disc brake *n.* a brake in which two pads rub against a flat disc.

discern (dɪˈsɜːn) *vb.* to see or be aware of (something) clearly. —disˈcernible *adj.*

discerning (dɪˈsɜːnɪŋ) *adj.* having or showing good judgment. —diˈscernment *n.*

discharge *vb.* (dɪsˈtʃɑːdʒ). **1.** to release or allow to go. **2.** to dismiss (someone) from duty or employment. **3.** to fire (a gun). **4.** to cause to pour forth: *the boil discharges pus.* **5.** to remove (the cargo) from a boat, etc.; unload. **6.** to meet the demands of (an office, obligation, etc.). **7.** to relieve oneself of (a responsibility or debt). **8.** *Physics.* to take or supply electrical current from (a cell or battery). **9.** *Law.* to release (a prisoner from custody, etc.). ~*n.* (ˈdɪstʃɑːdʒ, dɪsˈtʃɑːdʒ). **10.** something that is discharged. **11.** dismissal or release from an office, job, institution, etc. **12.** a pouring forth of a fluid; emission. **13.** *Physics.* a conduction of electricity through a gas.

disciple (dɪˈsaɪpᵊl) *n.* **1.** a follower of the doctrines of a teacher. **2.** one of the personal followers of Christ during his earthly life.

disciplinarian (ˌdɪsɪplɪˈnɛərɪən) *n.* a person who practises strict discipline.

disciplinary (ˈdɪsɪˌplɪnərɪ) *adj.* of or imposing discipline; corrective.

discipline (ˈdɪsɪplɪn) *n.* **1.** training imposed for the improvement of physical powers, self-control, etc. **2.** systematic training in obedience. **3.** the state of improved behaviour resulting from such training. **4.** punishment. **5.** a branch of learning or instruction. ~*vb.* **6.** to improve or attempt to improve the behaviour or orderliness of (oneself or another) by training, conditions, or rules. **7.** to punish.

disc jockey *n.* a person who announces and plays recorded pop music on a radio programme or at a disco.

disclaim (dɪsˈkleɪm) *vb.* **1.** to deny (responsibility for or knowledge of something). **2.** to give up (any claim to).

disclaimer (dɪsˈkleɪmə) *n.* a repudiation or denial.

disclose (dɪsˈkləʊz) *vb.* **1.** to make known. **2.** to allow to be seen. —**dis'closure** *n.*

disco (ˈdɪskəʊ) *n., pl.* **-cos.** **1.** an occasion at which people dance to pop records. **2.** a nightclub or other public place where such dances are held. **3.** mobile equipment for providing music for a disco.

discolour *or U.S.* **discolor** (dɪsˈkʌlə) *vb.* to change in colour; fade or stain. —**dis,col'or'ation** *n.*

discomfit (dɪsˈkʌmfɪt) *vb.* **1.** to make uneasy or confused. **2.** to frustrate the plans of. —**dis'comfiture** *n.*

discomfort (dɪsˈkʌmfət) *n.* **1.** an inconvenience, distress, or mild pain. **2.** something that disturbs or deprives of ease.

discommode (ˌdɪskəˈməʊd) *vb.* to cause inconvenience. —**,discom'modious** *adj.*

discompose (ˌdɪskəmˈpəʊz) *vb.* to disturb; disconcert. —**,discom'posure** *n.*

disconcert (ˌdɪskənˈsɜːt) *vb.* to disturb the confidence or self-possession of; upset, embarrass, or take aback. —**,discon'certing** *adj.*

disconnect (ˌdɪskəˈnɛkt) *vb.* **1.** to undo or break the connection between two things. **2.** to stop the supply of (gas or electricity to a building). —**,discon'nection** *n.*

disconnected (ˌdɪskəˈnɛktɪd) *adj.* (of speech or ideas) not logically connected; incoherent.

disconsolate (dɪsˈkɒnsəlɪt) *adj.* sad beyond comfort. —**dis'consolately** *adv.*

discontent (ˌdɪskənˈtɛnt) *n.* lack of contentment, as with one's condition or lot in life. —**,discon'tented** *adj.* —**,discon'tentedly** *adv.*

discontinue (ˌdɪskənˈtɪnjuː) *vb.* **-uing, -ued.** to come or bring to an end; stop.

discontinuous (ˌdɪskənˈtɪnjʊəs) *adj.* characterized by interruptions; intermittent. —**,disconti'nuity** *n.*

discord (ˈdɪskɔːd) *n.* **1.** lack of agreement or harmony between people. **2.** harsh confused sounds. **3.** a combination of musical notes that lacks harmony.

discordant (dɪsˈkɔːdˈnt) *adj.* **1.** at variance; disagreeing. **2.** harsh in sound; inharmonious. —**dis'cordance** *n.*

discotheque (ˈdɪskəˌtɛk) *n.* same as **disco**.

discount *vb.* (dɪsˈkaʊnt, ˈdɪskaʊnt). **1.** to leave (something) out of account as being unreliable, prejudiced, or irrelevant. **2.** to deduct (an amount or percentage) from the price of something. ~*n.* (ˈdɪskaʊnt). **3.** a deduction from the full amount of a price. **4. at a discount.** below the regular price.

discountenance (dɪsˈkaʊntɪnəns) *vb.* to make (someone) ashamed or confused.

discourage (dɪsˈkʌrɪdʒ) *vb.* **1.** to deprive of the will to persist in something. **2.** to oppose by expressing disapproval. —**dis'couragement** *n.* —**dis'couraging** *adj.*

discourse *n.* (ˈdɪskɔːs, dɪsˈkɔːs). **1.** conversation. **2.** a formal treatment of a subject in speech or writing. ~*vb.* (dɪsˈkɔːs). **3.** (foll. by *on* or *upon*) to speak or write (about) at length.

discourteous (dɪsˈkɜːtɪəs) *adj.* showing bad manners; rude. —**dis'courteously** *adv.* —**dis'courtesy** *n.*

discover (dɪˈskʌvə) *vb.* **1.** to be the first to find or find out about. **2.** to learn about for the first time. **3.** to find after study or search. —**dis'coverer** *n.*

discovery (dɪˈskʌvərɪ) *n., pl.* **-eries. 1.** the act of discovering. **2.** a person, place, or thing that has been discovered.

discredit (dɪsˈkrɛdɪt) *vb.* **1.** to damage the reputation of (someone). **2.** to cause (an idea) to be disbelieved or distrusted. ~*n.* **3.** something that causes disgrace. —**dis'creditable** *adj.*

discreet (dɪˈskriːt) *adj.* **1.** careful to avoid embarrassment, esp. by keeping confidences secret; tactful. **2.** unobtrusive. —**dis'creetly** *adv.*

discrepancy (dɪˈskrɛpənsɪ) *n., pl.* **-cies.** a conflict or variation between facts, figures, or claims. —**dis'crepant** *adj.*

discrete (dɪsˈkriːt) *adj.* separate or distinct. —**dis'creteness** *n.*

discretion (dɪˈskrɛʃən) *n.* **1.** the quality of behaving so as to avoid social embarrassment or distress. **2.** freedom or authority to make judgments and to act as one sees fit: *use your own discretion.* **3. age** *or* **years of discretion.** the age at which one is thought able to manage one's own affairs. —**dis'cretionary** *adj.*

discriminate (dɪˈskrɪmɪˌneɪt) *vb.* **1.** (usu. foll. by *against* or *in favour of*) to single out a particular person or group, etc., for special disfavour or favour. **2.** (foll. by *between* or *among*) to recognize or understand the difference (between). —**dis'crimi,nating** *adj.*

discrimination (dɪˌskrɪmɪˈneɪʃən) *n.* **1.** unfair treatment of a person, racial group, minority, etc., based on prejudice. **2.** subtle appreciation in matters of taste. **3.** the ability to see fine distinctions.

discriminatory (dɪˈskrɪmɪnətrɪ) *adj.* based on prejudice.

discursive (dɪsˈkɜːsɪv) *adj.* passing from one topic to another.

discus (ˈdɪskəs) *n. Field sports.* a disc-shaped object with a heavy middle, thrown by athletes.

discuss (dɪˈskʌs) *vb.* **1.** to consider (something) by talking it over. **2.** to treat (a subject) in speech or writing. —**disˈcussion** *n.*

disdain (dɪsˈdeɪn) *n.* **1.** a feeling of superiority and dislike; contempt. ~*vb.* **2.** to refuse with disdain: *she disdained to reply.* —**disˈdainful** *adj.* —**disˈdainfully** *adv.*

disease (dɪˈziːz) *n.* **1.** an illness or sickness. **2.** a corresponding condition in plants. —**disˈeased** *adj.*

diseconomy (ˌdɪsɪˈkɒnəmɪ) *n. Econ.* a disadvantage, such as higher costs, resulting from the scale on which an enterprise operates.

disembark (ˌdɪsɪmˈbɑːk) *vb.* to land or cause to land from a ship, aircraft, or bus. —**disembarkation** (dɪsˌɛmbɑːˈkeɪʃən) *n.*

disembodied (ˌdɪsɪmˈbɒdɪd) *adj.* **1.** lacking a body. **2.** seeming not to be attached to or come from anyone. —**disemˈbodiment** *n.*

disembowel (ˌdɪsɪmˈbaʊəl) *vb.* **-elling, -elled** *or U.S.* **-eling, -eled.** to remove the entrails of. —**disemˈbowelment** *n.*

disenchant (ˌdɪsɪnˈtʃɑːnt) *vb.* to free (someone) from or as if from an enchantment; disillusion. —**disenˈchantment** *n.*

disengage (ˌdɪsɪnˈgeɪdʒ) *vb.* **1.** to release or become released from a connection, obligation, etc. **2.** *Mil.* to withdraw from close action. —**disenˈgagement** *n.*

disentangle (ˌdɪsɪnˈtæŋgᵊl) *vb.* **1.** to release from entanglement or confusion. **2.** to unravel or work out. —**disenˈtanglement** *n.*

disequilibrium (ˌdɪsiːkwɪˈlɪbrɪəm) *n.* a loss or absence of stability or balance.

disestablish (ˌdɪsɪˈstæblɪʃ) *vb.* to deprive (a church, custom, institution, etc.) of established status. —**disesˈtablishment** *n.*

disfavour *or U.S.* **disfavor** (dɪsˈfeɪvə) *n.* **1.** disapproval or dislike. **2.** the state of being disapproved of or disliked.

disfigure (dɪsˈfɪgə) *vb.* to spoil the appearance or shape of. —**disˈfigurement** *n.*

disfranchise (dɪsˈfræntʃaɪz) *or* **disenfranchise** *vb.* to deprive (a person) of the right to vote or other rights of citizenship. —**disfranchisement** (dɪsˈfræntʃɪzmənt) *n.*

disgorge (dɪsˈgɔːdʒ) *vb.* **1.** to throw out (food) from the throat; vomit. **2.** to discharge (contents).

disgrace (dɪsˈgreɪs) *n.* **1.** a condition of shame, loss of reputation, or dishonour. **2.** a shameful person or thing. **3.** exclusion from confidence or trust: *he is in disgrace with his father.* ~*vb.* **4.** to bring shame upon (oneself or others). —**disˈgraceful** *adj.* —**disˈgracefully** *adv.*

disgruntled (dɪsˈgrʌntᵊld) *adj.* sulky or discontented. —**disˈgruntlement** *n.*

disguise (dɪsˈgaɪz) *vb.* **1.** to change the appearance or manner in order to conceal the identity of (someone or something). **2.** to misrepresent (something) in order to obscure its actual nature or meaning. ~*n.* **3.** a mask, costume, or manner that disguises. **4.** the state of being disguised. —**disˈguised** *adj.*

disgust (dɪsˈgʌst) *vb.* **1.** to sicken or fill with loathing. ~*n.* **2.** a great loathing or distaste. —**disˈgusted** *adj.* —**disˈgusting** *adj.*

dish (dɪʃ) *n.* **1.** a container used for holding or serving food, esp. an open shallow container. **2.** the food in a dish. **3.** a particular kind of food. **4.** something resembling a dish. **5.** short for **dish aerial.** **6.** *Informal.* an attractive person. ~*vb.* **7.** to make concave. **8.** *Brit. informal.* to ruin or spoil. ~See also **dish out, dish up.**

dishabille (ˌdɪsæˈbiːl) *or* **deshabille** *n.* the state of being partly dressed.

dish aerial *n. Brit.* a microwave aerial, used esp. in radar, radio telescopes, and satellite broadcasting, consisting of a concave dish-shaped reflector.

disharmony (dɪsˈhɑːmənɪ) *n.* lack of agreement or harmony. —**disharmonious** (ˌdɪshɑːˈməʊnɪəs) *adj.*

dishcloth (ˈdɪʃˌklɒθ) *n.* a cloth for washing dishes.

dishearten (dɪsˈhɑːtᵊn) *vb.* to weaken or destroy the hope, courage, or enthusiasm of. —**disˈheartened** *adj.* —**disˈheartening** *adj.*

dishevelled *or U.S.* **disheveled** (dɪˈʃɛvᵊld) *adj.* (of a person's hair, clothes, or general appearance) disordered and untidy.

dishonest (dɪsˈɒnɪst) *adj.* not honest or fair. —**disˈhonestly** *adv.* —**disˈhonesty** *n.*

dishonour *or U.S.* **dishonor** (dɪsˈɒnə) *vb.* **1.** to treat with disrespect. **2.** to refuse to pay (a cheque, etc.). ~*n.* **3.** a lack of honour or respect. **4.** a state of shame or disgrace. **5.** something that causes a loss of honour. —**disˈhonourable** *adj.* —**disˈhonourably** *adv.*

dish out *vb.* **1.** *Informal.* to distribute. **2. dish it out.** to inflict punishment.

dish up *vb.* to serve (food).

dishwasher (ˈdɪʃˌwɒʃə) *n.* a machine for washing dishes, cutlery, etc.

dishwater (ˈdɪʃˌwɔːtə) *n.* **1.** water in which dishes have been washed. **2. like dishwater.** (of tea) very weak.

dishy (ˈdɪʃɪ) *adj.* **dishier, dishiest.** *Informal, chiefly Brit.* good-looking.

disillusion (ˌdɪsɪˈluːʒən) *vb.* **1.** to destroy the illusions or false ideas of (someone). ~*n. also* **disillusionment.** **2.** the state of being disillusioned.

disincentive (ˌdɪsɪnˈsɛntɪv) *n.* something that acts as a deterrent.

disinclined (,dɪsɪn'klaɪnd) *adj.* unwilling.
—**disinclination** (,dɪsɪnklɪ'neɪʃən) *n.*

disinfect (,dɪsɪn'fɛkt) *vb.* to rid of harmful
germs, esp. by chemical means. —,**disin-
'fection** *n.*

disinfectant (,dɪsɪn'fɛktənt) *n.* a substance
that destroys harmful germs.

disinformation (,dɪsɪnfə'meɪʃən) *n.* false
information intended to mislead.

disingenuous (,dɪsɪn'dʒɛnjuəs) *adj.* not
sincere. —,**disin'genuously** *adv.*

disinherit (,dɪsɪn'hɛrɪt) *vb. Law.* to deprive
(an heir) of inheritance. —,**disin'heri-
tance** *n.*

disintegrate (dɪs'ɪntɪ,greɪt) *vb.* **1.** to
break into fragments; shatter. **2.** to lose
cohesion; break up: *the marriage disinte-
grated.* **3.** *Physics.* **a.** to undergo nuclear
fission or include nuclear fission in. **b.**
same as **decay** (sense 3). —**dis,inte'gration** *n.*

disinter (,dɪsɪn'tɜː) *vb.* -**terring, -terred. 1.**
to dig up. **2.** to bring to light; expose.

disinterested (dɪs'ɪntrɪstɪd) *adj.* **1.** free
from bias; objective. **2.** *Not universally
accepted.* feeling or showing a lack of interest; uninterested. —**dis'interest** *n.*
Usage. In spoken and sometimes written
English, *disinterested* (impartial) is used
where *uninterested* (showing or feeling lack
of interest) is meant. The difference in
meaning between the two words is helpful
in avoiding confusion, and should be preserved: *a disinterested judge; she was uninterested in public reaction.*

disjointed (dɪs'dʒɔɪntɪd) *adj.* having no coherence; disconnected.

disjunctive (dɪs'dʒʌŋktɪv) *adj.* serving to
disconnect or separate.

disk (dɪsk) *n.* **1.** *Chiefly U.S. & Canad.*
same as **disc. 2.** *Computers.* a storage device, consisting of a stack of plates coated
with a magnetic layer, which rotates rapidly as a single unit.

disk drive *n. Computers.* the unit that controls the mechanism for handling a floppy
disk.

dislike (dɪs'laɪk) *vb.* **1.** to consider unpleasant or disagreeable. ~*n.* **2.** a feeling
of aversion.

dislocate ('dɪslə,keɪt) *vb.* **1.** to displace (a
bone or joint) from its normal position. **2.**
to disrupt or shift out of place. —,**dis-
lo'cation** *n.*

dislodge (dɪs'lɒdʒ) *vb.* to remove (something) from a previously fixed position.

disloyal (dɪs'lɔɪəl) *adj.* not loyal; deserting
one's allegiance. —**dis'loyalty** *n.*

dismal ('dɪzməl) *adj.* **1.** causing gloom or
depression. **2.** *Informal.* of poor quality.
—'**dismally** *adv.*

dismantle (dɪs'mæntᵊl) *vb.* **1.** to take
apart. **2.** to demolish piece by piece.

dismay (dɪs'meɪ) *vb.* **1.** to fill with alarm

or depression. ~*n.* **2.** consternation or
agitation.

dismember (dɪs'mɛmbə) *vb.* **1.** to remove
the limbs of. **2.** to cut to pieces. —**dis-
'memberment** *n.*

dismiss (dɪs'mɪs) *vb.* **1.** to discharge from
employment. **2.** to allow (someone) to
leave. **3.** to put out of one's mind; no longer
think about. **4.** to decline further hearing
to (a claim or lawsuit). **5.** *Cricket.* to bowl
out (a side) for a particular number of runs.
—**dis'missal** *n.* —**dis'missive** *adj.*

dismount (dɪs'maʊnt) *vb.* **1.** to get off a
horse or bicycle. **2.** to take apart.

disobedient (,dɪsə'biːdɪənt) *adj.* refusing to
obey. —,**diso'bedience** *n.*

disobey (,dɪsə'beɪ) *vb.* to neglect or refuse
to obey (someone, an order, etc.).

disobliging (,dɪsə'blaɪdʒɪŋ) *adj.* unwilling
to help; unaccommodating.

disorder (dɪs'ɔːdə) *n.* **1.** a state of untidiness and disorganization. **2.** public violence or rioting. **3.** an illness. —**dis'ordered** *adj.*

disorderly (dɪs'ɔːdəlɪ) *adj.* **1.** untidy and
disorganized. **2.** uncontrolled; unruly. **3.**
Law. violating public peace.

disorganize *or* -**ise** (dɪs'ɔːgə,naɪz) *vb.* to
disrupt the arrangement or system of.
—**dis,organi'zation** *or* -**i'sation** *n.*

disorientate (dɪs'ɔːrɪɛn,teɪt) *or* **disorient**
vb. to cause (someone) to lose his bearings.
—**dis,orien'tation** *n.*

disown (dɪs'əʊn) *vb.* to deny any connection with (someone).

disparage (dɪ'spærɪdʒ) *vb.* **1.** to speak
contemptuously of. **2.** to damage the reputation of. —**dis'paragement** *n.* —**dis'par-
aging** *adj.*

disparate ('dɪspərɪt) *adj.* utterly different
in kind. —**disparity** (dɪ'spærɪtɪ) *n.*

dispassionate (dɪs'pæʃənɪt) *adj.* uninflu-
enced by emotion; objective. —**dis'passionately** *adv.*

dispatch *or* **despatch** (dɪ'spætʃ) *vb.* **1.** to
send off to a destination or to perform a
task. **2.** to carry out (a duty or task)
promptly. **3.** to murder. ~*n.* **4.** an official
communication or report, sent in haste. **5.**
a report sent to a newspaper by a correspondent. **6.** murder. **7. with dispatch.**
quickly.

dispatch rider *n.* a motorcyclist or (formerly) horseman who carries dispatches.

dispel (dɪ'spɛl) *vb.* -**pelling, -pelled.** to disperse or drive away.

dispensable (dɪ'spɛnsəbᵊl) *adj.* not essential; expendable.

dispensary (dɪ'spɛnsərɪ) *n., pl.* -**ries.** a
place where medicine is dispensed.

dispensation (,dɪspɛn'seɪʃən) *n.* **1.** the act
of distributing or dispensing. **2.** *Chiefly
R.C. Church.* permission to dispense with an
obligation of church law. **3.** any exemption

from an obligation. **4.** an administrative system. **5.** the ordering of life and events by God.

dispense (dɪˈspɛns) vb. **1.** to distribute in portions. **2.** to prepare and distribute (medicine), esp. on prescription. **3.** to administer (the law, etc.). **4. dispense with.** to do away with or manage without. —**disˈpenser** n.

disperse (dɪˈspɜːs) vb. **1.** to scatter over a wide area. **2.** to leave or cause to leave a gathering. **3.** to separate (light) into its different wavelengths. **4.** to spread (news, etc.). **5.** to separate (particles) throughout a solid, liquid, or gas. —**disˈpersal** or **disˈpersion** n.

dispirit (dɪˈspɪrɪt) vb. to make downhearted. —**disˈpirited** adj. —**disˈpiriting** adj.

displace (dɪsˈpleɪs) vb. **1.** to move from the usual location. **2.** to remove from office.

displaced person n. a person forced from his home or country, esp. by war or revolution.

displacement (dɪsˈpleɪsmənt) n. **1.** the act of displacing. **2.** the weight or volume displaced by a body in a fluid.

display (dɪˈspleɪ) vb. **1.** to show or exhibit. **2.** to disclose; reveal. ~n. **3.** the act of exhibiting or displaying. **4.** something exhibited or displayed. **5.** an exhibition. **6.** *Electronics.* a device capable of representing information visually, as on a screen. **7.** *Zool.* a pattern of behaviour by which an animal attracts attention while courting, defending its territory, etc.

displease (dɪsˈpliːz) vb. to annoy or offend (someone). —**displeasure** (dɪsˈplɛʒə) n.

disport (dɪˈspɔːt) vb. **disport oneself.** to indulge oneself in pleasure.

disposable (dɪˈspəʊzəbᵊl) adj. **1.** designed for disposal after use: *disposable cups.* **2.** available for use if needed: *disposable assets.*

disposal (dɪˈspəʊzᵊl) n. **1.** the act or means of getting rid of something. **2. at one's disposal.** available for use.

dispose (dɪˈspəʊz) vb. **1.** (foll. by *of*) **a.** to deal with or settle. **b.** to give, sell, or transfer to another. **c.** to throw away. **d.** to kill. **2.** to make willing or receptive. **3.** to place in a certain order.

disposition (ˌdɪspəˈzɪʃən) n. **1.** a person's usual temperament. **2.** a tendency or habit. **3.** arrangement; layout.

dispossess (ˌdɪspəˈzɛs) vb. to take away (something, esp. property) from. —**ˌdispos'sessed** adj. —**ˌdispos'session** n.

disproportion (ˌdɪsprəˈpɔːʃən) n. lack of proportion or equality.

disproportionate (ˌdɪsprəˈpɔːʃənɪt) adj. out of proportion; unequal. —**ˌdispro'portionately** adv.

disprove (dɪsˈpruːv) vb. to show (an assertion or claim) to be incorrect.

dispute vb. (dɪˈspjuːt). **1.** to argue or quarrel about (something). **2.** to doubt the validity of. **3.** to fight over possession of. ~n. (dɪˈspjuːt, ˈdɪspjuːt). **4.** an argument. —**ˌdispu'tation** n. —**ˌdispu'tatious** adj.

disqualify (dɪsˈkwɒlɪˌfaɪ) vb. **-fying, -fied.** **1.** to debar from a contest. **2.** to make ineligible, as for entry to an examination. —**dis,qualifi'cation** n.

disquiet (dɪsˈkwaɪət) n. **1.** a feeling of anxiety or uneasiness. ~vb. **2.** to make (someone) anxious. —**disˈquieting** adj. —**disˈquietude** n.

disregard (ˌdɪsrɪˈɡɑːd) vb. **1.** to give little or no attention to; ignore. ~n. **2.** lack of attention or respect.

disrepair (ˌdɪsrɪˈpɛə) n. the condition of being worn out or in poor working order.

disreputable (dɪsˈrɛpjʊtəbᵊl) adj. having or causing a bad reputation. —**disˈreputably** adv.

disrepute (ˌdɪsrɪˈpjuːt) n. a loss or lack of good reputation.

disrespect (ˌdɪsrɪˈspɛkt) n. contempt; lack of respect. —**disre'spectful** adj.

disrobe (dɪsˈrəʊb) vb. to undress.

disrupt (dɪsˈrʌpt) vb. to interrupt the progress of. —**disˈruption** n. —**disˈruptive** adj.

dissatisfy (dɪsˈsætɪsˌfaɪ) vb. **-fying, -fied.** to fail to satisfy; disappoint. —**ˌdissatis'faction** n.

dissect (dɪˈsɛkt, daɪ-) vb. **1.** to cut open and examine (a dead body). **2.** to examine critically and minutely. —**disˈsection** n.

dissemble (dɪˈsɛmbᵊl) vb. to conceal one's real motives or emotions by pretence. —**disˈsembler** n.

disseminate (dɪˈsɛmɪˌneɪt) vb. to scatter about. —**disˌsemi'nation** n.

dissension (dɪˈsɛnʃən) n. disagreement, esp. when leading to a quarrel.

dissent (dɪˈsɛnt) vb. **1.** to disagree. **2.** *Christianity.* to reject the doctrines of an established church. ~n. **3.** a difference of opinion. **4.** *Christianity.* separation from an established church. —**disˈsenter** n. —**disˈsenting** adj.

Dissenter (dɪˈsɛntə) n. *Christianity, chiefly Brit.* a Protestant who refuses to conform to the established church.

dissentient (dɪˈsɛnʃənt) adj. dissenting from the opinion of the majority.

dissertation (ˌdɪsəˈteɪʃən) n. **1.** a written thesis, usually required for a higher degree. **2.** a long formal speech.

disservice (dɪsˈsɜːvɪs) n. an ill turn; wrong.

dissident (ˈdɪsɪdənt) adj. **1.** disagreeing; dissenting. ~n. **2.** a person who disagrees, esp. with the government. —**ˈdissidence** n.

dissimilar (dɪˈsɪmɪlə) *adj.* not alike; different. —ˌdissimiˈlarity *n.*

dissimulate (dɪˈsɪmjʊˌleɪt) *vb.* to conceal one's real feelings by pretence. —disˌsimuˈlation *n.*

dissipate (ˈdɪsɪˌpeɪt) *vb.* 1. to waste or squander. 2. to scatter or break up.

dissipated (ˈdɪsɪˌpeɪtɪd) *adj.* indulging without restraint in the pursuit of pleasure; debauched.

dissipation (ˌdɪsɪˈpeɪʃən) *n.* 1. the process of dissipating. 2. unrestrained indulgence in physical pleasures.

dissociate (dɪˈsəʊʃɪˌeɪt, -sɪ-) *vb.* 1. to break the association between (people, organizations, etc.). 2. to regard or treat as separate. —disˌsociˈation *n.*

dissoluble (dɪˈsɒljʊbˀl) *adj.* same as **soluble.** —disˌsoluˈbility *n.*

dissolute (ˈdɪsəˌluːt) *adj.* given to dissipation; debauched.

dissolution (ˌdɪsəˈluːʃən) *n.* 1. destruction by breaking up and dispersing. 2. the termination of a meeting or assembly, such as Parliament. 3. the termination of a formal or legal relationship, such as a business or marriage.

dissolve (dɪˈzɒlv) *vb.* 1. to become or cause to become liquid; melt. 2. to bring to an end. 3. to dismiss (a meeting, Parliament, etc.). 4. to collapse emotionally: *to dissolve into tears.* 5. to lose or cause to lose distinctness. 6. *Films, television.* to fade out one scene and replace with another to make two scenes merge imperceptibly.

dissonance (ˈdɪsənəns) *n.* 1. a discordant combination of sounds. 2. lack of agreement or consistency. —ˈdissonant *adj.*

dissuade (dɪˈsweɪd) *vb.* to deter (someone) by persuasion from a course of action, policy, etc. —disˈsuasion *n.*

dissyllable (dɪˈsɪləbˀl) *or* **disyllable** *n.* a word of two syllables. —**dissyllabic** (ˌdɪsɪˈlæbɪk) *or* **disyllabic** (ˌdaɪsɪˈlæbɪk) *adj.*

distaff (ˈdɪstɑːf) *n.* the rod on which wool, flax, etc., is wound for spinning.

distaff side *n.* the female side of a family.

distance (ˈdɪstəns) *n.* 1. the space between two points. 2. the state of being apart. 3. a distant place. 4. remoteness in manner. 5. **the distance.** the most distant part of the visible scene. 6. **go the distance.** *Boxing.* to complete a bout without being knocked out. 7. **keep one's distance.** to maintain a reserved attitude to another person. ~*vb.* 8. **distance oneself** *or* **be distanced from.** to separate oneself or be separated mentally from. 9. to outstrip.

distant (ˈdɪstənt) *adj.* 1. far apart. 2. separated by a specified distance: *five miles distant.* 3. apart in relationship: *a distant cousin.* 4. going to a faraway place. 5.

remote in manner; aloof. 6. abstracted: *a distant look.* —ˈdistantly *adv.*

distaste (dɪsˈteɪst) *n.* a dislike; aversion.

distasteful (dɪsˈteɪstful) *adj.* unpleasant or offensive. —disˈtastefulness *n.*

distemper[1] (dɪsˈtempə) *n.* a highly contagious viral disease of animals, esp. dogs.

distemper[2] (dɪsˈtempə) *n.* 1. paint mixed with water, glue, size, etc.: used for poster, mural, and scene painting. ~*vb.* 2. to paint (something) with distemper.

distend (dɪsˈtɛnd) *vb.* to expand by pressure from within; swell; inflate. —disˈtensible *adj.* —disˈtension *n.*

distich (ˈdɪstɪk) *n. Prosody.* a unit of two verse lines.

distil *or U.S.* **distill** (dɪsˈtɪl) *vb.* **-tilling, -tilled.** 1. to subject to or obtain by distillation. 2. to give off (a substance) in drops. 3. to extract the essence of.

distillate (ˈdɪstɪlɪt) *n.* a concentrated essence.

distillation (ˌdɪstɪˈleɪʃən) *n.* 1. the process of evaporating a liquid and condensing its vapour. 2. purification or separation of mixtures by using different evaporation rates or boiling points of their components. 3. a concentrated essence.

distiller (dɪsˈtɪlə) *n.* a person or company that makes spirits.

distillery (dɪsˈtɪlərɪ) *n., pl.* **-eries.** a place where alcoholic drinks are made by distillation.

distinct (dɪsˈtɪŋkt) *adj.* 1. easily sensed or understood; clear. 2. not the same; different. 3. sharp; clear. 4. recognizable; unequivocal. —disˈtinctly *adv.*

distinction (dɪsˈtɪŋkʃən) *n.* 1. the act of distinguishing or differentiating. 2. a distinguishing feature. 3. the state of being different or distinguishable. 4. special honour, recognition, or fame. 5. excellence of character. 6. a symbol of honour or rank.

distinctive (dɪsˈtɪŋktɪv) *adj.* easily recognizable; characteristic. —disˈtinctively *adv.* —disˈtinctiveness *n.*

distingué (dɪsˈtæŋɡeɪ) *adj.* distinguished or noble.

distinguish (dɪsˈtɪŋɡwɪʃ) *vb.* 1. (foll. by *between* or *among*) to make, show, or recognize a difference (between or among); differentiate (between). 2. to be a distinctive feature of; characterize. 3. to make out; perceive. 4. **distinguish oneself.** to make oneself noteworthy. —disˈtinguishable *adj.* —disˈtinguishing *adj.*

distinguished (dɪsˈtɪŋɡwɪʃt) *adj.* 1. noble or dignified in appearance. 2. famous.

distort (dɪsˈtɔːt) *vb.* 1. to twist out of shape; deform. 2. to alter or misrepresent (facts). 3. *Electronics.* to reproduce or amplify (a signal) inaccurately. —disˈtorted *adj.* —disˈtortion *n.*

distract (dɪ'strækt) vb. **1.** to draw the attention of (a person) away from something. **2.** to confuse or trouble (a person). **3.** to amuse or entertain.

distraction (dɪ'strækʃən) n. **1.** something that diverts the attention. **2.** something that serves as an entertainment. **3.** mental turmoil.

distrain (dɪ'strein) vb. Law. to seize (personal property) as security for a debt. —**dis'traint** n.

distrait (dɪ'strei) adj. absent-minded; abstracted.

distraught (dɪ'strɔːt) adj. distracted or agitated.

distress (dɪ'stres) vb. **1.** to cause mental pain to; upset badly. ~n. **2.** mental pain; anguish. **3.** physical or financial trouble. **4.** in distress. in dire need of help. —**dis'tressing** adj. —**dis'tressingly** adv.

distressed (dɪ'strest) adj. **1.** much troubled; upset. **2.** in financial difficulties; poor. **3.** (of furniture or fabric) having signs of ageing artificially applied.

distributary (dɪ'strɪbjʊtrɪ) n., pl. -taries. one of several outlet streams draining a river, esp. on a delta.

distribute (dɪ'strɪbjuːt) vb. **1.** to give out in shares; dispense. **2.** to hand out or deliver.

distribution (ˌdɪstrɪ'bjuːʃən) n. **1.** the act of distributing. **2.** arrangement or location. **3.** the process of satisfying the demand for goods and services.

distributive (dɪ'strɪbjʊtɪv) adj. **1.** characterized by or relating to distribution. **2.** Maths. of a rule that the same result is produced when multiplication is performed on a set of numbers as when performed on the members of the set individually.

distributor (dɪ'strɪbjʊtə) n. **1.** a wholesaler engaged in the distribution of goods to retailers in a specific area. **2.** the device in a petrol engine that distributes the electric current to the sparking plugs.

district ('dɪstrɪkt) n. **1.** an area of land regarded as an administrative or geographical unit. **2.** any region or area: country districts; a shopping district.

district high school n. (in New Zealand) a school in a rural area providing both primary and secondary education.

district nurse n. (in Britain) a nurse appointed to attend patients in their homes within a particular district.

distrust (dɪs'trʌst) vb. **1.** to regard as untrustworthy. ~n. **2.** suspicion; doubt. —**dis'trustful** adj.

disturb (dɪ'stɜːb) vb. **1.** to intrude on; interrupt. **2.** to disarrange. **3.** to upset; trouble. **4.** to inconvenience. —**dis'turbing** adj. —**dis'turbingly** adv.

disturbance (dɪ'stɜːbəns) n. **1.** an interruption or intrusion. **2.** an unruly outburst or tumult.

disturbed (dɪ'stɜːbd) adj. Psychiatry. emotionally upset, troubled, or maladjusted.

disunite (ˌdɪsjuː'naɪt) vb. to set at variance; estrange. —**dis'union** n. —**dis'unity** n.

disuse (dɪs'juːs) n. the condition of being unused; neglect.

disyllable ('daɪˌsɪləb°l) n. same as **dissyllable**.

ditch (dɪtʃ) n. **1.** a narrow channel dug in the earth for drainage or irrigation. ~vb. **2.** Slang. to abandon.

dither ('dɪðə) vb. **1.** Chiefly Brit. to be uncertain or indecisive. **2.** Chiefly U.S. to be agitated. ~n. **3.** Chiefly Brit. a state of indecision or agitation. —**'ditherer** n. —**'dithery** adj.

dithyramb ('dɪθɪˌræm, -ˌræmb) n. **1.** (in ancient Greece) a passionate choral hymn in honour of Dionysus. **2.** any utterance or a piece of writing that resembles this. —ˌdithy'rambic adj.

ditto ('dɪtəʊ) n., pl. -tos. **1.** the aforementioned; the above; the same. Used in lists, etc., to avoid repetition, and symbolized by two small marks (ˌ) placed under the thing repeated. ~adv. **2.** in the same way.

ditty ('dɪtɪ) n., pl. -ties. a short simple song or poem.

diuretic (ˌdaɪjʊ'retɪk) n. a drug that increases the flow of urine.

diurnal (daɪ'ɜːn°l) adj. **1.** happening during the day or daily. **2.** (of animals) active during the day.

diva ('diːvə) n., pl. -vas or -ve (-vɪ). a distinguished female singer; prima donna.

divalent (daɪ'veilənt, 'daɪˌveɪ-) adj. Chem. **1.** having a valency of two. **2.** having two valencies. —**di'valency** n.

divan (dɪ'væn) n. **a.** a backless sofa or couch. **b.** a bed resembling such a couch.

dive (daɪv) vb. diving, dived or U.S. dove (dəʊv), dived. **1.** to plunge headfirst into water. **2.** (of a submarine or diver) to submerge under water. **3.** to fly in a steep nose-down descending path. **4.** to rush or reach for quickly: he dived for the ball. **5.** (foll. by in or into) **a.** to put (one's hand) quickly or forcefully (into). **b.** to start doing (something) enthusiastically. ~n. **6.** a headlong plunge into water. **7.** the act of diving. **8.** a steep nose-down descent of an aircraft or a bird. **9.** Slang. a disreputable bar or club.

dive bomber n. a military aircraft designed to release bombs on a target during a dive. —**'dive-bomb** vb.

diver ('daɪvə) n. **1.** a person who works or explores underwater. **2.** a person who dives for sport.

diverge (daɪ'vɜːdʒ) vb. **1.** to separate and go in different directions. **2.** to be at variance; differ. **3.** to deviate (from a pre-

scribed course). —**di'vergence** n. —**di-
'vergent** adj.

divers ('daɪvəz) det. Archaic or literary.
various; sundry.

diverse (daɪ'vɜːs, 'daɪvɜːs) adj. 1. having
variety; assorted. 2. distinct in kind.

diversify (daɪ'vɜːsɪˌfaɪ) vb. -**fying, -fied.** 1.
to create different forms of; vary. 2. (of an
enterprise) to vary (products or operations)
in order to spread risk or expand.
—**di,versifi'cation** n.

diversion (daɪ'vɜːʃən) n. 1. the act of diverting from a specified course. 2. Chiefly
Brit. an official detour used by traffic when
a main route is closed. 3. something that
distracts from business, etc.; amusement.
—**di'versionary** adj.

diversity (daɪ'vɜːsɪtɪ) n. 1. the quality of
being different or varied. 2. a point of
difference.

divert (daɪ'vɜːt) vb. 1. to deflect. 2. to
entertain; amuse. 3. to distract the attention of.

diverticulitis (ˌdaɪvəˌtɪkjʊ'laɪtɪs) n. an illness causing abdominal pain, resulting from
inflammation within pouches that have
formed in the wall of the colon.

divertimento (dɪˌvɜːtɪ'mɛntəʊ) n., pl. -**ti**
(-tɪ). a piece of entertaining music.

divertissement (dɪ'vɜːtɪsmənt) n. a brief
entertainment or diversion.

divest (daɪ'vɛst) vb. 1. to strip (of
clothes). 2. to deprive or dispossess.

divide (dɪ'vaɪd) vb. 1. to separate into
parts. 2. to share or be shared out in parts.
3. to disagree or cause to disagree: the
whole village was divided over the issue.
4. to keep apart or be a boundary between.
5. to categorize; classify. 6. to calculate
how many times one number can be contained in another. ~n. 7. Chiefly U.S. &
Canad. an area of high ground separating
drainage basins. 8. a division; split.

dividend ('dɪvɪˌdɛnd) n. 1. a sum of money
representing part of the profit made, paid
by a company to its shareholders. 2. something extra; a bonus. 3. a number to be
divided by another number.

divider (dɪ'vaɪdə) n. a screen placed so as to
divide a room into separate areas.

dividers (dɪ'vaɪdəz) pl. n. compasses with
two pointed arms, used for measuring lines
or dividing them.

divination (ˌdɪvɪ'neɪʃən) n. the art or practice of discovering future events or unknown things, as though by supernatural
powers.

divine (dɪ'vaɪn) adj. 1. of God or a god. 2.
godlike. 3. Informal. splendid; perfect.
~n. 4. a priest who is learned in theology.
~vb. 5. to discover (something) by intuition or guessing. —**di'vinely** adv. —**di-
'viner** n.

diving bell n. a diving apparatus with an
open bottom, supplied with compressed air.

diving board n. a platform from which
swimmers may dive.

diving suit n. a waterproof suit used by
divers, having a helmet and an air supply.

divining rod n. a forked twig said to
move when held over ground in which water or metal is to be found.

divinity (dɪ'vɪnɪtɪ) n., pl. -**ties.** 1. the state
of being divine. 2. a god. 3. theology.

divisible (dɪ'vɪzɪbəl) adj. capable of being
divided. —**di,visi'bility** n.

division (dɪ'vɪʒən) n. 1. the act of dividing
or sharing out. 2. one of the parts into
which something is divided. 3. a part of an
organization that has been made into a unit
for administrative or other reasons. 4. a
formal vote in Parliament. 5. a difference
of opinion. 6. the mathematical operation
of dividing. 7. Army. a major formation
containing the necessary arms to sustain
independent combat. —**di'visional** adj.

division sign n. the symbol ÷, placed
between the dividend and the divisor to
indicate division, as in $10 \div 6 = 2$.

divisive (dɪ'vaɪsɪv) adj. tending to cause
disagreement or dissension.

divisor (dɪ'vaɪzə) n. a number to be divided
into another number.

divorce (dɪ'vɔːs) n. 1. the legal ending of a
marriage. 2. a separation, esp. one that is
total. ~vb. 3. to separate or be separated
by divorce. 4. to remove or separate.

divorcée (dɪvɔː'siː) or (masc.) **divorcé** (dɪ-
'vɔːseɪ) n. a person who is divorced.

divulge (daɪ'vʌldʒ) vb. to make known; disclose. —**di'vulgence** n.

divvy ('dɪvɪ) Informal. ~n., pl. -**vies.** 1.
Brit. a dividend. ~vb. -**vying, -vied.** 2.
(foll. by up) to divide and share.

dixie ('dɪksɪ) n. Chiefly mil. a large metal
pot for cooking.

Dixie ('dɪksɪ) n. the southern states of the
U.S. Also called: **Dixieland.**

DIY or **d.i.y.** (in Britain) do-it-yourself.

dizzy ('dɪzɪ) adj. -**zier, -ziest.** 1. feeling
giddy. 2. mentally confused. 3. tending to
cause giddiness or bewilderment. ~vb.
-**zying, -zied.** 4. to make dizzy. —**'dizzily**
adv. —**'dizziness** n.

DJ or **dj** 1. disc jockey. 2. dinner jacket.

djinni or **djinny** (dʒɪ'niː, 'dʒɪnɪ) n., pl. **djinn**
(dʒɪn). same as **jinni.**

dl decilitre.

DLitt or **DLit** 1. Doctor of Letters. 2.
Doctor of Literature.

dm decimetre.

DM Deutsche Mark.

DMus Doctor of Music.

DNA deoxyribonucleic acid, the main constituent of the chromosomes of all organisms.

D-notice *n. Brit.* an official notice sent to newspapers prohibiting the publication of certain security information.

do[1] (duː; *unstressed* dʊ, də) *vb.* **does, doing, did, done.** **1.** to perform or complete (a deed or action): *to do a portrait.* **2.** to be suitable; suffice. **3.** to provide; serve: *this restaurant doesn't do lunch on Sundays.* **4.** to make tidy, elegant, or ready: *to do one's hair.* **5.** to improve: *that hat does nothing for you.* **6.** to find an answer to (a problem or puzzle). **7.** to conduct oneself: *do as you please.* **8.** to cause or produce: *complaints do nothing to help.* **9.** to give or render: *do me a favour.* **10.** to work at, esp. as a course of study or a job. **11.** to perform (a play, etc.); act. **12.** to mimic. **13.** to travel at a specified speed, esp. as a maximum. **14.** to travel (a distance). **15.** used: **a.** to form questions: *do you agree?* **b.** to intensify positive statements and commands: *I do like your new house; do hurry!* **c.** to form negative statements or commands: *do not leave me here alone!* **d.** to replace an earlier verb: *he likes you as much as I do.* **16.** *Informal.* to visit (a place) as a tourist. **17.** *Slang.* to serve (a period of time) as a prison sentence. **18.** *Informal.* to cheat or rob. **19.** *Slang.* **a.** to arrest. **b.** to convict of a crime. **20.** *Slang, chiefly Brit.* to assault. **21.** *Slang.* to take or use (drugs). **22. make do.** to manage with whatever is available. ~*n., pl.* **dos** *or* **do's.** **23.** *Informal, chiefly Brit. & N.Z.* a festive gathering; party. **24. do's and don'ts.** *Informal.* rules. ~See also **do away with, do by,** etc.

do[2] (dəʊ) *n., pl.* **dos.** same as **doh.**

doable ('duːəb'l) *adj.* capable of being done.

do away with *vb.* **1.** to kill or destroy. **2.** to abolish.

Doberman pinscher ('dəʊbəmən 'pɪnʃə) *or* **Doberman** *n.* a large dog with a glossy black-and-tan coat.

do by *vb.* to treat in the manner specified: *he felt badly done by.*

doc (dɒk) *n. Informal.* same as **doctor.**

docile ('dəʊsaɪl) *adj.* easy to manage; submissive. —'**docilely** *adv.* —**docility** (dəʊ-'sɪlɪtɪ) *n.*

dock[1] (dɒk) *n.* **1.** an enclosed area of water where ships are loaded, unloaded, or repaired. **2.** a wharf or pier. ~*vb.* **3.** to moor or be moored at a dock. **4.** to link (two spacecraft) together in space or (of two spacecraft) to link together in space.

dock[2] (dɒk) *vb.* **1.** to remove part of (an animal's tail) by cutting through the bone. **2.** to deduct (an amount) from (a person's wages).

dock[3] (dɒk) *n.* an enclosed space in a court of law where the accused person sits or stands.

dock[4] (dɒk) *n.* a weed with broad leaves.

docker ('dɒkə) *n. Brit.* a man employed in the loading or unloading of ships.

docket ('dɒkɪt) *n.* **1.** *Chiefly Brit.* a piece of paper accompanying a package or other delivery, stating contents, delivery instructions, etc. ~*vb.* **2.** to fix a docket to (a package, etc.).

dockyard ('dɒk,jɑːd) *n.* a place with docks and equipment where ships are built or repaired.

doctor ('dɒktə) *n.* **1.** a person licensed to practise medicine. **2.** a person who has been awarded a higher academic degree in any field of knowledge. **3.** *Chiefly U.S. & Canad.* a person licensed to practise dentistry or veterinary medicine. ~*vb.* **4.** *Informal.* to practise medicine. **5.** to make different in order to deceive. **6.** to poison or drug (food or drink). **7.** *Informal.* to castrate (a cat, dog, etc.). —'**doctoral** *adj.*

doctorate ('dɒktrɪt) *n.* the highest academic degree in any field of knowledge.

doctrinaire (,dɒktrɪ'nɛə) *adj.* stubbornly insistent on the observation of the niceties of a theory without regard to practicality.

doctrine ('dɒktrɪn) *n.* **1.** a body of teachings of a religious, political, or philosophical group. **2.** a principle or body of principles that is taught or advocated. —**doctrinal** (dɒk'traɪn'l) *adj.*

docudrama ('dɒkju,drɑːmə) *n.* a film or television programme based on true events, presented in a dramatized form.

document *n.* ('dɒkjumənt). **1.** a piece of paper, booklet, etc., providing information, esp. of an official nature. ~*vb.* ('dɒkju-,mɛnt). **2.** to record or report (something) in detail, as in the press or on television. **3.** to support (a claim) with evidence.

documentary (,dɒkju'mɛntrɪ) *n., pl.* -**ries.** **1.** a film or television programme presenting the facts about a particular subject. **2.** of or based on documents: *documentary evidence.*

documentation (,dɒkjumɛn'teɪʃən) *n.* **1.** the act of supplying with documents or references. **2.** the documents or references supplied.

dodder ('dɒdə) *vb.* to move unsteadily; totter. —'**dodderer** *n.* —'**doddery** *adj.*

doddle ('dɒd'l) *n. Brit. informal.* something easily accomplished.

dodecagon (dəʊ'dɛkə,gɒn) *n.* a polygon with twelve sides.

dodecahedron (,dəʊdɛkə'hiːdrən) *n.* a solid figure with twelve plane faces.

dodge (dɒdʒ) *vb.* **1.** to avoid (a blow, discovery, etc.) by moving suddenly. **2.** to evade by cleverness or trickery. ~*n.* **3.** a plan contrived to deceive. **4.** a sudden evasive movement.

Dodgem ('dɒdʒəm) *n. Trademark.* an electrically propelled vehicle driven and bumped against similar cars in a rink at a funfair.

dodger ('dɒdʒə) n. a person who evades or shirks something.

dodgy ('dɒdʒɪ) adj. **dodgier, dodgiest.** Brit., Austral., & N.Z. informal. **1.** difficult or dangerous. **2.** unreliable; tricky.

dodo ('dəʊdəʊ) n., pl. **dodos** or **dodoes. 1.** a large flightless extinct bird. **2. as dead as a dodo.** irretrievably defunct or out of date.

do down vb. to belittle or humiliate: don't do yourself down.

doe (dəʊ) n., pl. **does** or **doe.** the female of the deer, hare, or rabbit.

DOE (in Britain) Department of the Environment.

doek (dʊk) n. S. African informal. a square of cloth worn on the head.

doer ('duːə) n. an active or energetic person.

does (dʌz) vb. third person singular of the present tense of **do**[1].

doff (dɒf) vb. to take off or lift (one's hat) in salutation.

do for vb. Informal. **1.** to cause the ruin, death, or defeat of. **2.** to do housework for. **3. do well for oneself.** to thrive or succeed.

dog (dɒg) n. **1.** a domesticated canine mammal occurring in many different breeds. **2.** any other member of the dog family, such as the dingo or coyote. **3.** the male of animals of the dog family. **4.** a mechanical device for gripping. **5.** Informal. a fellow; chap: you lucky dog! **6.** U.S. & Canad. informal. something unsatisfactory or inferior. **7. a dog's life.** a wretched existence. **8. dog eat dog.** ruthless competition. **9. like a dog's dinner.** dressed smartly and ostentatiously. **10. put on the dog.** U.S. & Canad. informal. to behave pretentiously. ~vb. **dogging, dogged. 11.** to follow (someone) closely. **12.** to trouble; plague. ~See also **dogs.**

dog biscuit n. a hard biscuit for dogs.

dog box n. N.Z. informal. same as **doghouse** (sense 2).

dogcart ('dɒg,kɑːt) n. a light horse-drawn two-wheeled vehicle.

dog collar n. **1.** a collar for a dog. **2.** Informal. a clerical collar.

dog days pl. n. the hottest period of the summer.

doge (dəʊdʒ) n. (formerly) the chief magistrate of Venice or Genoa.

dog-eared adj. **1.** (of a book) having pages folded down at the corner. **2.** shabby or worn.

dog-end n. Informal. a cigarette end.

dogfight ('dɒg,faɪt) n. **1.** close-quarters combat between fighter aircraft. **2.** any rough fight.

dogfish ('dɒg,fɪʃ) n., pl. **-fish** or **-fishes.** a small shark.

dogged ('dɒgɪd) adj. obstinately determined; tenacious. —**'doggedly** adv. —**'doggedness** n.

doggerel ('dɒgərəl) n. poorly written, usually comic, verse.

doggo ('dɒgəʊ) adv. **lie doggo.** Brit. informal. to hide and keep quiet.

doggy or **doggie** ('dɒgɪ) n., pl. **-gies. 1.** a child's word for a **dog.** ~adj. **-gier, -giest. 2.** of or like a dog. **3.** fond of dogs.

doggy bag n. a bag in which leftovers from a meal may be taken away for a dog.

doghouse ('dɒg,haʊs) n. **1.** U.S. & Canad. a kennel. **2. in the doghouse.** Informal. in disfavour.

dogie, dogy, or **dogey** ('dəʊgɪ) n., pl. **-gies** or **-geys.** U.S. & Canad. a motherless calf.

dog in the manger n. a person who prevents others from using something he has no use for.

dogleg ('dɒg,lɛg) n. a sharp bend.

dogma ('dɒgmə) n. a doctrine or system of doctrines proclaimed by authority as true.

dogmatic (dɒg'mætɪk) adj. **1.** (of a statement or opinion) forcibly asserted as if unchallengeable. **2.** (of a person) prone to making such statements. —**dog'matically** adv. —**'dogma,tism** n.

do-gooder n. Informal. a well-intentioned person, esp. a naive or impractical one.

dog paddle n. a swimming stroke in which the hands are paddled in imitation of a swimming dog.

dog rose n. a wild rose with pink or white flowers.

dogs (dɒgz) pl. n. **1. go to the dogs.** Informal. to go to ruin physically or morally. **2. let sleeping dogs lie.** to leave things undisturbed. **3. the dogs.** Brit. informal. greyhound racing.

dogsbody ('dɒgz,bɒdɪ) n., pl. **-bodies.** Informal. a person who carries out menial tasks for others.

dog-tired adj. Informal. exhausted.

dogtooth violet ('dɒg,tuːθ) n. either of two plants, a European plant with purple flowers, or a North American plant with yellow flowers.

dogtrot ('dɒg,trɒt) n. a gently paced trot.

dogwatch ('dɒg,wɒtʃ) n. either of two watches aboard ship, from four to six p.m. or from six to eight p.m.

doh or **do** (dəʊ) n. Music. **1.** the note D. **2.** (in tonic sol-fa) the first degree of any major scale.

doily or **doyley** ('dɔɪlɪ) n., pl. **-lies** or **-leys.** a decorative mat of lace or lacelike paper, etc., laid on plates.

do in vb. Slang. **1.** to kill. **2.** to exhaust.

doings ('duːɪŋz) n. **1.** (functioning as pl.) deeds or actions. **2.** (functioning as sing.) Informal. anything of which the name is not known or is left unsaid.

do-it-yourself n. the practice of constructing and repairing things oneself, esp. as a hobby.

doldrums ('dɒldrəmz) n. **the. 1.** a depressed state of mind. **2.** a state of inactivity. **3.** a belt of sea along the equator noted for absence of winds.

dole (dəʊl) n. **1.** (usually preceded by the) Brit. informal. money received from the state while out of work. **2. on the dole.** Brit. informal. receiving such money. ~vb. **3.** (foll. by out) to distribute (something), esp. in small portions.

doleful ('dəʊlfʊl) adj. dreary; mournful. —'**dolefully** adv. —'**dolefulness** n.

doll (dɒl) n. **1.** a small model of a human being, used as a toy. **2.** Slang. a girl or young woman, esp. a pretty one.

dollar ('dɒlə) n. the standard monetary unit of the U.S., Canada, and various other countries.

dollop ('dɒləp) n. Informal. a semisolid lump.

doll up vb. Slang. to dress in a stylish or showy manner: all dolled up.

dolly ('dɒlɪ) n., pl. **-lies. 1.** a child's word for a **doll. 2.** Films, etc. a wheeled support on which a camera may be mounted. **3.** Also called: **dolly bird.** Slang, chiefly Brit. an attractive and fashionable girl.

dolman sleeve ('dɒlmən) n. a sleeve that is very wide at the armhole and tapers to a tight wrist.

dolmen ('dɒlmɛn) n. a prehistoric monument consisting of a horizontal stone supported by vertical stones, thought to be a tomb.

dolomite ('dɒlə,maɪt) n. a mineral consisting of calcium magnesium carbonate.

dolorous ('dɒlərəs) adj. causing or involving pain or sorrow.

dolphin ('dɒlfɪn) n. a mammal smaller than a whale and larger than a porpoise, with a beaklike snout.

dolphinarium (,dɒlfɪ'nɛərɪəm) n. an aquarium for dolphins, esp. one in which they give public displays.

dolt (dəʊlt) n. a stupid person. —'**doltish** adj.

domain (də'meɪn) n. **1.** a field of knowledge or activity **2.** land under one ruler or government.

dome (dəʊm) n. **1.** a hemispherical roof. **2.** something shaped like this.

domed (dəʊmd) adj. shaped like a dome.

Domesday Book or **Doomsday Book** ('duːmz,deɪ) n. History. the record of a survey of the land of England carried out by the commissioners of William I in 1086.

domestic (də'mɛstɪk) adj. **1.** of the home or family. **2.** enjoying home or family life. **3.** (of an animal) bred or kept as a pet or for the supply of food. **4.** of one's own country or a specific country: domestic and foreign affairs. ~n. **5.** a household servant. —**do'mestically** adv.

domesticate (də'mɛstɪ,keɪt) vb. **1.** to bring or keep (wild animals or plants) under control or cultivation. **2.** to accustom (someone) to home life. —**do,mesti'cation** n.

domesticity (,dəʊmɛ'stɪsɪtɪ) n., pl. **-ties. 1.** home life. **2.** devotion to home life.

domestic science n. the study of cooking, needlework, and other household skills.

domicile ('dɒmɪ,saɪl) n. **1.** a dwelling place. **2.** a permanent legal residence. ~vb. **3.** to establish (someone) in a dwelling place. —**domiciliary** (,dɒmɪ'sɪlɪərɪ) adj.

dominant ('dɒmɪnənt) adj. **1.** having primary authority or influence. **2.** predominant: the dominant topic of the day. **3.** Genetics. (in a pair of genes) designating the gene that produces a particular character in an organism. ~n. **4.** Music. the fifth degree of a scale. —'**dominance** n.

dominate ('dɒmɪ,neɪt) vb. **1.** to control or govern. **2.** to tower above (surroundings). **3.** to predominate in. —'**domi,nating** adj. —,**domi'nation** n.

domineering (,dɒmɪ'nɪərɪŋ) adj. arrogant; tyrannical.

Dominican[1] (də'mɪnɪkən) n. **1.** a friar or nun of an order founded by Saint Dominic. ~adj. **2.** of the Dominican order.

Dominican[2] (də'mɪnɪkən) adj. **1.** of the Dominican Republic or Dominica. ~n. **2.** a person from the Dominican Republic or Dominica.

dominion (də'mɪnjən) n. **1.** rule; authority. **2.** the land governed by one ruler or government. **3.** (formerly) a self-governing division of the British Empire.

domino[1] ('dɒmɪ,nəʊ) n., pl. **-noes.** a small rectangular block marked with dots, used in dominoes.

domino[2] ('dɒmɪ,nəʊ) n., pl. **-noes** or **-nos.** a large hooded cloak worn with an eye mask at a masquerade.

dominoes ('dɒmɪ,nəʊz) n. (functioning as sing.) a game in which dominoes with matching halves are laid together.

domkop ('dɒm,kɒp) n. S. African slang. an idiot; thickhead.

don[1] (dɒn) vb. **donning, donned.** to put on (clothing).

don[2] (dɒn) n. **1.** Brit. a member of the teaching staff at a university or college. **2.** a Spanish gentleman or nobleman.

Don (dɒn) n. a Spanish title equivalent to Mr.

Doña ('dɒnjə) n. a Spanish title equivalent to Mrs or Madam.

donate (dəʊ'neɪt) vb. to give (something), esp. to a charity.

donation (dəʊ'neɪʃən) n. **1.** the act of donating. **2.** a contribution.

donder ('dondə) S. African slang. ~vb. **1.** to beat (someone) up. ~n. **2.** a wretch; swine.

done (dʌn) vb. **1.** the past participle of **do**[1]. **2. be** or **have done with.** to end relations with. ~interj. **3.** an expression of agreement, as on the settlement of a bargain. ~adj. **4.** completed. **5.** cooked enough. **6.** used up. **7.** socially acceptable: the done thing. **8.** Informal. cheated; tricked. **9. done for.** Informal. **a.** dead or almost dead. **b.** in serious difficulty. **10. done in** or **up.** Informal. exhausted.

doner kebab ('dɒnə) n. a dish of grilled minced lamb, served in a split slice of unleavened bread.

donga ('dɒŋgə) n. S. African, Austral., & N.Z. a steep-sided gully created by soil erosion.

donjon ('dʌndʒən) n. the heavily fortified central tower of a castle.

Don Juan ('dɒn 'dʒuːən) n. a successful seducer of women.

donkey ('dɒŋkɪ) n. **1.** a long-eared member of the horse family. **2.** a person who is considered to be stupid or stubborn.

donkey jacket n. a thick hip-length jacket, usually navy blue, with a waterproof panel across the shoulders.

donkey's years pl. n. Informal. a long time.

donkey-work n. **1.** groundwork. **2.** drudgery.

Donna ('dɒnə) n. an Italian title equivalent to Madam.

donnish ('dɒnɪʃ) adj. resembling a university don; pedantic or fussy.

donor ('dəʊnə) n. **1.** a person who makes a donation. **2.** Med. a person who gives blood, organs, etc., for use in the treatment of another person.

donor card n. a card carried to show that the body parts specified may be used for transplants after the carrier's death.

Don Quixote ('dɒn 'kiː'həʊtɪ; 'kwɪksət) n. an impractical idealist.

don't (dəʊnt) do not.

doodle ('duːd³l) Informal. ~vb. **1.** to scribble or draw aimlessly. ~n. **2.** a shape or picture drawn aimlessly.

doodlebug ('duːd³l,bʌg) n. a robot bomb invented by the Germans in World War II. Also called: **V-1.**

doom (duːm) n. **1.** death or a terrible fate. ~vb. **2.** to destine or condemn to death or a terrible fate.

doomsday or **domesday** ('duːmz,deɪ) n. **1.** the day on which the Last Judgment will occur. **2.** any day of reckoning.

door (dɔː) n. **1.** a hinged or sliding panel for closing the entrance to a room, cupboard, etc. **2.** a doorway or entrance. **3.** a means of access or escape: a door to success. **4. lay at someone's door.** to lay (the blame or responsibility) on someone. **5. out of doors.** in the open air.

doorjamb ('dɔː,dʒæm) n. one of the two vertical posts forming the sides of a door frame. Also called: **doorpost.**

doorman ('dɔː,mæn, -mən) n., pl. **-men.** a man employed to be on duty at the doors of certain public buildings.

doormat ('dɔː,mæt) n. **1.** a mat, placed at an entrance, for wiping dirt from shoes. **2.** Informal. a person who offers little resistance to ill-treatment.

doorstep ('dɔː,stɛp) n. **1.** a step in front of a door. **2.** Informal. a thick slice of bread.

doorstop ('dɔː,stɒp) n. a device which prevents a door from moving or from striking a wall.

door-to-door adj. **1.** (of selling) from one house to the next. **2.** (of journeys) direct.

doorway ('dɔː,weɪ) n. an opening into a building or room.

dope (dəʊp) n. **1.** Slang. an illegal drug, usually cannabis. **2.** a drug, esp. one administered to a racehorse or greyhound to affect its performance. **3.** Informal. a slow-witted person. **4.** Informal. confidential information. **5.** a thick liquid, such as a lubricant. ~vb. **6.** to administer a drug to.

dopey or **dopy** ('dəʊpɪ) adj. **dopier, dopiest.** **1.** Informal. half-asleep, as when under the influence of a drug. **2.** Slang. silly.

doppelgänger ('dɒp³l,gɛŋə) n. Legend. a ghostly duplicate of a living person.

Doppler effect ('dɒplə) n. a change in the apparent frequency of a sound or light wave as a result of relative motion between the observer and the source.

Doric ('dɒrɪk) adj. of or denoting a classical order of architecture characterized by a heavy fluted column and a simple capital.

dormant ('dɔːmənt) adj. **1.** temporarily quiet, inactive, or not being used. **2.** Biol. alive but in a resting condition. —**'dormancy** n.

dormer or **dormer window** ('dɔːmə) n. a window that projects from a sloping roof.

dormitory ('dɔːmɪtrɪ) n., pl. **-ries.** **1.** a large room, esp. at a school, containing several beds. **2.** U.S. a building, esp. at a college, providing living accommodation. **3.** (modifier) Brit. denoting an area from which most of the residents commute to work: a dormitory suburb.

Dormobile ('dɔːməʊ,biːl) n. Trademark. a vanlike vehicle specially equipped for living in while travelling.

dormouse ('dɔː,maʊs) n., pl. **-mice.** a small rodent resembling a mouse with a furry tail.

dorp (dɔːp) n. S. African. a small town or village.

dorsal (ˈdɔːsəl) adj. Anat., zool. relating to the back.

dory (ˈdɔːrɪ) n., pl. **-ries.** a spiny-finned food fish. Also called: **John Dory.**

dose (dəʊs) n. **1.** a specific quantity of a medicine taken at one time. **2.** Informal. something unpleasant to experience: a dose of influenza. **3.** the total energy of radiation absorbed. **4.** Slang. a sexually transmitted infection. ~vb. **5.** to administer a dose to (someone). —ˈdosage n.

dosing strip n. (in New Zealand) an area for treating dogs suspected of having hydatid disease.

doss down (dɒs) vb. Brit. slang. to sleep, esp. on a makeshift bed.

dosshouse (ˈdɒsˌhaʊs) n. Brit. slang. a cheap lodging house for homeless people.

dossier (ˈdɒsɪˌeɪ) n. a collection of papers about a subject or person.

dot (dɒt) n. **1.** a small round mark; spot; point. **2.** the symbol (·) used, in combination with the symbol for dash (—), in Morse code. **3. on the dot.** at exactly the arranged time. ~vb. **dotting, dotted. 4.** to mark with a dot. **5.** to scatter or intersperse: bushes dotting the plain. **6. dot one's i's and cross one's t's.** Informal. to pay meticulous attention to detail.

dotage (ˈdəʊtɪdʒ) n. feebleness of mind as a result of old age.

dotard (ˈdəʊtəd) n. a person who is weak-minded through senility.

dote (dəʊt) vb. (foll. by on or upon) to love to an excessive or foolish degree.

dotterel (ˈdɒtrəl) n. a plover with white bands around the head and neck.

dottle (ˈdɒtəl) n. the tobacco left in a pipe after smoking.

dotty (ˈdɒtɪ) adj. **-tier, -tiest.** Slang, chiefly Brit. slightly crazy. —ˈdottiness n.

double (ˈdʌbəl) adj. **1.** as much again in size, strength, number, etc.: a double portion. **2.** composed of two equal or similar parts. **3.** designed for two users: a double room. **4.** folded in two; composed of two layers. **5.** stooping: bent double. **6.** ambiguous: a double meaning. **7.** false, deceitful, or hypocritical: a double life. **8.** (of flowers) having more than the normal number of petals. **9.** Music. (of an instrument) sounding an octave lower: a double bass. ~adv. **10.** twice over; twofold. ~n. **11.** twice the number, amount, size, etc. **12.** a double measure of spirits. **13.** a duplicate or counterpart, esp. a person who closely resembles another. **14.** a bet on two horses in different races in which any winnings from the first race are placed on the horse in the later race. **15. at** or **on the double.** quickly or immediately. ~vb. **16.** to make or become twice as much. **17.** to bend or

fold (material, etc.). **18.** to play two parts or serve two roles. **19.** to turn sharply. **20.** Bridge. to make a call that will double certain scoring points if the preceding bid becomes the contract. **21.** (foll. by for) to act as substitute. ~See also **double back, doubles, double up.** —ˈdoubler n.

double agent n. a spy employed by two mutually antagonistic countries.

double back vb. to go back in the opposite direction: to double back on one's tracks.

double-barrelled or U.S. **-barreled** adj. **1.** (of a gun) having two barrels. **2.** Brit. (of surnames) having hyphenated parts.

double bass (beɪs) n. a stringed instrument, the largest and lowest member of the violin family.

double-breasted adj. (of a garment) having overlapping fronts.

double-check vb. to check again; verify.

double chin n. a fold of fat under the chin.

double cream n. thick cream with a high fat content.

double-cross vb. **1.** to cheat or betray. ~n. **2.** an instance of double-crossing; betrayal.

double-dealing n. action characterized by treachery or deceit.

double-decker n. **1.** Chiefly Brit. a bus with two passenger decks. **2.** Informal. **a.** a thing or structure with two layers. **b.** (as modifier): a double-decker sandwich.

double Dutch n. Brit. informal. incomprehensible talk; gibberish.

double-edged adj. **1.** (of a remark) having two possible interpretations, esp. being malicious though apparently innocuous. **2.** (of a knife) having a cutting edge on either side of the blade.

double entendre (ɑːnˈtɑːndrə) n. a word or phrase that can be interpreted in two ways, esp. with one meaning that is indelicate.

double entry n. a book-keeping system in which any commercial transaction is entered as a debit in one account and as a credit in another.

double glazing n. two panes of glass in a window, fitted to reduce heat loss.

double-jointed adj. having unusually flexible joints.

double knitting n. a medium thickness of knitting wool.

double negative n. a construction, considered ungrammatical, in which two negatives are used where one is needed, as in I wouldn't never have believed it.
Usage. There are two contexts where double negatives are found. An adjective with negative force is often used with a negative in order to express a meaning somewhere between positive and negative: it is not an uncommon sight. Two negatives are also

found together where they reinforce each other rather than conflict: *he never went back, not even to collect his belongings.* These two uses of a double negative are acceptable. A third case, illustrated by *I shouldn't wonder it it didn't rain today*, has the force of a weak positive statement (*I expect it to rain today*) and is common in informal English.

double pneumonia *n*. pneumonia affecting both lungs.

double-quick *adj*. **1.** very quick; rapid. ~*adv*. **2.** in a very quick or rapid manner.

doubles ('dʌb³lz) *n*. (*functioning as sing.*) a game between two pairs of players.

double standard *n*. a set of principles that allows greater freedom to one person or group than to another.

doublet ('dʌblɪt) *n*. **1.** (formerly) a man's close-fitting jacket, with or without sleeves. **2. a.** a pair of similar things. **b.** one of such a pair.

double take *n*. (esp. in comedy) a delayed reaction by a person to a remark or situation.

double talk *n*. deceptive or ambiguous talk.

doublethink ('dʌb³l,θɪŋk) *n*. deliberate, perverse, or unconscious acceptance of conflicting facts or principles.

double time *n*. **1.** a doubled wage rate sometimes paid for overtime work. **2.** *Music.* two beats per bar.

double up *vb*. **1.** to bend or cause to bend in two. **2.** to share a room or bed designed for one person or family.

doubloon (dʌ'bluːn) *n*. a former Spanish gold coin.

doubly ('dʌblɪ) *adv*. **1.** to or in a double degree, quantity, or measure. **2.** in two ways.

doubt (daut) *n*. **1.** uncertainty about the truth, facts, or existence of something. **2.** an unresolved difficulty or point. **3. give someone the benefit of the doubt.** to presume innocent someone suspected of guilt. **4. no doubt.** almost certainly. ~*vb*. **5.** to be inclined to disbelieve. **6.** to distrust or be suspicious of. —'**doubter** *n*. **Usage.** Where a clause follows *doubt* in a positive statement, the conjunction may be *whether, that,* or *if. Whether* (*I doubt whether he is there*) is universally accepted; *that* (*I doubt that he is there*) is less widely accepted and *if* (*I doubt if he is there*) is usually restricted to informal contexts. In negative statements, *doubt* is followed by *that: I do not doubt that he is telling the truth.*

doubtful ('dautful) *adj*. **1.** unlikely; improbable. **2.** feeling doubt; uncertain. —'**doubtfully** *adv*. —'**doubtfulness** *n*.

doubtless ('dautlıs) *adv*. **1.** certainly. **2.** probably.

douche (duːʃ) *n*. **1.** a stream of water directed onto or into the body for cleansing or medical purposes. **2.** an instrument for applying a douche. ~*vb*. **3.** to cleanse or treat by means of a douche.

dough (dǝʊ) *n*. **1.** a thick mixture of flour and water or milk, used for making bread, pastry, etc. **2.** *Slang.* money.

doughnut ('dǝʊnʌt) *n*. a small cake of sweetened dough cooked in hot fat.

doughty ('dautɪ) *adj*. **-tier, -tiest.** hardy; resolute.

do up *vb*. **1.** to wrap and make into a bundle: *to do up a parcel.* **2.** to fasten or be fastened. **3.** to renovate or redecorate.

dour (dʊǝ) *adj*. sullen. —'**dourness** *n*.

douse *or* **dowse** (daus) *vb*. **1.** to drench with water or other liquid. **2.** to put out (a light).

dove (dʌv) *n*. **1.** a bird with a heavy body, small head, and short legs. **2.** *Politics.* a person opposed to war.

dovecote ('dʌv,kǝʊt) *or* **dovecot** ('dʌv,kɒt) *n*. a structure for housing pigeons.

dove-grey *adj*. greyish-brown.

dovetail ('dʌv,teɪl) *n*. **1.** Also called: **dovetail joint.** a joint containing wedge-shaped tenons. ~*vb*. **2.** to fit together closely or neatly.

dowager ('dauǝdʒǝ) *n*. **1. a.** a widow possessing property or a title obtained from her husband. **b.** (*as modifier*): *the dowager duchess.* **2.** a wealthy or dignified elderly woman.

dowdy ('daudɪ) *adj*. **-dier, -diest.** (esp. of a woman or a woman's dress) shabby or old-fashioned. —'**dowdily** *adv*. —'**dowdiness** *n*.

dowel ('dauǝl) *n*. a wooden or metal peg that fits into two corresponding holes to join two adjacent parts.

dower ('dauǝ) *n*. **1.** the life interest in a part of her husband's estate allotted to a widow by law. **2.** *Archaic.* a dowry.

dower house *n*. a house for the use of a widow, often on her deceased husband's estate.

do with *vb*. **1. could** *or* **can do with.** to find useful; benefit from: *I could do with a good night's sleep.* **2. have to do with.** to be involved in or connected with. **3. to do with.** concerning; related to. **4.** to put or place: *what did you do with my coat?*

do without *vb*. to manage without.

down[1] (daun) *prep*. **1.** used to indicate movement from a higher to a lower position. **2.** at a lower or further level or position on, in, or along: *he ran down the street.* ~*adv*. **3.** downwards; at or to a lower level or position. **4.** used with many verbs when the result of the verb's action is to lower or destroy its object: *knock down.* **5.** used with several verbs to indicate intensity or completion: *calm down.* **6.** immediately: *cash down.* **7.** on paper: *write this down.* **8.** arranged; scheduled. **9.** away from a more important place. **10.** reduced to a state of lack: *down to the last pound.* **11.** lacking a specified amount: *3 down.* **12.** lower in price. **13.** from an earlier to a later time. **14.** to a finer state: *to grind down.* **15.** *Sport.* being a specified number of points or goals behind an opponent. **16.** (of a person) being inactive, owing to illness: *down with flu.* **17. down with...!** away with...!: *down with the king!* ~*adj.* **18.** depressed. **19.** relating to a train from a more important place or one regarded as higher: *the down line.* **20.** made in cash: *a down payment.* ~*vb.* **21.** *Informal.* to drink, esp. quickly. **22.** to bring (someone) down, esp. by tackling. ~*n.* **23.** a poor period: *ups and downs.* **24. have a down on.** *Informal.* to bear ill will towards.

down² (daʊn) *n.* **1.** soft fine feathers. **2.** soft fine hair. —**'downy** *adj.*

down-and-out *adj.* **1.** without any means of livelihood; poor and, often, socially outcast. ~*n.* **2.** a person who is destitute and, often, homeless.

downbeat ('daʊn,biːt) *n.* **1.** *Music.* the first beat of a bar. ~*adj. Informal.* **2.** depressed; gloomy. **3.** relaxed.

downcast ('daʊn,kɑːst) *adj.* **1.** dejected. **2.** (of the eyes) directed downwards.

downer ('daʊnə) *n. Slang.* **1.** a barbiturate, tranquillizer, or narcotic. **2. on a downer.** in a state of depression.

downfall ('daʊn,fɔːl) *n.* **1.** a sudden loss of position or reputation. **2.** the cause of this.

downgrade ('daʊn,ɡreɪd) *vb.* to reduce in importance or value.

downhearted (,daʊn'hɑːtɪd) *adj.* discouraged; dejected.

downhill ('daʊn'hɪl) *adj.* **1.** going or sloping down. ~*adv.* **2.** towards the bottom of a hill; downwards. **3. go downhill.** *Informal.* to deteriorate.

Downing Street ('daʊnɪŋ) *n.* the prime minister or the British Government.

down-market *adj.* cheap, having little prestige, and poor in quality.

down payment *n.* the deposit paid on an item purchased on hire-purchase, mortgage, etc.

downpour ('daʊn,pɔː) *n.* a heavy continuous fall of rain.

downright ('daʊn,raɪt) *adv., adj.* extreme or extremely: *downright rude.*

downs (daʊnz) *pl. n.* rolling upland, esp. in the chalk areas of S England.

downside ('daʊnsaɪd) *n.* the disadvantageous aspect of a situation: *the downside of twentieth-century living.*

Down's syndrome (daʊnz) *n. Pathol.* a genetic disorder characterized by a flat face and nose, slanting eyes, and mental retardation.

downstairs ('daʊn'stɛəz) *adv.* **1.** down the stairs; to or on a lower floor. ~*n.* **2.** a lower or ground floor.

downstream ('daʊn'striːm) *adv., adj.* in or towards the lower part of a stream; with the current.

down-to-earth *adj.* sensible; practical; realistic.

downtown ('daʊn'taʊn) *Chiefly U.S., Canad., & N.Z.* ~*n.* **1.** the central or lower part of a city, esp. the main commercial area. ~*adv.* **2.** towards, to, or into this area.

downtrodden ('daʊn,trɒd'n) *adj.* oppressed and lacking the will to resist.

down under *Informal.* ~*n.* **1.** Australia or New Zealand. ~*adv.* **2.** in or to Australia or New Zealand.

downward ('daʊnwəd) *adj.* **1.** descending from a higher to a lower level, condition, or position. ~*adv.* **2.** same as **downwards.** —**'downwardly** *adv.*

downwards ('daʊnwədz) *or* **downward** *adv.* **1.** from a higher to a lower place, level, etc. **2.** from an earlier time or source to a later.

downwind ('daʊn'wɪnd) *adv., adj.* in the same direction towards which the wind is blowing; with the wind from behind.

dowry ('daʊərɪ) *n., pl.* **-ries.** the property brought by a woman to her husband at marriage.

dowse (daʊz) *vb.* to search for underground water or minerals using a divining rod. —**'dowser** *n.*

doxology (dɒk'sɒlədʒɪ) *n., pl.* **-gies.** a hymn, verse, or form of words in Christian liturgy glorifying God.

doyen ('dɔɪən) *n.* the senior member of a group, profession, or society. —**doyenne** (dɔɪ'ɛn) *fem. n.*

doz. dozen.

doze (dəʊz) *vb.* **1.** to sleep lightly or intermittently. **2.** (foll. by *off*) to fall into a light sleep. ~*n.* **3.** a short sleep.

dozen ('dʌz'n) *det.* **1.** twelve or a group of twelve: *two dozen oranges.* ~*n., pl.* **dozens** *or* **dozen.** **2. talk nineteen to the dozen.** to talk without stopping. —**'dozenth** *adj.*

dozy ('dəʊzɪ) *adj.* **dozier, doziest.** **1.** drowsy. **2.** *Brit. informal.* stupid.

DP **1.** data processing. **2.** displaced person.

DPhil *or* **DPh** Doctor of Philosophy.

DPP (in Britain) Director of Public Prosecutions.

Dr **1.** Doctor. **2.** Drive.

drab (dræb) *adj.* **drabber, drabbest.** **1.** dull; dingy. **2.** cheerless; dreary. **3.** light olive-brown. —**'drabness** *n.*

drachm (dræm) *n. Brit.* one eighth of a fluid ounce.

drachma ('drækmə) *n., pl.* **-mas** *or* **-mae**

(-miː). **1.** the standard monetary unit of Greece. **2.** a silver coin of ancient Greece.

draconian (dreɪˈkəʊnɪən) *adj.* harsh.

draft (drɑːft) *n.* **1.** a plan, sketch, or drawing of something. **2.** a preliminary outline of a book, speech, etc. **3.** a written order for payment of money by a bank. **4.** *U.S.* selection for compulsory military service. **5.** detachment of personnel from one place to another, esp. for a specific task. ~*vb.* **6.** to draw up an outline or plan of. **7.** to detach (personnel) from one place to another, esp. for a specific task. **8.** *U.S.* to select for compulsory military service. ~*n., vb.* **9.** *U.S.* same as **draught.**

drag (dræg) *vb.* **dragging, dragged. 1.** to pull with force, esp. along the ground. **2.** (foll. by *away* or *from*) to persuade (someone) or force (oneself) to come away. **3.** to trail on the ground. **4.** to bring (oneself or someone else) with effort or difficulty. **5.** to linger behind. **6.** (often foll. by *on* or *out*) to last, prolong, or be prolonged tediously: *his talk dragged on for hours.* **7.** to search (a river) with a dragnet or hook. **8.** *Informal.* to draw (on a cigarette). **9. drag one's feet.** *Informal.* to act with deliberate slowness. ~*n.* **10.** an implement, such as a dragnet, used for dragging. **11.** a person or thing that slows up progress. **12.** *Aeronautics.* the resistance to the motion of a body passing through air. **13.** *Informal.* a person or thing that is very tedious. **14.** women's clothes worn by a man (esp. in **in drag**). **15.** *Informal.* a draw on a cigarette. ~See also **drag up.**

draggle (ˈdræg²l) *vb.* to make or become wet or dirty by trailing on the ground.

dragnet (ˈdrægˌnɛt) *n.* a net used to scour the bottom of a pond or river, as when searching for something.

dragoman (ˈdrægəʊmən) *n., pl.* **-mans** or **-men.** (in Middle Eastern countries) a professional interpreter or guide.

dragon (ˈdrægən) *n.* **1.** a mythical fire-breathing monster with a scaly reptilian body, wings, claws, and a long tail. **2.** *Informal.* a fierce woman. **3. chase the dragon.** *Slang.* to smoke opium or heroin.

dragonfly (ˈdrægənˌflaɪ) *n., pl.* **-flies.** a brightly coloured insect with a long slender body and two pairs of wings.

dragoon (drəˈguːn) *n.* **1.** a heavily armed cavalryman. ~*vb.* **2.** to coerce; force.

drag race *n.* a race in which specially built or modified cars or motorcycles are timed over a measured course. —**drag racing** *n.*

drag up *vb. Informal.* to revive (an unpleasant fact or story).

drain (dreɪn) *n.* **1.** a pipe or channel that carries off water or sewage. **2.** a cause of continuous diminution in resources or energy: *a drain on one's resources.* **3. down the drain.** wasted. ~*vb.* **4.** (often foll. by *off*)

to draw off or remove (liquid) from. **5.** (often foll. by *away*) to flow (away) or filter (off). **6.** to dry or be emptied as a result of liquid running off or flowing away. **7.** to drink the entire contents of (a glass or cup). **8.** to make constant demands on (resources, energy, etc.); exhaust. **9.** (of a river) to carry off the surface water from (an area).

drainage (ˈdreɪnɪdʒ) *n.* **1.** the process or a method of draining. **2.** a system of watercourses or drains.

draining board *n.* a sloping grooved surface at the side of a sink, used for draining washed dishes.

drainpipe (ˈdreɪnˌpaɪp) *n.* a pipe for carrying off rainwater or sewage.

drainpipes (ˈdreɪnˌpaɪps) *pl. n.* very narrow trousers.

drake (dreɪk) *n.* the male of a duck.

dram (dræm) *n.* **1.** a small amount of spirits, esp. whisky. **2.** one sixteenth of an ounce (avoirdupois). **3.** *U.S.* one eighth of an apothecaries' ounce; 60 grains.

drama (ˈdrɑːmə) *n.* **1.** a work to be performed by actors; play. **2.** the genre of literature represented by works intended for the ...age. **3.** the art of the writing and production of plays. **4.** a situation that is highly emotional, tragic, or turbulent.

dramatic (drəˈmætɪk) *adj.* **1.** of drama. **2.** like a drama in suddenness, emotional impact, etc. **3.** striking; effective. **4.** acting or performed in a flamboyant way. —**dra-ˈmatically** *adv.*

dramatics (drəˈmætɪks) *n.* **1.** (*functioning as sing. or pl.*) the art of acting or producing plays. **2.** (*usually functioning as pl.*) exaggerated, theatrical behaviour.

dramatis personae (ˈdrɑːmətɪs pəˈsəʊnaɪ) *pl. n.* the characters in a play.

dramatist (ˈdræmətɪst) *n.* a playwright.

dramatize or **-tise** (ˈdræməˌtaɪz) *vb.* **1.** to put into dramatic form. **2.** to express (something) in a dramatic or exaggerated way. —ˌdramatiˈzation *or* -tiˈsation *n.*

drank (dræŋk) *vb.* the past tense of **drink.**

drape (dreɪp) *vb.* **1.** to cover with material or fabric, usually in folds. **2.** to hang or arrange, esp. in folds. **3.** to place casually and loosely. ~See also **drapes.**

draper (ˈdreɪpə) *n. Brit.* a dealer in fabrics and sewing materials.

drapery (ˈdreɪpərɪ) *n., pl.* **-peries. 1.** fabric or clothing arranged and draped. **2.** (*pl.*) curtains. **3.** fabrics and cloth collectively.

drapes (dreɪps) *pl. n. Chiefly U.S. & Canad.* curtains.

drastic (ˈdræstɪk) *adj.* extreme or forceful; severe. —**ˈdrastically** *adv.*

drat (dræt) *interj. Slang.* an exclamation of annoyance.

draught or *U.S.* **draft** (drɑːft) *n.* **1.** a current of air, esp. in an enclosed space. **2.**

a. the act of pulling a load by a vehicle or animal. **b.** (*as modifier*): *a draught horse.* **3.** a portion of liquid to be drunk, esp. a dose of medicine. **4.** an instance of drinking; a gulp or swallow. **5. on draught.** (of beer) drawn from a cask. **6.** one of the flat discs used in the game of draughts. U.S. and Canad. equivalent: **checker. 7. feel the draught.** to be short of money.

draught beer *n.* beer stored in a cask.

draughtboard ('drɑːft,bɔːd) *n.* a square board divided into 64 squares, used for playing draughts.

draughts (drɑːfts) *n.* (*functioning as sing.*) a game for two players using a draughtboard and 12 draughtsmen each.

draughtsman *or* *U.S.* **draftsman** ('drɑːftsmən) *n., pl.* **-men. 1.** a person employed to prepare detailed scale drawings of machinery, buildings, etc. **2.** a person skilled in drawing. **3.** *Brit.* any of the flat discs used in the game of draughts. U.S. and Canad. equivalent: **checker.** —'**draughtsman,ship** *n.*

draughty *or* *U.S.* **drafty** ('drɑːftɪ) *adj.* **draughtier, draughtiest** *or* *U.S.* **draftier, draftiest.** exposed to draughts of air. —'**draughtily** *adv.* —'**draughtiness** *n.*

draw (drɔː) *vb.* **drawing, drew, drawn. 1.** to depict or sketch (a figure, picture, etc.) in lines, as with a pencil or pen. **2.** to cause (a person or thing) to move towards one or away from a place by pulling. **3.** to bring, take, or pull (something) out, as from a drawer, holster, etc. **4.** to take (liquid) out of a cask, etc., by means of a tap. **5.** to move, esp. in a specified direction: *to draw alongside.* **6.** to attract: *to draw attention.* **7.** to cause to flow: *to draw blood.* **8.** to formulate or derive: *to draw conclusions.* **9.** (of a chimney) to induce or allow a draught to carry off smoke. **10.** to take from a source: *to draw money from the bank.* **11.** to earn: *draw interest.* **12.** to choose at random. **13.** *Archery.* to bend (a bow) by pulling the string. **14.** (of tea) to steep in boiling water. **15.** to disembowel. **16.** to cause (pus) to discharge from an abscess or wound. **17.** (of two teams or contestants) to finish a game with an equal number of points; tie. **18.** *Naut.* (of a vessel) to require (a specified depth) in which to float. ~*n.* **19.** *Informal.* an event, act, etc., that attracts a large audience. **20.** a raffle or lottery. **21.** something taken at random, as a ticket in a lottery. **22.** a contest or game ending in a tie. ~See also **drawback, draw in,** etc.

drawback ('drɔː,bæk) *n.* **1.** a disadvantage or hindrance. ~*vb.* **draw back. 2.** to retreat. **3.** to turn aside from an undertaking.

drawbridge ('drɔː,brɪdʒ) *n.* a bridge that may be raised to prevent access or to enable vessels to pass.

drawer *n.* **1.** (drɔː). a boxlike container in a

chest, table, etc., made for sliding in and out. **2.** ('drɔːə). a person or thing that draws.

drawers (drɔːz) *pl. n. Old-fashioned.* an undergarment worn below the waist.

draw in *vb.* **1.** (of a train) to arrive at a station. **2. the nights are drawing in.** the hours of daylight are becoming shorter.

drawing ('drɔːɪŋ) *n.* **1.** a picture or plan made by means of lines on a surface, esp. with a pencil or pen. **2.** the art of making drawings; draughtsmanship.

drawing pin *n. Brit.* a short tack with a broad smooth head for fastening papers to a drawing board, etc.

drawing room *n.* a room where visitors are received and entertained.

drawl (drɔːl) *vb.* **1.** to speak or utter (words) slowly, esp. prolonging the vowel sounds. ~*n.* **2.** the way of speech of someone who drawls. —'**drawling** *adj.*

drawn (drɔːn) *vb.* **1.** the past participle of **draw.** ~*adj.* **2.** haggard, tired, or tense in appearance.

draw off *vb.* to cause (a liquid) to flow from something.

draw on *vb.* **1.** to use or exploit (a source, fund, etc.). **2.** to come near: *winter draws on.* **3.** to lead (someone) further; entice (someone).

draw out *vb.* **1.** to extend. **2.** to cause (a person) to talk freely. **3.** (foll. by *of*) to elicit (information) (from). **4.** (of hours of daylight) to become longer. **5.** (of a train) to leave a station.

drawstring ('drɔː,strɪŋ) *n.* a cord run through a hem around an opening, so that when it is pulled tighter, the opening closes.

draw up *vb.* **1.** (of a vehicle) to come to a halt. **2.** to formulate and write out: *to draw up a contract.* **3. draw oneself up.** to straighten oneself.

dray (dreɪ) *n.* a low cart used for carrying heavy loads.

dread (drɛd) *vb.* **1.** to anticipate with apprehension or terror. ~*n.* **2.** great fear. **3.** *Slang.* a Rastafarian.

dreadful ('drɛdfʊl) *adj.* **1.** extremely disagreeable, shocking, or bad. **2.** extreme: *a dreadful waste of time.* —'**dreadfully** *adv.*

dreadnought ('drɛd,nɔːt) *n.* a battleship armed with heavy guns.

dream (driːm) *n.* **1.** mental activity, usually an imagined series of events, occurring during sleep. **2.** a sequence of imaginative thoughts indulged in while awake. **3.** a cherished hope; aspiration. **4.** a vain hope. **5.** a person or thing that is as pleasant or seemingly unreal as a dream. ~*vb.* **dreaming, dreamt** (drɛmt) *or* **dreamed. 6.** to experience (a dream). **7.** to indulge in daydreams. **8.** to be unrealistic. **9.** (foll. by *of* or *about*) to have an image (of) or fantasy (about) in or as if in a dream. **10.** (foll. by *of*) to consider the possibility (of). ~*adj.* **11.** ideal: *dream kitchen.* —'**dreamer** *n.*

dream up *vb.* to invent by ingenuity and imagination: *to dream up an excuse.*

dreamy ('dri:mɪ) *adj.* **dreamier, dreamiest. 1.** vague or impractical. **2.** relaxing; gentle: *dreamy music.* **3.** *Informal.* wonderful. —'**dreamily** *adv.* —'**dreaminess** *n.*

dreary ('drɪərɪ) *adj.* **drearier, dreariest.** sad or dull; boring. —'**drearily** *adv.* —'**dreariness** *n.*

dredge¹ (drɛdʒ) *n.* **1.** a machine used to scoop or suck up material from a riverbed, etc. ~*vb.* **2.** to remove material from (a riverbed, etc.) by means of a dredge. **3.** to search for (a submerged object) with or as if with a dredge. —'**dredger** *n.*

dredge² (drɛdʒ) *vb.* to sprinkle (food) with flour, etc. —'**dredger** *n.*

dredge up *vb. Informal.* to bring (something) to notice, esp. with effort and from an obscure source.

dregs (drɛgz) *pl. n.* **1.** solid particles that settle at the bottom of some liquids. **2.** the worst or most despised elements: *the dregs of society.*

drench (drɛntʃ) *vb.* **1.** to make completely wet. **2.** to give medicine to (an animal). ~*n.* **3.** a dose of medicine given to an animal. —'**drenching** *n., adj.*

Dresden ('drɛzdªn) *or* **Dresden china** *n.* delicate and decorative porcelain made near Dresden, East Germany.

dress (drɛs) *vb.* **1.** to put clothes on. **2.** to put on formal clothes. **3.** to arrange merchandise in (a shop window). **4.** to arrange (the hair). **5.** to apply protective covering to (a wound). **6.** to cover (a salad) with dressing. **7.** to prepare (fowl or fish) by cleaning, gutting, etc. **8.** to put a finish on (stone, metal, etc.). **9.** *Mil.* to bring (troops) into line or (of troops) to come into line: *dress ranks.* ~*n.* **10.** a one-piece garment for a woman or girl, consisting of a skirt and bodice. **11.** complete style of clothing: *military dress.* **12.** (*modifier*) suitable for a formal occasion: *a dress shirt.* ~See also **dress up.**

dressage ('drɛsɑːʒ) *n.* **a.** the training of a horse to perform manoeuvres in response to the rider's body signals. **b.** the manoeuvres performed.

dress circle *n.* the first gallery in a theatre.

dresser¹ ('drɛsə) *n.* **1.** a set of shelves, usually also with cupboards, for storing or displaying dishes. **2.** *U.S.* a chest of drawers.

dresser² ('drɛsə) *n.* **1.** a person who dresses in a specified way: *a fashionable dresser.* **2.** *Theatre.* a person employed to assist actors with their costumes. **3.** *Brit.* a person who assists a surgeon.

dressing ('drɛsɪŋ) *n.* **1.** a sauce for salad. **2.** *U.S. & Canad.* same as **stuffing** (sense 2). **3.** a covering for a wound. **4.** fertilizer spread on land. **5.** size used for stiffening textiles.

dressing-down *n. Informal.* a severe scolding.

dressing gown *n.* a robe worn before dressing or for lounging.

dressing room *n.* **1.** *Theatre.* a room backstage where an actor changes and makes up. **2.** any room used for changing clothes.

dressing table *n.* a piece of bedroom furniture with a mirror and a set of drawers.

dressmaker ('drɛs,meɪkə) *n.* a person who makes clothes for women. —'**dress-,making** *n.*

dress rehearsal *n.* **1.** the last rehearsal of a play, using costumes, lighting, etc., as for the first night. **2.** any full-scale practice.

dress shirt *n.* a man's evening shirt, worn as part of formal evening dress.

dress suit *n.* a man's evening suit.

dress up *vb.* **1.** to attire (oneself or another) in smart, glamorous, or stylish clothes. **2.** to put fancy dress on. **3.** to improve the appearance or impression of: *to dress up the facts.*

dressy ('drɛsɪ) *adj.* **dressier, dressiest. 1.** (of clothes or occasions) elegant. **2.** (of persons) dressing stylishly. —'**dressiness** *n.*

drew (druː) *vb.* the past tense of **draw.**

drey *or* **dray** (dreɪ) *n.* a squirrel's nest.

dribble ('drɪbªl) *vb.* **1.** to flow or allow to flow in a thin stream or drops. **2.** to allow saliva to trickle from the mouth. **3.** (in soccer, basketball, hockey, etc.) to propel (the ball) by repeatedly tapping it with the hand, foot, or a stick. ~*n.* **4.** a small quantity of liquid falling in drops or flowing in a thin stream. **5.** a small supply. **6.** an act of dribbling. —'**dribbler** *n.*

driblet *or* **dribblet** ('drɪblɪt) *n.* a small amount.

dried (draɪd) *vb.* past of **dry.**

drier¹ ('draɪə) *adj.* a comparative of **dry.**

drier² ('draɪə) *n.* same as **dryer¹.**

driest ('draɪɪst) *adj.* a superlative of **dry.**

drift (drɪft) *vb.* **1.** to be carried along by currents of air or water. **2.** to move aimlessly from one place or activity to another. **3.** to wander away from a fixed course or point. **4.** (of snow) to accumulate in heaps. ~*n.* **5.** something piled up by the wind or current, as a snowdrift. **6.** tendency or meaning: *the drift of the argument.* **7.** a general movement or development: *the drift of workers away from the countryside.* **8.** the extent to which a vessel or aircraft is driven off course by winds, etc. **9.** a general tendency of a mass of water to flow in the direction of the prevailing winds. **10.** a controlled four-wheel skid used to take bends at high speed.

drifter ('drɪftə) n. **1.** a person who moves aimlessly from place to place. **2.** a boat used for drift-net fishing.

drift net n. a fishing net that is allowed to drift with the tide.

driftwood ('drɪft,wʊd) n. wood floating on or washed ashore by the sea or other body of water.

drill[1] (drɪl) n. **1.** a machine or tool for boring holes. **2.** *Mil.* training in procedures or movements, as for parades. **3.** strict and often repetitious training. **4.** *Informal.* correct procedure. ~vb. **5.** to pierce, bore, or cut (a hole) in (material) with or as if with a drill. **6.** to instruct or be instructed in military procedures or movements. **7.** to teach by rigorous exercises or training.

drill[2] (drɪl) n. **1.** a machine for planting seeds in rows. **2.** a furrow in which seeds are sown. **3.** a row of seeds planted by means of a drill. ~vb. **4.** to plant (seeds) by means of a drill.

drill[3] (drɪl) n. a hard-wearing cotton cloth, used for uniforms.

drill[4] (drɪl) n. a monkey of W Africa, related to the mandrill.

drilling platform n. a structure which supports the machinery and equipment, together with the stores, etc., required for drilling an offshore oil well.

drilling rig n. **1.** the complete machinery, equipment, and structures needed to drill an oil well. **2.** a mobile drilling platform used for exploratory offshore drilling.

drily ('draɪlɪ) adv. same as **dryly**.

drink (drɪŋk) vb. **drinking, drank, drunk**. **1.** to swallow (a liquid). **2.** to consume alcohol, esp. to excess. **3.** to bring (oneself) into a specified condition by consuming alcohol: *he drank himself to death*. **4.** (foll. by *to*) to drink a toast. **5. drink someone's health.** to salute someone with a toast. **6.** to soak up (liquid). **7.** (foll. by *in*) to pay close attention to. ~n. **8.** liquid suitable for drinking. **9.** a portion of liquid for drinking. **10.** alcohol or its habitual or excessive consumption. **11. the drink.** *Informal.* the sea. —'**drinkable** adj. —'**drinker** n.

drink-driving n. (*modifier*) relating to driving a car after drinking alcohol: *a drink-driving charge*.

drip (drɪp) vb. **dripping, dripped. 1.** to fall or let fall in drops. ~n. **2.** the falling of drops of liquid. **3.** the sound made by falling drops. **4.** *Informal.* an inane, insipid person. **5.** *Med.* an apparatus for the intravenous drop-by-drop administration of a solution.

drip-dry adj. **1.** designating clothing that will dry free of creases if hung up when wet. ~vb. **-drying, -dried. 2.** to dry or become dry thus.

drip-feed vb. **-feeding, -fed. 1.** to feed (someone) a liquid drop by drop, esp. intravenously. ~n. **2.** same as **drip** (sense 5).

dripping ('drɪpɪŋ) n. the fat that exudes from meat while it is being roasted or fried.

drive (draɪv) vb. **driving, drove, driven. 1.** to guide the movement of (a vehicle). **2.** to transport or be transported in a vehicle. **3.** to compel to work excessively hard. **4.** to goad into a specified state: *pressure of work drove him to despair.* **5.** to push or propel. **6.** to cause (an object) to make (a hole or crack). **7.** to move rapidly by striking or throwing with force. **8.** *Sport.* to hit (a ball) very hard and straight. **9.** *Golf.* to strike (the ball) with a driver. **10.** to chase (game) from cover. **11.** to rush or dash violently, esp. against an obstacle. **12.** to transact with vigour: *he drives a hard bargain.* **13. drive home. a.** to cause to penetrate to the fullest extent. **b.** to make clear by special emphasis. ~n. **14.** a journey in a driven vehicle. **15.** a road for vehicles, esp. a private road leading to a house. **16.** a united effort towards a common goal. **17.** *Brit.* a large gathering of people to play cards. **18.** energy, ambition, or initiative. **19.** *Psychol.* a motive or interest, such as sex or ambition. **20.** a sustained and powerful military offensive. **21.** the means by which force, motion, etc., is transmitted in a mechanism: *fluid drive.* **22.** *Sport.* a hard straight shot or stroke.

drive at vb. *Informal.* to intend or mean: *what are you driving at?*

drive-in adj. **1.** denoting a public facility or service used by patrons in their cars: *a drive-in bank.* ~n. **2.** *Chiefly U.S. & Canad.* a cinema used in such a manner.

drivel ('drɪv²l) n. **1.** foolish talk. ~vb. **-elling, -elled** or U.S. **-eling, -eled. 2.** to speak foolishly. **3.** to allow (saliva) to flow from the mouth.

driven ('drɪv²n) vb. the past participle of **drive.**

driver ('draɪvə) n. **1.** a person who drives a vehicle. **2. in the driver's seat.** in a position of control. **3.** *Golf.* a club used for tee shots.

driveway ('draɪv,weɪ) n. a path for vehicles, often connecting a house with a public road.

driving licence n. an official document authorizing a person to drive a motor vehicle.

drizzle ('drɪz²l) n. **1.** very light rain. ~vb. **2.** to rain lightly. —'**drizzly** adj.

droll (drəʊl) adj. amusing in a quaint manner; comical. —'**drollery** n. —'**drolly** adv.

dromedary ('drʌmədərɪ) n., pl. **-daries.** a camel with a single hump.

drone[1] (drəʊn) *n.* **1.** a male honeybee whose sole function is to mate with the queen. **2.** a person who lives off the work of others.

drone[2] (drəʊn) *vb.* **1.** to make a monotonous low dull sound. **2.** (foll. by *on*) to talk in a monotonous tone, esp. without stopping. ~*n.* **3.** a monotonous low dull sound. **4.** a single-reed pipe in a set of bagpipes.

drool (druːl) *vb.* **1.** (foll. by *over*) to show excessive enthusiasm for or pleasure in. **2.** same as **drivel** (senses 2 and 3).

droop (druːp) *vb.* **1.** to sag or allow to sag, as from weakness. **2.** to be overcome by weariness. —'**drooping** *adj.*

drop (drɒp) *n.* **1.** a small quantity of liquid forming a round shape. **2.** a very small quantity of liquid: *a drop of tea*. **3.** something shaped like a drop: *peppermint drops; pearl drops*. **4.** the act of falling. **5.** a decrease in amount or value. **6.** the vertical distance that anything may fall. **7.** the act of unloading troops or supplies by parachute. ~*vb.* **dropping, dropped**. **8.** (of liquids) to fall or allow to fall in globules. **9.** to fall or allow (something) to fall vertically. **10.** to sink or fall to the ground, as from a blow or weariness. **11.** (foll. by *back, behind*, etc.) to move in a specified manner or direction. **12.** (foll. by *in* or *by*) *Informal.* to pay someone a casual visit. **13.** to decrease in amount, strength, or value. **14.** to sink to a lower position. **15.** (foll. by *into*) to pass easily into a condition: *to drop into a habit*. **16.** to mention casually: *to drop a hint*. **17.** to leave out in speaking: *to drop one's h's*. **18.** to set down (passengers or goods). **19.** to send: *drop me a line*. **20.** to discontinue: *let's drop the matter*. **21.** to cease to associate with. **22.** (of animals) to give birth to (offspring). **23.** *Slang, chiefly U.S. & Canad.* to lose (money). **24.** *Sport.* to omit (a player) from a team. **25.** to lose (a game or point). ~See also **drop off, drop out, drops**. —'**droplet** *n.*

drop curtain *n. Theatre.* a curtain that can be raised and lowered onto the stage.

drop-in *n.* (*modifier*) denoting a social service or meeting place provided where people may attend if and when they please.

drop off *vb.* **1.** to grow smaller or less. **2.** to set down (passengers or goods). **3.** *Informal.* to fall asleep.

dropout ('drɒp,aʊt) *n.* **1.** a student who does not complete a course of study. **2.** a person who rejects conventional society. ~*vb.* **drop out.** (often foll. by *of*) **3.** to abandon or withdraw (from a school, job, etc.).

dropper ('drɒpə) *n.* a small tube with a rubber bulb at one end for dispensing drops of liquid.

droppings ('drɒpɪŋz) *pl. n.* the dung of certain animals, such as rabbits or birds.

drops (drɒps) *pl. n.* any liquid medication applied by means of a dropper.

drop scone *n.* a flat spongy cake made by dropping a spoonful of batter on a hot griddle.

dropsy ('drɒpsɪ) *n.* an illness in which watery fluid collects in the tissues or in a body cavity. —'**dropsical** *adj.*

droshky ('drɒʃkɪ) *or* **drosky** ('drɒskɪ) *n., pl.* **-kies.** an open four-wheeled carriage, formerly used in Russia.

dross (drɒs) *n.* **1.** the scum formed on the surfaces of molten metals. **2.** worthless matter; waste.

drought (draʊt) *n.* a prolonged period of scanty rainfall.

drove[1] (drəʊv) *vb.* the past tense of **drive**.

drove[2] (drəʊv) *n.* **1.** a herd of livestock being driven together. **2.** (*pl.*) a moving crowd of people.

drover ('drəʊvə) *n.* a person who drives sheep or cattle.

drown (draʊn) *vb.* **1.** to die or kill by immersion in liquid. **2.** to get rid of (one's sorrows) temporarily by drinking alcohol. **3.** to drench thoroughly. **4.** (sometimes foll. by *out*) to render (a sound) inaudible by making a loud noise.

drowse (draʊz) *vb.* to be sleepy, dull, or sluggish.

drowsy ('draʊzɪ) *adj.* **drowsier, drowsiest.** **1.** heavy with sleepiness. **2.** inducing sleep; soporific. —'**drowsily** *adv.* —'**drowsiness** *n.*

drub (drʌb) *vb.* **drubbing, drubbed.** **1.** to beat as with a stick. **2.** to defeat utterly, as in a contest. —'**drubbing** *n.*

drudge (drʌdʒ) *n.* **1.** a person who works hard at wearisome menial tasks. ~*vb.* **2.** to toil at such tasks.

drudgery ('drʌdʒərɪ) *n.* hard, menial, and monotonous work.

drug (drʌg) *n.* **1.** any substance used in the treatment, prevention, or diagnosis of disease. **2.** a chemical substance, esp. a narcotic, taken for the effects it produces. **3. drug on the market.** a commodity available in excess of demand. ~*vb.* **drugging, drugged. 4.** to mix a drug with (food or drink). **5.** to administer a drug to (a person or an animal) in order to induce sleepiness or unconsciousness.

drug addict *n.* a person who is dependent on narcotic drugs.

drugget ('drʌgɪt) *n.* a coarse fabric used as a floor covering.

druggist ('drʌgɪst) *n. U.S. & Canad.* a pharmacist.

drugstore ('drʌg,stɔː) *n. U.S. & Canad.* a shop where medical prescriptions are made up and a wide variety of goods and usually light meals are sold.

Druid ('druːɪd) *n.* a member of an ancient

order of priests in Gaul, Britain, and Ireland in the pre-Christian era. **—Dru'idic** *or* **Dru'idical** *adj.*

drum (drʌm) *n.* **1.** a percussion instrument sounded by striking a skin stretched across the opening of a hollow cylinder. **2.** the sound produced by a drum. **3.** an object that resembles a drum in shape, such as a large spool or a cylindrical container. **4.** same as **eardrum.** ~*vb.* **drumming, drummed. 5.** to play (music) on a drum. **6.** to tap rhythmically or regularly. **7.** to instil by constant repetition: *these facts had been drummed into him.* ~See also **drum up. —'drummer** *n.*

drumbeat ('drʌm,biːt) *n.* the sound made by beating a drum.

drumhead ('drʌm,hɛd) *n.* the part of a drum that is struck.

drum machine *n.* a synthesizer programmed to reproduce the sound of percussion instruments.

drum major *n.* the noncommissioned officer who commands the corps of drums of a military band and who is in command of both the drums and the band when paraded together.

drum majorette (,meɪdʒəˈrɛt) *n.* a girl who marches at the head of a procession, twirling a baton.

drumstick ('drʌm,stɪk) *n.* **1.** a stick used for playing a drum. **2.** the lower joint of the leg of a cooked fowl.

drum up *vb.* to obtain (support or business) by solicitation or canvassing.

drunk (drʌŋk) *vb.* **1.** the past participle of **drink.** ~*adj.* **2.** intoxicated with alcohol to the extent of losing control over normal functions. **3.** overwhelmed by strong influence or emotion. ~*n.* **4.** a person who is drunk.

drunkard ('drʌŋkəd) *n.* a person who is frequently or habitually drunk.

drunken ('drʌŋkən) *adj.* **1.** intoxicated. **2.** habitually drunk. **3.** caused by or relating to alcoholic intoxication: *a drunken brawl.* **—'drunkenly** *adv.* **—'drunkenness** *n.*

drupe (druːp) *n.* a fleshy fruit with a stone, such as the peach, plum, or cherry.

dry (draɪ) *adj.* **drier, driest** *or* **dryer, dryest. 1.** lacking moisture; not wet. **2.** having little or no rainfall. **3.** having the water drained away or evaporated: *a dry river.* **4.** not providing milk: *a dry cow.* **5.** (of the eyes) free from tears. **6.** *Informal.* thirsty. **7.** eaten without butter, jam, etc.: *dry toast.* **8.** (of wine) not sweet. **9.** consisting of solid as opposed to liquid substances. **10.** lacking interest: *a dry book.* **11.** lacking warmth: *a dry greeting.* **12.** (of humour) shrewd and keen in a sarcastic or laconic way. **13.** prohibiting the sale of alcoholic liquor: *a dry area.* ~*vb.* **drying, dried. 14.** to make or become dry. **15.** to preserve

(food) by removing the moisture. ~*n., pl.* **drys** *or* **dries. 16.** *Brit. informal.* a Conservative politician who is a hardliner. ~See also **dry out, dry up. —'dryness** *n.*

dryad ('draɪəd, -æd) *n. Greek myth.* a nymph of the woods.

dry battery *n.* an electric battery consisting of two or more dry cells.

dry cell *n.* an electric cell in which the electrolyte is in the form of a paste to prevent it from spilling.

dry-clean *vb.* to clean (clothes, etc.) with a solvent other than water. **—,dry-'cleaner** *n.* **—,dry-'cleaning** *n.*

dry dock *n.* a dock that can be pumped dry for work on a ship's bottom.

dryer¹ ('draɪə) *n.* an apparatus for removing moisture by forced draught, heating, or centrifuging.

dryer² ('draɪə) *adj.* same as **drier¹.**

dry fly *n. Angling.* **a.** an artificial fly designed to be floated on the surface of the water. **b.** (*as modifier*): *dry-fly fishing.*

dry ice *n.* solid carbon dioxide used as a refrigerant.

dryly *or* **drily** ('draɪlɪ) *adv.* in a dry manner.

dry measure *n.* a unit or system of units for measuring dry goods.

dry out *vb.* **1.** to make or become dry. **2.** to undergo or cause to undergo treatment for alcoholism or drug addiction.

dry rot *n.* **1.** crumbling and drying of timber, caused by certain fungi. **2.** a fungus causing this decay.

dry run *n. Informal.* a rehearsal.

dry-stone *adj.* (of a wall) made without mortar.

dry up *vb.* **1.** to become unproductive; fail. **2.** to dry (dishes, cutlery, etc.) with a tea towel after they have been washed. **3.** *Informal.* to stop speaking.

DSc Doctor of Science.

DSC *Mil.* Distinguished Service Cross.

DSM *Mil.* Distinguished Service Medal.

DSO *Brit. mil.* Distinguished Service Order.

DSW (in New Zealand) Department of Social Welfare.

DT's *Informal.* delirium tremens.

dual ('djuːəl) *adj.* **1.** relating to or denoting two. **2.** twofold; double. **—duality** (djuː'ælɪtɪ) *n.*

dual carriageway *n. Brit.* a road on which traffic travelling in opposite directions is separated by a central strip of turf or concrete.

dub¹ (dʌb) *vb.* **dubbing, dubbed. 1.** to give (a person or place) a name or nickname. **2.** to make (a person) a knight by tapping him on the shoulder with a sword.

dub² (dʌb) *vb.* **dubbing, dubbed. 1.** to provide (a film) with a new soundtrack, esp. in a different language. **2.** to provide (a film or tape) with a soundtrack. ~*n.* **3.** *Music.* a style of record production associated with reggae, involving exaggeration of instrumental parts, the use of echo, etc.

dubbin ('dʌbɪn) *n. Brit.* a greasy preparation applied to leather to soften it and make it waterproof.

dubious ('djuːbɪəs) *adj.* **1.** marked by or causing doubt. **2.** uncertain; doubtful. **3.** of doubtful quality; untrustworthy. —**dubiety** (djuː'baɪɪtɪ) *n.* —**'dubiously** *adv.*

ducal ('djuːkᵊl) *adj.* of a duke.

ducat ('dʌkət) *n.* a former European gold or silver coin.

duchess ('dʌtʃɪs) *n.* **1.** the wife or widow of a duke. **2.** a woman who holds the rank of duke in her own right.

duchy ('dʌtʃɪ) *n., pl.* **duchies.** the territory of a duke or duchess.

duck¹ (dʌk) *n., pl.* **ducks** or **duck.** **1.** a water bird with short legs, webbed feet, and a broad blunt bill. **2.** the flesh of this bird, used as food. **3.** the female of such a bird. **4.** Also: **ducks.** *Brit. informal.* dear: used as a term of address. **5.** *Cricket.* a score of nothing. **6. like water off a duck's back.** without effect.

duck² (dʌk) *vb.* **1.** to move (the head or body) quickly downwards, to escape observation or evade a blow. **2.** to plunge suddenly under water. **3.** *Informal.* to dodge or escape (a duty, etc.).

duck-billed platypus *n.* an amphibious mammal of E Australia with dense fur, a broad bill and tail, and webbed feet.

duckboard ('dʌk,bɔːd) *n.* a board laid so as to form a path over muddy ground.

duckling ('dʌklɪŋ) *n.* a young duck.

ducks and drakes *n. (functioning as sing.)* **1.** a game in which a flat stone is bounced across the surface of water. **2. play ducks and drakes with.** *Informal.* to use recklessly; squander.

ducky or **duckie** ('dʌkɪ) *n., pl.* **duckies.** *Brit. informal.* dear: a term of endearment.

duct (dʌkt) *n.* **1.** a tube, pipe, or canal by means of which a fluid or gas is conveyed. **2.** a bodily passage conveying secretions or excretions.

ductile ('dʌktaɪl) *adj.* **1.** (of a metal) able to be hammered into sheets or drawn out into wires. **2.** easily led or influenced. —**ductility** (dʌk'tɪlɪtɪ) *n.*

ductless gland ('dʌktlɪs) *n. Anat.* same as **endocrine gland.**

dud (dʌd) *Informal.* ~*n.* **1.** a person or thing that proves ineffectual. **2.** (*pl.*) Old-fashioned. clothes. ~*adj.* **3.** bad or useless.

dude (djuːd) *n. Informal.* **1.** *Western U.S. & Canad.* a city dweller, esp. one holidaying on a ranch. **2.** *U.S. & Canad.* a dandy. **3.** *U.S. & Canad.* a fellow; chap.

dudgeon ('dʌdʒən) *n.* **in high dudgeon.** angry or resentful.

due (djuː) *adj.* **1.** expected or scheduled to be present or arrive. **2.** immediately payable. **3.** owed as a debt. **4.** fitting; proper. **5. due to.** attributable to or caused by. ~*n.* **6.** something that is owed, required, or due. **7. give a person his due.** to allow a person what is deserved or acknowledge his good points. ~*adv.* **8.** directly or exactly: *due north.*
Usage. There is considerable controversy over the use of *due to* as an equivalent to *because of.* Careful users of English prefer *because of* or *owing to.* The use of *due to* to mean *caused by,* as in *the error was due to carelessness,* is perfectly acceptable but *owing to* is not ordinarily used in this way.

duel ('djuːəl) *n.* **1.** a formal prearranged combat with deadly weapons between two people, to settle a quarrel. ~*vb.* **duelling, duelled** or *U.S.* **dueling, dueled.** **2.** to fight in a duel. —**'duellist** *n.*

duenna (djuː'ɛnə) *n.* (esp. in Spain) an elderly woman acting as chaperon to girls.

dues (djuːz) *pl. n.* charges for membership of a club or organization.

duet (djuː'ɛt) *n.* **1.** a musical composition for two performers. **2.** a pair of performers. —**du'ettist** *n.*

duff¹ (dʌf) *n.* a pudding boiled in a cloth bag.

duff² (dʌf) *vb.* **1.** (foll. by *up*) *Brit. slang.* to beat (a person) severely. **2.** *Golf, informal.* to bungle (a shot). ~*adj.* **3.** *Brit. informal.* bad or useless: *a duff engine.*

duffel or **duffle** ('dʌfᵊl) *n.* **1.** same as **duffel coat. 2.** a heavy woollen cloth.

duffel bag *n.* a cylindrical drawstring canvas bag.

duffel coat *n.* a wool coat, usually with a hood and fastened with toggles.

duffer ('dʌfə) *n. Informal.* a dull or incompetent person.

dug¹ (dʌg) *vb.* past of **dig.**

dug² (dʌg) *n.* a teat or udder.

dugong ('duːgɒŋ) *n.* a whalelike mammal occurring in tropical waters.

dugout ('dʌg,aʊt) *n.* **1.** a canoe made by hollowing out a log. **2.** *Mil.* a covered excavation dug to provide shelter. **3.** (at a sports ground) the covered bench where managers and substitutes sit.

duiker or **duyker** ('daɪkə) *n., pl.* **-kers** or **-ker. 1.** a small African antelope. **2.** *S. African.* a long-tailed cormorant.

duke (djuːk) *n.* **1.** a nobleman of high rank. **2.** the prince or ruler of a small principality or duchy. —**dukedom** *n.*

dulcet ('dʌlsɪt) *adj.* (of a sound) soothing or pleasant.

dulcimer ('dʌlsɪmə) *n.* a tuned percussion instrument consisting of a set of strings stretched over a sounding board and struck with hammers.

dull (dʌl) *adj.* **1.** lacking in interest. **2.** slow to understand; stupid. **3.** (of a blade) lacking sharpness. **4.** (of an ache) not acute, intense, or piercing. **5.** (of weather) not bright or clear. **6.** lacking in spirit; listless. **7.** (of colour) lacking brilliance; sombre. **8.** not loud or clear; muffled. ~*vb.* **9.** to make or become dull. —**'dullness** *n.* —**'dully** *adv.*

dullard ('dʌləd) *n.* a dull or stupid person.

dulse (dʌls) *n.* a seaweed with large red edible fronds.

duly ('dju:lɪ) *adv.* **1.** in a proper manner. **2.** at the proper time.

dumb (dʌm) *adj.* **1.** lacking the power to speak. **2.** lacking the power of human speech: *dumb animals.* **3.** temporarily bereft of the power to speak: *struck dumb.* **4.** done or performed without speech. **5.** *Informal.* **a.** dim-witted. **b.** foolish. —**'dumbly** *adv.*

dumbbell ('dʌm,bɛl) *n.* **1.** an exercising weight consisting of a short bar with a heavy ball or disc at either end. **2.** *Slang, chiefly U.S. & Canad.* a fool.

dumbfound *or* **dumfound** (dʌm'faʊnd) *vb.* to strike dumb with astonishment; amaze.

dumb show *n.* meaningful gestures.

dumbstruck ('dʌm,strʌk) *adj.* temporarily deprived of speech through shock or surprise.

dumbwaiter ('dʌm,weɪtə) *n.* **1.** *Brit.* **a.** a stand placed near a dining table to hold food. **b.** a revolving circular tray placed on a table to hold food. **2.** a lift for carrying food, rubbish, etc., between floors.

dumdum ('dʌm,dʌm) *or* **dumdum bullet** *n.* a soft-nosed bullet that expands on impact and inflicts extensive wounds.

dummy ('dʌmɪ) *n., pl.* **-mies. 1.** a figure representing the human form, used for displaying clothes, as a target, etc. **2.** a copy of an object, often lacking some essential feature of the original. **3.** *Slang.* a stupid person. **4.** a person who appears to act for himself while acting on behalf of another. **5.** *Bridge.* **a.** the hand exposed on the table by the declarer's partner and played by the declarer. **b.** the declarer's partner. **6.** *Brit.* a rubber teat for babies to suck. **7.** (*modifier*) counterfeit; sham.

dummy run *n.* an experimental run; practice; rehearsal.

dump (dʌmp) *vb.* **1.** to drop or let fall heavily or in a mass. **2. a.** *Informal.* to dispose of (something or someone) without subtlety or proper care. **b.** to dispose of (nuclear waste). **3.** *Commerce.* to market (goods) in bulk and at low prices, esp. abroad, in order to maintain a high price in the home market. **4.** *Computers.* to record (the contents of the memory) on a storage device at a series of points during a com-

puter run. ~*n.* **5.** a place where waste materials are dumped. **6.** *Informal.* a dirty, unattractive place. **7.** *Mil.* a place where weapons or supplies are stored.

dumpling ('dʌmplɪŋ) *n.* **1.** a small ball of dough cooked and served with stew. **2.** a round pastry case filled with fruit: *apple dumpling.* **3.** *Informal.* a short plump person.

dumps (dʌmps) *pl. n.* **down in the dumps.** *Informal.* in a state of melancholy or depression.

dumpy ('dʌmpɪ) *adj.* **dumpier, dumpiest.** short and plump.

dun¹ (dʌn) *vb.* **dunning, dunned. 1.** to press (a debtor) for payment. ~*n.* **2.** a demand for payment.

dun² (dʌn) *adj.* **dunner, dunnest.** brownish-grey.

dunce (dʌns) *n.* a person who is stupid or slow to learn.

dunderhead ('dʌndə,hɛd) *n.* a slow-witted person.

dune (dju:n) *n.* a mound or ridge of drifted sand.

dung (dʌŋ) *n.* excrement of animals; manure.

dungarees (,dʌŋgə'ri:z) *pl. n.* trousers with a bib attached.

dungeon ('dʌndʒən) *n.* a prison cell, often underground.

dunghill ('dʌŋ,hɪl) *n.* a heap of dung.

dunk (dʌŋk) *vb.* **1.** to dip (a biscuit, etc.) in a drink or soup before eating it. **2.** to submerge (something) in liquid.

dunlin ('dʌnlɪn) *n.* a small sandpiper with a brown back.

dunnock ('dʌnək) *n.* same as **hedge sparrow.**

duo ('dju:əʊ) *n., pl.* **duos. 1.** a pair of performers. **2.** *Informal.* a pair of closely connected individuals.

duodecimal (,dju:əʊ'dɛsɪməl) *adj.* relating to twelve or twelfths.

duodenum (,dju:əʊ'di:nəm) *n., pl.* **-na** (-nə) *or* **-nums.** the first part of the small intestine, just below the stomach. —,**duo'denal** *adj.*

duologue *or* U.S. (*sometimes*) **duolog** ('dju:ə,lɒg) *n.* a part or all of a play in which the speaking roles are limited to two actors.

dupe (dju:p) *vb.* **1.** to deceive; cheat; fool. ~*n.* **2.** a person who is easily deceived.

duple ('dju:p'l) *adj.* **1.** same as **double. 2.** *Music.* having two beats in a bar.

duplex ('dju:plɛks) *n.* **1.** *U.S. & Canad.* **a.** an apartment on two floors. **b.** a semidetached house. ~*adj.* **2.** having two parts.

duplicate *adj.* ('dju:plɪkɪt). **1.** copied exactly from an original. **2.** existing as a pair or in pairs. ~*n.* ('dju:plɪkɪt). **3.** an exact copy. **4.** something additional of the same kind. **5. in duplicate.** in two exact copies.

~*vb.* ('dju:plɪˌkeɪt). **6.** to make a replica of. **7.** to do again (something that has already been done). **8.** to make double. —ˌdupli'cation *n.* —'dupliˌcator *n.*

duplicity (dju:'plɪsɪtɪ) *n.* deception; double-dealing.

Dur. Durham.

durable ('djʊərəb³l) *adj.* long-lasting; enduring. —ˌdura'bility *n.*

durable goods *pl. n.* goods that require infrequent replacement. Also called: **durables.**

duration (djʊ'reɪʃən) *n.* the length of time that something lasts.

durbar ('dɜ:bɑː, ˌdɜ:'bɑː) *n.* **a.** (formerly) the court of a native ruler or a governor in India. **b.** a reception at such a court.

duress (djʊ'rɛs, djʊə-) *n.* compulsion by use of force or threat: *he agreed to be chairman under duress.*

during ('djʊərɪŋ) *prep.* throughout or within the limit of (a period of time).

dusk (dʌsk) *n.* the time just before nightfall when it is almost dark.

dusky ('dʌskɪ) *adj.* **duskier, duskiest. 1.** dark in colour. **2.** dim or shadowy. —'duskily *adv.* —'duskiness *n.*

dust (dʌst) *n.* **1.** dry fine powdery material, such as particles of dirt. **2.** the remains of a dead person. **3. kick up a dust.** *Informal.* to raise a disturbance. **4. shake the dust off one's feet.** to depart angrily. **5. throw dust in someone's eyes.** to confuse or mislead someone. ~*vb.* **6.** to remove dust from (furniture) by wiping. **7.** to sprinkle (something) with dust or some other powdery substance.

dustbin ('dʌstˌbɪn) *n.* a large, usually cylindrical container for household rubbish.

dust bowl *n.* a dry area in which the surface soil is exposed to wind erosion.

dustcart ('dʌstˌkɑːt) *n.* a road vehicle for collecting refuse.

dust cover *n.* **1.** same as **dustsheet. 2.** same as **dust jacket.**

duster ('dʌstə) *n.* a cloth used for dusting.

dust jacket *or* **cover** *n.* a removable paper cover used to protect a book.

dustman ('dʌstmən) *n., pl.* **-men.** *Brit.* a man whose job is to collect household refuse.

dustpan ('dʌstˌpæn) *n.* a short-handled hooded shovel into which dust is swept from floors.

dustsheet ('dʌstˌʃiːt) *n. Brit.* a large cloth used to protect furniture from dust.

dust-up *n. Informal.* a fight or argument.

dusty ('dʌstɪ) *adj.* **dustier, dustiest. 1.** covered with dust. **2.** (of a colour) tinged with grey.

Dutch (dʌtʃ) *n.* **1.** the language of the Netherlands. **2. the Dutch.** (*functioning as pl.*) the people of the Netherlands. ~*adj.* **3.** of

the Netherlands, its inhabitants, or their language. ~*adv.* **4. go Dutch.** *Informal.* to go on an outing where each person pays his own expenses.

Dutch auction *n.* an auction in which the price is lowered by stages until a buyer is found.

Dutch barn *n. Brit.* a farm building consisting of a steel frame and a curved roof.

Dutch courage *n.* false courage gained from drinking alcohol.

Dutch elm disease *n.* a fungal disease of elm trees.

Dutchman ('dʌtʃmən) *n., pl.* **-men. 1.** a person from the Netherlands. **2.** *S. African offensive.* an Afrikaner.

Dutch oven *n.* **1.** an iron or earthenware container with a cover, used for stews, etc. **2.** a metal box, open in front, for cooking in front of an open fire.

Dutch treat *n. Informal.* an outing where each person pays his own expenses.

Dutch uncle *n. Informal.* a person who criticizes or reproves frankly and severely.

duteous ('dju:tɪəs) *adj. Formal or archaic.* dutiful; obedient.

dutiable ('dju:tɪəb³l) *adj.* (of goods) requiring payment of duty.

dutiful ('dju:tɪful) *adj.* showing or resulting from a sense of duty. —'dutifully *adv.*

duty ('dju:tɪ) *n., pl.* **-ties. 1.** a task that a person is bound to perform for moral or legal reasons. **2.** respect or obedience owed to parents, older people, etc. **3.** the force that binds one morally or legally to one's obligations. **4.** a government tax, esp. on imports. **5. on** (*or* **off**) **duty.** at (*or* not at) work.

duty-bound *adj.* morally obliged.

duty-free *adj., adv.* with exemption from customs or excise duties.

duty-free shop *n.* a shop, esp. at an airport, that sells certain goods at duty-free prices.

duvet ('du:veɪ) *n.* same as **continental quilt.**

duvet jacket *n.* a down-filled jacket.

dwaal (dwɑːl) *n. S. African.* a state of befuddlement; daze.

dwarf (dwɔːf) *n., pl.* **dwarfs** *or* **dwarves** (dwɔːvz). **1.** an abnormally undersized person. **2.** (*modifier*) denoting an animal or plant much below the average size for the species. **3.** (in folklore) a small ugly manlike creature, often possessing magical powers. ~*vb.* **4.** to cause (someone or something) to seem small by being much larger.

dwell (dwɛl) *vb.* **dwelling, dwelt** *or* **dwelled.** *Formal, literary.* to live as a permanent resident. —'dweller *n.*

dwelling ('dwɛlɪŋ) *n. Formal, literary.* a place of residence.

dwell on *or* **upon** *vb.* to think, speak, or write at length about (something).

dwindle ('dwɪnd²l) *vb.* to grow less in size, intensity, or number.

Dy *Chem.* dysprosium.

dye (daɪ) *n.* **1.** a staining or colouring substance. **2.** the colour produced by dyeing. ~*vb.* **dyeing, dyed. 3.** to colour or stain (fabric, hair, etc.) by the application of a dye. —'**dyer** *n.*

dyed-in-the-wool *adj.* uncompromising or unchanging in attitude or opinion.

dying ('daɪɪŋ) *vb.* **1.** the present participle of **die¹**. ~*adj.* **2.** relating to or occurring at the moment of death: *a dying wish.*

dyke¹ *or esp. U.S.* **dike** (daɪk) *n.* **1.** an embankment to prevent flooding. **2.** a ditch. **3.** *Scot.* a dry-stone wall. ~*vb.* **4.** to enclose or drain (land) with a dyke.

dyke² *or* **dike** (daɪk) *n. Slang.* a lesbian.

dynamic (daɪ'næmɪk) *adj.* **1.** characterized by force of personality, ambition, and energy. **2.** of or concerned with energy or forces that produce motion. —**dy-** '**namically** *adv.*

dynamics (daɪ'næmɪks) *n.* **1.** (*functioning as sing.*) the branch of mechanics concerned with the forces that change or produce the motions of bodies. **2.** (*functioning as pl.*) those forces that produce change in any field or system. **3.** (*functioning as pl.*) *Music.* the various degrees of loudness called for in performance.

dynamism ('daɪnə,mɪzəm) *n.* the forcefulness of an energetic personality.

dynamite ('daɪnə,maɪt) *n.* **1.** an explosive consisting of nitroglycerin mixed with an absorbent substance. **2.** *Informal.* a spectacular or potentially dangerous person or thing: *the new singer is dynamite.* ~*vb.* **3.** to mine or blow (something) up with dynamite.

dynamo ('daɪnə,məʊ) *n., pl.* **-mos.** a device for converting mechanical energy into electrical energy.

dynamoelectric (,daɪnəməʊɪ'lɛktrɪk) *adj.* of the conversion of mechanical into electrical energy or vice versa.

dynamometer (,daɪnə'mɒmɪtə) *n.* an instrument for measuring mechanical power.

dynast ('dɪnəst) *n.* a ruler, esp. a hereditary one.

dynasty ('dɪnəstɪ) *n., pl.* **-ties. 1.** a sequence of hereditary rulers. **2.** any sequence of powerful leaders of the same family. —**dynastic** (dɪ'næstɪk) *adj.*

dyne (daɪn) *n.* the cgs unit of force; the force that imparts an acceleration of 1 centimetre per second per second to a mass of 1 gram.

dysentery ('dɪs²ntrɪ) *n.* infection of the intestine causing severe diarrhoea with mucus and blood.

dysfunction (dɪs'fʌŋkʃən) *n. Med.* any disturbance or abnormality in the function of an organ or part.

dyslexia (dɪs'lɛksɪə) *n.* a developmental disorder causing impaired ability to read. —**dys'lexic** *adj., n.*

dysmenorrhoea *or esp. U.S.* **dysmenorrhea** (,dɪsmɛnə'rɪə) *n.* painful or difficult menstruation.

dyspepsia (dɪs'pɛpsɪə) *n.* indigestion. —**dys'peptic** *adj., n.*

dysprosium (dɪs'prəʊsɪəm) *n.* a metallic element of the lanthanide series. Symbol: Dy

dystrophy ('dɪstrəfɪ) *n.* See **muscular dystrophy.**

dz. dozen.

E

e *or* **E** (iː) *n., pl.* **e's, E's,** *or* **Es.** the fifth letter of the English alphabet.

e *Maths.* a number used as the base of natural logarithms. Approximate value: 2.718 282...

E **1.** *Music.* the third note of the scale of C major. **2.** East. **3.** English. **4.** *Physics.* **a.** energy. **b.** electromotive force.

E- *prefix.* used with numbers indicating an EC standard, as of pack size or recognized food additive.

each (iːtʃ) *det.* **1.** every (one) of two or more considered individually: *each day; each gave according to his ability.* ~*adv.* **2.** for, to, or from each one; apiece: *four apples each.* **3. each other.** one another. **4. each way.** (of a bet) made on a horse or other contestant either winning or coming second or third.
Usage. see **everyone.**

eager (ˈiːgə) *adj.* showing or feeling great desire; keen. —ˈ**eagerly** *adv.* —ˈ**eagerness** *n.*

eager beaver *n. Informal.* an extremely hard-working person.

eagle (ˈiːgʲl) *n.* **1.** a bird of prey with large broad wings and strong soaring flight. **2.** *Golf.* a score of two strokes under par for a hole.

eagle-eyed *adj.* having keen or piercing eyesight.

eaglet (ˈiːglɪt) *n.* a young eagle.

ear[1] (ɪə) *n.* **1.** the organ of hearing. **2.** the external, visible part of the ear. **3.** sensitivity to musical or other sounds: *a good ear for music.* **4.** attention; consideration: *lend me your ears.* **5. all ears.** listening carefully. **6. fall on deaf ears.** to be ignored. **7. in one ear and out the other.** heard but unheeded. **8. keep** *or* **have one's ear to the ground.** to be well informed about current trends. **9. out on one's ear.** *Informal.* dismissed unceremoniously. **10. play by ear. a.** *Informal.* to act according to the demands of a situation. **b.** to play without written music. **11. turn a deaf ear.** to be deliberately unresponsive. **12. up to one's ears.** *Informal.* deeply involved.

ear[2] (ɪə) *n.* the part of a cereal plant, such as wheat or barley, that contains the seeds.

earache (ˈɪərˌeɪk) *n.* pain in the ear.

eardrum (ˈɪəˌdrʌm) *n.* the thin membrane separating the external ear from the middle ear.

earl (ɜːl) *n.* (in Britain) a nobleman ranking below a marquess and above a viscount. —ˈ**earldom** *n.*

Earl Marshal *n.* (in Britain) an officer who presides over the College of Heralds and organizes ceremonies.

early (ˈɜːlɪ) *adj., adv.* **-lier, -liest. 1.** before the expected or usual time. **2.** in the first part of a period. **3.** in a period far back in time. **4.** in the near future.

Early English *n.* a style of architecture used in England in the 12th and 13th centuries, characterized by lancet arches and tracery.

earmark (ˈɪəˌmɑːk) *vb.* **1.** to set (something) aside for a specific purpose. **2.** to make an identification mark on the ear of (a domestic animal). ~*n.* **3.** such a mark of identification.

earn (ɜːn) *vb.* **1.** to gain or be paid (money) in return for work. **2.** to acquire or deserve through behaviour or action: *this action earned the condemnation of the world's press.* **3.** (of securities or investments) to gain (interest or profit). —ˈ**earner** *n.*

earnest[1] (ˈɜːnɪst) *adj.* **1.** serious in mind or intention. ~*n.* **2. in earnest.** with serious or sincere intentions. —ˈ**earnestly** *adv.* —ˈ**earnestness** *n.*

earnest[2] (ˈɜːnɪst) *n.* a part payment given in advance as a guarantee of the remainder, esp. to confirm a contract.

earnings (ˈɜːnɪŋz) *pl. n.* **1.** money earned. **2.** profits or investment income.

earphone (ˈɪəˌfəʊn) *n.* a device or one of a pair of devices for converting electric currents into sound, worn over the ear.

ear-piercing *adj.* loud or shrill.

earplug (ˈɪəˌplʌg) *n.* a piece of soft material placed in the ear to keep out noise or water.

earring (ˈɪəˌrɪŋ) *n.* an ornament for the lobe of the ear.

earshot (ˈɪəˌʃɒt) *n.* the range within which sound may be heard: *out of earshot.*

ear-splitting *adj.* loud or shrill.

earth (ɜːθ) *n.* **1.** (*sometimes cap.*) the planet that we live on, the third planet from the sun, the only one on which life is known to exist. **2.** the inhabitants of this planet. **3.** land; ground. **4.** soil. **5.** the hole in which a fox lives. **6.** a connection between an electric circuit and the earth. **7. come down to earth.** to return to reality. **8. on earth.** (used for emphasis): *what on earth are you doing?* **9. run to earth.** to hunt down: *they ran him to earth on the Costa del Sol.* ~*vb.* **10.** to connect (a circuit) to earth. ~See also **earth up.**

earthbound (ˈɜːθˌbaʊnd) *adj.* **1.** confined to the earth. **2.** heading towards the earth.

earth closet *n.* a type of lavatory in which earth is used to cover excreta.

earthen ('ɜːθən) *adj.* made of earth or baked clay: *earthen pots.*

earthenware ('ɜːθən‚wɛə) *n.* dishes, mugs, etc., made of baked clay.

earthly ('ɜːθlɪ) *adj.* **-lier, -liest. 1.** of the earth as opposed to heaven; materialistic; worldly. **2.** *Informal.* conceivable or possible: *they haven't got an earthly chance of winning.*

earthquake ('ɜːθ‚kweɪk) *n.* a series of vibrations at the earth's surface caused by movement of the earth's crust.

earth science *n.* any science, such as geology, concerned with the structure, age, etc., of the earth.

earth up *vb.* to cover (part of a plant) with soil to protect it from frost, light, etc.

earthward ('ɜːθwəd) *adj.* directed towards the earth.

earthwards ('ɜːθwədz) *adv.* towards the earth.

earthwork ('ɜːθ‚wɜːk) *n.* a fortification made of earth.

earthworm ('ɜːθ‚wɜːm) *n.* any of numerous worms which burrow in the soil.

earthy ('ɜːθɪ) *adj.* **earthier, earthiest. 1.** of or like earth. **2.** unrefined, coarse, or crude. —**'earthiness** *n.*

ear trumpet *n.* a trumpet-shaped instrument held to the ear: an old form of hearing aid.

earwig ('ɪə‚wɪg) *n.* an insect with pincers at the tip of its abdomen.

ease (iːz) *n.* **1.** lack of difficulty. **2.** freedom from discomfort or worry. **3.** rest, leisure, or relaxation. **4.** freedom from poverty. **5. at ease. a.** *Mil.* (of a soldier) standing in a relaxed position with the feet apart. **b.** in a relaxed attitude or frame of mind. ~*vb.* **6.** to make or become less difficult or severe. **7.** to relieve (a person) of worry or care. **8.** to move into or out of a place or situation with careful manipulation. **9.** (often foll. by *off* or *up*) to lessen or cause to lessen in severity, pressure, tension, or strain.

easel ('iːz³l) *n.* a frame for supporting an artist's canvas, a display, or a blackboard.

easement ('iːzmənt) *n. Property law.* the right of making limited use of a neighbour's land, as for a right of way.

easily ('iːzɪlɪ) *adv.* **1.** with ease; without difficulty. **2.** almost certainly: *easily the best.*

east (iːst) *n.* **1.** the direction along a line of latitude towards the sunrise, at 90° to north. **2. the east.** any area lying in or towards the east. ~*adj.* **3.** situated in, moving towards, or facing the east. **4.** (esp. of the wind) from the east. ~*adv.* **5.** in, to, or towards the east.

East (iːst) *n.* **the. 1.** the continent of Asia;

the Orient. **2.** the countries under Communist rule in the E hemisphere. ~*adj.* **3.** of or denoting the eastern part of a country or region.

eastbound ('iːst‚baʊnd) *adj.* going towards the east.

Easter ('iːstə) *n.* **1.** *Christianity.* a festival, in the spring, commemorating the Resurrection of Christ. **2.** the time of the year when this is celebrated.

Easter egg *n.* a chocolate egg given at Easter.

easterly ('iːstəlɪ) *adj.* **1.** of or in the east. ~*adv., adj.* **2.** towards the east. **3.** from the east: *an easterly wind.*

eastern ('iːstən) *adj.* **1.** situated in or towards the east. **2.** facing or moving towards the east.

eastern hemisphere *n.* the half of the globe that contains Europe, Asia, Africa, and Australia.

eastward ('iːstwəd) *adj., adv. also* **eastwards. 1.** towards the east. ~*n.* **2.** the eastward part, direction, etc.

easy ('iːzɪ) *adj.* **easier, easiest. 1.** not difficult. **2.** free from pain, care, or anxiety. **3.** tolerant and undemanding; easy-going. **4.** readily influenced; pliant: *an easy victim.* **5.** moderate: *an easy pace.* **6.** *Informal.* ready to fall in with any suggestion made: *you decide what to do, I'm easy.* ~*adv.* **7.** *Informal.* in an easy or relaxed manner. **8. easy does it.** *Informal.* go slowly and carefully. **9. go easy.** to exercise moderation: *go easy on the salt, it's bad for your heart.* **10. take it easy. a.** to avoid stress or undue hurry. **b.** to remain calm. —**'easiness** *n.*
Usage. Easy is not usually used as an adverb except in certain set phrases: *to take it easy; easy does it.* Where a fixed expression is not involved, the usual adverbial form of *easy* is used: *this polish goes on more easily* (not *easier*) *than the other.*

easy chair *n.* a comfortable upholstered armchair.

easy-going ('iːzɪ'gəʊɪŋ) *adj.* relaxed in manner or attitude; very tolerant.

eat (iːt) *vb.* **eating, ate, eaten. 1.** to take (food) into the mouth and swallow it. **2.** (often foll. by *away, into,* or *up*) to destroy or use up partly or wholly: *the damp had eaten away the woodwork.* **3.** to take (a meal): *we eat at six.* **4.** *Informal.* to cause to worry; make anxious: *what's eating you?* ~See also **eat out, eat up.** —**'eater** *n.*

eatable ('iːtəb³l) *adj.* fit or suitable for eating.

eating ('iːtɪŋ) *n.* **1.** food in relation to quality or taste: *this fruit makes excellent eating.* ~*adj.* **2.** suitable for eating uncooked: *eating apples.*

eat out *vb.* to eat at a restaurant.

eat up *vb.* **1.** to eat or consume entirely:

eat up your breakfast. **2.** *Informal.* to affect grossly: *eaten up by jealousy.*

eau de Cologne (ˌəʊ də kəˈləʊn) *n.* See **cologne.**

eau de vie (ˌəʊ də ˈviː) *n.* brandy or other spirits.

eaves (iːvz) *pl. n.* the edge of a sloping roof that overhangs the walls.

eavesdrop (ˈiːvzˌdrɒp) *vb.* **-dropping, -dropped.** to listen secretly to private conversation. —**ˈeaves,dropper** *n.*

ebb (ɛb) *vb.* **1.** (of tide water) to flow back or recede. **2.** to fall away or decline. ~*n.* **3.** the flowing back of the tide from high to low water. **4. at a low ebb.** in a state of weakness.

ebony (ˈɛbənɪ) *n., pl.* **-onies.** **1.** the hard dark wood of various tropical and subtropical trees. **2.** a black colour.

ebullient (ɪˈbʌljənt) *adj.* overflowing with enthusiasm or excitement. —**eˈbullience** *n.*

EC European Community.

eccentric (ɪkˈsɛntrɪk) *adj.* **1.** unconventional or odd. **2.** situated away from the centre or the axis. **3.** not having a common centre: *eccentric circles.* ~*n.* **4.** a person who deviates from normal behaviour. —**ecˈcentrically** *adv.*

eccentricity (ˌɛksɛnˈtrɪsɪtɪ) *n., pl.* **-ties.** **1.** unconventional behaviour. **2.** deviation from a circular path or orbit.

ecclesiastic (ɪˌkliːzɪˈæstɪk) *n.* **1.** a clergyman. ~*adj.* **2.** of or associated with the Christian Church or clergy.

ecclesiastical (ɪˌkliːzɪˈæstɪkˀl) *adj.* of or relating to the Christian Church.

ECG electrocardiogram.

echelon (ˈɛʃəˌlɒn) *n.* **1.** a level of power, influence, or responsibility: *the upper echelons.* **2.** *Mil.* a formation in which units follow one another but are offset to allow each a line of fire ahead.

echidna (ɪˈkɪdnə) *n.* a spine-covered egg-laying mammal of Australia and New Guinea, with a long snout and claws. Also called: **spiny anteater.**

echinoderm (ɪˈkaɪnəʊˌdɜːm) *n.* any of various marine animals with a five-part symmetrical body, such as starfish, sea urchins, and sea cucumbers.

echo (ˈɛkəʊ) *n., pl.* **-oes.** **1. a.** the reflection of sound by a solid object. **b.** the sound so reflected. **2.** a repetition or imitation of another's opinions. **3.** something that evokes memories. **4.** the signal reflected by a radar target. ~*vb.* **-oing, -oed.** **5.** to resound or cause to resound with an echo. **6.** (of sounds) to repeat by echoes; reverberate. **7.** (of persons) to repeat (words or opinions) in imitation, agreement, or flattery. —**ˈechoing** *adj.*

echo chamber *n.* a room with walls that reflect sound, used for acoustic measure-

ments and as a recording studio when echo effects are required.

echoic (ɛˈkəʊɪk) *adj.* **1.** of or like an echo. **2.** sounding like something else; imitative.

echolocation (ˌɛkəʊləʊˈkeɪʃən) *n.* determination of an object's position by measuring the time taken for an echo to return from it.

echo sounder *n.* a navigation device that determines depth by measuring the time taken for a pulse of sound to reach the sea bed and for the echo to return. —**echo sounding** *n.*

éclair (eɪˈklɛə, ɪˈklɛə) *n.* a finger-shaped cake of choux pastry, filled with cream and covered with chocolate.

éclat (eɪˈklɑː) *n.* **1.** brilliant success or effect. **2.** showy display. **3.** acclaim.

eclectic (ɪˈklɛktɪk) *adj.* **1.** selecting from various styles, ideas, or methods. **2.** composed of elements so selected. ~*n.* **3.** a person who favours an eclectic approach. —**eˈclectically** *adv.* —**eclecticism** (ɪˈklɛktɪˌsɪzəm) *n.*

eclipse (ɪˈklɪps) *n.* **1.** the obscuring of one celestial body by another. A solar eclipse occurs when the moon passes between the sun and the earth; a **lunar eclipse** when the earth passes between the sun and the moon. **2.** a loss of importance, power, or fame: *the management has suffered an eclipse.* ~*vb.* **3.** to cause an eclipse of. **4.** to overshadow or surpass.

ecliptic (ɪˈklɪptɪk) *n. Astron.* the great circle on the celestial sphere representing the apparent annual path of the sun relative to the stars.

eclogue (ˈɛklɒg) *n.* a short poem on a rural theme.

eco- *combining form.* denoting ecology or ecological: *ecocide; ecosphere.*

ecology (ɪˈkɒlədʒɪ) *n.* the study of the relationships between living organisms and their environment. —**ecological** (ˌiːkəˈlɒdʒɪkˀl) *adj.* —**eˈcologist** *n.*

econ. economic(s).

economic (ˌiːkəˈnɒmɪk, ˌɛkə-) *adj.* **1.** of or relating to an economy, economics, or finance. **2.** *Brit.* capable of being produced, operated, or sold for profit; profitable. **3.** *Informal.* inexpensive; cheap.

economical (ˌiːkəˈnɒmɪkˀl, ˌɛkə-) *adj.* **1.** using the minimum required; not wasteful. **2.** frugal; thrifty. —**ecoˈnomically** *adv.*

economics (ˌiːkəˈnɒmɪks, ˌɛkə-) *n.* **1.** (*functioning as sing.*) the social science concerned with the production and consumption of goods and services and the commercial activities of a society. **2.** (*functioning as pl.*) financial aspects.

economist (ɪˈkɒnəmɪst) *n.* a person who specializes in economics.

economize *or* **-ise** (ɪˈkɒnəˌmaɪz) *vb.* to limit or reduce (expense or waste). —**eˌconomiˈzation** *or* **-iˈsation** *n.*

economy (ɪˈkɒnəmɪ) *n., pl.* **-mies.** **1.** careful management of resources; thrift. **2.** a means or instance of this. **3.** the complex of activities concerned with the production, distribution, and consumption of goods and services. **4.** the management of the resources, finances, income, and expenditure of a community, business enterprise, etc. **5.** a class of air travel, cheaper than first class. **6.** (*modifier*) purporting to offer a larger quantity for a lower price: *an economy pack.*

ecosystem (ˈiːkəʊˌsɪstəm, ˈɛkəʊ-) *n. Ecology.* a system involving the interactions between a community and its nonliving environment.

ecru (ˈɛkruː) *adj.* greyish-yellow.

ecstasy (ˈɛkstəsɪ) *n., pl.* **-sies.** **1.** a state of exalted delight or joy; rapture. **2.** *Slang.* 3,4-methylenedioxymethamphetamine: a powerful drug which acts as a stimulant and which can produce hallucinations. —**ecstatic** (ɛkˈstætɪk) *adj.*

ECT electroconvulsive therapy.

ectoplasm (ˈɛktəʊˌplæzəm) *n. Spiritualism.* the substance that supposedly exudes from the body of a medium during a trance. —ˌ**ectoˈplasmic** *adj.*

ECU (ˈeɪkjuː) *n.* European Currency Unit: a unit of currency based on the composite value of several different currencies in the Common Market.

ecumenical (ˌiːkjuˈmɛnɪkᵊl, ˌɛk-) *adj.* **1.** of or relating to the Christian Church throughout the world. **2.** tending to promote unity among Churches. —ˌ**ecuˈmenically** *adv.*

eczema (ˈɛksɪmə) *n. Pathol.* a skin inflammation with blisters that scale, crust, or weep, often accompanied by intense itching.

ed. **1.** edited. **2.** (*pl.* **eds.**) edition. **3.** (*pl.* **eds.**) editor. **4.** educated. **5.** education.

Edam (ˈiːdæm) *n.* a round yellow cheese with a red waxy covering.

eddy (ˈɛdɪ) *n., pl.* **-dies.** **1.** a movement in air, water, or other fluid in which the current doubles back on itself. ~*vb.* **-dying, -died.** **2.** to move or cause to move against the main current.

edelweiss (ˈeɪdᵊlˌvaɪs) *n.* a small alpine flowering plant having white woolly leaves surrounding the flowers.

Eden (ˈiːdᵊn) *n.* **1.** Also called: **Garden of Eden.** *Bible.* the garden in which Adam and Eve were placed at the Creation. **2.** a place of great delight or contentment.

edentate (iːˈdɛnteɪt) *n.* **1.** any of an order of mammals which have few or no teeth, such as anteaters, sloths, and armadillos. ~*adj.* **2.** of or relating to this order.

edge (ɛdʒ) *n.* **1.** a border, brim, or margin. **2.** a line along which two faces or surfaces of a solid meet. **3.** the sharp cutting side of a blade. **4.** keenness, sharpness, or urgency. **5. have the edge on.** to have a slight advantage over. **6. on edge.** nervously irritable or excited. **7. set (someone's) teeth on edge.** to make (someone) acutely irritated. ~*vb.* **8.** to provide an edge or border for. **9.** to shape or trim the edge or border of (something). **10.** (foll. by *in, through,* etc.) to push (one's way) gradually. **11.** to sharpen (a knife, etc.).

edgeways (ˈɛdʒˌweɪz) *or esp. U.S. & Canad.* **edgewise** (ˈɛdʒˌwaɪz) *adv.* **1.** with the edge forwards or uppermost. **2.** on, by, with, or towards the edge. **3. get a word in edgeways.** to interrupt a conversation in which someone else is talking continuously.

edging (ˈɛdʒɪŋ) *n.* anything placed along an edge to finish it, esp. as an ornament.

edgy (ˈɛdʒɪ) *adj.* **edgier, edgiest.** nervous, irritable, tense, or anxious. —ˈ**edginess** *n.*

edible (ˈɛdɪbᵊl) *adj.* fit to be eaten; eatable. —ˌ**ediˈbility** *n.*

edict (ˈiːdɪkt) *n.* a decree or order issued by any authority.

edifice (ˈɛdɪfɪs) *n.* **1.** a building, esp. a large or imposing one. **2.** an elaborate organization.

edify (ˈɛdɪˌfaɪ) *vb.* **-fying, -fied.** to improve the morality or understanding of (a person) by instruction. —ˌ**edifiˈcation** *n.* —ˈ**ediˌfying** *adj.*

edit (ˈɛdɪt) *vb.* **1.** to prepare (text) for publication by checking and improving its accuracy or clarity. **2.** to be in charge of (a publication, esp. a periodical). **3.** to prepare (a film, tape, etc.) by rearranging or selecting material. **4.** (often foll. by *out*) to remove (parts of a text, film, etc.).

edition (ɪˈdɪʃən) *n.* **1.** one of a number of printings of a book or other publication, issued at separate times with alterations or amendments. **2.** *Printing.* the entire number of copies of a book or other publication printed at one time.

editor (ˈɛdɪtə) *n.* **1.** a person who edits. **2.** a person in overall charge of a newspaper or periodical. **3.** a person in charge of one section of a newspaper or periodical. **4.** a person in overall control of a television or radio programme. —ˈ**editorˌship** *n.*

editorial (ˌɛdɪˈtɔːrɪəl) *adj.* **1.** of editing or editors. **2.** of or expressed in an editorial. ~*n.* **3.** an article in a newspaper expressing the opinion of the editor or the publishers. —ˌ**ediˈtorially** *adv.*

EDP electronic data processing.

EDT Eastern Daylight Time.

educate (ˈɛdjʊˌkeɪt) *vb.* **1.** to impart knowledge by formal instruction to (a pupil); teach. **2.** to provide schooling for. **3.** to improve or develop (a person, taste, skills, etc.). —ˈ**educable** *adj.* —ˌ**educaˈbility** *n.* —ˈ**educative** *adj.*

educated (ˈɛdjʊˌkeɪtɪd) *adj.* **1.** having an

education, esp. a good one. **2.** displaying culture, taste, and knowledge. **3.** based on experience: *an educated guess.*

education (ˌɛdjuˈkeɪʃən) *n.* **1.** the process of acquiring knowledge. **2.** the knowledge acquired. **3.** the process of imparting knowledge, esp. at a school, college, or university. **4.** the theory of teaching and learning. —ˌeduˈcational *adj.* —ˌeduˈcationalist *or* ˌeduˈcationist *n.*

Edwardian (ɛdˈwɔːdɪən) *adj.* of or characteristic of the reign of King Edward VII (1901–10).

EEC European Economic Community (the Common Market).

EEG electroencephalogram.

eel (iːl) *n.* a fish with a long snakelike body, a smooth slimy skin, and reduced fins.

e'en (iːn) *adv., n. Poetic or archaic.* short for **even²** or **evening.**

e'er (ɛə) *adv. Poetic or archaic.* short for **ever.**

eerie (ˈɪərɪ) *adj.* **eerier, eeriest.** uncannily frightening or disturbing; weird. —ˈeerily *adv.* —ˈeeriness *n.*

efface (ɪˈfeɪs) *vb.* **1.** to obliterate or make dim: *to efface a memory.* **2.** to make (oneself) inconspicuous. **3.** to rub out; erase. —efˈfacement *n.*

effect (ɪˈfɛkt) *n.* **1.** a change or state of affairs produced by a cause; result. **2.** power to influence or produce a result. **3.** the condition of being operative: *problems arose in putting the proposals into effect.* **4.** the overall impression. **5.** basic meaning or purpose: *comments to the effect that it was disgraceful; words to that effect.* **6.** an impression, usually contrived: *he's only doing it for effect.* **7. in effect.** for all practical purposes: *in effect, there is no alternative.* **8. take effect.** to begin to produce results. ~*vb.* **9.** to cause to occur; accomplish.

effective (ɪˈfɛktɪv) *adj.* **1.** producing a desired result. **2.** operative. **3.** impressive: *an effective speech.* **4.** (of a military force) equipped and prepared for action. —efˈfectively *adv.* —efˈfectiveness *n.*

effects (ɪˈfɛkts) *pl. n.* **1.** personal belongings. **2.** lighting, sounds, etc., to accompany a stage, film, or broadcast production.

effectual (ɪˈfɛktjʊəl) *adj.* **1.** producing an intended result; effective. **2.** (of documents, etc.) having legal force. —efˈfectually *adv.*

effeminate (ɪˈfɛmɪnɪt) *adj.* (of a man) displaying characteristics typical of a woman. —efˈfeminacy *n.*

efferent (ˈɛfərənt) *adj. Physiol.* carrying outwards, esp. from the brain or spinal cord.

effervescent (ˌɛfəˈvɛsənt) *adj.* **1.** (of a liquid) giving off bubbles of gas. **2.** (of a

person or a person's behaviour) lively and enthusiastic. —ˌefferˈvescence *n.*

effete (ɪˈfiːt) *adj.* **1.** weak or decadent. **2.** (of animals or plants) no longer capable of reproduction. —efˈfeteness *n.*

efficacious (ˌɛfɪˈkeɪʃəs) *adj.* producing an intended result; effective. —**efficacy** (ˈɛfɪkəsɪ) *n.*

efficient (ɪˈfɪʃənt) *adj.* functioning or producing effectively and with the least waste of effort; competent. —efˈficiency *n.* —efˈficiently *adv.*

effigy (ˈɛfɪdʒɪ) *n., pl.* **-gies. 1.** a portrait, esp. as a monument. **2.** a crude representation of someone, as a focus for contempt or ridicule: *the prime minister was burned in effigy.*

efflorescence (ˌɛflɔːˈrɛsᵊns) *n.* **1.** a bursting forth or flowering. **2.** *Chem., geol.* a change that occurs as a result of loss of water or crystallization. **3.** a powdery substance formed in this way. —ˌefˈfloˈrescent *adj.*

effluence (ˈɛfluəns) *or* **efflux** (ˈɛflʌks) *n.* **1.** a flowing out. **2.** something that flows out.

effluent (ˈɛfluənt) *n.* **1.** liquid discharged as waste, as from an industrial plant or sewage works. **2.** a stream that flows out of another body of water. ~*adj.* **3.** flowing out.

effluvium (ɛˈfluːvɪəm) *n., pl.* **-via** (-vɪə). an unpleasant smell, as a gaseous waste or decaying matter.

effort (ˈɛfət) *n.* **1.** physical or mental exertion. **2.** a determined attempt. **3.** achievement: *a great literary effort.* —ˈeffortless *adj.*

effrontery (ɪˈfrʌntərɪ) *n., pl.* **-eries.** shameless or insolent boldness.

effusion (ɪˈfjuːʒən) *n.* **1.** an unrestrained outpouring in speech or words. **2.** a being poured out.

effusive (ɪˈfjuːsɪv) *adj.* extravagantly demonstrative of emotion; gushing. —efˈfusively *adv.* —efˈfusiveness *n.*

EFL English as a Foreign Language.

eft (ɛft) *n. Dialect or archaic.* a newt.

EFTA (ˈɛftə) European Free Trade Association.

EFTPOS (ˈɛftpɒs) electronic funds transfer at point of sale.

e.g. for example.

egad (iːˈgæd) *interj. Archaic.* a mild oath.

egalitarian (ɪˌgælɪˈtɛərɪən) *adj.* **1.** denoting or upholding the equality of mankind. ~*n.* **2.** an adherent of egalitarian principles. —eˌgaliˈtarianˌism *n.*

egg (ɛg) *n.* **1.** the oval or round reproductive body laid by the females of birds, reptiles, and other creatures, containing a developing embryo. **2.** a hen's egg used as food. **3.** any female reproductive cell; ovum. **4. put all one's eggs in one basket.**

to stake everything on a single venture. **5.** **teach one's grandmother to suck eggs.** *Informal.* to presume to teach someone something that he knows already. **6. with egg on one's face.** *Informal.* made to look ridiculous.

egg cup *n.* a small cup for holding a boiled egg.

egghead (ˈɛgˌhɛd) *n. Informal.* an intellectual person.

eggnog (ˌɛgˈnɒg) *n.* a drink made of raw eggs, milk, sugar, spice, and brandy or rum. Also called: **egg flip.**

egg on *vb.* to encourage (someone) to do something foolish or daring.

eggplant (ˈɛgˌplɑːnt) *n. U.S. & Canad.* same as **aubergine.**

eggshell (ˈɛgˌʃɛl) *n.* **1.** the hard porous outer layer of a bird's egg. **2.** (*modifier*) (of paint) having a very slight sheen.

eglantine (ˈɛglənˌtaɪn) *n.* same as **sweetbrier.**

ego (ˈiːgəʊ) *n., pl.* **egos. 1.** the self of an individual person; the conscious subject. **2.** egotism; conceit.

egocentric (ˌiːgəʊˈsɛntrɪk) *adj.* self-centred. —ˌegocen'tricity *n.*

egoism (ˈiːgəʊˌɪzəm, ˈɛg-) *or* **egotism** (ˈiːgəˌtɪzəm, ˈɛg-) *n.* **1.** excessive concern for one's own interests. **2.** an excessively high opinion of oneself. —ˈegoist *or* ˈegotist *n.* —ˌego'istic *or* ˌego'tistic *adj.*

ego trip *n. Informal.* something undertaken to boost a person's own image of himself.

egregious (ɪˈgriːdʒəs) *adj.* outstandingly bad; flagrant.

egress (ˈiːgrɛs) *n.* **1.** the act of going out. **2.** a way out; exit. **3.** the right to go out.

egret (ˈiːgrɪt) *n.* a wading bird like a heron, with long white feathery plumes.

Egyptian (ɪˈdʒɪpʃən) *adj.* **1.** of or relating to Egypt. **2.** of or characteristic of the ancient Egyptians, their language, or their culture. ~*n.* **3.** a person from Egypt. **4.** the language of the ancient Egyptians.

Egyptology (ˌiːdʒɪpˈtɒlədʒɪ) *n.* the study of the culture of ancient Egypt. —ˌEgyp'tologist *n.*

eh (eɪ) *interj.* an exclamation used to express questioning surprise or to seek repetition or confirmation.

eider *or* **eider duck** (ˈaɪdə) *n.* a large sea duck of the N hemisphere.

eiderdown (ˈaɪdəˌdaʊn) *n.* **1.** the breast down of the female eider duck, used, esp. formerly, for stuffing quilts or other kinds of bed covers. **2.** a thick, warm cover for a bed, stuffed with down.

eight (eɪt) *n.* **1.** the cardinal number that is the sum of one and seven. **2.** a numeral, 8, VIII, representing this number. **3.** something consisting of eight units. **4.** *Rowing.* **a.** a racing shell propelled by eight oarsmen.

b. the crew. ~*det.* **5.** amounting to eight. —**eighth** (eɪtθ) *adj., n.*

eighteen (ˈeɪˈtiːn) *n.* **1.** the cardinal number that is the sum of ten and eight. **2.** a numeral, 18, XVIII, representing this number. **3.** something consisting of 18 units. ~*det.* **4.** amounting to eighteen. —**'eigh'teenth** *adj., n.*

eightfold (ˈeɪtˌfəʊld) *adj.* **1.** having eight times as many. **2.** composed of eight parts. ~*adv.* **3.** by eight times as much.

eightsome reel (ˈeɪtsəm) *n.* a Scottish dance for eight people.

eighty (ˈeɪtɪ) *n., pl.* **eighties. 1.** the cardinal number that is the product of ten and eight. **2.** a numeral, 80, LXXX, representing this number. **3.** (*pl.*) the numbers 80-89, esp. the 80th to the 89th year of a person's life or of a century. **4.** something consisting of 80 units. ~*det.* **5.** amounting to eighty. —**'eightieth** *adj., n.*

einsteinium (aɪnˈstaɪnɪəm) *n.* a radioactive metallic element artificially produced from plutonium. Symbol: Es

eisteddfod (aɪˈstɛdfəd) *n.* a Welsh festival with competitions in music, poetry, drama, and art.

either (ˈaɪðə, ˈiːðə) *det.* **1.** one or the other (of two): *either is acceptable.* **2.** both one and the other: *at either end of the table.* ~*conj.* **3.** used preceding two or more possibilities joined by "or". ~*adv.* **4.** (*with a negative*) used to indicate that the clause immediately preceding is a partial reiteration of a previous clause: *John isn't a liar, but he isn't exactly honest either.* **Usage.** *Either* is followed by a singular verb in good usage: *either of these books is useful.* Care should be taken in using *either* to mean *both* or *each* because of possible ambiguity, as in: *a ship could be moored on either side of the channel.* Agreement between verb and subject in *either...or...* constructions follows the pattern for *neither...nor...* See **neither.**

ejaculate (ɪˈdʒækjʊˌleɪt) *vb.* **1.** to discharge (semen) in orgasm. **2.** *Literary.* to utter abruptly; blurt out. —eˌjacu'lation *n.* —e'jaculatory *adj.*

eject (ɪˈdʒɛkt) *vb.* **1.** to force out; expel or emit. **2.** to compel (a person) to leave; evict. **3.** to leave an aircraft rapidly in mid-flight, using an ejection seat. —e'jection *n.* —e'jective *adj.* —e'jector *n.*

ejection seat *or* **ejector seat** *n.* a seat, esp. in a military aircraft, that ejects the occupant in an emergency.

eke out (iːk) *vb.* **1.** to make (a supply) last for a long time by frugal use. **2.** to support (existence) with difficulty. **3.** to add to (something insufficient), esp. with difficulty.

elaborate *adj.* (ɪˈlæbərɪt). **1.** with a lot of fine details; complex. ~*vb.* (ɪˈlæbəˌreɪt). **2.** (often foll. by *on* or *upon*) to add detail to an account; expand upon. **3.** to work out in detail; develop. —e**'laborately** adv. —e,**labo'ration** n.

élan (eɪˈlɑːn) n. style and vigour.

eland (ˈiːlənd) n. a large spiral-horned antelope of southern Africa.

elapse (ɪˈlæps) vb. (of time) to pass by.

elastic (ɪˈlæstɪk) adj. **1.** capable of returning to its original shape after stretching, compression, or other deformation. **2.** adaptable or tolerant: *they take an elastic view of what counts as right.* **3.** quick to recover from fatigue or dejection. **4.** springy: *an elastic walk.* **5.** made of elastic. ~n. **6.** tape, cord, or fabric containing flexible rubber. —e**'lastically** adv. —e**'lasticated** adj. —**elas'ticity** n.

elastic band n. a rubber band.

elate (ɪˈleɪt) vb. to fill with high spirits, pride, or optimism. —e**'lated** adj. —e**'latedly** adv. —e**'lation** n.

elbow (ˈɛlbəʊ) n. **1.** the joint between the upper arm and the forearm. **2.** the part of a garment that covers the elbow. ~vb. **3.** to make (one's way) by shoving or jostling. **4.** to knock or shove (someone) with one's elbow.

elbow grease n. *Facetious.* vigorous physical labour, esp. hard rubbing.

elbow room n. sufficient scope to move or to function.

elder[1] (ˈɛldə) adj. **1.** born earlier; senior. ~n. **2.** an older person; one's senior. **3.** a senior member of a tribe, who has authority. **4.** (in certain Protestant Churches) a lay officer.

elder[2] (ˈɛldə) n. a shrub or small tree with clusters of small white flowers and dark purple berry-like fruits.

elderberry (ˈɛldəˌbɛrɪ) n., pl. **-ries.** **1.** the fruit of the elder. **2.** same as **elder**[2].

elderly (ˈɛldəlɪ) adj. (of people) quite old; past middle age. —**'elderliness** n.

elder statesman n. a respected influential older person, esp. a politician.

eldest (ˈɛldɪst) adj. oldest, esp. the oldest child.

El Dorado (ɛl dɒˈrɑːdəʊ) n. **1.** a fabled city in South America, supposedly rich in treasure. **2.** Also: **eldorado.** any place of great riches or fabulous opportunity.

eldritch (ˈɛldrɪtʃ) adj. *Poetic, Scot.* unearthly; weird.

elect (ɪˈlɛkt) vb. **1.** to choose (someone) by voting. **2.** to choose or decide: *he elected not to go.* ~adj. **3.** voted into office but not yet installed: *the President elect.* **4.** chosen; elite. —e**'lectable** adj.

elect. or **elec.** **1.** electric(al). **2.** electricity.

election (ɪˈlɛkʃən) n. **1.** the selection by vote of a person or persons for a position, esp. a political office. **2.** a public vote. **3.** the act or an instance of choosing.

electioneer (ɪˌlɛkʃəˈnɪə) vb. to be active in a political election or campaign. —e,**lectioneering** n., adj.

elective (ɪˈlɛktɪv) adj. **1.** of or based on selection by vote. **2.** having the power to elect. **3.** optional.

elector (ɪˈlɛktə) n. **1.** someone who is eligible to vote in an election. **2.** (cap.) (in the Holy Roman Empire) any of the German princes who were entitled to elect a new emperor. —e**'lectoral** adj.

electorate (ɪˈlɛktərɪt) n. **1.** the body of all qualified voters. **2.** the rank or territory of an elector of the Holy Roman Empire.

electric (ɪˈlɛktrɪk) adj. **1.** produced by, producing, transmitting, or powered by electricity. **2.** very tense or exciting: *the atmosphere was electric.* ~n. **3.** (pl.) electric appliances.

Usage. see **electronic.**

electrical (ɪˈlɛktrɪkˀl) adj. of or concerned with electricity. —e**'lectrically** adv.

Usage. see **electronic.**

electrical engineering n. the branch of engineering concerned with practical applications of electricity and electronics. —**electrical engineer** n.

electric chair n. (in the U.S.) an electrified chair for executing criminals.

electric eel n. an eel-like freshwater fish of N South America, able to stun or kill its prey with a powerful electric shock.

electric eye n. same as **photocell.**

electric field n. *Physics.* a region of space surrounding a charged particle within which another charged particle experiences a force.

electric guitar n. an electrically amplified guitar.

electrician (ɪlɛkˈtrɪʃən, ˌiːlɛk-) n. a person whose occupation is to install and repair electrical equipment.

electricity (ɪlɛkˈtrɪsɪtɪ, ˌiːlɛk-) n. **1.** a form of energy associated with stationary or moving electrons, ions, or other charged particles. **2.** the science of electricity. **3.** an electric current. **4.** emotional tension or excitement.

electrify (ɪˈlɛktrɪˌfaɪ) vb. **-fying, -fied.** **1.** to adapt or equip (a system, device, etc.) for operation by electrical power. **2.** to charge with or subject to electricity. **3.** to startle or excite intensely. —e,**lectrifi'cation** n.

electro (ɪˈlɛktrəʊ) n., pl. **-tros.** short for **electroplate.**

electro- or sometimes before a vowel **electr-** combining form. electric or electrically: *electrodynamic.*

electrocardiograph (ɪˌlɛktrəʊˈkɑːdɪəʊˌgrɑːf) n. an instrument for making tracings (**electrocardiograms**) recording the electrical activity of the heart.

electrocute (ɪˈlɛktrəˌkjuːt) vb. to kill or

execute (someone) by an electric shock. —**e₁lectro'cution** n.

electrode (ɪˈlɛktrəʊd) n. a conductor through which an electric current enters or leaves an electrolyte, an electric arc, or an electronic valve or tube.

electrodynamics (ɪˌlɛktrəʊdaɪˈnæmɪks) n. (functioning as sing.) the branch of physics concerned with the interactions between electrical and mechanical forces.

electroencephalograph (ɪˌlɛktrəʊɛnˈsɛfələˌgrɑːf) n. an instrument for making tracings (**electroencephalograms**) recording the electrical activity of the brain.

electrolysis (ɪlɛkˈtrɒlɪsɪs) n. **1.** the conduction of electricity by an electrolyte, esp. the use of this process to induce chemical changes. **2.** the destruction of living tissue, such as hair roots, by an electric current.

electrolyte (ɪˈlɛktrəʊˌlaɪt) n. a solution or molten substance that conducts electricity. —**electrolytic** (ɪˌlɛktrəʊˈlɪtɪk) adj.

electromagnet (ɪˌlɛktrəʊˈmægnɪt) n. a magnet consisting of a coil of wire wound round an iron core through which a current is passed.

electromagnetic (ɪˌlɛktrəʊmægˈnɛtɪk) adj. **1.** of or operated by an electromagnet. **2.** of or relating to electromagnetism. —**e₁lectro'magnetically** adv.

electromagnetism (ɪˌlɛktrəʊˈmægnɪˌtɪzəm) n. magnetism produced by electric current.

electromotive (ɪˌlɛktrəʊˈməʊtɪv) adj. of or producing an electric current.

electromotive force n. Physics. **1.** a source of energy that can cause current to flow in an electrical circuit. **2.** the rate at which energy is drawn from such a source when unit current flows through the circuit, measured in volts.

electron (ɪˈlɛktrɒn) n. Physics. an elementary particle in all atoms that has a negative electrical charge.

electronegative (ɪˌlɛktrəʊˈnɛgətɪv) adj. Physics. **1.** having a negative charge. **2.** tending to gain or attract electrons.

electronic (ɪlɛkˈtrɒnɪk, ˌiːlɛk-) adj. **1.** of or concerned with electronics or electrons. **2.** making use of electronic systems: electronic shopping. —**elec'tronically** adv.
Usage. Electronic is used to refer to equipment, such as television sets, computers, etc., in which current is controlled by transistors, valves, etc., and also to these components themselves. Electrical is used in a more general sense, often to refer to the use of energy: an electrical appliance. Electric, in many cases used interchangeably with electrical, is often restricted to the description of devices or to concepts relating to the flow of current: electric fire.

electronics (ɪlɛkˈtrɒnɪks, ˌiːlɛk-) n. (functioning as sing.) the science and technology

concerned with the development, behaviour, and applications of devices and circuits that are operated by the actions of electrons.

electron microscope n. a powerful microscope that uses electrons, rather than light, to produce a magnified image.

electron tube n. an electrical device in which a flow of electrons between electrodes takes place.

electronvolt (ɪˌlɛktrɒnˈvəʊlt) n. Physics. a unit of energy equal to the work done on an electron accelerated through a potential difference of 1 volt.

electroplate (ɪˈlɛktrəʊˌpleɪt) vb. **1.** to plate (an object) by electrolysis. ~n. **2.** electroplated articles collectively.

electropositive (ɪˌlɛktrəʊˈpɒzɪtɪv) adj. Physics. **1.** having a positive electric charge. **2.** tending to release electrons.

electrostatics (ɪˌlɛktrəʊˈstætɪks) n. (functioning as sing.) the branch of physics concerned with static electricity. —**e₁lectro'static** adj.

elegant (ˈɛlɪgənt) adj. **1.** tasteful in dress, style, or design. **2.** dignified and graceful. **3.** cleverly simple. —**'elegance** n.

elegiac (ˌɛlɪˈdʒaɪək) adj. **1.** of or like an elegy. **2.** lamenting; mournful. —**el-e'giacally** adv.

elegy (ˈɛlɪdʒɪ) n., pl. **-gies.** a mournful poem or song, esp. a lament for the dead.

element (ˈɛlɪmənt) n. **1.** one of the fundamental components making up a whole. **2.** Chem. any of the 105 known substances that cannot be separated into simple substances by chemical means. **3.** a distinguishable section of a social group. **4.** the most favourable environment for an animal or plant. **5.** the situation in which a person is happiest: she was in her element at the keyboard. **6.** a metal part in an electrical device, such as a heater, that changes the electric current into heat. **7.** one of the four substances thought in ancient and medieval cosmology to constitute the universe (earth, air, water, or fire). **8.** (pl.) atmospheric conditions, esp. wind, rain, and cold. **9.** (pl.) the basic principles of something. **10.** Christianity. the bread and wine in the Eucharist.

elemental (ˌɛlɪˈmɛntˀl) adj. **1.** fundamental; basic. **2.** of or like primitive powerful natural forces or passions. **3.** denoting or relating to wind, rain, or other atmospheric conditions.

elementary (ˌɛlɪˈmɛntrɪ) adj. denoting or relating to the first principles of a subject; introductory or fundamental.

elementary particle n. Physics. any of several entities, such as electrons, neutrons, or protons, that are less complex than atoms.

elementary school n. **1.** Brit. same as

primary school. **2.** *U.S. & Canad.* a state school for the first six to eight years of a child's education.

elephant ('ɛlɪfənt) *n., pl.* **-phants** *or* **-phant.** the largest living four-legged animal which has a long flexible nose (**trunk**) and two tusks of ivory. The **African elephant** has large flapping ears and a less humped back than the **Indian elephant** of S and SE Asia.

elephantiasis (ˌɛlɪfən'taɪəsɪs) *n. Pathol.* a skin disease, caused by parasitic worms, in which the affected parts of the body become extremely enlarged.

elephantine (ˌɛlɪ'fæntaɪn) *adj.* resembling an elephant, esp. in being huge, clumsy, or ponderous.

elevate ('ɛlɪˌveɪt) *vb.* **1.** to lift (something) to a higher place. **2.** to raise (someone or something) in rank or status. **3.** to put (someone) on a higher cultural plane; uplift.

elevation (ˌɛlɪ'veɪʃən) *n.* **1.** the act of elevating or the state of being elevated. **2.** the height of something, esp. above sea level. **3.** a raised area; height. **4.** a drawing to scale of the external face of a building.

elevator ('ɛlɪˌveɪtə) *n.* **1.** a person or thing that elevates. **2.** a mechanical hoist. **3.** *U.S. & Canad.* a lift. **4.** *Chiefly U.S. & Canad.* a building for storing grain.

eleven (ɪ'lɛvᵊn) *n.* **1.** the cardinal number that is the sum of ten and one. **2.** a numeral, 11, XI, representing this number. **3.** something consisting of 11 units. **4.** (*functioning as sing. or pl.*) a team of 11 players in football, cricket, etc. —**e'leventh** *adj., n.*

eleven-plus *n.* (in Britain, esp. formerly) an examination taken by children aged 11 or 12 that determines the type of secondary education a child will be given.

elevenses (ɪ'lɛvᵊnzɪz) *pl. n.* (*sometimes functioning as sing.*) *Brit. informal.* a mid-morning snack.

elf (ɛlf) *n., pl.* **elves.** (in folklore) a small mischievous fairy. —**'elfish** *or* **'elvish** *adj.*

elfin ('ɛlfɪn) *adj.* small and delicate: *elfin features.*

elicit (ɪ'lɪsɪt) *vb.* to give rise to; evoke: *to elicit a sharp retort.*

elide (ɪ'laɪd) *vb.* to omit a syllable or vowel from a spoken word.

eligible ('ɛlɪdʒəbᵊl) *adj.* **1.** fit, worthy, or qualified, as for office. **2.** *Old-fashioned.* desirable as a spouse. —ˌeligi'bility *n.*

eliminate (ɪ'lɪmɪˌneɪt) *vb.* **1.** to get rid of. **2.** to leave out of consideration; ignore. **3.** to remove (a competitor or team) from a contest. **4.** *Slang.* to murder (someone) in cold blood. —eˌlimi'nation *n.*

elision (ɪ'lɪʒən) *n.* omission of a syllable or vowel from a spoken word.

elite *or* **élite** (ɪ'liːt, eɪ-) *n.* (*sometimes functioning as pl.*) the most powerful, rich, or gifted members of a group or community.

elitism (ɪ'liːtɪzəm, eɪ-) *n.* **1.** the belief that society should be governed by a small group of people who are superior to everyone else. **2.** pride in being one of an elite. —e'litist *n., adj.*

elixir (ɪ'lɪksə) *n.* **1.** an imaginary substance that is supposed to be capable of prolonging life and changing base metals into gold. **2.** a liquid medicine with syrup.

Elizabethan (ɪˌlɪzə'biːθən) *adj.* **1.** of or relating to the reign of Queen Elizabeth I of England (1558-1603). **2.** of the style of architecture used in England during the reign of Queen Elizabeth I.

elk (ɛlk) *n., pl.* **elks** *or* **elk.** a large deer of N Europe and Asia with broad antlers.

ellipse (ɪ'lɪps) *n.* a closed curve shaped like a flattened circle, formed by an inclined plane through a cone.

ellipsis (ɪ'lɪpsɪs) *n., pl.* **-ses** (-siːz). **1.** the omission of a word or words from a sentence. **2.** *Printing.* three dots (...) indicating an omission.

ellipsoid (ɪ'lɪpsɔɪd) *n. Geom.* a surface whose plane sections are ellipses or circles.

elliptical (ɪ'lɪptɪkᵊl) *or* **elliptic** *adj.* **1.** oval-shaped. **2.** (of speech or writing) obscure or ambiguous.

elm (ɛlm) *n.* **1.** a tree with serrated leaves and winged fruits. **2.** its hard heavy wood.

elocution (ˌɛlə'kjuːʃən) *n.* the art of speaking clearly in public. —ˌelo'cutionary *adj.* —ˌelo'cutionist *n.*

elongate ('iːlɒŋgeɪt) *vb.* to make or become longer; stretch. —**'elongated** *adj.* —ˌelon-'gation *n.*

elope (ɪ'ləʊp) *vb.* (of two people) to run away secretly to get married.

eloquence ('ɛləkwəns) *n.* **1.** the ability to speak or write in a skilful and convincing way. **2.** the art of speaking or writing in such a way.

eloquent ('ɛləkwənt) *adj.* **1.** (of speech or writing) fluent and persuasive. **2.** visibly or vividly expressive: *an eloquent yawn.* —**'eloquently** *adv.*

else (ɛls) *det.* **1.** in addition; more: *there is nobody else here.* **2.** other; different: *where else could he be?* ~*adv.* **3. or else.** **a.** if not, then: *go away or else I won't finish my work.* **b.** or something terrible will result: used as a threat: *sit down, or else!* *Usage.* The possessive of the expressions *anybody else, everybody else,* etc., is formed by adding *'s* to *else: somebody else's letter.* *Who else* is an exception in that *whose else* is an acceptable alternative to *who else's: whose else can it be?* or *who else's can it be?*

elsewhere (ˌɛls'wɛə) *adv.* in or to another place.

ELT English Language Teaching.

elucidate (ɪˈluːsɪˌdeɪt) vb. to make (something obscure or difficult) clear; clarify. —eˌluciˈdation n. —eˈluciˌdative adj.

elude (ɪˈluːd) vb. 1. to escape from (someone or something) by cleverness or quickness. 2. to escape discovery or understanding by; baffle: the solution eluded her. —elusion (ɪˈluːʒən) n.

elusive (ɪˈluːsɪv) adj. 1. difficult to catch. 2. difficult to remember. ~Also: eˈlusory. —eˈlusiveness n.

elver (ˈɛlvə) n. a young eel.

elves (ɛlvz) n. the plural of elf.

elvish (ˈɛlvɪʃ) adj. same as elfish: see elf.

Elysium (ɪˈlɪzɪəm) n. 1. Greek myth. the dwelling place of the blessed after death. 2. a state or place of perfect bliss.

em (ɛm) n. Printing. the square of a body of any size of type, used as a unit of measurement.

emaciated (ɪˈmeɪsɪˌeɪtɪd) adj. abnormally thin. —eˌmaciˈation n.

emanate (ˈɛməˌneɪt) vb. to issue or proceed from or as from a source: these ideas emanate from Henry Kissinger; a dim light emanated from the room. —ˌemaˈnation n.

emancipate (ɪˈmænsɪˌpeɪt) vb. to free (a person or section of society) from social, political, or legal restrictions. —eˈmanciˌpated adj. —eˌmanciˈpation n.

emasculate (ɪˈmæskjʊˌleɪt) vb. 1. to remove the testicles of; castrate. 2. to deprive (someone or something) of power or strength. —eˈmasculated adj. —eˌmascuˈlation n.

embalm (ɪmˈbɑːm) vb. to treat (a dead body) with preservatives. —emˈbalmment n.

embankment (ɪmˈbæŋkmənt) n. a man-made ridge of earth or stone that carries a road or railway or confines a waterway.

embargo (ɛmˈbɑːɡəʊ) n., pl. -goes. 1. a government order prohibiting the departure or arrival of merchant ships in the ports of a country. 2. any legal stoppage of commerce. 3. a restraint or prohibition. ~vb. -going, -goed. 4. to lay an embargo upon.

embark (ɛmˈbɑːk) vb. 1. to board (a ship or aircraft). 2. (usually foll. by on or upon) to begin a new project or venture. —ˌembarˈkation n.

embarrass (ɪmˈbærəs) vb. 1. to cause (someone) to feel ashamed or self-conscious. 2. to involve (someone) in financial difficulties. 3. Archaic. to hamper. —emˈbarrassed adj. —emˈbarrassing adj. —emˈbarrassingly adv. —emˈbarrassment n.

embassy (ˈɛmbəsɪ) n., pl. -sies. 1. the residence or place of business of an ambassador. 2. an ambassador and his entourage collectively. 3. any important or official mission.

embattled (ɪmˈbætˀld) adj. 1. prepared for battle. 2. beset with difficulties.

embed (ɪmˈbɛd) vb. -bedding, -bedded. 1. (usually foll. by in) to fix or become fixed firmly in a surrounding solid mass. 2. to fix or retain (a thought or idea) in the mind.

embellish (ɪmˈbɛlɪʃ) vb. 1. to beautify; adorn. 2. to make (a story) more interesting by adding often fictitious detail. —emˈbellishment n.

ember (ˈɛmbə) n. a glowing or smouldering piece of coal or wood, as in a dying fire.

embezzle (ɪmˈbɛzˀl) vb. to steal (money or property that has been entrusted to one). —emˈbezzlement n. —emˈbezzler n.

embitter (ɪmˈbɪtə) vb. to make (a person) bitter. —emˈbittered adj. —emˈbitterment n.

emblazon (ɪmˈbleɪzˀn) vb. 1. to portray heraldic arms on. 2. to make bright or splendid, as with colours or flowers. 3. to proclaim or publicize: her feat was emblazoned on the front page. —emˈblazoned adj. —emˈblazonment n.

emblem (ˈɛmbləm) n. a visible object or representation that symbolizes a quality, type, or group. —ˌemblemˈatic adj.

embody (ɪmˈbɒdɪ) vb. -bodying, -bodied. 1. to be an example of or express (an idea, principle, or other abstract concept). 2. (often foll. by in) to collect in a comprehensive whole. —emˈbodiment n.

embolden (ɪmˈbəʊldˀn) vb. to make bold.

embolism (ˈɛmbəˌlɪzəm) n. the blocking of a blood vessel by an embolus.

embolus (ˈɛmbələs) n., pl. -li (-ˌlaɪ). a blood clot, air bubble or other stoppage that blocks a small blood vessel.

emboss (ɪmˈbɒs) vb. to mould or carve (a decoration) on (a surface) so that it stands out from the surface. —emˈbossed adj. —emˈbossment n.

embrace (ɪmˈbreɪs) vb. 1. (of a person) to clasp (another person) in the arms, or (of two people) to clasp each other, as in affection or greeting; hug. 2. to accept eagerly: to embrace new ideas. 3. to comprise: the proposal embraces many previous suggestions. ~n. 4. the act of embracing.

embrasure (ɪmˈbreɪʒə) n. 1. a door or window having splayed sides on the interior. 2. an opening in a battlement or fortified wall, for shooting through. —emˈbrasured adj.

embrocation (ˌɛmbrəʊˈkeɪʃən) n. a liniment or lotion.

embroider (ɪmˈbrɔɪdə) vb. 1. to do decorative needlework on something, such as a tablecloth or piece of clothing. 2. to add fictitious detail to (a story). —emˈbroiderer n.

embroidery (ɪmˈbrɔɪdərɪ) n., pl. -deries. 1. the art or a piece of decorative needlework done usually on cloth or canvas. **2.** embellishment in reporting a story.

embroil (ɪmˈbrɔɪl) vb. **1.** to involve oneself or another person in problems or difficulties. **2.** to throw (affairs) into confusion; complicate. **—emˈbroilment** n.

embryo (ˈɛmbrɪˌəʊ) n., pl. **-bryos. 1.** an unborn animal or human being in the early stages of development, in humans up to approximately the end of the second month of pregnancy. **2.** something in an early stage of development: an embryo of an idea.

embryology (ˌɛmbrɪˈɒlədʒɪ) n. the scientific study of embryos.

embryonic (ˌɛmbrɪˈɒnɪk) adj. **1.** of or relating to an embryo. **2.** in an early stage.

emend (ɪˈmɛnd) vb. to make corrections or improvements in (a text). **—emenˈdation** n.

Usage. see **amend.**

emerald (ˈɛmərəld, ˈɛmrəld) n. **1.** a green transparent variety of beryl: highly valued as a gem. **2.** its clear green colour.

Emerald Isle n. the. Poetic. Ireland.

emerge (ɪˈmɜːdʒ) vb. (often foll. by from) **1.** to come into view, as from concealment or obscurity. **2.** to come out of or live through (a difficult experience, etc.). **3.** to become apparent: it emerged that she was in London all the time. **—eˈmergence** n. **—eˈmergent** adj.

emergency (ɪˈmɜːdʒənsɪ) n., pl. **-cies. 1.** an unforeseen or sudden occurrence, esp. of danger demanding immediate action. **2.** N.Z. a reserve player. **3. state of emergency.** a condition, declared by a government, in which martial law applies.

emeritus (ɪˈmɛrɪtəs) adj. retired, but retaining one's title on an honorary basis: a professor emeritus.

emery (ˈɛmərɪ) n. a hard greyish-black mineral used for smoothing and polishing.

emery board n. a strip of cardboard coated with crushed emery, for filing one's nails.

emetic (ɪˈmɛtɪk) adj. **1.** causing vomiting. ~n. **2.** a substance that causes vomiting.

EMF electromotive force.

emigrate (ˈɛmɪˌɡreɪt) vb. to leave one's native country to settle in another. **—ˈemigrant** n., adj. **—ˌemiˈgration** n.

émigré (ˈɛmɪˌɡreɪ) n. someone who has left his native country for political reasons.

eminence (ˈɛmɪnəns) n. **1.** a position of superiority or fame. **2.** a high or raised piece of ground.

Eminence (ˈɛmɪnəns) n., pl. **-nences.** (preceded by Your or His) a title used to address or refer to a cardinal.

éminence grise (ˌeɪmɪnɒns ˈɡriːz) n., pl. **éminences grises** (ˌeɪmɪnɒns ˈɡriːz). a person who wields power and influence unofficially.

eminent (ˈɛmɪnənt) adj. distinguished, powerful, and famous.

emir (ɛˈmɪə) n. (in the Islamic world) an independent ruler or chieftain. **—eˈmirate** n.

emissary (ˈɛmɪsərɪ) n., pl. **-saries.** an agent sent on a mission by a government or head of state.

emission (ɪˈmɪʃən) n. **1.** the act of emitting something. **2.** energy, in the form of heat, light, radio waves, etc., emitted from a source. **3.** a discharge; something emitted. **—eˈmissive** adj.

emit (ɪˈmɪt) vb. **emitting, emitted. 1.** to give or send forth (heat, light, or a smell). **2.** to utter (a sound).

Emmenthal or **Emmental** (ˈɛmənˌtɑːl) n. a hard Swiss cheese with holes in it.

emollient (ɪˈmɒljənt) adj. **1.** softening or soothing to the skin. ~n. **2.** any preparation that has this effect.

emolument (ɪˈmɒljʊmənt) n. profit from employment; fees or wages.

emote (ɪˈməʊt) vb. to display exaggerated emotion, as in acting.

emotion (ɪˈməʊʃən) n. any strong feeling, as of joy or fear.

emotional (ɪˈməʊʃənˀl) adj. **1.** of or denoting emotion or the emotions. **2.** readily or excessively affected by emotion. **3.** appealing to or arousing emotion: an emotional argument. **—eˈmotionalˌism** n. **—eˈmotionally** adv.

emotive (ɪˈməʊtɪv) adj. **1.** tending or designed to arouse emotion. **2.** of or characterized by emotion.

empanel (ɪmˈpænˀl) vb. **-elling, -elled** or U.S. **-eling, -eled.** Law. to enter on a list (names of persons for jury service).

empathy (ˈɛmpəθɪ) n. the power of imaginatively entering into and understanding another person's feelings. **—ˌempaˈthetic** adj.

emperor (ˈɛmpərə) n. a monarch who rules an empire.

emperor penguin n. an Antarctic penguin with orange-yellow patches on the neck: the largest penguin.

emphasis (ˈɛmfəsɪs) n., pl. **-ses** (-siːz). **1.** special importance or significance given to something, such as an object or idea. **2.** stress on a particular syllable, word, or phrase in speaking. **3.** force or intensity of expression.

emphasize or **-ise** (ˈɛmfəˌsaɪz) vb. to give emphasis or prominence to; stress.

emphatic (ɪmˈfætɪk) adj. **1.** expressed, spoken, or done with emphasis. **2.** forceful and positive: an emphatic personality. **3.** important or significant: the emphatic points in an argument. **—emˈphatically** adv.

emphysema (ˌɛmfɪˈsiːmə) n. Pathol. a condition in which the air sacs of the lungs are grossly enlarged.

empire ('ɛmpaɪə) n. 1. a group of peoples and territories under the rule of a single person or sovereign state. 2. supreme power; sovereignty. 3. a large industrial organization that is directed or owned by one person.

empire-builder n. Informal. a person who seeks extra power by increasing the number of his staff. —'empire-,building n., adj.

empirical (ɛm'pɪrɪk³l) adj. 1. derived from experiment and observation rather than from theory or from first principles by logic. 2. (of medical treatment) based on practical experience rather than scientific proof. —em'pirically adv.

empiricism (ɛm'pɪrɪ,sɪzəm) n. Philosophy. the doctrine that all knowledge derives from experience. —em'piricist n.

emplacement (ɪm'pleɪsmənt) n. 1. a prepared position for a gun. 2. the act of putting something in place.

emplane (ɪm'pleɪn) vb. to board or put on board an aeroplane.

employ (ɪm'plɔɪ) vb. 1. to engage the services of (a person) in return for money; hire. 2. to provide work or occupation for; keep busy. 3. to use as a means: to employ secret measures to achieve one's ends. ~n. 4. the state of being employed: the company has 20000 workers in its employ. —em'ployable adj.

employee or U.S. **employe** (ɛm'plɔɪiː, ,ɛmplɔɪ'iː) n. a person who is hired to work for another in return for payment.

employer (ɪm'plɔɪə) n. a person or company that employs workers.

employment (ɪm'plɔɪmənt) n. 1. the act of employing or state of being employed. 2. a person's work or occupation.

emporium (ɛm'pɔːrɪəm) n., pl. -riums or -ria (-rɪə). a large retail shop with a wide variety of merchandise.

empower (ɪm'paʊə) vb. to give (someone) the power or authority to do something.

empress ('ɛmprɪs) n. 1. the wife or widow of an emperor. 2. a woman who rules an empire.

empty ('ɛmptɪ) adj. -tier, -tiest. 1. containing nothing. 2. without inhabitants; unoccupied. 3. without purpose, substance, or value: an empty life. 4. insincere or trivial: empty words. 5. Informal. drained of energy or emotion. 6. Maths, logic. (of a set or class) containing no members. ~vb. -tying, -tied. 7. to make or become empty. 8. to remove (the contents) of something: to empty the rubbish out of the bin. ~n., pl. -ties. 9. an empty container, esp. a bottle. —'emptiness n.

empty-handed adj. having gained noth-

ing: they returned from the talks empty-handed.

empty-headed adj. lacking sense; frivolous.

empyrean (,ɛmpaɪ'riːən) n. 1. Archaic. the highest part of the heavens. 2. Poetic. the sky. —,empy'real adj.

emu ('iːmjuː) n. a large Australian flightless bird with long legs.

emulate ('ɛmjʊ,leɪt) vb. to attempt to equal or surpass by imitating. —,emu'lation n. —'emulative adj. —'emu,lator n.

emulous ('ɛmjʊləs) adj. 1. desiring to equal or surpass another. 2. arising from emulation.

emulsify (ɪ'mʌlsɪ,faɪ) vb. -fying, -fied. to make or form into an emulsion. —e'mulsi,fier n. —e,mulsifi'cation n.

emulsion (ɪ'mʌlʃən) n. 1. a mixture of two liquids one of which is dispersed in the other. 2. Photog. a light-sensitive coating for paper or film. 3. a type of water-based paint. —e'mulsive adj.

en (ɛn) n. Printing. a unit of measurement, half the width of an em.

enable (ɪn'eɪb³l) vb. 1. to provide (someone) with the means, opportunity, or authority (to do something). 2. to make possible: the porous shell enables oxygen to pass in.

enact (ɪn'ækt) vb. 1. to establish by law; decree: to enact a bill. 2. to represent as in a play. —en'actment n.

enamel (ɪ'næməl) n. 1. a coloured glassy coating on the surface of articles made of metal, glass, or pottery. 2. an enamel-like paint or varnish. 3. the hard white substance that covers each tooth. ~vb. -elling, -elled or U.S. -eling, -eled. 4. to decorate or cover with or as if with enamel.

enamoured or U.S. **enamored** (ɪn'æməd) adj. (foll. by of) inspired with love; captivated.

en bloc (ɒn 'blɒk) adv. as a whole; all together.

enc. 1. enclosed. 2. enclosure.

encamp (ɪn'kæmp) vb. Formal. to set up or cause to set up in a camp. —en'campment n.

encapsulate (ɪn'kæpsjʊ,leɪt) vb. 1. to enclose or be enclosed as in a capsule. 2. to put in a concise form; abridge. —en,capsu'lation n.

encase (ɪn'keɪs) vb. to place or enclose as in a case. —en'casement n.

encaustic (ɪn'kɒstɪk) Ceramics, etc. ~adj. 1. decorated by burning colours onto or into a surface. ~n. 2. the process or a product of burning in colours.

enceinte (ɒn'sænt) adj. pregnant.

encephalitis (,ɛnsɛfə'laɪtɪs) n. inflammation of the brain. —**encephalitic** (,ɛnsɛfə-'lɪtɪk) adj.

encephalogram (ɛnˈsɛfələˌgræm) n. short for **electroencephalogram**; see **electroencephalograph**.

enchain (ɪnˈtʃeɪn) vb. **1.** to bind with chains. **2.** to captivate (the attention).

enchant (ɪnˈtʃɑːnt) vb. **1.** to delight; charm. **2.** to cast a spell on; bewitch. —**en'chanted** adj. —**en'chantment** n. —**en'chantress** fem. n.

encircle (ɪnˈsɜːkˈl) vb. to form a circle around; surround. —**en'circlement** n.

enclave (ˈɛnkleɪv) n. a part of a country entirely surrounded by foreign territory.

enclose (ɪnˈkləʊz) vb. **1.** to surround completely: the garden is enclosed with a seven foot fence. **2.** to include along with something else: I have enclosed a cheque for ten pounds.

enclosure (ɪnˈkləʊʒə) n. **1.** the act of enclosing or state of being enclosed. **2.** an area of land enclosed as by a fence. **3.** something, such as a cheque, enclosed with a letter.

encomium (ɛnˈkəʊmɪəm) n., pl. **-miums** or **-mia** (-mɪə). a formal expression of praise.

encompass (ɪnˈkʌmpəs) vb. **1.** to enclose within a circle; surround. **2.** to include comprehensively: this book encompasses the whole range of knowledge.

encore (ˈɒŋkɔː) interj. **1.** again: used by an audience to demand a short extra performance. ~n. **2.** an extra performance in response to enthusiastic demand. ~vb. **3.** to demand an extra performance of or by.

encounter (ɪnˈkaʊntə) vb. **1.** to meet (someone) unexpectedly. **2.** to meet (an enemy) in battle or contest. **3.** to be faced with: we encountered many difficulties on our journey. ~n. **4.** a casual or unexpected meeting. **5.** a contest.

encourage (ɪnˈkʌrɪdʒ) vb. **1.** to inspire (someone) with the confidence (to do something). **2.** to stimulate (something or someone) by approval or help. —**en'couragement** n. —**en'couraging** adj.

encroach (ɪnˈkrəʊtʃ) vb. (often foll. by on or upon) to intrude gradually on someone's rights or on a piece of land. —**en'croachment** n.

encrust (ɪnˈkrʌst) vb. to cover (a surface) with a layer of something, such as jewels or ice —ˌencrus'tation n.

encumber (ɪnˈkʌmbə) vb. **1.** to hinder or impede; hamper: she was encumbered with heavy parcels; his stupidity encumbers his efforts to learn. **2.** to burden, as with debts.

encumbrance (ɪnˈkʌmbrəns) n. a thing that impedes or is burdensome; hindrance.

ency., encyc., or **encycl.** encyclopedia.

encyclical (ɛnˈsɪklɪkˈl) n. **1.** a letter sent by the pope to all Roman Catholic bishops. ~adj. **2.** (of letters) for general circulation.

encyclopedia or **encyclopaedia** (ɛnˌsaɪkləʊˈpiːdɪə) n. a book or set of books, often in alphabetical order, that contains facts about many different subjects or about one particular subject.

encyclopedic or **encyclopaedic** (ɛnˌsaɪkləʊˈpiːdɪk) adj. (of knowledge or information) very full and thorough; comprehensive.

end (ɛnd) n. **1.** one of the two extreme points of something, such as a road. **2.** the surface at one of the two extreme points of an object: a pencil with a rubber at one end. **3.** the extreme extent or limit of something: that hedge marks the end of my garden. **4.** the most distant place or time that can be imagined: the ends of the earth. **5.** the last part of something: I cried at the end of the film. **6.** a remnant or fragment: a cigarette end. **7.** death; destruction. **8.** the purpose of an action: she'll stop at nothing to achieve her ends. **9.** Sport. either of the two defended areas of a playing field. **10. in the end.** finally. **11. make (both) ends meet.** to spend no more than the money one has. **12. no end (of).** Informal. (used for emphasis): I had no end of work. **13. on end.** Informal. without pause or interruption. **14. the end.** Slang. the worst, esp. beyond the limits of endurance. ~vb. **15.** to bring or come to a finish; conclude. **16. end it all.** Informal. to commit suicide. ~See also **end up.**

endanger (ɪnˈdeɪndʒə) vb. to put in danger; risk —**en'dangered** adj.

endear (ɪnˈdɪə) vb. to cause to be beloved. —**en'dearing** adj.

endearment (ɪnˈdɪəmənt) n. an affectionate word or phrase.

endeavour or U.S. **endeavor** (ɪnˈdɛvə) vb. **1.** to try (to do something). ~n. **2.** an effort to do something.

endemic (ɛnˈdɛmɪk) adj. present within a localized area or peculiar to a particular group of people: an endemic disease. —**en'demically** adv.

ending (ˈɛndɪŋ) n. **1.** the act of bringing to or reaching an end. **2.** the last part of something. **3.** the final part of a word.

endive (ˈɛndaɪv) n. a plant with crisp curly leaves, used in salads.

endless (ˈɛndlɪs) adj. **1.** having no end; eternal or infinite. **2.** continuing too long or continually recurring. **3.** with the ends joined: an endless belt. —**'endlessly** adv.

endmost (ˈɛndˌməʊst) adj. nearest the end.

endocrine (ˈɛndəʊˌkraɪn) adj. of or denoting endocrine glands or their secretions.

endocrine gland n. any of the glands that secrete hormones directly into the bloodstream, such as the pituitary.

endogenous (ɛnˈdɒdʒɪnəs) adj. Biol. developing or originating from within.

endorsation (ˌɛndɔːˈseɪʃən) n. Canad. approval or support.

endorse *or* **indorse** (ɪn'dɔːs) *vb.* **1.** to give approval or sanction to. **2.** to sign the back of (a document) to specify the payee. **3.** *Chiefly Brit.* to record a conviction on (a driving licence). —**en'dorsement** *n.*

endow (ɪn'daʊ) *vb.* **1.** to provide with or bequeath a source of permanent income. **2.** **endowed with.** provided (with qualities, characteristics, etc.).

endowment (ɪn'daʊmənt) *n.* **1.** the money given to an institution, such as a hospital. **2.** the act or process of endowing. **3.** (*usually pl.*) natural talents or qualities.

endowment assurance *or* **insurance** *n.* a life insurance that pays a specified sum directly to the policyholder at a designated date or to his beneficiary should he die before this date.

endpaper ('ɛnd,peɪpə) *n.* either of two leaves at the front and back of a book pasted to the inside of the cover.

end product *n.* the final result of a process.

endue (ɪn'djuː) *vb.* **-duing, -dued.** (usually foll. by *with*) to provide with some quality or trait.

end up *vb.* **1.** to turn out to be. **2.** to arrive (somewhere) by a roundabout route.

endurance (ɪn'djʊərəns) *n.* **1.** the capacity, state, or an instance of enduring. **2.** the ability to withstand strain or hardship.

endure (ɪn'djʊə) *vb.* **1.** to undergo (strain or hardship) without yielding; bear. **2.** to tolerate. **3.** to last. —**en'durable** *adj.*

enduring (ɪn'djʊərɪŋ) *adj.* permanent; lasting.

endways ('ɛnd,weɪz) *or esp. U.S. & Canad.* **endwise** ('ɛnd,waɪz) *adv.* **1.** having the end forwards or upwards. ~*adj.* **2.** standing or lying end to end.

enema ('ɛnɪmə) *n. Med.* **1.** the injection of liquid into the rectum to evacuate the bowels, medicate, or nourish. **2.** the liquid so injected.

enemy ('ɛnəmɪ) *n., pl.* **-mies. 1.** a person hostile or opposed to a policy, cause, person, or group. **2.** an adversary; opposing military force. **3.** a hostile nation or people. **4.** something that harms or opposes.

energetic (,ɛnə'dʒɛtɪk) *adj.* showing energy; vigorous. —,**ener'getically** *adv.*

energize *or* **-ise** ('ɛnə,dʒaɪz) *vb.* to cause to have energy; invigorate.

energy ('ɛnədʒɪ) *n., pl.* **-gies. 1.** capacity for intense activity; vigour. **2.** intensity or vitality of action or expression; forcefulness. **3.** *Physics.* the capacity to do work and overcome resistance.

enervate ('ɛnə,veɪt) *vb.* to deprive of strength or vitality. —'**ener,vating** *adj.* —,**ener'vation** *n.*

enfant terrible (,ɒnfɒn tə'riːblə) *n., pl.* **enfants terribles** (,ɒnfɒn tə'riːblə). a person who is unconventional or indiscreet.

enfeeble (ɪn'fiːb'l) *vb.* to make (someone or something) weak. —**en'feeblement** *n.*

enfilade (,ɛnfɪ'leɪd) *Mil.* ~*n.* **1.** gunfire directed along the length of a formation. ~*vb.* **2.** to attack (a formation) with enfilade.

enfold (ɪn'fəʊld) *vb.* **1.** to cover (something) by wrapping something else around it. **2.** to embrace.

enforce (ɪn'fɔːs) *vb.* **1.** to ensure that (a law or decision) is obeyed. **2.** to impose (obedience) as by force. **3.** to emphasize or reinforce (an argument). —**en'forceable** *adj.* —**en'forcement** *n.*

enfranchise (ɪn'fræntʃaɪz) *vb.* **1.** to grant (someone) the right to vote. **2.** to free as from slavery. **3.** (in England) to give (a town or city) the right to be represented in Parliament. —**en'franchisement** *n.*

Eng. 1. England. **2.** English.

engage (ɪn'geɪdʒ) *vb.* **1.** to employ (someone). **2.** to reserve (a room, seat, etc.). **3.** to involve (a person or his attention) intensely. **4.** to draw (somebody) into conversation. **5.** to take part: *she engages in many sports.* **6.** to promise (to do something). **7.** *Mil.* to begin a battle with (an enemy). **8.** to bring (part of a machine or other mechanism) into operation. **9.** to undergo or cause to undergo interlocking, as of the components of a driving mechanism, such as a gear train.

engaged (ɪn'geɪdʒd) *adj.* **1.** pledged to be married. **2.** occupied or busy: *the toilet is engaged.* **3.** (of a telephone line) in use.

engagement (ɪn'geɪdʒmənt) *n.* **1.** a business or social appointment. **2.** a pledge of marriage. **3.** a limited period of employment, esp. in the performing arts. **4.** a battle.

engaging (ɪn'geɪdʒɪŋ) *adj.* pleasing, charming, or winning. —**en'gagingly** *adv.*

engender (ɪn'dʒɛndə) *vb.* to produce or cause (a particular feeling, atmosphere, or situation) to occur.

engine ('ɛndʒɪn) *n.* **1.** any machine designed to convert energy into mechanical work. **2.** a railway locomotive.

engineer (,ɛndʒɪ'nɪə) *n.* **1.** a person trained in any branch of engineering. **2.** *U.S. & Canad.* the driver of a railway locomotive. **3.** an officer responsible for a ship's engines. **4.** a member of the armed forces trained in engineering and construction work. ~*vb.* **5.** to cause or plan (an event or situation) in a clever or devious manner. **6.** to design or construct as a professional engineer.

engineering (,ɛndʒɪ'nɪərɪŋ) *n.* the profession of applying scientific principles to the design and construction of engines, cars, buildings, bridges, roads, and electrical machines.

English ('ɪŋglɪʃ) *n.* **1.** the official language

of Britain, the U.S., most of the Commonwealth, and certain other countries. **2. the English.** (*functioning as pl.*) the people of England collectively. ~*adj.* **3.** of or relating to England, its people, or the English language.
Usage. The United Kingdom consists of England, Scotland, Wales, and Northern Ireland. *England* or *English* should not be used to mean *Britain* or *British* as these usages are offensive to Scottish, Welsh, and Irish people.

English horn *n. Music.* see **cor anglais.**

Englishman (ˈɪŋglɪʃmən) *or* (*fem.*) **Englishwoman** *n., pl.* **-men** *or* **-women.** a person from England.

engorge (ɪnˈɡɔːdʒ) *vb.* **1.** to eat (food) greedily. **2.** *Pathol.* to congest with blood.

engrave (ɪnˈɡreɪv) *vb.* **1.** to carve or etch (a design or inscription) onto (a block, plate, or other printing surface). **2.** to print (designs or characters) from a plate so made. **3.** to fix deeply or permanently in the mind. —**enˈgraver** *n.*

engraving (ɪnˈɡreɪvɪŋ) *n.* **1.** the art of an engraver. **2.** a printing surface that has been engraved. **3.** a print made from this.

engross (ɪnˈɡrəʊs) *vb.* **1.** to occupy one's attention completely; absorb. **2.** to write out in large legible handwriting or in legal form. —**enˈgrossed** *adj.* —**enˈgrossing** *adj.*

engulf (ɪnˈɡʌlf) *vb.* **1.** to immerse, plunge or swallow up: *flames engulfed the house.* **2.** (*often passive*) to overwhelm: *engulfed by debts.*

enhance (ɪnˈhɑːns) *vb.* to intensify or increase in quality, value or power; improve. —**enˈhancement** *n.*

enigma (ɪˈnɪɡmə) *n.* a person, thing, or situation that is mysterious or puzzling. —**enigmatic** (ˌɛnɪɡˈmætɪk) *adj.* —ˌenigˈmatically *adv.*

enjoin (ɪnˈdʒɔɪn) *vb.* **1.** to order (someone) to do something. **2.** to impose (a particular kind of behaviour) on someone. **3.** *Law.* to prohibit (a person) from some act by an injunction.

enjoy (ɪnˈdʒɔɪ) *vb.* **1.** to receive pleasure from; take joy in. **2.** to have the benefit of; use. **3.** to have as a condition; experience. **4. enjoy oneself.** to have a good time. —**enˈjoyable** *adj.* —**enˈjoyably** *adv.* —**enˈjoyment** *n.*

enkindle (ɪnˈkɪndˈl) *vb.* **1.** to set on fire. **2.** to excite or arouse.

enlarge (ɪnˈlɑːdʒ) *vb.* **1.** to make or grow larger; increase or expand. **2.** to make (a photographic print) larger. **3. enlarge on** *or* **upon.** to speak or write (about) in greater detail. —**enˈlargement** *n.* —**enˈlarger** *n.*

enlighten (ɪnˈlaɪtˈn) *vb.* **1.** to give information or understanding to; instruct. **2.** to

free from prejudice, ignorance, or superstition. —**enˈlightened** *adj.*

enlightenment (ɪnˈlaɪtˈnmənt) *n.* the act of enlightening or the state of being enlightened.

enlist (ɪnˈlɪst) *vb.* **1.** to enter the armed forces. **2.** to engage or secure (a person or his support) for a cause or venture. —**enˈlistment** *n.*

enliven (ɪnˈlaɪvˈn) *vb.* to make lively, cheerful, or bright. —**enˈlivening** *adj.*

en masse (ɒn ˈmæs) *adv.* in a group or mass; as a whole; all together.

enmesh (ɪnˈmɛʃ) *vb.* to catch in or as if in a net; entangle.

enmity (ˈɛnmɪtɪ) *n., pl.* **-ties.** a feeling of hostility or ill will, as between enemies.

ennoble (ɪˈnəʊbˈl) *vb.* **1.** to make (something) noble; dignify. **2.** to raise (someone) to a noble rank. —**enˈnoblement** *n.*

ennui (ˈɒnwiː) *n.* a feeling of boredom and dissatisfaction resulting from lack of activity or excitement.

enormity (ɪˈnɔːmɪtɪ) *n., pl.* **-ties.** **1.** the quality of extreme wickedness. **2.** an act of great wickedness. **3.** *Not universally accepted.* vastness of size or extent.

enormous (ɪˈnɔːməs) *adj.* unusually large in size, extent, or degree. —**eˈnormously** *adv.*

enough (ɪˈnʌf) *det.* **1.** sufficient to answer a need or demand. **2. that's enough!** that will do: used to stop someone behaving in a particular way. ~*adv.* **3.** as much as necessary. **4.** very or quite; rather. **5.** especially: *oddly enough.* **6.** just adequately; tolerably: *he did it well enough.*

en passant (ɒn pæˈsɑːnt) *adv.* in passing; by the way.

enquire (ɪnˈkwaɪə) *vb.* same as **inquire.** —**enˈquiry** *n.*

enrage (ɪnˈreɪdʒ) *vb.* to put (someone) into a rage. —**enˈraged** *adj.*

enrapture (ɪnˈræptʃə) *vb.* to fill (someone) with delight; enchant.

enrich (ɪnˈrɪtʃ) *vb.* **1.** to increase the wealth of. **2.** to improve in quality, colour or flavour. —**enˈriched** *adj.* —**enˈrichment** *n.*

enrol *or* *U.S.* **enroll** (ɪnˈrəʊl) *vb.* **-rolling, -rolled. 1.** to record (someone's name) in a list. **2.** to become or cause to become a member; enlist. —**enˈrolment** *n.*

en route (ɒn ˈruːt) *adv.* on or along the way.

ensconce (ɪnˈskɒns) *vb.* to settle firmly or comfortably.

ensemble (ɒnˈsɒmbˈl) *n.* **1.** all the parts of something considered together. **2.** a person's complete costume; outfit. **3.** the cast of a play. **4.** *Music.* a group of musicians playing together.

enshrine (ɪn'ʃraɪn) vb. **1.** to enclose as in a shrine. **2.** to hold as sacred; cherish.

enshroud (ɪn'ʃraʊd) vb. to cover or hide as with a shroud.

ensign ('ɛnsaɪn) n. **1.** (also 'ɛnsən). a flag flown by a ship to indicate nationality. **2.** any flag, standard, or banner. **3.** (in the U.S. Navy) a commissioned officer of the lowest rank. **4.** (formerly, in the British infantry) a commissioned officer of the lowest rank.

ensilage ('ɛnsɪlɪdʒ) n. **1.** the process of storing green fodder in a silo. **2.** silage.

enslave (ɪn'sleɪv) vb. to make a slave of (someone). —**en'slavement** n.

ensnare (ɪn'snɛə) vb. to catch or trap as in a snare. —**en'snarement** n.

ensue (ɪn'sjuː) vb. **-suing, -sued. 1.** to come next. **2.** to occur as a consequence; result. —**en'suing** adj.

en suite (ɒn 'swiːt) adv. forming a unit: a room with a bathroom en suite.

ensure (ɛn'ʃʊə) or esp. U.S. **insure** vb. **1.** to make certain or sure; guarantee. **2.** to make safe or secure; protect.

ENT Med. ear, nose, and throat.

entablature (ɛn'tæblətʃə) n. Archit. the part of a classical temple above the columns, having an architrave, a frieze, and a cornice.

entail (ɪn'teɪl) vb. **1.** to bring about or impose inevitably: this task entails careful thought. **2.** Property law. to restrict (the descent of an estate) to designated heirs. ~n. **3.** Property law. **a.** an entailed estate. **b.** the order of descent for an entailed estate.

entangle (ɪn'tæŋgᵊl) vb. **1.** to catch or involve in or as if in a tangle; ensnare or enmesh. **2.** to make complicated; confuse. **3.** to involve in difficulties. —**en'tanglement** n.

entente (ɒn'tɒnt) n. short for **entente cordiale.**

entente cordiale (kɔːdɪ'ɑːl) n. a friendly understanding between two or more countries.

enter ('ɛntə) vb. **1.** to come or go into (a particular place). **2.** to penetrate or pierce: the bullet entered her leg. **3.** to join (a party or organization). **4.** to become involved or take part (in): to enter a competition; to enter into an agreement. **5.** to record (an item, a name, etc.) in a journal, list, etc. **6.** to present or submit: to enter a proposal. **7.** Theatre. to come on stage: enter Juliet. **8.** to begin; start: to enter upon a new career. **9.** to place (evidence) before a court of law.

enteric (ɛn'tɛrɪk) adj. intestinal.

enter into vb. **1.** to be considered as a necessary part of (one's plans). **2.** to be in sympathy with.

enteritis (ˌɛntə'raɪtɪs) n. inflammation of the intestine.

enterprise ('ɛntəˌpraɪz) n. **1.** a company or firm. **2.** a project or undertaking, esp. one that requires boldness or effort. **3.** boldness and energy.

enterprising ('ɛntəˌpraɪzɪŋ) adj. full of boldness and initiative. —**'enterˌprising-ly** adv.

entertain (ˌɛntə'teɪn) vb. **1.** to provide amusement for (a person or audience). **2.** to show hospitality to (guests). **3.** to consider (an idea or suggestion).

entertainer (ˌɛntə'teɪnə) n. any person who entertains, esp. professionally.

entertaining (ˌɛntə'teɪnɪŋ) adj. diverting; amusing.

entertainment (ˌɛntə'teɪnmənt) n. an act, production, etc., that entertains.

enthral or U.S. **enthrall** (ɪn'θrɔːl) vb. **-thralling, -thralled.** to hold the attention or interest of (someone). —**en'thralling** adj. —**en'thralment** n.

enthrone (ɛn'θrəʊn) vb. **1.** to place (someone) on a throne. **2.** to praise or honour. —**en'thronement** n.

enthuse (ɪn'θjuːz) vb. to feel or show or cause to feel or show enthusiasm.

enthusiasm (ɪn'θjuːzɪˌæzəm) n. ardent and lively interest or eagerness.

enthusiast (ɪn'θjuːzɪˌæst) n. a person motivated by enthusiasm; fanatic. —**enˌthusi-'astic** adj. —**enˌthusi'astically** adv.

entice (ɪn'taɪs) vb. to attract by exciting hope or desire; tempt. —**en'ticement** n. —**en'ticing** adj.

entire (ɪn'taɪə) adj. **1.** whole; complete. **2.** without reservation or exception. **3.** not broken or damaged. **4.** undivided; continuous. —**en'tirely** adv.

entirety (ɪn'taɪərɪtɪ) n., pl. **-ties. 1.** completeness. **2.** a thing that is entire. **3. in its entirety.** as a whole.

entitle (ɪn'taɪtᵊl) vb. **1.** to give (a person) the right to do or have something; qualify; allow. **2.** to give a name or title to (a book, film, etc.). —**en'titlement** n.

entity ('ɛntɪtɪ) n., pl. **-ties. 1.** something having real or distinct existence. **2.** existence or being.

entomb (ɪn'tuːm) vb. **1.** to place (a corpse) in a tomb; bury. **2.** to serve as a tomb for. —**en'tombment** n.

entomology (ˌɛntə'mɒlədʒɪ) n. the branch of science concerned with the study of insects. —**entomological** (ˌɛntəmə'lɒdʒɪkᵊl) adj. —ˌ**ento'mologist** n.

entourage ('ɒntʊˌrɑːʒ) n. a group of people who assist an important person or group of people.

entr'acte (ɒn'trækt) n. **1.** an interval between two acts of a play. **2.** (esp. formerly) an entertainment during such an interval.

entrails ('εntreɪlz) pl. n. **1.** the internal organs of a person or animal; intestines. **2.** the innermost parts of anything.

entrance[1] ('εntrəns) n. **1.** the act of entering; entry. **2.** a place for entering, such as a door. **3.** the right of entering. **4.** the coming of an actor onto a stage.

entrance[2] (ɪn'trɑːns) vb. **1.** to fill with delight; enchant. **2.** to put into a trance. —**en'trancement** n. —**en'trancing** adj.

entrant ('εntrənt) n. a person who enters a university, competition, etc.

entrap (ɪn'træp) vb. **-trapping, -trapped.** **1.** to catch as in a trap. **2.** to trick into danger or difficulty. —**en'trapment** n.

entreat (ɪn'triːt) vb. to ask (someone) earnestly to do something.

entreaty (ɪn'triːtɪ) n., pl. **-treaties.** an earnest request or petition; plea.

entrecôte ('ɒntrə,kəʊt) n. a beefsteak cut from between the ribs.

entrée ('ɒntreɪ) n. **1.** the right of entry. **2.** a dish served before a main course. **3.** Chiefly U.S. the main course.

entrench (ɪn'trεntʃ) vb. **1.** to fix or establish firmly: strongly entrenched ideas. **2.** to construct a defensive position by digging trenches around it. —**en'trenched** adj. —**en'trenchment** n.

entrepreneur (,ɒntrəprə'nɜː) n. the owner of a business who, by risk and initiative, attempts to make profits. —,entre-pre'neurial adj.

entropy ('εntrəpɪ) n., pl. **-pies.** **1.** a thermodynamic quantity that changes by an amount equal to the heat absorbed or emitted divided by the thermodynamic temperature. **2.** lack of pattern or organization; disorder.

entrust (ɪn'trʌst) vb. **1.** (usually foll. by with) to invest or charge (with a duty or responsibility). **2.** (often foll. by to) to put (something) into the care of someone.

entry ('εntrɪ) n., pl. **-tries.** **1.** the act of entering; entrance. **2.** a place for entering, such as a door. **3.** the right of entering. **4.** the act of recording an item in a journal, account, etc. **5.** an item so recorded. **6.** a person, horse, car, etc., entering a competition. **7.** the competitors collectively.

entwine (ɪn'twaɪn) vb. to twist together or around (something else).

E number n. any of a series of numbers with the prefix E indicating a specific food additive recognized by the EC.

enumerate (ɪ'njuːmə,reɪt) vb. **1.** to name one by one; list. **2.** to count. **3.** Canad. to compile (the voting list) for an area. —e,numer'ation n. —e'numerative adj. —e'nume,rator n.

enunciate (ɪ'nʌnsɪ,eɪt) vb. **1.** to pronounce (words) clearly. **2.** to state precisely or formally. —e,nunci'ation n.

enuresis (,εnjʊ'riːsɪs) n. involuntary discharge of urine, esp. during sleep. —enuretic (,εnjʊ'rεtɪk) adj.

envelop (ɪn'vεləp) vb. to cover, surround, or enclose. —en'velopment n.

envelope ('εnvə,ləʊp, 'ɒn-) n. **1.** a flat covering of paper, that can be sealed, used to enclose a letter, etc. **2.** any covering or wrapper. **3.** Biol. any enclosing structure, such as a shell or skin. **4.** the bag enclosing gas in a balloon. **5.** Maths. a curve or surface that is tangential to each one of a group of curves or surfaces.

enviable ('εnvɪəb[l]) adj. exciting envy; fortunate or privileged. —'enviably adv.

envious ('εnvɪəs) adj. feeling, showing, or resulting from envy. —'enviously adv.

environment (ɪn'vaɪrənmənt) n. **1.** external conditions or surroundings in which people live. **2.** Ecology. the external surroundings in which a plant or animal lives, which influence its development. —en,viron'mental adj.

environmentalist (ɪn,vaɪrən'mεntəlɪst) n. a person concerned with the protection and preservation of the natural environment.

environs (ɪn'vaɪrənz) pl. n. a surrounding area, esp. the outskirts of a city.

envisage (ɪn'vɪzɪdʒ) vb. **1.** to form a mental image of; visualize. **2.** to conceive of as a possibility in the future.

envoy[1] ('εnvɔɪ) n. **1.** a diplomat ranking next below an ambassador. **2.** a messenger or representative.

envoy[2] ('εnvɔɪ) n. a brief concluding stanza in a ballade.

envy ('εnvɪ) n., pl. **-vies.** **1.** a feeling of discontent aroused by the possessions, achievements, or qualities of another. **2.** an object of envy. ~vb. **-vying, -vied.** **3.** to be envious of (a person or thing). —'envyingly adv.

enzyme ('εnzaɪm) n. any of a group of complex proteins, that act as catalysts in specific biochemical reactions. —enzymatic (,εnzaɪ'mætɪk) adj.

Eocene ('iːəʊ,siːn) adj. of an epoch of geological time about 55 million years ago.

Eolithic (,iːəʊ'lɪθɪk) adj. of or denoting the early part of the Stone Age, characterized by the use of crude stone tools.

EP n. an extended-play gramophone record.

epaulette ('εpə,lεt) n. a piece of ornamental material on the shoulder of a garment, esp. a military uniform.

epergne (ɪ'pɜːn) n. an ornamental centrepiece for a table.

ephedrine (ɪ'fεdrɪn) n. an alkaloid used for the treatment of asthma and hay fever.

ephemeral (ɪ'fεmərəl) adj. lasting only for a short time.

epic ('εpɪk) n. **1.** a long narrative poem recounting the deeds of a legendary hero. **2.** a book, poem, or film having qualities associated with an epic. ~*adj.* **3.** of or characteristic of an epic.

epicene (ˈɛpɪˌsiːn) *adj.* **1.** having the characteristics of both sexes. **2.** sexless. **3.** effeminate.

epicentre *or U.S.* **epicenter** (ˈɛpɪˌsɛntə) *n.* the point on the earth's surface immediately above the origin of an earthquake.

epicure (ˈɛpɪˌkjʊə) *n.* a person who enjoys consuming good food and drink. —ˈepicurˌism *n.*

epicurean (ˌɛpɪkjʊˈriːən) *adj.* **1.** devoted to sensual pleasures, esp. food and drink. ~*n.* **2.** an epicure; gourmet. —ˌepicuˈreanism *n.*

Epicurean (ˌɛpɪkjʊˈriːən) *adj.* **1.** of or relating to the philosophy of Epicurus, who held that the highest good is pleasure. ~*n.* **2.** a follower of the philosophy of Epicurus. —ˌEpicuˈreanism *n.*

epidemic (ˌɛpɪˈdɛmɪk) *adj.* **1.** (esp. of a disease) affecting many persons in an area. ~*n.* **2.** a widespread occurrence of a disease. **3.** a rapid development or spread of something: *an epidemic of strikes.* —ˌepiˈdemically *adv.*

epidemiology (ˌɛpɪˌdiːmɪˈɒlədʒɪ) *n.* the branch of medical science concerned with epidemic diseases. —ˌepiˌdemiˈologist *n.*

epidermis (ˌɛpɪˈdɜːmɪs) *n.* the thin protective outer layer of the skin. —ˌepiˈdermal *adj.*

epidiascope (ˌɛpɪˈdaɪəˌskəʊp) *n.* an optical device for projecting a magnified image onto a screen.

epidural (ˌɛpɪˈdjʊərəl) *adj.* **1.** upon or outside the outermost membrane covering the brain and spinal cord (**dura mater**). ~*n.* **2 a.** injection of anaesthetic into the space outside the dura mater, the outermost membrane enveloping the spinal cord. **b.** anaesthesia induced by this method.

epiglottis (ˌɛpɪˈɡlɒtɪs) *n.* a thin flap that covers the entrance to the larynx during swallowing. —ˌepiˈglottal *adj.*

epigram (ˈɛpɪˌɡræm) *n.* **1.** a witty remark. **2.** a short poem with a witty ending. —ˌepigramˈmatic *adj.*

epigraph (ˈɛpɪˌɡrɑːf) *n.* **1.** a quotation at the beginning of a book. **2.** an inscription on a monument or building.

epilepsy (ˈɛpɪˌlɛpsɪ) *n.* a disorder of the central nervous system characterized by periodic loss of consciousness with or without convulsions.

epileptic (ˌɛpɪˈlɛptɪk) *adj.* **1.** of or having epilepsy. ~*n.* **2.** a person who has epilepsy.

epilogue (ˈɛpɪˌlɒɡ) *n.* **1.** a speech addressed to the audience by an actor at the end of a play. **2.** a short postscript to any literary work.

Epiphany (ɪˈpɪfənɪ) *n., pl.* **-nies.** a Christian festival held on Jan. 6, commemorating, in

the Western Church, the manifestation of Christ to the Magi.

episcopacy (ɪˈpɪskəpəsɪ) *n., pl.* **-cies. 1.** government of a Church by bishops. **2.** same as **episcopate.**

episcopal (ɪˈpɪskəpˀl) *adj.* of, denoting, governed by, or relating to bishops.

Episcopal (ɪˈpɪskəpˀl) *adj.* of or denoting the Episcopal Church of Scotland and the U.S.

episcopalian (ɪˌpɪskəˈpeɪlɪən) *adj. also* **episcopal. 1.** practising or advocating Church government by bishops. ~*n.* **2.** an advocate of such Church government. —eˌpiscoˈpalianism *n.*

Episcopalian (ɪˌpɪskəˈpeɪlɪən) *adj.* **1.** belonging to or denoting the Episcopal Church. ~*n.* **2.** a member of this Church.

episcopate (ɪˈpɪskəpɪt) *n.* **1.** the office, status, or term of office of a bishop. **2.** bishops collectively.

episode (ˈɛpɪˌsəʊd) *n.* **1.** an event or series of events. **2.** any of the sections into which a novel, radio programme, or television programme is divided. **3.** an incident that forms part of a narrative but may be a digression from the main story.

episodic (ˌɛpɪˈsɒdɪk) *or* **episodical** *adj.* **1.** resembling or relating to an episode. **2.** irregular or sporadic. —ˌepiˈsodically *adv.*

epistemology (ɪˌpɪstɪˈmɒlədʒɪ) *n.* the theory of knowledge, esp. the critical study of its validity, methods, and scope. —**epistemological** (ɪˌpɪstɪməˈlɒdʒɪkˀl) *adj.* —eˌpisteˈmologist *n.*

epistle (ɪˈpɪsˀl) *n.* **1.** *Sometimes humorous.* a letter. **2.** a literary work in letter form, esp. a poem.

Epistle (ɪˈpɪsˀl) *n.* **1.** *New Testament.* any of the letters written by the apostles. **2.** a reading from one of the Epistles, part of the Eucharistic service in many Christian Churches.

epistolary (ɪˈpɪstələrɪ) *adj.* **1.** relating to, conducted by, or contained in letters. **2.** (of a novel) presented in the form of a series of letters.

epitaph (ˈɛpɪˌtɑːf) *n.* **1.** a commemorative inscription on a tombstone. **2.** a commemorative speech or written passage.

epithelium (ˌɛpɪˈθiːlɪəm) *n., pl.* **-lia** (-lɪə). an animal cellular tissue covering the external and internal surfaces of the body. —ˌepiˈthelial *adj.*

epithet (ˈɛpɪˌθɛt) *n.* a descriptive word or phrase added to a person's name. —ˌepiˈthetic *adj.*

epitome (ɪˈpɪtəmɪ) *n.* **1.** a person or thing that is a typical example of a characteristic or class; personification. **2.** a summary, esp. of a written work.

epitomize *or* **-ise** (ɪˈpɪtəˌmaɪz) *vb.* to be or make an epitome of.

EPNS electroplated nickel silver.

epoch ('iːpɒk) n. **1.** the beginning of a new or distinctive period. **2.** a long period of time marked by some predominant characteristic; era. **3.** Geol. a unit of time within a period during which a series of rocks is formed. —**epochal** ('ɛpɒk°l) adj.

eponym ('ɛpənɪm) n. the name of the person from which the name of a place or thing is derived. —**eponymous** (ɪ'pɒnɪməs) adj.

EPOS electronic point of sale.

epoxy (ɪ'pɒksɪ) Chem. ~adj. **1.** of or containing an oxygen atom joined to two different groups that are themselves joined to other groups. **2.** of or consisting of an epoxy resin. ~n., pl. **epoxies. 3.** an epoxy resin.

epoxy resin n. a tough resistant thermosetting synthetic resin, used in laminates and adhesives.

Epsom salts ('ɛpsəm) n. (functioning as sing. or pl.) a medicinal preparation of hydrated magnesium sulphate, used to empty the bowels.

equable ('ɛkwəb°l) adj. **1.** even-tempered; placid. **2.** unvarying; uniform: an equable climate. —**equably** adv.

equal ('iːkwəl) adj. **1.** identical in size, quantity, degree, or intensity. **2.** having identical privileges, rights, or status. **3.** having uniform effect or application: equal opportunities. **4.** evenly balanced or proportioned. **5.** (usually foll. by to) having the necessary strength, ability, or means (for): to be equal to one's work. ~n. **6.** a person or thing equal to another. ~vb. **equalling, equalled** or U.S. **equaling, equaled. 7.** to be equal to; match. **8.** to make or do something equal to: to equal the world record. —**equally** adv.
Usage. Equally should not be followed by as: the two were equally important not the two were equally as important.

equality (ɪ'kwɒlɪtɪ) n., pl. **-ties.** the state of being equal.

equalize or **-ise** ('iːkwə,laɪz) vb. **1.** to make equal or uniform. **2.** (in sports) to reach the same score as one's opponent or opponents. —**equalization** or **-i'sation** n.

equal opportunity n. the offering of employment or promotion equally to all, without discrimination as to sex, race, colour, etc.

equanimity (,ɛkwə'nɪmɪtɪ) n. calmness of mind or temper; composure.

equate (ɪ'kweɪt) vb. **1.** to make or regard as equivalent. **2.** Maths. to indicate the equality of; form an equation from. —**e'quatable** adj.

equation (ɪ'kweɪʒən) n. **1.** a mathematical statement that two expressions are equal. **2.** the act of equating. **3.** a representation of a chemical reaction using symbols of the elements.

equator (ɪ'kweɪtə) n. **1.** an imaginary circle around the earth at an equal distance from the North Pole and the South Pole. **2.** Astron. See **celestial equator.**

equatorial (,ɛkwə'tɔːrɪəl) adj. of, like, or existing at or near the equator.

equerry (ɪ'kwɛrɪ) n., pl. **-ries.** an officer of the royal household who acts as a personal attendant to a member of the royal family.

equestrian (ɪ'kwɛstrɪən) adj. **1.** of or relating to horses and riding. **2.** on horseback; mounted. ~n. **3.** a person skilled in riding. —**e'questrian,ism** n.

equiangular (,iːkwɪ'æŋgjʊlə) adj. having all angles equal.

equidistant (,iːkwɪ'dɪstənt) adj. equally distant. —**,equi'distance** n.

equilateral (,iːkwɪ'lætərəl) adj. **1.** having all sides of equal length. ~n. **2.** a geometric figure having all sides of equal length.

equilibrium (,iːkwɪ'lɪbrɪəm) n., pl. **-ria** (-rɪə). **1.** a stable condition in which forces cancel one another. **2.** a state of mental and emotional balance; composure.

equine ('ɛkwaɪn) adj. of or resembling a horse.

equinoctial (,iːkwɪ'nɒkʃəl) adj. **1.** relating to or occurring at an equinox. ~n. **2.** a storm at or near an equinox. **3.** same as **celestial equator.**

equinoctial circle or **line** n. same as **celestial equator.**

equinox ('iːkwɪ,nɒks) n. either of the two occasions when day and night are of equal length: the **vernal equinox** occurs around March 21 and the **autumnal equinox** around Sept. 23.

equip (ɪ'kwɪp) vb. **equipping, equipped. 1.** to furnish (with necessary supplies). **2.** to provide with abilities, understanding, etc.: her son was never equipped to be a scholar.

equipage ('ɛkwɪpɪdʒ) n. **1.** the stores and equipment of a military unit. **2.** a horse-drawn carriage with liveried footmen.

equipment (ɪ'kwɪpmənt) n. **1.** an equipping. **2.** the items so provided. **3.** a set of tools or devices used for a particular purpose; kit.

equipoise ('ɛkwɪ,pɔɪz) n. **1.** even balance of weight; equilibrium. **2.** a counterbalance.

equitable ('ɛkwɪtəb°l) adj. **1.** fair; just. **2.** Law. relating to or valid in equity, as distinct from law. —**'equitably** adv.

equitation (,ɛkwɪ'teɪʃən) n. riding and horsemanship.

equities ('ɛkwɪtɪz) pl. n. same as **ordinary shares.**

equity ('ɛkwɪtɪ) n., pl. **-ties. 1.** the quality of being impartial; fairness. **2.** Law. a system of jurisprudence founded on principles of natural justice and fair conduct that supplements common law.

Equity ('ɛkwɪtɪ) *n. Brit.* the actors' trade union.

equiv. equivalent.

equivalent (ɪ'kwɪvələnt) *adj.* **1.** equal in value, quantity, significance, etc. **2.** having the same or a similar effect or meaning. ~*n.* **3.** something that is equivalent. —e'**quivalence** *n.*

equivocal (ɪ'kwɪvək²l) *adj.* **1.** capable of varying interpretations; ambiguous. **2.** deliberately misleading or vague. **3.** of doubtful character or sincerity. —e'**quivocally** *adv.*

equivocate (ɪ'kwɪvə,keɪt) *vb.* to use equivocal language in order to deceive someone or to avoid speaking the truth. —e,quivo'**cation** *n.* —e'**quivo,cator** *n.*

er (ə, ɜː) *interj.* a sound made when hesitating in speech.

Er *Chem.* erbium.

ER 1. Queen Elizabeth. **2.** King Edward.

era ('ɪərə) *n.* **1.** a period of time considered as distinctive; epoch. **2.** an extended period of time measured from a fixed point: *the Christian era.* **3.** the beginning of a new or distinctive period. **4.** *Geol.* a major division of time.

eradicate (ɪ'rædɪ,keɪt) *vb.* to destroy (something) completely; root out. —e'**radicable** *adj.* —e,radi'**cation** *n.* —e'**radi,cator** *n.*

erase (ɪ'reɪz) *vb.* **1.** to obliterate or rub out (something written). **2.** to destroy all traces of (something). **3.** to remove (a recording) from (magnetic tape). —e'**rasable** *adj.*

eraser (ɪ'reɪzə) *n.* an object, such as a piece of rubber, for erasing something written.

erasure (ɪ'reɪʒə) *n.* **1.** an erasing. **2.** the place or mark where something has been erased.

erbium ('ɜːbɪəm) *n.* a soft silvery-white element of the lanthanide series of metals. Symbol: Er

ere (ɛə) *conj., prep. Poetic.* before.

erect (ɪ'rɛkt) *adj.* **1.** upright in posture or position. **2.** *Physiol.* (of the penis, clitoris, or nipples) firm or rigid after swelling with blood, esp. as a result of sexual excitement. ~*vb.* **3.** to build. **4.** to raise to an upright position. **5.** to found or form; set up. —e'**rection** *n.*

erectile (ɪ'rɛktaɪl) *adj. Physiol.* (of an organ, such as the penis) capable of becoming erect.

eremite ('ɛrɪ,maɪt) *n.* a Christian hermit. —**eremitic** (,ɛrɪ'mɪtɪk) *adj.*

erg (ɜːg) *n.* the cgs unit of work or energy.

ergo ('ɜːgəʊ) *conj.* therefore.

ergonomics (,ɜːgə'nɒmɪks) *n.* (*functioning as sing.*) the study of the relationship between workers and their environment. —,ergo'**nomic** *adj.*

ergot ('ɜːgət, -gɒt) *n.* **1.** a disease of a cereal, such as rye, caused by a fungus. **2.** the dried fungus used in medicine.

Erin ('ɪərɪn, 'ɛərɪn) *n. Archaic or poetic.* Ireland.

ermine ('ɜːmɪn) *n., pl.* **-mines** *or* **-mine.** **1.** the stoat in northern regions, where it has a white winter coat. **2.** the fur of this animal, used to trim state robes of judges, nobles, etc.

erne *or* **ern** (ɜːn) *n.* a fish-eating sea eagle.

Ernie ('ɜːnɪ) *n.* (in Britain) a computer that randomly selects winning numbers of Premium Bonds.

erode (ɪ'rəʊd) *vb.* **1.** to wear down or away or become worn down or away. **2.** to deteriorate or cause to deteriorate.

erogenous (ɪ'rɒdʒɪnəs) *adj.* **1.** sensitive to sexual stimulation. **2.** arousing sexual desire or giving sexual pleasure.

erosion (ɪ'rəʊʒən) *n.* the wearing away of rocks or soil by the action of water, ice, or wind. —e'**rosive** *or* e'**rosional** *adj.*

erotic (ɪ'rɒtɪk) *adj.* of, concerning, or arousing sexual desire or giving sexual pleasure. —e'**rotically** *adv.*

erotica (ɪ'rɒtɪkə) *pl. n.* explicitly sexual literature or art.

eroticism (ɪ'rɒtɪ,sɪzəm) *n.* **1.** erotic quality or nature. **2.** the use of sexually arousing symbolism in literature or art. **3.** sexual excitement or desire.

err (ɜː) *vb.* **1.** to make a mistake. **2.** to sin.

errand ('ɛrənd) *n.* **1.** a short trip to get or do something for someone. **2.** the purpose of such a trip.

errant ('ɛrənt) *adj.* **1.** *Archaic or literary.* wandering in search of adventure: *a knight errant.* **2.** erring or straying from the right course. —'**errantry** *n.*

erratic (ɪ'rætɪk) *adj.* **1.** irregular or unpredictable: *erratic behaviour.* **2.** having no fixed course. ~*n.* **3.** a rock that has been transported by glacial action. —er'**ratically** *adv.*

erratum (ɪ'rɑːtəm) *n., pl.* **-ta** (-tə). an error in writing or printing.

erroneous (ɪ'rəʊnɪəs) *adj.* based on or containing error; incorrect. —er'**roneously** *adv.*

error ('ɛrə) *n.* **1.** a mistake or inaccuracy. **2.** an incorrect belief or wrong judgment. **3.** the condition of deviating from accuracy or correctness. **4.** *Maths, statistics.* a measure of the difference between some quantity and an approximation of it.

ersatz ('ɛəzæts) *adj.* **1.** made in imitation. ~*n.* **2.** an ersatz substance.

Erse (ɜːs) *n.* **1.** Gaelic. ~*adj.* **2.** of or relating to the Gaelic language.

erstwhile ('ɜːst,waɪl) *adj.* **1.** former. ~*adv.* **2.** *Archaic.* formerly.

eruct (ɪˈrʌkt) *or* **eructate** *vb.* to belch. —**eructation** (ˌiːrʌkˈteɪʃən, ˌiːrʌk-) *n.*

erudite (ˈɛrʊˌdaɪt) *adj.* having or showing scholarship; learned. —**erudition** (ˌɛrʊˈdɪʃən) *n.*

erupt (ɪˈrʌpt) *vb.* **1.** to eject (steam, water, and volcanic material) violently or (of volcanic material, etc.) to be so ejected. **2.** (of a blemish) to appear on the skin. **3.** to burst forth suddenly and violently. —eˈruptive *adj.* —eˈruption *n.*

erysipelas (ˌɛrɪˈsɪpɪləs) *n.* an acute disease of the skin, with fever and raised purplish patches.

erythrocyte (ɪˈrɪθrəʊˌsaɪt) *n.* a red blood cell that transports oxygen through the body.

Es *Chem.* einsteinium.

escalate (ˈɛskəˌleɪt) *vb.* to increase or be increased in extent, intensity, or magnitude. —ˌescaˈlation *n.*

escalator (ˈɛskəˌleɪtə) *n.* a moving staircase consisting of stair treads fixed to a conveyor belt.

escalator clause *n.* a clause in a contract stipulating an adjustment in wages, prices, etc., esp. in relation to the cost of living.

escallop (ɛˈskɒləp) *n.* same as **scallop.**

escalope (ˈɛskəˌlɒp) *n.* a thin slice of meat, usually veal.

escapade (ˈɛskəˌpeɪd) *n.* an adventure, esp. mischievous or unlawful.

escape (ɪˈskeɪp) *vb.* **1.** to get away or break free from (confinement). **2.** to manage to avoid (something dangerous, unpleasant, or difficult). **3.** (of gases, liquids, etc.) to leak gradually. **4.** to elude; be forgotten by: *the figure escapes me.* **5.** to be articulated involuntarily from: *a cry escaped his lips.* ~*n.* **6.** the act of escaping or state of having escaped. **7.** avoidance of injury, harm, etc. **8.** a means of escape. **9.** a means of distraction or relief: *hill walking provides an escape for city dwellers.* **10.** a leakage. —esˌcapˈee *n.*

escapement (ɪˈskeɪpmənt) *n.* a mechanism used in timepieces to provide periodic impulses to the pendulum or balance.

escape road *n.* a road, as on a hill, into which a car can be driven if the brakes fail.

escape velocity *n.* the minimum velocity necessary for a particle, space vehicle, etc. to escape from the gravitational field of the earth or other celestial body.

escapism (ɪˈskeɪpɪzəm) *n.* an inclination to retreat from unpleasant reality, as through fantasy. —esˈcapist *n.*, *adj.*

escapologist (ˌɛskəˈpɒlədʒɪst) *n.* an entertainer who specializes in freeing himself from chains, ropes, etc. —escaˈpology *n.*

escarpment (ɪˈskɑːpmənt) *n.* **1.** the long continuous steep face of a ridge or moun-

tain. **2.** a steep artificial slope in front of a fortified place.

eschatology (ˌɛskəˈtɒlədʒɪ) *n.* the branch of theology concerned with the end of the world. —**eschatological** (ˌɛskətəˈlɒdʒɪkᵊl) *adj.*

escheat (ɪsˈtʃiːt) *Law.* ~*n.* **1.** formerly, the reversion of property to the Crown or feudal lord in the absence of legal heirs. **2.** the property so reverting. ~*vb.* **3.** to take (land) or (of land) to revert by escheat.

eschew (ɪsˈtʃuː) *vb.* to keep clear of or abstain from (something disliked or harmful); avoid. —esˈchewal *n.*

escort *n.* (ˈɛskɔːt). **1.** one or more persons or vehicles accompanying another or others for protection or as a mark of honour. **2.** a person who accompanies another of the opposite sex on a social occasion. ~*vb.* (ɪsˈkɔːt). **3.** to accompany or attend as an escort.

escritoire (ˌɛskrɪˈtwɑː) *n.* a writing desk with compartments and drawers.

escudo (ɛˈskuːdəʊ) *n.*, *pl.* **-dos.** the standard monetary unit of Portugal.

esculent (ˈɛskjʊlənt) *n.* **1.** any edible substance. ~*adj.* **2.** edible.

escutcheon (ɪsˈkʌtʃən) *n.* **1.** a shield, esp. displaying a coat of arms. **2. blot on one's escutcheon.** a stain on one's honour.

Eskimo (ˈɛskɪˌməʊ) *n.* **1.** (*pl.* **-mos** *or* **-mo**) a member of a group of peoples who live in N Canada, Greenland, Alaska, and E Siberia. The Eskimos are more properly referred to as the **Inuit.** **2.** the language of these peoples. ~*adj.* **3.** of or relating to the Eskimos.

Eskimo dog *n.* a large powerful breed of dog with a long thick coat and curled tail, used by the Eskimos to pull sledges.

ESN educationally subnormal.

esoteric (ˌɛsəʊˈtɛrɪk) *adj.* understood by only a small number of people, esp. because they have a special knowledge. —ˌesoˈterically *adv.*

ESP extrasensory perception.

esp. especially.

espadrille (ˌɛspəˈdrɪl) *n.* a light canvas shoe with a braided cord sole.

espalier (ɪˈspæljə) *n.* **1.** a shrub or fruit tree trained to grow flat. **2.** the trellis on which such plants are trained.

esparto *or* **esparto grass** (ɛˈspɑːtəʊ) *n.*, *pl.* **-tos.** any of various grasses of S Europe and N Africa, used to make ropes, mats, etc.

especial (ɪˈspɛʃəl) *adj. Formal.* same as **special.**
Usage. Special is always used in preference to *especial* when the sense is one of being out of the ordinary: *a special lesson.* Special is also used when something is referred to as being for a particular purpose: *the word was specially underlined for you.* Where an idea of pre-eminence or individuality is in-

volved, either *especial* or *special* may be used: *he is especially* (or *specially*) *good at his job.*

especially (ɪ'speʃəlɪ) *adv.* **1.** particularly: *I love fruit, especially apples.* **2.** more than usually.

Esperanto (ˌɛspə'ræntəʊ) *n.* an international artificial language. —ˌEspe'rantist *n., adj.*

espionage ('ɛspɪəˌnɑːʒ) *n.* **1.** the use of spies to obtain secret information, esp. by governments. **2.** the act of spying.

esplanade (ˌɛsplə'neɪd) *n.* a long open level stretch of ground, esp. beside the seashore or in front of a fortified place.

espousal (ɪ'spaʊz°l) *n.* **1.** adoption or support: *an espousal of new beliefs.* **2.** (*sometimes pl.*) *Archaic.* a marriage or betrothal ceremony.

espouse (ɪ'spaʊz) *vb.* **1.** to adopt or give support to (a cause, ideal, etc.). **2.** *Archaic.* (esp. of a man) to marry.

espresso (ɛ'sprɛsəʊ) *n., pl.* -sos. **1.** coffee made by forcing steam or boiling water through ground coffee. **2.** a machine for making coffee in this way.

esprit (ɛ'spriː) *n.* spirit, liveliness, or wit.

esprit de corps (ɛ'spriː də 'kɔː) *n.* consciousness of and pride in belonging to a particular group.

espy (ɪ'spaɪ) *vb.* **espying, espied.** to catch sight of; detect.

Esq. esquire.

esquire (ɪ'skwaɪə) *n.* **1.** *Chiefly Brit.* a title of respect, usually abbreviated *Esq.,* placed after a man's name. **2.** (in medieval times) the attendant of a knight.

ESRO ('ɛzrəʊ) *n.* European Space Research Organization.

essay *n.* ('ɛseɪ; *sense 2 also* ɛ'seɪ). **1.** a short literary composition. **2.** an attempt. ~*vb.* (ɛ'seɪ). **3.** to attempt (something).

essayist ('ɛseɪɪst) *n.* a person who writes essays.

essence ('ɛsns) *n.* **1.** the basic, central, and most important feature of something which determines its identity. **2.** the most distinctive element of a thing. **3.** a concentrated liquid used to flavour food. **4.** a perfume. **5. in essence.** essentially. **6. of the essence.** vitally important.

essential (ɪ'sɛnʃəl) *adj.* **1.** vitally important; absolutely necessary. **2.** basic; fundamental. ~*n.* **3.** something fundamental or indispensable. —es'sentially *adv.*

essential oil *n.* any of various volatile oils in plants, having the odour or flavour of the plant from which they are extracted.

EST **1.** (in the U.S. and Canada) Eastern Standard Time. **2.** electric-shock treatment.

est. **1.** established. **2.** estimate(d).

establish (ɪ'stæblɪʃ) *vb.* **1.** to create or set

up (an organization, etc.) on a permanent basis. **2.** to make secure or permanent in a certain place, job, etc. **3.** to prove correct: *establish a fact.* **4.** to cause (a principle) to be accepted: *establish a precedent.* **5.** to give (a Church) the status of a national institution.

establishment (ɪ'stæblɪʃmənt) *n.* **1.** the act of establishing or state of being established. **2. a.** a business organization or other institution. **b.** a place of business. **3.** the staff of an organization. **4.** a body of employees.

Establishment (ɪ'stæblɪʃmənt) *n.* the. a group of people having authority within a society: usually seen as conservative.

estate (ɪ'steɪt) *n.* **1.** a large piece of landed property, esp. in the country. **2.** *Chiefly Brit.* a large area of property development, esp. of new houses or factories. **3.** *Law.* property or possessions, esp. of a deceased person. **4.** an order or class in a political community: the lords spiritual (**first estate**), lords temporal or peers (**second estate**), and commons (**third estate**).

estate agent *n.* **1.** *Brit.* an agent concerned with the valuation, lease, and sale of property. **2.** the administrator of a large landed property.

estate car *n. Brit.* a car which has a long body with a door at the back end and luggage space behind the rear seats.

estate duty *n.* same as **death duty.**

esteem (ɪ'stiːm) *vb.* **1.** to have great respect or high regard for (someone). **2.** *Formal.* to judge or consider: *I esteem him nothing but a fool.* ~*n.* **3.** high regard or respect; good opinion. —es'teemed *adj.*

ester ('ɛstə) *n. Chem.* a compound produced by the reaction between an acid and an alcohol.

estimable ('ɛstɪməb°l) *adj.* worthy of respect.

estimate *vb.* ('ɛstɪˌmeɪt). **1.** to form an approximate idea of (size, cost, etc.); calculate roughly. **2.** to form an opinion about; judge. **3.** to submit (an approximate price) for (a job) to a prospective client. ~*n.* ('ɛstɪmɪt). **4.** an approximate calculation. **5.** a statement of the likely charge for certain work. **6.** an opinion. —'estiˌmator *n.*

estimation (ˌɛstɪ'meɪʃən) *n.* **1.** a considered opinion; judgment. **2.** the act of estimating.

estrange (ɪ'streɪndʒ) *vb.* to antagonize (someone previously friendly); alienate. —es'tranged *adj.* —es'trangement *n.*

estuary ('ɛstjʊərɪ) *n., pl.* -aries. the widening channel of a river where it nears the sea. —'estuarine *adj.*

ETA estimated time of arrival.

et al. **1.** and elsewhere. **2.** and others.

etc. et cetera.

et cetera *or* **etcetera** (ɪt 'sɛtrə) *n. and vb.*

substitute. **1.** and the rest; and others; and so forth. **2.** or the like; or something similar.

Usage. Since *et cetera* (or *etc.*) means *and other things, and* is not used before *etc.* because it would be repeating the idea. The repetition of *etc.*, as in *notebooks, etc., etc.*, is avoided in formal contexts.

etceteras (ɪtˈsetrəz) *pl. n.* miscellaneous extra things or persons.

etch (ɛtʃ) *vb.* **1.** to wear away the surface of (a metal, glass, etc.) by the action of an acid. **2.** to cut (a design or pattern) on (a metal or other printing plate) by the action of acid. **3.** to imprint vividly: *the horror of the crash was etched on her memory.* —ˈetcher *n.*

etching (ˈetʃɪŋ) *n.* **1.** the art or process of preparing or printing etched designs. **2.** an etched plate. **3.** an impression made from an etched plate.

eternal (ɪˈtɜːnˀl)) *adj.* **1.** without beginning or end; lasting for ever. **2.** (*often cap.*) a name applied to God. **3.** unchanged by time: *eternal truths.* **4.** seemingly unceasing: *eternal bickering.* —eˈternally *adv.*

eternal triangle *n.* an emotional or sexual relationship in which there are conflicts between a man and two women or a woman and two men.

eternity (ɪˈtɜːnɪtɪ) *n., pl.* **-ties.** **1.** endless or infinite time. **2.** the state of being eternal. **3.** the timeless existence after death. **4.** a seemingly endless period of time: *I waited for what seemed like an eternity.*

eternity ring *n.* a ring given as a token of lasting affection, esp. one set all around with stones to symbolize continuity.

ethane (ˈiːθeɪn) *n.* a flammable gaseous alkane obtained from natural gas and petroleum: used as a fuel.

ethanoic acid (ˌɛθəˈnəʊɪk) *n.* same as **acetic acid.**

ethanol (ˈɛθəˌnɒl) *n.* same as **alcohol** (sense 1).

ethene (ˈɛθiːn) *n.* same as **ethylene.**

ether (ˈiːθə) *n.* **1.** a colourless volatile highly flammable liquid: used as a solvent and anaesthetic. **2.** the medium formerly believed to fill all space and to transmit electromagnetic waves. **3.** the upper regions of the atmosphere; clear sky. ~Also (for senses 2 and 3): **aether.**

ethereal (ɪˈθɪərɪəl) *adj.* **1.** extremely delicate or refined. **2.** heavenly; spiritual. —eˈthereally *adv.*

ethic (ˈɛθɪk) *n.* a moral principle or set of moral values held by an individual or group.

ethical (ˈɛθɪkˀl) *adj.* **1.** of or based on a system of moral beliefs about right and wrong. **2.** in accordance with principles of professional conduct. **3** of or relating to ethics. —ˈethically *adv.*

ethics (ˈɛθɪks) *n.* **1.** (*functioning as pl.*) a code of behaviour, esp. of a particular group, profession, or individual. **2.** (*functioning as pl.*) the moral fitness of a decision, course of action, etc. **3.** (*functioning as sing.*) the study of the moral value of human conduct.

Ethiopian (ˌiːθɪˈəʊpɪən) *adj.* **1.** of Ethiopia. ~*n.* **2.** a person from Ethiopia.

ethnic (ˈɛθnɪk) *or* **ethnical** *adj.* **1.** of or relating to a human group having racial, religious, and linguistic characteristics in common. **2.** characteristic of another culture, esp. a peasant one: *ethnic music.* —ˈethnically *adv.*

ethnocentric (ˌɛθnəʊˈsɛntrɪk) *adj.* of or relating to the belief that one's own nation, culture, or group is intrinsically superior. —**ethnocentricity** (ˌɛθnəʊsɛnˈtrɪsɪtɪ) *n.*

ethnology (ɛθˈnɒlədʒɪ) *n.* the branch of anthropology that deals with races and peoples and their relations to one another. —**ethnological** (ˌɛθnəˈlɒdʒɪkˀl) *adj.* —ethˈnologist *n.*

ethos (ˈiːθɒs) *n.* the distinctive spirit and attitudes of a people, culture, etc.

ethyl (ˈiːθaɪl, ˈɛθɪl) *n.* (*modifier*) of, consisting of, or containing the monovalent group C_2H_5-.

ethyl alcohol *n.* same as **alcohol** (sense 1).

ethylene (ˈɛθɪˌliːn) *or* **ethene** (ˈɛθiːn) *n.* a colourless flammable gaseous alkene used to make polythene and other chemicals.

etiolate (ˈiːtɪəʊˌleɪt) *vb.* **1.** *Bot.* to whiten (a green plant) through lack of sunlight. **2.** to become or cause to become pale and weak. —ˌetioˈlation *n.*

etiology (ˌiːtɪˈɒlədʒɪ) *n., pl.* **-gies.** **1.** the study of causation. **2.** the study of the cause of diseases. —**etiological** (ˌiːtɪəˈlɒdʒɪkˀl) *adj.*

etiquette (ˈɛtɪˌkɛt) *n.* **1.** the customs or rules of behaviour regarded as correct in social life. **2.** a conventional code of practice in certain professions.

Eton collar (ˈiːtˀn) *n.* a broad stiff white collar worn outside a Eton jacket.

Eton crop *n.* a very short mannish hairstyle worn by women in the 1920s.

Eton jacket *n.* a waist-length jacket, open in front, formerly worn by pupils of Eton College.

Etruscan (ɪˈtrʌskən) *n.* **1.** a member of an ancient people of Etruria in central Italy. **2.** the language of the Etruscans. ~*adj.* **3.** of Etruria or the Etruscans.

étude (ˈeɪtjuːd) *n.* a short musical composition for a solo instrument, esp. for exercise or exploiting virtuosity.

etymology (ˌɛtɪˈmɒlədʒɪ) *n., pl.* **-gies.** **1.** the study of the sources and development of words. **2.** an account of the source and development of a word. —**etymological** (ˌɛtɪməˈlɒdʒɪkᵊl) adj. —ˌ**ety'mologist** n.

Eu Chem. europium.

eucalyptus (ˌjuːkəˈlɪptəs) or **eucalypt** ('juːkəˌlɪpt) n., pl. **-lyptuses, -lypti** (-ˈlɪptaɪ), or **-lypts.** any of a mostly Australian genus of trees, widely cultivated for timber and gum, and for the medicinal oil in their leaves (**eucalyptus oil**).

Eucharist ('juːkərɪst) n. **1.** the Christian sacrament commemorating Christ's Last Supper by the consecration of bread and wine. **2.** the consecrated elements of bread and wine. —ˌ**Eucha'ristic** adj.

Euclidean or **Euclidian** (juːˈklɪdɪən) adj. denoting a system of geometry based on the rules of Euclid, 3rd-century B.C. Greek mathematician.

eugenics (juːˈdʒɛnɪks) n. (functioning as sing.) the study of methods of improving the human race, esp. by selective breeding. —**eu'genic** adj. —**eu'genically** adv. —**eu'genicist** n.

eulogize or **-gise** ('juːləˌdʒaɪz) vb. to praise (a person or thing) highly in speech or writing. —ˌ**eulo'gistic** adj.

eulogy ('juːlədʒɪ) n., pl. **-gies.** **1.** a speech or piece of writing praising a person or thing, esp. a person who has recently died. **2.** high praise.

eunuch ('juːnək) n. a man who has been castrated, esp. (formerly) a guard in a harem.

euphemism ('juːfɪˌmɪzəm) n. an inoffensive word or phrase substituted for one considered offensive or upsetting, such as departed for dead. —ˌ**euphe'mistic** adj. —ˌ**euphe'mistically** adv.

euphonious (juːˈfəʊnɪəs) adj. pleasing to the ear.

euphonium (juːˈfəʊnɪəm) n. a brass musical instrument with four valves.

euphony ('juːfənɪ) n., pl. **-nies.** a pleasing sound, esp. in speech.

euphoria (juːˈfɔːrɪə) n. a feeling of great elation, esp. when exaggerated. —**euphoric** (juːˈfɒrɪk) adj.

euphuism ('juːfjuːˌɪzəm) n. an artificial high-flown prose style. —ˌ**euphu'istic** adj.

Eur. Europe(an).

Eurasian (juəˈreɪʒən) adj. **1.** of Europe and Asia. **2.** of mixed European and Asian descent. ~n. **3.** a person of mixed European and Asian descent.

Euratom (juəˈrætəm) n. European Atomic Energy Community.

eureka (juˈriːkə) interj. an exclamation of triumph on discovering or solving something.

eurhythmics or **-rythmics** U.S. **eurythmics** (juːˈrɪðmɪks) n. (functioning as sing.) a system of training through physical movement to music.

Euro- ('juərəʊ) or before a vowel **Eur-** combining form. Europe or European.

European (ˌjuərəˈpɪən) adj. **1.** of or relating to Europe. **2.** native to Europe. ~n. **3.** a person from Europe. **4.** a person of European descent. **5.** S. African. any White person. —ˌ**Euro'pean,ism** n.

European Community or **European Economic Community** n. formal names for the **Common Market.**

europium (juˈrəʊpɪəm) n. a silvery-white element of the lanthanide series. Symbol: Eu

Eustachian tube (juːˈsteɪʃən) n. a tube that connects the middle ear with the pharynx and equalizes the pressure between the two sides of the eardrum.

euthanasia (ˌjuːθəˈneɪzɪə) n. the act of killing someone painlessly, esp. to relieve suffering from an incurable illness.

eV electronvolt.

evacuate (ɪˈvækjʊˌeɪt) vb. **1.** to send (people) away (from a place of danger) to a place of safety: children in London were evacuated to the country during the Second World War. **2.** to make empty. **3.** Physiol. to discharge (waste) from (the body). —e,**vacu'ation** n. —e,**vacu'ee** n.

evade (ɪˈveɪd) vb. **1.** to get away from or avoid (imprisonment, captors, etc.). **2.** to get around, shirk, or dodge (the law, a duty, etc.). **3.** to avoid answering (a question).

evaluate (ɪˈvæljʊˌeɪt) vb. **1.** to ascertain or set the value of. **2.** to judge the quality of. —e,**valu'ation** n.

evanesce (ˌɛvəˈnɛs) vb. Formal. to fade gradually from sight; vanish.

evanescent (ˌɛvəˈnɛsᵊnt) adj. quickly fading away; ephemeral or transitory. —ˌ**eva'nescence** n.

evangelical (ˌiːvænˈdʒɛlɪkᵊl) Christianity. ~adj. **1.** of or following from the Gospels. **2.** of certain Protestant sects which emphasize personal conversion and faith in atonement through the death of Christ as a means of salvation. ~n. **3.** a member of an evangelical sect. —ˌ**evan'gelicalism** n. —ˌ**evan'gelically** adv.

evangelism (ɪˈvændʒɪˌlɪzəm) n. the practice of spreading the Christian gospel.

evangelist (ɪˈvændʒɪlɪst) n. a preacher, sometimes itinerant. —e,**vange'listic** adj.

Evangelist (ɪˈvændʒɪlɪst) n. any of the writers of the Gospels: Matthew, Mark, Luke, or John.

evangelize or **-lise** (ɪˈvændʒɪˌlaɪz) vb. to preach the Christian gospel (to). —e,**vangeli'zation** or **-li'sation** n.

evaporate (ɪˈvæpəˌreɪt) vb. **1.** to change from a liquid or solid to a vapour. **2.** to lose or cause to lose liquid by vaporization leaving a more concentrated residue. —e'**vaporable** adj. —e,**vapo'ration** n.

evaporated milk n. thick unsweetened

tinned milk from which some of the water has been evaporated.

evasion (ɪ'veɪʒən) *n.* **1.** the act of evading, esp. a duty, responsibility, etc., by cunning or illegal means: *tax evasion*. **2.** cunning or deception used to dodge a question, duty, etc.

evasive (ɪ'veɪsɪv) *adj.* **1.** seeking to evade; not straightforward: *an evasive answer*. **2.** avoiding or seeking to avoid trouble or difficulties: *evasive action*. —e'**vasively** *adv.*

eve (iːv) *n.* **1.** the evening or day before some special event. **2.** the period immediately before an event: *the eve of war*. **3.** *Archaic.* evening.

even[1] ('iːvᵊn) *adj.* **1.** level and regular; flat. **2.** on the same level or in the same plane (as). **3.** without fluctuation; regular; constant. **4.** not easily excited; calm: *an even temper.* **5.** equally balanced between two sides. **6.** equal in number, quantity, etc. **7. a.** (of a number) divisible by two. **b.** indicated by such a number: *the even pages.* **8.** denoting alternatives, events, etc., that have an equal probability: *an even chance of winning or losing.* **9.** equal, as in score; level. **10. even money** *or* **evens.** a bet in which the winnings are exactly the same as the amount staked. **11. get even (with).** *Informal.* to exact revenge (on); settle accounts (with). ~*adv.* **12.** (intensifier; used to suggest that the content of a statement is unexpected or paradoxical): *even an idiot can do that.* **13.** (intensifier; used with comparative forms): *even better.* **14.** used to introduce a word that is stronger and more accurate than one already used: *they appeared satisfied, even happy, with the outcome.* **15.** used preceding a hypothesis to emphasize that whether or not the condition is fulfilled, the statement remains valid: *even if she died he wouldn't care.* **16. even so.** in spite of any assertion to the contrary; nevertheless. **17. even though.** despite the fact that. ~See also **even out, even up.** —'**evenly** *adv.* —'**evenness** *n.*

even[2] ('iːvᵊn) *n. Archaic.* **1.** eve. **2.** evening.

even-handed *adj.* fair; impartial.

evening ('iːvnɪŋ) *n.* **1.** the latter part of the day, esp. from late afternoon until nightfall. **2.** the latter or concluding period: *the evening of one's life.* ~*adj.* **3.** of or in the evening.

evening dress *n.* clothes for a formal occasion during the evening.

evening primrose *n.* a plant having yellow flowers that open in the evening.

evening star *n.* a planet, usually Venus, seen shining brightly in the west just after sunset.

even out *vb.* to make or become even, as by the removal of bumps, inequalities, etc.

evensong ('iːvᵊn,sɒŋ) *n. Church of Eng-*

land. the daily evening service. Also called: **Evening Prayer.**

event (ɪ'vɛnt) *n.* **1.** anything that takes place, esp. something important; an incident. **2.** the actual or final outcome (esp. in **in the event**). **3.** any one contest in a sporting programme. **4. at all events** *or* **in any event.** whatever happens. **5. in the event of.** if (such a thing) happens. **6. in the event that.** if it should happen that.

eventful (ɪ'vɛntfʊl) *adj.* full of exciting or important incidents.

eventide ('iːvᵊn,taɪd) *n. Archaic or poetic.* evening.

eventing (ɪ'vɛntɪŋ) *n. Chiefly Brit.* riding competitions (esp. **three-day events**), usually involving cross-country riding, jumping, and dressage.

eventual (ɪ'vɛntʃʊəl) *adj.* happening in due course; ultimate. —e'**ventually** *adv.*

eventuality (ɪ,vɛntʃʊ'ælɪtɪ) *n., pl.* **-ties.** a possible event, occurrence, or result.

eventuate (ɪ'vɛntʃʊ,eɪt) *vb.* (often foll. by *in*) to result ultimately (in).

even up *vb.* to make or become equal.

ever ('ɛvə) *adv.* **1.** at any time: *did you ever meet her?* **2.** always: *ever optimistic.* **3.** used to give emphasis: *come as fast as ever you can.* **4.** *Informal, chiefly Brit.* (intensifier, in **ever so, ever such,** and **ever such a**).

evergreen ('ɛvə,griːn) *adj.* **1.** (of certain trees and shrubs) bearing foliage throughout the year. ~*n.* **2.** an evergreen tree or shrub.

everlasting (,ɛvə'lɑːstɪŋ) *adj.* **1.** never coming to an end; eternal. **2.** lasting so long or occurring so often as to become tedious. ~*n.* **3.** eternity. **4.** a type of flower that retains its colour when dried. —,ever-'**lastingly** *adv.*

evermore (,ɛvə'mɔː) *adv.* all time to come.

every ('ɛvrɪ) *det.* **1.** each one without exception: *every person in the room.* **2.** the greatest or best possible: *every hope.* **3.** each: *every third day.* **4. every bit.** (used in comparisons with *as*) just; equally. **5. every other.** each alternate.

everybody ('ɛvrɪ,bɒdɪ) *pron.* every person; everyone.
Usage. see **everyone.**

everyday ('ɛvrɪ,deɪ) *adj.* **1.** happening each day. **2.** commonplace or usual. **3.** suitable for or used on ordinary days.

Everyman ('ɛvrɪ,mæn) *n.* the ordinary person; common man.

everyone ('ɛvrɪ,wʌn) *pron.* every person; everybody.
Usage. *Anybody, anyone, everybody, everyone, none, no-one, nobody, somebody, someone,* and *each* should strictly function as singular: *everyone nodded his head* (not *their heads*). The use of *their* in such constructions is, however, common.

everything (ˈɛvrɪˌθɪŋ) *pron.* **1.** the whole; all things: *everything went smoothly.* **2.** the thing that is most important: *money isn't everything.*

everywhere (ˈɛvrɪˌwɛə) *adv.* to or in all parts or places.

evict (ɪˈvɪkt) *vb.* to expel (a tenant) from property by process of law; turn out. —**eˈviction** *n.*

evidence (ˈɛvɪdəns) *n.* **1.** ground for belief or disbelief; data on which to base proof. **2.** a mark or sign that makes evident. **3.** *Law.* matter produced before a court of law in an attempt to prove or disprove a point in issue. **4. in evidence.** on display; apparent. ~*vb.* **5.** to make evident; show clearly.

evident (ˈɛvɪdənt) *adj.* easy to see or understand; apparent. —**ˈevidently** *adv.*

evidential (ˌɛvɪˈdɛnʃəl) *adj.* of, serving as, or based on evidence. —ˌevi**ˈdentially** *adv.*

evil (ˈiːvʲl) *adj.* **1.** morally wrong; wicked. **2.** causing harm. **3.** very unpleasant: *an evil smell.* ~*n.* **4.** wickedness. **5.** a force of wickedness. —**ˈevilly** *adv.* —**ˈevilness** *n.*

evildoer (ˈiːvʲlˌduːə) *n.* a person who does evil. —**ˈevilˌdoing** *n.*

evil eye *n.* **the.** a look superstitiously supposed to have the power of inflicting harm.

evince (ɪˈvɪns) *vb.* to make evident; show (something) clearly.

eviscerate (ɪˈvɪsəˌreɪt) *vb.* to remove the internal organs of; disembowel. —eˌviscerˈation *n.*

evocation (ˌɛvəˈkeɪʃən) *n.* the act of evoking. —**evocative** (ɪˈvɒkətɪv) *adj.*

evoke (ɪˈvəʊk) *vb.* **1.** to call or summon up (a memory, feeling, etc.), esp. from the past. **2.** to provoke; elicit.

evolution (ˌiːvəˈluːʃən) *n.* **1.** *Biol.* a gradual change in the characteristics of a population of animals or plants over successive generations. **2.** a gradual development, esp. to a more complex form. **3.** the act of throwing off, as heat, gas, vapour, etc. **4.** *Mil.* an exercise carried out in accordance with a set procedure. —ˌevo**ˈlutionary** *adj.*

evolve (ɪˈvɒlv) *vb.* **1.** to develop gradually. **2.** (of animal or plant species) to undergo evolution. **3.** to give off (heat, gas, vapour, etc.).

ewe (juː) *n.* a female sheep.

ewer (ˈjuːə) *n.* a large jug with a wide mouth.

ex¹ (ɛks) *prep.* **1.** *Finance.* excluding; without: *ex dividend.* **2.** *Commerce.* sold from: *ex warehouse.*

ex² (ɛks) *n. Informal.* one's former wife or husband.

ex- *prefix.* **1.** out of; outside; from: *exodus.* **2.** former: *ex-wife.*

exacerbate (ɛkˈsæsəˌbeɪt) *vb.* to make (pain, emotion, or a situation) worse. —exˌacerˈbation *n.*

exact (ɪɡˈzækt) *adj.* **1.** correct in every detail; strictly accurate. **2.** precise, as opposed to approximate. **3.** based on measurement and the formulation of laws: *an exact science.* ~*vb.* **4.** to force (payment of); extort. **5.** to demand as a right; insist upon.

exacting (ɪɡˈzæktɪŋ) *adj.* making rigorous or excessive demands.

exaction (ɪɡˈzækʃən) *n.* **1.** an exacting. **2.** an extortion. **3.** a sum or payment exacted.

exactitude (ɪɡˈzæktɪˌtjuːd) *n.* the quality of being exact; precision; accuracy.

exactly (ɪɡˈzæktlɪ) *adv.* **1.** in an exact manner; accurately or precisely. **2.** in every respect; just. **3.** just so! precisely!

exaggerate (ɪɡˈzædʒəˌreɪt) *vb.* **1.** to regard or represent as greater than is true. **2.** to make greater, more noticeable, etc. —exˈaggerˌated *adj.* —exˈaggerˌatedly *adv.* —exˌaggerˈation *n.*

exalt (ɪɡˈzɔːlt) *vb.* **1.** to elevate in rank, dignity, etc. **2.** to praise highly. **3.** to fill with joy or delight. —exˈalted *adj.* —ˌexalˈtation *n.*

exam (ɪɡˈzæm) *n.* short for **examination.**

examination (ɪɡˌzæmɪˈneɪʃən) *n.* **1.** the act of examining. **2.** *Education.* written exercises, oral questions, or practical tasks set to test a candidate's knowledge and skill. **3.** *Med.* physical inspection of a patient. **4.** *Law.* the formal interrogation of a person on oath.

examine (ɪɡˈzæmɪn) *vb.* **1.** to inspect carefully or in detail; investigate. **2.** *Education.* to test the knowledge of (a candidate) in (a subject) by written or oral questions. **3.** *Med.* to investigate the state of health of (a patient). **4.** *Law.* to interrogate (a person) formally on oath. —exˌamiˈnee *n.* —exˈaminer *n.*

example (ɪɡˈzɑːmpʲl) *n.* **1.** a specimen that is typical of its group; sample. **2.** a person, action, or thing that is worthy of imitation. **3.** a precedent or model. **4.** a punishment or the person punished regarded as a warning to others. **5. for example.** as an illustration.

exasperate (ɪɡˈzɑːspəˌreɪt) *vb.* to cause great irritation to. —exˈasperˌated *adj.* —exˈasperˌating *adj.* —exˌasperˈation *n.*

ex cathedra (ˈɛks kəˈθiːdrə) *adj., adv.* **1.** with authority. **2.** *R.C. Church.* (of doctrines of faith or morals) defined by the pope as infallibly true.

excavate (ˈɛkskəˌveɪt) *vb.* **1.** to unearth (buried objects) methodically to discover information about the past. **2.** to remove (soil) by digging. **3.** to make (a hole) in (solid matter) by hollowing. —ˌexcaˈvation *n.* —ˈexcaˌvator *n.*

exceed (ɪkˈsiːd) vb. **1.** to be greater in degree or quantity. **2.** to go beyond the limit of.

exceedingly (ɪkˈsiːdɪŋlɪ) adv. very; extremely.

excel (ɪkˈsɛl) vb. **-celling, -celled. 1.** to be superior to (another or others); surpass. **2.** (foll. by in or at) to be outstandingly good.

excellence (ˈɛksələns) n. the quality of being exceptionally good. —**'excellent** adj.

Excellency (ˈɛksələnsɪ) or **Excellence** n., pl. **-lencies** or **-lences.** (usually preceded by Your, His, or Her) a title used to address a high-ranking official, such as an ambassador.

except (ɪkˈsɛpt) prep. **1.** Also: **except for.** other than; apart from. **2. except that.** (conj.) but for the fact that. ~conj. **3.** Archaic. unless. ~vb. **4.** to leave out; exclude.

excepting (ɪkˈsɛptɪŋ) prep. except.

exception (ɪkˈsɛpʃən) n. **1.** the act of excepting or fact of being excepted; omission. **2.** anything excluded from or not in conformance with a general rule, principle, class, etc. **3. take exception.** (usually foll. by to) to make objections to.

exceptionable (ɪkˈsɛpʃənəbˀl) adj. open to objection.

exceptional (ɪkˈsɛpʃənˀl) adj. **1.** forming an exception. **2.** having much more than average intelligence, ability, or skill.

excerpt n. (ˈɛksɜːpt). **1.** a passage taken from a book, speech, etc.; extract. ~vb. (ɛkˈsɜːpt). **2.** to take (a passage) from a book, speech, etc. —**ex'cerption** n.

excess n. (ɪkˈsɛs). **1.** the state or act of going beyond normal or permitted limits. **2.** an immoderate or abnormal amount. **3.** the amount, number, etc., by which one thing exceeds another. **4.** overindulgence or intemperance. **5. in excess of.** more than. **6. to excess.** immoderately. ~adj. (ˈɛksɛs). **7.** more than normal, necessary, or permitted: excess weight. —**ex'cessive** adj. —**ex'cessively** adv.

excess luggage or **baggage** n. luggage that is more in weight or number of pieces than an airline, etc., will carry free.

exchange (ɪksˈtʃeɪndʒ) vb. **1.** to give up or transfer (one thing) for an equivalent. **2.** to give and receive (information, ideas, etc.). **3.** to replace (one thing) with another, esp. to replace unsatisfactory goods. ~n. **4.** the act of exchanging. **5.** anything given or received as an equivalent or substitute for something else. **6.** an argument. **7.** Also called: **telephone exchange.** a centre in which telephone lines are interconnected. **8.** a place where securities or commodities are traded, esp. by brokers or merchants. **9.** the system by which commercial debts are settled, esp. by bills of exchange, without direct payment of money. **10.** a transfer of sums of money of equivalent value, as between different currencies. —**ex'changeable** adj.

exchange rate n. the rate at which the currency unit of one country may be exchanged for that of another.

exchequer (ɪksˈtʃɛkə) n. (often cap.) Government. (in Britain and certain other countries) the accounting department of the Treasury.

excise[1] (ˈɛksaɪz) n. **1.** a tax on goods, such as spirits, produced for the home market. **2.** Brit. that section of the government service responsible for the collection of excise, now the Board of Customs and Excise.

excise[2] (ɪkˈsaɪz) vb. **1.** to delete (a passage). **2.** to remove (an organ or part) surgically. —**excision** (ɪkˈsɪʒən) n.

exciseman (ˈɛksaɪzˌmæn) n., pl. **-men.** Brit. (formerly) a government agent who collected excise and prevented smuggling.

excitable (ɪkˈsaɪtəbˀl) adj. easily excited; volatile. —**ex,cita'bility** n.

excite (ɪkˈsaɪt) vb. **1.** to arouse (a person), esp. to pleasurable anticipation or nervous agitation. **2.** to arouse (an emotion, response, etc.); evoke. **3.** to cause; stir up: to excite suspicion. **4.** to arouse sexually. **5.** Physiol. to cause a response in (an organ, tissue, or part). **6.** to raise (an atom, molecule, etc.) to a higher energy level. —**ex'cited** adj. —**ex'citedly** adv.

excitement (ɪkˈsaɪtmənt) n. **1.** the state of being excited. **2.** a person or thing that excites.

exciting (ɪkˈsaɪtɪŋ) adj. causing excitement; stirring; stimulating. —**ex'citingly** adv.

exclaim (ɪkˈskleɪm) vb. to cry out or speak suddenly or excitedly, as from surprise, delight, horror, etc.

exclamation (ˌɛkskləˈmeɪʃən) n. **1.** an abrupt or excited cry or utterance. **2.** the act of exclaiming. —**exclamatory** (ɪkˈsklæmətrɪ) adj.

exclamation mark or U.S. **point** n. the punctuation mark ! used after exclamations and vehement commands.

exclude (ɪkˈskluːd) vb. **1.** to keep out; prevent from entering. **2.** to leave out of consideration. —**ex'clusion** n.

excluding (ɪkˈskluːdɪŋ) prep. excepting.

exclusive (ɪkˈskluːsɪv) adj. **1.** excluding all else. **2.** not shared: exclusive rights. **3.** catering for a privileged minority, esp. a fashionable clique. **4. exclusive to.** limited to; found only in. **5.** not including the numbers, dates, etc., mentioned. **6. exclusive of.** except for; not taking account of. ~n. **7.** a story reported in only one newspaper. —**ex'clusively** adv. —**ex'clusiveness** or **exclusivity** (ˌɛkskluːˈsɪvɪtɪ) n.

excommunicate (ˌɛkskəˈmjuːnɪˌkeɪt) vb. to sentence (a member of the Church) to exclusion from membership and the sacraments of the Church. —**,excom,muni'cation** n.

excoriate (ik'skɔːrɪ,eɪt) vb. 1. to strip skin from (a person or animal). 2. to censure severely. —**ex,cori'ation** n.

excrement ('ɛkskrɪmənt) n. waste matter discharged from the body; faeces. —**excremental** (,ɛkskrɪ'mɛnt³l) adj.

excrescence (ik'skrɛs³ns) n. a protuberance, esp. an outgrowth from a part of the body. —**ex'crescent** adj.

excreta (ik'skriːtə) pl. n. urine and faeces discharged from the body.

excrete (ik'skriːt) vb. to discharge (waste matter, such as urine, sweat, or faeces) from the body. —**ex'cretion** n. —**ex'cretory** adj.

excruciating (ik'skruːʃɪ,eɪtɪŋ) adj. 1. unbearably painful; agonizing. 2. Humorous. very bad: an excruciating pun. —**ex'cruci,atingly** adv.

exculpate ('ɛkskʌl,peɪt) vb. to free from blame or guilt.

excursion (ik'skɜːʃən) n. a short outward and return journey, esp. for sightseeing, etc.; outing.

excursive (ik'skɜːsɪv) adj. tending to digress; rambling.

excuse vb. (ik'skjuːz). 1. to put forward a reason or justification for (an action, fault, or offending person). 2. to pardon (a person) or overlook (a fault). 3. to make allowances for: to excuse someone's ignorance. 4. to exempt from a task, obligation, etc. 5. to allow to leave. 6. **be excused.** Euphemistic. to go to the lavatory. 7. **excuse me!** an expression used to catch someone's attention or to apologize for an interruption, disagreement, etc. ~n. (ik'skjuːs). 8. an explanation offered in defence of some fault or as a reason for not fulfilling an obligation, etc. —**ex'cusable** adj.

ex-directory adj. Chiefly Brit. not listed in a telephone directory by request.

execrable ('ɛksɪkrəb³l) adj. of very poor quality. —**'execrably** adv.

execrate ('ɛksɪ,kreɪt) vb. 1. to loathe; detest. 2. to denounce. 3. to curse (a person or thing). —**,exe'cration** n.

execute ('ɛksɪ,kjuːt) vb. 1. to put (a condemned person) to death. 2. to carry out; accomplish. 3. to produce: to execute a drawing. 4. Law. to render (a deed) effective, as by signing. 5. to carry out the terms of (a contract, will, etc.). —**'exe,cuter** n.

execution (,ɛksɪ'kjuːʃən) n. 1. the act of executing. 2. the carrying out or undergoing of a sentence of death. 3. the manner in which something is performed; technique.

executioner (,ɛksɪ'kjuːʃənə) n. an official charged with carrying out the death sentence.

executive (ig'zɛkjʊtɪv) n. 1. a person or group responsible for the administration of a project or business. 2. the branch of government responsible for carrying out laws, decrees, etc. ~adj. 3. having the function of carrying plans, orders, laws, etc., into effect. 4. Informal. very expensive or exclusive: executive housing.

executor (ig'zɛkjʊtə) n. Law. a person appointed by a testator to carry out his will. —**ex,ecu'torial** adj. —**ex'ecutrix** fem. n.

exegesis (,ɛksɪ'dʒiːsɪs) n., pl. **-ses** (-siːz). explanation of a text, esp. of the Bible.

exemplar (ig'zɛmplə, -plɑː) n. 1. a person or thing to be copied; model. 2. a typical specimen; example.

exemplary (ig'zɛmplərɪ) adj. 1. fit for imitation; model. 2. serving as a warning; admonitory. 3. representative; typical.

exemplify (ig'zɛmplɪ,faɪ) vb. **-fying, -fied.** 1. to show by example. 2. to serve as an example of. —**ex,emplifi'cation** n.

exempt (ig'zɛmpt) vb. 1. to release (someone) from an obligation, tax, etc. ~adj. 2. not subject to an obligation, tax, etc. —**ex'emption** n.

exequies ('ɛksɪkwɪz) pl. n., sing. **-quy.** funeral rites.

exercise ('ɛksə,saɪz) n. 1. physical exertion, esp. for training or keeping fit. 2. mental or other activity, esp. to develop a skill. 3. a set of movements, tasks, etc., designed to improve or test one's ability. 4. the performance of a function: the exercise of one's rights. 5. (usually pl.) Mil. a manoeuvre or simulated combat operation. ~vb. 6. to put into use; employ. 7. to take exercise or perform exercises. 8. to practise using in order to develop or train. 9. to make use of: to exercise one's rights. 10. (often passive) to worry or vex: to be exercised about a decision. 11. Mil. to carry out simulated combat, manoeuvres, etc. —**'exer,ciser** n.

exert (ig'zɜːt) vb. 1. to use (influence, authority, etc.) forcefully or effectively. 2. **exert oneself.** to make a special effort. —**ex'ertion** n.

exeunt ('ɛksɪ,ʌnt) Latin. they go out: used as a stage direction.

exeunt omnes ('ɒmneɪz) Latin. they all go out: used as a stage direction.

ex gratia ('greɪʃə) adj. given as a favour where no legal obligation exists: an ex gratia payment.

exhale (ɛks'heɪl, ig'zeɪl) vb. 1. to expel (breath or smoke) from the lungs; breathe out. 2. to give off (air, fumes, etc.) or (of air, etc.) to be given off. —**,exha'lation** n.

exhaust (ig'zɔːst) vb. 1. to tire out. 2. to use up (supplies or resources) totally. 3. to empty (a container) by drawing off (the contents). 4. to develop or discuss (a topic) so thoroughly that no more remains to be said. **5.** to remove gas from (a vessel, etc.). ~*n.* **6.** gases ejected from an engine as waste products. **7.** the parts of an engine through which exhausted gases pass. —**ex'hausted** *adj.* —**ex'haustible** *adj.*

exhaustion (ɪgˈzɔːstʃən) *n.* **1.** extreme tiredness. **2.** the act of exhausting or state of being exhausted.

exhaustive (ɪgˈzɔːstɪv) *adj.* comprehensive; thorough. —**ex'haustively** *adv.*

exhibit (ɪgˈzɪbɪt) *vb.* **1.** to display (something) to the public. **2.** to show: *the child exhibited signs of distress.* ~*n.* **3.** an object exhibited to the public. **4.** *Law.* a document or object produced in court as evidence. —**ex'hibitor** *n.*

exhibition (ˌɛksɪˈbɪʃən) *n.* **1.** a public display of art, skills, etc. **2.** the act of exhibiting or the state of being exhibited. **3. make an exhibition of oneself.** to behave so foolishly that one attracts public attention. **4.** *Brit.* a scholarship awarded to a student at a university or school.

exhibitioner (ˌɛksɪˈbɪʃənə) *n. Brit.* a student who has been awarded an exhibition.

exhibitionism (ˌɛksɪˈbɪʃəˌnɪzəm) *n.* **1.** a compulsive desire to attract attention to oneself. **2.** a compulsive desire to expose one's genitals publicly. —ˌexhiˈbitionist *n.*

exhilarate (ɪgˈzɪləˌreɪt) *vb.* to make lively and cheerful. —**ex,hilaˈration** *n.*

exhort (ɪgˈzɔːt) *vb.* to urge (someone) earnestly. —**ex'hortative** *or* **ex'hortatory** *adj.* —,**exhor'tation** *n.*

exhume (ɛksˈhjuːm) *vb.* to dig up (something buried, esp. a corpse). —**exhumation** (ˌɛkshjuːˈmeɪʃən) *n.*

exigency (ˈɛksɪdʒənsɪ, ɪgˈzɪdʒənsɪ) *n., pl.* **-gencies.** **1.** (*often pl.*) an urgent demand or need. **2.** an emergency. —**'exigent** *adj.*

exiguous (ɪgˈzɪgjʊəs, ɪkˈsɪg-) *adj.* scanty; meagre. —**exiguity** (ˌɛksɪˈgjuːɪtɪ) *n.*

exile (ˈɛgzaɪl, ˈɛksaɪl) *n.* **1.** a prolonged, usually enforced absence from one's country. **2.** the official expulsion of a person from his native land. **3.** a person banished or living away from his country. ~*vb.* **4.** to expel from one's country; banish.

exist (ɪgˈzɪst) *vb.* **1.** to have being or reality; be. **2.** to eke out a living. **3.** to be living; live. **4.** to be present under specified conditions or in a specified place. —**ex'isting** *adj.*

existence (ɪgˈzɪstəns) *n.* **1.** the fact or state of existing; being. **2.** the continuance of life; living. **3.** everything that exists. —**ex'istent** *adj.*

existential (ˌɛgzɪˈstɛnʃəl) *adj.* **1.** of or relating to existence, esp. human existence. **2.** *Philosophy.* known by experience rather than reason. **3.** of or relating to existentialism.

existentialism (ˌɛgzɪˈstɛnʃəˌlɪzəm) *n.* a modern philosophical movement stressing

personal experience and responsibility of the individual, who is seen as a free agent. —,**exis'tentialist** *adj., n.*

exit (ˈɛgzɪt, ˈɛksɪt) *n.* **1.** a way out. **2.** the act of going out. **3.** *Theatre.* the act of going offstage. **4.** *Brit.* a point at which vehicles may leave or join a motorway. ~*vb.* **5.** to go away or out; depart. **6.** *Theatre.* to go offstage: used as a stage direction.

exocrine (ˈɛksəʊˌkraɪn) *adj.* of a gland, such as the sweat gland, that discharges its product through a duct.

exodus (ˈɛksədəs) *n.* the departure of a large number of people.

Exodus (ˈɛksədəs) *n.* **the.** the departure of the Israelites from Egypt.

ex officio (ˈɛks əˈfɪʃɪəʊ) *adv., adj.* by right of position or office.

exonerate (ɪgˈzɒnəˌreɪt) *vb.* to absolve from blame or a criminal charge. —**ex,oner'ation** *n.*

exorbitant (ɪgˈzɔːbɪtˀnt) *adj.* (of prices, demands, etc.) excessive; immoderate. —**ex'orbitantly** *adv.*

exorcise *or* **-cize** (ˈɛksɔːˌsaɪz) *vb.* to expel (evil spirits) from (a person or place), by prayers and religious rites. —**'exorcism** *n.* —**'exorcist** *n.*

exordium (ɛkˈsɔːdɪəm) *n., pl.* **-diums** *or* **-dia** (-dɪə). an introductory part, esp. of a speech or treatise.

exoskeleton (ˌɛksəʊˈskɛlɪtˀn) *n.* the protective or supporting structure covering the outside of the body of many animals, for example insects or crabs.

exotic (ɪgˈzɒtɪk) *adj.* **1.** originating in a foreign country; not native. **2.** having a strange allure or beauty. ~*n.* **3.** an exotic thing, esp. a plant. —**ex'otically** *adv.*

exotica (ɪgˈzɒtɪkə) *pl. n.* exotic objects, esp. as a collection.

expand (ɪkˈspænd) *vb.* **1.** to make or become greater in extent, size, or scope. **2.** to spread out; unfold. **3.** (often foll. by *on*) to enlarge (on a story, topic, etc.). **4.** to become increasingly relaxed, friendly, and talkative. **5.** *Maths.* to express (a function or expression) as the sum or product of terms. —**ex'pandable** *adj.*

expanse (ɪkˈspæns) *n.* an uninterrupted wide area; stretch: *an expanse of blue sky.*

expansible (ɪkˈspænsəbˀl) *adj.* able to expand or be expanded.

expansion (ɪkˈspænʃən) *n.* **1.** the act of expanding. **2.** the amount by which something expands. **3.** an increase or development, esp. in the activities of a company.

expansionism (ɪkˈspænʃəˌnɪzəm) *n.* the practice of expanding the economy or territory of a country. —**ex'pansionist** *n., adj.*

expansive (ɪkˈspænsɪv) *adj.* **1.** able or tending to expand. **2.** wide; extensive. **3.**

friendly, open, and talkative. **—ex¹pan-siveness** n.

expatiate (ɪkˈspeɪʃɪˌeɪt) vb. (foll. by on or upon) to speak or write at length (on a topic). **—ex¹pati¹ation** n.

expatriate (ɛksˈpætrɪt) adj. 1. resident outside one's native country. 2. exiled. ~n. 3. a person living outside his native country 4. an exile. **—ex¹patri¹ation** n.

expect (ɪkˈspɛkt) vb. 1. to regard as likely. 2. to look forward to or be waiting for. 3. to require (something) as an obligation: *the teacher expects us to work late.* 4. **be expecting.** *Informal.* to be pregnant.

expectancy (ɪkˈspɛktənsɪ) n. 1. something expected, esp. on the basis of a norm: *his life expectancy was 30 years.* 2. anticipation; expectation.

expectant (ɪkˈspɛktənt) adj. 1. expecting or hopeful. 2. pregnant. **—ex¹pectantly** adv.

expectation (ˌɛkspɛkˈteɪʃən) n. 1. the state of expecting or of being expected. 2. (usually pl.) something looked forward to, whether feared or hoped for. 3. an attitude of expectancy or hope.

expectorant (ɪkˈspɛktərənt) Med. ~adj. 1. helping the bringing up of phlegm from the respiratory passages. ~n. 2. an expectorant medicine.

expectorate (ɪkˈspɛktəˌreɪt) vb. to cough up (phlegm from the respiratory passages); spit. **—ex¹pecto¹ration** n.

expediency (ɪkˈspiːdɪənsɪ) or **expedience** n., pl. -encies or -ences. 1. appropriateness; suitability. 2. the use of methods that are advantageous rather than fair or just.

expedient (ɪkˈspiːdɪənt) adj. 1. suitable to the circumstances; appropriate. 2. inclined towards methods that are advantageous rather than fair or just. ~n. 3. something that achieves a particular purpose.

expedite (ˈɛkspɪˌdaɪt) vb. 1. to facilitate the progress of; hasten. 2. to do quickly.

expedition (ˌɛkspɪˈdɪʃən) n. 1. an organized journey or voyage, esp. for exploration. 2. the people and equipment comprising an expedition. 3. promptness. **—ˌexpe¹ditionary** adj.

expeditious (ˌɛkspɪˈdɪʃəs) adj. done with speed and efficiency; prompt; quick.

expel (ɪkˈspɛl) vb. **-pelling, -pelled.** 1. to drive out with force. 2. to dismiss from a school, club, etc., permanently.

expend (ɪkˈspɛnd) vb. to spend or use up (time, energy, or money).

expendable (ɪkˈspɛndəbˀl) adj. 1. not worth preserving. 2. able to be sacrificed to achieve an objective, esp. a military one.

expenditure (ɪkˈspɛndɪtʃə) n. 1. something expended, esp. money. 2. the amount expended.

expense (ɪkˈspɛns) n. 1. a particular payment of money; expenditure. 2. money needed for individual purchases; cost. 3. (pl.) money spent in the performance of a job, etc. 4. something requiring money for its purchase or upkeep. 5. **at the expense of.** to the detriment of.

expense account n. 1. an arrangement by which an employee's expenses are refunded by his employer. 2. a record of such expenses.

expensive (ɪkˈspɛnsɪv) adj. high-priced; costly; dear. **—ex¹pensiveness** n.

experience (ɪkˈspɪərɪəns) n. 1. direct personal participation. 2. a particular incident, feeling, etc., that a person has undergone. 3. accumulated knowledge, esp. of practical matters. ~vb. 4. to participate in or undergo. 5. to be moved by; feel.

experienced (ɪkˈspɪərɪənst) adj. skilful or knowledgeable from extensive participation.

experiential (ɪkˌspɪərɪˈɛnʃəl) adj. *Philosophy.* relating to or derived from experience.

experiment n. (ɪkˈspɛrɪmənt) 1. a test or investigation to provide evidence for or against a hypothesis. 2. an attempt at something new or original. ~vb. (ɪkˈspɛrɪˌmɛnt). 3. to make an experiment or experiments. **—ex¹perimen¹tation** n. **—ex¹peri¹menter** n.

experimental (ɪkˌspɛrɪˈmɛntˀl) adj. 1. relating to, based on, or having the nature of experiment. 2. tentative or provisional. **—ex¹peri¹mentally** adv.

expert (ˈɛkspɜːt) n. 1. a person who has extensive skill or knowledge in a particular field. ~adj. 2. skilful or knowledgeable. 3. of, involving, or done by an expert. **—¹expertly** adv.

expertise (ˌɛkspɜːˈtiːz) n. special skill, knowledge, or judgment.

expiate (ˈɛkspɪˌeɪt) vb. to atone for (sin or wrongdoing); make amends for. **—ˌexpi¹ation** n.

expiration (ˌɛkspɪˈreɪʃən) n. 1. the finish of something; expiry. 2. the act, process, or sound of breathing out. **—expiratory** (ɪkˈspaɪərətrɪ) adj.

expire (ɪkˈspaɪə) vb. 1. to finish or run out; come to an end. 2. to breathe out (air). 3. to die.

expiry (ɪkˈspaɪərɪ) n., pl. -ries. a coming to an end, esp. of a contract period.

explain (ɪkˈspleɪn) vb. 1. to make (something) comprehensible, esp. by giving a clear and detailed account of it. 2. to justify or attempt to justify (oneself) by reasons for one's actions. 3. **explain away.** to offer excuses or reason for (mistakes).

explanation (ˌɛkspləˈneɪʃən) n. 1. the act of explaining. 2. something that explains.

explanatory (ɪkˈsplænətrɪ) adj. serving or intended to serve as an explanation.

expletive (ɪkˈspliːtɪv) n. an exclamation or

swearword; an oath or sound expressing emotion rather than meaning.

explicable ('ɛksplɪkəb³l, ɪk'splɪk-) *adj.* capable of being explained.

explicate ('ɛksplɪˌkeɪt) *vb. Formal.* to make clear; explain. —ˌexpli'cation *n.*

explicit (ɪk'splɪsɪt) *adj.* 1. precisely and clearly expressed, leaving nothing to implication. 2. leaving little to the imagination; graphically detailed. 3. openly expressed. —ex'plicitly *adv.*

explode (ɪk'spləʊd) *vb.* 1. to burst with great violence; blow up. 2. (of a gas) to undergo a sudden violent expansion as a result of a fast chemical or nuclear reaction. 3. to react suddenly or violently with emotion. 4. (esp. of a population) to increase rapidly. 5. to show (a theory, etc.) to be baseless.

exploit *n.* ('ɛksplɔɪt). 1. a notable deed or feat. ~*vb.* (ɪk'splɔɪt). 2. to take advantage of (a person, situation, etc.) for one's own ends. 3. to make the best use of. —ˌexploi'tation *n.* —ex'ploiter *n.*

explore (ɪk'splɔː) *vb.* 1. to examine or investigate, esp. systematically. 2. to travel into (unfamiliar regions), esp. for scientific purposes. —**exploration** (ˌɛksplɔː'reɪʃən) *n.* —**exploratory** (ɪk'splɒrətrɪ) *adj.* —ex'plorer *n.*

explosion (ɪk'spləʊʒən) *n.* 1. an exploding. 2. a violent release of energy resulting from a rapid chemical or nuclear reaction. 3. a sudden or violent outburst of activity, noise, emotion, etc. 4. a rapid increase.

explosive (ɪk'spləʊsɪv) *adj.* 1. able, liable, or tending to explode. 2. potentially violent: *an explosive situation.* ~*n.* 3. a substance capable of exploding. —ex'plosiveness *n.*

expo ('ɛkspəʊ) *n., pl.* -pos. short for exposition (sense 3).

exponent (ɪk'spəʊnənt) *n.* 1. (usually foll. by *of*) a person who advocates (an idea, cause, etc.). 2. a person or thing that explains or interprets. 3. *Maths.* a number or variable placed as a superscript to another number indicating how many times the number is to be multiplied by itself.

exponential (ˌɛkspəʊ'nɛnʃəl) *adj.* 1. *Maths.* of or involving numbers raised to an exponent. 2. *Informal.* very rapid. —ˌexpo'nentially *adv.*

export *n.* ('ɛkspɔːt). 1. (*often pl.*) goods or services sold to a foreign country. ~*vb.* (ɪk'spɔːt, 'ɛkspɔːt). 2. to sell (goods or services) or ship (goods) to a foreign country. —ex'porter *n.*

expose (ɪk'spəʊz) *vb.* 1. to uncover (something previously covered). 2. to reveal (something previously hidden), esp. when disreputable. 3. (foll. by *to*) to make vulnerable (to attack or criticism). 4. to leave (a person or thing) unprotected in a poten-

tially harmful situation. 5. (foll. by *to*) to give (a person) an introduction to or experience of something new. 6. *Photog.* to subject (a film) to light. 7. expose oneself. to display one's sexual organs in public.

exposé (ɛks'pəʊzeɪ) *n.* the bringing of a scandal, crime, etc., to public notice.

exposed (ɪk'spəʊzd) *adj.* 1. not concealed; displayed for viewing. 2. without shelter from the elements. 3. vulnerable.

exposition (ˌɛkspə'zɪʃən) *n.* 1. a systematic explanation of a subject. 2. the act of expounding or setting forth a viewpoint. 3. a large public exhibition. 4. *Music.* the first statement of the themes of a movement.

expository (ɪk'spɒzɪtrɪ) *adj.* explanatory.

ex post facto ('ɛks pəʊst 'fæktəʊ) *adj.* having retrospective effect.

expostulate (ɪk'spɒstjʊˌleɪt) *vb.* (usually foll. by *with*) to reason (with), esp. in order to dissuade. —ex,postu'lation *n.* —ex'postulatory *adj.*

exposure (ɪk'spəʊʒə) *n.* 1. the act of exposing or the condition of being exposed. 2. lack of shelter from the weather, esp. the cold. 3. *Photog.* a. the act of exposing a film to light. b. an area on a film that has been exposed. 4. *Photog.* a. the intensity of light falling on a film multiplied by the time for which it is exposed. b. a combination of lens aperture and shutter speed used in taking a photograph. 5. appearance before the public, as on television.

exposure meter *n. Photog.* an instrument for measuring the intensity of light so that suitable camera settings can be determined.

expound (ɪk'spaʊnd) *vb.* to explain (a theory) in detail.

express (ɪk'sprɛs) *vb.* 1. to transform (ideas) into words; utter. 2. to show: *her face expressed disapproval.* 3. to indicate through a symbol or formula. 4. to squeeze out juice, etc. 5. express oneself. to communicate one's thoughts or ideas. ~*adj.* 6. explicitly stated. 7. particular. 8. of or for rapid transportation of people, mail, etc. ~*n.* 9. a fast train stopping at only a few stations. 10. *Chiefly U.S. & Canad.* a system for sending mail rapidly. ~*adv.* 11. by express delivery. —ex'pressible *adj.*

expression (ɪk'sprɛʃən) *n.* 1. transforming ideas into words. 2. a showing of emotion without words. 3. communication of emotion through music, painting, etc. 4. a look on the face that indicates mood or emotion. 5. the choice of words, intonation, etc., in communicating. 6. a particular phrase used conventionally to express something. 7. *Maths.* a variable, function, or some combination of these. —ex'pressionless *adj.*

expressionism (ɪk'sprɛʃəˌnɪzəm) *n.* an artistic and literary movement in the early 20th century, which sought to express emotions rather than to represent the physical world. —**ex'pressionist** n., adj.

expressive (ɪk'sprɛsɪv) adj. 1. of or full of expression. 2. (foll. by of) suggestive (of): a look expressive of love. 3. having a particular meaning or force.

expressway (ɪk'sprɛs,weɪ) n. a motorway.

expropriate (ɛks'prəʊprɪ,eɪt) vb. to deprive (an owner) of (property). —**ex,propri'ation** n. —**ex'propri,ator** n.

expulsion (ɪk'spʌlʃən) n. the act of expelling or the fact of being expelled. —**ex'pulsive** adj.

expunge (ɪk'spʌndʒ) vb. to delete or erase; blot out. —**expunction** (ɪk'spʌŋkʃən) n.

expurgate ('ɛkspə,geɪt) vb. to amend (a piece of writing) by removing (offensive sections). —,**expur'gation** n. —'**expur,gator** n.

exquisite (ɪk'skwɪzɪt, 'ɛkskwɪzɪt) adj. 1. showing unusual delicacy and craftsmanship. 2. extremely beautiful. 3. sensitive; discriminating: exquisite taste. 4. intense or sharp in feeling: exquisite pain. —**ex'quisitely** adv.

ex-serviceman or (fem.) **ex-servicewoman** n., pl. -**men** or -**women**. a person who has served in the armed forces.

extant (ɛk'stænt, 'ɛkstənt) adj. still in existence; surviving.

extemporaneous (ɪk,stɛmpə'reɪnɪəs) or **extemporary** (ɪk'stɛmpərərɪ) adj. spoken or performed without preparation. —**ex,tempo'raneously** or **ex'temporarily** adv.

extempore (ɪk'stɛmpərɪ) adv., adj. without planning or preparation.

extemporize or -**rise** (ɪk'stɛmpə,raɪz) vb. to perform, speak, or compose (an act, speech, or piece of music) without preparation. —**ex,tempori'zation** or -**ri'sation** n.

extend (ɪk'stɛnd) vb. 1. to draw out or be drawn out; stretch. 2. to last for a certain time: his schooling extended for three years. 3. to reach a certain point in time or distance: the land extends five miles. 4. to exist or occur: the trees extended throughout the area. 5. to increase (a building) in size. 6. to broaden the meaning or scope of: the law was extended. 7. to present or offer: to extend greetings. 8. to stretch forth (an arm, etc.). —**ex'tendible** or **ex'tendable** adj.

extended family n. a social unit in which parents, children, grandparents, and other relatives live as a family unit.

extensible (ɪk'stɛnsɪb'l) adj. capable of being extended.

extension (ɪk'stɛnʃən) n. 1. the act of extending or the condition of being extended. 2. a room or rooms added to an existing building. 3. something that can be extended or that extends another object: an extension ladder. 4. the length, range, etc., of something. 5. an additional telephone connected to the same line as another. 6. a delay in the date originally set for payment of a debt or completion of a contract. 7. a service by which the facilities of an educational establishment are offered to outsiders.

extensive (ɪk'stɛnsɪv) adj. 1. having a large extent, area, degree, etc. 2. widespread. —**ex'tensively** adv.

extensor (ɪk'stɛnsə) n. any muscle that stretches or extends an arm, leg, or other part of the body.

extent (ɪk'stɛnt) n. 1. the range over which something extends. 2. an area or volume.

extenuate (ɪk'stɛnjʊ,eɪt) vb. to represent (an offence or fault) as less serious than it appears, by giving reasons that partly excuse it. —**ex'tenu,ating** adj. —**ex,tenu-'ation** n.

exterior (ɪk'stɪərɪə) n. 1. a part or surface that is on the outside. 2. the outward appearance of a person. 3. a film scene shot outside. ~adj. 4. of, situated on, suitable for the outside. 5. coming or acting from without.

exterior angle n. 1. an angle of a polygon contained between one side extended and the adjacent side. 2. any of the four angles formed outside two straight lines by a straight line cutting across them.

exterminate (ɪk'stɜːmɪ,neɪt) vb. to destroy (living things) completely. —**ex,termi'nation** n. —**ex'termi,nator** n.

external (ɪk'stɜːn'l) adj. 1. of, situated on, or suitable for the outside. 2. coming or acting from without. 3. of or involving foreign nations. 4. of or designating a medicine applied to the outside of the body. 5. Anat. situated on or near the outside of the body. 6. (of a student) studying a university subject, but not attending a university. ~n. 7. (often pl.) an external circumstance or aspect, esp. one that is superficial. —,**exter'nality** n. —**ex'ternally** adv.

externalize or -**ise** (ɪk'stɜːnə,laɪz) vb. to make external; give outward shape or expression to. —**ex,ternali'zation** or -**i'sation** n.

extinct (ɪk'stɪŋkt) adj. 1. (of an animal or plant species) having died out. 2. quenched or extinguished. 3. (of a volcano) no longer liable to erupt.

extinction (ɪk'stɪŋkʃən) n. 1. the act of making extinct or the state of being extinct. 2. the act of extinguishing or the state of being extinguished. 3. complete destruction.

extinguish (ɪk'stɪŋgwɪʃ) vb. 1. to put out or quench (a fire or light). 2. to remove or destroy entirely. —**ex'tinguishable** adj. —**ex'tinguisher** n.

extirpate ('ɛkstə,peɪt) vb. 1. to destroy

completely. **2.** to pull up; uproot. —**,extir'pation** n.

extol or U.S. **extoll** (ɪkˈstəʊl) vb. **-tolling, -tolled.** to praise lavishly; exalt.

extort (ɪkˈstɔːt) vb. to secure (money or favours) by intimidation, violence, or the misuse of authority. —**ex'tortion** n.

extortionate (ɪkˈstɔːʃənɪt) adj. **1.** (of prices) excessive. **2.** (of persons) using extortion. —**ex'tortionately** adv.

extra (ˈɛkstrə) adj. **1.** being more than what is usual or expected; additional. ~n. **2.** a person or thing that is additional. **3.** something for which an additional charge is made. **4.** an additional edition of a newspaper. **5.** Films. a person temporarily engaged, usually for crowd scenes. **6.** Cricket. a run not scored from the bat. ~adv. **7.** unusually; exceptionally.

extra- prefix. outside or beyond an area or scope: extrasensory; extraterritorial.

extract vb. (ɪkˈstrækt). **1.** to pull out or uproot by force. **2.** to remove or separate. **3.** to derive (pleasure, information, etc.) from some source. **4.** Informal. to extort (money, etc.). **5.** to obtain (a substance) from a material by digestion, distillation, mechanical separation, etc. **6.** to copy out (an article, passage, etc.) from a publication. **7.** to determine the value of (the root of a number). ~n. (ˈɛkstrækt). **8.** something extracted, such as a passage from a book, etc. **9.** a preparation containing the concentrated essence of a material. —**ex'traction** n. —**ex'tractive** adj. —**ex-'tractor** n.

extracurricular (,ɛkstrəkəˈrɪkjʊlə) adj. not part of the set curriculum.

extradite (ˈɛkstrə,daɪt) vb. **1.** to surrender (an alleged offender) for trial to a foreign state. **2.** to obtain the extradition of. —**'extra,ditable** adj. —**,extra'dition** n.

extramarital (,ɛkstrəˈmærɪtˀl) adj. (esp. of sexual relations) occurring outside marriage.

extramural (,ɛkstrəˈmjʊərəl) adj. connected with but outside the normal courses of a university or college.

extraneous (ɪkˈstreɪnɪəs) adj. **1.** not essential. **2.** not pertinent; irrelevant. **3.** coming from outside.

extraordinary (ɪkˈstrɔːdˀnrɪ) adj. **1.** very unusual or surprising. **2.** not in an established manner or order. **3.** employed for particular purposes. —**ex'traordinarily** adv.

extrapolate (ɪkˈstræpə,leɪt) vb. Maths. to estimate (a value of a function or measurement) beyond the known values, by the extension of a curve. —**ex,trapo'lation** n.

extrasensory (,ɛkstrəˈsɛnsərɪ) adj. of or relating to extrasensory perception.

extrasensory perception n. the sup-

posed ability to obtain information without the use of normal sensory channels.

extravagant (ɪkˈstrævɪgənt) adj. **1.** spending money excessively. **2.** going beyond usual bounds: extravagant praise. **3.** exorbitant in price. —**ex'travagance** n.

extravaganza (ɪk,strævəˈgænzə) n. **1.** an elaborately staged light entertainment. **2.** any fanciful display, literary composition, etc.

extreme (ɪkˈstriːm) adj. **1.** being of a high or the highest degree or intensity. **2.** immoderate. **3.** very strict or severe; drastic. **4.** farthest or outermost. ~n. **5.** (often pl.) either of the two limits of a scale or range. **6. go to extremes.** to be unreasonable in speech or action. **7. in the extreme.** to the highest or further degree: her manner was friendly in the extreme. —**ex'tremely** adv.

extreme unction n. R.C. Church. a sacrament in which a person who dying is anointed by a priest.

extremist (ɪkˈstriːmɪst) n. **1.** a person who favours or resorts to immoderate methods, esp. in being politically radical. ~adj. **2.** of or characterized by immoderate actions, opinions, etc. —**ex'tremism** n.

extremity (ɪkˈstrɛmɪtɪ) n., pl. **-ties. 1.** the farthest point. **2.** the greatest degree. **3.** an extreme condition, as of misfortune. **4.** (pl.) hands and feet.

extricate (ˈɛkstrɪ,keɪt) vb. to free from complication or difficulty; disentangle. —**'extricable** adj. —**,extri'cation** n.

extrinsic (ɛkˈstrɪnsɪk) adj. **1.** not included within; extraneous. **2.** originating or acting from outside. —**ex'trinsically** adv.

extrovert (ˈɛkstrə,vɜːt) Psychol. ~adj. **1.** concerned more with external reality than inner feelings. ~n. **2.** such a person. —**'extro,verted** adj.

extrude (ɪkˈstruːd) vb. **1.** to squeeze or force out. **2.** to produce (moulded sections of plastic, metal, etc.) by forcing through a shaped die. —**ex'truded** adj. —**ex'trusion** n.

exuberant (ɪgˈzjuːbərənt) adj. **1.** full of vigour and high spirits. **2.** growing luxuriantly or in profusion. —**ex'uberance** n.

exude (ɪgˈzjuːd) vb. **1.** to release or be released through pores, incisions, etc., as sweat or sap. **2.** to make apparent by mood or behaviour. —**exudation** (,ɛksjʊ-'deɪʃən) n.

exult (ɪgˈzʌlt) vb. to be joyful or jubilant. —**exultation** (,ɛgzʌlˈteɪʃən) n. —**ex'ultant** adj.

eye (aɪ) n. **1.** the organ of sight in man and animals. **2.** (often pl.) the ability to see; vision. **3.** the external part of an eye, often including the area around it. **4.** a look, glance, or gaze. **5.** attention or observation. **6.** ability to judge or appreciate: an eye for antiques. **7.** (often pl.) opinion, judgment, or authority: *in the eyes of the law.* **8.** resembling an eye, such as the bud on a potato tuber. **9.** a small hole, as at one end of a sewing needle. **10.** a small area of calm in the centre of a hurricane or tornado. **11. all eyes.** *Informal.* acutely vigilant. **12. (all) my eye.** *Informal.* nonsense. **13. an eye for an eye.** retributive or vengeful justice. **14. have eyes for.** to be interested in. **15. in one's mind's eye.** imagined or remembered vividly. **16. in the public eye.** exposed to public curiosity. **17. keep an eye on.** to take care of. **18. keep an eye open** *or* **out (for).** to watch with special attention (for). **19. keep one's eyes skinned** *or* **peeled.** to watch vigilantly (for). **20. clap, lay,** *or* **set eyes on.** to see: *I haven't clapped eyes on her all day.* **21. look (someone) in the eye.** to look openly and without embarrassment at (someone). **22. make sheep's eyes (at).** *Old-fashioned.* to ogle amorously. **23. more than meets the eye.** hidden motives, meaning, or facts. **24. see eye to eye (with).** to agree (with). **25. shut one's eyes (to)** *or* **turn a blind eye (to).** to pretend not to notice. **26. up to one's eyes (in).** extremely busy (with). **27. with an eye to.** with the intention of. **28. with one's eyes open.** in full knowledge of all the facts. **29. with one's eyes shut.** with great ease, esp. through familiarity. ~*vb.* **eyeing** *or* **eying, eyed. 30.** to look at carefully or warily. ~See also **eye up.** —'eyeless *adj.* —'eye,like *adj.*

eyeball ('aɪ,bɔːl) *n.* **1.** the entire ball-shaped part of the eye. **2. eyeball to eyeball.** in close confrontation.

eyebrow ('aɪ,braʊ) *n.* **1.** the bony ridge over each eye. **2.** the arch of hair on this ridge. **3. raise an eyebrow.** to show doubt or disapproval.

eye-catching *adj.* tending to attract attention; striking. —'eye-,catcher *n.*

eye dog *n.* *N.Z.* a dog trained to control sheep by staring fixedly at them.

eyeful ('aɪ,fʊl) *n.* *Informal.* **1.** a view or gaze. **2.** an attractive sight, esp. a woman.

eyeglass ('aɪ,glɑːs) *n.* a lens for aiding defective vision.

eyehole ('aɪ,həʊl) *n.* **1.** the cavity that contains the eyeball. **2.** a hole to look through; peephole.

eyelash ('aɪ,læʃ) *n.* any of the short hairs that grow from the edge of the eyelids.

eyelet ('aɪlɪt) *n.* **1.** a small hole for a lace or cord to be passed through. **2.** a small metal ring reinforcing such a hole.

eyelevel ('aɪ,lɛv°l) *adj.* level with a person's eyes: *an eyelevel grill.*

eyelid ('aɪ,lɪd) *n.* either of the two folds of skin that can be moved to cover the eyes.

eyeliner ('aɪ,laɪnə) *n.* a cosmetic used to outline the eyes.

eye-opener *n.* *Informal.* something startling or revealing.

eyepiece ('aɪ,piːs) *n.* the lens in an optical instrument nearest the eye of the observer.

eye shadow *n.* a coloured cosmetic worn on the upper eyelids.

eyeshot ('aɪ,ʃɒt) *n.* range of vision; view.

eyesight ('aɪ,saɪt) *n.* the ability to see.

eyesore ('aɪ,sɔː) *n.* something very ugly.

eyestrain ('aɪ,streɪn) *n.* fatigue or irritation of the eyes, from excessive use or from uncorrected defects of vision.

eyetooth (,aɪ'tuːθ) *n., pl.* -**teeth. 1.** either of the two canine teeth in the upper jaw. **2. give one's eyeteeth for.** to go to any lengths to achieve or obtain (something).

eye up *vb.* to look at (someone) in a way that indicates sexual interest.

eyewash ('aɪ,wɒʃ) *n.* **1.** a lotion for the eyes. **2.** *Informal.* nonsense; rubbish.

eyewitness ('aɪ,wɪtnɪs) *n.* a person present at an event who can describe what happened.

eyrie ('ɪərɪ, 'ɛərɪ, 'aɪərɪ) *n.* **1.** the nest of an eagle, built in a high inaccessible place. **2.** any high isolated position.

F

f or **F** (ɛf) *n.*, *pl.* **f's**, **F's**, or **Fs.** the sixth letter of the English alphabet.

f 1. *Music.* forte: an instruction to play loudly. 2. *Physics.* frequency. 3. *Maths.* function (of). 4. *Physics.* femto-.

f, f/, or **f:** f- number.

F 1. *Music.* the fourth note of the scale of C major. 2. Fahrenheit. 3. farad(s). 4. *Chem.* fluorine. 5. *Physics.* force. 6. franc(s).

f. or **F.** 1. fathom(s). 2. female. 3. *Grammar.* feminine. 4. (*pl.* **ff.** or **FF.**) folio. 5. (*pl.* **ff.**) following (page).

fa (fɑː) *n. Music.* same as **fah.**

FA (in Britain) Football Association.

Fabian ('feɪbɪən) *adj.* 1. cautious; using delaying tactics as a policy. ~*n.* 2. a member of the Fabian Society which seeks to establish socialism by gradual reforms. —'**Fabian,ism** *n.*

fable ('feɪb²l) *n.* 1. a short moral story, esp. one with animals as characters. 2. a false, fictitious, or improbable account. 3. a story about mythical characters or events. 4. legends or myths collectively.

fabled ('feɪb²ld) *adj.* made famous in fable.

Fablon ('fæblɒn) *n. Trademark.* a brand of adhesive-backed plastic used for covering surfaces.

fabric ('fæbrɪk) *n.* 1. any cloth made from yarn or fibres by weaving, knitting, or felting. 2. a structure or framework: *the fabric of society.* 3. the walls, floor, and roof of a building.

fabricate ('fæbrɪ,keɪt) *vb.* 1. to make or build. 2. to invent (a story or lie). —,**fabri'cation** *n.*

fabulous ('fæbjʊləs) *adj.* 1. almost unbelievable; astounding; legendary. 2. *Informal.* extremely good. 3. of or based upon fable: *a fabulous beast.* —'**fabulously** *adv.*

façade (fə'sɑːd) *n.* 1. the front of a building. 2. a front or outer appearance, esp. a deceptive one.

face (feɪs) *n.* 1. the front of the head from the forehead to the lower jaw. 2. **a.** one's expression: *a sad face.* **b.** a distorted expression to indicate disgust or defiance. 3. appearance or pretence (esp. in **put a bold, good, bad,** etc., **face on**). 4. dignity (esp. in **lose** or **save face**). 5. *Informal.* impudence. 6. the front or main side of an object, building, etc. 7. the dial of a clock or watch. 8. the functional side of an object, as of a tool or playing card. 9. the exposed area of a mine from which coal or ore may be mined. 10. Also called: **type-face.** *Printing.* the style of the type. 11. **in the face of.** despite. 12. **on the face of it.** to all appearances. 13. **set one's face against.** to oppose with determination. 14. **show one's face.** to make an appearance. 15. **to someone's face.** directly and openly. ~*vb.* 16. to look or be situated (in a specified direction). 17. to be opposite. 18. to be confronted by. 19. to provide with a surface of a different material. ~See also **face up to.**

face card *n.* a court card.

faceless ('feɪslɪs) *adj.* without identity; anonymous.

face-lift *n.* cosmetic surgery for tightening sagging skin and smoothing wrinkles on the face.

facer ('feɪsə) *n. Brit. informal.* a difficulty or problem.

face-saving *adj.* maintaining dignity or prestige. —'**face-,saver** *n.*

facet ('fæsɪt) *n.* 1. any of the surfaces of a cut gemstone. 2. an aspect, as of a personality.

facetious (fə'siːʃəs) *adj.* joking, or trying to be amusing, esp. at inappropriate times. —**fa'cetiously** *adv.*

face up to *vb.* to accept (an unpleasant fact or reality).

face value *n.* apparent worth or meaning: *she took the remark at face value.*

facia ('feɪʃə) *n.* same as **fascia.**

facial ('feɪʃəl) *adj.* 1. of the face. ~*n.* 2. a beauty treatment for the face. —'**facially** *adv.*

facile ('fæsaɪl) *adj.* (of a remark, argument, etc.) superficial and showing lack of real thought.

facilitate (fə'sɪlɪ,teɪt) *vb.* to assist the progress of. —**fa,cili'tation** *n.*

facility (fə'sɪlɪtɪ) *n.*, *pl.* **-ties.** 1. ease of action or performance. 2. ready skill or ease. 3. (*often pl.*) the means or equipment needed for an activity.

facing ('feɪsɪŋ) *n.* 1. a piece of material used esp. to conceal the seam of a garment. 2. (*usually pl.*) contrasting collar and cuffs on a jacket. 3. an outer layer of material applied to the surface of a wall.

facsimile (fæk'sɪmɪlɪ) *n.* 1. an exact copy. 2. a telegraphic system for transmitting an exact copy of a document.

fact (fækt) *n.* 1. an event or thing known to have happened or existed. 2. a truth that can be proved from experience or observation. 3. a piece of information. 4. **after** (*or* before) **the fact.** *Criminal law.* after (*or* before) the commission of the offence. **5. as a matter of fact** *or* **in fact.** in reality or actuality. **6. fact of life.** an inescapable truth, esp. an unpleasant one. See also **facts of life.**

faction (ˈfækʃən) *n.* **1.** a small dissenting group of people within a larger body. **2.** strife within a group. —**ˈfactional** *adj.*

factitious (fækˈtɪʃəs) *adj.* artificial rather than natural.

factor (ˈfæktə) *n.* **1.** an element that contributes to a result. **2.** *Maths.* one of two or more integers whose product is a given integer: *2 and 3 are factors of 6.* **3.** (in Scotland) the manager of an estate.

factorial (fækˈtɔːrɪəl) *Maths.* ~*n.* **1.** the product of all the integers from one to a given integer. ~*adj.* **2.** of factorials or factors.

factorize *or* **-rise** (ˈfæktəˌraɪz) *vb. Maths.* to resolve (an integer) into factors. —ˌfactoriˈzation *or* -riˈsation *n.*

factory (ˈfæktrɪ) *n., pl.* **-ries.** a building or buildings containing a plant assembly for the manufacture of goods.

factory farm *n.* a farm in which animals are intensively reared using modern industrial methods. —**factory farming** *n.*

factory ship *n.* a vessel that processes fish supplied by a fleet.

factotum (fækˈtəʊtəm) *n.* a person employed to do all kinds of work.

facts of life *pl. n.* **the.** the details of sexual behaviour and reproduction.

factual (ˈfæktʃʊəl) *adj.* **1.** of facts. **2.** real; actual. —**ˈfactually** *adv.*

faculty (ˈfæk²ltɪ) *n., pl.* **-ties. 1.** one of the inherent powers of the mind or body, such as memory, sight, or hearing. **2.** any ability or power. **3. a.** a department within a university or college. **b.** its staff. **c.** *Chiefly U.S. & Canad.* all the staff of a university, school, or college.

fad (fæd) *n. Informal.* **1.** an intense but short-lived fashion. **2.** a personal whim. —**ˈfaddish** *or* **ˈfaddy** *adj.*

fade (feɪd) *vb.* **1.** to lose or cause to lose brightness, colour, or strength. **2.** (usually foll. by *away* or *out*) to vanish slowly.

fade in *vb.* to increase gradually, as vision or sound in a film or broadcast.

fade out *vb.* to decrease gradually, as vision or sound in a film or broadcast.

faeces *or esp. U.S.* **feces** (ˈfiːsiːz) *pl. n.* bodily waste matter discharged through the anus. —**faecal** *or esp. U.S.* **fecal** (ˈfiːk²l) *adj.*

Faeroese *or* **Faroese** (ˌfɛərəʊˈiːz) *adj.* **1.** of the Faeroes, islands in the N Atlantic, their inhabitants, or their language. ~*n.* **2.** the language of the Faeroes. **3.** (*pl.* **-ese**) a person from the Faeroes.

faff (fæf) *vb.* (often foll. by *about*) *Brit. informal.* to dither or fuss.

fag[1] (fæg) *n.* **1.** *Informal.* a boring or wearisome task. **2.** *Brit.* (esp. formerly) a young public school boy who performs menial chores for an older boy. ~*vb.* **fagging, fagged. 3.** (often foll. by *out*) *Informal.* to become or make exhausted by hard work **4.** *Brit.* to do menial chores in a public school.

fag[2] (fæg) *n. Brit. slang.* a cigarette.

fag[3] (fæg) *n. Slang, chiefly U.S. & Canad.* short for **faggot**[2].

fag end *n.* **1.** the last and worst part. **2.** *Brit. informal.* the stub of a cigarette.

faggot[1] *or esp. U.S.* **fagot** (ˈfægət) *n.* **1.** a ball of chopped liver bound with herbs and bread. **2.** a bundle of sticks.

faggot[2] (ˈfægət) *n. Slang, chiefly U.S. & Canad.* a male homosexual.

fah *or* **fa** (fɑː) *n. Music.* **1.** the note F. **2.** (in tonic sol-fa) the fourth degree of any major scale.

Fah. *or* **Fahr.** Fahrenheit.

Fahrenheit (ˈfærənˌhaɪt) *adj.* of or measured according to the scale of temperature in which 32° represents the melting point of ice and 212° the boiling point of water.

faïence (faɪˈɑːns) *n.* tin-glazed earthenware.

fail (feɪl) *vb.* **1.** to be unsuccessful in an attempt. **2.** to stop operating. **3.** to judge or be judged as being below the officially accepted standard required in (a course or examination). **4.** to prove disappointing or useless to (someone). **5.** to neglect or be unable (to do something). **6.** to go bankrupt. ~*n.* **7.** a failure to attain the required standard. **8. without fail.** definitely.

failing (ˈfeɪlɪŋ) *n.* **1.** a weak point. ~*prep.* **2.** in default of: *failing a solution, the problem will have to wait.*

fail-safe *adj.* **1.** designed to return to a safe condition in the event of a failure or malfunction. **2.** safe from failure; foolproof.

failure (ˈfeɪljə) *n.* **1.** the act or an instance of failing. **2.** a person or thing that is unsuccessful. **3.** nonperformance of something required or expected. **4.** cessation of normal operation: *a power failure.* **5.** an insufficiency: *crop failure.* **6.** the fact of not reaching the required standard in an examination or test. **7.** bankruptcy.

fain (feɪn) *adv.* **1.** *Archaic.* gladly. ~*adj.* **2.** *Obs.* **a.** willing. **b.** compelled.

faint (feɪnt) *adj.* **1.** lacking clarity, brightness, or volume. **2.** lacking conviction or force. **3.** feeling dizzy or weak. **4.** timid (esp. in **faint-hearted**). ~*vb.* **5.** to lose consciousness. ~*n.* **6.** a sudden loss of consciousness. —**ˈfaintly** *adv.*

fair[1] (fɛə) *adj.* **1.** free from discrimination

or dishonesty. **2.** in conformity with rules. **3.** light in colour. **4.** beautiful. **5.** quite good. **6.** unblemished. **7.** (of the wind) favourable. **8.** fine or cloudless. **9. fair and square.** in a correct or just way. ~*adv.* **10.** in a fair way. **11.** absolutely or squarely; quite. —**'fairness** *n.*

fair² (fɛə) *n.* **1.** a travelling entertainment with sideshows, rides, and amusements. **2.** an exhibition of goods produced by a particular industry to promote business.

fairground ('fɛə,graʊnd) *n.* an open space used for a fair.

fairing ('fɛərɪŋ) *n.* an external metal structure fitted around parts of an aircraft, car, etc., to reduce drag.

Fair Isle *n.* an intricate multicoloured knitted pattern.

fairly ('fɛəlɪ) *adv.* **1.** moderately. **2.** as deserved; justly. **3.** positively: *the hall fairly rang with applause.*

fair play *n.* a conventional standard of honourable behaviour.

fair sex *n.* **the.** women collectively.

fairway ('fɛə,weɪ) *n.* **1.** (on a golf course) the mown areas between tees and greens. **2.** *Naut.* a navigable channel.

fair-weather *adj.* not reliable in difficult situations: *fair-weather friend.*

fairy ('fɛərɪ) *n., pl.* **fairies. 1.** an imaginary supernatural being with magical powers. **2.** *Slang.* a male homosexual.

fairy godmother *n.* a benefactress.

fairyland ('fɛərɪ,lænd) *n.* **1.** the imaginary domain of the fairies. **2.** an enchanted or wonderful place.

fairy lights *pl. n.* small coloured electric bulbs used as decoration, esp. on a Christmas tree.

fairy ring *n.* a ring of dark grass caused by fungi.

fairy tale *or* **story** *n.* **1.** a story about fairies or other mythical beings. **2.** a highly improbable account.

fait accompli (,feɪt ə'kɒmpliː) *n.* something already done and beyond alteration.

faith (feɪθ) *n.* **1.** strong belief in something, esp. without proof. **2.** a specific system of religious beliefs. **3.** complete confidence or trust, as in a person or remedy. **4.** loyalty. **5. bad faith.** dishonesty. **6. good faith.** honesty. ~*adj.* **7.** using or relating to the supposed ability to cure bodily ailments by means of religious faith: *a faith healer.*

faithful ('feɪθfʊl) *adj.* **1.** remaining true or loyal. **2.** maintaining sexual loyalty to one's lover or spouse. **3.** consistently reliable. **4.** accurate. ~*n.* **5. the faithful. a.** the believers in a religious faith. **b.** loyal followers. —**'faithfully** *adv.* —**'faithfulness** *n.*

faithless ('feɪθlɪs) *adj.* treacherous or disloyal.

fake (feɪk) *vb.* **1.** to cause (something not

genuine) to appear real or more valuable by fraud. **2.** to pretend to have (an illness, emotion, etc.). ~*n.* **3.** an object, person, or act that is not genuine. ~*adj.* **4.** not genuine.

fakir ('feɪkɪə, fə'kɪə) *n.* **1.** a member of any religious order of Islam. **2.** a Hindu holy man.

falcon ('fɔːlkən) *n.* a type of bird of prey that can be trained to hunt small game.

falconry ('fɔːlkənrɪ) *n.* **1.** the art of training falcons to hunt. **2.** the sport of hunting with falcons. —**'falconer** *n.*

fall (fɔːl) *vb.* **falling, fell, fallen. 1.** to descend by the force of gravity from a higher to a lower place. **2.** to drop suddenly from an erect position. **3.** to collapse to the ground. **4.** to become less or lower in number or quality. **5.** to slope downwards. **6.** to be badly wounded or killed. **7.** to yield to temptation or sin. **8.** to yield to attack. **9.** to lose power or status. **10.** to pass into a specified condition: *fall asleep.* **11.** to adopt a despondent expression: *her face fell.* **12.** to occur; take place: *night fell.* **13.** to occur at a specified place: *the accent falls on the last syllable.* **14.** (foll. by *to*) to be inherited (by). **15. fall short. a.** to prove inadequate. **b.** (often foll. by *of*) to fail to reach (a standard). ~*n.* **16.** an instance of falling. **17.** something that falls: *a fall of snow.* **18.** *Chiefly U.S. & Canad.* autumn. **19.** (*often pl.*) a waterfall. **20.** a decrease in value or number. **21.** a decline in status or importance. **22.** a capture or overthrow: *the fall of the city.* **23.** *Wrestling.* a scoring move, pinning both shoulders of one's opponent to the floor for a specified period. ~See also **fall about, fall away,** etc.

Fall (fɔːl) *n.* **the.** *Theol.* Adam's sin of disobedience and the state of innate sinfulness following from this for himself and all mankind.

fall about *vb.* to laugh in an uncontrolled manner.

fallacy ('fæləsɪ) *n., pl.* **-cies. 1.** an incorrect or misleading notion based on inaccurate facts or invalid reasoning. **2.** unsound reasoning. —**fallacious** (fə'leɪʃəs) *adj.*

fall away *vb.* **1.** to become less: *their supporters fell away.* **2.** to slope down.

fall back *vb.* **1.** to retreat. **2.** (foll. by *on* or *upon*) to have recourse (to).

fall behind *vb.* **1.** to fail to keep up. **2.** to·be in arrears, as with a payment.

fall down *vb.* **1.** to drop suddenly or collapse. **2.** (often foll. by *on*) *Informal.* to fail.

fallen ('fɔːlən) *vb.* **1.** the past participle of **fall.** ~*adj.* **2.** having sunk in reputation: *a fallen woman.* **3.** killed in battle.

fall for *vb.* **1.** to become infatuated with (a person). **2.** to be deceived by (a lie or trick).

fall guy *n. Informal.* **1.** the victim of a confidence trick. **2.** a scapegoat.

fallible ('fælɪb'l) *adj.* **1.** capable of being mistaken. **2.** liable to mislead. —ˌfalli'bility *n.*

fall in *vb.* **1.** to collapse. **2.** to adopt a military formation, esp. as a soldier taking his place in a line. **3.** (often foll. by *with*) **a.** to meet and join. **b.** to agree with or support a person or suggestion.

falling star *n. Informal.* a meteor.

fall off *vb.* **1.** to drop unintentionally to the ground from (a high object, bicycle, etc.). **2.** to diminish in size or intensity.

fall on *vb.* **1.** to attack or snatch (an army, booty, etc.). **2. fall on one's feet.** to emerge unexpectedly well from a difficult situation.

Fallopian tube (fə'ləʊpɪən) *n.* either of a pair of slender tubes through which ova pass from the ovaries to the uterus in female mammals.

fallout ('fɔːlˌaʊt) *n.* **1.** radioactive material in the atmosphere following a nuclear explosion. ~*vb.* **fall out. 2.** *Informal.* to disagree. **3.** to occur. **4.** *Mil.* to leave a disciplinary formation.

fallow[1] ('fæləʊ) *adj.* (of land) left unseeded after being ploughed to regain fertility for a crop.

fallow[2] ('fæləʊ) *adj.* light yellowish-brown.

fallow deer *n.* a species of deer with a reddish coat with white spots in summer.

fall through *vb.* to fail.

fall to *vb.* **1.** to begin some activity, as eating, working, or fighting. **2.** to devolve on (a person): *the task fell to me.*

false (fɔːls) *adj.* **1.** not in accordance with the truth or facts. **2.** irregular or invalid: *a false start.* **3.** untruthful: *a false account.* **4.** artificial; fake. **5.** misleading or deceptive. **6.** treacherous. **7.** forced or insincere: *a false smile.* **8.** based on mistaken ideas. ~*adv.* **9.** in a dishonest manner (esp. in **play someone false**). —'falsely *adv.* —'falseness *n.*

falsehood ('fɔːls,hʊd) *n.* **1.** the quality of being untrue. **2.** a lie.

false pretences *pl. n.* **under false pretences.** so as to mislead people about one's true intentions.

falsetto (fɔːl'sɛtəʊ) *n., pl.* **-tos.** a voice pitch higher than normal, esp. of a male tenor.

falsies ('fɔːlsɪz) *pl. n. Informal.* pads worn to exaggerate the size of a woman's breasts.

falsify ('fɔːlsɪ,faɪ) *vb.* **-fying, -fied.** to make (a report or evidence) false by alteration in order to deceive. —**falsification** (ˌfɔːlsɪfɪ'keɪʃən) *n.*

falsity ('fɔːlsɪtɪ) *n., pl.* **-ties. 1.** the state of being false. **2.** a lie.

falter ('fɔːltə) *vb.* **1.** to be hesitant, weak, or unsure. **2.** to move unsteadily. **3.** to utter hesitantly. —'faltering *adj.*

fame (feɪm) *n.* **1.** the state of being widely known or recognized. **2.** *Archaic.* public report.

famed (feɪmd) *adj.* famous or renowned.

familial (fə'mɪlɪəl) *adj.* of or relating to the family.

familiar (fə'mɪlɪə) *adj.* **1.** well-known. **2.** frequent or customary: *a familiar excuse.* **3.** (foll. by *with*) acquainted. **4.** friendly; intimate. **5.** more intimate than is acceptable; presumptuous. ~*n.* **6.** a supernatural spirit supposed to attend a witch. **7.** a friend. —**fa'miliarly** *adv.* —**familiarity** (fəˌmɪlɪ'ærɪtɪ) *n.*

familiarize *or* **-rise** (fə'mɪljəˌraɪz) *vb.* to make (oneself or someone else) fully acquainted with a particular subject. —**faˌmiliari'zation** *or* **-ri'sation** *n.*

family ('fæmɪlɪ, 'fæmlɪ) *n., pl.* **-lies. 1.** a social group consisting of parents and their offspring. **2.** one's wife or husband and one's children. **3.** one's children. **4.** a group descended from a common ancestor. **5.** all the people living together in one household. **6.** any group of related things or beings, esp. when scientifically categorized. **7.** *Biol.* any of the taxonomic groups into which an order is divided and which contains one or more genera. **8. in the family way.** *Informal.* pregnant.

Family Allowance *n.* **1.** (in Britain) a former name for **child benefit. 2.** (in Canada) an allowance paid by the Federal Government to the parents of dependent children.

family benefit *n. N.Z.* a child allowance paid to the mothers of children under 18.

family credit *n. Brit.* an allowance paid to families whose earnings from full-time work are low.

family man *n.* a man who is married and has children, esp. one who is devoted to his family.

family name *n.* a surname, esp. when regarded as representing the family honour.

family planning *n.* the control of the number of children in a family, esp. by the use of contraceptives.

family support *n. N.Z.* a top-up of family income in certain circumstances where there are dependent children.

family tree *n.* a chart showing the genealogical relationships of a family.

famine ('fæmɪn) *n.* a severe shortage of food.

famish ('fæmɪʃ) *vb.* **be famished** *or* **famishing.** to be very hungry.

famous ('feɪməs) *adj.* **1.** known to or recognized by many people. **2.** *Informal.* excellent; splendid. —'famously *adv.*

fan[1] (fæn) *n.* **1.** any device for creating a current of air, esp. a rotating device of blades attached to a central hub. **2.** a folding semicircular series of flat segments of paper or ivory, waved in the hand to cool oneself. **3.** something shaped like such a fan, such as the tail of certain birds. ~*vb.* **fanning, fanned. 4.** to cause a current of air to blow upon, as by means of a fan. **5.** to agitate or move (air) with or as if with a fan. **6.** (often foll. by *out*) to spread out in the shape of a fan.

fan² (fæn) *n.* a devotee of a pop star, sport, or hobby.

fanatic (fə'nætɪk) *n.* **1.** a person whose enthusiasm for something is extreme. **2.** *Informal.* a person devoted to a particular hobby or pastime. ~*adj. also* **fanatical. 3.** excessively dedicated. —**fa'natically** *adv.* —**fa'nati,cism** *n.*

fan belt *n.* the belt that drives a cooling fan in a car engine.

fancier ('fænsɪə) *n.* a person with a special interest in something: *a pigeon fancier.*

fanciful ('fænsɪfʊl) *adj.* **1.** not based on fact. **2.** made in a curious or imaginative way. **3.** indulging in fancy. —**'fancifully** *adv.*

fan club *n.* an organized group of admirers of a particular pop singer or star.

fancy ('fænsɪ) *adj.* **-cier, -ciest. 1.** special, unusual, and elaborate. **2.** (often used ironically) superior in quality. **3.** higher than expected: *fancy prices.* ~*n., pl.* **-cies. 4.** a sudden capricious idea. **5.** a sudden or irrational liking for a person or thing. **6.** imagination. ~*vb.* **-cying, -cied. 7.** to picture in the imagination. **8.** to suppose: *I fancy it will rain.* **9.** (reflexive) to have a high opinion of oneself. **10.** *Informal.* to have a wish for. **11.** *Brit. informal.* to be physically attracted to (another person). ~*interj.* **12.** Also: **fancy that!** an exclamation of surprise. —**'fancily** *adv.*

fancy dress *n.* costume worn at parties, representing a historical or fictional figure.

fancy-free *adj.* not in love.

fancy goods *pl. n.* small decorative gifts.

fancy man *n. Slang.* **1.** a woman's lover. **2.** a pimp.

fancy woman *n. Slang.* a mistress or prostitute.

fancywork ('fænsɪ,wɜːk) *n.* ornamental needlework.

fandango (fæn'dæŋgəʊ) *n., pl.* **-gos.** an old Spanish dance in triple time.

fanfare ('fænfɛə) *n.* a flourish or short tune played on brass instruments.

fang (fæŋ) *n.* **1.** the long pointed tooth of a poisonous snake through which poison is injected. **2.** the canine tooth of a carnivorous mammal.

fanjet ('fæn,dʒɛt) *n.* same as **turbofan.**

fanlight ('fæn,laɪt) *n.* a semicircular window over a door or window.

fanny ('fænɪ) *n., pl.* **-nies.** *Slang.* **1.** *Brit.*

taboo. the female genitals. **2.** *Chiefly U.S. & Canad.* the buttocks.

fantail ('fæn,teɪl) *n.* **1.** a breed of domestic pigeon having a large tail like a fan. **2.** a flycatcher of Australia, New Zealand, and SE Asia with a broad fan-shaped tail.

fantasia (fæn'teɪzɪə) *n.* **1.** any musical composition of a free or improvisatory nature. **2.** a potpourri of popular tunes.

fantasize *or* **-sise** ('fæntə,saɪz) *vb.* to indulge in extravagant or fantastic daydreams (about something).

fantastic (fæn'tæstɪk) *adj.* **1.** strange or fanciful in appearance or conception. **2.** unrealistic or absurd. **3.** *Informal.* very large or very good.

fantasy ('fæntəsɪ) *n., pl.* **-sies. 1.** imagination unrestricted by reality. **2.** a whimsical or far-fetched notion. **3.** a daydream. **4.** a highly elaborate imaginative creation. **5.** literature with a large fantasy content. **6.** *Music.* same as **fantasia.**

fan vaulting *n. Archit.* vaulting having ribs that radiate like those of a fan from the top of a capital.

far (fɑː) *adv., adj.* **farther** *or* **further, farthest** *or* **furthest. 1.** at, to, or from a great distance. **2.** at or to a remote time: *far in the future.* **3.** to a considerable degree: *far better.* **4. as far as. a.** to the degree or extent that. **b.** to the distance or place of. **c.** *Informal.* with reference to. **5. by far.** by a considerable margin. **6. far and away.** by a very great margin. **7. far and wide.** everywhere. **8. go far. a.** to be successful. **b.** to be sufficient or last long: *the wine didn't go far.* **9. go too far.** to exceed reasonable limits. **10. so far. a.** up to the present moment. **b.** up to a certain point, extent, or degree. ~*adj.* **11.** remote in space or time: *in the far past.* **12.** extending a great distance. **13.** more distant: *the far end of the room.* **14. far from.** in a degree or state remote from: *he is far from happy.*

farad ('færəd) *n. Physics.* the derived SI unit of electric capacitance.

faraway ('fɑːrə,weɪ) *adj.* **1.** very distant. **2.** absent-minded.

farce (fɑːs) *n.* **1.** a broadly humorous play based on improbable situations. **2.** the genre of comedy of this kind. **3.** a ludicrous situation or action. —**'farcical** *adj.*

fare (fɛə) *n.* **1.** the sum charged or paid for conveyance in a bus, train, or plane. **2.** a paying passenger. **3.** a range of food and drink. ~*vb.* **4.** to get on (as specified): *he fared well.*

Far East *n.* **the.** the countries of E Asia. —**Far Eastern** *adj.*

fare stage *n.* **1.** a section of a bus journey for which a set charge is made. **2.** the bus stop marking the end of such a section.

farewell (,fɛə'wɛl) *interj.* **1.** goodbye;

adieu. ~*n.* **2.** a parting salutation. **3.** an act of departure.

far-fetched *adj.* unlikely.

far-flung *adj.* **1.** widely distributed. **2.** far distant; remote.

farinaceous (ˌfærɪˈneɪʃəs) *adj.* **1.** having a mealy texture. **2.** containing starch.

farm (fɑːm) *n.* **1.** a tract of land, usually with a house and buildings, cultivated as a unit or used to rear livestock. **2.** a unit of land or water devoted to the growing or rearing of some particular type of fruit, animal, or fish: *a salmon farm.* ~*vb.* **3. a.** to cultivate (land). **b.** to rear (stock) on a farm. **4.** to engage in agricultural work as a way of life. **5.** to collect the moneys due and retain the profits from (a tax district or business). ~See also **farm out.**

farmer (ˈfɑːmə) *n.* a person who owns or manages a farm.

farm hand *n.* a person who is hired to work on a farm.

farmhouse (ˈfɑːmˌhaʊs) *n.* a house attached to a farm.

farming (ˈfɑːmɪŋ) *n.* the business or skill of agriculture.

farm out *vb.* **1.** to send (work) to be done by another person or firm. **2.** to put (a child) into the care of a private individual.

farmstead (ˈfɑːmˌstɛd) *n.* a farm and its main buildings.

farmyard (ˈfɑːmˌjɑːd) *n.* an area surrounded by or adjacent to farm buildings.

far-off *adj.* remote in space or time; distant.

far-out *adj. Slang.* **1.** bizarre or avant-garde. **2.** wonderful.

far-reaching *adj.* extensive in influence, effect, or range.

farrier (ˈfærɪə) *n. Chiefly Brit.* a person who shoes horses.

farrow (ˈfærəʊ) *n.* **1.** a litter of piglets. ~*vb.* **2.** (of a sow) to give birth to (a litter).

far-seeing *adj.* having shrewd judgment.

far-sighted *adj.* **1.** possessing prudence and foresight. **2.** long-sighted.

fart (fɑːt) *Taboo.* ~*n.* **1.** an emission of intestinal gas from the anus. ~*vb.* **2.** to break wind.

farther (ˈfɑːðə) *adv.* **1.** to or at a greater distance in space or time. **2.** in addition. ~*adj.* **3.** more distant or remote in space or time. **4.** additional.
Usage. *Farther* and *farthest* are preferred when referring to literal distance: *the farthest planet. Further* and *furthest* are preferred for figurative senses: *nothing could be further from the truth.*

farthermost (ˈfɑːðəˌməʊst) *adj.* most distant or remote.

farthest (ˈfɑːðɪst) *adv.* **1.** to or at the greatest distance in space or time. ~*adj.* **2.** most distant in space or time. **3.** most

extended.
Usage. see **farther.**

farthing (ˈfɑːðɪŋ) *n.* a former British coin worth a quarter of an old penny.

farthingale (ˈfɑːðɪŋˌgeɪl) *n.* a hoop worn under skirts, esp. in the Elizabethan period.

fasces (ˈfæsiːz) *pl. n., sing.* **-cis** (-sɪs). (in ancient Rome) a bundle of rods containing an axe with its blade protruding; a symbol of a magistrate's power.

fascia *or* **facia** (ˈfeɪʃɪə) *n., pl.* **-ciae** (-ʃɪˌiː). **1.** the flat surface above a shop window. **2.** *Archit.* a flat band or surface. **3.** *Brit.* the outer panel which covers the dashboard of a motor vehicle.

fascinate (ˈfæsɪˌneɪt) *vb.* **1.** to attract and delight by arousing interest. **2.** to render motionless, as by arousing terror or awe. —ˈfasciˌnating *adj.* —ˌfasciˈnation *n.*

Fascism (ˈfæʃɪzəm) *n.* **1.** the authoritarian nationalistic political movement in Italy (1922–43). **2.** (*sometimes not cap.*) any ideology or movement like this. —ˈFascist *n., adj.*

fashion (ˈfæʃən) *n.* **1.** style in clothes or behaviour, esp. the latest style. **2.** manner of performance: *in a striking fashion.* **3. after** *or* **in a fashion.** in some manner, but not very well: *I mended it, after a fashion.* ~*vb.* **4.** to form or shape.

fashionable (ˈfæʃənəbʰl) *adj.* **1.** conforming to fashion; in vogue. **2.** of or patronized by people of fashion: *a fashionable café.* —ˈfashionably *adv.*

fast¹ (fɑːst) *adj.* **1.** acting or moving or capable of acting or moving quickly. **2.** accomplished in or lasting a short time. **3.** adapted to or facilitating rapid movement: *the fast lane.* **4.** (of a clock or watch) indicating a time in advance of the correct time. **5.** given to an active dissipated life. **6.** firmly fixed, fastened, or shut. **7.** steadfast; constant (esp. in **fast friends**). **8.** that will not fade. **9.** *Photog.* requiring a relatively short exposure. **10. a fast one.** *Informal.* an unscrupulous trick (esp. in **pull a fast one**). ~*adv.* **11.** quickly; rapidly. **12.** soundly; deeply: *fast asleep.* **13.** firmly; tightly: *stuck fast.* **14. play fast and loose.** to behave in an insincere or unreliable manner.

fast² (fɑːst) *vb.* **1.** to abstain from eating, esp. as a religious observance. ~*n.* **2.** a period of fasting.

fast-breeder reactor *n.* a nuclear reactor that produces more fissionable material than it consumes.

fasten (ˈfɑːsᵊn) *vb.* **1.** to make or become secure or joined. **2.** to close by fixing firmly in place or locking. **3.** (usually foll. by *on* or *upon*) to direct (one's attention) in a concentrated way. **4.** (usually foll. by *on*) to take a firm hold of. —ˈfastener *n.*

fastening ('fɑːsᵊnɪŋ) *n.* something that fastens, such as a clasp or lock.

fast food *n.* food, such as hamburgers, that is prepared and served very quickly.

fastidious (fæ'stɪdɪəs) *adj.* **1.** excessively particular about details. **2.** easily disgusted. —**fas'tidiously** *adv.* —**fas'tidiousness** *n.*

fast lane *n.* **1.** the outside lane on a motorway for overtaking or travelling fast. **2.** *Informal.* the quickest but most competitive route to success.

fastness ('fɑːstnɪs) *n.* a stronghold; fortress.

fast-track *adj.* taking the quickest but most competitive route to success or personal advancement: *fast-track executives.*

fat (fæt) *adj.* **fatter, fattest 1.** having more flesh on the body than is thought necessary or desirable; overweight. **2.** containing a lot of fat: *fat bacon.* **3.** thick: *a fat volume.* **4.** profitable. **5.** fertile or productive. **6.** *Slang.* very little or none (esp. in **a fat chance, a fat lot of good**). ~*n.* **7.** extra or unwanted flesh on the body. **8.** a greasy or oily substance obtained from animals or plants and used in cooking. **9. the fat is in the fire.** an action has been taken from which dire consequences are expected. **10. the fat of the land.** the best that is obtainable. —'**fatless** *adj.* —'**fatness** *n.*

fatal ('feɪtᵊl) *adj.* **1.** resulting in death: *a fatal accident.* **2.** bringing ruin. —'**fatally** *adv.*

fatalism ('feɪtə,lɪzəm) *n.* the belief that all events are predetermined so that man is powerless to alter his destiny. —'**fatalist** *n.* —,**fatal'istic** *adj.* —,**fatal'istically** *adv.*

fatality (fə'tælɪtɪ) *n., pl.* **-ties. 1.** a death caused by an accident or disaster. **2.** the power of causing death or disaster.

fate (feɪt) *n.* **1.** the ultimate agency that predetermines the course of events. **2.** the inevitable fortune that befalls a person or thing. **3.** death or downfall.

fated ('feɪtɪd) *adj.* **1.** destined: *we were fated to dislike each other.* **2.** doomed to death or destruction.

fateful ('feɪtfʊl) *adj.* having important, and usually disastrous, consequences. —'**fatefully** *adv.*

fathead ('fæt,hɛd) *n. Informal.* a stupid person; fool. —'**fat,headed** *adj.*

father ('fɑːðə) *n.* **1.** a male parent. **2.** a person who founds a line or family; forefather. **3.** any male acting in a paternal capacity. **4.** a male who originates something: *the father of modern psychology.* **5.** a leader of an association or council: *a city father.* ~*vb.* **6.** to procreate (offspring). **7.** to create, found, etc. —'**fatherhood** *n.*

Father ('fɑːðə) *n.* **1.** God. **2.** any of the early writers on Christian doctrine. **3.** a title used for Christian priests.

father-in-law *n., pl.* **fathers-in-law.** the father of one's wife or husband.

fatherland ('fɑːðə,lænd) *n.* a person's native country.

fatherly ('fɑːðəlɪ) *adj.* kind or protective, like a father.

Father's Day *n.* a day observed in honour of fathers.

fathom ('fæðəm) *n.* **1.** a unit of length equal to six feet, used to measure depths of water. ~*vb.* **2.** to penetrate (a mystery or problem). **3.** to measure the depth of. —'**fathomable** *adj.*

fathomless ('fæðəmlɪs) *adj.* too deep or difficult to fathom.

fatigue (fə'tiːɡ) *n.* **1.** physical or mental exhaustion due to exertion. **2.** the weakening of a material subjected to alternating stresses. **3.** any of the mainly domestic duties performed by military personnel. **4.** (*pl.*) special clothing worn to carry out such duties. ~*vb.* **-tiguing, -tigued. 5.** to make or become weary or exhausted.

fat stock *n.* livestock fattened and ready for market.

fatten ('fætᵊn) *vb.* to grow or cause to grow fat or fatter. —'**fattening** *adj.*

fatty ('fætɪ) *adj.* **-tier, -tiest. 1.** containing or derived from fat. **2.** greasy; oily. ~*n., pl.* **-ties. 3.** *Informal.* a fat person.

fatty acid *n.* any of a class of organic acids some of which, such as stearic acid, are found in animal or vegetable fats.

fatuity (fə'tjuːɪtɪ) *n., pl.* **-ties. 1.** complacent silliness. **2.** a fatuous remark.

fatuous ('fætjʊəs) *adj.* complacently silly. —'**fatuously** *adv.*

faucet ('fɔːsɪt) *n.* **1.** a tap fitted to a barrel. **2.** *U.S. & Canad.* a tap.

fault (fɔːlt) *n.* **1.** a failing or defect; flaw. **2.** a mistake or error. **3.** responsibility for something wrong. **4.** *Geol.* a fracture in the earth's crust with displacement of the rocks on either side. **5.** *Tennis, squash, etc.* an invalid serve. **6.** (in showjumping) a penalty mark for failing to clear, or refusing, a fence. **7. at fault.** guilty of error; culpable. **8. find fault with.** to seek out minor imperfections in. **9. to a fault.** excessively. ~*vb.* **10.** *Geol.* to undergo or cause to undergo a fault. **11.** to criticize or blame. —'**faultless** *adj.* —'**faultlessly** *adv.*

fault-finding *n.* continual criticism.

faulty ('fɔːltɪ) *adj.* **faultier, faultiest.** defective or imperfect. —'**faultily** *adv.* —'**faultiness** *n.*

faun (fɔːn) *n.* (in Roman legend) a rural god represented as a man with a goat's ears, horns, tail, and hind legs.

fauna ('fɔːnə) *n., pl.* **-nas** *or* **-nae** (-niː). all the animal life of a given place or time.

faux pas (ˌfəʊ ˈpɑː) *n., pl.* **faux pas** (ˌfəʊ ˈpɑːz). a social blunder.

favour *or U.S.* **favor** (ˈfeɪvə) *n.* **1.** an approving attitude; goodwill. **2.** an act performed out of goodwill or generosity. **3.** partiality. **4. in** (*or* **out of**) **favour.** regarded with approval (*or* disapproval). **5. in favour of. a.** approving. **b.** to the benefit of. ~*vb.* **6.** to regard with especial kindness. **7.** to treat with partiality. **8.** to support; advocate. **9.** *Informal.* to resemble: *he favours his father.*

favourable *or U.S.* **favorable** (ˈfeɪvərəbᵊl) *adj.* **1.** advantageous, encouraging, or promising. **2.** giving consent. —ˈ**favourably** *or U.S.* ˈ**favorably** *adv.*

favourite *or U.S.* **favorite** (ˈfeɪvərɪt) *adj.* **1.** most liked. ~*n.* **2.** a person or thing regarded with especial preference or liking. **3.** *Sport.* a competitor thought likely to win.

favouritism *or U.S.* **favoritism** (ˈfeɪvərɪˌtɪzəm) *n.* the practice of giving special treatment to a person or group.

fawn¹ (fɔːn) *n.* **1.** a young deer aged under one year. ~*adj.* **2.** light greyish-brown.

fawn² (fɔːn) *vb.* (often foll. by *on* or *upon*) **1.** to seek attention (from someone) by cringing and flattering. **2.** (esp. of dogs) to try to please by a show of extreme friendliness. —ˈ**fawning** *adj.*

fax (fæks) *n.* **1.** short for **facsimile.** ~*vb.* **2.** to send (a document) by a telegraphic facsimile system.

FBI (in the U.S.) Federal Bureau of Investigation.

FD Defender of the Faith: one of the titles of the British sovereign.

Fe *Chem.* iron.

fealty (ˈfiːəltɪ) *n., pl.* **-ties.** (in feudal society) the loyalty sworn to a lord by his vassal.

fear (fɪə) *n.* **1.** a feeling of distress or alarm caused by impending danger or pain. **2.** a cause of this feeling. **3.** awe; reverence: *fear of God.* **4.** possibility: *little fear of them refusing.* **5. no fear.** *Informal.* certainly not. ~*vb.* **6.** to be afraid (to do something) or of (a person or thing). **7.** to revere; respect. **8.** to be politely sorry: *I fear that you have not won.* **9.** (foll. by *for*) to feel anxiety about something. —ˈ**fearless** *adj.* —ˈ**fearlessly** *adv.*

fearful (ˈfɪəfʊl) *adj.* **1.** afraid. **2.** causing fear. **3.** *Informal.* very unpleasant. —ˈ**fearfully** *adv.*

fearsome (ˈfɪəsəm) *adj.* frightening.

feasible (ˈfiːzəbᵊl) *adj.* able to be done; possible. —ˌ**feasiˈbility** *n.* —ˈ**feasibly** *adv.*

feast (fiːst) *n.* **1.** a large and sumptuous meal. **2.** a periodic religious celebration. **3.** something extremely pleasing: *a feast for the eyes.* ~*vb.* **4. a.** to eat a feast. **b.** (usually foll. by *on*) to enjoy the eating of.

5. to give a feast to. **6.** to delight: *feast one's eyes.*

feat (fiːt) *n.* a remarkable, skilful, or daring action.

feather (ˈfɛðə) *n.* **1.** any of the flat light structures forming the plumage of birds, each consisting of a shaft with barbs on either side. **2. feather in one's cap.** a cause for pleasure at one's achievements. ~*vb.* **3.** to fit, cover, or supply with feathers. **4.** *Rowing.* to turn (an oar) parallel to the water between strokes, in order to lessen wind resistance. **5. feather one's nest.** to provide oneself with comforts. —ˈ**feathered** *adj.* —ˈ**feathery** *adj.*

feather bed *n.* **1.** a mattress filled with feathers or down. ~*vb.* **featherbed, -bedding, -bedded. 2.** to pamper; spoil.

featherbrain (ˈfɛðəˌbreɪn) *n.* a frivolous or forgetful person. —ˈ**featherˌbrained** *adj.*

featherweight (ˈfɛðəˌweɪt) *n.* **1.** something very light or of little importance. **2.** a professional boxer weighing up to 126 pounds or an amateur boxer weighing up to 57 kg. **3.** an amateur wrestler weighing up to 137 pounds.

feature (ˈfiːtʃə) *n.* **1.** any one of the parts of the face, such as the nose, chin, or mouth. **2.** a prominent or distinctive part, as of a landscape. **3.** the principal film in a cinema programme. **4.** an item appearing at intervals in a newspaper or magazine. **5.** a prominent story in a newspaper. ~*vb.* **6.** to have as a feature or make a feature of. **7.** to give prominence to. —ˈ**featureless** *adj.*

Feb. February.

febrile (ˈfiːbraɪl) *adj.* of or relating to fever; feverish.

February (ˈfɛbrʊərɪ) *n., pl.* **-aries.** the second month of the year.

feckless (ˈfɛklɪs) *adj.* feeble; weak; ineffectual.

fecund (ˈfiːkənd, ˈfɛk-) *adj.* **1.** fertile. **2.** intellectually productive. —**fecundity** (fɪˈkʌndɪtɪ) *n.*

fecundate (ˈfiːkənˌdeɪt, ˈfɛk-) *vb.* to make fruitful; fertilize.

fed (fɛd) *vb.* the past of **feed.**

federal (ˈfɛdərəl) *adj.* **1.** of a form of government in which power is divided between one central and several regional governments. **2.** of the central government of a federation. —ˈ**federaˌlism** *n.* —ˈ**federalist** *n., adj.*

Federal (ˈfɛdərəl) *adj.* of or supporting the Union government during the American Civil War.

Federal Government *n.* the national government of a federated state, such as that of Canada located in Ottawa.

federalize *or* **-lise** (ˈfɛdərəˌlaɪz) *vb.* **1.** to unite in a federal union. **2.** to subject to federal control. —**,federali'zation** or -li'**sation** n.

federate vb. ('fɛdə,reɪt). 1. to unite in a federal union. ~adj. ('fɛdərɪt). 2. federated. —'**federative** adj.

federation (,fɛdə'reɪʃən) n. 1. the union of several provinces, states, etc. 2. any alliance or confederacy.

fed up adj. Informal. annoyed or bored.

fee (fiː) n. 1. a payment asked by professional people or public servants for their services. 2. a charge made for a privilege: an entrance fee. 3. Property law. an interest in land capable of being inherited. The interest can be with unrestricted rights (**fee simple**) or restricted (**fee tail**).

feeble ('fiːb°l) adj. 1. lacking in physical or mental strength. 2. unconvincing: feeble excuses. —'**feebly** adv.

feeble-minded adj. mentally defective.

feed (fiːd) vb. **feeding, fed. 1.** to give food to: to feed the cat. 2. to give as food: to feed meat to the cat. 3. to eat food: the horses feed at noon. 4. to provide food for. 5. to provide what is necessary for the continued existence, operation, or growth of: feed one's imagination; the flames were fed by the escaping gas. ~n. 6. the act of feeding. 7. food, esp. that of animals or babies. 8. Informal. a meal.

feedback ('fiːd,bæk) n. 1. the return of part of the output of an electronic circuit to its input. 2. the return of part of the sound output of a loudspeaker to the microphone, so that a high-pitched whistle is produced. 3. information in response to an inquiry or experiment.

feeder ('fiːdə) n. 1. a child's feeding bottle or bib. 2. a tributary channel. 3. a road or transport service that links secondary areas to the main traffic network.

feel (fiːl) vb. **feeling, felt. 1.** to have a physical or emotional sensation of (something): to feel anger. 2. to become aware of or examine (something) by touching. 3. to sense (esp. in **feel (it) in one's bones**). 4. to believe: she felt it was right. 5. (foll. by for) to show compassion (towards). 6. (often foll. by up) Slang. to pass one's hands over the sexual organs of. 7. **feel like**. to have an inclination (for something or doing something). 8. **feel up to**. to be fit enough for (something or doing something). ~n. 9. the act of feeling. 10. an impression: a homely feel. 11. the sense of touch. 12. an instinctive aptitude: she's got a feel for this sort of work.

Usage. The verbs feel, look, and smell can be followed by an adverb or an adjective according to the sense in which they are used. Where a quality of the subject is involved, an adjective is used: I feel sick; he looks strong. For other senses an adverb would be used: she feels strongly about that; I must look closely at his record.

feeler ('fiːlə) n. 1. an organ in certain animals, such as an antenna, that is sensitive to touch. 2. a remark designed to probe the reactions of others.

feeling ('fiːlɪŋ) n. 1. an emotional reaction: a feeling of panic. 2. (pl.) emotional sensitivity (esp. in **hurt the feelings of**). 3. an emotional disturbance, esp. anger: a lot of bad feeling. 4. intuitive appreciation and understanding: a feeling for words. 5. an intuition: I had a feeling that something was wrong. 6. opinion; view: what is his feeling on the matter? 7. sympathy; pity. 8. **a.** the ability to experience physical sensations, such as heat. **b.** the sensation so experienced. 9. atmosphere; impression: a feeling of warmth. —'**feelingly** adv.

feet (fiːt) n. 1. the plural of **foot. 2. be run** or **rushed off one's feet**. to be very busy. 3. **feet of clay**. a weakness that is not widely known. 4. **have** (or **keep**) one's **feet on the ground**. to be practical and reliable. 5. **put one's feet up**. to take a rest. 6. **stand on one's own feet**. to be independent. 7. **sweep off one's feet**. to fill with enthusiasm.

feign (feɪn) vb. to pretend: to feign innocence. —**feigned** adj.

feint[1] (feɪnt) n. 1. a mock attack or movement designed to distract an adversary, as in boxing or fencing. ~vb. 2. to make a feint.

feint[2] (feɪnt) n. Printing. a narrow rule used for ruled paper.

feldspar ('fɛld,spɑː, 'fɛl,spɑː) or **felspar** n. a hard mineral that is the principal constituent of igneous rocks. —**feldspathic** (fɛld'spæθɪk, fɛl'spæθ-) or **fel'spathic** adj.

felicitate (fɪ'lɪsɪ,teɪt) vb. to congratulate. —**fe,lici'tation** n.

felicity (fɪ'lɪsɪtɪ) n., pl. -**ties. 1.** happiness. 2. appropriate expression or style. —**fe'licitous** adj.

feline ('fiːlaɪn) adj. 1. of or belonging to the cat family. 2. like a cat, esp. in stealth or grace. ~n. 3. any member of the cat family; a cat. —**felinity** (fɪ'lɪnɪtɪ) n.

fell[1] (fɛl) vb. the past tense of **fall**.

fell[2] (fɛl) vb. 1. to cut or knock down: to fell a tree. 2. Needlework. to fold under and sew flat (the edges of a seam).

fell[3] (fɛl) adj. 1. Archaic. cruel or deadly. 2. **one fell swoop**. a single destructive action or occurrence.

fell[4] (fɛl) n. (often pl.) Scot. & N English. a mountain, hill, or moor.

fellatio (fɪ'leɪʃɪəʊ) n. a sexual activity in which the penis is stimulated by the partner's mouth.

felloe ('fɛləʊ) or **felly** ('fɛlɪ) n., pl. -**loes** or -**lies**. a segment or the whole rim of a wooden wheel.

fellow ('fɛləʊ) n. 1. a man or boy. 2. (often pl.) a companion; associate. 3. a member of the governing body at any of various universities or colleges. **4.** a postgraduate research student. **5.** a person in the same group, class, or condition. **6.** one of a pair; counterpart.

Fellow ('fɛləʊ) n. a member of any of various learned societies.

fellow feeling n. sympathy existing between people who have shared similar experiences.

fellowship ('fɛləʊ,ʃɪp) n. **1.** the state of sharing mutual interests or activities. **2.** a society of people sharing mutual interests or activities. **3.** companionship; friendship. **4.** *Education.* a financed research post providing study facilities.

fellow traveller n. a non-Communist who sympathizes with Communism.

felon ('fɛlən) n. *Criminal law.* (formerly) a person who has committed a felony.

felony ('fɛlənɪ) n., pl. **-nies.** *Criminal law.* (formerly) a serious crime, such as murder or arson. —**felonious** (fɪ'ləʊnɪəs) adj.

felspar ('fɛl,spɑː) n. same as **feldspar.**

felt[1] (fɛlt) vb. the past of **feel.**

felt[2] (fɛlt) n. **1.** a matted fabric of wool, made by working the fibres together under pressure. ~vb. **2.** to make into or cover with felt. **3.** to become matted.

felt-tip pen n. a pen whose writing point is made from pressed fibres.

fem. 1. female. **2.** feminine.

female ('fiːmeɪl) adj. **1.** of the sex producing offspring. **2.** of or characteristic of a woman. **3.** (of reproductive organs such as the ovary and carpel) capable of producing female gametes. **4.** (of flowers) lacking stamens. **5.** having an internal cavity into which a projecting male counterpart can be fitted: *a female thread.* ~n. **6.** a female animal or plant.

feminine ('fɛmɪnɪn) adj. **1.** characteristic of a woman. **2.** possessing qualities considered typical of or appropriate to a woman. **3.** effeminate; womanish. **4.** *Grammar.* belonging to a gender of nouns that includes all kinds of referents as well as some female referents. —,**femi'ninity** n.

feminism ('fɛmɪ,nɪzəm) n. a doctrine or movement that advocates equal rights for women. —'**feminist** n., adj.

femme fatale (,fæm fə'tɑːl) n., pl. **femmes fatales** (,fæm fə'tɑːlz). an alluring or seductive woman who causes men distress.

femur ('fiːmə) n., pl. **femurs** or **femora** ('fɛmərə). the thighbone. —'**femoral** adj.

fen (fɛn) n. low-lying flat marshy land.

fence (fɛns) n. **1.** a barrier that encloses an area such as a garden or field, usually made of posts connected by wire rails or boards. **2.** *Slang.* a dealer in stolen property. **3.** an obstacle for a horse to jump in steeplechasing or showjumping. **4.** *Machinery.* a guard or guide, esp. in a circular saw

or plane. **5.** (**sit**) **on the fence.** (to be) unwilling to commit oneself. ~vb. **6.** to construct a fence on or around (a piece of land). **7.** (foll. by *in* or *off*) to close in or separate off with or as if with a fence. **8.** to fight using swords or foils. **9.** to evade a question.

fencing ('fɛnsɪŋ) n. **1.** the sport of fighting with foils. **2.** materials used for making fences.

fend (fɛnd) vb. **1.** (foll. by *for*) to give support (to someone, esp. oneself). **2.** (usually foll. by *off*) to ward off or turn aside (blows, questions, etc.).

fender ('fɛndə) n. **1.** a low metal frame which confines falling coals to the hearth. **2.** a soft but solid object, such as a coil of rope, hung over the side of a vessel to prevent damage when docking. **3.** *U.S. & Canad.* the wing of a car.

fenestration (,fɛnɪ'streɪʃən) n. the arrangement of windows in a building.

Fenian ('fiːnɪən, 'fiːnjən) n. (formerly) a member of an Irish revolutionary organization founded to fight for an independent Ireland. —'**Fenianism** n.

fennel ('fɛn*l) n. a strong-smelling yellow-flowered umbelliferous plant whose seeds, leaves, and root are used in cookery.

fenugreek ('fɛnjʊ,griːk) n. a heavily scented Mediterranean leguminous plant cultivated for its aromatic seeds.

feoff (fiːf) n. same as **fief.**

feral ('fɪərəl) adj. **1.** (of animals and plants) existing in a wild state. **2.** savage; brutal.

fermata (fə'mɑːtə) n., pl. **-tas** or **-te** (-tɪ). *Music.* same as **pause** (sense 4).

ferment n. ('fɜːmɛnt). **1.** commotion; unrest. **2.** any substance, such as yeast, that causes fermentation. ~vb. (fə'mɛnt). **3.** to undergo or cause to undergo fermentation.

fermentation (,fɜːmɛn'teɪʃən) n. a chemical reaction in which an organic molecule splits into simpler substances, esp. the conversion of sugar into ethyl alcohol by yeast.

fermium ('fɜːmɪəm) n. an element artificially produced by neutron bombardment of plutonium. Symbol: Fm

fern (fɜːn) n. a flowerless plant with roots, stems, and fronds that reproduces by spores. —'**ferny** adj.

ferocious (fə'rəʊʃəs) adj. savagely fierce or cruel. —**ferocity** (fə'rɒsɪtɪ) n.

ferret ('fɛrɪt) n. **1.** a domesticated albino variety of the polecat bred for hunting rats and rabbits. ~vb. **2.** to hunt (rabbits or rats) with ferrets. **3.** to search around. **4. ferret out. a.** to drive from hiding. **b.** to find by persistent investigation.

ferric ('fɛrɪk) adj. of or containing iron in the trivalent state.

Ferris wheel ('fɛrɪs) n. a fairground wheel with seats freely suspended from its rim.

ferroconcrete (ˌfɛrəʊ'kɒŋkriːt) *n.* same as **reinforced concrete**.

ferrous ('fɛrəs) *adj.* of or containing iron in the divalent state.

ferruginous (fə'ruːdʒɪnəs) *adj.* 1. (of minerals, rocks, etc.) containing iron. 2. rust-coloured.

ferrule ('fɛruːl) *n.* a metal ring or cap placed over the end of a stick for added strength.

ferry ('fɛrɪ) *n.*, *pl.* **-ries.** 1. a boat for transporting passengers and usually vehicles across a body of water, esp. as a regular service. 2. such a service. ~*vb.* **-rying, -ried.** 3. to transport or go by ferry. 4. to convey (passengers or goods). —'**ferryman** *n.*

fertile ('fɜːtaɪl) *adj.* 1. capable of producing offspring. 2. (of land) capable of an abundant growth of plants. 3. *Biol.* capable of development. 4. producing many offspring; prolific. 5. highly productive: *a fertile brain.* 6. *Physics.* (of a substance) able to be transformed into fissile or fissionable material. —**fertility** (fɜː'tɪlɪtɪ) *n.*

fertilize *or* **-lise** ('fɜːtɪˌlaɪz) *vb.* 1. to provide (an animal or plant) with sperm or pollen to bring about fertilization. 2. to supply (soil) with nutrients. 3. to make fertile. —ˌ**fertili'zation** *or* **-li'sation** *n.*

fertilizer *or* **-liser** ('fɜːtɪˌlaɪzə) *n.* any substance, such as manure, added to soil to increase its productivity.

fervent ('fɜːvənt) *or* **fervid** ('fɜːvɪd) *adj.* intensely sincere and passionate. —'**fervently** *adv.*

fervour *or* *U.S.* **fervor** ('fɜːvə) *n.* great intensity of feeling or belief.

fescue ('fɛskjuː) *n.* a widely grown pasture and lawn grass.

festal ('fɛstˀl) *adj.* festive.

fester ('fɛstə) *vb.* 1. to form or cause to form pus. 2. to rot; decay. 3. to grow worse and develop increasing bitterness or hatred: *his anger festered inwardly.*

festival ('fɛstɪvˀl) *n.* 1. a day or period set aside for celebration. 2. an organized series of special events and performances: *a festival of drama.*

festive ('fɛstɪv) *adj.* appropriate to or characteristic of a holiday or celebration.

festivity (fɛs'tɪvɪtɪ) *n.*, *pl.* **-ties.** 1. happy celebration; merriment. 2. (*pl.*) celebrations.

festoon (fɛ'stuːn) *n.* 1. a decorative chain of flowers or ribbons suspended in loops. 2. a representation of this, as in architecture. ~*vb.* 3. to decorate with festoons. 4. to form into festoons.

feta ('fɛtə) *n.* a Greek white sheep cheese.

fetch[1] (fɛtʃ) *vb.* 1. to go after and bring back. 2. to cost or sell for (a certain price). 3. to utter (a sigh or groan). 4. *Informal.* to deal (a blow or slap). 5. **fetch and carry.**

to perform menial tasks. ~*n.* 6. a trick or stratagem.

fetch[2] (fɛtʃ) *n.* the ghost or apparition of a living person.

fetching ('fɛtʃɪŋ) *adj. Informal.* attractive.

fetch up *vb.* 1. *Informal.* to arrive or end up. 2. *Slang.* to vomit food.

fête *or* **fete** (feɪt) *n.* 1. an event, usually outdoors, with stalls, competitions, etc., held to raise money for charity. ~*vb.* 2. to honour or entertain regally.

fetid ('fɛtɪd, 'fiː-) *adj.* having a stale nauseating smell, as of decay.

fetish ('fɛtɪʃ, 'fiː-) *n.* 1. something, esp. an inanimate object, that is believed to have magical powers. 2. a. a form of behaviour in which sexual satisfaction is derived from handling an object. b. any object that is involved in such behaviour. 3. any object, activity, etc., to which one is excessively devoted. —'**fetish,ism** *n.* —'**fetishist** *n.*

fetlock ('fɛtˌlɒk) *n.* 1. a projection behind and above a horse's hoof. 2. the tuft of hair growing from this part.

fetter ('fɛtə) *n.* 1. (*often pl.*) a chain or bond fastened round the ankle. 2. (*usually pl.*) a check or restraint. ~*vb.* 3. to restrict. 4. to bind in fetters.

fettle ('fɛtˀl) *n.* state of health or spirits (esp. in **in fine fettle**).

fetus *or* **foetus** ('fiːtəs) *n.*, *pl.* **-tuses.** the embryo of a mammal in the later stages of development. —'**fetal** *or* '**foetal** *adj.*

feu (fjuː) *n. Scots Law.* a right to the use of land in return for a fixed annual payment (**feu duty**).

feud (fjuːd) *n.* 1. long and bitter hostility between two families, clans, or individuals. ~*vb.* 2. to carry on a feud.

feudal ('fjuːdˀl) *adj.* of or characteristic of feudalism.

feudalism ('fjuːdəˌlɪzəm) *n.* the legal and social system in medieval Europe, in which vassals were protected by their lords, and were required to serve under them in war. Also called: **feudal system**.

fever ('fiːvə) *n.* 1. an abnormally high body temperature, accompanied by a fast pulse rate, shivering, and nausea. 2. any of various diseases characterized by a high temperature. 3. intense nervous excitement. ~*vb.* 4. to affect with or as if with fever. —'**fevered** *adj.*

feverish ('fiːvərɪʃ) *adj.* 1. suffering from fever. 2. in a state of restless excitement. —'**feverishly** *adv.*

fever pitch *n.* a state of intense excitement.

few (fjuː) *det.* 1. hardly any: *few men are so cruel.* 2. (preceded by *a*) a small number of: *a few drinks.* 3. **a good few.** *Informal.* several. 4. **few and far between.** scarce. 5. **quite a few.** *Informal.* several.

fey (feɪ) *adj.* **1.** whimsically strange. **2.** clairvoyant. **3.** *Chiefly Scot.* doomed.

fez (fez) *n., pl.* **fezzes.** an originally Turkish brimless red cap, shaped like a truncated cone and with a tassel.

ff *Music.* fortissimo. See **f**

ff. and the following (pages, lines, etc.).

fiancé *or (fem.)* **fiancée** (fɪˈɒnseɪ) *n.* a person who is engaged to be married.

fiasco (fɪˈæskəʊ) *n., pl.* **-cos** *or* **-coes.** a ridiculous or humiliating failure.

fiat (ˈfaɪət) *n.* **1.** official sanction. **2.** an arbitrary order.

fib (fɪb) *n.* **1.** a trivial and harmless lie. ~*vb.* **fibbing, fibbed.** **2.** to tell such a lie. —ˈfibber *n.*

fibre *or U.S.* **fiber** (ˈfaɪbə) *n.* **1.** a natural or synthetic thread that may be spun into yarn. **2.** essential substance or nature. **3.** strength of character (esp. in **moral fibre**). **4.** a fibrous substance, such as bran, as part of someone's diet: *dietary fibre.* —ˈfibrous *adj.*

fibreboard (ˈfaɪbəˌbɔːd) *n.* a building material made of compressed wood.

fibreglass (ˈfaɪbəˌɡlɑːs) *n.* **1.** material consisting of matted fine glass fibres, used as insulation. **2.** a light strong material made by bonding fibreglass with a synthetic resin; used for boats and car bodies.

fibre optics *n. (functioning as sing.)* the transmission of information modulated on light down very thin flexible fibres of glass. —**fibre optic** *adj.*

fibril (ˈfaɪbrɪl) *n.* a small fibre.

fibrillation (ˌfaɪbrɪˈleɪʃən) *n.* **1.** a local and uncontrollable twitching of muscle fibres. **2.** irregular twitchings of the muscular wall of the heart.

fibrin (ˈfɪbrɪn) *n.* a white insoluble elastic protein formed when blood clots.

fibroid (ˈfaɪbrɔɪd) *adj.* **1.** *Anat.* (of structures or tissues) containing or resembling fibres. ~*n.* **2.** a benign tumour derived from fibrous connective tissue.

fibrosis (faɪˈbrəʊsɪs) *n.* the formation of an abnormal amount of fibrous tissue.

fibrositis (ˌfaɪbrəˈsaɪtɪs) *n.* inflammation of white fibrous tissue, esp. of muscle sheaths.

fibula (ˈfɪbjʊlə) *n., pl.* **-lae** (-ˌliː) *or* **-las.** the outer and thinner of the two bones between the knee and ankle of the human leg. —ˈfibular *adj.*

fiche (fiːʃ) *n.* See **microfiche.**

fickle (ˈfɪk²l) *adj.* changeable in purpose, affections, etc. —ˈfickleness *n.*

fiction (ˈfɪkʃən) *n.* **1.** literary works invented by the imagination, such as novels. **2.** an invented story or explanation. **3.** *Law.* something assumed to be true for the sake of convenience, though probably false. —ˈfictional *adj.*

fictionalize *or* **-lise** (ˈfɪkʃənəˌlaɪz) *vb.* to make into fiction.

fictitious (fɪkˈtɪʃəs) *adj.* **1.** not genuine: *a fictitious name.* **2.** of or in fiction.

fiddle (ˈfɪd²l) *n.* **1.** *Informal or disparaging.* the violin. **2.** a violin played as a folk instrument. **3.** *Brit. informal.* a dishonest action or scheme. **4. on the fiddle.** *Informal.* engaged in an illegal or fraudulent undertaking. **5. fit as a fiddle.** *Informal.* in very good health. **6. play second fiddle.** *Informal.* to play a subordinate part. ~*vb.* **7.** to play (a tune) on the fiddle. **8.** (often foll. by *with*) to move or touch (something) restlessly or nervously. **9.** (often foll. by *about* or *around*) *Informal.* to waste time. **10.** *Informal.* to do (something) by illegal or dishonest means. **11.** *Informal.* to falsify (accounts).

fiddle-faddle (ˈfɪd²lˌfæd²l) *n., interj.* nonsense.

fiddler (ˈfɪdlə) *n.* **1.** a person who plays the fiddle. **2.** a small burrowing crab. **3.** *Informal.* a petty rogue.

fiddlesticks (ˈfɪd²lˌstɪks) *interj.* an expression of annoyance or disagreement.

fiddling (ˈfɪdlɪŋ) *adj.* insignificant.

fiddly (ˈfɪdlɪ) *adj.* **-dlier, -dliest.** small and awkward to do or handle.

fidelity (fɪˈdɛlɪtɪ) *n., pl.* **-ties.** **1.** loyalty to a person, belief, or cause. **2.** faithfulness to one's spouse or lover. **3.** accuracy in reporting detail. **4.** *Electronics.* the degree to which an amplifier or radio accurately reproduces the input signal.

fidget (ˈfɪdʒɪt) *vb.* **1.** to move about restlessly. **2.** (often foll. by *with*) to make restless or uneasy movements (with something). ~*n.* **3.** (*often pl.*) a state of restlessness: *he's got the fidgets.* **4.** a person who fidgets. —ˈfidgety *adj.*

fiduciary (fɪˈduːʃɪrɪ) *Law.* ~*n.* **1.** a person bound to act for another's benefit, as a trustee. ~*adj.* **2. a.** having the nature of a trust. **b.** of or relating to a trust or trustee.

fie (faɪ) *interj. Obs. or facetious.* an exclamation of distaste or mock dismay.

fief (fiːf) *n.* (in feudal Europe) the property or fee granted to a vassal by his lord in return for service.

field (fiːld) *n.* **1.** an area of uncultivated grassland; meadow. **2.** a piece of cleared land used for pasture or growing crops. **3.** a marked off area on which sports or athletic competitions are held. **4.** an area that is rich in minerals or other natural resources: *a coalfield.* **5. a.** all the competitors in a competition. **b.** the competitors in a competition excluding the favourite. **6.** a battlefield. **7.** *Cricket.* the fielders collectively. **8.** a wide or open expanse: *a field of snow.* **9.** an area of human activity or knowledge: *his field is physics.* **10.** a place away from the laboratory or classroom

where practical work is done. **11. the sur-**
face or background, as of a flag. **12.** *Phys-*
ics. In full: **field of force.** the region surrounding a body, such as a magnet, within
which it can exert a force on another similar body not in contact with it. **13. play**
the field. *Informal.* to disperse one's interests among a number of activities, people,
or objects. *~adj.* **14.** *Mil.* of equipment or
personnel for operations in the field: *a field*
gun. *~vb.* **15.** *Sport.* to catch or return
(the ball) as a fielder. **16.** *Sport.* to send (a
player or team) onto the field to play. **17.**
Sport. (of a player or team) to act or take
turn as a fielder or fielders. **18.** *Informal.*
to deal with successfully: *field a question.*

field day *n.* **1.** *Mil.* a day devoted to
manoeuvres or exercises. **2.** *Informal.* a
day or time of exciting activity.

fielder ('fiːldə) *n. Cricket, etc.* a member of
the fielding side.

field event *n.* a competition, such as the
discus, that takes place on a field as opposed to the track.

fieldfare ('fiːld,fɛə) *n.* a type of large
thrush.

field glasses *pl. n.* binoculars.

field hockey *n. U.S. & Canad.* hockey
played on a field, as distinguished from ice
hockey.

field marshal *n.* an officer holding the
highest rank in certain armies.

fieldmouse ('fiːld,maʊs) *n., pl.* **-mice.** a
nocturnal mouse of woods and fields that
has yellowish-brown fur.

field officer *n.* an officer holding the
rank of major, lieutenant colonel, or colonel.

fieldsman ('fiːldzmən) *n., pl.* **-men.** *Cricket.*
a fielder.

field sports *pl. n.* sports carried on in the
countryside, such as hunting or fishing.

field trip *n.* an expedition, as by students,
to study something at first hand.

fieldwork ('fiːld,wɜːk) *n. Mil.* a temporary
structure used in fortifying a place or position.

field work *n.* an investigation made in the
field as opposed to the classroom or laboratory. —**field worker** *n.*

fiend (fiːnd) *n.* **1.** an evil spirit. **2.** a cruel,
brutal, or spiteful person. **3.** *Informal.* a
person who is intensely interested in or
fond of something: *a fresh-air fiend.*
—'**fiendish** *adj.* —'**fiendishly** *adv.*

Fiend (fiːnd) *n.* **the.** the devil; Satan.

fierce (fiəs) *adj.* **1.** having a violent and
unrestrained nature. **2.** wild or turbulent.
3. intense or strong. —'**fiercely** *adv.*

fiery ('faɪərɪ) *adj.* **fierier, fieriest. 1.** composed of or like fire: *clouds of fiery gas; a*
fiery red. **2.** easily angered: *a fiery temper.*
3. (of food) producing a burning sensation.
—'**fierily** *adv.* —'**fieriness** *n.*

fiesta (fɪˈɛstə) *n.* (esp. in Spain and Latin
America) **1.** a religious festival or celebration. **2.** a carnival.

FIFA ('fiːfə) International Association Football Federation.

fife (faɪf) *n.* a small high-pitched flute, used
esp. in military bands.

fifteen ('fɪf'tiːn) *n.* **1.** the cardinal number
that is the sum of ten and five. **2.** a numeral, 15, XV, representing this number. **3.**
something represented by or consisting of
15 units. **4.** a rugby football team. *~det.*
5. amounting to fifteen: *fifteen jokes.*
—'**fif'teenth** *adj., n.*

fifth (fɪfθ) *adj., n.* See **five.**

fifth column *n.* any group that secretly
helps the enemies of its own country or
organization. —**fifth columnist** *n.*

fifty ('fɪftɪ) *n., pl.* **-ties. 1.** the cardinal
number that is the product of ten and five.
2. a numeral, 50, L, representing this number. **3.** something represented by or consisting of 50 units. *~det.* **4.** amounting to
fifty: *fifty people.* —'**fiftieth** *adj., n.*

fifty-fifty *adj., adv. Informal.* in equal
parts.

fig (fɪg) *n.* **1.** a soft sweet fruit full of tiny
seeds, which grows on a **fig tree.** **2.** something negligible: *I don't care a fig for your*
opinion.

fig. 1. figurative(ly). **2.** figure.

fight (faɪt) *vb.* **fighting, fought. 1.** to
struggle against (an enemy) in battle or
physical combat. **2.** to struggle to overcome or destroy: *to fight racism.* **3.** to
carry on (a battle or contest). **4.** to uphold
(a cause) by struggling: *to fight for free-*
dom. **5.** to make (a way) by fighting. **6.**
fight it out. to contend until a decisive
result is obtained. **7. fight shy.** to avoid.
~n. **8.** a battle. **9.** a quarrel or contest.
10. resistance (esp. in **put up a fight**). **11.**
a boxing match. *~See also* **fight off.**

fighter ('faɪtə) *n.* **1.** a professional boxer.
2. a person who has determination. **3.** *Mil.*
an armed aircraft for destroying other aircraft.

fighting chance *n.* a slight chance of
success dependent on a struggle.

fight off *vb.* **1.** to repulse; repel. **2.** to
struggle to avoid or repress: *to fight off a*
cold.

fig leaf *n.* a representation of a leaf of the
fig tree used in sculpture to cover the genitals of nude figures.

figment ('fɪgmənt) *n.* a fantastic notion or
fabrication: *a figment of the imagination.*

figuration (,fɪgəˈreɪʃən) *n.* **1.** ornamentation. **2.** a figurative representation. **3.** the
act of decorating with a design.

figurative ('fɪgərətɪv) *adj.* **1.** involving a
figure of speech; not literal; metaphorical.
2. using or filled with figures of speech.
—'**figuratively** *adv.*

figure 309 **film**

figure ('fɪgə) *n.* **1.** a written symbol for a number. **2.** an amount expressed numerically. **3.** (*pl.*) calculations with numbers. **4.** visible shape or form; outline. **5.** a slim bodily shape (esp. in **keep** *or* **lose one's figure**). **6.** a well-known person: *a national figure.* **7.** the impression created by a person's behaviour: *she cut a poor figure.* **8.** a representation in painting or sculpture, esp. of the human form. **9.** an illustration or diagram in a text. **10.** a decorative pattern. **11.** a predetermined set of movements in dancing or skating. **12.** *Geom.* any combination of points, lines, curves, or planes. **13.** *Music.* a characteristic short pattern of notes. ~*vb.* **14.** to calculate (sums or amounts). **15.** *U.S., Canad., & N.Z. informal.* to consider. **16.** (usually foll. by *in*) to be included: *his name figures in the article.* **17.** *Informal.* to accord with expectation: *it figures that he wouldn't come.* ~See also **figure out.**

figured ('fɪgəd) *adj.* **1.** decorated with a design. **2.** *Music.* ornamental.

figurehead ('fɪgəˌhɛd) *n.* **1.** a person nominally having a prominent position, but no real authority. **2.** a carved bust on the bow of some sailing vessels.

figure of speech *n.* an expression of language, such as metaphor, by which the literal meaning of a word is not employed.

figure out *vb. Informal.* to work out; solve or understand.

figure skating *n.* ice skating in which the skater traces outlines of selected patterns. —**figure skater** *n.*

figurine (ˌfɪgəˈriːn) *n.* a small carved or moulded figure; statuette.

filament ('fɪləmənt) *n.* **1.** the thin wire inside a light bulb that emits light. **2.** *Electronics.* a high-resistance wire forming the cathode in some valves. **3.** a single strand of fibre. **4.** *Bot.* the stalk of a stamen. —**filamentary** (ˌfɪləˈmɛntrɪ) *adj.*

filbert ('fɪlbət) *n.* the edible rounded brown nuts of the cultivated hazel.

filch (fɪltʃ) *vb.* to steal small amounts.

file¹ (faɪl) *n.* **1.** a folder or box used to keep documents in order. **2.** the documents, etc., kept in this way. **3.** documents or information about a specific subject or person. **4.** a line of people in marching formation, one behind another. **5.** *Computers.* an organized collection of related records. **6. on file.** recorded for reference, as in a file. ~*vb.* **7.** to place (a document) in a file. **8.** to place (a legal document) on public or official record. **9.** to bring (a suit, esp. a divorce suit) in a court of law. **10.** to submit (copy) to a newspaper. **11.** to march or walk in a file or files.

file² (faɪl) *n.* **1.** a hand tool consisting of a steel blade with small cutting teeth on its faces: used for shaping or smoothing. ~*vb.* **2.** to shape or smooth (a surface) with a file.

filial ('fɪljəl) *adj.* of or suitable to a son or daughter: *filial affection.*

filibuster ('fɪlɪˌbʌstə) *n.* **1.** the process of obstructing legislation by means of long speeches. **2.** a legislator who engages in such obstruction. ~*vb.* **3.** to obstruct (legislation) with such delaying tactics.

filigree ('fɪlɪˌgriː) *n.* **1.** delicate ornamental work of twisted gold, silver, or other wire. ~*adj.* **2.** made of filigree.

filings ('faɪlɪŋz) *pl. n.* shavings or particles removed by a file: *iron filings.*

Filipino (ˌfɪlɪˈpiːnəʊ) *n., pl.* -**nos.** **1.** a person from the Philippines. ~*adj.* **2.** of or relating to the Philippines or their inhabitants.

fill (fɪl) *vb.* (often foll. by *up*) **1.** to make or become full. **2.** to occupy the whole of. **3.** to plug (a gap or crevice). **4.** to meet (a requirement or need) satisfactorily. **5.** to cover (a page or blank space) with writing or drawing. **6.** to hold and perform the duties of (an office or position). **7.** to appoint or elect an occupant to (an office or position). **8. fill the bill.** *Informal.* to be suitable or adequate. ~*n.* **9. one's fill.** the quantity needed to satisfy one. ~See also **fill in, fill out,** etc.

filler ('fɪlə) *n.* **1.** a paste used for filling in cracks or holes in a surface before painting. **2.** *Journalism.* an item to fill space between more important articles.

fillet ('fɪlɪt) *n.* **1.** a piece of boneless meat or fish. **2.** a thin strip of ribbon or lace worn in the hair or around the neck. **3.** *Archit.* a narrow flat moulding. ~*vb.* **4.** to cut or prepare (meat or fish) as a fillet.

fill in *vb.* **1.** to complete (a form or drawing). **2.** to act as a substitute. **3.** to put material into (a hole) as to make it level with a surface. **4.** *Informal.* to give (a person) fuller details.

filling ('fɪlɪŋ) *n.* **1.** the substance or thing used to fill a space or container: *pie filling.* **2.** *Dentistry.* any of various substances for inserting into the prepared cavity of a tooth. ~*adj.* **3.** (of food or a meal) substantial and satisfying.

filling station *n.* a place where petrol and other supplies for motorists are sold.

fillip ('fɪlɪp) *n.* **1.** something that adds stimulation or enjoyment. **2.** the action of holding a finger towards the palm with the thumb and suddenly releasing it with a snapping sound.

fill out *vb.* **1.** to make or become plumper, thicker, or rounder. **2.** to make more substantial. **3.** *Chiefly U.S. & Canad.* to fill in (a form or application).

fill up *vb.* **1.** to complete (a form or application). **2.** to make or become full.

filly ('fɪlɪ) *n., pl.* -**lies.** **1.** a young female horse. **2.** *Informal.* a lively young woman.

film (fɪlm) *n.* **1. a.** a photographed sequence

of images of moving objects providing the optical illusion of continuous movement when projected onto a screen. **b.** a form of entertainment composed of such a sequence of images. **2.** a thin flexible strip of cellulose coated with a photographic emulsion, used to make negatives and transparencies. **3.** a thin coating or layer. **4.** a thin sheet of any material, as of plastic for packaging. **5.** a fine haze, mist, or blur. ~*vb.* **6. a.** to photograph with a cine camera. **b.** to make a film of (a screenplay or event). **7.** (often foll. by *over*) to cover or become covered with a film.

filmset ('film,set) *vb.* **-setting, -set.** *Brit.* to set (type matter) by exposing type characters onto photographic film from which printing plates are made.

film star *n.* a popular film actor or actress.

film strip *n.* a strip of film composed of different images projected separately as slides.

filmy ('filmi) *adj.* **filmier, filmiest. 1.** transparent or gauzy. **2.** hazy; blurred. —'**filmily** *adv.* —'**filminess** *n.*

Filofax ('failəu,fæks) *n. Trademark.* a type of loose-leaf ring binder, used as a portable personal filing system.

filter ('filtə) *n.* **1.** a porous substance, such as paper or sand, that allows fluid to pass but retains solid particles. **2.** any device containing such a porous substance, esp. a tip on the mouth end of a cigarette. **3.** any electronic or acoustic device that blocks signals of certain frequencies while allowing others to pass. **4.** any transparent disc of gelatin or glass used to reduce the intensity of given frequencies from the light leaving a lamp or entering a camera. **5.** *Brit.* a traffic signal which permits vehicles to turn either left or right when the main signals are red. ~*vb.* **6.** (often foll. by *out*) to remove or separate (particles) from (a liquid or gas) by a filter. **7** (foll. by *through*) to pass (through a filter or something like a filter).

filter out *or* **through** *vb.* to become known gradually; leak.

filter paper *n.* a porous paper used for filtering liquids.

filter tip *n.* **1.** an attachment to the mouth end of a cigarette for trapping impurities. **2.** a cigarette with such an attachment. —'**filter-,tipped** *adj.*

filth (filθ) *n.* **1.** foul or disgusting dirt; refuse. **2.** vulgarity or obscenity. —'**filthiness** *n.* —'**filthy** *adj.*

filtrate ('filtreit) *n.* **1.** a liquid or gas that has been filtered. ~*vb.* **2.** to filter. —**fil'tration** *n.*

fin (fin) *n.* **1.** any of the winglike projections from a fish's body enabling it to balance and swim. **2.** *Brit.* a vertical surface to which the rudder is attached at the rear

of an aeroplane. **3.** (*pl.*) a swimmer's flippers. —**finned** *adj.*

fin. 1. finance. **2.** financial.

finagle (fi'neig°l) *vb. Informal.* to use or achieve by craftiness or trickery. —**fi'nagler** *n.*

final ('fain°l) *adj.* **1.** of or occurring at the end; last. **2.** having no possibility of further discussion, action, or change. ~*n.* **3.** a deciding contest between the winners of previous rounds in a competition. ~*See* also **finals.** —**fi'nality** *n.* —'**finally** *adv.*

finale (fi'nɑːli) *n.* the concluding part of a dramatic performance or musical composition.

finalist ('fainəlist) *n.* a contestant who has reached the last stage of a competition.

finalize *or* **-lise** ('fainə,laiz) *vb.* to put into final form; settle. —,**finali'zation** *or* **-li'sation** *n.*

finals ('fain°lz) *pl. n.* **1.** the deciding part of a competition. **2.** *Education.* the last examinations in an academic course.

finance (fi'næns, 'fainæns) *n.* **1.** the system of money, credit, and investment. **2.** funds or the provision of funds. **3.** (*pl.*) financial condition. ~*vb.* **4.** to provide or obtain funds for.

financial (fi'nænfəl, fai-) *adj.* **1.** of or relating to finance or finances. **2.** of or relating to people who manage money. **3.** *Austral. & N.Z. informal.* having money; in funds. —**fi'nancially** *adv.*

financial year *n. Brit.* any annual accounting period, such as that of the British Government which ends on April 5.

financier (fi'nænsiə, fai-) *n.* a person who is engaged in large-scale financial operations.

finch (fintʃ) *n.* any of various songbirds with a short stout bill, such as the bullfinch or chaffinch.

find (faind) *vb.* **finding, found. 1.** to discover by chance. **2.** to discover by search or effort. **3.** to realize: *he found that nobody knew.* **4.** to consider: *I find this wine a little sour.* **5.** to experience or feel: *found comfort in his words.* **6.** *Law.* to determine an issue and pronounce a verdict (upon): *the court found the accused guilty.* **7.** to reach (a target): *the bullet found its mark.* **8.** to provide, esp. with difficulty. **9. find one's feet.** to become capable or confident. ~*n.* **10.** a person or thing that is found, esp. a valuable discovery.

finder ('faində) *n.* **1.** a person or thing that finds. **2.** a small telescope fitted to a larger one. **3.** *Photog.* short for **viewfinder.**

finding ('faindiŋ) *n.* (*often pl.*) the conclusion reached after an inquiry or investigation.

find out *vb.* **1.** to gain knowledge of (something); learn. **2.** to detect the crime, deception, etc., of (someone).

fine¹ (fain) *adj.* **1.** very good of its kind. **2.**

superior in skill: *a fine violinist.* **3.** (of weather) clear and dry. **4.** *Informal.* quite well: *I feel fine.* **5.** satisfactory; acceptable: *that's fine by me.* **6.** of delicate or careful workmanship. **7.** abstruse or subtle: *a fine point.* **8.** very thin or slender: *fine hair.* **9.** very small: *fine print.* **10.** (of edges or blades) sharp. **11.** ornate, showy, or smart. **12.** good-looking. **13.** *Informal.* disappointing or terrible: *a fine mess.* ~*adv.* **14.** *Informal.* all right: *that suits me fine.* **15.** finely. ~*vb.* **16.** (often foll. by *down* or *away*) to make or become smaller, finer, thinner, etc. —'**finely** *adv.*

fine² (faɪn) *n.* **1.** an amount of money exacted as a penalty. **2. in fine.** in conclusion. ~*vb.* **3.** to impose a fine on.

fine art *n.* **1.** art produced chiefly for its appeal to the sense of beauty. **2.** (*often pl.*) any of the fields in which such art is produced, such as painting, sculpture, and engraving.

fine-drawn *adj.* **1.** (of arguments or distinctions) subtle. **2.** (of wire) drawn out until very fine.

finery ('faɪnərɪ) *n.* elaborate or showy decoration, esp. clothing and jewellery.

fines herbes ('fiːnz 'ɛːb) *pl. n.* finely chopped mixed herbs, used to flavour omelettes.

finespun (faɪn'spʌn) *adj.* **1.** spun or drawn out to a fine thread. **2.** excessively subtle.

finesse (fɪ'nɛs) *n.* **1.** elegant skill. **2.** subtlety and tact in handling difficult situations. **3.** *Bridge, whist.* an attempt to win a trick when opponents hold a high card in the suit led by playing a lower card. ~*vb.* **4.** to bring about with finesse. **5.** to play (a card) as a finesse.

fine-tooth comb *or* **fine-toothed comb** *n.* **1.** a comb with fine teeth set closely together. **2. go over with a fine-tooth(ed) comb.** to examine very thoroughly.

fine-tune *vb.* to make fine adjustments to (something) so that it works really well.

finger ('fɪŋɡə) *n.* **1.** any of the digits of the hand, often excluding the thumb. **2.** the part of a glove made to cover a finger. **3.** something that resembles a finger in shape or function. **4.** a quantity of liquid in a glass as deep as a finger is wide. **5. get one's finger out.** *Brit. informal.* to begin or speed up activity, esp. after initial delay. **6. put one's finger on.** to identify precisely. **7. put the finger on.** *U.S. & N.Z. informal.* to inform on or identify, esp. for the police. **8. twist around one's little finger.** to have easy and complete influence over. ~*vb.* **9.** to touch or manipulate with the fingers; handle. **10.** to use one's fingers in playing (a musical instrument). —'**fingerless** *adj.*

fingerboard ('fɪŋɡə,bɔːd) *n.* the long strip of hard wood on a violin, guitar, etc., upon which the strings are stopped by the fingers.

finger bowl *n.* a small bowl of water for rinsing the fingers at table during a meal.

fingering ('fɪŋɡərɪŋ) *n.* **1.** the technique of using one's fingers in playing a musical instrument. **2.** the numerals in a musical part indicating this.

fingernail ('fɪŋɡə,neɪl) *n.* a thin horny translucent plate covering part of the upper surface of the end of each finger.

fingerprint ('fɪŋɡə,prɪnt) *n.* **1.** an impression of the pattern of ridges on the inner surface of the end of each finger and thumb. ~*vb.* **2.** to take an inked impression of the fingerprints of (a person). **3.** to take a sample of the DNA of (a person).

fingerstall ('fɪŋɡə,stɔːl) *n.* a protective covering for a finger.

fingertip ('fɪŋɡə,tɪp) *n.* **1.** the end of a finger. **2. have at one's fingertips.** to know or understand thoroughly.

finicky ('fɪnɪkɪ) *or* **finicking** *adj.* **1.** excessively particular; fussy. **2.** overelaborate.

finis ('fɪnɪs) *n.* the end: used at the end of books.

finish ('fɪnɪʃ) *vb.* **1.** to bring to an end; conclude or stop. **2.** to be at or come to the end; use up. **3.** to bring to a desired or complete condition. **4.** to put a particular surface texture on (wood, cloth, or metal). **5.** (often foll. by *off*) to destroy or defeat completely. **6.** (foll. by *with*) to end a relationship. ~*n.* **7.** the final stage or part; end. **8.** death or absolute defeat. **9.** the surface texture of wood, cloth, or metal. **10.** a thing or event that completes.

finishing school *n.* a private school for girls that teaches social graces.

finite ('faɪnaɪt) *adj.* **1.** having limits in size, space, or time. **2.** *Maths, logic.* having a countable number of elements. **3.** *Grammar.* denoting any form of a verb inflected for person, number, and tense.

Finn (fɪn) *n.* a person from Finland.

Finnish ('fɪnɪʃ) *adj.* **1.** of or characteristic of Finland, the Finns, or their language. ~*n.* **2.** the official language of Finland.

fino ('fiːnəʊ) *n.* a very dry sherry.

fiord (fjɔːd) *n.* same as **fjord.**

fipple flute ('fɪpˀl) *n.* an end-blown flute with a plug (**fipple**) at the mouthpiece, such as the recorder or flageolet.

fir (fɜː) *n.* a pyramidal coniferous tree with single needle-like leaves and erect cones.

fire ('faɪə) *n.* **1.** the state of combustion in which inflammable material burns, producing heat, flames, and often smoke. **2.** burning coal or wood, esp. in a hearth to heat a room. **3.** a destructive uncontrolled burning that destroys building, crops, etc. **4.** an electric or gas device for heating a room. **5.** the act of discharging weapons. **6.** a rapid volley: *a fire of questions.* **7.** intense passion; ardour. **8. catch fire.** to ignite. **9. on fire. a.** burning. **b.** ardent or eager. **10. open fire.** to start firing a gun, artillery, etc. **11. play with fire.** to be involved in something risky. **12. set fire to** *or* **set on fire. a.** to ignite. **b.** to arouse or excite. **13. set the Thames on fire.** *Informal.* to cause a great sensation. **14. under fire.** being attacked, as by weapons or by harsh criticism. ~*vb.* **15.** to discharge (a firearm). **16.** to detonate (an explosive device). **17.** *Informal.* to dismiss from employment. **18.** *Ceramics.* to bake in a kiln to harden the clay. **19.** to kindle or be kindled. **20.** (of an internal-combustion engine) undergo ignition. **21.** to provide with fuel. **22.** to arouse to strong emotion. **23.** to glow or cause to glow.

fire alarm *n.* a device to give warning of fire.

firearm ('faɪərˌɑːm) *n.* a weapon, such as a pistol, from which a projectile can be discharged by an explosion.

fireball ('faɪəˌbɔːl) *n.* **1.** ball-shaped lightning. **2.** the hot ionized gas at the centre of a nuclear explosion. **3.** a large bright meteor. **4.** *Slang.* an energetic person.

firebomb ('faɪəˌbɒm) *n.* same as **incendiary** (sense 5).

firebrand ('faɪəˌbrænd) *n.* **1.** a piece of burning wood. **2.** a person who causes unrest.

firebreak ('faɪəˌbreɪk) *n.* a strip of open land in a forest to stop the advance of a fire.

firebrick ('faɪəˌbrɪk) *n.* a heat-resistant brick, used for lining furnaces, flues, and fireplaces.

fire brigade *n. Chiefly Brit.* an organized body of firemen.

fire clay *n.* a heat-resistant clay used in making firebricks and furnace linings.

firecracker ('faɪəˌkrækə) *n.* a small cardboard container filled with explosive powder.

firedamp ('faɪəˌdæmp) *n.* an explosive mixture of hydrocarbons, chiefly methane, formed in coal mines.

firedog ('faɪəˌdɒg) *n.* an andiron.

fire door *n.* a door made of noncombustible material that prevents a fire spreading within a building.

fire-eater *n.* **1.** a performer who simulates the swallowing of fire. **2.** a belligerent person.

fire engine *n.* a vehicle that carries firemen and fire-fighting equipment to a fire.

fire escape *n.* a metal staircase or ladder on the outside of a building for escape in the event of fire.

fire-extinguisher *n.* a portable device for spraying water, foam, or powder to extinguish a fire.

firefly ('faɪəˌflaɪ) *n., pl.* **-flies.** a beetle that glows in the dark.

fireguard ('faɪəˌgɑːd) *n.* a screen made of wire mesh put before an open fire to protect against sparks.

fire hydrant *n.* an outlet from a water main in the street, from which firemen can draw water.

fire irons *pl. n.* metal fireside implements; poker, shovel, and tongs.

fireman ('faɪəmən) *n., pl.* **-men.** **1.** a person who fights fires; member of a fire brigade. **2.** (on steam locomotives) the man who stokes the fire. **3.** a stoker.

fireplace ('faɪəˌpleɪs) *n.* an open recess at the base of a chimney for a fire; hearth.

fire power *n. Mil.* the amount of fire that can be delivered by a unit or weapon.

fire raiser *n.* a person who deliberately sets fire to property. —**fire raising** *n.*

fire ship *n.* a vessel loaded with explosives, set on fire and left to drift among an enemy's warships.

fireside ('faɪəˌsaɪd) *n.* the hearth.

fire station *n.* a building where fire-fighting vehicles and equipment are stationed.

firetrap ('faɪəˌtræp) *n.* a building that would burn easily or one without fire escapes.

firewater ('faɪəˌwɔːtə) *n.* any alcoholic spirit.

firework ('faɪəˌwɜːk) *n.* a device in which combustible materials are ignited to produce coloured sparks and sometimes bangs.

fireworks ('faɪəˌwɜːks) *pl. n.* **1.** a show in which fireworks are let off. **2.** *Informal.* a burst of temper.

firing ('faɪərɪŋ) *n.* **1.** the process of baking ceramics in a kiln. **2.** a discharge of a firearm. **3.** something used as fuel.

firing line *n.* **1.** *Mil.* the positions from which fire is delivered. **2.** the leading or most vulnerable position in an activity.

firm[1] (fɜːm) *adj.* **1.** not soft or yielding to a touch or pressure. **2.** securely in position; stable. **3.** definitely established: *a firm date.* **4.** having determination or strength: *firm leadership.* ~*adv.* **5.** in an unyielding manner: *he stood firm.* ~*vb.* **6.** to make or become firm. —**firmly** *adv.* —**firmness** *n.*

firm[2] (fɜːm) *n.* **1.** a business partnership. **2.** any commercial enterprise.

firmament ('fɜːməmənt) *n. Literary.* the sky; heavens.

first (fɜːst) *adj.* **1.** coming before all others. **2.** preceding all others in order; 1st. **3.** rated, graded, or ranked above all other levels. **4.** denoting the lowest forward ratio of a gearbox in a motor vehicle. **5.** *Music.* denoting the highest voice part in a chorus or one of the sections of an orchestra: *the first violins.* ~*n.* **6.** the person or thing coming before all others. **7.** the beginning; outset. **8.** *Education, chiefly Brit.* an honours degree of the highest class. **9.** the lowest forward ratio of a gearbox in a motor vehicle. ~*adv.* **10.** Also: **firstly.** before anything else: *do this first.* **11.** for the first time: *I've loved you since I first saw you.*

first aid *n.* immediate medical assistance given in an emergency.

first-born *adj.* **1.** eldest of the children in a family. ~*n.* **2.** the eldest child in a family.

first class *n.* **1.** the class or grade of the best or highest value or quality. ~*adj.* **2.** of the best or highest class or grade. **3.** excellent. **4.** of or denoting the most comfortable class of accommodation in a hotel, aircraft, or train. **5.** (in Britain) of letters that are handled faster than second-class letters. ~*adv.* **first-class.** **6.** by first-class mail, means of transportation, etc.

first-day cover *n. Philately.* an envelope postmarked on the first day of the issue of its stamps.

first-degree burn *n. Pathol.* the least severe type of burn, in which the skin surface is red and painful.

first-foot *Chiefly Scot.* ~*n.* **1.** the first person to enter a household in the New Year. ~*vb.* **2.** to visit (someone) as first-foot. —'**first-'footing** *n.*

first fruits *pl. n.* **1.** the first results or profits of an undertaking. **2.** fruit that ripens first.

first-hand *adj., adv.* **1.** from the original source. **2. at first hand.** directly.

first lady *n.* (*often caps.*) (in the U.S.) the wife of the president.

firstly ('fɜːstlɪ) *adv.* same as **first.**

first mate *n.* an officer second in command to the captain of a merchant ship.

first night *n.* the first public performance of a play or other production.

first offender *n.* a person convicted of a criminal offence for the first time.

first officer *n.* same as **first mate.**

first person *n.* a grammatical category of pronouns and verbs used by the speaker to refer to himself.

first-rate *adj.* of the best quality; excellent.

firth (fɜːθ) *n.* a narrow inlet of the sea.

fiscal ('fɪskˀl) *adj.* **1.** of or relating to government finances, esp. tax revenues. **2.** of financial matters.

fish (fɪʃ) *n., pl.* **fish** *or* **fishes.** **1.** a cold-blooded animal with a backbone, gills, and usually fins and a skin covered in scales, that lives in water. **2.** the flesh of fish used as food. **3.** *Informal.* a person of little emotion or intelligence. **4. drink like a fish.** to drink alcohol to excess. **5. have**

other fish to fry. to have other more important concerns. **6. like a fish out of water.** ill at ease in an unfamiliar situation. ~*vb.* **7.** to attempt to catch fish. **8.** to fish in (a particular area of water). **9.** to grope for and find with some difficulty: *I fished the book out of the bottom of my bag.* **10.** (foll. by *for*) to seek something indirectly: *to fish for compliments.*

fish cake *n.* a fried flattened ball of flaked fish mixed with mashed potatoes.

fisherman ('fɪʃəmən) *n., pl.* **-men.** a person who fishes as a profession or for sport.

fishery ('fɪʃərɪ) *n., pl.* **-eries.** **1. a.** the industry of catching, processing, and selling fish. **b.** a place where this is carried on. **2.** a place where fish are reared. **3.** a fishing ground.

fish-eye lens *n. Photog.* a lens with a highly curved protruding front that covers almost 180°.

fishfinger ('fɪʃ'fɪŋgə) *n.* an oblong piece of fish coated in breadcrumbs.

fishing ('fɪʃɪŋ) *n.* the occupation of catching fish.

fishing rod *n.* a long tapered flexible pole for use with a fishing line and, usually, a reel.

fish meal *n.* ground dried fish used as feed for farm animals or as a fertilizer.

fishmonger ('fɪʃ,mʌŋgə) *n. Chiefly Brit.* a retailer of fish.

fishnet ('fɪʃ,nɛt) *n.* an open mesh fabric resembling netting.

fishplate ('fɪʃ,pleɪt) *n.* a flat piece of metal joining one rail or beam to the next, esp. on railway tracks.

fishtail ('fɪʃ,teɪl) *n.* a nozzle having a long narrow slot at the top, placed over a Bunsen burner to produce a thin fanlike flame.

fishwife ('fɪʃ,waɪf) *n., pl.* **-wives.** a coarse scolding woman.

fishy ('fɪʃɪ) *adj.* **fishier, fishiest.** **1.** of or suggestive of fish. **2.** *Informal.* suspicious or questionable. —'**fishily** *adv.*

fissile ('fɪsaɪl) *adj.* **1.** *Brit.* capable of undergoing nuclear fission. **2.** tending to split.

fission ('fɪʃən) *n.* **1.** the act or process of splitting into parts. **2.** *Biol.* a form of asexual reproduction involving a division into two or more equal parts. **3.** short for **nuclear fission.** —'**fissionable** *adj.*

fissure ('fɪʃə) *n.* any long narrow cleft or crack, esp. in a rock.

fist (fɪst) *n.* a hand with the fingers clenched into the palm, as for hitting.

fisticuffs ('fɪstɪ,kʌfs) *pl. n.* combat with the fists.

fistula ('fɪstjʊlə) *n. Pathol.* an abnormal opening between one hollow organ and another or between a hollow organ and the surface of the skin.

fit[1] (fɪt) *vb.* **fitting, fitted.** **1.** to be appropriate or suitable for. **2.** to be of the correct size or shape for. **3.** to adjust in order to make appropriate. **4.** to try clothes on (someone) in order to make adjustments if necessary. **5.** to make competent or ready. **6.** to correspond with the facts or circumstances. ~*adj.* **fitter, fittest.** **7.** appropriate. **8.** in good health. **9.** worthy or deserving. ~*n.* **10.** the manner in which something fits. ~See also **fit in, fit out.** —'**fitly** *adv.* —'**fitness** *n.*

fit[2] (fɪt) *n.* **1.** a sudden attack or convulsion, such as an epileptic seizure. **2.** a sudden short burst or spell: *a fit of coughing; fits of depression.* **3. by** *or* **in fits (and starts).** in spasmodic spells. **4. have a fit.** *Informal.* to become very angry.

fitful ('fɪtful) *adj.* occurring in irregular spells. —'**fitfully** *adv.*

fit in *vb.* **1.** to give a place or time to (someone or something). **2.** to belong or conform, esp. after adjustment.

fitment ('fɪtmənt) *n.* **1.** an accessory attached to a machine. **2.** *Chiefly Brit.* a detachable part of the furnishings of a room.

fit out *vb.* to equip.

fitted ('fɪtɪd) *adj.* **1.** designed for excellent fit: *a fitted bodice.* **2.** (of a carpet) covering a floor completely. **3. a.** (of furniture) built to fit a particular space. **b.** (of a room) equipped with fitted furniture. **4.** (of sheets) having ends that are elasticated to fit tightly over a mattress.

fitter ('fɪtə) *n.* **1.** a person who is skilled in the assembly and adjustment of machinery. **2.** a person who fits a garment for a particular person.

fitting ('fɪtɪŋ) *adj.* **1.** appropriate or proper. ~*n.* **2.** an accessory or part. **3.** (*pl.*) furnishings or accessories in a building. **4.** the trying on of clothes so that they can be adjusted to fit. —'**fittingly** *adv.*

five (faɪv) *n.* **1.** the cardinal number that is the sum of four and one. **2.** a numeral, 5, V, representing this number. **3.** the amount or quantity that is one greater than four. **4.** something representing or consisting of five units, such as a playing card with five symbols on it. ~*det.* **5.** amounting to five. ~See also **fives.** —**fifth** (fɪfθ) *adj., n.*

five-eighth *n. Austral. & N.Z.* a rugby player positioned between the halfbacks and three-quarters.

fivefold ('faɪv,fəʊld) *adj.* **1.** having five times as many or as much. **2.** composed of five parts. ~*adv.* **3.** five times as many or as much.

fivepins ('faɪv,pɪnz) *n.* (*functioning as sing.*) a bowling game played esp. in Canada.

fiver ('faɪvə) *n. Brit. informal.* a five-pound note.

fives (faɪvz) *n.* (*functioning as sing.*) a ball game similar to squash but played with bats or the hands.

fix (fɪks) *vb.* **1.** to make or become firm, stable, or secure. **2.** to place permanently. **3.** to settle definitely; decide. **4.** to hold or direct (eyes, etc.) steadily. **5.** to rivet or transfix: *he fixed the woman with his gaze.* **6.** to make rigid: *to fix one's jaw.* **7.** to repair. **8.** *Informal.* to influence (a person, etc.) unfairly, as by bribery. **9.** *Informal.* to give (someone) his just deserts: *that'll fix him.* **10.** *Informal, chiefly U.S. & Canad.* to prepare: *to fix a meal.* **11.** *Photog.* to treat (a film, plate, or paper) with fixer to make the image permanent. **12.** to convert (atmospheric nitrogen) into nitrogen compounds. **13.** *Slang.* to inject a narcotic drug. ~*n.* **14.** *Informal.* a predicament; dilemma. **15.** the ascertaining of the navigational position, as of a ship, by radar, etc. **16.** *Slang.* an injection of a narcotic. ~See also **fix up.**

fixation (fɪk'seɪʃən) *n.* **1.** a preoccupation or obsession. **2.** *Psychol.* a strong attachment of a person to another person or an object in early life. **3.** *Chem.* the conversion of nitrogen in the air into a compound, esp. a fertilizer. —**fix'ated** *adj.*

fixative ('fɪksətɪv) *n.* **1.** a fluid sprayed over drawings to prevent smudging. **2.** a substance added to a perfume to make it less volatile.

fixed (fɪkst) *adj.* **1.** attached or placed so as to be immovable. **2.** stable: *fixed prices.* **3.** steadily directed: *a fixed expression.* **4.** established as to relative position: *a fixed point.* **5.** always at the same time. **6.** (of ideas) firmly maintained. **7.** *Informal.* equipped or provided for, as with money or possessions. **8.** *Informal.* illegally arranged: *a fixed trial.* —**fixedly** ('fɪksɪdlɪ) *adv.*

fixed star *n.* an extremely distant star that appears to be almost stationary.

fixer ('fɪksə) *n.* **1.** *Photog.* a solution used to make an image permanent. **2.** *Slang.* a person who makes arrangements, esp. illegally.

fixity ('fɪksɪtɪ) *n., pl.* **-ties.** the state or quality of being fixed.

fixture ('fɪkstʃə) *n.* **1.** an object firmly fixed in place, esp. a household appliance. **2.** a person regarded as fixed in a particular place or position. **3.** *Chiefly Brit.* **a.** a sports match. **b.** the date of it.

fix up *vb.* **1.** to arrange. **2.** (often foll. by *with*) to provide.

fizz (fɪz) *vb.* **1.** to make a hissing or bubbling sound. **2.** (of a drink) to produce bubbles of carbon dioxide. ~*n.* **3.** a hissing or bubbling sound. **4.** effervescence. **5.** any effervescent drink. —'**fizzy** *adj.* —'**fizziness** *n.*

fizzle ('fɪz²l) *vb.* **1.** to make a hissing or bubbling sound. **2.** (often foll. by *out*) *In-*

formal. to fail or die out, esp. after a promising start.

fjord (fjɔːd) *n.* a long narrow inlet of the sea between high cliffs, esp. in Norway.

FL *or* **Fla.** Florida.

fl. **1.** floor. **2.** fluid.

flab (flæb) *n.* unsightly or unwanted fat on the body.

flabbergast (ˈflæbəˌgɑːst) *vb.* (*usually passive*) *Informal.* to amaze utterly; astound.

flabby (ˈflæbɪ) *adj.* **-bier, -biest.** **1.** loose or yielding: *flabby muscles.* **2.** having flabby flesh. **3.** weak. —**ˈflabbiness** *n.*

flaccid (ˈflæksɪd) *adj.* soft and limp. —**flacˈcidity** *n.*

flag[1] (flæg) *n.* **1.** a piece of cloth often attached to a pole, used as an emblem or for signalling. **2.** *Brit., Austral., & N.Z.* the part of a taximeter that is raised when a taxi is for hire. ~*vb.* **flagging, flagged.** **3.** to mark with a tag or sticker. **4.** (often foll. by *down*) to signal (a vehicle) to stop. **5.** to send (information) by flag.

flag[2] (flæg) *n.* any of various plants that have long swordlike leaves, esp. an iris.

flag[3] (flæg) *vb.* **flagging, flagged.** **1.** to lose enthusiasm or energy. **2.** to become limp; droop. —**ˈflagging** *adj.*

flag[4] (flæg) *n.* **1.** short for **flagstone.** ~*vb.* **flagging, flagged.** **2.** to pave with flagstones.

flag day *n.* a day on which money is collected by a charity and small stickers are given to contributors.

flagellate *vb.* (ˈflædʒɪˌleɪt). **1.** to whip. ~*adj.* (ˈflædʒɪlɪt). **2.** possessing one or more flagella. **3.** whiplike. —**ˌflagelˈlation** *n.*

flagellum (fləˈdʒɛləm) *n., pl.* **-la** (-lə) *or* **-lums.** **1.** *Biol.* a long whiplike outgrowth that acts as an organ of movement. **2.** *Bot.* a long thin shoot or runner.

flageolet (ˌflædʒəˈlɛt) *n.* a high-pitched musical instrument of the recorder family.

flag of convenience *n.* a foreign flag flown by a ship registered in that country to gain financial or legal advantage.

flagon (ˈflægən) *n.* **1.** a large bottle of wine, cider, etc. **2.** a container for liquids with a handle, spout, and narrow neck.

flagpole (ˈflægˌpəʊl) *or* **flagstaff** (ˈflægˌstɑːf) *n.* a pole on which a flag is flown.

flagrant (ˈfleɪgrənt) *adj.* openly outrageous. —**ˈflagrancy** *n.*

flagship (ˈflægˌʃɪp) *n.* **1.** a ship aboard which the commander of a fleet is quartered. **2.** the most important ship belonging to a shipping company.

flagstone (ˈflægˌstəʊn) *n.* a flat slab of hard stone for paving.

flag-waving *n. Informal.* an emotional appeal to patriotic feeling.

flail (fleɪl) *n.* **1.** an implement used for threshing grain, consisting of a long handle with a free-swinging bar attached to it. ~*vb.* **2.** to beat with or as if with a flail. **3.** to thresh about: *with arms flailing.*

flair (flɛə) *n.* **1.** natural ability; talent. **2.** originality and stylishness.

flak (flæk) *n.* **1.** anti-aircraft fire. **2.** adverse criticism.

flake (fleɪk) *n.* **1.** a small thin piece chipped off an object or substance. **2.** a small piece: *a flake of snow.* ~*vb.* **3.** to peel or cause to peel off in flakes. **4.** to break into small thin pieces: *simmer the fish until it flakes easily.* —**ˈflaky** *adj.*

flake out *vb. Informal.* to collapse or fall asleep as through extreme exhaustion.

flambé (ˈflɑːmbeɪ) *adj.* (of food) served in flaming brandy, etc.

flamboyant (flæmˈbɔɪənt) *adj.* **1.** elaborate or extravagant; showy. **2.** exuberant or ostentatious: *flamboyant gestures.* —**flamˈboyance** *n.*

flame (fleɪm) *n.* **1.** a hot luminous body of burning gas coming in flickering streams from burning material. **2.** (*often pl.*) the state of burning: *to burst into flames.* **3.** a strong reddish-orange colour. **4.** intense passion. ~*vb.* **5.** to burn brightly. **6.** to become red or fiery. **7.** to become angry or excited.

flamenco (fləˈmɛŋkəʊ) *n., pl.* **-cos.** a very rhythmical type of dance music for vocal soloist and guitar.

flame-thrower *n.* a weapon that ejects a stream or spray of burning fluid.

flaming (ˈfleɪmɪŋ) *adj.* **1.** burning with flames. **2.** glowing brightly. **3.** intense; heated: *a flaming row.* **4.** *Informal.* damned: *you flaming idiot.*

flamingo (fləˈmɪŋgəʊ) *n., pl.* **-gos** *or* **-goes.** a large wading bird with pink-and-red plumage and long thin legs.

flammable (ˈflæməbˀl) *adj.* easily set on fire; inflammable. —**ˌflammaˈbility** *n.*
Usage. Either *flammable* or *inflammable* can be used when referring to the properties of materials. *Flammable* is, however, often preferred for warning labels as there is less likelihood of misunderstanding (*inflammable* being sometimes taken to mean *not flammable*). The word that does mean *not flammable* is *nonflammable.*

flan (flæn) *n.* an open pastry or sponge tart filled with fruit or a savoury mixture.

flange (flændʒ) *n.* a projecting collar or rim on an object for strengthening it or for attaching it to another object.

flank (flæŋk) *n.* **1.** the side of a man or animal between the ribs and the hip. **2.** a cut of beef from the flank. **3.** the side of a naval or military formation. ~*vb.* **4.** to be positioned at the side of (a person or thing).

flannel (ˈflænˀl) *n.* **1.** a soft light woollen fabric used for clothing. **2.** (*pl.*) trousers made of flannel. **3.** *Brit.* a small piece of towelling cloth used to wash the face. **4.** *Brit. informal.* evasive talk that avoids giving any commitment or direct answer. *~vb.* **-nelling, -nelled** *or U.S.* **-neling, -neled. 5.** *Brit. informal.* to flatter or talk evasively.

flannelette (ˌflænˈlɛt) *n.* a cotton imitation of flannel.

flap (flæp) *vb.* **flapping, flapped. 1.** to move backwards and forwards or up and down, like a bird's wings in flight. **2.** *Informal.* to become agitated or flustered. *~n.* **3.** the action of or noise made by flapping. **4.** a piece of material attached at one edge and usually used to cover an opening, as on a pocket. **5.** a hinged section of an aircraft wing that is raised or lowered to control the aircraft's speed. **6.** *Informal.* a state of panic or agitation.

flapjack (ˈflæpˌdʒæk) *n.* a chewy biscuit made with rolled oats.

flapper (ˈflæpə) *n.* (in the 1920s) a young unconventional woman.

flare (flɛə) *vb.* **1.** to burn with an unsteady or sudden bright flame. **2.** (of temper, violence, or trouble) to break out suddenly. **3.** to spread outwards from a narrow to a wider shape. *~n.* **4.** an unsteady flame. **5.** a sudden burst of flame. **6. a.** a blaze of light used to illuminate, signal distress, alert, etc. **b.** the device producing such a blaze. **7.** a spreading shape.

flare up *vb.* **1.** to burst suddenly into fire. **2.** *Informal.* to burst into anger.

flash (flæʃ) *n.* **1.** a sudden short blaze of intense light or flame. **2.** a sudden occurrence or display, esp. one suggestive of brilliance: *a flash of understanding.* **3.** a very brief time: *over in a flash.* **4.** a short unscheduled news announcement. **5.** *Chiefly Brit.* an emblem on a uniform or vehicle to identify its military formation. **6.** *Photog.* short for **flashlight. 7. flash in the pan.** a project, person, etc., that enjoys only short-lived success. *~adj.* **8.** *Informal.* ostentatious or vulgar. **9.** *Informal.* relating to the criminal underworld. **10.** brief and rapid: *flash freezing.* *~vb.* **11.** to burst or cause to burst suddenly into flame. **12.** to emit or cause to emit light suddenly or intermittently. **13.** to move very fast. **14.** to come rapidly (into the mind or vision). **15. a.** to signal very fast: *to flash a message.* **b.** to signal by use of a light, such as car headlights. **16.** *Informal.* to display ostentatiously: *to flash money around.* **17.** *Informal.* to show briefly. **18.** *Brit. slang.* to expose oneself indecently. —ˈflasher *n.*

flashback (ˈflæʃˌbæk) *n.* a transition in a novel, film, etc., to an earlier event.

flashbulb (ˈflæʃˌbʌlb) *n.* *Photog.* a small light bulb that produces a bright flash of light.

flash flood *n.* a sudden short-lived torrent.

flashing (ˈflæʃɪŋ) *n.* a weatherproof material used to cover the joins in a roof.

flashlight (ˈflæʃˌlaɪt) *n.* **1.** *Photog.* the brief bright light emitted by a flashbulb. **2.** *Chiefly U.S. & Canad.* a torch.

flash point *n.* **1.** the lowest temperature at which the vapour above a liquid can be ignited. **2.** a critical time beyond which a situation will inevitably erupt into violence.

flashy (ˈflæʃɪ) *adj.* **flashier, flashiest.** gaudy and ostentatious. —ˈflashily *adv.* —ˈflashiness *n.*

flask (flɑːsk) *n.* **1.** a bottle with a narrow neck, esp. used in a laboratory. **2.** a small flat container for alcoholic drink designed to be carried in a pocket. **3.** See **vacuum flask.**

flat¹ (flæt) *adj.* **flatter, flattest. 1.** horizontal; level: *a flat roof.* **2.** even or smooth: *a flat surface.* **3.** lying stretched out at full length. **4.** (of a tyre) deflated. **5.** (of shoes) having an unraised heel. **6.** without qualification; total: *a flat denial.* **7.** fixed: *a flat rate.* **8.** neither more nor less; exact: *a flat thirty minutes.* **9.** unexciting: *a flat joke.* **10.** without variation or emotion: *a flat voice.* **11.** (of drinks) having lost effervescence. **12.** (of a battery) fully discharged. **13.** (of paint) without gloss. **14.** *Music.* **a.** denoting a note that has been lowered in pitch by one chromatic semitone: *B flat.* **b.** (of an instrument, voice, etc.) out of tune by being too low in pitch. *~adv.* **15.** in or into a level or flat position: *he held his hand out flat.* **16.** completely; absolutely. **17.** exactly: *in three minutes flat.* **18.** *Music.* **a.** lower than a standard pitch. **b.** too low in pitch: *she sings flat.* **19. fall flat (on one's face).** to fail to achieve a desired effect. **20. flat out.** *Informal.* with maximum speed and effort. *~n.* **21.** a flat object or part. **22.** (*often pl.*) low-lying land, esp. a marsh. **23.** (*often pl.*) a mud bank exposed at low tide. **24.** *Music.* **a.** an accidental that lowers the pitch of a note by one semitone. Usual symbol: ♭ **b.** a note affected by this accidental. **25.** *Theatre.* a wooden frame covered with painted canvas, used to form part of a stage setting. **26.** a punctured car tyre. **27.** (*often cap.;* preceded by *the*) *Chiefly Brit.* the season of flat racing. —ˈflatly *adv.*

flat² (flæt) *n.* a set of rooms forming a home entirely on one floor of a building.

flatfish (ˈflætˌfɪʃ) *n., pl.* **-fish** *or* **-fishes.** a sea fish, such as the sole, which has a flat body with both eyes on the uppermost side.

flat-footed (ˌflætˈfʊtɪd) *adj.* **1.** having less than the usual degree of arching in the insteps of the feet. **2.** *Informal.* clumsy or insensitive.

flatiron (ˈflætˌaɪən) *n.* (formerly) an iron

for pressing clothes that was heated by being placed on a stove.

flatlet ('flætlɪt) n. a small flat.

flat racing n. the racing of horses on racecourses without jumps.

flat spin n. **1.** an aircraft spin in which the longitudinal axis is more nearly horizontal than vertical. **2.** *Informal.* a state of confusion.

flatten ('flæt²n) vb. **1.** to make or become flat or flatter. **2.** *Informal.* **a.** to knock down or injure. **b.** to crush or subdue.

flatter ('flætə) vb. **1.** to praise insincerely, esp. in order to win favour. **2.** to show to advantage: *that dress flatters her.* **3.** to make (a person) appear more attractive than in reality. **4.** to gratify the vanity of (a person). **5. flatter oneself.** to believe, perhaps mistakenly, something good about oneself. —'**flatterer** n.

flattery ('flætərɪ) n., pl. **-teries.** excessive or insincere praise.

flatulent ('flætjulənt) adj. **1.** suffering from or caused by too much gas in the stomach or intestines. **2.** pretentious. —'**flatulence** n.

flatworm ('flæt,wɜːm) n. a worm, such as a tapeworm, with a flattened body.

flaunt (flɔːnt) vb. to display (possessions, oneself, etc.) ostentatiously.
Usage. see **flout.**

flautist ('flɔːtɪst) n. a player of the flute.

flavour or U.S. **flavor** ('fleɪvə) n. **1.** taste perceived in food or liquid in the mouth. **2.** a distinctive quality or atmosphere. ~vb. **3.** to impart a flavour to. —'**flavourless** or U.S. '**flavorless** adj.

flavouring or U.S. **flavoring** ('fleɪvərɪŋ) n. a substance used to flavour food.

flaw (flɔː) n. **1.** an imperfection or blemish. **2.** a mistake in something that makes it invalid: *a flaw in the argument.* —**flawed** adj. —'**flawless** adj.

flax (flæks) n. **1.** a plant that has blue flowers and is cultivated for its seeds and the fibres of its stems. **2.** this fibre, made into linen fabrics. **3.** N.Z. a swamp plant producing a fibre that is used by Maoris for decorative work, baskets, etc.

flaxen ('flæksən) adj. **1.** of flax. **2.** pale yellow: *flaxen hair.*

flay (fleɪ) vb. **1.** to strip off the skin of, esp. by whipping. **2.** to attack with savage criticism.

flea (fliː) n. **1.** a small wingless jumping insect feeding on the blood of mammals and birds. **2. flea in one's ear.** *Informal.* a sharp rebuke.

fleabite ('fliː,baɪt) n. **1.** the bite of a flea. **2.** a slight annoyance or discomfort.

flea-bitten adj. **1.** bitten by or infested with fleas. **2.** *Informal.* shabby or decrepit.

flea market n. an open-air market selling cheap second-hand goods.

fleapit ('fliː,pɪt) n. *Informal.* a shabby cinema or theatre.

fleck (flɛk) n. **1.** a small marking or streak. **2.** a speck: *a fleck of dust.* ~vb. **3.** to speckle.

fled (flɛd) vb. the past of **flee.**

fledged (flɛdʒd) adj. **1.** (of young birds) able to fly. **2.** qualified and competent: *a fully fledged instructor.*

fledgling or **fledgeling** ('flɛdʒlɪŋ) n. a young bird that has grown feathers.

flee (fliː) vb. **fleeing, fled. 1.** to run away from (a place, danger, etc.). **2.** to run or move quickly.

fleece (fliːs) n. **1.** the coat of wool that covers a sheep. **2.** the wool removed from a sheep at one shearing. **3.** sheepskin or a fabric with soft pile, used as a lining for coats, etc. ~vb. **4.** to defraud or charge exorbitantly. **5.** same as **shear** (sense 1). —'**fleecy** adj.

fleet[1] (fliːt) n. **1.** a number of warships organized as a tactical unit. **2.** all the warships of a nation. **3.** a number of vehicles under the same ownership.

fleet[2] (fliːt) adj. rapid in movement; swift.

fleet chief petty officer n. a noncommissioned officer in a navy.

fleeting ('fliːtɪŋ) adj. rapid and soon passing: *a fleeting glimpse.* —'**fleetingly** adv.

Fleming ('flɛmɪŋ) n. a person from Flanders or Flemish-speaking Belgium.

Flemish ('flɛmɪʃ) n. **1.** one of the two official languages of Belgium. **2. the Flemish.** *(functioning as pl.)* the Flemings collectively. ~adj. **3.** of or characteristic of Flanders, the Flemings, or their language.

flesh (flɛʃ) n. **1.** the soft part of the body of an animal or human, esp. muscular tissue. **2.** *Informal.* excess weight; fat. **3.** the edible tissue of animals as opposed to that of fish or, sometimes, fowl. **4.** the thick soft part of a fruit or vegetable. **5.** the human body and its physical or sensual nature as opposed to the soul. **6.** mankind in general. **7.** a yellowish-pink colour. **8. in the flesh.** in person; actually present. **9. one's own flesh and blood.** one's own family.

fleshly ('flɛʃlɪ) adj. **-lier, -liest. 1.** relating to the body; carnal: *fleshly desire.* **2.** worldly as opposed to spiritual.

fleshpots ('flɛʃ,pɒts) pl. n. Often facetious. **1.** luxurious living. **2.** places where bodily desires are gratified.

flesh wound (wuːnd) n. a wound affecting superficial tissues.

fleshy ('flɛʃɪ) adj. **fleshier, fleshiest. 1.** plump. **2.** resembling flesh. **3.** *Bot.* (of some fruits) thick and pulpy. —'**fleshiness** n.

fleur-de-lis or **fleur-de-lys** (,flɜːdə'liː) n., pl. **fleurs-de-lis** or **fleurs-de-lys** (,flɜːdə'liːz). a representation of a lily with three distinct petals.

flew (fluː) *vb.* the past tense of **fly**[1].

flews (fluːz) *pl. n.* the fleshy hanging upper lip of a bloodhound or similar dog.

flex (flɛks) *n.* **1.** *Brit.* a flexible insulated electric cable. ~*vb.* **2.** to bend. **3.** to contract (a muscle) or (of a muscle) to contract.

flexible ('flɛksɪb'l) *adj.* **1.** able to be bent easily without breaking. **2.** adaptable to changing circumstances. —,**flexi'bility** *n.* —'**flexibly** *adv.*

flexitime ('flɛksɪ,taɪm) *n.* a system permitting flexibility of working hours at the beginning or end of the day, provided an agreed total is worked.

flibbertigibbet ('flɪbətɪ,dʒɪbɪt) *n.* an irresponsible, silly, gossipy person.

flick (flɪk) *vb.* **1.** to touch or move with or as if with the finger or hand in a quick jerky movement. **2.** (foll. by *through*) to look at (a book or magazine) quickly or idly. ~*n.* **3.** a tap or quick stroke with the fingers, a whip, etc.

flicker ('flɪkə) *vb.* **1.** to shine with an unsteady or intermittent light. **2.** to move quickly to and fro. ~*n.* **3.** an unsteady or brief light. **4.** a brief or faint indication of emotion.

flick knife *n.* a knife with a retractable blade that springs out when a button is pressed.

flicks (flɪks) *pl. n. Slang, old-fashioned.* the cinema.

flier *or* **flyer** ('flaɪə) *n.* **1.** a person or thing that flies or moves very fast. **2.** an aviator.

flight[1] (flaɪt) *n.* **1.** the act or manner of flying. **2.** a journey made by a flying animal or object. **3.** a group of flying birds or aircraft. **4.** an aircraft flying on a scheduled journey. **5.** a mental soaring above the everyday world: *a flight of fancy.* **6.** a feather or plastic attachment to an arrow or dart. **7.** a set of stairs between one landing and the next.

flight[2] (flaɪt) *n.* **1.** the act of running away, as from danger. **2. put to flight.** to cause to run away. **3. take (to) flight.** to run away.

flight deck *n.* **1.** the crew compartment in an airliner. **2.** the upper deck of an aircraft carrier from which aircraft take off.

flightless ('flaɪtlɪs) *adj.* (of certain birds and insects) unable to fly.

flight lieutenant *n.* a junior commissioned officer in an air force.

flight recorder *n.* an electronic device in an aircraft for storing information concerning its performance in flight. It is often used to determine the cause of a crash. Also called: **black box.**

flight sergeant *n.* a noncommissioned officer in an air force.

flighty ('flaɪtɪ) *adj.* **flightier, flightiest.** frivolous and irresponsible. —'**flightiness** *n.*

flimsy ('flɪmzɪ) *adj.* **-sier, -siest. 1.** not strong or substantial. **2.** light and thin: *a flimsy dress.* **3.** unconvincing; weak: *a flimsy excuse.* —'**flimsily** *adv.* —'**flimsiness** *n.*

flinch (flɪntʃ) *vb.* **1.** to draw back suddenly, as from pain; wince. **2.** (foll. by *from*) to shrink from; avoid: *he never flinched from his duty.*

fling (flɪŋ) *vb.* **flinging, flung. 1.** to throw with force. **2.** to put or send without warning: *to fling someone into jail.* **3.** to move or go hurriedly or violently: *he flung his arms up.* **4.** to put (something) somewhere hurriedly or carelessly. **5.** (usually foll. by *into*) to apply (oneself) with vigour (to). ~*n.* **6.** a short spell of self-indulgent enjoyment. **7.** a vigorous Scottish reel: *a Highland fling.*

flint (flɪnt) *n.* **1.** a very hard stone that produces sparks when struck with steel. **2.** any piece of flint, esp. one used as a primitive tool. **3.** a small piece of an iron alloy, used in cigarette lighters. —'**flinty** *adj.*

flintlock ('flɪnt,lɒk) *n.* an obsolete gun in which the powder was lit by a spark produced by a flint.

flip (flɪp) *vb.* **flipping, flipped. 1.** to throw (something light or small) carelessly. **2.** to throw (an object such as a coin) so that it turns in the air. **3.** (foll. by *through*) to look at (a book or magazine) idly. **4.** Also: **flip one's lid.** *Slang.* to fly into an emotional outburst. ~*n.* **5.** a snap or tap, usually with the fingers. **6.** any alcoholic drink containing beaten egg. ~*adj.* **7.** *Informal.* flippant or pert.

flip-flop *n.* a rubber-soled sandal attached to the foot by a thong between the big toe and the next toe.

flippant ('flɪpənt) *adj.* treating serious matters with inappropriate light-heartedness or lack of respect. —'**flippancy** *n.*

flipper ('flɪpə) *n.* **1.** the flat broad limb of seals, whales, and other aquatic animals specialized for swimming. **2.** (*often pl.*) either of a pair of rubber paddle-like devices worn on the feet as an aid in swimming.

flirt (flɜːt) *vb.* **1.** to behave amorously towards someone without emotional commitment. **2.** (foll. by *with*) to deal playfully or carelessly (with something dangerous or serious). ~*n.* **3.** a person who flirts. —**flir'tation** *n.* —**flir'tatious** *adj.*

flit (flɪt) *vb.* **flitting, flitted. 1.** to fly or move along rapidly and lightly. **2.** to pass quickly: *a memory flitted into his mind.* **3.** *Scot. & N English dialect.* to move house. **4.** *Brit. informal.* to depart hurriedly and stealthily in order to avoid debts. ~*n.* **5.** the act of flitting.

flitch
319
floss

flitch (flɪtʃ) *n.* a side of pork salted and cured.

flitter ('flɪtə) *vb.* same as **flutter.**

flittermouse ('flɪtə,maʊs) *n., pl.* **-mice.** *Dialect.* a bat.

float (fləʊt) *vb.* **1.** to rest on the surface of a fluid without sinking. **2.** to move lightly or freely across a surface or through air or water. **3.** to move about aimlessly, esp. in the mind: *vague ideas floated through his head.* **4. a.** to launch (a commercial enterprise, etc.). **b.** to offer for sale on the stock market. **5.** *Finance.* to allow (a currency) to fluctuate against other currencies. ~*n.* **6.** *Angling.* an indicator attached to a baited line that moves when a fish bites. **7.** a structure allowing an aircraft to land on water. **8.** a motor vehicle used to carry a tableau in a parade. **9.** a small delivery vehicle: *a milk float.* **10.** *Austral. & N.Z.* a vehicle for transporting horses. **11.** a sum of money used to cover small expenses or provide change. **12.** the hollow floating ball of a ballcock.

floatation (fləʊ'teɪʃən) *n.* same as **flotation.**

floating ('fləʊtɪŋ) *adj.* **1.** moving about; not settled: *a floating population.* **2.** (of an organ or part) displaced or abnormally movable: *a floating kidney.* **3.** uncommitted: *floating voters.* **4.** *Finance.* **a.** (of capital) available for current use. **b.** (of a currency) free to fluctuate against other currencies.

floating rib *n.* a lower rib not attached to the breastbone.

floats (fləʊts) *pl. n. Theatre.* footlights.

flocculent ('flɒkjʊlənt) *adj.* like wool; in tufts. —**'flocculence** *n.*

flock[1] (flɒk) *n.* (*sometimes functioning as pl.*) **1.** a group of animals of one kind, esp. sheep or birds. **2.** a large number of people. **3.** a body of Christians regarded as the pastoral charge of a priest. ~*vb.* **4.** to gather together or move in large numbers.

flock[2] (flɒk) *n.* **1.** waste from fabrics such as cotton or wool used for stuffing mattresses. **2.** very small tufts of wool applied to wallpaper to give a raised pattern.

floe (fləʊ) *n.* See **ice floe.**

flog (flɒg) *vb.* **flogging, flogged. 1.** to beat harshly, esp. with a whip or stick. **2.** *Brit. slang.* to sell. **3. flog a dead horse.** *Chiefly Brit.* to waste one's energy.

flood (flʌd) *n.* **1.** an overflowing of water on an area that is normally dry. **2.** a great outpouring: *a flood of words.* **3.** the rising of the tide from low to high water. **4.** *Theatre.* short for **floodlight.** ~*vb.* **5.** (of water) to cover (land) or (of land) to be covered. **6.** to fill to overflowing: *cheap goods flooded the market.* **7.** to flow; surge: *relief flooded through him.* **8.** to supply excess petrol to (a petrol engine) so that it cannot work properly. **9.** to bleed profusely from the womb.

Flood (flʌd) *n. Old Testament. the.* the flood from which Noah and his family and livestock were saved in the ark (Genesis 7–8).

floodgate ('flʌd,geɪt) *n.* **1.** a gate used to control the flow of water. **2.** (*often pl.*) a control against an outpouring of emotion.

floodlight ('flʌd,laɪt) *n.* **1.** a lamp that casts a broad intense light, used in the theatre or to illuminate sports grounds or the exterior of buildings. ~*vb.* **-lighting, -lit. 2.** to illuminate by floodlight.

floor (flɔː) *n.* **1.** the inner lower surface of a room. **2.** a storey of a building. **3.** a flat bottom surface: *the sea floor.* **4.** that part of a legislative hall in which debate is conducted. **5.** the right to speak in a legislative body (esp. in **get, have,** *or* **be given the floor**). **6.** a minimum limit. ~*vb.* **7.** to cover with or construct a floor. **8.** to knock to the ground. **9.** *Informal.* to disconcert or defeat.

floorboard ('flɔː,bɔːd) *n.* one of the boards forming a floor.

floor plan *n.* a scale drawing of the arrangement of rooms on one floor of a building.

floor show *n.* a series of entertainments, such as singing and dancing, in a nightclub.

floozy, floozie, *or* **floosie** ('fluːzɪ) *n., pl.* **-zies** *or* **-sies.** *Slang.* a disreputable woman.

flop (flɒp) *vb.* **flopping, flopped. 1.** to bend, fall, or collapse loosely or carelessly. **2.** to fall or move with a sudden noise. **3.** *Informal.* to fail: *the scheme flopped.* ~*n.* **4.** the act of flopping. **5.** *Informal.* a complete failure. —**'floppy** *adj.*

floppy disk *n.* a flexible magnetic disk that stores data in the memory of a digital computer.

flora ('flɔːrə) *n.* all the plant life of a given place or time.

floral ('flɔːrəl) *adj.* decorated with or consisting of flowers or patterns of flowers.

Florentine ('florən,taɪn) *adj.* **1.** of or relating to Florence, in Italy. ~*n.* **2.** a person from Florence.

floret ('flɔːrɪt) *n.* a small flower, esp. one of many making up a composite flower.

floribunda (,florɪ'bʌndə) *n.* a cultivated hybrid rose whose flowers grow in large sprays.

florid ('florɪd) *adj.* **1.** having a red or flushed complexion. **2.** excessively ornate; flowery.

florin ('florɪn) *n.* a former British coin, equivalent to ten (new) pence.

florist ('florɪst) *n.* a person who grows or deals in flowers.

floss (flɒs) *n.* **1.** fine silky fibres, such as those obtained from silkworm cocoons. **2.** See **dental floss.** —**'flossy** *adj.*

flotation *or* **floatation** (fləʊˈteɪʃən) *n.* the launching or financing of a commercial enterprise by bond or share issues.

flotilla (fləˈtɪlə) *n.* a small fleet or a fleet of small vessels.

flotsam (ˈflɒtsəm) *n.* **1.** wreckage from a ship found floating. **2. flotsam and jetsam. a.** odds and ends. **b.** homeless or vagrant people.

flounce[1] (flaʊns) *vb.* **1.** to move or go with emphatic movements. ~*n.* **2.** the act of flouncing.

flounce[2] (flaʊns) *n.* an ornamental gathered ruffle on a garment.

flounder[1] (ˈflaʊndə) *vb.* **1.** to move with difficulty, as in mud. **2.** to behave or speak in an awkward, confused way.

flounder[2] (ˈflaʊndə) *n., pl.* **-der** *or* **-ders.** an edible flatfish.

flour (ˈflaʊə) *n.* **1.** a powder prepared by grinding grain, esp. wheat. ~*vb.* **2.** to sprinkle (food or utensils) with flour. —ˈ**floury** *adj.*

flourish (ˈflʌrɪʃ) *vb.* **1.** to thrive; prosper. **2.** to be at the peak of development. **3.** to wave with sweeping strokes. ~*n.* **4.** a dramatic waving or sweeping movement: *he drew his knife with a flourish.* **5.** an ornamental curly line in writing. **6.** a grandiose passage of music. —ˈ**flourishing** *adj.*

flout (flaʊt) *vb.* to show contempt (for).
Usage. Confusion sometimes arises between *flout* and *flaunt* although the meanings of the words are quite different. *Flout,* to defy or disregard, is typically used in relation to law or authority: *be prepared to flout convention — serve red wine with your fish course. Flaunt* implies a deliberate and ostentatious displaying of possessions, abilities, etc.: *she flaunted her large engagement ring.*

flow (fləʊ) *vb.* **1.** (of liquids) to move in a stream. **2.** (of blood; electricity, etc.) to circulate. **3.** to move steadily and smoothly: *traffic flowing down the street.* **4.** to be produced effortlessly: *ideas flowed from her pen.* **5.** to hang freely: *her hair flowed down her back.* **6.** to be abundant: *wine flows at their parties.* **7.** (of tide water) to rise. ~*n.* **8.** the act, rate, or manner of flowing: *a fast flow.* **9.** a continuous stream or discharge. **10.** the advancing of the tide.

flow chart *or* **sheet** *n.* a diagrammatic representation of the sequence of operations in an industrial process, computer program, etc.

flower (ˈflaʊə) *n.* **1.** the part of a plant that is, usually, brightly coloured, and quickly fades, producing seeds. **2.** a plant grown for its colourful flowers. **3.** the best or finest part. **4. in flower.** with flowers open. ~*vb.* **5.** to produce flowers; bloom. **6.** to reach full growth or maturity.

flowered (ˈflaʊəd) *adj.* decorated with flowers or a floral design.

flowerpot (ˈflaʊəˌpɒt) *n.* a pot in which plants are grown.

flowery (ˈflaʊərɪ) *adj.* **1.** decorated with flowers or floral patterns. **2.** (of language or style) elaborate. —ˈ**floweriness** *n.*

flown (fləʊn) *vb.* the past participle of **fly**[1].

flu (fluː) *n. Informal.* short for **influenza.**

fluctuate (ˈflʌktjʊˌeɪt) *vb.* to change frequently and erratically: *prices fluctuated.* —ˌ**fluctuˈation** *n.*

flue (fluː) *n.* a shaft, tube, or pipe, as in a chimney, used to carry off smoke or gas.

fluent (ˈfluːənt) *adj.* **1.** able to speak or write with ease: *a fluent reader; fluent in French.* **2.** spoken or written with ease. —ˈ**fluency** *n.* —ˈ**fluently** *adv.*

fluff (flʌf) *n.* **1.** soft light particles, such as the down of cotton or wool. **2.** *Informal.* a mistake, esp. in speaking or reading lines. ~*vb.* **3.** to make or become soft and puffy. **4.** *Informal.* to make a mistake in performing. —ˈ**fluffiness** *n.* —ˈ**fluffy** *adj.*

fluid (ˈfluːɪd) *n.* **1.** a substance, such as a liquid or gas, that can flow and has no fixed shape. ~*adj.* **2.** capable of flowing and easily changing shape. **3.** constantly changing or apt to change. —**fluˈidity** *n.*

fluid ounce *n.* **1.** *Brit.* one twentieth of an Imperial pint. **2.** *U.S.* one sixteenth of a U.S. pint.

fluke[1] (fluːk) *n.* an accidental stroke of luck. —ˈ**fluky** *adj.*

fluke[2] (fluːk) *n.* **1.** a flat bladelike projection at the end of the arm of an anchor. **2.** either of the two lobes of the tail of a whale.

fluke[3] (fluːk) *n.* any parasitic flatworm, such as the liver fluke.

flummery (ˈflʌmərɪ) *n., pl.* **-meries. 1.** *Informal.* meaningless flattery. **2.** *Chiefly Brit.* a cold pudding of oatmeal and milk.

flummox (ˈflʌməks) *vb.* to perplex or bewilder.

flung (flʌŋ) *vb.* the past of **fling.**

flunk (flʌŋk) *vb. Informal, chiefly U.S., Canad., & N.Z.* to fail (an examination, course, etc.).

flunky *or* **flunkey** (ˈflʌŋkɪ) *n., pl.* **flunkies** *or* **flunkeys. 1.** a servile follower. **2.** a person who performs menial tasks. **3.** a manservant in livery.

fluor (ˈfluːɔ) *n.* same as **fluorspar.**

fluoresce (ˌfluəˈrɛs) *vb.* to exhibit fluorescence.

fluorescence (ˌfluəˈrɛsəns) *n.* **1.** *Physics.* the emission of light from atoms or molecules that are bombarded by particles, such as electrons, or by radiation from a separate source. **2.** the radiation emitted as a result of fluorescence. —ˌ**fluoˈrescent** *adj.*

fluorescent lamp *n.* a lamp in which ultraviolet radiation from an electrical gas discharge causes a thin layer of phosphor on a tube's inside surface to fluoresce.

fluoridate ('flʊərɪˌdeɪt) *vb.* to add fluoride to (water) as protection against tooth decay. —ˌfluori'dation *n.*

fluoride ('flʊəˌraɪd) *n.* any compound containing fluorine and another element or radical.

fluorinate ('flʊərɪˌneɪt) *vb.* to treat or combine with fluorine. —ˌfluori'nation *n.*

fluorine ('flʊəriːn) *n.* a toxic pungent pale yellow gas that is the most reactive of all the elements. Symbol: F

fluoroscopy (flʊə'rɒskəpɪ) *n.* same as **radioscopy.**

fluorspar ('flʊəˌspɑː), **fluor,** *or* U.S. & Canad. **fluorite** *n.* a white or colourless mineral, consisting of calcium fluoride in crystalline form: the chief ore of fluorine.

flurry ('flʌrɪ) *n., pl.* **-ries.** **1.** a sudden commotion. **2.** a light gust of wind or rain or fall of snow. ~*vb.* **-rying, -ried.** **3.** to confuse or bewilder.

flush¹ (flʌʃ) *vb.* **1.** to blush or cause to blush. **2.** to send a volume of water quickly through (a pipe) or into (a toilet) for cleansing. **3.** (*usually passive*) to elate: *flushed with success.* ~*n.* **4.** a rosy colour, esp. in the cheeks. **5.** a sudden flow, as of water. **6.** a feeling of elation: *in the first flush of enthusiasm.* **7.** freshness: *the flush of youth.*

flush² (flʌʃ) *adj.* **1.** level with another surface. **2.** *Informal.* having plenty of money. ~*adv.* **3.** so as to be level.

flush³ (flʌʃ) *vb.* to rouse (game) and put to flight.

flush⁴ (flʌʃ) *n.* (in poker and similar games) a hand containing only one suit.

fluster ('flʌstə) *vb.* **1.** to make or become nervous or upset. ~*n.* **2.** a state of confusion or agitation.

flute (fluːt) *n.* **1.** a wind instrument consisting of a tube of wood or metal with holes in the side stopped either by the fingers or keys. The breath is directed across a mouth hole in the side. **2.** *Archit.* a rounded shallow groove. ~*vb.* **3.** to produce or utter (sounds) in the tone of a flute. **4.** to make grooves in. —'**fluty** *adj.*

fluting ('fluːtɪŋ) *n.* a design or decoration of flutes on a column.

flutter ('flʌtə) *vb.* **1.** to wave rapidly. **2.** (of birds or butterflies) to flap the wings. **3.** to move with an irregular motion. **4.** *Pathol.* (of the heart) to beat abnormally rapidly. **5.** to move about restlessly. ~*n.* **6.** a quick flapping or vibrating motion. **7.** a state of nervous excitement or confusion. **8.** excited interest; stir. **9.** *Brit. informal.* a modest bet. **10.** *Pathol.* an abnormally rapid beating of the heart. **11.** *Electronics.* a

slow variation in pitch in a sound-reproducing system.

fluvial ('fluːvɪəl) *adj.* of or occurring in a river: *fluvial deposits.*

flux (flʌks) *n.* **1.** a flow or discharge. **2.** continuous change; instability. **3.** a substance mixed with a metal oxide to assist in fusion. **4.** *Physics.* **a.** the rate of flow of particles, energy, or a fluid. **b.** the strength of a field in a given area: *magnetic flux.*

fly¹ (flaɪ) *vb.* **flying, flew, flown.** **1.** (of birds, aircraft, etc.) to move through the air using aerodynamic forces. **2.** to travel over (an area of land or sea) in an aircraft. **3.** to operate (an aircraft). **4.** to float, flutter, display or be displayed in the air: *they flew the flag.* **5.** to transport or be transported through the air by aircraft, wind, etc. **6.** to move very quickly or suddenly: *the door flew open.* **7.** to pass swiftly: *time flies.* **8.** to escape from (an enemy or a place); flee. **9.** (foll. by *at* or *upon*) to attack a person. **10. fly a kite.** to release information or take a step in order to test public opinion. **11. fly high.** *Informal.* to have a high aim. **12. let fly.** *Informal.* **a.** to lose one's temper: *she really let fly at him.* **b.** to throw (an object). ~*n., pl.* **flies.** **13.** (*often pl.*) a closure that conceals a zip, buttons, or other fastening, as on trousers. **14.** a flap forming the entrance to a tent. **15.** (*pl.*) *Theatre.* the space above the stage, used for storing scenery.

fly² (flaɪ) *n., pl.* **flies.** **1.** any two-winged insect, esp. the housefly, characterized by active flight. **2.** any of various similar but unrelated insects, such as the dragonfly. **3.** *Angling.* a lure made from a fish-hook dressed with feathers to resemble a fly. **4. fly in the ointment.** *Informal.* a slight flaw that detracts from value or enjoyment. **5. fly on the wall.** a person who watches others, while not being noticed himself. **6. there are no flies on him, her,** etc. *Informal.* he, she, etc., is no fool.

fly³ (flaɪ) *adj. Slang, chiefly Brit.* knowing and sharp; smart.

flyaway ('flaɪəˌweɪ) *adj.* **1.** (of hair or clothing) fine and fluttering. **2.** frivolous.

flyblown ('flaɪˌbləʊn) *adj.* **1.** covered with blowfly eggs. **2.** contaminated; tainted.

fly-by-night *Informal.* ~*adj.* **1.** unreliable or untrustworthy, esp. in finance. ~*n.* **2.** an untrustworthy person.

flyer ('flaɪə) *n.* same as **flier.**

fly-fish *vb. Angling.* to fish using artificial flies as lures. —'**fly-ˌfishing** *n.*

flying ('flaɪɪŋ) *adj.* **1.** hurried: *a flying visit.* **2.** designed for fast action. **3.** hanging, waving, or floating freely: *flying hair.* ~*n.* **4.** the act of piloting, navigating, or travelling in an aircraft.

flying boat *n.* a seaplane in which the fuselage consists of a hull that provides buoyancy.

flying buttress *n.* a buttress supporting a wall by an arch that transmits the thrust outwards and downwards.

flying colours *pl. n.* conspicuous success; triumph: *he passed his test with flying colours.*

flying fish *n.* a fish of warm and tropical seas, with enlarged winglike pectoral fins used for gliding above the water.

flying fox *n.* **1.** any large fruit bat of tropical Africa and Asia. **2.** *Austral. & N.Z.* a cable mechanism used for transportation across a river, gorge, etc.

flying officer *n.* a junior commissioned officer in an air force.

flying saucer *n.* any unidentified disc-shaped flying object alleged to come from outer space.

flying squad *n.* a small group of police or soldiers ready to move into action quickly.

flying start *n.* **1.** a start to a race in which the competitor is already travelling at speed as he passes the starting line. **2.** any promising beginning.

flying wing *n.* (in Canadian football) the twelfth player, who has a variable position behind the scrimmage line.

flyleaf ('flaɪ‚liːf) *n., pl.* **-leaves.** the inner leaf of the endpaper of a book.

flyover ('flaɪ‚əʊvə) *n. Brit.* an intersection of two roads at which one is carried over the other by a bridge.

flypaper ('flaɪ‚peɪpə) *n.* paper with a sticky and poisonous coating, hung up to trap flies.

fly-past *n.* a ceremonial flight of aircraft over a given area.

fly sheet *n.* a piece of canvas drawn over the ridgepole of a tent to form an outer roof.

fly spray *n.* a liquid used to destroy flies, sprayed from an aerosol.

flyweight ('flaɪ‚weɪt) *n.* **1. a.** a professional boxer weighing up to 112 pounds. **b.** an amateur boxer weighing up to 51 kg. **2.** an amateur wrestler weighing up to 115 pounds.

flywheel ('flaɪ‚wiːl) *n.* a heavy wheel that smooths the operation of a machine by making it work at a steady speed.

Fm *Chem.* fermium.

FM frequency modulation.

f-number *n. Photog.* the ratio of the effective diameter of a lens to its focal length.

foal (fəʊl) *n.* **1.** the young of a horse or related animal. ~*vb.* **2.** to give birth to (a foal).

foam (fəʊm) *n.* **1.** a mass of small bubbles of gas formed on the surface of a liquid, such as by agitation. **2.** frothy saliva. **3.** any of a number of light cellular solids made by creating bubbles of gas in a material such as plastic or rubber, when it is liquid. ~*vb.* **4.** to produce or cause to produce foam; froth. **5.** to be very angry (esp. in **foam at the mouth**). —'**foamy** *adj.*

fob (fɒb) *n.* **1.** a chain by which a pocket watch is attached to a waistcoat. **2.** a small pocket in a man's waistcoat, for holding a watch.

f.o.b. *or* **FOB** *Commerce.* free on board.

fob off *vb.* **fobbing, fobbed. 1.** to pretend to satisfy (a person) with lies or excuses. **2.** to dispose of (goods) by trickery.

focal ('fəʊk°l) *adj.* **1.** of or relating to a focus. **2.** situated at or measured from the focus.

focal length *n.* the distance from the focal point of a lens or mirror to the surface of the mirror or the centre of the lens.

focal point *n.* **1.** the point where the rays of light from a lens or mirror meet. **2.** the centre of attention or interest.

focus ('fəʊkəs) *n., pl.* **-cuses** *or* **-ci** (-saɪ). **1.** a point of convergence of light or sound waves, or a point from which they appear to diverge. **2.** same as **focal point** or **focal length. 3.** *Optics.* the state of an optical image when it is distinct or the state of an instrument producing this image. **4.** a point upon which attention or activity is concentrated. **5.** *Geom.* a fixed reference point on the concave side of a conic section, used when defining its eccentricity. ~*vb.* **-cusing, -cused** *or* **-cussing, -cussed. 6.** to bring or come to a focus or into focus. **7.** (often foll. by *on*) to concentrate.

fodder ('fɒdə) *n.* bulk feed for livestock, esp. hay or straw.

foe (fəʊ) *n. Formal or literary.* an enemy.

FoE *or* **FOE** Friends of the Earth.

foetid ('fɛtɪd, 'fiː-) *adj.* same as **fetid.**

foetus ('fiːtəs) *n., pl.* **-tuses.** same as **fetus.**

fog (fɒg) *n.* **1.** a mass of droplets of condensed water vapour suspended in the air, often greatly reducing visibility. **2.** *Photog.* a blurred area on a developed negative, print, or transparency. ~*vb.* **fogging, fogged. 3.** to envelop or become enveloped with or as if with fog. —'**foggy** *adj.*

fogbound ('fɒg‚baʊnd) *adj.* prevented from operation by fog.

foghorn ('fɒg‚hɔːn) *n.* a mechanical instrument sounded at intervals as a warning to ships in fog.

fogy *or* **fogey** ('fəʊgɪ) *n., pl.* **-gies** *or* **-geys.** an extremely old-fashioned person (esp. in **old fogy**). —'**fogyish** *or* '**fogeyish** *adj.*

foible ('fɔɪb°l) *n.* a slight peculiarity or minor weakness; idiosyncrasy.

foil[1] (fɔɪl) *vb.* to baffle or frustrate (a person or an attempt).

foil[2] (fɔɪl) *n.* **1.** metal in the form of very thin sheets. **2.** a person or thing that gives contrast to another.

foil[3] (fɔɪl) *n.* a light slender flexible sword tipped by a button.

foist (fɔɪst) *vb.* (often foll. by *off* or *on*) to pass off (something inferior) as genuine or valuable.

fold[1] (fəʊld) *vb.* **1.** to bend double so that one part covers another. **2.** to bring together and intertwine (the arms or legs). **3.** (often foll. by *up* or *in*) to enclose in a surrounding material. **4.** (foll. by *in*) to clasp (a person) in the arms. **5.** Also: **fold in.** to mix (ingredients) by gently turning one over the other with a spoon. **6.** *Informal.* to collapse; fail. ~*n.* **7.** a piece or section that has been folded. **8.** a mark, crease, or hollow made by folding. **9.** a bend in stratified rocks that results from movements within the earth's crust.

fold[2] (fəʊld) *n.* **1.** a small enclosure for sheep. **2.** a church or the members of it.

folder (ˈfəʊldə) *n.* a binder or file for holding loose papers.

folding door *n.* a door with two or more vertical hinged leaves that can be folded one against another.

foliaceous (ˌfəʊlɪˈeɪʃəs) *adj.* **1.** like a leaf. **2.** *Geol.* consisting of thin layers.

foliage (ˈfəʊlɪɪdʒ) *n.* **1.** the green leaves of a plant. **2.** sprays of leaves used for decoration.

foliation (ˌfəʊlɪˈeɪʃən) *n.* **1.** *Bot.* **a.** the process of producing leaves. **b.** the state of being in leaf. **2.** a leaflike decoration.

folio (ˈfəʊlɪəʊ) *n., pl.* **-lios. 1.** a sheet of paper folded in half to make two leaves for a book. **2.** a book of the largest common size made up of such sheets. **3. a.** a leaf of paper numbered on the front side only. **b.** the page number of a book. ~*adj.* **4.** of or made in the largest book size, common esp. in earlier centuries: *a folio edition.*

folk (fəʊk) *n., pl.* **folk** or **folks. 1.** (*functioning as pl.; often pl. in form*) people in general, esp. those of a particular group or class: *country folk.* **2.** (*functioning as pl.; usually pl. in form*) *Informal.* members of a family. **3.** (*functioning as sing.*) *Informal.* short for **folk music. 4.** a people or tribe. ~*adj.* **5.** originating from or traditional to the common people of a country: *a folk song.*

folk dance *n.* **1.** a traditional rustic dance. **2.** music for such a dance.

folk etymology *n.* the gradual change in the form of a word through the influence of a more familiar word, as for example *crayfish* from its Middle English form *crevis.*

folklore (ˈfəʊkˌlɔː) *n.* the unwritten literature of a people as expressed in stories and songs.

folk music *n.* **1.** music that is passed on from generation to generation. **2.** any music composed in this idiom.

folk song *n.* **1.** a song which has been handed down among the common people. **2.** a modern song which reflects the folk idiom. **—folk singer** *n.*

folksy (ˈfəʊksɪ) *adj.* **-sier, -siest.** of or like ordinary people; simple and unpretentious, sometimes affectedly so.

follicle (ˈfɒlɪkəl) *n.* any small sac or cavity in the body: *hair follicle.* **—follicular** (fɒˈlɪkjʊlə) *adj.*

follow (ˈfɒləʊ) *vb.* **1.** to go or come after. **2.** to accompany: *she followed her sister everywhere.* **3.** to come after as a logical or natural consequence. **4.** to keep to the course or track of. **5.** to act in accordance with: *to follow instructions.* **6.** to accept the ideas or beliefs of (a previous authority). **7.** to understand (an explanation). **8.** to have a keen interest in: *to follow athletics.*

follower (ˈfɒləʊə) *n.* **1.** a person who accepts the teachings of another: *a follower of Marx.* **2.** a supporter, as of a sport or team.

following (ˈfɒləʊɪŋ) *adj.* **1.** about to be mentioned. **2.** (of winds or currents) moving in the same direction as a vessel. ~*n.* **3.** a group of supporters or enthusiasts.

follow-on *Cricket.* ~*n.* **1.** an immediate second innings forced on a team scoring a prescribed number of runs fewer than its opponents in the first innings. ~*vb.* **follow on. 2.** to play a follow-on.

follow up *vb.* **1.** to investigate (a person, evidence, etc.) closely. **2.** to continue (action) after a beginning, esp. to increase its effect. ~*n.* **follow-up. 3.** something done to reinforce an initial action.

folly (ˈfɒlɪ) *n., pl.* **-lies. 1.** the quality of being foolish. **2.** a foolish action, idea, etc. **3.** a building in the form of a castle, temple, etc., built to satisfy a fancy.

foment (fəˈmɛnt) *vb.* to encourage or instigate (trouble, discord, etc.). **—fomentation** (ˌfəʊmɛnˈteɪʃən) *n.*

fond (fɒnd) *adj.* **1.** (foll. by *of*) having a liking (for). **2.** loving; tender. **3.** indulgent: *a fond mother.* **4.** (of hopes, wishes, etc.) cherished but unlikely to be realized. **—ˈfondly** *adv.* **—ˈfondness** *n.*

fondant (ˈfɒndənt) *n.* **1.** a thick flavoured paste of sugar and water. **2.** a sweet made of this mixture.

fondle (ˈfɒndəl) *vb.* to touch or stroke tenderly.

fondue (ˈfɒndjuː) *n.* a Swiss dish, consisting of melted cheese into which small pieces of bread are dipped.

font (fɒnt) *n.* a large bowl in a church for baptismal water.

fontanelle or chiefly U.S. **fontanel** (ˌfɒntəˈnɛl) *n. Anat.* any of the soft membranous gaps between the bones of the skull in a fetus or infant.

food (fuːd) *n.* **1.** any substance that can be taken into the body by a living organism and changed into energy and body tissue. **2.** nourishment in more or less solid form: *food and drink.*

food chain n. *Ecology.* a series of organisms in a community, each member of which feeds on another in the chain and is in turn eaten.

food poisoning n. an acute illness caused by food that is contaminated by bacteria.

foodstuff ('fuːdˌstʌf) n. any substance that can be used as food.

fool[1] (fuːl) n. **1.** a person who lacks sense or judgment. **2.** a person who is made to appear ridiculous. **3.** (formerly) a professional jester living in a royal or noble household. **4. act** *or* **play the fool.** to deliberately act foolishly. ~vb. **5.** to deceive (someone), esp. in order to make ridiculous. **6.** (foll. by *with, around with,* or *about with*) *Informal.* to act or play (with) irresponsibly or aimlessly. **7.** to speak or act in a playful or jesting manner.

fool[2] (fuːl) n. *Chiefly Brit.* a dessert made from a purée of fruit with cream.

foolery ('fuːlərɪ) n., pl. **-eries.** foolish behaviour.

foolhardy ('fuːlˌhɑːdɪ) adj. **-hardier, -hardiest.** heedlessly rash or adventurous. —'**fool,hardily** adv. —'**fool,hardiness** n.

foolish ('fuːlɪʃ) adj. **1.** unwise; silly. **2.** ridiculous or absurd. —'**foolishly** adv. —'**foolishness** n.

foolproof ('fuːlˌpruːf) adj. *Informal.* **1.** proof against failure. **2.** (esp. of machines, etc.) proof against human misuse or error.

foolscap ('fuːlsˌkæp) n. *Chiefly Brit.* a size of paper, 13½ by 17 inches.

fool's errand n. a fruitless undertaking.

fool's paradise n. illusory happiness.

foot (fʊt) n., pl. **feet. 1.** the part of the leg below the ankle joint that is in contact with the ground during standing and walking. **2.** the part of a garment covering a foot. **3.** a unit of length equal to 12 inches (0.3048 metre). **4.** any part resembling a foot in form or function: *the foot of a chair.* **5.** the lower part of something; bottom: *the foot of a hill; the foot of the list.* **6.** *Archaic.* infantry. **7.** *Prosody.* a group of two or more syllables in which one syllable has the major stress, forming the basic unit of poetic rhythm. **8. one foot in the grave.** *Informal.* near to death. **9. on foot.** walking. **10. put one's best foot forward. a.** to try to do one's best. **b.** to hurry. **11. put one's foot down.** *Informal.* to act firmly. **12. put one's foot in it.** *Informal.* to blunder tactlessly. **13. under foot.** on the ground; beneath one's feet. ~vb. **14. foot it. a.** to walk. **b.** to dance. **15. foot the bill.** to pay the entire cost of something. ~See also **feet.** —'**footless** adj.

footage ('fʊtɪdʒ) n. **1.** a length in feet. **2.** the extent of film exposed.

foot-and-mouth disease n. a highly infectious viral disease of cattle, pigs, sheep, and goats, in which blisters form in the mouth and on the feet.

football ('fʊtˌbɔːl) n. **1.** any of various games played with a ball in which two teams compete to kick, head or propel the ball into each other's goal. **2.** the ball used in any of these games. —'**foot,baller** n.

football pools pl. n. same as **pools.**

footbridge ('fʊtˌbrɪdʒ) n. a narrow bridge for the use of pedestrians.

footfall ('fʊtˌfɔːl) n. the sound of a footstep.

foothill ('fʊtˌhɪl) n. (*often pl.*) a relatively low hill at the foot of a mountain.

foothold ('fʊtˌhəʊld) n. **1.** a ledge or other place where a foot can be securely positioned, as during climbing. **2.** a secure position from which further progress may be made.

footing ('fʊtɪŋ) n. **1.** basis or foundation: *get this on an official footing.* **2.** the relationship between two people or groups: *on an equal footing.* **3.** a secure grip by or for the feet.

footle ('fuːt^əl) vb. (often foll. by *around* or *about*) *Informal.* to loiter aimlessly. —'**footling** adj.

footlights ('fʊtˌlaɪts) pl. n. *Theatre.* lights set in a row along the front of the stage floor.

footloose ('fʊtˌluːs) adj. free to go or do as one wishes.

footman ('fʊtmən) n., pl. **-men.** a male servant in livery.

footnote ('fʊtˌnəʊt) n. a note printed at the bottom of a page.

footpad ('fʊtˌpæd) n. *Archaic.* a highwayman, on foot rather than horseback.

footpath ('fʊtˌpɑːθ) n. a narrow path for walkers only.

footplate ('fʊtˌpleɪt) n. *Chiefly Brit.* a platform in the cab of a locomotive on which the crew stand to operate the controls.

footprint ('fʊtˌprɪnt) n. an indentation or outline of the foot on a surface.

footsie ('fʊtsɪ) n. *Informal.* flirtation involving the touching together of feet.

footsore ('fʊtˌsɔː) adj. having sore or tired feet, esp. from much walking.

footstep ('fʊtˌstɛp) n. **1.** a step in walking. **2.** the sound made by walking. **3.** a footmark. **4. follow in someone's footsteps.** to continue the example of another.

footstool ('fʊtˌstuːl) n. a low stool used for supporting the feet of a seated person.

footwear ('fʊtˌwɛə) n. anything worn to cover the feet.

footwork ('fʊtˌwɜːk) n. skilful use of the feet, as in sports or dancing.

fop (fɒp) n. a man who is excessively concerned with fashion. —'**foppery** n. —'**foppish** adj.

for (fɔː; *unstressed* fə) *prep*. **1.** directed or belonging to: *there's a phone call for you.* **2.** to the advantage of: *I only did it for you.* **3.** in the direction of: *heading for the border.* **4.** over a span of (time or distance): *working for six days.* **5.** in favour of: *vote for me.* **6.** in order to get: *I do it for money.* **7.** designed to meet the needs of: *these kennels are for puppies.* **8.** at a cost of: *I got it for 10p.* **9.** in place of: *a substitute for the injured player.* **10.** because of: *she wept for pure relief.* **11.** with regard to the usual characteristics of: *it's cool for this time of year.* **12.** concerning: *desire for money.* **13.** as being: *I know that for a fact.* **14.** at a specified time: *a date for the next evening.* **15.** to do or partake of: *an appointment for supper.* **16.** in the duty or task of: *that's for him to say.* **17.** to allow of: *too big a job for us to handle.* **18.** despite: *she's a good wife, for all her nagging.* **19.** in order to preserve, retain, etc.: *to fight for survival.* **20.** as a direct equivalent to: *word for word.* **21.** in order to become or enter: *to train for the priesthood.* **22.** in recompense for: *I paid for it last week.* **23. for it.** *Brit. informal.* liable for punishment or blame: *you'll be for it if she catches you.* ~*conj.* **24.** because; seeing that: *I couldn't stay, for the area was violent.*

for- *prefix*. **1.** rejecting or prohibiting: *forbid.* **2.** false or falsely: *forswear.*

Usage. The difference in meaning between the prefixes *for-* and *fore-* helps to distinguish between pairs of similar words like *forbear, forebear* and *forgo, forego. For-* has the sense of "not" or "not allowing" so that *forbear* means "not to do something" and *forgo* means "to deny oneself something". *Fore-* has the sense "before, earlier", hence *forebear* means "one who has gone before, i.e., an ancestor", and *forego* means "to go or have happened before", as in *a foregone conclusion.*

forage (ˈfɒrɪdʒ) *n*. **1.** food for horses or cattle, esp. hay or straw. **2.** the act of searching for food or provisions. ~*vb*. **3.** to search (the countryside or a town) for food, etc. **4.** to obtain by searching about.

forage cap *n*. a soldier's undress cap.

foramen (fɒˈreɪmɛn) *n., pl.* **-ramina** (-ˈræmɪnə) *or* **-ramens.** a natural hole, esp. one in a bone through which nerves pass.

forasmuch as (fərəzˈmʌtʃ) *conj. Archaic or legal.* seeing that; since.

foray (ˈfɒreɪ) *n*. **1.** a short raid or incursion. **2.** a first attempt or new undertaking.

forbade (fəˈbæd, -ˈbeɪd) *or* **forbad** (fəˈbæd) *vb.* the past tense of **forbid.**

forbear[1] (fɔːˈbɛə) *vb.* **-bearing, -bore, -borne.** to cease or refrain (from doing something). —**forˈbearance** *n*.

forbear[2] (ˈfɔːˌbɛə) *n*. same as **forebear.**

forbid (fəˈbɪd) *vb.* **-bidding, -bade** *or* **-bad,** **-bidden** *or* **-bid.** to prohibit (a person) in a forceful or authoritative manner (from doing or having something).

forbidding (fəˈbɪdɪŋ) *adj.* severe, unfriendly, or threatening.

forbore (fɔːˈbɔː) *vb.* the past tense of **forbear**[1].

forborne (fɔːˈbɔːn) *vb.* the past participle of **forbear**[1].

force[1] (fɔːs) *n*. **1.** strength or power: *the force of the blow.* **2.** exertion or the use of exertion against a person or thing that resists. **3.** *Physics.* an influence that changes a body from a state of rest to one of motion or changes its rate of motion. Symbol: *F* **4. a.** intellectual or moral influence: *the force of his argument.* **b.** a person or thing with such influence: *he was a force in the land.* **5.** vehemence or intensity: *she spoke with great force.* **6.** a group of people organized for particular duties or tasks: *a workforce; police force.* **7. in force. a.** (of a law) having legal validity. **b.** in great strength or numbers. ~*vb*. **8.** to compel (a person, group, etc.) to do something through effort, superior strength, etc. **9.** to acquire or produce through effort, superior strength, etc.: *to force a confession.* **10.** to propel or drive despite resistance. **11.** to break down or open (a lock, door, etc.). **12.** to impose or inflict: *he forced his views on them.* **13.** to cause (plants or farm animals) to grow at an increased rate. **14.** to strain to the utmost: *to force the voice.*

force[2] (fɔːs) *n*. (in N England) a waterfall.

forced (fɔːst) *adj.* **1.** done because of force: *forced labour.* **2.** false or unnatural: *a forced smile.* **3.** due to an emergency: *a forced landing.*

force-feed *vb.* **-feeding, -fed.** to force (a person or animal) to swallow food.

forceful (ˈfɔːsful) *adj.* **1.** powerful. **2.** persuasive or effective. —**ˈforcefully** *adv.*

forcemeat (ˈfɔːsˌmiːt) *n*. a mixture of chopped ingredients used for stuffing.

forceps (ˈfɔːsɛps) *n., pl.* **-ceps.** a surgical instrument in the form of a pair of pincers.

forcible (ˈfɔːsəbᵊl) *adj.* **1.** done by, involving, or having force. **2.** convincing or effective: *a forcible argument.* —**ˈforcibly** *adv.*

ford (fɔːd) *n*. **1.** a shallow area in a river that can be crossed by car, on horseback, etc. ~*vb*. **2.** to cross (a river) over a shallow area. —**ˈfordable** *adj.*

fore (fɔː) *adj.* **1.** (*usually in combination*) at, in, or towards the front: *the forelegs of a horse.* ~*n*. **2.** the front part. **3. fore and aft.** located at both ends of a vessel: *a fore-and-aft rig.* **4. to the fore.** to the front or conspicuous position.

fore- *prefix*. **1.** before in time or rank: *forefather.* **2.** at or near the front: *forecourt.*

Usage. see **for-.**

forearm[1] ('fɔːr,ɑːm) n. the part of the arm from the elbow to the wrist.

forearm[2] (fɔːr'ɑːm) vb. to prepare or arm (someone) in advance.

forebear or **forbear** ('fɔː,bɛə) n. an ancestor.

foreboding (fɔː'bəudɪŋ) n. a strong feeling that something bad is going to happen.

forecast ('fɔː,kɑːst) vb. **-casting, -cast** or **-casted.** 1. to predict or calculate (weather, events, etc.), in advance. ~n. 2. a statement of probable future weather calculated from meteorological data. 3. a prediction. —'**fore,caster** n.

forecastle, fo'c's'le, or **fo'c'sle** ('fəuks°l) n. the part of a vessel at the bow, formerly where the crew was quartered.

foreclose (fɔː'kləuz) vb. Law. to take possession of property bought with borrowed money because repayment has not been made: *the bank foreclosed on me.* —**foreclosure** (fɔː'kləuʒə) n.

forecourt ('fɔː,kɔːt) n. a courtyard in front of a building, as one in a filling station.

forefather ('fɔː,fɑːðə) n. an ancestor.

forefinger ('fɔː,fɪŋgə) n. the finger next to the thumb. Also called: **index finger.**

forefoot ('fɔː,fut) n., pl. **-feet.** either of the front feet of an animal.

forefront ('fɔː,frʌnt) n. 1. the extreme front. 2. the position of most prominence or action.

foregather (fɔː'gæðə) vb. same as **forgather.**

forego[1] (fɔː'gəu) vb. **-going, -went, -gone.** to precede in time, place, etc.

forego[2] (fɔː'gəu) vb. **-going, -went, -gone.** same as **forgo.**

foregoing (fɔː'gəuɪŋ) adj. (esp. of writing or speech) going before; preceding.

foregone conclusion ('fɔː,gɒn) n. an inevitable result.

foreground ('fɔː,graund) n. 1. the part of a scene nearest the viewer. 2. a conspicuous position.

forehand ('fɔː,hænd) Tennis, squash, etc. ~adj. 1. (of a stroke) made with the palm of the hand facing the direction of the stroke. ~n. 2. a forehand stroke.

forehead ('fɒrɪd, 'fɔː,hɛd) n. the part of the face between the natural hairline and the eyes.

foreign ('fɒrɪn) adj. 1. of, located in, or coming from another country, area, or people. 2. dealing or concerned with another country, area, or people: *a foreign office.* 3. not familiar; strange. 4. in an abnormal place or position: *foreign matter.*

foreigner ('fɒrɪnə) n. 1. a person from a foreign country. 2. an outsider.

foreign minister or **secretary** n. (often caps.) a cabinet minister who is responsible

for a country's dealings with other countries.

foreign office n. the ministry of a country that is concerned with dealings with other states.

foreknowledge (fɔː'nɒlɪdʒ) n. knowledge of something before it actually happens.

foreleg ('fɔː,lɛg) n. either of the front legs of an animal.

forelock ('fɔː,lɒk) n. a lock of hair growing or falling over the forehead.

foreman ('fɔːmən) n., pl. **-men.** 1. a person who supervises other workmen. 2. Law. the principal juror.

foremast ('fɔː,mɑːst) n. the mast nearest the bow of a vessel.

foremost ('fɔː,məust) adj., adv. first in time, place, rank, etc.

forenoon ('fɔː,nuːn) n. the daylight hours before noon.

forensic (fə'rɛnsɪk) adj. used in or connected with a court of law. —**fo'rensically** adv.

forensic medicine n. the application of medical knowledge to the purposes of the law, as in determining the cause of death.

foreordain (,fɔːrɔː'deɪn) vb. to determine (events, etc.) in the future.

forepaw ('fɔː,pɔː) n. either of the front feet of an animal.

foreplay ('fɔː,pleɪ) n. sexual stimulation before intercourse.

forerunner ('fɔː,rʌnə) n. 1. a person or thing that precedes another. 2. a person or thing coming in advance to herald the arrival of someone or something.

foresail ('fɔː,seɪl) n. the main sail on the foremast of a vessel.

foresee (fɔː'siː) vb. **-seeing, -saw, -seen.** to see or know beforehand. —**fore'seeable** adj.

foreshadow (fɔː'ʃædəu) vb. to show, indicate, or suggest in advance; presage.

foreshore ('fɔː,ʃɔː) n. the part of the shore that lies between the limits for high and low tides.

foreshorten (fɔː'ʃɔːt°n) vb. to represent (a line, form, or object) as shorter than it really is in accordance with perspective.

foresight ('fɔː,saɪt) n. 1. provision for or insight into future problems, needs, etc. 2. the front sight on a firearm.

foreskin ('fɔː,skɪn) n. Anat. the prepuce.

forest ('fɒrɪst) n. 1. a large wooded area having a thick growth of trees and plants. 2. the trees of such an area. 3. N.Z. an area planted with pines or other trees that are not native to the country. —**'forested** adj.

forestall (fɔː'stɔːl) vb. to delay, stop, or guard against beforehand.

forestation (,fɒrɪ'steɪʃən) n. the planting of trees over a wide area.

forester (ˈfɒrɪstə) n. a person skilled in forestry or in charge of a forest.

forestry (ˈfɒrɪstrɪ) n. 1. the science of planting and caring for trees. 2. the management of forests.

foretaste (ˈfɔːˌteɪst) n. an early but limited experience of something to come.

foretell (fɔːˈtɛl) vb. -telling, -told. to tell or indicate (an event, a result, etc.) beforehand.

forethought (ˈfɔːˌθɔːt) n. thoughtful anticipation of future events: I wished I'd had the forethought to bring a flask of coffee.

foretoken (ˈfɔːˌtəʊkən) n. a sign of a future event.

for ever or **forever** (fəˈrɛvə) adv. 1. without end; everlastingly. 2. at all times.

forewarn (fɔːˈwɔːn) vb. to warn beforehand.

foreword (ˈfɔːˌwɜːd) n. an introductory statement to a book.

forfeit (ˈfɔːfɪt) n. 1. something lost or given up as a penalty for a fault, mistake, etc. ~vb. 2. to lose or be liable to lose in consequence of a mistake, fault, etc. ~adj. 3. surrendered or liable to be surrendered as a penalty. —ˈforfeiture n.

forgather or **foregather** (fɔːˈgæðə) vb. to gather together; assemble.

forgave (fəˈgeɪv) vb. the past tense of **forgive**.

forge[1] (fɔːdʒ) n. 1. a place in which metal is worked by heating and hammering; smithy. 2. a hearth or furnace used for heating metal. ~vb. 3. to shape (metal) by heating and hammering. 4. to make a fraudulent imitation of (a signature, etc.). —ˈforger n.

forge[2] (fɔːdʒ) vb. 1. to move at a steady pace. 2. **forge ahead**. to increase speed or progress; take the lead.

forgery (ˈfɔːdʒərɪ) n., pl. -geries. 1. the act of reproducing something for a fraudulent purpose. 2. something forged, such as an antique.

forget (fəˈgɛt) vb. -getting, -got, -gotten. 1. to fail to remember (someone or something once known). 2. to neglect, either by mistake or on purpose. 3. to leave behind by mistake. 4. **forget oneself. a.** to act in an improper manner. **b.** to be unselfish. —forˈgettable adj.

forgetful (fəˈgɛtfʊl) adj. 1. tending to forget. 2. inattentive (to) or neglectful (of). —forˈgetfully adv.

forget-me-not n. a low-growing plant with clusters of small blue flowers.

forgive (fəˈgɪv) vb. -giving, -gave, -given. 1. to cease to feel anger and resentment towards (a person who has offended) or at (an offending deed). 2. to pardon (a mistake). 3. to free from (a debt).

forgiveness (fəˈgɪvnɪs) n. the act of forgiving or the state of being forgiven.

forgiving (fəˈgɪvɪŋ) adj. willing to forgive.

forgo or **forego** (fɔːˈgəʊ) vb. -going, -went, -gone. to give up or do without.

forgot (fəˈgɒt) vb. 1. the past tense of **forget**. 2. Archaic or dialect. a past participle of **forget**.

forgotten (fəˈgɒtˀn) vb. a past participle of **forget**.

fork (fɔːk) n. 1. a small usually metal implement with long thin prongs on the end of a handle, used for lifting food to the mouth. 2. a larger similar-shaped agricultural tool, used for lifting, digging, etc. 3. a pronged part of any machine, device, etc. 4. (of a road, river, etc.) **a.** a division into two or more branches. **b.** the point where the division begins. **c.** such a branch. ~vb. 5. to pick up, dig, etc., with a fork. 6. to be divided into two or more branches. 7. to take one or other branch at a fork in a road, etc.

forked (fɔːkt) adj. 1. having a fork or forklike parts. 2. zigzag: forked lightning.

fork-lift truck n. a vehicle with two horizontal prongs that can be raised and lowered for transporting and unloading goods.

fork out vb. Slang. to pay, esp. with reluctance.

forlorn (fəˈlɔːn) adj. 1. miserable or cheerless. 2. forsaken. 3. desperate: the last forlorn attempt. —forˈlornly adv.

forlorn hope n. 1. a hopeless enterprise. 2. a faint hope.

form (fɔːm) n. 1. the shape or configuration of something. 2. a visible person or animal. 3. the particular mode in which a thing or person manifests itself: water in the form of ice. 4. a type or kind: imprisonment is a form of punishment. 5. a printed document, esp. one with spaces in which to insert facts or answers. 6. physical or mental condition. 7. the previous record of a horse, athlete, etc. 8. Brit. slang. a criminal record. 9. Education, chiefly Brit. a group of children who are taught together. 10. procedure; etiquette: good form. 11. a prescribed order of words. 12. Brit. a bench. 13. a hare's nest. 14. any of the various ways in which a word may be spelt or inflected. ~vb. 15. to give shape to or to take shape, esp. a particular shape. 16. to come or bring into existence: ice formed on the lake. 17. to make or construct or be made or constructed. 18. to train or mould by instruction or example. 19. to acquire or develop: to form a habit; to form an opinion. 20. to be an element of: this plank will form a bridge.

formal (ˈfɔːməl) adj. 1. of or following established conventions: a formal document; formal language. 2. characterized by conventional forms of ceremony and behaviour: a formal dinner. 3. suitable for occasions organized according to conventional ceremony: formal dress. 4. methodical; organized: *a formal approach to the subject.* **5.** symmetrical in form: *a formal garden.* **6.** relating to the form of something as distinguished from its substance. **7.** logically deductive: *formal proof.* —**'formally** *adv.*

formaldehyde (fɔː'mældɪˌhaɪd) *n.* a colourless poisonous pungent gas, used as formalin and in synthetic resins.

formalin ('fɔːməlɪn) *n.* a solution of formaldehyde in water, used as a disinfectant and as a preservative for biological specimens.

formalism ('fɔːməˌlɪzəm) *n.* scrupulous or excessive adherence to outward form at the expense of content. —**'formalist** *n.*

formality (fɔː'mælɪtɪ) *n., pl.* **-ties.** **1.** a requirement of custom or etiquette: *let's get the formalities over.* **2.** a necessary procedure without real effect: *the interview was just a formality.* **3.** strict observance of ceremony.

formalize *or* **-lise** ('fɔːməˌlaɪz) *vb.* **1.** to make official or valid. **2.** to give a definite form to. —**ˌformali'zation** *or* **-li'sation** *n.*

format ('fɔːmæt) *n.* **1.** the shape, size, and general appearance of a publication. **2.** style or arrangement, as of a television programme. **3.** *Computers.* the arrangement of data to comply with a computer's input device. ~*vb.* **-matting, -matted.** **4.** to arrange in a specified format.

formation (fɔː'meɪʃən) *n.* **1.** the act of giving or taking form or existence. **2.** something that is formed. **3.** the manner in which something is arranged. **4.** an arrangement of people or things acting as a unit, such as a troop of soldiers. **5.** a series of rocks with certain characteristics in common.

formative ('fɔːmətɪv) *adj.* **1.** of or relating to formation, development, or growth: *formative years.* **2.** shaping; moulding: *a formative experience.*

former ('fɔːmə) *adj.* **1.** belonging to or occurring in an earlier time: *former glory.* **2.** having been at a previous time: *a former colleague.* ~*n.* **3. the former.** the first or first mentioned of two.

formerly ('fɔːməlɪ) *adv.* in the past.

Formica (fɔː'maɪkə) *n. Trademark.* a hard laminated plastic used esp. for heat-resistant surfaces.

formic acid ('fɔːmɪk) *n.* an acid derived from ants.

formidable ('fɔːmɪdəb'l) *adj.* **1.** arousing fear or dread. **2.** extremely difficult to defeat, overcome, manage, etc. —**'formidably** *adv.*

formless ('fɔːmlɪs) *adj.* without a definite shape or form; amorphous.

formula ('fɔːmjʊlə) *n., pl.* **-las** *or* **-lae** (-ˌliː). **1.** a group of letters, numbers, or other symbols which represents a mathematical or scientific rule. **2.** an established form of words, as used in religious ceremonies, legal proceedings, etc. **3.** a method or rule for doing something, often one proved to be successful. **4.** *U.S. & Canad.* a powder used to make a milky drink for babies. **5.** *Motor racing.* the category in which a car competes, judged according to engine size. —**formulaic** (ˌfɔːmjʊ'leɪɪk) *adj.*

formulary ('fɔːmjʊlərɪ) *n., pl.* **-laries.** a book of prescribed formulas.

formulate ('fɔːmjʊˌleɪt) *vb.* **1.** to express in a formula. **2.** to plan or describe precisely and clearly. —**ˌformu'lation** *n.*

fornicate ('fɔːnɪˌkeɪt) *vb.* to commit fornication. —**'forniˌcator** *n.*

fornication (ˌfɔːnɪ'keɪʃən) *n.* voluntary sexual intercourse outside marriage.

forsake (fə'seɪk) *vb.* **-saking, -sook, -saken.** **1.** to withdraw support or friendship from. **2.** to give up (something valued or enjoyed).

forsooth (fə'suːθ) *adv. Archaic.* in truth; indeed.

forswear (fɔː'swɛə) *vb.* **-swearing, -swore, -sworn.** **1.** to reject or renounce with determination. **2.** to perjure (oneself).

forsythia (fɔː'saɪθɪə) *n.* a shrub with yellow flowers which appear in spring before the foliage.

fort (fɔːt) *n.* **1.** a fortified enclosure, building, or position. **2. hold the fort.** *Informal.* to keep things in operation during someone's absence.

forte[1] ('fɔːteɪ) *n.* something at which a person excels.

forte[2] ('fɔːtɪ) *adv. Music.* loudly.

forth (fɔːθ) *adv.* **1.** *Formal or archaic.* forward, out, or away: *they put forth their conclusions; they set forth for the New World.* **2. and so forth.** and so on.

forthcoming (ˌfɔːθ'kʌmɪŋ) *adj.* **1.** about to appear or happen: *his forthcoming book.* **2.** available. **3.** (of a person) willing to be communicative.

forthright ('fɔːθˌraɪt) *adj.* direct and outspoken.

forthwith (ˌfɔːθ'wɪθ) *adv.* at once.

fortification (ˌfɔːtɪfɪ'keɪʃən) *n.* **1.** the act of fortifying. **2.** (*pl.*) walls, mounds, etc., used to fortify a place.

fortify ('fɔːtɪˌfaɪ) *vb.* **-fying, -fied.** **1.** to make (a place) defensible, as by building walls. **2.** to strengthen physically, mentally, or morally. **3.** to add alcohol to (wine), in order to produce sherry, port, etc. **4.** to increase the nutritious value of (a food), as by adding vitamins.

fortissimo (fɔː'tɪsɪˌməʊ) *adv. Music.* very loudly.

fortitude ('fɔːtɪˌtjuːd) *n.* strength and firmness of mind.

fortnight ('fɔːtˌnaɪt) *n.* a period of 14 consecutive days; two weeks.

fortnightly ('fɔːtˌnaɪtlɪ) *Chiefly Brit.* ~*adj.*

1. occurring or appearing once each fortnight. ~*adv.* **2.** once a fortnight.

FORTRAN (ˈfɔːtræn) *n.* a high-level computer programming language.

fortress (ˈfɔːtrɪs) *n.* a large fort or fortified town.

fortuitous (fɔːˈtjuːɪtəs) *adj.* happening by chance, esp. by a lucky chance. —**forˈtuitously** *adv.*

fortunate (ˈfɔːtʃənɪt) *adj.* **1.** having good luck. **2.** occurring by good luck. —**ˈfortunately** *adv.*

fortune (ˈfɔːtʃən) *n.* **1.** wealth or material prosperity. **2.** a power regarded as being responsible for human affairs. **3.** luck, esp. when favourable. **4.** (*often pl.*) a person's destiny.

fortune-teller *n.* a person who claims to predict events in other people's lives.

forty (ˈfɔːtɪ) *n., pl.* **-ties. 1.** the cardinal number that is the product of ten and four. **2.** a numeral, 40, XL, representing this number. **3.** something representing or consisting of 40 units. ~*det.* **4.** amounting to forty: *forty thieves.* —**ˈfortieth** *adj., n.*

forty winks *n.* (*functioning as sing. or pl.*) *Informal.* a short light sleep; nap.

forum (ˈfɔːrəm) *n.* **1.** a meeting or medium for the open discussion of subjects of public interest. **2.** (in ancient Roman cities) an open space serving as a marketplace and centre of public business.

forward (ˈfɔːwəd) *adj.* **1.** directed or moving ahead. **2.** at, in, or near the front. **3.** presumptuous or impudent. **4.** well developed or advanced. **5.** of or relating to the future or favouring change. **6.** *Commerce.* relating to fulfilment at a future date. ~*n.* **7.** an attacking player in any of various sports, such as soccer. ~*adv.* **8.** same as **forwards.** ~*vb.* **9.** to send on to an ultimate destination: *the letter was forwarded.* **10.** to advance or promote: *to forward one's career.*

forwards (ˈfɔːwədz) *or* **forward** *adv.* **1.** towards or at a place ahead or in advance, esp. in space but also in time. **2.** towards the front.

fosse *or* **foss** (fɒs) *n.* a ditch or moat, esp. one dug as a fortification.

fossick (ˈfɒsɪk) *vb. Austral. & N.Z.* **1.** to search for gold or precious stones in abandoned workings, rivers, etc. **2.** to search for (something).

fossil (ˈfɒsˀl) *n.* **1.** remains of a plant or animal that existed in a past geological age, occurring in the form of mineralized bones, shells, etc. ~*adj.* **2.** of, like, or being a fossil. **3.** formed by the decomposition of prehistoric organisms: *fossil fuel.*

fossil fuel *n.* any naturally occurring fuel, such as coal, formed by the decomposition of prehistoric organisms.

fossilize *or* **-lise** (ˈfɒsɪˌlaɪz) *vb.* **1.** to con-

vert or be converted into a fossil. **2.** to become antiquated or inflexible.

foster (ˈfɒstə) *vb.* **1.** to promote the growth or development of. **2.** to bring up (a child not one's own). ~*adj.* **3.** of or involved in the fostering of a child: *foster home.* —**ˈfostering** *n.*

fought (fɔːt) *vb.* the past of **fight.**

foul (faʊl) *adj.* **1.** offensive to the senses; revolting. **2.** stinking. **3.** full of dirt or offensive matter. **4.** obscene; vulgar: *foul language.* **5.** unfair: *to resort to foul means.* **6.** (of weather) unpleasant. **7.** blocked with dirt or foreign matter: *a foul drain.* **8.** *Informal.* disgustingly bad. ~*n.* **9.** *Sport.* a violation of the rules. ~*vb.* **10.** to make dirty or polluted. **11.** to become or cause to become entangled. **12.** to become or cause to become clogged. **13.** *Sport.* to commit a foul against (an opponent). ~*adv.* **14. fall foul of.** to come into conflict with.

foul play *n.* **1.** unfair conduct, esp. with violence. **2.** a violation of the rules in a game.

foul up *vb.* **1.** *Informal.* to bungle. **2.** to contaminate. **3.** to block or choke.

found¹ (faʊnd) *vb.* the past of **find.**

found² (faʊnd) *vb.* **1.** to bring into being or establish (something, such as an institution). **2.** to lay the foundation of (a building). **3.** (foll. by *on* or *upon*) to have a basis (in). —**ˈfounder** *n.*

found³ (faʊnd) *vb.* **1.** to cast (metal or glass) by melting and pouring into a mould. **2.** to make (articles) in this way. —**ˈfounder** *n.*

foundation (faʊnˈdeɪʃən) *n.* **1.** that on which something is founded. **2.** (*often pl.*) a construction below the ground that distributes the load of a building, wall, etc. **3.** the base on which something stands. **4.** the act of founding. **5.** an endowment for the support of an institution, such as a college. **6.** an institution supported by an endowment. **7.** a cosmetic used as a base for make-up.

foundation stone *n.* a stone laid at a ceremony to mark the foundation of a new building.

founder (ˈfaʊndə) *vb.* **1.** (of a ship) to sink. **2.** to break down or fail: *the project foundered.* **3.** to sink into or become stuck in soft ground. **4.** (of a horse) to stumble or go lame.

foundling (ˈfaʊndlɪŋ) *n.* an abandoned infant whose parents are not known.

foundry (ˈfaʊndrɪ) *n., pl.* **-ries.** a place in which metal castings are produced.

fount¹ (faʊnt) *n.* **1.** *Poetic.* a spring or fountain. **2.** a source.

fount² (faʊnt, fɒnt) *n. Printing.* a complete set of type of one style and size.

fountain (ˈfaʊntɪn) *n.* **1.** a jet or spray of water. **2.** a structure from which such a jet or a number of such jets spurt. **3.** a natural spring of water. **4.** a cascade of sparks, lava, etc. **5.** a principal source.

fountainhead ('fauntɪn,hɛd) n. a principal or original source.

fountain pen n. a pen the nib of which is supplied with ink from a cartridge or a reservoir in its barrel.

four (fɔː) n. **1.** the cardinal number that is the sum of three and one. **2.** a numeral, 4, IV, representing this number. **3.** something representing or consisting of four units. **4.** *Rowing.* **a.** a racing shell propelled by four oarsmen. **b.** the crew of such a shell. ~det. **5.** amounting to four: *four times.* —**fourth** adj., n.

fourfold ('fɔː,fəʊld) adj. **1.** equal to or having four times as many or as much. **2.** composed of four parts. ~adv. **3.** by or up to four times as many or as much.

four-in-hand n. a road vehicle drawn by four horses and driven by one driver.

four-letter word n. any of several short English words referring to sex or excrement: regarded generally as offensive or obscene.

four-poster n. a bed with posts at each corner supporting a canopy and curtains.

fourscore (,fɔː'skɔː) det. Archaic. eighty.

foursome ('fɔːsəm) n. **1.** a set of four. **2.** *Golf.* a game between two pairs of players.

foursquare (,fɔː'skwɛə) adv. **1.** squarely; firmly. ~adj. **2.** solid and strong.

four-stroke adj. designating an internal-combustion engine in which the piston makes four strokes for every explosion.

fourteen ('fɔː'tiːn) n. **1.** the cardinal number that is the sum of ten and four. **2.** a numeral, 14, XIV, representing this number. **3.** something represented by or consisting of 14 units. ~det. **4.** amounting to fourteen: *fourteen cats.* —**four'teenth** adj., n.

fourth dimension n. **1.** the dimension of time, which in addition to three spatial dimensions specifies the position of a point or particle. **2.** the concept in science fiction of an extra dimension. —**fourth-di'mensional** adj.

fourth estate n. the press.

fowl (faʊl) n. **1.** a domesticated bird such as a chicken. **2.** any other bird that is used as food or hunted as game. **3.** the meat of fowl. **4.** Archaic. a bird. ~vb. **5.** to hunt or snare wildfowl.

fox (fɒks) n., pl. **foxes** or **fox**. **1.** a doglike wild animal with a pointed muzzle and a bushy tail. **2.** its reddish-brown or grey fur. **3.** a person who is cunning and sly. ~vb. **4.** Informal. to perplex or deceive. **5.** to cause (paper) to become discoloured with spots or (of paper) to become discoloured.

foxglove ('fɒks,glʌv) n. a plant with spikes of purple or white thimble-like flowers.

foxhole ('fɒks,həʊl) n. Mil. a small pit dug to provide shelter against hostile fire.

foxhound ('fɒks,haʊnd) n. a breed of short-haired hound, usually kept for hunting foxes.

fox-hunting n. the sport of hunting foxes with hounds.

fox terrier n. either of two breeds of small tan-black-and-white terrier, the wire-haired and the smooth.

foxtrot ('fɒks,trɒt) n. **1.** a ballroom dance in quadruple time. ~vb. **-trotting, -trotted.** **2.** to perform this dance.

foxy ('fɒksɪ) adj. **foxier, foxiest. 1.** of or resembling a fox, esp. in craftiness. **2.** reddish-brown. —**foxily** adv. —**foxiness** n.

foyer ('fɔɪeɪ) n. an entrance hall as in a hotel, theatre, or cinema.

fp forte-piano.

FP 1. fire plug. **2.** freezing point.

Fr 1. Christianity: **a.** Father. **b.** Frater. **2.** Chem. francium.

fr. 1. franc. **2.** from.

fracas ('frækɑː) n. a noisy quarrel; brawl.

fraction ('frækʃən) n. **1.** Maths. a ratio of two expressions or numbers other than zero. **2.** any part or subdivision. **3.** a small piece; fragment. **4.** Chem. a component of a mixture separated by distillation. —**'fractional** adj. —**'fractionally** adv.

fractious ('frækʃəs) adj. peevishly irritable.

fracture ('fræktʃə) n. **1.** breaking, esp. the breaking or cracking of a bone. ~vb. **2.** to break, esp. to break (a bone) or (of a bone) to become broken. —**'fractural** adj.

fragile ('frædʒaɪl) adj. **1.** able to be broken easily. **2.** in a weakened physical state. —**fragility** (frə'dʒɪlɪtɪ) n.

fragment n. ('frægmənt). **1.** a piece broken off. **2.** an incomplete piece: *fragments of a novel.* ~vb. (fræg'mɛnt). **3.** to break into fragments. —,**fragmen'tation** n.

fragmentary ('frægməntrɪ) adj. made up of fragments; disconnected.

fragrance ('freɪgrəns) n. **1.** a pleasant odour. **2.** the state of being fragrant.

fragrant ('freɪgrənt) adj. having a pleasant smell.

frail (freɪl) adj. **1.** physically weak and delicate. **2.** fragile: *a frail craft.* **3.** easily tempted.

frailty ('freɪltɪ) n., pl. **-ties. 1.** physical or moral weakness. **2.** (often pl.) a fault symptomatic of moral weakness.

frame (freɪm) n. **1.** an open structure that gives shape and support to something, such as a building. **2.** an enclosing case or border into which something is fitted: *the frame of a picture.* **3.** the system around which something is built up: *the frame of government.* **4.** the structure of the human body. **5.** a condition; state (esp. in **frame**

of mind). **6.** one of a series of exposures on film used in making motion pictures. **7.** a television picture scanned by electron beams at a particular frequency. **8.** *Snooker, etc.* **a.** the wooden triangle used to set up the balls. **b.** the balls when set up. **c.** a single game. **9.** short for **cold frame. 10.** *Slang.* a frame-up. ~*vb.* **11.** to construct by fitting parts together. **12.** to draw up the plans: *to frame a policy.* **13.** to compose: *to frame a reply.* **14.** to provide or enclose with a frame: *to frame a picture.* **15.** *Slang.* to conspire to incriminate (someone) on a false charge.

frame of reference *n.* **1.** a set of standards that determines behaviour. **2.** any set of planes or curves, such as the three coordinate axes, used to locate a point in space.

frame-up *n. Slang.* a conspiracy to incriminate someone on a false charge.

framework ('freɪm,wɜːk) *n.* **1.** a structural plan or basis of a project. **2.** a structure supporting something.

franc (fræŋk) *n.* the standard monetary unit of France and various other countries.

franchise ('fræntʃaɪz) *n.* **1.** (usually preceded by *the*) the right to vote, esp. for a member of parliament. **2.** any exemption, privilege, or right granted by a public authority. **3.** *Commerce.* authorization granted to a distributor to market a manufacturer's products. ~*vb.* **4.** *Commerce, chiefly U.S. & Canad.* to grant (a person, firm, etc.) a franchise.

Franciscan (fræn'sɪskən) *n.* a member of a Christian religious order of friars or nuns founded by Saint Francis of Assisi.

francium ('frænsɪəm) *n.* an unstable radioactive element of the alkali-metal group. Symbol: Fr

Franco- ('fræŋkəʊ) *combining form.* indicating France or French: *Franco-Prussian.*

frank (fræŋk) *adj.* **1.** honest and straightforward in speech or attitude. **2.** outspoken or blunt. **3.** open; undisguised: *frank interest.* ~*vb.* **4.** *Chiefly Brit.* to put a mark on (a letter), ensuring free carriage. ~*n.* **5.** an official mark affixed to a letter ensuring free delivery. —'**frankly** *adv.* —'**frankness** *n.*

Frank (fræŋk) *n.* a member of the West Germanic peoples who in the late 4th century A.D. gradually conquered most of Gaul.

Frankenstein ('fræŋkɪn,staɪn) *n.* a thing that destroys its creator. Also called: **Frankenstein's monster.**

frankfurter ('fræŋk,fɜːtə) *n.* a smoked sausage of pork or beef.

frankincense ('fræŋkɪn,sɛns) *n.* an aromatic gum resin burnt as incense.

Frankish ('fræŋkɪʃ) *n.* **1.** the ancient West Germanic language of the Franks. ~*adj.* **2.** of the Franks or their language.

frantic ('fræntɪk) *adj.* **1.** distracted with

fear, pain, joy, etc. **2.** marked by or showing frenzy: *frantic efforts.* —'**frantically** *adv.*

frappé ('fræpeɪ) *adj.* (esp. of drinks) chilled.

fraternal (frə'tɜːnˀl) *adj.* **1.** of a brother; brotherly. **2.** designating twins that developed from two separate fertilized ova. —**fra'ternally** *adv.*

fraternity (frə'tɜːnɪtɪ) *n., pl.* **-ties.** **1.** a body of people united in interests, aims, etc. **2.** brotherliness. **3.** *U.S. & Canad.* a society of male students.

fraternize *or* **-nise** ('frætə,naɪz) *vb.* (often foll. by *with*) to associate on friendly terms. —,**fraterni'zation** *or* **-ni'sation** *n.*

fratricide ('frætrɪ,saɪd) *n.* **1.** the act of killing one's brother. **2.** a person who kills his brother. —,**fratri'cidal** *adj.*

Frau (frau) *n., pl.* **Frauen** ('frauən) *or* **Fraus.** a married German woman: a title equivalent to *Mrs.*

fraud (frɔːd) *n.* **1.** deliberate deception or cheating intended to gain an advantage. **2.** an act of such deception. **3.** *Informal.* a person who acts in a false or deceitful way.

fraudulent ('frɔːdjʊlənt) *adj.* **1.** acting with intent to deceive. **2.** proceeding from fraud. —'**fraudulence** *n.*

fraught (frɔːt) *adj.* **1.** (foll. by *with*) filled: *a venture fraught with peril.* **2.** *Informal.* showing or producing tension or anxiety.

Fräulein ('frɔɪlaɪn) *n., pl.* **-lein** *or* **-leins.** an unmarried German woman: a title equivalent to *Miss.*

fray[1] (freɪ) *n.* **1.** a noisy quarrel or brawl. **2.** any challenging conflict.

fray[2] (freɪ) *vb.* **1.** to wear away into loose threads, esp. at an edge. **2.** to make or become strained or irritated.

frazil ('freɪzɪl) *n.* small pieces of ice that form in water moving turbulently enough to prevent the formation of a sheet of ice.

frazzle ('fræzˀl) *n. Informal.* the state of being exhausted: *worn to a frazzle.*

freak (friːk) *n.* **1.** a person, animal, or plant that is abnormal or deformed. **2.** an object, event, etc., that is abnormal. **3.** *Informal.* a person who acts or dresses in a markedly unconventional way. **4.** *Informal.* a person who is ardently fond of something specified: *a jazz freak.* ~*adj.* **5.** abnormal: *a freak storm.* —'**freakish** *adj.* —'**freaky** *adj.*

freak out *vb. Informal.* to be or cause to be in a heightened emotional state.

freckle ('frɛkˀl) *n.* **1.** a small brownish spot on the skin. ~*vb.* **2.** to mark or become marked with freckles. —'**freckled** *adj.*

free (friː) *adj.* **freer, freest. 1.** able to act at will; not under compulsion or restraint. **2.** not enslaved or confined. **3.** (foll. by *from*) not subject (to): *free from pain.* **4.**

(of a country, etc.) independent. **5.** exempt from external direction: *free will.* **6.** not subject to conventional constraints: *free verse.* **7.** not exact or literal: *a free translation.* **8.** provided without charge: *free entertainment.* **9.** (often foll. by *of* or *with*) ready or generous in using or giving: *free with advice.* **10.** not occupied or in use; available: *a free cubicle.* **11.** (of a person) not busy. **12.** open or available to all. **13.** not fixed or joined; loose: *the free end of a chain.* **14.** without obstruction or impediment: *free passage.* **15.** *Chem.* chemically uncombined: *free nitrogen.* **16. free and easy.** casual or tolerant. **17. make free with.** to behave too familiarly towards. ~*adv.* **18.** in a free manner; freely. **19.** without charge or cost. ~*vb.* **freeing, freed. 20.** to set at liberty; release. **21.** to remove obstructions or impediments from. **22.** (often foll. by *of* or *from*) to relieve or rid (of obstacles, pain, etc.). —'**freely** *adv.*

-free *adj. combining form.* free from: *trouble-free; lead-free petrol.*

freebie ('friːbɪ) *n. Slang.* something provided without charge.

freeboard ('friːˌbɔːd) *n.* the space or distance between the deck of a vessel and the waterline.

freebooter ('friːˌbuːtə) *n.* a pirate.

freeborn ('friːˌbɔːn) *adj.* not born in slavery.

Free Church *n. Chiefly Brit.* any Protestant Church other than the Established Church.

freedman ('friːdˌmæn) *n., pl.* **-men.** a man who has been freed from slavery.

freedom ('friːdəm) *n.* **1.** the state of being free, esp. to enjoy political and civil liberties. **2.** (usually foll. by *from*) exemption or immunity: *freedom from taxation.* **3.** liberation, as from slavery. **4.** the right or privilege of unrestricted access: *the freedom of a city.* **5.** self-government or independence. **6.** the power to order one's own actions. **7.** ease or frankness of manner. **8.** excessive familiarity.

free enterprise *n.* an economic system in which commercial organizations compete for profit with little state control.

free fall *n.* **1.** free descent of a body in which gravity is the only force acting on it. **2.** the part of a parachute descent before the parachute opens.

free-for-all *n. Informal.* a disorganized brawl or argument involving all those present.

free hand *n.* **1.** unrestricted freedom to act: *they gave her a free hand to run her department.* ~*adj., adv.* **freehand. 2.** (done) by hand without the use of guiding instruments.

freehold ('friːˌhəʊld) *Property law.* ~*n.* **1.** tenure by which land is held without restrictions and for life. ~*adj.* **2.** of or held by freehold. —'**free,holder** *n.*

free house *n. Brit.* a public house not bound to sell only one brewer's products.

free kick *n. Soccer.* a place kick awarded for a foul or infringement.

freelance ('friːˌlɑːns) *n.* **1.** a self-employed person, esp. a writer or artist, who is hired to do specific assignments. ~*vb.* **2.** to work as a freelance. ~*adj., adv.* **3.** of or as a freelance.

freeloader ('friːˌləʊdə) *n. Slang.* a person who habitually depends on others for food, shelter, etc.

free love *n.* sexual relationships without fidelity to a single partner.

freeman ('friːmən) *n., pl.* **-men. 1.** a person who is not a slave. **2.** a person who enjoys a privilege, such as the freedom of a city.

free-market *adj.* denoting an economic system which allows supply and demand to regulate prices and wages.

Freemason ('friːˌmeɪsˀn) *n.* a member of a widespread secret order, pledged to brotherliness and mutual aid. Sometimes shortened to **Mason.** —'**Free,masonry** *n.*

free-range *adj. Chiefly Brit.* kept or produced in natural conditions.

freesia ('friːzɪə) *n.* a bulbous plant with tubular fragrant flowers.

free space *n.* a region that has no gravitational and electromagnetic fields.

freestanding (ˌfriːˈstændɪŋ) *adj.* not attached to or supported by another object.

freestyle ('friːˌstaɪl) *n.* **1.** a competition, as in swimming, in which each participant may use a style of his or her choice. **2.** Also called: **all-in wrestling.** a style of professional wrestling with no internationally agreed set of rules.

freethinker (ˌfriːˈθɪŋkə) *n.* a person who forms his ideas independently of authority, esp. in matters of religion.

free trade *n.* international trade that is free of such government interference as protective tariffs.

free verse *n.* unrhymed verse without a metrical pattern.

freeway ('friːˌweɪ) *n. U.S.* an expressway.

freewheel (ˌfriːˈwiːl) *n.* **1.** a device in the rear hub of a bicycle wheel that permits it to rotate freely while the pedals are stationary. ~*vb.* **2.** to coast.

free will *n.* **1.** the apparent human ability to make choices that are not externally determined. **2.** the ability to make a choice without outside coercion: *he left of his own free will.*

Free World *n.* **the.** the non-Communist countries collectively.

freeze (friːz) *vb.* **freezing, froze, frozen. 1.** to change (a liquid) into a solid as a result of a reduction in temperature, or (of a liquid) to solidify in this way. **2.** to cover or become covered with ice. **3.** to fix fast or become fixed (to something) because of frost. **4.** to preserve (food) by subjection to extreme cold. **5.** to feel or cause to feel the effects of extreme cold. **6.** to die of extreme cold. **7.** to become or make motionless through fear, shock, etc. **8.** to cause (moving film) to stop at a particular frame. **9.** to become formal, haughty, etc., in manner. **10.** to fix (prices, incomes, etc.) at a particular level. **11.** to forbid by law the exchange or collection of (loans, assets, etc.). ~*n.* **12.** the act of freezing or state of being frozen. **13.** *Meteorol.* a spell of temperatures below freezing point. **14.** the fixing of incomes, prices, etc., by legislation.

freeze-dry *vb.* **-drying, -dried.** to preserve (a substance) by rapid freezing and subsequently drying in a vacuum.

freezer ('fri:zə) *n.* an insulated cabinet for cold-storage of perishable foodstuffs.

freezing point *n.* the temperature below which a liquid turns into a solid.

freight (freit) *n.* **1. a.** commercial transport. **b.** the price charged for such transport. **c.** goods transported by this means. **2.** *Chiefly Brit.* a ship's cargo or part of it. ~*vb.* **3.** to transport (goods) by freight. **4.** to load with goods for transport.

freighter ('freitə) *n.* a ship or aircraft designed for transporting cargo.

French (frɛntʃ) *n.* **1.** the official language of France: also an official language of Switzerland, Belgium, Canada, and certain other countries. **2. the French.** (*functioning as pl.*) the people of France collectively. ~*adj.* **3.** of France, the French, or their language.

French bread *n.* white bread in a long slender loaf.

French Canadian *n.* a Canadian citizen whose native language is French.

French chalk *n.* a variety of talc used to mark cloth or remove grease stains.

French dressing *n.* a salad dressing made from oil and vinegar with seasonings.

French fries *pl. n. Chiefly U.S. & Canad.* chips.

French horn *n. Music.* a valved brass instrument coiled into a spiral.

Frenchify ('frɛntʃɪ,faɪ) *vb.* **-fying, -fied.** *Informal.* to make or become French in appearance, etc.

French leave *n.* an unauthorized absence or departure.

French letter *n. Brit. slang.* a condom.

French polish *n.* a shellac varnish for wood, giving a high gloss.

French seam *n.* a seam in which the edges are enclosed.

French windows *pl. n. Brit.* a pair of casement windows extending to floor level and opening onto a balcony or garden.

frenetic (frɪ'nɛtɪk) *adj.* distracted or frantic. —**fre'netically** *adv.*

frenzy ('frɛnzɪ) *n., pl.* **-zies. 1.** violent mental derangement. **2.** wild excitement or agitation. **3.** a bout of wild or agitated activity: *a frenzy of preparations.* —**'frenzied** *adj.*

Freon ('fri:ɒn) *n. Trademark.* any of a group of gas or liquid chemical compounds of methane with chlorine and fluorine: used as refrigerants, aerosol propellants, and solvents.

frequency ('fri:kwənsɪ) *n., pl.* **-cies. 1.** the state of being frequent. **2.** the number of times that an event occurs within a given period. **3.** *Physics.* the number of times that a periodic function or vibration repeats itself in a specified time.

frequency distribution *n.* statistical data arranged to show the frequency with which the possible values of a variable occur.

frequency modulation *n.* a method of transmitting information by varying the frequency |of | the |carrier wave in accord-|ance with| the amplitude of the input signal.

frequent *adj.* ('fri:kwənt). **1.** recurring at short intervals. **2.** habitual. ~*vb.* (frɪ'kwɛnt). **3.** to visit habitually. —**'frequently** *adv.*

frequentative (frɪ'kwɛntətɪv) *Grammar.* ~*adj.* **1.** denoting a verb or an affix meaning repeated action. ~*n.* **2.** a frequentative verb or affix.

fresco ('frɛskəʊ) *n., pl.* **-coes** *or* **-cos. 1.** a method of wall-painting using watercolours on wet plaster. **2.** a painting done in this way.

fresh (frɛʃ) *adj.* **1.** newly made, acquired, etc. **2.** novel; original: *a fresh outlook.* **3.** most recent: *fresh developments.* **4.** further; additional: *fresh supplies.* **5.** not canned, frozen, or otherwise preserved. **6.** (of water) not salt. **7.** bright and clear: *a fresh morning.* **8.** chilly or invigorating: *a fresh breeze.* **9.** not tired; alert. **10.** not worn or faded: *fresh colours.* **11.** having a healthy or ruddy appearance. **12.** just arrived: *fresh from the presses.* **13.** youthful or inexperienced. **14.** *Informal.* presumptuous or disrespectful. ~*adv.* **15.** recently: *fresh-cut flowers.* —**'freshly** *adv.* —**'freshness** *n.*

freshen ('frɛʃən) *vb.* **1.** to make or become fresh or fresher. **2.** (often foll. by *up*) to refresh (oneself), esp. by washing. **3.** (of the wind) to increase.

fresher ('frɛʃə) *or* **freshman** ('frɛʃmən) *n., pl.* **-ers** *or* **-men.** a first-year student at college or university.

freshet ('frɛʃɪt) *n.* **1.** the sudden overflowing of a river. **2.** a stream of fresh water emptying into the sea.

freshwater ('freʃ,wɔːtə) n. (modifier) of or living in fresh water.

fret¹ (frɛt) vb. **fretting, fretted. 1.** to distress or be distressed. **2.** to rub or wear away. **3.** to feel or give annoyance or vexation. ~n. **4.** a state of irritation or anxiety.

fret² (frɛt) n. **1.** a repetitive geometrical figure, esp. one used as an ornamental border. ~vb. **fretting, fretted. 2.** to ornament with fret or fretwork.

fret³ (frɛt) n. any of several small metal bars set across the fingerboard of a musical instrument, such as a guitar, as a guide to fingering.

fretful ('frɛtful) adj. peevish, irritable, or upset. —'**fretfully** adv.

fret saw n. a fine-toothed saw with a long thin narrow blade, used for cutting designs in thin wood or metal.

fretwork ('frɛt,wɜːk) n. decorative geometrical carving or openwork.

Freudian ('frɔɪdɪən) adj. of or relating to Sigmund Freud (1856–1939), Austrian psychiatrist, or his ideas. —'**Freudian,ism** n.

Freudian slip n. a slip of the tongue that may reveal an unconscious thought.

Fri. Friday.

friable ('fraɪəbᵊl) adj. easily broken up. —,**fria'bility** n.

friar ('fraɪə) n. a member of any of various men's religious orders of the Roman Catholic Church.

friar's balsam n. a compound with a camphor-like smell, used as an inhalant.

friary ('fraɪərɪ) n., pl. **-aries.** a house of friars.

fricassee ('frɪkəsɪ) n. stewed meat, esp. chicken or veal, served in a thick white sauce.

fricative ('frɪkətɪv) n. **1.** a consonant produced by friction of breath through a partly closed mouth, such as (f) or (z). ~adj. **2.** relating to or denoting a fricative.

friction ('frɪkʃən) n. **1.** a resistance encountered when one body moves relative to another body with which it is in contact. **2.** the act of rubbing one object against another. **3.** disagreement or conflict. —'**frictional** adj.

Friday ('fraɪdɪ) n. **1.** the sixth day of the week; fifth day of the working week. **2.** See **man Friday.**

fridge (frɪdʒ) n. short for **refrigerator.**

fried (fraɪd) vb. the past of **fry¹.**

friend (frɛnd) n. **1.** a person known well to another and regarded with liking, affection, and loyalty. **2.** an ally in a fight or cause. **3.** a patron or supporter. **4. make friends** (**with**). to become friendly (with). —'**friendless** adj. —'**friendship** n.

Friend (frɛnd) n. a member of the Society of Friends; Quaker.

friendly ('frɛndlɪ) adj. **-lier, -liest. 1.**

showing or expressing liking, goodwill, or trust. **2.** on the same side; not hostile. **3.** tending or disposed to help or support. ~n., pl. **-lies. 4.** Sport. a match played for its own sake. —'**friendliness** n.

friendly society n. Brit. an association of people who pay regular dues in return for old-age pensions, sickness benefits, etc.

frier ('fraɪə) n. same as **fryer.** See **fry¹.**

frieze (friːz) n. **1.** any ornamental band on a wall. **2.** Archit. the horizontal band between the architrave and cornice of a classical temple.

frigate ('frɪgɪt) n. **1.** Brit. a warship smaller than a destroyer. **2.** a medium-sized warship of the 18th and 19th centuries.

fright (fraɪt) n. **1.** sudden fear or alarm. **2.** a sudden alarming shock. **3.** Informal. a grotesque or ludicrous person or thing.

frighten ('fraɪtᵊn) vb. **1.** to terrify; scare. **2.** to drive or force to go (away, off, out, in, etc.) by making afraid. —'**frighteningly** adv.

frightful ('fraɪtful) adj. **1.** very alarming or horrifying. **2.** unpleasant, annoying, or extreme: a frightful hurry. —'**frightfully** adv.

frigid ('frɪdʒɪd) adj. **1.** formal or stiff in behaviour or temperament. **2.** (esp. of women) lacking sexual responsiveness. **3.** characterized by physical coldness: a frigid zone. —**fri'gidity** n.

frill (frɪl) n. **1.** a gathered strip of cloth sewn on at one edge only, as ornament. **2.** (often pl.) Informal. a superfluous or pretentious thing; affectation: he made a plain speech with no frills. —**frilled** adj. —'**frilly** adj.

fringe (frɪndʒ) n. **1.** an edging consisting of hanging threads, tassels, etc. **2.** an outer edge; periphery. **3.** (modifier) unofficial; not conventional in form: fringe theatre. **4.** Chiefly Brit. a section of the front hair cut short over the forehead. ~vb. **5.** to adorn with a fringe. **6.** to be a fringe for.

fringe benefit n. an additional advantage, esp. a benefit that supplements an employee's regular pay.

frippery ('frɪpərɪ) n., pl. **-peries. 1.** ornate or showy clothing or adornment. **2.** trifles; trivia.

Frisian ('frɪʒən) n. **1.** a language spoken in the NW Netherlands. **2.** a speaker of this language. ~adj. **3.** of or relating to this language or its speakers.

frisk (frɪsk) vb. **1.** to leap, move about, or act in a playful manner. **2.** Informal. to search (someone) by feeling for concealed weapons, etc. ~n. **3.** a playful movement. **4.** Informal. an instance of frisking a person.

frisky ('frɪskɪ) adj. **friskier, friskiest.** lively, high-spirited, or playful. —'**friskily** adv.

frisson ('friːsɒn) *n.* a shiver; thrill.

fritter[1] ('frɪtə) *vb.* (usually foll. by *away*) to waste: *to fritter away time.*

fritter[2] ('frɪtə) *n.* a piece of food, such as apple, that is dipped in batter and fried in deep fat.

frivolous ('frɪvələs) *adj.* **1.** not serious or sensible in content, attitude, or behaviour. **2.** unworthy of serious or sensible treatment: *frivolous details.* —**frivolity** (frɪ-'vɒlɪtɪ) *n.*

frizz (frɪz) *vb.* **1.** (of hair) to form or cause (hair) to form tight curls. ~*n.* **2.** hair that has been frizzed. —**'frizzy** *adj.*

frizzle[1] ('frɪz'l) *vb.* **1.** to form (hair) into tight crisp curls. ~*n.* **2.** a tight curl.

frizzle[2] ('frɪz'l) *vb.* to scorch or be scorched until crisp or shrivelled up.

frock (frɒk) *n.* **1.** a girl's or woman's dress. **2.** a loose garment, such as a peasant's smock.

frock coat *n.* a man's skirted coat, as worn in the 19th century.

frog[1] (frɒg) *n.* **1.** an amphibian having a short squat tailless body with a moist smooth skin and very long hind legs specialized for hopping. **2. a frog in one's throat.** phlegm on the vocal cords that affects one's speech.

frog[2] (frɒg) *n.* (*often pl.*) a decorative fastening of looped braid, as on a military uniform. —**'frogging** *n.*

frog[3] (frɒg) *n.* horny material in the centre of the sole of a horse's foot.

frogman ('frɒgmən) *n., pl.* **-men.** a swimmer equipped with a rubber suit, flippers, and breathing equipment for working underwater.

frogmarch ('frɒg,mɑːtʃ) *Chiefly Brit.* ~*n.* **1.** a method of carrying a resisting person in which each limb is held and the victim is face downwards. ~*vb.* **2.** to carry in a frogmarch or cause to move forward unwillingly.

frogspawn ('frɒg,spɔːn) *n.* a mass of frogs' eggs surrounded by protective jelly.

frolic ('frɒlɪk) *n.* **1.** a light-hearted occasion. **2.** light-hearted activity; gaiety. ~*vb.* **-icking, -icked. 3.** to caper about.

from (frɒm; *unstressed* frəm) *prep.* **1.** indicating the original location, situation, etc.: *from behind the bushes.* **2.** in a period of time starting at: *he lived from 1910 to 1970.* **3.** indicating the distance between two things or places: *a hundred miles from here.* **4.** indicating a lower amount: *from five to fifty pounds.* **5.** showing the model of: *painted from life.* **6.** used with a verbal noun to mark prohibition, etc.: *nothing prevents him from leaving.* **7.** because of: *exhausted from his walk.*
Usage. see **off.**

frond (frɒnd) *n.* **1.** the compound leaf of a fern. **2.** the leaf of a palm.

front (frʌnt) *n.* **1.** that part or side that is forward, or most often seen or used. **2.** a position or place directly before or ahead. **3.** the beginning, opening, or first part. **4.** the position of leadership. **5.** a promenade at a seaside resort. **6.** *Mil.* **a.** the total area in which opposing armies face each other. **b.** the space in which a military unit is operating. **7.** *Meteorol.* the dividing line between two air masses of different origins. **8.** outward aspect: *a bold front.* **9.** *Informal.* a business or other activity serving as a respectable cover for another, usually criminal, organization. **10.** Also called: **front man.** a nominal leader of an organization. **11.** a particular field of activity: *on the wages front.* **12.** a group of people with a common goal: *a national liberation front.* ~*adj.* **13.** of, at, or in the front. ~*vb.* **14.** to face (onto). **15.** to be a front of or for. **16.** to appear as a presenter in (a television show). **17.** to be the leader of (a band) on stage.

frontage ('frʌntɪdʒ) *n.* **1.** the façade of a building or the front of a plot of ground. **2.** the extent of the front of a shop, plot of land, etc.

frontal ('frʌnt'l) *adj.* **1.** of, at, or in the front. **2.** of or relating to the forehead.

front bench *n.* the leadership of either the Government or Opposition in the House of Commons or in various other legislative assemblies. —**front-'bencher** *n.*

frontier ('frʌntɪə, frʌn'tɪə) *n.* **1.** the region of a country bordering on another or a line marking such a boundary. **2.** the edge of the settled area of a country. **3.** (*often pl.*) the limit of knowledge in a particular field.

frontispiece ('frʌntɪ,piːs) *n.* an illustration facing the title page of a book.

frontrunner ('frʌnt,rʌnə) *n. Informal.* the leader or a favoured contestant in a race or election.

frost (frɒst) *n.* **1.** a white deposit of ice particles. **2.** an atmospheric temperature of below freezing point, producing this deposit. ~*vb.* **3.** to cover with frost. **4.** to kill or damage (plants) with frost.

frostbite ('frɒst,baɪt) *n.* destruction of tissues, esp. of the fingers, ears, toes, and nose, by freezing. —**'frost,bitten** *adj.*

frosted ('frɒstɪd) *adj.* (of glass) having the surface roughened so that it cannot be seen through clearly.

frosting ('frɒstɪŋ) *n. Chiefly U.S. & Canad.* icing.

frosty ('frɒstɪ) *adj.* **frostier, frostiest. 1.** characterized by frost: *a frosty night.* **2.** covered by frost. **3.** lacking warmth or enthusiasm: *a frosty reception.* —**'frostily** *adv.* —**'frostiness** *n.*

froth (frɒθ) *n.* **1.** a mass of small bubbles of air or a gas in a liquid. **2.** a mixture of saliva and air bubbles formed at the lips in certain diseases, such as rabies. ~*vb.* **3.** to produce or cause to produce froth. —'**frothy** *adj.*

frown (fraʊn) *vb.* **1.** to draw the brows together and wrinkle the forehead in worry, anger, or concentration. **2.** (foll. by *on* or *upon*) to look disapprovingly (upon). ~*n.* **3.** the act of frowning. **4.** a look of disapproval or displeasure.

frowsty ('fraʊstɪ) *adj.* ill-smelling; stale; musty.

frowzy *or* **frowsy** ('fraʊzɪ) *adj.* **frowzier, frowziest,** *or* **frowsier, frowsiest. 1.** slovenly or unkempt in appearance. **2.** ill-smelling; frowsty.

froze (frəʊz) *vb.* the past tense of **freeze.**

frozen ('frəʊzᵊn) *vb.* **1.** the past participle of **freeze.** ~*adj.* **2.** turned into or covered with ice. **3.** killed or stiffened by extreme cold. **4.** (of food) preserved by a freezing process. **5. a.** (of prices or wages) arbitrarily pegged at a certain level. **b.** (of business assets) not convertible into cash. **6.** motionless: *he was frozen with horror.*

FRS (in Britain) Fellow of the Royal Society.

fructose ('frʌktəʊs) *n.* a crystalline sugar occurring in honey and many fruits.

frugal ('fruːgᵊl) *adj.* **1.** practising economy; thrifty. **2.** not costly; meagre. —**fru-'gality** *n.* —'**frugally** *adv.*

fruit (fruːt) *n.* **1.** *Bot.* the ripened ovary of a flowering plant, containing one or more seeds. **2.** any fleshy part of a plant that supports the seeds and is edible, such as the strawberry. **3.** any plant product useful to man, including grain and vegetables. **4.** (*often pl.*) the result of an action or effort. ~*vb.* **5.** to bear fruit.

fruiterer ('fruːtərə) *n. Chiefly Brit.* a fruit dealer or seller.

fruitful ('fruːtfʊl) *adj.* **1.** producing good and useful results: *a fruitful discussion.* **2.** bearing fruit in abundance. —'**fruitfully** *adv.*

fruition (fruː'ɪʃən) *n.* **1.** the attainment of something worked for or desired. **2.** the act or condition of bearing fruit.

fruitless ('fruːtlɪs) *adj.* **1.** yielding nothing of value; unproductive. **2.** without fruit. —'**fruitlessly** *adv.*

fruit machine *n. Brit.* a gambling machine that pays out when certain combinations of diagrams, usually of fruit, appear on a dial.

fruit sugar *n.* same as **fructose.**

fruity ('fruːtɪ) *adj.* **fruitier, fruitiest. 1.** of or like fruit. **2.** (of a voice) mellow or rich. **3.** *Informal, chiefly Brit.* full of earthy humour. —'**fruitiness** *n.*

frump (frʌmp) *n.* a woman who is dowdy and unattractive. —'**frumpish** *or* '**frumpy** *adj.*

frustrate (frʌ'streɪt) *vb.* **1.** to hinder or prevent (the efforts, plans, or desires) of. **2.** to upset or anger (a person) by presenting insuperable difficulties: *the lack of facilities depressed and frustrated him.* —**frus'trating** *adj.* —**frus'tration** *n.*

frustrated (frʌ'streɪtɪd) *adj.* dissatisfied or unfulfilled.

frustum ('frʌstəm) *n., pl.* **-tums** *or* **-ta** (-tə). *Geom.* the part of a solid, such as a cone or pyramid, contained between the base and a plane parallel to the base that intersects the solid.

fry[1] (fraɪ) *vb.* **frying, fried. 1.** to cook or be cooked in fat or oil, usually over direct heat. ~*n., pl.* **fries. 2.** a dish of something fried, esp. the offal of a specified animal: *pig's fry.* **3.** Also: **fry-up.** *Brit. informal.* a dish of mixed fried food. —'**fryer** *or* '**frier** *n.*

fry[2] (fraɪ) *pl. n.* **1.** the young of various species of fish. **2.** See **small fry.**

frying pan *n.* **1.** a long-handled shallow pan used for frying. **2. out of the frying pan into the fire.** from a bad situation to a worse one.

f-stop ('ɛf,stɒp) *n.* any of the settings for the f-number of a camera.

ft. foot *or* feet.

fuchsia ('fjuːʃə) *n.* a shrub widely cultivated for its showy drooping purple, red, or white flowers.

fuck (fʌk) *Taboo.* ~*vb.* **1.** to have sexual intercourse with (someone). ~*n.* **2.** an act of sexual intercourse. **3.** *Slang.* a partner in sexual intercourse. **4. not give a fuck.** not to care at all. ~*interj.* **5.** *Offensive.* an expression of strong disgust or anger. —'**fucking** *n., adj., adv.*

fuck off *vb. Offensive taboo slang.* to go away.

fuck up *vb. Offensive taboo slang.* to make a mess of (something).

fuddle ('fʌdᵊl) *vb.* **1.** to cause to be confused or intoxicated. ~*n.* **2.** a confused state.

fuddy-duddy ('fʌdɪ,dʌdɪ) *n., pl.* **-dies.** *Informal.* a person, esp. an elderly one, who is extremely conservative or dull.

fudge[1] (fʌdʒ) *n.* a soft sweet made from sugar, butter, and milk.

fudge[2] (fʌdʒ) *vb.* to make (an issue or problem) less clear deliberately; misrepresent.

fuel (fjʊəl) *n.* **1.** any substance burned for heat or power, such as coal or petrol. **2.** the material that produces energy in a nuclear reactor. **3.** something that nourishes or builds up emotion or action. ~*vb.* **fuelling, fuelled** *or U.S.* **fueling, fueled. 4.** to supply with or receive fuel.

fuel cell *n.* a cell in which chemical energy is converted directly into electrical energy.

fug (fʌg) *n. Chiefly Brit.* a hot stale atmosphere. —'**fuggy** *adj.*

fugitive ('fjuːdʒɪtɪv) *n.* **1.** a person who

flees. ~*adj.* **2.** fleeing, esp. from arrest or pursuit. **3.** not permanent; fleeting.

fugue (fjuːg) *n.* a musical form consisting of a theme repeated above or below the continuing first statement. —**'fugal** *adj.*

Führer *or* **Fuehrer** ('fjʊərə) *n.* a leader; the title taken by Hitler.

-ful *suffix.* **1.** full of or characterized by: *painful; restful.* **2.** enough to fill the thing specified: *mouthful.*
Usage. Where the amount held by a spoon, etc., is used as a rough unit of measurement, the correct form is *spoonful*, as in: *take a spoonful of this medicine every day.* The plural of a word like spoonful is *spoonfuls* and not *spoonsful.*

fulcrum ('fʊlkrəm) *n., pl.* **-crums** *or* **-cra** (-krə). the pivot about which a lever turns.

fulfil *or U.S.* **fulfill** (fʊl'fɪl) *vb.* **-filling,** **-filled.** **1.** to bring about the achievement of (a desire or promise). **2.** to carry out (a request). **3.** to satisfy (demands or conditions). **4. fulfil oneself.** to achieve one's potential. —**ful'filment** *or U.S.* **ful'fillment** *n.*

full¹ (fʊl) *adj.* **1.** holding as much as possible. **2.** abundant in supply: *full of energy.* **3.** having consumed enough food or drink. **4.** (esp. of the face or figure) rounded or plump. **5.** complete: *a full dozen.* **6.** with all privileges or rights: *a full member.* **7.** (foll. by *of*) engrossed (with): *full of his own projects.* **8.** *Music.* powerful or rich in volume and sound. **9.** (of a skirt) containing a large amount of fabric. **10. full of oneself.** full of pride or conceit. **11. full up.** filled to capacity. ~*adv.* **12.** completely; entirely. **13.** directly; right: *he hit him full in the stomach.* **14.** very; extremely (esp. in **full well**). ~*n.* **15. in full.** without omitting or shortening. **16. to the full.** thoroughly; fully. —**'fullness** *or esp. U.S.* **'fulness** *n.*

full² (fʊl) *vb.* to make (cloth) more compact during manufacture through shrinking and beating.

fullback ('fʊl,bæk) *n. Soccer, hockey, & rugby.* a defensive player.

full-blooded *adj.* **1.** having great vigour or enthusiasm. **2.** (esp. of horses) of unmixed ancestry.

full-blown *adj.* fully developed.

full-bodied *adj.* having a full rich flavour or quality.

fuller's earth ('fʊləz) *n.* a natural absorbent clay used for fulling cloth.

full-frontal *adj. Informal.* exposing the genitals to full view.

full house *n.* **1.** a theatre filled to capacity. **2.** (in bingo) the set of numbers needed to win.

full-length *n. (modifier)* **1.** showing the complete human figure. **2.** not abridged.

full moon *n.* the phase of the moon when it is visible as a fully illuminated disc.

full pitch *or* **toss** *n. Cricket.* a bowled ball that reaches the batsman without bouncing.

full-scale *n. (modifier)* **1.** (of a plan) of actual size. **2.** using all resources; all-out.

full stop *n.* the punctuation mark (.) used at the end of a sentence and after abbreviations. Also called (esp. U.S. and Canad.): **period.**

full-time *adj.* **1.** for the entire time appropriate to an activity: *a full-time job.* ~*adv.* **full time.** **2.** on a full-time basis: *he works full time.*

fully ('fʊlɪ) *adv.* **1.** to the greatest degree or extent. **2.** amply; adequately. **3.** at least: *it was fully an hour before she came.*

fully fashioned *adj.* (of stockings or knitwear) shaped and seamed so as to fit closely.

fulmar ('fʊlmə) *n.* a heavily built short-tailed sea bird of polar regions.

fulminate ('fʌlmɪ,neɪt) *vb.* (often foll. by *against*) to criticize or denounce angrily and vehemently. —**,fulmi'nation** *n.*

fulsome ('fʊlsəm) *adj.* distastefully excessive or insincere: *fulsome compliments.*

fumble ('fʌmb'l) *vb.* **1.** (often foll. by *for* or *with*) to use the hands clumsily or grope about blindly. **2.** to say or do awkwardly. ~*n.* **3.** the act of fumbling.

fume (fjuːm) *vb.* **1.** to be overcome with anger or fury. **2.** to give off (fumes) or (of fumes) to be given off, esp. during a chemical reaction. **3.** to treat with fumes. ~*n.* **4.** (often *pl.*) a pungent or toxic vapour, gas, or smoke.

fumigate ('fjuːmɪ,geɪt) *vb.* to treat (something contaminated) with fumes. —**,fumi'gation** *n.*

fun (fʌn) *n.* **1.** a source of enjoyment, amusement or diversion. **2.** pleasure, gaiety, or merriment. **3.** jest or sport (esp. in **in** *or* **for fun**). **4. make fun of** *or* **poke fun at.** to ridicule or deride.

function ('fʌŋkʃən) *n.* **1.** the natural action or intended purpose of a person or thing. **2.** an official or formal social gathering. **3.** a factor dependent upon another or other factors. **4.** *Maths.* a quantity, the value of which depends on the varying value of another quantity. ~*vb.* **5.** to operate; work. **6.** (foll. by *as*) to perform the action or role (of something or someone else).

functional ('fʌŋkʃən'l) *adj.* **1.** of or performing a function. **2.** practical rather than decorative. **3.** working. **4.** *Med.* affecting a function of an organ without structural change. —**'functionally** *adv.*

functionalism ('fʌŋkʃənə,lɪzəm) *n.* the theory that the form of a thing should be determined by its use. —**'functionalist** *n., adj.*

functionary ('fʌŋkʃənərɪ) *n., pl.* **-aries.** a

person acting in an official capacity, as for a government; an official.

fund (fʌnd) n. **1.** a reserve of money set aside for a certain purpose. **2.** a supply or store of something; stock. ~vb. **3.** to provide money to. **4.** to convert (short-term debt) into long-term debt bearing fixed interest. ~See also **funds.**

fundamental (ˌfʌndəˈmɛntʳl) adj. **1.** of or forming a foundation; basic. **2.** essential; primary. ~n. **3.** a principle that serves as the basis of an idea or system. **4.** the lowest note of a harmonic series. —ˌfundaˈmentally adv.

fundamentalism (ˌfʌndəˈmɛntəˌlɪzəm) n. **1.** Christianity. the view that the Bible is literally true. **2.** Islam. a movement favouring strict observance of Islamic law. —ˌfundaˈmentalist n., adj.

fundamental particle n. same as **elementary particle.**

funds (fʌndz) pl. n. money that is readily available.

funeral (ˈfjuːnərəl) n. **1.** a ceremony at which a dead person is buried or cremated. **2.** Informal. problem; affair: that's your funeral. ~adj. **3.** of or for a funeral. —ˈfunerary adj.

funeral director n. an undertaker.

funereal (fjuːˈnɪərɪəl) adj. suggestive of a funeral; gloomy or mournful. —fuˈnereally adv.

funfair (ˈfʌnˌfɛə) n. Brit. an amusement park.

fungicide (ˈfʌndʒɪˌsaɪd) n. a substance that destroys fungi. —ˌfungiˈcidal adj.

fungoid (ˈfʌŋɡɔɪd) adj. resembling a fungus.

fungous (ˈfʌŋɡəs) adj. appearing suddenly and spreading quickly like a fungus.

fungus (ˈfʌŋɡəs) n., pl. **fungi** (ˈfʌŋɡaɪ) or **funguses.** any of a division of plants that do not have leaves or roots, and reproduce by spores, including moulds, yeasts, and mushrooms. —**fungal** adj.

funicular (fjuːˈnɪkjʊlə) n. a railway up the side of a mountain, consisting of two cars at either end of a cable passing round a driving wheel at the summit. Also called: **funicular railway.**

funk¹ (fʌŋk) Informal, chiefly Brit. ~n. **1.** Also called: **blue funk.** a state of nervousness, fear, or depression. **2.** a coward. ~vb. **3.** to avoid doing something through fear.

funk² (fʌŋk) n. a type of Black dance music with a strong beat.

funky (ˈfʌŋkɪ) adj. **-kier, -kiest.** (of jazz or pop) passionate; soulful.

funnel (ˈfʌnʳl) n. **1.** a hollow utensil with a wide mouth tapering to a small hole, used for pouring liquids into a narrow-necked vessel. **2.** a smokestack, as on a steamship. ~vb. **-nelling, -nelled** or U.S. **-neling,**

-neled. 3. to move or cause to move through or as if through a funnel.

funny (ˈfʌnɪ) adj. **-nier, -niest. 1.** causing amusement or laughter; humorous. **2.** peculiar; odd. **3.** suspicious or dubious (esp. in **funny business**). **4.** Informal. faint or ill. —ˈfunnily adv. —ˈfunniness n.

funny bone n. a sensitive area near the elbow where the nerve is close to the surface of the skin.

fur (fɜː) n. **1.** the dense coat of fine silky hairs on many mammals. **2.** the skin of certain animals, with the hair left on. **3.** a garment made of fur. **4. make the fur fly.** to cause a scene or disturbance. **5.** Informal. a whitish coating on the tongue, caused by illness. **6.** Brit. a deposit on the insides of waterpipes or kettles, caused by hard water. ~vb. **furring, furred. 7.** (often foll. by up) to cover or become covered with a furlike deposit.

furbelow (ˈfɜːbɪˌləʊ) n. **1.** a flounce or ruffle. **2.** (often pl.) showy ornamentation.

furbish (ˈfɜːbɪʃ) vb. (often foll. by up) to brighten up; renovate.

furcate (ˈfɜːkeɪt) vb. **1.** to divide into two parts. ~adj. **2.** forked: furcate branches. —furˈcation n.

Furies (ˈfjʊərɪz) pl. n., sing. **Fury.** Classical myth. the goddesses of vengeance, who pursued unpunished criminals.

furious (ˈfjʊərɪəs) adj. **1.** extremely angry or annoyed. **2.** violent or unrestrained, as in speed or energy. —ˈfuriously adv.

furl (fɜːl) vb. to roll up (an umbrella, flag, or sail) neatly and securely.

furlong (ˈfɜːˌlɒŋ) n. a unit of length equal to 220 yards (201.168 metres).

furlough (ˈfɜːləʊ) n. leave of absence from military duty.

furnace (ˈfɜːnɪs) n. **1.** an enclosed chamber in which heat is produced to destroy refuse or smelt ores. **2.** a very hot place.

furnish (ˈfɜːnɪʃ) vb. **1.** to provide (a house or room) with furniture, etc. **2.** to supply.

furnishings (ˈfɜːnɪʃɪŋz) pl. n. furniture, carpets, and fittings with which a room or house is furnished.

furniture (ˈfɜːnɪtʃə) n. **1.** the movable articles that equip a room or house. **2.** the equipment necessary for a ship or factory. **3.** locks and handles for use on doors.

furore (fjʊˈrɔːrɪ) or esp. U.S. **furor** (ˈfjʊərɔː) n. a very angry or excited reaction by people to something: the present furore over drugs.

furrier (ˈfʌrɪə) n. a person who makes or sells fur garments.

furrow (ˈfʌrəʊ) n. **1.** a long narrow trench made in the ground by a plough. **2.** any long deep groove, esp. a deep wrinkle on the forehead. ~vb. **3.** to become wrinkled. **4.** to make furrows in (land).

furry ('fɜːrɪ) *adj.* **-rier, -riest.** like or covered with fur or something furlike.

further ('fɜːðə) *adv.* **1.** in addition; furthermore. **2.** to a greater degree or extent. **3.** to or at a more advanced point. **4.** to or at a greater distance in time or space. ~*adj.* **5.** additional; more. **6.** more distant or remote in time or space. ~*vb.* **7.** to assist the progress of (something). —'**furtherance** *n.*

Usage. see **farther.**

further education *n.* (in Britain) formal education beyond school other than at a university or polytechnic.

furthermore ('fɜːðə,mɔː) *adv.* in addition.

furthest ('fɜːðɪst) *adv.* **1.** to the greatest degree or extent. **2.** to or at the greatest distance in time or space; farthest. ~*adj.* **3.** most distant in time or space; farthest.

Usage. see **farther.**

furtive ('fɜːtɪv) *adj.* characterized by stealth; sly and secretive. —'**furtively** *adv.*

fury ('fjʊərɪ) *n., pl.* **-ries. 1.** violent anger. **2.** an outburst of such anger. **3.** uncontrolled violence: *the fury of the storm.* **4.** a person with a violent temper. **5.** See **Furies. 6. like fury.** *Informal.* energetically; powerfully.

furze (fɜːz) *n.* gorse. —'**furzy** *adj.*

fuse[1] *or U.S.* **fuze** (fjuːz) *n.* **1.** a lead containing an explosive, used to fire an explosive charge. ~*vb.* **2.** to equip with such a fuse. —'**fuseless** *adj.*

fuse[2] (fjuːz) *n.* **1.** a protective device for safeguarding electric circuits, containing a wire that melts and breaks the circuit when the current exceeds a certain value. ~*vb.* **2.** *Brit.* to fail or cause to fail as a result of a fuse blowing. **3.** to equip (a plug or circuit) with a fuse. **4.** to join or become combined. **5.** to become or cause to become liquid, esp. by the action of heat. **6.** to unite or become united by melting.

fuselage ('fjuːzɪ,lɑːʒ) *n.* the main body of an aircraft.

fusible ('fjuːzəbʰl) *adj.* capable of being melted.

fusilier (,fjuːzɪ'lɪə) *n.* (formerly) an infantryman armed with a light musket: a term still used in the names of certain British regiments.

fusillade (,fjuːzɪ'leɪd) *n.* **1.** a rapid continual discharge of firearms. **2.** a sudden outburst, as of criticism.

fusion ('fjuːʒən) *n.* **1.** the act or process of melting together. **2.** something produced by fusing. **3.** a kind of popular music that is a blend of two or more styles, such as jazz and funk. **4.** See **nuclear fusion.**

fuss (fʌs) *n.* **1.** nervous activity or agitation. **2.** complaint or objection: *he made a fuss over the bill.* **3.** an exhibition of affection or admiration: *they made a great fuss over the new baby.* ~*vb.* **4.** to worry unnecessarily. **5.** to be excessively concerned over trifles. **6.** (usually foll. by *over*) to show great or excessive concern or affection (for). **7.** to bother (a person).

fusspot ('fʌs,pɒt) *n. Brit. informal.* a person who fusses unnecessarily.

fussy ('fʌsɪ) *adj.* **fussier, fussiest. 1.** inclined to fuss. **2.** very particular about detail. **3.** overelaborate. —'**fussily** *adv.*

fustian ('fʌstɪən) *n.* **1.** (formerly) a hardwearing fabric of cotton mixed with flax or wool. **2.** pompous talk or writing.

fusty ('fʌstɪ) *adj.* **-tier, -tiest. 1.** smelling of damp or mould. **2.** old-fashioned. —'**fustiness** *n.*

futile ('fjuːtaɪl) *adj.* **1.** having no effective result; unsuccessful. **2.** pointless; trifling. —**futility** (fjuː'tɪlɪtɪ) *n.*

future ('fjuːtʃə) *n.* **1.** the time yet to come. **2.** undetermined events that will occur in that time. **3.** the condition of a person or thing at a later date. **4.** *Grammar.* a tense of verbs used when the action described is to occur after the time of utterance. **5. in future.** from now on. ~*adj.* **6.** that is yet to come or be. **7.** of or expressing time yet to come. **8.** destined to become. **9.** *Grammar.* in or denoting the future as a tense of verbs. ~See also **futures.**

future perfect *Grammar.* ~*adj.* **1.** denoting a tense of verbs describing an action that will have been performed by a certain time. ~*n.* **2.** the future perfect tense.

futures ('fjuːtʃəz) *pl. n.* commodities bought or sold at an agreed price for delivery at a specified future date.

futurism ('fjuːtʃə,rɪzəm) *n.* an art movement that replaced traditional aesthetic values with the characteristics of the machine age. —'**futurist** *n., adj.*

futuristic (,fjuːtʃə'rɪstɪk) *adj.* **1.** of design or technology that appears to belong to some future time. **2.** of futurism.

futurity (fjuː'tjʊərɪtɪ) *n., pl.* **-ties. 1.** future. **2.** a future event.

futurology (,fjuːtʃə'rɒlədʒɪ) *n.* the study or prediction of the future of mankind.

fuzz[1] (fʌz) *n.* a mass or covering of fine or curly hairs, fibres, etc.

fuzz[2] (fʌz) *n. Slang.* the police or a policeman.

fuzzy ('fʌzɪ) *adj.* **fuzzier, fuzziest. 1.** of, resembling, or covered with fuzz. **2.** unclear or distorted. **3.** (of hair) tightly curled. —'**fuzzily** *adv.* —'**fuzziness** *n.*

G

g *or* **G** (dʒiː) *n., pl.* **g's, G,s** *or* **Gs.** the seventh letter of the English alphabet.

g **1.** gallon(s). **2.** gram(s). **3.** acceleration due to gravity.

G **1.** *Music.* the fifth note of the scale of C major. **2.** gravity. **3.** good. **4.** *Slang, chiefly U.S.* grand (a thousand dollars or pounds).

Ga *Chem.* gallium.

GA *or* **Ga.** Georgia.

gab (gæb) *Informal.* ~*vb.* **gabbing, gabbed. 1.** to talk idly or too much; chatter. ~*n.* **2.** idle talk. **3. gift of the gab.** ability to talk glibly or persuasively.

gabble ('gæbᵊl) *vb.* **1.** to speak rapidly and indistinctly. ~*n.* **2.** rapid and indistinct speech.

gaberdine ('gæbə,diːn, ˌgæbə'diːn) *n.* **1.** a twill-weave worsted, cotton, or viscose fabric. **2.** a coat or other garment made of this.

gable ('geɪbᵊl) *n.* the triangular upper part of a wall between the sloping ends of a ridged roof. —**'gabled** *adj.*

gad (gæd) *vb.* **gadding, gadded.** (often foll. by *about* or *around*) to go about in search of pleasure; gallivant.

gadabout ('gædə,baʊt) *n. Informal.* a person who restlessly seeks amusement.

gadfly ('gæd,flaɪ) *n., pl.* **-flies. 1.** a large fly that bites livestock. **2.** a constantly irritating person.

gadget ('gædʒɪt) *n.* a small mechanical device or appliance. —**'gadgetry** *n.*

gadoid ('geɪdɔɪd) *adj.* **1.** of or belonging to the cod family of marine fishes. ~*n.* **2.** any gadoid fish.

gadolinium (ˌgædə'lɪnɪəm) *n.* a silvery-white metallic element of the rare-earth group. Symbol: Gd

gadwall ('gæd,wɔːl) *n., pl.* **-walls** *or* **-wall.** a duck related to the mallard. The male has a grey body and black tail.

gadzooks (gæd'zuːks) *interj. Archaic.* a mild oath.

Gael (geɪl) *n.* a Gaelic-speaker of Scotland, Ireland, or the Isle of Man. —**'Gaeldom** *n.*

Gaelic ('geɪlɪk, 'gæ-) *n.* **1.** any of the closely related Celtic languages of Scotland, Ireland, or the Isle of Man. ~*adj.* **2.** of the Celtic people of Scotland, Ireland, or the Isle of Man, or their language.

gaff¹ (gæf) *n.* **1.** *Angling.* a stiff pole with a stout hook attached for landing large fish. **2.** *Naut.* a spar hoisted to support a fore-and-aft sail. ~*vb.* **3.** *Angling.* to hook or land (a fish) with a gaff.

gaff² (gæf) *n.* **blow the gaff.** *Brit. slang.* to divulge a secret.

gaffe (gæf) *n.* a social blunder.

gaffer ('gæfə) *n.* **1.** an old man: often used affectionately. **2.** *Informal, chiefly Brit.* a boss or foreman. **3.** *Informal.* the senior electrician on a television or film set.

gag¹ (gæg) *vb.* **gagging, gagged. 1.** to stop up (a person's mouth), usually with a piece of cloth, to prevent him from speaking or crying out. **2.** to deprive of free speech. **3.** to retch or cause to retch. **4.** to struggle for breath; choke. ~*n.* **5.** something, usually a piece of cloth, stuffed into or tied across the mouth. **6.** any restraint on free speech. **7.** *Parliamentary procedure.* same as **closure** (sense 3).

gag² (gæg) *Informal.* ~*n.* **1.** a joke, usually one told by a professional comedian. **2.** a hoax or practical joke. ~*vb.* **gagging, gagged. 3.** to tell jokes.

gaga ('gɑːgɑː) *adj. Informal.* **1.** senile; doting. **2.** slightly crazy.

gage¹ (geɪdʒ) *n.* **1.** something given as security; pledge. **2.** (formerly) a glove or other object thrown down to indicate a challenge to combat.

gage² (geɪdʒ) *n.* short for **greengage.**

gage³ (geɪdʒ) *n., vb.* *U.S.* same as **gauge.**

gaggle ('gægᵊl) *n.* **1.** a flock of geese. **2.** *Informal.* a disorderly group of people.

gaiety ('geɪətɪ) *n., pl.* **-ties. 1.** the condition of being merry. **2.** festivity; merrymaking. **3.** colourful bright appearance.

gaily ('geɪlɪ) *adv.* **1.** in a lively manner; merrily. **2.** with bright colours.

gain (geɪn) *vb.* **1.** to acquire (something desirable); obtain. **2.** to win in competition: *to gain the victory.* **3.** to increase, improve, or advance: *the car gained speed.* **4.** (usually foll. by *on* or *upon*) to get nearer (to) or catch up (on). **5.** to get to; reach: *the steamer gained port.* **6.** (of a timepiece) to become or be too fast. ~*n.* **7.** something won or acquired; profit; advantage. **8.** an increase in size or amount. **9.** a gaining; attainment; acquisition. **10.** *Electronics.* the ratio of the output signal of an amplifier to the input signal, usually measured in decibels.

gainful ('geɪnful) *adj.* profitable; lucrative. —**'gainfully** *adv.*

gainsay (geɪn'seɪ) *vb.* **-saying, -said.** *Archaic or literary.* to deny; contradict.

gait (geɪt) *n.* **1.** manner of walking. **2.** (of

horses and dogs) the pattern of footsteps at a particular speed, such as a trot.

gaiter (ˈgeɪtə) n. (often pl.). a cloth or leather covering for the leg or ankle.

gal (gæl) n. Slang. a girl.

gal. gallon.

gala (ˈgɑːlə, ˈgeɪlə) n. 1. a celebration; festival. 2. Chiefly Brit. a sporting occasion with competitions in several events: a swimming gala.

galactic (gəˈlæktɪk) adj. of the Galaxy or other galaxies.

galantine (ˈgælən,tiːn) n. a dish of white meat which is boned, cooked, and served cold in jelly.

galaxy (ˈgæləksɪ) n., pl. **-axies.** 1. a star system held together by gravitational attraction. 2. a splendid gathering of famous or distinguished people.

Galaxy (ˈgæləksɪ) n. **the.** the spiral galaxy that contains the solar system. Also called: the **Milky Way.**

gale (geɪl) n. 1. a strong wind, specifically one of force 8 on the Beaufort scale. 2. (often pl.) a loud outburst: gales of laughter.

galena (gəˈliːnə) or **galenite** (gəˈliːnaɪt) n. a soft bluish-grey mineral consisting of lead sulphide: the chief source of lead.

Galia melon (ˈgæliə) n. a kind of melon with a raised network texture on the skin and aromatic flesh.

gall[1] (gɔːl) n. 1. Informal. impudence. 2. bitterness; rancour. 3. something bitter or disagreeable. 4. Physiol., obs. same as **bile.**

gall[2] (gɔːl) n. 1. a sore on the skin caused by chafing. 2. something that causes annoyance. 3. annoyance. ~vb. 4. to chafe (the skin) by rubbing. 5. to annoy.

gall[3] (gɔːl) n. an abnormal outgrowth in plant tissue caused by parasitic insects, fungi, or bacteria.

gall. gallon.

gallant adj. (ˈgælənt). 1. brave and noble. 2. (gəˈlænt, ˈgælənt). (of a man) attentive to women; chivalrous. 3. imposing; stately: a gallant ship. ~n. (ˈgælənt, gəˈlænt). 4. a woman's lover or suitor. 5. a dashing or fashionable young man who pursues women. —'**gallantly** adv.

gallantry (ˈgæləntrɪ) n., pl. **-ries.** 1. conspicuous courage. 2. polite attentiveness to women. 3. a gallant action or phrase.

gall bladder n. a muscular sac, attached to the liver, that stores bile.

galleon (ˈgæliən) n. a large, three-masted sailing ship used from the 15th to the 18th centuries.

gallery (ˈgælərɪ) n., pl. **-leries.** 1. a covered passageway open on one or both sides. 2. a balcony running along or around the inside wall of a church, hall, or other building. 3. Theatre. **a.** an upper floor that projects from the rear and contains the cheapest seats. **b.** the audience seated there. **4. a** long narrow room: a shooting gallery. **5.** a room or building for exhibiting works of art. **6.** an underground passage. **7.** a group of spectators, as at a golf match. **8. play to the gallery.** to try to gain approval by appealing to popular taste.

galley (ˈgælɪ) n. **1.** a ship propelled by oars or sails, used in ancient or medieval times. **2.** the kitchen of a ship, boat, or aircraft. **3.** Printing. **a.** a tray for holding composed type. **b.** short for **galley proof.**

galley proof n. a printer's proof taken from type in a galley, used to make corrections before the type is made up into pages.

galley slave n. **1.** a criminal or slave forced to row in a galley. **2.** Informal. a drudge.

galliard (ˈgæljəd) n. **1.** a lively dance in triple time for two persons, popular in the 16th and 17th centuries. **2.** music for this dance.

Gallic (ˈgælɪk) adj. **1.** French. **2.** of ancient Gaul or the Gauls.

Gallicism (ˈgælɪ,sɪzəm) n. a word or idiom borrowed from French.

gallinaceous (,gælɪˈneɪʃəs) adj. of an order of birds, including poultry, pheasants, and grouse, having a heavy rounded body.

galling (ˈgɔːlɪŋ) adj. annoying or bitterly humiliating.

gallium (ˈgæliəm) n. a silvery metallic element used in high-temperature thermometers and semiconductors. Symbol: Ga

gallivant (ˈgælɪ,vænt) vb. to go about in search of pleasure.

gallon (ˈgælən) n. **1.** Brit. a unit of capacity equal to 4.55 litres. **2.** U.S. a unit of capacity equal to 3.79 litres.

gallop (ˈgæləp) vb. **1.** (of a horse) to run fast with a two-beat stride in which all four legs are off the ground at once. **2.** to ride (a horse) at a gallop. **3.** to move or progress rapidly. ~n. **4.** the fast two-beat gait of horses. **5.** a galloping.

gallows (ˈgæləʊz) n., pl. **-lowses** or **-lows.** **1.** a wooden structure consisting of two upright posts with a crossbeam, used for hanging criminals. **2. the gallows.** execution by hanging.

gallstone (ˈgɔːl,stəʊn) n. a small hard mass formed in the gall bladder or its ducts.

Gallup Poll (ˈgæləp) n. a sampling of the views of a representative cross section of the population, usually used to forecast voting.

galop (ˈgæləp) n. **1.** a 19th-century dance in quick duple time. **2.** music for this dance.

galore (gəˈlɔː) det. in abundance: food and drink galore.

galoshes (gəˈlɒʃɪz) pl. n. (sometimes sing.) a pair of waterproof overshoes.

galumph (gə'lʌmpf, -'lʌmf) *vb. Informal.* to leap or move about clumsily or joyfully.

galvanic (gæl'vænɪk) *adj.* **1.** of or producing an electric current by chemical means, as in a battery. **2.** *Informal.* stimulating, startling, or energetic.

galvanism ('gælvə‚nɪzəm) *n. Obs.* electricity produced by chemical means, as in a battery.

galvanize *or* **-ise** ('gælvə‚naɪz) *vb.* **1.** to stimulate; excite; startle. **2.** to cover (metal) with a protective zinc coating. **3.** to stimulate by an electric current. —‚**galvani'zation** *or* **-i'sation** *n.*

galvanometer (‚gælvə'nɒmɪtə) *n.* a sensitive instrument for detecting or measuring small electric currents.

gambit ('gæmbɪt) *n.* **1.** *Chess.* an opening move in which a piece, usually a pawn, is sacrificed to gain an advantageous position. **2.** an opening line or move intended to gain an advantage.

gamble ('gæmb³l) *vb.* **1.** to play games of chance to win money or prizes. **2.** to risk or bet (something) on the outcome of an event or sport. **3.** (often foll. by *on*) to act with the expectation of: *to gamble on its being a sunny day.* **4.** (often foll. by *away*) to lose by gambling. ~*n.* **5.** a risky act or venture. **6.** a bet or wager. —'**gambler** *n.* —'**gambling** *n.*

gamboge (gæm'bəʊdʒ, -'buːʒ) *n.* a gum resin obtained from a tropical Asian tree, used as a yellow pigment and as a purgative.

gambol ('gæmb³l) *vb.* **-bolling, -bolled** *or U.S.* **-boling, -boled. 1.** to jump about playfully; frolic. ~*n.* **2.** a gambolling; frolic.

game¹ (geɪm) *n.* **1.** an amusement or pastime. **2.** a contest with rules. **3.** a single period of play in such a contest. **4.** the score needed to win a contest. **5.** a single contest in a series; match. **6.** (*pl.; often cap.*) an event consisting of various sporting contests, usually in athletics: *Olympic Games.* **7.** equipment needed for playing certain games: *a compendium of games.* **8.** style or ability in playing a game. **9.** a proceeding practised like a game: *the game of politics.* **10.** an activity undertaken in a spirit of levity: *marriage is just a game to him.* **11.** wild animals, birds, or fish, hunted for sport or food. **12.** the flesh of such animals, used as food. **13.** an object of pursuit: *fair game.* **14.** *Informal.* work or occupation. **15.** *Informal.* a trick or scheme: *what's your game?* **16.** *Slang, chiefly Brit.* prostitution: *on the game.* **17. give the game away.** to reveal one's intentions or a secret. **18. make (a) game of.** to make fun of; mock. **19. play the game.** to behave fairly. **20. the game is up.** the scheme or trick has been found out and so cannot succeed. ~*adj.* **21.** *Informal.* full of fighting spirit; plucky. **22.** (usually foll. by *for*) *Informal.* prepared or ready; willing:

I'm game for a try. ~*vb.* **23.** to play games of chance for money; gamble. —'**gamely** *adv.* —'**gameness** *n.*

game² (geɪm) *adj.* lame: *a game leg.*

gamecock ('geɪm‚kɒk) *n.* a cock bred and trained for fighting.

gamekeeper ('geɪm‚kiːpə) *n.* a person employed to take care of game on an estate.

game laws *pl. n.* laws governing the hunting and preservation of game.

gamesmanship ('geɪmzmən‚ʃɪp) *n. Informal.* the art of winning by cunning practices without actually cheating.

gamester ('geɪmstə) *n.* a gambler.

gamete ('gæmiːt, gə'miːt) *n.* a cell that can fuse with another in reproduction. —**gametic** (gə'metɪk) *adj.*

gamin ('gæmɪn) *n.* a street urchin.

gamine ('gæmiːn) *n.* a slim and boyish girl or young woman.

gaming ('geɪmɪŋ) *n.* gambling.

gamma ('gæmə) *n.* the third letter in the Greek alphabet (Γ, γ).

gamma radiation *n.* electromagnetic radiation of shorter wavelength and higher energy than x-rays.

gamma rays *pl. n.* streams of gamma radiation.

gammon ('gæmən) *n.* **1.** a cured or smoked ham. **2.** the hindquarter of a side of bacon.

gammy ('gæmɪ) *adj.* **-mier, -miest.** *Brit. slang.* (of the leg) lame.

gamp (gæmp) *n. Brit. informal.* an umbrella.

gamut ('gæmət) *n.* **1.** entire range or scale, as of emotions. **2.** *Music.* **a.** a scale. **b.** the whole range of notes.

gamy *or* **gamey** ('geɪmɪ) *adj.* **gamier, gamiest.** having the smell or flavour of game.

gander ('gændə) *n.* **1.** a male goose. **2.** *Informal.* a quick look: *take a gander.*

gang¹ (gæŋ) *n.* **1.** a group of people who associate together, usually for criminal purposes. **2.** an organized group of workmen. **3.** a set of tools arranged to work in coordination. ~*vb.* **4.** to become or act as a gang. ~See also **gang up.**

gang² (gæŋ) *vb. Scot.* to go or walk.

gangland ('gæŋ‚lænd, -lənd) *n.* the criminal underworld.

gangling ('gæŋglɪŋ) *or* **gangly** *adj.* lanky and awkward in movement.

ganglion ('gæŋglɪən) *n., pl.* **-glia** (-glɪə) *or* **-glions.** a collection of nerve cells outside the brain and spinal cord. —‚**gangli'onic** *adj.*

gangplank ('gæŋ‚plæŋk) *n. Naut.* a portable bridge for boarding and leaving a ship.

gangrene ('gæŋgriːn) *n.* **1.** decay of tissue due to the blood supply being interrupted by disease or injury. ~*vb.* **2.** to affect or become affected with gangrene. —**gangrenous** ('gæŋgrɪnəs) *adj.*

gangster ('gæŋstə) *n.* a member of an organized gang of criminals.

gangue (gæŋ) *n.* valueless material in an ore.

gang up *vb.* (often foll. by *on* or *against*) *Informal.* to combine in a group (against).

gangway ('gæŋ,weɪ) *n.* **1.** same as **gangplank.** **2.** an opening in a ship's side to take a gangplank. **3.** *Brit.* an aisle between rows of seats. ~*interj.* **4.** clear a path!

gannet ('gænɪt) *n.* **1.** a heavily built marine bird with white plumage and dark wingtips. **2.** *Slang.* a greedy person.

ganoid ('gænɔɪd) *adj.* **1.** (of the scales of certain fishes) consisting of an inner bony layer covered with an enamel-like substance. **2.** (of a fish) having such scales. ~*n.* **3.** a ganoid fish.

gantry ('gæntrɪ) *n., pl.* **-tries. 1.** a bridgelike framework used to support something, such as a travelling crane or signals over a railway track. **2.** the framework tower used to position and service a large rocket on its launching pad.

gaol (dʒeɪl) *n., vb. Brit.* same as **jail.** —**'gaoler** *n.*

gap (gæp) *n.* **1.** a break or opening in something. **2.** a break in continuity; interruption; interval. **3.** *Chiefly U.S.* a gorge or ravine. **4.** a divergence or difference; disparity: *the generation gap.* —**'gappy** *adj.*

gape (geɪp) *vb.* **1.** to stare in wonder with the mouth open. **2.** to open the mouth wide, as in yawning. **3.** to be or become wide open: *the crater gaped under his feet.* ~*n.* **4.** a wide opening. **5.** a stare of astonishment. —**'gaping** *adj.*

garage ('gærɑːʒ, -rɪdʒ) *n.* **1.** a building used to house motor vehicles. **2.** an establishment in which vehicles are sold and repaired, and which also sells petrol and diesel oil. ~*vb.* **3.** to put into or keep in a garage.

garage sale *n.* a sale of household items held at a person's home, usually in the garage.

garb (gɑːb) *n.* **1.** clothes, usually the distinctive attire of an occupation or group: *clerical garb.* **2.** external appearance. ~*vb.* **3.** to clothe.

garbage ('gɑːbɪdʒ) *n.* **1.** worthless, useless, or unwanted matter. **2.** *U.S. & Canad.* rubbish.

garble ('gɑːbᵊl) *vb.* **1.** to jumble (a story or quotation) unintentionally. **2.** to distort the meaning of (a text) by making misleading omissions.

garçon (gɑːˈsɒn) *n.* a waiter.

garda ('gɑːdə) *n., pl.* **gardaí** ('gɑːdɪ). a member of the police force of the Republic of Ireland.

garden ('gɑːdᵊn) *n.* **1.** *Brit.* an area of land usually next to a house, for growing flowers, fruit, or vegetables. **2.** (*often pl.*) a cultivated area of land open to the public, sometimes part of a park: *botanical gardens.* **3. lead (a person) up the garden path.** *Informal.* to mislead or deceive. ~*vb.* **4.** to work in or take care of (a garden or plot of land). —**'gardener** *n.* —**'gardening** *n.*

garden centre *n.* a place where gardening tools and equipment, and plants are sold.

garden city *n. Brit.* a planned town of limited size surrounded by countryside.

gardenia (gɑːˈdiːnɪə) *n.* **1.** an evergreen shrub or tree cultivated for its large fragrant waxy white flowers. **2.** its flower.

gargantuan (gɑːˈgæntjʊən) *adj.* huge; enormous.

gargle ('gɑːgᵊl) *vb.* **1.** to rinse the mouth and throat with (a liquid) by slowly breathing out through the liquid. ~*n.* **2.** the liquid used for gargling. **3.** the sound made by gargling.

gargoyle ('gɑːgɔɪl) *n.* a waterspout carved in the form of a grotesque face or figure and projecting from a roof gutter.

garish ('gɛərɪʃ) *adj.* crudely bright or colourful; gaudy. —**'garishly** *adv.* —**'garishness** *n.*

garland ('gɑːlənd) *n.* **1.** a wreath of flowers and leaves worn round the head or neck or hung up. ~*vb.* **2.** to adorn with a garland or garlands.

garlic ('gɑːlɪk) *n.* the bulb of a plant of the onion family, made up of small, pungent, strong-smelling segments, that are used in cooking. —**'garlicky** *adj.*

garment ('gɑːmənt) *n.* **1.** (*often pl.*) an article of clothing. **2.** outer covering.

garner ('gɑːnə) *vb.* to gather or store as in a granary.

garnet ('gɑːnɪt) *n.* a hard glassy red, yellow, or green silicate mineral: its red form is used as a gemstone.

garnish ('gɑːnɪʃ) *vb.* **1.** to decorate; trim. **2.** to decorate (food) with something to improve its appearance or flavour. ~*n.* **3.** a decoration; trimming. **4.** something added to food to improve its appearance or its flavour.

garret ('gærɪt) *n.* an attic in a house.

garrison ('gærɪsᵊn) *n.* **1.** the troops who maintain and guard a base or fort. **2.** the place itself. ~*vb.* **3.** to station (troops) in (a fort or base).

garrotte *or* **garotte** (gəˈrɒt) *n.* **1.** a Spanish method of execution by strangling. **2.** a cord, wire, or iron collar, used to strangle someone. ~*vb.* **3.** to execute with the garrotte. **4.** to strangle.

garrulous ('gærʊləs) *adj.* constantly chattering; talkative. —**'garrulousness** *or* **garrulity** (gæˈruːlɪtɪ) *n.*

garter ('gɑːtə) *n.* **1.** a band, usually of elastic, worn round the leg to hold up a sock or stocking. **2.** *U.S. & Canad.* a suspender.

Garter ('gɑːtə) *n.* **the Order of the Garter.** the highest order of British knighthood.

garter stitch *n.* knitting in which all the rows are knitted in plain stitch.

gas (gæs) *n., pl.* **gases** *or* **gasses.** **1.** a substance which does not resist change of shape and will expand indefinitely to fill any container. **2.** any substance that is gaseous at room temperature and atmospheric pressure. **3.** a fossil fuel in the form of a gas, used as a source of heat. **4.** a gaseous anaesthetic. **5.** *Mining.* firedamp or the explosive mixture of firedamp and air. **6.** *U.S., Canad., Austral., & N.Z.* petrol. **7. step on the gas.** *Informal.* **a.** to accelerate a motor vehicle. **b.** to hurry. **8.** a poisonous gas used against an enemy or rioters. **9.** *Informal.* idle talk or boasting. **10.** *Slang.* an entertaining person or thing: *his latest record is a gas.* ~*vb.* **gases** *or* **gasses, gassing, gassed. 11.** to subject to gas fumes so as to asphyxiate or render unconscious. **12.** *Informal.* to talk in an idle or boastful way.

gasbag ('gæs,bæg) *n. Informal.* a person who talks idly or too much.

gas chamber *or* **oven** *n.* an airtight room which is filled with poison gas to kill people or animals.

gaseous ('gæsɪəs, -ʃəs, -ʃɪəs, 'geɪ-) *adj.* of or like a gas.

gas gangrene *n.* gangrene resulting from infection of a wound by bacteria that cause gas bubbles in the surrounding tissues.

gash (gæʃ) *vb.* **1.** to make a long deep cut in; slash. ~*n.* **2.** a long deep cut.

gasholder ('gæs,həʊldə) *n.* a large tank for storing gas prior to distribution to users.

gasify ('gæsɪ,faɪ) *vb.* **-fying, -fied.** to change into a gas. —,gasifi'cation *n.*

gasket ('gæskɪt) *n.* a piece of paper, rubber, or metal sandwiched between the faces of a metal joint to provide a seal.

gaslight ('gæs,laɪt) *n.* **1.** a lamp in which light is produced by burning gas. **2.** the light produced by such a lamp.

gasman ('gæs,mæn) *n., pl.* **-men.** a man employed to read household gas meters and install or repair gas fittings, etc.

gas mask *n.* a mask fitted with a chemical filter to protect the wearer from breathing in harmful gases.

gas meter *n.* an apparatus for measuring and recording the amount of gas passed through it.

gasoline *or* **gasolene** ('gæsə,liːn) *n. U.S. & Canad.* petrol.

gasometer (gæs'ɒmɪtə) *n.* same as **gasholder.**

gasp (gɑːsp) *vb.* **1.** to draw in the breath sharply or with difficulty. **2.** (foll. by *after* or *for*) to crave. **3.** to utter breathlessly. ~*n.* **4.** a short convulsive intake of breath.

gas ring *n.* a hollow perforated metal ring fed with gas for cooking.

gassy ('gæsɪ) *adj.* **-sier, -siest. 1.** filled with, containing, or resembling gas. **2.** *Informal.* full of idle or vapid talk. —'gassiness *n.*

gastric ('gæstrɪk) *adj.* of the stomach.

gastric juice *n.* a digestive fluid secreted by the stomach.

gastric ulcer *n.* an ulcer of the mucous membrane lining the stomach.

gastritis (gæs'traɪtɪs) *n.* inflammation of the stomach.

gastroenteritis (,gæstrəʊ,entə'raɪtɪs) *n.* inflammation of the stomach and intestines.

gastronomy (gæs'trɒnəmɪ) *n.* the art of good eating. —**gastronomic** (,gæstrə-'nɒmɪk) *adj.*

gastropod ('gæstrə,pɒd) *or* **gasteropod** *n.* a mollusc, such as a snail, whelk, or slug, having a single flattened muscular foot. —**gastropodous** (gæs'trɒpədəs) *adj.*

gasworks ('gæs,wɜːks) *n. (functioning as sing.)* a plant in which coal gas is made.

gate (geɪt) *n.* **1.** a movable barrier, usually hinged, for closing an opening in a wall or fence. **2.** an opening where there is a gate. **3.** any means of entrance or access. **4. a.** the number of people admitted to a sporting event or entertainment. **b.** the total entrance money received from them. **5.** *Electronics.* a circuit having one or more input terminals and one output terminal, the output being determined by the combination of input signals. **6.** a slotted metal frame that controls the positions of the gear lever in a motor vehicle.

gâteau ('gætəʊ) *n., pl.* **-teaux** (-təʊz). a large rich layered cake.

gate-crash *vb. Informal.* to gain entry to (a party or other event) without invitation. —'gate-,crasher *n.*

gatehouse ('geɪt,haʊs) *n.* a building at or above a gateway.

gate-leg table *or* **gate-legged table** *n.* a table with leaves supported by hinged legs that can swing back to let the leaves drop from the frame.

gateway ('geɪt,weɪ) *n.* **1.** an entrance that may be closed by a gate. **2.** a means of entry or access: *Bombay, gateway to India.*

gather ('gæðə) *vb.* **1.** to assemble. **2.** to collect or be collected gradually. **3.** to learn from information given; conclude. **4.** to pick or harvest. **5.** to bring close (to). **6.** to increase gradually in force, speed, or intensity. **7.** to wrinkle (one's brow). **8.** to prepare or make ready: *to gather one's wits.* **9.** to draw (material) into small folds or tucks. **10.** (of a boil or other sore) to come to a head; form pus. ~*n.* **11.** a small fold in material; tuck.

gathering ('gæðərɪŋ) *n.* **1.** a group of people or things that are gathered together; assembly. **2.** *Sewing.* a series of gathers in material.

GATT (gæt) *n.* General Agreement on Tariffs and Trade.

gauche (gəʊʃ) *adj.* lacking ease of manner; socially awkward. —**gaucherie** (ˌgəʊʃəˈriː, 'gəʊʃərɪ) *n.*

gaucho ('gaʊtʃəʊ) *n., pl.* **-chos.** a cowboy of the South American pampas.

gaudy ('gɔːdɪ) *adj.* **gaudier, gaudiest.** bright or colourful in a vulgar manner. —'**gaudily** *adv.* —'**gaudiness** *n.*

gauge (geɪdʒ) *vb.* **1.** to measure the amount or condition of. **2.** to estimate; judge. ~*n.* **3.** a scale or standard of measurement. **4.** an instrument for measuring a quantity: *a pressure gauge.* **5.** a standard or means for assessing. **6.** capacity or extent. **7.** the diameter of the barrel of a gun. **8.** the thickness of sheet metal or the diameter of wire. **9.** the distance between the rails of a railway track or between parallel wheels. **10.** a measure of the fineness of woven or knitted fabric. —'**gaugeable** *adj.*

Gaul (gɔːl) *n.* **1.** a native of ancient Gaul. **2.** a Frenchman.

gaunt (gɔːnt) *adj.* **1.** bony and emaciated in appearance. **2.** (of places) bleak or desolate. —'**gauntness** *n.*

gauntlet[1] ('gɔːntlɪt) *n.* **1.** a medieval armoured glove. **2.** a heavy glove with a long cuff. **3. take up** (*or* **throw down**) **the gauntlet.** to accept (*or* offer) a challenge.

gauntlet[2] ('gɔːntlɪt) *n.* **run the gauntlet. a.** to be forced to run between, and be struck by, two rows of men: a former military punishment. **b.** to endure an onslaught, as of criticism.

gauss (gaʊs) *n., pl.* **gauss.** the cgs unit of magnetic flux density.

gauze (gɔːz) *n.* **1.** a transparent, loosely-woven cloth. **2.** any thin openwork material, such as wire. —'**gauzy** *adj.*

gave (geɪv) *vb.* the past tense of **give.**

gavel ('gæv²l) *n.* a small hammer used by a judge, auctioneer, or chairman to call for order or attention.

gavotte *or* **gavot** (gəˈvɒt) *n.* **1.** an old formal dance in quadruple time. **2.** music for this dance.

gawk (gɔːk) *vb.* **1.** to stare stupidly; gape. ~*n.* **2.** a clumsy stupid person.

gawky ('gɔːkɪ) *adj.* **gawkier, gawkiest.** clumsy or ungainly; awkward. —'**gawkiness** *n.*

gawp (gɔːp) *vb.* (often foll. by *at*) *Brit. slang.* to stare stupidly; gape.

gay (geɪ) *adj.* **1. a.** homosexual. **b.** (*as n.*): *a group of gays.* **2.** carefree and merry: *a gay temperament.* **3.** brightly coloured: *a gay hat.* **4.** licentious. —'**gayness** *n.*

gaze (geɪz) *vb.* **1.** to look long and fixedly. ~*n.* **2.** a fixed look.

gazebo (gəˈziːbəʊ) *n., pl.* **-bos** *or* **-boes.** a summerhouse or pavilion with a good view.

gazelle (gəˈzɛl) *n., pl.* **-zelles** *or* **-zelle.** a small graceful usually fawn-coloured antelope of Africa and Asia.

gazette (gəˈzɛt) *n.* **1.** a newspaper. **2.** *Brit.* an official publication containing announcements. ~*vb.* **3.** *Brit.* to announce something in a gazette.

gazetteer (ˌgæzɪˈtɪə) *n.* a book or section of a book that lists and describes places.

gazump (gəˈzʌmp) *vb. Brit.* to raise the price of a house after agreeing a price verbally with (an intending buyer).

GB Great Britain.

GBE (Knight or Dame) Grand Cross of the British Empire (a Brit. title).

GBH grievous bodily harm.

GC George Cross (a Brit. award for bravery).

GCB (Knight) Grand Cross of the Bath (a Brit. title).

GCE (in Britain) **1.** General Certificate of Education. **2.** *Informal.* any subject taken for a GCE examination.

GCMG (Knight or Dame) Grand Cross of the Order of St Michael and St George (a Brit. title).

GCSE (in Britain) General Certificate of Secondary Education.

GCVO (Knight or Dame) Grand Cross of the Royal Victorian Order (a Brit. title).

Gd *Chem.* gadolinium.

GDP gross domestic product.

Ge *Chem.* germanium.

gear (gɪə) *n.* **1.** a toothed wheel that engages with another or with a rack in order to change the speed or direction of transmitted motion. **2.** a mechanism for transmitting motion by gears. **3.** the engagement or particular setting of a system of gears: *in gear; high gear.* **4.** clothing or personal belongings. **5.** equipment for a particular task. **6. out of gear.** out of order. ~*vb.* **7.** to adapt (one thing) so as to fit in with another: *to gear our output to current demand.* **8.** to equip with or connect by gears.

gearbox ('gɪəˌbɒks) *n.* the metal casing enclosing a set of gears in a motor vehicle.

gearing ('gɪərɪŋ) *n.* a system of gears designed to transmit motion.

gear lever *or U.S. & Canad.* **gearshift** ('gɪəˌʃɪft) *n.* a lever used to engage or change gears in a motor vehicle.

gearwheel ('gɪəˌwiːl) *n.* same as **gear** (sense 1).

gecko ('gɛkəʊ) *n., pl.* **geckos** *or* **geckoes.** a small tropical lizard.

gee[1] (dʒiː) *interj.* an exclamation to a horse to encourage it to start or go faster. Also: **gee up!**

gee[2] (dʒiː) *interj. U.S. & Canad. informal.* a mild exclamation. Also: **gee whiz.**

geelbek (ˈxiːlˌbɛk) *n. S. African.* an edible marine fish with yellow jaws.

geese (giːs) *n.* the plural of **goose**[1].

geezer (ˈgiːzə) *n. Informal.* a man, usually an eccentric old man.

Geiger counter (ˈgaɪgə) *or* **Geiger-müller counter** (ˈmʊlə) *n.* an instrument for detecting and measuring radiation.

geisha (ˈgeɪʃə) *n., pl.* **-sha** *or* **-shas.** a professional female companion for men in Japan, trained in music, dancing, and conversation.

gel (dʒɛl) *n.* a jelly-like colloid in which a liquid is dispersed through a solid: *nondrip paint is a gel.* ~*vb.* **gelling, gelled. 2.** to become or cause to become a gel. **3.** same as **jell.**

gelatin (ˈdʒɛlətɪn) *or* **gelatine** (ˈdʒɛləˌtiːn) *n.* **1.** a clear water-soluble protein made by boiling animal hides and bones: used in foods, glue, and photographic emulsions. **2.** an edible jelly made of this.

gelatinize *or* **-ise** (dʒɪˈlætɪˌnaɪz) *vb.* to make or become gelatinous. —**geˌlatiniˈzation** *or* **-iˈsation** *n.*

gelatinous (dʒɪˈlætɪnəs) *adj.* of or like jelly.

geld (gɛld) *vb.* **gelding, gelded** *or* **gelt** (gɛlt). to castrate (a horse or other animal).

gelding (ˈgɛldɪŋ) *n.* a castrated male horse.

gelignite (ˈdʒɛlɪgˌnaɪt) *n.* a type of dynamite used for blasting.

gem (dʒɛm) *n.* **1.** a precious stone used as a decoration; jewel. **2.** a highly-valued person or thing. ~*vb.* **gemming, gemmed. 3.** to ornament with gems. —**ˈgemmy** *adj.*

geminate *adj.* (ˈdʒɛmɪnɪt, -ˌneɪt). **1.** combined in pairs: *a geminate leaf.* ~*vb.* (ˈdʒɛmɪˌneɪt). **2.** to arrange or be arranged in pairs. —**ˌgemiˈnation** *n.*

Gemini (ˈdʒɛmɪˌnaɪ, -ˌniː) *n.* the third sign of the zodiac; the Twins.

gemma (ˈdʒɛmə) *n., pl.* **-mae** (-miː). a budlike outgrowth in mosses that detaches from the parent and grows into a new individual.

gen (dʒɛn) *n. Brit. informal.* information: *give me the gen on your latest project.* See also **gen up.**

Gen. General.

-gen *suffix forming nouns.* **1.** producing or that which produces: *hydrogen.* **2.** something produced: *carcinogen.*

gendarme (ˈʒɒndɑːm) *n.* a member of the French police force.

gender (ˈdʒɛndə) *n.* **1.** the classification of nouns in certain languages as masculine, feminine, or neuter. **2.** *Informal.* the state of being male, female, or neuter.

gene (dʒiːn) *n.* a unit composed of DNA forming part of a chromosome, by which inherited characteristics are transmitted from parent to offspring.

-gene *suffix forming nouns.* same as **-gen.**

genealogy (ˌdʒiːnɪˈælədʒɪ) *n., pl.* **-gies. 1.** the direct descent of an individual or group from an ancestor. **2.** the study of the evolutionary development of animals and plants. **3.** a chart showing the descent of an individual or group. —**genealogical** (ˌdʒiːnɪəˈlɒdʒɪkᵊl) *adj.* —**ˌgeneˈalogist** *n.*

general (ˈdʒɛnərəl, ˈdʒɛnrəl) *adj.* **1.** common; widespread. **2.** of, affecting, or including all or most of the members of a group. **3.** not specialized: *general office work.* **4.** including various or miscellaneous items: *general knowledge; a general store.* **5.** not definite; vague: *the general idea.* **6.** true in most cases; usual. **7.** highest in authority or rank: *general manager; consul general.* ~*n.* **8.** a very senior military officer. **9.** the head of a religious order. **10. in general.** generally; mostly or usually.

general anaesthetic *n.* See **anaesthesia.**

general election *n.* **1.** an election in which representatives are chosen in all constituencies of a state. **2.** *U.S. & Canad.* a national, state, or provincial election.

generalissimo (ˌdʒɛnərəˈlɪsɪˌməʊ, ˌdʒɛnrə-) *n., pl.* **-mos.** a supreme commander of combined armed forces.

generality (ˌdʒɛnəˈrælɪtɪ) *n., pl.* **-ties. 1.** a principle or observation having general application. **2.** the state of being general. **3.** *Archaic.* the majority.

generalization *or* **-isation** (ˌdʒɛnrəlaɪˈzeɪʃən) *n.* **1.** a principle or statement with general application. **2.** a generalizing.

generalize *or* **-ise** (ˈdʒɛnrəˌlaɪz) *vb.* **1.** to form (general principles or conclusions) from (specific instances); infer. **2.** to speak in generalities. **3.** (*usually passive*) to make widely used or known.

generally (ˈdʒɛnrəlɪ) *adv.* **1.** usually; as a rule. **2.** commonly or widely. **3.** not specifically; broadly.

general practitioner *n.* a doctor who does not specialize but has a medical practice (**general practice**) in which he treats all illnesses.

general-purpose *adj.* having a variety of uses.

general staff *n.* officers who assist commanders in the planning and execution of military operations.

general strike *n.* a strike by all or most of the workers of a country, area, or town.

generate (ˈdʒɛnəˌreɪt) *vb.* to produce or bring into being; create.

generation (ˌdʒɛnəˈreɪʃən) *n.* **1.** production or reproduction. **2.** a successive stage in descent of people or animals. **3.** the average time between two generations of a species: about 35 years for humans. **4.** all the people of approximately the same age. **5.** production of electricity or heat. **6.** (*modifier*) belonging to a specified generation or stage of development: *a third-generation American; a second-generation computer.*

generation gap *n.* the difference in outlook and the lack of understanding between people of different generations.

generative (ˈdʒɛnərətɪv) *adj.* **1.** of production. **2.** capable of producing or originating.

generator (ˈdʒɛnəˌreɪtə) *n.* **1.** a device for converting mechanical energy into electrical energy. **2.** an apparatus for producing a gas.

generic (dʒɪˈnɛrɪk) *adj.* **1.** of a whole class or group; general. **2.** *Biol.* of a genus: *the generic name.*

generosity (ˌdʒɛnəˈrɒsɪtɪ) *n., pl.* **-ties.** **1.** the quality of being generous. **2.** a generous act.

generous (ˈdʒɛnərəs, ˈdʒɛnrəs) *adj.* **1.** ready to give freely; unselfish. **2.** free from pettiness in character and mind. **3.** full or plentiful: *a generous portion.* —ˈ**generously** *adv.*

genesis (ˈdʒɛnɪsɪs) *n., pl.* **-ses** (-ˌsiːz). a beginning or origin of anything.

Genesis (ˈdʒɛnɪsɪs) *n.* the first book of the Bible.

genetic (dʒɪˈnɛtɪk) *adj.* of genetics, genes, or the origin of something. —geˈnetically *adv.*

genetic code *n. Biochem.* the order in which the four nucleic acid bases of DNA are arranged in the molecule for transmitting genetic information to the cells.

genetic engineering *n.* alteration of the DNA of a cell as a means of manufacturing animal proteins or producing new breeds of plants or animals.

genetic fingerprinting *n.* the use of a person's unique pattern of DNA, which can be obtained from blood, saliva, or tissue, as a means of identification. —**genetic fingerprint** *n.*

genetics (dʒɪˈnɛtɪks) *n.* (*functioning as sing.*) the study of heredity and variation in organisms. —geˈneticist *n.*

Geneva Convention (dʒɪˈniːvə) *n.* the international agreement formulated in 1864 at Geneva, establishing a code for wartime treatment of the sick, wounded, and prisoners of war.

genial (ˈdʒiːnjəl, -nɪəl) *adj.* **1.** cheerful, easy-going, and friendly. **2.** pleasantly warm, so as to give life, growth, or health. —**geniality** (ˌdʒiːnɪˈælɪtɪ) *n.* —ˈ**genially** *adv.*

genie (ˈdʒiːnɪ) *n., pl.* **-nies** *or* **-nii** (-nɪˌaɪ). **1.** (in fairy stories) a servant who appears by

magic and fulfils a person's wishes. **2.** same as **jinni.**

genital (ˈdʒɛnɪtˀl) *adj.* of the sexual organs or reproduction.

genitals (ˈdʒɛnɪtˀlz) *or* **genitalia** (ˌdʒɛnɪˈteɪlɪə, -ˈteɪljə) *pl. n.* the external sexual organs.

genitive (ˈdʒɛnɪtɪv) *Grammar.* ~*adj.* **1.** denoting a grammatical case used to indicate a relation of ownership or association. ~*n.* **2. a.** the genitive case. **b.** a word in this case.

genius (ˈdʒiːnɪəs, -njəs) *n., pl.* **-uses** *or* (*for sense 5*) **genii** (ˈdʒiːnɪˌaɪ). **1.** a person with exceptional ability in a particular subject or activity. **2.** such ability. **3.** the distinctive spirit of something. **4.** a person considered as exerting influence of a certain sort: *an evil genius.* **5.** *Roman myth.* **a.** the guiding spirit who attends a person from birth to death. **b.** the guardian spirit of a place.

genocide (ˈdʒɛnəʊˌsaɪd) *n.* the deliberate killing of a people or nation. —ˌgenoˈcidal *adj.*

genre (ˈʒɑːnrə) *n.* **1.** kind or type of literary, musical, or artistic work. **2.** a kind of painting depicting incidents from everyday life.

gent (dʒɛnt) *n. Informal.* short for **gentleman.**

genteel (dʒɛnˈtiːl) *adj.* **1.** affectedly proper, refined, or polite. **2.** respectable, polite, and well-bred. **3.** appropriate to polite or fashionable society. —genˈteelly *adv.*

gentian (ˈdʒɛnʃən) *n.* a mountain plant with usually blue showy flowers.

gentian violet *n.* a violet solution used as an antiseptic and in the treatment of burns.

Gentile (ˈdʒɛntaɪl) *n.* **1.** a person who is not a Jew. **2.** a heathen or pagan. ~*adj.* **3.** not Jewish. **4.** pagan or heathen.

gentility (dʒɛnˈtɪlɪtɪ) *n., pl.* **-ties.** **1.** respectability and good manners. **2.** affected politeness. **3.** noble birth or ancestry.

gentle (ˈdʒɛntˀl) *adj.* **1.** mild or kindly in character. **2.** temperate; moderate: *a gentle breeze.* **3.** gradual: *a gentle slope.* **4.** easily controlled; tame. **5.** *Archaic.* of good breeding; noble: *gentle blood.* **6.** *Archaic.* gallant; chivalrous. —ˈ**gentleness** *n.* —ˈ**gently** *adv.*

gentlefolk (ˈdʒɛntˀlˌfəʊk) *or* **gentlefolks** *pl. n.* people regarded as being of good breeding.

gentleman (ˈdʒɛntˀlmən) *n., pl.* **-men.** **1.** a man who comes from a family of high social position. **2.** a cultured, courteous, and well-bred man. **3.** a polite name for a man. —ˈ**gentlemanly** *adj.*

gentrification (ˌdʒɛntrɪfɪˈkeɪʃən) *n. Brit.* a process by which middle-class people take up residence in a traditionally working-class area, changing its character. —ˈ**gentriˌfy** *vb.*

gentry ('dʒɛntrɪ) n. 1. Brit. persons just below the nobility in social rank. 2. people of a particular class, usually one considered to be inferior.

gents (dʒɛnts) n. (functioning as sing.) Brit. informal. a men's public lavatory.

genuflect ('dʒɛnjʊˌflɛkt) vb. to bend the knee as a sign of reverence or deference. —ˌgenuˈflection or esp. Brit. ˌgenuˈflexion n.

genuine ('dʒɛnjʊɪn) adj. 1. not fake; authentic. 2. sincere. —ˈgenuinely adv. —ˈgenuineness n.

gen up vb. genning, genned. (often foll. by on) Brit. informal. to make or become fully informed (about).

genus ('dʒiːnəs) n., pl. genera ('dʒɛnərə) or genuses. 1. Biol. a group into which a family of animals or plants is divided and which contains one or more species. 2. Logic. a class of objects that can be divided into two or more groups. 3. a class or group.

geocentric (ˌdʒiːəʊˈsɛntrɪk) adj. 1. having the earth as its centre. 2. measured as from the centre of the earth.

geode ('dʒiːəʊd) n. a cavity, lined with crystals, within a rock. —geodic (dʒɪˈɒdɪk) adj.

geodesic (ˌdʒiːəʊˈdɛsɪk, -ˈdiː-) adj. 1. relating to the geometry of curved surfaces. ~n. 2. the shortest line between two points on a curved surface.

geodesy (dʒɪˈɒdɪsɪ) n. the study of the shape and size of the earth. —geˈodesist n.

geog. 1. geographic(al). 2. geography.

geographical mile n. same as nautical mile.

geography (dʒɪˈɒgrəfɪ) n., pl. -phies. 1. the study of the earth's surface, including physical features, climate, and population. 2. the physical features of a region. —geˈographer n. —geographical (ˌdʒɪəˈgræfɪkəl) or ˌgeoˈgraphic adj.

geoid ('dʒiːɔɪd) n. the earth considered as a hypothetical ellipsoid with its surface corresponding to the mean sea level.

geol. 1. geologic(al). 2. geologist. 3. geology.

geology (dʒɪˈɒlədʒɪ) n. 1. the study of the origin, structure, and composition of the earth. 2. the geological features of an area. —geological (ˌdʒɪəˈlɒdʒɪkəl) or ˌgeoˈlogic adj. —geˈologist n.

geometric (ˌdʒɪəˈmɛtrɪk) or geometrical adj. 1. of geometry. 2. consisting of or characterized by geometric forms, such as circles, triangles, and straight lines. —ˌgeoˈmetrically adv.

geometric progression n. a sequence of numbers, each of which differs from the succeeding one by a constant ratio, as 1, 2, 4, 8, ...

geometry (dʒɪˈɒmɪtrɪ) n. the branch of mathematics concerned with points, lines, curves, and surfaces. —geˌomeˈtrician n.

Geordie ('dʒɔːdɪ) n. Brit. 1. a person from Tyneside. 2. the Tyneside dialect.

George Cross (dʒɔːdʒ) n. a British award for bravery, esp. of civilians.

georgette or **georgette crepe** (dʒɔːˈdʒɛt) n. a thin crepe fabric.

Georgian ('dʒɔːdʒən) adj. 1. of any of the kings of Great Britain called George, or their reigns (1714-1830; 1910-52): Georgian architecture. 2. of the Georgian SSR, its people, or their language. 3. of Georgia, U.S., or its inhabitants. 4. (of furniture) in the style prevalent in Britain during the 18th century. ~n. 5. the official language of the Georgian SSR. 6. a person from the Georgian SSR. 7. a person from Georgia, U.S.

geostationary (ˌdʒiːəʊˈsteɪʃənərɪ) adj. (of a satellite) orbiting so as to remain over the same point on the earth's surface.

geothermal (ˌdʒiːəʊˈθɜːməl) adj. of or using the heat in the earth's interior.

geotropism (dʒɪˈɒtrəˌpɪzəm) n. the response of a plant part to the force of gravity. —geotropic (ˌdʒiːəʊˈtrɒpɪk) adj.

geranium (dʒɪˈreɪnɪəm) n. 1. a cultivated plant of the pelargonium family, having scarlet, pink, or white showy flowers. 2. a plant having divided leaves and pink or purplish flowers.

gerbil ('dʒɜːbɪl) n. a burrowing rodent of the deserts of Asia and Africa.

gerfalcon ('dʒɜːˌfɔːlkən, -ˌfɔːkən) n. same as gyrfalcon.

geriatrics (ˌdʒɛrɪˈætrɪks) n. (functioning as sing.) the branch of medicine concerned with the diseases affecting elderly people. —ˌgeriˈatric n., adj. —ˌgeriaˈtrician n.

germ (dʒɜːm) n. 1. a microorganism, usually one that causes disease. 2. (often pl.) the beginning form of something which may develop: the germs of revolution. 3. a simple structure that can develop into a complete organism.

german ('dʒɜːmən) adj. 1. having the same parents as oneself: brother-german. 2. being a first cousin: cousin-german.

German ('dʒɜːmən) n. 1. the language of East and West Germany and Austria and one of the languages of Switzerland. 2. a person from East or West Germany. ~adj. 3. of Germany, its people, or their language.

germander (dʒɜːˈmændə) n. a European plant having two-lipped flowers with a very small upper lip.

germane (dʒɜːˈmeɪn) adj. (usually foll. by to) relevant.

Germanic (dʒɜːˈmænɪk) n. 1. a branch of the Indo-European family of languages that includes English, German, and the Scandinavian languages. 2. the language from

which these languages developed. ~*adj*.
3. of this group of languages. **4.** of the
German language or any people that speaks
a Germanic language. **5.** (formerly) German.

germanium (dʒɜːˈmeɪnɪəm) *n*. a brittle grey
metalloid element that is a semiconductor:
used in transistors. Symbol: Ge

German measles *n*. (*functioning as
sing*.) same as **rubella**.

German shepherd dog *n*. same as **Alsatian**.

German silver *n*. same as **nickel silver**.

germ cell *n*. a sexual reproductive cell.

germicide (ˈdʒɜːmɪˌsaɪd) *n*. a substance
that kills germs. —ˌgermiˈcidal *adj*.

germinal (ˈdʒɜːmɪnᵊl) *adj*. **1.** of or like
germs or a germ cell. **2.** of or in the earliest
stage of development.

germinate (ˈdʒɜːmɪˌneɪt) *vb*. **1.** to sprout
or to cause (a seed) to sprout. **2.** to grow or
cause to grow; develop. —ˈgerminative
adj. —ˌgermiˈnation *n*.

germ warfare *n*. the military use of
disease-spreading bacteria against an enemy.

gerontology (ˌdʒɛrɒnˈtɒlədʒɪ) *n*. the scientific study of ageing and the problems of
elderly people. —ˌgeronˈtologist *n*.

gerrymander (ˈdʒɛrɪˌmændə) *vb*. **1.** to divide the constituencies of (a voting area) so
as to give one party an unfair advantage.
~*n*. **2.** a gerrymandering.

gerund (ˈdʒɛrənd) *n*. a noun formed from a
verb, ending in -*ing*, denoting an action or
state.

gerundive (dʒɪˈrʌndɪv) *n*. (in Latin grammar) an adjective formed from a verb, with
the sense "that should be done".

gesso (ˈdʒɛsəʊ) *n*. plaster used for painting
or in sculpture.

Gestapo (gɛˈstɑːpəʊ) *n*. the secret state police of Nazi Germany.

gestate (ˈdʒɛsteɪt) *vb*. **1.** to carry (developing young) in the womb during pregnancy. **2.** to develop (a plan or idea) in the
mind. **3.** to be gestating. —gesˈtation *n*.

gesticulate (dʒɛˈstɪkjʊˌleɪt) *vb*. to express
by or make gestures. —geˌsticuˈlation *n*.

gesture (ˈdʒɛstʃə) *n*. **1.** a motion of the
hands, head, or body to express or emphasize an idea or emotion. **2.** something said
or done to indicate intention, or as a formality. ~*vb*. **3.** to gesticulate. —ˈgestural
adj.

get (gɛt) *vb*. **getting, got**. **1.** to come into
possession of; receive or earn. **2.** to bring
or fetch. **3.** to contract (an illness). **4.** to
capture or seize: *the police got him*. **5.** to
become or cause to become as specified: *to
get one's hair cut; get wet*. **6.** to prepare: *to
get a meal*. **7.** to hear or understand: *I
didn't get your meaning*. **8.** to learn or
master by study. **9.** (often foll. by *to*) to

come (to) or arrive (at): *we got home safely*.
10. to catch or enter: *to get a train*. **11.** to
persuade: *get him to leave*. **12.** to reach by
calculation: *add 2 and 2 and you will get 4*.
13. to receive a broadcast signal. **14.** to
communicate with (a person or place), as by
telephone. **15.** (foll. by *to*) *Informal*. to
have an emotional effect (on): *that music
really gets me*. **16.** *Informal*. to annoy: *her
voice gets me*. **17.** *Informal*. to baffle. **18.**
Informal. to hit: *the blow got him in the
back*. **19.** *Informal*. to be revenged on. **20.**
Informal. to have the better of: *your extravagant habits will get you in the end*.
21. (foll. by present participle) *Informal*. to
begin: *get moving*. **22.** (used as a command) *Informal*. go! **23. get with child**.
Archaic. to make pregnant. ~*n*. **24.** *Brit.
slang*. same as **git**. ~See also **get about,
get across**, etc.

get about *or* **around** *vb*. **1.** to move
around. **2.** to be socially active. **3.** (of
news or rumour) to circulate.

get across *vb*. to be or cause to be understood.

get at *vb*. **1.** to gain access to. **2.** to
imply: *what are you getting at?* **3.** to annoy
persistently; criticize: *stop getting at him*.
4. to try to influence by bribery or threats:
*someone had got at the witness before the
trial*.

get away *vb*. **1.** to escape; leave. **2.** to
start. **3. get away with**. **a.** to steal and
escape with (something). **b.** to do (something wrong) without being caught or punished. ~*interj*. **4.** an exclamation of disbelief. ~*n*. **getaway**. **5.** the act of escaping,
usually by criminals. **6.** (*modifier*) used to
escape: *a getaway car*.

get back *vb*. **1.** to regain. **2.** (often foll.
by *to*) to return to a former state or activity. **3.** (foll. by *at*) to retaliate (against). **4.
get one's own back**. *Informal*. to get one's
revenge.

get by *vb*. **1.** to go past or overtake. **2.**
Informal. to manage in spite of difficulties.
3. to be just acceptable. **4.** to be accepted
or permitted: *that book will never get by
the authorities*.

get in *vb*. **1.** to enter a vehicle. **2.** to
arrive. **3.** to bring inside: *get the milk in*.
4. to insert or slip in: *he got his suggestion
in before anyone else*. **5.** to gather (crops).
6. to be elected. **7.** to get a place at university or college. **8.** (foll. by *on*) to join in (an
activity).

get off *vb*. **1.** to escape the consequences
of an action. **2.** to be or cause to be acquitted. **3.** to leave or move away from or
cause to leave or move away from (a thing
or place). **4.** to remove: *get your coat off*.
5. to go to sleep. **6.** to send (letters) or (of
letters) to be sent. **7. get off with**. *Brit.
informal*. to begin a romantic or sexual
relationship (with).

get on *vb.* **1.** Also: **get onto.** to board or cause to board (a vehicle). **2.** to grow late or (of time) to elapse: *it's getting on and I must go.* **3.** to grow old. **4.** (foll. by *for*) to approach (a time, age, or amount): *she is getting on for seventy.* **5.** to make progress, manage, or fare: *how did you get on in your exam?* **6.** (often foll. by *with*) to have a friendly relationship: *he gets on well with people.* **7.** (foll. by *with*) to continue to do: *get on with your work!*

get out *vb.* **1.** to leave or escape or cause to leave or escape. **2.** to make or become known. **3.** to express with difficulty. **4.** to gain something, usually of significance or value: *she got a confession out of him; what do we get out of the deal?* **5.** (foll. by *of*) to avoid or cause to avoid: *she always gets out of swimming.*

get over *vb.* **1.** to cross or surmount (something). **2.** to recover from (an illness or shock). **3.** to overcome (a problem). **4.** to appreciate fully: *I can't get over seeing you again.* **5.** to communicate effectively. **6.** (foll. by *with*) to bring (something necessary but unpleasant) to an end: *let's get this job over with quickly.*

get round *or* **around** *vb.* **1.** to circumvent or overcome. **2.** *Informal.* to win over; cajole: *she can get round anyone.* **3.** (foll. by *to*) to come to at length: *I'll get round to that job in an hour.* **4.** (of information or gossip) to circulate.

get through *vb.* **1.** to succeed or cause to succeed in an examination or test. **2.** to bring or come to a destination after overcoming problems: *we got through the blizzards to the survivors.* **3.** to contact by telephone. **4.** to use up (money or supplies). **5.** to complete or cause to complete (a task or process): *to get a bill through Parliament.* **6.** (foll. by *to*) to succeed in making (a person) understand: *I can't get through to him.*

get-together *n.* **1.** *Informal.* a small informal social gathering. ~*vb.* **get together.** **2.** (of people) to meet socially. **3.** to discuss in order to reach an agreement.

get up *vb.* **1.** to rise or cause to rise from bed. **2.** to rise to one's feet; stand up. **3.** to ascend or cause to ascend. **4.** to intensify or cause to intensify: *the wind got up at noon.* **5.** *Informal.* to dress in a particular way, usually elaborately. **6.** *Informal.* to devise or create: *to get up an entertainment for Christmas.* **7.** *Informal.* to study or improve one's knowledge of: *I must get up my history.* **8.** (foll. by *to*) *Informal.* to be involved in: *he's always getting up to mischief.* ~*n.* **get-up.** *Informal.* **9.** a costume or outfit.

get-up-and-go *n.* *Informal.* energy or drive.

geyser ('giːzə; *U.S.* 'gaɪzər) *n.* **1.** a spring

that discharges steam and hot water. **2.** *Brit.* a domestic gas water heater.

ghastly ('gɑːstlɪ) *adj.* **-lier, -liest. 1.** *Informal.* very unpleasant. **2.** deathly pale. **3.** *Informal.* extremely unwell. **4.** terrifying; horrible. ~*adv.* **5.** unhealthily; sickly: *ghastly pale.* —'**ghastliness** *n.*

ghat (gɔːt) *n.* (in India) **1.** stairs leading down to a river. **2.** a mountain pass.

ghee (giː) *n.* clarified butter used in Indian cookery.

gherkin ('gɜːkɪn) *n.* a small pickled cucumber.

ghetto ('getəʊ) *n., pl.* **-tos** *or* **-toes. 1.** an area of slums inhabited by a deprived minority. **2.** an area or community that is segregated or isolated. **3.** an area in a European city to which Jews were formerly restricted.

ghetto blaster *n.* *Informal.* a large portable cassette recorder with built-in speakers.

ghillie ('gɪlɪ) *n.* same as **gillie.**

ghost (gəʊst) *n.* **1.** the disembodied spirit of a dead person, supposed to haunt the living. **2.** a faint trace: *a ghost of a smile.* **3.** a faint secondary image in an optical instrument, esp. one on a television screen. **4.** give up the ghost. to die. ~*vb.* **5.** short for **ghostwrite.** —'**ghost,like** *adj.* —'**ghostly** *adj.*

ghost town *n.* a deserted town.

ghostwrite ('gəʊst,raɪt) *vb.* **-writing, -wrote, -written.** to write (an article or book) on behalf of a person who is then credited as author. —'**ghost,writer** *n.*

ghoul (guːl) *n.* **1.** a person interested in morbid or disgusting things. **2.** (in Muslim legend) a demon that eats corpses. —'**ghoulish** *adj.* —'**ghoulishly** *adv.*

GHQ *Mil.* General Headquarters.

ghyll (gɪl) *n.* same as **gill³.**

GI *n., pl.* **GIs** *or* **GI's.** *U.S. informal.* **1.** a soldier in the U.S. Army. ~*adj.* **2.** of or for the U.S. armed forces.

giant ('dʒaɪənt) *n.* **1.** Also (fem.): **giantess** ('dʒaɪəntɪs). a mythical figure of superhuman size and strength. **2.** a person or thing of exceptional size, ability, or importance. ~*adj.* **3.** remarkably large. **4.** (of an atom or ion or its structure) having large numbers of particles present in a crystal lattice, with each particle exerting a strong force of attraction on those near to it: all metals have a giant structure.

giant panda *n.* See **panda.**

gibber ('dʒɪbə) *vb.* to utter rapidly and unintelligibly; prattle.

gibberish ('dʒɪbərɪʃ) *n.* rapid, incomprehensible talk; nonsense.

gibbet ('dʒɪbɪt) *n.* **1. a.** a wooden structure like a gallows, from which the bodies of executed criminals were formerly hung to public view. **b.** a gallows. ~*vb.* **2.** to hang on a gibbet. **3.** to expose to public scorn.

gibbon ('gɪbˀn) *n.* a small agile tree-dwelling ape of the forests of S Asia.

gibbous ('gɪbəs) *adj.* **1.** (of the moon or a planet) more than half but less than fully illuminated. **2.** hunchbacked. **3.** bulging.

gibe *or* **jibe** (dʒaɪb) *vb.* **1.** to jeer or scoff (at); taunt. ~*n.* **2.** a jeer; taunt.

giblets ('dʒɪblɪts) *pl. n.* (*sometimes sing.*) the gizzard, liver, heart, and neck of a fowl.

gidday (gə'daɪ) *interj. Austral. & N.Z. informal.* same as **good day.**

giddy ('gɪdɪ) *adj.* **-dier, -diest.** **1.** affected with a reeling sensation; dizzy. **2.** tending to cause dizziness. **3.** impulsive; scatter-brained. —'**giddiness** *n.*

gie (giː) *vb. Scot.* to give.

gift (gɪft) *n.* **1.** a present. **2.** a special ability or power; talent. **3.** the power or right to give: *in the gift of.* **4. look a gift-horse in the mouth.** to find fault with a gift or favour. ~*vb.* **5.** to present (something) as a gift to (a person).

gifted ('gɪftɪd) *adj.* having natural talent or aptitude: *a gifted musician.*

giftwrap ('gɪft,ræp) *vb.* **-wrapping, -wrapped.** to wrap (a gift) attractively.

gig[1] (gɪg) *n.* **1.** a light open two-wheeled one-horse carriage. **2.** *Naut.* a light ship's boat. **3.** a long light rowing boat, used for racing.

gig[2] (gɪg) *n.* **1.** a single performance by jazz or pop musicians. ~*vb.* **gigging, gigged.** **2.** to play a gig or gigs.

giga- ('gɪgə, 'gaɪgə) *combining form.* **1.** denoting 10^9: *gigavolt.* **2.** *Computers.* denoting 2^{30}: *gigabyte.*

gigantic (dʒaɪ'gæntɪk) *adj.* enormous. —**gi'gantically** *adv.*

giggle ('gɪgˀl) *vb.* **1.** to laugh nervously or foolishly. ~*n.* **2.** such a laugh. **3.** *Informal.* an amusing person or thing. —'**giggly** *adj.*

gigolo ('ʒɪgə,ləʊ) *n., pl.* **-los.** a man who is kept by an older woman to be her escort or lover.

gigot ('dʒɪgət) *n.* a leg of lamb or mutton.

gild (gɪld) *vb.* **gilding, gilded** *or* **gilt.** **1.** to cover with or as if with gold. **2. gild the lily. a.** to adorn unnecessarily something already beautiful. **b.** to praise someone excessively. **3.** to give a falsely attractive appearance to.

gill[1] (gɪl) *n.* **1.** the breathing organ of most aquatic animals. **2.** a radiating structure on the underside of the cap of a mushroom. —**gilled** *adj.*

gill[2] (dʒɪl) *n.* a unit of liquid measure equal to one quarter of a pint.

gill[3] *or* **ghyll** (gɪl) *n. Dialect.* **1.** a narrow stream; rivulet. **2.** a wooded ravine.

gillie *or* **ghillie** ('gɪlɪ) *n., pl.* **-lies.** *Scot.* a sportsman's attendant or guide for hunting or fishing.

gills (gɪlz) *pl. n.* **1.** (*sometimes sing.*) the wattle of birds such as domestic fowl. **2.** a person's cheeks and jowls. **3. green about the gills.** *Informal.* looking or feeling sick.

gilt[1] (gɪlt) *vb.* **1.** past of **gild.** ~*n.* **2.** gold or a substance like it, used in gilding. **3.** a gilt-edged security. ~*adj.* **4.** covered with gilt; gilded.

gilt[2] (gɪlt) *n.* a young sow.

gilt-edged *adj.* denoting government securities on which interest payments and final repayments are guaranteed.

gimbals ('dʒɪmbˀlz, 'gɪm-) *pl. n.* a device, consisting of two or three pivoted rings at right angles to each other, that allows a ship's instrument to remain level despite the ship's movement.

gimcrack ('dʒɪm,kræk) *adj.* **1.** showy but cheap; shoddy. ~*n.* **2.** a cheap showy object.

gimlet ('gɪmlɪt) *n.* **1.** a small hand tool with a pointed spiral tip, used for boring holes in wood. ~*adj.* **2. gimlet-eyed.** having a piercing glance.

gimmick ('gɪmɪk) *n. Informal.* something designed to attract attention or publicity. —'**gimmickry** *n.* —'**gimmicky** *adj.*

gimp (gɪmp) *n.* a tapelike trimming.

gin[1] (dʒɪn) *n.* an alcoholic drink distilled from malted grain and flavoured with juniper berries.

gin[2] (dʒɪn) *n.* **1.** a machine in which a vertical shaft is turned by horses driving a horizontal beam in a circle. **2.** a machine of this type used for separating seeds from raw cotton. **3.** a noose of thin strong wire for catching small mammals. ~*vb.* **ginning, ginned.** **4.** to free (cotton) of seeds with a gin. **5.** to snare (game) with a gin.

gin[3] (gɪn) *vb.* **ginning, gan** (gæn), **gun** (gʌn). *Archaic.* to begin.

ginger ('dʒɪndʒə) *n.* **1.** the underground stem of a tropical plant, powdered and used as a spice or sugared and eaten as a sweet. **2.** a light reddish-brown colour. **3.** *Informal.* vigour. —'**gingery** *adj.*

ginger ale *n.* a nonalcoholic fizzy drink flavoured with ginger extract.

ginger beer *n.* a drink made by fermenting a mixture of syrup and root ginger.

gingerbread ('dʒɪndʒə,brɛd) *n.* **1.** a moist brown cake or biscuit flavoured with ginger. **2.** showy but unsubstantial ornamentation.

ginger group *n. Chiefly Brit.* a group within a larger group that enlivens or radicalizes its parent body.

gingerly ('dʒɪndʒəlɪ) *adv.* **1.** carefully or cautiously. ~*adj.* **2.** careful or cautious.

ginger snap *or* **nut** *n.* a crisp biscuit flavoured with ginger.

gingham ('gɪŋəm) *n.* a cotton fabric, usually woven in a checked or striped design.

gingivitis (,dʒɪndʒɪ'vaɪtɪs) *n.* inflammation of the gums.

ginkgo ('gɪŋkgəʊ) *n., pl.* **-goes.** an ornamental Chinese tree with fan-shaped leaves and fleshy yellow fruit.

ginormous (dʒaɪ'nɔːməs) *adj. Informal.* very large.

gin palace (dʒɪn) *n.* (formerly) a gaudy drinking house.

gin rummy (dʒɪn) *n.* a version of rummy in which a player may finish if the odd cards in his hand total less than ten points.

ginseng ('dʒɪnsɛŋ) *n.* the forked aromatic root of a plant of China and N America or a substance obtained from this, believed to possess tonic and energy-giving properties.

gip (dʒɪp) *n.* same as **gyp.**

Gipsy ('dʒɪpsɪ) *n., pl.* **-sies.** (*sometimes not cap.*) same as **Gypsy.**

giraffe (dʒɪ'rɑːf, -'ræf) *n.* a large ruminant mammal of the African savannas: the tallest mammal, with very long legs and neck and a spotted yellowy skin.

gird (gɜːd) *vb.* **girding, girded** *or* **girt. 1.** to put a belt or girdle around (the waist or hips). **2.** to secure with or as if with a belt: *to gird on one's armour.* **3.** to surround. **4.** **gird (up) one's loins.** to prepare oneself for action.

girder ('gɜːdə) *n.* a large timber or steel beam used in the construction of bridges and buildings.

girdle[1] ('gɜːd⁰l) *n.* **1.** a woman's elastic corset covering the waist and hips. **2.** anything that surrounds. **3.** a belt. **4.** *Anat.* an encircling structure or part: *the pelvic girdle.* ~*vb.* **5.** to put a girdle on or around. **6.** to surround.

girdle[2] ('gɜːd⁰l) *n. Scot. & N English dialect.* same as **griddle.**

girl (gɜːl) *n.* **1.** a female child. **2.** a young woman. **3.** *Informal.* a sweetheart or girlfriend. **4.** *Informal.* a woman of any age. **5.** a female employee, usually a servant. —'girl,hood *n.* —'girlish *adj.*

girlfriend ('gɜːl,frɛnd) *n.* **1.** a female friend with whom a person is romantically or sexually involved. **2.** any female friend.

Girl Guide *n.* See **Guide.**

girlie ('gɜːlɪ) *n.* (*modifier*) *Informal.* featuring nude or scantily dressed women: *a girlie magazine.*

giro ('dʒaɪrəʊ) *n., pl.* **-ros. 1.** a system of transferring money within a bank or post office, directly from one account into another. **2.** *Brit. informal.* a social security payment by giro cheque.

girt[1] (gɜːt) *vb.* past of **gird.**

girt[2] (gɜːt) *vb.* to bind or encircle; gird.

girth (gɜːθ) *n.* **1.** the distance around something; circumference. **2.** a band around a

horse's belly to keep the saddle in position.

gist (dʒɪst) *n.* the point or substance of a matter.

git (gɪt) *n. Brit. slang.* a contemptible person.

give (gɪv) *vb.* **giving, gave, given. 1.** to present (something that is one's own) voluntarily to another. **2.** (often foll. by *for*) to transfer (something, usually money) in exchange or payment: *to give fifty pounds for a painting.* **3.** to hand over temporarily to another: *I give the porter my bags.* **4.** to grant or provide: *give me some advice.* **5.** to administer: *to give a reprimand.* **6.** to award or attribute: *they gave her the blame.* **7.** to be a source of: *he gives no trouble.* **8.** to impart: *to give news.* **9.** to utter or emit: *to give a shout.* **10.** to perform, make, or do: *the car gave a jolt.* **11.** to sacrifice or devote: *he gave his life for his country.* **12.** to concede: *I will give you this game.* **13.** *Informal.* to happen: *what gives?* **14.** (often foll. by *to*) to cause; lead: *she gave me to believe that she would come.* **15.** to organize or put on (an entertainment). **16.** to yield or break under pressure: *this seat will give if you sit on it.* **17.** **give or take.** plus or minus: *three thousand, give or take a few hundred.* ~*n.* **18.** tendency to yield under pressure; resilience. ~See also **give away, give in,** etc. —'giver *n.*

give-and-take *n.* **1.** mutual concessions and cooperation. **2.** a smoothly flowing exchange of ideas and talk.

give away *vb.* **1.** to donate as a gift. **2.** to reveal. **3.** to present (a bride) formally to her husband in a marriage ceremony. ~*n.* **giveaway. 4.** a usually unintentional disclosure. **5.** (*modifier*) very cheap or free: *giveaway prices; a giveaway supplement.*

give in *vb.* **1.** to yield; admit defeat. **2.** to hand (something) in.

given ('gɪv⁰n) *vb.* **1.** past participle of **give.** ~*adj.* **2.** specific or previously stated. **3.** assumed as a premise. **4.** *Maths.* known or determined independently: *a given volume.* **5.** **given to.** inclined to.

give off *vb.* to emit or discharge: *the mothballs gave off an acrid odour.*

give out *vb.* **1.** to emit or discharge. **2.** to make known: *he gave out that he would resign.* **3.** to distribute: *they gave out leaflets.* **4.** to become exhausted; fail: *the light gave out.*

give over *vb.* **1.** to transfer to the custody of another. **2.** to set aside for a specific purpose: *the day was given over to work.* **3.** *Informal.* to cease: *give over fighting!*

give up *vb.* **1.** to abandon hope (for). **2.** to renounce or relinquish (something): *I have given up smoking; he gave up his job.* **3.** to surrender: *the escaped convict gave himself up.* **4.** to admit defeat or failure.

5. to devote completely (to): *she gave herself up to caring for the sick.*

gizzard ('gızəd) *n.* the thick-walled part of a bird's stomach, in which hard food is broken up.

glacé ('glæsı) *adj.* **1.** crystallized or candied: *glacé cherries.* **2.** (of leather or cloth) having a glossy finish.

glacial ('gleısıəl, -ʃəl) *adj.* **1.** characterized by masses of ice. **2.** of or produced by a glacier. **3.** extremely cold; icy. **4.** unfriendly.

glacial period *n.* **1.** any period of time during which a large part of the earth's surface was covered with ice, due to the advance of glaciers. **2.** (*often caps.*) the Pleistocene epoch.

glaciate ('gleısı,eıt) *vb.* **1.** to cover with glaciers or masses of ice. **2.** to subject to the effects of glaciers. —,**glaci'ation** *n.*

glacier ('glæsıə, 'gleıs-) *n.* a slowly moving mass of ice formed by an accumulation of snow.

glad (glæd) *adj.* **gladder, gladdest. 1.** happy and pleased. **2.** causing happiness. **3.** (foll. by *to*) very willing: *he was glad to help.* —'**gladly** *adv.* —'**gladness** *n.*

gladden ('glæd'n) *vb.* to make or become glad.

glade (gleıd) *n.* an open place in a forest.

glad eye *n. Informal.* an inviting or seductive glance: *give someone the glad eye.*

gladiator ('glædı,eıtə) *n.* (in ancient Rome) a man trained to fight in arenas to provide entertainment. —**gladiatorial** (,glædıə-'tɔːrıəl) *adj.*

gladiolus (,glædı'əυləs) *n., pl.* **-lus, -li** (-laı), or **-luses.** a plant having sword-shaped leaves and spikes of funnel-shaped brightly coloured flowers.

glad rags *pl. n. Informal.* best clothes.

gladsome ('glædsəm) *adj. Archaic.* joyous or cheerful.

glair (glɛə) *n.* **1.** white of egg, used as a size, glaze, or adhesive. **2.** any substance like or made from this.

glamour *or U.S.* (*sometimes*) **glamor** ('glæmə) *n.* **1.** alluring charm; fascination. **2.** fascinating beauty. —'**glamorize** *or* -**ise** *vb.* —'**glamorous** *adj.*

glance (glɑːns) *vb.* **1.** to look hastily or briefly. **2.** (foll. by *over or through*) to look over briefly: *to glance through a report.* **3.** to glint or gleam: *the sun glanced on the water.* **4.** (usually foll. by *off*) to be deflected (off an object struck) at an oblique angle: *the arrow glanced off the tree.* ~*n.* **5.** a hasty or brief look. **6.** a flash or glint of light. **7.** a glancing off. —'**glancing** *adj.*

gland (glænd) *n.* **1.** an organ that synthesizes and secretes chemical substances for the body to use or eliminate. **2.** an organ in plants that synthesizes and secretes a particular substance.

glanders ('glændəz) *n.* (*functioning as sing.*) a highly infectious, often fatal disease of horses, characterized by inflammation and ulceration of the air passages, skin, and lymph glands.

glandular ('glændjυlə) *adj.* of, like, or affecting a gland or glands.

glandular fever *n.* an acute infectious viral disease characterized by fever, sore throat, and painful swollen lymph nodes.

glare (glɛə) *vb.* **1.** to stare angrily. **2.** (of light or colour) to be too bright. ~*n.* **3.** an angry stare. **4.** a dazzling light or brilliance.

glaring ('glɛərıŋ) *adj.* **1.** conspicuous: *a glaring omission.* **2.** dazzling or garish. —'**glaringly** *adv.*

glasnost ('glæs,nɒst) *n.* a policy of public frankness and accountability, esp. that developed in the USSR under Mikhail Gorbachov.

glass (glɑːs) *n.* **1.** a hard brittle transparent or translucent solid, consisting of metal silicates or similar compounds. **2.** something made of glass, such as a drinking vessel or a mirror. **3.** the amount contained in a drinking glass: *he drank a glass of wine.* **4.** glassware collectively. ~*vb.* **5.** to fit or cover with glass.

glass-blowing *n.* the process of shaping a mass of molten glass by blowing air into it through a tube. —'**glass-,blower** *n.*

glasses ('glɑːsız) *pl. n.* a pair of lenses for correcting faulty vision, in a frame that rests on the nose and hooks behind the ears.

glasshouse ('glɑːs,haυs) *n.* **1.** *Brit.* same as **greenhouse. 2.** *Informal, chiefly Brit.* a military detention centre.

glass wool *n.* fine glass fibres in a wool-like mass, used in insulation and filtering.

glassy ('glɑːsı) *adj.* **glassier, glassiest. 1.** like glass in smoothness or transparency. **2.** expressionless: *a glassy stare.*

Glaswegian (glæz'wiːdʒən) *adj.* **1.** of Glasgow, a city in Scotland, or its inhabitants. ~*n.* **2.** a person from Glasgow. **3.** the Glasgow dialect.

glaucoma (glɔː'kəυmə) *n.* an eye disease in which increased pressure in the eyeball causes gradual loss of sight. —**glau'comatous** *adj.*

glaze (gleız) *vb.* **1.** to fit or cover with glass. **2.** *Ceramics.* to cover with a vitreous coating, rendering impervious to liquid. **3.** to cover (foods) with a shiny coating, such as beaten egg or syrup. **4.** to make glossy or shiny. **5.** (sometimes foll. by *over*) to become glassy: *his eyes were glazing over.* ~*n.* **6.** *Ceramics.* **a.** a vitreous coating. **b.** the substance used to produce this. **7.** a smooth lustrous finish on a fabric. **8.** something used to give a glossy surface to foods: *a syrup glaze.* **—glazed** *adj.* **—'glazing** *n.*

glazier ('gleɪzɪə) *n.* a person who fits windows or doors with glass. **—'glaziery** *n.*

gleam (gliːm) *n.* **1.** a small beam or glow of light. **2.** a brief or dim indication: *a gleam of hope.* *~vb.* **3.** to send forth a small beam of light. **4.** to appear briefly. **—'gleaming** *adj.*

glean (gliːn) *vb.* **1.** to gather (something) bit by bit: *to glean information.* **2.** to gather (the useful remnants of a crop) after harvesting. **—'gleaner** *n.*

gleanings ('gliːnɪŋz) *pl. n.* things which are gleaned.

glebe (gliːb) *n. Brit.* land granted to a clergyman as part of his benefice.

glee (gliː) *n.* **1.** great merriment; joy. **2.** a type of song sung by three or more unaccompanied voices.

gleeful ('gliːfʊl) *adj.* full of glee; merry. **—'gleefully** *adv.* **—'gleefulness** *n.*

glen (glɛn) *n.* a deep narrow mountain valley.

glengarry (glɛn'gærɪ) *n., pl.* **-ries.** a brimless Scottish cap with a crease down the crown.

glib (glɪb) *adj.* **glibber, glibbest.** fluent and easy, often in an insincere or deceptive way: *glib promises.* **—'glibly** *adv.* **—'glibness** *n.*

glide (glaɪd) *vb.* **1.** to move easily and smoothly. **2.** to pass gradually and imperceptibly: *to glide into sleep.* **3.** (of an aircraft) to land without engine power. **4.** to fly a glider. **5.** to cause to glide. *~n.* **6.** a smooth easy movement. **7.** a manoeuvre in which an aircraft descends gently without engine power. **—'gliding** *adj., n.*

glider ('glaɪdə) *n.* an aircraft which does not use an engine, but flies by floating on air currents.

glide time *n. N.Z.* same as **flexitime.**

glimmer ('glɪmə) *vb.* **1.** (of a light) to glow faintly or flickeringly. **2.** to be indicated faintly: *hope glimmered in his face.* *~n.* **3.** a glow or twinkle of light. **4.** a faint indication.

glimpse (glɪmps) *n.* **1.** a brief or incomplete view: *to catch a glimpse of the sea.* **2.** a vague indication. *~vb.* **3.** to catch sight of momentarily.

glint (glɪnt) *vb.* **1.** to gleam brightly. *~n.* **2.** a bright gleam.

glissade (glɪ'sɑːd, -'seɪd) *n.* **1.** a gliding step in ballet. **2.** a controlled slide down a snow slope. *~vb.* **3.** to perform a glissade.

glisten ('glɪs⁰n) *vb.* **1.** (of a wet or glossy surface) to gleam by reflecting light. **2.** (of light) to reflect brightly: *the sunlight glistens on wet leaves.*

glitch (glɪtʃ) *n.* a sudden malfunction in an electronic system.

glitter ('glɪtə) *vb.* **1.** (of a surface) to reflect light in bright flashes. **2.** (of light) to be reflected in bright flashes. **3.** (usually foll. by *with*) to be showy or glamorous with: *the show glitters with famous actors.* *~n.* **4.** sparkle or brilliance. **5.** show and glamour. **6.** tiny pieces of shiny decorative material. **7.** *Canad.* ice formed from freezing rain. **—'glittering** *adj.* **—'glittery** *adj.*

glitzy ('glɪtsɪ) *adj.* **glitzier, glitziest.** *Slang.* showily attractive.

gloaming ('gləʊmɪŋ) *n. Scot. or poetic.* twilight or dusk.

gloat (gləʊt) *vb.* **1.** (often foll. by *over*) to look (at) or think (of) with malicious pleasure. *~n.* **2.** a gloating.

glob (glɒb) *n. Informal.* a rounded mass of thick fluid.

global ('gləʊb⁰l) *adj.* **1.** worldwide. **2.** comprehensive; total. **—'globally** *adv.*

globe (gləʊb) *n.* **1.** a sphere on which a map of the world is drawn. **2. the globe.** the earth. **3.** a spherical object, such as a glass lampshade or fishbowl.

globeflower ('gləʊb,flaʊə) *n.* a plant having yellow, white, or orange spherical flowers.

globetrotter ('gləʊb,trɒtə) *n.* a habitual worldwide traveller. **—'globe,trotting** *n., adj.*

globular ('glɒbjʊlə) *adj.* **1.** shaped like a globe or globule. **2.** consisting of globules.

globule ('glɒbjuːl) *n.* a small globe, usually a drop of liquid.

globulin ('glɒbjʊlɪn) *n.* a simple protein found in living tissue.

glockenspiel ('glɒkən,spiːl, -,ʃpiːl) *n.* a percussion instrument consisting of tuned metal plates played with a pair of small hammers.

gloom (gluːm) *n.* **1.** partial or total darkness. **2.** depression or melancholy. *~vb.* **3.** to make or become gloomy.

gloomy ('gluːmɪ) *adj.* **gloomier, gloomiest.** **1.** dark or dismal. **2.** causing depression or gloom: *gloomy news.* **3.** despairing; sad. **—'gloomily** *adv.* **—'gloominess** *n.*

glorify ('glɔːrɪ,faɪ) *vb.* **-fying, -fied.** **1.** to make glorious. **2.** to exalt in worship. **3.** to extol. **4.** to make (something) seem more splendid than it is. **—,glorifi'cation** *n.*

glorious ('glɔːrɪəs) *adj.* **1.** having or full of glory; illustrious. **2.** conferring glory: *a glorious victory.* **3.** brilliantly beautiful. **4.** delightful or enjoyable. **—'gloriously** *adv.* **—'gloriousness** *n.*

glory ('glɔːrɪ) *n., pl.* **-ries.** **1.** exaltation, praise, or honour. **2.** something worthy of praise: *crowning glory.* **3.** adoration or worship: *glory be to God.* **4.** splendour: *the glory of the king's reign.* **5.** the beauty and bliss of heaven. **6.** extreme happiness or prosperity. **7.** a saint's halo. *~vb.* **-rying, -ried.** **8.** (often foll. by *in*) to triumph or exalt.

glory box *n. Austral. & N.Z.* a box in which a young woman stores her trousseau.

glory hole *n.* a cupboard or storeroom, usually one which is very untidy.

Glos Gloucestershire.

gloss[1] (glɒs) *n.* **1.** lustre or sheen of a surface. **2.** a superficially attractive appearance. **3.** a paint giving a shiny finish. **4.** a cosmetic used to give a sheen. ~*vb.* **5.** to make glossy. **6.** (often foll. by *over*) to conceal (an error, failing, or awkward moment) by minimizing it.

gloss[2] (glɒs) *n.* **1.** an explanatory comment added in the margin or text of a manuscript or book. ~*vb.* **2.** to add glosses to.

glossary (ˈglɒsərɪ) *n., pl.* **-ries.** an alphabetical list of technical or special words in a book, with explanations.

glossy (ˈglɒsɪ) *adj.* **glossier, glossiest. 1.** smooth and shiny; lustrous. **2.** superficially attractive. **3.** (of a magazine) produced on shiny paper. —**ˈglossily** *adv.* —**ˈglossiness** *n.*

glottal stop *n.* a speech sound produced by tightly closing and then opening the glottis.

glottis (ˈglɒtɪs) *n., pl.* **-tises** *or* **-tides** (-tɪˌdiːz). the vocal apparatus of the larynx, consisting of the vocal cords and the opening between them. —**ˈglottal** *adj.*

glove (glʌv) *n.* **1.** (*often pl.*) a shaped covering for the hand with individual sheaths for each finger and the thumb. **2.** a protective hand cover worn in various sports, such as boxing. ~*vb.* **3.** to cover with or as if with gloves.

glover (ˈglʌvə) *n.* a maker or seller of gloves.

glow (gləʊ) *n.* **1.** light emitted as a result of great heat. **2.** a steady light without flames. **3.** brilliance of colour. **4.** brightness of complexion. **5.** a feeling of wellbeing or satisfaction. **6.** intensity of emotion. ~*vb.* **7.** to emit a steady light without flames. **8.** to shine intensely. **9.** to experience a feeling of wellbeing or satisfaction: *to glow with pride.* **10.** (esp. of the complexion) to show a strong bright colour. **11.** to be very hot.

glower (ˈglaʊə) *vb.* **1.** to stare angrily. ~*n.* **2.** an angry stare.

glow-worm *n.* a European beetle, the females and larvae of which have organs producing a soft greenish light.

gloxinia (glɒkˈsɪnɪə) *n.* a tropical plant cultivated for its white, red, or purple bell-shaped flowers.

glucose (ˈgluːkəʊz, -kəʊs) *n.* a white crystalline sugar found in plant and animal tissues.

glue (gluː) *n.* **1.** a natural or synthetic adhesive. ~*vb.* **gluing** *or* **glueing, glued. 2.** to join or stick together as with glue. **3.**

(foll. by *to*) to pay full attention to: *her eyes were glued to the TV screen.* —**ˈgluey** *adj.*

glue-sniffing *n.* the inhaling of the fumes of certain types of glue to produce intoxicating or hallucinatory effects. —**ˈglueˌsniffer** *n.*

glum (glʌm) *adj.* **glummer, glummest.** morose or sullen; gloomy. —**ˈglumly** *adv.* —**ˈglumness** *n.*

glut (glʌt) *n.* **1.** an excessive supply. **2.** a glutting or being glutted. ~*vb.* **glutting, glutted. 3.** to feed or fill beyond capacity. **4.** to supply (a market) with a commodity in excess of the demand for it.

gluten (ˈgluːt²n) *n.* a protein present in cereal grains, such as wheat.

glutinous (ˈgluːtɪnəs) *adj.* gluelike in texture; sticky.

glutton[1] (ˈglʌt²n) *n.* **1.** someone who eats and drinks too much. **2.** a person who has a great capacity for something: *a glutton for punishment.* —**ˈgluttonous** *adj.*

glutton[2] (ˈglʌt²n) *n.* same as **wolverine.**

gluttony (ˈglʌtənɪ) *n., pl.* **-tonies.** the act or practice of eating too much.

glyceride (ˈglɪsəˌraɪd) *n.* an ester of glycerol.

glycerin (ˈglɪsərɪn) *or* **glycerine** (ˈglɪsərɪn, ˌglɪsəˈriːn) *n.* a nontechnical name for **glycerol.**

glycerol (ˈglɪsəˌrɒl) *n.* a colourless odourless syrupy liquid: a by-product of soap manufacture, used as a solvent, antifreeze, sweetener (**E422**), and in explosives.

glycogen (ˈglaɪkəʊdʒən) *n.* a starchlike carbohydrate consisting of glucose units: the form in which carbohydrate is stored in animals. —**glycogenic** (ˌglaɪkəʊˈdʒɛnɪk) *adj.*

glycolysis (glaɪˈkɒlɪsɪs) *n. Biochem.* the breakdown of glucose by enzymes, with the release of energy.

GM (in Britain) George Medal.

gm gramme.

G-man *n., pl.* **G-men.** *U.S. slang.* an FBI agent.

GMT Greenwich Mean Time.

gnarled (nɑːld) *or* **gnarly** *adj.* rough, twisted, and knobby, usually through age.

gnash (næʃ) *vb.* **1.** to grind (the teeth) together in pain or anger. ~*n.* **2.** the act of gnashing.

gnat (næt) *n.* a small fragile biting two-winged insect.

gnaw (nɔː) *vb.* **gnawing, gnawed; gnawed** *or* **gnawn. 1.** to bite or chew constantly so as to wear away bit by bit. **2.** to form by gnawing: *to gnaw a hole.* **3.** to erode (something). **4.** (often foll. by *at*) to cause constant distress or anxiety (to).

gneiss (naɪs) *n.* a coarse-grained layered metamorphic rock.

gnome (nəʊm) *n.* **1.** a legendary creature

said to live in the depths of the earth and guard buried treasure. **2.** the statue of a gnome in a garden. **3.** *Facetious.* an international banker or financier: *gnomes of Zürich.*

gnomic ('nəʊmɪk, 'nɒm-) *adj.* of aphorisms; pithy.

gnostic ('nɒstɪk) *adj.* of or having knowledge.

Gnosticism ('nɒstɪˌsɪzəm) *n.* a religious movement characterized by a belief in intuitive spiritual knowledge: regarded as a heresy by the Christian Church. —'**Gnostic** *n., adj.*

GNP gross national product.

gnu (nuː) *n., pl.* **gnus** or **gnu.** a sturdy antelope of the African savannas, having an oxlike head.

go (gəʊ) *vb.* **going, went, gone.** **1.** to move or proceed to or from a place: *go home.* **2.** to depart: *we'll have to go at eleven.* **3.** to start in a race: often used in commands. **4.** to make regular journeys: *this train service goes to the east coast.* **5.** to operate or function: *the radio won't go.* **6.** to do or become as specified: *his face went red; the gun went bang.* **7.** to be or continue to be in a specified state: *to go hungry.* **8.** to lead or proceed as specified: *this path goes to the river; go to sleep.* **9.** (takes an infinitive) to serve or contribute: *this letter goes to prove my point.* **10.** to follow a specified course; fare: *the lecture went badly.* **11.** to be allotted to a particular purpose or recipient: *his money went on drink.* **12.** to be sold: *the necklace went for fifty pounds.* **13.** to be ranked: *this meal is good as my meals go.* **14.** to blend or harmonize: *that colour doesn't go with your hair.* **15.** (foll. by *by* or *under*) to be known (by a name or disguise). **16.** to have a usual place: *those books go on this shelf.* **17.** (of words or music) to be expressed or sung: *how does that song go?* **18.** to fail or break down: *my eyesight is going; the ladder went at the critical moment.* **19.** to die: *the old man went at 2 a.m.* **20.** (often foll. by *by*) **a.** (of time or distance) to elapse: *the hours go by so slowly.* **b.** to be guided (by). **21.** to occur: *happiness does not always go with riches.* **22.** to be eliminated or given up: *this entry must go to save space.* **23.** to be spent or finished: *all his money has gone.* **24.** to attend: *go to school.* **25.** to join a stated profession: *go on the stage.* **26.** (foll. by *to*) to have recourse (to): *to go to arbitration.* **27.** (foll. by *to*) to subject or put oneself (to): *she goes to great pains to please him.* **28.** to proceed up to or beyond certain limits: *you will go too far one day.* **29.** to be acceptable: *anything goes.* **30.** to carry authority: *what the boss says goes.* **31.** *Nonstandard.* to say: *Then she goes, "shut up!"* **32.** (foll. by *into*) to be contained in: *four goes into twelve three times.*

33. (often foll. by *for*) to endure or last out: *we can't go for much longer without water.* **34. be going.** to intend or be about to start (doing or happening): *what's going to happen to us?* **35. go and.** *Informal.* to be so foolish or unlucky as to: *then she had to go and lose her hat.* **36. go it alone.** *Informal.* to act or proceed without help. **37. go one better.** *Informal.* to surpass or outdo (someone). **38. let go. a.** to relax one's hold (on); release. **b.** to discuss or consider no further. **39. let oneself go. a.** to act in an uninhibited manner. **b.** to lose interest in one's appearance. **40. to go. a.** remaining. **b.** *U.S. & Canad. informal.* (of food sold in a restaurant) for taking away. ~*n., pl.* **goes.** **41.** the act of going. **42.** an attempt: *he had a go at the stamp business.* **43.** an attack, usually verbal: *she had a real go at them.* **44.** a turn: *it's my go next.* **45.** *Informal.* the quality of being active and energetic: *she has a lot of go.* **46.** *Informal.* hard or energetic work: *it's all go.* **47.** *Informal.* a success: *he made a go of it.* **48. from the word go.** *Informal.* from the very beginning. **49. no go.** *Informal.* impossible or futile: *it's no go, I'm afraid.* **50. on the go.** *Informal.* active and energetic. ~*adj.* **51.** *Informal.* functioning and ready for action: *all systems are go.* ~See also **go about, go against,** etc.

go about *vb.* **1.** to busy oneself with: *to go about one's duties.* **2.** to tackle (a problem or task). **3.** to circulate: *there's a lot of flu going about.*

goad (gəʊd) *n.* **1.** a sharp pointed stick for driving cattle. **2.** a spur or incitement. ~*vb.* **3.** to drive as if with a goad; spur.

go against *vb.* **1.** to be contrary to (principles or beliefs). **2.** to be unfavourable to (a person): *the case went against him.*

go-ahead *n.* **1.** (usually preceded by *the*) *Informal.* permission to proceed. ~*adj.* **2.** enterprising or ambitious.

goal (gəʊl) *n.* **1.** an aim or object. **2.** the end point of a journey or race. **3.** *Sport.* the space into which players try to propel the ball or puck to score. **4.** *Sport.* **a.** a successful attempt at scoring. **b.** the score so made. —'**goalless** *adj.*

goalie ('gəʊlɪ) *n. Informal.* a goalkeeper.

goalkeeper ('gəʊlˌkiːpə) *n. Sport.* a player at the goal whose duty is to prevent the ball or puck from entering it.

goal line *n. Sport.* the line marking each end of the pitch, on which the goals stand.

goalpost ('gəʊlˌpəʊst) *n.* **1.** either of two uprights supporting the crossbar of a goal. **2. move the goalposts.** to change the aims of an activity to ensure the desired results.

goat (gəʊt) *n.* **1.** a sure-footed ruminant mammal with hollow horns. **2.** *Informal.* a lecherous man. **3.** a foolish person. **4. get someone's goat.** *Slang.* to annoy someone. —'**goatish** *adj.*

go at *vb.* **1.** to make an energetic attempt at (something). **2.** to attack vehemently.

goatee (gəʊˈtiː) *n.* a pointed tuftlike beard.

goatherd (ˈgəʊtˌhɜːd) *n.* a person employed to tend or herd goats.

goatskin (ˈgəʊtˌskɪn) *n.* **1.** the hide of a goat. **2.** something made from this, such as leather or a container for wine.

goatsucker (ˈgəʊtˌsʌkə) *n. U.S. & Canad.* same as **nightjar.**

gob[1] (gɒb) *n.* **1.** a lump or chunk of a soft substance. ~*vb.* **gobbing, gobbed. 2.** *Brit. informal.* to spit.

gob[2] (gɒb) *n. Slang, chiefly Brit.* the mouth.

go back *vb.* **1.** to return. **2.** (often foll. by *to*) to originate (in): *the links with France go back to the Norman Conquest.* **3.** (foll. by *on*) to change one's mind about; repudiate: *go back on one's word.*

gobbet (ˈgɒbɪt) *n.* a chunk or lump.

gobble[1] (ˈgɒbᵊl) *vb.* (often foll. by *up*) to eat (food) hastily and greedily.

gobble[2] (ˈgɒbᵊl) *n.* **1.** the loud rapid gurgling sound made by male turkeys. ~*vb.* **2.** to make this sound.

gobbledegook *or* **gobbledygook** (ˈgɒbᵊldɪˌguːk) *n.* pretentious or unintelligible language or jargon.

gobbler (ˈgɒblə) *n. Informal.* a male turkey.

go-between *n.* a person who acts as intermediary for two people or groups.

goblet (ˈgɒblɪt) *n.* a drinking vessel with a base and stem but without handles.

goblin (ˈgɒblɪn) *n.* (in folklore) a small grotesque creature, malevolent towards human beings.

goby (ˈgəʊbɪ) *n., pl.* **-by** *or* **-bies.** a small spiny-finned fish having ventral fins modified into a sucker.

go by *vb.* **1.** to pass: *as the years go by.* **2.** to be guided by: *in the darkness we could only go by the stars; don't go by appearances.* ~*n.* **go-by. 3.** *Slang.* a deliberate snub or slight: *she gave me the go-by.*

go-cart *n.* same as **go-kart.**

god (gɒd) *n.* **1.** a supernatural being, worshipped as the controller of the universe or some aspect of life or as the personification of some force. **2.** an image of such a deity. **3.** a person or thing to which excessive attention is given: *money was his god.* **4.** a man who has qualities regarded as making him superior to other men. **5.** (*pl.*) the gallery of a theatre. —**goddess** *fem. n.*

God (gɒd) *n.* **1.** the sole Supreme Being, Creator and ruler of all, in monotheistic religions. ~*interj.* **2.** an oath or exclamation of surprise or annoyance.

godchild (ˈgɒdˌtʃaɪld) *n., pl.* **-children.** a person who is sponsored by adults at baptism.

goddaughter (ˈgɒdˌdɔːtə) *n.* a female godchild.

godetia (gəˈdiːʃə) *n.* a plant grown for its showy flowers.

godfather (ˈgɒdˌfɑːðə) *n.* **1.** a male godparent. **2.** the head of a Mafia family or other criminal ring.

God-fearing *adj.* pious; devout.

godforsaken (ˈgɒdfəˌseɪkən) *adj.* desolate; dreary; forlorn.

Godhead (ˈgɒdˌhɛd) *n.* **1.** the nature and condition of being God. **2. the Godhead.** God.

godless (ˈgɒdlɪs) *adj.* **1.** wicked or unprincipled. **2.** irreligious. —**godlessness** *n.*

godly (ˈgɒdlɪ) *adj.* **-lier, -liest.** religious; pious; devout. —**godliness** *n.*

godmother (ˈgɒdˌmʌðə) *n.* a female godparent.

godown (ˈgəʊˌdaʊn) *n.* (in the Far East) a warehouse.

godparent (ˈgɒdˌpɛərənt) *n.* a person who stands sponsor to a child at baptism.

godsend (ˈgɒdˌsɛnd) *n.* a person or thing that comes unexpectedly but is very welcome.

godson (ˈgɒdˌsʌn) *n.* a male godchild.

Godspeed (ˈgɒdˈspiːd) *interj., n.* an expression of good wishes for a person's safe journey and success.

godwit (ˈgɒdwɪt) *n.* a shore bird having long legs and an upturned bill.

goer (ˈgəʊə) *n.* **1.** a person who attends something regularly: *a filmgoer.* **2.** an energetic person.

go for *vb.* **1.** to go somewhere in order to have or fetch: *he went for a drink.* **2.** to seek to obtain: *I'd go for that job if I were you.* **3.** to like: *I really go for that idea of yours.* **4.** to attack. **5.** to be considered to be of a stated importance or value: *his experience went for nothing when he was made redundant.*

go-getter *n. Informal.* an ambitious enterprising person. —**go-ˈgetting** *adj.*

goggle (ˈgɒgᵊl) *vb.* **1.** to stare with bulging eyes. **2.** (of the eyes) to bulge. ~*n.* **3.** a bulging stare. **4.** (*pl.*) close-fitting protective spectacles. —**ˈgoggle-ˌeyed** *adj.*

gogglebox (ˈgɒgᵊlˌbɒks) *n. Brit. slang.* a television set.

go-go dancer *n.* a scantily dressed woman who performs erotic dance routines in a nightclub or bar.

Goidelic (gɔɪˈdɛlɪk) *n.* **1.** the group of Celtic languages, consisting of Irish Gaelic, Scottish Gaelic, and Manx. ~*adj.* **2.** of this group of languages.

go in *vb.* **1.** (of the sun) to become hidden behind a cloud. **2. go in for. a.** to enter as a competitor. **b.** to adopt as an activity or principle: *she went in for nursing.*

going (ˈgəʊɪŋ) *n.* **1.** a departure. **2.** the condition of the ground with regard to walking or riding: *muddy going.* **3.** *Infor-*

mal. speed or progress: *we made good going on the trip.* ~*adj.* **4.** thriving: *a going concern.* **5.** current or accepted: *the going rate.* **6.** available: *the best going.*

going-over *n., pl.* **goings-over.** *Informal.* **1.** a thorough examination or investigation. **2.** a scolding or thrashing.

goings-on *pl. n. Informal.* actions or events, usually when mysterious or disapproved of.

go into *vb.* **1.** to start a career in: *to go into publishing.* **2.** to investigate. **3.** to discuss: *we won't go into that now.* **4.** to be admitted to: *she went into hospital.* **5.** to enter a specified state: *she went into hysterics.*

goitre *or U.S.* **goiter** ('gɔɪtə) *n. Pathol.* a swelling of the thyroid gland in the neck.

go-kart *n.* a small four-wheeled motor vehicle, used for racing.

gold (gəʊld) *n.* **1.** a bright yellow precious metal: used as a monetary standard and in jewellery and plating. Symbol: Au **2.** a coin or coins made of this metal. **3.** money; wealth. **4.** something precious or beautiful. **5.** short for **gold medal.** ~*adj.* **6.** deep yellow.

goldcrest ('gəʊld,krɛst) *n.* a small warbler having a bright yellow-and-black crown.

gold-digger *n.* **1.** a person who prospects or digs for gold. **2.** *Informal.* a woman who uses her sexual attractions to get gifts and money.

gold dust *n.* gold in the form of small particles or powder.

golden ('gəʊldən) *adj.* **1.** of the colour of gold: *golden hair.* **2.** made of or containing gold: *a golden statue.* **3.** happy or prosperous: *golden days.* **4.** (*sometimes cap.*) (of anniversaries) the 50th: *Golden Jubilee; golden wedding.* **5.** *Informal.* very successful or destined for success: *the golden girl of tennis.* **6.** very valuable or advantageous: *a golden opportunity.*

golden age *n.* the most flourishing and outstanding period in the history of an art or nation: *the golden age of poetry.*

golden eagle *n.* a large mountain eagle of the N hemisphere, having golden-brown plumage on the back.

golden handshake *n. Informal.* money given to an employee, either on retirement or to compensate for loss of employment.

golden mean *n.* the middle course between extremes.

golden retriever *n.* a breed of retriever with a silky wavy coat of a golden colour.

goldenrod (ˌgəʊldən'rɒd) *n.* a plant having spikes of small yellow flowers.

golden rule *n.* **1.** the rule of conduct, formulated by Christ, that one should do as one would wish to be done by. **2.** any important principle.

golden syrup *n. Brit.* a light golden-coloured treacle.

goldfinch ('gəʊld,fɪntʃ) *n.* a European finch, the male of which has yellow-and-black wings.

goldfish ('gəʊld,fɪʃ) *n., pl.* **-fish** *or* **-fishes.** a gold or orange-red freshwater fish, widely kept as a pond or aquarium fish.

gold foil *n.* thin gold sheet that is thicker than gold leaf.

gold leaf *n.* very thin gold sheet made by rolling or hammering gold and used for gilding.

gold medal *n.* a medal of gold, awarded to the winner of a competition or race.

gold plate *n.* **1.** a thin coating of gold, usually produced by electroplating. **2.** tableware made of gold. —ˌ**gold-'plate** *vb.*

gold rush *n.* a large-scale migration of people to a territory where gold has been found.

goldsmith ('gəʊld,smɪθ) *n.* a person who makes or sells articles made from gold.

gold standard *n.* a monetary system in which the basic currency unit equals a specified weight of gold.

golf (gɒlf) *n.* **1.** a game played on a large open course, the object of which is to hit a ball using clubs, with as few strokes as possible, into each of usually 18 holes. ~*vb.* **2.** to play golf. —**golfer** *n.*

golf club *n.* **1.** a long-shafted club used to strike a golf ball. **2. a.** an association of golf players. **b.** the premises of such an association.

golf course *or* **links** *n.* an area of ground laid out for golf.

Goliath (gə'laɪəθ) *n.* a Biblical giant.

golliwog ('gɒlɪ,wɒg) *n.* a soft doll with a black face, usually made of cloth.

golly ('gɒlɪ) *interj.* an exclamation of mild surprise.

goloshes (gə'lɒʃɪz) *pl. n.* same as **galoshes.**

gonad ('gɒnæd) *n.* an animal organ in which reproductive cells are produced, such as a testis or ovary.

gondola ('gɒndələ) *n.* **1.** a long narrow flat-bottomed boat with a high ornamented stem: traditionally used on the canals of Venice. **2.** a car suspended from an airship, balloon, or cable car.

gondolier (ˌgɒndə'lɪə) *n.* a man who rows a gondola.

gone (gɒn) *vb.* **1.** the past participle of **go.** ~*adj.* **2.** ended; past. **3.** lost; ruined. **4.** dead. **5.** used up. **6.** *Informal.* having been pregnant (for a specified time): *six months gone.* **7.** (usually foll. by *on*) *Slang.* in love (with).

goner ('gɒnə) *n. Slang.* a person about to die or a thing beyond help or recovery.

gonfalon ('gɒnfələn) *n.* a banner hanging

from a crossbar, usually ending in streamers.

gong (gɒŋ) *n.* **1.** a rimmed metal disc that produces a note when struck. **2.** *Brit. slang.* a medal.

gonorrhoea *or esp. U.S.* **gonorrhea** (ˌgɒnəˈrɪə) *n.* a venereal disease characterized by inflammation and a discharge from the genital organs.

goo (guː) *n. Informal.* **1.** a sticky substance. **2.** sickly sentiment.

good (gʊd) *adj.* **better, best.** **1.** having admirable, pleasing, superior, or positive qualities: *a good teacher.* **2.** morally excellent; virtuous: *a good man.* **3.** suitable for a purpose: *a good winter coat.* **4.** beneficial: *vegetables are good for you.* **5.** not ruined or decayed: *the meat is still good.* **6.** kindly or generous: *you are good to him.* **7.** valid or genuine: *I would not do this without good reason.* **8.** honourable or held in high esteem: *a good family.* **9.** financially sound: *a good investment.* **10.** competent or talented: *he's good at science.* **11.** obedient or well-behaved: *a good dog.* **12.** reliable or recommended: *a good make of clothes.* **13.** giving material pleasure: *the good life.* **14.** complete; full: *I took a good look round the house.* **15.** opportune: *a good time to ask for a rise.* **16.** satisfying or enjoyable: *a good rest.* **17.** newest or of the best quality: *keep the good plates for guests.* **18.** fairly large, extensive, or long: *a good distance away.* **19.** ample: *a good supply of food.* **20. as good as.** virtually; practically: *as good as new.* ~*interj.* **21.** an exclamation of approval or pleasure. ~*n.* **22.** moral or material advantage; benefit or profit: *what is the good of worrying?* **23.** positive moral qualities; virtue. **24.** (*sometimes cap.*) moral qualities seen as an abstract entity: *the conflict between Good and Evil.* **25.** a good thing. **26. for good** (**and all**). forever; permanently: *I have left them for good.* **27. good for** *or* **on you.** well done or well said: a term of congratulation. **28. make good. a.** to recompense or repair damage or injury. **b.** to be successful. **c.** to fulfil (something intended or promised). ~See also **goods.**

Good Book *n.* the Bible.

goodbye (ˌgʊdˈbaɪ) *interj.* **1.** farewell: an expression used on parting. ~*n.* **2.** a parting; farewell: *I said my goodbyes.*

good day *interj.* an expression of greeting or farewell used during the day.

good-for-nothing *n.* **1.** an irresponsible or worthless person. ~*adj.* **2.** irresponsible; worthless.

Good Friday *n.* the Friday before Easter, observed by Christians as a commemoration of the Crucifixion of Jesus.

goodies (ˈgʊdɪz) *pl. n.* any things considered particularly desirable.

goodly (ˈgʊdlɪ) *adj.* **-lier, -liest.** **1.** considerable: *a goodly amount.* **2.** *Obs.* attractive, pleasing, or fine. —ˈ**goodliness** *n.*

good morning *interj.* an expression of greeting or farewell used in the morning.

good-natured *adj.* tolerant and kindly.

goodness (ˈgʊdnɪs) *n.* **1.** the quality of being good. **2.** kindness. **3.** virtue. ~*interj.* **4.** an exclamation of surprise.

good night *interj.* an expression of farewell, used in the evening or at night.

goods (gʊdz) *pl. n.* **1.** movable personal property. **2.** merchandise. **3.** *Chiefly Brit.* freight. **4. deliver the goods.** *Informal.* to do that which is expected or required. **5. have the goods on someone.** *U.S. & Canad. slang.* to know something incriminating about someone.

Good Samaritan *n.* a person who helps another in difficulty or distress.

Good Shepherd *n. New Testament.* a title given to Jesus Christ in John 10:11-12.

good-tempered *adj.* of a tolerant, kindly, and generous disposition.

good turn *n.* a helpful and friendly act.

goodwill (ˌgʊdˈwɪl) *n.* **1.** benevolence; kindly feeling. **2.** willingness or acquiescence. **3.** the popularity and good reputation of a well-established business, considered as a valuable asset.

goody (ˈgʊdɪ) *interj.* **1.** a child's exclamation of pleasure. ~*n., pl.* **goodies. 2.** *Informal.* the hero in a film or book. **3.** See **goodies.**

goody-goody *n., pl.* **-goodies. 1.** *Informal.* a smugly virtuous person. ~*adj.* **2.** smugly virtuous.

gooey (ˈguːɪ) *adj.* **gooier, gooiest.** *Informal.* **1.** sticky, soft, and often sweet. **2.** sentimental.

goof (guːf) *Informal.* ~*n.* **1.** a foolish error. **2.** a stupid person. ~*vb.* **3.** to bungle (something); botch. **4.** (often foll. by *about* or *around*) to fool (around); mess (about).

go off *vb.* **1.** to stop functioning: *the lights suddenly went off.* **2.** to explode. **3.** (of an alarm) to sound. **4.** to occur as specified: *the meeting went off well.* **5.** to leave (a place): *the actors went off stage.* **6.** to fall asleep. **7.** *Brit. informal.* (of food) to become stale or rotten. **8.** *Brit. informal.* to stop liking.

goofy (ˈguːfɪ) *adj.* **goofier, goofiest.** *Informal.* foolish; silly. —ˈ**goofiness** *n.*

googly (ˈguːglɪ) *n., pl.* **-lies.** *Cricket.* a ball bowled so as to change direction unexpectedly on the bounce.

goon (guːn) *n.* **1.** a stupid person. **2.** *U.S. informal.* a hired thug.

go on *vb.* **1.** to continue or proceed. **2.** to happen: *there's something strange going on.* **3.** *Theatre.* to make an entrance on stage. **4.** to talk. **5.** to criticize or nag: *stop going on at me!*

goosander (guːˈsændə) *n.* a duck of Europe

and North America, having a dark head and white body in the male, and a sharp serrated beak.

goose[1] (guːs) *n., pl.* **geese.** 1. a web-footed long-necked migratory bird typically larger than a duck. 2. the female of such a bird, as opposed to the male (gander). 3. *Informal.* a silly person. 4. the flesh of the goose, used as food. 5. **cook someone's goose.** *Informal.* to spoil someone's chances or plans completely.

goose[2] (guːs) *Slang.* ~*vb.* 1. to prod (a person) playfully in the bottom. ~*n., pl.* **gooses.** 2. such a prod.

gooseberry ('guzbərɪ, -brɪ) *n., pl.* **-ries.** 1. the edible yellow-green berries of a Eurasian shrub. 2. **play gooseberry.** *Brit. informal.* to be an unwanted single person accompanying a couple.

goose flesh *n.* the bumpy condition of the skin due to cold or fear, in which the muscles at the base of the hair follicles contract, making the hair bristle. Also: **goose pimples.**

goosegog ('guzgɒg) *n. Brit. informal.* a gooseberry.

goose step *n.* 1. a military march step in which the leg is swung rigidly to an exaggerated height. ~*vb.* **goose-step, -stepping, -stepped.** 2. to march in goose step.

go out *vb.* 1. to be extinguished or cease to function: *the fire has gone out.* 2. to cease to be fashionable or popular: *that style went out ages ago!* 3. (of a broadcast) to be transmitted. 4. to go to entertainments or social functions. 5. (usually foll. by *with* or *together*) to spend time (with someone) regularly as a couple.

go over *vb.* 1. to be received in a specified manner: *the concert went over well.* 2. to examine and emend or repair as necessary: *he went over the accounts; can you go over my car, please?* 3. to rehearse or revise: *I'll go over my lines before the play.*

gopher ('gəufə) *n.* 1. an American burrowing rodent having wide cheek pouches. 2. same as **ground squirrel.** 3. a burrowing tortoise of North America.

Gordian knot ('gɔːdɪən) *n.* **cut the Gordian knot.** to solve a complicated problem by bold or forceful action.

gore[1] (gɔː) *n.* blood shed from a wound.

gore[2] (gɔː) *vb.* (of an animal) to pierce or stab (a person or another animal) with a horn or tusk.

gore[3] (gɔː) *n.* 1. a tapering piece of material in a garment, sail, or umbrella. ~*vb.* 2. to make into or with a gore or gores. —**gored** *adj.*

gorge (gɔːdʒ) *n.* 1. a deep ravine. 2. the contents of the stomach. 3. *Archaic.* the gullet. 4. **make one's gorge rise.** to induce feelings of disgust or resentment. ~*vb.* 5.

to eat (food) ravenously. 6. to stuff (oneself) with food.

gorgeous ('gɔːdʒəs) *adj.* 1. strikingly beautiful or attractive. 2. *Informal.* extremely pleasant or fine: *gorgeous weather.* —**gorgeously** *adv.*

Gorgon ('gɔːgən) *n.* 1. *Greek myth.* one of three monstrous sisters who had live snakes for hair, and were so horrifying that anyone looking on them was turned to stone. 2. (*often not cap.*) *Informal.* an ugly, fierce, or unpleasant woman.

Gorgonzola (,gɔːgən'zəulə) *n.* a semihard blue-veined cheese of sharp flavour.

gorilla (gə'rɪlə) *n.* the largest anthropoid ape, inhabiting the forests of central W Africa. It is stocky with a short muzzle and coarse dark hair.

gormless ('gɔːmlɪs) *adj. Brit. informal.* stupid; dull.

go round *vb.* 1. to be sufficient: *is there enough food to go round?* 2. to circulate (in): *measles is going round the school.* 3. to be long enough to encircle: *will that belt go round you?*

gorse (gɔːs) *n.* an evergreen shrub which has yellow flowers and thick green spines instead of leaves. —**gorsy** *adj.*

gory ('gɔːrɪ) *adj.* **gorier, goriest.** 1. horrific or bloodthirsty: *a gory tale.* 2. involving bloodshed: *a gory battle.* 3. covered in gore. —**goriness** *n.*

gosh (gɒʃ) *interj.* an exclamation of mild surprise or wonder.

goshawk ('gɒs,hɔːk) *n.* a large, swift, short-winged hawk.

gosling ('gɒzlɪŋ) *n.* a young goose.

go-slow *n. Brit.* a deliberate slowing of the rate of production by workers as a tactic in industrial conflict.

gospel ('gɒsp'l) *n.* 1. Also called: **gospel truth.** an unquestionable truth: *to take someone's word as gospel.* 2. a doctrine held to be of great importance. 3. Black religious music originating in the churches of the Southern U.S. 4. the story of Christ's life and teachings.

Gospel ('gɒsp'l) *n.* one of the first four books of the New Testament, namely Matthew, Mark, Luke, and John.

gossamer ('gɒsəmə) *n.* 1. a very fine fabric. 2. a filmy cobweb often seen on foliage or floating in the air.

gossip ('gɒsɪp) *n.* 1. idle chat. 2. a conversation involving chatter about other people. 3. a person who habitually talks about others, usually maliciously. ~*vb.* 4. (often foll. by *about*) to talk idly or maliciously (about other people). —**gossipy** *adj.*

got (gɒt) *vb.* 1. the past of **get.** 2. **have got. a.** to possess. **b.** (*takes an infinitive*) used to express necessity: *I've got to get a new coat.*

Goth (gɒθ) *n.* **1.** a member of an East Germanic people who invaded many parts of the Roman Empire from the 3rd to the 5th century. **2.** a rude or barbaric person.

Gothic (ˈgɒθɪk) *adj.* **1.** of or resembling the style of architecture used in W Europe from the 12th to the 16th centuries, characterized by pointed arches, ribbed vaults, and flying buttresses. **2.** (*sometimes not cap.*) of or in a literary style characterized by gloom, horror, and the supernatural, popular in the late 18th century. **3.** of the Goths or their language. **4.** (*sometimes not cap.*) primitive and barbarous. ~*n.* **5.** Gothic architecture or art. **6.** the extinct language of the ancient Goths. **7.** a heavy ornate script typeface much used from about the 15th to 18th centuries. —ˈGothiˌcism *n.*

go through *vb.* **1.** to be approved: *the amendment went through.* **2.** to use up; exhaust: *we went through our supplies in a day.* **3.** to examine: *he went through the figures.* **4.** to suffer: *she went through great pain.* **5.** to rehearse or revise: *go through the details again.* **6.** to search: *she went through the cupboards.* **7.** (foll. by *with*) to bring to a successful conclusion, often by persistence.

go together *vb.* **1.** to be mutually suited; harmonize: *the colours go well together.* **2.** *Informal.* (of two people) to be romantically involved with each other.

gotten (ˈgɒtən) *vb. U.S.* a past participle of **get.**

gouache (guˈɑːʃ) *n.* **1.** a painting technique using opaque watercolours bound with glue. **2.** the paint used in this technique. **3.** a painting done by this method.

Gouda (ˈgaʊdə) *n.* a flat round mild Dutch cheese, orig. made in the town of Gouda.

gouge (gaʊdʒ) *vb.* **1.** (usually foll. by *out*) to scoop or force (something) out of its position. **2.** (sometimes foll. by *out*) to cut (a hole or groove) in (something) with a pointed object. ~*n.* **3.** a type of chisel with a curved blade for cutting holes or grooves. **4.** a mark or groove made by gouging.

goulash (ˈguːlæʃ) *n.* a rich stew, originating in Hungary and highly seasoned with paprika.

go up *vb.* **1.** to move to a higher place or level: *prices are going up.* **2.** to be destroyed: *the house went up in flames.*

gourd (gʊəd) *n.* **1.** the fruit of a plant of the cucumber family, whose dried shells are used for ornaments or drinking cups. **2.** a plant bearing this fruit. **3.** a container made from a dried gourd shell.

gourmand (ˈgʊəmənd) *n.* a person devoted to eating and drinking, usually to excess.

gourmet (ˈgʊəmeɪ) *n.* a connoisseur of good food and drink.

gout (gaʊt) *n.* **1.** a disease characterized by painful inflammation of certain joints, esp. of the big toe. **2.** *Archaic.* a drop or splash. —ˈgouty *adj.*

Gov. *or* **gov.** **1.** government. **2.** governor.

govern (ˈgʌvən) *vb.* **1.** to direct and control the policy and affairs of (an organization or nation); rule. **2.** to exercise restraint over; control: *to govern one's temper.* **3.** to decide or determine (something): *what governed his decision to leave?* **4.** (of a word) to determine the inflection of (another word). —ˈgovernable *adj.*

governance (ˈgʌvənəns) *n.* **1.** government, control, or authority. **2.** the action, manner, or system of governing.

governess (ˈgʌvənɪs) *n.* a woman employed in a private household to teach and train the children.

government (ˈgʌvənmənt, ˈgʌvəmənt) *n.* **1.** the exercise of political authority over a country or state. **2.** the system by which a country or state is ruled: *tyrannical government.* **3.** (*sometimes cap.*) the executive policy-making body of a country or state. **4.** regulation; direction. —**governmental** (ˌgʌvənˈmɛntˀl, ˌgʌvəˈmɛntl) *adj.*

governor (ˈgʌvənə) *n.* **1.** an official governing a province or region. **2.** the representative of the Crown in a British colony. **3.** *Brit.* the senior administrator of a society, institution, or prison. **4.** the chief executive of a U.S. state. **5.** a device that automatically controls the speed of an engine. **6.** *Brit. informal.* one's father or employer. —ˈgovernorˌship *n.*

governor general *n., pl.* **governors general** *or* **governor generals.** **1.** the representative of the Crown in a Commonwealth dominion. **2.** *Brit.* a governor with authority over other governors.

Govt Government.

go with *vb.* **1.** to accompany. **2.** to blend or harmonize: *that new wallpaper goes well with the furniture.* **3.** to belong with: *a company car goes with the job.* **4.** (of two people) to be romantically involved with each other.

go without *vb. Chiefly Brit.* to be denied or deprived of (something): *if you don't like your tea, you can go without.*

gown (gaʊn) *n.* **1.** a woman's long formal dress. **2.** a surgeon's overall. **3.** a loose wide official robe worn by clergymen, judges, lawyers, and academics. **4.** the members of a university collectively.

goy (gɔɪ) *n., pl.* **goyim** (ˈgɔɪɪm) *or* **goys.** *Slang.* a Jewish word for a **Gentile.**

GP general practitioner.

GPO general post office.

grab (græb) *vb.* **grabbing, grabbed.** **1.** to seize hold of (something). **2.** to seize illegally or unscrupulously. **3.** to take (food, drink, or rest) hurriedly: *to grab a meal.* **4.** *Informal.* to interest; impress. ~*n.* **5.** a grabbing. **6.** a mechanical device for gripping objects.

grace (greɪs) n. **1.** elegance and beauty of movement, form, or expression. **2.** a pleasing or charming quality. **3.** goodwill or favour. **4.** a delay granted for the completion of a task or payment of a debt. **5.** courtesy; decency. **6.** *Christian theol.* the free and unmerited favour of God shown towards man. **7.** a short prayer of thanks for a meal. **8. airs and graces.** affected manner. **9. with (a) bad grace.** unwillingly or grudgingly. **10. with (a) good grace.** willingly or ungrudgingly. ~vb. **11.** to add grace: *flowers graced the room.* **12.** to honour or favour: *to grace a party with one's presence.*

Grace (greɪs) n. (preceded by *Your, His,* or *Her*) a title of a duke, duchess, or archbishop.

grace-and-favour n. (*modifier*) *Brit.* (of a house or flat) owned by the sovereign and granted rent-free to someone.

graceful ('greɪsfʊl) adj. characterized by beauty of movement, style, or form. —'**gracefully** adv. —'**gracefulness** n.

graceless ('greɪslɪs) adj. **1.** lacking manners. **2.** lacking elegance.

grace note n. *Music.* a merely ornamental note, usually printed in small type.

Graces ('greɪsɪz) pl. n. *Greek myth.* three sister goddesses, givers of charm and beauty.

gracious ('greɪʃəs) adj. **1.** showing kindness and courtesy. **2.** condescendingly polite. **3.** characterized by elegance, ease, and indulgence: *gracious living.* **4.** compassionate. ~interj. **5.** an expression of mild surprise or wonder. —'**graciously** adv. —'**graciousness** n.

gradation (grə'deɪʃən) n. **1.** a series of systematic stages; gradual progression. **2.** (*often pl.*) a stage in such a series or progression. **3.** an arranging in stages or a gradual progression. —**gra'date** vb. —**gra'dational** adj.

grade (greɪd) n. **1.** a position or degree in a scale of quality, rank, or size. **2.** a group of people or things of the same category. **3.** a stage in a course of progression. **4.** a mark or rating indicating a student's level of achievement. **5.** *U.S. & Canad.* a class or year in a school. **6. make the grade.** *Informal.* **a.** to reach the required standard. **b.** to succeed. ~vb. **7.** to arrange according to quality or rank. **8.** to give a grade to. **9.** to change or blend (something) gradually; merge. **10.** to level (ground or a road) to a suitable gradient.

gradient ('greɪdɪənt) n. **1.** Also (esp. U.S.): **grade.** a sloping part of a railway, road, or path. **2.** Also (esp. U.S. and Canad.): **grade.** a measure of the steepness of such a slope. **3.** a measure of the change in something, such as the angle of a curve, over a specified distance.

gradual ('grædjʊəl) adj. occurring, developing, or moving in small stages: *a gradual improvement; a gradual slope.* —'**gradually** adv.

gradualism ('grædjʊəˌlɪzəm) n. the policy of seeking to change something gradually. —'**gradualist** n., adj.

graduate n. ('grædjʊɪt). **1.** a person who holds a university or college degree. **2.** *U.S. & Canad.* a student who has completed a course of studies at a high school and has received a diploma. **3.** *U.S. & Canad.* same as **postgraduate.** ~vb. ('grædjʊˌeɪt). **4.** to receive a degree or diploma. **5.** to mark (a measuring flask or instrument) with units of measurement. **6.** to group according to type or quality. **7.** (often foll. by *to*) to change by degrees (from something to something else).

graduation (ˌgrædjʊ'eɪʃən) n. **1.** a graduating or being graduated. **2.** the ceremony at which degrees and diplomas are conferred. **3.** a mark or marks indicating measure on an instrument or container.

Graeco-Roman or esp. U.S. **Greco-Roman** (ˌgriːkəʊ'rəʊmən) adj. having Greek and Roman influences.

graffiti (græ'fiːtɪ) pl. n. (*sometimes functioning as sing.*) drawings or words scribbled or sprayed on walls or posters.

graft[1] (grɑːft) n. **1. a.** a small piece of tissue from one plant that is made to unite with another plant so that they grow together as one. **b.** a plant produced by this method. **2.** *Surgery.* a piece of tissue transplanted to an area of the body in need of the tissue. **3.** grafting. ~vb. **4.** to join part of one plant onto another plant so that they grow together as one. **5.** to transplant (tissue) or (of tissue) to be transplanted. **6.** to attach or incorporate or become attached or incorporated: *modern methods grafted onto old ideas.*

graft[2] (grɑːft) n. **1.** *Informal.* hard work. **2.** the obtaining of money by taking advantage of one's position. ~vb. **3.** *Informal.* to work hard. **4.** to acquire by or practise graft.

Grail (greɪl) n. See **Holy Grail.**

grain (greɪn) n. **1.** the small hard seedlike fruit of a cereal plant. **2.** a mass of such fruits gathered for food. **3.** cereal plants in general. **4.** a small hard particle: *a grain of sand.* **5. a.** the arrangement of the fibres, layers, or particles in wood, leather, or stone. **b.** the pattern or texture resulting from this. **6.** a very small amount: *a grain of truth.* **7. go against the grain.** to be contrary to one's natural inclinations. ~vb. **8.** to form or cause to form into grains. **9.** to give a granular or roughened appearance or texture to. **10.** to paint or stain in imitation of the grain of wood or leather. —'**grainy** *adj.*

grallatorial (ˌgrælə'tɔːrɪəl) *adj.* of or relating to long-legged wading birds.

gram *or* **gramme** (græm) *n.* a metric unit of mass equal to one thousandth of a kilogram.

gram. 1. grammar. 2. grammatical.

gramineous (grə'mɪnɪəs) *adj.* of or like grass. Also: **graminaceous** (ˌgræmɪ'neɪʃəs).

graminivorous (ˌgræmɪ'nɪvərəs) *adj.* (of animals) feeding on grass.

grammar ('græmə) *n.* 1. the branch of linguistics that deals with the form, function, and order of words. 2. a systematic description of the generally accepted rules of a language. 3. a book containing such a description. 4. one's language with regard to observance of the grammatical rules: *the teacher told him to watch his grammar.*

grammarian (grə'mɛərɪən) *n.* a person who studies or writes about grammar for a living.

grammar school *n.* 1. *Brit.* (esp. formerly) a secondary school providing an education with an academic bias. 2. *U.S.* same as **elementary school.** 3. *Austral.* a private school, usually one controlled by a church. 4. *N.Z.* a secondary school forming part of the public education system.

grammatical (grə'mætɪkˀl) *adj.* 1. of grammar. 2. (of a sentence) following the rules of grammar. —**gram'matically** *adv.*

gramme (græm) *n.* same as **gram.**

gramophone ('græmə,fəʊn) *n.* an old-fashioned type of record player.

grampus ('græmpəs) *n., pl.* -**puses.** 1. a dolphin-like mammal with a blunt snout. 2. a person who puffs or breathes heavily.

gran (græn) *n. Informal.* a grandmother.

granary ('grænərɪ; *U.S.* 'greɪnərɪ) *n., pl.* -**ries.** 1. a building for storing threshed grain. 2. a region that produces a large amount of grain.

grand (grænd) *adj.* 1. large or impressive in size or appearance; magnificent: *grand scenery; a grand feast.* 2. dignified or haughty. 3. designed to impress: *grand gestures.* 4. *Informal.* excellent; wonderful. 5. comprehensive; complete: *a grand total.* 6. worthy of respect: *a grand old man.* 7. most important; chief: *the grand arena.* ~*n.* 8. See **grand piano.** 9. (*pl.* **grand**) *Slang.* a thousand pounds or dollars. —'**grandly** *adv.*

grand- *prefix.* (in designations of kinship) one generation older or younger than: *grandfather; grandson.*

grandam ('grændəm, -dæm) *or* **grandame** ('grændeɪm, -dəm) *n. Archaic.* a grandmother.

grandchild ('græn,tʃaɪld) *n., pl.* -**children.** the son or daughter of one's child.

granddad ('græn,dæd) *or* **granddaddy**

n., pl. -**dads** *or* -**daddies.** *Informal.* a grandfather.

granddaughter ('græn,dɔːtə) *n.* a daughter of one's son or daughter.

grand duke *n.* a prince or nobleman who rules a territory, state, or principality. —**grand duchess** *fem. n.* —**grand duchy** *n.*

grande dame (grɒnd'dɑːm) *n.* a woman regarded as the most experienced or venerable member of her profession or group.

grandee (græn'diː) *n.* 1. a high-ranking Spanish or Portuguese noble. 2. a person of high station.

grandeur ('grændʒə) *n.* 1. personal greatness, dignity, or nobility. 2. magnificence; splendour.

grandfather ('græn,fɑːðə, 'grænd-) *n.* the father of one's father or mother.

grandfather clock *n.* a long-pendulum clock in a tall standing wooden case.

grandiloquent (græn'dɪləkwənt) *adj.* pompous or inflated in language. —**gran'diloquence** *n.*

grandiose ('grændɪ,əʊs) *adj.* 1. pretentiously grand. 2. on a large or impressive scale. —**grandiosity** (ˌgrændɪ'ɒsɪtɪ) *n.*

grand jury *n. Law, chiefly U.S.* a jury which investigates accusations of crime to ascertain whether the evidence is adequate to bring a prosecution.

grandma ('græn,mɑː), **grandmama,** *or* **grandmamma** ('grænmə,mɑː) *n. Informal.* a grandmother.

grand mal (grɒn 'mæl) *n.* a form of epilepsy characterized by loss of consciousness and violent convulsions.

grandmaster ('grænd,mɑːstə) *n.* a leading exponent of any of various arts, such as chess.

grandmother ('græn,mʌðə, 'grænd-) *n.* the mother of one's father or mother.

Grand National *n.* **the.** an annual steeplechase run at Aintree, Liverpool.

grandnephew ('græn,nɛvjuː, -,nɛfjuː, 'grænd-) *n.* a great-nephew.

grandniece ('græn,niːs, 'grænd-) *n.* a great-niece.

grand opera *n.* an opera that has a serious plot and no spoken dialogue.

grandpa ('græn,pɑː) *or* **grandpapa** ('grænpə,pɑː) *n. Informal.* a grandfather.

grandparent ('græn,pɛərənt, 'grænd-) *n.* the father or mother of either of one's parents.

grand piano *n.* a large piano in which the strings are arranged horizontally.

Grand Prix (ˌgrɒn 'priː) *n.* any of a series of formula motor races to determine the annual Drivers' World Championship.

grandsire ('græn,saɪə, 'grænd-) *n. Archaic.* a grandfather.

grandson ('grænsʌn, 'grænd-) *n.* a son of one's son or daughter.

grandstand ('græn₁stænd, 'grænd-) *n.* the main block of seats commanding the best view at a sports ground.

grand tour *n.* **1.** (formerly) an extended tour of continental Europe. **2.** *Informal.* a sightseeing trip or tour of inspection.

grange (greɪndʒ) *n. Chiefly Brit.* a farmhouse or country house with its farm buildings.

granite ('grænɪt) *n.* a very hard igneous rock consisting of quartz and feldspars: widely used for building.

granivorous (græ'nɪvərəs) *adj.* (of animals) feeding on seeds and grain.

granny *or* **grannie** ('grænɪ) *n., pl.* **-nies.** *Informal.* a grandmother.

granny flat *n.* self-contained accommodation in or adjoining a house, suitable for an elderly parent.

granny knot *n.* a reef knot with the ends crossed the wrong way, making it liable to slip or jam.

grant (grɑːnt) *vb.* **1.** to consent to perform or fulfil: *to grant a wish.* **2.** to permit as a favour: *to grant an interview.* **3.** to admit as true: *I grant it was a stupid mistake.* **4.** to bestow formally. **5. take for granted. a.** to accept (something) as true and not requiring verification. **b.** to take advantage of (something) without due appreciation. ~*n.* **6.** a sum of money provided by a government or public fund to a person or organization for a specific purpose. **7.** a privilege or right that has been granted.

Granth (grʌnt) *n.* the sacred scripture of the Sikhs.

grant-in-aid *n., pl.* **grants-in-aid.** a sum of money granted by one government to a lower level of government for a programme.

granular ('grænjʊlə) *adj.* **1.** of, like, or containing granules. **2.** having a grainy surface. —**granularity** (₁grænjʊ'lærɪtɪ) *n.*

granulate ('grænjʊ₁leɪt) *vb.* **1.** to make into grains: *granulated sugar.* **2.** to make or become roughened in surface texture. —₁**granu'lation** *n.*

granule ('grænjuːl) *n.* a small grain.

grape (greɪp) *n.* a round, sweet, juicy berry with a purple or green skin: eaten raw, dried to make raisins, currants, or sultanas, or used to make wine.

grapefruit ('greɪp₁fruːt) *n., pl.* **-fruit** *or* **-fruits.** a large round citrus fruit with yellow rind and juicy slightly bitter edible pulp.

grape hyacinth *n.* a plant with clusters of rounded blue flowers like tiny grapes.

grapeshot ('greɪp₁ʃɒt) *n.* ammunition for cannons consisting of a cluster of iron balls that scatter after firing.

grapevine ('greɪp₁vaɪn) *n.* **1.** a vine cultivated for its grapes. **2.** *Informal.* an unofficial means of relaying information from person to person.

graph (grɑːf) *n.* **1.** a drawing showing the relation between certain sets of numbers or quantities by means of a series of dots or lines plotted with reference to a set of axes. ~*vb.* **2.** to draw or represent in a graph.

-graph *n. combining form.* **1.** an instrument that writes or records: *telegraph.* **2.** a writing or record: *autograph.* —**graphic** *or* **-graphical** *adj. combining form.* —**graphically** *adv. combining form.*

graphic ('græfɪk) *or* **graphical** *adj.* **1.** vividly described: *a graphic account of the disaster.* **2.** of writing: *graphic symbols.* **3.** *Maths.* of or using a graph: *a graphic representation of the figures.* —'**graphically** *adv.*

graphic arts *pl. n.* the visual arts based on drawing or the use of line.

graphics ('græfɪks) *n.* **1.** (*functioning as sing.*) the process or art of drawing in accordance with mathematical rules. **2.** (*functioning as pl.*) the illustrations in a magazine or book, or in a television or film production. **3.** (*functioning as pl.*) *Computers.* information displayed in the form of diagrams or graphs.

graphite ('græfaɪt) *n.* a soft black form of carbon used in pencils, as a lubricant, and as a moderator in nuclear reactors.

graphology (græ'fɒlədʒɪ) *n.* the study of handwriting, usually to analyse the writer's character. —**gra'phologist** *n.*

graph paper *n.* paper printed with intersecting lines for drawing graphs or diagrams.

-graphy *n. combining form.* indicating: **1.** a form of writing or representing: *calligraphy; photography.* **2.** an art or descriptive science: *choreography; oceanography.*

grapnel ('græpn°l) *n.* **1.** a device with several hooks at one end, which is used to grasp or secure an object. **2.** a small anchor with several hooks.

grapple ('græp°l) *vb.* **1.** to come to grips with (someone) in hand-to-hand combat. **2.** (foll. by *with*) to try to cope (with): *to grapple with a problem.* **3.** to secure with a grapple. ~*n.* **4.** a hook or instrument by which something is secured, such as a grapnel. **5. a.** a gripping or seizing, as in wrestling. **b.** a grip or hold.

grappling iron *or* **hook** *n.* a grapnel.

grasp (grɑːsp) *vb.* **1.** to grip (something) firmly as with the hands. **2.** (sometimes foll. by *at*) to try to seize. **3.** to understand. ~*n.* **4.** a grip or clasp, as of a hand. **5.** total rule or possession. **6.** understanding; comprehension.

grasping ('grɑːspɪŋ) *adj.* greedy; avaricious.

grass (grɑːs) *n.* **1.** any of a family of plants having jointed stems sheathed by long narrow leaves, such as cereals and bamboo. **2.** a small plant of this family eaten by animals or used for lawns or sports fields. **3.** a lawn. **4.** pasture land. **5.** *Slang.* marijuana. **6.** *Brit. slang.* a person who informs, usually on criminals. **7. let the grass grow under one's feet.** to waste time or opportunity. ~*vb.* **8.** to cover or become covered with grass. **9.** to feed with grass. **10.** (usually foll. by *on*) *Brit. slang.* to inform (on someone), usually to the police. —'**grassy** *adj.*

grass hockey *n.* in W Canada, field hockey, as contrasted with ice hockey.

grasshopper ('grɑːsˌhɒpə) *n.* an insect with long hind legs adapted for leaping.

grassland ('grɑːsˌlænd) *n.* **1.** land covered with grass. **2.** pasture land.

grass roots *pl. n.* **1.** ordinary people as distinct from the leadership of a group or organization. **2.** the essentials.

grass snake *n.* a harmless European snake having a brownish-green body with variable markings.

grass widow or (*masc.*) **grass widower** *n.* a person whose husband or wife is regularly away for a time.

grate[1] (greɪt) *vb.* **1.** to reduce to shreds by rubbing against a rough surface: *to grate carrots.* **2.** to produce or cause to produce a harsh rasping sound by scraping (something) against another object or surface. **3.** (foll. by *on* or *upon*) to annoy. —'**grater** *n.*

grate[2] (greɪt) *n.* **1.** a framework of metal bars for holding fuel in a fireplace or furnace. **2.** a fireplace. **3.** same as **grating**[1].

grateful ('greɪtfʊl) *adj.* **1.** feeling or showing gratitude. **2.** pleasant or welcome: *a grateful rest.* —'**gratefully** *adv.*

gratify ('grætɪˌfaɪ) *vb.* **-fying, -fied. 1.** to satisfy or please. **2.** to indulge (a desire or whim). —ˌ**gratifiˈcation** *n.*

grating[1] ('greɪtɪŋ) *n.* a framework of metal bars in the form of a grille set into a wall or pavement.

grating[2] ('greɪtɪŋ) *adj.* **1.** (of sounds) harsh and rasping. **2.** annoying; irritating. ~*n.* **3.** (*often pl.*) something produced by grating.

gratis ('greɪtɪs, 'grætɪs, 'grɑːtɪs) *adv., adj.* without payment; free.

gratitude ('grætɪˌtjuːd) *n.* a feeling of thankfulness for gifts or favours.

gratuitous (grə'tjuːɪtəs) *adj.* **1.** given or received without charge or obligation. **2.** without cause; unjustified. —gra'**tuitously** *adv.* —gra'**tuitousness** *n.*

gratuity (grə'tjuːɪtɪ) *n., pl.* **-ties.** money given for services rendered; tip.

grav (græv) *n.* a unit of acceleration equal to the standard acceleration of free fall.

grave[1] (greɪv) *n.* **1.** a place for the burial of a corpse, usually underground. **2.** *Poetic.* (often preceded by *the*) death. **3. make**

(someone) **turn in his grave.** to do something that would have shocked a person now dead.

grave[2] *adj.* (greɪv) **1.** serious and solemn: *a grave look.* **2.** full of or threatening danger: *a grave situation.* **3.** important; crucial: *grave matters of state.* **4.** (of colours) sober or dull. **5.** (grɑːv). of an accent (`) over vowels, denoting that the letter is pronounced with a special quality (as in French), or in a manner that gives the vowel status as a syllable (as in English *agèd*). ~*n.* (grɑːv). **6.** a grave accent. —'**gravely** *adv.*

gravel ('græv²l) *n.* **1.** a mixture of rock fragments and pebbles that is coarser than sand. **2.** *Pathol.* small rough stones in the kidneys or bladder. ~*vb.* **-elling, -elled** or *U.S.* **-eling, -eled. 3.** to cover with gravel. **4.** to perplex.

gravelly ('grævəlɪ) *adj.* **1.** of, like, or full of gravel. **2.** (of a voice) harsh and grating.

graven ('greɪv²n) *adj.* strongly fixed.

graven image *n. Chiefly Bible.* a carved image used as an idol.

Graves (grɑːv) *n.* (*functioning as sing.*) (*sometimes not cap.*) a dry, usually white wine from the district around Bordeaux, France.

gravestone ('greɪvˌstəʊn) *n.* a stone marking a grave.

graveyard ('greɪvˌjɑːd) *n.* a cemetery or burial ground.

gravid ('grævɪd) *adj. Med.* pregnant.

gravimeter (grə'vɪmɪtə) *n.* **1.** an instrument for measuring the force of gravity. **2.** an instrument for measuring relative density. —**gravimetric** (ˌgrævɪ'mɛtrɪk) *adj.* —gra'**vimetry** *n.*

gravitate ('grævɪˌteɪt) *vb.* **1.** *Physics.* to move under the influence of gravity. **2.** (usually foll. by *to* or *towards*) to be influenced or drawn, as by strong impulses.

gravitation (ˌgrævɪ'teɪʃən) *n.* **1.** the force of attraction that bodies exert on one another as a result of their mass. **2.** the process or result of this interaction. —ˌ**gravi'tational** *adj.*

gravity ('grævɪtɪ) *n., pl.* **-ties. 1.** the force that attracts bodies towards the centre of a celestial body, such as the earth or moon. **2.** the property of having weight. **3.** same as **gravitation. 4.** seriousness or importance. **5.** solemn or dignified manner or conduct.

gravy ('greɪvɪ) *n., pl.* **-vies. a.** the juices that come from meat during cooking. **b.** the sauce made by thickening and flavouring these juices.

gravy boat *n.* a small boat-shaped vessel for serving gravy or sauce.

gravy train *n. Slang.* a job or scheme that produces good money or gains for little effort.

gray (greɪ) *adj., n., vb. Chiefly U.S.* grey.

grayling ('greɪlɪŋ) *n., pl.* **-ling** *or* **-lings**. a silvery-grey freshwater food fish resembling the salmon.

graze[1] (greɪz) *vb.* to allow (animals) to feed on growing plants or (of animals) to feed thus.

graze[2] (greɪz) *vb.* **1.** (often foll. by *against* or *along*) to brush (against) gently in passing. **2.** to break the skin of (a part of the body) by scraping. ~*n.* **3.** a grazing. **4.** an abrasion made by grazing.

grazier ('greɪzɪə) *n.* a rancher or farmer who keeps cattle or sheep on grazing land.

grazing ('greɪzɪŋ) *n.* land where grass is grown for livestock to feed upon.

grease (griːs, griːz) *n.* **1.** soft melted animal fat. **2.** any thick oily substance. ~*vb.* **3.** to soil, coat, or lubricate with grease. **4. grease the palm** (*or* **hand**) **of.** *Slang.* to bribe.

greasepaint ('griːs,peɪnt) *n.* theatrical make-up.

greasy ('griːsɪ, -zɪ) *adj.* **greasier, greasiest. 1.** coated or soiled with grease. **2.** containing or like grease. **3.** unctuous in manner. —'**greasiness** *n.*

greasy wool *n.* untreated wool still retaining the lanolin; used for waterproof clothing.

great (greɪt) *adj.* **1.** large in size. **2.** large in number: *a great crowd.* **3.** long in duration: *a great wait.* **4.** larger than others of its kind: *the great auk.* **5.** extreme or more than usual: *great worry.* **6.** of importance or consequence: *a great decision.* **7.** of exceptional talents or achievements: *a great writer.* **8.** heroic; noble: *great deeds.* **9.** illustrious or eminent: *a great history.* **10.** impressive or striking: *a great show of wealth.* **11.** active or enthusiastic: *a great reader.* **12.** (often foll. by *at*) skilful: *a great carpenter; you are great at singing.* **13.** *Informal.* excellent. —'**greatly** *adv.* —'**greatness** *n.*

great- *prefix.* (in designations of kinship) two generations older or younger than: *great-grandparent; great-grandchild.*

great auk *n.* an extinct large flightless auk.

great-aunt *n.* an aunt of one's father or mother; a grandparent's sister.

Great Britain *n.* the mainland part of the British Isles; England, Scotland, and Wales.

great circle *n.* a circular section of a sphere that has a radius equal to that of the sphere.

greatcoat ('greɪt,kəʊt) *n.* a heavy overcoat.

Great Dane *n.* a very large breed of dog with a short smooth coat.

great-nephew *n.* a son of one's nephew or niece; grandson of one's brother or sister. —,**great-**'**niece** *fem. n.*

Great Russian *n.* **1.** *Linguistics.* the Russian language. **2.** a member of the chief East Slavonic people of Russia. ~*adj.* **3.** of this people or their language.

Greats (greɪts) *pl. n.* (at Oxford University) **1.** the Honours course in classics and philosophy. **2.** the final examinations at the end of this course.

great seal *n.* (often *caps.*) the principal seal of a nation or sovereign, used to authenticate documents of the highest importance.

great tit *n.* a Eurasian bird with yellow-and-black underparts and a black-and-white head.

great-uncle *n.* an uncle of one's father or mother; a grandparent's brother.

Great War *n.* same as **World War I.**

greave (griːv) *n.* (often *pl.*) a piece of armour for the shin.

grebe (griːb) *n.* an aquatic bird with lobed toes and a vestigial tail.

Grecian ('griːʃən) *adj.* **1.** (of beauty or architecture) conforming to ancient Greek ideals. ~*adj., n.* **2.** same as **Greek.**

greed (griːd) *n.* **1.** excessive desire for food. **2.** any excessive desire.

greedy ('griːdɪ) *adj.* **greedier, greediest. 1.** excessively desirous of food. **2.** (foll. by *for*) eager (for): *greedy for success.* —'**greedily** *adv.*

Greek (griːk) *n.* **1.** the official language of Greece. **2.** a person from Greece. **3. it's** (**all**) **Greek to me.** *Informal.* I find it incomprehensible. ~*adj.* **4.** of Greece, the Greeks, or the Greek language.

Greek cross *n.* a cross with each of the four arms of the same length.

green (griːn) *n.* **1.** a colour, such as that of fresh grass, that lies between yellow and blue in the spectrum. **2.** something of this colour. **3.** a small area of grassy public land. **4.** an area of smooth turf kept for a special purpose: *a putting green.* **5.** (*pl.*) the leaves and stems of certain plants, eaten as a vegetable. **6.** (*sometimes cap.*) a person who supports environmentalist issues. ~*adj.* **7.** green in colour. **8.** vigorous; flourishing: *a green old age.* **9.** envious or jealous. **10.** inexperienced or gullible. **11.** characterized by foliage or green plants: *a green wood; a green salad.* **12.** denoting a unit of account used to make payments to agricultural producers within the EEC: *green pound.* **13.** (*sometimes cap.*) of or concerned with conservation and improvement of the environment: used in a political context. **14.** fresh, raw, or unripe: *green bananas.* **15.** unhealthily pale: *he was green after his boat trip.* **16.** (of meat) not smoked or cured: *green bacon.* **17.** (of timber) not dried or seasoned. ~*vb.* **18.** to make or become green. —'**greenish** *or* '**greeny** *adj.* —'**greenness** *n.*

green bean *n.* a bean plant having narrow green edible pods.

green belt *n.* a protected zone of parkland or open country surrounding a town or city.

green card *n.* an insurance document covering motorists against accidents abroad.

Green Cross Code *n. Brit.* a road safety code for children.

greenery ('griːnərɪ) *n., pl.* **-eries.** green foliage.

green-eyed *adj.* jealous or envious.

greenfinch ('griːn,fɪntʃ) *n.* a European finch, the male of which has olive-green plumage with yellow patches on the wings and tail.

green fingers *pl. n.* skill in growing plants.

greenfly ('griːn,flaɪ) *n., pl.* **-flies.** a green aphid commonly occurring as a pest on plants.

greengage ('griːn,geɪdʒ) *n.* a green sweet variety of plum.

greengrocer ('griːn,grəʊsə) *n. Chiefly Brit.* a retail trader in fruit and vegetables. —'**green,grocery** *n.*

greenhorn ('griːn,hɔːn) *n.* an inexperienced person; novice.

greenhouse ('griːn,haʊs) *n.* a building with glass walls and roof for the cultivation of plants under controlled conditions.

greenhouse effect *n.* the gradual rise in temperature in the earth's atmosphere due to heat being absorbed from the sun and being unable to leave the atmosphere.

greenkeeper ('griːn,kiːpə) *n.* a person responsible for maintaining a golf course or bowling green.

green light *n.* **1.** a signal to go. **2.** permission to proceed with a project.

green paper *n.* (*often caps.*) (in Britain) a government document containing policy proposals to be discussed.

green pepper *n.* the green unripe fruit of the sweet pepper, eaten as a vegetable.

green pound *n.* See **green** (sense 12).

greenroom ('griːn,ruːm, -,rʊm) *n.* (esp. formerly) a backstage room in a theatre where performers may rest or receive visitors.

greenshank ('griːn,ʃæŋk) *n.* a large European sandpiper with greenish legs.

greenstick fracture ('griːn,stɪk) *n.* a fracture in which the bone is partly bent and splinters only on the outer side of the bend.

greensward ('griːn,swɔːd) *n. Archaic or literary.* an area of fresh green turf.

green tea *n.* a tea made from leaves that have been dried quickly without fermenting.

Greenwich Mean Time ('grɪnɪdʒ) *n.* the local time of the 0° meridian passing through Greenwich, England: a basis for calculating times throughout most of the world.

greet¹ (griːt) *vb.* **1.** to address or meet with expressions of friendliness or welcome. **2.** to receive in a specified manner: *her remarks were greeted by silence.* **3.** to be immediately noticeable to: *the smell of bread greeted him.*

greet² (griːt) *Scot. or dialect.* ~*vb.* **1.** to weep; lament. ~*n.* **2.** weeping; lamentation.

greeting ('griːtɪŋ) *n.* **1.** the act or words of welcoming on meeting. **2.** (*pl.*) an expression of friendly salutation.

gregarious (grɪ'gɛərɪəs) *adj.* **1.** enjoying the company of others. **2.** (of animals) living together in herds or flocks. —**gre'gariousness** *n.*

Gregorian calendar (grɪ'gɔːrɪən) *n.* the revision of the calendar introduced in 1582 by Pope Gregory XIII and still widely used.

Gregorian chant *n.* same as **plainsong.**

gremlin ('gremlɪn) *n.* an imaginary imp jokingly blamed for malfunctions in machinery.

grenade (grɪ'neɪd) *n.* a small bomb filled with explosive or gas, thrown by hand or fired from a rifle.

grenadier (,grenə'dɪə) *n. Mil.* **1.** (in the British Army) a member of the senior regiment of infantry in the Household Brigade (the **Grenadier Guards**). **2.** (formerly) a soldier trained to throw grenades.

grew (gruː) *vb.* the past tense of **grow.**

grey *or U.S.* **gray** (greɪ) *adj.* **1.** of a colour between black and white. **2.** (of hair) having partly turned white. **3.** dismal or dark; gloomy. **4.** dull or boring. **5.** having grey hair. **6.** ancient; venerable. ~*n.* **7.** a grey colour. **8.** grey cloth or clothing. **9.** an animal, usually a horse, that is grey or whitish. ~*vb.* **10.** to become or make grey. —'**greyish** *adj.* —'**greyness** *n.*

Grey Friar *n.* a Franciscan friar.

greyhound ('greɪ,haʊnd) *n.* a tall slender swift breed of dog.

greylag *or* **greylag goose** ('greɪ,læg) *n.* a large grey Eurasian goose.

grey matter *n.* **1.** the grey nerve tissue of the brain and spinal cord. **2.** *Informal.* intellect.

grey squirrel *n.* a grey-furred squirrel, native to E North America but now common in Britain.

grid (grɪd) *n.* **1.** See **gridiron. 2.** a network of crossing parallel lines on a map, plan, or graph paper for locating points. **3. the grid.** the national network of cables or pipes by which electricity, gas, or water is distributed. **4.** *Electronics.* an electrode that controls the flow of electrons between the cathode and anode of a valve.

griddle ('grɪd'l) *n.* **1.** a thick round iron plate placed on top of a cooker and used to cook food. ~*vb.* **2.** to cook (food) on a griddle.

gridiron ('grɪd,aɪən) *n.* **1.** a utensil of parallel metal bars, used to grill food. **2.** the field of play in American football.

grief (griːf) *n.* **1.** deep or intense sorrow. **2.** something that causes keen distress. **3. come to grief.** *Informal.* to end unsuccessfully or disastrously.

grievance ('griːvᵊns) *n.* **1.** a real or imaginary cause for complaint. **2.** a feeling of resentment at having been unfairly treated.

grieve (griːv) *vb.* to feel or cause to feel great sorrow or distress. —**grieved** *adj.* —'**grieving** *n.*, *adj.*

grievous ('griːvəs) *adj.* **1.** very severe or painful: *a grievous injury.* **2.** very serious; heinous: *a grievous sin.* **3.** showing or marked by grief. **4.** causing grief. —'**grievously** *adv.*

grievous bodily harm *n. Criminal law.* serious injury caused by one person to another.

griffin ('grɪfɪn), **griffon**, *or* **gryphon** *n.* a mythical winged monster with an eagle's head and a lion's body.

griffon ('grɪfᵊn) *n.* **1.** a small wire-haired breed of dog. **2.** a large vulture having a pale plumage with black wings.

grill (grɪl) *vb.* **1.** to cook (food) by direct heat under a grill or over a hot fire, or (of food) to be cooked in this way. **2.** (*usually passive*) to torment with or as if with extreme heat: *grilled by the scorching sun.* **3.** *Informal.* to subject to relentless questioning. ~*n.* **4.** a device on a cooker that radiates heat downwards for grilling food. **5.** a gridiron for cooking food. **6.** grilled food. **7.** See **grillroom.** —**grilled** *adj.* —'**grilling** *n.*

grille *or* **grill** (grɪl) *n.* **1.** a metal or wooden grating, used as a screen or partition. **2.** Also called: **radiator grille.** a grating that lets cooling air into the radiator of a motor vehicle.

grillroom ('grɪl,ruːm, -,rʊm) *n.* a restaurant specializing in grilled foods.

grilse (grɪls) *n.*, *pl.* **grilses** *or* **grilse.** a salmon on its first return from the sea to fresh water.

grim (grɪm) *adj.* **grimmer, grimmest. 1.** stern; resolute: *grim determination.* **2.** harsh or forbidding: *a grim castle.* **3.** harshly ironic or sinister: *grim laughter.* **4.** cruel, severe, or ghastly: *a grim accident.* **5.** *Informal.* unpleasant; disagreeable. —'**grimly** *adv.* —'**grimness** *n.*

grimace (grɪ'meɪs) *n.* **1.** an ugly or distorted facial expression, as of wry humour, disgust, or pain. ~*vb.* **2.** to contort the face.

grimalkin (grɪ'mælkɪn, -'mɔːl-) *n.* an old female cat.

grime (graɪm) *n.* **1.** ingrained dirt, soot, or

filth. ~*vb.* **2.** to make very dirty. —'**grimy** *adj.* —'**griminess** *n.*

grin (grɪn) *vb.* **grinning, grinned. 1.** to smile broadly, revealing the teeth, or express (something) by such a smile: *to grin a welcome.* **2.** to draw back the lips revealing the teeth in a snarl or grimace. **3. grin and bear it.** *Informal.* to suffer hardship without complaint. ~*n.* **4.** a broad smile. **5.** a snarl or grimace. —'**grinning** *adj.*, *n.*

grind (graɪnd) *vb.* **grinding, ground. 1.** to reduce or be reduced to small particles by pounding or rubbing: *to grind corn.* **2.** to smooth, sharpen, or polish by friction: *to grind a knife.* **3.** (of two objects) to scrape or be scraped together with a harsh rasping sound. **4.** (often foll. by *down*) to oppress or tyrannize. **5.** to operate (a machine) by turning a handle. **6.** (foll. by *out*) to produce in a routine or uninspired manner: *he ground out his weekly article for the paper.* **7.** *Informal.* to study or work laboriously. ~*n.* **8.** *Informal.* laborious work or study. **9.** a specific size of ground particles. **10.** the act or sound of grinding.

grinder ('graɪndə) *n.* **1.** a machine that grinds. **2.** a molar tooth.

grindstone ('graɪnd,stəʊn) *n.* **1.** a revolving stone disc used for sharpening, grinding, or polishing. **2. keep** *or* **have one's nose to the grindstone.** to work hard and steadily.

grip (grɪp) *n.* **1.** a grasping and holding firmly: *he lost his grip on the slope.* **2.** the strength or way in which something is grasped: *a tight grip.* **3.** understanding or mastery of a subject or problem. **4. get** *or* **come to grips.** (often foll. by *with*) **a.** to deal with (a problem or subject). **b.** to tackle (an assailant). **5.** a handle. **6.** a travelling bag or holdall. **7.** a hairgrip. ~*vb.* **gripping, gripped. 8.** to take hold of firmly or tightly. **9.** to hold the interest or attention of: *to grip an audience.* —'**gripping** *adj.*

gripe (graɪp) *vb.* **1.** *Informal.* to complain persistently. **2.** to cause or suffer sudden intense pain in the bowels. ~*n.* **3.** (*usually pl.*) a sudden intense pain in the bowels; colic. **4.** *Informal.* a complaint.

grippe (grɪp) *n.* a former name for **influenza.**

grisly ('grɪzlɪ) *adj.* **-lier, -liest.** causing horror or dread; gruesome. —'**grisliness** *n.*

grist (grɪst) *n.* **1.** grain intended to be or that has been ground. **2. grist to** (*or* **for**) **the** (*or* **one's**) **mill.** anything that can be turned to profit or advantage.

gristle ('grɪsᵊl) *n.* cartilage present in meat. —'**gristly** *adj.*

grit (grɪt) *n.* **1.** small hard particles of sand, earth, or stone. **2.** coarse sandstone. **3.** indomitable courage or resolution. ~*vb.* **gritting, gritted. 4.** to clench or grind (the teeth) together. **5.** to cover (a surface, such as icy roads) with grit. —**'gritter** *n.* —**'gritty** *adj.*

grits (grɪts) *pl. n.* hulled or coarsely ground grain.

grizzle ('grɪz°l) *vb. Informal, chiefly Brit.* (esp. of a child) to fret; whine.

grizzled ('grɪz°ld) *adj.* **1.** streaked or mixed with grey. **2.** having grey hair.

grizzly ('grɪzlɪ) *adj.* **-zlier, -zliest.** **1.** greyish; grizzled. ~*n., pl.* **-zlies.** **2.** See **grizzly bear.**

grizzly bear *n.* a large N American variety of the brown bear: its fur has cream or white tips on the back, giving it a grizzled appearance.

groan (grəʊn) *n.* **1.** a long deep cry of pain, grief, or disapproval. **2.** a sound like a groan. **3.** *Informal.* a grumble or complaint. ~*vb.* **4.** to utter a long deep cry of pain, grief, or disapproval. **5.** to make a sound like a groan. **6.** (usually foll. by *beneath* or *under*) to be weighed down (by). **7.** *Informal.* to complain or grumble. —**'groaning** *adj., n.*

groat (grəʊt) *n.* an obsolete British silver coin worth four old pennies.

groats (grəʊts) *pl. n.* the hulled and crushed grain of various cereals.

grocer ('grəʊsə) *n.* a dealer in foodstuffs and household supplies.

groceries ('grəʊsərɪz) *pl. n.* merchandise sold by a grocer.

grocery ('grəʊsərɪ) *n., pl.* **-ceries.** the business or premises of a grocer.

grog (grɒg) *n.* **1.** diluted spirit, usually rum, as an alcoholic drink. **2.** *Austral. & N.Z. informal.* any alcoholic drink.

groggy ('grɒgɪ) *adj.* **-gier, -giest.** *Informal.* faint, weak, or dizzy. —**'grogginess** *n.*

grogram ('grɒgrəm) *n.* a coarse fabric of silk mixed with wool or mohair.

groin (grɔɪn) *n.* **1.** the part of the body where the abdomen joins the legs. **2.** *Chiefly U.S.* same as **groyne.** **3.** *Archit.* a curved edge formed where two intersecting vaults meet. ~*vb.* **4.** *Archit.* to build with groins.

grommet ('grɒmɪt) *or* **grummet** *n.* a rubber, plastic, or metal ring or eyelet.

groom (gruːm, grʊm) *n.* **1.** a person employed to clean and look after horses. **2.** See **bridegroom. 3.** an officer of a royal or noble household. ~*vb.* **4.** to make or keep (one's clothes or appearance) clean and tidy. **5.** to clean and smarten (a horse or other animal). **6.** to train for a particular task or occupation: *to groom someone for the Presidency.*

groomsman ('gruːmzmən, 'grʊmz-) *n., pl.* **-men.** a man who attends the groom at a wedding, usually the best man.

groove (gruːv) *n.* **1.** a long narrow furrow cut into a surface. **2.** the spiral channel in a gramophone record. **3.** a habitual existence or routine. ~*vb.* **4.** to form or cut a groove in.

groovy ('gruːvɪ) *adj.* **groovier, grooviest.** *Dated slang.* attractive, fashionable, or exciting.

grope (grəʊp) *vb.* **1.** (usually foll. by *for*) to feel about uncertainly (for something). **2.** (usually foll. by *for* or *after*) to search uncertainly (for a solution or expression). **3.** to find (one's way) by groping. **4.** *Slang.* to fondle (someone's) body in a sexual way. ~*n.* **5.** a groping.

grosbeak ('grəʊs,biːk, 'grɒs-) *n.* a finch with a large powerful bill.

grosgrain ('grəʊ,greɪn) *n.* a heavy ribbed silk or rayon fabric.

gros point (grəʊ) *n.* **1.** a cross-stitch in embroidery. **2.** work done in this stitch.

gross (grəʊs) *adj.* **1.** repulsively fat. **2.** with no deductions for tax or the weight of the container; total: *gross sales; 150kg gross weight.* **3.** very coarse or vulgar. **4.** outrageously wrong; flagrant: *gross inefficiency.* **5.** lacking in perception, sensitivity, or discrimination: *gross judgments.* **6.** thick; luxuriant. ~*n.* **7.** (*pl.* **gross**). twelve dozen. **8.** (*pl.* **grosses**). the entire amount or weight. ~*vb.* **9.** to earn as total revenue, before deductions. —**'grossly** *adv.* —**'grossness** *n.*

gross domestic product *n.* the total value of all goods and services produced domestically by a nation during a year.

gross national product *n.* the total value of all final goods and services produced annually by a nation. It is equivalent to gross domestic product plus net investment income from abroad.

gross profit *n. Accounting.* the difference between total revenue from sales and the total cost of purchases or materials.

grotesque (grəʊ'tɛsk) *adj.* **1.** strangely distorted; bizarre. **2.** of the grotesque in art. **3.** absurdly incongruous; ludicrous. ~*n.* **4.** an artistic style in which parts of human, animal, and plant forms are distorted and mixed, or a work of art in this style. **5.** a grotesque person or thing.

grotto ('grɒtəʊ) *n., pl.* **-toes** *or* **-tos.** **1.** a small picturesque cave. **2.** a construction in the form of a cave.

grotty ('grɒtɪ) *adj.* **-tier, -tiest.** *Brit. slang.* **1.** nasty or unattractive. **2.** in bad condition.

grouch (graʊtʃ) *Informal.* ~*vb.* **1.** to complain; grumble. ~*n.* **2.** a persistent complaint. **3.** a person who is always grumbling. —**'grouchy** *adj.*

ground[1] (graʊnd) *n.* **1.** the land surface. **2.** earth or soil. **3.** (*pl.*) the land around a building. **4.** (*sometimes pl.*) an area given over to a purpose: *football ground; fishing grounds.* **5.** land having a particular characteristic: *high ground.* **6.** matter for consideration or discussion: *the report covered a lot of ground.* **7.** a viewpoint, as in an argument or controversy: *give ground; stand one's ground; shift one's ground.* **8.** advantage, as in a competition: *gain ground; lose ground.* **9.** (*often pl.*) reason; justification: *grounds for complaint.* **10.** a substance applied to a wall or canvas to prevent it reacting with or absorbing the paint. **11.** the background colour of a painting. **12.** (*pl.*) sediment or dregs. **13.** *U.S. & Canad.* an electrical earth. **14. break new ground.** to do something that has not been done before. **15. common ground.** an agreed basis for identifying issues in an argument. **16. cut the ground from under someone's feet.** to anticipate someone's action or argument and thus deprive it of force. **17. (down) to the ground.** *Brit. informal.* completely; absolutely: *it suited him down to the ground.* **18. get (something) off the ground.** to start (something). **19. into the ground.** to exhaustion or excess. **20.** (*modifier*) on or concerned with the ground: *ground frost; ground forces.* ~*vb.* **21.** to place on the ground. **22.** to instruct in the basics. **23.** to provide a basis for; establish. **24.** to confine (an aircraft or pilot) to the ground. **25.** *U.S. & Canad.* to connect (a circuit or electrical device) to an earth. **26.** *Naut.* to run (a vessel) aground.

ground² (graʊnd) *vb.* **1.** past of **grind.** ~*adj.* **2.** having a surface produced by grinding. **3.** reduced to fine particles by grinding.

ground bass (beɪs) *n. Music.* a short melodic bass line that is repeated over and over again.

ground control *n.* the personnel and equipment on the ground that monitor the progress of aircraft or spacecraft.

ground cover *n.* dense low plants that grow over the surface of the ground.

ground floor *n.* the floor of a building level or almost level with the ground.

grounding ('graʊndɪŋ) *n.* a foundation, esp. the basic general knowledge of a subject.

ground ivy *n.* an aromatic creeping plant with scalloped leaves and purplish-blue flowers.

groundless ('graʊndlɪs) *adj.* without reason or justification: *his suspicions were groundless.*

groundnut ('graʊnd͵nʌt) *n.* **1.** the small edible underground tuber of a North American climbing plant. **2.** a peanut.

groundsel ('graʊnsəl) *n.* a weed with heads of small yellow flowers.

groundsheet ('graʊnd͵ʃiːt) *n.* a waterproof sheet placed on the ground in a tent to keep out damp.

groundsman ('graʊndzmən) *n., pl.* **-men.** a person employed to maintain a sports ground or park.

ground squirrel *n.* a burrowing rodent resembling a chipmunk, found in N America, E Europe, and Asia.

ground swell *n.* smooth heavy waves caused by a distant storm or earthquake.

groundwork ('graʊnd͵wɜːk) *n.* preliminary work as a foundation or basis.

group (gruːp) *n.* **1.** a number of people or things considered as a collective unit. **2.** a small band of players or singers, esp. of pop music. **3.** an association of companies under a single ownership. **4.** an air force unit larger than a squadron. **5.** *Chem.* two or more atoms that are bound together in a molecule and behave as a single unit: *a methyl group -CH₃.* **6.** a vertical column of elements in the periodic table that all have similar properties: *the halogen group.* ~*vb.* **7.** to place (things or people) in a group, or (of things or people) to form into a group.

group captain *n.* a middle-ranking officer in certain air forces.

groupie ('gruːpɪ) *n. Slang.* an ardent fan of a celebrity.

group therapy *n. Psychol.* the treatment of people by bringing them together to share their problems in group discussion.

grouse¹ (graʊs) *n., pl.* **grouse** *or* **grouses.** a game bird with a stocky body and feathered legs and feet.

grouse² (graʊs) *vb.* **1.** to grumble; complain. ~*n.* **2.** a persistent complaint.

grouse³ (graʊs) *adj. Austral. & N.Z. slang.* fine; excellent.

grout (graʊt) *n.* **1.** a thin mortar for filling joints between tiles or masonry. ~*vb.* **2.** to fill (joints) with grout.

grove (grəʊv) *n.* a small wood or group of trees.

grovel ('grɒvᵊl) *vb.* **-elling, -elled** *or U.S.* **-eling, -eled. 1.** to humble or abase oneself. **2.** to lie or crawl face downwards, as in fear or humility.

grow (grəʊ) *vb.* **growing, grew, grown. 1.** (of a living thing) to increase in size and develop physically: *warthogs grow up to 1.5m long; she decided to let her hair grow.* **2.** (of a plant) to exist: *nettles can grow almost anywhere.* **3.** (usually foll. by *from* or *out of*) to originate: *the idea for her novel grew out of a childhood memory.* **4.** to increase in size or degree: *the population grew rapidly.* **5.** (esp. of emotions or physical states) to develop or become gradually: *it was growing cold.* **6.** to cultivate (plants): *we tried growing leeks.* **7.** to let (hair or nails) develop: *he had grown a moustache.* ~See also **grow on, grow out of,** etc.

growing pains *pl. n.* pains in muscles or joints sometimes experienced by growing children.

growl (graʊl) *vb.* **1.** (of animals, esp. when hostile) to utter low rumbling sounds: *the* *dog growled.* **2.** to utter (words) in a gruff or angry manner. ~*n.* **3.** the act or sound of growling. —**'growlingly** *adv.*

grown (grəʊn) *adj.* developed or advanced: *fully grown; half-grown.*

grown-up *adj.* **1.** having reached maturity; adult. **2.** of or suitable for an adult. ~*n.* **3.** an adult.

grow on *vb.* to become progressively more acceptable or pleasant to.

grow out of *vb.* to become too big or mature for: *she soon grew out of her girlish ways.*

growth (grəʊθ) *n.* **1.** the process of growing. **2.** an increase in size, number, or significance. **3.** something grown or growing: *a new growth of hair.* **4.** any abnormal tissue, such as a tumour. **5.** (*modifier*) characterized by growth: *a growth industry.*

grow up *vb.* to reach maturity; become adult.

groyne *or esp. U.S.* **groin** (grɔɪn) *n.* a wall or breakwater built out from a shore to control erosion.

grub (grʌb) *vb.* **grubbing, grubbed. 1.** (often foll. by *up* or *out*) to search for and pull up (roots or stumps) by digging in the ground. **2.** to dig up the surface of (soil). **3.** (often foll. by *in* or *among*) to search carefully. ~*n.* **4.** the short legless larva of certain insects, esp. beetles. **5.** *Slang.* food.

grubby ('grʌbɪ) *adj.* **-bier, -biest.** dirty; slovenly. —**'grubbily** *adv.* —**'grubbiness** *n.*

grudge (grʌdʒ) *n.* **1.** a persistent feeling of resentment, esp. one due to an insult or injury. ~*vb.* **2.** to give unwillingly. **3.** to resent or envy (someone else's success or possessions). —**'grudging** *adj.*

gruel ('gruːəl) *n.* thin porridge made by boiling meal, esp. oatmeal, in water or milk.

gruelling *or U.S.* **grueling** ('gruːəlɪŋ) *adj.* extremely severe or tiring.

gruesome ('gruːsəm) *adj.* inspiring horror and disgust.

gruff (grʌf) *adj.* **1.** rough or surly in manner or speech. **2.** (of a voice) low and throaty. —**'gruffly** *adv.* —**'gruffness** *n.*

grumble ('grʌmb°l) *vb.* **1.** to utter (complaints) in a nagging way. **2.** to make low dull rumbling sounds. ~*n.* **3.** a complaint; grouse. **4.** a low rumbling sound. —**'grumbler** *n.* —**'grumbling** *adj., n.*

grumpy ('grʌmpɪ) *adj.* **grumpier, grumpiest.** peevish; sulky. —**'grumpily** *adv.* —**'grumpiness** *n.*

grunt (grʌnt) *vb.* **1.** (esp. of pigs) to emit a low short gruff noise. **2.** to express something gruffly: *he grunted his answer.* ~*n.* **3.** the characteristic low short gruff noise of pigs, or a similar sound, as of disgust.

Gruyère ('gruːjeə) *n.* a hard flat pale yellow cheese, with holes.

gryphon ('grɪf°n) *n.* same as **griffin.**

G-string *n.* **1.** a strip of cloth worn between the legs and attached to a waistband. **2.** *Music.* a string tuned to G.

G-suit *n.* a close-fitting pressurized garment that is worn by the crew of high-speed aircraft.

GT gran turismo: a touring car; usually a fast sports car with a hard fixed roof.

guanaco (gwɑːˈnɑːkəʊ) *n., pl.* **-cos.** a cud-chewing South American mammal related to the llama.

guano ('gwɑːnəʊ) *n., pl.* **-nos.** the dried excrement of fish-eating sea birds: used as a fertilizer.

guarantee (ˌgærənˈtiː) *n.* **1.** a formal assurance, esp. in writing, that a product or service will meet certain standards or specifications. **2.** a guarantor. **3.** something that makes a specified condition or outcome certain. **4.** same as **guaranty.** ~*vb.* **-teeing, -teed. 5.** to take responsibility for (someone else's debts or obligations). **6.** to serve as a guarantee for. **7.** to secure: *a small deposit will guarantee any dress.* **8.** (usually foll. by *from* or *against*) to undertake to protect or keep secure, as against injury or loss. **9.** to ensure: *good planning will guarantee success.* **10.** to promise or make certain.

guarantor (ˌgærənˈtɔː) *n.* a person who gives or is bound by a guarantee or guaranty.

guaranty ('gærəntɪ) *n., pl.* **-ties. 1.** a pledge of responsibility for fulfilling another person's obligations in case of that person's default. **2.** a thing given or taken as security for a guaranty.

guard (gɑːd) *vb.* **1.** to watch over or shield (a person or thing) from danger or harm; protect. **2.** to keep watch over (a prisoner or other potentially dangerous person or thing), as to prevent escape. **3.** to control: *to guard one's tongue.* **4.** (usually foll. by *against*) to take precautions. ~*n.* **5.** a person or group who protect or watch over people or things. **6.** a person or group of people, such as soldiers, who form a ceremonial escort. **7.** *Brit.* the official in charge of a train. **8.** the act or duty of protecting or supervising. **9.** a device or part of a machine designed to protect the user against injury. **10.** anything that provides protection: *a guard against infection.* **11.** the posture of defence or readiness in sports such as fencing and boxing. **12. off (one's) guard.** having one's defences down; unprepared. **13. on (one's) guard.** prepared to face danger or difficulties. **14. stand guard.** (of a sentry) to keep watch.

guarded ('gɑːdɪd) *adj.* cautious or noncommittal: *a guarded reply.* —**'guardedly** *adv.*

guardhouse ('gɑːd,haʊs) *or* **guardroom** ('gɑːd,ruːm,-,rʊm) *n. Mil.* a military police office in which prisoners can be detained.

guardian ('gɑːdɪən) *n.* **1.** one who looks after, protects, or defends: *the guardian of public morals.* **2.** someone legally appointed to manage the affairs of a person incapable of acting for himself, as a minor or person of unsound mind. —'**guardian,ship** *n.*

guardsman ('gɑːdzmən) *n., pl.* -**men.** **1.** a member of a regiment responsible for ceremonial duties. **2.** a guard.

guard's van *n. Railways, Brit. & N.Z.* the van in which the guard travels.

guava ('gwɑːvə) *n.* the edible fruit of a tropical American tree, having yellow skin and pink pulp.

gubernatorial (ˌgjuːbənəˈtɔːrɪəl) *adj. Chiefly U.S.* of or relating to a governor.

gudgeon[1] ('gʌdʒən) *n.* a small slender European freshwater fish: used as bait by anglers.

gudgeon[2] ('gʌdʒən) *n.* **1.** the socket of a hinge, which fits around the pin. **2.** *Naut.* one of two or more looplike sockets, into which the pins of a rudder are fitted.

guelder-rose ('gɛldəˌrəʊz) *n.* a Eurasian shrub with clusters of white flowers.

Guernsey ('gɜːnzɪ) *n.* **1.** a breed of dairy cattle producing rich creamy milk, originating from Guernsey, in the Channel Islands. **2.** (*not cap.*) a seaman's knitted woollen sweater.

guerrilla *or* **guerilla** (gəˈrɪlə) *n.* a member of an irregular usually politically motivated armed force that fights regular forces.

guess (gɛs) *vb.* **1.** to form an estimate or conclusion (about something), without proper knowledge: *guess what we're having for dinner.* **2.** to arrive at a correct estimate of (something) by guessing: *he guessed my age.* **3.** *Informal, chiefly U.S. & Canad.* to think or suppose (something): *I guess I'll go now.* ~*n.* **4.** an estimate or conclusion arrived at by guessing: *a bad guess.*

guesswork ('gɛsˌwɜːk) *n.* **1.** a set of conclusions or estimates arrived at by guessing. **2.** the process of making guesses.

guest (gɛst) *n.* **1.** a person who is entertained or taken out to eat and paid for by another. **2.** a person who receives hospitality at the home of another. **3.** a performer or speaker taking part in an event, show, or film by special invitation. **4.** a patron of a hotel or restaurant. ~*vb.* **5.** (in theatre and broadcasting) to be a guest: *to guest on a show.*

guesthouse ('gɛstˌhaʊs) *n.* a private home or boarding house offering accommodation.

guff (gʌf) *n. Slang.* ridiculous talk.

guffaw (gʌˈfɔː) *n.* **1.** a crude and boisterous laugh. ~*vb.* **2.** to laugh or express (something) in this way.

guidance ('gaɪdⁿns) *n.* **1.** leadership, instruction, or direction. **2.** counselling or advice on educational, vocational, or psychological matters.

guide (gaɪd) *vb.* **1.** to lead the way for (a person). **2.** to control the movement or course of; steer. **3.** to supervise or instruct (a person). **4.** to direct the affairs of (a person, company, or nation). **5.** to influence (a person) in his actions or opinions: *let truth guide you.* ~*n.* **6.** a person or thing that guides. **7.** a person, usually paid, who conducts tour expeditions. **8.** a model or criterion, as in moral standards or accuracy. **9.** same as **guidebook.** **10.** a book that explains the fundamentals of a subject or skill. **11.** any device that directs the motion of a tool or machine part.

Guide (gaɪd) *n.* a member of the organization for girls equivalent to the Scouts.

guidebook ('gaɪdˌbʊk) *n.* a handbook with information for visitors to a place.

guided missile *n.* a missile having a course controlled either by radio signals or by internal homing devices.

guide dog *n.* a dog specially trained to accompany a blind person, enabling that person to move about safely.

guideline ('gaɪdˌlaɪn) *n.* a principle put forward to set standards or determine a course of action.

guild (gɪld) *n.* **1.** an organization, club, or fellowship. **2.** (in medieval Europe) an association of men in the same trade or craft.

guilder ('gɪldə) *n., pl.* -**ders** *or* -**der.** **1.** the standard monetary unit of the Netherlands. **2.** any of various former coins of Germany, Austria, or the Netherlands.

guildhall ('gɪldˌhɔːl) *n. Brit.* **1.** the hall of a guild or corporation. **2.** a town hall.

guile (gaɪl) *n.* crafty character or behaviour. —'**guileful** *adj.* —'**guileless** *adj.*

guillemot ('gɪlɪˌmɒt) *n.* a northern oceanic diving bird with black-and-white plumage and a long narrow bill.

guillotine ('gɪləˌtiːn) *n.* **1.** a device for beheading people, consisting of a weighted blade set between two upright posts. **2.** a device with a blade for cutting paper or sheet metal. **3.** (in Parliament) a method of hastening the progress of a bill by dividing it into parts, which must be completely dealt with by a specified time. ~*vb.* **4.** to behead (a person) by guillotine. **5.** (in Parliament) to limit debate on (a bill) by the guillotine.

guilt (gɪlt) *n.* **1.** the fact or state of having done wrong. **2.** remorse or self-reproach caused by feeling that one has done something wrong.

guiltless ('gɪltlɪs) *adj.* free of all responsibility for wrongdoing or crime; innocent.

guilty ('gɪltɪ) *adj.* **guiltier, guiltiest.** **1.** responsible for an offence or misdeed. **2.** *Law.* judged to have committed an offence: *the accused was found guilty.* **3.** showing,

feeling, or characterized by guilt. —**'guilti-
ly** *adv.*

guinea ('gɪnɪ) *n.* **1.** the sum of £1.05 (21
shillings), used in quoting professional fees.
2. a former British gold coin worth this
amount.

guinea fowl *n.* a domestic bird with a
heavy rounded body and speckled plumage.

guinea pig *n.* **1.** a tailless S American
rodent, commonly kept as a pet or used in
scientific experiments. **2.** a person used for
experimentation.

guipure (gɪ'pjʊə) *n.* heavy lace that has its
pattern connected by threads, rather than
supported on a net mesh.

guise (gaɪz) *n.* **1.** semblance or pretence:
under the guise of friendship. **2.** external
appearance in general.

guitar (gɪ'tɑː) *n.* a plucked stringed instrument, usually with six strings, a flat back,
and a long neck with a fretted fingerboard.
—**gui'tarist** *n.*

Gulag ('guːlæg) *n.* the department of the
Soviet security service which runs prisons
and labour camps.

gulch (gʌltʃ) *n. U.S. & Canad.* a narrow
ravine with a fast stream running through
it.

gulf (gʌlf) *n.* **1.** a large deep bay. **2.** something that divides or separates people, such
as a lack of understanding.

Gulf Stream *n.* a warm ocean current
flowing northeastwards from the Gulf of
Mexico towards NW Europe.

gull (gʌl) *n.* a large sea bird with long pointed wings and a mostly white plumage.

gullet ('gʌlɪt) *n.* the muscular tube through
which food passes from the throat to the
stomach.

gullible ('gʌlɪb³l) *adj.* easily tricked. —**gul-
li'bility** *n.*

gully *or* **gulley** ('gʌlɪ) *n., pl.* **-lies** *or* **leys.**
1. a channel or small valley originally worn
away by running water. **2.** *Cricket.* **a.** a
fielding position slightly behind and to the
right of the batsman. **b.** a fielder in this
position.

gulp (gʌlp) *vb.* **1.** to swallow (food or
drink) rapidly in large mouthfuls. **2.** (foll.
by *back*) to stifle: *to gulp back sobs.* **3.** to
gasp or breathe in violently, for example
when nervous or when swimming. ~*n.* **4.**
the act of gulping. **5.** the quantity taken in
a gulp.

gum¹ (gʌm) *n.* **1.** a sticky substance obtained from certain plants, which hardens
on exposure to air and dissolves in water.
2. a sticky substance used as an adhesive;
glue. **3.** short for **chewing gum** or **bubble
gum. 4.** a gumtree. **5.** *Chiefly Brit.* a
gumdrop. ~*vb.* **gumming, gummed. 6.** to
stick (something) together or in place with
gum. ~See also **gum up.**

gum² (gʌm) *n.* the fleshy tissue that covers
the bases of the teeth.

gum arabic *n.* a gum obtained from certain acacia trees, used in the manufacture
of ink, food thickeners, and pills.

gumboil ('gʌm,bɔɪl) *n.* an abscess on the
gum.

gumboots ('gʌm,buːts) *pl. n.* same as **Wellington boots.**

gumdrop ('gʌm,drɒp) *n.* a small hard
transparent jelly-like sweet.

gummy¹ ('gʌmɪ) *adj.* **-mier, -miest. 1.**
sticky or tacky. **2.** producing gum.

gummy² ('gʌmɪ) *adj.* **-mier, -miest.** toothless.

gumption ('gʌmpʃən) *n. Brit. informal.*
common sense; resourcefulness; initiative.

gumtree ('gʌm,triː) *n.* **1.** any of various
trees that yield gum, such as the eucalyptus. **2. up a gumtree.** *Informal.* in an awkward position; in difficulties.

gum up *vb.* **1.** to cover (something) with
a gumlike substance. **2. gum up the works.**
Informal. to make a mess of something.

gun (gʌn) *n.* **1.** a weapon with a metallic
tube or barrel from which a missile is fired,
usually by force of an explosion. **2.** a member of a shooting party. **3.** a device used to
project something under pressure: *a spray
gun.* **4.** *U.S. slang.* a gunman. **5. jump the
gun.** *Informal.* to act prematurely. **6. stick
to one's guns.** *Informal.* to maintain one's
opinions or intentions in spite of opposition.
~*vb.* **gunning, gunned. 7.** (foll. by *down*)
to shoot (someone) with a gun. **8.** to press
hard on the accelerator of (an engine).
~See also **gun for.**

gunboat ('gʌn,bəʊt) *n.* a small ship carrying mounted guns.

gunboat diplomacy *n.* diplomacy conducted by threats of military intervention.

guncotton ('gʌn,kɒt³n) *n.* a form of cellulose nitrate used as an explosive.

gun dog *n.* **1.** a dog trained to locate or
retrieve birds or animals that have been
shot in a hunt. **2.** a dog belonging to any
breed traditionally used for these activities.

gunfire ('gʌn,faɪə) *n.* the repeated firing of
one or more guns.

gun for *vb.* **1.** to search for (someone) in
order to reprimand, punish, or kill him. **2.**
to try earnestly for (something): *he was
gunning for promotion.*

gunge (gʌndʒ) *n. Informal.* sticky or con-
gealed matter. —**'gungy** *adj.*

gunk (gʌŋk) *n. Informal.* slimy, oily, or
filthy matter.

gunman ('gʌnmən) *n., pl.* **-men.** a man who
uses a gun to commit a crime.

gunmetal ('gʌn,met³l) *n.* **1.** a type of
bronze containing copper, tin, and zinc.
~*adj.* **2.** dark grey.

gunnel ('gʌn³l) *n.* same as **gunwale.**

gunner ('gʌnə) n. a serviceman who works with, uses, or specializes in guns.

gunnery ('gʌnərɪ) n. the art and science of the efficient design and use of large guns.

gunny ('gʌnɪ) n. Chiefly U.S. **1.** a coarse hard-wearing fabric, made from jute and used for sacks. **2.** (pl. **-nies**) a sack made from this fabric.

gunpoint ('gʌn,pɔɪnt) n. **at gunpoint.** being under or using the threat of being shot.

gunpowder ('gʌn,paʊdə) n. an explosive mixture of potassium nitrate, charcoal, and sulphur.

gunrunning ('gʌn,rʌnɪŋ) n. the smuggling of guns and ammunition into a country. —'**gun,runner** n.

gunshot ('gʌn,ʃɒt) n. **1.** bullets fired from a gun. **2.** the sound of a gun being fired. **3.** the range of a gun: out of gunshot.

gunslinger ('gʌn,slɪŋə) n. Slang. a gun-fighter or gunman in the frontier days of the American West.

gunstock ('gʌn,stɒk) n. the wooden handle to which the barrel of a rifle is attached.

gunwale ('gʌnºl) n. Naut. the top of the side of a boat or ship.

guppy ('gʌpɪ) n., pl. **-pies.** a small brightly coloured freshwater fish of the Caribbean area: a popular aquarium fish.

gurgle ('gɜːgºl) vb. **1.** (of water) to make low bubbling noises when flowing. **2.** to make low throaty bubbling noises: the baby gurgled with delight. ~n. **3.** the sound of gurgling.

Gurkha ('gɜːkə) n. **1.** a member of a Hindu people living mainly in Nepal. **2.** a member of a Gurkha regiment in the British Army.

gurnard ('gɜːnəd) n., pl. **-nard** or **-nards.** a sea fish with a heavily armoured head and finger-like pectoral fins.

guru ('gʊruː) n. **1.** a Hindu or Sikh religious teacher or leader. **2.** a leader or adviser of a movement: the feminist guru.

gush (gʌʃ) vb. **1.** to pour out suddenly and profusely. **2.** to act or utter (something) in an overenthusiastic manner. ~n. **3.** a sudden copious flow of liquid. **4.** an extravagant and insincere expression of admiration. —'**gushing** or '**gushy** adj.

gusher ('gʌʃə) n. **1.** someone who gushes. **2.** a spurting oil well.

gusset ('gʌsɪt) n. a piece of material sewn into a garment to strengthen it.

gust (gʌst) n. **1.** a sudden blast of wind. **2.** a sudden rush of smoke or rain. **3.** an outburst of emotion. ~vb. **4.** to blow in gusts. —'**gusty** adj.

gusto ('gʌstəʊ) n. vigorous enjoyment: the aria was sung with great gusto.

gut (gʌt) n. **1.** same as **intestine. 2.** (pl.) the internal organs of a person or an animal. **3.** Slang. the belly; paunch. **4.** short for **catgut. 5.** a silky fibrous substance extracted from silkworms and used in the manufacture of fishing tackle. **6.** (pl.) Informal. courage, willpower, or daring; forcefulness. **7.** (pl.) Informal. the essential part: the guts of a problem. ~vb. **gutting, gutted. 8.** to remove the internal organs from (a dead animal or fish). **9.** (of a fire) to destroy the inside of (a building). ~adj. **10.** Informal. basic, essential, or natural: the gut problem; a gut reaction.

gutless ('gʌtlɪs) adj. Informal. lacking courage or determination.

gutsy ('gʌtsɪ) adj. **gutsier, gutsiest.** Slang. **1.** gluttonous; greedy. **2.** courageous; bold.

gutta-percha ('gʌtə'pɜːtʃə) n. a whitish rubber substance derived from various tropical Asian trees: used in electrical insulation and dentistry.

gutter ('gʌtə) n. **1.** a channel on the roof of a building or running alongside the kerb of a road, used to collect and carry away rainwater. **2.** Tenpin bowling. one of the channels running down either side of an alley. **3. the gutter.** a poverty-stricken, degraded, or criminal environment. ~vb. **4.** (of a candle) to melt away as the wax forms channels and runs down in drops. **5.** (of a flame) to flicker and be about to go out. —'**guttering** n.

gutter press n. the section of the popular press that seeks sensationalism in its coverage.

guttersnipe ('gʌtə,snaɪp) n. a child who spends most of his time in the streets, usually in a slum area.

guttural ('gʌtərəl) adj. **1.** Phonetics. pronounced at the back of the throat. **2.** harsh-sounding.

guy[1] (gaɪ) n. **1.** Informal. a man or boy. **2.** (pl.) Chiefly U.S. people of either sex: I'll see you guys next week. **3.** Brit. a crude model of Guy Fawkes, that is burnt on top of a bonfire on Guy Fawkes Day (November 5). ~vb. **4.** to make fun of (someone).

guy[2] (gaɪ) n. **1.** a rope, chain, or wire for anchoring, steadying, or guiding an object. ~vb. **2.** to anchor, steady, or guide (an object) with a guy or guys.

guzzle ('gʌzºl) vb. to eat or drink excessively or greedily.

gybe or **jibe** (dʒaɪb) Naut. ~vb. **1.** (of a fore-and-aft sail) to swing suddenly from one side of a ship or boat to the other. **2.** (of a ship or boat) to change course by letting the sail gybe. ~n. **3.** an instance of gybing.

gym (dʒɪm) n. short for **gymnasium** or **gymnastics.**

gymkhana (dʒɪm'kɑːnə) n. Chiefly Brit. an event in which horses and riders take part in various races and contests.

gymnasium (dʒɪm'neɪzɪəm) n. a large room containing equipment such as bars, weights, and ropes, for physical training.

gymnast ('dʒɪmnæst) *n.* a person who is skilled or trained in gymnastics. —**gym'nastic** *adj.*

gymnastics (dʒɪm'næstɪks) *n.* **1.** (*functioning as sing.*) practice or training in exercises that develop physical strength and agility. **2.** (*functioning as pl.*) gymnastic exercises.

gym shoes *pl. n.* same as **plimsolls.**

gymslip ('dʒɪm,slɪp) *n.* a tunic or pinafore dress formerly worn by schoolgirls as part of a school uniform.

gynaecology *or U.S.* **gynecology** (,gaɪnɪ'kɒlədʒɪ) *n.* the branch of medicine concerned with diseases and conditions specific to women. —**gynaecological** *or U.S.* **gyneco'logical** (,gaɪnɪkə'lɒdʒɪkˀl) *adj.* —**gynae'cologist** *or U.S.* **,gyne'cologist** *n.*

gyp *or* **gip** (dʒɪp) *n.* **give someone gyp.** *Brit. & N.Z. slang.* to cause someone severe pain: *his back was giving him gyp.*

gypsum ('dʒɪpsəm) *n.* a mineral used in making plaster of Paris.

Gypsy *or* **Gipsy** ('dʒɪpsɪ) *n., pl.* **-sies.** a member of a travelling people scattered throughout Europe and North America.

gyrate (dʒaɪ'reɪt) *vb.* to rotate or spiral about a fixed point or axis. —**gyration** (dʒaɪ'reɪʃən) *n.*

gyrfalcon ('dʒɜː,fɔːlkən) *n.* a very large rare falcon of northern regions.

gyro ('dʒaɪrəʊ) *n., pl.* **-ros.** short for **gyroscope.**

gyrocompass ('dʒaɪrəʊ,kʌmpəs) *n.* a nonmagnetic compass that uses a motor-driven gyroscope to indicate true north.

gyroscope ('dʒaɪrə,skəʊp) *n.* a device containing a disc rotating on an axis that can turn freely in any direction, so that the disc maintains the same position regardless of the movement of the surrounding structure.

H

h or **H** (eɪtʃ) n., pl. **h's**, **H's**, or **Hs**. the eighth letter of the English alphabet.

H Chem. hydrogen.

h. or **H.** 1. height. 2. hour.

ha¹ or **hah** (hɑː) interj. an exclamation expressing derision, triumph or surprise.

ha² hectare.

habeas corpus (ˈheɪbɪəs ˈkɔːpəs) n. Law. a writ ordering a person to be brought before a judge, so as to decide whether his detention is lawful.

haberdasher (ˈhæbəˌdæʃə) n. Brit. a dealer in small articles for sewing, such as buttons and ribbons. —**haber,dashery** n.

habiliments (həˈbɪlɪmənts) pl. n. dress or attire.

habit (ˈhæbɪt) n. 1. a tendency to act in a particular way. 2. established custom; usual practice. 3. mental disposition or attitude: a good working habit of mind. 4. the costume of a nun or monk.

habitable (ˈhæbɪtəb²l) adj. suitable to be lived in. —**,habita'bility** n.

habitant (ˈhæbɪt²nt) n. an early French settler in Canada or Louisiana or a descendant of one, esp. a farmer.

habitat (ˈhæbɪˌtæt) n. the natural home of an animal or plant.

habitation (ˌhæbɪˈteɪʃən) n. 1. occupation of a dwelling place: unfit for human habitation. 2. a dwelling place.

habit-forming adj. tending to become a habit or addiction.

habitual (həˈbɪtjʊəl) adj. 1. done regularly and repeatedly: the habitual Sunday walk. 2. by habit: a habitual drinker. —**ha'bitually** adv.

habituate (həˈbɪtjʊˌeɪt) vb. to accustom: habituated to the timetable. —**ha,bitu'ation** n.

habitué (həˈbɪtjʊˌeɪ) n. a frequent visitor to a place.

hachure (hæˈʃʊə) n. shading of short lines drawn on a map to indicate the degree of steepness of a hill.

hacienda (ˌhæsɪˈɛndə) n. (in Spanish-speaking countries) a ranch or large estate with a house on it.

hack¹ (hæk) vb. 1. to chop roughly or violently. 2. to cut and clear (a way) through undergrowth. 3. (in sport) to foul (an opposing player) by kicking his shins. 4. to cough in short dry bursts. ~n. 5. a cut or gash. 6. a tool, such as a pick. 7. a chopping blow. 8. a kick on the shins, as in rugby.

hack² (hæk) n. 1. a horse kept for riding, often one for hire. 2. Brit. a country ride on horseback. 3. a person who produces mediocre literary work. ~vb. 4. Brit. to ride (a horse) cross-country for pleasure. ~adj. 5. banal, mediocre, or unoriginal: hack writing.

hacker (ˈhækə) n. Slang. a computer enthusiast, esp. one who through a personal computer breaks into the computer system of a company or government. —**hackery** n.

hackles (ˈhæk²lz) pl. n. 1. anger or resentment: to make one's hackles rise. 2. the hairs or feathers on the back of the neck of certain animals or birds, which rise when they are angry.

hackney (ˈhæknɪ) n. 1. a taxi. 2. same as **hack²** (sense 1).

hackneyed (ˈhæknɪd) adj. (of a word or phrase) used so often as to be trite.

hacksaw (ˈhækˌsɔː) n. a small saw for cutting metal.

had (hæd) vb. past of **have**.

haddock (ˈhædək) n., pl. **-dock**. a North Atlantic food fish.

hadedah or **hadeda** (ˈhɑːdɪˌdɑː) n. a large grey-green S. African ibis.

Hades (ˈheɪdiːz) n. Greek myth. the underworld abode of the souls of the dead.

hadj (hædʒ) n. same as **hajj**.

hadji (ˈhædʒɪ) n., pl. **hadjis**. same as **hajji**.

hadn't (ˈhæd²nt) had not.

haemal or U.S. **hemal** (ˈhiːməl) adj. of the blood.

haematic or U.S. **hematic** (hiːˈmætɪk) adj. relating to or containing blood.

haematology or U.S. **hematology** (ˌhiːməˈtɒlədʒɪ) n. the branch of medical science concerned with the blood.

haemoglobin or U.S. **hemoglobin** (ˌhiːməʊˈɡləʊbɪn) n. a protein in red blood cells that carries oxygen from the lungs to the tissues.

haemophilia or U.S. **hemophilia** (ˌhiːməʊˈfɪlɪə) n. a hereditary disorder, usually affecting males, in which the blood does not clot properly. —**,haemo'philiac** n.

haemorrhage or U.S. **hemorrhage** (ˈhɛmərɪdʒ) n. 1. profuse bleeding from ruptured blood vessels. ~vb. 2. to bleed profusely.

haemorrhoids or U.S. **hemorrhoids** (ˈhɛməˌrɔɪdz) pl. n. Pathol. swollen veins in the wall of the anus.

haeremai (ˈhaɪrəˌmaɪ) interj. N.Z. an expression of greeting or welcome.

hafnium ('hæfniəm) n. a metallic element found in zirconium ores. Symbol: Hf

haft (hɑːft) n. the handle of an axe, knife, or dagger.

hag (hæg) n. **1.** an unpleasant or ugly old woman. **2.** a witch. —**'haggish** adj.

haggard ('hægəd) adj. looking careworn or gaunt.

haggis ('hægɪs) n. a Scottish dish made from sheep's or calf's offal, oatmeal, suet, and seasonings boiled in a skin made from the animal's stomach.

haggle ('hæg³l) vb. to bargain or wrangle (over a price); barter.

hagiography (,hægɪ'ɒgrəfɪ) n., pl. **-phies.** the writing of lives of the saints. —**,hagi-'ographer** n.

hagiology (,hægɪ'ɒlədʒɪ) n., pl. **-gies.** literature about the lives and legends of saints.

hag-ridden adj. tormented or distressed.

hah (hɑː) interj. same as **ha**[1].

ha-ha[1] ('hɑː'hɑː) or **haw-haw** ('hɔː'hɔː) interj. a written representation of the sound of laughter.

ha-ha[2] ('hɑːhɑː) n. a ditch, with one side made into a retaining wall, that borders a garden or park, and allows an uninterrupted view from within.

haiku ('haɪkuː) n., pl. **-ku.** a Japanese verse form in 17 syllables.

hail[1] (heɪl) n. **1.** small pellets of ice falling from thunderclouds. **2.** words, ideas, missiles, etc., directed with force and in great quantity: a hail of abuse. ~vb. **3.** to fall as hail: it's hailing. **4.** to fall or cause to fall like hail: blows hailed down on him.

hail[2] (heɪl) vb. **1.** to call out to; greet: she hailed John excitedly. **2.** to acclaim or acknowledge: they hailed him as their hero. **3.** to stop (a taxi) by shouting or gesturing. **4. hail from.** to be a native of: she hails from India. ~n. **5. within hailing distance.** within hearing range. ~interj. **6.** Poetic. an exclamation of greeting.

hail-fellow-well-met adj. genial and familiar in an offensive way.

Hail Mary n. R.C. Church. a prayer to the Virgin Mary.

hailstone ('heɪl,stəʊn) n. a pellet of hail.

hailstorm ('heɪl,stɔːm) n. a storm during which hail falls.

hair (heə) n. **1.** any of the threadlike outgrowths on the skin of mammals. **2.** a mass of such outgrowths, as on a person's head or an animal's body. **3.** Bot. a threadlike growth from the outer layer of a plant. **4.** a very small distance or margin: to lose by a hair. **5. get in someone's hair.** Informal. to annoy someone. **6. hair of the dog.** an alcoholic drink taken as a cure for a hangover. **7. let one's hair down.** to enjoy oneself without restraint. **8. not turn a hair.** to show no reaction. **9. split hairs.** to

make petty and unnecessary distinctions. —**'hairless** adj.

hairdo ('heə,duː) n., pl. **-dos.** the style of a person's hair.

hairdresser ('heə,dresə) n. **1.** a person who cuts and styles hair. **2.** a hairdresser's premises. —**'hair,dressing** n.

hairgrip ('heə,grɪp) n. Chiefly Brit. a small bent clasp used to fasten the hair.

hairline ('heə,laɪn) n. **1.** the natural margin formed by hair. **2. a.** a crack or line. **b.** (as modifier): a hairline crack.

hairpiece ('heə,piːs) n. a section of false hair added to one's real hair.

hairpin ('heə,pɪn) n. a thin U-shaped pin used to fasten the hair.

hairpin bend n. a bend in the road that curves very sharply.

hair-raising adj. causing horror; terrifying.

hair's-breadth n. an extremely small margin or distance.

hair shirt n. a shirt made of horsehair cloth worn against the skin as a penance.

hair slide n. a decorative clasp used to fasten the hair.

hairsplitting ('heə,splɪtɪŋ) n. **1.** the act of making petty distinctions. ~adj. **2.** characterized by petty distinctions.

hairspring ('heə,sprɪŋ) n. a fine spring in some clocks and watches which regulates the timekeeping.

hairstyle ('heə,staɪl) n. the cut and arrangement of the hair. —**'hair,stylist** n.

hair trigger n. a trigger that responds to the slightest pressure.

hairy ('heərɪ) adj. **hairier, hairiest. 1.** covered with hair. **2.** Slang. dangerous, exciting, and difficult. —**'hairiness** n.

hajj or **hadj** (hædʒ) n. the pilgrimage a Muslim makes to Mecca.

hajji or **hadji** ('hædʒɪ) n., pl. **hajjis** or **hadjis.** a Muslim who has made a pilgrimage to Mecca.

haka ('hɑːkə) n. N.Z. **1.** a Maori war chant accompanied by gestures. **2.** a similar chant by a sports team.

hake (heɪk) n., pl. **hake** or **hakes.** a food fish with a long body and a large head.

halal or **hallal** (hɑːˈlɑːl) n. meat from animals that have been slaughtered according to Muslim law.

halberd ('hælbəd) n. Hist. a tall spear that includes an axe blade and a pick.

halcyon ('hælsɪən) adj. peaceful, gentle, and calm: halcyon days.

hale (heɪl) adj. healthy and robust: hale and hearty.

half (hɑːf) n., pl. **halves** (hɑːvz). **1.** either of two equal or corresponding parts that together make up a whole. **2.** the fraction equal to one divided by two. **3.** half a pint, esp. of beer. **4.** Sport. one of two equal periods of play in a game. **5.** a half-price ticket. **6. by halves.** without being thorough: *we don't do things by halves.* **7. go halves.** to share expenses. *~det.* **8.** being a half or approximately a half: *half the kingdom.* *~adj.* **9.** incomplete: *he only did a half job on it.* *~adv.* **10.** to the amount or extent of a half. **11.** partially; to an extent: *half dead with exhaustion.* **12. by half.** to an excessive degree: *he's too arrogant by half.* **13. not half.** *Informal.* **a.** *Brit.* very; indeed: *he isn't half stupid.* **b.** yes, indeed.

half-and-half *adj.* half one thing and half another thing.

halfback ('hɑːf,bæk) *n. Sport.* a player positioned immediately behind the forwards.

half-baked *adj. Informal.* foolish; poorly planned: *half-baked ideas.*

half board *n.* the daily provision by a hotel of bed, breakfast, and evening meal.

half-bottle *n.* a bottle of spirits or wine that contains half the quantity of a standard bottle.

half-breed *n.* a person whose parents are of different races.

half-brother *n.* the son of either one's mother or father by another partner.

half-caste *n.* a person whose parents are of different races.

half-cock *n.* **go off at half-cock** *or* **half-cocked.** to fail because of inadequate preparation.

half-crown *or* **half-a-crown** *n.* a former British coin worth two shillings and sixpence (12½p).

half-cut *adj. Brit. slang.* rather drunk.

half-day *n.* a day when one works only in the morning or only in the afternoon.

half-dozen *n. six.*

half-hearted *adj.* without enthusiasm or determination. —,**half-'heartedly** *adv.*

half-hitch *n.* a knot made by passing the end of a piece of rope around itself and through the loop so made.

half-hour *n.* **1.** a period of 30 minutes. **2.** the point of time 30 minutes after the beginning of an hour. —,**half-'hourly** *adv., adj.*

half-life *n.* the time taken for radioactive material to lose half its radioactivity.

half-light *n.* a dim light, as at dawn or dusk.

half-mast *n.* the halfway position of a flag on a mast as a sign of mourning.

half measures *pl. n.* inadequate actions or solutions: *we don't want any half measures.*

half-moon *n.* **1.** the moon when half its face is illuminated. **2.** the time at which a half-moon occurs. **3.** something shaped like a half-moon.

half-nelson *n.* a wrestling hold in which a wrestler places an arm under his oppo-

nent's arm from behind and exerts pressure with his palm on the back of his opponent's neck.

halfpenny *or* **ha'penny** ('heɪpnɪ, 'hɑːf-,pɛnɪ) *n., pl.* **-pennies.** a former British coin worth half a penny.

half-pie *adj. N.Z. informal.* badly planned; not properly thought out: *a half-pie scheme.*

half-price *adj., adv.* for half the normal price: *half-price strawberries; children travel half-price.*

half-sister *n.* the daughter of either one's mother or father by another partner.

half term *n. Brit. education.* a short holiday midway through a term.

half-timbered *adj.* (of a building) having an exposed timber framework filled with brick or plaster.

half-time *n. Sport.* an interval between the two halves of a game.

half-title *n.* the first right-hand page of a book, with only the title on it.

halftone ('hɑːf,təʊn) *n.* a photographic illustration in which the image is composed of a large number of black and white dots.

half-track *n.* a vehicle with caterpillar tracks on the rear wheels.

half-truth *n.* a partially true statement. —,**half-'true** *adj.*

halfway (,hɑːf'weɪ) *adv., adj.* **1.** at or to half the distance. **2.** in or of an incomplete manner. **3. meet someone halfway.** to compromise with someone.

halfway house *n.* **1.** a place to rest midway on a journey. **2.** the halfway stage in any process: *adolescence is the halfway house between childhood and maturity.*

halfwit ('hɑːf,wɪt) *n.* a foolish or feeble-minded person. —,**half'witted** *adj.*

halibut ('hælɪbət) *n.* the largest flatfish: a very important food fish.

halitosis (,hælɪ'təʊsɪs) *n.* the condition of having offensive-smelling breath.

hall (hɔːl) *n.* **1.** an entry area to other rooms in a house. **2.** a building or room for public meetings, dances, etc. **3.** a residential building in a college or university. **4.** the great house of an estate; manor. **5.** a large dining room in a college or university. **6.** the large room of a castle or stately home.

hallelujah, halleluiah (,hælɪ'luːjə), *or* **alleluia** (,ælɪ'luːjə) *interj.* an exclamation of praise to God.

hallmark ('hɔːl,mɑːk) *n.* **1.** *Brit.* an official seal stamped on gold, silver, or platinum articles to guarantee purity and date of manufacture. **2.** a typical feature. **3.** a mark of authenticity or excellence. *~vb.* **4.** to stamp with a hallmark.

hallo (hə'ləʊ) *interj., n.* same as **hello.**

halloo (hə'luː) *interj.* a shout used to call hounds at a hunt.

hallowed ('hæləud) *adj.* **1.** regarded as holy: *hallowed ground.* **2.** worshipped; respected.

Hallowe'en *or* **Halloween** (ˌhæləu'iːn) *n.* Oct. 31, the eve of All Saints' Day.

hallucinate (hə'luːsɪˌneɪt) *vb.* to seem to see something that is not really there.

hallucination (həˌluːsɪ'neɪʃən) *n.* the experience of seeming to see something that is not really there. —**hal'lucinatory** *adj.*

hallucinogen (hə'luːsɪnəˌdʒen) *n.* any drug that causes hallucinations. —**halˌlucino-'genic** *adj.*

hallway ('hɔːlˌweɪ) *n.* an entrance area.

halo ('heɪləu) *n., pl.* -**loes** *or* -**los.** **1.** a ring of light around the head of a sacred figure. **2.** a circle of refracted light around the sun or moon. ~*vb.* -**loes** *or* -**los,** -**loing,** -**loed.** **3.** to surround with a halo.

halogen ('hæləˌdʒen) *n.* any of the nonmetallic chemical elements fluorine, chlorine, bromine, iodine, and astatine which form salts when combined with metal.

halt (hɔːlt) *n.* **1.** a temporary standstill. **2.** a military command to stop. **3.** *Chiefly Brit.* a minor railway station without a building. **4. call a halt to.** to put an end to; stop. ~*vb.* **5.** to come to a stop or bring (someone or something) to a stop.

halter ('hɔːltə) *n.* **1.** headgear for a horse, usually with a rope for leading. ~*vb.* **2.** to put a halter on (a horse).

halterneck ('hɔːltəˌnɛk) *n.* a woman's top or dress which fastens behind the neck, leaving the back and arms bare.

halting ('hɔːltɪŋ) *adj.* hesitant: *halting speech.*

halve (hɑːv) *vb.* **1.** to divide (something) into two equal parts. **2.** to reduce (something) by half, as by cutting. **3.** *Golf.* to draw with one's opponent on (a hole or round).

halyard *or* **halliard** ('hæljəd) *n. Naut.* a line for hoisting or lowering a sail, flag, or spar.

ham[1] (hæm) *n.* **1.** the rear of a pig between buttock and upper thigh. **2.** the meat from this part.

ham[2] (hæm) *n.* **1.** *Theatre, informal.* **a.** an actor who overacts and exaggerates the part. **b.** (*as modifier*): *a ham actor.* **2.** *Informal.* an amateur radio operator. ~*vb.* **hamming, hammed. 3. ham it up.** *Informal.* to overact.

hamba ('hæmbə) *interj. S. African, usually offensive.* go away.

hamburger ('hæmˌbɜːgə) *n.* a flat round of minced beef, often served in a bread roll.

ham-fisted *or* **ham-handed** *adj. Informal.* clumsy.

hamlet ('hæmlɪt) *n.* a small village.

hammer ('hæmə) *n.* **1.** a hand tool consisting of a heavy metal head on the end of a handle, used for driving in nails, beating metal, etc. **2.** the part of a gun that causes the bullet to shoot when the trigger is pulled. **3.** *Field sports.* **a.** a heavy metal ball attached to a flexible wire: thrown in competitions. **b.** the sport of throwing the hammer. **4.** an auctioneer's gavel. **5.** the striking mechanism in a piano. **6. come or go under the hammer.** to be on sale at auction. **7. hammer and tongs.** with great vigour and emotion. ~*vb.* **8.** to hit with or as if with a hammer. **9.** (foll. by *in* or *into*) to force (facts or ideas) into someone through constant repetition. **10.** to feel or sound like hammering: *the rain hammered down.* **11.** (foll. by *away*) to work at (something) constantly: *she hammered away at her essay for five hours.* **12.** *Brit.* to criticize severely. **13.** *Informal.* to defeat.

hammer and sickle *n.* the emblem on the flag of the Soviet Union, representing the industrial workers and the peasants.

hammerhead ('hæməˌhɛd) *n.* a fierce shark with a hammer-shaped head.

hammer out *vb.* to settle (differences) with great effort.

hammertoe ('hæməˌtəu) *n.* a condition causing the toe to be permanently bent at the joint.

hammock ('hæmək) *n.* a hanging bed of canvas or net.

hamper[1] ('hæmpə) *vb.* to impede the progress of (someone or something).

hamper[2] ('hæmpə) *n.* **1.** a large basket, usually with a cover. **2.** *Brit.* a selection of food and drink packed in a hamper or other container.

hamster ('hæmstə) *n.* a rodent with a stocky body, short tail, and cheek pouches.

hamstring ('hæmˌstrɪŋ) *n.* **1.** one of the tendons at the back of the knee. ~*vb.* -**stringing,** -**strung. 2.** to hinder.

hand (hænd) *n.* **1.** the part of the body at the end of the arm, consisting of a thumb, four fingers, and a palm. **2. a.** the cards dealt in one round of a card game. **b.** one round of a card game. **3.** an influence: *the hand of God.* **4.** a part in some activity: *he had a hand in the victory.* **5.** assistance: *can I give you a hand?* **6.** a pointer on a dial or gauge, esp. on a clock. **7.** consent to marry someone: *he asked for her hand in marriage.* **8.** a position indicated by its location to the side of an object or the observer: *on the right hand.* **9.** a contrasting aspect or condition: *on the other hand.* **10.** source: *a story heard at third hand.* **11.** a person who creates something: *a good hand at baking.* **12.** a manual worker. **13.** a member of a ship's crew. **14.** a person's handwriting: *the letter was in his own hand.* **15.** a round of applause: *let's give him a big hand.* **16.** a unit of length equalling four inches, used for measuring the height of horses. **17. by hand. a.** by manual rather than mechanical means. **b.** by messenger: *the letter was delivered by hand.* **18. from hand to mouth.** with no food or money in reserve: *living from hand to mouth.* **19. hand in glove.** in close association. **20. hand over fist.** steadily and quickly: *he makes money hand over fist.* **21. in hand. a.** under control. **b.** receiving attention: *the job in hand.* **c.** available in reserve: *he arrived with half an hour in hand.* **22. keep one's hand in.** to continue to practise something. **23. (near) at hand.** very close. **24. on hand.** close by; available. **25. out of hand. a.** beyond control. **b.** decisively, without possible reconsideration: *he rejected my suggestion out of hand.* **26. show one's hand.** to reveal one's plans. **27. to hand.** accessible. ~*vb.* **28.** to transmit or offer by the hand or hands. **29. hand it to someone.** to give credit to someone. ~See also **hand down, hand on,** etc., **hands.** —**'handless** *adj.*

handbag ('hænd,bæg) *n.* a woman's small bag carried to contain personal articles.

handball ('hænd,bɔːl) *n.* a game in which players strike a ball against a wall with their hands.

handbill ('hænd,bɪl) *n.* a small printed notice for distribution by hand.

handbook ('hænd,bʊk) *n.* a reference manual giving practical information on a subject.

handbrake ('hænd,breɪk) *n.* a brake operated by a hand lever.

handcart ('hænd,kɑːt) *n.* a simple cart pushed or drawn by hand.

handcrafted ('hænd,krɑːftɪd) *adj.* made by handicraft.

handcuff ('hænd,kʌf) *vb.* **1.** to put handcuffs on (a person). ~*n.* **2.** (*pl.*) a linked pair of locking metal rings used for securing prisoners.

hand down *vb.* **1.** to bequeath. **2.** to pass (an outgrown garment) on from one member of a family to a younger one. **3.** *U.S. & Canad. law.* to announce (a verdict).

handful ('hændfʊl) *n., pl.* **-fuls. 1.** the amount that can be held in the hand. **2.** a small number. **3.** *Informal.* a person or animal that is difficult to control.

handicap ('hændɪ,kæp) *n.* **1.** a physical, mental, or moral impairment. **2.** something that hampers or hinders. **3. a.** a contest in which competitors are given advantages or disadvantages in an attempt to equalize their chances. **b.** the advantage or disadvantage given. **4.** *Golf.* the number of strokes by which a player's averaged score exceeds par for the course. ~*vb.* **-capping, -capped. 5.** to be an impediment to (someone).

handicapped ('hændɪ,kæpt) *adj.* physically or mentally disabled.

handicraft ('hændɪ,krɑːft) *n.* **1.** a skill performed with the hands, such as weaving. **2.** the work so produced.

handiwork ('hændɪ,wɜːk) *n.* **1.** the result of someone's work or activity. **2.** work produced by hand.

handkerchief ('hæŋkətʃɪf, -tʃiːf) *n.* a small square of fabric used to wipe the nose.

handle ('hænd'l) *n.* **1.** the part of an object that is held or operated in order that it may be used. **2.** *Slang.* a person's name. **3.** a reason for doing something: *his background served as a handle for their mockery.* **4. fly off the handle.** *Informal.* to become suddenly extremely angry. ~*vb.* **5.** to hold, move, operate or touch with the hands. **6.** to control: *my wife handles my investments.* **7.** to manage successfully: *a secretary must be able to handle clients.* **8.** to discuss (a subject). **9.** to deal with in a specified way: *I was handled with great tact.* **10.** to trade or deal in (specified merchandise). **11.** to react in a specified way: *the car handles well.* —**'handling** *n.*

handlebars ('hænd'l,bɑːz) *pl. n.* a metal bar with handles at each end, used for steering a bicycle or motorcycle.

handler ('hændlə) *n.* **1.** a person who trains and controls an animal. **2.** a person who handles something: *a baggage handler.*

handmade (,hænd'meɪd) *adj.* made by hand, not by machine.

handmaiden ('hænd,meɪd'n) *or* **handmaid** *n. Archaic.* a female servant.

hand-me-down *n. Informal.* something, esp. an outgrown garment, passed down from one person to another.

hand on *vb.* to pass (something) to the next person in a succession.

hand-out *n.* **1.** clothing, food, or money given to a needy person. **2.** a leaflet, free sample, etc., given out to publicize something. **3.** a statement distributed to the press or an audience to confirm or replace an oral presentation. ~*vb.* **hand out. 4.** to distribute.

hand over *vb.* to surrender possession of or transfer (something).

hand-pick *vb.* to select (a person) with great care, as for a special job. —**,hand-'picked** *adj.*

handrail ('hænd,reɪl) *n.* a rail alongside a stairway, to provide support.

hands (hændz) *pl. n.* **1.** power or keeping: *your welfare is in his hands.* **2. change hands.** to pass from the possession of one person to another. **3. have one's hands full.** to be completely occupied. **4. off one's hands.** no longer one's responsibility. **5. on one's hands.** for which one is responsible: *I've got too much on my hands.* **6. wash one's hands of.** to have nothing more to do with. **7. win hands down.** to win easily.

handset ('hænd,sɛt) n. a telephone mouthpiece and earpiece mounted as a single unit.

handshake ('hænd,ʃeɪk) n. the act of grasping and shaking a person's hand, as a greeting or when agreeing on a deal.

handsome ('hændsəm) adj. 1. (esp. of a man) good-looking. 2. well-proportioned; stately: *a handsome room*. 3. liberal; generous: *a handsome allowance*.

hands-on adj. involving practical experience of equipment: *hands-on training in computers*.

handspring ('hænd,sprɪŋ) n. a gymnastic feat in which a person leaps forwards or backwards into a handstand and then onto his feet.

handstand ('hænd,stænd) n. the act of supporting the body on the hands in an upside-down position.

hand-to-hand adj., adv. (of combat) at close quarters.

hand-to-mouth adj., adv. with barely enough money or food to satisfy immediate needs.

handwork ('hænd,wɜːk) n. work done by hand rather than by machine.

handwriting ('hænd,raɪtɪŋ) n. 1. writing by hand rather than by typing or printing. 2. a person's characteristic writing style. —'**hand,written** adj.

handy ('hændɪ) adj. **handier, handiest.** 1. conveniently within reach. 2. easy to handle or use. 3. skilful with one's hands. —'**handily** adv.

handyman ('hændɪ,mæn) n., pl. -**men.** a man who is skilled in odd jobs.

hang (hæŋ) vb. **hanging, hung.** 1. to fasten or be fastened from above. 2. to place (something) in position as by a hinge so as to allow free movement: *to hang a door*. 3. to hover: *a pall of smoke hung over the city*. 4. (foll. by over) to worry: *the threat of redundancy hung over them*. 5. (p.t. & p.p. **hanged**) to suspend or be suspended by the neck until dead. 6. to decorate with something suspended, such as pictures. 7. to fasten to a wall: *to hang wallpaper*. 8. to exhibit or be exhibited in an art gallery. 9. to allow to droop: *to hang one's head*. 10. (of cloth or clothing) to drape: *her skirt hangs well*. 11. (p.t. & p.p. **hanged**) Slang. to damn: used in mild curses or interjections. 12. **hang fire.** to procrastinate. ~n. 13. the way in which something hangs. 14. Slang. a damn: *I don't give a hang*. 15. **get the hang of something.** Informal. to understand the technique of doing something. ~See also **hang about, hang back,** etc.

hang about or **around** vb. 1. to waste time; loiter. 2. (foll. by with) to frequent the company (of someone).

hangar ('hæŋə) n. a large building for storing aircraft.

hang back vb. to be reluctant to do something.

hangdog ('hæŋ,dɒg) adj. downcast, furtive, or guilty in appearance or manner.

hanger ('hæŋə) n. 1. same as **coat hanger.** 2. a person who hangs something: *paper-hanger*.

hanger-on n., pl. **hangers-on.** an unwanted follower.

hang-glider n. an unpowered aircraft consisting of a large cloth wing stretched over a light framework from which the pilot hangs in a harness. —'**hang-,gliding** n.

hangi ('hʌŋiː) n. N.Z. 1. an open-air cooking pit. 2. the food cooked in it. 3. the social gathering at the resultant meal.

hanging ('hæŋɪŋ) n. 1. the act or practice of putting a person to death by suspending the body by the neck. 2. a decorative drapery hung on a wall.

hangman ('hæŋmən) n., pl. -**men.** an official who carries out a sentence of hanging.

hangnail ('hæŋ,neɪl) n. a piece of skin partly torn away from the base or side of a fingernail.

hang on vb. 1. Informal. to wait: *hang on for a few minutes*. 2. to continue or persist with effort or difficulty. 3. to grasp or hold. 4. to depend on: *everything hangs on this deal*. 5. to listen attentively to: *he hangs on her every word*.

hang out vb. 1. to suspend, be suspended, or lean. 2. Informal. to frequent a place: *where does Richard hang out these days?* 3. **let it all hang out.** Informal, chiefly U.S. to relax completely; act or speak freely. ~n. **hang-out.** 4. Informal. a place that one frequents.

hangover ('hæŋ,əʊvə) n. the aftereffects of drinking too much alcohol.

hang together vb. 1. to be united. 2. to be consistent: *your statements don't quite hang together*.

hang up vb. 1. to replace (a telephone receiver) at the end of a conversation. 2. to put on a hook or hanger. ~n. **hang-up.** 3. Informal. an emotional or psychological preoccupation or problem.

hank (hæŋk) n. a loop, coil, or skein, as of rope or wool.

hanker ('hæŋkə) vb. (foll. by for or after) to have a yearning. —'**hankering** n.

hanky or **hankie** ('hæŋkɪ) n., pl. **hankies.** Informal. short for **handkerchief.**

hanky-panky ('hæŋkɪ'pæŋkɪ) n. Informal. 1. illicit sexual relations. 2. dubious or foolish behaviour.

Hanoverian (,hænə'vɪərɪən) adj. of or relating to the British royal house ruling from 1714 to 1901.

Hansard ('hænsɑːd) n. the official verbatim report of the proceedings of the British or Canadian parliament.

Hanseatic League (ˌhænsɪˈætɪk) n. a commercial organization of towns in N Germany formed in the 14th century to protect and control trade.

hansom (ˈhænsəm) n. a two-wheeled one-horse carriage with a fixed hood. Also called: **hansom cab.**

Hants (hænts) Hampshire.

Hanukkah (ˈhɑːnəkə, -nʊˌkɑː) n. same as **Chanukah.**

haphazard (hæpˈhæzəd) adj. done at random; careless; slipshod. —**hapˈhazardly** adv.

hapless (ˈhæplɪs) adj. unfortunate; wretched.

happen (ˈhæpᵊn) vb. 1. to take place; occur. 2. (foll. by to) (of some unforeseen event, such as death) to fall to the lot (of): *if anything happens to me it'll be your fault.* 3. to chance (to be or do something): *I happen to know him.* 4. to be the case, esp. by chance: *it happens that I know him.* **Usage.** see **occur.**

happening (ˈhæpənɪŋ, ˈhæpnɪŋ) n. 1. an event. 2. an improvised or spontaneous performance consisting of bizarre events.

happy (ˈhæpɪ) adj. -pier, -piest. 1. feeling or expressing joy; pleased. 2. causing joy or gladness: *the happiest day of my life.* 3. fortunate: *the happy position of not having to work.* —**ˈhappily** adv. —**ˈhappiness** n.

happy-go-lucky adj. carefree or easy-going.

hara-kiri (ˌhærəˈkɪrɪ) n. (formerly, in Japan) ritual suicide by disembowelment when disgraced or under sentence of death.

harangue (həˈræŋ) vb. 1. to address (a person or group) in an angry or forcefully persuasive way. ~n. 2. a forceful or angry speech.

harass (ˈhærəs, həˈræs) vb. to trouble, torment, or confuse by continual persistent attacks, questions, or problems. —**ˈharassed** adj. —**ˈharassment** n.

harbinger (ˈhɑːbɪndʒə) n. a person or thing that announces or indicates the approach of something: *a harbinger of doom.*

harbour or U.S. **harbor** (ˈhɑːbə) n. 1. a sheltered port. 2. a place of refuge or safety. ~vb. 3. to maintain secretly: *to harbour a grudge.* 4. to give shelter to: *to harbour a criminal.*

harbour master n. an official in charge of a harbour.

hard (hɑːd) adj. 1. firm or rigid. 2. difficult to do or understand: *a hard sum.* 3. showing or requiring considerable effort or application: *hard work.* 4. harsh; cruel: *a hard fate.* 5. causing pain, sorrow, or hardship: *hard times.* 6. tough or violent: *a hard man.* 7. forceful: *a hard knock.* 8. cool or uncompromising: *we took a long hard look at our profit factor.* 9. indisputable; real: *hard facts.* 10. (of water) con-

taining calcium salts which stop soap lathering freely. 11. practical, shrewd, or calculating: *he is a hard man in business.* 12. harsh: *hard light.* 13. (of currency) high and stable in exchange value. 14. (of alcoholic drink) being a spirit rather than a wine or beer. 15. (of a drug) highly addictive. 16. short for **hard-core.** 17. *Phonetics.* denoting the consonants *c* and *g* when they are pronounced as in *cat* and *got.* 18. politically extreme: *the hard left.* 19. **hard of hearing.** slightly deaf. 20. **hard up.** *Informal.* in need of money. ~adv. 21. with great energy or force: *the team always played hard.* 22. with great intensity: *she thought hard.* 23. **hard by.** close by. 24. **hard put (to it).** scarcely having the capacity (to do something). ~n. 25. **have a hard on.** *Taboo slang.* to have an erection of the penis. —**ˈhardness** n.

hard-and-fast adj. (of rules) invariable or strict.

hardback (ˈhɑːdˌbæk) n. 1. a book with stiff covers. ~adj. 2. of or denoting a hardback.

hard-bitten adj. *Informal.* tough and realistic.

hardboard (ˈhɑːdˌbɔːd) n. stiff board made in thin sheets of compressed sawdust and woodchips.

hard-boiled adj. 1. (of an egg) boiled until solid. 2. *Informal.* tough and realistic.

hard cash n. money or payment in money, as opposed to payment by cheque, credit, etc.

hard copy n. computer output printed on paper.

hard core n. 1. the members of a group who most resist change. 2. broken stones used to form a foundation for a road. ~adj. **hard-core.** 3. (of pornography) depicting sexual acts in explicit detail.

hard disk n. *Computers.* an inflexible disk in a sealed container.

harden (ˈhɑːdᵊn) vb. 1. to make or become hard; freeze, stiffen, or set. 2. to make or become tough or unfeeling. 3. to make or become stronger or firmer. 4. *Commerce.* (of prices or a market) to cease to fluctuate.

hardened (ˈhɑːdᵊnd) adj. toughened; seasoned: *a hardened criminal.*

hard-headed adj. tough, realistic, or shrewd; not moved by sentiment.

hardhearted (ˌhɑːdˈhɑːtɪd) adj. unkind or intolerant.

hardihood (ˈhɑːdɪˌhʊd) n. courage or daring.

hard labour n. *Criminal law.* (formerly) the penalty of compulsory physical labour imposed in addition to a sentence of imprisonment.

hard line n. an uncompromising policy. —**ˌhardˈliner** n.

hardly (ˈhɑːdlɪ) adv. 1. scarcely; barely: *we*

hardly knew the family. **2.** *Ironic.* not at all: *he will hardly incriminate himself.* **3.** with difficulty: *I can hardly keep my eyes open.*

Usage. Since *hardly, scarcely,* and *barely* already have negative force, it is not necessary to use another negative in the same clause: *he had hardly had* (not *he hadn't hardly had*) *time to think.*

hard pad *n.* (in dogs) an abnormal increase in the thickness of the foot pads: a sign of distemper.

hard palate *n.* the bony front part of the roof of the mouth.

hard-pressed *adj.* **1.** in difficulties. **2.** closely pursued.

hard science *n.* one of the natural or physical sciences, such as physics, chemistry, or biology.

hard sell *n.* an aggressive insistent technique of selling.

hardship ('hɑːdʃɪp) *n.* **1.** conditions of life difficult to endure. **2.** something that causes suffering.

hard shoulder *n. Brit.* a surfaced verge running along the edge of a motorway for emergency stops.

hardtack ('hɑːd,tæk) *n.* a kind of hard saltless biscuit, formerly eaten by sailors.

hardware ('hɑːd,wɛə) *n.* **1.** metal tools or implements, esp. cutlery or cooking utensils. **2.** *Computers.* the physical equipment used in a computer system. **3.** heavy military equipment, such as tanks and missiles.

hard-wired *adj.* (of a circuit or instruction) permanently wired into a computer.

hardwood ('hɑːd,wʊd) *n.* the wood of a deciduous tree such as oak, beech, or ash.

hardy ('hɑːdɪ) *adj.* **-dier, -diest. 1.** having a tough constitution; robust. **2.** (of plants) able to live out of doors throughout the winter. —'**hardiness** *n.*

hare (hɛə) *n., pl.* **hares** *or* **hare. 1.** a mammal which is larger than a rabbit and has longer ears and legs. ~*vb.* **2.** (foll. by *off* or *after*) *Brit. informal.* to run fast or wildly.

harebell ('hɛə,bɛl) *n.* a blue bell-shaped flower.

harebrained ('hɛə,breɪnd) *adj.* foolish; badly thought out: *harebrained schemes.*

harelip ('hɛə,lɪp) *n.* a slight split in the midline of the upper lip.

harem ('hɛərəm, hɑː'riːm) *n.* **1.** a Muslim man's wives and concubines collectively. **2.** the part of an Oriental house reserved for wives and concubines.

haricot bean *or* **haricot** ('hærɪkəʊ) *n.* a white edible bean, which can be dried.

hark (hɑːk) *vb.* to listen; pay attention: *Hark, the cocks are crowing.*

hark back *vb.* to return (to an earlier subject in speech or thought): *he keeps harking back to his music-hall days.*

harlequin ('hɑːlɪkwɪn) *n.* **1.** *Theatre.* a stock comic character, usually wearing a diamond-patterned multicoloured costume and a black mask. ~*adj.* **2.** in varied colours.

harlequinade (,hɑːlɪkwɪ'neɪd) *n.* **1.** *Theatre.* a play in which harlequin has a leading role. **2.** buffoonery.

harlot ('hɑːlət) *n.* a prostitute. —'**harlotry** *n.*

harm (hɑːm) *n.* **1.** physical, moral, or mental injury. ~*vb.* **2.** to injure physically, morally, or mentally.

harmful ('hɑːmfʊl) *adj.* causing or tending to cause harm; injurious.

harmless ('hɑːmlɪs) *adj.* not causing or tending to cause harm.

harmonic (hɑː'mɒnɪk) *adj.* **1.** of, producing, or characterized by harmony; harmonious. ~*n.* **2.** *Music.* overtone. ~See also **harmonics.** —**har'monically** *adv.*

harmonica (hɑː'mɒnɪkə) *n.* a small wind instrument in which reeds enclosed in a narrow oblong box are made to vibrate by blowing and sucking.

harmonics (hɑː'mɒnɪks) *n.* (*functioning as sing.*) the science of musical sounds.

harmonious (hɑː'məʊnɪəs) *adj.* **1.** (esp. of colours or sounds) fitting together well. **2.** agreeing. **3.** tuneful or melodious.

harmonium (hɑː'məʊnɪəm) *n.* a musical keyboard instrument in which air from pedal-operated bellows causes the reeds to vibrate.

harmonize *or* **-nise** ('hɑːmə,naɪz) *vb.* **1.** to sing or play in harmony, as with another singer or player. **2.** to make or become harmonious.

harmony ('hɑːmənɪ) *n., pl.* **-nies. 1.** *Music.* an agreeable combination of notes sounded simultaneously. **2.** agreement in action, opinion, or feeling. **3.** the way parts combine well together or into a whole.

harness ('hɑːnɪs) *n.* **1.** an arrangement of straps fitted to a horse so that it can be attached to a cart. **2.** something resembling this, for attaching something to a person's body: *a parachute harness.* **3. in harness.** at one's routine work. ~*vb.* **4.** to put a harness on (a horse or other animal). **5.** to control something in order to use its energy: *to harness the waves.*

harp (hɑːp) *n.* **1.** a large upright triangular stringed instrument played by plucking the strings with the fingers. ~*vb.* **2.** (foll. by *on*) to speak in a persistent and tedious manner (about a subject). —'**harpist** *n.*

harpoon (hɑː'puːn) *n.* **1.** a barbed missile attached to a long cord and hurled or fired when hunting whales, etc. ~*vb.* **2.** to spear with a harpoon.

harpsichord ('hɑːpsɪ,kɔːd) *n.* a stringed keyboard instrument, triangular in shape, with strings that are plucked mechanically.

harpy (ˈhɑːpɪ) *n., pl.* **-pies.** a cruel grasping woman.

harridan (ˈhærɪdᵊn) *n.* a scolding old woman; nag.

harrier[1] (ˈhærɪə) *n.* **1.** a cross-country runner. **2.** a smallish hound used originally for hare-hunting.

harrier[2] (ˈhærɪə) *n.* a bird of prey with broad wings and long legs and tail.

harrow (ˈhærəʊ) *n.* **1.** an implement used to break up clods of soil. ~*vb.* **2.** to draw a harrow over (land).

harrowing (ˈhærəʊɪŋ) *adj.* very distressing.

harry (ˈhærɪ) *vb.* **-rying, -ried.** to harass; worry.

harsh (hɑːʃ) *adj.* **1.** rough or grating to the senses. **2.** stern, severe, or cruel: *harsh punishment.* —ˈ**harshly** *adv.* —ˈ**harshness** *n.*

hart (hɑːt) *n., pl.* **harts** *or* **hart.** the male of the deer, esp. the red deer.

hartebeest (ˈhɑːtɪˌbiːst) *n.* a large African antelope with curved horns and a fawn-coloured coat.

harum-scarum (ˌhɛərəmˈskɛərəm) *adj.* **1.** reckless. ~*adv.* **2.** recklessly. ~*n.* **3.** an impetuous person.

harvest (ˈhɑːvɪst) *n.* **1.** the gathering of a ripened crop. **2.** the crop itself. **3.** the season for gathering crops. **4.** the product of an effort or action. ~*vb.* **5.** to gather (a ripened crop).

harvester (ˈhɑːvɪstə) *n.* **1.** a harvesting machine, esp. a combine harvester. **2.** a person who harvests.

harvest moon *n.* the full moon occurring nearest to the autumn equinox.

harvest mouse *n.* a very small reddish-brown mouse that lives in cornfields or hedgerows.

has (hæz) *vb.* third person singular of the present tense of **have.**

has-been *n. Informal.* a person who is no longer popular or successful.

hash[1] (hæʃ) *n.* **1.** a dish of diced cooked meat, vegetables, etc., reheated: *cornbeef hash.* **2.** a reworking of old material. **3. make a hash of.** *Informal.* to mess up or destroy. **4. settle someone's hash.** *Informal.* to subdue or silence someone.

hash[2] (hæʃ) *n. Slang.* short for **hashish.**

hashish (ˈhæʃiːʃ, -ɪʃ) *n.* a drug made from the dried flower tops of the hemp plant, smoked for its intoxicating effects.

hasn't (ˈhæzᵊnt) has not.

hasp (hɑːsp) *n.* a metal fastening consisting of a hinged strap with a slot that fits over a staple and is secured by a pin, bolt, or padlock.

hassle (ˈhæsᵊl) *Informal.* ~*n.* **1.** a great deal of trouble. **2.** a prolonged argument. ~*vb.* **3.** to cause annoyance or trouble to (someone); harass.

hassock (ˈhæsək) *n.* a firm upholstered cushion for kneeling on in church.

haste (heɪst) *n.* **1.** speed, esp. in an action. **2.** the act of hurrying in a careless manner. **3. make haste.** to hurry; rush. ~*vb.* **4.** *Poetic.* to hasten.

hasten (ˈheɪsᵊn) *vb.* **1.** to hurry or cause to hurry; rush. **2.** to be anxious (to say something).

hasty (ˈheɪstɪ) *adj.* **-tier, -tiest. 1.** rapid; swift; quick. **2.** too quick; rash. —ˈ**hastily** *adv.*

hat (hæt) *n.* **1.** a head covering, esp. one with a brim and a shaped crown. **2.** *Informal.* a role or capacity: *I'm wearing my teacher's hat today.* **3. keep something under one's hat.** to keep something secret. **4. pass the hat round.** to collect money for a cause. **5. take off one's hat to someone.** to admire or congratulate someone.

hatband (ˈhætˌbænd) *n.* a band or ribbon around the base of the crown of a hat.

hatch[1] (hætʃ) *vb.* **1.** to cause (the young of various animals, esp. birds) to emerge from the egg or (of young birds, etc.) to emerge from the egg. **2.** (of eggs) to break and release the young animal within. **3.** to contrive or devise (a plot).

hatch[2] (hætʃ) *n.* **1.** a covering for a hatchway. **2. a.** short for **hatchway. b.** a door in an aircraft or spacecraft. **3.** Also called: **serving hatch.** an opening in a wall between a kitchen and a dining area.

hatch[3] (hætʃ) *vb. Drawing, engraving, etc.* to mark (a figure, etc.) with fine parallel or crossed lines to indicate shading. —ˈ**hatching** *n.*

hatchback (ˈhætʃˌbæk) *n.* a car that has a sloping rear with a single door that is lifted to open.

hatchet (ˈhætʃɪt) *n.* **1.** a short axe used for chopping wood, etc. **2.** (*modifier*) narrow and sharp: *a hatchet face.* **3. bury the hatchet.** to cease hostilities and become reconciled.

hatchet man *n. Informal.* a person who carries out unpleasant tasks on behalf of an employer.

hatchway (ˈhætʃˌweɪ) *n.* an opening in the deck of a vessel to provide access below.

hate (heɪt) *vb.* **1.** to dislike (someone or something) intensely; detest. **2.** to be unwilling (to do something): *I hate to bother you.* ~*n.* **3.** intense dislike. **4.** *Informal.* a person or thing that is hated: *ironing is my pet hate.*

hateful (ˈheɪtful) *adj.* causing or deserving hate; loathsome.

hatred (ˈheɪtrɪd) *n.* intense dislike; enmity.

hatter (ˈhætə) *n.* **1.** a person who makes and sells hats. **2. mad as a hatter.** eccentric.

hat trick *n.* **1.** *Cricket.* the achievement of a bowler in taking three wickets with three successive balls. **2.** any achievement of three successive goals, victories, etc.

hauberk ('hɔːbɜːk) n. a long sleeveless coat of mail.

haughty ('hɔːtɪ) adj. **-tier, -tiest.** having or showing arrogance. —'**haughtily** adv. —'**haughtiness** n.

haul (hɔːl) vb. **1.** to drag (something) with effort. **2.** to transport, as in a lorry. **3.** Naut. to alter the course of (a vessel). ~n. **4.** the act of dragging with effort. **5.** goods obtained by theft or robbery. **6.** a distance of travelling: a long haul.

haulage ('hɔːlɪdʒ) n. **1.** the business of transporting goods. **2.** a charge for transporting goods.

haulier ('hɔːljə) n. Brit. a person or firm that transports goods by road.

haulm (hɔːm) n. the stalks of beans, peas, potatoes, etc., collectively.

haunch (hɔːntʃ) n. **1.** the human hip or fleshy hindquarter of an animal. **2.** the leg and loin of an animal, used for food.

haunt (hɔːnt) vb. **1.** to visit (a person or place) in the form of a ghost. **2.** to recur to the memory or thoughts of: he was haunted by the fear of insanity. **3.** to visit (a place) frequently. ~n. **4.** a place visited frequently.

haunted ('hɔːntɪd) adj. **1.** (of a place) frequented or visited by ghosts. **2.** (of a person) obsessed or worried.

haunting ('hɔːntɪŋ) adj. poignantly sentimental; eerily evocative.

hautboy ('əʊbɔɪ) n. Archaic. an oboe.

haute couture ('əʊt kuːˈtʊə) n. high fashion. .

hauteur (əʊˈtɜː) n. pride; haughtiness.

have (hæv) vb. **has, having, had. 1.** to possess: he has two cars; he has dark hair. **2.** to receive, take, or obtain: she had a present; have a look. **3.** to hold in the mind: to have an idea. **4.** to possess a knowledge of: I have no German. **5.** to experience: to have a shock. **6.** to suffer from: to have a cold. **7.** to gain control of or advantage over: you have me on that point. **8.** Slang. to cheat or outwit: I've been had. **9.** to show: have mercy on me. **10.** to take part in; hold: to have a conversation. **11.** to cause, compel, or require to (be, do, or be done): have my shoes mended. **12.** (foll. by to) used to express compulsion or necessity: I had to run quickly to escape him. **13.** to eat or drink. **14.** Taboo slang. to have sexual intercourse with. **15.** to tolerate or allow: I won't have all this noise. **16.** to receive as a guest: to have people to stay. **17.** to be pregnant with or bear (offspring). **18.** (takes a past participle) used to form past tenses: I have gone; I had gone. **19. have had it.** Informal. **a.** to be exhausted or killed. **b.** to have lost one's last chance. **20. have it off.** Taboo, Brit. slang. to have

sexual intercourse. ~n. **21.** (pl.) Informal. people who have wealth, security, etc.: the haves and the have-nots. ~See also **have on, have out,** etc.

haven ('heɪvˀn) n. **1.** a place of safety. **2.** a harbour for shipping.

haven't ('hævˀnt) have not.

have on vb. **1.** to wear: she had a blue dress on. **2.** to have a commitment: what do you have on this afternoon? **3.** Informal. to trick or tease: he's having you on. **4.** to have (information, esp. when incriminating) about (a person): she's got something on him.

have out vb. to settle (a matter), esp. by fighting or by frank discussion: we decided to have it out.

haver ('heɪvə) vb. **1.** Scot. & N English dialect. to talk nonsense. **2.** to dither.

haversack ('hævəˌsæk) n. a canvas bag carried on the back or shoulder.

have up vb. to cause to appear for trial: he was had up for breaking and entering.

havoc ('hævək) n. **1.** Informal. confusion; chaos. **2.** destruction; devastation; ruin. **3. play havoc with.** to cause a great deal of damage or confusion to.

haw¹ (hɔː) n. the fruit of the hawthorn.

haw² (hɔː) vb. **hum and haw.** to hesitate in speaking.

hawk¹ (hɔːk) n. **1.** a bird of prey with short rounded wings and a long tail. **2.** a person who advocates warlike policies. ~vb. **3.** to hunt with falcons or hawks. —'**hawkish** adj. —'**hawk,like** adj.

hawk² (hɔːk) vb. to offer (goods) for sale, as in the street.

hawk³ (hɔːk) vb. **1.** to clear the throat noisily. **2.** to force (phlegm) up from the throat.

hawker ('hɔːkə) n. a person who travels from place to place selling goods.

hawk-eyed adj. having extremely keen eyesight.

hawser ('hɔːzə) n. Naut. a large heavy rope.

hawthorn ('hɔːˌθɔːn) n. a thorny tree or shrub with white or pink flowers and reddish fruits.

hay (heɪ) n. **1.** grass cut and dried as fodder. **2. hit the hay.** Slang. to go to bed. **3. make hay while the sun shines.** to take full advantage of an opportunity.

hay fever n. an allergic reaction to pollen, which causes sneezing, runny nose, and watery eyes.

haystack ('heɪˌstæk) or **hayrick** n. a large pile of hay built in the open and covered with thatch.

haywire ('heɪˌwaɪə) adj. **go haywire.** Informal. to stop functioning properly.

hazard ('hæzəd) n. **1.** exposure or vulnerability to injury, loss, etc. **2. at hazard.** at risk; in danger. **3.** a thing likely to cause injury, loss, etc. **4.** *Golf.* an obstacle such as a bunker. ~*vb.* **5.** to risk. **6.** to venture (a guess).

hazardous ('hæzədəs) *adj.* involving great risk.

haze (heɪz) *n.* **1.** *Meteorol.* reduced visibility as a result of condensed water vapour, dust, etc., in the air. **2.** confused or unclear understanding or feeling.

hazel ('heɪz²l) *n.* **1.** a shrub with edible rounded nuts. ~*adj.* **2.** greenish-brown: *hazel eyes.*

hazelnut ('heɪz²l,nʌt) *n.* the nut of a hazel shrub, which has a smooth shiny hard shell.

hazy ('heɪzɪ) *adj.* **-zier, -ziest.** misty; indistinct; vague. —'**hazily** *adv.* —'**haziness** *n.*

Hb haemoglobin.

HB *Brit.* (of pencil lead) hard-black: denoting a medium-hard lead.

H-bomb *n.* short for **hydrogen bomb.**

he (hiː; *unstressed* iː) *pron.* refers to: **1.** a male person or animal. **2.** a person or animal of unknown or unspecified sex: *a member may vote as he sees fit.* ~*n.* **3.** a male person or animal: *a he-goat.*

He *Chem.* helium.

HE His *or* Her Excellency.

head (hɛd) *n.* **1.** the upper or front part of the body that contains the brain, eyes, mouth, nose, and ears. **2.** something resembling a head in form or function, such as the top of a tool. **3.** the person commanding most authority within a group or an organization. **4.** the position of leadership or command. **5.** the most forward part of a thing; front: *the head of a queue.* **6.** the highest part of a thing; upper end: *the head of the pass.* **7.** the froth on the top of a glass of beer. **8.** aptitude, intelligence, and emotions: *she has a good head for figures.* **9.** (*pl.* **head**) a person or animal considered as a unit: *the show was two pounds per head; six hundred head of cattle.* **10.** *Bot.* the top part of a plant, where the leaves or flowers grow in a cluster. **11.** a culmination or crisis: *increasing anti-British feeling came to a head in the 1890's.* **12.** the pus-filled tip of a pimple or boil. **13.** the source of a river or stream. **14.** a headland or promontory: *Beachy Head.* **15.** the side of a coin that usually bears a portrait of the head of a monarch, etc. **16.** a headline or heading. **17.** pressure of water or steam in an enclosed space. **18.** part of a computer or tape recorder that can read, write, or erase information. **19.** *Informal.* short for **headmaster, headmistress,** *or* **head teacher. 20.** *Informal.* short for **headache. 21. give someone his head.** to allow someone greater freedom or responsibility. **22. go to one's head. a.** (of an alcoholic drink) to make one tipsy. **b.** to make one conceited: *his success has gone to his head.* **23. head over heels (in love).** very much (in love). **24. keep one's head.** to remain calm. **25.**

not make head nor tail of. not to understand (a problem, etc.). **26. off one's head.** *Slang.* insane or delirious. **27. on one's own head.** at a one's own risk. **28. over someone's head. a.** to a higher authority: *he went straight to the director, over the head of his immediate boss.* **b.** beyond a person's comprehension. **29. put (our, their,** etc.) **heads together.** *Informal.* to consult together. **30. turn someone's head.** to make someone conceited. ~*vb.* **31.** to be at the front or top of: *to head the field.* **32.** to be in charge of. **33.** (often foll. by *for*) to go or cause to go (towards): *where are you heading?* **34.** *Soccer.* to propel (the ball) by striking it with the head. **35.** to provide with a heading. ~See also **head off, heads.**

headache ('hɛd,eɪk) *n.* **1.** a continuous pain in the head. **2.** *Informal.* any cause of worry, difficulty, or annoyance.

head-banger *n.* *Slang.* **1.** a person who shakes his head violently to the beat of heavy-metal music. **2.** a crazy or stupid person.

headboard ('hɛd,bɔːd) *n.* a vertical board at the head of a bed.

headdress ('hɛd,drɛs) *n.* any head covering, esp. an ornate one.

headed ('hɛdɪd) *adj.* **1.** having a head or heads: *two-headed; bullet-headed.* **2.** having a heading: *headed notepaper.*

header ('hɛdə) *n.* **1.** *Soccer.* the action of striking a ball with the head. **2.** *Informal.* a headlong fall or dive.

headfirst ('hɛd'fɜːst) *adv.* **1.** with the head foremost; headlong. **2.** rashly.

headgear ('hɛd,gɪə) *n.* hats collectively.

head-hunting *n.* **1.** the practice among certain peoples of removing the heads of enemies they have killed and preserving them as trophies. **2.** (of companies) the practice of actively searching for new high-level personnel. —'**head-,hunter** *n.*

heading ('hɛdɪŋ) *n.* **1.** a title for a page, chapter, etc. **2.** a main division, as of a speech. **3.** *Mining.* a horizontal tunnel.

headland ('hɛdlənd) *n.* a narrow area of land jutting out into a sea.

headlight ('hɛd,laɪt) *or* **headlamp** *n.* a powerful light on the front of a vehicle.

headline ('hɛd,laɪn) *n.* **1.** a phrase in heavy large type at the top of a newspaper or magazine article indicating the subject. **2.** (*pl.*) the main points of a television or radio news broadcast.

headlong ('hɛd,lɒŋ) *adv., adj.* **1.** with the head foremost; headfirst. **2.** with great haste.

headmaster (,hɛd'mɑːstə) *or* (*fem.*) **headmistress** *n.* the principal of a school.

head off *vb.* **1.** to intercept and force to change direction: *to head off the stampede.* **2.** to prevent or forestall.

head-on *adv., adj.* **1.** front foremost: *a head-on collision.* **2.** with directness or without compromise: *in his usual head-on fashion.*

headphones ('hɛd,fəʊnz) *pl. n.* two small sound receivers held against the ears by a flexible metallic strap passing over the head, worn to listen to the radio or recorded music without other people hearing it.

headquarters (,hɛd'kwɔːtəz) *pl. n.* (*sometimes functioning as sing.*) any centre from which operations are directed, as in the police.

headroom ('hɛd,rʊm, -,ruːm) *or* **headway** *n.* the height of a bridge, room, etc.; clearance.

heads (hɛdz) *adv.* with the side of a coin uppermost which has a portrait of a head on it.

headship ('hɛdʃɪp) *n.* the position or state of being a leader, esp. the head teacher of a school.

headshrinker ('hɛd,ʃrɪŋkə) *n. Slang.* a psychiatrist.

headstall ('hɛd,stɔːl) *n.* the part of a bridle that fits round a horse's head.

head start *n.* an initial advantage in a competitive situation.

headstone ('hɛd,stəʊn) *n.* a memorial stone at the head of a grave.

headstrong ('hɛd,strɒŋ) *adj.* self-willed; obstinate.

head teacher *n.* the principal of a school.

headwaters ('hɛd,wɔːtəz) *pl. n.* the tributary streams of a river in the area in which it rises.

headway ('hɛd,weɪ) *n.* **1.** progress: *he made no headway with the problem.* **2.** motion forward: *the vessel made no headway.* **3.** same as **headroom.**

headwind ('hɛd,wɪnd) *n.* a wind blowing directly against the course of an aircraft or ship.

heady ('hɛdɪ) *adj.* **headier, headiest. 1.** (of an experience or period of time) extremely exciting. **2.** (of alcoholic drink) intoxicating. **3.** rash; impetuous.

heal (hiːl) *vb.* **1.** (of a wound) to repair by natural processes, as by scar formation. **2.** to restore (someone) to health. **3.** to repair (a rift in a personal relationship or an emotional wound). —'**healer** *n.* —'**healing** *n., adj.*

health (hɛlθ) *n.* **1.** the state of being bodily and mentally vigorous and free from disease. **2.** the general condition of body and mind: *in poor health.* **3.** the condition of an organization, society, etc.: *the economic health of a nation.*

health centre *n.* the surgery and offices of the doctors in a district.

health food *n.* vegetarian food, produced without chemicals, eaten for its benefit to health.

healthful ('hɛlθfʊl) *adj.* same as **healthy** (senses 1–3).

health visitor *n.* (in Britain) a nurse employed to visit people such as mothers of babies and the elderly in their homes.

healthy ('hɛlθɪ) *adj.* **healthier, healthiest. 1.** having or showing good health. **2.** likely to produce good health. **3.** sound: *the company's finances are not very healthy.* **4.** *Informal.* considerable: *a healthy sum.* —'**healthily** *adv.* —'**healthiness** *n.*

heap (hiːp) *n.* **1.** a collection of articles or mass of material gathered in a pile. **2.** (*often pl.*) *Informal.* a large number or quantity. ~*adv.* **3. heaps.** much: *he was heaps better.* ~*vb.* **4.** to collect into a pile. **5.** to give abundantly: *the critics heaped him with praise.*

hear (hɪə) *vb.* **hearing, heard** (hɜːd). **1.** to perceive (a sound) with the sense of hearing. **2.** to listen to: *did you hear what I said?* **3.** to be informed (of something); receive information (about something): *I heard you were leaving.* **4.** *Law.* to give a hearing to (a case). **5.** (foll. by *of*) to allow: *she wouldn't hear of it.* **6. hear from.** to receive a letter or telephone call from. **7. hear! hear!** an exclamation of approval. —'**hearer** *n.*

hearing ('hɪərɪŋ) *n.* **1.** the sense by which sound is perceived. **2.** an opportunity for someone to be listened to. **3.** the range within which sound can be heard; earshot. **4.** the investigation of a matter by a court of law.

hearing aid *n.* a small amplifier worn by a partially deaf person in or behind the ear to improve hearing.

hearken ('hɑːkən) *vb. Archaic.* to listen.

hearsay ('hɪə,seɪ) *n.* gossip; rumour.

hearse (hɜːs) *n.* a large car used to carry a coffin at a funeral.

heart (hɑːt) *n.* **1.** a hollow muscular organ whose contractions pump the blood throughout the body. **2.** this organ considered as the centre of emotions, esp. love. **3.** tenderness or pity: *you have no heart.* **4.** courage or spirit. **5.** the most central part or important part: *the heart of the matter.* **6.** (of vegetables, such as cabbage) the inner compact part. **7.** the breast: *she held him to her heart.* **8.** a shape representing the heart, with two rounded lobes at the top meeting in a point at the bottom. **9. a.** a red heart-shaped symbol on a playing card. **b.** a card with one or more of these symbols or (*when pl.*) the suit of cards so marked. **10. break someone's heart.** to cause someone to grieve very deeply, esp. by ending a love affair. **11. by heart.** by memorizing. **12. have a change of heart.** to experience a profound change of outlook or attitude. **13. have one's heart in one's mouth.** to be full of apprehension, excitement, or fear. **14. have the heart.** to have the necessary will or callousness (to do something): *I didn't have the heart to tell him.* **15. set one's heart on something.** to have something as one's ambition. **16. take heart.** to become encouraged. **17. take something to heart.** to take something seriously or be upset about something. **18. wear one's heart on one's sleeve.** to show one's feelings openly. **19. with all one's heart.** deeply and sincerely.

heartache ('hɑːtˌeɪk) *n.* intense anguish or mental suffering.

heart attack *n.* an instance of abnormal heart functioning causing sudden severe chest pain.

heartbeat ('hɑːtˌbiːt) *n.* one complete pulsation of the heart.

heartbreak ('hɑːtˌbreɪk) *n.* intense and overwhelming grief, esp. after the end of a love affair. —'**heartˌbreaking** *adj.* —'**heartˌbroken** *adj.*

heartburn ('hɑːtˌbɜːn) *n.* a burning sensation beneath the breastbone caused by inflammation of the gullet.

hearten ('hɑːt'n) *vb.* to make cheerful. —'**heartening** *adj.*

heart failure *n.* **1.** a condition in which the heart is unable to pump an adequate amount of blood to the tissues. **2.** sudden stopping of the heartbeat, resulting in death.

heartfelt ('hɑːtˌfelt) *adj.* sincerely and strongly felt.

hearth (hɑːθ) *n.* **1.** the floor of a fireplace. **2.** this as a symbol of the home.

heartless ('hɑːtlɪs) *adj.* unkind or cruel. —'**heartlessly** *adv.*

heart-rending *adj.* causing great mental pain and sorrow.

heart-searching *n.* examination of one's feelings or conscience.

heartstrings ('hɑːtˌstrɪŋz) *pl. n. Often facetious.* deep emotions: *a sentimental film that tugs at the heartstrings.*

heart-throb *n. Brit.* an object of infatuation, esp. a male film star or pop star.

heart-to-heart *adj.* **1.** (of a talk) concerned with personal problems or intimate feelings. ~*n.* **2.** an intimate conversation.

heart-warming *adj.* inspiring feelings of happiness.

heartwood ('hɑːtˌwʊd) *n.* the central core of dark hard wood in tree trunks, consisting of nonfunctioning tissue.

hearty ('hɑːtɪ) *adj.* **heartier, heartiest. 1.** warm and unreserved in manner. **2.** vigorous and heartfelt: *a hearty dislike.* **3.** (of a meal) substantial and nourishing. —'**heartily** *adv.*

heat (hiːt) *n.* **1.** the state of being hot. **2.** the energy transferred as a result of a difference in temperature. **3.** hot weather: *the heat of summer.* **4.** intensity of feeling: *the heat of rage.* **5.** the most intense part:

the heat of the battle. **6.** *Sport.* a preliminary eliminating contest in a competition. **7. in** *or* **on heat.** (of some female mammals) sexually receptive. ~*vb.* **8.** to make or become hot or warm. —'**heating** *n.*

heated ('hiːtɪd) *adj.* impassioned or highly emotional. —'**heatedly** *adv.*

heater ('hiːtə) *n.* a device for supplying heat.

heath (hiːθ) *n.* **1.** *Brit.* a large open area, usually with sandy soil, low shrubs, and heather. **2.** a low-growing evergreen shrub with small bell-shaped pink or purple flowers.

heathen ('hiːðən) *n., pl.* **-thens** *or* **-then. 1.** a person who does not acknowledge the God of Christianity, Judaism, or Islam; pagan. ~*adj.* **2.** of or relating to heathen peoples.

heather ('hɛðə) *n.* a low-growing evergreen shrub with clusters of small bell-shaped pinkish-purple or white flowers.

Heath Robinson (hiːθ 'rɒbɪns'n) *adj.* (of a mechanical device) absurdly complicated in design for a simple function.

heatstroke ('hiːtˌstrəʊk) *n.* same as **sunstroke.**

heat wave *n.* a spell of unusually hot weather.

heave (hiːv) *vb.* **heaving, heaved** *or* **hove. 1.** to lift or move (something) with a great effort. **2.** to throw (something heavy) with effort. **3.** to utter (a sigh) noisily or unhappily. **4.** to rise and fall heavily. **5.** (*p.t. & p.p.* **hove**) *Naut.* **a.** to move in a specified direction: *to heave in sight.* **b.** (of a vessel) to pitch or roll. **6.** to vomit or retch. ~*n.* **7.** the act of heaving.

heaven ('hɛv'n) *n.* **1.** the abode of God and the angels and of the righteous after death. **2.** (*pl.*) the sky. **3.** a place or state of happiness. **4.** (*sing. or pl.*) God or the gods, used in exclamatory phrases: *for heaven's sake.*

heavenly ('hɛv'nlɪ) *adj.* **1.** *Informal.* wonderful. **2.** of or occurring in space: *a heavenly body.* **3.** of or relating to heaven.

heave to *vb.* to stop (a vessel) or (of a vessel) to stop, as by trimming the sails.

heavy ('hɛvɪ) *adj.* **heavier, heaviest. 1.** of comparatively great weight. **2.** with a relatively high density: *lead is a heavy metal.* **3.** great in yield, quality, or quantity: *heavy traffic.* **4.** considerable: *heavy emphasis.* **5.** hard to fulfil: *heavy demands.* **6.** sad or dejected: *heavy at heart.* **7.** coarse or broad: *heavy features.* **8.** (of soil) with a high clay content. **9.** solid or fat: *a heavy build.* **10.** (of an industry) engaged in the large-scale manufacture of large objects or extraction of raw materials. **11.** serious; grave. **12.** *Mil.* (of guns, etc.) large and powerful. **13.** dull and uninteresting: *a heavy style.* **14.** excessive: *a heavy drinker.* **15.** (of cakes or bread) insufficiently

raised. **16.** deep and loud: *a heavy thud.*
17. (of music, literature, etc.) not immediately comprehensible or appealing. **18.**
Slang. (of rock music) having a powerful
beat. **19.** clumsy and slow: *heavy going.*
20. cloudy or overcast: *heavy skies.* **21.** not
easily digestible: *a heavy meal.* **22.** *Slang.*
using, or prepared to use, violence or brutality. *~n., pl.* **heavies. 23.** *Slang.* a large
strong man hired to threaten violence or
deter others by his presence. **24. a.** a villainous role. **b.** an actor who plays such a
part. **25. the heavies.** *Informal.* serious
newspapers. *~adv.* **26.** heavily: *time
hangs heavy.* —'**heavily** *adv.* —'**heaviness** *n.*

heavy-duty *n.* (*modifier*) made to withstand hard wear, bad weather, etc.

heavy-handed *adj.* clumsy; harsh and
oppressive.

heavy-hearted *adj.* sad; melancholy.

heavy hydrogen *n.* same as **deuterium.**

heavy metal *n.* a type of rock music with a
strong beat and amplified instrumental effects.

heavy water *n.* water formed of oxygen
and deuterium.

heavyweight ('hɛvɪˌweɪt) *n.* **1.** a professional boxer weighing over 175 pounds or
an amateur weighing over 81 kg. **2.** a professional wrestler weighing over 209
pounds or an amateur weighing over 220
pounds. **3.** a person who is heavier than
average. **4.** *Informal.* an important or highly influential person.

Heb. *or* **Hebr.** Hebrew (language).

Hebraic (hɪ'breɪk) *adj.* of or relating to the
Hebrews or their language or culture.

Hebrew ('hiːbruː) *n.* **1.** the ancient language of the Hebrews, revived as the official language of Israel. **2.** a member of an
ancient Semitic people; an Israelite. *~adj.*
3. of the Hebrews or their language.

heck (hɛk) *interj.* a mild exclamation of
surprise, irritation, etc.

heckle ('hɛkᵊl) *vb.* to interrupt (a public
speaker) with comments, questions, or
taunts. —'**heckler** *n.*

hectare ('hɛktɑː) *n.* one hundred ares
(10 000 square metres or 2.471 acres).

hectic ('hɛktɪk) *adj.* involving a great deal
of activity or excitement.

hector ('hɛktə) *vb.* **1.** to bully or torment.
~n. **2.** a blustering bully.

he'd (hiːd; *unstressed* iːd, hɪd, ɪd) he had *or*
he would.

hedge (hɛdʒ) *n.* **1.** a row of shrubs or
bushes forming a boundary. **2.** a barrier or
protection against something, esp. against
the risk of loss on an investment. *~vb.* **3.**
to avoid making a decision by making noncommittal statements. **4.** to guard against
the risk of loss in (a bet or disagreement),
by supporting the opposition as well.

hedgehog ('hɛdʒˌhɒg) *n.* a small mammal
with a protective covering of spines.

hedgehop ('hɛdʒˌhɒp) *vb.* **-hopping,
-hopped.** (of an aircraft) to fly close to the
ground, as in crop spraying. —'**hedgeˌhopping** *n.*

hedgerow ('hɛdʒˌrəʊ) *n.* a hedge of shrubs
or low trees bordering a field.

hedge sparrow *n.* a small brownish
songbird.

hedonism ('hiːdᵊˌnɪzəm, 'hɛd-) *n.* the doctrine that the pursuit of pleasure is the
most important thing in life. —'**hedonist**
n. —ˌhedon'**istic** *adj.*

heebie-jeebies ('hiːbɪ'dʒiːbɪz) *pl. n.* **the.**
Slang. nervous apprehension.

heed (hiːd) *n.* **1.** careful attention; notice:
take heed of these warnings. *~vb.* **2.** to
pay close attention to (a warning or piece of
advice).

heedless ('hiːdlɪs) *adj.* taking no notice;
careless or thoughtless. —'**heedlessly**
adv.

heehaw (ˌhiː'hɔː) *interj.* a representation of
the braying sound of a donkey.

heel[1] (hiːl) *n.* **1.** the back part of the foot.
2. the part of a stocking or sock designed to
fit the heel. **3.** the outer part of a shoe
underneath the heel. **4.** *Slang.* a contemptible person. **5. at one's heels.** following
closely behind one. **6. cool** *or* **kick one's
heels.** to be kept waiting. **7. down at heel.**
shabby. **8. take to one's heels.** to run off.
9. to heel. under control, as a dog walking
by a person's heel. *~vb.* **10.** to repair or
replace the heel of (a shoe or boot).

heel[2] (hiːl) *vb.* (of a vessel) to lean over; list.

heelball ('hiːlˌbɔːl) *n.* **a.** a mixture of beeswax and lampblack used by shoemakers.
b. a similar substance used to take brass
rubbings.

hefty ('hɛftɪ) *adj.* **heftier, heftiest.** *Informal.* **1.** big and strong. **2.** bulky or heavy:
a hefty package. **3.** involving a large
amount of money: *a hefty fine.*

hegemony (hɪ'gɛmənɪ) *n., pl.* **-nies.** domination of one power or state within a
league, confederation, etc.

Hegira ('hɛdʒɪrə) *n.* the flight of Mohammed
from Mecca to Medina in 622 A.D.; the starting point of the Muslim era.

heifer ('hɛfə) *n.* a young cow.

height (haɪt) *n.* **1.** the vertical distance
from the bottom of something to the top. **2.**
the vertical distance of a place above sea
level. **3.** relatively great altitude. **4.** the
topmost point; summit. **5.** the period of
greatest intensity: *the height of the battle.*
6. an extreme example: *the height of rudeness.*

heighten ('haɪtᵊn) *vb.* to make or become
more intense. —'**heightened** *adj.*

height of land *n.* *U.S. & Canad.* a ridge of
high ground dividing two river basins.

heinous (ˈheɪnəs, ˈhiː-) *adj.* evil; atrocious.

heir (ɛə) *n.* the person legally succeeding to the property of a deceased person. —ˈ**heiress** *fem. n.*

heir apparent *n., pl.* **heirs apparent.** a person whose right to succeed to certain property cannot be defeated.

heirloom (ˈɛəˌluːm) *n.* an object that has been in a family for generations.

heir presumptive *n. Property law.* a person who expects to succeed to an estate but whose right may be defeated by the birth of an heir nearer in blood to the ancestor.

held (hɛld) *vb.* past of **hold**[1].

helical (ˈhɛlɪkᵊl) *adj.* of or like a helix; spiral.

helicopter (ˈhɛlɪˌkɒptə) *n.* an aircraft, propelled by rotating overhead blades, that is capable of hovering, vertical flight, and horizontal flight in any direction.

heliograph (ˈhiːlɪəˌgrɑːf) *n.* an instrument with mirrors and a shutter used for sending messages in Morse code by reflecting the sun's rays.

heliotrope (ˈhiːlɪəˌtrəʊp, ˈhɛljə-) *n.* a plant with small fragrant purple flowers.

heliport (ˈhɛlɪˌpɔːt) *n.* an airport for helicopters.

helium (ˈhiːlɪəm) *n.* a very light colourless odourless inert gas. Symbol: He

helix (ˈhiːlɪks) *n., pl.* **helices** *or* **helixes.** a spiral.

hell (hɛl) *n.* **1.** (in Christianity and some other religions) the place or state of eternal punishment of the wicked after death. **2.** (in various religions and cultures) the abode of the spirits of the dead. **3.** *Informal.* a situation that causes suffering or extreme difficulty: *war is hell.* **4. come hell or high water.** *Informal.* whatever difficulties may arise. **5. for the hell of it.** *Informal.* for the fun of it. **6. give someone hell.** *Informal.* **a.** to give someone a severe reprimand or punishment. **b.** to be a torment to someone. **7. hell for leather.** at great speed. **8. the hell.** *Informal.* **a.** used for emphasis in such phrases as **what the hell. b.** an expression of strong disagreement: *the hell I will.* ~*interj.* **9.** *Informal.* an exclamation of anger or surprise.

he'll (hiːl; *unstressed* iːl, hɪl, ɪl) he will *or* he shall.

hellbent (ˌhɛlˈbɛnt) *adj. Informal.* rashly intent: *hellbent on revenge.*

hellebore (ˈhɛlɪˌbɔː) *n.* a plant with showy flowers and poisonous parts.

Hellene (ˈhɛliːn) *n.* a Greek.

Hellenic (hɛˈlɛnɪk, -ˈliː-) *adj.* **1.** of the Greeks or their language. **2.** of or relating to ancient Greece during the classical period (776-323 B.C.).

Hellenism (ˈhɛlɪˌnɪzəm) *n.* **1.** the principles and ideals of classical Greek civilization. **2.**

the spirit or national character of the Greeks. —ˈ**Hellenist** *n.*

Hellenistic (ˌhɛlɪˈnɪstɪk) *adj.* of Greek civilization during the period 323-30 B.C..

hellfire (ˈhɛlˌfaɪə) *n.* the torment of hell, envisaged as eternal fire.

hellish (ˈhɛlɪʃ) *adj. Informal.* very unpleasant.

hello, hallo, *or* **hullo** (hɛˈləʊ, hə-; ˈhɛləʊ) *interj.* **1.** an expression of greeting or surprise. **2.** a call used to attract attention. ~*n., pl.* **-los. 3.** the act of saying "hello".

Hell's Angel *n.* a member of a motorcycle gang noted for their lawless behaviour.

helm (hɛlm) *n.* **1.** *Naut.* the wheel or entire apparatus by which a vessel is steered. **2. at the helm.** in a position of leadership or control. —ˈ**helmsman** *n.*

helmet (ˈhɛlmɪt) *n.* a piece of protective headgear worn by soldiers, policemen, firemen, divers, etc.

helot (ˈhɛlət, ˈhiː-) *n.* a serf or slave.

help (hɛlp) *vb.* **1.** to assist (someone to do something). **2.** to contribute to: *to help the relief operations.* **3.** to improve a situation: *crying won't help.* **4. a.** to refrain from: *we can't help wondering who he is.* **b.** to be responsible for: *I can't help it if it rains.* **5.** to serve (a customer). **6. help oneself.** to take something, esp. food or drink, for oneself, without being served. ~*n.* **7.** the act of helping. **8.** a person or thing that helps, esp. a farm servant or domestic servant. **9.** a remedy: *there's no help for it.* ~*interj.* **10.** used to ask for assistance. ~See also **help out.** —ˈ**helper** *n.*

helpful (ˈhɛlpfʊl) *adj.* giving help. —ˈ**helpfully** *adv.* —ˈ**helpfulness** *n.*

helping (ˈhɛlpɪŋ) *n.* a single portion of food.

helpless (ˈhɛlplɪs) *adj.* **1.** unable to manage independently. **2.** made weak: *they were helpless from giggling.*

helpline (ˈhɛlpˌlaɪn) *n.* a telephone line set aside for callers to contact an organization for help with a problem.

helpmate (ˈhɛlpˌmeɪt) *or* **helpmeet** (ˈhɛlpˌmiːt) *n.* a companion and helper, esp. a spouse.

help out *vb.* to assist (someone) by sharing the burden or cost of something.

helter-skelter (ˈhɛltəˈskɛltə) *adj.* **1.** haphazard or careless. ~*adv.* **2.** in a haphazard or careless manner. ~*n.* **3.** *Brit.* a high spiral slide at a fairground.

hem[1] (hɛm) *n.* **1.** the bottom edge of a garment, folded under and stitched down. ~*vb.* **hemming, hemmed. 2.** to provide (a garment) with a hem. ~See also **hem in.**

hem[2] (hɛm) *n.* **1.** a representation of the sound of clearing the throat, used to gain attention. ~*vb.* **hemming, hemmed. 2.** to utter this sound. **3. hem and haw.** to hesitate in speaking.

he-man *n., pl.* **-men.** *Informal.* a strongly built muscular man.

hemi- *prefix.* half: *hemisphere.*

hem in *vb.* to enclose or confine (someone).

hemipterous (hɪˈmɪptərəs) *adj.* of an order of insects with sucking or piercing mouth-parts.

hemisphere (ˈhɛmɪˌsfɪə) *n.* one half of a sphere, esp. of the earth (**northern and southern hemisphere**) or of the brain. —**hemispherical** (ˌhɛmɪˈsfɛrɪkᵊl) *adj.*

hemline (ˈhɛmˌlaɪn) *n.* the level to which the hem of a skirt or dress hangs.

hemlock (ˈhɛmˌlɒk) *n.* a poisonous drug derived from a plant with spotted stems and small white flowers.

hemp (hɛmp) *n.* **1.** an Asian plant with tough fibres. **2.** the fibre of this plant, used to make canvas and rope. **3.** a narcotic drug obtained from this plant. —**hempen** *adj.*

hen (hɛn) *n.* the female of any bird, esp. of the domestic fowl.

hence (hɛns) *adv.* **1.** for this reason; therefore. **2.** from this time: *a year hence.* **3.** *Archaic.* from here.

henceforth (ˈhɛnsˈfɔːθ) *or* **henceforward** *adv.* from now on.

henchman (ˈhɛntʃmən) *n., pl.* **-men.** a faithful attendant or supporter.

henge (hɛndʒ) *n.* a circular monument, often containing a circle of stones, dating from the Neolithic and Bronze Ages.

henna (ˈhɛnə) *n.* **1.** a reddish dye, obtained from a shrub or tree of Asia and N Africa which is used to colour hair. ~*vb.* **2.** to dye (the hair) with henna.

hen party *n. Informal.* a party at which only women are present.

henpecked (ˈhɛnˌpɛkt) *adj.* (of a man) harassed by the persistent nagging of his wife.

henry (ˈhɛnrɪ) *n., pl.* **-ry, -ries,** *or* **-rys.** the derived SI unit of electric inductance. Symbol: H

hepatic (hɪˈpætɪk) *adj.* of the liver.

hepatitis (ˌhɛpəˈtaɪtɪs) *n.* inflammation of the liver.

heptagon (ˈhɛptəgən) *n.* a polygon with seven sides. —**heptagonal** (hɛpˈtægənᵊl) *adj.*

heptathlon (hɛpˈtæθlɒn) *n.* an athletic contest for women in which athletes compete in seven different events: 100 m hurdles, shot put, high jump, 200 m, long jump, javelin, and 800 m.

her (hɜː; *unstressed* hə, ə) *pron.* refers to: **1.** a female person or animal: *he loves her.* **2.** things personified as feminine, such as ships and nations. ~*det.* **3.** of, belonging to, or associated with her: *her hair.*

herald (ˈhɛrəld) *n.* **1.** a person who announces important news. **2.** *Often literary.*

a forerunner. ~*vb.* **3.** to precede: *his rise to power heralded the end of the liberal era.* **4.** to announce publicly. —**heraldic** (hɛˈrældɪk) *adj.*

heraldry (ˈhɛrəldrɪ) *n., pl.* **-ries.** the study of coats of arms, the tracing of genealogies, etc.

herb (hɜːb) *n.* **1.** a plant whose parts above ground die back at the end of the growing season. **2.** an aromatic plant, such as parsley or rosemary, that is used in cookery and medicine. —**herbal** *adj.* —**herby** *adj.*

herbaceous (hɜːˈbeɪʃəs) *adj.* designating plants that are fleshy rather than woody.

herbaceous border *n.* a flower bed that contains perennials rather than annuals.

herbage (ˈhɜːbɪdʒ) *n.* herbaceous plants collectively, esp. those on which animals graze.

herbalist (ˈhɜːbᵊlɪst) *n.* a person who grows or specializes in the use of medicinal herbs.

herbicide (ˈhɜːbɪˌsaɪd) *n.* a chemical that destroys plants, esp. weeds.

herbivore (ˈhɜːbɪˌvɔː) *n.* an animal that feeds on plants. —**herbivorous** (hɜːˈbɪvərəs) *adj.*

herculean (ˌhɜːkjʊˈliːən) *adj.* **1.** (of a task) requiring tremendous effort or strength. **2.** resembling Hercules, hero of classical myth, in strength or courage.

herd (hɜːd) *n.* **1.** a large group of mammals, esp. cattle living and feeding together. **2.** *Often disparaging.* a large group of people. ~*vb.* **3.** to collect or be collected into or as if into a herd.

herd instinct *n. Psychol.* the inborn tendency to associate with others and follow the group's behaviour.

herdsman (ˈhɜːdzmən) *n., pl.* **-men.** *Chiefly Brit.* a man who looks after a herd of animals.

here (hɪə) *adv.* **1.** in, at, or to this place, point, case, or respect: *we come here every summer.* **2. here and there.** at several places in or throughout an area. **3. here's to.** a formula used in proposing a toast. **4. neither here nor there.** of no relevance. ~*n.* **5.** this place: *they leave here tonight.*

hereabouts (ˈhɪərəˌbaʊts) *or* **hereabout** *adv.* in this region.

hereafter (ˌhɪərˈɑːftə) *adv.* **1.** *Formal or law.* in a subsequent part of this document, matter or case. **2.** at some time in the future. ~*n.* **3. the. a.** life after death. **b.** the future.

hereby (ˌhɪəˈbaɪ) *adv.* (used in official statements and documents) by means of or as a result of this.

hereditable (hɪˈrɛdɪtəbᵊl) *adj.* same as **heritable.**

hereditary (hɪˈrɛdɪtrɪ) *adj.* **1.** transmitted genetically from one generation to another. **2.** *Law.* descending to succeeding generations by inheritance.

heredity (hɪ'redɪtɪ) n., pl. -ties. the transmission from one generation to another of genetic factors that determine individual characteristics.

herein (,hɪər'ɪn) adv. Formal or law. in this place, matter, or document.

hereinafter (,hɪərɪn'ɑːftə) adv. Formal or law. from this point on in this document, matter, or case.

hereof (,hɪər'ɒv) adv. Formal or law. of or concerning this.

heresy ('herəsɪ) n., pl. -sies. 1. an opinion contrary to the principles of a religion. 2. any belief thought to be contrary to official or established theory.

heretic ('herətɪk) n. 1. Now chiefly R.C. Church. a person who maintains beliefs contrary to the established teachings of the Church. 2. a person who holds unorthodox opinions in any field. —**heretical** (hɪ'retɪk°l) adj.

hereto (,hɪə'tuː) adv. Formal or law. to this place, matter, or document.

heretofore (,hɪətʊ'fɔː) adv. Formal or law. until now.

hereupon (,hɪərə'pɒn) adv. following immediately after this; at this stage.

herewith (,hɪə'wɪð, -'wɪθ) adv. Formal. together with this: we send you herewith your statement of account.

heritable ('herɪtəb°l) adj. capable of being inherited.

heritage ('herɪtɪdʒ) n. 1. something inherited at birth. 2. anything that has been transmitted from the past or handed down by tradition. 3. the evidence of the past, such as historical sites, considered as the inheritance of present-day society.

hermaphrodite (hɜː'mæfrə,daɪt) n. an animal, flower, or person that has both male and female reproductive organs. —**hermaphroditic** (hɜː,mæfrə'dɪtɪk) adj.

hermetic (hɜː'metɪk) adj. sealed so as to be airtight. —**her'metically** adv.

hermit ('hɜːmɪt) n. a person living in solitude, esp. for religious reasons.

hermitage ('hɜːmɪtɪdʒ) n. 1. the dwelling of a hermit. 2. any retreat.

hermit crab n. a small crab that lives in empty shells of other shellfish.

hernia ('hɜːnɪə) n. protrusion of an organ or part through the lining of the body cavity in which it is normally situated.

hero ('hɪərəʊ) n., pl. -roes. 1. a man distinguished by exceptional courage, nobility, etc. 2. a man who is idealized for possessing superior qualities in any field. 3. the principal male character in a novel, play, etc.

heroic (hɪ'rəʊɪk) adj. 1. of, like, or befitting a hero. 2. courageous but desperate. 3. treating of heroes and their deeds. —**he'roically** adv.

heroics (hɪ'rəʊɪks) pl. n. extravagant or melodramatic language or behaviour.

heroin ('herəʊɪn) n. a highly addictive narcotic derived from morphine.

heroine ('herəʊɪn) n. 1. a woman distinguished by exceptional courage, nobility, etc. 2. a woman who is idealized for possessing superior qualities in any field. 3. the principal female character in a novel, play, etc.

heroism ('herəʊ,ɪzəm) n. the state or quality of being a hero.

heron ('herən) n. a wading bird with a long neck and grey or white plumage.

heronry ('herənrɪ) n., pl. -ries. a colony of breeding herons.

hero worship n. admiration for heroes or idealized persons.

herpes ('hɜːpiːz) n. any of several inflammatory diseases of the skin.

herpes simplex ('sɪmpleks) n. an acute viral disease causing clusters of watery blisters.

herpes zoster ('zɒstə) n. same as **shingles**.

Herr (heə) n., pl. **Herren** ('herən). a German title of address equivalent to Mr.

herring ('herɪŋ) n., pl. -rings or -ring. an important food fish of northern seas, with a long silver-coloured body.

herringbone ('herɪŋ,bəʊn) n. a pattern consisting of rows of short parallel strokes slanting in alternate directions to form a series of zigzags.

herring gull n. a common gull that has a white plumage with black-tipped wings.

hers (hɜːz) pron. 1. something belonging to her: hers is the nicest dress; that cat is hers. 2. of hers. belonging to her.

herself (hə'self) pron. 1. a. the reflexive form of she or her: she taught herself to type. b. (used for emphasis): the queen herself signed. 2. her normal self: she looks herself again after the operation. Usage. see **myself**.

Herts (hɑːts) Hertfordshire.

hertz (hɜːts) n., pl. **hertz**. the derived SI unit of frequency.

he's he is or he has.

hesitant ('hezɪt°nt) adj. wavering, hesitating, or irresolute. —**'hesitancy** n.

hesitate ('hezɪ,teɪt) vb. 1. to be slow in acting; be uncertain. 2. to be reluctant (to do something): I hesitate to use the word "squandered". 3. to stammer or pause in speaking. —,hesi'tation n.

hessian ('hesɪən) n. a coarse jute fabric similar to sacking.

hetero- combining form. other, another, or different: heterosexual.

heterodox ('hetərəʊ,dɒks) adj. at variance with established or accepted doctrines or beliefs. —**'hetero,doxy** n.

heterodyne ('hɛtərəʊˌdaɪn) *Electronics.* ~*vb.* **1.** to combine (two alternating signals) so as to produce two signals with frequencies corresponding to the sum and the difference of the original frequencies. ~*adj.* **2.** produced or operating by heterodyning two signals.

heterogeneous (ˌhɛtərəʊ'dʒiːnɪəs) *adj.* composed of unrelated parts. —**heterogeneity** (ˌhɛtərəʊdʒɪ'niːɪtɪ) *n.*

heteromorphic (ˌhɛtərəʊ'mɔːfɪk) *adj. Biol.* **1.** differing from the normal form. **2.** (esp. of insects) having different forms at different stages of the life cycle. —**heteromorphism** *n.*

heterosexual (ˌhɛtərəʊ'sɛksjʊəl) *n.* **1.** a person who is sexually attracted to members of the opposite sex. ~*adj.* **2.** (of a person) sexually attracted to members of the opposite sex. **3.** (of a sexual relationship) between a man and a woman. —**heteroˌsexuˈality** *n.*

het up *adj. Informal.* angry; excited: *don't get het up.*

heuristic (hjʊə'rɪstɪk) *adj.* (of a method of teaching) allowing students to learn things for themselves by trial and error.

hew (hjuː) *vb.* **hewing, hewed, hewed** *or* **hewn. 1.** to strike (stone or wood) with cutting blows, as with an axe. **2.** to carve (something) from a substance: *huge figures hewn out of stone.*

hex (hɛks) *n.* **a.** short for **hexadecimal notation. b.** (*as modifier*): *hex code.*

hexa- *or before a vowel* **hex-** *combining form.* six: *hexameter.*

hexadecimal notation (ˌhɛksə'dɛsɪməl) *n.* a number system with a base of 16, the numbers 10-15 being represented by the letters A-F.

hexagon ('hɛksəgən) *n. Geom.* a plane shape with six sides. —**hexˈagonal** *adj.*

hexagram ('hɛksəˌgræm) *n. Geom.* a star formed by extending the sides of a regular hexagon to meet at six points.

hexameter (hɛk'sæmɪtə) *n. Prosody.* a verse line consisting of six metrical feet.

hey (heɪ) *interj.* **1.** an expression indicating surprise, dismay, discovery, etc. **2. hey presto.** an exclamation used by conjurers at the climax of a trick.

heyday ('heɪˌdeɪ) *n.* the time of most power, popularity, or vigour: *he was a bit of a heart-throb in his heyday.*

Hf *Chem.* hafnium.

Hg *Chem.* mercury.

HGV (in Britain) heavy goods vehicle.

HH 1. His (*or* Her) Highness. **2.** His Holiness (title of the Pope).

hi (haɪ) *interj. Informal.* hello.

HI Hawaii.

hiatus (haɪ'eɪtəs) *n., pl.* **-tuses** *or* **-tus.** a break or interruption in continuity.

hiatus hernia *n.* protrusion of the stomach through the diaphragm at the hole for the gullet.

hibernate ('haɪbəˌneɪt) *vb.* (of some animals) to pass the winter in a dormant condition. —ˌhiberˈnation *n.*

Hibernia (haɪ'bɜːnɪə) *n. Poetic.* Ireland. —**Hiˈbernian** *adj., n.*

hibiscus (hɪ'bɪskəs) *n., pl.* **-cuses.** a plant with large brightly coloured flowers.

hiccup ('hɪkʌp) *n.* **1.** a spasm of the diaphragm producing a sudden breathing in of air resulting in a characteristic sharp sound. **2.** (*pl.*) the state of having such spasms. **3.** *Informal.* a minor difficulty. ~*vb.* **-cuping, -cuped** *or* **-cupping, -cupped. 4.** to make a hiccup or hiccups. ~Also: **hiccough** ('hɪkʌp).

hick (hɪk) *n. Informal, chiefly U.S. & Canad.* an unsophisticated country person.

hickory ('hɪkərɪ) *n., pl.* **-ries. 1.** a North American tree with edible nuts. **2.** the hard wood of this tree.

hidden ('hɪd'n) *vb.* **1.** the past participle of **hide¹.** ~*adj.* **2.** concealed or obscured: *a hidden meaning.*

hide¹ (haɪd) *vb.* **hiding, hid, hidden** *or* **hid. 1.** to conceal (oneself or an object) from view or discovery: *to hide from the police.* **2.** to obscure: *clouds hid the sun.* **3.** to keep (information or one's feelings) secret. ~*n.* **4.** *Brit.* a place of concealment, disguised to appear as part of its surrounding, used by hunters, birdwatchers, etc.

hide² (haɪd) *n.* the skin of an animal, either tanned or raw.

hide-and-seek *n.* a game in which one player covers his eyes while the others hide, and he then tries to find them.

hideaway ('haɪdəˌweɪ) *n.* a hiding place or secluded spot.

hidebound ('haɪdˌbaʊnd) *adj.* restricted by petty rules or a conservative attitude.

hideous ('hɪdɪəs) *adj.* extremely ugly or unpleasant.

hide-out *n.* a hiding place.

hiding¹ ('haɪdɪŋ) *n.* **1.** a state of concealment: *in hiding.* **2. hiding place.** a place of concealment.

hiding² ('haɪdɪŋ) *n. Informal.* a flogging; beating.

hie (haɪ) *vb.* **hieing** *or* **hying, hied.** *Archaic or poetic.* to hurry.

hierarchy ('haɪəˌrɑːkɪ) *n., pl.* **-chies. 1.** a system of persons or things arranged in a graded order. **2. the hierarchy.** the people in power in any organization. —ˌhierˈarchical *adj.*

hieroglyphic (ˌhaɪərə'glɪfɪk) *adj.* **1.** of or relating to a form of writing using picture symbols, as used in ancient Egypt. ~*n. also* **hieroglyph. 2.** a symbol that is difficult to decipher. **3.** a picture or symbol representing an object, idea, or sound.

hieroglyphics (ˌhaɪərəˈglɪfɪks) n. (functioning as sing. or pl.) 1. a form of writing, as used in ancient Egypt, in which pictures or symbols are used to represent objects, ideas, or sounds. 2. writing that is difficult to decipher.

hi-fi (ˈhaɪˌfaɪ) n. Informal. 1. a set of high-quality sound-reproducing equipment. 2. a. short for **high fidelity**. b. (as modifier): hi-fi equipment.

higgledy-piggledy (ˈhɪgºldɪˈpɪgºldɪ) adj., adv. Informal. in a jumble.

high (haɪ) adj. 1. being a relatively great distance from top to bottom: a high building. 2. situated at a relatively great distance above sea level: a high plateau. 3. being a specified distance from top to bottom: three feet high. 4. coming up to a specified level: knee-high. 5. being at its peak: high noon. 6. of greater than average height: a high collar. 7. greater than usual in intensity or amount: a high wind; high mileage. 8. (of a sound) acute in pitch. 9. (of food) slightly decomposed, regarded as enhancing the flavour of game. 10. very important: the high priestess. 11. intensely emotional: high drama. 12. elated; cheerful: high spirits. 13. Informal. under the influence of alcohol or drugs. 14. luxurious or extravagant: high life. 15. advanced in complexity: high finance. 16. formal and elaborate: High Mass. 17. **high and dry.** stranded; destitute. 18. **high and mighty.** Informal. arrogant. 19. **high opinion.** a favourable opinion. ~adv. 20. at or to a height: flying high. ~n. 21. a high level. 22. same as **anticyclone.** 23. **on a high.** Informal. a. in a state of intoxication by alcohol or drugs. b. in a state of great excitement and happiness.

highball (ˈhaɪˌbɔːl) n. Chiefly U.S. a long iced drink consisting of spirits with soda water, etc.

highbrow (ˈhaɪˌbraʊ) Often disparaging. ~n. 1. a person of scholarly tastes. ~adj. 2. appealing to highbrows.

highchair (ˈhaɪˌtʃɛə) n. a long-legged chair with a table-like tray, used for a child at mealtimes.

High Church n. 1. the movement within the Church of England stressing the importance of ceremony and ritual. ~adj. **High-Church.** 2. of or relating to this movement.

high commissioner n. the senior diplomatic representative sent by one Commonwealth country to another.

high country n. the. N.Z. sheep pastures in the foothills of the Southern Alps.

High Court n. (in England, Wales, Australia, and New Zealand) the supreme court dealing with civil law cases.

higher education n. education and training at colleges, universities, and polytechnics.

higher-up n. Informal. a person of higher rank.

highest common factor n. the largest number that divides equally into each member of a group of numbers.

high explosive n. an extremely powerful chemical explosive, such as TNT or gelignite.

highfalutin (ˌhaɪfəˈluːtɪn) adj. Informal. pompous or pretentious.

high fidelity n. a. the electronic reproduction of sound with little or no distortion. b. (as modifier): a high-fidelity amplifier.

high-flier or **high-flyer** n. 1. a person who is extremely ambitious. 2. a person of great ability in a career. —ˈhighˌflying adj.

high-flown adj. extravagant or pretentious: high-flown ideas.

high frequency n. a radio frequency lying between 30 and 3 megahertz.

High German n. the standard German language.

high-handed adj. tactlessly overbearing and inconsiderate. —ˌhigh-ˈhandedness n.

highjack (ˈhaɪˌdʒæk) vb., n. same as **hijack.**

high jump n. the. 1. an athletic event in which competitors have to jump over a high bar. 2. Brit. informal. a severe reprimand or punishment: you're for the high jump when your mother finds out.

Highland (ˈhaɪlənd) n. (modifier) of or denoting the Highlands, a mountainous region of NW Scotland. —ˈHighlander n.

Highland cattle n. cattle with shaggy reddish-brown hair and long horns.

Highland fling n. an energetic Scottish solo dance.

highlands (ˈhaɪləndz) n. relatively high ground.

high-level language n. a computer-programming language that is close to human language.

highlight (ˈhaɪˌlaɪt) n. 1. Also called: **high spot.** the most exciting or memorable part of something. 2. an area of the lightest tone in a painting or photograph. 3. (pl.) a lightened streak in the hair produced by bleaching. ~vb. 4. to bring emphasis to: this problem was highlighted in her book.

highly (ˈhaɪlɪ) adv. 1. extremely: highly disappointed. 2. with great approbation: they spoke highly of her.

highly strung or U.S. & Canad. **high-strung** adj. tense and easily upset.

High Mass n. a solemn and elaborate Mass.

high-minded adj. having high moral principles.

Highness (ˈhaɪnɪs) n. (preceded by Your, His, or Her) a title used to address or refer to a royal person.

high-pitched *adj.* (of a sound, esp. a voice) pitched high in tone.

high-powered *adj.* dynamic and energetic.

high-pressure *adj. Informal.* (of selling) persuasive in an aggressive and persistent manner.

high priest *n.* the head of a cult. —**high priestess** *fem. n.*

high-rise *adj.* of or relating to a building that has many storeys: *a high-rise block.*

high-risk *adj.* denoting a group or area that is particularly subject to a danger.

highroad (ˈhaɪˌrəʊd) *n.* a main road.

high school *n.* a secondary school.

high seas *pl. n.* the open seas, which are outside the authority of any one nation.

high season *n.* the most popular time of year at a holiday resort, etc.

high-spirited *adj.* vivacious, bold, or lively.

high tea *n. Brit.* an early evening meal consisting of a cooked dish, bread, cakes and tea.

high-tech *adj.* See **hi-tech.**

high-tension *n.* (*modifier*) carrying a relatively high voltage.

high tide *n.* the tide at its highest level.

high time *adv. Informal.* the latest possible time: *it's high time you left.*

high treason *n.* an act of treason directly affecting a sovereign or state.

high-water mark *n.* **1.** the level reached by sea water at high tide or a river in flood. **2.** the highest point of any process.

highway (ˈhaɪˌweɪ) *n.* **1.** a public road that everyone may use. **2.** *Chiefly U.S. & Canad.* a main road, esp. one that connects towns.

highwayman (ˈhaɪweɪmən) *n., pl.* **-men.** (formerly) a robber, usually on horseback, who held up travellers on public roads.

hijack *or* **highjack** (ˈhaɪˌdʒæk) *vb.* **1.** to seize control of or divert (a vehicle) while in transit: *to hijack an aircraft.* ~*n.* **2.** an instance of hijacking. —ˈhiˌjacker *or* ˈhighˌjacker *n.*

hike (haɪk) *vb.* **1.** to walk a long way in the country, usually for pleasure. **2.** to pull up; hitch up. **3.** (foll. by *up*) to raise (prices). ~*n.* **4.** a long walk. **5.** a rise in price. —ˈhiker *n.*

hilarious (hɪˈlɛərɪəs) *adj.* very funny. —hiˈlariously *adv.* —hilarity (hɪˈlærɪtɪ) *n.*

hill (hɪl) *n.* **1.** a natural elevation of the earth's surface, less high than a mountain. **2.** a heap or mound. **3.** an incline; slope. —ˈhilly *adj.*

hillbilly (ˈhɪlˌbɪlɪ) *n., pl.* **-lies. 1.** *Usually disparaging.* an unsophisticated person from the mountainous areas in the south-

eastern U.S. **2.** same as **country and western.**

hillock (ˈhɪlək) *n.* a small hill or mound.

hilt (hɪlt) *n.* **1.** the handle or shaft of a sword, dagger or knife. **2. to the hilt.** to the full: *he plays the role to the hilt.*

hilum (ˈhaɪləm) *n., pl.* **-la** (-lə). *Bot.* a scar on a seed marking its point of attachment to the seed vessel.

him (hɪm; *unstressed* ɪm) *pron.* refers to a male person or animal: *they needed him; she gave him an assignment.*

himself (hɪmˈsɛlf; *unstressed* ɪmˈsɛlf) *pron.* **1. a.** the reflexive form of *he* or *him*: *he introduced himself.* **b.** used for emphasis: *the king himself waved to me.* **2.** his normal self: *he seems himself once more.* **Usage.** see **myself.**

hind¹ (haɪnd) *adj.* **hinder, hindmost.** situated at the back: *a hind leg.*

hind² (haɪnd) *n., pl.* **hinds** *or* **hind.** the female of the deer, esp. the red deer.

hinder¹ (ˈhɪndə) *vb.* to get in the way of (someone or something).

hinder² (ˈhaɪndə) *adj.* situated at the back; posterior.

Hindi (ˈhɪndɪ) *n.* **1.** a language or group of dialects of N central India. **2.** a formal literary dialect of this language, the official language of India.

hindmost (ˈhaɪndˌməʊst) *adj.* furthest back; last.

hindquarters (ˈhaɪndˌkwɔːtəz) *pl. n.* the rear of a four-legged animal.

hindrance (ˈhɪndrəns) *n.* **1.** an obstruction or snag. **2.** the act of hindering.

hindsight (ˈhaɪndˌsaɪt) *n.* the ability to understand, after something has happened, what should have been done.

Hindu (ˈhɪnduː; hɪnˈduː) *n., pl.* **-dus. 1.** a person who practises Hinduism. ~*adj.* **2.** relating to Hinduism.

Hinduism (ˈhɪnduːˌɪzəm) *n.* the dominant religion of India, which involves the worship of many gods, a caste system, and belief in reincarnation.

Hindustani (ˌhɪnduːˈstɑːnɪ) *n.* a group of northern Indian languages that includes Hindi and Urdu.

hinge (hɪndʒ) *n.* **1.** a device for holding together two parts so that one can swing freely. ~*vb.* **2.** (foll. by *on*) to depend on: *the future of the company hinges on your decision.* **3.** to fit a hinge to (something). —**hinged** *adj.*

hinny (ˈhɪnɪ) *n., pl.* **-nies.** the offspring of a male horse and a female donkey.

hint (hɪnt) *n.* **1.** a suggestion given in an indirect or subtle manner. **2.** a helpful piece of advice. **3.** a small amount: *a hint of garlic.* ~*vb.* **4.** (sometimes foll. by *at*) to suggest indirectly: *this hints at the truth.*

hinterland (ˈhɪntəˌlænd) *n.* **1.** land lying

behind a coast or the shore of a river. **2.** an area near and dependent on a large city, esp. a port.

hip¹ (hɪp) *n.* either side of the body below the waist and above the thigh.

hip² (hɪp) *n.* the berry-like brightly coloured fruit of a rose bush. Also called: **rosehip.**

hip³ (hɪp) *interj.* an exclamation used to introduce cheers: *hip, hip, hurrah.*

hip⁴ (hɪp) *adj.* **hipper, hippest.** *Slang.* following the latest trends.

hip bath *n.* a portable bath in which the bather sits.

hipbone ('hɪpˌbəʊn) *n.* either of the two bones that form the sides of the pelvis.

hip-hop ('hɪpˌhɒp) *n.* a U.S. pop culture movement of the 1980s, comprising rap music, graffiti, and break dancing.

hippie *or* **hippy** ('hɪpɪ) *n.* (esp. during the 1960s) a person whose behaviour and dress imply a rejection of conventional values.

hippo ('hɪpəʊ) *n.*, *pl.* **-pos.** *Informal.* short for **hippopotamus.**

Hippocratic oath (ˌhɪpəʊ'krætɪk) *n.* an oath taken by a doctor to observe a code of medical ethics.

hippodrome ('hɪpəˌdrəʊm) *n.* **1.** a music hall, variety theatre, or circus. **2.** (in ancient Greece or Rome) an open-air course for horse and chariot races.

hippopotamus (ˌhɪpə'pɒtəməs) *n.*, *pl.* **-muses** *or* **-mi** (-ˌmaɪ). a very large mammal with thick wrinkled skin and short legs, which lives around the rivers of tropical Africa.

hippy¹ ('hɪpɪ) *adj.* **-pier, -piest.** *Informal.* having large hips.

hippy² ('hɪpɪ) *n.*, *pl.* **-pies.** same as **hippie.**

hipsters ('hɪpstəz) *pl. n. Brit.* trousers cut so that the top encircles the hips.

hire ('haɪə) *vb.* **1.** to acquire the temporary use of (a thing) or the services of (a person) in exchange for payment. **2.** to employ (a person) for wages. **3.** (foll. by *out*) to provide (something) or the services of (oneself or others) for payment. **4.** (foll. by *out*) *Chiefly Brit.* to pay independent contractors for (work to be done). ~*n.* **5.** the act of hiring. **6. for hire.** available to be hired.

hireling ('haɪəlɪŋ) *n. Disparaging.* a person who works only for money.

hire-purchase *n. Brit.* a system in which a buyer takes possession of merchandise on payment of a deposit and completes the purchase by paying a series of instalments while the seller retains ownership until the final instalment is paid.

hirsute ('hɜːsjuːt) *adj.* hairy.

his (hɪz; *unstressed* ɪz) *det.* **1.** of, belonging to, or associated with him: *his knee.* ~*pron.* **2.** something belonging to him: *his is on the left; that book is his.* **3. of his.** belonging to him.

Hispanic (hɪ'spænɪk) *adj.* **1.** of or derived from Spain or the Spanish. ~*n.* **2.** *U.S.* a U.S. citizen of Latin-American descent.

hiss (hɪs) *n.* **1.** a sound like that of a prolonged *s.* **2.** such a sound as an exclamation of contempt. ~*vb.* **3.** to utter a hiss. **4.** to express with a hiss: *she hissed her disapproval.* **5.** to show derision or anger towards (a speaker or performer) by hissing.

histamine ('hɪstəˌmiːn) *n.* a chemical compound released by the body tissues in allergic reactions.

histogram ('hɪstəˌɡræm) *n.* a statistical graph that represents the frequency of values of a quantity by vertical rectangles of varying heights and widths.

histology (hɪ'stɒlədʒɪ) *n.* the study of the tissues of an animal or plant.

historian (hɪ'stɔːrɪən) *n.* a person who writes or studies history.

historic (hɪ'stɒrɪk) *adj.* famous in history; significant: *a historic decision.*

Usage. A distinction is made between *historic* (important, significant) and *historical* (relating to history): *a historic decision; a historical perspective.*

historical (hɪ'stɒrɪkˀl) *adj.* **1.** occurring in history. **2.** based on history; *a historical novel.* **3.** belonging to or typical of the study of history: *historical methods.*

Usage. see **historic.**

historicism (hɪ'stɒrɪˌsɪzəm) *n.* **1.** the belief that natural laws govern historical events. **2.** excessive emphasis on history and past styles.

historicity (ˌhɪstə'rɪsɪtɪ) *n.* historical authenticity.

historiographer (hɪˌstɔːrɪ'ɒɡrəfə) *n.* a historian employed to write the history of a group or public institution. —**hiˌstori'ography** *n.*

history ('hɪstrɪ) *n.*, *pl.* **-ries.** **1.** a record or account of past events and developments. **2.** all that is preserved of the past, esp. in written form. **3.** the study of interpreting past events. **4.** the past events or previous experiences, of a place, thing, or person: *the house had a strange history.* **5.** a play that depicts historical events.

histrionic (ˌhɪstrɪ'ɒnɪk) *adj.* **1.** excessively dramatic: *histrionic gestures.* ~*n.* **2.** (*pl.*) melodramatic displays of temperament.

hit (hɪt) *vb.* **hitting, hit.** **1.** to deal a blow to (a person or thing). **2.** to come into violent contact with: *the car hit the tree.* **3.** to propel (a ball) by striking. **4.** *Cricket.* to score (runs). **5.** to affect (a person, place, or thing) adversely: *his illness hit him very hard.* **6.** to reach: *unemployment hit a new high.* **7. hit the bottle.** *Slang.* to start drinking excessive amounts of alcohol. **8. hit the road.** *Informal.* to set out on a journey. ~*n.* **9.** an impact or collision. **10.** a shot or blow that reaches its target. **11.** *Informal.* a person or thing that gains wide appeal: *she's a hit with everyone.* ~See also **hit off, hit on, hit out at.**

hit-and-run *adj.* denoting a motor-vehicle accident in which the driver leaves the scene without stopping to give assistance or inform the police.

hitch (hɪtʃ) *n.* **1.** a temporary or minor impediment. **2.** a knot that can be undone by pulling against the direction of the strain that holds it. ~*vb.* **3.** (foll. by *up*) to pull up (one's trousers, etc.) with a quick jerk. **4.** *Informal.* to obtain (a ride) by hitchhiking. **5.** to fasten with a knot or tie. **6. get hitched.** *Slang.* to get married.

hitchhike ('hɪtʃˌhaɪk) *vb.* to travel by obtaining free lifts in motor vehicles. —'**hitch**ˌ**hiker** *n.*

hi-tech *adj.* using sophisticated, esp. electronic technology.

hither ('hɪðə) *adv. Old-fashioned.* towards this place: *come hither.*

hitherto (ˌhɪðə'tuː) *adv.* until this time: *hitherto, there have been no problems.*

hit list *n. Informal.* **1.** a list of people to be murdered. **2.** a list of targets to be eliminated: *a hit list of pits to be closed.*

hit man *n.* a hired assassin.

hit off *vb.* **hit it off.** *Informal.* to have a good relationship with someone.

hit on *or* **upon** *vb.* to think of (an idea or a solution).

hit-or-miss *adj. Informal.* random; haphazard. Also: **hit-and-miss.**

hit out at *vb.* **1.** to direct blows forcefully and vigorously at (someone). **2.** to make a verbal attack upon (someone).

HIV human immunodeficiency virus.

hive (haɪv) *n.* **1.** a structure in which bees live. **2. hive of activity.** a place showing signs of great industry.

hive off *vb.* to transfer (profitable activities of a nationalized industry) back to private ownership.

hives (haɪvz) *n.* (*functioning as sing. or pl.*) *Pathol.* an allergic reaction in which itchy red or whitish raised patches develop on the skin.

HM Her (*or* His) Majesty.

HMI (in Britain) Her (*or* His) Majesty's Inspector; a government official who examines and supervises schools.

H.M.S. *or* **HMS** Her (*or* His) Majesty's Ship.

HMSO (in Britain) Her (*or* His) Majesty's Stationery Office.

HNC (in Britain) Higher National Certificate; a qualification recognized by many national technical and professional institutions.

HND (in Britain) Higher National Diploma;

a qualification in a technical subject equivalent to an ordinary degree.

Ho *Chem.* holmium.

hoar (hɔː) *adj. Archaic.* hoary.

hoard (hɔːd) *n.* **1.** an accumulated store of money, food, etc., hidden away for future use. ~*vb.* **2.** to gather or accumulate (money, food, etc.). —'**hoarder** *n.*

hoarding ('hɔːdɪŋ) *n.* a large board at the side of a road, used for displaying advertising posters.

hoarfrost ('hɔːˌfrɒst) *n.* a deposit of ice crystals formed on the ground by condensation at temperatures below freezing point.

hoarse (hɔːs) *adj.* having a husky voice, as through illness or too much shouting. —'**hoarsely** *adv.* —'**hoarseness** *n.*

hoary ('hɔːrɪ) *adj.* **hoarier, hoariest. 1.** having grey or white hair. **2.** ancient.

hoax (həʊks) *n.* **1.** a deception, esp. a practical joke. ~*vb.* **2.** to deceive or play a joke on (someone).

hob (hɒb) *n.* the flat top part of a cooking stove, or a separate flat surface, containing hotplates or burners.

hobble ('hɒbˁl) *vb.* **1.** to walk with a lame awkward movement. **2.** to fetter the legs of (a horse) in order to restrict its movement.

hobby ('hɒbɪ) *n., pl.* **-bies.** an activity pursued in one's spare time for pleasure or relaxation.

hobbyhorse ('hɒbɪˌhɔːs) *n.* **1.** a favourite topic: *on one's hobbyhorse.* **2.** a toy consisting of a stick with a figure of a horse's head at one end. **3.** a figure of a horse attached to a performer's waist in a morris dance.

hobgoblin (ˌhɒb'gɒblɪn) *n.* a mischievous goblin.

hobnail ('hɒbˌneɪl) *n. Old-fashioned.* **a.** a short nail with a large head for protecting the soles of heavy footwear. **b.** (*as modifier*): *hobnail boots.*

hobnob ('hɒbˌnɒb) *vb.* **-nobbing, -nobbed.** to socialize or talk informally: *hobnobbing with the aristocracy.*

hobo ('həʊbəʊ) *n., pl.* **-boes** *or* **-bos.** *Chiefly U.S. & Canad.* a tramp; vagrant.

Hobson's choice ('hɒbsˁnz) *n.* the choice of taking what is offered or nothing at all.

hock[1] (hɒk) *n.* the joint in the leg of a horse or similar animal that corresponds to the human ankle.

hock[2] (hɒk) *n.* a white wine from the German Rhine.

hock[3] (hɒk) *Informal.* ~*vb.* **1.** to pawn or pledge. ~*n.* **2. in hock. a.** in pawn. **b.** in prison. **c.** in debt.

hockey ('hɒkɪ) *n.* **1.** a game played on a field by two teams of 11 players who try to hit a ball into their opponents' goal using long sticks curved at the end. **2.** same as **ice hockey.**

hocus-pocus (ˈhəʊkəsˈpəʊkəs) n. Informal. trickery.

hod (hɒd) n. an open wooden box attached to a pole, for carrying bricks or mortar.

hodgepodge (ˈhɒdʒˌpɒdʒ) n. Chiefly U.S. & Canad. same as **hotchpotch**.

Hodgkin's disease (ˈhɒdʒkɪnz) n. a malignant disease that causes enlargement of the lymph nodes, spleen, and liver.

hoe (həʊ) n. 1. a long-handled implement used to loosen the soil or to weed. ~vb. **hoeing, hoed.** 2. to scrape or weed with a hoe.

hog (hɒg) n. 1. a castrated male pig. 2. U.S. & Canad. any mammal of the pig family. 3. Informal. a greedy person. 4. **go the whole hog.** Slang. to do something thoroughly or unreservedly. ~vb. **hogging, hogged.** 5. Slang. to take more than one's share of (something).

Hogmanay (ˌhɒgməˈneɪ) n. New Year's Eve in Scotland.

hogshead (ˈhɒgzˌhɛd) n. a large cask.

hogwash (ˈhɒgˌwɒʃ) n. nonsense.

ho-ho (ˈhəʊˈhəʊ) interj. a written representation of the sound of laughter.

hoick (hɔɪk) vb. to raise abruptly and sharply.

hoi polloi (ˈhɔɪ pəˈlɔɪ) n. the masses; the common people.

hoist (hɔɪst) vb. 1. to raise or lift up, esp. by mechanical means. ~n. 2. any apparatus or device for lifting things.

hoity-toity (ˌhɔɪtɪˈtɔɪtɪ) adj. Informal. arrogant or haughty.

hokonui (ˌhəʊkəˈnuːɪ) n. N.Z. illicit whisky.

hokum (ˈhəʊkəm) n. Slang, chiefly U.S. & Canad. 1. claptrap; bunk. 2. obvious sentimental material in a play or film.

hold¹ (həʊld) vb. **holding, held.** 1. to keep (an object or a person) with or within the hands or arms; clasp. 2. to support: to hold a drowning man's head above water. 3. to maintain or be maintained in a specified state: to hold firm. 4. to set aside or reserve: they will hold our tickets until tomorrow. 5. to restrain: hold that man until the police come. 6. to remain unbroken: that cable won't hold much longer. 7. (of the weather) to remain dry and bright. 8. to keep (the attention of): to hold an audience; to hold someone's attention. 9. to engage in or carry on: to hold a meeting. 10. to have the ownership or possession of: he holds a law degree; who's holding the ace? 11. to have responsibility for: to hold office. 12. to have the capacity for: the carton will hold eight books. 13. to be able to control the outward effects of drinking (alcohol): he can't hold his liquor. 14. to remain or cause to remain committed: hold him to his promise. 15. to claim: he holds that the theory is incorrect. 16. to remain valid or true: the old philosophies don't

hold nowadays. 17. to consider in a specified manner: I hold him very dear. 18. to defend successfully: hold the fort against the attack. 19. Music. to sustain the sound of (a note). ~n. 20. the act or a method of holding fast or grasping something or someone. 21. something to hold onto for support. 22. controlling influence: she has a hold on him. 23. **with no holds barred.** with all limitations removed. ~See also **hold back, hold down,** etc. —ˈholder n.

hold² (həʊld) n. the space in a ship or aircraft for storing cargo.

holdall (ˈhəʊldˌɔːl) n. Brit. a large strong travelling bag.

hold back vb. 1. to restrain (someone) or refrain from doing something: police held back the crowds; I held back from telling him the full truth. 2. to withhold: he held back part of the payment.

hold down vb. 1. to restrain or control someone. 2. Informal. to manage to keep: to hold down two jobs at once.

hold forth vb. to speak for a long time.

hold in vb. to curb, control, or conceal (one's feelings).

holding (ˈhəʊldɪŋ) n. 1. land held under a lease. 2. property to which the holder has legal title, such as land, stocks, or shares.

holding company n. a company with controlling shareholdings in one or more other companies.

holding paddock n. Austral. & N.Z. a paddock in which cattle or sheep are kept temporarily, as when awaiting sale.

hold off vb. 1. to keep (an attacker or attacking force) at a distance. 2. to refrain (from doing something): he held off making a final decision.

hold on vb. 1. to maintain a firm grasp (of something or someone). 2. (foll. by to) to keep or retain: hold on to those stamps as they'll soon be valuable. 3. Informal. to wait, esp. on the telephone.

hold out vb. 1. to offer (something). 2. to last: I hope my luck holds out. 3. to continue to stand firm, refusing to succumb to persuasion. 4. **hold out for.** to wait patiently for (the fulfilment of one's demands). 5. **hold out on someone.** Informal. to keep from telling someone some important information.

hold over vb. to defer or postpone: the decision has been held over until the next meeting.

hold-up n. 1. an armed robbery. 2. a delay; stoppage. ~vb. **hold up.** 3. to delay; hinder. 4. to support (an object). 5. to detain and rob someone, using a weapon. 6. to exhibit or present (something) as an example.

hold with vb. approve of: I don't hold with blood sports.

hole (həʊl) n. 1. an area hollowed out in a

solid. **2.** an opening in or through something. **3.** an animal's burrow. **4.** *Informal.* an unattractive town or other place. **5.** *Informal.* a fault or error: *there's a hole in your argument.* **6. pick holes in.** to point out faults in. **7.** *Slang.* a difficult and embarrassing situation. **8.** (on a golf course) any one of the divisions of a course (usually 18) represented by the distance between the tee and the cavity on the green into which the ball is to be played. **9. make a hole in.** to use a great amount of (one's money or food supply). ~*vb.* **10.** to make a hole or holes in (something). —'**holey** *adj.*

hole-and-corner *adj. Informal.* furtive or secretive.

hole in the heart *n.* a congenital defect of the heart, in which there is an abnormal opening in the partition between the left and right halves.

hole up *vb. Informal.* to go into hiding.

holiday ('hɒlɪˌdeɪ) *n.* **1.** (*often pl.*) *Chiefly Brit.* a period in which a break is taken from work or studies for rest or recreation. **2.** a day on which work is suspended by law or custom, such as a bank holiday. ~*vb.* **3.** *Chiefly Brit.* to spend a holiday.

holier-than-thou *adj.* offensively self-righteous.

Holiness ('həʊlɪnɪs) *n.* (preceded by *His* or *Your*) a title reserved for the pope.

holism ('həʊlɪzəm) *n.* **1.** the view that a whole is greater than the sum of its parts. **2.** (in medicine) consideration of the complete person in the treatment of disease. —**ho'listic** *adj.*

hollandaise sauce (ˌhɒlənˈdeɪz, ˈhɒlənˌdeɪz) *n.* a rich sauce of egg yolks, butter, vinegar, and lemon juice.

holler ('hɒlə) *Informal.* ~*vb.* **1.** to shout or yell. ~*n.* **2.** a shout; call.

hollow ('hɒləʊ) *adj.* **1.** having a hole or space within; not solid. **2.** concave: *hollow cheeks.* **3.** (of sounds) as if echoing in a hollow place. **4.** without substance or validity: *a hollow claim; a hollow laugh.* ~*adv.* **5. beat someone hollow.** *Brit. informal.* to defeat someone thoroughly. ~*n.* **6.** a cavity or space in something. **7.** a dip in the land. ~*vb.* (often foll. by *out*) **8.** to form a hole or cavity in. —'**hollowly** *adv.*

holly ('hɒlɪ) *n.* a tree or shrub with bright red berries and shiny evergreen leaves with prickly edges, used for Christmas decorations.

hollyhock ('hɒlɪˌhɒk) *n.* a tall plant with white, yellow, red, or purple flowers.

holmium ('hɒlmɪəm) *n.* a silver-white metallic element. Symbol: Ho

holm oak *n.* an evergreen oak tree with prickly leaves resembling holly.

holocaust ('hɒləˌkɔːst) *n.* destruction or loss of life on a massive scale.

hologram ('hɒləˌɡræm) *n.* a three-dimensional photographic image produced by means of a split laser beam.

holograph ('hɒləˌɡrɑːf) *n.* a book or document handwritten by its author.

holography (hɒˈlɒɡrəfɪ) *n.* the science or practice of producing holograms. —**holographic** (ˌhɒləˈɡræfɪk) *adj.* —ˌholo-'graphically *adv.*

hols (hɒlz) *pl. n. Brit. school slang.* holidays.

holster ('həʊlstə) *n.* a sheathlike leather case for a pistol, worn attached to a belt.

holt (həʊlt) *n.* the lair of an otter.

holy ('həʊlɪ) *adj.* **-lier, -liest. 1.** of or associated with God or a deity; sacred. **2.** devout or virtuous. —'**holiness** *n.*

Holy Communion *n. Christianity.* a church service in which people take bread and wine in remembrance of Christ's Last Supper and His atonement for the sins of the world.

Holy Ghost *n.* **the.** same as **Holy Spirit.**

Holy Grail *n.* **the.** (in medieval legend) the bowl used by Jesus at the Last Supper.

Holy Land *n.* **the.** Palestine.

holy of holies *n.* **1.** any place of special sanctity. **2.** the innermost compartment of the Jewish tabernacle.

holy orders *pl. n.* the status of an ordained Christian minister.

Holy See *n.* **the.** *R.C. Church.* the see of the pope as bishop of Rome.

Holy Spirit *n.* **the.** *Christianity.* the third person of the Trinity.

Holy Week *n. Christianity.* the week before Easter Sunday.

homage ('hɒmɪdʒ) *n.* a public show of respect or honour towards someone or something: *in his final number he paid homage to his hero Oscar Peterson.*

home (həʊm) *n.* **1.** the place where one lives. **2.** the country or area of one's birth. **3.** the place where something is invented or started: *the home of the cuckoo clock.* **4.** a building or organization set up to care for people in a certain category, such as orphans or the aged. **5.** *Sport.* one's own ground: *the match is at home.* **6.** the objective towards which a player strives in certain games and sports. **7. at home. a.** in one's own home or country. **b.** at ease. **c.** receiving visitors. **8. home and dry.** *Brit. slang.* definitely safe or successful. ~*adj.* **9.** of one's home, birthplace, or native country; domestic. **10.** (of an activity) done in one's house: *home taping.* **11.** *Sport.* played on one's own ground: *a home game.* ~*adv.* **12.** to or at home: *I'll be home tomorrow.* **13.** to or on the point: *that remark hit home.* **14.** to the fullest extent: *hammer the nail home.* **15. bring something home to someone.** to make something clear to someone. ~*vb.* **16.** (foll. by *in on*) to be directed towards (a goal or target). **17.** (of birds) to return home accurately from a distance. —**'homeless** *adj.*, *n.* —**'homelessness** *n.*

Home Counties *pl. n.* the counties surrounding London.

home economics *n.* (*functioning as sing. or pl.*) the study of diet, budgeting, child care, and other subjects concerned with running a home.

home farm *n. Brit.* a farm that was attached to and provided food for a large country house.

Home Guard *n.* a part-time military force of volunteers recruited for the defence of the United Kingdom in World War II.

home help *n. Brit.* a person employed by a local authority to do housework in a person's home.

homeland ('həʊm,lænd) *n.* **1.** the country from which the ancestors of a person or group came. **2.** the official name in S Africa for a **Bantustan.**

homely ('həʊmlɪ) *adj.* **-lier, -liest. 1.** characteristic of or suited to the ordinary home; unpretentious. **2.** (of a person) **a.** *Brit.* warm and domesticated. **b.** *Chiefly U.S. & Canad.* unattractive. —**'homeliness** *n.*

home-made *adj.* (esp. of foods) made at home or on the premises.

Home Office *n. Brit. government.* the department responsible for law and order, immigration, and other domestic affairs.

homeopathy *or* **homoeopathy** (,həmɪ-'ɒpəθɪ) *n.* a method of treating disease by the use of small amounts of a drug that produces symptoms of the disease in healthy people. —**homeopath** ('həʊmɪə,pæθ) *n.* —**homeopathic** (,həmɪə'pæθɪk) *adj.*

homeostasis *or* **homoeostasis** (,həmɪəʊ'steɪsɪs) *n.* the tendency of an organism to achieve a stable metabolic state by compensating automatically for violent changes in the environment and other disruptions.

Homeric (həʊ'mɛrɪk) *adj.* of or relating to Homer, Greek epic poet (circa 800 B.C.).

home rule *n.* self-government in domestic affairs.

Home Secretary *n. Brit. government.* the head of the Home Office.

homesick ('həʊm,sɪk) *adj.* melancholy at being away from home and family. —**'home,sickness** *n.*

homespun ('həʊm,spʌn) *adj.* (of philosophies or opinions) plain and unsophisticated.

homestead ('həʊm,stɛd, -stɪd) *n.* **1.** a farmhouse and the adjoining land. **2.** (in the western U.S. & Canada) a house and adjoining tract of land (originally often 160 acres) that was granted by the government for development as a farm. Homesteads are exempt from seizure or sale for debt.

homesteader ('həʊm,stɛdə) *n.* (in the western U.S. & Canada) a person who lives on and farms a homestead.

home truths *pl. n.* unpleasant facts told to a person about himself.

home unit *n. Austral. & N.Z.* a self-contained residence which is part of a block of such residences.

homeward ('həʊmwəd) *adj.* **1.** going home. *~adv. also* **homewards. 2.** towards home.

homework ('həʊm,wɜːk) *n.* **1.** school work done at home. **2.** any preparatory study.

homicide ('hɒmɪ,saɪd) *n.* **1.** the killing of a human being by another person. **2.** a person who kills another. —**,homi'cidal** *adj.*

homily ('hɒmɪlɪ) *n., pl.* **-lies.** a moralizing talk or piece of writing. —**,homi'letic** *adj.*

homing ('həʊmɪŋ) *n.* (*modifier*) **1.** *Zool.* denoting the ability to return home after travelling great distances. **2.** (of a missile) capable of guiding itself onto a target.

homing pigeon *n.* a pigeon developed for its homing instinct, used for racing.

hominid ('hɒmɪnɪd) *n.* **1.** any member of the family of primates that includes modern man and the extinct forerunners of man. *~adj.* **2.** of or belonging to this family.

hominoid ('hɒmɪ,nɔɪd) *adj.* **1.** of or like man; manlike. *~n.* **2.** a manlike animal.

hominy ('hɒmɪnɪ) *n. Chiefly U.S.* coarsely ground maize prepared as a food by boiling in milk or water.

homogeneous (,həmə'dʒiːnɪəs) *adj.* composed of similar parts. —**homogeneity** (,hɒmədʒɪ'niːɪtɪ) *n.*

homogenize *or* **-nise** (hɒ'mɒdʒɪ,naɪz) *vb.* **1.** to break up the fat globules in (milk) so that they are evenly distributed. **2.** to make homogeneous.

homogenous (hɒ'mɒdʒɪnəs) *adj.* having a similar structure because of common ancestry.

homograph ('hɒmə,grɑːf) *n.* a word spelt the same as another, but having a different meaning, such as *bear* (to carry) and *bear* (the animal).

homologous (hɒ'mɒləgəs) *adj.* **1.** having a related or similar position or structure. **2.** *Biol.* (of organs and parts) deriving from the same origin but having different functions: *the wing of a bat and the arm of a monkey are homologous.*

homology (hɒ'mɒlədʒɪ) *n.* the condition of being homologous.

homonym ('hɒmənɪm) *n.* a word pronounced and spelt the same as another, but having a different meaning, such as *novel* (a book) and *novel* (new).

homophobia (,həʊmə'fəʊbɪə) *n.* intense hatred or fear of homosexuals.

homophone ('hɒmə,fəʊn) *n.* a word pronounced the same as another, but having a different meaning or spelling or both, such as *bear* and *bare*.

Homo sapiens (ˈsæpɪˌɛnz) *n.* the name for modern man as a species.

homosexual (ˌhəʊməʊˈsɛksjʊəl, ˌhɒm-) *n.* **1.** a person who is sexually attracted to members of the same sex. ~*adj.* **2.** (of a person) sexually attracted to members of the same sex. **3.** (of a sexual relationship) between members of the same sex. —ˌhomoˌsexuˈality *n.*

homy *or esp. U.S.* **homey** (ˈhəʊmɪ) *adj.* **homier, homiest.** like a home; cosy.

Hon. Honourable (title).

hone (həʊn) *n.* **1.** a fine whetstone for sharpening. ~*vb.* **2.** to sharpen with or as if with a hone.

honest (ˈɒnɪst) *adj.* **1.** not given to lying, cheating, or stealing; trustworthy. **2.** just or fair: *honest wages.* **3.** genuine; sincere; without pretensions: *an honest attempt.*

honestly (ˈɒnɪstlɪ) *adv.* **1.** in an honest manner. **2.** truly: *I honestly don't believe it.*

honesty (ˈɒnɪstɪ) *n., pl.* **-ties. 1.** the condition of being honest. **2.** a plant with flattened silvery pods which are used for indoor decoration.

honey (ˈhʌnɪ) *n.* **1.** a sweet edible sticky substance made by bees from nectar. **2.** *Chiefly U.S. & Canad.* a term of endearment. **3.** *Informal, chiefly U.S. & Canad.* something very good of its kind: *a honey of a role.*

honeybee (ˈhʌnɪˌbiː) *n.* a bee widely domesticated as a source of honey and beeswax.

honeycomb (ˈhʌnɪˌkəʊm) *n.* a waxy structure, constructed by bees in a hive, that consists of many six-sided cells in which honey is stored.

honeydew (ˈhʌnɪˌdjuː) *n.* a sugary substance excreted by aphids and similar insects.

honeydew melon *n.* a melon with yellow skin and sweet pale flesh.

honeyed (ˈhʌnɪd) *adj. Poetic.* flattering or soothing: *honeyed words.*

honeymoon (ˈhʌnɪˌmuːn) *n.* **1.** a holiday taken by a newly married couple. **2.** the early, usually calm period of a relationship or enterprise. ~*vb.* **3.** to take a honeymoon. —ˈhoneyˌmooner *n.*

honeysuckle (ˈhʌnɪˌsʌkᵊl) *n.* a climbing shrub with sweet-smelling white, yellow, or pink flowers.

honk (hɒŋk) *n.* **1.** the sound made by a motor horn. **2.** the sound made by a goose. ~*vb.* **3.** to make or cause (something) to make a honking sound.

honky-tonk (ˈhɒŋkɪˌtɒŋk) *n.* **1.** *U.S. & Canad. slang.* a cheap disreputable nightclub or dance hall. **2.** a style of ragtime

piano-playing, esp. on a tinny-sounding piano.

honorarium (ˌɒnəˈrɛərɪəm) *n., pl.* **-iums** *or* **-ia** (-ɪə). a voluntary fee paid for a service which is usually free.

honorary (ˈɒnərərɪ) *adj.* **a.** held or given only as an honour, without the normal privileges or duties: *an honorary degree.* **b.** (of a secretary, treasurer, etc.) unpaid.

honorific (ˌɒnəˈrɪfɪk) *adj.* showing respect.

honour *or U.S.* **honor** (ˈɒnə) *n.* **1.** the quality of being firm in one's moral principles. **2. a.** fame or glory. **b.** a person who wins this for his country, school, etc. **3.** great respect or esteem, or an outward sign of this. **4.** a privilege or pleasure: *it is an honour to serve you.* **5.** (of a woman) chastity. **6.** *Bridge, whist.* any of the top four or five cards in a suit. **7.** *Golf.* the right to tee off first. **8. in honour of.** out of respect for. **9. on one's honour.** under a moral obligation. ~*vb.* **10.** to hold someone in respect. **11.** to give (someone) a symbol of honour. **12.** to accept and then pay (a cheque or bill). **13.** to keep (one's promise); fulfil (a previous agreement).

Honour (ˈɒnə) *n.* (preceded by *Your, His,* or *Her*) a title used to address or refer to certain judges.

honourable *or U.S.* **honorable** (ˈɒnərəbᵊl) *adj.* **1.** possessing high principles. **2.** worthy of honour or esteem. —ˈhonourably *adv.*

Honourable (ˈɒnərəbᵊl) *adj.* **the.** a title of respect placed before a name: used of various officials, of the children of certain peers, and in Parliament by one member speaking of another.

honours *or U.S.* **honors** (ˈɒnəz) *pl. n.* **1.** observances of respect, esp. at a funeral. **2.** (in a university degree course) a rank or mark of the highest academic standard: *an honours degree.* **3. do the honours.** to serve as host or hostess, as by serving food or drinks.

hooch (huːtʃ) *n. Informal.* alcoholic drink, esp. illicitly distilled spirits.

hood[1] (hʊd) *n.* **1.** a loose head covering either attached to a cloak or coat or made as a separate garment. **2.** *U.S. & Canad.* the bonnet of a car. **3.** the folding roof of a convertible car or a pram. ~*vb.* **4.** to cover with or as if with a hood. —ˈhooded *adj.* —ˈhoodˌlike *adj.*

hood[2] (hʊd) *n. Slang.* short for **hoodlum.**

hooded crow *n.* a crow that has a grey body and black head, wings, and tail.

hoodlum (ˈhuːdləm) *n.* **1.** a petty gangster. **2.** a lawless youth.

hoodoo (ˈhuːduː) *n., pl.* **-doos. 1.** same as **voodoo. 2.** *Informal.* bad luck. **3.** *Informal.* a person or thing that brings bad luck.

hoodwink (ˈhʊdˌwɪŋk) *vb.* to dupe; trick.

hooey (ˈhuːɪ) *n. Slang.* nonsense.

hoof (huːf) *n., pl.* **hooves** *or* **hoofs. 1.** the horny covering of the end of the foot in the horse, deer, and certain other mammals. ~*vb.* **2. hoof it.** *Slang.* to walk. —**hoofed** *adj.*

hoo-ha ('huːˌhɑː) *n.* a noisy commotion or fuss.

hook (hʊk) *n.* **1.** a curved piece of metal used to hang, hold, or pull something. **2.** something resembling a hook, such as a sharp bend in a river or a sharply curved strip of land. **3.** *Boxing.* a short swinging blow with the elbow bent. **4.** *Cricket, golf.* a shot that causes the ball to go to the player's left. **5. by hook or by crook.** by any means: *I'll get there by hook or by crook.* **6. hook, line, and sinker.** *Informal.* completely: *he fell for it hook, line, and sinker.* **7. let someone off the hook.** *Slang.* to free someone from obligation or guilt. **8. sling one's hook.** *Brit. slang.* to leave. ~*vb.* **9.** to fasten with or as if with a hook. **10.** to catch (a fish) on a hook. **11.** *Cricket, etc.* to play (a ball) with a hook. **12.** *Rugby.* to obtain and pass (the ball) backwards from a scrum, using the feet.

hookah ('hʊkə) *n.* an oriental pipe for smoking marijuana or tobacco, with a long flexible stem connected to a container of water through which smoke is drawn and cooled.

hooked (hʊkt) *adj.* **1.** bent like a hook. **2. hooked on. a.** *Slang.* addicted to: *hooked on cocaine.* **b.** obsessed with: *hooked on video games.*

hooker ('hʊkə) *n.* **1.** *Slang.* a prostitute. **2.** *Rugby.* a player in the front row of a scrum whose main job is to hook the ball.

hook-up *n.* the linking of broadcasting equipment or stations to transmit a special programme.

hookworm ('hʊkˌwɜːm) *n.* a bloodsucking worm with hooked mouthparts.

hooligan ('huːlɪgən) *n. Slang.* a rough lawless young person. —'**hooliganism** *n.*

hoop (huːp) *n.* **1.** a rigid circular band of metal or wood. **2.** a child's toy shaped like a hoop and rolled on the ground or whirled around the body. **3.** *Croquet.* any of the iron arches through which the ball is driven. **4.** a large ring often with paper stretched over it through which performers or animals jump in the circus. **5. go** *or* **be put through the hoops.** to be subjected to an ordeal. ~*vb.* **6.** to surround (something) with a hoop. —**hooped** *adj.*

hoopla ('huːplɑː) *n. Brit.* a fairground game in which a player tries to throw a hoop over an object and so win it.

hoopoe ('huːpuː) *n.* a bird having a pinkish-brown plumage with black-and-white wings and a fanlike crest.

hooray (huːˈreɪ) *interj., n.* same as **hurrah.**

Hooray Henry ('huːˌreɪ 'henrɪ) *n., pl.* **Hoo-**

ray Henries *or* **-rys.** a young upper-class man with affectedly hearty voice and manners.

hoot¹ (huːt) *n.* **1.** the mournful wavering cry of some owls. **2.** a similar sound, such as that of a car horn. **3.** a jeer of derision. **4.** *Informal.* an amusing person or thing. ~*vb.* **5.** to jeer or yell contemptuously at someone. **6.** to drive (speakers or performers on stage) off by hooting. **7.** to make a hoot. **8.** *Brit.* to blow (a horn).

hoot² (huːt) *n. Austral & N.Z. slang.* money.

hooter ('huːtə) *n. Chiefly Brit.* **1.** a device that hoots, such as a car horn. **2.** *Slang.* a nose.

Hoover ('huːvə) *n.* **1.** *Trademark.* a vacuum cleaner. ~*vb.* **2.** to vacuum-clean (a carpet).

hooves (huːvz) *n.* a plural of **hoof.**

hop¹ (hɒp) *vb.* **hopping, hopped. 1.** to jump forwards or upwards on one foot. **2.** (of frogs, birds, etc.) to move forwards in short jumps. **3.** to jump over something. **4.** *Informal.* to move quickly (in, on, out of, etc.): *hop on a bus.* **5. hop it.** *Brit. slang.* to go away. ~*n.* **6.** an instance of hopping. **7.** *Informal.* an informal dance. **8.** *Informal.* a short journey, usually in an aircraft. **9. on the hop.** *Informal.* **a.** active or busy: *he keeps me on the hop.* **b.** *Brit.* unawares or unprepared: *you've caught me on the hop.*

hop² (hɒp) *n.* a climbing plant with green conelike flowers. See also **hops.**

hope (həʊp) *n.* **1.** a feeling of desire for something, usually with confidence in the possibility of its fulfilment: *his hope for peace was justified.* **2.** a reasonable ground for this feeling: *there is still hope.* **3.** a person or thing that gives cause for hope. **4.** a thing, situation, or event that is desired: *my hope is that prices will fall.* ~*vb.* **5.** to desire (something), usually with some possibility of fulfilment: *I hope to tell you.* **6.** to trust or believe: *we hope that this is satisfactory.*

hopeful ('həʊpfʊl) *adj.* **1.** having or expressing hope. **2.** inspiring hope; promising. ~*n.* **3.** a person considered to be on the brink of success: *a young hopeful.*

hopefully ('həʊpfʊlɪ) *adv.* **1.** in a hopeful manner. **2.** *Informal.* it is hoped: *hopefully they will be married soon.*
Usage. The use of *hopefully* to mean "it is hoped that" is not liked by some people. It does, however, represent a construction already well-established in colloquial English.

hopeless ('həʊplɪs) *adj.* **1.** having or offering no hope. **2.** impossible to solve. **3.** *Informal.* without skill or ability: *I'm hopeless at maths.*

hopper ('hɒpə) *n.* **1.** a funnel-shaped device from which solid materials can be discharged into a receptacle below. **2.** a hopping insect.

hops (hɒps) *pl. n.* the dried flowers of the hop plant, used to give a bitter taste to beer.

hopscotch ('hɒpˌskɒtʃ) *n.* a children's game in which a player throws a stone to land in one of a pattern of squares marked on the ground and then hops over to it to pick it up.

horde (hɔːd) *n.* a vast crowd; throng; mob.

horehound ('hɔːˌhaʊnd) *n.* a plant that produces a bitter juice formerly used as a cough medicine.

horizon (həˈraɪzᵊn) *n.* **1.** the apparent line that divides the earth and the sky. **2.** (*pl.*) the limits of scope, interest, or knowledge.

horizontal (ˌhɒrɪˈzɒntᵊl) *adj.* **1.** parallel to the plane of the horizon; level; flat. **2.** *Econ.* relating to identical stages of commercial activity: *horizontal integration.* ~*n.* **3.** a horizontal plane, position, or line. —ˌhoriˈzontally *adv.*

hormone ('hɔːməʊn) *n.* **1.** a chemical substance produced in an endocrine gland and transported in the blood to a certain tissue, on which it has a specific effect. **2.** a similar substance produced by a plant that is essential for growth. **3.** a synthetic substance having the same effects. —horˈmonal *adj.*

horn (hɔːn) *n.* **1.** either of a pair of permanent bony outgrowths on the heads of animals such as cattle and antelopes. **2.** any hornlike projection, such as the eyestalk of a snail. **3.** the antler of a deer. **4.** the hard substance of which horns are made. **5.** a musical wind instrument made from horn. **6.** any musical instrument consisting of a pipe or tube of brass fitted with a mouthpiece. **7.** a device, as on a vehicle, for producing a warning or signalling noise. ~*vb.* **8.** to provide with a horn or horns. —**horned** *adj.*

hornbeam ('hɔːnˌbiːm) *n.* a tree with hard white wood.

hornbill ('hɔːnˌbɪl) *n.* a tropical bird having a very large bill with a bony protuberance.

hornblende ('hɔːnˌblɛnd) *n.* a green to black mineral containing aluminium, calcium, sodium, magnesium, and iron.

hornet ('hɔːnɪt) *n.* **1.** a large wasp that can inflict a severe sting. **2. hornet's nest.** a strongly unfavourable reaction: *I seem to have stirred up a hornet's nest.*

horn of plenty *n.* same as **cornucopia.**

hornpipe ('hɔːnˌpaɪp) *n.* **1.** a solo dance, traditionally performed by sailors. **2.** music for this dance.

horny ('hɔːnɪ) *adj.* **hornier, horniest. 1.** of, like, or hard as horn. **2.** *Slang.* aroused sexually.

horology (hɒˈrɒlədʒɪ) *n.* the art of making clocks and watches or of measuring time. —**horological** (ˌhɒrəˈlɒdʒɪkᵊl) *adj.*

horoscope ('hɒrəˌskəʊp) *n.* **1.** the prediction of a person's future based on the posi-

tions of the planets, sun, and moon at the time of birth. **2.** a diagram showing the positions of the planets, sun, and moon at a particular time and place.

horrendous (hɒˈrɛndəs) *adj.* same as **horrific.**

horrible ('hɒrɪbᵊl) *adj.* **1.** causing horror; dreadful. **2.** disagreeable. —**horribly** *adv.*

horrid ('hɒrɪd) *adj.* **1.** disagreeable; unpleasant: *a horrid meal.* **2.** *Informal.* unkind.

horrific (hɒˈrɪfɪk, hə-) *adj.* provoking horror; horrible. —**horˈrifically** *adv.*

horrify ('hɒrɪˌfaɪ) *vb.* **-fying, -fied.** to cause feelings of horror in (someone); shock (someone) greatly.

horror ('hɒrə) *n.* **1.** extreme fear; terror; dread. **2.** intense hatred. **3.** a thing or person causing fear, loathing, or distaste. **4.** (*modifier*) having a frightening subject: *a horror film.*

horrors ('hɒrəz) *pl. n.* **the.** *Slang.* a fit of depression or anxiety.

hors d'oeuvre (ɔː ˈdɜːvrə) *n., pl.* **hors d'oeuvre** or **hors d'oeuvres** ('dɜːvrə). an appetizer, usually served before the main meal.

horse (hɔːs) *n.* **1.** a solid-hoofed domesticated mammal used for pulling carts, etc., and for riding. **2.** the adult male of this species; stallion. **3.** (*functioning as pl.*) cavalry: *a regiment of horse.* **4.** *Gymnastics.* a padded apparatus on legs, used for vaulting. **5. be** *or* **get on one's high horse.** *Informal.* to act haughtily. **6. the horse's mouth.** the most reliable source: *I got it straight from the horse's mouth.*

horse around *or* **about** *vb. Informal.* to indulge in horseplay.

horseback ('hɔːsˌbæk) *n.* a horse's back: *on horseback.*

horsebox ('hɔːsˌbɒks) *n. Brit.* a van or trailer used for transporting horses.

horse brass *n.* a decorative brass ornament, originally attached to a horse's harness.

horse chestnut *n.* **1.** a tree with broad leaves and brown shiny inedible nuts enclosed in a spiky case. **2.** the nut of this tree.

horseflesh ('hɔːsˌflɛʃ) *n.* **1.** horses collectively: *a good judge of horseflesh.* **2.** the flesh of a horse as food.

horsefly ('hɔːsˌflaɪ) *n., pl.* **-flies.** a large fly which sucks the blood of horses, cattle, and people.

horsehair ('hɔːsˌheə) *n.* hair from the tail or mane of a horse, used in upholstery.

horse laugh *n.* a coarse or raucous laugh.

horseman ('hɔːsmən) *n., pl.* **-men. 1.** a man who is skilled in riding. **2.** a man riding a horse. —**'horsemanˌship** *n.* —**'horseˌwoman** *fem. n.*

horseplay (ˈhɔːsˌpleɪ) n. rough or rowdy play.

horsepower (ˈhɔːsˌpaʊə) n. a unit of power (equivalent to 745.7 watts), used to measure the power of an engine.

horseradish (ˈhɔːsˌrædɪʃ) n. a plant with a white strong-tasting root, which is used to make a sauce.

horse sense n. same as **common sense**.

horseshoe (ˈhɔːsˌʃuː) n. 1. a piece of iron shaped like a U nailed to the bottom of a horse's hoof to protect the foot. 2. an object of similar shape.

horsetail (ˈhɔːsˌteɪl) n. a plant with small dark toothlike leaves.

horsewhip (ˈhɔːsˌwɪp) n. 1. a whip with a long thong, used for managing horses. ~vb. -whipping, -whipped. 2. to flog (a person or animal) with such a whip.

horsy or **horsey** (ˈhɔːsɪ) adj. **horsier**, **horsiest**. 1. of or relating to horses: a horsy smell. 2. devoted to horses: the horsy set. 3. like a horse: a horsy face.

hortatory (ˈhɔːtətrɪ) or **hortative** (ˈhɔːtətɪv) adj. encouraging.

horticulture (ˈhɔːtɪˌkʌltʃə) n. the art of cultivating gardens. —ˌhortiˈcultural adj. —ˌhortiˈculturist n.

hosanna (həʊˈzænə) interj. an exclamation of praise to God.

hose[1] (həʊz) n. 1. a flexible pipe, for conveying a liquid or gas. ~vb. 2. to wash or water (a person or thing) with a hose.

hose[2] (həʊz) n. 1. stockings, socks, and tights collectively. 2. History. a man's garment covering the legs and reaching up to the waist.

hosiery (ˈhəʊzɪərɪ) n. stockings, socks, and knitted underclothing collectively.

hospice (ˈhɒspɪs) n. 1. a nursing home that specializes in caring for the terminally ill. 2. Archaic. a place of shelter for travellers, esp. one kept by a religious order.

hospitable (ˈhɒspɪtəb³l, hɒˈspɪt-) adj. welcoming to guests or strangers. —ˈhospitably adv.

hospital (ˈhɒspɪt³l) n. an institution for the medical or psychiatric care and treatment of patients.

hospitality (ˌhɒspɪˈtælɪtɪ) n., pl. -ties. kindness in welcoming strangers or guests.

hospitalize or **-lise** (ˈhɒspɪtəˌlaɪz) vb. to admit or send (a person) into a hospital. —ˌhospitaliˈzation or -liˈsation n.

hospitaller or U.S. **hospitaler** (ˈhɒspɪtələ) n. a member of a religious order dedicated to hospital work, ambulance services, etc.

host[1] (həʊst) n. 1. a person who receives or entertains guests, esp. in his own home. 2. the compere of a radio or television programme. 3. Biol. an animal or plant in or on which a parasite lives. 4. Old-fashioned. the owner or manager of an inn. ~vb. 5. to be the host of (a party or programme): to host one's own show.

host[2] (həʊst) n. a great number; multitude.

Host (həʊst) n. Christianity. the bread used in Holy Communion.

hostage (ˈhɒstɪdʒ) n. a person held by another or others as security for the fulfilment of certain terms.

hostel (ˈhɒst³l) n. 1. a building providing overnight accommodation, as for homeless people. 2. same as **youth hostel**. 3. Brit. a supervised lodging house for nurses, students, etc. —ˈhosteller or U.S. ˈhosteler n.

hostelry (ˈhɒstəlrɪ) n., pl. -ries. Archaic or facetious. an inn.

hostel school n. Canad. same as **residential school**.

hostess (ˈhəʊstɪs) n. 1. a woman acting as host. 2. a woman who receives and entertains patrons of a club, restaurant, or dance hall.

hostile (ˈhɒstaɪl) adj. 1. unfriendly and aggressive. 2. antagonistic; opposed: hostile to new developments. 3. of or relating to an enemy.

hostility (hɒˈstɪlɪtɪ) n., pl. -ties. 1. unfriendly and aggressive feelings or behaviour. 2. (pl.) fighting; warfare.

hot (hɒt) adj. **hotter, hottest**. 1. having a relatively high temperature. 2. having a temperature higher than desirable. 3. causing a burning sensation on the tongue: a hot curry. 4. expressing or feeling intense emotion, such as anger or lust. 5. (of a contest or conflict) intense or vehement. 6. recent; new: hot from the press. 7. much favoured: a hot favourite. 8. Informal. having a dangerously high level of radioactivity. 9. Slang. stolen or otherwise illegally obtained. 10. (of a colour) intense; striking: hot pink. 11. following closely: hot on the scent. 12. Informal. dangerous or unpleasant: they're making it hot for me here. 13. (in various games) very near the answer. 14. **hot on**. Informal. **a.** strict about: the police are hot on drunk driving. **b.** particularly knowledgeable about. 15. **hot under the collar**. Informal. aroused with anger, annoyance, or resentment. 16. **in hot water**. Informal. in trouble. ~See also **hot up**. —ˈhotly adv.

hot air n. Informal. empty and usually boastful talk.

hotbed (ˈhɒtˌbed) n. a place offering ideal conditions for the growth of an idea or activity, esp. one considered bad: a hotbed of crime.

hot-blooded adj. passionate or excitable.

hotchpotch (ˈhɒtʃˌpɒtʃ) or esp. U.S. & Canad. **hodgepodge** n. a jumbled mixture.

hot cross bun n. a yeast bun marked

with a cross and traditionally eaten on Good Friday.

hot dog n. a long roll split lengthways with a hot sausage inside.

hotel (həʊ'tɛl) n. a commercially run establishment providing lodging and meals for guests.

hotelier (hɒ'tɛljeɪ) n. an owner or manager of a hotel.

hotfoot ('hɒt,fʊt) adv. with all possible speed.

hot-gospeller n. Informal. a revivalist preacher with a highly enthusiastic delivery.

hot-headed adj. impetuous, rash, or hot-tempered. —,hot-'headedness n.

hothouse ('hɒt,haʊs) n. a greenhouse in which the temperature is maintained at a fixed level.

hot line n. a direct telephone link between heads of government for emergency use.

hot money n. capital that is transferred from one financial centre to another seeking the best opportunity for short-term gain.

hotplate ('hɒt,pleɪt) n. 1. an electrically heated plate on a cooker. 2. a portable device on which food can be kept warm.

hotpot ('hɒt,pɒt) n. Brit. a casserole of meat and vegetables covered with a layer of potatoes.

hot rod n. a car with an engine that has been modified to produce increased power.

hot seat n. 1. in the hot seat. Informal. in a difficult and responsible position. 2. U.S. slang. the electric chair.

hot stuff n. Informal. 1. a person, object, or activity considered attractive, exciting, or important. 2. pornographic or erotic books, plays, films, etc.

Hottentot ('hɒt'n,tɒt) n. 1. (pl. -tot or -tots) a member of a race of people of southern Africa which is now almost extinct. 2. any of the languages of this people.

hot up vb. hotting, hotted. Informal. 1. to make or become more exciting, active, or intense. 2. same as **soup up**.

hot-water bottle n. a rubber container, designed to be filled with hot water and used for warming a bed.

hound (haʊnd) n. 1. a dog used for hunting: a deerhound. 2. a despicable person. ~vb. 3. to pursue relentlessly: hounded by the press.

hour ('aʊə) n. 1. a period of time equal to 60 minutes; 1/24th of a day. 2. any of the points on the face of a clock or watch that indicate intervals of 60 minutes: the bus leaves on the hour. 3. the time. 4. the time allowed for or used for something: the lunch hour. 5. a special moment: our finest hour. 6. the distance covered in an hour:

we live an hour from the city. ~See also **hours**.

hourglass ('aʊə,glɑːs) n. a device consisting of two transparent sections linked by a narrow channel, containing a quantity of sand that takes an hour to trickle from one section to the other.

houri ('hʊərɪ) n., pl. -ris. (in Muslim belief) any of the nymphs of Paradise.

hourly ('aʊəlɪ) adj. 1. of, occurring, or done once every hour. 2. measured by the hour: an hourly rate. 3. frequent. ~adv. 4. once every hour. 5. by the hour: hourly paid. 6. frequently. 7. at any moment: we expect him hourly.

hours ('aʊəz) pl. n. 1. a period regularly appointed for work or business. 2. one's times of rising and going to bed: he keeps late hours. 3. an indefinite time: we talked for hours. 4. R.C. Church. prayers recited at seven specified times of the day.

house n. (haʊs), pl. **houses** ('haʊzɪz). 1. a building used as a home; dwelling. 2. the people in a house. 3. a building for some specific purpose: schoolhouse. 4. a family or dynasty: the House of York. 5. a commercial company: a publishing house. 6. a law-making body or the hall where it meets. 7. Astrol. any of the 12 divisions of the zodiac. 8. a division of a large school: house captain. 9. the audience in a theatre or cinema. 10. Informal. a brothel. 11. get on like a house on fire. Informal. (of people) to get on very well together. 12. on the house. (usually of drinks) paid for by the management. 13. put one's house in order. to settle or organize one's affairs. ~vb. (haʊz). 14. to provide (someone) with or serve (someone) as accommodation. 15. to contain or cover (something).

house arrest n. confinement to one's own home rather than in prison.

houseboat ('haʊs,bəʊt) n. a stationary boat used as a home.

housebound ('haʊs,baʊnd) adj. unable to leave one's house, usually because of illness.

housebreaking ('haʊs,breɪkɪŋ) n. Criminal law. the act of entering a building as a trespasser for an unlawful purpose. —'house,breaker n.

housecoat ('haʊs,kəʊt) n. a woman's loose robelike informal garment.

housefly ('haʊs,flaɪ) n., pl. -flies. a common fly often found in houses.

household ('haʊs,həʊld) n. 1. all the people living together in one house. 2. (modifier) relating to the running of a household: household management.

householder ('haʊs,həʊldə) n. a person who owns or rents a house.

household name or **word** n. a person or thing that is very well known.

housekeeper ('haʊsˌkiːpə) n. a person employed to run someone else's household.

housekeeping ('haʊsˌkiːpɪŋ) n. **1.** the running of a household. **2.** money allotted for this.

house lights pl. n. the lights in the auditorium of a theatre or cinema.

housemaid ('haʊsˌmeɪd) n. a female servant employed to do housework.

housemaid's knee n. a fluid-filled swelling of the kneecap.

houseman ('haʊsmən) n., pl. **-men**. Med. a junior doctor in a hospital.

house martin n. a swallow with a slightly forked tail.

House music or **House** n. a type of disco music of the late 1980s, based on funk, with fragments of other recordings edited in electronically.

House of Commons n. (in Britain and Canada) the lower chamber of Parliament.

House of Keys n. the lower chamber of the law-making body of the Isle of Man.

House of Lords n. (in Britain) the upper chamber of Parliament, composed of the peers of the realm.

house party n. **1.** a party, usually in a country house, at which guests are invited to stay for several days. **2.** the guests who are invited.

house-proud adj. excessively concerned with the appearance, cleanliness, and tidiness of one's house.

houseroom ('haʊsˌrʊm, -ˌruːm) n. **not give something houseroom.** not to want to have something in one's house.

housetops ('haʊsˌtɒps) pl. n. **shout** or **proclaim something from the housetops.** to announce something publicly.

house-train vb. Brit. to train (a pet) to urinate and defecate outside.

house-warming n. a party given after moving into a new home.

housewife ('haʊsˌwaɪf) n., pl. **-wives**. a woman who runs her own household and does not have a paid job. —**'housewifely** adj.

housework ('haʊsˌwɜːk) n. the work of running a home, such as cleaning, cooking, and shopping.

housing ('haʊzɪŋ) n. **1.** houses collectively. **2.** the job of providing people with accommodation. **3.** a part designed to contain and support a component or mechanism: a wheel housing.

hove (həʊv) vb. Chiefly naut. a past of **heave**.

hovel ('hɒvᵊl) n. a dirty or untidy dwelling place.

hover ('hɒvə) vb. **1.** to remain suspended in one place, as hawks do by rapidly beating their wings. **2.** to linger uncertainly in one place. **3.** to be in a state of indecision.

hovercraft ('hɒvəˌkrɑːft) n. a vehicle that is able to travel across both land and water on a cushion of air.

how (haʊ) adv. **1.** in what way, by what means: how did it happen? tell me how he did it. **2.** to what extent: how tall is he? **3.** how good, how well, what...like: how did she sing? how was the holiday? **4. how about?** used to suggest something: how about a cup of tea? **5. how are you?** what is your state of health? **6. how's that? a.** what is your opinion?: I'll give you it for a fiver - how's that? **b.** Cricket. Also written: **howzat** (haʊ'zæt). (an appeal to the umpire) is the batsman out?

howdah ('haʊdə) n. a seat for riding on an elephant's back.

however (haʊ'ɛvə) adv. **1.** still; nevertheless: I don't want to go - however, I will make the effort. **2.** by whatever means: get there however you can. **3.** (with an adjective or adverb) no matter how: however long it takes, finish it.

howitzer ('haʊɪtsə) n. a cannon with a short barrel and a steep angle of fire.

howl (haʊl) n. **1.** the long plaintive cry of a wolf or hound. **2.** a similar cry of pain or sorrow. **3.** a loud burst of laughter. ~vb. **4.** to express (something) in a howl or utter such cries. **5.** (of the wind, etc.) to make a wailing noise.

howl down vb. to prevent (a speaker) from being heard by shouting disapprovingly.

howler ('haʊlə) n. Informal. a glaring mistake.

howling ('haʊlɪŋ) adj. Informal. great: a howling success.

hoy (hɔɪ) interj. a cry used to attract someone's attention.

hoyden ('hɔɪdᵊn) n. a wild boisterous girl; tomboy. —**'hoydenish** adj.

HP or **h.p.** **1.** Brit. hire-purchase. **2.** horsepower.

HQ or **h.q.** headquarters.

hr hour.

HRH Her (or His) Royal Highness.

HRT hormone replacement therapy.

hub (hʌb) n. **1.** the central portion of a wheel, through which the axle passes. **2.** the focal point of a place.

hubble-bubble ('hʌbᵊl'bʌbᵊl) n. **1.** same as **hookah**. **2.** turmoil. **3.** a gargling sound.

hubbub ('hʌbʌb) n. **1.** a confused noise of many voices. **2.** tumult; uproar.

hubby ('hʌbɪ) n., pl. **-bies**. Informal. a husband.

hubris ('hjuːbrɪs) n. pride or arrogance. —**hu'bristic** adj.

huckster ('hʌkstə) n. **1.** a person who uses aggressive methods of selling. **2.** Now rare. a person who sells small articles or fruit in the street.

huddle ('hʌd³l) n. 1. a heaped or crowded mass of people or things. 2. **go into a huddle**. *Informal.* to have a private conference. ~*vb.* 3. (of a group of people) to crowd or nestle closely together. 4. (of a person) to hunch (oneself), as through cold.

hue (hjuː) n. 1. the feature of colour that enables an observer to classify it as red, blue, etc. 2. a shade of a colour.

hue and cry n. a loud public outcry.

huff (hʌf) n. 1. a passing mood of anger or resentment: *in a huff.* ~*vb.* 2. to blow or puff heavily. 3. *Draughts* to remove (an opponent's draught) from the board for failure to make a capture. 4. **huffing and puffing.** empty threats or objections; bluster. —'**huffy** *adj.* —'**huffily** *adv.*

hug (hʌg) *vb.* **hugging, hugged.** 1. to clasp (someone or something) tightly, usually with affection. 2. to keep close to (a shore or the kerb). ~*n.* 3. a tight or fond embrace.

huge (hjuːdʒ) *adj.* extremely large. —'**hugely** *adv.*

huggermugger ('hʌgə,mʌgə) *Archaic.* ~*n.* 1. confusion or secrecy. ~*adj., adv.* 2. in confusion.

Huguenot ('hjuːgə,nəʊ, -,nɒt) n. a French Calvinist of the 16th or 17th centuries.

huh (hʌ) *interj.* an exclamation of derision, bewilderment, or inquiry.

hui ('huːɪ) n. *N.Z.* 1. a Maori social gathering. 2. any party.

hula ('huːlə) n. a Hawaiian dance performed by a woman.

hulk (hʌlk) n. 1. the body of an abandoned ship. 2. *Disparaging.* a large ungainly person or thing.

hulking ('hʌlkɪŋ) *adj.* big and ungainly.

hull (hʌl) n. 1. the main body of a boat. 2. the outer covering of a fruit or seed such as a pea or bean. 3. the leaves round the stem of a strawberry, raspberry, or similar fruit. ~*vb.* 4. to remove the hulls from (fruit or seeds).

hullabaloo (,hʌləbə'luː) n., pl. **-loos.** a loud confused noise; commotion.

hullo (hʌ'ləʊ) *interj., n.* same as **hello.**

hum (hʌm) *vb.* **humming, hummed.** 1. to make a low continuous vibrating sound. 2. (of a person) to sing with the lips closed. 3. to utter an indistinct sound, as in hesitation. 4. *Slang.* to be in a state of feverish activity: *an area humming with shoppers.* 5. *Slang.* to smell unpleasant. 6. **hum and haw.** to hesitate in speaking. ~*n.* 7. a low continuous murmuring sound. 8. an unpleasant smell. ~*interj., n.* 9. an indistinct sound of hesitation.

human ('hjuːmən) *adj.* 1. of or relating to people: *human nature.* 2. having the qualities of people as opposed to animals, divine beings, or machines: *human failings.* 3. kind or considerate. ~*n.* 4. a human being.

human being n. a man, woman, or child.

humane (hjuː'meɪn) *adj.* 1. showing kindness and sympathy. 2. inflicting as little pain as possible: *a humane killing.* 3. civilizing or liberal: *humane studies.*

humanism ('hjuːmə,nɪzəm) n. the rejection of religion in favour of a belief in the advancement of humanity by its own efforts. —'**humanist** n., adj. —,**human'istic** adj.

humanitarian (hjuː,mænɪ'teərɪən) adj. 1. having the interests of mankind at heart. ~n. 2. a person who has the interests of mankind at heart. —**hu,mani'tarianism** n.

humanity (hjuː'mænɪtɪ) n., pl. **-ties.** 1. the human race. 2. the quality of being human. 3. kindness or mercy. 4. (pl.) the study of literature, philosophy, and the arts.

humanize or **-nise** ('hjuːmə,naɪz) vb. to make human or humane. —,**humani'zation** or **-ni'sation** n.

humankind (,hjuːmən'kaɪnd) n. the human race; humanity.

humanly ('hjuːmənlɪ) adv. by human powers or means: *as fast as is humanly possible.*

humanoid ('hjuːmə,nɔɪd) adj. 1. like a human being in appearance. ~n. 2. (in science fiction) a robot or creature resembling a human being.

human rights pl. n. the basic rights of individuals to liberty, justice, etc.

humble ('hʌmb³l) adj. 1. conscious of one's failings. 2. unpretentious; lowly: *a humble cottage; my humble opinion.* ~vb. 3. to cause to become humble; humiliate. —'**humbly** adv.

humble pie n. **eat humble pie.** to be forced to behave humbly; be humiliated.

humbug ('hʌm,bʌg) n. 1. *Brit.* a hard peppermint sweet with a striped pattern. 2. a person or thing that deceives. 3. nonsense.

humdinger ('hʌm,dɪŋə) n. *Slang.* an excellent person or thing.

humdrum ('hʌm,drʌm) adj. ordinary; dull.

humerus ('hjuːmərəs) n., pl. **-meri** (-mə,raɪ). the bone from the shoulder to the elbow. —'**humeral** adj.

humid ('hjuːmɪd) adj. moist; damp.

humidex ('hjuːmɪ,dɛks) n. *Canad.* a system of measuring discomfort showing the combined effect of humidity and temperature.

humidify (hjuː'mɪdɪ,faɪ) vb. **-fying, -fied.** to make the air in (a room) more humid or damp. —**hu'midi,fier** n.

humidity (hjuː'mɪdɪtɪ) n. 1. dampness. 2. a measure of the amount of moisture in the air.

humiliate (hjuː'mɪlɪ,eɪt) vb. to lower or hurt the dignity or pride of: *he humiliated her in front of her friends.* —**hu'mili,ating** adj. —**hu,mili'ation** n.

humility (hju:'mɪlɪtɪ) *n*. the quality of being humble.

hummingbird ('hʌmɪŋˌbɜːd) *n*. a very small American bird with a brilliant plumage, long slender bill, and powerful wings that hum as they vibrate.

hummock ('hʌmək) *n*. a hillock.

humorist ('hju:mərɪst) *n*. a person who speaks or writes in a humorous way.

humorous ('hju:mərəs) *adj*. funny; comical; amusing. —**'humorously** *adv*.

humour *or U.S.* **humor** ('hju:mə) *n*. **1.** the quality of being funny. **2.** the ability to appreciate or express things that are humorous: *a good sense of humour*. **3.** situations, speech, or writings that are humorous. **4.** a state of mind; mood: *good humour*. **5.** any of various fluids in the body: *aqueous humour*. ~*vb*. **6.** to indulge: *he bought it to humour his wife*. —**'humourless** *adj*.

hump (hʌmp) *n*. **1.** a rounded lump on the ground. **2.** a rounded deformity of the back. **3.** a rounded lump on the back of a camel or related animal. **4. the hump.** *Brit. informal*. a fit of sulking: *what's he got the hump about?* ~*vb*. **5.** *Slang*. to carry or heave.

humpback ('hʌmpˌbæk) *n*. **1.** same as **hunchback. 2.** Also called: **humpback whale.** a large whalebone whale with a hump on its back. **3.** Also called: **humpback bridge.** *Brit*. a road bridge with a sharp slope on either side. —**'humpˌbacked** *adj*.

humph (hʌmf) *interj*. an exclamation of annoyance or indecision.

humus ('hju:məs) *n*. a dark brown or black mass of partially decomposed plant and animal matter in the soil.

Hun (hʌn) *n*., *pl*. **Huns** *or* **Hun. 1.** a member of any of several Asiatic peoples who invaded the Roman Empire in the 4th and 5th centuries A.D. **2.** *Offensive, informal*. (esp. in World War I) a German.

hunch (hʌntʃ) *n*. **1.** an intuitive guess or feeling. **2.** same as **hump.** ~*vb*. **3.** to draw (oneself or one's shoulders) up or together.

hunchback ('hʌntʃˌbæk) *n*. a person who has an abnormal curvature of the spine. —**'hunchˌbacked** *adj*.

hundred ('hʌndrəd) *n*., *pl*. **-dreds** *or* **-dred. 1.** the cardinal number that is the product of ten and ten. **2.** a numeral, 100, C, representing this number. **3.** (*often pl*.) a large but unspecified number, amount, or quantity. **4.** (*pl*.) the 100 years of a specified century: *in the sixteen hundreds*. ~*det*. **5.** amounting to a hundred. —**'hundredth** *adj.*, *n*.

hundreds and thousands *pl. n*. tiny beads of coloured sugar, used in decorating cakes.

hundredweight ('hʌndrədˌweɪt) *n*., *pl*. **-weights** *or* **-weight. 1.** *Brit*. a unit of weight equal to 112 pounds (50.802 kg). **2.** *U.S. & Canad*. a unit of weight equal to 100 pounds (45.359 kg). **3.** a metric unit of weight equal to 50 kilograms.

hung (hʌŋ) *vb*. **1.** past of **hang** (except in the sense of *to execute*). ~*adj*. **2.** (of a parliament or jury) with no side having a clear majority. **3. hung over.** *Informal*. suffering the effects of a hangover.

Hungarian (hʌŋ'geərɪən) *n*. **1.** the official language of Hungary. **2.** a person from Hungary. ~*adj*. **3.** of or relating to Hungary, its people, or their language.

hunger ('hʌŋgə) *n*. **1.** a feeling of emptiness or weakness caused by lack of food. **2.** desire or craving: *a hunger for power*. ~*vb*. **3.** (foll. by *for* or *after*) to have a great desire (for).

hunger strike *n*. a voluntary fast undertaken, usually by a prisoner, as a means of protest.

hungry ('hʌŋgrɪ) *adj*. **-grier, -griest. 1.** desiring food. **2.** (foll. by *for*) having a craving, desire, or need for: *hungry for news*. **3.** expressing greed, craving, or desire: *hungry eyes*. —**'hungrily** *adv*.

hunk (hʌŋk) *n*. **1.** a large piece: *a hunk of cheese*. **2.** *Slang*. a sexually attractive man.

hunkers ('hʌŋkəz) *pl. n*. haunches.

hunt (hʌnt) *vb*. **1.** to seek out and kill (animals) for food or sport. **2.** (often foll. by *for*) to search (for): *to hunt for a book*. **3.** (often foll. by *down*) to track in an attempt to capture (someone): *to hunt down a criminal*. ~*n*. **4.** the act or an instance of hunting. **5.** a party organized for the pursuit of wild animals for sport. **6.** the members of such a party. —**'hunting** *n*.

hunter ('hʌntə) *n*. **1.** a person or animal that seeks out and kills or captures game. **2.** a person who looks carefully for something: *a bargain-hunter*. **3.** a horse used in hunting. **4.** a watch with a hinged metal lid or case to protect the glass.

huntsman ('hʌntsmən) *n*., *pl*. **-men. 1.** a person who hunts. **2.** a person who trains hounds and manages them during a hunt.

hurdle ('hɜːd³l) *n*. **1.** *Athletics*. one of a number of light barriers over which runners leap in certain events. **2.** an obstacle: *the next hurdle in his career*. ~*vb*. **3.** to jump (a hurdle). —**'hurdler** *n*.

hurdy-gurdy ('hɜːdɪˌgɜːdɪ) *n*., *pl*. **hurdy-gurdies.** a mechanical musical instrument, such as a barrel organ.

hurl (hɜːl) *vb*. **1.** to throw (something) with great force. **2.** to utter (something) with force; yell: *to hurl insults*.

hurling ('hɜːlɪŋ) *or* **hurley** *n*. a traditional Irish game resembling hockey.

hurly-burly ('hɜːlɪˈbɜːlɪ) *n*. confusion or commotion.

hurrah (hʊˈrɑː) *or* **hooray** *interj., n.* a cheer of joy or victory.

hurricane (ˈhʌrɪkˈn) *n.* a severe, often destructive storm, esp. a tropical cyclone.

hurricane lamp *n.* a paraffin lamp with a glass covering.

hurried (ˈhʌrɪd) *adj.* done with great or excessive haste. —ˈ**hurriedly** *adv.*

hurry (ˈhʌrɪ) *vb.* **-rying, -ried. 1.** to hasten; rush: *hurry home.* **2.** to speed up the completion or progress of: *if you hurry your work you will make mistakes.* ~*n.* **3.** haste. **4.** urgency or eagerness: *in my hurry to get here I forgot my glasses.* **5. in a hurry.** *Informal.* **a.** easily: *you won't beat him in a hurry.* **b.** willingly: *we won't go there again in a hurry.*

hurt (hɜːt) *vb.* **hurting, hurt. 1.** to cause physical or mental injury to: *don't hurt me.* **2.** to cause someone to feel pain: *my leg hurts.* **3.** *Informal.* to feel pain: *I'm hurting all over.* ~*n.* **4.** physical or mental pain or suffering. ~*adj.* **5.** injured or pained: *a hurt knee; a hurt look.* —ˈ**hurtful** *adj.*

hurtle (ˈhɜːtˈl) *vb.* to move very quickly or violently.

husband (ˈhʌzbənd) *n.* **1.** a woman's partner in marriage. ~*vb.* **2.** to use (resources, finances, etc.) thriftily.

husbandry (ˈhʌzbəndrɪ) *n.* **1.** farming. **2.** management of resources.

hush (hʌʃ) *vb.* **1.** to make silent; quieten; soothe. ~*n.* **2.** stillness; silence. ~*interj.* **3.** a plea or demand for silence. —**hushed** *adj.*

hush-hush *adj. Informal.* (esp. of official work) secret; confidential.

hush money *n. Slang.* money given to a person to ensure that something is kept secret.

hush up *vb.* to suppress information or rumours about (something).

husk (hʌsk) *n.* **1.** the outer covering of certain fruits and seeds. ~*vb.* **2.** to remove the husk from.

husky[1] (ˈhʌskɪ) *adj.* **huskier, huskiest. 1.** (of a voice) slightly hoarse. **2.** *Informal.* (of a man) big and strong. —ˈ**huskily** *adv.*

husky[2] (ˈhʌskɪ) *n., pl.* **huskies.** an Arctic sled dog with a thick coat and a curled tail.

hussar (hʊˈzɑː) *n.* a member of a light cavalry regiment.

hussy (ˈhʌsɪ, -zɪ) *n., pl.* **-sies.** a shameless or promiscuous woman.

hustings (ˈhʌstɪŋz) *pl. n.* the proceedings at a parliamentary election.

hustle (ˈhʌsˈl) *vb.* **1.** to shove (someone) roughly or furtively: *he hustled her out of sight.* **2.** to deal with (something) hurriedly: *to hustle legislation through.* **3.** *U.S. & Canad. slang.* (of a prostitute) to solicit clients. ~*n.* **4.** lively activity; bustle.

hut (hʌt) *n.* a small house or shelter.

hutch (hʌtʃ) *n.* a cage for small animals.

hyacinth (ˈhaɪəsɪnθ) *n.* a plant with bell-shaped sweet-smelling flowers.

hyaena (haɪˈiːnə) *n.* same as **hyena.**

hybrid (ˈhaɪbrɪd) *n.* **1.** an animal or plant resulting from a cross between two different types of animal or plant. **2.** anything of mixed ancestry. ~*adj.* **3.** of mixed origin.

hybridize *or* **-ise** (ˈhaɪbrɪˌdaɪz) *vb.* to produce or cause (species) to produce hybrids; crossbreed. —ˌ**hybridiˈzation** *or* **-iˈsation** *n.*

hydatid disease (ˈhaɪdətɪd) *n.* a condition caused by the presence of bladder-like cysts (**hydatids**) in the liver, lungs, or brain.

hydra (ˈhaɪdrə) *n.* **1.** a freshwater polyp with tentacles around the mouth. **2.** a persistent trouble.

hydrangea (haɪˈdreɪndʒə) *n.* a shrub with large clusters of white, pink, or blue flowers.

hydrant (ˈhaɪdrənt) *n.* an outlet from a water main, from which water can be tapped for fighting fires.

hydrate (ˈhaɪdreɪt) *Chem.* ~*n.* **1.** a compound containing water chemically combined with a substance: *chloral hydrate.* ~*vb.* **2.** to treat or impregnate (a substance) with water or (of a substance) to be treated or impregnated with water. —**hyˈdration** *n.*

hydraulic (haɪˈdrɒlɪk) *adj.* operated by pressure transmitted through a pipe by a liquid, such as water or oil. —**hyˈdraulically** *adv.*

hydraulics (haɪˈdrɒlɪks) *n.* (*functioning as sing.*) the study of the mechanical properties of fluids as they apply to practical engineering.

hydride (ˈhaɪdraɪd) *n. Chem.* a compound of hydrogen with another element.

hydro[1] (ˈhaɪdrəʊ) *n., pl.* **-dros.** *Brit.* a hotel offering facilities for hydropathic treatment.

hydro[2] (ˈhaɪdrəʊ) *adj.* short for **hydroelectric.**

hydro- *or before a vowel* **hydr-** *combining form.* **1.** indicating water or fluid: *hydrodynamics.* **2.** indicating hydrogen in a chemical compound: *hydrochloric acid.*

hydrocarbon (ˌhaɪdrəʊˈkɑːbˈn) *n. Chem.* a compound containing only carbon and hydrogen.

hydrocephalus (ˌhaɪdrəʊˈsɛfələs) *n.* accumulation of fluid within the cavities of the brain. —**hydrocephalic** (ˌhaɪdrəʊsɪˈfælɪk) *adj.*

hydrochloric acid (ˌhaɪdrəˈklɒrɪk) *n. Chem.* a solution of hydrogen chloride in water: a strong acid used in many industrial and laboratory processes.

hydrodynamics (ˌhaɪdrəʊdaɪˈnæmɪks, -dɪ-) *n.* (*functioning as sing.*) the branch of science concerned with the mechanical properties of fluids.

hydroelectric (ˌhaɪdrəʊˈlɛktrɪk) *adj.* **1.** generated by the pressure of falling water: *hydroelectric power.* **2.** of the generation of electricity by water pressure: *a hydroelectric scheme.* —**hydroelectricity** (ˌhaɪdrəʊlɛkˈtrɪsɪtɪ) *n.*

hydrofoil (ˈhaɪdrəˌfɔɪl) *n.* **1.** a fast light vessel the hull of which is raised out of the water on one or more pairs of fins. **2.** any of these fins.

hydrogen (ˈhaɪdrɪdʒən) *n. Chem.* a colourless gas that burns easily and is the lightest element in the universe. It occurs in water and in most organic compounds. Symbol: H —**hydrogenous** (haɪˈdrɒdʒɪnəs) *adj.*

hydrogenate (haɪˈdrɒdʒɪˌneɪt) *vb. Chem.* to combine (a substance) with hydrogen: *hydrogenated vegetable oil.* —ˌhydro-genˈation *n.*

hydrogen bomb *n.* an extremely powerful bomb in which energy is released by fusion of hydrogen nuclei to give helium nuclei.

hydrogen peroxide *n.* a colourless oily unstable liquid chemical used as a bleach.

hydrogen sulphide *n.* a colourless poisonous gas with an odour of rotten eggs.

hydrography (haɪˈdrɒgrəfɪ) *n.* the study of the oceans, seas, and rivers. —**hyˈdrographer** *n.* —**hydrographic** (ˌhaɪdrəˈgræfɪk) *adj.*

hydrology (haɪˈdrɒlədʒɪ) *n.* the study of the distribution, conservation, and use, of the water of the earth and its atmosphere.

hydrolysis (haɪˈdrɒlɪsɪs) *n. Chem.* a process of decomposition in which a compound reacts with water to produce other compounds.

hydrometer (haɪˈdrɒmɪtə) *n.* an instrument for measuring the density of a liquid.

hydropathy (haɪˈdrɒpəθɪ) *n.* a method of treating disease by the use of large quantities of water both internally and externally. —**hydropathic** (ˌhaɪdrəʊˈpæθɪk) *adj.*

hydrophilic (ˌhaɪdrəʊˈfɪlɪk) *adj. Chem.* tending to dissolve in or mix with water: *a hydrophilic colloid.*

hydrophobia (ˌhaɪdrəˈfəʊbɪə) *n.* **1.** same as **rabies.** **2.** (esp. of a person with rabies) a fear of drinking fluids. —ˌhydroˈphobic *adj.*

hydroplane (ˈhaɪdrəʊˌpleɪn) *n.* **1.** a motorboat that raises its hull out of the water at high speeds. **2.** a fin on the hull of a submarine for controlling its vertical motion.

hydroponics (ˌhaɪdrəʊˈpɒnɪks) *n. (functioning as sing.)* a method of growing plants in gravel, etc., through which water containing the necessary nutrients is pumped.

hydrosphere (ˈhaɪdrəˌsfɪə) *n.* the watery part of the earth's surface.

hydrostatics (ˌhaɪdrəʊˈstætɪks) *n. (functioning as sing.)* the branch of science concerned with the properties and behaviour of fluids that are not in motion. —ˌhydro-ˈstatic *adj.*

hydrotherapy (ˌhaɪdrəʊˈθɛrəpɪ) *n. Med.* the treatment of certain diseases by the external application of water.

hydrous (ˈhaɪdrəs) *adj.* containing water.

hydroxide (haɪˈdrɒksaɪd) *n. Chem.* a compound containing a hydroxyl group or ion.

hydroxyl (haɪˈdrɒksɪl) *n. (modifier) Chem.* of or containing the monovalent group -OH or the ion OH⁻: *a hydroxyl group or radical.*

hyena *or* **hyaena** (haɪˈiːnə) *n.* a meat-eating doglike mammal of Africa and S Asia.

hygiene (ˈhaɪdʒiːn) *n.* **1.** clean or healthy practices: *personal hygiene.* **2.** Also called: **hygienics.** the science concerned with the maintenance of health. —**hyˈgienic** *adj.* —**hyˈgienically** *adv.* —**ˈhygienist** *n.*

hygrometer (haɪˈgrɒmɪtə) *n.* an instrument for measuring humidity.

hygroscope (ˈhaɪgrəˌskəʊp) *n.* a device that indicates the humidity of the air without measuring it.

hygroscopic (ˌhaɪgrəˈskɒpɪk) *adj.* (of a substance) tending to absorb water from the air.

hymen (ˈhaɪmɛn) *n. Anat.* a membrane that partly covers the entrance to the vagina and is usually ruptured when sexual intercourse takes place for the first time.

hymenopterous (ˌhaɪmɪˈnɒptərəs) *adj.* of or belonging to an order of insects with two pairs of membranous wings.

hymn (hɪm) *n.* a Christian song of praise sung to God or a saint.

hymnal (ˈhɪmnəl) *n.* a book of hymns. Also: **hymn book.**

hymnody (ˈhɪmnədɪ) *n.* **1.** the composition or singing of hymns. **2.** hymns collectively.

hymnology (hɪmˈnɒlədʒɪ) *n.* the study of hymn composition. —**hymˈnologist** *n.*

hype (haɪp) *Slang.* ~*n.* **1.** intensive or exaggerated publicity or sales promotion. ~*vb.* **2.** to market or promote (a commodity) using intensive or exaggerated publicity.

hyped up *adj. Old-fashioned slang.* stimulated or excited by or as if by drug.

hyper (ˈhaɪpə) *adj. Informal.* overactive; overexcited.

hyper- *prefix.* above, over, or in excess: *hypercritical.*

hyperactive (ˌhaɪpərˈæktɪv) *adj.* abnormally active.

hyperbola (haɪˈpɜːbələ) *n. Geom.* a conic section formed by a plane that cuts a cone at a steeper angle to its base than its side.

hyperbole (haɪˈpɜːbəlɪ) *n.* a deliberate exaggeration used for effect: *he embraced her a thousand times.*

hyperbolic (ˌhaɪpəˈbɒlɪk) *or* **hyperbolical** *adj.* of a hyperbola or a hyperbole.

hypercritical (ˌhaɪpəˈkrɪtɪkᵊl) *adj.* excessively critical.

hyperglycaemia *or U.S.* **hyperglycemia** (ˌhaɪpəglaɪˈsiːmɪə) *n. Pathol.* an abnormally large amount of sugar in the blood.

hypermarket (ˈhaɪpəˌmɑːkɪt) *n.* a huge self-service store.

hypersensitive (ˌhaɪpəˈsɛnsɪtɪv) *adj.* **1.** having unduly vulnerable feelings. **2.** abnormally sensitive to an allergen, a drug, or high or low temperatures.

hypersonic (ˌhaɪpəˈsɒnɪk) *adj.* having a speed of at least five times the speed of sound.

hypertension (ˌhaɪpəˈtɛnʃən) *n. Pathol.* abnormally high blood pressure.

hypertrophy (haɪˈpɜːtrəfɪ) *n., pl.* **-phies.** enlargement of an organ or part resulting from an increase in the size of the cells.

hyperventilation (ˌhaɪpəˌvɛntɪˈleɪʃən) *n.* an increase in the rate of breathing at rest. —ˌhyperˈventiˌlate *vb.*

hyphen (ˈhaɪfᵊn) *n.* the punctuation mark (-), used to separate parts of compound words and between syllables of a word split between two consecutive lines.

hyphenate (ˈhaɪfᵊˌneɪt) *vb.* to separate (words) with a hyphen. —ˌhyphenˈation *n.*

hypnosis (hɪpˈnəʊsɪs) *n.* an artificially induced state of relaxation in which the mind is more than usually receptive to suggestion.

hypnotherapy (ˌhɪpnəʊˈθɛrəpɪ) *n.* the use of hypnosis in the treatment of emotional and mental problems.

hypnotic (hɪpˈnɒtɪk) *adj.* **1.** of or producing hypnosis or sleep. **2.** having an effect resembling hypnosis: *a hypnotic voice.* ~*n.* **3.** a drug that induces sleep. —**hypˈnotically** *adv.*

hypnotism (ˈhɪpnəˌtɪzəm) *n.* **1.** the practice of hypnosis. **2.** the process of inducing hypnosis. —ˈhypnotist *n.*

hypnotize *or* **-tise** (ˈhɪpnəˌtaɪz) *vb.* **1.** to induce hypnosis in (a person). **2.** to charm or beguile; fascinate.

hypo- *or before a vowel* **hyp-** *prefix.* beneath; less than: *hypodermic.*

hypoallergenic (ˌhaɪpəʊˌæləˈdʒɛnɪk) *adj.* not likely to cause an allergic reaction.

hypocaust (ˈhaɪpəˌkɔːst) *n.* an ancient Roman heating system in which hot air circulated under the floor and between double walls.

hypochondria (ˌhaɪpəˈkɒndrɪə) *n.* abnormal anxiety concerning one's health.

hypochondriac (ˌhaɪpəˈkɒndrɪˌæk) *n.* a person suffering from hypochondria.

hypocrisy (hɪˈpɒkrəsɪ) *n., pl.* **-sies.** **1.** the practice of claiming to have standards or beliefs that are contrary to one's real character or actual behaviour. **2.** an act or instance of this.

hypocrite (ˈhɪpəkrɪt) *n.* a person who pretends to be what he is not. —ˌhypoˈcritical *adj.*

hypodermic (ˌhaɪpəˈdɜːmɪk) *adj.* **1.** used for injecting. ~*n.* **2.** a hypodermic syringe or needle.

hypodermic syringe *n. Med.* a syringe consisting of a hollow cylinder, a piston, and a hollow needle, used for withdrawing blood samples or injecting drugs under the skin.

hypotension (ˌhaɪpəʊˈtɛnʃən) *n. Pathol.* abnormally low blood pressure.

hypotenuse (haɪˈpɒtɪˌnjuːz) *n.* the side in a right-angled triangle that is opposite the right angle.

hypothermia (ˌhaɪpəʊˈθɜːmɪə) *n. Pathol.* an abnormally low body temperature, as a result of exposure to cold weather.

hypothesis (haɪˈpɒθɪsɪs) *n., pl.* **-ses** (-ˌsiːz). a suggested explanation for a group of facts, accepted either as a basis for further verification or as likely to be true. —**hyˈpotheˌsize** *or* **-ise** *vb.*

hypothetical (ˌhaɪpəˈθɛtɪkᵊl) *adj.* assumed or thought to exist. —ˌhypoˈthetically *adv.*

hyssop (ˈhɪsəp) *n.* **1.** an aromatic herb used in folk medicine. **2.** a Biblical plant, used for sprinkling in the ritual practices of the Hebrews.

hysterectomy (ˌhɪstəˈrɛktəmɪ) *n., pl.* **-mies.** surgical removal of the womb.

hysteria (hɪˈstɪərɪə) *n.* **1.** a mental disorder marked by emotional outbursts and, often, symptoms such as paralysis. **2.** any frenzied emotional state, as of laughter or crying.

hysteric (hɪˈstɛrɪk) *n.* a hysterical person.

hysterical (hɪˈstɛrɪkᵊl) *adj.* **1.** suggesting hysteria: *hysterical cries.* **2.** suffering from hysteria. **3.** *Informal.* wildly funny. —**hysˈterically** *adv.*

hysterics (hɪˈstɛrɪks) *n. (functioning as pl. or sing.)* **1.** an attack of hysteria. **2.** *Informal.* wild uncontrollable bursts of laughter.

Hz hertz.

I

i or **I** (aɪ) *n., pl.* **i's, I's,** or **Is.** the ninth letter and third vowel of the English alphabet.

i the imaginary number √−1.

I[1] (aɪ) *pron.* used by a speaker or writer to refer to himself as the subject of a verb.

I[2] **1.** *Chem.* iodine. **2.** the Roman numeral for one.

I. 1. Independent. **2.** Institute. **3.** International. **4.** Island; Isle.

IA or **Ia.** Iowa.

iamb (ˈaɪæm) or **iambus** (aɪˈæmbəs) *n., pl.* **iambs** or **iambuses.** *Prosody.* a metrical foot of two syllables, a short one followed by a long one.

iambic (aɪˈæmbɪk) *Prosody.* ~*adj.* **1.** of or using an iamb. ~*n.* **2.** a metrical foot, line, or stanza consisting of iambs.

IBA (in Britain) Independent Broadcasting Authority.

Iberian (aɪˈbɪərɪən) *n.* **1.** a person from the Iberian Peninsula in SW Europe; a Spaniard or Portuguese. ~*adj.* **2.** of the Iberian Peninsula, its inhabitants, or any of their languages.

ibex (ˈaɪbɛks) *n., pl.* **ibexes** or **ibex.** a wild goat of the mountainous regions of Europe, Asia, and North Africa, which has large backward-curving horns.

ibid. (referring to a book, page, or passage previously cited) in the same place.

ibis (ˈaɪbɪs) *n., pl.* **ibises** or **ibis.** a large wading bird with a long thin curved bill.

Ibo (ˈiːbəʊ) *n.* **1.** (*pl.* **Ibos** or **Ibo**) a member of an African people of S Nigeria. **2.** their language.

ICBM intercontinental ballistic missile.

ice (aɪs) *n.* **1.** water that has frozen and become solid. **2.** a portion of ice cream. **3. break the ice.** to relax the atmosphere, esp. between strangers. **4. on ice.** in readiness or reserve. **5. on thin ice.** unsafe; dangerous. ~*vb.* **6.** (often foll. by *up* or *over*) to form ice; freeze. **7.** to cool or chill with ice. **8.** to cover (a cake) with icing. —**iced** *adj.*

ice age *n.* same as **glacial period.**

iceberg (ˈaɪsbɜːg) *n.* **1.** a large mass of ice floating in the sea. **2. tip of the iceberg.** the small visible part of a problem that is much larger.

iceberg lettuce *n.* a type of lettuce with very crisp pale leaves tightly enfolded.

icebox (ˈaɪsˌbɒks) *n.* **1.** a compartment in a refrigerator for making or storing ice. **2.** an insulated cabinet packed with ice for keeping food cold. **3.** *U.S. & Canad.* a refrigerator.

icebreaker (ˈaɪsˌbreɪkə) *n.* a ship designed to break through ice.

icecap (ˈaɪsˌkæp) *n.* a thick mass of glacial ice that permanently covers an area.

ice cream *n.* a sweet frozen food, made from cream, milk, or a custard base, flavoured in various ways.

ice field *n.* a large expanse of floating sea ice.

ice floe *n.* a sheet of ice, of variable size, floating in the sea.

ice hockey *n.* a game played on ice by two teams wearing skates, who try to drive a flat puck into their opponents' goal with long sticks.

Icelandic (aɪsˈlændɪk) *adj.* **1.** of Iceland, its people, or their language. ~*n.* **2.** the official language of Iceland.

ice lolly *n. Brit. informal.* a water ice or an ice cream on a stick.

ice pack *n.* **1.** a bag or folded cloth containing crushed ice, applied to a part of the body to reduce swelling. **2.** same as **pack ice.**

ice skate *n.* **1.** a boot with a steel blade fitted to the sole which enables the wearer to glide over ice. ~*vb.* **ice-skate. 2.** to glide over ice on ice skates. —**ˈice-ˌskater** *n.*

ichthyology (ˌɪkθɪˈɒlədʒɪ) *n.* the study of fishes. —**ichthyological** (ˌɪkθɪəˈlɒdʒɪkᵊl) *adj.* —**ˌichthyˈologist** *n.*

ICI Imperial Chemical Industries.

icicle (ˈaɪsɪkᵊl) *n.* a hanging spike of ice formed by dripping water freezing as it falls.

icing (ˈaɪsɪŋ) *n.* **1.** Also (esp. U.S. and Canad.): **frosting.** a mixture of sugar and water or egg whites used to coat and decorate cakes. **2. icing on the cake.** any unexpected extra or bonus. **3.** the formation of ice on a ship or aircraft.

icing sugar *n. Brit.* a very finely ground sugar used for making icing or sweets.

icon (ˈaɪkɒn) *n.* a picture of Christ, the Virgin Mary, or a saint, venerated in the Orthodox Church.

iconoclast (aɪˈkɒnəˌklæst) *n.* **1.** a person who attacks established or traditional ideas or principles. **2.** a destroyer of religious images or objects. —**iˌconoˈclastic** *adj.* —**iˈconoˌclasm** *n.*

icosahedron (ˌaɪkəsəˈhiːdrən) *n., pl.* **-drons** or **-dra** (-drə). a solid figure with 20 faces.

icy (ˈaɪsɪ) *adj.* **icier, iciest. 1.** made of,

covered with, or containing ice. **2.** like ice. **3.** freezing or very cold. **4.** cold or reserved in manner; aloof. —**'icily** adv. —**'iciness** n.

id (ɪd) n. Psychoanal. the primitive instincts and energies in the unconscious mind that underlie all psychological impulses.

ID 1. Idaho. **2.** identification.

I'd (aɪd) I had or I would.

idea (aɪ'dɪə) n. **1.** any product of mental activity; thought. **2.** the thought of something: the idea appals me. **3.** a belief; opinion. **4.** a scheme, intention, or plan. **5.** a vague notion; inkling: he had no idea of the truth. **6.** a person's conception of something: her idea of honesty is not the same as mine. **7.** aim or purpose: the idea of the game is to discover the murderer. **8.** Philosophy. (in Plato) a universal model of which all things in the same class are only imperfect imitations.

ideal (aɪ'dɪəl) n. **1.** a conception of something that is perfect. **2.** a person or thing considered to represent perfection. **3.** something existing only as an idea. ~adj. **4.** conforming to an ideal: he is the ideal person for the job. **5.** of, involving, or existing only as an idea; imaginary: an ideal world. —**i'deally** adv.

idealism (aɪ'dɪə,lɪzəm) n. **1.** belief in or striving towards ideals. **2.** the tendency to represent things in their ideal forms, rather than as they are. **3.** Philosophy. the doctrine that material objects and the external world do not exist in reality, but are creations of the mind. —**i'dealist** n. —**i,deal-'istic** adj.

idealize or **-ise** (aɪ'dɪə,laɪz) vb. to consider or represent (something) as ideal or more nearly perfect than is true. —**i,deali'zation** or **-i'sation** n.

idée fixe (,iːdeɪ 'fiːks) n., pl. **idées fixes** (,iːdeɪ 'fiːks). a fixed idea; obsession.

idem ('aɪdɛm, 'ɪdɛm) pron., adj. the same: used to refer to an article, chapter, or book previously cited.

identical (aɪ'dɛntɪk²l) adj. **1.** that is the same: we got the identical hotel room as last year. **2.** exactly alike or equal. **3.** (of twins) developed from a single fertilized ovum that has split into two, and thus of the same sex and very much alike. —**i'dentically** adv.

identification (aɪ,dɛntɪfɪ'keɪʃən) n. **1.** an identifying or being identified. **2.** something that identifies a person or thing.

identification parade n. a group of persons, including one suspected of a crime, assembled to discover whether a witness can identify the suspect.

identify (aɪ'dɛntɪ,faɪ) vb. **-fying, -fied. 1.** to prove or recognize as being a certain person or thing; determine the identity of. **2.** to consider or treat as the same. **3.** to

connect or associate closely: he was identified with a revolutionary group. **4.** (often foll. by with) to understand and sympathize with a person or group because one regards oneself as having characteristics in common with them. —**i'denti,fiable** adj.

Identikit (aɪ'dɛntɪ,kɪt) n. Trademark. a composite picture, assembled from descriptions given, of a person wanted by the police.

identity (aɪ'dɛntɪtɪ) n., pl. **-ties. 1.** the state of being a specified person or thing: the identity of the killer is still unknown. **2.** the individual characteristics by which a person or thing is recognized; individuality or personality. **3.** the state of being the same: linked by the identity of their tastes. **4.** Maths. Also called: **identity element.** a member of a set that when combined with any other member of the set, leaves it unchanged: the identity for multiplication of numbers is 1.

ideogram ('ɪdɪəʊ,græm) or **ideograph** ('ɪdɪəʊ,grɑːf) n. a character or symbol that directly represents a concept or thing, rather than the sounds that form its name.

ideology (,aɪdɪ'ɒlədʒɪ) n., pl. **-gies.** the doctrines, opinions, or way of thinking of a person, group, or nation. —**ideological** (,aɪdɪə'lɒdʒɪk²l) adj. —**,ide'ologist** n.

ides (aɪdz) n. (functioning as sing.) (in the ancient Roman calendar) the 15th day in March, May, July, and October and the 13th of the other months.

idiocy ('ɪdɪəsɪ) n., pl. **-cies. 1.** (not in technical usage) severe mental retardation. **2.** foolishness; stupidity. **3.** a foolish act or remark.

idiom ('ɪdɪəm) n. **1.** a group of words which, when used together, have a different meaning from the one suggested by the individual words, e.g. it was raining cats and dogs. **2.** linguistic usage that is grammatical and natural to native speakers. **3.** the characteristic vocabulary or usage of a specific person or group. **4.** the characteristic artistic style of an individual or school. —**idiomatic** (,ɪdɪə'mætɪk) adj.

idiosyncrasy (,ɪdɪəʊ'sɪŋkrəsɪ) n., pl. **-sies.** a personal peculiarity, habit, or type of behaviour; quirk. —**idiosyncratic** (,ɪdɪəʊsɪŋ-'krætɪk) adj.

idiot ('ɪdɪət) n. **1.** a person with severe mental retardation. **2.** a foolish or senseless person. —**idiotic** (,ɪdɪ'ɒtɪk) adj. —**,idi'otically** adv.

idle ('aɪd²l) adj. **1.** unemployed or unoccupied; inactive. **2.** not operating or being used. **3.** not wanting to work; lazy. **4.** frivolous or trivial: idle pleasures. **5.** ineffective or vain: it would be idle to look for a solution now. **6.** without basis; unfounded: idle rumours. ~vb. **7.** (often foll. by away) to waste or pass (time) in idleness; be idle. **8.** (of an engine) to run at low speed without transmitting any power. —**'idleness** n. —**'idler** n. —**'idly** adv.

idol ('aɪd'l) n. **1.** an image of a god used as an object of worship. **2.** an object of excessive devotion or admiration.

idolatry (aɪ'dɒlətrɪ) n. **1.** the worship of idols. **2.** excessive devotion or reverence. —i**'dolater** n. —i**'dolatrous** adj.

idolize or **-ise** ('aɪdə,laɪz) vb. **1.** to admire or revere greatly. **2.** to worship as an idol. —,**idoli'zation** or **-i'sation** n.

idyll or U.S. (sometimes) **idyl** ('ɪdɪl) n. **1.** a poem or prose work describing a simple, pleasant rural or pastoral scene. **2.** such a scene. —i**'dyllic** adj.

i.e. that is to say.

if (ɪf) conj. **1.** in the event that, or on condition that: if you try hard it might work. **2.** used to introduce an indirect question to which the answer is either yes or no; whether: I asked if I could help. **3.** even though: an attractive if awkward girl. **4.** used to introduce an unfulfilled wish, with only: if only you had told me. ~n. **5.** a condition or stipulation: I won't have any ifs or buts.

iffy ('ɪfɪ) adj. Informal. full of uncertainty.

igloo ('ɪgluː) n., pl. **-loos.** a dome-shaped Eskimo house, built of blocks of solid snow.

igneous ('ɪgnɪəs) adj. **1.** (of rocks) formed by volcanic action. **2.** of or like fire.

ignis fatuus ('ɪgnɪs 'fætjʊəs) n., pl. **ignes fatui** ('ɪgniːz 'fætjʊ,aɪ). same as **will-o'-the-wisp.**

ignite (ɪg'naɪt) vb. to catch fire or set fire to. —ig**'nitable** or ig**'nitible** adj.

ignition (ɪg'nɪʃən) n. **1.** an igniting or the process of igniting. **2.** the system used to ignite the fuel in an internal-combustion engine.

ignoble (ɪg'nəʊb'l) adj. **1.** dishonourable; base; despicable. **2.** of low birth or origins. —ig**'nobly** adv.

ignominy ('ɪgnə,mɪnɪ) n., pl. **-minies.** disgrace or public shame; dishonour. —,**igno'minious** adj.

ignoramus (,ɪgnə'reɪməs) n., pl. **-muses.** an ignorant person; fool.

ignorance ('ɪgnərəns) n. lack of knowledge or education; the state of being ignorant.

ignorant ('ɪgnərənt) adj. **1.** lacking in knowledge or education; unenlightened. **2.** (often foll. by of) lacking in awareness or knowledge (of): ignorant of the law. **3.** uncouth through lack of knowledge or awareness: an ignorant remark.

ignore (ɪg'nɔː) vb. to refuse to notice; disregard deliberately.

iguana (ɪ'gwɑːnə) n. a large tropical tree lizard of the W Indies and S America having a greyish-green body with a row of spines along the back.

ikebana (,iːkə'bɑːnə) n. the Japanese art of flower arrangement.

IL Illinois.

il- same as **in-[1]** and **in-[2]**.

ileum ('ɪlɪəm) n. the third and lowest part of the small intestine.

ilex ('aɪlɛks) n. **1.** same as **holly.** **2.** same as **holm oak.**

ilium ('ɪlɪəm) n., pl. **-ia** (-ɪə). the uppermost and widest of the three sections of the hipbone.

ilk (ɪlk) n. a type; class; sort: people of that ilk should not be allowed here.

ill (ɪl) adj. **worse, worst. 1.** not in good health; sick. **2.** bad, harmful, or hostile: ill effect; ill will. **3.** promising an unfavourable outcome: ill omen. **4.** ill at ease. unable to relax; uncomfortable. ~n. **5.** evil or harm; misfortune; trouble. ~adv. **6.** badly, wrongly: the title ill befits him. **7.** with difficulty; hardly: he can ill afford the money.

ill. **1.** illustrated. **2.** illustration.

Ill. Illinois.

I'll (aɪl) I will or I shall.

ill-advised adj. **1.** (of a person) acting without reasonable care or thought. **2.** (of a plan or action) badly thought out; unwise.

ill-bred adj. badly brought up; lacking good manners. —,**ill-'breeding** n.

ill-disposed adj. (often foll. by towards) unfriendly or unsympathetic; malicious.

illegal (ɪ'liːg'l) adj. unlawful; against the law. —il**'legally** adv. —,**ille'gality** n.

illegible (ɪ'lɛdʒɪb'l) adj. unable to be read or deciphered. —il,**legi'bility** n.

illegitimate (,ɪlɪ'dʒɪtɪmɪt) adj. **1.** born of parents who were not married to each other at the time of birth; bastard. **2.** illegal; unlawful. —,**ille'gitimacy** n.

ill-fated adj. doomed or unlucky.

ill-favoured adj. unattractive or repulsive in appearance.

ill-founded adj. not based on proper proof or evidence.

ill-gotten adj. obtained dishonestly or illegally: ill-gotten gains.

ill-health n. the condition of being unwell; poor health.

illiberal (ɪ'lɪbərəl) adj. **1.** narrow-minded; prejudiced; intolerant. **2.** not generous; mean. **3.** lacking in culture or refinement. —il,**liber'ality** n.

illicit (ɪ'lɪsɪt) adj. **1.** same as **illegal. 2.** not allowed or approved by the social customs of a country: illicit sexual relations.

illiterate (ɪ'lɪtərɪt) adj. **1.** unable to read and write. **2.** uneducated or ignorant: scientifically illiterate. ~n. **3.** an illiterate person. —il**'literacy** n.

ill-mannered adj. having bad manners; rude.

illness ('ɪlnɪs) n. **1.** a disease or indisposition; sickness. **2.** a state of ill health.

illogical (ɪ'lɒdʒɪk'l) adj. **1.** senseless or unreasonable. **2.** not following logical principles. —**illogicality** (ɪˌlɒdʒɪˈkælɪtɪ) *n.* —**illogically** *adv.*

ill-starred *adj.* unlucky; unfortunate; ill-fated.

ill-timed *adj.* happening at or done at an unsuitable time.

ill-treat *vb.* to treat (someone or something) cruelly or harshly; maltreat. —ˌ**ill-ˈtreatment** *n.*

illuminant (ɪˈluːmɪnənt) *n.* **1.** something that gives off light. ~*adj.* **2.** giving off light.

illuminate (ɪˈluːmɪˌneɪt) *vb.* **1.** to give light to; light up. **2.** to make easily understood; clarify: *the book illuminates many obscure points.* **3.** to decorate with lights. **4.** to decorate (an initial letter or manuscript) with designs of gold, silver, or bright colours. —**ilˈlumiˌnating** *adj.* —**ilˈluminative** *adj.*

illumination (ɪˌluːmɪˈneɪʃən) *n.* **1.** an illuminating or being illuminated. **2.** a source of light; lighting. **3.** (*pl.*) *Chiefly Brit.* lights used as decorations in streets or towns. **4.** the decoration in colours, gold, or silver used on some manuscripts.

illumine (ɪˈluːmɪn) *vb.* same as **illuminate.**

illusion (ɪˈluːʒən) *n.* **1.** a false appearance or deceptive impression of reality: *the mirror gives an illusion of depth.* **2.** a false or misleading idea or belief; delusion. —**ilˈlusory** *or* **ilˈlusive** *adj.*

illusionist (ɪˈluːʒənɪst) *n.* a conjurer; magician who performs sleight-of-hand tricks.

illustrate (ˈɪləˌstreɪt) *vb.* **1.** to clarify or explain by use of examples or comparisons. **2.** to be an example of. **3.** to explain or decorate (a book or text) with pictures. —ˈ**illusˌtrative** *adj.* —ˈ**illusˌtrator** *n.*

illustration (ˌɪləˈstreɪʃən) *n.* **1.** pictorial matter used to explain or decorate a text. **2.** an example: *an illustration of his ability.* **3.** an illustrating or being illustrated.

illustrious (ɪˈlʌstrɪəs) *adj.* glorious; famous and distinguished.

ill will *n.* hostile feeling; enmity; antagonism.

I'm (aɪm) I am.

im- same as **in-**[1] and **in-**[2].

image (ˈɪmɪdʒ) *n.* **1.** a representation of a person or thing, esp. in sculpture. **2.** an optical reproduction of an object, formed by the lens of an eye or camera or by a mirror. **3.** a person or thing that resembles another closely; double or copy. **4.** a mental picture; idea produced by the imagination or memory. **5.** the appearance or impression given to the public by a person or organization: *a politician's image.* **6.** a personification of a specified quality; epitome: *the image of good breeding.* **7.** a simile or metaphor. ~*vb.* **8.** to picture in the mind;

imagine. **9.** to mirror or reflect an image of. **10.** to portray or describe.

imagery (ˈɪmɪdʒrɪ, -dʒərɪ) *n., pl.* **-ries. 1.** figurative or descriptive language in a literary work. **2.** images collectively, esp. statues or carvings. **3.** mental images.

imaginary (ɪˈmædʒɪnərɪ, -dʒɪnrɪ) *adj.* **1.** existing in the imagination; unreal. **2.** *Maths.* relating to the square root of a negative number.

imagination (ɪˌmædʒɪˈneɪʃən) *n.* **1.** the faculty or action of producing mental images of what is not present or in one's experience. **2.** mental creative ability.

imaginative (ɪˈmædʒɪnətɪv) *adj.* **1.** produced by or showing a creative imagination. **2.** having a vivid imagination.

imagine (ɪˈmædʒɪn) *vb.* **1.** to form a mental image of. **2.** to think, believe, or guess: *I can't imagine what's happened to him.* —**imˈaginable** *adj.*

imago (ɪˈmeɪɡəʊ) *n., pl.* **imagoes** *or* **imagines** (ɪˈmædʒəˌniːz). an adult sexually mature insect.

imam (ɪˈmɑːm) *n. Islam.* **1.** a leader of congregational prayer in a mosque. **2.** the title of some Muslim leaders.

imbalance (ɪmˈbæləns) *n.* a lack of balance as in emphasis or proportion: *the political imbalance of the programme.*

imbecile (ˈɪmbɪˌsiːl) *n.* **1.** *Psychol.* a person of abnormally low intelligence. **2.** *Informal.* an extremely stupid person. ~*adj.* **3.** of or like an imbecile. **4.** stupid or senseless: *an imbecile thing to do.* —**imbecility** (ˌɪmbɪˈsɪlɪtɪ) *n.*

imbed (ɪmˈbɛd) *vb.* **-bedding, -bedded.** same as **embed.**

imbibe (ɪmˈbaɪb) *vb.* **1.** to drink (esp. alcoholic drinks). **2.** *Literary.* to take in or assimilate (ideas): *to imbibe the spirit of the Renaissance.*

imbroglio (ɪmˈbrəʊlɪˌəʊ) *n., pl.* **-glios.** a confusing and complicated situation.

imbue (ɪmˈbjuː) *vb.* **-buing, -bued.** (usually foll. by *with*) **1.** to instil or inspire (with ideals or principles). **2.** *Rare.* to saturate, esp. with dye.

IMF International Monetary Fund.

imitate (ˈɪmɪˌteɪt) *vb.* **1.** to copy the manner or style of or take as a model: *many writers imitated the language of Shakespeare.* **2.** to mimic or impersonate, esp. for humour. **3.** to make a copy or reproduction of; duplicate. —ˈ**imitable** *adj.* —ˈ**imiˌtator** *n.*

imitation (ˌɪmɪˈteɪʃən) *n.* **1.** the act or practice of imitating. **2.** an instance or product of imitating, such as a copy of the manner of a person. **3.** a copy of a genuine article; counterfeit. ~*adj.* **4.** made to resemble something which is usually superior or more expensive: *imitation leather.*

imitative (ˈɪmɪtətɪv) *adj.* **1.** imitating or

tending to copy. **2.** copying or reproducing an original, esp. in an inferior manner: *imitative painting.* **3.** same as **onomatopoeic.**

immaculate (ɪˈmækjʊlɪt) *adj.* **1.** completely clean or tidy: *his clothes were immaculate.* **2.** completely flawless: *an immaculate rendering of the symphony.* —**imˈmaculately** *adv.*

immanent (ˈɪmənənt) *adj.* **1.** inherent; remaining within. **2.** (of God) present throughout the universe. —**ˈimmanence** *n.*

immaterial (ˌɪməˈtɪərɪəl) *adj.* **1.** of no real importance; inconsequential. **2.** not formed of matter; spiritual.

immature (ˌɪməˈtjʊə, -ˈtʃʊə) *adj.* **1.** not fully grown or developed. **2.** without wisdom, insight, or emotional stability, due to lack of maturity. —**ˌimmaˈturity** *n.*

immeasurable (ɪˈmɛʒərəbəl) *adj.* too great to be measured; limitless. —**imˈmeasurably** *adv.*

immediate (ɪˈmiːdɪət) *adj.* **1.** taking place without delay: *an immediate reaction.* **2.** next or nearest in space, time, or relationship: *our immediate neighbour.* **3.** present; current: *the immediate problem is food.* —**imˈmediacy** *n.* —**imˈmediately** *adv.*

immemorial (ˌɪmɪˈmɔːrɪəl) *adj.* originating in the distant past; ancient: *this has been the custom since time immemorial.*

immense (ɪˈmɛns) *adj.* **1.** unusually large; huge. **2.** *Informal.* very good. —**imˈmensely** *adv.* —**imˈmensity** *n.*

immerse (ɪˈmɜːs) *vb.* **1.** (often foll. by *in*) to plunge or dip into liquid. **2.** (often passive; often foll. by *in*) to involve deeply; engross: *to immerse oneself in a problem.* **3.** to baptize by dipping the whole body into water. —**imˈmersion** *n.*

immersion heater *n.* an electrical device in a domestic hot-water tank for heating the water in which it is immersed.

immigrant (ˈɪmɪgrənt) *n.* a person who immigrates.

immigrate (ˈɪmɪˌgreɪt) *vb.* to come to a foreign country in order to settle there. —**ˌimmiˈgration** *n.*

imminent (ˈɪmɪnənt) *adj.* likely to happen soon. —**ˈimminence** *n.*

immiscible (ɪˈmɪsɪbəl) *adj.* (of liquids) incapable of being mixed: *oil and water are immiscible.* —**imˌmisciˈbility** *n.*

immobile (ɪˈməʊbaɪl) *adj.* **1.** not moving; motionless. **2.** not able to move or be moved; fixed. —**immobility** (ˌɪməʊˈbɪlɪtɪ) *n.*

immobilize *or* **-lise** (ɪˈməʊbɪˌlaɪz) *vb.* to make immobile: *to immobilize a car.* —**imˌmobiliˈzation** *or* **-liˈsation** *n.*

immoderate (ɪˈmɒdərɪt) *adj.* lacking in moderation; excessive: *immoderate demands.* —**imˈmoderately** *adv.*

immodest (ɪˈmɒdɪst) *adj.* **1.** indecent; improper. **2.** bold, impudent, or conceited. —**imˈmodesty** *n.*

immolate (ˈɪməʊˌleɪt) *vb.* to kill or offer as a sacrifice. —**ˌimmoˈlation** *n.*

immoral (ɪˈmɒrəl) *adj.* **1.** morally wrong; corrupt: *nuclear energy is dangerous and immoral.* **2.** sexually depraved or promiscuous: *an immoral seducer of young girls.* —**immorality** (ˌɪməˈrælɪtɪ) *n.* **Usage.** see **amoral.**

immortal (ɪˈmɔːtəl) *adj.* **1.** living forever. **2.** having everlasting fame; remembered throughout time. **3.** everlasting; perpetual. ~*n.* **4.** an immortal being. **5.** (*often pl.*) a person who is remembered enduringly, esp. an author. —**immortality** (ˌɪmɔːˈtælɪtɪ) *n.*

immortalize *or* **-ise** (ɪˈmɔːtəˌlaɪz) *vb.* **1.** to give everlasting fame to, as by treating in a literary work. **2.** to give immortality to.

immovable (ɪˈmuːvəbəl) *adj.* **1.** that cannot be moved; immobile. **2.** unyielding; steadfast. **3.** unaffected by feeling; impassive. **4.** unchanging; unalterable. **5.** *Law.* (of property) consisting of land or houses. —**imˌmovaˈbility** *n.* —**imˈmovably** *adv.*

immune (ɪˈmjuːn) *adj.* **1.** protected against a specific disease by inoculation or as the result of natural resistance. **2.** (foll. by *to*) unsusceptible (to) or secure (against): *immune to inflation.* **3.** exempt from obligation or penalty.

immunity (ɪˈmjuːnɪtɪ) *n., pl.* **-ties.** **1.** the ability of an organism to resist disease, by producing its own antibodies or as a result of inoculation. **2.** freedom from obligation or duty, esp. exemption from tax or legal liability.

immunize *or* **-nise** (ˈɪmjʊˌnaɪz) *vb.* to make immune, esp. by inoculation. —**ˌimmuniˈzation** *or* **-niˈsation** *n.*

immunodeficiency (ˌɪmjʊnəʊdɪˈfɪʃənsɪ) *n.* a deficiency in or breakdown of a person's immune system.

immunology (ˌɪmjʊˈnɒlədʒɪ) *n.* the branch of medicine concerned with the study of immunity. —**ˌimmunoˈlogical** *adj.* —**ˌimmuˈnologist** *n.*

immure (ɪˈmjʊə) *vb.* **1.** *Archaic or literary.* to imprison. **2.** to shut (oneself) away from society.

immutable (ɪˈmjuːtəbəl) *adj.* unchangeable or unchanging; ageless: *immutable laws.* —**imˌmutaˈbility** *n.*

imp (ɪmp) *n.* **1.** a small demon. **2.** a mischievous child.

imp. 1. imperative. **2.** imperfect.

impact *n.* (ˈɪmpækt). **1.** the act of one object striking another; collision. **2.** the force of a collision. **3.** the effect or impression made by something. ~*vb.* (ɪmˈpækt). **4.** to press (an object) firmly into (another object) or (of two objects) to be pressed firmly together. —**imˈpaction** *n.*

impacted (ɪmˈpæktɪd) *adj.* (of a tooth) unable to grow out because of being wedged against another tooth below the gum.

impair (ɪmˈpɛə) vb. to damage or weaken in strength or quality: *his hearing was impaired by an accident.* —**imˈpairment** n.

impala (ɪmˈpɑːlə) n., pl. **-las** or **-la.** an African antelope with lyre-shaped horns, that can move with enormous leaps.

impale (ɪmˈpeɪl) vb. (often foll. by *on, upon,* or *with*) to pierce through or fix with a sharp instrument: *they impaled his severed head on a spear.* —**imˈpalement** n.

impalpable (ɪmˈpælpəbˀl) adj. **1.** imperceptible to the touch: *impalpable shadows.* **2.** difficult to understand; abstruse. —**imˌpalpaˈbility** n.

impanel (ɪmˈpænˀl) vb. **-elling, -elled** or U.S. **-eling, -eled.** Chiefly U.S. to empanel.

impart (ɪmˈpɑːt) vb. **1.** to communicate (information or knowledge); tell. **2.** to give (a specified quality): *to impart flavour.*

impartial (ɪmˈpɑːʃəl) adj. fair; unbiased. —**impartiality** (ɪmˌpɑːʃɪˈælɪtɪ) n. —**imˈpartially** adv.

impassable (ɪmˈpɑːsəbˀl) adj. (of terrain or roads) not able to be travelled through or over. —**imˌpassaˈbility** n.

impasse (ˈæmpɑːs) n. a situation in which progress or escape is impossible.

impassioned (ɪmˈpæʃənd) adj. filled with passion; fiery; ardent: *an impassioned appeal.*

impassive (ɪmˈpæsɪv) adj. not feeling or expressing emotion; calm or reserved. —**imˈpassively** adv. —**impasˈsivity** n.

impasto (ɪmˈpæstəʊ) n. the technique of applying paint thickly, so that brush marks are evident.

impatience (ɪmˈpeɪʃəns) n. **1.** lack of patience; intolerance of or annoyance with anything that causes delay. **2.** restless eagerness to do or have something. —**imˈpatient** adj. —**imˈpatiently** adv.

impeach (ɪmˈpiːtʃ) vb. **1.** Brit. criminal law. to accuse of treason or serious crime. **2.** Chiefly U.S. to charge (a public official) with an offence committed in office. **3.** to challenge or question (a person's honesty or honour). —**imˈpeachable** adj. —**imˈpeachment** n.

impeccable (ɪmˈpɛkəbˀl) adj. without flaw or error; faultless: *an impeccable record.* —**imˈpeccably** adv.

impecunious (ˌɪmpɪˈkjuːnɪəs) adj. without money; penniless.

impedance (ɪmˈpiːdˀns) n. the total effective resistance in an electric circuit to the flow of an alternating current.

impede (ɪmˈpiːd) vb. to restrict or retard in action or progress; obstruct.

impediment (ɪmˈpɛdɪmənt) n. **1.** a hindrance or obstruction. **2.** a physical defect, esp. one of speech.

impedimenta (ɪmˌpɛdɪˈmɛntə) pl. n. any

objects that impede progress, esp. the baggage and equipment carried by an army.

impel (ɪmˈpɛl) vb. **-pelling, -pelled. 1.** to urge or force (a person) to an action. **2.** to push, drive, or force into motion.

impending (ɪmˈpɛndɪŋ) adj. (esp. of something threatening) about to happen.

impenetrable (ɪmˈpɛnɪtrəbˀl) adj. **1.** incapable of being passed through or penetrated: *an impenetrable forest.* **2.** incapable of being understood; incomprehensible. **3.** not receptive to ideas or influence: *impenetrable ignorance.* —**imˌpenetraˈbility** n. —**imˈpenetrably** adv.

impenitent (ɪmˈpɛnɪtənt) adj. not sorry or penitent; unrepentant. —**imˈpenitence** n.

imper. imperative.

imperative (ɪmˈpɛrətɪv) adj. **1.** extremely urgent; essential. **2.** commanding or authoritative: *an imperative tone of voice.* **3.** Grammar. denoting a mood of verbs used in giving orders. ~n. **4.** Grammar. the imperative mood.

imperceptible (ˌɪmpəˈsɛptɪbˀl) adj. too slight, subtle, or gradual to be noticed. —**ˌimperˈceptibly** adv.

imperf. imperfect.

imperfect (ɪmˈpɜːfɪkt) adj. **1.** having faults or errors. **2.** not complete. **3.** Grammar. denoting a tense of verbs describing continuous, incomplete, or repeated past actions. ~n. **4.** Grammar. the imperfect tense. —**imˈperfectly** adv.

imperfection (ˌɪmpəˈfɛkʃən) n. **1.** the state of being imperfect. **2.** a fault or defect.

imperial (ɪmˈpɪərɪəl) adj. **1.** of an empire, emperor, or empress. **2.** majestic; commanding. **3.** exercising supreme authority; imperious. **4.** (of weights or measures) conforming to the standards of a system formerly official in Great Britain.

imperialism (ɪmˈpɪərɪəˌlɪzəm) n. **1.** the policy or practice of extending a country's influence over other territories by conquest, colonization, or economic domination. **2.** an imperial system, authority, or government. —**imˈperialist** adj., n. —**imˌperialˈistic** adj.

imperil (ɪmˈpɛrɪl) vb. **-illing, -illed** or U.S. **-iling, -iled.** to put in danger.

imperious (ɪmˈpɪərɪəs) adj. domineering; overbearing. —**imˈperiously** adv.

impermanent (ɪmˈpɜːmənənt) adj. not permanent; fleeting. —**imˈpermanence** n.

impermeable (ɪmˈpɜːmɪəbˀl) adj. (of a substance) not allowing the passage of a fluid. —**imˌpermeaˈbility** n.

impermissible (ˌɪmpəˈmɪsɪbˀl) adj. not allowed.

impersonal (ɪmˈpɜːsənˀl) adj. **1.** without reference to any individual person; objective: *an impersonal assessment.* **2.** without human warmth or sympathy; unemotional: *an impersonal manner.* **3.** Grammar. **a.** (of a verb) having no subject, as in *it is raining*. **b.** (of a pronoun) not referring to a person. —**impersonality** (ɪmˌpɜːsəˈnælɪtɪ) *n.* —**im'personally** *adv.*

impersonate (ɪmˈpɜːsəˌneɪt) *vb.* **1.** to pretend to be (another person). **2.** to imitate the character or mannerisms of (another person) for entertainment. —**imˌperson'ation** *n.* —**im'person,ator** *n.*

impertinent (ɪmˈpɜːtɪnənt) *adj.* rude; insolent; impudent. —**im'pertinence** *n.*

imperturbable (ˌɪmpɜːˈtɜːbəbˀl) *adj.* not easily upset; calm; unruffled. —**imperˌturba'bility** *n.* —**imper'turbably** *adv.*

impervious (ɪmˈpɜːvɪəs) *adj.* **1.** not able to be penetrated; impermeable. **2.** (foll. by *to*) not able to be affected or influenced by: *impervious to argument.*

impetigo (ˌɪmpɪˈtaɪɡəʊ) *n.* a contagious skin disease causing spots or pimples.

impetuous (ɪmˈpɛtjʊəs) *adj.* **1.** acting without consideration; rash; impulsive. **2.** done in rashness or haste. —**impetuosity** (ɪmˌpɛtjuˈɒsɪtɪ) *n.*

impetus ('ɪmpɪtəs) *n., pl.* **-tuses. 1.** an incentive or impulse; stimulus. **2.** *Physics*. the force that starts a body moving or that tends to resist changes in its speed or direction once it is moving.

impi ('ɪmpɪ) *n., pl.* **-pi** or **-pies.** a group of Zulu warriors.

impiety (ɪmˈpaɪɪtɪ) *n.* lack of respect or religious reverence.

impinge (ɪmˈpɪndʒ) *vb.* (usually foll. by *on* or *upon*) to encroach or infringe: *to impinge on someone's time.* —**im'pingement** *n.*

impious ('ɪmpɪəs) *adj.* **1.** lacking piety or religious reverence. **2.** lacking respect.

impish ('ɪmpɪʃ) *adj.* of or like an imp; mischievous. —'**impishness** *n.*

implacable (ɪmˈplækəbˀl) *adj.* **1.** incapable of being appeased or pacified. **2.** inflexible; intractable. —**imˌplaca'bility** *n.* —**im'placably** *adv.*

implant *vb.* (ɪmˈplɑːnt). **1.** to fix firmly in the mind, instil: *to implant sound moral principles.* **2.** to plant or embed; fix firmly. **3.** *Surgery.* to graft or insert (a tissue or hormone) into the body. ~*n.* ('ɪmplɑːnt). **4.** anything implanted in the body, such as a tissue graft. —**implan'tation** *n.*

implausible (ɪmˈplɔːzəbˀl) *adj.* not easy to believe; unlikely. —**imˌplausi'bility** *n.*

implement *n.* ('ɪmplɪmənt). **1.** a piece of equipment; tool or utensil: *gardening implements.* ~*vb.* ('ɪmplɪˌmɛnt). **2.** to carry out; put into action: *to implement a plan.* —**ˌimplemen'tation** *n.*

implicate ('ɪmplɪˌkeɪt) *vb.* **1.** to show to be involved, esp. in a crime. **2.** to imply.

implication (ˌɪmplɪˈkeɪʃən) *n.* **1.** something that is implied. **2.** an implying or being implied.

implicit (ɪmˈplɪsɪt) *adj.* **1.** implied; ex-

pressed indirectly. **2.** absolute and unquestioning: *implicit trust.* **3.** contained, although not stated openly: *to bring out the anger implicit in the argument.* —**im'plicitly** *adv.*

implied (ɪmˈplaɪd) *adj.* hinted at or suggested; not directly expressed: *an implied criticism.*

implode (ɪmˈpləʊd) *vb.* to collapse inwards.

implore (ɪmˈplɔː) *vb.* to beg (someone) earnestly (to do something); plead for (something).

imply (ɪmˈplaɪ) *vb.* **-plying, -plied. 1.** to express or indicate by a hint; suggest. **2.** to suggest or involve as a necessary consequence.
Usage. see **infer.**

impolite (ˌɪmpəˈlaɪt) *adj.* discourteous; rude. —**ˌimpo'liteness** *n.*

impolitic (ɪmˈpɒlɪtɪk) *adj.* ill-advised; unwise.

imponderable (ɪmˈpɒndərəbˀl, -drəbˀl) *adj.* **1.** unable to be weighed or assessed. ~*n.* **2.** something difficult or impossible to assess.

import *vb.* (ɪmˈpɔːt, 'ɪmpɔːt). **1.** to bring in (esp. goods or services) from another country. **2.** *Rare.* to signify; mean: *to import doom.* ~*n.* ('ɪmpɔːt). **3.** (*often pl.*) something imported. **4.** importance: *a work of great import.* **5.** meaning. **6.** *Canad. slang.* a sportsman who is not native to the area where he plays. —**im'porter** *n.*

important (ɪmˈpɔːtˀnt) *adj.* **1.** of great significance, value, or consequence. **2.** of social significance; eminent; esteemed: *an important man in the town.* **3.** (usually foll. by *to*) of great concern (to); valued highly (by): *your wishes are important to me.* —**im'portance** *n.*
Usage. In a sentence such as *he changed the financial structure of the parent company and, more important, he altered its social policy*, some writers prefer *more important* to *more importantly.* This also applies to *first, second, last,* etc., which are often preferred to *firstly, secondly, lastly,* etc.; *first, he introduced the sonnet; second, he initiated poetic experiments; last and most important, he created an atmosphere of sincerity in his poetry.*

importation (ˌɪmpɔːˈteɪʃən) *n.* **1.** an importing or being imported. **2.** something imported.

importunate (ɪmˈpɔːtjʊnɪt) *adj.* persistent or demanding; insistent.

importune (ɪmˈpɔːtjuːn, ˌɪmpɔːˈtjuːn) *vb.* to harass with persistent requests; demand of (someone) insistently. —**impor'tunity** *n.*

impose (ɪmˈpəʊz) *vb.* (usually foll. by *on* or *upon*) **1.** to establish (a rule, condition, etc.) as something to be obeyed or complied with; enforce. **2.** to force (oneself) on others. **3.** to take advantage of (a person or

quality): *to impose on someone's kindness.*
4. *Printing.* to arrange (pages) in the correct
order for printing. **5.** to pass off deceptively.

imposing (ɪmˈpəʊzɪŋ) *adj.* grand or impressive: *an imposing building.*

imposition (ˌɪmpəˈzɪʃən) *n.* **1.** the act of imposing. **2.** something imposed, esp. unfairly on someone. **3.** a task set as a school punishment. **4.** the arrangement of pages for printing.

impossibility (ɪmˌpɒsəˈbɪlɪtɪ) *n., pl.* **-ties.** **1.** the state or quality of being impossible. **2.** something that is impossible.

impossible (ɪmˈpɒsəbºl) *adj.* **1.** incapable of being done, or of happening. **2.** absurd or inconceivable; unreasonable. **3.** *Informal.* intolerable; outrageous: *those children are impossible.* **—imˈpossibly** *adv.*

impostor (ɪmˈpɒstə) *n.* a person who deceives others, esp. by assuming a false identity.

imposture (ɪmˈpɒstʃə) *n.* deception, esp. by assuming a false identity.

impotent (ˈɪmpətənt) *adj.* **1.** lacking sufficient strength; ineffective or powerless. **2.** (of males) unable to perform sexual intercourse. **—ˈimpotence** *n.*

impound (ɪmˈpaʊnd) *vb.* **1.** to confine (an animal) in a pound. **2.** to take legal possession of; confiscate.

impoverish (ɪmˈpɒvərɪʃ) *vb.* to make poor or diminish the quality of: *to impoverish society by cutting the grant to the arts.* **—imˈpoverishment** *n.*

impracticable (ɪmˈpræktɪkəbºl) *adj.* **1.** incapable of being put into practice; not feasible. **2.** unsuitable for a desired use; unfit. **—imˌpracticaˈbility** *n.*

impractical (ɪmˈpræktɪkºl) *adj.* **1.** not practical or workable: *an impractical solution.* **2.** not having practical skills. **—impracticality** (ɪmˌpræktɪˈkælɪtɪ) *n.*

imprecate (ˈɪmprɪˌkeɪt) *vb.* **1.** to swear or curse. **2.** to invoke or bring down (evil or a curse). **—ˌimpreˈcation** *n.* **—ˈimpreˌcatory** *adj.*

imprecise (ˌɪmprɪˈsaɪs) *adj.* not precise; inexact or inaccurate. **—imprecision** (ˌɪmprɪˈsɪʒən) *n.*

impregnable (ɪmˈprɛɡnəbºl) *adj.* **1.** unable to be broken into or taken by force: *an impregnable castle.* **2.** unable to be affected or overcome: *impregnable self-confidence.* **—imˌpregnaˈbility** *n.*

impregnate (ˈɪmprɛɡˌneɪt) *vb.* **1.** to saturate, soak, or fill throughout. **2.** to imbue or permeate. **3.** to make pregnant; fertilize. **—ˌimpregˈnation** *n.*

impresario (ˌɪmprəˈsɑːrɪˌəʊ) *n., pl.* **-sarios.** the director or manager of a theatre or music company.

impress[1] *vb.* (ɪmˈprɛs). **1.** to make a strong, lasting, or favourable impression

on: *I am impressed by your work.* **2.** to imprint or stamp by pressure: *to impress a seal in wax.* **3.** (often foll. by *on*) to stress (something to a person); emphasize. *~n.* (ˈɪmprɛs). **4.** an impressing. **5.** a mark produced by impressing. **—imˈpressible** *adj.*

impress[2] (ɪmˈprɛs) *vb.* to force (a person) into service in the army or navy.

impression (ɪmˈprɛʃən) *n.* **1.** an effect produced in the mind by a person or thing: *I don't think I made a very good impression at the interview.* **2.** an imprint or mark produced by pressing. **3.** a vague idea or belief: *I had the impression we had met before.* **4.** a strong, favourable, or remarkable effect. **5.** *Printing.* **a.** the act or result of printing from type or plates. **b.** the number of copies of a publication printed at one time. **6.** an impersonation for entertainment.

impressionable (ɪmˈprɛʃənəbºl) *adj.* easily impressed or influenced: *an impressionable age.* **—imˌpressionaˈbility** *n.*

impressionism (ɪmˈprɛʃəˌnɪzəm) *n.* (*often cap.*) a style of painting developed in 19th-century France, with the aim of reproducing the immediate impression or mood of things, especially the effects of light and atmosphere, rather than form or structure. **—imˈpressionist** *n.* **—imˌpressionˈistic** *adj.*

impressive (ɪmˈprɛsɪv) *adj.* capable of impressing, esp. by size, magnificence, or importance. **—imˈpressively** *adv.*

imprimatur (ˌɪmprɪˈmeɪtə, -ˈmɑː-) *n.* sanction or approval for something to be printed, usually given by the Roman Catholic Church.

imprint *n.* (ˈɪmprɪnt). **1.** a mark or impression produced by pressing, printing, or stamping. **2.** the publisher's name and address, often with the date of publication, printed on the title page of a book. *~vb.* (ɪmˈprɪnt). **3.** to produce (a mark or impression) on (a surface) by pressing, printing, or stamping: *to imprint a seal on wax.* **4.** to establish firmly; impress: *to imprint the details on one's mind.*

imprison (ɪmˈprɪzən) *vb.* to confine in or as if in prison. **—imˈprisonment** *n.*

improbable (ɪmˈprɒbəbºl) *adj.* not likely or probable; doubtful; unlikely. **—imˌprobaˈbility** *n.* **—imˈprobably** *adv.*

improbity (ɪmˈprəʊbɪtɪ) *n., pl.* **-ties.** dishonesty or wickedness.

impromptu (ɪmˈprɒmptjuː) *adj.* **1.** unrehearsed; improvised. *~adv.* **2.** in a spontaneous or improvised way: *he spoke impromptu.* *~n.* **3.** something that is impromptu. **4.** a short piece of instrumental music resembling improvisation.

improper (ɪmˈprɒpə) *adj.* **1.** indecent; unseemly. **2.** irregular or incorrect. **—imˈproperly** *adv.*

improper fraction *n.* a fraction in which the numerator is greater than the denominator, as ⅞.

impropriety (ˌɪmprə'praɪɪtɪ) *n., pl.* **-ties.** **1.** indecency; indecorum. **2.** an improper act or use.

improve (ɪm'pruːv) *vb.* **1.** to make or become better in quality. **2.** (usually foll. by *on* or *upon*) to achieve a better standard or quality in comparison (with): *to improve on last year's crop.* —**im'provable** *adj.*

improvement (ɪm'pruːvmənt) *n.* **1.** the act of improving or the state of being improved. **2.** a change that improves something or adds to its value. **3.** *Austral. & N.Z.* a building on a piece of land, adding to its value.

improvident (ɪm'prɒvɪdənt) *adj.* **1.** not providing for the future; thriftless. **2.** incautious or rash. —**im'providence** *n.*

improvise ('ɪmprəˌvaɪz) *vb.* **1.** to do or make quickly from whatever is available, without previous planning. **2.** to perform (a play or piece of music) composing as one goes along. —ˌimprovi'sation *n.*

imprudent (ɪm'pruːd³nt) *adj.* rash, heedless, or indiscreet. —**im'prudence** *n.*

impudent ('ɪmpjʊdənt) *adj.* impertinent or insolent. —'**impudence** *n.* —'**impudently** *adv.*

impugn (ɪm'pjuːn) *vb.* to challenge or attack as false; criticize. —**im'pugnment** *n.*

impulse ('ɪmpʌls) *n.* **1.** an impelling force or motion; thrust; impetus. **2.** a sudden desire, whim, or inclination. **3.** an instinctive drive; urge. **4.** *Physics.* **a.** the product of a force acting on a body and the time for which it acts. **b.** the change in the momentum of a body as a result of a force acting upon it. **5.** *Physiol.* a stimulus transmitted in a nerve or muscle.

impulsive (ɪm'pʌlsɪv) *adj.* **1.** tending to act on impulse: *an impulsive man.* **2.** done on impulse. **3.** forceful, inciting, or impelling.

impunity (ɪm'pjuːnɪtɪ) *n., pl.* **-ties.** exemption from punishment or unpleasant consequences: *done with impunity.*

impure (ɪm'pjʊə) *adj.* **1.** combined with something else; tainted or adulterated. **2.** dirty or unclean. **3.** immoral; obscene.

impurity (ɪm'pjʊərɪtɪ) *n., pl.* **-ties.** **1.** the quality of being impure. **2.** an impure thing or element: *impurities in the water.*

impute (ɪm'pjuːt) *vb.* **1.** to attribute or ascribe (blame or a crime) to a person. **2.** to attribute to a source or cause: *I impute your success to nepotism.* —ˌimpu'tation *n.*

in (ɪn) *prep.* **1.** inside; within: *in the room.* **2.** at a place where there is: *in the shade.* **3.** indicating a state, situation, or condition: *in silence.* **4.** when (a period of time) has elapsed: *come back in one year.* **5.** using: *written in code.* **6.** wearing: *the man in the blue suit.* **7.** with regard to (a specified activity or occupation): *in journalism.* **8.** while performing the action of: *in crossing the street he was run over.* **9.** having as purpose: *in honour of the president.* **10.** (of certain animals) pregnant with: *in calf.* **11.** into: *she fell in the water.* **12. have it in one.** (often foll. by an infinitive) to have the ability (to do something). **13. in that** *or* **in so far as.** (*conj.*) because or to the extent that: *I regret my remark in that it upset you.* ~*adv.* **14.** in or into a particular place; indoors: *come in.* **15.** at one's home or place of work: *he's not in at the moment.* **16.** fashionable or popular: *bright colours are in this year.* **17.** in office or power: *the Conservatives got in at the last election.* **18.** so as to enclose: *block in.* **19.** (in certain games) so as to take one's turn of the play: *you have to get the other side out before you go in.* **20.** *Brit.* (of a fire) alight. **21.** indicating prolonged activity, esp. by a large number: *teach-in; sit-in.* **22. in for.** about to experience (something, esp. something unpleasant): *you're in for a shock.* **23. in on.** acquainted with or sharing in: *I was in on all his plans.* **24. in with.** friendly with. **25. have (got) it in for.** to wish or intend harm towards. ~*adj.* **26.** fashionable; modish: *the in thing to do.* ~*n.* **27. ins and outs.** the detailed points or facts (of a situation).

In *Chem.* indium.

IN Indiana.

in. inch(es).

in-¹, il-, im-, *or* **ir-** *prefix.* **a.** not; non-: *incredible; illegal; imperfect; irregular.* **b.** lack of: *inexperience.*

in-², il-, im-, *or* **ir-** *prefix.* in; into; towards; within; on: *infiltrate.*

inability (ˌɪnə'bɪlɪtɪ) *n.* the fact of not being able to do something.

in absentia *Latin.* (ɪn æb'sentɪə) *adv.* in the absence of (someone indicated).

inaccessible (ˌɪnæk'sesəb³l) *adj.* **1.** impossible or very difficult to reach: *the most inaccessible parts of the jungle.* **2.** (of a person) unapproachable. —ˌinac,cessi'bility *n.*

inaccuracy (ɪn'ækjʊrəsɪ) *n., pl.* **-cies.** **1.** lack of accuracy; imprecision. **2.** an error or mistake. —**in'accurate** *adj.*

inaction (ɪn'ækʃən) *n.* lack of action; inertia.

inactive (ɪn'æktɪv) *adj.* **1.** idle; not active. **2.** *Chem.* (of a substance) having little or no reactivity. —ˌinac'tivity *n.*

inadequate (ɪn'ædɪkwɪt) *adj.* **1.** not adequate; insufficient. **2.** not capable; incompetent. —**in'adequacy** *n.* —**in'adequately** *adv.*

inadmissible (ˌɪnəd'mɪsəb³l) *adj.* not allowable or acceptable.

inadvertent (ˌɪnəd'vɜːt³nt) *adj.* resulting from heedless action; unintentional. —ˌin-ad'vertence *n.* —ˌinad'vertently *adv.*

inadvisable (ˌɪnədˈvaɪzəbʰl) *adj.* unwise; not sensible.

inalienable (ɪnˈeɪljənəbʰl) *adj.* not able to be taken away or transferred to another: *the inalienable rights of the citizen.*

inamorata (ɪnˌæməˈrɑːtə) *or* (*masc.*) **inamorato** (ɪnˌæməˈrɑːtəʊ) *n., pl.* **-tas** *or* (*masc.*) **-tos.** a sweetheart or lover.

inane (ɪˈneɪn) *adj.* senseless or silly: *inane remarks.* —**inanity** (ɪˈnænɪtɪ) *n.*

inanimate (ɪnˈænɪmɪt) *adj.* lacking the qualities of living beings: *inanimate objects.*

inanition (ˌɪnəˈnɪʃən) *n.* emptiness or weakness, esp. from lack of food.

inapplicable (ˌɪnæˈplɪkəbʰl) *adj.* not suitable or relevant.

inapposite (ɪnˈæpəzɪt) *adj.* not appropriate; unsuitable. —**in'appositeness** *n.*

inappropriate (ˌɪnəˈprəʊprɪɪt) *adj.* not suitable or proper.

inapt (ɪnˈæpt) *adj.* **1.** inappropriate. **2.** lacking skill. —**in'apti,tude** *n.*

inarticulate (ˌɪnɑːˈtɪkjʊlɪt) *adj.* unable to express oneself clearly or well.

inasmuch as (ˌɪnəzˈmʌtʃ) *conj.* **1.** since; because. **2.** in so far as.

inattentive (ˌɪnəˈtɛntɪv) *adj.* not paying attention.

inaudible (ɪnˈɔːdəbʰl) *adj.* not loud enough to be heard.

inaugural (ɪnˈɔːgjʊrəl) *adj.* **1.** of or for an inauguration. ~*n.* **2.** a speech made at an inauguration.

inaugurate (ɪnˈɔːgjʊˌreɪt) *vb.* **1.** to begin officially or formally. **2.** to place in office formally and ceremonially. **3.** to open or celebrate the first public use of ceremonially: *to inaugurate a factory.* —**in,augu'ration** *n.* —**in'augu,rator** *n.*

inauspicious (ˌɪnɔːˈspɪʃəs) *adj.* unlucky.

inboard (ˈɪnˌbɔːd) *adj.* **1.** (of a boat's motor or engine) situated within the hull. **2.** situated close to the fuselage of an aircraft. ~*adv.* **3.** within the sides of or towards the centre of a vessel or aircraft.

inborn (ˈɪnˈbɔːn) *adj.* existing from birth; congenital; innate.

inbred (ˈɪnˈbrɛd) *adj.* **1.** produced as a result of inbreeding. **2.** deeply ingrained; innate: *inbred good manners.*

inbreed (ˈɪnˈbriːd) *vb.* **-breeding, -bred.** to breed from closely related individuals. —**'in'breeding** *n., adj.*

inbuilt (ˈɪnˈbɪlt) *adj.* (of a quality or feeling) present from the beginning: *inbuilt limitations.*

inc. 1. including. **2.** inclusive. **3.** income. **4.** increase.

Inc. (esp. U.S.) incorporated.

incalculable (ɪnˈkælkjʊləbʰl) *adj.* unable to be predicted or determined. —**in,calcula'bility** *n.*

incandescent (ˌɪnkænˈdɛsʰnt) *adj.* glowing

with heat; red-hot or white-hot. —**,incan'descence** *n.*

incandescent lamp *n.* a lamp that contains a filament which is electrically heated to incandescence.

incantation (ˌɪnkænˈteɪʃən) *n.* **1.** ritual chanting of magic words or sounds. **2.** a magic spell. —**in'cantatory** *adj.*

incapable (ɪnˈkeɪpəbʰl) *adj.* **1.** (foll. by *of*) not capable; lacking the ability to. **2.** powerless; helpless: *drunk and incapable.*

incapacitate (ˌɪnkəˈpæsɪˌteɪt) *vb.* to deprive of power, strength, or capacity; disable.

incapacity (ˌɪnkəˈpæsɪtɪ) *n., pl.* **-ties. 1.** lack of power, strength, or capacity; disability. **2.** *Law.* legal disqualification or ineligibility.

incarcerate (ɪnˈkɑːsəˌreɪt) *vb.* to confine or imprison. —**in,carcer'ation** *n.*

incarnate *adj.* (ɪnˈkɑːnɪt). **1.** possessing bodily form, esp. the human form: *a devil incarnate.* **2.** personified or typified: *stupidity incarnate.* ~*vb.* (ɪnˈkɑːneɪt). **3.** to give a bodily or concrete form to. **4.** to be representative or typical of.

incarnation (ˌɪnkɑːˈneɪʃən) *n.* **1.** the act of embodying or state of being embodied, esp. in human form. **2.** a person or thing that typifies some quality or idea.

Incarnation (ˌɪnkɑːˈneɪʃən) *n. Christian theol.* the assuming of a human body by Jesus as the Son of God.

incautious (ɪnˈkɔːʃəs) *adj.* (of a person or action) careless or rash.

incendiary (ɪnˈsɛndɪərɪ) *adj.* **1.** relating to the illegal burning of property or goods. **2.** tending to create strife or violence. **3.** designed to cause fires, as certain bombs. ~*n., pl.* **-aries. 4.** a person who illegally sets fire to property or goods; arsonist. **5.** a bomb that is designed to start fires. —**in'cendia,rism** *n.*

incense[1] (ˈɪnsɛns) *n.* **1.** an aromatic substance burnt for its fragrant odour, esp. in religious ceremonies. **2.** the odour or smoke so produced. ~*vb.* **3.** to burn incense to (a deity). **4.** to perfume or fumigate with incense.

incense[2] (ɪnˈsɛns) *vb.* to enrage greatly.

incentive (ɪnˈsɛntɪv) *n.* **1.** a motivating influence; stimulus. **2.** an additional payment made to employees to increase production. ~*adj.* **3.** inciting to action.

inception (ɪnˈsɛpʃən) *n.* the beginning of a project.

incessant (ɪnˈsɛsʰnt) *adj.* unceasing; continual. —**in'cessantly** *adv.*

incest (ˈɪnsɛst) *n.* sexual intercourse between two persons who are too closely related to marry. —**in'cestuous** *adj.*

inch (ɪntʃ) *n.* **1.** a unit of length equal to one twelfth of a foot or 2.54cm. **2.** *Meteorol.* the amount of rain or snow that would cover a surface to a depth of one inch. **3.** a very small distance, degree, or amount. **4. every inch.** in every way; completely: *every inch an aristocrat.* **5. inch by inch.** gradually; little by little. **6. within an inch of one's life.** almost to death. ~*vb.* **7.** to move or be moved very slowly or gradually: *the car inched forward.*

inchoate (ɪnˈkəʊeɪt) *adj.* **1.** just beginning. **2.** undeveloped; half-formed.

incidence (ˈɪnsɪdəns) *n.* **1.** extent or frequency of occurrence: *a high incidence of death from pneumonia.* **2.** *Physics.* the arrival of a beam of light or particles at a surface. **3.** *Geom.* the partial overlapping of two figures or a figure and a line.

incident (ˈɪnsɪdənt) *n.* **1.** an occurrence, event, or episode, esp. a minor, subsidiary, or related one. **2.** a relatively insignificant event that might have serious consequences. **3.** a public disturbance. ~*adj.* **4.** (foll. by *to*) likely to occur in connection with: *the dangers are incident to a policeman's job.* **5.** (of a beam of light or particles) arriving at or striking a surface.

incidental (ˌɪnsɪˈdɛntᵊl) *adj.* **1.** happening in connection with or resulting from something more important. **2.** secondary or minor: *incidental expenses.* ~*n.* **3.** (*often pl.*) a minor expense, event, or action. —**ˌinciˈdentally** *adv.*

incidental music *n.* background music for a film or play.

incinerate (ɪnˈsɪnəˌreɪt) *vb.* to burn up completely; reduce to ashes. —**inˌcinerˈation** *n.*

incinerator (ɪnˈsɪnəˌreɪtə) *n.* a furnace or other device for incinerating something.

incipient (ɪnˈsɪpɪənt) *adj.* just starting to be or happen.

incise (ɪnˈsaɪz) *vb.* to cut into (something) with a sharp tool.

incision (ɪnˈsɪʒən) *n.* a cut, esp. one made during a surgical operation.

incisive (ɪnˈsaɪsɪv) *adj.* keen, penetrating, or sharp.

incisor (ɪnˈsaɪzə) *n.* a sharp cutting tooth at the front of the mouth.

incite (ɪnˈsaɪt) *vb.* to stir up or provoke to action. —**inˈcitement** *n.*

incivility (ˌɪnsɪˈvɪlɪtɪ) *n., pl.* **-ties.** **1.** rudeness. **2.** an impolite act or remark.

incl. **1.** including. **2.** inclusive.

inclement (ɪnˈklɛmənt) *adj.* (of weather) stormy or severe. —**inˈclemency** *n.*

inclination (ˌɪnklɪˈneɪʃən) *n.* **1.** a particular disposition or tendency; a liking: *I've no inclination for such dull work.* **2.** the degree of incline from a horizontal or vertical plane. **3.** a slope or slant. **4.** *Surveying.* the angular distance of the horizon below the plane of observation.

incline *vb.* (ɪnˈklaɪn). **1.** to deviate from a vertical or horizontal plane; slope or slant. **2.** to have or cause to have a certain tendency or disposition: *that does not incline me to think that you are right.* **3.** to bend or lower (part of the body, esp. the head). **4. incline one's ear.** to listen favourably. ~*n.* (ˈɪnklaɪn). **5.** an inclined surface or slope. —**inˈclined** *adj.*

inclined plane *n.* a sloping plane used to enable a load to be raised or lowered by pushing or sliding, which requires less force than lifting.

include (ɪnˈkluːd) *vb.* **1.** to have as part of the whole; be made up of or contain. **2.** to put in as part of a set, group, or category.

inclusion (ɪnˈkluːʒən) *n.* **1.** an including or being included. **2.** something included.

inclusive (ɪnˈkluːsɪv) *adj.* **1.** (foll. by *of*) including: *capital inclusive of profit.* **2.** including the limits specified: *Monday to Friday inclusive.* **3.** comprehensive.

incognito (ˌɪnkɒgˈniːtəʊ) *adv., adj.* **1.** under an assumed name or appearance; in disguise. ~*n., pl.* **-tos.** **2.** a person who is incognito. **3.** the pretended identity of such a person.

incognizant (ɪnˈkɒgnɪzənt) *adj.* (foll. by *of*) unaware of. —**inˈcognizance** *n.*

incoherent (ˌɪnkəʊˈhɪərənt) *adj.* **1.** not logically connected or ordered. **2.** unable to express oneself clearly. —**ˌincoˈherence** *n.*

income (ˈɪnkʌm, ˈɪnkəm) *n.* the total amount of money earned from work or obtained from other sources over a given period of time.

income support *n.* (in Britain) an allowance paid by the government to people with a very low income.

income tax *n.* a personal tax levied on annual income.

incoming (ˈɪnˌkʌmɪŋ) *adj.* **1.** coming in; entering. **2.** about to come into office; succeeding.

incommensurable (ˌɪnkəˈmɛnʃərəbᵊl) *adj.* **1.** incapable of being judged, measured, or compared. **2.** *Maths.* not having a common divisor other than 1, such as 2 and $\sqrt{-5}$. —**ˌincomˌmensuraˈbility** *n.*

incommensurate (ˌɪnkəˈmɛnʃərɪt) *adj.* **1.** (often foll. by *with*) inadequate; disproportionate: *gains incommensurate with the risk involved.* **2.** incommensurable.

incommode (ˌɪnkəˈməʊd) *vb.* to bother, disturb, or inconvenience.

incommodious (ˌɪnkəˈməʊdɪəs) *adj.* inconveniently small; cramped.

incommunicado (ˌɪnkəˌmjuːnɪˈkɑːdəʊ) *adv., adj.* not permitted to communicate with other people, as while in solitary confinement.

incomparable (ɪnˈkɒmpərəbᵊl) *adj.* beyond or above comparison; unequalled. —**inˈcomparably** *adv.*

incompatible (ˌɪnkəmˈpætəbᵊl) *adj.* incapable of existing together in harmony; conflicting or inconsistent. —**incom‚pati'bil-ity** n.

incompetent (ɪn'kɒmpɪtənt) adj. **1.** not possessing the necessary ability or skill to carry out a task. **2.** Law. not legally qualified: an incompetent witness. ~n. **3.** an incompetent person. —**in'competence** n.

incomplete (‚ɪnkəm'pliːt) adj. **1.** not finished. **2.** not whole.

incomprehension (ɪn‚kɒmprɪ'hɛnʃən) n. inability to understand. —**in‚compre'hensible** adj.

inconceivable (‚ɪnkən'siːvəbᵊl) adj. unable to be imagined or considered. —**‚incon‚ceiva'bility** n.

inconclusive (‚ɪnkən'kluːsɪv) adj. not conclusive or decisive.

incongruous (ɪn'kɒŋgrʊəs) adj. out of place; inappropriate: an incongruous figure among the tourists. —**in'congruously** adv. —**incongruity** (‚ɪnkɒŋ'gruːɪtɪ) n.

inconnu ('ɪnkənjuː, -nuː) n. Canad. a whitefish of arctic waters.

inconsequential (ɪn‚kɒnsɪ'kwɛnʃəl) or **inconsequent** (ɪn'kɒnsɪkwənt) adj. **1.** not following logically as a consequence. **2.** trivial or insignificant. —**in‚conse'quentially** adv.

inconsiderable (‚ɪnkən'sɪdərəbᵊl) adj. **1.** relatively small. **2.** not worth considering; insignificant. —**incon'siderably** adv.

inconsiderate (‚ɪnkən'sɪdərɪt) adj. lacking in care or thought for others; thoughtless. —**‚incon'siderateness** n.

inconsistent (‚ɪnkən'sɪstənt) adj. **1.** unstable or changeable in behaviour or mood. **2.** containing contradictory elements: an inconsistent argument. **3.** not in accordance: actions inconsistent with high office. —**‚incon'sistency** n.

inconsolable (‚ɪnkən'səʊləbᵊl) adj. that cannot be comforted. —**‚incon'solably** adv.

inconspicuous (‚ɪnkən'spɪkjʊəs) adj. not easily noticed or seen; attracting little attention.

inconstant (ɪn'kɒnstənt) adj. **1.** not constant; variable. **2.** fickle. —**in'constancy** n.

incontestable (‚ɪnkən'tɛstəbᵊl) adj. not able to be disputed.

incontinent (ɪn'kɒntɪnənt) adj. **1.** unable to control the bladder and bowels. **2.** lacking self-restraint, esp. sexually. —**in'continence** n.

incontrovertible (ɪn‚kɒntrə'vɜːtəbᵊl) adj. absolutely certain; undeniable. —**in‚contro'vertibly** adv.

inconvenience (‚ɪnkən'viːnɪəns) n. **1.** a state or instance of trouble or difficulty. ~vb. **2.** to cause trouble or difficulty to (a person). —**‚incon'venient** adj.

incorporate vb. (ɪn'kɔːpə‚reɪt). **1.** to include or be included as part of a united

whole. **2.** to form a united whole or mass; merge or blend. **3.** to form into a corporation. ~adj. (ɪn'kɔːpərɪt). **4.** incorporated. —**in'corpo‚rated** adj. —**in‚corpo'ration** n.

incorporeal (‚ɪnkɔː'pɔːrɪəl) adj. without material form, substance, or existence. —**incorporeity** (ɪn‚kɔːpə'riːɪtɪ) n.

incorrect (‚ɪnkə'rɛkt) adj. **1.** wrong: an incorrect answer. **2.** not proper: incorrect behaviour. —**‚incor'rectly** adv.

incorrigible (ɪn'kɒrɪdʒəbᵊl) adj. (of a person or behaviour) beyond correction or reform; incurably bad. —**in‚corrigi'bility** n. —**in'corrigibly** adv.

incorruptible (‚ɪnkə'rʌptəbᵊl) adj. **1.** incapable of being corrupted; honest. **2.** not subject to decay. —**‚incor‚rupti'bility** n.

increase vb. (ɪn'kriːs). **1.** to make or become greater in size, degree, or frequency. ~n. ('ɪnkriːs). **2.** an increasing or becoming increased. **3.** the amount by which something increases. **4. on the increase.** increasing, esp. in frequency. —**in'creasingly** adv.

incredible (ɪn'krɛdəbᵊl) adj. **1.** unbelievable. **2.** Informal. marvellous; amazing. —**in‚credi'bility** n. —**in'credibly** adv.

incredulity (‚ɪnkrɪ'djuːlɪtɪ) n. unwillingness to believe; scepticism.

incredulous (ɪn'krɛdjʊləs) adj. not prepared or willing to believe something; unbelieving.

increment ('ɪnkrɪmənt) n. **1.** the amount by which something increases. **2.** Maths. a small positive or negative change in a variable or function. —**incremental** (‚ɪnkrɪ'mɛntᵊl) adj.

incriminate (ɪn'krɪmɪ‚neɪt) vb. **1.** to imply or suggest the guilt of (someone). **2.** to charge (someone) with a crime. —**in‚crimi'nation** n. —**in'criminatory** adj.

incrust (ɪn'krʌst) vb. same as **encrust**.

incubate ('ɪnkjʊ‚beɪt) vb. **1.** (of birds) to hatch (eggs) by sitting on them. **2.** to cause (bacteria) to develop, esp. in an incubator or culture medium. **3.** (of disease germs) to remain inactive in an animal or human before causing disease. **4.** to develop gradually. —**‚incu'bation** n.

incubator ('ɪnkjʊ‚beɪtə) n. **1.** Med. an apparatus used to care for prematurely born babies. **2.** an apparatus for hatching birds' eggs or growing bacterial cultures.

incubus ('ɪnkjʊbəs) n., pl. **-bi** (-‚baɪ) or **-buses.** **1.** a demon believed in folklore to have sexual intercourse with sleeping women. **2.** a nightmare.

inculcate ('ɪnkʌl‚keɪt, ɪn'kʌlkeɪt) vb. to instil (an idea, habit, or value) in a person by insistent repetition. —**‚incul'cation** n.

inculpate ('ɪnkʌl‚peɪt, ɪn'kʌlpeɪt) vb. to incriminate.

incumbency (ɪn'kʌmbənsɪ) n., pl. **-cies.** the office, duty, or tenure of an incumbent.

incumbent (ɪnˈkʌmbənt) *adj.* **1.** *Formal.* (often foll. by *on* or *upon* and an infinitive) resting on one as a duty; obligatory: *it is incumbent on me to attend.* ~*n.* **2.** a person who holds an office, esp. a clergyman holding a benefice.

incur (ɪnˈkɜː) *vb.* **-curring, -curred.** to bring (something undesirable) upon oneself.

incurable (ɪnˈkjʊərəbºl) *adj.* **1.** not capable of being cured or changed: *an incurable disease; incurable optimism.* ~*n.* **2.** a person with an incurable disease. —**in,cura'bility** *n.* —**in'curably** *adv.*

incurious (ɪnˈkjʊərɪəs) *adj.* indifferent or uninterested. —**in'curiously** *adv.*

incursion (ɪnˈkɜːʃən) *n.* **1.** a sudden or brief invasion. **2.** an inroad or encroachment: *buying a car made a considerable incursion into our savings.* —**incursive** (ɪnˈkɜːsɪv) *adj.*

ind. 1. independent. **2.** index. **3.** indicative. **4.** indirect. **5.** industrial.

Ind. 1. Independent. **2.** India. **3.** Indian. **4.** Indiana. **5.** Indies.

indaba (ɪnˈdɑːbə) *n.* **1.** (among native peoples of southern Africa) a meeting to discuss a serious topic. **2.** *S. African informal.* a matter of concern or for discussion; problem.

indebted (ɪnˈdɛtɪd) *adj.* **1.** owing gratitude for help or favours; obligated. **2.** owing money. —**in'debtedness** *n.*

indecent (ɪnˈdiːsºnt) *adj.* **1.** morally or sexually offensive. **2.** unseemly or improper: *they married in indecent haste.* —**in'decency** *n.* —**in'decently** *adv.*

indecipherable (ˌɪndɪˈsaɪfərəbºl) *adj.* not able to be read.

indecisive (ˌɪndɪˈsaɪsɪv) *adj.* **1.** unable to make decisions; wavering. **2.** not decisive or conclusive: *an indecisive argument.* —**indecision** (ˌɪndɪˈsɪʒən) *or* ,**inde'cisiveness** *n.*

indeed (ɪnˈdiːd) *adv.* **1.** certainly; actually: *indeed, it may never happen.* **2.** truly; very: *that is indeed amazing.* **3.** in fact; what is more: *a comfortable, indeed wealthy family.* ~*interj.* **4.** an expression of doubt or surprise.

indef. indefinite.

indefatigable (ˌɪndɪˈfætɪɡəbºl) *adj.* unable to be tired out; unflagging. —,**inde'fatigably** *adv.*

indefensible (ˌɪndɪˈfɛnsəbºl) *adj.* **1.** (of behaviour or statements) unable to be justified or supported. **2.** (of places or buildings) incapable of defence against attack. —,**inde,fensi'bility** *n.*

indefinable (ˌɪndɪˈfaɪnəbºl) *adj.* not able to be fully described or explained.

indefinite (ɪnˈdɛfɪnɪt) *adj.* **1.** without exact limits; indeterminate: *an indefinite number.* **2.** vague or unclear. —**in'definitely** *adv.*

indefinite article *n. Grammar.* a determiner that does not limit or specify the noun to which it refers, such as *a, an,* or *some.*

indelible (ɪnˈdɛlɪbºl) *adj.* **1.** incapable of being erased or obliterated. **2.** making indelible marks: *indelible ink.* —**in'delibly** *adv.*

indelicate (ɪnˈdɛlɪkɪt) *adj.* **1.** coarse, crude, or rough. **2.** offensive, embarrassing, or tasteless. —**in'delicacy** *n.*

indemnify (ɪnˈdɛmnɪˌfaɪ) *vb.* **-fying, -fied. 1.** to secure against loss, damage, or liability; insure. **2.** to compensate for loss or damage; reimburse. —**in,demnifi'cation** *n.*

indemnity (ɪnˈdɛmnɪtɪ) *n., pl.* **-ties. 1.** compensation for loss or damage; reimbursement. **2.** insurance against loss or damage. **3.** legal exemption from penalties incurred.

indent *vb.* (ɪnˈdɛnt). **1.** to place (written matter) in from the margin. **2.** to write out (a document) in duplicate. **3.** *Chiefly Brit.* (foll. by *for, on,* or *upon*) to order (goods, esp. foreign merchandise) by an official order form. **4.** to notch (an edge or border); make jagged. **5.** to bind (an apprentice) by indenture. ~*n.* (ˈɪnˌdɛnt). **6.** *Chiefly Brit.* an official order for goods, esp. foreign merchandise.

indentation (ˌɪndɛnˈteɪʃən) *n.* **1.** a hollow, notch, or cut, as on an edge or on a coastline. **2.** an indenting or being indented. **3.** Also: **indention.** the leaving of space or the amount of space left between a margin and the start of an indented line.

indenture (ɪnˈdɛntʃə) *n.* **1.** a deed, contract, or sealed agreement. **2.** (often *pl.*) a contract binding an apprentice to his master. ~*vb.* **3.** to enter into an agreement by indenture. **4.** to bind (an apprentice) by indenture.

independent (ˌɪndɪˈpɛndənt) *adj.* **1.** free from the influence or control of others. **2.** not dependent on anything else for function or validity; separate. **3.** not relying on the support, esp. financial support, of others. **4.** capable of acting for oneself or on one's own: *a very independent little girl.* **5.** of or having a private income large enough to enable one to live without working: *independent means.* **6.** *Maths.* (of a variable) not dependent on another variable. ~*n.* **7.** an independent person or thing. **8.** a politician who does not represent any political party. —,**inde'pendence** *n.* —,**inde'pendently** *adv.*

independent school *n.* (in Britain) a school that is neither financed nor controlled by the government or local authorities.

indescribable (ˌɪndɪˈskraɪbəbºl) *adj.* beyond description; too intense or extreme for words. —,**inde'scribably** *adv.*

indestructible (ˌɪndɪˈstrʌktəbºl) *adj.* not able to be destroyed; very strong.

indeterminate (ˌɪndɪˈtɜːmɪnɪt) *adj.* **1.** uncertain in extent, amount, or nature. **2.** left doubtful; inconclusive: *an indeterminate reply*. **3.** *Maths*. **a.** having no numerical meaning, as %. **b.** (of an equation) having more than one variable and an unlimited number of solutions. —**inde'terminable** *adj*. —**inde'terminacy** *n*.

index ('ɪndɛks) *n., pl*. **-dexes** *or* **-dices** (-dɪˌsiːz). **1.** an alphabetical list of names or subjects mentioned in a text, usually at the back, and indicating where they are referred to. **2.** a file or catalogue, as in a library, which enables a book or reference to be found. **3.** an indication or sign. **4.** a pointer, needle, or other indicator on an instrument. **5.** *Maths*. **a.** same as **exponent**. **b.** a superscript number placed to the left of a radical sign indicating the root to be extracted: *the index of $\sqrt[3]{8}$ is 3*. **6.** a number indicating the level of wages or prices as compared with some standard value. **7.** a number or ratio indicating a specific characteristic or property: *refractive index*. ~*vb*. **8.** to put an index in (a book). **9.** to enter (a word or item) in an index. **10.** to make index-linked.

indexation (ˌɪndɛk'seɪʃən) *or* **index-linking** *n*. the act of making wages, pensions, or interest rates index-linked.

index finger *n*. the finger next to the thumb. Also called: **forefinger**.

index-linked *adj*. (of pensions, wages, or interest rates) directly related to the cost-of-living index and rising or falling accordingly.

Indiaman ('ɪndɪəmən) *n., pl*. **-men**. (formerly) a merchant ship engaged in trade with India.

Indian ('ɪndɪən) *n*. **1.** a person from the Republic of India, a subcontinent of Asia. **2.** an American Indian. ~*adj*. **3.** of India, its inhabitants, or any of their languages. **4.** of the American Indians or any of their languages.

Indian club *n*. a heavy bottle-shaped club, usually swung in pairs for exercise.

Indian corn *n*. same as **maize**.

Indian file *n*. same as **single file**.

Indian hemp *n*. same as **hemp**.

Indian ink *or esp. U.S. & Canad*. **India ink** ('ɪndɪə) *n*. a black ink made from lampblack.

Indian list *n. Informal*. (in Canada) a list of persons to whom spirits may not be sold.

Indian summer *n*. **1.** a period of unusually warm weather, esp. in the autumn. **2.** a period of tranquillity or of renewed productivity towards the end of something, esp. a person's life.

India paper *n*. a thin soft opaque printing paper originally made in the Orient.

Indic ('ɪndɪk) *adj*. **1.** of a branch of Indo-European consisting of many of the languages of India, including Sanskrit, Hindi, and Urdu. ~*n*. **2.** this group of languages.

indicate ('ɪndɪˌkeɪt) *vb*. **1.** to be or give a sign or symptom of; imply: *cold hands indicate a warm heart*. **2.** to point out or show. **3.** to state briefly; suggest. **4.** (of measuring instruments) to show a reading of. **5.** (*usually passive*) to recommend or require: *surgery seems to be indicated for this patient*. —**indi'cation** *n*.

indicative (ɪn'dɪkətɪv) *adj*. **1.** (foll. by *of*) acting as a sign of; suggesting: *indicative of trouble ahead*. **2.** *Grammar*. denoting a mood of verbs used to make a statement. ~*n*. **3.** *Grammar*. the indicative mood.

indicator ('ɪndɪˌkeɪtə) *n*. **1.** something that acts as a sign or indication: *an indicator of public opinion*. **2.** an instrument or device, such as a gauge, that registers or measures something. **3.** a device for indicating that a motor vehicle is about to turn left or right, esp. two pairs of lights that flash. **4.** *Chem*. a substance used to indicate the completion of a chemical reaction, usually by a change of colour.

indices ('ɪndɪˌsiːz) *n*. a plural of **index**.

indict (ɪn'daɪt) *vb*. to charge (a person) formally with a crime, esp. in writing; accuse. —**in'dictable** *adj*.

indictment (ɪn'daɪtmənt) *n*. **1.** *Criminal law*. a formal charge of crime, esp. in writing; accusation. **2.** a serious criticism; denunciation: *a striking indictment of our educational system*.

indie ('ɪndɪ) *n. Informal*. an independent record company.

indifference (ɪn'dɪfrəns) *n*. **1.** lack of concern or interest: *years of official indifference*. **2.** lack of importance; insignificance: *a matter of indifference to me*.

indifferent (ɪn'dɪfrənt) *adj*. **1.** (often foll. by *to*) showing no concern or interest: *he was indifferent to my pleas*. **2.** unimportant; immaterial. **3. a.** of only average standard or quality; mediocre. **b.** not at all good; poor. **4.** showing or having no preferences; impartial.

indigenous (ɪn'dɪdʒɪnəs) *adj*. (often foll. by *to*) originating or occurring naturally (in a country or area); native: *the indigenous population*.

indigent ('ɪndɪdʒənt) *adj*. so poor as to lack even necessities; very needy. —**'indigence** *n*.

indigestible (ˌɪndɪ'dʒɛstəbʰl) *adj*. difficult or impossible to digest. —**ˌindiˌgesti'bility** *n*.

indigestion (ˌɪndɪ'dʒɛstʃən) *n*. difficulty in digesting food, accompanied by stomach pain, heartburn, and belching.

indignant (ɪn'dɪgnənt) *adj*. feeling or showing indignation. —**in'dignantly** *adv*.

indignation (ˌɪndɪg'neɪʃən) *n*. anger aroused by something felt to be unfair, unworthy, or wrong.

indignity (ɪnˈdɪgnɪtɪ) n., pl. **-ties.** injury to one's self-esteem or dignity; humiliation.

indigo (ˈɪndɪˌgəʊ) n., pl. **-gos** or **-goes.** 1. a blue dye originally obtained from plants but now made synthetically. ~adj. 2. deep violet-blue.

indirect (ˌɪndɪˈrɛkt) adj. 1. not going in a direct course or line; roundabout: an indirect route. 2. not done or caused directly; secondary: indirect benefits. 3. not coming straight to the point; devious: an indirect question.

indirect object n. Grammar. the person or thing indirectly affected by the action of a verb and its direct object, as John in the sentence I bought John a newspaper.

indirect speech n. same as **reported speech.**

indirect tax n. a tax levied on goods or services which is paid indirectly by being added to the price.

indiscernible (ˌɪndɪˈsɜːnəbᵊl) adj. not able or scarcely able to be seen.

indiscipline (ɪnˈdɪsɪplɪn) n. lack of discipline.

indiscreet (ˌɪndɪˈskriːt) adj. not discreet; incautious or tactless.

indiscretion (ˌɪndɪˈskrɛʃən) n. 1. the lack of discretion. 2. an indiscreet act or remark.

indiscriminate (ˌɪndɪˈskrɪmɪnɪt) adj. 1. lacking discrimination or careful choice; random: indiscriminate slaughter. 2. jumbled; confused: an indiscriminate mixture. —ˌindisˈcriminately adv. —ˌindisˌcriminaˈnation n.

indispensable (ˌɪndɪˈspɛnsəbᵊl) adj. absolutely necessary; essential: in my job a telephone is indispensable. —ˌindisˌpensaˈbility n.

indisposed (ˌɪndɪˈspəʊzd) adj. 1. sick or ill. 2. unwilling. —indisposition (ˌɪndɪspəˈzɪʃən) n.

indisputable (ˌɪndɪˈspjuːtəbᵊl) adj. beyond doubt; certain.

indistinct (ˌɪndɪˈstɪŋkt) adj. unable to be seen or heard clearly. —ˌindisˈtinctly adv.

indistinguishable (ˌɪndɪˈstɪŋgwɪʃəbᵊl) adj. so similar as to be difficult to tell apart.

indite (ɪnˈdaɪt) vb. Archaic. to put into words and write.

indium (ˈɪndɪəm) n. a rare soft silvery metallic element. Symbol: In

individual (ˌɪndɪˈvɪdjʊəl) adj. 1. of, relating to, or meant for a single person or thing: individual tuition. 2. separate or distinct from others of its kind; specific: please mark the individual pages. 3. characterized by unusual and striking qualities; unique. ~n. 4. a single person, esp. when regarded as distinct from others: the freedom of the individual. 5. Biol. a single animal or plant, esp. as distinct from a

species. 6. Informal. a person: a most obnoxious individual. —ˌindiˈvidually adv.

individualism (ˌɪndɪˈvɪdjʊəˌlɪzəm) n. 1. the principle of leading one's life in one's own way. 2. egoism. 3. same as **laissez faire.** —ˌindiˈvidualist n. —ˈindiˌvidualiˈistic adj.

individuality (ˌɪndɪˌvɪdjʊˈælɪtɪ) n., pl. **-ties.** 1. distinctive or unique character or personality: a work of great individuality. 2. the qualities that distinguish one person or thing from another. 3. a separate existence.

individualize or **-ise** (ˌɪndɪˈvɪdjʊəˌlaɪz) vb. to make individual or distinctive in character.

indivisible (ˌɪndɪˈvɪzəbᵊl) adj. 1. unable to be divided. 2. Maths. leaving a remainder when divided by a given number.

indoctrinate (ɪnˈdɒktrɪˌneɪt) vb. to teach (someone) systematically to accept a doctrine or opinion uncritically. —inˌdoctriˈnation n.

Indo-European (ˈɪndəʊ-) adj. 1. of a family of languages that includes most of the European and some of the Asian languages. ~n. 2. the Indo-European family of languages.

indolent (ˈɪndələnt) adj. disliking work; lazy; idle. —ˈindolence n.

indomitable (ɪnˈdɒmɪtəbᵊl) adj. (of a quality) difficult or impossible to defeat or discourage: indomitable pride; an indomitable spirit.

Indonesian (ˌɪndəʊˈniːzɪən) adj. 1. of Indonesia, a republic in SE Asia, its people, or their language. ~n. 2. a person from Indonesia.

indoor (ˈɪnˌdɔː) adj. situated, happening, or used inside a building: an indoor pool.

indoors (ˌɪnˈdɔːz) adv., adj. inside or into a building.

indorse (ɪnˈdɔːs) vb. same as **endorse.**

indrawn (ˌɪnˈdrɔːn) adj. drawn or pulled in: an indrawn breath.

indubitable (ɪnˈdjuːbɪtəbᵊl) adj. not able to be doubted; definite. —inˈdubitably adv.

induce (ɪnˈdjuːs) vb. 1. to persuade or use influence on. 2. to cause or bring about. 3. Med. to cause (labour) to begin by the use of drugs or other means. 4. Logic, obs. to draw (a general conclusion) from particular instances. 5. to produce (an electromotive force or electrical current) by induction. 6. to transmit (magnetism) by induction. —inˈducible adj.

inducement (ɪnˈdjuːsmənt) n. 1. the act of inducing. 2. a means of inducing; incentive.

induct (ɪnˈdʌkt) vb. 1. to bring in formally or install in a job, rank, or position. 2. (foll. by to or into) to introduce to or initiate in knowledge of (a profession).

inductance (ɪnˈdʌktəns) n. the property of an electric circuit as a result of which an electromotive force is created by a change of current in the same or in a neighbouring circuit.

induction (ɪnˈdʌkʃən) *n.* **1.** an inducting or being inducted. **2.** the act of inducing (labour). **3.** (in an internal-combustion engine) the drawing in of mixed air and fuel from the carburettor to the cylinder. **4.** *Logic.* a process of reasoning by which a general conclusion is drawn from particular instances. **5.** the process by which electrical or magnetic properties are transferred, without physical contact, from one circuit or body to another. **6.** a formal introduction or entry into an office or position. —**inˈductional** *adj.*

induction coil *n.* a transformer for producing a high voltage from a low voltage. It consists of a soft-iron core, a primary coil of few turns, and a concentric secondary coil of many turns.

inductive (ɪnˈdʌktɪv) *adj.* **1.** of or operated by electrical or magnetic induction. **2.** *Logic.* of or using induction: *inductive reasoning.*

inductor (ɪnˈdʌktə) *n.* a device designed to create inductance in an electrical circuit.

indue (ɪnˈdjuː) *vb.* **-duing, -dued.** same as **endue**.

indulge (ɪnˈdʌldʒ) *vb.* **1.** (often foll. by *in*) to yield to or gratify (a whim or desire for): *to indulge in new clothes.* **2.** to yield to the wishes of; pamper: *to indulge a child.* **3.** to allow (oneself) the pleasure of something: *he indulged himself.* **4.** *Informal.* to take alcoholic drink.

indulgence (ɪnˈdʌldʒəns) *n.* **1.** an indulging or being indulgent. **2.** a pleasure that is indulged in. **3.** liberal or tolerant treatment. **4.** something granted as a favour or privilege. **5.** *R.C. Church.* a remission of the temporal punishment for sin after its guilt has been forgiven.

indulgent (ɪnˈdʌldʒənt) *adj.* indulging or tending to indulge; kind or lenient often to excess. —**inˈdulgently** *adv.*

industrial (ɪnˈdʌstrɪəl) *adj.* **1.** of or derived from industry. **2.** employed or used in industry. **3.** relating to or concerned with industry: *industrial conditions.*

industrial action *n. Brit.* action, such as a strike or go-slow, taken by employees in industry to protest about pay, working conditions, or redundancies.

industrial estate *n. Brit.* an area of land set aside for industrial and business use.

industrialism (ɪnˈdʌstrɪəˌlɪzəm) *n.* an organization of society characterized by large-scale manufacturing industry rather than trade or farming.

industrialist (ɪnˈdʌstrɪəlɪst) *n.* a person who owns or controls large amounts of money or property in industry.

industrialize *or* **-lise** (ɪnˈdʌstrɪəˌlaɪz) *vb.* to develop industry on a large scale in (a country or region). —**inˌdustrialiˈzation** *or* **-liˈsation** *n.*

industrious (ɪnˈdʌstrɪəs) *adj.* hardworking; diligent.

industry (ˈɪndəstrɪ) *n., pl.* **-tries. 1.** the work and process involved in manufacture: *Japanese industry is making increasing use of robots.* **2.** a branch of commercial enterprise concerned with the manufacture of a specified product: *the steel industry.* **3.** the quality of working hard; diligence.

inebriate *vb.* (ɪnˈiːbrɪˌeɪt). **1.** to make drunk; intoxicate. ~*n.* (ɪnˈiːbrɪt). **2.** a person who is drunk, esp. habitually. ~*adj.* (ɪnˈiːbrɪt) *also* **inebriated. 3.** drunk, esp. habitually. —**inˌebriˈation** *n.*

inedible (ɪnˈɛdɪbʲl) *adj.* not fit to be eaten. **Usage.** *Inedible* does not mean exactly the same as *uneatable*. *Inedible* implies that something is of a sort not suitable for eating, while *uneatable* implies that it is so disgusting as to be beyond eating.

ineducable (ɪnˈɛdjukəbʲl) *adj.* incapable of being educated, esp. on account of mental retardation.

ineffable (ɪnˈɛfəbʲl) *adj.* too great or intense to be expressed in words; unutterable. —**inˈeffably** *adv.*

ineffective (ˌɪnɪˈfɛktɪv) *adj.* having no effect.

ineffectual (ˌɪnɪˈfɛktʃʊəl) *adj.* having no effect or an inadequate effect: *ineffectual struggles.*

inefficient (ˌɪnɪˈfɪʃənt) *adj.* wasteful, incompetent, or ineffective. —**ˌinefˈficiency** *n.*

inelegant (ɪnˈɛlɪgənt) *adj.* lacking elegance or refinement.

ineligible (ɪnˈɛlɪdʒəbʲl) *adj.* not qualified for or entitled to something.

ineluctable (ˌɪnɪˈlʌktəbʲl) *adj.* incapable of being avoided; inescapable.

inept (ɪnˈɛpt) *adj.* **1.** awkward, clumsy, or incompetent. **2.** not suitable or fitting; out of place. —**inˈeptiˌtude** *n.*

inequable (ɪnˈɛkwəbʲl) *adj.* **1.** unfair. **2.** not uniform.

inequality (ˌɪnɪˈkwɒlɪtɪ) *n., pl.* **-ties. 1.** the lack of equality. **2.** an instance of this. **3.** lack of smoothness or regularity of a surface. **4.** *Maths.* a statement indicating that the value of one quantity or expression is not equal to another.

inequitable (ɪnˈɛkwɪtəbʲl) *adj.* unjust or unfair.

ineradicable (ˌɪnɪˈrædɪkəbʲl) *adj.* not able to be removed or rooted out: *an ineradicable disease.*

inert (ɪnˈɜːt) *adj.* **1.** with no inherent power to move or to resist motion. **2.** inactive, lazy, or sluggish. **3.** having only a limited ability to react chemically; unreactive.

inertia (ɪnˈɜːʃə) *n.* **1.** the state of being

inert; disinclination to move or act. **2.** *Physics.* the tendency of a body to remain still or continue moving unless a force is applied to it. —**in'ertial** *adj.*

inertia selling *n.* the illegal practice of sending unrequested goods to householders, followed by a bill for the goods if they do not return them.

inescapable (ˌɪnɪ'skeɪpəbʰl) *adj.* not able to be avoided.

inessential (ˌɪnɪ'sɛnʃəl) *adj.* **1.** not necessary. ~*n.* **2.** an unnecessary thing.

inestimable (ɪn'ɛstɪməbʰl) *adj.* not able to be estimated; immeasurable.

inevitable (ɪn'ɛvɪtəbʰl) *adj.* **1.** unavoidable; sure to happen; certain. **2.** *Informal.* so regular as to be predictable: *the inevitable cup of tea.* ~*n.* **3.** (often preceded by *the*) something that is unavoidable. —**in₁evi-ta'bility** *n.* —**in'evitably** *adv.*

inexact (ˌɪnɪg'zækt) *adj.* not exact or accurate.

inexcusable (ˌɪnɪk'skjuːzəbʰl) *adj.* too bad to be justified or tolerated.

inexhaustible (ˌɪnɪg'zɔːstəbʰl) *adj.* incapable of being used up; endless.

inexorable (ɪn'ɛksərəbʰl) *adj.* **1.** (of a person) not able to be moved by entreaty or persuasion. **2.** (of a thing) that cannot be prevented from continuing or progressing; relentless: *an inexorable trend.* —**in'exorably** *adv.*

inexpensive (ˌɪnɪk'spɛnsɪv) *adj.* not expensive; cheap.

inexperience (ˌɪnɪk'spɪərɪəns) *n.* lack of experience. —**ˌinex'perienced** *adj.*

inexpert (ɪn'ɛkspɜːt) *adj.* not expert; lacking skill.

inexpiable (ɪn'ɛkspɪəbʰl) *adj.* (of sin) incapable of being atoned for; unpardonable.

inexplicable (ˌɪnɪk'splɪkəbʰl) *adj.* not able to be explained.

inexpressible (ˌɪnɪk'sprɛsəbʰl) *adj.* (of a feeling) too strong to be expressed in words.

in extremis *Latin.* (ɪn ɪk'striːmɪs) *adv.* **1.** in dire straits. **2.** at the point of death.

inextricable (ˌɪnɛks'trɪkəbʰl) *adj.* **1.** not able to be escaped from: *an inextricable dilemma.* **2.** not able to be disentangled or separated: *an inextricable knot.* —**ˌinex-'tricably** *adv.*

inf. 1. Also: **Inf.** infantry. **2.** infinitive. **3.** informal. **4.** information.

infallible (ɪn'fæləbʰl) *adj.* **1.** incapable of error. **2.** not liable to fail; certain: *an infallible cure.* **3.** (of the Pope) incapable of error in setting forth matters of doctrine on faith and morals. —**in₁falli'bility** *n.* —**in'fallibly** *adv.*

infamous ('ɪnfəməs) *adj.* having a bad reputation; notorious.

infamy ('ɪnfəmɪ) *n., pl.* **-mies. 1.** the state

of being infamous. **2.** an infamous act or event.

infancy ('ɪnfənsɪ) *n., pl.* **-cies. 1.** the state or period of being an infant. **2.** an early stage of growth or development: *this research is still in its infancy.* **3.** *Law.* the state or period of being a minor.

infant ('ɪnfənt) *n.* **1.** a very young child; baby. **2.** *Law.* same as **minor** (sense 4). **3.** *Brit.* a young schoolchild. **4.** (*modifier*) **a.** of or relating to young children or infancy. **b.** designed or intended for young children: *infant school.* ~*adj.* **5.** in an early stage of development: *an infant science.*

infanta (ɪn'fæntə) *n.* **1.** (formerly) a daughter of a king of Spain or Portugal. **2.** the wife of an infante.

infante (ɪn'fæntɪ) *n.* (formerly) any son of a king of Spain or Portugal, except the heir to the throne.

infanticide (ɪn'fæntɪˌsaɪd) *n.* the killing of an infant.

infantile ('ɪnfənˌtaɪl) *adj.* **1.** like a child in action or behaviour; childishly immature. **2.** of infants or infancy.

infantile paralysis *n.* same as **poliomyelitis.**

infantry ('ɪnfəntrɪ) *n., pl.* **-tries.** soldiers who fight on foot.

infant school *n. Brit.* a school for children aged between 5 and 7.

infatuate (ɪn'fætjʊˌeɪt) *vb.* to inspire or fill with an intense and unreasoning passion. —**in₁fatu'ation** *n.*

infatuated (ɪn'fætjʊˌeɪtɪd) *adj.* (often foll. by *with*) carried away by an intense and unreasoning passion for someone.

infect (ɪn'fɛkt) *vb.* **1.** to cause infection in; contaminate (a person or thing) with a germ or virus or its consequent disease. **2.** to taint or contaminate. **3.** to affect, esp. adversely, with an opinion or feeling as if by contagion: *I was infected by his pessimism.*

infection (ɪn'fɛkʃən) *n.* **1.** contamination of a person or thing by a germ or virus or its consequent disease. **2.** the resulting physical condition. **3.** an infectious disease. **4.** something that infects.

infectious (ɪn'fɛkʃəs) *adj.* **1.** (of a disease) capable of being transmitted without actual contact; caused by microorganisms, such as bacteria or viruses. **2.** causing or transmitting infection. **3.** tending to spread from one person to another: *infectious mirth.*

infectious hepatitis *n.* an acute viral disease causing inflammation of the liver, fever, and jaundice.

infectious mononucleosis *n.* same as **glandular fever.**

infelicity (ˌɪnfɪ'lɪsɪtɪ) *n., pl.* **-ties. 1.** the state or quality of being unhappy or unfortunate. **2.** an instance of bad luck; misfortune. **3.** something, esp. a remark or expression, that is inapt. —ˌinfeˈlicitous adj.

infer (ɪnˈfɜː) vb. -ferring, -ferred. 1. to conclude by reasoning from evidence; deduce. 2. Not universally accepted. to imply or suggest. —inˈferable or inˈferrable adj.
Usage. The use of infer in the sense of imply often occurs in both speech and writing but it is wise to avoid this if possible.

inference (ˈɪnfərəns) n. 1. the act or process of reaching a conclusion by reasoning from evidence. 2. an inferred conclusion or deduction.

inferential (ˌɪnfəˈrɛnʃəl) adj. of or based on inference.

inferior (ɪnˈfɪərɪə) adj. 1. lower in value or quality. 2. lower in rank, position, or status; subordinate. 3. of poor quality; second-rate. 4. lower in position; situated beneath. 5. Printing. (of a character) printed at the foot of an ordinary character. ~n. 6. a person inferior to another, esp. in rank. —inferiority (ɪnˌfɪərɪˈɒrɪtɪ) n.

inferiority complex n. Psychiatry. a disorder arising from a feeling of inferiority to others, characterized by aggressiveness or extreme shyness.

infernal (ɪnˈfɜːnºl) adj. 1. of or relating to hell. 2. wicked and cruel; diabolic; fiendish: infernal experiments. 3. Informal. irritating: stop that infernal noise.

inferno (ɪnˈfɜːnəʊ) n., pl. -nos. 1. (sometimes cap.; usually preceded by the) hell; the infernal region. 2. a place or situation resembling hell, usually because it is crowded and noisy. 3. a raging fire.

infertile (ɪnˈfɜːtaɪl) adj. 1. not capable of producing offspring; sterile. 2. (of land) not productive; barren. —infertility (ˌɪnfəˈtɪlɪtɪ) n.

infest (ɪnˈfɛst) vb. (of vermin or parasites) to inhabit or overrun (a place, plant, etc.) in unpleasantly large numbers: the place was infested by rats. —ˌinfesˈtation n.

infidel (ˈɪnfɪdºl) n. 1. a person who has no religious belief; unbeliever. 2. a person who rejects a specific religion, esp. Christianity or Islam. ~adj. 3. of unbelievers or unbelief.

infidelity (ˌɪnfɪˈdɛlɪtɪ) n., pl. -ties. 1. unfaithfulness to another, esp. one's husband or wife. 2. an act or instance of unfaithfulness.

infield (ˈɪnˌfiːld) n. 1. Cricket. the area of the field near the pitch. 2. Baseball. the area of the playing field enclosed by the base lines. —ˈinˌfielder n.

infighting (ˈɪnˌfaɪtɪŋ) n. 1. rivalry or quarrelling between members of the same group or organization. 2. Boxing. combat at close quarters.

infiltrate (ˈɪnfɪlˌtreɪt) vb. 1. Mil. to pass undetected through (an enemy-held line or position). 2. to enter or cause to enter (an organization) gradually and in secret, so as to gain influence or control: they infiltrated the party structure. 3. to pass (a liquid or gas) through (a substance) by filtering or (of a liquid or gas) to pass through (a substance) by filtering. —ˌinfilˈtration n. —ˈinfilˌtrator n.

infin. infinitive.

infinite (ˈɪnfɪnɪt) adj. 1. having no limits or boundaries in time, space, extent, or size. 2. extremely or immeasurably great or numerous: infinite wealth. 3. Maths. having an unlimited or uncountable number of digits, factors, or terms. —ˈinfinitely adv.

infinitesimal (ˌɪnfɪnɪˈtɛsɪməl) adj. 1. infinitely or immeasurably small. 2. Maths. of or involving a small change in the value of a variable that approaches zero as a limit. ~n. 3. Maths. an infinitesimal quantity.

infinitive (ɪnˈfɪnɪtɪv) n. Grammar. a form of the verb which is not inflected for tense or person and is used without a particular subject. In English, the infinitive usually consists of the word to followed by the verb.

infinitude (ɪnˈfɪnɪˌtjuːd) n. 1. the state or quality of being infinite. 2. an infinite extent or quantity.

infinity (ɪnˈfɪnɪtɪ) n., pl. -ties. 1. the state or quality of being infinite. 2. endless time, space, or quantity. 3. an infinitely great number or amount. 4. Maths. the concept of a value greater than any finite numerical value.

infirm (ɪnˈfɜːm) adj. weak in health or body, esp. from old age.

infirmary (ɪnˈfɜːmərɪ) n., pl. -ries. a place for the treatment of the sick or injured; hospital.

infirmity (ɪnˈfɜːmɪtɪ) n., pl. -ties. 1. the state or quality of being infirm. 2. physical weakness or debility; frailty.

infix (ɪnˈfɪks, ˈɪnˌfɪks) vb. 1. to fix firmly in. 2. to instil or impress on the mind by repetition. —ˌinfixˈation or infixion (ɪnˈfɪkʃən) n.

in flagrante delicto (ɪn fləˈɡræntɪ dɪˈlɪktəʊ) adv. Chiefly law. in the very act of committing the offence; red-handed.

inflame (ɪnˈfleɪm) vb. 1. to arouse or become aroused to violent emotion, esp. anger. 2. to increase or intensify; aggravate. 3. to produce inflammation in (a tissue, organ, or part) or (of a tissue, organ, or part) to become inflamed. 4. to set or be set on fire.

inflammable (ɪnˈflæməbºl) adj. 1. liable to catch fire; flammable. 2. easily aroused to anger or passion. —inˌflammaˈbility n.
Usage. see flammable.

inflammation (ˌɪnfləˈmeɪʃən) n. 1. the reaction of living tissue to injury or infection, characterized by heat, redness, swelling, and pain. **2.** an inflaming or being inflamed.

inflammatory (ɪnˈflæmətrɪ) *adj.* **1.** tending to arouse violence or strong emotion. **2.** characterized by or caused by inflammation.

inflatable (ɪnˈfleɪtəbˀl) *adj.* **1.** capable of being inflated. ~*n.* **2.** any object, made of strong plastic or rubber, which can be inflated.

inflate (ɪnˈfleɪt) *vb.* **1.** to expand or cause to expand by filling with gas or air. **2.** to give an impression of greater importance than is justified; puff up: *to have an inflated opinion of oneself.* **3.** to cause inflation of (prices or money) or (of prices or money) to undergo inflation.

inflation (ɪnˈfleɪʃən) *n.* **1.** an inflating or being inflated. **2.** *Econ.* a progressive increase in the general level of prices brought about by an increase in the amount of money in circulation or by increases in costs. **3.** *Informal.* the rate of increase of prices. —in**ˈflationary** *adj.*

inflect (ɪnˈflɛkt) *vb.* **1.** *Grammar.* to change (the form of a word) by inflection. **2.** to change (the voice) in tone or pitch; modulate. **3.** to bend or curve. —in**ˈflective** *adj.*

inflection *or* **inflexion** (ɪnˈflɛkʃən) *n.* **1.** modulation of the voice. **2.** *Grammar.* a change in the form of a word, signalling change in such grammatical functions as tense or number. **3.** an angle or bend. **4.** an inflecting or being inflected. **5.** *Maths.* a change in curvature from concave to convex or vice versa. —in**ˈflectional** *or* in**ˈflexional** *adj.*

inflexible (ɪnˈflɛksəbˀl) *adj.* **1.** obstinate; unyielding: *dogmatically inflexible in the face of change.* **2.** unalterable; fixed: *inflexible schedules.* **3.** rigid; stiff: *inflexible joints.* —in**ˌflexiˈbility** *n.*

inflict (ɪnˈflɪkt) *vb.* **1.** (often foll. by *on* or *upon*) to impose (something unwelcome or unpleasant, such as pain) upon (a person). **2.** to deal out (a blow or wound). —in**ˈfliction** *n.* —in**ˈflictor** *n.*

in-flight *adj.* provided during flight in an aircraft: *in-flight meals.*

inflorescence (ˌɪnflɔːˈrɛsəns) *n.* **1.** the part of a plant that consists of the flower-bearing stalks. **2.** the arrangement of the flowers on the stalks. **3.** the process of flowering; blossoming.

inflow (ˈɪnˌfləʊ) *n.* **1.** something, such as a liquid or gas, that flows in. **2.** the act of flowing in; influx.

influence (ˈɪnfluəns) *n.* **1.** an effect of one person or thing on another. **2.** the power of a person or thing to have such an effect. **3.** power resulting from ability, wealth, or position. **4.** a person or thing having influence. **5. under the influence.** *Informal.* drunk. ~*vb.* **6.** to persuade or induce. **7.**

to have an effect upon (actions or events); affect.

influential (ˌɪnfluˈɛnʃəl) *adj.* having or exerting influence.

influenza (ˌɪnfluˈɛnzə) *n.* a highly contagious viral disease characterized by fever, muscular pains, and inflammation of the breathing passages.

influx (ˈɪnˌflʌks) *n.* **1.** the arrival or entry of many people or things. **2.** the act of flowing in; inflow.

info (ˈɪnfəʊ) *n. Informal.* short for **information.**

inform (ɪnˈfɔːm) *vb.* **1.** (often foll. by *of* or *about*) to give information to; tell. **2.** (often foll. by *of* or *about*) to make knowledgeable (about) or familiar (with). **3.** (often foll. by *against* or *on*) to give information incriminating someone, esp. to the police. **4.** to impart some essential or formative characteristic to. **5.** to animate or inspire. —in**ˈformed** *adj.*

informal (ɪnˈfɔːməl) *adj.* **1.** not of a formal, official, or stiffly conventional nature; relaxed and friendly: *an informal interview.* **2.** appropriate to everyday life or use rather than formal occasions: *informal clothes.* **3.** (of speech or writing) appropriate to ordinary conversation rather than to formal written language. —**informality** (ˌɪnfɔːˈmælɪtɪ) *n.* —in**ˈformally** *adv.*

informant (ɪnˈfɔːmənt) *n.* a person who gives information.

information (ˌɪnfəˈmeɪʃən) *n.* **1.** knowledge acquired in any manner; facts. **2.** *Computers.* **a.** the meaning given to data by the way it is interpreted. **b.** same as **data** (sense 2).

information technology *n.* the production, storage, and communication of information using computers and microelectronics.

information theory *n.* the study of the processes of communication and the transmission of information.

informative (ɪnˈfɔːmətɪv) *adj.* providing information; instructive.

informer (ɪnˈfɔːmə) *n.* a person who informs against someone, esp. a criminal.

infra dig (ˈɪnfrə ˈdɪg) *adj. Informal.* beneath one's dignity.

infrared (ˌɪnfrəˈrɛd) *adj.* **1.** of or using rays with a wavelength just beyond the red end of the visible spectrum. ~*n.* **2.** the infrared part of the spectrum.

infrasonic (ˌɪnfrəˈsɒnɪk) *adj.* having a frequency below the range audible to the human ear.

infrastructure (ˈɪnfrəˌstrʌktʃə) *n.* **1.** the basic structure of an organization or system. **2.** the stock of facilities, services, and equipment in a country, including factories, roads, and schools, that are needed for it to function properly.

infrequent (ɪnˈfriːkwənt) *adj.* not happening often; only occasional. —**in'frequently** *adv.*

infringe (ɪn'frɪndʒ) *vb.* **1.** to violate or break (a law or agreement). **2.** (foll. by *on* or *upon*) to encroach or trespass on: *the children infringed on our privacy.* —**in'fringement** *n.*

infuriate (ɪn'fjʊərɪˌeɪt) *vb.* to anger; annoy. —**in'furiˌating** *adj.* —**in'furiˌatingly** *adv.*

infuse (ɪn'fjuːz) *vb.* **1.** (often foll. by *into*) to instil or impart (a quality). **2.** (foll. by *with*) to inspire: *she infused them with new hope.* **3.** to soak or be soaked in order to extract flavour or other properties.

infusible (ɪn'fjuːzəbˀl) *adj.* that cannot be fused or melted. —**inˌfusi'bility** *n.*

infusion (ɪn'fjuːʒən) *n.* **1.** the act of infusing. **2.** something infused. **3.** an extract obtained by soaking.

ingenious (ɪn'dʒiːnjəs) *adj.* made or contrived with skill and originality; clever.

ingénue ('ænʒeɪˌnjuː) *n.* an artless, innocent, or inexperienced young woman, esp. as a role played by an actress.

ingenuity (ˌɪndʒɪ'njuːɪtɪ) *n.* inventive talent; cleverness.

ingenuous (ɪn'dʒɛnjʊəs) *adj.* **1.** naive, artless, or innocent. **2.** candid; frank; straightforward.

ingest (ɪn'dʒɛst) *vb.* to take (food or liquid) into the body. —**in'gestion** *n.*

ingle ('ɪŋgˀl) *n. Archaic or dialect.* a fire in a room or a fireplace.

inglenook ('ɪŋgˌnʊk) *n. Brit.* a corner by a fireplace; chimney corner.

ingoing ('ɪnˌgəʊɪŋ) *adj.* going in; entering.

ingot ('ɪŋgət) *n.* a piece of metal cast in a form suitable for storage, usually a bar.

ingrained *or* **engrained** (ɪn'greɪnd) *adj.* **1.** (of a habit, feeling, or belief) deeply impressed or instilled. **2.** (esp. of dirt) worked into or through the fibre or pores.

ingratiate (ɪn'greɪʃɪˌeɪt) *vb.* (often foll. by *with*) to act so as to bring (oneself) into favour with (someone). —**in'gratiˌating** *adj.*

ingratitude (ɪn'grætɪˌtjuːd) *n.* lack of gratitude; ungratefulness.

ingredient (ɪn'griːdɪənt) *n.* a component of a mixture or compound, esp. in cooking.

ingress ('ɪngrɛs) *n.* **1.** the act of going or coming in. **2.** the right or permission to enter.

ingrowing ('ɪnˌgrəʊɪŋ) *adj.* (esp. of a toenail) growing abnormally into the flesh.

ingrown ('ɪnˌgrəʊn, ɪn'grəʊn) *adj.* (esp. of a toenail) grown abnormally into the flesh.

inhabit (ɪn'hæbɪt) *vb.* to live or dwell in; occupy. —**in'habitable** *adj.*

inhabitant (ɪn'hæbɪtənt) *n.* a person or animal that is a permanent resident of a particular place or region.

inhalant (ɪn'heɪlənt) *n.* a medicinal preparation inhaled for its therapeutic effect.

inhale (ɪn'heɪl) *vb.* to draw (breath, smoke, or vapour) into the lungs; breathe in. —**inhalation** (ˌɪnhə'leɪʃən) *n.*

inhaler (ɪn'heɪlə) *n.* a device for sending out therapeutic vapours for inhalation, esp. one for relieving nasal congestion.

inharmonious (ˌɪnhɑː'məʊnɪəs) *adj.* lacking harmony; discordant; disagreeing.

inhere (ɪn'hɪə) *vb.* (foll. by *in*) to be an inseparable part (of).

inherent (ɪn'hɪərənt, -'hɛr-) *adj.* existing as an inseparable part; intrinsic. —**in'herently** *adv.*

inherit (ɪn'hɛrɪt) *vb.* **1.** to receive money, property, or a title by succession or under a will. **2.** to receive (a characteristic) from an earlier generation by heredity: *he inherited the disease from his father.* **3.** to receive (a position or situation) from a predecessor: *the government inherited a work economy.* —**in'heritor** *n.*

inheritable (ɪn'hɛrɪtəbˀl) *adj.* **1.** capable of being transmitted by heredity from one generation to a later one. **2.** capable of being inherited.

inheritance (ɪn'hɛrɪtəns) *n.* **1.** *Law.* **a.** hereditary succession to an estate or title. **b.** the right of an heir to succeed on the death of an ancestor. **2.** the act of inheriting. **3.** something inherited or to be inherited; heritage. **4.** the fact of receiving characteristics from an earlier generation by heredity.

inhibit (ɪn'hɪbɪt) *vb.* **1.** to restrain or hinder (an impulse or desire). **2.** to prohibit or prevent: *it inhibits progress.* **3.** *Chem.* to stop, prevent, or decrease the rate of (a chemical reaction). —**in'hibited** *adj.*

inhibition (ˌɪnɪ'bɪʃən, ˌɪnhɪ-) *n.* **1.** an inhibiting or being inhibited. **2.** *Psychol.* a mental condition in which the expression and behaviour of an individual become restricted by emotional resistance. **3.** the process of stopping or retarding a chemical reaction.

inhospitable (ˌɪnhɒ'spɪtəbˀl, ɪn'hɒs-) *adj.* **1.** not hospitable; unfriendly. **2.** (of a place or climate) not easy to live in; harsh.

inhuman (ɪn'hjuːmən) *adj.* **1.** Also: **inhumane** (ˌɪnhjuː'meɪn). unfeeling; cruel; brutal. **2.** not human.

inhumanity (ˌɪnhjuː'mænɪtɪ) *n., pl.* **-ties.** **1.** lack of humane qualities. **2.** an inhumane act.

inimical (ɪ'nɪmɪkˀl) *adj.* **1.** adverse or unfavourable: *inimical to change.* **2.** not friendly; hostile.

inimitable (ɪ'nɪmɪtəbˀl) *adj.* incapable of being imitated; unique. —**in'imitably** *adv.*

iniquity (ɪ'nɪkwɪtɪ) *n., pl.* **-ties.** **1.** lack of justice or righteousness; wickedness. **2.** a wicked act; sin. —**in'iquitous** *adj.*

initial (ɪ'nɪʃəl) *adj.* **1.** of or at the beginning.

~*n.* **2.** the first letter of a word, esp. a person's name. **3.** *Printing.* a large letter set at the beginning of a chapter or work. ~*vb.* **-tialling, -tialled** *or U.S.* **-tialing, -tialed. 4.** to sign with one's initials, esp. to indicate approval; endorse. —**in'itial·ly** *adv.*

initiate *vb.* (ɪˈnɪʃɪˌeɪt). **1.** to begin or set going: *to initiate peace talks.* **2.** to accept (new members) into an organization or social group, through often secret ceremonies. **3.** to teach fundamentals of a skill or knowledge to. ~*n.* (ɪˈnɪʃɪɪt, -ˌeɪt). **4.** a person who has been initiated, esp. recently. **5.** a beginner; novice. —**i,niti'ation** *n.* —**in'iti,ator** *n.*

initiative (ɪˈnɪʃɪətɪv) *n.* **1.** a first step; commencing move: *a peace initiative.* **2.** the right or power to initiate something: *he has the initiative.* **3.** enterprise: *try to show some initiative.* **4. on one's own initiative.** without being prompted.

inject (ɪnˈdʒɛkt) *vb.* **1.** *Med.* to introduce (a fluid) into the body (of a person or animal) by means of a syringe. **2.** (foll. by *into*) to introduce (a new element): *to inject humour into a scene.* —**in'jection** *n.*

injudicious (ˌɪndʒuˈdɪʃəs) *adj.* showing poor judgment; unwise.

injunction (ɪnˈdʒʌŋkʃən) *n.* **1.** *Law.* an order issued by a court to a person or group, esp. to refrain from some act. **2.** an authoritative command. —**in'junctive** *adj.*

injure (ˈɪndʒə) *vb.* **1.** to hurt physically or mentally. **2.** to do wrong to (a person), esp. by an injustice. —**'injured** *adj.*

injurious (ɪnˈdʒʊərɪəs) *adj.* **1.** causing harm. **2.** abusive, slanderous, or libellous.

injury (ˈɪndʒərɪ) *n.*, *pl.* **-ries. 1.** physical hurt. **2.** a specific instance of this: *a leg injury.* **3.** harm done to the feelings.

injury time *n. Football, rugby, etc.* extra playing time added on to compensate for time spent attending to injured players during the match.

injustice (ɪnˈdʒʌstɪs) *n.* **1.** unfairness; lack of justice. **2.** an unjust act.

ink (ɪŋk) *n.* **1.** a black or coloured liquid used for printing, writing, and drawing. **2.** a dark brown fluid squirted into the water for self-concealment by an octopus or cuttlefish. ~*vb.* **3.** to mark with ink. **4.** to coat (a printing surface) with ink.

inkling (ˈɪŋklɪŋ) *n.* a hint; vague idea or suspicion.

inkstand (ˈɪŋkˌstænd) *n.* a stand or tray on which are kept writing tools and containers for ink.

inkwell (ˈɪŋkˌwɛl) *n.* a small container for ink, often fitted into the surface of a desk.

inky (ˈɪŋkɪ) *adj.* **inkier, inkiest. 1.** like ink, esp. in colour; dark or black. **2.** of or stained with ink. —**'inkiness** *n.*

inlaid (ɪnˈleɪd) *adj.* **1.** set in another material so that the surfaces are smooth and flat, as a design in wood. **2.** having such a design: *an inlaid table.*

inland *adj.* (ˈɪnlənd). **1.** of or in the interior of a country or region, away from a sea or border. **2.** *Chiefly Brit.* operating within a country or region; domestic: *inland trade.* ~*n.* (ˈɪnˌlænd, -lənd). **3.** the interior of a country or region. ~*adv.* (ˈɪnˌlænd, -lənd). **4.** towards or into the interior of a country or region.

Inland Revenue *n.* (in Britain and New Zealand) a government department that administers and collects major direct taxes, such as income tax.

in-law *n.* **1.** a relative by marriage. ~*adj.* **2.** related by marriage: *a father-in-law.*

inlay *vb.* (ɪnˈleɪ), **-laying, -laid. 1.** to decorate (an article, esp. of furniture) by inserting pieces of wood, ivory, or metal so that the surfaces are smooth and flat. ~*n.* (ˈɪnˌleɪ). **2.** *Dentistry.* a filling shaped to fit a cavity. **3.** decoration made by inlaying. **4.** an inlaid article.

inlet (ˈɪnlɪt) *n.* **1.** a narrow strip of water which goes from a sea or lake into the land or between two islands. **2.** a passage or valve through which a substance, esp. a fluid, enters a machine.

in loco parentis Latin. (ɪn ˈlɒkəʊ pəˈrɛntɪs) in place of a parent: said of a person acting in a parental capacity.

inmate (ˈɪnˌmeɪt) *n.* a person who is confined to an institution such as a prison or hospital.

inmost (ˈɪnˌməʊst) *adj.* same as **innermost.**

inn (ɪn) *n.* a pub or small hotel providing food and accommodation.

innards (ˈɪnədz) *pl. n. Informal.* the internal organs of the body, esp. the entrails.

innate (ɪˈneɪt, ˈɪneɪt) *adj.* existing from birth, rather than acquired; natural; inborn: *an innate talent.* —**in'nately** *adv.*

inner (ˈɪnə) *adj.* **1.** happening or located inside or further inside: *an inner room.* **2.** of the mind or spirit: *inner calm.* **3.** more profound; less apparent: *the inner meaning.* **4.** exclusive or private: *inner regions of the party.* ~*n.* **5.** *Archery.* **a.** the red innermost ring on a target. **b.** a shot which hits this ring.

inner city *n.* the parts of a city in or near its centre, where there are often social and economic problems such as unemployment and inadequate housing.

inner man *or* (*fem.*) **inner woman** *n.* **1.** the mind or soul. **2.** *Jocular.* the stomach.

innermost (ˈɪnəˌməʊst) *adj.* **1.** furthest within; central. **2.** most intimate or private.

inner tube *n.* an inflatable rubber tube inside a pneumatic tyre casing.

innings (ˈɪnɪŋz) *n.* **1.** (*functioning as sing.*)

Cricket, baseball. **a.** the batting turn of a player or team. **b.** the runs scored during such a turn. **2.** a period of opportunity or action.

innkeeper ('ɪn,kiːpə) *n.* an owner or manager of an inn.

innocence ('ɪnəsəns) *n.* the quality or state of being innocent.

innocent ('ɪnəsənt) *adj.* **1.** not tainted with evil; sinless; pure. **2.** not guilty of a particular crime; blameless. **3.** (foll. by *of*) free of; lacking: *innocent of all knowledge of history.* **4.** harmless or innocuous: *an innocent game.* **5.** naive or artless. ~*n.* **6.** an innocent person, esp. a young child or a naive adult. —'**innocently** *adv.*

innocuous (ɪ'nɒkjʊəs) *adj.* having no adverse or harmful effect; harmless.

innovate ('ɪnə,veɪt) *vb.* to invent or begin to apply new methods or ideas. —'**inno,vative** *or* '**inno,vatory** *adj.* —'**inno,vator** *n.*

innovation (,ɪnə'veɪʃən) *n.* **1.** something newly introduced, such as a new method or device. **2.** the act of innovating.

innuendo (,ɪnjʊ'endəʊ) *n., pl.* **-dos** *or* **-does.** an indirect or subtle reference, esp. one which is malicious, derogatory, or disapproving; insinuation.

Innuit ('ɪnjuːɪt) *n.* same as **Inuit.**

innumerable (ɪ'njuːmərəb'l) *adj.* too many to be counted; extremely numerous. —**in-'numerably** *adv.*

innumerate (ɪ'njuːmərɪt) *adj.* having no knowledge or understanding of mathematics or science. —**in'numeracy** *n.*

inoculate (ɪ'nɒkjʊ,leɪt) *vb.* **1.** to inject a vaccine or serum into (a person or animal) in order to create immunity to a disease. **2.** to introduce (microorganisms, esp. bacteria) into (a culture medium). —**in,ocu-'lation** *n.*

inoffensive (,ɪnə'fɛnsɪv) *adj.* causing no harm or annoyance; unobjectionable.

inoperable (ɪn'ɒpərəb'l) *adj. Surgery.* that cannot safely be operated on: *an inoperable tumour.*

inopportune (ɪn'ɒpə,tjuːn) *adj.* badly timed or inappropriate.

inordinate (ɪn'ɔːdɪnɪt) *adj.* **1.** exceeding normal limits; excessive: *an inordinate number of old people died of cold this winter.* **2.** unrestrained, as in behaviour or emotion: *inordinate fury.* —**in'ordinately** *adv.*

inorganic (,ɪnɔː'gænɪk) *adj.* **1.** not having the structure or characteristics of living organisms; not organic. **2.** of or denoting chemical compounds that do not contain carbon. **3.** not resulting from or produced by growth; artificial: *inorganic fertilizers.*

inorganic chemistry *n.* the branch of chemistry concerned with the elements and compounds which do not contain carbon.

inpatient ('ɪn,peɪʃənt) *n.* a patient living in the hospital where he is being treated.

input ('ɪn,pʊt) *n.* **1.** that which is put in. **2.** a resource required for industrial production, such as money, labour, or power. **3.** *Computers.* the data fed into a computer. ~*vb.* **4.** to insert (data) into a computer.

inquest ('ɪn,kwɛst) *n.* **1.** an official inquiry, esp. into the cause of an unexplained, sudden, or violent death, held by a coroner. **2.** *Informal.* an investigation or discussion.

inquietude (ɪn'kwaɪɪ,tjuːd) *n.* restlessness, uneasiness, or anxiety.

inquire *or* **enquire** (ɪn'kwaɪə) *vb.* **1. a.** to seek information (about); ask: *she inquired his age; she inquired about rates of pay.* **b.** (foll. by *of*) to ask (a person) for information: *I'll inquire of my aunt when she is coming.* **2.** (often foll. by *into*) to make an investigation. —**in'quirer** *or* **en'quirer** *n.* —**in'quiry** *or* **en'quiry** *n.*

inquisition (,ɪnkwɪ'zɪʃən) *n.* **1.** a deep or searching inquiry. **2.** an official inquiry, esp. one held by a jury before an officer of the Crown. —**,inqui'sitional** *adj.*

Inquisition (,ɪnkwɪ'zɪʃən) *n. History.* a tribunal of the Roman Catholic Church (1232–1820) founded to suppress heresy.

inquisitive (ɪn'kwɪzɪtɪv) *adj.* **1.** excessively curious, esp. about other people's business; prying. **2.** eager to learn; inquiring. —**in-'quisitively** *adv.* —**in'quisitiveness** *n.*

inquisitor (ɪn'kwɪzɪtə) *n.* **1.** a person who inquires, esp. deeply, searchingly, or ruthlessly. **2.** (*often cap.*) an officer of the Inquisition.

inquisitorial (ɪn,kwɪzɪ'tɔːrɪəl) *adj.* **1.** of or resembling inquisition or an inquisitor. **2.** offensively curious; prying. **in,quisi'torially** *adv.*

in re (ɪn 'reɪ) *prep.* in the matter of; concerning.

INRI Jesus of Nazareth, king of the Jews (the inscription placed over Christ's head during the Crucifixion).

inroad ('ɪn,rəʊd) *n.* **1.** a sudden hostile attack; raid. **2.** an encroachment or intrusion: *my gambling has made great inroads on my savings.*

inrush ('ɪn,rʌʃ) *n.* a sudden and overwhelming inward flow; influx.

ins. 1. inches. **2.** insurance.

insane (ɪn'seɪn) *adj.* **1.** mentally ill; crazy; of unsound mind. **2.** irresponsible; very foolish; stupid: *an insane plan.* —**in'sanely** *adv.*

insanitary (ɪn'sænɪtrɪ) *adj.* dirty; unhealthy.

insanity (ɪn'sænɪtɪ) *n., pl.* **-ties. 1.** the state of being insane. **2.** utter folly; stupidity.

insatiable (ɪn'seɪʃəb'l, -ʃɪə-) *adj.* not able to be satisfied; greedy or unappeasable. —**in-,satia'bility** *n.* —**in'satiably** *adv.*

inscribe (ɪnˈskraɪb) vb. **1.** to mark or engrave (words, symbols, or letters) on (a surface such as stone or paper). **2.** to enter (a name) on a list. **3.** to write one's name, and sometimes a brief dedication, on (a book or work of art) before presentation to another person. **4.** to draw (a geometric construction) inside another construction so that the two are in contact at as many points as possible but do not intersect.

inscription (ɪnˈskrɪpʃən) n. **1.** something inscribed, esp. words carved or engraved on a coin, tomb, or ring. **2.** a signature or brief dedication in a book or on a work of art.

inscrutable (ɪnˈskruːtəbˀl) adj. mysterious or enigmatic; incomprehensible. —**in,scruta'bility** n.

insect (ˈɪnsɛkt) n. **1.** a small air-breathing invertebrate with a body divided into head, thorax, and abdomen, three pairs of legs, and (in most species) two pairs of wings. **2.** (loosely) any similar invertebrate, such as a spider, tick, or centipede.

insecticide (ɪnˈsɛktɪˌsaɪd) n. a substance used to destroy insect pests. —**in,secti'cidal** adj.

insectivore (ɪnˈsɛktɪˌvɔː) n. **1.** any of an order of small primitive mammals which feed on invertebrates. The group includes shrews, moles, and hedgehogs. **2.** any animal or plant that feeds on insects. —**,insec'tivorous** adj.

insecure (ˌɪnsɪˈkjʊə) adj. **1.** anxious or afraid; not confident or certain. **2.** not adequately protected: an insecure fortress. **3.** unstable or shaky. —**,inse'curity** n.

inseminate (ɪnˈsɛmɪˌneɪt) vb. to impregnate (a female) with semen. —**in,semi'nation** n.

insensate (ɪnˈsɛnseɪt, -sɪt) adj. **1.** lacking sensation or consciousness. **2.** insensitive; unfeeling. **3.** foolish; senseless.

insensible (ɪnˈsɛnsɪbˀl) adj. **1.** lacking sensation or consciousness. **2.** (foll. by of or to) unaware of or indifferent to: insensible to suffering. **3.** same as **imperceptible**. —**in,sensi'bility** n.

insensitive (ɪnˈsɛnsɪtɪv) adj. unaware of or not responsive to other people's feelings.

inseparable (ɪnˈsɛprəbˀl) adj. **1.** constantly together because of mutual liking: the two girls became inseparable friends. **2.** too closely connected to be separated.

insert vb. (ɪnˈsɜːt). **1.** to place or fit (something) inside something else. **2.** to introduce into text or a speech. ~n. (ˈɪnsɜːt). **3.** something inserted, esp. a printed sheet bearing advertising, placed loose between the leaves of a magazine.

insertion (ɪnˈsɜːʃən) n. **1.** the act of inserting. **2.** something inserted, such as an advertisement in a newspaper.

in-service adj. denoting training that is given to employees during the course of employment: an in-service course.

inset vb. (ɪnˈsɛt), **-setting**, **-set**. **1.** to place in or within; insert. ~n. (ˈɪnˌsɛt). **2.** something inserted. **3.** Printing. a small map or diagram set within the borders of a larger one.

inshore (ˈɪnˈʃɔː) adj. **1.** in or on the water, but close to the shore: inshore weather. ~adv., adj. **2.** towards the shore from the water: we swam inshore; an inshore wind.

inside n. (ˈɪnˈsaɪd). **1.** the inner side or part of something. **2.** the side of a path away from the road. **3.** (also pl.) Informal. the stomach and bowels. **4.** inside out. with the inside facing outwards. **5.** know inside out. to know thoroughly. ~prep. (ˌɪnˈsaɪd). **6.** in or to the interior of; within. **7.** in a period of time less than: I'll be back inside an hour. ~adj. (ˈɪnˌsaɪd). **8.** on or of the inside: an inside door. **9.** arranged or provided by someone within an organization, esp. illicitly: inside information. ~adv. (ˌɪnˈsaɪd). **10.** on, in, or to the inside; indoors. **11.** Slang. in or into prison.

inside job n. Informal. a crime committed with the assistance of someone employed by or trusted by the victim.

insider (ˌɪnˈsaɪdə) n. a member of a specified group or organization who therefore has exclusive information about it.

insider dealing n. the illegal practice of a person on the stock exchange or in the civil service taking advantage of early confidential information in order to deal in shares for personal profit.

insidious (ɪnˈsɪdɪəs) adj. working in a subtle or apparently harmless way, but nevertheless dangerous or deadly: insidious propaganda; an insidious illness. —**in'sidiously** adv. —**in'sidiousness** n.

insight (ˈɪnˌsaɪt) n. **1.** the ability to perceive clearly or deeply the inner nature of things. **2.** a penetrating understanding, as of a complex situation or problem.

insignia (ɪnˈsɪgnɪə) n., pl. **-nias** or **-nia**. a badge or emblem of membership, office, or dignity.

insignificant (ˌɪnsɪgˈnɪfɪkənt) adj. having little or no importance; trivial or relatively small. —**,insig'nificance** n.

insincere (ˌɪnsɪnˈsɪə) adj. lacking sincerity; hypocritical. —**,insin'cerely** adv. —**insincerity** (ˌɪnsɪnˈsɛrɪtɪ) n.

insinuate (ɪnˈsɪnjʊˌeɪt) vb. **1.** to suggest indirectly by allusion, hints, or innuendo. **2.** to get (someone, esp. oneself) into a position by gradual manoeuvres: insinuating himself into her favour.

insinuation (ɪnˌsɪnjʊˈeɪʃən) n. **1.** an indirect or devious hint or suggestion. **2.** an act or the practice of insinuating.

insipid (ɪnˈsɪpɪd) adj. **1.** lacking spirit or

interest; boring. **2.** lacking taste; unpalatable. —**,insi'pidity** n.

insist (ɪn'sɪst) vb. (often foll. by on or upon) **1.** to make a determined demand (for): he insisted on his rights. **2.** to express a convinced belief (in) or assertion (of): I insist that he is innocent.

insistent (ɪn'sɪstənt) adj. **1.** making continual and persistent demands. **2.** demanding attention; compelling: the insistent cry of a bird. —**in'sistence** n. —**in'sistently** adv.

in situ Latin. (ɪn 'sɪtjuː) adv., adj. in the original position.

in so far or U.S. **insofar** (,ɪnsəʊ'fɑː) adv. (usually foll. by as) to the degree or extent (that).

insole ('ɪn,səʊl) n. **1.** the inner sole of a shoe or boot. **2.** a loose additional inner sole used to give extra warmth or to make a shoe fit.

insolent ('ɪnsələnt) adj. insulting; disrespectful. —**'insolence** n. —**'insolently** adv.

insoluble (ɪn'sɒljʊb°l) adj. **1.** incapable of being dissolved. **2.** incapable of being solved. —**in,solu'bility** n.

insolvent (ɪn'sɒlvənt) adj. **1.** unable to pay debts; bankrupt. ~n. **2.** a person who is insolvent; bankrupt. —**in'solvency** n.

insomnia (ɪn'sɒmnɪə) n. chronic inability to sleep. —**in'somni,ac** n., adj.

insomuch (,ɪnsəʊ'mʌtʃ) adv. **1.** (foll. by as or that) to such an extent or degree. **2.** (foll. by as) because of the fact (that); inasmuch (as).

insouciant (ɪn'suːsɪənt) adj. carefree or unconcerned; light-hearted. —**in'souciance** n.

inspan (ɪn'spæn) vb. **-spanning, -spanned.** Chiefly S. African. **1.** to harness (animals) to (a vehicle); yoke. **2.** to press (people) into service.

inspect (ɪn'spɛkt) vb. **1.** to examine closely, esp. for faults or errors. **2.** to examine officially. —**in'spection** n.

inspector (ɪn'spɛktə) n. **1.** a person who inspects, esp. an official who examines for compliance with regulations or standards. **2.** a police officer ranking below a superintendent and above a sergeant.

inspectorate (ɪn'spɛktərɪt) n. **1.** the position or duties of an inspector. **2.** a body of inspectors.

inspiration (,ɪnspɪ'reɪʃən) n. **1.** stimulation of the mind or feelings to activity or creativity. **2.** a person or thing that causes this state. **3.** an inspired idea or action. —**in-spi'rational** adj.

inspire (ɪn'spaɪə) vb. **1.** to stimulate (a person) to activity or creativity. **2.** (foll. by with or to) to arouse (with a particular emotion or to a particular reaction): he inspires confidence.

inst. instant (this month).

instability (,ɪnstə'bɪlɪtɪ) n. lack of stability or steadiness.

install (ɪn'stɔːl) vb. **1.** to place (equipment) in position and connect and adjust it for use. **2.** to place (a person) formally in a position or rank. **3.** to settle (a person, esp. oneself) in a position or state: she installed herself in an armchair. —**installation** (,ɪnstə'leɪʃən) n.

installment plan n. U.S. same as **hire-purchase.** Also (Canad.): **instalment plan.**

instalment or U.S. **installment** (ɪn'stɔːlmənt) n. **1.** one of the portions into which a debt is divided for payment at regular intervals. **2.** a portion of something that is issued, broadcast, or published in parts.

instance ('ɪnstəns) n. **1.** a case or particular example. **2. for instance.** as an example. **3.** a specified stage in proceedings; step: in the first instance. **4.** urgent request or demand: at the instance of. ~vb. **5.** to cite as an example.

instant ('ɪnstənt) n. **1.** a very brief time; moment. **2.** a particular moment: at the same instant. ~adj. **3.** immediate. **4.** (of foods) that can be prepared very quickly and easily: instant coffee. **5.** urgent or pressing. **6.** of the present month: a letter of the 7th instant.

instantaneous (,ɪnstən'teɪnɪəs) adj. occurring or done in an instant; immediate: instantaneous death. —**,instan'taneously** adv.

instantly ('ɪnstəntlɪ) adv. immediately; at once.

instead (ɪn'stɛd) adv. **1.** as a replacement or substitute for the person or thing mentioned. **2. instead of.** in place of or as an alternative to.

instep ('ɪn,stɛp) n. **1.** the middle section of the human foot, forming the arch between the ankle and toes. **2.** the part of a shoe or stocking covering this.

instigate ('ɪnstɪ,geɪt) vb. **1.** to bring about by incitement: to instigate rebellion. **2.** to urge on to some action. —**,insti'gation** n. —**'insti,gator** n.

instil or U.S. **instill** (ɪn'stɪl) vb. **-stilling, -stilled. 1.** to introduce (an idea or feeling) gradually. **2.** Rare. to pour in or inject drop by drop. —**,instil'lation** n. —**in'stiller** n.

instinct ('ɪnstɪŋkt) n. **1.** the inborn tendency of a person or animal to behave in a particular way without the need for thought: maternal instinct. **2.** natural reaction: my first instinct was to hit him. **3.** intuition: she knew by instinct that he was lying. —**in'stinctive** adj. —**in'stinctively** adv.

institute ('ɪnstɪ,tjuːt) vb. **1.** to organize; establish. **2.** to initiate: to institute a practice. **3.** to install in a position or office.

~*n.* **4.** an organization founded for particular work, especially research or teaching. **5.** the building where such an organization is situated. **6.** a rule, custom, or precedent.

institution (ˌɪnstɪˈtjuːʃən) *n.* **1.** an instituting or being instituted. **2.** an organization founded for a specific purpose, such as a hospital or college. **3.** an established custom, law, or principle: *the institution of marriage.* **4.** *Informal.* a well-established person or feature: *he has become a local institution.*

institutional (ˌɪnstɪˈtjuːʃənᵊl) *adj.* **1.** of or relating to an institution: *institutional care.* **2.** dull, routine, and uniform: *institutional meals.* —ˌinstiˈtutionalˌism *n.*

institutionalize (ˌɪnstɪˈtjuːʃənəˌlaɪz) *vb.* **1.** to place in an institution. **2.** (*often passive*) to subject (a person) to institutional life, often causing apathy and dependence on routine. **3.** to make or become an institution: *institutionalized religion.*

instruct (ɪnˈstrʌkt) *vb.* **1.** to direct to do something; order. **2.** to teach (someone) how to do (something).

instruction (ɪnˈstrʌkʃən) *n.* **1.** a direction; order. **2.** the process or act of teaching; education. —inˈstructional *adj.*

instructions (ɪnˈstrʌkʃənz) *pl. n.* clear and detailed information, in written form, on how to do something: *read the instructions before you switch on the engine.*

instructive (ɪnˈstrʌktɪv) *adj.* serving to instruct or enlighten; conveying information.

instructor (ɪnˈstrʌktə) *n.* **1.** someone who instructs; teacher. **2.** *U.S. & Canad.* a college teacher ranking below assistant professor. —inˈstructress *fem. n.*

instrument (ˈɪnstrəmənt) *n.* **1.** a tool or implement, esp. one used for precision work. **2.** *Music.* any of various devices that can be played to produce musical sounds. **3.** an important factor in something: *her evidence was an instrument in his arrest.* **4.** *Informal.* a person used by another to gain an end. **5.** a device for measuring, indicating, or controlling: *the pilot watched the panel of instruments.* **6.** a formal legal document.

instrumental (ˌɪnstrəˈmɛntᵊl) *adj.* **1.** serving as a means or factor. **2.** of or done with an instrument: *instrumental error.* **3.** played by or composed for musical instruments.

instrumentalist (ˌɪnstrəˈmɛntəlɪst) *n.* a person who plays a musical instrument.

instrumentation (ˌɪnstrəmɛnˈteɪʃən) *n.* **1.** the instruments specified in a musical score or arrangement. **2.** same as **orchestration**. **3.** the use or provision of instruments or tools.

instrument panel *n.* a panel on which instruments are mounted in a vehicle or on a machine.

insubordinate (ˌɪnsəˈbɔːdɪnɪt) *adj.* not submissive to authority; disobedient or rebellious. —**insubordination** (ˌɪnsəˌbɔːdɪˈneɪʃən) *n.*

insubstantial (ˌɪnsəbˈstænʃəl) *adj.* **1.** not substantial; flimsy, fine, or slight. **2.** imaginary; unreal.

insufferable (ɪnˈsʌfərəbᵊl) *adj.* intolerable; unendurable. —inˈsufferably *adv.*

insufficient (ˌɪnsəˈfɪʃənt) *adj.* not enough for a particular purpose; inadequate. —ˌinsufˈficiency *n.* —ˌinsufˈficiently *adv.*

insular (ˈɪnsjʊlə) *adj.* **1.** not responsive to change or new influences; narrowminded. **2.** of or like an island. —insularity (ˌɪnsjʊˈlærɪtɪ) *n.*

insulate (ˈɪnsjʊˌleɪt) *vb.* **1.** to prevent the transmission of electricity, heat, or sound to or from (a place or body) by surrounding with a nonconducting material. **2.** to isolate or set apart. —ˈinsuˌlator *n.*

insulation (ˌɪnsjʊˈleɪʃən) *n.* **1.** material used to insulate something. **2.** the act of insulating.

insulin (ˈɪnsjʊlɪn) *n.* a hormone, secreted in the pancreas, that controls the amount of sugar in the blood.

insult *vb.* (ɪnˈsʌlt). **1.** to treat or speak to rudely; offend. ~*n.* (ˈɪnsʌlt). **2.** an offensive remark or action. **3.** a person or thing producing the effect of an insult: *some television is an insult to intelligence.*

insuperable (ɪnˈsuːpərəbᵊl) *adj.* incapable of being overcome; insurmountable. —inˌsuperaˈbility *n.*

insupportable (ˌɪnsəˈpɔːtəbᵊl) *adj.* **1.** incapable of being endured; intolerable. **2.** incapable of being upheld or justified; indefensible: *an insupportable accusation.*

insurance (ɪnˈʃʊərəns) *n.* **1. a.** the business of providing financial protection in the event of loss, damage, or death. **b.** the state of having such protection. **c.** Also called: **insurance policy.** the policy providing such protection. **d.** the amount paid by the insurance company in the event of loss, damage, or death. **e.** the amount paid in return for such protection. **2.** a means of safeguarding against risk or injury.

insure (ɪnˈʃʊə) *vb.* **1.** (*often foll. by against*) to guarantee or protect (against risk or loss). **2.** (*often foll. by against*) to issue (a person) with an insurance policy or take out an insurance policy (on): *his house was heavily insured against fire.* **3.** *Chiefly U.S.* same as **ensure.** —inˈsurable *adj.* —inˌsuraˈbility *n.*

insured (ɪnˈʃʊəd) *n.* **the.** the person covered by an insurance policy.

insurer (ɪnˈʃʊərə) *n.* a person or company that sells insurance.

insurgent (ɪnˈsɜːdʒənt) *adj.* **1.** rebellious or

in revolt against an established authority.
~*n.* **2.** a person who takes part in a rebellion. —**in'surgence** *n.*

insurmountable (,ɪnsə'maʊntəb°l) *adj.* impossible to overcome: *insurmountable problems.*

insurrection (,ɪnsə'rɛkʃən) *n.* the act of rebelling against an established authority; insurgence. —,**insur'rectionist** *n., adj.*

int. 1. internal. **2.** Also: **Int.** international.

intact (ɪn'tækt) *adj.* untouched; left complete or perfect. —**in'tactness** *n.*

intaglio (ɪn'tɑːlɪ,əʊ) *n., pl.* **-lios** *or* **-li** (-ljiː). **1.** a seal or gem ornamented with an engraved design. **2.** a design carved into the surface of the material used. —**intagliated** (ɪn'tɑːlɪ,eɪtɪd) *adj.*

intake ('ɪn,teɪk) *n.* **1.** a thing or a quantity taken in: *an intake of students.* **2.** the act of taking in. **3.** the opening through which fluid enters a pipe or fuel or air enters an engine.

intangible (ɪn'tændʒɪb°l) *adj.* **1.** incapable of being perceived by touch. **2.** vague or indefinable; difficult for the mind to grasp: *intangible ideas.* —**in,tangi'bility** *n.*

integer ('ɪntɪdʒə) *n.* any positive or negative whole number or zero, as opposed to a number with fractions or decimals.

integral ('ɪntɪgrəl) *adj.* **1.** (often foll. by *to*) being an essential part (of a whole). **2.** whole; complete. **3.** *Maths.* **a.** of or involving an integral. **b.** involving or being an integer. ~*n.* **4.** *Maths.* the sum of a large number of minute quantities, summed either between stated limits (**definite integral**) or in the absence of limits (**indefinite integral**).

integral calculus *n.* the branch of calculus concerned with the determination of integrals and their use in solving differential equations.

integrand ('ɪntɪ,grænd) *n.* a mathematical function to be integrated.

integrate ('ɪntɪ,greɪt) *vb.* **1.** to make or be made into a whole; incorporate or be incorporated. **2.** to designate (an institution) for use by all races or groups; desegregate. **3.** to amalgamate (a racial or religious group) with an existing community. **4.** *Maths.* to determine the integral of a function or variable. —,**inte'gration** *n.*

integrated circuit *n.* a very small electronic circuit consisting of an assembly of elements made from a single chip of semiconducting material.

integrity (ɪn'tɛgrɪtɪ) *n.* **1.** adherence to moral principles; honesty. **2.** the quality of being unimpaired; soundness. **3.** unity; wholeness: *cultural integrity.*

integument (ɪn'tɛgjʊmənt) *n.* any outer protective covering, such as a skin, rind, or shell. —**in,tegu'mental** *or* **in,tegu'mentary** *adj.*

intellect ('ɪntɪ,lɛkt) *n.* **1.** the ability to understand, think, and reason. **2.** a particular person's mind or intelligence, esp. a brilliant one: *his intellect is wasted on that job.* **3.** *Informal.* a person who has a brilliant mind.

intellectual (,ɪntɪ'lɛktjʊəl) *adj.* **1.** of, involving, or appealing to the intellect: *intellectual literature.* **2.** having a highly developed intellect. ~*n.* **3.** a person who has a highly developed intellect. —,**intel,lectu'ality** *n.* —,**intel'lectually** *adv.*

intelligence (ɪn'tɛlɪdʒəns) *n.* **1.** the ability to understand, learn, and think things out quickly. **2.** *Old-fashioned.* news; information. **3.** the collection of secret information, esp. for military purposes. **4.** a group or department that gathers or deals with such information.

intelligence quotient *n.* a measure of the intelligence of a person. The quotient is calculated by dividing a person's mental age by his actual age and multiplying the result by 100.

intelligent (ɪn'tɛlɪdʒənt) *adj.* **1.** having or showing intelligence; clever: *an intelligent child; an intelligent guess.* **2.** (of computerized functions, weapons, etc.) able to initiate or modify action in the light of ongoing events. —**in'telligently** *adv.*

intelligentsia (ɪn,tɛlɪ'dʒɛntsɪə) *n.* (usually preceded by *the*) the educated or intellectual people in a society.

intelligible (ɪn'tɛlɪdʒəb°l) *adj.* able to be understood; comprehensible. —**in,telligi'bility** *n.*

intemperate (ɪn'tɛmpərɪt) *adj.* **1.** drinking alcohol too much or too often. **2.** unrestrained: *intemperate rage.* **3.** extreme or severe: *an intemperate climate.* —**in'temperance** *n.*

intend (ɪn'tɛnd) *vb.* **1.** to propose or plan (something or to do something); have as one's purpose: *I intend to go out.* **2.** (often foll. by *for*) to design or destine (for a certain purpose or person): *the money was intended for you.* **3.** to mean to express or indicate: *no criticism was intended.*

intended (ɪn'tɛndɪd) *adj.* **1.** planned or future. ~*n.* **2.** *Informal.* a person whom one is to marry; fiancé or fiancée.

intense (ɪn'tɛns) *adj.* **1.** of very great force, strength, degree, or amount: *intense heat.* **2.** characterized by deep or forceful feelings: *an intense person.* —**in'tensely** *adv.* —**in'tenseness** *n.*

intensifier (ɪn'tɛnsɪ,faɪə) *n.* a word, esp. an adjective or adverb, that intensifies the meaning of the word or phrase that it modifies, for example *very* or *extremely.*

intensify (ɪn'tɛnsɪ,faɪ) *vb.* **-fying, -fied.** to make or become intense or more intense. —**intensification** (ɪn,tɛnsɪfɪ'keɪʃən) *n.*

intensity (ɪn'tɛnsɪtɪ) *n., pl.* **-ties. 1.** the

state or quality of being intense. **2.** extreme force, degree, or amount. **3.** *Physics.* the amount or degree of strength of electricity, heat, light, or sound per unit area of volume.

intensive (ɪnˈtɛnsɪv) *adj.* **1.** of or characterized by intensity; thorough: *intensive training.* **2.** using one specified factor more than others: *labour-intensive.* **3.** *Agriculture.* designed to increase production from a particular area: *an intensive agricultural programme.* **4.** *Grammar.* of a word giving emphasis, for example *very* in *the very same.* —in**ˈtensively** *adv.* —in**ˈtensiveness** *n.*

intensive care *n.* thorough, continuously supervised treatment of an acutely ill patient in a hospital.

intent (ɪnˈtɛnt) *n.* **1.** something that is intended; aim; purpose. **2.** *Law.* the will or purpose to commit a crime: *lurking with intent.* **3. to all intents and purposes.** in almost every respect; virtually. ~*adj.* **4.** having one's attention firmly fixed; absorbed: *an intent look.* **5.** (foll. by *on* or *upon*) having the fixed intention of; strongly resolved on: *intent on getting it right.* —in**ˈtently** *adv.* —in**ˈtentness** *n.*

intention (ɪnˈtɛnʃən) *n.* something intended; a plan, idea, or purpose: *she had no intention of going; motivated by good intentions.*

intentional (ɪnˈtɛnʃənˈl) *adj.* done on purpose; deliberate. —in**ˈtentionally** *adv.*

inter (ɪnˈtɜː) *vb.* **-terring, -terred.** to place (a body) in the earth; bury.

inter- *prefix.* **1.** between or among: *international.* **2.** together, mutually, or reciprocally: *interdependent; interchange.*

interact (ˌɪntərˈækt) *vb.* to act on or in close relation with each other. —inter**ˈaction** *n.* —inter**ˈactive** *adj.*

inter alia Latin. (ˈɪntər ˈeɪlɪə) *adv.* among other things.

interbreed (ˌɪntəˈbriːd) *vb.* **-breeding, -bred. 1.** to breed within a single family or strain so as to produce particular characteristics in the offspring. **2.** same as **cross-breed** (sense 1).

intercede (ˌɪntəˈsiːd) *vb.* to act as a mediator in order to end a disagreement; plead on another's behalf: *to intercede in the strike; I interceded for him with his father.*

intercept *vb.* (ˌɪntəˈsɛpt). **1.** to stop or seize on the way from one place to another; prevent from arriving or proceeding. **2.** *Maths.* to mark off or include (part of a line, curve, plane, or surface) between two points or lines. ~*n.* (ˈɪntəˌsɛpt). **3.** *Maths.* **a.** a point at which two figures intersect. **b.** the distance from the origin to the point at which a line, curve, or surface cuts a coordinate axis. —inter**ˈception** *n.* —inter**ˈceptor** *n.*

intercession (ˌɪntəˈsɛʃən) *n.* **1.** the act of

interceding. **2.** prayer offered to God on behalf of others. —inter**ˈcessor** *n.*

interchange *vb.* (ˌɪntəˈtʃeɪndʒ). **1.** to change places or cause to change places; exchange; switch. ~*n.* (ˈɪntəˌtʃeɪndʒ). **2.** the act of interchanging; exchange. **3.** a motorway junction of interconnecting roads and bridges designed to prevent streams of traffic crossing one another. —inter**ˈchangeable** *adj.* —inter**ˈchangeably** *adv.*

inter-city *adj.* (in Britain) denoting a fast rail service between main towns.

intercom (ˈɪntəˌkɒm) *n.* an internal telephone system for communicating within a building or vehicle.

intercommunicate (ˌɪntəkəˈmjuːnɪˌkeɪt) *vb.* **1.** to communicate mutually. **2.** (of two rooms) to interconnect. —ˌintercomˌmuniˈcation *n.*

intercommunion (ˌɪntəkəˈmjuːnjən) *n.* association between Churches, involving esp. mutual reception of Holy Communion.

interconnect (ˌɪntəkəˈnɛkt) *vb.* to connect with one another. —interconˈnected *adj.* —ˌinterconˈnection *n.*

intercontinental (ˌɪntəˌkɒntɪˈnɛntˈl) *adj.* travelling between or linking continents.

intercourse (ˈɪntəˌkɔːs) *n.* **1.** same as **sexual intercourse. 2.** communication or dealings between individuals or groups.

interdenominational (ˌɪntədɪˌnɒmɪˈneɪʃənˈl) *adj.* among or involving more than one denomination of the Christian Church.

interdepartmental (ˌɪntəˌdiːpɑːtˈmɛntˈl) *adj.* of or between different departments.

interdependent (ˌɪntədɪˈpɛndənt) *adj.* dependent on one another. —ˌinterdeˈpendence *n.*

interdict *n.* (ˈɪntəˌdɪkt). **1.** *R.C. Church.* the exclusion of a person or place from certain sacraments, although not from communion. **2.** *Law.* an official prohibition or restraint. ~*vb.* (ˌɪntəˈdɪkt). **3.** to place under legal or ecclesiastical sanction; prohibit or forbid. —interˈdiction *n.* —ˌinterˈdictory *adj.*

interdisciplinary (ˌɪntəˈdɪsɪˌplɪnərɪ) *adj.* involving two or more academic disciplines.

interest (ˈɪntrɪst) *n.* **1.** curiosity or concern about something or someone. **2.** the power of causing this: *to have great interest.* **3.** something in which one is interested; a hobby or pursuit. **4.** (*often pl.*) advantage: *in one's own interest.* **5.** (*often pl.*) a right, share, or claim, esp. in a business or property. **6.** money paid for the use of credit or borrowed money: *he borrowed money at 25 per cent interest.* **7.** (*often pl.*) a group of people with common aims: *the landed interest.* ~*vb.* **8.** to arouse the curiosity or concern of. **9.** to cause to become interested or involved in something.

interested (ˈɪntrɪstɪd) *adj.* **1.** showing or having interest. **2.** personally involved: *the* *interested parties met to discuss the business.*

interesting (ˈɪntrɪstɪŋ) *adj.* causing interest; absorbing. —**ˈinterestingly** *adv.*

interface *n.* (ˈɪntəˌfeɪs). **1.** *Physical chem.* a surface that forms the boundary between two liquids or chemical phases that cannot be mixed. **2.** a common boundary between two things: *the interface between technology and design.* **3.** an electrical circuit linking one device, esp. a computer, with another. ~*vb.* (ˌɪntəˈfeɪs). **4.** to connect or be connected with by interface.

interfacing (ˈɪntəˌfeɪsɪŋ) *n.* **1.** a piece of fabric sewn beneath the facing of a garment to give shape and firmness. **2.** same as **interlining.**

interfere (ˌɪntəˈfɪə) *vb.* **1.** (often foll. by *in*) to meddle: *your mother always interferes in our business.* **2.** (foll. by *with*) to clash with; hinder: *child-bearing may interfere with your career.* **3.** (foll. by *with*) *Euphemistic.* to assault sexually. **4.** *Physics.* to produce or cause to produce interference. —**ˌinterˈfering** *adj.*

interference (ˌɪntəˈfɪərəns) *n.* **1.** the act of interfering. **2.** *Physics.* the meeting of two waves which reinforce or neutralize each other depending on whether they are in or out of phase. **3.** any undesired signal that interferes with the reception of radio waves.

interferon (ˌɪntəˈfɪərɒn) *n. Biochem.* a protein made by cells in response to virus infection that prevent the growth of the virus.

interfuse (ˌɪntəˈfjuːz) *vb.* **1.** to mix or become mixed; intermingle. **2.** to blend or fuse together. —**ˌinterˈfusion** *n.*

interim (ˈɪntərɪm) *adj.* **1.** temporary or provisional: *interim measures to deal with the emergency.* ~*n.* **2. in the interim.** during the intervening time.

interior (ɪnˈtɪərɪə) *n.* **1.** a part or region that is inside: *the interior of the earth.* **2.** the central area of a country or continent, furthest from the sea. **3.** a picture of the inside of a room or building. **4.** the inside of a building or room, with respect to design and decoration. ~*adj.* **5.** of, situated on, or suitable for the inside; inner. **6.** coming or acting from within; internal. **7.** of a nation's domestic affairs; internal. **8.** mental or spiritual: *interior development.*

interior angle *n.* an angle of a polygon contained between two adjacent sides.

interior decoration *n.* **1.** the decoration and furnishings of the interior of a room or house. **2.** Also called: **interior design.** the art or business of planning this.

interj. interjection.

interject (ˌɪntəˈdʒɛkt) *vb.* to interpose abruptly; interrupt with: *she interjected clever remarks.*

interjection (ˌɪntəˈdʒɛkʃən) *n.* a word or phrase which is used on its own and which expresses sudden emotion; exclamation.

interlace (ˌɪntəˈleɪs) *vb.* to join together by crossing over, as if woven: *interlaced fingers.*

interlard (ˌɪntəˈlɑːd) *vb.* to insert in or occur throughout: *to interlard one's writing with foreign phrases.*

interlay (ˌɪntəˈleɪ) *vb.* **-laying, -laid.** to insert (layers) between; interpose: *to interlay gold among the silver.*

interleaf (ˈɪntəˌliːf) *n., pl.* **-leaves.** a blank leaf inserted between the other leaves of a book. —**ˌinterˈleave** *vb.*

interleukin (ˌɪntəˈluːkɪn) *n.* a substance obtained from white blood cells that stimulates their activity against infection and may by used to fight some forms of cancer.

interline[1] (ˌɪntəˈlaɪn) *or* **interlineate** (ˌɪntəˈlɪnɪˌeɪt) *vb.* to write or print (matter) between the lines of (a text or book).

interline[2] (ˌɪntəˈlaɪn) *vb.* to provide (a part of a garment) with a second lining, esp. of stiffened material.

interlining (ˈɪntəˌlaɪnɪŋ) *n.* the material used to interline parts of garments.

interlink (ˌɪntəˈlɪŋk) *vb.* to connect together.

interlock *vb.* (ˌɪntəˈlɒk). **1.** to join or be joined firmly together. ~*n.* (ˈɪntəˌlɒk). **2.** a device used to prevent a mechanism from operating independently or unsafely. **3.** a closely knitted fabric. ~*adj.* (ˈɪntəˌlɒk). **4.** closely knitted.

interlocutor (ˌɪntəˈlɒkjʊtə) *n.* a person who takes part in a conversation.

interlocutory (ˌɪntəˈlɒkjʊtrɪ) *adj.* **1.** *Law.* pronounced during the course of legal proceedings; provisional: *an interlocutory injunction.* **2.** of dialogue; conversational.

interloper (ˈɪntəˌləʊpə) *n.* a person who interferes in other people's affairs; intruder.

interlude (ˈɪntəˌluːd) *n.* **1.** a period of time or different activity between longer periods or events; interval. **2. a.** a pause between the acts of a play. **b.** a brief piece of music or other entertainment performed during this pause.

intermarry (ˌɪntəˈmærɪ) *vb.* **-rying, -ried.** **1.** (of different races, religions, or social groups) to become connected by marriage. **2.** to marry within one's own family or tribe. —**ˌinterˈmarriage** *n.*

intermediary (ˌɪntəˈmiːdɪərɪ) *n., pl.* **-aries.** **1.** a person who tries to bring about agreement between two parties in dispute. **2.** a medium or means. ~*adj.* **3.** acting as an intermediary. **4.** intermediate.

intermediate *adj.* (ˌɪntəˈmiːdɪt). **1.** occurring between two points or extremes; in between. ~*n.* (ˌɪntəˈmiːdɪt). **2.** something intermediate. **3.** a substance formed between the first and final stages of a chemical process. ~*vb.* (ˌɪntəˈmiːdɪˌeɪt). **4.** to act as an intermediary. —ˌinter**ˌmedi**ˈation *n.*

interment (ɪnˈtɜːmənt) *n.* an interring; burial.

intermezzo (ˌɪntəˈmɛtsəʊ) *n., pl.* -zos *or* -zi (-tsiː). **1.** a short piece of instrumental music performed between the acts of a play or opera. **2. a.** a short composition between two longer movements in an extended musical work. **b.** a similar composition intended for independent performance.

interminable (ɪnˈtɜːmɪnəbᵊl) *adj.* seemingly endless because of monotony: *an interminable lecture.* —in**ˈterminably** *adv.*

intermingle (ˌɪntəˈmɪŋgᵊl) *vb.* to mix together.

intermission (ˌɪntəˈmɪʃən) *n.* a pause, esp. an interval between parts of a film, play, etc.

intermittent (ˌɪntəˈmɪtᵊnt) *adj.* occurring at regular or irregular intervals; not continuous. —**ˌinter**ˈmittently *adv.*

intern *vb.* (ɪnˈtɜːn). **1.** to confine within a country or a limited area, esp. during wartime. ~*n.* (ˈɪntɜːn), *also* **interne.** **2.** *Chiefly U.S* a medical student or recent graduate undergoing practical training in a working environment. —in**ˈternment** *n.*

internal (ɪnˈtɜːnᵊl) *adj.* **1.** of, situated on, or suitable for the inside; inner. **2.** coming or acting from within an organization: *an internal reorganization.* **3.** spiritual or mental: *internal conflict.* **4.** of a nation's domestic affairs: *internal politics.* **5.** affecting or relating to the inside of the body: *internal bleeding.* —in**ˈternally** *adv.*

internal-combustion engine *n.* an engine in which power is produced by the explosion of a fuel-and-air mixture within the cylinders.

international (ˌɪntəˈnæʃənᵊl) *adj.* **1.** of or involving two or more nations. **2.** controlling or legislating for several nations: *an international court.* **3.** available for use by all nations: *international waters.* ~*n.* **4.** *Sport.* **a.** a contest between two national teams. **b.** a member of a national team. —ˌinter**ˈnation**ˈality *n.* —ˌinter**ˈnational**ly *adv.*

International (ˌɪntəˈnæʃənᵊl) *n.* any of several international socialist organizations.

internationalism (ˌɪntəˈnæʃənəˌlɪzəm) *n.* the ideal or practice of cooperation and understanding for the good of all nations. —**ˌinter**ˈnationalist *n.*

International Phonetic Alphabet *n.* a series of signs and letters for the representation of human speech sounds.

internecine (ˌɪntəˈniːsaɪn) *adj.* destructive to both sides: *internecine war.*

internee (ˌɪntɜːˈniː) *n.* a person who is interned.

internist (ɪnˈtɜːnɪst) *n.* a physician who specializes in internal medicine.

interpenetrate (ˌɪntəˈpɛnɪˌtreɪt) *vb.* to penetrate (something) thoroughly; pervade. —ˌinter**ˌpene**ˈtration *n.*

interplanetary (ˌɪntəˈplænɪtrɪ) *adj.* between planets.

interplay (ˈɪntəˌpleɪ) *n.* the reciprocal action and reaction of things on each other.

Interpol (ˈɪntəˌpɒl) International Criminal Police Organization: an association of over 100 national police forces, devoted chiefly to fighting international crime.

interpolate (ɪnˈtɜːpəˌleɪt) *vb.* **1.** to insert (a comment or passage) into (a conversation or text). **2.** *Maths.* to estimate (a value of a function) between the values already known. —in**ˌterpo**ˈlation *n.*

interpose (ˌɪntəˈpəʊz) *vb.* **1.** to place (something) between or among other things. **2.** to interrupt (with comments or questions). **3.** to put forward so as to interrupt: *he ended the discussion by interposing a veto.* —ˌinterpo**ˈsition** *n.*

interpret (ɪnˈtɜːprɪt) *vb.* **1.** to explain the meaning of; elucidate. **2.** to construe the significance of: *to interpret a smile as an invitation.* **3.** to convey the meaning of (a poem, song, etc.) in performance. **4.** to act as an interpreter; translate orally. —in**ˈterpretive** *adj.*

interpretation (ɪnˌtɜːprɪˈteɪʃən) *n.* **1.** the act or result of interpreting or explaining. **2.** the expression of a person's conception of a play, dance, or other work of art through acting or performing. **3.** explanation, as of a historical site, provided by the use of original objects, visual display material, etc.

interpreter (ɪnˈtɜːprɪtə) *n.* **1.** a person who translates orally from one language into another. **2.** *Computers.* a program that translates a statement in a source program to machine language and executes it before translating and executing the next statement.

interpretive centre *n.* a building situated at a place of interest, such as a country park or historical site, that provides information about the next. showing videos, exhibiting objects, etc.

interracial (ˌɪntəˈreɪʃəl) *adj.* between or among people of different races.

interregnum (ˌɪntəˈrɛgnəm) *n., pl.* -nums *or* -na (-nə). a period when a state lacks its usual government, esp. the interval between the end of one ruler's reign and the beginning of the next. —ˌinter**ˈregnal** *adj.*

interrelate (ˌɪntərɪˈleɪt) *vb.* to connect (two or more things) or (of two or more things) to become connected to each other: *these courses interrelate; all three factors are interrelated.* —ˌinterre**ˈlation** *n.* —ˌinterre**ˈlation**ˌship *n.*

interrogate (ɪnˈtɛrəˌgeɪt) vb. to question (someone) closely. —inˌterroˈgation n. —inˈterroˌgator n.

interrogative (ˌɪntəˈrɒgətɪv) adj. 1. asking or having the nature of a question: an interrogative look. 2. used in asking a question: an interrogative pronoun. ~n. 3. an interrogative word, phrase, sentence, or construction.

interrogatory (ˌɪntəˈrɒgətrɪ) adj. 1. expressing or involving a question. ~n., pl. -tories. 2. a question or interrogation.

interrupt (ˌɪntəˈrʌpt) vb. 1. to break into (a conversation or discussion) by questions or comment. 2. to break the continuity of (an action or event) or hinder (a person) by intrusion. —ˌinterˈrupted adj. —ˌinterˈruptive adj.

interrupter or **interruptor** (ˌɪntəˈrʌptə) n. a device for opening and closing an electric circuit.

interruption (ˌɪntəˈrʌpʃən) n. 1. something that interrupts, such as a comment or question. 2. an interval or intermission. 3. the act of interrupting or the state of being interrupted.

interscholastic (ˌɪntəskəˈlæstɪk) adj. occurring between two or more schools: an interscholastic competition.

intersect (ˌɪntəˈsɛkt) vb. 1. to divide or mark off (a place, area, or surface) by passing through or across. 2. (esp. of roads) to cross (each other).

intersection (ˌɪntəˈsɛkʃən) n. 1. a point at which things intersect, esp. a road junction. 2. the act of intersecting or the state of being intersected. 3. Maths. a. a point or set of points common to two or more geometric figures. b. the set of elements that are common to two sets. —ˌinterˈsectional adj.

interspace (ˌɪntəˈspeɪs) vb. to make or occupy a space between.

intersperse (ˌɪntəˈspɜːs) vb. 1. to scatter among, between, or on. 2. to mix (something) with other things scattered here and there. —interspersion (ˌɪntəˈspɜːʃən) n.

interstellar (ˌɪntəˈstɛlə) adj. between or among stars.

interstice (ɪnˈtɜːstɪs) n. (usually pl.) 1. a small gap or crack between things. 2. Physics. the space between adjacent atoms in a crystal lattice.

intertwine (ˌɪntəˈtwaɪn) vb. to twist together.

interval (ˈɪntəvəl) n. 1. the period of time between two events. 2. the distance between two things. 3. Brit. a short period between parts of a play, concert, etc.; intermission. 4. Music. the difference of pitch between two notes. 5. **at intervals. a.** now and then: turn the chicken at intervals. **b.** with a certain amount of space between: plant the seeds at intervals of six inches.

intervene (ˌɪntəˈviːn) vb. 1. (often foll. by in) to come between two people or groups in order to prevent conflict or settle a dispute. 2. (foll. by in or between) to come or be among or between. 3. (of an event) to disturb or hinder a course of action: neither bill became law because the general election intervened.

intervention (ˌɪntəˈvɛnʃən) n. the act of intervening, esp. by one state in the affairs of another. —ˌinterˈventionist n., adj.

interview (ˈɪntəˌvjuː) n. 1. a formal discussion, esp. one in which an employer assesses a job applicant. 2. a conversation in which a well-known person is asked about his or her views, career, etc., by a reporter. ~vb. 3. to conduct an interview with (someone). —ˌinterviewˈee n. —ˈinterˌviewer n.

interwar (ˌɪntəˈwɔː) adj. of or happening in the period between World War I and World War II.

interweave (ˌɪntəˈwiːv) vb. -weaving, -wove or -weaved; -woven or -weaved. to weave together; connect intimately.

intestate (ɪnˈtɛsteɪt, -tɪt) adj. 1. (of a person) not having made a will. ~n. 2. a person who dies without having made a will. —inˈtestacy n.

intestine (ɪnˈtɛstɪn) n. the part of the alimentary canal between the stomach and the anus. See **large intestine, small intestine**. —inˈtestinal adj.

intimacy (ˈɪntɪməsɪ) n., pl. -cies. 1. close or warm friendship; personal relationship. 2. (often pl.) Euphemistic. sexual relations.

intimate[1] (ˈɪntɪmɪt) adj. 1. characterized by a close or warm personal relationship: an intimate friend. 2. deeply personal, private, or secret. 3. Euphemistic. having sexual relations . 4. (of knowledge) extensive and detailed. 5. having a friendly quiet atmosphere: an intimate nightclub. ~n. 6. a close friend. —ˈintimately adv.

intimate[2] (ˈɪntɪˌmeɪt) vb. to make (something) known in an indirect way: she had already intimated her disapproval. —ˌintiˈmation n.

intimidate (ɪnˈtɪmɪˌdeɪt) vb. to frighten (someone) by threats, esp. in order to subdue or influence. —inˈtimiˌdating adj. —inˌtimiˈdation n.

into (ˈɪntuː; unstressed ˈɪntə) prep. 1. to the inner part of: they went into the house. 2. to the middle of so as to be surrounded by: into the bushes. 3. against; up against: he drove into a wall. 4. used to indicate the result of a change: he changed into a monster. 5. Maths. used to indicate division: three into six is two. 6. Informal. interested in: I'm really into Freud.

intolerable (ɪnˈtɒlərəbᵊl) adj. more than can be endured. —inˈtolerably adv.

intolerant (ɪnˈtɒlərənt) adj. refusing to accept practices and beliefs that differ from one's own. —**in'tolerance** n.

intonation (ˌɪntəʊ'neɪʃən) n. 1. the sound pattern produced by variations in the voice. 2. the act of intoning. 3. *Music.* the capacity to play or sing in tune. —ˌinto'national adj.

intone (ɪn'təʊn) *or* **intonate** ('ɪntəʊˌneɪt) vb. 1. to speak or recite (a chant or prayer) in a monotonous tone. 2. to speak with a particular tone.

in toto Latin. (ɪn 'təʊtəʊ) adv. totally; entirely.

intoxicant (ɪn'tɒksɪkənt) n. 1. something, such as an alcoholic drink, that causes intoxication. ~adj. 2. causing intoxication.

intoxicate (ɪn'tɒksɪˌkeɪt) vb. 1. (of an alcoholic drink) to make (a person) drunk; inebriate. 2. to stimulate or excite to a point beyond self-control. —**in'toxiˌcating** adj.

intoxication (ɪnˌtɒksɪ'keɪʃən) n. 1. drunkenness; inebriation. 2. great elation.

intractable (ɪn'træktəb'l) adj. 1. (of a person) difficult to influence or direct. 2. (of a problem or illness) difficult to solve, alleviate, or cure. —**inˌtracta'bility** n. —**in'tractably** adv.

intramural (ˌɪntrə'mjʊərəl) adj. *Chiefly U.S. & Canad.* operating within or involving those within boundaries, esp. of a school or college: *intramural sports.*

intransigent (ɪn'trænsɪdʒənt) adj. 1. uncompromising; obstinately maintaining an attitude. ~n. 2. an intransigent person, esp. in politics. —**in'transigence** n.

intransitive (ɪn'trænsɪtɪv) adj. denoting a verb that does not require a direct object. —**in'transitively** adv.

intrapreneur (ˌɪntrəprə'nɜː) n. a person who while remaining within a larger organization uses entrepreneurial skills to develop new services or systems as a subsidiary of the organization.

intrauterine (ˌɪntrə'juːtəraɪn) adj. situated within the womb.

intrauterine device n. a contraceptive device in the shape of a coil, inserted into the womb.

intravenous (ˌɪntrə'viːnəs) adj. *Anat.* within a vein: *an intravenous injection.* —ˌintra'venously adv.

in-tray n. a tray used in offices for incoming letters or documents requiring attention.

intrepid (ɪn'trepɪd) adj. fearless; daring; bold. —ˌintre'pidity n. —**in'trepidly** adv.

intricate ('ɪntrɪkɪt) adj. 1. difficult to sort out; involved: *an intricate problem.* 2. full of complicated detail: *intricate patterns.* —'intricacy n. —'intricately adv.

intrigue vb. (ɪn'triːg), **-triguing**, **-trigued**. 1. to make interested or curious: *the idea seemed to intrigue her.* 2. to plot secretly

or dishonestly; conspire. ~n. (ɪn'triːg, 'ɪntriːg). 3. secret plotting. 4. a secret love affair. —**in'triguing** adj. —**in'triguingly** adv.

intrinsic (ɪn'trɪnsɪk) adj. 1. essential to the real nature of a thing; inherent: *dependency is an intrinsic part of love.* 2. *Anat.* situated within or peculiar to a part: *intrinsic muscles.* —**in'trinsically** adv.

intro ('ɪntrəʊ) n., pl. **-tros.** *Informal.* short for **introduction.**

introduce (ˌɪntrə'djuːs) vb. 1. to present (someone) by name (to another person). 2. to present (a radio or television programme). 3. (foll. by *to*) to cause to experience for the first time: *to introduce a visitor to beer.* 4. to present for consideration or approval: *to introduce a bill in parliament.* 5. to bring into use; establish: *to introduce decimal currency.* 6. (foll. by *with*) to start: *he introduced his talk with some music.* —ˌintro'ducible adj.

introduction (ˌɪntrə'dʌkʃən) n. 1. the act of introducing. 2. a presentation of one person to another or others. 3. a preliminary part, as of a book or musical composition. 4. a book that explains the basic facts about a particular subject to a beginner.

introductory (ˌɪntrə'dʌktrɪ) adj. serving as an introduction; preliminary.

introit ('ɪntrɔɪt) n. *R.C. Church, Church of England.* a short prayer said or sung as the celebrant is entering the sanctuary to celebrate Mass or Holy Communion.

introspection (ˌɪntrə'spekʃən) n. the examining of one's own thoughts, impressions, and feelings. —ˌintro'spective adj.

introversion (ˌɪntrə'vɜːʃən) n. *Psychol.* the directing of interest inwards towards one's own thoughts and feelings rather than towards the external world or making social contacts.

introvert ('ɪntrəˌvɜːt) *Psychol.* ~adj. 1. concerned more with one's inner feelings than with external reality. ~n. 2. such a person. —'introˌverted adj.

intrude (ɪn'truːd) vb. (foll. by *on* or *upon*) to put forward or interpose (oneself or one's views) abruptly or without invitation. —**in'truder** n.

intrusion (ɪn'truːʒən) n. 1. the act of intruding; an unwelcome visit, etc.: *an intrusion on one's privacy.* 2. **a.** the forcing of molten rock into spaces in the overlying strata. **b.** molten rock formed in this way. —**in'trusive** adj.

intrust (ɪn'trʌst) vb. same as **entrust.**

intuition (ˌɪntjʊ'ɪʃən) n. instinctive knowledge of or belief about something without conscious reasoning: *my intuition told me to stay away.* —**intu'itional** adj.

intuitive (ɪn'tjuːɪtɪv) adj. of, possessing, or resulting from intuition: *an intuitive awareness.* —**in'tuitively** adv.

Inuit or **Innuit** ('ınjuːɪt) n., pl. -**it** or -**its**. an Eskimo of North America or Greenland.

Inuktitut (ɪ'nʊktə,tʊt) n. Canad. the language of the Inuit.

inundate ('ınʌn,deɪt) vb. **1.** to cover completely with water; swamp. **2.** to overwhelm, as if with a flood: to be inundated with requests. —,**inun'dation** n.

inure (ɪ'njʊə) vb. **be inured** or **inure oneself to something.** to be or become hardened to something. —**in'urement** n.

invade (ɪn'veɪd) vb. **1.** to enter (a country or territory) by military force. **2.** to occupy in large numbers: the town was invaded by football supporters. **3.** to encroach upon (privacy, etc.). —**in'vader** n.

invalid[1] ('ınvə,liːd, -lıd) n. **1.** a person who is disabled or chronically ill. ~adj. **2.** sick; disabled. ~vb. **3.** Chiefly Brit. to dismiss (a member of the armed forces) from active service because of illness. —'**invalid-,ism** n.

invalid[2] (ın'vælıd) adj. **1.** not valid; having no legal force: an invalid cheque. **2.** (of an argument, result, etc.) not valid because it has been based on a mistake. —,**inva'lidity** n. —**in'validly** adv.

invalidate (ın'vælı,deɪt) vb. **1.** to prove (an argument, result, etc.) to be wrong. **2.** to take away the legal force of (a contract). —**in,vali'dation** n.

invaluable (ın'væljʊəb'l) adj. having great value that is impossible to calculate; priceless.

invariable (ın'vɛərɪəb'l) adj. unchanging; always the same. —**in'variably** adv.

invasion (ın'veɪʒən) n. **1.** the act of invading with armed forces. **2.** any intrusion: an invasion of privacy. —**invasive** (ın-'veɪsɪv) adj.

invective (ın'vɛktɪv) n. a verbal attack, esp. of a bitterly abusive or sarcastic kind.

inveigh (ın'veɪ) vb. (foll. by against) to criticize (something) harshly.

inveigle (ın'veɪg'l) vb. to coax or manipulate (someone) into an action or situation. —**in'veiglement** n.

invent (ın'vɛnt) vb. **1.** to create or devise (a machine, game, etc.). **2.** to make up (a story, excuse, etc.). —**in'ventor** n.

invention (ın'vɛnʃən) n. **1.** the act of inventing. **2.** something that is invented. **3.** creative power; inventive skill. **4.** Euphemistic. a fabrication; lie: his story is a malicious invention.

inventive (ın'vɛntɪv) adj. creative; ingenious; resourceful.

inventory ('ınvəntrı) n., pl. -**tories**. **1.** a detailed list of articles, goods, etc., in a particular place. ~vb. -**torying, -toried**. **2.** to enter (items) in an inventory; make a list of.

inverse (ın'vɜːs, 'ınvɜːs) adj. **1.** opposite in effect, sequence, direction, etc. **2.** Maths. (of a relationship) containing two variables such that an increase in one results in a decrease in the other. ~n. **3.** Maths. an inverse element.

inversion (ın'vɜːʃən) n. **1.** the act of inverting or state of being inverted. **2.** something inverted, esp. a reversal of order, mutual functions, etc.: an inversion of their previous relationship. —**in'versive** adj.

invert vb. (ın'vɜːt). **1.** to turn upside down or inside out. **2.** to reverse in effect, sequence, or direction. ~n. ('ınvɜːt). **3.** a homosexual. —**in'vertible** adj.

invertebrate (ın'vɜːtıbrıt) n. **1.** any animal without a backbone, such as an insect, worm, or octopus. ~adj. **2.** of or designating invertebrates.

inverted comma n. same as **quotation mark**.

invest (ın'vɛst) vb. **1.** (often foll. by in) to put (money into an enterprise) with the expectation of profit. **2.** (often foll. by in) to devote (time, effort, etc., to a project). **3.** (foll. by in) Informal. to buy: she invested in a new dress. **4.** (often foll. by in) to install someone (in an official position). **5.** to give power or authority to: to invest new rights in the monarchy. **6.** (foll. by in or with) to provide (a person with qualities): he was invested with great common sense. **7.** (foll. by with) Usually poetic. to cover, as if with a coat: when spring invests the trees with leaves. —**in'vestor** n.

investigate (ın'vɛstı,geɪt) vb. to inquire into (a situation or problem) thoroughly in order to discover the truth: the inspector had come to investigate a murder; we set out to investigate the mood of the community. —**in'vesti,gative** adj. —**in'vesti,gator** n.

investigation (ın,vɛstı'geɪʃən) n. a careful search or examination in order to discover facts.

investiture (ın'vɛstıtʃə) n. the act of presenting someone with an official title.

investment (ın'vɛstmənt) n. **1.** the act of investing. **2.** money invested. **3.** something, such as a business, in which money is invested.

investment trust n. a financial enterprise that invests its subscribed capital in a wide range of securities for its investors' benefit.

inveterate (ın'vɛtərıt) adj. **1.** deep-rooted or ingrained: an inveterate feeling of hostility. **2.** confirmed in a habit or practice: an inveterate smoker. —**in'veteracy** n.

invidious (ın'vıdıəs) adj. likely to cause resentment or unpopularity: an invidious task.

invigilate (ın'vıdʒı,leıt) vb. Brit. to supervise people who are sitting an examination, esp. to prevent cheating. —**in,vigi'lation** n. —**in'vigi,lator** n.

invigorate (ɪn'vɪgə,reɪt) vb. to give vitality and vigour to; refresh: *to be invigorated by fresh air.* —**in'vigor,ating** adj.

invincible (ɪn'vɪnsəb°l) adj. incapable of being defeated: *an army of invincible strength.* —**in,vinci'bility** n. —**in'vincibly** adv.

inviolable (ɪn'vaɪələb°l) adj. that must not be violated; sacred: *an inviolable oath.* —**in,viola'bility** n.

inviolate (ɪn'vaɪəlɪt) adj. free from violation, injury, disturbance, etc. —**in'violacy** n.

invisible (ɪn'vɪzəb°l) adj. 1. not able to be seen by the eye: *invisible rays.* 2. concealed from sight; hidden. 3. *Econ.* relating to services, such as insurance and freight, rather than goods: *invisible earnings.* —**in,visi'bility** n. —**in'visibly** adv.

invitation (,ɪnvɪ'teɪʃən) n. 1. a request to attend a dance, meal, etc. 2. the card or paper on which an invitation is written.

invite vb. (ɪn'vaɪt). 1. to ask (a person) in a friendly or polite way (to do something, attend an event, etc.). 2. to make a request for, esp. publicly or formally: *to invite applications.* 3. to bring on or provoke: *you invite disaster by your actions.* 4. to tempt. ~n. ('ɪnvaɪt). 5. *Informal.* an invitation.

inviting (ɪn'vaɪtɪŋ) adj. tempting; alluring; attractive.

in vitro (ɪn 'viːtrəʊ) adv., adj. (of biological processes or reactions) made to occur outside the body of the organism in an artificial environment.

invocation (,ɪnvə'keɪʃən) n. 1. the act of invoking. 2. a prayer to God or another deity asking for help, forgiveness, etc. —**invocatory** (ɪn'vɒkətrɪ) adj.

invoice ('ɪnvɔɪs) n. 1. a document issued by a seller to a buyer listing the goods or services supplied and stating the sum of money due. ~vb. 2. to present (a customer) with an invoice.

invoke (ɪn'vəʊk) vb. 1. to call on (God or another deity) for help, inspiration, etc. 2. to put (a law or penalty) into use: *the union invoked the dispute procedure.* 3. to implore or beg (help, etc.). 4. to summon (a spirit) by uttering magic words.

involuntary (ɪn'vɒləntrɪ) adj. 1. carried out without one's conscious wishes; unintentional. 2. *Physiol.* (esp. of a movement or muscle) performed or acting without conscious control. —**in'voluntarily** adv.

involute ('ɪnvə,luːt) adj. also **involuted.** 1. complex, intricate, or involved. 2. rolled inwards or curled in a spiral. ~n. 3. *Geom.* the curve described by the free end of a thread as it is wound around another curve on the same plane.

involve (ɪn'vɒlv) vb. 1. to include as a necessary part. 2. to have an effect on: *the investigation involved many innocent people.* 3. to implicate: *many people were involved in the crime.* 4. to make complicated: *the situation was further involved by her disappearance.* —**in'volvement** n.

invulnerable (ɪn'vʌlnərəb°l) adj. incapable of being wounded or damaged. —**in,vulnera'bility** n.

inward ('ɪnwəd) adj. 1. directed towards the middle of something. 2. situated within; inside. 3. of the mind or spirit: *inward meditation.* ~adv. 4. same as **inwards.**

inwardly ('ɪnwədlɪ) adv. 1. within the private thoughts or feelings; secretly: *inwardly troubled, he kept smiling.* 2. not aloud: *to laugh inwardly.* 3. in or on the inside; internally.

inwards ('ɪnwədz) or **inward** adv. towards the inside or middle of something.

inwrought (,ɪn'rɔːt) adj. worked or woven into material, esp. decoratively.

Io *Chem.* ionium.

iodide ('aɪə,daɪd) n. a compound containing an iodine atom, such as methyl iodide.

iodine ('aɪə,diːn) n. *Chem.* a bluish-black element found in seaweed and used in medicine, photography, and dyeing. Symbol: I

iodize or **-dise** ('aɪə,daɪz) vb. to treat with iodine. —**,iodi'zation** or **-di'sation** n.

IOM Isle of Man.

ion ('aɪən, -ɒn) n. an electrically charged atom or group of atoms formed by the loss or gain of one or more electrons.

ion exchange n. the process in which ions are exchanged between a solution and an insoluble solid. It is used to soften water.

ionic (aɪ'ɒnɪk) adj. of or in the form of ions.

Ionic (aɪ'ɒnɪk) adj. of an order of classical architecture distinguished by ornamental scrolls on the capitals.

ionize or **-ise** ('aɪə,naɪz) vb. to change or become changed into ions. —**,ioni'zation** or **-i'sation** n.

ionosphere (aɪ'ɒnə,sfɪə) n. a region of ionized layers of air in the earth's upper atmosphere, which reflects radio waves. —**ionospheric** (aɪ,ɒnə'sferɪk) adj.

iota (aɪ'əʊtə) n. 1. the ninth letter in the Greek alphabet (Ι, ι). 2. a very small amount; jot: *I don't feel one iota of guilt.*

IOU n. a written promise or reminder to pay a debt.

IOW Isle of Wight.

IPA International Phonetic Alphabet.

ipecac ('ɪpɪ,kæk) or **ipecacuanha** (,ɪpɪ,kækjʊ'ænə) n. a drug prepared from the dried roots of a South American plant, used to induce vomiting.

ipso facto ('ɪpsəʊ 'fæktəʊ) adv. by that very fact or act.

IQ intelligence quotient.

Ir *Chem.* iridium.

IRA Irish Republican Army.

Iranian (ɪ'reɪnɪən) n. 1. a person from Iran, in SW Asia. 2. a branch of the Indo-

European family of languages, including Persian. ~*adj.* **3.** of Iran, its inhabitants, or their language.

Iraqi (ɪˈrɑːkɪ) *adj.* **1.** of Iraq, in SW Asia, its inhabitants, or their language. ~*n., pl.* -**qis.** **2.** a person from Iraq.

irascible (ɪˈræsɪbᵊl) *adj.* easily angered; irritable. —**i,rasci'bility** *n.* —**i'rascibly** *adv.*

irate (aɪˈreɪt) *adj.* very angry; furious.

ire (ˈaɪə) *n. Literary.* anger.

iridaceous (ˌɪrɪˈdeɪʃəs) *adj.* of or belonging to the iris family.

iridescent (ˌɪrɪˈdɛsᵊnt) *adj.* having or displaying a spectrum of colours that shimmer and change. —**iri'descence** *n.*

iridium (aɪˈrɪdɪəm, ɪˈrɪd-) *n.* a hard yellowish-white chemical element that occurs in platinum ores and is used as an alloy with platinum. Symbol: Ir

iris (ˈaɪrɪs) *n.* **1.** the coloured muscular membrane in the eye that surrounds and controls the size of the pupil. **2.** a tall plant with long pointed leaves and large flowers.

Irish (ˈaɪrɪʃ) *adj.* **1.** of Ireland, its people, their Celtic language, or their dialect of English. ~*n.* **2. the Irish.** (*functioning as pl.*) the people of Ireland. **3.** same as **Irish Gaelic. 4.** the dialect of English spoken in Ireland.

Irish coffee *n.* hot coffee mixed with Irish whiskey and topped with double cream.

Irish Gaelic *n.* the Celtic language of Ireland.

Irish moss *n.* same as **carrageen.**

irk (ɜːk) *vb.* to irritate, vex, or annoy.

irksome (ˈɜːksəm) *adj.* annoying, tiresome, or tedious.

iron (ˈaɪən) *n.* **1.** a strong silvery-white metallic element, widely used for structural and engineering purposes. Symbol: Fe **2.** any of certain tools made of iron, esp. a small electrically heated device with a weighted flat bottom for pressing clothes. **3.** any of various golf clubs with metal heads. **4.** a splintlike support for a malformed leg. **5.** great strength or resolve: *a will of iron.* **6. strike while the iron is hot.** to act at an opportune moment. ~*adj.* **7.** very hard or merciless: *iron determination.* **8.** very strong: *an iron constitution.* ~*vb.* **9.** to smooth (clothes or fabric) by removing (creases) using a heated iron. ~See also **iron out, irons.**

Iron Age *n.* the period that began in the Middle East about 1100 B.C. during which iron tools and weapons were used.

ironclad *adj.* **1.** covered or protected with iron: *an ironclad warship.* ~*n.* (ˈaɪənˌklæd). **2.** a large wooden 19th-century warship with armoured plating.

Iron Curtain *n.* the guarded border between the countries of the Soviet bloc and the rest of Europe.

ironic (aɪˈrɒnɪk) *or* **ironical** *adj.* of, characterized by, or using irony. —**i'ronically** *adv.*

ironing board *n.* a narrow board, usually on legs, with a suitable covering on which to iron clothes.

iron lung *n.* an airtight metal cylinder enclosing the entire body up to the neck and providing artificial respiration.

iron maiden *n.* a medieval instrument of torture, consisting of a hinged case (often shaped in the form of a woman) lined with iron spikes.

ironmaster (ˈaɪənˌmɑːstə) *n. Brit.* a manufacturer of iron.

ironmonger (ˈaɪənˌmʌŋɡə) *n. Brit.* a person who deals in hardware. —**'iron,mongery** *n.*

iron out *vb.* to settle (a problem or difficulty) as a result of negotiations or discussions.

iron pyrites (ˈpaɪraɪts) *n.* same as **pyrite.**

iron rations *pl. n.* emergency food supplies, esp. for military personnel in action.

irons (ˈaɪənz) *pl. n.* **1.** fetters or chains. **2. have several irons in the fire.** to be involved in many projects.

ironstone (ˈaɪənˌstəʊn) *n.* **1.** any rock consisting mainly of an iron-bearing ore. **2.** a tough durable earthenware.

ironwood (ˈaɪənˌwʊd) *n.* **1.** any of various trees, such as hornbeam, with exceptionally hard wood. **2.** the wood of any of these trees.

ironwork (ˈaɪənˌwɜːk) *n.* work done in iron, esp. decorative work.

ironworks (ˈaɪənˌwɜːks) *n.* (*sometimes functioning as sing.*) a building in which iron is smelted, cast, or wrought.

irony (ˈaɪrənɪ) *n., pl.* -**nies. 1.** the mildly sarcastic use of words to imply the opposite of what they normally mean. **2.** a situation or result that is the direct opposite of what was expected or intended.

irradiate (ɪˈreɪdɪˌeɪt) *vb.* **1.** *Physics.* to subject to or treat with light or other electromagnetic radiation. **2.** to make clear or bright intellectually or spiritually; illumine. **3.** same as **radiate** (sense 1). —**ir,radi'ation** *n.*

irrational (ɪˈræʃənᵊl) *adj.* **1.** inconsistent with reason; illogical; absurd. **2.** incapable of reasoning. **3.** *Maths.* (of an equation or expression) involving radicals or fractional exponents. —**ir,ration'ality** *n.* —**ir'rationally** *adv.*

irrational number *n.* any real number that cannot be expressed as the ratio of two integers, such as π.

irreconcilable (ɪˈrɛkᵊnˌsaɪləbᵊl) *adj.* not able to be brought into agreement; opposed; incompatible. —**ir,recon,cila'bility** *n.*

irrecoverable (ˌɪrɪˈkʌvərəbᵊl) *adj.* not able to be recovered, remedied, or rectified.

irredeemable (ˌɪrɪˈdiːməbᵊl) adj. 1. (of bonds or shares) incapable of being bought back directly or paid off. 2. (of paper money) not convertible into coin. 3. irreparable; hopeless.

irredentist (ˌɪrɪˈdɛntɪst) n. a person who favours the acquisition of territory that was once part of his country. —ˌirreˈdentism n.

irreducible (ˌɪrɪˈdjuːsɪbᵊl) adj. not able to be brought to a simpler or reduced form. —ˌirreˌduciˈbility n.

irrefutable (ɪˈrɛfjʊtəbᵊl, ˌɪrɪˈfjuːtəbᵊl) adj. impossible to deny or disprove.

irregular (ɪˈrɛgjʊlə) adj. 1. uneven in shape, position, arrangement, etc. 2. not occurring at expected or equal intervals: an irregular pulse. 3. not conforming to accepted practice or routine; unconventional. 4. (of a word) not following the usual pattern of formation in a language. 5. (of troops) not belonging to regular forces. ~n. 6. a soldier not in a regular army. —irregularity (ɪˌrɛgjʊˈlærɪtɪ) n. —irˈregularly adv.

irrelevant (ɪˈrɛləvənt) adj. not connected with the matter at hand. —irˈrelevance or irˈrelevancy n.

irreligious (ˌɪrɪˈlɪdʒəs) adj. 1. lacking religious faith. 2. indifferent or opposed to religion.

irremediable (ˌɪrɪˈmiːdɪəbᵊl) adj. not able to be remedied; incurable.

irremovable (ˌɪrɪˈmuːvəbᵊl) adj. not able to be removed. —ˌirreˌmovaˈbility n.

irreparable (ɪˈrɛpərəbᵊl) adj. not able to be put right or remedied: irreparable damage to her reputation. —irˌreparaˈbility n.

irreplaceable (ˌɪrɪˈpleɪsəbᵊl) adj. not able to be replaced: an irreplaceable antique.

irrepressible (ˌɪrɪˈprɛsəbᵊl) adj. not capable of being repressed, controlled, or restrained. —ˌirreˌpressiˈbility n. —ˌirreˈpressibly adv.

irreproachable (ˌɪrɪˈprəʊtʃəbᵊl) adj. blameless; faultless. —ˌirreˌproachaˈbility n.

irresistible (ˌɪrɪˈzɪstəbᵊl) adj. 1. not able to be resisted or refused; overpowering: an irresistible impulse. 2. very fascinating or alluring: an irresistible woman. —ˌirreˌsistiˈbility n. —ˌirreˈsistibly adv.

irresolute (ɪˈrɛzəˌluːt) adj. unable to make decisions; hesitating. —irˌresoˈlution n.

irrespective (ˌɪrɪˈspɛktɪv) adj. **irrespective of.** without taking account of; regardless of.

irresponsible (ˌɪrɪˈspɒnsəbᵊl) adj. 1. not showing or done with due care for the consequences of one's actions or attitudes; reckless. 2. not capable of bearing responsibility. —ˌirreˌsponsiˈbility n. —ˌirreˈsponsibly adv.

irretrievable (ˌɪrɪˈtriːvəbᵊl) adj. not able to be retrieved, recovered, or repaired. —ˌirreˌtrievaˈbility n. —ˌirreˈtrievably adv.

irreverence (ɪˈrɛvərəns) n. 1. lack of due respect; disrespect. 2. a disrespectful remark or act. —irˈreverent adj.

irreversible (ˌɪrɪˈvɜːsəbᵊl) adj. not able to be reversed or put right again: the damage may be irreversible. —ˌirreˈversibly adv.

irrevocable (ɪˈrɛvəkəbᵊl) adj. not able to be changed or undone: an irrevocable loss. —irˈrevocably adv.

irrigate (ˈɪrɪˌgeɪt) vb. 1. to supply (land) with water through ditches or pipes, esp. to promote the growth of food crops. 2. Med. to bathe or wash out (a bodily part or wound). —ˌirriˈgation n. —ˈirriˌgator n.

irritable (ˈɪrɪtəbᵊl) adj. 1. easily annoyed or angered. 2. (of all living organisms) capable of responding to such stimuli as heat, light, and touch. 3. Pathol. abnormally sensitive. —ˌirritaˈbility n.

irritant (ˈɪrɪtənt) adj. 1. causing irritation; irritating. ~n. 2. something that irritates, esp. a substance that causes a part of the body to become tender or inflamed.

irritate (ˈɪrɪˌteɪt) vb. 1. to annoy or anger (someone). 2. Biol. to stimulate (an organ) to respond in a characteristic manner. 3. Pathol. to cause (a bodily organ or part) to become inflamed or tender. —ˌirriˈtation n.

irrupt (ɪˈrʌpt) vb. to enter forcibly or suddenly. —irˈruption n. —irˈruptive adj.

is (ɪz) vb. third person singular of the present tense of **be.**

isallobar (aɪˈsæləˌbɑː) n. a line on a map connecting places with equal pressure changes.

ISBN International Standard Book Number.

isinglass (ˈaɪzɪŋˌglɑːs) n. 1. a gelatin made from the air bladders of freshwater fish. 2. same as **mica.**

Isl. 1. Island. 2. Isle.

Islam (ˈɪzlɑːm) n. 1. Also called: **Islamism.** the religion of Muslims, teaching that there is only one God and that Mohammed is his prophet. 2. **a.** Muslims collectively and their civilization. **b.** the countries where the Muslim religion is predominant. —Isˈlamic adj.

island (ˈaɪlənd) n. 1. a mass of land that is completely surrounded by water. 2. something isolated, detached, or surrounded: a traffic island.

islander (ˈaɪləndə) n. a person who lives on an island.

isle (aɪl) n. Poetic except when cap. and part of place name. an island, esp. a small one.

islet (ˈaɪlɪt) n. a small island.

ism (ˈɪzəm) n. Informal, often used to show contempt. a doctrine, system, or practice, esp. one whose name ends in -ism: communism; fascism.

isn't (ˈɪzᵊnt) is not.

iso- *or before a vowel* **is-** *combining form.* equal or identical: *isomagnetic.*

isobar (ˈaɪsəʊˌbɑː) *n.* **1.** a line on a map connecting places of equal atmospheric pressure. **2.** *Physics.* any of two or more atoms that have the same mass number but different atomic numbers. —**ˌisoˈbaric** *adj.* —**ˈisobarˌism** *n.*

isochronal (aɪˈsɒkrənᵊl) *or* **isochronous** *adj.* **1.** equal in length of time. **2.** occurring at equal time intervals. —**iˈsochroˌnism** *n.*

isohel (ˈaɪsəʊˌhɛl) *n.* a line on a map connecting places with an equal period of sunshine.

isohyet (ˌaɪsəʊˈhaɪɪt) *n.* a line on a map connecting places having equal rainfall.

isolate (ˈaɪsəˌleɪt) *vb.* **1.** to place apart; cause to be alone. **2.** *Med.* to quarantine (a person or animal) having a contagious disease. **3.** to obtain (a compound) in an uncombined form. —**ˌisoˈlation** *n.*

isomer (ˈaɪsəmə) *n. Chem.* a substance with the same molecules as another but a different atomic arrangement. —**isomeric** (ˌaɪsəˈmɛrɪk) *adj.*

isometric (ˌaɪsəʊˈmɛtrɪk) *or* **isometrical** *adj.* **1.** having equal dimensions or measurements. **2.** *Physiol.* of or relating to muscular contraction that does not produce shortening of the muscle. **3.** (of a method of projecting a drawing in three dimensions) having the three axes equally inclined and all lines drawn to scale. —**ˌisoˈmetrically** *adv.*

isomorphism (ˌaɪsəʊˈmɔːˌfɪzəm) *n.* **1.** *Biol.* similarity of form, as in different generations of the same life cycle. **2.** *Chem.* the existence of two or more substances of different composition in a similar crystalline form. **3.** *Maths.* a one-to-one correspondence between the elements of two or more sets. —**ˈisoˌmorph** *n.* —**ˌisoˈmorphic** *or* **ˌisoˈmorphous** *adj.*

isosceles (aɪˈsɒsɪˌliːz) *adj.* (of a triangle) having two sides of equal length.

isotherm (ˈaɪsəʊˌθɜːm) *n.* a line on a map linking places of equal temperature. Also called: **isothermal, isothermal line.**

isotope (ˈaɪsəˌtəʊp) *n.* one of two or more atoms with the same atomic number but different atomic weights. —**isotopic** (ˌaɪsəˈtɒpɪk) *adj.* —**isotopy** (aɪˈsɒtəpɪ) *n.*

isotropic (ˌaɪsəʊˈtrɒpɪk) *or* **isotropous** (aɪˈsɒtrəpəs) *adj.* having uniform physical properties, such as elasticity or conduction in all directions. —**iˈsotropy** *n.*

Israeli (ɪzˈreɪlɪ) *n., pl.* **-lis** *or* **-li.** **1.** a person from Israel, in SW Asia. *~adj.* **2.** of Israel or its inhabitants.

Israelite (ˈɪzrɪəˌlaɪt) *n. Bible.* a member of the ethnic group claiming descent from Jacob; a Hebrew.

issue (ˈɪʃjuː) *n.* **1.** the act of sending or giving out something. **2.** something issued, such as an edition of stamps or a magazine. **3.** the act of emerging; outflow. **4.** something flowing out, such as a river. **5.** a place of outflow; outlet. **6.** the descendants of a person; offspring. **7.** a topic of interest or discussion. **8.** an important subject requiring a decision. **9.** a consequence; result. **10. at issue. a.** under discussion. **b.** in disagreement. **11. force the issue.** to compel decision on some matter. **12. join issue.** to join in controversy. **13. take issue.** to disagree. *~vb.* **-suing, -sued.** **14.** to come forth or emerge. **15.** to send out; put into circulation. **16.** to publish. **17.** to be a consequence; result. **18.** (foll. by *in*) to end or terminate. **19.** (foll. by *with*) to supply officially with. —**ˈissuable** *adj.*

isthmus (ˈɪsməs) *n., pl.* **-muses** *or* **-mi** (-maɪ). a narrow strip of land connecting two relatively large land areas. —**ˈisthmoid** *adj.*

it (ɪt) *pron.* (*subjective or objective*) **1.** refers to a nonhuman, animal, plant, or inanimate thing, or sometimes to a small baby: *it looks dangerous; give it a bone.* **2.** refers to something unspecified or implied or to a previous or understood clause, phrase, or word: *it is impossible; I knew it.* **3.** used to represent human life or experience in respect of the present situation: *how's it going?; to brazen it out.* **4.** used as the subject of impersonal verbs: *it is raining; it's Tuesday.* **5.** *Informal.* the crucial or ultimate point: *the steering failed and I thought that was it.* *~n.* **6.** *Informal.* **a.** sexual intercourse. **b.** sex appeal.

i.t.a. *or* **ITA** initial teaching alphabet: a partly phonetic alphabet used to teach reading.

Italian (ɪˈtæljən) *n.* **1.** the official language of Italy and one of the official languages of Switzerland. **2.** a person from Italy. *~adj.* **3.** of Italy, its inhabitants, or their language.

Italianate (ɪˈtæljəˌneɪt) *or* **Italianesque** (ɪˌtæljəˈnɛsk) *adj.* Italian in style or character.

italic (ɪˈtælɪk) *adj.* **1.** of or denoting a style of printing type in which the characters slant to the right. *~n.* **2.** (*often pl.*) italic type or print.

italicize *or* **-ise** (ɪˈtælɪˌsaɪz) *vb.* to print (text) in italic type. —**iˌtaliciˈzation** *or* **-iˈsation** *n.*

itch (ɪtʃ) *n.* **1.** an irritation or tickling sensation of the skin. **2.** a restless desire. **3.** any skin disorder, such as scabies, characterized by intense itching. *~vb.* **4.** to feel an irritating or tickling sensation. **5.** to have a restless desire (to do something): *I was itching to get away.* **6. have itchy feet.** to be restless; have a desire to travel. —**ˈitchy** *adj.* —**ˈitchiness** *n.*

it'd ('ɪt'd) it would *or* it had.

item ('aɪtəm) *n.* **1.** a thing or unit, esp. one included in a list or collection. **2.** *Bookkeeping.* an entry in an account. **3.** a piece of information: *a news item.*

itemize *or* **-ise** ('aɪtə‚maɪz) *vb.* to put on a list or make a list of. —‚itemi'zation *or* -i'sation *n.*

iterate ('ɪtə‚reɪt) *vb.* to say or do again. —‚iter'ation *n.* —'iterative *adj.*

itinerant (aɪ'tɪnərənt) *adj.* **1.** working for a short time in various places, esp. as a casual labourer. ~*n.* **2.** an itinerant worker or other person.

itinerary (aɪ'tɪnərərɪ) *n., pl.* **-aries. 1.** a detailed plan of travel; route. **2.** a record of a journey. **3.** a guidebook for travellers.

-itis *suffix forming nouns.* indicating inflammation of a specified part: *tonsillitis.*

it'll ('ɪt'l) it will *or* it shall.

its (ɪts) *det.* **1.** of, belonging to, or associated in some way with it: *its left rear wheel; I can see its logical consequence.* ~*pron.* **2.** something belonging to it: *its is over there.*
Usage. The possessive adjective and pronoun *its* is never written with an apostrophe: *the cat has hurt its ear.* The contraction of *it is* (or *it has*), *it's,* always has an apostrophe: *it's a pity that the cat has hurt its ear.*

it's (ɪts) it is *or* it has.
Usage. see **its.**

itself (ɪt'sɛlf) *pron.* **1. a.** the reflexive form of *it: the dog scratched itself.* **b.** (used for emphasis): *even the money itself won't con-*

vince me. **2.** its normal or usual self: *my cat doesn't seem itself these days.*

ITV (in Britain) Independent Television.

IU(C)D intrauterine (contraceptive) device.

I've (aɪv) I have.

ivories ('aɪvərɪz) *pl. n. Slang.* **1.** the keys of a piano. **2.** the teeth. **3.** dice.

ivory ('aɪvərɪ) *n., pl.* **-ries. 1.** a hard smooth creamy white type of bone that makes up a major part of the tusks of elephants. ~*adj.* **2.** yellowish-white. —'ivory-‚like *adj.*

ivory tower ('taʊə) *n.* seclusion or withdrawal from practical matters or from the problems of everyday life. —‚ivory-'towered *adj.*

IVR International Vehicle Registration.

ivy ('aɪvɪ) *n., pl.* **ivies. 1.** a woody climbing or trailing plant with evergreen leaves and black berry-like fruits. **2.** any of various other climbing or creeping plants, such as the poison ivy.

ixia ('ɪksɪə) *n.* a southern African plant of the iris family with showy ornamental funnel-shaped flowers.

-ize *or* **-ise** *suffix.* **1.** to make or become: *legalize, crystallize.* **2.** to affect in a specified way: *hypnotize.* **3.** to act according to some principle, practice, policy etc.: *economize.*
Usage. In Britain and the U.S. *-ize* is the preferred ending for many verbs, but *-ise* is equally acceptable in British English. Certain words (chiefly those not formed by adding the suffix to an existing word) are, however always spelt with *-ise* in both Britain and the U.S.: *advertise, revise.*

J

j *or* **J** (dʒeɪ) *n., pl.* **j's, J's,** *or* **Js.** the tenth letter of the English alphabet.

J joule(s).

jab (dʒæb) *vb.* **jabbing, jabbed. 1.** to poke sharply. **2.** to punch with quick short blows. ~*n.* **3.** a sharp poke. **4.** a quick short punch. **5.** *Informal.* an injection: *a polio jab.*

jabber (ˈdʒæbə) *vb.* **1.** to speak very quickly and excitedly; chatter. ~*n.* **2.** quick, excited chatter.

jabot (ˈʒæbəʊ) *n.* a frill or ruffle on the front of a blouse or shirt.

jacaranda (ˌdʒækəˈrændə) *n.* a tropical American tree with sweet-smelling wood and pale purple flowers.

jack (dʒæk) *n.* **1.** a mechanical device used to raise a heavy weight, such as a motor vehicle. **2.** a playing card with a picture of a pageboy on it. **3.** *Bowls.* a small white bowl at which the players aim with their own bowls. **4.** *Electrical engineering.* a socket designed for the insertion of a plug. **5.** a flag flown at the bow of a ship, showing the ship's nationality. **6.** Also called: **jackstone.** one of the pieces used in the game of jacks. **7. every man jack.** everyone without exception. ~See also **jack in, jacks, jack up.**

jackal (ˈdʒækəl) *n.* a wild doglike animal of Africa and Asia, which has a yellowish-grey coat, long legs, and pointed ears and which feeds on the decaying flesh of dead animals.

jackanapes (ˈdʒækəˌneɪps) *n.* (*functioning as sing.*) an impertinent person.

jackass (ˈdʒækˌæs) *n.* **1.** a male donkey. **2.** a fool.

jackboot (ˈdʒækˌbuːt) *n.* **1.** a leather military boot, reaching up to or above the knee. **2. under the jackboot of.** under the harsh rule of.

jackdaw (ˈdʒækˌdɔː) *n.* a large black-and-grey bird of Europe and Asia, which is related to the crow.

jacket (ˈdʒækɪt) *n.* **1.** a short coat with a front opening and long sleeves. **2.** same as **dust jacket. 3.** the skin of a potato.

Jack Frost *n.* frost represented as a person.

jack in *vb. Slang.* to abandon (an attempt or enterprise).

jack-in-office *n.* a self-important petty official.

jack-in-the-box *n.* a toy consisting of a figure on a tight spring in a box, which springs out when the lid is opened.

jackknife (ˈdʒækˌnaɪf) *n., pl.* **-knives. 1.** a knife with a blade that can be folded into the handle. **2.** a dive in which the diver bends at the waist in midair. ~*vb.* **3.** (of an articulated lorry) to go out of control in such a way that the trailer swings round at a sharp angle to the cab.

jack of all trades *n., pl.* **jacks of all trades.** a person who can do many different kinds of work; handyman.

jackpot (ˈdʒækˌpɒt) *n.* **1.** the most valuable prize or an accumulated stake that may be won in a game or lottery. **2. hit the jackpot.** *Informal.* to achieve great success through luck.

jack rabbit *n.* a hare of W North America with long hind legs and large ears.

jacks (dʒæks) *n.* (*functioning as sing.*) a game in which bone or metal pieces are thrown and then picked up between throws of a small ball. Also called: **jackstones.**

Jack Tar *n. Now chiefly literary.* a sailor.

jack up *vb.* **1.** to raise (a heavy weight, such as a motor vehicle) with a jack. **2.** *Slang.* to inject oneself with a drug. **3.** to increase (prices or salaries).

Jacobean (ˌdʒækəˈbɪən) *adj.* **1.** *History.* relating to James I of England and Ireland or to the period of his rule (1603–25). **2.** of the style of furniture or architecture current at this time.

Jacobite (ˈdʒækəˌbaɪt) *n. History.* a supporter of James II of England, Scotland, and Ireland and his descendants.

Jacquard (ˈdʒækɑːd) *n.* **1.** a fabric in which the design is incorporated into the weave. **2.** a loom on which this fabric is produced.

Jacuzzi (dʒəˈkuːzɪ) *n. Trademark.* a large circular bath fitted with a mechanism that makes the water swirl around.

jade¹ (dʒeɪd) *n.* **1.** a hard, usually green, semiprecious stone used for making ornaments and jewellery. ~*adj.* **2.** of the colour of green jade.

jade² (dʒeɪd) *n. Old-fashioned.* a disreputable woman.

jaded (ˈdʒeɪdɪd) *adj.* tired and unenthusiastic; weary.

Jaffa (ˈdʒæfə, ˈdʒɑː-) *n.* a large orange with a thick skin.

jag¹ (dʒæg) *n. Informal.* same as **jab** (sense 5).

jag² (dʒæg) *n. Slang.* **1.** a bout of drinking. **2.** a period of uncontrolled activity: *a crying jag.*

jagged ('dʒægɪd) *adj.* having an uneven edge with sharp points.

jaguar ('dʒægjʊə) *n.* a large catlike animal of south and central America, similar to the leopard but with larger spots on its coat.

jail *or* **gaol** (dʒeɪl) *n.* **1.** a prison. ~*vb.* **2.** to confine (someone) in prison.

jailbird *or* **gaolbird** ('dʒeɪl,bɜːd) *n.* a person who is or has often been in jail.

jailer *or* **gaoler** ('dʒeɪlə) *n.* a person in charge of prisoners in a jail.

jake (dʒeɪk) *adj.* **she's jake.** *Austral. & N.Z. slang.* it is all right.

jalap ('dʒæləp) *n.* the dried and powdered root of a Mexican climbing plant, used as a purgative.

jalopy (dʒə'lopɪ) *n., pl.* **-lopies.** *Informal.* a dilapidated old car.

jalousie ('ʒælʊˌziː) *n.* a window blind or shutter made of horizontal slats of wood.

jam¹ (dʒæm) *vb.* **jamming, jammed. 1.** to cram or wedge (a thing or people) into a place or against a thing: *to jam paper into an incinerator.* **2.** to crowd, pack, or congest: *cars jammed the roads.* **3.** to make or become stuck or locked. **4.** (foll. by *on*) to activate suddenly: *to jam on the brakes.* **5.** *Radio.* to prevent the clear reception of (radio communications) by transmitting other signals on the same frequency. **6.** *Slang.* to play in a jam session. ~*n.* **7.** a crowd or congestion in a confined space: *a traffic jam.* **8.** *Informal.* a difficult situation: *to help a friend out of a jam.* **9.** same as **jam session.**

jam² (dʒæm) *n.* a food made from fruit boiled with sugar until the mixture sets, used for spreading on bread.

jamb (dʒæm) *n.* a side post of a doorframe or window frame.

jamboree (ˌdʒæmbə'riː) *n.* **1.** a party or spree. **2.** a large gathering of Scouts.

jammy ('dʒæmɪ) *adj.* **-mier, -miest. 1.** covered with jam. **2.** *Brit. slang.* lucky: *you jammy so-and-so!*

jam-packed *adj.* filled to capacity.

jam session *n. Slang.* an improvised performance by jazz or rock musicians.

Jan. January.

jandal ('dʒændəl) *n. N.Z.* same as **flip-flop.**

jangle ('dʒæŋgəl) *vb.* **1.** to make or cause (something) to make a harsh unpleasant ringing noise. **2.** to produce an irritating or unpleasant effect on: *the accident jangled his nerves.*

janitor ('dʒænɪtə) *n. Chiefly Scot., U.S., & Canad.* the caretaker of a school, university, hospital, or apartment block.

January ('dʒænjʊərɪ) *n., pl.* **-aries.** the first month of the year.

japan (dʒə'pæn) *n.* **1.** a glossy black lacquer, originally from the Orient, which is used on wood or metal. ~*vb.* **-panning,**

-**panned. 2.** to lacquer (something) with japan.

Japanese (ˌdʒæpə'niːz) *adj.* **1.** of Japan, its people, or their language. ~*n.* **2.** (*pl.* -**nese**) a person from Japan. **3.** the official language of Japan.

jape (dʒeɪp) *n.* a joke or prank.

japonica (dʒə'pɒnɪkə) *n.* **1.** a Japanese shrub with red flowers and yellowish fruit. **2.** same as **camellia.**

jar¹ (dʒɑː) *n.* **1.** a wide-mouthed container that is usually cylindrical and made of glass. **2.** *Brit. informal.* a glass of beer.

jar² (dʒɑː) *vb.* **jarring, jarred. 1.** to have an irritating or unpleasant effect: *their laughing jarred on his nerves.* **2.** to vibrate or cause (something) to vibrate. **3.** to make or cause (something) to make a harsh unpleasant noise. **4.** to clash: *our beliefs jar.* ~*n.* **5.** a jolt or shock. —**jarring** *adj.*

jardinière (ˌdʒɑːdɪ'njɛə) *n.* **1.** an ornamental pot or stand for plants. **2.** a garnish of fresh vegetables for a dish of meat.

jargon ('dʒɑːgən) *n.* **1.** specialized language concerned with a particular subject, profession, or group. **2.** pretentious language.

jasmine ('dʒæzmɪn) *n.* a shrub or climbing plant with sweet-smelling white, yellow, or red flowers.

jasper ('dʒæspə) *n.* a red, yellow, brown, or dark green opaque variety of quartz, used as a gemstone and for ornamental decoration.

jaundice ('dʒɔːndɪs) *n.* **1.** a condition in which the skin becomes yellow due to the abnormal presence of bile pigments in the blood. ~*vb.* **2.** to distort (someone's judgment) adversely: *jealousy had jaundiced his mind.* **3.** to affect (someone) with or as if with jaundice. —**jaundiced** *adj.*

jaunt (dʒɔːnt) *n.* **1.** a short pleasurable excursion; outing. ~*vb.* **2.** to go on such an excursion.

jaunting car *n.* a light two-wheeled one-horse car, formerly widely used in Ireland.

jaunty ('dʒɔːntɪ) *adj.* **-tier, -tiest. 1.** sprightly and cheerful: *a jaunty step.* **2.** smart: *a jaunty hat.* —**jauntily** *adv.*

Javanese (ˌdʒɑːvə'niːz) *adj.* **1.** of the island of Java, in Indonesia. ~*n.* **2.** (*pl.* -**nese**) a person from Java. **3.** the language of Java.

javelin ('dʒævlɪn) *n.* **1.** a long pointed spear thrown in a sports competition. **2.** **the javelin.** the sport of throwing the javelin.

jaw (dʒɔː) *n.* **1.** either of the two bony structures in the head that hold the teeth and frame the mouth. **2.** the lower part of the face below the mouth. **3.** either of a pair of hinged or sliding parts of a machine or tool that are designed to grip an object. **4.** *Slang.* a long conversation. ~*vb.* **5.** *Slang.* to chat; gossip.

jawbone ('dʒɔːˌbəʊn) *n.* the bone in the lower jaw of a person or animal.

jaws (dʒɔːz) *pl. n.* **1.** the narrow opening of some confined place such as a gorge. **2.** a dangerous or threatening position: *the jaws of death.*

jay (dʒeɪ) *n.* a bird of Europe and Asia with a pinkish-brown body and blue-and-black wings.

jaywalking ('dʒeɪˌwɔːkɪŋ) *n.* the act of crossing a road in a dangerous or careless manner. —'**jay**ˌ**walker** *n.*

jazz (dʒæz) *n.* **1.** a kind of popular music of Black American origin, which has an exciting rhythm and usually features a lot of improvisation. **2.** *Slang.* other related things: *legal papers and all that jazz.* ~*vb.* **3.** to play or dance to jazz music.

jazz up *vb. Informal.* **1.** to liven up (a piece of music) with jazzy qualities. **2.** to make (something) more colourful, appealing, or lively.

jazzy ('dʒæzɪ) *adj.* **-zier, -ziest. 1.** colourful and stylish: *a jazzy tie.* **2.** of or like jazz.

JCB *n. Trademark.* a machine with a hydraulically operated shovel on the front and a digger arm on the back, used in building.

jealous ('dʒɛləs) *adj.* **1.** suspicious or fearful of being displaced by a rival. **2.** envious: *jealous of her success.* **3.** (foll. by *of*) possessive and watchful in the protection of: *jealous of one's reputation.* **4.** resulting from jealousy: *a jealous rage.* —'**jealously** *adv.*

jealousy ('dʒɛləsɪ) *n., pl.* **-ousies.** the state or quality of being jealous.

Jean Baptiste (ˌʒɒn bæ'tiːst) *n. Canad. slang.* a French Canadian.

jeans (dʒiːnz) *pl. n.* trousers for casual wear, usually made of denim.

Jeep (dʒiːp) *n. Trademark.* a small road vehicle with four-wheel drive.

jeer (dʒɪə) *vb.* **1.** to laugh or scoff (at a person or thing). ~*n.* **2.** a cry of derision. —'**jeering** *adj., n.*

Jehovah (dʒɪ'həʊvə) *n. Bible.* a personal name of God.

Jehovah's Witness *n.* a member of a Christian Church of American origin, the followers of which believe that the end of the present world system of government is near.

jejune (dʒɪ'dʒuːn) *adj.* **1.** simple and unsophisticated. **2.** dull and uninteresting: *a jejune film.*

jejunum (dʒɪ'dʒuːnəm) *n. Anat.* the part of the small intestine between the duodenum and the ileum.

Jekyll and Hyde ('dʒɛkᵊl; haɪd) *n.* a person with two distinct personalities, one good and the other evil.

jell *or* **gel** (dʒɛl) *vb.* **1.** to become thick and

jelly-like. **2.** to take on a definite form: *his ideas have jelled.*

jellaba *or* **jellabah** ('dʒɛləbə) *n.* a loose cloak with a hood, worn by many Arab men.

jelly ('dʒɛlɪ) *n., pl.* **-lies. 1.** a fruit-flavoured clear dessert set with gelatin. **2.** a food made from the juice of fruit boiled with sugar, usually spread on bread. **3.** a savoury food preparation set with gelatin. ~*vb.* **-lying, -lied. 4.** to prepare (food) in a jelly. —'**jellied** *adj.* —'**jelly**-ˌ**like** *adj.*

jellyfish ('dʒɛlɪˌfɪʃ) *n., pl.* **-fish.** a sea creature with an umbrella-shaped body and trailing tentacles.

jemmy ('dʒɛmɪ) *or U.S.* **jimmy** *n., pl.* **-mies.** a short steel crowbar, used by burglars to prise open doors and windows.

jenny ('dʒɛnɪ) *n., pl.* **-nies. 1.** the female of certain animals or birds, such as a donkey, ass, or wren. **2.** short for **spinning jenny.**

jeopardize *or* **-ise** ('dʒɛpəˌdaɪz) *vb.* to put (something) in danger; risk: *he jeopardized his job by being persistently late.*

jeopardy ('dʒɛpədɪ) *n.* danger of injury, loss, or death: *his health was in jeopardy.*

jerbil ('dʒɜːbɪl) *n.* same as **gerbil.**

jerboa (dʒɜː'bəʊə) *n.* a small rodent of Asia and N Africa, with long hind legs specialized for jumping.

jeremiad (ˌdʒɛrɪ'maɪəd) *n.* a long mournful complaint.

jerk¹ (dʒɜːk) *vb.* **1.** to move with an irregular or spasmodic motion. **2.** to throw, twist, pull, or push (something) abruptly or spasmodically. ~*n.* **3.** an abrupt or spasmodic movement. **4.** an irregular jolting motion: *the car moved with a jerk.* **5.** *Slang, chiefly U.S. & Canad.* a stupid or ignorant person.

jerk² (dʒɜːk) *vb.* to preserve (beef) by cutting it into thin strips and drying it in the sun.

jerkin ('dʒɜːkɪn) *n.* a short jacket.

jerky ('dʒɜːkɪ) *adj.* **jerkier, jerkiest.** having an irregular jolting motion: *the bus ride was a bit jerky.* —'**jerkily** *adv.* —'**jerkiness** *n.*

Jerry ('dʒɛrɪ) *n., pl.* **-ries.** *Brit. slang.* **1.** a German. **2.** Germans collectively.

jerry-built *adj.* (of houses) built badly with cheap materials. —'**jerry**ˌ**builder** *n.*

jerry can *n.* a flat-sided can used for storing or transporting motor fuel or water.

jersey ('dʒɜːzɪ) *n.* **1.** a knitted garment covering the upper part of the body. **2.** a machine-knitted slightly elastic cloth of wool, silk, or nylon, used for clothing.

Jersey ('dʒɜːzɪ) *n.* a breed of reddish-brown dairy cattle producing milk with a high butterfat content.

Jerusalem artichoke (dʒə'ruːsələm) *n.* a small yellowish-white vegetable that grows underground.

jest (dʒɛst) *n.* **1.** something done or said for amusement; joke. **2.** playfulness; fun: *spo-*

ken in jest. ~*vb.* **3.** to act or speak in an amusing way.

jester ('dʒɛstə) *n.* a professional clown employed by a king or nobleman during the Middle Ages.

Jesuit ('dʒɛzjʊɪt) *n.* a member of a Roman Catholic religious order founded by Ignatius Loyola in 1534. —,**Jesu'itical** *adj.*

Jesus ('dʒiːzəs) *n.* **1.** Also called: **Jesus Christ, Jesus of Nazareth.** the founder of Christianity, believed by Christians to be the Son of God. ~*interj.* **2.** *Taboo slang.* an oath expressing intense surprise or dismay.

jet¹ (dʒɛt) *n.* **1.** a thin stream of liquid or gas forced out of a small hole. **2.** an outlet or nozzle through which such a stream is forced out. **3.** a jet-propelled aircraft. ~*vb.* **jetting, jetted.** **4.** to come out in a jet: *water jetted from the hose.* **5.** to transport or be transported by jet aircraft.

jet² (dʒɛt) *n.* a hard black mineral that takes a brilliant polish and is used in jewellery.

jet-black *adj.* deep black.

jet engine *n.* an engine that uses jet propulsion for forward thrust, esp. one fitted to an aircraft.

jet lag *n.* a general feeling of fatigue often experienced by aircraft passengers who have crossed several time zones in relatively few hours.

jet-propelled *adj.* **1.** driven by jet propulsion. **2.** *Informal.* very fast.

jet propulsion *n.* propulsion by means of a jet of air or gas, esp. when the exhaust gases provide the forward thrust.

jetsam ('dʒɛtsəm) *n.* **1.** the portion of a ship's cargo thrown overboard to lighten her during a storm. **2.** See **flotsam** (sense 2).

jet set *n.* rich and fashionable people who travel widely for pleasure. —'**jet,setter** *n.* —'**jet-,setting** *n., adj.*

jettison ('dʒɛtɪs'n, -z'n) *vb.* **1.** to abandon: *to jettison old clothes.* **2.** to throw (cargo) overboard.

jetty ('dʒɛtɪ) *n., pl.* **-ties.** **1.** a structure built from a shore out into the water to direct currents or protect a harbour. **2.** a landing pier; dock.

Jew (dʒuː) *n.* **1.** a descendant of the ancient Israelites. **2.** a person whose religion is Judaism. **3.** *Offensive.* a miserly person. —'**Jewess** *fem. n.*

jewel ('dʒuːəl) *n.* **1.** a precious or semiprecious stone; gem. **2.** a person or thing regarded as precious or special. **3.** a gemstone used as part of the machinery of a watch. ~*vb.* **-elling, -elled** or *U.S.* **-eling, -eled.** **4.** to decorate (something) with jewels.

jeweller or *U.S.* **jeweler** ('dʒuːələ) *n.* a person who makes, sells, and repairs jewellery.

jewellery or *U.S.* **jewelry** ('dʒuːəlrɪ) *n.* objects such as rings, necklaces, or bracelets, worn for decoration.

Jewish ('dʒuːɪʃ) *adj.* of Jews or Judaism.

Jewry ('dʒʊərɪ) *n.* Jews collectively.

jew's-harp *n.* a small musical instrument held between the teeth and played by plucking a steel tongue with one's finger.

Jezebel ('dʒɛzə,bɛl) *n.* a shameless or scheming woman.

jib¹ (dʒɪb) *n.* **1.** *Naut.* any triangular sail set forward of the foremast of a vessel. **2. the cut of one's jib.** one's manner or style.

jib² (dʒɪb) *vb.* **jibbing, jibbed.** *Chiefly Brit.* **1.** (of an animal) to stop short and refuse to go forwards: *the horse jibbed at the jump.* **2. jib at.** to object to: *I thought she would jib at the new working methods.* **3.** *Naut.* same as **gybe.**

jib³ (dʒɪb) *n.* the projecting arm of a crane.

jib boom *n.* *Naut.* a spar forming an extension of the bowsprit of a ship.

jibe¹ (dʒaɪb) *vb., n.* *Naut.* same as **gybe.**

jibe² (dʒaɪb) *vb.* same as **gibe.**

jiffy ('dʒɪfɪ) or **jiff** *n., pl.* **jiffies** or **jiffs.** *Informal.* a very short time: *I'll be back in a jiffy.*

Jiffy bag *n. Trademark.* a large padded envelope.

jig (dʒɪg) *n.* **1.** a lively folk dance. **2.** music for this dance. **3.** a mechanical device that holds and locates a component during machining. ~*vb.* **jigging, jigged.** **4.** to dance a jig. **5.** to jerk up and down rapidly. **6.** to drill or cut (a workpiece) in a jig.

jigger ('dʒɪgə) *n.* a small whisky glass.

jiggered ('dʒɪgəd) *adj. Informal.* damned; blowed: *I'm jiggered if he'll get away with it.*

jiggery-pokery ('dʒɪgərɪ'pəʊkərɪ) *n. Informal, chiefly Brit.* dishonest or deceitful behaviour.

jiggle ('dʒɪg'l) *vb.* **1.** to move up and down or to and fro with a short jerky motion. ~*n.* **2.** a short jerky motion.

jigsaw ('dʒɪg,sɔː) *n.* **1.** Also called: **jigsaw puzzle.** a puzzle in which the player has to put together a picture that has been cut into irregularly shaped interlocking pieces. **2.** a mechanical saw with a fine steel blade for cutting along curved or irregular lines in sheets of material.

jilt (dʒɪlt) *vb.* to leave or reject (a lover) without previous warning.

Jim Crow ('dʒɪm 'krəʊ) *n. U.S.* **1.** the policy or practice of segregating Black people. **2.** *Offensive.* a Black person.

jimjams ('dʒɪm,dʒæmz) *pl. n.* **1.** *Slang.* same as **delirium tremens.** **2.** a state of nervous tension or anxiety.

jingle ('dʒɪŋg'l) *vb.* **1.** to ring lightly and repeatedly. ~*n.* **2.** a sound of metal jingling. **3.** a short song or tune used to advertise a product on radio or television or in a cinema.

jingo ('dʒɪŋgəʊ) *n., pl.* **-goes. 1.** a person who boasts loudly of his patriotism and favours an aggressive warlike foreign policy. **2. by jingo.** *Old-fashioned.* an exclamation of surprise.

jingoism ('dʒɪŋgəʊ,ɪzəm) *n.* aggressive patriotism. —,**jingo'istic** *adj.*

jink (dʒɪŋk) *vb.* to move swiftly in order to dodge someone: *when they saw me they jinked behind the trees.*

jinks (dʒɪŋks) *pl. n.* **high jinks.** boisterous or mischievous behaviour.

jinni, jinnee, *or* **djinni** (dʒɪˈniː) *n., pl.* **jinn** *or* **djinn** (dʒɪn). a spirit in Muslim mythology that could take on human or animal form.

jinx (dʒɪŋks) *n.* **1.** an unlucky force, person, or thing. ~*vb.* **2.** to be or put a jinx on.

jitterbug ('dʒɪtə,bʌg) *n.* **1.** a fast jerky American dance that was popular in the 1940s. ~*vb.* **-bugging, -bugged. 2.** to dance the jitterbug.

jitters ('dʒɪtəz) *pl. n.* **the.** *Informal.* a feeling of extreme nervousness experienced before an important event: *I had a bad case of the jitters before the audition.* —'**jittery** *adj.*

jive (dʒaɪv) *n.* **1.** a lively jerky dance that was popular in the 1940s and 1950s. **2.** *Slang, chiefly U.S.* misleading or deceptive talk. ~*vb.* **3.** to dance the jive. **4.** *Slang, chiefly U.S.* to mislead or deceive (someone). —'**jiver** *n.*

Jnr Junior.

job (dʒɒb) *n.* **1.** an occupation; paid employment. **2.** a piece of work; task. **3.** an object worked on or a result produced from working: *you made a good job of the paintwork.* **4.** a duty: *her job was to cook the dinner.* **5.** *Informal.* a difficult task: *I had a job to contact him.* **6.** a state of affairs: *to make the best of a bad job.* **7.** *Informal.* a crime, esp. a robbery. **8. just the job.** exactly what is required. **9. on the job.** actively engaged in one's employment. ~*vb.* **jobbing, jobbed. 10.** to do piecework or casual jobs. —'**jobber** *n.* —'**jobbing** *adj.* —'**jobless** *adj.*

Jobcentre ('dʒɒb,sentə) *or* **job centre** *n.* *Brit.* a government office in which people can consult displayed advertisements of available jobs.

job lot *n.* a miscellaneous collection of articles sold together.

Job's comforter (dʒəʊbz) *n.* a person who, while pretending to be sympathetic, succeeds only in adding to someone's distress.

job sharing *n.* an arrangement by which a job is shared by two part-time workers.

Jock (dʒɒk) *n. Slang.* a Scot.

jockey ('dʒɒkɪ) *n.* **1.** a person who rides horses in races, esp. as a profession. ~*vb.*

2. to ride (a horse) in a race. **3. jockey for position.** to try to obtain an advantage by skilful manoeuvring.

jockstrap ('dʒɒk,stræp) *n.* an elasticated belt with a pouch to support the genitals, worn by male athletes. Also called: **athletic support.**

jocose (dʒəˈkəʊs) *adj.* playful or humorous. —jo'**cosely** *adv.*

jocular ('dʒɒkjʊlə) *adj.* **1.** (of a person) often joking; good-humoured. **2.** (of a remark) meant lightly or humorously. —**jocularity** (,dʒɒkjʊ'lærɪtɪ) *n.* —'**jocularly** *adv.*

jocund ('dʒɒkənd) *adj. Literary.* cheerful; merry.

jodhpurs ('dʒɒdpəz) *pl. n.* riding breeches, loose-fitting around the thighs and tight-fitting from the knees to the ankles.

jog (dʒɒg) *vb.* **jogging, jogged. 1.** to run at a gentle pace for physical exercise. **2.** (foll. by *along*) to continue in a plodding way: *she has no ambition, she just jogs along.* **3.** to nudge slightly. **4. jog someone's memory.** to remind someone of something. ~*n.* **5.** the act of jogging. **6.** a slight nudge. —'**jogger** *n.* —'**jogging** *n.*

joggle ('dʒɒg°l) *vb.* **1.** to shake or move with a slightly jolting motion. ~*n.* **2.** the act of joggling.

jog trot *n.* an easy bouncy gait, midway between a walk and a trot.

john (dʒɒn) *n. Slang, chiefly U.S. & Canad.* a toilet.

John Bull *n.* **1.** England represented as a person. **2.** a typical Englishman.

johnny ('dʒɒnɪ) *n., pl.* **-nies.** *Brit. informal.* a man or boy; chap.

Johnny Canuck (kəˈnʌk) *n. Canad. informal.* **1.** Canada represented as a person. **2.** a typical Canadian.

joie de vivre (ʒwɑː də ˈviːvrə) *n.* joy of living; enjoyment of life.

join (dʒɔɪn) *vb.* **1.** to come or bring together. **2.** to become a member of (a club, organization, or society). **3.** to meet (someone) as a companion: *I'll join you later.* **4.** to become part of: *join the queue.* **5.** to unite (two people) in marriage. **6.** to connect (two points), for example with a straight line. ~*n.* **7.** a joint; seam. ~See also **join in, join up.**

joiner ('dʒɔɪnə) *n. Chiefly Brit.* a person skilled in making finished woodwork, such as windows and stairs.

joinery ('dʒɔɪnərɪ) *n.* **1.** the skill or craft of a joiner. **2.** work made by a joiner.

join in *vb.* to take part in (an activity).

joint (dʒɔɪnt) *n.* **1.** a junction of two or more parts or objects. **2.** *Anat.* the junction between two or more bones. **3.** a piece of meat suitable for roasting. **4.** *Slang.* a building or place, for example a bar or nightclub. **5.** *Slang.* a cannabis cigarette.

6. out of joint. a. (of a bone) knocked out of its normal position. **b.** *Informal.* out of order. *~adj.* **7.** shared by or belonging to two or more people: *joint property.* *~vb.* **8.** to provide (something) with a joint or joints. **9.** to cut or divide (meat) into joints. —'**jointed** *adj.* —'**jointly** *adv.*

joint-stock company *n. Brit.* a business enterprise whose capital is owned jointly by shareholders.

jointure ('dʒɔɪntʃə) *n. Law.* property settled on a wife by her husband for her use after his death.

join up *vb.* **1.** to become a member of a military organization; enlist. **2.** to connect (two or more things).

joist (dʒɔɪst) *n.* a beam made of timber, steel, or reinforced concrete, used in the construction of floors or roofs.

jojoba (həʊ'həʊbə) *n.* a shrub with seeds that contain an oil which is used in cosmetics.

joke (dʒəʊk) *n.* **1.** a humorous story. **2.** something that is said or done for fun. **3.** a ridiculous or humorous circumstance. **4.** a person or thing inspiring ridicule or amusement. **5. no joke.** a situation that is difficult or serious: *it's no joke trying to bring up a child on your own.* *~vb.* **6.** to tell jokes. **7.** to speak or act facetiously. **8. joking apart.** seriously: said after there has been joking in a discussion. —'**jokey** *adj.* —'**jokingly** *adv.*

joker ('dʒəʊkə) *n.* **1.** a person who jokes a lot. **2.** *Slang.* an incompetent person: *that joker earns a lot more than me.* **3.** an extra playing card in a pack, which in many card games can replace any other card.

jollification (,dʒɒlɪfɪ'keɪʃən) *n.* a merry festivity.

jollity ('dʒɒlɪtɪ) *n.* the condition of being jolly.

jolly ('dʒɒlɪ) *adj.* **-lier, -liest. 1.** full of good humour. **2.** having or provoking gaiety and merrymaking. *~adv.* **3.** *Brit.* extremely: *that's jolly kind of you.* *~vb.* **-lying, -lied.** **4.** (foll. by *along*) *Informal.* to try to keep (someone) cheerful by flattery or coaxing. —'**jolliness** *n.*

Jolly Roger *n.* the traditional pirate flag, consisting of a white skull and crossbones on a black background.

jolt (dʒəʊlt) *vb.* **1.** to bump against (someone or something) with a jarring blow. **2.** to move in a jerking manner. **3.** to surprise or shock: *it jolted me seeing them just then.* *~n.* **4.** a sudden jerking movement. **5.** an emotional shock.

Jonah ('dʒəʊnə) *n.* a person believed to bring bad luck to those around him.

jonquil ('dʒɒŋkwɪl) *n.* a kind of narcissus with long sweet-smelling yellow or white flowers.

josh (dʒɒʃ) *Slang, chiefly U.S. & Canad.*

~vb. **1.** to tease (someone). *~n.* **2.** a teasing joke.

joss (dʒɒs) *n.* a Chinese idol.

joss stick *n.* a stick of dried perfumed paste, giving off a sweet smell when burnt as incense.

jostle ('dʒɒs°l) *vb.* **1.** to bump or push (someone) roughly. **2.** to compete with someone: *jostling for first place.* *~n.* **3.** the act of jostling.

jot (dʒɒt) *vb.* **jotting, jotted. 1.** (foll. by *down*) to write a brief note of: *jot down this message.* *~n.* **2.** the least bit: *I don't care a jot whether she comes or not.*

jotter ('dʒɒtə) *n.* a small notebook.

jotting ('dʒɒtɪŋ) *n.* something jotted down.

joual (ʒwɑːl) *n.* nonstandard Canadian French dialect, as associated with ill-educated speakers.

joule (dʒuːl) *n.* the derived SI unit of work or energy. Symbol: J

journal ('dʒɜːn°l) *n.* **1.** a newspaper or magazine. **2.** a book in which a record of a person's daily activities is recorded.

journalese (,dʒɜːn°'liːz) *n.* a superficial style of writing regarded as typical of newspapers and magazines.

journalism ('dʒɜːn°,lɪzəm) *n.* **1.** the profession of collecting, writing, and publishing news through newspapers and magazines or by radio and television. **2.** newspapers and magazines collectively. —'**journalist** *n.* —,**journa**'**listic** *adj.*

journey ('dʒɜːnɪ) *n.* **1.** the act of travelling from one place to another. **2. a.** the distance travelled in a journey. **b.** the time taken to make a journey. *~vb.* **3.** to make a journey.

journeyman ('dʒɜːnɪmən) *n., pl.* **-men. 1.** a qualified craftsman who works at his trade in the employment of another. **2.** a competent workman.

joust (dʒaʊst) *History.* *~n.* **1.** a combat with lances between two mounted knights. *~vb.* **2.** to take part in such a tournament.

Jove (dʒəʊv) *n.* **1.** Jupiter (the god). **2. by Jove.** *Old-fashioned.* an exclamation of surprise or excitement.

jovial ('dʒəʊvɪəl) *adj.* happy and cheerful. —'**joviality** (,dʒəʊvɪ'ælɪtɪ) *n.* —'**jovially** *adv.*

jowl[1] (dʒaʊl) *n.* **1.** the lower jaw. **2.** (*pl.*) cheeks. **3. cheek by jowl.** See **cheek.** —'**jowled** *adj.*

jowl[2] (dʒaʊl) *n.* fatty flesh hanging from the lower jaw.

joy (dʒɔɪ) *n.* **1.** a deep feeling of happiness and contentment. **2.** something causing such a feeling. **3.** *Brit. informal.* success; satisfaction: *I went for a loan, but got no joy.*

joyful ('dʒɔɪfʊl) *adj.* **1.** full of joy; elated. **2.** expressing or producing joy: *a joyful look; a joyful occasion.* —'**joyfully** *adv.*

joyless ('dʒɔɪlɪs) *adj.* having or producing no joy or pleasure.

joyous ('dʒɔɪəs) *adj.* **1.** having a happy nature or mood. **2.** joyful.

joy ride *n.* **1.** a ride taken for pleasure in a stolen car, usually driven recklessly. ~*vb.* **joy-ride, -riding, -rode, -ridden. 2.** to take such a ride. —'**joyriding** *n.*

joystick ('dʒɔɪˌstɪk) *n.* the control lever of an aircraft or a computer.

JP Justice of the Peace.

Jr Junior.

jube (dʒuːb) *n. Austral. & N.Z. informal.* same as **jujube.**

jubilant ('dʒuːbɪlənt) *adj.* feeling or expressing great joy.

jubilation (ˌdʒuːbɪˈleɪʃən) *n.* a feeling of great happiness.

jubilee ('dʒuːbɪˌliː) *n.* **1.** a special anniversary, esp. a 25th or 50th one. **2.** a time of rejoicing.

Judaic (dʒuːˈdeɪɪk) *adj.* of the Jews or Judaism.

Judaism ('dʒuːdeɪˌɪzəm) *n.* **1.** the religion of the Jews, based on the Old Testament and the Talmud. **2.** the religious and cultural traditions of the Jews.

Judas ('dʒuːdəs) *n.* a person who betrays a friend; traitor.

judder ('dʒʌdə) *Informal, chiefly Brit.* ~*vb.* **1.** to shake or vibrate: *the car juddered to a halt.* ~*n.* **2.** a shaking or vibrating motion.

judge (dʒʌdʒ) *n.* **1.** a public official with authority to hear cases and pass sentences in a court of law. **2.** a person appointed to determine the result of a competition. **3.** a person whose opinion on a particular subject is usually reliable: *a good judge of character.* ~*vb.* **4.** to hear and decide upon (a case at law). **5.** to pass judgment on (someone). **6.** to decide (something) after inquiry. **7.** to determine the result of (a competition). **8.** to appraise (something) critically. **9.** to believe (something to be the case): *he judged that it was safe to proceed.*

judgment *or* **judgement** ('dʒʌdʒmənt) *n.* **1.** the faculty of being able to make critical distinctions and achieve a balanced viewpoint. **2. a.** the verdict pronounced by a court of law. **b.** an obligation arising as a result of such a verdict. **3.** the formal decision of one or more judges of a competition. **4.** a particular decision formed in a case in dispute. **5.** criticism or censure. **6.** **against one's better judgment.** contrary to what one thinks is sensible. —**judgmental** *or* **judgemental** (dʒʌdʒˈmentˀl) *adj.*

Judgment ('dʒʌdʒmənt) *n.* same as **Last Judgment.**

Judgment Day *n.* the occasion of the Last Judgment by God at the end of the world.

judicature ('dʒuːdɪkətʃə) *n.* **1.** the administration of justice. **2.** the office, function, or power of a judge. **3.** a group of judges.

judicial (dʒuːˈdɪʃəl) *adj.* **1.** of judges, courts, or the administration of justice. **2.** having qualities appropriate to a judge: *a judicial mind.* —**ju'dicially** *adv.*

judiciary (dʒuːˈdɪʃɪərɪ) *n.* the branch of the central authority in a state that administers justice.

judicious (dʒuːˈdɪʃəs) *adj.* having or showing good judgment; sensible.

judo ('dʒuːdəʊ) *n.* a sport derived from jujitsu, in which the object is to force an opponent to submit using the minimum of physical effort.

jug (dʒʌg) *n.* **1.** a container for holding or pouring liquids, usually with a handle and a lip. **2.** the amount of liquid held by a jug. **3.** *Slang.* jail. ~*vb.* **jugging, jugged. 4.** to stew (hare) in an earthenware container.

juggernaut ('dʒʌgəˌnɔːt) *n.* **1.** *Brit.* a very large heavy lorry. **2.** any terrible force that demands complete self-sacrifice.

juggle ('dʒʌgˀl) *vb.* **1.** to throw and catch (several objects) continuously so that most are in the air at the same time. **2.** to manipulate (facts or figures) to suit one's purpose. **3.** to keep (several activities) in progress at the same time. —'**juggler** *n.*

jugular ('dʒʌgjʊlə) *n.* a large vein in the neck that carries blood to the heart from the head. Also called: **jugular vein.**

juice (dʒuːs) *n.* **1.** any liquid that occurs naturally in or is secreted by plant or animal tissue: *orange juice.* **2.** *Informal.* **a.** petrol. **b.** electricity.

juicy ('dʒuːsɪ) *adj.* **juicier, juiciest. 1.** full of juice. **2.** provocatively interesting; spicy: *juicy gossip.*

jujitsu (dʒuːˈdʒɪtsuː) *n.* the traditional Japanese system of unarmed self-defence, perfected by the samurai.

juju ('dʒuːˌdʒuː) *n.* **1.** a magic charm or fetish used in parts of west Africa by certain tribes. **2.** the power associated with a juju.

jujube ('dʒuːdʒuːb) *n.* a chewy sweet made of flavoured gelatin.

jukebox ('dʒuːkˌbɒks) *n.* an automatic record player in which records may be selected by inserting coins and pressing appropriate buttons.

jukskei ('jʊkˌskeɪ) *n. S. African.* a game in which a peg is thrown over a fixed distance at a stake driven into the ground.

Jul. July.

Julian calendar ('dʒuːljən) *n.* the calendar introduced by Julius Caesar in 46 B.C., in which leap years occurred every fourth year and in every centenary year.

julienne (ˌdʒuːlɪˈɛn) *adj.* **1.** (of vegetables or meat) cut into thin shreds. ~*n.* **2.** a clear soup containing thinly shredded vegetables.

July (dʒuːˈlaɪ) *n., pl.* **-lies.** the seventh month of the year.

jumble (ˈdʒʌmbʰl) *vb.* **1.** to mingle (objects) in a state of disorder. **2.** to remember (something) in a confused form. *~n.* **3.** a disordered mass or state. **4.** *Brit.* articles donated for a jumble sale.

jumble sale *n. Brit.* a sale, usually of second-hand articles, in aid of charity.

jumbo (ˈdʒʌmbəʊ) *n.* **1.** (*modifier*) *Informal.* very large: *a jumbo box of detergent.* **2.** (*pl.* **-bos**) short for **jumbo jet.**

jumbo jet *n. Informal.* a type of large jet-propelled airliner.

jump (dʒʌmp) *vb.* **1.** to leap or spring into the air by using the muscles in the legs and feet. **2.** to leap over (an obstacle): *to jump a gap.* **3.** to cause to leap over an obstacle: *to jump a horse over a hedge.* **4.** to proceed hastily: *she jumped into a taxi.* **5.** to jerk with astonishment or surprise: *she jumped when she heard the explosion.* **6.** (of prices) to rise suddenly or abruptly. **7.** to pass over (intervening matter): *she jumped a few lines and then continued reading.* **8.** to change (from one subject to another). **9.** (of a train) to come off (the rails). **10.** (of the stylus of a record player) to be jerked out of the groove. **11.** *Slang.* to be lively: *the party was jumping.* **12.** *Informal.* to attack without warning: *thieves jumped the old man.* **13.** *Informal.* (of a driver or a motor vehicle) to pass through (a red traffic light). **14. jump down someone's throat.** *Informal.* to speak sharply to someone. **15. jump to it.** *Informal.* to begin something quickly and efficiently. *~n.* **16.** the act or an instance of jumping. **17.** a space, distance, or obstacle to be jumped. **18.** *Sport.* any of several contests involving a jump: *the high jump.* **19.** a sudden rise: *the jump in prices last month.* **20.** a sudden change from one subject to another: *the professor made an unexpected jump in his lecture.* **21.** a sudden jerk, as a reaction of surprise. **22.** a step or degree: *one jump ahead.* **23.** *Films.* a break in continuity in the normal sequence of shots. **24. take a running jump.** *Brit. informal.* a contemptuous expression of dismissal. *~See also* **jump at, jump on.**

jump at *vb.* to be glad to accept: *I would jump at the chance of going.*

jumped-up *adj. Informal.* having suddenly risen in significance and appearing arrogant: *a jumped-up office boy.*

jumper¹ (ˈdʒʌmpə) *n.* **1.** *Chiefly Brit.* a knitted garment covering the upper part of the body. **2.** *U.S. & Canad.* a pinafore dress.

jumper² (ˈdʒʌmpə) *n.* **1.** a short piece of wire used to make an electrical connection,

usually temporarily. **2.** a person or animal that jumps.

jump jet *n. Informal.* a fixed-wing jet aircraft that is capable of landing and taking off vertically.

jump leads (liːdz) *pl. n.* two heavy cables used to start a motor vehicle with a flat battery by connecting the flat battery to the battery of another vehicle.

jump on *vb. Informal.* to reprimand or attack (someone) suddenly and forcefully.

jump-start *vb.* **1.** to start the engine of (a motor vehicle) by pushing or rolling it and then engaging the gears or (of a motor vehicle) to start in this way. *~n.* **2.** the act of starting a motor vehicle in this way.

jump suit *n.* a one-piece garment of combined trousers and top.

jumpy (ˈdʒʌmpɪ) *adj.* **jumpier, jumpiest.** **1.** nervous or apprehensive. **2.** moving jerkily.

Jun. 1. June. **2.** Junior.

junction (ˈdʒʌŋkʃən) *n.* **1.** a place where several routes, lines, or roads meet, link, or cross each other: *a railway junction.* **2.** a point on a motorway where traffic may leave or join it. **3.** *Electronics.* a point where wires are joined.

juncture (ˈdʒʌŋktʃə) *n.* a point in time, esp. a critical one: *we don't want to risk an industrial dispute at this juncture.*

June (dʒuːn) *n.* the sixth month of the year.

jungle (ˈdʒʌŋgʰl) *n.* **1.** a forest area in a hot country with luxuriant vegetation. **2.** any dense or tangled vegetation. **3.** a place of intense struggle for survival: *the concrete jungle.*

junior (ˈdʒuːnjə) *adj.* **1.** lower in rank or position: *a junior partner.* **2.** younger in years: *my sister is junior to me by ten years.* **3.** *Brit.* of schoolchildren between the ages of 7 and 11 approximately. **4.** *U.S.* of the third year of a four-year course at college or high school. *~n.* **5.** a person holding a low rank or position. **6.** a person younger than a particular person: *she married a man eight years her junior.* **7.** *Brit.* a junior schoolchild. **8.** *U.S.* a junior student.

Junior (ˈdʒuːnjə) *adj. Chiefly U.S.* being the younger: usually used after a name to distinguish between two people of the same name: *Douglas Fairbanks, Junior.*

juniper (ˈdʒuːnɪpə) *n.* a low-growing evergreen shrub or tree with purple berries which are used as a flavouring in making gin.

junk¹ (dʒʌŋk) *n.* **1.** discarded objects collectively. **2.** *Informal.* **a.** rubbish generally. **b.** nonsense: *the play was absolute junk.* **3.** *Slang.* narcotic drugs, esp. heroin.

junk² (dʒʌŋk) *n.* a Chinese sailing boat with a flat bottom and square sails.

junket (ˈdʒʌŋkɪt) *n.* **1.** a sweet dessert made of flavoured milk set with rennet. **2.**

a feast. **3.** an excursion made by a public official and paid for out of public funds. ~*vb.* **4.** to have a feast. **5.** (of a public official) to go on an excursion paid for out of public funds.

junk food *n.* food with a low nutritional value.

junkie ('dʒʌŋkɪ) *n. Informal.* a drug addict.

junta ('dʒʌntə) *n.* (functioning as sing. or pl.) a group of military officers holding the power in a country after a revolution.

Jupiter ('dʒuːpɪtə) *n.* **1.** the king of the Roman gods. **2.** the largest planet.

Jurassic (dʒʊ'ræsɪk) *adj. Geol.* of the geological period about 180 million years ago, during which dinosaurs flourished.

juridical (dʒʊ'rɪdɪkˀl) *adj.* of law or the administration of justice; legal.

jurisdiction (ˌdʒʊərɪs'dɪkʃən) *n.* **1.** the right or power to administer justice and to apply laws. **2.** the exercise or extent of such right or power. **3.** authority in general.

jurisprudence (ˌdʒʊərɪs'pruːdˀns) *n.* the science or philosophy of law.

jurist ('dʒʊərɪst) *n.* a person who is expert in the science of law.

juror ('dʒʊərə) *n.* a member of a jury.

jury ('dʒʊərɪ) *n., pl.* **-ries. 1.** a group of twelve people sworn to deliver a true verdict according to the evidence upon a case presented in a court of law. **2.** a group of people appointed to judge a competition.

jury box *n.* an enclosure where the jury sits in a court of law.

jury-rigged *adj. Chiefly naut.* set up in a makeshift manner.

just (dʒʌst) *adv.* **1.** used to indicate an action performed in the very recent past: *I have just closed the door.* **2.** at this very instant: *he's just coming in to land.* **3.** no more than; only: *just an ordinary car.* **4.** exactly: *that's just what I mean.* **5.** barely: *he just got there in time.* **6. just about. a.** at the point of starting (to do something). **b.** almost: *I've just about had enough.* **7. just a moment, second,** *or* **minute.** an expression requesting someone to wait for a short time. **8. just now. a.** a short time ago: *he left on the bus just now.* **b.** at the present time: *we're very busy just now.* **9. just so. a.** an expression used to indicate

agreement. **b.** arranged with precision: *when we arrived everything was just so.* ~*adj.* **10.** fair or impartial in action or judgment: *a just decision.* **11.** rightly given: *a just reward.* **12.** well-founded: *just criticism.* —'**justly** *adv.* —'**justness** *n.*

justice ('dʒʌstɪs) *n.* **1.** the quality of being just. **2.** the administration of law according to prescribed and accepted principles. **3.** conformity to the law. **4.** a judge. **5.** short for **justice of the peace. 6.** good reason: *she complained bitterly, and with justice.* **7. bring to justice.** to capture, try, and punish (a criminal). **8. do justice to. a.** to show to full advantage: *the picture did not do justice to her beauty.* **b.** to show full appreciation of (something) by action: *he did justice to the meal.* **9. do oneself justice.** to make full use of one's abilities: *he didn't do himself justice in the exam.*

justice of the peace *n.* a magistrate who is authorized to act as a judge in a local court of law.

justiciary (dʒʌ'stɪʃɪərɪ) *n., pl.* **-aries.** an administrator of justice; judge.

justify ('dʒʌstɪˌfaɪ) *vb.* **-fying, -fied. 1.** to prove (something) to be just or valid; show (something) to be reasonable: *his behaviour justifies our suspicion.* **2.** to show (someone) to be free from blame; absolve. **3.** to arrange (text) when typing or printing so that both margins are straight. —'**justiˌfiable** *adj.* —'**justiˌfiably** *adv.* —**justification** (ˌdʒʌstɪfɪ'keɪʃən) *n.*

jut (dʒʌt) *vb.* **jutting, jutted.** (foll. by *out*) to stick out beyond the surface or main part of something.

jute (dʒuːt) *n.* a fibre obtained from the bark of an East Indian plant and used in making rope, sacks, and mats.

juvenile ('dʒuːvɪˌnaɪl) *adj.* **1.** young, youthful, or immature. **2.** suitable for young people: *juvenile pastimes.* ~*n.* **3.** a young person. **4.** an actor who performs youthful roles.

juvenile delinquent *n.* a young person who is guilty of a crime. —**juvenile delinquency** *n.*

juxtapose (ˌdʒʌkstə'pəʊz) *vb.* to place (things or ideas) close together or side by side. —ˌ**juxtapo'sition** *n.*

K

k or **K** (keɪ) *n.*, *pl.* **k's**, **K's**, or **Ks.** the 11th letter of the English alphabet.

K **1.** kelvin(s). **2.** *Chess.* king. **3.** *Chem.* potassium. **4.** one thousand. **5.** *Computers.* originally or strictly, a unit of 1024 words, bits, or bytes.

Kaffir (ˈkæfə) *n.* **1.** *Offensive.* (in Africa) a Black African. **2.** an old name for the Xhosa language.

kaftan or **caftan** (ˈkæftæn) *n.* a long coat-like garment worn by men in eastern countries and by women and men in western countries.

kahawai (ˈkɑːhəwaɪ, ˈkɑːwaɪ) *n.* a New Zealand food and game fish.

kai (kaɪ) *n.* *N.Z. informal.* food.

kaiser (ˈkaɪzə) *n.* *History.* a German or Austro-Hungarian emperor.

kaka (ˈkɑːkə) *n.* a green parrot of New Zealand with a long compressed bill.

kakapo (ˈkɑːkəˌpəʊ) *n.*, *pl.* **-pos.** a ground-living parrot of New Zealand that resembles an owl.

kalashnikov (kəˈlæʃnɪˌkɒf) *n.* a Russian-made sub-machine-gun used by terrorists and guerrillas.

kale (keɪl) *n.* a variety of cabbage with crinkled leaves.

kaleidoscope (kəˈlaɪdəˌskəʊp) *n.* a tube-shaped toy that contains loose pieces of coloured paper or glass reflected by mirrors so that various symmetrical patterns form when the tube is twisted. —**kaleidoscopic** (kəˌlaɪdəˈskɒpɪk) *adj.*

kalends (ˈkælɪndz) *pl. n.* same as **calends.**

kaleyard (ˈkeɪlˌjɑːd) *n.* *Scot.* a vegetable garden.

Kamasutra (ˌkɑːməˈsuːtrə) *n.* **the.** an ancient Hindu text on erotic pleasure.

kamikaze (ˌkæmɪˈkɑːzɪ) *n.* **1.** (in World War II) a Japanese pilot who performed suicidal missions. **2.** (*modifier*) (of an action) undertaken or (of a person) undertaking an action in the knowledge that it will result in the death or injury of the person performing it: *a kamikaze attack.*

Kamloops trout (ˈkæmluːps) *n.* a bright silvery rainbow trout common in British Columbia, Canada.

Kan. Kansas.

kangaroo (ˌkæŋgəˈruː) *n.*, *pl.* **-roos.** a large Australian animal with powerful hind legs used for leaping and, in the female, a pouch for carrying her babies in.

kangaroo court *n.* an unofficial court, for example one set up by strikers to judge strikebreakers.

kaolin (ˈkeɪəlɪn) *n.* a fine white clay used in making porcelain and as a poultice.

kapok (ˈkeɪpɒk) *n.* a silky fibre obtained from a tropical tree and used for stuffing pillows and padding sleeping bags.

kaput (kæˈpʊt) *adj.* *Informal.* **a.** ruined: *now all our plans are kaput.* **b.** broken: *this record player seems to be kaput.*

karakul (ˈkærəkʰl) *n.* **1.** a sheep of central Asia the lambs of which have soft curled dark hair. **2.** the fur prepared from these lambs.

karate (kəˈrɑːtɪ) *n.* a Japanese system of unarmed combat, in which punches, chops, and kicks are made with the hands, feet, elbows, and legs.

Karitane (ˌkærɪˈtɑːnɪ) *n.* *N.Z.* a nurse for babies; nanny.

karma (ˈkɑːmə) *n.* *Hinduism, Buddhism.* the totality of a person's actions in one life seen as affecting or deciding his fate in the next.

karoo or **karroo** (kəˈruː) *n.*, *pl.* **-roos.** a dry tableland of southern Africa, with semidesert vegetation.

kart (kɑːt) *n.* same as **go-kart.**

kasbah or **casbah** (ˈkæzbɑː) *n.* the citadel of a North African city.

katydid (ˈkeɪtɪˌdɪd) *n.* a large green grasshopper of North America.

kauri (ˈkaʊrɪ) *n.* a New Zealand coniferous tree cultivated for its wood and resin.

kayak (ˈkaɪæk) *n.* **1.** a canoe-like boat used by Eskimos, consisting of a frame covered with animal skins. **2.** a fibreglass or canvas-covered canoe of similar design.

kazoo (kəˈzuː) *n.*, *pl.* **-zoos.** a simple musical instrument, consisting of a metal tube open at both ends with a membrane-covered hole in one side, which vibrates with a buzzing sound when the player hums into it.

KBE Knight Commander of the Order of the British Empire.

kbyte *Computers.* kilobyte.

kcal kilocalorie.

kea (ˈkɛə) *n.* a large parrot of New Zealand with a brownish-green plumage.

kebab (kəˈbæb) *n.* a dish consisting of small pieces of meat and vegetables, usually threaded onto skewers and grilled.

kedge (kɛdʒ) *Naut.* ~*vb.* **1.** to draw (a ship) along by hauling in on the cable of a light anchor, or (of a ship) to be drawn in this fashion. ~*n.* **2.** a light anchor used for kedging.

kedgeree (ˌkɛdʒəˈriː) *n. Chiefly Brit.* a dish consisting of rice, fish, and eggs.

keek (kiːk) *n., vb. Scot.* same as **peep**[1].

keel (kiːl) *n.* **1.** one of the main lengthways steel or timber pieces along the base of a ship, to which the frames are fastened. **2. on an even keel.** well balanced; steady.

keelhaul (ˈkiːlˌhɔːl) *vb.* **1.** to rebuke (someone) harshly. **2.** to drag (someone) under the keel of a ship as a punishment.

keel over *vb.* **1.** (of an object) to turn upside down; capsize. **2.** *Informal.* (of a person) to collapse suddenly.

keelson *or* **kelson** (ˈkɛlsən) *n.* a lengthways beam fastened to the keel of a ship for strength.

keen[1] (kiːn) *adj.* **1.** eager or enthusiastic. **2.** (foll. by *on*) fond of; devoted to: *keen on golf.* **3.** intellectually acute: *a keen wit.* **4.** (of sight, smell, or hearing) capable of recognizing fine distinctions. **5.** (of a knife or blade) having a sharp cutting edge. **6.** extremely cold and penetrating: *a keen wind.* **7.** intense or strong: *a keen desire.* **8.** *Chiefly Brit.* extremely low so as to be competitive: *keen prices.* —ˈ**keenly** *adv.* —ˈ**keenness** *n.*

keen[2] (kiːn) *vb.* **1.** to lament the dead. ~*n.* **2.** a lament for the dead.

keep (kiːp) *vb.* **keeping, kept. 1.** to have or retain possession of (something). **2.** to have temporary charge of: *keep my watch for me.* **3.** to store in a customary place: *I keep my books in the desk.* **4.** to remain or cause (someone or something) to remain in a specified state or condition: *keep quiet.* **5.** to continue or cause (someone) to continue: *keep in step.* **6.** to look after or maintain for use, pleasure, or profit: *to keep chickens.* **7.** to support (someone) financially. **8.** to detain (someone). **9.** not to give away: *to keep a secret.* **10.** (of food) to stay in good condition for a certain time: *fish doesn't keep very well.* **11.** to observe (a religious festival) with rites or ceremonies. **12.** to maintain by writing regular records in: *to keep a diary.* **13.** to stay (in, on, or at a place or position): *keep to the path.* **14.** to associate with: *to keep bad company.* **15.** *Chiefly Brit.* to have habitually in stock: *this shop keeps all kinds of wool.* **16. how are you keeping?** are you well? ~*n.* **17.** the cost of food and other everyday expense: *to pay one's keep.* **18.** the main tower within the walls of a medieval castle or fortress. **19. for keeps.** *Informal.* permanently. ~See also **keep at, keep away,** etc.

keep at *vb.* **1.** to persist in (an activity). **2.** to compel (a person) to continue doing (a task).

keep away *vb.* (often foll. by *from*) to refrain or prevent (someone) from going (somewhere).

keep back *vb.* to refuse to reveal (something).

keep down *vb.* **1.** to hold (a group of people) under control. **2.** to cause (numbers or costs) not to increase. **3.** to lie low. **4.** to cause (food) to stay in the stomach; not vomit.

keeper (ˈkiːpə) *n.* **1.** a person in charge of animals in a zoo. **2.** a person in charge of a museum, collection, or section of a museum. **3.** a person in charge of other people, such as a warder in a jail. **4.** short for **goalkeeper** or **wicketkeeper.**

keep fit *n.* exercises designed to promote physical fitness if performed regularly.

keep from *vb.* **1.** to restrain (oneself or someone else) from (doing something). **2.** to preserve or protect (someone) from (something).

keeping (ˈkiːpɪŋ) *n.* **1. in keeping with.** suitable or appropriate to or for. **2. out of keeping with.** unsuitable or inappropriate to or for.

keep off *vb.* **1.** to stay or cause (someone) to stay at a distance (from). **2.** not to eat or drink or to prevent (someone) from eating or drinking (something). **3.** to avoid or cause (someone) to avoid (a topic).

keep on *vb.* **1.** to persist in (doing something): *keep on running.* **2.** to continue to employ: *the firm kept on only ten men.* **3.** (foll. by *about*) to persist in talking about. **4.** (foll. by *at*) to nag (a person).

keep out *vb.* **1.** to remain or cause (someone) to remain outside. **2.** (foll. by *of*) **a.** to cause (someone) to remain unexposed to (an unpleasant situation). **b.** to avoid: *keep out of trouble.*

keepsake (ˈkiːpˌseɪk) *n.* a gift kept in memory of the giver.

keep to *vb.* **1.** to adhere to: *to keep to a promise.* **2.** to be confined to: *she kept to her bed when she had flu.* **3. keep oneself to oneself.** to avoid the company of others. **4. keep to oneself. a.** to avoid the company of others. **b.** to refrain from disclosing (information).

keep up *vb.* **1.** to maintain (prices, standards, or one's morale) at the present level. **2.** to maintain in good condition. **3. keep up with. a.** to maintain a pace set by (someone). **b.** to remain informed about: *to keep up with developments.* **c.** to remain in contact with (someone). **4. keep up with the Joneses.** *Informal.* to compete with one's friends or neighbours in material possessions.

keg (kɛg) *n.* a small barrel in which beer is transported and stored.

kelp (kɛlp) *n.* a large brown seaweed rich in iodine and potash.

kelpie (ˈkɛlpɪ) *n.* (in Scottish folklore) a water spirit in the form of a horse.

kelson (ˈkɛlsən) *n.* same as **keelson.**

kelt (kɛlt) *n.* a salmon that has recently spawned.

Kelt (kɛlt) *n.* same as **Celt**.

kelvin ('kɛlvɪn) *n. Physics.* the basic SI unit of thermodynamic temperature.

Kelvin scale *n. Physics.* a thermodynamic temperature scale in which the zero is absolute zero.

ken (kɛn) *n.* **1. beyond one's ken.** beyond one's range of knowledge. ~*vb.* **kenning, kenned** *or* **kent.** **2.** *Scot. & northern English dialect.* to know.

kendo ('kɛndəʊ) *n.* the Japanese art of fencing with pliable bamboo poles or, sometimes, real swords.

kennel ('kɛn²l) *n.* **1.** a hutlike shelter for a dog. **2.** (*pl.*) an establishment where dogs are bred, trained, or boarded. ~*vb.* **-nelling, -nelled** *or U.S.* **-neling, -neled. 3.** to keep (a dog) in a kennel.

kepi ('keɪpiː) *n.* a military cap with a circular top and a horizontal peak.

kept (kɛpt) *vb.* **1.** past of **keep. 2. kept woman** *or* **man.** a person financially supported by someone in return for sexual favours.

kerb *or U.S. & Canad.* **curb** (kɜːb) *n.* a line of stone or concrete forming an edge between a pavement and a roadway.

kerb crawling *n.* the act of driving slowly beside a kerb in order to entice someone into the car for sexual purposes. —**kerb crawler** *n.*

kerbstone *or U.S. & Canad.* **curbstone** ('kɜːb,stəʊn) *n.* one of a series of stones that form a kerb.

kerchief ('kɜːtʃɪf) *n.* a piece of cloth worn over the head or round the neck.

kerel ('kɛərəl) *n. S. African.* a young man.

kerfuffle (kə'fʌf³l) *n. Informal, chiefly Brit.* a commotion.

kermes ('kɜːmɪz) *n.* the dried bodies of female scale insects, used as a red dyestuff.

kernel ('kɜːn²l) *n.* **1.** the edible seed of a nut or fruit within the shell or stone. **2.** the grain of a cereal, such as wheat, consisting of the seed in a hard husk. **3.** the central or essential part of something: *the kernel of the plan.*

kerosene ('kɛrə,siːn) *n. Chiefly U.S. & Canad.* same as **paraffin** (sense 1).

kestrel ('kɛstrəl) *n.* a small falcon that feeds on small animals such as mice.

ketch (kɛtʃ) *n.* a two-masted sailing ship.

ketchup ('kɛtʃəp) *n.* a thick cold sauce containing vinegar: *tomato ketchup.*

ketone ('kiːtəʊn) *n. Chem.* any of a class of compounds with the general formula R²COR.

kettle ('kɛt²l) *n.* **1.** a metal container with a handle and spout, for boiling water. **2. a different kettle of fish.** a different matter

entirely. **3. a fine kettle of fish.** a difficult or awkward situation.

kettledrum ('kɛt²l,drʌm) *n.* a percussion instrument consisting of a hollow bowl shape covered with a skin or membrane and supported on a tripod.

key[1] (kiː) *n.* **1.** a specially shaped metal instrument, for moving the bolt of a lock so as to lock or unlock a door, suitcase, etc. **2.** an instrument that is turned to operate a valve, clock winding mechanism, etc. **3.** any of a set of levers pressed to operate a typewriter, computer, or musical keyboard instrument. **4.** a scale of musical notes that starts at one specific note. **5.** something that is crucial in providing an explanation or interpretation. **6.** (*modifier*) of great importance: *a key issue.* **7.** a means of achieving a desired end: *the key to happiness.* **8.** a list of explanations of symbols, codes, or abbreviations. **9.** pitch: *he spoke in a low key.* ~*vb.* **10.** (foll. by *to*) to harmonize with: *to key one's actions to the prevailing mood.* **11.** to adjust or fasten (something) with a key or some similar device. **12.** same as **keyboard.** ~See also **key in.**

key[2] (kiː) *n.* same as **cay**.

keyboard ('kiː,bɔːd) *n.* **1.** a set of keys on a typewriter, computer, or musical keyboard instrument. ~*vb.* **2.** to set (text) in type using a keyboard machine. —'**key,boarder** *n.*

keyed up *adj.* very excited or nervous.

key grip *n.* the person in charge of moving and setting up camera tracks and scenery in a film or television studio.

keyhole ('kiː,həʊl) *n.* an opening in a lock through which a key may be passed to engage the lock mechanism.

key in *vb.* to enter (information or instructions) into a computer by means of a keyboard.

key money *n.* a sum of money required from a new tenant of a house or flat before he moves in.

Keynesian ('keɪnzɪən) *adj.* of the economic theories of J.M. Keynes, who argued that governments should fund public works to maintain full employment, accepting if necessary the consequence of inflation.

keynote ('kiː,nəʊt) *n.* **1. a.** a central or determining idea in a speech or literary work. **b.** (*as modifier*): *a keynote speech.* **2.** the note upon which a scale or key is based.

keypad ('kiː,pæd) *n.* a small panel with a set of buttons for operating a teletext system, electronic calculator, etc.

keyring ('kiː,rɪŋ) *n.* a metal ring, often decorative, for keeping keys on.

key signature *n. Music.* a group of sharps or flats at the beginning of each stave line to indicate the key.

keystone (ˈkiːˌstəʊn) *n.* **1.** the central stone at the top of an arch. **2.** something that is necessary to connect other related things.

kg kilogram(s).

KG (in Britain) Knight of the Order of the Garter.

KGB the Soviet secret police.

khaki (ˈkɑːkɪ) *adj.* **1.** dull yellowish-brown. ~*n.* **2.** a hard-wearing fabric of this colour, used for military uniforms.

khan (kɑːn) *n.* a title of respect in Afghanistan and central Asia.

kHz kilohertz.

kia ora (ˌkiːə ˈɔːrə) *interj.* N.Z. good luck!

kibbutz (kɪˈbʊts) *n., pl.* **kibbutzim** (ˌkɪbʊtˈsiːm). a farm, factory, or other workplace in Israel, owned and administered communally by its members.

kibosh (ˈkaɪˌbɒʃ) *n.* **put the kibosh on.** *Slang.* to put a stop to.

kick (kɪk) *vb.* **1.** to drive, push, or hit with the foot or feet. **2.** to strike out with the feet, as in swimming. **3.** to raise a leg high, as in dancing. **4.** (of a firearm) to recoil when fired. **5.** *Soccer.* to score (a goal) by a kick. **6.** *Informal.* to object or resist: *she's for ever kicking against the system.* **7.** *Informal.* to be active and in good health: *alive and kicking.* **8.** *Informal.* to free oneself of (an addiction): *to kick the heroin habit.* **9. kick someone upstairs.** to promote someone to a higher but effectively powerless position. ~*n.* **10.** a thrust or blow with the foot. **11.** any of certain rhythmic leg movements used in swimming. **12.** the recoil of a firearm. **13.** *Informal.* an exciting effect: *we get a kick out of going to the races; she only does it for kicks.* **14.** *Informal.* power or force. **15. kick in the teeth.** *Slang.* a humiliating rebuff. ~See also **kick about, kick off,** etc.

kick about *or* **around** *vb. Informal.* **1.** to treat (someone) harshly. **2.** to discuss (ideas) informally. **3.** to wander aimlessly. **4.** to lie neglected or forgotten: *there's a copy of that book kicking about somewhere.*

kickback (ˈkɪkˌbæk) *n.* **1.** a strong reaction. **2.** part of an income paid to a person in return for an opportunity to make a profit, often by some illegal arrangement.

kick off *vb.* **1.** to start play in a game of football by kicking the ball from the centre of the field. **2.** *Informal.* to commence (a discussion, event, etc.). ~*n.* **kickoff. 3. a.** the kick that officially starts a game of football. **b.** the time when the first kick is due to take place. **4.** *Informal.* the time when an event is due to begin.

kick out *vb. Informal.* to dismiss (someone) or throw (someone) out forcefully.

kickstand (ˈkɪkˌstænd) *n.* a short metal bar on a motorcycle, which when kicked into a vertical position holds the cycle upright when stationary.

kick-start *n. also* **kick-starter. 1.** a pedal on a motorcycle that is kicked downwards to start the engine. ~*vb.* **2.** to start (a motorcycle) in this way.

kick up *vb. Informal.* to cause (trouble).

kid[1] (kɪd) *n.* **1.** a young goat. **2.** soft smooth leather made from the hide of a kid. **3.** *Informal.* **a.** a young person; child. **b.** (*modifier*) younger: *my kid brother.* ~*vb.* **kidding, kidded. 4.** (of a goat) to give birth to (young).

kid[2] (kɪd) *vb.* **kidding, kidded.** *Informal.* **1.** to tease or deceive (someone) for fun. **2.** to fool (oneself) into believing something: *don't kid yourself that no-one else knows.* —ˈkidder *n.*

kiddie (ˈkɪdɪ) *n. Informal.* a child.

kid gloves *pl. n.* **handle someone with kid gloves.** to treat someone with great tact.

kidnap (ˈkɪdnæp) *vb.* **-napping, -napped** *or U.S.* **-naping, -naped.** to capture and hold (a person), usually for ransom. —ˈkidnapper *or U.S.* **-naper** *n.*

kidney (ˈkɪdnɪ) *n.* **1.** either of two bean-shaped organs at the back of the abdominal cavity. They filter waste products from the blood, which are excreted as urine. **2.** the kidneys of certain animals used as food.

kidney bean *n.* a reddish-brown kidney-shaped bean, eaten as a vegetable.

kidney machine *n.* a machine carrying out the functions of damaged human kidneys.

kidology (kɪˈdɒlədʒɪ) *n. Brit. informal.* the practice of bluffing or deception in order to gain a psychological advantage over someone.

kill (kɪl) *vb.* **1.** to cause the death of (a person or animal). **2.** to put an end to: *to kill someone's interest.* **3.** to make (time) pass quickly while waiting for something. **4.** *Informal.* to cause (someone) pain or discomfort: *my shoes are killing me.* **5.** *Informal.* to quash or veto: *the bill was killed in the House of Lords.* **6.** *Informal.* to overcome (someone) with attraction, laughter, or surprise: *she was dressed to kill.* **7. kill oneself.** *Informal.* to overexert oneself. **8. kill two birds with one stone.** to achieve two results with one action. ~*n.* **9.** the act of causing death at the end of a hunt or bullfight. **10.** the animal or animals killed during a hunt. **11. in at the kill.** present when something comes to a dramatic end with unpleasant results for someone else. —ˈkiller *n.*

killer whale *n.* a ferocious black-and-white toothed whale, most common in cold seas.

killing (ˈkɪlɪŋ) *Informal.* ~*adj.* **1.** very tiring: *a killing pace.* **2.** extremely funny. **3.** causing death; fatal. ~*n.* **4.** the act of causing death; slaying. **5. make a killing.** to make a sudden financial gain.

killjoy ('kıl,dʒɔı) n. a person who spoils other people's pleasure.

kiln (kıln) n. a large oven for burning, drying, or processing something, such as porcelain or bricks.

kilo ('ki:ləʊ) n., pl. **kilos.** short for **kilogram** or **kilometre.**

kilo- prefix. **1.** denoting 10³ (1000): kilometre. **2.** (in computers) denoting 2¹⁰ (1024): kilobyte. In computer usage, kilo- is restricted to sizes of storage (e.g. kilobit) when it means 1024; in other computer contexts it retains its usual meaning of 1000.

kilobyte ('kılə,baıt) n. Computers. 1024 bytes.

kilocalorie ('kılə,kælərı) n. same as **Calorie.**

kilocycle ('kılə,saık³l) n. an old word for kilohertz.

kilogram or **kilogramme** ('kılə,græm) n. **1.** one thousand grams. **2.** the basic SI unit of mass.

kilohertz ('kılə,hɜːts) n. one thousand hertz; one thousand cycles per second.

kilojoule ('kılə,dʒuːl) n. one thousand joules.

kilolitre or U.S. **kiloliter** ('kılə,liːtə) n. one thousand litres.

kilometre or U.S. **kilometer** ('kılə,miːtə, kı'lɒmıtə) n. one thousand metres.

kiloton ('kılə,tʌn) n. **1.** one thousand tons. **2.** an explosive power equal to the power of 1000 tons of TNT.

kilovolt ('kılə,vəʊlt) n. one thousand volts.

kilowatt ('kılə,wɒt) n. one thousand watts.

kilowatt-hour n. a unit of energy equal to the work done by a power of 1000 watts in one hour.

kilt (kılt) n. **1.** a knee-length pleated tartan skirt, worn by men in Highland dress and by women and girls. ~vb. **2.** to put pleats in (cloth). —'**kilted** adj.

kimono (kı'məʊnəʊ) n., pl. **-nos.** a loose sashed ankle-length garment with wide sleeves, worn in Japan.

kin (kın) n. **1.** a person's relatives collectively. **2.** See **next of kin.**

kind¹ (kaınd) adj. **1.** considerate, friendly, and helpful: a kind neighbour; a kind thought. **2.** cordial; courteous: kind regards.

kind² (kaınd) n. **1.** a class or group having characteristics in common: two of a kind. **2.** essential nature or character: the difference is one of kind rather than degree. **3. in kind. a.** (of payment) in goods or services rather than in money. **b.** with something of the same sort: to return an insult in kind. **4. kind of.** to a certain extent; loosely: kind of hard; a kind of socialist. **5. of a**

kind. of poorer quality or standard than is wanted or expected.

Usage. It is wise to try to avoid a mixture of plural and singular constructions with kind and sort, as in those kinds (not kind) of buildings seem badly designed or these sorts (not sort) of distinctions are becoming blurred.

kindergarten ('kındə,gɑːt³n) n. a school for young children, usually between the ages of 4 and 6.

kind-hearted adj. kindly; readily sympathetic.

kindle ('kınd³l) vb. **1.** to set (a fire) alight or (of a fire) to start to burn. **2.** to arouse or be aroused: the project kindled his interest.

kindling ('kındlıŋ) n. material for starting a fire, such as dry wood or straw.

kindly ('kaındlı) adj. **-lier, -liest. 1.** having a warm-hearted nature. **2.** pleasant: a kindly climate. ~adv. **3.** in a considerate or humane way. **4.** please: will you kindly behave yourself! **5. not take kindly to.** to react unfavourably towards. —'**kindliness** n.

kindness ('kaındnıs) n. **1.** the quality of being kind. **2.** a kind or helpful act.

kindred ('kındrıd) adj. **1.** having similar qualities. **2.** related by blood or marriage. **3. kindred spirit.** a person with whom one has something in common. ~n. **4.** relationship by blood or marriage. **5.** similarity in character. **6.** a person's relatives collectively.

kine (kaın) pl. n. Archaic. cows or cattle.

kinematics (,kını'mætıks) n. (functioning as sing.) Physics. the study of the motion of bodies without reference to mass or force. —,**kine'matic** adj.

kinetic (kı'nɛtık) adj. relating to or caused by motion. —**ki'netically** adv.

kinetic art n. art, such as sculpture, that moves or has moving parts.

kinetic energy n. Physics. the energy of motion of a body equal to the work it would do if it were brought to rest.

kinetics (kı'nɛtıks) n. (functioning as sing.) Physics. the branch of mechanics concerned with the study of bodies in motion.

king (kıŋ) n. **1.** a male ruler of a monarchy. **2.** a ruler or chief: king of the fairies. **3.** a person, animal, or thing considered as the best or most important of its kind: king of the jungle. **4.** a playing card with a picture of a king on it. **5.** the most important chess piece. **6.** Draughts. a piece which has moved entirely across the board and been crowned and which may therefore move backwards as well as forwards. —'**kingship** n.

King Charles spaniel (tʃɑːlz) n. a small spaniel with a black-and-tan coat.

kingcup (ˈkɪŋˌkʌp) n. Brit. a yellow-flowered plant; marsh marigold.

kingdom (ˈkɪŋdəm) n. 1. a territory or state ruled by a king or queen. 2. any of the three groups into which natural objects may be divided: the animal, plant, and mineral kingdoms. 3. an area of activity: the kingdom of the mind.

kingfisher (ˈkɪŋˌfɪʃə) n. a fish-eating bird with a greenish-blue and orange plumage.

kingklip (ˈkɪŋˌklɪp) n. an edible eel-like marine fish of S. Africa.

king-of-arms n., pl. **kings-of-arms.** a person holding the highest rank of heraldic office.

kingpin (ˈkɪŋˌpɪn) n. 1. the most important person in an organization. 2. a pivot pin that provides a steering joint in a motor vehicle.

king-size or **king-sized** adj. larger than a standard size.

kink (kɪŋk) n. 1. a twist or bend in something such as a rope or hair. 2. a flaw or quirk in someone's personality.

kinky (ˈkɪŋkɪ) adj. **kinkier, kinkiest. 1.** Slang. given to unusual or deviant sexual practices. 2. tightly looped or curled.

kinsfolk (ˈkɪnzˌfəʊk) pl. n. one's family or relatives.

kinship (ˈkɪnʃɪp) n. 1. blood relationship. 2. the state of having common characteristics.

kinsman (ˈkɪnzmən) n., pl. **-men.** a relation by blood or marriage. —ˈkinsˌwoman fem. n.

kiosk (ˈkiːɒsk) n. 1. a small booth from which cigarettes, newspapers, and sweets are sold. 2. Chiefly Brit. a telephone box.

kip (kɪp) Brit. slang. ~n. 1. sleep: to get some kip. 2. a bed. ~vb. **kipping, kipped. 3.** to sleep or take a nap. 4. **kip down.** to sleep in a makeshift bed.

kipper (ˈkɪpə) n. 1. a herring that has been cleaned, salted, and smoked. ~vb. 2. to cure (a herring) by salting and smoking it.

kirk (kɜːk) n. Scot. a church.

Kirsch (kɪəʃ) or **Kirschwasser** (ˈkɪəʃˌvɑːsə) n. a brandy distilled from black cherries.

kismet (ˈkɪzmɛt, ˈkɪs-) n. fate or destiny.

kiss (kɪs) vb. 1. to touch with the lips as an expression of love, greeting or respect. 2. to join lips with another person as an act of love or desire. 3. to touch lightly: the sunlight kissed her cheek. ~n. 4. a caress with the lips. 5. a light touch. —ˈkissable adj.

kissagram (ˈkɪsəˌgræm) n. a greetings service in which a person is employed to present greetings by kissing the person celebrating.

kiss curl n. Brit. a circular curl of hair pressed flat against the cheek or forehead.

kisser (ˈkɪsə) n. Slang. the mouth or face.

kiss of life n. **the.** mouth-to-mouth resuscitation in which a person blows gently into the mouth of an unconscious person.

kit[1] (kɪt) n. 1. a set of tools or supplies for use together or for a purpose: a first-aid kit. 2. the container for such a set. 3. a set of parts sold ready to be assembled: a model aeroplane kit. 4. clothing and other personal effects, such as those of a soldier: a safari kit. ~See also **kit out.**

kit[2] (kɪt) n. N.Z. a shopping bag made of string.

kitbag (ˈkɪtˌbæg) n. a canvas or other bag for a serviceman's kit.

kitchen (ˈkɪtʃɪn) n. a room equipped for preparing and cooking food.

kitchenette (ˌkɪtʃɪˈnɛt) n. a small kitchen or part of a room equipped for use as a kitchen.

kitchen garden n. a garden where vegetables and sometimes also fruit are grown.

kitchen tea n. Austral. & N.Z. a party held before a wedding to which guests bring kitchen equipment as presents.

kite (kaɪt) n. 1. a light frame covered with a thin material flown in the wind at the end of a length of string. 2. a bird of prey with a long forked tail and large wings.

Kite mark n. Brit. the official mark in the form of a kite on articles approved by the British Standards Institution.

kith (kɪθ) n. **kith and kin.** one's friends and relations.

kit out or **up** vb. **kitting, kitted.** Chiefly Brit. to provide (someone or something) with clothes, furniture, or equipment.

kitsch (kɪtʃ) n. tawdry, vulgarized, or pretentious art or literature, usually with popular appeal. —ˈkitschy adj.

kitten (ˈkɪtⁿn) n. 1. a young cat. 2. **have kittens.** Brit. informal. to react with disapproval or anxiety: she had kittens when she got the bill.

kittenish (ˈkɪtⁿnɪʃ) adj. lively and coyly flirtatious.

kittiwake (ˈkɪtɪˌweɪk) n. an oceanic gull with pale grey black-tipped wings and a square-cut tail.

kitty[1] (ˈkɪtɪ) n., pl. **-ties.** a diminutive or affectionate name for a **kitten** or **cat.**

kitty[2] (ˈkɪtɪ) n., pl. **-ties. 1.** the pool in certain gambling games. 2. any shared fund of money.

kiwi (ˈkiːwiː) n., pl. **kiwis. 1.** a nocturnal flightless bird of New Zealand having a long beak, stout legs, and no tail. 2. Informal except in N.Z. a New Zealander. 3. N.Z. informal. a lottery.

kiwi fruit n. an edible fruit with a fuzzy brown skin and green flesh.

kJ kilojoule.

klaxon (ˈklæksⁿn) n. a type of loud horn

used on fire engines and ambulances as a warning signal.

kleptomania (ˌklɛptəʊˈmeɪnɪə) n. Psychol. a strong impulse to steal. —ˌklepto-ˈmaniˌac n.

klipspringer (ˈklɪpˌsprɪŋə) n. a small agile antelope inhabiting rocky regions of Africa south of the Sahara.

km kilometre.

knack (næk) n. 1. a skilful way of doing something. 2. an innate talent or aptitude.

knacker (ˈnækə) Brit. ~n. 1. a person who buys up old horses for slaughter. ~vb. 2. Slang. to tire: she was knackered after the climb.

knapsack (ˈnæpˌsæk) n. a canvas or leather bag carried strapped on the back or shoulder.

knapweed (ˈnæpˌwiːd) n. any of several plants with purplish thistle-like flowers.

knave (neɪv) n. 1. Archaic. a dishonest man. 2. Cards. the jack. —ˈknavish adj.

knavery (ˈneɪvərɪ) n., pl. -eries. dishonest conduct; trickery.

knead (niːd) vb. 1. to work and press (a soft substance, such as dough) into a smooth mixture with the hands. 2. to squeeze or press with the hands. —ˈkneader n.

knee (niː) n. 1. the joint of the leg between the thigh and the lower leg. 2. the area around this joint. 3. the upper surface of a sitting person's thigh: the child sat on her mother's knee. 4. the part of a garment that covers the knee. 5. **bring someone to his knees.** to force someone into submission. ~vb. **kneeing, kneed.** 6. to strike, nudge, or push with the knee.

kneecap (ˈniːˌkæp) n. 1. Anat. a small flat triangular bone in front of and protecting the knee. ~vb. **-capping, -capped.** 2. (of terrorists) to shoot (a person) in the kneecap.

knee-deep adj. 1. so deep as to reach or cover the knees. 2. a. sunk to the knees: knee-deep in sand. b. deeply involved: knee-deep in work.

knee-high adj. as high as the knee.

knee-jerk n. 1. Physiol. a sudden involuntary kick of the lower leg caused by a sharp tap on the tendon just below the kneecap. ~modifier. **kneejerk.** 2. made or occurring as a predictable and automatic response: a kneejerk reaction.

kneel (niːl) vb. **kneeling, knelt** or **kneeled.** 1. to rest, fall, or support oneself on one's knees. ~n. 2. the act or position of kneeling. —ˈkneeler n.

knell (nɛl) n. 1. the sound of a bell rung to announce a death or a funeral. 2. something that indicates death or destruction. ~vb. 3. to ring a knell. 4. to proclaim by a tolling bell.

knelt (nɛlt) vb. past of **kneel.**

knew (njuː) vb. the past tense of **know.**

knickerbockers (ˈnɪkəˌbɒkəz) pl. n. baggy breeches fastened with a band at the knee or above the ankle.

knickers (ˈnɪkəz) pl. n. a woman's or girl's undergarment covering the lower trunk and having separate legs or leg-holes.

knick-knack (ˈnɪkˌnæk) n. a small ornament or trinket.

knife (naɪf) n., pl. **knives** (naɪvz). 1. a cutting instrument or weapon consisting of a sharp-edged blade of metal fitted into a handle. ~vb. 2. to stab or kill with a knife. —ˈknifeˌlike adj.

knife edge n. 1. the sharp cutting edge of a knife. 2. a critical point in the development of a situation.

knight (naɪt) n. 1. a man who has been given a knighthood in recognition of his achievements. 2. (in medieval Europe) a person who served his lord as a mounted and heavily armed soldier. 3. a chess piece, usually shaped like a horse's head. 4. a champion of a lady or of a cause or principle. ~vb. 5. to make (a man) a knight.

knight errant n., pl. **knights errant.** (esp. in medieval romance) a knight who wanders in search of deeds of courage, chivalry, etc. —**knight errantry** n.

knighthood (ˈnaɪthʊd) n. an honorary title given to a man by the British sovereign in recognition of his achievements.

knightly (ˈnaɪtlɪ) adj. of, resembling, or befitting a knight. —ˈknightliness n.

knit (nɪt) vb. **knitting, knitted** or **knit.** 1. to make (a garment) by looping (wool) using long eyeless needles or a knitting machine. 2. to join together closely. 3. to draw (the brows) together or (of the brows) to come together, as in frowning or concentrating. ~n. 4. a fabric made by knitting. —ˈknitter n.

knitting (ˈnɪtɪŋ) n. knitted work or the process of producing it.

knitwear (ˈnɪtˌwɛə) n. sweaters or other knitted clothes.

knives (naɪvz) n. the plural of **knife.**

knob (nɒb) n. 1. a rounded projection from a surface, such as a rotating switch on a radio. 2. a rounded handle of a door or drawer. 3. a small amount of butter or lard. —ˈknobbly adj. —ˈknobˌlike adj.

knock (nɒk) vb. 1. to give a blow or push to. 2. to rap sharply with the knuckles: to knock at the door. 3. to make by striking: to knock a hole in the wall. 4. to collide (with). 5. to bring into a certain condition by hitting: to knock someone unconscious. 6. Informal. to criticize adversely. 7. to emit a regular banging sound as a result of a fault: the engine was knocking badly. 8. **knock on the head.** to prevent the further development of (a plan). ~n. 9. a. a blow, push, or rap: he gave the table a knock. b.

the sound so caused. **10.** the sound of knocking in an engine or bearing. **11.** *Informal.* a misfortune, rebuff, or setback. **12.** *Informal.* criticism. ~See also **knock about, knock back,** etc.

knock about *or* **around** *vb.* **1.** to wander or travel about: *he's knocked about the world.* **2.** (foll. by *with*) to associate. **3.** to treat brutally: *he knocks his wife about.* **4.** to consider or discuss informally. ~*adj.* **knockabout.** **5.** boisterous: *knockabout farce.*

knock back *vb. Informal.* **1.** to drink quickly. **2.** to cost: *how much did the meal knock you back?* **3.** to reject or refuse: *you can't knock back such an offer.* ~*n.* **knockback.** **4.** *Slang.* a refusal or rejection.

knock down *vb.* **1.** to strike to the ground with a blow, as in boxing. **2.** (in auctions) to declare an article sold. **3.** to demolish. **4.** *Informal.* to reduce (a price). ~*adj.* **knockdown.** **5.** powerful: *a knockdown argument.* **6.** *Chiefly Brit.* cheap: *a knockdown price.* **7.** easily dismantled: *knockdown furniture.*

knocker ('nɒkə) *n.* **1.** a metal object attached to a door by a hinge and used for knocking. **2.** (*usually pl.*) *Slang.* a female breast.

knock-knees *pl. n.* legs that are bent inwards at the knees. —,knock'kneed *adj.*

knock off *vb.* **1.** *Informal.* to finish work: *we knocked off an hour early.* **2.** *Informal.* to make or do hastily or easily: *to knock off a novel in a week.* **3.** *Informal.* to take (an amount) off the price of (an article): *I'll knock off 10% if you pay cash.* **4.** *Slang.* to kill. **5.** *Slang.* to stop doing something, used as a command: *knock it off!*

knock-on *Rugby.* ~*n.* **1.** the infringement of playing the ball forward with the hand or arm. ~*vb.* **knock on.** **2.** to play (the ball) forward with the hand or arm.

knock-on effect *n.* the indirect result of an action or decision.

knockout ('nɒk,aʊt) *n.* **1.** the act of rendering someone unconscious. **2.** *Boxing.* a blow that renders an opponent unable to continue after the referee has counted to ten. **3.** a competition in which competitors are eliminated progressively. **4.** *Informal.* a person or thing that is very impressive or attractive: *she's a knockout.* ~*vb.* **knock out.** **5.** to render (someone) unconscious. **6.** *Boxing.* to defeat (an opponent) by a knockout. **7.** to destroy: *the radars were completely knocked out.* **8.** to eliminate from a knockout competition. **9.** *Informal.* to amaze: *I was knocked out by that new song.*

knock up *vb.* **1.** Also: **knock together.** *Informal.* to assemble quickly: *to knock up a set of shelves.* **2.** *Brit. informal.* to waken: *to knock someone up early.* **3.** *Slang.* to make pregnant. **4.** to practise before a

game of tennis, squash, or badminton. ~*n.* **knock-up.** **5.** a practice session at tennis, squash, or badminton.

knoll (nəʊl) *n.* a small rounded hill.

knot (nɒt) *n.* **1.** a fastening formed by looping and tying pieces of rope, cord, or string. **2.** a tangle, as in hair. **3.** a decorative bow, as of ribbon. **4.** a small cluster or huddled group. **5.** a bond: *the marriage knot.* **6. a.** a hard mass of wood where a branch joins the trunk of a tree. **b.** a cross section of this visible in timber. **7.** a sensation of constriction, caused by tension or nervousness: *his stomach was tying itself in knots.* **8.** a unit of speed used by ships and aircraft, equal to one nautical mile per hour. **9. at a rate of knots.** very fast. **10. tie someone in knots.** to completely perplex someone. ~*vb.* **knotting, knotted.** **11.** to tie or fasten in a knot. **12.** to form into a knot. **13.** to entangle or become entangled. —'**knotted** *adj.* —'**knotless** *adj.*

knothole ('nɒt,həʊl) *n.* a hole in a piece of wood where a knot has been.

knotty ('nɒtɪ) *adj.* **-tier, -tiest.** **1.** full of knots. **2.** extremely difficult or intricate: *a knotty problem.*

know (nəʊ) *vb.* **knowing, knew, known.** **1.** to be or feel certain of the truth or accuracy of (a fact, answer, or piece of information). **2.** to be acquainted with: *she's known him five years.* **3.** to have a grasp of: *he knows French.* **4.** to understand or be aware of (something, or how to do or be something): *I know how to repair that.* **5.** to experience: *to know poverty.* **6.** to be intelligent, informed, or sensible enough (to do something): *she knew not to go home yet.* **7.** to be able to distinguish: *to know right from wrong.* **8. know what's what.** to know how one thing or things in general work. **9. you never know.** things are uncertain. ~*n.* **10. in the know.** *Informal.* aware or informed. —'**knowable** *adj.*

know-all *n. Informal, disparaging.* a person who pretends or appears to know a lot more than other people.

know-how *n. Informal.* ingenuity, aptitude, or skill.

knowing ('nəʊɪŋ) *adj.* **1.** suggesting secret knowledge: *she gave him a knowing glance.* **2.** wise, shrewd, or clever. **3.** deliberate. —'**knowingly** *adv.* —'**knowingness** *n.*

knowledge ('nɒlɪdʒ) *n.* **1.** the facts or experiences known by a person or group of people. **2.** the state of knowing. **3.** specific information about a subject. **4. to my knowledge.** as I understand it.

knowledgeable *or* **knowledgable** ('nɒlɪdʒəb°l) *adj.* possessing or showing much knowledge; well-informed. —'**knowledgeably** *or* '**knowledgably** *adv.*

known (nəʊn) *vb.* **1.** the past participle of

know. ~*adj.* **2.** identified: *a known criminal.*

knuckle (ˈnʌkʰl) *n.* **1.** a joint of a finger. **2.** the knee joint of a calf or pig. **3. near the knuckle.** *Informal.* approaching indecency. ~See also **knuckle down, knuckle under.**

knuckle down *vb. Informal.* to apply oneself diligently: *to knuckle down to some work.*

knuckle-duster *n.* (*often pl.*) a metal bar or set of linked rings fitted over the knuckles for inflicting injury by a blow with the fist.

knuckle under *vb.* to give way under pressure or authority; yield.

knurl (nɜːl) *n.* a small ridge, often one of a series.

KO *or* **k.o.** (ˈkeɪˈəʊ) *vb.* **KO'ing, KO'd; k.o.'ing, k.o.'d.** **1.** to knock out. ~*n., pl.* **KO's** *or* **k.o.'s.** a knockout.

koala *or* **koala bear** (kəʊˈɑːlə) *n.* a slow-moving Australian tree-dwelling marsupial with dense greyish fur.

kohl (kəʊl) *n.* a cosmetic powder used to darken the area around the eyes.

kohlrabi (kəʊlˈrɑːbɪ) *n., pl.* **-bies.** a type of cabbage whose thickened stem is eaten as a vegetable.

kokanee (kəʊˈkænɪ) *n.* a freshwater salmon of lakes and rivers in W North America.

kola (ˈkəʊlə) *n.* same as **cola.**

kolkhoz (kɒlˈhɔːz) *n.* a Russian collective farm.

komatik (ˈkəʊmætɪk) *n. Canad.* a sledge with wooden runners and crossbars bound with rawhide.

kook (kuːk) *n. U.S. & Canad. informal.* an eccentric or foolish person. —ˈ**kooky** *or* ˈ**kookie** *adj.*

kookaburra (ˈkʊkəˌbʌrə) *n.* a large Australian kingfisher with a cackling cry.

kopeck (ˈkəʊpɛk) *n.* a Soviet monetary unit worth one hundredth of a rouble.

Koran (kɔːˈrɑːn) *n.* the sacred book of Islam, believed by Muslims to be the infallible word of God dictated to Mohammed. —**Ko'ranic** *adj.*

Korean (kəˈriːən) *adj.* **1.** of Korea in SE Asia, its people, or their language. ~*n.* **2.** a person from Korea. **3.** the official language of North and South Korea.

kosher (ˈkəʊʃə) *adj.* **1.** *Judaism.* conforming to religious law: esp. (of food) prepared in accordance with the dietary laws. **2.** *Informal.* legitimate, genuine, or proper. ~*n.* **3.** kosher food.

kowhai (ˈkəʊwaɪ) *n.* a small tree of New Zealand and Chile with clusters of yellow flowers.

kowtow (ˌkaʊˈtaʊ) *vb.* **1.** to touch the forehead to the ground in deference. **2.** to be servile (towards). ~*n.* **3.** the act of kowtowing.

kph kilometres per hour.

Kr *Chem.* krypton.

kraal (krɑːl) *n.* **1.** a Southern African hut village surrounded by a stockade. **2.** *S. African.* an enclosure for livestock.

krans (krɑːns) *n. S. African.* a sheer rock face.

kremlin (ˈkrɛmlɪn) *n.* the citadel of any Russian city.

Kremlin (ˈkrɛmlɪn) *n.* the central government of the Soviet Union.

krill (krɪl) *n., pl.* **krill.** a small shrimplike crustacean.

krona (ˈkrəʊnə) *n., pl.* **-nor** (-nə). the standard monetary unit of Sweden.

krone (ˈkrəʊnə) *n., pl.* **-ner** (-nə). the standard monetary unit of Denmark or Norway.

krugerrand (ˈkruːgəˌrænd) *n.* a one-ounce gold coin minted in South Africa.

krypton (ˈkrɪptɒn) *n.* an inert gaseous element occurring in trace amounts in air and used in fluorescent lights and lasers. Symbol: Kr

KS Kansas.

Kt Knight.

kudos (ˈkjuːdɒs) *n.* (*functioning as sing.*) acclaim, glory, or prestige.

kudu *or* **koodoo** (ˈkuːduː) *n.* either of two spiral-horned African antelopes.

Ku Klux Klan (ˌkuː klʌks ˈklæn) *n.* a secret organization of White Protestant Americans who use violence against Blacks and Jews. —**Ku Klux Klanner** (ˈklænə) *n.*

kukri (ˈkʊkrɪ) *n.* a heavy curved knife used by Gurkhas.

kulak (ˈkuːlæk) *n.* a property-owning Russian peasant.

kumera *or* **kumara** (ˈkuːmərə) *n. N.Z.* the sweet potato.

kümmel (ˈkʊməl) *n.* a German liqueur flavoured with aniseed and cumin.

kumquat (ˈkʌmkwɒt) *n.* a citrus fruit resembling a very small orange.

kung fu (ˈkʌŋ ˈfuː) *n.* a Chinese martial art combining principles of karate and judo.

kuri (ˈkuːrɪ) *n. N.Z.* a mongrel dog.

kW kilowatt.

kwashiorkor (ˌkwæʃɪˈɔːkə) *n.* severe malnutrition of young children, caused by not eating enough protein.

kWh kilowatt-hour.

KWIC (kwɪk) keyword in context.

KWOC (kwɒk) keyword out of context.

KY *or* **Ky.** Kentucky.

kyle (kaɪl) *n. Scot.* a narrow strait or channel: *Kyle of Lochalsh.*

L

l *or* **L** (εl) *n., pl.* **l's, L's,** *or* **Ls.** **1.** the 12th letter of the English alphabet. **2.** something shaped like an L.
l litre.
L **1.** large. **2.** Latin. **3.** learner driver. **4.** Usually written: £ pound. **5.** the Roman numeral for 50.
L. *or* **l.** **1.** lake. **2.** left. **3.** length. **4.** (*pl.* **LL.** *or* **ll.**) line.
la (lɑː) *n. Music.* same as **lah.**
La *Chem.* lanthanum.
LA **1.** Los Angeles. **2.** Also: **La.** Louisiana.
laager (ˈlɑːɡə) *n.* (in Africa) a camp defended by a circular formation of wagons.
lab (læb) *n. Informal.* short for **laboratory.**
Lab. *Politics.* Labour.
label (ˈleɪbəl) *n.* **1.** a piece of card or other material attached to an object to show its contents, ownership, use, or destination. **2.** a brief descriptive term given to a person, group, or school of thought: *the label "Romantic" is applied to many kinds of poetry.* ~*vb.* **-belling, -belled** *or U.S.* **-beling, -beled.** **3.** to fasten a label to. **4.** to describe or classify in a word or phrase.
labial (ˈleɪbɪəl) *adj.* **1.** of or near the lips. **2.** *Phonetics.* relating to a speech sound made using the lips. ~*n.* **3.** *Phonetics.* a speech sound such as English *p* or *m,* that involves the lips.
labiate (ˈleɪbɪˌeɪt, -ɪt) *n.* **1.** any of a family of plants with square stems, aromatic leaves, and a two-lipped flower, such as mint or thyme. ~*adj.* **2.** of this family.
labium (ˈleɪbɪəm) *n., pl.* **-bia** (-bɪə). **1.** a lip or liplike structure. **2.** any one of the four lip-shaped folds of the vulva.
laboratory (ləˈbɒrətrɪ; *U.S.* ˈlæbrəˌtɔːrɪ) *n., pl.* **-ries.** a building or room equipped for conducting scientific research or for teaching practical science.
laborious (ləˈbɔːrɪəs) *adj.* involving great exertion or long effort. —**laˈboriously** *adv.*
labour *or U.S.* **labor** (ˈleɪbə) *n.* **1.** productive work, esp. physical toil done for wages. **2.** the people involved in this, as opposed to management. **3.** difficult work or a difficult job. **4.** the final stage of pregnancy, leading to childbirth. ~*vb.* **5.** to perform labour; work. **6.** to strive or work hard (for something). **7.** (usually foll. by *under*) to be burdened (by) or be at a disadvantage (because of): *to labour under a misapprehension.* **8.** to make one's way with difficulty. **9.** to deal with too persistently: *to labour a point.*

Labour Day *n.* a public holiday in honour of labour, held in Britain on May 1.
laboured *or U.S.* **labored** (ˈleɪbəd) *adj.* showing effort.
labourer *or U.S.* **laborer** (ˈleɪbərə) *n.* a person engaged in physical work.
labour exchange *n. Brit.* an old name for employment office.
Labour Party *n.* **1.** the major left-wing political party in Britain, which believes in democratic socialism and social equality. **2.** any similar party in various other countries.
Labrador *or* **Labrador retriever** (ˈlæbrəˌdɔː) *n.* a powerfully-built breed of dog with a short dense black or golden coat.
laburnum (ləˈbɜːnəm) *n.* a small ornamental tree that has clusters of yellow drooping flowers. It is highly poisonous.
labyrinth (ˈlæbərɪnθ) *n.* **1.** a mazelike network of tunnels or paths, either natural or man-made. **2.** any complex or confusing system. **3.** the interconnecting cavities of the internal ear. —ˌlabyˈrinthine *adj.*
lac (læk) *n.* a resinous substance secreted by certain insects (**lac insects**), used in the manufacture of shellac.
lace (leɪs) *n.* **1.** a delicate decorative fabric made from threads woven in an open web of patterns. **2.** a cord or string drawn through eyelets to fasten a shoe or garment. ~*vb.* **3.** to fasten (shoes) with a lace. **4.** to draw (a cord or thread) through holes as when tying shoes. **5.** to add a dash of spirits to (a beverage). **6.** to intertwine; interlace.
lacerate (ˈlæsəˌreɪt) *vb.* **1.** to tear (the flesh) jaggedly. **2.** to hurt (the feelings). —ˌlacerˈation *n.*
lace up *vb.* **1.** to fasten (clothes or footwear) with laces. ~*adj.* **lace-up.** **2.** (of footwear) to be fastened with laces. ~*n.* **lace-up.** **3.** a lace-up shoe or boot.
lachrymal (ˈlækrɪməl) *adj.* same as **lacrimal.**
lachrymose (ˈlækrɪˌməʊs) *adj.* **1.** given to weeping; tearful. **2.** mournful; sad.
lacing (ˈleɪsɪŋ) *n. Informal.* a severe beating.
lack (læk) *n.* **1.** an insufficiency, shortage, or absence of something required or desired: *lack of privacy.* ~*vb.* **2.** (often foll. by *in* or *for*) to be deficient (in) or have need (of): *lacking in taste.*
lackadaisical (ˌlækəˈdeɪzɪkəl) *adj.* **1.** lacking vitality and purpose. **2.** lazy, esp. in a dreamy way.

lackey (ˈlækı) *n.* **1.** a servile follower; hanger-on. **2.** a liveried male servant or valet.

lacklustre *or U.S.* **lackluster** (ˈlæk,lʌstə) *adj.* lacking force, brilliance, or vitality.

laconic (ləˈkɒnık) *adj.* (of a person's speech) using few words; terse. —**la-ˈconically** *adv.*

lacquer (ˈlækə) *n.* **1.** a hard glossy coating made by dissolving natural or synthetic resins in a solvent that evaporates quickly. **2.** a black resinous substance, obtained from certain trees (**lacquer trees**), used to give a hard glossy finish to wooden furniture. **3.** a clear sticky substance for spraying onto the hair to hold a style in place. ~*vb.* **4.** to apply lacquer to.

lacrimal *or* **lachrymal** (ˈlækrıməl) *adj.* of or relating to tears or to the glands that secrete tears.

lacrosse (ləˈkrɒs) *n.* a sport in which two teams try to propel a ball into each other's goal using long-handled pouched sticks.

lactate[1] (ˈlækteıt) *n.* an ester or salt of lactic acid.

lactate[2] (ˈlækteıt) *vb.* (of mammals) to secrete milk.

lactation (lækˈteıʃən) *n.* **1.** the secretion of milk from the mammary glands. **2.** the period during which milk is secreted.

lacteal (ˈlæktıəl) *adj.* **1.** of or like milk. **2.** (of lymphatic vessels) conveying or containing chyle. ~*n.* **3.** any of the lymphatic vessels that convey chyle from the small intestine to the blood.

lactic (ˈlæktık) *adj.* relating to or derived from milk.

lactic acid *n.* a colourless syrupy acid found in sour milk and used as a preservative (**E270**) for foodstuffs.

lactose (ˈlæktəʊs) *n.* a white crystalline sugar occurring in milk.

lacuna (ləˈkjuːnə) *n., pl.* **-nae** (-niː) *or* **-nas.** a gap or space in a book or manuscript.

lacy (ˈleısı) *adj.* **lacier, laciest.** of or like lace.

lad (læd) *n.* **1.** a boy or young man. **2.** *Informal.* any male.

ladder (ˈlædə) *n.* **1.** a portable framework with two long parallel pieces of wood, metal, or rope connected by steps, for climbing up or down. **2.** any system thought of as having a series of ascending stages: *the social ladder.* **3.** *Chiefly Brit.* a line of connected stitches that have come undone in tights or stockings. ~*vb.* **4.** *Chiefly Brit.* to cause a line of interconnected stitches in (stockings) to undo, as by snagging, or (of a stocking) to come undone in this way.

ladder back *n.* a chair in which the back is made of horizontal slats between two uprights.

lade *vb.* (leıd) *vb.* **lading, laded, laden** *or*

laded. **1.** to put cargo on board (a ship) or (of a ship) to take on cargo. **2.** (foll. by *with*) to burden or load.

laden (ˈleıd³n) *vb.* **1.** a past participle of **lade.** ~*adj.* **2.** loaded. **3.** burdened.

la-di-da *or* **lah-di-dah** (ˌlɑːdıˈdɑː) *adj. Informal.* affected or pretentious in speech or manners.

ladies *or* **ladies' room** *n.* (*functioning as sing.*) *Informal.* a women's public toilet.

lading (ˈleıdıŋ) *n.* a load; cargo; freight.

ladle (ˈleıd³l) *n.* **1.** a long-handled spoon with a deep bowl for serving soup, stew, etc. ~*vb.* **2.** to serve out as with a ladle.

ladle out *vb. Informal.* to distribute (money, gifts, etc.) generously.

lady (ˈleıdı) *n., pl.* **-dies.** **1.** a woman regarded as having the characteristics of a good family and high social position. **2.** a polite name for a woman. ~*adj.* **3.** female: *a lady doctor.*

Lady (ˈleıdı) *n., pl.* **-dies.** **1.** (in Britain) a title of honour borne by various classes of women of the peerage. **2. Our Lady.** a title of the Virgin Mary.

ladybird (ˈleıdı,bɜːd) *n.* a small red beetle with black spots.

Lady Day *n.* March 25, the feast of the Annunciation of the Virgin Mary: a quarter day in England, Wales, and Ireland.

lady-in-waiting *n., pl.* **ladies-in-waiting.** a lady who attends a queen or princess.

lady-killer *n. Informal.* a man who is or believes he is irresistible to women.

ladylike (ˈleıdı,laık) *adj.* like or befitting a lady; refined and fastidious.

Ladyship (ˈleıdıʃıp) *n.* (preceded by *Your* or *Her*) a title used to address or refer to a peeress except a duchess.

lady's-slipper *n.* an orchid with reddish or purple flowers.

lag[1] (læg) *vb.* **lagging, lagged.** **1.** (often foll. by *behind*) to hang (back) or fall (behind) in movement, progress, or development. **2.** to fall away in strength or intensity. ~*n.* **3.** a slowing down or falling behind. **4.** the interval of time between two events, esp. between an action and its effect.

lag[2] (læg) *n. Slang.* a convict or ex-convict.

lag[3] (læg) *vb.* **lagging, lagged.** **1.** to cover (a pipe, cylinder, or boiler) with lagging to prevent loss of heat. ~*n.* **2.** the insulating casing of a steam cylinder or boiler.

lager (ˈlɑːgə) *n.* a light-bodied beer.

laggard (ˈlægəd) *n.* a person who lags behind.

lagging (ˈlægıŋ) *n.* insulating material wrapped around pipes, boilers, or tanks to prevent loss of heat.

lagoon (ləˈguːn) *n.* a body of water cut off from the open sea by coral reefs or sand bars.

lah (lɑː) *n. Music.* (in tonic sol-fa) the sixth note of any major scale.

laid (leɪd) *vb.* the past of **lay**[1].

laid-back *adj.* relaxed in style or character.

laid paper *n.* paper with a regular mesh impressed upon it.

lain (leɪn) *vb.* the past participle of **lie**[2].

lair (lɛə) *n.* **1.** the resting place of a wild animal. **2.** *Informal.* a place of seclusion or hiding.

laird (lɛəd) *n. Scot.* a landowner, esp. of a large estate.

laissez faire or **laisser faire** (ˌleseɪ ˈfɛə) *n.* the doctrine of unrestricted freedom in commerce, esp. for private interests.

laity (ˈleɪtɪ) *n.* **1.** laymen, as distinguished from clergymen. **2.** all the people who do not belong to a specific profession.

lake[1] (leɪk) *n.* an expanse of water entirely surrounded by land.

lake[2] (leɪk) *n.* **1.** a bright pigment produced by combining organic colouring matter with an inorganic compound. **2.** a red dye obtained by combining a metallic compound with cochineal.

Lake District *n.* a region of lakes and mountains in NW England. Also called: **Lakeland, the Lakes.**

lake trout *n.* a yellow-spotted trout of the Great Lakes region of Canada.

lakh (lɑːk) *n.* (in India) 100 000, esp. referring to this sum of rupees.

lam[1] (læm) *vb.* **lamming, lammed.** *Slang.* to thrash or beat.

lam[2] (læm) *n.* **on the lam.** *U.S. & Canad. slang.* making an escape.

lama (ˈlɑːmə) *n.* a Buddhist priest or monk in Mongolia or Tibet.

lamb (læm) *n.* **1.** the young of a sheep. **2.** the meat of a young sheep eaten as food. **3.** someone who is innocent, gentle, and good. ~*vb.* **4.** (of a ewe) to give birth.

Lamb (læm) *n.* **the.** a title given to Christ.

lambaste (læmˈbeɪst) or **lambast** (læmˈbæst) *vb.* **1.** to beat (someone) severely. **2.** to reprimand (someone).

lambent (ˈlæmbənt) *adj.* **1.** (of a flame or light) flickering softly over a surface. **2.** (of wit or humour) light or brilliant. —**ˈlambency** *n.*

lambskin (ˈlæmˌskɪn) *n.* the skin of a lamb, usually with the wool still on, used to make coats, slippers, etc.

lame (leɪm) *adj.* **1.** disabled or crippled in the legs or feet. **2.** weak; unconvincing: *a lame excuse.* ~*vb.* **3.** to make lame. —**ˈlamely** *adv.* —**ˈlameness** *n.*

lamé (ˈlɑːmeɪ) *n.* a fabric interwoven with threads of metal.

lame duck *n.* a person who is unable to cope without the help of other people.

lament (ləˈmɛnt) *vb.* **1.** to feel or express

sorrow, remorse, or regret (for or over). ~*n.* **2.** an expression of sorrow. **3.** a poem or song in which a death is lamented. —ˌlamenˈtation *n.*

lamentable (ˈlæməntəbˀl) *adj.* deplorable or distressing. —**ˈlamentably** *adv.*

lamented (ləˈmɛntɪd) *adj.* grieved for: usually said of someone dead.

lamina (ˈlæmɪnə) *n., pl.* **-nae** (-ˌniː). a thin plate, esp. of bone or mineral. —**ˈlaminar** *adj.*

laminate *vb.* (ˈlæmɪˌneɪt). **1.** to make (material in sheet form) by bonding together thin sheets. **2.** to split or be split into thin sheets. **3.** to beat or press (metal) into thin sheets. **4.** to cover with a thin sheet of material. ~*n.* (ˈlæmɪˌneɪt, -nɪt). **5.** a material made by bonding sheets together. ~*adj.* (ˈlæmɪˌneɪt, -nɪt). **6.** composed of lamina; laminated. —ˌlamiˈnation *n.*

laminated (ˈlæmɪˌneɪtɪd) *adj.* **1.** composed of many layers bonded together. **2.** covered with a thin protective layer of plastic.

Lammas (ˈlæməs) *n.* Aug. 1, formerly observed in England as a harvest festival: a quarter day in Scotland.

lamp (læmp) *n.* **1.** a device that produces illumination: *an electric lamp; a gas lamp; an oil lamp.* **2.** a device that produces radiation, esp. for therapeutic purposes: *an ultraviolet lamp.*

lampblack (ˈlæmpˌblæk) *n.* a fine black soot used as a pigment in paint and ink.

lampoon (læmˈpuːn) *n.* **1.** a satire ridiculing a person. ~*vb.* **2.** to attack or satirize (someone) in a lampoon. —**lamˈpooner** or **lamˈpoonist** *n.*

lamppost (ˈlæmpˌpəʊst) *n.* a metal or concrete pole supporting a lamp in a street.

lamprey (ˈlæmprɪ) *n.* an eel-like fish with a round sucking mouth for clinging to and feeding on the blood of other fish.

Lancastrian (læŋˈkæstrɪən) *n.* **1.** a person from Lancashire or Lancaster. **2.** a supporter of the house of Lancaster in the Wars of the Roses (1455-85). ~*adj.* **3.** of Lancashire or Lancaster. **4.** of the house of Lancaster.

lance (lɑːns) *n.* **1.** a long weapon with a pointed head used by horsemen. ~*vb.* **2.** to pierce (an abscess or boil) with a lancet. **3.** to pierce with or as with a lance.

lance corporal *n.* a noncommissioned officer of the lowest rank in the British Army.

lanceolate (ˈlɑːnsɪəˌleɪt, -lɪt) *adj.* narrow and tapering to a point at each end, as certain leaves.

lancer (ˈlɑːnsə) *n.* (formerly) a cavalryman armed with a lance.

lancers (ˈlɑːnsəz) *n.* (*functioning as sing.*) **1.** a quadrille. **2.** music for this dance.

lancet (ˈlɑːnsɪt) *n.* **1.** a pointed surgical knife with two sharp edges. **2.** short for **lancet arch** or **lancet window.**

lancet arch *n.* a narrow acutely pointed arch.

lancet window *n.* a narrow window with a lancet arch.

lancewood (ˈlɑːns,wʊd) *n.* a New Zealand tree with slender leaves.

Lancs (læŋks) Lancashire.

land (lænd) *n.* **1.** the solid part of the surface of the earth as distinct from seas and lakes. **2.** ground, esp. with reference to its use or quality: *arable land.* **3.** rural or agricultural areas: *life on the land.* **4.** *Law.* ground owned as property. **5.** a country, region, or area: *native land.* ~*vb.* **6.** to come down or bring (something) down to earth after a flight or jump. **7.** to transfer (something) or go from a ship to the shore: *land the cargo.* **8.** to come to or touch shore. **9.** (in Canada) to be legally admitted to the country as an immigrant. **10.** *Angling.* to retrieve (a hooked fish) from the water. **11.** *Informal.* to obtain: *to land a job.* **12.** *Informal.* to deliver (a blow or punch). ~See also **land up.** —ˈ**landless** *adj.*

land agent *n.* a person in charge of a landed estate.

landau (ˈlændɔː) *n.* a four-wheeled horse-drawn carriage with two folding hoods.

landed (ˈlændɪd) *adj.* **1.** owning land: *landed gentry.* **2.** consisting of land: *a landed estate.*

landfall (ˈlænd,fɔːl) *n.* the act of sighting or nearing land, esp. from the sea.

land girl *n.* a girl or woman who does farm work, esp. in wartime.

land-holder *n.* a person who owns or occupies land. —ˈ**land-,holding** *adj., n.*

landing (ˈlændɪŋ) *n.* **1.** the floor area at the top of a flight of stairs. **2.** the act of coming to land, esp. after a sea voyage. **3.** a place of disembarkation.

landing field *n.* an area of land on which aircraft land and from which they take off.

landing gear *n.* the undercarriage of an aircraft.

landlady (ˈlænd,leɪdɪ) *n., pl.* **-dies. 1.** a woman who owns and leases property. **2.** a woman who owns or runs a lodging house or pub.

landlocked (ˈlænd,lɒkt) *adj.* (of a country) completely surrounded by land.

landlord (ˈlænd,lɔːd) *n.* **1.** a man who owns and leases property. **2.** a man who owns or runs a lodging house or pub.

landlubber (ˈlænd,lʌbə) *n. Naut.* any person without experience at sea.

landmark (ˈlænd,mɑːk) *n.* **1.** a prominent object in or feature of a particular landscape. **2.** an important or unique decision, event, fact, or discovery: *the discovery of penicillin was a landmark in medicine.*

landmass (ˈlænd,mæs) *n.* a large continu-

ous area of land, as opposed to seas or islands.

land mine *n. Mil.* an explosive device placed in the ground, usually detonated when someone steps on it or drives over it.

landowner (ˈlænd,əʊnə) *n.* a person who owns land. —ˈ**land,owning** *n., adj.*

landscape (ˈlænd,skeɪp) *n.* **1.** an extensive area of scenery as viewed from a single place. **2.** a painting, drawing, or photograph depicting natural scenery. ~*vb.* **3.** to improve the natural features of (an area of land).

landscape gardening *n.* the art of laying out grounds in imitation of natural scenery. —**landscape gardener** *n.*

landslide (ˈlænd,slaɪd) *n.* **1.** Also called: **landslip. a.** the sliding of a large mass of rocks and soil down the side of a mountain or cliff. **b.** the material dislodged in this way. **2.** an overwhelming electoral victory.

land up *vb.* to arrive at a final point or condition.

landward (ˈlændwəd) *adj.* **1.** lying, facing, or moving towards land. **2.** in the direction of the land. ~*adv. also* **landwards. 3.** towards land.

lane (leɪn) *n.* **1.** a narrow road between buildings, hedges, or fences. **2.** any well-defined track or course, as for traffic in a road, or for ships or aircraft. **3.** one of the parallel strips into which a running track or swimming bath is divided for races.

lang. language.

language (ˈlæŋgwɪdʒ) *n.* **1.** a system of expression by spoken sounds or conventional symbols. **2.** the faculty for the use of such systems. **3.** the language of a particular nation or people. **4.** any other means of communicating: *the language of love.* **5.** the specialized vocabulary used by a particular group: *medical language.* **6.** a particular manner or style of verbal expression: *your language is disgusting.* **7.** *Computers.* See **programming language.**

language laboratory *n.* a room in a school or college equipped with tape recorders, etc., for learning foreign languages.

languid (ˈlæŋgwɪd) *adj.* **1.** lacking energy or enthusiasm. **2.** sluggish; inactive. —ˈ**languidly** *adv.*

languish (ˈlæŋgwɪʃ) *vb.* **1.** to suffer deprivation, hardship, or neglect: *to languish in prison.* **2.** to lose or diminish in strength or energy. **3.** (often foll. by *for*) to be listless with desire; pine. —ˈ**languishing** *adj.*

languor (ˈlæŋgə) *n.* **1.** laziness or weariness. **2.** dreaminess and relaxation. **3.** oppressive stillness. —ˈ**languorous** *adj.*

lank (læŋk) *adj.* **1.** (of hair) long and limp. **2.** thin or gaunt.

lanky (ˈlæŋkɪ) *adj.* **lankier, lankiest.** ungracefully tall and thin. —ˈ**lankiness** *n.*

lanolin (ˈlænəlɪn) *n.* a yellowish sticky substance extracted from wool: used in some ointments.

lantern ('læntən) n. 1. a light with a transparent protective case. 2. a structure on top of a dome or roof with windows for light or air. 3. the upper part of a lighthouse that houses the light.

lantern jaw n. a long hollow jaw that gives the face a drawn appearance. —'**lantern-,jawed** adj.

lanthanide series ('lænθə,naɪd) n. a class of 15 chemically related elements (**lanthanides**) with atomic numbers from 57 (lanthanum) to 71 (lutetium).

lanthanum ('lænθənəm) n. a silvery-white metallic element of the lanthanide series: used in electronic devices and glass manufacture. Symbol: La

lanyard ('lænjəd) n. 1. a cord worn around the neck to hold a whistle or knife. 2. Naut. a line for extending or tightening rigging.

laodicean (,leɪəʊdɪ'sɪən) adj. indifferent, esp. in religious matters.

lap[1] (læp) n. 1. the area formed by the upper surface of the thighs of a seated person. 2. a protected place or environment: in the lap of luxury. 3. the part of a person's clothing that covers the lap. 4. **drop in someone's lap.** to give someone the responsibility of.

lap[2] (læp) n. 1. one circuit of a racecourse or track. 2. a stage or part of a journey. 3. **a.** an overlapping part. **b.** the extent of overlap. ~vb. **lapping, lapped.** 4. to overtake (an opponent) in a race so as to be one or more circuits ahead. 5. to wrap or fold (around or over): he lapped a bandage around his wrist. 6. to envelop in: he lapped his wrist in a bandage. 7. to place or lie partly or completely over or project beyond. 8. (usually passive) to envelop or surround with comfort, love, or peace: lapped in luxury.

lap[3] (læp) vb. **lapping, lapped.** 1. (of small waves) to wash against (the shore or a boat) with light splashing sounds. 2. (often foll. by up) (esp. of animals) to scoop (a liquid) into the mouth with the tongue. ~n. 3. the act or sound of lapping. ~See also **lap up.**

lapdog ('læp,dɒg) n. a small pet dog.

lapel (lə'pɛl) n. the part on the front of a garment, such as a jacket, that folds back towards the shoulders.

lapidary ('læpɪdərɪ) n., pl. **-daries.** 1. a person who cuts, polishes, sets, or deals in gemstones. ~adj. 2. of or relating to gemstones or the work of a lapidary.

lapis lazuli ('læpɪs 'læzjʊ,laɪ) n. 1. a brilliant blue mineral used as a gemstone. 2. its deep blue colour.

lap joint n. a joint made by overlapping parts and fastening them together.

lap of honour n. a ceremonial circuit of a racing track by the winner of a race.

Lapp (læp) n. 1. Also: **Laplander.** a member of a nomadic people living chiefly in N Scandinavia. 2. the language of this people. ~adj. 3. of this people or their language.

lappet ('læpɪt) n. 1. a small hanging flap or piece of lace. 2. a lobelike hanging structure in some invertebrate animals.

lapse (læps) n. 1. a temporary drop in standard as a result of forgetfulness or lack of concentration. 2. a moment or instance of bad behaviour, esp. by someone who is usually well-behaved. 3. a break in occurrence or usage: a lapse of five weeks between letters. 4. a gradual decline to a lower degree, condition, or state: a lapse from high office. 5. Law. the termination of some right, interest, or privilege, as by neglecting to claim, exercise, or renew it. ~vb. 6. to drop in standard or fail to maintain a norm. 7. to decline gradually in status, condition, or degree. 8. to be discontinued, esp. through negligence. 9. (usually foll. by into) to drift (into a condition): to lapse into sleep. 10. (often foll. by from) to turn away (from beliefs or norms). 11. (of time) to slip away. —**lapsed** adj.

laptop ('læp,tɒp) n. (modifier) (of a computer) small and light enough to be held on the user's lap.

lap up vb. 1. to eat or drink. 2. to accept (information or attention) eagerly: he laps up stories.

lapwing ('læp,wɪŋ) n. a bird of the plover family with a crested head. Also called: **peewit.**

larboard ('lɑːbəd) n., adj. Naut. an old word for **port**[2].

larceny ('lɑːsɪnɪ) n., pl. **-nies.** Law. theft. —'**larcenist** n.

larch (lɑːtʃ) n. 1. a coniferous tree with needle-like leaves and egg-shaped cones. 2. the wood of this tree.

lard (lɑːd) n. 1. the soft white fat obtained from pigs and prepared for use in cooking. ~vb. 2. to prepare (lean meat or poultry) by inserting small strips of bacon or fat before cooking. 3. to add unnecessary material to (speech or writing).

larder ('lɑːdə) n. a room or cupboard, used as a store for food.

lardy cake ('lɑːdɪ) n. Brit. a sweet cake made of bread dough, lard, sugar, and dried fruit.

large (lɑːdʒ) adj. 1. having a relatively great size, quantity, or extent; big. 2. of wide or broad scope, capacity, or range; comprehensive: large change. ~n. 3. **at large. a.** (of a dangerous criminal or wild animal) free; not confined. **b.** as a whole; in general. **c.** in full detail. —'**largeness** n.

large intestine n. the part of the alimentary canal consisting of the caecum, colon, and rectum.

largely ('lɑːdʒlɪ) *adv.* principally; to a great extent.

large-scale *adj.* **1.** wide-ranging or extensive. **2.** (of maps and models) constructed or drawn to a big scale.

largess *or* **largesse** (lɑː'dʒes) *n.* the generous giving of gifts, favours, or money.

largish ('lɑːdʒɪʃ) *adj.* fairly large.

largo ('lɑːgəʊ) *Music.* ~*adv.* **1.** slowly and stately. ~*n., pl.* -**gos.** **2.** a piece or passage to be performed in this way.

lariat ('lærɪət) *n. U.S. & Canad.* **1.** a lasso. **2.** a rope for tethering animals.

lark[1] (lɑːk) *n.* a small brown songbird, esp. the skylark.

lark[2] (lɑːk) *Informal.* ~*n.* **1.** a carefree adventure or frolic. **2.** a harmless piece of mischief. ~*vb.* **3. lark about.** to have a good time frolicking or playing pranks. —'**larkish** *or* '**larky** *adj.*

larkspur ('lɑːkˌspɜː) *n.* a plant with blue, pink, or white spurred flowers.

larva ('lɑːvə) *n., pl.* -**vae** (-viː). an immature free-living form of many animals that develops into a different adult form by metamorphosis. —'**larval** *adj.*

laryngeal (ˌlærɪn'dʒɪəl) *adj.* of or relating to the larynx.

laryngitis (ˌlærɪn'dʒaɪtɪs) *n.* inflammation of the larynx.

larynx ('lærɪŋks) *n.* a hollow organ forming part of the air passage to the lungs: it contains the vocal cords.

lasagne *or* **lasagna** (lə'zænjə, -'sæn-) *n.* **1.** a form of pasta consisting of wide flat sheets. **2.** a dish made from layers of lasagne, meat, and cheese.

lascivious (lə'sɪvɪəs) *adj.* **1.** lustful; lecherous. **2.** producing sexual desire. —**las'civiously** *adv.*

laser ('leɪzə) *n.* a device for converting light of mixed frequencies into an intense narrow beam of light of the same frequency.

laser printer *n.* a quiet, high-quality computer printer which uses a laser beam shining on light-sensitive paper to produce characters.

lash[1] (læʃ) *n.* **1.** a sharp cutting blow from a whip. **2.** the flexible end of a whip. **3.** an eyelash. ~*vb.* **4.** to hit (a person or thing) sharply with a whip, esp. formerly as punishment. **5.** (of rain or waves) to beat forcefully against. **6.** to attack (someone) with words of ridicule or scolding. **7.** to flick or wave sharply to and fro: *the panther lashed his tail.* **8.** to urge as with a whip: *to lash the audience into a violent mood.* ~See also **lash out.**

lash[2] (læʃ) *vb.* to bind or secure with rope, string, or cord.

lashing[1] ('læʃɪŋ) *n.* **1.** a flogging. **2.** a scolding.

lashing[2] ('læʃɪŋ) *n.* rope, string, or cord used for binding or securing.

lashings ('læʃɪŋz) *pl. n. Brit. informal.* large amounts; lots: *lashings of cream.*

lash out *vb.* **1.** to burst into or resort to verbal or physical attack. **2.** *Informal.* to spend (money) extravagantly.

lass (læs) *n.* a girl or young woman.

Lassa fever ('læsə) *n.* a serious viral disease of Central West Africa, characterized by high fever and muscular pains.

lassie ('læsɪ) *n. Informal.* a little lass; girl.

lassitude ('læsɪˌtjuːd) *n.* physical or mental weariness.

lasso (læ'suː, 'læsəʊ) *n., pl.* -**sos** *or* -**soes.** **1.** a long rope with a running noose at one end, esp. used for roping horses and cattle. ~*vb.* -**soing,** -**soed.** **2.** to catch as with a lasso. —**las'soer** *n.*

last[1] (lɑːst) *adj.* **1.** being, happening, or coming at the end or after all others. **2.** most recent: *last Thursday.* **3.** only remaining: *one's last cigarette.* **4.** most extreme; utmost. **5.** least suitable or likely: *he was the last person I would have chosen.* ~*adv.* **6.** after all others. **7.** most recently: *he was last seen in the mountains.* **8.** as the last or latest item. ~*n.* **9. the last. a.** a person or thing that is last. **b.** the final moment; end. **10.** the final appearance, mention, or occurrence: *we've seen the last of him.* **11. at last.** in the end; finally. **12. at long last.** finally, after difficulty or delay.

last[2] (lɑːst) *vb.* **1.** to remain in being (for a length of time); continue: *his hatred lasted for several years.* **2.** to be sufficient for the needs of (a person) for (a length of time): *it will last us until Friday.* **3.** to remain fresh, uninjured, or unaltered (for a certain time): *she lasted for three hours underground.* ~See also **last out.**

last[3] (lɑːst) *n.* the wooden or metal form on which a shoe or boot is made or repaired.

last-ditch *adj.* done as a last resort: *a last-ditch effort.*

lasting ('lɑːstɪŋ) *adj.* permanent or enduring.

Last Judgment *n.* **the.** *Theol.* God's verdict on the destinies of all human beings at the end of the world.

lastly ('lɑːstlɪ) *adv.* **1.** at the end or at the last point. **2.** finally.

last-minute *adj.* given or done at the latest possible time: *last-minute preparations.*

last name *n.* same as **surname.**

last out *vb.* **1.** to be sufficient for one's needs: *will our supplies last out?* **2.** to endure or survive: *some old people don't last out the winter.*

last rites *pl. n. Christianity.* religious rites for those close to death.

last straw *n.* a small incident, irritation, or

setback that coming after others is too much to cope with.

Last Supper n. **the.** the meal eaten by Christ with his disciples on the night before his Crucifixion.

lat. latitude.

Lat. Latin.

latch (lætʃ) n. **1.** a fastening for a gate or door that consists of a bar that may be slid or lowered into a groove, hole, or notch. **2.** a spring-loaded door lock that can be opened by a key from outside. ~vb. **3.** to fasten, fit, or be fitted as with a latch.

latchkey child ('lætʃ,kiː) n. a child who has to let himself in at home after school, as his parents are out at work.

latch on vb. Informal. **1.** (often foll. by to) to attach oneself (to): to latch on to new ideas. **2.** to understand: it took me a while to latch on.

late (leɪt) adj. **1.** occurring or arriving after the correct or expected time: the train was late. **2.** occurring or being at a relatively advanced time: a late marriage. **3.** towards or near the end: the late evening. **4.** at an advanced time in the evening or at night: it was late. **5.** recent: his late remarks on industry. **6.** having died recently: my late grandfather. **7.** former: the late manager of this firm. **8. of late.** recently. ~adv. **9.** after the correct or expected time: he arrived late. **10.** at a relatively advanced age: she married late. **11.** recently: as late as yesterday he was selling books. **12. late in the day. a.** at a late or advanced stage. **b.** too late. —**lateness** n.

lateen (lə'tiːn) adj. Naut. denoting a rig with a triangular sail bent to a yard hoisted to the head of a low mast.

Late Greek n. the Greek language from about the 3rd to the 8th centuries A.D.

Late Latin n. the form of written Latin used from the 3rd to the 7th centuries A.D.

lately ('leɪtlɪ) adv. in recent times; of late.

latent ('leɪt³nt) adj. lying hidden and not yet developed within a person or thing. —**latency** n.

later ('leɪtə) adj., adv. **1.** the comparative of **late.** ~adv. **2.** afterwards.

lateral ('lætərəl) adj. **1.** of or relating to the side or sides. ~n. **2.** a lateral object, part, passage, or movement. —**laterally** adv.

lateral thinking n. a way of solving problems by apparently illogical methods.

latest ('leɪtɪst) adj., adv. **1.** the superlative of **late.** ~adj. **2.** most recent, modern, or new: the latest fashions. ~n. **3. at the latest.** no later than the time specified.

latex ('leɪtɛks) n. a milky fluid produced by many plants which is used in the manufacture of rubber.

lath (lɑːθ) n., pl. **laths** (lɑːðz, lɑːθs). one of several thin narrow strips of wood used as a supporting framework for plaster or tiles.

lathe (leɪð) n. a machine for shaping metal or wood, in which the workpiece is turned against a fixed tool.

lather ('lɑːðə) n. **1.** foam formed by soap or detergent in water. **2.** foamy sweat, as of a horse. **3.** Informal. a state of agitation. ~vb. **4.** to coat or become coated with lather. **5.** to form a lather. **6.** Informal. to beat; flog. —**lathery** adj.

Latin ('lætɪn) n. **1.** the language of ancient Rome and the Roman Empire. **2.** a member of any of those peoples whose languages are derived from Latin. ~adj. **3.** of or relating to the Latin language. **4.** of or relating to those peoples whose languages are derived from Latin. **5.** of or relating to the Roman Catholic Church.

Latin America n. those areas of South and Central America whose official languages are Spanish and Portuguese.

latish ('leɪtɪʃ) adj., adv. rather late.

latitude ('lætɪ,tjuːd) n. **1. a.** an angular distance measured in degrees north or south of the equator. **b.** (often pl.) a region considered with regard to its distance from the equator. **2.** scope for freedom of action and thought. —**latitudinal** adj.

latitudinarian (,lætɪ,tjuːdɪ'nɛərɪən) adj. **1.** liberal, esp. in religious matters. ~n. **2.** a person with latitudinarian views.

latrine (lə'triːn) n. a toilet, as in a barracks or camp.

latter ('lætə) adj. **1.** near or nearer the end: the latter part of a film. **2.** more advanced in time or sequence; later. ~n. **3. the latter.** the second or second mentioned of two.

Usage. Latter is used when only two items are in question: he gave the money to Christopher and not to John, the latter being less in need of it. Last-named is used to refer to the last-named of three or more items.

latter-day adj. present-day; modern.

latterly ('lætəlɪ) adv. recently; lately.

lattice ('lætɪs) n. **1.** Also called: **latticework.** an open framework of strips of wood or metal, arranged to form an ornamental pattern. **2.** a gate, screen, or fence formed of such a framework. **3.** an array of atoms, ions, or molecules in a crystal or an array of points indicating their positions in space. ~vb. **4.** to make, adorn, or supply with a lattice. —**latticed** adj.

laud (lɔːd) Literary. ~vb. **1.** to praise or glorify. ~n. **2.** praise or glorification.

laudable ('lɔːdəb³l) adj. deserving praise; commendable. —**lauda'bility** n. —**laudably** adv.

laudanum ('lɔːd³nəm) n. a tincture of opium.

laudatory ('lɔːdətrɪ) adj. (of speech or writing) expressing praise.

laugh (lɑːf) vb. **1.** to express mirth or amusement, typically by producing an inarticulate voiced noise. **2.** to utter or express with laughter: *he laughed his derision at the play.* **3.** to bring or force (someone, esp. oneself) into a certain condition by laughter: *he laughed himself sick.* **4. laugh at.** to make fun (of); jeer (at). **5. laugh up one's sleeve.** to laugh secretly. ~*n.* **6.** the act or an instance of laughing. **7.** a manner of laughter. **8.** *Informal.* a person or thing that causes laughter: *that holiday was a laugh.* **9. the last laugh.** final success after previous defeat. ~*See* also **laugh off.** —'**laughingly** *adv.*

laughable ('lɑ:fəbªl) *adj.* **1.** producing scorn; ludicrous. **2.** arousing laughter.

laughing gas *n.* nitrous oxide used as an anaesthetic: it may cause laughter and exhilaration when inhaled.

laughing stock *n.* an object of humiliating ridicule.

laugh off *vb.* to treat (something serious or difficult) lightly.

laughter ('lɑ:ftə) *n.* the action of or noise produced by laughing.

launch[1] (lɔ:ntʃ) *vb.* **1.** to move (a vessel) into the water, esp. for the first time. **2. a.** to start off or set in motion: *to launch a scheme.* **b.** to put (a new product) on the market. **3.** to involve (oneself) totally and enthusiastically: *to launch oneself into work.* **4.** to set (a rocket, missile, or spacecraft) into motion. **5. launch into.** to start talking or writing (about). **6.** (usually foll. by *out*) to start (out) on a new enterprise. ~*n.* **7.** an act or instance of launching. —'**launcher** *n.*

launch[2] (lɔ:ntʃ) *n.* an open motorboat.

launching pad *or* **launch pad** *n.* a platform from which a spacecraft, rocket, or missile is launched.

launder ('lɔ:ndə) *vb.* **1.** to wash and often also iron (clothes and linen). **2.** to make (money illegally obtained) appear to be legally gained by passing it through foreign banks or legitimate enterprises.

Launderette (ˌlɔːndəˈrɛt, lɔːnˈdrɛt) *Brit. & N.Z. trademark.* an establishment where clothes can be washed and dried, using coin-operated machines. Also called (U.S., Canad., and N.Z.): **Laundromat.**

laundry ('lɔːndrɪ) *n., pl.* **-dries.** **1.** a place where clothes and linen are washed and ironed. **2.** the clothes or linen to be laundered or that have been laundered.

laureate ('lɔːrɪɪt) *adj.* **1.** *Literary.* crowned with laurel leaves as a sign of honour. ~*n.* **2.** short for **poet laureate.** —'**laureate,ship** *n.*

laurel ('lɒrəl) *n.* **1.** a small Mediterranean evergreen tree with glossy leaves. **2.** (*pl.*) a wreath of laurel, worn on the head as an emblem of victory or honour in classical times. **3.** (*pl.*) honour, distinction, or fame. **4. look to one's laurels.** to be on guard

against one's rivals. **5. rest on one's laurels.** to be satisfied with what one has already achieved and stop striving for further success.

Laurentian (lɔːˈrɛnʃən) *adj.* of or near the St Lawrence River.

Laurentian Shield *n.* same as **Canadian Shield.**

lav (læv) *n. Brit. informal.* short for **lavatory.**

lava ('lɑːvə) *n.* **1.** molten rock flowing from volcanoes. **2.** any rock formed by the solidification of lava.

lavatorial (ˌlævəˈtɔːrɪəl) *adj.* characterized by frequent reference to excretion: *lavatorial humour.*

lavatory ('lævətrɪ) *n., pl.* **-ries.** same as **toilet.**

lavender ('lævəndə) *n.* **1.** a shrub or plant cultivated for its mauve or blue flowers and as the source of a fragrant oil (**oil of lavender**). **2.** its dried flowers, used to perfume clothes. **3.** a pale or light bluish-purple colour.

lavender water *n.* a light perfume made from lavender.

lavish ('lævɪʃ) *adj.* **1.** great in quantity or richness: *lavish decoration.* **2.** very generous in giving. **3.** extravagant; wasteful: *lavish expenditure.* ~*vb.* **4.** to give or to spend very generously or in great quantities. —'**lavishly** *adv.*

law (lɔː) *n.* **1.** a rule or set of rules regulating the relationship between the state and its subjects, and the conduct of subjects towards one another. **2.** a rule or body of rules made by the legislature or other authority. **3.** the condition and control enforced by such rules. **4. law and order.** the policy of strict enforcement of the law, esp. against crime and violence. **5.** a rule of conduct: *a law of etiquette.* **6. the law. a.** the legal or judicial system. **b.** the profession or practice of law. **c.** *Informal.* the police or a policeman. **7.** Also called: **law of nature.** a generalization based on a recurring fact or event. **8.** the science or knowledge of law; jurisprudence. **9.** a general principle, formula, or rule in mathematics, science, or philosophy: *the laws of thermodynamics.* **10. the Law.** the laws contained in the first five books of the Old Testament. **11. go to law.** to resort to legal proceedings on some matter. **12. lay down the law.** to speak in an authoritative manner.

law-abiding *adj.* obeying the laws: *a law-abiding citizen.*

lawbreaker ('lɔːˌbreɪkə) *n.* a person who breaks the law. —'**law,breaking** *n., adj.*

lawful ('lɔːfʊl) *adj.* allowed, recognized, or sanctioned by law; legal. —'**lawfully** *adv.*

lawgiver ('lɔːˌgɪvə) *n.* **1.** the giver of a code

of laws. **2.** Also called: **lawmaker.** a maker of laws. —**'law,giving** *n., adj.*

lawless (*'lɔːlɪs*) *adj.* **1.** breaking the law, esp. in a wild or violent way: *lawless violence*. **2.** not having laws. —**'lawlessness** *n.*

Law Lords *pl. n.* members of the House of Lords who sit as the highest court of appeal.

lawn[1] (lɔːn) *n.* a flat area of mown grass.

lawn[2] (lɔːn) *n.* a fine linen or cotton fabric.

lawn mower *n.* a hand-operated or power-operated machine for cutting grass on lawns.

lawn tennis *n.* **1.** tennis played on a grass court. **2.** same as **tennis**.

lawrencium (lɒ'rɛnsɪəm) *n.* an element artificially produced from californium. Symbol: Lr

lawsuit (*'lɔː,suːt*) *n.* a proceeding in a court of law brought by one party against another.

lawyer (*'lɔːjə, 'lɔɪə*) *n.* a member of the legal profession, esp. a solicitor.

lax (læks) *adj.* lacking firmness; not strict. —**'laxity** *n.*

laxative (*'læksətɪv*) *n.* **1.** a medicine that eases the emptying of the bowels. ~*adj.* **2.** easing the emptying of the bowels.

lay[1] (leɪ) *vb.* **laying, laid. 1.** to put in a low or horizontal position; cause to lie: *to lay a cover on a bed.* **2.** to place, put, or be in a particular state or position: *he laid his finger on his lips.* **3.** to establish as a basis: *to lay a foundation for discussion.* **4.** to place in position: *to lay a carpet.* **5.** to arrange (a table) for a meal. **6.** to prepare (a fire) by arranging fuel in the grate. **7.** (of birds, esp. the domestic hen) to produce (eggs). **8.** to put forward: *he laid his case before the magistrate.* **9.** to attribute: *all the blame was laid on him.* **10.** to arrange, devise, or prepare: *to lay a trap.* **11.** to make (a bet) with (someone): *I lay you five to one on Prince.* **12.** *Taboo slang.* to have sexual intercourse with. **13. lay bare.** to reveal or explain: *he laid bare his plans.* **14. lay hold of.** to seize or grasp. **15. lay oneself open.** to make oneself vulnerable (to criticism or attack). **16. lay open.** to reveal or disclose. ~*n.* **17.** the manner or position in which something lies or is placed. **18.** *Taboo slang.* **a.** an act of sexual intercourse. **b.** a sexual partner. ~See also **lay aside**, **lay down**, etc.
Usage. The verb *lay* is used with an object and *lie* without one: *the soldier laid down his arms; the book was lying on the table.*

lay[2] (leɪ) *vb.* the past tense of **lie**[2].

lay[3] (leɪ) *adj.* **1.** of or involving people who are not clergymen. **2.** nonprofessional or nonspecialist.

lay[4] (leɪ) *n.* a short narrative poem, esp. one intended to be sung.

layabout (*'leɪə,baʊt*) *n.* a lazy person; loafer.

lay aside *vb.* **1.** to store or reserve for future use. **2.** to abandon or reject.

lay-by *n. Brit.* a place for drivers to stop at the side of a main road.

lay down *vb.* **1.** to place on the ground or a surface. **2.** to sacrifice: *to lay down one's life.* **3.** to formulate (a rule or principle). **4.** to record (plans) on paper. **5.** to store or stock: *to lay down wine.*

layer (*'leɪə*) *n.* **1.** a single thickness of some substance, such as a stratum or a coating on a surface. **2.** a laying hen. **3.** *Horticulture.* a shoot or branch that forms its own root while still attached to the parent plant. ~*vb.* **4.** to form or make a layer of (something). **5.** to take root or cause to take root as a layer.

layette (leɪ'ɛt) *n.* a complete set of clothing, bedclothes, and other accessories for a newborn baby.

lay figure *n.* **1.** an artist's jointed dummy, used esp. for studying effects of drapery. **2.** a person considered to be subservient or unimportant.

lay in *vb.* to accumulate and store: *we must lay in food for the party.*

lay into *vb. Informal.* to attack or scold (someone) severely.

layman (*'leɪmən*) *or (fem.)* **laywoman** *n., pl.* **-men** *or* **-women. 1.** a person who is not a clergyman. **2.** a person who does not have specialized knowledge of a subject: *science for the layman.*

lay off *vb.* **1.** to suspend (an employee) from work with the intention of re-employing later. **2.** *Informal.* to leave (a person, thing, or activity) alone: *lay off me, will you!* ~*n.* **lay-off. 3.** a period of imposed unemployment.

lay on *vb.* **1.** to provide or supply: *to lay on entertainment.* **2. lay it on thick.** *Slang.* to exaggerate, esp. when flattering.

lay out *vb.* **1.** to arrange or spread out. **2.** to prepare (a corpse) for burial. **3.** to plan or design: *to lay out a garden.* **4.** *Informal.* to spend (money), esp. lavishly. **5.** *Informal.* to knock (someone) unconscious. ~*n.* **layout. 6.** the arrangement or plan of something, such as a building. **7.** the arrangement of written material and photographs in a book, newspaper, or magazine.

lay reader *n.* **1.** *Church of England.* a person licensed to conduct religious services other than the Eucharist. **2.** *R.C. Church.* a layman chosen to read the epistle at Mass.

lay up *vb.* **1.** to store or reserve for future use. **2.** *Informal.* to confine through illness: *laid up with a bad cold.*

laze (leɪz) *vb.* **1.** to be idle or lazy. **2.** (often foll. by *away*) to spend (time) in idleness. ~*n*. **3.** the act or an instance of idling.

lazy ('leɪzɪ) *adj*. **lazier, laziest. 1.** not inclined to work or exert oneself. **2.** encouraging or causing inactivity. **3.** moving in a sluggish manner: *a lazy river.* —**'lazily** *adv*. —**'laziness** *n*.

lazybones ('leɪzɪˌbəʊnz) *n. Informal.* a lazy person.

lb pound (weight).

lbw *Cricket.* leg before wicket.

lc 1. in the place cited. **2.** *Printing.* lower case.

LCD 1. liquid crystal display. **2.** Also: **lcd.** lowest common denominator.

lcm *or* **LCM** lowest common multiple.

lea (liː) *n.* **1.** *Poetic.* a meadow or field. **2.** grassland.

LEA Local Education Authority.

leach (liːtʃ) *vb.* **1.** to remove or be removed from a substance by a liquid passing through it. **2.** to lose soluble substances by the action of a liquid passing through.

lead¹ (liːd) *vb.* **leading, led. 1.** to show the way to (an individual or a group) by going with or ahead: *lead the party into the garden.* **2.** to guide or be guided by holding or pulling: *he led the horse by its reins.* **3.** to cause to act, feel, think, or behave in a certain way: *he led me to believe that he would go.* **4.** (of a road, route, or way) to serve as the means of reaching a place. **5.** to guide, control, or direct: *to lead an army.* **6.** to direct the course of (water, a rope, or wire) along or as if along a channel. **7.** to have the principal part in (something): *to lead a discussion.* **8.** to go at the head of or have the top position in (something): *he leads his class in geography.* **9.** (foll. by *with*) to have as the most important item: *the newspaper led with the royal birth.* **10.** *Music, Brit.* to play first violin in (an orchestra). **11.** to pass or spend: *I lead a miserable life.* **12.** to begin a round of cards by putting down (the first card). ~*n.* **13.** the first, foremost, or most prominent place. **14.** example or leadership: *the class followed the teacher's lead.* **15.** an advantage over others: *the runner had a lead of twenty yards.* **16.** an indication; clue: *the police are following up several leads.* **17.** a leash. **18.** the act of playing the first card in a round of cards or the card so played. **19.** the principal role in a play, film, or other production, or the person playing such a role. **20.** the most important news story in a newspaper: *the scandal was the lead in the papers.* **21.** a wire, cable, or other conductor for making an electrical connection. ~*adj.* **22.** acting as a leader or lead: *lead singer.* ~See also **lead off, lead on,** etc.

lead² (lɛd) *n.* **1.** a heavy toxic bluish-white metallic element: used in alloys, cable sheaths, paints, and as a radiation shield.

Symbol: Pb **2. a.** graphite used for drawing. **b.** a thin stick of this as the core of a pencil. **3.** a lead weight suspended on a line, used to take soundings of the depth of water. **4.** lead weights or shot, as used in cartridges or fishing lines. **5.** a thin strip of lead for holding small panes of glass or pieces of stained glass. **6.** (*pl.*) **a.** thin sheets or strips of lead used as a roof covering. **b.** a roof covered with such sheets. **7.** Also called: **leading.** *Printing.* a thin strip of type metal, used esp. formerly for spacing between lines. ~*adj.* **8.** of, relating to, or containing lead. ~*vb.* **9.** to surround, cover, or secure with lead or leads.

leaden ('lɛdən) *adj.* **1.** heavy or sluggish: *leaden steps.* **2.** gloomy, spiritless, or lifeless. **3.** made of lead. **4.** of a dull greyish colour: *a leaden sky.*

leader ('liːdə) *n.* **1.** a person who rules, guides, or inspires others; head. **2.** *Music.* the principal first violinist of an orchestra who acts as the conductor's deputy. **3.** the leading horse or dog in a team. **4.** *Chiefly Brit.* the leading editorial in a newspaper. Also: **leading article. 5.** a strip of blank film or tape at the beginning of a reel. **6.** *Bot.* any of the long slender shoots that grow from the stem or branch of a tree. —**'leader,ship** *n.*

lead-in ('liːdˌɪn) *n.* an introduction to a subject.

leading ('liːdɪŋ) *adj.* **1.** principal or primary: *the leading role.* **2.** in the first position: *the leading car.*

leading aircraftman *n. Brit. Air Force.* the rank above aircraftman. —**leading aircraftwoman** *fem. n.*

leading light *n.* an important or outstanding person in an organization or campaign.

leading note *n. Music.* same as **subtonic.**

leading question *n.* a question put in such a way as to suggest the desired answer, such as *What do you think of the horrible effects of pollution?*

lead off (liːd) *vb.* to begin.

lead on (liːd) *vb.* to lure or entice (someone), esp. into trouble or wrongdoing.

lead pencil (lɛd) *n.* a pencil containing a thin stick of a graphite compound.

lead poisoning (lɛd) *n.* acute or chronic poisoning by lead.

lead time (liːd) *n. Manufacturing.* the time between the design of a product and its production.

lead up to (liːd) *vb.* **1.** to act as a preliminary or introduction to. **2.** to approach (a topic) gradually or cautiously.

leaf (liːf) *n., pl.* **leaves** (liːvz). **1.** one of the flat usually green blades attached to the stem of a plant. **2.** leaves collectively. **3. in leaf.** (of shrubs or trees) having a full complement of leaves. **4.** one of the sheets of paper in a book. **5.** a hinged, sliding, or detachable part, such as an extension to a table. **6. take a leaf out of** (*or* **from**) **someone's book.** to imitate someone in a particular course of action. **7. turn over a new leaf.** to begin a new and improved course of behaviour. ~*vb.* **8.** (usually foll. by *through*) to turn (pages) casually or hurriedly. **9.** (of plants) to produce leaves. —'**leafless** *adj.*

leafage ('liːfɪdʒ) *n.* the leaves of plants.

leaflet ('liːflɪt) *n.* **1.** a printed and usually folded sheet of paper for distribution, usually free, for advertising or information. **2.** one of the divisions of a compound leaf. **3.** any small leaf. ~*vb.* **4.** to distribute leaflets (to).

leaf mould *n.* a rich soil consisting of decayed leaves.

leafy ('liːfɪ) *adj.* **leafier, leafiest. 1.** covered with leaves. **2.** resembling a leaf or leaves.

league[1] (liːg) *n.* **1.** an association of people or nations formed to promote the interests of its members. **2.** an association of sporting clubs that organizes matches between member teams. **3.** a class, category, or level: *he is not in the same league.* **4. in league** (**with**). working or planning together with. ~*vb.* **leaguing, leagued. 5.** to form or be formed into a league.

league[2] (liːg) *n.* an obsolete unit of distance of varying length: commonly equal to 3 miles.

leak (liːk) *n.* **1. a.** a crack or hole that allows the accidental escape or entrance as of fluid or light. **b.** such escaping or entering fluid or light. **2.** the loss of current from an electrical conductor because of faulty insulation. **3.** a disclosure of secret information. **4.** the act or an instance of leaking. **5.** *Slang.* urination. ~*vb.* **6.** to enter or escape or allow to enter or escape through a crack or hole. **7.** to disclose (secret information) or (of secret information) to be disclosed. —'**leaky** *adj.*

leakage ('liːkɪdʒ) *n.* **1.** the act or an instance of leaking. **2.** something that escapes or enters by a leak.

lean[1] (liːn) *vb.* **leaning; leant** *or* **leaned. 1.** (foll. by *against, on,* or *upon*) to rest or cause to rest against a support. **2.** to bend or cause to bend from an upright position. **3.** (foll. by *to* or *towards*) to have or express a tendency or preference. ~*n.* **4.** the condition of bending from an upright position. ~See also **lean on.**

lean[2] (liːn) *adj.* **1.** (esp. of a person) having no surplus flesh or bulk. **2.** (of meat) having little or no fat. **3.** (of a period) sparse, difficult, or causing hardship: *the lean years.* ~*n.* **4.** the part of meat that contains little or no fat. —'**leanness** *n.*

leaning ('liːnɪŋ) *n.* a tendency or inclination.

lean on *vb.* **1.** *Informal.* to put pressure on (someone) as by threats. **2.** to depend on (someone) for help and advice.

leant (lɛnt) *vb.* past of **lean**[1].

lean-to *n., pl.* **-tos.** a building with a sloping roof attached to another building or a wall.

leap (liːp) *vb.* **leaping; leapt** (lɛpt) *or* **leaped. 1.** to jump suddenly from one place to another. **2.** (often foll. by *at*) to move or react quickly. **3.** to jump over. ~*n.* **4.** the act of jumping. **5.** an abrupt change or increase: *a leap in costs.* **6. a leap in the dark.** an action performed without knowledge of the consequences. **7. by leaps and bounds.** with unexpectedly rapid progress.

leapfrog ('liːp,frɒg) *n.* **1.** a children's game in which each player in turn leaps over the others' bent backs. ~*vb.* **-frogging, -frogged. 2. a.** to play leapfrog. **b.** to leap over (something). **3.** to advance by jumps or stages.

leap year *n.* a calendar year of 366 days, February 29 (**leap day**) being the additional day, that occurs every four years.

learn (lɜːn) *vb.* **learning; learnt** (lɜːnt) *or* **learned** (lɜːnd). **1.** to gain knowledge of (something) or acquire skill in (some art or practice). **2.** to memorize (something). **3.** to gain by experience, example, or practice: *she learned how to cope over the years.* **4.** (often foll. by *of* or *about*) to become informed; find out: *his parents learnt of the accident by chance.* —'**learnable** *adj.* —'**learner** *n.*

learned ('lɜːnɪd) *adj.* **1.** having great knowledge. **2.** involving or characterized by scholarship: *learned journals.*

learning ('lɜːnɪŋ) *n.* knowledge gained by studying.

lease (liːs) *n.* **1.** a contract by which an owner grants the use of buildings or land to another person for a named period, usually for rent. **2.** a prospect of renewed energy, health, or happiness: *a new lease of life.* ~*vb.* **3.** to give or take (land or buildings) by lease.

leasehold ('liːs,həʊld) *n.* **1.** land or property held under a lease. **2.** the holding of such property under lease. —'**lease,holder** *n.*

leash (liːʃ) *n.* **1.** a length of leather or chain used to walk or control a dog or other animal; lead. **2. straining at the leash.** eagerly impatient to begin something. ~*vb.* **3.** to control as by a leash.

least (liːst) *det.* **1. the.** the superlative of **little:** *you have the least talent of anyone.* **2. at least.** if nothing else: *you should at least try.* **3. at the least.** at the minimum: *at the least you should earn a hundred pounds.* **4. not in the least.** not at all: *I don't mind in the least.* ~*adv.* **5. the**

least. superlative of **little:** *they travel the least.* ~*adj.* **6.** of very little importance.

leastways ('liːst,weɪz) *or U.S. & Canad.* **leastwise** *adv. Informal.* at least; anyway.

leather ('lɛðə) *n.* **1.** the skin of an animal made smooth and flexible by tanning and removing the hair. ~*adj.* **2.** made of leather. ~*vb.* **3.** to cover with leather. **4.** to whip as with a leather strap.

leatherjacket ('lɛðə,dʒækɪt) *n.* the tough-skinned larva of certain craneflies, which destroy the roots of grasses.

leathery ('lɛðərɪ) *adj.* having the appearance or texture of leather, esp. in toughness.

leave[1] (liːv) *vb.* **leaving, left. 1.** to go away (from a person or place). **2.** to cause to remain behind, often by mistake, in a place: *he often leaves his keys in his coat.* **3.** to cause to be or remain in a specified state: *paying the bill left him penniless.* **4.** to stop attending or belonging to a particular organization or institution: *to leave a political movement.* **5.** to break off from consuming or doing something: *the things we have left undone.* **6.** to result in; cause: *childhood problems often leave emotional scars.* **7.** to allow (someone) to do something without interfering: *leave the shopping to her.* **8.** to be survived by (members of one's family): *he leaves a wife and two children.* **9.** to bequeath: *he left his investments to his children.* **10.** to have as a remainder: *37−14 leaves 23.* **11. leave (someone) alone. a.** to stop annoying (someone). **b.** to permit to stay or be alone. ~See also **leave off, leave out.**

leave[2] (liːv) *n.* **1.** permission to be absent, as from work: *leave of absence.* **2.** the duration of such absence: *ten days' leave.* **3.** permission to do something: *he was granted leave to speak.* **4. on leave.** officially excused from work or duty. **5. take (one's) leave (of).** to say farewell (to).

leaven ('lɛv'n) *n. also* **leavening. 1.** any substance, such as yeast, that produces fermentation in dough and causes it to rise. **2.** an influence that produces a gradual change. ~*vb.* **3.** to cause fermentation in (dough). **4.** to spread through, causing a gradual change.

leave off *vb.* **1.** to stop; cease. **2.** to stop wearing or using.

leave out *vb.* to omit or exclude: *we'll have to leave out the next scene.*

leaves (liːvz) *n.* the plural of **leaf.**

leave-taking *n.* a departing; a farewell.

leavings ('liːvɪŋz) *pl. n.* something remaining, such as food on a plate, residue, or refuse.

Lebensraum ('leɪbənz,raʊm) *n.* territory claimed by a nation or state because it is necessary for survival or growth.

lecherous ('lɛtʃərəs) *adj.* (of a man) having or showing strong and uncontrolled sexual desire. —**'lecher** *n.* —**'lechery** *n.*

lecithin ('lɛsɪθɪn) *n. Biochem.* a yellow-brown compound found in plant and animal tissues, esp. egg yolk: used in making cosmetics and inks, and as an emulsifier and stabilizer (**E322**) in foods.

lectern ('lɛktən) *n.* a sloping reading desk, esp. in a church.

lecture ('lɛktʃə) *n.* **1.** a talk on a particular subject given or read to an audience. **2.** a lengthy rebuke or scolding. ~*vb.* **3.** to give or read a lecture (to an audience or class). **4.** to rebuke (someone) at length. —**'lecturer** *n.* —**'lectureship** *n.*

led (lɛd) *vb.* the past of **lead**[1].

LED *Electronics.* light-emitting diode: a semiconductor that gives out light when an electric current is applied to it.

ledge (lɛdʒ) *n.* **1.** a narrow horizontal surface that projects from a wall or window. **2.** a narrow shelflike projection on a cliff or mountain.

ledger ('lɛdʒə) *n. Book-keeping.* the principal book in which the commercial transactions of a company are recorded.

ledger line *n. Music.* a short line above or below the staff used to indicate the pitch of notes higher or lower than the range of the staff.

lee (liː) *n.* **1.** a sheltered part or side; the side away from the direction from which the wind is blowing. ~*adj.* **2.** *Naut.* on, at, or towards the side away from the wind: *on a lee shore.*

leech (liːtʃ) *n.* **1.** a worm which has a sucker at each end of the body and feeds on the blood or tissues of other animals. **2.** a person who lives off another person; parasite.

leek (liːk) *n.* a vegetable of the onion family with a slender white bulb and broad flat overlapping leaves: the national emblem of Wales.

leer (lɪə) *vb.* **1.** to give a sneering or suggestive look or grin. ~*n.* **2.** such a look.

leery ('lɪərɪ) *adj.* **leerier, leeriest. 1.** *Now chiefly dialect.* knowing or sly. **2.** *Slang.* (foll. by *of*) suspicious or wary.

lees (liːz) *pl. n.* the sediment from an alcoholic drink.

leet (liːt) *n. Scot.* a list of candidates for an office.

leeward ('liːwəd; *Naut.* 'luːəd) *Chiefly naut.* ~*adj.* **1.** of, in, or moving to the quarter towards which the wind blows. ~*n.* **2.** the side towards the lee. ~*adv.* **3.** towards the lee.

leeway ('liː,weɪ) *n.* **1.** room for free movement within limits, as in action or expenditure. **2.** sideways drift of a boat or aircraft.

left[1] (lɛft) *adj.* **1.** of or designating the side

of something or someone that faces west when the front is turned towards the north. **2.** worn on a left hand or foot. **3.** of or relating to the political left. ~*adv.* **4.** on or in the direction of the left. ~*n.* **5.** a left side, direction, position, area, or part. **6.** (*often cap.*) the people who support the political ideals of socialism rather than capitalism. **7.** *Boxing.* **a.** a blow with the left hand. **b.** the left hand.

left² (lɛft) *vb.* the past of **leave¹**.

left-hand *adj.* **1.** of, on, or towards the left. **2.** for the left hand.

left-handed *adj.* **1.** using the left hand with greater ease than the right. **2.** performed with the left hand. **3.** designed for use by the left hand. **4.** awkward or clumsy. **5.** ambiguous or insincere: *a left-handed compliment.* **6.** turning from right to left; anticlockwise. ~*adv.* **7.** with the left hand. —ˌ**left-ˈhander** *n.*

leftist (ˈlɛftɪst) *adj.* **1.** of or relating to the political left or its principles. ~*n.* **2.** a person who supports the political left. —ˈ**leftism** *n.*

left-luggage office *n. Brit.* a place at a railway station or airport where luggage may be left for a small charge.

leftover (ˈlɛftˌəʊvə) *n.* **1.** (*often pl.*) an unused portion, as of material or of cooked food. ~*adj.* **2.** left as an unused portion.

leftward (ˈlɛftwəd) *adj., adv. also* **leftwards.** on or towards the left.

left wing *n.* **1.** (*often cap.*) the more radical or progressive section, esp. of a political party. **2.** *Sports.* **a.** the left-hand side of the field. **b.** a player positioned in this area in certain games. ~*adj.* **left-wing. 3.** of, belonging to, or relating to the political left wing. —ˌ**left-ˈwinger** *n.*

lefty (ˈlɛftɪ) *n., pl.* **lefties.** *Informal.* **1.** a left-winger. **2.** *Chiefly U.S. & Canad.* a left-handed person.

leg (lɛg) *n.* **1.** either of the two lower limbs in humans, or any similar structure in animals that is used for movement or support. **2.** this part of an animal, used for food: *leg of lamb.* **3.** something similar to a leg in appearance or function, such as one of the supports of a chair. **4.** a branch of a forked object. **5.** the part of a garment that covers the leg. **6.** a section of a journey. **7.** a single stage, lap, or length in a relay race. **8.** one of a series of games, matches, or parts of games. **9.** *Cricket.* the side of the field to the left of and behind a right-handed batsman as he faces the bowler. **10. not have a leg to stand on.** *Informal.* to have no reasonable basis for an opinion or argument. **11. on his, its,** etc., **last legs.** (of a person or thing) worn out; exhausted. **12. pull someone's leg.** *Informal.* to tease or make fun of someone. **13. shake a leg.** *Informal.* to hurry up. **14. stretch one's legs.** to stand up or walk around, esp. after

sitting for some time. ~*vb.* **legging, legged. 15. leg it.** *Informal.* to walk, run, or hurry.

legacy (ˈlɛgəsɪ) *n., pl.* **-cies. 1.** money or personal property left to someone by a will. **2.** something handed down by a predecessor.

legal (ˈliːgªl) *adj.* **1.** established by or founded upon law; lawful. **2.** of or relating to law. **3.** relating to or characteristic of lawyers. —ˈ**legally** *adv.*

legal aid *n.* financial assistance available to people who are unable to meet the full cost of legal proceedings.

legalese (ˌliːgəˈliːz) *n.* the conventional language in which legal documents are written.

legalism (ˈliːgəˌlɪzəm) *n.* strict adherence to the letter of the law. —ˈ**legalist** *n., adj.* —ˌ**legalˈistic** *adj.*

legality (lɪˈgælɪtɪ) *n., pl.* **-ties.** the state or quality of being legal or lawful.

legalize *or* **-ise** (ˈliːgəˌlaɪz) *vb.* to make lawful or legal. —ˌ**legaliˈzation** *or* **-iˈsation** *n.*

legal tender *n.* currency that a creditor must by law accept to pay a debt.

legate (ˈlɛgɪt) *n.* a messenger, esp. one representing the Pope.

legation (lɪˈgeɪʃən) *n.* **1.** a diplomatic mission headed by a minister. **2.** the official residence and office of a diplomatic minister.

legato (lɪˈgɑːtəʊ) *Music.* ~*adv.* **1.** smoothly and evenly. ~*n., pl.* **-tos. 2.** a style of playing with no gaps between notes.

leg before wicket *n. Cricket.* a dismissal on the grounds that a batsman has been struck on the leg by a bowled ball that otherwise would have hit the wicket. Abbrev.: **lbw.**

legend (ˈlɛdʒənd) *n.* **1.** a popular story handed down from earlier times which may or may not be true. **2.** such stories collectively. **3.** modern stories about a famous person which may or may not be true: *the Monroe legend.* **4.** a person whose fame makes him seem exceptional: *a legend in his own lifetime.* **5.** an inscription, as on a coin or beneath a coat of arms. **6.** an explanation on a table, map, or chart, of the symbols used.

legendary (ˈlɛdʒəndrɪ) *adj.* **1.** of or relating to legend. **2.** celebrated or described in legend: *legendary knights of long ago.* **3.** very famous: *legendary skill.*

legerdemain (ˌlɛdʒədəˈmeɪn) *n.* **1.** same as **sleight of hand. 2.** cunning deception.

leger line (ˈlɛdʒə) *n.* same as **ledger line.**

leggings (ˈlɛgɪŋz) *pl. n.* **1.** an extra outer covering for the lower legs. **2.** close-fitting trousers for women or children.

leggy (ˈlɛgɪ) *adj.* **1.** having unusually long

legs. **2.** (of a plant) having a long weak stem.

leghorn (ˈlɛɡˌhɔːn) n. **1.** a type of Italian wheat straw that is woven into hats. **2.** any hat made from this straw.

Leghorn (lɛˈɡɔːn) n. a breed of domestic fowl.

legible (ˈlɛdʒəbᵊl) adj. (of handwriting) able to be read. —ˌlegiˈbility n. —ˈlegibly adv.

legion (ˈliːdʒən) n. **1.** a unit in the ancient Roman army of infantry with supporting cavalry of three to six thousand men. **2.** any large military force: the French Foreign Legion. **3.** (often pl.) any very large number. —ˈlegionary adj., n.

legionnaire (ˌliːdʒəˈnɛə) n. (often cap.) a member of a legion.

Legionnaire's disease (ˌliːdʒəˈnɛəz) n. a serious bacterial infection, with symptoms similar to pneumonia.

legislate (ˈlɛdʒɪsˌleɪt) vb. **1.** to make or pass laws. **2.** to bring into effect by legislation. —ˈlegisˌlator n.

legislation (ˌlɛdʒɪsˈleɪʃən) n. **1.** the act or process of making laws. **2.** the laws so made.

legislative (ˈlɛdʒɪslətɪv) adj. **1.** of or relating to legislation or a legislature. **2.** having the power or function of legislating: a legislative assembly.

legislature (ˈlɛdʒɪsˌleɪtʃə) n. a body of persons empowered to make and repeal laws.

legitimate adj. (lɪˈdʒɪtɪmɪt). **1.** authorized by or in accordance with law: legitimate business. **2.** based on correct or acceptable principles of reasoning: a legitimate argument. **3.** (of a child) born of parents legally married to each other. **4.** of, relating to, or ruling by hereditary right: a legitimate monarch. **5.** of or relating to serious drama as distinct from films, television, or vaudeville. ~vb. (lɪˈdʒɪtɪˌmeɪt). **6.** to make, pronounce, or show to be legitimate. —leˈgitimacy n. —leˈgitimately adv.

legitimize or **-mise** (lɪˈdʒɪtɪˌmaɪz) vb. to make (something) legitimate; legalize. —leˌgitimiˈzation or -miˈsation n.

Lego (ˈlɛɡəʊ) n. Trademark. a construction toy consisting of plastic bricks that fit together with studs.

leg-pull n. Brit. informal. a practical joke.

legroom (ˈlɛɡˌruːm) n. room to move one's legs comfortably, as in a car.

leguaan (ˈlɛɡuˌɑːn) n. a large amphibious S African lizard.

legume (ˈlɛɡjuːm, lɪˈɡjuːm) n. **1.** the fruit of leguminous plants; a pod. **2.** any of various table vegetables, esp. beans or peas.

leguminous (lɪˈɡjuːmɪnəs) adj. of or relating to any family of flowering plants having pods (or legumes) as fruits.

lei (leɪ) n. (in Hawaii) a garland of flowers, worn around the neck.

Leics Leicestershire.

leisure (ˈlɛʒə) n. **1.** time or opportunity for ease, relaxation, or hobbies. **2. at leisure. a.** having free time. **b.** not occupied. **c.** without hurrying. **3. at one's leisure.** when one has free time. —ˈleisured adj.

leisure centre n. a building providing facilities, such as a swimming pool, gym, and café, for a range of leisure pursuits.

leisurely (ˈlɛʒəlɪ) adj. **1.** unhurried; relaxed. ~adv. **2.** in a relaxed way. —ˈleisureliness n.

leitmotiv or **leitmotif** (ˈlaɪtməʊˌtiːf) n. **1.** Music. a recurring melodic phrase used to suggest a character, thing, or idea. **2.** an often repeated image in a literary work.

lekker (ˈlɛkə) adj. S. African slang. pleasing, enjoyable, or likable.

lemming (ˈlɛmɪŋ) n. **1.** a small rodent of northern and arctic regions, noted for rushing into the sea in large groups and drowning. **2.** a member of any group following an unthinking course towards destruction.

lemon (ˈlɛmən) n. **1.** a yellow oval edible fruit with juicy acidic flesh that grows on an evergreen tree in warm and tropical regions. **2.** a pale yellow colour. **3.** Slang. a person or thing considered to be useless or defective. —ˈlemony adj.

lemonade (ˌlɛməˈneɪd) n. a drink made from lemon juice, sugar, and water or from carbonated water, citric acid, and sweetener.

lemon sole n. a European flatfish valued as food.

lemon squash n. Brit. a drink made from a sweetened lemon concentrate and water.

lemur (ˈliːmə) n. an animal of Madagascar, related to the monkeys, with a foxy face and long tail, that lives in trees and is active at night.

lend (lɛnd) vb. **lending, lent. 1.** to permit the use of (something) on the condition that it is returned. **2.** to provide (money) temporarily, often at interest. **3.** to contribute (something, esp. some abstract quality): her presence lent beauty. **4. lend an ear.** to listen. **5. lend oneself** or **itself.** to be appropriate for: the novel lends itself to serialization. —ˈlender n.

length (lɛŋθ) n. **1.** the extent or measurement of something from end to end. **2.** a specified distance, esp. between two positions: the length of a race. **3.** a period of time, as between specified limits or moments. **4.** a piece of something narrow and long: a length of tubing. **5.** the quality, state, or fact of being long rather than short. **6.** (usually pl.) the amount of trouble taken in doing something: to go to great length. **7.** Prosody, phonetics. the duration of a vowel or syllable. **8. at length. a.** after a long interval or period of time. **b.** in great detail.

lengthen (ˈlɛŋθən) *vb.* to make or become longer.

lengthways (ˈlɛŋθˌweɪz) *or* **lengthwise** *adv., adj.* in, according to, or along the direction of length.

lengthy (ˈlɛŋθɪ) *adj.* **lengthier, lengthiest.** very long or tiresome. —ˈ**lengthily** *adv.* —ˈ**lengthiness** *n.*

lenient (ˈliːnɪənt) *adj.* tolerant, not strict or severe. —ˈ**leniency** *n.* —ˈ**leniently** *adv.*

lenity (ˈlɛnɪtɪ) *n., pl.* **-ties.** the state or quality of being lenient.

lens (lɛnz) *n.* **1.** a piece of glass or other transparent material with a curved surface or surfaces, used to bring together or spread rays of light passing through it: used in cameras, telescopes, and spectacles. **2.** *Anat.* a transparent structure in the eye, behind the iris, that focuses images on the retina.

lent (lɛnt) *vb.* the past of **lend.**

Lent (lɛnt) *n. Christianity.* the period from Ash Wednesday to Easter Saturday, observed as a time of penance and fasting. —ˈ**Lenten** *adj.*

lentil (ˈlɛntɪl) *n.* any of the small seeds of a leguminous Asian plant, which are cooked and eaten in soups and vegetable dishes.

lento (ˈlɛntəʊ) *Music.* ~*adv.* **1.** slowly. ~*n., pl.* **-tos.** **2.** a movement or passage performed slowly.

Leo (ˈliːəʊ) *n. Astrol.* the fifth sign of the zodiac: the Lion.

leonine (ˈliːəˌnaɪn) *adj.* of or like a lion.

leopard (ˈlɛpəd) *n.* a large African and Asian mammal of the cat family, usually having a tawny yellow coat with black spots. Also called: **panther.**

leotard (ˈliːəˌtɑːd) *n.* a tight-fitting garment covering the body from the shoulders to the thighs and worn by acrobats, ballet dancers, and people doing exercises.

leper (ˈlɛpə) *n.* **1.** a person who has leprosy. **2.** a person who is avoided.

lepidopteran (ˌlɛpɪˈdɒptərən) *n., pl.* **-terans** *or* **-tera** (-tərə). **1.** any of a large order of insects, including the butterflies and moths, typically having two pairs of wings covered with fragile scales. ~*adj.* also **lepidopterous. 2.** of this order.

lepidopterist (ˌlɛpɪˈdɒptərɪst) *n.* a person who studies or collects moths and butterflies.

leprechaun (ˈlɛprəˌkɔːn) *n.* (in Irish folklore) a mischievous elf.

leprosy (ˈlɛprəsɪ) *n. Pathol.* a chronic infectious disease, characterized by painful inflamed lumps beneath the skin and disfigurement and wasting of affected parts. —ˈ**leprous** *adj.*

lepton (ˈlɛptɒn) *n. Physics.* any of a group of elementary particles with weak interactions.

lesbian (ˈlɛzbɪən) *n.* **1.** a female homosexual. ~*adj.* **2.** of or characteristic of lesbians. —ˈ**lesbianism** *n.*

lese-majesty (ˈliːzˈmædʒɪstɪ) *n.* **1.** an offence against the sovereign power in a state; treason. **2.** a slight against authority or position.

lesion (ˈliːʒən) *n.* **1.** any structural change in an organ or tissue resulting from injury or disease. **2.** an injury or wound.

less (lɛs) *det.* **1.** the comparative of **little** (sense 1): *less sugar; less spirit than before.* **2.** *Not universally accepted.* fewer. **3.** (usually preceded by *no*) lower in rank or importance: *no less a man than the president.* **4. less of.** to a smaller extent or degree: *we see less of John these days.* ~*adv.* **5.** the comparative of **a little:** *she walks less than she should.* ~*prep.* **6.** subtracting; minus: *three weeks less a day.*

lessee (lɛˈsiː) *n.* a person to whom a lease is granted.

lessen (ˈlɛsᵊn) *vb.* to make or become less.

lesser (ˈlɛsə) *adj.* not as great in quantity, size, or worth.

lesson (ˈlɛsᵊn) *n.* **1. a.** a unit, or single period of instruction in a subject; class. **b.** the content of such a unit. **2.** material assigned for individual study. **3.** something from which useful knowledge or principles can be learned; example: *his patience is a lesson to us all.* **4.** an experience that serves as a warning or example: *let that be a lesson to you.* **5.** a passage of Scripture read aloud from the Bible during a church service.

lessor (ˈlɛsə, lɛˈsɔː) *n.* a person who grants a lease of property.

lest (lɛst) *conj.* **1.** so as to prevent any possibility that: *keep down lest anyone see us.* **2.** in case: *he was alarmed lest she should find out.*

let[1] (lɛt) *vb.* **letting, let. 1.** to allow: *she lets him roam around.* **2.** used as an auxiliary to express: **a.** a request, proposal, or command, or to convey a warning or threat: *let's get on; just let me catch you here again!* **b.** an assumption or hypothesis: *let "a" equal "b".* **c.** resigned acceptance of the inevitable: *let the worst happen.* **3.** to allow someone to rent (property or accommodation). **4.** to allow or cause the movement of (something) in a specified direction: *to let air out of a tyre.* **5. let alone.** not to mention: *I can't afford wine, let alone champagne.* **6. let alone** *or* **be.** stop annoying or interfering with: *let the poor cat alone.* **7. let go.** to relax one's hold (on). **8. let loose.** to allow (a person or animal) to leave or escape. ~*n.* **9.** *Brit.* the act of letting property or accommodation. ~See also **let down, let off,** etc.

let[2] (lɛt) *n.* **1.** *Tennis, squash, etc.* a minor infringement or obstruction of the ball, requiring a point to be replayed. **2. without let or hindrance.** without obstruction.

let down *vb.* **1.** to fail to satisfy the expectations of (someone); disappoint. **2.** to lower. **3.** to shorten (the hem) so as to lengthen (a dress, skirt, or trousers). **4.** to deflate: *to let down a tyre.* ~*n.* **letdown. 5.** a disappointment.

lethal ('li:θəl) *adj.* able to cause or causing death. —**'lethally** *adv.*

lethargy ('lɛθədʒɪ) *n., pl.* -**gies. 1.** sluggishness or dullness. **2.** an abnormal lack of energy. —**lethargic** (lɪ'θɑːdʒɪk) *adj.* —**le-'thargically** *adv.*

let off *vb.* **1.** to excuse from (work or other responsibilities): *I'll let you off homework for a week.* **2.** *Informal.* to allow to get away without or with less than the expected punishment: *I'll let you off with a warning this time.* **3.** to explode or fire (a bomb, gun, or firework). **4.** to release (liquid, air, or steam).

let on *vb. Informal.* **1.** to allow (something, such as a secret) to be known; reveal. **2.** to pretend: *she let on she didn't know me.*

let out *vb.* **1.** to emit: *to let out a howl.* **2.** to allow to leave; release. **3.** to reveal (a secret). **4.** to make (property) available for people to rent. **5.** to make (a garment) larger, as by reducing the seams. ~*n.* **letout. 6.** a chance to escape.

letter ('lɛtə) *n.* **1.** a written or printed message, usually enclosed in an envelope and sent by post. **2.** any of a set of conventional symbols used in writing or printing a language: character of the alphabet. **3.** the strict meaning of an agreement or document; exact wording: *the letter of the law.* **4. to the letter.** precisely: *I followed her instructions to the letter.* ~*vb.* **5.** to write or mark letters on (a sign). —**'lettering** *n.*

letter bomb *n.* an explosive device in an envelope or parcel that explodes when the envelope or parcel is opened.

letter box *n. Chiefly Brit.* **1.** a slot through which letters are delivered to a building. **2.** Also called: **pillar box, postbox.** a public box into which letters and postcards are put for collection.

lettered ('lɛtəd) *adj.* **1.** well educated. **2.** printed or marked with letters.

letterhead ('lɛtə,hɛd) *n.* a sheet of writing paper with the name and address of a person, company, or organization printed at the top.

letter of credit *n.* a letter issued by a bank entitling the bearer to draw money from other banks.

letterpress ('lɛtə,prɛs) *n.* a method of printing in which ink is transferred from raised surfaces to paper by pressure.

letters ('lɛtəz) *n.* (*functioning as sing. or pl.*) **1.** literary knowledge, ability, or learning: *a man of letters.* **2.** literary culture in general.

letters patent *pl. n.* See **patent** (senses 1, 3).

lettuce ('lɛtɪs) *n.* a plant cultivated in many varieties for its large edible leaves, which are eaten in salads.

let up *vb.* **1.** to diminish or stop. **2.** (foll. by *on*) *Informal.* to be less harsh (towards someone). ~*n.* **let-up. 3.** *Informal.* a lessening.

leucocyte ('lu:kə,saɪt) *n.* any of the various large white cells in the blood of vertebrates.

leukaemia *or esp. U.S.* **leukemia** (lu:-'kiːmɪə) *n.* an acute or chronic disease characterized by extreme overproduction of white blood cells.

levee[1] ('lɛvɪ) *n. U.S.* **1.** an embankment alongside a river, produced naturally or constructed to prevent flooding. **2.** a quay.

levee[2] ('lɛvɪ, 'lɛveɪ) *n.* a formal reception held by a sovereign just after rising from bed.

level ('lɛv°l) *adj.* **1.** on a horizontal plane. **2.** having a surface of completely equal height. **3.** being of the same height as something else: *the sunflowers were level with the porch roof.* **4.** equal to or even with (something or someone else): *production will keep level with population growth.* **5.** not inconsistent or irregular: *a level pulse.* **6. one's level best.** the best one can do. ~*vb.* -**elling, -elled** *or U.S.* -**eling, -eled. 7.** (sometimes foll. by *off*) to make (a surface) horizontal, level, or even. **8.** to make (two or more people or things) equal, as in position or status. **9.** to raze to the ground. **10.** to direct (a gaze, accusation, or criticism) emphatically at someone. **11.** (often foll. by *at*) to aim (a weapon) horizontally. ~*n.* **12.** a horizontal line or plane. **13.** a device, such as a spirit level, for determining whether a surface is horizontal. **14.** position or status in a scale of values: *low-level nuclear waste.* **15.** amount or degree of progress; stage: *primary school level.* **16.** a specified vertical position: *roof level.* **17.** a horizontal line or plane from which measurement of height is based: *sea level.* **18.** a flat even surface or area of land. **19.** a degree or intensity reached on a measurable or notional scale: *noise level.* **20. on the level.** *Informal.* sincere or genuine.

level crossing *n. Brit.* a point at which a railway and a road cross.

level-headed *adj.* even-tempered, balanced, and reliable.

lever ('liːvə) *n.* **1.** a rigid bar pivoted about a fulcrum, used to transfer a force to a load and usually to provide a mechanical advantage. **2.** a bar, such as a crowbar, used to move a heavy object or to prise something open. **3.** a means of exerting pressure in order to accomplish something: *industrial action may be threatened as a political lever*. ~*vb*. **4.** to prise or move (an object) with a lever.

leverage ('li:vərɪdʒ) *n*. **1.** the action of a lever. **2.** the mechanical advantage gained by using a lever. **3.** strategic advantage.

leveret ('levərɪt) *n*. a young hare.

leviathan (lɪ'vaɪəθən) *n*. **1.** *Bible*. a sea monster. **2.** any huge or powerful thing.

Levis ('li:vaɪz) *pl. n. Trademark*. denim jeans.

levitate ('levɪ,teɪt) *vb*. to rise or cause to rise and float in the air, usually by using supernatural powers. —,levi'tation *n*.

levity ('levɪtɪ) *n., pl*. **-ties**. the quality of being light-hearted about serious matters.

levy ('levɪ) *vb*. **levying, levied**. **1.** to impose and collect (a tax, tariff, or fine). **2.** to conscript troops for service. ~*n., pl*. **levies**. **3. a.** the act of imposing and collecting a tax, tariff, or fine. **b.** the money so raised. **4.** troops conscripted for service.

lewd (lu:d) *adj*. characterized by or intended to excite crude sexual desire; obscene.

lexical ('leksɪk³l) *adj*. **1.** of or relating to the vocabulary of a language. **2.** of or relating to a lexicon. —'lexically *adv*.

lexicography (,leksɪ'kɒgrəfɪ) *n*. the process or profession of writing or compiling dictionaries. —,lexi'cographer *n*.

lexicon ('leksɪkən) *n*. **1.** a dictionary, esp. one of an ancient language such as Greek. **2.** the vocabulary of a language or of an individual.

ley (leɪ, li:) *n*. land temporarily under grass.

Leyden jar ('laɪd³n) *n. Physics*. an early type of capacitor consisting of a glass jar with the lower part of the inside and outside coated with tinfoil.

Li *Chem*. lithium.

liability (,laɪə'bɪlɪtɪ) *n., pl*. **-ties**. **1.** the state of being liable. **2.** a financial obligation. **3.** a person or thing that is a hindrance or disadvantage.

liable ('laɪəb³l) *adj*. **1.** legally obliged or responsible; answerable. **2.** given to or at risk from a condition: *liable to colds*. **3.** *Not universally accepted*. probable or likely: *it's liable to happen soon*.

liaise (lɪ'eɪz) *vb*. (usually foll. by *with*) to communicate and maintain contact with.

liaison (lɪ'eɪzɒn) *n*. **1.** communication and contact between groups or units. **2.** a secretive or adulterous sexual relationship.

liana (lɪ'ɑːnə) *n*. a woody climbing and twining plant of tropical forests.

liar ('laɪə) *n*. a person who tells lies.

lib (lɪb) *n. Informal*. short for **liberation**: used in the name of certain movements: *women's lib; gay lib*.

Lib. Liberal.

libation (laɪ'beɪʃən) *n*. **a.** the pouring-out of

wine in honour of a deity. **b.** the wine so poured out.

libel ('laɪb³l) *n*. **1.** *Law*. the publication of something false which damages a person's reputation. **2.** any damaging or unflattering representation or statement. ~*vb*. **-belling, -belled** or *U.S*. **-beling, -beled**. **3.** *Law*. to make or publish a false damaging statement or representation about (a person). —'libellous or 'libelous *adj*.

liberal ('lɪbərəl, 'lɪbrəl) *adj*. **1.** relating to or having social and political views that favour progress and reform. **2.** giving and generous in temperament or behaviour. **3.** tolerant of other people. **4.** abundant; lavish: *a liberal helping of cream*. **5.** not strict; free: *a liberal translation*. **6.** (of an education) designed to develop general cultural interests and intellectual ability. ~*n*. **7.** a person who has liberal ideas or opinions. —'liberalism *n*. —'liberally *adv*.

Liberal ('lɪbərəl, 'lɪbrəl) *n*. **1.** a member or supporter of a political party that favours progress and reform. ~*adj*. **2.** of or relating to such a party.

liberality (,lɪbə'rælɪtɪ) *n., pl*. **-ties**. **1.** generosity; bounty. **2.** the quality or condition of being broad-minded.

liberalize or **-ise** ('lɪbərə,laɪz, 'lɪbrə-) *vb*. to make or become liberal. —,liberali'zation or **-i'sation** *n*.

liberate ('lɪbə,reɪt) *vb*. **1.** to free (someone) from social prejudices or injustices. **2.** to give liberty to; make free. **3.** to release (a country) from enemy occupation. —,libe'ration *n*. —'liber,ator *n*.

liberated ('lɪbə,reɪtɪd) *adj*. **1.** not bound by traditional sexual and social roles: *a liberated woman*. **2.** given liberty. **3.** released from enemy occupation.

libertine ('lɪbə,tiːn, -,taɪn) *n*. **1.** a person who is promiscuous and unscrupulous. ~*adj*. **2.** promiscuous and unscrupulous.

liberty ('lɪbətɪ) *n., pl*. **-ties**. **1.** the power of choosing, thinking, and acting for oneself; freedom from control or restriction. **2.** the right or privilege of access to a particular place; freedom. **3.** (*often pl*.) a social action regarded as being familiar, forward, or improper. **4. at liberty**. free, unoccupied, or unrestricted. **5. take liberties (with)**. to be overfamiliar (towards someone).

libidinous (lɪ'bɪdɪnəs) *adj*. characterized by excessive sexual desire. —li'bidinously *adv*.

libido (lɪ'biːdəʊ) *n., pl*. **-dos**. **1.** *Psychoanal*. psychic energy from the id. **2.** sexual urge or desire. —**libidinal** (lɪ'bɪdɪn³l) *adj*.

Libra ('liːbrə) *n. Astrol*. the seventh sign of the zodiac: the scales.

librarian (laɪ'breərɪən) *n*. a person in charge of or assisting in a library. —li'brarian-,ship *n*.

library ('laɪbrərɪ) *n., pl*. **-braries**. **1.** a room or set of rooms where books and other literary materials are kept. **2.** a collection of literary materials, films, tapes, or gramophone records, kept for borrowing or reference. **3.** the building or institution that houses such a collection. **4.** a set of books published as a series, often in a similar format. **5.** *Computers.* a collection of standard programs, usually stored on disk.

libretto (lɪˈbrɛtəʊ) *n., pl.* **-tos** *or* **-ti** (-tiː). a text written for an opera. —**liˈbrettist** *n.*

lice (laɪs) *n.* the plural of **louse.**

licence *or U.S.* **license** (ˈlaɪsəns) *n.* **1.** a document giving official permission to do something. **2.** formal permission or exemption. **3.** intentional disregard of conventional rules to achieve a certain effect: *poetic licence.* **4.** excessive freedom.

license (ˈlaɪsəns) *vb.* **1.** to grant or give a licence for (something, such as the sale of alcohol). **2.** to give permission to or for. —**ˈlicensable** *adj.*

licensee (ˌlaɪsənˈsiː) *n.* a person who holds a licence, esp. one to sell alcoholic drink.

licentiate (laɪˈsɛnʃɪɪt) *n.* a person who holds a certificate of competence to practise a certain profession.

licentious (laɪˈsɛnʃəs) *adj.* sexually unrestrained or promiscuous. —**liˈcentiousness** *n.*

lichee (ˌlaɪˈtʃiː) *n.* same as **lychee.**

lichen (ˈlaɪkən, ˈlɪtʃən) *n.* any of various small plants which are formed by the association of a fungus and an alga that grow in patches on tree trunks, bare ground, rocks, and stone walls.

lich gate *or* **lych gate** (lɪtʃ) *n.* a roofed gate to a churchyard, formerly used as a temporary shelter for a coffin.

licit (ˈlɪsɪt) *adj.* lawful; permitted.

lick (lɪk) *vb.* **1.** to pass the tongue over in order to taste, wet, or clean. **2.** to flicker over or round (something): *the flames licked around the door.* **3.** *Informal.* **a.** to defeat. **b.** to thrash. **4. lick into shape.** to put into a satisfactory condition. **5. lick one's wounds.** to retire after a defeat. ~*n.* **6.** an instance of passing the tongue over something. **7.** a small amount: *a lick of paint.* **8.** *Informal.* a hit; blow. **9.** *Informal.* a fast pace: *he was going at quite a lick.* **10. a lick and a promise.** something hastily done, esp. a hurried wash.

licorice (ˈlɪkərɪs) *n. U.S. & Canad.* same as **liquorice.**

lid (lɪd) *n.* **1.** a removable or hinged cover: *a saucepan lid.* **2.** short for **eyelid. 3. put the** (**tin**) **lid on.** *Informal.* to put an end to. —**ˈlidded** *adj.*

lido (ˈliːdəʊ) *n., pl.* **-dos.** *Brit.* a public place of recreation, including a swimming pool.

lie[1] (laɪ) *vb.* **lying, lied. 1.** to speak untruthfully with intent to mislead or deceive. **2.** to convey a false impression or practise

deception: *the camera does not lie.* ~*n.* **3.** an untrue statement deliberately used to mislead. **4.** something that is deliberately intended to deceive. **5. give the lie to. a.** to disprove. **b.** to accuse of lying. **Usage.** see **lay**[1].

lie[2] (laɪ) *vb.* **lying, lay, lain. 1.** (often foll. by *down*) to place oneself or be in a prostrate position, horizontal to the ground. **2.** to be situated, esp. on a horizontal surface: *the pencil is lying on the desk; India lies to the south of Russia.* **3.** to be and remain (in a particular state or condition): *to lie dormant.* **4.** to stretch or extend: *the city lies before us.* **5.** (usually foll. by *in*) to exist or consist in: *strength lies in unity.* **6.** (foll. by *with*) to be or rest (with): *the ultimate decision lies with you.* ~*n.* **7.** the manner, place, or style in which something is situated. **8.** the hiding place or lair of an animal. **9. lie of the land.** the way in which a situation is developing. ~See also **lie down, lie in.**

lied (liːd) *n., pl.* **lieder** (ˈliːdə). *Music.* a musical setting for solo voice and piano of a romantic or lyrical poem.

lie detector *n. Informal.* a device used to measure the blood pressure, pulse rate, etc., of someone being questioned, which is thought to increase when the person is lying.

lie down *vb.* **1.** to place oneself or be in a horizontal position in order to rest. **2.** to accept without protest or opposition: *I won't take bureaucratic bullying lying down.* ~*n.* **lie-down. 3.** a rest.

liege (liːdʒ) *adj.* **1.** (of a lord) owed feudal allegiance: *liege lord.* **2.** (of a vassal or servant) owing feudal allegiance: *a liege subject.* **3.** faithful; loyal. ~*n.* **4.** a liege lord. **5.** a subject.

lie in *vb.* **1.** to remain in bed late in the morning. ~*n.* **lie-in. 2.** a long stay in bed in the morning.

lien (ˈliːən, liːn) *n. Law.* a right to retain possession of another's property until a debt is paid.

lieu (ljuː, luː) *n.* **in lieu of.** instead of.

lieutenant (lɛfˈtɛnənt; *U.S.* luːˈtɛnənt) *n.* **1.** a junior officer in the army or navy, or in the U.S. police force. **2.** a person who holds an office in subordination to or in place of a superior. —**lieuˈtenancy** *n.*

lieutenant colonel *n.* an officer in an army, air force, or marine corps.

lieutenant commander *n.* an officer in a navy.

lieutenant general *n.* a senior officer in an army, air force, or marine corps.

lieutenant governor *n.* **1.** a deputy governor. **2.** (in Canada) the representative of the Crown in a province.

life (laɪf) *n., pl.* **lives** (laɪvz). **1.** the state or quality that distinguishes living beings from dead ones, characterized chiefly by metabolism, growth, and the ability to reproduce and respond to stimuli. **2.** the period between birth and death or between birth and the present time. **3.** a living person or being: *to save a life*. **4.** the remainder or extent of one's life. **5.** *Informal.* a sentence of imprisonment for life, now taken to be approximately fifteen years. **6.** the amount of time that something is active or functioning: *the life of a battery*. **7.** a present condition, state, or mode of existence: *my life is very dull here*. **8.** a biography. **9.** a characteristic state or mode of existence: *town life*. **10.** the sum or course of human events and activities. **11.** liveliness or high spirits: *full of life*. **12.** a source of strength, animation, or vitality: *he was the life of the show*. **13.** all living things, taken as a whole: *there is no life on Mars; plant life*. **14. a matter of life and death.** a matter of extreme urgency. **15. as large as life.** *Informal.* real and living. **16. not on your life.** *Informal.* certainly not. **17. to the life.** (of a copy of a painting or drawing) resembling the original exactly. **18. true to life.** faithful to reality.

life assurance *n.* insurance that provides for a sum of money to be paid to the policyholder at a certain age or to the widow or children on the death of the policyholder. Also called: **life insurance.**

life belt *n.* an inflatable ring used to keep a person afloat when in danger of drowning.

lifeblood ('laɪf,blʌd) *n.* **1.** the blood vital to life. **2.** something that is essential in order to exist, develop, or be successful.

lifeboat ('laɪf,bəʊt) *n.* a boat used for rescuing people at sea or escaping from a sinking ship.

life buoy *n.* a buoyant device for keeping people afloat in an emergency.

life cycle *n.* the series of changes occuring in each generation of an animal or plant.

lifeguard ('laɪf,gɑːd) *n.* a person at a beach or pool to guard people against drowning.

life jacket *n.* an inflatable sleeveless jacket worn to keep a person afloat when in danger of drowning.

lifeless ('laɪflɪs) *adj.* **1.** inanimate; dead. **2.** having no vitality or animation. **3.** unconscious.

lifelike ('laɪf,laɪk) *adj.* closely resembling or representing life.

lifeline ('laɪf,laɪn) *n.* **1.** a rope used for lifesaving. **2.** a single means of contact, communication, or support on which a person or an area relies.

lifelong ('laɪf,lɒŋ) *adj.* lasting for or as if for a lifetime.

life peer *n. Brit.* a peer whose title lapses at his death.

life preserver *n.* **1.** *Brit.* a bludgeon kept for self-defence. **2.** *U.S. & Canad.* a life belt or life jacket.

lifer ('laɪfə) *n. Informal.* a prisoner sentenced to imprisonment for life.

life raft *n.* a raft for emergency use at sea.

life-saver *n.* **1.** same as **lifeguard. 2.** *Informal.* a person or thing that gives help in time of need. —'**life-,saving** *adj., n.*

life science *n.* any of the sciences concerned with the structure and behaviour of living organisms, such as biology, botany, or zoology.

life-size *or* **life-sized** *adj.* representing actual size.

lifestyle ('laɪf,staɪl) *n.* a set of attitudes, habits, and possessions regarded as fashionable and desirable or associated with a particular person or group.

life-support *adj.* of or providing the equipment to sustain life in an unnatural environment, such as in space, or in severe illness.

lifetime ('laɪf,taɪm) *n.* the length of time a person is alive.

lift (lɪft) *vb.* **1.** to rise or cause to rise upwards to a higher place: *to lift a sack*. **2.** to move upwards: *to lift one's eyes*. **3.** to raise in status or estimation: *his position lifted him from the common crowd*. **4.** to revoke or cancel: *to lift tax restrictions*. **5.** to take (plants or underground crops) out of the ground for harvesting. **6.** to disappear by lifting or as if by lifting: *the fog lifted*. **7.** *Informal.* to plagiarize (music or a piece of writing). ~*n.* **8.** the act or an instance of lifting. **9.** the power or force available or used for lifting. **10. a.** *Brit.* a platform, compartment, or cage raised or lowered in a vertical shaft to transport people or goods to another floor in a building. **b.** See **chair lift, ski lift. 11.** a ride in a car or other vehicle for part or all of a passenger's journey. **12.** a rise in morale or feeling of cheerfulness. **13.** aid; help.

liftoff ('lɪft,ɒf) *n.* the initial movement of a rocket from its launching pad.

ligament ('lɪgəmənt) *n. Anat.* a band of tough tissue that connects various bones or cartilages.

ligature ('lɪgətʃə, -,tʃʊə) *n.* **1.** the act of binding or tying up. **2.** a link, bond, or tie. **3.** *Printing.* a character of two or more joined letters, such as fi, ffi. **4.** *Music.* a slur or the group of notes connected by it. ~*vb.* **5.** to bind with a ligature.

light[1] (laɪt) *n.* **1.** the medium of illumination that makes sight possible. **2.** electromagnetic radiation that is capable of causing a visual sensation. **3.** anything that illuminates, such as a lamp or candle. **4.** See **traffic light. 5.** a particular quality or type of light: *a good light for reading*. **6. a.** daylight. **b.** daybreak; dawn. **7.** anything that lets in light, such as a window. **8.** an aspect or view: *he saw it in a different light.* **9.** mental understanding or spiritual insight: *suddenly he saw the light.* **10.** an outstanding person: *a leading light of the movement.* **11.** brightness of countenance, esp. a sparkle in the eyes. **12. a.** something that ignites, such as a spark or flame. **b.** something used for igniting, such as a match. **13.** See **lighthouse. 14. come to light.** to become known or visible. **15. in (the) light of.** taking into account. **16. see the light.** to understand. **17. see the light (of day). a.** to come into being. **b.** to come to public notice. ~*adj.* **18.** full of light; well-lighted. **19.** (of a colour) pale; not dark: *light blue.* ~*vb.* **lighting, lighted** *or* **lit. 20.** to ignite. **21.** (often foll. by *up*) to illuminate or cause to illuminate. **22.** to guide or lead by light. ~See also **light up.** —'**lightish** *adj.*

light² (laɪt) *adj.* **1.** not heavy; weighing relatively little. **2.** relatively low in density, strength, amount, degree, etc.: *light rain; light metal.* **3.** lacking sufficient weight. **4.** without burdens, difficulties, or problems: *a light heart.* **5.** graceful or agile: *light fingers.* **6.** not bulky or clumsy: *light weapons.* **7.** not serious or profound; entertaining: *light music.* **8.** frivolous or capricious. **9.** loose in morals. **10.** dizzy or unclear: *a light head.* **11.** (of bread or cake) spongy or well leavened. **12.** easily digested: *a light meal.* **13.** relatively low in alcohol: *a light wine.* **14.** (of a vessel, lorry, or other transport) **a.** designed to carry light loads. **b.** not loaded. **15.** carrying light arms or equipment: *light infantry.* **16. make light of.** to treat as insignificant or trifling. ~*adv.* **17.** with little equipment or luggage: *to travel light.* ~*vb.* **lighting, lighted** *or* **lit. 18.** (esp. of birds) to settle or land after flight. **19.** (foll. by *on* or *upon*) to discover by chance. ~See also **lights.** —'**lightish** *adj.* —'**lightly** *adv.* —'**lightness** *n.*

light bulb *n.* a hollow rounded glass fitting containing a gas and a thin metal filament that gives out light when an electric current is passed through it.

lighten¹ ('laɪt²n) *vb.* **1.** to become or make light. **2.** to shine; glow. **3.** (of lightning) to flash.

lighten² ('laɪt²n) *vb.* **1.** to make or become less heavy. **2.** to make or become less burdensome. **3.** to make or become more cheerful or lively.

lighter¹ ('laɪtə) *n.* a small portable device for lighting cigarettes, etc.

lighter² ('laɪtə) *n.* a flat-bottomed barge used in loading or unloading a ship.

light-fingered *adj.* skilful at thieving, esp. by picking pockets.

light flyweight *n.* **1.** an amateur boxer weighing not more than 48 kg. **2.** an amateur wrestler weighing not more than 48 kg.

light-footed *adj.* having a light tread.

light-headed *adj.* **1.** giddy; feeling faint or slightly delirious. **2.** frivolous.

light-hearted *adj.* cheerful or carefree in mood or disposition. —,**light-'heartedly** *adv.*

light heavyweight *n.* **1. a.** a professional boxer weighing 160–175 pounds. **b.** an amateur boxer weighing 75–81 kg. **2. a.** a professional wrestler weighing not more than 198 pounds. **b.** an amateur wrestler weighing not more than 90 kg.

lighthouse ('laɪt,haʊs) *n.* a tower with a light to guide and warn ships of obstructions.

lighting ('laɪtɪŋ) *n.* **1.** the act or quality of illumination. **2.** the apparatus for and design of artificial light effects to a stage, film, or television set.

lighting-up time *n.* the time when vehicles are required by law to have their lights on.

light middleweight *n.* an amateur boxer weighing 67–71 kg.

lightning ('laɪtnɪŋ) *n.* **1.** a flash of light in the sky caused by a discharge of electricity. **2.** (*modifier*) fast and sudden: *a lightning raid.*

lightning conductor *or* **rod** *n.* a metal strip attached to the highest part of a building to provide a safe path to earth for lightning discharges.

light pen *n.* a penlike photoelectric device that in conjunction with a computer can be used to draw lines or identify symbols on a VDU screen.

lights (laɪts) *pl. n.* the lungs of sheep, bullocks, and pigs, used for feeding pets.

lightship ('laɪt,ʃɪp) *n.* a moored ship equipped as a lighthouse.

lights out *n.* the time when those resident at an institution, such as soldiers in barracks, are expected to retire to bed.

light up *vb.* **1.** to illuminate. **2.** to make or become cheerful or animated: *her face lit up when they arrived.* **3.** to light a cigarette or pipe.

lightweight ('laɪt,weɪt) *adj.* **1.** of relatively light weight. **2.** not serious. ~*n.* **3.** a person or animal of relatively light weight. **4. a.** a professional boxer weighing 130–135 pounds. **b.** an amateur boxer weighing 57–60 kg. **5. a.** a professional wrestler weighing not more than 154 pounds. **b.** an amateur wrestler weighing not more than 68 kg. **6.** *Informal.* a person of little importance or influence.

light welterweight *n.* an amateur boxer weighing 60–63.5 kg.

light year *n. Astron.* the distance travelled by light in one mean solar year, i.e. 9.4607×10^{15} metres.

ligneous ('lignɪəs) *adj.* of or resembling wood.

lignite ('lignaɪt) *n.* a brown sedimentary rock with woody texture: used as a fuel.

lignum vitae ('lignəm 'vaɪtiː) *n.* a tropical American tree with heavy resinous wood.

like[1] (laɪk) *adj.* **1.** similar; resembling. ~*prep.* **2.** similar to; similarly to; in the manner of: *acting like a maniac; he's so like his father.* **3.** such as: *there are lots of games—like draughts, for instance.* ~*adv.* **4.** *Dialect.* likely. ~*conj.* **5.** *Not universally accepted.* as though; as if: *you look like you've just seen a ghost.* **6.** *Not universally accepted.* in the same way as: *she doesn't dance like you do.* ~*n.* **7.** the equal or counterpart of a person or thing. **8. the like.** similar things: *dogs, foxes, and the like.* **9. the likes** or **like of.** people or things similar to (someone or something specified): *we don't want the likes of you around here.*

like[2] (laɪk) *vb.* **1.** to find (something) enjoyable or find it enjoyable (to do something). **2.** to be fond of. **3.** to prefer or wish (to do something): *we would like you to go.* **4.** to feel disposed or inclined; choose; wish. ~*n.* **5.** (*usually pl.*) a favourable feeling, desire, or preference. —'**likable** or '**likeable** *adj.*

likelihood ('laɪklɪ‚hʊd) *n.* chance; probability.

likely ('laɪklɪ) *adj.* **1.** tending or inclined; apt: *likely to rain.* **2.** probable: *a likely result.* **3.** appropriate for a purpose or activity. ~*adv.* **4.** probably or presumably. **5. not likely.** *Informal.* definitely not.

like-minded *adj.* agreeing in opinions.

liken ('laɪkən) *vb.* to see or represent as the same or similar; compare.

likeness ('laɪknɪs) *n.* **1.** the condition of being alike. **2.** an image created of a person or thing. **3.** an imitative appearance; semblance.

likewise ('laɪk‚waɪz) *adv.* **1.** in addition; moreover; also. **2.** similarly.

liking ('laɪkɪŋ) *n.* **1.** fondness. **2.** a preference, inclination, or pleasure.

lilac ('laɪlək) *n.* **1.** a shrub or small tree that has large sprays of purple or white fragrant flowers. ~*adj.* **2.** light purple.

Lilliputian (‚lɪlɪ'pjuːʃən) *n.* **1.** a tiny person or being. ~*adj.* **2.** tiny; very small.

Lilo ('laɪ‚ləʊ) *n., pl.* **-los.** *Trademark.* a type of inflatable plastic mattress.

lilt (lɪlt) *n.* **1.** a pleasing musical quality in a speaking voice. **2.** (in music) a jaunty rhythm. **3.** a graceful rhythmic motion. ~*vb.* **4.** (of a voice, tune, or song) to rise and fall in a pleasant way. **5.** to move gracefully and rhythmically. —'**lilting** *adj.*

lily ('lɪlɪ) *n., pl.* **lilies. 1.** any perennial plant of a N temperate genus, such as the tiger lily, with scaly bulbs and showy white or coloured flowers. **2.** the bulb or flower of any of these plants. **3.** any of various similar plants, such as the water lily.

lily-livered *adj.* cowardly; timid.

lily of the valley *n., pl.* **lilies of the valley.** a small plant with spikes of fragrant white bell-shaped flowers.

limb[1] (lɪm) *n.* **1.** an arm, leg, or wing. **2.** any of the main branches of a tree. **3. out on a limb. a.** in a precarious or questionable position. **b.** *Brit.* isolated, esp. because of unpopular opinions. —'**limbless** *adj.*

limb[2] (lɪm) *n.* the apparent outer edge of the sun, a moon, or a planet.

limber[1] ('lɪmbə) *adj.* **1.** capable of being easily bent; pliant. **2.** able to move or bend the body freely; agile.

limber[2] ('lɪmbə) *n.* **1.** part of a gun carriage, consisting of an axle, pole, and two wheels. ~*vb.* **2.** to attach the limber (to a gun).

limber up *vb.* (esp. in sports) to exercise in preparation.

limbo[1] ('lɪmbəʊ) *n., pl.* **-bos. 1.** (*often cap.*) *R.C. Church.* (formerly) the supposed region intermediate between heaven and hell for the unbaptized. **2.** an imaginary place for lost, forgotten, or unwanted persons or things. **3.** an unknown intermediate place or condition: *in limbo.*

limbo[2] ('lɪmbəʊ) *n., pl.* **-bos.** a West Indian dance in which dancers lean backwards and pass under a horizontal bar which is gradually lowered.

lime[1] (laɪm) *n.* **1.** *Agriculture.* calcium hydroxide spread as a dressing on acidic land. ~*vb.* **2.** to spread a calcium compound upon (land).

lime[2] (laɪm) *n.* the round oval fruit of a small Asian citrus tree with acid fleshy pulp rich in vitamin C.

lime[3] (laɪm) *n.* a European linden tree planted for ornament.

lime-green *adj.* greenish-yellow.

limekiln ('laɪm‚kɪln) *n.* a kiln in which calcium carbonate is burned to produce quicklime.

limelight ('laɪm‚laɪt) *n.* **1. the.** a position of public attention or notice: *in the limelight.* **2. a.** a type of lamp, formerly used in stage lighting, in which lime is heated to white heat. **b.** brilliant white light produced in this way.

limerick ('lɪmərɪk) *n.* a form of comic verse consisting of five lines.

limestone ('laɪm‚stəʊn) *n.* rock consisting mainly of calcium carbonate: used as a building stone and in making cement.

limey ('laɪmɪ) *n. U.S. & Canad. slang.* **1.** a British person. **2.** a British sailor or ship.

limit ('lɪmɪt) *n.* **1.** (*sometimes pl.*) the ultimate extent, degree, or amount of something: *the limit of endurance.* **2.** (*often pl.*)

the boundary or edge of a specific area: *the city limits.* **3.** the largest quantity or amount allowed. **4. the limit.** *Informal.* a person or thing that is intolerably exasperating. ~*vb.* **5.** to restrict or confine, as to area, extent, or time. —'**limitable** *adj.*

limitation (ˌlɪmɪˈteɪʃən) *n.* **1.** something that limits a quality or achievement. **2.** the act of limiting or the condition of being limited.

limited ('lɪmɪtɪd) *adj.* **1.** having a limit; restricted. **2.** without fullness or scope; narrow. **3.** (of governing powers or sovereignty) restricted, by or as if by a constitution, laws, or an assembly: *limited government.* **4.** *Chiefly Brit.* (of a business enterprise) owned by shareholders whose liability for the enterprise's debts is restricted.

limn (lɪm) *vb.* to represent in drawing or painting.

limousine ('lɪməˌziːn, ˌlɪməˈziːn) *n.* any large and luxurious car.

limp[1] (lɪmp) *vb.* **1.** to walk with an uneven step, esp. with a weak or injured leg. **2.** to advance in a labouring or faltering manner. ~*n.* **3.** an uneven walk or progress. —'**limping** *adj., n.*

limp[2] (lɪmp) *adj.* **1.** not firm or stiff. **2.** not energetic or vital. **3.** (of the binding of a book) not stiffened with boards. —'**limply** *adv.*

limpet ('lɪmpɪt) *n.* **1.** a sea creature that has a conical shell and clings tightly to rocks with its muscular foot. **2.** (*modifier*) denoting certain weapons that are attached to their targets by magnetic or adhesive properties and resist removal: *limpet mines.*

limpid ('lɪmpɪd) *adj.* **1.** clear or transparent. **2.** (of speech or writing) clear and easy to understand. —**lim'pidity** *n.*

limy[1] ('laɪmɪ) *adj.* **limier, limiest.** of, like, or smeared with birdlime.

limy[2] ('laɪmɪ) *adj.* **limier, limiest.** of or tasting of lime (the fruit).

linage ('laɪnɪdʒ) *n.* **1.** the number of lines in written or printed matter. **2.** payment according to the number of lines.

linchpin ('lɪntʃˌpɪn) *n.* **1.** a pin placed through an axle to keep a wheel in position. **2.** a person or thing regarded as essential: *the linchpin of the company.*

Lincs (lɪŋks) Lincolnshire.

linctus ('lɪŋktəs) *n., pl.* **-tuses.** a soothing syrupy cough mixture.

linden ('lɪndən) *n.* a large tree with heart-shaped leaves and fragrant yellowish flowers. See also **lime**[3].

line[1] (laɪn) *n.* **1.** a narrow continuous mark, as one made by a pencil or brush. **2.** a thin indented mark or wrinkle. **3.** a straight or curved continuous trace having no breadth that is produced by a moving point. **4.** a boundary: *the county line.* **5.** *Sport.* **a.** a white band indicating division on a field or track. **b.** a mark or imaginary mark at which a race begins or ends. **6.** a specified point of change or limit: *the dividing line between sanity and madness.* **7.** the edge or contour of a shape: *the line of a building.* **8.** anything long, flexible, and thin, such as a wire or string: *a fishing line.* **9.** a telephone connection: *a direct line to New York.* **10.** a conducting wire, cable, or circuit for electric-power transmission or telecommunications. **11.** a system of travel or transportation: *a shipping line.* **12.** a route between two points on a railway. **13.** *Chiefly Brit.* a railway track. **14.** a course or direction of movement or advance: *the line of flight of a bullet.* **15.** a course or method of action or behaviour: *take a new line with him.* **16.** a policy or prescribed course of action or way of thinking: *bring into line.* **17.** a field of study, interest, or occupation: *this book is in your line.* **18.** alignment; true: *in line.* **19.** one kind of product or article: *a nice line in hats.* **20.** a row of people or things. **21.** a row of words printed or written across a page. **22.** a unit of verse consisting of words in a single row. **23.** one of a number of narrow horizontal bands forming a television picture. **24.** *Music.* any of the five horizontal marks that make up the stave. **25.** the most forward defensive position: *the front line.* **26.** a formation of ships or soldiers abreast of each other. **27.** the combatant forces of certain armies and navies. **28.** *U.S. & Canad.* a queue. **29. all along the line.** at every stage in a series. **30. draw the line (at).** to object (to) or set a limit (on): *her father draws the line at her coming in after midnight.* **31. drop someone a line.** to send someone a short note. **32. get a line on.** *Informal.* to obtain information about. **33. in line for.** to be a candidate for: *he's in line for a directorship.* **34. in line with.** conforming to. **35. lay** *or* **put on the line. a.** to speak frankly and directly. **b.** to risk (one's career or reputation) on something. ~*vb.* **36.** to mark with a line or lines. **37.** to be or put as a border to: *tulips lined the lawns.* **38.** to place in or form a row, series, or alignment. ~See also **lines, line-up.** —**lined** *adj.*

line[2] (laɪn) *vb.* **1.** to attach an inside covering to (a garment or curtain). **2.** to cover or fit the inside of: *to line the walls with books.* **3.** to fill: *line one's pockets with money.*

lineage ('lɪnɪɪdʒ) *n.* direct descent from an ancestor.

lineal ('lɪnɪəl) *adj.* **1.** being in a direct line of descent from an ancestor. **2.** of or derived from direct descent. **3.** linear.

lineament ('lɪnɪəmənt) *n.* (*often pl.*) a facial outline or distinctive feature.

linear ('lɪnɪə) *adj.* **1.** of, in, along, or relating to a line. **2.** of or relating to length. **3.**

resembling, represented by, or consisting of a line or lines. —**linearity** (ˌlɪnɪ'ærɪtɪ) n.

linear measure n. a unit or system of units for the measurement of length.

lineation (ˌlɪnɪ'eɪʃən) n. 1. the act of marking with lines. 2. an arrangement of lines.

line drawing n. a drawing made with lines only.

linen ('lɪnɪn) n. 1. a hard-wearing fabric woven from the spun fibres of flax. 2. yarn or thread spun from flax fibre. 3. things, such as sheets or tablecloths, made from linen cloth or from cotton.

line of fire n. the flight path of a missile discharged from a firearm.

line printer n. an electromechanical device that prints a line of characters at a time: used in printing and in computer systems.

liner[1] ('laɪnə) n. 1. a passenger ship or aircraft, esp. one that is part of a commercial fleet. 2. Also called: **eyeliner**. a cosmetic used to outline the eyes.

liner[2] ('laɪnə) n. something used as a lining: *a plastic bin liner.*

lines (laɪnz) pl. n. 1. the words of a theatrical role: *he forgot his lines.* 2. *Informal, chiefly Brit.* a marriage certificate: *marriage lines.* 3. a school punishment of writing the same sentence or phrase out a specified number of times. 4. **read between the lines.** to understand or find an implicit meaning in addition to the obvious one.

linesman ('laɪnzmən) n., pl. **-men.** an official who helps the referee or umpire in various sports, by indicating when the ball has gone out of play.

line-up n. 1. a row or arrangement of people or things for a particular purpose: *the line-up for the football match.* 2. the members of such a row or arrangement. ~vb. **line up.** 3. to form, put into, or organize a line-up.

ling[1] (lɪŋ) n., pl. **ling** or **lings.** a northern coastal food fish with a long slender body.

ling[2] (lɪŋ) n. heather.

linger ('lɪŋgə) vb. 1. to delay or prolong departure. 2. to remain just alive for some time before death. 3. to spend a long time doing or considering something. —**'lingering** adj.

lingerie ('lænʒərɪ) n. women's underwear and nightwear.

lingo ('lɪŋgəʊ) n., pl. **-goes.** *Informal.* any foreign or unfamiliar language or jargon.

lingua franca ('lɪŋgwə 'fræŋkə) n., pl. **lingua francas** or **linguae francae** ('lɪŋgwiː 'frænsiː). 1. a language used for communication among people of different mother tongues. 2. any system of communication providing mutual understanding.

lingual ('lɪŋgwəl) adj. 1. *Anat.* of the tongue. 2. *Rare.* of language or languages.

3. articulated with the tongue. —**'lingually** adv.

linguist ('lɪŋgwɪst) n. 1. a person who is skilled in foreign languages. 2. a person who studies linguistics.

linguistic (lɪŋ'gwɪstɪk) adj. 1. of language. 2. of linguistics. —**lin'guistically** adv.

linguistics (lɪŋ'gwɪstɪks) n. (*functioning as sing.*) the scientific study of language.

liniment ('lɪnɪmənt) n. a medicated liquid, usually containing an oil, applied to the skin to relieve pain or stiffness.

lining ('laɪnɪŋ) n. 1. material used to line a garment or curtain. 2. any interior covering: *the stomach lining.*

link (lɪŋk) n. 1. any of the separate rings, loops, or pieces that form a chain. 2. an emotional or logical relationship between people or things; association. 3. a connecting part or episode. 4. any of various types of communications connection: *a rail link; radio link.* 5. a unit of length equal to one hundredth of a chain. ~vb. 6. (often foll. by *up*) to connect with or as if with links. 7. to connect by association.

linkage ('lɪŋkɪdʒ) n. 1. the act of linking or the state of being linked. 2. a system of links.

linkman ('lɪŋkmən) n., pl. **-men.** a presenter of a television or radio programme consisting of a number of outside broadcasts from different locations.

links (lɪŋks) pl. n. short for **golf links.** See **golf course.**

link-up n. a joining together of two systems or groups.

linnet ('lɪnɪt) n. a brownish finch: the male has a red breast and forehead.

lino ('laɪnəʊ) n. short for **linoleum.**

linocut ('laɪnəʊˌkʌt) n. 1. a design cut in relief on a block of linoleum. 2. a print made from such a block.

linoleum (lɪ'nəʊlɪəm) n. a floor covering made of hessian or jute coated with powdered cork.

Linotype ('laɪnəʊˌtaɪp) n. *Trademark.* a typesetting machine that casts an entire line on one piece of metal.

linseed ('lɪnˌsiːd) n. the seed of flax.

linseed oil n. a yellow oil extracted from seeds of the flax plant. It is used in making oil paints, printer's ink, linoleum, and varnish.

linsey-woolsey ('lɪnzɪ'wʊlzɪ) n. a thin rough fabric of linen and wool or cotton.

lint (lɪnt) n. 1. an absorbent cotton or linen fabric with the nap raised on one side, used to dress wounds. 2. shreds of yarn or cloth.

lintel ('lɪnt²l) n. a horizontal beam, as over a door or window.

lion ('laɪən) n. 1. a large predatory mammal of the cat family found in Africa and India, with a tawny yellow coat and, in the male, a shaggy mane. **2.** a courageous strong person. **3. the lion's share.** the largest portion. —'**lioness** *fem. n.*

lion-hearted *adj.* very brave; courageous.

lionize *or* **-ise** ('laɪəˌnaɪz) *vb.* to treat as or make into a celebrity.

lip (lɪp) *n.* **1.** *Anat.* either of the two fleshy folds surrounding the mouth. **2.** any structure resembling a lip, such as the rim of a jug. **3.** *Slang.* impudent talk or backchat. **4. bite one's lip.** to stifle one's feelings. **5. keep a stiff upper lip.** to maintain one's composure during a time of trouble. **6. lick** *or* **smack one's lips.** to anticipate or recall something with glee or relish.

lip-read ('lɪpˌriːd) *vb.* **-reading, -read** (-ˌrɛd). to interpret (words) by lip-reading.

lip-reading *n.* a method used by the deaf to comprehend spoken words by interpreting movements of the speaker's lips. —'**lip-ˌreader** *n.*

lip service *n.* support or respect expressed but not practised.

lipstick ('lɪpˌstɪk) *n.* a cosmetic for colouring the lips, usually in the form of a stick.

liquefy ('lɪkwɪˌfaɪ) *vb.* **-fying, -fied.** (esp. of a gas) to become or cause to become liquid. —**liquefaction** (ˌlɪkwɪ'fækʃən) *n.*

liqueur (lɪ'kjʊə) *n.* a highly flavoured sweetened spirit, intended to be drunk after a meal.

liquid ('lɪkwɪd) *n.* **1.** a substance in a physical state in which it does not resist change of shape but does resist change of size. ~*adj.* **2.** of or being a liquid: *liquid wax.* **3.** shining, transparent, or brilliant: *liquid eyes.* **4.** flowing, fluent, or smooth. **5.** (of assets) in the form of money or easily convertible into money. —**li'quidity** *n.*

liquidate ('lɪkwɪˌdeɪt) *vb.* **1.** to settle or pay off (a debt or claim). **2.** to terminate the operations of (a commercial firm) by assessment of debts and appropriation of assets to settle them. **3.** to convert (assets) into cash. **4.** to eliminate or kill. —'**liquiˌdator** *n.*

liquidation (ˌlɪkwɪ'deɪʃən) *n.* **1. a.** the winding-up of a business firm by selling its assets to pay off its debts. **b. go into liquidation.** (of a business firm) to have its affairs so terminated. **2.** destruction; elimination.

liquid crystal display *n.* a display of numbers, as on a calculator, using cells containing a liquid with crystalline properties, that change their reflectivity when an electric field is applied to them.

liquidize *or* **-dise** ('lɪkwɪˌdaɪz) *vb.* **1.** to make or become liquid; liquefy. **2.** to pulverize (food) in a liquidizer so as to produce a fluid.

liquidizer *or* **-diser** ('lɪkwɪˌdaɪzə) *n.* a kitchen appliance with blades for puréeing food.

liquid measure *n.* a unit or system of units for measuring volumes of liquids or their containers.

liquid oxygen *n.* oxygen liquefied by cooling: used in rocket fuels.

liquid paraffin *n.* an oily liquid obtained by petroleum distillation and used as a laxative.

liquor ('lɪkə) *n.* **1.** spirits or other alcoholic drinks. **2.** any liquid in which food has been cooked.

liquorice *or* *U.S. & Canad.* **licorice** ('lɪkərɪs, -ərɪʃ) *n.* **1.** the dried root of a Mediterranean plant, used as a laxative and in confectionery. **2.** a sweet having a liquorice flavour.

lira ('lɪərə) *n., pl.* **lire** ('lɪərɪ) *or* **liras.** **1.** the standard monetary unit of Italy. **2.** the standard monetary unit of Turkey.

lisle (laɪl) *n.* a strong fine cotton thread or fabric.

lisp (lɪsp) *n.* **1.** a speech defect in which *s* and *z* are pronounced like the *th* sounds in English *thin* and *then* respectively. ~*vb.* **2.** to speak or pronounce (something) with a lisp.

lissom *or* **lissome** ('lɪsəm) *adj.* supple in the limbs or body; lithe; agile.

list[1] (lɪst) *n.* **1.** an item-by-item record of names or things, usually written one under the other. ~*vb.* **2.** to make a list of. **3.** to include in a list. —'**listing** *n.*

list[2] (lɪst) *vb.* **1.** (esp. of ships) to lean over to one side. ~*n.* **2.** the act or an instance of leaning to one side.

listed building *n.* (in Britain) a building protected from demolition or alteration because of its special historical or architectural interest.

listen ('lɪsᵊn) *vb.* **1.** to concentrate on hearing something. **2.** to take heed; pay attention: *I warned you but you wouldn't listen.* —'**listener** *n.*

listen in *vb.* (often foll. by *on* or *to*) to listen secretly to a conversation or communication.

listeriosis (lɪˌstɪərɪ'əʊsɪs) *n.* a serious form of food poisoning, caused by bacteria of the genus *Listeria.* Its symptoms can include meningitis.

listless ('lɪstlɪs) *adj.* having or showing no interest or energy. —'**listlessly** *adv.*

list price *n.* the selling price of merchandise as quoted in a catalogue or advertisement.

lists (lɪsts) *pl. n.* **1.** *History.* the enclosed field of combat at a tournament. **2.** any arena of conflict or controversy. **3. enter the lists.** to engage in a conflict or controversy.

lit (lɪt) *vb.* the past of **light**[1] and **light**[2].

lit. 1. literal(ly). **2.** literary. **3.** literature.

litany ('lɪtənɪ) *n., pl.* **-nies. 1.** *Christianity.*

a prayer consisting of a series of invocations, each followed by the same response. **2.** any tedious recital.

litchi (ˌlaɪˈtʃiː) *n.* same as **lychee.**

liter (ˈliːtə) *n. U.S.* same as **litre.**

literacy (ˈlɪtərəsɪ) *n.* **1.** the ability to read and write. **2.** the ability to use language proficiently.

literal (ˈlɪtərəl) *adj.* **1.** in exact accordance with the explicit meaning of a word or text. **2.** word for word: *a literal translation.* **3.** dull, factual, or prosaic. **4.** true; actual. ~*n.* **5.** a misprint or misspelling in a text. —ˈ**literally** *adv.*

literalism (ˈlɪtərəlˌɪzəm) *n.* the tendency to take words and statements in their literal sense. —ˈ**literalist** *n.*

literary (ˈlɪtrərɪ) *adj.* **1.** of or characteristic of literature: *a literary style.* **2.** knowledgeable about literature. **3.** (of a word) formal; not colloquial. —ˈ**literariness** *n.*

literate (ˈlɪtərɪt) *adj.* **1.** able to read and write. **2.** educated; learned. ~*n.* **3.** a literate person.

literati (ˌlɪtəˈrɑːtiː) *pl. n.* literary or scholarly people.

literature (ˈlɪtərɪtʃə, ˈlɪtrɪ-) *n.* **1.** written material such as poetry, novels, or essays. **2.** the body of written work of a particular culture or people: *Scandinavian literature.* **3.** written or printed matter of a particular type or genre: *scientific literature.* **4.** the art or profession of a writer. **5.** *Informal.* printed matter on any subject.

lithe (laɪð) *adj.* flexible or supple.

lithium (ˈlɪθɪəm) *n.* a soft silvery element of the alkali metal series: the lightest known metal. Symbol: Li

litho (ˈlaɪθəʊ) *n., pl.* **-thos,** *adj., adv.* short for **lithograph, lithograph, lithographic,** or **lithographically.**

lithograph (ˈlɪθəˌɡrɑːf) *n.* **1.** a print made by lithography. ~*vb.* **2.** to reproduce (pictures or text) by lithography. —**lithographic** (ˌlɪθəˈɡræfɪk) *adj.* —ˌ**lithoˈgraphically** *adv.*

lithography (lɪˈθɒɡrəfɪ) *n.* a method of printing from a metal or stone surface on which the printing areas are made ink-receptive. —**liˈthographer** *n.*

litigant (ˈlɪtɪɡənt) *n.* a party to a lawsuit.

litigate (ˈlɪtɪˌɡeɪt) *vb.* **1.** to bring or contest (a claim or action) in a lawsuit. **2.** to engage in legal proceedings. —ˈ**litiˌgator** *n.*

litigation (ˌlɪtɪˈɡeɪʃən) *n.* the process of bringing or contesting a lawsuit.

litigious (lɪˈtɪdʒəs) *adj.* frequently going to law.

litmus (ˈlɪtməs) *n.* a soluble powder obtained from certain lichens. It turns red under acid conditions and blue under basic conditions. Absorbent paper treated with it (**litmus paper**) is used as an indicator.

litotes (ˈlaɪtəʊˌtiːz) *n., pl.* **-tes.** understatement for effect, as in "She was not a little upset" meaning "She was extremely upset".

litre *or U.S.* **liter** (ˈliːtə) *n.* one cubic decimetre.

litter (ˈlɪtə) *n.* **1.** small refuse or waste materials carelessly dropped in public places. **2.** a disordered or untidy collection of objects. **3.** a group of animals produced at one birth. **4.** straw or hay used as bedding for animals. **5.** a means of conveying people, esp. sick or wounded people, consisting of a light bed or seat held between parallel sticks. ~*vb.* **6.** to make (a place) untidy by strewing (refuse). **7.** to scatter (objects) about or (of objects) to lie around or upon (anything) in an untidy fashion. **8.** (of animals) to give birth to (offspring). **9.** to provide (an animal) with straw or hay for bedding.

litter lout *or U.S. & Canad.* **litterbug** (ˈlɪtəˌbʌɡ) *n. Slang.* a person who tends to drop refuse in public places.

little (ˈlɪtˈl) *det.* **1.** a small quantity, extent, or duration of: *the little hope there is left; little damage was done.* **2. make little of.** to regard or treat as insignificant; dismiss. **3. think little of.** to have a low opinion of. ~*adj.* **4.** of small or less than average size. **5.** young: *a little boy.* **6.** endearingly familiar: *my husband's little ways.* **7.** contemptible, mean, or disagreeable: *your filthy little mind.* ~*adv.* **8.** (usually preceded by *a*) to a small extent or degree; not a lot: *to laugh a little.* **9.** (*used preceding a verb*) not at all, or hardly: *he little realized his fate.* **10.** not much or often: *we go there very little now.* **11. little by little.** by small degrees. ~See also **less, lesser, least.**

little people *pl. n. Folklore.* small supernatural beings, such as elves.

littoral (ˈlɪtərəl) *adj.* **1.** of or by the shore. ~*n.* **2.** a coastal region.

liturgy (ˈlɪtədʒɪ) *n., pl.* **-gies.** the forms of public services officially prescribed by a Church. —**liˈturgical** *adj.*

livable *or* **liveable** (ˈlɪvəbˈl) *adj.* (foll. by *with*) tolerable or pleasant to live (with).

live[1] (lɪv) *vb.* **1.** to show the characteristics of life; be alive. **2.** to remain alive or in existence. **3.** to exist in a specified way: *to live poorly.* **4.** to reside or dwell: *to live in London.* **5.** to continue or last: *the pain still lives in her memory.* **6.** (foll. by *on, upon,* or *by*) to support one's style of life; subsist: *to live by writing.* **7.** (foll. by *with*) to endure the effects (of a crime or mistake). **8.** to pass or spend (one's life). **9.** to enjoy life to the full: *he knows how to live.* **10.** to put into practice in one's daily life; express: *he lives religion every day.* **11. live and let live.** to be tolerant. ~See also **live down, live in,** etc.

live² (laɪv) *adj.* **1.** showing the characteristics of life. **2.** of current interest; controversial: *a live issue.* **3.** actual: *a real live cowboy.* **4.** (of a coal or ember) glowing or burning. **5.** loaded or capable of exploding: *a live bomb.* **6.** *Radio, television.* transmitted at the time of performance, rather than being a recording: *a live show.* **7.** (of a record) recorded during a performance. **8.** connected to a source of electric power: *a live circuit.* ~*adv.* **9.** during, at, or in the form of a live performance.

live down (lɪv) *vb.* to withstand the effects of (a crime or mistake) by waiting until others forget or forgive it.

live in (lɪv) *vb.* **1.** to dwell at one's place of employment, as in a hotel. ~*adj.* **live-in.** **2.** resident: *a live-in nanny; her live-in boyfriend.*

livelihood ('laɪvlɪ‚hʊd) *n.* occupation or employment.

livelong ('lɪv‚lɒŋ) *adj. Chiefly poetic.* long or seemingly long: *all the livelong day.*

lively ('laɪvlɪ) *adj.* **-lier, -liest. 1.** full of life or vigour. **2.** vivacious or animated. **3.** vivid. —'**liveliness** *n.*

liven ('laɪvⁿn) *vb.* (usually foll. by *up*) to make or become lively; enliven.

liver¹ ('lɪvə) *n.* **1.** a large glandular organ which processes nutrients for use by the body and which secretes bile and removes certain poisons. **2.** the liver of certain animals used as food. **3.** a reddish-brown colour.

liver² ('lɪvə) *n.* a person who lives in a specified way: *a fast liver.*

liveried ('lɪvərɪd) *adj.* wearing livery.

liverish ('lɪvərɪʃ) *adj.* **1.** *Informal.* having a disorder of the liver. **2.** disagreeable; peevish.

liver sausage *n.* a sausage containing liver.

liverwort ('lɪvə‚wɜːt) *n.* a plant growing in wet places and resembling green seaweeds or leafy mosses.

livery ('lɪvərɪ) *n., pl.* **-eries. 1.** the identifying uniform of a servant. **2.** distinctive dress or outward appearance. **3.** the stabling, keeping, or hiring out of horses for money.

lives (laɪvz) *n.* the plural of **life.**

livestock ('laɪv‚stɒk) *n.* (*functioning as sing. or pl.*) cattle, horses, and similar animals kept on a farm.

live together (lɪv) *vb.* (of an unmarried couple) to dwell in the same house; cohabit.

live up (lɪv) *vb.* (foll. by *to*) to fulfil (an expectation, obligation, or principle).

live wire (laɪv) *n.* **1.** *Informal.* an energetic or enterprising person. **2.** a wire carrying an electric current.

livid ('lɪvɪd) *adj.* **1.** *Informal.* angry or furious. **2.** of a greyish colour.

living ('lɪvɪŋ) *adj.* **1.** possessing life; not dead or inanimate. **2.** currently in use or valid: *living language.* **3.** seeming to be real: *a living image.* **4.** (of animals or plants) existing in the present age. **5.** very: *the living daylights.* ~*n.* **6.** the condition of being alive. **7.** the manner of one's life: *fast living.* **8.** one's financial means. **9.** *Church of England.* a benefice. **10.** (*modifier*) of or like everyday life: *living conditions.* **11.** (*modifier*) of or involving those now alive: *in living memory.*

living room *n.* a room in a private house or flat used for relaxation and entertainment.

living wage *n.* a wage adequate for a worker to live on and support a family in reasonable comfort.

lizard ('lɪzəd) *n.* a reptile with an elongated body, four limbs, and a long tail.

ll. lines (of written matter).

llama ('lɑːmə) *n.* a domesticated South American mammal of the camel family, that is used as a beast of burden and is valued for its hair, flesh, and hide.

LLB Bachelor of Laws.

lo (ləʊ) *interj.* look! see! (now often in **lo and behold**).

loach (ləʊtʃ) *n.* a carplike freshwater fish with a long narrow body and barbels around the mouth.

load (ləʊd) *n.* **1.** something to be borne or conveyed; weight. **2.** the amount borne or conveyed. **3.** something that weighs down, oppresses, or burdens: *that's a load off my mind.* **4.** *Electronics.* the power delivered by a machine, generator, or circuit. **5.** an external force applied to a component or mechanism. **6. a load of.** *Informal.* a quantity of: *a load of nonsense.* **7. get a load of.** *Informal.* to pay attention to. ~*vb.* **8.** to place or receive (cargo or goods) upon (a ship or vehicle). **9.** to burden or oppress. **10.** to supply in abundance: *load with gifts.* **11.** to cause to be biased: *to load a question.* **12.** to put an ammunition charge into (a firearm). **13.** *Photog.* to position (a film) in (a camera). **14.** to weight or bias (a roulette wheel or dice). **15.** *Computers.* to transfer (a program) to a memory. ~See also **loads.** —'**loader** *n.*

loaded ('ləʊdɪd) *adj.* **1.** carrying a load. **2.** (of dice or a roulette wheel) weighted or otherwise biased. **3.** (of a question or statement) containing a hidden trap or implication. **4.** charged with ammunition. **5.** *Slang.* wealthy. **6.** *Slang, chiefly U.S. & Canad.* drunk.

loads (ləʊdz) *pl. n. Informal.* (often foll. by *of*) a lot.

loadstar ('ləʊd‚stɑː) *n.* same as **lodestar.**

loadstone ('ləʊd‚stəʊn) *n.* same as **lodestone.**

loaf¹ (ləʊf) *n., pl.* **loaves** (ləʊvz). **1.** a

shaped mass of baked bread. **2.** any shaped or moulded mass of food, such as sugar or cooked meat. **3.** *Slang.* the head; sense: *use your loaf!*

loaf[2] (ləʊf) *vb.* to loiter or lounge around in an idle way.

loafer ('ləʊfə) *n.* **1.** a person who avoids work; idler. **2.** *Chiefly U.S. & Canad.* a moccasin-like shoe.

loam (ləʊm) *n.* rich soil consisting of sand, clay, and decaying organic material. —'**loamy** *adj.*

loan (ləʊn) *n.* **1.** the act of lending: *the loan of a car.* **2.** property lent, esp. money lent at interest for a period of time. **3. on loan.** lent out; borrowed. ~*vb.* **4.** to lend (something, esp. money).

loath *or* **loth** (ləʊθ) *adj.* (usually foll. by *to*) reluctant or unwilling.

loathe (ləʊð) *vb.* to feel strong hatred or disgust for.

loathing ('ləʊðɪŋ) *n.* abhorrence; disgust.

loathsome ('ləʊðsəm) *adj.* causing loathing; abhorrent.

loaves (ləʊvz) *n.* the plural of **loaf**[1].

lob (lɒb) *Sport.* ~*n.* **1.** a ball struck or bowled in a high arc. ~*vb.* **lobbing, lobbed. 2.** to hit or kick (a ball) in a high arc. **3.** *Informal.* to throw.

lobar ('ləʊbə) *adj.* of or affecting a lobe.

lobate ('ləʊbeɪt) *adj.* with or like lobes.

lobby ('lɒbɪ) *n., pl.* -**bies. 1.** a room or corridor used as an entrance hall or vestibule. **2.** *Chiefly Brit.* a hall in a legislative building used for meetings between legislators and members of the public. **3.** *Chiefly Brit.* one of two corridors in a legislative building in which members vote. **4.** a group of persons who attempt to influence legislators on behalf of a particular interest. ~*vb.* -**bying, -bied. 5.** to attempt to influence (legislators) in the formulation of policy.

lobbyist ('lɒbɪɪst) *n.* a person employed by a particular interest to lobby.

lobe (ləʊb) *n.* **1.** any rounded projection forming part of a larger structure. **2.** the fleshy lower part of the external ear. **3.** any subdivision of a bodily organ.

lobelia (ləʊ'biːlɪə) *n.* a plant with red, blue, white, or yellow five-lobed flowers with the three lower lobes forming a lip.

lobola (lɔː'bɔːlə) *n.* (in southern Africa) an African custom by which a bridegroom's family makes a payment in cattle or cash to the bride's family shortly before the marriage.

lobotomy (ləʊ'bɒtəmɪ) *n., pl.* -**mies.** surgical cutting of nerves in the frontal lobe of the brain: used in the treatment of severe mental disorders.

lobscouse ('lɒb₁skaʊs) *n.* a sailor's stew of meat, vegetables, and hardtack.

lobster ('lɒbstə) *n., pl.* -**sters** *or* -**ster. 1.** a large crustacean found on rocky sea shores and with the first pair of limbs modified as large pincers. **2.** its edible flesh.

lobster pot *n.* a round basket made of open slats, used to catch lobsters.

local ('ləʊk°l) *adj.* **1.** characteristic of or associated with a particular locality or area. **2.** of or relating to a particular place or point in space. **3.** *Med.* of, affecting, or confined to a limited area or part: *a local anaesthetic.* **4.** (of a train or bus) stopping at all stations or stops. ~*n.* **5.** an inhabitant of a specified locality: *the locals support him.* **6.** *Brit. informal.* a pub close to one's home. —'**locally** *adv.*

local anaesthetic *n. Med.* See **anaesthesia.**

local authority *n. Brit. & N.Z.* the governing body of a county or district.

locale (ləʊ'kɑːl) *n.* the place where something happens or has happened.

local government *n.* government of the affairs of counties, towns, and districts by locally elected political bodies.

locality (ləʊ'kælɪtɪ) *n., pl.* -**ties. 1.** a neighbourhood or area. **2.** the site or scene of an event.

localize *or* -**ise** ('ləʊkə₁laɪz) *vb.* to restrict or confine (something) to a particular place.

locate (ləʊ'keɪt) *vb.* **1.** to discover the whereabouts of; find. **2.** to situate or place: *located on the edge of the city.* **3.** *U.S. & Canad.* to become established or settled.

location (ləʊ'keɪʃən) *n.* **1.** a site or position; situation. **2.** the act of locating or the state of being located. **3.** a place outside a studio where filming is done: *shot on location.* **4.** (in South Africa) a Black African or Coloured township.

loc. cit. (in textual annotation) loco citato.

loch (lɒx) *n.* **1.** *Scot.* a lake. **2.** a long narrow arm of the sea in Scotland.

loci ('ləʊsaɪ) *n.* the plural of **locus.**

lock[1] (lɒk) *n.* **1.** a device fitted to a door, drawer, lid, etc., to keep it closed and prevent unauthorized access. **2.** a section of a canal or river that may be closed off by gates to control the water level and the raising and lowering of vessels that pass through it. **3.** the jamming or fastening together of parts. **4.** *Brit.* the extent to which a vehicle's front wheels will turn: *this car has a good lock.* **5.** a mechanism that detonates the charge of a gun. **6. lock, stock, and barrel.** completely; entirely. **7.** any wrestling hold in which a wrestler seizes a part of his opponent's body. **8.** Also called: **lock forward.** *Rugby.* a player in the second row of the scrum. ~*vb.* **9.** to fasten (a door, gate, etc.) or (of a door, etc.) to become fastened so as to prevent entry or exit. **10.** to secure (a building) by locking all doors and windows. **11.** to fix or become fixed together securely or inextricably. **12.** to become or cause to become rigid or immovable: *the front wheels of the car locked.* **13.** to clasp or entangle (someone or each other) in a struggle or embrace. ~See also **lock out, lock up.**

lock² (lɒk) *n.* **1.** a strand or curl of hair. **2.** (*pl.*) *Chiefly literary.* hair.

locker (ˈlɒkə) *n.* a small compartment that may be locked, as for temporarily storing clothes and valuables.

locket (ˈlɒkɪt) *n.* a small ornamental case, usually on a necklace or chain, that holds a picture or keepsake.

lockjaw (ˈlɒkˌdʒɔː) *n. Pathol.* a nontechnical name for **trismus** and (often) **tetanus.**

lock out *vb.* **1.** to prevent from entering by locking a door. **2.** to prevent (employees) from working during an industrial dispute, as by closing a factory. ~*n.* **lockout.** **3.** the closing of a place of employment by an employer, in order to bring pressure on employees to agree to terms.

locksmith (ˈlɒkˌsmɪθ) *n.* a person who makes or repairs locks.

lock up *vb.* **1.** to imprison or confine. **2.** to lock or secure the doors and windows of (a building). ~*n.* **lockup. 3.** a jail. **4.** *Brit.* a small shop with no attached quarters for the owner. **5.** *Brit.* a garage or store separate from the main premises. ~*adj.* **lockup. 6.** *Brit. & N.Z.* (of premises) without living quarters: *a lock-up shop.*

loco¹ (ˈləʊkəʊ) *n. Informal.* a locomotive.

loco² (ˈləʊkəʊ) *adj. Slang, chiefly U.S.* insane.

locomotion (ˌləʊkəˈməʊʃən) *n.* the act or power of moving.

locomotive (ˌləʊkəˈməʊtɪv) *n.* **1.** a self-propelled engine used for pulling trains. ~*adj.* **2.** of locomotion.

locum (ˈləʊkəm) *n. Chiefly Brit.* a person who stands in temporarily for a doctor or clergyman.

locus (ˈləʊkəs) *n., pl.* **loci.** *Maths.* a set of points or lines whose location satisfies or is determined by one or more specified conditions: *the locus of points equidistant from a given point is a circle.*

locust (ˈləʊkəst) *n.* **1.** an insect, related to the grasshopper, of warm and tropical regions, which travels in vast swarms, stripping large areas of vegetation. **2.** a North American leguminous tree with prickly branches; the carob tree.

locution (ləʊˈkjuːʃən) *n.* **1.** a word, phrase, or expression. **2.** manner or style of speech.

lode (ləʊd) *n.* a vein of metallic ore.

lodestar (ˈləʊdˌstɑː) *n.* **1.** a star, esp. the North Star, used in navigation or astronomy as a point of reference. **2.** something that serves as a guide.

lodestone (ˈləʊdˌstəʊn) *n.* **1. a.** magnetite

that is naturally magnetic. **b.** a piece of this, which can be used as a magnet. **2.** a person or thing regarded as a focus of attraction.

lodge (lɒdʒ) *n.* **1.** *Chiefly Brit.* a small house at the entrance to the grounds of a country mansion, usually occupied by a gatekeeper. **2.** a house or cabin used occasionally, as for some seasonal activity: *a ski lodge.* **3.** a room for the use of porters in a university or college. **4.** a local branch of certain societies. **5.** a beaver's home. ~*vb.* **6.** to provide or be provided with rented accommodation. **7.** to live temporarily in rented accommodation. **8.** to implant or embed or be implanted or embedded: *the bullet lodged close to his spine.* **9.** to deposit or leave for safety or storage: *documents lodged with my solicitor.* **10.** to bring (a charge or accusation) against someone: *to lodge a complaint.* **11.** (often foll. by *in* or *with*) to place (authority or power) in the control (of someone).

lodger (ˈlɒdʒə) *n.* a person who pays rent in return for accommodation in someone else's house.

lodging (ˈlɒdʒɪŋ) *n.* **1.** a temporary residence. **2.** (*pl.*) a rented room or rooms in another person's house.

loess (ˈləʊɪs) *n.* a fine-grained soil, found esp. in river valleys, originally deposited by the wind.

loft (lɒft) *n.* **1.** the space inside a roof. **2.** a gallery, esp. one for the choir in a church. **3.** a room over a stable used to store hay. **4.** a raised house or coop in which pigeons are kept. **5.** *Golf.* **a.** the angle from the vertical made by the club face to give elevation to a ball. **b.** the height reached by a struck ball. ~*vb.* **6.** *Sport.* to strike or kick (a ball) high in the air.

lofty (ˈlɒftɪ) *adj.* **loftier, loftiest. 1.** of majestic or imposing height. **2.** exalted or noble. **3.** haughty or supercilious. —**loftily** *adv.* —**loftiness** *n.*

log¹ (lɒg) *n.* **1.** a section of the trunk or a main branch of a tree, when stripped of branches. **2. a.** a detailed record of a voyage of a ship or aircraft. **b.** a record of the hours flown by pilots and aircrews. **c.** a book in which these records are made; logbook. **3.** a device consisting of a float with an attached line, formerly used to measure the speed of a ship. **4. sleep like a log.** to sleep without stirring or being disturbed. ~*vb.* **logging, logged. 5.** to saw logs from (trees). **6.** to enter (a distance or event) in a logbook or log.

log² (lɒg) *n.* short for **logarithm.** **Usage.** In mathematical usage *log* is followed by a subscript number indicating the base. The absence of this number implies that the logarithm is a common logarithm.

loganberry (ˈləʊgənbərɪ) *n., pl.* **-ries.** a

purplish-red fruit, similar to a raspberry, that grows on a trailing prickly plant.

logarithm ('lɒgə,rɪðəm) *n.* the exponent indicating the power to which a fixed number, the base, must be raised to obtain a given number or variable. —,loga'rithmic *adj.*

logbook ('lɒg,bʊk) *n.* **1.** a book containing the official record of trips made by a ship or aircraft. **2.** *Brit. informal.* the registration document of a car.

loggerhead ('lɒgə,hɛd) *n.* **1.** a large-headed turtle occurring in most seas. **2. at loggerheads.** engaged in dispute or confrontation.

loggia ('lɒdʒə) *n.* a covered gallery on the side of a building.

logging ('lɒgɪŋ) *n.* the work of felling, trimming, and transporting timber. —'logger *n.*

logic ('lɒdʒɪk) *n.* **1.** the branch of philosophy concerned with analysing the patterns of reasoning. **2.** a particular system or method of reasoning. **3.** reasoned thought or argument, as distinguished from irrationality. **4.** the relationship and interdependence of a series of events or facts. **5.** *Electronics, computers.* the principles underlying the units in a computer system that produce results from data.

logical ('lɒdʒɪkˀl) *adj.* **1.** relating to or characteristic of logic. **2.** using or deduced from the principles of logic: *a logical conclusion.* **3.** capable of or using clear or valid reasoning. **4.** reasonable because of facts or events: *the logical candidate.* —'logically *adv.*

logician (lɒ'dʒɪʃən) *n.* a person who specializes in or is skilled at logic.

logistics (lɒ'dʒɪstɪks) *n.* (*functioning as sing. or pl.*) the detailed planning and organization of a large complex operation, such as a military campaign. —lo'gistic *or* lo'gistical *adj.* —lo'gistically *adv.*

log jam *n. Chiefly U.S. & Canad.* **1.** a blockage caused by the crowding together of logs floating in a river. **2.** a deadlock.

logo ('ləʊgəʊ, 'lɒg-) *n., pl.* -os. a trademark, company emblem, or similar device.

-logy *n. combining form.* **1.** indicating the science or study of: *musicology.* **2.** indicating writing or discourse: *trilogy; phraseology; martyrology.* —logical *or* -logic *adj. combining form.* —logist *n. combining form.*

loin (lɔɪn) *n.* **1.** *Anat.* the lower back and sides between the pelvis and the ribs. **2.** a cut of meat from this part of an animal. ~See also **loins.**

loincloth ('lɔɪn,klɒθ) *n.* a piece of cloth worn round the loins.

loins (lɔɪnz) *pl. n.* **1.** the hips and the inner surface of the legs where they join the body. **2.** *Euphemistic.* the genitals.

loiter ('lɔɪtə) *vb.* to stand or act aimlessly or idly.

loll (lɒl) *vb.* **1.** to lie, lean, or lounge in a lazy manner. **2.** to hang or allow to hang loosely.

lollipop ('lɒlɪ,pɒp) *n.* **1.** a boiled sweet or toffee stuck on a small wooden stick. **2.** *Brit.* an ice lolly.

lollipop man *or* **lady** *n. Brit. informal.* a person holding a circular sign on a pole who stops traffic so that children may cross the road.

lollop ('lɒləp) *vb. Chiefly Brit.* to walk or run with a clumsy or relaxed bouncing movement.

lolly ('lɒlɪ) *n., pl.* -lies. **1.** *Informal.* a lollipop. **2.** *Brit.* short for **ice lolly. 3.** *Brit., Austral., & N.Z. slang.* money. **4.** *Austral. & N.Z. informal.* a sweet.

London pride ('lʌndən) *n.* a saxifrage plant with a rosette of leaves and pink flowers.

lone (ləʊn) *adj.* **1.** unaccompanied; solitary: *a lone figure.* **2.** isolated: *a lone house.* **3.** unmarried or widowed: *a lone parent.*

lonely ('ləʊnlɪ) *adj.* -lier, -liest. **1.** unhappy as a result of being without companions. **2.** causing or resulting from the state of being alone: *a lonely existence.* **3.** isolated or unfrequented: *lonely moorland.* —'loneliness *n.*

lonely hearts *adj.* of or for people who wish to meet a congenial companion or marriage partner: *a lonely hearts advertisement.*

loner ('ləʊnə) *n. Informal.* a person who prefers to be alone.

lonesome ('ləʊnsəm) *adj.* **1.** *Chiefly U.S. & Canad.* lonely. **2.** causing feelings of loneliness: *an owl's lonesome cry.*

long¹ (lɒŋ) *adj.* **1.** having relatively great extent in space or duration in time. **2.** of a specified extent or duration: *three hours long.* **3.** consisting of a large number of items or parts: *a long list.* **4.** having greater than the average or expected range, extent, or duration: *a long match.* **5.** seeming to occupy a greater time than is really so: *she spent a long afternoon waiting.* **6.** *Informal.* (foll. by *on*) plentifully supplied or endowed (with): *long on good ideas.* **7.** *Phonetics, prosody.* (of a vowel) of relatively considerable duration. **8.** from end to end; lengthwise. **9.** *Finance.* having large holdings of securities or commodities in anticipation of rising prices. **10. in the long run.** ultimately; after or over a period of time. ~*adv.* **11.** for a certain time or period: *how long will it last?* **12.** for or during an extensive period of time: *long into the next year.* **13.** a considerable amount of time: *long before I met you; long ago.* **14. as** *or* **so long as. a.** for or during just the length of time that. **b.** provided that; if. ~n. **15.** anything that is long. **16. before long.** soon. **17. for long.** for a long time. **18. the long and the short of it.** the essential points or facts. —'**longish** adj.

long[2] (lɒŋ) vb. (foll. by for or an infinitive) to have a strong desire.

long. longitude.

long- adv. (in combination) for or lasting a long time: long-established; long-lasting.

longboat ('lɒŋ,bəʊt) n. the largest boat carried aboard a commercial ship.

longbow ('lɒŋ,bəʊ) n. a large powerful hand-drawn bow.

long-distance n. (modifier) **1.** covering relatively long distances: a long-distance driver. **2.** (of telephone calls) connecting points a relatively long way apart.

longevity (lɒn'dʒɛvɪtɪ) n. long life.

longhand ('lɒŋ,hænd) n. ordinary handwriting, as opposed to typing or shorthand.

longing ('lɒŋɪŋ) n. **1.** a prolonged unfulfilled desire. ~adj. **2.** having or showing desire: a longing look. —'**longingly** adv.

longitude ('lɒndʒɪ,tjuːd, 'lɒŋgɪ-) n. distance in degrees east or west of the prime meridian at 0°.

longitudinal (,lɒndʒɪ'tjuːdɪn²l, ,lɒŋgɪ-) adj. **1.** of longitude or length. **2.** placed or extended lengthways.

long johns pl. n. Informal. long underpants.

long jump n. an athletic contest of covering the farthest distance with a running jump from a fixed mark.

long-lived adj. having long life, existence, or currency.

long-playing adj. of or relating to an LP.

long-range adj. **1.** of or extending into the future: a long-range weather forecast. **2.** (of vehicles, aircraft, or weapons) capable of covering great distances.

longship ('lɒŋ,ʃɪp) n. a narrow open boat with oars and a square sail, used by the Vikings.

longshore drift ('lɒŋ,ʃɔː) n. the movement of material along a beach, caused by the fact that waves approach the shore at an oblique angle.

longshoreman ('lɒŋ,ʃɔːmən) n., pl. -men. U.S. & Canad. a docker.

long shot n. **1.** a bet against heavy odds. **2.** an undertaking, guess, or possibility with little chance of success. **3. by a long shot.** by any means: he still hasn't finished by a long shot.

long-sighted adj. **1.** able to see distant objects in focus. **2.** far-sighted.

long-standing adj. existing for a long time.

long-suffering adj. enduring trouble or unhappiness without complaint.

long-term adj. lasting or extending over a long time: long-term prospects.

longtime ('lɒŋ,taɪm) adj. of long standing: his longtime friend.

long ton n. See **ton**[1] (sense 1).

long wave n. a radio wave with a wavelength greater than 1000 metres.

longways ('lɒŋ,weɪz) or U.S. & Canad. **longwise** adv. lengthways.

long-winded (,lɒŋ'wɪndɪd) adj. tiresomely long. —,**long-'windedness** n.

loo (luː) n., pl. **loos.** Brit. informal. a toilet.

loofah ('luːfə) n. the dried fibrous interior of a type of gourd, used as a sponge.

look (lʊk) vb. **1.** (often foll. by at) to direct the eyes (towards): to look at the sea. **2.** (often foll. by at) to direct one's attention (towards): let's look at the circumstances. **3.** to give the impression of being; seem: that looks interesting. **4.** to face in a particular direction: the house looks north. **5.** to expect or hope (to do something): I look to hear from you soon. **6.** (foll. by for) to search or seek: I looked for you everywhere. **7.** (foll. by into) to carry out an investigation. **8.** to direct a look at (someone) in a specified way: she looked her rival up and down. **9.** to accord in appearance with (something): to look one's age. **10. look alive, lively, sharp,** or **smart.** to hurry up; get busy. **11. look here.** an expression used to attract someone's attention or add emphasis to a statement. ~n. **12.** an instance of looking: a look of despair. **13.** a view or sight (of something): let's have a look. **14.** (often pl.) appearance to the eye or mind; aspect: the look of innocence; I don't like the looks of this place. **15.** style; fashion: the new look for spring. ~conj. **16.** an expression demanding attention or showing annoyance: look, I've had enough of this. ~See also **look after, look back,** etc. —'**looker** n.

Usage. see **feel.**

look after vb. to take care of.

lookalike ('lʊkə,laɪk) n. a person or thing that is the double of another, often well-known, person or thing.

look back vb. **1.** to cast one's mind to the past. **2. never looked back.** was extremely successful: after his first book was published, he never looked back.

look down vb. (foll. by on or upon) to express or show contempt (for).

look forward to vb. to wait or hope for, esp. with pleasure.

look-in Informal. ~n. **1.** a chance to be chosen or join in: she never got a look-in. ~vb. **look in. 2.** to pay a short visit.

looking glass n. a mirror.

look on vb. **1.** to be a spectator at an event or incident. **2.** to consider or regard: she looked on the affair as a joke. —,**looker-'on** n.

lookout ('lʊk,aʊt) n. **1.** the act of keeping watch against danger or for an opportunity:

on the lookout. **2.** a person or persons keeping such a watch, as on a ship. **3.** a strategic point from which a watch is kept. **4.** *Informal.* worry or concern: *that's his lookout.* **5.** *Chiefly Brit.* chances or prospect: *a poor lookout.* ~*vb.* **look out.** **6.** to be careful. **7.** to be on the watch: *look out for my mother at the station.* **8.** to search for and find: *I've looked out the books you asked for.* **9.** (foll. by *on* or *over*) to face in a particular direction: *the house looks out over the moor.*

look over *vb.* **1.** to inspect or examine. ~*n.* **look-over. 2.** an inspection.

look-see *n. Slang.* a brief inspection or look.

look up *vb.* **1.** to discover (something required to be known) by checking in a reference book. **2.** to improve: *things are looking up.* **3.** (foll. by *to*) to have respect (for): *I looked up to her because of her wisdom.* **4.** to visit (a person): *I'll look you up when I'm in town.*

loom[1] (luːm) *n.* an apparatus for weaving yarn into cloth.

loom[2] (luːm) *vb.* **1.** to come into view indistinctly with an enlarged and often threatening aspect. **2.** (of an event) to seem ominously close.

loon (luːn) *n. U.S. & Canad.* a diver (the bird).

loony ('luːnɪ) *Slang.* ~*adj.* **loonier, looniest. 1.** lunatic; insane. **2.** foolish or ridiculous. ~*n., pl.* **loonies. 3.** a foolish or insane person.

loop (luːp) *n.* **1.** the round or oval shape formed by a line that curves around to cross itself. **2.** any round or oval-shaped thing that is closed or nearly closed. **3.** *Electronics.* a closed circuit through which a signal can circulate. **4.** a flight manoeuvre in which an aircraft flies in a complete vertical circle. **5.** a continuous strip of cinema film or tape. **6.** *Computers.* a series of instructions in a program, performed repeatedly until some specified condition is satisfied. ~*vb.* **7.** to make a loop in or of (a line, string, or thread). **8.** to fasten or encircle with a loop. **9.** Also: **loop the loop.** to cause (an aircraft) to perform a loop or (of an aircraft) to perform a loop.

loophole ('luːp,həʊl) *n.* an ambiguity or omission, as in a law, by which one can avoid a penalty or responsibility.

loopy ('luːpɪ) *adj.* **loopier, loopiest.** *Informal.* slightly mad, crazy.

loose (luːs) *adj.* **1.** free or released from confinement or restraint. **2.** not close, compact, or tight in structure or arrangement. **3.** not fitted or fitting closely: *loose clothing is cooler.* **4.** not bundled, fastened, or put in a container: *loose nails.* **5.** inexact; imprecise: *a loose translation.* **6.** (of cash) readily available: *loose change.* **7.** promiscuous, immoral, or dissolute. **8.** lacking a

sense of responsibility or propriety: *loose talk.* ~*n.* **9. the loose.** *Rugby.* the part of play when the forwards close round the ball in a ruck or loose scrum. **10. on the loose.** free from confinement or restraint. ~*adv.* **11.** in a loose manner; loosely. ~*vb.* **12.** to set free or release, as from restraint or obligation: *until that hold of law is loosed.* **13.** to unfasten or untie: *he loosed the strap.* **14.** to make or become less strict, tight, firmly attached, or compact. **15.** to let fly (a bullet, arrow, or other missile). —'**loosely** *adv.* —'**looseness** *n.*

loosebox ('luːs,bɒks) *n.* an enclosed stall with a door in which an animal can be kept.

loose-jointed *adj.* supple and easy in movement.

loose-leaf *adj.* (of a binder) capable of being opened to allow removal and addition of pages.

loosen ('luːs²n) *vb.* **1.** to make or become less tight or fixed: *loosen the screws.* **2.** (often foll. by *up*) to make or become less firm, compact, or rigid: *loosen up the soil.* **3.** to untie. **4.** (often foll. by *up*) to make or become less strict or severe: *as sexual attitudes loosened up.*

loot (luːt) *n.* **1.** goods stolen in wartime or during riots. **2.** *Informal.* money. ~*vb.* **3.** to rob (a city) during war or riots. **4.** to steal (money or goods) during war or riots. —'**looter** *n.*

lop (lɒp) *vb.* **lopping, lopped.** (usually foll. by *off*) **1.** to sever (parts) from a tree or body. **2.** to cut out or eliminate from as excessive.

lope (ləʊp) *vb.* **1.** to move or run with a long swinging stride or gait. ~*n.* **2.** a long steady gait or stride.

lop-eared *adj.* (of animals) having ears that droop.

lopsided (,lɒp'saɪdɪd) *adj.* greater in weight, height, or size on one side.

loquacious (lɒ'kweɪʃəs) *adj.* having a tendency to talk a great deal. —**loquacity** (lɒ-'kwæsɪtɪ) *n.*

lord (lɔːd) *n.* **1.** a person who has power or authority over others, such as a monarch or master. **2.** a male member of the nobility. **3.** (in medieval Europe) a feudal superior. **4. my lord.** a respectful form of address used to a judge, bishop, or nobleman. ~*vb.* **5. lord it over someone.** to act in a superior manner towards someone.

Lord (lɔːd) *n.* **1.** *Christianity.* a title given to God or Jesus Christ. **2.** *Brit.* a title given to certain male peers. **3.** *Brit.* a title given to certain high officials and judges. ~*interj.* **4.** an exclamation of dismay or surprise: *Good Lord!*

Lord Chancellor *n. Brit. government.* the cabinet minster who is head of the judiciary and Speaker of the House of Lords.

Lord Chief Justice *n.* (in England and

Wales) the judge who is second only to the Lord Chancellor and president of one division of the High Court of Justice.

Lord Lieutenant *n.* **1.** (in Britain) the representative of the Crown in a county. **2.** (formerly) the British viceroy in Ireland.

lordly ('lɔːdlɪ) *adj.* **-lier, -liest. 1.** haughty; arrogant; proud. **2.** of or suitable to a lord. **—'lordliness** *n.*

Lord Mayor *n.* the mayor in the City of London and in certain other boroughs.

Lord Privy Seal *n.* (in Britain) the senior cabinet minister without official duties.

Lords (lɔːdz) *n.* **the.** short for **House of Lords.**

lordship ('lɔːdʃɪp) *n.* the position or authority of a lord.

Lordship ('lɔːdʃɪp) *n.* (preceded by *Your* or *His*) *Brit.* a title used to address or refer to a bishop, a judge of the high court, or any peer except a duke.

Lord's Prayer *n.* **the.** the prayer taught by Jesus Christ to his disciples.

Lords Spiritual *pl. n.* (in Britain) the Anglican archbishops and senior bishops who are members of the House of Lords.

Lord's Supper *n.* **the.** same as **Holy Communion.**

Lords Temporal *pl. n.* **the.** (in Britain) peers other than bishops in their capacity as members of the House of Lords.

lore (lɔː) *n.* collective knowledge or wisdom on a particular subject.

lorgnette (lɔːˈnjet) *n.* a pair of spectacles or opera glasses mounted on a handle.

lorry ('lɒrɪ) *n., pl.* **-ries.** a large motor vehicle designed to carry heavy loads.

lose (luːz) *vb.* **losing, lost. 1.** to part with or come to be without, as through theft, accident, or carelessness. **2.** to fail to keep or maintain: *to lose one's balance.* **3.** to suffer the loss or deprivation of: *to lose a parent.* **4.** to get rid off: *try to lose weight.* **5.** to fail to get or make use of: *to lose a chance.* **6.** to be defeated, as in a fight or game. **7.** to fail to see, hear, or understand: *I lost the gist of his speech.* **8.** to waste: *to lose money gambling.* **9.** to wander from so as to be unable to find: *to lose one's way.* **10.** to cause the loss of: *his delay lost him the battle.* **11.** to allow to go astray or out of sight: *we lost him in the crowd.* **12.** to absorb or engross: *he was lost in contemplation.* **13.** to cause the death or destruction of: *two men were lost in the attack.* **14.** to outdistance or escape from: *he soon lost his pursuers.* **15.** (of a timepiece) to run slow (by a specified amount).

lose out *vb. Informal.* **1.** to be defeated or unsuccessful. **2. lose out on.** to fail to secure or make use of: *we lost out on the sale.*

loser ('luːzə) *n.* **1.** a person or thing that loses. **2.** *Informal.* a person or thing that

seems destined to be taken advantage of or fail: *a born loser.*

losing ('luːzɪŋ) *adj.* unprofitable; failing: *the business was a losing concern.*

loss (lɒs) *n.* **1.** the act or an instance of losing. **2.** the disadvantage or deprivation resulting from losing: *a loss of reputation.* **3.** the person, thing, or amount lost: *a large loss.* **4. at a loss. a.** uncertain what to do; bewildered. **b.** with income less than outlay: *the firm was running at a loss.*

loss leader *n.* an article offered below cost to attract customers.

lost (lɒst) *vb.* **1.** the past of **lose.** ~*adj.* **2.** unable to be found or recovered. **3.** unable to find one's way. **4.** confused or bewildered: *he is lost in discussions of theory.* **5.** (sometimes foll. by *on*) not utilized, noticed, or understood (by): *rational arguments are lost on her.* **6.** no longer possessed or existing because of defeat, misfortune, or the passage of time: *a lost art.* **7.** (foll. by *in*) engrossed (in): *he was lost in his book.* **8.** morally fallen: *a lost woman.* **9.** damned: *a lost soul.*

lost cause *n.* a cause with no chance of success.

lot (lɒt) *pron.* **1.** (*functioning as sing. or pl.*; preceded by *a*) a great number or quantity: *a lot to do; a lot of people.* ~*n.* **2.** a collection of things or people: *a nice lot of youngsters.* **3.** destiny or fortune: *it falls to my lot to be poor.* **4.** any object, such as a straw or slip of paper, drawn from others at random to make a selection or choice: *draw lots; cast lots.* **5.** the use of lots in making a choice: *chosen by lot.* **6.** an item or set of items for sale in an auction. **7.** *Chiefly U.S. & Canad.* an area of land: *a parking lot.* **8. a bad lot.** an unpleasant or disreputable person. **9. cast** *or* **throw in one's lot with someone.** to join with voluntarily and share the fortunes of someone. **10. the lot.** the entire amount or number. ~*adv.* **11.** (preceded by *a*) *Informal.* to a considerable extent, degree, or amount: *to delay a lot.* ~See also **lots.**

loth (ləʊθ) *adj.* same as **loath.**

Lothario (ləʊˈθɑːrɪˌəʊ) *n., pl.* **-os.** a seducer.

lotion ('ləʊʃən) *n.* a liquid preparation having a soothing, cleansing, or antiseptic action, applied to the skin.

lots (lɒts) *Informal.* ~*pl. n.* **1.** (often foll. by *of*) great numbers or quantities: *lots of people; to eat lots.* ~*adv.* **2.** a great deal.

lottery ('lɒtərɪ) *n., pl.* **-teries. 1.** a game of chance in which tickets are sold, which may later qualify the holder for a prize. **2.** an endeavour the success of which is regarded as a matter of luck.

lotto ('lɒtəʊ) *n.* a game of chance in which numbers are drawn and called out, while the players cover the corresponding numbers on cards, the winner being the first to cover all the numbers or a particular row.

lotus ('ləʊtəs) n. 1. (in Greek mythology) a fruit that induces dreamy forgetfulness in those who eat it. 2. any of several water lilies of tropical Africa and Asia, regarded as sacred. 3. a symbolic representation of such a plant.

lotus-eater n. one who lives in lazy forgetfulness.

lotus position n. a seated cross-legged position with each foot on top of the opposite thigh, used in yoga and meditation.

loud (laʊd) adj. 1. (of sound) relatively great in volume: a loud shout. 2. making or able to make sounds of relatively great volume: a loud voice. 3. insistent and emphatic: loud protests. 4. (of colours or patterns) harsh to look at. 5. noisy, vulgar, and offensive. ~adv. 6. in a loud manner. 7. **out loud.** audibly. —'**loudly** adv. —'**loudness** n.

loud-hailer n. a portable loudspeaker with a built-in amplifer and microphone.

loudspeaker (ˌlaʊd'spiːkə) n. a device for converting electrical signals into sounds.

lough (lɒx, lɒk) n. 1. Irish. a lake. 2. a long narrow arm of the sea in Ireland.

lounge (laʊndʒ) vb. 1. (often foll. by about or around) to sit, lie, walk, or stand in a relaxed manner. 2. to pass (time) lazily or idly. ~n. 3. a communal room in a hotel, ship, or airport, used for waiting or relaxing in. 4. Chiefly Brit. a living room in a private house. 5. Brit. a more expensive bar in a pub or hotel. 6. the act of lounging.

lounge suit n. a man's suit of matching jacket and trousers worn for the normal business day.

lour ('laʊə) vb. same as **lower²**.

lourie ('laʊrɪ) n. a type of African bird with bright plumage.

louse (laʊs) n. 1. (pl. **lice**) a wingless bloodsucking insect which infests man and some animals. 2. (pl. **louses**) Slang. an unpleasant or mean person.

louse up vb. Slang. to ruin or spoil.

lousy ('laʊzɪ) adj. **lousier, lousiest.** 1. Slang. very mean or unpleasant. 2. Slang. inferior or bad. 3. Slang. ill or unwell. 4. infested with lice.

lout (laʊt) n. a crude or oafish person; boor. —'**loutish** adj.

louvre or U.S. **louver** ('luːvə) n. **a.** any of a set of horizontal slats in a door or window, sloping outwards to throw off rain and admit air. **b.** the slats and frame supporting them. —'**louvred** or U.S. '**louvered** adj.

lovage ('lʌvɪdʒ) n. a European herb with greenish-white flowers.

love (lʌv) vb. 1. to have a great fondness and affection for a person or thing. 2. to have passionate desire for a particular person. 3. to like or desire (to do something) very much. ~n. 4. an intense emotion of affection, warmth, and regard towards a person or thing. 5. a deep feeling of sexual attraction and desire. 6. wholehearted liking for or pleasure in something. 7. a beloved person: often used as an endearment. 8. Brit. informal. a term of address, not necessarily for a person regarded as likable. 9. (in tennis, squash, etc.) a score of zero. 10. **fall in love.** to become in love. 11. **for love or money.** by any means. 12. **in love.** in a state of strong emotional attachment and usually sexual attraction. 13. **make love to. a.** to have sexual intercourse with. **b.** Now archaic. to court. —'**lovable** or '**loveable** adj.

lovebird ('lʌvˌbɜːd) n. any of several small African parrots often kept as cagebirds.

lovebite ('lʌvˌbaɪt) n. a temporary red mark left on a person's skin by a partner's biting or sucking it during lovemaking.

love child n. Euphemistic. a child whose parents have not been married to each other.

loveless ('lʌvlɪs) adj. without love: a loveless marriage.

love-lies-bleeding n. a plant with drooping spikes of small red flowers.

love life n. the part of a person's life consisting of romantic or sexual relationships.

lovelorn ('lʌvˌlɔːn) adj. miserable because of unrequited love or unhappiness in love.

lovely ('lʌvlɪ) adj. **-lier, -liest.** 1. very attractive or beautiful. 2. highly pleasing or enjoyable: a lovely time. ~n., pl. **-lies.** 3. Slang. a lovely woman. —'**loveliness** n.

lovemaking ('lʌvˌmeɪkɪŋ) n. 1. sexual play and activity between lovers, including sexual intercourse. 2. Archaic. courtship.

lover ('lʌvə) n. 1. a person who has a sexual relationship with another person outside marriage. 2. (often pl.) either of the people involved in a love affair. 3. someone who loves a specified person or thing: a cat-lover.

lovesick ('lʌvˌsɪk) adj. pining or languishing because of love. —'**love,sickness** n.

lovey-dovey (ˌlʌvɪ'dʌvɪ) adj. making a sentimental or showy display of affection.

loving ('lʌvɪŋ) adj. feeling or showing love and affection. —'**lovingly** adv.

loving cup n. a large two-handled cup out of which people drink in turn at a banquet.

low¹ (ləʊ) adj. 1. having a relatively small distance from base to top: a low building. 2. situated at a relatively short distance above the ground, sea level, or the horizon: low cloud. 3. of less than usual height, depth, degree, or cost: low temperature; low prices. 4. (of numbers) small. 5. involving or containing a relatively small amount of something: a low supply. 6. having little value or quality: of low grade. 7. coarse or vulgar: a low conversation. 8. inferior in culture or status. 9. in a physically or mentally depressed or weakened state. **10. low-necked:** *a low dress.* **11.** with a hushed tone: *a low whisper.* **12.** *Music.* of or having a relatively low pitch. **13.** (of latitudes) situated not far north or south of the equator. **14.** having little or no money. **15.** unfavourable: *a low opinion.* **16.** deep: *a low bow.* **17.** (of a gear) providing a relatively low forward speed for a given engine speed. ~*adv.* **18.** in a low position, level, degree, or intensity: *to bring someone low.* **19.** at a low pitch; deep: *to sing low.* **20.** cheaply: *to buy low.* **21. lay low. a.** to cause to fall by a blow. **b.** to overcome, defeat, or destroy. **22. lie low.** to keep or be concealed or quiet. ~*n.* **23.** a low position, level, or degree: *an all-time low.* **24.** an area of low atmospheric pressure; a depression. —'**lowness** *n.*

low² (ləʊ) *n. also* **lowing. 1.** the sound uttered by cattle; moo. ~*vb.* **2.** to make or express by a low or moo.

lowborn (ˌləʊˈbɔːn) *adj. Now rare.* of ignoble or common parentage.

lowbrow ('ləʊˌbraʊ) *Disparaging.* ~*n.* **1.** a person who has uncultivated or nonintellectual tastes. ~*adj.* **2.** of or for such a person.

Low Church *n.* the school of thought in the Church of England stressing evangelical beliefs and practices. —ˌ**Low**-'**Church** *adj.*

low comedy *n.* comedy characterized by slapstick and physical action.

Low Countries *pl. n.* Belgium, Luxembourg, and the Netherlands.

low-down *Informal.* ~*adj.* **1.** mean, underhand, or despicable. ~*n.* **lowdown. 2. the.** information.

lower¹ ('ləʊə) *adj.* **1.** being below one or more other things: *the lower shelf.* **2.** reduced in amount or value: *a lower price.* **3. Lower.** *Geol.* denoting the early part of a period or formation. ~*vb.* **4.** to bring, put, or cause to move down: *lower one's eyes.* **5.** to reduce or bring down in estimation, dignity, or value: *to lower oneself.* **6.** to reduce or be reduced: *to lower one's confidence.* **7.** to make quieter or reduce the pitch of. **8.** to become less.

lower² *or* **lour** ('laʊə) *vb.* (of the sky or weather) to be overcast and menacing. —'**lowering** *or* '**louring** *adj.*

lower case ('ləʊə) *n.* (in printing) small letters, as opposed to capital letters. —ˌ**lower**-'**case** *adj.*

lower class ('ləʊə) *n.* the class with the lowest position in society. —ˌ**lower**-'**class** *adj.*

lower house ('ləʊə) *n.* one of the houses of a parliament that has two chambers: usually the larger and more representative.

lowest common denominator *n. Maths.* the smallest integer or polynomial that is exactly divisible by each denominator of a set of fractions.

lowest common multiple *n. Maths.* the smallest number or quantity that is exactly divisible by each member of a set of numbers or quantities.

low frequency *n.* any radio frequency lying between 300 and 30 kilohertz.

Low German *n.* a language of N Germany, spoken in rural areas.

low-key *or* **low-keyed** *adj.* **1.** having a low intensity or tone. **2.** restrained or subdued.

lowland ('ləʊlənd) *n.* **1.** relatively low ground. **2.** (*often pl.*) a low generally flat region. ~*adj.* **3.** of a lowland or lowlands. —'**lowlander** *n.*

Lowland ('ləʊlənd) *n.* (*modifier*) of the Lowlands, a low generally flat region of S Central Scotland or the dialects of English spoken there. —'**Lowlander** *n.*

lowly ('ləʊlɪ) *adj.* **-lier, -liest. 1.** humble or low in position, rank, or status. **2.** simple, unpretentious, or plain. —'**lowliness** *n.*

Low Mass *n.* a simplified form of Mass that is spoken rather than sung.

low-minded *adj.* having a vulgar or crude mind. —ˌ**low**-'**mindedness** *n.*

low-pitched *adj.* **1.** pitched low in tone. **2.** (of a roof) with a shallow slope.

low profile *n.* a position or attitude deliberately avoiding prominence or publicity.

low-spirited *adj.* depressed or dejected.

low-tech *adj.* **1.** of or using low technology. **2.** in the style of interior design using items associated with low technology.

low technology *n.* simple unsophisticated technology that is limited to the production of basic necessities.

low tide *n.* the tide when it is at its lowest level or the time at which it reaches this.

low water *n.* **1.** low tide. **2.** the state of any stretch of water at its lowest level.

loyal ('lɔɪəl) *adj.* **1.** faithful to one's friends, country, or government. **2.** of or expressing loyalty. —'**loyally** *adv.*

loyalist ('lɔɪəlɪst) *n.* a patriotic supporter of his sovereign or government. —'**loyalism** *n.*

Loyalist ('lɔɪəlɪst) *n.* (in Northern Ireland) any of the Protestants wishing to retain Ulster's link with Britain.

loyalty ('lɔɪəltɪ) *n., pl.* **-ties. 1.** the quality of being loyal. **2.** a feeling of friendship or duty towards someone or something.

lozenge ('lɒzɪndʒ) *n.* **1.** *Med.* a medicated tablet held in the mouth until it has dissolved. **2.** *Geom.* a rhombus.

LP *n.* a record, usually 12 inches in diameter, which is played at 33⅓ revolutions per minute and normally holds about 20 or 25 minutes of sound on each side.

L-plate *n. Brit.* a red "L" on a white square

fixed to the front and back of a motor vehicle to show that the driver has not passed the driving test.

Lr *Chem.* lawrencium.

LSD *n.* lysergic acid diethylamide; an illegal hallucinogenic drug.

L.S.D., £.s.d., *or* **l.s.d.** pounds, shillings, pence.

Lt Lieutenant.

Ltd Limited (Liability).

Lu *Chem.* lutetium.

lubber (ˈlʌbə) *n.* **1.** a big, awkward, or stupid person. **2.** short for **landlubber.** —ˈlubberly *adj., adv.* —ˈlubberliness *n.*

lubricant (ˈluːbrɪkənt) *n.* a lubricating substance, such as oil.

lubricate (ˈluːbrɪˌkeɪt) *vb.* **1.** to cover or treat with an oily substance so as to lessen friction. **2.** to make greasy, slippery, or smooth. —ˌlubriˈcation *n.*

lubricious (luːˈbrɪʃəs) *adj. Formal or literary.* lewd.

lucerne (luːˈsɜːn) *n. Brit.* same as **alfalfa.**

lucid (ˈluːsɪd) *adj.* **1.** readily understood; clear. **2.** shining or glowing. **3.** of or relating to a period of normality between periods of insanity or delirium. —luˈcidity *n.* —ˈlucidly *adv.*

Lucifer (ˈluːsɪfə) *n.* Satan.

luck (lʌk) *n.* **1.** events that are beyond control and seem subject to chance; fortune. **2.** success or good fortune. **3. down on one's luck.** having so little luck as to be suffering hardships. **4. no such luck.** *Informal.* unfortunately not. **5. try one's luck.** to attempt something that is uncertain.

luckless (ˈlʌklɪs) *adj.* unfortunate; unlucky.

lucky (ˈlʌkɪ) *adj.* **luckier, luckiest. 1.** having or bringing good fortune. **2.** happening by chance, esp. as desired. —ˈluckily *adv.*

lucky dip *n. Brit.* a box filled with sawdust containing small prizes for which children search.

lucrative (ˈluːkrətɪv) *adj.* profitable.

lucre (ˈluːkə) *n. Usually facetious.* money or wealth: *filthy lucre.*

Luddite (ˈlʌdaɪt) *n. Brit.* **1.** any of the textile workers opposed to mechanization, who organized machine-breaking between 1811 and 1816. **2.** any opponent of industrial change or innovation. ~*adj.* **3.** of the Luddites.

ludicrous (ˈluːdɪkrəs) *adj.* absurd or ridiculous. —ˈludicrously *adv.*

ludo (ˈluːdəʊ) *n. Brit.* a simple board game in which players advance counters by throwing dice.

luff (lʌf) *vb.* **1.** *Naut.* to head (a sailing vessel) into the wind so that her sails flap. **2.** to move the jib of (a crane) in order to shift a load.

lug¹ (lʌg) *vb.* **lugging, lugged.** to carry or drag (something heavy) with great effort.

lug² (lʌg) *n.* **1.** a projecting piece by which something is connected, supported, or lifted. **2.** *Informal or Scot.* an ear.

luggage (ˈlʌgɪdʒ) *n.* suitcases, trunks, and bags.

lugger (ˈlʌgə) *n. Naut.* a small working boat with a four-sided fore-and-aft sail.

lugubrious (luˈguːbrɪəs) *adj.* excessively mournful.

lugworm (ˈlʌgˌwɜːm) *n.* a worm living in burrows on sandy shores: much used as bait.

lukewarm (ˌluːkˈwɔːm) *adj.* **1.** (of a liquid) moderately warm; tepid. **2.** having or expressing little enthusiasm or conviction.

lull (lʌl) *vb.* **1.** to soothe (a person or animal) by soft sounds or motions. **2.** to calm (someone or someone's fears or suspicions) by deception. ~*n.* **3.** a short period of calm.

lullaby (ˈlʌləˌbaɪ) *n., pl.* **-bies.** a quiet song to lull a child to sleep.

lumbago (lʌmˈbeɪgəʊ) *n.* pain in the lower back; backache.

lumbar (ˈlʌmbə) *adj.* of, in, or near the part of the body between the lowest ribs and the hipbones.

lumbar puncture *n. Med.* insertion of a hollow needle into the lower spinal cord to withdraw fluid for diagnosis.

lumber¹ (ˈlʌmbə) *n.* **1.** *Brit.* useless household articles that are stored away. **2.** *Chiefly U.S. & Canad.* logs; sawn timber. ~*vb.* **3.** *Brit. informal.* to burden with something unpleasant or tedious. **4.** to fill up or encumber with useless household articles. **5.** *Chiefly U.S. & Canad.* to convert trees into marketable timber.

lumber² (ˈlʌmbə) *vb.* to move or proceed in an awkward heavy manner. —ˈlumbering *adj.*

lumberjack (ˈlʌmbəˌdʒæk) *n.* (esp. in North America) a person whose work involves felling trees and transporting the timber.

luminary (ˈluːmɪnərɪ) *n., pl.* **-naries. 1.** a famous person who enlightens or influences others. **2.** *Literary.* something, such as the sun or moon, that gives off light.

luminescence (ˌluːmɪˈnesəns) *n. Physics.* the emission of light at low temperatures by any process other than incandescence. —ˌlumiˈnescent *adj.*

luminous (ˈluːmɪnəs) *adj.* **1.** reflecting or giving off light: *luminous colours.* **2.** (*not in technical use*) luminescent: *luminous paint.* **3.** enlightening or wise. —luminosity (ˌluːmɪˈnɒsɪtɪ) *n.*

lump¹ (lʌmp) *n.* **1.** a small solid mass without definite shape. **2.** *Pathol.* any small swelling or tumour. **3.** *Informal.* an awkward, heavy, or stupid person. **4. the lump.** *Brit.* self-employed workers in the building trade considered collectively. **5.** (*modifier*) in the form of a lump or lumps: *lump sugar.* **6. a lump in one's throat.** a tight dry feeling in one's throat, usually caused by great emotion. ~*vb.* **7.** to grow into lumps or become lumpy. **8.** (often foll. by *together*) to consider as a single group, often without justification.

lump² (lʌmp) *vb. Informal.* to tolerate or put up with: *you'll just have to lump it.*

lumpectomy (ˌlʌmˈpɛktəmɪ) *n., pl.* **-mies.** the surgical removal of a tumour in a breast.

lumpish (ˈlʌmpɪʃ) *adj.* stupid, clumsy, or heavy. —**ˈlumpishness** *n.*

lump sum *n.* a relatively large sum of money, paid at one time.

lumpy (ˈlʌmpɪ) *adj.* **lumpier, lumpiest.** full of or having lumps. —**ˈlumpiness** *n.*

lunacy (ˈluːnəsɪ) *n., pl.* **-cies. 1.** (formerly) any severe mental illness. **2.** foolishness.

lunar (ˈluːnə) *adj.* of, occurring on, or used on the moon: *lunar module.*

lunatic (ˈluːnətɪk) *adj.* **1.** *Archaic.* insane. **2.** foolish; eccentric. ~*n.* **3.** a person who is insane.

lunatic asylum *n. Offensive.* a home or hospital for the mentally ill.

lunatic fringe *n.* the members of a group who adopt views regarded as extreme.

lunch (lʌntʃ) *n.* **1.** a meal eaten during the middle of the day. ~*vb.* **2.** to eat lunch.

luncheon (ˈlʌntʃən) *n.* a lunch, often a formal one.

luncheon meat *n.* a ground mixture of meat (often pork) and cereal, usually tinned.

luncheon voucher *n.* a voucher worth a specified amount issued to employees and accepted by some restaurants as payment for food.

lunchroom (ˈlʌntʃˌruːm) *n. Chiefly Canad.* a room where lunch is served or where students or employees may eat lunches they bring.

lung (lʌŋ) *n.* the part of the body that allows an animal or bird to breathe air. Humans have two lungs, contained within the chest cavity.

lunge (lʌndʒ) *n.* **1.** a sudden forward motion. **2.** *Fencing.* a thrust made by advancing the front foot and straightening the back leg. ~*vb.* **3.** to move with a lunge. **4.** *Fencing.* to make a lunge.

lungfish (ˈlʌŋˌfɪʃ) *n., pl.* **-fish** or **-fishes.** a freshwater fish with an air-breathing lung.

lupin (ˈluːpɪn) *n.* a plant with large spikes of brightly coloured flowers and flattened pods.

lupine (ˈluːpaɪn) *adj.* of or like a wolf.

lupus (ˈluːpəs) *n.* an ulcerous skin disease.

lurch¹ (lɜːtʃ) *vb.* **1.** to lean or tilt suddenly to one side. **2.** to stagger. ~*n.* **3.** a lurching.

lurch² (lɜːtʃ) *n.* **leave someone in the lurch.** to desert someone in trouble.

lurcher (ˈlɜːtʃə) *n.* a crossbred hunting dog trained to hunt silently.

lure (lʊə) *vb.* **1.** (sometimes foll. by *away* or *into*) to tempt or attract by the promise of reward. ~*n.* **2.** a person or thing that lures. **3.** *Angling.* a brightly coloured artificial spinning bait. **4.** *Falconry.* a feathered decoy to which small pieces of meat can be attached.

lurid (ˈlʊərɪd) *adj.* **1.** vivid in shocking detail; sensational. **2.** horrible in savagery or violence. **3.** glaring in colour. —**ˈluridly** *adv.*

lurk (lɜːk) *vb.* **1.** to move stealthily or be concealed, as for evil purposes. **2.** to be present in an unobtrusive way; be latent.

lurking (ˈlɜːkɪŋ) *adj.* lingering but almost unacknowleged: *a lurking suspicion.*

luscious (ˈlʌʃəs) *adj.* **1.** extremely pleasurable to taste or smell. **2.** very attractive.

lush¹ (lʌʃ) *adj.* **1.** (of vegetation) abounding in lavish growth. **2.** luxurious, elaborate, or opulent.

lush² (lʌʃ) *n. Slang, chiefly U.S. & Canad.* an alcoholic.

lust (lʌst) *n.* **1.** a strong sexual desire. **2.** a strong desire or drive: *a lust for power.* ~*vb.* **3.** (often foll. by *after* or *for*) to have a lust (for). —**ˈlustful** *adj.* —**ˈlustfully** *adv.*

lustre *or U.S.* **luster** (ˈlʌstə) *n.* **1.** reflected light; sheen. **2.** radiance or brilliance of light. **3.** great splendour of accomplishment or beauty. **4.** a shiny metallic surface on some pottery and porcelain. —**ˈlustrous** *adj.*

lusty (ˈlʌstɪ) *adj.* **lustier, lustiest. 1.** having or characterized by robust health. **2.** strong or invigorating. —**ˈlustily** *adv.* —**ˈlustiness** *n.*

lute (luːt) *n.* an ancient plucked stringed instrument with a long fingerboard and a body shaped like a sliced pear.

lutetium (luːˈtiːʃɪəm) *n.* a silvery-white metallic element of the lanthanide series. Symbol: Lu

Lutheran (ˈluːθərən) *n.* **1.** a follower of Luther (1483-1546), German leader of the Reformation, or a member of a Lutheran Church. ~*adj.* **2.** of or relating to Luther, his doctrines, or any of the Churches that follow these doctrines. —**ˈLutheranism** *n.*

lux (lʌks) *n., pl.* **lux.** the SI unit of illumination.

luxe (lʌks, lʊks) *n.* See **de luxe.**

luxuriant (lʌgˈzjʊərɪənt) *adj.* **1.** rich and abundant; lush. **2.** very elaborate or ornate. —**luxˈuriance** *n.* —**luxˈuriantly** *adv.*

luxuriate (lʌgˈzjʊərɪˌeɪt) *vb.* **1.** (foll. by *in*)

to take self-indulgent pleasure; revel. **2.** to flourish profusely.

luxurious (lʌgˈzjʊərɪəs) *adj.* **1.** characterized by luxury. **2.** enjoying or devoted to luxury.

luxury (ˈlʌkʃərɪ) *n., pl.* **-ries. 1.** indulgence in and enjoyment of rich, comfortable, and sumptuous living. **2.** something considered an indulgence rather than a necessity. **3.** (*modifier*) relating to, indicating, or supplying luxury: *a luxury liner.*

LV luncheon voucher.

lyceum (laɪˈsɪəm) *n.* (now chiefly in the names of buildings) a public building for events such as concerts and lectures.

lychee (ˌlaɪˈtʃiː) *n.* the fruit of a Chinese tree, which has a whitish juicy pulp.

lych gate (lɪtʃ) *n.* same as **lich gate.**

Lycra (ˈlaɪkrə) *n. Trademark.* a synthetic elastic fabric and fibre used for tight-fitting garments, such as swimming costumes.

lye (laɪ) *n.* **1.** a caustic solution obtained from wood ash. **2.** a concentrated solution of sodium hydroxide or potassium hydroxide.

lying (ˈlaɪɪŋ) *vb.* the present participle of **lie¹** and **lie².**

lying-in *n., pl.* **lyings-in.** confinement in childbirth.

lymph (lɪmf) *n.* the almost colourless fluid, containing chiefly white blood cells, that comes from the tissues of the body. —**lymˈphatic** *adj.*

lymphatic system *n.* a network of fine vessels by which lymph circulates throughout the body.

lymph node *n.* any of many bean-shaped masses of tissue in the lymphatic system that help to protect against infection.

lymphocyte (ˈlɪmfəʊˌsaɪt) *n.* a type of white blood cell.

lynch (lɪntʃ) *vb.* (of a mob) to kill (a person) for some supposed offence without a trial. —**ˈlynching** *n.*

lynx (lɪŋks) *n., pl.* **lynxes** *or* **lynx.** a mammal of the cat family, with grey-brown mottled fur, tufted ears, and a short tail.

lynx-eyed *adj.* having keen sight.

lyre (ˈlaɪə) *n.* an ancient Greek U-shaped stringed instrument, similar to a harp but plucked with a plectrum.

lyrebird (ˈlaɪəˌbɜːd) *n.* either of two pheasant-like Australian birds: during courtship displays, the male spreads its tail into the shape of a lyre.

lyric (ˈlɪrɪk) *adj.* **1.** (of poetry) **a.** expressing the writer's personal feelings. **b.** having the form and manner of a song. **2.** of or relating to such poetry. **3.** (of a singing voice) light and melodic. ~*n.* **4.** a short poem of songlike quality. **5.** (*pl.*) the words of a popular song. —**ˈlyrically** *adv.*

lyrical (ˈlɪrɪkˀl) *adj.* **1.** same as **lyric** (senses 1, 2). **2.** enthusiastic; effusive.

lyricism (ˈlɪrɪˌsɪzəm) *n.* **1.** the quality or style of lyric poetry. **2.** emotional outpouring.

lyricist (ˈlɪrɪsɪst) *n.* a person who writes the words for a song, opera, or musical.

M

m *or* **M** (εm) *n.*, *pl.* **m's, M's,** *or* **Ms.** the 13th letter of the English alphabet.

m 1. metre(s). 2. mile(s). 3. milli-. 4. million. 5. minute(s).

M 1. mach. 2. *Currency.* mark(s). 3. medium. 4. mega-. 5. (in Britain) motorway. 6. the Roman numeral for 1000.

m. 1. male. 2. married. 3. masculine. 4. meridian. 5. month.

M. 1. Majesty. 2. Master. 3. (in titles) Member. 4. (*pl.* **MM.** *or* **MM**) *French.* Monsieur.

ma (mɑː) *n. Informal.* a mother.

MA 1. Massachusetts. 2. Master of Arts.

ma'am (mæm, mɑːm; *unstressed* məm) *n.* short for **madam**: used as a title of respect.

mac *or* **mack** (mæk) *n. Brit. informal.* a mackintosh.

Mac (mæk) *n. Chiefly U.S. & Canad.* an informal term of address to a man.

macabre (mə'kɑːbrə) *adj.* gruesome; ghastly; grim.

macadam (mə'kædəm) *n.* a road made of compressed layers of small broken stones, esp. one bound together with tar or asphalt. —**ma'cadam,ize** *or* -,**ise** *vb.*

macaque (mə'kɑːk) *n.* any of various Asian and African monkeys with cheek pouches and either a short tail or no tail.

macaroni (,mækə'rəʊnɪ) *n.*, *pl.* -**nis** *or* -**nies.** 1. pasta tubes made from wheat flour. 2. (in 18th-century Britain) a dandy.

macaroon (,mækə'ruːn) *n.* a sweet biscuit made of ground almonds.

macaw (mə'kɔː) *n.* a large tropical American parrot with a long tail and brilliant plumage.

mace[1] (meɪs) *n.* 1. a club with a spiked metal head used in the Middle Ages. 2. a ceremonial staff carried by certain officials.

mace[2] (meɪs) *n.* a spice made from the dried outer casing of the nutmeg.

macebearer (,meɪs,bɛərə) *n.* a person who carries a mace in processions or ceremonies.

macerate ('mæsə,reɪt) *vb.* 1. to soften or be softened by soaking. 2. to become or cause to become thin. —,**macer'ation** *n.*

Mach (mæk) *n.* short for **Mach number.**

machete (mə'ʃɛtɪ, -'tʃeɪ-) *n.* a broad heavy knife used for cutting or as a weapon.

Machiavellian (,mækɪə'vɛlɪən) *adj.* cunning, amoral, and opportunist. —,**Machia-'vellian,ism** *n.*

machinate ('mækɪ,neɪt) *vb.* to contrive, plan, or devise (schemes, plots, etc.). —,**machi'nation** *n.*

machine (mə'ʃiːn) *n.* 1. an assembly of components arranged so as to perform a particular task and usually powered by electricity. 2. a vehicle, such as a car or aircraft. 3. a system within an organization that controls activities and policies: *the party machine.* ~*vb.* 4. to shape, cut, or make (something) using a machine. —**ma'chinable** *adj.*

machine gun *n.* 1. a rapid-firing automatic gun, using small-arms ammunition. ~*vb.* **machine-gun, -gunning, -gunned.** 2. to shoot or fire at with a machine gun.

machine language *n.* instructions for a computer in binary or hexadecimal code.

machinery (mə'ʃiːnərɪ) *n.*, *pl.* -**eries.** 1. machines, machine parts, or machine systems collectively. 2. the mechanism of a machine.

machine shop *n.* a workshop in which machine tools are operated.

machine tool *n.* a power-driven machine, such as a lathe, for cutting and shaping metal, wood, or plastic.

machinist (mə'ʃiːnɪst) *n.* 1. a person who operates machines to cut or process materials. 2. a maker or repairer of machines.

machismo (mæ'kɪzməʊ, -'tʃɪz-) *n.* strong or exaggerated masculinity.

Mach number (mæk) *n.* (*often not cap.*) the ratio of the speed of a body in a particular medium to the speed of sound in that medium.

macho ('mætʃəʊ) *adj.* 1. strongly or exaggeratedly masculine. ~*n.*, *pl.* **machos.** 2. machismo.

mack (mæk) *n. Brit. informal.* same as **mac.**

mackerel ('mækrəl) *n.*, *pl.* -**rel** *or* -**rels.** an edible sea fish with a greenish-blue body marked with wavy dark bands on the back.

mackintosh *or* **macintosh** ('mækɪn,tɒʃ) *n.* 1. a raincoat made of rubberized cloth. 2. such cloth. 3. any raincoat.

macramé (mə'krɑːmɪ) *n.* a type of ornamental work made by knotting and weaving coarse thread.

macro- *or before a vowel* **macr-** *combining form.* large, long, or great: *macroscopic.*

macrobiotics (,mækrəʊbaɪ'ɒtɪks) *n.* (*functioning as sing.*) a dietary system which advocates whole grains and vegetables grown without chemical additives. —,**macrobi'otic** *adj.*

macrocarpa (ˌmækrəʊˈkɑːpə) *n.* a large New Zealand coniferous tree.

macrocosm (ˈmækrəˌkɒzəm) *n.* a complex structure, such as the universe or society, regarded as a whole.

macromolecule (ˌmækrəʊˈmɒlɪˌkjuːl) *n.* any very large molecule, such as a protein or synthetic polymer.

macron (ˈmækrɒn) *n.* a mark (¯) placed over a letter to represent a long vowel.

macroscopic (ˌmækrəʊˈskɒpɪk) *adj.* **1.** large enough to be visible to the naked eye. **2.** comprehensive; concerned with large units.

macula (ˈmækjʊlə) *n., pl.* **-ulae** (-jʊˌliː). *Anat.* a small spot or area of distinct colour, such as a freckle.

mad (mæd) *adj.* **madder, maddest. 1.** mentally deranged; insane. **2.** senseless; foolish. **3.** (often foll. by *at*) *Informal.* angry. **4.** (foll. by *about, on,* or *over*) wildly enthusiastic (about) or fond (of). **5.** extremely excited or confused; frantic: *a mad rush.* **6.** (of animals) **a.** unusually ferocious: *a mad buffalo.* **b.** afflicted with rabies. **7. like mad.** *Informal.* with great energy, enthusiasm, or haste. —ˈ**madness** *n.*

madam (ˈmædəm) *n., pl.* **madams** *or* (for sense 1) **mesdames. 1.** a polite term of address for a woman. **2.** a woman who runs a brothel. **3.** *Brit. informal.* a precocious or pert girl.

madame (ˈmædəm) *n., pl.* **mesdames.** a French title equivalent to *Mrs.*

madcap (ˈmædˌkæp) *adj.* **1.** impulsive, reckless, or lively. *~n.* **2.** an impulsive, reckless, or lively person.

madden (ˈmædᵊn) *vb.* to make or become mad or angry. —ˈ**maddening** *adj.*

madder (ˈmædə) *n.* **1.** a plant with small yellow flowers and a red fleshy root. **2.** a dark reddish-purple dye formerly obtained from its root. **3.** an artificial pigment of this colour.

made (meɪd) *vb.* **1.** the past of **make.** *~adj.* **2.** produced or shaped as specified: *handmade.* **3. get** *or* **have it made.** *Informal.* to be assured of success.

Madeira (məˈdɪərə) *n.* a fortified white wine from Madeira, an island in the N Atlantic.

mademoiselle (ˌmædmwəˈzɛl) *n., pl.* **mesdemoiselles. 1.** a French title equivalent to *Miss.* **2.** a French teacher or governess.

made-up *adj.* **1.** invented; fictional. **2.** wearing make-up. **3.** put together. **4.** (of a road) surfaced with tarmac or concrete.

madhouse (ˈmædˌhaʊs) *n. Informal.* **1.** a mental hospital. **2.** a state of uproar or confusion.

madly (ˈmædlɪ) *adv.* **1.** in an insane or foolish manner. **2.** with great speed and energy. **3.** *Informal.* extremely or excessively: *I love you madly.*

madman (ˈmædmən) *or* (*fem.*) **madwoman** *n., pl.* **-men** *or* **-women.** a person who is insane.

Madonna (məˈdɒnə) *n.* **1.** *Chiefly R.C. Church.* the Virgin Mary. **2.** (*sometimes not cap.*) a picture or statue of the Virgin Mary.

madrigal (ˈmædrɪgᵊl) *n.* a type of 16th- or 17th-century part song for unaccompanied voices. —ˈ**madrigalist** *n.*

maelstrom (ˈmeɪlstrəʊm) *n.* a large powerful whirlpool.

maenad (ˈmiːnæd) *n.* **1.** *Classical history.* a female disciple of Dionysus, Greek god of wine. **2.** a frenzied woman.

maestro (ˈmaɪstrəʊ) *n., pl.* **-tri** (-trɪ) *or* **-tros. 1.** a distinguished music teacher, conductor, or musician. **2.** any master of an art.

mae west (meɪ) *n. Slang.* an inflatable life jacket.

Mafia (ˈmæfɪə) *n.* **the.** a secret criminal organization founded in Sicily, and carried to the U.S. by Italian immigrants.

mafioso (ˌmæfɪˈəʊsəʊ) *n., pl.* **-sos** *or* **-si** (-sɪ). a member of the Mafia.

magazine (ˌmægəˈziːn) *n.* **1.** a periodic paperback publication containing written pieces and illustrations. **2.** a television or radio programme made up of short nonfictional items. **3.** a metal case holding several cartridges used in some automatic firearms. **4.** a place for storing weapons, explosives, or military equipment. **5.** a stock of ammunition. **6.** a rack for automatically feeding slides through a projector.

magenta (məˈdʒɛntə) *adj.* deep purplish-red.

maggot (ˈmægət) *n.* the limbless larva of various insects, esp. the housefly and blowfly. —ˈ**maggoty** *adj.*

magi (ˈmeɪdʒaɪ) *pl. n., sing.* **magus** (ˈmeɪgəs). **1.** See **magus. 2. the three Magi.** *Christianity.* the wise men from the East who came to do homage to the infant Jesus (Matthew 2:1–12).

magic (ˈmædʒɪk) *n.* **1.** the supposed invocation of supernatural powers to influence events; sorcery. **2.** tricks done to entertain; conjuring. **3.** any mysterious or extraordinary quality or power. **4. like magic.** very quickly. *~adj. also* **magical. 5.** of magic. **6.** possessing or considered to possess mysterious powers. **7.** unaccountably enchanting. **8.** *Informal.* wonderful; marvellous. *~vb.* **-icking, -icked. 9.** to transform or produce as if by magic. **10.** (foll. by *away*) to cause to disappear as if by magic. —ˈ**magically** *adv.*

magician (məˈdʒɪʃən) *n.* **1.** a conjurer. **2.** a person with magic powers.

magic lantern *n.* an early type of slide projector.

magisterial (ˌmædʒɪˈstɪərɪəl) *adj.* **1.** commanding; authoritative. **2.** of a magistrate. —**,magis'terially** adv.

magistracy ('mædʒɪstrəsɪ) n., pl. -**cies**. **1.** the office or function of a magistrate. **2.** magistrates collectively.

magistrate ('mædʒɪ,streɪt) n. **1.** a public officer concerned with the administration of law. **2.** same as **justice of the peace**.

magistrates' court n. (in England) a court that deals with minor crimes, certain civil actions, and preliminary hearings.

magma ('mægmə) n., pl. -**mas** or -**mata** (-mətə). hot molten rock within the earth's crust which sometimes finds its way to the surface where it solidifies to form igneous rock.

Magna Carta ('mægnə 'kɑːtə) n. English history. the charter granted by King John at Runnymede in 1215, recognizing the rights and privileges of the barons, church, and freemen.

magnanimous (mæg'nænɪməs) adj. generous and noble. —**magnanimity** (,mægnə-'nɪmɪtɪ) n. —**mag'nanimously** adv.

magnate ('mægneɪt) n. a person of power and rank, esp. in industry.

magnesia (mæg'niːzɪə) n. a white tasteless substance used as an antacid and laxative; magnesium oxide.

magnesium (mæg'niːzɪəm) n. a light silvery-white metallic element that burns with an intense white flame. Symbol: Mg

magnet ('mægnɪt) n. **1.** a piece of iron, steel, or lodestone that has the property of attracting iron to it. **2.** a person or thing that exerts a great attraction.

magnetic (mæg'nɛtɪk) adj. **1.** of, producing, or operated by means of magnetism. **2.** of or like a magnet. **3.** capable of being magnetized. **4.** exerting a powerful attraction: a magnetic personality. —**mag'netically** adv.

magnetic disk n. a computer storage disk.

magnetic field n. an area around a magnet in which its power of attraction is felt.

magnetic mine n. a mine which detonates when a magnetic field such as that generated by the metal of a ship's hull is detected.

magnetic needle n. a slender magnetized rod used in certain instruments, such as the magnetic compass, for indicating the direction of a magnetic field.

magnetic north n. the direction in which a compass needle points, at an angle from the direction of true (geographic) north.

magnetic pole n. either of two variable points on the earth's surface towards which a magnetic needle points.

magnetic storm n. a sudden severe disturbance of the earth's magnetic field, caused by emission of charged particles from the sun.

magnetic tape n. a long plastic strip coated with a magnetic substance, and used to record sound or video signals or to store information in computers.

magnetism ('mægnɪ,tɪzəm) n. **1.** the property of attraction displayed by magnets. **2.** the branch of physics concerned with magnetic phenomena. **3.** powerful personal charm.

magnetite ('mægnɪ,taɪt) n. a black magnetizable mineral that is an important source of iron.

magnetize or -**ise** ('mægnɪ,taɪz) vb. **1.** to make (a substance or object) magnetic. **2.** to attract strongly. —**'magnet,izable** or -**,isable** adj. —**,magneti'zation** or -**i'sation** n.

magneto (mæg'niːtəʊ) n., pl. -**tos**. a small electric generator in which the magnetic field is produced by a permanent magnet.

magnetron ('mægnɪ,trɒn) n. an electronic valve used with a magnetic field to generate microwave oscillations, esp. for use in radar.

Magnificat (mæg'nɪfɪ,kæt) n. Christianity. the hymn of the Virgin Mary (Luke 1:46-55), used as a canticle.

magnification (,mægnɪfɪ'keɪʃən) n. **1.** the act of magnifying or the state of being magnified. **2.** the degree to which something is magnified. **3.** a magnified copy of something.

magnificent (mæg'nɪfɪsˀnt) adj. **1.** splendid or impressive in appearance. **2.** superb or very fine: a magnificent performance. —**mag'nificence** n. —**mag'nificently** adv.

magnify ('mægnɪ,faɪ) vb. -**fying**, -**fied**. **1.** to increase in apparent size, as through the action of a lens or microscope. **2.** to exaggerate: don't magnify your troubles. **3.** Archaic. to glorify.

magnifying glass or **magnifier** ('mægnɪ-,faɪə) n. a convex lens used to produce an enlarged image of an object.

magniloquent (mæg'nɪləkwənt) adj. (of speech) lofty in style; grandiloquent. —**mag'niloquence** n.

magnitude ('mægnɪ,tjuːd) n. **1.** relative importance: a problem of the first magnitude. **2.** relative size or extent. **3.** Astron. the apparent brightness of a celestial body expressed on a numerical scale on which bright stars have a low value.

magnolia (mæg'nəʊlɪə) n. an Asian and North American tree or shrub with white, pink, purple, or yellow showy flowers.

magnox ('mægnɒks) n. an alloy composed mainly of magnesium, used in fuel elements of some nuclear reactors (**magnox reactors**).

magnum ('mægnəm) n., pl. -**nums**. a wine bottle of twice the normal size.

magnum opus n. a great work of art or

literature, esp. the greatest single work of an artist.

magpie ('mæg‚paɪ) n. **1.** a bird of the crow family with black-and-white plumage, a long tail, and a chattering call. **2.** Brit. a person who hoards small objects.

magus ('meɪgəs) n., pl. **magi**. **1.** a Zoroastrian priest. **2.** an astrologer or magician of ancient times.

Magyar ('mægjɑː) n. **1.** (pl. **-yars**) a member of the main ethnic group of Hungary. **2.** the Hungarian language. ~adj. **3.** of the Magyars or their language.

maharajah or **maharaja** (‚mɑːhə'rɑːdʒə) n. an Indian prince, esp. any of the rulers of the former native states.

maharani or **maharanee** (‚mɑːhə'rɑːniː) n. the wife of a maharajah.

maharishi (‚mɑːhə'riːʃɪ, mə'hɑːrɪʃɪ) n. Hinduism. a teacher of religious and mystical knowledge.

mahatma (mə'hɑːtmə) n. (sometimes cap.) a person revered for his holiness or wisdom.

mahjong or **mah-jongg** (‚mɑː'dʒɒŋ) n. a game of Chinese origin, usually played by four people, using tiles bearing various designs.

mahogany (mə'hɒgənɪ) n., pl. **-nies**. **1.** the hard reddish-brown wood of any of several tropical trees. ~adj. **2.** reddish-brown.

mahout (mə'haʊt) n. (in India and the East Indies) an elephant driver or keeper.

maid (meɪd) n. **1.** a female servant. **2.** Archaic or literary. a young unmarried girl; maiden.

maiden ('meɪd²n) n. **1.** Archaic or literary. a young unmarried girl, esp. a virgin. **2.** Horse racing. a horse that has never won a race. **3.** (modifier) unmarried: a maiden aunt. **4.** (modifier) first; earliest: a maiden voyage. —'**maiden‚hood** n. —'**maidenly** adj.

maidenhair fern ('meɪd²n‚hɛə) n. a fern with delicate hairlike fronds of small pale green leaflets.

maidenhead ('meɪd²n‚hɛd) n. **1.** the hymen. **2.** virginity; maidenhood.

maiden name n. a woman's surname before marriage.

maiden over n. Cricket. an over in which no runs are scored.

maid of honour n. **1.** an unmarried lady attending a queen or princess. **2.** U.S. & Canad. the principal unmarried attendant of a bride.

maidservant ('meɪd‚sɜːvənt) n. a female servant.

mail¹ (meɪl) n. **1.** letters and packages transported and delivered by the post office. **2.** the postal system. **3.** a single collection or delivery of mail. **4.** a train, ship, or aircraft that carries mail. ~vb. **5.** Chiefly U.S. & Canad. to send by mail.

mail² (meɪl) n. flexible armour consisting of riveted metal rings or links. —**mailed** adj.

mailbag ('meɪl‚bæg) n. a large bag for transporting or delivering mail.

mail coach n. Hist. a fast stagecoach designed primarily for carrying mail.

mailing list n. a register of names and addresses to which information or advertising matter is sent by post.

mail order n. a system of buying and selling goods by post.

mailshot ('meɪl‚ʃɒt) n. a posting of circulars, leaflets, or other advertising to a selected large number of people at once.

maim (meɪm) vb. to mutilate, cripple, or disable.

main (meɪn) adj. **1.** chief or principal. ~n. **2.** a principal pipe or line in a system used to distribute water, electricity, or gas. **3.** (pl.) the main distribution network for water, gas, or electricity. **4.** great strength or force (now esp. in (**with**) **might and main**). **5.** Literary. the open ocean. **6.** Archaic. the mainland. **7. in the main.** on the whole.

mainbrace ('meɪn‚breɪs) n. Naut. **1.** the rope that controls the movement of the spar of a ship's mainsail. **2. splice the mainbrace.** See **splice**.

main clause n. Grammar. a clause that can stand alone as a sentence.

mainframe ('meɪn‚freɪm) n. Computers. a high-speed general-purpose computer, with a large store capacity.

mainland ('meɪnlənd) n. the main part of a land mass as opposed to an island.

main line n. **1.** Railways. the trunk route between two points, usually fed by branch lines. ~vb. **mainline**. **2.** Slang. to inject a drug into a vein.

mainly ('meɪnlɪ) adv. for the most part; principally.

mainmast ('meɪn‚mɑːst) n. Naut. the chief mast of a sailing vessel with two or more masts.

mainsail ('meɪn‚seɪl; Naut. 'meɪns²l) n. Naut. the largest and lowermost sail on the mainmast.

mainspring ('meɪn‚sprɪŋ) n. the chief cause or motive of something.

mainstay ('meɪn‚steɪ) n. a chief support.

mainstream ('meɪn‚striːm) n. the main current (of a river or cultural trend).

mainstreeting ('meɪn‚striːtɪŋ) n. Canad. the practice of a politician walking about a town or city to try to gain votes.

maintain (meɪn'teɪn) vb. **1.** to continue or retain; keep in existence. **2.** to keep in proper or good condition. **3.** to enable (a person) to support a style of living: the money maintained us for a month. **4.** (takes a clause as object) to assert: she maintained that the plan was bound to fail.

5. to defend against contradiction; uphold: *she maintained her innocence.*

maintenance ('meɪntɪnəns) *n.* **1.** the act of maintaining or the state of being maintained. **2.** a means of support; livelihood. **3.** *Law.* financial provision ordered to be made by way of periodical payments or a lump sum, as for a spouse after a divorce.

maisonette (,meɪzə'nɛt) *n.* a flat with more than one floor.

maître d'hôtel (,mɛtrə dəʊ'tɛl) *n., pl.* **maîtres d'hôtel.** a head waiter.

maize (meɪz) *n.* a tall annual grass cultivated for its yellow edible grains, which are used for food and as a source of oil.

Maj. Major.

majesty ('mædʒɪstɪ) *n.* **1.** great stateliness of bearing; grandeur. **2.** supreme power or authority. —**ma'jestic** *adj.* —**ma'jestically** *adv.*

Majesty ('mædʒɪstɪ) *n., pl.* **-ties.** (preceded by *Your, His, Her,* or *Their*) a title used to address or refer to a sovereign or the wife or widow of a sovereign.

majolica (mə'dʒɒlɪkə, mə'jɒl-) *or* **maiolica** (mə'jɒlɪkə) *n.* a type of porous pottery glazed with bright metallic oxides that was extensively made in Renaissance Italy.

major ('meɪdʒə) *n.* **1.** a middle-ranking military officer. **2.** (often preceded by *the*) *Music.* a major key, chord, mode, or scale. **3.** a person who has reached the age of legal majority. **4.** *U.S., Canad., Austral., & N.Z.* the principal field of study of a student. ~*adj.* **5.** of greater size, number, or importance. **6.** very serious or significant. **7.** main or principal. **8.** *Music.* (of a scale) **a.** having notes separated by a whole tone, except for the third and fourth degrees, and seventh and eighth degrees, which are separated by a semitone. **b.** of or based on the major scale: *a major key.* ~*vb.* **9.** (usually foll. by *in*) *U.S., Canad., Austral., & N.Z.* to do one's principal study (in a particular subject): *to major in English literature.*

major-domo (-'dəʊməʊ) *n., pl.* **-mos.** the chief steward or butler of a great household.

majorette (,meɪdʒə'rɛt) *n.* one of a group of girls who practise formation marching and baton twirling.

major general *n.* a senior military officer.

majority (mə'dʒɒrɪtɪ) *n., pl.* **-ties.** **1.** the greater number or part of something. **2.** (in an election) the number of votes or seats by which the strongest party or candidate beats the combined opposition or the runner-up. **3.** the largest party or group that votes together in an assembly. **4.** full legal age. **5. in the majority.** forming or part of the greater number of something.

make (meɪk) *vb.* **making, made. 1.** to bring

into being by shaping, changing, or combining materials or ideas; form. **2.** to draw up; establish: *to make one's will.* **3.** to bring about or produce: *don't make a noise.* **4.** to compel or induce: *please make him go away.* **5.** to appoint: *they made him chairman.* **6.** to come into a specified state or condition: *to make merry.* **7.** to become: *he will make a good teacher.* **8.** to cause or ensure the success of: *your news has made my day.* **9.** to amount to: *5 and 5 make 10.* **10.** to serve as or be suitable for: *that piece of cloth will make a coat.* **11.** to prepare for use: *to make a bed.* **12.** to be the essential element in: *charm makes a good salesman.* **13.** to carry out, effect, or do. **14.** (foll. by *to, as if to,* or *as though to*) to act with the intention or with a show of doing something: *he made as if to hit her.* **15.** to use for a specified purpose: *I will make this town my base.* **16.** to deliver: *to make a speech.* **17.** to consider to be: *what time do you make it?* **18.** to cause to seem or represent as being. **19.** to acquire: *to make friends.* **20.** to engage in: *to make war.* **21.** to travel: *we can make a hundred miles by nightfall.* **22.** to arrive in time for: *he didn't make the first act of the play.* **23.** to win or score. **24.** *Informal.* to gain a place or position on or in: *to make the headlines.* **25. make a day, night,** etc., **of it.** to cause an activity to last a day, night, etc. **26. make eyes at.** to flirt with or ogle. **27. make it.** *Informal.* to be successful. **28. make like.** *Slang, chiefly U.S. & Canad.* **a.** to imitate. **b.** to pretend. ~*n.* **29.** manufacturer; brand. **30.** the way in which something is made. **31. on the make.** *Slang.* out for profit or conquest. ~See also **make away, make for,** etc. —'**maker** *n.*

make away *vb.* **1.** to depart in haste. **2. make away with. a.** to steal. **b.** to kill or get rid of.

make believe *vb.* **1.** to pretend. ~*n.* **make-believe. 2.** a fantasy or pretence.

make for *vb.* **1.** to head towards. **2.** to prepare to attack. **3.** to help bring about.

make of *vb.* to interpret as the meaning of: *what do you make of it all?*

make off *vb.* **1.** to go or run away in haste. **2. make off with.** to steal or abduct.

make out *vb.* **1.** to perceive. **2.** to understand. **3.** to write out: *he made out a cheque.* **4.** to attempt to establish or prove: *he made me out to be a liar.* **5.** to pretend: *he made out that he could cook.* **6.** to manage.

Maker ('meɪkə) *n.* a title given to God.

makeshift ('meɪk,ʃɪft) *adj.* serving as a temporary substitute.

make-up *n.* **1.** cosmetics, such as powder or lipstick. **2.** the cosmetics used by an actor to adapt his appearance. **3.** the arrangement of the parts of something. **4.** mental or physical constitution. ~*vb.*

make up. 5. to form or constitute: *these arguments make up the case for the defence.* **6.** to devise or compose, sometimes with the intent to deceive: *to make up an excuse.* **7.** to supply what is lacking in; complete: *these extra people will make up our numbers.* **8.** (foll. by *for*) to compensate or atone (for). **9.** to settle (differences) amicably (often in **make it up**). **10.** to apply cosmetics to (the face). **11. make up to.** *Informal.* **a.** to make friendly overtures to. **b.** to flirt with.

makeweight ('meɪk,weɪt) *n.* **1.** something put on a scale to make up a required weight. **2.** an unimportant person or thing added to make up a lack.

making ('meɪkɪŋ) *n.* **1.** the act or process of producing something. **2. be the making of.** to cause the success of. **3. in the making.** in the process of becoming or being made.

makings ('meɪkɪŋz) *pl. n.* potentials, qualities, or materials: *he had the makings of a leader.*

mal- *combining form.* bad or badly; wrong or wrongly: *maladjusted; malfunction.*

malachite ('mælə,kaɪt) *n.* a green mineral used as a source of copper, and for making ornaments.

maladjustment (,mælə'dʒʌstmənt) *n. Psychol.* a failure to meet the demands of society, such as coping with problems and social relationships. —,**malad'justed** *adj.*

maladminister (,mæləd'mɪnɪstə) *vb.* to administer badly, inefficiently, or dishonestly. —,**malad,minis'tration** *n.*

maladroit (,mælə'drɔɪt) *adj.* clumsy, awkward, or tactless. —,**mala'droitly** *adv.* —,**mala'droitness** *n.*

malady ('mælədɪ) *n., pl.* **-dies.** any disease or illness.

malaise (mæ'leɪz) *n.* a feeling of unease, mild sickness, or depression.

malapropism ('mæləprɒp,ɪzəm) *n.* the comic misuse of a word by confusion with one of similar sound, as in *under the affluence of alcohol.*

malaria (mə'lɛərɪə) *n.* a disease with recurring attacks of fever, caused by the bite of a mosquito. —**ma'larial** *adj.*

malarkey (mə'lɑːkɪ) *n. Slang.* nonsense; rubbish.

Malay (mə'leɪ) *n.* **1.** a member of a people living chiefly in Malaysia and Indonesia. **2.** the language of this people. ~*adj.* **3.** of the Malays or their language.

Malayan (mə'leɪən) *adj.* **1.** of or from the Malay peninsula in SE Asia. ~*n.* **2.** a person from the Malay peninsula.

malcontent ('mælkən,tɛnt) *n.* a person who is discontented with the existing situation.

male (meɪl) *adj.* **1.** of the sex that can fertilize female reproductive cells. **2.** of or

characteristic of a man. **3.** for or composed of men or boys: *a male choir.* **4.** (of flowers) bearing stamens but lacking a pistil. **5.** *Electronics, engineering.* having a projecting part or parts that fit into a hollow counterpart: *a male plug.* ~*n.* **6.** a male person, animal, or plant. —'**maleness** *n.*

male chauvinism *n.* the belief, held by certain men, that men are superior to women. —**male chauvinist** *n., adj.*

malediction (,mælɪ'dɪkʃən) *n.* the utterance of a curse against someone or something. —,**male'dictory** *adj.*

malefactor ('mælɪ,fæktə) *n.* a criminal; wrongdoer. —,**male'faction** *n.*

malevolent (mə'lɛvələnt) *adj.* wishing evil to others; malicious. —**ma'levolence** *n.* —**ma'levolently** *adv.*

malfeasance (mæl'fiːz²ns) *n. Law.* wrongful or illegal behaviour, esp. by a public official.

malformation (,mælfɔː'meɪʃən) *n.* **1.** the condition of being faulty or abnormal in form or shape. **2.** *Pathol.* a deformity, esp. when congenital. —**mal'formed** *adj.*

malfunction (mæl'fʌŋkʃən) *vb.* **1.** to function imperfectly or fail to function. ~*n.* **2.** failure to function or defective functioning.

malice ('mælɪs) *n.* the desire to do harm or cause mischief. —**ma'licious** *adj.*

malice aforethought *n. Law.* a deliberate intention to do something unlawful.

malign (mə'laɪn) *adj.* **1.** evil in influence, intention, or effect. ~*vb.* **2.** to slander or defame.

malignant (mə'lɪgnənt) *adj.* **1.** seeking to harm others. **2.** tending to cause great harm; injurious. **3.** *Pathol.* (of a tumour) uncontrollable or resistant to therapy. —**ma'lignancy** *n.*

malignity (mə'lɪgnɪtɪ) *n.* the condition of being malign or deadly.

malinger (mə'lɪŋgə) *vb.* to pretend or exaggerate illness, esp. to avoid work. —**ma'lingerer** *n.*

mall (mɔːl, mæl) *n.* **1.** a shaded avenue, esp. one open to the public. **2.** a street or shopping centre closed to vehicles.

mallard ('mælɑːd) *n., pl.* **-lard** *or* **-lards.** a common N hemisphere duck, the male of which has a dark green head.

malleable ('mælɪəb³l) *adj.* **1.** (esp. of metal) able to be worked, hammered, or shaped without breaking. **2.** able to be influenced. —,**mallea'bility** *n.* —'**malleably** *adv.*

mallet ('mælɪt) *n.* **1.** a hammer with a large, often wooden head. **2.** a long stick with a head like a hammer used to strike the ball in croquet or polo.

mallow ('mæləʊ) *n.* any of a group of European plants, having purple, pink, or white flowers.

malmsey ('mɑːmzɪ) *n.* a sweet Madeira wine.

malnutrition (ˌmælnjuːˈtrɪʃən) n. physical weakness resulting from insufficient food or unbalanced diet.

malodorous (mælˈəʊdərəs) adj. having a bad smell.

malpractice (mælˈpræktɪs) n. illegal, unethical, or negligent professional conduct.

malt (mɔːlt) n. 1. cereal grain, such as barley, that is kiln-dried after it has germinated by soaking in water. 2. See **malt whisky.** ~vb. 3. to make into or become malt. —'**malty** adj.

Maltese (mɔːlˈtiːz) adj. 1. of Malta, an island in the Mediterranean, its inhabitants, or their language. ~n. 2. (pl. **-tese**) a person from Malta. 3. the language of Malta.

Maltese cross n. a cross with triangular arms that taper towards the centre, sometimes having indented outer sides.

Malthusian (mælˈθjuːzɪən) adj. of the theory stating that increases in population tend to exceed increases in the food supply and that therefore sexual restraint should be exercised.

maltose ('mɔːltəʊz) n. a sugar formed by the action of enzymes on starch.

maltreat (mælˈtriːt) vb. to treat badly, cruelly, or violently. —**malˈtreatment** n.

malt whisky n. whisky made from malted barley.

malversation (ˌmælvɜːˈseɪʃən) n. Rare. professional or public misconduct.

mam (mæm) n. Informal or dialect. same as **mother.**

mama or esp. U.S. **mamma** (məˈmɑː) n. Old-fashioned, informal. same as **mother.**

mamba ('mæmbə) n. a poisonous tropical African tree snake.

mambo ('mæmbəʊ) n., pl. **-bos.** a modern Latin American dance resembling the rumba.

mammal ('mæməl) n. any warm-blooded vertebrate animal, the female of which produces milk to feed her young. —**mammalian** (mæˈmeɪlɪən) adj., n.

mammary gland ('mæmərɪ) n. any of the milk-producing glands in mammals, such as a woman's breast or a cow's udder.

mammon ('mæmən) n. wealth regarded as a source of evil and corruption, personified in the New Testament as a false god (**Mammon**).

mammoth ('mæməθ) n. 1. a large extinct elephant with a hairy coat and long curved tusks. ~adj. 2. gigantic.

man (mæn) n., pl. **men.** 1. an adult male human being, as distinguished from a woman. 2. a human being of either sex; person: all men are born equal. 3. human beings collectively; mankind. 4. a human being regarded as representative of a particular period or category: medieval man; Neanderthal man. 5. an adult male human being

with qualities associated with the male, such as courage or virility: take it like a man. 6. a subordinate, servant, or employee. 7. (usually pl.) a member of the armed forces who is not an officer, (as in **officers and men**). 8. a member of a group or team. 9. a husband, boyfriend, or male lover. 10. a movable piece in various games, such as draughts. 11. S. African slang. any person. 12. **as one man.** with unanimous action or response. 13. **he's your man.** he's the person needed. 14. **man and boy.** from childhood. 15. **sort out the men from the boys.** to discover who can cope with difficult or dangerous situations and who cannot. 16. **to a man.** without exception. ~vb. **manning, manned.** 17. to provide with sufficient men for operation or defence. 18. to take one's place at or near in readiness for action. —'**manhood** n.

Usage. The use of words ending in -man is avoided as implying a male in job advertisements, where sexual discrimination is illegal, and in many other contexts where a term that does not refer specifically to either sex is available, such as salesperson, barperson, camera operator.

Man. Manitoba.

manacle ('mænəkˀl) n. 1. (usually pl.) a shackle, handcuff, or fetter, used to secure a prisoner or convict. ~vb. 2. to put manacles on.

manage ('mænɪdʒ) vb. 1. to be in charge (of); administer: to manage a shop. 2. to succeed in being able (to do something); contrive. 3. to have room or time for: can you manage dinner tomorrow? 4. to exercise control or domination over. 5. to struggle on despite difficulties, esp. financial ones. 6. to wield or handle (a weapon). —'**manageable** adj.

management ('mænɪdʒmənt) n. 1. the people responsible for running an organization or business. 2. managers or employers collectively. 3. the technique or practice of managing or controlling.

manager ('mænɪdʒə) n. 1. a person who manages an organization or business. 2. a person who controls the business affairs of an actor or entertainer. 3. a person in charge of a sports team. —ˌ**manage'ress** fem. n.

managerial (ˌmænɪˈdʒɪərɪəl) adj. of a manager or management.

mañana (məˈnjɑːnə) n., adv. a. tomorrow. b. some other and later time.

man-at-arms n., pl. **men-at-arms.** a soldier, esp. a medieval soldier.

manatee (ˌmænəˈtiː) n. a large plant-eating mammal occurring in tropical coastal waters of the Atlantic.

Manchu (mænˈtʃuː) n., pl. **-chus** or **-chu.** a member of a Mongoloid people of Manchuria, a region of NE China, who conquered

China in the 17th century, ruling until 1912.

Mancunian (mæŋˈkjuːnɪən) *n.* **1.** a person from Manchester, a city in NW England. ~*adj.* **2.** of Manchester.

mandala (ˈmændələ) *n. Hindu & Buddhist art.* a circular design symbolizing the universe.

mandarin (ˈmændərɪn) *n.* **1.** (in the Chinese Empire) a member of a senior grade of the bureaucracy. **2.** a high-ranking official with extensive powers. **3.** a person of standing and influence, as in literary or intellectual circles. **4.** a small citrus fruit resembling the tangerine.

Mandarin Chinese *or* **Mandarin** *n.* the official language of China since 1917.

mandate (ˈmændeɪt) *n.* **1.** an official or authoritative command. **2.** *Politics.* the political authority given to a government or an elected representative through an electoral victory. **3.** (*often cap.*) Also: **mandated territory.** (formerly) a territory administered by one country on behalf of an international body. ~*vb.* **4.** to assign (territory) to a nation under a mandate. **5.** to delegate authority to.

mandatory (ˈmændətrɪ) *adj.* **1.** having the nature or powers of a mandate. **2.** obligatory; compulsory. —ˈ**mandatorily** *adv.*

mandible (ˈmændɪbˀl) *n.* **1.** the lower jawbone in vertebrates. **2.** either of the jawlike mouthparts of an insect. **3.** either part of the bill of a bird, esp. the lower part.

mandolin (ˌmændəˈlɪn) *n.* a musical instrument with four pairs of strings stretched over a small light body: usually played with a plectrum.

mandrake (ˈmændreɪk) *n.* a plant with a forked root. It was formerly thought to have magic powers and a narcotic was prepared from its root.

mandrel *or* **mandril** (ˈmændrəl) *n.* **1.** a spindle on which the piece being worked on is supported during machining. **2.** a shaft on which a machining tool is mounted.

mandrill (ˈmændrɪl) *n.* a monkey of W Africa. The male has red and blue markings on its face and buttocks.

mane (meɪn) *n.* **1.** the long hair that grows from the neck in such mammals as the lion and horse. **2.** long thick human hair. —**maned** *adj.*

manège *or* **manege** (mæˈneɪʒ) *n.* **1.** the art of training horses and riders. **2.** a riding school.

maneuver (məˈnuːvə) *n., vb. U.S.* same as **manoeuvre.**

man Friday *n.* **1.** a loyal male servant or assistant. **2.** Also: **girl Friday, person Friday.** any factotum, esp. in an office.

manful (ˈmænful) *adj.* resolute, strong; manly. —ˈ**manfully** *adv.*

manganese (ˈmæŋɡəˌniːz) *n.* a brittle greyish-white metallic element: used in making steel. Symbol: Mn

mange (meɪndʒ) *n.* a skin disease of domestic animals, characterized by itching and loss of hair.

mangelwurzel (ˈmæŋɡˀlˌwɜːzˀl) *n.* a variety of beet with a large yellowish root.

manger (ˈmeɪndʒə) *n.* a trough or box in a stable or barn from which horses or cattle feed.

mangetout (ˌmɒnʒˈtuː) *n.* a variety of garden pea with an edible pod.

mangle[1] (ˈmæŋɡˀl) *vb.* **1.** to mutilate or destroy by cutting, crushing, or tearing. **2.** to ruin; spoil. —ˈ**mangled** *adj.*

mangle[2] (ˈmæŋɡˀl) *n.* **1.** a machine for pressing or squeezing water out of washed clothes, consisting of two heavy rollers between which the clothes are passed. ~*vb.* **2.** to put through a mangle.

mango (ˈmæŋɡəʊ) *n., pl.* **-goes** *or* **-gos.** the egg-shaped edible fruit of a tropical Asian tree, with a smooth rind and sweet juicy flesh.

mangrove (ˈmæŋɡrəʊv, ˈmæn-) *n.* a tropical evergreen tree or shrub with intertwining aerial roots that forms dense thickets along coasts.

mangy (ˈmeɪndʒɪ) *adj.* **-gier, -giest. 1.** having or caused by mange. **2.** scruffy or shabby. —ˈ**mangily** *adv.* —ˈ**manginess** *n.*

manhandle (ˈmænˌhændˀl) *vb.* **1.** to handle or push (someone) about roughly. **2.** to move or do by manpower rather than by machinery.

manhole (ˈmænˌhəʊl) *n.* a hole with a detachable cover, through which a person can enter a sewer or pipe to inspect or repair it.

man-hour *n.* a unit of work in industry, equal to the work done by one person in one hour.

manhunt (ˈmænˌhʌnt) *n.* an organized search, usually by police, for a wanted man or fugitive.

mania (ˈmeɪnɪə) *n.* **1.** a mental disorder characterized by great or violent excitement. **2.** obsessional enthusiasm or partiality. —**manic** (ˈmænɪk) *adj., n.*

-mania *n. combining form.* indicating extreme or abnormal excitement aroused by something: *kleptomania.*

maniac (ˈmeɪnɪˌæk) *n.* **1.** a wild disorderly person. **2.** a person who has a great craving or enthusiasm for something. —**maniacal** (məˈnaɪəkˀl) *adj.*

manic-depressive (ˌmænɪkdɪˈpresɪv) *Psychiatry.* ~*adj.* **1.** denoting a mental disorder characterized by an alternation between extreme euphoria and deep depression. ~*n.* **2.** a person afflicted with this disorder.

manicure (ˈmænɪˌkjʊə) *n.* **1.** cosmetic care of the hands and fingernails, as by trimming the nails. ~*vb.* **2.** to care for (the hands and fingernails) in this way. —'**mani,curist** n.

manifest ('mænɪ,fɛst) adj. **1.** easily noticed, obvious. ~vb. **2.** to show plainly. **3.** to be evidence of. **4.** (of a disembodied spirit) to appear in visible form. ~n. **5.** a customs document containing particulars of a ship and its cargo. **6.** a list of cargo and passengers on an aeroplane. —,**manife's-tation** n.

manifesto (,mænɪ'fɛstəu) n., pl. **-toes** or **-tos.** a public declaration of intent or policy as issued by a political party.

manifold ('mænɪ,fəuld) adj. Formal. **1.** of several different kinds; multiple. **2.** having many different forms or features. ~n. **3.** a pipe with a number of inlets or outlets, esp. one in a car engine.

manikin ('mænɪkɪn) n. a little man; dwarf or child.

manila or **manilla** (mə'nɪlə) n. a strong usually brown paper used to make envelopes.

man in the street n. the average person.

manipulate (mə'nɪpjʊ,leɪt) vb. **1.** to handle or use skilfully. **2.** to control (something or someone) cleverly or deviously. —**ma,nipu'lation** n.

mankind (,mæn'kaɪnd) n. **1.** human beings collectively. **2.** men collectively.

manly ('mænlɪ) adj. **-lier, -liest. 1.** possessing qualities, such as vigour or courage, generally regarded as appropriate to a man; masculine. **2.** characteristic of a man. —'**manliness** n.

man-made adj. made by man; artificial.

manna ('mænə) n. **1.** Bible. the miraculous food which sustained the Israelites in the wilderness (Exodus 16:14–36). **2.** a windfall (esp. in **manna from heaven**).

manned (mænd) adj. having a human staff or crew: a manned spaceflight.

mannequin ('mænɪkɪn) n. **1.** a woman who wears the clothes displayed at a fashion show; model. **2.** a life-size dummy of the human body used to fit or display clothes.

manner ('mænə) n. **1.** a way of doing or being. **2.** a person's bearing and behaviour. **3.** the style or customary way of doing something: sculpture in the Greek manner. **4.** type or kind. **5. in a manner of speaking.** in a way; so to speak. **6. to the manner born.** naturally fitted to a specified role or activity.

mannered ('mænəd) adj. **1.** having idiosyncrasies or mannerisms; affected. **2.** having manners as specified: ill-mannered.

mannerism ('mænə,rɪzəm) n. **1.** a distinctive and individual gesture or trait. **2.** adherence to a distinctive or affected manner, esp. in art or literature.

mannerly ('mænəlɪ) adj. well-mannered; polite. —'**mannerliness** n.

manners ('mænəz) pl. n. **1.** social conduct. **2.** a socially acceptable way of behaving.

mannish ('mænɪʃ) adj. (of a woman) displaying qualities regarded as typical of a man.

manoeuvre or U.S. **maneuver** (mə'nu:və) n. **1.** a contrived, complicated, and possibly deceptive plan or action. **2.** a movement or action requiring dexterity and skill. **3.** (pl.) military or naval exercises, usually on a large scale. **4.** a change in course of a ship or aircraft, esp. a complicated one. ~vb. **5.** to contrive or accomplish with skill or cunning. **6.** to manipulate situations in order to gain some end. **7.** to perform a manoeuvre or manoeuvres. —**ma'noeuvrable** or U.S. **ma'neuverable** adj. —**ma,noeuvra'bility** or U.S. **ma,neuvera'bility** n.

man-of-war n., pl. **men-of-war. 1.** a warship. **2.** short for **Portuguese man-of-war.**

manor ('mænə) n. **1.** (in medieval Europe) the lands and property controlled by a lord. **2.** a manor house. **3.** a landed estate. **4.** Brit. slang. a police district. —**manorial** (mə'nɔːrɪəl) adj.

manor house n. a large country house, esp. one that was originally part of a medieval manor.

manpower ('mæn,pauə) n. the number of people needed or available for a job.

manqué ('mɒŋkeɪ) adj. unfulfilled; would-be: an actor manqué.

mansard ('mænsɑːd) n. a roof having two slopes on both sides and both ends, the lower slopes being steeper than the upper.

manse (mæns) n. (in certain Christian Churches) the house provided for a minister.

manservant ('mæn,sɜːvənt) n., pl. **menservants.** a male servant, esp. a valet.

mansion ('mænʃən) n. **1.** a large and imposing house. **2.** (pl.) Brit. a block of flats.

manslaughter ('mæn,slɔːtə) n. Law. the unlawful but not deliberately planned killing of one human being by another.

mantel ('mænt²l) n. a wooden or stone frame around a fireplace.

mantelpiece ('mænt²l,piːs) n. a shelf above a fireplace often forming part of the mantel. Also: **mantel shelf, chimneypiece.**

mantilla (mæn'tɪlə) n. a woman's lace or silk scarf covering the shoulders and head, worn esp. in Spain.

mantis ('mæntɪs) n., pl. **-tises** or **-tes** (-tiːz). a carnivorous insect with a long body and large eyes that rests with the first pair of legs raised as if in prayer. Also: **praying mantis.**

mantissa (mæn'tɪsə) n. the fractional part of a common logarithm: the mantissa of 2.4771 is .4771.

mantle ('mænt²l) n. **1.** Archaic. a loose wrap or cloak. **2.** anything that covers completely or envelops. **3.** a small mesh dome used to increase illumination in a gas or oil lamp by becoming incandescent. **4.** *Geol.* the part of the earth between the crust and the core. ~*vb.* **5.** to spread over or become spread over.

mantra ('mæntrə, 'mʌn-) *n.* **1.** *Hinduism.* a Vedic psalm of praise. **2.** *Hinduism, Buddhism.* any sacred word or syllable used as an object of concentration.

manual ('mænjʊəl) *adj.* **1.** of a hand or hands. **2.** operated or done by hand. **3.** physical as opposed to mental: *manual labour.* **4.** by human labour rather than automatic or computer-aided means. ~*n.* **5.** a book of instructions or information. **6.** *Music.* one of the keyboards on an organ. —'**manually** *adv.*

manufacture (,mænjʊ'fæktʃə) *vb.* **1.** to process or make (a product) from a raw material, esp. as a large-scale operation using machinery. **2.** to invent or concoct (evidence, an excuse, etc.). ~*n.* **3.** the production of goods, esp. by industrial processes. —,manu'facturer *n.* —,manu'facturing *n., adj.*

manuka ('mɑːnʊkə) *n.* a New Zealand tree with strong elastic wood and aromatic leaves.

manumit (,mænjʊ'mɪt) *vb.* -mitting, -mitted. to free from slavery. —**manumission** (,mænjʊ'mɪʃən) *n.*

manure (mə'njʊə) *n.* **1.** animal excrement used as a fertilizer. ~*vb.* **2.** to spread manure upon (fields or soil).

manuscript ('mænjʊ,skrɪpt) *n.* **1.** a book or other document written by hand. **2.** the original handwritten or typed version of a book or article as submitted by an author for publication.

Manx (mæŋks) *adj.* **1.** of the Isle of Man (an island in the Irish Sea) or its inhabitants. ~*n.* **2.** an almost extinct Celtic language of the Isle of Man. **3. the Manx.** (*functioning as pl.*) the people of the Isle of Man. —'**Manxman** *n.* —'**Manx,woman** *n.*

Manx cat *n.* a short-haired tailless variety of cat.

many ('mɛnɪ) *det.* **1. a.** a large number of: *many times; too many to count.* **b.** (*as pron.; functioning as pl.*): *many are seated already; take as many as you want.* **2.** (foll. by *a, an,* or *another,* and a sing. noun) each of a considerable number of: *many a man.* ~*n.* **3. the many.** the majority of mankind, esp. the common people.

Maoism ('maʊɪzəm) *n.* Communism as interpreted in the theories and policies of Mao Tse-tung (1893–1976), Chinese statesman. —'**Maoist** *n., adj.*

Maori ('maʊrɪ) *n.* **1.** (*pl.* -ris *or* -ri) a member of the Polynesian people living in New Zealand since before the arrival of European settlers. **2.** the language of this peo-

ple. ~*adj.* **3.** of this people or their language.

map (mæp) *n.* **1.** a diagrammatic representation of the earth's surface or part of it, showing the geographical distributions or positions of features such as roads, towns, relief and rainfall. **2.** a diagrammatic representation of the stars or of the surface of a celestial body. **3.** *Maths.* same as **function.** **4. put on the map.** to make (a town or company) well-known. ~*vb.* **mapping, mapped. 5.** to make a map of. **6.** *Maths.* to represent or transform (a function, figure, or set). ~See also **map out.**

maple ('meɪpˀl) *n.* **1.** any of various trees or shrubs with winged seeds borne in pairs and lobed leaves. **2.** the hard wood of any of these trees. ~See also **sugar maple.**

maple leaf *n.* the leaf of the maple tree, the national emblem of Canada.

maple syrup *n.* a very sweet syrup made from the sap of the sugar maple.

map out *vb.* to plan or design.

mapping ('mæpɪŋ) *n. Maths.* same as **function.**

maquis (mɑː'kiː) *n., pl.* -quis (-'kiː). (*often cap.*) **1.** the French underground movement that fought against the German occupying forces in World War II. **2.** a member of this movement.

mar (mɑː) *vb.* **marring, marred.** to cause harm to; spoil or impair.

Mar. March.

marabou ('mærə,buː) *n.* **1.** a large black-and-white African stork. **2.** a down feather of this bird, used to trim garments.

maraca (mə'rækə) *n.* a shaken percussion instrument, usually one of a pair, consisting of a gourd or plastic shell filled with dried seeds or pebbles.

marae (mə'raɪ) *n. N.Z.* a traditional Maori meeting place.

maraschino (,mærə'skiːnəʊ, -'ʃiːnəʊ) *n.* a liqueur made from a type of sour cherry having a taste like bitter almonds.

maraschino cherry *n.* a cherry preserved in maraschino.

marathon ('mærəθən) *n.* **1.** a race on foot of 26 miles 385 yards (42.195 kilometres). **2.** any long or arduous task.

maraud (mə'rɔːd) *vb.* to wander or raid in search of plunder. —**ma'rauder** *n.* —**ma'rauding** *adj.*

marble ('mɑːbˀl) *n.* **1.** a hard limestone rock, which usually has a mottled appearance and can be given a high polish. **2.** a block or work of art of marble. **3.** a small round glass ball used in playing marbles. ~*vb.* **4.** to mottle with variegated streaks in imitation of marble. —'**marbled** *adj.*

marbles ('mɑːbˀlz) *n.* (*functioning as sing.*) a game in which marbles are rolled at one another, similar to bowls.

marbling ('mɑːblɪŋ) *n.* **1.** a mottled effect

or pattern resembling marble. 2. the streaks of fat in lean meat.

marc (mɑːk) *n.* 1. the remains of grapes or other fruit that have been pressed for wine-making. 2. a brandy distilled from these.

marcasite ('mɑːkə,saɪt) *n.* 1. a pale yellow form of iron pyrites used in jewellery. 2. a cut and polished form of steel used for making jewellery.

march¹ (mɑːtʃ) *vb.* 1. to walk with stately or regular steps, usually in a procession or military formation. 2. to make (a person or group) proceed. 3. to traverse by marching. ~*n.* 4. a regular stride. 5. a long or exhausting walk. 6. advance; progression (as of time). 7. a distance covered by marching. 8. a piece of music, as for a march. 9. **steal a march on.** to gain an advantage over, esp. by a trick. —'**marcher** *n.*

march² (mɑːtʃ) *n.* a border or boundary or the land lying along it, often of disputed ownership.

March (mɑːtʃ) *n.* the third month of the year.

March hare *n.* a hare during its breeding season in March, noted for its wild and excitable behaviour (esp. in **mad as a March hare**).

marching orders *pl. n.* 1. military orders, giving instructions about a march. 2. *Informal.* dismissal, esp. from employment.

marchioness ('mɑːʃənɪs) *n.* 1. a woman who holds the rank of marquis. 2. the wife or widow of a marquis.

marchpane ('mɑːtʃ,peɪn) *n. Archaic.* marzipan.

Mardi Gras ('mɑːdɪ 'grɑː) *n.* the festival of Shrove Tuesday, celebrated in some cities with great revelry.

mare¹ (mɛə) *n.* the adult female of a horse or zebra.

mare² ('mɑːreɪ) *n., pl.* **maria** ('mɑːrɪə). a huge dry plain on the surface of the moon or Mars, visible as dark markings.

mare's-nest ('mɛəz,nɛst) *n.* a discovery imagined to be important but proving worthless.

margarine (,mɑːdʒə'riːn, ,mɑːg-) *n.* a substitute for butter, prepared from vegetable and animal fats.

marge (mɑːdʒ) *n. Brit. informal.* margarine.

margin ('mɑːdʒɪn) *n.* 1. an edge or rim; border. 2. the blank space surrounding the text on a page. 3. an additional amount or one beyond the minimum necessary: *they won by a small margin; a margin of error.* 4. a limit. 5. *Econ.* the minimum return below which an enterprise becomes unprofitable.

marginal ('mɑːdʒɪnˀl) *adj.* 1. of, in, on, or forming a margin. 2. close to a limit, esp. a lower limit: *marginal legal ability.* 3. not considered central or important; insignifi-

cant. 4. *Econ.* relating to goods or services produced and sold at the margin of profitability: *marginal cost.* 5. *Politics, chiefly Brit. & N.Z.* of or designating a constituency in which elections tend to be won by small margins: *a marginal seat.* 6. designating agricultural land on the edge of fertile areas. ~*n.* 7. *Politics, chiefly Brit. & N.Z.* a marginal constituency. —'**marginally** *adv.*

marginalia (,mɑːdʒɪ'neɪlɪə) *pl. n.* notes in the margin of a book, manuscript, or letter.

margrave ('mɑː,greɪv) *n.* a German nobleman ranking above a count.

marguerite (,mɑːgə'riːt) *n.* a garden plant with flowers resembling large daisies.

marigold ('mærɪ,gəʊld) *n.* any of various plants cultivated for their yellow or orange flowers.

marijuana *or* **marihuana** (,mærɪ'wɑːnə) *n.* the dried leaves and flowers of the hemp plant, used as a drug, esp. in cigarettes.

marimba (mə'rɪmbə) *n.* a percussion instrument consisting of a set of hardwood plates placed over tuned metal resonators, played with soft-headed sticks.

marina (mə'riːnə) *n.* a harbour for yachts and other pleasure boats.

marinade (,mærɪ'neɪd) *n.* 1. a mixture of oil, wine, vinegar, etc., in which meat or fish is soaked before cooking. 2. meat or fish soaked in this. ~*vb.* 3. same as **marinate.**

marinate ('mærɪ,neɪt) *vb.* to soak in marinade.

marine (mə'riːn) *adj.* 1. of, found in, or relating to the sea. 2. of shipping or navigation. 3. used or adapted for use at sea. ~*n.* 4. a soldier trained to serve on land or at sea. 5. a country's shipping or navy collectively: *the merchant marine.*

mariner ('mærɪnə) *n.* a seaman.

marionette (,mærɪə'nɛt) *n.* a puppet whose limbs are moved by strings.

marital ('mærɪtˀl) *adj.* of or relating to marriage. —'**maritally** *adv.*

maritime ('mærɪ,taɪm) *adj.* 1. of or relating to shipping. 2. of, near, or living near the sea.

marjoram ('mɑːdʒərəm) *n.* a plant with sweet-scented leaves, used for seasoning food and in salads.

mark¹ (mɑːk) *n.* 1. a visible impression on a surface, such as a spot or scratch. 2. a sign, symbol, or other indication that distinguishes something. 3. a written or printed symbol, as for punctuation. 4. a letter, number, or percentage used to grade academic work. 5. a thing that indicates position; marker. 6. a desired standard: *up to the mark.* 7. an indication of some quality: *a mark of respect.* 8. a target or goal. 9. impression or influence: *this book displays the mark of its author's admiration of*

Kafka. **10.** (*often cap.*) (in trade names) a model, brand, or type. **11. make one's mark.** to achieve recognition. **12. on your mark** *or* **marks.** a command given to runners in a race to prepare themselves at the starting line. ~*vb.* **13.** to make or receive (a visible impression, trace, or stain) on (a surface). **14.** to characterize or distinguish. **15.** (often foll. by *off* or *out*) to set boundaries or limits (on). **16.** to select, designate, or doom: *to mark someone as a criminal.* **17.** to label, esp. to indicate price. **18.** to pay attention to: *mark my words.* **19.** to observe; notice. **20.** to grade or evaluate (scholastic work). **21.** to stay close to (an opponent) to hamper his play. **22. mark time. a.** to move the feet alternately as in marching but without advancing. **b.** to wait for something more interesting to happen. ~See also **markdown, mark-up.** —'**marker** *n.*

mark² (mɑːk) *n.* **1.** See **Deutschmark.** **2.** the standard monetary unit of East Germany.

markdown ('mɑːkˌdaʊn) *n.* **1.** a price reduction. ~*vb.* **mark down.** **2.** to reduce in price.

marked (mɑːkt) *adj.* **1.** obvious or noticeable. **2.** singled out, esp. as the target of attack: *a marked man.* —**markedly** ('mɑːkɪdlɪ) *adv.*

market ('mɑːkɪt) *n.* **1.** an occasion at which people meet to buy and sell merchandise. **2.** a place at which a market is held. **3.** the trading opportunities provided by a particular group of people: *the foreign market.* **4.** demand for a particular product. **5.** short for **stock market.** **6. be in the market for.** to wish to buy. **7. on the market.** available for purchase. **8. seller's** (*or* **buyer's**) **market.** a market characterized by excess demand (or supply) and thus favourable to sellers (or buyers). ~*vb.* **9.** to offer or produce for sale. —'**marketable** *adj.*

market garden *n. Chiefly Brit.* a place where fruit and vegetables are grown for sale. —**market gardener** *n.*

marketing ('mɑːkɪtɪŋ) *n.* the part of a business which controls the way that goods or services are sold.

market maker *n. Stock Exchange.* someone who uses his firm's money to create a market for a stock: formerly done by a jobber, but a market maker can deal directly with the public.

marketplace ('mɑːkɪtˌpleɪs) *n.* **1.** a place where a public market is held. **2.** the commercial world of buying and selling.

market price *n.* the prevailing price at which goods may be bought or sold.

market research *n.* the study of influences upon customer behaviour and the analysis of market characteristics and trends.

market town *n. Chiefly Brit.* a town that holds a market, esp. an agricultural centre.

marking ('mɑːkɪŋ) *n.* **1.** the arrangement of colours on an animal or plant. **2.** assessment and correction of pupils' or students' written work by teachers.

marksman ('mɑːksmən) *n., pl.* **-men.** a person skilled in shooting. —'**marksmanship** *n.*

mark-up *n.* **1.** an amount added to the cost of a commodity to provide the seller with a profit. ~*vb.* **mark up.** **2.** to add a percentage for profit to the cost of (a commodity).

marl (mɑːl) *n.* a fine-grained rock consisting of clay, limestone, and silt: used as a fertilizer. —'**marly** *adj.*

marlin ('mɑːlɪn) *n., pl.* **-lin** *or* **-lins.** a large fish with a very long upper jaw, found in warm and tropical seas.

marlinespike *or* **marlinspike** ('mɑːlɪnˌspaɪk) *n. Naut.* a pointed metal tool used in separating strands of rope.

marmalade ('mɑːməˌleɪd) *n.* jam made from citrus fruits, esp. oranges.

marmoreal (mɑːˈmɔːrɪəl) *adj.* of or like marble.

marmoset ('mɑːməˌzɛt) *n.* a small South American monkey with a long hairy tail.

marmot ('mɑːmət) *n.* any of various burrowing rodents of Europe, Asia, and North America. They are heavily built and have coarse fur.

maroon¹ (məˈruːn) *vb.* **1.** to abandon ashore, esp. on an island. **2.** to isolate without resources.

maroon² (məˈruːn) *adj.* dark purplish-red.

marque (mɑːk) *n.* a brand of product, esp. of a car.

marquee (mɑːˈkiː) *n.* a large tent used for entertainment, exhibition, etc.

marquess ('mɑːkwɪs) *n.* **1.** (in the British Isles) a nobleman ranking between a duke and an earl. **2.** See **marquis.**

marquetry ('mɑːkɪtrɪ) *n., pl.* **-quetries.** a pattern of inlaid veneers of wood or metal used chiefly as ornamentation in furniture.

marquis ('mɑːkwɪs, mɑːˈkiː) *n., pl.* **-quises** *or* **-quis.** (in various countries) a nobleman ranking above a count, corresponding to a British marquess.

marquise (mɑːˈkiːz) *n.* **1.** (in various countries) a marchioness. **2.** a gemstone cut in a pointed oval shape.

marram grass ('mærəm) *n.* a grass that grows on sandy shores: often planted to stabilize sand dunes.

marriage ('mærɪdʒ) *n.* **1.** the state or relationship of being husband and wife: *the institution of marriage.* **2.** the contract made by a man and woman to live as husband and wife. **3.** the ceremony formalizing this union; wedding.

marriageable ('mærɪdʒəb'l) *adj.* suitable for marriage, usually with reference to age.

marriage guidance *n.* advice given to couples who have problems in their married life.

married ('mærɪd) *adj.* **1.** having a husband or wife. **2.** of marriage or married persons. ~*n.* **3.** (*usually pl.*) a married person (esp. in **young marrieds**).

marrow ('mærəʊ) *n.* **1.** the fatty tissue that fills the cavities of bones. **2.** *Brit.* short for **vegetable marrow.**

marrowfat ('mærəʊ,fæt) *or* **marrow pea** *n.* a variety of large pea.

marry[1] ('mærɪ) *vb.* **-rying, -ried. 1.** to take (someone as one's husband or wife) in marriage. **2.** to join or give in marriage. **3.** (sometimes foll. by *up*) to fit together or align (two things); join.

marry[2] ('mærɪ) *interj. Archaic.* an exclamation of surprise or anger.

Mars (mɑːz) *n.* **1.** the Roman god of war. **2.** the fourth planet from the sun.

Marsala (mɑːˈsɑːlə) *n.* a dark sweet dessert wine from Marsala, a port in Sicily.

Marseillaise (,mɑːseɪˈjeɪz, -səˈleɪz) *n.* **the.** the French national anthem.

marsh (mɑːʃ) *n.* low poorly drained land that is wet, muddy, and sometimes flooded. —'**marshy** *adj.*

marshal ('mɑːʃəl) *n.* **1.** (in some armies and air forces) an officer of the highest rank. **2.** an officer who organizes or controls ceremonies or public events. **3.** (formerly in England) an officer of the royal family or court. ~*vb.* **-shalling, -shalled** *or U.S.* **-shaling, -shaled. 4.** to arrange in order: *to marshal the facts.* **5.** to assemble and organize (people or vehicles) in readiness for onward movement. **6.** to guide or lead, esp. in a ceremonious way. —'**marshalcy** *n.*

marshalling yard *n. Railways.* a place where railway wagons are shunted and made up into trains.

Marshal of the Royal Air Force *n.* the highest rank in the Royal Air Force.

marsh gas *n.* a gas largely composed of methane formed when plants decay in the absence of air.

marshmallow (,mɑːʃˈmæləʊ) *n.* a spongy pink or white sweet.

marsh mallow *n.* a plant that grows in salt marshes and has pale pink flowers. It was formerly used to make marshmallows.

marsupial (mɑːˈsjuːpɪəl) *n.* **1.** any mammal whose young are born in an immature state and continue development in a pouch on the mother's body. They include the opossums and kangaroos. ~*adj.* **2.** of or like a marsupial.

mart (mɑːt) *n.* a market or trading centre.

Martello tower (mɑːˈtɛləʊ) *n.* a small circular tower for coastal defence.

marten ('mɑːtɪn) *n., pl.* **-tens** *or* **-ten. 1.** any of several agile weasel-like mammals with bushy tails and golden-brown to blackish fur. **2.** the highly valued fur of these animals.

martial ('mɑːʃəl) *adj.* of or characteristic of war, soldiers, or the military life.

martial art *n.* any of various philosophies and techniques of self-defence originating in the Far East, such as judo or karate.

martial law *n.* rule of law maintained by the military in the absence of civil law.

Martian ('mɑːʃən) *adj.* **1.** of the planet Mars. ~*n.* **2.** an inhabitant of Mars, in science fiction.

martin ('mɑːtɪn) *n.* a bird of the swallow family with a square or slightly forked tail.

martinet (,mɑːtɪˈnɛt) *n.* a person who maintains strict discipline.

martingale ('mɑːtɪn,geɪl) *n.* a strap from the reins to the girth of a horse, preventing it from carrying its head too high.

martini (mɑːˈtiːnɪ) *n.* **1.** (*often cap.*) *Trademark.* an Italian vermouth. **2.** a cocktail of gin and vermouth.

Martinmas ('mɑːtɪnməs) *n.* the feast of St Martin on Nov. 11; a quarter day in Scotland.

martyr ('mɑːtə) *n.* **1.** a person who suffers death rather than renounce his religious beliefs. **2.** a person who suffers greatly or dies for a cause or belief. **3. a martyr to.** suffering constantly from: *a martyr to rheumatism.* ~*vb.* **4.** to make a martyr of. —'**martyrdom** *n.*

marvel ('mɑːv'l) *vb.* **-velling, -velled** *or U.S.* **-veling, -veled. 1.** to be filled with surprise or wonder. ~*n.* **2.** something that causes wonder.

marvellous *or U.S.* **marvelous** ('mɑːv'ləs) *adj.* **1.** causing great wonder or surprise; extraordinary. **2.** excellent; splendid. —'**marvellously** *or U.S.* '**marvelously** *adv.*

Marxism ('mɑːksɪzəm) *n.* the economic and political theories of Karl Marx (1818–83), German political philosopher, holding that class struggle is the basic agency of historical change, and that capitalism will be superseded by communism. —'**Marxist** *n., adj.*

marzipan ('mɑːzɪ,pæn) *n.* a paste made from ground almonds, sugar, and egg whites.

masc. masculine.

mascara (mæˈskɑːrə) *n.* a cosmetic for darkening the eyelashes.

mascot ('mæskət) *n.* a person, animal, or thing considered to bring good luck.

masculine ('mæskjʊlɪn) *adj.* **1.** possessing qualities or characteristics considered typical of or appropriate to a man; manly. **2.** unwomanly. **3.** *Grammar.* denoting a gender of nouns that includes some male animate things. **4.** *Prosody.* denoting a rhyme between pairs of single final stressed syllables. —ˌ**mascuˈlinity** *n.*

maser (ˈmeɪzə) *n.* a device for amplifying microwaves, working on the same principle as a laser.

mash (mæʃ) *n.* **1.** a soft pulpy mass. **2.** *Agriculture.* a feed of bran, meal, or malt mixed with water and fed to horses, cattle, or poultry. **3.** *Brit. informal.* mashed potatoes. ~*vb.* **4.** to beat or crush into a mash. —**mashed** *adj.*

mask (mɑːsk) *n.* **1.** any covering for the whole or a part of the face worn for amusement, protection, or disguise. **2.** behaviour that hides one's true feelings: *a mask of indifference.* **3.** a moulded likeness of a face or head, such as a death mask. **4.** *Surgery.* a sterile gauze covering for the nose and mouth worn to minimize the spread of germs. **5.** a device placed over the nose and mouth to facilitate or prevent inhalation of a gas. **6.** the face or head of an animal such as a fox. ~*vb.* **7.** to cover with or put on a mask. **8.** to conceal; disguise: *to mask an odour.* —**masked** *adj.*

masking tape *n.* an adhesive tape used to protect surfaces surrounding an area to be painted.

masochism (ˈmæsəˌkɪzəm) *n.* **1.** *Psychiatry.* a condition in which pleasure, esp. sexual pleasure, is derived from pain or from being humiliated. **2.** a tendency to take pleasure from one's own suffering. —ˈ**masochist** *n., adj.* —ˌ**masoˈchistic** *adj.*

mason (ˈmeɪsᵊn) *n.* a person skilled in building with stone.

Mason (ˈmeɪsᵊn) *n.* short for **Freemason.**

Masonic (məˈsɒnɪk) *adj.* of Freemasons or Freemasonry.

masonry (ˈmeɪsənrɪ) *n.* **1.** the craft of a mason. **2.** stonework or brickwork.

Masonry (ˈmeɪsənrɪ) *n.* short for **Freemasonry.**

masque (mɑːsk) *n.* a dramatic entertainment of the 16th to 17th centuries, consisting of dancing, dialogue, and song. —ˈ**masquer** *n.*

masquerade (ˌmæskəˈreɪd) *n.* **1.** a deceptive show; pretence. **2.** a party at which the guests wear masks and costumes. ~*vb.* **3.** to pretend to be someone or something else.

mass (mæs) *n.* **1.** a large coherent body of matter without a definite shape. **2.** a collection of the component parts of something: *a mass of fibres.* **3.** a large amount or number, as of people. **4.** the main part or majority. **5.** the size of a body; bulk. **6.** *Physics.* a physical quantity expressing the amount of matter in a body. **7.** (in painting or drawing) an area of unified colour, shade, or intensity. ~(*modifier*) **8.** done or occurring on a large scale: *mass hysteria.* **9.** consisting of a mass or large number, esp. of people: *a mass meeting.* ~*vb.* **10.** to form (people or things) or (of people or things) to join together into a mass. ~See also **masses.**

Mass (mæs, mɑːs) *n.* **1.** (in the Roman Catholic Church and certain other Christian churches) the celebration of the Eucharist. **2.** a musical setting of parts of the Eucharistic service.

Mass. Massachusetts.

massacre (ˈmæsəkə) *n.* **1.** the wanton or savage killing of large numbers of people. **2.** *Informal.* an overwhelming defeat. ~*vb.* **3.** to kill indiscriminately in large numbers. **4.** *Informal.* to defeat overwhelmingly.

massage (ˈmæsɑːʒ) *n.* **1.** the act of kneading or rubbing parts of the body to promote circulation, suppleness, or relaxation. ~*vb.* **2.** to give a massage to. **3.** to manipulate (statistics or evidence) to produce a desired result.

massasauga (ˌmæsəˈsɔːgə) *n.* a North American venomous snake with a horny rattle at the end of the tail.

masses (ˈmæsɪz) *pl. n.* **1.** (preceded by *the*) the body of common people. **2.** (often foll. by *of*) *Informal, chiefly Brit.* great numbers or quantities: *masses of food.*

masseur (mæˈsɜː) *or* (*fem.*) **masseuse** (mæˈsɜːz) *n.* a person who gives massages.

massif (ˈmæsiːf) *n.* a series of connected masses of rock forming a mountain range.

massive (ˈmæsɪv) *adj.* **1.** (of objects) large, bulky, heavy, and usually solid. **2.** impressive or imposing. **3.** intensive or considerable: *a massive dose.* —ˈ**massively** *adv.*

mass-market *adj.* of, for, or appealing to a large number of people; popular: *mass-market paperbacks.*

mass media *pl. n.* the means of communication that reach large numbers of people, such as television, newspapers, and radio.

mass noun *n.* a noun that refers to an extended substance rather than to each of a set of objects, e.g., *water* as opposed to *lake.*

mass number *n.* the total number of protons and neutrons in the nucleus of an atom.

mass-produce *vb.* to manufacture standardized goods on a large scale by means of extensive mechanization. —ˌ**mass-proˈduced** *adj.*

mass spectrometer *n.* an instrument for analysing the composition of a sample of material, in which ions, produced from the sample, are separated by electric or magnetic fields according to their ratios of charge to mass.

mast[1] (mɑːst) *n.* **1.** *Naut.* any vertical spar for supporting sails, radar equipment, etc., above the deck of a vessel. **2.** any upright pole used as a support: *a television mast.* **3. before the mast.** *Naut.* as an apprentice seaman.

mast² (mɑːst) *n.* the fruit of forest trees, such as beech or oak, used as food for pigs.

mastaba ('mæstəbə) *n.* a mudbrick superstructure above tombs in ancient Egypt.

mastectomy (mæ'stɛktəmɪ) *n., pl.* **-mies.** the surgical removal of a breast.

master ('mɑːstə) *n.* **1.** the man in authority, such as the head of a household, the employer of servants, or the owner of slaves or animals. **2.** a person with exceptional skill at a certain thing. **3.** a person who has complete control of a situation. **4.** a craftsman fully qualified to practise his trade and to train others. **5.** an original copy or tape from which duplicates are made. **6.** a player of a game, esp. chess or bridge, who has won a specified number of tournament games. **7.** a highly regarded teacher or leader. **8.** a graduate holding a master's degree. **9.** the chief officer aboard a merchant ship. **10.** *Chiefly Brit.* a male teacher. **11.** the superior person or side in a contest. **12.** (*often cap.*) the heir apparent of a Scottish viscount or baron: *the Master of Ballantrae.* ~(*modifier*) **13.** overall or controlling: *master plan.* **14.** designating a mechanism that controls others: *master switch.* **15.** main; principal: *master bedroom.* ~*vb.* **16.** to become thoroughly proficient in. **17.** to overcome; defeat.

Master ('mɑːstə) *n.* a title of address for a boy who is not old enough to be called *Mr.*

masterful ('mɑːstəfʊl) *adj.* **1.** having or showing mastery. **2.** fond of playing the master; imperious. —'**masterfully** *adv.*

master key *n.* a key that opens all the locks of a set; passkey.

masterly ('mɑːstəlɪ) *adj.* showing the skill befitting a master; expert.

mastermind ('mɑːstə,maɪnd) *vb.* **1.** to plan and direct (a complex undertaking). ~*n.* **2.** a person of great intelligence, esp. one who directs an undertaking.

Master of Arts *n.* a degree, usually postgraduate and in a nonscientific subject, or its holder.

master of ceremonies *n.* a person who presides over a public ceremony, formal dinner, or entertainment, introducing the events and performers.

Master of Science *n.* a degree, usually postgraduate and in a scientific subject, or its holder.

Master of the Rolls *n.* (in England) the senior civil judge in the country and the head of the Public Record Office.

masterpiece ('mɑːstə,piːs) *or* **masterwork** ('mɑːstə,wɜːk) *n.* **1.** an outstanding work or performance. **2.** the most outstanding piece of work of an artist or craftsman.

masterstroke ('mɑːstə,strəʊk) *n.* an outstanding piece of strategy, skill, or talent.

mastery ('mɑːstərɪ) *n., pl.* **-teries. 1.** outstanding skill; expertise. **2.** the power of command; control.

masthead ('mɑːst,hɛd) *n.* **1.** *Naut.* the head of a mast. **2.** the name of a newspaper or periodical printed at the top of the front page.

mastic ('mæstɪk) *n.* **1.** an aromatic resin obtained from a Mediterranean tree and used to make varnishes and lacquers. **2.** any of several putty-like substances used as a filler, adhesive, or seal.

masticate ('mæstɪ,keɪt) *vb.* to chew (food). —,**masti'cation** *n.*

mastiff ('mæstɪf) *n.* a breed of large powerful short-haired dog, usually fawn or brindled.

mastitis (mæ'staɪtɪs) *n.* inflammation of a breast or an udder.

mastodon ('mæstə,dɒn) *n.* an extinct elephant-like mammal.

mastoid ('mæstɔɪd) *adj.* **1.** shaped like a nipple or breast. ~*n.* **2.** a nipple-like projection of the temporal bone behind the ear. **3.** *Informal.* mastoiditis.

mastoiditis (,mæstɔɪ'daɪtɪs) *n.* inflammation of the mastoid.

masturbate ('mæstə,beɪt) *vb.* to fondle the genitals of (oneself or another) to cause sexual pleasure. —,**mastur'bation** *n.*

mat¹ (mæt) *n.* **1.** a thick flat piece of fabric used as a floor covering, a place to wipe one's shoes, etc. **2.** a smaller pad of material used to protect a surface from heat or scratches from an object placed upon it. **3.** a large piece of thick padded material put on the floor as a surface for wrestling, gymnastics, etc. ~*vb.* **matting, matted. 4.** to tangle or become tangled into a dense mass.

mat² (mæt) *adj.* having a dull, lustreless, or roughened surface.

matador ('mætə,dɔː) *n.* the bullfighter armed with a sword, who attempts to kill the bull.

matai ('mɑːtaɪ) *n.* a New Zealand tree, the wood of which is used for building timber.

match¹ (mætʃ) *n.* **1.** a formal game or sports event in which people or teams compete. **2.** a person or thing able to provide competition for another: *she's met her match.* **3.** a person or thing that resembles, harmonizes with, or is equivalent to another. **4.** a person or thing that is an exact copy or equal of another. **5.** a partnership between a man and a woman, as in marriage. **6.** a person regarded as a possible partner in marriage. ~*vb.* **7.** to fit (parts) together. **8.** (sometimes foll. by *up*) to resemble, harmonize with, or equal (one another or something else). **9.** (sometimes foll. by *with* or *against*) to compare in order to determine which is the superior. **10.** (often foll. by *with* or *against*) to arrange a

competition between. 11. to find a match for. —**'matching** *adj.*

match² (mætʃ) *n.* **1.** a thin strip of wood or cardboard tipped with a chemical that ignites when scraped against a rough or specially treated surface. **2.** a fuse used to fire cannons' explosives.

matchbox ('mætʃ,bɒks) *n.* a small box for holding matches.

matchless ('mætʃlɪs) *adj.* unequalled.

matchmaker ('mætʃ,meɪkə) *n.* a person who introduces people in the hope that they will form a couple. —**'match,making** *n., adj.*

match play *n. Golf.* scoring according to the number of holes won and lost.

match point *n. Sport.* the final point needed to win a match.

matchstick ('mætʃ,stɪk) *n.* **1.** the wooden part of a match. ~*adj.* **2.** (esp. of drawn figures) thin and straight: *matchstick men.*

matchwood ('mætʃ,wʊd) *n.* **1.** wood suitable for making matches. **2.** splinters.

mate¹ (meɪt) *n.* **1.** the sexual partner of an animal. **2.** a marriage partner. **3. a.** *Informal, chiefly Brit., Austral., & N.Z.* a friend: often used to any male in direct address. **b.** an associate or colleague: *a classmate.* **4.** one of a pair of matching items. **5.** *Naut.* any officer below the master on a commercial ship. **6.** (in some trades) an assistant: *a plumber's mate.* ~*vb.* **7.** to pair (a male and female animal) or (of animals) to pair for reproduction. **8.** to marry. **9.** to join as a pair.

mate² (meɪt) *n., vb. Chess.* same as **checkmate.**

mater ('meɪtə) *n. Brit. slang.* mother: often used facetiously.

material (mə'tɪərɪəl) *n.* **1.** the substance of which a thing is made; component matter. **2.** things needed for a particular activity: *writing materials.* **3.** ideas or notes that a finished work may be based on. **4.** cloth. ~*adj.* **5.** composed of physical substance. **6.** of or affecting economic or physical wellbeing: *material ease.* **7.** of physical rather than spiritual interests. **8.** (often foll. by *to*) relevant. ~See also **materials.**

materialism (mə'tɪərɪə,lɪzəm) *n.* **1.** interest in and desire for money or possessions rather than spiritual or ethical values. **2.** *Philosophy.* the doctrine that matter is the only reality. —**ma'terialist** *n.* —**ma,terial'istic** *adj.*

materialize *or* **-ise** (mə'tɪərɪə,laɪz) *vb.* **1.** *Not universally accepted.* to become fact; actually happen. **2.** to appear or cause to appear after being invisible: *trees materialized out of the gloom.* **3.** to take shape; become tangible. —**ma,teriali'zation** *or* **-i'sation** *n.*

materially (mə'tɪərɪəlɪ) *adv.* to a significant extent; considerably.

materials (mə'tɪərɪəlz) *pl. n.* the equipment necessary for a particular activity.

materiel *or* **matériel** (mə,tɪərɪ'ɛl) *n.* the materials and equipment of an organization, esp. of a military force.

maternal (mə'tɜːn²l) *adj.* **1.** of or characteristic of a mother. **2.** related through the mother's side of the family: *his maternal uncle.* —**ma'ternally** *adv.*

maternity (mə'tɜːnɪtɪ) *n.* **1.** motherhood. **2.** motherliness. **3.** (*modifier*) relating to pregnant women: *maternity leave.*

mate's rates *pl. n. N.Z. informal.* reduced charges offered to a friend or colleague: *a plumber friend did the job at mate's rates.*

matey ('meɪtɪ) *adj. Brit. informal.* friendly or intimate.

math (mæθ) *n. U.S. & Canad. informal.* short for **mathematics.**

mathematical (,mæθə'mætɪk²l) *adj.* **1.** using, used in, or relating to mathematics. **2.** having the precision of mathematics. —**,mathe'matically** *adv.*

mathematician (,mæθəmə'tɪʃən) *n.* an expert or specialist in mathematics.

mathematics (,mæθə'mætɪks) *n.* **1.** (*functioning as sing.*) a group of related sciences, including algebra, geometry, and calculus, which use a specialized notation to study number, quantity, shape, and space. **2.** (*functioning as sing. or pl.*) numerical calculations involved in the solution of a problem.

maths (mæθs) *n.* (*functioning as sing.*) *Brit. informal.* short for **mathematics.**

matinée ('mætɪ,neɪ) *n.* an afternoon performance of a play or film.

matinée coat *or* **jacket** *n.* a short coat for a baby.

matins ('mætɪnz) *n.* (*functioning as sing. or pl.*) *Christianity.* an early morning service in various Churches.

matriarch ('meɪtrɪ,ɑːk) *n.* the female head of a tribe or family. —**'matri,archal** *adj.*

matriarchy ('meɪtrɪ,ɑːkɪ) *n., pl.* **-chies.** a form of social organization in which a female is head of the family or society, and descent and kinship are traced through the female line.

matricide ('mætrɪ,saɪd, 'meɪ-) *n.* **1.** the act of killing one's mother. **2.** a person who kills his mother. —**,matri'cidal** *adj.*

matriculate (mə'trɪkjʊ,leɪt) *vb.* to enrol or be enrolled in a college or university. —**ma,tricu'lation** *n.*

matrilineal (,mætrɪ'lɪnɪəl, ,meɪ-) *adj.* relating to descent through the female line.

matrimony ('mætrɪmənɪ) *n., pl.* **-nies. 1.** the state of being married. **2.** the ceremony of marriage. —**matrimonial** (,mætrɪ'məʊnɪəl) *adj.*

matrix ('meɪtrɪks) *n., pl.* **matrices** ('meɪtrɪ,siːz) *or* **matrixes. 1.** a substance, situation, or environment in which something has its origin, takes form, or is enclosed. **2.** the rock in which fossils or pebbles are embedded. **3.** a mould, esp. one used in printing. **4.** *Maths.* a rectangular array of elements set out in rows and columns.

matron ('meɪtrən) *n.* **1.** a staid or dignified married woman. **2.** a woman in charge of the domestic or medical arrangements in an institution. **3.** *Brit.* (formerly) the administrative head of the nursing staff in a hospital. —'**matronly** *adj.*

matron of honour *n., pl.* **matrons of honour.** a married woman attending a bride.

matt *or* **matte** (mæt) *adj.* same as **mat²**.

matted ('mætɪd) *adj.* tangled into a thick mass.

matter ('mætə) *n.* **1.** that which makes up something, esp. a physical object; material. **2.** substance that occupies space and has mass, as distinguished from substance that is mental or spiritual. **3.** substance of a specified type: *vegetable matter.* **4.** (sometimes foll. by *of* or *for*) thing; affair; concern; question: *a matter of taste.* **5.** a quantity or amount: *a matter of a few pence.* **6.** the content of written or verbal material as distinct from its style or form. **7.** written material in general: *advertising matter.* **8.** a secretion or discharge, such as pus. **9. for that matter.** as regards that. **10. no matter. a.** regardless of; irrespective of: *no matter what the excuse, you must not be late.* **b.** *interj.* it is unimportant. **11. the matter.** wrong; the trouble: *there's nothing the matter.* ~*vb.* **12.** to be of consequence or importance.

matter of fact *n.* **1. as a matter of fact.** actually; in fact. ~*adj.* **matter-of-fact. 2.** unimaginative or emotionless: *he gave a matter-of-fact account of the murder.*

matting ('mætɪŋ) *n.* a coarsely woven fabric used as a floor covering and packing material.

mattock ('mætək) *n.* a type of large pick that has one flat, horizontal end to its blade, used for loosening soil.

mattress ('mætrɪs) *n.* a large flat cushion with a strong cover, filled with cotton, foam rubber, etc., and often including coiled springs, used as a bed or as part of a bed.

maturate ('mætjʊˌreɪt) *vb.* **1.** to mature or bring to maturity. **2.** (of a wound etc.) to discharge pus. —ˌ**matu'ration** *n.*

mature (mə'tjʊə) *adj.* **1.** fully developed physically or mentally; grown-up. **2.** (of plans or theories) fully considered; perfected. **3.** due or payable: *a mature insurance policy.* **4.** (of fruit, wine, or cheese) ripe or fully aged. ~*vb.* **5.** to make or become mature. **6.** (of bills or bonds) to become due for payment or repayment. —**ma'turity** *n.*

matzo ('mætsəʊ) *n., pl.* **matzos.** a large very

thin biscuit of unleavened bread, traditionally eaten by Jews during Passover.

maudlin ('mɔːdlɪn) *adj.* foolishly tearful or sentimental, as when drunk.

maul (mɔːl) *vb.* **1.** to handle clumsily; paw. **2.** to batter or tear. ~*n.* **3.** a heavy two-handed hammer. **4.** *Rugby.* a loose scrum.

maunder ('mɔːndə) *vb.* to move, talk, or act aimlessly or idly.

Maundy money ('mɔːndɪ) *n.* specially minted coins given by the British sovereign in a symbolic almsgiving ceremony on the Thursday before Easter (**Maundy Thursday**).

mausoleum (ˌmɔːsə'lɪəm) *n.* a large stately tomb.

mauve (məʊv) *adj.* light purple.

maverick ('mævərɪk) *n.* **1.** a person of independent or unorthodox views. **2.** (in the U.S. and Canada) an unbranded stray calf.

maw (mɔː) *n.* the mouth, throat, or stomach of an animal, esp. of a voracious animal.

mawkish ('mɔːkɪʃ) *adj.* falsely sentimental, esp. in a weak or maudlin way. —'**mawkishness** *n.*

max. maximum.

maxi ('mæksɪ) *adj.* **1.** (of a garment) very long. **2.** large or considerable.

maxilla (mæk'sɪlə) *n., pl.* **-lae** (-liː). **1.** the upper jawbone in vertebrates. **2.** any part of the mouth in insects and other arthropods. —**max'illary** *adj.*

maxim ('mæksɪm) *n.* a brief expression of a general truth, principle, or rule of conduct.

maximal ('mæksɪməl) *adj.* of or being a maximum; the greatest possible.

maximize *or* **-ise** ('mæksɪˌmaɪz) *vb.* to make as high or great as possible; increase to a maximum. —ˌ**maximi'zation** *or* **-i'sation** *n.*

maximum ('mæksɪməm) *n., pl.* **-mums** *or* **-ma** (-mə). **1.** the greatest possible amount or degree. **2.** the highest value of a variable quantity. ~*adj.* **3.** of, being, or showing a maximum or maximums.

maxwell ('mækswəl) *n.* the cgs unit of magnetic flux.

may¹ (meɪ) *vb. past* **might.** used as an auxiliary to indicate or express: **1.** that permission is requested by or granted to someone: *he may go.* **2.** (often foll. by *well*) possibility: *the rope may well break.* **3.** ability or capacity, esp. in questions: *may I help you?* **4.** a strong wish: *long may she reign.*

Usage. In written English, *may* is used rather than *can* when the idea of permission rather than ability is involved. So when the sense required is *he is allowed to do it,* the expression *he may do it* is more appropriate thean *he can do it.* In spoken English, however, *can* is often used where the correct use of *may* results in forms that are considered to be awkward. *Can't I?* is preferred for this reason to *mayn't I?* in speech. The difference between *may* and *might* is one of emphasis: *he might be coming* usually indicates less certainty than *he may be coming*. Similarly, *might I have it?* is felt to be more hesitant than *may I have it?*

may² *or* **may tree** (meɪ) *n. Brit.* same as **hawthorn.**

May (meɪ) *n.* the fifth month of the year.

Maya ('maɪə) *n.* **1.** (*pl.* **-ya** *or* **-yas**) a member of an American Indian people of Central America, once having an advanced civilization. **2.** the language of this people. —'**Mayan** *n., adj.*

maybe ('meɪ,biː) *adv.* perhaps.

Mayday ('meɪ,deɪ) *n.* the international radiotelephone distress signal.

May Day *n.* the first day of May, traditionally a celebration of the coming of spring: in some countries now a holiday in honour of workers.

mayfly ('meɪ,flaɪ) *n., pl.* **-flies.** a short-lived insect with large transparent wings.

mayhem ('meɪhɛm) *n.* **1.** any violent destruction or confusion. **2.** *Law.* the maiming of a person.

mayn't ('meɪənt, meɪnt) may not.

mayonnaise (,meɪə'neɪz) *n.* a thick creamy sauce made from egg yolks, oil, and vinegar.

mayor (mɛə) *n.* the civic head of a municipal council in many countries. —'**mayoral** *adj.*

mayoralty ('mɛərəltɪ) *n., pl.* **-ties.** the office or term of office of a mayor.

mayoress ('mɛərɪs) *n.* **1.** *Chiefly Brit.* the wife of a mayor. **2.** a female mayor.

maypole ('meɪ,pəʊl) *n.* a tall pole around which people dance during May-Day celebrations.

May queen *n.* a girl chosen to preside over May-Day celebrations.

maze (meɪz) *n.* **1.** a complex network of paths or passages designed to puzzle those walking through it. **2.** a similar system represented diagrammatically as a pattern of lines. **3.** any confusing network of streets or paths. **4.** a state of confusion.

mazurka (mə'zɜːkə) *n.* **1.** a Polish national dance in triple time. **2.** music for this dance.

MB 1. Bachelor of Medicine. **2.** *Computers.* megabyte.

MBE Member of the Order of the British Empire (a Brit. title).

MC 1. Master of Ceremonies. **2.** (in the U.S.) Member of Congress. **3.** (in Britain) Military Cross.

MCC (in Britain) Marylebone Cricket Club.

MCh Master of Surgery.

Md *Chem.* mendelevium.

MD 1. Doctor of Medicine. **2.** Managing Director. **3.** Also: **Md.** Maryland.

MDT (in the U.S. and Canada) Mountain Daylight Time.

me¹ (miː; *unstressed* mɪ) *pron.* (*objective*) **1.** refers to the speaker or writer: *that shocks me.* ~*n.* **2.** *Informal.* the personality of the speaker or writer or something that expresses it: *the real me.*
Usage. Although technically *I, he, she,* etc. is required after the verb *to be, it is me* (or *him, her,* etc.) sounds more natural than *it is I.* The use of *me,* etc., before an *-ing* form of the verb (*he disapproved of me coming*) is common, but strictly the possessive form is correct: *he disapproved of my coming.*

me² (miː) *n.* same as **mi.**

ME 1. Also: **Me.** Maine. **2.** Middle English. **3.** myalgic encephalomyelitis: painful muscles and general weakness sometimes persisting long after a viral illness.

mea culpa ('meɪɑː 'kʊlpɑː) an acknowledgment of guilt.

mead¹ (miːd) *n.* a wine made from fermented honey, often with spices added.

mead² (miːd) *n. Archaic or poetic.* a meadow.

meadow ('mɛdəʊ) *n.* **1.** an area of grassland, often used for hay or for grazing of animals. **2.** a low-lying piece of grassland, often near a river.

meadowsweet ('mɛdəʊ,swiːt) *n.* a plant with dense heads of small fragrant cream-coloured flowers.

meagre *or U.S.* **meager** ('miːgə) *adj.* **1.** deficient in amount, quality, or extent. **2.** thin or emaciated.

meal¹ (miːl) *n.* **1.** any of the regular occasions, such as breakfast or dinner, when food is served and eaten. **2.** the food served and eaten. **3. make a meal of.** *Informal.* to perform (a task) with unnecessarily great effort.

meal² (miːl) *n.* **1.** the edible part of a grain or pulse (excluding wheat) ground to a coarse powder. **2.** *Scot.* oatmeal. **3.** *Chiefly U.S.* maize flour. —'**mealy** *adj.*

mealie ('miːlɪ) *n.* (*often pl.*) *S. African.* same as **maize.**

meals-on-wheels *n.* (*functioning as sing.*) (in Britain) a service taking hot meals to the elderly or infirm in their own homes.

meal ticket *n. Slang.* a person or situation providing a source of livelihood or income.

mealy-mouthed *adj.* hesitant or afraid to speak plainly; not outspoken.

mean¹ (miːn) *vb.* **meaning, meant. 1.** to intend to convey or express. **2.** to intend: *she didn't mean to hurt it.* **3.** to say or do in all seriousness: *the boss means what he says.* **4.** (often foll. by *for*) to destine or design (for a certain person or purpose): *she was meant for greater things.* **5.** to denote; signify; represent. **6.** to produce; cause: *the weather will mean long traffic* *delays.* **7.** to foretell: *those dark clouds mean rain.* **8.** to have the importance of: *money means nothing to him.* **9. mean well.** to have good intentions.

mean² (miːn) *adj.* **1.** *Chiefly Brit.* miserly, ungenerous, or petty. **2.** despicable, ignoble, or callous: *a mean action.* **3.** poor or shabby: *a mean abode.* **4.** *Informal, chiefly U.S. & Canad.* bad-tempered; vicious. **5.** *Informal.* ashamed: *he felt mean about not letting the children stay out late.* **6.** *Slang.* excellent; skilful: *he plays a mean trombone.* **7. no mean. a.** of high quality: *no mean performer.* **b.** difficult: *no mean feat.* —'**meanly** *adv.* —'**meanness** *n.*

mean³ (miːn) *n.* **1.** the middle point, state, or course between limits or extremes. **2.** *Maths.* **a.** the mid-point between the highest and lowest number in a set. **b.** the average. ~*adj.* **3.** intermediate in size or quantity. **4.** occurring halfway between extremes or limits; average.

meander (mɪˈændə) *vb.* **1.** to follow a winding course. **2.** to wander without definite aim or direction. ~*n.* **3.** a curve or bend, as in a river. **4.** a winding course or movement.

mean deviation *n. Statistics.* the difference between an observed value of a variable and its mean.

meanie *or* **meany** (ˈmiːnɪ) *n. Informal.* **1.** *Chiefly Brit.* a miserly person. **2.** *Chiefly U.S.* a nasty ill-tempered person.

meaning (ˈmiːnɪŋ) *n.* **1.** the sense or significance of a word, sentence, or symbol. **2.** the inner, symbolic, or true interpretation, value, or message: *the meaning of life.* ~*adj.* **3.** expressive of some sense or intention: *a meaning look.*

meaningful (ˈmiːnɪŋfʊl) *adj.* **1.** having great meaning or validity. **2.** eloquent; expressive: *a meaningful silence.*

meaningless (ˈmiːnɪŋlɪs) *adj.* futile or empty of meaning.

means (miːnz) *n.* **1.** (*functioning as sing. or pl.*) the medium, method, or instrument used to obtain a result or achieve an end: *a means of communication.* **2.** (*functioning as pl.*) income: *a man of means.* **3. by all means.** without hesitation or doubt; certainly. **4. by means of.** with the use or help of. **5. by no** *or* **not by any means.** on no account; in no way.

means test *n.* the checking of a person's income to determine whether he qualifies for financial aid.

meant (mɛnt) *vb.* past of **mean¹**.

meantime (ˈmiːnˌtaɪm) *n.* **1.** the intervening period: *in the meantime.* ~*adv.* **2.** same as **meanwhile.**

Usage. In formal usage, *in the meantime* is preferred to *meantime*, although *meantime* is very common in informal spoken English. The most usual one-word form of the adverb in written English is *meanwhile: in the*

meantime (or *meanwhile* not *meantime*), *she had not been idle.*

mean time *or* **mean solar time** *n.* the times, at a particular place, measured so as to give 24-hour days (mean solar days) throughout a year.

meanwhile (ˈmiːnˌwaɪl) *adv.* **1.** during the intervening period. **2.** at the same time, esp. in another place.
Usage. see **meantime.**

meany (ˈmiːnɪ) *n., pl.* **meanies.** same as **meanie.**

measles (ˈmiːz²lz) *n.* (*functioning as sing.*) a highly contagious viral disease common in children, characterized by fever and a rash of small red spots. See also **German measles.**

measly (ˈmiːzlɪ) *adj.* **-slier, -sliest. 1.** *Informal.* meagre in quality or quantity. **2.** having or relating to measles.

measure (ˈmɛʒə) *n.* **1.** the extent, quantity, amount, or degree of something, as determined by measurement or calculation. **2.** a device for measuring distance, volume, etc., such as a graduated scale or container. **3.** a system or unit of measurement: *metric measure.* **4.** degree or extent: *a measure of freedom.* **5.** (*often pl.*) a particular action intended to achieve an effect. **6.** a legislative bill, act, or resolution. **7.** *Music.* another word for **bar¹** (sense 11). **8.** *Prosody.* poetic rhythm or cadence; metre. **9.** a metrical foot. **10.** *Archaic.* a dance. **11. for good measure.** as an extra precaution or beyond requirements. **12. made to measure.** (of clothes) made to fit an individual purchaser. ~*vb.* **13.** (often foll. by *up*) to determine the size, amount, etc., of by measurement. **14.** to make a measurement. **15.** to estimate or determine. **16.** to function as a measurement of: *the ohm measures electrical resistance.* **17.** to bring into competition or conflict with: *he measured his strength against that of his opponent.* **18.** to be as specified in extent, amount, etc.: *the room measures six feet.* ~See also **measure up.** —'**measurable** *adj.*

measured (ˈmɛʒəd) *adj.* **1.** slow or stately. **2.** carefully considered; deliberate.

measurement (ˈmɛʒəmənt) *n.* **1.** the act or process of measuring. **2.** an amount, extent, or size determined by measuring. **3.** a system of measures based on a particular standard.

measures (ˈmɛʒəz) *pl. n.* rock strata that contain a particular type of deposit: *coal measures.*

measure up *vb.* (usually foll. by *to*) to fulfil (expectations or standards).

meat (miːt) *n.* **1.** the flesh of animals used as food. **2.** the essence or gist. —'**meatless** *adj.*

meatball (ˈmiːtˌbɔːl) *n.* minced beef, shaped into a ball before cooking.

meaty ('miːtɪ) *adj.* **meatier, meatiest. 1.** of, like, or full of meat. **2.** heavily built; fleshy or brawny. **3.** full of import or interest: *a meaty discussion.*

Mecca ('mɛkə) *n.* (*sometimes not cap.*) a place that attracts many visitors.

mech. 1. mechanical. **2.** mechanics.

mechanic (mɪ'kænɪk) *n.* a person skilled in maintaining or operating machinery or motors.

mechanical (mɪ'kænɪk³l) *adj.* **1.** made, performed, or operated by machinery. **2.** concerned with machines or machinery. **3.** relating to or operated by physical forces. **4.** of or concerned with mechanics. **5.** (of a gesture or response) automatic; lacking thought or feeling. **—me'chanically** *adv.*

mechanical drawing *n.* a drawing to scale of a machine or architectural plan from which dimensions can be taken.

mechanical engineering *n.* the branch of engineering concerned with the design, construction, and operation of machines.

mechanics (mɪ'kænɪks) *n.* **1.** (*functioning as sing.*) the branch of science concerned with the equilibrium or motion of bodies. **2.** (*functioning as sing.*) the science of designing, constructing, and operating machines. **3.** the technical aspects of something.

mechanism ('mɛkə,nɪzəm) *n.* **1.** a system of moving parts that performs some function, esp. in a machine. **2.** any mechanical device or part of such a device. **3.** a process or technique: *the defence mechanism.* **—,mecha'nistic** *adj.*

mechanize *or* **-ise** ('mɛkə,naɪz) *vb.* **1.** to equip (a factory or industry) with machinery. **2.** to make mechanical or automatic. **3.** to equip (an army) with motorized or armoured vehicles. **—,mechani'zation** *or* **-i'sation** *n.*

med. 1. medical. **2.** medicine. **3.** medieval. **4.** medium.

MEd Master of Education.

medal ('mɛd³l) *n.* a small flat piece of metal bearing an inscription or image, given as an award or in commemoration of some outstanding event.

medallion (mɪ'dæljən) *n.* **1.** a round ornament worn on a chain round the neck. **2.** a large medal. **3.** a decorative device resembling a medal, used in architecture.

medallist *or U.S.* **medalist** ('mɛd³lɪst) *n. Chiefly sport.* a winner of a medal or medals.

meddle ('mɛd³l) *vb.* (foll. by *with* or *in*) to interfere annoyingly. **—'meddler** *n.* **—'meddlesome** *adj.*

media ('miːdɪə) *n.* **1.** a plural of **medium. 2.** the mass media collectively. **Usage.** see **medium.**

mediaeval (,mɛdɪ'iːv³l) *adj.* same as **medieval.**

media event *n.* an event that is staged for or exploited by the mass media.

medial ('miːdɪəl) *adj.* of or situated in the middle. **—'medially** *adv.*

median ('miːdɪən) *n.* **1.** a middle point, plane, or part. **2.** *Geom.* a straight line joining one vertex of a triangle to the midpoint of the opposite side. **3.** *Statistics.* the middle value in a frequency distribution, below and above which lie values with equal total frequencies.

mediate *vb.* ('miːdɪ,eɪt). **1.** (usually foll. by *between* or *in*) to intervene (between parties or in a dispute) in order to bring about agreement. **2.** to resolve (differences) by mediation. **3.** to be in an intermediate position. *~adj.* ('miːdɪɪt). **4.** occurring as a result of or dependent upon mediation. **—,medi'ation** *n.* **—'medi,ator** *n.*

medic ('mɛdɪk) *n. Informal.* a doctor, medical orderly, or medical student.

medical ('mɛdɪk³l) *adj.* **1.** of or relating to the science of medicine or to the treatment of patients without surgery. *~n.* **2.** *Informal.* a medical examination. **—'medically** *adv.*

medical certificate *n.* **1.** a document stating the result of a satisfactory medical examination. **2.** a doctor's certificate giving evidence of a person's unfitness for work.

medicament (mɪ'dɪkəmənt) *n.* a medicine.

medicate ('mɛdɪ,keɪt) *vb.* **1.** to treat (a patient) with a medicine. **2.** to add a medication to (a bandage or shampoo). **—'medicative** *adj.*

medication (,mɛdɪ'keɪʃən) *n.* **1.** treatment with drugs or remedies. **2.** a drug or remedy.

medicinal (mɪ'dɪsɪn³l) *adj.* relating to or having therapeutic properties. **—me'dicinally** *adv.*

medicine ('mɛdɪsɪn, 'mɛdsɪn) *n.* **1.** any substance used in treating or alleviating the symptoms of disease. **2.** the science of preventing, diagnosing, or curing disease. **3.** any nonsurgical branch of medical science. **4. take one's medicine.** to accept a deserved punishment.

medicine man *n.* (among certain peoples) a person believed to have supernatural powers of healing.

medico ('mɛdɪ,kəʊ) *n., pl.* **-cos.** *Informal.* a doctor or medical student.

medieval *or* **mediaeval** (,mɛdɪ'iːv³l) *adj.* **1.** of, relating to, or in the style of the Middle Ages. **2.** *Informal.* old-fashioned; primitive. **—,medi'evalist** *or* ,medi-'aevalist *n.*

Medieval Greek *n.* the Greek language from the 7th to 13th century A.D.

Medieval Latin *n.* the Latin language as used throughout Europe in the Middle Ages.

mediocre (ˌmiːdɪˈəʊkə) adj. average or ordinary in quality. —**mediocrity** (ˌmiːdɪˈɒkrɪtɪ) n.

meditate (ˈmɛdɪˌteɪt) vb. 1. (foll. by on or upon) to think about something deeply. 2. to reflect deeply on spiritual matters. 3. to plan, consider, or think of doing (something). —ˈ**meditative** adj. —ˈ**medi**ˌ**tator** n.

meditation (ˌmɛdɪˈteɪʃən) n. 1. the act of meditating; reflection. 2. contemplation of spiritual matters, esp. as a religious practice.

Mediterranean (ˌmɛdɪtəˈreɪnɪən) n. 1. short for the **Mediterranean Sea,** the sea between S Europe, N Africa, and SW Asia. ~adj. 2. of, relating to, or near the Mediterranean Sea.

medium (ˈmiːdɪəm) adj. 1. midway between extremes; average. ~n., pl. -**dia** or -**diums.** 2. a middle state, degree, or condition: the happy medium. 3. an intervening substance or agency for transmitting or producing an effect. 4. a means for communicating information or news to the public. 5. a person who can supposedly communicate with the dead. 6. the substance or surroundings in which an organism naturally lives or grows. 7. Art. the category of a work of art, as determined by its materials: her works in the photographic medium.
Usage. Media should not be used as a singular noun when referring to a medium of mass communication: television is a valuable medium (not media) for advertising.

medium wave n. a radio wave with a wavelength between 100 and 1000 metres.

medlar (ˈmɛdlə) n. the fruit of a small Eurasian tree, which resembles the crab apple and is not edible until it has begun to decay.

medley (ˈmɛdlɪ) n. 1. a mixture of various elements. 2. a musical composition consisting of various tunes arranged as a continuous whole. 3. Swimming. a race in which a different stroke is used for each length.

medulla (mɪˈdʌlə) n., pl. -**las** or -**lae** (-liː). 1. Anat. the innermost part of an organ or structure. 2. Anat. the lower stalklike section of the brain. 3. Bot. the central pith of a plant stem. —**me**ˈ**dullary** adj.

medusa (mɪˈdjuːzə) n., pl. -**sas** or -**sae** (-ziː). jellyfish.

meek (miːk) adj. patient, long-suffering, or submissive. —ˈ**meekly** adv.

meerkat (ˈmɪəˌkæt) n. a South African mongoose.

meerschaum (ˈmɪəʃəm) n. 1. a white, heat-resistant, claylike mineral. 2. a tobacco pipe with a bowl made of this mineral.

meet[1] (miːt) vb. **meeting, met.** 1. to come together (with), either by design or by accident; encounter. 2. to come into contact with (something or each other). 3. to come

to or be at the place of arrival of: to meet a train. 4. to make the acquaintance of or be introduced to (someone or each other). 5. (of people) to gather together for a purpose: the committee meets once a month. 6. to come into the presence of (someone or each other) as opponents. 7. to cope with effectively; satisfy: to meet someone's demands. 8. (sometimes foll. by with) to experience; suffer: he met his death in a road accident. 9. **more to this than meets the eye.** there is more involved in this than appears. ~n. 10. the assembly of hounds and huntsmen prior to a hunt. 11. a sports meeting.

meet[2] (miːt) adj. Archaic. proper, fitting, or correct.

meeting (ˈmiːtɪŋ) n. 1. an act of coming together; encounter. 2. an assembly or gathering. 3. a sporting competition, as of athletes, or of horse racing.

mega (ˈmɛgə) adj. Slang. extremely good, great, or successful.

mega- combining form. 1. denoting 10^6: megawatt. 2. (in computer technology) denoting 2^{20} (1 048 576): megabyte. 3. large or great: megalith. 4. Informal. greatest: megastar.

megabyte (ˈmɛgəˌbaɪt) n. Computers. 2^{20} or 1 048 576 bytes.

megadeath (ˈmɛgəˌdɛθ) n. the death of a million people, esp. in a nuclear war or attack.

megahertz (ˈmɛgəˌhɜːts) n., pl. **megahertz.** one million hertz.

megajoule (ˈmɛgəˌdʒuːl) n. one million joules.

megalith (ˈmɛgəlɪθ) n. a stone of great size, esp. one forming part of a prehistoric monument. —ˌ**mega**ˈ**lithic** adj.

megalomania (ˌmɛgələʊˈmeɪnɪə) n. 1. a mental illness characterized by delusions of power. 2. Informal. a craving for power. —ˌ**megalo**ˈ**maniac** adj., n.

megaphone (ˈmɛgəˌfəʊn) n. a funnel-shaped instrument used to amplify the voice.

megapode (ˈmɛgəˌpəʊd) n. any of various ground-living birds of Australia, New Guinea, and adjacent islands. Their eggs incubate in mounds of sand or rotting vegetation.

megaton (ˈmɛgəˌtʌn) n. an explosive power, esp. of a nuclear weapon, equal to the power of one million tons of TNT.

megawatt (ˈmɛgəˌwɒt) n. one million watts.

meiosis (maɪˈəʊsɪs) n., pl. -**ses** (-ˌsiːz). a type of cell division in which reproductive cells are produced, each containing half the chromosome number of the parent nucleus.

melamine (ˈmɛləˌmiːn) n. a colourless crystalline compound used in making synthetic resins.

melancholia (ˌmɛlənˈkəʊlɪə) *n.* an old name for depression.

melancholy (ˈmɛlənkəlɪ) *n., pl.* **-cholies. 1.** a tendency to gloominess or depression. **2.** a sad thoughtful state of mind. ~*adj.* **3.** characterized by, causing, or expressing sadness. —**melancholic** (ˌmɛlənˈkɒlɪk) *adj., n.*

melange *or* **mélange** (meɪˈlɒnʒ) *n.* a mixture; confusion.

melanin (ˈmɛlənɪn) *n.* a black pigment present in the hair, skin, and eyes of man and animals.

melanoma (ˌmɛləˈnəʊmə) *n., pl.* **-mas** *or* **-mata** (-mətə). *Pathol.* a tumour composed of darkly pigmented cells.

Melba toast (ˈmɛlbə) *n.* very thin crisp toast.

meld (mɛld) *vb.* to merge.

melee *or* **mêlée** (ˈmɛleɪ) *n.* a noisy riotous fight or brawl.

mellifluous (mɪˈlɪflʊəs) *adj.* (of sounds or utterances) smooth or honeyed; sweet.

mellow (ˈmɛləʊ) *adj.* **1.** (esp. of fruits) full-flavoured; sweet; ripe. **2.** (esp. of wines) well-matured. **3.** (esp. of colours or sounds) soft or rich. **4.** kind-hearted, esp. through maturity or old age. **5.** genial, as through the effects of alcohol. **6.** (of soil) soft and loamy. ~*vb.* **7.** to make or become mellow.

melodeon (mɪˈləʊdɪən) *n. Music.* **1.** a small accordion. **2.** a keyboard instrument like a harmonium.

melodic (mɪˈlɒdɪk) *adj.* **1.** of or relating to melody. **2.** melodious. —**meˈlodically** *adv.*

melodious (mɪˈləʊdɪəs) *adj.* **1.** tuneful and pleasant to the ear. **2.** of or relating to melody; melodic. —**meˈlodiousness** *n.*

melodrama (ˈmɛləˌdrɑːmə) *n.* **1.** a play or film characterized by extravagant action and emotion. **2.** overdramatic emotion or behaviour. —**melodramatic** (ˌmɛlədrəˈmætɪk) *adj.* —ˌmelodraˈmatics *pl. n.*

melody (ˈmɛlədɪ) *n., pl.* **-dies. 1.** *Music.* a succession of notes forming a distinctive sequence; tune. **2.** sounds that are pleasant because of tone or arrangement, esp. words of poetry.

melon (ˈmɛlən) *n.* the large edible fruit of various trailing plants, which has a hard rind and juicy flesh.

melt (mɛlt) *vb.* **1.** to change from a solid into a liquid as a result of the action of heat. **2.** to dissolve: *these scones melt in the mouth.* **3.** (often foll. by *away*) to disappear; fade. **4.** (often foll. by *into*) to blend or cause to blend gradually. **5.** to make or become emotional or sentimental; soften. —ˈmeltingly *adv.*

meltdown (ˈmɛltˌdaʊn) *n.* (in a nuclear reactor) the melting of the fuel rods, with the possible escape of radioactivity.

melting point *n.* the temperature at which a solid turns into a liquid.

melting pot *n.* a place or situation in which many races, ideas, etc., are mixed.

meltwater (ˈmɛltˌwɔːtə) *n.* melted snow or ice.

member (ˈmɛmbə) *n.* **1.** a person who belongs to a group or organization such as a club or political party. **2.** any part of a plant or animal, such as a limb or petal.

Member of Parliament *n.* a member of the House of Commons or similar legislative body, as in many Commonwealth countries.

membership (ˈmɛmbəʃɪp) *n.* **1.** the members of an organization collectively. **2.** the number of members. **3.** the state of being a member.

membrane (ˈmɛmbreɪn) *n.* a pliable sheetlike tissue that covers, lines, or connects plant and animal organs or cells. —**membranous** (ˈmɛmbrənəs) *adj.*

memento (mɪˈmɛntəʊ) *n., pl.* **-tos** *or* **-toes.** something that reminds one of past events; a souvenir.

memento mori (ˈmɔːriː) *n., pl.* **memento mori.** an object intended to remind people of death.

memo (ˈmɛməʊ) *n., pl.* **memos.** short for **memorandum.**

memoir (ˈmɛmwɑː) *n.* a biography or historical account, esp. one based on personal knowledge.

memoirs (ˈmɛmwɑːz) *pl. n.* **1.** a collection of reminiscences about a period or series of events, written from personal experience. **2.** an autobiography.

memorabilia (ˌmɛmərəˈbɪlɪə) *pl. n., sing.* **-rabile** (-ˈræbɪlɪ). objects connected with famous people or events.

memorable (ˈmɛmərəbˀl) *adj.* worth remembering or easily remembered. —ˈmemorably *adv.*

memorandum (ˌmɛməˈrændəm) *n., pl.* **-dums** *or* **-da** (-də). **1.** a written statement, record, or communication. **2.** a note of things to be remembered. **3.** *Law.* a short written summary of the terms of a transaction.

memorial (mɪˈmɔːrɪəl) *adj.* **1.** serving to preserve the memory of the dead or a past event. ~*n.* **2.** something, such as a statue, serving as a remembrance of someone or something.

memorize *or* **-ise** (ˈmɛməˌraɪz) *vb.* to commit to memory; learn by heart.

memory (ˈmɛmərɪ) *n., pl.* **-ries. 1.** the ability of the mind to store and recall past sensations, thoughts, and knowledge: *he can do it from memory.* **2.** the sum of everything retained by the mind. **3.** a particular recollection of an event or person. **4.** the time over which recollection extends: *within his memory.* **5.** commemoration: *in memory of our leader.* **6.** the state of being remembered, as after death. **7.** a part of a computer in which information is stored.

memsahib ('mɛm,saːıb) n. (formerly, in India) a term of respect used for a European married woman.

men (mɛn) n. the plural of **man**.

menace ('mɛnɪs) vb. **1.** to threaten with violence or danger. ~n. **2.** a threat; a source of danger. **3.** Informal. a nuisance. —'**menacing** adj.

ménage (meɪ'naːʒ) n. a household.

ménage à trois (meɪ'naːʒ aː 'trwaː) n., pl. **ménages à trois** (meɪ'naːʒ aː 'trwaː) a sexual arrangement involving a married couple and the lover of one of them.

menagerie (mɪ'nædʒərɪ) n. a collection of wild animals kept for exhibition.

mend (mɛnd) vb. **1.** to repair (something broken or not working). **2.** to heal or recover. **3.** to improve; become better. ~n. **4.** a mended area, esp. on a garment. **5. on the mend.** becoming better, esp. in health.

mendacity (mɛn'dæsɪtɪ) n. the tendency to be untruthful. —**mendacious** (mɛn'deɪʃəs) adj.

mendelevium (,mɛndɪ'liːvɪəm) n. an artificially produced radioactive element. Symbol: Md

Mendel's laws ('mɛnd³lz) pl. n. the principles of heredity proposed by Gregor Mendel (1822–84), Austrian monk and botanist. —'**Mendel,ism** n.

mendicant ('mɛndɪkənt) adj. **1.** begging. **2.** (of a member of a religious order) dependent on charity for food. ~n. **3.** a mendicant friar. **4.** a beggar.

meneer (mə'nɪə) n. a S. African title of address equivalent to sir or Mr.

menfolk ('mɛn,fəʊk) pl. n. men collectively, esp. the men of a particular family.

menhir ('mɛnhɪə) n. a single standing stone, dating from prehistoric times.

menial ('miːnɪəl) adj. **1.** involving or doing boring work of low status. ~n. **2.** a domestic servant.

meninges (mɪ'nɪndʒiːz) pl. n., sing. **meninx** ('miːnɪŋks). the three membranes that envelop the brain and spinal cord.

meningitis (,mɛnɪn'dʒaɪtɪs) n. inflammation of the membranes that surround the brain or spinal cord, caused by infection.

meniscus (mɪ'nɪskəs) n., pl. **-nisci** (-'nɪsaɪ) or **-niscuses. 1.** the curved upper surface of a liquid standing in a tube, produced by the surface tension. **2.** a crescent-shaped lens.

menopause ('mɛnəʊ,pɔːz) n. the period during which a woman's menstrual cycle ceases, normally at an age of 45 to 50. —,**meno'pausal** adj.

menorah (mɪ'nɔːrə) n. Judaism. a seven-branched candelabrum used as an emblem of Judaism.

menses ('mɛnsiːz) n., pl. **menses**. same as **menstruation**.

menstruate ('mɛnstrʊ,eɪt) vb. to undergo menstruation. —'**menstrual** adj.

menstruation (,mɛnstrʊ'eɪʃən) n. the approximately monthly discharge of blood from the womb in nonpregnant women of childbearing age.

mensuration (,mɛnsjə'reɪʃən) n. **1.** the study of the measurement of geometric magnitudes such as length. **2.** the act or process of measuring.

mental ('mɛnt³l) adj. **1.** of, done by, or involving the mind. **2.** affected by mental illness: a mental patient. **3.** concerned with mental illness: a mental hospital. **4.** Slang. insane. —'**mentally** adv.

mental handicap n. any intellectual disability resulting from injury to or abnormal development of the brain. —**mentally handicapped** adj.

mentality (mɛn'tælɪtɪ) n., pl. **-ties.** a way of thinking; mental inclination or character.

menthol ('mɛnθɒl) n. an organic compound found in peppermint oil and used as an antiseptic, in inhalants, and as a painkiller. —'**mentho,lated** adj.

mention ('mɛnʃən) vb. **1.** to refer to or speak about briefly or incidentally. **2.** to acknowledge or honour. **3. not to mention** (**something**). to say nothing of (something too obvious to mention). ~n. **4.** a recognition or acknowledgment. **5.** a slight reference or allusion.

mentor ('mɛntɔː) n. an adviser or guide.

menu ('mɛnjuː) n. **1.** a list of dishes served at a meal or that can be ordered in a restaurant. **2.** a list of options displayed on a visual display unit from which the operator can choose.

MEP (in Britain) Member of the European Parliament.

Mephistopheles (,mɛfɪ'stɒfɪ,liːz) n. a devil in medieval mythology to whom Faust sold his soul. —**Mephistophelean** (,mɛfɪstə-'fiːlɪən) adj.

mercantile ('mɜːkən,taɪl) adj. of trade or traders; commercial.

Mercator projection (mɜː'keɪtə) n. a way of drawing maps in which latitude and longitude form a rectangular grid, scale being exaggerated with increasing distance from the equator.

mercenary ('mɜːsɪnərɪ, -sɪnrɪ) adj. **1.** influenced by greed or desire for gain. **2.** of or relating to a mercenary or mercenaries. ~n., pl. **-naries. 3.** a soldier hired to fight for a foreign army.

mercerize or **-ise** ('mɜːsə,raɪz) vb. to treat (cotton yarn) with an alkali to make it strong and shiny.

merchandise ('mɜːtʃəndaɪz) n. **1.** commercial goods; commodities. ~vb. **2.** to engage in the commercial purchase and sale of (goods or services); trade.

merchant ('mɜːtʃənt) n. **1.** a person who buys and sells goods for profit; trader. **2.** *Chiefly Scot., U.S., & Canad.* a person engaged in retail trade. **3.** *Slang.* a person dealing in something undesirable: *a gossip merchant.* **4.** *(modifier)* **a.** of the merchant navy: *a merchant sailor.* **b.** of or concerned with trade: *a merchant ship.*

merchant bank n. *Brit.* a financial institution that deals primarily with foreign trade and business finance. —**merchant banker** n.

merchantman ('mɜːtʃəntmən) n., pl. -**men.** a merchant ship.

merchant navy n. the ships or crew engaged in a nation's commercial shipping.

merciful ('mɜːsɪfʊl) adj. showing or giving mercy; compassionate. —'**mercifully** adv.

merciless ('mɜːsɪlɪs) adj. without mercy; pitiless, cruel, or heartless. —'**mercilessly** adv.

mercurial (mɜːˈkjʊərɪəl) adj. **1.** volatile; lively: *a mercurial temperament.* **2.** of or containing mercury.

mercuric (mɜːˈkjʊərɪk) adj. of or containing mercury in the divalent state.

mercurous ('mɜːkjʊrəs) adj. of or containing mercury in the monovalent state.

mercury ('mɜːkjʊrɪ) n., pl. -**ries.** a heavy silvery-white toxic liquid metallic element: used in thermometers, barometers, mercury-vapour lamps, and dental amalgams. Symbol: Hg

Mercury ('mɜːkjʊrɪ) n. **1.** *Roman myth.* the messenger of the gods. **2.** the second smallest planet and the nearest to the sun.

mercy ('mɜːsɪ) n., pl. -**cies. 1.** compassionate treatment of or attitude towards an offender or enemy who is in one's power. **2.** the power to show mercy. **3.** a relieving or welcome occurrence. **4. at the mercy of.** in the power of.

mercy killing n. same as **euthanasia.**

mere¹ (mɪə) adj. being nothing more than something specified: *a mere child.* —'**merely** adv.

mere² (mɪə) n. *Dialect or archaic.* a lake.

meretricious (ˌmɛrɪˈtrɪʃəs) adj. superficially or garishly attractive but of no real value.

merganser (mɜːˈɡænsə) n., pl. -**sers** or -**ser.** a large crested marine diving duck.

merge (mɜːdʒ) vb. **1.** to combine, esp. so as to become part of a larger whole. **2.** to blend or cause to blend; fuse.

merger ('mɜːdʒə) n. the act of merging, esp. the combination of two or more companies.

meridian (məˈrɪdɪən) n. **1.** one of the imaginary lines joining the north and south poles at right angles to the equator, designated by degrees of longitude from 0° at Greenwich to 180°. **2.** the peak; zenith: *the meridian of his achievements.*

meridional (məˈrɪdɪənˀl) adj. **1.** of or along a meridian. **2.** of or in the south, esp. of Europe.

meringue (məˈræŋ) n. **1.** stiffly beaten egg whites mixed with sugar and baked. **2.** a small cake of this mixture.

merino (məˈriːnəʊ) n., pl. -**nos. 1.** a breed of sheep with long fine wool. **2.** the yarn made from this wool.

merit ('mɛrɪt) n. **1.** worth or superior quality; excellence. **2.** *(often pl.)* a good or admirable quality or act. **3.** a mark of worth or excellence. **4. on its merits.** on its intrinsic qualities or virtues. ~vb. **5.** to be worthy of; deserve.

meritocracy (ˌmɛrɪˈtɒkrəsɪ) n., pl. -**cies.** a social system based on rule by persons of superior talents or intellect.

meritorious (ˌmɛrɪˈtɔːrɪəs) adj. praiseworthy; showing merit.

merlin ('mɜːlɪn) n. a small falcon with dark plumage.

mermaid ('mɜːˌmeɪd) n. an imaginary sea creature with a woman's head and upper body and a fish's tail. —'**mer,man** *masc.* n.

merry ('mɛrɪ) adj. -**rier,** -**riest. 1.** cheerful; jolly. **2.** *Brit. informal.* slightly drunk. **3. make merry.** to revel; be festive. —'**merrily** adv. —'**merriment** n.

merry-go-round n. **1.** a fairground roundabout. **2.** a whirl of activity.

merrymaking ('mɛrɪˌmeɪkɪŋ) n. fun, revelry, or festivity. —'**merry,maker** n.

mésalliance (mɛˈzælɪəns) n. a marriage with a person of lower social status.

mescal (mɛˈskæl) n. a spineless globe-shaped cactus of Mexico and the southwestern U.S.

mescaline ('mɛskəˌliːn) n. a hallucinogenic drug derived from the button-like top of the mescal cactus.

mesdames ('meɪˌdæm) n. the plural of **madame** and **madam** (sense 1).

mesdemoiselles (ˌmeɪdmwəˈzɛl) n. the plural of **mademoiselle.**

mesembryanthemum (mɪzˌɛmbrɪˈænθɪməm) n. a plant with fleshy leaves and bright flowers with rayed petals.

mesh (mɛʃ) n. **1.** a network; net. **2.** an open space between the strands of a network. **3.** *(often pl.)* the strands surrounding these spaces. **4.** anything that ensnares or holds like a net. ~vb. **5.** to entangle or become entangled. **6.** (of gear teeth) to engage. **7.** to work in harmony.

mesmerize or -**ise** ('mɛzməˌraɪz) vb. **1.** *Archaic.* to hypnotize. **2.** to hold (someone) as if spellbound. —'**mesmer,ism** n.

Mesolithic (ˌmɛsəʊˈlɪθɪk) adj. of the middle period of the Stone Age, in Europe from about 12 000 to 3000 B.C.

meson ('miːzɒn) *n.* any of a group of elementary particles that has a mass between those of an electron and a proton.

mesosphere ('mɛsəʊ,sfɪə) *n.* the atmospheric layer above the stratosphere.

Mesozoic (,mɛsəʊ'zəʊɪk) *adj. Geol.* of or denoting a geological era that began 225 000 000 years ago and lasted about 155 000 000 years; the era of the dinosaurs.

mess (mɛs) *n.* **1.** a state of confusion or untidiness, esp. if dirty or unpleasant. **2.** *Informal.* a dirty or untidy person or thing. **3.** *Archaic.* a portion of soft or semiliquid food. **4.** a place where service personnel eat or take recreation. **5.** a group of people, usually servicemen, who eat together. ~*vb.* **6.** (often foll. by *up*) to muddle or dirty. **7.** (often foll. by *with*) to interfere; meddle. **8.** (often foll. by *with* or *together*) *Mil.* to group together for eating.

mess about *or* **around** *vb.* **1.** to occupy oneself trivially; potter. **2.** to interfere or meddle (with). **3.** (often foll. by *with*) *Chiefly U.S.* to engage in adultery.

message ('mɛsɪdʒ) *n.* **1.** a communication from one person or group to another. **2.** an implicit meaning, as in a work of art. **3.** a religious or political belief that someone attempts to communicate to others: *the Christian message of salvation.* **4. get the message.** *Informal.* to understand.

messages ('mɛsɪdʒɪz) *pl. n. Scot. & NE English dialect.* household shopping.

messenger ('mɛsɪndʒə) *n.* a person who takes messages from one person or group to another.

Messiah (mɪ'saɪə) *n.* **1.** *Judaism.* the awaited king of the Jews, to be sent by God to free them. **2.** *Christianity.* Jesus Christ, when regarded in this role. **3.** a liberator of a country or people. —**Messianic** (,mɛsɪ-'ænɪk) *adj.*

messieurs ('mɛsəz) *n.* the plural of **monsieur.**

mess jacket *n.* a waist-length jacket, worn by officers in the mess for formal dinners.

mess kit *n. Mil.* eating utensils used esp. in the field.

Messrs ('mɛsəz) *n.* the plural of **Mr.**

messy ('mɛsɪ) *adj.* **messier, messiest.** dirty, confused, or untidy. —**'messily** *adv.* —**'messiness** *n.*

met (mɛt) *vb.* past of **meet**[1].

met. **1.** meteorological. **2.** metropolitan.

metabolism (mɪ'tæbə,lɪzəm) *n.* the chemical processes that occur in living organisms, resulting in growth, production of energy, and elimination of waste. —**metabolic** (,mɛtə'bɒlɪk) *adj.*

metabolize *or* **-ise** (mɪ'tæbə,laɪz) *vb.* to produce or be produced by metabolism.

metacarpus (,mɛtə'kɑːpəs) *n., pl.* **-pi** (-paɪ). the set of five long bones in the hand between the wrist and the fingers. —**,meta'carpal** *adj., n.*

metal ('mɛt°l) *n.* **1. a.** a chemical element, such as iron or copper, that is lustrous and ductile, forms positive ions, and is a good conductor of heat and electricity. **b.** an alloy, such as brass or steel, containing one or more of these elements. **2.** short for **road metal. 3.** (*pl.*) the rails of a railway. ~*adj.* **4.** made of metal. ~*vb.* **-alling, -alled** *or U.S.* **-aling, -aled. 5.** to fit or cover with metal. **6.** to make or mend (a road) with road metal.

metallic (mɪ'tælɪk) *adj.* **1.** of or consisting of metal. **2.** suggestive of a metal: *a metallic click; metallic lustre.*

metalliferous (,mɛt°'lɪfərəs) *adj.* containing a metallic element.

metallography (,mɛtə'lɒgrəfɪ) *n.* the study of the composition and structure of metals.

metalloid ('mɛtə,lɔɪd) *n.* a nonmetallic element, such as arsenic or silicon, that has some of the properties of a metal.

metallurgy (mɛ'tælədʒɪ) *n.* the scientific study of the extraction and alloying of metals and of their structure and properties. —**metallurgist** (mɛ'tælədʒɪst, 'mɛtə,lɜː-dʒɪst) *n.*

metalwork ('mɛt°l,wɜːk) *n.* **1.** the craft of working in metal. **2.** articles made from metal. —**'metal,worker** *n.*

metamorphic (,mɛtə'mɔːfɪk) *adj.* **1.** of metamorphosis or metamorphism. **2.** (of rocks) altered considerably from the original structure and composition by pressure and heat.

metamorphism (,mɛtə'mɔːfɪzəm) *n.* **1.** the process by which metamorphic rocks are formed. **2.** same as **metamorphosis.**

metamorphose (,mɛtə'mɔːfəʊz) *vb.* to change from one state or thing into something different.

metamorphosis (,mɛtə'mɔːfəsɪs) *n., pl.* **-ses** (-,siːz). **1.** a complete change of physical form or substance. **2.** a complete change of character or appearance. **3.** *Zool.* the change of form that accompanies transformation into an adult in certain animals, for example the butterfly or frog.

metaphor ('mɛtəfə) *n.* a figure of speech in which a word or phrase is applied to an object or action that it does not literally denote in order to imply a resemblance, for example *he is a lion in battle.* —**metaphorical** (,mɛtə'fɒrɪk°l) *adj.* —**metaphorically** (,mɛtə'fɒrɪkəlɪ) *adv.*

metaphysical (,mɛtə'fɪzɪk°l) *adj.* **1.** of metaphysics. **2.** (popularly) abstract, abstruse, or unduly theoretical.

Metaphysical (,mɛtə'fɪzɪk°l) *adj.* denoting certain 17th-century poets who combined intense feeling with elaborate imagery.

metaphysics (,mɛtə'fɪzɪks) *n.* (*functioning as sing.*) **1.** the philosophical study of the nature of reality. **2.** (popularly) abstract or subtle discussion or reasoning.

metastasis (mɪˈtæstəsɪs) n., pl. **-ses** (-ˌsiːz). Pathol. the spreading of a disease, esp. cancer, from one part of the body to another.

metatarsus (ˌmɛtəˈtɑːsəs) n., pl. **-si** (-saɪ). the set of five long bones in the foot between the toes and the ankle. —ˌmeta'tarsal adj., n.

metathesis (mɪˈtæθəsɪs) n., pl. **-ses** (-ˌsiːz). the transposition of two sounds or letters in a word or of two words in a sentence.

metazoan (ˌmɛtəˈzəʊən) n. **1.** any animal having a body composed of many cells: includes all animals except sponges and protozoans. ~adj. **2.** of the metazoans.

mete (miːt) vb. (usually foll. by out) Formal. to distribute or allot (something, often unpleasant).

meteor (ˈmiːtɪə) n. **1.** a small meteoroid that has entered the earth's atmosphere. **2.** Also: **shooting star.** the bright streak of light appearing in the sky due to a meteoroid burning up because of friction as it falls through the atmosphere.

meteoric (ˌmiːtɪˈɒrɪk) adj. **1.** of or relating to meteors. **2.** like a meteor in brilliance, speed, or transience. —ˌmete'orically adv.

meteorite (ˈmiːtɪəˌraɪt) n. the rocklike remains of a meteoroid that has fallen on earth.

meteoroid (ˈmiːtɪəˌrɔɪd) n. any of the small celestial bodies that are thought to orbit the sun. When they enter the earth's atmosphere, they become visible as meteors.

meteorol. or **meteor.** **1.** meteorological. **2.** meteorology.

meteorology (ˌmiːtɪəˈrɒlədʒɪ) n. the study of the earth's atmosphere, esp. of weather-forming processes and for weather forecasting. —**meteorological** (ˌmiːtɪərəˈlɒdʒɪkˀl) adj. —ˌmeteor'ologist n.

meter[1] (ˈmiːtə) n. **1.** any device that measures and records a quantity, such as of gas, current, or voltage that has passed through it during a specified period. **2.** See **parking meter.** ~vb. **3.** to measure (a rate of flow) with a meter.

meter[2] (ˈmiːtə) n. U.S. same as **metre**[1] and **metre**[2].

-meter n. combining form. **1.** indicating an instrument for measuring: barometer. **2.** Prosody. indicating a verse having a specified number of feet: pentameter.

methadone (ˈmɛθəˌdəʊn) n. a drug similar to morphine but less habit-forming.

methane (ˈmiːθeɪn) n. a colourless odourless flammable gas, the main constituent of natural gas.

methane series n. a series of saturated hydrocarbons with the general formula C_nH_{2n+2}.

methanol (ˈmɛθəˌnɒl) n. a colourless poisonous liquid used as a solvent and fuel. Also: **methyl alcohol.**

methinks (mɪˈθɪŋks) vb. past **methought.** (takes a clause as object) Archaic. it seems to me.

method (ˈmɛθəd) n. **1.** a way of doing something, esp. a systematic or regular one. **2.** orderliness of thought or action. **3.** (often pl.) the techniques of a particular field or subject.

Method (ˈmɛθəd) n. (sometimes not cap.) an acting technique in which the actor bases his role on the inner motivation of the character played.

methodical (mɪˈθɒdɪkˀl) adj. characterized by method or orderliness; systematic. —me'thodically adv.

Methodist (ˈmɛθədɪst) n. **1.** a member of any of the Christian Nonconformist denominations that derive from the beliefs and practices of John Wesley and his followers. ~adj. **2.** of or relating to Methodists or their Church. —'Method,ism n.

methodology (ˌmɛθəˈdɒlədʒɪ) n., pl. **-gies.** **1.** the system of methods and principles used in a particular discipline. **2.** the philosophical study of method. —**methodological** (ˌmɛθədəˈlɒdʒɪkˀl) adj.

methought (mɪˈθɔːt) vb. Archaic. the past tense of **methinks.**

meths (mɛθs) n. Chiefly Brit., Austral., & N.Z. informal. methylated spirits.

methyl (ˈmiːθaɪl, ˈmɛθɪl) n. (modifier) of or containing the monovalent group of atoms CH_3.

methyl alcohol n. same as **methanol.**

methylate (ˈmɛθɪˌleɪt) vb. to mix with methanol.

methylated spirits n. (functioning as sing. or pl.) alcohol that has been rendered undrinkable by the addition of methanol and a violet dye. Also: **methylated spirit.**

methylene (ˈmɛθɪˌliːn) n. (modifier) of, consisting of, or containing the divalent group of atoms $=CH_2$: a methylene group or radical.

meticulous (mɪˈtɪkjʊləs) adj. very precise about details; painstaking. —me'ticulously adv.

métier (ˈmɛtɪeɪ) n. **1.** a profession or trade. **2.** a person's strong point or speciality.

Métis (meɪˈtiːs) n., pl. **-tis** (-ˈtiːs, -ˈtiːz). a person of mixed parentage, esp. the offspring of a North American Indian and a French Canadian. —**Métisse** (meɪˈtiːs) fem. n.

metonymy (mɪˈtɒnɪmɪ) n., pl. **-mies.** the substitution of a word referring to an attribute for the thing that is meant, e.g. the crown, used to refer to a monarch.

metre[1] or U.S. **meter** (ˈmiːtə) n. the basic SI unit of length equal to approximately 1.094 yards.

metre[2] *or U.S.* **meter** ('miːtə) *n.* **1.** *Prosody.* the rhythmic arrangement of syllables in verse, usually according to the number and kind of feet in a line. **2.** *Music, chiefly U.S.* the rhythmic arrangement of the beat in a piece of music.

metre-kilogram-second *n.* See **mks units.**

metric ('mɛtrɪk) *adj.* of or relating to the metre or metric system.

metrical ('mɛtrɪk²l) *or* **metric** *adj.* **1.** of or relating to measurement. **2.** of or in poetic metre. —'**metrically** *adv.*

metricate ('mɛtrɪˌkeɪt) *vb.* to convert (a measuring system or instrument) to metric units. —ˌ**metri'cation** *n.*

metric system *n.* any decimal system of units based on the metre. For scientific purposes SI units are used.

metric ton *n.* (not in technical use) a tonne.

metro ('mɛtrəʊ) *n., pl.* -**ros.** an urban, usually underground, railway system in certain cities, such as Paris.

metronome ('mɛtrəˌnəʊm) *n.* a device which indicates the tempo of music by producing a clicking sound from a pendulum with an adjustable period of swing.

metropolis (mɪ'trɒpəlɪs) *n.* the main city of a country or region.

metropolitan (ˌmɛtrə'pɒlɪtən) *adj.* **1.** of or characteristic of a metropolis. **2.** constituting a city and its suburbs. **3.** of or belonging to the home territories of a country, as opposed to overseas territories: *metropolitan France.* ~*n.* **4.** *Christianity.* the senior clergyman, esp. an archbishop, in charge of an ecclesiastical province. **5.** an inhabitant of a large city.

-metry *n. combining form.* indicating the process or science of measuring: *geometry.* —**metric** *adj. combining form.*

mettle ('mɛt²l) *n.* **1.** courage; spirit. **2.** character. **3. on one's mettle.** roused to making one's best efforts.

MeV million electronvolts (10⁶ electronvolts).

mevrou (mə'frəʊ) *n.* a S. African title of address equivalent to *madam* or *Mrs.*

mew[1] (mjuː) *n.* **1.** the characteristic high-pitched cry of a cat. ~*vb.* **2.** to make such a sound.

mew[2] (mjuː) *n.* a seagull.

mewl (mjuːl) *vb.* **1.** (esp. of a baby) to cry weakly; whimper. ~*n.* **2.** such a cry.

mews (mjuːz) *n. (functioning as sing. or pl.) Chiefly Brit.* a yard or street lined by buildings originally used as stables but now often converted into dwellings.

Mex. 1. Mexican. **2.** Mexico.

Mexican ('mɛksɪkən) *adj.* **1.** of or relating to Mexico, in Central America. ~*n.* **2.** a person from Mexico.

mezzanine ('mɛzəˌniːn, 'mɛtsəˌniːn) *n.* an intermediate storey, esp. a low one between the ground and first floor of a building.

mezzo ('mɛtsəʊ) *adv. Music.* moderately; quite: *mezzo piano.*

mezzo-soprano *n., pl.* -**nos.** **1.** a female voice intermediate between a soprano and contralto. **2.** a singer with such a voice.

mezzotint ('mɛtsəʊˌtɪnt) *n.* **1.** a method of engraving a copper plate by scraping and burnishing the roughened surface. **2.** a print made from a plate so treated.

mf *Music.* moderately loud.

mg milligram.

Mg *Chem.* magnesium.

M. Glam Mid Glamorgan.

Mgr 1. manager. **2.** monseigneur. **3.** monsignor.

MHz megahertz.

mi *or* **me** (miː) *n. Music.* (in tonic sol-fa) the third degree of any major scale.

MI 1. Michigan. **2.** Military Intelligence.

MI5 Military Intelligence, section five; the counterintelligence agency of the British Government.

MI6 Military Intelligence, section six; the intelligence and espionage agency of the British Government.

miaow (mɪ'aʊ, mjaʊ) *vb.* **1.** (of a cat) to make a characteristic crying sound. ~*interj.* **2.** an imitation of this sound.

miasma (mɪ'æzmə) *n., pl.* -**mata** (-mətə) *or* -**mas.** an unwholesome or foreboding atmosphere.

mica ('maɪkə) *n.* any of a group of minerals consisting of silicates of aluminium or potassium found in flakelike crystals. They have a high resistance to electricity and heat.

mice (maɪs) *n.* the plural of **mouse.**

Mich. 1. Michaelmas. **2.** Michigan.

Michaelmas ('mɪk²lməs) *n.* Sept. 29, the feast of St Michael the archangel; in England, Ireland, and Wales, one of the four quarter days.

Michaelmas daisy *n. Brit.* a composite plant with small purple, pink, or white flowers in autumn.

Mick (mɪk) *n. (sometimes not cap.) Offensive slang.* an Irishman.

mickey ('mɪkɪ) *n.* **take the mickey (out of).** *Informal.* to tease.

Mickey Finn *n. Slang.* a drink containing a drug to make the drinker unconscious.

mickle ('mɪk²l) *or* **muckle** ('mʌk²l) *Archaic or Scot. & N English dialect.* ~*adj.* **1.** great or abundant. ~*adv.* **2.** much; greatly. ~*n.* **3.** a great amount.

micro ('maɪkrəʊ) *n., pl.* -**os.** short for **microcomputer** and **microprocessor.**

micro- *or* **micr-** *combining form.* **1.** small or minute: *microdot.* **2.** involving the use of a microscope: *microscopy*. **3.** denoting one millionth of a unit: *microsecond*.

microbe ('maɪkrəʊb) *n.* any microscopic organism, esp. a disease-causing bacterium. —**mi'crobial** *or* **mi'crobic** *adj.*

microbiology (ˌmaɪkrəʊbaɪ'ɒlədʒɪ) *n.* the branch of biology involving the study of microorganisms.

microchemistry (ˌmaɪkrəʊ'kemɪstrɪ) *n.* chemical experimentation with minute quantities of material.

microchip ('maɪkrəʊˌtʃɪp) *n.* same as **chip** (sense 6).

microcircuit ('maɪkrəʊˌsɜːkɪt) *n.* a miniature electronic circuit in which a number of permanently connected components are contained in one small chip of semiconducting material.

microcomputer (ˌmaɪkrəʊkəm'pjuːtə) *n.* a computer in which the central processing unit is contained in one or more silicon chips.

microcosm ('maɪkrəʊˌkɒzəm) *n.* **1.** a miniature representation of something. **2.** man regarded as epitomizing the universe. —ˌmicro'cosmic *adj.*

microdot ('maɪkrəʊˌdɒt) *n.* a greatly reduced photographic copy (about the size of a pinhead) of a document.

microelectronics (ˌmaɪkrəʊɪlek'trɒnɪks) *n.* (*functioning as sing.*) the branch of electronics concerned with microcircuits.

microfiche ('maɪkrəʊˌfiːʃ) *n.* a sheet of film, usually the size of a filing card, on which publications can be recorded in miniaturized form.

microfilm ('maɪkrəʊˌfɪlm) *n.* **1.** a strip of film on which books or documents can be recorded in miniaturized form. ~*vb.* **2.** to photograph (a page or document) on microfilm.

microlight ('maɪkrəʊˌlaɪt) *n.* a very small private aircraft with large wings.

micrometer (maɪ'krɒmɪtə) *n.* an instrument for the accurate measurement of small distances or angles.

microminiaturization *or* **-isation** (ˌmaɪkrəʊˌmɪnɪtʃəraɪ'zeɪʃən) *n.* the production and use of very small electronic components.

micron ('maɪkrɒn) *n.* a unit of length equal to one millionth of a metre.

microorganism (ˌmaɪkrəʊ'ɔːgəˌnɪzəm) *n.* any organism, such as a virus or bacterium, of microscopic size.

microphone ('maɪkrəˌfəʊn) *n.* a device for converting sound into electrical energy.

microprocessor (ˌmaɪkrəʊ'prəʊsesə) *n. Computers.* a single integrated circuit which acts as the central processing unit in a small computer.

microscope ('maɪkrəˌskəʊp) *n.* **1.** an optical instrument that uses a lens or combination of lenses to produce a magnified image of a small, close object. **2.** any instrument,

such as the electron microscope, for producing a magnified visual image of a small object.

microscopic (ˌmaɪkrə'skɒpɪk) *adj.* **1.** too small to be seen except with a microscope. **2.** very small; minute. **3.** of or using a microscope. —ˌmicro'scopically *adv.*

microsecond ('maɪkrəʊˌsekənd) *n.* one millionth of a second.

microstructure ('maɪkrəʊˌstrʌktʃə) *n.* structure on a microscopic scale, such as that of a metal or a cell.

microsurgery (ˌmaɪkrəʊ'sɜːdʒərɪ) *n.* intricate surgery performed using a special microscope and miniature precision instruments.

microwave ('maɪkrəʊˌweɪv) *n.* **1.** electromagnetic radiation in the wavelength range 0.3 to 0.001 metres: used in radar and cooking. **2.** short for **microwave oven**. ~*vb.* **3.** to cook in a microwave oven.

microwave detector *n. N.Z.* a device used by police for recording the speed of a motorist.

microwave oven *n.* an oven which uses microwaves to cook food quickly.

micturate ('mɪktjʊˌreɪt) *vb.* to urinate. —**micturition** (ˌmɪktjʊ'rɪʃən) *n.*

mid[1] (mɪd) *n. Archaic.* the middle.

mid[2] *or* **'mid** (mɪd) *prep. Poetic.* amid.

mid- *combining form.* indicating a middle part, point, time, or position: *midday; mid-April; mid-Victorian.*

midair (ˌmɪd'ɛə) *n.* some point above ground level, in the air.

midday ('mɪd'deɪ) *n.* the middle of the day; noon.

midden ('mɪd³n) *n. Archaic or dialect.* a dunghill or pile of refuse.

middle ('mɪd³l) *adj.* **1.** equally distant from the ends or outer edge of something; central. **2.** intermediate in status or situation: *middle management.* **3.** between the early and late parts of a time sequence. **4.** not extreme, esp. in size; medium. ~*n.* **5.** an area or point equal in distance from the ends or edge or in time between the early and late parts. **6.** an intermediate part or section, such as the waist.

middle age *n.* the period of life between youth and old age, usually considered to occur between the ages of 40 and 60. —ˌmiddle-'aged *adj.*

Middle Ages *n.* **the.** *European history.* **1.** (broadly) the period from the fall of the W Roman Empire in 476 A.D. to the Italian Renaissance. **2.** (narrowly) the period from about 1000 A.D. to the 15th century.

Middle America *n.* the U.S. middle class, esp. those groups that are politically conservative.

middlebrow ('mɪd³lˌbraʊ) *Disparaging.* ~*n.* **1.** a person with conventional tastes

and limited cultural appreciation. ~*adj.*
2. of or appealing to middlebrows.

middle C *n. Music.* the note written on the first ledger line below the treble staff or the first ledger line above the bass staff.

middle class *n.* **1.** the social class between the working and upper classes. It consists of business and professional people. ~*adj.* **middle-class. 2.** of or characteristic of the middle class.

middle ear *n.* the sound-conducting part of the ear immediately inside the eardrum.

Middle East *n.* the area around the E Mediterranean, esp. Israel and the Arab countries from Turkey to North Africa and eastwards to Iran. —**Middle Eastern** *adj.*

Middle English *n.* the English language from about 1100 to about 1450.

Middle High German *n.* High German from about 1200 to about 1500.

Middle Low German *n.* Low German from about 1200 to about 1500.

middleman (ˈmɪd²lˌmæn) *n., pl.* **-men. 1.** a trader engaged in the distribution of goods from producer to consumer. **2.** an intermediary.

middle name *n.* **1.** a name between a person's first name and surname. **2.** a characteristic quality for which a person is known: *caution is my middle name.*

middle-of-the-road *adj.* **1.** not extreme, esp. in political views; moderate. **2.** of or denoting popular music of wide general appeal.

middle school *n. Brit.* a school for children aged between 8 or 9 and 12 or 13.

middleweight (ˈmɪd²lˌweɪt) *n.* **1.** a professional boxer weighing up to 160 pounds or an amateur weighing up to 75 kg. **2.** a professional wrestler weighing up to 176 pounds or an amateur weighing up to 82 kg.

middling (ˈmɪdlɪŋ) *adj.* **1.** mediocre in quality or size. **2. fair to middling.** neither good nor bad, esp. in health. ~*adv.* **3.** *Informal.* moderately: *middling well.*

Middx. Middlesex.

midfield (ˌmɪdˈfiːld) *n. Soccer.* the area between the two opposing defences.

midge (mɪdʒ) *n.* a mosquito-like insect occurring in dancing swarms, esp. near water. —ˈ**midgy** *adj.*

midget (ˈmɪdʒɪt) *n.* **1.** a dwarf whose skeleton and features are of normal proportions. **2.** something small of its kind.

mid-heavyweight *n.* a professional wrestler weighing up to 209 pounds or an amateur weighing up to 100kg.

midi- *combining form.* of medium or middle size or length: *midibus.*

midi system (ˈmɪdɪ) *n.* a complete set of compact hi-fi sound equipment designed as a single unit.

midland (ˈmɪdlənd) *adj.* the central or inland part of a country.

Midlands (ˈmɪdləndz) *n.* (*functioning as pl. or sing.*) **the.** the central counties of England.

midmost (ˈmɪdˌməʊst) *adj., adv.* in the middle or midst.

midnight (ˈmɪdˌnaɪt) *n.* **1.** the middle of the night; 12 o'clock at night. **2. burn the midnight oil.** to work or study late into the night.

midnight sun *n.* the sun visible at midnight during the summer inside the Arctic and Antarctic circles.

mid-off *n. Cricket.* the fielding position on the off side closest to the bowler.

mid-on *n. Cricket.* the fielding position on the on side closest to the bowler.

midpoint (ˈmɪdˌpɔɪnt) *n.* **1.** the point on a line equally distant from either end. **2.** a point in time halfway between the beginning and end of an event.

midriff (ˈmɪdrɪf) *n.* **1.** the middle part of the human body between waist and chest. **2.** *Anat.* same as **diaphragm** (sense 1).

midshipman (ˈmɪdˌʃɪpmən) *n., pl.* **-men.** a junior naval officer.

midships (ˈmɪdˌʃɪps) *adv., adj. Naut.* See **amidships.**

midst (mɪdst) *n.* **1. in our midst.** among us. **2. in the midst of.** surrounded by; at a point during.

midsummer (ˈmɪdˈsʌmə) *n.* **1.** the middle or height of summer. **2.** same as **summer solstice.**

Midsummer Day *or* **Midsummer's Day** *n.* June 24, the feast of St John the Baptist; in England, Ireland, and Wales, one of the four quarter days.

midway *adj.* (ˈmɪdˌweɪ). **1.** in or at the middle of the distance; halfway. ~*adv.* (ˌmɪdˈweɪ). **2.** to the middle of the distance.

midweek (ˈmɪdˈwiːk) *n.* the middle of the week.

Midwest (ˈmɪdˈwɛst) *n.* the N central part of the U.S. —ˈ**Mid**ˈ**western** *adj.*

mid-wicket *n. Cricket.* the fielding position on the on side, roughly the same distance from both wickets, and halfway towards the boundary.

midwife (ˈmɪdˌwaɪf) *n., pl.* **-wives** (-ˌwaɪvz). a nurse qualified to deliver babies and to care for women before, during, and after childbirth. —**midwifery** (ˈmɪdˌwɪfərɪ) *n.*

midwinter (ˈmɪdˈwɪntə) *n.* **1.** the middle or depth of winter. **2.** same as **winter solstice.**

mien (miːn) *n. Literary.* a person's manner, bearing, or appearance.

miff (mɪf) *vb. Informal.* to take offence or offend. —**miffed** *adj.*

might¹ (maɪt) *vb.* used as an auxiliary: **1.** making the past tense or subjunctive mood of **may**[1]: *he might have come.* **2.** (often foll. by *well*) expressing possibility: *he might well come.* In this sense *might* looks to the future and functions as a weak form of *may.* See **may**[1] (sense 2).

might[2] (maɪt) *n.* **1.** great power, strength, or vigour. **2.** (**with**) **might and main.** See **main.**

mighty ('maɪtɪ) *adj.* **mightier, mightiest. 1.** powerful or strong. **2.** very large; vast. **3.** very great in extent or importance. ~*adv.* **4.** *Informal, chiefly U.S. & Canad.* very: *mighty tired.* —'**mightily** *adv.* —'**mightiness** *n.*

mignonette (,mɪnjə'nɛt) *n.* a plant with spikes of small fragrant greenish-white flowers.

migraine ('miːgreɪn, 'maɪ-) *n.* a throbbing headache usually affecting only one side of the head and commonly accompanied by nausea and visual disturbances.

migrant ('maɪgrənt) *n.* **1.** a person or animal that moves from one place to another. ~*adj.* **2.** moving from one place to another: *migrant workers.*

migrate (maɪ'greɪt) *vb.* **1.** to go from one place to settle in another, esp. in a foreign country. **2.** (of living creatures, esp. birds) to journey between different habitats at specific times of the year. —**mi'gration** *n.* —**migratory** ('maɪgrətrɪ) *adj.*

mikado (mɪ'kɑːdəʊ) *n., pl.* -**dos.** (often *cap.*) *Archaic.* the Japanese emperor.

mike (maɪk) *n. Informal.* a microphone.

mil (mɪl) *n.* **1.** a unit of length equal to one thousandth of an inch. **2.** *Photog.* short for **millimetre:** *35-mil film.*

milady (mɪ'leɪdɪ) *n., pl.* -**dies.** (formerly) a continental title for an English gentlewoman.

milch (mɪltʃ) *n. modifier* (esp. of cattle) yielding milk.

mild (maɪld) *adj.* **1.** (of a taste or sensation) not strong; bland. **2.** gentle or temperate in character, climate, or behaviour. **3.** not extreme; moderate: *mild amusement.* **4.** feeble; unassertive: *a mild protest.* ~*n.* **5.** *Brit.* a dark beer flavoured with fewer hops than bitter.

mildew ('mɪl,djuː) *n.* **1.** a disease of plants caused by a parasitic fungus. **2.** same as **mould**[2]. ~*vb.* **3.** to affect or become affected with mildew. —'**mil,dewy** *adj.*

mild steel *n.* strong tough steel containing a small quantity of carbon.

mile (maɪl) *n.* **1.** Also: **statute mile.** a unit of length used in English-speaking countries, equal to 1760 yards. 1 mile is equivalent to 1.60934 kilometres. **2.** See **nautical mile. 3.** (often *pl.*) *Informal.* a great distance; great deal: *he missed by a mile.* **4.** a race extending over a mile. ~*adv.* **5. miles.** very much: *that's miles better.*

mileage ('maɪlɪdʒ) *n.* **1.** a distance expressed in miles. **2.** the total number of miles that a motor vehicle has travelled. **3.** the number of miles a motor vehicle will travel on one gallon of fuel. **4.** *Informal.* use, benefit, or service provided by something.

mileometer *or* **milometer** (maɪ'lɒmɪtə) *n.* a device that records the number of miles that a vehicle has travelled.

milepost ('maɪl,pəʊst) *n. Chiefly U.S. & Canad.* a signpost that shows the distance in miles to or from a place.

miler ('maɪlə) *n.* an athlete, horse, etc., that runs or specializes in races of one mile.

milestone ('maɪl,stəʊn) *n.* **1.** a stone pillar that shows the distance in miles to or from a place. **2.** a significant event in a life or history.

milfoil ('mɪl,fɔɪl) *n.* same as **yarrow.**

milieu ('miːljɜː) *n., pl.* **milieus** *or* **milieux** ('miːljɜːz). surroundings, location, or setting.

militant ('mɪlɪtənt) *adj.* **1.** aggressive or vigorous, esp. in the support of a cause. **2.** warring; engaged in warfare. ~*n.* **3.** a militant person. —'**militancy** *n.* —'**militantly** *adv.*

militarism ('mɪlɪtə,rɪzəm) *n.* **1.** military spirit; pursuit of military ideals. **2.** a belief in maintaining a strong military organization in aggressive readiness for war. —'**militarist** *n.*

military ('mɪlɪtrɪ) *adj.* **1.** of or relating to the armed forces or war. **2.** of or characteristic of soldiers. ~*n., pl.* -**taries** *or* -**tary. 3.** (preceded by *the*) the armed services, esp. the army. —'**militarily** *adv.*

military police *n.* a corps within an army that performs police duties.

militate ('mɪlɪ,teɪt) *vb.* (usually foll. by *against* or *for*) (of facts or events) to have influence or effect: *the evidence militated against his release.*

militia (mɪ'lɪʃə) *n.* a body of citizen (as opposed to professional) soldiers enlisted for service in emergency only. —**mi'litiaman** *n.*

milk (mɪlk) *n.* **1. a.** a whitish fluid secreted by the mammary glands of mature female mammals and used for feeding their young. **b.** the milk of cows, goats, etc., used by man as a food. **2.** any similar fluid, such as the juice of a coconut. ~*vb.* **3.** to draw milk from the udder of (an animal). **4.** to extract as much money, help, or value as possible from: *to milk a situation of its news value.* —'**milker** *n.* —'**milkiness** *n.* —'**milky** *adj.*

milk-and-water *adj.* weak, feeble, or insipid.

milk bar *n.* a snack bar at which milk drinks and light refreshments are served.

milk chocolate *n.* chocolate that has

been made with milk, having a creamy taste.

milk float *n. Brit.* a small electrically powered vehicle used to deliver milk to houses.

milkmaid ('mɪlk,meɪd) *n.* a girl or woman who milks cows.

milkman ('mɪlkmən) *n., pl.* **-men.** a man who delivers milk to people's houses.

milk of magnesia *n.* a suspension of magnesium hydroxide in water, used as an antacid and laxative.

milk pudding *n. Chiefly Brit.* a pudding made by cooking milk with a grain, esp. rice.

milk round *n. Brit.* **1.** a route along which a milkman regularly delivers milk. **2.** a regular series of visits, esp. as made by recruitment officers from industry to colleges.

milk run *n. Aeronautics, informal.* a routine and uneventful flight.

milk shake *n.* a cold frothy drink made of milk, flavouring, and sometimes ice cream, whisked together.

milksop ('mɪlk,sɒp) *n.* a feeble or ineffectual man or youth.

milk tooth *n.* any of the first teeth to come through; a baby tooth.

Milky Way *n.* **the.** the diffuse band of light stretching across the night sky that consists of millions of distant stars.

mill (mɪl) *n.* **1.** a factory. **2.** any of various processing or manufacturing machines, esp. one that grinds, presses, or rolls. **3.** a small device for grinding solids: *a pepper mill.* **4. go or be put through the mill.** to have an unpleasant experience or ordeal. ~*vb.* **5.** to grind, press, or otherwise process in or as if in a mill. **6.** to groove or flute the edge of (a coin). **7.** (often foll. by *about* or *around*) to move about in a confused manner.

millennium (mɪ'lɛnɪəm) *n., pl.* **-niums** or **-nia** (-nɪə). **1. the.** *Christianity.* the period of a thousand years of Christ's awaited reign upon earth. **2.** any period of one thousand years. **3.** a time of peace and happiness, esp. in the distant future. —**mil'lennial** *adj.*

millepede ('mɪlɪ,piːd) *n.* same as **millipede.**

miller ('mɪlə) *n.* a person who keeps, operates, or works in a mill, esp. a corn mill.

miller's thumb *n.* a small freshwater European fish with a flattened body.

millesimal (mɪ'lɛsɪməl) *adj.* **1. a.** denoting a thousandth. **b.** (*as n.*): *a millesimal.* **2.** of or consisting of a thousandth.

millet ('mɪlɪt) *n.* a cereal grass cultivated for its edible grain and as animal fodder.

milli- *prefix.* denoting 10^{-3}: *millimetre.*

milliard ('mɪljɑːd) *n. Brit.* (no longer in technical use) a thousand million.

millibar ('mɪlɪ,bɑː) *n.* a unit of atmospheric pressure equal to 100 newtons per square metre.

milligram or **milligramme** ('mɪlɪ,græm) *n.* one thousandth of a gram.

millilitre or *U.S.* **milliliter** ('mɪlɪ,liːtə) *n.* one thousandth of a litre.

millimetre or *U.S.* **millimeter** ('mɪlɪ,miːtə) *n.* one thousandth of a metre.

milliner ('mɪlɪnə) *n.* a person who makes or sells women's hats. —**'millinery** *n.*

million ('mɪljən) *n., pl.* **-lions** or **-lion. 1.** the cardinal number that is the product of 1000 multiplied by 1000: 1 000 000; 10^6. **2.** (*often pl.*) *Informal.* an extremely large but unspecified number: *I have millions of things to do.* —**'millionth** *n., adj.*

millionaire (,mɪljə'nɛə) *n.* a person whose assets are worth at least a million of the standard monetary units of his country. —,**million'airess** *fem. n.*

millipede or **millepede** ('mɪlɪ,piːd) *n.* a small crawling animal with a cylindrical many-segmented body, each segment of which bears two pairs of legs.

millisecond ('mɪlɪ,sɛkənd) *n.* one thousandth of a second.

millpond ('mɪl,pɒnd) *n.* a pool which provides water to turn a millwheel.

millrace ('mɪl,reɪs) *n.* the current of water that turns a millwheel.

millstone ('mɪl,stəʊn) *n.* **1.** one of a pair of heavy flat stones that are rotated one against the other to grind grain. **2.** a heavy burden, such as a responsibility or obligation.

millstream ('mɪl,striːm) *n.* a stream of water used to turn a millwheel.

millwheel ('mɪl,wiːl) *n.* a wheel, esp. a waterwheel, that drives a mill.

milometer (maɪ'lɒmɪtə) *n.* same as **mileometer.**

milord (mɪ'lɔːd) *n.* (formerly) a continental title used for an English gentleman.

milt (mɪlt) *n.* the testis, sperm, or semen of a fish.

mime (maɪm) *n.* **1.** a theatrical technique of acting using only gesture and bodily movement and not words. **2.** a performer specializing in this. **3.** a dramatic presentation using such a technique. ~*vb.* **4.** to express (an idea or message) in actions or gestures without speech. **5.** (of musicians) to perform as if singing or playing music that is actually prerecorded. —**'mimer** *n.*

Mimeograph ('mɪmɪə,grɑːf) *n.* **1.** *Trademark.* an office machine for printing multiple copies from a stencil. ~*vb.* **2.** to print copies using this machine.

mimetic (mɪ'mɛtɪk) *adj.* **1.** of or relating to imitation. **2.** *Biol.* of or showing mimicry.

mimic ('mɪmɪk) *vb.* **-icking, -icked. 1.** to imitate (a person or manner), esp. for satirical effect; ape. **2.** to take on the appearance of: *certain flies mimic wasps.* **3.** to copy closely or in a servile manner. ~*n.* **4.** a person or an animal, such as a parrot, that is clever at mimicking.

mimicry ('mɪmɪkrɪ) *n., pl.* **-ries. 1.** the act or art of copying or imitating closely; mimicking. **2.** *Biol.* the resemblance shown by one animal species to another, which protects it from predators.

mimosa (mɪ'məʊsə, -zə) *n.* a tropical shrub with ball-like clusters of typically yellow flowers.

min. 1. minimum. **2.** minute *or* minutes.

Min. 1. Minister. **2.** Ministry.

mina ('maɪnə) *n.* same as **myna.**

minaret (ˌmɪnə'rɛt, 'mɪnəˌrɛt) *n.* a slender tower of a mosque with one or more balconies.

minatory ('mɪnətrɪ) *adj.* threatening or menacing.

mince (mɪns) *vb.* **1.** to chop, grind, or cut into very small pieces. **2.** to soften or moderate: *I didn't mince my words.* **3.** to walk or speak in an affected dainty manner. ~*n.* **4.** *Chiefly Brit.* minced meat. —'**mincer** *n.*

mincemeat ('mɪnsˌmiːt) *n.* **1.** a mixture of dried fruit and spices used esp. for filling pies. **2. make mincemeat of.** *Informal.* to defeat completely.

mince pie *n.* a small round pastry tart filled with mincemeat.

mincing ('mɪnsɪŋ) *adj.* (of a person) affectedly elegant in gait, manner, or speech.

mind (maɪnd) *n.* **1.** the part of a person responsible for thought, feelings, and intention. **2.** intelligence as opposed to feelings or wishes. **3.** recollection or remembrance: *it comes to mind.* **4.** a person considered as an intellectual being: *great minds.* **5.** condition, state, or manner of feeling or thought: *a depressed state of mind.* **6.** an inclination, desire, or purpose: *I have a mind to go.* **7.** attention or thoughts: *keep your mind on your work.* **8.** a sound mental state; sanity: *she's out of her mind.* **9. change one's mind.** to alter one's decision or opinion. **10. in two minds.** undecided; wavering. **11. make up one's mind.** to decide (something or to do something). **12. on one's mind.** in one's thoughts. ~*vb.* **13.** to take offence at: *do you mind if I smoke?* **14.** to pay attention to (something): *to mind one's own business.* **15.** to make certain; ensure: *mind you tell her.* **16.** to take care of: *mind the shop.* **17.** to be cautious or careful about (something): *mind how you go.* ~See also **mind out.**

minded ('maɪndɪd) *adj.* having a mind, inclination, or intention as specified: *politically minded.*

minder ('maɪndə) *n.* **1.** *Slang.* an aide or assistant, esp. one employed as a bodyguard or public relations officer for someone. **2.** short for **child minder.**

mindful ('maɪndfʊl) *adj.* (usually foll. by *of*)

keeping aware; heedful: *mindful of your duty.*

mindless ('maɪndlɪs) *adj.* **1.** stupid or careless. **2.** requiring little or no intellectual effort. **3.** heedless: *mindless of the danger.* —'**mindlessly** *adv.* —'**mindlessness** *n.*

mind out *vb. Brit.* to be careful or pay attention.

mind-reader *n.* a person seemingly able to make out the thoughts of another.

mind's eye *n.* the imagination.

mine[1] (maɪn) *pron.* **1.** something or someone belonging to or associated with me: *mine is best.* **2. of mine.** belonging to or associated with me. ~*det.* **3.** *Archaic.* same as **my:** *mine eyes; mine host.*

mine[2] (maɪn) *n.* **1.** a place where minerals, esp. coal, ores, or precious stones are dug from the ground. **2.** any deposit of ore or minerals. **3.** a lucrative source or abundant supply: *a mine of information.* **4.** a type of bomb designed to destroy ships, vehicles, or personnel, usually laid beneath the ground or in water. ~*vb.* **5.** to dig into (the earth) for (minerals). **6.** to dig (minerals) from the ground. **7.** to make (a hole or tunnel) by digging or boring. **8.** to place explosive mines in position below the surface of (the sea or land).

mine dump *n. S. African.* a large mound of residue, esp. from gold-mining operations.

minefield ('maɪnˌfiːld) *n.* **1.** an area of ground or water containing explosive mines. **2.** a subject or situation full of hidden problems.

minelayer ('maɪnˌleɪə) *n.* a warship or aircraft for carrying and laying mines.

miner ('maɪnə) *n.* a person who works in a mine, esp. a coal mine.

mineral ('mɪnərəl, 'mɪnrəl) *n.* **1.** a naturally occurring solid inorganic substance with a characteristic chemical composition and structure. **2.** any inorganic matter. **3.** any substance obtained by mining, esp. a metal ore. **4.** (*often pl.*) *Brit.* short for **mineral water. 5.** *Brit.* a soft drink containing carbonated water and flavourings. ~*adj.* **6.** of, containing, or resembling minerals.

mineral acid *n.* any acid which can be produced from a mineral.

mineralogy (ˌmɪnə'rælədʒɪ) *n.* the scientific study of minerals. —**mineralogical** (ˌmɪnərə'lɒdʒɪkᵊl) *adj.* —ˌminer'alogist *n.*

mineral water *n.* water containing dissolved mineral salts or gases.

minestrone (ˌmɪnɪ'strəʊnɪ) *n.* a soup made from a variety of vegetables and pasta.

minesweeper ('maɪnˌswiːpə) *n.* a naval vessel equipped to clear mines.

Ming (mɪŋ) *adj.* of or relating to Chinese porcelain from the time of the Ming dynasty, which ruled China from 1368 to 1644.

mingle (ˈmɪŋgˀl) vb. **1.** to mix or cause to mix. **2.** (often foll. by *with*) to come into close association.

mingy (ˈmɪndʒɪ) adj. **-gier, -giest.** *Brit. informal.* miserly or niggardly.

mini (ˈmɪnɪ) adj. **1.** small; miniature. **2.** (of a skirt or dress) very short; thigh-length. ~n., pl. **minis. 3.** something very small of its kind, esp. a miniskirt.

mini- *combining form.* smaller or shorter than the standard size: *minibus; miniskirt.*

miniature (ˈmɪnɪtʃə) n. **1.** a model or representation on a very small scale. **2.** a very small painting, esp. a portrait. **3. in miniature.** on a small scale. ~adj. **4.** greatly reduced in size. **5.** on a small scale. —ˈminiaturist n.

miniaturize or **-ise** (ˈmɪnɪtʃəˌraɪz) vb. to make or construct (something, esp. electronic components) to a very small size.

minibus (ˈmɪnɪˌbʌs) n. a small bus.

minicab (ˈmɪnɪˌkæb) n. *Brit.* an ordinary car used as a taxi.

minicomputer (ˌmɪnɪkəmˈpjuːtə) n. a small digital computer which is more powerful than a microcomputer.

minim (ˈmɪnɪm) n. **1.** a unit of fluid measure equal to one sixtieth of a drachm; a drop. **2.** *Music.* a note with the time value of half a semibreve.

minimalism (ˈmɪnɪməˌlɪzəm) n. **1.** a type of music based on the repetition of simple elements. **2.** design or style using the simplest and fewest elements to create the maximum effect. —ˈminimalist adj., n.

minimize or **-ise** (ˈmɪnɪˌmaɪz) vb. **1.** to reduce to or estimate at the least possible degree or amount. **2.** to rank or treat at less than the true worth; belittle.

minimum (ˈmɪnɪməm) n., pl. **-mums** or **-ma** (-mə). **1.** the least possible amount, degree, or quantity. **2.** the least amount recorded, allowed, or reached. **3.** (*modifier*) being the least possible, recorded, or allowed: *minimum age.* ~adj. **4.** of or relating to a minimum or minimums. —ˈminimal adj. —ˈminimally adv.

minimum lending rate n. the minimum rate at which a central bank, such as the Bank of England, will lend money.

minimum wage n. the lowest wage that an employer is permitted to pay by law or union contract.

mining (ˈmaɪnɪŋ) n. **1.** the act, process, or industry of extracting coal or ores from the earth. **2.** *Mil.* the process of laying mines.

minion (ˈmɪnjən) n. a servile follower or subordinate.

miniseries (ˈmɪnɪˌsɪəriːz) n., pl. **-series.** a television programme in several parts that is shown on consecutive days over a short period.

miniskirt (ˈmɪnɪˌskɜːt) n. a very short skirt.

minister (ˈmɪnɪstə) n. **1.** (esp. in Presbyter-

ian and some Nonconformist Churches) a clergyman. **2.** a head of a government department. **3.** any diplomatic agent accredited to a foreign government or head of state. **4.** a person who acts as the agent or servant of a person or thing. ~vb. **5.** (often foll. by *to*) to attend to the needs (of); take care (of). —**ministerial** (ˌmɪnɪˈstɪərɪəl) adj.

minister of state n. (in the British Parliament) a minister, usually below cabinet rank, appointed to assist a senior minister.

Minister of the Crown n. *Brit.* any Government minister of cabinet rank.

ministration (ˌmɪnɪˈstreɪʃən) n. **1.** the act or an instance of serving or giving aid. **2.** the act or an instance of ministering religiously.

ministry (ˈmɪnɪstrɪ) n., pl. **-tries. 1.** the profession or duties of a minister of religion. **2.** ministers considered as a group. **3.** the tenure of a minister. **4. a.** a government department headed by a minister. **b.** the buildings of such a department.

mink (mɪŋk) n., pl. **mink** or **minks. 1.** a mammal of Europe, Asia, and North America, resembling a large stoat. **2.** its highly valued fur. **3.** a garment made of this, esp. a woman's coat or stole.

Minn. Minnesota.

minneola (ˌmɪnɪˈəʊlə) n. a juicy citrus fruit that is a cross between a tangerine and a grapefruit.

minnow (ˈmɪnəʊ) n., pl. **-nows** or **-now.** a small slender European freshwater fish.

Minoan (mɪˈnəʊən) adj. of or denoting the Bronze Age culture of Crete from about 3000 B.C. to about 1100 B.C.

minor (ˈmaɪnə) adj. **1.** lesser or secondary in amount or importance. **2.** below the age of legal majority. **3.** *Music.* **a.** (of a scale) having a semitone between the second and third and fifth and sixth degrees (**natural minor**). **b.** relating to or employing notes from the minor scale: *the key of D minor; minor seventh.* ~n. **4.** a person below the age of legal majority. **5.** *U.S. & Canad. education.* a subsidiary subject. **6.** *Music.* a minor key, chord, mode, or scale. ~vb. **7.** (usually foll. by *in*) *U.S. education.* to take a minor.

minority (maɪˈnɒrɪtɪ, mɪ-) n., pl. **-ties. 1.** the smaller of two parts, factions, or groups. **2.** a group that is different, esp. racially or politically, from a larger group of which it is a part. **3. a.** the state of being a minor. **b.** the period during which a person is below legal age. **4.** (*modifier*) relating to or being a minority: *a minority opinion.*

minster (ˈmɪnstə) n. *Brit.* any of certain cathedrals and large churches, usually originally connected to a monastery.

minstrel (ˈmɪnstrəl) n. **1.** a medieval singer

and musician. **2.** a performer in a minstrel show.

minstrel show *n.* a theatrical entertainment consisting of songs and dances performed by actors wearing black face make-up.

mint[1] (mɪnt) *n.* **1.** any of various plants with aromatic leaves used for seasoning and flavouring. **2.** a sweet flavoured with mint. —**'minty** *adj.*

mint[2] (mɪnt) *n.* **1.** a place where money is coined by governmental authority. **2.** a very large amount of money. ~*adj.* **3. in mint condition.** in perfect condition; as if new. ~*vb.* **4.** to make (coins) by stamping metal. **5.** to invent (esp. phrases or words).

minuet (ˌmɪnjʊ'ɛt) *n.* **1.** a stately court dance of the 17th and 18th centuries in triple time. **2.** music for this dance.

minus ('maɪnəs) *prep.* **1.** reduced by the subtraction of: *four minus two* (written 4 – 2). **2.** *Informal.* deprived of; lacking: *minus the trimmings.* ~*adj.* **3. a.** indicating or involving subtraction: *a minus sign.* **b.** Also: **negative.** less than zero: *a minus number.* **4.** *Education.* slightly below the standard of a particular grade: *a B minus.* **5.** denoting a negative electric charge. ~*n.* **6.** short for **minus sign. 7.** a negative quantity. **8.** *Informal.* something detrimental or negative.

minuscule ('mɪnəˌskjuːl) *adj.* very small.

minus sign *n.* the symbol –, indicating subtraction or a negative quantity.

minute[1] ('mɪnɪt) *n.* **1.** 60 seconds; one sixtieth of an hour. **2.** a measure of angle equal to one sixtieth of a degree. **3.** any very short period of time; moment. **4.** the distance that can be travelled in a minute: *it's only two minutes away.* **5. up to the minute.** the very latest or newest. ~*vb.* **6.** to record in minutes: *to minute a meeting.* ~See also **minutes.**

minute[2] (maɪ'njuːt) *adj.* **1.** very small; tiny. **2.** unimportant; petty. **3.** precise or detailed. —**mi'nutely** *adv.*

minutes ('mɪnɪts) *pl. n.* an official record of the proceedings of a meeting or conference.

minute steak ('mɪnɪt) *n.* a small piece of steak that can be cooked quickly.

minutiae (mɪ'njuːʃɪˌiː) *pl. n., sing.* **-tia** (-ʃɪə). small, precise, or trifling details.

minx (mɪŋks) *n.* a bold, flirtatious, or scheming woman.

Miocene ('maɪəˌsiːn) *adj. Geol.* of the epoch of geological time about 25 million years ago.

miracle ('mɪrək³l) *n.* **1.** an event contrary to the laws of nature and attributed to a supernatural cause. **2.** any amazing or wonderful event. **3.** a marvellous example of something: *a miracle of engineering.*

miracle play *n.* a medieval play based on a biblical story or the life of a saint.

miraculous (mɪ'rækjʊləs) *adj.* **1.** like a miracle; marvellous. **2.** surprising or remarkable.

mirage (mɪ'rɑːʒ) *n.* **1.** an image of a distant object or sheet of water, often inverted or distorted, caused by atmospheric refraction by hot air. **2.** something illusory.

mire ('maɪə) *n.* **1.** a boggy or marshy area. **2.** mud, muck, or dirt. ~*vb.* **3.** to sink or cause to sink in a mire. **4.** to make dirty or muddy.

mirror ('mɪrə) *n.* **1.** a surface, such as glass coated with a metal film, that reflects an image of an object placed in front of it. **2.** a thing that reflects or depicts something else. ~*vb.* **3.** to reflect, represent, or depict faithfully: *he mirrors his teacher's ideals.*

mirror ball *n.* a large revolving ball covered with small pieces of mirror glass so that it reflects light in changing patterns: used in discos and ballrooms.

mirror image *n.* an image or object that has left and right reversed as if seen in a mirror.

mirth (mɜːθ) *n.* laughter, gaiety, or merriment. —**'mirthful** *adj.* —**'mirthless** *adj.*

MIRV (mɜːv) multiple independently targeted re-entry vehicle: a missile that has several warheads, each one being aimed at a different target.

mis- *prefix.* **1.** wrong or bad; wrongly or badly: *misunderstanding; mislead.* **2.** lack of; not: *mistrust.*

misadventure (ˌmɪsəd'vɛntʃə) *n.* **1.** an unlucky event; misfortune. **2.** *Law.* accidental death not due to crime or negligence.

misaligned (ˌmɪsə'laɪnd) *adj.* not properly aligned; out of true. —**misa'lignment** *n.*

misalliance (ˌmɪsə'laɪəns) *n.* an unsuitable alliance or marriage.

misanthrope ('mɪzənˌθrəʊp) *or* **misanthropist** (mɪ'zænθrəpɪst) *n.* a person who dislikes or distrusts people in general. —**misanthropic** (ˌmɪzən'θrɒpɪk) *adj.* —**misanthropy** (mɪ'zænθrəpɪ) *n.*

misapply (ˌmɪsə'plaɪ) *vb.* **-plying, -plied.** to apply wrongly or badly. —**misapplication** (ˌmɪsæplɪ'keɪʃən) *n.*

misapprehend (ˌmɪsæprɪ'hɛnd) *vb.* to misunderstand. —**misapprehension** (ˌmɪsæprɪ'hɛnʃən) *n.*

misappropriate (ˌmɪsə'prəʊprɪˌeɪt) *vb.* to take (money) for a wrong or dishonest use; embezzle or steal. —**misap,propri'ation** *n.*

misbegotten (ˌmɪsbɪ'gɒt³n) *adj.* **1.** conceived, planned, or designed badly or with dishonourable motives or aims. **2.** *Literary or dialect.* illegitimate; bastard.

misbehave (ˌmɪsbɪ'heɪv) *vb.* to behave badly. —**misbehaviour** *or U.S.* **misbehavior** (ˌmɪsbɪ'heɪvjə) *n.*

miscalculate (ˌmɪs'kælkjʊˌleɪt) *vb.* to calculate wrongly. —**miscalcu'lation** *n.*

miscall (ˌmɪsˈkɔːl) *vb.* to call by the wrong name.

miscarriage (mɪsˈkærɪdʒ) *n.* **1.** (*also* ˈmɪskær-). spontaneous expulsion of a fetus from the womb, esp. before the 20th week of pregnancy. **2.** an act of mismanagement or failure: *a miscarriage of justice.*

miscarry (mɪsˈkærɪ) *vb.* **-rying, -ried.** **1.** to expel a fetus prematurely from the womb. **2.** to fail.

miscast (ˌmɪsˈkɑːst) *vb.* **-casting, -cast.** (*often passive*) to cast (a role or an actor) in (a play or film) inappropriately: *Falstaff was miscast; he was miscast as Othello.*

miscegenation (ˌmɪsɪdʒɪˈneɪʃən) *n.* interbreeding of races, esp. where differences of colour are involved.

miscellaneous (ˌmɪsəˈleɪnɪəs) *adj.* composed of or containing a variety of things; mixed.

miscellany (mɪˈsɛlənɪ; *U.S.* ˈmɪsəˌleɪnɪ) *n., pl.* **-nies.** (*sometimes pl.*) a miscellaneous collection of items, esp. essays or poems.

mischance (mɪsˈtʃɑːns) *n.* **1.** bad luck. **2.** a stroke of bad luck.

mischief (ˈmɪstʃɪf) *n.* **1.** wayward but not malicious behaviour that causes trouble or irritation. **2.** a playful inclination to behave in this way. **3.** injury or harm caused by a person or thing. **4.** a source of trouble or difficulty.

mischievous (ˈmɪstʃɪvəs) *adj.* **1.** inclined to acts of mischief. **2.** teasing; slightly malicious. **3.** intended to cause harm. —ˈ**mischievously** *adv.*

miscible (ˈmɪsɪbʰl) *adj.* capable of mixing: *miscible with water.* —ˌ**misciˈbility** *n.*

misconception (ˌmɪskənˈsɛpʃən) *n.* a false or mistaken view, opinion, or attitude.

misconduct (mɪsˈkɒndʌkt) *n.* behaviour, such as adultery or professional negligence, that is regarded as immoral or unethical.

misconstrue (ˌmɪskənˈstruː) *vb.* **-struing, -strued.** to interpret mistakenly. —**misconstruction** (ˌmɪskənˈstrʌkʃən) *n.*

miscreant (ˈmɪskrɪənt) *n.* a wrongdoer or villain.

misdeal (ˌmɪsˈdiːl) *vb.* **-dealing, -dealt** (-ˈdɛlt). **1.** to deal out cards incorrectly. ~*n.* **2.** a faulty deal.

misdeed (ˌmɪsˈdiːd) *n.* an evil or illegal action.

misdemeanour *or U.S.* **misdemeanor** (ˌmɪsdɪˈmiːnə) *n.* **1.** a minor wrongdoing. **2.** *Criminal law.* (formerly) an offence less serious than a felony.

misdirect (ˌmɪsdɪˈrɛkt) *vb.* to give (a person) wrong directions or instructions. —ˌ**misdiˈrection** *n.*

mise en scène (ˌmiːz ɒn ˈseɪn) *n.* **1.** the stage setting and scenery in a play. **2.** the environment of an event.

miser (ˈmaɪzə) *n.* a person who hoards mon-

ey or possessions, often living miserably. —ˈ**miserly** *adj.*

miserable (ˈmɪzərəbʰl) *adj.* **1.** unhappy or depressed; wretched. **2.** causing misery or discomfort: *a miserable life.* **3.** sordid or squalid: *miserable living conditions.* **4.** mean; stingy. —ˈ**miserableness** *n.* —ˈ**miserably** *adv.*

misericord (mɪˈzɛrɪˌkɔːd) *n.* a ledge projecting from the underside of the hinged seat of a choir stall in a church, on which the occupant can support himself while standing.

misery (ˈmɪzərɪ) *n., pl.* **-eries.** **1.** intense unhappiness or suffering. **2.** a cause of such unhappiness. **3.** squalid or poverty-stricken conditions. **4.** *Brit. informal.* a person who is habitually depressed: *he is such a misery.*

misfire (ˌmɪsˈfaɪə) *vb.* **1.** (of a firearm) to fail to fire as expected. **2.** (of a motor engine or vehicle) to fail to fire at the appropriate time. **3.** to fail to operate or occur as intended. ~*n.* **4.** the act or an instance of misfiring.

misfit (ˈmɪsˌfɪt) *n.* **1.** a person not suited to a particular social environment. **2.** something that does not fit or fits badly.

misfortune (mɪsˈfɔːtʃən) *n.* **1.** bad luck. **2.** an unfortunate event.

misgiving (mɪsˈgɪvɪŋ) *n.* (*often pl.*) a feeling of uncertainty, apprehension, or doubt.

misgovern (ˌmɪsˈgʌvən) *vb.* to govern badly. —ˌ**misˈgovernment** *n.*

misguided (ˌmɪsˈgaɪdɪd) *adj.* mistaken or unwise in opinion or action.

mishandle (ˌmɪsˈhændʰl) *vb.* to handle or treat badly or inefficiently.

mishap (ˈmɪshæp) *n.* an unfortunate accident.

mishear (ˌmɪsˈhɪə) *vb.* **-hearing, -heard** (-ˈhɜːd). to fail to hear correctly.

mishit *Sport.* ~*n.* (ˈmɪsˌhɪt). **1.** a faulty shot or stroke. ~*vb.* (ˌmɪsˈhɪt), **-hitting, -hit.** **2.** to hit (a ball) with a faulty stroke.

mishmash (ˈmɪʃˌmæʃ) *n.* a confused collection or mixture.

misinform (ˌmɪsɪnˈfɔːm) *vb.* to give incorrect information to. —**misinformation** (ˌmɪsɪnfəˈmeɪʃən) *n.*

misinterpret (ˌmɪsɪnˈtɜːprɪt) *vb.* to interpret badly, misleadingly, or incorrectly. —ˌ**misinˌterpreˈtation** *n.*

misjudge (ˌmɪsˈdʒʌdʒ) *vb.* to judge wrongly or unfairly. —ˌ**misˈjudgment** *or* ˌ**misˈjudgement** *n.*

mislay (mɪsˈleɪ) *vb.* **-laying, -laid.** to lose (something) temporarily, esp. by forgetting where it is.

mislead (mɪsˈliːd) *vb.* **-leading, -led.** to give false or confusing information to. —**misˈleading** *adj.*

mismanage (ˌmɪsˈmænɪdʒ) *vb.* to organize,

run, or handle (something) badly or wrongly. —,**mis'management** n.

mismatch (,mɪs'mætʃ) vb. **1.** to match badly, esp. in marriage. ~n. **2.** a bad match.

misnamed (,mɪs'neɪmd) adj. badly or incorrectly named.

misnomer (,mɪs'nəʊmə) n. **1.** an incorrect or unsuitable name for a person or thing. **2.** the use of the wrong name.

misogyny (mɪ'sɒdʒɪnɪ, maɪ-) n. hatred of women. —**mi'sogynist** n. —**mi'sogynous** adj.

misplace (,mɪs'pleɪs) vb. **1.** to put (something) in the wrong place, esp. to lose (something) temporarily by forgetting where it was placed. **2.** (often passive) to bestow (trust or affection) unadvisedly.

misprint n. (,mɪs,prɪnt). **1.** an error in printing. ~vb. (,mɪs'prɪnt). **2.** to print (a letter) incorrectly.

misprision (mɪs'prɪʒən) n. Law. the concealment of the commission of a felony or an act of treason.

mispronounce (,mɪsprə'naʊns) vb. to pronounce (a word) wrongly. —**mispronunciation** (,mɪsprə,nʌnsɪ'eɪʃən) n.

misquote (,mɪs'kwəʊt) vb. to quote inaccurately. —,**misquo'tation** n.

misread (,mɪs'riːd) vb. -**reading**, -**read** (-'rɛd). **1.** to read incorrectly. **2.** to misinterpret.

misrepresent (,mɪsrɛprɪ'zɛnt) vb. to represent wrongly or inaccurately.

misrule (,mɪs'ruːl) vb. **1.** to govern inefficiently or without justice. ~n. **2.** inefficient or unjust government. **3.** disorder.

miss[1] (mɪs) vb. **1.** to fail to reach, hit, meet, find, or attain (some aim or target). **2.** to fail to be present for: to miss an appointment. **3.** to fail to see, hear, understand, or perceive. **4.** to fail to take advantage of: to miss an opportunity. **5.** to discover or regret the loss or absence of: she missed him. **6.** to escape or avoid (something, esp. a danger), usually narrowly: he missed death by inches. ~n. **7.** a failure to reach, hit, etc. **8. give (something) a miss.** Informal. to avoid (something): give the pudding a miss. ~See also **miss out.**

miss[2] (mɪs) n. Informal. an unmarried woman or girl.

Miss (mɪs) n. a title of an unmarried woman or girl, usually used before the surname. **Usage.** When reference is made to two or more unmarried women with the same surname, the Misses Smith is more formal than the Miss Smiths. See also **Ms.**

Miss. Mississippi.

missal ('mɪs'l) n. R.C. Church. a book containing the prayers and rites of the Masses for a complete year.

misshapen (,mɪs'ʃeɪp'n) adj. badly shaped; deformed.

missile ('mɪsaɪl) n. **1.** any object or weapon that is thrown, launched, or fired at a target. **2.** a rocket with an exploding warhead, used as a weapon.

missing ('mɪsɪŋ) adj. **1.** not present; absent or lost. **2.** not able to be traced and not known to be dead: nine men were missing after the attack.

missing link n. **1.** any missing section or part in a series. **2.** (usually preceded by the) a hypothetical extinct animal, formerly thought to be intermediate between the apes and man.

mission ('mɪʃən) n. **1.** a specific task or duty assigned to a person or group of people. **2.** a person's vocation. **3.** a group of persons representing or working for a particular country or organization in a foreign country. **4.** a group of people sent by a church to a foreign country to do religious and social work. **5.** a building in which missionary work is performed. **6.** the dispatch of aircraft or spacecraft to achieve a particular task. **7.** a charitable centre that offers shelter or aid to the destitute or underprivileged.

missionary ('mɪʃənərɪ) n., pl. -**aries**. a member of a religious mission.

missis or **missus** ('mɪsɪz, -ɪs) n. **1.** (usually preceded by the) Informal. one's wife or the wife of the person addressed or referred to. **2.** an informal term of address for a woman.

missive ('mɪsɪv) n. a formal or official letter.

miss out vb. **1.** to leave out; overlook. **2.** (often foll. by on) to fail to take part in something enjoyable or beneficial: you missed out on the celebrations.

misspell (,mɪs'spɛl) vb. -**spelling**, -**spelt** or -**spelled**. to spell (a word or words) wrongly.

misspend (,mɪs'spɛnd) vb. -**spending**, -**spent**. to spend thoughtlessly or wastefully.

missy ('mɪsɪ) n., pl. **missies**. Informal. an affectionate or disparaging form of address to a girl.

mist (mɪst) n. **1.** a thin fog. **2.** a fine spray of liquid, such as that produced by an aerosol container. **3.** condensed water vapour on a surface. **4.** something that causes haziness or lack of clarity, such as a film of tears. ~vb. **5.** to cover or be covered with mist. —'**misty** adj. —'**mistiness** n.

mistake (mɪ'steɪk) n. **1.** an error or blunder. **2.** a misconception or misunderstanding. ~vb. -**taking**, -**took**, -**taken**. **3.** to misunderstand; misinterpret: she mistook his meaning. **4.** (foll. by for) to interpret as or confuse with: she mistook his direct manner for honesty. **5.** to choose badly or incorrectly: he mistook his path.

mistaken (mɪ'steɪkən) adj. **1.** wrong in

opinion or judgment. **2.** arising from error in opinion or judgment: *a mistaken viewpoint.*

mister (ˈmɪstə) *n.* (*sometimes cap.*) an informal form of address for a man.

Mister (ˈmɪstə) *n.* the full form of **Mr.**

mistime (ˌmɪsˈtaɪm) *vb.* to time (an action or utterance) wrongly.

mistle thrush *or* **missel thrush** (ˈmɪsᵊl) *n.* a large European thrush with a brown back and spotted breast.

mistletoe (ˈmɪsᵊlˌtəʊ) *n.* a Eurasian evergreen shrub with waxy white berries: grows as a parasite on various trees.

mistook (mɪˈstʊk) *vb.* the past tense of **mistake.**

mistral (ˈmɪstrəl, mɪˈstrɑːl) *n.* a strong cold dry northerly wind of S France.

mistreat (ˌmɪsˈtriːt) *vb.* to treat badly. —ˌmisˈtreatment *n.*

mistress (ˈmɪstrɪs) *n.* **1.** a woman who has a continuing sexual relationship with a man she is not married to. **2.** a woman in a position of authority, ownership, or control. **3.** a woman having control over something specified: *mistress of her own destiny.* **4.** *Chiefly Brit.* short for **schoolmistress.**

mistrial (mɪsˈtraɪəl) *n.* a trial made void because of some error.

mistrust (ˌmɪsˈtrʌst) *vb.* **1.** to have doubts or suspicions about (someone or something). ~*n.* **2.** distrust. —ˌmisˈtrustful *adj.* —ˌmisˈtrustfully *adv.*

misunderstand (ˌmɪsʌndəˈstænd) *vb.* **-standing, -stood.** to fail to understand properly.

misunderstanding (ˌmɪsʌndəˈstændɪŋ) *n.* **1.** a failure to understand properly. **2.** a disagreement.

misunderstood (ˌmɪsʌndəˈstʊd) *adj.* not properly or sympathetically understood: *a misunderstood adolescent.*

misuse *n.* (ˌmɪsˈjuːs), *also* **misusage. 1.** erroneous, improper, or unorthodox use: *misuse of words.* **2.** cruel or inhumane treatment. ~*vb.* (ˌmɪsˈjuːz), **3.** to use wrongly. **4.** to treat badly or harshly.

mite¹ (maɪt) *n.* any of numerous very small creatures of the spider family some of which live as parasites.

mite² (maɪt) *n.* **1.** a very small particle, creature, or object. **2.** a very small sum of money. **3.** a mite. *Informal.* somewhat: *he's a mite foolish.*

mitigate (ˈmɪtɪˌgeɪt) *vb.* to make or become less severe or harsh; moderate. —ˈmitiˌgating *adj.* —ˌmitiˈgation *n.*

mitosis (maɪˈtəʊsɪs, mɪ-) *n.* a method of cell division, in which the nucleus divides into two daughter nuclei, each containing the same number of chromosomes as the parent nucleus.

mitre *or U.S.* **miter** (ˈmaɪtə) *n.* **1.** *Christianity.* the liturgical headdress of a bishop or abbot, consisting of a tall pointed cleft cap. **2.** *Also:* **mitre joint.** a corner joint formed by cutting bevels of equal angles at the ends of each piece of material. ~*vb.* **3.** to make a mitre joint between (two pieces of material). **4.** to confer a mitre upon: *a mitred abbot.*

mitt (mɪt) *n.* **1.** a glovelike hand covering that does not cover the fingers. **2.** short for **mitten. 3.** *Slang.* a hand. **4.** a baseball glove.

mitten (ˈmɪtᵊn) *n.* a glove with one section for the thumb and a single section for the fingers.

mix (mɪks) *vb.* **1.** to combine or blend into one mass. **2.** to become or have the capacity to become combined or joined: *some chemicals do not mix.* **3.** to form (something) by combining constituents: *to mix cement.* **4.** to do at the same time: *to mix study and pleasure.* **5.** to be outgoing in social situations: *Pauline mixed well.* **6.** *Music.* to balance and adjust (individual performers' parts) to make an overall sound by electronic means. ~*n.* **7.** the result of mixing; mixture. **8.** a mixture of ingredients, esp. one commercially prepared for making a cake. **9.** *Music.* the sound produced by mixing. ~*See also* **mix-up.** —**mixed** *adj.*

mixed bag *n. Informal.* something composed of diverse elements, characteristics, or people.

mixed blessing *n.* an event or situation with both advantages and disadvantages.

mixed doubles *pl. n. Tennis, badminton.* a doubles game with a man and a woman as partners on each side.

mixed farming *n.* combined arable and livestock farming (on **mixed farms**).

mixed grill *n.* a dish of several kinds of grilled meat, tomatoes, and mushrooms.

mixed marriage *n.* a marriage between persons of different races or religions.

mixed metaphor *n.* a combination of incongruous metaphors, as *when the Nazi jackboots sing their swan song.*

mixed-up *adj.* in a state of mental confusion.

mixer (ˈmɪksə) *n.* **1.** *Informal.* a person considered in relation to his ability to mix socially. **2.** a kitchen appliance, usually electrical, used for mixing foods. **3.** a drink such as ginger ale or fruit juice used in preparing cocktails.

mixture (ˈmɪkstʃə) *n.* **1.** something mixed; a result of mixing. **2.** a combination of different things, such as feelings: *she watched with a mixture of disgust and fascination.* **3.** *Chem.* a substance consisting of two or more substances mixed together without any chemical bonding between them.

mix-up *n.* **1.** a confused condition or

situation. ~*vb.* **mix up. 2.** to make into a mixture. **3.** to confuse: *Tom mixes John up with Bill.* **4.** (foll. by *in* or *with; usually passive*) to involve (in an activity or group, esp. one that is illegal): *mixed up in the drugs racket.*

mizzenmast ('mɪz²n,mɑːst; *Naut.* 'mɪz²n-məst) *n. Naut.* (on a vessel with three or more masts) the third mast from the bow.

mks units *pl. n.* a metric system of units based on the metre, kilogram, and second; it forms the basis of the SI units.

ml 1. mile. **2.** millilitre.

ML Medieval Latin.

MLitt Master of Letters.

Mlle *or* **Mile.,** *pl.* **Mlles** *or* **Mlles.** the French equivalent of *Miss.*

MLR minimum lending rate.

mm millimetre.

Mme, *pl.* **Mmes.** the French equivalent of *Mrs.*

MMus Master of Music.

Mn *Chem.* manganese.

MN Minnesota.

mnemonic (nɪ'mɒnɪk) *adj.* **1.** aiding or meant to aid one's memory. ~*n.* **2.** something, such as a verse, to assist memory. —**mne'monically** *adv.*

mo (məʊ) *n. Informal, chiefly Brit.* short for **moment** (sense 1).

Mo *Chem.* molybdenum.

MO 1. Medical Officer. **2.** Also: **Mo.** Missouri.

m.o. *or* **MO 1.** mail order. **2.** money order.

moa ('məʊə) *n.* any of various recently extinct large flightless birds of New Zealand resembling the ostrich.

moan (məʊn) *n.* **1.** a low prolonged mournful sound expressive of suffering or pleading. **2.** any similar sound, esp. that made by the wind. **3.** *Informal.* a grumble or complaint. ~*vb.* **4.** to utter in a low mournful manner. **5.** to make a sound like a moan. **6.** *Informal.* to grumble or complain. —'**moaner** *n.*

moat (məʊt) *n.* a wide water-filled ditch surrounding a fortified place, such as a castle.

mob (mɒb) *n.* **1.** a riotous or disorderly crowd of people. **2.** *Informal.* any group of people. **3.** the masses. **4.** *Slang.* a gang of criminals. **5.** *Austral. & N.Z.* a flock or herd of animals. **6. mobs of.** *Austral. & N.Z. informal.* lots of. ~*vb.* **mobbing, mobbed. 7.** to attack in a group resembling a mob. **8.** to surround, esp. in order to acclaim.

mobcap ('mɒb,kæp) *n.* a woman's 18th-century cotton cap with a pouched crown.

mobile ('məʊbaɪl) *adj.* **1.** having freedom of movement; movable. **2.** changing quickly in expression: *a mobile face.* **3.** *Sociol.* (of individuals or social groups) moving

within and between classes, occupations, and localities. ~*n.* **4.** a sculpture suspended in midair with delicately balanced parts that are set in motion by air currents. —**mobility** (məʊ'bɪlɪtɪ) *n.*

mobilize *or* **-lise** ('məʊbɪ,laɪz) *vb.* **1.** to prepare for war or another emergency by organizing (resources and armed services). **2.** to organize for a purpose. —,**mobili'zation** *or* -li'sation *n.*

moccasin ('mɒkəsɪn) *n.* a shoe of soft leather originally worn by North American Indians.

mocha ('mɒkə) *n.* **1.** a dark brown coffee originally imported from the port of Mocha in Arabia. **2.** a flavouring made from coffee and chocolate.

mock (mɒk) *vb.* **1.** to behave with scorn or contempt towards (a person or thing). **2.** to imitate, esp. in fun; mimic. **3.** to deceive, disappoint, or delude. **4.** to defy or frustrate. ~*n.* **5.** a counterfeit; imitation. **6.** (*often pl.*) *Informal.* (in England and Wales) school examinations taken as practice before public exams. ~*adj.* **7.** sham or counterfeit. **8.** serving as an imitation or substitute, esp. for practice purposes: *a mock battle.* ~See also **mock-up.** —'**mocking** *n., adj.*

mockers ('mɒkəz) *pl. n.* **put the mockers on.** *Informal.* to ruin the chances of success of.

mockery ('mɒkərɪ) *n., pl.* **-eries. 1.** ridicule, contempt, or derision. **2.** an imitation or pretence, esp. a derisive one. **3.** a person or thing that is mocked. **4.** a person, thing, or action that is inadequate.

mock-heroic *adj.* (of a literary work, esp. a poem) imitating the style of heroic poetry in order to satirize an unheroic subject.

mockingbird ('mɒkɪŋ,bɜːd) *n.* an American songbird which can mimic the song of other birds.

mock orange *n.* a shrub with white fragrant flowers like those of the orange.

mock turtle soup *n.* an imitation turtle soup made from a calf's head.

mock-up *n.* a working full-scale model of a machine or apparatus for test or research purposes.

mod[1] (mɒd) *n. Brit.* a member of a group of teenagers, originally in the mid-1960s, noted for their clothes-consciousness.

mod[2] (mɒd) *n.* an annual Highland Gaelic meeting with musical and literary competitions.

MOD (in Britain) Ministry of Defence.

mod. 1. moderate. **2.** modern.

modal ('məʊd²l) *adj.* **1.** of or relating to mode or manner. **2.** *Grammar.* (of a verb form or auxiliary verb) expressing a distinction of mood, such as that between possibility and actuality: *in English, "can" and* *"might"* are modal verbs. **3.** *Music.* of or relating to a mode. **—modality** (məʊˈdælɪtɪ) *n.*

mod cons *pl. n. Informal.* modern conveniences, such as hot water and heating.

mode (məʊd) *n.* **1.** a manner or way of doing, acting, or existing. **2.** the current fashion or style. **3.** *Music.* any of the various scales of notes within one octave.

model (ˈmɒdˀl) *n.* **1.** a representation, usually on a smaller scale, of something such as a device or structure. **2. a.** a standard to be imitated. **b.** (*as modifier*): *a model wife.* **3.** a representative form, style, or pattern. **4.** a person who poses for a sculptor, painter, or photographer. **5.** a person who wears clothes to display them to prospective buyers; mannequin. **6.** a design or style of a particular product. ~*vb.* **-elling, -elled** *or U.S.* **-eling, -eled. 7.** to make a model of (something or someone). **8.** to form in clay or wax; mould. **9.** to display (clothing and accessories) as a mannequin. **10.** to plan or create according to a model or models.

modem (ˈməʊdɛm) *n. Computers.* a device for connecting two computers by a telephone line, consisting of a modulator that converts computer signals into audio signals and a corresponding demodulator.

moderate *adj.* (ˈmɒdərɪt). **1.** not extreme or excessive. **2.** not violent; mild or temperate. **3.** of average quality or extent: *moderate success.* ~*n.* (ˈmɒdərɪt). **4.** a person who holds moderate views, esp. in politics. ~*vb.* (ˈmɒdəˌreɪt). **5.** to become or cause to become less extreme or violent. **6.** to preside over a meeting, discussion, etc.

moderation (ˌmɒdəˈreɪʃən) *n.* **1.** the state or an instance of being moderate. **2.** the act of moderating. **3. in moderation.** within moderate or reasonable limits.

moderato (ˌmɒdəˈrɑːtəʊ) *adv. Music.* **1.** at a moderate tempo. **2.** with restraint: *allegro moderato.*

moderator (ˈmɒdəˌreɪtə) *n.* **1.** *Presbyterian Church.* a minister appointed to preside over a Church court, synod, or general assembly. **2.** a presiding officer at a public or legislative assembly. **3.** a material, such as heavy water, used for slowing down neutrons in nuclear reactors.

modern (ˈmɒdən) *adj.* **1.** of the present or a recent time; contemporary. **2.** of contemporary styles or schools of art, literature, and music, esp. those of an experimental kind. ~*n.* **3.** a contemporary person. **—moˈdernity** *n.*

Modern English *n.* the English language since about 1450.

modernism (ˈmɒdəˌnɪzəm) *n.* modern tendencies, thoughts, or styles, or support of these. **—ˈmodernist** *n., adj.*

modernize *or* **-ise** (ˈmɒdəˌnaɪz) *vb.* **1.** to make modern in style, methods, or equipment: *to modernize rolling stock.* **2.** to

adopt modern ways or ideas. **—ˌmoderniˈzation** *or* **-iˈsation** *n.*

modern pentathlon *n.* an athletic contest consisting of five different events: horse riding with jumps, fencing with electric épée, freestyle swimming, pistol shooting, and cross-country running.

modest (ˈmɒdɪst) *adj.* **1.** having a humble opinion of oneself or one's accomplishments. **2.** reserved or shy. **3.** not ostentatious or pretentious. **4.** not extreme or excessive. **5.** decorous or decent. **—ˈmodestly** *adv.* **—ˈmodesty** *n.*

modicum (ˈmɒdɪkəm) *n.* a small amount.

modifier (ˈmɒdɪˌfaɪə) *n. Grammar.* a word or phrase that qualifies the sense of another word; for example, the noun *alarm* is a modifier of *clock* in *alarm clock.*
Usage. Nouns are frequently used in English to modify other nouns: *police officer; chicken farm.* They should be used with restraint, however, esp. when the appropriate adjective can be used: *lunar research* (not *moon research*).

modify (ˈmɒdɪˌfaɪ) *vb.* **-fying, -fied. 1.** to change or alter slightly. **2.** to make less extreme or uncompromising. **3.** *Grammar.* (of a word or phrase) to bear the relation of modifier to (another word or phrase). **—ˌmodifiˈcation** *n.*

modish (ˈməʊdɪʃ) *adj.* in the current fashion or style. **—ˈmodishly** *adv.*

modiste (məʊˈdiːst) *n.* a fashionable dressmaker or milliner.

modulate (ˈmɒdjʊˌleɪt) *vb.* **1.** to change the tone, pitch, or volume of (one's voice). **2.** to adjust or regulate the degree of. **3.** *Music.* to change from one key to another. **4.** *Physics, electronics.* to superimpose the amplitude, frequency, or phase of a wave or signal onto another wave or signal. **—ˌmoduˈlation** *n.*

module (ˈmɒdjuːl) *n.* **1.** a standard self-contained unit or item, such as an assembly of electronic components or a standardized piece of furniture, that can be used in combination with other units. **2.** *Astronautics.* a self-contained separable unit making up a spacecraft. **3.** *Education.* a short course of study that together with other such courses counts towards a qualification. **—ˈmodular** *adj.*

modulus (ˈmɒdjʊləs) *n., pl.* **-li** (-ˌlaɪ). *Physics.* a coefficient expressing a specified property, for instance elasticity, of a specified substance.

modus operandi (ˈməʊdəs ˌɒpəˈrændaɪ) *n., pl.* **modi operandi** (ˈməʊdaɪ ˌɒpəˈrændaɪ). procedure; method of operating.

modus vivendi (ˈməʊdəs vɪˈvɛndaɪ) *n., pl.* **modi vivendi** (ˈməʊdaɪ vɪˈvɛndaɪ). a working arrangement between conflicting interests; practical compromise.

mog (mɒg) *or* **moggy** *n., pl.* **mogs** *or* **moggies.** *Brit. slang.* a cat.

mogul ('məʊgʌl) *n.* an important or powerful person.

Mogul ('məʊgʌl) *adj.* of or relating to a Muslim dynasty of Indian emperors established in 1526.

MOH (in Britain) Medical Officer of Health.

mohair ('məʊ,hɛə) *n.* **1.** the long soft silky hair of the Angora goat. **2.** a fabric made from yarn of this hair and cotton or wool.

Mohammedan (məʊ'hæmɪdᵊn) *n., adj.* another word (not in Muslim use) for **Muslim.**

mohican (məʊ'hiːkən) *n.* a punk hairstyle in which the head is shaved at the sides and the remaining strip of hair is worn stiffly erect.

moiety ('mɔɪtɪ) *n., pl.* **-ties. 1.** a half. **2.** one of two parts or divisions of something.

moire (mwɑː) *n.* a fabric, usually silk, with a watered effect.

moiré ('mwɑːreɪ) *adj.* **1.** with a watered or wavelike pattern. ~*n.* **2.** such a pattern, impressed on fabrics. **3.** any fabric with such a pattern. **4.** Also: **moiré pattern.** a pattern seen when two geometrical patterns, such as grids, are visually superimposed.

moist (mɔɪst) *adj.* **1.** slightly damp or wet. **2.** saturated with or suggestive of moisture.

moisten ('mɔɪsᵊn) *vb.* to make or become moist.

moisture ('mɔɪstʃə) *n.* water diffused as vapour or condensed on or in objects.

moisturize *or* **-ise** ('mɔɪstʃə,raɪz) *vb.* to add moisture to (the air or the skin). —'**moistur,izer** *or* -**,iser** *n.*

moke (məʊk) *n. Brit. slang.* a donkey.

mol *Chem.* mole³.

mol. 1. molecular. **2.** molecule.

molar ('məʊlə) *n.* **1.** any of the back teeth specialized for grinding in man and other mammals. ~*adj.* **2.** of any of these teeth.

molasses (mə'læsɪz) *n.* (functioning as sing.) **1.** the thick brown uncrystallized bitter syrup obtained from sugar during refining. **2.** U.S. & Canad. same as **treacle** (sense 1).

mold (məʊld) *n., vb. U.S.* same as **mould.**

mole¹ (məʊl) *n. Pathol.* a small dark raised spot on the skin.

mole² (məʊl) *n.* **1.** a small burrowing mammal with velvety, typically dark fur and forearms specialized for digging. **2.** *Informal.* a spy who has infiltrated an organization and become a trusted member of it.

mole³ (məʊl) *n.* the basic SI unit of amount of substance; the amount that contains as many elementary entities as there are atoms in 0.012 kilogram of carbon-12.

mole⁴ (məʊl) *n.* **1.** a breakwater. **2.** a harbour protected by a breakwater.

molecular (mə'lɛkjʊlə) *adj.* of or relating to molecules.

molecular compound *n.* a compound in which the atoms are linked by covalent bonds to form molecules.

molecular formula *n.* a chemical formula indicating the number and type of atoms in a molecule, but not its structure: NH_3 *is the molecular formula of ammonia.*

molecular weight *n.* the sum of all the atomic weights of the atoms in a molecule.

molecule ('mɒlɪ,kjuːl) *n.* **1.** the simplest unit of a chemical compound that can exist, consisting of two or more atoms held together by chemical bonds. **2.** a very small particle.

molehill ('məʊl,hɪl) *n.* **1.** the small mound of earth thrown up by a burrowing mole. **2. make a mountain out of a molehill.** to exaggerate an unimportant matter out of all proportion.

molest (mə'lɛst) *vb.* **1.** to disturb or annoy (someone) by hostile interference. **2.** to accost or attack, (esp. a woman or child) with the intention of assaulting sexually. —**molestation** (,məʊlɛ'steɪʃən) *n.* —**mo-'lester** *n.*

moll (mɒl) *n. Slang.* **1.** the female accomplice of a gangster. **2.** a prostitute.

mollify ('mɒlɪ,faɪ) *vb.* **-fying, -fied.** to pacify; soothe. —,**mollifi'cation** *n.*

mollusc *or U.S.* **mollusk** ('mɒləsk) *n.* any of various invertebrates with a soft unsegmented body and often a shell. The group includes snails, slugs, clams, mussels, squid, and octopuses.

mollycoddle ('mɒlɪ,kɒdᵊl) *vb.* **1.** to treat with indulgent care; pamper. ~*n.* **2.** a pampered person.

Molotov cocktail ('mɒlə,tɒf) *n.* an elementary incendiary weapon, usually a bottle of petrol with a short delay fuse or wick; petrol bomb.

molt (məʊlt) *vb., n. U.S.* same as **moult.**

molten ('məʊltən) *adj.* liquefied; melted.

molto ('mɒltəʊ) *adv. Music.* very: *allegro molto; molto adagio.*

molybdenum (mɒ'lɪbdɪnəm) *n.* a very hard silvery-white metallic element used in alloys, esp. to harden and strengthen steels. Symbol: Mo

mom (mɒm) *n. Informal, chiefly U.S. & Canad.* same as **mother.**

moment ('məʊmənt) *n.* **1.** a short indefinite period of time. **2.** a specific instant or point in time: *at that moment the phone rang.* **3. the moment.** the present point of time: *at the moment it's fine.* **4.** import, significance, or value: *a matter of greatest moment.* **5.** *Physics.* **a.** a tendency to produce motion, esp. rotation about a point or axis. **b.** the product of a physical quantity, such as force or mass, and its distance from a fixed reference point.

momentary ('məʊməntrɪ) *adj.* lasting for only a moment; temporary. —'**momentarily** *adv.*

moment of truth *n.* a moment when a person or thing is put to the test.

momentous (məʊ'mɛntəs) *adj.* of great significance. —**mo'mentousness** *n.*

momentum (məʊ'mɛntəm) *n., pl.* **-ta** (-tə) *or* **-tums.** **1.** *Physics.* the product of a body's mass and its velocity. **2.** the impetus of a moving body. **3.** driving power or strength.

momma ('mɒmə) *n. Chiefly U.S.* an informal or childish word for **mother.**

Mon. Monday.

mon- *combining form.* See **mono-.**

monad ('mɒnæd, 'məʊ-) *n.* **1.** *Philosophy.* any fundamental singular metaphysical entity. **2.** a single-celled organism. **3.** an atom, ion, or radical with a valency of one.

monandrous (mɒ'nændrəs) *adj.* **1.** having only one male sexual partner over a period of time. **2.** *Biol.* having only one stamen (in each flower).

monarch ('mɒnək) *n.* a sovereign head of state, esp. a king, queen, or emperor, who rules usually by hereditary right. —**monarchical** (mɒ'nɑːkɪkᵊl) *or* **mo'narchic** *adj.* —'**monarchism** *n.* —'**monarchist** *n., adj.*

monarchy ('mɒnəkɪ) *n., pl.* **-chies.** **1.** a form of government in which supreme authority is vested in a single and usually hereditary figure, such as a king. **2.** a country reigned over by a monarch.

monastery ('mɒnəstrɪ) *n., pl.* **-teries.** the residence of a religious community, esp. of monks.

monastic (mə'næstɪk) *adj.* **1.** of or relating to monasteries, monks, or nuns. **2.** resembling this sort of life; ascetic. —**monasticism** (mə'næstɪ,sɪzəm) *n.*

monatomic (,mɒnə'tɒmɪk) *adj. Chem.* **1.** (of an element) consisting of single atoms. **2.** (of a compound or molecule) having only one atom or group that can be replaced in a reaction.

Monday ('mʌndɪ) *n.* the second day of the week; first day of the working week.

monetarism ('mʌnɪtə,rɪzəm) *n.* **1.** the theory that inflation is caused by an excess quantity of money in an economy. **2.** an economic policy based on this theory and a belief in the efficiency of free market forces. —'**monetarist** *n., adj.*

monetary ('mʌnɪtrɪ) *adj.* of money or currency.

money ('mʌnɪ) *n.* **1.** a medium of exchange that functions as legal tender. **2.** the official currency, in the form of banknotes or coins, issued by a government. **3.** (*Law or archaic. pl.* **moneys** *or* **monies**) a financial sum or income. **4.** an unspecified amount of wealth: *money to lend.* **5. for one's money.** in one's opinion. **6. one's money's worth.** full value for the money one has paid for something. **7. put money on.** to place a bet on.

moneybags ('mʌnɪ,bægz) *n.* (*functioning as sing.*) *Informal.* a very rich person.

moneychanger ('mʌnɪ,tʃeɪndʒə) *n.* a person engaged in the business of exchanging currencies or money.

moneyed *or* **monied** ('mʌnɪd) *adj.* having a great deal of money; rich.

money-grubbing *adj. Informal.* seeking greedily to obtain money. —'**money-,grubber** *n.*

moneylender ('mʌnɪ,lɛndə) *n.* a person who lends money at interest as a living.

moneymaker ('mʌnɪ,meɪkə) *n.* **1.** a person who is intent on accumulating money. **2.** a person or thing that is or might be profitable. —'**money,making** *adj., n.*

money-spinner *n. Informal.* an enterprise, idea, or thing that is a source of wealth.

monger ('mʌngə) *n.* **1.** a trader or dealer: *ironmonger.* **2.** a promoter of something: *warmonger.*

mongol ('mɒngᵊl) *n.* (not in technical use) a person affected by Down's syndrome. —'**mongo,loid** *n., adj.*

Mongolian (mɒŋ'gəʊlɪən) *adj.* **1.** of Mongolia, a region in E Central Asia, its people, or their language. ~*n.* **2.** a person from Mongolia. **3.** the language of Mongolia.

mongolism ('mɒŋgə,lɪzəm) *n. Pathol.* a former name (not in technical use) for **Down's syndrome.**

Mongoloid ('mɒŋgə,lɔɪd) *adj.* of a major racial group of mankind, characterized by yellowish skin, straight black hair, and slanting eyes: includes most of the people of Asia, the American Indians, and the Eskimos.

mongoose ('mɒŋ,guːs) *n., pl.* **-gooses.** a small long-tailed predatory mammal of Asia and Africa that kills snakes.

mongrel ('mʌŋgrəl) *n.* **1.** a plant or animal, esp. a dog, of mixed or unknown breeding. ~*adj.* **2.** of mixed origin, breeding, or character.

monied ('mʌnɪd) *adj.* same as **moneyed.**

monies ('mʌnɪz) *n. Law, archaic.* a plural of **money.**

monism ('mɒnɪzəm) *n. Philosophy.* the doctrine that reality consists of only one basic substance or element, such as mind or matter. —'**monist** *n., adj.*

monition (məʊ'nɪʃən) *n.* a warning or caution.

monitor ('mɒnɪtə) *n.* **1.** a person or piece of equipment that warns, checks, controls, or keeps a continuous record of something. **2.** *Education.* a pupil assisting a teacher with various duties. **3.** a television set or loudspeaker used in a studio for checking what is being transmitted or recorded. **4.** a large predatory lizard inhabiting warm regions of Africa, Asia, and Australia. ~*vb.* **5.** to act as a monitor of. **6.** to observe or record (the condition or performance of a person or thing). **7.** to check (a broadcast) for acceptable quality or content. —**monitorial** (ˌmɒnɪˈtɔːrɪəl) *adj.*

monitory ('mɒnɪtrɪ) *adj.* warning or admonishing.

monk (mʌŋk) *n.* a male member of a religious community bound by vows of poverty, chastity, and obedience. —'**monkish** *adj.*

monkey ('mʌŋkɪ) *n.* **1.** any of numerous long-tailed primates excluding lemurs and tarsiers. **2.** any primate except man. **3.** a naughty or mischievous child. **4.** *Slang.* £500 or $500. ~*vb.* **5.** (usually foll. by *around, with,* etc.) to meddle, fool, or tinker.

monkey business *n. Informal.* mischievous, suspect, or dishonest behaviour or acts.

monkey nut *n. Brit.* a peanut.

monkey puzzle *n.* a South American coniferous tree with branches shaped like a candelabrum and stiff sharp leaves.

monkey tricks or *U.S.* **monkey shines** *pl. n. Informal.* mischievous behaviour or acts.

monkey wrench *n.* a wrench with adjustable jaws.

monkshood ('mʌŋkshʊd) *n.* a poisonous plant with hooded blue-purple flowers.

mono ('mɒnəʊ) *adj.* **1.** short for **monophonic.** ~*n.* **2.** monophonic sound.

mono- or before a vowel **mon-** *combining form.* **1.** one; single: *monorail.* **2.** indicating that a chemical compound contains a single specified atom or group: *monoxide.*

monobasic (ˌmɒnəʊˈbeɪsɪk) *adj. Chem.* (of an acid, such as hydrogen chloride) having only one replaceable hydrogen atom per molecule.

monochromatic (ˌmɒnəʊkrəʊˈmætɪk) *adj.* (of light or other electromagnetic radiation) having only one wavelength.

monochrome ('mɒnəˌkrəʊm) *adj.* **1.** *Photog., T.V.* black-and-white. ~*n.* **2.** a painting or drawing done in a range of tones of a single colour.

monocle ('mɒnək°l) *n.* a lens for correcting defective vision of one eye, held in position by the facial muscles. —'**monocled** *adj.*

monocline ('mɒnəʊˌklaɪn) *n.* a fold in stratified rocks in which the strata are inclined in the same direction from the horizontal. —ˌmono'**clinal** *adj., n.*

monoclinic (ˌmɒnəʊˈklɪnɪk) *adj. Crystallog.* of the crystal system characterized by three unequal axes, one pair of which are not at right angles to each other.

monoclonal antibody (ˌmɒnəʊˈkləʊn°l) *n.*

an antibody produced from a single clone of cells grown in a culture.

monocotyledon (ˌmɒnəʊˌkɒtɪˈliːd°n) *n.* any flowering plant with a single embryonic seed leaf, such as the grasses, lilies, palms, and orchids.

monocular (mɒˈnɒkjʊlə) *adj.* having or intended for the use of only one eye.

monody ('mɒnədɪ) *n., pl.* **-dies.** **1.** (in Greek tragedy) an ode sung by a single actor. **2.** *Music.* a style of composition consisting of a single vocal part, usually with accompaniment. —'**monodist** *n.*

monoecious (mɒˈniːʃəs) *adj.* **1.** (of some flowering plants) having the male and female reproductive organs in separate flowers on the same plant. **2.** (of some animals and lower plants) hermaphrodite.

monogamy (mɒˈnɒgəmɪ) *n.* the state or practice of having only one husband or wife at a time. —**mo'nogamous** *adj.*

monogram ('mɒnəˌɡræm) *n.* a design of one or more letters, esp. initials, on clothing, stationery, etc.

monograph ('mɒnəˌɡrɑːf) *n.* a paper, book, or other work concerned with a single subject or aspect of a subject.

monolingual (ˌmɒnəʊˈlɪŋɡwəl) *adj.* knowing or expressed in only one language.

monolith ('mɒnəlɪθ) *n.* **1.** a large block of stone or anything that resembles one in appearance, solidity, or size. **2.** a statue, obelisk, or column cut from one block of stone. —ˌmono'**lithic** *adj.*

monologue ('mɒnəˌlɒg) *n.* **1.** a long speech made by one actor in a play or film; soliloquy. **2.** a dramatic piece for a single performer. **3.** any long speech by one person, esp. when interfering with conversation.

monomania (ˌmɒnəʊˈmeɪnɪə) *n.* an obsession with one thing or idea. —ˌmono'**maniac** *n., adj.*

monomer ('mɒnəmə) *n. Chem.* a compound whose molecules can join together to form a polymer.

monomial (mɒˈnəʊmɪəl) *n. Maths.* an expression consisting of a single term, such as 5*ax.*

mononucleosis (ˌmɒnəʊˌnjuːklɪˈəʊsɪs) *n.* **infectious mononucleosis.** same as **glandular fever.**

monophonic (ˌmɒnəʊˈfɒnɪk) *adj.* (of a system of broadcasting, recording, or reproducing sound) using only one channel between source and loudspeaker. Often shortened to **mono.**

monoplane ('mɒnəʊˌpleɪn) *n.* an aeroplane with only one pair of wings.

monopolize or **-lise** (məˈnɒpəˌlaɪz) *vb.* **1.** to have full control or use of, to the exclusion of others. **2.** to hold a monopoly of (a market or commodity).

monopoly (məˈnɒpəlɪ) *n., pl.* **-lies.** **1.** exclusive control of the market supply of a product or service. **2. a.** an enterprise exercising this control. **b.** the product or service so controlled. **3.** *Law.* the exclusive right granted to a person or company by the state to trade in a specified commodity or area. **4.** exclusive control, possession, or use of something. —**mo'nopolist** *n.* —**mo-ˌnopo'listic** *adj.*

Monopoly (mə'nɒpəlɪ) *n. Trademark.* a board game for two to six players who deal in "property" as they move tokens around the board.

monorail ('mɒnəʊˌreɪl) *n.* a single-rail railway.

monosaccharide (ˌmɒnəʊ'sækəˌraɪd) *n.* a simple sugar, such as glucose, that cannot be broken down into other sugars.

monosodium glutamate (ˌmɒnəʊ'səʊdɪəm 'gluːtəˌmeɪt) *n.* a substance which enhances protein flavours: used as a food additive.

monosyllable ('mɒnəˌsɪləbᵊl) *n.* a word of one syllable. —**monosyllabic** (ˌmɒnəsɪ-'læbɪk) *adj.*

monotheism ('mɒnəʊˌθiːˌɪzəm) *n.* the belief or doctrine that there is only one God. —'**monoˌtheist** *n., adj.* —ˌ**monothe'istic** *adj.*

monotone ('mɒnəˌtəʊn) *n.* **1.** a single unvaried pitch level in speech or sound. **2.** speech without change of pitch. **3.** lack of variety in style or expression. ~*adj.* **4.** unvarying.

monotonous (mə'nɒtənəs) *adj.* tedious, esp. because of repetition. —**mo'notonously** *adv.*

monotony (mə'nɒtənɪ) *n., pl.* **-nies.** **1.** wearisome routine; dullness. **2.** lack of variety in pitch or cadence.

monovalent (ˌmɒnəʊ'veɪlənt) *adj. Chem.* **1.** having a valency of one. **2.** having only one valency. —ˌ**mono'valence** *or* ˌ**mono-'valency** *n.*

monoxide (mɒ'nɒksaɪd) *n.* an oxide that contains one oxygen atom per molecule.

Monseigneur (ˌmɒnsen'jɜː) *n., pl.* **Messeigneurs** (ˌmeɪsen'jɜː). a title given to French prelates and princes.

monsieur (məs'jɜː) *n., pl.* **messieurs.** a French title of address equivalent to *sir* or *Mr.*

Monsignor (mɒn'siːnjə) *n., pl.* **Monsignors** *or* **Monsignori** (ˌmɒnsiː'njɔːriː). *R.C. Church.* an ecclesiastical title attached to certain offices.

monsoon (mɒn'suːn) *n.* **1.** a seasonal wind of S Asia from the southwest in summer and from the northeast in winter. **2.** the rainy season when the SW monsoon blows, from about April to October.

mons pubis ('mɒnz 'pjuːbɪs) *n., pl.* **montes pubis** ('mɒntiːz). the fatty flesh in human males over the junction of the pubic bones.

monster ('mɒnstə) *n.* **1.** an imaginary beast, usually frightening in appearance.

2. a person, animal, or plant with a marked deformity. **3.** a cruel, wicked, or inhuman person. **4.** a very large person, animal, or thing.

monstrance ('mɒnstrəns) *n. R.C. Church.* a vessel in which the consecrated Host is exposed for adoration.

monstrosity (mɒn'strɒsɪtɪ) *n., pl.* **-ties.** **1.** an outrageous or ugly person or thing. **2.** the state or quality of being monstrous.

monstrous ('mɒnstrəs) *adj.* **1.** hideous or unnatural in size or character. **2.** (of plants and animals) abnormal in structure. **3.** outrageous, atrocious, or shocking. **4.** huge. **5.** of or like a monster. —'**monstrously** *adv.*

mons veneris ('mɒnz 'vɛnərɪs) *n., pl.* **montes veneris** ('mɒntiːz). the fatty flesh in human females over the junction of the pubic bones.

Mont. Montana.

montage (mɒn'tɑːʒ) *n.* **1.** the creation of pictures from miscellaneous elements, such as other pictures or photographs. **2.** such a composition. **3.** a method of film editing by juxtaposition or partial superimposition of several shots to form a single image. **4.** a film sequence of this kind.

month (mʌnθ) *n.* **1.** one of the twelve divisions (**calendar months**) of the calendar year. **2.** a period of time extending from one date to a corresponding date in the next calendar month. **3.** a period of four weeks or of 30 days.

monthly ('mʌnθlɪ) *adj.* **1.** occurring, done, or payable once every month. **2.** lasting or valid for a month. ~*adv.* **3.** once a month. ~*n., pl.* **-lies.** **4.** a book or periodical published once a month.

monument ('mɒnjʊmənt) *n.* **1.** something, such as a statue or building, erected in commemoration of a person or event. **2.** a tomb or tombstone. **3.** an exceptional example: *his lecture was a monument of tedium.*

monumental (ˌmɒnjʊ'mɛntᵊl) *adj.* **1.** like a monument, esp. in large size, endurance, or importance. **2.** of or being a monument. **3.** *Informal.* extreme: *monumental stupidity.*

moo (muː) *vb.* **1.** (of a cow) to make a characteristic deep long sound; low. ~*interj.* **2.** this sound.

mooch (muːtʃ) *vb. Slang.* **1.** (often with *around*) to loiter or walk aimlessly. **2.** to cadge.

mood[1] (muːd) *n.* **1.** a temporary state of mind or temper: *a cheerful mood.* **2.** a sullen or gloomy state of mind, esp. when temporary: *she's in a mood.* **3.** a prevailing atmosphere or feeling. **4. in the mood.** inclined to do or have (something).

mood[2] (muːd) *n. Grammar.* a form of a verb indicating whether the verb expresses a fact (indicative mood), a wish or supposition (subjunctive mood), or a command (imperative mood).

moody ('muːdɪ) *adj.* **moodier, moodiest.**
1. sullen, sulky, or gloomy. **2.** temperamental or changeable. —'**moodily** *adv.*
—'**moodiness** *n.*

Moog (muːg) *n. Music, trademark.* a type of synthesizer.

mooi (mɔɪ) *adj. S. African slang.* pleasing; nice.

mooli ('muːlɪ) *n.* a type of large white radish.

moon (muːn) *n.* **1.** the natural satellite of the earth. **2.** this satellite as it is seen during its revolution around the earth, esp. at one of its phases: *new moon; full moon.*
3. any natural satellite of a planet. **4.** a month. **5. over the moon.** *Informal.* extremely happy; ecstatic. ~*vb.* **6.** (often foll. by *away* or *around*) to be idle in a listless way or to idle (time) away.
—'**moonless** *adj.*

moonbeam ('muːnˌbiːm) *n.* a ray of moonlight.

moon-faced *adj.* having a round face.

moonlight ('muːnˌlaɪt) *n.* **1.** light from the sun received on earth after reflection by the moon. **2.** (*modifier*) illuminated by the moon: *a moonlight walk.* ~*vb.* **-lighting, -lighted. 3.** *Informal.* to work at a secondary job, esp. at night and illegally.
—'**moon,lighter** *n.*

moonlight flit *n. Brit. informal.* a hurried departure at night to avoid paying rent.

moonlit ('muːnlɪt) *adj.* illuminated by the moon.

moonscape ('muːnˌskeɪp) *n.* the surface of the moon or a representation of it.

moonshine ('muːnˌʃaɪn) *n.* **1.** moonlight. **2.** *U.S. & Canad.* illegally distilled or smuggled whisky. **3.** foolish talk or thought.

moonshot ('muːnˌʃɒt) *n.* the launching of a spacecraft to the moon.

moonstone ('muːnˌstəʊn) *n.* a white translucent form of feldspar, used as a gem.

moonstruck ('muːnˌstrʌk) *adj.* deranged or mad.

moony ('muːnɪ) *adj.* **moonier, mooniest.**
Informal. dreamy or listless.

moor[1] (mʊə, mɔː) *n.* an expanse of open ground, usually covered with heather, coarse grass, and bracken.

moor[2] (mʊə, mɔː) *vb.* to secure (a ship or boat) with cables, ropes, or anchors or (of a ship or boat) to be secured in this way.
—'**moorage** *n.*

Moor (mʊə, mɔː) *n.* a member of a Muslim people of North Africa who ruled Spain between the 8th and 15th centuries.
—'**Moorish** *adj.*

moorhen ('mʊəˌhɛn, 'mɔː-) *n.* a waterfowl with black plumage and a red bill.

mooring ('mʊərɪŋ, 'mɔː-) *n.* **1.** a place for

anchoring a vessel. **2.** (*pl.*) *Naut.* the ropes and anchors used in mooring a vessel.

moorland ('mʊələnd) *n. Brit.* an area of moor.

moose (muːs) *n., pl.* **moose.** a large North American deer with large flattened antlers; the American elk.

moot (muːt) *adj.* **1.** subject or open to debate: *a moot point.* ~*vb.* **2.** to suggest or bring up for debate. ~*n.* **3.** (in Anglo-Saxon England) a local administrative assembly.

mop (mɒp) *n.* **1.** a tool with a long handle and a head made of twists of cotton or sponge, used for washing or polishing floors, and for washing dishes. **2.** something resembling this, such as a tangle of hair. ~*vb.* **mopping, mopped. 3.** to clean or soak up as with a mop. ~See also **mop up.**

mope (məʊp) *vb.* **1.** to be gloomy or apathetic. **2.** to move or act in an aimless way. ~*n.* **3.** a gloomy person.

moped ('məʊped) *n. Brit.* a light motorcycle not over 50cc.

mopes (məʊps) *pl. n.* **the.** low spirits.

mopoke ('məʊˌpəʊk) *n.* **1.** a small spotted owl of Australia and New Zealand. **2.** *Austral. & N.Z. slang.* a slow or lugubrious person.

moppet ('mɒpɪt) *n.* same as **poppet.**

mop up *vb.* **1.** to clean with a mop. **2.** *Informal.* to complete (a task). **3.** *Mil.* to clear (remaining enemy forces) after a battle, by killing them or taking them prisoner.

moquette (mɒ'kɛt) *n.* a thick velvety fabric used for carpets and upholstery.

moraine (mɒ'reɪn) *n.* a mass of debris, carried by glaciers and forming ridges and mounds when deposited.

moral ('mɒrəl) *adj.* **1.** concerned with or relating to the distinction between good and bad or right and wrong behaviour: *moral sense.* **2.** based on a sense of right and wrong: *moral duty.* **3.** having psychological rather than physical effects: *moral support.* ~*n.* **4.** the lesson to be obtained from a fable or event. **5.** (*pl.*) principles of behaviour in accordance with standards of right and wrong. —'**morally** *adv.*

morale (mɒ'rɑːl) *n.* the degree of confidence or optimism of a person or group.

moralist ('mɒrəlɪst) *n.* **1.** a person who seeks to regulate the morals of others. **2.** a person who lives in accordance with moral principles. —,**moral'istic** *adj.*

morality (mə'rælɪtɪ) *n., pl.* **-ties. 1.** the quality of being moral. **2.** conformity, or degree of conformity, to moral ideals. **3.** a system of moral principles.

morality play *n.* a medieval type of drama concerned with the conflict between personified virtues and vices.

moralize *or* **-lise** ('mɒrəˌlaɪz) *vb.* **1.** to

make moral pronouncements. **2.** to interpret or explain in a moral sense. **3.** to improve the morals of.

moral philosophy *n.* the branch of philosophy dealing with ethics.

morass (məˈræs) *n.* **1.** a tract of swampy low-lying land. **2.** a disordered, confusing, or muddled state of affairs.

moratorium (ˌmɒrəˈtɔːrɪəm) *n., pl.* **-ria** (-rɪə) *or* **-riums.** **1.** a legally authorized postponement of the payment of a debt. **2.** an agreed suspension of activity.

moray (mɒˈreɪ) *n.* a voracious marine coastal eel marked with brilliant colours.

morbid (ˈmɔːbɪd) *adj.* **1.** having an unusual interest in death or unpleasant events. **2.** gruesome. **3.** relating to or characterized by disease. **—morˈbidity** *n.* **—ˈmorbidly** *adv.*

mordant (ˈmɔːd²nt) *adj.* **1.** sarcastic or caustic. *~n.* **2.** a substance used in dyeing to fix colours. **3.** an acid or other corrosive fluid used to etch lines on a printing plate.

more (mɔː) *det.* **1.** the comparative of **much** or **many:** *more joy than you know; even more are dying.* **2.** additional; further: *no more bananas.* **3. more of.** to a greater extent or degree: *more of a nuisance.* *~adv.* **4.** used to form the comparative of some adjectives and adverbs: *more quickly.* **5.** the comparative of **much:** *people listen to the radio more now.* **6. more or less. a.** as an estimate; approximately. **b.** to an unspecified extent or degree: *the party was ruined, more or less.* **Usage.** see **most.**

moreish *or* **morish** (ˈmɔːrɪʃ) *adj. Informal.* (of food) causing a desire for more.

morel (mɒˈrɛl) *n.* an edible mushroom with a pitted cap.

morello (məˈrɛləʊ) *n., pl.* **-los.** a variety of small dark sour cherry.

moreover (mɔːˈrəʊvə) *adv.* in addition to what has already been said.

morepork (ˈmɔːˌpɔːk) *n. Chiefly N.Z.* same as **mopoke.**

mores (ˈmɔːreɪz) *pl. n.* the customs and conventions embodying the fundamental values of a community.

morganatic (ˌmɔːɡəˈnætɪk) *adj.* of or designating a marriage between a person of high rank and a person of low rank, by which the latter is not elevated to the higher rank and any children have no rights to inherit the higher party's titles or property.

morgue (mɔːɡ) *n.* **1.** a mortuary. **2.** *Informal.* a store of clippings and back numbers used for reference in a newspaper.

moribund (ˈmɒrɪˌbʌnd) *adj.* **1.** near death. **2.** without force or vitality.

Morisco (məˈrɪskəʊ) *n., pl.* **-cos** *or* **-coes.** **1.** a Spanish Moor. *~adj.* **2.** Moorish.

morish (ˈmɔːrɪʃ) *adj.* same as **moreish.**

Mormon (ˈmɔːmən) *n.* **1.** a member of the Church of Jesus Christ of Latter-day Saints, founded in 1830 in New York by Joseph Smith. *~adj.* **2.** of the Mormons, their Church, or their beliefs. **—ˈMormonism** *n.*

morn (mɔːn) *n. Poetic.* morning.

mornay (ˈmɔːneɪ) *adj.* denoting a cheese sauce: *eggs mornay.*

morning (ˈmɔːnɪŋ) *n.* **1.** the first part of the day, ending at noon. **2.** daybreak; dawn. **3. the morning after.** *Informal.* the aftereffects of excess, esp. a hangover. **4.** (*modifier*) of or in the morning: *morning coffee.*

morning dress *n.* formal day dress for men, comprising a cutaway frock coat (**morning coat**), usually with grey trousers and top hat.

morning-glory *n., pl.* **-ries.** a tropical climbing plant with trumpet-shaped blue, pink, or white flowers, which close in late afternoon.

mornings (ˈmɔːnɪŋz) *adv. Informal.* in the morning, esp. regularly, or during every morning.

morning sickness *n.* nausea occurring shortly after rising in early pregnancy.

morning star *n.* a planet, usually Venus, seen just before sunrise.

Moroccan (məˈrɒkən) *adj.* **1.** of or denoting Morocco, a kingdom in NW Africa, or its inhabitants. *~n.* **2.** a person from Morocco.

morocco (məˈrɒkəʊ) *n.* a fine soft leather made from goatskins.

moron (ˈmɔːrɒn) *n.* **1.** a foolish or stupid person. **2.** a person having an intelligence quotient of between 50 and 70. **—moronic** (məˈrɒnɪk) *adj.*

morose (məˈrəʊs) *adj.* ill-tempered or gloomy. **—moˈrosely** *adv.*

morpheme (ˈmɔːfiːm) *n. Linguistics.* a speech element having a meaning or grammatical function that cannot be subdivided into further such elements.

morphine (ˈmɔːfiːn) *or* **morphia** (ˈmɔːfɪə) *n.* a drug extracted from opium: used in medicine as an anaesthetic and sedative.

morphology (mɔːˈfɒlədʒɪ) *n.* the form and structure of anything, esp. organisms or words. **—morphological** (ˌmɔːfəˈlɒdʒɪk²l) *adj.*

morris dance (ˈmɒrɪs) *n.* an old English folk dance usually performed by men (**morris men**) adorned with bells.

morrow (ˈmɒrəʊ) *n.* (usually preceded by *the*) *Archaic or poetic.* **1.** the next day. **2.** the morning.

Morse code (mɔːs) *n.* a code used internationally for transmitting messages. Letters and numbers are represented by groups of dots and dashes, or by shorter and longer sounds.

morsel (ˈmɔːs²l) *n.* **1.** a small slice or mouthful of food. **2.** a small piece; bit.

mortal (ˈmɔːtʰl) *adj.* **1.** (of living beings, esp. humans) subject to death. **2.** of or involving life or the world. **3.** causing death; fatal: *a mortal blow.* **4.** deadly or unrelenting: *a mortal enemy.* **5.** of or like the fear of death: *mortal terror.* **6.** great or very intense: *mortal pain.* **7.** conceivable or possible: *there was no mortal reason to go.* **8.** *Slang.* long and tedious: *for three mortal hours.* ~*n.* **9.** a mortal being. **10.** *Informal.* a person: *a mean mortal.* —ˈ**mortally** *adv.*

mortality (mɔːˈtælɪtɪ) *n., pl.* -**ties.** **1.** the condition of being mortal. **2.** great loss of life, as in war or disaster. **3.** the number of deaths in a given period.

mortal sin *n. Christianity.* a sin regarded as involving total loss of grace.

mortar (ˈmɔːtə) *n.* **1.** a mixture of cement or lime or both with sand and water, used as a bond between bricks or stones. **2.** a cannon with a short barrel that fires shells in high arcs. **3.** a vessel, usually bowl-shaped, in which substances are crushed with a pestle. ~*vb.* **4.** to join (bricks or stones) with mortar. **5.** to fire on with mortars.

mortarboard (ˈmɔːtəˌbɔːd) *n.* **1.** a black tasselled academic cap with a flat square top. **2.** a small square board with a handle on the underside for carrying mortar.

mortgage (ˈmɔːgɪdʒ) *n.* **1.** a conditional pledging of property, such as a house, as security for the repayment of a loan. **2.** the deed effecting such a transaction. **3.** the loan itself. ~*vb.* **4.** to convey (property) by mortgage.

mortician (mɔːˈtɪʃən) *n. Chiefly U.S.* same as **undertaker.**

mortify (ˈmɔːtɪˌfaɪ) *vb.* -**fying,** -**fied.** **1.** to humiliate or cause to feel shame. **2.** *Christianity.* to subdue and bring under control (one's emotions, the body, etc.) by self-denial. **3.** to become gangrenous. —**mortification** (ˌmɔːtɪfɪˈkeɪʃən) *n.* —ˈ**morti‚fying** *adj.*

mortise *or* **mortice** (ˈmɔːtɪs) *n.* **1.** a slot or recess cut into a piece of wood or stone to receive a matching projection (tenon) on another piece, or a mortise lock. ~*vb.* **2.** to cut a slot or recess in (a piece of wood or stone) **3.** to join (two pieces of wood or stone) by means of a mortise and tenon.

mortise lock *n.* a lock set into the edge of a door so that the mechanism of the lock is enclosed by the door.

mortuary (ˈmɔːtʃʊərɪ) *n., pl.* -**aries.** a building where dead bodies are kept before cremation or burial.

mosaic (məˈzeɪɪk) *n.* a design or decoration made up of small pieces of coloured glass or stone.

Mosaic (məʊˈzeɪɪk) *adj.* of or relating to Moses or the laws and traditions ascribed to him.

moselle (məʊˈzɛl) *n.* a German white wine from the valley of the river Moselle.

mosey (ˈməʊzɪ) *vb. Informal.* (often foll. by *along* or *on*) to amble.

Moslem (ˈmɒzləm) *n., pl.* -**lems** *or* -**lem,** *adj.* same as **Muslim.**

mosque (mɒsk) *n.* a Muslim place of worship.

mosquito (məˈskiːtəʊ) *n., pl.* -**toes** *or* -**tos.** a two-winged insect, the females of which pierce the skin of man and animals to suck their blood.

mosquito net *n.* a fine curtain or net to keep mosquitoes out.

moss (mɒs) *n.* **1.** a very small flowerless plant typically growing in dense mats on trees, rocks, or moist ground. **2.** *Scot. & N English.* a peat bog or marsh. —ˈ**mossy** *adj.*

mossie (ˈmɒsɪ) *n.* same as **cape sparrow.**

moss rose *n.* a variety of rose that has a mossy stem and fragrant pink flowers.

most (məʊst) *det.* **1.** a great majority of; nearly all: *most of it is finished.* **2. the most.** the superlative of **many** and **much:** *you have the most money.* **3. at (the) most.** at the maximum: *that girl is four at the most.* **4. make the most of.** to use to the best advantage: *she made the most of the chance.* ~*adv.* **5. the most.** used to form the superlative of some adjectives and adverbs: *the most beautiful daughter of all.* **6.** the superlative of **much.** **7.** very; exceedingly: *a most absurd story.*
Usage. The meanings of *most* and *mostly* should not be confused. In *she was most affected by the news, most* is equivalent to *very* and is generally acceptable. In *she was mostly affected by the news,* the implication is that there was something else, in addition to the news, which affected her, although less so. *More* and *most* should also be distinguished when used in comparisons. *More* applies to cases involving two persons, objects, etc., *most* to cases involving three or more: *John is the more intelligent of the two; he is the most intelligent of the students.*

mostly (ˈməʊstlɪ) *adv.* **1.** almost entirely; chiefly. **2.** on many or most occasions; usually.

Most Reverend *n.* (in Britain) a courtesy title applied to archbishops.

mot (məʊ) *n.* short for **bon mot.**

MOT **1.** *Brit. & N.Z.* Ministry of Transport (*Brit.,* now Transport Industries). **2.** *Brit.* the MOT test or test certificate.

mote (məʊt) *n.* a tiny speck.

motel (məʊˈtɛl) *n.* a roadside hotel for motorists.

motet (məʊˈtɛt) *n.* a polyphonic religious song for choir.

moth (mɒθ) *n.* any of numerous chiefly nocturnal insects resembling butterflies, that typically have stout bodies with antennae of various shapes (but not clubbed).

mothball ('mɒθˌbɔːl) *n.* **1.** a small ball of camphor or naphthalene placed in stored clothing to repel clothes moths. **2. put in mothballs.** to postpone work on (a project or activity). ~*vb.* **3.** to take (something) out of operation but maintain it for future use. **4.** to postpone work on (a project or activity).

moth-eaten *adj.* **1.** decayed, decrepit, or outdated. **2.** eaten away by or as if by moths.

mother ('mʌðə) *n.* **1.** a female who has given birth to offspring. **2.** (*often cap., esp. as a term of address*) a person's own mother. **3.** motherly qualities, such as maternal affection: *it appealed to the mother in her.* **4.** a female or thing that creates, nurtures, or protects something. **5.** a title given to certain members of female religious orders. **6.** (*modifier*) native or innate: *mother wit.* ~*vb.* **7.** to give birth to or produce. **8.** to nurture or protect. —'**motherless** *adj.* —'**motherly** *adj.*

Mother Carey's chicken ('kɛərɪz) *n.* same as **stormy petrel.**

mother country *n.* **1.** the original country of colonists or settlers. **2.** a person's native country.

Mother Goose *n.* the imaginary author of a collection of nursery rhymes.

motherhood ('mʌðəˌhʊd) *n.* the state of being a mother.

Mothering Sunday ('mʌðərɪŋ) *n. Brit.* the fourth Sunday in Lent, when mothers traditionally receive presents from their children. Also called: **Mother's Day.**

mother-in-law *n., pl.* **mothers-in-law.** the mother of one's wife or husband.

motherland ('mʌðəˌlænd) *n.* a person's native country.

mother-of-pearl *n.* a hard iridescent substance that forms the inner layer of the shells of certain molluscs, such as the oyster.

Mother's Day *n.* **1.** See **Mothering Sunday.** **2.** *U.S. & Canad.* the second Sunday in May, observed as a day in honour of mothers.

mother superior *n., pl.* **mother superiors** *or* **mothers superior.** the head of a community of nuns.

mother tongue *n.* the language first learned by a child.

mothproof ('mɒθˌpruːf) *adj.* **1.** (esp. of clothes) chemically treated so as to repel clothes moths. ~*vb.* **2.** to make mothproof.

motif (məʊ'tiːf) *n.* **1.** a distinctive idea, esp. a theme elaborated on in a piece of music or literature. **2.** a recurring shape in a design.

3. a single decoration, such as a symbol or name on a piece of clothing.

motion ('məʊʃən) *n.* **1.** the process of continual change in the position of an object; movement. **2.** a movement or action, esp. of part of the human body; a gesture. **3. a.** the capacity for movement. **b.** a manner of movement, esp. walking; gait. **4.** a formal proposal to be discussed and voted on in a debate or meeting. **5.** *Brit.* **a.** the evacuation of the bowels. **b.** excrement. **6. go through the motions.** to do something mechanically or without sincerity. **7. set in motion.** to make operational or start functioning. ~*vb.* **8.** to signal or direct (a person) by a movement or gesture. —'**motionless** *adj.*

motion picture *n. U.S. & Canad.* a film; movie.

motivate ('məʊtɪˌveɪt) *vb.* to give incentive to. —ˌ**moti'vation** *n.*

motive ('məʊtɪv) *n.* **1.** the reason for a certain course of action, whether conscious or unconscious. **2.** same as **motif** (sense 2). ~*adj.* **3.** of or causing motion: *a motive force.*

motive power *n.* **1.** any source of energy used to produce motion. **2.** the means of supplying power to an engine or vehicle.

mot juste (ˌməʊ 'ʒuːst) *n., pl.* **mots justes** (ˌməʊ 'ʒuːst). the appropriate word or expression.

motley ('mɒtlɪ) *adj.* **1.** made up of disparate elements. **2.** multicoloured. ~*n.* **3.** *History.* the costume of a jester.

motocross ('məʊtəˌkrɒs) *n.* the sport of motorcycle racing across rough ground.

motor ('məʊtə) *n.* **1.** the engine, esp. an internal-combustion engine, of a vehicle. **2.** a machine that converts energy, esp. electrical energy, into mechanical energy. **3.** *Chiefly Brit.* a car. ~*adj.* **4.** producing or causing motion. **5.** powered by or relating to a motor. ~*vb.* **6.** to travel by car. **7.** *Informal.* to move fast. —'**motoˌrize** *or* **-ise** *vb.*

motorbicycle ('məʊtəˌbaɪsɪkʰl) *n.* **1.** a motorcycle. **2.** a moped.

motorbike ('məʊtəˌbaɪk) *n. Informal.* a motorcycle.

motorboat ('məʊtəˌbəʊt) *n.* any boat powered by a motor.

motorcade ('məʊtəˌkeɪd) *n.* a procession of cars carrying important people.

motorcar ('məʊtəˌkɑː) *n.* a more formal word for **car.**

motorcycle ('məʊtəˌsaɪkʰl) *n.* a two-wheeled vehicle that is driven by a petrol engine. —'**motorˌcyclist** *n.*

motorist ('məʊtərɪst) *n.* a driver of a car.

motorman ('məʊtəmən) *n., pl.* **-men.** the driver of an electric train.

motor scooter *n.* a light motorcycle with small wheels and an enclosed engine.

motor vehicle *n.* a road vehicle driven by an engine.

motorway ('məʊtə‚weɪ) *n. Brit.* a dual carriageway for fast-moving traffic, with no stopping permitted and no crossroads.

Motown ('məʊ‚taʊn) *n.* music combining rhythm and blues and pop.

motte (mɒt) *n. History.* a mound on which a castle was built.

MOT test *n.* (in Britain) a compulsory annual test of the roadworthiness of motor vehicles over a certain age.

mottle ('mɒt²l) *vb.* to colour with streaks or blotches of different shades. —'**mottled** *adj.*

motto ('mɒtəʊ) *n., pl.* -**toes** *or* -**tos.** 1. a short saying expressing the guiding maxim or ideal of a family or organization, esp. when part of a coat of arms. 2. a verse or maxim contained in a paper cracker. 3. a quotation prefacing a book or chapter of a book.

mould¹ *or U.S.* **mold** (məʊld) *n.* 1. a shaped cavity used to give a definite form to fluid or plastic material. 2. a frame on which something may be constructed. 3. something made in or on a mould. 4. shape, form, design, or pattern. 5. specific nature, character, or type. ~*vb.* 6. to make in a mould. 7. to shape or form, as by using a mould. 8. to influence or direct: *to mould opinion.*

mould² *or U.S.* **mold** (məʊld) *n.* a coating or discoloration caused by various fungi that develop in a damp atmosphere on food, fabrics, and walls.

mould³ *or U.S.* **mold** (məʊld) *n.* loose soil, esp. when rich in organic matter.

mouldboard *or U.S.* **moldboard** ('məʊld‚bɔːd) *n.* the curved blade of a plough, which turns over the furrow.

moulder *or U.S.* **molder** ('məʊldə) *vb.* (often foll. by *away*) to crumble or cause to crumble, as through decay.

moulding *or U.S.* **molding** ('məʊldɪŋ) *n.* 1. a shaped outline, such as one used on cornices. 2. a shaped strip made of wood or stone.

mouldy *or U.S.* **moldy** ('məʊldɪ) *adj.* -**dier,** -**diest.** 1. covered with mould. 2. stale or musty, esp. from age or lack of use. 3. *Slang.* boring; dull.

moult *or U.S.* **molt** (məʊlt) *vb.* 1. (of birds and animals) to shed (feathers, hair, or cuticle) so that they can be replaced by a new growth. ~*n.* 2. the periodic process of moulting.

mound (maʊnd) *n.* 1. a raised mass of earth, debris, etc. 2. any heap or pile. 3. a small natural hill. 4. an artificial ridge of earth, stone, etc., as used for defence.

mount¹ (maʊnt) *vb.* 1. to climb or ascend (stairs or a slope). 2. to get up on (a horse, a platform, etc.). 3. (often foll. by *up*) to

increase; accumulate: *excitement mounted.* 4. to fix onto a backing, setting, or support: *to mount a photograph.* 5. to organize and stage (a campaign, a play, etc.). ~*n.* 6. a backing, setting, or support onto which something is fixed. 7. a horse for riding.

mount² (maʊnt) *n.* a mountain or hill: used in literature and (when cap.) in proper names: *Mount Everest.*

mountain ('maʊntɪn) *n.* 1. a natural upward projection of the earth's surface, higher and steeper than a hill. 2. a huge heap or mass: *a mountain of papers.* 3. anything of great quantity or size. 4. a surplus of a commodity, esp. in the European Community: *a butter mountain.*

mountain ash *n.* any of various trees, such as the rowan, with clusters of small white flowers and bright red berries.

mountain bike *n.* a type of bicycle with straight handlebars and heavy-duty tyres.

mountain cat *n.* any of various wild feline mammals, such as the bobcat, lynx, or puma.

mountaineer (‚maʊntɪ'nɪə) *n.* 1. a person who climbs mountains. ~*vb.* 2. to climb mountains. —‚**mountain'eering** *n.*

mountain goat *n.* any wild goat inhabiting mountainous regions.

mountain lion *n.* a puma.

mountainous ('maʊntɪnəs) *adj.* 1. having many mountains: *a mountainous region.* 2. like a mountain, esp. in size.

mountain sickness *n.* nausea, headache, and shortness of breath caused by climbing to high altitudes.

mountebank ('maʊntɪ‚bæŋk) *n.* 1. (formerly) a person who sold quack medicines in public places. 2. a charlatan; fake.

mounted ('maʊntɪd) *adj.* riding horses: *mounted police.*

Mountie *or* **Mounty** ('maʊntɪ) *n., pl.* **Mounties.** *Informal.* a member of the Royal Canadian Mounted Police.

mounting ('maʊntɪŋ) *n.* same as **mount¹** (sense 6).

mourn (mɔːn) *vb.* to feel or express sadness for the death or loss of (someone or something). —'**mourner** *n.*

mournful ('mɔːnful) *adj.* 1. evoking grief; sorrowful. 2. gloomy; sad. —'**mournfully** *adv.*

mourning ('mɔːnɪŋ) *n.* 1. sorrow or grief, esp. over a death. 2. the conventional symbols of grief, such as the wearing of black. 3. the period of time during which a death is officially mourned. ~*adj.* 4. of or relating to mourning.

mouse *n.* (maʊs), *pl.* **mice** (maɪs). 1. any of numerous small long-tailed rodents that are similar to but smaller than rats. 2. a quiet, timid, or cowardly person. 3. *Computers.* a hand-held device used to control cursor movements and computing functions without keying. ~vb. (mauz). **4.** to stalk and catch (mice).

mouser ('mauzə, 'mausə) n. a cat or other animal that is used to catch mice.

mousetrap ('maus,træp) n. **1.** a spring-loaded trap for killing mice. **2.** *Brit. informal.* cheese of indifferent quality.

moussaka (mu'sɑːkə) n. a dish originating in the Balkan States, consisting of meat, aubergines, and tomatoes, topped with cheese sauce.

mousse (muːs) n. **1.** a light creamy dessert made with eggs, cream, and fruit set with gelatin. **2.** a similar dish made from fish or meat. **3.** short for **styling mousse**.

moustache or U.S. **mustache** (mə'stɑːʃ) n. unshaved hair growing on the upper lip.

mousy or **mousey** ('mausı) adj. **mousier**, **mousiest**. **1.** resembling a mouse, esp. in hair colour. **2.** shy or ineffectual. —'**mousiness** n.

mouth n. (mauθ), pl. **mouths** (mauðz). **1.** the opening through which many animals take in food and issue vocal sounds. **2.** the visible part of the mouth; lips. **3.** a person regarded as a consumer of food: *four mouths to feed.* **4.** a particular manner of speaking: *a foul mouth.* **5.** *Informal.* boastful, rude, or excessive talk: *he is all mouth.* **6.** the point where a river issues into a sea or lake. **7.** an opening, such as that of a bottle, tunnel, or gun. **8. down in the mouth.** in low spirits. ~vb. (mauð). **9.** to speak or say (something) insincerely, esp. in public. **10.** to form (words) with movements of the lips but without speaking.

mouthful ('mauθ,ful) n., pl. **-fuls**. **1.** as much as is held in the mouth at one time. **2.** a small quantity, as of food. **3.** a long word or phrase that is difficult to say. **4.** *Brit. informal.* an abusive response.

mouth organ n. same as **harmonica**.

mouthpiece ('mauθ,piːs) n. **1.** the part of a wind instrument into which the player blows. **2.** the part of a telephone receiver into which a person speaks. **3.** a person or publication expressing the views of an organization.

mouthwash ('mauθ,wɒʃ) n. a medicated solution for gargling and cleansing the mouth.

mouthwatering ('mauθ,wɔːtərɪŋ) adj. (of food) making one want to eat it, because it looks or smells delicious.

movable or **moveable** ('muːvəb°l) adj. **1.** able to be moved; not fixed. **2.** (of a festival, esp. Easter) varying in date from year to year. ~n. **3.** (often pl.) a movable article, esp. a piece of furniture.

move (muːv) vb. **1.** to go or take from one place to another; change in position. **2.** to change (one's dwelling or place of business). **3.** to be or cause to be in motion; stir. **4.** (of machines) to work or operate. **5.** to cause (to do something); prompt: *public*

opinion *moved the government to action.* **6.** to begin to act: *move soon or we'll lose the order.* **7.** to associate oneself with a specified social circle: *to move in exalted spheres.* **8.** to make progress. **9.** to arouse affection, pity, or compassion in; touch. **10.** (in board games) to change the position of (a piece). **11.** (of merchandise) to be disposed of by being bought. **12.** to suggest (a proposal) formally, as in debating or parliamentary procedure. **13.** to cause (the bowels) to evacuate or (of the bowels) to be evacuated. ~n. **14.** the act of moving; movement. **15.** one of a sequence of actions, usually part of a plan; manoeuvre. **16.** the act of moving one's residence or place of business. **17.** (in board games) **a.** a player's turn to move his piece. **b.** a manoeuvre of a piece. **18. get a move on.** *Informal.* to hurry up. **19. on the move.** travelling from place to place.

move in vb. **1.** Also: **move into.** to start to live or be based in (a new residence or place of business). **2.** (often foll. by *on*) *Informal.* to try to gain power or influence (over).

movement ('muːvmənt) n. **1.** the act, process, or an instance of moving. **2.** the manner of moving. **3. a.** a group of people with a common ideology. **b.** the organized action of such a group. **4.** a trend or tendency. **5.** the driving and regulating mechanism of a watch or clock. **6.** (often pl.) a person's location and activities during a specific time. **7. a.** the evacuation of the bowels. **b.** the matter evacuated. **8.** *Music.* a principal self-contained section of a large-scale work, such as a symphony.

mover ('muːvə) n. **1.** Informal. a person, business, idea, etc., that is advancing or progressing. **2.** a person who moves a proposal, as in a debate. **3.** U.S. & Canad. a removal firm or a person who works for one.

movie ('muːvɪ) n. Informal. same as **film** (sense 1).

moving ('muːvɪŋ) adj. **1.** arousing or touching the emotions. **2.** changing or capable of changing position. —'**movingly** adv.

moving staircase or **stairway** n. an escalator.

mow (məu) vb. **mowing**, **mowed**, **mowed** or **mown**. **1.** to cut down (grass or crops). **2.** to cut the growing vegetation of (a field or lawn). —'**mower** n.

mow down vb. to kill in large numbers, esp. by gunfire.

mown (məun) vb. the past participle of **mow**.

mozzarella (,mɒtsə'rɛlə) n. a moist white curd cheese originally made in Italy from buffalo milk.

mp *Music.* moderately soft.

MP 1. Member of Parliament. 2. Military Police. 3. Mounted Police.

mpg miles per gallon.

mph miles per hour.

MPhil Master of Philosophy.

Mr ('mɪstə) *n., pl.* **Messrs.** a title used before a man's name or before some office that he holds: *Mr Brown; Mr President.*

Mrs ('mɪsɪz) *n., pl.* **Mrs** *or* **Mesdames.** a title used before the name of a married woman. **Usage.** see **Ms.**

Ms (mɪz) *n.* a title used before the name of a woman to avoid indicating whether she is married or not.

Usage. *Ms* as a form of address, while not universally liked, has gained wide acceptance in recent years. It fulfils the need for a title corresponding to *Mr* in contexts where it is undesirable or irrelevant to distinguish between married and unmarried women or where a woman's marital status is not known.

MS 1. Mississippi. 2. multiple sclerosis.

MS. *or* **ms.,** *pl.* **MSS.** *or* **mss.** manuscript.

MSc Master of Science.

MSC (in Britain) Manpower Services Commission.

MSG monosodium glutamate.

MST (in the U.S. and Canada) Mountain Standard Time.

Mt Mount: *Mt Everest.*

MT Montana.

MTech (in the U.S. and Canada) Master of Technology.

much (mʌtʃ) *det.* 1. (*usually used with a negative*) a great quantity or amount: *there isn't much honey left.* 2. **a bit much.** *Informal.* rather excessive. 3. **make much of. a.** (*used with a negative*) to make sense of: *he couldn't make much of her babble.* **b.** to give importance to: *she made much of this fact.* 4. **not much of.** not to any appreciable degree or extent: *he's not much of an actor.* 5. **not up to much.** *Informal.* of a low standard: *this beer is not up to much.* ~*adv.* 6. considerably: *they're much better now.* 7. practically; nearly: *it's much the same.* 8. (*usually used with a negative*) often; a great deal: *it doesn't happen much in this country.* 9. (**as**) **much as.** even though; although: *much as I'd like to, I can't come.* ~See also **more** and **most.**

muchness ('mʌtʃnɪs) *n.* **much of a muchness.** *Brit.* very similar.

mucilage ('mjuːsɪlɪdʒ) *n.* 1. a sticky preparation, such as gum, used as an adhesive. 2. a glutinous substance secreted by certain plants. —**mucilaginous** (ˌmjuːsɪ'lædʒɪnəs) *adj.*

muck (mʌk) *n.* 1. farmyard dung or decaying vegetable matter. 2. dirt or filth. 3. *Slang, chiefly Brit.* rubbish. 4. **make a muck of.** *Slang, chiefly Brit.* to ruin or spoil. ~*vb.* 5. to spread manure upon

(fields). 6. to soil or pollute. 7. (*usually foll. by up*) *Brit. slang.* to ruin or spoil. 8. (*often foll. by out*) to clear muck from. —**'mucky** *adj.*

muck about *vb. Brit. slang.* 1. to waste time; misbehave. 2. (*often foll. by with*) to interfere with, annoy, or waste the time of.

muck in *vb. Brit. slang.* to share duties or work (with other people).

muckraking ('mʌkˌreɪkɪŋ) *n.* seeking out and exposing scandal concerning public figures. —**'muck,raker** *n.*

mucksweat ('mʌkˌswet) *n. Brit. informal.* profuse sweat.

mucous membrane *n.* a mucus-secreting membrane that lines body cavities or passages.

mucus ('mjuːkəs) *n.* the slimy protective secretion of the mucous membranes. —**mucosity** (mjuː'kɒsɪtɪ) *n.* —**'mucous** *adj.*

mud (mʌd) *n.* 1. soft wet earth, as found on the ground after rain or at the bottom of ponds. 2. (**someone's**) **name is mud.** *Informal.* (someone) is disgraced. 3. **throw mud at.** *Informal.* slander; vilify. ~*adj.* 4. made from mud or dried mud.

mud bath *n.* 1. a medicinal bath in heated mud. 2. a dirty or muddy occasion or state.

muddle ('mʌd²l) *vb.* 1. (*often foll. by up*) to mix up (objects or items). 2. to confuse. ~*n.* 3. a state of physical or mental confusion. —**'muddled** *adj.*

muddleheaded (ˌmʌd²l'hedɪd) *adj.* mentally confused or vague.

muddle through *vb. Chiefly Brit.* to succeed in spite of lack of organization.

muddy ('mʌdɪ) *adj.* **-dier, -diest.** 1. covered or filled with mud. 2. not clear or bright: *muddy colours.* 3. cloudy: *a muddy liquid.* 4. (esp. of thoughts) confused or vague. ~*vb.* **-dying, -died.** 5. to become or cause to become muddy. —**'muddily** *adv.* —**'muddiness** *n.*

mud flat *n.* an area of low muddy land that is covered at high tide but not at low tide.

mud flow *n.* the rapid downhill movement of a mass of mud, typically in the shape of a tongue.

mudguard ('mʌdˌgɑːd) *n.* a curved part of a bicycle or other vehicle attached above the wheels to reduce the amount of water or mud thrown up by them.

mudpack ('mʌdˌpæk) *n.* a cosmetic astringent paste containing fuller's earth.

mudslinging ('mʌdˌslɪŋɪŋ) *n.* casting malicious slurs on an opponent, esp. in politics. —**'mud,slinger** *n.*

muesli ('mjuːzlɪ) *n.* a mixture of rolled oats, nuts, and fruit, eaten with milk.

muezzin (muː'ɛzɪn) *n. Islam.* the official of

a mosque who calls the faithful to prayer from the minaret.

muff[1] (mʌf) *n.* an open-ended cylinder of fur or cloth into which the hands are placed for warmth.

muff[2] (mʌf) *vb.* **1.** to perform (an action) awkwardly. **2.** to bungle (a shot or catch).

muffin (ˈmʌfɪn) *n.* **1.** *Brit.* a thick round baked yeast roll, usually toasted and served with butter. **2.** *U.S. & Canad.* a small cup-shaped sweet bread roll, usually eaten hot with butter.

muffin man *n. Brit.* (formerly) an itinerant seller of muffins.

muffle (ˈmʌfᵊl) *vb.* **1.** (often foll. by *up*) to wrap up in a scarf or coat esp. for warmth. **2.** to deaden (a sound or noise), esp. by wrapping. **3.** to prevent (the expression of something) by (someone).

muffler (ˈmʌflə) *n.* **1.** a thick scarf worn for warmth. **2.** *U.S. & Canad.* a device to deaden sound, esp. one on a car exhaust; silencer.

mufti (ˈmʌftɪ) *n.* civilian dress, esp. as worn by a person who normally wears a military uniform.

mug[1] (mʌg) *n.* **1.** a large drinking cup with a handle, usually cylindrical and made of earthenware. **2.** Also called: **mugful.** the quantity held by a mug or its contents.

mug[2] (mʌg) *n.* **1.** *Slang.* a person's face or mouth. **2.** *Slang.* a gullible person, esp. one who is swindled easily. **3. a mug's game.** a worthless activity. ~*vb.* **mugging, mugged. 4.** *Informal.* to attack or rob (someone) violently. —ˈ**mugger** *n.*

muggins (ˈmʌgɪnz) *n.* (*functioning as sing.*) *Brit. slang.* **a.** a simpleton. **b.** a title used humorously to refer to oneself.

muggy (ˈmʌgɪ) *adj.* **-gier, -giest.** (of weather or air) unpleasantly warm and humid. —ˈ**mugginess** *n.*

mug shot *n. Informal.* a photograph of a person's face, esp. one resembling a police-file picture.

mug up *vb. Brit. slang.* to study (a subject) hard, esp. for an exam.

Muhammadan (muˈhæmədᵊn) *n., adj.* (not in Muslim use) same as **Muslim.**

mujaheddin or **mujahedeen** (ˌmuːdʒəhəˈdiːn) *pl. n.* (preceded by *the*) fundamentalist Muslim guerrillas.

mukluk (ˈmʌklʌk) *n.* a soft boot, usually of sealskin, worn by Inuits.

mulatto (mjuːˈlætəʊ) *n., pl.* **-tos** or **-toes.** a person having one Black and one White parent.

mulberry (ˈmʌlbərɪ, -brɪ) *n., pl.* **-ries. 1.** a tree with edible blackberry-like fruit, the leaves of which are used to feed silkworms. **2.** the fruit of any of these trees. ~*adj.* **3.** dark purple.

mulch (mʌltʃ) *n.* **1.** a mixture of half-rotten vegetable matter and peat used to protect

the roots of plants or enrich the soil. ~*vb.* **2.** to cover (the surface of land) with mulch.

mule[1] (mjuːl) *n.* **1.** the sterile offspring of a male donkey and a female horse, used as a beast of burden. **2.** a machine that spins cotton into yarn.

mule[2] (mjuːl) *n.* a backless shoe or slipper.

muleteer (ˌmjuːlɪˈtɪə) *n.* a person who drives mules.

mulish (ˈmjuːlɪʃ) *adj.* stubborn; obstinate.

mull[1] (mʌl) *vb.* (often foll. by *over*) to study or ponder.

mull[2] (mʌl) *vb.* to heat (wine or ale) with sugar and spices. —**mulled** *adj.*

mull[3] (mʌl) *n. Scot.* a promontory.

mullah (ˈmʌlə) *n.* (formerly) a Muslim scholar, teacher, or religious leader.

mullet (ˈmʌlɪt) *n.* any of various marine food fishes such as the red mullet.

mulligatawny (ˌmʌlɪgəˈtɔːnɪ) *n.* a curry-flavoured soup of Anglo-Indian origin.

mullion (ˈmʌlɪən) *n.* a slender vertical bar between the casements or panes of a window. —ˈ**mullioned** *adj.*

multi- *combining form.* **1.** many or much: *multimillion.* **2.** more than one: *multistorey.*

multicoloured (ˈmʌltɪˌkʌləd) *adj.* having many colours.

multicultural (ˌmʌltɪˈkʌltʃərəl) *adj.* of or for the cultures of several different races.

multifarious (ˌmʌltɪˈfɛərɪəs) *adj.* having many parts of great variety.

multiflora rose (ˌmʌltɪˈflɔːrə) *n.* a climbing rose with clusters of small fragrant flowers.

multiform (ˈmʌltɪˌfɔːm) *adj.* having many shapes or forms.

multilateral (ˌmʌltɪˈlætərəl) *adj.* **1.** of or involving more than two nations or parties: *a multilateral pact.* **2.** having many sides.

multilingual (ˌmʌltɪˈlɪŋgwəl) *adj.* **1.** able to speak more than two languages. **2.** written or expressed in more than two languages.

multimedia (ˌmʌltɪˈmiːdɪə) *pl. n.* the combined use of media such as television and slides.

multimillionaire (ˌmʌltɪˌmɪljəˈnɛə) *n.* a person with a fortune of several million pounds, dollars, etc.

multinational (ˌmʌltɪˈnæʃənᵊl) *adj.* **1.** (of a large business company) operating in several countries. ~*n.* **2.** such a company.

multiparous (mʌlˈtɪpərəs) *adj.* producing many offspring at one birth.

multiple (ˈmʌltɪpᵊl) *adj.* **1.** having or involving more than one part, individual, or element. ~*n.* **2.** the product of a given number or polynomial and any other one: *6 is a multiple of 2.* —ˈ**multiply** *adv.*

multiple-choice *adj.* having a number of possible given answers out of which the correct one must be chosen.

multiple sclerosis *n.* a chronic progressive disease of the central nervous system, resulting in speech and visual disorders, tremor, muscular incoordination, and partial paralysis.

multiplex ('mʌltɪˌplɛks) *adj.* having many elements; complex.

multiplicand (ˌmʌltɪplɪ'kænd) *n.* a number to be multiplied by another number, the **multiplier.**

multiplication (ˌmʌltɪplɪ'keɪʃən) *n.* **1.** a mathematical operation, equivalent to adding a number to itself a specified number of times. For instance, 4 multiplied by 3 equals 12 (i.e. 4+4+4). **2.** the act of multiplying or state of being multiplied.

multiplication sign *n.* the symbol ×, placed between numbers to be multiplied.

multiplication table *n.* a table giving the results of multiplying two numbers together.

multiplicity (ˌmʌltɪ'plɪsɪtɪ) *n., pl.* **-ties. 1.** a large number or great variety. **2.** the state of being multiple.

multiplier ('mʌltɪˌplaɪə) *n.* a number by which another number (the **multiplicand**) is multiplied.

multiply ('mʌltɪˌplaɪ) *vb.* **-plying, -plied. 1.** to increase or cause to increase in number, quantity, or degree. **2.** to combine (two numbers or quantities) by multiplication. **3.** to increase in number by reproduction.

multipurpose (ˌmʌltɪ'pɜːpəs) *adj.* having many uses: *a multipurpose gadget.*

multiracial (ˌmʌltɪ'reɪʃəl) *adj.* comprising people of many races. —ˌ**multi**'**racialism** *n.*

multistage ('mʌltɪˌsteɪdʒ) *adj.* (of a rocket or missile) having several stages, each of which can be jettisoned after it has burnt out.

multistorey (ˌmʌltɪ'stɔːrɪ) *adj.* (of a building) having many storeys.

multitrack ('mʌltɪˌtræk) *adj.* (in sound recording) using tape containing two or more tracks.

multitude ('mʌltɪˌtjuːd) *n.* **1.** a large gathering of people. **2. the.** the common people. **3.** a large number. —ˌ**multi**'**tudinous** *adj.*

multi-user *adj.* (of a computer) capable of being used by several people at once.

mum[1] (mʌm) *n.* **1.** *Informal, chiefly Brit.* same as **mother. 2.** *Austral. & N.Z. informal.* same as **wife.**

mum[2] (mʌm) *adj.* **1.** silent. ~*n.* **2. mum's the word.** keep quiet (about something).

mumble ('mʌmb'l) *vb.* **1.** to utter indistinctly, as with the mouth partly closed. ~*n.* **2.** an indistinct or low utterance or sound.

mumbo jumbo ('mʌmbəʊ) *n., pl.* **mumbo jumbos. 1.** foolish religious ritual or incantation. **2.** meaningless or unnecessarily complicated language. **3.** an object of superstitious awe or reverence.

mummer ('mʌmə) *n.* one of a group of masked performers in a folk play or mime.

mummery ('mʌmərɪ) *n., pl.* **-meries. 1.** a performance by mummers. **2.** hypocritical or ostentatious ceremony.

mummify ('mʌmɪˌfaɪ) *vb.* **-fying, -fied.** to preserve (a body) as a mummy. —ˌ**mummifi**'**cation** *n.*

mummy[1] ('mʌmɪ) *n., pl.* **-mies.** an embalmed body as prepared for burial in ancient Egypt.

mummy[2] ('mʌmɪ) *n., pl.* **-mies.** *Chiefly Brit.* a child's word for **mother.**

mumps (mʌmps) *n.* (*functioning as sing. or pl.*) an acute contagious viral disease in which the glands below the ear swell and are painful.

munch (mʌntʃ) *vb.* to chew (food) steadily, esp. with a crunching noise.

mundane (mʌn'deɪn) *adj.* **1.** everyday, ordinary, or banal. **2.** relating to the world or worldly matters.

mung bean (mʌŋ) *n.* an E Asian bean plant grown for forage and for its edible seeds which are used as a source of bean sprouts for cookery.

municipal (mjuː'nɪsɪp'l) *adj.* of or relating to a town or city or its local government.

municipality (mjuːˌnɪsɪ'pælɪtɪ) *n., pl.* **-ties. 1.** a city, town, or district enjoying local self-government. **2.** the governing body of such a unit.

munificent (mjuː'nɪfɪsənt) *adj.* **1.** (of a person) generous; bountiful. **2.** (of a gift) liberal. —**mu**'**nificence** *n.*

muniments ('mjuːnɪmənts) *pl. n. Law.* the title deeds and other documentary evidence relating to the title to land.

munitions (mjuː'nɪʃənz) *pl. n.* (*sometimes sing.*) military equipment and stores, esp. ammunition.

muon ('mjuːɒn) *n.* a positive or negative elementary particle with a mass 207 times that of an electron.

mural ('mjʊərəl) *n.* **1.** a large painting on a wall. ~*adj.* **2.** of or relating to a wall. —'**muralist** *n.*

murder ('mɜːdə) *n.* **1.** the unlawful premeditated killing of one human being by another. **2.** *Informal.* something dangerous, difficult, or unpleasant: *driving around London is murder.* **3. cry blue murder.** *Informal.* to make an outcry. **4. get away with murder.** *Informal.* to do as one pleases. ~*vb.* **5.** to kill (someone) unlawfully with premeditation or during the commission of a crime. **6.** *Informal.* to destroy; ruin: *he murdered that soliloquy.* **7.** *Informal.* to beat decisively: *the home team murdered their opponents.* —'**murderer** *n.* —'**murderess** *fem. n.* —'**murderous** *adj.*

murk (mɜːk) *n.* gloomy darkness.

murky ('mɜːkɪ) *adj.* **murkier, murkiest. 1.** gloomy or dark. **2.** cloudy or impenetrable as with smoke or fog. **3.** obscure and suspicious; shady: *murky goings-on; her murky past.* —'**murkily** *adv.* —'**murkiness** *n.*

murmur ('mɜːmə) *n.* **1.** a continuous low indistinct sound, as of distant voices. **2.** an indistinct utterance: *a murmur of satisfaction.* **3.** a complaint; grumble: *he made no murmur at my suggestion.* **4.** *Med.* any abnormal soft blowing sound heard usually over the chest: *a heart murmur.* ~*vb.* **5.** to utter (something) in a murmur. **6.** to complain. —'**murmuring** *n., adj.* —'**murmurous** *adj.*

murrain ('mʌrɪn) *n.* any plaguelike disease in cattle.

mus. 1. museum. **2.** music. **3.** musical.

MusB *or* **MusBac** Bachelor of Music.

muscat ('mʌskət) *n.* **1.** any of various grapevines that produce sweet white grapes used for making wine or raisins. **2.** same as **muscatel.**

muscatel (,mʌskə'tɛl) *n.* **1.** a rich sweet wine made from muscat grapes. **2.** the grape or raisin from a muscat vine.

muscle ('mʌsəl) *n.* **1.** a tissue composed of bundles of elongated cells capable of contraction and relaxation to produce movement in an organ or part. **2.** an organ composed of muscle tissue. **3.** strength or force. ~*vb.* **4.** (often foll. by *in* or *on*) *Informal.* to force one's way (in).

muscle-bound *adj.* having overdeveloped and inelastic muscles.

muscleman ('mʌsəl,mæn) *n., pl.* -**men.** 1. a man with highly developed muscles. **2.** a henchman employed to intimidate or use violence upon victims.

Muscovite ('mʌskə,vaɪt) *n.* **1.** a person from Moscow. ~*adj.* **2.** of or relating to Moscow.

muscular ('mʌskjʊlə) *adj.* **1.** having well-developed muscles; brawny. **2.** of, relating to, or consisting of muscle. —**muscularity** (,mʌskjʊ'lærɪtɪ) *n.*

muscular dystrophy *n.* a genetic disease characterized by progressive deterioration and wasting of muscle fibres.

musculature ('mʌskjʊlətʃə) *n.* the arrangement of muscles in an organ, part, or organism.

MusD *or* **MusDoc** Doctor of Music.

muse[1] (mjuːz) *vb.* (sometimes foll. by *on* or *about*) to reflect (about) or ponder (on), usually in silence.

muse[2] (mjuːz) *n.* (often preceded by *the*) a goddess that inspires a creative artist, esp. a poet.

Muse (mjuːz) *n. Greek myth.* any of nine sister goddesses, each of whom was regarded as the protectress of a different art or science.

museum (mjuː'zɪəm) *n.* a building where objects of historical, artistic, or scientific interest are exhibited and preserved.

museum piece *n. Informal.* a person or thing regarded as antiquated.

mush[1] (mʌʃ) *n.* **1.** a soft pulpy mass or consistency. **2.** *Informal.* cloying sentimentality.

mush[2] (mʌʃ) *Canad.* ~*interj.* **1.** an order to dogs in a sled team to start up or go faster. ~*vb.* **2.** to travel by or drive a dogsled.

mushroom ('mʌʃrʊm) *n.* **1.** an edible fungus consisting of a cap at the end of a stem. **2.** something resembling a mushroom in shape or rapid growth. ~*vb.* **3.** to grow rapidly: *demand mushroomed overnight.*

mushroom cloud *n.* the large mushroom-shaped cloud produced by a nuclear explosion.

mushy ('mʌʃɪ) *adj.* **mushier, mushiest. 1.** soft and pulpy. **2.** *Informal.* excessively sentimental.

music ('mjuːzɪk) *n.* **1.** an art form consisting of sequences of sounds organized melodically, harmonically, and rhythmically. **2.** such sounds, esp. when produced by singing or musical instruments. **3.** any written or printed representation of musical sounds. **4.** any sequence of sounds perceived as pleasing or harmonious. **5. face the music.** *Informal.* to confront the consequences of one's actions.

musical ('mjuːzɪkəl) *adj.* **1.** of or used in music. **2.** harmonious; melodious: *musical laughter.* **3.** talented in or fond of music. **4.** involving or set to music. ~*n.* **5.** a play or film having dialogue interspersed with songs and dances. —**musicality** (,mjuːzɪ'kælɪtɪ) *n.* —'**musically** *adv.*

musical box *n.* a box containing a mechanical instrument that plays tunes when the box is opened.

musical chairs *n.* (*functioning as sing.*) a game in which whenever the music stops, the player who fails to find a chair is out of the game.

music centre *n.* a single hi-fi unit containing a turntable, radio, and cassette player.

music hall *n. Chiefly Brit.* **1.** a variety entertainment consisting of songs and comic turns. **2.** a theatre at which such entertainments are staged.

musician (mjuː'zɪʃən) *n.* a person who plays or composes music, esp. as a profession. —**mu'sicianship** *n.*

musicology (,mjuːzɪ'kɒlədʒɪ) *n.* the scholarly study of music. —,**musi'cologist** *n.*

musk (mʌsk) *n.* **1.** a strong-smelling glandular secretion of the male musk deer, used in perfumery. **2.** any similar substance produced by animals, plants, or manufactured synthetically.

musk deer *n.* a small central Asian mountain deer. The male secretes musk.

muskeg ('mʌs,kɛg) *n. Chiefly Canad.* an area of undrained boggy land.

musket (ˈmʌskɪt) n. a long-barrelled muzzle-loading shoulder gun, a forerunner of the rifle. —ˌmuskeˈteer n.

muskmelon (ˈmʌskˌmɛlən) n. any of several varieties of melon, such as the cantaloupe and honeydew.

musk ox n. a large ox, which has a dark shaggy coat, downward-curving horns, and emits a musky smell.

muskrat (ˈmʌskˌræt) n., pl. -rats or -rat. 1. a North American beaver-like amphibious rodent. 2. the brown fur of this animal.

musk rose n. a Mediterranean rose, cultivated for its white musk-scented flowers.

musky (ˈmʌskɪ) adj. muskier, muskiest. resembling the smell of musk; having a heady or pungent sweet aroma. —ˈmuskiness n.

Muslim (ˈmʊzlɪm, ˈmʌz-) or **Moslem** n., pl. -lims or -lim. 1. a follower of the religion of Islam. ~adj. 2. of or relating to Islam.

muslin (ˈmʌzlɪn) n. a fine plain-weave cotton fabric.

musquash (ˈmʌskwɒʃ) n. same as **muskrat**, esp. the fur.

muss (mʌs) vb. U.S. & Canad. informal. (often foll. by up) to make untidy; rumple.

mussel (ˈmʌsˀl) n. any of various bivalves, esp. the edible mussel, which has a dark slightly elongated shell and lives attached to rocks.

must[1] (mʌst) vb. used as an auxiliary to express or indicate: 1. obligation or necessity: I must go to the bank. In this sense, must does not form a negative. If used with a negative infinitive it indicates obligatory prohibition. 2. the probable correctness of a statement: he must be there by now. 3. inevitability: all good things must come to an end. 4. resolution: I must finish this. 5. conviction or certainty on the part of the speaker: you must be joking. ~n. 6. an essential or necessary thing: strong shoes are a must for hill walking.

must[2] (mʌst) n. the pressed juice of grapes or other fruit ready for fermentation.

mustache (məˈstɑːʃ) n. U.S. same as **moustache**.

mustachio (məˈstɑːʃɪˌəʊ) n., pl. -chios. (often pl.) Often humorous. a moustache, esp. when bushy or elaborately shaped. —musˈtachioed adj.

mustang (ˈmʌstæŋ) n. a small breed of horse, often wild or half wild, found in the southwestern U.S.

mustard (ˈmʌstəd) n. 1. any of several plants with yellow flowers and slender pods: cultivated for their pungent seeds. 2. a paste made from the powdered seeds of any of these plants and used as a condiment. 3. a brownish-yellow colour.

mustard and cress n. seedlings of white mustard and garden cress, used in salads, and as a garnish.

mustard gas n. an oily liquid whose poisonous vapour is used in chemical warfare. It causes blindness, burns, and sometimes death.

mustard plaster n. Med. a mixture of powdered black mustard seeds applied to the skin for its counterirritant effects.

muster (ˈmʌstə) vb. 1. to call (people, esp. soldiers) or (of people) to be called together for duty or inspection. 2. (sometimes foll. by up) to summon or gather: to muster one's arguments. ~n. 3. an assembly of military personnel for duty or inspection. 4. a collection, assembly, or gathering. 5. **pass muster.** to be acceptable.

musty (ˈmʌstɪ) adj. -tier, -tiest. 1. smelling or tasting old, stale, or mouldy. 2. old-fashioned, dull, or hackneyed: musty ideas. —ˈmustily adv. —ˈmustiness n.

mutable (ˈmjuːtəbˀl) adj. able to or tending to change. —ˌmutaˈbility n.

mutant (ˈmjuːtˀnt) n. 1. an animal, organism, or gene that has undergone mutation. ~adj. 2. of mutation.

mutate (mjuːˈteɪt) vb. to undergo or cause to undergo mutation.

mutation (mjuːˈteɪʃən) n. 1. a change or alteration. 2. a change in the chromosomes or genes of a cell which may affect the structure and development of the resultant offspring. 3. a physical characteristic, or the organism resulting from this type of chromosomal change.

mute (mjuːt) adj. 1. not giving out sound or speech; silent. 2. unable to speak; dumb. 3. unspoken or unexpressed. 4. (of a letter in a word) silent. ~n. 5. a person who is unable to speak. 6. any of various devices used to soften the tone of stringed or brass instruments. 7. a silent letter. ~vb. 8. to reduce the volume of (a musical instrument) by means of a mute or soft pedal. 9. to subdue the strength of (a colour, lighting, emotion, or activity): their criticism was muted; a muted blue shirt. —ˈmutely adv. —ˈmuteness n.

mute swan n. a Eurasian swan with a pure white plumage and an orange-red bill.

muti (ˈmuːtɪ) n. S. African. medicine, esp. herbal.

mutilate (ˈmjuːtɪˌleɪt) vb. 1. to deprive of a limb or essential part; maim. 2. to expurgate or otherwise damage (a text). —ˌmutiˈlation n. —ˈmutiˌlator n.

mutineer (ˌmjuːtɪˈnɪə) n. a person who mutinies.

mutinous (ˈmjuːtɪnəs) adj. 1. openly rebellious. 2. characteristic or indicative of mutiny.

mutiny (ˈmjuːtɪnɪ) n., pl. -nies. 1. open rebellion against constituted authority, esp. by seamen or soldiers against their officers. ~vb. -nying, -nied. 2. to engage in mutiny.

mutt (mʌt) n. Slang. 1. a foolish or stupid person. 2. a mongrel dog.

mutter ('mʌtə) *vb.* **1.** to utter (something) in a low and indistinct tone. **2.** to grumble. ~*n.* **3.** a muttered sound or complaint. —'**muttering** *n.*, *adj.*

mutton ('mʌt²n) *n.* **1.** the flesh of mature sheep, used as food. **2. mutton dressed as lamb.** an older person dressed up to look young.

muttonchops ('mʌt²n,tʃɒps) *pl. n.* side whiskers trimmed in the shape of chops.

muttonhead ('mʌt²n,hɛd) *n. Slang.* a stupid or ignorant person; fool.

mutual ('mjuːtʃʊəl) *adj.* **1.** experienced or expressed by each of two or more people about the other; reciprocal: *mutual distrust.* **2.** *Informal.* common to or shared by both: *a mutual friend.* **3.** denoting an organization, such as an insurance company, in which the policyholders or investors share the profits and expenses and there are no shareholders. —**mutuality** (,mjuːtʃʊ'ælɪtɪ) *n.* —'**mutually** *adv.*
Usage. *Mutual* was originally used when only two people, or groups of people, were concerned, but is nowadays often extended to cover more than two and to mean "common" rather than "reciprocal": *several of the group felt that this course would be in their mutual interest.* It is used especially in instances where "common" might be ambiguous: *he sent an emissary who was a mutual friend to ask me to reconsider my decision.*

Muzak ('mjuːzæk) *n. Trademark.* recorded light music played in places such as restaurants and factories.

muzzle ('mʌz²l) *n.* **1.** the projecting part of an animal's face, usually the jaws and nose. **2.** a guard or strap fitted over an animal's nose and jaws to prevent it biting or eating. **3.** the front end of a gun barrel. ~*vb.* **4.** to prevent from being heard or noticed. **5.** to put a muzzle on (an animal).

muzzy ('mʌzɪ) *adj.* **-zier, -ziest. 1.** blurred or hazy. **2.** confused or befuddled. —'**muzzily** *adv.* —'**muzziness** *n.*

MW 1. megawatt. **2.** *Radio.* medium wave.

Mx *Physics.* maxwell.

my (maɪ) *det.* **1.** of, belonging to, or associated with the speaker or writer (me): *my own ideas.* **2.** used in various forms of address: *my lord.* ~*interj.* **3.** an exclamation of surprise or awe: *my, how you've grown!*

mycelium (maɪ'siːlɪəm) *n.*, *pl.* **-lia** (-lɪə). the mass forming the body of a fungus.

Mycenaean (,maɪsɪ'niːən) *adj.* of or relating to the Aegean civilization of Mycenae, a city in S Greece (1400 to 1100 B.C.).

mycology (maɪ'kɒlədʒɪ) *n.* the study of fungi.

myelin ('maɪɪlɪn) *n.* a white tissue forming an insulating sheath around certain nerve fibres.

myeloma (,maɪəʊ'ləʊmə) *n.*, *pl.* **-mas** *or* **-mata** (-mətə). a tumour of the bone marrow.

myna, mynah, *or* **mina** ('maɪnə) *n.* a tropical Asian starling which can mimic human speech.

Mynheer (mə'nɪə) *n.* a Dutch title of address equivalent to *Sir* or *Mr.*

myocardium (,maɪəʊ'kɑːdɪəm) *n.*, *pl.* **-dia** (-dɪə). the muscular tissue of the heart. —,**myo'cardial** *adj.*

myopia (maɪ'əʊpɪə) *n.* inability to see distant objects clearly because the images are focused in front of the retina; shortsightedness. —**myopic** (maɪ'ɒpɪk) *adj.*

myriad ('mɪrɪəd) *adj.* **1.** innumerable. ~*n.* (*also used in pl.*) **2.** a large indefinite number.

myriapod ('mɪrɪə,pɒd) *n.* an arthropod with a long segmented body and many walking limbs, such as a centipede.

myrmidon ('mɜːmɪ,dɒn, -d²n) *n.* a follower or henchman.

myrrh (mɜː) *n.* the aromatic resin of an African or Asian shrub or tree, used in perfume, incense, and medicine.

myrtle ('mɜːt²l) *n.* an evergreen shrub with pink or white flowers and aromatic blueblack berries.

myself (maɪ'sɛlf) *pron.* **1.** the reflexive form of *I* or *me.* **2.** I or me in person, as distinct from anyone else: *I myself know of no answer.* **3.** my usual self: *I'm not myself today.*
Usage. The use of *myself* for *I* or *me* is often the result of an attempt to be elegant or correct. However *myself* is best used when it follows *I* or *me* in the same clause: *I cut myself,* but *he gave it to me* (not *myself*). The same is true of the other reflexives. This rule does allow sentences such as *he wrote it himself* (unassisted) and *he himself wrote it* (without an intermediary), when these reinforce a previous reference to the same person.

mysterious (mɪ'stɪərɪəs) *adj.* **1.** characterized by or indicative of mystery. **2.** puzzling, curious. —**mys'teriously** *adv.*

mystery ('mɪstrɪ) *n.*, *pl.* **-teries. 1.** an unexplained or inexplicable event or phenomenon. **2.** a person or thing that arouses curiosity or suspense because of an unknown, obscure, or enigmatic quality. **3.** a story or film which arouses suspense and curiosity because of facts concealed. **4.** a religious rite, such as the Eucharist in Christianity.

mystery play *n.* (in the Middle Ages) a type of drama based on the life of Christ.

mystery tour *n.* an excursion to an unspecified destination.

mystic ('mɪstɪk) *n.* **1.** a person who achieves mystical experience. ~*adj.* **2.** same as **mystical.**

mystical ('mɪstɪkᵊl) *adj.* **1.** relating to or characteristic of mysticism. **2.** *Christianity.* having a sacred significance that is beyond human understanding. **3.** having occult or metaphysical significance. —'**mystically** *adv.*

mysticism ('mɪstɪˌsɪzəm) *n.* **1.** belief in or experience of a reality beyond normal human understanding or experience. **2.** the use of prayer and meditation in an attempt to achieve direct intuitive experience of the divine.

mystify ('mɪstɪˌfaɪ) *vb.* **-fying, -fied. 1.** to confuse, bewilder, or puzzle. **2.** to make obscure. —ˌmystifi'**cation** *n.* —'**mysti-**ˌfying *adj.*

mystique (mɪ'stiːk) *n.* an aura of mystery, power, and awe that surrounds a person or thing.

myth (mɪθ) *n.* **1. a.** a story about superhuman beings of an earlier age, usually of how natural phenomena or social customs came into existence. **b.** same as **mythology** (senses 1, 3). **2.** a person or thing whose existence is fictional or unproven.

myth. 1. mythological. **2.** mythology.

mythical ('mɪθɪkᵊl) *or* **mythic** *adj.* **1.** of or relating to myth. **2.** imaginary or fictitious. —'**mythically** *adv.*

mythology (mɪ'θɒlədʒɪ) *n., pl.* **-gies. 1.** myths collectively, esp. those associated with a particular culture or person. **2.** a body of stories about a person, institution, etc. **3.** the study of myths. —**mythological** (ˌmɪθə'lɒdʒɪkᵊl) *adj.*

myxoedema *or U.S.* **myxedema** (ˌmɪk-sɪ'diːmə) *n.* a disease resulting from underactivity of the thyroid gland, characterized by puffy eyes, face, and hands and mental sluggishness.

myxomatosis (ˌmɪksəmə'təʊsɪs) *n.* an infectious and usually fatal viral disease of rabbits causing swellings and tumours.

N

n *or* **N** (ɛn) *n.*, *pl.* **n's**, **N's**, *or* **Ns.** the 14th letter of the English alphabet.

n¹ 1. nano-. **2.** neutron.

n² (ɛn) *det.* an indefinite number: *there are n objects in the box.* —**nth** (ɛnθ) *adj.*

N 1. *Chess.* knight. **2.** newton(s). **3.** *Chem.* nitrogen. **4.** North. **5.** nuclear: *N plant.*

n. 1. neuter. **2.** noun.

N. 1. National(ist). **2.** Navy. **3.** New. **4.** Norse.

Na *Chem.* sodium.

NA North America.

NAAFI *or* **Naafi** (ˈnæfɪ) *n.* **1.** Navy, Army, and Air Force Institutes. **2.** a canteen or shop run by this organization for military personnel.

naartjie (ˈnɑːtʃɪ) *n. S. African.* a tangerine.

nab (næb) *vb.* **nabbing, nabbed.** *Informal.* **1.** to arrest (someone). **2.** to catch (someone) doing something wrong.

nabob (ˈneɪbɒb) *n.* **1.** *Informal.* a rich or important person. **2.** (formerly) a European who made a fortune in India. **3.** same as **nawab.**

nacre (ˈneɪkə) *n.* same as **mother-of-pearl.** —**nacreous** (ˈneɪkrɪəs) *adj.*

nadir (ˈneɪdɪə, ˈnæ-) *n.* **1.** the point in the sky directly below an observer and opposite the zenith. **2.** the lowest point of anything.

nae (neɪ) *or* **na** (nɑː) *det., adv. Scot.* same as **no²** *or* **not.**

naevus *or* *U.S.* **nevus** (ˈniːvəs) *n., pl.* **-vi** (-vaɪ) a birthmark or mole.

naff (næf) *adj. Brit. slang.* inferior or useless.

nag¹ (næg) *vb.* **nagging, nagged. 1.** to scold or find fault constantly. **2.** (foll. by *at*) to be a constant source of discomfort or worry to. ~*n.* **3.** a person who nags. —ˈ**nagging** *adj., n.*

nag² (næg) *n.* **1.** *Often disparaging.* a horse. **2.** a small riding horse.

naiad (ˈnaɪæd) *n., pl.* **-ads** *or* **-ades** (-əˌdiːz). *Greek myth.* a water nymph.

naïf (nɑːˈiːf) *adj.* same as **naive.**

nail (neɪl) *n.* **1.** a piece of metal with a point at one end and a head at the other, hit with a hammer to join two objects together. **2.** the horny covering of the upper tips of the fingers and toes. **3. hit the nail on the head.** to say something exactly correct or accurate. **4. on the nail.** at once: *she paid on the nail.* ~*vb.* **5.** to attach (something) with nails. **6.** *Informal.* to arrest or catch (someone).

nailfile (ˈneɪlˌfaɪl) *n.* a small metal file, used to trim the nails.

nail polish *or* **varnish** *or esp. U.S.* **enamel** *n.* a cosmetic lacquer applied to the nails.

naive, naïve (nɑːˈiːv, naɪˈiːv), *or* **naïf** *adj.* **1.** innocent and credulous. **2.** lacking developed powers of reasoning or criticism: *a naive argument.* —**naˈively, naˈively,** *or* **naˈïfly** *adv.*

naivety (naɪˈiːvtɪ), **naiveté,** *or* **naïveté** (ˌnɑːiːvˈteɪ) *n.* the state or quality of being naive.

naked (ˈneɪkɪd) *adj.* **1.** having the body unclothed. **2.** having no covering: *a naked flame.* **3.** with no concealment: *the naked facts.* **4.** unaided by special equipment: *visible to the naked eye.* **5.** with no protection. —ˈ**nakedly** *adv.* —ˈ**nakedness** *n.*

namby-pamby (ˌnæmbɪˈpæmbɪ) *adj.* insipidly sentimental or prim.

name (neɪm) *n.* **1.** a word or term by which a person or thing is known. **2.** mere outward appearance as opposed to fact: *ruler in name only.* **3.** an abusive word or phrase considered descriptive of someone: *to call someone names.* **4.** reputation, usually good reputation: *he's made quite a name for himself.* **5.** a famous person: *a big name in the music world.* **6. in the name of. a.** for the sake of: *in the name of peace.* **b.** by the authority of: *in the name of the law.* **7. name of the game.** the most significant or important aspect of something. **8. to one's name.** in one's possession: *I haven't a penny to my name.* ~*vb.* **9.** to give a name to. **10.** to refer to by name; cite: *he named three French poets.* **11.** to ban (an MP) from the House of Commons by mentioning him formally by name as being guilty of disorderly conduct. **12.** to fix or specify: *they have named a date for the meeting.* **13.** to appoint: *he was named Journalist of the Year.* **14. name names.** to cite people in order to blame or accuse them. **15. name the day.** to choose the day for one's wedding.

name day *n. R.C. Church.* the feast day of a saint whose name one bears.

name-dropping *n. Informal.* the practice of referring to famous people as though they were friends, in order to impress others.

nameless (ˈneɪmlɪs) *adj.* **1.** without a name. **2.** unspecified: *persons who shall remain nameless.* **3.** too horrible to mention: *nameless terror.*

namely (ˈneɪmlɪ) *adv.* that is to say.

nameplate ('neɪm‚pleɪt) n. a panel on or next to a door bearing the occupant's name and, sometimes, profession.

namesake ('neɪm‚seɪk) n. a person or thing with the same name as another.

nan bread or **naan** (nɑːn) n. (in Indian cookery) a slightly leavened bread in a large flat leaf shape.

nancy ('nænsɪ) n., pl. **-cies.** an effeminate or homosexual boy or man. Also called: **nance, nancy boy.**

nankeen (næŋ'kiːn) n. **1.** a buff-coloured cotton fabric. ~adj. **2.** pale greyish-yellow.

nanny ('nænɪ) n., pl. **-nies. 1.** a child's nursemaid. **2.** Also: **nana, nan.** a child's word for **grandmother.**

nanny goat n. a female goat.

nano- ('nænəʊ) combining form. denoting one billionth (10^{-9}): nanosecond.

nap[1] (næp) vb. **napping, napped. 1.** to sleep for a short while; doze. **2. catch someone napping.** to catch someone off guard. ~n. **3.** a doze.

nap[2] (næp) n. the raised fibres of velvet or similar cloth.

nap[3] (næp) n. **1.** a card game similar to whist. **2.** Horse racing. a tipster's choice for a certain winner. ~vb. **napping, napped. 3.** Horse racing. to name (a horse) as a likely winner.

napalm ('neɪpɑːm, 'næ-) n. **1.** a thick and highly incendiary liquid, used in firebombs and flame-throwers. ~vb. **2.** to attack (people or places) with napalm.

nape (neɪp) n. the back of the neck.

naphtha ('næfθə, 'næp-) n. Chem. a liquid mixture distilled from coal tar or petroleum: used as a solvent and in petrol.

naphthalene ('næfθə‚liːn, 'næp-) n. Chem. a white crystalline substance distilled from coal tar or petroleum, used in mothballs, dyes, and explosives.

napkin ('næpkɪn) n. **1.** a piece of cloth or paper used while eating to protect the clothes or to wipe the mouth. **2.** same as **nappy. 3.** same as **sanitary towel.**

nappy ('næpɪ) n., pl. **-pies.** Brit. a piece of soft absorbent material wrapped around the waist and between the legs of a baby to absorb its excrement.

narcissism ('nɑːsɪ‚sɪzəm) n. an exceptional interest in or admiration for oneself. —‚narcis'sistic adj.

narcissus (nɑː'sɪsəs) n., pl. **-cissi** (-'sɪsaɪ). a yellow, orange, or white flower with a crown surrounded by spreading segments.

narcosis (nɑː'kəʊsɪs) n. unconsciousness caused by a narcotic or general anaesthetic.

narcotic (nɑː'kɒtɪk) n. **1.** a drug, such as opium or morphine, that produces numbness and drowsiness. ~adj. **2.** of narcotics or narcosis.

nard (nɑːd) n. **1.** same as **spikenard. 2.** a plant whose aromatic roots were formerly used in medicine.

nark (nɑːk) Slang. ~n. **1.** Brit., Austral., & N.Z. an informer or spy: copper's nark. **2.** Brit. someone who complains in an irritating or whining manner. ~vb. **3.** Brit., Austral., & N.Z. to annoy.

narky ('nɑːkɪ) adj. **narkier, narkiest.** Slang. irritable, complaining, or sarcastic.

narrate (nə'reɪt) vb. **1.** to tell (a story); relate. **2.** to speak in accompaniment of (a film). —**nar'rator** n.

narration (nə'reɪʃən) n. **1.** a narrating. **2.** a narrated account or story.

narrative ('nærətɪv) n. **1.** an account of events. **2.** the part of a literary work that relates events. ~adj. **3.** telling a story: a narrative poem. **4.** of narration: narrative art.

narrow ('nærəʊ) adj. **1.** small in breadth in comparison to length. **2.** limited in range or extent: in a narrow sense. **3.** limited in outlook: a narrow mind. **4.** with little margin: a narrow escape. ~vb. **5.** to make or become narrow. ~See also **narrows.** —'narrowly adv. —'narrowness n.

narrow boat n. a long bargelike canal boat.

narrow gauge n. **1.** a railway track with less than 56½ inches between the lines. ~adj. **narrow-gauge. 2.** denoting a railway with a narrow gauge.

narrow-minded adj. bigoted, intolerant, or prejudiced. —‚narrow-'mindedness n.

narrows ('nærəʊz) pl. n. a narrow part of a strait, river, or current.

narwhal ('nɑːwəl) n. an arctic whale, the male of which has a long spiral tusk.

NASA ('næsə) (in the U.S.) National Aeronautics and Space Administration.

nasal ('neɪz'l) adj. **1.** of the nose. **2.** (of a sound) pronounced with air passing through the nose. **3.** (of a voice) characterized by nasal sounds. —'nasally adv.

nasalize or **-lise** ('neɪzə‚laɪz) vb. to pronounce or speak nasally.

nascent ('næs'nt, 'neɪ-) adj. starting to grow or develop.

nasturtium (nə'stɜːʃəm) n. a plant with yellow, red, or orange trumpet-shaped flowers.

nasty ('nɑːstɪ) adj. **-tier, -tiest. 1.** unpleasant: a nasty smell. **2.** dangerous or painful: a nasty wound. **3.** (of a person) spiteful or ill-natured. ~n., pl. **-ties. 4.** something unpleasant: a video nasty. —'nastily adv. —'nastiness n.

nat. 1. national. **2.** nationalist.

natal ('neɪt'l) adj. of or relating to birth.

nation ('neɪʃən) n. a large body of people of one or more cultures or races, organized into a single state: the Australian nation.

national ('næʃən'l) adj. **1.** of a nation as a

whole. **2.** characteristic of a particular nation: *the national dress of Poland.* ~*n.* **3.** a citizen of a particular country: *Greek nationals.* **4.** a national newspaper. —'**nationally** *adv.*

national anthem *n.* a patriotic song adopted by a nation for use on public occasions.

national debt *n.* the total outstanding borrowings of a nation's central government.

national grid *n. Brit.* **1.** a network of high-voltage power lines linking major electric power stations. **2.** the arrangement of vertical and horizontal lines on an ordnance survey map.

National Health Service *n.* (in Britain) the system of national medical services, financed mainly by taxation.

national insurance *n.* (in Britain) state insurance based on contributions from employees and employers, providing payments to the unemployed, the sick, and the retired.

nationalism ('næʃənə,lɪzəm) *n.* **1.** a policy of national independence. **2.** patriotism, sometimes to an excessive degree. —'**nationalist** *n., adj.* —,**national'istic** *adj.*

nationality (,næʃə'nælɪtɪ) *n., pl.* -**ties. 1.** the fact of being a citizen of a particular nation. **2.** a nation.

nationalize *or* -**lise** ('næʃənə,laɪz) *vb.* to put (an industry or a company) under state control. —,**nationali'zation** *or* -**li'sation** *n.*

national park *n.* an area of countryside protected by a national government for its scenic or environmental importance.

national service *n. Chiefly Brit.* compulsory military service.

National Socialism *n. German history.* the doctrines and practices of the Nazis, involving the supremacy of Hitler, anti-Semitism, state control of the economy, and national expansion. —**National Socialist** *n., adj.*

national superannuation *n. N.Z.* a government pension paid to people of 65 years and over; retirement pension.

National Trust *n.* (in Britain) an organization concerned with the preservation of historic buildings and areas of natural beauty.

nationwide ('neɪʃən,waɪd) *adj.* covering or available to the whole of a nation; national.

native ('neɪtɪv) *adj.* **1.** relating to a place where a person was born: *native language.* **2.** natural or inborn: *native wit.* **3.** born in a specified place: *a native Indian.* **4.** (foll. by *to*) originating in: *tigers are native to India.* **5.** relating to the original inhabitants of a country: *the native art of New Zealand.* **6. go native.** (of a settler) to adopt the lifestyle of the local population.

~*n.* **7.** a person born in a specified place: *a native of Geneva.* **8.** an indigenous animal or plant: *the llama is a native of Peru.* **9.** a member of the original people of a country, as opposed to colonial immigrants.

nativity (nə'tɪvɪtɪ) *n., pl.* -**ties.** birth or origin.

Nativity (nə'tɪvɪtɪ) *n.* **1.** the birth of Christ. **2.** the feast of Christmas commemorating this.

NATO *or* **Nato** ('neɪtəʊ) North Atlantic Treaty Organization: an international organization established for purposes of collective security.

natter ('nætə) *Chiefly Brit. informal.* ~*vb.* **1.** to talk idly and at length; chatter. ~*n.* **2.** a long idle chat.

natterjack ('nætə,dʒæk) *n.* a greyish-brown toad with reddish warty lumps.

natty ('nætɪ) *adj.* -**tier**, -**tiest.** *Informal.* smart; spruce. —'**nattily** *adv.*

natural ('nætʃrəl) *adj.* **1.** of, existing in, or produced by nature: *natural science; natural cliffs.* **2.** in accordance with human nature. **3.** as is normal or to be expected: *the natural course of events.* **4.** not acquired; inborn: *a natural talent.* **5.** being so through inborn qualities: *a natural leader.* **6.** genuine or spontaneous. **7.** lifelike: *she looked more natural without make-up.* **8.** not affected by man; wild: *in the natural state this animal is not ferocious.* **9.** being or made from organic material; not synthetic: *a natural fibre like wool.* **10.** born out of wedlock: *his natural son.* **11.** related by blood: *her natural parents.* **12.** *Music.* not sharp or flat: *F natural.* ~*n.* **13.** *Informal.* a person or thing regarded as certain for success or selection: *the horse was a natural for first place.* **14.** *Music.* **a.** an accidental cancelling a previous sharp or flat. **b.** a note affected by this accidental. —'**naturalness** *n.*

natural gas *n.* a gaseous mixture, consisting mainly of methane, found below ground; used widely as a fuel.

natural history *n.* the study of animals and plants in the wild state.

naturalism ('nætʃrə,lɪzəm) *n.* a movement in art and literature advocating detailed realism. —,**natural'istic** *adj.*

naturalist ('nætʃrəlɪst) *n.* **1.** a person who studies botany or zoology. **2.** a person who advocates or practises naturalism.

naturalize *or* -**lise** ('nætʃrə,laɪz) *vb.* **1.** to give citizenship to (a person of foreign birth). **2.** to cause (a foreign word or custom) to be adopted in another place. **3.** to introduce (a plant or animal from another region) and cause it to adapt to local conditions. —,**naturali'zation** *or* -**li'sation** *n.*

natural logarithm *n.* a logarithm which has the irrational number e as a base.

naturally ('nætʃrəlɪ) *adv.* **1.** of course;

surely. **2.** in a natural or normal way. **3.** instinctively.

natural number *n.* a positive integer, such as 1, 2, 3, 4, and so on.

natural philosophy *n.* physics.

natural resources *pl. n.* naturally occurring materials such as coal, oil, and minerals.

natural science *n.* any of the sciences dealing with the study of the physical world, including biology, physics, chemistry, and geology, or these sciences collectively.

natural selection *n.* a process resulting in the survival of those animals or plants that are best adapted to their environment.

natural wastage *n.* the reduction in number of employees through not replacing those who leave, rather than by dismissing employees or making them redundant.

nature ('neɪtʃə) *n.* **1.** fundamental qualities; essential character. **2.** the whole system of the existence, forces, and events of the physical world that are not controlled by man. **3.** disposition: *a sweet nature.* **4.** the basic biological needs of the body. **5.** sort: *a problem of a serious nature.* **6. by nature.** innately. **7. call of nature.** *Informal.* the need to urinate or defecate. **8. in the nature of.** essentially; by way of: *this call is in the nature of a reminder.*

nature reserve *n.* an area of land that is preserved and managed in order to protect its animal and plant life.

nature study *n.* the study of animals and plants by direct observation.

nature trail *n.* a path through countryside, signposted to draw attention to natural features of interest.

naturism ('neɪtʃə,rɪzəm) *n.* same as **nudism.** —'**naturist** *n., adj.*

naught (nɔːt) *n.* **1.** *Archaic or literary.* nothing. **2.** *Chiefly U.S.* same as **nought.** ~*adv.* **3.** *Archaic or literary.* not at all: *it matters naught.*

naughty ('nɔːtɪ) *adj.* **-tier, -tiest. 1.** (usually of children) mischievous or disobedient. **2.** mildly indecent; titillating: *naughty pictures.* —'**naughtily** *adv.* —'**naughtiness** *n.*

nausea ('nɔːzɪə, -sɪə) *n.* **1.** the feeling that precedes vomiting. **2.** revulsion.

nauseate ('nɔːzɪ,eɪt, -sɪ-) *vb.* **1.** to arouse feelings of revulsion in (someone). **2.** to cause (someone) to feel sick. —'**nause,ating** *adj.*

nauseous ('nɔːzɪəs, -sɪəs) *adj.* **1.** as if about to be sick: *I feel nauseous.* **2.** sickening.

nautical ('nɔːtɪkᵊl) *adj.* of ships, navigation, or sailors.

nautical mile *n.* a unit of length, used in navigation, equal to 1852 metres (6076.103 feet).

nautilus ('nɔːtɪləs) *n., pl.* **-luses** *or* **-li** (-,laɪ). a sea creature with a shell and tentacles.

naval ('neɪv³l) *adj.* **1.** of or having a navy. **2.** of or relating to ships.

nave¹ (neɪv) *n.* the central space in a church.

nave² (neɪv) *n.* the hub of a wheel.

navel ('neɪv³l) *n.* the slight hollow in the centre of the abdomen, where the umbilical cord was attached.

navel orange *n.* a sweet orange that has a navel-like hollow at the top.

navigable ('nævɪgəb³l) *adj.* **1.** wide, deep, or safe enough to be sailed through: *a navigable river.* **2.** that can be steered: *a navigable raft.*

navigate ('nævɪ,geɪt) *vb.* **1.** to direct or plot the course of (a ship or an aircraft). **2.** to travel over or through (water, air, or land) in a ship, aircraft, or vehicle. **3.** *Informal.* to direct (oneself) carefully or safely: *he navigated his way to the bar.* **4.** (of a passenger in a vehicle) to give directions to the driver. —,**navi'gation** *n.* —,**navi'gational** *adj.* —'**navi,gator** *n.*

navvy ('nævɪ) *n., pl.* **-vies.** *Brit. informal.* a labourer on a building site or road.

navy ('neɪvɪ) *n., pl.* **-vies. 1.** the warships of a nation. **2.** the branch of a country's armed services comprising such ships, their crews, and all their supporting services. ~*adj.* **3.** short for **navy-blue.**

navy-blue *adj.* dark blue.

nawab (nə'wɑːb) *n.* (formerly) a Muslim ruler or powerful landowner in India.

nay (neɪ) *interj.* **1.** same as **no**¹: archaic or dialect except in voting. ~*n.* **2.** a person who votes against a motion. ~*adv.* **3.** used for emphasis: *there were hundreds, nay, thousands of people there.*

Nazarene (,næzə'riːn) *n.* **1.** an old name for a Christian or (when preceded by *the*) for Jesus Christ. **2.** a person from Nazareth in N Israel. ~*adj.* **3.** of Nazareth.

Nazi ('nɑːtsɪ) *n., pl.* **-zis. 1.** a member of the National Socialist German Workers' Party, which seized political control in Germany in 1933 under Adolf Hitler. ~*adj.* **2.** of or relating to the Nazis. —'**Nazism** *n.*

Nb *Chem.* niobium.

NB 1. Nebraska. **2.** New Brunswick. **3.** note well.

NC North Carolina.

NCO noncommissioned officer.

Nd *Chem.* neodymium.

ND *or* **N.Dak.** North Dakota.

NDT (in Canada) Newfoundland Daylight Time.

Ne *Chem.* neon.

NE northeast(ern).

ne- *combining form.* See **neo-**: *Nearctic.*

Neanderthal man (nɪ'ændə,tɑːl) *n.* a type

of primitive man of late Palaeolithic Europe.

neap (niːp) *n.* short for **neap tide.**

Neapolitan (ˌnɪəˈpɒlɪtᵊn) *n.* **1.** a person from Naples, a city in SW Italy. ~*adj.* **2.** of Naples.

neap tide *n.* a tide that occurs at the first and last quarter of the moon when there is the smallest rise and fall in tidal level.

near (nɪə) *prep.* **1.** at or to a place or time not far away from. ~*adv.* **2.** at or to a place or time not far away. **3.** short for **nearly:** *I was damn near killed.* ~*adj.* **4.** at or in a place or time not far away: *in the near future.* **5.** with little margin: *a near escape.* **6.** closely connected or intimate: *a near relation.* ~*vb.* **7.** to draw close (to): *we're nearing home.* ~*n.* **8.** the left side of a horse or vehicle. —**'nearness** *n.*

nearby *adj.* ('nɪəˌbaɪ), *adv.* (ˌnɪəˈbaɪ). not far away; close at hand.

Near East *n.* same as **Middle East.**

nearly ('nɪəlɪ) *adv.* **1.** almost. **2. not nearly.** nowhere near: *not nearly enough.*

near miss *n.* **1.** a bomb or shot that does not quite hit the target. **2.** any attempt that just fails to succeed. **3.** an incident in which two aircraft or vehicles narrowly avoid collision.

nearside ('nɪəˌsaɪd) *n.* **1.** *Chiefly Brit.* the side of a vehicle that is nearer the kerb. **2.** the left side of an animal.

near-sighted (ˌnɪəˈsaɪtɪd) *adj.* same as **short-sighted.**

near thing *n. Informal.* an event or action whose outcome is nearly a failure, nearly a success, or nearly a disaster.

neat (niːt) *adj.* **1.** clean and tidy. **2.** smoothly or competently done: *a neat job.* **3.** (of alcoholic drinks) undiluted. **4.** *Slang, chiefly U.S. & Canad.* admirable; excellent. —**'neatly** *adv.* —**'neatness** *n.*

neaten ('niːtᵊn) *vb.* to make neat.

neath *or* **'neath** (niːθ) *prep. Archaic.* short for **beneath.**

neb (nɛb) *n. Archaic or dialect.* the beak of a bird or the nose of an animal.

Nebr. Nebraska.

nebula ('nɛbjʊlə) *n., pl.* **-lae** (-ˌliː) *Astron.* a mass of particles and gases visible as a hazy luminous or dark patch. —**'nebular** *adj.*

nebulous ('nɛbjʊləs) *adj.* lacking definite form or content; vague.

necessaries ('nɛsɪsərɪz) *pl. n.* essential items: *the necessaries of life.*

necessarily ('nɛsɪsərɪlɪ, ˌnɛsɪ'sɛrɪlɪ) *adv.* **1.** as a certainty: *he won't necessarily come.* **2.** inevitably: *I was necessarily detained.*

necessary ('nɛsɪsərɪ) *adj.* **1.** indispensable; required. **2.** inevitable: *the necessary consequences.* ~*n.* **3.** (preceded by *the*) *Informal.* the money required for a particular purpose. **4. do the necessary.** *Infor-*

mal. to do something that is necessary in a particular situation. ~See also **necessaries.**

necessitate (nɪ'sɛsɪˌteɪt) *vb.* to compel or require.

necessitous (nɪ'sɛsɪtəs) *adj.* very needy.

necessity (nɪ'sɛsɪtɪ) *n., pl.* **-ties. 1.** something needed: *necessities of life.* **2.** a set of circumstances that inevitably requires a certain result: *it is a matter of necessity to wear formal clothes when meeting the Queen.* **3.** the state or quality of being obligatory or unavoidable. **4.** urgent requirement. **5.** poverty or want. **6. of necessity.** inevitably.

neck (nɛk) *n.* **1.** the part of the body connecting the head with the rest of the body. **2.** the part of a garment around the neck. **3.** the narrow part of something, such as a bottle or violin. **4.** the length of a horse's head and neck taken as the distance by which one horse beats another in a race: *to win by a neck.* **5.** *Informal.* impudence. **6. get it in the neck.** *Informal.* to be reprimanded or punished severely. **7. neck and neck.** absolutely level in a race or competition. **8. neck of the woods.** *Informal.* a particular area: *what brings you to this neck of the woods?* **9. save someone's neck.** *Informal.* to help someone out of a difficult or dangerous situation. **10. stick one's neck out.** *Informal.* to risk criticism or ridicule by speaking one's mind. ~*vb.* **11.** (of two people) *Informal.* to kiss each other passionately.

neckband ('nɛkˌbænd) *n.* a band around the neck of a garment.

neckerchief ('nɛkətʃɪf, -ˌtʃiːf) *n.* a piece of cloth worn round the neck.

necklace ('nɛklɪs) *n.* **1.** a decorative chain, band, or cord, often with beads or jewels, worn around the neck, usually by women. **2.** (in South Africa) a tyre soaked in petrol, placed round a person's neck, and set on fire in order to burn the person to death.

neckline ('nɛkˌlaɪn) *n.* the shape or position of the upper edge of a dress or top.

necktie ('nɛkˌtaɪ) *n. U.S.* same as **tie** (sense 8).

necromancy ('nɛkrəʊˌmænsɪ) *n.* black magic; sorcery. —**'necroˌmancer** *n.*

necrophilia (ˌnɛkrəʊ'fɪlɪə) *n.* sexual attraction for or sexual intercourse with dead bodies.

necropolis (nɛ'krɒpəlɪs) *n.* a cemetery.

necrosis (nɛ'krəʊsɪs) *n.* **1.** *Biol., Med.* the death of cells in the body, as from an interruption of the blood supply. **2.** *Bot.* death of plant tissue due to disease or frost. —**necrotic** (nɛ'krɒtɪk) *adj.*

nectar ('nɛktə) *n.* **1.** a sugary fluid produced by flowers and collected by bees. **2.**

Classical myth. the drink of the gods. **3.** any delicious drink.

nectarine ('nɛktərɪn) *n.* a smooth-skinned variety of peach.

ned (nɛd) *n. Slang.* a hooligan.

NEDC National Economic Development Council. Also (informal): **Neddy** ('nɛdɪ).

neddy ('nɛdɪ) *n., pl.* **-dies.** a child's word for a **donkey.**

née *or* **nee** (neɪ) *adj.* indicating the maiden name of a married woman: *Jane Bloggs, née Blandish.*

need (niːd) *vb.* **1.** to be in want of: *to need money.* **2.** to be obliged: *you need to do more work.* **3.** used to express necessity or obligation and does not add *-s* when used with singular nouns or pronouns: *need he go?* ~*n.* **4.** the condition of lacking something: *he has need of a new coat.* **5.** a requirement: *the need for vengeance.* **6.** necessity: *no need to be frightened.* **7.** distress: *a friend in need.* **8.** poverty or destitution: *the money will go to those areas where need is greatest.* ~See also **needs.**

needful ('niːdfʊl) *adj.* **1.** necessary; required. ~*n.* **2. the needful.** *Informal.* what is necessary, usually money.

needle ('niːd°l) *n.* **1.** a pointed slender piece of metal with a hole in it through which thread is passed for sewing. **2.** a rod with a point at one end, used in knitting. **3.** same as **stylus. 4.** *Med.* the long hollow pointed part of a hypodermic syringe, which is inserted into the body. **5.** a long narrow stiff leaf: *pine needles.* **6.** a pointer on the scale of a measuring instrument. **7.** short for **magnetic needle. 8.** *Informal.* anger or intense rivalry, usually in a sporting encounter. **9. have** *or* **get the needle.** *Brit. informal.* to be annoyed. ~*vb.* **10.** *Informal.* to goad or provoke.

needlecord ('niːd°l,kɔːd) *n.* a finely-ribbed corduroy fabric.

needlepoint ('niːd°l,pɔɪnt) *n.* **1.** embroidery done on canvas. **2.** lace made by needles on a paper pattern.

needless ('niːdlɪs) *adj.* not required; unnecessary. —**'needlessly** *adv.*

needlewoman ('niːd°l,wʊmən) *n., pl.* **-women.** a woman who does needlework.

needlework ('niːd°l,wɜːk) *n.* sewing and embroidery.

needs (niːdz) *adv.* **1.** (preceded or foll. by *must*) of necessity: *we must needs go.* ~*pl. n.* **2.** what is required: *his needs are modest.*

needy ('niːdɪ) *adj.* **needier, neediest.** in need of financial support; poor.

ne'er (nɛə) *adv. Poetic.* never.

ne'er-do-well *n.* **1.** an irresponsible or lazy person. ~*adj.* **2.** useless; worthless: *your ne'er-do-well schemes.*

nefarious (nɪ'fɛərɪəs) *adj.* evil; wicked.

neg. negative.

negate (nɪ'geɪt) *vb.* **1.** to invalidate: *that negates all our efforts.* **2.** to deny the existence of.

negation (nɪ'geɪʃən) *n.* **1.** the opposite or absence of something. **2.** a negative thing or condition. **3.** a negating.

negative ('nɛgətɪv) *adj.* **1.** expressing a refusal or denial: *a negative answer.* **2.** lacking positive qualities, such as enthusiasm or optimism. **3.** measured in a direction opposite to that regarded as positive. **4.** *Med.* indicating absence of the condition for which a test was made. **5.** same as **minus** (sense 3b). **6.** *Physics.* **a.** (of an electric charge) having the same electrical charge as an electron. **b.** (of a body or system) having a negative electric charge; having an excess of electrons. **7.** short for **electronegative. 8.** of a photographic negative. ~*n.* **9.** a statement or act of denial or refusal. **10.** a word or expression with a negative meaning, such as *not.* **11.** *Photog.* a piece of photographic film, exposed and developed, bearing an image with a reversal of tones or colours, from which positive prints are made. **12.** a quantity less than zero. **13. in the negative.** indicating denial or refusal. —**'negatively** *adv.*

negativism ('nɛgətɪv,ɪzəm) *n.* **1.** a tendency to be unconstructively critical. **2.** any sceptical system of thought. —**'negativist** *n., adj.*

neglect (nɪ'glɛkt) *vb.* **1.** to fail to give due care or attention to: *to neglect a child.* **2.** to fail (to do something) through carelessness: *he neglected to tell her.* **3.** to disregard: *to neglect one's duty.* ~*n.* **4.** lack of due care or attention: *the child starved through neglect.* **5.** the state of being neglected.

neglectful (nɪ'glɛktfʊl) *adj.* careless; negligent.

negligee *or* **negligée** ('nɛglɪ,ʒeɪ) *n.* a woman's light, usually lace-trimmed dressing gown.

negligent ('nɛglɪdʒənt) *adj.* **1.** lacking attention or concern. **2.** careless or nonchalant. —**'negligence** *n.* —**'negligently** *adv.*

negligible ('nɛglɪdʒəb°l) *adj.* so small or unimportant as to be not worth considering.

negotiable (nɪ'gəʊʃəb°l) *adj.* **1.** able to be negotiated: *salary is negotiable.* **2.** (of a bill of exchange or promissory note) legally transferable.

negotiate (nɪ'gəʊʃɪ,eɪt) *vb.* **1.** to talk with others in order to reach (an agreement). **2.** to succeed in passing round or over (a place or a problem). —**ne,goti'ation** *n.* —**ne'goti,ator** *n.*

Negress ('niːgrɪs) *n.* a female Negro.

negritude ('niːgrɪ,tjuːd, 'nɛg-) *n.* **1.** the fact of being a Negro. **2.** awareness and cultivation of Negro culture.

Negro ('niːgrəʊ) *n., pl.* **-groes. 1.** a member

of any of the dark-skinned peoples of Africa and their descendants elsewhere. ~*adj*. 2. of Negroes.

Negroid ('niːgrɔɪd) *adj*. 1. of or belonging to one of the major racial groups of mankind, characterized by brown-black skin, crisp curly hair, a short broad nose, and full lips. ~*n*. 2. a member of this racial group.

neigh (neɪ) *n*. 1. the high-pitched cry of a horse. ~*vb*. 2. to make this sound.

neighbour *or U.S.* **neighbor** ('neɪbə) *n*. 1. a person who lives near or next to another. 2. a person, thing, or country near or next to another. ~*vb*. 3. (often foll. by *on*) to be or live close (to). —'**neighbouring** *or U.S.* '**neighboring** *adj*.

neighbourhood *or U.S.* **neighborhood** ('neɪbəˌhʊd) *n*. 1. the immediate environment; surroundings. 2. a district where people live. 3. the people in a district. 4. (*modifier*) in and for a district: *a neighbourhood watch scheme*. 5. **in the neighbourhood of**. approximately.

neighbourly *or U.S.* **neighborly** ('neɪbəlɪ) *adj*. kind, friendly, or helpful.

neither ('naɪðə, 'niːðə) *det*. 1. not one nor the other (of two): *neither option appeals to me; neither can win*. ~*conj*. 2. **a.** (used preceding alternatives joined by *nor*) not: *neither John nor Mary went*. **b.** same as **nor** (sense 2). ~*adv*. 3. *Not standard*. same as **either** (sense 4).
Usage. In a sentence that uses *neither...nor* to distinguish two subjects, the verb should be in the singular if both subjects are in the singular: *neither Jack nor John has done the work*. Where the subjects are different in number, the verb usually agrees with the subject nearest to it: *neither they nor Jack was able to come*.

nelson ('nɛlsən) *n*. a wrestling hold in which a wrestler places his arm or arms under his opponent's arm or arms from behind and exerts pressure with his palms on the back of his opponent's neck.

nematode ('nɛməˌtəʊd) *n*. a slender unsegmented cylindrical worm.

nemesis ('nɛmɪsɪs) *n., pl*. **-ses** (-ˌsiːz). any agency of retribution and vengeance.

neo- *or sometimes before a vowel* **ne-** *combining form*. new, recent, or a modern form: *neoclassicism*.

neoclassicism (ˌniːəʊˈklæsɪˌsɪzəm) *n*. a late 18th- and early 19th-century style in architecture and art, based on classical models. —**neoclassical** (ˌniːəʊˈklæsɪkˀl) *adj*.

neodymium (ˌniːəʊˈdɪmɪəm) *n. Chem*. a toxic silvery-white metallic element of the lanthanide series. Symbol: Nd

Neolithic (ˌniːəˈlɪθɪk) *adj. Geol*. of the cultural period that lasted in Europe from about 4000 to 2400 B.C. and was characterized by primitive farming and the use of polished stone and flint tools and weapons.

neologism (nɪˈɒləˌdʒɪzəm) *n*. a newly coined word, or an established word used in a new sense.

neon ('niːɒn) *n*. 1. *Chem*. a colourless odourless rare gas, used in illuminated signs and lights. Symbol: Ne 2. (*modifier*) of or illuminated by neon: *neon sign*.

neonatal (ˌniːəʊˈneɪtˀl) *adj*. relating to the first few weeks of a baby's life. —'**neoˌnate** *n*.

neon light *n*. a glass tube containing neon, which gives a pink or red glow when a voltage is applied.

neophyte ('niːəʊˌfaɪt) *n*. 1. a beginner. 2. a person newly converted to a religious faith. 3. a novice in a religious order.

Nepali (nɪˈpɔːlɪ) *or* **Nepalese** (ˌnɛpəˈliːz) *n*. 1. the official language of Nepal. 2. (*pl*. **-pali, -palis,** *or* **-palese**) a person from Nepal. ~*adj*. 3. of Nepal, its inhabitants, or their language.

nephew ('nɛvjuː, 'nɛf-) *n*. a son of one's sister or brother.

nephritis (nɪˈfraɪtɪs) *n*. inflammation of a kidney.

nepotism ('nɛpəˌtɪzəm) *n*. favouritism shown to relatives or close friends by those with power.

Neptune ('nɛptjuːn) *n*. 1. the Roman god of the sea. 2. the eighth planet from the sun.

neptunium (nɛpˈtjuːnɪəm) *n. Chem*. a silvery metallic element synthesized in the production of plutonium. Symbol: Np

nerine (nɪˈraɪnɪ) *n*. a plant, originally from South Africa, with pink, red, or orange flowers.

nervate ('nɜːveɪt) *adj*. (of leaves) having veins.

nerve (nɜːv) *n*. 1. a cordlike bundle of fibres that conducts impulses between the brain and other parts of the body. 2. bravery and determination. 3. **lose one's nerve.** to lose self-confidence and become afraid about what one is doing. 4. *Informal*. impudence: *what a nerve*. 5. **strain every nerve.** to make every effort (to do something). ~*vb*. 6. **nerve oneself.** to prepare oneself (to do something difficult or unpleasant). ~See also **nerves**.

nerve cell *n*. same as **neuron**.

nerve centre *n*. 1. a group of nerve cells associated with a specific function. 2. a centre of control: *the nerve centre of the BBC*.

nerve gas *n*. a poisonous gas which has a paralysing effect and which can be fatal.

nerveless ('nɜːvlɪs) *adj*. 1. (of a person) fearless. 2. (of fingers) without feeling; numb.

nerve-racking *or* **nerve-wracking** *adj*. very distressing or harrowing.

nerves (nɜːvz) *pl. n. Informal*. 1. the imagined source of emotional control: *my nerves* *won't stand it.* **2.** anxiety or tension: *she's all nerves.* **3. get on someone's nerves.** to irritate someone.

nervous ('nɜːvəs) *adj.* **1.** excitable; highly strung. **2.** apprehensive or worried. **3.** of or containing nerves: *nervous tissue.* **4.** affecting the nerves: *a nervous disease.* —**'nervously** *adv.* —**'nervousness** *n.*

nervous breakdown *n.* a mental illness in which the patient ceases to function properly, often accompanied by severely impaired concentration, anxiety, and lack of self-esteem.

nervous system *n.* the apparatus that controls the thoughts, feelings, and movements of animals, and which consists of a network of nerve cells (see **neuron**).

nervy ('nɜːvɪ) *adj.* **nervier, nerviest.** *Brit. informal.* excitable or nervous.

-ness *suffix forming nouns chiefly from adjectives and participles.* indicating state, condition, or quality: *greatness; selfishness.*

nest (nɛst) *n.* **1.** a place or structure in which birds or other animals lay eggs or give birth to young. **2.** a cosy or secluded place. **3.** a set of things of graduated sizes, designed to fit together: *a nest of tables.* ~*vb.* **4.** (of a bird or other animal) to make or inhabit a nest. **5.** *Computers.* to position (data) within other data at different ranks or levels.

nest egg *n.* a fund of money kept in reserve; savings.

nestle ('nɛsᵊl) *vb.* **1.** to snuggle or cuddle closely. **2.** to be in a sheltered position: *houses nestling on the hillside.*

nestling ('nɛstlɪŋ, 'nɛslɪŋ) *n.* a young bird not yet able to fly.

net¹ (nɛt) *n.* **1.** an openwork fabric of string, thread, or wire; mesh. **2.** a piece of net, used to protect or hold things or to trap animals. **3.** a strategy intended to trap people: *the murderer slipped through the police net.* **4.** *Tennis, badminton, volleyball.* a strip of net that divides the playing area into two equal parts. **5.** the goal in soccer or hockey. ~*vb.* **netting, netted.** **6.** to catch (a fish or other animal) in a net.

net² *or* **nett** (nɛt) *adj.* **1.** remaining after all deductions, as for taxes and expenses: *net profit.* **2.** (of weight) excluding the weight of wrapping or container. **3.** final; conclusive: *a net result.* ~*vb.* **netting, netted.** **4.** to yield or earn (a sum) as clear profit.

netball ('nɛt,bɔːl) *n.* a game for two teams of seven players (usually women). Points are scored by shooting the ball through a net hanging from a ring at the top of a pole.

nether ('nɛðə) *adj.* lower or under: *nether regions.*

nethermost ('nɛðə,məʊst) *adj.* lowest.

nether world *n.* **1.** the underworld. **2.** hell. ~Also called: **nether regions.**

net profit *n.* gross profit minus all operating expenses such as wages and overheads.

nett (nɛt) *adj., vb.* same as **net²**.

netting ('nɛtɪŋ) *n.* a fabric or structure made of net.

nettle ('nɛtᵊl) *n.* **1.** a plant having spiky leaves with stinging hairs. **2. grasp the nettle.** to attempt something with boldness and courage. ~*vb.* **3.** to irritate.

nettle rash *n.* a skin condition, usually caused by an allergy, in which itchy red or whitish raised patches appear.

network ('nɛt,wɜːk) *n.* **1.** an interconnected group or system: *a network of shops.* **2.** a system of intersecting lines, roads, veins, etc. **3.** *Radio & TV.* a group of broadcasting stations that all transmit the same programme at the same time. **4.** *Electronics, computers.* a system of interconnected components or circuits. ~*vb.* **5.** *Radio & TV.* to broadcast (a programme) over a network.

neural ('njʊərəl) *adj.* of a nerve or the nervous system.

neuralgia (njʊ'rældʒə) *n.* severe pain along a nerve. —**neu'ralgic** *adj.*

neuritis (njʊ'raɪtɪs) *n.* inflammation of a nerve or nerves.

neurology (njʊ'rɒlədʒɪ) *n. Med.* the study of the nervous system. —**neurological** (,njʊərə'lɒdʒɪkᵊl) *adj.* —**neu'rologist** *n.*

neuron ('njʊərɒn) *or* **neurone** ('njʊərəʊn) *n.* a cell specialized to conduct nerve impulses.

neurosis (njʊ'rəʊsɪs) *n., pl.* **-ses** (-siːz). a mental disorder producing hysteria, anxiety, depression, or obsessive behaviour.

neurosurgery (,njʊərəʊ'sɜːdʒərɪ) *n. Med.* the branch of surgery concerned with the nervous system. —**neuro'surgeon** *n.* —**,neuro'surgical** *adj.*

neurotic (njʊ'rɒtɪk) *adj.* **1.** tending to be emotionally unstable. **2.** afflicted by neurosis. ~*n.* **3.** a person afflicted with a neurosis or tending to be emotionally unstable.

neuter ('njuːtə) *adj.* **1.** *Grammar.* denoting a gender of nouns which are neither male nor female. **2.** (of animals and plants) sexually underdeveloped. ~*n.* **3.** *Grammar.* **a.** the neuter gender. **b.** a neuter noun. **4.** a sexually underdeveloped female insect, such as a worker bee. **5.** a castrated animal. ~*vb.* **6.** to castrate (an animal).

neutral ('njuːtrəl) *adj.* **1.** not taking any side in a war or dispute. **2.** of or belonging to a neutral party or country. **3.** of no distinctive quality or type. **4.** (of a colour) **a.** having no hue: *neutral shoe cream.* **b.** dull, but harmonizing with most other colours, for example fawn or grey. **5.** same as **neuter** (sense 2). **6.** *Chem.* neither acidic nor alkaline. **7.** *Physics.* having zero charge or potential. ~*n.* **8.** a neutral person or nation. **9.** the position of the controls of a gearbox that leaves the gears unconnected to the engine. —**neutrality** (nju:'trælıtı) *n.*

neutralize *or* **-ise** ('nju:trə,laız) *vb.* **1.** to render ineffective by counteracting. **2.** to make electrically or chemically neutral. **3.** to make (a country) neutral by international agreement: *the great powers neutralized Belgium in the 19th century.* —,**neutrali-'zation** *or* -**i'sation** *n.*

neutrino (nju:'tri:nəʊ) *n., pl.* -**nos.** *Physics.* an elementary particle with zero rest mass and a spin of ½.

neutron ('nju:trɒn) *n. Physics.* a neutral elementary particle of about the same mass as a proton.

neutron bomb *n.* a nuclear weapon, designed to cause little blast or radioactive contamination, which destroys all life in the target area.

Nev. Nevada.

never ('nɛvə) *adv.* **1.** at no time; not ever. **2.** certainly not; not at all. **3.** Also: **well I never!** surely not!
Usage. In good usage, *never* is not used with simple past tenses to mean *not,* e.g. *I was asleep at midnight, so I did not see* (not *never saw*) *her go.*

nevermore (,nɛvə'mɔ:) *adv. Literary.* never again.

never-never *n.* **the.** *Brit. informal.* the hire-purchase system of buying.

never-never land *n.* an imaginary idyllic place.

nevertheless (,nɛvəðə'lɛs) *adv.* in spite of that; however; yet.

new (nju:) *adj.* **1.** recently made, brought into being, or acquired: *a new dress.* **2.** of a kind never before existing; novel: *a new concept in marketing.* **3.** recently discovered: *a new comet.* **4.** recently introduced to or inexperienced in a place or situation: *new to this game.* **5.** fresh; additional: *send some new troops.* **6.** unknown: *this is new to me.* **7.** (of a cycle) beginning again: *a new year.* **8.** (of crops) harvested early: *new potatoes.* **9.** changed for the better: *she returned a new woman.* ~*adv.* **10.** recently, newly: *new-laid eggs.* ~See also **news.** —'**newish** *adj.* —'**newness** *n.*

New Age Music *or* **New Age** *n.* a type of gentle, melodic popular music originating in the U.S. in the late 1980s, which takes in elements of jazz, folk, and classical music and is played largely on synthesizers and acoustic instruments.

newborn ('nju:,bɔ:n) *adj.* recently or just born.

New Canadian *n. Canad.* a recent immigrant to Canada.

new chum *n. Austral. & N.Z. informal.* a recent British immigrant.

newcomer ('nju:,kʌmə) *n.* a person who

has recently arrived or started to participate in something.

newel ('nju:əl) *n.* **1.** Also called: **newel post.** the post at the top or bottom of a flight of stairs that supports the handrail. **2.** the central pillar of a winding staircase.

newfangled ('nju:'fæŋg²ld) *adj.* objectionably or unnecessarily modern.

New Jerusalem *n. Christianity.* heaven.

New Latin *n.* the form of Latin used since the Renaissance, mainly for scientific names.

newly ('nju:lı) *adv.* **1.** recently. **2.** again; anew: *newly raised hopes.*

newlyweds ('nju:lı,wɛdz) *pl. n.* a recently married couple.

new maths *n. (functioning as sing.) Brit.* an approach to mathematics in which basic set theory is introduced at an elementary level.

new moon *n.* the moon when it appears as a narrow crescent at the beginning of its cycle.

news (nju:z) *n. (functioning as sing.)* **1.** important or interesting new happenings. **2.** information about such events, reported in the mass media. **3. the news.** a television or radio programme presenting such information. **4.** interesting or important new information: *that's news to me.* **5.** a person or thing widely reported in the mass media: *she is news in the film world.*

newsagent ('nju:z,eıdʒənt) *or U.S.* **newsdealer** *n.* a shopkeeper who sells newspapers and magazines.

newscast ('nju:z,kɑ:st) *n.* a radio or television broadcast of the news. —'**news-,caster** *n.*

news conference *n.* same as **press conference.**

newsflash ('nju:z,flæʃ) *n.* a brief item of important news, which interrupts a radio or television programme.

newsletter ('nju:z,lɛtə) *n.* a periodical bulletin issued to members of a group.

newspaper ('nju:z,peıpə) *n.* a weekly or daily publication consisting of folded sheets and containing news, features, and advertisements.

newspeak ('nju:,spi:k) *n.* the language of politicians and officials regarded as deliberately ambiguous and misleading.

newsprint ('nju:z,prınt) *n.* an inexpensive wood-pulp paper used for newspapers.

newsreader ('nju:z,ri:də) *n.* a news announcer on radio or television.

newsreel ('nju:z,ri:l) *n.* a short film with a commentary which presents current events.

newsroom ('nju:z,ru:m, -,rʊm) *n.* a room in a newspaper office or broadcasting station where news is received and prepared for publication or broadcasting.

newsstand ('nju:z,stænd) *n.* a portable stand from which newspapers are sold.

New Style *n.* the present method of reckoning dates using the Gregorian calendar.

newsworthy ('nju:z,wɜːðɪ) *adj.* sufficiently interesting to be reported as news.

newsy ('nju:zɪ) *adj.* **newsier, newsiest.** (of a letter) full of news.

newt (nju:t) *n.* a small amphibious creature with a long slender body and tail and short legs.

New Testament *n.* the part of the Christian Bible dealing with the life and teachings of Christ and his followers.

newton ('nju:t²n) *n.* the SI unit of force that gives an acceleration of 1 metre per second per second to a mass of 1 kilogram.

new town *n.* (in Britain) a town planned as a complete unit and built with government sponsorship.

New World *n.* **the.** the Americas; the western hemisphere.

New Year *n.* the first day or days of the year in various calendars, usually a holiday.

New Year's Day *n.* January 1, celebrated as a holiday in many countries.

New Year's Eve *n.* December 31.

next (nɛkst) *adj.* **1.** immediately following: *send in the next patient.* **2.** immediately adjoining: *the next room.* **3.** closest to in degree: *the next-best thing.* ~*adv.* **4.** at a time immediately to follow: *the patient to be examined next.* **5. next to. a.** adjacent to: *the house next to ours.* **b.** following in degree: *next to my wife, I love you most.* **c.** almost: *next to nothing.* ~*prep.* **6.** next to.

next door *adj., adv.* in, at, or to the adjacent house or flat: *my next-door neighbour; she lives next door.*

next of kin *n.* a person's closest relative.

nexus ('nɛksəs) *n., pl.* **nexus. 1.** a means of connection; link; bond. **2.** a connected group or series.

NF (in Britain) National Front.

Nfld. *or* **NF** Newfoundland.

ngati ('nɑːtiː) *n., pl.* **ngati.** *N.Z.* a tribe or clan.

NH New Hampshire.

NHS (in Britain) National Health Service.

Ni *Chem.* nickel.

NI (in Britain) National Insurance.

nib (nɪb) *n.* the writing point of a pen.

nibble ('nɪb²l) *vb.* (often foll. by *at*) **1.** (of small animals) to take small repeated bites (of). **2.** (of a person) to take dainty or cautious bites: *to nibble at a cake.* **3.** to bite gently: *he nibbled her ear lobe.* ~*n.* **4.** *Informal.* a light hurried meal. **5.** a nibbling.

nibs (nɪbz) *n.* **his** *or* **her nibs.** *Slang.* a mock title used of an important or self-important person.

nice (naɪs) *adj.* **1.** pleasant. **2.** kind: *a nice gesture.* **3.** good or satisfactory: *they made a nice job of it.* **4.** subtle; precise: *a nice distinction.* —'**nicely** *adv.* —'**niceness** *n.*

nicety ('naɪsɪtɪ) *n., pl.* **-ties. 1.** a subtle point: *a nicety of etiquette.* **2.** a refinement or delicacy: *the niceties of first-class travel.* **3. to a nicety.** precisely.

niche (nɪtʃ, niːʃ) *n.* **1.** a recess in a wall for a statue or ornament. **2.** a position exactly suitable for the person occupying it: *he found his niche in politics.*

Nichrome ('naɪkrəʊm) *n. Trademark.* an alloy containing nickel, iron, and chromium, used in electrical heating elements and furnaces.

nick (nɪk) *n.* **1.** a small notch or cut. **2.** *Brit. slang.* a prison or police station. **3.** *Informal.* condition: *in good nick.* **4. in the nick of time.** just in time. ~*vb.* **5.** to chip or cut (something or oneself). **6.** *Slang, chiefly Brit.* **a.** to steal (something). **b.** to arrest (someone).

nickel ('nɪk²l) *n.* **1.** *Chem.* a silvery-white metallic element that is often used in alloys. Symbol: Ni **2.** a U.S. or Canadian coin worth five cents.

nickelodeon (,nɪkə'ləʊdɪən) *n. U.S.* an early type of jukebox.

nickel silver *n.* an alloy containing copper, zinc, and nickel.

nicker ('nɪkə) *n., pl.* **-er.** *Brit. slang.* a pound sterling.

nick-nack ('nɪk,næk) *n.* same as **knick-knack.**

nickname ('nɪk,neɪm) *n.* **1.** a familiar, pet, or derisory name given to a person or place. ~*vb.* **2.** to call (a person or place) by a nickname: *Bruce Springsteen, nicknamed the Boss.*

nicotine ('nɪkə,tiːn) *n.* a poisonous alkaloid found in tobacco. —**nicotinic** (,nɪkə-'tɪnɪk) *adj.*

nictitating membrane ('nɪktɪ,teɪtɪŋ) *n.* (in reptiles, birds, and some mammals) a thin fold of skin under the eyelid that can be drawn across the eye.

niece (niːs) *n.* a daughter of one's sister or brother.

niff (nɪf) *Brit. slang.* ~*n.* **1.** a stink. ~*vb.* **2.** to stink. —'**niffy** *adj.*

nifty ('nɪftɪ) *adj.* **-tier, -tiest.** *Informal.* pleasing, apt, or stylish.

niggard ('nɪgəd) *n.* a stingy person.

niggardly ('nɪgədlɪ) *adj.* **1.** stingy. **2.** meagre: *a niggardly salary.* —'**niggardliness** *n.*

nigger ('nɪgə) *n.* **1.** *Offensive.* a Negro or other dark-skinned person. **2. nigger in the woodpile.** a hidden snag.

niggle ('nɪg²l) *vb.* **1.** to irritate or worry (someone). **2.** to find fault continually; fuss. ~*n.* **3.** a small worry or doubt. **4.** a trivial objection or complaint. —'**niggling** *adj.*

nigh (naɪ) *adj., adv., prep. Archaic, poetic, or dialect.* near.

night (naɪt) *n.* **1.** the period of darkness that occurs each 24 hours, between sunset and sunrise. **2.** (*modifier*) of, occurring, or working at night: *a night nurse.* **3.** the period between sunset and bedtime; evening. **4.** the time between bedtime and morning. **5.** an evening designated for a specific activity: *parents' night.* **6.** nightfall or dusk. **7. make a night of it.** to celebrate the whole evening. ~See also **nights.**

nightcap ('naɪt,kæp) *n.* **1.** a bedtime drink. **2.** a soft cap formerly worn in bed.

nightclub ('naɪt,klʌb) *n.* a place of entertainment open until late at night, usually offering food, drink, a floor show and dancing.

nightdress ('naɪt,drɛs) *n. Brit.* a loose dress worn in bed by women or girls.

nightfall ('naɪt,fɔːl) *n.* the approach of darkness; dusk.

nightgown ('naɪt,gaʊn) *n.* same as **nightdress.**

nightie ('naɪtɪ) *n. Informal.* short for **nightdress.**

nightingale ('naɪtɪŋ,geɪl) *n.* a brownish bird which is well known for its musical song, usually heard at night.

nightjar ('naɪt,dʒɑː) *n.* a nocturnal bird with large eyes.

nightlife ('naɪt,laɪf) *n.* the entertainment and social activities available at night in a town or city: *the New York nightlife.*

night-light *n.* a dim light burning at night.

nightlong ('naɪt,lɒŋ) *adj., adv.* throughout the night.

nightly ('naɪtlɪ) *adj.* **1.** happening each night. ~*adv.* **2.** each night.

nightmare ('naɪt,mɛə) *n.* **1.** a terrifying or deeply distressing dream. **2.** a terrifying or unpleasant experience. **3.** a thing that is feared: *my nightmare is being buried alive.* —'**night,marish** *adj.*

nights (naɪts) *adv. Informal.* at night or on most nights: *he works nights.*

night safe *n.* a safe built into the outside wall of a bank, in which customers can deposit money when the bank is closed.

night school *n.* an educational institution that holds classes in the evening.

nightshade ('naɪt,ʃeɪd) *n.* a plant of the family that includes the deadly nightshade.

nightshirt ('naɪt,ʃɜːt) *n.* a long loose shirtlike garment worn in bed mainly by men and boys.

night soil *n. Archaic.* human excrement collected at night from cesspools or privies.

nightspot ('naɪt,spɒt) *n. Informal.* a nightclub.

night-time *n.* the time from sunset to sunrise.

night watch *n.* **1.** a watch or guard kept at night for security. **2.** the period of time this watch is kept. **3.** a night watchman.

night watchman *n.* a person who keeps guard at night on a factory or other building.

nihilism ('naɪɪ,lɪzəm) *n.* a total denial of all established authority and institutions. —'**nihilist** *n., adj.* —,**nihil'istic** *adj.*

-nik *suffix forming nouns.* indicating a person associated with a particular state or quality: *beatnik.*

nil (nɪl) *n.* nothing: used esp. as a score in games.

nimble ('nɪmbəl) *adj.* **1.** agile and quick in movement. **2.** mentally alert or acute. —'**nimbly** *adv.*

nimbus ('nɪmbəs) *n., pl.* **-bi** (-baɪ) *or* **-buses.** a dark grey rain cloud.

nincompoop ('nɪnkəm,puːp, 'nɪŋ-) *n.* a stupid person.

nine (naɪn) *n.* **1.** the cardinal number that is the sum of one and eight. **2.** a numeral, 9, IX, representing this number. **3.** something consisting of nine units. **4. dressed up to the nines.** *Informal.* elaborately dressed. **5. 999.** (in Britain) the telephone number of the emergency services. ~*det.* **6.** amounting to nine. —**ninth** (naɪnθ) *adj., n.*

nine-days wonder *n.* something that arouses great interest, but only for a short period.

ninefold ('naɪn,fəʊld) *adj.* **1.** having nine times as many. **2.** having nine parts. ~*adv.* **3.** by nine times as much.

ninepins ('naɪn,pɪnz) *n.* (*functioning as sing.*) the game of skittles.

nineteen ('naɪn'tiːn) *n.* **1.** the cardinal number that is the sum of ten and nine. **2.** a numeral, 19, XIX, representing this number. **3.** something consisting of nineteen units. **4. talk nineteen to the dozen.** to talk very fast. ~*det.* **5.** amounting to nineteen. —'**nine'teenth** *adj., n.*

nineteenth hole *n. Golf, slang.* the bar in a golf clubhouse.

ninety ('naɪntɪ) *n., pl.* **-ties. 1.** the cardinal number that is the product of ten and nine. **2.** a numeral, 90, XC, representing this number. **3.** (*pl.*) the numbers 90–99, esp. the 90th to the 99th year of a person's life or of a century. **4.** something consisting of ninety units. ~*det.* **5.** amounting to ninety. —'**ninetieth** *adj., n.*

ninny ('nɪnɪ) *n., pl.* **-nies.** a stupid person.

niobium (naɪ'əʊbɪəm) *n. Chem.* a white superconductive metallic element. Symbol: Nb

nip[1] (nɪp) *vb.* **nipping, nipped. 1.** to pinch or squeeze. **2.** (foll. by *along, up, out,* etc.) *Brit. informal.* to hurry; dart. **3.** to bite lightly. **4.** (of the cold) to affect (someone) with a stinging sensation. **5.** to check the

growth of (something): *nip it in the bud.*
~*n.* **6.** a pinch or light bite. **7.** coldness: *a nip in the air.*

nip² (nɪp) *n.* a small drink of spirits.

nipper ('nɪpə) *n. Informal, chiefly Brit.* a child.

nipple ('nɪp³l) *n.* the small projection in the centre of each breast, which in females contains the outlet of the milk ducts.

nippy ('nɪpɪ) *adj.* **-pier, -piest. 1.** (of weather) frosty or chilly. **2.** *Brit. informal.* **a.** quick; nimble. **b.** (of a motor vehicle) small and relatively powerful.

nirvana (nɪə'vɑːnə, nɜː-) *n. Buddhism, Hinduism.* the ultimate state of spiritual enlightenment and bliss attained by extinction of all desires and individual existence.

Nissen hut ('nɪs³n) *n.* a tunnel-shaped military shelter made of corrugated steel.

nit¹ (nɪt) *n.* the egg or larva of a louse.

nit² (nɪt) *n. Informal, chiefly Brit.* short for **nitwit.**

nit-picking *Informal.* ~*n.* **1.** a concern with insignificant details, usually with the intention of finding fault. ~*adj.* **2.** showing such concern; fussy.

nitrate ('naɪtreɪt) *Chem.* ~*n.* **1.** a salt or ester of nitric acid. **2.** a fertilizer containing nitrate salts. ~*vb.* **3.** to treat with nitric acid or a nitrate. **4.** to convert or be converted into a nitrate. —**ni'tration** *n.*

nitre or *U.S.* **niter** ('naɪtə) *n. Chem.* same as **potassium nitrate.**

nitric ('naɪtrɪk) *adj. Chem.* of or containing nitrogen.

nitric acid *n. Chem.* a colourless corrosive liquid widely used in industry.

nitride ('naɪtraɪd) *n.* a compound of nitrogen with a more electropositive element.

nitrify ('naɪtrɪˌfaɪ) *vb.* **-fying, -fied.** *Chem.* **1.** to treat (a substance) or cause (a substance) to react with nitrogen. **2.** to treat (soil) with nitrates. **3.** to convert (ammonium compounds) into nitrates by oxidation. —**ˌnitrifi'cation** *n.*

nitrite ('naɪtraɪt) *n.* a salt or ester of nitrous acid.

nitro- or before a vowel **nitr-** *combining form.* indicating that: **1.** a chemical compound contains the univalent group, -NO₂: *nitrobenzene.* **2.** a chemical compound is a nitrate ester: *nitrocellulose.*

nitrogen ('naɪtrədʒən) *n. Chem.* a colourless odourless gaseous element that forms four-fifths of the air and is an essential part of all animal and plant life. Symbol: N —**nitrogenous** (naɪ'trɒdʒɪnəs) *adj.*

nitrogen cycle *n.* the natural cycle by which nitrates in the soil, derived from dead organic matter, are absorbed by plants and reduced to nitrates again when the plants and the animals feeding on them die and decay.

nitrogen fixation *n.* the conversion of

atmospheric nitrogen into nitrogen compounds by soil bacteria.

nitroglycerin (ˌnaɪtrəʊ'glɪsərɪn) or **nitroglycerine** (ˌnaɪtrəʊ'glɪsəˌriːn) *n. Chem.* a thick pale yellow explosive liquid made from glycerol and nitric and sulphuric acids.

nitrous ('naɪtrəs) *adj. Chem.* derived from or containing nitrogen in a low valency state.

nitrous acid *n. Chem.* a weak acid known only in solution and in the form of nitrite salts.

nitrous oxide *n. Chem.* a colourless gas used as an anaesthetic.

nitty-gritty ('nɪtɪ'grɪtɪ) *n.* **the.** *Informal.* the basic facts of a matter or situation.

nitwit ('nɪtˌwɪt) *n. Informal.* a stupid person.

NJ New Jersey.

NM or **N. Mex.** New Mexico.

no¹ (nəʊ) *interj.* **1.** used to express denial, disagreement, or refusal. ~*n., pl.* **noes** or **nos. 2.** an answer or vote of *no.* **3.** a person who votes in the negative.

no² (nəʊ) *det.* **1.** not any, not a, or not one: *I have no money; no excuse.* **2.** not at all: *he's no fool.* **3.** (foll. by comparative adjectives and adverbs) not: *no taller than a child.* **4. no way!** an expression of emphatic refusal or denial.

No¹ or **Noh** (nəʊ) *n., pl.* **No** or **Noh.** the stylized classic drama of Japan, using music and dancing.

No² *Chem.* nobelium.

No. or **no.,** *pl.* **Nos.** or **nos.** number.

n.o. *Cricket.* not out.

nob (nɒb) *n. Slang, chiefly Brit.* a person of wealth or social distinction.

no-ball *n. Cricket.* an improperly bowled ball, for which the batting side scores a run.

nobble ('nɒb³l) *vb. Brit. slang.* **1.** to disable (a racehorse) to stop it from winning. **2.** to outwit (a person) by underhand means. **3.** to bribe or threaten (a person). **4.** to steal.

nobelium (nəʊ'biːlɪəm) *n. Chem.* a radioactive element produced artificially from curium. Symbol: No

Nobel prize (nəʊ'bɛl) *n.* a prize for outstanding contributions to chemistry, physics, physiology and medicine, literature, economics, and peace that may be awarded annually.

nobility (nəʊ'bɪlɪtɪ) *n.* **1.** the quality of being noble; dignity. **2.** the class of people who hold titles and high social rank.

noble ('nəʊb³l) *adj.* **1.** having or showing high moral qualities: *a noble deed.* **2.** belonging to a class of people who hold titles and high social rank. **3.** imposing; magnificent: *a noble palace.* **4.** *Chem.* (of certain metals) resisting oxidation. ~*n.* **5.** a person who holds a title and high social rank. —**'nobly** adv.

noble gas n. any of the unreactive gaseous elements helium, neon, argon, krypton, xenon, and radon.

nobleman ('nəʊblˌmən) or (fem.) **noblewoman** n., pl. **-men** or **-women**. a person of noble rank; peer; aristocrat.

noblesse oblige (nəʊ'blɛs əʊ'bliːʒ) n. Often ironic. the obligation of nobility to be honourable and kind.

nobody ('nəʊbədɪ) pron. **1.** no person; no-one. ~n., pl. **-bodies. 2.** an insignificant person.
Usage. see **everyone**.

nock (nɒk) n. **1.** a notch on an arrow that fits on the bowstring. **2.** a groove at either end of a bow that holds the bowstring.

no-claim bonus n. a reduction on an insurance premium, usually one covering a motor vehicle, if no claims have been made within a specified period. Also called: **no-claims bonus.**

nocturnal (nɒk'tɜːnᵊl) adj. **1.** of the night. **2.** (of animals) active at night.

nocturne ('nɒktɜːn) n. a short dreamy piece of music.

nod (nɒd) vb. **nodding, nodded. 1.** to lower and raise (the head) briefly, to express agreement or greeting. **2.** to express by nodding: she nodded approval. **3.** to sway or bend forwards and back. **4.** to let the head fall forwards through drowsiness; be drowsy. **5. nodding acquaintance.** a slight knowledge (of a subject or person). ~n. **6.** a quick down-and-up movement of the head, in agreement. **7. land of Nod.** an imaginary land of sleep.

noddle ('nɒdᵊl) n. Informal, chiefly Brit. the head or brains.

noddy ('nɒdɪ) n., pl. **-dies. 1.** a tropical tern with a dark plumage. **2.** a fool.

node (nəʊd) n. **1.** a knot or knob. **2.** Bot. the point on a plant stem from which the leaves grow. **3.** Physics. a point in a vibrating body at which there is practically no vibration. **4.** Maths. a point at which a curve crosses itself. **5.** Astron. either of the two points at which the orbit of a body intersects the path of the sun or the orbit of another body. **6.** Anat. any natural bulge or swelling: lymph node. —**'nodal** adj.

nod off vb. Informal. to fall asleep.

nodule ('nɒdjuːl) n. **1.** a small rounded lump, knot, or node. **2.** a knoblike growth on the root of a plant such as clover, which contains nitrogen-fixing bacteria. —**'nodular** adj.

Noel or **Noël** (nəʊ'ɛl) n. (in carols and on cards) same as **Christmas.**

nog (nɒg) n. an alcoholic drink containing beaten egg.

noggin ('nɒgɪn) n. **1.** Informal. the head. **2.** a small quantity of spirits.

no-go area n. a district in a town that is barricaded off and which the police or army can only enter by force.

noise (nɔɪz) n. **1.** a sound, usually a loud or disturbing one. **2.** clamour; din. **3.** an undesired electrical disturbance in a signal. **4.** (pl.) conventional utterances conveying a reaction: sympathetic noises. ~vb. **5. be noised abroad.** (of news or gossip) to be spread.

noiseless ('nɔɪzlɪs) adj. making little or no sound. —**'noiselessly** adv.

noisette (nwɑː'zɛt) n. a hazelnut chocolate.

noisome ('nɔɪsəm) adj. **1.** (of smells) offensive. **2.** harmful or poisonous.

noisy ('nɔɪzɪ) adj. **noisier, noisiest. 1.** making a lot of noise. **2.** (of a place) full of noise. —**'noisily** adv.

nomad ('nəʊmæd) n. **1.** a member of a tribe who move from place to place to find pasture and food. **2.** a wanderer. —**no'madic** adj.

no-man's-land n. land between boundaries, esp. an unoccupied zone between opposing forces.

nom de plume ('nɒm də 'pluːm) n., pl. **noms de plume** ('nɒm də 'pluːm). same as **pen name.**

nomenclature (nəʊ'mɛnklətʃə) n. the system of names used in a particular subject.

nominal ('nɒmɪnᵊl) adj. **1.** in name only: the nominal leader. **2.** very small in comparison with real worth: a nominal fee.

nominalism ('nɒmɪnᵊˌlɪzəm) n. the philosophical theory that a general word, such as dog, is merely a name and does not denote a real object. —**'nominalist** n.

nominal value n. same as **par value.**

nominate ('nɒmɪˌneɪt) vb. **1.** to propose (someone) as a candidate. **2.** to appoint (someone) to an office or position. —ˌnomi'nation n.

nominative ('nɒmɪnətɪv) Grammar. ~adj. **1.** denoting a case of nouns and pronouns in some languages such as Latin, that identifies the subject of a verb. ~n. **2. a.** the nominative case. **b.** a word in this case.

nominee (ˌnɒmɪ'niː) n. a person who is nominated to an office or as a candidate.

non- prefix. indicating: **1.** negation: nonexistent. **2.** refusal or failure: noncooperation. **3.** exclusion from a specified class: nonfiction. **4.** lack or absence: nonevent.

nonage ('nəʊnɪdʒ) n. **1.** Law. the state of being under full legal age. **2.** immaturity.

nonagenarian (ˌnəʊnədʒɪ'nɛərɪən) n. a person who is from 90 to 99 years old.

nonagon ('nɒnəˌgɒn) n. a polygon having nine sides. —**nonagonal** (nɒn'ægənᵊl) adj.

---

nonaddictive   **nonaggression**   **nonalcoholic**

nonaligned (ˌnɒnəˈlaɪnd) *adj.* (of a country) not part of a major alliance or power bloc. —ˌnonaˈlignment *n.*

nonce (nɒns) *n.* **for the nonce.** for the present.

nonce word *n.* a word coined for a single occasion.

nonchalant (ˈnɒnʃələnt) *adj.* casually unconcerned or indifferent. —ˈnonchalance *n.* —ˈnonchalantly *adv.*

non-com (ˈnɒnˌkɒm) *n.* short for **noncommissioned officer.**

noncombatant (nɒnˈkɒmbətənt) *n.* a member of the armed forces whose duties do not include fighting, such as a chaplain or surgeon.

noncommissioned officer (ˌnɒnkəˈmɪʃənd) *n.* (in the armed forces) a person who is appointed as a subordinate officer, from the lower ranks, rather than by a commission.

noncommittal (ˌnɒnkəˈmɪtˀl) *adj.* not committing oneself to any particular opinion.

non compos mentis (ˈnɒn ˈkɒmpəs ˈmɛntɪs) *adj.* of unsound mind.

nonconductor (ˌnɒnkənˈdʌktə) *n.* a substance that is a poor conductor of heat, electricity, or sound.

nonconformist (ˌnɒnkənˈfɔːmɪst) *n.* **1.** a person who does not conform to generally accepted patterns of behaviour or thought. ~*adj.* **2.** (of behaviour or ideas) not conforming to accepted patterns. —ˌnonconˈformity *n.*

Nonconformist (ˌnɒnkənˈfɔːmɪst) *n.* **1.** a Protestant who does not belong to the Church of England. ~*adj.* **2.** of or denoting Nonconformists.

noncontributory (ˌnɒnkənˈtrɪbjʊtrɪ) *adj.* denoting a pension scheme for employees, the premiums of which are paid entirely by the employer.

nondescript (ˈnɒndɪˌskrɪpt) *adj.* having no outstanding features.

none (nʌn) *pron.* (*functioning as sing. or pl.*) **1.** not any: *none of us went; none of it looks edible.* **2.** no-one; nobody: *there were none to tell the tale.* **3. none the.** (*foll. by a comparative adj.*) in no degree: *she was none the worse for her ordeal.* **Usage.** see **everyone.**

nonentity (nɒnˈɛntɪtɪ) *n., pl.* **-ties.** an insignificant person or thing.

nonetheless (ˌnʌnðəˈlɛs) *adv.* nevertheless.

nonevent (ˌnɒnɪˈvɛnt) *n.* a disappointing or insignificant occurrence which was expected to be important.

nonferrous (nɒnˈfɛrəs) *adj.* denoting a metal other than iron.

nonflammable (nɒnˈflæməbˀl) *adj.* not easily set on fire.

nonintervention (ˌnɒnɪntəˈvɛnʃən) *n.* refusal to intervene in the affairs of others.

nonmetal (nɒnˈmɛtˀl) *n. Chem.* a chemical element that forms acidic oxides and is a poor conductor of heat and electricity. —**nonmetallic** (ˌnɒnmɪˈtælɪk) *adj.*

nonmoral (nɒnˈmɒrəl) *adj.* not involving morality; neither moral nor immoral.

no-nonsense (ˌnəʊˈnɒnsəns) *adj.* sensible, practical, and straightforward: *a severe no-nonsense look.*

nonpareil (ˈnɒnpərəl, ˌnɒnpəˈreɪl) *n.* a person or thing that is unsurpassed.

nonplussed *or U.S.* **nonplused** (nɒnˈplʌst) *adj.* perplexed.

nonproliferation (ˌnɒnprəˌlɪfərˈeɪʃən) *n.* limitation of the production or spread of something such as nuclear or chemical weapons.

nonrepresentational (ˌnɒnrɛprɪzɛnˈteɪʃənˀl) *adj. Art.* same as **abstract.**

---

nonbeliever	nondrip	nonoperational
nonbelligerent	nondriver	nonparticipation
non-Catholic	nonessential	nonpartisan
non-Christian	nonexecutive	nonparty
nonclassified	nonexistent	nonpaying
noncombustible	nonfattening	nonpayment
noncommercial	nonfiction	nonplaying
noncommunicable	nonfulfilment	nonpractising
noncommunist	nonfunctional	nonprofessional
noncompetitive	nongovernmental	non-profit-making
noncompliance	noninfectious	nonracial
noncompulsory	nonintellectual	nonreader
noncontagious	noniron	nonrecognition
noncontroversial	nonmalignant	nonrenewable
noncooperation	nonmember	nonresident
noncustodial	non-native	nonreturnable
nondenominational	non-negotiable	nonscientific
nondiscrimination	non-nuclear	nonsectarian
nondrinker	nonobservance	nonsegregated

nonsense ('nonsəns) *n.* **1.** something that has or makes no sense; unintelligible language. **2.** foolish behaviour: *she'll stand no nonsense.* —**nonsensical** (non'sɛnsɪkᵊl) *adj.*

non sequitur ('non 'sɛkwɪtə) *n.* a statement having little or no relevance to what preceded it.

nonstandard (non'stændəd) *adj.* denoting words, expressions, or pronunciations that are not regarded as correct by educated native speakers of a language.

nonstarter (non'stɑːtə) *n.* a person or an idea that has little chance of success.

nonstick ('non'stɪk) *adj.* (of saucepans, etc.) coated with a substance that prevents food sticking to them.

nonstop ('non'stop) *adj., adv.* without a stop: *a nonstop flight; she talks nonstop.*

non-U (non'juː) *adj. Brit. informal.* (of language or behaviour) not characteristic of the upper classes.

nonunion (non'juːnjən) *adj.* **1.** (of a company) not employing union labour: *a nonunion shop.* **2.** not belonging to a trade union.

nonvoter (non'vəʊtə) *n.* **1.** a person who does not vote. **2.** a person not eligible to vote.

nonvoting (non'vəʊtɪŋ) *adj. Finance.* (of shares) not entitling the holder to vote at company meetings.

noodle ('nuːdᵊl) *n. U.S. & Canad. slang.* the head.

noodles ('nuːdᵊlz) *pl. n.* ribbon-like strips of pasta.

nook (nʊk) *n.* **1.** a corner or recess. **2.** a secluded or sheltered place.

noon (nuːn) *n.* the middle of the day; 12 o'clock.

noonday ('nuːn,deɪ) *n.* midday; noon.

no-one *or* **no one** *pron.* no person; nobody.
Usage. see **everyone.**

noose (nuːs) *n.* **1.** a loop in the end of a rope, tied with a slipknot, such as one used to hang people. **2. put one's head in a noose.** to bring about one's own downfall.

nor (nɔː; *unstressed* nə) *conj.* **1.** (used to join alternatives, the first of which is preceded by *neither*) and not: *neither up nor down.* **2.** (foll. by a verb) and not...either: *I'm not rich nor am I famous.*
Usage. see **neither.**

nordic ('nɔːdɪk) *adj. Skiing.* of competitions in cross-country racing and ski-jumping.

Nordic ('nɔːdɪk) *adj.* of the tall blond blue-eyed long-headed people of Scandinavia.

norm (nɔːm) *n.* a standard that is required, desired, or regarded as normal.

normal ('nɔːmᵊl) *adj.* **1.** usual; regular; typical: *the normal level.* **2.** free from mental or physical disorder. **3.** *Geom.* same as **perpendicular** (sense 1). ~*n.* **4.** the usual, regular, or typical state, degree, or form. **5.** *Geom.* a perpendicular line or plane. —**normality** (nɔː'mælɪtɪ) *or esp. U.S.* '**normalcy** *n.*

normalize *or* **-ise** ('nɔːmə,laɪz) *vb.* **1.** to make or become normal. **2.** to bring into conformity with a standard. —,**normali'zation** *or* **-i'sation** *n.*

normally ('nɔːməlɪ) *adv.* **1.** as a rule; usually. **2.** in a normal manner.

Norman ('nɔːmən) *n.* **1.** a person from Normandy in N France, esp. one of the people who conquered England in 1066. **2.** same as **Norman French.** ~*adj.* **3.** of the Normans or their dialect of French. **4.** denoting or having the style of architecture used in Britain from the Norman Conquest in 1066 until the 12th century, with rounded arches and massive masonry walls.

Norman French *n.* the medieval Norman and English dialect of Old French.

normative ('nɔːmətɪv) *adj.* of or establishing a norm or standard: *normative grammar.*

Norn (nɔːn) *n. Norse myth.* any of the three virgin goddesses of fate.

Norse (nɔːs) *adj.* **1.** of ancient and medieval Scandinavia. **2.** of Norway. ~*n.* **3. a.** the N group of Germanic languages spoken in Scandinavia. **b.** any one of these languages, esp. in their ancient or medieval forms.

Norseman ('nɔːsmən) *n., pl.* **-men.** same as **Viking.**

north (nɔːθ) *n.* **1.** one of the four cardinal points of the compass, at 0° or 360°, that is opposite south. **2.** the direction along a meridian towards the North Pole. **3.** the direction in which a compass needle points; magnetic north. **4. the north.** (*often cap.*) any area lying in or towards the north. ~*adj.* **5.** in or towards the north. **6.** from the north: *a north wind.* ~*adv.* **7.** in, to, or towards the north.

North (nɔːθ) *n.* **the. 1.** the northern part of England, generally regarded as reaching the southern boundaries of Yorkshire, Derbyshire, and Cheshire. **2.** (in the U.S.) the

nonsexist	nonspecialist	nontransferable
nonsexual	nonswimmer	nonverbal
nonslip	nontaxable	nonvintage
nonsmoker	nonteaching	nonviolence
nonsoluble	nontechnical	nonviolent
nonspeaking	nontoxic	non-White

states north of the Mason-Dixon Line that were known as the Free States during the Civil War. **3.** the economically and technically advanced countries of the world. ~*adj.* **4.** of or denoting the northern part of a country or area.

Northants (nɔːˈθænts) Northamptonshire.

North Country *n.* **the.** same as **North** (sense 1).

northeast (ˌnɔːθˈiːst; *Naut.* ˌnɔːrˈiːst) *n.* **1.** the direction midway between north and east. **2. the northeast.** (*often cap.*) any area lying in or towards the northeast. ~*adj. also* **northeastern. 3.** (*sometimes cap.*) of or denoting that part of a country or area which lies in the northeast. **4.** in, towards, or facing the northeast. **5.** from the northeast: *a northeast wind.* ~*adv.* **6.** in, to, or towards the northeast. —ˌnorthˈeasterly *adj., adv., n.*

Northeast (ˌnɔːθˈiːst) *n.* **the.** the northeastern part of England, esp. Northumberland and Durham.

northeaster (ˌnɔːθˈiːstə; *Naut.* ˌnɔːrˈiːstə) *n.* a strong wind or storm from the northeast.

northerly (ˈnɔːðəlɪ) *adj.* **1.** of or in the north. ~*adv., adj.* **2.** towards the north. **3.** from the north: *a northerly wind.*

northern (ˈnɔːðən) *adj.* **1.** of, in, or towards the north. **2.** from the north. **3.** (*sometimes cap.*) of or characteristic of the North. —ˈnorthernˌmost *adj.*

Northerner (ˈnɔːðənə) *n.* a person from the north of a country or area.

northern hemisphere *n.* that half of the globe lying north of the equator.

northern lights *pl. n.* same as **aurora borealis.**

Northman (ˈnɔːθmən) *n., pl.* **-men.** same as **Viking.**

North Pole *n.* the northernmost point on the earth's axis, at a latitude of 90°N, which has very low temperatures.

North-Sea gas *n.* (in Britain) natural gas obtained from deposits below the North Sea.

North Star *n.* **the.** same as **Pole Star.**

Northumb. Northumberland.

northward (ˈnɔːθwəd; *Naut.* ˈnɔːðəd) *adj., adv. also* **northwards. 1.** towards the north. ~*n.* **2.** the northward part or direction.

northwest (ˌnɔːθˈwɛst; *Naut.* ˌnɔːˈwɛst) *n.* **1.** the direction midway between north and west. **2.** (*often cap.*) any area lying in or towards the northwest. ~*adj. also* **northwestern. 3.** (*sometimes cap.*) of or denoting that part of a country or area which lies in the northwest. **4.** in or towards the northwest. **5.** in, to, or towards the northwest. —ˌnorthˈwesterly *adj., adv., n.*

Northwest (ˌnɔːθˈwɛst) *n.* **the.** the north-

western part of England, esp. Lancashire and the Lake District.

northwester (ˌnɔːθˈwɛstə; *Naut.* ˌnɔːˈwɛstə) *n.* a strong wind or storm from the northwest.

Norwegian (nɔːˈwiːdʒən) *adj.* **1.** of Norway, its language, or its people. ~*n.* **2.** the language of Norway. **3.** a person from Norway.

Nos. *or* **nos.** numbers.

nose (nəʊz) *n.* **1.** the organ situated above the mouth, used for smelling and breathing. **2.** the sense of smell. **3.** the odour or bouquet of something such as wine. **4.** instinctive skill in finding something: *he had a nose for good news stories.* **5.** the front part of a vehicle. **6. get up someone's nose.** *Informal.* to annoy someone. **7. keep one's nose clean.** to stay out of trouble. **8. look down one's nose at.** *Informal.* to be disdainful of. **9. pay through the nose.** *Informal.* to pay a high price. **10. put someone's nose out of joint.** *Informal.* to make someone envious by doing what he would have liked to do or had expected to do. **11. rub someone's nose in it.** *Informal.* to remind someone unkindly of a failing or error. **12. turn up one's nose at.** *Informal.* to show contempt for. **13. win by a nose.** to win by a narrow margin. **14. with one's nose in the air.** haughtily. ~*vb.* **15.** (foll. by *out*) to discover (a secret) by prying. **16.** to move forward slowly and carefully: *we nosed the car into the garage.* **17.** (foll. by *around* or *about*) to pry or snoop.

nosebag (ˈnəʊzˌbæg) *n.* a bag containing feed, fastened around the head of a horse.

noseband (ˈnəʊzˌbænd) *n.* the part of a horse's bridle that goes around the nose.

nosebleed (ˈnəʊzˌbliːd) *n.* bleeding from the nose.

nose cone *n.* the cone-shaped front section of a missile or spacecraft.

nose dive *n.* **1.** (of an aircraft) a sudden plunge with the nose pointing downwards. **2.** *Informal.* a sudden drop: *prices took a nose dive.* ~*vb.* **nose-dive. 3.** to take a nose dive.

nosegay (ˈnəʊzˌgeɪ) *n.* a small bunch of flowers; posy.

nosey (ˈnəʊzɪ) *adj.* same as **nosy.**

nosh (nɒʃ) *Slang.* ~*n.* **1.** food. ~*vb.* **2.** to eat.

nosh-up *n. Brit. slang.* a large meal.

nostalgia (nɒˈstældʒə, -dʒɪə) *n.* **1.** a sentimental yearning for the past. **2.** homesickness. —**nosˈtalgic** *adj.* —**nosˈtalgically** *adv.*

nostril (ˈnɒstrɪl) *n.* either of the two openings at the end of the nose.

nostrum (ˈnɒstrəm) *n.* **1.** a quack medicine. **2.** a favourite remedy.

nosy *or* **nosey** (ˈnəʊzɪ) *adj.* **nosier, nosi-**

est. *Informal.* prying or inquisitive. —**'nosiness** *n.*

nosy parker *n. Informal, chiefly Brit.* a prying person.

not (nɒt) *adv.* **1.** used to negate the sentence, phrase, or word that it modifies: *I will not stand for it.* **2. not that.** which is not to say that: *he's left me — not that I care.*

nota bene (ˈnəʊtə ˈbiːnɪ) note well; take note.

notable (ˈnəʊtəbᵊl) *adj.* **1.** worthy of being noted; remarkable; distinguished. ~*n.* **2.** a notable person. —ˌnota'bility *n.* —'notably *adv.*

notary public *or* **notary** (ˈnəʊtərɪ) *n., pl.* **notaries public** *or* **notaries.** a public official, usually a solicitor, who is legally authorized to attest and certify documents.

notation (nəʊˈteɪʃən) *n.* a series of signs or symbols used to represent quantities or elements in a specialized system such as music or mathematics.

notch (nɒtʃ) *n.* **1.** a V-shaped cut; nick. **2.** *Informal.* a step or level: *my esteem for her went up a notch.* ~*vb.* **3.** to cut a notch in. **4.** (foll. by *up*) *Informal.* to score or achieve: *he notched up a victory.*

note (nəʊt) *n.* **1.** a brief record in writing for future reference. **2.** a brief informal letter. **3.** an official written communication, as from a government or from a doctor. **4.** a critical comment or explanation in a book. **5.** short for **banknote.** **6.** a particular feeling or atmosphere: *a note of sarcasm.* **7.** a distinctive vocal sound, as of a type of animal. **8.** a written symbol representing the pitch and duration of a musical sound. **9.** *Chiefly Brit.* a musical sound of a particular pitch. **10.** *Chiefly Brit.* a key on a piano, organ, or other keyboard instrument. **11.** a sound used as a signal or warning: *the note to retreat was sounded.* **12.** short for **promissory note. 13. of note. a.** distinguished or famous. **b.** important: *nothing of note.* **14. strike the right note.** to behave appropriately. **15. take note of.** to pay attention to. ~*vb.* **16.** to notice; perceive; pay attention to: *they noted every movement.* **17.** to make a written note of: *she noted the date in her diary.* **18.** to remark upon: *I note that you do not wear shoes.*

notebook (ˈnəʊtˌbʊk) *n.* a book for writing in.

notecase (ˈnəʊtˌkeɪs) *n.* same as **wallet.**

noted (ˈnəʊtɪd) *adj.* celebrated; famous: *a noted sculptor.*

notelet (ˈnəʊtlɪt) *n.* a folded card with a printed design on the front, for writing a short letter.

notepaper (ˈnəʊtˌpeɪpə) *n.* paper for writing letters.

noteworthy (ˈnəʊtˌwɜːðɪ) *adj.* worthy of notice; notable.

nothing (ˈnʌθɪŋ) *pron.* **1.** not anything: *I saw nothing.* **2.** a matter of no importance: *don't worry, it's nothing.* **3.** absence of meaning, value, or worth: *to amount to nothing.* **4.** zero; nought. **5. have** *or* **be nothing to do with.** to have no connection with. **6. nothing but.** no more than; only. **7. nothing doing.** *Informal.* an expression of dismissal or refusal. **8. nothing less than.** downright; truly: *nothing less than tragic.* **9. think nothing of something.** to regard something as easy or natural. ~*adv.* **10.** not at all: *he looked nothing like his brother.* ~*n.* **11.** *Informal.* a person or thing of no importance or significance. *Usage. Nothing* always takes a singular verb in correct usage, although a plural verb is often heard in sentences such as *nothing but books were on the shelf.*

nothingness (ˈnʌθɪŋnɪs) *n.* **1.** nonexistence. **2.** unconsciousness. **3.** total insignificance.

notice (ˈnəʊtɪs) *n.* **1.** observation; attention: *to escape notice.* **2. take notice.** to pay attention. **3. take no notice of.** to ignore or disregard. **4.** a displayed placard or announcement giving information. **5.** advance notification of something such as intention to end a contract of employment: *I handed in my notice this morning.* **6. at short notice.** with very little notification. **7.** a theatrical or literary review: *the play received very good notices.* ~*vb.* **8.** to become aware (of); perceive; note. **9.** to point out or remark upon.

noticeable (ˈnəʊtɪsəbᵊl) *adj.* easily seen or detected. —'noticeably *adv.*

notice board *n. Brit.* a board on which notices are displayed.

notifiable (ˈnəʊtɪˌfaɪəbᵊl) *adj.* denoting certain infectious diseases, outbreaks of which must be reported to the public health authorities.

notification (ˌnəʊtɪfɪˈkeɪʃən) *n.* **1.** the act of notifying someone of something. **2.** a formal announcement.

notify (ˈnəʊtɪˌfaɪ) *vb.* **-fying, -fied.** to tell: *you should notify the bank of your change of address.*

notion (ˈnəʊʃən) *n.* **1.** a vague idea; impression. **2.** an idea or opinion. **3.** a whim.

notional (ˈnəʊʃənᵊl) *adj.* not real; hypothetical or imaginary: *a notional tax credit.*

notorious (nəʊˈtɔːrɪəs) *adj.* well known for some bad reason. —**notoriety** (ˌnəʊtəˈraɪɪtɪ) *n.* —**no'toriously** *adv.*

not proven (ˈprəʊvᵊn) *adj.* a verdict in Scottish courts, given when there is insufficient evidence to convict the accused.

no-trump *Cards.* ~*n.* **1.** a bid or hand without trumps. ~*adj.* **2.** (of a hand) suitable for playing without trumps.

Notts (nɒts) Nottinghamshire.

notwithstanding (ˌnɒtwɪθˈstændɪŋ) *prep.*
1. in spite of. ~*adv.* **2.** nevertheless.

nougat (ˈnuːgɑː) *n.* a hard chewy pink or white sweet containing chopped nuts.

nought (nɔːt) *n.* **1.** same as **zero.** ~*n., adj., adv.* **2.** same as **naught.**

noughts and crosses *n.* (*functioning as sing.*) *Brit.* a game in which two players, one using a nought, the other a cross, alternately mark squares formed by two pairs of crossed lines, the winner being the first to get three of his symbols in a row.

noun (naʊn) *n.* a word that refers to a person, place, or thing.

nourish (ˈnʌrɪʃ) *vb.* **1.** to provide (a person or animal) with the food necessary for life and growth. **2.** to encourage or foster (an idea or feeling). —ˈnourishing *adj.*

nourishment (ˈnʌrɪʃmənt) *n.* **1.** a nourishing substance; food. **2.** a nourishing or being nourished.

nous (naʊs) *n. Old-fashioned Brit. slang.* common sense.

nouveau riche (ˌnuːvəʊ ˈriːʃ) *n., pl.* **nouveaux riches** (ˌnuːvəʊ ˈriːʃ). a person who has become wealthy recently and is regarded as vulgar.

nouvelle cuisine (ˈnuːvɛl kwiˈziːn) *n.* a style of preparing food, often raw or only lightly cooked, with unusual combinations of flavours.

Nov. November.

nova (ˈnəʊvə) *n., pl.* **-vae** (-viː) *or* **-vas.** a star that undergoes an explosion and fast increase of brightness, then gradually decreases to its original brightness.

novel[1] (ˈnɒvəl) *n.* a long fictional story in prose, dealing with character, action, and thought.

novel[2] (ˈnɒvəl) *adj.* fresh; new; original: *a novel suggestion.*

novelette (ˌnɒvəˈlɛt) *n.* a short novel, usually one regarded as slight, trivial, or sentimental.

novelist (ˈnɒvəlɪst) *n.* a writer of novels.

novella (nəʊˈvɛlə) *n., pl.* **-las** *or* **-le** (-leɪ). a short narrative tale or short novel.

novelty (ˈnɒvəltɪ) *n., pl.* **-ties. 1.** the quality of being new and interesting. **2.** a new or unusual experience. **3.** a small cheap toy or trinket.

November (nəʊˈvɛmbə) *n.* the eleventh month of the year.

novena (nəʊˈviːnə) *n., pl.* **-nae** (-niː). *R.C. Church.* a devotion consisting of prayers or services on nine consecutive days.

novice (ˈnɒvɪs) *n.* **1.** a beginner. **2.** a person who has entered a religious order but has not yet taken vows.

novitiate *or* **noviciate** (nəʊˈvɪʃɪɪt, -ˌeɪt) *n.* **1.** the period of being a novice. **2.** the part

of a monastery or convent where the novices live.

now (naʊ) *adv.* **1.** at or for the present time. **2.** immediately: *do it now.* **3.** in these times; nowadays. **4.** given the present circumstances: *now we'll have to stay to the end.* **5. a.** used as a hesitation word: *now, I can't really say.* **b.** used for emphasis: *now listen to this.* **c.** used at the end of a command: *run along now.* **6. just now. a.** very recently: *he left just now.* **b.** very soon: *I'm going just now.* **7. now and again** *or* **then.** occasionally. **8. now now!** an exclamation used to tell someone off or to calm someone. ~*conj.* **9.** (often foll. by *that*) seeing that: *now you're here, you can help me.* ~*n.* **10.** the present time: *now is the time to go.*

nowadays (ˈnaʊəˌdeɪz) *adv.* in these times: *most companies use computers nowadays.*

Nowel *or* **Nowell** (nəʊˈɛl) *n.* same as **Noel.**

nowhere (ˈnəʊwɛə) *adv.* **1.** in, at, or to no place; not anywhere. **2. getting nowhere.** *Informal.* making no progress. **3. nowhere near.** far from; not nearly. ~*n.* **4. in the middle of nowhere.** (of a place) completely isolated.

nowise (ˈnəʊˌwaɪz) *adv.* in no way; not at all.

nowt (naʊt) *n. N English dialect.* nothing.

noxious (ˈnɒkʃəs) *adj.* poisonous or harmful.

nozzle (ˈnɒzˀl) *n.* a projecting spout from which fluid is discharged.

Np *Chem.* neptunium.

NS **1.** New Style (method of reckoning dates). **2.** Nova Scotia.

NSPCC (in Britain) National Society for the Prevention of Cruelty to Children.

NST (in Canada) Newfoundland Standard Time.

NT **1.** (in Britain) National Trust. **2.** New Testament.

-n't not: added to *be* or *have,* or auxiliary verbs: *can't; don't; isn't.*

nth (ɛnθ) *adj.* See n^2.

nuance (njuːˈɑːns, ˈnjuːɑːns) *n.* a subtle difference, as in colour, meaning, or tone.

nub (nʌb) *n.* the point or gist: *the nub of a story.*

nubble (ˈnʌbˀl) *n.* a small lump. —ˈnubbly *adj.*

nubile (ˈnjuːbaɪl) *adj.* (of a young woman) **1.** sexually attractive. **2.** old enough or mature enough for marriage.

nuclear (ˈnjuːklɪə) *adj.* **1.** of an atomic nucleus: *nuclear fission.* **2.** of atoms or nuclear energy: *a nuclear weapon; nuclear war.*

nuclear bomb *n.* a bomb whose force is due to uncontrolled nuclear fusion or fission.

nuclear energy *n. Chem., physics.* energy released during a nuclear reaction as a result of fission or fusion.

nuclear family *n. Sociol., anthropol.* a family consisting only of parents and their offspring.

nuclear fission *n. Nuclear physics.* the splitting of an atomic nucleus, either spontaneously or by bombardment by a neutron: used in atomic bombs and nuclear power plants.

nuclear fusion *n. Nuclear physics.* the combination of two nuclei to form a heavier nucleus with the release of energy: used in hydrogen bombs.

nuclear physics *n.* (*functioning as sing.*) the branch of physics concerned with the structure of the nucleus and the behaviour of its particles.

nuclear power *n.* power produced by a nuclear reactor.

nuclear reaction *n. Physics.* a process in which the structure and energy content of an atomic nucleus is changed by interaction with another nucleus or particle.

nuclear reactor *n. Nuclear physics.* a device in which a nuclear reaction is maintained and controlled to produce nuclear energy.

nuclear winter *n.* a period of low temperatures and little light that has been suggested would occur after a nuclear war.

nucleate *adj.* ('nju:klɪt, -ˌeɪt). **1.** having a nucleus. ~*vb.* ('nju:klɪˌeɪt). **2.** to form a nucleus.

nuclei ('nju:klɪˌaɪ) *n.* the plural of **nucleus.**

nucleic acid (nju:ˈkliːɪk, -ˈkleɪ-) *n. Biochem.* a complex compound with a high molecular weight: a vital constituent of all living cells.

nucleon ('nju:klɪˌɒn) *n. Physics.* a proton or neutron.

nucleonics (ˌnju:klɪˈɒnɪks) *n.* (*functioning as sing.*) the branch of physics concerned with the applications of nuclear energy. —ˌnucle'onic *adj.*

nucleus ('nju:klɪəs) *n., pl.* **-clei. 1.** a central thing around which others are grouped; core. **2.** a centre of growth or development: *the nucleus of an idea.* **3.** *Physics.* the positively charged centre of an atom, made of protons and neutrons, about which electrons orbit. **4.** *Biol.* the part of a cell that contains the chromosomes and associated molecules that control the characteristics and growth of the cell. **5.** *Chem.* a fundamental group of atoms in a molecule serving as the base structure for related compounds.

nude (nju:d) *adj.* **1.** completely undressed. ~*n.* **2.** a naked figure in painting, sculpture, or photography. **3. in the nude.** naked. —'nudity *n.*

nudge (nʌdʒ) *vb.* **1.** to push (someone) gently with the elbow to get attention. **2.**

to push (something or someone) lightly: *as I drove out, I just nudged the gatepost.* ~*n.* **3.** a gentle poke or push.

nudism ('nju:dɪzəm) *n.* the practice of not wearing clothes, for reasons of health. —'nudist *n., adj.*

nugatory ('nju:gətrɪ) *adj.* **1.** of little value; trifling. **2.** not valid: *a nugatory law.*

nugget ('nʌgɪt) *n.* **1.** a small lump of gold in its natural state. **2.** something small but valuable: *a nugget of information.*

nuisance ('nju:səns) *n.* a person or thing that causes annoyance or bother.

nuke (nju:k) *Slang, chiefly U.S.* ~*vb.* **1.** to attack with nuclear weapons. ~*n.* **2.** a nuclear bomb.

null (nʌl) *adj.* **1. null and void.** without legal force. **2. null set.** *Maths.* a set with no members. —'nullity *n.*

nullify ('nʌlɪˌfaɪ) *vb.* **-fying, -fied. 1.** to make (something) ineffective; cancel out. **2.** to make (something) legally void. —ˌnullifi'cation *n.*

numb (nʌm) *adj.* **1.** deprived of feeling through cold, shock, or fear. **2.** unable to move; paralysed. ~*vb.* **3.** to make numb; deaden, shock, or paralyse. —'numbly *adv.* —'numbness *n.*

number ('nʌmbə) *n.* **1.** a concept of quantity that is or can be derived from a single unit, a sum of units, or zero. **2.** the symbol used to represent a number; numeral. **3.** a numeral or string of numerals used to identify a person or thing: *a telephone number.* **4.** the person or thing so identified: *she was number seven in the race.* **5.** sum or quantity: *a large number of people.* **6.** one of a series, as of a magazine. **7.** a self-contained piece of pop or jazz music. **8.** a group of people: *he was not one of our number.* **9.** *Informal.* an admired article: *that little number is by Dior.* **10.** *Grammar.* classification of words depending on how many persons or things are referred to. **11. any number of.** many. **12. beyond** *or* **without number.** innumerable. **13. have someone's number.** *Informal.* to have discovered someone's true character or intentions. **14. one's number is up.** *Brit. informal.* one is about to die. ~*vb.* **15.** to assign a number to: *number the pages of your essay.* **16.** to add up to; total: *the guests numbered seventy.* **17.** to include in a group: *they were numbered among the worst hit.* **18. one's days are numbered.** something unpleasant, such as death, is likely to happen to one soon.

number crunching *n. Computers.* the large-scale processing of numerical data.

numberless ('nʌmbəlɪs) *adj.* too many to be counted.

number one *n.* **1.** *Informal.* oneself: *look after number one.* **2.** *Informal.* the best-selling pop record in any one week. ~*adj.*

3. first in importance, urgency, or quality: *number one priority.*

numberplate ('nʌmbə,pleɪt) *n.* a plate on the front or back of a motor vehicle showing the registration number.

Number Ten *n.* 10 Downing Street, the British prime minister's official London residence.

numbskull ('nʌm,skʌl) *n.* same as **numskull.**

numeral ('njuːmərəl) *n.* a symbol or group of symbols used to express a number.

numerate ('njuːmərɪt) *adj.* able to do basic arithmetic. —'**numeracy** *n.*

numeration (,njuːmə'reɪʃən) *n.* **1.** the act or process of numbering or counting. **2.** a system of numbering.

numerator ('njuːmə,reɪtə) *n. Maths.* the number above the line in a fraction.

numerical (njuː'mɛrɪkʰl) *adj.* measured or expressed in numbers: *numerical value.* —**nu'merically** *adv.*

numerology (,njuːmə'rɒlədʒɪ) *n.* the study of numbers and of their supposed influence on human affairs.

numerous ('njuːmərəs) *adj.* **1.** many: *on numerous occasions.* **2.** having many parts: *a numerous collection.*

numinous ('njuːmɪnəs) *adj.* **1.** arousing spiritual or religious emotions. **2.** mysterious or awe-inspiring.

numismatics (,njuːmɪz'mætɪks) *n.* (*functioning as sing.*) the study or collection of coins or medals. —**numismatist** (njuː'mɪzmətɪst) *n.*

numskull *or* **numbskull** ('nʌm,skʌl) *n.* a stupid person.

nun (nʌn) *n.* a female member of a religious order.

nuncio ('nʌnʃɪ,əʊ, -sɪ-) *n., pl.* **-cios.** *R.C. Church.* a papal ambassador.

nunnery ('nʌnərɪ) *n., pl.* **-neries.** a convent.

nunny bag ('nʌnɪ) *n. Canad.* (in Newfoundland) a small sealskin haversack.

nuptial ('nʌpʃəl, -tʃəl) *adj.* relating to marriage: *nuptial vows.*

nuptials ('nʌpʃəlz, -tʃəlz) *pl. n.* a wedding.

nurd (nɜːd) *n. Slang.* a stupid and feeble person. —'**nurdish** *adj.*

nurse (nɜːs) *n.* **1.** a person trained to tend the sick and infirm and assist doctors. **2.** short for **nursemaid.** ~*vb.* **3.** to tend (the sick). **4.** (of a woman) to feed (a baby) at the breast. **5.** (of a baby) to feed at its mother's breast. **6.** to try to cure (an ailment). **7.** to clasp fondly: *she nursed the child in her arms.* **8.** to harbour; foster: *to nurse a grudge.* —'**nursing** *n., adj.*

nursemaid ('nɜːs,meɪd) *or* **nurserymaid** *n.* a woman employed to look after children.

nursery ('nɜːsrɪ) *n., pl.* **-ries. 1.** a room in a house, set apart for children. **2.** an establishment providing daycare for babies and young children. **3.** a place where plants and young trees are grown for sale.

nurseryman ('nɜːsrɪmən) *n., pl.* **-men.** a person who owns or works in a nursery in which plants are grown.

nursery rhyme *n.* a short traditional verse or song for children.

nursery school *n.* a school for young children, usually from three to five years old.

nursery slopes *pl. n.* gentle slopes used by beginners in skiing.

nursery stakes *pl. n.* a race for two-year-old horses.

nursing home *n.* a private hospital or home for aged or infirm persons.

nurture ('nɜːtʃə) *n.* **1.** the act or process of promoting the development of a child or young plant. ~*vb.* **2.** to promote the development of (a child or young plant). **3.** to encourage the development of (a person, project, or idea).

nut (nʌt) *n.* **1.** a dry one-seeded fruit that grows inside a hard shell. **2.** the edible inner part of such a fruit. **3.** *Slang.* an eccentric or insane person. **4.** *Slang.* the head. **5.** a small piece of metal with a hole in it, that screws on to a bolt. **6.** *Brit.* a small piece of coal. **7. do one's nut.** *Brit. slang.* to be very angry. **8. off one's nut.** *Slang.* mad or foolish. **9. a hard** *or* **tough nut to crack.** a person or thing that presents difficulties. ~See also **nuts.**

nutcase ('nʌt,keɪs) *n. Slang.* an insane person.

nutcracker ('nʌt,krækə) *n.* a device for cracking the shells of nuts. Also: **nutcrackers.**

nuthatch ('nʌt,hætʃ) *n.* a songbird that feeds on insects, seeds, and nuts.

nutmeg ('nʌt,mɛg) *n.* a spice made from the seed of a tropical tree.

nutria ('njuːtrɪə) *n.* coypu fur.

nutrient ('njuːtrɪənt) *n.* **1.** a substance that provides nourishment. ~*adj.* **2.** providing nourishment.

nutriment ('njuːtrɪmənt) *n.* a substance providing nourishment.

nutrition (njuː'trɪʃən) *n.* **1.** the process in animals and plants of taking in and absorbing nutrients. **2.** a nourishing. **3.** the study of nutrition. —**nu'tritional** *adj.* —**nu'tritionist** *n.*

nutritious (njuː'trɪʃəs) *adj.* nourishing.

nutritive ('njuːtrɪtɪv) *adj.* of nutrition; nutritious.

nuts (nʌts) *adj. Slang.* **1.** insane. **2. nuts about.** very fond of or enthusiastic about.

nuts and bolts *pl. n. Informal.* the essential or practical details.

nutshell ('nʌt,ʃɛl) *n.* **in a nutshell.** in essence; briefly.

nutter ('nʌtə) *n. Brit. slang.* an insane person.

nutty ('nʌtɪ) *adj.* **-tier, -tiest.** **1.** containing nuts. **2.** like nuts. **3.** *Slang.* insane. **4.** **nutty about.** *Informal.* very enthusiastic about. —'**nuttiness** *n.*

nux vomica ('nʌks 'vɒmɪkə) *n.* the seed of a tree, which contains strychnine.

nuzzle ('nʌz²l) *vb.* to push or rub gently with the nose or snout.

NV Nevada.

NW northwest(ern).

NWT Northwest Territories (of Canada).

NY *or* **N.Y.** New York.

NYC New York City.

nylon ('naɪlɒn) *n.* a synthetic material used for clothing, stockings, and other products.

nylons ('naɪlɒnz) *pl. n.* stockings made of nylon.

nymph (nɪmf) *n.* **1.** *Myth.* a spirit of nature, represented as a beautiful maiden. **2.** *Chiefly poetic.* a beautiful young woman. **3.** a wingless larval form resembling that of the adult in the development of certain insects.

nymphet ('nɪmfɪt) *n.* a girl who is sexually precocious and desirable.

nympho ('nɪmfəʊ) *n., pl.* **-phos.** *Informal.* short for **nymphomaniac.**

nymphomaniac (ˌnɪmfə'meɪnɪæk) *n.* a woman who has a neurotic compulsion to have sexual intercourse with many men. —ˌ**nympho'mania** *n.*

N.Z., NZ, *or* **N. Zeal.** New Zealand.

O

o *or* **O** (əʊ) *n., pl.* **o's, O's,** *or* **Os. 1.** the 15th letter of the English alphabet. **2.** same as **nought.**

O¹ 1. *Chem.* oxygen. **2.** Old.

O² (əʊ) *interj.* same as **oh:** *O God! O for the wings of a dove!*

o. *or* **O. 1.** octavo. **2.** old.

O. Ocean.

o' (ə) *prep. Informal or archaic.* shortened form of **of:** *a cup o' tea.*

oaf (əʊf) *n.* a stupid or clumsy person. —**'oafish** *adj.*

oak (əʊk) *n.* **1.** a large forest tree with hard wood, acorns as fruits, and lobed leaves. **2.** the wood of this tree, used as building timber and for making furniture. —**'oaken** *adj.*

oak apple *or* **gall** *n.* a brownish round lump or ball produced on oak trees by certain wasps.

Oaks (əʊks) *n.* (*functioning as sing.*) **the.** a horse race for fillies held annually at Epsom.

oakum (ˈəʊkəm) *n.* loose fibre obtained by unravelling old rope, used esp. for caulking seams in wooden ships.

OAP (in Britain) old age pension *or* pensioner.

oar (ɔː) *n.* **1.** a long pole with a broad blade, used for rowing a boat. **2. put** *or* **stick one's oar in.** to interfere or interrupt.

oarsman (ˈɔːzmən) *n., pl.* **-men.** a man who rows. —**'oarsmanship** *n.*

oasis (əʊˈeɪsɪs) *n., pl.* **-ses** (-siːz). **1.** a fertile patch in a desert. **2.** a place or situation offering relief in the midst of difficulty or dullness.

oast (əʊst) *n. Chiefly Brit.* **1.** a kiln for drying hops. **2.** Also called: **oast house.** a building containing such kilns.

oat (əʊt) *n.* **1.** a hard cereal grown as food. **2.** (*usually pl.*) the edible grain of this cereal. **3. sow one's (wild) oats.** to indulge in adventure or promiscuity during youth. —**'oaten** *adj.*

oatcake (ˈəʊtˌkeɪk) *n.* a thin unleavened biscuit made of oatmeal.

oath (əʊθ) *n., pl.* **oaths** (əʊðz). **1.** a solemn promise, esp. to tell the truth in a court of law. **2.** the form of such a promise. **3.** an offensive or blasphemous expression; a swearword. **4. on** *or* **under oath.** having made a solemn promise to tell the truth, esp. in a court of law.

oatmeal (ˈəʊtˌmiːl) *n.* **1.** a coarse flour made by grinding oats. ~*adj.* **2.** greyishyellow.

ob. (on tombstones) he (*or* she) died.

obbligato (ˌɒblɪˈɡɑːtəʊ) *Music.* ~*adj.* **1.** not to be omitted in performance. ~*n., pl.* **-tos. 2.** an essential part or accompaniment: *with oboe obbligato.*

obdurate (ˈɒbdjʊrɪt) *adj.* not easily moved; hardhearted or obstinate. —**'obduracy** *n.*

OBE Officer of the Order of the British Empire.

obedient (əˈbiːdɪənt) *adj.* obeying or willing to obey. —**o'bedience** *n.* —**o'bediently** *adv.*

obeisance (əʊˈbeɪsəns) *n.* **1.** an attitude of respect or homage. **2.** a gesture of respect, such as a curtsy. —**o'beisant** *adj.*

obelisk (ˈɒbɪlɪsk) *n.* **1.** a four-sided stone pillar that tapers towards a pyramidal top. **2.** *Printing.* same as **dagger** (sense 2).

obese (əʊˈbiːs) *adj.* very fat. —**o'besity** *n.*

obey (əˈbeɪ) *vb.* **1.** to carry out (instructions or orders); be obedient. **2.** to behave or act in accordance with: *to obey one's conscience.*

obfuscate (ˈɒbfʌsˌkeɪt) *vb.* **1.** to obscure or darken. **2.** to confuse or bewilder. —ˌob**fus'cation** *n.* —**'obfusˌcatory** *adj.*

obituary (əˈbɪtjʊərɪ) *n., pl.* **-aries.** a published announcement of a death, usually with a short biography of the dead person. —**o'bituarist** *n.*

obj. 1. objection. **2.** *Grammar.* object(ive).

object¹ (ˈɒbdʒɪkt) *n.* **1.** a thing that can be touched or seen. **2.** a person or thing seen as a focus for feelings, actions, or thought: *the object of her dislike.* **3.** an aim or purpose. **4.** *Philosophy.* that which can be perceived by the mind, as contrasted with the thinking subject. **5.** *Grammar.* a noun, pronoun, or noun phrase that receives the action of a verb or is governed by a preposition. **6. no object.** not a hindrance or obstacle: *money is no object.*

object² (əbˈdʒɛkt) *vb.* **1.** to state as an objection. **2.** (often foll. by *to*) to state an objection (to); present an argument (against). —**ob'jector** *n.*

objection (əbˈdʒɛkʃən) *n.* **1.** an expression or feeling of opposition or dislike. **2.** a reason for objecting.

objectionable (əbˈdʒɛkʃənəb²l) *adj.* unpleasant, offensive, or obnoxious.

objective (əbˈdʒɛktɪv) *adj.* **1.** having existence independent of the mind; real. **2.** undistorted by personal feelings or bias: *an objective opinion.* **3.** of or relating to actual facts as opposed to thoughts or feelings: *objective evidence.* **4.** *Grammar.* denoting a case of nouns and pronouns, that identifies the direct object of a verb or preposition. ~*n.* **5.** a goal; aim. **6.** an actual fact; reality. **7.** *Grammar.* the objective case. **8.** *Optics.* the lens nearest to the object observed in an optical instrument. —**objectival** (ˌɒbdʒɛkˈtaɪvəl) *adj.* —**obˈjectively** *adv.* —ˌobjecˈtivity *n.*

object lesson *n.* a practical demonstration of some principle or ideal.

objet d'art (ˌɒbʒeɪ ˈdɑː) *n.*, *pl.* **objets d'art** (ˌɒbʒeɪ ˈdɑː). a small object considered to be of artistic worth.

oblate (ˈɒbleɪt) *adj.* *Geom.* (of a spheroid) flattened at the poles: *the earth is an oblate sphere.*

oblation (ɒˈbleɪʃən) *n.* **1.** *Christianity.* the offering of bread and wine to God at Communion. **2.** any offering made for religious purposes. —**obˈlational** *adj.*

obligate (ˈɒblɪˌgeɪt) *vb.* to bind (someone) morally or legally to do something: *I felt obligated to pay for the damage.* —**obˈligative** *adj.*

obligation (ˌɒblɪˈgeɪʃən) *n.* **1.** a moral or legal duty. **2.** the binding power of such a duty. **3.** indebtedness for a service or favour.

obligatory (ɒˈblɪgətrɪ) *adj.* legally or morally binding; required or compulsory.

oblige (əˈblaɪdʒ) *vb.* **1.** to compel (someone) by legal, moral, or physical means to do something. **2.** to make indebted or grateful to someone by doing a favour: *I am obliged to you for your help.* **3.** to do a favour to (someone): *she obliged the guests with a song.*

obliging (əˈblaɪdʒɪŋ) *adj.* willing to be helpful; accommodating. —**oˈbligingly** *adv.*

oblique (əˈbliːk) *adj.* **1.** at an angle; slanting; sloping. **2.** *Geom.* (of lines or planes) neither perpendicular nor parallel to one another. **3.** indirect or evasive. **4.** *Grammar.* denoting any case other than the nominative or vocative. ~*n.* **5.** something that is oblique. **6.** same as **solidus.** —**oˈbliquely** *adv.* —**oˈbliqueness** *n.*

oblique angle *n.* an angle that is not a right angle or any multiple of a right angle.

obliterate (əˈblɪtəˌreɪt) *vb.* to destroy every trace of; wipe out completely. —**oˌbliteˈration** *n.*

oblivion (əˈblɪvɪən) *n.* **1.** the condition of being forgotten or disregarded: *old crafts such as thatching are gradually sinking into oblivion.* **2.** the state of being unaware or unconscious: *the oblivion of sleep.*

oblivious (əˈblɪvɪəs) *adj.* (usually foll. by *of*) unaware or forgetful. —**obˈliviousness** *n.*

oblong (ˈɒbˌlɒŋ) *adj.* **1.** having an elongat-

ed, rectangular shape. ~*n.* **2.** a figure or object having this shape.

obloquy (ˈɒbləkwɪ) *n.*, *pl.* **-quies.** **1.** verbal abuse or censure. **2.** disgrace brought about by this.

obnoxious (əbˈnɒkʃəs) *adj.* extremely unpleasant. —**obˈnoxiousness** *n.*

oboe (ˈəʊbəʊ) *n.* a double-reeded woodwind instrument with a penetrating nasal tone. —ˈoboist *n.*

obs. obsolete.

obscene (əbˈsiːn) *adj.* **1.** offensive to accepted standards of decency or modesty. **2.** *Law.* tending to deprave or corrupt: *obscene publications.* **3.** disgusting; repulsive. —**obscenity** (əbˈsɛnɪtɪ) *n.*

obscure (əbˈskjʊə) *adj.* **1.** unclear or indistinct: *an obscure shape.* **2.** not well known: *an obscure opera.* **3.** not easily understood: *an obscure point of theology.* ~*vb.* **4.** to make unclear or vague. **5.** to cover or cloud over. —**obscuration** (ˌɒbskjʊˈreɪʃən) *n.* —**obˈscurity** *n.*

obsequies (ˈɒbsɪkwɪz) *pl. n.*, *sing.* **-quy.** funeral rites.

obsequious (əbˈsiːkwɪəs) *adj.* ingratiating or servile; fawning. —**obˈsequiousness** *n.*

observance (əbˈzɜːvəns) *n.* **1.** the observing of a law or custom. **2.** a ritual, ceremony, or practice, esp. of a religion.

observant (əbˈzɜːvənt) *adj.* paying close attention to detail; watchful or perceptive.

observation (ˌɒbzəˈveɪʃən) *n.* **1.** the act or power of observing; the state of being observed. **2.** a comment or remark. **3.** detailed examination of something before analysis, diagnosis, or interpretation: *the patient was under observation.* **4.** the facts learned from observing. —ˌobserˈvational *adj.*

observatory (əbˈzɜːvətrɪ) *n.*, *pl.* **-ries.** a building specially designed and equipped for meteorological and astronomical observation.

observe (əbˈzɜːv) *vb.* **1.** to see; perceive: *we have observed that you steal.* **2.** to watch or pay attention to (something) carefully. **3.** to make scientific observations of (something). **4.** to make a comment or remark: *the speaker observed that times had changed.* **5.** to abide by or keep (a law or custom). —**obˈservable** *adj.* —**obˈserver** *n.*

obsess (əbˈsɛs) *vb.* (often passive and foll. by *with* or *by*) to preoccupy completely; haunt. —**obˈsessive** *adj.*

obsession (əbˈsɛʃən) *n.* **1.** *Psychiatry.* a persistent idea or impulse, often associated with anxiety and mental illness. **2.** any persistent preoccupation, idea, or feeling. —**obˈsessional** *adj.*

obsidian (ɒbˈsɪdɪən) *n.* a dark glassy volcanic rock.

obsolescent (,ɒbsə'lɛsᵊnt) adj. becoming obsolete or out of date. —,**obso'lescence** n.

obsolete ('ɒbsə,liːt) adj. no longer used; out of date.

obstacle ('ɒbstək°l) n. a person or thing that obstructs or hinders progress.

obstetrician (,ɒbstɪ'trɪʃən) n. a doctor who specializes in obstetrics.

obstetrics (ɒb'stɛtrɪks) n. (functioning as sing.) the branch of medicine concerned with pregnancy and childbirth. —**ob'stetric** adj.

obstinate ('ɒbstɪnɪt) adj. **1.** holding stubbornly to a particular opinion or course of action. **2.** resisting treatment; persistent: an obstinate fever. —'**obstinacy** n. —'**obstinately** adv.

obstreperous (əb'strɛpərəs) adj. noisy, boisterous, or unruly.

obstruct (əb'strʌkt) vb. **1.** to block (a way) with an obstacle. **2.** to make (progress or activity) difficult; impede. **3.** to block a clear view of. —**ob'structive** adj., n. —**ob'structiveness** n.

obstruction (əb'strʌkʃən) n. **1.** a person or thing that obstructs. **2.** an obstructing or being obstructed. **3.** Sport. the act of unfairly impeding an opposing player.

obstructionist (əb'strʌkʃənɪst) n. a person who deliberately obstructs legal or parliamentary business. —**ob'structionism** n.

obtain (əb'teɪn) vb. **1.** to gain possession of; get. **2.** to be customary or accepted: a new law obtains in this case. —**ob'tainable** adj.

obtrude (əb'truːd) vb. **1.** to push (oneself or one's opinions) on others in an unwelcome way. **2.** to be or make unpleasantly noticeable. —**obtrusion** (əb'truːʒən) n.

obtrusive (əb'truːsɪv) adj. **1.** obtruding or tending to obtrude. **2.** sticking out; protruding. —**ob'trusiveness** n.

obtuse (əb'tjuːs) adj. **1.** mentally slow or emotionally insensitive. **2.** Maths. (of an angle) between 90° and 180°. **3.** not sharp or pointed; of blunt shape. —**ob'tuseness** n.

obverse ('ɒbvɜːs) n. **1.** a counterpart or opposite. **2.** the side of a coin that bears the main design. **3.** the front, top, or main surface of anything.

obviate ('ɒbvɪ,eɪt) vb. to anticipate and prevent (a problem or difficulty) by effective measures: he destroyed the letter to obviate any suspicion that might fall on him.

obvious ('ɒbvɪəs) adj. easy to see or understand; evident. —'**obviously** adv. —'**obviousness** n.

ocarina (,ɒkə'riːnə) n. a small egg-shaped wind instrument with a mouthpiece and finger holes.

occasion (ə'keɪʒən) n. **1.** a particular happening or event or the time at which it happens. **2.** (sometimes foll. by for) a need or reason (to do or be something); grounds: I had no occasion to complain. **3.** a suitable time or opportunity (to do something). **4.** a special event, time, or celebration: the party was quite an occasion. **5. on occasion.** every so often. **6. rise to the occasion.** to meet the special demands of a situation. ~vb. **7.** to cause, esp. incidentally.

occasional (ə'keɪʒənᵊl) adj. **1.** happening from time to time; not frequent or regular. **2.** of, for, or on special occasions. —**oc'casionally** adv.

Occident ('ɒksɪdənt) n. the western hemisphere, esp. Europe and America. —**Occidental** (,ɒksɪ'dɛntᵊl) adj.

occiput ('ɒksɪ,pʌt) n. the back of the head or skull. —**oc'cipital** adj.

occlude (ə'kluːd) vb. **1.** to block or stop up (a passage or opening); obstruct. **2.** to shut in or out. **3.** Chem. (of a solid) to absorb and retain (a gas or other substance). —**oc'clusion** n.

occluded front n. Meteorol. the front formed when the cold front of a depression overtakes a warm front, raising the warm air from ground level.

occult (ɒ'kʌlt, 'ɒkʌlt) adj. **1.** involving mystical or supernatural phenomena or powers. **2.** beyond ordinary human understanding. **3.** secret or esoteric. ~n. **4. the occult.** the knowledge and study of occult phenomena and powers.

occupancy ('ɒkjʊpənsɪ) n., pl. **-cies. 1.** the act of occupying; taking or keeping possession of a property. **2.** the period of time during which one is an occupant of a property.

occupant ('ɒkjʊpənt) n. a person or thing occupying a dwelling, position, or place.

occupation (,ɒkjʊ'peɪʃən) n. **1.** a person's job or profession. **2.** any activity on which time is spent by a person. **3.** an occupying or being occupied. **4.** the control of a country by a foreign military power. —,**occu'pational** adj.

occupational therapy n. Med. creative activity, such as a craft or hobby, to help a patient recover from an illness.

occupier ('ɒkjʊ,paɪə) n. Brit. a person who is in possession or occupation of a house or land.

occupy ('ɒkjʊ,paɪ) vb. **-pying, -pied. 1.** to live, stay or work in (a house, flat or office). **2.** (often passive) to keep (a person or his mind) busy. **3.** (often passive) to take up (time or space): this seat is occupied. **4.** to take and hold possession of forcibly: students occupied the college buildings. **5.** to fill or hold (a position or office).

occur (ə'kɜː) vb. **-curring, -curred. 1.** to happen; take place. **2.** to be found or be present; exist. **3. occur to.** to come into the mind of; suggest itself to.

Usage. It is best not to use *occur* and *happen* of prearranged events: *the wedding took place* (not *occurred* or *happened*) *in the afternoon.*

occurrence (əˈkʌrəns) *n.* **1.** something that occurs; a happening; event. **2.** the act or fact of occurring: *a crime of frequent occurrence.*

ocean (ˈəʊʃən) *n.* **1.** the body of salt water covering about 70 per cent of the earth's surface. **2.** one of the five principal divisions of this, the Atlantic, Pacific, Indian, Arctic, and Antarctic. **3.** a huge quantity or expanse: *an ocean of replies.* **4.** *Literary.* the sea. —**oceanic** (ˌəʊʃɪˈænɪk) *adj.*

ocean-going *adj.* (of a ship or boat) suited for travel on the open ocean.

oceanography (ˌəʊʃəˈnɒɡrəfɪ) *n.* the study of oceans and their environment. —**oceanographer** *n.*

ocelot (ˈɒsɪˌlɒt, ˈəʊ-) *n.* a large cat of Central and South America that has a dark-spotted yellow-grey coat.

och (ɒx) *interj. Scot. & Irish.* an expression of surprise, annoyance, or disagreement.

ochre *or U.S.* **ocher** (ˈəʊkə) *n.* **1.** a yellow or reddish-brown earth used as a pigment. ~*adj.* **2.** moderate yellow-orange to orange.

o'clock (əˈklɒk) *adv.* used after a number to specify an hour: *four o'clock in the morning.*

OCR optical character reader *or* recognition.

oct. octavo.

Oct. October.

octagon (ˈɒktəɡən) *n.* a polygon having eight sides. —**octagonal** (ɒkˈtæɡənᵊl) *adj.*

octahedron (ˌɒktəˈhiːdrən) *n., pl.* **-drons** *or* **-dra** (-drə). a solid figure having eight plane faces.

octane (ˈɒkteɪn) *n.* a liquid hydrocarbon found in petroleum.

octane number *or* **rating** *n.* a number indicating the antiknock quality of a petrol.

octave (ˈɒktɪv) *n.* **1. a.** the musical interval between the first note and the eighth note of a major or minor scale. **b.** the higher of these two notes. **c.** the series of notes filling this interval. **2.** *Prosody.* a rhythmic group of eight lines of verse.

octavo (ɒkˈteɪvəʊ) *n., pl.* **-vos.** **1.** a book size resulting from folding a sheet of paper of a standard size to form eight leaves. **2.** a book or sheet of this size.

octet (ɒkˈtɛt) *n.* **1.** any group of eight, esp. singers or musicians. **2.** a piece of music composed for eight performers.

October (ɒkˈtəʊbə) *n.* the tenth month of the year.

octogenarian (ˌɒktəʊdʒɪˈnɛərɪən) *n.* **1.** a person between 80 and 89 years old. ~*adj.* **2.** of an octogenarian.

octopus (ˈɒktəpəs) *n., pl.* **-puses.** a sea creature with a soft oval body and eight long suckered tentacles.

ocular (ˈɒkjʊlə) *adj.* of or relating to the eyes or sight.

oculist (ˈɒkjʊlɪst) *n.* an old name for an ophthalmologist.

OD (ˌəʊˈdiː) *Informal.* ~*n.* **1.** an overdose of a drug. ~*vb.* **OD'ing, OD'd.** **2.** to take an overdose of a drug.

odalisque (ˈəʊdəlɪsk) *n.* a female slave in a harem.

odd (ɒd) *adj.* **1.** unusual or peculiar. **2.** occasional or incidental: *odd jobs.* **3.** leftover or additional: *odd bits of wool.* **4. a.** not divisible by two. **b.** indicated by an odd number: *graphs are on odd pages.* **5.** being part of a pair or set when the other or others are missing: *an odd sock.* **6.** somewhat more than the round numbers specified: *fifty-odd pounds: ten pounds and some odd change.* **7.** out of the way: *in odd corners.* **8. odd man out.** a person or thing excluded from others forming a group or unit. ~See also **odds.** —**oddly** *adv.* —**oddness** *n.*

oddball (ˈɒdˌbɔːl) *n. Informal.* a strange or eccentric person.

oddity (ˈɒdɪtɪ) *n., pl.* **-ties.** **1.** an odd person or thing. **2.** an odd characteristic; peculiarity.

oddment (ˈɒdmənt) *n.* (*often pl.*) an odd piece or thing; leftover.

odds (ɒdz) *pl. n.* **1.** (foll. by *on* or *against*) the probability, expressed as a ratio, that something will or will not happen: *the odds against the outsider are a hundred to one.* **2.** the difference, expressed as a ratio, between the money placed on a bet and the amount that would be received as winning payment: *he was offering odds of five to one.* **3.** the likelihood that a certain state of affairs will be so: *the odds are that he is drunk.* **4.** the advantage that one contender is judged to have over another: *all the odds are in his favour.* **5. it makes no odds.** *Brit.* it does not matter. **6. at odds.** in conflict or at variance. **7. over the odds.** more than is expected or necessary.

odds and ends *pl. n.* miscellaneous articles.

odds-on *adj.* having a better than even chance of winning.

ode (əʊd) *n.* a lyric poem, usually addressed to a particular subject, with lines of varying lengths and metres.

odious (ˈəʊdɪəs) *adj.* offensive; hateful. —**odiousness** *n.*

odium (ˈəʊdɪəm) *n.* widespread dislike or disapproval of a person or action.

odometer (ɒˈdɒmɪtə, əʊ-) *n. U.S. & Canad.* same as **mileometer.**

odoriferous (ˌəʊdəˈrɪfərəs) *adj.* having or giving off a fragrant odour.

odour or U.S. **odor** ('əudə) n. **1.** a particular and distinctive scent or smell. **2.** repute or regard (in **in good odour**, **in bad odour**). —'**odorous** adj. —'**odourless** adj.

odyssey ('ɒdɪsɪ) n. a long eventful journey.

OECD Organization for Economic Cooperation and Development.

oedema or **edema** (ɪ'diːmə) n., pl. **-mata** (-mətə). Pathol. an abnormal accumulation of fluid in the tissues of the body, causing swelling.

Oedipus complex ('iːdɪpəs) n. Psychoanal. the usually unconscious sexual desire of a child, esp. a male child, for the parent of the opposite sex. —'**oedipal** adj.

o'er (ɔː, 'əuə) prep., adv. Poetic. over.

oesophagus (iː'sɒfəgəs) n., pl. **-gi** (-ˌgaɪ). the tube through which food travels from the throat to the stomach; gullet. —**oesophageal** (iːˌsɒfə'dʒiːəl) adj.

oestrogen ('iːstrədʒən, 'ɛstrə-) n. a female sex hormone that controls the reproductive cycle, and prepares the body for pregnancy.

oestrus ('iːstrəs, 'ɛstrəs) n. a regularly occurring period of fertility and sexual receptivity in the reproductive cycle of most female mammals, except humans; heat.

of (ɒv) prep. **1.** belonging to; situated in or coming from; because of: citizens of London; to die of hunger. **2.** used after words or phrases expressing quantities: a pint of milk. **3.** specifying an amount or value: a height of two metres. **4.** made up of, containing, or characterized by: a rod of iron; a man of some depth. **5.** used with a verbal noun to link it with a following noun that is either the subject or the object of the verb: the breathing of a fine swimmer (subject); the breathing of clean air (object). **6.** at a given distance or space of time from: within a mile of the town; within ten minutes of leaving. **7.** used to indicate identity or closer definition: the city of Naples; a speech on the subject of archaeology. **8.** about; concerning: think of me. **9.** U.S. before the hour of: a quarter of nine.

off (ɒf) prep. **1.** so as to be no longer in contact with something: to lift a cup off the table. **2.** so as to be no longer attached to or associated with something else: to take the tax off potatoes. **3.** away from: we swerved off the road. **4.** situated near to or leading away from: just off the High Street. **5.** no longer having a liking for: I've gone off you. **6.** no longer using: he has been taken off the antibiotics. ~adv. **7.** so as to deactivate or disengage: turn off the radio. **8. a.** so as to get rid of: sleep off a hangover. **b.** as a reduction in price: he took ten per cent off. **9.** spent away from work or other duties: take the afternoon off. **10.** away; at a distance: the girl ran off; the ship was 10 miles off. **11.** away in the future: August is less than a week off. **12.** so as to be no longer taking place: the match has been called off. **13.** removed from contact with something: she took her clothes off. **14. off and on.** now and then: he comes here off and on. ~adj. **15.** not on; no longer operating: turn the television off. **16.** cancelled or postponed: the meeting is off. **17.** in a specified condition, esp. regarding money or provisions: I'd be better off without this job; how are you off for money? **18.** not up to the usual standard: an off year for good wine. **19.** no longer on the menu: haddock is off. **20.** (of food or drink) having gone bad or sour: this milk is off. ~n. **21.** Cricket. the side of the field to the right of a right-handed batsman when he is facing the bowler.

Usage. Off is best not followed by from or of: he stepped off (not off of) the platform. It is also best to avoid using the word in the place of from: they bought apples from (rather than off) the man.

off. **1.** office. **2.** officer. **3.** official.

offal ('ɒf'l) n. **1.** the edible internal parts of an animal, such as the heart or liver. **2.** refuse; rubbish.

offbeat ('ɒfˌbiːt) adj. unusual, unconventional, or eccentric.

off colour adj. **1.** Chiefly Brit. slightly ill; unwell. **2.** indecent or indelicate; risqué.

offcut ('ɒfˌkʌt) n. a piece of paper, wood, or fabric remaining after the main pieces have been cut; remnant.

offence or U.S. **offense** (ə'fɛns) n. **1.** a breaking of a law or rule; crime. **2.** annoyance or anger. **3.** a cause of annoyance or anger. **4.** attack; assault. **5. give offence.** to cause annoyance or anger. **6. take offence.** to feel hurt or offended.

offend (ə'fɛnd) vb. **1.** to hurt the feelings of (a person); insult. **2.** to be disagreeable to; disgust: the smell offended him. **3.** to commit a crime. —**of'fender** n. —**of'fending** adj.

offensive (ə'fɛnsɪv) adj. **1.** unpleasant or disgusting to the senses: an offensive smell. **2.** causing annoyance or anger; insulting. **3.** for the purpose of attack rather than defence. ~n. **4.** (usually preceded by the) an attitude or position of aggression. **5.** an attack or hostile action. —**of'fensively** adv.

offer ('ɒfə) vb. **1.** to present for acceptance or rejection: I offered him a cup of tea. **2.** to provide: this stream offers the best fishing. **3.** to present itself: if an opportunity should offer. **4.** to be willing (to do something): he offered to help me. **5.** to put forward (a proposal, information, or opinion) for consideration: have you any advice to offer? **6.** to present for sale. **7.** to propose as payment; bid. **8.** (often foll. by up) to present (a prayer or sacrifice) as an act of worship. **9.** to show readiness for: to offer resistance. ~n. **10.** something that is

offered. **11.** the act of offering. **12. on
offer.** for sale at a reduced price.

offering (ˈɒfərɪŋ) n. **1.** something that is
offered. **2.** a contribution to the funds of a
religious organization. **3.** a sacrifice to a
god.

offertory (ˈɒfətrɪ) n., pl. **-tories.** Christianity. **1.** the part of a church service when
the bread and wine for communion are offered for consecration. **2.** the collection of
money at this service. **3.** the prayers said
or sung while the worshippers' offerings
are being brought to the altar.

offhand (ˌɒfˈhænd) adj. also **offhanded,**
adv. **1.** curt or casual in manner: offhand
behaviour. **2.** without preparation; impromptu: I can't give you an answer offhand. —ˌoffˈhandedness n.

office (ˈɒfɪs) n. **1.** a room, set of rooms, or
building in which business, professional
duties or clerical work are carried out. **2.** a
room or department of an organization
dealing with particular business: the architect's office approved the plans. **3.** the
group of persons working in an office: it
was a happy office until she came. **4.** (cap.
when part of a name) a government department or agency: Office of Fair Trading. **5.** a
position of trust or authority, as in a government: to run for office. **6.** duty or function: the office of an administrator. **7.**
(often pl.) something done for another:
through his good offices. **8.** a place where
tickets, information, or some service can be
obtained: a ticket office. **9.** Christianity.
(often pl.) a religious ceremony or service.
10. in (or **out of**) **office.** (of a government)
in (or out of) power.

officer (ˈɒfɪsə) n. **1.** a person in the armed
services, or on a nonnaval ship, who holds a
position of authority. **2.** a policeman. **3.** a
person holding a position of authority in a
government or organization.

official (əˈfɪʃəl) adj. **1.** of an office or position of authority: in an official capacity. **2.**
sanctioned by or derived from authority: an
official statement. **3.** formal or ceremonial:
an official dinner. ~n. **4.** a person holding
a position of authority. —**ofˈficially** adv.

officialdom (əˈfɪʃəldəm) n. officials or bu-
reaucrats collectively.

officialese (əˌfɪʃəˈliːz) n. language typical
of official documents, esp. when wordy or
pompous.

Official Receiver n. an officer appointed
by the government to deal with the affairs
of a bankrupt person or company.

officiate (əˈfɪʃɪˌeɪt) vb. **1.** to perform the
duties of an office; act in an official capacity. **2.** to conduct a religious or other ceremony. —**ofˌficiˈation** n. —**ofˈficiˌator** n.

officious (əˈfɪʃəs) adj. offering unwanted
advice or services; interfering. —**of-
ˈficiousness** n.

offing (ˈɒfɪŋ) n. **1.** the part of the sea that

can be seen from the shore. **2. in the
offing.** not far off; likely to occur soon.

off key adj., adv. **1.** Music. out of tune.
2. out of keeping; not quite suitable or
fitting.

off-licence n. Brit. **1.** a shop or a counter
in a shop where alcoholic drink is sold for
consumption elsewhere. **2.** a licence permitting such sales.

off-line adj. (of computer equipment) not
directly connected to or controlled by the
central processing unit of a computer.

off-load vb. to get rid of (something unpleasant), usually by giving it to someone
else.

off-peak adj. (of services) used at times
other than those of greatest demand.

off-putting adj. Brit. informal. arousing
dislike; distracting or disconcerting.

offset n. (ˈɒfˌsɛt). **1. a.** a printing method
in which the impression is made onto a
surface, such as a rubber roller, which
transfers it to the paper. **b.** (as modifier):
offset letterpress. **2.** Bot. a short runner in
certain plants that produces roots and
shoots at the tip. ~vb. (ˌɒfˈsɛt), **-setting,
-set. 3.** to counterbalance or compensate
for. **4.** to print (something) using the offset
process.

offshoot (ˈɒfˌʃuːt) n. **1.** a shoot growing
from the main stem of a plant. **2.** something that has developed from something
else.

offshore (ˌɒfˈʃɔː) adj., adv. **1.** away from
or at some distance from the shore. ~adj.
2. sited or conducted at sea: offshore industries.

offside adj., adv. (ˌɒfˈsaɪd). **1.** Sport. in a
position illegally ahead of the ball when it
is played. ~n. (ˈɒfˌsaɪd). **2.** (usually preceded by the) Chiefly Brit. the side of a
vehicle nearest the centre of the road.

offspring (ˈɒfˌsprɪŋ) n. **1.** the immediate
descendant or descendants of a person or
animal. **2.** a product, outcome, or result.

off-the-peg adj. (of clothing) ready to
wear; not produced especially for the person buying.

oft (ɒft) adv. Archaic or poetic. short for
often.

often (ˈɒfən) adv. **1.** frequently; much of
the time. **2. as often as not.** quite frequently. **3. every so often.** occasionally.
4. more often than not. in more than half
the instances.

ogee arch (ˈəʊdʒiː) n. a pointed arch made
with an S-shaped curve on each side.

ogle (ˈəʊgəl) vb. to stare at (someone) lust-
fully.

ogre (ˈəʊgə) n. **1.** (in folklore) a man-eating
giant. **2.** any monstrous or cruel person.
—**ˈogreish** adj. —**ˈogress** fem. n.

oh (əʊ) interj. an exclamation of surprise,
pain, pleasure, fear, or annoyance.

OH Ohio.

ohm (əʊm) *n.* the SI unit of electric resistance.

OHMS (in Britain and the Commonwealth) On Her (*or* His) Majesty's Service.

oil (ɔɪl) *n.* **1.** any of a number of viscous liquids with a smooth sticky feel, which are usually flammable, insoluble in water, and are obtained from plants, animals, or mineral deposits by synthesis. **2.** same as **petroleum. 3.** a substance derived from petroleum and used for lubrication. **4.** *Brit.* paraffin as a domestic fuel. **5.** (*often pl.*) oil colour or paint. **6.** an oil painting. ~*vb.* **7.** to lubricate with oil or apply oil to. **8. oil the wheels.** to make things run smoothly.

oil cake *n.* compressed linseed from which the oil has been extracted, used as livestock feed.

oilcloth (ˈɔɪlˌklɒθ) *n.* cloth made waterproof by treating with oil or a synthetic resin.

oilfield (ˈɔɪlˌfiːld) *n.* an area containing reserves of oil.

oilfired (ˈɔɪlˌfaɪəd) *adj.* using oil as fuel.

oil paint *n.* a thick paint made of pigment ground in linseed oil.

oil painting *n.* **1.** a picture painted with oil paints. **2.** the art of painting with oil paints.

oil rig *n.* a structure used as a base when drilling an oil well.

oilskin (ˈɔɪlˌskɪn) *n.* **1.** a cotton fabric treated with oil to make it waterproof. **2.** (*often pl.*) a protective outer garment of this fabric.

oil slick *n.* a mass of floating oil covering an area of water.

oil well *n.* a well bored into the earth or sea bed to a supply of oil.

oily (ˈɔɪlɪ) *adj.* **oilier, oiliest. 1.** soaked or covered with oil. **2.** of, containing, or like oil. **3.** flatteringly servile or fawning. —ˈoiliness *n.*

oink (ɔɪŋk) *interj.* the grunt of a pig or an imitation of this.

ointment (ˈɔɪntmənt) *n.* a smooth greasy substance applied to the skin to heal or protect, or as a cosmetic.

OK Oklahoma.

O.K. (ˌəʊˈkeɪ) *Informal.* ~*interj.* **1.** an expression of approval or agreement. ~*adj., adv.* **2.** in good or satisfactory condition. ~*vb.* **O.K.ing** (ˌəʊˈkeɪɪŋ), **O.K.ed** (ˌəʊˈkeɪd). **3.** to approve or endorse. ~*n., pl.* **O.K.s. 4.** approval or agreement.

okapi (əʊˈkɑːpɪ) *n., pl.* **-pis** *or* **-pi.** an African mammal related to the giraffe, but with a shorter neck, a reddish coat, and white stripes on the legs.

okay (ˌəʊˈkeɪ) *interj., adj., adv., vb., n.* same as **O.K.**

Okla. Oklahoma.

okra (ˈəʊkrə) *n.* a tall plant with long green pods that are used as food.

old (əʊld) *adj.* **1.** having lived or existed for a long time: *an old man; an old tradition.* **2.** of or relating to advanced years or a long life: *old age.* **3.** decrepit or senile. **4.** worn with age or use: *old clothes.* **5.** having lived or existed for a specified period: *six years old.* **6.** earlier or earliest of two or more things with the same name: *the old edition; the Old Testament.* **7.** designating the form of a language in which the earliest known records are written: *Old English.* **8.** familiar through long acquaintance or repetition: *an old friend; an old excuse.* **9.** (often preceded by *good*) dear: used as a term of affection or familiarity: *good old George.* **10.** skilled through long experience (esp. in **an old hand**). **11.** out of date; unfashionable. **12.** remote in origin or time of origin: *an old culture.* **13.** former; previous: *my old house was small.* **14.** of long standing: *an old member.* **15.** sensible, wise, or mature: *old beyond one's years.* **16.** very: *a high old time.* **17. good old days.** an earlier period of time regarded as better than the present. ~*n.* **18.** an earlier or past time: *in days of old.* —ˈoldish *adj.* —ˈoldness *n.*

old age pension *n.* a former name for **retirement pension.** —**old age pensioner** *n.*

Old Bailey (ˈbeɪlɪ) *n.* the Central Criminal Court of England.

old boy *n.* **1.** (*sometimes caps.*) *Brit.* a male ex-pupil of a school. **2.** *Informal, chiefly Brit.* **a.** a familiar form of address used to refer to a man. **b.** an old man.

old country *n.* the country of origin of an immigrant or an immigrant's ancestors.

olden (ˈəʊldⁿn) *adj. Archaic or poetic.* old: *in olden days.*

Old English *n.* the English language of the Anglo-Saxons, spoken from the fifth century A.D. to about 1100. Also called: **Anglo-Saxon.**

Old English sheepdog *n.* a breed of large sheepdog with a thick shaggy coat.

old-fashioned *adj.* **1.** belonging to or favoured by former times; outdated: *old-fashioned ideas.* **2.** favouring or adopting the styles or ideas of a former time: *an old-fashioned romantic.*

old flame *n. Informal, old-fashioned.* a former sweetheart.

Old French *n.* the French language in its earliest forms, from about the 9th century up to about 1400.

old guard *n.* **1.** a group that works for a long-established or old-fashioned cause. **2.** the conservative element in a party or group.

old hat *adj.* old-fashioned or trite.

Old High German *n.* a group of West

Germanic dialects that developed into modern German; High German up to about 1200.

oldie ('əʊldɪ) n. Informal. an old joke, song, film or person.

old lady n. Informal. one's mother or wife.

old maid n. **1.** a woman regarded as unlikely ever to marry; spinster. **2.** Informal. a prim, fussy, or excessively cautious person.

old man n. **1.** Informal. one's father or husband. **2.** an affectionate form of address used to a man.

old master n. **1.** one of the great European painters of the period 1500 to 1800. **2.** a painting by one of these.

old moon n. a phase of the moon between last quarter and new moon, when it appears as a waning crescent.

Old Nick (nɪk) n. Informal. Satan.

old school n. a group of people favouring traditional or conservative ideas or practices.

old school tie n. the system of mutual help supposed to operate among the former pupils of public schools.

Old Style n. the former method of reckoning dates using the Julian calendar.

Old Testament n. the first part of the Christian Bible, containing the sacred Scriptures of the Hebrews.

old-time adj. of or relating to a former time; old-fashioned: old-time dancing.

old wives' tale n. a belief, usually superstitious or foolish, passed on by word of mouth as a piece of traditional wisdom.

old woman n. **1.** Informal. one's mother or wife. **2.** a timid, fussy, or cautious person. —ˌold-'womanish adj.

Old World n. that part of the world that was known before the discovery of the Americas; the eastern hemisphere.

old-world adj. of or characteristic of former times; quaint or traditional.

oleaginous (ˌəʊlɪ'ædʒɪnəs) adj. like or producing oil; oily.

oleander (ˌəʊlɪ'ændə) n. an evergreen Mediterranean shrub with fragrant white, pink, or purple flowers.

O level n. Brit. **1.** the basic level of the General Certificate of Education. **2.** a pass in a particular subject at O level: he has eight O levels.

olfactory (ɒl'fæktrɪ) adj. of the sense of smell.

oligarch ('ɒlɪˌgɑːk) n. a member of an oligarchy.

oligarchy ('ɒlɪˌgɑːkɪ) n., pl. **-chies. 1.** government by a small group of people. **2.** a state or organization so governed. **3.** a small body of individuals ruling such a state or organization. —ˌoli'garchic or ˌoli'garchical adj.

Oligocene ('ɒlɪgəʊˌsiːn, ɒ'lɪg-) adj. Geol. of the epoch of geological time about 35 million years ago.

olive ('ɒlɪv) n. **1.** an evergreen Mediterranean tree. **2.** the fruit of this tree, eaten as a relish or pressed to make olive oil. ~adj. **3.** yellow-green.

olive branch n. peace offering: to hold out the olive branch.

olive-green adj. deep yellowish-green.

olive oil n. a green or yellow oil pressed from ripe olives and used in cooking and medicines.

Olympiad (ə'lɪmpɪˌæd) n. **1.** a staging of the modern Olympic Games. **2.** an international contest in chess or other games.

Olympian (ə'lɪmpɪən) adj. **1.** of Mount Olympus or the classical Greek gods. **2.** majestic or godlike. ~n. **3.** a god of Mount Olympus.

Olympic (ə'lɪmpɪk) adj. of the Olympic Games.

Olympic Games n. (functioning as sing. or pl.) **1.** an ancient Greek festival, held every fourth year in honour of Zeus, consisting of games and festivities. **2.** Also called: **the Olympics.** the modern revival of these games, consisting of international athletic and sporting contests held every four years in a selected country.

OM Order of Merit (a Brit. title).

ombudsman ('ɒmbʊdzmən) n., pl. **-men.** an official who investigates citizens' complaints against the government or its servants.

omega ('əʊmɪgə) n. **1.** the 24th and last letter of the Greek alphabet (Ω, ω). **2.** the ending or last of a series.

omelette or esp. U.S. **omelet** ('ɒmlɪt) n. a dish of beaten eggs cooked in a flat pan and often folded round a savoury filling.

omen ('əʊmən) n. **1.** a thing or occurrence regarded as a sign of future happiness or disaster. **2.** prophetic significance: bird of ill omen.

ominous ('ɒmɪnəs) adj. foreboding evil. —'ominously adv.

omission (əʊ'mɪʃən) n. **1.** something that has been omitted or neglected. **2.** an omitting or having been omitted.

omit (əʊ'mɪt) vb. **omitting, omitted. 1.** to fail to include; leave out. **2.** to fail (to do something).

omnibus ('ɒmnɪˌbʌs, -bəs) n., pl. **-buses. 1.** a bus. **2.** a collection of works by one author or several works on a similar topic, reprinted in one volume. ~adj. **3.** consisting of or dealing with several different things at once: an omnibus programme.

omnipotent (ɒm'nɪpətənt) adj. having very great or unlimited power. —om'nipotence n.

omnipresent (ˌɒmnɪ'prɛzənt) adj. (esp. of a god) present in all places at the same time. —ˌomni'presence n.

omniscient (ɒmˈnɪsɪənt) *adj.* knowing or seeming to know everything. —**omˈniscience** *n.*

omnivorous (ɒmˈnɪvərəs) *adj.* **1.** eating any type of food. **2.** taking in or assimilating everything indiscriminately: *an omnivorous reader.* —**omnivore** (ˈɒmnɪˌvɔː) *n.* —**omˈnivorousness** *n.*

on (ɒn) *prep.* **1.** in contact with the surface of; at the upper surface of: *an apple on the ground; a mark on the tablecloth.* **2.** attached to: *a puppet on a string.* **3.** carried with: *I've no money on me.* **4.** near to or along the side of: *a house on the sea.* **5.** within the time limits of (a day or date): *he arrived on Thursday.* **6.** being performed upon or relayed through the medium of: *a waltz played on the violin; what's on television?* **7.** at the occasion of: *on his retirement.* **8.** immediately after or at the same time as: *on entering I spotted him.* **9.** through the use of: *he lives on bread; cars run on petrol.* **10. a.** regularly taking (a drug): *she's on the pill.* **b.** addicted to: *he's on heroin.* **11.** by means of (a mode of transport): *on foot; on horseback.* **12.** in the process or course of: *on a journey; on strike.* **13.** concerned with or relating to: *a programme on jazz.* **14.** (of a statement or action) having a basis or grounds: *I have it on good authority.* **15.** charged to: *the drinks are on me.* **16.** staked as a bet: *ten pounds on that horse.* **17.** (used with an adj. preceded by *the*) indicating the manner or way in which an action is carried out: *on the sly; on the cheap.* ~*adv.* **18.** in operation; functioning: *the radio's been on all night.* **19.** attached to, surrounding, or placed in contact with something: *the girl had nothing on.* **20.** taking place: *what's on tonight?* **21.** continuously or persistently: *don't keep on about it; the play went on all afternoon.* **22.** towards or forwards: *we drove on towards London; march on!* **23. on and off.** intermittently; from time to time. **24. on and on.** without ceasing; continually. ~*adj.* **25.** functioning; operating: *the on position on a radio.* **26.** *Informal.* performing: *I'm on in five minutes.* **27.** *Informal.* definitely taking place: *the match is on for Friday.* **28.** *Informal.* tolerable, practicable or acceptable: *your plan just isn't on.* **29. on at.** *Informal.* nagging: *she was always on at her husband.* ~*n.* **30.** *Cricket.* the side of the field to the left of and behind a right-handed batsman.

onager (ˈɒnədʒə) *n., pl.* **-gri** (-ˌgraɪ) *or* **-gers.** a wild ass of Persia.

onanism (ˈəʊnəˌnɪzəm) *n.* **1.** withdrawal in sexual intercourse before ejaculation. **2.** masturbation.

ONC (in Britain) Ordinary National Certificate.

once (wʌns) *adv.* **1.** one time; on one occasion only. **2.** at some past time, but no longer: *I could speak French once.* **3.** by one degree (of relationship): *a cousin once removed.* **4.** ever; at all: *if you once forget it.* **5. once and for all.** conclusively; for the last time. **6. once in a while.** occasionally; now and then. **7. once or twice.** a few times. **8. once upon a time.** used to begin fairy tales and children's stories. ~*conj.* **9.** as soon as: *once you begin, you'll enjoy it.* ~*n.* **10.** one occasion or case: *you may do it, this once.* **11. all at once. a.** suddenly. **b.** simultaneously. **12. at once. a.** immediately. **b.** simultaneously. **13. for once.** this time, even if at no other time.

once-over *n. Informal.* a quick examination or appraisal.

oncoming (ˈɒnˌkʌmɪŋ) *adj.* coming nearer in space or time; approaching.

oncogene (ˈɒŋkəʊˌdʒiːn) *n.* a gene present in all cells, that when abnormally activated can cause cancer.

OND (in Britain) Ordinary National Diploma.

one (wʌn) *det.* **1.** single; lone; not two or more: *one drink; one at a time.* **2.** only; unique: *he's the one man who can do it; one of a kind.* **3.** a specified (person or thing) as distinct from another or others of its kind: *raise one hand and then the other; which one is correct?* **4.** a certain, indefinite, or unspecified (time): *one day you'll be sorry.* **5.** *Informal.* an emphatic word for **a** or **an**: *it was one hell of a fight.* **6.** (**all**) **in one.** combined; united. **7. all one.** of no consequence: *it's all one to me.* **8. at one.** (often foll. by *with*) in a state of agreement or harmony. **9. one and all.** everyone, without exception. **10. one by one.** one at a time; individually. **11. one or two.** a few. ~*pron.* **12.** an indefinite person regarded as typical of every person: *one can't say any more than that.* **13.** any indefinite person: *one can catch fine trout in this stream.* ~*n.* **14.** the smallest natural number and first cardinal number. **15.** a numeral, 1 or I, representing this number. **16.** *Informal.* a joke or story: *have you heard the one about the actress and the bishop?* **17.** something consisting of one unit or represented by the number one.

Usage. Where the pronoun *one* is repeated, as in *one might think one would be unwise to say that, he* is sometimes substituted: *one might think he would be unwise to say that.* It is best to avoid *one* followed by *he* if there would be any ambiguity: *he* in this case could refer either to the same person as *one* or to some other person.

one another *pron.* each other; each one the other: *they dislike one another.*

one-armed bandit *n. Informal.* a fruit machine operated by pulling down a lever at one side.

one-horse *adj. Informal.* small or insignificant: *a one-horse town.*

one-liner *n. Informal.* a short joke or witty remark.

oneness (ˈwʌnnɪs) *n.* **1.** agreement. **2.** uniqueness. **3.** sameness.

one-night stand *n.* **1.** a performance given only once at any one place. **2.** *Informal.* a sexual encounter lasting only one evening or night.

one-off *n. Brit.* something that happens or is made only once.

onerous (ˈɒnərəs, ˈəʊ-) *adj.* laborious or burdensome. —**ˈonerousness** *n.*

oneself (wʌnˈsɛlf) *pron.* **1.** the reflexive form of *one.* **2.** one's normal or usual self: *one doesn't feel oneself after such an experience.*

one-sided *adj.* **1.** considering or favouring only one side of a matter or problem: *a one-sided account.* **2.** having all the advantage on one side: *a one-sided race.*

one-stop *adj.* having or providing a range of related services or goods in one place: *a one-stop shop.*

one-time *adj.* at some time in the past; former.

one-to-one *adj.* **1.** (of two or more things) corresponding exactly. **2.** denoting a relationship or encounter in which someone is involved with only one other person: *one-to-one tuition.* **3.** *Maths.* involving the pairing of each member of one set with only one member of another set, without remainder.

one-track *adj. Informal.* obsessed with one idea or subject: *a one-track mind.*

one-up *adj. Informal.* having an advantage or lead over another. —**ˌone-ˈupmanship** *n.*

one-way *adj.* **1.** moving or allowing travel in one direction only: *one-way traffic.* **2.** involving no reciprocal obligation or action: *a one-way relationship.*

ongoing (ˈɒnˌgəʊɪŋ) *adj.* in progress; continuing: *ongoing projects.*

onion (ˈʌnjən) *n.* **1.** a vegetable with an edible bulb having a pungent odour and taste. **2. know one's onions.** *Brit. slang.* to be fully acquainted with a subject. —**ˈoniony** *adj.*

on-line *adj.* (of computer equipment) directly connected to and controlled by the central processing unit of a computer.

onlooker (ˈɒnˌlʊkə) *n.* a person who observes without taking part. —**ˈonˌlooking** *adj.*

only (ˈəʊnlɪ) *adj.* **1.** alone of its or their kind: *the only men left in town were too old to bear arms.* **2.** (of a child) having no brothers or sisters. **3.** unique by virtue of superiority; best: *flying is the only way to travel.* **4. one and only.** incomparable: *the one and only Diana Ross.* ~*adv.* **5.** without anyone or anything else being included; alone: *you have one choice only; only a genius can do that.* **6.** merely or just: *it's only Henry.* **7.** no more or no greater than: *we met only an hour ago.* **8.** merely: *I returned, only to find him gone.* **9.** not earlier than; not until: *I only found out yesterday.* **10. if only** *or* **if...only.** used to introduce a wish or hope. **11. only too.** *adj.* extremely: *he was only too pleased to help.* ~*conj.* **12.** but; however: *play outside, only don't go into the street.*
Usage. In informal English, *only* is often used to connect sentences: *it would have been possible, only he was not present at the time.* This use is avoided in formal contexts: *it would have been possible had he been present.* In formal speech and writing, *only* is placed directly before the word or words that it modifies: *she could interview only three applicants in the morning.* In all but the most formal contexts it is acceptable to put *only* before the verb: *she could only interview three applicants in the morning.*

o.n.o. or near(est) offer.

onomatopoeia (ˌɒnəˌmætəˈpiːə) *n.* the formation or use of a word whose sound imitates the sound of the noise or action represented, such as *hiss.* —**ˌonoˌmatoˈpoeic** *or* **onomatopoetic** (ˌɒnəˌmætəpəʊˈɛtɪk) *adj.*

onrush (ˈɒnˌrʌʃ) *n.* a forceful forward rush or flow; surge.

onset (ˈɒnˌsɛt) *n.* a start; beginning.

onshore (ˈɒnˈʃɔː) *adj., adv.* **1.** towards the land: *an onshore gale.* **2.** on land; not at sea.

onside (ˌɒnˈsaɪd) *adj., adv. Sport.* (of a player) in a legal position, as when behind the ball or with a required number of opponents between oneself and the opposing team's goal line.

onslaught (ˈɒnˌslɔːt) *n.* a violent attack.

Ont. Ontario.

onto *or* **on to** (ˈɒntʊ) *prep.* **1.** to a position that is on: *step onto the train.* **2.** having become aware of (something): *the police are onto us.* **3.** into contact with: *get onto the factory.*
Usage. *Onto* is generally accepted as a word in its own right. *On to* is still used, however, where *on* is considered to be part of the verb: *he moved on to the next platform* as contrasted with *he jumped onto the next platform.*

ontology (ɒnˈtɒlədʒɪ) *n. Philosophy.* the study of the nature of being. —**ontological** (ˌɒntəˈlɒdʒɪkᵊl) *adj.*

onus (ˈəʊnəs) *n., pl.* **onuses.** a responsibility, task, or burden.

onward (ˈɒnwəd) *adj.* **1.** directed or moving forward. ~*adv. also* **onwards. 2.** continuing; progressing.

onyx (ˈɒnɪks) *n.* a kind of quartz with alternating coloured layers, used as a gemstone.

oodles (ˈuːdˀlz) *pl. n. Informal.* great quantities: *oodles of money.*

Ookpik (ˈuːkpɪk) *n. Canad. trademark.* a sealskin doll resembling an owl, used abroad as a symbol of Canadian handicrafts.

oolite (ˈəʊəˌlaɪt) *n.* a limestone made up of tiny grains of calcium carbonate. —**oolitic** (ˌəʊəˈlɪtɪk) *adj.*

oomiak *or* **oomiac** (ˈuːmɪˌæk) *n.* same as **umiak.**

oompah (ˈuːmˌpɑː) *n.* a representation of the sound made by a deep brass instrument, esp. in brass band music.

oomph (ʊmf) *n. Informal.* enthusiasm, vigour, or energy.

oops (ʊps, uːps) *interj.* an exclamation of surprise or of apology when someone has a slight accident or makes a mistake.

ooze[1] (uːz) *vb.* **1.** to flow or leak out slowly; seep. **2.** to exude or emit moisture. **3.** to overflow with (a feeling or quality): *to ooze charm.* ~*n.* **4.** a slow flowing or leaking. —**oozy** *adj.*

ooze[2] (uːz) *n.* a soft thin mud, such as that found at the bottom of a lake, river, or sea.

op. opus.

opacity (əʊˈpæsɪtɪ) *n., pl.* **-ties. 1.** the state or quality of being opaque. **2.** obscurity of meaning; unintelligibility.

opal (ˈəʊpˀl) *n.* a precious stone, usually milky or bluish in colour, with iridescent reflections.

opalescent (ˌəʊpəˈlɛsˀnt) *adj.* iridescent like opal. —**opaˈlescence** *n.*

opaque (əʊˈpeɪk) *adj.* **1.** not able to be seen through; not transparent or translucent. **2.** hard to understand; unintelligible.

op. cit. (in textual annotations) in the work cited.

OPEC (ˈəʊpɛk) Organization of Petroleum-Exporting Countries.

open (ˈəʊpˀn) *adj.* **1.** not closed, fastened, or blocked up. **2.** not enclosed, covered, or wrapped. **3.** extended, expanded, or unfolded: *an open flower.* **4.** ready for business: *the shops are open till five.* **5.** (of a job) available: *the position is no longer open.* **6.** unobstructed by buildings or trees: *open countryside.* **7.** free to all to join in, enter, or use: *an open competition.* **8.** (of a season or period) not restricted for purposes of hunting game of various kinds. **9.** not decided or finalized: *an open question.* **10.** ready to consider new ideas: *an open mind.* **11.** frank; candid. **12.** liberal or generous: *an open hand.* **13.** undisguised; manifest: *open disregard of the law.* **14.** unprotected; susceptible: *you will leave yourself open to attack.* **15.** having spaces or gaps: *open ranks; an open texture.* **16.** *Music.* **a.** (of a string) not stopped with the finger. **b.** (of a note) played on such a string. **17.** *Sport.* (of a goal or court) unguarded or relatively unprotected. **18.** (of a wound) exposed to the air. ~*vb.* **19.** to make or become open: *to open a window.* **20.** to make or become accessible or unobstructed: *to open a road; to open a parcel.* **21.** to extend, expand, or unfold: *to open a newspaper.* **22.** to set or be set in action; start: *to open the batting; to open a shop.* **23.** to arrange for (a bank account), usually by making an initial deposit. **24.** to declare open ceremonially or officially. ~*n.* **25. the open.** any wide or unobstructed area. **26.** *Sport.* a competition which all may enter. —**ˈopener** *n.* —**ˈopenly** *adv.* —**ˈopenness** *n.*

open air *n.* the place or space where the air is unenclosed; outdoors.

open-and-shut *adj.* easily decided or solved; obvious: *an open-and-shut case.*

opencast mining (ˈəʊpˀnˌkɑːst) *n. Brit.* mining by excavating from the surface.

open day *n.* a special occasion on which a school, university, or other institution is open for the public to visit.

open-ended *adj.* without definite limits; unrestricted: *an open-ended contract.*

open-eyed *adj.* **1.** with the eyes wide open, as in amazement. **2.** watchful; alert.

open-handed *adj.* generous.

open-hearted *adj.* **1.** kindly; generous. **2.** frank; candid.

open-heart surgery *n.* surgical repair of the heart during which the heart is exposed and the blood circulation is maintained mechanically.

open house *n.* a situation in which people allow friends or visitors to come to their house whenever they want to.

opening (ˈəʊpənɪŋ) *n.* **1.** the act of making or becoming open. **2.** a hole or gap. **3.** the beginning or first part of something. **4.** the first performance of a theatrical production. **5.** an opportunity or chance.

opening time *n. Brit.* the time at which public houses can legally open for business.

open letter *n.* a letter, esp. one of protest, addressed to an individual but published in a newspaper or magazine for all to read.

open-minded *adj.* having a mind receptive to new ideas; unprejudiced.

open-mouthed *adj.* gaping in surprise.

open-plan *adj.* having no or few dividing walls between areas: *an open-plan office.*

open prison *n.* a prison in which the prisoners are not locked up, thus extending the range of work they can do.

open secret *n.* something that is supposed to be secret but is widely known.

Open University *n.* (in Britain) a university teaching by means of television and radio lectures, correspondence courses, and summer schools.

open up *vb.* **1.** to make or become accessible: *the motorway opened up the remoter* *areas.* **2.** to speak freely or without self-restraint. **3.** to start firing a gun or guns. **4.** *Informal.* (of a motor vehicle) to accelerate.

open verdict *n.* a finding by a coroner's jury of death without stating the cause.

opera[1] ('ɒpərə, 'ɒprə) *n.* **1.** a dramatic work in which most or all of the text is sung to orchestral accompaniment. **2.** the branch of music or drama relating to operas. **3.** a theatre where opera is performed.

opera[2] ('ɒpərə) *n.* a plural of **opus.**

operable ('ɒpərəb'l, 'ɒprə-) *adj.* **1.** capable of being treated by a surgical operation. **2.** capable of being operated. **3.** capable of being put into practice. —**opera'bility** *n.*

opera glasses *pl. n.* small low-powered binoculars used by audiences in theatres.

opera house *n.* a theatre specially designed for the performance of operas.

operand ('ɒpə,rænd) *n. Maths.* a quantity, variable, or function upon which an operation is performed.

operate ('ɒpə,reɪt) *vb.* **1.** to function or cause to function. **2.** to control the functioning of. **3.** to manage, direct, or run (a business or system). **4.** to perform a surgical operation (upon a person or animal). **5.** to produce a desired effect. **6.** to conduct military or naval operations.

operatic (,ɒpə'rætɪk) *adj.* **1.** of or relating to opera. **2.** overdramatic or exaggerated.

operating theatre *or U.S.* **room** *n.* a room in which surgical operations are performed.

operation (,ɒpə'reɪʃən) *n.* **1.** the act or method of operating. **2.** the condition of being in action: *similar schemes are in operation elsewhere.* **3.** an action or series of actions done to produce a particular result. **4.** *Surgery.* a surgical procedure carried out to remove, replace, or repair a diseased or damaged part of the body. **5.** a military or naval campaign or manoeuvre. **6.** *Maths.* any procedure, such as addition, in which a number is derived from another number or numbers by applying specific rules.

operational (,ɒpə'reɪʃən²l) *adj.* **1.** of or relating to an operation. **2.** in working order and ready for use.

operations research *n.* the analysis of problems in business and industry. Also called: **operational research.**

operative ('ɒpərətɪv) *adj.* **1.** in force, effect, or operation. **2.** (of a word) particularly relevant or significant: *"if" is the operative word.* **3.** of or relating to a surgical operation. ~*n.* **4.** a worker with a special skill.

operator ('ɒpə,reɪtə) *n.* **1.** a person who operates a machine or instrument, esp. a telephone switchboard. **2.** a person who runs a business. **3.** a financial speculator. **4.** *Informal.* a person who manipulates affairs and other people. **5.** *Maths.* any symbol, term or letter used to indicate or express a specific operation or process.

operculum (əʊ'pɜːkjʊləm) *n., pl.* -**la** (-lə) *or* -**lums.** a covering flap or lidlike structure in animals or plants.

operetta (,ɒpə'rɛtə) *n.* a type of comic or light-hearted opera.

ophthalmia (ɒf'θælmɪə) *n.* inflammation of the eyeball or conjunctiva.

ophthalmic (ɒf'θælmɪk) *adj.* of or relating to the eye.

ophthalmic optician *n.* See **optician.**

ophthalmology (,ɒfθæl'mɒlədʒɪ) *n.* the branch of medicine concerned with the eye and its diseases. —**ophthal'mologist** *n.*

ophthalmoscope (ɒf'θælmə,skəʊp) *n.* an instrument for examining the interior of the eye.

opiate ('əʊpɪɪt) *n.* **1.** a narcotic or sedative drug containing opium. **2.** something that has a tranquillizing or stupefying effect.

opine (əʊ'paɪn) *vb.* to hold or express an opinion: *he opined that it was a mistake.*

opinion (ə'pɪnjən) *n.* **1.** belief not founded on certainty or proof but on what seems probable. **2.** evaluation or estimation of a person or thing. **3.** an evaluation or judgment given by an expert: *a medical opinion.* **4. a matter of opinion.** a point open to question.

opinionated (ə'pɪnjə,neɪtɪd) *adj.* holding obstinately to one's own opinions; dogmatic.

opinion poll *n.* same as **poll** (sense 3).

opium ('əʊpɪəm) *n.* **1.** an addictive narcotic drug made from the seed capsules of the opium poppy: used in medicine as a painkiller and sedative. **2.** something having a tranquillizing or stupefying effect.

opossum (ə'pɒsəm) *n., pl.* -**sums** *or* -**sum.** **1.** a thick-furred American marsupial, with a long snout and a hairless prehensile tail. **2.** *Austral. & N.Z.* a similar Australian animal, such as a phalanger.

opp. opposite.

opponent (ə'pəʊnənt) *n.* a person who opposes another in a contest, battle, or argument.

opportune ('ɒpə,tjuːn) *adj.* **1.** happening at a time that is suitable or advantageous: *an opportune interruption.* **2.** (of time) suitable for a particular purpose: *an opportune moment.*

opportunist (,ɒpə'tjuːnɪst) *n.* **1.** a person who adapts his actions to take advantage of opportunities and circumstances without regard for principles. ~*adj.* **2.** taking advantage of opportunities and circumstances in this way. —**oppor'tunism** *n.* —**opportu'nistic** *adj.*

opportunity (,ɒpə'tjuːnɪtɪ) *n., pl.* -**ties.** **1.** a favourable combination of circumstances. **2.** a good chance or prospect.

opposable (ə'pəʊzəb'l) *adj.* **1.** capable of being opposed. **2.** (of the thumb) capable of touching the tip of all the other fingers.

oppose (ə'pəʊz) *vb.* **1.** to be against (something) in speech or action; resist strongly. **2.** to contrast or counterbalance. **3.** to place opposite or facing. —**op'posing** *adj.*

opposite ('ɒpəzɪt, -sɪt) *adj.* **1.** situated on the other or further side. **2.** facing or going in contrary directions: *opposite ways.* **3.** completely different; exactly contrary. **4.** *Maths.* (of a side in a triangle) facing a specified angle. ~*n.* **5.** a person or thing that is opposite; antithesis. ~*prep.* **6.** facing; across from. ~*adv.* **7.** in an opposite position: *she lives opposite.* —**'oppositeness** *n.*

opposite number *n.* a person holding an equivalent position in another group or organization.

opposition (,ɒpə'zɪʃən) *n.* **1.** an opposing or being opposed. **2.** hostility, resistance or disagreement. **3.** a person or group antagonistic or opposed to another. **4.** a political party or group opposed to the ruling party or government. **5.** *Astrol.* a diametrically opposite position of two heavenly bodies.

oppress (ə'prɛs) *vb.* **1.** to subjugate by cruelty or force. **2.** to make anxious or uncomfortable. —**op'pression** *n.* —**op'pressor** *n.*

oppressive (ə'prɛsɪv) *adj.* **1.** cruel, harsh, or tyrannical. **2.** constricting or depressing. **3.** (of weather) hot and humid. —**op'pressiveness** *n.*

opprobrium (ə'prəʊbrɪəm) *n.* **1.** the state of being abused or scornfully criticized. **2.** a cause of disgrace or shame. —**op'probrious** *adj.*

oppugn (ə'pjuːn) *vb.* to call into question; dispute.

opt (ɒpt) *vb.* (often foll. by *for*) to show preference (for) or choose (to do something).

optic ('ɒptɪk) *adj.* of the eye or vision.

optical ('ɒptɪk'l) *adj.* **1.** of or involving light or optics. **2.** of the eye or the sense of sight; optic. **3.** (of a lens) helping vision.

optical character reader *n.* a computer device enabling letters and numbers to be optically scanned and input to a storage device.

optical fibre *n.* a thin flexible glass fibre used in fibre optics to transmit information.

optician (ɒp'tɪʃən) *n.* a general name used to refer to: **a.** an **ophthalmic optician.** one qualified to examine the eyes and prescribe and supply spectacles and contact lenses. **b.** a **dispensing optician.** one who supplies and fits spectacle frames and lenses, but is not qualified to prescribe lenses.

optics ('ɒptɪks) *n.* (*functioning as sing.*) the science dealing with light and vision.

optimism ('ɒptɪ,mɪzəm) *n.* **1.** the tendency to take the most hopeful view in all matters. **2.** the doctrine of the ultimate triumph of good over evil. —**'optimist** *n.* —**,opti'mistic** *adj.* —**,opti'mistically** *adv.*

optimize *or* **-mise** ('ɒptɪ,maɪz) *vb.* to make the most of.

optimum ('ɒptɪməm) *n., pl.* **-ma** (-mə) *or* **-mums.** **1.** the most favourable conditions or best compromise possible. ~*adj.* **2.** most favourable or advantageous; best: *optimum conditions.*

option ('ɒpʃən) *n.* **1.** an act of choosing or deciding. **2.** the power or liberty to choose. **3.** an exclusive right, usually for a limited period, to buy or sell something at a future date: *a six-month option on the Canadian rights to this book.* **4.** something that is or may be chosen. **5. keep** *or* **leave one's options open.** to not commit oneself. **6. soft option.** an easy alternative.

optional ('ɒpʃən'l) *adj.* possible but not compulsory; open to choice.

optometrist (ɒp'tɒmɪtrɪst) *n.* a person qualified to examine the eyes and prescribe and supply spectacles and contact lenses. —**op'tometry** *n.*

opt out *vb.* (often foll. by *of*) to choose not to be involved (in) or part (of).

opulent ('ɒpjʊlənt) *adj.* **1.** having or indicating wealth. **2.** abundant or plentiful. —**'opulence** *n.*

opus ('əʊpəs) *n., pl.* **opuses** *or* **opera.** an artistic creation, esp. a musical work by a particular composer, numbered in order of publication: *Beethoven's opus 61.*

or (ɔː) *conj.* used to join: **1.** alternatives: *do you want to go out or stay at home?* **2.** rephrasings of the same thing: *twelve, or a dozen.*

Usage. see **and, either.**

OR Oregon.

oracle ('ɒrək'l) *n.* **1.** a shrine in ancient Greece or Rome at which gods were consulted through the medium of a priest or priestess for advice or prophecy. **2.** a prophecy or statement made by an oracle. **3.** any person believed to indicate future action with infallible authority.

Oracle ('ɒrək'l) *n. Trademark.* Optional Reception of Announcements by Coded Line Electronics: the teletext service of Independent Television.

oracular (ɒ'rækjʊlə) *adj.* **1.** of or like an oracle. **2.** wise and prophetic. **3.** mysterious or ambiguous.

oral ('ɔːrəl, 'ɒrəl) *adj.* **1.** spoken or verbal; using spoken words. **2.** of or for use in the mouth: *an oral thermometer.* **3.** (of a drug) to be taken by mouth: *an oral contraceptive.* ~*n.* **4.** an examination in which the questions and answers are spoken rather than written. —**'orally** *adv.*

orange ('ɒrɪndʒ) *n.* **1.** a round reddish-yellow juicy citrus fruit. **2.** the evergreen tree on which it grows. ~*adj.* **3.** of a colour between red and yellow.

orangeade (ˌɒrɪndʒˈeɪd) *n.* a usually fizzy orange-flavoured drink.

orange blossom *n.* the flowers of the orange tree, traditionally worn by brides.

Orangeman (ˈɒrɪndʒmən) *n., pl.* **-men.** a member of a political society founded in Ireland in 1795 to uphold Protestantism.

orangery (ˈɒrɪndʒərɪ, -dʒrɪ) *n., pl.* **-eries.** a conservatory or greenhouse in which orange trees are grown in cooler climates.

orang-utan (ˌɔːræŋˈuːtæn) *or* **orang-outang** (ˌɔːræŋˈuːtæŋ) *n.* a large ape of the forests of Sumatra and Borneo, with shaggy reddish-brown hair and long arms.

oration (ɔːˈreɪʃən) *n.* **1.** a formal or ceremonial public speech. **2.** any lengthy or pompous speech.

orator (ˈɒrətə) *n.* a person who gives an oration, esp. one skilled in rhetoric.

oratorio (ˌɒrəˈtɔːrɪəʊ) *n., pl.* **-rios.** a musical composition for soloists, chorus, and orchestra, based on a religious theme.

oratory[1] (ˈɒrətrɪ) *n.* the art or skill of public speaking.

oratory[2] (ˈɒrətrɪ) *n., pl.* **-ries.** a small room or building, set apart for private prayer.

orb (ɔːb) *n.* **1.** an ornamental sphere with a cross on top, carried by a king or queen in important ceremonies. **2.** a sphere; globe. **3.** *Poetic.* the eye. **4.** *Obs. or poetic.* a heavenly body, such as the sun.

orbit (ˈɔːbɪt) *n.* **1.** the curved path followed by something, such as a heavenly body or spacecraft, in its motion around another body. **2.** a range or sphere of action or influence. **3.** the eye socket. ~*vb.* **4.** to move around (a heavenly body) in an orbit. **5.** to send (a satellite or spacecraft) into orbit. —ˈ**orbital** *adj.*

Orcadian (ɔːˈkeɪdɪən) *n.* **1.** a person from the Orkneys. ~*adj.* **2.** of the Orkneys.

orchard (ˈɔːtʃəd) *n.* an area of land on which fruit trees are grown.

orchestra (ˈɔːkɪstrə) *n.* **1.** a large group of musicians whose members play a variety of different instruments. **2.** Also called: **orchestra pit.** the space, in front of or under the stage, reserved for musicians in a theatre. —**orchestral** (ɔːˈkestrəl) *adj.*

orchestrate (ˈɔːkɪˌstreɪt) *vb.* **1.** to score or arrange (a piece of music) for orchestra. **2.** to arrange (something) in order to produce a particular result: *he orchestrated the whole event.* —ˌ**orches'tration** *n.*

orchid (ˈɔːkɪd) *n.* a plant having flowers of unusual shapes and beautiful colours, usually with one lip-shaped petal which is larger than the other two.

ordain (ɔːˈdeɪn) *vb.* **1.** to consecrate (someone) as a priest. **2.** to decree, order, or enact with authority. —**or'dainment** *n.*

ordeal (ɔːˈdiːl) *n.* **1.** a severe or trying experience. **2.** *History.* a method of trial in which the accused person was subjected to physical danger.

order (ˈɔːdə) *n.* **1.** a state in which everything is arranged logically, comprehensibly, or naturally. **2.** an arrangement of things in succession; sequence: *alphabetical order.* **3.** an established or customary system of society: *after 1945 a new world order was constructed.* **4.** a peaceful or harmonious condition of society: *order reigned in the streets.* **5.** a social class or rank: *the lower orders.* **6.** *Biol.* a grouping that ranks below a class and above a family in animal or plant classification. **7.** an instruction that must be obeyed; command. **8.** kind or sort: *skills of the highest order.* **9. a.** an instruction to supply something in return for payment. **b.** the thing supplied. **10.** a written instruction to pay money: *a banker's order.* **11.** a procedure followed by an assembly or meeting. **12.** (*usually cap.*) Also called: **religious order.** a religious community who bind themselves by vows in order to devote themselves to the pursuit of religious aims. **13.** a group of people distinguished by a particular honour awarded for service or merit. **14.** a style of architecture, usually one of the five major classical styles of architecture classified by the type of columns used. **15.** *Christianity.* **a.** any rank in the Christian clergy. **b.** the office of an ordained Christian minister. **16. a tall order.** something difficult or demanding. **17. in order. a.** in sequence. **b.** properly arranged. **c.** appropriate or fitting. **18. in order that.** (*conj.*) so that. **19. in order to.** (*prep.*) so that it is possible to: *to eat in order to live.* **20. keep order.** to maintain or enforce order. **21. on order.** having been ordered but not yet delivered. **22. out of order. a.** not in sequence. **b.** not working. **c.** not following the rules or customary procedure. **23. to order.** according to a buyer's specifications. ~*vb.* **24.** to give a command (to do something). **25.** to request (something) to be supplied in return for payment. **26.** to command to move or go (to a specified place): *they ordered her into the house.* **27.** to arrange (things) in their proper places. ~*interj.* **28.** an exclamation demanding that orderly behaviour be restored.

orderly (ˈɔːdəlɪ) *adj.* **1.** tidy, methodical, or well-organized. **2.** well-behaved; law-abiding. ~*n., pl.* **-lies. 3.** *Med.* a male hospital attendant. **4.** *Mil.* a soldier whose duty is to carry orders or perform minor tasks for a more senior officer. —ˈ**orderliness** *n.*

Order of Merit *n. Brit.* an order awarded for outstanding achievement in any field.

order paper *n.* a list indicating the order of business, esp. in Parliament.

ordinal (ˈɔːdɪnˀl) *or* **ordinal number** *n.* a

number indicating relative position in a sequence, such as *first, second, third.*

ordinance (ˈɔːdɪnəns) *n.* an authoritative regulation, decree, or practice.

ordinarily (ˈɔːdᵊnrɪlɪ) *adv.* in ordinary circumstances; usually; normally.

ordinary (ˈɔːdᵊnrɪ) *adj.* **1.** customary or usual. **2.** familiar, everyday, or unexceptional. **3.** uninteresting or commonplace. ~*n., pl.* **-naries. 4.** *R.C. Church.* the parts of the Mass that do not vary from day to day. **5. out of the ordinary.** unusual.

Ordinary level *n.* same as **O level.**

ordinary rating *n.* a rank in the Royal Navy equivalent to that of a private in the army.

ordinary seaman *n.* a seaman of the lowest rank.

ordinary shares *pl. n. Brit.* shares issued by a company entitling their holders to a dividend according to the profits of the company and to a claim on net assets.

ordinate (ˈɔːdɪnɪt) *n. Maths.* the vertical coordinate of a point in a two-dimensional system of coordinates.

ordination (ˌɔːdɪˈneɪʃən) *n.* the act or ceremony of making someone a member of the clergy.

ordnance (ˈɔːdnəns) *n.* **1.** weapons and other military supplies. **2. the.** a government department dealing with military supplies.

Ordnance Survey *n.* the British government organization that produces detailed maps of Britain and Ireland.

Ordovician (ˌɔːdəʊˈvɪʃən) *adj. Geol.* of the period of geological time about 500 million years ago.

ordure (ˈɔːdjʊə) *n.* excrement; dung.

ore (ɔː) *n.* rock or mineral from which valuable substances such as metals can be extracted.

Oreg. Oregon.

oregano (ˌɒrɪˈɡɑːnəʊ) *n.* a sweet-smelling herb used as seasoning.

organ (ˈɔːɡən) *n.* **1.** a musical keyboard instrument in which sound is produced by means of pipes of different lengths, through which air is forced. **2.** a part in animals and plants that is adapted to perform a particular function. **3.** a means of communication, such as a newspaper issued by a specialist group or party. **4.** *Euphemistic.* a penis.

organdie (ˈɔːɡəndɪ) *n.* a fine, slightly stiff cotton fabric.

organ-grinder *n.* an entertainer who plays a barrel organ in the streets.

organic (ɔːˈɡænɪk) *adj.* **1.** of, produced by, or found in plants or animals. **2.** relating to an organ or organs of an animal or plant. **3.** of or grown with fertilizers or pesticides produced from animal or vegetable matter. **4.** of or belonging to the class of chemical compounds that are formed from carbon. **5.** systematically arranged or organized: *an organic whole.* **—orˈganically** *adv.*

organic chemistry *n.* the branch of chemistry dealing with carbon compounds.

organism (ˈɔːɡəˌnɪzəm) *n.* **1.** an animal or plant. **2.** anything resembling a living creature in structure, behaviour, or complexity.

organist (ˈɔːɡənɪst) *n.* a person who plays the organ.

organization *or* **-isation** (ˌɔːɡənaɪˈzeɪʃən) *n.* **1.** an organized group of people, such as a club, society, union, or business. **2.** the act of organizing. **3.** the administrative or executive structure of a political party or business. **—ˌorganiˈzational** *or* **-iˈsational** *adj.*

organize *or* **-ise** (ˈɔːɡəˌnaɪz) *vb.* **1.** to form (parts or elements of something) into a structured whole; coordinate or arrange methodically. **2.** to make plans and arrange for (something). **3.** to enlist (the workers in a factory or business) in a trade union: *organized labour.* **4.** to form an organization or trade union. **—ˈorganˌizer** *or* **-ˌiser** *n.*

organza (ɔːˈɡænzə) *n.* a thin stiff fabric of silk, cotton, or synthetic fibre.

orgasm (ˈɔːɡæzəm) *n.* the most intense point during sexual excitement. **—orˈgasmic** *adj.*

orgy (ˈɔːdʒɪ) *n., pl.* **-gies. 1.** a wild party involving promiscuous sexual activity and excessive drinking. **2.** an act of immoderate or frenzied indulgence: *an orgy of destruction.* **—ˌorgiˈastic** *adj.*

oriel window *or* **oriel** (ˈɔːrɪəl) *n.* a window built out from the wall of a house at an upper level.

orient *n.* (ˈɔːrɪənt). **1.** *Poetic.* the east. ~*vb.* (ˈɔːrɪˌɛnt). **2.** to adjust or align (oneself or one's ideas) according to surroundings or circumstances. **3.** to position or set (a map or chart) with relation to the points of the compass or other specific directions. **4. be oriented to** *or* **towards.** to have a particular interest in; concentrate one's efforts on: *the union is oriented towards welfare capitalism.*

Orient (ˈɔːrɪənt) *n.* **the.** East Asia.

oriental (ˌɔːrɪˈɛntᵊl) *adj.* eastern.

Oriental (ˌɔːrɪˈɛntᵊl) *adj.* **1.** of the Orient. ~*n.* **2.** a person from the Orient.

orientate (ˈɔːrɪɛnˌteɪt) *vb. Not universally accepted.* same as **orient.**

orientation (ˌɔːrɪɛnˈteɪʃən) *n.* **1.** the adjustment or alignment of oneself or one's ideas to surroundings or circumstances. **2.** positioning with relation to the points of the compass or other specific directions. **3.** *Chiefly U.S. & Canad.* information or training needed to understand a new situation or environment: *an orientation course.*

orienteering (ˌɔːrɪɛnˈtɪərɪŋ) *n.* a sport in

which contestants race on foot over a cross-country course consisting of checkpoints found with the aid of a map and compass.

orifice ('ɒrɪfɪs) n. an opening; vent or aperture.

orig. 1. origin. **2.** original(ly).

origami (ˌɒrɪ'gɑːmɪ) n. the art, originally Japanese, of folding paper intricately into decorative shapes.

origin ('ɒrɪdʒɪn) n. **1.** a primary source; root: *the origin of a word.* **2.** the beginning of something; starting point: *the origin of the war.* **3.** (*pl.*) ancestry or parentage. **4.** *Maths.* the point at which the horizontal and vertical axes intersect.

original (ə'rɪdʒɪnˀl) adj. **1.** first; earliest; initial: *my original idea was to do it all myself.* **2.** fresh and unusual; novel: *an original concept.* **3.** able to think of or carry out new ideas or concepts: *a very original writer.* **4.** being the first and genuine form of something, from which a copy or translation is made: *translated from the original French.* ~n. **5.** the first and genuine form of something, from which others are copied or translated: *the original is in the British Museum.* **6.** a person or thing used as a model in art or literature. —**originality** (əˌrɪdʒɪ'nælɪtɪ) n. —**o'riginally** adv.

original sin n. a state of sin believed by some Christians to be inborn in all human beings as a result of Adam's disobedience.

originate (ə'rɪdʒɪˌneɪt) vb. to come or bring (something) into being. —**origination** (əˌrɪdʒɪ'neɪʃən) n. —**o'rigiˌnator** n.

oriole ('ɔːrɪˌəʊl) n. a songbird with a long pointed bill and a mostly yellow-and-black plumage.

ormolu ('ɔːməˌluː) n. a gold-coloured alloy of copper, tin, or zinc, used to decorate furniture and other articles.

ornament n. ('ɔːnəmənt). **1.** anything that adorns someone or something; decoration. **2.** decorations collectively: *she was totally without ornament.* **3.** a small decorative object: *a china ornament.* **4.** a person whose character or talent makes them an asset to society or the group to which they belong: *an ornament of the firm.* ~vb. ('ɔːnəˌmɛnt). **5.** to furnish with ornaments or act as an ornament to; adorn. —**ornamental** (ˌɔːnə'mɛntˀl) adj. —**ornamentation** (ˌɔːnəmɛn'teɪʃən) n.

ornate (ɔː'neɪt) adj. **1.** heavily or elaborately decorated. **2.** (of style in writing) overelaborate; using many literary expressions. —**or'nately** adv.

ornithology (ˌɔːnɪ'θɒlədʒɪ) n. the study of birds. —**ornithological** (ˌɔːnɪθə'lɒdʒɪkˀl) adj. —**orni'thologist** n.

orotund ('ɒrəʊˌtʌnd) adj. **1.** (of the voice) resonant; booming. **2.** (of speech or writing) pompous; containing many long or formal words.

orphan ('ɔːfən) n. **1.** a child whose parents are dead. ~vb. **2.** to deprive (someone) of his parents.

orphanage ('ɔːfənɪdʒ) n. an institution for orphans and abandoned children.

orrery ('ɒrərɪ) n., pl. **-ries.** a mechanical model of the solar system in which the planets can be moved around the sun.

orris ('ɒrɪs) n. **1.** a kind of iris that has fragrant roots. **2.** Also: **orrisroot.** the root of this plant prepared and used as perfume.

orthodontics (ˌɔːθəʊ'dɒntɪks) n. (*functioning as sing.*) the branch of dentistry concerned with correcting irregularities of the teeth. —**ortho'dontic** adj. —**ortho'dontist** n.

orthodox ('ɔːθəˌdɒks) adj. conforming with traditional or established standards in religion, behaviour, or attitudes. —**'orthoˌdoxy** n.

Orthodox ('ɔːθəˌdɒks) adj. of the Orthodox Church of Eastern Europe.

Orthodox Church n. the Christian Church dominant in Eastern Europe, with the Greek Patriarch of Constantinople as its head.

orthography (ɔː'θɒgrəfɪ) n. **1.** spelling considered to be correct. **2.** the study of spelling. —**orthographic** (ˌɔːθəʊ'græfɪk) adj.

orthopaedics or U.S. **orthopedics** (ˌɔːθəʊ'piːdɪks) n. (*functioning as sing.*) the branch of surgery concerned with disorders of the bones and joints. —**ortho'paedic** or U.S. **ortho'pedic** adj. —**ortho'paedist** or U.S. **ortho'pedist** n.

ortolan ('ɔːtələn) n. a European songbird eaten as a delicacy.

Os Chem. osmium.

OS 1. Ordnance Survey. **2.** outsize(d).

Oscar ('ɒskə) n. any of several small gold statuettes awarded annually in the U.S. for outstanding achievements in films.

oscillate ('ɒsɪˌleɪt) vb. **1.** to swing repeatedly back and forth. **2.** to waver between two extremes of opinion, attitude, or behaviour. **3.** *Physics.* (of an electric current) to vary between minimum and maximum values. —**oscillation** (ˌɒsɪ'leɪʃən) n. —**'oscilˌlator** n.

oscilloscope (ɒ'sɪləˌskəʊp) n. an instrument that produces a visual representation of an oscillating electric current on the screen of a cathode-ray tube.

osier ('əʊzɪə) n. **1.** a willow tree whose flexible branches or twigs are used for making baskets and furniture. **2.** a twig or branch from this tree.

osmium ('ɒzmɪəm) n. a very hard brittle bluish-white metal, the heaviest known element. Symbol: Os

osmosis (ɒz'məʊsɪs) n. **1.** the diffusion of liquids through a membrane until they are mixed. **2.** the process by which people influence each other gradually and subtly.

osprey (ˈɒspreɪ) *n.* a large fish-eating bird of prey, with a dark back and whitish head and underparts.

osseous (ˈɒsɪəs) *adj.* consisting of, containing, or like bone.

ossify (ˈɒsɪˌfaɪ) *vb.* **-fying, -fied. 1.** to change into bone; harden. **2.** to become rigid, inflexible, or unprogressive: *a bureaucratic and ossified system.* —**ossification** (ˌɒsɪfɪˈkeɪʃən) *n.*

ostensible (ɒˈstɛnsɪbᵊl) *adj.* apparent; seeming; alleged: *the ostensible cause of the war.* —**os'tensibly** *adv.*

ostensive (ɒˈstɛnsɪv) *adj.* directly showing or pointing out: *an ostensive definition.*

ostentation (ˌɒstɛnˈteɪʃən) *n.* pretentious, showy, or vulgar display. —**ˌosten'tatious** *adj.* —**ˌosten'tatiously** *adv.*

osteoarthritis (ˌɒstɪəʊɑːˈθraɪtɪs) *n.* chronic inflammation of the joints, causing pain and stiffness.

osteopathy (ˌɒstɪˈɒpəθɪ) *n.* a system of healing based on the manipulation of bones or muscle. —**osteopath** (ˈɒstɪəˌpæθ) *n.*

osteoporosis (ˌɒstɪəʊpɔːˈrəʊsɪs) *n.* brittleness of the bones, caused by lack of calcium.

ostler (ˈɒslə) *n. Archaic.* a stableman at an inn.

ostracize *or* **-ise** (ˈɒstrəˌsaɪz) *vb.* to exclude or banish (a person) from a particular group or from society. —**'ostracism** *n.*

ostrich (ˈɒstrɪtʃ) *n.* **1.** a large fast-running flightless African bird with powerful two-toed feet and dark feathers. **2.** a person who refuses to recognize an unpleasant truth.

OT Old Testament.

OTC (in Britain) Officers' Training Corps.

other (ˈʌðə) *det.* **1.** being the remaining (one or ones) in a group of which one or some have been specified: *I'll read the other sections of the paper later; one walks while the other rides.* **2.** being a different one or ones from the one or ones already specified or understood: *no other man but you.* **3.** additional; further: *I need one other thing.* **4. every other.** every alternate: *it buzzes every other minute.* **5. other than. a.** apart from: *a lady other than his wife.* **b.** different from: *he couldn't be other than what he is.* **6. or other.** (preceded by a word or phrase with *some*) used to add vagueness to the preceding word or phrase: *he's somewhere or other; for some reason or other.* **7. the other day.** a few days ago. ~*pron.* **8.** another person or thing: *show me one other.* ~*adv.* **9.** otherwise; differently: *they couldn't behave other than they do.* —**'otherness** *n.*

other ranks *pl. n. Chiefly Brit.* (in the

armed forces) all those who do not hold a commissioned rank.

otherwise (ˈʌðəˌwaɪz) *conj.* **1.** or else; if not, then: *go home — otherwise your mother will worry.* ~*adv.* **2.** differently: *I wouldn't have thought otherwise.* **3.** in other respects: *an otherwise hopeless situation.* ~*adj.* **4.** different: *the facts are otherwise.* ~*pron.* **5. or otherwise.** or not; or the opposite: *I have no ideas, brilliant or otherwise.*

otherworldly (ˌʌðəˈwɜːldlɪ) *adj.* of or concerned with the spiritual world.

otiose (ˈəʊtɪˌəʊs, -ˌəʊz) *adj.* serving no useful purpose: *otiose language.*

OTT *Brit. slang.* over the top.

otter (ˈɒtə) *n.* a small freshwater fish-eating animal with smooth brown fur, a streamlined body, and webbed feet.

ottoman (ˈɒtəmən) *n., pl.* **-mans.** a low padded seat without back or arms, usually in the form of a chest.

Ottoman (ˈɒtəmən) *adj.* **1.** *History.* of the Ottomans or the Ottoman Empire, the former Turkish empire which lasted from the late 13th century until the end of World War I. ~*n., pl.* **-mans. 2.** a member of a Turkish people forming this empire.

ou (əʊ) *n. S. African slang.* a man.

OU 1. the Open University. **2.** Oxford University.

oubaas (ˈəʊˌbɑːs) *n. S. African.* a man in authority.

ouch (aʊtʃ) *interj.* an exclamation of sharp sudden pain.

ought¹ (ɔːt) *vb.* (foll. by *to*) used to express: **1.** duty or obligation: *you ought to pay.* **2.** advisability: *you ought to see a doctor.* **3.** probability or expectation: *you ought to finish this by Friday.* **4.** a desire on the part of the speaker: *you ought to come next week.* **Usage.** In careful English, *ought* is not used with *did* or *had*. *I ought not to do it*, not *I didn't ought to do it; I ought not to have done it*, not *I hadn't ought to have done it.*

ought² (ɔːt) *n.* same as **nought** (zero).

oughtn't (ˈɔːtᵊnt) ought not.

Ouija board *or* **Ouija** (ˈwiːdʒə) *n. Trademark.* a board on which are marked the letters of the alphabet. Answers to questions are spelt out by a pointer and are supposedly formed by spirits during seances.

ouma (ˈəʊmɑː) *n. S. African.* **1.** grandmother, often as a title with a surname. **2.** *Slang.* any elderly woman.

ounce (aʊns) *n.* **1.** a unit of weight equal to one sixteenth of a pound. **2.** short for **fluid ounce. 3.** a small amount: *he hasn't an ounce of sense.*

oupa (ˈəʊpɑː) *n. S. African.* **1.** grandfather, often as a title with a surname. **2.** *Slang.* any elderly man.

our ('aʊə) *det.* **1.** of, belonging to, or associated with us: *our parents.* **2.** a formal word for *my* used by monarchs.

Our Father *n.* same as the **Lord's Prayer.**

ours ('aʊəz) *pron.* **1.** something belonging to us: *ours have blue tags; the brown car is ours.* **2. of ours.** belonging to us.

ourself (aʊə'sɛlf) *pron. Archaic.* a formal word for *myself* used by monarchs.

ourselves (aʊə'sɛlvz) *pron.* **1. a.** the reflexive form of *we* or *us*: *we hurt ourselves.* **b.** used for emphasis: *we ourselves will finish it.* **2.** our usual selves: *we are not ourselves today.* **3.** *Not standard.* used instead of *we* or *us* in compound noun phrases: *other people and ourselves.*

ousel ('uːz²l) *n.* same as **ouzel.**

oust (aʊst) *vb.* to force (someone) out of a position; supplant or expel.

out (aʊt) *adv., adj.* **1.** away from a place; outside: *get out at once; she rushed out of the house.* **2.** used to indicate exhaustion or extinction: *the sugar's run out; put the light out.* **3.** absent from one's home or place of work for a short time: *I came while you were out.* **4.** public; revealed: *the secret is out.* **5.** available to the public: *the book is being brought out next May.* **6.** (of the sun, stars, or moon) visible. **7.** in bloom: *the roses are out now.* **8.** not in fashion, favour, or current usage: *long skirts are out this year.* **9.** excluded from consideration: *that plan is out.* **10.** not allowed: *smoking on duty is out.* **11.** not working: *the radio's out.* **12.** on strike. **13.** out of consciousness: *she passed out.* **14.** used to indicate a burst of activity as indicated by a verb: *fever broke out.* **15.** out of existence: *the mistakes were scored out.* **16.** to the fullest extent: *spread out.* **17.** loudly; clearly: *calling out.* **18.** (foll. by *for* or *to*) desirous of or intent on (something or doing something): *I'm out for as much money as I can get; they're out to get me.* **19.** to a conclusion; completely: *he worked it out.* **20.** (*preceded by a superlative*) existing: *the friendliest dog out.* **21.** used up: *our supplies are completely out.* **22.** inaccurate or discrepant: *out by six pence.* **23.** not in office or authority: *he was voted out.* **24.** (of a period of time) completed: *before the year is out.* **25.** *Obs.* (of a young woman) in or into society: *Lucinda had a large party when she came out.* **26.** *Sport.* (of a player) dismissed from play. **27. out of. a.** at or to a point outside: *out of his reach.* **b.** away from; not in: *stepping out of line; out of focus.* **c.** because of; motivated by: *out of jealousy.* **d.** from (a material or source): *made out of plastic.* **e.** no longer having any (of a substance or material): *we're out of sugar.* **f.** no longer in a specified state or condition: *out of work; out of practice.* ~*adj.* **28.** directed or indicating direction outwards: *the out tray.* ~*prep.* **29.** Non-

standard *or U.S.* out of; out through: *he ran out the door.* ~*interj.* **30. a.** an exclamation of dismissal. **b.** (in signalling and radio) an expression used to signal that the speaker is signing off: *over and out!* **31. out with it.** a command to someone to make something known immediately, without missing any details. ~*n.* **32.** *Chiefly U.S.* a method of escape from a difficult situation. **33.** *Baseball.* an instance of causing a batter or base runner to be out.

out- **1.** excelling or surpassing in a particular action: *outlast; outlive.* **2.** at or from a point away; outside: *outpost; outpatient.* **3.** going away, outward: *outcrop; outgrowth.*

outage ('aʊtɪdʒ) *n.* a period of power failure.

out-and-out *adj.* absolute; thorough: *an out-and-out cheat.*

outback ('aʊt,bæk) *n.* the remote bush country of Australia.

outbid (,aʊt'bɪd) *vb.* **-bidding, -bidded** *or* **-bid.** to offer a higher price than (another person).

outboard motor ('aʊt,bɔːd) *n.* a portable petrol engine that can be attached externally to the stern of a boat to propel it.

outbreak ('aʊt,breɪk) *n.* a sudden occurrence of disease or war.

outbuilding ('aʊt,bɪldɪŋ) *n.* same as **outhouse.**

outburst ('aʊt,bɜːst) *n.* **1.** a sudden strong expression of emotion. **2.** a sudden period of violent activity: *an outburst of drunken violence.*

outcast ('aʊt,kɑːst) *n.* a person who is rejected or excluded from a particular group or from society.

outclass (,aʊt'klɑːs) *vb.* to surpass (someone) in performance or quality.

outcome ('aʊt,kʌm) *n.* the result or consequence of something.

outcrop ('aʊt,krɒp) *n.* part of a rock formation that sticks out of the earth.

outcry ('aʊt,kraɪ) *n., pl.* **-cries.** a widespread or vehement protest.

outdated (,aʊt'deɪtɪd) *adj.* old-fashioned or obsolete.

outdistance (,aʊt'dɪstəns) *vb.* **1.** to surpass (someone) in a particular activity. **2.** to leave (other competitors) behind in a race.

outdo (,aʊt'duː) *vb.* **-doing, -did, -done.** to surpass (someone) in performance.

outdoor ('aʊt,dɔː) *adj.* **1.** taking place, existing, or intended for use in the open air: *outdoor games; outdoor clothes.* **2.** fond of the outdoors: *he's the outdoor type.*

outdoors (,aʊt'dɔːz) *adv.* **1.** in the open air; outside. ~*n.* **2.** the world outside or far away from buildings; the open air.

outer ('aʊtə) *adj.* **1.** exterior; external. **2.** further from the middle. ~*n.* **3.** *Archery.*

a. the white outermost ring on a target. **b.** a shot that hits this ring.

outermost ('aʊtəˌməʊst) *adj.* furthest from the centre or middle.

outer space *n.* space beyond the atmosphere of the earth.

outface (aʊt'feɪs) *vb.* to subdue or disconcert (someone) by staring.

outfield ('aʊtˌfiːld) *n.* **1.** *Cricket.* the area of the field far from the pitch. **2.** *Baseball.* the area of the playing field beyond the lines connecting first, second, and third bases. —'out,fielder *n.*

outfit ('aʊtˌfɪt) *n.* **1.** a set of clothes worn together. **2.** *Informal.* a group of people working together as a unit. **3.** a set of equipment for a particular task; kit.

outfitter ('aʊtˌfɪtə) *n. Old-fashioned.* a supplier of men's clothes.

outflank (ˌaʊt'flæŋk) *vb.* **1.** to go around and beyond the flank of (an opposing army). **2.** to get the better of (someone).

outflow ('aʊtˌfləʊ) *n.* **1.** anything that flows out, such as liquid or money. **2.** the amount that flows out.

outfox (ˌaʊt'fɒks) *vb.* to surpass (someone) in cunning.

outgoing ('aʊtˌgəʊɪŋ) *adj.* **1.** leaving: *outgoing mail; the outgoing president.* **2.** friendly and sociable.

outgoings ('aʊtˌgəʊɪŋz) *pl. n.* expenses.

outgrow (ˌaʊt'grəʊ) *vb.* **-growing, -grew, -grown.** **1.** to grow too large for (clothes or shoes). **2.** to lose (a way of behaving or thinking) in the course of becoming more mature. **3.** to grow larger or faster than (someone).

outgrowth ('aʊtˌgrəʊθ) *n.* **1.** a thing growing out of a main body; offshoot. **2.** a natural development, result, or consequence.

outhouse ('aʊtˌhaʊs) *n.* a building near to, but separate from, a main building.

outing ('aʊtɪŋ) *n.* a trip or excursion.

outlandish (aʊt'lændɪʃ) *adj.* grotesquely unconventional; bizarre.

outlast (ˌaʊt'lɑːst) *vb.* to last longer than.

outlaw ('aʊtˌlɔː) *n.* **1.** a criminal who is a fugitive from the law. ~*vb.* **2.** to declare (a person) to be an outlaw. **3.** to ban.

outlay ('aʊtˌleɪ) *n.* an expenditure of money, effort, or time.

outlet ('aʊtlɪt) *n.* **1.** a means of expressing one's feelings: *an outlet for his anger.* **2. a.** a market for a product. **b.** a shop or organization selling the goods of a particular producer or wholesaler. **3.** an opening permitting escape or release.

outline ('aʊtˌlaɪn) *n.* **1.** a general explanation or description of something, which does not give all the details. **2.** (*usually pl.*) the important features of something. **3.** the line by which an object or figure is or

appears to be bounded. **4.** a drawing showing only the external lines of an object. ~*vb.* **5.** to draw the outline of (something). **6.** to give the main features or general idea of (something).

outlive (ˌaʊt'lɪv) *vb.* **1.** to live longer than (someone). **2.** to live beyond (a date or period): *he outlived the century.*

outlook ('aʊtˌlʊk) *n.* **1.** a mental attitude. **2.** the probable condition or outcome of something; prospect: *the weather outlook.* **3.** the view from a place.

outlying ('aʊtˌlaɪɪŋ) *adj.* far out from a central point.

outmanoeuvre *or U.S.* **outmaneuver** (ˌaʊtmə'nuːvə) *vb.* to gain an advantage over (someone) by skilful manoeuvring.

outmatch (ˌaʊt'mætʃ) *vb.* to surpass or outdo (someone).

outmoded (ˌaʊt'məʊdɪd) *adj.* no longer fashionable or widely accepted.

outnumber (ˌaʊt'nʌmbə) *vb.* to exceed in number: *we outnumbered them twelve to one.*

out of bounds *adj., adv.* **1.** (foll. by *to*) not to be entered by; barred to: *out of bounds to civilians.* **2.** outside specified or prescribed limits.

out-of-date *adj., adv.* outmoded; old-fashioned.

out of doors *adv.* in the open air; outside.

out of pocket *adj.* having lost money: *I was £10 out of pocket after paying for their drinks.*

out-of-the-way *adj.* **1.** remote or secluded. **2.** unusual.

outpace (ˌaʊt'peɪs) *vb.* **1.** to go faster than (someone). **2.** to surpass or outdo (someone).

outpatient ('aʊtˌpeɪʃənt) *n.* a patient who receives treatment at a hospital but who is not staying there.

outpost ('aʊtˌpəʊst) *n.* **1.** *Mil.* a settlement stationed at a distance from the area occupied by a major formation. **2.** an outlying settlement or position.

outpouring ('aʊtˌpɔːrɪŋ) *n.* **1.** (*pl.*) a passionate outburst. **2.** the amount of something that pours out.

output ('aʊtˌpʊt) *n.* **1.** the amount produced: *a weekly output.* **2.** *Electronics.* the power, voltage, or current delivered by a circuit or component. **3.** *Computers.* the information produced by a computer. ~*vb.* **-putting, -putted** *or* **-put.** **4.** *Computers.* to cause (data) to be emitted as output.

outrage ('aʊtˌreɪdʒ) *n.* **1.** deep indignation, anger, or resentment. **2.** an extremely vicious or cruel act; gross violation of decency, morality, or honour. ~*vb.* **3.** to cause deep indignation, anger, or resentment in (someone).

outrageous (aʊt'reɪdʒəs) *adj.* **1.** immoderate in behaviour. **2.** grossly offensive to decency, morality, or honour; shocking or unacceptable. **—out'rageously** adv.

outrank (ˌaʊt'ræŋk) vb. to be of higher rank than (someone).

outré ('uːtreɪ) adj. eccentric or bizarre; outrageous.

outrider ('aʊtˌraɪdə) n. a person who rides a motorcycle or horse in front of or beside a car or carriage as an attendant or guard.

outrigger ('aʊtˌrɪgə) n. **1.** a framework projecting over the side of a boat or canoe to provide stability. **2.** a boat or canoe equipped with such a framework.

outright adj. ('aʊtˌraɪt). **1.** complete; total: an outright villain. **2.** straightforward; direct: outright hostility. ~adv. (ˌaʊt'raɪt). **3.** completely: the government has banned it outright. **4.** openly: ask outright. **5.** instantly: he was killed outright.

outrun (ˌaʊt'rʌn) vb. **-running, -ran, -run. 1.** to run faster or further than (someone). **2.** to exceed (something).

outsell (ˌaʊt'sɛl) vb. **-selling, -sold.** to be sold in greater quantities than (another product).

outset ('aʊtˌsɛt) n. a start; beginning: this plan was a failure from the outset.

outshine (ˌaʊt'ʃaɪn) vb. **-shining, -shone.** to surpass (someone) in excellence.

outside prep. (ˌaʊt'saɪd). **1.** on or to the exterior of: outside the house. **2.** beyond the limits of: outside his capabilities. **3.** apart from; other than: no-one knows outside us. ~adj. ('aʊtˌsaɪd). **4.** situated on the exterior: an outside lavatory. **5.** remote; unlikely: an outside chance. **6.** coming from outside a particular group or organization: outside influences. ~adv. (ˌaʊt'saɪd). **7.** outside a specified thing or place; out of doors. **8.** Slang. not in prison. ~n. ('aʊtˌsaɪd). **9.** the external side or surface of something. **10. at the outside.** Informal. at the very most: two days at the outside.
Usage. In careful usage, outside and inside are preferred to outside of and inside of: she waits outside (not outside of) the school.

outside broadcast n. Radio, television. a broadcast not made from a studio.

outsider (ˌaʊt'saɪdə) n. **1.** a person excluded from a group. **2.** a contestant thought unlikely to win a race.

outsize ('aʊtˌsaɪz) adj. also **outsized. 1.** very large or larger than normal. ~n. **2.** an outsize garment or person.

outskirts ('aʊtˌskɜːts) pl. n. outlying areas.

outsmart (ˌaʊt'smɑːt) vb. Informal. same as **outwit.**

outspan ('aʊtˌspæn) S. African. ~n. **1.** an area on a farm kept available for travellers to rest and refresh their animals. ~vb. **-spanning, -spanned. 2.** to unharness or unyoke (animals).

outspoken (ˌaʊt'spəʊkən) adj. **1.** candid or bold in speech. **2.** spoken candidly: her outspoken comments.

outspread ('aʊtˌsprɛd) adj. spread or stretched out; extended or expanded.

outstanding (ˌaʊt'stændɪŋ) adj. **1.** superior; excellent. **2.** prominent, remarkable, or striking. **3.** unsettled, unpaid, or unresolved. **—ˌout'standingly** adv.

outstation ('aʊtˌsteɪʃən) n. a station or post in a remote region.

outstay (ˌaʊt'steɪ) vb. same as **overstay.**

outstretch (ˌaʊt'strɛtʃ) vb. to extend or expand; stretch out.

outstrip (ˌaʊt'strɪp) vb. **-stripping, -stripped. 1.** to surpass (someone) in a particular activity. **2.** to go faster than (someone).

outtake ('aʊtˌteɪk) n. an unreleased take from a recording session, film, or television programme.

outvote (ˌaʊt'vəʊt) vb. to defeat (someone) by a majority of votes.

outward ('aʊtwəd) adj. **1.** apparent or superficial: outward appearances. **2.** of or relating to the outside: outward shape. **3.** (of a journey) away from a place to which one intends to return. ~adv. also **outwards. 4.** in an outward direction; towards the outside. **—'outwardly** adv.

outweigh (ˌaʊt'weɪ) vb. **1.** to be more important, significant, or influential than. **2.** to be heavier than.

outwit (ˌaʊt'wɪt) vb. **-witting, -witted.** to gain an advantage over (someone) by cunning or ingenuity.

outworks ('aʊtˌwɜːks) pl. n. defences which lie outside main defensive works.

ouzel or **ousel** ('uːzˀl) n. same as **dipper** (the bird).

ouzo ('uːzəʊ) n., pl. **ouzos.** a strong aniseed-flavoured alcoholic drink from Greece.

ova ('əʊvə) n. the plural of **ovum.**

oval ('əʊvˀl) adj. **1.** egg-shaped. ~n. **2.** anything that is oval in shape, such as a sports ground.

ovary ('əʊvərɪ) n., pl. **-ries. 1.** a reproductive organ in women and female animals in which eggs are produced. **2.** Bot. the lower part of a pistil, containing the ovules. **—ovarian** (əʊ'vɛərɪən) adj.

ovate ('əʊveɪt) adj. shaped like an egg.

ovation (əʊ'veɪʃən) n. an enthusiastic reception with prolonged applause.

oven ('ʌvˀn) n. an enclosed heated compartment or receptacle for baking or roasting food, drying substances, or firing ceramics.

over ('əʊvə) prep. **1.** directly above; on the top of; across the top or upper surface of: over one's head. **2.** on or to the other side of: over the river. **3.** during or throughout (a period of time). **4.** throughout the whole extent of: to travel over England. **5.** by means of (an instrument of telecommunication): *over the radio.* **6.** more than: *over a century ago.* **7.** concerning; about: *an argument over nothing.* **8.** while occupied in: *discussing business over dinner.* **9.** having recovered from the effects of: *she is not over her husband's death yet.* **10. all over someone.** *Informal.* extremely affectionate or attentive towards someone. **11. over and above.** added to; in addition to. ~*adv.* **12.** in a state, condition, or position over something: *to climb over.* **13.** so as to cause (someone) to fall: *knocking over a policeman.* **14.** at or to a point across an intervening space. **15.** covering the whole area: *the world over.* **16.** from beginning to end: *to read a document over.* **17. all over. a.** finished. **b.** over one's entire body. **c.** typically: *that's you all over.* **18. over again.** once more. **19. over and over (again).** repeatedly. ~*interj.* **20.** (in signalling and radio) it is now your turn to speak. ~*adj.* **21.** finished; no longer in progress: *the fight is over.* ~*adv., adj.* **22.** remaining; surplus: *with six left over.* ~*n.* **23.** *Cricket.* **a.** a series of six or eight balls bowled by a bowler from the same end of the pitch. **b.** the play during this.

over- *prefix.* **1.** excessive or excessively: *overcharge; overdue.* **2.** superior in rank: *overlord.* **3.** indicating location or movement above: *overhang.* **4.** downwards from above: *overthrow.*

overact (ˌəʊvərˈækt) *vb.* to act in an exaggerated manner.

overall *adj.* (ˈəʊvərˌɔːl). **1.** from one end to the other: *the overall length.* **2.** including everything; total: *the overall cost.* ~*adv.* (ˌəʊvərˈɔːl). **3.** in general; on the whole. ~*n.* (ˈəʊvərˌɔːl). **4.** *Brit.* a coat-shaped work garment worn over ordinary clothes as a protection against dirt. **5.** (*pl.*) work trousers with a front flap or jacket attached, worn over ordinary clothes as a protection against dirt and wear.

overarm (ˈəʊvərˌɑːm) *Sport, esp. cricket.* ~*adj.* **1.** bowled, thrown, or performed with the arm raised above the shoulder. ~*adv.* **2.** with the arm raised above the shoulder.

overawe (ˌəʊvərˈɔː) *vb.* to subdue (someone) by affecting him with a feeling of awe.

overbalance (ˌəʊvəˈbæləns) *vb.* to lose one's balance.

overbearing (ˌəʊvəˈbɛərɪŋ) *adj.* **1.** domineering or dictatorial. **2.** of particular or

overriding importance: *an overbearing need.*

overblown (ˌəʊvəˈbləʊn) *adj.* inflated or excessive: *overblown pride.*

overboard (ˈəʊvəˌbɔːd) *adv.* **1.** from on board a vessel into the water. **2. go overboard.** *Informal.* **a.** to be extremely enthusiastic. **b.** to go to extremes. **3. throw overboard.** to reject or abandon (an idea or a plan).

overcast (ˈəʊvəˌkɑːst) *adj.* (of the sky or weather) cloudy.

overcharge (ˌəʊvəˈtʃɑːdʒ) *vb.* to charge too high a price.

overcoat (ˈəʊvəˌkəʊt) *n.* a warm heavy coat worn in cold weather.

overcome (ˌəʊvəˈkʌm) *vb.* **-coming, -came, -come.** **1.** (of an emotion or a feeling) to affect (someone) strongly or make (someone) powerless: *overcome by exhaustion.* **2.** to deal successfully with or control (a problem or feeling). **3.** to defeat (someone) in a conflict.

overdo (ˌəʊvəˈduː) *vb.* **-doing, -did, -done.** **1.** to do (something) to excess. **2.** to exaggerate or overplay (something). **3.** to cook (something) too long. **4. overdo it** *or* **things.** to overtax one's strength.

overdose *n.* (ˈəʊvəˌdəʊs). **1.** an excessive dose of a drug. ~*vb.* (ˌəʊvəˈdəʊs). **2.** to take an excessive dose of a drug.

overdraft (ˈəʊvəˌdrɑːft) *n.* **1.** a withdrawal of money in excess of the credit balance in one's bank account. **2.** the amount of money withdrawn thus.

overdraw (ˌəʊvəˈdrɔː) *vb.* **-drawing, -drew, -drawn. a. be overdrawn.** to have drawn money from one's bank account in excess of the credit balance. **b.** to draw money from (one's bank account) in excess of the credit balance.

overdress *vb.* (ˌəʊvəˈdrɛs). **1.** to dress too elaborately or formally. ~*n.* (ˈəʊvəˌdrɛs). **2.** a dress that may be worn over a jumper or blouse.

overdrive (ˈəʊvəˌdraɪv) *n.* a very high gear in a motor vehicle, used at high speeds to reduce wear.

overdue (ˌəʊvəˈdjuː) *adj.* past the due time for arrival, occurrence, or payment.

overestimate *vb.* (ˌəʊvərˈɛstɪˌmeɪt). **1.** to estimate too highly. ~*n.* (ˌəʊvərˈɛstɪmɪt). **2.** an estimate that is too high. **—overestimation** (ˌəʊvərˌɛstɪˈmeɪʃən) *n.*

overflow *vb.* (ˌəʊvəˈfləʊ), **-flowing,**

overabundance	overconfident	overemphasize
overactive	overcook	overenthusiastic
overambitious	overcrowded	overexcited
overanxious	overdeveloped	overexert
overburden	overeager	overexpose
overcautious	overeat	overfeed
overcompensate	overemotional	overfill

-flowed, -flown. 1. to flow over (a brim). **2.** to be filled beyond capacity so as to spill over. **3.** (foll. by *with*) to be filled with an emotion: *overflowing with love.* **4.** to spread over; flood. ~*n.* (ˈəʊvəˌfləʊ). **5.** something that overflows, usually a liquid. **6.** an outlet that enables surplus liquid to be drained off. **7.** the amount by which a limit or capacity is exceeded.

overgraze (ˌəʊvəˈgreɪz) *vb.* to graze (land) too intensively so that it is damaged and no longer provides nourishment.

overgrown (ˌəʊvəˈgrəʊn) *adj.* covered over with plants or weeds: *an overgrown path.*

overhang *vb.* (ˌəʊvəˈhæŋ), **-hanging, -hung. 1.** to project or hang over beyond (something). ~*n.* (ˈəʊvəˌhæŋ). **2.** an overhanging part or object.

overhaul *vb.* (ˌəʊvəˈhɔːl). **1.** to examine (a system or an idea) carefully for faults. **2.** to make repairs or adjustments to (a vehicle or machine). **3.** to overtake (a vehicle or person). ~*n.* (ˈəʊvəˌhɔːl). **4.** a thorough examination and repair.

overhead (ˈəʊvəˌhed, ˌəʊvəˈhed) *adj., adv.* above head height.

overhead projector *n.* a projector that throws an enlarged image of a transparency onto a surface above and behind the person using it.

overheads (ˈəʊvəˌhedz) *pl. n.* the general costs of running a business, such as rent, electricity, and stationery.

overhear (ˌəʊvəˈhɪə) *vb.* **-hearing, -heard** (-ˈhɜːd). to hear (a speaker or remark) unintentionally or without the knowledge of the speaker.

overheat (ˌəʊvəˈhiːt) *vb.* **1.** to make or become too hot. **2.** to make (someone) very agitated or irritated. **3.** to stimulate (the economy) excessively.

overjoyed (ˌəʊvəˈdʒɔɪd) *adj.* extremely pleased.

overkill (ˈəʊvəˌkɪl) *n.* **1.** a capability to kill or destroy which far exceeds that necessary to achieve victory. **2.** any treatment that is greater than that required: *the media coverage of this event amounts to overkill.*

overlap *vb.* (ˌəʊvəˈlæp), **-lapping, -lapped. 1.** (of two things) to extend or lie partly over (each other). **2.** to coincide partly in time or subject: *our holidays overlap by two days.* ~*n.* (ˈəʊvəˌlæp). **3.** a part that overlaps. **4.** the amount or length of something overlapping.

overlay *vb.* (ˌəʊvəˈleɪ), **-laying, -laid. 1.** to cover (a surface) with an applied decoration: *ebony overlaid with silver.* ~*n.* (ˈəʊvəˌleɪ). **2.** something that is laid over

something else; a covering. **3.** an applied decoration or layer, for example of gold leaf.

overleaf (ˌəʊvəˈliːf) *adv.* on the other side of the page.

overlie (ˌəʊvəˈlaɪ) *vb.* **-lying, -lay, -lain. 1.** to lie on (something or someone). **2.** to smother (a baby or newborn animal) by lying on it.

overload *vb.* (ˌəʊvəˈləʊd). **1.** to put too large a load on or in (something). ~*n.* (ˈəʊvəˌləʊd). **2.** an excessive load.

overlook (ˌəʊvəˈlʊk) *vb.* **1.** to fail to notice (something). **2.** to disregard (misbehaviour or a fault) deliberately or indulgently. **3.** to give a view of (something) from above: *the house overlooks the bay.*

overlord (ˈəʊvəˌlɔːd) *n.* a supreme lord or master.

overly (ˈəʊvəlɪ) *adv.* too; excessively.

overmuch (ˌəʊvəˈmʌtʃ) *adv., adj.* too much; very much.

overnight *adv.* (ˌəʊvəˈnaɪt). **1.** during the night. **2.** in or as if in the course of one night; suddenly: *the situation changed overnight.* ~*adj.* (ˈəʊvəˌnaɪt). **3.** done in, occurring in, or lasting the night: *an overnight stop.* **4.** staying for one night: *an overnight guest.* **5.** for use during a single night: *an overnight bag.* **6.** occurring in or as if in the course of one night; sudden: *an overnight success.*

overpass (ˈəʊvəˌpɑːs) *n.* same as **flyover** (the road).

overplay (ˌəʊvəˈpleɪ) *vb.* **1.** to overemphasize (something). **2. overplay one's hand.** to overestimate the worth or strength of one's position.

overpower (ˌəʊvəˈpaʊə) *vb.* **1.** to conquer or subdue (someone) by superior force. **2.** to have such a strong effect on (someone) as to make him helpless or ineffective: *the smell overpowered me.* —ˌover'powering *adj.*

overprint *vb.* (ˌəʊvəˈprɪnt). **1.** to print (additional matter or another colour) onto (something already printed). ~*n.* (ˈəʊvəˌprɪnt). **2.** additional matter or another colour printed onto something already printed.

overrate (ˌəʊvəˈreɪt) *vb.* to have too high an opinion of.

overreach (ˌəʊvəˈriːtʃ) *vb.* **1.** to defeat or thwart (oneself) by attempting to do or gain too much. **2.** to gain an advantage over (someone) by trickery.

overreact (ˌəʊvərɪˈækt) *vb.* to react excessively. —**overreaction** (ˌəʊvərɪˈækʃən) *n.*

override (ˌəʊvəˈraɪd) *vb.* **-riding, -rode,**

overfond	overpaid	overpriced
overfull	overpopulated	overprotective
overindulge	overpopulation	

-ridden. 1. to set aside or disregard (a person or a person's decisions) with superior authority or power. **2.** to supersede or replace (something). —,over'riding *adj.*

overrule (,əʊvə'ruːl) *vb.* **1.** to disallow the arguments of (a person) by the use of authority. **2.** to rule or decide against (an argument or decision).

overrun (,əʊvə'rʌn) *vb.* **-running, -ran, -run. 1.** to spread over (a place) rapidly: *the city is overrun by rats.* **2.** to conquer (territory) rapidly by force of number. **3.** to extend or run beyond a limit: *the meeting overran by an hour.*

overseas *adv.* (,əʊvə'siːz). **1.** across the sea; abroad. ~*adj.* ('əʊvə'siːz). **2.** of, to, from, or situated in countries across the sea. ~*n.* (,əʊvə'siːz). **3.** (*functioning as sing.*) *Informal.* a foreign country or foreign countries collectively.

oversee (,əʊvə'siː) *vb.* **-seeing, -saw, -seen.** to watch over and direct (someone or something); supervise. —'over,seer *n.*

oversew (,əʊvə'səʊ) *vb.* **-sewing, -sewed; -sewn** *or* **-sewed.** to sew (two edges) with stitches that pass over them both.

oversexed (,əʊvə'sɛkst) *adj.* having an excessive preoccupation with sexual activity.

overshadow (,əʊvə'ʃædəʊ) *vb.* **1.** to make (someone or something) seem insignificant or less important by comparison. **2.** to cast a gloom over (an occasion).

overshoe ('əʊvə,ʃuː) *n.* a protective shoe worn over an ordinary shoe.

overshoot (,əʊvə'ʃuːt) *vb.* **-shooting, -shot.** to go beyond (a mark or target): *the plane overshot the runway.*

overshot ('əʊvə,ʃɒt) *adj.* (of a water wheel) driven by a flow of water that passes over the wheel.

oversight ('əʊvə,saɪt) *n.* a mistake made through failure to notice something.

oversleep (,əʊvə'sliːp) *vb.* **-sleeping, -slept.** to sleep beyond the intended time for getting up.

overspend (,əʊvə'spɛnd) *vb.* **-spending, -spent.** to spend more than one can afford.

overspill ('əʊvə,spɪl) *n.* an arrangement by which people from overcrowded cities are rehoused in smaller towns.

overstate (,əʊvə'steɪt) *vb.* to state (something) too strongly; overemphasize. —'over,statement *n.*

overstay (,əʊvə'steɪ) *vb.* **overstay one's welcome.** to stay as a guest longer than pleases the host or hostess.

overstep (,əʊvə'stɛp) *vb.* **-stepping, -stepped.** to go beyond (a certain limit).

overstrung (,əʊvə'strʌŋ) *adj.* too highly strung; tense.

oversubscribe (,əʊvəsəb'skraɪb) *vb.* to subscribe or apply for (something) in excess of the available supply.

overt (əʊ'vɜːt) *adj.* done or shown in an open and obvious way: *overt hostility.* —əʊ'vertly *adv.*

overtake (,əʊvə'teɪk) *vb.* **-taking, -took, -taken. 1.** *Chiefly Brit.* to move past (another vehicle or person) travelling in the same direction. **2.** to do better than (someone) after catching up with him. **3.** to come upon (someone) suddenly or unexpectedly: *night overtook him.*

overtax (,əʊvə'tæks) *vb.* **1.** to impose too great a strain on (oneself). **2.** to tax (people) too heavily.

over the top *adj. Brit. slang.* excessive; beyond the usual or acceptable bounds of behaviour.

overthrow *vb.* (,əʊvə'θrəʊ), **-throwing, -threw, -thrown. 1.** to bring about the downfall of (a ruler or government) by force. **2.** to replace (standards or values). ~*n.* ('əʊvə,θrəʊ). **3.** downfall; destruction.

overtime ('əʊvə,taɪm) *n.* **1.** work at a regular job done in addition to regular working hours. **2.** pay for such work. ~*adv.* **3.** in addition to one's regular working hours: *to work overtime.*

overtone ('əʊvə,təʊn) *n.* **1.** an additional meaning or hint: *overtones of despair.* **2.** *Music, acoustics.* any of the tones, with the exception of the principal or lowest one, that make up a musical sound.

overture ('əʊvə,tjʊə) *n.* **1.** *Music.* a piece of orchestral music played at the beginning of an opera, oratorio, or ballet, musical comedy, or film, often containing the main musical themes of the work. **2.** (*pl.*) opening moves towards a new relationship or agreement: *friendly overtures.*

overturn (,əʊvə'tɜːn) *vb.* **1.** to turn over or upside down. **2.** to overrule or reverse (a legal decision). **3.** to overthrow or destroy (a government).

overview ('əʊvə,vjuː) *n.* a general survey.

overweening (,əʊvə'wiːnɪŋ) *adj.* (of opinions or qualities) excessive; immoderate: *overweening pride.*

overweight (,əʊvə'weɪt) *adj.* weighing more than is usual, allowed, or healthy.

overwhelm (,əʊvə'wɛlm) *vb.* **1.** to overpower the thoughts, emotions, or senses of (someone): *overwhelmed by horror.* **2.** to overcome (people) with irresistible force: *the army overwhelmed the city.* —,over-'whelming *adj.* —,over'whelmingly *adv.*

overwork *vb.* (,əʊvə'wɜːk). **1.** to work too hard or too long. **2.** to use (something)

too much: *to overwork an excuse.* ~*n.*
('əʊvə,wɜːk). **3.** excessive work.

overwrought (,əʊvə'rɔːt) *adj.* full of nervous tension; agitated.

oviduct ('əʊvɪ,dʌkt) *n. Anat.* the tube
through which eggs are conveyed from an
ovary.

oviform ('əʊvɪ,fɔːm) *adj. Biol.* shaped like
an egg.

ovine ('əʊvaɪn) *adj.* of or resembling a
sheep.

oviparous (əʊ'vɪpərəs) *adj. Zool.* producing
eggs that hatch outside the body of the
mother.

ovoid ('əʊvɔɪd) *adj.* egg-shaped.

ovulate ('ɒvjʊ,leɪt) *vb. Biol.* to produce or
discharge eggs from an ovary. —**ovulation**
(,ɒvjʊ'leɪʃən) *n.*

ovule ('ɒvjuːl) *n.* **1.** *Bot.* the part of a plant
that contains the egg cell and develops into
the seed after fertilization. **2.** *Zool.* an immature ovum.

ovum ('əʊvəm) *n., pl.* **ova.** an unfertilized
female egg cell.

owe (əʊ) *vb.* **1.** to be under an obligation to
pay (someone) to the amount of: *you owe
me a pound.* **2.** to be in debt: *he still owes
for his house.* **3.** (foll. by *to*) to have as a
result of: *I owe my success to my teacher.*
4. to feel an obligation to do or give: *I owe
you an apology.*

owing ('əʊɪŋ) *adj.* **1.** owed; due. **2. owing
to.** because of; on account of.
Usage. see **due.**

owl (aʊl) *n.* a bird of prey which has a flat
face, large eyes, and a small hooked beak,
and which is active at night. —'**owlish**
adj.

own (əʊn) *det.* (*preceded by a possessive*)
1. used to emphasize that something belongs to a particular person: *John's own
idea; I'll use my own.* **2. come into one's
own.** to fulfil one's potential. **3. hold one's
own.** to have the necessary ability to deal
successfully with a situation: *she can hold
her own in an argument.* **4. on one's own.
a.** without help. **b.** by oneself; alone. ~*vb.*
5. to have (something) as one's possession.
6. (often foll. by *up, to,* or *up to*) to confess
or admit; acknowledge. —'**owner** *n.*
—'**ownership** *n.*

owner-occupier *n.* someone who owns the
house in which he lives.

own goal *n.* **1.** *Soccer.* a goal scored by a
player accidentally playing the ball into his
own team's net. **2.** *Informal.* any action
that results in disadvantage to the person
who took it or to his associates.

ox (ɒks) *n., pl.* **oxen.** a castrated bull used
for pulling heavy loads and for meat.

oxalic acid (ɒk'sælɪk) *n.* a colourless poisonous acid found in many plants.

Oxbridge ('ɒks,brɪdʒ) *n.* the British universities of Oxford and Cambridge considered together.

oxen ('ɒksən) *n.* the plural of **ox.**

oxeye ('ɒks,aɪ) *n.* a daisy-like flower with
yellow rays and a dark centre.

Oxfam ('ɒks,fæm) Oxford Committee for
Famine Relief.

oxidation (,ɒksɪ'deɪʃən) *n.* the act or process of oxidizing.

oxide ('ɒksaɪd) *n.* a compound of oxygen
with another element.

oxidize *or* **-ise** ('ɒksɪ,daɪz) *vb.* to undergo
or cause (a substance) to undergo a chemical reaction with oxygen, as in burning or
rusting. —,**oxidi'zation** *or* -**i'sation** *n.*

Oxon ('ɒksən) Oxfordshire.

Oxon. (in degree titles) of Oxford University.

Oxonian (ɒk'səʊnɪən) *adj.* **1.** of Oxford or
Oxford University. ~*n.* **2.** a member of
Oxford University. **3.** a person from Ox-
ford, a city in England.

oxtail ('ɒks,teɪl) *n.* the tail of an ox, used in
soups and stews.

oxyacetylene (,ɒksɪə'setɪ,liːn) *n.* a mixture of oxygen and acetylene, used in blow-
lamps for cutting or welding metals at high
temperatures.

oxygen ('ɒksɪdʒən) *n.* a colourless odourless gaseous element essential to life processes and to combustion. Symbol: O

oxygenate ('ɒksɪdʒɪ,neɪt) *vb.* to treat or
combine with oxygen: *to oxygenate blood.*

oxygen tent *n. Med.* a transparent enclosure covering a bedridden patient, into
which oxygen is released to aid breathing.

oxymoron (,ɒksɪ'mɔːrɒn) *n.* a figure of
speech in which contradictory terms are
used together, for example *cruel kindness.*

oyez *or* **oyes** ('əʊ'jes) *interj.* a cry usually
uttered three times by a public crier or
court official, for silence and attention.

oyster ('ɔɪstə) *n.* **1.** an edible shellfish of
which some types produce pearls. **2. the
world is your oyster.** you are in a position
where there is every possible chance of
personal advancement and satisfaction.
~*adj.* **3.** greyish-white.

oystercatcher ('ɔɪstə,kætʃə) *n.* a wading
bird with black-and-white plumage and a
long stout red bill.

oz *or* **oz.** ounce.

ozone ('əʊzəʊn) *n.* **1.** a form of oxygen
with a strong odour, formed by an electric
discharge in the atmosphere. **2.** *Informal.*
clean bracing air, as found at the seaside.

P

p or **P** (piː) n., pl. **p's**, **P's**, or **Ps**. 1. the 16th letter of the English alphabet. 2. **mind one's p's and q's.** to be careful to behave correctly and use polite language.

p 1. (in Britain) penny or pence. 2. *Music.* quietly.

P 1. *Chem.* phosphorus. 2. (on road signs) parking. 3. *Chess.* pawn.

p. 1. (pl. **pp.**) page. 2. per.

pa (pɑː) n. *Informal.* father.

Pa *Chem.* protactinium.

PA 1. Also: **Pa.** Pennsylvania. 2. personal assistant. 3. public-address system.

p.a. yearly.

pace[1] (peɪs) n. 1. a. a single step in walking. b. the distance covered by a step. 2. speed of walking or running. 3. rate of proceeding at some other activity: *to live at a fast pace.* 4. manner of walking; gait. 5. **keep pace with.** to proceed at the same speed as. 6. **put someone through his paces.** to test someone's ability. 7. **set the pace.** to determine the speed at which a group proceeds. ~vb. 8. to set the pace for (the competitors) in a race. 9. to walk with regular slow or fast paces, often in anxiety or impatience: *to pace up and down.* 10. (foll. by *out*) to measure by paces.

pace[2] ('peɪsɪ) prep. with due respect to: used to express polite disagreement.

pacemaker ('peɪsˌmeɪkə) n. 1. an electronic device implanted in the body, next to the heart, in order to regulate the heartbeat. 2. a competitor who leads the other competitors during part of a race, causing that part of the race to be run at a particular speed.

pachyderm ('pækɪˌdɜːm) n. a large thick-skinned mammal, such as an elephant or rhinoceros.

pacific (pə'sɪfɪk) adj. tending to bring peace; peaceful.

Pacific (pə'sɪfɪk) n. 1. Also called: **Pacific Ocean.** the world's largest and deepest ocean, lying between Asia and Australia and North and South America. ~adj. 2. of the Pacific Ocean or its islands.

pacifier ('pæsɪˌfaɪə) n. *U.S. & Canad.* a baby's dummy.

pacifism ('pæsɪˌfɪzəm) n. the belief that violence of any kind is unjustifiable and that one should not participate in war. —'**pacifist** n., adj.

pacify ('pæsɪˌfaɪ) vb. **-fying, -fied.** to bring or restore (a person or country) to a state of peace or calm. —**pacification** (ˌpæsɪfɪ-ˈkeɪʃən) n.

pack[1] (pæk) n. 1. a bundle or load carried on the back of a person or an animal. 2. *Chiefly Brit.* a complete set of playing cards. 3. a group of animals that hunt together: *a pack of hounds.* 4. *Rugby.* the forwards of a team. 5. an organized group of Cub Scouts or Brownie Guides. 6. *Chiefly U.S. & Canad.* same as **packet** (sense 1). 7. any collection of people or things: *a pack of lies.* 8. same as **rucksack** or **backpack.** 9. Also called: **face pack.** a cream treatment that cleanses and tones the skin. ~vb. 10. to put (articles) in (a container), such as clothes in a suitcase. 11. to roll (articles) up into a bundle. 12. to press tightly together; cram: *the hall was packed out.* 13. (foll. by *off*) to send away hastily: *the children were packed off to bed.* 14. *Slang.* to be capable of inflicting (a blow): *he packs a mean punch.* 15. *U.S. informal.* to carry (a gun) habitually. 16. **send someone packing.** *Informal.* to dismiss someone abruptly. ~See also **pack in, pack up.**

pack[2] (pæk) vb. to fill (a committee, jury, or audience) with one's own supporters.

package ('pækɪdʒ) n. 1. a wrapped or boxed object or group of objects. 2. a. a proposition, offer, or thing for sale in which separate items are presented together as a unit. b. (as modifier): *a package holiday.* 3. *U.S. & Canad.* same as **packet** (sense 1). ~vb. 4. to put (something) into a package. —'**packaging** n.

packet ('pækɪt) n. 1. a container made of cardboard, paper, or plastic, often together with its contents: *a packet of biscuits.* 2. a small parcel. 3. Also: **packet boat.** a boat that transports mail, passengers, or goods on a fixed short route. 4. *Slang.* a large sum of money: *to cost a packet.*

packhorse ('pækˌhɔːs) n. a horse used to transport goods.

pack ice n. a large area of floating ice, consisting of pieces that have become massed together.

pack in vb. *Informal.* to stop doing (something): *that's enough noise, pack it in.*

packing ('pækɪŋ) n. material, such as paper or plastic, used to cushion packed goods.

packthread ('pækˌθrɛd) n. a strong thread for sewing or tying up packages.

pack up vb. 1. to put (articles) away in a proper or suitable place. 2. *Informal.* to stop doing (something). 3. (of a machine) to fail to operate; break down.

pact (pækt) *n.* a formal agreement between two or more parties.

pad[1] (pæd) *n.* **1.** a thick piece of soft material used to make something comfortable, give it shape, or protect it. **2.** a number of sheets of paper fastened together along one edge. **3.** the fleshy cushion-like underpart of an animal's paw. **4.** a level surface or flat-topped structure, such as a launching pad. **5.** the floating leaf of the water lily. **6.** *Slang.* a person's residence. ~*vb.* **padding, padded. 7.** to line, stuff, or fill (something) out with soft material, in order to make it comfortable, give it shape, or protect it. **8. pad out.** to lengthen (a speech or piece of writing) with unnecessary words or pieces of information.

pad[2] (pæd) *vb.* **padding, padded. 1.** to walk with a soft or muffled step. **2.** to travel (a route) on foot; tramp: *to pad around the country.*

padded cell *n.* a room with padded walls in a psychiatric hospital, in which violent patients are placed.

padding ('pædɪŋ) *n.* **1.** any soft material used to pad something. **2.** unnecessary words or information put into a speech or written work to make it longer.

paddle[1] ('pæd²l) *n.* **1.** a short light oar with a flat blade at one or both ends, used without a rowlock. **2.** a blade of a water wheel or paddle wheel. **3.** a paddle wheel used to propel a boat. ~*vb.* **4.** to propel (a boat) with a paddle. **5.** to swim with short rapid strokes, like a dog. **6.** *U.S. & Canad. informal.* to spank.

paddle[2] ('pæd²l) *vb.* **1.** to walk barefoot in shallow water. **2.** to dabble (one's fingers, hands, or feet) in water. ~*n.* **3.** the act of paddling in water.

paddle steamer *n.* a ship propelled by paddle wheels turned by a steam engine.

paddle wheel *n.* a large wheel fitted with paddles, turned by an engine to propel a ship.

paddock ('pædək) *n.* **1.** a small enclosed field, usually near a house or stable. **2.** (in horse racing) the enclosure in which horses are paraded and mounted before a race.

paddy[1] ('pædɪ) *n., pl.* **-dies.** Also: **paddy field.** a field planted with rice. **2.** rice as a growing crop or when harvested but not yet milled.

paddy[2] ('pædɪ) *n., pl.* **-dies.** *Brit. informal.* a fit of temper.

padlock ('pæd,lɒk) *n.* **1.** a detachable lock with a pivoted U-shaped bar, which can be used to secure a door or lid by passing this bar through a ring or hoop. ~*vb.* **2.** to fasten (something) with a padlock.

padre ('pɑːdrɪ) *n.* *Informal.* a chaplain to the armed forces.

paean ('piːən) *n.* a song of praise, triumph, or joy.

paediatrician *or U.S.* **pediatrician** (,piːdɪə'trɪʃən) *n.* a doctor who specializes in children's diseases.

paediatrics *or U.S.* **pediatrics** (,piːdɪ'ætrɪks) *n.* (*functioning as sing.*) the branch of medicine concerned with children and their diseases. —,**paedi'atric** *or U.S.* ,**pedi'atric** *adj.*

paedophile *or U.S.* **pedophile** ('piːdəʊ,faɪl) *n.* a person who is sexually attracted to children.

paedophilia *or U.S.* **pedophilia** (,piːdəʊ'fɪlɪə) *n.* the condition of being sexually attracted to children.

paella (pɑɪ'ɛlə) *n.* a Spanish dish made from rice, shellfish, chicken, and vegetables.

pagan ('peɪgən) *n.* **1.** a person who is not a Christian, Jew, or Muslim. **2.** a person without any religion; heathen. ~*adj.* **3.** of pagans. **4.** irreligious. —'**paganism** *n.*

page[1] (peɪdʒ) *n.* **1.** one side of one of the leaves of a book, newspaper, or magazine. **2.** one of the leaves of a book, newspaper, or magazine. **3.** an episode, phase, or period: *a glorious page in our history.*

page[2] (peɪdʒ) *n.* **1.** a boy employed to run errands for the guests in a hotel or club. **2.** a youth in attendance at official functions or ceremonies, such as weddings. **3.** *Medieval history.* a boy in training for knighthood. ~*vb.* **4.** to call out the name of (a person), often using a loudspeaker system, so as to give him a message.

pageant ('pædʒənt) *n.* **1.** an outdoor show portraying scenes from history. **2.** any magnificent display or procession.

pageantry ('pædʒəntrɪ) *n.* spectacular display or ceremony.

pageboy ('peɪdʒ,bɔɪ) *n.* **1.** a smooth medium-length hairstyle with the ends of the hair curled under. **2.** same as **page**[2].

pagination (,pædʒɪ'neɪʃən) *n.* the numbering of the pages of a book, manuscript, etc. in sequence.

pagoda (pə'gəʊdə) *n.* a Far Eastern temple, usually an ornate pyramid-shaped tower with many storeys.

paid (peɪd) *vb.* **1.** past of **pay. 2. put paid to.** *Chiefly Brit. & N.Z.* to end or destroy: *breaking his leg put paid to his hopes of running in the Olympics.*

pail (peɪl) *n.* **1.** a bucket. **2.** Also called: **pailful.** the amount contained in a pail: *a pail of water.*

pain (peɪn) *n.* **1.** physical hurt or discomfort caused by injury or illness. **2.** emotional suffering or mental distress. **3. on pain of.** subject to the penalty of: *they were ordered not to cross the borders, on pain of death.* **4.** Also called: **pain in the neck.** *Informal.* a person or thing that is annoying or irritating. ~*vb.* **5.** to cause (a person) hurt, grief, or anxiety. **6.** *Informal.* to annoy; irritate. ~See also **pains**. —'**pain-less** *adj.*

pained (peɪnd) *adj.* having or suggesting pain or distress: *a pained expression.*

painful ('peɪnfʊl) *adj.* **1.** causing pain; distressing: *a painful duty.* **2.** affected with pain: *a painful toe.* **3.** tedious or difficult: *progress is rather painful.* **4.** *Informal.* extremely bad: *a painful performance.* —'**painfully** *adv.*

painkiller ('peɪn,kɪlə) *n.* a pill or other form of medicine that relieves pain.

pains (peɪnz) *pl. n.* care or trouble: *she takes great pains with her work.*

painstaking ('peɪnz,teɪkɪŋ) *adj.* extremely careful as to fine detail. —'**pains,takingly** *adv.*

paint (peɪnt) *n.* **1.** a substance used for decorating or protecting a surface, usually consisting of a solid pigment suspended in a liquid that dries to form a hard coating. **2.** a dry film of paint on a surface. **3.** *Informal.* face make-up. ~*vb.* **4.** to make (a picture) of (a figure, landscape, etc.) with paint applied to paper or canvas. **5.** to coat (a surface) with paint, as in decorating. **6.** to apply (liquid) to (a surface): *she painted the cut with antiseptic.* **7.** to apply make-up to (the face). **8.** to describe vividly in words: *she paints a dismal picture of the future.* **9. paint the town red.** *Informal.* to celebrate uninhibitedly.

paintbrush ('peɪnt,brʌʃ) *n.* a brush used to apply paint.

painted lady *n.* a butterfly with pale brownish-red mottled wings.

painter[1] ('peɪntə) *n.* **1.** a person who paints surfaces of buildings as a trade. **2.** an artist who paints pictures.

painter[2] ('peɪntə) *n.* a rope attached to the bow of a boat for tying it up.

painting ('peɪntɪŋ) *n.* **1.** a picture produced by using paint. **2.** the art of producing pictures by applying paints to paper or canvas. **3.** the act of applying paint to a surface.

pair (pɛə) *n.* **1.** two identical or similar things matched for use together: *a pair of socks.* **2.** two people, animals, or things used or grouped together: *a pair of horses; a pair of scoundrels.* **3.** an object considered to be two identical or similar things joined together: *a pair of trousers.* **4.** a male and a female animal of the same species kept for breeding purposes. **5.** *Parliament.* two opposed members who both agree not to vote on a specified motion. **6.** two playing cards of the same denomination. **7.** one member of a matching pair: *I can't find the pair to this glove.* ~*vb.* **8.** to group (people or things) in matching pairs. **9.** (foll. by *off*) to separate into groups of two.
Usage. Like other collective nouns, *pair* takes a singular or a plural verb according to whether it is seen as a unit or as a

collection of two things: *the pair of cuff links was gratefully received; that pair* (those two people) *are on very good terms.*

paisley pattern *or* **paisley** ('peɪzlɪ) *n.* a pattern of small curving shapes with intricate detailing. **2.** a fine wool fabric traditionally printed with this pattern.

pajamas (pə'dʒɑːməz) *pl. n.* U.S. pyjamas.

pakeha ('pɑːkɪ,hɑː) *n., pl.* **pakeha** *or* **pakehas.** *N.Z.* a person of European descent, as distinct from a Maori.

Paki ('pækɪ) *Brit. slang, offensive.* ~*n.* **1.** a Pakistani or person of Pakistani descent. ~*adj.* **2.** Pakistani or of Pakistani descent.

Pakistani (,pɑːkɪ'stɑːnɪ) *adj.* **1.** of or relating to Pakistan. ~*n.* **2.** a person from Pakistan.

pal (pæl) *Informal.* ~*n.* **1.** a close friend; comrade. ~*vb.* **palling, palled. 2. pal up with.** to become friends with.

palace ('pælɪs) *n.* **1.** the official residence of a king, queen, president, or archbishop. **2.** a large and richly furnished building resembling a royal palace.

paladin ('pælədɪn) *n.* **1.** one of the legendary twelve peers of Charlemagne's court. **2.** (formerly) a knight who did battle for a king or queen.

Palaeocene *or* U.S. **Paleocene** ('pælɪəʊ,siːn) *adj. Geol.* of the epoch of geological time about 65 million years ago.

palaeography *or* U.S. **paleography** (,pælɪ'ɒgrəfɪ) *n.* the study of ancient handwriting.

Palaeolithic *or* U.S. **Paleolithic** (,pælɪəʊ-'lɪθɪk) *adj.* of the period from about 2.5 to 3 million years ago until about 12 000 B.C., during which primitive man emerged and unpolished chipped stone tools were made.

palaeontology *or* U.S. **paleontology** (,pælɪɒn'tɒlədʒɪ) *n.* the study of past geological periods and fossils. —,**palaeon-'tologist** *or* U.S. ,**paleon'tologist** *n.*

Palaeozoic *or* U.S. **Paleozoic** (,pælɪəʊ-'zəʊɪk) *adj. Geol.* of an era of geological time that lasted from about 600 million years ago to 230 million years ago.

palanquin *or* **palankeen** (,pælən'kiːn) *n.* (formerly, in the Orient) a covered bed in which someone could be carried on the shoulders of four men.

palatable ('pælətəb'l) *adj.* **1.** (of food or drink) pleasant to taste. **2.** (of an experience or idea) acceptable or satisfactory.

palate ('pælɪt) *n.* **1.** the roof of the mouth. **2.** the sense of taste: *she had no palate for the wine.*

palatial (pə'leɪʃəl) *adj.* like a palace; sumptuous.

palatinate (pə'lætɪnɪt) *n.* a territory ruled by a palatine prince or noble or a count palatine.

palatine ('pælə,taɪn) *adj.* possessing royal prerogatives: *a count palatine.*

palaver (pə'lɑːvə) n. tedious or time-consuming business; fuss: *all the palaver of filling in forms.*

pale[1] (peɪl) adj. 1. (of a colour) whitish: *pale blue.* 2. (of a person or a person's complexion) having a whitish appearance, usually because of illness, shock, or fear. 3. lacking brightness or colour: *pale morning light.* ~vb. 4. to make or become pale or paler. —**paleness** n.

pale[2] (peɪl) n. 1. a wooden post or strip used in fences. 2. an enclosing barrier, such as a fence made of pales. 3. **beyond the pale.** outside the limits of social convention.

paleface ('peɪl,feɪs) n. a derogatory term for a White person, said to have been used by North American Indians.

Palestinian (,pælɪ'stɪnɪən) adj. 1. of Palestine, a former country in the Middle East. ~n. 2. a person from this area.

palette ('pælɪt) n. 1. a flat piece of wood or plastic used by artists to mix paints. 2. the range of colours characteristic of a particular artist or school of painting: *a restricted palette.*

palette knife n. a spatula with a thin flexible blade used in painting or cookery.

palindrome ('pælɪn,drəʊm) n. a word or phrase that reads the same backwards or forwards, such as *able was I ere I saw Elba.*

paling ('peɪlɪŋ) n. 1. a fence made of pales. 2. pales collectively. 3. a single pale.

palisade (,pælɪ'seɪd) n. 1. a fence made of stakes driven into the ground. 2. one of the stakes used in such a fence.

pall[1] (pɔːl) n. 1. a cloth covering spread over a coffin. 2. a coffin at a funeral ceremony. 3. a dark heavy covering: *the clouds formed a pall over the sky.* 4. a depressing atmosphere: *her bereavement cast a pall on the party.*

pall[2] (pɔːl) vb. (foll. by on) to become boring to: *history classes palled on me.*

palladium (pə'leɪdɪəm) n. Chem. a rare silvery-white element of the platinum metal group, used in jewellery. Symbol: Pd

pallbearer ('pɔːl,beərə) n. a person who helps to carry or who escorts the coffin at a funeral.

pallet[1] ('pælɪt) n. a straw-filled mattress or bed.

pallet[2] ('pælɪt) n. 1. an instrument with a handle and a flat, sometimes flexible, blade used for shaping pottery. 2. a portable platform for storing and moving goods.

palliasse ('pælɪ,æs) n. a straw-filled mattress; pallet.

palliate ('pælɪ,eɪt) vb. 1. to lessen the severity of (pain or disease) without curing it. 2. to cause (an offence) to seem less serious; excuse.

palliative ('pælɪətɪv) adj. 1. relieving without curing. ~n. 2. something that palliates something, such as a sedative drug.

pallid ('pælɪd) adj. lacking colour, brightness, or vigour: *a pallid complexion; a pallid performance.*

pallor ('pælə) n. paleness of complexion, usually because of illness, shock, or fear.

pally ('pælɪ) adj. -lier, -liest. Informal. on friendly terms.

palm[1] (pɑːm) n. 1. the inner part of the hand from the wrist to the base of the fingers. 2. the part of a glove that covers the palm. 3. **in the palm of one's hand.** at one's mercy. ~vb. 4. to hide (something) in the hand, for example in conjuring tricks. ~See also **palm off.**

palm[2] or **palm tree** (pɑːm) n. any of several tropical or subtropical trees that have a straight unbranched trunk crowned with long pointed leaves.

palmate ('pælmeɪt) adj. shaped like an open hand: *palmate leaves.*

palmetto (pæl'mɛtəʊ) n., pl. -tos. a small palm tree with fan-shaped leaves.

palmistry ('pɑːmɪstrɪ) n. the process or art of predicting someone's future by examining the lines and bumps on his hand. —**palmist** n.

palm off vb. 1. to offer or sell fraudulently: *to palm off a counterfeit coin.* 2. to divert (someone) in order to be rid of him: *I palmed the unwelcome visitor off on John.*

palm oil n. an oil obtained from the fruit of certain palm trees, used as an edible fat and in soap.

Palm Sunday n. the Sunday before Easter, commemorating Christ's entry into Jerusalem.

palmy ('pɑːmɪ) adj. **palmier, palmiest.** 1. prosperous, flourishing, or luxurious: *a palmy life.* 2. covered with palm trees: *a palmy beach.*

palomino (,pælə'miːnəʊ) n., pl. -nos. a golden or cream horse with a white mane and tail.

palpable ('pælpəb'l) adj. 1. easily perceived by the senses or the mind; obvious: *a palpable lie.* 2. (of a feeling or an atmosphere) so intense as to seem capable of being touched. —**palpably** adv.

palpate ('pælpeɪt) vb. Med. to examine (an area of the body) by touching. —**palpation** (pæl'peɪʃən) n.

palpitate ('pælpɪ,teɪt) vb. 1. (of the heart) to beat rapidly. 2. to flutter or tremble. —**palpitation** (,pælpɪ'teɪʃən) n.

palsy ('pɔːlzɪ) Pathol. ~n. 1. paralysis of a specified type: *cerebral palsy.* ~vb. -sying, -sied. 2. to paralyse (someone).

paltry ('pɔːltrɪ) adj. -trier, -triest. insignificant, worthless, or petty.

pampas ('pæmpəs) n. (functioning as sing.) the extensive grassy plains of temperate South America.

pampas grass *n.* a South American grass, widely cultivated for its large feathery silver-coloured flower branches.

pamper ('pæmpə) *vb.* to treat (someone) with excessive indulgence or care; spoil.

pamphlet ('pæmflɪt) *n.* a brief publication, usually with a paper cover and often on a subject of current interest.

pamphleteer (ˌpæmflɪ'tɪə) *n.* a person who writes or issues pamphlets.

pan¹ (pæn) *n.* **1.** a wide long-handled metal container used in cooking. **2.** any of various similar containers used in industry, etc. **3.** either of the two dishlike receptacles on a set of scales. **4.** *Brit.* the bowl of a lavatory. **5.** a natural or artificial hollow in the ground: *a saltpan.* ~*vb.* **panning, panned. 6.** to sift gold from (a river) in a shallow pan. **7.** *Informal.* to criticize harshly: *the critics panned his new play.* ~See also **pan out.**

pan² (pæn) *vb.* **panning, panned. 1.** to move (a film camera) or (of a film camera) to be moved so as to follow a moving object or obtain a panoramic effect. ~*n.* **2.** the act of panning.

pan- *combining form.* including or relating to all parts or members: *Pan-American.*

panacea (ˌpænə'sɪə) *n.* a remedy for all diseases or problems.

panache (pə'næʃ) *n.* a dashing manner; swagger: *he rides with panache.*

panama hat *or* **panama** ('pænə,mɑː) *n.* a straw hat with a rounded crown and a wide brim.

Pan-American *adj.* of North, South, and Central America collectively.

panatella (ˌpænə'tɛlə) *n.* a long slender cigar.

pancake ('pæn,keɪk) *n.* **1.** a thin flat cake made from batter and fried on both sides. **2.** Also called: **pancake landing.** an aircraft landing made by levelling out a few feet from the ground and then dropping onto it.

Pancake Day *n.* Shrove Tuesday, when people traditionally eat pancakes.

panchromatic (ˌpænkrəʊ'mætɪk) *adj. Photog.* (of an emulsion or film) sensitive to all colours.

pancreas ('pæŋkrɪəs) *n.* a large gland, situated behind the stomach, that secretes insulin and an alkaline juice containing digestive enzymes. —**pancreatic** (ˌpæŋkrɪ'ætɪk) *adj.*

panda ('pændə) *n.* **1.** Also called: **giant panda.** a large black-and-white bearlike animal that inhabits the bamboo forests of China. **2.** Also called: **lesser** *or* **red panda.** a raccoon-like animal of the mountain forests of S Asia, with a reddish-brown coat and ringed tail.

panda car *n. Brit.* a police patrol car.

pandemic (pæn'dɛmɪk) *adj.* (of a disease) affecting people over a wide geographical area.

pandemonium (ˌpændɪ'məʊnɪəm) *n.* wild confusion; uproar.

pander ('pændə) *vb.* **1.** (foll. by *to*) to indulge (a person or his desires). ~*n.* **2.** a person who procures a sexual partner for someone.

pandit ('pændɪt) *n. Hinduism.* same as **pundit** (sense 2).

p & p *Brit.* postage and packing.

pane (peɪn) *n.* a sheet (of glass).

panegyric (ˌpænɪ'dʒɪrɪk) *n.* a formal speech or piece of writing that praises a person or event.

panel ('pæn°l) *n.* **1.** a flat section of a surface, such as a door or wall. **2.** any distinct section of something formed from a sheet of material, such as part of a car body. **3.** a piece of material inserted in a garment. **4. a.** a group of people selected to act as a team in a quiz, to discuss a topic before an audience, etc. **b.** (*as modifier*): *a panel game.* **5.** *Law.* **a.** a list of jurors. **b.** the people on a jury. **6.** short for **instrument panel.** ~*vb.* **-elling, -elled** *or* U.S. **-eling, -eled. 7.** to furnish or decorate (something) with panels.

panelling *or* U.S. **paneling** ('pæn°lɪŋ) *n.* panels collectively, for example on a wall or ceiling.

panellist *or* U.S. **panelist** ('pæn°lɪst) *n.* a member of a panel, usually on radio or television.

panel van *n. Austral. & N.Z.* a small van.

pang (pæŋ) *n.* a sudden sharp feeling of loneliness, physical pain, or hunger.

pangolin (pæŋ'gəʊlɪn) *n.* an animal of tropical countries with a scaly body and a long snout for feeding on ants and termites. Also called: **scaly anteater.**

panic ('pænɪk) *n.* **1.** a sudden overwhelming feeling of terror or anxiety, sometimes affecting a whole group of people. **2.** (*modifier*) of or resulting from such terror: *panic measures.* ~*vb.* **-icking, -icked. 3.** to feel or cause (someone) to feel panic. —**'panicky** *adj.*

panicle ('pænɪk°l) *n.* a loose, irregularly branched cluster of flowers, as in the oat.

panic-stricken *adj.* affected by panic.

panjandrum (pæn'dʒændrəm) *n.* a pompous self-important official.

pannier ('pænɪə) *n.* **1.** one of a pair of bags slung either side of the back wheel of a bicycle or motorcycle. **2.** one of a pair of large baskets slung over a beast of burden.

panoply ('pænəplɪ) *n.* a complete or magnificent array: *there was a full panoply of relatives at the wedding.*

panorama (ˌpænə'rɑːmə) *n.* **1.** an extensive unbroken view in all directions. **2.** a wide or comprehensive survey of a subject. **3.** a picture of a scene unrolled before spectators a part at a time so as to appear continuous. —**panoramic** (ˌpænəˈræmɪk) adj.

pan out vb. 1. Informal. to work out; result: the meeting didn't pan out as expected. 2. (of gravel) to yield gold by panning.

panpipes (ˈpænˌpaɪps) pl. n. a musical wind instrument made of a number of tubes of graduated lengths bound together.

pansy (ˈpænzɪ) n., pl. -sies. 1. a garden plant having flowers with rounded white, yellow, or purple velvety petals. 2. Offensive slang. an effeminate or homosexual man or boy.

pant (pænt) vb. 1. to breathe with noisy gasps after exertion. 2. to say (something) while breathing in this way. 3. (foll. by for) to have a frantic desire for. ~n. 4. the act of panting.

pantaloons (ˌpæntəˈluːnz) pl. n. baggy trousers gathered at the ankles.

pantechnicon (pænˈtɛknɪkən) n. Brit. a large van used for furniture removals.

pantheism (ˈpænθɪˌɪzəm) n. 1. the belief that God is identical with the material universe or the forces of nature. 2. readiness to worship all gods. —**pantheist** n. —ˌpanthe'**istic** adj.

pantheon (ˈpænθɪən) n. 1. (in ancient Greece or Rome) a temple erected to honour all the gods. 2. a building commemorating a nation's dead heroes.

panther (ˈpænθə) n. a leopard, usually a black one.

panties (ˈpæntɪz) pl. n. women's or children's underpants.

pantihose (ˈpæntɪˌhəʊz) pl. n. Austral. women's tights.

pantile (ˈpænˌtaɪl) n. a roofing tile, with an S-shaped cross section.

panto (ˈpæntəʊ) n., pl. -tos. Brit. informal. short for **pantomime** (sense 1).

pantograph (ˈpæntəˌɡrɑːf) n. 1. an instrument consisting of pivoted levers for copying drawings or maps to any scale. 2. a similar instrument mounted on a train roof to convey current from an overhead wire.

pantomime (ˈpæntəˌmaɪm) n. 1. (in Britain) a play based on a fairy tale and usually performed at Christmas time. 2. a theatrical entertainment in which words are replaced by gestures and bodily actions. 3. Informal, chiefly Brit. a confused or farcical situation.

pantry (ˈpæntrɪ) n., pl. -tries. a small room or large cupboard in which food is kept.

pants (pænts) pl. n. 1. Brit. an undergarment with two leg holes, covering the body from the waist or hips to the thighs. 2. U.S. & Canad. trousers. 3. **bore** or **scare the pants off someone**. Informal. to bore or scare someone very much.

panty hose (ˈpæntɪ) pl. n. U.S. women's tights.

pap[1] (pæp) n. 1. a soft or semiliquid food for babies or invalids. 2. worthless or oversimplified entertainment or information. 3. S. African. maize porridge.

pap[2] (pæp) n. Archaic or Scot. & N English dialect. a nipple or teat.

papa (pəˈpɑː) n. Old-fashioned, informal. father.

papacy (ˈpeɪpəsɪ) n., pl. -cies. 1. the office or term of office of a pope. 2. the system of government in the Roman Catholic Church that has the pope as its head.

papal (ˈpeɪpᵊl) adj. of the pope or the papacy.

paparazzo (ˌpæpəˈrætsəʊ) n., pl. -razzi (-ˈrætsiː). a freelance photographer who specializes in candid-camera shots of famous people.

papaya (pəˈpaɪə) n. a large green fruit with a sweet yellow flesh, that grows on a West Indian tree.

paper (ˈpeɪpə) n. 1. a flexible material made from wood pulp or other fibrous material and formed into flat thin sheets suitable for writing on, decorating walls, or wrapping parcels. 2. (pl.) documents, such as a passport, for establishing the identity of the bearer. 3. (pl.) the collected diaries, letters, etc., of a person's private or public life. 4. short for **newspaper** or **wallpaper**. 5. a lecture or an essay on a specific subject. 6. a set of examination questions. 7. **on paper**. in theory, as opposed to fact: the project looks impressive enough on paper. ~adj. 8. made of paper: paper cups do not last long. 9. existing only as recorded on paper but not yet in practice: paper expenditure. ~vb. 10. to cover (walls) with wallpaper. ~See also **paper over**. —ˈ**papery** adj.

paperback (ˈpeɪpəˌbæk) n. 1. a book with covers made of flexible card. ~adj. 2. of a paperback or publication of paperbacks.

paperboy (ˈpeɪpəˌbɔɪ) or **papergirl** n. a boy or girl employed to deliver newspapers to people's homes.

paper chase n. a cross-country run in which a runner lays a trail of paper for others to follow.

paperclip (ˈpeɪpəˌklɪp) n. a bent wire clip for holding sheets of paper together.

paperhanger (ˈpeɪpəˌhæŋə) n. a person who hangs wallpaper as an occupation.

paperknife (ˈpeɪpəˌnaɪf) n., pl. -knives. a knife-shaped object with a blunt blade for opening sealed envelopes.

paper money n. banknotes, rather than coins.

paper over vb. to conceal (something unpleasant or difficult).

paperweight (ˈpeɪpəˌweɪt) n. a small heavy object placed on top of loose papers to prevent them from scattering.

paperwork (ˈpeɪpəˌwɜːk) n. clerical work, such as the writing of reports or letters.

papier-mâché (ˌpæpjeɪˈmæʃeɪ) n. **1.** a hard substance made of layers of paper mixed with paste and moulded when moist. ~adj. **2.** made of papier-mâché.

papilla (pəˈpɪlə) n., pl. **-lae** (-liː). Biol. a small projection of tissue at the base of a hair, tooth, or feather. —**paˈpillary** adj.

papist (ˈpeɪpɪst) n., adj. Usually offensive. same as **Roman Catholic.**

papoose (pəˈpuːs) n. an American Indian baby.

paprika (ˈpæprɪkə, pəˈpriː-) n. a mild powdered seasoning made from red peppers.

Pap test or **smear** (pæp) n. Med. an examination of stained cells in a specimen taken from the neck or lining of the womb for detection of cancer.

papyrus (pəˈpaɪrəs) n., pl. **-ri** (-raɪ) or **-ruses. 1.** a tall water plant of S Europe and N and central Africa. **2.** a kind of paper made from the stem of this plant, used by the ancient Egyptians, Greeks, and Romans. **3.** an ancient document written on this paper.

par (pɑː) n. **1.** the usual or average state or condition: I feel a bit below par today. **2. on a par with.** equal or equivalent to: his latest film puts him on a par with the Hollywood greats. **3.** Golf. a standard score for a hole or course that a good player should make: par for the course was 72. **4.** Finance. the established value of the unit of one national currency in terms of the unit of another. **5.** Commerce. short for **par value.** ~adj. **6. par for the course.** to be expected; typical.

par. 1. paragraph. **2.** parenthesis.

para (ˈpærə) n. Informal. **1.** a paratrooper. **2.** a paragraph.

para- or before a vowel **par-** prefix. **1.** beside; near: parameter. **2.** beyond: parapsychology. **3.** resembling: paratyphoid fever.

parable (ˈpærəbᵊl) n. a short story that uses familiar situations to illustrate a religious or ethical point.

parabola (pəˈræbələ) n. Geom. an open plane curve formed by the intersection of a cone by a plane parallel to its side. —**parabolic** (ˌpærəˈbɒlɪk) adj.

paracetamol (ˌpærəˈsiːtəˌmɒl, -ˈsɛtə-) n. a mild pain-relieving drug.

parachute (ˈpærəˌʃuːt) n. **1.** a device consisting of a large fabric canopy connected to a harness, used to slow down the descent of a person or package from an aircraft. ~vb. **2.** to land or to drop (supplies or troops) by parachute from an aircraft. —**ˈparaˌchutist** n.

parade (pəˈreɪd) n. **1.** an ordered march or procession, for example of troops being inspected. **2.** a conspicuous display: to make a parade of one's grief. **3.** a public promenade or street of shops. ~vb. **4.** to walk or march, esp. in a procession. **5.** to exhibit or flaunt: he was parading his medals.

parade ground n. a place where soldiers assemble regularly for inspection or display.

paradigm (ˈpærəˌdaɪm) n. a pattern, model, or example.

paradise (ˈpærəˌdaɪs) n. **1.** heaven; the abode of the righteous after death. **2.** the Garden of Eden. **3.** any place or condition that fulfils all one's desires.

paradise duck n. a New Zealand duck with bright plumage.

paradox (ˈpærəˌdɒks) n. **1.** a seemingly absurd or self-contradictory statement that is or may be true: religious truths are often expressed in paradox. **2.** a self-contradictory proposition, such as I always tell lies. **3.** a person or thing that is made up of contradictory elements. —**ˌparaˈdoxical** adj. —**ˌparaˈdoxically** adv.

paraffin (ˈpærəfɪn) n. **1.** a liquid mixture distilled from petroleum or shale and used as an aircraft fuel, in domestic heaters, and as a solvent. **2.** Chem. any saturated hydrocarbon with the general formula C_nH_{2n+2}

paraffin wax n. a white waxlike substance distilled from petroleum and used in making candles and as a sealing agent.

paragon (ˈpærəgən) n. a model of excellence or perfection: a paragon of virtue.

paragraph (ˈpærəˌɡrɑːf) n. **1.** a section of a piece of writing, usually devoted to one idea, which begins on a new line and is often indented. **2.** Printing. the character ¶, used to indicate the beginning of a new paragraph. ~vb. **3.** to form (a piece of writing) into paragraphs.

parakeet (ˈpærəˌkiːt) n. a small colourful parrot with a long tail.

parallax (ˈpærəˌlæks) n. an apparent change in the position of an object resulting from a change in position of the observer.

parallel (ˈpærəˌlɛl) adj. **1.** separated by an equal distance at every point: parallel walls. **2.** corresponding; similar: parallel situations. **3.** Computers. operating on several items of information or instructions at the same time. ~n. **4.** Maths. one of a set of parallel lines or planes. **5.** something very similar or corresponding to something else. **6.** a comparison; similarity between two things. **7.** Also called: **parallel of latitude.** any of the imaginary lines around the earth parallel to the equator, marking degrees of latitude. **8.** Printing. the character ‖, used as a reference mark. ~vb. **9.** to be a parallel to; correspond to: your experience parallels mine.

parallel bars pl. n. Gymnastics. a pair of

wooden bars on upright posts used for various exercises.

parallelepiped (ˌpærəˌlɛlɪˈpaɪpɛd) *n. Geom.* a solid shape whose six faces are parallelograms.

parallelism (ˈpærəˌlɛlɪzəm) *n.* **1.** the state of being parallel. **2.** a close likeness; similarity.

parallelogram (ˌpærəˈlɛləˌɡræm) *n. Geom.* a plane figure whose opposite sides are parallel and equal in length.

paralyse or *U.S.* **-lyze** (ˈpærəˌlaɪz) *vb.* **1.** *Pathol.* to affect (someone) with paralysis. **2.** to make (someone) immobile: *paralysed with fright.*

paralysis (pəˈrælɪsɪs) *n.* **1.** *Pathol.* impairment or loss of voluntary muscle function or sensation in all or part of the body. **2.** a state of inactivity: *paralysis of industry by strikes.*

paralytic (ˌpærəˈlɪtɪk) *adj.* **1.** of or relating to paralysis. **2.** *Brit. informal.* very drunk. ~*n.* **3.** a person who is paralysed.

paramecium (ˌpærəˈmiːsɪəm) *n.*, *pl.* **-cia** (-sɪə). a unicellular animal which lives in ponds, puddles, and sewage filters and swims by means of cilia.

paramedic (ˌpærəˈmɛdɪk) *n.* a person, such as a laboratory technician, who supplements the work of the medical profession.

paramedical (ˌpærəˈmɛdɪk'l) *adj.* supplementing the work of the medical profession.

parameter (pəˈræmɪtə) *n.* **1.** *Maths.* an arbitrary constant that determines the specific form of a mathematical expression, such as a and b in $y = ax^2 + b$. **2.** *Informal.* any constant or limiting factor: *a designer must work within the parameters of budget and practicality.*

paramilitary (ˌpærəˈmɪlɪtrɪ) *adj.* denoting a group of personnel with military structure working in support of military forces or as a guerilla or terrorist group.

paramount (ˈpærəˌmaʊnt) *adj.* of the greatest importance.

paramour (ˈpærəˌmʊə) *n. Old-fashioned.* an adulterous lover.

paranoia (ˌpærəˈnɔɪə) *n.* **1.** a mental disorder characterized by delusions of grandeur or of persecution. **2.** *Informal.* intense fear or suspicion, usually when unfounded. —ˈpara,noid or ˌparaˈnoiac *adj., n.*

paranormal (ˌpærəˈnɔːməl) *adj.* **1.** beyond normal scientific explanation. ~*n.* **2. the.** paranormal happenings or matters generally.

parapet (ˈpærəpɪt) *n.* **1.** a low wall or railing along the edge of a balcony or roof. **2.** *Mil.* a rampart or mound of sandbags in front of a trench to conceal and protect troops from fire.

paraphernalia (ˌpærəfəˈneɪlɪə) *n.* miscellaneous articles or equipment.

paraphrase (ˈpærəˌfreɪz) *n.* **1.** an expression of a statement or text in other words. ~*vb.* **2.** to put (a statement or text) into other words; restate.

paraplegia (ˌpærəˈpliːdʒə) *n. Pathol.* paralysis of the lower half of the body. —ˌparaˈplegic *adj., n.*

parapsychology (ˌpærəsaɪˈkɒlədʒɪ) *n.* the study of mental phenomena such as telepathy.

Paraquat (ˈpærəˌkwɒt) *n. Trademark.* an extremely poisonous weedkiller.

parasite (ˈpærəˌsaɪt) *n.* **1.** an animal or plant that lives in or on another from which it obtains nourishment. **2.** a person who habitually lives at the expense of others; sponger. —**parasitic** (ˌpærəˈsɪtɪk) *adj.*

parasol (ˈpærəˌsɒl) *n.* an umbrella-like sunshade.

paratrooper (ˈpærəˌtruːpə) *n.* a member of the paratroops.

paratroops (ˈpærəˌtruːps) *pl. n.* troops trained to be dropped by parachute into a battle area.

paratyphoid fever (ˌpærəˈtaɪfɔɪd) *n.* a disease resembling but less severe than typhoid fever.

parboil (ˈpɑːˌbɔɪl) *vb.* to boil (food) until partially cooked.

parcel (ˈpɑːs'l) *n.* **1.** something wrapped up; a package. **2.** a quantity of some commodity offered for sale; lot. **3.** a distinct portion of land. ~*vb.* **-celling, -celled** or *U.S.* **-celing, -celed.** **4.** (foll. by *up*) to wrap (something) up into a parcel. **5.** (foll. by *out*) to divide (something) into portions.

parch (pɑːtʃ) *vb.* **1.** to deprive (something) of water; dry up: *the sun parches the fields.* **2.** to make (someone) very thirsty: *I was parched after the run.*

parchment (ˈpɑːtʃmənt) *n.* **1.** the skin of certain animals, such as sheep, treated to form a material for writing on. **2.** a manuscript made of this material. **3.** a stiff yellowish paper resembling parchment.

pardon (ˈpɑːd'n) *vb.* **1.** to forgive (a person) for (an offence or mistake): *to pardon someone; to pardon a fault.* ~*n.* **2.** forgiveness. **3.** official release from punishment for a crime. ~*interj.* **4.** Also: **pardon me, I beg your pardon. a.** sorry; excuse me. **b.** what did you say? —ˈpardonable *adj.*

pare (pɛə) *vb.* **1.** to peel (the outer layer) from (something): *to pare apples.* **2.** to cut the edges from (one's nails). **3.** to decrease bit by bit: *to pare down expenses.*

parent (ˈpɛərənt) *n.* **1.** a father or mother. **2.** a person acting as a father or mother; guardian. **3.** a plant or animal that has produced one or more plants or animals. —**parental** (pəˈrɛntəl) *adj.* —ˈparenthood *n.*

parentage ('pɛərəntɪdʒ) *n.* ancestry; family.

parent company *n.* a company that owns a number of smaller companies.

parenthesis (pə'rɛnθɪsɪs) *n., pl.* **-ses** (-ˌsiːz). **1.** a phrase inserted into a passage, often as an explanation, and marked off by brackets or dashes. **2.** Also called: **bracket**. either of a pair of characters (), used to enclose such a phrase. —**parenthetical** (ˌpærən-'θɛtɪk³l) *adj.* —ˌparen'thetically *adv.*

parenting ('pɛərəntɪŋ) *n.* the activity of bringing up children.

parent-teacher association *n.* an organization consisting of the parents of children at a school and their teachers formed in order to promote better understanding between them.

par excellence (paːr ˌɛksə'lɒns) *adv.* beyond comparison: *she is a hostess par excellence.*

parfait (paː'feɪ) *n.* a dessert consisting of layers of ice cream, fruit, and sauce, topped with whipped cream, and served in a tall glass.

pariah (pə'raɪə) *n.* a social outcast.

parietal (pə'raɪɪt³l) *adj. Anat., biol.* of or forming the walls of a bodily cavity: *the parietal bones of the skull.*

paring ('pɛərɪŋ) *n.* something that has been cut off something.

parish ('pærɪʃ) *n.* **1.** an area that has its own church and clergyman. **2.** the people who live in a parish. **3.** (in England and, formerly, Wales) the smallest unit of local government.

parish clerk *n.* a person who assists in various church duties.

parish council *n.* (in England and, formerly, Wales) the administrative body of a parish. See **parish** (sense 3).

parishioner (pə'rɪʃənə) *n.* a person who lives in a particular parish.

parish register *n.* a book in which the births, baptisms, marriages, and deaths in a parish are recorded.

parity ('pærɪtɪ) *n.* **1.** equality, for example of rank or pay. **2.** close or exact equivalence. **3.** *Finance.* equivalence between the units of currency of two countries.

park (paːk) *n.* **1.** a large area of land preserved in a natural state for recreational use by the public. **2.** a piece of open land in a town with public amenities. **3.** a large area of land forming a private estate. **4.** an area designed to accommodate a number of related enterprises: *a business park.* **5.** *U.S. & Canad.* a playing field or sports stadium. **6. the park.** *Brit. informal.* the pitch in soccer. ~*vb.* **7.** to stop and leave (a vehicle) temporarily. **8.** *Informal.* to leave or put (someone or something) somewhere: *park yourself in front of the fire.* —ˈparking *n.*

parka ('paːkə) *n.* a long jacket with a quilted lining and a fur-trimmed hood.

parkin ('paːkɪn) *n. Brit.* a moist spicy ginger cake containing oatmeal.

parking meter *n.* a coin-operated timing device beside a parking space that indicates how long a vehicle may be left parked.

parking ticket *n.* the notice of a fine served on a motorist for a parking offence.

Parkinson's disease ('paːkɪnsənz) *or* **Parkinsonism** *n.* a disorder of the central nervous system which causes tremor, rigidity, and impaired muscular coordination.

Parkinson's law *n.* the notion that work expands to fill the time available for its completion.

parkland ('paːkˌlænd) *n.* grassland with scattered trees.

parky ('paːkɪ) *adj.* **parkier, parkiest.** *Brit. informal.* (of the weather) chilly.

parlance ('paːləns) *n.* a particular manner of speaking: *political parlance.*

parley ('paːlɪ) *n.* **1.** a discussion, for example between enemies to decide terms of surrender. ~*vb.* **2.** to have a parley, usually with an enemy.

parliament ('paːləmənt) *n.* an assembly of the representatives of a political nation or people, usually the highest law-making authority.

Parliament ('paːləmənt) *n.* **1.** the highest law-making authority in Britain, consisting of the House of Commons, the House of Lords, and the sovereign. **2.** the equivalent law-making authority in another country.

parliamentarian (ˌpaːləmən'tɛərɪən) *n.* an expert in parliamentary procedures.

parliamentary (ˌpaːlə'mɛntrɪ) *adj.* **1.** of or from a parliament: *a parliamentary decree.* **2.** conforming to the procedures of a parliament: *parliamentary conduct.*

parlour *or U.S.* **parlor** ('paːlə) *n.* **1.** *Old-fashioned.* a living room for receiving visitors in. **2.** a room or shop equipped as a place of business: *an ice-cream parlour.*

parlous ('paːləs) *adj. Archaic or humorous.* dangerous: *the parlous state of the roof.*

Parmesan cheese *or* **Parmesan** ('paːmɪˌzæn) *n.* a hard strong-flavoured cheese used grated on pasta dishes and soups.

parochial (pə'rəʊkɪəl) *adj.* **1.** narrow in outlook; provincial. **2.** of or relating to a parish. —**pa'rochial.ism** *n.*

parody ('pærədɪ) *n., pl.* **-dies. 1.** a musical, literary, or other composition that mimics the style of another composer, author, etc., in a humorous way. **2.** something so badly done as to seem like an intentional mockery. ~*vb.* **-dying, -died. 3.** to make a parody of. —ˈparodist *n.*

parole (pə'rəʊl) *n.* **1.** the freeing of a prisoner before his sentence has expired, on condition that he behaves well. **2.** a promise given by a prisoner to behave well if granted liberty or partial liberty. **3. on parole.** conditionally released from prison. ~*vb.* **4.** to place (a person) on parole.

parotid gland (pə'rɒtɪd) *n. Anat.* either of a pair of glands in front of and below the ears.

paroxysm ('pærək,sɪzəm) *n.* **1.** an uncontrollable outburst of laughter, or jealousy. **2.** *Pathol.* **a.** a sudden attack or recurrence of a disease. **b.** a fit or convulsion. —,**parox'ysmal** *adj.*

parquet ('pɑːkeɪ) *n.* **1.** a floor covering made of pieces of parquetry. ~*vb.* **2.** to cover (a floor) with parquetry.

parquetry ('pɑːkɪtrɪ) *n.* a geometric pattern of inlaid pieces of wood, used to cover floors.

parr (pɑː) *n.* a salmon up to two years of age.

parricide ('pærɪ,saɪd) *n.* **1.** a person who kills one of his parents. **2.** the act of killing either of one's parents. —,**parri'cidal** *adj.*

parrot ('pærət) *n.* **1.** a tropical bird with a short hooked bill, bright plumage, and an ability to mimic human speech. **2.** a person who repeats or imitates someone else's words. ~*vb.* **3.** to repeat or imitate (someone else's words) without understanding them.

parrot fever *n.* same as **psittacosis.**

parry ('pærɪ) *vb.* **-rying, -ried. 1.** to ward off (an attack) by blocking or deflecting, as in fencing. **2.** to avoid answering (questions) in a clever way. ~*n., pl.* **-ries. 3.** an instance of parrying. **4.** a skilful evasion of a question.

parse (pɑːz) *vb.* to analyse (a sentence or the words in a sentence) grammatically.

parsec ('pɑː,sɛk) *n.* a unit of astronomical distance equivalent to 3.0857×10^{16} metres or 3.262 light years.

parsimony ('pɑːsɪmənɪ) *n.* extreme caution in spending. —**parsimonious** (,pɑːsɪ'məun-ɪəs) *adj.*

parsley ('pɑːslɪ) *n.* a herb with curled pleasant-smelling leaves, used for seasoning and decorating food.

parsnip ('pɑːsnɪp) *n.* a long tapering cream-coloured root vegetable.

parson ('pɑːs²n) *n.* **1.** a parish priest in the Church of England. **2.** any clergyman.

parsonage ('pɑːs²nɪdʒ) *n.* the residence of a parson, provided by the parish.

parson's nose *n.* the rump of a fowl when cooked.

part (pɑːt) *n.* **1.** a piece or portion. **2.** one of several equal divisions: *mix two parts flour to one part water.* **3.** an actor's role in a play. **4.** a person's duty: *everyone must do his part.* **5.** (*pl.*) region; area: *he's well known in these parts.* **6.** *Anat.* an area of the body. **7.** a component that can be replaced in a vehicle or machine. **8.** *U.S. &*

Canad. same as **parting** (sense 2). **9.** *Music.* a melodic line assigned to one or more instrumentalists or singers. **10. for my part.** as far as I am concerned. **11. for the most part.** generally. **12. in part.** to some degree; partly. **13. on the part of.** on behalf of. **14. part and parcel of.** an essential ingredient of. **15. play a part. a.** to pretend to be what one is not. **b.** (foll. by *in*) to have something to do with: *to play a part in the king's downfall.* **16. take part in.** to participate in. **17. take someone's part.** to support someone, for example in an argument. **18. take something in good part.** to respond to (teasing or criticism) with good humour. ~*vb.* **19.** to divide or separate from one another: *to part the curtains; the seams parted when I washed the dress.* **20.** to go away or cause (people) to go away from one another: *the couple parted amicably.* **21.** (foll. by *with*) to give up: *I wouldn't part with my Mini.* **22.** (foll. by *from*) to cause (someone) to give up: *he's not easily parted from his cash.* **23.** to split: *the path parts here.* **24.** to arrange (the hair) in such a way that a line of scalp is left showing. ~*adv.* **25.** to some extent; partly: *part woman, part child.* ~See also **parts.**

partake (pɑː'teɪk) *vb.* **-taking, -took, -taken. 1.** (foll. by *of*) to take (food or drink). **2.** (foll. by *in*) to participate in.

parterre (pɑː'tɛə) *n.* **1.** a formally patterned flower garden. **2.** the pit of a theatre.

Parthian shot ('pɑːθɪən) *n.* a hostile remark or gesture delivered while departing.

partial ('pɑːʃəl) *adj.* **1.** relating to only a part; not complete: *a partial eclipse.* **2.** biased: *a partial judge.* **3.** (foll. by *to*) having a particular liking for. —**partiality** (,pɑːʃɪ'ælɪtɪ) *n.* —**'partially** *adv.*
Usage. In strict usage, a difference is sometimes made between the meanings of *partially* "not fully or completely", and *partly* "concerning only a part" or "in part". The distinction can be helpful in a sentence such as *the book, which was written partly in English and partly in French, was only partially completed when he died.*

participate (pɑː'tɪsɪ,peɪt) *vb.* (foll. by *in*) to become actively involved in. —**par'ticipant** *n.* —**participation** (pɑː,tɪsɪ'peɪʃən) *n.* —**par'ticipatory** *adj.*

participle ('pɑːtɪsɪp²l) *n.* a form of a verb that is used in compound tenses or as an adjective. See also **present participle, past participle.** —,**parti'cipial** *adj.*

particle ('pɑːtɪk²l) *n.* **1.** an extremely small piece or amount: *food particles; it doesn't make a particle of difference.* **2.** *Grammar.* an uninflected part of speech, such as an interjection or preposition. **3.** *Physics.* a minute piece of matter, such as an electron or proton.

parti-coloured or U.S. **particolored** ('pɑːtɪˌkʌləd) adj. having different colours in different parts.

particular (pə'tɪkjʊlə) adj. **1.** of or belonging to a single or specific person, thing, or category: the particular demands of the job. **2.** exceptional or marked: a matter of particular importance. **3.** providing specific details or circumstances: a particular account. **4.** difficult to please; fussy. ~n. **5.** a separate distinct item that helps to form a generalization: moving from the general to the particular. **6.** an item of information; detail: complete in every particular. **7. in particular.** especially or exactly: there's one person in particular who may be able to help. —**par'ticularly** adv.

particularity (pəˌtɪkjʊ'lærɪtɪ) n., pl. **-ties.** **1.** great attentiveness to detail. **2.** the state or quality of being particular as opposed to general; individuality.

particularize or **-ise** (pə'tɪkjʊləˌraɪz) vb. to give details about (something). —**parˌticulari'zation** or **-i'sation** n.

parting ('pɑːtɪŋ) n. **1.** a departure or leave-taking. **2.** Brit. the line of scalp showing when sections of hair are combed in opposite directions. **3.** the act of dividing (something).

partisan (ˌpɑːtɪ'zæn, 'pɑːtɪˌzæn) n. **1.** a person who supports a particular cause or party. **2.** a member of an armed resistance group within occupied territory. ~adj. **3.** excessively devoted to a particular cause or party; one-sided. —**ˌparti'sanship** n.

partition (pɑː'tɪʃən) n. **1.** a large screen or thin wall that divides a room in two. **2.** the division of a country into two or more independent countries. ~vb. **3.** (foll. by off) to separate (a room) into sections.

partitive ('pɑːtɪtɪv) Grammar. ~adj. **1.** (of a noun) referring to part of something. The phrase some of the butter is a partitive construction. ~n. **2.** a partitive word, such as some or any.

partly ('pɑːtlɪ) adv. not completely.

partner ('pɑːtnə) n. **1.** either member of a couple in a relationship. **2.** a member of a business partnership. **3.** one of a pair of dancers or players on the same side in a game: my bridge partner. **4.** an ally or companion: a partner in crime. ~vb. **5.** to be the partner of (someone).

partnership ('pɑːtnəʃɪp) n. **1.** a contractual relationship between two or more people or organizations in a joint business venture. **2.** the condition of being a partner.

part of speech n. Grammar. a class of words, such as a noun, verb, or adjective, sharing important syntactic or semantic features.

partook (pɑː'tʊk) vb. the past tense of **partake.**

partridge ('pɑːtrɪdʒ) n., pl. **-tridges** or **-tridge.** a game bird with an orange-brown head, greyish neck, and a short rust-coloured tail.

parts (pɑːts) pl. n. abilities or talents: a man of many parts.

part song n. a song composed in harmonized parts.

part-time adj. **1.** for less than the normal full working time: a part-time job. ~adv. **part time.** **2.** on a part-time basis: he works part time. —**ˌpart-'timer** n.

parturient (pɑː'tjʊərɪənt) adj. giving birth.

parturition (ˌpɑːtjʊ'rɪʃən) n. the process of giving birth.

party ('pɑːtɪ) n., pl. **-ties.** **1.** a social gathering for pleasure, often held as a celebration. **2.** a group of people associated in some activity: a rescue party. **3.** a group of people organized together to further a common political aim. **4.** the person or people taking part in legal proceedings: a party to the action. **5.** Informal, humorous. a person: he's an odd old party. ~vb. **-ties, -tying, -tied.** **6.** Informal. to celebrate; revel.

party line n. **1.** the policies of a political party. **2.** a telephone line serving two or more subscribers.

party wall n. Property law. a wall separating two properties.

par value n. the value imprinted on the face of a share certificate or bond at the time of its issue.

parvenu or (fem.) **parvenue** ('pɑːvəˌnjuː) n. a person who, having risen socially or economically, is considered to be an upstart.

pas (pɑː) n., pl. **pas.** a dance step.

pascal ('pæskˀl) n. the derived SI unit of pressure; the pressure exerted on an area of 1 square metre by a force of 1 newton.

paschal ('pæskˀl) adj. **1.** of or relating to the Passover. **2.** of or relating to Easter.

pas de deux (pɑː də 'dɜː) n., pl. **pas de deux.** Ballet. a dance for two people.

pasha ('pɑːʃə) n. (formerly) a high official of the Ottoman Empire: placed after a name when used as a title.

pas op ('pɑːs ˌɒp) interj. S. African. beware.

pasqueflower ('pɑːskˌflaʊə) n. a small purple-flowered plant of Europe and Asia.

pass (pɑːs) vb. **1.** to go by or past (a person or thing). **2.** to run, extend, or lead (through, over, or across): the route passes through the city. **3.** to go through or cause (something) to go through (an obstacle or barrier): to pass a needle through cloth. **4.** to move onwards or over: he passed his hand over her face. **5.** to exceed: this victory passes all expectations. **6.** to gain or cause (someone) to gain an adequate mark or grade in (a test or examination). **7.** (of time) to elapse or to allow (time) to elapse:

we passed the time talking. **8.** to take place: *what passed at the meeting?* **9.** to transfer or exchange or be transferred or exchanged: *the bomb passed from hand to hand.* **10.** to transfer or be transferred by inheritance: *the house passed to the younger son.* **11.** (of a law-making body) to agree to (a law or proposal): *the assembly passed 10 resolutions.* **12.** to pronounce (judgment): *the court passed sentence.* **13.** to go without comment: *the insult passed unnoticed.* **14.** to opt not to answer a question or not to make a bid or a play in card games. **15.** to discharge (waste matter or blood in the waste matter) from the body. **16.** to come to an end or disappear: *his anger soon passed.* **17.** (foll. by *for* or *as*) to be likely to be mistaken for (someone or something else): *you could easily pass for your sister.* **18.** *Sport.* to hit, kick, or throw (the ball) to another player. **19. pass away** *or* **on.** *Euphemistic.* to die. ~*n.* **20.** a route through a range of mountains where there is a gap between peaks. **21.** a permit, licence, or authorization to do something without restriction. **22.** *Mil.* a document authorizing leave of absence. **23.** *Brit.* the passing of a college or university examination to a satisfactory standard but not as high as honours. **24.** *Informal.* an attempt to invite sexual intimacy: *he made a pass at his secretary.* **25.** *Sport.* the transfer of a ball from one player to another. **26.** *Bridge, etc.* an instance of opting not to answer a question or not to make a bid or a play in card games. **27. a pretty pass.** a bad state of affairs. ~See also **pass off, pass out,** etc.

pass. passive.

passable (ˈpɑːsəb^əl) *adj.* **1.** adequate or acceptable: *a passable but not outstanding speech.* **2.** (of an obstacle) capable of being crossed. —ˈ**passably** *adv.*

passage (ˈpæsɪdʒ) *n.* **1.** a channel or opening through or by which someone or something may pass. **2.** a hall or lobby. **3.** a section of a written work, speech, or piece of music. **4.** a journey by ship. **5.** the act or process of passing from one place or condition to another: *passage of a gas through a liquid.* **6.** the permission, right, or freedom to pass: *to be denied passage through a country.* **7.** the enactment of a law by a law-making body.

passageway (ˈpæsɪdʒ,weɪ) *n.* a long narrow space in a building or between buildings; passage.

passbook (ˈpɑːs,bʊk) *n.* **1.** a book issued by a building society for keeping a record of deposits and withdrawals. **2.** a book issued with some bank accounts for keeping a record of deposits and withdrawals. **3.** *S. African.* an official identity document.

passé (ˈpæseɪ) *adj.* out-of-date: *passé ideas.*

passenger (ˈpæsɪndʒə) *n.* **1.** a person

travelling in a vehicle driven by someone else. **2.** *Chiefly Brit.* a member of a team who is not participating fully in the work: *there's no room for passengers on this project.*

passer-by (ˌpɑːsəˈbaɪ) *n., pl.* **passers-by.** a person who is walking past someone or something.

passerine (ˈpæsə,raɪn) *adj.* **1.** of or belonging to an order of perching birds that includes the larks, finches, and starlings. ~*n.* **2.** any bird of this order.

passim (ˈpæsɪm) *adv.* throughout: used to indicate that what is referred to occurs frequently in a particular piece of writing.

passing (ˈpɑːsɪŋ) *adj.* **1.** momentary: *a passing fancy.* **2.** casual: *a passing reference.* ~*n.* **3.** *Euphemistic.* death. **4.** the ending of something: *the passing of the silent film.* **5. in passing.** incidentally: *he mentioned your visit in passing.*

passion (ˈpæʃən) *n.* **1.** intense sexual love. **2.** a strong enthusiasm for something: *a passion for poetry.* **3.** any strongly felt emotion, such as love, hate, or envy. **4.** the object of an intense desire or enthusiasm: *jazz is his passion.* —ˈ**passionless** *adj.*

Passion (ˈpæʃən) *n.* the sufferings of Christ from the Last Supper to his death on the cross.

passionate (ˈpæʃənɪt) *adj.* **1.** showing intense sexual desire. **2.** capable of or revealing intense emotion: *a passionate plea.* —ˈ**passionately** *adv.*

passionflower (ˈpæʃən,flaʊə) *n.* a tropical plant with red, yellow, greenish, or purple showy flowers.

passion fruit *n.* the edible egg-shaped fruit of the passionflower.

Passion play *n.* a play about the Passion of Christ.

passive (ˈpæsɪv) *adj.* **1.** not active in an activity or organization. **2.** unresisting and receptive to outside forces; submissive. **3.** *Grammar.* denoting a form of verbs used to indicate that the subject is the recipient of the action, as *was broken* in *The glass was broken by a boy.* **4.** *Chem.* (of a substance) chemically unreactive. ~*n.* **5.** *Grammar.* the passive form of a verb. —ˈ**passively** *adv.* —**pasˈsivity** *n.*

passive resistance *n.* resistance to a government, authority, or the law by nonviolent acts such as fasting, peaceful demonstrations, or refusing to cooperate.

passive smoking *n.* the inhaling of smoke from other people's cigarettes by a nonsmoker.

passkey (ˈpɑːs,kiː) *n.* **1.** a private key; latchkey. **2.** same as **master key** or **skeleton key.**

pass law *n.* (in South Africa) a law restricting the movement of Black Africans.

pass off *vb.* **1.** to present (something or

oneself) under false pretences: *he passed the fake diamonds off as real.* **2.** to come to a gradual end; disappear: *eventually the pain passed off.* **3.** to take place: *the meeting passed off without disturbance.*

pass out *vb.* **1.** *Informal.* to become unconscious; faint. **2.** *Brit.* (of an officer cadet) to qualify for a military commission.

pass over *vb.* **1.** to take no notice of; disregard: *they passed me over in the last round of promotions.* **2.** not to discuss: *we shall pass over your former faults.*

Passover ('pɑːsˌəuvə) *n.* an eight-day Jewish festival commemorating the sparing of the Israelites in Egypt.

passport ('pɑːspɔːt) *n.* **1.** an official document issued by a government, identifying an individual and granting him permission to travel abroad. **2.** a quality or asset that gains a person admission or acceptance: *a good education is the passport to success.*

pass up *vb. Informal.* to let (something) go by; ignore: *I won't pass up this opportunity.*

password ('pɑːsˌwɜːd) *n.* a secret word or phrase that ensures admission by proving identity or membership.

past (pɑːst) *adj.* **1.** no longer in existence: *past happiness.* **2.** denoting the time that has elapsed at the present moment: *the past history of the world.* **3.** denoting a specific unit of time that immediately precedes the present one: *the past month.* **4.** denoting a person who has formerly held a position: *a past president.* **5.** *Grammar.* denoting a tense of verbs that is used in describing actions, events, or states that have been begun or completed at the time of utterance. ~*n.* **6. the past.** the period of time that has elapsed: *forget the past.* **7.** the history of a person or nation. **8.** an earlier disreputable period of a person's life: *a man with a past.* **9.** *Grammar.* **a.** the past tense. **b.** a verb in the past tense. ~*adv.* **10.** at a time before the present; ago: *three years past.* ~*prep.* **11.** beyond in time: *it's past midnight.* **12.** beyond in place or position: *the library is past the church.* **13.** beyond or above the reach, limit, or scope of: *his foolishness is past comprehension.* **14. not put it past someone.** to consider someone capable of (a particular action): *I wouldn't put it past her to cheat.* **15. past it.** *Informal.* unable to perform the tasks one could do when one was younger.

pasta ('pæstə) *n.* a type of food, such as spaghetti, that is made from a flour and water dough and formed into different shapes.

paste (peɪst) *n.* **1.** a soft mixture, such as toothpaste. **2.** an adhesive made from water and flour or starch, used for joining pieces of paper. **3.** a preparation of fish or meat that has been pounded to a creamy mass, for spreading on bread: *anchovy*

paste. **4.** dough for making pastry. **5.** a hard shiny glass used for making imitation gems. ~*vb.* **6.** to attach by or as if by using paste: *he pasted posters onto the wall.* **7.** *Slang.* to thrash or beat (someone); defeat.

pasteboard ('peɪstˌbɔːd) *n.* a stiff board formed from layers of paper pasted together.

pastel ('pæst²l) *n.* **1. a.** a crayon made of ground pigment bound with gum. **b.** a drawing done with such crayons. **2.** a pale delicate colour. ~*adj.* **3.** (of a colour) pale and delicate: *pastel blue.*

pastern ('pæstən) *n.* the part of a horse's foot between the fetlock and the hoof.

paste-up *n. Printing.* a sheet of paper or board on which are pasted artwork and proofs for photographing prior to making a plate.

pasteurize *or* **-ise** ('pɑːstjəˌraɪz) *vb.* to destroy bacteria (in beverages, such as milk or beer, or solid foods, such as cheese or crab meat) by a special heating process. —ˌpasteuri'zation *or*-i'sation *n.*

pastiche (pæ'stiːʃ) *n.* a work of art that mixes styles or copies the style of another artist.

pastille ('pæstɪl) *n.* a small fruit-flavoured and sometimes medicated sweet.

pastime ('pɑːsˌtaɪm) *n.* an activity or entertainment which makes time pass pleasantly.

past master *n.* a person with a talent for or experience in a particular activity: *a past master at chess.*

pastor ('pɑːstə) *n.* a clergyman in charge of a congregation.

pastoral ('pɑːstərəl) *adj.* **1.** of or depicting rural life or scenery. **2.** (of land) used for pasture. **3.** of or relating to a clergyman or his duties. **4.** of or relating to shepherds or their work. ~*n.* **5.** a literary work, picture, or piece of music portraying rural life. **6.** a letter from a bishop to the clergy or people of his diocese.

pastorale (ˌpæstə'rɑːl) *n., pl.* **-rales.** a musical composition that evokes rural life.

pastoralism ('pɑːstərəlˌɪzəm) *n.* a system of agriculture in dry grassland regions based on raising stock such as cattle, sheep, or goats. —'pastoralist *n.*

pastorate ('pɑːstərɪt) *n.* **1.** the office or term of office of a pastor. **2.** a group of pastors.

past participle *n.* a form of verb that is used to form compound past tenses and passive forms of the verb and to modify nouns: *given* is the past participle of *give.*

pastrami (pə'strɑːmɪ) *n.* highly seasoned smoked beef.

pastry ('peɪstrɪ) *n.* **1.** a dough of flour, water, and fat. **2.** baked foods, such as tarts, made with this dough. **3.** (*pl.* **-tries**) an individual cake or pie.

pasturage ('pɑːstʃərɪdʒ) n. **1.** the business of grazing cattle. **2.** same as **pasture**.

pasture ('pɑːstʃə) n. **1.** land covered with grass, suitable for grazing by farm animals. **2.** the grass growing on this land.

pasty[1] ('peɪstɪ) adj. **pastier, pastiest.** (of the complexion) pale and unhealthy-looking.

pasty[2] ('pæstɪ) n., pl. **pasties.** a round of pastry folded over a filling of meat and vegetables.

pat[1] (pæt) vb. **patting, patted. 1.** to hit (someone or something) lightly with the palm of one's hand. **2.** to shape or smooth (something) with a flat instrument or the palm of one's hand. **3. pat someone on the back.** Informal. to congratulate someone. ~n. **4.** a gentle tap or stroke. **5.** a small lump of something soft, such as butter. **6. pat on the back.** Informal. a gesture or word indicating approval.

pat[2] (pæt) adv. **1.** Also: **off pat.** exactly or fluently memorized: he had the answers off pat. **2. stand pat.** Chiefly U.S. & Canad. to stick firmly to a belief or decision. ~adj. **3.** exactly right; apt: a pat reply. **4.** too exactly fitting; glib: a pat answer to a difficult problem.

patch (pætʃ) n. **1.** a piece of material used to cover a hole in a garment or to make a sewn-on pocket. **2.** a small plot of land. **3.** Med. a protective covering for an injured eye. **4.** a small contrasting section: a patch of cloud in the blue sky. **5.** a scrap; remnant. **6.** the area patrolled by a particular policeman. **7. a bad patch.** a difficult time. **8. not a patch on.** not nearly as good as. ~vb. **9.** to mend (a garment) with a patch or patches. **10.** (foll. by together) to produce (something) by piecing parts together hurriedly or carelessly. **11.** (foll. by up) **a.** to mend (something) hurriedly or carelessly. **b.** to settle (a quarrel or differences).

patchwork ('pætʃˌwɜːk) n. **1.** needlework done by sewing pieces of different materials together. **2.** something made up of various parts.

patchy ('pætʃɪ) adj. **patchier, patchiest. 1.** irregular in quality, occurrence or intensity: a patchy essay. **2.** having or forming patches.

pate (peɪt) n. Old-fashioned or humorous. the head or the crown of the head.

pâté ('pæteɪ) n. a spread of finely minced meat, fish, or vegetables often served as a starter.

pâté de foie gras (də fwɑː grɑː) n. a smooth rich paste made from the liver of specially fattened geese.

patella (pə'tɛlə) n., pl. **-lae** (-liː). Anat. kneecap. —**pa'tellar** adj.

paten ('pæt²n) n. a plate, usually made of silver or gold, used for the bread at Communion.

patent ('peɪt²nt, 'pæt²nt) n. **1. a.** an official document granting an inventor or company the sole right to make, use, and sell an invention for a limited period. **b.** the right granted by such a document. **2.** an invention protected by a patent. ~adj. **3.** open or available for inspection: letters patent. **4.** ('peɪt²nt). obvious: their scorn was patent to everyone. **5.** concerning protection of or appointment by a patent. **6.** (of food, drugs, etc.) made or held under a patent. ~vb. **7.** to obtain a patent for (an invention).

patent leather ('peɪt²nt) n. leather processed with lacquer to give a hard glossy surface.

patently ('peɪt²ntlɪ) adv. obviously: he was patently bored.

patent medicine ('peɪt²nt) n. a medicine with a patent, available without a prescription.

Patent Office ('pæt²nt) n. a government department that issues patents.

pater ('peɪtə) n. Brit. slang. father.

paternal (pə'tɜːn²l) adj. **1.** of or like a father; fatherly: paternal love. **2.** related through one's father: his paternal grandfather. —**pa'ternally** adv.

paternalism (pə'tɜːnəˌlɪzəm) n. an attitude of a government or other authority that denies personal responsibility to the people for whom it is responsible. —**pa,ternal'istic** adj.

paternity (pə'tɜːnɪtɪ) n. **1.** the fact or state of being a father. **2.** descent or derivation from a father.

paternity suit n. legal proceedings, usually brought by an unmarried mother, in order to gain legal recognition that a particular man is the father of her child.

Paternoster (ˌpætə'nɒstə) n. R.C. Church. the Lord's Prayer.

path (pɑːθ) n., pl. **paths** (pɑːðz). **1.** a road or way, often a narrow trodden track. **2.** a surfaced walk, for example through a garden. **3.** the course or direction in which something moves: the path of a whirlwind. **4.** a course of conduct: the path of virtue.

pathetic (pə'θɛtɪk) adj. **1.** arousing pity or sympathy. **2.** distressingly inadequate or unsuccessful: the old man sat huddled before a pathetic fire; a pathetic attempt. —**pa'thetically** adv.

pathetic fallacy n. (in literature) the presentation of inanimate objects in nature as possessing human feelings.

pathogen ('pæθəˌdʒɛn) n. any agent, such as a bacterium, that can cause disease. —**ˌpatho'genic** adj.

pathological (ˌpæθə'lɒdʒɪk²l) adj. **1.** of or relating to pathology. **2.** Informal. compulsively motivated: a pathological liar.

pathology (pə'θɒlədʒɪ) n. the branch of

medicine concerned with the cause, origin, and nature of disease. —**pa'thologist** n.

pathos ('peɪθɒs) n. the quality or power, for example in literature or speech, of arousing feelings of pity or sorrow.

pathway ('pɑːθˌweɪ) n. a path.

patience ('peɪʃəns) n. 1. tolerant and even-tempered perseverance. 2. the capacity for calmly enduring pain or difficult situations, etc. 3. Brit. a card game for one player only.

patient ('peɪʃənt) adj. 1. enduring difficult situations with even temper. 2. persevering or diligent: a patient worker. ~n. 3. a person who is receiving medical care. —**'patiently** adv.

patina ('pætɪnə) n. 1. a film formed on the surface of a metal, such as the green oxidation of bronze or copper. 2. the sheen on a surface of something, such as an antique, caused by much handling.

patio ('pætɪˌəʊ) n., pl. **-tios**. 1. a paved area adjoining a house. 2. an open inner courtyard in a Spanish or Spanish-American house.

patisserie (pə'tiːsərɪ) n. 1. a shop where fancy pastries are sold. 2. such pastries.

patois ('pætwɑː) n., pl. **patois** ('pætwɑːz). 1. a regional dialect of a language, usually considered substandard. 2. the jargon of a particular group.

patrial ('peɪtrɪəl) n. (in Britain, formerly) a person with a right by statute to live in the United Kingdom, and so not subject to immigration control.

patriarch ('peɪtrɪˌɑːk) n. 1. the male head of a tribe or family. 2. Bible. any of the men regarded as the fathers of the human race or of the Hebrew people. 3. a. R.C. Church. the pope. b. Eastern Orthodox Church. a highest-ranking bishop. 3. a venerable old man. —**ˌpatri'archal** adj.

patriarchate ('peɪtrɪˌɑːkɪt) n. the office, jurisdiction or residence of a patriarch.

patriarchy ('peɪtrɪˌɑːkɪ) n. 1. a form of social organization in which a male is the head of the family and descent, kinship, and title are traced through the male line. 2. (pl. **-chies**) a society governed by such a system.

patrician (pə'trɪʃən) n. 1. a member of the nobility of ancient Rome. 2. an aristocrat. 3. a person of refined conduct and tastes. ~adj. 4. (in ancient Rome) of or relating to patricians. 5. aristocratic.

patricide ('pætrɪˌsaɪd) n. 1. a person who kills his father. 2. the act of killing one's father. —**ˌpatri'cidal** adj.

patrimony ('pætrɪmənɪ) n., pl. **-nies**. an inheritance from one's father or other ancestor.

patriot ('peɪtrɪət, 'pæt-) n. a person who vigorously supports his country and its way

of life. —**ˌpatri'otic** adj. —**ˌpatri'otical-ly** adv. —**'patriot,ism** n.

patrol (pə'trəʊl) n. 1. the action of going round an area or building at regular intervals for purposes of security or observation. 2. a person or group that carries out such an action. 3. a group of soldiers or ships involved in patrolling a particular area. 4. a division of a troop of Scouts or Guides. ~vb. **-trolling**, **-trolled**. 5. to engage in a patrol of (a place).

patrol car n. a police car used for patrolling streets.

patron ('peɪtrən) n. 1. a person who financially supports artists, writers, musicians, or charities; protector or benefactor. 2. a regular customer of a shop, hotel, etc.

patronage ('pætrənɪdʒ) n. 1. the support or custom given by a patron. 2. (in politics) the practice of making appointments to office. 3. a condescending manner.

patronize or **-ise** ('pætrəˌnaɪz) vb. 1. to treat (someone) in a condescending way. 2. to act as a patron by supporting (an artist, etc.) or bringing trade to (a shop, etc.). —**'patron,izing** or **-,ising** adj. —**'patron-,izingly** or **-,isingly** adv.

patron saint n. a saint regarded as the particular guardian of a country or a group of people.

patronymic (ˌpætrə'nɪmɪk) n. a name derived from one's father's or a male ancestor's name.

patter¹ ('pætə) vb. 1. to walk with quick soft steps. 2. to make a quick succession of light tapping sounds. ~n. 3. a quick succession of light tapping sounds, as of feet: the patter of mice.

patter² ('pætə) n. 1. the glib rapid speech of comedians or salesmen. 2. quick idle talk; chatter. 3. the jargon of a particular group. ~vb. 4. to speak glibly and rapidly.

pattern ('pæt²n) n. 1. an arrangement of repeated or corresponding parts or decorative motifs. 2. a plan or diagram used in making something: a paper pattern for a dress. 3. a model worthy of imitation: a pattern of kindness. 4. a representative sample. ~vb. 5. (foll. by after or on) to model: his behaviour is patterned on his father's.

patty ('pætɪ) n., pl. **-ties**. a small meat pie.

paua ('pɑːʊə) n. an edible shellfish of New Zealand, which has an iridescent shell used for jewellery.

paucity ('pɔːsɪtɪ) n. smallness of amount or number.

paunch (pɔːntʃ) n. a protruding belly or abdomen. —**'paunchy** adj.

pauper ('pɔːpə) n. 1. a person who is extremely poor. 2. (formerly) a person supported by public charity.

pause (pɔːz) vb. 1. to cease an action temporarily. **2.** to hesitate: *she replied without pausing.* ~*n.* **3.** a temporary stop or rest in speech or action. **4.** *Music.* a continuation of a note or rest beyond its normal length. **5. give someone pause.** to cause someone to hesitate.

pavane *or* **pavan** (pəˈvæn) *n.* **1.** a slow and stately dance of the 16th and 17th centuries. **2.** music for this dance.

pave (peɪv) *vb.* **1.** to cover (a road or area of ground) with a firm surface suitable for travelling on, for example with paving stones or concrete. **2. pave the way for.** to prepare or make easier: *to pave the way for future development.*

pavement (ˈpeɪvmənt) *n.* **1.** a hard-surfaced path for pedestrians, alongside and a little higher than a road. **2.** the material used in paving. **3.** *U.S.* the surface of a road.

pavilion (pəˈvɪljən) *n.* **1.** *Brit.* a building at a sports ground, esp. a cricket pitch, in which players can wash and change. **2.** a summerhouse or other decorative shelter. **3.** an open building or temporary structure used for exhibitions. **4.** a large ornate tent.

paving (ˈpeɪvɪŋ) *n.* **1.** a paved surface; pavement. **2.** material used for a pavement.

pavlova (pævˈləʊvə) *n.* a meringue cake topped with whipped cream and fruit.

paw (pɔː) *n.* **1.** any of the feet of a four-legged mammal, bearing claws or nails. **2.** *Informal.* a hand. ~*vb.* **3.** to scrape or hit with the paws. **4.** *Informal.* to touch or caress (someone) in a clumsy, rough, or overfamiliar manner.

pawl (pɔːl) *n.* a pivoted lever shaped to engage with a ratchet wheel to prevent motion in a particular direction.

pawn¹ (pɔːn) *vb.* **1.** to deposit (an article) as security for the repayment of a loan from a pawnbroker. **2.** to stake: *to pawn one's honour.* ~*n.* **3.** an article deposited as security. **4.** the condition of being so deposited: *in pawn.*

pawn² (pɔːn) *n.* **1.** a chess man of the lowest value. **2.** a person manipulated by another.

pawnbroker (ˈpɔːnˌbrəʊkə) *n.* a dealer licensed to lend money at interest on the security of personal property, which can be sold if the loan is not repaid within a specified period. —ˈpawnˌbroking *n.*

pawnshop (ˈpɔːnˌʃɒp) *n.* the premises of a pawnbroker.

pawpaw (ˈpɔːˌpɔː) *n.* same as **papaya.**

pax (pæks) *n.* **1.** *Chiefly R.C. Church.* the kiss of peace. ~*interj.* **2.** *Brit. school slang.* a call signalling a desire to end hostilities.

pay (peɪ) *vb.* **paying, paid. 1.** to settle (a debt or obligation) by giving or doing something: *he paid his creditors.* **2.** to give

(money) to (a person) in return for goods or services: *they pay their workers well.* **3.** to profit or benefit (a person): *it pays one to be honest.* **4.** to give (a compliment, regards, attention, etc.). **5.** to make (a visit or call). **6.** to give compensation or make amends: *she paid dearly for her mistake.* **7.** to yield a return of: *the shares pay 15 per cent.* **8. pay one's way. a.** to contribute one's share of expenses. **b.** to remain solvent without outside help. ~*n.* **9.** money given in return for work or services; a salary or wage. **10. in the pay of.** employed by. ~See also **pay back, pay for,** etc.

payable (ˈpeɪəbᵊl) *adj.* **1.** (often foll. by *on*) to be paid: *payable on the third of each month.* **2.** that is capable of being paid.

pay back *vb.* **1.** to retaliate against: *to pay someone back for an insult.* **2.** to repay (a loan).

pay bed *n.* a bed in a hospital used by a patient who is paying for treatment.

PAYE (in Britain and New Zealand) pay as you earn; a system by which income tax is paid by employers directly to the government.

payee (peɪˈiː) *n.* the person to whom a cheque, money order, etc., is made out.

pay for *vb.* **1.** to make payment for. **2.** to suffer or be punished, as for a mistake.

paying guest *n. Euphemistic.* a lodger.

payload (ˈpeɪˌləʊd) *n.* **1.** that part of a cargo earning revenue. **2.** the passengers, cargo, or bombs carried by an aircraft. **3.** the explosive power of a warhead, bomb, etc., carried by a missile or aircraft.

paymaster (ˈpeɪˌmɑːstə) *n.* an official responsible for the payment of wages and salaries.

payment (ˈpeɪmənt) *n.* **1.** the act of paying. **2.** a sum of money paid. **3.** something given in return; punishment or reward.

pay off *vb.* **1.** to pay (a person) all that is due in wages and dismiss them from employment. **2.** to pay the complete amount of (a debt). **3.** to turn out to be effective: *the gamble paid off.* **4.** *Informal.* to give a bribe to. ~*n.* **payoff. 5.** the final settlement, esp. in retribution. **6.** *Informal.* the climax, consequence, or outcome of events, a story, etc. **7.** the final payment of a debt. **8.** *Informal.* a bribe.

payola (peɪˈəʊlə) *n. Informal.* a bribe given to secure special treatment, esp. to a disc jockey to promote a commercial product.

pay out *vb.* **1.** to spend (money) on a particular thing. **2.** to release (a rope) gradually, hand over hand.

payphone (ˈpeɪˌfəʊn) *n.* a coin-operated telephone.

payroll (ˈpeɪˌrəʊl) *n.* a list of employees, specifying the salary or wage of each.

payslip (ˈpeɪˌslɪp) *n.* a note given to an

employee each week or month stating how much money he has earned and how much tax, national insurance, etc., has been deducted.

pay up *vb.* to pay (money) promptly, in full, or on demand.

Pb *Chem.* lead.

pc 1. per cent. **2.** postcard.

PC 1. (in Britain) Police Constable. **2.** (in Britain) Privy Council(lor). **3.** (in Canada) Progressive Conservative.

pd paid.

Pd *Chem.* palladium.

PDSA (in Britain) People's Dispensary for Sick Animals.

PDT (in the U.S. and Canada) Pacific Daylight Time.

PE physical education.

pea (piː) *n.* **1.** an annual climbing plant with green pods containing green seeds. **2.** the seed of this plant, eaten as a vegetable.

peace (piːs) *n.* **1.** the state existing during the absence of war. **2.** a treaty marking the end of a war. **3.** a state of harmony between people or groups. **4.** law and order within a state: *a breach of the peace.* **5.** absence of mental anxiety: *peace of mind.* **6.** a state of stillness, silence, or serenity. **7. at peace. a.** dead: *the old lady is at peace now.* **b.** in a state of harmony, friendship, or serenity. **8. hold** *or* **keep one's peace.** to keep silent. **9. keep the peace.** to maintain law and order.

peaceable ('piːsəbᵊl) *adj.* **1.** inclined towards peace. **2.** tranquil; calm.

peaceful ('piːsful) *adj.* **1.** not in a state of war or disagreement. **2.** calm; tranquil. —'**peacefully** *adv.*

peacemaker ('piːs,meɪkə) *n.* a person who establishes peace, esp. between others.

peace offering *n.* something given in order to maintain or bring about peace: *I bought Mum some flowers as a peace offering.*

peace pipe *n.* a long decorated pipe smoked by North American Indians, esp. as a token of peace.

peacetime ('piːs,taɪm) *n.* a period without war; time of peace.

peach (piːtʃ) *n.* **1.** a soft juicy fruit with a downy reddish-yellow skin, yellowish-orange sweet flesh, and a single stone which grows on a small tree. **2.** *Informal.* a person or thing that is especially pleasing: *that was a peach of a shot!* ~*adj.* **3.** pinkish-yellow to orange.

peach melba *n.* a dessert made of halved peaches, vanilla ice cream, and raspberries.

peachy ('piːtʃɪ) *adj.* **peachier, peachiest.** of or like a peach, esp. in colour or texture.

peacock ('piː,kɒk) *n., pl.* **-cocks** *or* **-cock.** **1.** a large bird of the pheasant family, the male of which has a crested head and a very large fanlike tail with blue and green eyelike spots. **2.** a vain strutting person. —'**pea,hen** *fem. n.*

pea-green *adj.* yellowish-green.

peak (piːk) *n.* **1.** a pointed end, edge, or projection: *the peak of a roof.* **2.** the pointed summit of a mountain. **3.** a mountain with a pointed summit. **4.** the point of greatest development, strength, etc.: *the peak of his career.* **5.** a projecting piece on the front of some caps. ~*vb.* **6.** to form or reach or cause to form or reach a peak. ~*adj.* **7.** of or relating to a period of greatest use or demand: *peak viewing hours.*

peaked (piːkt) *adj.* having a peak; pointed.

peak load *n.* the maximum load on an electrical power-supply system.

peaky ('piːkɪ) *adj.* **peakier, peakiest.** pale and sickly.

peal (piːl) *n.* **1.** a long loud echoing sound, as of bells, thunder, or laughter. ~*vb.* **2.** to sound with a peal or peals.

peanut ('piː,nʌt) *n.* a leguminous plant with edible nutlike seeds used for food and as a source of oil. See also **peanuts.**

peanut butter *n.* a brownish oily paste made from peanuts.

peanuts ('piː,nʌts) *n. Slang.* a trifling amount of money.

pear (pɛə) *n.* a sweet juicy fruit with a narrow top and a rounded base that grows on a tree of the rose family.

pearl (pɜːl) *n.* **1.** a hard smooth greyish-white rounded structure occurring on the inner surface of the shell of a clam or oyster; much valued as a gem. **2.** See **mother-of-pearl. 3.** a person or thing that is like a pearl, esp. in beauty or value. ~*adj.* **4.** of, made of, or set with pearl or mother-of-pearl. **5.** having the shape or colour of a pearl. ~*vb.* **6.** to set with or as if with pearls. **7.** to shape into or assume a pearl-like form or colour. **8.** to dive for pearls.

pearl barley *n.* barley ground into small round grains, used esp. in soups and stews.

pearly ('pɜːlɪ) *adj.* **pearlier, pearliest. 1.** resembling a pearl, esp. in lustre. **2.** decorated with pearls or mother-of-pearl.

Pearly Gates *pl. n. Informal.* the entrance to heaven.

pearly king *or* (*fem.*) **pearly queen** *n.* the London costermonger whose ceremonial clothes display the most lavish collection of pearl buttons.

peasant ('pɛzᵊnt) *n.* **1.** a member of a class of low social status that depends on agricultural labour as a means of subsistence. **2.** *Informal.* an uncouth or uncultured person.

peasantry ('pɛzᵊntrɪ) *n.* peasants as a class.

pease (piːz) *n., pl.* **pease.** *Archaic or dialect.* same as **pea.**

pease pudding *n.* (esp. in Britain) a dish

of split peas that have been soaked and boiled.

peasouper (ˌpiːˈsuːpə) *n.* **1.** *Informal, chiefly Brit.* dense dirty yellowish fog. **2.** *Canad. slang.* a French Canadian.

peat (piːt) *n.* a compact brownish deposit of partially decomposed vegetable matter found in uplands and bogs and used as a fuel (when dried) and as a fertilizer.

pebble (ˈpɛb³l) *n.* **1.** a small smooth rounded stone, esp. one worn by the action of water. ~*vb.* **2.** to cover with pebbles. —ˈ**pebbly** *adj.*

pebble dash *n. Brit.* a finish for external walls consisting of small stones embedded in plaster.

pecan (pɪˈkæn, ˈpiːkən) *n.* a smooth oval nut with a sweet oily kernel that grows on hickory trees in the Southern U.S.

peccadillo (ˌpɛkəˈdɪləʊ) *n., pl.* -los *or* -loes. a petty sin or fault.

peccary (ˈpɛkərɪ) *n., pl.* -ries *or* -ry. a piglike mammal of forests of southern North America, Central and South America.

peck¹ (pɛk) *vb.* **1.** to strike with the beak or with a pointed instrument. **2.** to dig (a hole, etc.) by pecking. **3.** (of birds) to pick up (corn, worms, etc.) by pecking. **4.** *Informal.* to kiss (a person) quickly and lightly. **5. peck at.** to eat slowly and reluctantly: *peck at food.* ~*n.* **6.** a quick light blow, esp. from a bird's beak. **7.** a mark made by such a blow. **8.** *Informal.* a quick light kiss.

peck² (pɛk) *n.* **1.** a unit of dry measure equal to 8 quarts or one quarter of a bushel. **2.** a large quantity or number.

pecker (ˈpɛkə) *n.* **keep one's pecker up.** *Brit. slang.* to remain cheerful.

peckish (ˈpɛkɪʃ) *adj. Informal, chiefly Brit.* feeling slightly hungry.

pectin (ˈpɛktɪn) *n. Biochem.* a water-soluble carbohydrate that occurs in ripe fruit: used in the manufacture of jams because of its ability to gel.

pectoral (ˈpɛktərəl) *adj.* **1.** of or relating to the chest, breast, or thorax: *pectoral fins.* **2.** worn on the breast or chest: *a pectoral medallion.* ~*n.* **3.** a pectoral organ or part, esp. a muscle or fin.

pectoral fin *n.* a fin, just behind the head in fishes, that helps to control the direction of movement.

peculate (ˈpɛkjʊˌleɪt) *vb.* to embezzle (public money). —ˌ**pecuˈlation** *n.*

peculiar (pɪˈkjuːlɪə) *adj.* **1.** strange or unusual; odd: *a peculiar idea.* **2.** distinct from others; special. **3.** (foll. by *to*) belonging characteristically or exclusively (to): *peculiar to North America.*

peculiarity (pɪˌkjuːlɪˈærɪtɪ) *n., pl.* -ties. **1.** a strange or unusual habit or characteristic. **2.** a distinguishing trait, etc., that is characteristic of a particular person; idiosyncrasy. **3.** the state or quality of being peculiar.

pecuniary (pɪˈkjuːnɪərɪ) *adj.* **1.** of or relating to money. **2.** *Law.* (of an offence) involving a monetary penalty.

pedagogue *or U.S.* (*sometimes*) **pedagog** (ˈpɛdəˌgɒg) *n.* a teacher, esp. a pedantic one. —ˌ**pedaˈgogic** *adj.*

pedagogy (ˈpɛdəˌgɒdʒɪ) *n.* the principles, practice, or profession of teaching.

pedal¹ (ˈpɛd³l) *n.* **1.** any foot-operated lever, esp. one of the two levers that drive the chainwheel of a bicycle, the foot brake, clutch control, or accelerator of a car, or one of the levers on an organ or piano. ~*vb.* -alling, -alled *or U.S.* -aling, -aled. **2.** to propel (a bicycle, etc.) by operating the pedals. **3.** to operate the pedals of an organ, piano, etc.

pedal² (ˈpiːd³l) *adj.* of the foot or feet.

pedant (ˈpɛd³nt) *n.* a person who relies too much on academic learning or who is concerned chiefly with insignificant detail. —**pedantic** (pɪˈdæntɪk) *adj.* —pe'**dantical**-ly *adv.*

pedantry (ˈpɛd³ntrɪ) *n., pl.* -ries. the habit or an instance of being a pedant, esp. in the minute observance of petty rules or details.

peddle (ˈpɛd³l) *vb.* **1.** to go from place to place selling (goods, esp. small articles). **2.** to sell (illegal drugs, esp. narcotics). **3.** to advocate (an idea or information) persistently: *to peddle a new philosophy.*

pederasty *or* **paederasty** (ˈpɛdəˌræstɪ) *n.* homosexual relations between men and boys. —ˈ**peder,ast** *or* ˈ**paeder,ast** *n.*

pedestal (ˈpɛdɪst³l) *n.* **1.** a base that supports something, such as a statue. **2. put someone on a pedestal.** to admire someone very much.

pedestrian (pɪˈdɛstrɪən) *n.* **1.** a person travelling on foot; walker. ~*adj.* **2.** dull; commonplace: *a pedestrian style.*

pedestrian crossing *n. Brit.* a path across a road marked as a crossing for pedestrians.

pedestrianize *or* -ise (pɪˈdɛstrɪəˌnaɪz) *vb.* to convert (a street or shopping area) into an area for the use of pedestrians only.

pedicure (ˈpɛdɪˌkjʊə) *n.* treatment of the feet, either by a medical expert or a beautician.

pedigree (ˈpɛdɪˌgriː) *n.* **1.** the line of descent of a purebred animal. **2.** a document recording this. **3.** a genealogical table, esp. one indicating pure ancestry.

pediment (ˈpɛdɪmənt) *n.* a low-pitched gable, esp. one that is triangular as used in classical architecture.

pedlar *or esp. U.S.* **peddler** (ˈpɛdlə) *n.* a person who peddles; hawker.

pedometer (pɪˈdɒmɪtə) *n.* a device that records the number of steps taken in walking and hence the distance travelled.

peduncle (pɪˈdʌŋk³l) *n.* **1.** the stalk of a plant bearing a flower cluster or solitary flower. **2.** *Anat., pathol.* any stalklike structure. —**peduncular** (pɪˈdʌŋkjʊlə) *adj.*

pee (piː) *Informal.* ~*vb.* **peeing,.peed. 1.** to urinate. ~*n.* **2.** urine. **3.** the act of urinating.

peek (piːk) *vb.* **1.** to glance quickly or furtively. ~*n.* **2.** such a glance.

peel (piːl) *vb.* **1.** to remove (the skin or rind) of (a fruit or vegetable). **2.** (of a surface) to lose its outer covering of paint, etc. **3.** (of a person or part of the body) to shed skin in flakes or (of skin) to be shed in flakes, esp. as a result of sunburn. ~*n.* **4.** the skin or rind of a fruit, etc.

peeling (ˈpiːlɪŋ) *n.* a strip of skin, rind, bark, etc., that has been peeled off: *a potato peeling.*

peel off *vb.* **1.** to remove or be removed by peeling: *I peeled some moss off the wood.* **2.** *Slang.* to undress.

peen (piːn) *n.* the end of a hammer head opposite the striking face, often rounded or wedge-shaped.

peep¹ (piːp) *vb.* **1.** to look furtively or secretly, as through a small opening or from a hidden place. **2.** to appear partially or briefly: *the sun peeped through the clouds.* ~*n.* **3.** a quick or furtive look. **4.** the first appearance: *the peep of dawn.*

peep² (piːp) *vb.* **1.** (esp. of young birds) to utter shrill small noises. ~*n.* **2.** a peeping sound.

Peeping Tom *n.* a man who furtively observes women undressing.

peepshow (ˈpiːpˌʃəʊ) *n.* a box containing a series of pictures that can be seen through a small hole.

peer¹ (pɪə) *n.* **1.** a member of a nobility. **2.** a person who holds any of the five grades of the British nobility: duke, marquess, earl, viscount, and baron. **3.** an equal in social standing, rank, age, etc.: *to be tried by one's peers.*

peer² (pɪə) *vb.* **1.** to look intently or as if with difficulty: *to peer into the distance.* **2.** to appear dimly: *the sun peered through the fog.*

peerage (ˈpɪərɪdʒ) *n.* **1.** the whole body of peers; aristocracy. **2.** the position, rank, or title of a peer.

peeress (ˈpɪərɪs) *n.* **1.** the wife or widow of a peer. **2.** a woman holding the rank of a peer in her own right.

peer group *n.* a social group composed of individuals of approximately the same age.

peerless (ˈpɪəlɪs) *adj.* having no equals; matchless.

peeve (piːv) *Informal.* ~*vb.* **1.** to irritate, annoy. ~*n.* **2.** something that irritates; vexation. —**peeved** *adj.*

peevish (ˈpiːvɪʃ) *adj.* fretful or irritable. —**peevishly** *adv.*

peewit *or* **pewit** (ˈpiːwɪt) *n.* same as **lapwing.**

peg (pɛg) *n.* **1.** a small cylindrical pin or bolt used to join two parts together. **2.** a pin driven into a surface: used to mark scores, define limits, support coats, etc. **3.** *Music.* any of several pins on a stringed instrument which can be turned so as to tune strings wound around them. **4.** Also called: **clothes peg.** *Brit.* a split or hinged pin for fastening wet clothes to a line to dry. **5.** *Brit.* a small drink of spirits. **6.** an opportunity or pretext for doing something: *a peg on which to hang a theory.* **7. bring** *or* **take (someone) down a peg.** to lower the pride of (someone). **8. off the peg.** *Chiefly Brit.* (of clothes) ready-to-wear, as opposed to tailor-made. ~*vb.* **pegging, pegged. 9.** to insert a peg into. **10.** to secure with pegs: *to peg a tent.* **11.** to mark (a score) with pegs, as in some card games. **12.** *Chiefly Brit.* to work steadily: *he pegged away at his job for years.* **13.** to stabilize something, such as the price of a commodity, at a fixed level.

pegboard (ˈpɛgˌbɔːd) *n.* **1.** a board with holes into which small pegs can be fitted, used for playing certain games or keeping a score. **2.** hardboard with a row of holes in which articles may be hung, as for display.

peg leg *n. Informal.* **1.** an artificial leg. **2.** a person with an artificial leg.

peg out *vb.* **1.** *Informal.* to collapse or die. **2.** to mark or secure with pegs: *to peg out one's claims to a piece of land.*

PEI Prince Edward Island.

peignoir (ˈpeɪnwɑː) *n.* a woman's dressing gown.

pejorative (pɪˈdʒɒrətɪv, ˈpiːdʒər-) *adj.* **1.** (of a word or expression) having an unpleasant or disparaging sense. ~*n.* **2.** a pejorative word or expression.

peke (piːk) *n. Informal.* a Pekingese dog.

Pekingese (ˌpiːkɪŋˈiːz) *or* **Pekinese** (ˌpiːkəˈniːz) *n.* **1.** (*pl.* **-ese**) a small dog with a long straight coat, curled plumed tail, and short wrinkled muzzle. **2.** the dialect of Mandarin Chinese spoken in Peking. **3.** (*pl.* **-ese**) a person from Peking, in NE China. ~*adj.* **4.** of Peking or its people.

pelargonium (ˌpɛləˈgəʊnɪəm) *n.* a plant with circular or lobed leaves and red, pink, or white aromatic flowers: includes many cultivated geraniums.

pelf (pɛlf) *n. Contemptuous.* money or wealth.

pelican (ˈpɛlɪkən) *n.* a large water bird with a long straight flattened bill and a pouch for holding fish.

pelican crossing *n.* a type of road crossing with a pedestrian-operated traffic-light system.

pelisse (pɛˈliːs) *n.* a usually fur-trimmed cloak or loose coat.

pellagra (pəˈleɪgrə, -ˈlæ-) *n. Pathol.* a disease caused by a diet lacking a vitamin of the B complex, characterized by scaling of the skin, diarrhoea and mental disorder.

pellet ('pɛlɪt) *n.* **1.** a small round ball, esp. of compressed matter. **2. a.** an imitation bullet used in toy guns. **b.** a piece of small shot. **3.** a small pill.

pell-mell ('pɛl'mɛl) *adv.* **1.** in a confused headlong rush: *the hounds ran pell-mell into the yard.* **2.** in a disorderly manner: *the things were piled pell-mell in the room.*

pellucid (pɛ'luːsɪd) *adj.* **1.** transparent or translucent. **2.** extremely clear in style and meaning.

pelmet ('pɛlmɪt) *n.* a board or piece of fabric fixed above a window to conceal the curtain rail.

pelota (pə'lotə) *n.* a game played by two players who use a basket strapped to their wrists or a wooden racket to propel a ball against a specially marked wall.

pelt¹ (pɛlt) *vb.* **1.** to throw (missiles) at (someone or something). **2.** (foll. by *along,* etc.) to hurry. **3.** to rain heavily. ~*n.* **4.** a blow. **5. at full pelt.** very quickly: *she ran down the street at full pelt.*

pelt² (pɛlt) *n.* **1.** the skin of a fur-bearing animal, esp. when it has been removed from the carcass. **2.** the hide of an animal, stripped of hair.

pelvis ('pɛlvɪs) *n.* **1.** the large funnel-shaped structure at the lower end of the trunk of most vertebrates. **2.** the bones that form this structure. —**'pelvic** *adj.*

pen¹ (pɛn) *n.* **1.** an implement for writing or drawing using ink, with a metal nib attached to a holder. See also **ballpoint, fountain pen. 2. the pen.** writing as an occupation. ~*vb.* **penning, penned. 3.** to write or compose (a letter).

pen² (pɛn) *n.* **1.** an enclosure in which domestic animals are kept. **2.** any place of confinement. ~*vb.* **penning, penned** *or* **pent. 3.** to enclose (animals) in a pen.

pen³ (pɛn) *n. U.S. & Canad. informal.* short for **penitentiary** (sense 1).

pen⁴ (pɛn) *n.* a female swan.

Pen. Peninsula.

penal ('piːnºl) *adj.* **1.** of or relating to punishment. **2.** used or designated as a place of punishment: *a penal institution.* —**'penally** *adv.*

penal code *n.* the body of the laws that relate to crime and its punishment.

penalize *or* **-ise** ('piːnə,laɪz) *vb.* **1.** to impose a penalty on (someone), as for breaking a law or rule. **2.** to inflict a disadvantage on: *why should I be penalized just because I'm a woman?* —**,penali'zation** *or* **-i'sation** *n.*

penalty ('pɛnºltɪ) *n., pl.* **-ties. 1.** a legal punishment, such as a term of imprisonment or a fine. **2.** loss, suffering, or other unfortunate result of one's own action, error, etc: *I made a wrong decision and I had*

to pay the penalty. **3.** *Sport, games, etc.* a handicap awarded against a player or team for illegal play, such as a free shot at goal by the opposing team.

penalty box *n.* Also called: **penalty area.** *Soccer.* a rectangular area in front of the goal, within which a penalty is awarded for a foul by the defending team. **2.** *Ice hockey.* a bench for players serving time penalties.

penance ('pɛnəns) *n.* **1.** voluntary self-punishment to make amends for a sin. **2.** *R.C. Church.* a sacrament in which repentant sinners are absolved on condition of confession of their sins to a priest and of performing a penance.

pence (pɛns) *n.* a plural of **penny.**

penchant ('pɒnʃɒn) *n.* strong inclination or liking; bent or taste.

pencil ('pɛnsºl) *n.* **1.** a thin cylindrical instrument used for writing or drawing, consisting of a rod of graphite encased in wood and sharpened. ~*vb.* **-cilling, -cilled** *or U.S.* **-ciling, -ciled. 2.** to draw, colour, write, or mark with a pencil.

pendant ('pɛndənt) *n.* **a.** an ornament that hangs from a piece of jewellery. **b.** a necklace with such an ornament.

pendent ('pɛndənt) *adj.* **1.** dangling. **2.** jutting.

pending ('pɛndɪŋ) *prep.* **1.** while waiting for. ~*adj.* **2.** not yet decided, confirmed, or finished. **3.** imminent: *these developments have been pending for some time.*

pendulous ('pɛndjʊləs) *adj.* hanging downwards, esp. so as to swing from side to side.

pendulum ('pɛndjʊləm) *n.* **1.** a body mounted so that it can swing freely under the influence of gravity. **2.** such a device used to regulate a clock mechanism.

penetrate ('pɛnɪ,treɪt) *vb.* **1.** to find or force a way into or through (something). **2.** to diffuse through (a substance, etc.); permeate. **3.** to see through: *their eyes could not penetrate the fog.* **4.** (of a man) to insert the penis into the vagina of (a woman). **5.** to grasp the meaning of (a principle, etc.). —**'penetrable** *adj.*

penetrating ('pɛnɪ,treɪtɪŋ) *adj.* tending to or able to penetrate: *a penetrating mind; a penetrating voice.*

penetration (,pɛnɪ'treɪʃən) *n.* **1.** the act or an instance of penetrating. **2.** the ability or power to penetrate. **3.** keen insight or perception.

pen friend *n.* a person with whom one exchanges letters, often a person in another country whom one has not met.

penguin ('pɛŋgwɪn) *n.* a flightless marine bird of cool southern, esp. Antarctic, regions with webbed feet and wings modified as flippers for swimming.

penicillin (,pɛnɪ'sɪlɪn) *n.* an antibiotic used to treat diseases caused by bacteria.

peninsula (pɪˈnɪnsjʊlə) n. a narrow strip of land projecting into a sea or lake from the mainland. —**penˈinsular** adj.

penis (ˈpiːnɪs) n., pl. **-nises** or **-nes** (-niːz). the male organ of copulation in higher vertebrates, also used for urinating in many mammals. —**penile** (ˈpiːnaɪl) adj.

penitent (ˈpɛnɪtənt) adj. **1.** feeling regret for one's sins; repentant. ~n. **2.** a person who is penitent. —**ˈpenitence** n.

penitential (ˌpɛnɪˈtɛnʃəl) adj. of, showing, or as a penance.

penitentiary (ˌpɛnɪˈtɛnʃərɪ) n., pl. **-ries**. **1.** (in the U.S. and Canada) a state or federal prison. ~adj. **2.** of or for penance. **3.** used for punishment and reformation: penitentiary measures.

penknife (ˈpɛnˌnaɪf) n., pl. **-knives**. a small knife with one or more blades that fold into the handle.

penmanship (ˈpɛnmənʃɪp) n. style or technique of writing by hand.

pen name n. a name used by a writer instead of his real name; nom de plume.

pennant (ˈpɛnənt) n. **1.** a long flag, esp. one flown from vessels as identification or for signalling. **2.** Chiefly U.S., Canad., & Austral. a flag serving as an emblem of championship in certain sports.

penniless (ˈpɛnɪlɪs) adj. very poor; almost totally without money.

pennon (ˈpɛnən) n. **1.** a long flag, often tapering and divided at the end, originally a knight's personal flag. **2.** a small tapering or triangular flag borne on a ship or boat.

penny (ˈpɛnɪ) n., pl. **pennies** or **pence** (pɛns). **1.** Brit. **a.** a bronze coin worth one hundredth of a pound. **b.** (before 1971) a bronze or copper coin worth one twelfth of a shilling. **2.** (pl. **pennies**). U.S. & Canad. a cent. **3.** Informal, chiefly Brit. the least amount of money: I don't have a penny. **4. a pretty penny.** Informal. a considerable sum of money. **5. spend a penny.** Brit. informal. to urinate. **6. the penny dropped.** Informal, chiefly Brit. the explanation of something was finally realized.

Penny Black n. the first adhesive postage stamp, issued in Britain in 1840.

penny-dreadful n., pl. **-fuls**. Brit. informal. a cheap, often lurid book or magazine.

penny-farthing n. Brit. an early type of bicycle with a large front wheel and a small rear wheel.

penny-pinching adj. **1.** excessively careful with money; miserly. ~n. **2.** miserliness. —**ˈpenny-ˌpincher** n.

pennyroyal (ˌpɛnɪˈrɔɪəl) n. a Eurasian plant with hairy leaves and small mauve flowers, yielding an aromatic oil used in medicine.

penny-wise adj. **penny-wise and pound-foolish.** careful or thrifty in small matters but wasteful in large ventures.

pennywort (ˈpɛnɪˌwɜːt) n. a Eurasian rock plant with whitish-green tubular flowers and rounded leaves.

pennyworth (ˈpɛnɪˌwɜːθ) n. **1.** the amount that can be bought for a penny. **2.** a small amount: he hasn't got a pennyworth of sense.

penology (piːˈnɒlədʒɪ) n. the study of the punishment of criminals and of prison management.

pen pal n. same as **pen friend**.

penpusher (ˈpɛnˌpʊʃə) n. a person whose work involves a lot of boring paperwork. —**ˈpenˌpushing** adj., n.

pension¹ (ˈpɛnʃən) n. **1.** a regular payment made by the state or a former employer to a person who has retired or to a widowed or disabled person. ~vb. **2.** to grant a pension to. —**ˈpensionable** adj. —**ˈpensioner** n.

pension² (ˈpɒnsjɒn) n. (in France and some other countries) a relatively cheap boarding house.

pension off vb. to cause (someone) to retire from a job and pay him a pension.

pensive (ˈpɛnsɪv) adj. deeply or seriously thoughtful, often with a tinge of sadness. —**ˈpensively** adv.

pent (pɛnt) vb. past of **pen²**.

penta- combining form. five: pentagon; pentameter.

pentacle (ˈpɛntək³l) n. same as **pentagram**.

pentagon (ˈpɛntəˌgɒn) n. a polygon having five sides. —**pentagonal** (pɛnˈtæɡən³l) adj.

Pentagon (ˈpɛntəˌgɒn) n. a five-sided building that houses the headquarters of the U.S. Department of Defense.

pentagram (ˈpɛntəˌɡræm) n. a star-shaped figure with five points.

pentameter (pɛnˈtæmɪtə) n. a line of poetry consisting of five metrical feet.

Pentateuch (ˈpɛntəˌtjuːk) n. the first five books of the Old Testament. —**ˌPentaˈteuchal** adj.

pentathlon (pɛnˈtæθlən) n. any of various athletic contests consisting of five different events. See also **modern pentathlon**.

pentatonic scale (ˌpɛntəˈtɒnɪk) n. Music. any of several scales consisting of five notes.

Pentecost (ˈpɛntɪˌkɒst) n. a Christian festival occurring on Whit Sunday commemorating the descent of the Holy Ghost on the apostles.

Pentecostal (ˌpɛntɪˈkɒst³l) adj. of or relating to any of various Christian groups that emphasize the charismatic aspects of Christianity and adopt a fundamental attitude to the Bible.

penthouse (ˈpɛntˌhaʊs) n. a luxurious flat or maisonette built onto the top floor or roof of a block of flats.

pent-up *adj.* not released; repressed: *pent-up emotions.*

penultimate (pɪˈnʌltɪmɪt) *adj.* next to the last.

penumbra (pɪˈnʌmbrə) *n., pl.* **-brae** (-briː) *or* **-bras.** **1.** a fringe region of half shadow resulting from the partial obstruction of light by an opaque object. **2.** *Astron.* the lighter and outer region of a sunspot. —**peˈnumbral** *adj.*

penurious (pɪˈnjʊərɪəs) *adj.* **1.** niggardly with money. **2.** lacking money or means.

penury (ˈpɛnjʊrɪ) *n.* **1.** extreme poverty. **2.** extreme scarcity.

peon (ˈpiːɒn) *n.* a Spanish-American farm labourer or unskilled worker.

peony (ˈpiːənɪ) *n., pl.* **-nies.** a garden plant with large pink, red, white, or yellow flowers.

people (ˈpiːpᵊl) *n.* (*usually functioning as pl.*) **1.** persons collectively or in general. **2.** a group of persons considered together: *blind people.* **3.** (*pl.* **peoples**) the persons living in a particular country: *the French people.* **4.** one's family: *he took her home to meet his people.* **5. the people. a.** the mass of persons without special distinction or privileges. **b.** the body of persons in a country who are entitled to vote. ~*vb.* **6.** to provide with or as if with people or inhabitants.
Usage. see **person.**

pep (pɛp) *n.* **1.** high spirits, energy, or vitality. **2. pep up.** to stimulate; invigorate: *to pep up a party.*

peplum (ˈpɛpləm) *n., pl.* **-lums** *or* **-la** (-lə) a flared ruffle attached to the waist of a garment.

pepper (ˈpɛpə) *n.* **1.** a sharp hot condiment obtained from the ground berry-like fruits of an East Indian climbing plant. **2.** Also called: **capsicum.** a tropical fruit used as a vegetable and a condiment, which can have either a mild or a pungent taste. ~*vb.* **3.** to season with pepper. **4.** to sprinkle liberally; dot: *his prose was peppered with alliteration.* **5.** to pelt with small missiles.

pepper-and-salt *adj.* **1.** (of a fabric) marked with a fine mixture of black and white. **2.** (of hair) streaked with grey.

peppercorn (ˈpɛpəˌkɔːn) *n.* the small dried berry of the pepper plant.

peppercorn rent *n.* a rent that is very low or nominal.

pepper mill *n.* a small hand mill used to grind peppercorns.

peppermint (ˈpɛpəˌmɪnt) *n.* **1.** a mint plant with purple or white flowers and downy leaves, which yield a pungent oil, used as a flavouring. **2.** a sweet flavoured with peppermint.

peppery (ˈpɛpərɪ) *adj.* **1.** flavoured with or tasting of pepper. **2.** quick-tempered; irritable.

pep pill *n. Informal.* a tablet containing a stimulant drug.

pepsin (ˈpɛpsɪn) *n.* an enzyme produced in the stomach, which, when activated by acid, breaks down proteins.

pep talk *n. Informal.* an enthusiastic talk designed to increase confidence, production, cooperation, etc.

peptic (ˈpɛptɪk) *adj.* **1.** of or aiding digestion. **2.** of or caused by pepsin or the action of the digestive juices: *a peptic ulcer.*

per (pɜː) *det.* **1.** for every: *three pence per pound.* ~*prep.* **2.** by; through. **3. as per.** according to: *as per specifications.* **4. as per usual** *or* **as per normal.** *Informal.* as usual.

peradventure (ˌpɛrədˈvɛntʃə, ˌpɜːr-) *Archaic.* ~*adv.* **1.** by chance; perhaps. ~*n.* **2.** chance or doubt.

perambulate (pəˈræmbjʊˌleɪt) *vb.* to walk about (a place). —**perˌambuˈlation** *n.*

perambulator (pəˈræmbjʊˌleɪtə) *n.* same as **pram.**

per annum (pər ˈænəm) *adv.* every year or by the year.

percale (pəˈkeɪl, -ˈkɑːl) *n.* a close-textured woven cotton fabric, used esp. for sheets.

per capita (pə ˈkæpɪtə) *adj., adv.* of or for each person: *what is the average wage per capita?*

perceive (pəˈsiːv) *vb.* **1.** to become aware of (something) through the senses; recognize or observe. **2.** to come to comprehend; grasp. —**perˈceivable** *adj.*

per cent (pə ˈsɛnt) *adv.* **1.** in or for every hundred. ~*n. also* **percent.** **2.** a percentage or proportion.

percentage (pəˈsɛntɪdʒ) *n.* **1.** proportion or rate per hundred parts. **2.** any proportion in relation to the whole: *a small percentage of the population.* **3.** *Informal.* profit or advantage.

percentile (pəˈsɛntaɪl) *n.* one of 99 actual or notional values of a variable dividing its distribution into 100 groups with equal frequencies.

perceptible (pəˈsɛptəbᵊl) *adj.* able to be perceived; noticeable or recognizable. —**perˌceptiˈbility** *n.*

perception (pəˈsɛpʃən) *n.* **1.** the act or the effect of perceiving. **2.** insight or intuition gained by perceiving. **3.** the ability or capacity to perceive. **4.** way of perceiving; view: *advertising affects the customer's perception of a product.* —**perceptual** (pəˈsɛptjʊəl) *adj.*

perceptive (pəˈsɛptɪv) *adj.* **1.** quick at perceiving; observant. **2.** able to perceive. —**perˈceptively** *adv.* —**ˌpercepˈtivity** *or* **perˈceptiveness** *n.*

perch[1] (pɜːtʃ) *n.* **1.** a pole, branch, or other resting place above ground on which a bird roosts. **2.** any raised resting place. **3.** same as **rod** (sense 5). ~*vb.* **4.** to alight, rest, or cause to rest on or as if on a perch: *the bird perched on the branch; the cap was perched on his head.*

perch² (pɜːtʃ) *n., pl.* **perch** or **perches**. a spiny-finned freshwater food fish of Europe and North America.

perchance (pəˈtʃɑːns) *adv. Archaic or poetic.* **1.** perhaps; possibly. **2.** by chance; accidentally.

percipient (pəˈsɪpɪənt) *adj.* quick at perceiving; observant. —**perˈcipience** *n.*

percolate (ˈpɜːkəˌleɪt) *vb.* **1.** to pass or ooze through (something) with very small holes in it: *rain percolated through the roof.* **2.** to spread gradually: *word percolated through to us.* **3.** to make (coffee) or (of coffee) to be made in a percolator. —**ˌpercoˈlation** *n.*

percolator (ˈpɜːkəˌleɪtə) *n.* a coffeepot in which boiling water is forced up through a tube and filters down through the coffee grounds into a container.

percussion (pəˈkʌʃən) *n.* **1.** the striking of one body against another, as the hammer of a firearm against a percussion cap. **2.** *Music.* percussion instruments collectively. —**perˈcussive** *adj.*

percussion cap *n.* a detonator consisting of a paper or thin metal cap containing material that explodes when struck.

percussion instrument *n.* a musical instrument, such as the drums, that produces a sound when struck directly, as with a stick or mallet.

percussionist (pəˈkʌʃənɪst) *n. Music.* a person who plays percussion instruments.

perdition (pəˈdɪʃən) *n.* **1.** *Christianity.* final and irrevocable spiritual ruin; damnation. **2.** same as **hell.**

peregrinate (ˈpɛrɪgrɪˌneɪt) *vb.* to travel or wander about from place to place. —**ˌperegriˈnation** *n.*

peregrine falcon *n.* a European falcon with dark plumage on the back and wings and lighter underparts.

peremptory (pəˈrɛmptərɪ) *adj.* **1.** urgent or commanding: *a peremptory ring on the bell.* **2.** not able to be remitted or debated; decisive. **3.** dogmatic.

perennial (pəˈrɛnɪəl) *adj.* **1.** lasting throughout the year or through many years. ~*n.* **2.** a plant that continues its growth for at least three years.

perestroika (ˌpɛrəˈstrɔɪkə) *n.* the policy of restructuring the Soviet economy and institutions under Gorbachov.

perfect *adj.* (ˈpɜːfɪkt). **1.** having all essential elements. **2.** unblemished; faultless: *a perfect gemstone.* **3.** correct or precise: *perfect timing.* **4.** utter or absolute: *a perfect stranger.* **5.** excellent in all respects: *a perfect day.* **6.** *Maths.* exactly divisible into equal integral or polynomial roots: *36 is a perfect square.* **7.** *Grammar.* denoting

a tense of verbs used in describing an action that has been completed. ~*n.* (ˈpɜːfɪkt). **8.** *Grammar.* the perfect tense. ~*vb.* (pəˈfɛkt). **9.** to improve to one's satisfaction: *he is in Paris to perfect his French.* **10.** to make fully accomplished. —**ˈperfectly** *adv.*

Usage. see **unique.**

perfectible (pəˈfɛktəbʔl) *adj.* capable of becoming or being made perfect. —**perˌfectiˈbility** *n.*

perfection (pəˈfɛkʃən) *n.* the act of perfecting or the state or quality of being perfect.

perfectionism (pəˈfɛkʃəˌnɪzəm) *n.* the demand for the highest standard of excellence. —**perˈfectionist** *n., adj.*

perfect pitch *n.* same as **absolute pitch.**

perfidious (pəˈfɪdɪəs) *adj.* treacherous or deceitful. —**ˈperfidy** *n.*

perforate (ˈpɜːfəˌreɪt) *vb.* **1.** to make a hole or holes in (something). **2.** to punch rows of holes between (stamps) for ease of separation. —**perforable** (ˈpɜːfərəbʔl) *adj.* —**ˈperfoˌrator** *n.*

perforation (ˌpɜːfəˈreɪʃən) *n.* **1.** a hole or holes made in something. **2.** any of a series of punched holes, as those between individual stamps.

perforce (pəˈfɔːs) *adv.* by necessity; unavoidably.

perform (pəˈfɔːm) *vb.* **1.** to carry out (an action). **2.** to fulfil: *to perform someone's request.* **3.** to present (a play or concert): *the group performed Hamlet.* —**perˈformable** *adj.* —**perˈformer** *n.*

performance (pəˈfɔːməns) *n.* **1.** the act, process, or art of performing. **2.** an artistic or dramatic production: *last night's performance was terrible.* **3.** manner or quality of functioning: *a machine's performance.* **4.** *Informal.* mode of conduct or behaviour, esp. when distasteful: *what did you mean by that performance at the restaurant?*

perfume *n.* (ˈpɜːfjuːm). **1.** a liquid cosmetic prepared from a mixture of alcohol and essential oils extracted from flowers or made synthetically, and worn for its pleasant smell. **2.** a fragrant smell. ~*vb.* (pəˈfjuːm). **3.** to impart a perfume to. —**ˈperfumed** *adj.*

perfumer (pəˈfjuːmə) *n.* a person who makes or sells perfume. —**perˈfumery** *n.*

perfunctory (pəˈfʌŋktərɪ) *adj.* done only as a matter of routine: *he gave his wife a perfunctory kiss.* —**perˈfunctorily** *adv.* —**perˈfunctoriness** *n.*

pergola (ˈpɜːgələ) *n.* a horizontal trellis or framework, supported on posts, that carries climbing plants.

perhaps (pəˈhæps) *adv.* possibly; maybe.

perianth (ˈpɛrɪˌænθ) *n.* the outer part of a flower.

pericardium (ˌpɛrɪˈkɑːdɪəm) *n., pl.* **-dia**

(-dɪə). the membranous sac enclosing the heart. —**peri'cardial** or **peri'cardi-ac** adj.

pericarp ('pɛrɪˌkɑːp) n. the part of a fruit enclosing the seed that develops from the wall of the ovary.

perigee ('pɛrɪˌdʒiː) n. the point in its orbit when the moon or a satellite is nearest the earth.

perihelion (ˌpɛrɪ'hiːlɪən) n., pl. -lia (-lɪə). the point in its orbit when a planet or comet is nearest the sun.

peril ('pɛrɪl) n. exposure to risk or harm; danger or jeopardy. —**'perilous** adj.

perimeter (pə'rɪmɪtə) n. 1. Maths. a. the curve or line enclosing a plane area. b. the length of this curve or line. 2. any boundary around something.

perinatal (ˌpɛrɪ'neɪtˀl) adj. of or occurring in the period from about three months before to one month after birth.

perineum (ˌpɛrɪ'niːəm) n., pl. -nea (-'niːə). the region of the body between the anus and the genitals. —**peri'neal** adj.

period ('pɪərɪəd) n. 1. a portion of time of indefinable length: he spent a period away from home. 2. a portion of time specified in some way: Picasso's blue period. 3. an occurrence of menstruation. 4. Geol. a unit of geological time during which a system of rocks is formed: the Jurassic period. 5. a division of time at school, college, or university when a particular subject is taught. 6. Physics, maths. the time taken to complete one cycle of a regularly recurring phenomenon. 7. Chem. one of the horizontal rows of elements in the periodic table. 8. Chiefly U.S. & Canad. same as full stop. ~adj. 9. dating from or in the style of an earlier time: period costume.

periodic (ˌpɪərɪ'ɒdɪk) adj. happening or recurring at intervals or in cycles. —**peri'odically** adv. —**periodicity** (ˌpɪərɪə'dɪsɪtɪ) n.

periodical (ˌpɪərɪ'ɒdɪkˀl) n. 1. a publication issued at regular intervals, usually monthly or weekly. ~adj. 2. of or relating to such publications. 3. periodic or occasional.

periodic law n. the principle that the chemical properties of the elements are periodic functions of their atomic numbers.

periodic table n. a table of the elements, arranged in order of increasing atomic number, based on the periodic law.

peripatetic (ˌpɛrɪpə'tɛtɪk) adj. 1. travelling from place to place. 2. Brit. employed in two or more educational establishments and travelling from one to another: a peripatetic football coach. ~n. 3. a peripatetic person.

peripheral (pə'rɪfərəl) adj. 1. not relating to the most important part of something; incidental. 2. of or relating to a periphery.

~n. 3. Computers. any device, such as a disk drive, concerned with input/output or storage.

periphery (pə'rɪfərɪ) n., pl. -eries. 1. the outermost boundary of an area. 2. the outside surface of something.

periphrasis (pə'rɪfrəsɪs) n., pl. -rases (-rəˌsiːz). a roundabout way of expressing something; circumlocution.

periscope ('pɛrɪˌskəʊp) n. an optical instrument that enables the user to view objects that are not in the direct line of vision, such as one in a submarine for looking above the surface of the water. They use a system of mirrors or prisms to reflect the light.

perish ('pɛrɪʃ) vb. 1. to be destroyed or die. 2. to cause to suffer: we were perished with cold. 3. to rot or cause to rot: leather perishes if exposed to bad weather.

perishable ('pɛrɪʃəbˀl) adj. 1. liable to rot. ~n. 2. (often pl.) a perishable article, esp. food.

perishing ('pɛrɪʃɪŋ) adj. 1. Informal. (of weather) extremely cold. 2. Slang. confounded, blasted: it's a perishing nuisance!

peristalsis (ˌpɛrɪ'stælsɪs) n., pl. -ses (-siːz). Physiol. the wave-like involuntary muscular contractions of the walls of the digestive tract. —**peri'staltic** adj.

peritoneum (ˌpɛrɪtə'niːəm) n., pl. -nea (-'niːə) or -neums. a serous sac that lines the walls of the abdominal cavity and covers the abdominal organs. —**perito'neal** adj.

peritonitis (ˌpɛrɪtə'naɪtɪs) n. inflammation of the peritoneum.

periwig ('pɛrɪˌwɪg) n. a wig formerly worn by men.

periwinkle[1] ('pɛrɪˌwɪŋkˀl) n. an edible marine gastropod with a spirally coiled shell.

periwinkle[2] ('pɛrɪˌwɪŋkˀl) n. a Eurasian evergreen plant with trailing stems and blue flowers.

perjure ('pɜːdʒə) vb. Criminal law. to commit perjury. —**'perjurer** n.

perjury ('pɜːdʒərɪ) n., pl. -juries. Criminal law. the deliberate giving of false evidence while under oath.

perk[1] (pɜːk) n. Brit. informal. short for **perquisite**.

perk[2] (pɜːk) vb. Informal. short for **percolate** (sense 3).

perk up vb. 1. to make or become more cheerful, hopeful, or lively. 2. to rise or cause to rise briskly: the dog's ears perked up.

perky ('pɜːkɪ) adj. perkier, perkiest. 1. jaunty; lively. 2. confident; spirited.

perm[1] (pɜːm) n. 1. a hairstyle produced by treatment with chemicals which gives long-lasting waves or curls. ~vb. 2. to give a perm to (hair).

perm² (pɜːm) n. Informal. short for **permutate, permutation** (sense 4).

permafrost ('pɜːməˌfrɒst) n. ground that is permanently frozen.

permanent ('pɜːmənənt) adj. 1. existing or intended to exist for an indefinite period: a permanent structure. 2. not expected to change: a permanent condition. —'permanence n. —'permanently adv.

permanent wave n. same as **perm¹**.

permanent way n. Chiefly Brit. the track of a railway, including the sleepers and rails.

permanganate (pəˈmæŋgəˌneɪt) n. a salt of an acid containing manganese, used as a disinfectant.

permeable ('pɜːmɪəbᵊl) adj. capable of being permeated, esp. by liquids. —ˌpermeaˈbility n.

permeate ('pɜːmɪˌeɪt) vb. 1. to penetrate or pervade (a substance or area): a lovely smell permeated the room. 2. to pass through or cause to pass through by osmosis or diffusion: to permeate a membrane. —ˌpermeˈation n.

Permian ('pɜːmɪən) adj. Geol. of the period of geological time about 280 million years ago.

permissible (pəˈmɪsəbᵊl) adj. permitted; allowable. —perˌmissiˈbility n.

permission (pəˈmɪʃən) n. authorization to do something.

permissive (pəˈmɪsɪv) adj. tolerant or lenient, esp. in sexual matters: a permissive society. —perˈmissiveness n.

permit vb. (pəˈmɪt), -mitting, -mitted. 1. to grant permission to do something: you are permitted to smoke. 2. to consent to: she will not permit him to come. 3. to allow the possibility (of): his work permits him to relax nowadays. ~n. ('pɜːmɪt). 4. an official document granting authorization.

permutate ('pɜːmjʊˌteɪt) vb. to alter the sequence or arrangement (of): endlessly permutating three basic designs.

permutation (ˌpɜːmjʊˈteɪʃən) n. 1. Maths. an ordered arrangement of the numbers or terms of a set into specified groups: the permutations of a, b, and c, taken two at a time, are ab, ba, ac, ca, bc, cb. 2. a combination of items made by reordering. 3. a transformation. 4. a fixed combination for selections of results on football pools.

pernicious (pəˈnɪʃəs) adj. 1. wicked or malicious: pernicious lies. 2. causing grave harm; deadly.

pernicious anaemia n. a severe form of anaemia characterized by a reduction of the red blood cells, weakness, and a sore tongue.

pernickety (pəˈnɪkɪtɪ) adj. Informal. 1. excessively precise; fussy. 2. (of a task) requiring close attention.

peroration (ˌpɛrəˈreɪʃən) n. the concluding part of a speech in which points made previously are summed up.

peroxide (pəˈrɒksaɪd) n. 1. hydrogen peroxide as a hair bleach. 2. any of a class of metallic oxides, such as sodium peroxide, Na₂O₂. 3. (modifier) of, bleached with, or resembling peroxide: a peroxide blonde. ~vb. 4. to bleach (the hair) with peroxide.

perpendicular (ˌpɜːpənˈdɪkjʊlə) adj. 1. at right angles. 2. denoting the style of English Gothic architecture characterized by vertical lines. 3. upright; vertical. ~n. 4. Geom. a line or plane perpendicular to another. —**perpendicularity** (ˌpɜːpənˌdɪkjuˈlærɪtɪ) n.

perpetrate ('pɜːpɪˌtreɪt) vb. to perform or be responsible for (a deception or crime). —ˌperpeˈtration n. —'perpeˌtrator n.

perpetual (pəˈpɛtjʊəl) adj. 1. eternal; permanent. 2. seemingly ceaseless because often repeated: your perpetual complaints. —perˈpetually adv.

perpetual motion n. motion of a hypothetical mechanism that continues indefinitely without any external source of energy.

perpetuate (pəˈpɛtjʊˌeɪt) vb. to cause to continue: to perpetuate misconceptions. —perˌpetuˈation n.

perpetuity (ˌpɜːpɪˈtjuːɪtɪ) n., pl. -ties. 1. eternity. 2. the state of being perpetual. 3. something perpetual, such as a pension that is payable indefinitely. 4. in perpetuity. for ever.

perplex (pəˈplɛks) vb. 1. to puzzle; bewilder; confuse. 2. to complicate: to perplex an issue. —perˈplexing adj.

perplexity (pəˈplɛksɪtɪ) n., pl. -ties. 1. the state of being perplexed. 2. something that perplexes.

perquisite ('pɜːkwɪzɪt) n. 1. an incidental benefit gained from a certain type of employment, such as the use of a company car. 2. a customary tip. 3. something expected or regarded as an exclusive right.

perry ('pɛrɪ) n., pl. -ries. an alcoholic drink made from fermented pear juice.

per se ('pɜː 'seɪ) adv. by or in itself; intrinsically.

persecute ('pɜːsɪˌkjuːt) vb. 1. to oppress, harass, or maltreat (someone), esp. because of race or religion. 2. to bother (someone) persistently. —ˌperseˈcution n. —'perseˌcutor n.

perseverance (ˌpɜːsɪˈvɪərəns) n. continued steady belief or efforts; persistence.

persevere (ˌpɜːsɪˈvɪə) vb. (often foll. by in) to show perseverance.

Persian ('pɜːʃən) adj. 1. of ancient Persia or modern Iran, their inhabitants, or their languages. ~n. 2. a person from Persia (now Iran). 3. the language of Iran or Persia in any of its ancient or modern forms.

Persian cat *n.* a long-haired variety of domestic cat.

Persian lamb *n.* **1.** a black loosely curled fur from the karakul lamb. **2.** a karakul lamb.

persiflage ('pɜːsɪˌflɑːʒ) *n.* light frivolous conversation or writing.

persimmon (pɜː'sɪmən) *n.* a sweet red tropical fruit, which is edible when completely ripe.

persist (pə'sɪst) *vb.* **1.** (often foll. by *in*) to continue obstinately despite opposition. **2.** to continue without interruption: *the rain persisted through the night.*

persistent (pə'sɪstənt) *adj.* **1.** showing persistence. **2.** unrelenting: *your persistent questioning.* —**per'sistence** *n.* —**per'sistently** *adv.*

person ('pɜːsʔn) *n., pl.* **persons. 1.** an individual human being. **2.** the body of a human being: *guns hidden on his person.* **3.** a grammatical category into which pronouns and forms of verbs are subdivided depending on whether they refer to the speaker, the person addressed, or some other individual or thing. **4. in person.** actually present: *the author will be there in person.*
Usage. *People* is the word usually used to refer to more than one person: *there were a hundred people at the reception. Persons* is rarely used, except in official English: *several persons were interviewed.*

-person *n. combining form.* sometimes used instead of *-man* and *-woman* or *-lady: chairperson.*
Usage. see **-man.**

persona (pɜː'səʊnə) *n., pl.* **-nae** (-niː). the personality that a person adopts and presents to other people.

personable ('pɜːsənəbʔl) *adj.* pleasant in appearance and personality.

personage ('pɜːsənɪdʒ) *n.* **1.** an important or distinguished person. **2.** any person.

personal ('pɜːsənʔl) *adj.* **1.** of the private aspects of a person's life: *personal letters.* **2.** of a person's body, its care, or its appearance: *personal hygiene.* **3.** undertaken by an individual: *a personal appearance by a celebrity.* **4.** referring to a person's individual personality or intimate affairs in an offensive way: *personal remarks.* **5.** having the attributes of an individual conscious being: *a personal God.* **6.** of grammatical person. **7.** *Law.* of movable property, such as money.

personal column *n.* a newspaper column containing personal messages and advertisements.

personal computer *n.* a small computer used for word processing or computer games.

personality (ˌpɜːsə'nælɪtɪ) *n., pl.* **-ties. 1.** *Psychol.* distinctive characteristics by

means of which an individual is recognized as being unique. **2.** the distinctive character of a person that makes him socially attractive: *a salesman needs a lot of personality.* **3.** a well-known person in a certain field, such as entertainment. **4.** a remarkable person: *the old fellow is a real personality.* **5.** (*often pl.*) a personal remark: *the discussion degenerated into personalities.*

personalize *or* **-ise** ('pɜːsənəˌlaɪz) *vb.* **1.** to base (an argument or discussion) around people's characters rather than on abstract arguments. **2.** to mark (stationery or clothing) with a person's initials or name. **3.** same as **personify.**

personally ('pɜːsənəlɪ) *adv.* **1.** without the help of others: *I'll attend to it personally.* **2.** in one's own opinion: *personally, I hate onions.* **3.** as if referring to oneself: *to take the insults personally.* **4.** as a person: *we like him personally, but professionally he's incompetent.*

personal pronoun *n.* a pronoun such as *I, you, he, she, we,* and *they* that represents a definite person or thing.

personal stereo *n.* a small audio cassette player worn attached to a belt and used with lightweight headphones.

persona non grata (pɜː'səʊnə nɒn 'grɑːtə) *n., pl.* **personae non gratae** (pɜː'səʊniː nɒn 'grɑːtiː). an unacceptable person.

personate ('pɜːsəˌneɪt) *vb. Criminal law.* to assume the identity of (another person) with intent to deceive. —ˌperson'ation *n.*

personify (pɜː'sɒnɪˌfaɪ) *vb.* **-fying, -fied. 1.** to attribute human characteristics to (a thing or abstraction). **2.** to represent (an abstract quality) in human or animal form. **3.** (of a person or thing) to represent (an abstract quality), as in art. **4.** to be the embodiment of: *she is meanness personified.* —**personification** (pɜːˌsɒnɪfɪ'keɪʃən) *n.*

personnel (ˌpɜːsə'nɛl) *n.* **1.** the people employed in an organization or for a service. **2.** the department in an organization that appoints, or keeps records of employees.

perspective (pə'spɛktɪv) *n.* **1.** a way of regarding situations or facts and judging their relative importance. **2.** the proper or accurate point of view or the ability to see it; objectivity: *try to get some perspective on your troubles.* **3.** the art of drawing on a flat surface to give the effect of solidity and relative distance and sizes. **4.** the appearance of objects or buildings relative to each other, as determined by their distance from the viewer.

Perspex ('pɜːspɛks) *n. Trademark.* any of various clear acrylic resins.

perspicacious (ˌpɜːspɪ'keɪʃəs) *adj.* acutely perceptive or discerning. —**perspicacity** (ˌpɜːspɪ'kæsɪtɪ) *n.*

perspicuous (pə'spɪkjʊəs) *adj.* (of speech

or writing) easily understood; lucid. —**perspicuity** (ˌpɜːspɪˈkjuːɪtɪ) n.

perspiration (ˌpɜːspəˈreɪʃən) n. **1.** the salty fluid secreted by the sweat glands of the skin; sweat. **2.** the act of sweating.

perspire (pəˈspaɪə) vb. to sweat.

persuade (pəˈsweɪd) vb. **1.** to induce, urge, or prevail upon (someone) successfully: he finally persuaded them to buy it. **2.** to cause to believe; convince: even with the evidence, the police were not persuaded. —**perˈsuadable** adj.

persuasion (pəˈsweɪʒən) n. **1.** the act of persuading or of trying to persuade. **2.** the power to persuade. **3.** a set of beliefs; creed: the Roman Catholic persuasion; a young woman of radical persuasion.

persuasive (pəˈsweɪsɪv) adj. having the power or tending to persuade: a persuasive salesman. —**perˈsuasively** adv.

pert (pɜːt) adj. **1.** saucy, impudent, or forward. **2.** jaunty: a pert little hat.

pertain (pəˈteɪn) vb. (often foll. by to) **1.** to have reference or relevance: the notes pertaining to the case. **2.** to be appropriate. **3.** to belong (to) or be a part (of).

pertinacious (ˌpɜːtɪˈneɪʃəs) adj. **1.** doggedly resolute in purpose or belief. **2.** stubbornly persistent. —**pertinacity** (ˌpɜːtɪˈnæsɪtɪ) n.

pertinent (ˈpɜːtɪnənt) adj. relating to the matter at hand; relevant. —**ˈpertinence** or **ˈpertinency** n.

perturb (pəˈtɜːb) vb. **1.** to disturb the composure of; trouble. **2.** to throw into disorder.

perturbation (ˌpɜːtəˈbeɪʃən) n. **1.** the act of perturbing or the state of being perturbed. **2.** a cause of disturbance.

peruke (pəˈruːk) n. a wig for men in the 17th and 18th centuries.

peruse (pəˈruːz) vb. **1.** to read or examine with care. **2.** to browse or read in a leisurely way. —**peˈrusal** n.

pervade (pɜːˈveɪd) vb. to spread through or throughout. —**pervasion** (pɜːˈveɪʒən) n. —**pervasive** (pɜːˈveɪsɪv) adj.

perverse (pəˈvɜːs) adj. **1.** deliberately deviating from what is regarded as normal, good, or proper. **2.** wayward or contrary; obstinate. —**perˈversely** adv. —**perˈversity** n.

perversion (pəˈvɜːʃən) n. **1.** any abnormal means of obtaining sexual satisfaction. **2.** the act of perverting or the state of being perverted.

pervert vb. (pəˈvɜːt). **1.** to use wrongly or badly. **2.** to interpret wrongly or badly; distort. **3.** to lead (someone) into deviant or perverted beliefs or behaviour; corrupt. **4.** to debase. ~n. (ˈpɜːvɜːt). **5.** a person who practises sexual perversion. —**perˈverted** adj.

pervious (ˈpɜːvɪəs) adj. **1.** able to be pen-

etrated; permeable: pervious soil. **2.** receptive to new ideas, etc.; open-minded.

peseta (pəˈseɪtə) n. the standard monetary unit of Spain.

pesky (ˈpɛskɪ) adj. **peskier, peskiest.** U.S. & Canad. informal. troublesome.

peso (ˈpeɪsəʊ) n., pl. -sos (-səʊz). the standard monetary unit of Bolivia, Chile, Colombia, Cuba, the Dominican Republic, Mexico, the Philippines, and Uruguay.

pessary (ˈpesərɪ) n., pl. -ries. Med. **1.** a device worn in the vagina, either as a support for the uterus or as a contraceptive. **2.** a vaginal suppository.

pessimism (ˈpesɪˌmɪzəm) n. **1.** the tendency to expect the worst in all things. **2.** the doctrine of the ultimate triumph of evil over good. —**ˈpessimist** n. —**ˌpessiˈmistic** adj. —**ˌpessiˈmistically** adv.

pest (pest) n. **1.** an annoying person or thing; nuisance. **2.** any organism that damages crops, or injures or irritates livestock or man.

pester (ˈpestə) vb. to annoy or nag (someone) continually.

pesticide (ˈpestɪˌsaɪd) n. a chemical used for killing pests, esp. insects.

pestilence (ˈpestɪləns) n. any deadly infectious disease, such as the plague.

pestilent (ˈpestɪlənt) adj. **1.** annoying; irritating. **2.** highly destructive morally or physically. **3.** likely to cause infectious disease. —**pestilential** (ˌpestɪˈlenʃəl) adj.

pestle (ˈpesˀl) n. a club-shaped instrument for grinding or pounding substances in a mortar.

pet[1] (pet) n. **1.** a tame animal kept for companionship or pleasure. **2.** a person who is fondly indulged; favourite: teacher's pet. ~adj. **3.** kept as a pet: a pet dog. **4.** of or for pet animals: pet food. **5.** particularly cherished: a pet hatred. ~vb. **petting, petted. 6.** to treat (a person or animal) as a pet; pamper. **7.** to pat or stroke (a person or animal). **8.** Informal. (of two people) to caress each other in an erotic manner.

pet[2] (pet) n. a fit of sulkiness.

petal (ˈpetˀl) n. any of the brightly-coloured leaflike parts which form the head of a flower. —**ˈpetalled** adj.

petard (pɪˈtɑːd) n. **1.** (formerly) a device containing explosives used to breach a wall or door. **2. hoist with one's own petard.** being the victim of one's own schemes.

peter out (ˈpiːtə) vb. to gradually come to an end: the cash petered out in three months.

Peter Pan n. a youthful or immature man.

pethidine (ˈpeθɪˌdiːn) n. a white crystalline water-soluble drug used to relieve pain.

petiole (ˈpetɪˌəʊl) n. the stalk which attaches a leaf to a plant.

petit bourgeois (ˈpetɪ ˈbuəʒwɑː) n., pl. **pe-**

tits bourgeois ('buɔʒwɑːz). the lower middle class.

petite (pə'tiːt) *adj.* (of a woman) small, delicate, and dainty.

petit four ('petɪ 'fɔː) *n., pl.* **petits fours** ('fɔːz). any of various very small fancy cakes and biscuits.

petition (pɪ'tɪʃən) *n.* **1.** a written document signed by a large number of people demanding some form of action from a government or other authority. **2.** any formal request to a higher authority. **3.** *Law.* a formal application in writing made to a court asking for some specific judicial action: *a petition for divorce.* ~*vb.* **4.** to address or present a petition to (a government or to someone in authority): *to petition Parliament.* **5.** (foll. by *for*) to seek by petition: *to petition for a change in the law.* —**pe'titionary** *adj.*

petit mal ('petɪ 'mæl) *n.* a mild form of epilepsy characterized by periods of loss of consciousness for up to 30 seconds.

petit point ('petɪ 'pɔɪnt) *n.* **1.** a small diagonal needlepoint stitch used for fine detail. **2.** work done with such stitches.

petrel ('petrəl) *n.* a sea bird with a hooked bill and tubular nostrils, such as an albatross, storm petrel, or shearwater.

Petri dish ('piːtrɪ) *n.* a shallow dish used in laboratories, esp. for producing cultures of bacteria.

petrify ('petrɪˌfaɪ) *vb.* **-fying, -fied. 1.** to stun or daze, as with fear. **2.** to convert (organic material) into stone. **3.** to make or become unable to change or develop: *a society petrified by convention.* —**ˌpetrifi'cation** *n.*

petrochemical (ˌpetrəʊ'kemɪk²l) *n.* a substance, such as acetone, obtained from petroleum. —**ˌpetro'chemistry** *n.*

petrodollar (ˌpetrəʊˌdɒlə) *n.* money earned by a country by the exporting of petroleum.

petrol ('petrəl) *n.* a volatile flammable liquid obtained from petroleum and used as a fuel for internal-combustion engines.

petrolatum (ˌpetrə'leɪtəm) *n.* a translucent jellylike substance obtained from petroleum; used as a lubricant and in medicine as an ointment base.

petrol bomb *n.* a simple grenade consisting of a bottle filled with petrol. A piece of cloth is put in the neck of the bottle and set alight just before the bomb is thrown.

petroleum (pə'trəʊlɪəm) *n.* a dark-coloured thick flammable crude oil occurring in sedimentary rocks, consisting mainly of hydrocarbons: the source of petrol and paraffin.

petroleum jelly *n.* same as **petrolatum**.

petrol station *n. Brit.* same as **filling station**.

petticoat ('petɪˌkəʊt) *n.* a woman's underskirt.

pettifogger ('petɪˌfɒgə) *n.* **1.** a lawyer who conducts unimportant cases, esp. one who resorts to trickery. **2.** any person who quibbles. —**'pettiˌfogging** *adj.*

pettish ('petɪʃ) *adj.* peevish; petulant. —**'pettishness** *n.*

petty ('petɪ) *adj.* **-tier, -tiest. 1.** trivial; trifling: *petty details.* **2.** narrow-minded; mean: *petty spite.* **3.** minor or subordinate in rank: *petty officialdom.* —**'pettily** *adv.* —**'pettiness** *n.*

petty cash *n.* a small cash fund for minor incidental expenses.

petty officer *n.* a noncommissioned officer in the navy.

petulant ('petjʊlənt) *adj.* irritable or upset in a peevish way. —**'petulance** *n.* —**'petulantly** *adv.*

petunia (pɪ'tjuːnɪə) *n.* a tropical American plant with pink, white, or purple funnel-shaped flowers.

pew (pjuː) *n.* **1.** (in a church) **a.** a long benchlike seat with a back, used by the congregation. **b.** an enclosed compartment reserved for the use of a family or group. **2.** *Brit. informal.* a seat: *take a pew.*

pewter ('pjuːtə) *n.* **1.** an alloy containing tin, lead, sometimes copper and antimony. **2.** plate or kitchen utensils made from pewter.

pfennig ('fenɪg) *n.* a German monetary unit worth one hundredth of a mark.

PG a film certified for viewing by anyone, but which contains scenes that may be unsuitable for children, for whom parental guidance is necessary.

pH *n.* potential of hydrogen; a measure of the acidity or alkalinity of a solution.

phaeton ('feɪt²n) *n.* a light four-wheeled horse-drawn carriage with or without a top.

phagocyte ('fægəˌsaɪt) *n.* a cell or protozoan that engulfs particles, such as microorganisms.

phalanger (fə'lændʒə) *n.* an Australian marsupial with dense fur and a long tail.

phalanx ('fælæŋks) *n., pl.* **phalanxes** or **phalanges** (fæ'lændʒiːz). **1.** any closely ranked unit or mass of people: *the police formed a phalanx to protect the embassy.* **2.** a number of people united for a common purpose. **3.** an ancient Greek battle formation of infantry in close ranks.

phallic ('fælɪk) *adj.* of or resembling a phallus: *a phallic symbol.*

phallus ('fæləs) *n., pl.* **-li** (-laɪ) or **-luses. 1.** same as **penis**. **2.** an image of the penis as a symbol of reproductive power.

phantasm ('fæntæzəm) *n.* **1.** a phantom. **2.** an illusory perception of a person or thing. —**phan'tasmal** *adj.*

phantasmagoria (ˌfæntæzmə'gɔːrɪə) *n. Psychol.* a shifting medley of real or imagined figures, as in a dream. —**phantasmagoric** (ˌfæntæzmə'gɒrɪk) *adj.*

phantasy ('fæntəsɪ) *n., pl.* -**sies**. *Archaic.* same as **fantasy.**

phantom ('fæntəm) *n.* **1.** an apparition or spectre. **2.** the visible representation of something abstract, esp. as in a dream or hallucination: *the phantom of liberty.* ~*adj.* **3.** deceptive or unreal: *a phantom army marching through the sky.*

Pharaoh ('fɛərəʊ) *n.* the title of the ancient Egyptian kings.

Pharisee ('færɪˌsiː) *n.* **1.** a member of an ancient Jewish sect teaching strict observance of Jewish traditions. **2.** (*often not cap.*) a self-righteous or hypocritical person. —**Pharisaic** (ˌfærɪ'seɪɪk) *adj.*

pharmaceutical (ˌfɑːmə'sjuːtɪk°l) *adj.* of or relating to drugs or pharmacy.

pharmaceutics (ˌfɑːmə'sjuːtɪks) *n.* (*functioning as sing.*) same as **pharmacy** (sense 1).

pharmacist ('fɑːməsɪst) *n.* a person qualified to prepare and dispense drugs.

pharmacology (ˌfɑːmə'kɒlədʒɪ) *n.* the science or study of drugs, including their characteristics, action, and uses. —**pharmacological** (ˌfɑːməkə'lɒdʒɪk°l) *adj.* —ˌ**pharma-**ˈ**cologist** *n.*

pharmacopoeia (ˌfɑːməkə'piːə) *n.* an authoritative book containing a list of medicinal drugs with their uses, preparation and dosages.

pharmacy ('fɑːməsɪ) *n., pl.* -**cies**. **1.** the preparing and dispensing of drugs. **2.** a dispensary.

pharyngitis (ˌfærɪn'dʒaɪtɪs) *n.* inflammation of the pharynx; sore throat.

pharynx ('færɪŋks) *n., pl.* **pharynges** (fæ-'rɪndʒiːz) *or* **pharynxes.** the part of the alimentary canal between the mouth and the oesophagus. —**pharyngeal** (ˌfærɪn-'dʒiːəl) *adj.*

phase (feɪz) *n.* **1.** any distinct or characteristic period or stage in a sequence of events: *there were two phases to the revolution.* **2.** *Astron.* one of the recurring shapes of the portion of the moon, Mercury, or Venus illuminated by the sun. **3.** *Physics.* a particular stage in a periodic process or phenomenon. **4. in phase.** (of two waveforms) reaching corresponding phases at the same time. **5. out of phase.** (of two waveforms) not in phase. ~*vb.* **6.** to do, arrange, or introduce gradually or in stages: *the withdrawal was phased over several months.*

phase in *vb.* to introduce in a gradual or cautious manner: *the legislation was phased in over two years.*

phase out *vb.* to discontinue or withdraw gradually.

PhD Doctor of Philosophy.

pheasant ('fɛz°nt) *n.* a long-tailed bird with a brightly-coloured plumage in the

male: native to Asia but introduced elsewhere.

phenobarbitone (ˌfiːnəʊ'bɑːbɪˌtəʊn) *or* **phenobarbital** (ˌfiːnəʊ'bɑːbɪt°l) *n.* a sedative used to treat insomnia and epilepsy.

phenol ('fiːnɒl) *n.* a white crystalline derivative of benzene, used as an antiseptic and disinfectant and in the manufacture of resins, explosives, and pharmaceuticals.

phenomena (fɪ'nɒmɪnə) *n.* a plural of **phenomenon.**

phenomenal (fɪ'nɒmɪn°l) *adj.* **1.** of or relating to a phenomenon. **2.** extraordinary; outstanding: *a phenomenal achievement.* —**phe**ˈ**nomenally** *adv.*

phenomenalism (fɪ'nɒmɪnəˌlɪzəm) *n. Philosophy.* the doctrine that all knowledge comes from sense perception. —**phe**ˈ**nomenalist** *n., adj.*

phenomenon (fɪ'nɒmɪnən) *n., pl.* -**ena** (-ɪnə) *or* -**enons**. **1.** anything that can be perceived as an occurrence or fact by the senses. **2.** any remarkable occurrence or person.

Usage. *Phenomena* should not be treated as if it were singular. Correct usage is to employ *phenomenon* with a singular verb and *phenomena* with a plural: *that is an interesting phenomenon* (not *phenomena*); *several new phenomena were recorded in his notes.*

phenyl ('fiːnaɪl) *n.* (*modifier*) of, containing, or consisting of the monovalent group C_6H_5, derived from benzene: *a phenyl group.*

phew (fjuː) *interj.* an exclamation of relief, surprise, disbelief or weariness.

phial ('faɪəl) *n.* a small bottle for liquid medicine.

phil. 1. philharmonic. **2.** philosophy.

philadelphus (ˌfɪlə'dɛlfəs) *n.* a shrub grown for its strongly scented showy flowers.

philander (fɪ'lændə) *vb.* (of a man) to flirt with women. —**phi**ˈ**landerer** *n.*

philanthropy (fɪ'lænθrəpɪ) *n., pl.* -**pies**. **1.** the practice of performing charitable or benevolent actions. **2.** love of mankind in general. —**philanthropic** (ˌfɪlən'θrɒpɪk) *adj.* —**phi**ˈ**lanthropist** *n.*

philately (fɪ'lætəlɪ) *n.* the collection and study of postage stamps. —**phi**ˈ**latelist** *n.*

philharmonic (ˌfɪlhɑː'mɒnɪk) *adj.* **1.** fond of music. ~*n.* **2.** (*cap. when part of a name*) a specific philharmonic choir, orchestra, or society.

philippic (fɪ'lɪpɪk) *n.* a bitter verbal attack.

Philippine ('fɪlɪˌpiːn) *n., adj.* same as **Filipino.**

philistine ('fɪlɪˌstaɪn) *n.* **1.** a person who is hostile towards culture and the arts. ~*adj.* **2.** boorishly uncultured. —**philistinism** ('fɪlɪstɪˌnɪzəm) *n.*

Philistine ('fɪlɪˌstaɪn) *n.* a member of the

non-Semitic people who inhabited ancient Palestine.

philology (fɪˈlɒlədʒɪ) n. (no longer in scholarly use) comparative and historical linguistics. —**philological** (ˌfɪləˈlɒdʒɪkᵊl) adj. —**phiˈlologist** n.

philosopher (fɪˈlɒsəfə) n. 1. a student, teacher, or devotee of philosophy. 2. a person who is patient, wise, and stoical.

philosopher's stone n. a substance thought by alchemists to be capable of changing base metals into gold.

philosophize or **-phise** (fɪˈlɒsəˌfaɪz) vb. 1. to make philosophical pronouncements and speculations. 2. to explain philosophically. —**phiˈloso,phizer** or -ˌ**phiser** n.

philosophy (fɪˈlɒsəfɪ) n., pl. **-phies**. 1. the academic discipline concerned with making explicit the nature and significance of beliefs and investigating the intelligibility of concepts by means of rational argument. 2. the particular doctrines of a specific individual or school relating to these issues: *the philosophy of Descartes*. 3. any system of beliefs, values, or tenets. 4. a personal outlook or viewpoint. 5. the ability to remain calm through upsets and difficulties. —**philosophical** (ˌfɪləˈsɒfɪkᵊl) adj.

philtre or U.S. **philter** (ˈfɪltə) n. a drink supposed to arouse desire.

phlebitis (flɪˈbaɪtɪs) n. inflammation of a vein. —**phlebitic** (flɪˈbɪtɪk) adj.

phlegm (flɛm) n. 1. the thick yellowish substance secreted by the walls of the respiratory tract. 2. apathy; stolidity; indifference. 3. calmness. —**ˈphlegmy** adj.

phlegmatic (flɛɡˈmætɪk) adj. 1. having an unemotional disposition. 2. not easily excited.

phloem (ˈfləʊɛm) n. the plant tissue that acts as a path for the distribution of food substances to all parts of the plant.

phlox (flɒks) n., pl. **phlox** or **phloxes**. a plant with clusters of white, red, or purple flowers.

phobia (ˈfəʊbɪə) n. Psychiatry. an intense and irrational fear of a given situation or thing. —**ˈphobic** adj., n.

Phoenician (fəˈnɪʃən) n. 1. a person from Phoenicia. ~adj. 2. of Phoenicia, an ancient E Mediterranean maritime country, or the Phoenicians.

phoenix (ˈfiːnɪks) n. a legendary Arabian bird said to set fire to itself and rise anew from the ashes every 500 years.

phone (fəʊn) n., vb. short for **telephone**.

phonecard (ˈfəʊnˌkɑːd) n. 1. a public telephone that is operated by a special card instead of coins. 2. the card used.

phone-in n. a radio or television programme in which listeners' or viewers' questions or comments are telephoned to the studio and broadcast live as part of a discussion.

phoneme (ˈfəʊniːm) n. Linguistics. one of the set of speech sounds in any given language that serve to distinguish one word from another. —**phonemic** (fəˈniːmɪk) adj.

phonemics (fəˈniːmɪks) n. (functioning as sing.) the classification and analysis of the phonemes of a language.

phonetic (fəˈnɛtɪk) adj. 1. of phonetics. 2. denoting any perceptible distinction between one speech sound and another. 3. conforming to pronunciation: *phonetic spelling*. —**phoˈnetically** adv.

phonetics (fəˈnɛtɪks) n. (functioning as sing.) the study of speech processes, including the production, perception, and analysis of speech sounds.

phoney or esp. U.S. **phony** (ˈfəʊnɪ) Informal. ~adj. **-nier, -niest**. 1. not genuine; fake: *a phoney name*; *a phoney diamond*. 2. (of a person) insincere or pretentious. ~n., pl. **-neys** or esp. U.S. **-nies**. 3. an insincere or pretentious person. 4. something that is not genuine; a fake.

phonograph (ˈfəʊnəˌɡrɑːf) n. 1. an early form of record player capable of recording and reproducing sound on wax cylinders. 2. U.S. & Canad. a record player.

phonology (fəˈnɒlədʒɪ) n., pl. **-gies**. 1. the study of the sound system of a language or of languages in general. 2. such a sound system. —**phonological** (ˌfəʊnəˈlɒdʒɪkᵊl, ˌfɒn-) adj.

phooey (ˈfuːɪ) interj. Informal. an exclamation of scorn or contempt.

phosphate (ˈfɒsfeɪt) n. 1. any salt or ester of any phosphoric acid. 2. (often pl.) chemical fertilizer containing phosphorous compounds. —**phosphatic** (fɒsˈfætɪk) adj.

phosphor (ˈfɒsfə) n. a substance capable of emitting light when irradiated with particles of electromagnetic radiation.

phosphoresce (ˌfɒsfəˈrɛs) vb. to exhibit phosphorescence.

phosphorescence (ˌfɒsfəˈrɛsəns) n. 1. Physics. a fluorescence that persists after the bombarding radiation producing it has stopped. 2. the light emitted in phosphorescence. —**phospho'rescent** adj.

phosphoric (fɒsˈfɒrɪk) adj. of or containing phosphorus in the pentavalent state.

phosphorous (ˈfɒsfərəs) adj. of or containing phosphorus in the trivalent state.

phosphorus (ˈfɒsfərəs) n. a toxic flammable nonmetallic element which appears luminous in the dark. It exists in two forms, white and red. Symbol: P

photo (ˈfəʊtəʊ) n., pl. **-tos**. short for **photograph**.

photo- combining form. 1. of or produced by light: *photosynthesis*. 2. indicating a photographic process: *photolithography*.

photocell (ˈfəʊtəʊˌsɛl) n. a cell which produces a current or voltage when exposed to light or other electromagnetic radiation.

photocopier (ˈfəʊtəʊˌkɒpɪə) n. a machine using light-sensitive photographic materials to reproduce written, printed, or graphic work.

photocopy (ˈfəʊtəʊˌkɒpɪ) n., pl. -copies. 1. a photographic reproduction of written, printed, or graphic work. ~vb. -copying, -copied. 2. to reproduce (written, printed, or graphic work) on photographic material.

photoelectric (ˌfəʊtəʊɪˈlɛktrɪk) adj. of or concerned with electric or electronic effects caused by light or other electromagnetic radiation. —**photoelectricity** (ˌfəʊtəʊɪlɛkˈtrɪsɪtɪ) n.

photoengraving (ˌfəʊtəʊɪnˈɡreɪvɪŋ) n. 1. a photomechanical process for producing letterpress printing plates. 2. a print made from such a plate. —ˌphotoenˈgrave vb.

photo finish n. a finish of a race in which contestants are so close that a photograph is needed to decide the result.

photoflash (ˈfəʊtəʊˌflæʃ) n. same as **flashbulb**.

photoflood (ˈfəʊtəʊˌflʌd) n. a highly incandescent electric lamp used for indoor photography and television.

photogenic (ˌfəʊtəʊˈdʒɛnɪk) adj. 1. (esp. of a person) having a general facial appearance that looks attractive in photographs. 2. Biol. producing or emitting light.

photograph (ˈfəʊtəˌɡrɑːf) n. 1. an image of an object, person or scene in the form of a print or slide recorded by a camera. ~vb. 2. to take a photograph of (an object, person or scene).

photographic (ˌfəʊtəˈɡræfɪk) adj. 1. of or like photography or a photograph. 2. (of a person's memory) able to retain facts or appearances in precise detail. —ˌphotoˈgraphically adv.

photography (fəˈtɒɡrəfɪ) n. 1. the process of recording images on sensitized material by the action of light or other radiant energy. 2. the art, practice, or occupation of taking photographs. —phoˈtographer n.

photogravure (ˌfəʊtəʊɡrəˈvjʊə) n. any of various methods in which an etched metal plate for printing is produced by the use of photography.

photolithography (ˌfəʊtəʊlɪˈθɒɡrəfɪ) n. a lithographic printing process using photographically made plates. —ˌphotoliˈthographer n.

photometer (fəʊˈtɒmɪtə) n. an instrument used to measure the intensity of light.

photometry (fəʊˈtɒmɪtrɪ) n. the branch of physics concerned with the measurement of the intensity of light. —phoˈtometrist n.

photomontage (ˌfəʊtəʊmɒnˈtɑːʒ) n. 1. the combination of several photographs to produce a composite picture. 2. a composite picture so produced.

photon (ˈfəʊtɒn) n. a quantum of electromagnetic radiation energy, such as light, having both particle and wave behaviour.

photosensitive (ˌfəʊtəʊˈsɛnsɪtɪv) adj. sensitive to electromagnetic radiation, esp. light.

Photostat (ˈfəʊtəʊˌstæt) n. 1. Trademark. a type of photocopying machine or process. 2. any copy made by such a machine. ~vb. -statting or -stating, -statted or -stated. 3. to make a Photostat copy (of).

photosynthesis (ˌfəʊtəʊˈsɪnθɪsɪs) n. (in plants) the synthesis of organic compounds from carbon dioxide and water using light energy absorbed by chlorophyll. —ˌphotoˈsynthesize or -sise vb. —photosynthetic (ˌfəʊtəʊsɪnˈθɛtɪk) adj.

phototropism (ˌfəʊtəʊˈtrəʊpɪzəm) n. the growth of plants towards a source of light. —ˌphotoˈtropic adj.

phrasal verb n. a phrase that consists of a verb plus an adverb or preposition, esp. one the meaning of which cannot be deduced from its parts, such as take in meaning deceive.

phrase (freɪz) n. 1. a group of words forming a unit of meaning in a sentence. 2. an idiomatic or original expression. 3. Music. a small group of notes forming a coherent unit of melody. ~vb. 4. to express orally or in a phrase. 5. Music. to divide (a melodic line or part) into musical phrases, esp. in performance. —ˈphrasal adj.

phraseology (ˌfreɪzɪˈɒlədʒɪ) n., pl. -gies. the manner in which words or phrases are used.

phrenology (frɪˈnɒlədʒɪ) n. (formerly) the study of the shape and size of the skull as a means of finding out a person's character and mental ability. —**phrenological** (ˌfrɛnəˈlɒdʒɪkˀl) adj. —phreˈnologist n.

phut (fʌt) Informal. ~n. 1. a representation of a muffled explosive sound. ~adv. 2. go phut. to break down or collapse.

phylactery (fɪˈlæktərɪ) n., pl. -teries. Judaism. either of the pair of square cases containing biblical passages, worn by Jewish men on the left arm and head during weekday morning prayers.

phylum (ˈfaɪləm) n., pl. -la. a major taxonomic division of the animals and plants that contain one or more classes.

physical (ˈfɪzɪkˀl) adj. 1. of the body, as distinguished from the mind or spirit. 2. of material things or nature: the physical universe. 3. of or concerned with matter and energy. 4. of or relating to physics. —ˈphysically adv.

physical education n. training and practice in sports and gymnastics.

physical geography n. the branch of geography that deals with the natural features of the earth's surface.

physical jerks pl. n. Brit. informal. repetitive keep-fit exercises.

physical science n. any of the sciences concerned with nonliving matter, such as physics, chemistry, astronomy, and geology.

physician (fɪ'zɪʃən) n. **1.** a medical doctor. **2.** Archaic. a healer.

physicist ('fɪzɪsɪst) n. a person versed in or studying physics.

physics ('fɪzɪks) n. (functioning as sing.) **1.** the branch of science concerned with the properties of matter and energy and the relationships between them. **2.** physical properties of behaviour: the physics of the electron.

physiognomy (ˌfɪzɪ'ɒnəmɪ) n. **1.** a person's features considered as an indication of personality. **2.** the outward appearance of something.

physiography (ˌfɪzɪ'ɒɡrəfɪ) n. same as **physical geography**.

physiology (ˌfɪzɪ'ɒlədʒɪ) n. **1.** the branch of science concerned with the functioning of organisms. **2.** the processes and functions of all or part of an organism. —ˌphysi'ologist n. —physiological (ˌfɪzɪə'lɒdʒɪk°l) adj.

physiotherapy (ˌfɪzɪəʊ'θɛrəpɪ) n. the treatment of disease or injury by physical means, such as massage or exercises, rather than by drugs. —ˌphysio'therapist n.

physique (fɪ'ziːk) n. the general appearance of the body with regard to size, shape, and muscular development.

pi (paɪ) n., pl. **pis**. **1.** the 16th letter in the Greek alphabet (Π, π). **2.** Maths. a number that is the ratio of the circumference of a circle to its diameter. Approximate value: 3.141 592... ; symbol: π

pia mater ('paɪə 'meɪtə) n. the innermost of the three membranes that cover the brain and spinal cord.

pianissimo (pɪə'nɪsɪˌməʊ) adj., adv. Music. to be performed very quietly. Symbol: pp

pianist ('pɪənɪst) n. a person who plays the piano.

piano[1] (pɪ'ænəʊ) n., pl. **-anos**. a musical stringed instrument played by depressing keys that cause hammers to strike the strings and produce audible vibrations.

piano[2] ('pjɑːnəʊ) adj., adv. Music. to be performed softly.

piano accordion (pɪ'ænəʊ) n. an accordion in which the right hand plays a piano-like keyboard. —**piano accordionist** n.

pianoforte (pɪˌænəʊ'fɔːtɪ) n. the full name for **piano**[1].

Pianola (pɪə'nəʊlə) n. Trademark. a type of mechanical piano, the music for which is encoded in perforations in a paper roll.

piazza (pɪ'ætsə) n. **1.** a large open square in an Italian town. **2.** Chiefly Brit. a covered passageway or gallery.

pibroch ('piːbrɒx) n. a form of music for Scottish bagpipes, consisting of a theme and variations.

pic (pɪk) n., pl. **pics** or **pix**. Informal. a photograph or illustration.

pica ('paɪkə) n. **1.** a size of printer's type giving 6 lines to the inch. **2.** a typewriter type size having 10 characters to the inch.

picador ('pɪkəˌdɔː) n. Bullfighting. a horseman who wounds the bull with a lance to weaken it.

picaresque (ˌpɪkə'rɛsk) adj. of or relating to a type of fiction in which the hero, a rogue, goes through a series of episodic adventures.

picayune (ˌpɪkə'juːn) adj. U.S. & Canad. informal. **1.** of small value or importance. **2.** mean; petty. ~n. **3.** any coin of little value, such as a five-cent piece. **4.** an unimportant person or thing.

piccalilli ('pɪkəˌlɪlɪ) n. a pickle of mixed vegetables in a mustard sauce.

piccanin ('pɪkəˌnɪn) n. S. African informal. a Black African child.

piccaninny or esp. U.S. **pickaninny** (ˌpɪkə'nɪnɪ) n., pl. **-nies**. Offensive. a small Black or Aboriginal child.

piccolo ('pɪkəˌləʊ) n., pl. **-los**. a woodwind instrument an octave higher than the flute.

pick[1] (pɪk) vb. **1.** to choose (someone or something) carefully; select. **2.** to gather (fruit, berries, or crops) from (a tree, bush, or field). **3.** to remove loose particles from (the teeth, nose, or nails). **4.** to pierce, dig, or break up (a hard surface) with a pick. **5.** (foll. by at) to nibble (at) without appetite. **6.** to separate (strands or fibres), as in weaving. **7.** to provoke (an argument or fight) deliberately. **8.** to steal (money or valuables) from (a person's pocket). **9.** to open (a lock) with an instrument other than a key. **10.** to make (one's way) carefully on foot: they picked their way through the rubble. **11. pick and choose.** to select fastidiously or fussily. ~n. **12.** freedom or right of selection: take your pick. **13.** a person or thing that is chosen first or preferred: the pick of the bunch. ~See also **pick off, pick on**, etc.

pick[2] (pɪk) n. **1.** a tool with a handle carrying a long steel head curved and tapering to a point at one or both ends, used for loosening soil or breaking rocks. **2.** any tool used for picking, such as an ice pick or toothpick. **3.** a plectrum.

pickaback ('pɪkəˌbæk) n., adv. same as **piggyback**.

pickaxe or U.S. **pickax** ('pɪkˌæks) n. a large pick.

picket ('pɪkɪt) n. **1.** an individual or group standing outside an establishment to make a protest, or to dissuade strikebreakers from entering. **2.** a small detachment of troops positioned to give early warning of attack. **3.** a pointed stake that is driven

into the ground to support a fence. ~*vb.*
4. to post or act as pickets at (an establishment). **5.** to guard (a main body or place) by using or acting as a picket.

picket fence *n.* a fence consisting of pickets driven into the ground.

picket line *n.* a line of people acting as pickets.

pickings ('pɪkɪŋz) *pl. n.* (*sometimes sing.*) money or profits acquired easily.

pickle ('pɪk⁹l) *n.* **1.** (*often pl.*) vegetables, such as onions and cucumbers, preserved in vinegar, brine, or a similar solution. **2.** any food preserved in this way. **3.** a liquid or marinade, such as spiced vinegar, for preserving vegetables, meat, or fish. **4.** *Informal.* an awkward or difficult situation: *to be in a pickle.* ~*vb.* **5.** to preserve or treat in a pickling liquid.

pickled ('pɪk⁹ld) *adj.* **1.** (of food) preserved in a pickling liquid. **2.** *Informal.* intoxicated; drunk.

pick-me-up *n. Informal.* a tonic, esp. a special drink taken as a stimulant.

pick off *vb.* to aim at and shoot (people or things) one by one.

pick on *vb.* to select (someone) for something unpleasant, esp. in order to bully or blame.

pick out *vb.* **1.** to select for use or special consideration, as from a group. **2.** to distinguish (an object from its surroundings), as in painting: *she picked out the woodwork in white.* **3.** to recognize (a person or thing): *we picked out his face among the crowd.* **4.** to play (a tune) tentatively, as by ear.

pickpocket ('pɪk,pɒkɪt) *n.* a person who steals from the pockets of others in public places.

pick-up *n.* **1.** a small truck with an open body used for light deliveries. **2.** *Informal.* a casual acquaintance, usually one made with sexual intentions. **3.** *Informal.* **a.** a stop to collect passengers or goods. **b.** the people or things collected. **4.** an electromagnetic transducer, such as that to which a record player stylus is attached, which converts vibrations into electrical signals. ~*vb.* **pick up. 5.** to gather up in the hand or hands. **6.** to raise (oneself) after a fall or setback. **7.** to obtain or purchase: *she picked up nice shoes in the sales.* **8.** to improve in health or condition: *the market began to pick up.* **9.** to learn gradually or as one goes along: *I picked up dressmaking very quickly.* **10.** to resume; return to. **11.** to accept the responsibility for paying (a bill). **12.** to collect or give a lift to (passengers or goods). **13.** *Informal.* to become acquainted with, esp. with a view to having sexual relations. **14.** *Informal.* to arrest. **15.** to receive (sounds or signals).

picky ('pɪkɪ) *adj.* **pickier, pickiest.** *Informal.* fussy; finicky.

picnic ('pɪknɪk) *n.* **1.** an excursion on which people bring food to be eaten in the open air. **2.** an informal meal eaten out-of-doors. **3.** *Informal.* an easy or agreeable task. ~*vb.* **-nicking, -nicked. 4.** to eat or take part in a picnic. —'**picnicker** *n.*

pico- *prefix.* denoting 10^{-12}: *picofarad.*

Pict (pɪkt) *n.* a member of any of the peoples who lived in N Britain in the first to the fourth centuries A.D. —'**Pictish** *adj.*

pictograph ('pɪktə,grɑːf) *n.* **1.** a picture or symbol standing for a word or group of words, as in written Chinese. **2.** a chart on which symbols are used to represent values. —,**picto'graphic** *adj.*

pictorial (pɪk'tɔːrɪəl) *adj.* **1.** relating to, consisting of, or expressed by pictures. ~*n.* **2.** a periodical containing many pictures.

picture ('pɪktʃə) *n.* **1.** a visual representation of a person, thing, or scene produced on a surface, as in a photograph or painting. **2.** a mental image: *a clear picture of events.* **3.** a situation considered as an observable scene: *the political picture.* **4.** a person or thing resembling another: *he was the picture of his father.* **5.** a person or scene typifying a particular state: *the picture of despair.* **6.** the image on a television screen. **7.** a motion picture. **8.** **the pictures.** *Chiefly Brit.* a cinema or film show. **9. in the picture.** informed about a situation. ~*vb.* **10.** to visualize or imagine. **11.** to describe or depict vividly. **12.** to put in a picture or make a picture of: *they were pictured sitting on the rocks.*

picture moulding *or* **picture rail** *n.* the rail near the top of a wall from which pictures are hung.

picturesque (,pɪktʃə'resk) *adj.* **1.** visually pleasing, as in being striking or quaint: *a picturesque view.* **2.** (of language) graphic; vivid.

picture window *n.* a large window having a single pane of glass, usually facing a view.

piddle ('pɪd⁹l) *vb.* **1.** *Informal.* to urinate. **2.** (often foll. by *away*) to spend (one's time) aimlessly; fritter.

piddling ('pɪdlɪŋ) *adj. Informal.* petty; trifling; trivial.

pidgin ('pɪdʒɪn) *n.* a language made up of elements of two or more other languages and used, often for trading purposes, between the speakers of other languages.

pidgin English *n.* a pidgin in which one of the languages involved is English.

pie (paɪ) *n.* **1.** a baked sweet or savoury filling in a pastry-lined dish, often covered with a pastry crust. **2. pie in the sky.** illusory hope or promise of some future good.

piebald ('paɪ,bɔːld) *adj.* **1.** marked in two

colours, esp. black and white. ~n. **2.** a black-and-white horse.

piece (piːs) n. **1.** an amount or portion forming a separate mass or structure; bit: *a piece of wood.* **2.** a small part, item, or amount broken off or separated from a whole: *a piece of bread.* **3.** an instance or occurrence: *a piece of luck.* **4.** an example or specimen of a style or type: *a beautiful piece of Dresden.* **5.** a literary, musical, or artistic composition. **6.** a coin: *a fifty-pence piece.* **7.** a firearm or cannon. **8.** a small object used in playing various games: *a chess piece.* **9. go to pieces.** (of a person) to lose control of oneself; have a breakdown. ~vb. **10.** (often foll. by *together*) to fit or assemble piece by piece. **11.** (often foll. by *up*) to patch or make up (a garment) by adding pieces.

pièce de résistance (ˌpjɛs də rɪˈziːstɒns) n. the principal or most outstanding item in a series.

piece goods pl. n. goods, esp. fabrics, made in standard widths and lengths.

piecemeal (ˈpiːsˌmiːl) adv. **1.** bit by bit; gradually. ~adj. **2.** fragmentary or unsystematic: *a piecemeal approach.*

piece of eight n., pl. **pieces of eight.** a former Spanish coin worth eight reals.

piecework (ˈpiːsˌwɜːk) n. work paid for according to the quantity produced.

pie chart n. a circular graph divided into sectors proportional to the sizes of the quantities represented.

pied (paɪd) adj. having markings of two or more colours.

pied-à-terre (ˌpjeɪtɑːˈtɛə) n., pl. **pieds-à-terre** (ˌpjeɪtɑːˈtɛə). a flat or other lodging for occasional use.

pie-eyed adj. Slang. drunk.

pier (pɪə) n. **1.** a structure with a deck that is built out over water, and used as a landing place or promenade. **2.** a pillar or support that bears heavy loads. **3.** the part of a wall between two adjacent openings.

pierce (pɪəs) vb. **1.** to form or cut (a hole) in (something) as with a sharp instrument. **2.** to thrust into sharply: *the thorn pierced his heel.* **3.** to force (a way) through (something). **4.** (of light) to shine through (darkness). **5.** (of sounds or cries) to sound sharply through (the silence). **6.** to penetrate: *piercing cold.* —ˈ**piercing** adj.

pier glass n. a tall narrow mirror, designed to hang on the wall between windows.

Pierrot (ˈpɪərəʊ) n. a male character from French pantomime with a whitened face, white costume, and pointed hat.

pietism (ˈpaɪɪˌtɪzəm) n. exaggerated piety.

piety (ˈpaɪtɪ) n., pl. **-ties. 1.** dutiful devotion to God and observance of religious principles. **2.** the quality of being pious. **3.** a pious action or saying.

piezoelectric effect (paɪˌiːzəʊɪˈlɛktrɪk) or **piezoelectricity** (paɪˌiːzəʊɪlɛkˈtrɪsɪtɪ) n. Physics. **a.** the production of electricity by applying a mechanical stress to certain crystals. **b.** the converse effect in which stress is produced in a crystal as a result of an applied voltage.

piffle (ˈpɪfˀl) n. Informal. nonsense.

piffling (ˈpɪflɪŋ) adj. Informal. worthless; trivial.

pig (pɪg) n. **1.** a wild or domesticated mammal typically having a long head with a movable snout and a thick bristle-covered skin. **2.** Informal. a dirty, greedy, or bad-mannered person. **3.** Offensive slang. a policeman. **4.** a mass of metal cast into a simple shape. **5.** Brit. informal. something that is difficult or unpleasant. **6. a pig in a poke.** something bought or received without prior sight or knowledge. **7. make a pig of oneself.** Informal. to overeat. ~vb. **pigging, pigged. 8.** (of a sow) to give birth. **9.** Also: **pig it.** Informal. to live in squalor.

pigeon[1] (ˈpɪdʒɪn) n. **1.** a bird with a heavy body, small head, short legs, and long pointed wings. **2.** Slang. a victim or dupe.

pigeon[2] (ˈpɪdʒɪn) n. Brit. informal. concern or responsibility: *that's your pigeon, John.*

pigeonhole (ˈpɪdʒɪnˌhəʊl) n. **1.** a small compartment, as in a bureau, for filing papers. ~vb. **2.** to classify or categorize. **3.** to put aside or defer.

pigeon-toed adj. having the toes or feet turned inwards.

piggery (ˈpɪgərɪ) n., pl. **-geries.** a place where pigs are kept.

piggish (ˈpɪgɪʃ) adj. like a pig, esp. in appetite or manners. —ˈ**piggishness** n.

piggy (ˈpɪgɪ) n., pl. **-gies. 1.** a child's word for a **pig.** ~adj. **-gier, -giest. 2.** same as **piggish.**

piggyback (ˈpɪgɪˌbæk) or **pickaback** n. **1.** a ride on the back and shoulders of another person. ~adv., adj. **2.** on the back and shoulders of another person.

piggy bank n. a child's coin bank shaped like a pig with a slot for coins.

pig-headed adj. stupidly stubborn.

pig iron n. crude iron produced in a blast furnace and poured into moulds.

Pig Islander n. N.Z. informal. a New Zealander.

piglet (ˈpɪglɪt) n. a young pig.

pigment (ˈpɪgmənt) n. **1.** any substance used to impart colour to paint or dye. **2.** a substance occurring in plant or animal tissue and producing a characteristic colour. —ˈ**pigmentary** adj.

pigmentation (ˌpɪgmənˈteɪʃən) n. coloration in plants, animals, or man caused by the presence of pigments.

Pigmy (ˈpɪgmɪ) n., pl. **-mies.** same as **Pygmy.**

pigskin ('pɪg,skɪn) n. 1. the skin of the domestic pig. 2. leather made of this skin. 3. *U.S. & Canad. informal.* a football.

pigsty ('pɪg,staɪ) *or U.S. & Canad.* **pigpen** n., pl. **-sties.** 1. a pen for pigs; sty. 2. *Brit.* an untidy place.

pigswill ('pɪg,swɪl) n. waste food or other edible matter fed to pigs.

pigtail ('pɪg,teɪl) n. a plait of hair or one of two plaits on either side of the face.

pike¹ (paɪk) n., pl. **pike** or **pikes.** large predatory freshwater fish with a broad flat snout, strong teeth, and an elongated body covered with small scales.

pike² (paɪk) n. a medieval weapon consisting of a metal spearhead joined to a long pole. —**'pikeman** n.

pikestaff ('paɪk,stɑːf) n. the wooden handle of a pike.

pilaster (pɪ'læstə) n. a shallow rectangular column attached to the face of a wall. —**pi'lastered** adj.

pilau (pɪ'laʊ) *or* **pilaf** ('pɪlæf) n. a dish originating from the East, consisting of rice flavoured with spices and cooked in stock, to which meat, poultry, or fish may be added.

pilchard ('pɪltʃəd) n. a European food fish of the herring family, with a rounded body covered with large scales.

pile¹ (paɪl) n. 1. a collection of objects laid on top of one another. 2. *Informal.* a large amount: *a pile of money; piles of work.* 3. same as **pyre.** 4. a large building or group of buildings. 5. *Physics.* a nuclear reactor. ~vb. 6. (often foll. by *up*) to collect or be collected into a pile: *snow piled up in the drive.* 7. (foll. by *in, into, off, out,* etc.) to move in a group, often in a hurried manner: *to pile off the bus.* 8. **pile it on.** *Informal.* to exaggerate. ~See also **pile up.**

pile² (paɪl) n. a long heavy beam driven into the ground as a foundation for a structure.

pile³ (paɪl) n. the yarns in a fabric that stand up or out from the weave, as in carpeting or velvet.

pile-driver n. a machine that drives piles into the ground.

piles (paɪlz) pl. n. haemorrhoids.

pile up vb. 1. to gather or be gathered in a pile. ~n. **pile-up.** 2. *Informal.* a multiple collision of vehicles.

pilfer ('pɪlfə) vb. to steal (minor items), esp. in small quantities.

pilgrim ('pɪlgrɪm) n. 1. a person who undertakes a journey to a sacred place. 2. any wayfarer.

pilgrimage ('pɪlgrɪmɪdʒ) n. 1. a journey to a shrine or other sacred place. 2. a journey or long search made for exalted or sentimental reasons.

Pilgrim Fathers or **Pilgrims** pl. n. **the.** the English Puritans who founded Plymouth Colony in SE Massachusetts (1620).

pill (pɪl) n. 1. a small round or oval mass of a medicinal substance, intended to be swallowed whole. 2. **the pill.** *Informal.* an oral contraceptive. 3. something unpleasant that must be endured: *her reinstatement was a bitter pill to swallow.*

pillage ('pɪlɪdʒ) vb. 1. to loot or plunder (a town). ~n. 2. the act of pillaging. 3. something obtained by pillaging; booty.

pillar ('pɪlə) n. 1. an upright structure of stone, brick or metal, used as a support; column. 2. something resembling this: *a pillar of smoke.* 3. a prominent supporter: *a pillar of the Church.* 4. **from pillar to post.** from one place to another.

pillar box n. (in Britain) a red pillar-shaped public letter box situated on a pavement.

pillbox ('pɪl,bɒks) n. 1. a box for pills. 2. a small enclosed fortified emplacement, made of reinforced concrete. 3. a small round hat.

pillion ('pɪljən) n. 1. a seat or place behind the rider of a motorcycle or horse. ~adv. 2. on a pillion: *to ride pillion.*

pillory ('pɪlərɪ) n., pl. **-ries.** 1. a wooden framework into which offenders were formerly locked by the neck and wrists and exposed to public abuse and ridicule. ~vb. **-rying, -ried.** 2. to expose to public scorn or ridicule. 3. to punish by putting in a pillory.

pillow ('pɪləʊ) n. 1. a cloth case stuffed with feathers or foam rubber used to support the head during sleep. ~vb. 2. to rest (one's head) on or as if on a pillow.

pillowcase ('pɪləʊ,keɪs) or **pillowslip** ('pɪləʊ,slɪp) n. a removable washable cover of cotton or other fabric for a pillow.

pilot ('paɪlət) n. 1. a person who is qualified to operate an aircraft or spacecraft in flight. 2. a person employed to steer or guide a ship into or out of a port. 3. a person who acts as a guide. 4. (*modifier*) serving as a test or trial: *a pilot project.* 5. (*modifier*) serving as a guide: *a pilot beacon.* ~vb. 6. to act as pilot of. 7. to control the course of. 8. to guide or lead (a project or people).

pilot light n. a small auxiliary flame that ignites the main burner of a gas appliance.

pilot officer n. the most junior commissioned rank in certain air forces.

pimento (pɪ'mɛntəʊ) n., pl. **-tos.** same as **allspice** or **pimiento.**

pimiento (pɪ'mjɛntəʊ, -'mɛn-) n., pl. **-tos.** a Spanish pepper with a red fruit used as a vegetable.

pimp (pɪmp) n. 1. a man who obtains customers for a prostitute or brothel, in return for a share of the earnings. ~vb. 2. to act as a pimp.

pimpernel ('pɪmpə,nɛl, -n'l) n. a plant, such

as the scarlet pimpernel, typically having small star-shaped flowers.

pimple ('pımp°l) *n.* a small round usually inflamed swelling of the skin.   —'**pimpled** *adj.*   —'**pimply** *adj.*

pin (pın) *n.* **1.** a short stiff straight piece of wire with a pointed end and a rounded head: used mainly for fastening. **2.** short for **cotter pin, hairpin, rolling pin,** or **safety pin. 3.** a peg or dowel. **4.** a pin-shaped brooch. **5.** (in various bowling games) a usually club-shaped wooden object set up in groups as a target. **6.** a clip on a hand grenade that prevents its detonation until removed or released. **7.** *Golf.* the flagpole marking the hole on a green. **8.** (*usually pl.*) *Informal.* a leg. ~*vb.* **pinning, pinned. 9.** to attach, hold, or fasten with or as if with a pin or pins. **10.** to transfix with a pin, spear, etc. **11. pin (something) on someone.** *Informal.* to place the blame for (something) on someone: *he pinned the charge on his accomplice.* ~See also **pin down.**

pinafore ('pınə,fɔː) *n.* **1.** *Chiefly Brit.* an apron with a bib. **2.** a dress with a sleeveless bodice or bib top, worn over a jumper or blouse.

pinball ('pın,bɔːl) *n.* a game in which the player shoots a small ball through several hazards on a table or electrically operated machine.

pince-nez ('pæns,neı) *n., pl.* **pince-nez.** glasses that are held in place only by means of a clip over the bridge of the nose.

pincers ('pınsəz) *pl. n.* **1.** a gripping tool consisting of two hinged arms and curved jaws that close on the workpiece. **2.** the jointed grasping arms of animals such as crabs.

pinch (pıntʃ) *vb.* **1.** to press (something, esp. flesh) tightly between a finger and thumb. **2.** to squeeze or painfully press upon (a part of the body): *these shoes pinch.* **3.** to cause stinging pain to: *the cold pinched his face.* **4.** to make thin or drawn-looking, as from grief or lack of food. **5.** (usually foll. by *off, out,* or *back*) to remove the tips of (a plant shoot) to correct or encourage growth. **6.** *Informal.* to steal. **7.** *Informal.* to arrest. ~*n.* **8.** a squeeze or sustained nip. **9.** the quantity of a substance, such as salt, that can be taken between a thumb and finger. **10.** painful or extreme stress or need: *the pinch of poverty.* **11. at a pinch.** if absolutely necessary.

pinchbeck ('pıntʃ,bek) *n.* **1.** an alloy of copper and zinc, used as imitation gold. ~*adj.* **2.** sham or cheap.

pincushion ('pın,kuʃən) *n.* a small cushion in which pins are stuck ready for use.

pin down *vb.* **1.** to force (someone) to make a decision or carry out a promise. **2.** to define clearly: *a suspicion that he couldn't quite pin down.*

pine¹ (paın) *n.* **1.** an evergreen tree of the N hemisphere, with long needle-shaped leaves and brown cones. **2.** the light-coloured wood of this tree.

pine² (paın) *vb.* **1.** (often foll. by *for*) to feel great longing or desire; yearn. **2.** (often foll. by *away*) to become ill or thin through worry or longing.

pineal gland *or* **body** ('pınıəl) *n.* a pea-sized organ situated at the base of the brain.

pineapple ('paın,æp°l) *n.* an oval yellow-fleshed fruit with a thick hard skin that grows on a tropical American plant.

pine cone *n.* the seed-producing structure of a pine tree.

pine marten *n.* a mammal of N European and Asian coniferous woods, with dark brown fur and a creamy-yellow patch on the throat.

ping (pıŋ) *n.* **1.** a short high-pitched sound, as of a bullet striking metal. ~*vb.* **2.** to make such a noise.

pinger ('pıŋə) *n.* a device that makes a pinging sound, esp. one that can be preset to ring at a particular time.

Ping-Pong ('pıŋ,pɒŋ) *n. Trademark.* same as **table tennis.**

pinhead ('pın,hed) *n.* **1.** the head of a pin. **2.** *Informal.* a stupid person. —'**pin,headed** *adj.*

pinhole ('pın,həʊl) *n.* a small hole made with or as if with a pin.

pinion¹ ('pınjən) *n.* **1.** *Chiefly poetic.* a bird's wing. **2.** the outer part of a bird's wing including the flight feathers. ~*vb.* **3.** to hold or bind (the arms) of (a person) so as to immobilize him. **4.** to confine.

pinion² ('pınjən) *n.* a cogwheel that engages with a larger wheel or rack.

pink¹ (pıŋk) *n.* **1.** a pale reddish colour. **2.** a plant, such as the garden pink, with pink, red, or white fragrant flowers. **3. in the pink.** in good health. ~*adj.* **4.** of the colour pink. **5.** *Brit. informal.* left-wing. ~*vb.* **6.** same as **knock** (sense 7). —'**pinkish** *or* '**pinky** *adj.*

pink² (pıŋk) *vb.* to cut with pinking shears.

pinkie *or* **pinky** ('pıŋkı) *n., pl.* **-ies.** *Scot., U.S., & Canad.* the little finger.

pinking shears *pl. n.* scissors with a serrated edge on one or both blades, giving a wavy edge to material cut, thus preventing fraying.

pin money *n.* a small amount of extra money saved or earned for incidental expenses.

pinnace ('pınıs) *n.* a ship's boat.

pinnacle ('pınək°l) *n.* **1.** the highest point of fame or success. **2.** a towering peak, as of a mountain. **3.** a slender spire on the top of a buttress, gable, or tower.

pinnate ('pıneıt) *adj.* (of compound leaves)

having leaflets growing opposite each other in pairs.

pinny ('pɪnɪ) *n., pl.* **-nies.** a child's or informal name for **pinafore** (sense 1).

pinpoint ('pɪn,pɔɪnt) *vb.* **1.** to locate or identify exactly: *we've pinpointed the fault.* ~*n.* **2.** (*modifier*) exact: *pinpoint accuracy.*

pinprick ('pɪn,prɪk) *n.* a small irritation or annoyance.

pins and needles *n.* (*functioning as sing.*) *Informal.* a tingling sensation in a part of the body.

pinstripe ('pɪn,straɪp) *n.* (in textiles) a very narrow stripe in fabric or the fabric itself.

pint (paɪnt) *n.* **1.** a unit of liquid measure of capacity equal to one eighth of a gallon. 1 Brit. pint is equal to 0.568 litre, 1 U.S. pint to 0.473 litre. **2.** *Brit. informal.* a pint of beer.

pinta ('paɪntə) *n. Informal.* a pint of milk.

pintail ('pɪn,teɪl) *n., pl.* **-tails** *or* **-tail.** a greyish-brown duck with a pointed tail.

pintle ('pɪnt'l) *n.* a pin or bolt forming the pivot of a hinge.

pinto ('pɪntəʊ) *U.S. & Canad.* ~*adj.* **1.** marked with patches of white; piebald. ~*n., pl.* **-tos.** **2.** a pinto horse.

pint-size *or* **pint-sized** *adj. Informal.* very small.

pin tuck *n.* a narrow, ornamental fold, as used on shirt fronts and dress bodices.

pin-up *n.* **1.** *Informal.* a picture of a sexually attractive person, often when partially or totally undressed. **2.** *Slang.* a person who has appeared in such a picture. **3.** a photograph of a famous personality.

pinwheel ('pɪn,wiːl) *n.* same as **Catherine wheel.**

Pinyin ('pɪn'jɪn) *n.* a system of spelling used to transliterate Chinese characters into the Roman alphabet.

pion ('paɪɒn) *or* **pi meson** *n. Physics.* any of three subatomic particles which are classified as mesons.

pioneer (,paɪə'nɪə) *n.* **1.** an explorer or settler of a new land or region. **2.** an innovator or developer of something new. ~*vb.* **3.** to be a pioneer (in or of). **4.** to initiate or develop: *to pioneer a medical programme.*

pious ('paɪəs) *adj.* **1.** religious or devout. **2.** marked by false reverence; sanctimonious. —'**piousness** *n.*

pip¹ (pɪp) *n.* the seed of a fleshy fruit, such as an apple or pear.

pip² (pɪp) *n.* **1.** a short high-pitched sound, a sequence of which is used as a time signal on radio. **2.** any of the spots on a playing card, dice or domino. **3.** *Informal.* the emblem worn on the shoulder by junior officers in the British Army, indicating their rank.

pip³ (pɪp) *n.* **1.** a contagious disease of poultry. **2.** *Facetious slang.* a minor human ailment. **3.** *Brit. slang.* a bad temper or depression: *she gives me the pip.*

pip⁴ (pɪp) *vb.* **pipping, pipped.** *Brit. slang.* **pip (someone) at the post.** to defeat (someone) whose success seems certain.

pipe (paɪp) *n.* **1.** a long tube used to convey water, oil or gas. **2. a.** a small bowl with an attached tubular stem, in which tobacco or other substances are smoked. **b.** the amount of tobacco that fills the bowl of a pipe. **3. put that in your pipe and smoke it.** *Informal.* accept that fact if you can. **4.** *Zool., bot.* any of various hollow organs, such as the respiratory passage of certain animals. **5. a.** any musical instrument whose sound production results from the vibration of an air column in a simple tube. **b.** any of the tubular devices on an organ. **6. the pipes.** See **bagpipes.** **7.** a boatswain's whistle. ~*vb.* **8.** to play (music) on a pipe. **9.** to summon or lead by a pipe: *to pipe the dancers.* **10.** to utter (something) shrilly. **11.** to convey (water, gas, etc.) by a pipe or pipes. **12.** to force cream or icing through a shaped nozzle to decorate food. ~See also **pipe down, pipe up.**

pipeclay ('paɪp,kleɪ) *n.* a fine white pure clay, used in the manufacture of tobacco pipes and pottery and for whitening leather and similar materials.

pipe cleaner *n.* a short length of thin wires twisted so as to hold tiny tufts of yarn: used to clean the stem of a tobacco pipe.

piped music *n.* light music played through amplifiers as background music in a shop, restaurant or factory.

pipe down *vb. Informal.* to stop talking or making noise.

pipe dream *n.* a fanciful or impossible plan or hope.

pipeline ('paɪp,laɪn) *n.* **1.** a long pipe used to transport oil or gas. **2.** a medium of communication, esp. a private one. **3. in the pipeline.** in the process of being completed, delivered, or produced.

pipe organ *n.* same as **organ** (the musical instrument).

piper ('paɪpə) *n.* a person who plays a pipe or bagpipes.

pipette (pɪ'pɛt) *n.* a slender glass tube for transferring or measuring out known volumes of liquid.

pipe up *vb.* to speak up, esp. in a shrill voice.

pipi ('pɪpiː) *n., pl.* **pipi** *or* **pipis.** **1.** an edible shellfish of New Zealand. **2.** an Australian mollusc of sandy beaches widely used as bait.

piping ('paɪpɪŋ) *n.* **1.** pipes collectively, as in the plumbing of a house. **2.** a cord of icing or whipped cream often used to decorate desserts and cakes. **3.** a thin strip of covered cord or material, used to edge hems or cushions. **4.** a shrill voice or whistling sound. ~*adj.* **5.** making a shrill sound. **6.** **piping hot.** extremely hot.

pipistrelle (ˌpɪpɪˈstrɛl) *n.* any of a genus of small brownish bats occurring in most parts of the world.

pipit (ˈpɪpɪt) *n.* a small songbird with a brownish speckled plumage and a long tail.

pippin (ˈpɪpɪn) *n.* any of several varieties of eating apple.

pipsqueak (ˈpɪpˌskwiːk) *n. Informal.* a person or thing that is insignificant or contemptible.

piquant (ˈpiːkənt, -kɑːnt) *adj.* **1.** having a spicy taste. **2.** lively or stimulating to the mind. —ˈ**piquancy** *n.*

pique (piːk) *n.* **1.** a feeling of resentment or irritation, as from having one's pride wounded. ~*vb.* **piquing, piqued. 2.** to cause to feel resentment or irritation. **3.** to excite (curiosity or interest).

piqué (ˈpiːkeɪ) *n.* a close-textured fabric of cotton, silk, or spun rayon woven with lengthwise ribs.

piquet (pɪˈkɛt, -ˈkeɪ) *n.* a card game for two people played with a reduced pack.

piracy (ˈpaɪrəsɪ) *n., pl.* **-cies. 1.** *Brit.* robbery on the seas. **2.** a felony, such as robbery or hijacking, committed aboard a ship or aircraft. **3.** the unauthorized use of patented or copyrighted material or ideas.

piranha (pɪˈrɑːnə) *n.* a small fierce freshwater fish of tropical America, with strong jaws and sharp teeth.

pirate (ˈpaɪrɪt) *n.* **1.** a person who commits piracy. **2.** a vessel used by pirates. **3.** a person who illicitly uses or appropriates someone else's literary, artistic, or other work. **4.** a person or group of people who broadcast illegally. ~*vb.* **5.** to use, appropriate, or reproduce (artistic work, ideas, etc.) illicitly. —**piratic** (paɪˈrætɪk) *or* pi-ˈ**ratical** *adj.*

pirouette (ˌpɪruˈɛt) *n.* **1.** a body spin, esp. in dancing, on the toes or the ball of the foot. ~*vb.* **2.** to perform a pirouette.

piscatorial (ˌpɪskəˈtɔːrɪəl) *adj.* of or relating to fish, fishing, or fishermen.

Pisces (ˈpaɪsiːz, ˈpɪ-) *n. Astrol.* the twelfth sign of the zodiac, the Fishes.

pisciculture (ˈpɪsɪˌkʌltʃə) *n.* the rearing and breeding of fish under controlled conditions.

piscine (ˈpɪsaɪn) *adj.* of or resembling a fish.

piss (pɪs) *Taboo.* ~*vb.* **1.** to urinate. **2.** to discharge as or in one's urine: *to piss blood.* ~*n.* **3.** an act of urinating. **4.** urine.

pissed (pɪst) *adj. Brit. taboo slang.* drunk.

piss off *vb. Taboo slang.* **1.** to annoy or disappoint. **2.** *Chiefly Brit.* to go away: often used to dismiss a person.

pistachio (pɪˈstɑːʃɪˌəʊ) *n., pl.* **-chios.** a Mediterranean nut with a hard shell and an edible green kernel.

piste (piːst) *n.* a slope or course for skiing.

pistil (ˈpɪstɪl) *n.* the female reproductive part of a flower.

pistillate (ˈpɪstɪlɪt) *adj.* (of plants) having pistils.

pistol (ˈpɪstəl) *n.* a short-barrelled handgun.

pistol-whip *vb.* **-whipping, -whipped.** *U.S.* to beat or strike with a pistol barrel.

piston (ˈpɪstən) *n.* a disc or cylindrical part that slides to and fro in a hollow cylinder. In an internal-combustion engine it is attached by a pivoted connecting rod to a crankshaft or flywheel, thus converting up-and-down motion into rotation.

pit[1] (pɪt) *n.* **1.** a large, usually deep opening in the ground. **2.** a mine or excavation, esp. for coal. **3.** a concealed danger or difficulty. **4. the pit.** hell. **5.** the area that is occupied by the orchestra in a theatre, located in front of the stage. **6.** an enclosure for fighting animals or birds. **7.** *Anat.* **a.** a small natural depression on the surface of a body, organ, or part. **b.** the floor of any natural bodily cavity: *the pit of the stomach.* **8.** *Pathol.* a pockmark. **9.** an area at the side of a motor-racing track for servicing or refuelling vehicles. **10.** the back of the ground floor of a theatre. **11.** same as **pitfall** (sense 2). ~*vb.* **pitting, pitted. 12.** (often foll. by *against*) to match in opposition, esp. as antagonists. **13.** to mark or become marked with pits. **14.** to place or bury in a pit.

pit[2] (pɪt) *Chiefly U.S. & Canad.* ~*n.* **1.** the stone of various fruits. ~*vb.* **pitting, pitted. 2.** to extract the stone from (a fruit).

pitapat (ˈpɪtəˌpæt) *adv.* **1.** with quick light taps. ~*n.* **2.** such taps.

pitch[1] (pɪtʃ) *vb.* **1.** to hurl or throw (something); fling. **2.** to set up: *pitch a tent.* **3.** to set the level, character, or slope of. **4.** to slope or fall forwards or downwards. **5.** (of a vessel) to dip and raise its bow and stern alternately. **6.** (foll. by *up*) *Cricket.* to bowl (a ball) so that it bounces near the batsman. **7.** *Music.* to sing or play (a note or interval) accurately. ~*n.* **8.** the degree of elevation or depression. **9.** the angle of descent of a downward slope. **10.** *Chiefly Brit.* (in many sports) the field of play. **11.** the distance between corresponding points or adjacent threads on a screw thread. **12.** the pitching motion of a ship. **13.** *Music.* the quality of the sound of a note that results from the frequency of the vibrations producing it: the higher the frequency, the higher the sound. **14.** the act or manner of pitching a ball, as in cricket, etc. **15.** *Chiefly Brit.* a vendor's station on a pavement. **16.** *Slang.* a persuasive sales talk, esp. one routinely repeated. ~See also **pitch in, pitch into.**

pitch[2] (pɪtʃ) *n.* **1.** a thick sticky substance formed from coal tar and used for paving or waterproofing. **2.** any of various similar substances, such as asphalt, occurring as natural deposits. ~*vb.* **3.** to apply pitch to (something).

pitch-black *adj.* extremely dark; unlit: *the room was pitch-black.*

pitchblende (ˈpɪtʃˌblɛnd) *n.* a blackish mineral which is the principal source of uranium and radium.

pitch-dark *adj.* extremely or completely dark.

pitched battle *n.* a fierce fight.

pitcher[1] (ˈpɪtʃə) *n.* a large jug, usually rounded with a narrow neck, used mainly for holding water.

pitcher[2] (ˈpɪtʃə) *n. Baseball.* the player on the fielding team who throws the ball to the batter.

pitcher plant *n.* a plant with leaves modified to form pitcher-like organs that attract and trap insects, which are then digested.

pitchfork (ˈpɪtʃˌfɔːk) *n.* **1.** a long-handled fork with two or three long curved prongs for tossing hay. ~*vb.* **2.** to use a pitchfork on (something).

pitch in *vb.* to cooperate or contribute.

pitch into *vb. Informal.* to attack (someone) physically or verbally.

pitch pine *n.* a pine tree of North America: a source of turpentine and pitch.

pitch pipe *n.* a small pipe that sounds a note. It is used for establishing the correct starting note for unaccompanied singing.

piteous (ˈpɪtɪəs) *adj.* exciting or deserving pity. —**ˈpiteousness** *n.*

pitfall (ˈpɪtˌfɔːl) *n.* **1.** an unsuspected difficulty or danger. **2.** a trap in the form of a concealed pit, designed to catch men or wild animals.

pith (pɪθ) *n.* **1.** the soft white lining inside the rind of fruits such as the orange. **2.** the essential part: *the pith of the matter was in those two phrases.* **3.** the soft spongy tissue in the centre of the stem of certain plants.

pithead (ˈpɪtˌhɛd) *n.* the top of a mine shaft and the buildings and hoisting gear around it.

pith helmet *n.* a lightweight hat made of the pith of the sola, an E Indian swamp plant, that is worn for protection from the sun.

pithy (ˈpɪθɪ) *adj.* **pithier, pithiest. 1.** terse and full of meaning or substance. **2.** of, resembling, or full of pith. —**ˈpithiness** *n.*

pitiable (ˈpɪtɪəbʲl) *adj.* exciting or deserving pity or contempt. —**ˈpitiableness** *n.*

pitiful (ˈpɪtɪfʊl) *adj.* **1.** arousing or deserving pity. **2.** arousing or deserving contempt. —**ˈpitifully** *adv.* —**ˈpitifulness** *n.*

pitiless (ˈpɪtɪlɪs) *adj.* having or showing little or no pity or mercy. —**ˈpitilessly** *adv.*

piton (ˈpiːtɒn) *n. Mountaineering.* a metal spike that may be driven into a crevice and used to secure a rope.

pits (pɪts) *pl. n. Slang.* the worst possible person, place, or thing.

pittance (ˈpɪtʲns) *n.* a very small amount of money.

pitter-patter (ˈpɪtəˌpætə) *n.* **1.** the sound of light rapid taps or pats, as of raindrops. ~*vb.* **2.** to make such a sound.

pituitary (pɪˈtjuːɪtərɪ) *or* **pituitary gland** *n.* the master endocrine gland at the base of the brain. It secretes hormones affecting skeletal growth, development of the sex glands, and the functioning of the other endocrine glands.

pity (ˈpɪtɪ) *n., pl.* **pities. 1.** sorrow felt for the sufferings of another. **2. have** (*or* **take**) **pity on.** to have sympathy or show mercy for. **3.** a cause of regret: *what a pity you can't come.* ~*vb.* **pitying, pitied. 4.** to feel pity for. —**ˈpitying** *adj.*

più (pjuː) *adv. Music.* more: *più allegro.*

pivot (ˈpɪvət) *n.* **1.** a short shaft or pin supporting something that turns. **2.** a person or thing upon which progress or success depends. ~*vb.* **3.** to mount on or provide with a pivot or pivots. **4.** to turn on a pivot.

pivotal (ˈpɪvətʲl) *adj.* **1.** of or acting as a pivot. **2.** of crucial importance.

pix (pɪks) *n.* a plural of **pic.**

pixie *or* **pixy** (ˈpɪksɪ) *n., pl.* **pixies.** (in folklore) a fairy or elf.

pizza (ˈpiːtsə) *n.* a dish of Italian origin consisting of a baked disc of dough covered with cheese, tomatoes, herbs, etc.

pizzazz *or* **pizazz** (pəˈzæz) *n. Informal.* an attractive combination of energy and style.

pizzicato (ˌpɪtsɪˈkɑːtəʊ) *Music.* ~*adj., adv.* (in music for the violin family) to be plucked with the finger.

Pl. (in street names) Place.

plaas (plɑːs) *n. S. African.* a farm.

placard (ˈplækɑːd) *n.* **1.** a notice for public display; poster. ~*vb.* **2.** to post placards on or in.

placate (pləˈkeɪt) *vb.* to pacify or appease (someone). —**plaˈcatory** *adj.*

place (pleɪs) *n.* **1.** a particular point or part of space or of a surface, esp. that occupied by a person or thing. **2.** a geographical point, such as a town or city. **3.** a position or rank in a sequence or order. **4.** an open square lined with houses in a city or town. **5.** space or room. **6.** a house or living quarters. **7.** any building or area set aside for a specific purpose. **8.** the point reached in reading or speaking: *to lose one's place.* **9.** right or duty: *it is your place to give a speech.* **10.** appointment, position, or job: *a place at college.* **11.** position,

condition, or state: *if I were in your place.*
12. a space or seat, as at a dining table. **13.**
Maths. the relative position of a digit in a
number. **14. all over the place.** in disorder
or disarray. **15. go places.** *Informal.* to
become successful. **16. in** (*or* **out of**)
place. in (*or* out of) the proper or customary position. **17. in place of. a.** instead of;
in lieu of: *go in place of my sister.* **b.** in
exchange for: *he gave her it in place of her
ring.* **18. know one's place.** to be aware of
one's inferior position. **19. put someone in
his** (*or* **her**) **place.** to humble someone who
is arrogant, conceited, etc. **20. take place.**
to happen or occur. **21. take the place of.**
to be a substitute for. ~*vb.* **22.** to put in a
particular or appropriate place. **23.** to find
or indicate the place of. **24.** to identify or
classify by linking with an appropriate context: *to place a face.* **25.** to make (an order
or bet). **26.** to find a home or job for
(someone). **27.** (often foll. by *with*) to put
under the care (of). **28.** *Brit.* (of a racehorse, greyhound, athlete, etc.) to arrive in
first, second, third, or sometimes fourth
place.

placebo (pləˈsiːbəʊ) *n., pl.* **-bos** *or* **-boes.**
Med. an inactive substance administered to
a patient usually to compare its effects with
those of a real drug but sometimes for the
psychological benefit to the patient through
his believing he is receiving treatment.

place kick *n. Rugby, American football,
etc.* a kick in which the ball is placed in
position before it is kicked.

placement (ˈpleɪsmənt) *n.* **1.** the act of
placing or the state of being placed. **2.**
arrangement or position. **3.** the process of
finding employment.

placenta (pləˈsɛntə) *n., pl.* **-tas** *or* **-tae** (-tiː).
the organ formed in the womb of most
mammals during pregnancy, providing oxygen and nutrients for the fetus. —**pla-
ˈcental** *adj.*

place setting *n.* the cutlery, crockery,
and glassware laid for one person at a
dining table.

placid (ˈplæsɪd) *adj.* having a calm appearance or nature: *placid waters; a placid disposition.* —**placidity** (pləˈsɪdɪtɪ) *or* **plac-
idness** *n.* —**ˈplacidly** *adv.*

placket (ˈplækɪt) *n. Dressmaking.* an opening or slit at the waist of a dress or skirt for
buttons or zips or for access to a pocket.

plagiarize *or* **-ise** (ˈpleɪdʒəˌraɪz) *vb.* to
steal (ideas or passages) from (another
work or author). —**ˈplagiaˌrism** *n.* —**ˈpla-
giaˌrizer** *or* **-iser** *n.*

plague (pleɪg) *n.* **1.** any widespread and
usually highly contagious disease with a
high fatality rate. **2.** an infectious disease
of rodents transmitted to man by the bite of
the rat flea. **3.** something that afflicts or
harasses. **4.** *Informal.* a nuisance. ~*vb.*

plaguing, plagued. 5. to afflict or harass.
6. *Informal.* to annoy.

plaice (pleɪs) *n., pl.* **plaice** *or* **plaices.** a
European flatfish with an oval brown body
marked with red or orange spots and valued
as a food fish.

plaid (plæd, pleɪd) *n.* **1.** a long piece of
tartan cloth worn over the shoulder as part
of Highland costume. **2.** a crisscross weave
or cloth.

Plaid Cymru (ˌplaɪd ˈkʌmrɪ) *n.* the Welsh
nationalist party.

plain (pleɪn) *adj.* **1.** flat or smooth; level.
2. not complicated; clear: *the plain truth.*
3. honest or straightforward. **4.** lowly, esp.
in social rank or education. **5.** without
adornment: *a plain coat.* **6.** (of fabric)
without pattern or of simple untwilled
weave. **7.** not good-looking. **8.** *Knitting.* of
or done in plain. ~*n.* **9.** a level or almost
level tract of country. **10.** a simple stitch in
knitting made by passing the wool round
the front of the needle. ~*adv.* **11.** clearly
or simply: *just plain tired.* —**ˈplainly** *adv.*
—**ˈplainness** *n.*

plainchant (ˈpleɪnˌtʃɑːnt) *n.* same as **plainsong.**

plain chocolate *n.* chocolate with a
slightly bitter flavour and dark colour.

plain clothes *pl. n.* ordinary clothes, as
distinguished from uniform, worn by a detective on duty.

plain flour *n.* flour to which no raising
agent has been added.

plain sailing *n.* **1.** *Informal.* smooth or
easy progress. **2.** *Naut.* sailing in a body of
water that is unobstructed; clear sailing.

plainsong (ˈpleɪnˌsɒŋ) *n.* the style of unison unaccompanied vocal music used in the
medieval Church, esp. in Gregorian chant.

plain-spoken *adj.* candid; frank; blunt.

plaint (pleɪnt) *n.* **1.** *Archaic.* a complaint or
lamentation. **2.** *Law.* a statement in writing of grounds of complaint made to a court
of law.

plaintiff (ˈpleɪntɪf) *n.* a person who brings a
civil action in a court of law.

plaintive (ˈpleɪntɪv) *adj.* expressing melancholy; mournful. —**ˈplaintively** *adv.*

plait (plæt) *n.* **1.** a length of hair that has
been plaited. ~*vb.* **2.** to intertwine
(strands or strips) in a pattern.

plan (plæn) *n.* **1.** a scheme or method for
doing or achieving something. **2.** a drawing
to scale of a horizontal section through a
building taken at a given level. **3.** an outline or sketch. ~*vb.* **planning, planned.**
4. to form a plan (for) or make plans (for).
5. to make a plan of (a building). **6.** to
intend.

planchette (plɑːnˈʃɛt) *n.* a device that
writes messages under supposed spirit
guidance.

plane[1] (pleɪn) *n.* **1.** *Maths.* a flat surface in

which a straight line joining any two of its points lies entirely on that surface. **2.** a level surface. **3.** a level of existence or attainment. **4.** an aeroplane. ~*adj.* **5.** level or flat. **6.** *Maths.* lying entirely in one plane. ~*vb.* **7.** (of a boat) to skim over the water at high speed.

plane² (plem) *n.* **1.** a tool with a steel blade for smoothing timber. ~*vb.* **2.** to smooth (timber) using a plane. **3.** (often foll. by *off*) to remove using a plane.

planet ('plænɪt) *n.* any of the nine celestial bodies, Mercury, Venus, earth, Mars, Jupiter, Saturn, Uranus, Neptune, or Pluto, that revolve around the sun in elliptical orbits. —'**planetary** *adj.*

planetarium (,plænɪ'tɛərɪəm) *n., pl.* -**iums** or -**ia** (-ɪə). **1.** an instrument for projecting images of the sun, moon, stars, and planets onto a domed ceiling. **2.** a building in which such an instrument is housed.

planetoid ('plænɪ,tɔɪd) *n.* See **asteroid.**

plane tree *or* **plane** (plem) *n.* a tree with ball-shaped heads of fruit and leaves with pointed lobes.

plank (plæŋk) *n.* **1.** a stout length of sawn timber. **2.** one of the policies in a political party's programme. **3. walk the plank.** to be forced by pirates to walk to one's death off the end of a plank jutting out from the side of a ship.

planking ('plæŋkɪŋ) *n.* a number of planks.

plankton ('plæŋktən) *n.* the organisms inhabiting the surface layer of a sea or lake, consisting of small drifting plants and animals.

plant (plɑːnt) *n.* **1.** any living organism that typically synthesizes its food from inorganic substances, lacks specialized sense organs, and has no powers of locomotion. **2.** such an organism that is smaller than a shrub or tree. **3.** the land, building, and equipment used in an industry or business. **4.** a factory or workshop. **5.** mobile mechanical equipment for construction or road-making. **6.** *Informal.* a thing positioned secretly for discovery by another, often in order to incriminate an innocent person. ~*vb.* **7.** (often foll. by *out*) to set (seeds or crops) into (ground) to grow. **8.** to place firmly in position: *I planted my chair beside hers.* **9.** *Slang.* to deliver (a blow or kiss). **10.** *Informal.* to position or hide, often in order to deceive or observe. **11.** *Informal.* to hide or secrete, usually for some illegal purpose or in order to incriminate someone.

plantain¹ ('plæntɪn) *n.* a plant with a rosette of broad leaves and a slender spike of small greenish flowers.

plantain² ('plæntɪn) *n.* a large tropical plant with a green-skinned banana-like fruit which is eaten as a staple food in many tropical regions.

plantation (plæn'teɪʃən) *n.* **1.** an estate, esp. in tropical countries, where cash crops such as rubber or coffee are grown on a large scale. **2.** a group of cultivated trees or plants. **3.** (formerly) a colony or group of settlers.

planter ('plɑːntə) *n.* **1.** the owner or manager of a plantation. **2.** a decorative pot for house plants.

plantigrade ('plæntɪ,greɪd) *adj.* walking on the entire sole of the foot, as humans and bears do.

plaque (plæk, plɑːk) *n.* **1.** an ornamental or commemorative inscribed tablet. **2.** Also called: **dental plaque.** a filmy deposit on teeth consisting of mucus, bacteria, food, etc.

plasma ('plæzmə) *n.* **1.** the clear yellowish fluid portion of blood or lymph in which the corpuscles and cells are suspended. **2.** a sterilized preparation of such fluid, taken from the blood, for use in transfusions. **3.** a former name for **protoplasm. 4.** *Physics.* a hot ionized gas containing positive ions and free electrons.

plaster ('plɑːstə) *n.* **1.** a mixture of lime, sand, and water that is applied to a wall or ceiling as a soft paste that hardens when dry. **2.** *Brit.* an adhesive strip of material for dressing a cut or wound. **3.** short for **mustard plaster** or **plaster of Paris.** ~*vb.* **4.** to coat (a wall or ceiling) with plaster. **5.** to apply like plaster: *she plastered make-up on her face; the walls were plastered with posters.* **6.** to cause to lie flat or to adhere: *his hair was plastered down to his eyebrows.* —'**plasterer** *n.*

plasterboard ('plɑːstə,bɔːd) *n.* a thin rigid board, made of plaster compressed between two layers of fibreboard, used to form or cover walls.

plastered ('plɑːstəd) *adj. Slang.* drunk.

plaster of Paris *n.* a white powder that sets to a hard solid when mixed with water, used for making sculptures and casts, as an additive for lime plasters, and for making casts for setting broken limbs.

plastic ('plæstɪk) *n.* **1.** any one of a large number of synthetic materials that can be moulded when soft and then set. ~*adj.* **2.** made of plastic. **3.** easily influenced. **4.** capable of being moulded or formed. **5.** of moulding or modelling: *the plastic arts.* **6.** *Slang.* superficially attractive yet unoriginal or artificial: *plastic food.* —**plasticity** (plæ'stɪsɪtɪ) *n.*

plastic bomb *n.* a bomb consisting of plastic explosive fitted around a detonator.

plastic bullet *n.* a solid PVC cylinder fired by the police in riot control.

plastic explosive *n.* an adhesive jelly-like explosive substance.

Plasticine ('plæstɪ,siːn) *n. Trademark.* a soft coloured material used, esp. by children, for modelling.

plasticize *or* **-cise** (ˈplæstɪˌsaɪz) *vb.* to make or become plastic.

plasticizer *or* **-ciser** (ˈplæstɪˌsaɪzə) *n.* a substance added to a plastic material to soften it and improve flexibility.

plastic surgery *n.* the branch of surgery concerned with the repair or re-formation of missing, injured, or malformed tissues or parts. —**plastic surgeon** *n.*

plate (pleɪt) *n.* **1.** a shallow dish made of porcelain, earthenware, glass, etc., on which food is served. **2.** Also called: **plateful.** the contents of a plate. **3.** a shallow dish for receiving a collection in church. **4.** flat metal of uniform thickness obtained by rolling. **5.** a thin coating of metal usually on another metal. **6.** dishes or cutlery made of gold or silver. **7.** a sheet of metal, plastic or rubber having a printing surface produced by a process such as stereotyping. **8.** a print taken from such a sheet or from a woodcut. **9.** a thin flat sheet of a substance, such as metal or glass. **10.** a small piece of metal or plastic designed to bear an inscription and to be fixed to another surface. **11.** *Photog.* a sheet of glass coated with photographic emulsion on which an image can be formed by exposure to light. **12.** *Informal.* same as **denture** (sense 1). **13.** *Anat.* any flat platelike structure. **14.** a cup awarded to the winner of a sporting contest, esp. a horse race. **15.** any of the rigid layers of the earth's crust. **16. on a plate.** acquired without trouble: *he was handed the job on a plate.* **17. on one's plate.** waiting to be done or dealt with: *she has a lot on her plate at the moment.* ~*vb.* **18.** to coat (a surface, usually metal) with a thin layer of other metal, as by electrolysis. **19.** to cover with metal plates, as for protection. **20.** to form (metal) into plate, usually by rolling.

plateau (ˈplætəʊ) *n., pl.* **-eaus** *or* **-eaux** (-əʊz). **1.** a wide mainly level area of elevated land. **2.** a relatively long period of stability; levelling off: *the rising prices reached a plateau.*

plated (ˈpleɪtɪd) *adj.* coated with a layer of metal.

plate glass *n.* glass formed into a thin sheet by rolling, used for windows.

platelayer (ˈpleɪtˌleɪə) *n. Brit.* a workman who lays and maintains railway track.

platelet (ˈpleɪtlɪt) *n.* a minute particle occurring in the blood of vertebrates and involved in the clotting of the blood.

platen (ˈplætˀn) *n.* **1.** a flat plate in a printing press that presses the paper against the type. **2.** the roller on a typewriter, against which the keys strike.

platform (ˈplætfɔːm) *n.* **1.** a raised floor or other horizontal surface. **2.** a raised area at a railway station, from which passengers have access to the trains. **3.** See **drilling platform.** **4.** the declared aims of a

political party. **5.** the thick raised sole of some shoes.

platform ticket *n.* a ticket for admission to railway platforms but not for travel.

plating (ˈpleɪtɪŋ) *n.* **1.** a coating or layer of material, esp. metal. **2.** a layer or covering of metal plates.

platinum (ˈplætɪnəm) *n.* a silvery-white metallic element, very resistant to heat and chemicals: used in jewellery, laboratory apparatus, electrical contacts, dentistry, electroplating, and as a catalyst. Symbol: Pt

platinum blonde *n.* a girl or woman with silvery blonde hair.

platitude (ˈplætɪˌtjuːd) *n.* a trite or unoriginal remark. —**ˌplatiˈtudinous** *adj.*

Platonic (pləˈtɒnɪk) *adj.* **1.** of Plato or his teachings. **2.** (*often not cap.*) free from physical desire: *Platonic love.*

Platonism (ˈpleɪtəˌnɪzəm) *n.* the teachings of Plato (?427–?347 B.C.), Greek philosopher, and his followers. —**ˈPlatonist** *n.*

platoon (pləˈtuːn) *n. Mil.* a subunit of a company, usually comprising three sections of ten to twelve men.

platteland (ˈplatəˌlant) *n.* **the.** (in South Africa) the area outside the cities and chief towns.

platter (ˈplætə) *n.* a large shallow usually oval dish or plate.

platypus (ˈplætɪpəs) *n., pl.* **-puses.** See **duck-billed platypus.**

plaudit (ˈplɔːdɪt) *n.* (*usually pl.*) **1.** an expression of enthusiastic approval. **2.** a round of applause.

plausible (ˈplɔːzɪbˀl) *adj.* **1.** apparently reasonable, valid or true: *a plausible excuse.* **2.** apparently trustworthy or believable: *a plausible speaker.* —**ˌplausiˈbility** *n.* —**ˈplausibly** *adv.*

play (pleɪ) *vb.* **1.** to occupy oneself in (a sport or recreation). **2.** to contend against (someone) in a sport or game: *Ed played Tony at chess.* **3.** to fulfil or cause to fulfil (a particular role) in a team game: *he plays in the defence.* **4.** (often foll. by *about* or *around*) to behave carelessly: *he plays about with her affections.* **5.** (often foll. by *at*) to act the part (of) in or as in a dramatic piece. **6.** to perform (a dramatic piece). **7.** to be able to perform on (a musical instrument): *she plays the harp.* **8.** to reproduce (a piece of music or note) on an instrument. **9.** to emit or cause to emit: *he played the hose onto the garden.* **10.** to cause (a radio, etc.) to emit sound. **11.** to move freely or quickly: *lights played on the scenery.* **12.** *Stock Exchange.* to speculate for gain in (a market). **13.** *Angling.* to tire (a hooked fish) by alternately letting out and reeling in the line. **14.** to put (a card) into play. **15.** to gamble. **16. play fair** (*or* **false**). (often foll. by *with*) to act fairly (*or* unfairly). **17. play for time.** to cause delay so as to gain time to one's own advantage. **18. play into the hands of.** to act directly to the advantage of (an opponent). ~*n.* **19.** a dramatic piece written for performance by actors. **20.** the performance of a dramatic piece. **21.** games or other activity undertaken for pleasure. **22.** conduct: *fair play.* **23.** the playing of a game or the time during which a game is in progress: *rain stopped play.* **24.** gambling. **25.** activity or operation: *the play of the imagination.* **26.** freedom of movement: *too much play in the rope.* **27.** free or rapidly shifting motion: *the play of light on the water.* **28.** fun or jest: *I only did it in play.* **29. in** (or **out of**) **play.** (of a ball in a game) in (or not in) a position for continuing play according to the rules. **30. make a play for.** *Informal.* to make an obvious attempt to gain (something). ~See also **play along, playback.** —'**playable** *adj.*

play along *vb.* to cooperate (with) temporarily: *I'll play along with them for the moment.*

playback ('pleɪ,bæk) *n.* **1.** the playing of a recording on magnetic tape. ~*vb.* **play back. 2.** to play (a recording) on (a magnetic tape) by means of a tape recorder.

playbill ('pleɪ,bɪl) *n.* a poster or bill advertising a play.

playboy ('pleɪ,bɔɪ) *n.* a rich man who devotes himself to such pleasures as nightclubs and female company.

play down *vb.* to minimize the importance of: *she played down the problems of the company.*

player ('pleɪə) *n.* **1.** a person who plays in or is skilled at some game or sport. **2.** a person who plays a musical instrument. **3.** an actor.

player piano *n.* a mechanical piano; Pianola.

playful ('pleɪfʊl) *adj.* **1.** full of high spirits and fun: *a playful kitten.* **2.** good-natured and humorous: *a playful remark.* —'**playfully** *adv.*

playgoer ('pleɪ,gəʊə) *n.* a person who goes often to the theatre.

playground ('pleɪ,graʊnd) *n.* an outdoor area for children's play, either with equipment such as swings and slides, or adjoining a school.

playgroup ('pleɪ,gruːp) *n.* a regular meeting of small children for supervised creative play.

playhouse ('pleɪ,haʊs) *n.* a theatre.

playing field *n. Chiefly Brit.* a field or open space used for sport.

playlist ('pleɪ,lɪst) *n.* a list of records chosen for playing, as on a radio station.

playmate ('pleɪ,meɪt) *n.* a companion in play or recreation.

play off *vb.* **1.** (usually foll. by *against*) to manipulate: *to play one person off*

against another. **2.** to take part in a play-off. ~*n.* **play-off. 3.** *Sport.* an extra contest to decide the winner when there is a tie. **4.** *Chiefly U.S. & Canad.* a contest or series of games to determine a championship.

play on *vb.* to exploit (the feelings or weakness of another): *he played on my sympathy.*

play on words *n.* same as **pun.**

playpen ('pleɪ,pen) *n.* a small portable enclosure in which a young child can safely be left to play.

playschool ('pleɪ,skuːl) *n.* an informal nursery group for preschool children.

plaything ('pleɪ,θɪŋ) *n.* **1.** a toy. **2.** a person regarded or treated as a toy.

playtime ('pleɪ,taɪm) *n.* a time for play or recreation, such as a school break.

play up *vb.* **1.** to highlight: *to play up one's best features.* **2.** *Brit. informal.* to behave irritatingly (towards). **3.** to hurt; give (one) trouble: *my back's playing up again.* **4. play up to. a.** to support (another actor) in a performance. **b.** to try to please by flattery.

playwright ('pleɪ,raɪt) *n.* a writer of plays.

plaza ('plɑːzə) *n.* **1.** an open public square, usually in Spain. **2.** *Chiefly U.S. & Canad.* a modern shopping complex.

PLC *or* **plc** Public Limited Company.

plea (pliː) *n.* **1.** an earnest appeal. **2.** *Law.* a statement by or on behalf of a defendant. **3.** an excuse: *a plea of poverty.*

plead (pliːd) *vb.* **pleading, pleaded, plead** (plɛd), *or esp. Scot. & U.S.* **pled. 1.** (sometimes foll. by *with*) to appeal earnestly (to). **2.** to give as an excuse: *to plead poverty.* **3.** *Law.* to declare oneself to be (guilty or not guilty) to the charge. **4.** *Law.* to present (a case) in a court of law. **5.** to address a court as an advocate.

pleadings ('pliːdɪŋz) *pl. n. Law.* the formal written statements presented by the plaintiff and defendant in a lawsuit.

pleasant ('plezᵊnt) *adj.* **1.** pleasing; enjoyable. **2.** having pleasing manners or appearance. —'**pleasantly** *adv.*

pleasantry ('plezᵊntrɪ) *n., pl.* **-ries. 1.** (often *pl.*) a polite or jocular remark: *they exchanged pleasantries.* **2.** agreeable jocularity.

please (pliːz) *vb.* **1.** to give pleasure or satisfaction to (a person). **2.** to be the will of: *if it pleases you; the court pleases.* **3. if you please.** if you wish, sometimes used in ironic exclamation. **4. pleased with.** happy because of. **5. please oneself.** to do as one likes. ~*adv.* **6.** used in making polite requests or pleading. **7. yes please.** a polite phrase used to accept an offer or invitation. —**pleased** *adj.*

pleasing ('pliːzɪŋ) *adj.* giving pleasure.

pleasurable ('plɛʒərəb³l) *adj.* enjoyable or agreeable. —'**pleasurably** *adv.*

pleasure ('plɛʒə) *n.* **1.** an enjoyable sensation or emotion: *the pleasure of hearing good music.* **2.** something that gives enjoyment: *his garden was his only pleasure.* **3.** amusement or enjoyment. **4.** *Euphemistic.* sexual gratification: *he took his pleasure of her.* **5.** a person's preference.

pleat (pliːt) *n.* **1.** a fold formed by doubling back fabric and pressing or stitching into place. ~*vb.* **2.** to arrange (material) in pleats.

pleb (plɛb) *n. Brit. informal, often offensive.* a common vulgar person.

plebeian (plə'biːən) *adj.* **1.** of the common people. **2.** unrefined; vulgar: *plebeian tastes.* ~*n.* **3.** one of the common people, usually of ancient Rome. **4.** a coarse or vulgar person.

plebiscite ('plɛbɪ,saɪt, -sɪt) *n.* a direct vote by all the electorate on an issue of national importance.

plectrum ('plɛktrəm) *n., pl.* **-tra** (-trə) *or* **-trums.** an implement for plucking the strings of a guitar or similar instrument.

pled (plɛd) *vb. U.S. or (esp. in legal usage) Scot.* a past of **plead.**

pledge (plɛdʒ) *n.* **1.** a solemn promise or agreement. **2. a.** security for the payment of a debt or the performance of an obligation. **b.** the condition of being security: *in pledge.* **3.** a token: *a pledge of good faith.* **4.** an assurance of support or goodwill, given by drinking a toast: *we drank a pledge to their success.* **5. take** or **sign the pledge.** to vow not to drink alcohol. ~*vb.* **6.** to promise solemnly. **7.** to bind by or as if by a pledge: *I was pledged to secrecy.* **8.** to give or offer (one's word or property) as a guarantee. **9.** to drink a toast to (a person or cause).

Pleiocene ('plaɪəʊ,siːn) *adj., n.* same as **Pliocene.**

Pleistocene ('plaɪstə,siːn) *adj. Geol.* of the epoch of geological time about 600 000 years ago.

plenary ('pliːnərɪ, 'plɛn-) *adj.* **1.** full or complete: *plenary powers.* **2.** (of an assembly) attended by all the members.

plenipotentiary (,plɛnɪpə'tɛnʃərɪ) *adj.* **1.** (usually of a diplomat) invested with full authority. ~*n., pl.* **-aries. 2.** a person, usually a diplomat invested with full authority to transact business.

plenitude ('plɛnɪ,tjuːd) *n.* **1.** abundance. **2.** fullness; completeness.

plenteous ('plɛntɪəs) *adj.* **1.** ample; abundant: *a plenteous supply.* **2.** producing abundantly: *a plenteous harvest.*

plentiful ('plɛntɪfʊl) *adj.* **1.** ample; abundant. **2.** having or yielding an abundance: *a plentiful year.* —'**plentifully** *adv.*

plenty ('plɛntɪ) *n., pl.* **-ties. 1.** (often foll. by *of*) a great number or amount; lots: *plenty of time.* **2.** ample supplies: *an age of plenty.* ~*det.* **3.** very many; ample: *plenty of people hate spiders.* ~*adv.* **4.** *Informal.* fully: *the coat was plenty big enough.*

pleonasm ('pliːə,næzəm) *n. Rhetoric.* **1.** the use of more words than necessary, such as *a tiny little child.* **2.** an unnecessary word or phrase. —,**pleo'nastic** *adj.*

plethora ('plɛθərə) *n.* an excess; overabundance.

pleura ('plʊərə) *n., pl.* **pleurae** ('plʊəriː). the thin transparent membrane enveloping the lungs. —'**pleural** *adj.*

pleurisy ('plʊərɪsɪ) *n.* inflammation of the pleura, making breathing painful. —**pleuritic** (plʊ'rɪtɪk) *adj., n.*

plexus ('plɛksəs) *n., pl.* **-uses** *or* **-us.** a complex network of nerves or blood vessels.

pliable ('plaɪəb³l) *adj.* easily bent, influenced, or altered. —,**plia'bility** *n.*

pliant ('plaɪənt) *adj.* **1.** easily bent; supple. **2.** adaptable; easily influenced. —'**pliancy** *n.*

pliers ('plaɪəz) *pl. n.* a gripping tool consisting of two hinged arms usually with serrated jaws.

plight[1] (plaɪt) *n.* a condition of extreme hardship or danger.

plight[2] (plaɪt) *vb.* **1.** to promise formally. **2. plight one's troth.** to make a promise to marry.

Plimsoll line ('plɪmsəl) *n.* a line on the hull of a ship showing the level that the water should reach if the ship is properly loaded.

plimsolls ('plɪmsəlz) *pl. n. Brit.* light rubber-soled canvas sports shoes.

plinth (plɪnθ) *n.* **1.** the rectangular block that forms the base of a column, pedestal, or pier. **2.** a base on which a statue stands.

Pliocene *or* **Pleiocene** ('plaɪəʊ,siːn) *adj. Geol.* of the epoch of geological time about 10 million years ago.

PLO Palestine Liberation Organization.

plod (plɒd) *vb.* **plodding, plodded. 1.** to walk with heavy slow steps. **2.** to work slowly and perseveringly. ~*n.* **3.** the act of plodding. —'**plodder** *n.*

plonk[1] (plɒŋk) *vb.* **1.** (often foll. by *down*) to drop or be dropped heavily: *he plonked the money on the table.* ~*n.* **2.** the act or sound of plonking.

plonk[2] (plɒŋk) *n. Informal.* inferior wine.

plonker ('plɒŋkə) *n. Slang.* a stupid person.

plop (plɒp) *n.* **1.** the sound made by an object dropping into water without a splash. ~*vb.* **plopping, plopped. 2.** to fall or cause to fall with a plop: *the stone plopped into the water.* ~*adv.* **3.** with a plop: *to go plop.*

plosive ('pləʊsɪv) *Phonetics.* ~*adj.* **1.** pronounced with a sudden release of breath. ~*n.* **2.** a plosive consonant.

plot¹ (plɒt) n. **1.** a secret plan for an illegal purpose. **2.** the story of a play, novel, or film. ~vb. **plotting, plotted. 3.** to plan secretly; conspire. **4.** to mark (a course) on a map. **5.** to make a plan or map of. **6. a.** to locate (points) on a graph by means of coordinates. **b.** to draw (a curve) through these points. **7.** to construct the plot of (a play, novel, or film). —'**plotter** n.

plot² (plɒt) n. a small piece of land: a vegetable plot.

plough or esp. U.S. **plow** (plau) n. **1.** an agricultural implement for cutting or turning over the earth. **2.** a similar implement, such as a device for clearing snow. ~vb. **3.** to till (the soil) with a plough. **4.** to make (furrows or grooves) in (something) with or as if with a plough. **5.** (sometimes foll. by through) to move (through something) in the manner of a plough. **6.** (foll. by through) to work at slowly or perseveringly. **7.** (foll. by into or through) (of a vehicle) to run uncontrollably into something.

Plough (plau) n. **the.** the group of the seven brightest stars in the constellation Ursa Major.

ploughman or esp. U.S. **plowman** ('plaumən) n., pl. **-men.** a man who ploughs.

ploughshare or esp. U.S. **plowshare** ('plau̩ʃɛə) n. the cutting blade of a plough.

plover ('plʌvə) n. a shore bird with a round head, straight bill, and large pointed wings.

plow (plau) n., vb. U.S. same as **plough.**

ploy (plɔɪ) n. a manoeuvre designed to gain advantage in a situation.

pluck (plʌk) vb. **1.** to pull off (feathers or fruit) from (a fowl or tree). **2.** (sometimes foll. by at) to pull or tug. **3.** (foll. by off, away, etc.) Archaic. to pull (something) forcibly or violently (from something or someone). **4.** to sound (the strings) of (a musical instrument) with the fingers or a plectrum. **5.** Slang. to swindle. ~n. **6.** courage. **7.** a pull or tug. **8.** the heart, liver, and lungs of an animal used for food.

pluck up vb. to muster (courage).

plucky ('plʌkɪ) adj. **pluckier, pluckiest.** courageous. —'**pluckily** adv. —'**pluckiness** n.

plug (plʌg) n. **1.** a piece of solid material used to stop up holes or waste pipes. **2.** a device having one or more pins to which an electric cable is attached: used to make an electrical connection when inserted into a socket. **3.** See **spark plug. 4.** a cake or piece of tobacco for chewing. **5.** Informal. a favourable mention of a product or show, as on television. ~vb. **plugging, plugged. 6.** to stop up (a hole or gap) with or as if with a plug. **7.** Informal. to make favourable and frequent mentions of (a product or show), as on television. **8.** Slang. to shoot: he plugged six rabbits. **9.** Slang. to punch.

10. (foll. by along, away, etc.) Informal. to work steadily.

plug in vb. to connect (an electrical appliance) with a power source by means of an electrical plug.

plum (plʌm) n. **1.** an edible oval purple, yellow, or green fruit with an oval stone, that grows on a small tree. **2.** a raisin, as used in a cake or pudding. **3.** Informal. something of a superior or desirable kind. ~adj. **4.** dark reddish-purple.

plumage ('pluːmɪdʒ) n. the feathers of a bird.

plumb (plʌm) n. **1.** a lead weight suspended at the end of a line and used to determine water depth or whether a structure, such as a wall, is vertical. **2. out of plumb.** not vertical. ~adv. **3.** vertical or perpendicular. **4.** Informal, chiefly U.S. utterly: plumb stupid. **5.** Informal. exactly. ~vb. **6.** to test the alignment of or make vertical with a plumb line. **7.** to experience (the worst extremes of): to plumb the depths of despair. **8.** to understand (something obscure): to plumb a mystery. **9.** to connect (a device) to a water pipe or drainage system.

plumber ('plʌmə) n. a person who fits and repairs pipes and fixtures for water, drainage, or gas.

plumbing ('plʌmɪŋ) n. **1.** the trade or work of a plumber. **2.** the pipes and fixtures used in a water, drainage, or gas installation.

plumb line n. a string with a metal weight, or **plumb bob,** at one end, used to determine depth or whether a structure, such as a wall, is vertical.

plume (pluːm) n. **1.** a large or ornamental feather. **2.** a feather or feathers worn as a badge or ornament in a headband or hat. **3.** something like a plume: a plume of smoke. ~vb. **4.** to adorn with plumes. **5.** (of a bird) to preen (itself or its feathers). **6.** (foll. by on or upon) to pride (oneself).

plummet ('plʌmɪt) vb. **1.** to drop down; plunge. ~n. **2.** the weight on a plumb line. **3.** a weight attached to a fishing-line.

plummy ('plʌmɪ) adj. **-mier, -miest. 1.** of, full of, or like plums. **2.** Brit. informal. (of a voice) deep, rich, and usually affected. **3.** Brit. informal. choice; desirable.

plump¹ (plʌmp) adj. **1.** full or rounded; chubby: a plump turkey. ~vb. **2.** (often foll. by up or out) to make or become plump: to plump up a pillow. —'**plumpness** n.

plump² (plʌmp) vb. **1.** (often foll. by down, into, etc.) to drop or fall suddenly and heavily. **2. plump for.** to choose one out of a number. ~n. **3.** a heavy abrupt fall or the sound of this. ~adv. **4.** suddenly or heavily. **5.** straight down; directly: the plane landed plump in the middle of the *field.* **6.** in a blunt, direct, or decisive manner.

plum pudding *n. Brit.* a boiled or steamed pudding made with flour, suet, and dried fruit.

plumy (ˈpluːmɪ) *adj.* **plumier, plumiest. 1.** feathery. **2.** covered or adorned with feathers.

plunder (ˈplʌndə) *vb.* **1.** to steal (valuables or goods) from (a place) by force, usually in wartime; loot. **2.** to steal (choice or desirable things) from (a place): *to plunder an orchard.* ~*n.* **3.** anything plundered; booty. **4.** a plundering; pillage.

plunge (plʌndʒ) *vb.* **1.** (usually foll. by *into*) to thrust or throw (something or oneself): *they plunged into the sea.* **2.** to throw or be thrown into a certain condition: *the room was plunged into darkness.* **3.** (usually foll. by *into*) to involve or become involved deeply (in). **4.** to move swiftly or impetuously. **5.** to descend very suddenly or steeply: *a plunging neckline.* **6.** *Informal.* to gamble heavily. ~*n.* **7.** a leap or dive. **8.** *Informal.* a swim; dip. **9.** a pitching motion. **10. take the plunge.** *Informal.* to decide to do something risky which cannot be altered later.

plunger (ˈplʌndʒə) *n.* **1.** a rubber suction cup used to clear blocked drains. **2.** a device with a plunging motion; piston.

plunk (plʌŋk) *vb.* **1.** to pluck (the strings) of (an instrument) or (of an instrument) to produce a twanging sound when played. **2.** (often foll. by *down*) to drop or be dropped heavily. ~*n.* **3.** the act or sound of plunking.

pluperfect (pluːˈpɜːfɪkt) *Grammar.* ~*adj.* **1.** denoting a tense of verbs used in relating past events where the action had already occurred at the time of the action of a main verb that is itself in a past tense. In English this is a compound tense formed with *had* plus the past participle. ~*n.* **2.** the pluperfect tense.

plural (ˈplʊərəl) *adj.* **1.** of or consisting of more than one. **2.** denoting a word indicating more than one. ~*n.* **3.** *Grammar.* **a.** the plural number. **b.** a plural form.

pluralism (ˈplʊərəˌlɪzəm) *n.* **1.** the holding by a person of more than one office. **2.** the existence in a society of groups with distinctive ethnic origin, cultures, or religions. —ˈpluralist *n., adj.* —ˌpluralˈistic *adj.*

plurality (plʊəˈrælɪtɪ) *n., pl.* -ties. **1.** the state of being plural. **2.** *Maths.* a number greater than one. **3.** a large number. **4.** a majority.

pluralize *or* -ise (ˈplʊərəˌlaɪz) *vb.* to make or become plural.

plus (plʌs) *prep.* **1.** increased by the addition of: *four plus two.* **2.** with the addition of: *a good job, plus a new car.* ~*adj.* **3.** indicating addition: *a plus sign.* **4.** *Maths.* same as **positive** (sense 7). **5.** on the posi-

tive part of a scale. **6.** indicating the positive side of an electrical circuit. **7.** involving advantage: *a plus factor.* **8.** *Informal.* having a value above that stated: *she had charm plus.* **9.** slightly above a specified standard: *he received a B+ for his essay.* ~*n.* **10.** the symbol +, indicating addition. **11.** a positive quantity. **12.** *Informal.* something positive or to the good. **13.** a gain, surplus, or advantage. ~*Mathematical symbol:* +

Usage. *Plus, together with,* and *along with* do not create compound subjects in the way that *and* does: the number of the verb depends on that of the subject to which *plus, together with,* or *along with* is added: *this task, plus all the others, was* (not *were*) *undertaken by the government.*

plus fours *pl. n.* men's baggy knickerbockers reaching below the knee, now only worn for hunting or golf.

plush (plʌʃ) *n.* **1.** a fabric with a long soft pile. ~*adj.* **2.** Also: **plushy.** *Informal.* luxurious; costly.

Pluto (ˈpluːtəʊ) *n.* **1.** *Greek myth.* the god of the underworld; Hades. **2.** the second smallest planet.

plutocracy (pluːˈtɒkrəsɪ) *n., pl.* -cies. **1.** government by the wealthy. **2.** a state ruled by the wealthy. **3.** a group that exercises power by virtue of its wealth. —plutocratic (ˌpluːtəˈkrætɪk) *adj.*

plutocrat (ˈpluːtəˌkræt) *n.* a member of a plutocracy.

plutonic (pluːˈtɒnɪk) *adj.* (of igneous rocks) formed from molten rock that has cooled and solidified below the earth's surface.

plutonium (pluːˈtəʊnɪəm) *n.* a toxic radioactive metallic element. Symbol: Pu

pluvial (ˈpluːvɪəl) *adj.* of or due to the action of rain; rainy.

ply¹ (plaɪ) *vb.* **plying, plied. 1.** to work at (a job or trade). **2.** to use (a tool). **3.** (usually foll. by *with*) to provide (with) or subject (to) repeatedly or persistently: *he plied us with drink; he plied me with questions.* **4.** to work steadily. **5.** (of a ship) to travel regularly along (a route): *to ply the trade routes.*

ply² (plaɪ) *n., pl.* **plies. 1.** a layer, fold, or thickness, as of yarn or wood. **2.** one of the strands twisted together to make rope or yarn.

Plymouth Brethren (ˈplɪməθ) *pl. n.* a Puritanical religious sect with no organized ministry.

plywood (ˈplaɪˌwʊd) *n.* a board made of thin layers of wood glued together under pressure, with the grain of one layer at right angles to that of the next.

Pm *Chem.* promethium.

PM 1. Paymaster. **2.** Postmaster. **3.** Prime Minister.

p.m. 1. after noon. 2. postmortem (examination).

PMG 1. Paymaster General. 2. Postmaster General.

PMS premenstrual syndrome.

PMT premenstrual tension.

pneumatic (njʊˈmætɪk) *adj.* 1. of or concerned with air, gases, or wind. 2. operated by compressed air: *pneumatic drill*. 3. containing compressed air: *a pneumatic tyre*.

pneumatics (njuˈmætɪks) *n.* (*functioning as sing.*) the branch of physics concerned with the mechanical properties of air and other gases.

pneumonia (njuːˈməʊnɪə) *n.* inflammation of one or both lungs.

po (pəʊ) *n., pl.* **pos.** *Brit. informal.* a chamber pot.

Po *Chem.* polonium.

PO 1. petty officer. 2. Pilot Officer. 3. Also: **p.o.** postal order. 4. Post Office.

poach¹ (pəʊtʃ) *vb.* 1. to catch (game or fish) illegally by trespassing on private property. 2. to encroach on (another person's rights or duties) or steal (an idea, employee, or player). —**poacher** *n.*

poach² (pəʊtʃ) *vb.* to simmer (food) very gently in liquid.

pock (pɒk) *n.* 1. a pustule resulting from smallpox. 2. a pockmark.

pocket (ˈpɒkɪt) *n.* 1. a small pouch in a garment for carrying small articles. 2. any pouch resembling this. 3. a cavity in the earth, such as one containing ore. 4. a small isolated area: *a pocket of resistance*. 5. any of the six holes with pouches or nets at the corners and sides of a billiard table. 6. **in one's pocket.** under one's control. 7. **in** *or* **out of pocket.** having made a profit or loss. ~*adj.* 8. small: *a pocket edition*. ~*vb.* 9. to put into one's pocket. 10. to take secretly or unlawfully; steal. 11. (*usually passive*) to confine as if in a pocket. 12. to receive (an insult) without retaliating. 13. to conceal or suppress: *he pocketed his pride and asked for help.* 14. *Billiards.* to drive (a ball) into a pocket.

pocketbook (ˈpɒkɪtˌbʊk) *n. Chiefly U.S.* a small case for money and papers.

pocket borough *n.* (before the Reform Act of 1832) an English borough constituency controlled by one person or family.

pocketful (ˈpɒkɪtfʊl) *n., pl.* **-fuls.** as much as a pocket will hold.

pocketknife (ˈpɒkɪtˌnaɪf) *n., pl.* **-knives.** a small knife with one or more blades that fold into the handle; penknife.

pocket money *n.* 1. *Brit.* a small weekly sum of money given to children by parents. 2. money for incidental expenses.

pockmark (ˈpɒkˌmɑːk) *n.* a pitted scar left on the skin after the healing of a smallpox or similar pustule. —**ˈpockˌmarked** *adj.*

poco (ˈpəʊkəʊ) *or* **un poco** *adj., adv. Music.* to a small degree: *poco rit.*

pod (pɒd) *n.* 1. **a.** the fruit of a leguminous plant, consisting of a long two-valved case that contains seeds. **b.** the seedcase as distinct from the seeds. ~*vb.* **podding, podded.** 2. to remove the pod from.

podgy (ˈpɒdʒɪ) *adj.* **podgier, podgiest.** short and fat; chubby. —**ˈpodginess** *n.*

podium (ˈpəʊdɪəm) *n., pl.* **-diums** *or* **-dia** (-dɪə). 1. a small raised platform used by conductors or speakers. 2. a plinth that supports a colonnade or wall.

poem (ˈpəʊɪm) *n.* 1. a composition in verse, using such techniques as metre, rhyme, or alliteration. 2. a literary composition that is not in verse but exhibits the intensity of imagination and language common to it: *a prose poem.* 3. anything like a poem in beauty or effect.

poesy (ˈpəʊɪzɪ) *n. Archaic.* poetry.

poet (ˈpəʊɪt) *or* (*sometimes when fem.*) **poetess** *n.* 1. a writer of poetry. 2. a person with great imagination and creativity.

poetaster (ˌpəʊɪˈtæstə, -ˈteɪ-) *n.* a writer of inferior verse.

poetic (pəʊˈɛtɪk) *or* **poetical** *adj.* 1. of poetry or poets. 2. like poetry, as in being expressive or imaginative. 3. recounted in verse.

poetic justice *n.* fitting retribution.

poetic licence *n.* justifiable departure from conventional rules of form or fact, as in poetry.

poet laureate *n., pl.* **poets laureate.** *Brit.* the poet appointed as court poet of Britain.

poetry (ˈpəʊɪtrɪ) *n.* 1. poems collectively. 2. the art or craft of writing poems. 3. poetic qualities, spirit, or feeling.

po-faced *adj.* wearing a disapproving stern expression.

pogey *or* **pogy** (ˈpəʊɡɪ) *n., pl.* **pogeys** *or* **pogies.** *Canad. slang.* 1. financial or other relief given to the unemployed by the government; dole. 2. unemployment insurance. 3. the office distributing relief to the unemployed.

pogo stick (ˈpəʊɡəʊ) *n.* a pole with steps for the feet and a spring at the bottom, so that the user can bounce up, down, and along on it.

pogrom (ˈpɒɡrəm) *n.* an organized persecution and massacre.

poi (pɔɪ) *n. N.Z.* a ball of woven New Zealand flax swung rhythmically by Maori women while performing poi dances.

poi dance *n. N.Z.* a women's formation dance that involves singing and manipulating a poi.

poignant (ˈpɔɪnjənt, -nənt) *adj.* 1. sharply painful to the feelings. 2. cutting: *poignant* *wit.* **3.** pertinent in mental appeal: *a poignant subject.* —**'poignancy** *n.*

poinsettia (pɔɪnˈsɛtɪə) *n.* a shrub of Mexico and Central America, widely cultivated for its showy scarlet leaves.

point (pɔɪnt) *n.* **1.** a dot or tiny mark. **2.** a location or position. **3.** a dot used in writing or printing, such as a decimal point or a full stop. **4.** the sharp tapered end of anything. **5.** *Maths.* a geometric element having a position located by coordinates, but no magnitude. **6.** a promontory. **7.** a specific condition or degree: *freezing point.* **8.** a moment: *at that point he left.* **9.** a reason or aim: *what is the point of this exercise?* **10.** an essential element in an argument: *I take your point.* **11.** a detail or item. **12.** a characteristic: *he has his good points.* **13.** (*often pl.*) any of the extremities, such as the tail, ears, or feet, of a domestic animal. **14.** (*often pl.*) *Ballet.* the tip of the toes. **15.** a single unit for measuring something such as value, or of scoring in a game. **16.** *Printing.* a unit of measurement equal to one twelfth of a pica. **17.** *Navigation.* one of the 32 marks on the compass indicating direction. **18.** *Cricket.* a fielding position at right angles to the batsman on the off side. **19.** either of the two electrical contacts that make or break the circuit in the distributor of a motor vehicle. **20.** *Brit.* (*often pl.*) a movable section of railway track used to direct a train from one line to another. **21.** *Brit.* short for **power point. 22.** *Boxing.* a mark awarded for a scoring blow or knockdown. **23.** **at** *or* **on the point of.** on the verge of: *on the point of leaving.* **24.** **beside the point.** irrelevant. **25.** **make a point of. a.** to make a habit of (something). **b.** to do (something) because one thinks it important. **26.** **to the point.** relevant. **27.** **up to a point.** not completely. ~*vb.* **28.** (usually foll. by *at* or *to*) to indicate the location or direction of by extending (a finger or other pointed object) towards it. **29.** (usually foll. by *at* or *to*) to indicate a specific person or thing among several: *all evidence pointed to Donald as the murderer.* **30.** to direct or face in a specific direction: *point me in the right direction.* **31.** (of gun dogs) to indicate the place where game is lying by standing rigidly with the muzzle turned in its direction. **32.** to finish or repair the joints of (brickwork) with mortar or cement. ~See also **point out.**

point-blank *adj.* **1.** aimed or fired at a very close target; at nearly zero range. **2.** plain or blunt: *a point-blank question.* ~*adv.* **3.** directly or straight. **4.** bluntly.

point duty *n.* the stationing of a policeman at a road junction to control traffic.

pointed (ˈpɔɪntɪd) *adj.* **1.** having a point. **2.** cutting or incisive: *pointed wit.* **3.** obviously directed at a particular person: *a pointed remark.* **4.** emphasized or evident: *pointed ignorance.* —**'pointedly** *adv.*

pointer (ˈpɔɪntə) *n.* **1.** an indicator on a measuring instrument. **2.** a rod used to point to parts of a map or chart. **3.** a breed of large smooth-coated gun dog. **4.** a helpful hint.

pointillism (ˈpwæntɪˌlɪzəm) *n.* a technique of painting of some impressionists, in which dots of unmixed colour are juxtaposed so that from a distance they fuse in the viewer's eye. —**'pointillist** *n., adj.*

pointing (ˈpɔɪntɪŋ) *n.* the act or process of repairing or finishing joints in brickwork with mortar.

pointless (ˈpɔɪntlɪs) *adj.* without meaning, purpose, or force.

point of no return *n.* a point at which an irreversible commitment must be made to an action.

point of order *n., pl.* **points of order.** a question in a meeting as to whether the rules of procedure are being broken.

point of view *n., pl.* **points of view. 1.** a position from which something is observed. **2.** a mental viewpoint or attitude.

point out *vb.* to indicate or specify.

point-to-point *n. Brit.* a steeplechase organized by a hunt.

poise (pɔɪz) *n.* **1.** composure or dignity. **2.** physical balance. **3.** stability. ~*vb.* **4.** to be or cause to be balanced or suspended. **5.** to hold in readiness: *to poise a lance.*

poison (ˈpɔɪzᵊn) *n.* **1.** a substance that causes death or injury when swallowed or absorbed. **2.** something that destroys or corrupts. ~*vb.* **3.** to give poison to. **4.** to add poison to. **5.** to taint or infect with poison. **6.** (foll. by *against*) to turn (a person's mind) against: *he poisoned her mind against me.* —**'poisoner** *n.*

poison ivy *n.* a North American climbing plant that causes an itching rash on contact.

poisonous (ˈpɔɪzᵊnəs) *adj.* **1.** having the effects or qualities of a poison. **2.** corruptive or malicious.

poison-pen letter *n.* an abusive, usually anonymous, letter written in malice.

poke[1] (pəʊk) *vb.* **1.** to jab or prod, as with the elbow or a stick. **2.** to make (a hole) by poking. **3.** (sometimes foll. by *at*) to thrust (at). **4.** (usually foll. by *in, through, etc.*) to stick out: *don't poke your tongue out at me.* **5.** to stir (a fire) by poking. **6.** (often foll. by *about* or *around*) to search or pry. **7.** **poke one's nose into.** to interfere with or meddle in. ~*n.* **8.** a jab or prod.

poke[2] (pəʊk) *n.* **1.** *Dialect.* a pocket or bag. **2. a pig in a poke.** See **pig.**

poker[1] (ˈpəʊkə) *n.* a metal rod with a handle for stirring a fire.

poker[2] (ˈpəʊkə) *n.* a card game of bluff and skill in which players bet on the hands dealt.

poker face *n. Informal.* an expressionless

face, as that of a poker player trying to hide the value of his cards. —'**poker,faced** adj.

pokerwork ('pəυkə,wɜːk) n. the art of producing pictures or designs on wood by charring it with a heated tool.

poky ('pəυkı) adj. **pokier, pokiest.** (esp. of rooms) small and cramped. —'**pokiness** n.

pol. 1. political. **2.** politics.

polar ('pəυlə) adj. **1.** at, near, or of either of the earth's poles or the area inside the Arctic or Antarctic Circles. **2.** of or having a pole or poles. **3.** directly opposite in tendency or nature.

polar bear n. a white bear of coastal regions of the North Pole.

polar circle n. the Arctic or Antarctic Circle.

polarity (pəυ'lærıtı) n., pl. **-ties. 1.** the condition of a body in which it has opposing physical properties, usually magnetic poles or electric charge. **2.** the particular state of a part that has polarity: *an electrode with positive polarity.* **3.** the state of having two directly opposite tendencies or opinions.

polarization or **-isation** (,pəυləraı'zeıʃən) n. **1.** the condition of acquiring or giving polarity. **2.** *Physics.* the condition in which waves of light or other radiation are restricted to certain directions of vibration.

polarize or **-ise** ('pəυlə,raız) vb. **1.** to acquire or give polarity or polarization. **2.** to cause (people) to adopt directly opposite opinions: *to polarize opinion.*

Polaroid ('pəυlə,rɔıd) n. *Trademark.* **1.** a type of plastic sheet that can polarize light: used in sunglasses to eliminate glare. **2. Polaroid Camera.** a camera that produces a finished print by means of a developing and processing technique that occurs inside the camera and takes only a few seconds.

polder ('pəυldə, 'pɒl-) n. a stretch of land reclaimed from the sea.

pole[1] (pəυl) n. **1.** a long slender rounded piece of wood, metal, or other material. **2.** same as **rod** (sense 5). **3. up the pole.** *Brit., Austral., & N.Z. informal.* **a.** slightly mad. **b.** in a predicament. ~vb. **4.** to punt (a boat).

pole[2] (pəυl) n. **1.** either end of the earth's axis of rotation. See also **North Pole, South Pole.** **2.** *Physics.* **a.** either of the two regions at the ends of a magnet to which the lines of force converge. **b.** either of two points at which there are opposite electric charges. **3.** either of two directly opposite tendencies or opinions. **4. poles apart.** having widely divergent opinions or tastes.

Pole (pəυl) n. a person from Poland.

poleaxe or U.S. **poleax** ('pəυl,æks) n. **1.** an axe formerly used in battle or used by a butcher. ~vb. **2.** to hit or fell with or as if with a poleaxe.

polecat ('pəυl,kæt) n., pl. **-cats** or **-cat. 1.** a

dark brown mammal like a weasel that gives off a foul smell. **2.** *U.S.* a skunk.

polemic (pə'lɛmık) adj. *also* **polemical. 1.** of or involving dispute or controversy. ~n. **2.** a dispute or controversy. —**polemicist** (pə'lɛmısıst) n.

polemics (pə'lɛmıks) n. (*functioning as sing.*) the art or practice of dispute or argument.

pole position n. **1.** (in motor racing) the starting position on the inside of the front row, generally considered the best one. **2.** an advantageous starting position.

pole star n. a guiding principle or rule.

Pole Star n. **the.** the star closest to the N celestial pole.

pole vault n. **1. the.** a field event in which competitors try to clear a high bar with the aid of a very flexible long pole. ~vb. **pole-vault. 2.** to perform or compete in the pole vault. —'**pole-,vaulter** n.

police (pə'liːs) n. **1.** (often preceded by *the*) the organized civil force of a state for keeping law and order. **2.** (*functioning as pl.*) the members of such a force collectively. **3.** an organized body with a similar function: *security police.* ~vb. **4.** to regulate or control by means of a police force or similar body.

police dog n. a dog trained to help the police.

policeman (pə'liːsmən) or (*fem.*) **policewoman** n., pl. **-men** or **-women.** a member of a police force.

police state n. a state in which a repressive government keeps control through the police.

police station n. the office of the police force of a district.

policy[1] ('pɒlısı) n., pl. **-cies. 1.** a plan of action adopted by a person, group, or government. **2.** wisdom or prudence.

policy[2] ('pɒlısı) n., pl. **-cies.** a document containing an insurance contract. —'**policy,holder** n.

polio ('pəυlıəυ) n. short for **poliomyelitis.**

poliomyelitis (,pəυlıəυ,maıə'laıtıs) n. an acute infectious viral disease, affecting the brain and spinal cord, causing paralysis.

polish ('pɒlıʃ) vb. **1.** to make or become smooth and shiny by rubbing. **2.** to perfect or complete. **3.** to make or become elegant or refined. ~n. **4.** a finish or gloss. **5.** a substance used to produce a shiny surface. **6.** elegance or refinement.

Polish ('pəυlıʃ) adj. **1.** of Poland, its people, or their language. ~n. **2.** the official language of Poland.

polished ('pɒlıʃt) adj. **1.** accomplished: *a polished actor.* **2.** impeccably or professionally done: *a polished performance.*

polish off vb. *Informal.* **1.** to finish completely. **2.** to dispose of or kill.

polish up vb. **1.** to make or become

smooth and shiny by polishing. **2.** to improve (something) by working at it: *he's polishing up his German.*

Politburo ('pɒlɪtˌbjʊərəʊ) *n.* the executive and policy-making committee of a Communist Party.

polite (pə'laɪt) *adj.* **1.** having good manners; courteous. **2.** cultivated or refined: *polite society.* —**po'litely** *adv.* —**po'liteness** *n.*

politic ('pɒlɪtɪk) *adj.* **1.** artful or shrewd: *a politic manager.* **2.** crafty; cunning: *a politic old scoundrel.* **3.** wise or prudent: *a politic choice.* **4.** *Archaic.* political. ~See also **body politic.**

political (pə'lɪtɪk'l) *adj.* **1.** of the state, government, or public administration. **2.** of or dealing with politics: *a political person.* **3.** of the parties and the partisan aspects of politics. —**po'litically** *adv.*

political prisoner *n.* a person imprisoned for holding particular political beliefs.

political science *n.* the study of the state, government, and politics. —**political scientist** *n.*

politician (ˌpɒlɪ'tɪʃən) *n.* a person actively engaged in politics, usually a full-time professional member of a deliberative assembly.

politicize *or* **-ise** (pə'lɪtɪˌsaɪz) *vb.* **1.** to make political in character or awareness. **2.** to take part in political discussion or activity. —**po,litici'zation** *or* **-i'sation** *n.*

politics ('pɒlɪtɪks) *n.* **1.** (*functioning as sing.*) the art and science of government. **2.** (*functioning as pl.*) political activities or affairs: *party politics.* **3.** (*functioning as sing.*) the business or profession of politics. **4.** (*functioning as sing. or pl.*) any activity concerned with the acquisition of power: *company politics are often vicious.* **5.** (*functioning as pl.*) political opinions or sympathies: *his conservative politics.*

polity ('pɒlɪtɪ) *n., pl.* **-ties. 1.** a form of government of a state, church, or society. **2.** a politically organized state, church, or society.

polka ('pɒlkə) *n.* **1.** a 19th-century dance in fast duple time. **2.** music for this dance. ~*vb.* **-kaing, -kaed. 3.** to dance a polka.

polka dot *n.* one of a pattern of small circular regularly spaced spots on a fabric.

poll (pəʊl) *n.* **1.** the casting, recording, or counting of votes in an election; a voting. **2.** the result of such a voting: *a heavy poll.* **3.** Also called: **opinion poll.** a canvassing of a representative sample of people on some question in order to determine the general opinion. **4.** the head. ~*vb.* **5.** to receive (a certain number of votes). **6.** to receive, take, or record the votes of: *he polled the whole town.* **7.** to canvass (a person, group, or area) as part of a survey of opinion. **8.** to cast (a vote) in an election. **9.** to

clip or shear. **10.** to remove or cut short the horns of (cattle).

pollack *or* **pollock** ('pɒlək) *n., pl.* **-lacks, -lack** *or* **-locks, -lock.** a food fish related to the cod, found in northern seas.

pollard ('pɒləd) *n.* **1.** an animal that has shed its horns or has had them removed. **2.** a tree that has had its branches cut back to encourage a more bushy growth. ~*vb.* **3.** to make into a pollard.

pollen ('pɒlən) *n.* a substance produced by the anthers of seed-bearing plants, consisting of numerous fine grains containing the male fertilizing cells.

pollen count *n.* a measure of the pollen present in the air over a 24-hour period, often published as a warning to hay fever sufferers.

pollinate ('pɒlɪˌneɪt) *vb.* to transfer pollen from the anthers to the stigma of (a flower). —**,polli'nation** *n.*

polling booth *n.* a semienclosed space in which a voter stands to mark a ballot paper during an election.

polling station *n.* a building designated as the place to which voters go during an election to cast their votes.

pollster ('pəʊlstə) *n.* a person who conducts opinion polls.

poll tax *n.* a tax levied per head of adult population, esp. (in Scotland from 1989 and England and Wales from 1990) a tax levied by a local authority to pay for council services, replacing domestic rates.

pollutant (pə'luːt'nt) *n.* a substance that pollutes, usually the chemical waste of an industrial process.

pollute (pə'luːt) *vb.* **1.** to contaminate with poisonous or harmful substances. **2.** to make morally corrupt. —**pol'lution** *n.*

polo ('pəʊləʊ) *n.* **1.** a game like hockey played on horseback with long-handled mallets and a wooden ball. **2.** short for **water polo. 3.** Also called: **polo neck.** a collar on a garment, rolled over to fit closely round the neck.

polonaise (ˌpɒlə'neɪz) *n.* **1.** a stately Polish dance. **2.** music for this dance.

polonium (pə'ləʊnɪəm) *n.* a rare radioactive element found in trace amounts in uranium ores. Symbol: Po

poltergeist ('pɒltəˌgaɪst) *n.* a spirit believed to manifest its presence by noises and acts of mischief, such as throwing objects about.

poltroon (pɒl'truːn) *n.* a complete coward.

poly ('pɒlɪ) *n., pl.* **polys.** *Informal.* short for **polytechnic.**

poly- *combining form.* **1.** many or much: *polyhedron.* **2.** having an excessive number or amount: *polyphagia.*

polyandry ('pɒlɪˌændrɪ) *n.* the practice or condition of having more than one husband at the same time. —**,poly'androus** *adj.*

polyanthus (ˌpɒlɪˈænθəs) *n., pl.* **-thuses.** a hybrid garden primrose with brightly coloured flowers.

polychromatic (ˌpɒlɪkrəʊˈmætɪk) *adj.* **1.** having various colours. **2.** (of radiation) containing more than one wavelength.

polyester (ˌpɒlɪˈɛstə) *n.* a synthetic polymer used to make plastics and textile fibres.

polyethylene (ˌpɒlɪˈɛθɪˌliːn) *n.* same as **polythene.**

polygamy (pəˈlɪɡəmɪ) *n.* the practice of having more than one wife or husband at the same time. **—poˈlygamist** *n.* **—poˈlygamous** *adj.*

polyglot (ˈpɒlɪˌɡlɒt) *adj.* **1.** able to speak many languages. **2.** written in or using many languages. **~n.** **3.** a person who can speak many languages.

polygon (ˈpɒlɪˌɡɒn) *n.* a closed plane figure with three or more sides and angles. **—polygonal** (pəˈlɪɡənˈl) *adj.*

polygraph (ˈpɒlɪˌɡrɑːf) *n.* an instrument for recording involuntary physiological activities such as pulse rate, often used as a lie detector.

polygyny (pəˈlɪdʒɪnɪ) *n.* the practice or condition of having more than one wife at the same time. **—poˈlygynous** *adj.*

polyhedron (ˌpɒlɪˈhiːdrən) *n., pl.* **-drons** or **-dra** (-drə). a solid figure consisting of four or more plane faces. **—ˌpolyˈhedral** *adj.*

polymath (ˈpɒlɪˌmæθ) *n.* a person of great and varied learning.

polymer (ˈpɒlɪmə) *n.* a natural or synthetic compound that has large molecules made up of many relatively simple repeated units.

polymeric (ˌpɒlɪˈmɛrɪk) *adj.* of or being a polymer: *a polymeric compound.*

polymerization or **-isation** (ˌpɒlɪməraɪˈzeɪʃən) *n.* the act or process of forming a polymer. **—ˈpolymerˌize** or **-ˌise** *vb.*

polymorphous (ˌpɒlɪˈmɔːfəs) or **polymorphic** *adj.* having, taking, or passing through many different forms or stages.

Polynesian (ˌpɒlɪˈniːʒən, -ʒɪən) *adj.* **1.** of Polynesia, its people, or any of their languages. **~n.** **2.** a person from Polynesia. **3.** any of the languages of Polynesia.

polynomial (ˌpɒlɪˈnəʊmɪəl) *adj.* **1.** consisting of two or more terms. **~n.** **2.** an algebraic expression consisting of the sum of a number of terms.

polyp (ˈpɒlɪp) *n.* **1.** *Zool.* a small sea creature that has a hollow cylindrical body with a ring of tentacles around the mouth. **2.** *Pathol.* a small growth on the surface of a mucous membrane.

polyphonic (ˌpɒlɪˈfɒnɪk) *adj. Music.* composed of several different parts; contrapuntal.

polyphony (pəˈlɪfənɪ) *n., pl.* **-nies.** polyphonic style of composition or a piece of music using it.

polystyrene (ˌpɒlɪˈstaɪriːn) *n.* a plastic obtained by polymerizing styrene; used for insulating and packing.

polysyllable (ˈpɒlɪˌsɪləbˈl) *n.* a word having more than two syllables. **—polysyllabic** (ˌpɒlɪsɪˈlæbɪk) *adj.*

polytechnic (ˌpɒlɪˈtɛknɪk) *n.* **1.** *Brit.* a college offering advanced courses in many fields at and below degree standard. **~adj.** **2.** of or relating to technical instruction.

polytheism (ˈpɒlɪθiːˌɪzəm, ˌpɒlɪˈθiːɪzəm) *n.* belief in more than one god. **—ˌpolytheˈistic** *adj.* **—ˈpolyˌtheist** *n.*

polythene (ˈpɒlɪˌθiːn) *n.* a light thermoplastic material made from ethylene.

polyunsaturated (ˌpɒlɪʌnˈsætʃəˌreɪtɪd) *adj.* of a class of animal and vegetable fats that do not contain cholesterol.

polyurethane (ˌpɒlɪˈjʊərəˌθeɪn) *n.* a synthetic material mainly used as a foam for packing.

polyvinyl chloride *n.* See **PVC.**

pomace (ˈpʌmɪs) *n.* apple pulp left after pressing for juice.

pomade (pəˈmɑːd) *n.* a perfumed oil put on the hair.

pomander (pəʊˈmændə) *n.* **1.** a mixture of aromatic substances in a round container, used to perfume drawers or cupboards. **2.** a container for such a mixture.

pomegranate (ˈpɒmɪˌɡrænɪt, ˈpɒmˌɡrænɪt) *n.* the fruit of an Asian tree, which has tough reddish rind, juicy red pulp, and many seeds.

pomelo (ˈpɒmɪˌləʊ) *n., pl.* **-los.** the edible yellow fruit, like a grapefruit, of a tropical tree.

Pomeranian (ˌpɒməˈreɪnɪən) *n.* a breed of toy dog with a long straight silky coat.

pomfret (ˈpʌmfrɪt, ˈpɒm-) or **pomfret-cake** *n.* a small black rounded liquorice sweet.

pommel (ˈpʌməl, ˈpɒm-) *n.* **1.** the raised part on the front of a saddle. **2.** a knob at the top of a sword. **~vb.** **-melling, -melled** or *U.S.* **-meling, -meled.** **3.** same as **pummel.**

pommy (ˈpɒmɪ) *n., pl.* **-mies.** (*sometimes cap.*) *Slang.* a word used by Australians and New Zealanders for a British person. Sometimes shortened to **pom.**

pomp (pɒmp) *n.* **1.** stately or splendid display. **2.** ostentatious display.

pom-pom (ˈpɒmpɒm) *n.* an automatic rapid-firing gun.

pompon (ˈpɒmpɒn) *n.* **1.** a decorative ball of tufted silk or wool. **2.** the small round flower head of some dahlias and chrysanthemums.

pompous (ˈpɒmpəs) *adj.* **1.** too consciously dignified or self-important. **2.** too consciously grand in style: *a pompous speech.*

—**pomposity** (pɒmˈpɒsɪtɪ) *n.* —ˈ**pompously** *adv.*

ponce (pɒns) *Offensive slang, chiefly Brit.* ~*n.* **1.** an effeminate man. **2.** same as **pimp.** ~*vb.* **3.** (often foll. by *around* or *about*) to act like a ponce.

poncho (ˈpɒntʃəʊ) *n., pl.* **-chos.** a cloak of a kind originally worn in South America, made of a piece of cloth with a hole in the middle for the head.

pond (pɒnd) *n.* a pool of still water.

ponder (ˈpɒndə) *vb.* (sometimes foll. by *on* or *over*) to consider thoroughly or deeply. —ˈ**ponderable** *adj.*

ponderous (ˈpɒndərəs) *adj.* **1.** heavy; huge. **2.** (of movement) lumbering or graceless. **3.** dull or laborious: *a ponderous speech.*

pondok (ˈpɒndɒk) *or* **pondokie** *n.* (in southern Africa) a crudely made house or shack.

pondweed (ˈpɒndˌwiːd) *n.* a plant which grows in ponds and slow streams.

pong (pɒŋ) *Brit. informal.* ~*n.* **1.** a stink. ~*vb.* **2.** to stink. —ˈ**pongy** *adj.*

ponga (ˈpɒŋə) *n.* a tall New Zealand tree fern with large leathery leaves.

poniard (ˈpɒnjəd) *n.* a small slender dagger.

pontiff (ˈpɒntɪf) *n.* a title now confined to the pope.

pontifical (pɒnˈtɪfɪkᵊl) *adj.* **1.** of a pontiff. **2.** pompous or dogmatic in manner.

pontificate *vb.* (pɒnˈtɪfɪˌkeɪt). **1.** to speak in a pompous or dogmatic manner. **2.** to officiate as a pontiff. ~*n.* (pɒnˈtɪfɪkɪt). **3.** the office or term of office of a pope.

pontoon[1] (pɒnˈtuːn) *n.* a floating platform used to support a bridge.

pontoon[2] (pɒnˈtuːn) *n.* a card game in which players try to obtain sets of cards never worth more than 21 points.

pony (ˈpəʊnɪ) *n., pl.* **-nies.** a breed of small horse.

ponytail (ˈpəʊnɪˌteɪl) *n.* a hairstyle in which the hair is gathered together by a band at the back of the head and hangs down like a tail.

pony trekking *n.* the pastime of riding ponies cross-country.

poodle (ˈpuːdᵊl) *n.* a breed of dog with curly hair, which is usually clipped.

poof (pʊf, puːf) *n. Brit. offensive slang.* a male homosexual.

pooh (puː) *interj.* an exclamation of disdain, scorn, or disgust.

pooh-pooh (ˈpuːˈpuː) *vb.* to express disdain or scorn for.

pool[1] (puːl) *n.* **1.** a small body of still water. **2.** a small body of spilt liquid: *a pool of blood.* **3.** a deep part of a stream or river. **4.** See **swimming pool.**

pool[2] (puːl) *n.* **1.** a communal combination of resources or funds: *a typing pool.* **2.** the combined stakes of the betters in many gambling games. **3.** *Commerce.* a group of producers who agree to maintain output levels and high prices. **4.** a billiard game in which the object is to pot all the balls with the cue ball. ~*vb.* **5.** to combine (resources or money) into a common fund.

pools (puːlz) *pl. n.* **the.** *Brit.* an organized nationwide mainly postal gambling pool betting on the result of football matches.

poop (puːp) *n. Naut.* a raised structure or deck at the stern of a sailing ship.

pooped (puːpt) *adj. U.S. & Canad. slang.* exhausted; tired: *he was pooped after the race.*

poor (pʊə, pɔː) *adj.* **1.** not having enough money to live on. **2.** inadequate: *a poor salary.* **3.** (sometimes foll. by *in*) deficient in (something): *a region poor in wild flowers.* **4.** inferior: *poor quality.* **5.** disappointing or disagreeable: *a poor play.* **6.** deserving of pity; unlucky: *poor John is ill.* **7. poor man's (something).** a (cheaper) substitute for (something).

poorhouse (ˈpʊəˌhaʊs, ˈpɔː-) *n.* same as **workhouse.**

poor law *n. English history.* a law providing for support of the poor from parish funds.

poorly (ˈpʊəlɪ, ˈpɔː-) *adv.* **1.** badly. ~*adj.* **2.** *Informal.* rather ill.

poort (pʊət) *n.* (in South Africa) a steep narrow mountain pass.

poor White *n. Often offensive.* a poverty-stricken White person, usually in the southern U.S. and South Africa.

pop[1] (pɒp) *vb.* **popping, popped. 1.** to make or cause to make a light sharp explosive sound. **2.** to burst with such a sound. **3.** (often foll. by *in, out, etc.*) *Informal.* to come (to) or go (from) briefly or suddenly. **4.** (of the eyes) to protrude. **5.** to place with a sudden movement: *she popped a pill into her mouth.* **6.** *Informal.* to pawn. **7. pop the question.** *Informal.* to propose marriage. ~*n.* **8.** a light sharp explosive sound. **9.** *Informal.* a fizzy drink. ~*adv.* **10.** with a pop. ~See also **pop off.**

pop[2] (pɒp) *n.* **1.** music of general appeal, esp. among young people, that usually has a strong rhythm and uses electrical amplification. ~*adj.* **2.** of or playing pop music: *a pop group.* **3.** *Informal.* short for **popular.**

pop[3] (pɒp) *n. Informal.* **1.** father. **2.** an old man.

pop. **1.** popular(ly). **2.** population.

pop art *n.* a movement in modern art that uses the methods, styles, and themes of popular culture and mass media.

popcorn (ˈpɒpˌkɔːn) *n.* maize kernels that puff up and burst when heated.

pope (pəʊp) *n.* (*often cap.*) the bishop of Rome as head of the Roman Catholic Church.

popery (ˈpəʊpərɪ) *n. Offensive.* Roman Catholicism.

popeyed (ˈpɒpˌaɪd) *adj.* **1.** having bulging eyes. **2.** staring in astonishment.

popgun (ˈpɒpˌgʌn) *n.* a toy gun that fires a pellet or cork by means of compressed air.

popinjay (ˈpɒpɪnˌdʒeɪ) *n.* a conceited or talkative person.

popish (ˈpəʊpɪʃ) *adj. Offensive.* of or characteristic of Roman Catholicism.

poplar (ˈpɒplə) *n.* a tree with triangular leaves, catkins, and light soft wood.

poplin (ˈpɒplɪn) *n.* a strong plain-woven fabric, usually of cotton, with fine ribbing.

pop off *vb. Informal.* **1.** to depart suddenly. **2.** to die suddenly.

poppadom *or* **poppadum** (ˈpɒpədəm) *n.* a thin round crisp fried Indian bread.

popper (ˈpɒpə) *n. Brit. informal.* a press stud.

poppet (ˈpɒpɪt) *n.* a term of affection for a small child or sweetheart.

popping crease *n. Cricket.* a line in front of and parallel with the wicket at or behind which the batsman stands.

poppy (ˈpɒpɪ) *n., pl.* **-pies. 1.** a plant with showy red, orange, or white flowers and a milky sap. **2.** a drug, such as opium, obtained from these plants. **3.** an artificial red poppy worn to mark Remembrance Sunday. ~*adj.* **4.** reddish-orange.

poppycock (ˈpɒpɪˌkɒk) *n. Informal.* nonsense.

Poppy Day *n. Informal.* Remembrance Sunday.

populace (ˈpɒpjʊləs) *n.* (*sometimes functioning as pl.*) the common people; masses.

popular (ˈpɒpjʊlə) *adj.* **1.** widely liked or admired. **2.** liked by a person or group: *I'm not very popular with her.* **3.** prevailing among the general public: *popular discontent.* —**popularity** (ˌpɒpjʊˈlærɪtɪ) *n.*

popular front *n.* (*often cap.*) a left-wing group or party opposed to fascism.

popularize *or* **-ise** (ˈpɒpjʊləˌraɪz) *vb.* **1.** to make popular. **2.** to make easily understandable. —ˌpopulariˈzation *or* -iˈsation *n.*

populate (ˈpɒpjʊˌleɪt) *vb.* **1.** (*often passive*) to live in; inhabit. **2.** to provide with inhabitants.

population (ˌpɒpjʊˈleɪʃən) *n.* **1.** (*sometimes functioning as pl.*) all the inhabitants of a place. **2.** the number of such inhabitants. **3.** (*sometimes functioning as pl.*) all the people of a particular class in a place: *the Chinese population of New York.* **4.** the act or process of providing a place with inhabitants.

populist (ˈpɒpjʊlɪst) *n.* a politician who claims to support the interests of the ordinary people.

populous (ˈpɒpjʊləs) *adj.* containing many inhabitants.

porangi (ˈpɔːræŋɪ) *adj. N.Z. informal.* crazy; mad.

porcelain (ˈpɔːslɪn) *n.* **1.** a translucent ceramic material. **2.** an object made of this or such objects collectively.

porch (pɔːtʃ) *n.* a structure projecting from the doorway of a house and forming a covered entrance.

porcine (ˈpɔːsaɪn) *adj.* of or like pigs.

porcupine (ˈpɔːkjʊˌpaɪn) *n.* a large rodent with a covering of protective quills.

pore[1] (pɔː) *vb.* **1.** (foll. by *over*) to examine or study closely or intently: *he pored over his notes.* **2.** (foll. by *over, on,* or *upon*) to think deeply (about).

pore[2] (pɔː) *n.* **1.** a small opening in the skin or outer surface of an animal or plant through which fluids may pass. **2.** any small hole, such as a space in a rock.

pork (pɔːk) *n.* the flesh of pigs used as food.

porker (ˈpɔːkə) *n.* a pig fattened for pork.

pork pie *n.* a pie filled with minced pork.

porky (ˈpɔːkɪ) *adj.* **porkier, porkiest. 1.** of or like pork. **2.** *Informal.* fat; obese.

porn (pɔːn) *or* **porno** (ˈpɔːnəʊ) *n., adj. Informal.* short for **pornography** or **pornographic.**

pornography (pɔːˈnɒgrəfɪ) *n.* writings, pictures, or films designed to be sexually exciting. —**porˈnographer** *n.* —**pornographic** (ˌpɔːnəˈgræfɪk) *adj.*

porous (ˈpɔːrəs) *adj.* **1.** able to absorb air or fluids. **2.** *Biol., geol.* having pores. —**porosity** (pɔːˈrɒsɪtɪ) *n.*

porphyry (ˈpɔːfɪrɪ) *n., pl.* **-ries.** a reddish-purple rock consisting of large crystals of feldspar in a finer mass of minerals. —ˌporphyˈritic *adj.*

porpoise (ˈpɔːpəs) *n., pl.* **-poise** *or* **-poises.** a small mammal of the whale family with a blunt snout.

porridge (ˈpɒrɪdʒ) *n.* **1.** a dish made from oatmeal or other cereal, cooked in water or milk. **2.** *Slang.* imprisonment.

porringer (ˈpɒrɪndʒə) *n.* a small dish, often with a handle, for soup or porridge.

port[1] (pɔːt) *n.* a town or place alongside navigable water where ships can load and unload.

port[2] (pɔːt) *n.* **1.** the left side of an aircraft or ship when facing the bow. ~*vb.* **2.** to turn or be turned towards the port.

port[3] (pɔːt) *n.* a sweet fortified wine.

port[4] (pɔːt) *n. Naut.* **a.** an opening with a watertight door in the side of a ship, for access to the holds. **b.** See **porthole.**

portable (ˈpɔːtəbəl) *adj.* **1.** able to be easily carried or moved. ~*n.* **2.** an article designed to be easily carried or moved, such as a television or typewriter. —ˌportaˈbility *n.*

portage ('pɔːtɪdʒ) *n.* **1.** the transporting of boats and supplies overland between navigable waterways. **2.** the route used for such transport. ~*vb.* **3.** to transport (boats and supplies) thus.

portal ('pɔːt³l) *n.* an entrance, gateway, or doorway, usually a large and impressive one.

portcullis (pɔːt'kʌlɪs) *n.* an iron grating suspended vertically in the gateway of a castle or town and able to be lowered so as to bar the entrance.

portend (pɔː'tɛnd) *vb.* to be an omen of; foreshadow: *those clouds portend rain.*

portent ('pɔːtɛnt) *n.* **1.** a sign of a future event; omen. **2.** great or ominous significance: *a cry of dire portent.* **3.** a marvel.

portentous (pɔː'tɛntəs) *adj.* **1.** of great or ominous significance. **2.** self-important or pompous: *portentous speechifying.*

porter¹ ('pɔːtə) *n.* a man employed to carry luggage at a railway station or hotel. —'**porterage** *n.*

porter² ('pɔːtə) *n. Chiefly Brit.* a doorman or gatekeeper of a building.

porter³ ('pɔːtə) *n. Brit.* a dark sweet ale brewed from black malt.

porterhouse ('pɔːtə,haʊs) *n.* a thick choice beef steak. Also called: **porterhouse steak.**

portfolio (pɔːt'fəʊlɪəʊ) *n., pl.* **-os. 1.** a flat case for carrying maps, drawings, or papers. **2.** the contents of such a case, such as drawings or photographs, that show recent work. **3.** the responsibilities or role of the head of a government department: *the portfolio for foreign affairs.* **4. Minister without portfolio.** a cabinet minister who is not responsible for a government department. **5.** a list of investments held by an investor.

porthole ('pɔːt,həʊl) *n.* a small opening with a watertight cover in the side of a vessel, to admit light and air.

portico ('pɔːtɪkəʊ) *n., pl.* **-coes** or **-cos.** a porch or covered walkway consisting of a roof supported by columns.

portion ('pɔːʃən) *n.* **1.** a part of a whole. **2.** a part allotted or belonging to a person or group. **3.** a helping of food served to one person. **4.** *Law.* a dowry. **5.** a person's lot or destiny. ~*vb.* **6.** to divide up; share out. **7.** to give a share to (a person).

portly ('pɔːtlɪ) *adj.* **-lier, -liest.** stout or rather fat.

portmanteau (pɔːt'mæntəʊ) *n., pl.* **-teaus** or **-teaux** (-təʊz). (formerly) a large travelling case made of stiff leather that opens out into two compartments.

portmanteau word *n.* a word made by joining together the beginning and end of two other words, such as *brunch.* Also called: **blend.**

portrait ('pɔːtrɪt, -treɪt) *n.* **1.** a painting, drawing, or photograph of a person, often

only of the face. **2.** a description. —'**portraitist** *n.*

portraiture ('pɔːtrɪtʃə) *n.* **1.** the making of portraits. **2. a.** a portrait. **b.** portraits collectively. **3.** a description.

portray (pɔː'treɪ) *vb.* **1.** to make a portrait of. **2.** to describe. **3.** to play the part of (a character) in a play or film. —**por-'trayal** *n.*

Portuguese (,pɔːtjʊ'giːz) *n.* **1.** the official language of Portugal and Brazil. **2.** (*pl.* **-guese**) a person from Portugal. ~*adj.* **3.** of Portugal, its people, or their language.

Portuguese man-of-war *n.* a large jellyfish with a sail-like float and long stinging tentacles.

pose (pəʊz) *vb.* **1.** to adopt or cause to adopt a physical attitude for an artist or photographer. **2.** (often foll. by *as*) to present oneself (as something one is not). **3.** to affect an attitude in order to impress others. **4.** to put forward or ask: *to pose a question.* ~*n.* **5.** a physical attitude adopted for an artist or photographer. **6.** behaviour adopted for effect.

poser¹ ('pəʊzə) *n.* **1.** a person who poses. **2.** *Informal.* a person who likes to be seen in trendy clothes in fashionable places.

poser² ('pəʊzə) *n.* a baffling question.

poseur (pəʊ'zɜː) *n.* a person who affects an attitude in order to impress others.

posh (pɒʃ) *adj. Informal, chiefly Brit.* **1.** smart or elegant. **2.** upper-class.

posit ('pɒzɪt) *vb.* to assume or suggest as fact or the factual basis for an argument: *to posit a national scale of values.*

position (pə'zɪʃən) *n.* **1.** place or location: *he took up a position to the rear.* **2.** the proper or usual place. **3.** the way in which a person or thing is placed; arrangement. **4.** *Mil.* a place occupied for tactical reasons. **5.** point of view; stand: *what's your position on this issue?* **6.** social status, esp. high social standing. **7.** a post of employment; job. **8.** *Sport.* the part of a playing area where a player is placed. **9. in a position.** (foll. by an infinitive) able (to). ~*vb.* **10.** to put in the proper or usual place; locate. —**po'sitional** *adj.*

positive ('pɒzɪtɪv) *adj.* **1.** expressing certainty or affirmation: *a positive answer.* **2.** possessing actual qualities; real: *a positive benefit.* **3.** tending to emphasize what is good; constructive: *positive criticism.* **4.** tending towards progress or improvement: *this is seen as a positive development.* **5.** *Philosophy.* constructive rather than sceptical. **6.** *Informal.* complete; downright: *a positive joy.* **7.** *Maths.* having a value greater than zero: *a positive number.* **8.** *Grammar.* denoting the unmodified form of an adjective as opposed to its comparative or superlative form. **9.** *Physics.* (of an electric charge) having an opposite charge to that of an electron. **10.** *Physics.* short for **electropositive**. **11.** *Med.* (of the result of an examination or test) indicating the presence of a suspected condition or organism. ~*n.* **12.** something positive. **13.** *Maths.* a quantity greater than zero. **14.** *Photog.* a print showing an image whose colours and tones correspond to those of the original subject. **15.** *Grammar.* the positive degree of an adjective or adverb. **16.** a positive object, such as a terminal in a cell. —'**positively** *adv.* —'**positiveness** *n.*

positive discrimination *n.* the provision of special opportunities for a disadvantaged group.

positive vetting *n.* the checking of a person's background, political affiliation, and activities to assess his suitability for a position that may involve national security.

positivism ('pɒzɪtɪ,vɪzəm) *n.* a system of philosophy that accepts only observable phenomena and objective facts as sources of knowledge. —'**positivist** *n., adj.*

positron ('pɒzɪ,trɒn) *n. Physics.* the antiparticle of the electron, having the same mass but an equal and opposite charge.

poss. 1. possession. **2.** possessive. **3.** possible. **4.** possibly.

posse ('pɒsɪ) *n.* **1.** *U.S.* a group of men in a district on whom the sheriff may call for assistance. **2.** (in W Canada), a troop of horses and riders who perform at rodeos.

possess (pə'zɛs) *vb.* **1.** to have as one's property; own. **2.** to have as a quality or attribute: *to possess courage.* **3.** to gain control over or dominate: *whatever possessed you to come?* —**pos'sessor** *n.*

possessed (pə'zɛst) *adj.* **1.** (foll. by *of*) owning or having: *possessed of talent.* **2.** under the influence of a powerful force, such as a spirit or strong emotion: *possessed by fury.*

possession (pə'zɛʃən) *n.* **1.** a possessing or being possessed: *in possession of the crown.* **2.** anything that is possessed. **3.** (*pl.*) wealth or property. **4.** the state of being controlled by or as if by evil spirits. **5.** the occupancy of land or property: *to take possession of a house.* **6.** a territory subject to a foreign state. **7.** *Sport.* control of the ball by a player: *he got possession in his own half.*

possessive (pə'zɛsɪv) *adj.* **1.** of possession. **2.** showing an excessive desire to possess or dominate: *a possessive husband.* **3.** *Grammar.* denoting a form of a noun or pronoun used to convey possession, as *my* or *Harry's.* ~*n.* **4.** *Grammar.* **a.** the possessive case. **b.** a word in the possessive case. —**pos'sessiveness** *n.*

possibility (,pɒsɪ'bɪlɪtɪ) *n., pl.* -**ties.** **1.** the state of being possible. **2.** anything that is possible. **3.** a competitor or candidate with a chance of success. **4.** (*often pl.*) a future prospect or potential: *the idea has possibilities.*

possible ('pɒsɪb'l) *adj.* **1.** capable of existing, happening, or proving true. **2.** capable of being done: *it is not possible to finish in three weeks.* **3.** having potential: *the idea is a possible money-spinner.* **4.** feasible but less than probable: *it is possible that man will live on Mars.* **5.** same as **possibility** (sense 3).

possibly ('pɒsɪblɪ) *adv.* **1.** perhaps or maybe. **2.** by any means; at all: *he can't possibly come.*

possum ('pɒsəm) *n.* **1.** *Informal.* an opossum. **2.** *Austral. & N.Z.* a phalanger. **3.** **play possum.** to pretend to be dead, ignorant, or asleep in order to deceive an opponent.

post[1] (pəʊst) *n.* **1.** a length of wood, metal, or concrete fixed upright to serve as a support, marker, or point of attachment. **2.** *Horse racing.* **a.** either of two upright poles marking the beginning and end of a racecourse. **b.** the finish of a horse race. ~*vb.* **3.** (sometimes foll. by *up*) to put up (a notice) in a public place. **4.** to publish (a name) on a list.

post[2] (pəʊst) *n.* **1.** a position to which a person is appointed; job. **2.** a position to which a soldier or guard is assigned for duty. **3.** a permanent military establishment. **4.** *Brit.* either of two military bugle calls (**first post** and **last post**) giving notice of the time to retire for the night. ~*vb.* **5.** to assign to or station at a particular place or position. **6.** *Chiefly Brit.* to transfer (someone) to a different unit or place on taking up a new appointment.

post[3] (pəʊst) *n.* **1.** *Chiefly Brit.* letters or packages that are transported and delivered by the Post Office; mail. **2.** *Chiefly Brit.* a single collection or delivery of mail. **3.** *Brit.* an official system of mail delivery. **4.** *Brit.* a postbox or post office: *take this to the post.* ~*vb.* **5.** *Chiefly Brit.* to send by post. **6.** *Book-keeping.* **a.** to enter (an item) in a ledger. **b.** (often foll. by *up*) to enter all paper items in (a ledger). **7.** to inform of the latest news: *keep us posted.*

post- *prefix.* **1.** after in time; following: *postgraduate.* **2.** behind: *postorbital.*

postage ('pəʊstɪdʒ) *n.* the charge for delivering a piece of mail.

postage stamp *n.* a printed paper label for attaching to mail as an official indication that the required postage has been paid.

postal ('pəʊst'l) *adj.* of a Post Office or the mail-delivery service.

postal order *n.* a money order obtainable and payable at a post office.

postbag ('pəʊst,bæg) *n.* **1.** *Chiefly Brit.* a mailbag. **2.** the mail received by a magazine, radio programme, or public figure.

postbox ('pəʊst,bɒks) *n.* same as **letterbox** (sense 2).

postcard ('pəʊst,kɑːd) n. a card, often with a picture on one side (**picture postcard**), for sending a message by post without an envelope.

post chaise n. a four-wheeled horse-drawn coach formerly used as a rapid means of carrying mail and passengers.

postcode ('pəʊst,kəʊd) n. a code of letters and digits used as part of a postal address.

postdate (pəʊst'deɪt) vb. **1.** to write a future date on (a cheque or document). **2.** to assign a date to (an event or period) that is later than its previously assigned date. **3.** to be or occur at a later date than.

poster ('pəʊstə) n. **1.** a placard posted in a public place as an advertisement. **2.** a large printed picture.

poste restante ('pəʊst rɪ'stænt) n. a post-office department where mail is kept until collected.

posterior (pɒ'stɪərɪə) adj. **1.** at the back of or behind something. **2.** coming after in a series or time. ~n. **3.** the buttocks.

posterity (pɒ'stɛrɪtɪ) n. **1.** future generations. **2.** all of one's descendants.

postern ('pɒstən) n. a back door or gate.

post-free adv., adj. **1.** Brit. with the postage prepaid. **2.** free of postal charge.

postgraduate (pəʊst'grædjuət) n. **1.** a person who is studying for a more advanced qualification after obtaining a university degree. **2.** (modifier) of or for postgraduates.

posthaste ('pəʊst'heɪst) adv. with great haste.

posthumous ('pɒstjʊməs) adj. **1.** happening after one's death. **2.** (of a book) published after the author's death. **3.** (of a child) born after the father's death. —**'posthumously** adv.

postilion or **postillion** (pɒ'stɪljən) n. a person who rides the near horse of a team drawing a coach.

postimpressionism (,pəʊstɪm'prɛʃə,nɪzəm) n. a movement in painting in France at the end of the 19th century which rejected impressionism but adapted its use of pure colour to paint with greater subjective emotion. —,**postim'pressionist** n., adj.

postman ('pəʊstmən) or (fem.) **post-woman** n., pl. -**men** or -**women**. a person who delivers mail as a profession.

postmark ('pəʊst,mɑːk) n. **1.** a mark stamped on mail by postal officials, usually showing the date and place of posting. ~vb. **2.** to put such a mark on (mail).

postmaster ('pəʊst,mɑːstə) or (fem.) **postmistress** n. an official in charge of a local post office.

postmaster general n., pl. **postmasters general.** the executive head of the postal service.

postmeridian (,pəʊstmə'rɪdɪən) adj. of or in the afternoon.

postmortem (pəʊst'mɔːtəm) adj. **1.** occurring after death. ~n. **2.** In full: **postmortem examination.** dissection and examination of a dead body to determine the cause of death. **3.** analysis of a recent event: a postmortem on a game of chess.

postnatal (pəʊst'neɪt'l) adj. occurring after childbirth: postnatal depression.

post office n. a building where stamps are sold and postal business is conducted.

Post Office n. a government department responsible for postal services.

postoperative (pəʊst'ɒpərətɪv) adj. of or occurring in the period after a surgical operation.

postpaid ('pəʊst'peɪd) adv., adj. with the postage prepaid.

postpone (pəʊst'pəʊn, pə'spəʊn) vb. to put off or delay until a future time. —**post'ponement** n.

postpositive (pəʊst'pɒzɪtɪv) adj. (of an adjective) placed after the word it modifies.

postprandial (pəʊst'prændɪəl) adj. after a meal.

postscript ('pəʊs,skrɪpt, 'pəʊst-) n. a message added at the end of a letter, after the signature.

postulant ('pɒstjʊlənt) n. an applicant, usually for admission to a religious order.

postulate vb. ('pɒstjʊ,leɪt). **1.** to assume to be true as the basis of an argument; take for granted. **2.** to ask, demand, or claim. ~n. ('pɒstjʊlɪt). **3.** something postulated. —,**postu'lation** n.

posture ('pɒstʃə) n. **1.** a position or attitude of the body. **2.** a characteristic manner of bearing the body: good posture. **3.** a mental attitude: a cooperative posture. **4.** a state or condition. **5.** an affected attitude; pose. ~vb. **6.** to assume or cause to assume a bodily attitude. **7.** to assume an affected attitude; pose. —**'postural** adj.

postviral (fatigue) syndrome (pəʊst-'vaɪrəl) n. a condition following a viral infection, characterized by fatigue, weakness, headaches, impaired balance, sight, and hearing, and an inability to concentrate.

postwar (pəʊst'wɔː) adj. occurring or existing after a war.

posy ('pəʊzɪ) n., pl. -**sies.** a small bunch of flowers.

pot¹ (pɒt) n. **1.** a round deep container, often having a handle and lid, used for cooking and other domestic purposes. **2.** the amount that a pot will hold; potful. **3.** the money in the pool in gambling games. **4.** a handmade piece of pottery. **5.** Billiards, etc. a shot by which a ball is pocketed. **6.** a chamber pot. **7.** (often pl.) Informal. a large sum of money. **8.** Informal. a cup or other trophy. **9.** short for **flowerpot, teapot. 10.** See **potbelly. 11. go to pot.** to go to ruin. ~vb. **potting, potted. 12.** to put or preserve (food) in a pot. **13.**

to put (a plant) in soil in a flowerpot. **14.** to shoot (game) for food rather than for sport. **15.** to shoot casually or without careful aim. **16.** *Billiards, etc.* to pocket (a ball). **17.** *Informal.* to capture or win.

pot[2] (pɒt) *n. Slang.* cannabis used as a drug.

potable ('pəʊtəb°l) *adj.* drinkable.

potage (pəʊ'tɑːʒ) *n.* thick soup.

potash ('pɒtˌæʃ) *n.* **1.** potassium carbonate, used as a fertilizer. **2.** a compound containing potassium: *chloride of potash.*

potassium (pə'tæsɪəm) *n.* a light silvery element of the alkali metal group. Symbol: K

potassium nitrate *n.* a crystalline compound used in gunpowders, fertilizers, and as a preservative for foods (E252).

potation (pəʊ'teɪʃən) *n.* **1.** the act of drinking. **2.** a drink, usually alcoholic.

potato (pə'teɪtəʊ) *n., pl.* **-toes. a.** a plant widely cultivated for its edible tubers. **b.** the starchy tuber of this plant, cooked and eaten as a vegetable.

potato beetle *n.* same as **Colorado beetle.**

potato crisp *n.* same as **crisp** (sense 8).

potbelly ('pɒtˌbɛlɪ) *n., pl.* **-lies. 1.** a bulging belly. **2.** a person with such a belly.

potboiler ('pɒtˌbɔɪlə) *n. Informal.* an artistic work of little merit produced quickly to make money.

pot-bound *adj.* (of a pot plant) having roots too big for its pot, so that it can grow no further.

poteen ('pɒtiːn) *or* **poitín** (pɒ'tʃiːn) *n.* (in Ireland) illicit spirit.

potent ('pəʊt°nt) *adj.* **1.** having great strength; powerful. **2.** (of arguments) persuasive or forceful. **3.** highly effective: *a potent poison.* **4.** (of a male) capable of having sexual intercourse. —**'potency** *n.*

potentate ('pəʊt°nˌteɪt) *n.* a ruler or monarch.

potential (pə'tɛnʃəl) *adj.* **1. a.** possible but not yet actual. **b.** capable of being or becoming; latent. ~*n.* **2.** latent but unrealized ability: *Jones has great potential as a manager.* **3.** In full: **electric potential.** the work required to transfer a unit positive electric charge from an infinite distance to a given point. —**po'tentially** *adv.*

potential difference *n.* the difference in electric potential between two points in an electric field, measured in volts.

potentiality (pəˌtɛnʃɪ'ælɪtɪ) *n., pl.* **-ties.** latent capacity for becoming or developing.

pother ('pɒðə) *n.* a commotion or fuss.

potherb ('pɒtˌhɜːb) *n.* a plant whose leaves, flowers, or stems are used in cooking.

pothole ('pɒtˌhəʊl) *n.* **1.** a deep hole in a limestone area. **2.** a hole produced in a road surface by wear or weathering.

potholing ('pɒtˌhəʊlɪŋ) *n. Brit.* the sport of exploring underground caves. —**'potˌholer** *n.*

pothook ('pɒtˌhʊk) *n.* **1.** an S-shaped hook for suspending a pot over a fire. **2.** an S-shaped mark in handwriting.

pothunter ('pɒtˌhʌntə) *n.* **1.** a hunter who shoots without regard to the rules of sport. **2.** *Informal.* a person who enters competitions solely to win prizes.

potion ('pəʊʃən) *n.* a drink of medicine, poison, or some supposedly magic liquid.

potluck ('pɒt'lʌk) *n. Informal.* **1.** whatever food happens to be available. **2.** whatever is available: *to take potluck.*

potpourri (ˌpəʊ'pʊərɪ) *n., pl.* **-ris. 1.** a fragrant mixture of dried flower petals. **2.** a miscellany or medley.

pot roast *n.* meat cooked slowly in a covered pot with very little liquid.

potsherd ('pɒtˌʃɜːd) *n.* a broken piece of pottery.

pot shot *n.* **1.** a shot taken without careful aim. **2.** a shot fired at quarry within easy range.

pottage ('pɒtɪdʒ) *n.* a thick soup.

potted ('pɒtɪd) *adj.* **1.** grown in a pot. **2.** cooked or preserved in a pot: *potted shrimps.* **3.** *Informal.* abridged: *a potted history.*

potter[1] ('pɒtə) *n.* a person who makes pottery.

potter[2] ('pɒtə) *or esp. U.S. & Canad.* **putter** *vb.* **1.** (often foll. by *about* or *around*) to busy oneself in an aimless but pleasant manner. **2.** (often foll. by *along* or *about*) to move with little energy or direction: *to potter about town.*

Potteries ('pɒtərɪz) *pl. n.* **the.** (*sometimes functioning as sing.*) a region of W central England, in Staffordshire, in which the china industries are concentrated.

potter's wheel *n.* a device with a horizontal rotating disc, on which clay is shaped by hand.

pottery ('pɒtərɪ) *n., pl.* **-teries. 1.** articles made from baked clay. **2.** a place where such articles are made. **3.** the craft or business of making such articles.

potting shed *n.* a building in which plants are put in flowerpots.

potty[1] ('pɒtɪ) *adj.* **-tier, -tiest.** *Brit. informal.* **1.** slightly crazy. **2.** trivial or insignificant. **3.** (foll. by *about*) very keen (on). —**'pottiness** *n.*

potty[2] ('pɒtɪ) *n., pl.* **-ties.** a child's chamber pot.

pouch (paʊtʃ) *n.* **1.** a small bag. **2.** a saclike structure in various animals, such as the cheek fold in rodents. ~*vb.* **3.** to place in or as if in a pouch. **4.** to make or be made into a pouch.

pouf *or* **pouffe** (puːf) *n.* a large solid cushion used as a seat.

poulterer ('pəʊltərə) n. a dealer in poultry.

poultice ('pəʊltɪs) n. Med. a moist and often heated dressing applied to inflamed skin.

poultry ('pəʊltrɪ) n. domestic fowls collectively.

pounce (paʊns) vb. 1. (often foll. by on or upon) to spring or swoop, as in capturing prey. ~n. 2. a pouncing; a spring or swoop.

pound¹ (paʊnd) vb. 1. (sometimes foll. by on or at) to strike heavily and repeatedly. 2. to beat to a pulp; pulverize. 3. (foll. by out) to produce, as by typing heavily. 4. to move with heavy steps. 5. to throb heavily.

pound² (paʊnd) n. 1. an avoirdupois unit of weight divided into 16 ounces and equal to 0.453 592 kilograms. 2. a troy unit of weight divided into 12 ounces and equal to 0.373 242 kilograms. 3. the standard monetary unit of the United Kingdom, divided into 100 pence. Official name: **pound sterling.** 4. the standard monetary unit of various other countries, such as Ireland, Cyprus, and Malta.

pound³ (paʊnd) n. an enclosure for keeping officially removed vehicles or stray dogs.

poundage ('paʊndɪdʒ) n. 1. a charge of so much per pound of weight. 2. a charge of so much per pound sterling.

-pounder ('paʊndə) n. 1. something weighing a specified number of pounds: a 200-pounder. 2. something worth a specified number of pounds: a ten-pounder. 3. a gun that discharges a shell weighing a specified number of pounds: a two-pounder.

pour (pɔː) vb. 1. to flow or cause to flow in a stream. 2. to emit profusely: the words poured out of her. 3. to rain heavily. 4. to move together in large numbers; swarm: the fans poured onto the pitch.

pourboire ('pʊəbwɑː) n. a tip; gratuity.

pout (paʊt) vb. 1. to thrust out (the lips), as when sullen, or (of the lips) to be thrust out. 2. to swell out; protrude. ~n. 3. a pouting.

pouter ('paʊtə) n. a breed of domestic pigeon with a crop that can be greatly puffed out.

poverty ('pɒvətɪ) n. 1. the condition of being without adequate food or money. 2. scarcity: a poverty of wit. 3. inferior quality or inadequacy: the poverty of the soil.

poverty-stricken adj. suffering from extreme poverty.

poverty trap n. the situation of being unable to raise one's living standard because of depending on state benefits which are reduced if one gains any extra income.

pow (paʊ) interj. an exclamation imitative of a collision or explosion.

POW prisoner of war.

powder ('paʊdə) n. 1. a substance in the form of tiny loose particles. 2. a preparation in this form, such as gunpowder or face powder. ~vb. 3. to turn into powder; pulverize. 4. to cover or sprinkle with or as if with powder. —**powdery** adj.

powder keg n. 1. a small barrel to hold gunpowder. 2. a potential source of violence or disaster.

powder puff n. a soft pad used to apply cosmetic powder to the skin.

powder room n. a ladies' cloakroom.

power ('paʊə) n. 1. ability to do something. 2. (often pl.) a specific ability or faculty. 3. political, financial, or social force or influence. 4. control or a position of control. 5. a state with political, industrial, or military strength. 6. a person or group that has control, influence, or authority. 7. a prerogative or privilege: the power of veto. 8. legal authority: power of attorney. 9. Maths. the value of a number or quantity raised to some exponent. 10. Physics, engineering. a measure of the rate of doing work expressed as the work done per unit time. 11. the rate at which electrical energy is fed into or taken from a device or system, measured in watts. 12. mechanical energy as opposed to manual labour. 13. a particular form of energy: nuclear power. 14. the magnifying capacity of a lens or optical system. 15. Informal. a great deal: a power of good. 16. **the powers that be.** established authority. ~vb. 17. to supply with power. ~adj. 18. producing or using mechanical or electrical energy: a power tool.

powerboat ('paʊə,bəʊt) n. a fast powerful motorboat.

power cut n. a temporary interruption in the supply of electrical power.

powerful ('paʊəfʊl) adj. 1. having great power. 2. extremely effective: a powerful drug. —**powerfully** adv. —**powerfulness** n.

powerhouse ('paʊə,haʊs) n. 1. an electrical generating station. 2. Informal. a forceful person or thing.

powerless ('paʊəlɪs) adj. without power or authority. —**powerlessness** n.

power of attorney n. 1. legal authority to act for another person. 2. the document conferring such authority.

power point n. an electrical socket mounted on or recessed into a wall.

power station n. an electrical generating station.

power steering n. a form of steering on vehicles in which the turning of the steering wheel is assisted by power from the engine.

powwow ('paʊ,waʊ) n. 1. a talk or meeting. 2. a meeting of North American Indians. ~vb. 3. to hold a powwow.

pox (pɒks) n. 1. a disease accompanied by skin pustules. 2. (usually preceded by the) Informal. syphilis.

pp 1. past participle. **2.** (in signing documents on behalf of someone else) by delegation to. **3.** *Music.* very quietly.

pp. pages.

PPS 1. parliamentary private secretary. **2.** additional postscript.

PQ 1. (in Canada) Parti Québecois. **2.** Province of Quebec.

pr, *pl.* **prs.** pair.

Pr *Chem.* praseodymium.

PR 1. proportional representation. **2.** public relations.

pr. 1. price. **2.** pronoun.

practicable (ˈpræktɪkəbʰl) *adj.* **1.** capable of being done; feasible. **2.** usable. —ˌpracticaˈbility *n.* Usage. see practical.

practical (ˈpræktɪkʰl) *adj.* **1.** involving or concerned with experience or actual use, rather than theory. **2.** concerned with ordinary affairs, work, and daily living: *a survivor must be practical.* **3.** adapted or adaptable for use: *penicillin became a practical antibiotic.* **4.** involving or trained by practice: *practical skills.* **5.** being such for all general purposes; virtual: *it's a practical certainty.* ~*n.* **6.** an examination or lesson in a practical subject. —ˌpractiˈcality *n.* —ˈpractically *adv.* Usage. *Practical* refers to a person, idea, project, etc., as being more concerned with or relevant to practice than theory: *he is a very practical person; the idea had no practical application.* *Practicable* refers to a project or idea as being capable of being done or put into effect: *the plan was expensive, yet practicable.*

practical joke *n.* a trick intended to make someone look foolish. —**practical joker** *n.*

practice (ˈpræktɪs) *n.* **1.** a usual or customary action. **2.** repetition of an activity in order to gain skill: *piano practice.* **3.** the condition of being skilful in an activity through repetition: *in practice; out of practice.* **4.** the exercise of a profession: *he set up practice as a lawyer.* **5.** the act of doing something: *he put his plans into practice.*

practise or *U.S.* **practice** (ˈpræktɪs) *vb.* **1.** to do repeatedly so as to gain skill. **2.** to do (something) regularly: *they practise torture.* **3.** to observe or pursue (something): *to practise Buddhism.* **4.** to work at (a profession): *he practises law.*

practitioner (prækˈtɪʃənə) *n.* a person who practises a profession or art.

praetor (ˈpriːtə, -tɔː) *n.* (in ancient Rome) a senior magistrate ranking just below the consuls. —**praeˈtorian** *adj., n.*

pragmatic (prægˈmætɪk) *adj.* **1.** advocating behaviour that is dictated by practical consequences rather than by theory. **2.** *Philosophy.* of pragmatism. —**pragˌmatiˈcality** *n.*

pragmatism (ˈprægməˌtɪzəm) *n.* **1.** action or policy dictated by the practical consequences rather than by theory. **2.** *Philosophy.* the doctrine that the content of a concept consists only in its practical applicability. —ˈpragmatist *n., adj.*

prairie (ˈprɛərɪ) *n.* (*often pl.*) a treeless grassy plain of the central U.S. and S Canada.

prairie dog *n.* a rodent that lives in large complex burrows in the N American prairies.

praise (preɪz) *n.* **1.** the act of expressing admiration or approval. **2.** **sing someone's praises.** to praise someone highly. ~*vb.* **3.** to express admiration or approval for. **4.** to proclaim the glory of (a god) with homage and thanksgiving.

praiseworthy (ˈpreɪzˌwɜːðɪ) *adj.* deserving of praise; commendable.

praline (ˈprɑːliːn) *n.* a sweet made of nuts with caramelized sugar.

pram (præm) *n. Brit.* a four-wheeled carriage for a baby.

prance (prɑːns) *vb.* **1.** to swagger or strut. **2.** (of a horse) to move with high springing steps. ~*n.* **3.** a prancing.

prang (præŋ) *Slang, chiefly Brit.* ~*n.* **1.** a crash in an aircraft or car. ~*vb.* **2.** to crash or damage (an aircraft or car).

prank (præŋk) *n.* a mischievous trick. —ˈprankster *n.*

praseodymium (ˌpreɪzɪəʊˈdɪmɪəm) *n.* a silvery-white element of the lanthanide series of metals. Symbol: Pr

prat (præt) *n. Slang.* an incompetent or ineffectual person.

prate (preɪt) *vb.* **1.** to talk idly and at length; chatter. ~*n.* **2.** chatter.

prattle (ˈprætʰl) *vb.* **1.** to talk or utter in a foolish or childish way. ~*n.* **2.** foolish or childish talk.

prawn (prɔːn) *n.* a small edible shellfish.

praxis (ˈpræksɪs) *n.* **1.** the practice of a profession or field of study, as opposed to the theory. **2.** accepted practice or custom.

pray (preɪ) *vb.* **1.** to utter prayers (to God or other object of worship). **2.** to beg or implore. ~*adv.* **3.** *Archaic.* I beg you; please: *pray, leave us alone.*

prayer[1] (prɛə) *n.* **1.** a thanksgiving or an appeal for something spoken to one's God. **2.** the practice of praying. **3.** (*often pl.*) a form of devotion spent mainly praying: *morning prayers.* **4.** a form of words used in praying: *the Lord's Prayer.* **5.** something prayed for. **6.** an earnest request or entreaty.

prayer[2] (ˈpreɪə) *n.* a person who prays.

prayer book (prɛə) *n.* a book of prayers used in church or for private devotions.

prayer mat (prɛə) *n.* the small carpet on which a Muslim kneels while praying.

prayer wheel (prɛə) *n. Buddhism.* (in Tibet) a cylinder inscribed with prayers, each turning of which is counted as an uttered prayer.

praying mantis n. same as **mantis**.

pre- prefix. before in time or position: predate; pre-eminent.

preach (priːtʃ) vb. **1.** to make known (religious truth) or give religious instruction in (sermons). **2.** to advocate (something) in a moralizing way.

preacher ('priːtʃə) n. a person who preaches, usually a Protestant clergyman.

preamble (priː'æmbᵊl) n. a preliminary or introductory statement.

prearrange (ˌpriːə'reɪndʒ) vb. to arrange beforehand. —ˌprear'ranged adj. —ˌprear'rangement n.

prebend ('prɛbənd) n. **1.** the allowance paid by a cathedral or collegiate church to a canon or member of the chapter. **2.** the land or tithe from which this is paid. —**prebendal** (prɪ'bɛndᵊl) adj.

prebendary ('prɛbəndrɪ) n., pl. **-daries.** a canon or chapter member of a cathedral or collegiate church who holds a prebend.

Precambrian or **Pre-Cambrian** (priː-'kæmbrɪən) adj. Geol. of the earliest geological era, lasting from about 4500 million years ago to 600 million years ago.

precancerous (priː'kænsərəs) adj. of, relating to, or denoting a growth that though not yet malignant will become so unless treated.

precarious (prɪ'kɛərɪəs) adj. (of a position or situation) dangerous or insecure.

precaution (prɪ'kɔːʃən) n. an action taken to avoid a dangerous or undesirable event. —**pre'cautionary** adj.

precede (prɪ'siːd) vb. to go or be before (someone or something) in time, place, or rank.

precedence ('prɛsɪdəns) n. **1.** the ceremonial order of priority to be observed on formal occasions: the officers sat according to precedence. **2.** a right to preferential treatment: I take precedence over you.

precedent n. ('prɛsɪdənt). **1.** Law. a judicial decision that serves as an authority for deciding a later case. **2.** an example used to justify later similar occurrences. ~adj. (prɪ'siːdᵊnt, 'prɛsɪdənt). **3.** preceding.

precentor (prɪ'sɛntə) n. a person who leads the singing in church services.

precept ('priːsɛpt) n. **1.** a rule of conduct. **2.** a rule for morals; maxim. **3.** Law. a writ or warrant. —**pre'ceptive** adj.

preceptor (prɪ'sɛptə) n. Rare. an instructor. —**preceptorial** (ˌpriːsɛp'tɔːrɪəl) adj.

precession (prɪ'sɛʃən) n. **1.** the act of preceding. **2.** the motion of a spinning body, in which the axis of rotation sweeps out a cone.

precinct ('priːsɪŋkt) n. **1.** an enclosed area or building marked by a fixed boundary. **2.** an area in a town closed to traffic: a shopping precinct. **3.** U.S. a district of a city for administrative or police purposes.

precincts ('priːsɪŋkts) pl. n. the surrounding region or area.

preciosity (ˌprɛʃɪ'ɒsɪtɪ) n., pl. **-ties.** fastidiousness or affectation.

precious ('prɛʃəs) adj. **1.** beloved; dear; cherished. **2.** very costly or valuable. **3.** very fastidious or affected in speech, manners, or behaviour. **4.** Informal. worthless: you and your precious ideas! ~adv. **5.** Informal. very: there's precious little left.

precious metal n. gold, silver, or platinum.

precious stone n. a rare mineral, such as diamond, ruby, or opal that is highly valued as a gemstone.

precipice ('prɛsɪpɪs) n. the steep sheer face of a cliff or crag.

precipitant (prɪ'sɪpɪtənt) adj. **1.** hasty or impulsive; rash. **2.** rushing or falling rapidly.

precipitate vb. (prɪ'sɪpɪˌteɪt). **1.** to cause to happen too soon. **2.** to throw as from a height. **3.** to cause (moisture) to condense and fall as snow or rain or (of moisture) to condense and fall thus. **4.** Chem. to undergo or cause to undergo a process in which a dissolved substance separates from solution as a suspension of solid particles. ~adj. (prɪ'sɪpɪtɪt). **5.** rushing ahead. **6.** done rashly or hastily. ~n. (prɪ'sɪpɪtɪt). **7.** Chem. a precipitated solid.

precipitation (prɪˌsɪpɪ'teɪʃən) n. **1.** Meteorol. **a.** rain, hail, snow, or sleet formed by condensation of water vapour in the atmosphere. **b.** the falling of these on the earth's surface. **2.** the formation of a chemical precipitate. **3.** a precipitating or being precipitated. **4.** rash haste.

precipitous (prɪ'sɪpɪtəs) adj. **1.** like a precipice; very steep. **2.** hasty or precipitate.

precis or **précis** ('preɪsiː) n., pl. **precis** or **précis** ('preɪsiːz). **1.** a summary of a text. ~vb. **2.** to make a precis of.

precise (prɪ'saɪs) adj. **1.** strictly correct in amount or value: a precise sum. **2.** particular: this precise moment. **3.** operating with total accuracy: precise instruments. **4.** strict in observing rules or standards. —**pre'cisely** adv.

precision (prɪ'sɪʒən) n. **1.** the quality of being precise; accuracy. **2.** (modifier) characterized by accuracy: precision grinding.

preclude (prɪ'kluːd) vb. to prevent or make impossible, usually beforehand.

precocious (prɪ'kəʊʃəs) adj. **1.** ahead in development of some faculty or characteristic. **2.** of or showing unusually early development: a precocious feat. —**precocity** (prɪ'kɒsɪtɪ) n.

precognition (ˌpriːkɒg'nɪʃən) n. Psychol.

the alleged ability to foresee future events.

preconceive (ˌpriːkənˈsiːv) vb. to form an idea of beforehand. —**preconception** (ˌpriːkənˈsɛpʃən) n.

precondition (ˌpriːkənˈdɪʃən) n. a necessary or required condition; prerequisite.

precursor (prɪˈkɜːsə) n. 1. a forerunner. 2. a predecessor.

pred. predicate.

predacious (prɪˈdeɪʃəs) adj. (of animals) habitually hunting and killing other animals for food.

predate (priːˈdeɪt) vb. 1. to write a date on (a document) that is earlier than the actual date. 2. to be or occur at an earlier date than.

predator (ˈprɛdətə) n. a carnivorous animal.

predatory (ˈprɛdətrɪ) adj. 1. (of animals) habitually hunting and killing other animals for food. 2. of or given to plundering or robbing.

predecease (ˌpriːdɪˈsiːs) vb. to die before (another person).

predecessor (ˈpriːdɪˌsɛsə) n. 1. a person who precedes another, as in an office. 2. something that precedes something else. 3. an ancestor.

predestination (priːˌdɛstɪˈneɪʃən) n. Christian theol. the act of God foreordaining everything.

predestine (priːˈdɛstɪn) or **predestinate** vb. 1. to determine beforehand. 2. Christian theol. (of God) to foreordain (any event).

predetermine (ˌpriːdɪˈtɜːmɪn) vb. 1. to determine beforehand. 2. to influence or bias.

predicable (ˈprɛdɪkəbˀl) adj. capable of being predicated.

predicament (prɪˈdɪkəmənt) n. an embarrassing or difficult situation.

predicant (ˈprɛdɪkənt) adj. 1. of preaching. ~n. 2. a member of a religious order founded for preaching, usually a Dominican.

predicate vb. (ˈprɛdɪˌkeɪt). 1. to declare or affirm. 2. to imply or connote. 3. Logic. to assert (something) about the subject of a proposition. ~n. (ˈprɛdɪkɪt). 4. Grammar. the part of a sentence in which a statement is made about the subject of a sentence. 5. Logic. something that is asserted about the subject of a proposition. —ˌprediˈcation n. —preˈdicative adj.

predict (prɪˈdɪkt) vb. to make a declaration about in advance; foretell. —preˈdictable adj. —preˈdictably adv. —preˈdictor n.

prediction (prɪˈdɪkʃən) n. 1. the act of predicting. 2. something predicted; a forecast.

predikant (ˌprɛdɪˈkænt) n. a minister in the Dutch Reformed Church in South Africa.

predilection (ˌpriːdɪˈlɛkʃən) n. a predisposition or preference.

predispose (ˌpriːdɪˈspəʊz) vb. (often foll. by to or towards) to incline or make (someone) susceptible to something beforehand. —ˌpredispoˈsition n.

predominant (prɪˈdɒmɪnənt) adj. 1. having power or influence over others. 2. prevailing. —preˈdominance n. —preˈdominantly adv.

predominate (prɪˈdɒmɪˌneɪt) vb. 1. (often foll. by over) to have power or influence. 2. to prevail or preponderate.

pre-eminent (prɪˈɛmɪnənt) adj. extremely eminent; outstanding. —pre-ˈeminence n.

pre-empt (prɪˈɛmpt) vb. to get or do (something) in advance of or to the exclusion of others.

pre-emption (prɪˈɛmpʃən) n. Law. the purchase of or right to buy property in advance of others.

pre-emptive (prɪˈɛmptɪv) adj. Mil. designed to reduce or destroy an enemy's attacking strength before it can be used: a pre-emptive strike.

preen (priːn) vb. 1. (of birds) to keep (feathers) in good condition by arranging and cleaning with the bill. 2. to smarten (oneself) carefully. 3. (usually foll. by on) to pride or congratulate (oneself).

pref. 1. preface. 2. prefatory. 3. preference. 4. preferred. 5. prefix.

prefab (ˈpriːˌfæb) n. a prefabricated building, usually a small house.

prefabricate (priːˈfæbrɪˌkeɪt) vb. to manufacture sections of (a building) so that they can be rapidly assembled.

preface (ˈprɛfɪs) n. 1. a statement written as an introduction to a book, usually explaining its scope, intention, or method; foreword. 2. anything introductory. ~vb. 3. to provide with a preface. 4. to act as a preface to.

prefatory (ˈprɛfətrɪ) adj. of or serving as a preface; introductory.

prefect (ˈpriːfɛkt) n. 1. (in some countries) the chief administrative officer in a department. 2. Brit. a senior pupil in a school given limited power to help maintain discipline.

prefecture (ˈpriːfɛkˌtjʊə) n. the office, position, or area of authority of a prefect.

prefer (prɪˈfɜː) vb. **-ferring, -ferred.** 1. to like better or value more highly: I prefer to stand. 2. Law. to put (charges) before a court or magistrate for consideration and judgment. 3. (often passive) to promote over another or others.

preferable (ˈprɛfərəbˀl) adj. preferred or more desirable. —ˈpreferably adv.

preference (ˈprɛfərəns, ˈprɛfrəns) n. 1. a preferring. 2. a person or thing preferred.

preference shares pl. n. Brit. shares issued by a company and giving their holders a prior right over ordinary shareholders to payment of dividend.

preferential (ˌprɛfə'rɛnʃəl) *adj.* 1. showing or resulting from preference. 2. giving or receiving preference.

preferment (prɪ'fɜːmənt) *n.* promotion to a higher position or office.

prefigure (priː'fɪgə) *vb.* 1. to represent or suggest in advance. 2. to imagine beforehand.

prefix *n.* ('priːfɪks). 1. *Grammar.* a letter or group of letters that precedes the word to which it is attached, such as *un-* in *unhappy.* 2. something coming or placed before. ~*vb.* (priː'fɪks, 'priːfɪks). 3. to put or place before. 4. *Grammar.* to add (a letter or group of letters) as a prefix to the beginning of a word.

pregnant ('prɛgnənt) *adj.* 1. carrying a fetus or fetuses within the womb. 2. full of meaning or significance: *a pregnant pause.* —**'pregnancy** *n.*

prehensile (prɪ'hɛnsaɪl) *adj.* adapted for grasping by wrapping around a support: *a prehensile tail.*

prehistoric (ˌpriːhɪ'stɒrɪk) *adj.* of man's development before the appearance of the written word. —**pre'history** *n.*

preindustrial (ˌpriːɪn'dʌstrɪəl) *adj.* of a time before the mechanization of industry.

prejudge (priː'dʒʌdʒ) *vb.* to judge beforehand without sufficient evidence.

prejudice ('prɛdʒʊdɪs) *n.* 1. an opinion formed beforehand. 2. the act or condition of holding such opinions. 3. intolerance of or dislike for people of a specific race, religion, or group. 4. harm resulting from prejudice. 5. **without prejudice.** *Law.* without detriment to an existing right or claim. ~*vb.* 6. to cause to be prejudiced. 7. to harm by prejudice.

prejudicial (ˌprɛdʒʊ'dɪʃəl) *adj.* causing prejudice; damaging.

prelacy ('prɛləsɪ) *n., pl.* **-cies.** 1. **a.** the office or status of a prelate. **b.** prelates collectively. 2. *Often offensive.* government of the Church by prelates.

prelate ('prɛlɪt) *n.* a Church dignitary of high rank, such as a bishop.

preliminaries (prɪ'lɪmɪnərɪz) *pl. n.* same as **prelims.**

preliminary (prɪ'lɪmɪnərɪ) *adj.* 1. occurring before or in preparation; introductory. ~*n., pl.* **-naries.** 2. a preliminary event. 3. an eliminating contest held before a main competition.

prelims ('priːlɪmz, prə'lɪmz) *pl. n.* 1. the pages of a book, such as the title page and contents, before the main text. 2. the first public examinations in some universities.

prelude ('prɛljuːd) *n.* 1. **a.** the introductory section of a fugue or first movement of a suite. **b.** a short piece of music for piano or organ. 2. an introduction or preceding

event. ~*vb.* 3. to act as a prelude to (something). 4. to introduce by a prelude.

premarital (priː'mærɪt'l) *adj.* occurring before marriage: *premarital sex.*

premature (ˌprɛmə'tjʊə, 'prɛmə,tjʊə) *adj.* 1. occurring or existing before the normal or expected time. 2. impulsive or hasty: *a premature judgment.* 3. (of an infant) born before the date when it was due to be born.

premedication (ˌpriːmɛdɪ'keɪʃən) *n. Surgery.* any drugs given to prepare a patient for a general anaesthetic.

premeditate (prɪ'mɛdɪ,teɪt) *vb.* to plan (something) beforehand. —**pre,medi'tation** *n.*

premenstrual (priː'mɛnstrʊəl) *adj.* of or occurring before a menstrual period.

premenstrual tension *or* **syndrome** *n.* symptoms, such as nervous tension, that may be experienced because of hormonal changes in the days before a menstrual period starts.

premier ('prɛmjə) *n.* 1. a prime minister. 2. a head of government of a Canadian province or Australian state. ~*adj.* 3. first in importance or rank: *the premier competition.* 4. first in occurrence; earliest.

premiere ('prɛmɪ,ɛə, 'prɛmɪə) *n.* 1. the first public performance of a film, play, or opera. ~*vb.* 2. to give a premiere of: *the show was premiered on Broadway.*

premise *or* **premiss** ('prɛmɪs) *n. Logic.* a statement that is assumed to be true and is used as a basis for an argument.

premises ('prɛmɪsɪz) *pl. n.* 1. a piece of land together with its buildings. 2. *Law.* (in a deed) the matters referred to previously.

premium ('priːmɪəm) *n.* 1. an amount paid in addition to a standard rate, price, or wage; bonus. 2. the amount to be paid for an insurance policy. 3. the amount above the usual value at which something sells. 4. great value or regard: *to put a premium on honesty.* 5. **at a premium. a.** in great demand, usually because of scarcity. **b.** at a higher price than usual.

Premium Savings Bonds *pl. n.* (in Britain) bonds issued by the Treasury, on which no interest is paid, but there is a monthly draw for cash prizes. Also called: **premium bonds.**

premolar (priː'məʊlə) *n.* a tooth between the canine and first molar in adult humans.

premonition (ˌprɛmə'nɪʃən) *n.* an intuition of a future occurrence; foreboding. —**premonitory** (prɪ'mɒnɪtrɪ) *adj.*

prenatal (priː'neɪt'l) *adj.* before birth; during pregnancy.

preoccupy (priː'ɒkjʊ,paɪ) *vb.* **-pying, -pied.** to engross the thoughts or mind of. —**pre,occu'pation** *n.*

preordain (ˌpriːɔː'deɪn) *vb.* to ordain or decree beforehand.

prep (prɛp) *n. Informal.* short for **preparation** (sense 4).

prep. **1.** preparation. **2.** preparatory. **3.** preposition.

prepacked (priː'pækt) *adj.* (of goods) sold already wrapped or packed.

preparation (ˌprɛpə'reɪʃən) *n.* **1.** a preparing or being prepared. **2.** (*often pl.*) a measure done in order to prepare for something: *to make preparations for something.* **3.** something that is prepared, such as a medicine. **4. a.** homework. **b.** the period reserved for this.

preparatory (prɪ'pærətrɪ) *adj.* **1.** serving to prepare. **2.** introductory. **3. preparatory to.** before: *a drink preparatory to eating.*

preparatory school *n.* **1.** (in Britain) a private school for children between the ages of 6 and 13, generally preparing pupils for public school. **2.** (in the U.S.) a private secondary school preparing pupils for college.

prepare (prɪ'pɛə) *vb.* **1.** to make ready in advance for some use, event, or action: *to prepare a meal; to prepare to go.* **2.** to put together using parts or ingredients; construct. **3.** to equip or outfit, as for an expedition. **4. be prepared.** (*foll. by an infinitive*) to be willing and able: *I'm not prepared to say.*

prepay (priː'peɪ) *vb.* **-paying, -paid.** to pay for in advance. **—pre'payment** *n.*

preponderant (prɪ'pɒndərənt) *adj.* greater in amount, force, or influence. **—pre'ponderance** *n.*

preponderate (prɪ'pɒndə,reɪt) *vb.* (often foll. by *over*) to be more powerful, important, or numerous (than).

preposition (ˌprɛpə'zɪʃən) *n.* a word or group of words used before a noun or pronoun to relate it to another element of a sentence, for example *in* in *he is in the car.* **—ˌprepo'sitional** *adj.*
Usage. The rule that a sentence should not end in a preposition (*they are the people I hate talking to*) is very often broken in the interests of natural-sounding English.

prepossess (ˌpriːpə'zɛs) *vb.* **1.** to preoccupy or engross mentally. **2.** to make a favourable impression in advance. **—ˌprepos'session** *n.*

prepossessing (ˌpriːpə'zɛsɪŋ) *adj.* creating a good impression; attractive.

preposterous (prɪ'pɒstərəs) *adj.* contrary to nature or sense; absurd.

prep school *n. Informal.* See **preparatory school.**

prepuce (ˈpriːpjuːs) *n.* **1.** the retractable fold of skin covering the tip of the penis; foreskin. **2.** a similar fold of skin covering the tip of the clitoris.

Pre-Raphaelite (ˌpriː'ræfəlaɪt) *n.* **1.** a member of a society of painters founded in 1848 to revive the fidelity to nature and realistic colour considered typical of Italian painting before Raphael. *~adj.* **2.** of or in the manner of Pre-Raphaelite painting and painters.

prerecord (ˌpriːrɪ'kɔːd) *vb.* to record (music or a programme) in advance so that it can be played or broadcast later. **—ˌprere'corded** *adj.*

prerequisite (priː'rɛkwɪzɪt) *adj.* **1.** required as a prior condition. *~n.* **2.** something required as a prior condition.

prerogative (prɪ'rɒɡətɪv) *n.* an exclusive privilege or right.

pres. **1.** present (time). **2.** presidential.

Pres. President.

presage *n.* (ˈprɛsɪdʒ). **1.** a portent; omen. **2.** a foreboding. *~vb.* (ˈprɛsɪdʒ, prɪ'seɪdʒ). **3.** to have a foreboding of. **4.** to give a forewarning of; portend: *what does it presage for the future?*

presbyopia (ˌprɛzbɪ'əʊpɪə) *n.* a progressively diminishing ability of the eye to focus.

presbyter (ˈprɛzbɪtə) *n.* **1.** (in some episcopal Churches) an official with administrative and priestly duties. **2.** (in the Presbyterian Church) an elder. **—ˌpresby'terial** *adj.*

presbyterian (ˌprɛzbɪ'tɪərɪən) *adj.* **1.** of or designating Church government by presbyters or elders. *~n.* **2.** an upholder of this type of Church government. **—ˌpresby'terianism** *n.*

Presbyterian (ˌprɛzbɪ'tɪərɪən) *adj.* **1.** of any of various Protestant Churches governed by presbyters or elders. *~n.* **2.** a member of a Presbyterian Church. **—ˌPresby'terianism** *n.*

presbytery (ˈprɛzbɪtərɪ) *n., pl.* **-teries. 1.** *Presbyterian Church.* a local Church court. **2.** the part of a church east of the choir; a sanctuary. **3.** presbyters or elders collectively. **4.** *R.C. Church.* the residence of a parish priest.

preschool (priː'skuːl) *adj.* of or provided for children before the age at which they must go to school: *a preschool playgroup.*

prescience (ˈprɛsɪəns) *n.* knowledge of events before they happen; foresight. **—ˈprescient** *adj.*

prescribe (prɪ'skraɪb) *vb.* **1.** to lay down as a rule. **2.** *Med.* to recommend the use of (a drug or other remedy).

prescript (ˈpriːskrɪpt) *n.* something laid down or prescribed.

prescription (prɪ'skrɪpʃən) *n.* **1. a.** written instructions from a doctor for the preparation and use of a medicine to be issued to a patient. **b.** the medicine prescribed. **2.** prescribing.

prescriptive (prɪ'skrɪptɪv) *adj.* **1.** making or giving directions or rules. **2.** based on long-standing custom.

presence ('prɛzəns) n. **1.** a being present. **2.** immediate proximity: *in his presence*. **3.** impressive personal appearance or bearing: *he had great physical presence*. **4.** an invisible spirit felt to be nearby: *I felt a presence in the room*.

presence of mind n. the ability to stay calm and act sensibly in a crisis.

present¹ ('prɛzⁿnt) adj. **1.** existing at the time at which something is spoken or written. **2.** being in a specified place: *the murderer is present in this room*. **3.** now being dealt with or discussed: *the present author*. **4.** *Grammar*. denoting a tense of verbs used when the action or event described is happening at the time of utterance. ~n. **5.** *Grammar*. the present tense. **6. at present.** now. **7. for the present.** for now; temporarily. **8. the present.** the time being; now. ~See also **presents**.

present² n. ('prɛzⁿnt). **1.** a gift. ~vb. (prɪ'zɛnt). **2.** to introduce (a person) to another. **3.** to introduce to the public: *to present a play*. **4.** to introduce and compere (a radio or television show). **5.** to show; exhibit: *he presented a brave face to the world*. **6.** to bring or suggest to the mind: *to present a problem*. **7.** to put forward; submit: *to present a proposal*. **8.** to give or offer formally: *to present one's compliments; to present a prize*. **9.** to hand over for action or payment: *to present a bill*. **10.** to depict in a particular way: *the actor presented Hamlet as a very young man*. **11.** to aim (a weapon). **12. present arms.** to salute someone with one's weapon.

presentable (prɪ'zɛntəbⁿl) adj. **1.** fit to be seen by or introduced to other people. **2.** fit to be shown or offered. —**pre,senta'bility** n.

presentation (,prɛzⁿn'teɪʃən) n. **1.** a presenting or being presented. **2.** the manner of presenting. **3.** a formal offering, as of a gift. **4.** a performance or representation, as of a play.

present-day n. (*modifier*) of the modern day; current: *I don't like present-day fashions*.

presenter (prɪ'zɛntə) n. *Radio, television*. a person who introduces and comperes a show and links the items in it.

presentiment (prɪ'zɛntɪmənt) n. a sense of something about to happen; premonition.

presently ('prɛzⁿntlɪ) adv. **1.** soon. **2.** *Chiefly Scot., U.S., & Canad.* at the moment.

present participle ('prɛzⁿnt) n. a participial form of verbs used adjectivally when the action it describes is happening at the same time as that of the main verb of a sentence.

present perfect ('prɛzⁿnt) adj., n. *Grammar*. another term for **perfect** (senses 7, 8).

presents ('prɛzⁿnts) pl. n. *Law*. used in a

deed or document to refer to itself: *know all men by these presents*.

preservative (prɪ'zɜːvətɪv) n. **1.** something that preserves, usually a chemical added to foods. ~adj. **2.** that preserves.

preserve (prɪ'zɜːv) vb. **1.** to keep safe from danger or harm; protect. **2.** to protect from decay: *to preserve old buildings*. **3.** to maintain; keep up: *to preserve a façade of indifference*. **4.** to treat (something, such as food) in order to prevent it from decomposition or chemical change. **5.** to rear and protect (game) in restricted places for hunting or fishing. ~n. **6.** a special domain: *archaeology is the preserve of specialists*. **7.** (*usually pl.*) fruit preserved by cooking with sugar. **8.** an area where game is reared for private hunting or fishing. —**preservation** (,prɛzə'veɪʃən) n.

preset (priː'sɛt) vb. **1.** to set (the controls of a piece of equipment) before the time at which it is to work. ~adj. **2.** (of equipment) with the controls set in advance.

preside (prɪ'zaɪd) vb. **1.** to sit in or hold a position of authority, as over a meeting. **2.** to exercise authority; control.

presidency ('prɛzɪdənsɪ) n., pl. **-cies.** the office, dignity, or term of a president.

president ('prɛzɪdənt) n. **1.** (*often cap.*) the head of state of a republic, esp. of the U.S. **2.** (in the U.S.) the head of a company, corporation, or university. **3.** a person who presides over a meeting. **4.** the head of certain establishments of higher education. —**presidential** (,prɛzɪ'dɛnʃəl) adj.

presidium (prɪ'sɪdɪəm) n. (*often cap.*) (in Communist countries) a permanent administrative committee.

press¹ (prɛs) vb. **1.** to apply weight, force, or steady pressure (to): *he pressed the button on the camera*. **2.** to squeeze or compress so as to alter in shape. **3.** to iron (clothing) so as to smooth out creases. **4.** to make (objects) from soft material by pressing with a mould. **5.** to squeeze; embrace: *she pressed his hand*. **6.** to extract or force out (juice) by pressure (from). **7.** to force or compel: *colonial powers could be pressed to carry out their mission*. **8.** to urge (someone) insistently: *they pressed for an answer*. **9.** to plead or put forward strongly: *to press a claim*. **10.** to be urgent: *time presses*. **11.** to have little of: *we're hard pressed for time*. **12.** (sometimes foll. by *on* or *forward*) to hasten or advance in a forceful manner: *they pressed on with their journey*. **13.** to crowd; push: *shoppers press along the pavements*. ~n. **14.** any machine that exerts pressure to form or cut materials or to extract liquids or compress solids. **15.** See **printing press.** **16.** the art or process of printing. **17. go to press.** to go to be printed: *when is this book going to press?* **18. the press.** news media collectively, esp. newspapers. **19.** the opinions and reviews in the newspapers: *the play received a poor press.* **20.** the act of pressing or state of being pressed. **21.** a crowd: *a press of people at the exit.* **22.** a cupboard for storing clothes or linen.

press² (pres) *vb.* **1.** to recruit (men) by forcible measures for military service. **2.** to use for a purpose other than intended: *press into service.*

press agent *n.* a person employed to obtain favourable publicity for an individual or organization.

press conference *n.* an interview for reporters given by a politician, film star, or someone in the news.

press gallery *n.* an area for newspaper reporters, esp. in a legislative assembly.

press gang *n.* **1.** (formerly) a group of men used to press civilians for service in the navy or army. ~*vb.* **press-gang.** **2.** to force (a person) to join the navy or army by a press gang. **3.** to induce (a person) to do something by forceful persuasion.

pressing ('prɛsɪŋ) *adj.* **1.** demanding immediate attention. ~*n.* **2.** a large number of gramophone records produced at one time.

press stud *n.* a fastening device in which one part with a projecting knob snaps into a hole on another part, used esp. on clothing.

press-up *n.* an exercise in which the body is raised from and lowered to the floor by the arms only, the trunk being kept straight.

pressure ('prɛʃə) *n.* **1.** the state of pressing or being pressed. **2.** the exertion of force by one body on the surface of another. **3.** a moral force that compels: *to bring pressure to bear.* **4.** urgent claims or demands: *to work under pressure.* **5.** a burdensome condition that is hard to bear: *the pressure of grief.* **6.** the force applied to a unit area of a surface, measured in pascals, millibars, torrs, or atmospheres. ~*vb.* **7.** to constrain or compel, as by moral force.

pressure cooker *n.* an airtight pot in which food may be cooked quickly by steam under pressure. —'**pressure-ˌcook** *vb.*

pressure group *n.* a group of people who seek to influence legislators or public opinion.

pressurize *or* **-ise** ('prɛʃəˌraɪz) *vb.* **1.** to make insistent demands of (someone); coerce. **2.** to increase the pressure in (an enclosure, such as an aircraft cabin) in order to maintain approximately atmospheric pressure when the external pressure is low. —ˌpressuriˈzation *or* -iˈsation *n.*

Prestel ('prɛstɛl) *n. Trademark.* (in Britain) the Post Office public viewdata service.

prestidigitation (ˌprɛstɪˌdɪdʒɪˈteɪʃən) *n.* same as **sleight of hand.** —ˌprestiˈdigiˌtator *n.*

prestige (prɛˈstiːʒ) *n.* **1.** high status or reputation achieved through success, influence, or position. **2.** the power to impress. —**prestigious** (prɛˈstɪdʒəs) *adj.*

presto ('prɛstəʊ) *Music.* ~*adv.* **1.** very fast. ~*n., pl.* **-tos.** **2.** a passage to be played very quickly.

prestressed concrete (ˌpriːˈstrɛst) *n.* concrete that contains stretched steel wires.

presumably (prɪˈzjuːməblɪ) *adv.* one supposes that: *presumably she'll arrive today.*

presume (prɪˈzjuːm) *vb.* **1.** to take (something) for granted; assume. **2.** to dare (to do something): *do you presume to copy my work?* **3.** (foll. by *on* or *upon*) to rely or depend: *don't presume on his agreement.* **4.** (foll. by *on* or *upon*) to take advantage (of): *don't presume upon his good nature too far.* —**presumedly** (prɪˈzjuːmɪdlɪ) *adv.* —preˈsuming *adj.*

presumption (prɪˈzʌmpʃən) *n.* **1.** the act of presuming. **2.** bold or insolent behaviour. **3.** a belief or assumption based on reasonable evidence. **4.** a basis on which to presume. —preˈsumptive *adj.*

presumptuous (prɪˈzʌmptjʊəs) *adj.* characterized by presumption; bold; forward.

presuppose (ˌpriːsəˈpəʊz) *vb.* **1.** to take for granted. **2.** to require as a necessary prior condition: *all arguments make use of logic and presuppose it.* —**presupposition** (ˌpriːsʌpəˈzɪʃən) *n.*

pretence *or U.S.* **pretense** (prɪˈtɛns) *n.* **1.** the act of pretending. **2.** a false display; affectation. **3.** a claim, esp. a false one, to a right, title, or distinction. **4.** make-believe. **5.** a pretext.

pretend (prɪˈtɛnd) *vb.* **1.** to claim or allege (something untrue): *he pretended that he was ill.* **2.** to make believe: *you pretend to be Ophelia.* **3.** (foll. by *to*) to present a claim, esp. a dubious one: *to pretend to the throne.*

pretender (prɪˈtɛndə) *n.* a person who mounts a claim, as to a throne or title.

pretension (prɪˈtɛnʃən) *n.* (*often pl.*) a false claim to merit, worth, or importance.

pretentious (prɪˈtɛnʃəs) *adj.* **1.** making claim to distinction or importance, esp. undeservedly. **2.** ostentatious.

preterite *or esp. U.S.* **preterit** ('prɛtərɪt) *Grammar.* ~*n.* **1.** a tense of verbs used to relate past action, as *jumped, swam.* **2.** a verb in this tense. ~*adj.* **3.** denoting this tense.

preternatural (ˌpriːtəˈnætʃrəl) *adj.* **1.** beyond what is ordinarily found in nature; abnormal. **2.** supernatural.

pretext ('priːtɛkst) *n.* a fictitious reason given in order to conceal the real one: *he put them off on one pretext or another.*

prettify ('prɪtɪˌfaɪ) *vb.* **-fying, -fied.** to make pretty, esp. in a trivial fashion.

pretty ('prɪtɪ) *adj.* **-tier, -tiest.** **1.** pleasing or appealing in a delicate or graceful way. **2.** dainty, neat, or charming. **3.** *Informal, often ironical.* excellent, grand, or fine: *here's a pretty mess!* **4. sitting pretty.** *Informal.* in a favourable state. ~*adv.* **5.** *Informal.* fairly; somewhat: *I'm pretty certain.* —'**prettily** *adv.* —'**prettiness** *n.*

pretty-pretty *adj. Informal.* excessively or ostentatiously pretty.

pretzel ('prɛtsəl) *n.* a brittle savoury biscuit in the form of a knot.

prevail (prɪ'veɪl) *vb.* **1.** (often foll. by *over* or *against*) to prove superior; gain mastery: *skill will prevail.* **2.** to be the most important feature; be prevalent: *a mood of sadness prevailed.* **3.** to exist widely; be in force: *the condition that now prevails.* **4. prevail on** *or* **upon.** to succeed in persuading: *she prevailed upon him to come to the party.*

prevailing (prɪ'veɪlɪŋ) *adj.* **1.** generally accepted; widespread: *the prevailing opinion.* **2.** most frequent; predominant: *the prevailing wind is from the north.*

prevalent ('prɛvələnt) *adj.* widespread or current. —'**prevalence** *n.*

prevaricate (prɪ'værɪ,keɪt) *vb.* to speak or act falsely or evasively with intent to deceive. —pre,vari'cation *n.* —pre'vari,cator *n.*

prevent (prɪ'vɛnt) *vb.* **1.** to keep from happening; hinder. **2.** (often foll. by *from*) to keep (someone from doing something). —pre'ventable *or* pre'ventible *adj.* —pre-'vention *n.*

Usage. *Prevent* in the sense of definition 2, above, is in strict usage followed either by *from* or by the possessive case: *there is nothing to prevent Mary from going* or *there is nothing to prevent Mary's going.* The use of *prevent* in a construction such as *there is nothing to prevent Mary going* is regarded as less acceptable and less formal.

preventive (prɪ'vɛntɪv) *adj.* **1.** tending or intended to prevent or hinder. **2.** *Med.* tending to prevent disease. ~*n.* **3.** something that serves to prevent. **4.** *Med.* any drug or agent that tends to prevent disease. Also: **preventative.** —pre'vention *n.*

preview ('priː,vjuː) *n.* **1.** an advance showing before public presentation of a film, art exhibition, or play. ~*vb.* **2.** to view in advance.

previous ('priːvɪəs) *adj.* **1.** existing or coming before something else. **2.** *Informal.* taking place or done too soon; premature: *your congratulations are a bit previous.* **3. previous to.** before. —'**previously** *adv.*

prewar (,priː'wɔː, 'priː,wɔː) *adj.* of or occurring in the period before a war, esp. before World War I or II.

prey (preɪ) *n.* **1.** an animal hunted or captured by another for food. **2.** a person or thing that becomes the victim of a hostile person, influence, or emotion. **3. bird** *or*

beast of prey. a bird or animal that preys on others for food. ~*vb.* (often foll. by *on* or *upon*) **4.** to hunt food by killing other animals. **5.** to make a victim (of others), as by profiting at their expense. **6.** to exert a depressing or obsessive effect (on the mind or spirits).

price (praɪs) *n.* **1.** the sum in money or goods for which anything is or may be bought or sold. **2.** the cost at which anything is obtained. **3.** *Gambling.* odds. **4. at any price.** whatever the price or cost. **5. at a price.** at a high price. **6. what price (something)?** what are the chances of (something) happening now? ~*vb.* **7.** to fix the price of. **8.** to discover the price of.

price-fixing *n.* the setting of prices by agreement among producers and distributors.

priceless ('praɪslɪs) *adj.* **1.** of inestimable worth; invaluable. **2.** *Informal.* extremely amusing.

pricey ('praɪsɪ) *adj.* **pricier, priciest.** *Informal.* expensive.

prick (prɪk) *vb.* **1.** to make (a small hole) in (something) by piercing lightly with a sharp point. **2.** to cause or have a piercing or stinging sensation. **3.** to cause to feel a sharp emotional pain: *knowledge of such poverty pricked his conscience.* **4.** to outline by dots or punctures. **5.** (usually foll. by *up*) to rise or raise erect: *the dog pricked his ears up.* **6. prick up one's ears.** to start to listen attentively; become interested. ~*n.* **7.** the act of pricking or the sensation of being pricked. **8.** a mark made by a sharp point; puncture. **9.** a sharp emotional pain: *a prick of conscience.* **10.** *Slang, taboo.* a penis. **11.** *Slang, offensive.* a despicable man.

prickle ('prɪkˀl) *n.* **1.** *Bot.* a pointed thornlike growth on a stem or leaf. **2.** a pricking or stinging sensation. ~*vb.* **3.** to feel a stinging sensation.

prickly ('prɪklɪ) *adj.* **-lier, -liest.** **1.** having or covered with prickles. **2.** stinging. **3.** irritable.

prickly heat *n.* a rash of small itchy spots on the skin that occurs in very hot weather.

prickly pear *n.* **1.** any of various tropical cactuses with edible oval fruit. **2.** the fruit of any of these plants.

pride (praɪd) *n.* **1.** a feeling of honour and self-respect; a sense of personal worth. **2.** excessive self-esteem; conceit. **3.** a source of pride: *his garden was his pride and joy.* **4.** satisfaction in one's own or another's success or achievements. **5.** the better or superior part of something; flower. **6.** a group (of lions). **7. pride of place.** the most important position. ~*vb.* **8.** (foll. by *on* or *upon*) to take pride in (oneself) for.

prie-dieu (priː'djɜː) *n.* an upright frame with a ledge for kneeling upon, for use when praying.

priest (pri:st) *n.* **1.** (in the Christian Church) a person ordained to administer the sacraments and preach. **2.** a minister of any religion. **3.** an official who offers sacrifice on behalf of the people and performs other religious ceremonies. —'**priestess** *fem. n.* —'**priest,hood** *n.* —'**priestly** *adj.*

prig (prɪg) *n.* a person who is smugly self-righteous and narrow-minded. —'**priggish** *adj.* —'**priggishness** *n.*

prim (prɪm) *adj.* **primmer, primmest.** affectedly proper, precise, or formal. —'**primly** *adv.*

prima ballerina ('pri:mə) *n.* a leading female ballet dancer.

primacy ('praɪməsɪ) *n., pl.* **-cies.** **1.** the state of being first in rank, grade, or order. **2.** *Christianity.* the office, rank, or jurisdiction of a primate.

prima donna ('pri:mə 'dɒnə) *n., pl.* **prima donnas. 1.** a leading female operatic star. **2.** *Informal.* a temperamental person.

prima facie ('praɪmə 'feɪʃɪ) *adv.* at first sight; as it seems at first.

primal ('praɪml) *adj.* **1.** first or original. **2.** chief or most important.

primarily ('praɪmərəlɪ) *adv.* **1.** principally; chiefly; mainly. **2.** at first; originally.

primary ('praɪmərɪ) *adj.* **1.** first in importance. **2.** first in position or time, as in a series. **3.** fundamental; basic. **4.** being the first stage; elementary. **5.** of or relating to the education of children up to the age of 11. **6.** (of the flight feathers of a bird's wing) outer and longest. **7.** being the part of an electric circuit in which a changing current induces a current in a neighbouring circuit: *a primary coil.* ~*n., pl.* **-ries. 8.** a person or thing that is first in rank, occurrence, or importance. **9.** (in the U.S.) a preliminary election in which the voters of a state nominate a candidate for office. Full name: **primary election. 10.** short for **primary colour** or **primary school. 11.** any of the outer and longest flight feathers of a bird's wing. **12.** a primary coil, winding, inductance, or current in an electric circuit.

primary accent *or* **stress** *n. Linguistics.* the strongest accent in a word.

primary colour *n.* **1.** any of three colours (usually red, green, and blue) that can be mixed to match any other colour, excluding black. **2.** any one of the colours red, yellow, green, or blue. All other colours look like a mixture of two or more of these colours.

primary school *n.* **1.** (in England and Wales) a school for children below the age of 11. **2.** (in Scotland) a school for children below the age of 12. **3.** (in the U.S. and Canad.) a school equivalent to the first three or four grades of elementary school.

primate ('praɪmeɪt) *n.* **1.** an archbishop.

2. any of an order of mammals including lemurs, apes, and man.

prime (praɪm) *adj.* **1.** first in quality: *prime beef.* **2.** fundamental; original. **3.** first in importance; chief: *of prime importance.* ~*n.* **4.** the time when a thing is at its best. **5.** a period of power, vigour, and activity: *a man in the prime of life.* **6.** *Maths.* short for **prime number.** ~*vb.* **7.** to prepare (something). **8.** to apply a primer, such as paint or size, to (a surface). **9.** to fill (a pump) with its working fluid, in order to expel air from it before starting. **10.** to insert a primer into (a gun or mine) before detonating or firing. **11.** to provide with facts beforehand; brief.

prime meridian *n.* the 0° meridian from which the other meridians are calculated, usually taken to pass through Greenwich.

prime minister *n.* the head of a parliamentary government.

prime number *n.* an integer that cannot be divided into other integers but is only divisible by itself or 1, such as 2, 3, 7, and 11.

primer[1] ('praɪmə) *n.* an introductory text, such as a school textbook.

primer[2] ('praɪmə) *n.* **1.** a device, such as a tube containing explosive, for detonating the main charge in a gun or mine. **2.** a substance, such as paint, applied to a surface as a base or sealer.

primeval (praɪ'mi:vl) *adj.* of or belonging to the first ages of the world.

primitive ('prɪmɪtɪv) *adj.* **1.** of or belonging to the beginning; original. **2.** characteristic of an early state, esp. in being crude or uncivilized: *a primitive dwelling.* **3.** *Biol.* of, relating to, or resembling an early stage in development: *primitive amphibians.* ~*n.* **4.** a primitive person or thing. **5.** a painter of any era whose work appears childlike or untrained. **6.** a work by such an artist.

primogeniture (,praɪməʊ'dʒenɪtʃə) *n.* **1.** the state of being a first-born. **2.** *Law.* the right of an eldest son to succeed to the estate of his ancestor.

primordial (praɪ'mɔ:dɪəl) *adj.* existing at or from the beginning; primeval.

primp (prɪmp) *vb.* to dress (oneself) carefully in fine clothes.

primrose ('prɪm,rəʊz) *n.* **1.** a wild plant which has pale yellow flowers in spring. **2.** Also called: **primrose yellow.** a light yellow colour. ~*adj.* **3.** of or abounding in primroses. **4.** of the colour primrose.

primrose path *n.* (often preceded by *the*) a pleasurable way of life.

primula ('prɪmjʊlə) *n.* any of a genus of plants with white, yellow, pink, or purple funnel-shaped flowers with five spreading petals.

Primus ('praɪməs) *n. Trademark.* a portable

paraffin cooking stove, used esp. by campers.

prince (prɪns) *n*. **1.** (in Britain) a son of the sovereign. **2.** a nonreigning male member of a sovereign family. **3.** the monarch of a small territory. **4.** any monarch. **5.** a nobleman in various countries. **6.** an outstanding member of a specified group: *a merchant prince.*

prince consort *n*. the husband of a female sovereign, who is himself a prince.

princely (ˈprɪnslɪ) *adj*. **-lier, -liest. 1.** generous or lavish. **2.** of or characteristic of a prince.

Prince of Wales (weɪlz) *n*. the eldest son and heir apparent of the British sovereign.

princess (prɪnˈsɛs) *n*. **1.** (in Britain) a daughter of the sovereign. **2.** a nonreigning female member of a sovereign family. **3.** the wife and consort of a prince.

princess royal *n*. the eldest daughter of a British sovereign.

principal (ˈprɪnsɪp^əl) *adj*. **1.** first in importance, rank, or value. ~*n*. **2.** a person who is first in importance. **3.** the head of a school or other educational institution. **4.** *Law*. **a.** a person who engages another to act as his agent. **b.** an active participant in a crime. **c.** the person primarily liable to fulfil an obligation. **5.** the leading performer in a play. **6.** *Finance*. **a.** capital or property, as contrasted with income. **b.** the original amount of a debt on which interest is calculated. —ˈ**principally** *adv*.

principal boy *n*. the leading male role in a pantomime, played by a woman.

principality (ˌprɪnsɪˈpælɪtɪ) *n., pl*. **-ties.** a territory ruled by a prince or from which a prince draws his title.

principal parts *pl. n. Grammar*. the main inflected forms of a verb, from which all other inflections may be deduced.

principle (ˈprɪnsɪp^əl) *n*. **1.** a standard or rule of personal conduct: *he'd stoop to anything - he has no principles.* **2.** a set of such moral rules: *a man of principle.* **3.** a fundamental or general truth: *the principle of equality.* **4.** the essence of something: *the male principle.* **5.** a source; origin: *principle of life.* **6.** a law concerning a natural phenomenon or the behaviour of a system: *the principle of the conservation of mass.* **7.** *Chem.* a constituent of a substance that gives the substance its characteristics. **8. in principle.** in theory. **9. on principle.** because of a principle.

prink (prɪŋk) *vb*. **1.** to dress (oneself) finely. **2.** to preen oneself.

print (prɪnt) *vb*. **1.** to reproduce (text or pictures) by applying ink to paper. **2.** to produce or reproduce (a manuscript) in print, as for publication. **3.** to write (words or letters) in the style of printed matter. **4.** to mark (a surface) by pressing (something)

onto it. **5.** to produce a photographic print from (a negative). **6.** to fix in the mind or memory. ~*n*. **7.** printed matter, such as newsprint. **8.** a printed publication, such as a book. **9. in print. a.** in printed or published form. **b.** (of a book) offered for sale by the publisher. **10. out of print.** no longer available from a publisher. **11.** a design or picture printed from an engraved plate or wood block. **12.** printed text, esp. with regard to the typeface: *small print.* **13.** a positive photographic image produced from a negative image on film. **14.** a fabric with a printed design. **15.** a mark made by pressing something onto a surface. **16.** See **fingerprint.** ~See also **print out.**

printed circuit *n*. an electronic circuit in which certain components and the connections between them are formed by etching a metallic coating on a thin insulating board.

printer (ˈprɪntə) *n*. **1.** a person or business engaged in printing. **2.** a machine that prints. **3.** *Computers*. an output device for printing results on paper.

printing (ˈprɪntɪŋ) *n*. **1.** the business or art of producing printed matter. **2.** printed text. **3.** all the copies of a book printed at one time. **4.** a form of writing in which letters resemble printed letters.

printing press *n*. any of various machines used for printing.

print out *vb*. **1.** (of a computer output device) to produce (printed information). ~*n*. **print-out. 2.** such printed information.

prior[1] (ˈpraɪə) *adj*. **1.** previous. **2. prior to.** before; until.

prior[2] (ˈpraɪə) *n*. **1.** the superior of a community in certain religious orders. **2.** the deputy head of a monastery or abbey. —ˈ**prioress** *fem. n*.

priority (praɪˈɒrɪtɪ) *n., pl*. **-ties. 1.** the condition of being prior; precedence. **2.** the right of precedence. **3.** something given specified attention: *my first priority.*

priory (ˈpraɪərɪ) *n., pl*. **-ories.** a religious house governed by a prior.

prise *or* **prize** (praɪz) *vb*. to force open or out by levering.

prism (ˈprɪzəm) *n*. **1.** a transparent polygonal solid, often having triangular ends and rectangular sides, for dispersing light into a spectrum. **2.** *Maths*. a polyhedron having parallel bases and sides that are parallelograms.

prismatic (prɪzˈmætɪk) *adj*. **1.** of or produced by a prism. **2.** exhibiting bright spectral colours: *prismatic light.*

prison (ˈprɪz^ən) *n*. **1.** a public building used to house convicted criminals and accused persons awaiting trial. **2.** any place of confinement.

prisoner (ˈprɪzənə) *n*. **1.** a person kept in custody as a punishment for a crime, while awaiting trial, or for some other reason. **2.**

a person confined by any of various restraints: *we are all prisoners of time.* **3. take (someone) prisoner.** to capture and hold (someone) as a prisoner.

prisoner of war *n.* a serviceman captured by an enemy in time of war.

prissy ('prɪsɪ) *adj.* **-sier, -siest.** prim and prudish. —**'prissily** *adv.*

pristine ('prɪstaɪn, -tiːn) *adj.* **1.** of or involving the earliest period or state; original. **2.** completely new, clean, and pure.

privacy ('praɪvəsɪ, 'prɪvəsɪ) *n.* **1.** the condition of being private. **2.** secrecy.

private ('praɪvɪt) *adj.* **1.** not widely or publicly known: *they had private reasons for the decision.* **2.** confidential; secret: *a private conversation.* **3.** not for general or public use: *a private bathroom.* **4.** of or provided by a private individual or organization rather than by the state: *private medicine.* **5.** having no public office, rank, or position: *a private man.* **6.** (of a place) quiet and secluded: *the garden is completely private.* ~*n.* **7.** a soldier of the lowest rank in many armies and marine corps. **8. in private.** in secret. —**'privately** *adv.*

private bill *n.* a bill presented to Parliament on behalf of a private individual or corporation.

private company *n.* a limited company that does not issue shares for public subscription.

private detective *n.* an individual hired to do detective work on behalf of a client.

privateer (ˌpraɪvə'tɪə) *n.* **1.** an armed privately owned vessel commissioned for war service. **2.** a Commander of a privateer.

private eye *n. Informal.* a private detective.

private income *n.* income from sources other than employment, such as investment.

private member *n.* a member of a legislative assembly not having an appointment in the government.

private member's bill *n.* a parliamentary bill sponsored by a Member of Parliament who is not a government minister.

private parts *or* **privates** *pl. n. Euphemistic.* the genitals.

private school *n.* a school controlled by a private body, accepting mostly fee-paying pupils.

private sector *n.* the part of a country's economy that consists of privately owned enterprises.

privation (praɪ'veɪʃən) *n.* loss or lack of the necessities of life.

privative ('prɪvətɪv) *adj.* **1.** causing privation. **2.** *Grammar.* expressing lack or absence, as for example *-less* and *un-*.

privatize *or* **-ise** ('praɪvɪˌtaɪz) *vb.* to take into, or return to, private ownership, a company or concern that has previously been

owned by the state. —**'privati,zation** *or* **-i,sation** *n.*

privet ('prɪvɪt) *n.* a bushy shrub with oval dark green leaves, used for hedges.

privilege ('prɪvɪlɪdʒ) *n.* **1.** a benefit, immunity, or advantage granted under certain conditions to a person, group, or class. ~*vb.* **2.** to bestow a privilege upon.

privileged ('prɪvɪlɪdʒd) *adj.* enjoying or granted as a privilege or privileges.

privy ('prɪvɪ) *adj.* **privier, priviest. 1. privy to.** participating in the knowledge of something secret. **2.** *Archaic.* secret; hidden. ~*n., pl.* **privies. 3.** a toilet, esp. an outside one.

Privy Council *n.* **1.** the private council of the British sovereign. **2.** (in Canada) a ceremonial body of advisers of the governor general. —**Privy Councillor** *n.*

privy purse *n.* (*often cap.*) an allowance voted by Parliament for the private expenses of the monarch.

privy seal *n.* (*often cap.*) (in Britain) a seal affixed to certain documents issued by royal authority.

prize[1] (praɪz) *n.* **1.** something, such as a trophy, given to the winner of a contest or competition. **2.** something given to the winner of any game of chance, lottery, etc. **3.** something striven for.

prize[2] (praɪz) *vb.* to value highly.

prizefight ('praɪzˌfaɪt) *n.* a boxing match for a prize or purse. —**'prize,fighter** *n.*

pro[1] (prəʊ) *adv.* **1.** in favour of a motion, issue, or course of action. ~*prep.* **2.** in favour of. ~*n., pl.* **pros. 3.** (*usually pl.*) an argument or vote in favour of a proposal or motion. See also **pros and cons.**

pro[2] (prəʊ) *n., pl.* **pros,** *adj. Informal.* **1.** short for **professional. 2.** a prostitute.

PRO public relations officer.

pro-[1] *prefix.* **1.** in favour of; supporting: *pro-Chinese.* **2.** acting as a substitute for: *proconsul; pronoun.*

pro-[2] *prefix.* before in time or position; anterior; forward: *proboscis.*

probability (ˌprobə'bɪlɪtɪ) *n., pl.* **-ties. 1.** the condition of being probable. **2.** an event or other thing that is probable. **3.** *Statistics.* a measure of the degree of confidence one may have in the occurrence of an event.

probable ('probəbᵊl) *adj.* **1.** likely to be or to happen but not necessarily so. **2.** most likely: *the probable cause of the accident.* ~*n.* **3.** a person who is likely to be chosen for a team, event, etc.

probably ('probəblɪ) *adv.* in all likelihood or probability: *I'll probably see you tomorrow.*

probate ('prəʊbɪt, -beɪt) *n.* **1.** the process of officially proving the validity of a will. **2.** the official certificate stating a will to be genuine.

probation (prəˈbeɪʃən) n. 1. a system of dealing with offenders by placing them under the supervision of a probation officer. 2. **on probation. a.** under the supervision of a probation officer. **b.** undergoing a test or trial period, as of a person's character or abilities. —**proˈbationary** adj.

probationer (prəˈbeɪʃənə) n. a person on probation.

probation officer n. an officer of a court who supervises offenders placed on probation.

probe (prəʊb) vb. 1. to search into closely. 2. to examine (something) with or as if with a probe. ~n. 3. Surgery. a slender instrument for exploring a wound, etc. 4. a thorough inquiry, such as one into corrupt practices. 5. See **space probe**.

probity (ˈprəʊbɪtɪ) n. honesty; uprightness; integrity.

problem (ˈprɒbləm) n. 1. any thing, matter, or person that is difficult to deal with. 2. a puzzle or question set for solution. 3. Maths. a statement requiring a solution usually by means of several operations. 4. (modifier) designating a literary work that deals with difficult moral questions: a problem play.

problematic (ˌprɒbləˈmætɪk) or **problematical** adj. difficult to solve or deal with; uncertain.

proboscis (prəʊˈbɒsɪs) n. 1. a long flexible trunk or snout, as of an elephant. 2. the elongated mouthpart of certain insects.

procedure (prəˈsiːdʒə) n. 1. a way of acting or progressing, esp. an established method. 2. the established form of conducting the business of a legislature. —**proˈcedural** adj.

proceed (prəˈsiːd) vb. 1. to advance or carry on, esp. after stopping. 2. (often foll. by with) to continue: he proceeded with his reading. 3. (often foll. by against) to institute or carry on a legal action. 4. to originate; arise: evil proceeds from the heart.

proceeding (prəˈsiːdɪŋ) n. 1. an act or course of action. 2. (pl.) the events of an occasion: millions watched the proceedings on television. 3. (pl.) the minutes of the meetings of a society. 4. (pl.) legal action; litigation.

proceeds (ˈprəʊsiːdz) pl. n. the amount of money obtained from an event or activity.

process¹ (ˈprəʊsɛs) n. 1. a series of actions which produce a change or development: the process of digestion. 2. a method of doing or producing something. 3. progress or course of time. 4. **in the process of.** during or in the course of. 5. a. a summons to appear in court. b. an action at law. 6. a natural outgrowth or projection of a part or organism. ~vb. 7. to subject to a routine procedure; handle. 8. to treat or prepare by a special method, esp. to treat (food) in order to preserve it: to process cheese. 9. Computers. to perform operations on (data) in order to obtain the required information.

process² (prəˈsɛs) vb. to proceed in a procession.

procession (prəˈsɛʃən) n. 1. the act of proceeding in a regular formation. 2. a group of people or vehicles moving forwards in an orderly, regular, or ceremonial manner.

processional (prəˈsɛʃənəl) adj. 1. of or suitable for a procession. ~n. 2. Christianity. a hymn sung as the clergy enter church.

processor (ˈprəʊsɛsə) n. 1. Computers. same as **central processing unit**. 2. a person or thing that carries out a process.

proclaim (prəˈkleɪm) vb. 1. to announce publicly: the Government proclaimed a state of emergency. 2. to indicate plainly: the display proclaimed the designer's art. —**proclamation** (ˌprɒkləˈmeɪʃən) n.

proclivity (prəˈklɪvɪtɪ) n., pl. -**ties.** a tendency or inclination.

procrastinate (prəʊˈkræstɪˌneɪt) vb. to put off (an action) until later; delay. —**proˌcrastiˈnation** n. —**proˈcrastiˌnator** n.

procreate (ˈprəʊkrɪˌeɪt) vb. (of people or animals) to produce (offspring). —**ˈprocreˌative** adj. —**ˌprocreˈation** n.

Procrustean (prəʊˈkrʌstɪən) adj. designed to produce conformity by ruthless methods.

proctor (ˈprɒktə) n. a member of the staff of certain universities having duties including the enforcement of discipline. —**proctorial** (prɒkˈtɔːrɪəl) adj.

procurator fiscal (ˈprɒkjʊˌreɪtə) n. (in Scotland) a legal officer who performs the functions of public prosecutor and coroner.

procure (prəˈkjʊə) vb. 1. to obtain or acquire; secure. 2. to obtain (women or girls) to act as prostitutes. —**proˈcurement** n.

procurer (prəˈkjʊərə) n. a person who procures, esp. one who procures women as prostitutes.

prod (prɒd) vb. **prodding, prodded.** 1. to poke with or as if with a pointed object. 2. to rouse (someone) to action. ~n. 3. the act or an instance of prodding. 4. a reminder.

prodigal (ˈprɒdɪgˌl) adj. 1. recklessly wasteful or extravagant. 2. lavish: prodigal of compliments. ~n. 3. a person who spends lavishly or squanders money. —**ˌprodiˈgality** n.

prodigious (prəˈdɪdʒəs) adj. 1. vast in size, extent, or power. 2. wonderful or amazing.

prodigy (ˈprɒdɪdʒɪ) n., pl. -**gies.** 1. a person, esp. a child, of unusual or marvellous talents. 2. anything that is a cause of wonder.

produce vb. (prə'djuːs). **1.** to bring (something) into existence; yield. **2.** to make: *she produced a delicious dinner.* **3.** to give birth to. **4.** to present to view: *to produce evidence.* **5.** to bring before the public: *he produced a film last year.* **6.** to act as producer of. ~n. ('prɒdjuːs). **7.** anything produced; a product. **8.** agricultural products collectively: *farm produce.* —**pro'ducible** *adj.*

producer (prə'djuːsə) n. **1.** a person or thing that produces. **2.** *Brit.* a person responsible for the artistic direction of a play. **3.** *U.S. & Canad.* a person who organizes the stage production of a play, including the finance and management. **4.** the person who takes overall administrative responsibility for a film or television programme.

product ('prɒdʌkt) n. **1.** something produced by a natural, mechanical, or industrial process. **2.** a result or consequence: *their skill was the product of hours of training.* **3.** *Maths.* the result of the multiplication of two or more numbers or quantities.

production (prə'dʌkʃən) n. **1.** the act of producing. **2.** anything that is produced; a product. **3.** the amount produced or the rate at which it is produced. **4.** *Econ.* the creation or manufacture of goods and services. **5.** any work created as a result of literary or artistic effort. **6.** the presentation of a play, opera, etc. **7.** *Brit.* the artistic direction of a play.

productive (prə'dʌktɪv) adj. **1.** producing or having the power to produce; fertile. **2.** yielding favourable results. **3.** *Econ.* producing goods and services that have exchange value: *productive assets.* **4.** (foll. by *of*) resulting in: *productive of good results.* —**productivity** (,prɒdʌk'tɪvɪtɪ) n.

proem ('prəʊɛm) n. an introduction or preface.

Prof. Professor.

profane (prə'feɪn) adj. **1.** having or indicating irreverence or disrespect for a divinity or something sacred. **2.** not designed for religious purposes; secular. **3.** coarse or blasphemous: *profane language.* ~vb. **4.** to treat (something sacred) with irreverence. **5.** to put to an unworthy use. —**profanation** (,prɒfə'neɪʃən) n.

profanity (prə'fænɪtɪ) n., pl. **-ties. 1.** the state or quality of being profane. **2.** vulgar or irreverent action or speech.

profess (prə'fɛs) vb. **1.** to affirm or acknowledge: *to profess ignorance; to profess a belief in God.* **2.** to claim (something), often insincerely or falsely: *to profess to be a skilled driver.* **3.** to receive or be received into a religious order, as by taking vows. —**pro'fessed** adj.

profession (prə'fɛʃən) n. **1.** an occupation that requires special training, such as law or medicine. **2.** the body of people in such

an occupation. **3.** an avowal; declaration: *professions of concern.* **4.** a declaration of faith, esp. as made on entering a religious order.

professional (prə'fɛʃənˀl) adj. **1.** of, suitable for, or engaged in as a profession. **2.** engaging in an activity as a means of livelihood. **3.** extremely competent in a job. **4.** undertaken or performed by people who are paid. ~n. **5.** a professional person. —**pro'fessiona,lism** n. —**pro'fessionally** adv.

professor (prə'fɛsə) n. **1.** the principal teacher holding a university chair. **2.** *Chiefly U.S. & Canad.* any teacher in a university or college. **3.** a person who professes his opinions or beliefs. —**professorial** (,prɒfɪ'sɔːrɪəl) adj. —**pro'fessorship** n.

proffer ('prɒfə) vb. to offer for acceptance.

proficient (prə'fɪʃənt) adj. skilled; expert. —**pro'ficiency** n.

profile ('prəʊfaɪl) n. **1.** a side view or outline, esp. of a human head. **2.** a short biographical sketch.

profit ('prɒfɪt) n. **1.** (*often pl.*) excess of revenues over outlays and expenses in a business enterprise. **2.** the monetary gain derived from a transaction. **3.** a gain, benefit, or advantage. ~vb. **4.** to gain profit.

profitable ('prɒfɪtəbˀl) adj. making profit. —**,profita'bility** n.

profit and loss n. *Book-keeping.* an account showing the year's revenue and expense items and indicating gross and net profit or loss.

profiteer (,prɒfɪ'tɪə) n. **1.** a person who makes excessive profits by charging exorbitant prices for goods in short supply. ~vb. **2.** to make excessive profits.

profit-sharing n. a system in which a portion of the net profit of a business is distributed to its employees.

profligate ('prɒflɪgɪt) adj. **1.** shamelessly immoral. **2.** wildly extravagant or wasteful. ~n. **3.** a profligate person. —**profligacy** ('prɒflɪgəsɪ) n.

pro forma ('prəʊ 'fɔːmə) adj. **1.** prescribing a set form or procedure. ~adv. **2.** performed in a set manner.

profound (prə'faʊnd) adj. **1.** having, showing, or requiring great knowledge or understanding: *a profound treatise.* **2.** situated at or extending to a great depth. **3.** strongly felt; intense: *profound silence.* **4.** thoroughgoing; extensive: *profound changes.* —**pro'foundly** adv. —**profundity** (prə'fʌndɪtɪ) n.

profuse (prə'fjuːs) adj. **1.** plentiful or abundant: *profuse compliments.* **2.** (*often* foll. by *in*) free or generous in the giving (of): *profuse in thanks.* —**pro'fusely** adv. —**pro'fusion** n.

progenitor (prəʊ'dʒɛnɪtə) n. **1.** a direct ancestor. **2.** an originator or founder.

progeny ('prɒdʒɪnɪ) *n., pl.* **-nies. 1.** offspring; descendants. **2.** a result or outcome.

progesterone (prəʊ'dʒɛstə,rəʊn) *n.* a steroid hormone, secreted in the ovary, that prepares and maintains the uterus for pregnancy.

prognosis (prɒg'nəʊsɪs) *n., pl.* **-noses** (-'nəʊsiːz). **1.** *Med.* a prediction of the course or outcome of a disease. **2.** any prediction.

prognosticate (prɒg'nɒstɪ,keɪt) *vb.* **1.** to foretell (future events). **2.** to indicate or suggest beforehand. **—prog,nosti'cation** *n.* **—prog'nosti,cator** *n.*

program ('prəʊgræm) *n.* **1.** a sequence of coded instructions enabling a computer to perform specified logical and arithmetical operations on data. ~*vb.* **-gramming, -grammed. 2.** to arrange (data) so that it can be processed by a computer. **3.** to write a program. **—'programmer** *n.*

programmable *or* **programable** (prəʊ-'græməbəl) *adj.* capable of being programmed for computer processing.

programme *or U.S.* **program** ('prəʊgræm) *n.* **1.** a written or printed list of the events and performers in a public performance. **2.** a performance presented at a scheduled time on radio or television. **3.** a specially arranged selection of things to be done: *what's the programme for this afternoon?* **4.** a plan, schedule, or procedure: *the development of a nuclear power programme.* ~*vb.* **-gramming, -grammed** *or U.S.* **-graming, -gramed. 5.** to design or schedule (something) as a programme. **—,program'matic** *adj.*

programming language *n.* a language system by which instructions to a computer are coded, that is mutually comprehensible to user and computer.

progress *n.* ('prəʊgrɛs). **1.** movement forwards, esp. towards a place or objective. **2.** satisfactory development or advance. **3.** advance towards completion or perfection. **4. in progress.** taking place. ~*vb.* (prə-'grɛs). **5.** to move forwards or onwards. **6.** to move towards completion or perfection.

progression (prə'grɛʃən) *n.* **1.** the act of progressing; advancement. **2.** the act or an instance of moving from one thing in a sequence to the next. **3.** *Maths.* a sequence of numbers in which each term differs from the succeeding term by a constant relation.

progressive (prə'grɛsɪv) *adj.* **1.** of or relating to progress. **2.** progressing by steps or degrees. **3.** favouring or promoting political or social reform: *a progressive policy.* **4.** (esp. of a disease) advancing in severity, complexity, or extent. **5.** (of a dance, card game, etc.) involving a regular change of partners. ~*n.* **6.** a person who advocates political progress or reform. **—pro'gressively** *adv.*

prohibit (prə'hɪbɪt) *vb.* **1.** to forbid by law or other authority. **2.** to hinder or prevent. **—pro'hibitor** *n.*

prohibition (,prəʊɪ'bɪʃən) *n.* **1.** the act of prohibiting or state of being prohibited. **2.** an order or decree that prohibits. **3.** a policy of legally forbidding the manufacture, sale, or consumption of alcoholic beverages. **—,prohi'bitionist** *n.*

Prohibition (,prəʊɪ'bɪʃən) *n.* the period (1920–33) when the manufacture, sale, and transportation of intoxicating liquors was banned in the U.S. **—,Prohi'bitionist** *n.*

prohibitive (prə'hɪbɪtɪv) *adj.* **1.** prohibiting or tending to prohibit. **2.** (esp. of prices) tending or designed to discourage sale or purchase.

project *n.* ('prɒdʒɛkt). **1.** a proposal, scheme, or design. **2.** a detailed study of a particular subject. ~*vb.* (prə'dʒɛkt). **3.** to propose or plan. **4.** to throw forwards. **5.** to jut out. **6.** to make a prediction based on known data and observations. **7.** to transport in the imagination: *to project oneself into the future.* **8.** to cause (an image) to appear on a surface. **9.** to cause (one's voice) to be heard clearly at a distance.

projectile (prə'dʒɛktaɪl) *n.* **1.** an object designed to be shot forward, such as a shell, rocket, or bullet. ~*adj.* **2.** designed to be hurled forwards. **3.** projecting forwards.

projection (prə'dʒɛkʃən) *n.* **1.** the act of projecting or the state of being projected. **2.** a part that juts out. **3.** the representation of a line, figure, or solid on a given plane as it would be seen from a particular direction or in accordance with an accepted set of rules. **4.** a prediction based on known evidence and observations. **5.** the process of showing film on a screen.

projectionist (prə'dʒɛkʃənɪst) *n.* a person responsible for the operation of film projection machines.

projector (prə'dʒɛktə) *n.* an apparatus for projecting photographic images, film, or slides onto a screen.

prolapse ('prəʊlæps, prəʊ'læps) *Pathol.* ~*n.* **1.** Also: **prolapsus** (prəʊ'læpsəs). the sinking or falling down of an organ or part. ~*vb.* **2.** (of an organ or part) to sink from its normal position.

prolate ('prəʊleɪt) *adj.* having a polar diameter of greater length than the equatorial diameter.

prole (prəʊl) *n., adj. Disparaging, slang, chiefly Brit.* short for **proletarian.**

proletariat (,prəʊlɪ'tɛərɪət) *n.* the lower or working class. **—,prole'tarian** *adj., n.*

proliferate (prə'lɪfə,reɪt) *vb.* **1.** to grow or reproduce (new parts, such as cells) rapidly. **2.** to increase rapidly in numbers. **—pro,lifer'ation** *n.*

prolific (prə'lɪfɪk) *adj.* **1.** producing fruit or offspring in abundance. **2.** producing a

constant creative output: *a prolific novelist.*
3. (often foll. by *in* or *of*) rich or fruitful.
—**pro'lifically** *adv.*

prolix ('prəʊlɪks, prəʊ'lɪks) *adj.* (of a speech
or book) so long as to be boring.
—**pro'lixity** *n.*

prologue *or U.S.* (*often*) **prolog** ('prəʊlɒg)
n. **1.** an introduction to a play or speech.
2. a preliminary act or event.

prolong (prə'lɒŋ) *vb.* to lengthen; extend.
—**prolongation** (ˌprəʊlɒŋ'geɪʃən) *n.*

prom (prɒm) *n.* **1.** *Brit.* short for **promenade** (sense 1) or **promenade concert.** **2.**
U.S. & Canad. informal. a formal dance held
at a high school or college.

PROM (prɒm) *n. Computers.* Programmable
Read Only Memory.

promenade (ˌprɒmə'nɑːd) *n.* **1.** *Chiefly
Brit.* a public walk, esp. at a seaside resort.
2. a leisurely walk for pleasure or display.
~*vb.* **3.** to take a promenade in or through
(a place). **4.** to display or exhibit (someone
or oneself) on or as if on a promenade.

promenade concert *n.* a concert at
which some of the audience stand rather
than sit.

promethium (prə'miːθɪəm) *n.* an artificial
radioactive element of the lanthanide series. Symbol: Pm

prominent ('prɒmɪnənt) *adj.* **1.** jutting or
projecting outwards. **2.** standing out from
its surroundings; noticeable. **3.** widely
known; eminent. —**'prominence** *n.*

promiscuous (prə'mɪskjʊəs) *adj.* **1.** indulging in casual sexual relationships. **2.**
consisting of different elements mingled indiscriminately. —**promiscuity** (ˌprɒmɪ-
'skjuːɪtɪ) *n.*

promise ('prɒmɪs) *vb.* **1.** to give an assurance of (something to someone): *I promise
that I will come.* **2.** to undertake to give
(something to someone): *he promised me a
car for my birthday.* **3.** to cause people to
expect that one is likely (to be or do something): *she promises to be a fine soprano.*
4. to assure (someone) of the inevitability
of something: *there'll be trouble, I promise
you.* ~*n.* **5.** an assurance given by one
person to another guaranteeing to do or not
to do something. **6.** indication of forthcoming excellence: *a writer showing considerable promise.*

Promised Land *n.* **1.** *Bible.* the land of
Canaan. **2.** any longed-for place where one
expects to find greater happiness.

promising ('prɒmɪsɪŋ) *adj.* showing promise of future success.

promissory note *n. Commerce.* a document containing a signed promise to pay a
stated sum of money to a specified person.

promo ('prəʊməʊ) *n., pl.* **-mos.** *Informal.*
something used to promote a product, such
as a videotape film used to promote a pop
record.

promontory ('prɒməntrɪ) *n., pl.* **-ries.** a
high point of land that juts out into the sea.

promote (prə'məʊt) *vb.* **1.** to encourage
the progress of. **2.** to raise to a higher
rank, status, or office. **3.** to work for: *to
promote reform.* **4.** to encourage the sale of
(a product) by advertising. —**pro'motion**
n. —**pro'motional** *adj.*

promoter (prə'məʊtə) *n.* **1.** a person who
helps to organize, develop, or finance an
undertaking. **2.** a person who organizes
and finances a sporting event, esp. a boxing
match.

prompt (prɒmpt) *adj.* **1.** performed without delay. **2.** quick or ready to act or
respond. ~*adv.* **3.** *Informal.* punctually:
at 9 o'clock prompt. ~*vb.* **4.** to urge
(someone to do something). **5.** to remind
(an actor) of lines forgotten during a performance. **6.** to refresh the memory of. **7.**
to give rise to by suggestion: *his affairs will
prompt discussion.* ~*n.* **8.** anything that
serves to remind. —**'promptly** *adv.*
—**'promptness** *n.*

prompter ('prɒmptə) *n.* a person offstage
who reminds the actors of forgotten lines.

promulgate ('prɒməlˌgeɪt) *vb.* **1.** to put
into effect (a law or decree) by announcing
it officially. **2.** to make widespread.
—ˌ**promul'gation** *n.* —**'promulˌgator** *n.*

pron. 1. pronoun. **2.** pronunciation.

prone (prəʊn) *adj.* **1.** having a tendency to
be affected by or do something: *prone to
hay fever.* **2.** lying flat or face downwards;
prostrate.

prong (prɒŋ) *n.* a sharply pointed end of an
instrument, such as on a fork.

pronominal (prəʊ'nɒmɪn'l) *adj.* relating to
or playing the part of a pronoun.

pronoun ('prəʊˌnaʊn) *n.* one of a class of
words that serves to replace a noun or noun
phrase that has already been or is about to
be mentioned.

pronounce (prə'naʊns) *vb.* **1.** to utter or
speak (a sound or sounds). **2.** to utter
(words) in the correct way. **3.** to proclaim
officially: *I now pronounce you man and
wife.* **4.** to declare as one's judgment: *to
pronounce the death sentence upon someone.* —**pro'nounceable** *adj.*

pronounced (prə'naʊnst) *adj.* strongly
marked or indicated: *a pronounced change.*

pronouncement (prə'naʊnsmənt) *n.* a
public or official announcement.

pronto ('prɒntəʊ) *adv. Informal.* at once.

pronunciation (prəˌnʌnsɪ'eɪʃən) *n.* **1.** the
act, instance, or manner of pronouncing
sounds. **2.** the supposedly correct manner
of pronouncing sounds in a given language.

proof (pruːf) *n.* **1.** any evidence that establishes or helps to establish the truth, validity, or quality of something. **2.** *Law.* the
whole body of evidence upon which the
verdict of a court is based. **3.** *Maths, logic.*

a sequence of steps or statements that establishes the truth of a proposition. **4.** the act of testing the truth of something. **5.** a trial impression of printed matter for the correction of errors. **6.** *Photog.* a trial print from a negative. **7.** the alcoholic strength of proof spirit. ~*adj.* **8.** (foll. by *against*) able to withstand; resistant (to): *the roof is proof against rain.* **9.** having the alcoholic strength of proof spirit. ~*vb.* **10.** to take a proof from (type matter). **11.** to render (something) proof, esp. to waterproof.

proofread (ˈpruːˌriːd) *vb.* **-reading, -read** (-ˌrɛd). to read (printer's proofs) and mark errors to be corrected. —ˈproofˌreader *n.*

proof spirit *n.* (in Britain) an alcoholic beverage that contains a standard percentage of alcohol.

prop¹ (prɒp) *vb.* **propping, propped.** (often foll. by *up*) **1.** to support with a rigid object, such as a stick. **2.** (often foll. by *against*) to place or lean. **3.** to sustain or support. ~*n.* **4.** something that gives rigid support, such as a stick. **5.** a person or thing giving support, as of a moral nature.

prop² (prɒp) *n.* short for **property** (sense 6).

prop³ (prɒp) *n. Informal.* a propeller.

prop. 1. proper(ly). **2.** property. **3.** proposition. **4.** proprietor.

propaganda (ˌprɒpəˈgændə) *n.* **1.** the organized promotion of certain information or allegations, to assist or damage the cause of a government or movement. **2.** such information or allegations. —ˌpropaˈgandist *n., adj.*

propagate (ˈprɒpəˌgeɪt) *vb.* **1.** *Biol.* to reproduce; breed. **2.** *Horticulture.* to produce (plants) by layering, grafting, or cuttings. **3.** to spread (information or ideas). **4.** *Physics.* to transmit, esp. in the form of a wave: *to propagate sound.* —ˌpropaˈgation *n.* —ˈpropaˌgator *n.*

propane (ˈprəʊpeɪn) *n.* a flammable gaseous alkane found in petroleum and used as a fuel.

propel (prəˈpɛl) *vb.* **-pelling, -pelled.** to impel, drive, or cause to move forwards. —proˈpellant *n., adj.*

propeller (prəˈpɛlə) *n.* a device having blades radiating from a central hub that is rotated to produce thrust to propel a ship or aircraft.

propensity (prəˈpɛnsɪtɪ) *n., pl.* **-ties.** a natural tendency: *we recognize our own propensity to evil.*

proper (ˈprɒpə) *adj.* **1.** appropriate or usual: *in its proper place.* **2.** suited to a particular purpose: *use the proper knife to cut the bread.* **3.** correct in behaviour: *proper young ladies.* **4.** excessively moral: *a self-righteous sense of what is proper.* **5.** real or genuine: *a proper job.* **6.** *Brit. informal.* complete; utter: *I felt a proper fool.* —ˈproperly *adv.*

proper fraction *n.* a fraction in which the numerator has a lower absolute value than the denominator, as ½.

proper noun *or* **name** *n.* the name of a person, place, or object, as for example *Iceland, Patrick,* or *Uranus.*

property (ˈprɒpətɪ) *n., pl.* **-ties. 1.** something owned, such as land. **2.** *Law.* the right to possess, use, and dispose of anything. **3.** possessions collectively. **4.** land or real estate. **5.** a quality or attribute, such as the density of a material. **6.** any movable object used on the set of a stage play or film.

prophecy (ˈprɒfɪsɪ) *n., pl.* **-cies. 1. a.** a message of divine truth revealing God's will. **b.** the act of uttering such a message. **2.** a prediction or guess. **3.** the function or activity of a prophet.

prophesy (ˈprɒfɪˌsaɪ) *vb.* **-sying, -sied.** to foretell (something) by or as if by divine inspiration.

prophet (ˈprɒfɪt) *n.* **1.** a person who supposedly speaks by divine inspiration. **2.** a person who predicts the future: *a prophet of doom.* **3.** a spokesman for some cause: *a prophet of socialism.* —ˈprophetess *fem. n.*

Prophet (ˈprɒfɪt) *n.* **the.** the principal designation of Mohammed as the founder of Islam.

prophetic (prəˈfɛtɪk) *adj.* **1.** of or relating to a prophet or prophecy. **2.** of the nature of a prophecy. —proˈphetically *adv.*

prophylactic (ˌprɒfɪˈlæktɪk) *adj.* **1.** protecting from or preventing disease. ~*n.* **2.** a prophylactic drug or device.

propinquity (prəˈpɪŋkwɪtɪ) *n.* nearness in time, place, or relationship.

propitiate (prəˈpɪʃɪˌeɪt) *vb.* to appease (a god or person); make well disposed. —proˈpitiable *adj.* —proˌpitiˈation *n.* —proˈpitiˌator *n.* —proˈpitiatory *adj.*

propitious (prəˈpɪʃəs) *adj.* **1.** favourable or auspicious: *a propitious time.* **2.** favourably inclined: *conditions are propitious for development.*

proponent (prəˈpəʊnənt) *n.* a person who argues in favour of something or puts forward a proposal.

proportion (prəˈpɔːʃən) *n.* **1.** relative magnitude or extent; ratio: *a large proportion of our revenue comes from advertisements.* **2.** correct relationship between parts; symmetry. **3.** a part considered with respect to the whole: *the proportion of women in the total workforce.* **4.** (*pl.*) dimensions or size: *a building of vast proportions.* **5.** *Maths.* a relationship between four numbers in which the ratio of the first pair equals the ratio of the second pair. ~*vb.* **6.** to adjust in relative amount or size. **7.** to cause to be harmonious in relationship of parts.

proportional (prəˈpɔːʃənˀl) *adj.* **1.** of, involving, or being in proportion. ~*n.* **2.**

Maths. an unknown term in a proportion: *in a/b = c/x, x is the fourth proportional.* —**pro'portionally** *adv.*

proportional representation *n.* representation of parties in an elective body in proportion to the votes they win.

proportionate (prə'pɔːʃənɪt) *adj.* being in proper proportion. —**pro'portionately** *adv.*

proposal (prə'pəʊz²l) *n.* **1.** the act of proposing. **2.** something proposed, as a plan. **3.** an offer of marriage.

propose (prə'pəʊz) *vb.* **1.** to put forward (a plan) for consideration. **2.** to nominate (someone), as for a position. **3.** to intend (to do something): *I propose to leave town now.* **4.** to announce the drinking of (a toast). **5.** (often foll. by *to*) to make an offer of marriage.

proposition (ˌprɒpə'zɪʃən) *n.* **1.** a proposal for consideration. **2.** *Logic.* a statement that affirms or denies something and is capable of being true or false. **3.** *Maths.* a statement or theorem, usually containing its proof. **4.** *Informal.* a person or matter to be dealt with: *he's a difficult proposition.* **5.** *Informal.* an invitation to engage in sexual intercourse. ~*vb.* **6.** to propose a plan to (someone), esp. to engage in sexual intercourse.

propound (prə'paʊnd) *vb.* to put forward for consideration.

proprietary (prə'praɪɪtrɪ) *adj.* **1.** of or belonging to property or proprietors. **2.** privately owned and controlled. **3.** *Med.* denoting a drug manufactured and distributed under a trade name.

proprietor (prə'praɪətə) *n.* an owner of a business establishment. —**proprietorial** (prəˌpraɪə'tɔːrɪəl) *adj.* —**pro'prietress** *fem. n.*

propriety (prə'praɪətɪ) *n., pl.* **-ties. 1.** the quality or state of being appropriate or fitting. **2.** conformity to the prevailing standard of behaviour, speech, or morality. **3. the proprieties.** the standards of behaviour considered correct by polite society.

propulsion (prə'pʌlʃən) *n.* **1.** the act of propelling or the state of being propelled. **2.** a propelling force. —**propulsive** (prə'pʌlsɪv) *adj.*

pro rata ('prəʊ 'rɑːtə) *adv., adj.* in proportion.

prorogue (prə'rəʊg) *vb.* to discontinue the meetings of (a legislative body) without dissolving it. —**prorogation** (ˌprəʊrə'geɪʃən) *n.*

prosaic (prəʊ'zeɪɪk) *adj.* **1.** lacking imagination; dull. **2.** having the characteristics of prose. —**pro'saically** *adv.*

pros and cons *pl. n.* the various arguments for and against a motion or course of action.

proscenium (prə'siːnɪəm) *n., pl.* **-nia** (-nɪə)

or **-niums.** the arch separating the stage from the auditorium together with the area immediately in front of the arch.

proscribe (prəʊ'skraɪb) *vb.* **1.** to condemn or prohibit (something). **2.** to outlaw; banish; exile. —**proscription** (prəʊ'skrɪpʃən) *n.* —**pro'scriptive** *adj.*

prose (prəʊz) *n.* **1.** spoken or written language distinguished from poetry by its lack of a marked metrical structure. **2.** a passage set for translation into a foreign language. **3.** commonplace or dull talk. ~*vb.* **4.** to speak or write in a tedious style.

prosecute ('prɒsɪˌkjuːt) *vb.* **1.** to bring a criminal action against (a person). **2. a.** to seek redress by legal proceedings. **b.** to institute or conduct a prosecution. **3.** to continue to do (a task, etc.). —**prose,cutor** *n.*

prosecution (ˌprɒsɪ'kjuːʃən) *n.* **1.** the act of prosecuting or the state of being prosecuted. **2.** the institution and conduct of legal proceedings against a person. **3.** the lawyers acting for the Crown to put the case against a person. **4.** the carrying on of something begun.

proselyte ('prɒsɪˌlaɪt) *n.* a person newly converted from one religion or belief to another. —**proselytism** ('prɒsɪlɪˌtɪzəm) *n.*

proselytize or **-ise** ('prɒsɪlɪˌtaɪz) *vb.* to convert (someone) from one religion or belief to another.

prosody ('prɒsədɪ) *n.* **1.** the study of poetic metre and of the art of versification. **2.** the patterns of stress and intonation in a language. —**prosodic** (prə'sɒdɪk) *adj.* —**'prosodist** *n.*

prospect *n.* ('prɒspekt). **1.** (*sometimes pl.*) a probability of future success: *a job with prospects.* **2.** a view or scene. **3.** expectation, or what one expects: *she was excited at the prospect of living in London.* ~*vb.* (prə'spekt). **4.** (sometimes foll. by *for*) to explore (a region) for gold or other valuable minerals.

prospective (prə'spektɪv) *adj.* **1.** future: *prospective customers.* **2.** expected or likely: *the prospective loss.* —**pro'spectively** *adv.*

prospector (prə'spektə) *n.* a person who searches for gold or other valuable minerals.

prospectus (prə'spektəs) *n., pl.* **-tuses. 1.** a formal statement giving details of a forthcoming event, such as the issue of shares. **2.** a brochure giving details of courses, as at a school.

prosper ('prɒspə) *vb.* to thrive, do well, or be successful.

prosperity (prɒ'sperɪtɪ) *n.* the condition of prospering; success or wealth.

prosperous ('prɒspərəs) *adj.* **1.** flourishing; prospering. **2.** wealthy.

prostate ('prɒsteɪt) *n.* a gland in male

mammals that surrounds the neck of the bladder. Also called: **prostate gland.**

prosthesis (ˈprɒsθɪsɪs) n., pl. -ses (-ˌsiːz). Surgery. **a.** the replacement of a missing bodily part with an artificial substitute. **b.** an artificial part such as a limb, eye, or tooth. —**prosthetic** (prɒsˈθɛtɪk) adj.

prostitute (ˈprɒstɪˌtjuːt) n. **1.** a woman who engages in sexual intercourse for money. **2.** a man who engages in such activity, esp. in homosexual practices. ~vb. **3.** to offer (oneself or another) in sexual intercourse for money. **4.** to offer (oneself or one's talent) for unworthy purposes. —ˌprostiˈtution n.

prostrate adj. (ˈprɒstreɪt). **1.** lying face downwards, as in submission. **2.** physically or emotionally exhausted. ~vb. (prɒˈstreɪt). **3.** to cast (oneself) down, as in submission. **4.** to make helpless or exhausted. —**prosˈtration** n.

prosy (ˈprəʊzɪ) adj. **prosier, prosiest.** dull, tedious, or long-winded. —**ˈprosily** adv.

Prot. 1. Protectorate. **2.** Protestant.

protactinium (ˌprəʊtækˈtɪnɪəm) n. a toxic radioactive metallic element. Symbol: Pa

protagonist (prəʊˈtægənɪst) n. **1.** Not universally accepted. a supporter of a cause or party. **2.** the principal character in a play or story.

protea (ˈprəʊtɪə) n. an African shrub having flowers with coloured bracts arranged in showy heads.

protean (prəʊˈtiːən, ˈprəʊtɪən) adj. readily taking on various shapes or forms; variable.

protect (prəˈtɛkt) vb. **1.** to defend from trouble, harm, or loss. **2.** Econ. to assist (domestic industries) by tariffs on imports.

protection (prəˈtɛkʃən) n. **1.** the act of protecting or the condition of being protected. **2.** something that protects. **3. a.** the imposition of duties on imports, for the protection of domestic industries. **b.** Also called: **protectionism.** the system or theory of such restrictions. **4.** Informal. Also called: **protection money.** money demanded by gangsters for freedom from attack. —**proˈtectionˌism** n. —**proˈtectionist** n., adj.

protective (prəˈtɛktɪv) adj. giving, tending to, or capable of giving protection. —**proˈtectively** adv. —**proˈtectiveness** n.

protector (prəˈtɛktə) n. **1.** a person or thing that protects. **2.** History. a person who exercised royal authority during the minority, absence, or incapacity of the monarch. —**proˈtectress** fem. n.

protectorate (prəˈtɛktərɪt) n. **1.** a territory largely controlled by a stronger state. **2.** the office or period of office of a protector.

protégé or (fem.) **protégée** (ˈprɒtɪˌʒeɪ) n. a person who is protected and aided by the patronage of another.

protein (ˈprəʊtiːn) n. any of a large group of nitrogenous compounds that are essential constituents of all living organisms.

pro tempore Latin. (ˈprəʊ ˈtɛmpərɪ) adv., adj. for the time being. Often shortened to **pro tem** (prəʊ ˈtɛm).

protest n. (ˈprəʊtɛst). **1.** public, often organized, manifestation of dissent. **2.** a formal or solemn objection. **3.** a formal statement declaring that a debtor has dishonoured a bill. **4.** the act of protesting. ~vb. (prəˈtɛst). **5.** (sometimes foll. by against, at, about, etc.) to make a strong objection (to something, esp. a supposed injustice or offence). **6.** to disagree; object: "I'm O.K." she protested. **7.** to assert in a formal or solemn manner. **8.** Chiefly U.S. to object forcefully to: leaflets protesting Dr King's murder. —**proˈtestant** adj., n. —**proˈtester** or **proˈtestor** n.

Protestant (ˈprɒtɪstənt) n. **1.** an adherent of the religious system or any of its churches that separated from the Roman Catholic Church in the sixteenth century. ~adj. **2.** of or relating to Protestants. —**ˈProtestanˌtism** n.

protestation (ˌprɒtɛsˈteɪʃən) n. **1.** the act of protesting. **2.** a strong declaration.

protium (ˈprəʊtɪəm) n. the most common isotope of hydrogen, with a mass number of 1.

proto- or sometimes before a vowel **prot-** combining form. **1.** first: protomartyr. **2.** original: prototype.

protocol (ˈprəʊtəˌkɒl) n. **1.** the formal etiquette and procedure for state and diplomatic ceremonies. **2.** a record of an agreement, esp. in international negotiations.

proton (ˈprəʊtɒn) n. a stable, positively charged elementary particle, found in atomic nuclei in numbers equal to the atomic number of the element.

protoplasm (ˈprəʊtəˌplæzəm) n. Biol. the living contents of a cell: a complex translucent colourless substance. —**ˌprotoˈplasmic** adj.

prototype (ˈprəʊtəˌtaɪp) n. **1.** one of the first units manufactured of a product, which is tested so that the design can be changed if necessary. **2.** a person or thing that serves as an example of a type.

protozoan (ˌprəʊtəˈzəʊən) n., pl. -zoa (-ˈzəʊə). a minute invertebrate, such as the amoeba. Also: protozoon.

protract (prəˈtrækt) vb. to lengthen or extend (a speech, occasion, or situation). —**proˈtracted** adj. —**proˈtraction** n.

protractor (prəˈtræktə) n. an instrument for measuring angles, usually a semicircular transparent plastic sheet graduated in degrees.

protrude (prəˈtruːd) vb. **1.** to thrust forwards or outwards. **2.** to project. —**proˈtrusion** n. —**proˈtrusive** adj.

protuberant (prə'tjuːbərənt) *adj.* swelling out; bulging. **—pro'tuberance** *n.*

proud (praud) *adj.* **1.** pleased or satisfied with oneself, one's possessions, or achievements, or another's achievements or qualities; *proud of one's family; very proud of her new car.* **2.** feeling honoured or gratified by some distinction. **3.** haughty; arrogant. **4.** characterized by or proceeding from a sense of pride: *a proud moment.* **5.** having a proper sense of self-respect: *too proud to accept charity.* **6.** (of a surface or edge) projecting or protruding. ~*adv.* **7. do (someone) proud.** to entertain (someone) on a grand scale: *they did us proud at the hotel.* **—'proudly** *adv.*

proud flesh *n.* a mass of tissue formed around a healing wound.

prove (pruːv) *vb.* **proving, proved; proved** *or* **proven.** **1.** to demonstrate the truth or validity of (something): *the autopsy proved that she had been drowned.* **2.** to establish that (someone or something) has a particular quality: *his advice proved sound.* **3.** *Law.* to establish the genuineness of (a will). **4.** to show (oneself) able or courageous. **5.** to be found to be: *this has proved useless.* **—'provable** *adj.*

proven ('pruːv°n, 'prəu-) *vb.* **1.** a past participle of **prove. 2.** See **not proven.** ~*adj.* **3.** tried; tested: *a proven method.*

provenance ('provinəns) *n.* a place of origin, as of a work of art.

Provençal (,provɒn'saːl) *adj.* **1.** of Provence, in SE France. ~*n.* **2.** a language of Provence. **3.** a person from Provence.

provender ('provində) *n.* **1.** fodder for livestock. **2.** food in general.

proverb ('provɜːb) *n.* a short memorable saying that expresses a truth or gives a warning. An example is *"half a loaf is better than none".*

proverbial (prə'vɜːbiəl) *adj.* **1.** well-known because commonly or traditionally referred to. **2.** of or resembling a proverb. **—pro'verbially** *adv.*

provide (prə'vaid) *vb.* **1.** to furnish or supply. **2.** to afford; yield: *this meeting provides an opportunity to talk.* **3.** (often foll. by *for* or *against*) to take careful precautions: *he provided against financial ruin by wise investment.* **4.** (foll. by *for*) to supply means of support (to): *he provides for his family.* **5.** (of a person, law, etc.) to state as a condition; stipulate. **—pro'vider** *n.*

providence ('providəns) *n.* **1.** the foreseeing protection and care given by God or some other force. **2.** the foresight or care exercised by a person in the management of his affairs.

Providence ('providəns) *n. Christianity.* God, esp. as showing foreseeing care of his creatures.

provident ('providənt) *adj.* **1.** exercising foresight in the management of one's affairs. **2.** characterized by foresight.

providential (,provi'denfəl) *adj.* characteristic of or presumed to proceed from or as if from divine providence.

provident society *n.* same as **friendly society.**

providing (prə'vaidiŋ) *or* **provided** *conj.* on the condition or understanding (that): *I'll play, providing you pay me.*

province ('provins) *n.* **1.** a territory governed as a unit of a country or empire. **2.** (*pl.;* usually preceded by *the*) those parts of a country lying outside the capital and regarded as outside the mainstream of sophisticated culture. **3.** an area of learning, activity, etc. **4.** the extent of a person's activities or office.

provincewide ('provins,waid) *Canad.* ~*adj.* **1.** covering or available to the whole of a province: *a provincewide referendum.* ~*adv.* **2.** throughout a province: *an advertising campaign to go provincewide.*

provincial (prə'vinfəl) *adj.* **1.** of or connected with a province. **2.** characteristic of or connected with the provinces. **3.** having attitudes and opinions supposedly common to people living in the provinces; unsophisticated. **4.** *N.Z.* denoting a football team representing a province. ~*n.* **5.** a person lacking the sophistications of city life. **6.** a person from a province or the provinces. **—pro'vincia,lism** *n.*

provision (prə'viʒən) *n.* **1.** the act of supplying something. **2.** something supplied. **3.** preparations: *she didn't make any provision for her children.* **4.** (*pl.*) food and other necessities. **5.** a stipulation incorporated in a document. ~*vb.* **6.** to supply with provisions.

provisional (prə'viʒən°l) *adj.* subject to later alteration; temporary or conditional: *a provisional decision.* **—pro'visionally** *adv.*

Provisional (prə'viʒən°l) *n.* a member of the Provisional IRA or Sinn Féin.

proviso (prə'vaizəu) *n., pl.* **-sos** *or* **-soes.** **1.** a conditional clause, as in a contract. **2.** a condition or stipulation. **—pro'visory** *adj.*

provocation (,provə'keifən) *n.* **1.** the act of provoking or inciting. **2.** something that causes indignation or anger.

provocative (prə'vokətiv) *adj.* serving or intended to provoke or incite, esp. to anger or sexual desire: *a provocative look; a provocative remark.* **—pro'vocatively** *adv.*

provoke (prə'vəuk) *vb.* **1.** to anger or infuriate. **2.** to incite or stimulate. **3.** to promote (anger or indignation) in a person. **4.** to bring about: *the accident provoked an inquiry.* **—pro'voking** *adj.*

provost ('provəst) *n.* **1.** the head of certain university colleges or schools. **2.** (formerly) the principal magistrate of a Scottish burgh.

provost marshal (prə'vɔu) *n.* the officer in charge of military police in a camp or city.

prow (prau) *n.* the bow of a vessel.

prowess ('prauis) *n.* 1. outstanding or superior skill or ability. 2. bravery or fearlessness, esp. in battle.

prowl (praul) *vb.* 1. (sometimes foll. by *around* or *about*) to move stealthily around (a place) as if in search of prey or plunder. ~*n.* 2. the act of prowling. 3. **on the prowl.** moving around stealthily.

prox. proximo (next month).

proximate ('prɔksɪmɪt) *adj.* 1. next or nearest in space or time. 2. very near; close. 3. immediately preceding or following in a series. 4. approximate.

proximity (prɔk'sɪmɪtɪ) *n.* 1. nearness in space or time. 2. nearness or closeness in a series.

proxy ('prɔksɪ) *n., pl.* **proxies.** 1. a person authorized to act on behalf of someone else; agent: *to vote by proxy.* 2. the authority, esp. in the form of a document, to act on behalf of someone else.

prude (pru:d) *n.* a person who is excessively modest, prim, or proper, esp. regarding sex. —**'prudery** *n.* —**'prudish** *adj.*

prudent ('pru:d⁰nt) *adj.* 1. discreet or cautious in managing one's activities. 2. practical and careful in providing for the future. 3. exercising good judgment. —**'prudence** *n.* —**'prudently** *adv.*

prudential (pru:'dɛnʃəl) *adj.* showing prudence: *prudential reasons.* —**pru'dential-ly** *adv.*

prune¹ (pru:n) *n.* a purplish-black partially dried plum.

prune² (pru:n) *vb.* 1. to remove (dead or superfluous twigs or branches) from (a tree or shrub) by cutting off. 2. to remove (anything undesirable or superfluous) from (something, such as a book).

prurient ('pruərɪənt) *adj.* 1. unusually interested in sexual thoughts or practices. 2. exciting lustfulness. —**'prurience** *n.*

Prussian ('prʌʃən) *adj.* 1. of, relating to, or characteristic of Prussia, a former German state, esp. of its formal military tradition. ~*n.* 2. a German from Prussia.

prussic acid ('prʌsɪk) *n.* the extremely poisonous solution of hydrogen cyanide.

pry (praɪ) *vb.* **prying, pried.** (often foll. by *into*) to make an impertinent or uninvited inquiry (about a private matter).

PS 1. Also: **ps.** postscript. 2. private secretary.

psalm (sɑ:m) *n.* 1. (*often cap.*) any of the sacred songs that constitute a book (Psalms) of the Old Testament. 2. any sacred song.

psalmist ('sɑ:mɪst) *n.* a composer of psalms.

psalmody ('sɑ:mədɪ, 'sæl-) *n., pl.* **-dies.** the singing of psalms or hymns.

Psalter ('sɔːltə) *n.* 1. the Book of Psalms. 2. a book containing a version of Psalms.

psaltery ('sɔːltərɪ) *n., pl.* **-teries.** an ancient stringed instrument played by plucking strings.

PSBR (in Britain) public sector borrowing requirement; the money required by the public sector of the economy for items not financed from income.

psephology (sɛ'fɒlədʒɪ) *n.* the statistical and sociological study of elections. —**pse'phologist** *n.*

pseud (sju:d) *n.* 1. *Informal.* a false or pretentious person. ~*adj.* 2. pseudo.

pseudo ('sju:dəu) *adj. Informal.* not genuine.

pseudo- *or sometimes before a vowel* **pseud-** *combining form.* false, pretending, or unauthentic: *pseudo-intellectual.*

pseudonym ('sju:də,nɪm) *n.* a fictitious name adopted, esp. by an author. —**,pseudo'nymity** *n.* —**pseudonymous** (sju:'dɒnɪməs) *adj.*

psittacosis (,sɪtə'kəusɪs) *n.* a viral disease of parrots that can be transmitted to man.

psoriasis (sə'raɪəsɪs) *n.* a skin disease characterized by reddish spots and patches covered with silvery scales.

psst (pst) *interj.* an exclamation of beckoning, esp. one made surreptitiously.

PST (in the U.S. and Canada) Pacific Standard Time.

PSV public service vehicle.

psyche ('saɪkɪ) *n.* the human mind or soul.

psychedelic (,saɪkɪ'dɛlɪk) *adj.* 1. relating to or denoting altered perceptions, as through the use of hallucinogenic drugs. 2. *Informal.* having the vivid colours and complex patterns popularly associated with the visual effects of psychedelic states.

psychiatry (saɪ'kaɪətrɪ) *n.* the branch of medicine concerned with the diagnosis and treatment of mental disorders. —**psychiatric** (,saɪkɪ'ætrɪk) *adj.* —**psy'chiatrist** *n.*

psychic ('saɪkɪk) *adj.* 1. **a.** outside the possibilities defined by natural laws, as mental telepathy. **b.** (of a person) sensitive to forces not recognized by natural laws. ~*n.* 2. a person who has psychic powers. —**'psychical** *adj.*

psycho ('saɪkəu) *n., pl.* **-chos,** *adj. Informal.* same as **psychopath** or **psychopathic.**

psycho- *or sometimes before a vowel* **psych-** *combining form.* indicating the mind or psychological or mental processes: *psychology; psychosomatic.*

psychoanalyse *or esp. U.S.* **-lyze** (,saɪkəu'ænə,laɪz) *vb.* to examine or treat (a person) by psychoanalysis.

psychoanalysis (ˌsaɪkəʊəˈnælɪsɪs) n. a method of treating mental and emotional disorders by revealing and investigating the role of the unconscious mind. —**psychoanalyst** (ˌsaɪkəʊˈæ ɪəlɪst) n. —**psychoanalytic** (ˌsaɪkəʊˌænəˈlɪtɪk) or ˌ**psycho**ˌ**ana**ˈ**lytical** adj.

psychogenic (ˌsaɪkəʊˈdʒenɪk) adj. Psychol. (esp. of disorders or symptoms) of mental, rather than organic, origin.

psychological (ˌsaɪkəˈlɒdʒɪk²l) adj. 1. of or relating to psychology. 2. of or relating to the mind or mental activity. 3. affecting the mind. —**psycho**ˈ**logically** adv.

psychological moment n. the most appropriate time for producing a desired effect.

psychological warfare n. the military application of psychology, esp. to influence morale in time of war.

psychology (saɪˈkɒlədʒɪ) n., pl. -gies. 1. the scientific study of all forms of human and animal behaviour. 2. Informal. the mental make-up of an individual. —**psy**ˈ**chologist** n.

psychopath (ˈsaɪkəʊˌpæθ) n. a person afflicted with a personality disorder characterized by a tendency to commit antisocial and sometimes violent acts. —ˌ**psycho**ˈ**pathic** adj.

psychopathology (ˌsaɪkəʊpəˈθɒlədʒɪ) n. the scientific study of mental disorders.

psychopathy (saɪˈkɒpəθɪ) n. any mental disorder or disease.

psychosis (saɪˈkəʊsɪs) n., pl. -choses (-ˈkəʊsiːz). any form of severe mental disorder in which the individual's contact with reality becomes highly distorted. —**psychotic** (saɪˈkɒtɪk) adj.

psychosomatic (ˌsaɪkəʊsəˈmætɪk) adj. of disorders, such as stomach ulcers, thought to be caused by psychological factors such as stress.

psychotherapy (ˌsaɪkəʊˈθerəpɪ) n. the treatment of nervous disorders by psychological methods. —ˌ**psycho**ˌ**thera**ˈ**peutic** adj. —ˌ**psycho**ˈ**therapist** n.

psych up (saɪk) vb. to prepare (oneself or another) mentally for a contest, performance, or action.

pt 1. part. 2. point. 3. port.

Pt Chem. platinum.

PT physical training.

pt. pint.

PTA Parent-Teacher Association.

Pte. Mil. private.

pterodactyl (ˌterəˈdæktɪl) n. an extinct flying reptile with membranous wings.

PTO or **pto** please turn over.

Ptolemaic (ˌtɒlɪˈmeɪk) adj. of or relating to Ptolemy, the 2nd-century A.D. Greek astronomer, or to his conception that the earth lay at the centre of the universe.

ptomaine or **ptomain** (ˈtəʊmeɪn) n. any of a group of alkaloid substances formed by decaying organic matter.

Pu Chem. plutonium.

pub (pʌb) n. 1. Chiefly Brit. a building with a bar licensed for the sale and consumption of alcoholic drink. 2. Austral. & N.Z. a hotel.

pub. 1. public. 2. publication. 3. published. 4. publisher. 5. publishing.

pub-crawl n. Informal, chiefly Brit. a drinking tour of a number of pubs.

puberty (ˈpjuːbətɪ) n. the period at the beginning of adolescence when the sex glands become functional. —ˈ**pubertal** adj.

pubes (ˈpjuːbiːz) n., pl. **pubes**. 1. the region above the external genital organs. 2. pubic hair. 3. the plural of **pubis**.

pubescent (pjuːˈbes²nt) adj. 1. arriving or arrived at puberty. 2. covered with down, as some plants and animals. —**pu**ˈ**bescence** n.

pubic (ˈpjuːbɪk) adj. of or relating to the pubes or pubis: pubic hair.

pubis (ˈpjuːbɪs) n., pl. -bes. one of the three sections of the hipbone that forms part of the pelvis.

public (ˈpʌblɪk) adj. 1. of or concerning the people as a whole. 2. open to all: public gardens. 3. performed or made openly: public proclamation. 4. well-known: a public figure. 5. maintained at the expense of, serving, or for the use of a community: a public library. 6. open, acknowledged, or notorious: a public scandal. 7. go public. (of a private company) to offer shares for sale to the public. ~n. 8. the community or people in general. 9. a section of the community: the racing public. —ˈ**publicly** adv.

public-address system n. a system of microphones, amplifiers, and loudspeakers for increasing the sound level at public gatherings.

publican (ˈpʌblɪkən) n. (in Britain) a person who keeps a public house.

publication (ˌpʌblɪˈkeɪʃən) n. 1. the publishing of a printed work. 2. any printed work offered for sale. 3. the act of making information known to the public.

public company n. a limited company whose shares may be purchased by the public.

public convenience n. a public lavatory.

public enemy n. a notorious person, such as a criminal, who is regarded as a menace to the public.

public house n. 1. Brit. a pub. 2. U.S. & Canad. an inn, tavern, or small hotel.

publicist (ˈpʌblɪsɪst) n. a person who publicizes something, such as a press agent or journalist.

publicity (pʌˈblɪsɪtɪ) n. 1. the technique or

the information used to attract public attention to people or products. **2.** public interest so aroused.

publicize or **-ise** ('pʌblɪˌsaɪz) vb. to bring to public notice; advertise.

public lending right n. the right of authors to receive payment when their books are borrowed from public libraries.

public prosecutor n. Law. an official in charge of prosecuting important cases.

public relations n. (functioning as sing. or pl.) the practice of creating, promoting, or maintaining goodwill and a favourable image among the public towards an institution, public body, or business.

public school n. **1.** (in England and Wales) a private independent fee-paying secondary school. **2.** in certain Canadian provinces, a public elementary school as distinguished from a separate school. **3.** any school that is part of a free local educational system.

public sector n. the part of an economy which consists of state-owned institutions, including nationalized industries and services provided by local authorities.

public servant n. **1.** an elected or appointed holder of a public office. **2.** Austral. & N.Z. a civil servant.

public service n. Austral. & N.Z. the civil service.

public-spirited adj. having or showing active interest in the good of the community.

public utility n. an enterprise that provides services, such as water or electricity, to the public.

publish ('pʌblɪʃ) vb. **1.** to produce and issue (printed matter) for sale. **2.** to have one's written work issued for publication. **3.** to announce formally or in public.

publisher ('pʌblɪʃə) n. **1.** a company or person engaged in publishing books, periodicals, music, etc. **2.** U.S. & Canad. the proprietor of a newspaper.

puce (pjuːs) adj. purplish-brown.

puck[1] (pʌk) n. a small disc of hard rubber used in ice hockey.

puck[2] (pʌk) n. a mischievous or evil spirit. —'**puckish** adj.

pucker ('pʌkə) vb. **1.** to gather (a soft surface, such as the skin) into wrinkles or (of such a surface) to be so gathered. ~n. **2.** a wrinkle or crease.

pudding ('pʊdɪŋ) n. **1.** a sweetened, usually cooked dessert, made in many forms and containing various ingredients. **2.** a savoury dish, usually consisting partially of pastry or batter: steak-and-kidney pudding. **3.** the dessert course in a meal. **4.** a sausage-like mass of meat: black pudding.

puddle ('pʌd'l) n. **1.** a small pool of water, esp. of rain. **2.** a worked mixture of wet clay and sand that is impervious to water.

~vb. **3.** to make (clay, etc.) into puddle. **4.** to subject (iron) to puddling. —'**puddly** adj.

pudendum (pjuː'dɛndəm) n., pl. **-da** (-də). (often pl.) the human external genital organs collectively, esp. of a female.

pudgy ('pʌdʒɪ) adj. **pudgier, pudgiest.** Chiefly U.S. podgy. —'**pudginess** n.

puerile ('pjʊəraɪl) adj. **1.** silly; immature. **2.** childish. —**puerility** (pjʊə'rɪlɪtɪ) n.

puerperal (pjuː'ɜːpərəl) adj. of or occurring during the period following childbirth.

puerperal fever n. a serious, formerly widespread, form of blood poisoning caused by infection during childbirth.

puff (pʌf) n. **1.** a short quick gust or emission, as of wind or smoke. **2.** the amount of wind or smoke released in a puff. **3.** the sound made by a puff. **4.** an instance of inhaling and expelling the breath as in smoking. **5.** a light pastry usually filled with cream and jam. **6.** one's breath: by the third flight of stairs she was out of puff. ~vb. **7.** to blow or breathe in short quick draughts. **8.** (often foll. by out) to cause to be out of breath. **9.** to take draws at (a cigarette). **10.** to move with or by the emission of puffs: the steam train puffed up the incline. **11.** (often foll. by up or out) to swell, as with air, pride, or as a result of injury. —'**puffy** adj.

puff adder n. a large venomous African viper that inflates its body when alarmed.

puffball ('pʌfˌbɔːl) n. a fungus with a round body that lets out a cloud of brown spores when mature.

puffin ('pʌfɪn) n. a northern diving bird with a black-and-white plumage and a brightly coloured vertically flattened bill.

puff pastry or U.S. **puff paste** n. a dough used for making a rich flaky pastry.

pug (pʌg) n. a small compact breed of dog with a smooth coat, lightly curled tail, and a short wrinkled nose.

pugilism ('pjuːdʒɪˌlɪzəm) n. the art, practice, or profession of fighting with the fists; boxing. —'**pugilist** n. —ˌpugi'**listic** adj.

pugnacious (pʌg'neɪʃəs) adj. ready and eager to fight; belligerent. —**pugnacity** (pʌg'næsɪtɪ) n.

pug nose n. a short stubby upturned nose. —'**pugˌnosed** adj.

puissance ('pjuːɪsəns, 'pwiːsɑːns) n. a competition in showjumping that tests a horse's ability to jump large obstacles.

puissant ('pjuːɪsˀnt) adj. Archaic or poetic. powerful.

puke (pjuːk) Slang. ~vb. **1.** to vomit. ~n. **2.** the act of vomiting. **3.** the matter vomited.

pukeko ('pʊkəkəʊ) n., pl. **-kos.** a New Zealand wading bird with bright plumage.

pukka or **pucka** ('pʌkə) adj. Anglo-Indian. proper; good; genuine.

pulchritude ('pʌlkrɪˌtjuːd) *n. Formal or literary.* physical beauty. —ˌpulchri'tudinous *adj.*

pule (pjuːl) *vb.* to cry plaintively; whimper.

pull (pʊl) *vb.* **1.** to exert force on (an object) so as to draw it towards the source of the force. **2.** to remove; extract: *to pull a tooth.* **3.** to rend or tear. **4.** to strain (a muscle or tendon). **5.** (usually foll. by *off*) *Informal.* to bring about: *to pull off a million-pound deal.* **6.** (often foll. by *on*) *Informal.* to draw out (a weapon) for use: *he pulled a knife on his attacker.* **7.** *Informal.* to attract: *the pop group pulled a crowd.* **8.** (usually foll. by *on* or *at*) to drink or inhale deeply: *to pull at one's pipe.* **9.** to make (a grimace): *to pull a face.* **10.** (foll. by *away, out, over,* etc.) to move (a vehicle) or (of a vehicle) to be moved in a specified manner. **11.** to possess or exercise the power to move: *this car doesn't pull well on hills.* **12.** *Printing.* to take (a proof) from type. **13.** *Golf, baseball, etc.* to hit (a ball) away from the direction in which the player intended to hit it. **14.** *Cricket.* to hit (a ball) to the leg side. **15.** to row (a boat) or take a stroke of (an oar) in rowing. **16. pull a fast one.** *Slang.* to play a sly trick. **17. pull apart** *or* **to pieces.** to criticize harshly. **18. pull (one's) punches.** to restrain the force of one's criticisms or blows. ~*n.* **19.** an act or an instance of pulling or being pulled. **20.** the force or effort used in pulling: *the pull of the moon affects the tides.* **21.** the act or an instance of taking in drink or smoke. **22.** *Printing.* a proof taken from type. **23.** something used for pulling, such as a handle. **24.** *Informal.* special advantage or influence: *his uncle is chairman of the company, so he has quite a lot of pull.* **25.** *Informal.* the power to attract attention or support. **26.** a single stroke of an oar in rowing. **27.** the act of pulling the ball in golf, cricket, etc. ~See also **pull down, pull in,** etc.

pull down *vb.* to destroy or demolish: *the old houses were pulled down.*

pullet ('pʊlɪt) *n.* a young hen of the domestic fowl, less than one year old.

pulley ('pʊlɪ) *n.* a wheel with a grooved rim in which a belt, chain, or piece of rope runs in order to lift or lower heavy loads or change the direction of a pull.

pull in *vb.* **1.** (often foll. by *to*) to reach a destination: *the train pulled in at the station.* **2.** Also: **pull over.** (of a motor vehicle) to draw in to the side of the road. **3.** to attract: *his appearance will pull in the crowds.* **4.** *Brit. slang.* to arrest. **5.** to earn or gain (money): *he pulls in twenty thousand a year.*

Pullman ('pʊlmən) *n., pl.* **-mans.** a luxurious railway coach.

pull off *vb.* to succeed in performing (a difficult feat).

pull out *vb.* **1.** to extract. **2.** to depart: *the train pulled out of the station.* **3.** *Mil.* to withdraw or be withdrawn: *the troops were pulled out of the ruined city.* **4.** (of a motor vehicle) **a.** to draw away from the side of the road. **b.** to draw out from behind another vehicle to overtake. **5.** to abandon a position or situation.

pullover ('pʊlˌəʊvə) *n.* a garment, esp. a sweater, that is pulled on over the head.

pull through *vb.* to survive or recover, esp. after a serious illness or crisis. Also: **pull round.**

pull together *vb.* **1.** to cooperate or work harmoniously. **2. pull oneself together.** *Informal.* to regain one's self-control or composure.

pull up *vb.* **1.** to remove by the roots. **2.** (often foll. by *with* or *on*) to move level (with) or ahead (of), esp. in a race. **3.** to stop: *the car pulled up suddenly.* **4.** to rebuke.

pulmonary ('pʌlmənərɪ, 'pʊl-) *adj.* **1.** of or affecting the lungs. **2.** having lungs or lunglike organs.

pulp (pʌlp) *n.* **1.** soft or fleshy plant tissue, such as the succulent part of a fleshy fruit. **2.** a moist mixture of cellulose fibres, as obtained from wood, from which paper is made. **3.** a magazine or book containing trite or sensational material, and usually printed on cheap rough paper. ~*vb.* **4.** to reduce (a material) to pulp or (of a material) to be reduced to pulp. —'**pulpy** *adj.*

pulpit ('pʊlpɪt) *n.* **1.** a raised platform in churches as the appointed place for preaching. **2.** (usually preceded by *the*) preaching or the clergy.

pulpwood ('pʌlpˌwʊd) *n.* pine, spruce, or any other soft wood used to make paper.

pulsar ('pʌlˌsɑː) *n.* any of a number of very small stars which emit regular pulses of polarized radiation.

pulsate (pʌl'seɪt) *vb.* **1.** to expand and contract with a rhythmical beat; throb. **2.** *Physics.* to vary in intensity or magnitude. **3.** to quiver or vibrate. —pul'sation *n.*

pulse[1] (pʌls) *n.* **1.** *Physiol.* **a.** the rhythmical contraction and expansion of an artery at each beat of the heart. **b.** a single such pulsation. **2.** *Physics, electronics.* a sudden change in a quantity, such as a voltage, that is normally constant in a system. **3.** a recurrent rhythmical series of beats or vibrations. **4.** bustle, vitality, or excitement: *the pulse of a city.* **5.** the feelings or thoughts of a group as they can be measured: *the pulse of the voters.* ~*vb.* **6.** to beat, throb, or vibrate.

pulse[2] (pʌls) *n.* the edible seeds of any of several leguminous plants, such as peas, beans, and lentils.

pulverize *or* **-ise** ('pʌlvəˌraɪz) *vb.* **1.** to reduce (a substance) to fine particles, as by grinding, or (of a substance) to be so reduced. **2.** to destroy completely. —**¡pulveri'zation** or **-i'sation** n.

puma ('pju:mə) n. a large American mammal of the cat family, with a plain greyish-brown coat and long tail.

pumice ('pʌmɪs) n. a light porous volcanic rock used for scouring and, in powdered form, for polishing. Also called: **pumice stone.**

pummel ('pʌmɐl) vb. **-melling, -melled** or U.S. **-meling, -meled.** to strike repeatedly with or as if with the fists.

pump[1] (pʌmp) n. **1.** any device for compressing, driving, raising, or reducing the pressure of a fluid, esp. by means of a piston or set of rotating impellers. ~vb. **2.** (sometimes foll. by *from, out,* etc.) to raise or drive (air, liquid, etc., esp. into or from something) with a pump. **3.** (usually foll. by *in* or *into*) to supply in large amounts: *to pump capital into a project.* **4.** to operate (something, esp. a handle) in the manner of a pump or (of something) to work in this way: *to pump the pedals of a bicycle.* **5.** to obtain (information) from (a person) by persistent questioning.

pump[2] (pʌmp) n. **1.** a low-cut low-heeled shoe, worn for dancing. **2.** a shoe with a rubber sole, used in games such as tennis; plimsoll.

pumpernickel ('pʌmpə₂nɪkʰl) n. a slightly sour black bread made of coarse rye flour.

pumpkin ('pʌmpkɪn) n. **1.** a large round fruit with a thick orange rind, pulpy flesh, and numerous seeds. **2.** the creeping plant that bears this fruit.

pun (pʌn) n. **1.** the use of words to exploit double meanings for humorous effect. An example is *"my dog's a champion boxer".* ~vb. **punning, punned.** **2.** to make puns.

punch[1] (pʌntʃ) vb. **1.** to strike at with a clenched fist. ~n. **2.** a blow with the fist. **3.** *Informal.* point or vigour: *his arguments lacked punch.*

punch[2] (pʌntʃ) n. **1.** a tool or machine for shaping, piercing, or engraving. **2.** *Computers.* a device for making holes in a card or paper tape. ~vb. **3.** to pierce, cut, stamp, shape, or drive with a punch.

punch[3] (pʌntʃ) n. a mixed drink containing fruit juice and, usually, alcoholic liquor, generally hot and spiced.

Punch (pʌntʃ) n. the main character in the children's puppet show **Punch and Judy.**

punchball ('pʌntʃ₂bɔːl) n. a stuffed or inflated ball or bag, supported or supported by a flexible rod, that is punched for exercise, esp. boxing training.

punchbowl ('pʌntʃ₂bəʊl) n. a large bowl for serving punch.

punch-drunk adj. dazed; stupefied, as from repeated blows to the head.

punched card or esp. U.S. **punch card** n.

Computers. a card on which data can be coded in the form of punched holes.

Punchinello (₂pʌntʃɪ'nɛləʊ) n., pl. **-los** or **-loes.** a clown from Italian puppet shows, the prototype of Punch.

punch line n. the line of a joke or funny story that gives it its point.

punch-up n. *Brit. informal.* a fight or brawl.

punchy ('pʌntʃɪ) adj. *Informal.* incisive or forceful: *a punchy leaflet.*

punctilious (pʌŋk'tɪlɪəs) adj. **1.** paying scrupulous attention to correctness in etiquette. **2.** attentive to detail. —**punc-'tiliously** adv.

punctual ('pʌŋktjʊəl) adj. **1.** arriving or taking place at an arranged time. **2.** (of a person) having the characteristic of always keeping to arranged times. —**¡punctu-'ality** n. —**'punctually** adv.

punctuate ('pʌŋktjʊ₂eɪt) vb. **1.** to insert punctuation marks into (a written text). **2.** to interrupt at frequent intervals: *a meeting punctuated by heckling.* **3.** to emphasize.

punctuation (₂pʌŋktjʊ'eɪʃən) n. **1.** the use of symbols not belonging to the alphabet to indicate intonation and meaning not otherwise conveyed in the written language. **2.** the symbols used for this purpose.

punctuation mark n. any of the signs used in punctuation, such as a comma.

puncture ('pʌŋktʃə) n. **1.** a small hole made by a sharp object. **2.** a perforation and loss of pressure in a pneumatic tyre. **3.** the act of puncturing or perforating. ~vb. **4.** to pierce a hole in (something) with a sharp object. **5.** to cause (something pressurized, esp. a tyre) to lose pressure by piercing, or (of a tyre) to collapse in this way.

pundit ('pʌndɪt) n. **1.** a self-appointed expert. **2.** a Brahman learned in Hindu religion, philosophy, or law.

pungent ('pʌndʒənt) adj. **1.** having an acrid smell or sharp bitter flavour. **2.** (of wit or satire) biting; caustic. —**'pungency** n.

punish ('pʌnɪʃ) vb. **1.** to force (someone) to undergo a penalty for some crime or misdemeanour. **2.** to inflict punishment for (some crime or misdemeanour). **3.** to treat harshly, esp. as by overexertion: *to punish a horse.* —**'punishing** adj.

punishment ('pʌnɪʃmənt) n. **1.** a penalty for a crime or offence. **2.** the act of punishing or state of being punished. **3.** *Informal.* rough treatment.

punitive ('pju:nɪtɪv) adj. relating to, involving, or with the intention of inflicting punishment: *a punitive expedition.*

punk (pʌŋk) n. **1.** a worthless person. **2. a.** a youth movement of the late 1970s, characterized by anti-Establishment slogans and the wearing of worthless articles such as safety pins for decoration. **b.** (*as modifi-*

er): *a punk record.* **3.** short for **punk rock.** ~*adj.* **4.** worthless; insignificant.

punka *or* **punkah** ('pʌŋkə) *n.* a fan made of palm leaves.

punk rock *n.* rock music in a style of the late 1970s, characterized by energy and aggressive lyrics and performance. —**punk rocker** *n.*

punnet ('pʌnɪt) *n. Chiefly Brit.* a small basket for fruit.

punster ('pʌnstə) *n.* a person who is fond of making puns.

punt[1] (pʌnt) *n.* **1.** an open flat-bottomed boat, propelled by a pole. ~*vb.* **2.** to propel (a punt) by pushing with a pole on the bottom of a river.

punt[2] (pʌnt) *n.* **1.** a kick in certain sports, such as rugby, in which the ball is released and kicked before it hits the ground. ~*vb.* **2.** to kick (a ball) using a punt.

punt[3] (pʌnt) *Chiefly Brit.* ~*vb.* **1.** to gamble; bet. ~*n.* **2.** a gamble or bet, esp. against the bank, as in roulette, or on horses.

punter ('pʌntə) *n.* **1.** a person who places a bet. **2.** *Informal.* any member of the public, esp. when a customer: *the punters flock into the sales.*

puny ('pju:nɪ) *adj.* **-nier, -niest.** small and weakly.

pup (pʌp) *n.* **1. a.** a young dog; puppy. **b.** the young of various other animals, such as the seal. ~*vb.* **pupping, pupped. 2.** (of dogs, seals, etc.) to give birth to (young).

pupa ('pju:pə) *n., pl.* **-pae** (-pi:) *or* **-pas.** an insect at the immobile nonfeeding stage of development between larva and adult. —**pupal** *adj.*

pupil[1] ('pju:p³l) *n.* a student who is taught by a teacher.

pupil[2] ('pju:p³l) *n.* the dark circular opening at the centre of the iris of the eye.

puppet ('pʌpɪt) *n.* **1.** a small doll or figure moved by strings attached to its limbs or by the hand inserted in its cloth body. **2.** a person or state that appears independent but is controlled by another.

puppeteer (,pʌpɪ'tɪə) *n.* a person who manipulates puppets.

puppy ('pʌpɪ) *n., pl.* **-pies. 1.** a young dog. **2.** *Informal, contemptuous.* a brash or conceited young man. —**puppyish** *adj.*

puppy fat *n.* fatty tissue that develops in childhood or adolesence and usually disappears with maturity.

purblind ('pɜ:,blaɪnd) *adj.* **1.** partly or nearly blind. **2.** lacking in understanding; obtuse.

purchase ('pɜ:tʃɪs) *vb.* **1.** to obtain (goods) by payment. **2.** to obtain by effort or sacrifice: *to purchase one's freedom.* ~*n.* **3.** something that is purchased. **4.** the act of buying. **5.** the mechanical advantage

achieved by a lever. **6.** a firm foothold or grasp. —**purchaser** *n.*

purdah ('pɜ:də) *n.* the custom in some Muslim and Hindu communities of keeping women in seclusion, with clothing that conceals them completely when they go out.

pure (pjʊə) *adj.* **1.** not mixed with any materials or elements of other kinds or from other sources. **2.** free from tainting or polluting matter: *pure water.* **3.** free from moral taint or defilement: *pure love.* **4.** complete: *a pure coincidence.* **5.** (of a subject) studied in its theoretical aspects rather than for its practical applications: *pure mathematics.* **6.** of unmixed descent. —**purely** *adv.* —**pureness** *n.*

purebred ('pjʊə'brɛd) *adj.* denoting a pure strain obtained through many generations of controlled breeding.

purée ('pjʊəreɪ) *n.* **1.** a smooth thick pulp of sieved fruit, vegetables, meat, or fish. ~*vb.* **-réeing, -réed. 2.** to make (foods) into a purée.

purgative ('pɜ:gətɪv) *Med.* ~*n.* **1.** a medicine for purging the bowels. ~*adj.* **2.** causing emptying of the bowels.

purgatory ('pɜ:gətrɪ) *n.* **1.** *Chiefly R.C. Church.* a state or place in which the souls of those who have died undergo limited suffering for their sins on earth before they go to heaven. **2.** a place or condition of temporary suffering or torment. —**purgatorial** *adj.*

purge (pɜ:dʒ) *vb.* **1.** to rid (something) of (impure elements). **2.** to rid (a state, organization, or political party) of (dissident people). **3. a.** to empty (the bowels) by evacuation of faeces. **b.** to cause (a person) to evacuate his bowels. **4. a.** to clear (a person) of a charge. **b.** to free (oneself) of guilt, as by atonement. **5.** to be purified. ~*n.* **6.** the act or process of purging. **7.** the elimination of opponents or dissidents from a state, organization, or political party. **8.** a purgative medicine.

purify ('pjʊərɪ,faɪ) *vb.* **-fying, -fied. 1.** to free (something) of contaminating or debasing matter. **2.** to free (a person) from sin or guilt. **3.** to make clean, as in a ritual. —**purification** *n.*

purism ('pjʊə,rɪzəm) *n.* excessive insistence on the correctness of usage or style, as in grammar or art. —**purist** *adj., n.* —**puristic** *adj.*

puritan ('pjʊərɪt³n) *n.* **1.** a person who adheres to strict moral or religious principles. ~*adj.* **2.** characteristic of a puritan. —**puritanism** *n.*

Puritan ('pjʊərɪt³n) (in the late 16th and 17th centuries) ~*n.* **1.** any of the extreme English Protestants who wished to purify the Church of England of most of its ceremony. ~*adj.* **2.** of or relating to the Puritans. —**Puritanism** *n.*

puritanical (,pjʊərɪ'tænɪk³l) *adj.* **1.** *Usually*

disparaging. strict in moral or religious outlook. **2.** (*sometimes cap.*) of or relating to a puritan or the Puritans. —ˌ**puri'tanically** *adv.*

purity ('pjʊərɪtɪ) *n.* the state or quality of being pure.

purl[1] (pɜːl) *n.* **1.** a knitting stitch made by doing a plain stitch backwards. **2.** a decorative border, as of lace. ~*vb.* **3.** to knit in purl stitch.

purl[2] (pɜːl) *vb.* (of a stream) to flow with a gentle swirling or rippling movement and a murmuring sound.

purlieu ('pɜːljuː) *n.* **1.** *English history.* land on the edge of a royal forest. **2.** (*usually pl.*) a neighbouring area; outskirts. **3.** (*often pl.*) a place one frequents; haunt.

purlin *or* **purline** ('pɜːlɪn) *n.* a horizontal beam that supports the rafters of a roof.

purloin (pɜː'lɔɪn) *vb.* to steal.

purple ('pɜːpᵊl) *n.* **1.** a colour between red and blue. **2.** cloth of this colour, often used to symbolize royalty or nobility. **3.** the official robe of a cardinal. ~*adj.* **4.** of the colour purple. **5.** (of writing) excessively elaborate: *purple prose.* —'**purplish** *adj.*

purple heart *n. Informal, chiefly Brit.* a heart-shaped purple tablet consisting mainly of amphetamine.

Purple Heart *n.* a decoration awarded to members of the U.S. Armed Forces for a wound received in action.

purport *vb.* (pɜː'pɔːt). **1.** to claim to be (true, official, etc.) by manner or appearance, esp. falsely. **2.** (of speech or writing) to signify or imply. ~*n.* ('pɜːpɔːt). **3.** meaning; significance.

purpose ('pɜːpəs) *n.* **1.** the reason for which anything is done, created, or exists. **2.** a fixed design or idea that is the object of an action. **3.** determination: *a man of purpose.* **4.** practical advantage or use: *to work to good purpose.* **5. on purpose.** intentionally. ~*vb.* **6.** to intend or determine to do (something).

purpose-built *adj.* made to serve a specific purpose.

purposeful ('pɜːpəsfʊl) *adj.* with a fixed and definite purpose; determined. —'**purposefully** *adv.*

purposely ('pɜːpəslɪ) *adv.* on purpose.

purposive ('pɜːpəsɪv) *adj.* **1.** having or indicating conscious intention. **2.** useful.

purr (pɜː) *vb.* **1.** (esp. of cats) to make a low vibrant sound, usually considered as expressing pleasure. **2.** to express (pleasure) by this sound or by a sound suggestive of purring. ~*n.* **3.** a purring sound.

purse (pɜːs) *n.* **1.** a small pouch for carrying money. **2.** *U.S. & Canad.* a woman's handbag. **3.** wealth; funds; resources. **4.** a sum of money that is offered as a prize. ~*vb.* **5.** to contract (the lips) into a small rounded shape.

purser ('pɜːsə) *n.* an officer aboard a ship who keeps the accounts.

purse strings *pl. n.* **hold the purse strings.** to control the expenditure of a particular family, group, etc.

pursuance (pə'sjuːəns) *n.* the carrying out of an action or plan.

pursue (pə'sjuː) *vb.* **-suing, -sued. 1.** to follow (a person, vehicle, or animal) in order to capture or overtake. **2.** to strive to attain (some desire or aim). **3.** to follow the precepts of (a plan or policy). **4.** to apply oneself to (studies or interests). **5.** to follow persistently or seek to become acquainted with: *what a wonderful feeling to be loved and pursued!* **6.** to continue to discuss or argue (a point or subject). —**pur'suer** *n.*

pursuit (pə'sjuːt) *n.* **1.** the act of pursuing. **2.** an occupation or pastime.

pursuivant ('pɜːsɪvənt) *n.* the lowest rank of heraldic officer.

purulent ('pjʊərʊlənt) *adj.* of, relating to, or containing pus. —'**purulence** *n.*

purvey (pə'veɪ) *vb.* to sell or provide (foodstuffs). —**pur'veyor** *n.*

purview ('pɜːvjuː) *n.* **1.** scope of operation. **2.** breadth or range of outlook.

pus (pʌs) *n.* the yellowish fluid that comes from inflamed or infected tissue.

push (pʊʃ) *vb.* **1.** (sometimes foll. by *off, away,* etc.) to apply steady force to in order to move. **2.** to thrust (one's way) through something, such as a crowd. **3.** (sometimes foll. by *for*) to be an advocate or promoter (of): *to push for acceptance of one's theories.* **4.** to spur or drive (oneself or another person) in order to achieve more effort or better results. **5.** *Informal.* to sell (narcotic drugs) illegally. ~*n.* **6.** the act of pushing; thrust. **7.** *Informal.* drive or determination. **8.** *Informal.* a special effort or attempt to get something done or finished. **9. the push.** *Informal, chiefly Brit.* dismissal from employment. ~See also **push about, push off,** etc.

push about *or* **around** *vb. Informal.* to bully: *don't let them push you around.*

push-bike *n. Brit. informal.* a bicycle.

push button *n.* **1.** an electrical switch operated by pressing a button. ~*modifier.* **push-button. 2.** operated by a push button: *a push-button radio.*

pushchair ('pʊʃˌtʃɛə) *n. Brit.* a chair-shaped carriage for a small child.

pushed (pʊʃt) *adj.* (often foll. by *for*) *Informal.* short of: *pushed for time.*

pusher ('pʊʃə) *n. Informal.* a person who sells illegal drugs.

pushing ('pʊʃɪŋ) *adv.* **1.** almost or nearly (a certain age, speed, etc.): *pushing fifty.* ~*adj.* **2.** aggressively ambitious.

push off *vb. Informal.* to go away; leave.

pushover ('pʊʃˌəʊvə) *n. Informal.* **1.** something that is easily achieved. **2.** a person, team, etc., that is easily taken advantage of or defeated.

push-start *vb.* **1.** to start (a motor vehicle) by pushing it, thus turning the engine. ~*n.* **2.** this process.

push through *vb.* to compel to accept: *the bill was pushed through Parliament.*

pushy ('puʃɪ) *adj.* **pushier, pushiest.** *Informal.* offensively assertive or ambitious.

pusillanimous (ˌpjuːsɪ'lænɪməs) *adj.* timid and cowardly. —**pusillanimity** (ˌpjuːsɪlə'nɪmɪtɪ) *n.*

puss (pus) *n.* **1.** *Informal.* a cat. **2.** *Slang.* a girl or woman.

pussy[1] ('pusɪ) *n., pl.* **pussies.** **1.** Also called: **pussycat.** *Informal.* a cat. **2.** *Taboo slang.* the female genitals.

pussy[2] ('pʌsɪ) *adj.* **-sier, -siest.** containing or full of pus.

pussyfoot ('pusɪˌfut) *vb.* *Informal.* **1.** to move about stealthily. **2.** to avoid committing oneself.

pussy willow ('pusɪ) *n.* a willow tree with silvery silky catkins.

pustulate ('pʌstjuˌleɪt) *vb.* to form into pustules.

pustule ('pʌstjuːl) *n.* a small inflamed raised area of skin containing pus. —**pustular** ('pʌstjulə) *adj.*

put (put) *vb.* **putting, put.** **1.** to cause to be (in a position or place): *to put a book on the table.* **2.** to cause to be (in a state, relation, or condition): *to put one's things in order.* **3.** to lay (blame, emphasis, trust, etc.) on a person or thing: *I put the blame on him.* **4.** to set or commit (to an action, task, or duty), esp. by force: *he put him to work.* **5.** (foll. by *at*) to estimate: *he put the distance at fifty miles.* **6.** (foll. by *to*) to utilize: *he put his knowledge to use.* **7.** to express: *to put it bluntly.* **8.** to make (an end or limit): *he put an end to the proceedings.* **9.** to present for consideration; propose: *he put the question to the committee.* **10.** to invest (money) in or expend (time or energy) on: *he put five thousand pounds into the project.* **11.** to throw or cast: *put the shot.* ~*n.* **12.** a throw, esp. in putting the shot. ~See also **put about, put across,** etc.

put about *vb.* **1.** to make widely known: *he put about the news of the air disaster.* **2.** *Naut.* to change course.

put across *vb.* to communicate comprehensively: *he couldn't put things across very well.*

put aside *vb.* **1.** to save: *to put money aside for a rainy day.* **2.** to disregard: *let us put aside our differences.*

putative ('pjuːtətɪv) *adj.* **1.** commonly regarded as being: *the putative father.* **2.** considered to exist or have existed; inferred: *a putative earlier form.*

put away *vb.* **1.** to save: *to put away*

money for the future. **2.** to lock up in a prison, mental institution, etc.: *they put him away for twenty years.* **3.** to eat or drink in large amounts.

put back *vb.* **1.** to return to its former place. **2.** to move to a later time: *the wedding was put back a fortnight.*

put down *vb.* **1.** to make a written record of. **2.** to repress: *to put down a rebellion.* **3.** to consider: *they put him down for an ignoramus.* **4.** to attribute: *the mistake was put down to inexperience.* **5.** to put (an animal) to death. **6.** *Slang.* to belittle or humiliate. ~*n.* **put-down.** **7.** a cruelly crushing remark.

put forward *vb.* **1.** to propose; suggest. **2.** to offer the name of; nominate.

put in *vb.* **1.** to devote (time or effort): *he put in three hours overtime last night.* **2.** (often foll. by *for*) to apply (for a job). **3.** to submit: *he put in his claims form.* **4.** *Naut.* to bring a vessel into port.

put off *vb.* **1.** to postpone: *they have put off the dance until tomorrow.* **2.** to evade (a person) by postponement or delay: *they tried to put him off, but he came anyway.* **3.** to cause aversion: *he was put off by her appearance.* **4.** to cause to lose interest in: *the accident put him off driving.*

put on *vb.* **1.** to clothe oneself in. **2.** to adopt (an attitude or feeling) insincerely: *his misery was just put on.* **3.** to present (a play or show). **4.** to add: *she put on weight.* **5.** to cause (an electrical device) to function. **6.** to wager (money) on a horse race or game. **7.** to impose: *to put a tax on cars.*

put out *vb.* **1. a.** to annoy; anger. **b.** to disturb; confuse. **2.** to extinguish (something, such as a fire or light). **3.** to be a source of inconvenience to: *I hope I'm not putting you out.* **4.** to publish; broadcast: *the authorities put out a leaflet.* **5.** to dislocate: *he put out his shoulder in the accident.* **6.** *Cricket, etc.* to dismiss (a player or team).

put over *vb.* *Informal.* to communicate (facts or information).

putrefy ('pjuːtrɪˌfaɪ) *vb.* **-fying, -fied.** (of organic matter) to rot and produce an offensive smell. —**putrefaction** (ˌpjuːtrɪ'fækʃən) *n.*

putrescent (pjuː'trɛsᵊnt) *adj.* becoming putrid; rotting. —**pu'trescence** *n.*

putrid ('pjuːtrɪd) *adj.* **1.** (of organic matter) in a state of decomposition: *putrid meat.* **2.** morally corrupt. **3.** sickening; foul: *a putrid smell.* **4.** *Informal.* deficient in quality or value: *a putrid film.* —**pu'tridity** *n.*

putsch (putʃ) *n.* a violent and sudden political revolt.

putt (pʌt) *Golf.* ~*n.* **1.** a stroke on the green with a putter to roll the ball into or near the hole. ~*vb.* **2.** to strike (the ball) in this way.

puttee (ˈpʌtɪ) *n.* (*often pl.*) a strip of cloth worn wound around the leg from the ankle to the knee.

putter (ˈpʌtə) *n. Golf.* a club with a short shaft for putting.

put through *vb.* **1.** to carry out to a conclusion: *he put through his plan.* **2.** to connect by telephone.

putting green (ˈpʌtɪŋ) *n.* (on a golf course) the area of closely mown grass where the hole is.

putty (ˈpʌtɪ) *n., pl.* **-ties. 1.** a stiff paste made of whiting and linseed oil used to fix glass into frames and fill cracks in woodwork. ~*vb.* **-tying, -tied. 2.** to fix or fill with putty.

put up *vb.* **1.** to build; erect: *to put up a statue.* **2.** to accommodate or be accommodated at: *can you put me up for tonight?* **3.** to increase (prices). **4.** to submit (a plan, case, etc.). **5.** to offer: *to put a house up for sale.* **6.** to give: *to put up a good fight.* **7.** to provide (money) for: *they put up five thousand for the new project.* **8.** to nominate or be nominated as a candidate: *he put up for president.* **9. put up to.** to incite to: *I wonder who put them up to it.* **10. put up with.** *Informal.* to endure; tolerate. ~*adj.* **put-up. 11.** dishonestly or craftily prearranged: *a put-up job.*

put upon *vb.* to presume on (a person's generosity or good nature): *he's always being put upon.*

puzzle (ˈpʌzˀl) *vb.* **1.** to perplex or be perplexed. **2. puzzle out.** to solve (a problem) by mental effort. **3. puzzle over.** to ponder about the cause of: *he puzzled over her absence.* ~*n.* **4.** a problem that cannot be easily solved. **5.** a toy, game, or question presenting a problem that requires skill or ingenuity for its solution. —ˈ**puzzlement** *n.* —ˈ**puzzler** *n.* —ˈ**puzzling** *adj.*

PVC polyvinyl chloride.

PW policewoman.

PWR pressurized-water reactor.

pyaemia *or* **pyemia** (paɪˈiːmɪə) *n.* blood poisoning characterized by pus-forming microorganisms in the blood.

pye-dog, pie-dog, *or* **pi-dog** (ˈpaɪˌdɒg) *n.* an ownerless half-wild Asian dog.

pygmy (ˈpɪgmɪ) *n., pl.* **-mies. 1.** an abnormally undersized person. **2.** something that is a very small example of its type. **3.** a person of little importance or significance. **4.** (*modifier*) very small.

Pygmy (ˈpɪgmɪ) *n., pl.* **-mies.** a member of one of the dwarf peoples of Equatorial Africa.

pyjamas *or U.S.* **pajamas** (pəˈdʒɑːməz) *pl. n.* loose-fitting nightclothes comprising a jacket or top and trousers.

pylon (ˈpaɪlən) *n.* a large vertical steel tower-like structure supporting high-tension electrical cables.

pyorrhoea *or esp. U.S.* **pyorrhea** (ˌpaɪəˈrɪə) *n.* a discharge of pus, esp. in disease of the gums or tooth sockets.

pyramid (ˈpɪrəmɪd) *n.* **1.** a huge masonry construction that has a square base and, as in the ancient Egyptian royal tombs, four sloping triangular sides. **2.** *Maths.* a solid figure having a polygonal base and triangular sides that meet in a common vertex. —**pyramidal** (pɪˈræmɪdˀl) *adj.*

pyramid selling *n.* the practice of selling distributors batches of goods which they then subdivide and sell to other distributors. This process continues until the final distributors are left with a stock that is unsaleable except at a loss.

pyre (ˈpaɪə) *n.* a pile of wood for cremating a corpse.

pyrethrum (paɪˈriːθrəm) *n.* **1.** a Eurasian chrysanthemum with white, pink, red, or purple flowers. **2.** an insecticide prepared from the dried flowers.

pyretic (paɪˈrɛtɪk) *adj. Pathol.* of, relating to, or characterized by fever.

Pyrex (ˈpaɪrɛks) *n. Trademark.* a variety of heat-resistant glassware used in cookery and chemical apparatus.

pyrite (ˈpaɪraɪt) *n.* a yellow mineral consisting of iron sulphide in cubic crystalline form. Formula: FeS_2

pyrites (paɪˈraɪtiːz; *in combination* ˈpaɪraɪts) *n., pl.* **-tes. 1.** same as **pyrite. 2.** any of a number of other disulphides of metals, esp. of copper and tin.

pyromania (ˌpaɪrəʊˈmeɪnɪə) *n. Psychiatry.* the uncontrollable impulse and practice of setting things on fire. —ˌ**pyroˈmaniˌac** *n., adj.*

pyrotechnics (ˌpaɪrəʊˈtɛknɪks) *n.* **1.** (*functioning as sing.*) the art of making fireworks. **2.** (*functioning as sing. or pl.*) a firework display. **3.** (*functioning as sing. or pl.*) brilliance of display, as in the performance of music. —ˌ**pyroˈtechnic** *adj.*

Pyrrhic victory (ˈpɪrɪk) *n.* a victory in which the victor's losses are as great as those of the defeated.

Pythagoras' theorem (paɪˈθægərəs) *n.* the theorem that in a right-angled triangle the square of the length of the hypotenuse equals the sum of the squares of the other two sides.

python (ˈpaɪθən) *n.* a large nonvenomous snake of Africa, S Asia, and Australia. It kills its prey by constriction.

pyx (pɪks) *n. Christianity.* any receptacle in which the Eucharistic Host is kept.

Q

q *or* **Q** (kjuː) *n., pl.* **q's, Q's,** *or* **Qs.** the 17th letter of the English alphabet.

Q 1. *Chess.* queen. 2. question.

q. 1. quart. 2. quarter. 3. question. 4. quire.

Q. 1. Quebec. 2. Queen. 3. question.

QC Queen's Counsel.

QED which was to be shown or proved

QM Quartermaster.

qr., *pl.* **qrs.** 1. quarter. 2. quire.

qt, *pl.* **qt** *or* **qts** quart.

q.t. **on the q.t.** *Informal.* secretly.

qua (kwɑː) *prep.* in the capacity of; by virtue of being.

quack¹ (kwæk) *vb.* 1. (of a duck) to utter a harsh guttural sound. 2. to make a noise like a duck. ~*n.* 3. the sound made by a duck.

quack² (kwæk) *n.* 1. an unqualified person who claims medical knowledge. 2. *Brit., Austral., & N.Z. informal.* a doctor. —**'quackery** *n.*

quad¹ (kwɒd) *n.* short for **quadrangle** (sense 2).

quad² (kwɒd) *n. Informal.* a quadruplet.

quad³ (kwɒd) *n.* 1. short for **quadraphonics.** ~*adj.* 2. short for **quadraphonic.**

Quadragesima (ˌkwɒdrə'dʒɛsɪmə) *n.* the first Sunday in Lent.

quadrangle ('kwɒd,ræŋg°l) *n.* 1. *Geom.* a plane figure consisting of four points connected by four lines. 2. a rectangular courtyard with buildings on all four sides. —**quadrangular** (kwɒ'dræŋgjʊlə) *adj.*

quadrant ('kwɒdrənt) *n.* 1. *Geom.* **a.** a quarter of the circumference of a circle. **b.** the area enclosed by two perpendicular radii of a circle. 2. a piece of a mechanism in the form of a quarter circle. 3. an instrument formerly used in astronomy and navigation for measuring the altitudes of stars.

quadraphonic (ˌkwɒdrə'fɒnɪk) *adj.* using four independent channels to reproduce or record sound. —**quadra'phonics** *n.*

quadrate ('kwɒdreɪt) *n.* 1. a cube or square, or a square or cubelike object. ~*vb.* 2. to make square or rectangular.

quadratic (kwɒ'drætɪk) *Maths.* ~*n.* 1. Also called: **quadratic equation.** an equation in which the variable is raised to the power of two, but nowhere raised to a higher power: *solve the quadratic equation* $2x^2-3x-6=3$. ~*adj.* 2. of or relating to the second power.

quadrennial (kwɒ'drɛnɪəl) *adj.* 1. occur-

ring every four years. 2. lasting four years.

quadri- *or before a vowel* **quadr-** *combining form.* four: *quadrilateral.*

quadrilateral (ˌkwɒdrɪ'lætərəl) *adj.* 1. having four sides. ~*n.* 2. a polygon having four sides.

quadrille (kwɒ'drɪl) *n.* 1. a square dance for four couples. 2. music for this dance.

quadrillion (kwɒ'drɪljən) *n.* 1. (in Britain, France, and Germany) the number represented as one followed by 24 zeros (10^{24}). 2. (in the U.S. and Canada) the number represented as one followed by 15 zeros (10^{15}).

quadriplegia (ˌkwɒdrɪ'pliːdʒɪə) *n.* paralysis of all four limbs. —ˌ**quadri'plegic** *adj., n.*

quadruped ('kwɒdrʊ,pɛd) *n.* an animal, esp. a mammal, that has all four limbs specialized for walking.

quadruple ('kwɒdrʊp°l, kwɒ'druːp°l) *vb.* 1. to multiply by four. ~*adj.* 2. four times as much or as many. 3. consisting of four parts. 4. *Music.* having four beats in each bar. ~*n.* 5. a quantity or number four times as great as another.

quadruplet ('kwɒdrʊplɪt, kwɒ'druːplɪt) *n.* one of four offspring born at one birth.

quadruplicate *adj.* (kwɒ'druːplɪkɪt). 1. fourfold or quadruple. ~*vb.* (kwɒ'druːplɪ,keɪt). 2. to multiply or be multiplied by four.

quaff (kwɒf) *vb.* to drink heartily or in one draught.

quagga ('kwægə) *n., pl.* **-gas** *or* **-ga.** a recently extinct zebra, striped only on the head and shoulders.

quagmire ('kwæg,maɪə) *n.* a soft wet area of land that gives way under the feet; bog.

quail¹ (kweɪl) *n., pl.* **quails** *or* **quail.** a small game bird of the partridge family.

quail² (kweɪl) *vb.* to shrink back with fear; cower.

quaint (kweɪnt) *adj.* attractively unusual, esp. in an old-fashioned style.

quake (kweɪk) *vb.* 1. to shake or tremble with or as with fear. 2. to convulse or quiver, as from instability. ~*n.* 3. a quaking. 4. *Informal.* an earthquake.

Quaker ('kweɪkə) *n.* a member of a Christian sect, the Society of Friends. —'**Quakerism** *n.*

qualification (ˌkwɒlɪfɪ'keɪʃən) *n.* 1. an ability, quality, or attribute, esp. one that fits a person to perform a particular job or task. **2.** a condition that modifies or limits; restriction. **3.** a qualifying or being qualified.

qualified (ˈkwɒlɪˌfaɪd) *adj.* **1.** having the abilities, qualities, or attributes necessary to perform a particular job or task. **2.** limited, modified, or restricted: *qualified praise.*

qualify (ˈkwɒlɪˌfaɪ) *vb.* **-fying, -fied. 1.** to provide or be provided with the abilities or attributes necessary for a task, office or duty: *his degree qualifies him for the job.* **2.** to moderate or restrict (something, esp. a statement). **3.** *Grammar.* to modify the sense of a word. See **modifier. 4.** to attribute a quality to; characterize: *the accident qualified as news.* **5.** to progress to the final stages of a competition, as by winning preliminary contests. —ˈqualiˌfier *n.*

qualitative (ˈkwɒlɪtətɪv) *adj.* involving or relating to distinctions based on quality.

qualitative analysis *n. Chem.* analysis of a substance to determine its constituents.

quality (ˈkwɒlɪtɪ) *n., pl.* **-ties. 1.** a distinguishing characteristic or attribute. **2.** the basic character or nature of something. **3.** a feature of personality. **4.** degree or standard of excellence. **5.** (formerly) high social status. **6.** musical tone colour; timbre. **7.** (*modifier*) excellent or superior: *a quality product.*

quality control *n.* control of the relative quality of a manufactured product, usually by testing samples.

qualm (kwɑːm) *n.* **1.** a sudden feeling of sickness or nausea. **2.** a pang of conscience; scruple. **3.** a sudden sensation of misgiving.

quandary (ˈkwɒndrɪ) *n., pl.* **-ries.** a difficult situation; predicament; dilemma.

quango (ˈkwæŋɡəʊ) *n., pl.* **-gos.** quasi-autonomous nongovernmental organization.

quantify (ˈkwɒntɪˌfaɪ) *vb.* **-fying, -fied.** to discover or express the quantity of. —ˈquantiˌfiable *adj.* —ˌquantifiˈcation *n.*

quantitative (ˈkwɒntɪtətɪv) *adj.* **1.** involving considerations of amount or size. **2.** capable of being measured.

quantitative analysis *n. Chem.* analysis of a substance to determine the proportions of its constituents.

quantity (ˈkwɒntɪtɪ) *n., pl.* **-ties. 1.** a specified or definite amount or number. **2.** the aspect of anything that can be measured, weighed, or counted. **3.** a large amount. **4.** *Maths.* an entity having a magnitude that may be denoted by a numerical expression.

quantity surveyor *n.* a person who estimates the cost of the materials and labour necessary for a construction job.

quantum (ˈkwɒntəm) *n., pl.* **-ta** (-tə). **1.** *Physics.* the smallest quantity of some physical property that a system can possess. **2.** amount or quantity, esp. a specific amount. ~*adj.* **3.** of or designating a major breakthrough or sudden advance: *a quantum leap forward.*

quantum theory *n.* a theory concerning the behaviour of physical systems based on the idea that they can only possess certain properties, such as energy and angular momentum, in discrete amounts (quanta).

quarantine (ˈkwɒrənˌtiːn) *n.* **1.** a period of isolation, esp. of persons or animals arriving from abroad, to prevent the spread of disease. ~*vb.* **2.** to isolate in or as if in quarantine.

quark (kwɑːk) *n. Physics.* the hypothetical elementary particle postulated to be a fundamental unit of all baryons and mesons.

quarrel (ˈkwɒrəl) *n.* **1.** an angry disagreement; argument. **2.** a cause of dispute; grievance. ~*vb.* **-relling, -relled** or *U.S.* **-reling, -reled.** (often foll. by *with*) **3.** to engage in a disagreement or dispute; argue. **4.** to find fault; complain.

quarrelsome (ˈkwɒrəlsəm) *adj.* inclined to quarrel or disagree.

quarry¹ (ˈkwɒrɪ) *n., pl.* **-ries. 1.** a place where stone is dug from the surface of the earth. ~*vb.* **-rying, -ried. 2.** to extract (stone) from a quarry.

quarry² (ˈkwɒrɪ) *n., pl.* **-ries. 1.** an animal that is being hunted; prey. **2.** anything pursued.

quarry tile *n.* an unglazed floor tile.

quart (kwɔːt) *n.* a unit of liquid measure equal to a quarter of a gallon or two pints (1.136 litres).

quarter (ˈkwɔːtə) *n.* **1.** one of four equal parts of something such as an object or quantity. **2.** the fraction equal to one divided by four (¼). **3.** *U.S. & Canad.* a 25-cent piece. **4.** a unit of weight equal to a quarter of a hundredweight. **5.** short for **quarter-hour. 6.** a fourth part of a year; three months. **7.** *Astron.* **a.** one fourth of the moon's period of revolution around the earth. **b.** either of two phases of the moon when half of the lighted surface is visible. **8.** *Informal.* a unit of weight equal to a quarter of a pound or 4 ounces. **9.** a region or district of a town or city: *the Spanish quarter.* **10.** a region, direction, or point of the compass. **11.** (*sometimes pl.*) an unspecified person or group of people: *the highest quarters.* **12.** mercy or pity, as shown to a defeated opponent: *he would give no quarter.* **13.** any of the four limbs of a quadruped. ~*vb.* **14.** to divide into four equal parts. **15.** (formerly) to dismember (a human body). **16.** to billet or be billeted in lodgings. **17.** *Heraldry.* to divide (a shield) into four separate bearings. ~*adj.* **18.** being or consisting of one of four equal parts. ~See also **quarters.**

quarterback (ˈkwɔːtəˌbæk) *n.* a player in American football who directs attacking play.

quarter day *n.* any of four days in the year when certain payments become due.

quarterdeck ('kwɔːtəˌdɛk) *n. Naut.* the after part of the upper deck of a ship, traditionally for official or ceremonial use.

quarterfinal (ˌkwɔːtə'faɪnᵊl) *n.* the round before the semifinal in a competition.

quarter-hour *n.* **1.** a period of 15 minutes. **2.** either of the points of time 15 minutes before or after the hour.

quarterlight ('kwɔːtəˌlaɪt) *n. Brit.* a small pivoted window in the door of a car.

quarterly ('kwɔːtəlɪ) *adj.* **1.** occurring, done, due, or issued at intervals of three months. ~*n., pl.* **-lies. 2.** a periodical issued every three months. ~*adv.* **3.** once every three months.

quartermaster ('kwɔːtəˌmɑːstə) *n.* **1.** a military officer responsible for accommodation, food, and equipment. **2.** a naval officer responsible for navigation.

quarters ('kwɔːtəz) *pl. n.* **1.** accommodation, esp. as provided for military personnel. **2.** the stations assigned to crew members of a warship: *general quarters.*

quarter sessions *n. (functioning as sing. or pl.)* (formerly) a court with limited jurisdiction, held four times a year.

quarterstaff ('kwɔːtəˌstɑːf) *n., pl.* **-staves** (-ˌsteɪvz). a stout iron-tipped wooden staff about 6ft. long, formerly used as a weapon.

quartet (kwɔː'tɛt) *n.* **1.** a group of four singers or instrumentalists or a piece of music composed for such a group. **2.** any group of four.

quarto ('kwɔːtəʊ) *n., pl.* **-tos.** a book size resulting from folding a sheet of paper into four leaves or eight pages.

quartz (kwɔːts) *n.* a hard glossy mineral consisting of crystalline silicon dioxide.

quartz clock *or* **watch** *n.* a clock or watch that is operated by a vibrating quartz crystal.

quartz crystal *n.* a thin plate or rod cut from a piece of quartz and ground so that it vibrates at a particular frequency.

quasar ('kweizɑː, -sɑː) *n.* any of a class of extremely distant starlike objects that are powerful sources of radio waves and other forms of energy.

quash (kwɒʃ) *vb.* **1.** to subdue forcefully and completely. **2.** to annul or make void (something, such as a law). **3.** to reject (something, for instance an indictment) as invalid.

quasi- *combining form.* **1.** almost but not really; seemingly: *a quasi-religious cult.* **2.** resembling but not actually being; so-called: *a quasi-scholar.*

quassia ('kwɒʃə) *n.* **1.** a tropical American tree with bitter bark and wood. **2.** the wood of this tree or a bitter compound extracted from it, used in insecticides.

quaternary (kwə'tɜːnərɪ) *adj.* consisting of fours or by fours.

Quaternary (kwə'tɜːnərɪ) *adj. Geol.* of the most recent period of geological time, which started about one million years ago.

quatrain ('kwɒtreɪn) *n.* a stanza or poem of four lines.

quatrefoil ('kætrəˌfɔɪl) *n.* **1.** a leaf composed of four leaflets. **2.** *Archit.* a carved ornament of four arcs about a common centre.

quattrocento (ˌkwætrəʊ'tʃɛntəʊ) *n.* the 15th century, esp. in reference to Renaissance Italian art.

quaver ('kweivə) *vb.* **1.** (esp. of the voice) to quiver or tremble. **2.** to say or sing (something) with a trembling voice. ~*n.* **3.** *Music.* a note having the time value of an eighth of a semibreve. **4.** a tremulous sound or note. —'**quavering** *adj.*

quay (kiː) *n.* a wharf built parallel to the shoreline.

Que. Quebec.

queasy ('kwiːzɪ) *adj.* **-sier, -siest. 1.** having the feeling that one is about to vomit; nauseous. **2.** feeling or causing uneasiness. —'**queasily** *adv.* —'**queasiness** *n.*

queen (kwiːn) *n.* **1.** a female sovereign who is the official ruler or head of state. **2.** the wife of a king. **3.** a woman, thing, or place considered the best or most important of her or its kind: *the queen of ocean liners.* **4.** *Slang.* an effeminate male homosexual. **5.** the only fertile female in a colony of bees, wasps, or ants. **6.** a playing card bearing the picture of a queen. **7.** the most powerful chess piece, able to move in a straight line in any direction. ~*vb.* **8.** *Chess.* to promote (a pawn) to a queen when it reaches the eighth rank. **9. queen it.** (often foll. by *over*) *Informal.* to behave in an overbearing manner. —'**queenly** *adj.*

Queen-Anne (ˌkwiːn'æn) *n.* an 18th-century style of furniture characterized by the use of curves.

queen consort *n.* the wife of a reigning king.

queen mother *n.* the widow of a former king who is also the mother of the reigning sovereign.

queen post *n.* one of a pair of vertical posts that connect the tie beam of a truss to the principal rafters.

Queen's Bench *n.* one of the divisions of the High Court of Justice.

Queensberry rules ('kwiːnzbərɪ) *pl. n.* the code of rules followed in modern boxing.

Queen's Counsel *n.* **1.** (in Britain) a barrister or advocate appointed Counsel to the Crown. **2.** (in Canada) an honorary title bestowed on lawyers with long experience.

Queen's English *n.* standard Southern British English.

queen's evidence *n. English law.* evidence given for the Crown against his former associates in crime by an accomplice.

Queen's Guide *or* **Scout** *n.* a Guide or Scout who has passed the highest tests of proficiency.

queen's highway *n.* **1.** (in Britain) any public road or right of way. **2.** (in Canada) a main road maintained by the provincial government.

queer (kwɪə) *adj.* **1.** not normal or usual; odd or strange. **2.** dubious; shady. **3.** faint, giddy, or queasy. **4.** *Informal, offensive.* homosexual. **5.** *Informal.* eccentric or slightly mad. *~n.* **6.** *Informal, offensive.* a homosexual. *~vb.* **7. queer someone's pitch.** *Informal.* to spoil or thwart someone's chances of something.

queer street *n.* **in queer street.** *Informal.* in a difficult situation, such as debt or bankruptcy.

quell (kwɛl) *vb.* **1.** to suppress (rebellion or unrest); subdue. **2.** to overcome or allay.

quench (kwɛntʃ) *vb.* **1.** to satisfy (one's thirst); slake. **2.** to put out; extinguish. **3.** to suppress or subdue. **4.** to cool (hot metal) by plunging it into cold water.

quern (kwɜːn) *n.* a stone hand mill for grinding corn.

querulous (ˈkwɛrjʊləs) *adj.* complaining; whining or peevish. —ˈ**querulously** *adv.*

query (ˈkwɪərɪ) *n., pl.* **-ries. 1.** a question, esp. one expressing doubt. **2.** a question mark. *~vb.* **-rying, -ried. 3.** to express uncertainty, doubt, or an objection concerning (something). **4.** to express as a query.

quest (kwɛst) *n.* **1.** a looking for or seeking; search. **2.** the object of a search; a goal or target. *~vb.* **3.** (foll. by *for* or *after*) to go in search of. **4.** to search for game.

question (ˈkwɛstʃən) *n.* **1.** a form of words addressed to a person in order to obtain an answer; interrogative sentence. **2.** a point at issue: *it's only a question of time.* **3.** a difficulty or uncertainty. **4. a.** an act of asking. **b.** an investigation into some problem. **5.** a motion presented for debate. **6. beyond (all) question.** beyond (any) doubt. **7. call something into question. a.** to make something the subject of disagreement. **b.** to cast doubt upon the validity or truth of something. **8. in question.** under discussion: *this is the man in question.* **9. out of the question.** beyond consideration; impossible. *~vb.* **10.** to put a question or questions to (a person); interrogate. **11.** to make (something) the subject of dispute. **12.** to express uncertainty; doubt.

questionable (ˈkwɛstʃənəbᵊl) *adj.* **1.** (esp. of a person's morality or honesty) dubious. **2.** of disputable value or authority. —ˈ**questionably** *adv.*

questioning (ˈkwɛstʃənɪŋ) *adj.* **1.** proceeding from or characterized by doubt or uncertainty. **2.** intellectually inquisitive: *a questioning mind.* *~n.* **3.** interrogation.

question mark *n.* **1.** the punctuation mark **?**, used at the end of questions. **2.** a doubt or uncertainty: *a question mark still hangs over their success.*

question master *n. Brit.* the chairman of a radio or television quiz or panel game.

questionnaire (ˌkwɛstʃəˈnɛə, ˌkɛs-) *n.* a set of questions on a form, used to collect statistical information or opinions from people.

question time *n.* (in parliamentary bodies of the British type) the time set aside each day for questions to government ministers.

queue (kjuː) *Chiefly Brit.* *~n.* **1.** a line of people or vehicles waiting for something. *~vb.* **queueing** *or* **queuing, queued. 2.** (often foll. by *up*) to form or remain in a line while waiting.

quibble (ˈkwɪbᵊl) *vb.* **1.** to make trivial objections. *~n.* **2.** a trivial objection or equivocation, esp. one used to avoid an issue. **3.** *Archaic.* a pun.

quiche (kiːʃ) *n.* a savoury flan with an egg custard filling to which cheese, bacon, or vegetables are added.

quick (kwɪk) *adj.* **1.** lasting or taking a short time. **2.** characterized by rapidity of movement or action; fast. **3.** immediate or prompt. **4.** eager or ready to perform (an action): *quick to criticize.* **5.** responsive to stimulation; alert; lively. **6.** easily excited or aroused. **7.** nimble in one's movements or actions; deft: *quick fingers.* *~n.* **8.** any area of sensitive flesh, esp. that under a nail. **9. cut someone to the quick.** to hurt someone's feelings deeply. **10. the quick.** *Archaic.* living people. *~adv.* **11.** *Informal.* in a rapid manner; swiftly. —ˈ**quickly** *adv.*

quick-change artist *n.* an actor or entertainer who undertakes several rapid changes of costume during a performance.

quicken (ˈkwɪkən) *vb.* **1.** to make or become faster; accelerate. **2.** to impart to or receive vigour or enthusiasm: *science quickens the imagination.* **3. a.** (of a fetus) to begin to show signs of life. **b.** (of a pregnant woman) to reach the stage of pregnancy at which movements of the fetus can be felt.

quick-freeze *vb.* **-freezing, -froze, -frozen.** to preserve (food) by subjecting it to rapid refrigeration.

quickie (ˈkwɪkɪ) *n.* *Informal.* anything made or done rapidly.

quicklime (ˈkwɪkˌlaɪm) *n.* a white caustic solid, mainly composed of calcium oxide, used in the manufacture of glass and steel.

quicksand (ˈkwɪkˌsænd) *n.* a deep mass of loose wet sand that sucks anything on top of it inextricably into it.

quickset ('kwɪkˌsɛt) *Chiefly Brit.* ~*adj.* **1.** (of plants or cuttings) set so as to form a hedge. ~*n.* **2.** a hedge composed of such plants.

quicksilver ('kwɪkˌsɪlvə) *n.* the metal mercury.

quickstep ('kwɪkˌstɛp) *n.* **1.** a modern ballroom dance in rapid quadruple time. **2.** music for this dance.

quick-tempered *adj.* easy to anger.

quick-witted *adj.* having a keenly alert mind. —ˌquick-'wittedness *n.*

quid[1] (kwɪd) *n., pl.* **quid**. *Brit. slang.* **1.** a pound (sterling). **2. be quids in.** to be in a very favourable or advantageous position.

quid[2] (kwɪd) *n.* a piece of tobacco for chewing.

quiddity ('kwɪdɪtɪ) *n., pl.* **-ties. 1.** the essential nature of something. **2.** a petty or trifling distinction.

quid pro quo ('kwɪd prəʊ 'kwəʊ) *n., pl.* **quid pro quos.** one thing, esp. an advantage or object, given in exchange for another.

quiescent (kwɪ'ɛs³nt) *adj.* quiet, inactive, or dormant. —qui'escence *n.*

quiet ('kwaɪət) *adj.* **1.** characterized by an absence of noise. **2.** calm or tranquil: *the sea is quiet tonight.* **3.** untroubled: *a quiet life.* **4.** not busy: *business is quiet today.* **5.** private; secret: *a quiet word with someone.* **6.** free from anger, impatience, or other extreme emotion. **7.** not showy: *quiet colours; a quiet wedding.* **8.** modest or reserved: *quiet humour.* ~*n.* **9.** the state of being silent, peaceful, or untroubled. **10. on the quiet.** without other people knowing. ~*vb.* **11.** to make or become calm or silent. —'quietly *adv.*

quieten ('kwaɪət³n) *vb. Chiefly Brit.* **1.** (often foll. by *down*) to make or become calm or silent. **2.** to allay (fear or doubts).

quietism ('kwaɪəˌtɪzəm) *n.* passivity and calmness of mind towards external events. —'quietist *n., adj.*

quietude ('kwaɪəˌtjuːd) *n.* quietness, peace, or tranquillity.

quietus (kwaɪ'iːtəs, -'eɪtəs) *n., pl.* **-tuses. 1.** a release from life; death. **2.** the discharge or settlement of debts or duties.

quiff (kwɪf) *n. Brit.* a tuft of hair brushed up above the forehead.

quill (kwɪl) *n.* **1. a.** any of the large stiff feathers of the wing or tail of a bird. **b.** the hollow stem of a feather. **2.** Also called: **quill pen.** a feather made into a pen. **3.** any of the stiff hollow spines of a porcupine or hedgehog.

quilt (kwɪlt) *n.* **1.** a cover for a bed, consisting of a soft filling sewn between two layers of material, usually with crisscross seams. **2.** a continental quilt; duvet. ~*vb.* **3.** to stitch together (two pieces of fabric) with (padding) between them. —'quilted *adj.*

quin (kwɪn) *n.* a quintuplet.

quince (kwɪns) *n.* the acid-tasting pear-shaped fruit of an Asian tree, used in preserves.

quincentenary (ˌkwɪnsɛn'tiːnərɪ) *n., pl.* **-naries.** a 500th anniversary. —**quincentennial** (ˌkwɪnsɛn'tɛnɪəl) *adj., n.*

quincunx ('kwɪnkʌŋks) *n.* a group of five objects arranged in the shape of a rectangle with one at each corner and the fifth in the centre.

quinine (kwɪ'niːn; *U.S.* 'kwaɪnaɪn) *n.* a bitter drug extracted from cinchona bark, used as a tonic and formerly in malaria therapy.

Quinquagesima (ˌkwɪŋkwə'dʒɛsɪmə) *n.* the Sunday preceding Lent.

quinquennial (kwɪŋ'kwɛnɪəl) *adj.* occurring once every five years or over a period of five years.

quinquereme (ˌkwɪŋkwɪ'riːm) *n.* an ancient Roman galley with five banks of oars.

quinsy ('kwɪnzɪ) *n.* inflammation of the tonsils and throat, with abscesses.

quint (kwɪnt) *n. U.S. & Canad.* a quintuplet.

quintal ('kwɪnt³l) *n.* **1.** a unit of weight equal to (esp. in Britain) 112 pounds or (esp. in U.S.) 100 pounds. **2.** a unit of weight equal to 100 kilograms.

quintessence (kwɪn'tɛsəns) *n.* **1.** the most perfect representation of a quality or state. **2.** an extract of a substance containing its principle in its most concentrated form. —**quintessential** (ˌkwɪn tɪ'sɛnʃəl) *adj.*

quintet (kwɪn'tɛt) *n.* **1.** a group of five singers or instrumentalists or a piece of music composed for such a group. **2.** any group of five.

quintillion (kwɪn'tɪljən) *n., pl.* **-lions** or **-lion. 1.** (in Britain, France, and Germany) the number represented as one followed by 30 zeros (10^{30}). **2.** (in the U.S. and Canada) the number represented as one followed by 18 zeros (10^{18}).

quintuple ('kwɪntjʊp³l, kwɪn'tjuːp³l) *vb.* **1.** to multiply by five. ~*adj.* **2.** five times as much or as many. **3.** consisting of five parts. ~*n.* **4.** a quantity or number five times as great as another.

quintuplet ('kwɪntjʊplɪt, kwɪn'tjuːplɪt) *n.* one of five offspring born at one birth.

quip (kwɪp) *n.* **1.** a witty saying. ~*vb.* **quipping, quipped. 2.** to make a quip.

quire ('kwaɪə) *n.* a set of 24 or 25 sheets of paper.

quirk (kwɜːk) *n.* **1.** a peculiarity of character; mannerism or foible. **2.** an unexpected twist or turn: *a quirk of fate.* —'quirky *adj.*

quisling ('kwɪzlɪŋ) *n.* a traitor who aids an occupying enemy force; collaborator.

quit (kwɪt) *vb.* **quitting, quitted,** or *esp. U.S.* **quit. 1.** to depart from; leave. **2.** to resign; give up (a job). **3.** (of a tenant) to move out of premises. **4.** *Chiefly U.S.* to desist or cease from (something or doing something). ~*adj.* **5.** (foll. by *of*) free from; released from. —**'quitter** *n.*

quitch *or* **quitch grass** (kwɪtʃ) *n.* same as **couch grass.**

quite (kwaɪt) *adv.* **1.** absolutely: *you're quite right.* **2.** (*not used with a negative*) somewhat: *she's quite pretty.* **3.** in actuality; truly. **4. quite a** *or* **an.** (*not used with a negative*) of an exceptional kind: *quite a girl.* **5. quite something.** a remarkable thing or person. **6.** an expression used to indicate agreement.

quits (kwɪts) *adj. Informal.* **1.** on an equal footing. **2. call it quits.** to end a dispute or contest, agreeing that honours are even.

quittance ('kwɪt°ns) *n.* **1.** release from debt or other obligation. **2.** a document certifying this.

quiver[1] ('kwɪvə) *vb.* **1.** to shake with a tremulous movement; tremble. ~*n.* **2.** a shaking or trembling. —**'quivering** *adj.*

quiver[2] ('kwɪvə) *n.* a case for arrows.

quixotic (kwɪk'sɒtɪk) *adj.* unrealistically optimistic or chivalrous. —**quix'otically** *adv.*

quiz (kwɪz) *n., pl.* **quizzes. 1.** an entertainment in which the knowledge of the players is tested by a series of questions. **2.** any set of quick questions designed to test knowledge. **3.** an investigation by close questioning. ~*vb.* **quizzing, quizzed. 4.** to investigate by close questioning; interrogate.

quizzical ('kwɪzɪk°l) *adj.* questioning and mocking or supercilious. —**'quizzically** *adv.*

quod (kwɒd) *n. Slang, chiefly Brit.* a jail.

quoin (kwɔɪn, kɔɪn) *n.* **1.** an external corner of a wall. **2.** a cornerstone. **3.** a wedge.

quoit (kɔɪt) *n.* a large ring used in the game of quoits.

quoits (kɔɪts) *pl. n.* (*usually functioning as sing.*) a game in which quoits are tossed at a stake in the ground in attempts to encircle it.

quondam ('kwɒndæm) *adj.* of an earlier time; former: *her quondam lover.*

quorate ('kwɔːˌreɪt) *adj.* having or being a quorum: *the meeting is now quorate.*

quorum ('kwɔːrəm) *n.* the minimum number of members required to be present in a meeting or assembly before any business can be transacted.

quota ('kwəʊtə) *n.* **1.** the share that is due from, due to, or allocated to a person or group. **2.** the prescribed number or quantity allowed, required, or admitted. |

quotation (kwəʊ'teɪʃən) *n.* **1.** a written or spoken passage repeated exactly in a later work, speech, or conversation, usually with an acknowledgment of its source. **2.** the act of quoting. **3.** an estimate of costs submitted by a contractor to a prospective client.

quotation mark *n.* either of the punctuation marks used to begin or end a quotation, respectively " and " or ' and '.

quote (kwəʊt) *vb.* **1.** to repeat words exactly from an earlier work, speech, or conversation, usually with an acknowledgment of their source. **2.** to put quotation marks round (words). **3.** to state a price for goods or a job of work. ~*n.* **4.** *Informal.* a quotation. **5.** (*often pl.*) *Informal.* a quotation mark. ~*interj.* **6.** an expression used to indicate that the words that follow are a quotation. —**'quotable** *adj.*

quoth (kwəʊθ) *vb. Archaic.* (used before *I, he,* or *she*) said.

quotidian (kwəʊ'tɪdɪən) *adj.* **1.** daily. **2.** commonplace. **3.** (esp. of fever) recurring daily.

quotient ('kwəʊʃənt) *n.* the result of the division of one number or quantity by another.

q.v. (denoting a cross-reference) which (word, item, etc.) see.

qwerty *or* **QWERTY keyboard** ('kwɜːtɪ) *n.* the standard English language typewriter keyboard with the characters q, w, e, r, t, and y at the top left of the keyboard.

R

r *or* **R** (ɑː) *n., pl.* **r's, R's,** *or* **Rs. 1.** the 18th letter of the English alphabet. **2.** See **three Rs, the.**

R 1. *Chem.* radical. **2.** Registered Trademark. **3.** *Physics, electronics.* resistance. **4.** *Chess.* rook.

r. 1. Also: **r** radius. **2.** *Cricket.* run(s).

R. 1. Regina. **2.** Rex. **3.** Also: **r.** right. **4.** River.

Ra *Chem.* radium.

RA 1. rear admiral. **2.** (in Britain) Royal Academician *or* Academy. **3.** (in Britain) Royal Artillery.

rabbet (ˈræbɪt) *n.* **1.** a groove cut into a piece of timber to receive a mating piece. ~*vb.* **2.** to cut a rabbet in (timber). **3.** to join (pieces of timber) using a rabbet.

rabbi (ˈræbaɪ) *n., pl.* **-bis. 1.** the spiritual leader of a Jewish congregation. **2.** an expert in or teacher of Jewish Law. —**rabbinical** (rəˈbɪnɪk²l) *adj.*

rabbit (ˈræbɪt) *n., pl.* **-bits** *or* **-bit. 1.** a common burrowing mammal with long ears and a short fluffy tail. **2.** *Brit. informal.* a poor performer at a game or sport. ~*vb.* **3.** to hunt rabbits. **4.** (often foll. by *on* or *away*) *Brit. informal.* to talk inconsequentially; ramble.

rabbit punch *n.* a short sharp blow to the back of the neck.

rabble (ˈræb²l) *n.* **1.** a disorderly crowd; mob. **2. the rabble.** *Contemptuous.* the common people.

rabble-rouser *n.* a person who stirs up the passions of the mob; demagogue. —**ˈrabble-ˌrousing** *adj., n.*

Rabelaisian (ˌræbəˈleɪzɪən) *adj.* of or like the work of François Rabelais, French writer, in broad, often bawdy humour and sharp satire.

rabid (ˈræbɪd) *adj.* **1.** having rabies. **2.** fanatical: *a rabid Tory.* —**rabidity** (rəˈbɪdɪtɪ) *n.*

rabies (ˈreɪbiːz) *n. Pathol.* a fatal infectious viral disease of the nervous system transmitted by the saliva of infected animals, esp. dogs.

RAC 1. Royal Armoured Corps. **2.** Royal Automobile Club.

raccoon *or* **racoon** (rəˈkuːn) *n., pl.* **-coons** *or* **-coon.** an American mammal with a pointed muzzle, long tail, and greyish-black fur with black bands around the tail and across the face.

race¹ (reɪs) *n.* **1.** a contest of speed, as in running or driving. **2.** any competition or

rivalry: *the arms race.* **3.** a rapid current of water. **4.** a channel of a stream: *a mill race.* **5.** *Austral. & N.Z.* a narrow passage through which sheep pass individually, as to a sheep dip. ~*vb.* **6.** to engage in a contest of speed with (another). **7.** to enter (an animal or vehicle) in a race: *to race pigeons.* **8.** to travel as fast as possible. **9.** to operate at a higher speed than normal: *my heart raced; the engine began to race.* ~See also **races.**

race² (reɪs) *n.* **1.** a group of people of common ancestry, distinguished from others by physical characteristics, such as hair type, colour of skin, or stature. **2. the human race.** human beings collectively. **3.** a group of animals or plants having common characteristics that distinguish them from other members of the same species.

racecourse (ˈreɪsˌkɔːs) *n.* a long broad track, over which horses are raced.

racehorse (ˈreɪsˌhɔːs) *n.* a horse specially bred for racing.

raceme (rəˈsiːm) *n.* a cluster of flowers in which the flowers are borne along the main stem.

race meeting *n.* a prearranged fixture for racing horses or greyhounds over a set course.

race relations *n.* (*functioning as pl.*) the relations between members of two or more human races within a single community.

race riot *n.* a riot involving ill-feeling or violence between people of different races.

races (ˈreɪsɪz) *pl. n.* **the races.** a series of contests of speed between horses or greyhounds over a set course.

racetrack (ˈreɪsˌtræk) *n.* **1.** a circuit used for races between cars, bicycles, or runners. **2.** *U.S. & Canad.* a racecourse.

racial (ˈreɪʃəl) *adj.* **1.** denoting or relating to the division of the human species into races. **2.** characteristic of any such group. —**ˈracially** *adv.*

racism (ˈreɪsɪzəm) *or* **racialism** (ˈreɪʃəˌlɪzəm) *n.* **1.** discriminatory, oppressive, abusive, or aggressive behaviour towards people because they belong to a different race. **2.** the belief that races have distinctive cultural characteristics determined by hereditary factors and that this endows some races with an intrinsic superiority. —**ˈracist** *or* **ˈracialist** *n., adj.*

rack¹ (ræk) *n.* **1.** a framework for holding, carrying, or displaying a specific load or object. **2.** a toothed bar designed to engage a pinion to form a mechanism that will adjust the position of something. **3. the rack.** an instrument of torture that stretched the body of the victim. **4.** *U.S. & Canad.* (in pool or snooker) the triangular frame used to arrange the balls for the opening shot. ~*vb.* **5.** to cause great suffering to: *guilt racked his conscience.* **6.** to torture on the rack. **7.** to place or arrange in or on a rack. **8. rack one's brains.** to try very hard to think of something.

rack² (ræk) *n.* destruction (obs. except in **go to rack and ruin**).

rack³ (ræk) *vb.* to clear (wine or beer) by siphoning it off from the dregs.

rack-and-pinion *n.* a device for converting rotary into linear motion and vice versa, in which a gearwheel (the pinion) engages with a flat toothed bar (the rack).

racket¹ ('rækɪt) *n.* **1.** a noisy disturbance; clamour; din. **2.** an illegal enterprise carried on for profit; fraud. **3.** *Slang.* a business or occupation: *what's your racket?* ~*vb.* **4.** (often foll. by *about*) to make a commotion. —**'rackety** *adj.*

racket² *or* **racquet** ('rækɪt) *n.* a bat consisting of an open network of taut strings in an oval frame with a handle, used in games such as tennis, badminton, and squash. ~See also **rackets**.

racketeer (,rækɪ'tɪə) *n.* a person engaged in illegal enterprises for profit. —**,racket'eering** *n.*

rackets ('rækɪts) *n.* (*functioning as sing.*) a game similar to squash.

rack railway *n.* a steep mountain railway with a middle rail fitted with a rack that engages a pinion on the locomotive to provide traction.

rack-rent *n.* an extortionate rent.

raconteur (,rækɒn'tɜ) *n.* a person skilled in telling stories.

racoon (rə'ku:n) *n., pl.* **-coons** *or* **-coon.** same as **raccoon**.

racquet ('rækɪt) *n.* same as **racket²**.

racy ('reɪsɪ) *adj.* **racier, raciest. 1.** lively and spirited in style. **2.** risqué; suggestive. —**'racily** *adv.* —**'raciness** *n.*

RADA ('rɑːdə) *n.* (in Britain) Royal Academy of Dramatic Art.

radar ('reɪdɑː) *n.* **1.** a method of detecting the position and velocity of a distant object by bouncing a narrow beam of extremely high-frequency radio pulses off it. **2.** the equipment used in such detection.

radar trap *n.* a device using radar to detect motorists who exceed the speed limit.

raddled ('ræd³ld) *adj.* (of a person) unkempt or run-down in appearance.

radial ('reɪdɪəl) *adj.* **1.** (esp. of lines) emanating from a common central point; arranged like the radii of a circle. **2.** of a radius or ray. **3.** short for **radial-ply**. ~*n.* **4.** a radial-ply tyre. —**'radially** *adv.*

radial-ply *adj.* (of a tyre) having the fabric cords in the outer casing running radially to enable the sidewalls to be flexible.

radian ('reɪdɪən) *n.* an SI unit of plane angle; the angle between two radii of a circle that cut off on the circumference an arc equal in length to the radius. 1 radian is equivalent to 57.296 degrees.

radiant ('reɪdɪənt) *adj.* **1.** sending out rays of light; bright; shining. **2.** characterized by health and happiness: *a radiant smile.* **3.** emitted as radiation: *radiant heat.* **4.** sending out heat by radiation: *a radiant heater.* ~*n.* **5.** a point or object that emits radiation. —**'radiance** *n.* —**'radiantly** *adv.*

radiant energy *n.* energy that is emitted or propagated in the form of particles or electromagnetic radiation.

radiate *vb.* ('reɪdɪ,eɪt). **1.** to emit (heat, light, or other forms of radiation) or (of heat, light, etc.) to be emitted as radiation. **2.** (esp. of lines) to spread out from a centre or be arranged in a radial pattern. **3.** (of a person) to show (an emotion such as happiness) to a great degree. ~*adj.* ('reɪdɪɪt). **4.** having rays or a radial structure.

radiation (,reɪdɪ'eɪʃən) *n.* **1.** *Physics.* **a.** the emission of energy as particles, electromagnetic waves or sound. **b.** the particles or waves emitted. **2.** the act or state of radiating or being radiated.

radiation sickness *n.* illness caused by overexposure of the body to radiation from radioactive material or x-rays.

radiator ('reɪdɪ,eɪtə) *n.* **1.** a device for heating a room or building, consisting of a series of pipes through which hot water passes. **2.** a device for cooling an internal-combustion engine, consisting of thin-walled tubes through which water passes.

radical ('rædɪk³l) *adj.* **1.** of the essential nature of a person or thing; fundamental: *a radical fault.* **2.** searching or thoroughgoing: *radical thought.* **3.** favouring or tending to produce fundamental changes in political, economic, or social conditions or institutions: *a radical party.* **4.** *Maths.* of or containing roots of numbers or quantities. ~*n.* **5.** a person who favours fundamental change in existing institutions or in political, social, or economic conditions. **6.** *Maths.* a root of a number or quantity, such as $\sqrt[3]{5}$, $\sqrt{x}$. **7.** *Chem.* an atom or group of atoms which belongs as a unit during chemical reactions. —**'radica,lism** *n.* —**'radically** *adv.*

radical sign *n.* the symbol $\sqrt{}$ placed before a number or quantity to indicate the extraction of a root, esp. a square root. The value of a higher root is indicated by a raised digit in front of the symbol, as in $\sqrt[3]{}$.

radicle ('rædɪk³l) *n. Bot.* **a.** the part of the embryo of seed-bearing plants that develops into the main root. **b.** a very small root or rootlike part.

radii ('reɪdɪ,aɪ) *n.* a plural of **radius**.

radio ('reɪdɪəʊ) *n., pl.* **-dios. 1.** the use of electromagnetic waves for broadcasting or two-way communication without the use of linking wires. **2.** an electronic device for converting radio signals into sounds. **3.** a communications device for sending and receiving messages using radio waves. **4.** sound broadcasting. ~*adj.* **5.** of, produced for, or using radio broadcasting or radio signals: *radio drama; a radio station.* **6.** of, using, or producing electromagnetic waves in the range used for radio signals: *radio astronomy.* ~*vb.* **7.** to transmit (a message) to (a person, place, or vehicle) by means of radio waves.

radio- *combining form.* denoting: **1.** radio. **2.** radioactivity or radiation: *radiocarbon; radiochemistry.*

radioactive (,reɪdɪəʊ'æktɪv) *adj.* showing, using, or concerned with radioactivity.

radioactivity (,reɪdɪəʊæk'tɪvɪtɪ) *n.* the spontaneous emission of radiation from atomic nuclei. The radiation can consist of alpha or beta particles, or gamma rays.

radio astronomy *n.* astronomy using a radio telescope to analyse signals received from radio sources in space.

radiocarbon (,reɪdɪəʊ'kɑːbˀn) *n.* a radioactive isotope of carbon, esp. carbon-14.

radiocarbon dating *n.* same as **carbon dating**.

radiochemistry (,reɪdɪəʊ'kemɪstrɪ) *n.* the chemistry of radioactive substances.

radio-controlled *adj.* remote-controlled by means of radio signals.

radio frequency *n.* any electromagnetic frequency that lies in the range 10 kilohertz to 300 000 megahertz and can be used for broadcasting.

radiogram ('reɪdɪəʊ,græm) *n. Brit.* an old-fashioned unit comprising a radio and record player.

radiograph ('reɪdɪəʊ,grɑːf) *n.* an image produced on a special photographic film or plate by radiation, usually by x-rays.

radiography (,reɪdɪ'ɒɡrəfɪ) *n.* the production of radiographs for use in medicine or industry. —,**radi'ographer** *n.*

radioisotope (,reɪdɪəʊ'aɪsətəʊp) *n.* a radioactive isotope.

radiology (,reɪdɪ'ɒlədʒɪ) *n.* the use of x-rays and radioactive substances in the diagnosis and treatment of disease. —,**radi'ologist** *n.*

radiopaging ('reɪdɪəʊ,peɪdʒɪŋ) *n.* a system whereby a person carrying a small radio receiver (**pager**) is alerted when it emits a signal in response to a call.

radioscopy (,reɪdɪ'ɒskəpɪ) *n.* examination of a person or object by means of a fluorescent screen and an x-ray source.

radiosonde ('reɪdɪəʊ,sɒnd) *n.* an airborne instrument to send meteorological information back to earth by radio.

radiotelegraphy (,reɪdɪəʊtɪ'lɛɡrəfɪ) *n.* telegraphy in which messages are transmitted by radio waves.

radiotelephone (,reɪdɪəʊ'tɛlɪ,fəʊn) *n.* a telephone which sends and receives messages using radio waves rather than wires. —**radiotelephony** (,reɪdɪəʊtɪ'lɛfənɪ) *n.*

radio telescope *n.* an instrument used in radio astronomy to pick up and analyse radio waves from space.

radiotherapy (,reɪdɪəʊ'θerəpɪ) *n.* the treatment of disease, esp. of cancer, by means of radiation.

radish ('rædɪʃ) *n.* a small pungent red-skinned root vegetable which is eaten raw in salads.

radium ('reɪdɪəm) *n.* a highly radioactive luminescent metallic element, found in pitchblende. Symbol: Ra

radius ('reɪdɪəs) *n., pl.* **-dii** *or* **-diuses. 1.** a straight line joining the centre of a circle or sphere to any point on the circumference. **2.** the length of this line. **3.** *Anat.* the outer, slightly shorter of the two bones of the forearm. **4.** a circular area of a size indicated by the length of its radius: *within a radius of four miles.*

radon ('reɪdɒn) *n.* a colourless radioactive element of the noble gas group. Symbol: Rn

RAF (*Not standard* ræf) Royal Air Force.

Rafferty ('ræfətɪ) *or* **Rafferty's rules** *pl. n. Austral. & N.Z. slang.* no rules at all.

raffia ('ræfɪə) *n.* a fibre obtained from the leaves of a type of palm tree, and used for weaving.

raffish ('ræfɪʃ) *adj.* unconventional or slightly disreputable; rakish.

raffle ('ræfˀl) *n.* **1.** a lottery, often to raise money for charity, in which the prizes are goods rather than money. ~*vb.* **2.** to offer as a prize in a raffle.

raft (rɑːft) *n.* a buoyant platform of logs, planks, or oil drums used as a vessel or moored platform.

rafter ('rɑːftə) *n.* any of the parallel sloping beams that form the framework of a roof.

rag[1] (ræg) *n.* **1.** a small piece of cloth, such as one torn from a discarded garment, or such pieces of cloth collectively. **2.** *Informal, contemptuous.* a newspaper. **3.** (*pl.*) old, torn, or worn-out clothing.

rag[2] (ræg) *vb.* **ragging, ragged. 1.** to make teasing remarks about (a person). **2.** *Brit.* to play rough practical jokes on. ~*n.* **3.** *Brit.* a boisterous practical joke. **4.** (in British universities and colleges) a period in which various events are organized to raise money for charity.

rag[3] (ræg) *n.* a piece of ragtime music.

ragamuffin ('ræɡə,mʌfɪn) *n.* a ragged unkempt child.

rag-and-bone man *n. Brit.* a man who

buys and sells discarded items, such as old clothing or furniture.

ragbag ('ræg,bæg) n. a confused assortment; jumble.

rage (reidʒ) n. **1.** intense anger; fury. **2.** a fashion or craze: *skateboards are all the rage again.* **3.** *Austral. & N.Z. informal.* a dance or party. ~vb. **4.** to feel or exhibit intense anger. **5.** (esp. of storms, fires, and battle) to move or surge with great violence.

ragged ('rægid) adj. **1.** (of clothes) worn to rags; tattered. **2.** (of a person) dressed in tattered clothes. **3.** neglected; untidy: *ragged weeds.* **4.** having a rough or uneven surface or edge; jagged.

ragged robin n. a plant that has pink or white flowers with ragged petals.

raglan ('ræglən) adj. **1.** (of a sleeve) joined to the garment by seams running diagonally from the collar to underneath the armpit. **2.** (of a garment) having this style of sleeve.

ragout (ræ'guː) n. a richly seasoned stew of meat and vegetables.

ragtag ('ræg,tæg) n. **ragtag and bobtail.** the common people; rabble.

ragtime ('ræg,taim) n. a style of jazz piano music with a syncopated melody.

rag trade n. *Informal.* the clothing business.

ragwort ('ræg,wɜːt) n. a plant with ragged leaves and yellow flowers.

raid (reid) n. **1.** a sudden surprise attack: *an air raid.* **2.** a surprise visit by police searching for criminals or illicit goods: *a fraud squad raid.* ~vb. **3.** to make a raid against (a person or thing). **4.** to sneak into (a place) in order to steal: *raiding the kitchen for a late-night snack.* —'**raider** n.

rail[1] (reil) n. **1.** a horizontal bar supported by vertical posts, functioning as a fence or barrier. **2.** a horizontal bar on which to hang things: *a picture rail.* **3.** one of a pair of parallel bars that serve as a running surface for the wheels of a train. **4.** railway: *travel by rail.* **5. go off the rails.** to start behaving in a way considered improper or eccentric. ~vb. **6.** (usually foll. by *in* or *off*) to fence (an area) with rails.

rail[2] (reil) vb. (foll. by *at* or *against*) to complain bitterly or vehemently.

rail[3] (reil) n. any of various small cranelike wading marsh birds.

railcard ('reil,kɑːd) n. *Brit.* an identity card, which people such as pensioners or young people can buy, entitling the holder to reduced rail fares.

railhead ('reil,hed) n. **1.** a terminal of a railway. **2.** the farthest point reached by completed track on an unfinished railway.

railing ('reiliŋ) n. (often pl.) a fence or balustrade that consists of rails.

raillery ('reiləri) n., pl. -**leries.** light-hearted ridicule.

railroad ('reil,rəʊd) n. **1.** *U.S.* a railway. ~vb. **2.** *Informal.* to force (a person) into (an action) with haste or by unfair means.

railway ('reil,wei) n. **1.** a track composed of a line of parallel metal rails fixed to sleepers, for trains to run on. **2.** any track for the wheels of a vehicle to run on: *a cable railway.* **3.** the rolling stock, buildings, and tracks used in such a transport system. **4.** the organization responsible for operating a railway network.

raiment ('reimənt) n. *Archaic or poetic.* clothing.

rain (rein) n. **1. a.** water falling from the sky in drops formed by the condensation of water vapour in the atmosphere. **b.** a fall of rain; shower. **2.** a large quantity of anything falling rapidly: *a rain of bullets.* **3. (come) rain or (come) shine.** regardless of circumstances. **4. right as rain.** *Brit. informal.* perfectly all right. ~vb. **5.** (with *it* as subject) to be the case that rain is falling. **6.** to fall or cause to fall like rain: *to rain abuse on someone.* **7. rained off.** cancelled or postponed on account of rain. *U.S. and Canad.* term: **rained out.** ~See also **rains.** —'**rainy** adj.

rainbow ('rein,bəʊ) n. a bow-shaped display in the sky of the colours of the spectrum, caused by the refraction and reflection of the sun's rays through rain.

rainbow trout n. a freshwater trout of North American origin, with black spots and two longitudinal red stripes.

raincoat ('rein,kəʊt) n. a coat made of a waterproof material.

rainfall ('rein,fɔːl) n. the amount of rain, hail, or snow in a specified place and time.

rainforest ('rein,fɒrist) n. dense forest found in tropical areas of heavy rainfall.

rains (reinz) pl. n. **the rains.** the season of heavy rainfall, esp. in the tropics.

rainwater ('rein,wɔːtə) n. pure water from rain.

rainy day n. a future time of need, esp. financial.

raise (reiz) vb. **1.** to elevate to a higher position or level; lift. **2.** to place in an upright position. **3.** to build: *to raise a barn.* **4.** to increase in amount, value, intensity, etc.: *we must raise our prices; to raise one's voice.* **5.** to advance in rank; promote. **6.** to arouse from sleep or death. **7.** to stir up: *to raise a mutiny.* **8. raise Cain. a.** to create a disturbance. **b.** to protest vehemently. **9.** to put forward for consideration: *to raise a question.* **10.** to collect or gather together: *raising money for charity; to raise an army.* **11.** to grow: *to raise a crop.* **12.** to bring up; rear: *to raise a family.* **13.** to cause to be expressed: *to raise a smile.* **14.** to bring to an end: *to raise a siege.* **15.** to cause (dough) to rise, as by the addition of yeast. **16.** to establish radio communications with: *we raised Moscow last night.* **17.** *Maths.* to multiply (a number) by itself a specified number of times: *8 is 2 raised to the power 3.* ~*n.* **18.** the act of raising. **19.** *Chiefly U.S. & Canad.* an increase in pay.

raised ('reɪzd) *adj.* higher than the surrounding area: *a raised platform.*

raisin ('reɪz°n) *n.* a dried grape.

raison d'être ('reɪzɒn 'dɛtrə) *n., pl.* **raisons d'être** ('reɪzɒn 'dɛtrə). reason or justification for existence.

raj (rɑːdʒ) *n.* **the Raj.** the British government in India before 1947.

rajah *or* **raja** ('rɑːdʒə) *n.* (in India, formerly) a ruler: sometimes used as a title preceding a name.

rake[1] (reɪk) *n.* **1.** a farm or garden tool consisting of a row of teeth set in a headpiece attached to a long shaft and used for gathering leaves or straw, or for smoothing loose earth. **2.** any of various implements similar in shape or function. ~*vb.* **3.** to scrape, gather, or remove (leaves, refuse, or hay) with a rake. **4.** to level or prepare (a surface) with a rake. **5.** (sometimes foll. by *out*) to clear (ashes) from (a fire). **6.** (foll. by *up* or *together*) to gather (items or people) with difficulty, as from a limited supply. **7.** (often foll. by *through* or *over*) to search or examine carefully. **8.** to scrape or graze: *the ship raked the side of the quay.* **9.** to direct (gunfire) along the length of (a target): *machine-guns raked the column.* ~See also **rake in, rake-off,** etc.

rake[2] (reɪk) *n.* a dissolute man, esp. one in fashionable society.

rake[3] (reɪk) *vb.* **1.** to slope from the vertical, esp. (of a ship's mast) towards the stern. **2.** to construct with a backward slope. ~*n.* **3.** the degree to which an object slopes.

rake in *vb. Informal.* to acquire (money) in large amounts.

rake-off *n. Slang.* a share of profits, esp. an illegal one.

rake up *vb.* to revive (something forgotten): *to rake up an old quarrel.*

rakish[1] ('reɪkɪʃ) *adj.* dissolute; profligate. —**'rakishly** *adv.*

rakish[2] ('reɪkɪʃ) *adj.* dashing; jaunty: *a hat set at a rakish angle.*

rallentando (ˌrælɛn'tændəʊ) *adj., adv. Music.* becoming slower.

rally[1] ('rælɪ) *vb.* **-lying, -lied. 1.** to bring (a group) into order, as after dispersal, or (of such a group) to come to order. **2.** to come or bring together for a common cause. **3.** to summon up (one's strength or spirits). **4.** to recover (sometimes only temporarily) from an illness. **5.** *Stock Exchange.* to increase sharply after a decline. **6.** *Tennis, squash, etc.* to exchange a series of shots before one player wins the point. ~*n., pl.* **-lies. 7.** a

large gathering of people for a common purpose. **8.** a marked recovery of strength, as during illness. **9.** *Stock Exchange.* a sharp increase in price or trading activity after a decline. **10.** *Tennis, squash, etc.* an exchange of several shots before one player wins the point. **11.** a type of motor competition over public roads. —**'rallier** *n.*

rally[2] ('rælɪ) *vb.* **-lying, -lied.** to mock or tease (someone) in a good-natured way.

rally round *vb.* to come to the aid of (someone); offer support.

ram (ræm) *n.* **1.** an uncastrated adult male sheep. **2.** a hydraulically or pneumatically driven piston. **3.** the falling weight of a pile driver. **4.** short for **battering ram.** ~*vb.* **ramming, rammed. 5.** (usually foll. by *into*) to force or drive, as by heavy blows: *to ram a post into the ground.* **6.** to crash violently. **7.** to stuff, cram, or thrust violently. **8. ram (something) down someone's throat.** to put forward or emphasize (an argument or idea) with excessive force.

RAM (ræm) *n. Computers.* random access memory: a temporary storage space which loses its contents when the computer is switched off.

Ramadan (ˌræmə'dɑːn) *n.* **1.** the ninth month of the Muslim year, 30 days long, during which strict fasting is observed from sunrise to sunset. **2.** the fast itself.

ramble ('ræmb°l) *vb.* **1.** to walk for relaxation, sometimes with no particular direction. **2.** to grow or develop in a random fashion. **3.** to speak or write in a confused disconnected style. ~*n.* **4.** a walk, esp. in the countryside. —**'rambling** *adj.*

rambler ('ræmblə) *n.* **1.** a person who takes country walks. **2.** a vigorous climbing and spreading rose.

RAMC Royal Army Medical Corps.

ramekin ('ræmɪkɪn) *n.* a small container for baking and serving one portion of food.

ramification (ˌræmɪfɪ'keɪʃən) *n.* **1.** a consequence or complication. **2.** a structure of branching parts. —**'ramify** *vb.*

ramp (ræmp) *n.* **1.** a slope that joins two surfaces at different levels, such as one designed to be used instead of steps for someone pushing a pram. **2.** a place where the level of a road surface changes because of road works. **3.** a movable stairway by which passengers enter and leave an aircraft. ~*vb.* **4.** to act in a violent or threatening manner (esp. in **ramp and rage**).

rampage *vb.* (ræm'peɪdʒ). **1.** to rush about in a violent disorderly fashion. ~*n.* ('ræmpeɪdʒ). **2. on the rampage.** behaving violently or destructively.

rampant ('ræmpənt) *adj.* **1.** unrestrained or violent in growth or spread. **2.** *Heraldry.* (of a beast) standing on the hind legs, the right foreleg raised above the left.

rampart ('ræmpɑːt) *n.* the surrounding embankment of a fort, often with a wall or parapets built on it.

rampike ('ræm,paik) n. Canad. a tall tree that has been burned bare of branches.

ramrod ('ræm,rɒd) n. a rod for cleaning the barrel of a gun or for ramming the charge of a muzzle-loading firearm into place.

ramshackle ('ræm,ʃæk³l) adj. (esp. of buildings) rickety, shaky, or derelict.

ran (ræn) vb. the past tense of **run**.

ranch (rɑːntʃ) n. 1. a large farm, esp. in North America, for rearing livestock, esp. cattle. 2. Chiefly U.S. & Canad. any large farm for the rearing of a particular kind of livestock or crop: a mink ranch. ~vb. 3. to run a ranch. —'rancher n.

rancherie ('rɑːntʃərɪ) n. (in British Columbia, Canada) a settlement of North American Indians.

rancid ('rænsɪd) adj. (of food, or a taste or smell) rank or sour; stale. —'rancidness or rancidity (ræn'sɪdɪtɪ) n.

rancour or U.S. **rancor** ('ræŋkə) n. bitter resentfulness or hostility. —'rancorous adj.

rand (rænd, rɒnt) n. the standard monetary unit of the Republic of South Africa.

R & B rhythm and blues.

R & D research and development.

random ('rændəm) adj. 1. lacking any definite plan or prearranged order; haphazard: a random selection. ~n. 2. **at random**. not following any prearranged order. —'randomly adv. —'randomness n.

random access n. a method of reading data from a computer file without having to read through the file from the beginning.

randy ('rændɪ) adj. **randier, randiest**. Informal, chiefly Brit. sexually eager or lustful. —'randily adv. —'randiness n.

ranee ('rɑːnɪ) n. same as **rani**.

rang (ræŋ) vb. the past tense of **ring**².

rangatira (,rʌŋgə'tɪərə) n. N.Z. a Maori chief of either sex.

range (reɪndʒ) n. 1. the limits within which a person or thing can function effectively: the range of vision. 2. the limits within which something can lie: a range of prices. 3. the total products of a manufacturer, designer, or stockist: the new spring range. 4. **a.** the maximum effective distance of a projectile fired from a weapon. **b.** the distance between a target and a weapon. 5. an area set aside for shooting practice or rocket testing. 6. the total distance which a ship, aircraft, or land vehicle is capable of covering without taking on fresh fuel. 7. the difference in pitch between the highest and lowest note of a voice or musical instrument. 8. Maths. the set of values that a function or variable can take. 9. U.S. & Canad. an extensive tract of open land on which livestock can graze. 10. a rank, row, or series of items. 11. a chain of mountains. 12. a large cooking stove with one or more ovens, usually heated by solid fuel. ~vb. 13. to establish or be situated in a line or series. 14. (often reflexive, foll. by with) to put into a specific category; classify: she ranged herself with the opposition. 15. to roam (over). 16. to fluctuate within specific limits: their ages range from 22 to 35. 17. to cover a specified period or specified things: her book ranged as far back as the Middle Ages.

rangefinder ('reɪndʒ,faɪndə) n. an instrument for determining how far away an object is, esp. in order to sight a gun or focus a camera.

ranger ('reɪndʒə) n. 1. (sometimes cap.) an official in charge of a forest, park, or nature reserve. 2. U.S. one of a body of armed troops employed to police a State or district: a Texas ranger.

Ranger or **Ranger Guide** ('reɪndʒə) n. Brit. a member of the senior branch of the Guides.

rangy ('reɪndʒɪ) adj. **rangier, rangiest**. having long slender limbs.

rani or **ranee** ('rɑːnɪ) n. the wife of a rajah.

rank¹ (ræŋk) n. 1. a position within a social organization: the rank of captain. 2. high social or other standing; status. 3. a line or row of people or things. 4. the position of an item in any ordering or sequence. 5. Brit. a place where taxis wait to be hired. 6. a line of people, esp. soldiers, positioned one beside the other. 7. **close ranks**. to maintain solidarity. 8. **pull rank**. to get one's own way by virtue of one's superior position. 9. **rank and file**. the great mass of any group, as opposed to the leadership. ~vb. 10. to arrange (people or things) in rows or lines. 11. to give or hold a specific position in an organization or group. 12. to arrange in sequence: to rank students by their test scores. 13. to be important; rate: money ranks low in her order of priorities.

rank² (ræŋk) adj. 1. showing vigorous and profuse growth: rank weeds. 2. highly offensive or disagreeable, esp. in smell or taste. 3. absolute; utter: a rank outsider.

rankle ('ræŋk³l) vb. to cause severe and continuous irritation, anger, or bitterness.

ransack ('rænsæk) vb. 1. to search through every part of (a place or thing). 2. to plunder; pillage.

ransom ('rænsəm) n. 1. the release of captured prisoners on payment of a stipulated price. 2. the price demanded for such a release. 3. **hold to ransom**. **a.** to keep (a prisoner) in confinement until payment is received. **b.** to attempt to force (a person) to comply with one's demands. ~vb. 4. to pay a stipulated price and so obtain the release of (prisoners). 5. to set free (prisoners) upon receiving the payment demanded. —'ransomer n.

rant (rænt) vb. 1. to utter (something) in

loud, violent, or bombastic tones. ~*n.* **2.** loud, declamatory, or extravagant speech. —'**ranting** *adj., n.*

RAOC Royal Army Ordnance Corps.

rap[1] (ræp) *vb.* **rapping, rapped. 1.** to strike (a fist, stick, etc.) against (something) with a sharp quick blow; knock. **2.** to knock loudly and sharply. **3.** to rebuke or criticize sharply. **4.** (foll. by *out*) to utter in sharp rapid speech: *to rap out orders.* **5.** *Slang.* to talk volubly. **6.** to perform a rhythmic monologue with musical backing. **7. rap over the knuckles.** to reprimand. ~*n.* **8.** a sharp quick blow or the sound produced by it. **9.** a sharp rebuke or criticism. **10.** a fast, rhythmic monologue over a musical backing. **11. take the rap.** *Slang.* to suffer the punishment for a crime, whether guilty or not. —'**rapper** *n.*

rap[2] (ræp) *n.* (*used with a negative*) the least amount.

rapacious (rə'peɪʃəs) *adj.* **1.** greedy or grasping. **2.** (of animals, esp. birds) subsisting by catching living prey. —**rapacity** (rə'pæsɪtɪ) *n.*

rape[1] (reɪp) *n.* **1.** the offence of forcing a person, esp. a woman, to submit to sexual intercourse against that person's will. **2.** any violation or abuse: *the rape of justice.* ~*vb.* **3.** to force (a person) to submit to sexual intercourse against that person's will. —'**rapist** *n.*

rape[2] (reɪp) *n.* a yellow-flowered plant cultivated for its seeds, **rapeseed,** which yield a useful oil, **rape oil,** and as a fodder plant.

rapid ('ræpɪd) *adj.* **1.** (of an action) taking or lasting a short time; quick. **2.** acting or moving quickly; fast: *a rapid worker.* —'**rapidly** *adv.* —**rapidity** (rə'pɪdɪtɪ) *or* '**rapidness** *n.*

rapids ('ræpɪdz) *pl. n.* part of a river where the water is very fast and turbulent.

rapier ('reɪpɪə) *n.* a long narrow two-edged sword used as a thrusting weapon.

rapine ('ræpaɪn) *n.* pillage or plundering.

rapport (ræ'pɔː) *n.* (often foll. by *with*) a sympathetic relationship or understanding.

rapprochement (ræ'prɒʃmɒn) *n.* a resumption of friendly relations, esp. between two countries.

rapscallion (ræp'skæljən) *n.* a rascal or rogue.

rapt (ræpt) *adj.* **1.** totally engrossed; spellbound: *rapt with wonder.* **2.** characterized by or proceeding from rapture: *a rapt smile.*

raptor ('ræptə) *n.* any bird of prey. —**rap**'**torial** *adj.*

rapture ('ræptʃə) *n.* **1.** extreme happiness or delight; joyous ecstasy. **2.** (*often pl.*) an expression of ecstatic joy. —'**rapturous** *adj.*

rare[1] (rɛə) *adj.* **1.** uncommon or unusual: *a rare word.* **2.** (of a gas, esp. the atmosphere at high altitudes) having a low density; thin; rarefied. **3.** showing uncommon excellence: *rare skill.*

rare[2] (rɛə) *adj.* (of meat) very lighty cooked.

rarebit ('rɛəbɪt) *n.* same as **Welsh rabbit.**

rare earth *n.* **1.** any oxide of a lanthanide. **2.** Also called: **rare-earth element.** any element of the lanthanide series.

rarefied ('rɛərɪˌfaɪd) *adj.* **1.** exalted in character; lofty: *a rarefied spiritual existence.* **2.** current within only a small group. **3.** thin: *air rarefied at altitude.*

rarefy ('rɛərɪˌfaɪ) *vb.* -**fying, -fied.** to make or become less dense; thin out.

rarely ('rɛəlɪ) *adv.* **1.** hardly ever; seldom. **2.** to an unusual degree; exceptionally.

raring ('rɛərɪŋ) *adj.* ready; willing; enthusiastic (esp. in **raring to go**).

rarity ('rɛərɪtɪ) *n., pl.* -**ties. 1.** something valued because it is uncommon. **2.** the state of being rare.

rascal ('rɑːskəl) *n.* **1.** a scoundrel or rogue. **2.** a mischievous child. —'**rascally** *adj.*

rase (reɪz) *vb.* same as **raze.**

rash[1] (ræʃ) *adj.* hasty, impetuous, or reckless. —'**rashly** *adv.* —'**rashness** *n.*

rash[2] (ræʃ) *n.* an outbreak of spots, swellings, or reddening on the skin, caused by illness or allergy.

rasher ('ræʃə) *n.* a thin slice of bacon or ham.

rasp (rɑːsp) *n.* **1.** a harsh grating noise. **2.** a coarse file with rows of raised teeth. ~*vb.* **3.** to scrape or rub (something) roughly, esp. with a rasp. **4.** to make a harsh grating noise. **5.** to irritate (one's nerves); grate (upon).

raspberry ('rɑːzbrɪ) *n., pl.* -**ries. 1.** the red fruits of a prickly shrub of Europe and North America. **2.** a spluttering noise made with the tongue and lips to express contempt: *she blew a loud raspberry.*

Rastafarian (ˌræstə'fɛərɪən) *n.* a believer in a religion of Jamaican origin that regards Ras Tafari, the former emperor of Ethiopia, Haile Selassie, as God. Often shortened to **Rasta.**

rat (ræt) *n.* **1.** a long-tailed rodent, similar to but larger than a mouse. **2.** *Informal.* someone who is disloyal or treacherous. **3. smell a rat.** to detect something suspicious. ~*vb.* **4.** (usually foll. by *on*) to betray (a person) or go back on (an agreement). **5.** to hunt and kill rats.

ratable *or* **rateable** ('reɪtəb²l) *adj.* **1.** able to be rated or evaluated. **2.** *Brit.* (of property) liable to payment of rates.

ratable value *or* **rateable value** *n. Brit.* a fixed value assigned to a property, used to assess the rates due on it.

ratan (ræ'tæn) *n.* same as **rattan.**

ratatat-tat ('rætəˌtæt'tæt) *or* **ratatat** ('rætə'tæt) *n.* the sound of knocking on a door.

ratatouille (ˌrætəˈtwiː) *n.* a vegetable casserole made of tomatoes, aubergines, etc., stewed slowly in oil.

ratbag (ˈrætˌbæg) *n. Slang.* an eccentric or despicable person.

ratchet (ˈrætʃɪt) *n.* **1.** a device in which a toothed rack or wheel is engaged by a pivoted lever which permits motion in one direction only. **2.** the toothed rack or wheel in such a device.

rate¹ (reɪt) *n.* **1.** a quantity or amount considered in relation to or measured against another quantity or amount: *a rate of 70 miles an hour.* **2.** a price or charge with reference to a standard or scale: *rate of interest.* **3.** a charge made per unit for a commodity or service. **4.** See **rates. 5.** the speed of progress or change; pace: *the rate of production has doubled.* **6.** relative quality; class or grade: *first-rate ideas.* **7. at any rate.** in any case; anyway. ~*vb.* **8.** to assign a position on a scale of relative values; rank: *he is rated fifth in the world.* **9.** to estimate the value of: *we rate your services highly.* **10.** to be worthy of; deserve: *this hotel does not rate four stars.* **11.** to consider; regard: *I rate him among my friends.* **12.** *Brit.* to assess the value of (property) for the purpose of local taxation.

rate² (reɪt) *vb.* to scold or criticize severely.

rate-cap (ˈreɪtˌkæp) *vb.* **-capping, -capped.** (in Britain) to impose on (a local authority) an upper limit on the rates it may levy. —ˈrate-ˌcapping *n.*

ratepayer (ˈreɪtˌpeɪə) *n. Brit.* a person who pays local rates, esp. a householder.

rates (reɪts) *pl. n. Brit.* a tax on property levied by a local authority.

rather (ˈrɑːðə) *adv.* **1.** fairly; somewhat: *she's rather pretty; it's rather dull.* **2.** to a limited extent: *I rather thought that was the case.* **3.** more truly or appropriately: *it's no cause for congratulation, but rather for concern.* **4.** more willingly; sooner: *I would rather not see you tomorrow.* ~*interj.* (ˈrɑːˈðɜː) **5.** an expression of strong affirmation: *Is it worth seeing? Rather!*
Usage. Both *would* and *had* are used with *rather* in sentences such as *I would rather* (or *had rather*) *go to the film than to the play. Had rather* is less common and now regarded as old-fashioned.

ratify (ˈrætɪˌfaɪ) *vb.* **-fying, -fied.** to give formal consent to. —ˌratifiˈcation *n.*

rating (ˈreɪtɪŋ) *n.* **1.** a classification according to order or grade; ranking. **2.** an ordinary seaman. **3.** the estimated financial or credit standing of a business enterprise or individual. **4.** *Radio & television.* the proportion of the total audience that tunes in to a specific programme.

ratio (ˈreɪʃɪəʊ) *n., pl.* **-tios. 1.** a measure of the relative size of two classes expressible as a proportion: *the ratio of boys to girls is 2 to 1.* **2.** *Maths.* a quotient of two numbers or quantities.

ration (ˈræʃən) *n.* **1.** a fixed allowance of something that is scarce, such as food or petrol in wartime. **2.** (*usually pl.*) a fixed daily allowance of food, as in the armed forces. ~*vb.* **3.** (often foll. by *out*) to distribute (provisions), esp. to an army. **4.** to restrict the distribution of (a commodity): *the government has rationed sugar.* —ˈrationing *n.*

rational (ˈræʃənˀl) *adj.* **1.** using reason or logic in thinking out a problem. **2.** sensible; reasonable. **3.** of sound mind; sane: *the patient seemed quite rational.* **4.** able to reason: *man is a rational being.* **5.** *Maths.* expressible as a ratio of two integers: *a rational number.* —ˌratioˈnality *n.* —ˈrationally *adv.*

rationale (ˌræʃəˈnɑːl) *n.* the fundamental reasons on which an action, decision, or belief is based.

rationalism (ˈræʃənəˌlɪzəm) *n.* reliance on reason rather than intuition or experience as the basis for beliefs or actions. —ˈrationalist *n.* —ˌrationalˈistic *adj.*

rationalize or **-ise** (ˈræʃənəˌlaɪz) *vb.* **1.** to justify (one's actions) with plausible reasons, esp. after the event. **2.** to apply logic or reason to (something). **3.** to get rid of unnecessary equipment or staff from (a workplace or industry), in order to make it more efficient. —ˌrationaliˈzation or -iˈsation *n.*

rational number *n.* any real number of the form *a/b*, where *a* and *b* are integers and *b* is not zero, as 7 or 7/3.

rat race *n.* a continual routine of hectic competitive activity: *working in the City is a real rat race.*

ratsbane (ˈrætsˌbeɪn) *n.* rat poison.

rattan or **ratan** (ræˈtæn) *n.* a climbing palm with tough stems used for wickerwork and canes.

ratter (ˈrætə) *n.* a dog or cat that catches and kills rats.

rattle (ˈrætˀl) *vb.* **1.** to make a rapid succession of short sharp sounds, as of loose pellets colliding when shaken in a container. **2.** to shake, producing such a sound. **3.** to send, move, or drive with such a sound: *the car rattled along the country road.* **4.** (foll. by *on* or *away*) to chatter idly: *he rattled on about his work.* **5.** (foll. by *off* or *out*) to recite perfunctorily or rapidly. **6.** *Informal.* to disconcert; make frightened or anxious. ~*n.* **7.** a rapid succession of short sharp sounds. **8.** a baby's toy filled with small pellets that rattle when shaken. —ˈrattly *adj.*

rattlesnake (ˈrætˀlˌsneɪk) *n.* a poisonous New World snake with a series of loose horny segments on the tail that are vibrated to produce a whirring sound.

rattletrap ('ræt°l,træp) *n. Informal.* a broken-down old vehicle, esp. an old car.

rattling ('rætlıŋ) *adv. Informal, old-fashioned.* very; exceptionally: *a rattling good lunch.*

ratty ('rætı) *adj.* **-tier, -tiest. 1.** *Brit. & N.Z. informal.* irritable; annoyed. **2.** *Informal.* (of the hair) straggly and greasy. —'**rattily** *adv.* —'**rattiness** *n.*

raucous ('rɔːkəs) *adj.* harshly or hoarsely loud.

raunchy ('rɔːntʃı) *adj.* **-chier, -chiest.** *Slang.* openly sexual; earthy.

ravage ('rævıdʒ) *vb.* **1.** to cause extensive damage to. ~*n.* **2.** (*often pl.*) destructive action: *the ravages of time.*

rave (reɪv) *vb.* **1.** to utter (something) in a wild or incoherent manner, as when delirious. **2.** (foll. by *over* or *about*) to write or speak (about) with great enthusiasm. ~*n.* **3.** *Informal.* an enthusiastically favourable review. **4.** Also called: **rave-up.** *Brit. slang.* a party.

ravel ('ræv°l) *vb.* **-elling, -elled** *or U.S.* **-eling, -eled. 1.** to tangle or become entangled. **2.** (*often foll. by out*) to tease out (the fibres of a fabric) or (of a fabric) to fray out in loose ends; unravel. **3.** (*usually foll. by out*) to disentangle: *to ravel out a complicated story.*

raven ('reɪv°n) *n.* **1.** a large bird of the crow family with a long wedge-shaped tail and shiny black feathers. **2.** a shiny black colour.

ravening ('rævənıŋ) *adj.* (of animals) hungrily searching for prey; predatory.

ravenous ('rævənəs) *adj.* **1.** famished; starving. **2.** rapacious; ravening. —'**ravenously** *adv.*

raver ('reɪvə) *n. Brit. slang.* a person who leads a wild or uninhibited social life.

ravine (rə'viːn) *n.* a deep narrow steep-sided valley.

raving ('reɪvıŋ) *adj.* **1. a.** delirious; frenzied. **b.** (*as adv.*): *raving mad.* **2.** *Informal.* great or exceptional: *a raving beauty.* ~*n.* **3.** (*usually pl.*) frenzied or wildly extravagant talk or utterances.

ravioli (,rævı'əʊlı) *n.* small squares of pasta containing a savoury filling, such as meat or cheese.

ravish ('rævıʃ) *vb.* **1.** (*often passive*) to enrapture. **2.** to rape. —'**ravishment** *n.*

ravishing ('rævıʃıŋ) *adj.* delightful; lovely; entrancing. —'**ravishingly** *adv.*

raw (rɔː) *adj.* **1.** (of food) not cooked. **2.** in an unfinished, natural, or unrefined state; not processed: *raw materials.* **3.** (of the skin or a wound) having the surface exposed or scraped away, esp. painfully. **4.** untrained, inexperienced, or immature: *a raw recruit.* **5.** not selected or modified: *raw statistics.* **6.** frank or realistic: *a raw picture of a marriage.* **7.** (of the weather) harshly cold and damp. **8.** *Informal.* unfair; unjust (esp. in **a raw deal**). ~*n.* **9. in the raw. a.** *Informal.* naked. **b.** in a natural state. **10. the raw.** *Brit. informal.* a sensitive point: *his criticism touched me on the raw.*

rawboned ('rɔː'bəʊnd) *adj.* having a lean bony physique.

rawhide ('rɔː,haɪd) *n.* **1.** untanned hide. **2.** a whip or rope made of strips of this.

ray¹ (reɪ) *n.* **1.** a narrow beam of light. **2.** a slight indication: *a ray of solace.* **3.** *Maths.* a straight line extending from a point. **4.** a thin beam of electromagnetic radiation or particles. **5.** any of a set of lines emerging from a central point. **6.** any of the spines that support the fin of a fish.

ray² (reɪ) *n.* a sea fish related to the sharks, with a flattened body and a long whiplike tail.

ray³ (reɪ) *n. Music.* (in tonic sol-fa) the second degree of any major scale.

rayon ('reɪɒn) *n.* a textile fibre or fabric made from cellulose.

raze *or* **rase** (reɪz) *vb.* to demolish (buildings, towns, etc.) completely.

razoo (rɑː'zuː) *n., pl.* **-zoos.** *Austral. & N.Z. informal.* an imaginary coin: *not a brass razoo left.*

razor ('reɪzə) *n.* an implement with a sharp blade, used esp. for shaving the face.

razorbill ('reɪzə,bıl) *n.* a common black-and-white auk with a deep narrow bill.

razor wire *n.* strong wire with pieces of sharp metal set across it at intervals.

razzle-dazzle ('ræz°l'dæz°l) *or* **razzma-tazz** ('ræzmə'tæz) *n. Slang.* **1.** noisy or showy fuss or activity. **2.** a spree or frolic.

Rb *Chem.* rubidium.

RC Roman Catholic.

Rd road.

re¹ (reɪ, riː) *n. Music.* same as **ray³**.

re² (riː) *prep.* with reference to: used esp. in the headings of business letters.

Usage. *Re* is acceptable in everyday business correspondence: *re your note of June 10; she spoke to me re your complaint.* In formal business correspondence, *re* is generally used only in a letter heading. In general English, *with reference to* or *about* should be used rather than *re*: *with reference to your letter; she spoke to me about your complaint.*

Re *Chem.* rhenium.

RE 1. Religious Education. **2.** Royal Engineers.

re- *prefix.* used with many main words to mean: **1.** return to a previous condition: *rebuild; react.* **2.** repetition of an action: *remarry.*

Usage. Verbs with *re-* indicate repetition or restoration. It is unnecessary to add an adverb such as *back* or *again*: *This must not recur* (not *recur again*).

reach (riːtʃ) *vb.* **1.** to arrive at or get to (a place): *to reach the office.* **2.** to extend as far as (a point or place): *to reach the ceiling; can you reach?* **3.** to come to (a certain condition or situation): *to reach the point of starvation.* **4.** to arrive at or amount to (an amount or value): *temperatures in Greece reached 35° C yesterday.* **5.** *Informal.* to pass or give (something to a person) with the outstretched hand. **6.** (foll. by *out, for,* or *after*) to make a movement (towards), as if to grasp or touch. **7.** to make contact or communication with (someone): *we tried to reach him all day.* ~*n.* **8.** the extent or distance of reaching: *within reach.* **9.** the range of influence or power. **10.** an open stretch of water, esp. on a river. —'**reachable** *adj.*

reach-me-down *adj.* cheaply ready-made or second-hand: *reach-me-down finery.*

react (rɪ'ækt) *vb.* **1.** (of a person or thing) to act in response to another person, a stimulus, or a situation. **2.** (foll. by *against*) to act in an opposing or contrary manner. **3.** *Physics.* to exert an equal force in the opposite direction to an acting force. **4.** *Chem.* to undergo a chemical reaction. —re'**active** *adj.* —**reactivity** (ˌriːæk-'tɪvɪtɪ) *n.*

reactance (rɪ'æktəns) *n.* the opposition to the flow of alternating current by the capacitance or inductance of an electrical circuit.

reactant (rɪ'æktənt) *n.* a substance that participates in a chemical reaction.

reaction (rɪ'ækʃən) *n.* **1.** a response to some foregoing action or stimulus. **2.** the reciprocal action of two things acting together. **3.** opposition to change, esp. political change. **4.** a response indicating a person's feelings. **5.** *Med.* any effect produced by a drug or by a substance (allergen) to which a person is allergic. **6.** *Chem.* a process that involves changes in the structure and energy content of atoms, molecules, or ions. **7.** the equal and opposite force that acts on a body whenever it exerts a force on another body.

reactionary (rɪ'ækʃənrɪ) *adj.* **1.** of or characterized by reaction, esp. against political or social change. ~*n., pl.* -**aries.** **2.** a person opposed to radical change.

reactivate (rɪ'æktɪˌveɪt) *vb.* to make (something) active again. —**re,acti'vation** *n.*

reactive (rɪ'æktɪv) *adj.* **1.** readily taking part in chemical reactions: *sodium is a reactive metal.* **2.** of or having a reactance. **3.** responsive to stimulus. —re'**actively** *adv.*

reactor (rɪ'æktə) *n.* short for **nuclear reactor.**

read (riːd) *vb.* **reading, read** (rɛd). **1.** to understand (something written or printed) by looking at and interpreting the written or printed characters. **2.** (often foll. by *out*) to speak aloud (something written or printed). **3.** to interpret the significance or meaning of: *to read a map.* **4.** to interpret (signs, characters, etc.) other than by visual means: *to read Braille.* **5.** to have sufficient knowledge of (a language) to understand the written word. **6.** to make out the true nature or mood of: *she could read his thoughts.* **7.** to interpret in a specified way: *it can be read as satire.* **8.** to have a certain wording: *the sentence reads as follows.* **9.** to undertake a course of study in (a subject): *to read history.* **10.** to gain knowledge by reading: *he read about the war; a well-read young woman.* **11.** to register or show: *the meter reads 100.* **12.** to put into a specified condition by reading: *I read my son to sleep.* **13.** to hear and understand, esp. when using a two-way radio: *we are reading you loud and clear.* **14.** *Computers.* to obtain (data) from a storage device, such as magnetic tape. ~*n.* **15.** matter suitable for reading: *this book is a very good read.* **16.** a spell of reading. ~See also **read in, read out,** etc.

readable ('riːdəb°l) *adj.* **1.** (of a style of writing) interesting or pleasant to read. **2.** (of handwriting or print) legible.

reader ('riːdə) *n.* **1.** a person who reads. **2.** *Chiefly Brit.* a member of staff below a professor but above a senior lecturer at a university. **3.** a book of texts for those learning a foreign language. **4.** a person who reads aloud in public. **5.** a person who reads and assesses the merit of manuscripts submitted to a publisher. **6.** a proofreader. **7.** short for **lay reader.**

readership ('riːdəʃɪp) *n.* all the readers collectively of a particular publication or author: *a readership of five million.*

reading ('riːdɪŋ) *n.* **1.** the act of a person who reads. **2.** ability to read: *her reading is good for a 6-year-old.* **3.** material for reading. **4.** a public recital of a literary work. **5.** the form of a particular word or passage in a given text, esp. where more than one version exists. **6.** an interpretation, as of a situation or something said. **7.** knowledge gained from books. **8.** a measurement indicated by a gauge or dial. **9.** *Parliamentary procedure.* one of the three stages in the passage of a bill through a legislative assembly. ~*adj.* **10.** of or for reading: *a reading lamp.*

read into (riːd) *vb.* to discern in or infer

---

reacquaint   readmission   readopt
readjust   readmit

from a statement (meanings not intended by the speaker or writer).

read out (riːd) *vb.* **1.** to read (something) aloud. **2.** to retrieve information from a computer memory or storage device. ~*n.* **read-out. 3. a.** the act of retrieving information from a computer. **b.** the information retrieved.

read up (riːd) *vb.* (often foll. by *on*) to acquire information about (a subject) by reading intensively.

read-write head ('riːd'raɪt) *n. Computers.* an electromagnet that can both read and write information on a magnetic tape or disk.

ready ('rɛdɪ) *adj.* **readier, readiest. 1.** in a state of completion or preparedness, as for use or action. **2.** prompt or eager: *a ready response; ready with complaints.* **3.** quick; intelligent: *a ready wit.* **4.** (foll. by *to*) on the point (of) or liable (to): *ready to collapse.* **5.** easily available: *a ready market.* ~*n.* **6.** *Informal.* See **ready money. 7. at the ready.** poised for use: *with pen at the ready.* ~*vb.* **readying, readied. 8.** to put in a state of readiness; prepare. —'**readily** *adv.* —'**readiness** *n.*

ready-made *adj.* **1.** made for purchase and immediate use by any customer. **2.** extremely convenient or ideally suited: *a ready-made solution.*

ready money *n.* funds for immediate use; cash. Also: **the ready, the readies.**

reafforest (ˌriːə'fɒrɪst) *vb.* to replant (an area that was formerly forested). —ˌre-afˌforest'ation *n.*

reagent (riː'eɪdʒənt) *n.* a substance for use in a chemical reaction.

real[1] (rɪəl) *adj.* **1.** existing or occurring in the physical world; not imaginary or theoretical. **2.** true; actual: *the real reason.* **3.** important or serious: *a real problem.* **4.** rightly so called: *a real friend.* **5.** not artificial: *real fur.* **6.** (of food or drink) made in a traditional way to ensure the best flavour. **7.** *Econ.* (of prices or incomes) considered in terms of purchasing power rather than nominal currency value. **8.** relating to immovable property such as land and buildings: *real estate.* **9.** *Maths.* involving or containing real numbers alone; having no imaginary part. **10. the real thing.** the genuine article, not a substitute.

real[2] (reɪ'ɑːl) *n.* a former small Spanish or Spanish-American silver coin.

real estate *n. Chiefly U.S. & Canad.* immovable property, esp. land and houses.

realism ('rɪəˌlɪzəm) *n.* **1.** awareness or acceptance of things as they are, as opposed to the abstract or ideal. **2.** a style in art that seeks to represent the familiar or typical in real life. **3.** *Philosophy.* the theory that physical objects continue to exist whether they are perceived or not. —'**realist** *n.* —ˌrea'listic *adj.*

reality (rɪ'ælɪtɪ) *n., pl.* **-ties. 1.** the state of things as they are or appear to be, rather than as one might wish them to be. **2.** something that is real. **3.** the state of being real. **4. in reality.** actually; in fact.

realize *or* **-ise** ('rɪəˌlaɪz) *vb.* **1.** to become conscious or aware of (something). **2.** (often passive) to bring (a plan or ambition) to fruition. **3.** (of goods or property) to sell for (a certain sum): *this table realized £800.* **4.** to convert (property or goods) into cash. **5.** to produce a complete work of art from an idea or draft. —ˌreali'zation *or* -i'sation *n.*

really ('rɪəlɪ) *adv.* **1.** in reality: *it's really quite harmless.* **2.** truly; genuinely: *really beautiful.* ~*interj.* **3.** an exclamation of dismay, doubt, surprise, etc.

realm (rɛlm) *n.* **1.** a kingdom: *peer of the realm.* **2.** a field of interest or study: *the realm of the occult.*

real number *n.* any rational or irrational number.

real tennis *n.* an ancient form of tennis played in a four-walled indoor court.

real-time *adj.* of a data-processing system in which a computer is on-line to a source of data and processes the data as it is generated.

realtor ('rɪəltə) *n. U.S. & Canad.* an estate agent.

realty ('rɪəltɪ) *n.* same as **real estate.**

ream (riːm) *n.* **1.** a number of sheets of paper, now equal to 500 or 516 sheets (20 quires). **2.** (often *pl.*) *Informal.* a large quantity, esp. of written matter: *he wrote reams.*

reap (riːp) *vb.* **1.** to cut or harvest (a crop) from (a field). **2.** to gain (something) as a reward for or result of some action.

reaper ('riːpə) *n.* **1.** a person who reaps or a machine for reaping. **2. the grim reaper.** death.

rear[1] (rɪə) *n.* **1.** the back part. **2.** the area or position that lies at the back: *a garden at the rear of the house.* **3.** *Informal.* the buttocks. **4. bring up the rear.** to be at the end; come last. **5.** (*modifier*) of or in the rear: *the rear side.*

rear[2] (rɪə) *vb.* **1.** to care for and educate (children) until maturity; raise. **2.** to breed (animals) or grow (plants). **3.** to place or lift (something) upright. **4.** (often foll. by *up*) (esp. of horses) to lift the front legs in the air and stand nearly upright. **5.** (often foll. by *up* or *over*) (esp. of tall buildings) to rise high; tower.

rear admiral *n.* a high-ranking naval officer.

rearguard (ˈrɪəˌɡɑːd) *n.* **1.** a body of troops who protect the rear of a military formation, esp. in retreat. **2. rearguard action.** an effort to prevent or postpone the inevitable.

rear light *or* **lamp** *n.* a red light, usually one of a pair, attached to the rear of a vehicle.

rearm (riːˈɑːm) *vb.* **1.** to arm again. **2.** to equip with better weapons. —**reˈarmament** *n.*

rearmost (ˈrɪəˌməʊst) *adj.* nearest the back; coming last.

rear-view mirror *n.* a mirror on a motor vehicle enabling the driver to see traffic behind him.

rearward (ˈrɪəwəd) *adj., adv.* Also (for adv. only): **rearwards.** towards or in the rear.

reason (ˈriːzʰn) *n.* **1.** a cause or motive, as for a belief or action. **2.** an argument in favour of or a justification for something. **3.** the faculty of rational argument, deduction, or judgment. **4.** sanity. **5. by reason of.** because of. **6. in** *or* **within reason.** within moderate or justifiable bounds. **7. it stands to reason.** it is logical or obvious. ~*vb.* **8.** to think logically or draw (logical conclusions) from facts or premises. **9.** (usually foll. by *with*) to seek to persuade by reasoning. **10.** (often foll. by *out*) to work out (a problem) by reasoning.
Usage. It is incorrect to say *the reason is because...* since *the reason is...* and *because* mean the same thing. *Because* should be replace by *that: the reason is that...*

reasonable (ˈriːzənəbʰl) *adj.* **1.** showing reason or sound judgment. **2.** having modest expectations; not making unfair demands. **3.** moderate in price. **4.** fair; average: *reasonable weather.* —**ˈreasonably** *adv.* —**ˈreasonableness** *n.*

reasoning (ˈriːzənɪŋ) *n.* **1.** the process of drawing conclusions from facts or evidence. **2.** the conclusions so reached.

reassure (ˌriːəˈʃʊə) *vb.* to relieve (someone) of anxieties; restore confidence to. —**ˌreasˈsurance** *n.* —**ˌreasˈsuring** *adj.*

rebate (ˈriːbeɪt) *n.* a refund of a fraction of the amount payable; discount.

rebel *vb.* (rɪˈbɛl), **-belling, -belled.** (often foll. by *against*) **1.** to resist openly or fight against the established government. **2.** to reject an accepted moral code or convention of behaviour. ~*n.* (ˈrɛbʰl). **3. a.** a person who rebels. **b.** (*as modifier*): *rebel troops.* **4.** a person who rejects some accepted moral code or convention of behaviour.

rebellion (rɪˈbɛljən) *n.* **1.** organized opposition to a government or other authority. **2.** rejection of an accepted moral code or convention of behaviour.

rebellious (rɪˈbɛljəs) *adj.* rebelling or showing a tendency towards rebellion. —**reˈbelliously** *adv.*

rebirth (riːˈbɜːθ) *n.* a revival or renaissance: *the rebirth of learning.*

rebound *vb.* (rɪˈbaʊnd) **1.** to spring back, as from a sudden impact. **2.** (of a plan or action) to misfire so as to hurt the perpetrator. ~*n.* (ˈriːbaʊnd). **3.** the act of rebounding. **4. on the rebound.** *Informal.* while recovering from rejection: *he married her on the rebound from an unhappy love affair.*

rebuff (rɪˈbʌf) *vb.* **1.** to snub and reject someone who offers help, advice, or sympathy or makes a suggestion or request. ~*n.* **2.** a blunt refusal; snub.

rebuke (rɪˈbjuːk) *vb.* **1.** to reprimand (someone). ~*n.* **2.** a reprimand.

rebus (ˈriːbəs) *n., pl.* **-buses.** a puzzle consisting of pictures and symbols representing syllables and words; the word *hear* might be represented by H and a picture of an ear.

rebut (rɪˈbʌt) *vb.* **-butting, -butted.** to disprove, esp. by offering a contrary argument. —**reˈbuttal** *n.*

recalcitrant (rɪˈkælsɪtrənt) *adj.* not willing to submit to, or cooperate with, authority. —**reˈcalcitrance** *n.*

recall (rɪˈkɔːl) *vb.* **1.** to bring back to mind; remember. **2.** to order to return. ~*n.* **3.** the act of recalling. **4.** the ability to remember things; recollection.

recant (rɪˈkænt) *vb.* to take back (a former belief or statement), esp. formally in public. —**recantation** (ˌriːkænˈteɪʃən) *n.*

recap *Informal.* ~*vb.* (ˈriːˌkæp, riːˈkæp), **-capping, -capped.** **1.** to recapitulate. ~*n.* (ˈriːˌkæp). **2.** a recapitulation.

recapitulate (ˌriːkəˈpɪtjʊˌleɪt) *vb.* to restate the main points of (an argument or speech).

recapitulation (ˌriːkəˌpɪtjʊˈleɪʃən) *n.* **1.** the act of recapitulating. **2.** *Music.* the repeating of earlier themes, esp. in the final section of a movement.

recapture (riːˈkæptʃə) *vb.* **1.** to relive vividly (a former experience or sensation): *re-captured images of the past.* **2.** to capture again. ~*n.* **3.** the act of recapturing.

recce (ˈrɛkɪ) *n., vb.* **-ceing, -ced** or **-ceed.** *Slang.* short for **reconnaissance** or **reconnoitre.**

recede (rɪˈsiːd) *vb.* **1.** to withdraw from a point or limit; go back: *the tide receded.* **2.** to become more distant: *hopes of rescue receded.* **3.** to slope backwards: *apes have receding foreheads.* **4.** (of a man's hair) to cease to grow at the temples and above the forehead.

receipt (rɪˈsiːt) *n.* **1.** a written acknowledgment by a receiver of money or goods that payment or delivery has been made. **2.** the act of receiving. **3.** (*usually pl.*) money taken in over a particular period, as by a shop. **4.** *Archaic.* a recipe.

receive (rɪˈsiːv) *vb.* **1.** to get (something offered or sent to one). **2.** to be informed of (news). **3.** to react to: *the book was well received.* **4.** to experience: *she received minor injuries.* **5.** to greet (guests). **6.** to have (an honour) bestowed: *he received the Order of the Garter.* **7.** to admit (a person) to a society or condition: *he was received into the priesthood.* **8.** to support or sustain (the weight of something). **9.** to convert (incoming radio or television signals) into sounds or pictures. **10.** *Tennis, etc.* to play at the other end from the server. **11.** *Chiefly Brit.* to buy and sell stolen goods.

received (rɪˈsiːvd) *adj.* generally accepted or believed: *received wisdom.*

Received Pronunciation *n.* the accent of standard Southern British English.

receiver (rɪˈsiːvə) *n.* **1.** a person appointed by a court to manage property after the owner has been declared bankrupt. **2.** *Chiefly Brit.* a person who receives stolen goods knowing that they have been stolen. **3.** the equipment in a telephone, radio, or television that converts the incoming signals into sounds or pictures. **4.** the detachable part of a telephone that is held to the ear.

receivership (rɪˈsiːvəʃɪp) *n. Law.* the condition of being administered by a receiver: *the company went into receivership.*

recent (ˈriːs²nt) *adj.* having appeared, happened, or been made not long ago. —ˈ**recently** *adv.*

Recent (ˈriːs²nt) *adj. Geol.* of the current geological epoch, which began about 10 000 years ago.

receptacle (rɪˈsɛptək²l) *n.* **1.** an object that holds something; container. **2.** *Bot.* the enlarged or modified tip of the flower stalk that bears the flower.

reception (rɪˈsɛpʃən) *n.* **1.** the act of receiving or state of being received. **2.** the

manner in which something is received: *a hostile reception.* **3.** a formal party for guests, esp. after a wedding. **4.** an area in an office, hotel, etc., where visitors are received or reservations dealt with. **5.** *Radio & television.* the quality of a received broadcast: *the reception was poor.*

receptionist (rɪˈsɛpʃənɪst) *n.* a person employed in an office or surgery to receive clients and arrange appointments.

reception room *n.* (esp. in property advertisements) a room in a private house suitable for entertaining guests.

receptive (rɪˈsɛptɪv) *adj.* able and willing to consider and accept new ideas or suggestions. —**receptivity** (ˌriːsɛpˈtɪvɪtɪ) or re-ˈ**ceptiveness** *n.*

recess (rɪˈsɛs, ˈriːsɛs). **1.** a space, such as an alcove, set back in a wall. **2.** (*often pl.*) a secluded or secret place: *recesses of the mind.* **3.** a cessation of business, such as the closure of Parliament during a vacation. **4.** *U.S. & Canad.* a break between classes at a school. ~*vb.* (rɪˈsɛs). **5.** to set (something) in a recess. **6.** to build a recess in (something).

recession (rɪˈsɛʃən) *n.* **1.** a temporary depression in economic activity or prosperity. **2.** the act of receding.

recessional (rɪˈsɛʃən²l) *n.* a hymn sung as the clergy and choir withdraw after a church service.

recessive (rɪˈsɛsɪv) *adj.* **1.** tending to recede. **2.** *Genetics.* (in a pair of genes) designating a gene that has a characteristic which will only be passed on if the other gene has the same characteristic.

recherché (rəˈʃɛəʃeɪ) *adj.* **1.** known only to connoisseurs; choice or rare. **2.** studiedly refined or elegant.

recidivism (rɪˈsɪdɪˌvɪzəm) *n.* habitual relapse into crime. —re**ˈcidivist** *n., adj.*

recipe (ˈrɛsɪpɪ) *n.* **1.** a list of ingredients and directions for making a particular dish. **2.** a method for achieving some desired objective: *a recipe for success.*

recipient (rɪˈsɪpɪənt) *n.* a person who or thing that receives.

reciprocal (rɪˈsɪprək²l) *adj.* **1.** given, done, or felt by each of two people or groups about or to the other; mutual: *reciprocal trade.* **2.** given or done in return: *a reciprocal favour.* **3.** (of a pronoun) indicating that action is given and received by each subject; for example, *each other* in *they started to shout at each other.* ~*n.* **4.** Also called: **inverse.** *Maths.* a number or quantity that when multiplied by a given number or quantity gives a product of one: *the reciprocal of 2 is 0.5.* —re**ˈciprocally** *adv.*

reciprocate (rɪˈsɪprəˌkeɪt) *vb.* **1.** to give or feel in return: *his affection was not recipro-*

---

recharge   recheck *cated.* **2.** (of a machine part) to move backwards and forwards. —**re,cipro'cation** *n.*

reciprocity (,rɛsɪ'prɒsɪtɪ) *n.* **1.** reciprocal action or relation. **2.** a mutual exchange of commercial or other privileges.

recital (rɪ'saɪt³l) *n.* **1.** a musical performance by a soloist or soloists. **2.** the act of reciting something learned or prepared. **3.** a narration or description.

recitation (,rɛsɪ'teɪʃən) *n.* **1.** the act of reciting from memory, esp. before an audience. **2.** something recited.

recitative (,rɛsɪtə'tiːv) *n.* a narrative passage in an opera or oratorio, reflecting the natural rhythms of speech.

recite (rɪ'saɪt) *vb.* **1.** to repeat (a poem or passage) aloud from memory before an audience. **2.** to give a detailed account of.

reck (rɛk) *vb. Archaic* (*used mainly with a negative*) **1.** to mind or care about (something): *to reck nought.* **2.** to concern or interest (someone).

reckless ('rɛklɪs) *adj.* having or showing no regard for danger or consequences: *a reckless driver.*

reckon ('rɛkən) *vb.* **1.** to calculate or compute. **2.** to include; count as part of a set or class. **3.** (*usually passive*) to consider: *he is reckoned clever.* **4.** *Informal.* to think; be of the opinion: *I reckon you don't know.* **5.** (foll. by *with* or *without*) to take into account or fail to take into account: *they reckoned without John.* **6.** (foll. by *on* or *upon*) to rely on or expect: *I reckon on your support.*

reckoning ('rɛkənɪŋ) *n.* **1.** counting or calculating: *by his reckoning, it had taken five hours.* **2.** settlement of an account or bill. **3.** retribution for one's actions: *the day of reckoning.*

reclaim (rɪ'kleɪm) *vb.* **1.** to regain possession of. **2.** to convert unusable or submerged land into land suitable for farming or building on. **3.** to recover (useful substances) from waste products. **4.** *Old-fashioned.* to convert (someone) from sin, folly, or vice. —**reclamation** (,rɛklə'meɪʃən) *n.*

recline (rɪ'klaɪn) *vb.* to rest in a leaning position.

reclining (rɪ'klaɪnɪŋ) *adj.* (of a seat) having a back that can be adjusted to slope at various angles.

recluse (rɪ'kluːs) *n.* a person who lives in seclusion; a hermit. —**re'clusive** *adj.*

recognition (,rɛkəg'nɪʃən) *n.* **1.** the act of recognizing. **2.** acceptance or acknowledgment. **3.** formal acknowledgment of a government or of the independence of a country. **4. in recognition of.** as a token of thanks for.

recognizance *or* **recognisance** (rɪ'kɒgnɪzəns) *n. Law.* **a.** an undertaking made before a court or magistrate by which a person promises to do something specified, such as to appear in court on a stated day. **b.** a sum of money pledged to the performance of such an act.

recognize *or* **-ise** ('rɛkəg,naɪz) *vb.* **1.** to identify (a person or thing) as someone or something previously seen or known; know again. **2.** to accept or be aware of (a fact or problem): *to recognize necessity.* **3.** to give formal acknowledgment of the status or legality of (something or someone, esp. a government or a representative). **4.** to make formal acknowledgment of (a claim or duty). **5.** to show approval or appreciation of (something). —**'recog,nizable** *or* **-isable** *adj.*

recoil *vb.* (rɪ'kɔɪl). **1.** to jerk back, as from an impact or violent thrust. **2.** (often foll. by *from*) to draw back in fear, horror, or disgust. **3.** (foll. by *on* or *upon*) to go wrong, esp. so as to hurt the perpetrator. ~*n.* (rɪ'kɔɪl, 'riːkɔɪl). **4.** the backward movement of a gun when fired. **5.** the act of recoiling.

recollect (,rɛkə'lɛkt) *vb.* to remember. —,**recol'lection** *n.*

recommend (,rɛkə'mɛnd) *vb.* **1.** to advise as the best course or choice. **2.** to praise or commend: *to recommend a new book.* **3.** to make attractive or advisable: *the trip has little to recommend it.* —**recommendation** (,rɛkəmɛn'deɪʃən) *n.*

recompense ('rɛkəm,pɛns) *vb.* **1.** to pay or reward for service, work, or help. **2.** to compensate for loss or injury. ~*n.* **3.** compensation for loss or injury. **4.** reward, remuneration, or repayment.

reconcile ('rɛkən,saɪl) *vb.* **1.** (*often passive;* usually foll. by *to*) to make (oneself or another) no longer opposed; cause to accept something unpleasant: *she reconciled herself to poverty.* **2.** to re-establish friendly relations with (a person or people) or between (people). **3.** to settle (a quarrel). **4.** to make (two apparently conflicting things) compatible or consistent with each other. —**reconciliation** (,rɛkən,sɪlɪ'eɪʃən) *n.*

recondite (rɪ'kɒndaɪt, 'rɛkən,daɪt) *adj.* **1.** requiring special knowledge; abstruse. **2.** dealing with abstruse or profound subjects.

recondition (,riːkən'dɪʃən) *vb.* to restore to good condition or working order: *a reconditioned engine.* —,**recon'ditioned** *adj.*

reconnaissance (rɪ'kɒnɪsəns) *n.* **1.** the process of obtaining information about the position, strength, and movements of an enemy. **2.** a preliminary inspection.

reconnoitre *or U.S.* **reconnoiter** (,rɛkə'nɔɪtə) *vb.* to make a reconnaissance of.

---

reconsider (ˌriːkənˈsɪdə) *vb.* to consider (something) again, with a view to changing one's policy or course of action. —ˌreconˌsiderˈation *n.*

reconstitute (riːˈkɒnstɪˌtjuːt) *vb.* 1. to restore (food) to its former state, as by adding water to a concentrate. 2. to reconstruct (something), esp. in a slightly different form. —ˌreconstiˈtution *n.*

reconstruct (ˌriːkənˈstrʌkt) *vb.* 1. to form again; rebuild. 2. to form a picture of (a past event, esp. a crime) by piecing together evidence. —ˌreconˈstruction *n.*

record *n.* (ˈrekɔːd). 1. an account in permanent form, esp. in writing, preserving knowledge or information. 2. (*often pl.*) information or data on a subject collected over a long period: *weather records.* 3. Also called: **disc.** a thin disc of a plastic material upon which sound has been recorded in a continuous spiral groove on each side. 4. the best or most outstanding amount, rate, height, etc., ever attained, as in some field of sport: *a world record.* 5. the sum of one's recognized achievements, career, or performance. 6. a list of crimes of which an accused person has previously been convicted. 7. anything serving as evidence or as a memorial: *the First World War is a record of human folly.* 8. *Computers.* a group of data or piece of information preserved as a unit in machine-readable form. 9. **for the record.** for the sake of strict factual accuracy. 10. **go on record.** to state one's views publicly. 11. **have a record.** to have previous criminal convictions. 12. **off the record.** confidential or confidentially. 13. **on record.** **a.** stated in a public document. **b.** publicly known. ~*vb.* (rɪˈkɔːd). 14. to set down in some permanent form so as to preserve the true facts of: *to record the minutes of a meeting.* 15. to make a recording of (music or speech) for later reproduction or broadcasting. 16. to show or register: *his face recorded his disappointment; this thermometer records how hot it is.*

recorded delivery *n.* a Post Office service by which an official record of posting and delivery is obtained for a letter or package.

recorder (rɪˈkɔːdə) *n.* 1. a person or machine that records. 2. short for **tape recorder.** 3. *Music.* a wind instrument, blown through the end with finger-holes and a reedlike tone. 4. (in England and Wales) a barrister or solicitor appointed to sit as a part-time judge in the crown court.

recording (rɪˈkɔːdɪŋ) *n.* 1. the process of storing sounds or visual signals for later use. 2. something that has been recorded, such as a radio programme.

record player *n.* a device for reproducing the sounds stored on a record. A stylus vibrates in accordance with the undulations of the walls of the groove in the rotating record, and its vibrations are converted into sound.

recount (rɪˈkaʊnt) *vb.* to tell the story or details of; narrate.

re-count *vb.* (riːˈkaʊnt). 1. to count again. ~*n.* (ˈriːˌkaʊnt). 2. a second or further count, esp. of votes in an election.

recoup (rɪˈkuːp) *vb.* 1. to regain or make good (a financial or other loss). 2. to reimburse or compensate (someone), as for a loss. —reˈcoupment *n.*

recourse (rɪˈkɔːs) *n.* 1. **have recourse to.** to turn to a person, organization, or course of action (when in difficulty). 2. a person, organization, or course of action that is turned to for help.

recover (rɪˈkʌvə) *vb.* 1. to find again or obtain the return of (something lost). 2. (of a person) to regain health, spirits, or composure. 3. to regain a former and better condition: *industry recovered after the war.* 4. to get back or make good (expense or loss). 5. *Law.* to gain (something) by the judgment of a court: *to recover damages.* 6. to obtain (useful substances) from waste. —reˈcoverable *adj.*

recovery (rɪˈkʌvərɪ) *n., pl.* **-eries.** 1. the act or process of recovering, esp. from sickness, a shock, or a setback. 2. restoration to a former and better condition. 3. the regaining of something lost. 4. the extraction of useful substances from waste.

recreant (ˈrekrɪənt) *n. Archaic.* a disloyal or cowardly person.

re-create (ˌriːkrɪˈeɪt) *vb.* to create anew; reproduce. —ˌre-creˈation *n.*

recreation (ˌrekrɪˈeɪʃən) *n.* 1. refreshment of health or spirits by relaxation and enjoyment. 2. an activity that promotes this. —ˌrecreˈational *adj.*

recrimination (rɪˌkrɪmɪˈneɪʃən) *n.* (*often pl.*) accusations made by two people or groups about each other: *bitter recriminations; bouts of recrimination.* —reˈcriminatory *adj.*

recrudesce (ˌriːkruːˈdes) *vb.* (of trouble or a disease) to break out or appear again after a period of quiet. —ˌrecruˈdescence *n.*

recruit (rɪˈkruːt) *vb.* 1. to enlist (people) for military service. 2. to enrol or obtain (members or support). ~*n.* 3. a newly joined member of a military service. 4. any new member or supporter. —reˈcruitment *n.*

rectal (ˈrektəl) *adj.* of the rectum.

rectangle (ˈrekˌtæŋgˀl) *n.* a shape with four

rectify ('rɛktɪˌfaɪ) vb. -fying, -fied. 1. to put right; correct. 2. to separate (a substance) from a mixture or refine (a substance) by distillation. 3. to convert (alternating current) into direct current. —ˌrectifiˈcation n. —ˈrectiˌfier n.

rectilinear (ˌrɛktɪˈlɪnɪə) adj. 1. in, moving in, or characterized by a straight line. 2. bounded by or formed of straight lines.

rectitude ('rɛktɪˌtjuːd) n. moral or religious correctness.

recto ('rɛktəʊ) n., pl. -tos. 1. the front of a sheet of printed paper. 2. the right-hand pages of a book.

rector ('rɛktə) n. 1. Church of England. a clergyman in charge of a parish in which he would, formerly, have received all the tithes. 2. R.C. Church. a cleric in charge of a college, religious house, or congregation. 3. Chiefly Brit. the head of certain schools, colleges, or universities. 4. (in Scotland) a high-ranking official in a university, elected by the students. —ˈrectorship n.

rectory ('rɛktərɪ) n., pl. -ries. the house of a rector.

rectum ('rɛktəm) n., pl. -tums or -ta. the lower part of the alimentary canal, ending in the anus.

recumbent (rɪˈkʌmbənt) adj. lying down; reclining.

recuperate (rɪˈkuːpəˌreɪt) vb. to recover from illness or exhaustion. —reˌcuperˈation n. —reˈcuperative adj.

recur (rɪˈkɜː) vb. -curring, -curred. 1. to happen or occur again. 2. (of a thought or feeling) to come back to the mind. —recurrence (rɪˈkʌrəns) n. —reˈcurrent adj. —reˈcurring adj.

recurring decimal n. a rational number that contains a pattern of digits repeated indefinitely after the decimal point: *1 divided by 11 gives the recurring decimal 0.09090909...*

recusant ('rɛkjʊzənt) n. 1. (in 16th to 18th century England) a Roman Catholic who did not attend the services of the Church of England. 2. any person who refuses to submit to authority. —ˈrecusancy n.

recycle (riːˈsaɪkˀl) vb. 1. to reprocess (something already used) for further use: *recycled paper.* 2. to pass (a substance) through a system again for further use.

red (rɛd) n. 1. any of a group of colours, such as that of a ripe tomato or fresh blood. 2. red cloth or clothing: *dressed in red.* 3. something that is red in colour, such as a red ball in snooker. 4. **in the red.** Informal. in debt. 5. **see red.** Informal. to become very angry. ~adj. **redder, reddest.** 6. of the colour red. 7. reddish in colour or having parts or marks that are reddish: *red hair; red deer.* 8. flushed in the face from anger or shame. 9. (of the eyes) bloodshot. 10. (of wine) made from black grapes and coloured by their skins. —ˈreddish adj. —ˈredness n.

Red (rɛd) Informal. ~adj. 1. revolutionary or socialist, esp. Communist. ~n. 2. a revolutionary or socialist, esp. a Communist.

red admiral n. a butterfly having black wings with red and white markings.

red blood cell n. same as **erythrocyte**.

red-blooded adj. Informal. vigorous; virile.

redbreast ('rɛdˌbrɛst) n. a bird with a red breast, esp. the Old World robin.

redbrick ('rɛdˌbrɪk) n. (modifier) of or relating to a British university founded in the late 19th or early 20th century.

red card n. Soccer. a piece of red pasteboard displayed by a referee to indicate that a player has been sent off.

red carpet n. very special treatment given to an important or honoured guest.

redcoat ('rɛdˌkəʊt) n. 1. (formerly) a British soldier. 2. Canad. informal. a Mountie.

red corpuscle n. same as **erythrocyte**.

Red Crescent n. a national branch of the Red Cross Society in a Muslim country.

Red Cross n. an international organization (**Red Cross Society**) which helps victims of war or natural disaster.

redcurrant (ˌrɛdˈkʌrənt) n. the small edible rounded red berry of a widely-cultivated European shrub.

red deer n. a large deer of Europe and Asia, which has a reddish-brown coat and a short tail.

redden ('rɛdˀn) vb. 1. to make or become red. 2. to blush, as with embarrassment.

redeem (rɪˈdiːm) vb. 1. to recover possession of by payment of a price or service. 2. to convert (bonds or shares) into cash. 3. to pay off (a loan or debt). 4. to recover (something mortgaged or pawned). 5. to exchange (coupons) for goods. 6. to fulfil (a promise). 7. to reinstate in someone's good opinion: *he redeemed himself by his altruistic action.* 8. to make amends for. 9. to recover from captivity, esp. by a money payment. 10. Christianity. (of Christ as Saviour) to free (humanity) from sin by death on the Cross. —reˈdeemable adj. —reˈdeemer n.

Redeemer (rɪˈdiːmə) n. **the.** Christianity. Jesus Christ.

redeeming (rɪˈdiːmɪŋ) adj. serving to compensate for faults or deficiencies: *he has no redeeming feature.*

redemption (rɪˈdɛmpʃən) n. 1. the act of

redeeming. **2.** the state of being redeemed. **3.** *Christianity.* deliverance from sin through the incarnation and death of Christ. —**re'demptive** *adj.*

Red Ensign *n.* the ensign of the British Merchant Navy. It has the Union Jack on a red background at the upper corner.

redeploy (ˌriːdɪ'plɔɪ) *vb.* to assign (people) to new positions or tasks. —ˌrede'ployment *n.*

redevelop (ˌriːdɪ'vɛləp) *vb.* to rebuild or renovate (an area or building). —ˌrede'veloper *n.* —ˌrede'velopment *n.*

redfish ('rɛdˌfɪʃ) *n.*, *pl.* -**fish** or -**fishes**. *Canad.* same as **kokanee.**

red flag *n.* **1.** a symbol of revolution. **2.** a warning of danger.

red-handed *adj.* in the act of committing a crime or doing something wrong: *caught red-handed.*

red hat *n.* the broad-brimmed crimson hat given to cardinals as the symbol of their rank.

redhead ('rɛdˌhɛd) *n.* a person with reddish hair. —'red,headed *adj.*

red herring *n.* anything that diverts attention from a topic or line of inquiry.

red-hot *adj.* **1.** (esp. of metal) heated to the temperature at which it glows red. **2.** extremely hot. **3.** keen, excited, or eager. **4.** furious: *red-hot anger.* **5.** very recent or topical: *red-hot information.*

red-hot poker *n.* a garden plant with spikes of red or yellow flowers.

Red Indian *n., adj. Offensive.* American Indian.

redistribution (ˌriːdɪstrɪ'bjuːʃən) *n.* **1.** the act of distributing again. **2.** a revision of the number of seats that each province has in the Canadian House of Commons, made every ten years.

red lead (lɛd) *n.* a bright-red poisonous insoluble oxide of lead.

red-letter day *n.* a memorably important or happy occasion.

red light *n.* **1.** a signal to stop, esp. a red traffic signal. **2.** a danger signal.

red-light district *n.* an area where many prostitutes work.

red meat *n.* any meat that is dark in colour, esp. beef and lamb.

redo (riː'duː) *vb.* -**doing,** -**did,** -**done.** **1.** to do over again. **2.** *Informal.* to redecorate: *we redid the house last summer.*

redolent ('rɛdəʊlənt) *adj.* **1.** (foll. by *of* or *with*) smelling of: *a room redolent of flowers.* **2.** (foll. by *of* or *with*) reminiscent or suggestive of: *a picture redolent of the 18th century.* —**'redolence** *n.*

redouble (rɪ'dʌb'l) *vb.* **1.** to make or become much greater, esp. in intensity: *to redouble one's efforts.* **2.** *Bridge.* to double (an opponent's double).

redoubt (rɪ'daʊt) *n.* **1.** a small fort defending a hilltop or pass. **2.** a stronghold.

redoubtable (rɪ'daʊtəb'l) *adj.* to be feared and respected; formidable. —**re'doubtably** *adv.*

redound (rɪ'daʊnd) *vb.* **1.** (foll. by *to*) to have an advantageous or disadvantageous effect on: *brave deeds redound to your credit.* **2.** (foll. by *on* or *upon*) to recoil or rebound.

redox ('riːdɒks) *n.* a chemical reaction between two substances, in which one is oxidized and the other reduced.

red pepper *n.* **1.** the ripe red fruit of the sweet pepper. **2.** cayenne pepper.

red rag *n.* a provocation; something that infuriates.

redress (rɪ'drɛs) *vb.* **1.** to put right (a wrong), esp. by compensation. **2.** to correct or adjust (esp. in **redress the balance**). ~*n.* **3.** the setting right of a wrong. **4.** compensation or reparation.

red salmon *n.* any salmon having reddish flesh.

redshank ('rɛdˌʃæŋk) *n.* a large common European sandpiper with red legs.

red shift *n.* a shift in the spectral lines of the spectrum of a star or galaxy towards the red end of the visible region relative to their position in the terrestrial spectrum. It is used to calculate the velocity of the object in relation to the earth.

redskin ('rɛdˌskɪn) *n. Informal, offensive.* an American Indian.

red squirrel *n.* a reddish-brown squirrel inhabiting woodlands of Europe and parts of Asia.

redstart ('rɛdˌstɑːt) *n.* **1.** a European songbird of the thrush family: the male has an orange-brown tail and breast. **2.** a North American warbler.

red tape *n.* obstructive official routine or procedure; time-consuming bureaucracy.

reduce (rɪ'djuːs) *vb.* **1.** to make or become smaller in size, number, or intensity. **2.** to bring into a certain condition: *to reduce a forest to ashes; he was reduced to tears.* **3.** to impoverish: *to be in reduced circumstances.* **4.** to bring into a state of submission; subjugate: *the whole country was reduced after three months.* **5.** to bring down the price of (a commodity). **6.** to lower the rank or status of; demote: *reduced to the ranks.* **7.** to set out systematically as an aid to understanding; simplify: *reducing the problem to three main issues.* **8.** *Maths.* to simplify the form of (an expression or

redesign   **rediscover**   **redraft**
redirect   **redistribute**   **redraw**

equation), esp. by substitution of one term by another. **9.** *Chem.* **a.** to undergo a chemical reaction with hydrogen. **b.** to lose oxygen atoms. **c.** to increase the number of electrons. **10.** *Cookery.* to thicken (a sauce) by boiling away some of its liquid. —**re'ducible** *adj.*

reduction (rɪ'dʌkʃən) *n.* **1.** the act of reducing. **2.** the amount by which something is reduced. **3.** a reduced form of an original, such as a copy of a document on a smaller scale. —**re'ductive** *adj.*

redundant (rɪ'dʌndənt) *adj.* **1.** deprived of one's job because it is no longer necessary or sufficiently profitable. **2.** surplus to requirements. —**re'dundancy** *n.*

reduplicate (rɪ'djuːplɪˌkeɪt) *vb.* **1.** to make double; repeat. **2.** to repeat (a word or syllable) to form a new word, sometimes with changes, as in *chitchat.*

redwood ('redˌwʊd) *n.* a giant Californian conifer with reddish bark.

re-echo (riː'ekəʊ) *vb.* **-oing, -oed.** to echo a sound that is already an echo; resound.

reed (riːd) *n.* **1.** a tall grass that grows in swamps and shallow water and has jointed hollow stalks. **2.** these stalks, esp. as used for thatching. **3.** *Music.* **a.** a thin piece of cane or metal in certain wind instruments, which vibrates producing a musical note when the instrument is blown. **b.** a wind instrument or organ pipe that sounds by means of a reed.

reedy ('riːdɪ) *adj.* **reedier, reediest. 1.** (of a place) full of reeds. **2.** having a tone like a reed instrument; shrill or piping. —**'reedily** *adv.* —**'reediness** *n.*

reef[1] (riːf) *n.* **1.** a ridge of rock, sand, or coral, lying just beneath the surface of the sea. **2.** a vein of ore, esp. one of gold-bearing quartz.

reef[2] (riːf) *Naut.* ~*n.* **1.** the part of a sail gathered in when sail area is reduced, as in a high wind. ~*vb.* **2.** to reduce the area of (sail) by taking in a reef.

reefer ('riːfə) *n.* **1.** Also called: **reefer jacket, reefing jacket.** a man's short heavy double-breasted woollen jacket. **2.** *Slang.* a hand-rolled cigarette containing cannabis.

reef knot *n.* a knot consisting of two overhand knots turned opposite ways.

reek (riːk) *vb.* **1.** to give off a strong unpleasant smell; stink. **2.** (often foll. by *of*) to be permeated (by): *their lyrics reek of pretentiousness.* **3.** *Chiefly dialect.* to give off smoke or fumes. ~*n.* **4.** a strong offen-

sive smell; stink. **5.** *Dialect.* smoke or steam.

reel[1] (riːl, rɪəl) *n.* **1.** a cylindrical object or frame that turns on an axis and onto which film, tape, wire, thread, etc., may be wound. **2.** such a device attached to a fishing rod, used for casting and winding in the line. ~*vb.* **3.** (foll. by *in* or *out*) to wind or draw with a reel: *to reel in a fish.*

reel[2] (riːl, rɪəl) *vb.* **1.** to sway, esp. under the shock of a blow or through dizziness or drunkenness. **2.** to whirl about or have the feeling of whirling about: *his brain reeled.*

reel[3] (riːl, rɪəl) *n.* any of various lively Scottish dances for a fixed number of couples who combine in square and circular formations.

reel off *vb.* to recite or write fluently and without apparent effort.

re-entry (riː'entrɪ) *n., pl.* **-tries. 1.** the act of coming back into a place, esp. a country. **2.** the return of a spacecraft into the earth's atmosphere.

reeve (riːv) *n.* **1.** *English history.* the local representative of the king in a shire until the early 11th century. **2.** (in medieval England) a steward who supervised the daily affairs of a manor. **3.** *Canad. government.* (in some provinces) a president of a local council.

ref (ref) *n. Informal.* the referee in a sport.

refectory (rɪ'fektrɪ) *n., pl.* **-ries.** a dining hall in a religious or academic institution.

refectory table *n.* a long narrow dining table supported by two trestles.

refer (rɪ'fɜː) *vb.* **-ferring, -ferred.** (often foll. by *to*). **1.** to make mention (of). **2.** to direct the attention of (someone) for information: *the reader is referred to the introduction.* **3.** to seek information (from): *he referred to his notes.* **4.** to be relevant or relate (to): *the question refers to the range of materials such devices can be made from.* **5.** to hand over for consideration or decision: *to refer a complaint to another department.* **6.** to direct (a patient or client) to another doctor or agency: *her GP referred her to a specialist.* —**referable** ('refərəbªl) or **referrable** (rɪ'fɜːrəbªl) *adj.* —**re'ferral** *n.*

Usage. The common practice of adding *back* to *refer* is unnecessary, since this meaning is already contained in the *re-* of *refer*: this *refers to* (not *back to*) what has already been said. However, when *refer* is used in the sense of passing a document or question for further consideration to the person from whom it was received, it may

re-educate	re-employ	re-establish
re-elect	re-enact	re-examination
re-election	re-enactment	re-examine
re-emerge	re-enter	refashion
re-emphasize	re-equip	

be appropriate to say *he referred the matter back.*

referee (ˌrɛfəˈriː) *n.* **1.** the umpire in various sports, esp. football and boxing. **2.** a person who is willing to testify to the character or capabilities of someone. ~*vb.* **-eeing, -eed. 3.** to act as a referee.

reference (ˈrɛfərəns, ˈrɛfrəns) *n.* **1.** the act of referring. **2.** direction to a passage elsewhere in a book or to another book. **3.** a book or passage referred to. **4.** a mention: *this book contains several references to the Civil War.* **5.** (*modifier*) containing information or facts: *a reference book.* **6.** a written testimonial regarding one's character or capabilities. **7.** a person referred to for such a testimonial. **8.** (foll. by *to*) relation or restriction, esp. to or by membership of a specific group: *without reference to sex or age.* **9. with reference to.** concerning. —**referential** (ˌrɛfəˈrɛnʃəl) *adj.*

referendum (ˌrɛfəˈrɛndəm) *n., pl.* **-dums** or **-da** (-də). submission of an issue of importance to the direct vote of the electorate.

refill *vb.* (riːˈfɪl). **1.** to fill (something) again. ~*n.* (ˈriːfɪl). **2.** a replacement supply of a substance in a permanent container. **3.** a second or subsequent filling. —**refillable** *adj.*

refine (rɪˈfaɪn) *vb.* **1.** to make free from impurities; purify. **2.** to separate (a mixture) into pure constituents, as in an oil refinery. **3.** to make elegant or subtly improved: *their theories are constantly being refined.*

refined (rɪˈfaɪnd) *adj.* **1.** elegant, cultured, or polite. **2.** subtle; discriminating. **3.** freed from impurities; purified.

refinement (rɪˈfaɪnmənt) *n.* **1.** the act of refining. **2.** precision of thought, expression, or manners. **3.** an improvement to something, such as a piece of equipment. **4.** a subtle point or distinction.

refinery (rɪˈfaɪnərɪ) *n., pl.* **-eries.** a factory for purifying a raw material, such as sugar or oil.

refit *vb.* (riːˈfɪt), **-fitting, -fitted. 1.** to make ready for use again by repairing or re-equipping. ~*n.* (ˈriːˌfɪt). **2.** a repair or re-equipping, as of a ship, for further use.

reflation (riːˈfleɪʃən) *n.* an increase in the supply of money and credit designed to encourage economic activity. —**reflate** *vb.* —**reflationary** *adj.*

reflect (rɪˈflɛkt) *vb.* **1.** (of a surface or object) to throw back (light, heat, or sound). **2.** (of a mirror) to form an image of (something) by reflection. **3.** to show: *his tactics reflect his desire for power.* **4.** to bring as a consequence: *their success reflected great credit on them.* **5.** (foll. by *on* or *upon*) to cause to be regarded in a specified way: *her behaviour reflects on the whole group.* **6.** (usually foll. by *on*) to consider carefully; ponder.

reflecting telescope *n.* a telescope in which the initial image is formed by a concave mirror.

reflection (rɪˈflɛkʃən) *n.* **1.** the act of reflecting. **2.** something reflected or the image so produced, as by a mirror. **3.** careful or long consideration. **4.** attribution of discredit or blame: *it's no reflection on you.* **5.** *Maths.* a transformation of a shape in which right and left, or top and bottom, are reversed.

reflective (rɪˈflɛktɪv) *adj.* **1.** characterized by quiet thought or contemplation. **2.** capable of reflecting: *a reflective surface.*

reflector (rɪˈflɛktə) *n.* **1.** a piece of glass or plastic, as on the back of a bicycle, that glows when light shines on it. **2.** a reflecting telescope.

reflex (ˈriːflɛks) *n.* **1.** an immediate involuntary response, such as coughing, evoked by a given stimulus. **2.** a mechanical response to a particular situation, involving no conscious decision. **3.** an image produced by reflection. ~*adj.* **4.** of or caused by a reflex: *a reflex action.* **5.** *Maths.* (of an angle) between 180° and 360°.

reflex camera *n.* a camera containing a mirror which directs the light from a lens to the viewfinder, so that the image seen closely resembles the image photographed.

reflexive (rɪˈflɛksɪv) *adj.* **1.** denoting a pronoun that refers back to the subject of a sentence or clause. Thus, in *that man thinks a great deal of himself,* the pronoun *himself* is reflexive. **2.** denoting a verb used with a reflexive pronoun as its direct object, as in *to dress oneself.* **3.** *Physiol.* of or relating to a reflex. ~*n.* **4.** a reflexive pronoun or verb.

reflexology (ˌriːflɛkˈsɒlədʒɪ) *n.* massage of the soles of the feet as a therapy in alternative medicine. —**reflexologist** *n.*

reform (rɪˈfɔːm) *vb.* **1.** to improve (an existing institution or law) by correction of abuses. **2.** to give up or cause to give up a bad habit or way of life. ~*n.* **3.** correction of abuses or malpractices: *reform of the divorce laws; social reforms.* **4.** improvement of morals or behaviour. —**reformative** *adj.* —**reformer** *n.*

reformation (ˌrɛfəˈmeɪʃən) *n.* **1.** the act of reforming or the state of being reformed. **2. the Reformation.** a religious movement in 16th-century Europe that began as an attempt to reform the Roman Catholic Church and resulted in the establishment of the Protestant Churches.

reformatory (rɪˈfɔːmətrɪ) *n., pl.* **-ries.** (formerly) a place where young offenders were sent for corrective training.

Reformed (rɪˈfɔːmd) *adj.* of or designating a Protestant Church, esp. the Calvinist.

refract (rɪˈfrækt) *vb.* to cause light, heat, or

sound to undergo refraction. **—re'fractive** *adj.* **—re'fractor** *n.*

refracting telescope *n.* a type of telescope in which the image is formed by a set of lenses. Also called: **refractor.**

refraction (rɪ'frækʃən) *n.* **1.** *Physics.* the change in direction of a wave, such as light or sound, in passing from one medium to another in which it has a different velocity. **2.** the amount by which a wave is refracted.

refractory (rɪ'fræktərɪ) *adj.* **1.** unmanageable or rebellious. **2.** *Med.* not responding to treatment. **3.** (of a material) able to withstand high temperatures without fusion or decomposition.

refrain[1] (rɪ'freɪn) *vb.* (usually foll. by *from*) to keep oneself from doing: *I carefully refrained from looking at him.*

refrain[2] (rɪ'freɪn) *n.* **1.** a regularly recurring melody, such as the chorus of a song. **2.** a much repeated saying or idea.

refrangible (rɪ'frændʒɪb°l) *adj.* able to be refracted.

refresh (rɪ'frɛʃ) *vb.* **1.** to revive or reinvigorate, as through rest, drink, or food. **2.** to stimulate (the memory). **3.** to replenish or enliven with something new. **—re'fresher** *n.* **—re'freshing** *adj.*

refreshment (rɪ'frɛʃmənt) *n.* **1.** the act of refreshing or the state of being refreshed. **2.** (*pl.*) snacks and drinks served as a light meal.

refrigerant (rɪ'frɪdʒərənt) *n.* **1.** a fluid capable of vaporizing at low temperatures: used as the working fluid of a refrigerator. ~*adj.* **2.** causing cooling or freezing.

refrigerate (rɪ'frɪdʒə,reɪt) *vb.* to chill or freeze, esp. in order to preserve. **—re,friger'ation** *n.*

refrigerator (rɪ'frɪdʒə,reɪtə) *n.* a cabinet or room for keeping food and drink cool. Informal name: **fridge.**

refuel (riː'fjuːəl) *vb.* **-elling, -elled** or *U.S.* **-eling, -eled.** to supply or be supplied with fresh fuel.

refuge ('rɛfjuːdʒ) *n.* **1.** shelter or protection, as from the weather or danger. **2.** a place, person, or thing that offers protection, help, or relief.

refugee (,rɛfju'dʒiː) *n.* a person who has fled from some danger, esp. war or political persecution.

refulgent (rɪ'fʌldʒənt) *adj. Literary.* shining, brilliant, or radiant. **—re'fulgence** *n.*

refund *vb.* (rɪ'fʌnd). **1.** to give back (money), as when an article purchased is unsatisfactory. **2.** to reimburse (a person). ~*n.* ('riː,fʌnd). **3.** return of money to a purchaser or the amount returned. **—re'fundable** *adj.*

refurbish (riː'fɜːbɪʃ) *vb.* to renovate and brighten up. **—re'furbishment** *n.*

refusal (rɪ'fjuːz°l) *n.* **1.** the act of refusing. **2.** the opportunity to reject or accept; option: *he gave me first refusal.*

refuse[1] (rɪ'fjuːz) *vb.* **1.** to decline to accept (something offered): *to refuse promotion.* **2.** to decline to give or allow (something) to (someone). **3.** to be determined not (to do something): *he refuses to talk about it.* **4.** (of a horse) to be unwilling to take (a jump).

refuse[2] ('rɛfjuːs) *n.* anything thrown away; rubbish.

refusenik *or* **refusnik** (rɪ'fjuːznɪk) *n.* a Jew in the USSR who has been refused permission to emigrate.

refute (rɪ'fjuːt) *vb.* to prove (a statement, theory, or charge) to be false or incorrect. **—,refu'tation** *n.*
Usage. *Refute* is often used incorrectly as a synonym of *deny.* To *deny* something is to state that it is untrue; to *refute* something is to assemble evidence in order to prove it untrue: *all he could do was deny the allegations since he was unable to refute them.*

regain (rɪ'geɪn) *vb.* **1.** to get back; recover. **2.** to reach again: *to regain the shore.*

regal ('riːg°l) *adj.* **1.** of or fit for a king or queen; royal. **2.** splendid and dignified; magnificent. **—re'gality** *n.* **—'regally** *adv.*

regale (rɪ'geɪl) *vb.* (usually foll. by *with*) **1.** to give delight or amusement to: *he regaled them with stories.* **2.** to provide with choice or abundant food or drink.

regalia (rɪ'geɪlɪə) *n.* (*pl.*, *sometimes functioning as sing.*) the ceremonial emblems or robes of royalty, high office, or a society.

regard (rɪ'gɑːd) *vb.* **1.** to look closely or attentively at (something or someone). **2.** to look upon or think of in a specified way: *she regarded her brother as her responsibility; we regard your work very highly.* **3.** to take notice of: *he has never regarded the conventions.* **4. as regards.** in respect of; concerning. ~*n.* **5.** respect or affection. **6.** a gaze; look. **7.** attention; heed: *he spends without regard to his bank balance.* **8.** reference or connection: *with regard to my complaint.* **9.** (*pl.*) good wishes or greetings; used at the close of a letter: *with kind regards, Bill.*

regardful (rɪ'gɑːdfʊl) *adj.* (often foll. by *of*) heedful (of).

regarding (rɪ'gɑːdɪŋ) *prep.* in respect of; on the subject of.

regardless (rɪ'gɑːdlɪs) *adj.* **1.** (usually foll. by *of*) taking no notice; heedless: *regardless of what the law says.* ~*adv.* **2.** disregarding drawbacks or difficulties: *carried on regardless.*

---

regatta (rɪˈgætə) *n.* an organized series of races of boats, esp. yachts or rowing boats.

regency (ˈriːdʒənsɪ) *n., pl.* **-cies. 1.** government by a regent. **2.** the office of a regent. **3.** a period when a regent is in power.

Regency (ˈriːdʒənsɪ) *adj.* of the regency (1811-20) of the Prince of Wales (later George IV) or the styles of architecture, furniture, etc. produced during it.

regenerate *vb.* (rɪˈdʒɛnəˌreɪt). **1.** to undergo moral, spiritual, or physical renewal. **2.** to come or bring into existence once again. **3.** to replace (lost or damaged tissues or organs) by new growth. ~*adj.* (rɪˈdʒɛnərɪt). **4.** morally, spiritually, or physically renewed or reborn. —**re-ˌgenerˈation** *n.* —**reˈgenerative** *adj.*

regent (ˈriːdʒənt) *n.* **1.** the ruler of a country during the childhood, absence, or incapacity of its monarch. **2.** *U.S. & Canad.* a member of the governing board of certain schools and colleges. ~*adj.* **3.** acting as a regent: *the Prince Regent.*

reggae (ˈrɛgeɪ) *n.* a type of popular music of Jamaican origin with four beats to the bar, the upbeat being strongly accented.

regicide (ˈrɛdʒɪˌsaɪd) *n.* **1.** the killing of a king. **2.** a person who kills a king.

regime (reɪˈʒiːm) *n.* **1.** a system of government or a particular administration: *a fascist regime.* **2.** a social system or order. **3.** *Med.* a regimen.

regimen (ˈrɛdʒɪˌmɛn) *n. Med.* a systematic course of therapy, often including a recommended diet.

regiment (ˈrɛdʒɪmənt) *n.* **1.** a military formation varying in size from a battalion to a number of battalions. **2.** a large number. —ˌregiˈmental *adj.*

regimentals (ˌrɛdʒɪˈmɛntˀlz) *pl. n.* **1.** the uniform and insignia of a regiment. **2.** military dress.

regimented (ˈrɛdʒɪˌmɛntɪd) *adj.* very strictly controlled: *the regimented lifestyle of the industrial world.* —ˌregimenˈtation *n.*

Regina (rɪˈdʒaɪnə) *n.* queen: now used chiefly in documents and inscriptions.

region (ˈriːdʒən) *n.* **1.** any large continuous part of a surface or space. **2.** an area considered as a unit for geographical, social, or cultural reasons. **3.** an administrative division of a country. **4.** a sphere of activity or interest. **5. in the region of.** approximately: *in the region of £150.* **6.** a part of the body: *the lumbar region.* —ˈregional *adj.*

register (ˈrɛdʒɪstə) *n.* **1.** an official list recording names, events, or transactions. **2.** the book in which such a list is written. **3.** a device that records data, totals sums of money, etc.: *a cash register.* **4.** *Music.* **a.** the timbre characteristic of a certain man-

ner of voice production. **b.** any of the stops on an organ in respect of its tonal quality: *the flute register.* **5.** a style of speaking or writing, such as slang, used in particular circumstances or social situations. ~*vb.* **6.** to enter (an event, person's name, ownership, etc.) in a register. **7.** to show on a scale or other measuring instrument: *the current didn't register on the meter.* **8.** to show in a person's face or bearing: *his face registered surprise.* **9.** *Informal.* to have an effect; make an impression: *the news of her uncle's death just did not register.* **10.** to have a letter or parcel insured against loss by the Post Office: *registered mail.* —**registration** (ˌrɛdʒɪˈstreɪʃən) *n.*

register office *n. Brit.* a government office where civil marriages are performed and births, marriages, and deaths are recorded.

registrar (ˌrɛdʒɪˈstrɑː) *n.* **1.** a person who keeps official records. **2.** an administrative official responsible for student records and enrolment in a college. **3.** *Brit. & N.Z.* a hospital doctor senior to a houseman but junior to a consultant.

registration document *n. Brit.* a document giving identification details of a vehicle, including its owner's name.

registration number *n.* a sequence of letters and numbers assigned to a motor vehicle when it is registered, displayed on numberplates at the front and rear.

registration plate *n. Austral. & N.Z.* the numberplate of a vehicle.

registry (ˈrɛdʒɪstrɪ) *n., pl.* **-tries. 1.** a place where registers are kept. **2.** the registration of a ship's country of origin: *a ship of Liberian registry.*

registry office *n. Brit.* same as **register office.**

Regius professor (ˈriːdʒɪəs) *n. Brit.* a person appointed by the Crown to a university chair founded by a royal patron.

regress *vb.* (rɪˈgrɛs). **1.** to revert to a former and worse condition. ~*n.* (ˈriːgrɛs). **2.** reversion to a former and worse condition. —**reˈgressive** *adj.*

regression (rɪˈgrɛʃən) *n.* **1.** *Psychol.* the adoption by an adult of behaviour more appropriate to a child. **2.** the act of regressing.

regret (rɪˈgrɛt) *vb.* **-gretting, -gretted. 1.** to feel sorry, repentant, or upset about. **2.** to express apology or distress: *we regret the inconvenience caused.* ~*n.* **3.** a sense of repentance, guilt, or sorrow. **4.** (*pl.*) a polite expression of refusal: *send my regrets.* —**reˈgretful** *adj.* —**reˈgrettable** *adj.* —**reˈgrettably** *adv.*

regular (ˈrɛgjʊlə) *adj.* **1.** normal, customary, or usual. **2.** according to a uniform principle, arrangement, or order. **3.** occurring at fixed or prearranged intervals: *a regular call on a customer.* **4.** following a set rule or normal practice. **5.** symmetrical in appearance; even: *regular features.* **6.** officially qualified or recognized: *he's not a regular doctor.* **7.** complete; utter: *a regular fool.* **8.** *U.S. & Canad. informal.* likable: *a regular guy.* **9.** of or serving in the permanent military services: *a regular soldier.* **10.** *Grammar.* following the usual pattern of formation in a language: *regular verbs.* **11.** *Maths.* (of a polygon) having all its sides and angles the same. **12.** *Informal.* not constipated: *eating fresh vegetables helps keep you regular.* **13.** subject to the rule of an established religious community: *canons regular.* ~*n.* **14.** a professional long-term serviceman in a military unit. **15.** *Informal.* a frequent customer, visitor, or member of an audience. —ˌregu'larity *n.* —'regularˌize *or* -ˌise *vb.* —'regularly *adv.*

regulate ('rɛgjʊˌleɪt) *vb.* **1.** to adjust (the amount of heat, sound, etc.) as required; control. **2.** to adjust (an instrument or appliance) so that it operates correctly. **3.** to bring into conformity with a rule, principle, or usage. —'regulatory *adj.*

regulation (ˌrɛgjʊ'leɪʃən) *n.* **1.** the act of regulating. **2.** a rule that governs procedure or behaviour. **3.** (*modifier*) as required by official rules: *regulation uniform.* **4.** (*modifier*) conventional or customary: *the regulation wife and two kids.*

regulator ('rɛgjʊˌleɪtə) *n.* **1.** the mechanism by which the speed of a clock is regulated. **2.** a mechanism, such as a governor valve, for controlling fluid flow, pressure, temperature, etc.

regurgitate (rɪ'gɜːdʒɪˌteɪt) *vb.* **1.** to vomit up (partially digested food). **2.** (of some birds and animals) to bring back (partly digested food) to the mouth to feed the young. —reˌgurgi'tation *n.*

rehabilitate (ˌriːə'bɪlɪˌteɪt) *vb.* **1.** to help (a disabled person or an ex-prisoner) to readapt to society or a new job, as by vocational guidance, retraining, or therapy. **2.** to restore to a former position or rank. **3.** to restore the good reputation of. —ˌrehaˌbili'tation *n.*

rehash (riː'hæʃ) *vb.* **1.** to use (old or already used ideas or material) in a slightly different form without real improvement. ~*n.* **2.** something consisting of rehashed material.

rehearse (rɪ'hɜːs) *vb.* **1.** to practise (a play, concert, etc.), in preparation for public performance. **2.** to run through; recite: *he rehearsed the grievances of the commit-*

tee. **3.** to train (a person) for public performance. —re'hearsal *n.* —re'hearser *n.*

Reich (raɪx) *n.* the former German state, esp. the Nazi dictatorship in Germany from 1933–45 (**Third Reich**).

reign (reɪn) *n.* **1.** the period during which a monarch is the official ruler of a country. **2.** a period during which a person or thing is dominant: *a reign of terror.* ~*vb.* **3.** to hold the position of sovereign. **4.** to predominate; prevail: *darkness reigns.* **5.** (*usually present participle*) to be the most recent winner of a contest, etc.: *the reigning champion.*

reimburse (ˌriːɪm'bɜːs) *vb.* to repay (someone) for (expenses, losses, or damages). —ˌreim'bursement *n.*

rein (reɪn) *n.* **1.** (*often pl.*) one of a pair of long straps, one end of which is fastened to the bit, used to control a horse. **2.** (*pl.*) a similar device used to control a very young child. **3.** means of control: *to take up the reins of government.* **4. give (a) free rein.** to allow considerable freedom; remove restraints. **5. keep a tight rein on.** to control carefully: *we have to keep a tight rein on expenditure.* ~*vb.* **6.** to restrain or halt with or as if with reins. ~See also **rein in.**

reincarnate (riː'ɪnkɑːˌneɪt) *vb.* (*often passive*) to be born again in a different body.

reincarnation (ˌriːɪnkɑː'neɪʃən) *n.* **1.** the belief that after death the soul is reborn in another body. **2.** embodiment again in a new form, as of a principle or idea.

reindeer ('reɪnˌdɪə) *n., pl.* **-deer** *or* **-deers.** a deer with large branched antlers in both sexes that inhabits the arctic regions.

reinforce (ˌriːɪn'fɔːs) *vb.* **1.** to give added strength or support to. **2.** to give added emphasis to; increase: *his rudeness reinforced my determination.* **3.** to give added support to (a military force) by providing more men or equipment. —ˌrein'forcement *n.*

reinforced concrete *n.* concrete with steel bars or mesh embedded in it to strengthen it.

rein in *vb.* to stop (a horse) by pulling on the reins.

reinstate (ˌriːɪn'steɪt) *vb.* to restore to a former rank or status. —ˌrein'statement *n.*

reiterate (riː'ɪtəˌreɪt) *vb.* to state again or repeatedly. —reˌiter'ation *n.*

reject *vb.* (rɪ'dʒɛkt). **1.** to refuse to accept, use, believe, etc. **2.** to pass over or throw out as useless. **3.** to rebuff (a person). **4.** (of an organism) to fail to accept (a

rehouse	reinterpret	reinvigorated
reimpose	reinterpretation	reissue
reinsert	reintroduce	
reinsure	reintroduction	

tissue graft or organ transplant). ~*n.* ('riːdʒɛkt). **5.** something rejected as imperfect, unsatisfactory, or useless. —**re'jection** *n.*

rejig (riːˈdʒɪg) *vb.* **-jigging, -jigged. 1.** to re-equip (a factory or plant). **2.** *Informal.* to manipulate in an unscrupulous way.

rejoice (rɪˈdʒɔɪs) *vb.* to feel or express great happiness. —**re'joicing** *n.*

rejoin[1] (riːˈdʒɔɪn) *vb.* to come together with (someone or something) again.

rejoin[2] (rɪˈdʒɔɪn) *vb.* to reply, esp. sharply or wittily.

rejoinder (rɪˈdʒɔɪndə) *n.* a reply, esp. a sharp or witty one.

rejuvenate (rɪˈdʒuːvɪˌneɪt) *vb.* to give new youth, restored vitality, or youthful appearance to. —**re,juve'nation** *n.*

relapse (rɪˈlæps) *vb.* **1.** to lapse back into a former state or condition, esp. an unhealthy or undesirable one. ~*n.* **2.** the act of relapsing. **3.** the return of ill health after an apparent or partial recovery.

relate (rɪˈleɪt) *vb.* **1.** to tell or narrate (a story). **2.** (often foll. by *to*) to form a connection (between two or more things) or (of something) to have reference (to something else). **3.** (often foll. by *to*) to form a sympathetic or significant relationship (with other people, things, etc.).

related (rɪˈleɪtɪd) *adj.* **1.** connected; associated. **2.** linked by kinship or marriage.

relation (rɪˈleɪʃən) *n.* **1.** the state of being related or the manner in which things are related. **2.** connection by blood or marriage; kinship. **3.** a person who is connected by blood or marriage; relative. **4. in** *or* **with relation to.** with reference to; in comparison with. **5.** the position or connection of one person or thing with regard to another. **6.** an account or narrative.

relations (rɪˈleɪʃənz) *pl. n.* **1.** social, political, or personal connections or dealings between or among individuals, groups, or nations. **2.** family or relatives. **3.** *Euphemistic.* sexual intercourse.

relationship (rɪˈleɪʃənʃɪp) *n.* **1.** the state of being related. **2.** association by blood or marriage; kinship. **3.** the mutual dealings, connections, or feelings that exist between two countries, people, or groups. **4.** an emotional or sexual affair.

relative ('rɛlətɪv) *adj.* **1.** having significance only in relation to something else: "*hot*" *is a relative term.* **2.** comparative: *relative comfort; relative density.* **3.** respective: *the relative qualities of speed and accuracy.* **4.** (foll. by *to*) in proportion to: *earnings relative to production.* **5.** relevant: *the facts relative to the enquiry.* **6.** *Grammar.* of a clause (**relative clause**) that modifies a noun or pronoun occurring earli-

er in the sentence. **7.** *Grammar.* of or belonging to a class of words, such as *who, which,* or *that,* which function as conjunctions introducing relative clauses. ~*n.* **8.** a person who is related by blood or marriage; relation. —**'relatively** *adv.*

relative atomic mass *n.* same as **atomic weight.**

relativity (ˌrɛləˈtɪvɪtɪ) *n.* **1.** either of two theories developed by Albert Einstein, the **special theory of relativity,** which requires that the laws of physics shall be the same as seen by any two different observers in uniform relative motion, and the **general theory of relativity,** which considers observers with relative acceleration and leads to a theory of gravitation. **2.** the state of being relative.

relax (rɪˈlæks) *vb.* **1.** to make or become less tense, looser, or less rigid. **2.** to take rest, as from work or effort. **3.** to make (rules or discipline) less strict. **4.** (of a person) to become less formal. **5.** to lessen the intensity of: *he relaxed his vigilance.* —**re'laxed** *adj.*

relaxation (ˌriːlækˈseɪʃən) *n.* **1.** rest or refreshment, as after work or effort; recreation. **2.** a form of recreation: *his relaxation is cricket.* **3.** the act of relaxing.

relay *n.* ('riːleɪ). **1.** a person or team of people relieving others, as on a shift. **2.** short for **relay race. 3.** an automatic device that controls a valve or switch, esp. one in which a small change in current or voltage controls the switching on or off of circuits. **4.** *Radio.* a combination of a receiver and transmitter designed to receive radio signals and retransmit them. ~*vb.* (rɪˈleɪ). **5.** to receive (news or information) and pass it on to others. **6.** to retransmit (a signal) by means of a relay. **7.** *Brit.* to broadcast (a performance or event) as it happens.

relay race *n.* a race between teams of contestants in which each contestant covers a specified portion of the distance.

release (rɪˈliːs) *vb.* **1.** to free (a person or animal) from captivity or imprisonment. **2.** to free (someone) from obligation or duty. **3.** to free (something) from (one's grip); let fall. **4.** to issue (a record, film, or book) for sale. **5.** to make (news or information) known. **6.** to allow (something) to move freely, as by undoing a catch or lock: *she released the handbrake.* **7.** to emit heat, energy, radiation, etc.: *the accident released a cloud of poisonous gas.* ~*n.* **8.** the act of freeing or state of being freed. **9.** the act of issuing for sale or publication. **10.** something issued for sale or public showing, esp. a film or a record: *a new release from Bob Dylan.* **11.** a news item made public: *a press release.*

relegate ('rɛlɪˌgeɪt) vb. **1.** to move to a position of less authority, importance, or status; demote. **2.** (usually passive) Chiefly Brit. to demote (a sports team) to a lower division. —ˌrele'gation n.

relent (rɪ'lɛnt) vb. **1.** to change one's mind about some decision, esp. a harsh one. **2.** to become milder or less severe.

relentless (rɪ'lɛntlɪs) adj. **1.** (of a person) harsh, pitiless, and unyielding. **2.** (of pace or intensity) sustained; unremitting.

relevant ('rɛlɪvənt) adj. having direct bearing on the matter in hand; pertinent. —'relevance n.

reliable (rɪ'laɪəb³l) adj. able to be trusted; dependable. —reˌlia'bility n. —re'liably adv.

reliance (rɪ'laɪəns) n. dependence, confidence, or trust. —re'liant adj.

relic ('rɛlɪk) n. **1.** something that has survived from the past, such as an object or custom. **2.** something valued for its past associations. **3.** (usually pl.) a remaining part or fragment. **4.** R.C. Church, Eastern Church. part of the body of a saint or his belongings, venerated as holy.

relict ('rɛlɪkt) n. Archaic. **1.** a widow. **2.** a relic.

relief (rɪ'liːf) n. **1.** a feeling of cheerfulness that follows the removal of anxiety, pain, or distress. **2.** deliverance from or alleviation of anxiety, pain, etc. **3.** money, food, or clothing given to people in special need: famine relief. **4.** a diversion from monotony. **5.** a person who replaces another at some task or duty. **6.** a bus, plane, etc., that carries additional passengers when a scheduled service is full. **7.** the act of freeing a besieged town or fortress: the relief of Mafeking. **8.** Also called: relievo. Sculpture, archit. the projection of figures from a flat surface, so that they are partly or wholly free of it. **9.** any vivid effect resulting from contrast: comic relief. **10.** variation in altitude in an area; difference between highest and lowest level. **11. on relief.** U.S. & Canad. (of people) in receipt of government aid because of personal need.

relief map n. a map that shows the shape and height of the land surface, usually by means of contours.

relieve (rɪ'liːv) vb. **1.** to bring alleviation of (pain, distress, etc.) to (someone). **2.** to bring assistance to (someone in need). **3.** to take over the duties of (someone). **4.** to free (someone) from an obligation. **5.** (foll. by of) to take from: the thief relieved him of his watch. **6.** to make (something) less unpleasant, arduous, or monotonous. **7.** to set off by contrast: black relieved with touches of white. **8.** to bring a relieving force to (a besieged town, etc.). **9. relieve oneself.** to urinate or defecate. —re'lieved adj.

religion (rɪ'lɪdʒən) n. **1.** belief in, worship of, or obedience to a supernatural power or powers considered to be divine or to have control of human destiny. **2.** any formal expression of such belief: the Christian religion. **3.** Chiefly R.C. Church. the way of life entered upon by monks and nuns: to enter religion.

religious (rɪ'lɪdʒəs) adj. **1.** of or concerned with religion. **2.** pious; devout; godly. **3.** scrupulous or conscientious. **4.** Christianity. of or relating to the way of life of monks and nuns. ~n. **5.** Christianity. a monk or nun. —re'ligiously adv.

relinquish (rɪ'lɪŋkwɪʃ) vb. **1.** to give up (a task or struggle); abandon. **2.** to renounce (a claim or right). **3.** to release one's hold on; let go. —re'linquishment n.

reliquary ('rɛlɪkwərɪ) n., pl. -quaries. a container for relics of saints.

relish ('rɛlɪʃ) vb. **1.** to savour or enjoy (an experience) to the full. **2.** to anticipate eagerly. ~n. **3.** liking or enjoyment: he accepted the challenge with relish. **4.** pleasurable anticipation: he didn't have much relish for the idea. **5.** an appetizing or spicy food, such as a pickle, added to a main dish to enhance its flavour. **6.** a zestful touch: there was a certain relish in all his writing.

relive (riː'lɪv) vb. to experience (a sensation or event) again, esp. in the imagination.

relocate (ˌriːləʊ'keɪt) vb. (esp. of an employee or a business) to move or be moved to a new place or site. —ˌrelo'cation n.

reluctance (rɪ'lʌktəns) n. **1.** lack of eagerness; unwillingness. **2.** Physics. a measure of the resistance of a closed magnetic circuit to a magnetic flux.

reluctant (rɪ'lʌktənt) adj. not eager; unwilling. —re'luctantly adv.

rely (rɪ'laɪ) vb. -lying, -lied. (foll. by on or upon) **1.** to be dependent (on): he relies on his charm. **2.** to have trust or confidence (in): you can rely on us.

remain (rɪ'meɪn) vb. **1.** to stay behind or in the same place: to remain at home. **2.** to continue to be: to remain cheerful. **3.** to be left, as after use or the passage of time. **4.** to be left to be done, said, etc.: it remains to be pointed out.

remainder (rɪ'meɪndə) n. **1.** a part or portion that is left, as after use or the passage of time: the remainder of the milk. **2.** Maths. **a.** the amount left over when one quantity cannot be exactly divided by another: for $10 \div 3$, the remainder is 1. **b.** the amount left over when one quantity is subtracted from another. **3.** a number of copies of a book left unsold when demand ceases, which are sold at a reduced price. ~*vb.* **4.** to sell (copies of a book) as a remainder.

remains (rɪ'meɪnz) *pl. n.* **1.** any pieces that are left unused or still extant, as after use, consumption, or the passage of time: *archaeological remains.* **2.** a corpse.

remake ('riː,meɪk) *n.* something that is made again, esp. a new version of an old film.

remand (rɪ'mɑːnd) *vb.* **1.** *Law.* to send (a prisoner or accused person) back into custody to await trial. ~*n.* **2.** the sending of a prisoner or accused person back into custody to await trial. **3. on remand.** in custody or on bail awaiting trial.

remand centre *n.* (in Britain) an institution where accused people are detained while awaiting trial.

remark (rɪ'mɑːk) *vb.* **1.** to pass a casual comment (about). **2.** to perceive; observe; notice. ~*n.* **3.** a brief casually expressed thought or opinion. **4.** notice, comment, or observation: *the event passed without remark.*

remarkable (rɪ'mɑːkəb°l) *adj.* **1.** worthy of note or attention: *a remarkable achievement.* **2.** striking or extraordinary: *a remarkable sight.* —**re'markably** *adv.*

REME ('riːmɪ) Royal Electrical and Mechanical Engineers.

remedial (rɪ'miːdɪəl) *adj.* **1.** providing or intended as a remedy; curative. **2.** of special teaching for slow learners: *remedial education.* —**re'medially** *adv.*

remedy ('rɛmɪdɪ) *n., pl.* **-dies.** (usually foll. by *for* or *against*) **1.** any drug or agent that cures a disease or controls its symptoms. **2.** anything that serves to cure defects, improve conditions, etc.: *a remedy for industrial disputes.* ~*vb.* **3.** to relieve or cure (a disease). **4.** to correct (a fault, error, etc.). —**remediable** (rɪ'miːdɪəb°l) *adj.*

remember (rɪ'mɛmbə) *vb.* **1.** to become aware of (something forgotten) again. **2.** to keep (an idea, intention, etc.) in one's mind: *remember to do one's shopping.* **3.** to give money to (someone), as in a will or in tipping. **4.** (foll. by *to*) to mention (a person's name) to another person, as by way of greeting: *remember me to your mother.* **5.** to commemorate: *to remember the dead of the wars.*

remembrance (rɪ'mɛmbrəns) *n.* **1.** a remembering or being remembered. **2.** a memento or keepsake. **3.** the act of honouring some past event or person.

Remembrance Day *n.* **1.** (in Britain) Remembrance Sunday. **2.** (in Canada) a statutory holiday observed on November 11 in memory of the dead of both World Wars.

Remembrance Sunday *n.* (in Britain) the Sunday closest to November 11th, on which the dead of both World Wars are commemorated.

remind (rɪ'maɪnd) *vb.* (usually foll. by *of*) to cause (a person) to remember (something or to do something); put (a person) in mind (of someone or something): *remind me to phone home; flowers remind me of holidays.* —**re'minder** *n.*

reminisce (,rɛmɪ'nɪs) *vb.* to talk or write about old times or past experiences.

reminiscence (,rɛmɪ'nɪsəns) *n.* **1.** the act of recalling or narrating past experiences. **2.** (*often pl.*) some past experience, event or feeling that is recalled.

reminiscent (,rɛmɪ'nɪs°nt) *adj.* **1.** (foll. by *of*) stimulating memories (of) or comparisons (with). **2.** characterized by reminiscence.

remiss (rɪ'mɪs) *adj.* lacking in attention to duty; negligent.

remission (rɪ'mɪʃən) *n.* **1.** a reduction of the term of imprisonment, as for good conduct. **2.** forgiveness for sin. **3.** release from penalty or obligation. **4.** lessening of intensity, as in the symptoms of a disease.

remit *vb.* (rɪ'mɪt), **-mitting, -mitted. 1.** to send (payment), as for goods or service, esp. by post. **2.** *Law.* to send back (a case) to a lower court for further consideration. **3.** to refrain from exacting or cancel (a penalty or punishment). **4.** to slacken or ease off; abate. **5.** *Archaic.* to forgive (crime or sins). ~*n.* ('riːmɪt, rɪ'mɪt). **6.** area of authority (of a committee, inquiry, etc.).

remittance (rɪ'mɪtəns) *n.* money sent, esp. by post, as payment.

remittent (rɪ'mɪt°nt) *adj.* (of a disease) periodically less severe.

remix *vb.* (riː'mɪks). **1.** to change the relative volume and prominence of the individual performer's parts of (a recording). ~*n.* ('riːmɪks). **2.** a remixed version of a recording.

remnant ('rɛmnənt) *n.* **1.** (*often pl.*) a part left over. **2.** a surviving trace or vestige: *a remnant of imperialism.* **3.** a piece of material from the end of a roll.

remonstrance (rɪ'mɒnstrəns) *n.* **1.** the act of remonstrating. **2.** a protest or reproof, esp. a petition protesting against something.

remonstrate ('rɛmən,streɪt) *vb.* to argue in protest or objection: *to remonstrate with the government.* —**,remon'stration** *n.*

remorse (rɪ'mɔːs) *n.* **1.** a sense of deep regret and guilt for some misdeed. **2.** pity; compassion. —**re'morseful** *adj.*

remote (rɪ'məʊt) *adj.* **1.** far away; distant.

2. far from civilization. **3.** distant in time. **4.** operated from a distance; remote-controlled: *a remote monitor.* **5.** distantly related or connected: *a remote cousin.* **6.** slight or faint: *I haven't the remotest idea.* **7.** (of a person's manner) aloof or abstracted. —**re'motely** *adv.*

remote control *n.* control of a system from a distance, as by radio or electrical signals. —**re'mote-con'trolled** *adj.*

remould *vb.* (ˌriːˈməʊld). **1.** to bond a new tread onto the casing of (a worn pneumatic tyre). ~*n.* (ˈriːˌməʊld). **2.** a tyre made by this process.

removal (rɪˈmuːvˀl) *n.* **1.** the act of removing or state of being removed. **2. a.** a change of residence. **b.** (*as modifier*): *a removal company.*

remove (rɪˈmuːv) *vb.* **1.** to take away and place elsewhere. **2.** to dismiss (someone) from office. **3.** to do away with; get rid of. **4.** *Formal.* to change the location of one's home or place of business. ~*n.* **5.** the act of removing, esp. (formal) a removal of one's residence or place of work. **6.** the degree of difference: *only one remove from madness.* **7.** *Brit.* (in certain schools) a class or form.

remunerate (rɪˈmjuːnəˌreɪt) *vb.* to reward or pay for work or service. —**re,muner'a-tion** *n.* —**re'munerative** *adj.*

renaissance (rəˈneɪsəns; *U.S. & Canad. also* ˈrɛnəˌsɒns) *n.* a revival or rebirth, esp. of culture and learning.

Renaissance (rəˈneɪsəns; *U.S. & Canad. also* ˈrɛnəˌsɒns) *n.* **1. the.** the great revival of art, literature, and learning in Europe in the 14th, 15th, and 16th centuries. ~*adj.* **2.** of or from the Renaissance.

renal (ˈriːnˀl) *adj.* of or near the kidney.

renascent (rɪˈnæsˀnt, -ˈneɪ-) *adj.* becoming active or vigorous again: *renascent nationalism.* —**re'nascence** *n.*

rend (rɛnd) *vb.* **rending, rent. 1.** to tear violently; rip. **2.** (of a noise or cry) to disturb (the silence) with a shrill or piercing tone.

render (ˈrɛndə) *vb.* **1.** to present or submit (something) for payment, approval, etc. **2.** to give or provide (aid, a service, etc.). **3.** to cause to become: *grief had rendered him simple-minded.* **4.** to portray (something), as in painting, music, or acting. **5.** to translate (something). **6.** to yield or give: *the tomb rendered up its secret.* **7.** to cover the surface of (brickwork, etc.) with a coat of plaster. **8.** (often foll. by *down*) to extract (fat) from (meat) by melting.

rendezvous (ˈrɒndɪˌvuː) *n.,* *pl.* **-vous** (-ˌvuːz). **1.** a meeting or an appointment to

meet at a specified time and place. **2.** a place where people meet. ~*vb.* **3.** to meet at a specified time or place.

rendition (rɛnˈdɪʃən) *n.* **1.** a performance of a musical composition, dramatic role, etc. **2.** a translation.

renegade (ˈrɛnɪˌɡeɪd) *n.* a person who deserts his cause or faith for another.

renege (rɪˈniːɡ, -ˈneɪɡ) *vb.* **1.** (often foll. by *on*) to go back (on one's promise). ~*vb., n.* **2.** *Cards.* same as **revoke.**

renew (rɪˈnjuː) *vb.* **1.** to take up again after a break. **2.** to begin (an activity) again; recommence. **3.** to restate or reaffirm (a promise). **4.** to make (a lease, guarantee, etc.) valid for a further period. **5.** to regain or recover (strength). **6.** to restore to a new or fresh condition. **7.** to replace (an old or worn-out part or piece). **8.** to replenish (a supply, etc.). —**re'newable** *adj.* —**re'newal** *n.*

rennet (ˈrɛnɪt) *n.* a substance prepared from the stomachs of calves and used for curdling milk to make cheese.

renounce (rɪˈnaʊns) *vb.* **1.** to give up formally (a claim or right): *to renounce a title.* **2.** to repudiate: *to renounce Christianity.* **3.** to give up (something) voluntarily: *to renounce one's old ways.*

renovate (ˈrɛnəˌveɪt) *vb.* to restore (something) to good condition. —**,reno'vation** *n.* —**'reno,vator** *n.*

renown (rɪˈnaʊn) *n.* widespread reputation, esp. good fame. —**re'nowned** *adj.*

rent[1] (rɛnt) *n.* **1.** a payment made periodically by a tenant to a landlord or owner for the occupation or use of land, buildings, equipment, etc. ~*vb.* **2.** to allow (a person) to use one's property in return for periodic payments. **3.** to occupy or use (property) in return for periodic payments. **4.** (often foll. by *at*) to be let or rented (for a specified amount).

rent[2] (rɛnt) *n.* **1.** a slit made by tearing. ~*vb.* **2.** the past of **rend.**

rental (ˈrɛntˀl) *n.* **1.** the amount paid or received as rent. ~*adj.* **2.** of or relating to rent.

rent boy *n.* a young male prostitute.

renunciation (rɪˌnʌnsɪˈeɪʃən) *n.* **1.** the act or an instance of renouncing. **2.** a formal declaration renouncing something.

rep[1] (rɛp) *n. Theatre.* short for **repertory company.**

rep[2] (rɛp) *n.* **1.** a sales representative. **2.** someone elected to represent a group of people: *the union rep.* **3.** *N.Z. informal.* a rugby player selected to represent his district.

---

renegotiate	reoccurrence	reorganization
renumber	reopen	reorganize
reoccupy	reorder	repaint

repair[1] (rɪ'pɛə) vb. **1.** to restore (something damaged or broken) to good condition or working order. **2.** to heal (a breach or division) in (something): *to repair a broken marriage.* **3.** to make amends for (a mistake, injury, etc.). ~n. **4.** the act, task, or process of repairing. **5.** a part that has been repaired. **6.** state or condition: *in good repair.* —**re'pairable** adj.

repair[2] (rɪ'pɛə) vb. (usually foll. by *to*) to go (to a place).

reparable ('rɛpərəb'l, 'rɛprə-) adj. able to be repaired or remedied.

reparation (ˌrɛpə'reɪʃən) n. **1.** the act or process of making amends. **2.** (*usually pl.*) compensation paid by a defeated nation after a war for the damage and injuries it caused.

repartee (ˌrɛpɑː'tiː) n. **1.** a sharp witty remark made as a reply. **2.** skill in making sharp witty replies.

repast (rɪ'pɑːst) n. a meal or the food provided at a meal.

repatriate vb. (riː'pætrɪˌeɪt). **1.** to send back (a person) to the country of his birth or citizenship. ~n. (riː'pætrɪt). **2.** a person who has been repatriated. —**reˌpatri'ation** n.

repay (rɪ'peɪ) vb. -**paying**, -**paid**. **1.** to refund or reimburse. **2.** to make a return for (something): *to repay kindness.* —**re'payable** adj. —**re'payment** n.

repeal (rɪ'piːl) vb. **1.** to cancel officially; revoke: *these laws were repealed.* ~n. **2.** annulment or withdrawal. —**re'pealable** adj.

repeat (rɪ'piːt) vb. **1.** to do or experience (something) again, esp. to say or write (something) again. **2.** to occur more than once: *the last figure repeats.* **3.** to say (the words or sounds) uttered by someone else; echo. **4.** to recite (a poem, etc.) from memory. **5.** (of food) to be tasted again after eating as the result of belching. **6.** to tell to another person (the secrets imparted to one by someone else). ~n. **7. a.** the act or an instance of repeating. **b.** (*as modifier*): *a repeat performance.* **8.** a word, action, pattern, etc., that is repeated. **9.** *Radio, television.* a broadcast of a programme which has been broadcast before. **10.** *Music.* a passage that is an exact restatement of the passage preceding it. —**re'peated** adj. —**re'peatedly** adv.

repeater (rɪ'piːtə) n. **1.** a gun capable of firing several shots without reloading. **2.** a clock or watch which strikes the hour or quarter-hour just past, when a spring is pressed.

repel (rɪ'pɛl) vb. -**pelling**, -**pelled**. **1.** to force or drive back (someone or something).

2. to cause (someone) to feel disgusted. **3.** to be effective in keeping away, controlling, or resisting: *a spray that repels flies.* **4.** to fail to mix with or absorb: *water and oil repel each other.* **5.** to reject or spurn (someone or something): *she repelled his advances.* —**re'pellent** n., adj.
Usage. see **repulse**.

repent (rɪ'pɛnt) vb. to feel remorse (for); show penitence (for). —**re'pentance** n. —**re'pentant** adj.

repercussion (ˌriːpə'kʌʃən) n. **1.** (*often pl.*) a result or consequence of an action or event: *the repercussions of the war are still felt.* **2.** an echo or reverberation.

repertoire ('rɛpəˌtwɑː) n. **1.** all the works that a company or performer is competent to perform. **2.** the entire stock of skills or techniques that someone or something, such as a computer, is capable of.

repertory ('rɛpətrɪ) n., pl. -**ries**. **1.** same as **repertoire** (sense 2). **2.** short for **repertory company**.

repertory company n. a theatrical company that performs plays from a repertoire.

repetition (ˌrɛpɪ'tɪʃən) n. **1.** the act or an instance of repeating; reiteration. **2.** a thing, word, action, etc., that is repeated. **3.** a replica or copy. —**ˌrepe'titious** adj. —**repetitive** (rɪ'pɛtɪtɪv) adj.

repine (rɪ'paɪn) vb. to be fretful or discontented.

replace (rɪ'pleɪs) vb. **1.** to take the place of; supersede. **2.** to substitute a person or thing for (another); put in place of: *to replace an old pair of shoes.* **3.** to restore (something) to its rightful place.

replacement (rɪ'pleɪsmənt) n. **1.** the act or process of replacing. **2.** a person or thing that replaces another.

replay n. ('riːˌpleɪ). **1.** a showing again of a sequence of action immediately after it happens. **2.** a second match between a pair or group of contestants, esp. one that takes place because the first match was drawn. ~vb. (riː'pleɪ). **3.** to play again (a record, sporting contest, etc.).

replenish (rɪ'plɛnɪʃ) vb. to make full or complete again by supplying what has been used up. —**re'plenishment** n.

replete (rɪ'pliːt) adj. **1.** (often foll. by *with*) well supplied (with); abounding (in). **2.** having one's appetite completely or excessively satisfied. —**re'pletion** n.

replica ('rɛplɪkə) n. an exact copy or reproduction, esp. on a smaller scale.

reply (rɪ'plaɪ) vb. -**plying**, -**plied**. **1.** to make answer (to) in words or writing or by an action; respond. **2.** to say (something) in answer: *he replied that he didn't want to*

---

come. ~*n., pl.* **-plies. 3.** an answer; response.

report (rɪˈpɔːt) *n.* **1.** an account prepared after investigation and published or broadcast. **2.** a statement made widely known; rumour: *according to report, he is not dead.* **3.** an account of the deliberations of a committee or other group of people: *a report of parliamentary proceedings.* **4.** *Brit.* a statement on the progress of each schoolchild. **5.** comment on a person's character or actions; reputation: *he is of good report here.* **6.** a sharp loud noise, esp. one made by a gun. ~*vb.* **7.** to give an account (of); describe. **8.** to give an account of the results of an investigation (into): *to report on housing conditions.* **9.** (of a committee or other group of people) to make a formal report on (a subject). **10.** to complain about (a person), esp. to a superior. **11.** to present (oneself) or be present at an appointed place or for a specific purpose: *report to the manager's office.* **12.** (foll. by *to*) to be responsible (to) and under the authority (of). **13.** to act as a reporter. —re'portedly *adv.*

reported speech *n.* a report of what someone said that gives the content of the speech without repeating the exact words.

reporter (rɪˈpɔːtə) *n.* a person employed to gather news for a newspaper or broadcasting organization.

repose¹ (rɪˈpəʊz) *n.* **1.** a state of quiet restfulness; peace or tranquillity. **2.** calmness or composure. ~*vb.* **3.** to lie or lay down at rest. **4.** to lie when dead, as in the grave.

repose² (rɪˈpəʊz) *vb.* to put (trust) in a person or thing.

repository (rɪˈpɒzɪtrɪ) *n., pl.* **-ries. 1.** a place or container in which things can be stored for safety. **2.** a person to whom a secret is entrusted; confidant.

repossess (ˌriːpəˈzɛs) *vb.* to take back possession of (property), esp. when the buyer has not kept up payments. —**repossession** (ˌriːpəˈzɛʃən) *n.*

reprehend (ˌrɛprɪˈhɛnd) *vb.* to find fault with; criticize.

reprehensible (ˌrɛprɪˈhɛnsɪbˀl) *adj.* open to criticism; blameworthy.

represent (ˌrɛprɪˈzɛnt) *vb.* **1.** to stand as an equivalent of; correspond to. **2.** to act as a substitute (for). **3.** to act as or be the authorized delegate or agent for (a person, country, etc.): *an MP represents his constituency.* **4.** to be a means of expressing: *letters represent the sounds of speech.* **5.** to display the characteristics of; typify: *romanticism in music is represented by Liszt.* **6.** to present an image of through a picture or sculpture; portray. **7.** to bring

clearly before the mind. **8.** to set forth in words; state or explain. **9.** to describe as having a specified character or quality: *he represented her as a saint.* **10.** to act out the part of on stage; portray.

representation (ˌrɛprɪzɛnˈteɪʃən) *n.* **1.** the act or an instance of representing or the state of being represented. **2.** anything that represents, such as a pictorial portrait. **3.** a body of representatives. **4.** (*often pl.*) a statement of facts, true or alleged, esp. one seeking changes, or making a complaint. —ˌrepresenˈtational *adj.*

representative (ˌrɛprɪˈzɛntətɪv) *n.* **1.** a person or thing that represents another. **2.** a person who represents and tries to sell the products or services of a firm. **3.** a typical example. **4.** a person representing a constituency in a legislative body. ~*adj.* **5.** serving to represent; symbolic. **6.** typical of a class or kind. **7.** including examples of all the interests, types, etc., in a group. **8.** acting as deputy for another. **9.** of or relating to the political representation of the people: *representative government.*

repress (rɪˈprɛs) *vb.* **1.** to keep (feelings) under control; restrain. **2.** to put into a state of subjugation: *to repress a people.* **3.** *Psychol.* to banish (unpleasant thoughts) from one's conscious mind. —re'pression *n.* —re'pressive *adj.*

reprieve (rɪˈpriːv) *vb.* **1.** to postpone the punishment of (a person, esp. one condemned to death). **2.** to give temporary relief to (a person or thing). ~*n.* **3.** a postponement of punishment. **4.** a warrant granting a postponement. **5.** a temporary relief from pain or harm; respite.

reprimand (ˈrɛprɪˌmɑːnd) *n.* **1.** a formal reproof or rebuke. ~*vb.* **2.** to admonish or rebuke, esp. formally.

reprint *n.* (ˈriːˌprɪnt). **1.** a reissue of a printed work. ~*vb.* (riːˈprɪnt). **2.** to print again.

reprisal (rɪˈpraɪzˀl) *n.* a taking of revenge; retaliation.

reproach (rɪˈprəʊtʃ) *vb.* **1.** to express disapproval (of someone's actions); rebuke. ~*n.* **2.** rebuke or censure; blame. **3.** disgrace or shame: *to bring reproach upon one's family.* **4. beyond reproach.** perfect; beyond criticism. —re'proachful *adj.*

reprobate (ˈrɛprəʊˌbeɪt) *adj.* **1.** morally unprincipled; bad. ~*n.* **2.** an unprincipled bad person.

reprobation (ˌrɛprəʊˈbeɪʃən) *n.* disapproval, blame, or censure.

reproduce (ˌriːprəˈdjuːs) *vb.* **1.** to make a copy or representation of; duplicate. **2.** *Biol.* to produce or cause to produce offspring. **3.** to bring back into existence; recreate. —ˌreproˈducible *adj.*

reproduction (ˌriːprəˈdʌkʃən) n. 1. *Biol.* any process by which an animal or plant produces one or more individuals similar to itself. 2. a copy of a work of art. 3. (*modifier*) made in imitation of an earlier style: *reproduction furniture*. 4. the quality of sound from an audio system. 5. the act or process of reproducing. —ˌreproˈductive *adj.*

reproof (rɪˈpruːf) n. a rebuke.

reprove (rɪˈpruːv) vb. to rebuke or scold. —reˈprovingly *adv.*

reptile (ˈrɛptaɪl) n. 1. any of the cold-blooded vertebrates covered by horny scales or plates, such as the tortoises, snakes, lizards, and crocodiles. 2. a grovelling insignificant person: *you miserable little reptile!* —reptilian (rɛpˈtɪlɪən) n., *adj.*

republic (rɪˈpʌblɪk) n. 1. a form of government in which the people or their elected representatives possess the supreme power. 2. a country in which the head of state is an elected or nominated president.

republican (rɪˈpʌblɪkən) *adj.* 1. of a republic. 2. supporting or advocating a republic. ~n. 3. a supporter or advocate of a republic. —reˈpublicanˌism n.

Republican (rɪˈpʌblɪkən) *adj.* 1. belonging to a Republican Party. 2. belonging to the Irish Republican Army. ~n. 3. a member or supporter of a Republican Party. 4. a member or supporter of the Irish Republican Army. —Reˈpublicanˌism n.

repudiate (rɪˈpjuːdɪˌeɪt) vb. 1. to reject the authority or validity of (something). 2. to refuse to acknowledge or pay (a debt). 3. to disown (a person). —reˌpudiˈation n.

repugnant (rɪˈpʌgnənt) *adj.* repellent to the senses; disgusting. —reˈpugnance n.

repulse (rɪˈpʌls) vb. 1. to drive back or ward off (an attacking force). 2. to reject with coldness or discourtesy: *she repulsed his advances*. ~n. 3. a driving back or warding off. 4. a cold discourteous rejection or refusal.
Usage. The verbs *repulse* and *repel* share the meaning of physically driving back or away, but they can be carefully distinguished in other senses. Although the related adjective *repulsive* has the meaning of causing feelings of disgust, *repulse* does not mean to drive away by arousing disgust. Instead, *repel* is normally used in this sense, and *repulse* is used when the required meaning is to reject coldly or drive away with discourtesy.

repulsion (rɪˈpʌlʃən) n. 1. a feeling of disgust or aversion. 2. *Physics.* a force separating two objects, such as the force between two like electric charges.

repulsive (rɪˈpʌlsɪv) *adj.* 1. disgusting or distasteful; loathsome. 2. *Physics.* of repulsion. —reˈpulsively *adv.*

reputable (ˈrɛpjʊtəbˀl) *adj.* of good reputation; trustworthy or respectable. —ˈreputably *adv.*

reputation (ˌrɛpjʊˈteɪʃən) n. 1. the estimation in which a person or thing is generally held; opinion. 2. a high opinion generally held about a person or thing; esteem. 3. notoriety or fame, esp. for some specified characteristic.

repute (rɪˈpjuːt) vb. 1. (*usually passive*) to consider (a person or thing) to be as specified: *he is reputed to be rich.* ~n. 2. public estimation: *a writer of little repute.*

reputed (rɪˈpjuːtɪd) *adj.* supposed: *reputed innocence.* —reˈputedly *adv.*

request (rɪˈkwɛst) vb. 1. to ask for or politely demand: *to request a bottle of wine.* ~n. 2. the act or an instance of asking for something. 3. something asked for. 4. **on request.** if asked for: *application forms are available on request.*

request stop n. a point on a route at which a bus stops only if signalled to do so.

Requiem (ˈrɛkwɪəm) n. 1. *R.C. Church.* a Mass celebrated for the dead. 2. a musical setting of this Mass.

require (rɪˈkwaɪə) vb. 1. to need. 2. to be a necessary condition: *this work requires precision.* 3. to insist upon. 4. to order or command: *to require someone to account for his actions.*

requirement (rɪˈkwaɪəmənt) n. 1. something demanded or imposed as an obligation. 2. a thing desired or needed.

requisite (ˈrɛkwɪzɪt) *adj.* 1. absolutely essential; indispensable. ~n. 2. something indispensable; necessity.

requisition (ˌrɛkwɪˈzɪʃən) n. 1. an authoritative or formal request or demand. 2. an official form on which such a demand is made. 3. the act of taking something over, esp. temporarily for military or public use. ~vb. 4. to demand and take for use, esp. by military or public authority.

requite (rɪˈkwaɪt) vb. to make return to (a person for a kindness or injury); repay with a similar action. —reˈquital n.

reredos (ˈrɪədɒs) n. a screen or wall decoration at the back of an altar.

rerun vb. (riːˈrʌn), **-running, -ran.** 1. to put on (a film or programme) again. 2. to run (a race) again. ~n. (ˈriːˌrʌn). 3. a repeat. 4. a race that is run again.

rescind (rɪˈsɪnd) vb. to annul or repeal.

rescission (rɪˈsɪʒən) n. a rescinding.

rescue (ˈrɛskjuː) vb. **-cuing, -cued.** 1. to

reprogram	reread	reroute
reprogrammable	rerecording	reschedule
republish	reroof	

bring (someone or something) out of danger or trouble; save. ~n. **2.** the act or an instance of rescuing. —**'rescuer** n.

research (rɪ'sɜːtʃ) n. **1.** systematic investigation to establish facts or collect information on a subject. ~vb. **2.** to carry out investigations into (a subject). —**re'searcher** n.

resemble (rɪ'zɛmb°l) vb. to possess some similarity to; be like. —**re'semblance** n.

resent (rɪ'zɛnt) vb. to feel bitter, indignant, or aggrieved at. —**re'sentful** adj. —**re'sentment** n.

reservation (ˌrɛzə'veɪʃən) n. **1.** something reserved, esp. a seat. **2.** (often pl.) a qualification or uncertainty that prevents one's wholehearted acceptance or approval. **3.** an area of land set aside, esp. (in the U.S. and Canada) for American Indian peoples. **4.** Brit. the strip of land between the two carriageways of a dual carriageway.

reserve (rɪ'zɜːv) vb. **1.** to keep back or set aside, esp. for future use. **2.** to keep for oneself; retain: I reserve the right to question these men later. **3.** to obtain or secure by advance arrangement: I have reserved two tickets. **4.** to delay announcing (a legal judgment). ~n. **5.** something kept back or set aside for future use. **6.** the state or condition of being reserved: I have plenty in reserve. **7.** a tract of land set aside for a special purpose: a nature reserve. **8.** Canad. an Indian reservation. **9.** Sport. a substitute. **10.** that part of a nation's armed services not in active service. **11.** coolness or formality of manner; reticence. **12.** (often pl.) Finance. money or assets held by a bank or business to meet future expenses.

reserved (rɪ'zɜːvd) adj. **1.** set aside for use by a particular person. **2.** cool or formal in manner; reticent.

reserve price n. Brit. the minimum price acceptable to the owner of property being auctioned or sold.

reservist (rɪ'zɜːvɪst) n. a member of a nation's military reserve.

reservoir ('rɛzə,vwɑː) n. **1.** a natural or artificial lake used for collecting and storing water for community use. **2.** a large supply of something: a reservoir of talent.

reshuffle (riː'ʃʌf°l) n. **1.** a reorganization of jobs in a government or cabinet. ~vb. **2.** to reorganize jobs or duties in a government.

reside (rɪ'zaɪd) vb. Formal. **1.** to live permanently (in a place); have one's home (in): he resides in London. **2.** (of things or qualities) to be inherently present (in); be vested (in): political power resides in military strength.

residence ('rɛzɪdəns) n. **1.** the place in which one resides; home. **2.** a large imposing house; mansion. **3.** the fact of residing in a place or a period of residing. **4. in residence. a.** actually resident: the Queen is in residence. **b.** designating a creative artist working for a set period at a college, gallery, etc.: writer in residence.

resident ('rɛzɪdənt) n. **1.** a person who resides in a place. **2.** a bird or animal that does not migrate. ~adj. **3.** living in a place; residing. **4.** living at a place in order to carry out a job or duty: a resident caretaker. **5.** (of birds and animals) not in the habit of migrating.

residential (ˌrɛzɪ'dɛnʃəl) adj. **1.** suitable for or used for residence: a residential area. **2.** relating to residence.

residential school n. a government boarding school in N Canada for Indian and Inuit students.

residual (rɪ'zɪdjʊəl) adj. **1.** of or being a remainder; leftover. ~n. **2.** something left over as a residue; remainder.

residue ('rɛzɪ,djuː) n. **1.** matter remaining after something has been removed. **2.** Law. what is left of an estate after the discharge of debts and distribution of specific gifts.

residuum (rɪ'zɪdjʊəm) n., pl. -ua (-jʊə). same as **residue.**

resign (rɪ'zaɪn) vb. **1.** to give up (a job, office, etc.). **2.** to reconcile (oneself) to: to resign oneself to death. **3.** to give up (a right, claim, etc.); relinquish.

resignation (ˌrɛzɪg'neɪʃən) n. **1.** the act of resigning. **2.** a formal document stating one's intention to resign. **3.** passive endurance of difficulties.

resigned (rɪ'zaɪnd) adj. having or showing resignation; enduring passively. —**resignedly** (rɪ'zaɪnɪdlɪ) adv.

resilient (rɪ'zɪlɪənt) adj. **1.** (of an object) capable of regaining its original shape or position after bending, stretching, or compression; elastic. **2.** (of a person) recovering easily and quickly from illness or misfortune. —**re'silience** n.

resin ('rɛzɪn) n. **1.** a solid or semisolid substance exuded from certain plants: pine resin. **2.** a similar substance produced synthetically. ~vb. **3.** to treat or coat with resin. —**'resinous** adj.

resist (rɪ'zɪst) vb. **1.** to stand firm against; not yield to: he resisted the changes. **2.** to be proof against: to resist corrosion. **3.** to refuse to comply with: to resist arrest. **4.** to refrain from, esp. in spite of temptation: I cannot resist chocolate. —**re'sistible** adj.

resistance (rɪ'zɪstəns) n. **1.** the act of resisting. **2.** the capacity to withstand something, esp. the body's natural capacity to withstand disease. **3.** the opposition to a flow of electric current through a circuit, component, or substance. **4.** any force that tends to retard or oppose motion: *wind resistance.* **5. line of least resistance.** the easiest, but not necessarily the best or most honourable, course of action. **6.** See **passive resistance.** —re'**sistant** *adj., n.*

Resistance (rɪ'zɪstəns) *n.* **the.** an illegal organization fighting for national liberty in a country under enemy occupation.

resistor (rɪ'zɪstə) *n.* an electrical component designed to introduce a known value of resistance into a circuit.

resit (riː'sɪt) *vb.* -**sitting, -sat. 1.** to sit (an examination) again. ~*n.* **2.** an examination which one must sit again.

resoluble (rɪ'zɒljʊb²l, 'rɛzəl-) *adj.* able to be resolved or analysed.

resolute ('rɛzə₁luːt) *adj.* firm in purpose or belief; steadfast; determined. —'**reso-₁lutely** *adv.*

resolution (₁rɛzə'luːʃən) *n.* **1.** firmness or determination. **2.** something resolved or determined; decision. **3.** a formal expression of opinion by a meeting. **4.** the act of separating something into its constituent elements. **5.** *Music.* the process in harmony whereby a dissonant note or chord is followed by a consonant one. **6.** the ability of a television to reproduce fine detail. **7.** *Physics.* Also called: **resolving power.** the ability of a telescope or microscope to produce separate images of closely placed objects.

resolve (rɪ'zɒlv) *vb.* **1.** to decide or determine firmly. **2.** to express (an opinion) formally, esp. by a vote. **3.** (usually foll. by *into*) to separate or cause to separate into (constituent parts). **4.** to find the answer or solution to. **5.** to explain away or dispel: *to resolve a doubt.* **6.** to bring to an end; conclude: *to resolve an argument.* **7.** *Music.* to follow (a dissonant note or chord) by one producing a consonance. **8.** *Physics.* to distinguish between (separate parts) of (an image) as in a microscope, telescope, or other optical instrument. ~*n.* **9.** something decided; resolution: *it was her resolve to work all day.* **10.** firmness of purpose; determination: *nothing can break his resolve.*

resolved (rɪ'zɒlvd) *adj.* fixed in purpose or intention; determined.

resonance ('rɛzənəns) *n.* **1.** the condition or quality of being resonant. **2.** sound produced by a body vibrating in sympathy with a neighbouring source of sound.

resonant ('rɛzənənt) *adj.* **1.** resounding or re-echoing. **2.** producing resonance: *resonant walls.* **3.** full of, or intensified by, resonance: *a resonant voice.*

resonate ('rɛzə₁neɪt) *vb.* to resound or cause to resound. —'**reso₁nator** *n.*

resort (rɪ'zɔːt) *vb.* **1.** (usually foll. by *to*) to have recourse (to) for help, use, etc.: *to resort to violence.* **2.** to go, esp. often or habitually: *to resort to the beach.* ~*n.* **3.** a place to which many people go for recreation, etc.: *a holiday resort.* **4.** the use of something as a means or aid. **5. last resort.** the last possible course of action open to one.

resound (rɪ'zaʊnd) *vb.* **1.** to ring or echo with sound; reverberate. **2.** to make a prolonged echoing noise. **3.** (of sounds) to echo or ring. **4.** to be widely famous: *his fame resounded throughout India.*

resounding (rɪ'zaʊndɪŋ) *adj.* **1.** clear and emphatic: *a resounding vote of confidence.* **2.** resonant; reverberating. —re'**sounding-ly** *adv.*

resource (rɪ'zɔːs, -'sɔːs) *n.* **1.** the ability to deal with problems; initiative or quick-wittedness: *a man of resource.* **2.** (*often pl.*) a source of economic wealth, esp. of a country or business enterprise: *natural resources.* **3.** something resorted to for aid or support: *resource centre.* **4.** a means of doing something; expedient: *flight was his only resource.*

resourceful (rɪ'zɔːsfʊl, -'sɔːs-) *adj.* ingenious, capable, and full of initiative. —re-'**sourcefulness** *n.*

respect (rɪ'spɛkt) *n.* **1.** an attitude of deference, admiration, or esteem. **2.** the state of being honoured or esteemed. **3.** a detail, point, or characteristic: *they differ in some respects.* **4. in respect of** *or* **with respect to.** in reference or relation to. **5.** consideration: *respect for people's feelings.* **6.** (*often pl.*) an expression of esteem or regard: *to pay one's respects.* ~*vb.* **7.** to have an attitude of esteem towards: *to respect one's elders.* **8.** to pay proper attention to or consideration to: *to respect Swiss neutrality.* —re'**specter** *n.*

respectable (rɪ'spɛktəb²l) *adj.* **1.** having or deserving the respect of other people. **2.** having good social standing or reputation, esp. as regards morals: *a respectable woman.* **3.** relatively or fairly good: *a respectable salary.* **4.** fit to be seen by other people; presentable. —re₁specta'**bility** *n.* —re'**spectably** *adv.*

respectful (rɪ'spɛktfʊl) *adj.* full of, showing, or giving respect.

respecting (rɪ'spɛktɪŋ) *prep.* concerning; regarding.

respective (rɪ'spɛktɪv) *adj.* belonging or relating separately to each of several people or things: *we went our respective ways.*

respectively (rɪ'spɛktɪvlɪ) *adv.* (in listing things that refer to another list) separately in the order given: *he gave Janet and John a cake and a sweet respectively.*

respiration (₁rɛspɪ'reɪʃən) *n.* **1.** the process in living organisms of taking in oxygen and giving out carbon dioxide. **2.** the breakdown of complex organic substances that takes place in the cells of animals and plants, producing energy and carbon dioxide. —**respiratory** (ˈrɛspɪrətrɪ) adj.

respirator (ˈrɛspɪˌreɪtə) n. 1. an apparatus for providing artificial respiration. 2. a device worn over the mouth and nose to prevent inhalation of noxious fumes.

respire (rɪˈspaɪə) vb. 1. to inhale and exhale (air); breathe. 2. to undergo respiration.

respite (ˈrɛspɪt, -paɪt) n. 1. a pause from exertion; interval of rest. 2. a temporary delay; reprieve. ~vb. 3. to grant a respite to.

resplendent (rɪˈsplɛndənt) adj. brilliant or splendid in appearance. —**reˈsplendence** n.

respond (rɪˈspɒnd) vb. 1. to state or utter (something) in reply. 2. to act in reply; react: to respond by issuing an invitation. 3. (foll. by to) to react favourably: this patient will respond to treatment.

respondent (rɪˈspɒndənt) n. Law. a person against whom a petition is brought.

response (rɪˈspɒns) n. 1. the act of responding; reply or reaction. 2. (usually pl.) Christianity. a short sentence or phrase recited or sung in reply to the priest at a church service. 3. a reaction to stimulation of the nervous system.

responsibility (rɪˌspɒnsɪˈbɪlɪtɪ) n., pl. -ties. 1. the state or position of being responsible. 2. a person or thing for which one is responsible.

responsible (rɪˈspɒnsɪbˀl) adj. 1. (usually foll. by for) having control or authority (over). 2. (foll. by to) being accountable for one's actions and decisions to: responsible to the manager. 3. (of a position, duty, etc.) involving decision and accountability. 4. (often foll. by for) being the agent or cause (of some action): responsible for a mistake. 5. rational and accountable for one's own actions. —**reˈsponsibly** adv.

responsive (rɪˈspɒnsɪv) adj. reacting or replying quickly or favourably, as to a suggestion or initiative. —**reˈsponsiveness** n.

rest¹ (rɛst) n. 1. relaxation from exertion or labour. 2. repose; sleep. 3. any relief or refreshment, as from worry. 4. calm; tranquillity. 5. death regarded as repose: eternal rest. 6. at rest. a. not moving. b. calm. c. dead. d. asleep. 7. a pause or interval. 8. a mark in a musical score indicating a pause of specific duration. 9. a thing or place on which to put something for support or to steady it. 10. lay to rest. to bury (a dead person). ~vb. 11. to become or make refreshed. 12. to position (oneself, etc.) for rest or relaxation. 13. to place for

support or steadying: to rest one's elbows on the table. 14. to be at ease; be calm. 15. to cease or cause to cease from motion or exertion. 16. to remain without further attention or action: let the matter rest. 17. to direct (one's eyes) or (of one's eyes) to be directed: her eyes rested on the child. 18. to depend or cause to depend; rely: the whole argument rests on one crucial fact. 19. Law. to finish the introduction of evidence in (a case). 20. to put pastry in a cool place to allow the gluten to contract.

rest² (rɛst) n. (usually preceded by the) 1. something left; remainder. 2. the others: the rest of the world. ~vb. 3. to continue to be (as specified); remain: rest assured.

rest area n. Austral. & N.Z. a motorist's stopping place, usually off a highway, equipped with tables and seats.

restaurant (ˈrɛstəˌrɒŋ, ˈrɛstrɒŋ) n. a place where meals are prepared and served to customers.

restaurant car n. Brit. a railway coach in which meals are served.

restaurateur (ˌrɛstərəˈtɜː) n. a person who owns or runs a restaurant.

rest-cure n. a rest taken as part of a course of medical treatment.

restful (ˈrɛstfʊl) adj. relaxing or soothing.

restitution (ˌrɛstɪˈtjuːʃən) n. 1. the act of giving back something that has been lost or stolen. 2. Law. compensation for loss or injury.

restive (ˈrɛstɪv) adj. 1. restless, nervous, or uneasy. 2. impatient of control or authority.

restless (ˈrɛstlɪs) adj. 1. unable to stay still or quiet. 2. worried; anxious; uneasy. 3. not restful: a restless night.

restoration (ˌrɛstəˈreɪʃən) n. 1. the act of restoring to a former or original condition, place, etc. 2. the giving back of something lost or stolen. 3. something restored, replaced, or reconstructed. 4. a model or representation of a ruin or extinct animal. 5. the Restoration. Brit. history. the re-establishment of the monarchy in 1660 or the reign of Charles II (1660–85).

restorative (rɪˈstɒrətɪv) adj. 1. tending to renew health, spirits, etc. ~n. 2. anything that restores or revives.

restore (rɪˈstɔː) vb. 1. to return (something) to its original or former condition. 2. to bring back to health or good spirits. 3. to return (something lost or stolen) to its owner. 4. to reintroduce or re-enforce: to restore discipline. 5. to reconstruct (a ruin, extinct animal, etc.). —**reˈstorer** n.

restrain (rɪˈstreɪn) vb. 1. to hold (someone) back from some action, esp. by force.

2. to deprive (someone) of liberty, as by imprisonment. **3.** to limit or restrict.

restrained (rɪˈstreɪnd) *adj.* not displaying emotion.

restraint (rɪˈstreɪnt) *n.* **1.** the ability to control one's impulses or passions. **2.** a restraining or being restrained. **3.** a restriction.

restrict (rɪˈstrɪkt) *vb.* (often foll. by *to*) to confine or keep within certain, often specified, limits. —**reˈstriction** *n.* —**reˈstrictive** *adj.*

restrictive practice *n. Brit.* **1.** a trading agreement against the public interest. **2.** a practice of a union or other group tending to limit the freedom of other workers or employers.

rest room *n. U.S. & Canad.* a toilet in a public building.

result (rɪˈzʌlt) *n.* **1.** the outcome or consequence of an action, policy, etc. **2.** a number or value obtained by solving a mathematical problem. **3.** (*often pl.*) the final score of a sporting contest. **4.** (*often pl.*) the mark or grade obtained in an examination. ~*vb.* **5.** (often foll. by *from*) to be the outcome or consequence (of). **6.** (foll. by *in*) to end (in a specified way): *to result in tragedy.*

resultant (rɪˈzʌltənt) *adj.* **1.** that results; resulting. ~*n.* **2.** *Maths, physics.* a single vector that is the vector sum of two or more other vectors, such as a force which results from two other forces acting on a single point.

resume (rɪˈzjuːm) *vb.* **1.** to begin again or go on with (something interrupted). **2.** to occupy again, take back, or recover: *to resume one's seat.*

résumé (ˈrɛzjʊˌmeɪ) *n.* **1.** a short descriptive summary, as of events. **2.** *U.S. & Canad.* a curriculum vitae.

resumption (rɪˈzʌmpʃən) *n.* the act of resuming or beginning again.

resurgent (rɪˈsɜːdʒənt) *adj.* rising again, as to new life or vigour: *resurgent nationalism.* —**reˈsurgence** *n.*

resurrect (ˌrɛzəˈrɛkt) *vb.* **1.** to bring or be brought back to life from death. **2.** to bring back into use or activity; revive.

resurrection (ˌrɛzəˈrɛkʃən) *n.* **1.** a return to life by a dead person. **2.** revival or renewal. **3.** (*usually cap.*) *Christian theol.* the rising again of Christ from the tomb three days after his death. **4.** (*usually cap.*) the rising again from the dead of all people at the Last Judgment.

resuscitate (rɪˈsʌsɪˌteɪt) *vb.* to restore to consciousness; revive. —**reˌsusciˈtation** *n.*

retail (ˈriːteɪl) *n.* **1.** the sale of goods individually or in small quantities to consumers. ~*adj.* **2.** of, relating to, or engaged in such selling: *retail prices.* ~*adv.* **3.** in small amounts or at a retail price. ~*vb.* **4.** to sell or be sold in small quantities to consumers. **5.** (rɪˈteɪl). to relate (gossip or scandal) in detail. —**ˈretailer** *n.*

retain (rɪˈteɪn) *vb.* **1.** to keep in one's possession. **2.** to be able to hold or contain: *soil that retains water.* **3.** (of a person) to be able to remember (something) without difficulty. **4.** to hold in position. **5.** *Law.* to engage the services of (a barrister) by payment of a preliminary fee.

retainer (rɪˈteɪnə) *n.* **1.** a fee paid in advance to secure first option on someone, esp. a barrister's services. **2.** a reduced rent paid for a flat, room, etc., to reserve it for future use. **3.** a servant who has been with a family for a long time.

retaining wall *n.* a wall constructed to hold back earth, loose rock, etc.

retake *vb.* (riːˈteɪk), **-taking, -took, -taken.** **1.** to take something, such as an examination or vote, again. **2.** to recapture: *to retake a fortress.* ~*n.* (ˈriːˌteɪk). **3.** *Films.* a rephotographed scene.

retaliate (rɪˈtælɪˌeɪt) *vb.* **1.** to repay some injury or wrong in kind. **2.** to cast (accusations) back upon a person. —**reˌtaliˈation** *n.* —**retaliatory** (rɪˈtælɪətrɪ) *adj.*

retard (rɪˈtɑːd) *vb.* to delay or slow down (the progress or speed) of (something). —**reˈtardant** *n., adj.* —**ˌretarˈdation** *n.*

retarded (rɪˈtɑːdɪd) *adj.* underdeveloped, esp. mentally.

retch (rɛtʃ, riːtʃ) *vb.* **1.** to undergo an involuntary spasm of ineffectual vomiting. ~*n.* **2.** an involuntary spasm of ineffectual vomiting.

retention (rɪˈtɛnʃən) *n.* **1.** the act of retaining or state of being retained. **2.** the capacity to remember. **3.** *Pathol.* the abnormal holding of something within the body, esp. fluid. —**reˈtentive** *adj.*

rethink *vb.* (riːˈθɪŋk), **-thinking, -thought.** **1.** to think about (something) again, esp. with a view to changing one's tactics or opinions. ~*n.* (ˈriːθɪŋk). **2.** the act or an instance of thinking again.

reticent (ˈrɛtɪsənt) *adj.* not communicative; not saying all that one knows. —**ˈreticence** *n.*

reticulate *adj.* (rɪˈtɪkjʊlɪt) **1.** in the form of a network or having a network of parts: *a reticulate leaf.* ~*vb.* (rɪˈtɪkjʊˌleɪt). **2.** to form or be formed into a net. —**reˌticuˈlation** *n.*

retina (ˈrɛtɪnə) *n., pl.* **-nas** *or* **-nae** (-ˌniː). the light-sensitive inner lining of the back of the eyeball. —**ˈretinal** *adj.*

---

restructure **restyle** **retell**

retinue ('rɛtɪˌnjuː) *n.* a body of aides and followers attending an important person.

retire (rɪ'taɪə) *vb.* **1.** to give up or to cause (a person) to give up work, esp. on reaching pensionable age. **2.** to go away, as into seclusion, esp. to rest. **3.** to go to bed. **4.** to withdraw from a sporting contest, esp. because of injury. **5.** to pull back (troops) from battle or (of troops) to fall back. —**re'tired** *adj.* —**re'tirement** *n.*

retirement pension *n. Brit.* a weekly payment made by the government to a retired man over 65 or a woman over 60.

retiring (rɪ'taɪərɪŋ) *adj.* shunning contact with others; shy; reserved.

retort[1] (rɪ'tɔːt) *vb.* **1.** to utter (something) quickly, wittily, or angrily, in response. **2.** to use (an argument) against its originator. ~*n.* **3.** a sharp, angry, or witty reply. **4.** an argument used against its originator.

retort[2] (rɪ'tɔːt) *n.* **1.** a glass vessel with a long tapering neck that is bent down, used for distillation. **2.** a vessel used for heating ores in the production of metals or heating coal to produce gas.

retouch (riː'tʌtʃ) *vb.* to restore, correct, or improve (a painting, photograph, make-up, etc.) with new touches.

retrace (rɪ'treɪs) *vb.* **1.** to go back over (one's steps, a route, etc.). **2.** to go over (a story, account, etc.) from the beginning.

retract (rɪ'trækt) *vb.* **1.** to draw in (a part or appendage): *the plane's undercarriage had not yet retracted.* **2.** to withdraw (a statement, opinion, charge, etc.) as invalid or unjustified. **3.** to go back on (a promise or agreement). —**re'traction** *n.*

retractile (rɪ'træktaɪl) *adj.* capable of being drawn in: *the retractile claws of a cat.*

retread *vb.* (riː'trɛd), -**treading**, -**treaded**. **1.** to bond a new tread onto (a worn tyre). ~*n.* ('riːˌtrɛd). **2.** a remoulded tyre.

retreat (rɪ'triːt) *vb.* **1.** *Mil.* to withdraw or retire in the face of or from action with an enemy. **2.** to retire or withdraw, as to seclusion or shelter. ~*n.* **3.** the act of retreating or withdrawing. **4.** *Mil.* **a.** a withdrawal or retirement in the face of the enemy. **b.** a bugle call signifying withdrawal or retirement. **5.** a place to which one may retire, esp. for religious contemplation. **6.** a period of seclusion, esp. for religious contemplation.

retrench (rɪ'trɛntʃ) *vb.* to reduce (costs); economize. —**re'trenchment** *n.*

retribution (ˌrɛtrɪ'bjuːʃən) *n.* punishment or vengeance for wrongdoing, sin, or harm. —**retributive** (rɪ'trɪbjutɪv) *adj.*

retrieve (rɪ'triːv) *vb.* **1.** to get or fetch back again; recover. **2.** to bring back to a more satisfactory state; revive. **3.** to res-

cue or save. **4.** to recover or make newly available (stored information) from a computer system. **5.** (of dogs) to find and fetch (shot birds and animals). **6.** to recall; remember. ~*n.* **7.** the chance of being retrieved: *beyond retrieve.* —**re'trievable** *adj.* —**re'trieval** *n.*

retriever (rɪ'triːvə) *n.* a dog trained to retrieve shot birds and animals.

retro ('rɛtrəʊ) *adj.* associated with or revived from the past: *retro fashion.*

retro- *prefix.* **1.** back or backwards: *retroactive.* **2.** located behind: *retrochoir.*

retroactive (ˌrɛtrəʊ'æktɪv) *adj.* effective from a date in the past: *retroactive legislation.*

retrograde ('rɛtrəʊˌɡreɪd) *adj.* **1.** moving or bending backwards. **2.** (esp. of order) reverse or inverse. **3.** tending towards an earlier worse condition; declining or deteriorating. ~*vb.* **4.** to go backwards or deteriorate.

retrogress (ˌrɛtrəʊ'ɡrɛs) *vb.* to go back to an earlier worse condition. —**retro'gression** *n.* —**retro'gressive** *adj.*

retrorocket ('rɛtrəʊˌrɒkɪt) *n.* a small auxiliary rocket on a larger rocket or a spacecraft, that produces thrust in the opposite direction to the direction of flight in order to decelerate.

retrospect ('rɛtrəʊˌspɛkt) *n.* **in retrospect.** when looking back on the past.

retrospective (ˌrɛtrəʊ'spɛktɪv) *adj.* **1.** looking backwards, esp. in time. **2.** applying to the past; retroactive. ~*n.* **3.** an exhibition of an artist's life's work.

retroussé (rə'truːseɪ) *adj.* (of a nose) turned up.

retsina (rɛt'siːnə) *n.* a Greek wine flavoured with resin.

return (rɪ'tɜːn) *vb.* **1.** to come back to a former place or state. **2.** to replace or restore. **3.** to repay with something of equivalent value: *return the compliment.* **4.** to earn or yield (profit or interest). **5.** to come back or revert in thought or speech: *I'll return to that later.* **6.** to recur or reappear: *the symptoms have returned.* **7.** to answer or reply. **8.** to vote into office; elect. **9.** *Law.* (of a jury) to deliver a verdict. **10.** *Ball games.* to hit, throw, or play (a ball) back. ~*n.* **11.** the act or an instance of coming back. **12.** something that is given or sent back, esp. unsatisfactory merchandise or a theatre ticket for resale. **13.** replacement or restoration. **14.** (*often pl.*) the yield or profit from an investment or venture. **15. in return.** in exchange. **16.** a recurrence or reappearance. **17.** a statement of one's taxable income (a **tax return**). **18.** (*often pl.*) a statement of the votes counted at an election.

19. an answer or reply. **20.** *Brit.* short for **return ticket. 21.** *Ball games.* the act of playing or throwing a ball back. **22.** (*modifier*) of, relating to, or characterized by a return: *a return visit.* **23. by return** (**of post**). *Brit.* by the next post back to the sender. **24. many happy returns** (**of the day**). a conventional birthday greeting. —**re'turnable** *adj.*

returned man *n. Austral. & Canad.* a soldier who has served abroad. Also (*Austral. & N.Z.*): **returned soldier.**

returning officer *n.* an official in charge of conducting an election in a constituency.

return ticket *n. Brit.* a ticket entitling a passenger to travel to his destination and back.

reunify (riː'juːnɪˌfaɪ) *vb.* **-fying, -fied.** to bring together again something previously divided. —**ˌreunifiˈcation** *n.*

reunion (riː'juːnjən) *n.* **1.** the act of coming together again. **2.** the state of having been brought together again. **3.** a gathering of relatives, friends, or former associates.

rev (rɛv) *Informal.* ~*n.* **1.** revolution per minute. ~*vb.* **revving, revved. 2.** (often foll. by *up*) to increase the speed of revolution of (an engine).

rev. 1. revise(d). **2.** revision.

Rev. Reverend.

revamp (riː'væmp) *vb.* to patch up or renovate.

Revd. Reverend.

reveal (rɪ'viːl) *vb.* **1.** to disclose or divulge (a secret). **2.** to expose to view or show (something concealed). **3.** (of God) to disclose (divine truths).

reveille (rɪ'vælɪ) *n.* a signal given by a bugle or drum to awaken soldiers or sailors in the morning.

revel ('rɛvəl) *vb.* **-elling, -elled** *or U.S.* **-eling, -eled. 1.** (foll. by *in*) to take pleasure or wallow: *to revel in success.* **2.** to take part in noisy festivities. ~*n.* **3.** (*often pl.*) an occasion of noisy merrymaking. —**'reveller** *n.*

revelation (ˌrɛvə'leɪʃən) *n.* **1.** the disclosure of a truth previously secret or obscure. **2.** a fact disclosed or revealed. **3.** *Christianity.* God's disclosure of his own nature and his purpose for mankind.

Revelation (ˌrɛvə'leɪʃən) *n.* (*popularly, often pl.*) the last book of the New Testament, containing visionary descriptions of heaven, and of the end of the world.

revelry ('rɛvəlrɪ) *n., pl.* **-ries.** noisy or unrestrained merrymaking.

revenge (rɪ'vɛndʒ) *n.* **1.** vengeance for wrongs or injury received. **2.** something done as a means of vengeance. ~*vb.* **3.** to

inflict equivalent injury or damage for (injury received). **4.** to take vengeance for (oneself or another); avenge. —**re'vengeful** *adj.*

revenue ('rɛvɪˌnjuː) *n.* **1.** any income, esp. that obtained by a government from taxation. **2.** a government department responsible for collecting taxes.

reverberate (rɪ'vɜːbəˌreɪt) *vb.* **1.** to resound or re-echo. **2.** to reflect or be reflected many times. —**reˌverberˈation** *n.*

revere (rɪ'vɪə) *vb.* to be in awe of and respect deeply.

reverence ('rɛvərəns) *n.* profound respect, esp. towards the sacred or divine. —**reverential** (ˌrɛvə'rɛnʃəl) *adj.*

Reverence ('rɛvərəns) *n.* (preceded by *Your* or *His*) a title sometimes used for a Roman Catholic priest.

reverend ('rɛvərənd) *adj.* **1.** worthy of reverence. **2.** relating to or designating a clergyman. ~*n.* **3.** *Informal.* a clergyman.

Reverend ('rɛvərənd) *adj.* a title of respect for a clergyman.

Usage. *Reverend* with a surname alone (*Reverend Smith*), as a term of address ("*Yes, Reverend*"), or in the salutation of a letter (*Dear Rev. Mr Smith*) are all considered to be wrong usage. Preferred are (*the*) *Reverend John Smith* or *Reverend Mr Smith* and *Dear Mr Smith.*

reverent ('rɛvərənt, 'rɛvrənt) *adj.* feeling or expressing reverence.

reverie ('rɛvərɪ) *n.* absent-minded daydreaming.

revers (rɪ'vɪə) *n., pl.* **-vers** (-'vɪəz). (*usually pl.*) the turned-back lining of part of a garment, esp. of a lapel or cuff.

reverse (rɪ'vɜːs) *vb.* **1.** to turn or set in an opposite direction, order, or position. **2.** to change into something different or contrary: *reverse one's policy.* **3.** to move or cause to move backwards or in an opposite direction: *to reverse a car.* **4.** to run (machinery) in the opposite direction to normal. **5.** to turn inside out. **6.** *Law.* to revoke or set aside (a judgment or decree); annul. **7. reverse the charge(s).** to make a telephone call at the recipient's expense. ~*n.* **8.** the opposite or contrary of something. **9.** the back or rear side of something. **10.** a change to an opposite position, state, or direction. **11.** a change for the worse; setback or defeat. **12.** the mechanism or gears by which machinery or a vehicle can be made to go backwards. **13.** the side of a coin bearing a secondary design. **14. in reverse.** in an opposite or backward direction. **15. the reverse of.** emphatically not; not at all: *he was the reverse of polite.* ~*adj.* **16.** opposite or contrary in direction,

---

retype   reupholster   reuse
reunite   reusable   revalue

position, order, nature, etc. **17.** operating or moving in a direction contrary to that which is usual. —**re'versal** *n.*

reversible (rɪ'vɜːsɪb'l) *adj.* **1.** capable of being reversed: *a reversible decision.* **2.** (of a garment) made so that either side may be used as the outer side.

reversing light *n.* a light on the rear of a motor vehicle to provide illumination when the vehicle is being reversed.

reversion (rɪ'vɜːʃən) *n.* **1.** a return to an earlier condition, practice, or belief. **2.** *Biol.* the return of individuals or organs to a more primitive condition or type.

revert (rɪ'vɜːt) *vb.* (foll. by *to*). **1.** to go back to a former practice, condition, belief, or topic. **2.** *Biol.* (of individuals or organs) to return to a more primitive, earlier, or simpler condition or type. **3.** *Property law.* (of an estate) to return to its former owner or his heirs.

review (rɪ'vjuː) *vb.* **1.** to examine again: *to review a situation.* **2.** to look back upon (a period of time or sequence of events): *he reviewed his achievements with pride.* **3.** to inspect, esp. formally or officially: *the general reviewed his troops.* **4.** *Law.* to re-examine (a decision) judicially. **5.** to write a critical assessment of (a book, film, concert, etc.), esp. as a profession. ~*n.* **6.** the act or an instance of reviewing. **7.** a general survey or report: *a review of the political situation.* **8.** a critical assessment of a book, film, concert, etc., esp. in a newspaper. **9.** a publication containing such articles. **10.** a second consideration; re-examination. **11.** a retrospective survey. **12.** a formal or official inspection. **13.** *Law.* a re-examination of a case. —**re'viewer** *n.*

revile (rɪ'vaɪl) *vb.* to use abusive or scornful language against (someone or something).

revise (rɪ'vaɪz) *vb.* **1.** to amend: *to revise one's opinion.* **2.** *Brit.* to reread (a subject or notes on it) so as to memorize it for an examination. **3.** to prepare a new edition of (a previously printed work).

Revised Version *n.* a revision of the Authorized Version of the Bible published between 1881 and 1885.

revision (rɪ'vɪʒən) *n.* **1.** the act or process of revising. **2.** *Brit.* the process of rereading a subject or notes on it for an examination. **3.** a corrected or new version of a book, article, etc.

revisory (rɪ'vaɪzərɪ) *adj.* of or having the power of revision.

revitalize *or* **-lise** (riː'vaɪt°ˌlaɪz) *vb.* to restore vitality or animation to.

revival (rɪ'vaɪv'l) *n.* **1.** a reviving or being revived. **2.** a renewed use or interest in (past customs or styles): *the Gothic revival.*

3. a new production of a play that has not been recently performed. **4.** a reawakening of religious faith.

revivalism (rɪ'vaɪvəˌlɪzəm) *n.* a movement that seeks to revive religious faith. —**re'vivalist** *n., adj.*

revive (rɪ'vaɪv) *vb.* **1.** to bring or be brought back to life, consciousness, or strength: *revived by a drop of whisky.* **2.** to give or assume new vitality. **3.** to make or become operative or active again: *the youth movement was revived.* **4.** *Theatre.* to mount a new production of (an old play).

revivify (rɪ'vɪvɪˌfaɪ) *vb.* **-fying, -fied.** to give new life to. —**re,vivifi'cation** *n.*

revoke (rɪ'vəʊk) *vb.* **1.** to take back or cancel (an agreement, will, etc.). **2.** *Cards.* to break a rule by failing to follow suit when able to do so. ~*n.* **3.** *Cards.* the act of revoking. —**revocation** (ˌrɛvə'keɪʃən) *n.*

revolt (rɪ'vəʊlt) *n.* **1.** a rebellion or uprising against authority. **2. in revolt.** in the state of rebelling. ~*vb.* **3.** to rise up in rebellion against authority. **4.** (*usually passive*) to feel or cause to feel revulsion, disgust, or abhorrence.

revolting (rɪ'vəʊltɪŋ) *adj.* nauseating, disgusting, or repulsive.

revolution (ˌrɛvə'luːʃən) *n.* **1.** the overthrow of a regime or political system by the governed. **2.** (in Marxist theory) the transition from one system of production in a society to the next. **3.** a far-reaching and drastic change, esp. in ideas or methods. **4. a.** movement in or as if in a circle. **b.** one complete turn in a circle: *33 revolutions per minute.* **5.** a cycle of successive events.

revolutionary (ˌrɛvə'luːʃənərɪ) *n., pl.* **-aries.** **1.** a person who advocates or engages in revolution. ~*adj.* **2.** of or like a revolution. **3.** advocating or engaged in revolution. **4.** radically new or different: *a revolutionary method of making plastics.*

revolutionize *or* **-ise** (ˌrɛvə'luːʃəˌnaɪz) *vb.* to bring about a radical change in.

revolve (rɪ'vɒlv) *vb.* **1.** to move or cause to move around a centre; rotate. **2.** to occur periodically or in cycles. **3.** to consider or be considered. **4.** (foll. by *around* or *about*) to be centred or focused upon: *Juliet's thoughts revolved around Romeo.* —**re'volvable** *adj.*

revolver (rɪ'vɒlvə) *n.* a pistol with a revolving cylinder that allows several shots to be fired without reloading.

revolving door *n.* a door that rotates about a vertical axis, esp. one with four leaves at right angles to each other.

revue (rɪ'vjuː) *n.* a light entertainment consisting of sketches, songs, etc.

revulsion (rɪ'vʌlʃən) *n.* a sudden violent

reaction in feeling, esp. one of extreme loathing.

reward (rɪ'wɔːd) n. **1.** something given in return for a deed or service rendered. **2.** a sum of money offered, esp. for help in finding a criminal or missing property. **3.** something received in return for good or evil; deserts. ~vb. **4.** to give something to (someone), esp. in gratitude for a service rendered.

rewarding (rɪ'wɔːdɪŋ) adj. giving personal satisfaction; gratifying.

rewarewa ('reɪwə'reɪwə) n. a tall New Zealand tree with reddish wood.

rewind (riː'waɪnd) vb. **-winding, -wound.** to wind back, esp. a film or tape, to the beginning.

rewire (riː'waɪə) vb. to provide (a house, engine, etc.) with new wiring.

reword (riː'wɜːd) vb. to alter the wording of; express differently.

rewrite vb. (riː'raɪt), **-writing, -wrote, -written. 1.** to write (material) again, esp. changing the words or form. ~n. ('riː,raɪt). **2.** something rewritten.

Rex (rɛks) n. king: now used chiefly in documents and inscriptions.

RFC 1. Royal Flying Corps. **2.** Rugby Football Club.

rh or **RH** right hand.

Rh 1. Chem. rhodium. **2.** See **Rh factor.**

rhapsodize or **-ise** ('ræpsə,daɪz) vb. to speak or write (something) with extravagant enthusiasm.

rhapsody ('ræpsədɪ) n., pl. **-dies. 1.** Music. a composition free in structure and highly emotional in character. **2.** an expression of ecstatic enthusiasm. —**rhapsodic** (ræp-'sɒdɪk) adj.

rhea (rɪə) n. a large fast-running flightless bird of South America, similar to the ostrich.

rhebuck ('riːbʌk) n., pl. **-bucks** or **-buck.** a southern African antelope with brownish-grey hair.

rhenium ('riːnɪəm) n. a silvery-white metallic element with a high melting point. Symbol: Re

rheostat ('rɪə,stæt) n. a variable resistor in an electrical circuit, such as one used to dim lights. —,**rheo'static** adj.

rhesus factor n. See **Rh factor.**

rhesus monkey n. a monkey of S Asia.

rhetoric ('rɛtərɪk) n. **1.** the art of using speech or writing to persuade or influence. **2.** speech that pretends to significance but lacks true meaning: mere rhetoric. —**rhetorical** (rɪ'tɒrɪkˀl) adj.

rhetorical question n. a question to which no answer is required: used for dramatic effect. An example is Who knows?

rheum (ruːm) n. a watery discharge from the eyes or nose. —**'rheumy** adj.

rheumatic (ruː'mætɪk) adj. **1.** of, caused by, or afflicted with rheumatism. ~n. **2.** a person afflicted with rheumatism. —**rheu-'matically** adv.

rheumatic fever n. a disease with inflammation and pain in the joints.

rheumatics (ruː'mætɪks) n. (functioning as sing.) Informal. rheumatism.

rheumatism ('ruːmə,tɪzəm) n. any painful disorder of joints, muscles, or connective tissue.

rheumatoid ('ruːmə,tɔɪd) adj. (of symptoms) resembling rheumatism.

rheumatoid arthritis n. a chronic disease characterized by inflammation and swelling of the joints.

Rh factor n. an antigen commonly found in human blood: the terms **Rh positive** and **Rh negative** are used to indicate its presence or absence.

rhinestone ('raɪn,stəʊn) n. an imitation diamond made of glass.

rhino ('raɪnəʊ) n., pl. **-nos** or **-no.** a rhinoceros.

rhinoceros (raɪ'nɒsərəs, -'nɒsrəs) n., pl. **-oses** or **-os.** a plant-eating mammal of SE Asia and Africa with one or two horns on the nose, a very thick skin, and a massive body.

rhizome ('raɪzəʊm) n. a thick horizontal underground stem whose buds develop into new plants.

rhodium ('rəʊdɪəm) n. a hard silvery-white metallic element, used to harden platinum and palladium. Symbol: Rh

rhododendron (,rəʊdə'dɛndrən) n. an evergreen shrub with clusters of showy red, purple, pink, or white flowers.

rhombohedron (,rɒmbəʊ'hiːdrən) n., pl. **-drons** or **-dra** (-drə). a six-sided prism whose sides are parallelograms.

rhomboid ('rɒmbɔɪd) n. **1.** a parallelogram having adjacent sides of unequal length. It resembles a rectangle but does not have 90° angles. ~adj. also **rhom'boidal. 2.** having such a shape.

rhombus ('rɒmbəs) n., pl. **-buses** or **-bi** (-baɪ). an oblique-angled parallelogram having four equal sides. —**'rhombic** adj.

rhubarb ('ruːbɑːb) n. **1.** a large-leaved plant with long green and red acid-tasting edible leafstalks, eaten sweetened and cooked. **2.** a related plant of central Asia, whose root can be dried and used as a laxative or astringent. ~interj., n., vb. **3.** the noise made by actors to simulate conversation, esp. by repeating the word rhubarb.

rhyme (raɪm) n. **1.** sameness of the final

sounds in lines of verse or in words. **2.** a word that is identical to another in its final sound: *"while" is a rhyme for "mile"*. **3.** a piece of poetry with corresponding sounds at the ends of the lines. **4. rhyme or reason.** sense, logic, or meaning. ~*vb.* **5.** to use (a word) or (of a word) to be used so as to form a rhyme. **6.** to put (a subject) into rhyme. **7.** to compose (verse) in a metrical structure.

rhymester ('raɪmstə) *n.* a poet, esp. one considered to be mediocre.

rhyming slang *n.* slang in which a word is replaced by another word or phrase that rhymes with it; e.g. *apples and pears* meaning *stairs*.

rhythm ('rɪðəm) *n.* **1.** any regular movement or beat: *the rhythm of her breathing*. **2. a.** the arrangement of the durations of and accents on the notes of a melody, usually laid out into regular groups (**bars**) of beats. **b.** any specific arrangement of such groupings; time: *waltz rhythm*. **3.** (in poetry) the arrangement of words into a sequence of stressed and unstressed or long and short syllables. —**rhythmical** ('rɪðmɪkˀl) *or* '**rhythmic** *adj.* —'**rhythmically** *adv.*

rhythm and blues *n.* (*functioning as sing.*) a kind of popular music of Black American origin, derived from and influenced by the blues.

rhythm method *n.* a method of contraception by restricting sexual intercourse to those days in a woman's menstrual cycle when conception is least likely to occur.

RI Rhode Island.

rialto (rɪ'æltəʊ) *n., pl.* **-tos.** a market or exchange.

rib[1] (rɪb) *n.* **1.** any of the elastic arches of bone that together form the chest wall and are attached to the spinal column. **2.** a cut of meat including one or more ribs. **3.** a part or element similar in function to a rib, such as a structural member in an aeroplane wing. **4.** one of a series of raised rows in knitted fabric. ~*vb.* **ribbing, ribbed. 5.** to provide or support with a rib or ribs. —**ribbed** *adj.*

rib[2] (rɪb) *vb.* **ribbing, ribbed.** *Informal.* to tease or ridicule. —'**ribbing** *n.*

RIBA Royal Institute of British Architects.

ribald ('rɪbˀld) *adj.* coarse or obscene in a humorous or mocking way. —'**ribaldry** *n.*

riband *or* **ribband** ('rɪbənd) *n.* a ribbon, esp. one awarded for some achievement.

ribbing ('rɪbɪŋ) *n.* **1.** a framework or structure of ribs. **2.** a pattern of ribs in knitted material.

ribbon ('rɪbˀn) *n.* **1.** a narrow strip of fine material used for trimming, tying, etc. **2.** something resembling a ribbon; a long strip. **3.** a long narrow strip of inked cloth or plastic used to produce print in a typewriter. **4.** (*pl.*) ragged strips or shreds: *his clothes were torn to ribbons*. **5.** a small strip of coloured cloth worn as a badge or as a symbol of an award.

ribbon development *n. Brit.* the building of houses along a main road.

ribbonwood ('rɪbˀn‚wʊd) *n.* a small evergreen tree of New Zealand. Its wood is used in furniture making.

ribcage ('rɪb‚keɪdʒ) *n.* the bony structure formed by the ribs that encloses the lungs.

riboflavin (‚raɪbəʊ'fleɪvɪn) *n.* a vitamin of the B complex that occurs in green vegetables, milk, fish, egg yolk, liver, and kidney: used as a yellow or orange food colouring (**E 101**). Also called: **vitamin B**$_2$.

ribonucleic acid (‚raɪbəʊnjuː'kliːɪk, -'kleɪk) *n.* the full name of **RNA.**

rice (raɪs) *n.* **1.** the edible grain of an erect grass that grows on wet ground in warm climates. ~*vb.* **2.** *U.S. & Canad.* to sieve (potatoes or other vegetables) to a coarse mashed consistency.

rice paper *n.* **1.** a thin edible paper made from rice straw. **2.** a thin Chinese paper made from the **rice-paper plant**, the pith of which is flattened into sheets.

rich (rɪtʃ) *adj.* **1.** owning a lot of money or property; wealthy. **2.** having an abundance of natural resources, minerals, etc.: *a land rich in metals*. **3.** producing abundantly; fertile: *rich soil*. **4.** well supplied (with desirable qualities); abundant (in): *a country rich with cultural interest*. **5.** luxuriant or prolific: *a rich growth of weeds*. **6.** (of food) having a large proportion of flavoursome or fatty ingredients. **7.** having a full-bodied flavour: *a rich ruby port*. **8.** (of colour) intense or vivid; deep: *a rich red*. **9.** (of sound or a voice) full, mellow, or resonant. **10.** (of a fuel-air mixture) containing a relatively high proportion of fuel. **11.** very amusing or ridiculous: *a rich joke*. —'**richness** *n.*

riches ('rɪtʃɪz) *pl. n.* wealth; an abundance of money or property.

richly ('rɪtʃlɪ) *adv.* **1.** in a rich or elaborate manner: *a richly decorated stairway*. **2.** fully and appropriately: *richly deserved contempt*.

Richter scale ('rɪxtə) *n.* a scale for expressing the magnitude of an earthquake, ranging from 0 to over 8.

rick[1] (rɪk) *n.* a large stack of hay, corn, etc.

rick[2] (rɪk) *n.* **1.** a wrench or sprain, as of the neck. ~*vb.* **2.** to wrench or sprain (a joint, the neck, etc.).

rickets ('rɪkɪts) *n.* (*functioning as sing. or pl.*) a disease mainly of children, caused by a deficiency of vitamin D and characterized by softening of developing bone, and hence bow legs.

rickety ('rɪkɪtɪ) *adj.* **1.** (of a structure or piece of furniture) likely to collapse or break. **2.** resembling or afflicted with rickets. —**'ricketiness** n.

rickrack or **ricrac** ('rɪk,ræk) n. a zigzag braid used for trimming.

rickshaw ('rɪkʃɔ:) or **ricksha** ('rɪkʃə) n. **1.** a small two-wheeled passenger vehicle drawn by one or two men, used in parts of Asia. **2.** a similar vehicle with three wheels, propelled by a man pedalling as on a tricycle.

ricochet ('rɪkə,ʃeɪ, 'rɪkə,ʃet) vb. **-cheting** (-,ʃeɪɪŋ), **-cheted** (-,ʃeɪd) or **-chetting** (-,ʃetɪŋ), **-chetted** (-,ʃetɪd). **1.** (esp. of a bullet) to rebound from a surface. ~n. **2.** the motion or sound of a rebounding object, esp. a bullet.

rid (rɪd) vb. **ridding, rid** or **ridded. 1.** (foll. by of) to relieve (oneself) of something disagreeable or undesirable; make (a place) free of. **2. get rid of.** to relieve or free oneself of (something unpleasant or undesirable).

riddance ('rɪd²ns) n. **good riddance.** relief at getting rid of someone or something.

ridden ('rɪd²n) vb. **1.** the past participle of **ride.** ~adj. **2.** afflicted or dominated by something specified: disease-ridden.

riddle[1] ('rɪd²l) n. **1.** a question, puzzle, or verse so phrased that ingenuity is required to find the answer or meaning. **2.** a puzzling person or thing. ~vb. **3.** to speak in riddles.

riddle[2] ('rɪd²l) vb. **1.** (usually foll. by with) to pierce or perforate with numerous holes: riddled with bullets. **2.** to put through a sieve; sift. ~n. **3.** a coarse sieve.

ride (raɪd) vb. **riding, rode, ridden. 1.** to sit on and control the movements of (a horse or other animal). **2.** to sit on and propel (a bicycle or similar vehicle). **3.** (often foll. by on or in) to travel on or in a vehicle: she rides to work on the bus. **4.** to travel over: they rode the countryside in search of shelter. **5.** to travel through or be carried across (sea, sky, etc.): the small boat rode the waves; the moon was riding high. **6.** U.S. & Canad. to cause to be carried: to ride someone out of town. **7.** (of a vessel) to lie at anchor. **8.** (usually passive) to tyrannize over or dominate: ridden by fear. **9.** Informal. to continue undisturbed: let it ride. **10. riding high.** confident, popular, and successful. ~n. **11.** a journey or outing on horseback or in a vehicle. **12.** a path for riding on horseback. **13.** transport in a vehicle; lift: can you give me a ride to the station? **14.** the type of movement experienced in a vehicle: a bumpy ride. **15. take for a ride.** Informal. to cheat, swindle, or deceive.

ride out vb. to endure successfully; survive (a storm, crisis, etc.).

rider ('raɪdə) n. **1.** a person or thing that rides. **2.** an additional clause, amendment, or stipulation added to a document.

ride up vb. to work away from the proper position: her new skirt rode up.

ridge (rɪdʒ) n. **1.** a long narrow raised land formation with sloping sides. **2.** any long narrow raised strip, as on a fabric or in ploughed land. **3.** the top of a roof at the junction of two sloping sides. **4.** Meteorol. an elongated area of high pressure. ~vb. **5.** to form into a ridge or ridges. —**'ridgy** adj.

ridgepole ('rɪdʒ,pəʊl) n. **1.** a timber along the ridge of a roof, to which the rafters are attached. **2.** the horizontal pole at the apex of a tent.

ridicule ('rɪdɪ,kju:l) n. **1.** language or behaviour intended to humiliate or mock. ~vb. **2.** to make fun of or mock.

ridiculous (rɪ'dɪkjʊləs) adj. worthy of or causing ridicule; absurd or laughable.

riding[1] ('raɪdɪŋ) n. the art or practice of horsemanship.

riding[2] ('raɪdɪŋ) n. **1.** (cap. when part of a name) any of the three former administrative divisions of Yorkshire: **North Riding, East Riding,** and **West Riding. 2.** Canad. an electoral constituency.

riding crop n. a short whip with a handle at one end for opening gates.

riesling ('ri:zlɪŋ, 'raɪz-) n. a medium-dry white wine.

rife (raɪf) adj. **1.** widespread or common. **2.** (foll. by with) abounding in: a system rife with errors.

riff (rɪf) n. Jazz, rock. a short repeated melodic figure used as an introduction or accompaniment.

riffle ('rɪf²l) vb. **1.** (often foll. by through) to flick rapidly through (pages of a book, etc.). ~n. **2.** U.S. & Canad. **a.** a rapid in a stream. **b.** a rocky shoal causing a rapid. **c.** a ripple on water. **3.** a riffling.

riffraff ('rɪf,ræf) n. (sometimes functioning as pl.) worthless people; rabble.

rifle[1] ('raɪf²l) n. **1.** a firearm having a long barrel with a spirally grooved interior, which gives the bullet a spinning motion and thus greater accuracy over a longer range. **2.** (pl.) a unit of soldiers equipped with rifles: the King's Own Rifles. ~vb. **3.** to cut spiral grooves inside the barrel of (a gun).

rifle[2] ('raɪf²l) vb. **1.** to search (a house or safe) and steal from it; ransack. **2.** to steal and carry off: to rifle goods.

rift (rɪft) n. **1.** a gap or space made by cleaving or splitting. **2.** a break in friendly relations between people or groups of people.

rift valley n. a long narrow valley resulting from the subsidence of land between two faults.

rig (rɪg) vb. **rigging, rigged. 1.** Naut. to equip (a vessel or mast) with (sails or rigging). **2.** to set up or prepare (something) hastily ready for use. **3.** to manipulate in a fraudulent manner, for profit or advantage: *to rig prices.* ~*n.* **4.** *Naut.* the arrangement of the sails and masts of a vessel. **5.** the installation used in drilling for and exploiting natural gas and oil deposits: *an oil rig.* **6.** apparatus or equipment. **7.** *U.S. & Canad.* an articulated lorry. ~See also **rig out, rig up.**

-rigged *adj.* (of a sailing vessel) having a rig of a certain kind: *schooner-rigged.*

rigging ('rɪgɪŋ) *n.* the ropes and cables supporting the masts, sails, etc., of a vessel.

right (raɪt) *adj.* **1.** morally or legally acceptable or correct: *right conduct.* **2.** correct or true: *the right answer.* **3.** appropriate, suitable, or proper: *the right man for the job.* **4.** most favourable or convenient: *the right time to act.* **5.** in a satisfactory condition: *things are right again now.* **6.** accurate: *the clock is right.* **7.** correct in opinion or judgment. **8.** sound in mind or body. **9.** of or on the side of something or someone that faces east when the front is turned towards the north. **10.** (*sometimes cap.*) conservative or reactionary: *the right wing of the party.* **11.** *Geom.* formed by or containing a line or plane perpendicular to another line or plane: *a right angle.* **12.** of or on the side of cloth worn or facing outwards. **13. in one's right mind.** sane. **14. she'll be right.** *Austral. & N.Z. informal.* that's all right; not to worry. **15. the right side of. a.** in favour with: *you'd better stay on the right side of him.* **b.** younger than: *she's still on the right side of fifty.* **16. too right.** *Austral. & N.Z. informal.* an exclamation of agreement. ~*adv.* **17.** correctly: *to guess right.* **18.** in the appropriate manner: *do it right next time!* **19.** straight or directly: *right to the top.* **20.** in the direction of the east from the point of view of a person or thing facing north. **21.** all the way: *the bus goes right into town; she worked right through the night.* **22.** without delay: *I'll be right over.* **23.** exactly or precisely: *right here.* **24.** fittingly: *it serves you right.* **25.** to good or favourable advantage: *it all came out right in the end.* ~*n.* **26.** a freedom or power that is morally or legally due to a person: *I know my rights.* **27.** anything that accords with the principles of legal or moral justice. **28. in the right.** the fact or state of being in accordance with reason, truth, or accepted standards. **29.** the right side, direction, position, or part: *the right of the army.* **30.** (*often cap.* and preceded by *the*) the supporters or advocates of conservatism or reaction. **31.** *Boxing.* a punch with the right hand. **32.** (*often pl.*) *Finance.* the privilege of a company's shareholders to subscribe for new issues of the company's shares on advantageous terms. **33. by right** *or* **rights.** properly: *by rights you should be in bed.* **34. in one's own right.** having a claim or title oneself

rather than through marriage or other connection. **35. to rights.** consistent with justice or orderly arrangement: *he put the matter to rights.* ~*vb.* **36.** to restore to or attain a normal, esp. an upright, position: *the raft righted in a few seconds.* **37.** to make (something) accord with truth or facts. **38.** to restore to an orderly state or condition. **39.** to compensate for or redress: *to right a wrong.* ~*interj.* **40.** an expression of agreement or compliance.

right angle *n.* **1.** an angle of 90° or π/2 radians. **2. at right angles.** perpendicular or perpendicularly. —'**right-,angled** *adj.*

right-angled triangle *n.* a triangle one angle of which is a right angle.

right away *adv.* without delay.

righteous ('raɪtʃəs) *adj.* **1.** moral, just, or virtuous: *a righteous man.* **2.** morally justifiable or right: *righteous indignation.* —'**righteousness** *n.*

rightful ('raɪtful) *adj.* **1.** in accordance with what is right. **2.** having a legally or morally just claim: *the rightful owner.* **3.** held by virtue of a legal or just claim: *my rightful property.* —'**rightfully** *adv.*

right-hand *adj.* **1.** of, on, or towards the right: *a right-hand bend.* **2.** for use by the right hand. **3. right-hand man.** one's most valuable assistant.

right-handed *adj.* **1.** using the right hand with greater skill or ease than the left. **2.** made for or by the right hand. **3.** turning from left to right.

rightist ('raɪtɪst) *adj.* **1.** of the political right or its principles. ~*n.* **2.** a supporter of the political right. —'**rightism** *n.*

rightly ('raɪtlɪ) *adv.* **1.** in accordance with the true facts. **2.** in accordance with justice or morality. **3.** with good reason: *he was rightly annoyed with her.*

right-minded *adj.* holding opinions or principles that accord with what is right or with the opinions of the speaker.

right of way *n., pl.* **rights of way. 1.** the right of one vehicle or vessel to take precedence over another. **2. a.** the legal right of someone to pass over another's land. **b.** the path used by this right.

Right Reverend *adj.* (in Britain) a title of respect for a bishop.

rightward ('raɪtwəd) *adj.* **1.** situated on or directed towards the right. ~*adv.* **2.** Also: **rightwards.** on or towards the right.

right whale *n.* a large grey or black whalebone whale with a large head.

right wing *n.* **1.** (*often cap.*) the conservative faction of a political body or party. **2.** *Sports.* **a.** the right-hand side of the field of play. **b.** a player positioned in this area in certain games. ~*adj.* **right-wing. 3.** of, belonging to, or relating to the right wing. —'**right-'winger** *n.*

rigid ('rɪdʒɪd) *adj.* **1.** physically inflexible

or stiff: *a rigid piece of plastic.* **2.** rigorously strict: *rigid rules.* —**ri'gidity** *n.*

rigmarole ('rɪgmə,rəʊl) *n.* **1.** any long complicated procedure. **2.** a set of incoherent or pointless statements.

rigor mortis ('rɪgə 'mɔːtɪs) *n.* the stiffness of joints and muscles of a dead body.

rigorous ('rɪgərəs) *adj.* **1.** harsh, strict, or severe: *rigorous discipline.* **2.** severely accurate: *rigorous book-keeping.* **3.** (esp. of weather) extreme or harsh.

rigour *or U.S.* **rigor** ('rɪgə) *n.* **1.** harsh but just treatment. **2.** a severe or cruel circumstance: *the rigours of famine.* **3.** strictness in judgment or conduct.

rig out *vb.* **1.** (often foll. by *with*) to equip (with): *his car is rigged out with gadgets.* **2.** to dress or be dressed: *rigged out smartly.* ~*n.* **rigout.** **3.** *Informal.* a person's clothing or costume.

rig up *vb.* to erect or construct, esp. as a temporary measure: *cameras were rigged up to televise the event.*

rile (raɪl) *vb.* **1.** to annoy or anger. **2.** *U.S. & Canad.* to agitate (a liquid, such as water).

rill (rɪl) *n.* a stream.

rim (rɪm) *n.* **1.** the raised edge of an object, esp. of something circular such as a cup. **2.** the outer part of a wheel, to which the tyre is attached.

rime[1] (raɪm) *n.* **1.** frost formed by the freezing of water droplets in fog onto solid objects. ~*vb.* **2.** to cover with rime or something resembling rime. —**'rimy** *adj.*

rime[2] (raɪm) *n., vb. Archaic.* same as **rhyme.**

rind (raɪnd) *n.* a hard outer layer or skin, as on bacon or cheese.

ring[1] (rɪŋ) *n.* **1.** a circular band of a precious metal worn upon the finger. **2.** any object or mark that is circular in shape. **3.** a circular path or course: *to run around in a ring.* **4.** a group of people or things standing or arranged so as to form a circle: *a ring of spectators.* **5.** a circular enclosure, esp. one where circus acts perform or livestock is sold at a market. **6.** a square raised platform, marked off by ropes, in which contestants box or wrestle. **7. the ring.** the sport of boxing. **8. throw one's hat in the ring.** to announce one's intention to be a candidate or contestant. **9.** a group of people, usually illegal, who cooperate to control the market in antiques, illicit drugs, etc. **10.** *Chem.* a closed loop of atoms in a molecule. **11.** one of the systems of circular bands orbiting the planets Saturn and Uranus. **12. run rings around.** *Informal.* to outclass completely. ~*vb.* **ringing, ringed.** **13.** to surround with, or as if with, or form a ring. **14.** to mark a bird with a ring or clip for subsequent identification. **15.** to fit a ring in the nose of (a bull, etc.) so that it

can be led easily. **16.** to cut a ring of bark off a tree. —**ringed** *adj.*

ring[2] (rɪŋ) *vb.* **ringing, rang, rung.** **1.** to emit or cause to emit a resonant sound, like that of a bell. **2.** to cause (a bell) to emit a ringing sound or (of a bell) to emit such a sound. **3.** (of a building or place) to be filled with sound: *the church rang with singing.* **4.** (foll. by *for*) to call by means of a bell: *to ring for the butler.* **5.** Also: **ring up.** *Chiefly Brit.* to call (a person) by telephone. **6.** (of the ears) to have the sensation of humming or ringing. **7. ring a bell.** to bring something to the mind or memory: *that rings a bell.* **8. ring down the curtain. a.** to lower the curtain at the end of a theatrical performance. **b.** (foll. by *on*) to put an end to (to). **9. ring true** (*or* **false**). to give the impression of being true (or false). ~*n.* **10.** the act of or a sound made by ringing. **11.** a sound produced by or suggestive of a bell. **12.** *Informal, chiefly Brit.* a telephone call. **13.** an inherent quality: *his explanation has the ring of sincerity.* ~See also **ring in, ring off,** etc.

Usage. Rang and *sang* are the correct forms of the past tenses of *ring* and *sing,* although *rung* and *sung* are still heard informally and dialectally: *he rung* (*rang*) *the bell.*

ring binder *n.* a loose-leaf binder with metal rings that can be opened to insert perforated paper.

ringdove ('rɪŋ,dʌv) *n.* a wood pigeon.

ringer ('rɪŋə) *n.* a person or thing that is almost identical to another. Also called: **dead ringer.**

ring finger *n.* the third finger, esp. of the left hand, on which a wedding ring is worn.

ring in *vb.* to accompany the arrival of with bells: *ring in the New Year.*

ringleader ('rɪŋ,liːdə) *n.* a person who leads others in unlawful or mischievous activity.

ringlet ('rɪŋlɪt) *n.* a lock of hair hanging down in a spiral curl. —**'ringleted** *adj.*

ring main *n.* a domestic electrical supply in which outlet sockets are connected to the mains supply through a continuous closed circuit (**ring circuit**).

ringmaster ('rɪŋ,mɑːstə) *n.* the master of ceremonies in a circus.

ring off *vb. Chiefly Brit.* to end a telephone conversation by replacing the receiver; hang up.

ring out *vb.* **1.** to accompany the departure of with bells: *ring out the old year.* **2.** to send forth a loud resounding noise.

ring road *n.* a main road that bypasses a town or town centre.

ringside ('rɪŋ,saɪd) *n.* **1.** the row of seats nearest a boxing or wrestling ring. **2.** any place affording a close uninterrupted view.

ring up *vb.* **1.** *Chiefly Brit.* to make a telephone call to. **2.** to record on a cash register. **3. ring up the curtain. a.** to begin a theatrical performance. **b.** (often foll. by *on*) to make a start on.

ringworm ('rɪŋ,wɜːm) *n.* a fungal infection of the skin producing itching circular patches.

rink (rɪŋk) *n.* **1.** an expanse of ice for skating on, esp. one that is artificially prepared and under cover. **2.** an area for roller-skating on. **3.** a building or enclosure for ice-skating or roller-skating. **4.** (in bowls or curling) a strip of grass or ice on which a game is played. **5.** (in bowls or curling) the players on one side in a game.

rinkhals ('rɪŋk,hæls) *n., pl.* **-hals** or **-halses.** a venomous snake of southern Africa, which can spit venom from a distance.

rink rat *n. Canad. slang.* a youth who helps with odd chores at an ice-hockey rink in return for free admission to games.

rinse (rɪns) *vb.* **1.** to remove soap, detergent, or shampoo from (clothes, dishes, or hair) by washing it out with clean water. **2.** to wash lightly, esp. without using soap. **3.** to cleanse the mouth by swirling water or mouthwash in it and then spitting the liquid out. **4.** to give a light tint to (hair). ~*n.* **5.** the act or an instance of rinsing. **6.** *Hairdressing.* a liquid preparation put on the hair when wet to give a tint to it: *a blue rinse.* —'**rinser** *n.*

riot ('raɪət) *n.* **1.** a disturbance made by an unruly mob or (in law) three or more persons. **2.** an occasion of boisterous merriment. **3.** *Slang.* a person who creates boisterous merriment. **4.** a dazzling display: *a riot of colour.* **5. read the riot act.** to reprimand severely. **6. run riot. a.** to behave without restraint. **b.** (of plants) to grow profusely. ~*vb.* **7.** to take part in a riot.

riotous ('raɪətəs) *adj.* **1.** like a riot or rioting. **2.** characterized by wanton revelry: *riotous living.* **3.** characterized by unrestrained merriment: *riotous laughter.*

riot shield *n.* a large shield used by police controlling crowds.

rip (rɪp) *vb.* **ripping, ripped. 1.** to tear or be torn violently or roughly. **2.** (foll. by *off* or *out*) to remove hastily or roughly. **3.** *Informal.* to move violently or hurriedly. **4. let rip.** to act or speak without restraint. ~*n.* **5.** a tear or split. ~See also **rip off.**

RIP may he, she, or they rest in peace.

riparian (raɪ'pɛərɪən) *adj.* of or on the bank of a river.

ripcord ('rɪp,kɔːd) *n.* a cord that when pulled opens a parachute from its pack.

ripe (raɪp) *adj.* **1.** mature enough to be eaten or used: *ripe cheese; a ripe banana.* **2.** fully developed in mind or body. **3.** resembling ripe fruit, esp. in redness or fullness: *a ripe complexion.* **4.** (foll. by *for*) ready or eager (to undertake or undergo an action). **5.** (foll. by *for*) suitable: *the time is*

not yet ripe. **6. ripe old age.** an elderly but healthy age.

ripen ('raɪp°n) *vb.* to make or become ripe.

rip off *Slang.* ~*vb.* **1.** to steal from or cheat (someone). **2.** to steal (something). ~*n.* **rip-off. 3.** a grossly overpriced article. **4.** the act of stealing or cheating.

riposte (rɪ'pɒst) *n.* **1.** a swift sharp reply. **2.** *Fencing.* a counterattack made immediately after a successful parry. ~*vb.* **3.** to make a riposte.

ripple ('rɪp°l) *n.* **1.** a slight wave on the surface of water. **2.** a sound reminiscent of water flowing quietly in ripples: *a ripple of laughter.* ~*vb.* **3.** to form ripples or flow with a waving motion. **4.** (of sounds) to rise and fall gently. —'**rippling** or '**ripply** *adj.*

rip-roaring *adj. Informal.* boisterous, noisy, and exciting.

ripsaw ('rɪp,sɔː) *n.* a handsaw for cutting along the grain of timber.

rise (raɪz) *vb.* **rising, rose, risen** ('rɪz°n). **1.** to get up from a lying, sitting, or kneeling position. **2.** to get out of bed, esp. to begin one's day: *he always rises early.* **3.** to move from a lower to a higher position or place. **4.** to ascend or appear above the horizon: *the sun is rising.* **5.** to increase in height or level: *the water rose.* **6.** to increase in strength, degree, etc.: *the wind is rising.* **7.** to increase in amount or value: *house prices are always rising.* **8.** to swell up: *dough rises.* **9.** to become erect, or rigid: *the hairs on his neck rose in fear.* **10.** to revolt: *the people rose against their oppressors.* **11.** to slope upwards: *the ground rises beyond the lake.* **12.** to be resurrected. **13.** to originate: *that river rises in the mountains.* **14.** (of a session of a court, legislative assembly, etc.) to come to an end. **15.** *Angling.* (of fish) to come to the surface of the water. **16.** (often foll. by *to*) *Informal.* to respond (to teasing, etc.). ~*n.* **17.** the act or an instance of rising. **18.** an increase in height. **19.** an increase in rank, status, or position. **20.** an increase in amount, cost, or value. **21.** an increase in degree or intensity. **22.** *Brit.* an increase in salary or wages. **23.** the vertical height of a step or of a flight of stairs. **24.** a piece of rising ground; slope. **25. get** or **take a rise out of.** *Slang.* to provoke an angry or petulant reaction from. **26. give rise to.** to cause the development of.

riser ('raɪzə) *n.* **1.** a person who rises from bed: *an early riser.* **2.** the vertical part of a stair.

risible ('rɪzɪb°l) *adj.* causing laughter; ridiculous.

rising ('raɪzɪŋ) *n.* **1.** a rebellion; revolt. ~*adj.* **2.** increasing in status or reputation: *a rising young politician.* **3.** growing up to adulthood: *the rising generation.*

rising damp n. seepage of moisture from the ground into the walls of buildings.

risk (rɪsk) n. **1.** the possibility of incurring misfortune or loss. **2.** a person or thing considered as a potential hazard: *that old heater must be a fire risk.* **3. at risk.** vulnerable. **4. take** *or* **run a risk.** to act without regard to the danger involved. ~vb. **5.** to expose to danger or loss. **6.** to act in spite of the possibility of (injury or loss): *to risk a fall in climbing.* —'**risky** adj.

risotto (rɪ'zɒtəʊ) n., pl. **-tos.** a dish of rice cooked in stock with tomatoes, cheese, chicken, etc.

risqué ('rɪskeɪ) adj. bordering on impropriety or indecency: *a risqué joke.*

rissole ('rɪsəʊl) n. a mixture of minced cooked meat coated in egg and breadcrumbs and fried.

ritardando (ˌrɪtɑː'dændəʊ) adj., adv. same as **rallentando.**

rite (raɪt) n. **1.** a formal act which forms part of a religious ceremony: *the rite of baptism.* **2.** a particular body of such acts, esp. of a particular Christian Church: *the Latin rite.*

ritual ('rɪtjʊəl) n. **1.** the prescribed form of a religious or other ceremony. **2.** such prescribed forms in general or collectively. **3.** stereotyped activity or behaviour. **4.** any formal act, institution, or procedure that is followed consistently: *the ritual of the law.* ~adj. **5.** of or like religious, social, or other rituals. —'**ritually** adv.

ritualism ('rɪtjʊəˌlɪzəm) n. exaggerated emphasis on the importance of rites and ceremonies. —ˌritual'**istic** adj. —ˌritual'**istically** adv.

ritzy ('rɪtsɪ) adj. **ritzier, ritziest.** *Slang.* luxurious or elegant.

rival ('raɪvᵊl) n. **1.** a person or group that competes with another for the same object or in the same field. **2.** a person or thing that is considered the equal of another: *she is without rival in the field of physics.* ~vb. **-valling, -valled** *or* U.S. **-valing, -valed. 3.** to be the equal or near equal of: *an empire that rivalled Rome.* **4.** to try to equal or surpass.

rivalry ('raɪvəlrɪ) n., pl. **-ries. 1.** the act of rivalling. **2.** the state of being a rival or rivals.

riven ('rɪvᵊn) adj. **1.** split asunder: *a tree riven by lightning.* **2.** torn apart: *riven to shreds.*

river ('rɪvə) n. **1.** a large natural stream of fresh water flowing along a definite course into the sea, a lake, or a larger river. **2.** any abundant stream or flow: *a river of blood.*

rivet ('rɪvɪt) n. **1.** a short metal pin for fastening two or more pieces together, having a head at one end, the other end being hammered flat after being passed through

holes in the pieces. ~vb. **2.** to join by riveting. **3.** (*often passive*) to cause to be fixed, as in fascinated attention or horror: *to be riveted to the spot.* —'**riveter** n. —'**riveting** adj.

rivulet ('rɪvjʊlɪt) n. a small stream.

rm 1. ream. **2.** room.

RM 1. Royal Mail. **2.** Royal Marines. **3.** (in Canada) Rural Municipality.

Rn *Chem.* radon.

RN 1. (in Canada) Registered Nurse. **2.** Royal Navy.

RNA n. *Biochem.* ribonucleic acid; any of a group of nucleic acids, present in all living cells, that play an essential role in the synthesis of proteins.

RNLI Royal National Lifeboat Institution.

roach¹ (rəʊtʃ) n., pl. **roaches** *or* **roach.** a European freshwater food fish with a deep compressed body and reddish tail fins.

roach² (rəʊtʃ) n. *Chiefly U.S. & Canad.* a cockroach.

road (rəʊd) n. **1. a.** an open way, usually surfaced, providing passage from one place to another. **b.** (*in combination*): *the roadside.* **2.** a street. **3.** a way, path, or course: *the road to fame.* **4.** (*often pl.*) *Naut.* a partly sheltered anchorage. **5. one for the road.** *Informal.* a last alcoholic drink before leaving. **6. on the road. a.** travelling about; on tour. **b.** leading a wandering life.

roadblock ('rəʊdˌblɒk) n. a barrier set up across a road by the police or military, in order to stop and check vehicles.

road-fund licence n. *Brit.* a licence showing that the tax payable in respect of a motor vehicle has been paid.

road hog n. *Informal.* a selfish or aggressive driver.

roadholding ('rəʊdˌhəʊldɪŋ) n. the extent to which a vehicle is stable and does not skid, esp. on bends or wet roads.

roadhouse ('rəʊdˌhaʊs) n. a pub or restaurant at the side of a road.

roadie ('rəʊdɪ) n. *Informal.* a person who transports and sets up equipment for a band or group.

road metal n. crushed rock or broken stone used to construct a road.

road show n. **1.** *Radio.* a live programme transmitted from a radio van taking a particular show on the road. **2.** a group of entertainers on tour.

roadstead ('rəʊdˌstɛd) n. *Naut.* same as **road.**

roadster ('rəʊdstə) n. *Old-fashioned.* an open car, esp. one seating only two.

road test n. **1.** a test of something, such as a vehicle in actual use. ~vb. **road-test. 2.** to test (a vehicle, etc.) in this way.

roadway ('rəʊdˌweɪ) n. the part of a road that is used by vehicles.

road works pl. n. repairs to a road or

cable under a road, esp. when forming a hazard or obstruction to traffic.

roadworthy ('rəʊd,wɜːðɪ) *adj.* (of a motor vehicle) mechanically sound; fit for use on the roads. —'**road,worthiness** *n.*

roam (rəʊm) *vb.* **1.** to walk about with no fixed purpose or direction. ~*n.* **2.** the act of roaming.

roan (rəʊn) *adj.* **1.** (of a horse) having a brown or black coat sprinkled with white hairs. ~*n.* **2.** a horse having such a coat.

roar (rɔː) *vb.* **1.** (of lions and other animals) to make loud growling cries. **2.** (of people) to utter (something) with a loud deep cry, as in anger or triumph. **3.** to laugh in a loud hearty unrestrained manner. **4.** (of the wind, waves, etc.) to blow or break loudly and violently, as during a storm. **5.** (of a fire) to burn fiercely with a roaring sound. ~*n.* **6.** a loud deep cry, uttered by a person or crowd, esp. in anger or triumph. **7.** a prolonged loud cry of certain animals, esp. lions. **8.** any similar noise made by a fire, the wind, waves, an engine, etc.

roaring ('rɔːrɪŋ) *adv.* **1.** noisily or boisterously: *roaring drunk.* ~*adj.* **2. a roaring trade.** a brisk and profitable business.

roast (rəʊst) *vb.* **1.** to cook (meat or other food) by dry heat, as in an oven or on a spit. **2.** to brown or dry (coffee or nuts) by exposure to heat. **3.** to be, become or make extremely hot. **4.** *Informal.* to criticize severely. ~*n.* **5.** something that has been roasted, esp. meat. ~*adj.* **6.** cooked by roasting: *roast parsnips.* —'**roaster** *n.*

roasting ('rəʊstɪŋ) *Informal.* ~*adj.* **1.** extremely hot. ~*n.* **2.** severe criticism.

rob (rɒb) *vb.* **robbing, robbed. 1.** to take something from (a person or place) illegally, esp. by or with force. **2.** to deprive unjustly: *to be robbed of an opportunity.* —'**robber** *n.*

robbery ('rɒbərɪ) *n., pl.* **-beries. 1.** *Criminal law.* the stealing of property from a person by using or threatening to use force. **2.** the act or an instance of robbing.

robe (rəʊb) *n.* **1.** any loose flowing garment, esp. the official gown of a peer, judge, or academic. **2.** a dressing gown or bathrobe. ~*vb.* **3.** to put a robe on (oneself or someone else).

robin ('rɒbɪn) *n.* **1.** Also called: **robin redbreast.** a small Old World songbird with a brown back and an orange-red breast and face. **2.** a North American thrush similar to but larger than the Old World robin.

robot ('rəʊbɒt) *n.* **1.** a machine programmed to perform specific tasks in a human manner, esp., popularly, one with a human shape. **2.** a person who works or behaves like a machine. **3.** *S. African.* a set of traffic lights. —ro'**botic** *adj.*

robust (rəʊ'bʌst, 'rəʊbʌst) *adj.* **1.** strong in

constitution. **2.** sturdily built: *a robust shelter.* **3.** requiring physical strength: *a robust sport.*

roc (rɒk) *n.* (in Arabian legend) a bird of enormous size and power.

rock[1] (rɒk) *n.* **1.** *Geol.* the mass of mineral matter that makes up part of the earth's crust; stone. **2.** any hard mass of mineral matter, such as a boulder. **3.** *U.S., Canad., & Austral.* a stone. **4.** a person or thing suggesting a rock, esp. in being dependable, unchanging, or providing firm foundation. **5.** *Brit.* a hard sweet, typically a long brightly coloured peppermint-flavoured stick, sold esp. in holiday resorts. **6.** *Slang.* a jewel, esp. a diamond. **7. on the rocks. a.** (of a marriage) in trouble; about to end. **b.** (of drinks, esp. whisky) served with ice.

rock[2] (rɒk) *vb.* **1.** to move or cause to move from side to side or backwards and forwards. **2.** to feel or cause to feel shock: *the scandal rocked the government.* **3.** to shake or move (something) violently. **4.** to dance to or play rock music. ~*n.* **5.** a rocking motion. **6.** Also called: **rock music.** rock and roll, or any of various styles of pop music with a heavy beat derived from it.

rockabilly ('rɒkə,bɪlɪ) *n.* a fast, spare style of White rock music which originated in the mid-1950s in the U.S. South.

rock and roll *or* **rock'n'roll** *n.* a type of pop music originating in the 1950s as a blend of rhythm and blues and country and western.

rock bottom *n.* the lowest possible level.

rock-bound *adj.* hemmed in or encircled by rocks. Also (poetic): **rock-girt.**

rock cake *n.* a small cake containing dried fruit and spice, with a rough surface supposed to resemble a rock.

rock crystal *n.* a pure transparent colourless quartz.

rock dove *or* **pigeon** *n.* a common dove from which domestic and feral pigeons are descended.

rocker ('rɒkə) *n.* **1.** any of various devices that operate with or transmit a rocking motion. **2.** a rocking chair. **3.** either of two curved supports on the legs of a chair on which it may rock. **4.** a rock music performer, fan, or song. **5. off one's rocker.** *Slang.* crazy.

rockery ('rɒkərɪ) *n., pl.* **-eries.** a garden constructed with rocks, esp. one where alpine plants are grown.

rocket ('rɒkɪt) *n.* **1.** a self-propelling device, usually cylindrical, which produces thrust by expelling through a nozzle the gases produced by burning fuel, such as one used as a firework or distress signal. **2.** any vehicle propelled by a rocket engine, esp. one used to carry a spacecraft or as a missile. **3.** *Brit. & N.Z. informal.* a severe reprimand: *you'll get a rocket.* ~*vb.* **4.** to propel (a missile or spacecraft) by means of a rocket. **5.** to move rapidly: *she rocketed to the top.*

rocketry ('rɒkɪtrɪ) *n.* the science and technology of the design and operation of rockets.

rock garden *n.* a garden featuring rocks or rockeries.

rocking chair *n.* a chair set on curving supports so that the sitter may rock backwards and forwards.

rocking horse *n.* a toy horse mounted on a pair of rocking supports on which a child can rock to and fro.

rock melon *n. U.S., Austral., & N.Z.* same as **cantaloupe.**

rock plant *n.* any plant that grows on rocks or in rocky ground.

rock rabbit *n. S. African.* a rodent-like mammal, the dassie or rock hyrax.

rock salmon *n. Brit.* a former term for dogfish when used as a food.

rock salt *n.* common salt as a naturally occurring solid mineral.

rock tripe *n. Canad.* any of various edible lichens that grow on rocks.

rocky[1] ('rɒkɪ) *adj.* **rockier, rockiest.** consisting of or abounding in rocks: *a rocky shore.* —**'rockiness** *n.*

rocky[2] ('rɒkɪ) *adj.* **rockier, rockiest.** weak, shaky, or unstable. —**'rockiness** *n.*

rococo (rə'kəukəu) *n. (often cap.)* **1.** an 18th-century style of architecture, decoration and music characterized by elaborate ornamentation. **2.** any florid or excessively ornamental style. ~*adj.* **3.** of or in the rococo style. **4.** florid or excessively elaborate.

rod (rɒd) *n.* **1.** a slim cylinder of metal, wood, etc. **2.** a stick or cane used to beat people as a punishment. **3.** any of various staffs of insignia or office. **4.** short for fishing rod. **5.** a unit of length equal to 5½ yards. **6.** *U.S. slang.* a pistol. —**'rod- ,like** *adj.*

rode (rəud) *vb.* the past tense of **ride.**

rodent ('rəud³nt) *n.* any of the relatively small mammals with constantly growing incisor teeth specialized for gnawing. The group includes rats, mice and squirrels. —**'rodent-,like** *adj.*

rodeo ('rəudɪ,əu) *n., pl.* **-deos.** a display of the skills of cowboys, including bareback riding.

rodomontade (,rɒdəmɒn'teɪd, -'tɑːd) *n. Literary.* boastful words or behaviour.

roe[1] (rəu) *n.* the ovary and eggs of a female fish.

roe[2] (rəu) *or* **roe deer** *n.* a small graceful deer of woodlands of Europe and Asia, with small antlers.

Rogation Days *pl. n.* the three days before Ascension Day.

roger ('rɒdʒə) *interj.* **1.** (used in signalling) message received and understood. **2.** an expression of agreement.

rogue (rəug) *n.* **1.** a dishonest or unprincipled person. **2.** a mischievous person, often a child. **3.** any inferior or defective specimen, esp. a defective crop plant. **4.** an animal of vicious character that leads a solitary life. —**'roguish** *adj.*

roguery ('rəugərɪ) *n., pl.* **-gueries. 1.** behaviour characteristic of a rogue. **2.** a roguish or mischievous act.

rogues' gallery *n.* a collection of portraits of known criminals kept by the police for identification purposes.

roister ('rɔɪstə) *vb.* to engage in noisy or unrestrained merrymaking. —**'roist- erer** *n.*

role *or* **rôle** (rəul) *n.* **1.** a part in a play, film, etc. **2.** function: *what is his role in the organization?*

roll (rəul) *vb.* **1.** to move or cause to move along by turning over and over. **2.** to move or cause to move along on wheels or rollers. **3.** to flow or cause to flow onwards in an undulating movement. **4.** (of animals) to turn onto the back and kick. **5.** to appear like a series of waves: *the hills roll down to the sea.* **6.** (foll. by *on, by,* etc.) to pass or elapse: *the years roll by.* **7.** to rotate or cause to rotate wholly or partially: *to roll one's eyes.* **8.** to curl, cause to curl, or make by curling into a ball, tube, or cylinder. **9.** (often foll. by *out*) to spread or cause to spread out flat or smooth as by a roller: *to roll pastry.* **10.** to make a deep prolonged reverberating sound: *the thunder rolled continuously.* **11.** to trill or cause to be trilled: *to roll one's r's.* **12.** (of a vessel, aircraft, or rocket) to turn from side to side around the longitudinal axis. **13.** to walk with a swaying gait, as when drunk. **14.** *Chiefly U.S.* to throw (dice). **15.** to operate or begin to operate: *the presses rolled.* ~*n.* **16.** the act or an instance of rolling. **17.** anything rolled up in a cylindrical form: *a roll of newspaper.* **18.** an official list or register, esp. of names: *an electoral roll.* **19.** a rounded mass: *rolls of flesh.* **20.** a small cake of bread for one person. **21.** a flat pastry or cake rolled up with a meat (**sausage roll**), jam (**jam roll**), or other filling. **22.** a swaying, rolling, or unsteady movement or gait. **23.** a deep prolonged reverberating sound: *a roll of thunder.* **24.** a trilling sound; trill. **25.** a very rapid beating of the sticks on a drum. **26.** a complete rotation about its longitudinal axis by an aircraft. **27. strike off the roll(s).** to expel from membership of a professional association. ~See also **roll in, roll on,** etc.

roll call *n.* the reading aloud of an official

list of names, those present responding when their names are read out.

rolled gold *n.* a metal, such as brass, coated with a thin layer of gold.

roller ('rəʊlə) *n.* **1.** a cylinder with an absorbent surface and a handle, used for spreading paint. **2.** Also called: **garden roller.** a heavy cast-iron cylinder on an axle to which a handle is attached; used for flattening lawns. **3.** a long heavy wave of the sea. **4.** a cylinder fitted on pivots, used to enable heavy objects to be easily moved. **5.** any of various rotating cylindrical devices, used for flattening, crushing, or spreading. **6.** a small cylinder onto which a woman's hair may be rolled to make it curl.

roller coaster *n.* (at a fair) a narrow railway with open carriages, sharp curves and steep inclines.

roller skate *n.* **1.** a device worn fastened to a shoe, with four small wheels that enable the wearer to glide swiftly over a floor. ~*vb.* **roller-skate.** **2.** to move on roller skates. —**roller skater** *n.*

roller towel *n.* **1.** a towel with the two ends sewn together, hung on a roller. **2.** a towel wound inside a roller enabling a clean section to be pulled out when needed.

rollicking ('rɒlɪkɪŋ) *adj.* boisterously carefree.

roll in *vb.* **1.** to arrive in large numbers. **2. be rolling in.** *Slang.* to have plenty of (wealth, money, etc.).

rolling ('rəʊlɪŋ) *adj.* **1.** having gentle rising and falling slopes: *rolling country.* **2.** progressing by stages or in succession: *a rolling strike.* **3.** subject to regular review and updating: *a rolling plan for overseas development.*

rolling mill *n.* **1.** a factory where metal ingots are passed between rollers to produce sheets or bars of the required shape. **2.** a machine having rollers that may be used for this purpose.

rolling pin *n.* a cylinder with handles at both ends used for rolling pastry out flat.

rolling stock *n.* the wheeled vehicles of a railway, including the locomotives and coaches.

rolling stone *n.* a restless or wandering person.

rollmop ('rəʊl,mɒp) *n.* a herring fillet rolled around onion slices and pickled.

rollneck ('rəʊl,nɛk) *adj.* (of a garment) having a high neck that may be rolled over.

roll on *vb.* **1.** *Brit.* used to express the wish that an eagerly anticipated event or date will come quickly: *roll on Saturday.* ~*adj.* **roll-on.** **2.** (of a deodorant) applied by means of a revolving ball fitted into the neck of the container.

roll-on/roll-off *adj.* denoting a ship designed so that vehicles can be driven straight on and straight off.

roll-top desk *n.* a desk having a slatted wooden panel that can be pulled down over the writing surface when not in use.

roll up *vb.* **1.** to form or cause to form a cylindrical shape: *to roll up a map.* **2.** *Informal.* to arrive. ~*n.* **roll-up.** **3.** *Brit. informal.* a cigarette made by hand from loose tobacco and cigarette papers.

roly-poly ('rəʊlɪ'pəʊlɪ) *adj.* **1.** plump or chubby. ~*n., pl.* **-lies.** **2.** *Brit.* a strip of suet pastry spread with jam, rolled up, and baked or steamed.

ROM (rɒm) *n. Computers.* read only memory: a storage device that holds data permanently and cannot be altered by the programmer.

rom. *Printing.* roman (type).

roman ('rəʊmən) *adj.* **1.** in or relating to the vertical style of printing type used for most printed matter. ~*n.* **2.** roman type.

Roman ('rəʊmən) *adj.* **1.** of Rome or its inhabitants in ancient or modern times. **2.** of Roman Catholicism or the Roman Catholic Church. ~*n.* **3.** a person from ancient or modern Rome.

Roman alphabet *n.* the alphabet evolved by the ancient Romans for writing Latin, used for writing most of the languages of W Europe, including English.

Roman candle *n.* a firework that produces a continuous shower of sparks punctuated by coloured balls of fire.

Roman Catholic *adj.* **1.** of the Roman Catholic Church. ~*n.* **2.** a member of this Church. —**Roman Catholicism** *n.*

Roman Catholic Church *n.* the Christian Church over which the pope presides.

romance *n.* (rə'mæns, 'rəʊmæns). **1.** a love affair. **2.** love, esp. romantic love idealized for its purity or beauty. **3.** a spirit of or inclination for adventure or mystery. **4.** a mysterious, exciting, sentimental, or nostalgic quality. **5.** a story or film dealing with events and characters remote from ordinary life. **6.** a story or film dealing with love, usually in an idealized or sentimental way. **7.** an extravagant, absurd, or fantastic account. **8.** a medieval narrative dealing with adventures of chivalrous heroes. ~*vb.* (rə'mæns). **9.** to tell or write extravagant or romantic fictions. **10.** to tell extravagant or improbable lies.

Romance (rə'mæns, 'rəʊmæns) *adj.* of or relating to the languages derived from Latin, including Italian, French, Spanish, Portuguese, and Romanian.

Romanesque (,rəʊmə'nɛsk) *adj.* of or in the style of architecture used in W and S Europe from the 9th to the 12th century, characterized by the rounded arch and massive-masonry wall construction.

Romanian (rəʊ'meɪnɪən) *n.* **1.** the official language of Romania, in SE Europe. **2.** a person from Romania. ~*adj.* **3.** of Romania, its people, or their language.

Roman nose *n.* a nose with a high prominent bridge.

Roman numerals *pl. n.* the letters used as numerals by the Romans, used occasionally today: I (= 1), V (= 5), X (= 10), L (= 50), C (= 100), D (= 500), and M (= 1000). VI = 6 (V + I) but IV = 4 (V − I).

romantic (rəʊˈmæntɪk) *adj.* **1.** of, like, or characterized by romance. **2.** evoking or given to thoughts and feelings of love, esp. idealized or sentimental love: *a romantic setting.* **3.** impractical, visionary, or idealistic: *a romantic scheme.* **4.** (*often cap.*) of or relating to a movement in European art, music, and literature in the late 18th and early 19th centuries, characterized by an emphasis on feeling and content rather than order and form. ~*n.* **5.** a person who is romantic, as in being idealistic, amorous, or soulful. **6.** a person who likes or produces artistic works in the style of romanticism. —**roˈmantically** *adv.*

romanticism (rəʊˈmæntɪˌsɪzəm) *n.* **1.** (*often cap.*) the spirit and style of the romantic art, music, and literature of the late 18th and early 19th centuries. **2.** romantic attitudes, ideals, or qualities. —**roˈmanticist** *n.*

romanticize *or* **-cise** (rəʊˈmæntɪˌsaɪz) *vb.* **1.** to make or become romantic. **2.** to describe or regard (something) in an unrealistic and idealized way: *her romanticized view of marriage.*

Romany (ˈrɒmənɪ, ˈrəʊ-) *n.* **1.** (*pl.* **-nies**) a Gypsy. **2.** the language of the Gypsies, belonging to the Indic branch of the Indo-European family.

Romeo (ˈrəʊmɪəʊ) *n., pl.* **Romeos.** an ardent male lover.

romp (rɒmp) *vb.* **1.** to play or run about wildly, boisterously, or joyfully. **2.** **romp home** (*or* **in**). to win a race or other competition easily. ~*n.* **3.** a noisy or boisterous game or prank.

rompers (ˈrɒmpəz) *pl. n.* **1.** Also called: **romper suit.** a one-piece baby garment combining trousers and a top. **2.** *N.Z.* a type of costume worn by schoolgirls for games and gymnastics.

rondavel (ˌrɒnˈdɑːvəl) *n. S. African.* a circular building, often thatched.

rondeau (ˈrɒndəʊ) *n., pl.* **-deaux** (-dəʊ, -dəʊz). a poem consisting of 13 or 10 lines with two rhymes and having the opening words of the first line used as an unrhymed refrain.

rondo (ˈrɒndəʊ) *n., pl.* **-dos.** a piece of music in which a refrain is repeated between episodes: often forms the last movement of a sonata or concerto.

roof (ruːf) *n., pl.* **roofs** (ruːfs, ruːvz). **1.** a structure that covers or forms the top of a building. **2.** the top covering of a vehicle, oven, or other structure: *the roof of a car.* **3.** *Anat.* any structure that covers an organ or part: *the roof of the mouth.* **4.** **hit** (*or* **go through**) **the roof.** *Informal.* to get extremely angry. **5. raise the roof.** *Informal.* to be very noisy. ~*vb.* **6.** to provide or cover with a roof or rooflike part.

roof garden *n.* a garden on a flat roof of a building.

roofing (ˈruːfɪŋ) *n.* material used to construct a roof.

roof rack *n.* a rack attached to the roof of a motor vehicle for carrying luggage.

rooftree (ˈruːfˌtriː) *n.* same as **ridgepole.**

rooikat (ˈrɔɪˌkæt, ˈrʊɪkæt) *n.* a South African lynx.

rooinek (ˈrɔɪˌnɛk, ˈrʊɪnɛk) *n. S. African, facetious.* an Englishman.

rook[1] (rʊk) *n.* **1.** a large crowlike Eurasian bird, with a black plumage and a whitish base to its bill. ~*vb.* **2.** *Slang.* to overcharge, swindle, or cheat.

rook[2] (rʊk) *n.* a chesspiece that may move any number of unoccupied squares in a straight line, horizontally or vertically; castle.

rookery (ˈrʊkərɪ) *n., pl.* **-eries. 1.** a group of nesting rooks. **2.** a colony of certain other birds or mammals, esp. penguins or seals.

rookie (ˈrʊkɪ) *n. Informal.* a newcomer, esp. a raw recruit in the army.

room (ruːm, rʊm) *n.* **1.** unoccupied or unobstructed space: *is there room to pass?* **2.** an area within a building enclosed by a floor, a ceiling, and walls. **3.** (*functioning as sing. or pl.*) the people present in a room: *the whole room was laughing.* **4.** (foll. by *for*) opportunity or scope: *room for manoeuvre.* **5.** (*pl.*) lodgings. ~*vb.* **6.** to occupy or share a room: *Jim and I used to room together.*

rooming house *n. U.S. & Canad.* a house having self-contained furnished rooms or flats for renting.

roommate (ˈruːmˌmeɪt, ˈrʊm-) *n.* a person with whom one shares a room.

room service *n.* service in a hotel providing food and drinks in guests' rooms.

roomy (ˈruːmɪ, ˈrʊmɪ) *adj.* **roomier, roomiest.** spacious. —ˈ**roominess** *n.*

roost (ruːst) *n.* **1.** a place, such as a perch where birds, esp. domestic fowl, rest or sleep. ~*vb.* **2.** to rest or sleep on a roost. **3.** to settle down or stay. **4. come home to roost.** to have unfavourable repercussions.

rooster (ˈruːstə) *n. Chiefly U.S. & Canad.* the male of the domestic fowl; a cock.

root[1] (ruːt) *n.* **1.** the part of a plant that anchors the rest of the plant in the ground and absorbs water and mineral salts from the soil. **2.** any plant part, such as a tuber, that resembles a root. **3.** the essential part or nature of something: *the root of the problem*. **4.** *Anat.* the embedded portion of a tooth, nail, hair, etc. **5.** origin or derivation. **6.** (*pl.*) a person's sense of belonging in a community or place, esp. the one in which he was born or brought up. **7.** *Linguistics.* the form of a word that remains after removal of all affixes. **8.** *Maths.* a quantity that when multiplied by itself a certain number of times equals a given quantity: *3 is a cube root of 27.* **9.** Also called: **solution.** *Maths.* a number that when substituted for the variable satisfies a given equation. **10.** *Austral. & N.Z. slang.* sexual intercourse. **11. root and branch.** entirely; utterly. ~*vb.* **12.** Also: **take root.** to establish a root and begin to grow. **13.** Also: **take root.** to become established, embedded, or effective. **14.** to embed with or as if with a root or roots. **15.** *Austral. & N.Z. slang.* to have sexual intercourse (with). ~See also **root out, roots.**

root² (ruːt) *vb.* **1.** (of a pig) to dig up the earth in search of food, using the snout. **2.** (foll. by *about, around, in,* etc.) *Informal.* to search vigorously but unsystematically.

root canal *n.* the passage in the root of a tooth through which its nerves and blood vessels enter.

root crop *n.* a crop, as of turnips or beets, cultivated for the food value of its roots.

root for *vb. Informal.* to give support to (a team or contestant), as by cheering.

rootle (ˈruːtʲl) *vb. Brit.* same as **root²**.

rootless (ˈruːtlɪs) *adj.* having no roots, esp. (of a person) having no ties with a particular place.

root mean square *n.* the square root of the average of the squares of a set of numbers or quantities: *the root mean square of 1, 2, and 4 is* $\sqrt{[(1^2 + 2^2 + 4^2)/3]} = \sqrt{7}$.

root out *vb.* to remove or eliminate completely: *we must root out inefficiency.*

roots (ruːts) *adj.* (of popular music) going back to the origins of a style, esp. in being unpretentious: *roots rock.*

rootstock (ˈruːtˌstɒk) *n.* same as **rhizome.**

rope (rəʊp) *n.* **1.** a fairly thick cord made of intertwined fibres or wire. **2.** a row of objects fastened to form a line: *a rope of pearls.* **3.** a filament or strand: *a rope of slime.* **4. know the ropes.** to have a thorough understanding of a particular activity. **5. the rope. a.** a rope noose used for hanging someone. **b.** death by hanging. ~*vb.* **6.** to bind, tie, or fasten with or as if with a rope. **7.** (usually foll. by *off*) to enclose or divide by means of a rope.

rope in *vb.* **1.** *Brit.* to persuade to take part in some activity. **2.** *U.S. & Canad.* to trick or entice into some activity.

ropy *or* **ropey** (ˈrəʊpɪ) *adj.* **ropier, ropiest.** *Brit. informal.* **1.** poor or unsatisfactory in

quality: *a ropy performance.* **2.** slightly unwell. —**ropiness** *n.*

Roquefort (ˈrɒkfɔː) *n.* a strong blue-veined cheese made from ewe's and goat's milk.

ro-ro (ˈrəʊrəʊ) *adj.* (of a ferry) roll-on/roll-off.

rorqual (ˈrɔːkwəl) *n.* a whalebone whale with a dorsal fin.

Rorschach test (ˈrɔːʃɑːk) *n. Psychol.* a personality test consisting of a number of unstructured inkblots for interpretation.

rosaceous (rəʊˈzeɪʃəs) *adj.* of or belonging to a family of plants typically having five-petalled flowers, which includes the rose, strawberry, blackberry, and many fruit trees.

rosary (ˈrəʊzərɪ) *n., pl.* **-saries.** *R.C. Church.* **a.** a series of prayers counted on a string of beads. **b.** a string of beads used to count these prayers as they are recited.

rose¹ (rəʊz) *n.* **1.** a shrub or climbing plant with prickly stems and fragrant flowers. **2.** the flower of any of these plants. **3.** any of various similar plants, such as the Christmas rose. **4.** a purplish-pink colour. **5.** a rose as the national emblem of England. **6.** a perforated cap fitted to a watering can or hose, causing the water to issue in a spray. **7. bed of roses.** a situation of comfort or ease.

rose² (rəʊz) *vb.* the past tense of **rise.**

rosé (ˈrəʊzeɪ) *n.* a pink wine.

roseate (ˈrəʊzɪˌeɪt) *adj.* **1.** of the colour rose or pink. **2.** excessively optimistic.

rosebay willowherb (ˈrəʊzˌbeɪ ˈwɪləʊˌhɜːb) *n.* a widespread perennial plant that has spikes of deep pink flowers.

rosebud (ˈrəʊzˌbʌd) *n.* the bud of a rose.

rose-coloured *adj.* **1.** excessively optimistic. **2. see through rose-coloured glasses** (*or* **spectacles**). to view in an excessively optimistic light.

rosehip (ˈrəʊzˌhɪp) *n.* the berry-like fruit of a rose plant.

rosemary (ˈrəʊzmərɪ) *n., pl.* **-maries.** an aromatic European shrub widely cultivated for its grey-green evergreen leaves, which are used in cookery and perfumes.

rose of Sharon (ˈʃærən) *n.* a creeping shrub with large yellow flowers.

rosette (rəʊˈzɛt) *n.* a decoration resembling a rose, esp. an arrangement of ribbons in a rose-shaped design worn as a badge or presented as a prize.

rose-water *n.* scented water made by the distillation of rose petals or by impregnation with oil of roses.

rose window *n.* a circular window with ornamental tracery radiating from the centre to form a symmetrical roselike pattern.

rosewood (ˈrəʊzˌwʊd) *n.* a hard dark wood with a roselike scent, used to make furniture.

rosin ('rɒzɪn) *n.* **1.** a translucent brittle substance produced in the distillation of crude turpentine and used for treating the bows of stringed instruments. ~*vb.* **2.** to treat or coat with rosin.

ROSPA ('rɒspə) *n.* (in Britain) Royal Society for the Prevention of Accidents.

roster ('rɒstə) *n.* **1.** a list or register, esp. one showing the order of people enrolled for duty. ~*vb.* **2.** to place on a roster.

rostrum ('rɒstrəm) *n., pl.* **-trums** or **-tra** (-trə). **1.** any platform on which public speakers stand. **2.** a platform in front of an orchestra on which the conductor stands.

rosy ('rəuzɪ) *adj.* **rosier, rosiest. 1.** of the colour rose or pink. **2.** having a healthy pink complexion: *rosy cheeks.* **3.** optimistic, esp. excessively so: *a rosy view of social improvements.* —**'rosiness** *n.*

rot (rɒt) *vb.* **rotting, rotted. 1.** to decay or cause to decay. **2.** to become weak or depressed, as through inertia or confinement: *rotting in prison.* ~*n.* **3.** the process of rotting or the state of being rotten. **4.** something decomposed. **5.** short for **dry rot. 6.** any of various plant or animal diseases which cause decay of the tissues. **7.** nonsense; rubbish.

rota ('rəutə) *n. Chiefly Brit.* a register of names showing the order in which people take their turn to perform certain duties.

rotary ('rəutərɪ) *adj.* **1.** operating by rotation. **2.** revolving. ~*n., pl.* **-ries. 3.** *U.S. & Canad.* a traffic roundabout.

Rotary Club *n.* any of the local clubs that form **Rotary International,** an international association of professional and business men founded in the U.S. in 1905 to promote community service. —**Rotarian** (rəu-'tɛərɪən) *n., adj.*

rotate (rəu'teɪt) *vb.* **1.** to turn or cause to turn around an axis; spin. **2.** to follow or cause to follow a set sequence. **3.** to regularly change the type of crop grown on a piece of land in order to preserve the fertility of the soil. —**ro'tation** *n.*

rote (rəut) *n.* **1.** a habitual or mechanical routine or procedure. **2. by rote.** by repetition; by heart.

rotgut ('rɒt,gʌt) *n. Facetious slang.* alcoholic drink, esp. spirits, of inferior quality.

rotisserie (rəu'tɪsərɪ) *n.* a rotating spit on which meat and poultry can be cooked.

rotor ('rəutə) *n.* **1.** the rotating part of a machine or device, such as the revolving arm of the distributor of an internal-combustion engine. **2.** a rotating device with blades projecting from a hub which produces thrust to lift a helicopter.

Rotovator ('rəutə,veɪtə) *n. Trademark.* a mechanical cultivator with rotary blades.

rotten ('rɒt²n) *adj.* **1.** decomposing, decaying, or putrid. **2.** breaking up, esp. through age or hard use: *rotten ironwork.* **3.** moral-ly corrupt. **4.** *Informal.* unpleasant: *rotten weather.* **5.** *Informal.* unsatisfactory: *rotten workmanship.* **6.** *Informal.* miserably unwell. **7.** *Informal.* distressed and embarrassed: *I felt rotten breaking the news to him.*

rotter ('rɒtə) *n. Slang, chiefly Brit.* a worthless or despicable person.

rotund (rəu'tʌnd) *adj.* **1.** rounded or spherical in shape. **2.** plump. **3.** sonorous or grandiloquent. —**ro'tundity** *n.* —**ro'tundly** *adv.*

rotunda (rəu'tʌndə) *n.* a circular building or room, esp. wih a dome.

rouble *or* **ruble** ('ru:b²l) *n.* the standard monetary unit of the Soviet Union.

roué ('ru:eɪ) *n.* a man who gives himself over to a sensual immoral life.

rouge (ru:ʒ) *n.* **1.** a red cosmetic for adding redness to the cheeks. ~*vb.* **2.** to apply rouge to.

rough (rʌf) *adj.* **1.** (of a surface) not smooth; uneven or irregular. **2.** (of ground) covered with scrub, boulders, etc. **3.** denoting or taking place on uncultivated ground: *rough grazing.* **4.** shaggy or hairy. **5.** turbulent: *a rough sea.* **6.** (of behaviour or character) rude, coarse, or violent. **7.** harsh or sharp: *rough words.* **8.** (of work, etc.) requiring physical rather than mental effort. **9.** *Informal.* ill: *he felt rough after an evening's drinking.* **10.** unfair: *rough luck.* **11.** harsh or grating to the ear. **12.** without refinement, luxury, etc. **13.** incomplete or rudimentary: *a rough draft.* **14.** (of a guess) approximate. ~*n.* **15.** rough ground. **16.** a sketch or preliminary piece of artwork. **17.** unfinished or crude state. **18. the rough.** *Golf.* the part of the course bordering the fairways where the grass is untrimmed. **19.** *Informal.* a violent person; thug. **20.** the unpleasant side of something: *to take the rough with the smooth.* ~*adv.* **21.** roughly. **22. sleep rough.** to spend the night in the open; be without shelter. ~*vb.* **23.** to make rough; roughen. **24.** (foll. by *out* or *in*) to prepare (a sketch, report, etc.) in preliminary form. **25. rough it.** *Informal.* to live without the usual comforts of life. ~See also **rough up.**

roughage ('rʌfɪdʒ) *n.* the coarse indigestible constituents of food, which provide bulk to the diet and aid digestion.

rough-and-ready *adj.* **1.** crude, unpolished, or hastily prepared, but sufficient for the purpose. **2.** (of a person) without formality or refinement.

rough-and-tumble *n.* **1.** a fight or scuffle without rules. ~*adj.* **2.** disorderly and without rules.

roughcast ('rʌf,kɑːst) *n.* **1.** a coarse plaster used to cover the surface of an external wall. ~*vb.* **-casting, -cast. 2.** to apply roughcast to (a wall).

rough diamond *n.* **1.** an unpolished diamond. **2.** an intrinsically trustworthy or good person with uncouth manners.

roughen ('rʌfᵊn) vb. to make or become rough.

rough-hew vb. -hewing, -hewed; -hewed or -hewn. to cut or shape roughly without finishing the surface.

roughhouse ('rʌf,haʊs) n. Slang. rough, disorderly, or noisy behaviour.

roughneck ('rʌf,nɛk) n. Slang. **1.** a rough or violent person; thug. **2.** a worker in an oil-drilling operation.

roughshod ('rʌf,ʃɒd) adj. **1.** (of a horse) shod with rough-bottomed shoes to prevent sliding. ~adv. **2. ride roughshod over.** to act with complete disregard for.

rough up vb. Informal. to beat up.

roulette (ruːˈlɛt) n. a gambling game in which a ball is dropped onto a spinning horizontal wheel divided into numbered slots, with players betting on the slot into which the ball will fall.

round (raʊnd) adj. **1.** having a flat circular shape, as a hoop. **2.** having the shape of a ball. **3.** curved; not angular. **4.** involving or using circular motion. **5.** complete: a round dozen. **6.** Maths. **a.** forming or expressed by a whole number, with no fraction. **b.** expressed to the nearest ten, hundred, or thousand: in round figures. **7.** (of speech) candid: a round assertion. ~n. **8.** a round shape or object. **9. in the round. a.** in full detail. **b.** Theatre. with the audience all round the stage. **10.** a session, as of a negotiation: a round of talks. **11.** a series: a giddy round of parties. **12. the daily round.** the usual activities of one's day. **13.** a stage of a competition: he was eliminated in the first round. **14.** (often pl.) a series of calls: a milkman's round. **15.** a playing of all the holes on a golf course. **16.** a single turn of play by each player, as in a card game. **17.** one of a number of periods in a boxing, wrestling, or other match. **18.** a single discharge by a gun. **19.** a bullet or other charge of ammunition. **20.** a number of drinks bought at one time for a group of people. **21. a.** a single slice of bread. **b.** a serving of sandwiches made from two complete slices of bread. **22.** a general outburst of applause. **23.** movement in a circle. **24.** Music. a part song in which the voices follow each other at equal intervals at the same pitch. **25. go the rounds.** (of information, infection, etc.) to be passed around. ~prep. **26.** surrounding, encircling, or enclosing: a band round her head. **27.** on all or most sides of: to look round one. **28.** on or outside the circumference or perimeter of. **29.** from place to place in: driving round Ireland. **30.** reached by making a partial circuit about: the shop round the corner. **31.** revolving about (a centre or axis): the earth's motion round its axis. ~adv. **32.** on all or most

sides. **33.** on or outside the circumference or perimeter: the racing track is two miles round. **34.** to all members of a group: pass the food round. **35.** in rotation or revolution: the wheels turn round. **36.** by a circuitous route: the road to the farm goes round by the pond. **37.** to a specific place: she came round to see me. **38. all year round.** throughout the year. ~vb. **39.** to make or become round. **40.** to move or cause to move with turning motion: to round a bend. ~See also **round down, round off,** etc.

roundabout ('raʊndə,baʊt) n. **1.** Brit. a revolving circular platform, often with seats, on which people ride for amusement; merry-go-round. **2.** a road junction in which traffic moves in one direction around a central island. ~adj. **3.** indirect; devious: she found out by roundabout methods. ~adv., prep. **round about. 4.** approximately: at round about 5 o'clock.

round dance n. **1.** a dance in which the dancers form a circle. **2.** a ballroom dance, such as the waltz, in which couples revolve.

round down vb. to lower (a number) to the nearest whole number or ten, hundred, or thousand below it.

roundel ('raʊndᵊl) n. **1.** a circular identifying mark on military aircraft. **2.** a small circular object, such as a window or medallion.

roundelay ('raʊndɪ,leɪ) n. a song in which a line or phrase is repeated as a refrain.

rounders ('raʊndəz) n. (functioning as sing.) Brit. a bat and ball game in which players run between posts after hitting the ball, scoring a **rounder** if they run round all four posts before the ball is retrieved.

Roundhead ('raʊnd,hɛd) n. English history. a supporter of Parliament against Charles I during the Civil War.

roundhouse ('raʊnd,haʊs) n. U.S. & Canad. a circular building in which railway locomotives are serviced.

roundly ('raʊndlɪ) adv. bluntly or thoroughly: this policy has been roundly criticized.

round off vb. (often foll. by with) to complete, esp. agreeably: we rounded off the evening with a brandy.

round on vb. to attack or reply to (someone) with sudden irritation or anger.

round robin n. **1.** a petition or protest with the signatures in a circle to disguise the order of signing. **2.** a tournament in which each player plays against every other player.

round-shouldered adj. denoting a faulty posture with drooping shoulders and a slight forward bending of the back.

round table n. a meeting of parties or people on equal terms for discussion.

Round Table n. the. **1.** (in Arthurian

legend) the table of King Arthur, shaped so that his knights could sit around it without any having precedence. **2.** one of an organization of clubs of young business and professional men who meet in order to further charitable work.

round-the-clock *adj.* (*or as adv.* **round the clock**) throughout the day and night.

round trip *n.* a trip to a place and back again, esp. returning by a different route.

round up *vb.* **1.** to gather together: *to round ponies up.* **2.** to raise (a number) to the nearest whole number or ten, hundred, or thousand above it. ~*n.* **roundup. 3.** the act of gathering together livestock, esp. cattle. **4.** any similar act of bringing together: *a roundup of today's news.*

roundworm ('raʊnd‚wɜːm) *n.* a worm that is a common intestinal parasite of man and pigs.

rouse (raʊz) *vb.* **1.** to wake up. **2.** to provoke: *to rouse someone's anger.* **3.** **rouse oneself.** to become energetic.

rousing ('raʊzɪŋ) *adj.* tending to excite; lively or vigorous: *a rousing chorus.*

roustabout ('raʊstə‚baʊt) *n.* an unskilled labourer on an oil rig.

rout[1] (raʊt) *n.* **1.** an overwhelming defeat. **2.** a disorderly retreat. **3.** a noisy rabble. ~*vb.* **4.** to defeat and cause to flee in confusion.

rout[2] (raʊt) *vb.* **1.** to dig up (something), esp. (of an animal) with the snout. **2.** (usually foll. by *out* or *up*) to find by searching. **3.** (usually foll. by *out*) to drive out: *they routed him out of bed at midnight.* **4.** to search, poke, or rummage.

route (ruːt) *n.* **1.** the choice of roads taken to get to a place. **2.** a regular journey travelled. ~*vb.* **3.** to send by a particular route.

routemarch ('ruːt‚mɑːtʃ) *n. Mil.* a long training march.

routine (ruːˈtiːn) *n.* **1.** a usual or regular method of procedure, esp. one that is unvarying. **2.** *Computers.* a program or part of a program performing a specific function: *an input routine.* **3.** a set sequence of dance steps. ~*adj.* **4.** relating to or characteristic of routine.

roux (ruː) *n.* a cooked mixture of fat and flour used as a basis for sauces.

rove (rəʊv) *vb.* **1.** to wander about (a place); roam. **2.** (of the eyes) to look around; wander. —'**rover** *n.*

row[1] (rəʊ) *n.* **1.** an arrangement of people or things in a line: *a row of chairs.* **2.** *Chiefly Brit.* a street, esp. one lined with identical houses. **3.** a line of seats in a cinema or theatre. **4.** a horizontal line of numbers. **5. in a row.** in succession; one after the other: *he won two gold medals in a row.*

row[2] (rəʊ) *vb.* **1.** to propel (a boat) by using oars. **2.** to carry (people or goods) in a rowing boat. **3.** to take part in the racing of rowing boats as a sport. ~*n.* **4.** an act, period, or distance of rowing. **5.** an excursion in a rowing boat.

row[3] (raʊ) *n.* **1.** a noisy quarrel. **2.** *Informal.* a controversy, esp. a political one: *a new row over NHS cuts.* **3.** a noisy disturbance: *we couldn't hear the music for the row next door.* **4.** a reprimand. ~*vb.* **5.** (often foll. by *with*) to quarrel noisily.

rowan ('rəʊən, 'raʊ-) *n.* a European tree with white flowers and red berries; mountain ash.

rowdy ('raʊdɪ) *adj.* **-dier, -diest. 1.** rough, noisy, or disorderly: *a rowdy gang of football supporters.* ~*n., pl.* **-dies. 2.** a person who behaves in such a fashion. —'**rowdily** *adv.*

rowel ('raʊəl) *n.* a small spiked wheel at the end of a spur.

rowing boat ('rəʊɪŋ) *n. Chiefly Brit.* a small pleasure boat propelled by oars. Usual U.S. and Canad. word: **rowboat.**

rowlock ('rɒlək) *n.* a swivelling device attached to the top of the side of a boat that holds an oar in place.

royal ('rɔɪəl) *adj.* **1.** of or befitting a king or queen; regal. **2.** (*often cap.*) supported by or in the service of royalty: *the Royal Society of St George.* **3.** being a member of a royal family. **4.** better, bigger, or more impressive than usual. ~*n.* **5.** (*sometimes cap.*) a member of a royal family. —'**royally** *adv.*

Royal Air Force *n.* the air force of Great Britain.

royal-blue *adj.* deep blue in colour.

royalist ('rɔɪəlɪst) *n.* **1.** a supporter of a monarch or monarchy. ~*adj.* **2.** of or relating to royalists. —'**royalism** *n.*

royal jelly *n.* a substance secreted by worker bees and fed to all larvae when very young and to larvae destined to become queens throughout their growth.

Royal Marines *pl. n. Brit.* a corps of soldiers specially trained in amphibious warfare.

Royal Navy *n.* the navy of Great Britain.

royalty ('rɔɪəltɪ) *n., pl.* **-ties. 1.** the rank, power, or position of a king or queen. **2.** royal persons individually or collectively. **3.** a percentage of the revenue from the sale of a book, performance of a work, use of a patented invention or of land, etc., paid to the author, inventor, or owner.

royal warrant *n.* an authorization to a tradesman to supply goods to a royal household.

RPI (in Britain) retail price index; a measure of the changes in the average level of retail prices of selected goods.

rpm revolutions per minute.

RR 1. Right Reverend. 2. *Canad. & U.S.* rural route.

RSA 1. Republic of South Africa. 2. (in New Zealand) Returned Services Association. 3. Royal Scottish Academy. 4. Royal Society of Arts.

RSFSR Russian Soviet Federative Socialist Republic.

RSI repetitive strain injury.

RSM regimental sergeant major.

RSPCA (in Britain) Royal Society for the Prevention of Cruelty to Animals.

RSVP please reply.

Rt Hon. Right Honourable: a title of respect for a Privy Councillor, certain peers, and the Lord Mayor or Lord Provost of certain cities.

Ru *Chem.* ruthenium.

rub (rʌb) *vb.* **rubbing, rubbed.** 1. to apply pressure and friction to (something) with a backward and forward motion. 2. to move (something) with pressure along, over, or against (a surface). 3. to chafe or fray. 4. to bring into a certain condition by rubbing: *rub it clean.* 5. to spread with pressure, esp. so that it can be absorbed: *she rubbed ointment into his back.* 6. to mix (fat) into flour with the fingertips, as in making pastry. 7. (foll. by *off, out, away,* etc.) to remove or be removed by rubbing: *the mark would not rub off.* 8. **rub it in.** to harp on something distasteful to a person. 9. **rub up the wrong way.** to annoy. ~*n.* 10. the act of rubbing. 11. (preceded by *the*) an obstacle or difficulty: *there's the rub.* ~See also **rub along, rub down,** etc.

rub along *vb. Brit.* 1. to continue in spite of difficulties. 2. to maintain an amicable relationship; not quarrel.

rubato (ruːˈbɑːtəʊ) *Music.* ~*n., pl.* **-tos.** 1. flexibility of tempo in performance. ~*adj., adv.* 2. to be played with a flexible tempo.

rubber¹ (ˈrʌbə) *n.* 1. an elastic material obtained from the latex of certain plants, esp. the rubber tree. 2. a similar substance produced synthetically. 3. *Chiefly Brit.* a piece of rubber used for erasing something written; eraser. 4. (*often pl.*) *Chiefly U.S. & Canad.* a rubber-coated waterproof overshoe. 5. *Slang.* a condom. 6. (*modifier*) made of or producing rubber: *a rubber ball; a rubber factory.* —**ˈrubbery** *adj.*

rubber² (ˈrʌbə) *n.* 1. Bridge, whist. a match of three games. 2. a series of matches or games in any of various sports.

rubber band *n.* a continuous loop of thin rubber, used to hold papers, etc., together.

rubberize *or* **-ise** (ˈrʌbəˌraɪz) *vb.* to coat or impregnate with rubber.

rubberneck (ˈrʌbəˌnɛk) *Slang.* ~*n.* 1. a person who stares or gapes inquisitively. 2. a sightseer or tourist. ~*vb.* 3. to stare in a naive or foolish manner.

rubber plant *n.* 1. a large house plant with glossy leathery leaves. 2. same as **rubber tree.**

rubber stamp *n.* 1. a device used for imprinting dates, signatures, etc., on forms, invoices, etc. 2. automatic authorization of a payment, proposal, etc. 3. a person or body that gives official approval to decisions taken elsewhere but has no real power. ~*vb.* **rubber-stamp.** 4. *Informal.* to approve automatically.

rubber tree *n.* a tropical tree cultivated for its latex, which is the major source of commercial rubber.

rubbing (ˈrʌbɪŋ) *n.* an impression taken of an incised or raised design by laying paper over it and rubbing with wax, graphite, etc.

rubbish (ˈrʌbɪʃ) *n.* 1. anything worthless, useless, or unwanted. 2. discarded or waste matter; refuse. 3. foolish words or speech; nonsense. ~*vb.* 4. *Informal.* to criticize; attack verbally. —**ˈrubbishy** *adj.*

rubble (ˈrʌbˀl) *n.* 1. pieces of broken stones or bricks. 2. debris from ruined buildings.

rub down *vb.* 1. to dry or clean (a horse, oneself, etc.) vigorously, esp. after exercise. 2. to make or become smooth by rubbing. 3. to prepare (a surface) for painting by rubbing it with sandpaper.

rubella (ruːˈbɛlə) *n.* a mild contagious viral disease characterized by cough, sore throat, and skin rash. Also called: **German measles.**

Rubicon (ˈruːbɪkən) *n.* 1. a stream in N Italy: in ancient times part of the Italian border. 2. **cross** (*or* **pass**) **the Rubicon.** to commit oneself irrevocably to some course of action.

rubicund (ˈruːbɪkənd) *adj.* of a reddish colour; rosy.

rubidium (ruːˈbɪdɪəm) *n.* a soft highly reactive radioactive metallic element used in electronic valves, photocells, and special glass. Symbol: Rb

ruble (ˈruːbˀl) *n.* same as **rouble.**

rub off *vb.* (often foll. by *on* or *onto*) to have an effect through close association: *her manners have rubbed off on you.*

rub out *vb.* 1. to remove or be removed with a rubber. 2. *U.S. slang.* to murder.

rubric (ˈruːbrɪk) *n.* 1. a set of rules of conduct or procedure, esp. one for the conduct of Christian church services. 2. a title, heading, or initial letter in a book, esp. one in red ink.

ruby (ˈruːbɪ) *n., pl.* **-bies.** 1. a deep red transparent precious variety of corundum: used as a gemstone, in lasers, and in watchmaking. 2. the deep-red colour of a ruby. 3. (*modifier*) denoting a fortieth anniversary: *our ruby wedding.*

RUC Royal Ulster Constabulary.

ruche (ruːʃ) *n.* a strip of pleated or frilled lace or ribbon used to decorate clothes.

ruck¹ (rʌk) *n.* 1. a large number or quantity

of undistinguished people or things. **2.** *Rugby.* a loose scrum that forms around the ball when it is on the ground.

ruck² (rʌk) *n.* **1.** a wrinkle, crease, or fold. ~*vb.* **2.** (usually foll. by *up*) to wrinkle or crease.

rucksack ('rʌk,sæk) *n.* a large bag, with two straps, carried on the back.

ruction ('rʌkʃən) *n. Informal.* **1.** an uproar; noisy or quarrelsome disturbance. **2.** (*pl.*) an unpleasant row; trouble.

rudder ('rʌdə) *n.* **1.** *Naut.* a pivoted vertical vane that projects into the water at the stern: used to steer a vessel. **2.** a vertical control surface attached to the rear of the fin used to steer an aircraft. —'**rudderless** *adj.*

ruddy ('rʌdɪ) *adj.* **-dier, -diest. 1.** (of the complexion) having a healthy reddish colour. **2.** red or pink: *a ruddy sky.* ~*adv., adj. Informal, chiefly Brit.* **3.** bloody; damned: *a ruddy fool.*

rude (ruːd) *adj.* **1.** insulting; discourteous; impolite. **2.** lacking refinement; uneducated. **3.** vulgar or obscene: *a rude joke.* **4.** roughly or crudely made: *we made a rude shelter on the island.* **5.** robust or sturdy: *in rude health.* **6.** unexpected and unpleasant: *a rude awakening.* —'**rudely** *adv.* —'**rudeness** *n.*

rudiment ('ruːdɪmənt) *n.* **1.** (*often pl.*) the first principles or elementary stages of a subject. **2.** (*often pl.*) a partially developed version of something. **3.** *Biol.* an organ or part that is incompletely developed or no longer functions. —**rudimentary** (,ruːdɪ-'mɛntrɪ) *adj.*

rue¹ (ruː) *vb.* **ruing, rued.** to feel sorrow, remorse, or regret for (one's wrongdoing, past events, etc.).

rue² (ruː) *n.* an aromatic shrub with bitter evergreen leaves formerly used in medicine.

rueful ('ruːful) *adj.* feeling or expressing sorrow or regret: *a rueful face.* —'**ruefully** *adv.*

ruff¹ (rʌf) *n.* **1.** a circular pleated or fluted cloth collar worn by men and women in the 16th and 17th centuries. **2.** a natural growth of long or coloured hair or feathers around the necks of certain animals or birds. **3.** a bird of the sandpiper family.

ruff² (rʌf) *n., vb. Cards.* same as **trump¹** (sense 1).

ruffian ('rʌfɪən) *n.* a violent or lawless person.

ruffle ('rʌf²l) *vb.* **1.** to disturb the smoothness of: *a breeze ruffling the water.* **2.** to annoy, irritate, or be annoyed or irritated. **3.** (of a bird) to erect its feathers in anger, display, etc. **4.** to flick cards or pages rapidly. ~*n.* **5.** a strip of pleated material used as a trim.

rufous ('ruːfəs) *adj.* reddish-brown.

rug (rʌg) *n.* **1.** a floor covering resembling a

small carpet. **2.** *Chiefly Brit.* a blanket, esp. one used for travellers. **3. pull the rug out from under.** to betray, expose, or leave defenceless.

rugby or **rugby football** ('rʌgbɪ) *n.* a form of football played with an oval ball in which the handling and carrying of the ball is permitted.

rugby league *n.* a form of rugby played between teams of 13 players, professionalism being allowed.

rugby union *n.* a form of rugby played only by amateurs, in teams of 15.

rugged ('rʌgɪd) *adj.* **1.** having an uneven or jagged surface. **2.** rocky or steep: *rugged scenery.* **3.** (of the face) strong-featured or furrowed. **4.** rough, sturdy, or determined in character. **5.** (of equipment or machines) designed to withstand rough treatment or use in rough conditions.

rugger ('rʌgə) *n. Informal, chiefly Brit.* rugby.

ruin ('ruːɪn) *n.* **1.** a destroyed or decayed building or town. **2.** the state of being destroyed or decayed. **3.** loss of wealth, status, or power, or something that causes such loss; downfall. **4.** something that is severely damaged: *his life was a ruin.* ~*vb.* **5.** to bring to ruin; destroy. **6.** to injure or spoil: *the town has been ruined with tower blocks.*

ruination (,ruːɪ'neɪʃən) *n.* **1.** the act of ruining or the state of being ruined. **2.** something that causes ruin.

ruinous ('ruːɪnəs) *adj.* **1.** causing ruin or destruction. **2.** more expensive than can reasonably be afforded: *high interest rates are ruinous for industry.* —'**ruinously** *adv.*

rule (ruːl) *n.* **1.** a principle, regulation, or direction concerning method or procedure, as for a court of law, or sport: *judges' rules; play according to the rules.* **2.** the exercise of governmental authority or control: *the rule of Caesar.* **3.** the period of time in which a monarch or government has power: *his rule lasted 100 days.* **4.** a customary form or procedure: *he made a morning swim his rule.* **5.** (usually preceded by *the*) the common order of things: *violence was the rule.* **6.** a device with a straight edge for guiding or measuring; ruler: *a carpenter's rule.* **7.** *Printing.* a long thin line or dash. **8.** *Christianity.* a systematic body of laws and customs followed by members of a religious order. **9.** *Law.* an order by a court or judge. **10. as a rule.** ordinarily. ~*vb.* **11.** to govern (people or a political unit). **12.** to decide authoritatively; decree: *the chairman ruled against the proposal.* **13.** to mark with straight parallel lines or one straight line. **14.** to restrain or control. **15.** to be customary or prevalent: *chaos rules in this school.* **16.** to be pre-eminent or superior: *football rules in the field of* *sport.* **17. rule the roost.** to be preeminent; be in charge.

rule of thumb *n.* a rough and practical approach, based on experience, rather than theory.

rule out *vb.* **1.** to dismiss from consideration. **2.** to make impossible; preclude.

ruler ('ru:lə) *n.* **1.** a person who rules or commands. **2.** a strip of wood, metal, or other material, having straight edges, used for measuring and drawing straight lines.

ruling ('ru:lɪŋ) *n.* **1.** a decision of someone in authority, such as a judge. ~*adj.* **2.** controlling or exercising authority. **3.** predominant.

rum[1] (rʌm) *n.* spirit made from sugar cane.

rum[2] (rʌm) *adj.* **rummer, rummest.** *Brit. slang.* strange; odd.

Rumanian (ru:'meɪnɪən) *n., adj.* same as **Romanian**.

rumba ('rʌmbə, 'rʊm-) *n.* **1.** a rhythmic and syncopated dance in duple time. **2.** music for this dance.

rumble ('rʌmb²l) *vb.* **1.** to make or cause to make a deep resonant sound: *thunder rumbled in the sky.* **2.** to move with such a sound: *the train rumbled along.* **3.** *Brit. slang.* to find out about (someone or something): *the police rumbled their plans.* ~*n.* **4.** a deep resonant sound. **5.** *U.S. & N.Z. slang.* a gang fight. —'**rumbling** *adj., n.*

rumbustious (rʌm'bʌstʃəs) *adj.* boisterous or unruly.

ruminant ('ru:mɪnənt) *n.* **1.** any of a suborder of mammals which chew the cud and have a stomach of four compartments, including deer, antelopes, cattle, sheep, and goats. **2.** any other animal that chews the cud, such as a camel. ~*adj.* **3.** of such mammals. **4.** meditating or contemplating in a slow quiet way.

ruminate ('ru:mɪ,neɪt) *vb.* **1.** (of ruminants) to chew (the cud). **2.** (sometimes foll. by *upon* or *on*) to meditate or ponder (upon). —,**rumi'nation** *n.* —'**ruminative** *adj.*

rummage ('rʌmɪdʒ) *vb.* **1.** (often foll. by *through*) to search untidily (through) while looking for something. ~*n.* **2.** an act of rummaging.

rummage sale *n. U.S. & Canad.* a jumble sale.

rummy ('rʌmɪ) *n.* a card game based on collecting sets and sequences.

rumour *or U.S.* **rumor** ('ru:mə) *n.* **1.** information, often a mixture of truth and untruth, passed around verbally. **2.** gossip or hearsay. ~*vb.* **3.** (*usually passive*) to pass around or circulate in the form of a rumour: *it is rumoured that the Queen is coming.*

rump (rʌmp) *n.* **1.** the rear part of a mammal's or birds body. **2.** a person's buttocks. **3.** Also called: **rump steak.** a cut of beef from the rump. **4.** an inferior remnant.

rumple ('rʌmp²l) *vb.* to make or become crumpled or dishevelled.

rumpus ('rʌmpəs) *n., pl.* **-puses.** a noisy, confused, or disruptive commotion.

run (rʌn) *vb.* **running, ran, run.** **1.** to move on foot at a rapid pace, esp. (of a two-legged creature) so that both feet are off the ground for part of each stride. **2.** to pass over (a distance or route) in running: *to run a mile.* **3.** to run in or finish a race in a particular position or fashion: *John is running third.* **4.** to perform as by running: *to run an errand.* **5.** to flee. **6.** to track down or hunt (an animal): *to run a fox to earth.* **7.** (often foll. by *over, round,* or *up*) to make a short trip or brief visit: *I'll run over this afternoon.* **8.** to move quickly and easily on wheels by rolling, or in any of certain other ways: *a sledge running over snow.* **9.** to move with a specified result: *to run a ship aground; run into a tree.* **10.** (often foll. by *over*) to move or pass or cause to move or pass quickly: *to run one's eyes over a page.* **11.** to force, thrust, or drive: *she ran a needle into her finger.* **12.** to drive or maintain and operate (a vehicle). **13.** to give a lift to (someone) in a vehicle: *he ran her to the station.* **14.** to travel regularly between places on a route: *the bus runs from Piccadilly to Golders Green.* **15.** to function or cause to function: *the engine is running smoothly.* **16.** to manage: *to run a company.* **17.** to extend or continue in a particular direction, for a particular duration, etc.: *the road runs north; the play ran for two years.* **18.** *Law.* to have legal force or effect: *the lease runs for two years.* **19.** to be subjected to, affected by, or incur: *to run a risk; run a temperature.* **20.** (often foll. by *to*) to tend or incline: *to run to fat.* **21.** to recur persistently or be inherent: *red hair runs in my family.* **22.** to cause or allow (liquids) to flow or (of liquids) to flow: *the well has run dry.* **23.** (of waves, tides, rivers, etc.) to rise high, surge, or be at a specified height: *a high sea was running.* **24.** to dissolve and spread: *the colours in my dress ran.* **25.** (of stitches) to unravel or (of a garment) to have stitches unravel. **26.** to spread or circulate quickly: *a rumour ran through the town.* **27.** to be stated or reported: *his story runs as follows.* **28.** to publish or be published in a newspaper or magazine: *they ran his story in the next issue.* **29.** (often foll. by *for*) *Chiefly U.S. & Canad.* to stand as a candidate for political or other office: *Jones is running for president.* **30.** to get past or through: *to run a blockade.* **31.** to smuggle (goods, esp. arms). **32.** (of fish) to migrate upstream from the sea, esp. in order to spawn. **33.** *Cricket.* to score (a run or number of runs) by hitting the ball and running between the wickets. ~*n.* **34.** an act, instance, or period of running. **35.** a gait, pace, or motion faster than a walk: *she* *went off at a run.* **36.** a distance covered by running or a period of running: *a run of ten miles.* **37.** a trip in a vehicle, esp. for pleasure: *to go for a run in the car.* **38.** free and unrestricted access: *we had the run of the house.* **39. a.** a period of time during which a machine or computer operates. **b.** the amount of work performed in such a period. **40.** a continuous or sustained period: *a run of good luck.* **41.** a continuous sequence of performances: *the play had a good run.* **42.** *Cards.* a sequence of winning cards in one suit: *a run of spades.* **43.** type, class, or category: *the usual run of graduates.* **44.** (usually foll. by *on*) a continuous and urgent demand: *a run on the dollar.* **45.** a series of unravelled stitches, esp. in tights; ladder. **46.** a steeply inclined course, esp. a snow-covered one used for skiing. **47.** an enclosure for domestic fowls or other animals: *a chicken run.* **48.** (esp. in Australia and New Zealand) a tract of land for grazing livestock. **49.** the migration of fish upstream in order to spawn. **50.** *Music.* a rapid scalelike passage of notes. **51.** *Cricket.* a score of one, normally achieved by both batsmen running from one end of the wicket to the other after one of them has hit the ball. **52.** *Baseball.* an instance of a batter touching all four bases safely, thereby scoring. **53. a run for one's money.** *Informal.* **a.** a close competition. **b.** pleasure or success from an activity. **54. in the long run.** as an eventual outcome. **55. on the run.** escaping from arrest; fugitive. **56. the runs.** *Slang.* diarrhoea. ~See also **runabout, run across,** etc.

runabout (ˈrʌnəˌbaʊt) *n.* **1.** a small light vehicle, esp. a car. ~*vb.* **run about.** **2.** to move busily from place to place.

run across *vb.* to meet unexpectedly by chance.

run along *vb.* to go away; leave.

run away *vb.* **1.** to take flight; escape. **2.** to go away; depart. **3.** (of a horse) to gallop away uncontrollably. **4. run away with. a.** to abscond or elope with: *he ran away with his boss's daughter.* **b.** to escape from the control of: *his enthusiasm ran away with him.* **c.** to win easily or be assured of victory in (a competition): *he ran away with the race.* ~*n.* **runaway.** **5. a.** a person or animal that runs away. **b.** (*as modifier*): *a runaway horse.* **6.** (*modifier*) rising rapidly, as prices: *runaway inflation.* **7.** (*modifier*) (of a race or victory) easily won.

run down *vb.* **1.** (of a device such as a clock or battery) to lose power gradually and cease to function. **2.** to decline or reduce in number or size: *the firm ran down its sales force.* **3.** to criticize adversely. **4.** to hit and knock to the ground with a moving vehicle. **5.** to pursue and find or capture: *to run down a fugitive.* ~*adj.* **rundown.** **6.** tired; exhausted. **7.** worn-out,

shabby, or dilapidated. ~*n.* **rundown.** **8.** a brief review, résumé, or summary. **9.** a reduction in number or size.

rune (ruːn) *n.* **1.** any of the characters of an ancient Germanic alphabet. **2.** any obscure piece of writing using mysterious symbols. —ˈ**runic** *adj.*

rung[1] (rʌŋ) *n.* **1.** one of the bars forming the steps of a ladder. **2.** a crosspiece between the legs of a chair, etc.

rung[2] (rʌŋ) *vb.* the past participle of **ring**[2].

run in *vb.* **1.** to run (an engine) gently, usually when it is new. **2.** *Informal.* to arrest. ~*n.* **run-in.** **3.** *Informal.* an argument or quarrel.

run into *vb.* **1.** to collide with or cause to collide with: *her car ran into a tree.* **2.** to encounter unexpectedly. **3.** to be beset by: *the project ran into difficulties.* **4.** to extend to: *debts running into thousands.*

runnel (ˈrʌnˀl) *n. Literary.* a small stream.

runner (ˈrʌnə) *n.* **1.** a person who runs, esp. an athlete. **2.** a messenger for a firm. **3.** a person or vessel engaged in smuggling. **4. a.** either of the strips of metal or wood on which a sledge runs. **b.** the blade of an ice skate. **5.** a roller or guide for a sliding component. **6.** *Bot.* a slender horizontal stem, as of the strawberry, that grows along the surface of the soil and produces new roots and shoots. **7.** a long strip of cloth used to decorate a table or as a rug.

runner bean *n.* the edible pod and seeds of a type of climbing bean plant.

runner-up *n., pl.* **runners-up.** a contestant finishing a race or competition in second place.

running (ˈrʌnɪŋ) *adj.* **1.** maintained continuously; incessant: *running commentary.* **2.** without interruption; consecutive: *he lectured for two hours running.* **3.** operating: *the running time of a train; running machinery.* **4.** accomplished at a run: *a running jump.* **5.** moving or slipping easily, as a rope or a knot. **6.** discharging pus: *a running sore.* **7. a.** flowing: *running water.* **b.** supplied through a tap: *hot and cold running water.* ~*n.* **8.** management or organization: *the running of a company.* **9.** operation or maintenance: *the running of a machine.* **10. in** (*or* **out of**) **the running.** in (or out of) a competition or competitive situation. **11. make the running.** to set the pace in a competition or race.

running board *n.* a footboard along the side of a vehicle, esp. an early motorcar.

running head *or* **title** *n. Printing.* a heading printed at the top of every page of a book.

running repairs *pl. n.* repairs that do not, or do not seriously, interrupt operations.

runny (ˈrʌnɪ) *adj.* **-nier, -niest. 1.** tending to flow; liquid. **2.** (of the nose) exuding mucus.

run off vb. **1.** to depart in haste. **2.** to produce quickly, as copies on a duplicating machine. **3.** to drain (liquid) or (of liquid) to be drained. **4. run off with. a.** to steal. **b.** to elope with. ~n. **run-off. 5.** an extra race, contest, election, etc., to decide the winner after a tie. **6.** N.Z. grazing land for cattle.

run-of-the-mill adj. ordinary, average, or undistinguished.

run on vb. **1.** to continue without interruption. ~n. **run-on. 2.** a word added at the end of a dictionary entry whose meaning can be easily inferred from the definition of the headword.

run out vb. **1.** (often foll. by of) to use up (a supply of something) or (of a supply) to be used up. **2. run out on.** Informal. to desert or abandon. **3.** Cricket. to dismiss (a running batsman) by breaking the wicket with the ball while he is running between the wickets.

run over vb. **1.** to knock down (a person) with a moving vehicle. **2.** to overflow. **3.** to examine hastily.

runt (rʌnt) n. **1.** the smallest and weakest young animal in a litter. **2.** an undersized or inferior person.

run through vb. **1.** to transfix with a sword or other weapon. **2.** to practise or rehearse: let's run through the plan. ~n. **run-through. 3.** a practice or rehearsal.

run to vb. to be sufficient for: my income doesn't run to luxuries.

run up vb. **1.** to amass; incur: to run up debts. **2.** to make by sewing together quickly. **3.** to hoist: to run up a flag. ~n. **run-up. 4.** a preliminary or preparatory period: the run-up to the election.

runway ('rʌn,weɪ) n. a hard level roadway where aircraft take off and land.

rupee (ruː'piː) n. the standard monetary unit of India, Pakistan, Sri Lanka, the Maldive Islands, Mauritius, the Seychelles, and Nepal.

rupture ('rʌptʃə) n. **1.** the act of breaking or the state of being broken. **2.** a breach of peaceful or friendly relations. **3.** Pathol. a hernia. ~vb. **4.** to break or burst. **5.** to affect or be affected with a hernia. **6.** to undergo or cause to undergo a breach in relations or friendship.

rural ('ruərəl) adj. in or of the countryside.

rural dean n. Chiefly Brit. a clergyman having authority over a group of parishes.

rural route n. U.S. & Canad. a mail service or route in a rural area.

rusbank ('rʊs,bæŋk) n. S. African. a wooden bench or settle without upholstery.

ruse (ruːz) n. an action intended to mislead, deceive, or trick.

rush¹ (rʌʃ) vb. **1.** to hurry or cause to hurry. **2.** to make a sudden attack upon (a person or place). **3.** (often foll. by at, in, or into) to proceed or approach in a reckless manner. **4. rush one's fences.** to act too hurriedly. **5.** to come, flow, swell, etc., quickly or suddenly: tears rushed to her eyes. **6.** U.S. & Canad. to make a concerted effort to secure the agreement or participation of (a person). ~n. **7.** the act or condition of rushing. **8.** a sudden surge towards someone or something: a gold rush. **9.** a sudden surge of sensation, esp. from a drug. **10.** a sudden demand. **11.** (usually pl.) (in film-making) the initial prints of a scene before editing. ~adj. **12.** requiring speed or urgency: a rush job.

rush² (rʌʃ) n. a plant which grows in wet places and has grasslike cylindrical leaves and small green or brown flowers. —'rushy adj.

rush hour n. a period at the beginning and end of the day when large numbers of people are travelling to or from work.

rush light or **candle** n. a narrow candle, formerly in use, made of the pith of various types of rush dipped in tallow.

rusk (rʌsk) n. light bread baked twice until it is brown, hard, and crisp: often given to babies.

russet ('rʌsɪt) n. **1.** any of various apples with rough brownish-red skins. ~adj. **2.** brown with a reddish tinge.

Russian ('rʌʃən) n. **1.** the official language of the Soviet Union. **2.** a person from Russia or (loosely) the Soviet Union. ~adj. **3.** of Russia or the Soviet Union, its people, or their language.

Russian roulette n. an act of bravado in which a person spins the cylinder of a revolver loaded with only one cartridge and presses the trigger with the barrel against his own head.

Russo- ('rʌsəʊ) combining form. Russia or Russian: Russo-Japanese.

rust (rʌst) n. **1.** a reddish-brown oxide coating formed on iron or steel by the action of oxygen and moisture. **2.** a strong brown colour, sometimes with a reddish or yellowish tinge. **3.** a fungal disease of plants which produces a reddish brown discolouration. **4.** any corrosive or weakening influence, esp. lack of use. ~vb. **5.** to become or cause to become coated with a layer of rust. **6.** to deteriorate as through lack of use: he allowed his talent to rust over the years.

rustic ('rʌstɪk) adj. **1.** of or living in the country; rural. **2.** having qualities ascribed to country life or people; simple; unsophisticated: rustic pleasures. **3.** crude, awkward, or uncouth. **4.** made of untrimmed branches: a rustic seat. ~n. **5.** a person from the country. —**rusticity** (rʌ'stɪsɪtɪ) n.

rusticate ('rʌstɪ,keɪt) vb. **1.** to retire to the country. **2.** to make or become rustic. **3.** Brit. to send (a student) down from university for a specified time as a punishment.

rustle[1] ('rʌsᵊl) *vb.* **1.** to make or cause to make a low crisp whispering sound, as of dry leaves or paper. ~*n.* **2.** such a sound or sounds.

rustle[2] ('rʌsᵊl) *vb. Chiefly U.S. & Canad.* to steal (livestock). —'**rustler** *n.*

rustle up *vb. Informal.* to prepare (a meal) rapidly, esp. at short notice.

rusty ('rʌstɪ) *adj.* **rustier, rustiest. 1.** affected by or consisting of rust: *a rusty machine.* **2.** of the colour rust. **3.** discoloured by age: *a rusty coat.* **4.** out of practice in a skill or subject. —'**rustily** *adv.* —'**rustiness** *n.*

rut[1] (rʌt) *n.* **1.** a groove or furrow in a soft road, caused by wheels. **2.** dreary or unchanging routine: *in a rut.*

rut[2] (rʌt) *n.* **1.** a recurrent period of sexual excitement in certain male ruminants. ~*vb.* **rutting, rutted. 2.** (of male ruminants) to be in a period of sexual excitement.

ruthenium (ruː'θiːnɪəm) *n.* a rare hard brittle white metallic element. Symbol: Ru

ruthless ('ruːθlɪs) *adj.* feeling or showing no mercy; hardhearted. —'**ruthlessly** *adv.* —'**ruthlessness** *n.*

rutted ('rʌtɪd) *adj.* (of a road) with many ruts; very uneven.

RV Revised Version (of the Bible).

rye (raɪ) *n.* **1.** a tall grasslike cereal grown for its light brown grain. **2.** the grain of this plant, used in making flour and whisky, and as a livestock food. **3.** Also called (esp. U.S.): **rye whiskey.** whisky distilled from rye. **4.** *U.S.* short for **rye bread.**

rye bread *n.* bread made entirely or partly from rye flour.

rye-grass *n.* any of various grasses with flattened flower spikes and hairless leaves, widely grown as animal fodder.

S

s or **S** (ɛs) n., pl. **s's, S's,** or **Ss.** 1. the 19th letter of the English alphabet. 2. something shaped like an S.

s second (of time).

S 1. South. 2. *Chem.* sulphur.

-'s *suffix.* 1. forming the possessive singular of nouns and some pronouns: *man's; one's.* 2. forming the possessive plural of nouns whose plurals do not end in *-s: children's.* (The possessive plural of nouns ending in *s* is formed by the addition of an apostrophe after the final *s: girls'.*) 3. forming the plural of numbers, letters, or symbols: *20's.* 4. *Informal.* contraction of *is* or *has: it's gone.* 5. *Informal.* contraction of *us* with *let: let's.*

SA 1. Salvation Army. 2. South Africa. 3. South America. 4. South Australia.

Sabbath ('sæbəθ) n. 1. Saturday, observed by Jews as the day of worship and rest. 2. Sunday, observed by Christians as the day of worship and rest.

sabbatical (sə'bætɪk'l) *adj.* 1. denoting a period of leave granted at intervals to university teachers for rest, study, or travel: *a sabbatical year.* ~*n.* 2. a sabbatical period.

SABC South African Broadcasting Corporation.

sable ('seɪb'l) n., pl. **-bles** or **-ble.** 1. a marten of N Asia, N Europe, and America, with dark brown luxuriant fur. 2. the highly valued fur of this animal. ~*adj.* 3. dark brown-to-black. 4. *Heraldry.* black.

sable antelope n. a large black E African antelope with long backward-curving horns.

sabot ('sæbəʊ) n. a heavy wooden or wooden-soled shoe.

sabotage ('sæbə,tɑːʒ) n. 1. the deliberate destruction or damage of equipment as by enemy agents or dissatisfied employees. 2. deliberate obstruction of or damage to a cause or effort. ~*vb.* 3. to destroy or disrupt by sabotage.

saboteur (,sæbə'tɜː) n. a person who commits sabotage.

sabre or U.S. **saber** ('seɪbə) n. 1. a stout single-edged cavalry sword with a curved blade. 2. a light sword used in fencing, with a narrow V-shaped blade.

sac (sæk) n. a pouch or pouchlike part in an animal or plant.

saccharin ('sækərɪn) n. a very sweet nonfattening sugar substitute.

saccharine ('sækə,riːn) *adj.* 1. excessively sweet or sentimental: *a saccharine smile.* 2. like or containing sugar or saccharin.

sacerdotal (,sæsə'dəʊt'l) *adj.* of priests or priestly office.

sachet ('sæʃeɪ) n. 1. a small sealed usually plastic envelope containing a small portion of a substance such as shampoo. 2. a small soft bag of perfumed powder, placed in drawers to scent clothing.

sack¹ (sæk) n. 1. a large bag made of coarse cloth or thick paper and used as a container. 2. the amount contained in a sack. 3. **the sack.** *Informal.* dismissal from employment. 4. *Slang.* bed. 5. **hit the sack.** *Slang.* to go to bed. ~*vb.* 6. *Informal.* to dismiss from employment. 7. to put into a sack or sacks. —'**sack,like** *adj.*

sack² (sæk) n. 1. the plundering of a captured town or city by an army or mob. ~*vb.* 2. to plunder and partially destroy (a town or city).

sack³ (sæk) n. *Archaic except in trademarks.* a dry white wine from Spain or the Canary Islands.

sackbut ('sæk,bʌt) n. a medieval form of trombone.

sackcloth ('sæk,klɒθ) n. 1. coarse cloth such as sacking. 2. garments made of such cloth, worn formerly to indicate mourning. 3. **sackcloth and ashes.** a public display of extreme grief.

sacking ('sækɪŋ) n. coarse cloth used for making sacks, woven from flax, hemp or jute.

sacrament ('sækrəmənt) n. 1. a symbolic religious ceremony in the Christian Church, such as baptism or communion. 2. (*often cap.*) Holy Communion. 3. something regarded as sacred. —**sacramental** (,sækrə'ment'l) *adj.*

sacred ('seɪkrɪd) *adj.* 1. exclusively devoted to a god or gods; holy. 2. regarded with reverence and respect, as if holy: *damage done in the sacred name of profit.* 3. connected with religion or intended for religious use: *sacred music.* 4. **sacred to.** dedicated to.

sacred cow n. *Informal.* a person, custom, belief, or institution regarded as being beyond criticism.

sacrifice ('sækrɪ,faɪs) n. 1. a surrender of something of value in order to gain something more desirable or prevent some evil. 2. a ritual killing of a person or animal as an offering to a god. 3. a symbolic offering of something to a god. 4. the person, animal, or object killed or offered. ~*vb.* 5. to make a sacrifice (of). **6.** *Chess.* to permit or force one's opponent to capture (a piece) as a tactical move. —**sacrificial** (ˌsækrɪˈfɪʃəl) *adj.*

sacrifice paddock *n.* *N.Z.* a grassed field which is allowed to be grazed completely so that it can be cultivated and resown later.

sacrilege (ˈsækrɪlɪdʒ) *n.* **1.** the desecration of anything regarded as sacred. **2.** the taking of anything sacred for secular use. —ˌsacriˈlegious *adj.*

sacristan (ˈsækrɪstən) *n.* **1.** a person in charge of the contents of a church. **2.** a sexton.

sacristy (ˈsækrɪstɪ) *n., pl.* **-ties.** a room attached to a church or chapel where the sacred objects and vestments are kept.

sacrosanct (ˈsækrəʊˌsæŋkt) *adj.* very sacred or holy; inviolable. —ˌsacroˈsanctity *n.*

sacrum (ˈseɪkrəm) *n., pl.* **-cra** (-krə). the large wedge-shaped bone in the lower part of the back.

sad (sæd) *adj.* **sadder, saddest.** **1.** feeling sorrow; unhappy. **2.** causing, suggesting, or expressive of such feelings: *a sad story: a sad expression.* **3.** deplorably bad: *her clothes were in a sad state.* —ˈsadly *adv.* —ˈsadness *n.*

sadden (ˈsædᵊn) *vb.* to make (someone) sad.

saddle (ˈsædᵊl) *n.* **1.** a seat for a rider, usually made of leather, placed on a horse's back and secured under the belly. **2.** a similar seat on a bicycle, motorcycle, or tractor. **3.** a cut of meat, esp. mutton, consisting of both loins. **4. in the saddle.** in a position of control. ~*vb.* **5.** (sometimes foll. by *up*) to put a saddle on (a horse). **6.** to burden: *I didn't ask to be saddled with this job.*

saddleback (ˈsædᵊlˌbæk) *n.* **1.** an animal with a marking resembling a saddle on its back. **2.** a hill with a concave upper outline. —ˈsaddle-ˌbacked *adj.*

saddlebag (ˈsædᵊlˌbæg) *n.* a pouch or small bag attached to the saddle of a horse, bicycle, or motorcycle.

saddle horse *n.* a horse trained for riding only.

saddler (ˈsædlə) *n.* a person who makes, deals in, or repairs saddles and other leather equipment for horses.

saddlery (ˈsædlərɪ) *n., pl.* **-dleries. 1.** saddles and harness for horses collectively. **2.** the work or place of work of a saddler.

saddle soap *n.* a soft soap used to preserve and clean leather.

saddletree (ˈsædᵊlˌtriː) *n.* the frame of a saddle.

Sadducee (ˈsædjuˌsiː) *n.* *Judaism.* a member of an ancient Jewish sect that denied the resurrection of the dead and accepted only the traditional written law.

sadhu (ˈsɑːduː) *n.* a Hindu wandering holy man.

sadism (ˈseɪdɪzəm) *n.* the gaining of pleasure, esp. sexual pleasure, from infliction of suffering on another person. —ˈsadist *n.* —**sadistic** (səˈdɪstɪk) *adj.* —**sadistically** (səˈdɪstɪkəlɪ) *adv.*

sadomasochism (ˌseɪdəʊˈmæsəˌkɪzəm) *n.* the combination of sadistic and masochistic elements in one person. —ˌsadoˈmasochist *n.* —ˌsadomasoˈchistic *adj.*

s.a.e. stamped addressed envelope.

safari (səˈfɑːrɪ) *n., pl.* **-ris.** an overland expedition for hunting or observing animals, esp. in Africa.

safari park *n.* an enclosed park in which wild animals are kept uncaged in the open and can be viewed by the public from cars or buses.

safe (seɪf) *adj.* **1.** giving security or protection from harm: *a safe place.* **2.** free from danger: *you'll be safe here.* **3.** taking or involving no risks: *a safe investment.* **4.** worthy of trust: *a safe companion.* **5.** not dangerous: *water safe to drink.* **6. on the safe side.** as a precaution. ~*n.* **7.** a strong metal container with a secure lock, for storing money or valuables. —ˈsafely *adv.*

safe-conduct *n.* **1.** a document giving official permission to travel through a dangerous region, esp. in time of war. **2.** the protection given by such a document.

safe-deposit *or* **safety-deposit** *n.* a place with facilities for the safe storage of money.

safeguard (ˈseɪfˌgɑːd) *n.* **1.** a person or thing that ensures protection against danger or harm. ~*vb.* **2.** to protect.

safekeeping (ˈseɪfˈkiːpɪŋ) *n.* protection: *the painting was removed for safekeeping.*

safety (ˈseɪftɪ) *n., pl.* **-ties.** the quality or state of being free from danger.

safety belt *n.* same as **seat belt.**

safety curtain *n.* a fireproof curtain that can be lowered to separate the auditorium from the stage in a theatre to prevent the spread of a fire.

safety lamp *n.* a miner's oil lamp designed to prevent it from igniting combustible gas.

safety match *n.* a match that will light only when struck against a specially prepared surface.

safety net *n.* **1.** a large net under a trapeze or high wire to catch performers if they fall. **2.** something which can be relied on for help in the event of difficulties.

safety pin *n.* a pin bent back on itself so that it forms a spring, with the point shielded by a guard when closed.

safety razor *n.* a razor with a guard over the blade or blades to protect the skin from deep cuts.

safety valve *n.* **1.** a valve in a boiler or

safflower ('sæflauə) n. a thistle-like plant with orange-yellow flowers, which yields a dye and an oil used in paints, medicines, and cooking.

saffron ('sæfrən) n. 1. a species of crocus having purple or white flowers with orange stigmas. 2. the dried stigmas of this plant, used for colouring or flavouring. ~adj. 3. orange to orange-yellow.

sag (sæg) vb. **sagging, sagged. 1.** to sink in the middle, as under weight or pressure: *the bed sags when I sit on it.* **2.** to fall in value: *prices sagged to a new low.* **3.** to hang unevenly. **4.** (of courage or spirits) to weaken. ~n. **5.** the act or state of sagging: *a sag in profits.* —**'saggy** adj.

saga ('sɑːgə) n. 1. a medieval Scandinavian prose narrative recounting the exploits of a hero or a family. 2. *Informal.* a long story or series of events.

sagacious (sə'geɪʃəs) adj. having or showing insight or wisdom. —**sa'gaciously** adv. —**sagacity** (sə'gæsɪtɪ) n.

sage[1] (seɪdʒ) n. 1. a man regarded as being very wise. ~adj. 2. very wise or prudent.

sage[2] (seɪdʒ) n. 1. a Mediterranean plant with grey-green leaves which are used in cooking for flavouring. 2. short for **sagebrush.**

sagebrush ('seɪdʒ,brʌʃ) n. an aromatic plant of W North America, with silver-green leaves and large clusters of small white flowers.

Sagittarius (,sædʒɪ'tɛərɪəs) n. *Astrol.* the ninth sign of the zodiac; the Archer.

sago ('seɪgəʊ) n. an edible starch obtained from the powdered pith of certain palm trees, used for puddings and as a thickening agent.

sahib ('sɑːhɪb) n. an Indian term of address equivalent to *sir,* formerly used as a mark of respect to a European man.

said (sɛd) adj. 1. (in documents) named or mentioned already. ~vb. 2. past of **say.**

sail (seɪl) n. 1. a sheet of canvas or other fabric, spread on rigging to catch the wind and propel a vessel over water. 2. a voyage on such a vessel: *a sail down the river.* 3. a vessel or vessels with sails. *to travel by sail.* 4. one of the revolving arms of a windmill. 5. **set sail.** to begin a voyage by water. 6. **under sail. a.** with sail hoisted. **b.** under way. ~vb. 7. to travel in a boat or ship: *we sailed to Le Havre.* 8. to begin a voyage: *we sail at 5 o'clock.* 9. (of a vessel) to move over the water. 10. to navigate a vessel: *he sailed the schooner up the channel.* 11. to sail over: *she sailed the Atlantic single-handed.* 12. (often foll. by *through*) to progress quickly or effortlessly: *we sailed through the exams.* 13. to move

along smoothly; glide. 14. (foll. by *in* or *into*) *Informal.* to make a violent attack on.

sailboard ('seɪl,bɔːd) n. the craft used for windsurfing, consisting of a moulded board to which a mast bearing a single sail is attached.

sailcloth ('seɪl,klɒθ) n. 1. any of various fabrics from which sails are made. 2. a canvas-like cloth used for clothing.

sailfish ('seɪl,fɪʃ) n., pl. **-fish** or **-fishes.** a large tropical game fish, with a long sail-like dorsal fin.

sailor ('seɪlə) n. 1. any member of a ship's crew, esp. one below the rank of officer. 2. a person considered as liable or not liable to seasickness: *a good sailor.*

sainfoin ('sænfɔɪn) n. a Eurasian plant with pink flowers, widely grown as a fodder crop.

saint (seɪnt) n. 1. a person who after death is formally recognized by a Christian Church as deserving special honour because of having lived a very holy life. 2. a very holy or good person. —**'sainthood** n. —**'saintlike** adj.

Saint Bernard ('bɜːnəd) n. a very large dog with a dense red-and-white coat, formerly used as a mountain rescue-dog.

sainted ('seɪntɪd) adj. 1. canonized. 2. like a saint. 3. hallowed or holy.

Saint John's wort ('dʒɒnz) n. a plant with yellow flowers.

Saint Leger ('lɛdʒə) n. **the.** an annual horse race for three-year-olds, run at Doncaster.

saintly ('seɪntlɪ) adj. like, relating to, or suitable for a saint. —**'saintliness** n.

Saint Vitus's dance ('vaɪtəsɪz) n. *Pathol.* a nontechnical name for **chorea.**

saithe (seɪθ) n. *Brit.* a dark-coloured food fish found in northern seas.

sake[1] (seɪk) n. 1. **for someone's** or **one's own sake.** for the benefit or interest of someone or oneself. 2. **for the sake of something.** for the purpose of obtaining or achieving something. 3. used in various exclamations of annoyance, impatience, or urgency: *for heaven's sake.*

sake[2] or **saki** ('sækɪ) n. a Japanese alcoholic drink made from fermented rice.

salaam (sə'lɑːm) n. 1. a Muslim greeting consisting of a deep bow with the right palm on the forehead. 2. a greeting signifying peace. ~vb. 3. to make a salaam (to).

salacious (sə'leɪʃəs) adj. 1. having an excessive interest in sex. 2. (of books, films, or jokes) erotic or bawdy. —**sa'laciousness** n.

salad ('sæləd) n. a dish of raw vegetables, often served with a dressing, eaten as a separate course or as part of a main course.

salad days pl. n. a period of youth and inexperience.

salad dressing *n.* a sauce for salad, such as oil and vinegar or mayonnaise.

salamander ('sælə,mændə) *n.* **1.** a tailed amphibian which resembles a lizard. **2.** a mythical reptile supposed to live in fire.

salami (sə'lɑːmɪ) *n.* a highly seasoned sausage, usually flavoured with garlic.

salaried ('sælərɪd) *adj.* earning or providing a salary: *a salaried worker; salaried employment.*

salary ('sælərɪ) *n., pl.* **-ries.** a fixed regular payment made by an employer, usually monthly, for professional or office work.

sale (seɪl) *n.* **1.** the exchange of goods or property for an agreed sum of money. **2.** the amount sold. **3.** an event at which goods are sold at reduced prices. **4.** an auction.

saleable *or U.S.* **salable** ('seɪləb°l) *adj.* fit for selling or capable of being sold. —,**salea'bility** *or U.S.* ,**sala'bility** *n.*

sale of work *n.* a sale of articles, often handmade, the proceeds of which go to a charity.

saleroom ('seɪl,ruːm) *n. Chiefly Brit.* a room where objects are displayed for sale by auction.

salesman ('seɪlzmən) *n., pl.* **-men.** **1.** Also called: **saleswoman** (*fem.*), **salesgirl** (*fem.*), *or* **salesperson.** a person who sells goods in a shop. **2.** short for **travelling salesman.**

salesmanship ('seɪlzmənʃɪp) *n.* the technique of or skill in selling.

sales talk *or* **pitch** *n.* persuasive talk used in selling.

salicylic acid (,sælɪ'sɪlɪk) *n.* a white crystalline substance used to make aspirin and as a fungicide.

salient ('seɪlɪənt) *adj.* **1.** conspicuous or striking: *a salient feature.* ~*n.* **2.** *Mil.* a projection of the forward line into enemy-held territory.

saline ('seɪlaɪn) *adj.* **1.** of or containing salt: *a saline taste.* **2.** *Med.* of or relating to saline: *a saline drip.* ~*n.* **3.** *Med.* a solution of sodium chloride and water. —**salinity** (sə'lɪnɪtɪ) *n.*

salinization *or* **-isation** (,sælɪnaɪ'zeɪʃən) *n.* the process by which salts accumulate in undrained land, adversely affecting its potential for plant growth.

saliva (sə'laɪvə) *n.* the watery fluid secreted by glands in the mouth, which aids digestion. —**sa'livary** *adj.*

salivate ('sælɪ,veɪt) *vb.* to secrete saliva, esp. an excessive amount. —,**sali'vation** *n.*

sallow ('sæləʊ) *adj.* (of human skin) of an unhealthy pale or yellowish colour. —'**sallowness** *n.*

sally ('sælɪ) *n., pl.* **-lies.** **1.** a sudden brief attack by troops. **2.** an excursion. **3.** a jocular retort. ~*vb.* **-lying, -lied.** **4.** to make a sudden violent attack. **5.** (often foll. by *forth*) to make an excursion. **6.** to come or set out in an energetic manner.

salmon ('sæmən) *n., pl.* **-ons** *or* **-on.** a large pink-fleshed fish which is highly valued for food and sport: salmon live in the sea but return to fresh water to spawn.

salmonella (,sælmə'nɛlə) *n., pl.* **-lae** (-,liː). a bacterium which causes food poisoning.

salmon ladder *n.* a series of steps designed to enable salmon to move upstream to their breeding grounds.

salon ('sælɒn) *n.* **1.** a room in a large house in which guests are received. **2.** an informal gathering of major literary, artistic, and political figures in a fashionable household. **3.** a commercial establishment in which hairdressers or fashion designers carry on their business. **4.** an art exhibition.

saloon (sə'luːn) *n.* **1.** *Brit.* a lounge bar. **2.** a large public room on a passenger ship. **3.** any large public room used for a purpose: *a billiard saloon.* **4.** *Chiefly U.S. & Canad.* a place where alcoholic drink is sold and consumed. **5.** a closed two-door or four-door car.

salsa ('sælsə) *n.* a type of Puerto Rican big-band dance music.

salsify ('sælsɪfɪ) *n., pl.* **-fies.** a Mediterranean plant with a long white edible root.

salt (sɔːlt) *n.* **1.** sodium chloride, a white crystalline substance, used for seasoning and preserving food. **2.** (*modifier*) preserved in or tasting of salt: *salt pork.* **3.** *Chem.* a crystalline solid compound formed from an acid by replacing its hydrogen with a metal. **4.** liveliness or pungency: *his wit added salt to the discussion.* **5.** an experienced sailor. **6. rub salt into someone's wounds.** to make an unpleasant situation even worse for someone. **7. salt of the earth.** a person or people regarded as the finest of their kind. **8. take something with a pinch of salt.** to regard something sceptically. **9. worth one's salt.** worthy of one's pay. ~*vb.* **10.** to season or preserve with salt. **11.** to scatter salt over (an iced road or path) to melt the ice. ~*adj.* **12.** not sour, sweet, or bitter; salty. ~See also **salt away, salts.** —'**salted** *adj.*

SALT (sɔːlt) Strategic Arms Limitation Talks *or* Treaty.

salt away *vb.* to hoard or save (money or valuables).

saltcellar ('sɔːlt,sɛlə) *n.* a small container for salt used at the table.

salt lick *n.* **1.** a place where wild animals go to lick salt deposits. **2.** a block of salt given to domestic animals to lick.

saltpetre *or U.S.* **saltpeter** (,sɔːlt'piːtə) *n.* same as **potassium nitrate.**

salts (sɔːlts) *pl. n.* **1.** *Med.* mineral salts used as a medicine. **2. like a dose of salts.** *Informal.* very quickly.

saltwater ('sɔːlt,wɔːtə) *adj.* of or inhabiting salt water, esp. the sea: *saltwater fishes.*

salty ('sɔːltɪ) *adj.* **saltier, saltiest. 1.** of, tasting of, or containing salt. **2.** (esp. of humour) sharp. —**'saltiness** *n.*

salubrious (sə'luːbrɪəs) *adj.* favourable to health. —**sa'lubrity** *n.*

Saluki (sə'luːkɪ) *n.* a tall hound with a smooth coat and long fringes on the ears and tail.

salutary ('sæljʊtrɪ) *adj.* **1.** promoting some good purpose; beneficial: *a salutary warning.* **2.** promoting health.

salutation (,sæljʊ'teɪʃən) *n.* a phrase or gesture that serves as a greeting.

salute (sə'luːt) *vb.* **1.** to greet with friendly words or gestures of respect, such as bowing. **2.** to acknowledge with praise: *we salute your gallantry.* **3.** *Mil.* to pay formal respect to (someone), as by raising the right hand to the forehead. ~*n.* **4.** the act of saluting. **5.** a formal military gesture of respect.

salvage ('sælvɪdʒ) *n.* **1.** the rescue of a ship or its cargo from loss at sea. **2.** the saving of any goods or property from destruction or waste. **3.** the goods or property so saved. **4.** compensation paid for the salvage of a ship or its cargo. ~*vb.* **5.** to save (goods or property) from shipwreck, destruction, or waste. **6.** to gain (something beneficial) from a failure. —**'salvageable** *adj.*

salvation (sæl'veɪʃən) *n.* **1.** a preserving from harm. **2.** a person or thing that preserves from harm. **3.** *Christianity.* spiritual deliverance from the consequences of sin.

Salvation Army *n.* a Christian body organized on quasi-military lines for evangelism and social work among the poor.

salve (sælv, sɑːv) *n.* **1.** an ointment for wounds. **2.** anything that heals or soothes. ~*vb.* **3.** to soothe, comfort, or appease.

salver ('sælvə) *n.* a tray on which something is presented.

salvia ('sælvɪə) *n.* any plant of the sage genus.

salvo ('sælvəʊ) *n., pl.* **-vos** or **-voes. 1.** a unison firing of guns, in battle or on a ceremonial occasion. **2.** an outburst of applause or questions.

sal volatile (,sæl vɒ'lætɪlɪ) *n.* a solution of ammonium carbonate, used as smelling salts.

SAM (sæm) surface-to-air missile.

Samaritan (sə'mærɪt'n) *n.* **1.** short for **Good Samaritan. 2.** a member of a voluntary organization (**the Samaritans**) whose aim is to help people in distress or despair.

samarium (sə'mɛərɪəm) *n.* a silvery metallic element of the rare-earth series. Symbol: Sm

samba ('sæmbə) *n., pl.* **-bas. 1.** a modern

ballroom dance from Brazil in bouncy duple time. **2.** music for this dance.

same (seɪm) *adj.* (usually preceded by *the*) **1.** being the very one: *she is wearing the same hat.* **2.** being the one previously referred to: *I didn't go for the same reason.* **3. a.** alike in kind or quantity: *two girls of the same age.* **b.** (*as n.*): *we'd like the same again.* **4.** unchanged in character or nature: *his attitude is the same as ever.* **5. all the same** *or* **just the same.** nevertheless; even so. **6. be all the same.** to be immaterial: *it's all the same to me.* ~*adv.* **7.** in the same way; similarly: *I feel the same about it.* —**'sameness** *n.*

Usage. The use of *same* as in *if you send us your order for the materials, we will deliver same tomorrow* is common in business and official English. In general English, however, this use of the word is avoided: *may I borrow your book? I'll return it* (not *same*) *tomorrow.*

samizdat ('sæmɪz,dæt) *n.* (in the Soviet Union) a system of secret printing and distribution of banned literature.

samosa (sə'məʊsə) *n.* (in Indian cookery) a small fried triangular spiced meat or vegetable pasty. Also (S. African): **samoosa** (sə'muːsə).

samovar ('sæmə,vɑː) *n.* a Russian metal tea urn in which the water is heated by an inner container.

Samoyed ('sæməʊ,jed) *n.* a white or cream medium-sized dog with a dense coat and a tightly curled tail.

sampan ('sæmpæn) *n.* a small flat-bottomed boat with oars, widely used in the Orient.

samphire ('sæm,faɪə) *n.* a Eurasian coastal plant with fleshy leaves and clusters of small flowers.

sample ('sɑːmp'l) *n.* **1.** a small part of anything, intended as being representative of the whole. ~*vb.* **2.** to take a sample or samples of. **3.** *Music.* **a.** to take a short extract from (one record) and mix it into a different backing track. **b.** to record (a sound) and feed it into a computerized synthesizer so that it can be reproduced at any pitch. —**'sampling** *n.*

sampler ('sɑːmplə) *n.* a piece of embroidery done to show the embroiderer's skill in using many different stitches.

Samson ('sæmsən) *n.* a man of outstanding physical strength.

samurai ('sæmʊ,raɪ) *n., pl.* **-rai.** a member of the aristocratic warrior caste of feudal Japan.

sanatorium (,sænə'tɔːrɪəm) *or U.S.* **sanitarium** *n., pl.* **-riums** *or* **-ria** (-rɪə). **1.** an institution for the treatment of invalids or convalescents. **2.** *Brit.* a room in a boarding school where sick pupils may be treated.

sanctify ('sæŋktɪ,faɪ) *vb.* **-fying, -fied. 1.**

to make holy. **2.** to free from sin. **3.** to sanction (an action or practice) as religiously binding: *to sanctify a marriage.* —ˌsanctifiˈcation *n.*

sanctimonious (ˌsæŋktɪˈməʊnɪəs) *adj.* pretending to be very pious or holy.

sanction (ˈsæŋkʃən) *n.* **1.** permission granted by authority. **2.** support or approval. **3.** something that gives binding force to a law, such as a penalty for breaking it or a reward for obeying it. **4.** a coercive measure, such as a boycott taken by one or more states against another guilty of violating international law. ~*vb.* **5.** to permit or give authority to. **6.** to confirm or ratify.

sanctity (ˈsæŋktɪtɪ) *n.* **1.** the condition of being sanctified; holiness. **2.** the condition of being inviolable: *the sanctity of human life.*

sanctuary (ˈsæŋktjʊərɪ) *n., pl.* **-aries. 1.** a holy place, such as a consecrated building or shrine. **2.** the holiest part of a sacred building, surrounding the main altar. **3.** a place of refuge or protection, esp., formerly, a church. **4.** refuge or safety: *he retreated to the sanctuary of his study.* **5.** a place, protected by law, where animals can live and breed without interference.

sanctum (ˈsæŋktəm) *n., pl.* **-tums** *or* **-ta** (-tə). **1.** a sacred or holy place. **2.** a room or place of total privacy.

sand (sænd) *n.* **1.** a powdery substance consisting of very small rock or mineral grains, found on the seashore and in deserts. **2.** (*pl.*) a large sandy area, esp. on the seashore or in a desert. ~*vb.* **3.** to smooth or polish the surface of (something) with sandpaper or a sander. **4.** to fill with sand: *the channel sanded up.*

sandal (ˈsændˀl) *n.* a light shoe consisting of a sole held on the foot by thongs or straps. —ˈsandalled *or U.S.* ˈsandaled *adj.*

sandalwood (ˈsændˀl‚wʊd) *n.* **1.** the hard light-coloured heartwood of a S Asian or Australian tree, which is used for carving and for incense, and which yields an aromatic oil used in perfumery. **2.** a tree yielding this wood.

sandbag (ˈsænd‚bæg) *n.* **1.** a sack filled with sand used to make a temporary defence against gunfire or floodwater, or as ballast. ~*vb.* **-bagging, -bagged. 2.** to protect or strengthen with sandbags.

sandbank (ˈsænd‚bæŋk) *or* **sand bar** *n.* a bank of sand in a sea or river, that may be exposed at low tide.

sandblast (ˈsænd‚blɑːst) *n.* **1.** a jet of sand blown from a nozzle under air or steam pressure. ~*vb.* **2.** to clean or decorate (a surface) with a sandblast. —ˈsand‚blaster *n.*

sandboy (ˈsænd‚bɔɪ) *n.* **happy as a sandboy.** very happy; high-spirited.

sand castle *n.* a mass of sand made into a castle-like shape by a child.

sander (ˈsændə) *n.* a power-driven tool for smoothing surfaces by rubbing with an abrasive disc.

sandman (ˈsænd‚mæn) *n., pl.* **-men.** (in folklore) a magical person supposed to put children to sleep by sprinkling sand in their eyes.

sand martin *n.* a small brown European songbird which nests in tunnels bored in sand or river banks.

sandpaper (ˈsænd‚peɪpə) *n.* **1.** a strong paper coated with sand or other abrasive material for smoothing or polishing a surface. ~*vb.* **2.** to smooth or polish (a surface) with sandpaper.

sandpiper (ˈsænd‚paɪpə) *n.* a wading shore bird with a long bill and slender legs.

sandpit (ˈsænd‚pɪt) *n.* a shallow pit or container holding sand for children to play in.

sandshoes (ˈsænd‚ʃuːz) *pl. n.* light canvas shoes with rubber soles.

sandstone (ˈsænd‚stəʊn) *n.* a sedimentary rock consisting mainly of sand grains, much used in building.

sandstorm (ˈsænd‚stɔːm) *n.* a strong wind that whips up clouds of sand, esp. in a desert.

sandwich (ˈsænwɪdʒ) *n.* **1.** two or more slices of bread, usually buttered, with a layer of food between them. ~*vb.* **2.** to place between two other things.

sandwich board *n.* one of two connected boards that are hung over the shoulders in front of and behind a person to display advertisements.

sandwich course *n.* an educational course consisting of alternate periods of study and industrial work.

sandy (ˈsændɪ) *adj.* **sandier, sandiest. 1.** resembling, containing, or covered with sand. **2.** (of hair) reddish-yellow. —ˈsandiness *n.*

sane (seɪn) *adj.* **1.** of sound mind; not mad. **2.** sensible or well-judged: *a sane policy.*

sang (sæŋ) *vb.* the past tense of **sing.**

sang-froid (ˌsɒŋˈfrwɑː) *n.* composure; self-possession.

sangoma (sæŋˈɡəʊmə) *n. S. African.* a witch doctor.

sangria (sæŋˈɡriːə) *n.* a Spanish drink of red wine, sugar, and orange or lemon juice.

sanguinary (ˈsæŋɡwɪnərɪ) *adj.* **1.** accompanied by much bloodshed. **2.** bloodthirsty. **3.** of or stained with blood.

sanguine (ˈsæŋɡwɪn) *adj.* **1.** cheerful and confident; optimistic. **2.** (of the complexion) ruddy.

Sanhedrin (ˈsænɪdrɪn) *n. Judaism.* the highest court and supreme council of the ancient Jewish nation.

sanitary (ˈsænɪtrɪ) *adj.* **1.** promoting

health by getting rid of dirt and germs. **2.** free from dirt or germs; hygienic.

sanitary towel *or esp. U.S.* **napkin** *n.* a pad worn externally by women during menstruation to absorb the flow of blood.

sanitation (ˌsænɪˈteɪʃən) *n.* **1.** the use of sanitary measures to maintain public health. **2.** drainage and disposal of sewage.

sanity (ˈsænɪtɪ) *n.* **1.** the state of being sane. **2.** good sense or soundness of judgment.

sank (sæŋk) *vb.* a past tense of **sink.**

sans-culotte (ˌsænzkjʊˈlɒt) *n.* a revolutionary extremist.

Sanskrit (ˈsænskrɪt) *n.* the classical literary language of India, used since ancient times for religious purposes. —**San'skritic** *adj.*

sans serif (sæn ˈsɛrɪf) *n.* a style of printer's typeface in which the characters have no serifs.

Santa Claus (ˈsæntə ˌklɔːz) *n.* the legendary patron saint of children, who brings presents to children on Christmas Eve, commonly identified with Saint Nicholas.

sap[1] (sæp) *n.* **1.** a thin liquid that circulates in a plant, carrying food and water. **2.** energy; vigour. **3.** *Slang.* a gullible person. ~*vb.* **sapping, sapped.** **4.** to drain of sap.

sap[2] (sæp) *n.* **1.** a deep and narrow trench used to approach or undermine an enemy position. ~*vb.* **sapping, sapped.** **2.** to undermine (an enemy position) by digging saps. **3.** to weaken or exhaust.

sapient (ˈseɪpɪənt) *adj. Often used ironically.* wise or sagacious. —**'sapience** *n.*

sapling (ˈsæplɪŋ) *n.* a young tree.

saponify (səˈpɒnɪˌfaɪ) *vb.* **-fying, -fied.** *Chem.* to convert (a fat) or (of a fat) to be converted into a soap by treatment with alkali. —**sa,ponifi'cation** *n.*

sapper (ˈsæpə) *n.* **1.** a soldier who digs trenches. **2.** (in the British Army) a private of the Royal Engineers.

sapphire (ˈsæfaɪə) *n.* **1.** a transparent blue precious stone. ~*adj.* **2.** of the blue colour of sapphire.

sappy (ˈsæpɪ) *adj.* **-pier, -piest.** **1.** (of plants) full of sap. **2.** full of energy or vitality.

saprophyte (ˈsæprəʊˌfaɪt) *n.* any plant, such as a fungus, that lives and feeds on dead organic matter.

saraband *or* **sarabande** (ˈsærəˌbænd) *n.* **1.** a stately slow Spanish dance in triple time. **2.** music for this dance.

Saracen (ˈsærəsən) *n.* **1.** an Arab or Muslim who opposed the crusades. ~*adj.* **2.** of the Saracens.

sarcasm (ˈsɑːkæzəm) *n.* **1.** mocking or ironic language intended to convey scorn or insult. **2.** the use or tone of such language.

sarcastic (sɑːˈkæstɪk) *adj.* **1.** full of or

showing sarcasm. **2.** given to the use of sarcasm. —**sar'castically** *adv.*

sarcoma (sɑːˈkəʊmə) *n., pl.* **-mata** (-mətə) *or* **-mas.** *Pathol.* a malignant tumour beginning in connective tissue.

sarcophagus (sɑːˈkɒfəgəs) *n., pl.* **-gi** (-ˌgaɪ) *or* **-guses.** a stone or marble coffin or tomb, esp. one bearing sculpture or inscriptions.

sardine (sɑːˈdiːn) *n., pl.* **-dine** *or* **-dines.** **1.** a small food fish, often preserved in tightly packed tins. **2. like sardines.** very closely crowded together.

sardonic (sɑːˈdɒnɪk) *adj.* mocking or scornful. —**sar'donically** *adv.*

sardonyx (ˈsɑːdənɪks) *n.* a variety of chalcedony with alternating reddish-brown and white parallel bands.

sargassum (sɑːˈgæsəm) *n.* a floating brown seaweed with ribbon-like fronds containing air sacs.

sarge (sɑːdʒ) *n. Informal.* sergeant.

sari *or* **saree** (ˈsɑːrɪ) *n., pl.* **-ris** *or* **-rees.** the traditional dress of Hindi women, consisting of a very long piece of cloth swathed around the body with one end over the shoulder.

sarking (ˈsɑːkɪŋ) *n. Scot., N English, & N.Z.* flat planking supporting the roof cladding of a building.

sarky (ˈsɑːkɪ) *adj.* **-kier, -kiest.** *Brit. informal.* sarcastic.

sarnie (ˈsɑːnɪ) *n. Brit. informal.* a sandwich.

sarong (səˈrɒŋ) *n.* a garment worn by Malaysian men and women, consisting of a long piece of cloth tucked around the waist or under the armpits.

sarsaparilla (ˌsɑːsəpəˈrɪlə) *n.* a nonalcoholic drink prepared from the roots of a tropical American climbing plant.

sartorial (sɑːˈtɔːrɪəl) *adj.* of men's clothes or tailoring.

SAS Special Air Service.

sash[1] (sæʃ) *n.* a long piece of cloth worn around the waist or over one shoulder, as a symbol of rank.

sash[2] (sæʃ) *n.* **1.** a frame that contains the panes of a window or door. **2.** a complete frame together with panes of glass.

sash cord *n.* a strong cord connecting a weight to the sliding half of a sash window.

sashimi (sɑːˈʃiːmɪ) *n.* a Japanese dish of thin fillets of raw fish.

sash window *n.* a window consisting of two sashes placed one above the other so that the window can be opened by sliding one frame over the front of the other.

Sask. Saskatchewan.

sassafras (ˈsæsəˌfræs) *n.* a tree of North America, whose aromatic dried root bark is used as a flavouring.

Sassenach (ˈsæsəˌnæx) *n. Scot. & occasionally Irish.* an English person or Lowland Scot.

sat (sæt) *vb.* past of **sit**.

Sat. Saturday.

Satan ('seɪt°n) *n.* the Devil, adversary of God, and tempter of mankind.

satanic (sə'tænɪk) *adj.* **1.** of Satan. **2.** supremely evil or wicked.

Satanism ('seɪt°ˌnɪzəm) *n.* the worship of Satan. —'**Satanist** *n., adj.*

satchel ('sætʃəl) *n.* a small bag, usually with a shoulder strap, used for carrying school books.

sate (seɪt) *vb.* **1.** to satisfy (a desire or appetite) fully. **2.** to satiate.

satellite ('sæt°ˌlaɪt) *n.* **1.** a heavenly body orbiting a planet or star: *the earth is a satellite of the sun.* **2.** a man-made device orbiting the earth or another planet, used in communications or to collect scientific information. **3.** a country controlled by or dependent on a more powerful one. **4.** (*modifier*) of, used in, or relating to the transmission of television signals from a satellite to the home: *a satellite dish aerial.*

satiable ('seɪʃɪəb°l) *adj.* capable of being satiated. —ˌsatia'bility *n.*

satiate ('seɪʃɪˌeɪt) *vb.* to provide with more than enough, so as to disgust or weary. —ˌsati'ation *n.*

satiety (sə'taɪɪtɪ) *n.* the state of being satiated.

satin ('sætɪn) *n.* **1.** a fabric, usually of silk or rayon, closely woven to give a smooth glossy surface on one side. **2.** (*modifier*) like satin in texture: *a satin finish.* —'**satiny** *adj.*

satinwood ('sætɪnˌwʊd) *n.* **1.** a hard wood with a satiny texture, used in fine furniture. **2.** the East Indian tree yielding this wood.

satire ('sætaɪə) *n.* **1.** a work in which topical issues, folly, or evil are held up to scorn by means of ridicule. **2.** the use of ridicule or irony to create such an effect. —**satirical** (sə'tɪrɪk°l) *adj.*

satirist ('sætərɪst) *n.* **1.** a writer of satire. **2.** a person who uses satire.

satirize or **-rise** ('sætəˌraɪz) *vb.* to ridicule (a person or thing) by means of satire. —ˌsatiri'zation or -ri'sation *n.*

satisfaction (ˌsætɪs'fækʃən) *n.* **1.** a satisfying or being satisfied. **2.** the pleasure obtained from the fulfilment of a desire. **3.** something that brings fulfilment. **4.** compensation for a wrong done.

satisfactory (ˌsætɪs'fæktrɪ) *adj.* **1.** adequate or suitable; acceptable. **2.** giving satisfaction. —ˌsatis'factorily *adv.*

satisfy ('sætɪsˌfaɪ) *vb.* -fying, -fied. **1.** to fulfil the desires or needs of (a person). **2.** to provide amply for (a need or desire). **3.** to convince. **4.** to dispel (a doubt). **5.** to fulfil the requirements of; comply with: *you must satisfy the terms of your lease.* —'**satisˌfiable** *adj.* —'**satisˌfying** *adj.*

satrap ('sætrəp) *n.* **1.** (in ancient Persia) a provincial governor. **2.** a subordinate ruler.

satsuma (sæt'suːmə) *n.* a small loose-skinned variety of orange with easily separable segments.

saturate ('sætʃəˌreɪt) *vb.* **1.** to soak completely. **2.** to fill so completely that no more can be added: *the police saturated the area with photographs of the wanted man.* **3.** *Chem.* to combine (a substance) or (of a substance) to be combined with the greatest possible amount of another substance.

saturation (ˌsætʃə'reɪʃən) *n.* a saturating or being saturated.

saturation point *n.* **1.** the point at which the maximum amount of a substance has been absorbed. **2.** the point at which some capacity is at its fullest; limit: *the market has reached saturation point.*

Saturday ('sætədɪ) *n.* the seventh and last day of the week.

Saturn ('sætɜːn) *n.* **1.** the Roman god of agriculture. **2.** the sixth planet from the sun, second largest in the solar system, around which revolve concentric rings.

Saturnalia (ˌsætə'neɪlɪə) *n., pl.* -**lia** or -**lias**. **1.** the ancient Roman festival of Saturn, renowned for its unrestrained merry-making. **2.** (*sometimes not cap.*) a period of wild revelry.

saturnine ('sætəˌnaɪn) *adj.* having a gloomy temperament or appearance.

satyr ('sætə) *n.* **1.** *Greek myth.* a lecherous woodland god represented as having a man's body with the ears, horns, tail, and legs of a goat. **2.** a man who has strong sexual desires.

sauce (sɔːs) *n.* **1.** any liquid or semiliquid preparation eaten with food to enhance its flavour. **2.** anything that adds interest or zest. **3.** *Informal.* impudent language or behaviour.

sauce boat *n.* a boat-shaped container for serving sauce in.

saucepan ('sɔːspən) *n.* a metal pan with a long handle and often a lid, used for cooking food.

saucer ('sɔːsə) *n.* **1.** a small round dish on which a cup is set. **2.** something shaped like a saucer. —'**saucerful** *n.*

saucy ('sɔːsɪ) *adj.* **saucier, sauciest. 1.** impertinent. **2.** pert; jaunty: *a saucy hat.* —'**sauciness** *n.*

sauerkraut ('saʊəˌkraʊt) *n.* finely shredded cabbage which has been fermented in brine.

sault (suː) *n. Canad.* a waterfall or rapids.

sauna ('sɔːnə) *n.* **1.** a Finnish-style hot steam bath, usually followed by a cold plunge. **2.** the place in which such a bath is taken.

saunter ('sɔːntə) *vb.* **1.** to walk in a casual

manner; stroll. ~*n.* **2.** a leisurely pace or stroll.

saurian ('sɔːrɪən) *adj.* of or resembling a lizard.

sausage ('sɒsɪdʒ) *n.* **1.** finely minced meat mixed with fat, cereal, and seasonings, and packed into a tube-shaped edible casing. **2.** an object shaped like a sausage. **3. not a sausage.** nothing at all.

sausage roll *n. Brit.* a roll of sausage meat in pastry.

sauté ('səʊteɪ) *vb.* **-téing** *or* **-téeing, -téed. 1.** to fry (food) quickly in a little fat. ~*n.* **2.** a dish of sautéed food. ~*adj.* **3.** sautéed until lightly brown: *sauté potatoes.*

savage ('sævɪdʒ) *adj.* **1.** wild; untamed: *savage beasts.* **2.** fierce or cruel: *a savage temper.* **3.** uncivilized; crude: *savage behaviour.* **4.** (of peoples) uncivilized or primitive: *a savage tribe.* **5.** (of terrain) wild and uncultivated. ~*n.* **6.** a member of an uncivilized or primitive society. **7.** a fierce or vicious person or animal. ~*vb.* **8.** to criticize violently. **9.** to attack ferociously and wound. —'**savagely** *adv.*

savagery ('sævɪdʒrɪ) *n., pl.* **-ries.** viciousness and cruelty.

savanna *or* **savannah** (sə'vænə) *n.* open grasslands, usually with scattered bushes or trees, in or near the tropics.

savant ('sævənt) *n.* a learned person; sage. —'**savante** *fem. n.*

save[1] (seɪv) *vb.* **1.** to rescue or preserve (a person or thing) from danger or harm. **2.** to avoid the spending, waste, or loss of (something): *you save time, money, and fuel with a microwave oven.* **3.** to deliver from sin; redeem. **4.** (often foll. by *up*) to set aside or reserve (money or goods) for future use: *I'm saving up for a car.* **5.** to treat with care so as to preserve. **6.** to prevent the necessity for: *he resigned to save them the trouble of sacking him.* **7.** *Sport.* to prevent (a goal) by stopping (a ball or puck). ~*n.* **8.** *Sport.* the act of saving a goal. **9.** *Computers.* an instruction to write information from the memory onto a tape or disk. —'**savable** *or* '**saveable** *adj.* —'**saver** *n.*

save[2] (seɪv) *Archaic.* ~*prep.* **1.** (often foll. by *for*) with the exception of. ~*conj.* **2.** but.

save as you earn *n.* (in Britain) a savings scheme operated by the government, in which regular deposits are made into a savings account from a salary.

saveloy ('sævɪˌlɔɪ) *n.* a highly seasoned smoked sausage made from salted pork.

saving ('seɪvɪŋ) *adj.* **1.** tending to rescue or preserve. **2. saving grace.** a redeeming or compensating quality. ~*n.* **3.** preservation or redemption. **4.** economy or avoidance of waste. **5.** anything saved. **6.** (*pl.*) money saved for future use. ~*prep.* **7.** with the exception of.

saviour *or U.S.* **savior** ('seɪvjə) *n.* a person who rescues another person or a thing from danger or harm.

Saviour *or U.S.* **Savior** ('seɪvjə) *n. Christianity.* Jesus Christ, regarded as the saviour of men from sin.

savoir-faire ('sævwɑː'fɛə) *n.* the ability to say and do the right thing in any situation.

savory ('seɪvərɪ) *n., pl.* **-vories.** an aromatic plant whose leaves are used in cooking.

savour *or U.S.* **savor** ('seɪvə) *n.* **1.** the taste or smell of something. **2.** a slight but distinctive quality or trace. ~*vb.* **3.** (foll. by *of*) to possess the taste or smell of. **4.** (foll. by *of*) to have a suggestion of: *her actions savoured of melodrama.* **5.** to relish or enjoy: *he savoured the word as he said it.*

savoury *or U.S.* **savory** ('seɪvərɪ) *adj.* **1.** attractive to the sense of taste or smell. **2.** salty or spicy: *a savoury dish.* **3.** pleasant or acceptable: *the less savoury episodes in her past.* ~*n., pl.* **-ries. 4.** *Chiefly Brit.* a savoury dish served as an hors d'oeuvre or dessert. —'**savouriness** *or U.S.* '**savoriness** *n.*

savoy (sə'vɔɪ) *n.* a cabbage with a compact head and wrinkled leaves.

savvy ('sævɪ) *Slang.* ~*vb.* **-vying, -vied. 1.** to understand. ~*n.* **2.** understanding or common sense.

saw[1] (sɔː) *n.* **1.** a cutting tool with a toothed metal blade or edge, either operated by hand or powered by electricity. ~*vb.* **sawing, sawed; sawed** *or* **sawn. 2.** to cut with or as if with a saw. **3.** to form by sawing. **4.** to move (an object) from side to side as if moving a saw.

saw[2] (sɔː) *vb.* the past tense of **see**[1].

saw[3] (sɔː) *n.* a wise saying, maxim, or proverb.

sawdust ('sɔːˌdʌst) *n.* particles of wood formed by sawing.

sawfish ('sɔːˌfɪʃ) *n., pl.* **-fish** *or* **-fishes.** a sharklike ray with a long serrated snout resembling a saw.

sawmill ('sɔːˌmɪl) *n.* a factory where timber is sawn into planks.

sawn (sɔːn) *vb.* a past participle of **saw**[1].

sawn-off *or esp. U.S.* **sawed-off** *adj.* (of a shotgun) having the barrel cut short to make concealment of the weapon easier.

sawyer ('sɔːjə) *n.* a person who saws timber for a living.

sax (sæks) *n. Informal.* short for **saxophone.**

saxifrage ('sæksɪˌfreɪdʒ) *n.* a rock plant with small white, yellow, purple, or pink flowers.

Saxon ('sæksən) *n.* **1.** a member of a West Germanic people who raided and settled parts of Britain in the fifth and sixth centuries A.D. **2.** any of the West Germanic dialects spoken by the ancient Saxons. ~*adj.* **3.** of the ancient Saxons or their language.

saxophone ('sæksə,fəʊn) *n.* a keyed single-reed wind instrument with a usually curved metal body. —**saxophonist** (sæk'sɒfənɪst) *n.*

say (seɪ) *vb.* **saying, said. 1.** to speak or utter. **2.** to express in words; tell: *I can't say what I feel.* **3.** to state (an opinion or fact) positively: *I say you are wrong.* **4.** to indicate or show: *the clock says ten to nine.* **5.** to recite: *to say grace.* **6.** to report or allege: *they say we shall have rain today.* **7.** to suppose: *let us say that he is lying.* **8.** to convey by means of artistic expression: *what does the artist have to say in this picture?* **9.** to make a case for: *there is much to be said for it.* **10. go without saying.** to be so obvious as to need no explanation. **11. to say the least.** at the very least. ~*adv.* **12.** approximately: *there were, say, 20 people present.* **13.** for example: *choose a number, say, four.* ~*n.* **14.** the right or chance to speak: *let him have his say.* **15.** authority, esp. to influence a decision: *he has a lot of say.*

SAYE (in Britain) save as you earn.

saying ('seɪɪŋ) *n.* a maxim, adage, or proverb.

Sb *Chem.* antimony.

Sc *Chem.* scandium.

SC South Carolina.

scab (skæb) *n.* **1.** the dried crusty surface of a healing skin wound or sore. **2.** a contagious disease of sheep, caused by a mite. **3.** a fungal disease of plants. **4.** *Disparaging.* a person who refuses to support a trade union's actions, and continues to work during a strike. **5.** a despicable person. ~*vb.* **scabbing, scabbed. 6.** to become covered with a scab. **7.** *Disparaging.* to work as a scab.

scabbard ('skæbəd) *n.* a holder for a sword or dagger.

scabby ('skæbɪ) *adj.* **-bier, -biest. 1.** *Pathol.* covered with scabs. **2.** *Informal.* despicable. —'**scabbiness** *n.*

scabies ('skeɪbiːz) *n.* a contagious skin infection caused by a mite, characterized by intense itching.

scabious ('skeɪbɪəs) *n.* a plant with showy blue, red, or whitish dome-shaped flower heads.

scabrous ('skeɪbrəs) *adj.* **1.** rough and scaly. **2.** indecent or lewd: *scabrous humour.*

scaffold ('skæfəld) *n.* **1.** a temporary framework used to support workmen and materials during the construction or repair of a building. **2.** a raised wooden platform on which criminals are executed.

scaffolding ('skæfəldɪŋ) *n.* **1.** a scaffold or scaffolds. **2.** the building materials used to make scaffolds.

scalar ('skeɪlə) *n.* **1.** a quantity, such as time or temperature, that has magnitude but not direction. ~*adj.* **2.** having magnitude but not direction.

scalawag ('skælə,wæg) *n.* same as **scally-wag.**

scald (skɔːld) *vb.* **1.** to burn with hot liquid or steam. **2.** to use boiling water on, so as to sterilize. **3.** to heat (a liquid) almost to boiling point. ~*n.* **4.** a burn caused by scalding.

scale¹ (skeɪl) *n.* **1.** one of the thin flat horny plates covering the bodies of fishes and reptiles. **2.** a thin flat piece or flake. **3.** a coating which sometimes forms in kettles and hot-water pipes in areas where the water is hard. **4.** tartar formed on the teeth. ~*vb.* **5.** to remove the scales or coating from. **6.** to peel off in flakes or scales. **7.** to cover or become covered with scales. —'**scaly** *adj.*

scale² (skeɪl) *n.* **1.** (*often pl.*) a machine or device for weighing. **2.** one of the pans of a balance. **3. tip** or **turn the scales. a.** to have a decisive influence. **b.** (foll. by *at*) to amount in weight to.

scale³ (skeɪl) *n.* **1.** a sequence of marks at regular intervals, used as a reference in making measurements. **2.** a measuring instrument with such a scale. **3.** the ratio between the size of something real and that of a representation of it: *the map has a scale of one centimetre to a kilometre.* **4.** a series of degrees or graded system of things: *a wage scale for carpenters.* **5.** a relative degree or extent: *he entertained on a grand scale.* **6.** *Music.* a sequence of notes taken in ascending or descending order, esp. within the compass of one octave. **7.** *Maths.* the notation of a given number system: *the decimal scale.* ~*vb.* **8.** to climb to the top of (a height) by or as if by a ladder. **9.** (usually foll. by *up* or *down*) to increase or reduce proportionately in size.

scalene ('skeɪliːn) *adj. Maths.* (of a triangle) having all sides of unequal length.

scallion ('skæljən) *n.* an onion, such as the spring onion, that has a small bulb and long leaves and is eaten in salads.

scallop ('skɒləp, 'skæl-) *n.* **1.** an edible marine mollusc with two fluted fan-shaped shells. **2.** a single shell of this mollusc. **3.** one of a series of curves along an edge. ~*vb.* **4.** to decorate (an edge) with scallops. —'**scalloping** *n.*

scallywag ('skælɪ,wæg) *n. Informal.* a scamp; rascal.

scalp (skælp) *n.* **1.** *Anat.* the skin and hair covering the top of the head. **2.** (among North American Indians) a part of this removed as a trophy from a slain enemy. ~*vb.* **3.** to cut the scalp from. **4.** *Informal, chiefly U.S.* to buy and resell so as to make a high or quick profit.

scalpel ('skælp°l) *n.* a small surgical knife with a very sharp thin blade.

scamp (skæmp) *n.* a mischievous person, esp. a child.

scamper ('skæmpə) *vb.* 1. to run about hurriedly or quickly. ~*n.* 2. the act of scampering.

scampi ('skæmpɪ) *n.* (*usually functioning as sing.*) large prawns, usually eaten fried in breadcrumbs.

scan (skæn) *vb.* **scanning, scanned.** 1. to scrutinize minutely. 2. to glance at quickly. 3. *Prosody.* to analyse (verse) by examining its rhythmical structure. 4. *Prosody.* (of a line or verse) to be metrically correct. 5. to examine or search (an area) by systematically moving a beam of light or electrons, or a radar or sonar beam over it. 6. *Med.* to obtain an image of (a part of the body) by means of ultrasound or a scanner. ~*n.* 7. an instance of scanning.

scandal ('skænd°l) *n.* 1. a disgraceful action or event: *his negligence was a scandal.* 2. shame or outrage arising from a disgraceful action or event. 3. malicious gossip. —'**scandalous** *adj.* —'**scandalously** *adv.*

scandalize or **-ise** ('skændə,laɪz) *vb.* to shock, as by improper behaviour.

scandalmonger ('skænd°l,mʌŋgə) *n.* a person who spreads or enjoys scandal or gossip.

Scandinavian (,skændɪ'neɪvɪən) *adj.* 1. of Scandinavia (Norway, Sweden, Denmark, and Iceland), its inhabitants, or their languages. ~*n.* 2. a person from Scandinavia. 3. the group of Germanic languages spoken by the Scandinavians.

scandium ('skændɪəm) *n.* a rare silvery-white metallic element. Symbol: Sc

scanner ('skænə) *n.* 1. an aerial or similar device designed to transmit or receive signals, esp. radar signals. 2. a device used in medical diagnosis to obtain an image of an internal organ or part.

scansion ('skænʃən) *n.* the metrical scanning of verse.

scant (skænt) *adj.* scarcely sufficient; meagre: *he paid her scant attention.*

scanty ('skæntɪ) *adj.* **scantier, scantiest.** 1. limited; barely enough. 2. inadequate. —'**scantily** *adv.* —'**scantiness** *n.*

scapegoat ('skeɪp,gəʊt) *n.* a person made to bear the blame for others.

scapula ('skæpjʊlə) *n., pl.* **-lae** (-liː) or **-las.** the technical name for **shoulder blade.**

scapular ('skæpjʊlə) *adj.* 1. *Anat.* of the scapula. ~*n.* 2. a loose sleeveless garment worn by monks over their habits.

scar[1] (skɑː) *n.* 1. a mark left on the skin following the healing of a wound. 2. a permanent effect on a person's character resulting from emotional distress. 3. a mark on a plant where a leaf was formerly attached. 4. a mark of damage. ~*vb.* **scarring, scarred.** 5. to mark or become marked with a scar.

scar[2] (skɑː) *n.* a bare craggy rock formation.

scarab ('skærəb) *n.* 1. the black dung-beetle, regarded by the ancient Egyptians as divine. 2. an image or carving of this beetle.

scarce (skɛəs) *adj.* 1. not common; rarely found. 2. insufficient to meet the demand. 3. **make oneself scarce.** *Informal.* to go away. ~*adv.* 4. *Archaic or literary.* scarcely.

scarcely ('skɛəslɪ) *adv.* 1. hardly at all. 2. *Often used ironically.* probably or definitely not: *that is scarcely justification for your actions.*
Usage. see **hardly.**

scarcity ('skɛəsɪtɪ) *n., pl.* **-ties.** inadequate supply.

scare (skɛə) *vb.* 1. to fill or be filled with fear or alarm. 2. (foll. by *away* or *off*) to drive away by frightening. ~*n.* 3. a sudden attack of fear or alarm: *I had a terrible scare.* 4. a period of general fear or alarm: *a rabies scare.*

scarecrow ('skɛə,krəʊ) *n.* 1. an object, usually in the shape of a man, made out of sticks and old clothes to scare birds away from crops. 2. *Informal.* a raggedly dressed person.

scaremonger ('skɛə,mʌŋgə) *n.* a person who starts or spreads rumours of disaster to frighten people. —'**scare,mongering** *n.*

scarf[1] (skɑːf) *n., pl.* **scarfs** or **scarves.** a square, triangular, or long narrow piece of cloth worn around the head, neck, or shoulders.

scarf[2] (skɑːf) *n., pl.* **scarfs.** 1. a joint between two pieces of timber made by notching the ends and strapping or gluing the two pieces together. ~*vb.* 2. to join (two pieces of timber) by means of a scarf.

scarify ('skɛərɪ,faɪ) *vb.* **-fying, -fied.** 1. *Surgery.* to make slight incisions in (the skin). 2. *Agriculture.* to break up and loosen (topsoil). 3. to wound with harsh criticism. —,**scarifi'cation** *n.*

scarlatina (,skɑːlə'tiːnə) *n.* the technical name for **scarlet fever.**

scarlet ('skɑːlɪt) *adj.* bright orange-red.

scarlet fever *n.* an acute contagious disease characterized by fever, a sore throat, and a red rash on the body.

scarp (skɑːp) *n.* 1. a steep slope or ridge of rock. 2. *Fortifications.* the side of a ditch cut nearest to a rampart.

scarper ('skɑːpə) *vb. Brit. slang.* to run away or escape.

scarves (skɑːvz) *n.* a plural of **scarf**[1].

scary ('skɛərɪ) *adj.* **scarier, scariest.** *Informal.* causing fear or alarm.

scat[1] (skæt) *vb.* **scatting, scatted.** (*usually imperative*) *Informal.* to go away in haste.

scat[2] (skæt) *n.* 1. a type of jazz singing

characterized by improvised vocal sounds instead of words. ~*vb.* **scatting, scatted.** **2.** to sing jazz in this way.

scathing ('skeɪðɪŋ) *adj.* harshly critical; scornful. —**'scathingly** *adv.*

scatology (skæ'tɒlədʒɪ) *n.* preoccupation with obscenity, esp. with references to excrement. —**scatological** (ˌskætə'lɒdʒɪkᵊl) *adj.*

scatter ('skætə) *vb.* **1.** to throw about in various directions: *his possessions were scattered all over the room.* **2.** to separate and move in various directions; disperse: *the crowd scattered when the alarm went off.* ~*n.* **3.** the act of scattering. **4.** a number of objects scattered about.

scatterbrain ('skætəˌbreɪn) *n.* a person who is incapable of serious thought or concentration. —**'scatterˌbrained** *adj.*

scatty ('skætɪ) *adj.* **-tier, -tiest.** *Brit. informal.* empty-headed or thoughtless. —**'scattiness** *n.*

scavenge ('skævɪndʒ) *vb.* to search for (anything usable) among discarded material.

scavenger ('skævɪndʒə) *n.* **1.** a person who collects things discarded by others. **2.** any animal that feeds on discarded or decaying matter.

SCE (in Scotland) Scottish Certificate of Education.

scenario (sɪ'nɑːrɪˌəʊ) *n., pl.* **-narios. 1.** a summary of the plot and characters of a play or film. **2.** an imagined sequence of future events.

scene (siːn) *n.* **1.** the place where an action or event, real or imaginary, occurs. **2.** an incident or situation, real or imaginary, esp. as described or represented. **3.** a division of an act of a play, in which the setting is fixed and the action is continuous. **4.** *Films.* a shot or series of shots that constitutes a unit of the action. **5.** the backcloths or screens used to represent a location in a play or film set. **6.** the view of a place or landscape. **7.** a display of emotion: *don't make a scene in front of everyone.* **8.** *Informal.* a specific activity or interest: *the fashion scene.* **9. behind the scenes. a.** backstage. **b.** in secret or in private.

scenery ('siːnərɪ) *n., pl.* **-eries. 1.** the natural features of a landscape. **2.** *Theatre.* the painted backcloths or screens used to represent a location in a theatre or studio.

scenic ('siːnɪk) *adj.* **1.** of or having beautiful natural scenery: *a scenic drive.* **2.** of the stage or stage scenery: *scenic design.*

scent (sent) *n.* **1.** a distinctive smell, esp. a pleasant one. **2.** a smell left in passing, by which a person or animal may be traced. **3.** a trail or series of clues by which something is followed: *on the scent of something big.* **4.** perfume. ~*vb.* **5.** to become aware of by smelling. **6.** to suspect: *I scent foul play.* **7.** to fill with odour or fragrance. —**'scented** *adj.*

sceptic *or U.S.* **skeptic** ('skɛptɪk) *n.* **1.** a person who habitually doubts generally accepted beliefs. **2.** a person who mistrusts people or ideas in general. —**'sceptical** *adj.* —**'sceptically** *adv.* —**'scepticism** *n.*

sceptre *or U.S.* **scepter** ('sɛptə) *n.* a ceremonial staff held by a monarch as the symbol of authority. —**'sceptred** *or U.S.* **'sceptered** *adj.*

schedule ('ʃɛdjuːl; *also, esp. U.S.* 'skɛdʒʊəl) *n.* **1.** a timed plan of procedure for a project. **2.** a list of details or items: *a schedule of fixed prices.* **3.** a timetable. ~*vb.* **4.** to make a schedule of or place in a schedule. **5.** to plan to occur at a certain time.

schema ('skiːmə) *n., pl.* **-mata** (-mətə). a plan, diagram, or scheme.

schematic (skɪ'mætɪk) *adj.* of or having the nature of a diagram or plan. —**sche'matically** *adv.*

schematize *or* **-ise** ('skiːmə,taɪz) *vb.* to form into or arrange in a scheme.

scheme (skiːm) *n.* **1.** a systematic plan for a course of action. **2.** a systematic arrangement of parts or features: *colour scheme.* **3.** a secret plot. **4.** a chart, diagram, or outline. **5.** *Chiefly Brit.* a plan formally adopted by a government or organization: *the state pension scheme.* ~*vb.* **6.** to plot (for) in an underhand manner. —**'schemer** *n.* —**'scheming** *adj., n.*

scherzo ('skɛətsəʊ) *n., pl.* **-zos** *or* **-zi** (-tsiː). a brisk lively piece of music, often the second or third movement in a sonata or symphony.

schilling ('ʃɪlɪŋ) *n.* the standard monetary unit of Austria.

schism ('sɪzəm, 'skɪz-) *n.* the division of a group, esp. a religious group, into opposing factions, due to differences in doctrine. —**schis'matic** *adj.*

schist (ʃɪst) *n.* a metamorphic rock that can be split into thin layers.

schizo ('skɪtsəʊ) *Informal.* ~*adj.* **1.** schizophrenic. ~*n., pl.* **-os. 2.** a schizophrenic person.

schizoid ('skɪtsɔɪd) *adj.* **1.** *Psychol.* having a personality disorder characterized by extreme shyness and oversensitivity. **2.** *Informal.* characterized by conflicting or contradictory ideas or attitudes. ~*n.* **3.** a person who has a schizoid personality.

schizophrenia (ˌskɪtsəʊ'friːnɪə) *n.* **1.** a psychotic disorder characterized by withdrawal from reality, hallucinations, or emotional instability. **2.** *Informal.* behaviour that seems to be motivated by contradictory or conflicting principles. —**schizophrenic** (ˌskɪtsəʊ'frɛnɪk) *adj., n.*

schmaltz (ʃmɔːlts) *n.* excessive sentimentality, esp. in music. —**'schmaltzy** *adj.*

schnapps (ʃnæps) *n.* (in Europe) any strong dry spirit, such as Dutch potato gin.

schnitzel (ˈʃnɪtsəl) *n.* a thin slice of meat, esp. veal.

scholar (ˈskɒlə) *n.* **1.** a learned person. **2.** a person who studies; pupil. **3.** a student receiving a scholarship. —ˈ**scholarly** *adj.*

scholarship (ˈskɒləʃɪp) *n.* **1.** academic achievement; learning gained by serious study. **2.** financial aid provided for a scholar because of academic merit.

scholastic (skəˈlæstɪk) *adj.* **1.** of schools, scholars, or education. **2.** (*often cap.*) of or relating to scholasticism. ~*n.* **3.** a scholarly person. **4.** (*often cap.*) a disciple or adherent of scholasticism.

scholasticism (skəˈlæstɪˌsɪzəm) *n.* (*sometimes cap.*) the system of philosophy, theology, and teaching that dominated medieval Europe and was based on the writings of Aristotle.

school¹ (skuːl) *n.* **1.** an institution or building at which people, usually children and young people, are taught. **2.** a faculty or department specializing in a particular subject: *a law school.* **3.** the staff and pupils of a school. **4.** a regular session of instruction in a school: *he stayed after school to do extra work.* **5.** a place or sphere of activity that instructs: *the school of hard knocks.* **6.** a group of artists, writers, or thinkers, linked by the same style, teachers, or methods. **7.** *Informal.* a group assembled for a common purpose, such as gambling: *a card school.* ~*vb.* **8.** to educate in or as in a school. **9.** to discipline or control.

school² (skuːl) *n.* a group of fishes or other aquatic animals that swim together.

schoolboy (ˈskuːlˌbɔɪ) *or* (*fem.*) **schoolgirl** *n.* a child attending school.

schoolhouse (ˈskuːlˌhaʊs) *n.* **1.** a building used as a school. **2.** a house attached to a school.

schooling (ˈskuːlɪŋ) *n.* education, esp. when received at school.

schoolmarm (ˈskuːlˌmɑːm) *n. Informal.* **1.** a woman schoolteacher. **2.** any woman considered to be prim or old-fashioned.

schoolmaster (ˈskuːlˌmɑːstə) *or* (*fem.*) **schoolmistress** *n.* a person who teaches in or runs a school.

schoolteacher (ˈskuːlˌtiːtʃə) *n.* a person who teaches in a school.

school year *n.* **1.** a twelve-month period, usually of three terms, during which pupils remain in the same class. **2.** the time during this period when the school is open.

schooner (ˈskuːnə) *n.* **1.** a sailing vessel with at least two masts, rigged fore-and-aft. **2.** *Brit.* a large glass for sherry. **3.** *U.S., Canad., Austral., & N.Z.* a large glass for beer.

schottische (ʃɒˈtiːʃ) *n.* **1.** a 19th-century German dance resembling a slow polka. **2.** music for this dance.

schuss (ʃʊs) *Skiing.* ~*n.* **1.** a straight high-speed downhill run. ~*vb.* **2.** to perform a schuss.

schwa (ʃwɑː) *n.* **1.** the neutral vowel sound occurring in unstressed syllables in English, as in *around* and *sofa.* **2.** the symbol (ə) used to represent this sound.

sciatic (saɪˈætɪk) *adj.* **1.** *Anat.* of the hip or the hipbone. **2.** of or afflicted with sciatica.

sciatica (saɪˈætɪkə) *n.* a form of neuralgia causing intense pain along the nerve running from the back of the thigh down to the calf of the leg.

science (ˈsaɪəns) *n.* **1.** the systematic study of the nature and behaviour of the physical universe, based on observation, experiment, and measurement. **2.** the knowledge so obtained. **3.** any particular branch of this knowledge: *medical science.* **4.** any body of knowledge organized in a systematic manner. **5.** skill or technique.

science fiction *n.* a literary genre that makes imaginative use of scientific knowledge or theories.

science park *n.* an area where scientific research and commercial development are carried on in cooperation.

scientific (ˌsaɪənˈtɪfɪk) *adj.* **1.** of, derived from, or used in science: *scientific equipment.* **2.** conforming with the systematic methods used in science. —ˌ**scien'tifically** *adv.*

scientist (ˈsaɪəntɪst) *n.* a person who studies or practises a science.

sci-fi (ˈsaɪˈfaɪ) *n.* short for **science fiction.**

scilicet (ˈsɪlɪˌsɛt) *adv.* namely; that is to say: used esp. in explaining an obscure text or supplying a missing word.

scimitar (ˈsɪmɪtə) *n.* a curved oriental sword.

scintilla (sɪnˈtɪlə) *n.* a minute amount; hint or trace.

scintillate (ˈsɪntɪˌleɪt) *vb.* **1.** to give off (sparks); sparkle. **2.** to talk or act with animation or brilliance. —ˈ**scintillating** *adj.* —ˌ**scintil'lation** *n.*

scintillation counter *n.* an instrument for measuring the intensity of high-energy radiation, by counting the flashes of light produced when particles collide with a fluorescent material.

scion (ˈsaɪən) *n.* **1.** a descendant or young member of a family. **2.** a shoot of a plant used to form a graft.

scissors (ˈsɪzəz) *pl. n.* a cutting instrument held in one hand, with two crossed blades pivoted so that they close together on what is to be cut.

sclera (ˈsklɪərə) *n.* the tough white fibrous membrane that forms the outer covering of the eyeball.

sclerosis (sklɪəˈrəʊsɪs) *n.*, *pl.* **-ses** (-siːz). *Pathol.* an abnormal hardening or thickening of body tissues, esp. of the nervous system or the inner wall of arteries.

sclerotic (sklɪəˈrɒtɪk) *adj.* **1.** of or relating to the sclera. **2.** of, relating to, or having sclerosis.

scoff[1] (skɒf) *vb.* **1.** (often foll. by *at*) to speak contemptuously (about); mock. ~*n.* **2.** an expression of derision; jeer. —ˈ**scoffing** *adj., n.*

scoff[2] (skɒf) *Informal, chiefly Brit.* ~*vb.* **1.** to eat (food) fast and greedily. ~*n.* **2.** food.

scold (skəʊld) *vb.* **1.** to find fault with or reprimand (a person) harshly. **2.** to use harsh or abusive language. ~*n.* **3.** a person, esp. a woman, who constantly scolds. —ˈ**scolding** *n.*

scollop (ˈskɒləp) *n., vb.* same as **scallop.**

sconce (skɒns) *n.* a bracket fixed to a wall for holding candles or lights.

scone (skɒn, skəʊn) *n.* a light doughy cake made from flour and fat, cooked in an oven or on a griddle.

scoop (skuːp) *n.* **1.** any of various spoonlike tools with a deep bowl, used for handling loose or soft materials such as flour or ice cream. **2.** the deep shovel of a mechanical digger. **3.** the quantity taken up by a scoop. **4.** the act of scooping or dredging. **5.** a news story reported in one newspaper before all the others. ~*vb.* **6.** (often foll. by *up*) to take up and remove (an object or substance) with or as if with a scoop. **7.** (often foll. by *out*) to hollow out with or as if with a scoop. **8.** to beat (rival newspapers) in uncovering a news item.

scoot (skuːt) *vb.* to go or leave quickly.

scooter (ˈskuːtə) *n.* **1.** a child's toy vehicle consisting of a low footboard mounted between two small wheels with a raised handlebar for steering. **2.** same as **motor scooter.**

scope (skəʊp) *n.* **1.** opportunity for exercising the faculties or abilities: *there is no scope for originality in this job.* **2.** range of view or grasp: *these ideas are beyond my scope.* **3.** the area covered by an activity or topic: *the scope of his thesis was vast.*

scorbutic (skɔːˈbjuːtɪk) *adj.* of or having scurvy.

scorch (skɔːtʃ) *vb.* **1.** to burn or become burnt slightly on the surface. **2.** to wither or parch from exposure to heat. **3.** *Informal.* to criticize harshly. ~*n.* **4.** a slight burn. **5.** a mark caused by the application of too great heat. —ˈ**scorching** *adj.*

scorcher (ˈskɔːtʃə) *n. Informal.* a very hot day.

score (skɔː) *n.* **1.** the total number of points made by a side or individual in a game. **2.** the act of scoring a point or points: *there was no score at the end of the*

first half. **3. the score.** *Informal.* the actual situation: *you don't know the score.* **4.** a group or set of twenty: *three score years and ten.* **5.** (*usually pl.; foll. by of*) lots: *I have scores of things to do.* **6.** *Music.* the printed form of a piece of music in which the parts for each musician are printed one under the other on separate staves. **7. a.** the incidental music for a film or play. **b.** the songs and music for a stage or film musical. **8.** a mark or scratch. **9.** a record of amounts due. **10.** an amount recorded as due. **11.** a reason: *the book was rejected on the score of length.* **12.** a grievance: *I have a score to settle with you.* **13. over the score.** *Informal.* excessive; unfair. ~*vb.* **14.** to gain (a point or points) in a game or contest. **15.** to make a total score of. **16.** to keep a record of the score (of). **17.** to be worth (a certain number of points) in a game: *red aces score twenty.* **18.** to make cuts or lines in or on. **19.** *Slang.* to obtain something desired, esp. to purchase an illegal drug. **20.** *Slang.* to be successful in seducing someone. **21.** to arrange (a piece of music) for specific instruments or voices. **22.** to write the music for (a film or play). **23.** to achieve (success or an advantage): *your idea scored with the boss.* —ˈ**scorer** *n.*

scoreboard (ˈskɔːˌbɔːd) *n. Sport.* a board for displaying the score of a game or match.

scorecard (ˈskɔːˌkɑːd) *n.* **1.** a card on which scores are recorded in games such as golf. **2.** a card identifying the players in a sports match, esp. cricket.

score off *vb.* to gain an advantage at someone else's expense.

scoria (ˈskɔːrɪə) *n., pl.* **-riae** (-rɪˌiː). **1.** a mass of solidified lava containing many cavities. **2.** refuse left after ore has been smelted.

scorn (skɔːn) *n.* **1.** open contempt for a person or thing. ~*vb.* **2.** to treat with contempt or derision. **3.** to reject with contempt. —ˈ**scornful** *adj.* —ˈ**scornfully** *adv.*

Scorpio (ˈskɔːpɪˌəʊ) *n. Astrol.* the eighth sign of the zodiac; the Scorpion.

scorpion (ˈskɔːpɪən) *n.* a creature of warm dry regions, which has an insect-like body with a long tail ending in a venomous sting.

Scot (skɒt) *n.* a person from Scotland.

Scot. **1.** Scotland. **2.** Scottish.

scotch (skɒtʃ) *vb.* **1.** to put an end to; crush: *bad weather scotched our plans.* **2.** to wound without killing.

Scotch[1] (skɒtʃ) *Not universally accepted.* ~*adj.* **1.** same as **Scottish.** ~*n.* **2. the.** (*functioning as pl.*) the Scots or their language.
Usage. In the north of England and in Scotland, *Scotch* is not used except in fixed expressions such as *Scotch whisky.* The use

of *Scotch* for *Scots* or *Scottish* is incorrect, esp. when applied to people.

Scotch² (skɒtʃ) *n.* whisky distilled in Scotland from fermented malted barley.

Scotch broth *n. Brit.* a thick soup made from mutton or beef stock, vegetables, and pearl barley.

Scotch egg *n. Brit.* a hard-boiled egg enclosed in a layer of sausage meat, covered in egg and crumbs, and fried.

Scotch mist *n.* **1.** a heavy wet mist. **2.** drizzle.

Scotch terrier *n.* same as **Scottish terrier.**

scot-free *adv., adj.* without harm or punishment.

Scotland Yard ('skɒtlənd) *n.* the headquarters of the police force of metropolitan London.

Scots (skɒts) *adj.* **1.** of Scotland, its people or their language. ~*n.* **2.** any of the English dialects spoken or written in Scotland.

Scotsman ('skɒtsmən) *or (fem.)* **Scotswoman** *n., pl.* **-men** *or* **-women.** a person from Scotland.

Scots pine *n.* **1.** a hardy coniferous tree of Europe and Asia, with blue-green needle-like leaves. **2.** the wood of this tree.

Scotticism ('skɒtɪˌsɪzəm) *n.* a Scottish expression or word.

Scottie ('skɒtɪ) *n., pl.* **-ties.** *Informal.* a Scottish terrier.

Scottish ('skɒtɪʃ) *adj.* of Scotland, its people, or their language.

Scottish terrier *n.* a small but sturdy long-haired terrier, usually with a black coat.

scoundrel ('skaʊndrəl) *n.* a worthless or villainous person.

scour¹ ('skaʊə) *vb.* **1.** to clean or polish (a surface) by hard rubbing with something rough. **2.** to clear (a channel) by the force of water. ~*n.* **3.** the act of scouring. —'**scourer** *n.*

scour² ('skaʊə) *vb.* **1.** to make a thorough and energetic search of: *we have scoured the archives for information.* **2.** to move swiftly or energetically over (land), as in search or pursuit.

scourge (skɜːdʒ) *n.* **1.** a person who or thing which causes affliction or suffering. **2.** a whip used for inflicting punishment. ~*vb.* **3.** to whip. **4.** to afflict.

Scouse (skaʊs) *Brit. informal.* ~*n.* **1.** a person from Liverpool. **2.** the Liverpool dialect. ~*adj.* **3.** of or from Liverpool.

scout (skaʊt) *n.* **1.** *Mil.* a person or unit sent to reconnoitre the position of the enemy. **2.** same as **talent scout.** **3.** the act or an instance of scouting. ~*vb.* **4.** to examine or observe (something) in order to obtain information. **5.** (foll. by *about* or *around*) to go in search of.

Scout *or* **scout** (skaʊt) *n.* a boy who is a member of the Scout Association, founded in 1908 by Lord Baden-Powell to promote outdoor activities and develop character. —'**Scouting** *n.*

scow (skaʊ) *n.* a flat-bottomed boat used for carrying freight.

scowl (skaʊl) *vb.* **1.** to draw one's brows together in an angry or bad-tempered expression. ~*n.* **2.** an angry or bad-tempered expression.

scrabble ('skræb³l) *vb.* **1.** (foll. by *about* or *at*) to scrape at or grope for with hands, feet, or claws. **2.** (foll. by *for*) to struggle to gain possession of. ~*n.* **3.** a scrabbling.

Scrabble ('skræb³l) *n. Trademark.* a board game in which words are formed by placing letter tiles in a pattern similar to a cross-word puzzle.

scrag (skræg) *n.* **1.** a thin or scrawny person or animal. **2.** the thin end of a neck of veal or mutton. ~*vb.* **scragging, scragged. 3.** *Informal.* to wring the neck of.

scraggy ('skrægɪ) *adj.* **-gier, -giest.** thin or scrawny. —'**scragginess** *n.*

scram¹ (skræm) *vb.* **scramming, scrammed.** *(often imperative) Informal.* to go away hastily.

scram² (skræm) *n.* **1.** an emergency shutdown of a nuclear reactor. ~*vb.* **scramming, scrammed. 2.** (of a nuclear reactor) to shut down or be shut down in an emergency.

scramble ('skræmb³l) *vb.* **1.** to climb or crawl hurriedly, esp. by using the hands to aid movement. **2.** to proceed hurriedly or in a disorderly fashion. **3.** (often foll. by *for*) to compete with others, often in a disordered manner. **4.** to jumble together in a haphazard manner. **5.** to cook (eggs that have been whisked up with milk) in a pan. **6.** *Mil.* (of a crew or aircraft) to take off quickly in an emergency. **7.** to make (speech) unintelligible during transmission by means of an electronic scrambler. ~*n.* **8.** the act of scrambling. **9.** a climb or trek over difficult ground. **10.** a disorderly struggle, as to gain possession of something. **11.** *Mil.* an immediate takeoff of crew or aircraft in an emergency. **12.** *Brit.* a motor-cycle race across rough open ground.

scrambler ('skræmblə) *n.* an electronic device that makes broadcast or telephone messages unintelligible without a special receiver.

scrap¹ (skræp) *n.* **1.** a small piece of something larger; fragment. **2.** waste material or used articles, often collected and reprocessed. **3.** (*pl.*) pieces of leftover food. ~*vb.* **scrapping, scrapped. 4.** to discard as useless.

scrap² (skræp) *Informal.* ~*n.* **1.** a fight or

argument. ~*vb.* **scrapping, scrapped. 2.** to quarrel or fight.

scrapbook ('skræp,buk) *n.* a book of blank pages in which to mount newspaper cuttings or pictures.

scrape (skreɪp) *vb.* **1.** to move (a rough or sharp object) across (a surface), as to smooth or clean. **2.** (often foll. by *away* or *off*) to remove (a layer) by rubbing. **3.** to produce a grating sound by rubbing against (something else). **4.** to injure or damage by scraping: *to scrape one's knee.* **5.** to be very economical (esp. in **scrimp and scrape**). **6.** to draw the foot backwards in making a bow. ~*n.* **7.** the act of scraping. **8.** a scraped place. **9.** a harsh or grating sound. **10.** *Informal.* an awkward or embarrassing predicament. **11.** *Informal.* a conflict or struggle. —'**scraper** *n.*

scrape through *vb.* to manage, succeed in, or survive with difficulty: *I just scraped through the exam.*

scrape together *or* **up** *vb.* to collect with difficulty: *to scrape together money for a new car.*

scrappy ('skræpɪ) *adj.* **-pier, -piest.** fragmentary; disjointed.

scratch (skrætʃ) *vb.* **1.** to mark or cut (the surface of something) with a rough or sharp instrument. **2.** (often foll. by *at, out,* or *off*) to tear or dig with the nails or claws. **3.** to scrape (the surface of the skin) with the nails to relieve itching. **4.** to chafe or irritate (the skin). **5.** to make or cause to make a grating sound. **6.** (sometimes foll. by *out*) to erase or cross out. **7.** to withdraw from a race or (U.S.) an election. ~*n.* **8.** the act of scratching. **9.** a slight injury. **10.** a mark made by scratching. **11.** a slight grating sound. **12.** (in a handicap sport) a competitor who has no allowance. **13. from scratch.** *Informal.* from the very beginning. **14. not up to scratch.** *Informal.* not up to standard. ~*adj.* **15.** put together hastily: *a scratch team.* **16.** (in a handicap sport) with no allowance. —'**scratchy** *adj.*

scratching ('skrætʃɪŋ) *n.* a percussive effect obtained by rotating a gramophone record manually.

scrawl (skrɔːl) *vb.* **1.** to write carelessly or hastily. ~*n.* **2.** careless or scribbled writing. —'**scrawly** *adj.*

scrawny ('skrɔːnɪ) *adj.* **scrawnier, scrawniest.** very thin and bony. —'**scrawniness** *n.*

scream (skriːm) *vb.* **1.** to utter or emit (a sharp piercing cry or sound), as of fear or pain. **2.** to laugh wildly. **3.** to utter with or as if with a scream: *she stood there and screamed abuse at him.* **4.** to be unpleasantly conspicuous: *bad news screaming out from the headlines.* ~*n.* **5.** a sharp piercing cry or sound, esp. of fear or pain. **6.** *Informal.* a person or thing that causes great amusement.

scree (skriː) *n.* a pile of rock fragments at the foot of a cliff or hill, often forming a sloping heap.

screech[1] (skriːtʃ) *n.* **1.** a shrill or high-pitched sound or cry. ~*vb.* **2.** to utter with or emit a screech. —'**screechy** *adj.*

screech[2] (skriːtʃ) *n. Canad. slang.* **1.** a dark rum. **2.** any strong cheap drink.

screech owl *n.* **1.** *Brit.* same as **barn owl. 2.** a small North American owl with a reddish-brown or grey plumage.

screed (skriːd) *n.* a long tiresome speech or piece of writing.

screen (skriːn) *n.* **1.** a light movable frame, panel, or partition serving to shelter, divide, or conceal. **2.** anything that shelters, protects, or conceals. **3.** a frame containing a mesh that is used to keep out insects. **4.** the blank surface of a television set or radar receiver, on which a visible image is formed. **5.** the white surface on which films or slides are projected. **6. the screen.** the film industry or films collectively. ~*vb.* **7.** (sometimes foll. by *off*) to shelter, protect, or conceal with or as if with a screen. **8.** to test or check (an individual or group) so as to determine suitability for a task or to detect the presence of a disease or weapons. **9.** to show (a film) in the cinema or show (a programme) on television.

screenplay ('skriːn,pleɪ) *n.* the script for a film, including instructions for sets and camera work.

screen process *n.* a method of printing by forcing ink through a fine mesh of silk or nylon, some parts of which have been treated so as not to let the ink pass.

screw (skruː) *n.* **1.** a metal pin with a head threaded evenly with a spiral ridge, which is used to fasten materials together by being firmly twisted into them. **2.** a threaded cylindrical rod that engages with a similarly threaded cylindrical hole. **3.** a thread in a cylindrical hole corresponding with that on the screw with which it is designed to engage. **4.** anything resembling a screw in shape. **5.** *Slang.* a prison guard. **6.** *Taboo slang.* an act of or partner in sexual intercourse. **7. have a screw loose.** *Informal.* to be insane. **8. put the screws on.** *Slang.* to use force or compulsion on. ~*vb.* **9.** to rotate (a screw or bolt) so as to drive it into or draw it out of a material. **10.** to twist or turn in the manner of a screw. **11.** to attach or fasten with or as if with a screw or screws. **12.** *Informal.* to take advantage of; cheat. **13.** (often foll. by *up*) *Informal.* to distort or contort: *he screwed his face into a scowl.* **14.** (often foll. by *from* or *out of*) *Informal.* to force out of; extort. **15.** *Taboo slang.* to have sexual intercourse (with). **16. have one's head screwed on the right way.** *Informal.* to be sensible. ~See also **screw up.**

screwball ('skru:,bɔːl) *Slang, chiefly U.S. & Canad.* ~*n.* **1.** an odd or eccentric person. ~*adj.* **2.** odd; eccentric.

screwdriver ('skru:,draɪvə) *n.* **1.** a tool used for turning screws, consisting of a long thin metal rod with a flattened tip that fits into a slot in the head of the screw. **2.** a drink consisting of orange juice and vodka.

screw top *n.* **1.** a bottle top that screws onto the bottle, allowing the bottle to be resealed after use. **2.** a bottle with such a top. —'**screw-,top** *adj.*

screw up *vb.* **1.** to twist out of shape or distort. **2.** to summon up (courage). **3.** *Informal.* to mishandle or bungle.

screwy ('skru:ɪ) *adj.* **screwier, screwiest.** *Informal.* odd, crazy, or eccentric.

scribble ('skrɪbʰl) *vb.* **1.** to write hastily or illegibly. **2.** to make meaningless or illegible marks (on). ~*n.* **3.** hasty careless writing. **4.** meaningless or illegible marks. —'**scribbler** *n.* —'**scribbly** *adj.*

scribe (skraɪb) *n.* **1.** a person who made handwritten copies of manuscripts or documents before the invention of printing. **2.** *Bible.* a recognized scholar and teacher of the Jewish Law.

scrim (skrɪm) *n.* a fine open-weave fabric, used in upholstery, lining, and bookbinding.

scrimmage ('skrɪmɪdʒ) *n.* **1.** a rough or disorderly struggle. ~*vb.* **2.** to engage in a scrimmage.

scrimp (skrɪmp) *vb.* (sometimes foll. by *on*) to be very sparing in the use (of): *I have to scrimp and save to get by.*

scrip (skrɪp) *n. Finance.* a certificate representing a claim to part of a share of stock.

script (skrɪpt) *n.* **1.** handwriting. **2.** a typeface which looks like a handwriting. **3.** an alphabet or system of writing: *Arabic script.* **4.** the text of a play or film for the use of performers. **5.** a candidate's answer paper in an examination. ~*vb.* **6.** to write a script for.

scripture ('skrɪptʃə) *n.* the sacred writings of a religion. —'**scriptural** *adj.*

Scripture ('skrɪptʃə) *n. Christianity.* the Old and New Testaments.

scriptwriter ('skrɪpt,raɪtə) *n.* a person who prepares scripts, esp. for a film. —'**script-,writing** *n.*

scrofula ('skrɒfjʊlə) *n.* (*no longer in technical use*) tuberculosis of the lymphatic glands. —'**scrofulous** *adj.*

scroll (skrəʊl) *n.* **1.** a roll of parchment or paper usually inscribed with writing. **2.** an ancient book in the form of a roll of parchment, papyrus, or paper. **3.** a decorative carving or moulding resembling a scroll. ~*vb.* **4.** *Computers.* to move (text) on a screen in order to view a section that cannot be fitted into a single display.

Scrooge (skru:dʒ) *n.* a mean or miserly person.

scrotum ('skrəʊtəm) *n., pl.* **-ta** (-tə) *or* **-tums.** the pouch of skin containing the testicles in most male mammals.

scrounge (skraʊndʒ) *vb. Informal.* to obtain or seek to obtain (something) by cadging or begging. —'**scrounger** *n.*

scrub[1] (skrʌb) *vb.* **scrubbing, scrubbed.** **1.** to rub (something) hard, with or as if with a brush, soap, and water, in order to clean it. **2.** to remove (dirt) by rubbing, esp. with a brush and water. **3.** (foll. by *up*) (of a surgeon) to wash the hands and arms thoroughly before operating. **4.** *Informal.* to delete or cancel. ~*n.* **5.** a scrubbing.

scrub[2] (skrʌb) *n.* **1.** vegetation consisting of stunted trees or bushes growing in a dry area. **2.** an area of dry land covered with such vegetation. **3.** a stunted or inferior person, animal, or thing. ~*adj.* **4.** stunted or inferior.

scrubber ('skrʌbə) *n.* **1.** *Offensive slang.* a promiscuous woman. **2.** an apparatus for purifying a gas.

scrubby ('skrʌbɪ) *adj.* **-bier, -biest. 1.** covered with or consisting of scrub. **2.** stunted. **3.** *Brit. informal.* shabby.

scruff[1] (skrʌf) *n.* the nape of the neck: *he grabbed the boy by the scruff of the neck.*

scruff[2] (skrʌf) *n. Informal.* an untidy scruffy person.

scruffy ('skrʌfɪ) *adj.* **scruffier, scruffiest.** unkempt or shabby.

scrum (skrʌm) *n.* **1.** *Rugby.* a formation in which players from each side form a tight pack and push against each other in an attempt to get the ball which is thrown on the ground between them. **2.** *Informal.* a disorderly struggle. ~*vb.* **scrumming, scrummed. 3.** (usually foll. by *down*) *Rugby.* to form a scrum.

scrum half *n. Rugby.* a player who puts in the ball at scrums and tries to get it away to his three-quarter backs.

scrummage ('skrʌmɪdʒ) *n., vb.* **1.** *Rugby.* same as **scrum. 2.** same as **scrimmage.**

scrump (skrʌmp) *vb. Dialect.* to steal (apples) from an orchard or garden.

scrumptious ('skrʌmpʃəs) *adj. Informal.* very pleasing; delicious.

scrumpy ('skrʌmpɪ) *n.* a rough dry cider, brewed esp. in the West Country of England.

scrunch (skrʌntʃ) *vb.* **1.** to crumple or crunch or be crumpled or crunched. ~*n.* **2.** the act or sound of scrunching.

scruple ('skru:pʰl) *n.* **1.** (*often pl.*) a doubt or hesitation as to what is morally right in a certain situation. ~*vb.* **2.** to have doubts (about), esp. on moral grounds.

scrupulous ('skru:pjʊləs) *adj.* **1.** taking great care to do what is morally right. **2.** very careful or precise. —'**scrupulously** *adv.*

scrutinize *or* **-nise** ('skru:tɪˌnaɪz) *vb.* to examine carefully or in minute detail.

scrutiny ('skru:tɪnɪ) *n., pl.* **-nies. 1.** close or minute examination. **2.** a searching look.

scuba ('skju:bə) *n.* an apparatus used in skin diving, consisting of cylinders containing compressed air attached to a breathing apparatus.

scud (skʌd) *vb.* **scudding, scudded. 1.** (esp. of clouds) to move along swiftly. **2.** *Naut.* to run before a gale. ~*n.* **3.** the act of scudding. **4.** spray, rain, or clouds driven by the wind.

scuff (skʌf) *vb.* **1.** to drag (one's feet) while walking. **2.** to scratch (a surface) or (of a surface) to become scratched. ~*n.* **3.** the act or sound of scuffing. **4.** a rubbed place caused by scuffing.

scuffle ('skʌf²l) *vb.* **1.** to fight in a disorderly manner. **2.** to move by shuffling. ~*n.* **3.** a disorderly struggle. **4.** the sound of scuffling.

scull (skʌl) *n.* **1.** a single oar moved from side to side over the stern of a boat to propel it. **2.** one of a pair of small oars, both of which are pulled by one oarsman. **3.** a racing boat propelled by a single oarsman pulling two oars. ~*vb.* **4.** to propel (a boat) with a scull. —'**sculler** *n.*

scullery ('skʌlərɪ) *n., pl.* **-leries.** *Chiefly Brit.* a small room where washing-up and other kitchen work is done.

scullion ('skʌljən) *n. Archaic.* a servant employed to do the rough work in a kitchen.

sculpt (skʌlpt) *vb.* same as **sculpture.**

sculptor ('skʌlptə) *or* (*fem.*) **sculptress** *n.* a person who practises sculpture.

sculpture ('skʌlptʃə) *n.* **1.** the art of making figures or designs by carving wood, moulding plaster, chiselling stone, or casting metals. **2.** works or a work made in this way. ~*vb.* **3.** to carve, cast, or fashion (a material) into figures or designs. **4.** to represent (a person or thing) by means of sculpture. **5.** to form in the manner of sculpture: *her delicately sculptured features.* **6.** to decorate with sculpture. —'**sculptural** *adj.*

scum (skʌm) *n.* **1.** a layer of impure or waste matter that forms on the surface of a liquid: *there was green scum over the pond.* **2.** waste matter. **3.** a worthless person or people. ~*vb.* **4.** to remove scum from. **5.** *Rare.* to form a layer of or become covered with scum. —'**scummy** *adj.*

scumbag ('skʌmˌbæg) *n. Slang.* an offensive or despicable person.

scungy ('skʌndʒɪ) *adj.* **scungier, scungiest.** *Austral. & N.Z. slang.* miserable; sordid.

scunner ('skʌnə) *Dialect, chiefly Scot.* ~*vb.* **1.** to produce a feeling of dislike in. ~*n.* **2.** a strong dislike (often in **take a scunner to**). **3.** an object of dislike.

scupper[1] ('skʌpə) *n. Naut.* a drain or spout in a ship's side allowing water on the deck to flow overboard.

scupper[2] ('skʌpə) *vb. Brit. slang.* **1.** to defeat or ruin: *our plans will be scuppered if he doesn't lend us the money.* **2.** to sink (one's ship) deliberately.

scurf (skɜ:f) *n.* **1.** same as **dandruff. 2.** any flaky or scaly matter sticking to or peeling off a surface. —'**scurfy** *adj.*

scurrilous ('skʌrɪləs) *adj.* untrue or unfair, insulting, and designed to damage a person's reputation: *scurrilous rumours.* —**scurrility** (skə'rɪlɪtɪ) *n.*

scurry ('skʌrɪ) *vb.* **-rying, -ried. 1.** to move about hurriedly. ~*n., pl.* **-ries. 2.** the act or sound of scurrying. **3.** a flurry of rain or snow.

scurvy ('skɜ:vɪ) *n.* **1.** a disease caused by a lack of vitamin C, characterized by anaemia, spongy gums, and bleeding beneath the skin. ~*adj.* **-vier, -viest. 2.** mean or despicable. —'**scurviness** *n.*

scut (skʌt) *n.* the short tail of animals such as the deer and rabbit.

scuttle[1] ('skʌt²l) *n.* same as **coal scuttle.**

scuttle[2] ('skʌt²l) *vb.* **1.** to run with short hasty steps. ~*n.* **2.** a hurried pace or run.

scuttle[3] ('skʌt²l) *vb.* **1.** *Naut.* to cause (a vessel) to sink by making holes in the sides or bottom. **2.** to give up (hopes or plans). ~*n.* **3.** *Naut.* a small hatch in a ship's deck or side.

Scylla ('sɪlə) *n.* **1.** *Gk myth.* a sea monster believed to drown sailors navigating the Straits of Messina. **2. between Scylla and Charybdis.** in a predicament in which avoidance of either of two dangers means exposure to the other.

scythe (saɪð) *n.* **1.** a long-handled tool for cutting grass or grain, with a curved sharpened blade that is swung parallel to the ground. ~*vb.* **2.** to cut (grass or grain) with a scythe.

SD *or* **S.Dak.** South Dakota.

SDI Strategic Defense Initiative.

Se *Chem.* selenium.

SE southeast(ern).

sea (si:) *n.* **1.** (usually preceded by *the*) the mass of salt water that covers three-quarters of the earth's surface. **2. a.** one of the smaller areas of this: *the Irish Sea.* **b.** a large inland area of water: *the Caspian Sea.* **3.** turbulence or swell: *heavy seas.* **4.** anything resembling the sea in size or apparent limitlessness: *a sea of faces.* **5. at sea. a.** on the ocean. **b.** in a state of confusion or bewilderment. **6. go to sea.** to become a sailor. **7. put out to sea.** to embark on a sea voyage.

sea anchor *n. Naut.* a device, usually a canvas-covered frame, dragged in the water behind a vessel to slow it down or reduce drifting.

sea anemone *n.* a marine animal with a round body and rings of petal-like tentacles which trap food from the water.

sea bird *n.* a bird that lives on or near the sea.

seaboard ('siː,bɔːd) *n.* land bordering on the sea.

seaborne ('siː,bɔːn) *adj.* 1. carried on or by the sea. 2. transported by ship.

sea breeze *n.* a breeze blowing inland from the sea.

sea cow *n.* 1. a dugong or manatee. 2. *Archaic.* a walrus.

sea dog *n.* an experienced or old sailor.

seafarer ('siː,fɛərə) *n.* 1. a traveller who goes by sea. 2. a sailor.

seafaring ('siː,fɛərɪŋ) *adj.* 1. travelling by sea. 2. working as a sailor. ~*n.* 3. the act of travelling by sea. 4. the work of a sailor.

seafood ('siː,fuːd) *n.* edible saltwater fish or shellfish.

seagoing ('siː,gəʊɪŋ) *adj.* built for travelling on the sea.

sea-green *adj.* bluish-green.

sea gull *n.* same as **gull** (the bird).

sea horse *n.* a small marine fish with a horselike head, which swims upright.

sea kale *n.* a European coastal plant with broad fleshy leaves and edible asparagus-like shoots.

seal¹ (siːl) *n.* 1. a special design impressed on a piece of wax, lead, or paper, and fixed to a letter or document as a mark of authentication. 2. a stamp or signet ring engraved with a design to form such an impression. 3. a substance, esp. wax, placed over an envelope or container, so that it cannot be opened without the seal being broken. 4. any substance or device used to close or fasten tightly. 5. anything that serves as a pledge or confirmation. 6. a decorative adhesive stamp: *a Christmas seal.* 7. **set one's seal on.** to endorse or approve. ~*vb.* 8. to affix a seal to. 9. to stamp with or as if with a seal. 10. to approve or authorize. 11. (sometimes foll. by *up*) to close or secure with or as if with a seal: *to seal one's lips.* 12. (foll. by *off*) to enclose or isolate (a place) completely. 13. to decide irrevocably: *your fate is sealed.* 14. to close tightly so as to render airtight or watertight. 15. to paint (a porous material) with a nonporous coating. —'**sealable** *adj.*

seal² (siːl) *n.* 1. a fish-eating mammal with four flippers, which lives in the sea but comes ashore to breed. 2. sealskin. ~*vb.* 3. to hunt seals.

sealant ('siːlənt) *n.* any substance, such as wax, used for sealing, esp. to make airtight or watertight.

sea legs *pl. n. Informal.* the ability to maintain one's balance on board ship and to resist seasickness.

sea level *n.* the level of the surface of the sea with respect to the land, taken to be the mean level between high and low tide.

sealing wax *n.* a hard material made of shellac and turpentine, which softens when heated and which is used to make a seal.

sea lion *n.* a large eared seal, often used as a performing animal.

Sea Lord *n.* (in Britain) a naval officer on the admiralty board of the Ministry of Defence.

sealskin ('siːl,skɪn) *n.* the skin or prepared fur of a seal, used to make garments.

seam (siːm) *n.* 1. the line along which pieces of fabric are joined by stitching. 2. a ridge or line made by joining two edges. 3. a stratum of coal or ore. 4. a mark or line like a seam, such as a wrinkle or scar. 5. (*modifier*) *Cricket.* of a style of bowling in which the bowler uses the stitched seam round the ball in order to make it swing in flight and after touching the ground: *a seam bowler.* ~*vb.* 6. to join together by or as if by a seam. 7. to mark or become marked with or as if with a seam or wrinkle. —'**seamless** *adj.*

seaman ('siːmən) *n., pl.* -**men.** 1. a man ranking below an officer in a navy. 2. a sailor.

seamanship ('siːmənʃɪp) *n.* skill in navigating and operating a vessel.

seamstress ('sɛmstrɪs) *n.* a woman who sews, esp. professionally.

seamy ('siːmɪ) *adj.* **seamier, seamiest.** showing the least pleasant aspect; sordid. —'**seaminess** *n.*

seance *or* **séance** ('seɪɒns) *n.* a meeting at which spiritualists attempt to communicate with the spirits of the dead.

seaplane ('siː,pleɪn) *n.* an aircraft that is designed to land on and take off from water.

seaport ('siː,pɔːt) *n.* a town or city with a harbour for seagoing vessels.

sear (sɪə) *vb.* 1. to scorch or burn the surface of. 2. to cause to wither.

search (sɜːtʃ) *vb.* 1. to look through (a place) thoroughly in order to find someone or something. 2. to examine (a person) for concealed objects. 3. to look at or examine (something) closely: *to search one's conscience.* 4. (foll. by *out*) to find by searching. 5. to make a search. 6. **search me.** *Informal.* I don't know. ~*n.* 7. a searching.

searching ('sɜːtʃɪŋ) *adj.* keenly penetrating: *a searching look.* —'**searchingly** *adv.*

searchlight ('sɜːtʃ,laɪt) *n.* 1. a device which projects a powerful beam of light that can be shone in any direction. 2. the beam of light produced by this device.

search warrant *n.* a legal order authorizing a constable to enter and search premises.

Sea Scout *n.* a member of the branch of

the Scouts which gives training in seamanship.

seashell ('siː,ʃɛl) *n.* the empty shell of a marine mollusc.

seashore ('siː,ʃɔː) *n.* land bordering on the sea.

seasick ('siː,sɪk) *adj.* suffering from nausea and dizziness caused by the motion of a ship at sea. —'**sea,sickness** *n.*

seaside ('siː,saɪd) *n.* an area bordering on the sea, esp. one regarded as a resort.

season ('siːz²n) *n.* **1.** one of the four divisions of the year (spring, summer, autumn, and winter), each of which has characteristic weather conditions. **2.** a period of the year characterized by particular conditions or activities: *the rainy season; the holiday season.* **3.** the period during which any particular species of animal, bird, or fish is legally permitted to be caught or killed: *open season on red deer.* **4.** any definite or indefinite period: *the busy season.* **5.** fitting or proper time. **6. in season. a.** (of game) permitted to be killed. **b.** (of fresh food) readily available. **c.** (of animals) on heat. **d.** at the appropriate time. ~*vb.* **7.** to add herbs, salt, pepper, or spice to (food) in order to enhance the flavour. **8.** to add zest to. **9.** (in the preparation of timber) to dry and harden. **10.** to make experienced: *seasoned troops.* **11.** to moderate or temper. —'**seasoned** *adj.*

seasonable ('siːzənəb²l) *adj.* **1.** suitable for the season: *a seasonable Christmas snow scene.* **2.** timely or opportune.

seasonal ('siːzən²l) *adj.* of or depending on a certain season or seasons of the year: *seasonal labour.* —'**seasonally** *adv.*

seasoning ('siːzənɪŋ) *n.* something that is added to food to enhance the flavour.

season ticket *n.* a ticket for a series of events or number of journeys, usually obtained at a reduced rate.

seat (siːt) *n.* **1.** a piece of furniture designed for sitting on, such as a chair. **2.** the part of a chair or other piece of furniture on which one sits. **3.** a place to sit in a theatre, esp. one that requires a ticket: *I have two seats for the film tonight.* **4.** the buttocks. **5.** the part of a garment covering the buttocks. **6.** the part or surface on which an object rests. **7.** the place or centre in which something is based: *a seat of learning.* **8.** a country mansion. **9.** a membership or the right to membership of a legislative or administrative body: *a seat on the Board.* **10.** *Chiefly Brit.* a parliamentary constituency. **11.** the manner in which a rider sits on a horse. ~*vb.* **12.** to bring to or place on a seat. **13.** to provide seats for: *the bus seats fifty people.* **14.** to set firmly in place. **15.** to fix or install in a position of power.

seat belt *n.* a belt worn in a car or aircraft to prevent someone being thrown forward in the event of a collision.

sea urchin *n.* a small sea animal with a round body enclosed in a spiny shell.

seaward ('siːwəd) *adv. also* **seawards. 1.** towards the sea. ~*adj.* **2.** directed or moving towards the sea.

seaweed ('siː,wiːd) *n.* any plant growing in the sea or on the seashore.

seaworthy ('siː,wɜːðɪ) *adj.* (of a ship) in a fit condition for a sea voyage. —'**sea,worthiness** *n.*

sebaceous (sɪ'beɪʃəs) *adj.* of, like, or secreting fat.

sebaceous glands *pl. n.* the small glands in the skin that secrete oil into hair follicles and onto most of the body surface.

sec[1] (sɛk) *adj.* (of wines) dry.

sec[2] (sɛk) *n. Informal.* short for **second**[2]: *wait a sec.*

sec[3] (sɛk) secant.

sec. 1. second (of time). **2.** secondary. **3.** secretary.

secant ('siːkənt) *n.* **1.** (in trigonometry) the ratio of the length of the hypotenuse to that of the adjacent side in a right-angled triangle; the reciprocal of cosine. **2.** a straight line that intersects a curve.

secateurs ('sɛkətəz) *pl. n. Chiefly Brit.* a small pair of shears for pruning.

secede (sɪ'siːd) *vb.* (often foll. by *from*) to make a formal withdrawal of membership from a political alliance, federation, or group.

secession (sɪ'sɛʃən) *n.* the act of seceding. —se'**cession,ism** *n.* —se'**cessionist** *n., adj.*

seclude (sɪ'kluːd) *vb.* **1.** to remove from contact with others. **2.** to shut off or screen from view.

secluded (sɪ'kluːdɪd) *adj.* **1.** kept apart from the company of others: *a secluded life.* **2.** private; sheltered: *a secluded garden.*

seclusion (sɪ'kluːʒən) *n.* **1.** a secluding or being secluded. **2.** a secluded place.

second[1] ('sɛkənd) *adj.* **1.** coming directly after the first in order; often written 2nd. **2.** graded or ranked between the first and third levels. **3.** alternate: *every second Thursday.* **4.** another of the same kind; additional: *a second opportunity.* **5.** resembling or comparable to a person or event from the past: *a second Wagner.* **6.** of subordinate importance or position; inferior. **7.** denoting the lowest but one gear in a motor vehicle. **8.** *Music.* denoting a musical part, voice, or instrument subordinate to or lower in pitch than another (the first): *the second tenors.* **9. at second hand.** by hearsay. ~*n.* **10.** a person or thing that is second. **11.** *Brit. education.* an honours degree of the second class. **12.** the lowest but one gear in a motor vehicle. **13.** (in boxing or duelling) an attendant who looks after a combatant. **14.** (*pl.*) goods of inferior quality. **15.** (*pl.*) *Informal.* a second helping of food. **16.** (*pl.*) the second course of a meal. ~*vb.* **17.** to give aid or backing to. **18.** (in boxing or duelling) to act as second to (a combatant). **19.** to express formal support for (a motion already proposed). ~*adv.* **20.** Also: **secondly.** in the second place.

second² ('sɛkənd) *n.* **1.** 1/60 of a minute of time. **2.** 1/60 of a minute of angle. **3.** a very short period of time.

second³ (sɪ'kɒnd) *vb. Brit.* to transfer (a person) temporarily to another post, position, or job. —**se'condment** *n.*

secondary ('sɛkəndrɪ) *adj.* **1.** coming next after the first. **2.** derived from or depending on what is primary or first: *a secondary source.* **3.** below the first in rank or importance. **4.** of or relating to the education of young people between the ages of 11 and 18: *secondary education.* ~*n., pl.* -**aries.** **5.** a person or thing that is secondary. **6.** a subordinate, deputy, or inferior.

secondary colour *n.* a colour formed by mixing two primary colours.

secondary picketing *n.* the picketing by striking workers of the premises of a firm that supplies or distributes goods to or from their employer.

second-best *adj.* **1.** next to the best. **2.** **come off second best.** *Informal.* to fail to win against someone. ~*n.* **second best.** **3.** an inferior alternative.

second chamber *n.* the upper house of a two-chamber system of government.

second childhood *n.* dotage; senility: *the old dear's in her second childhood and doesn't know what she's saying.*

second class *n.* **1.** the class or grade next in value, rank, or quality to the first. ~*adj.* **second-class.** **2.** of the class or grade next to the best in value, rank, or quality. **3.** shoddy or inferior. **4.** denoting the class of accommodation in a hotel or on a train, aircraft, or ship, lower in quality and price than first class. **5.** (of mail) sent by a cheaper type of postage and taking slightly longer to arrive than first-class mail. ~*adv.* **6.** by second-class mail, transport, etc.

Second Coming *n.* the prophesied return of Christ to earth at the Last Judgment.

second cousin *n.* the child of one's parent's first cousin.

second-degree burn *n. Pathol.* a burn in which blisters appear on the skin.

second fiddle *n. Informal.* a person who has a secondary status.

second floor *n. Brit.* the storey of a building immediately above the first and two floors up from the ground.

second hand *n.* a pointer on the face of a timepiece that indicates the seconds.

second-hand *adj.* **1.** previously owned or used. **2.** not from an original source or one's own experience: *a second-hand report.* **3.** dealing in or selling goods that are not new: *a second-hand car dealer.* ~*adv.* **4.** from a source of previously owned or used goods: *he prefers to buy second-hand.* **5.** not directly or from one's own experience: *he got the news second-hand.*

second lieutenant *n.* an officer holding the lowest commissioned rank in an army or navy.

secondly ('sɛkəndlɪ) *adv.* same as **second¹.**

second nature *n.* a habit or characteristic practised for so long that it seems to be part of one's character.

second person *n.* the form of a pronoun or verb used to refer to the person or people being addressed.

second-rate *adj.* **1.** not of the highest quality; mediocre. **2.** second in importance or rank: *a second-rate citizen.*

second sight *n.* the supposed ability to foresee the future or see actions taking place elsewhere.

second thoughts *pl. n.* a revised opinion or idea on a matter already considered.

second wind (wɪnd) *n.* **1.** the return of normal breathing following strenuous exertion. **2.** renewed ability to continue in an effort.

secrecy ('siːkrɪsɪ) *n., pl.* -**cies.** **1.** the state of being secret. **2.** the ability or tendency to keep things secret.

secret ('siːkrɪt) *adj.* **1.** kept hidden or separate from the knowledge of all or all but a few others. **2.** inclined to secrecy. **3.** operating without the knowledge of outsiders: *a secret society.* ~*n.* **4.** something kept or to be kept hidden. **5.** something unrevealed; a mystery: *the secrets of nature.* **6.** an underlying explanation or reason: *the secret of my success.* **7. in secret.** without the knowledge of others. —'**secretly** *adv.*

secret agent *n.* a person employed in spying, as for a government.

secretaire (,sɛkrɪ'tɛə) *n.* same as **escritoire.**

secretariat (,sɛkrɪ'tɛərɪət) *n.* **1. a.** an office responsible for the secretarial, clerical, and administrative affairs of a legislative body or international organization. **b.** the staff of such an office or department. **2.** the premises of a secretariat.

secretary ('sɛkrətrɪ) *n., pl.* -**taries.** **1.** a person who handles correspondence, keeps records, and does general clerical work for an individual or organization. **2.** the official manager of the day-to-day business of a society, club, or committee. **3.** (in Britain) a senior civil servant who assists a government minister. **4.** (in the U.S.) the head of a government administrative department. —**secretarial** (,sɛkrɪ'tɛərɪəl) *adj.*

secretary bird *n.* a large African long-legged bird of prey with a crest and a tail of long feathers.

secretary-general *n., pl.* **secretaries-general.** the chief administrative official of a legislative body or international organization.

secretary of state *n.* **1.** (in Britain) the head of a major government department. **2.** (in the U.S.) the head of the government department in charge of foreign affairs.

secrete[1] (sɪˈkriːt) *vb.* (of a cell, organ, or gland) to produce and release (a secretion). —**seˈcretory** *adj.*

secrete[2] (sɪˈkriːt) *vb.* to put in a hiding place.

secretion (sɪˈkriːʃən) *n.* **1.** a substance that is released from a cell, organ, or gland. **2.** the process involved in producing and releasing such a substance.

secretive (ˈsiːkrɪtɪv) *adj.* inclined to secrecy. —**ˈsecretively** *adv.*

secret police *n.* a police force that operates secretly to suppress opposition to the government.

secret service *n.* a government agency or department that conducts intelligence or counterintelligence operations.

sect (sɛkt) *n.* **1.** a subdivision of a larger religious or political group, esp. one regarded as extreme in its beliefs or practices. **2.** a group of people with a common interest or philosophy.

sectarian (sɛkˈtɛərɪən) *adj.* **1.** of or belonging to a sect. **2.** narrow-minded as a result of adherence to a particular sect. ~*n.* **3.** a member of a sect. —**secˈtarianism** *n.*

section (ˈsɛkʃən) *n.* **1.** a part cut off or separated from the main body of something. **2.** a part or subdivision of a piece of writing or a book: *the sports section of the newspaper.* **3.** one of several separate parts. **4.** a distinct part of a country or community which make something up. **5.** the act or process of cutting or separating by cutting. **6.** *Geom.* a plane surface formed by cutting through a solid. ~*vb.* **7.** to cut or divide into sections.

sectional (ˈsɛkʃənᵊl) *adj.* **1.** made of sections. **2.** of a section. **3.** concerned with a particular area or group within a country or community, esp. to the exclusion of others.

sector (ˈsɛktə) *n.* **1.** a part or subdivision, esp. of a society or an economy: *the private sector.* **2.** *Geom.* either portion of a circle bounded by two radii and the arc cut off by them. **3.** a portion into which an area is divided for military operations.

secular (ˈsɛkjʊlə) *adj.* **1.** relating to worldly as opposed to sacred things. **2.** not connected with religion or the church. **3.** (of clerics) not bound by religious vows to a monastic or other order. **4.** occurring once in an age or century.

secularism (ˈsɛkjʊləˌrɪzəm) *n.* the belief that religion should have no place in morality or education. —**ˈsecularist** *n., adj.*

secularize *or* **-rise** (ˈsɛkjʊləˌraɪz) *vb.* to change (something, such as education) so that it is no longer connected with religion or the Church. —**ˌseculariˈzation** *or* **-riˈsation** *n.*

secure (sɪˈkjʊə) *adj.* **1.** free from danger or damage. **2.** free from fear, doubt, or care. **3.** in safe custody. **4.** firmly held; stable. **5.** able to be relied on: *a secure investment.* ~*vb.* **6.** to obtain: *I will secure some good seats.* **7.** (often foll. by *against*) to make or become free from danger or fear. **8.** to make fast or firm. **9.** to guarantee (payment of a loan), as by giving security. —**seˈcurely** *adv.*

security (sɪˈkjʊərɪtɪ) *n., pl.* **-ties. 1.** the state of being secure. **2.** assured freedom from poverty or want: *he needs the security of a permanent job.* **3.** precautions taken to ensure against theft, espionage, or other danger. **4.** (*often pl.*) a certificate of ownership, such as a share, stock, or bond. **5.** something given or pledged to secure the fulfilment of a promise or obligation.

security risk *n.* someone or something thought to be a threat to state security.

sedan (sɪˈdæn) *n.* *U.S., Canad., & N.Z.* a saloon car.

sedan chair *n.* an enclosed chair for one passenger, carried on poles by two bearers, commonly used in the 17th and 18th centuries.

sedate[1] (sɪˈdeɪt) *adj.* **1.** calm and composed in manner. **2.** sober or decorous. —**seˈdately** *adv.*

sedate[2] (sɪˈdeɪt) *vb.* to administer a sedative to.

sedation (sɪˈdeɪʃən) *n.* **1.** a state of calm, esp. when brought about by sedatives. **2.** the administration of a sedative.

sedative (ˈsɛdətɪv) *adj.* **1.** having a soothing or calming effect. ~*n.* **2.** *Med.* a sedative drug or agent.

sedentary (ˈsɛdᵊntrɪ) *adj.* **1.** characterized by much sitting and very little exercise: *sedentary work.* **2.** tending to sit about without taking much exercise.

sedge (sɛdʒ) *n.* a coarse grasslike plant growing on wet ground. —**ˈsedgy** *adj.*

sedge warbler *n.* a European songbird of swampy areas, having a streaked brownish plumage with white eye stripes.

sediment (ˈsɛdɪmənt) *n.* **1.** matter that settles to the bottom of a liquid. **2.** material that has been deposited by water, ice, or wind. —**sedimentary** (ˌsɛdɪˈmɛntrɪ) *adj.*

sedition (sɪˈdɪʃən) *n.* speech, writing, or behaviour intended to encourage rebellion or resistance against the government. —**seˈditionary** *n., adj.* —**seˈditious** *adj.*

seduce (sɪˈdjuːs) *vb.* **1.** to persuade to

engage in sexual intercourse. **2.** to lead astray; tempt into wrongdoing. —**seduction** (sɪˈdʌkʃən) n.

seductive (sɪˈdʌktɪv) adj. tending to seduce or capable of seducing; enticing. —**seˈductively** adv. —**seˈductiveness** n.

sedulous (ˈsɛdjʊləs) adj. diligent; painstaking. —**sedulity** (sɪˈdjuːlɪtɪ) n.

sedum (ˈsiːdəm) n. a rock plant with thick fleshy leaves and clusters of white, yellow, or pink flowers.

see¹ (siː) vb. **seeing, saw, seen. 1.** to perceive with the eyes. **2.** to understand: I explained the problem but he could not see it. **3.** to perceive or be aware of: I hate to see you so unhappy. **4.** to view, watch, or attend: I saw a good film last night. **5.** to foresee: I can see what will happen if you don't help. **6.** to find out (a fact): see who is at the door. **7.** (sometimes foll. by to) to make sure (of something) or take care (of something): see that he gets to bed early; don't worry, I'll see to it. **8.** to consider, deliberate, or decide: see if you can come next week. **9.** to have experience of: he had seen much unhappiness in his life. **10.** to meet or pay a visit to: to see one's solicitor. **11.** to receive: the Prime Minister will see the deputation now. **12.** to frequent the company of: she is seeing a married man. **13.** to accompany: I saw her to the door. **14.** to refer to or look up: for further information see the appendix. **15.** (in gambling, esp. in poker) to match (another player's bet) or match the bet of (another player) by staking an equal sum. **16. see fit.** to consider it proper (to do something): I don't see fit to allow her to come here. **17. see you, see you later,** or **be seeing you.** an expression of farewell. ~See also **see about, see into,** etc.

see² (siː) n. the diocese of a bishop or the place within it where his cathedral is situated.

see about vb. **1.** to take care of: he couldn't see about the matter because he was ill. **2.** to investigate: to see about a new car.

seed (siːd) n. **1.** Bot. the mature fertilized part of a plant, containing an embryo ready for germination. **2.** seeds used for growing. **3.** the source, beginning, or origin of anything: the seeds of revolt. **4.** Chiefly Bible. descendants: the seed of Abraham. **5.** Sport. a seeded player. **6. go** or **run to seed. a.** (of plants) to produce and shed seeds after flowering. **b.** to lose vigour or usefulness. ~vb. **7.** to plant (seeds) in (soil). **8.** (of plants) to produce or shed seeds. **9.** to remove the seeds from (fruit or plants). **10.** to scatter certain substances, such as silver iodide, in (clouds) in order to cause rain. **11.** to arrange (the draw of a tournament) so that outstanding teams or

players will not meet in the early rounds. —**ˈseedless** adj.

seedbed (ˈsiːdˌbɛd) n. **1.** an area of soil prepared for the growing of seedlings before they are transplanted. **2.** the place where something develops: a seedbed of discontent.

seedling (ˈsiːdlɪŋ) n. a plant produced from a seed, esp. a very young plant.

seed pearl n. a tiny pearl, often imperfect.

seed pod n. a carpel or pistil enclosing the seeds of a plant, esp. a flowering plant.

seed vessel n. Bot. a dry hollow fruit containing seeds.

seedy (ˈsiːdɪ) adj. **seedier, seediest. 1.** shabby in appearance: seedy clothes. **2.** (of a plant) at the stage of producing seeds. **3.** Informal. physically unwell. —**ˈseediness** n.

seeing (ˈsiːɪŋ) n. **1.** the sense or faculty of sight. ~conj. **2.** (often foll. by that) in light of the fact (that).

see into vb. to discover the true nature of: I can't see into your thoughts.

seek (siːk) vb. **seeking, sought. 1.** (often foll. by for or after) to try to find by searching: to seek a solution. **2.** to try to obtain: to seek happiness. **3.** to try (to do something): I'm only seeking to help.

seek out vb. to search hard for and find (a specific person or thing): she sought out her friend from amongst the crowd.

seem (siːm) vb. **1.** to appear to the mind or eye; give the impression of: the car seems to be running well. **2.** to appear to be: there seems no need for all this nonsense. **3.** to have the impression: I seem to remember you were there too.

seeming (ˈsiːmɪŋ) adj. apparent but not actual or genuine. —**ˈseemingly** adv.

seemly (ˈsiːmlɪ) adj. **-lier, -liest.** proper or fitting.

seen (siːn) vb. the past participle of **see¹**.

see off vb. **1.** to be present at the departure of (a person making a journey). **2.** Informal. to cause to leave or depart, esp. by force.

seep (siːp) vb. to leak slowly as if through small openings. —**ˈseepage** n.

seer (sɪə) n. **1.** a person who can supposedly see into the future. **2.** a person who sees.

seersucker (ˈsɪəˌsʌkə) n. a light cotton, linen, or other fabric with a crinkled surface.

seesaw (ˈsiːˌsɔː) n. **1.** a plank balanced in the middle so that two people seated on the ends can ride up and down by pushing on the ground with their feet. **2.** an up-and-down or back-and-forth movement. ~vb. **3.** to move up and down or back and forth in such a manner.

seethe (siːð) vb. **1.** to boil or to foam as if boiling. **2.** to be in a state of extreme agitation, esp. through anger. —**'seething** *adj.*

see through *vb.* **1.** to help out in time of need or trouble. **2.** to remain with until the end or completion: *let's see the job through.* **3.** to perceive the true nature of: *I can see through your evasion.* ~*adj.* **see-through.** **4.** (esp. of clothing) partly or wholly transparent.

segment *n.* ('sɛgmənt). **1.** one of several parts or sections into which an object is divided. **2.** *Maths.* **a.** a part of a circle cut off by an intersecting line. **b.** a part of a sphere cut off by an intersecting plane or planes. ~*vb.* (sɛg'mɛnt). **3.** to cut or divide into segments. —**seg'mental** *adj.* —ˌsegmen'tation *n.*

segregate ('sɛgrɪ,geɪt) *vb.* **1.** to set apart from others or from the main group. **2.** to impose segregation on (a racial or minority group).

segregation (ˌsɛgrɪ'geɪʃən) *n.* **1.** a segregating or being segregated. **2.** *Sociol.* the practice or policy of creating separate facilities within the same society for the use of a racial or minority group. —ˌsegre'gational *adj.* —ˌsegre'gationist *n.*

seigneur (sɛ'njɜː) *n.* a feudal lord, esp. in France. —sei'gneurial *adj.*

seine (seɪn) *n.* **1.** a large fishing net that hangs vertically in the water by means of floats at the top and weights at the bottom. ~*vb.* **2.** to catch (fish) using this net.

seismic ('saɪzmɪk) *adj.* relating to or caused by earthquakes.

seismograph ('saɪzmə,grɑːf) *n.* an instrument that records the intensity and duration of earthquakes. —**seismographer** (saɪz'mɒgrəfə) *n.* —**seis'mography** *n.*

seismology (saɪz'mɒlədʒɪ) *n.* the branch of geology concerned with the study of earthquakes. —**seis'mologist** *n.*

seismometer (saɪz'mɒmɪtə) *n.* same as **seismograph.**

seize (siːz) *vb.* **1.** to take hold of forcibly or quickly; grab. **2.** (sometimes foll. by *on* or *upon*) to understand quickly: *she immediately seized his idea.* **3.** to affect or fill the mind of suddenly: *alarm seized the crowd.* **4.** to take legal possession of. **5.** to take by force or capture: *the army seized the undefended town.* **6.** to take immediate advantage of: *to seize an opportunity.* **7.** (often foll. by *up*) (of mechanical parts) to become jammed, esp. because of overheating.

seizure ('siːʒə) *n.* **1.** a seizing or being seized. **2.** *Pathol.* a sudden violent attack of an illness, such as an epileptic convulsion.

seldom ('sɛldəm) *adv.* rarely.

select (sɪ'lɛkt) *vb.* **1.** to choose (someone or something) in preference to another or others. ~*adj.* **2.** chosen in preference to others. **3.** limited as to membership or entry; exclusive: *a select gathering.* —se'lector *n.*

select committee *n.* (in Britain) a small committee of members of parliament, set up to investigate and report on a specified matter.

selection (sɪ'lɛkʃən) *n.* **1.** a selecting or being selected. **2.** a thing or number of things that have been selected. **3.** a range from which something may be selected: *a good selection of clothes.* **4.** *Biol.* the process by which certain organisms or individuals are reproduced and survive in preference to others.

selective (sɪ'lɛktɪv) *adj.* **1.** of or characterized by selection. **2.** tending to choose carefully or characterized by careful choice. —se'lectively *adv.* —seˌlec'tivity *n.*

selenium (sɪ'liːnɪəm) *n.* a nonmetallic element used in photocells, solar cells, and in xerography. Symbol: Se

self (sɛlf) *n., pl.* **selves.** **1.** the distinct individuality or identity of a person or thing. **2.** a person's typical bodily make-up or personal characteristics: *she's looking her old self again.* **3.** one's own welfare or interests: *he only thinks of self.* **4.** an individual's consciousness of his own identity or being. ~*pron.* **5.** *Not standard.* myself, yourself, himself, or herself: *seats for self and wife.*

self- *combining form.* used with many main words to mean: **1.** of oneself or itself: *self-defence.* **2.** by, to, in, due to, for, or from the self: *self-employed; self-respect.* **3.** automatic or automatically: *self-propelled.*

self-abnegation *n.* the denial of one's own interests in favour of the interests of others.

self-absorption *n.* preoccupation with oneself to the exclusion of others. —ˌself-ab'sorbed *adj.*

self-abuse *n.* same as **masturbation.**

self-addressed *adj.* addressed for return to the sender.

self-aggrandizement *n.* the act of increasing one's own power, wealth, or importance.

self-appointed *adj.* having assumed authority without the agreement of others: *a self-appointed critic.*

self-assertion *n.* the act of putting forward one's own opinions or demanding one's rights, esp. in an aggressive or confident manner. —ˌself-asˈsertive adj.

self-assurance n. confidence in oneself, one's abilities, or one's judgment. —ˌself-asˈsured adj.

self-catering adj. denoting accommodation in which the tenant provides and prepares his own food.

self-centred or U.S. **self-centered** adj. totally preoccupied with one's own concerns.

self-certification n. (in Britain) a formal assertion by a worker to his employer that absence from work for up to seven days was due to sickness.

self-coloured or U.S. **self-colored** adj. 1. having only a single and uniform colour: a self-coloured dress. 2. (of cloth or wool) having the natural or original colour.

self-confessed adj. according to one's own testimony or admission: a self-confessed liar.

self-confidence n. confidence in oneself, one's abilities, or one's judgment. —ˌself-ˈconfident adj.

self-conscious adj. embarrassed or ill at ease through being unduly aware of oneself as the object of the attention of others. —ˌself-ˈconsciously adv. —ˌself-ˈconsciousness n.

self-contained adj. 1. containing within itself all parts necessary for completeness. 2. (of a flat) having its own kitchen, bathroom, and toilet not shared by others.

self-control n. the ability to control one's feelings, emotions, or reactions. —ˌself-conˈtrolled adj.

self-deception or **self-deceit** n. the act or an instance of deceiving oneself.

self-defence or U.S. **self-defense** n. 1. the act or skill of defending oneself against physical attack. 2. the act of defending one's actions, ideas, or rights.

self-denial n. the denial or sacrifice of one's own desires. —ˌself-deˈnying adj.

self-determination n. 1. the ability to make a decision for oneself without influence from outside. 2. the right of a nation or people to determine its own form of government. —ˌself-deˈtermined adj.

self-discipline n. the act of controlling or power to control one's own feelings, desires, or behaviour. —ˌself-ˈdisciplined adj.

self-drive adj. denoting or relating to a hired vehicle that is driven by the hirer.

self-educated adj. educated through one's own efforts without formal instruction.

self-effacement n. the act of making oneself or one's actions inconspicuous because of modesty or timidity. —ˌselfefˈfacing adj.

self-employed adj. earning one's living in one's own business, rather than as the employee of another.

self-esteem n. respect for or a favourable opinion of oneself.

self-evident adj. so obvious that no proof or explanation is needed. —ˌself-ˈevidently adv.

self-explanatory adj. understandable without explanation; self-evident.

self-expression n. the expression of one's own personality or feelings, as in the creative arts. —ˌself-exˈpressive adj.

self-government n. the government of a country, nation, or community by its own people. —ˌself-ˈgoverning adj.

self-help n. the use of one's own abilities and resources to help oneself without relying on the assistance of others.

self-image n. one's own idea of oneself or sense of one's worth.

self-important adj. having an unduly high opinion of one's own importance. —ˌself-imˈportance n.

self-improvement n. the improvement of one's position, skills, or education by one's own efforts.

self-indulgent adj. tending to indulge one's own desires. —ˌself-inˈdulgence n.

self-interest n. 1. one's personal interest or advantage. 2. the pursuit of one's own interest. —ˌself-ˈinterested adj.

selfish (ˈsɛlfɪʃ) adj. 1. caring too much about oneself and not enough about others. 2. (of behaviour or attitude) motivated by self-interest. —ˈselfishly adv. —ˈselfishness n.

selfless (ˈsɛlflɪs) adj. having little concern for one's own interests. —ˈselflessly adv. —ˈselflessness n.

self-made adj. having achieved wealth or status by one's own efforts.

self-opinionated adj. adhering stubbornly to one's own opinions.

self-pity n. pity for oneself, esp. when greatly exaggerated. —ˌself-ˈpitying adj.

self-possessed adj. having control of

self-cleaning	self-doubt	self-inflicted
self-congratulation	self-examination	self-perpetuating
self-contradictory	self-focusing	self-pollination
self-defeating	self-fulfilling	self-portrait
self-delusion	self-hypnosis	
self-destruct	self-imposed	

one's emotions or behaviour, esp. in difficult situations. —,**self-pos'session** n.

self-preservation n. the instinctive behaviour that protects oneself from danger or injury.

self-propelled adj. (of a vehicle) provided with its own source of power rather than requiring an external means of propulsion. —,**self-pro'pelling** adj.

self-raising adj. (of flour) having a raising agent, such as baking powder, already added.

self-realization n. the fulfilment of one's own potential or abilities.

self-regard n. 1. concern for one's own interest. 2. proper esteem for oneself.

self-reliance n. reliance on oneself or one's own abilities. —,**self-re'liant** adj.

self-reproach n. the act of finding fault with or blaming oneself.

self-respect n. a proper sense of one's own dignity and integrity. —,**self-re'specting** adj.

self-restraint n. restraint imposed by oneself on one's own feelings, desires, or actions.

self-righteous adj. thinking oneself more virtuous than others. —,**self-'righteousness** n.

self-sacrifice n. the sacrifice of one's own interests for the wellbeing of others. —,**self-'sacri,ficing** adj.

selfsame ('sɛlf,seɪm) adj. the very same.

self-satisfied adj. complacently satisfied with oneself or one's own actions. —,**self-,satis'faction** n.

self-sealing adj. 1. (of an envelope) sealable by pressure alone. 2. (of a tyre) automatically sealing small punctures.

self-seeking n. 1. the act or an instance of seeking one's own profit or interest. ~adj. 2. having or showing an exclusive preoccupation with one's own profit or interest: a self-seeking attitude. —,**self-'seeker** n.

self-service adj. 1. of or denoting a shop or restaurant where the customer serves himself and then pays a cashier. ~n. 2. the practice of serving oneself and then paying a cashier.

self-serving adj. habitually seeking one's own advantage, esp. at the expense of others.

self-starter n. 1. an electric motor used to start an internal-combustion engine. 2. a person who is strongly motivated and shows initiative at work.

self-styled adj. using a title or name that one has given oneself, esp. without right or justification: a self-styled expert.

self-sufficient adj. able to provide for or support oneself without the help of others. —,**self-suf'ficiency** n.

self-supporting adj. 1. able to support or maintain oneself without the help of others. 2. able to stand up or hold firm without support, props, or attachments.

self-willed adj. stubbornly determined to have one's own way, esp. at the expense of others.

self-winding adj. (of a wristwatch) having a mechanism which winds itself automatically.

sell (sɛl) vb. **selling, sold.** 1. to exchange (something) for money. 2. to deal in (objects or property): he sells used cars. 3. to give up or surrender for a price or reward: to sell one's honour. 4. to promote the sale of (objects or property): publicity sells many products. 5. to gain acceptance of: to sell an idea. 6. to be in demand on the market: these dresses sell well. 7. **sell down the river.** Informal. to betray. 8. **sell oneself. a.** to convince someone else of one's potential or worth. **b.** to give up one's moral standards for a price or reward. 9. **sell someone short.** Informal. to belittle someone. ~n. 10. the act or an instance of selling: a soft sell. 11. Informal. a hoax or deception. ~See also **sell off, sell out, sell up.** —'**seller** n.

sell off vb. to sell (remaining items) at reduced prices.

Sellotape ('sɛlə,teɪp) n. 1. Trademark. a type of transparent adhesive tape. ~vb. 2. to seal or stick using adhesive tape.

sell out vb. 1. to dispose of (something) completely by selling. 2. Informal. to betray. ~n. **sellout.** 3. Informal. a performance of a play, film, or other form of entertainment for which all tickets are sold. 4. a commercial success. 5. Informal. a betrayal.

sell up vb. Chiefly Brit. to sell all one's goods or property.

selvage or **selvedge** ('sɛlvɪdʒ) n. a specially woven edge on a length of fabric to prevent it from unravelling. —'**selvaged** adj.

selves (sɛlvz) n. the plural of **self.**

semantic (sɪ'mæntɪk) adj. 1. of or relating to the meanings of words. 2. of or relating to semantics.

semantics (sɪ'mæntɪks) n. (functioning as sing.) the branch of linguistics that deals with the study of meaning.

semaphore ('sɛmə,fɔː) n. 1. a signalling device for conveying information by means of lights, flags, or movable arms. 2. a system of signalling by holding a flag in each hand and moving the arms to designated positions for each letter of the alphabet. ~*vb*. **3.** to signal (information) by means of semaphore.

semblance ('sɛmbləns) *n.* outward or superficial appearance.

semen ('siːmɛn) *n.* the thick whitish fluid containing spermatozoa that is secreted by the male reproductive organs and ejaculated from the penis.

semester (sɪ'mɛstə) *n. Chiefly U.S. & Canad.* either of two divisions of the academic year.

semi ('sɛmɪ) *n. Brit. informal.* short for **semidetached** (house).

semi- *prefix.* used with many main words to mean: **1.** half: *semicircle.* **2.** partly or almost: *semiprofessional.* **3.** occurring twice in a specified period: *semiweekly.* **Usage.** see **bi-.**

semiannual (ˌsɛmɪ'ænjuəl) *adj.* **1.** occurring every half-year. **2.** lasting for half a year.

semiarid (ˌsɛmɪ'ærɪd) *adj.* denoting land that lies on the edges of a desert but has a slightly higher rainfall (above 300 mm) so that some farming is possible.

semiautomatic (ˌsɛmɪˌɔːtə'mætɪk) *adj.* **1.** (of a firearm) self-loading but firing only one shot at each pull of the trigger. ~*n.* **2.** a semiautomatic firearm.

semibreve ('sɛmɪˌbriːv) *n. Music.* a note, now the longest in common use, having a time value that may be divided by any power of 2 to give all other notes.

semicircle ('sɛmɪˌsɜːkᵊl) *n.* **1.** one half of a circle. **2.** anything having the shape or form of half a circle. —**semicircular** (ˌsɛmɪ'sɜːkjʊlə) *adj.*

semicolon (ˌsɛmɪ'kəʊlən) *n.* the punctuation mark (;) used to separate clauses or items in a list, or to indicate a pause longer than that of a comma and shorter than that of a full stop.

semiconductor (ˌsɛmɪkən'dʌktə) *n.* a substance, such as silicon, which has an electrical conductivity that increases with temperature.

semiconscious (ˌsɛmɪ'kɒnʃəs) *adj.* not fully conscious. —ˌsemi'consciousness *n.*

semidetached (ˌsɛmɪdɪ'tætʃt) *adj.* **a.** (of a house) joined to another house on one side by a common wall. **b.** (*as n.*): *they live in a semidetached.*

semifinal (ˌsɛmɪ'faɪnᵊl) *n.* the round before the final in a competition. —ˌsemi'finalist *n.*

seminal ('sɛmɪnəl) *adj.* **1.** potentially capable of development. **2.** highly original

and influential: *a seminal artist.* **3.** of semen: *seminal fluid.* **4.** *Biol.* of seed.

seminar ('sɛmɪˌnɑː) *n.* **1.** a small group of students meeting regularly under the guidance of a tutor for study and discussion. **2.** one such meeting.

seminary ('sɛmɪnərɪ) *n., pl.* **-naries.** an academy for the training of priests. —**seminarian** (ˌsɛmɪ'nɛərɪən) *n.*

semiotics (ˌsɛmɪ'ɒtɪks) *n.* (*functioning as sing.*) the study of human communication, esp. communication using signs and symbols. —ˌsemi'otic *adj.*

semipermeable (ˌsɛmɪ'pɜːmɪəbᵊl) *adj.* (of a cell membrane) allowing small molecules to pass through but not large ones.

semiprecious (ˌsɛmɪ'prɛʃəs) *adj.* (of certain stones) having less value than a precious stone.

semiprofessional (ˌsɛmɪprə'fɛʃənᵊl) *adj.* **1.** (of a person) engaged in an activity or sport part time for pay. **2.** (of an activity or sport) engaged in by semiprofessional people. ~*n.* **3.** a semiprofessional person.

semiquaver ('sɛmɪˌkweɪvə) *n. Music.* a note having the time value of one-sixteenth of a semibreve.

semiskilled (ˌsɛmɪ'skɪld) *adj.* partly skilled or trained but not sufficiently so to perform specialized work.

Semite ('siːmaɪt) *n.* a member of the group of peoples who speak a Semitic language, such as the Jews and Arabs.

Semitic (sɪ'mɪtɪk) *n.* **1.** a group of languages that includes Arabic, Hebrew, and Aramaic. ~*adj.* **2.** belonging to this group of languages. **3.** of any of the peoples speaking a Semitic language, esp. the Jews or the Arabs. **4.** same as **Jewish.**

semitone ('sɛmɪˌtəʊn) *n.* the smallest interval between two notes in Western music represented on a piano by the difference in pitch between any two adjacent keys. —**semitonic** (ˌsɛmɪ'tɒnɪk) *adj.*

semitropical (ˌsɛmɪ'trɒpɪkᵊl) *adj.* bordering on the tropics; nearly tropical. —ˌsemi'tropics *pl. n.*

semivowel ('sɛmɪˌvaʊəl) *n. Phonetics.* a vowel-like sound that acts like a consonant, such as the sound of *w* in *well.*

semolina (ˌsɛmə'liːnə) *n.* the large hard grains of wheat left after flour has been milled, used for making puddings and pasta.

sempre ('sɛmprɪ) *adv. Music.* (of a tempo or volume) to be sustained throughout a piece or passage.

SEN (in Britain) State Enrolled Nurse.

---

semiautobiographical
semidarkness
semi-invalid

semiofficial
semipermanent
semiretired

semirigid
semiserious

Sen. *or* **sen.** **1.** senate. **2.** senator. **3.** senior.

Senate ('senɪt) *n.* **1.** the upper chamber of the legislatures of the U.S., Canada, Australia, and many other countries. **2.** the main governing body at some universities.

senator ('senətə) *n.* a member of a Senate. —**senatorial** (ˌsenə'tɔːrɪəl) *adj.*

send (send) *vb.* **sending, sent. 1.** to cause or order (a person or thing) to be taken, directed, or transmitted to another place: *to send a letter.* **2.** (foll. by *for*) to dispatch a request or command for (something): *he sent for a bottle of wine.* **3.** to cause to go to a place or point: *his blow sent the champion to the floor.* **4.** to bring to a state or condition: *this noise will send me mad.* **5.** to cause to happen or come: *misery sent by fate.* **6.** *Slang.* to move to excitement or rapture: *this music really sends me.* —**'sender** *n.*

send down *vb.* **1.** *Brit.* to expel from a university. **2.** *Informal.* to send to prison.

sendoff ('sendˌɒf) *n.* **1.** *Informal.* a demonstration of good wishes to a person about to set off on a journey or start a new career. ~*vb.* **send off. 2.** to dispatch (something, such as a letter). **3.** *Sport.* (of the referee) to dismiss (a player) from the field of play for some offence.

send up *Brit. informal.* ~*vb.* **1.** to make fun of by doing an imitation or parody. ~*n.* **send-up. 2.** a parody or imitation.

senescent (sɪ'nesᵊnt) *adj.* growing old. —**se'nescence** *n.*

seneschal ('senɪʃəl) *n.* a steward of the household of a medieval prince or nobleman.

senile ('siːnaɪl) *adj.* **1.** of old age. **2.** mentally or physically weak or infirm on account of old age. —**senility** (sɪ'nɪlɪtɪ) *n.*

senior ('siːnjə) *adj.* **1.** higher in rank or length of service. **2.** older in years: *senior citizens.* **3.** *Education.* of or designating more advanced or older pupils or students. ~*n.* **4.** a senior person.

Senior ('siːnjə) *adj. Chiefly U.S.* being older than another of the same name: *Charles Parker, Senior.*

senior aircraftman *n.* an ordinary rank in the Royal Air Force.

senior citizen *n. Euphemistic.* an old age pensioner.

seniority (ˌsiːnɪ'ɒrɪtɪ) *n., pl.* **-ties. 1.** the state of being senior. **2.** precedence in rank due to senior status.

senior service *n. Brit.* the Royal Navy.

senna ('senə) *n.* **1.** a tropical plant with yellow flowers and long pods. **2.** the dried leaves and pods of this plant, used as a laxative.

señor (se'njɔː) *n., pl.* **-ñors** *or* **-ñores** (-'njɔːrɛz). a Spanish term of address equivalent to *sir* or *Mr.*

señora (se'njɔːrə) *n.* a Spanish term of address equivalent to *madam* or *Mrs.*

señorita (ˌsenjɔː'riːtə) *n.* a Spanish term of address equivalent to *madam* or *Miss.*

sensation (sen'seɪʃən) *n.* **1.** the power of feeling things physically: *I had lost all sensation in my legs.* **2.** a physical feeling: *a tingling sensation in my left arm.* **3.** a general feeling or awareness: *a sensation of fear.* **4.** a state of general excitement: *his announcement caused a sensation.* **5.** anything that causes such a state: *your speech was a sensation.*

sensational (sen'seɪʃənᵊl) *adj.* **1.** causing or intended to cause intense feelings of shock, anger, or excitement: *sensational disclosures in the press.* **2.** *Informal.* extremely good: *a sensational skater.* **3.** of the senses or sensation. —**sen'sationally** *adv.*

sensationalism (sen'seɪʃənᵊˌlɪzəm) *n.* the use of sensational language or subject matter to arouse intense feelings of shock, anger, or excitement. —**sen'sationalist** *n.*

sense (sens) *n.* **1.** any of the faculties (sight, hearing, touch, taste, and smell) by which the mind receives information about the external world or the state of the body. **2.** the ability to perceive. **3.** a feeling perceived through one of the senses: *a sense of warmth.* **4.** a mental perception or awareness: *a sense of happiness.* **5.** moral discernment: *a sense of right and wrong.* **6.** (*sometimes pl.*) sound practical judgment or intelligence: *take leave of one's senses.* **7.** reason or purpose: *what is the sense of going out?* **8.** general meaning: *he couldn't understand every word but he got the sense of what they were saying.* **9.** specific meaning; definition: *in what sense are you using the word?* **10. make sense.** to be understandable or practical. ~*vb.* **11.** to perceive through the senses. **12.** to perceive or detect without the evidence of the senses: *he sensed that he was being watched.*

senseless ('senslɪs) *adj.* **1.** foolish: *a senseless plan.* **2.** unconscious. —**'senselessly** *adv.* —**'senselessness** *n.*

sense organ *n.* an organ or structure that receives stimuli and transmits them as sensations to the brain.

sensibility (ˌsensɪ'bɪlɪtɪ) *n., pl.* **-ties. 1.** the ability to perceive or feel. **2.** (*often pl.*) the capacity for being affected emotionally. **3.** (*usually pl.*) tendency to be influenced or offended: *his sensibility to criticism.*

sensible ('sensɪbᵊl) *adj.* **1.** having or showing good sense or judgment. **2.** (of clothing) serviceable; practical. **3.** capable of receiving sensation. **4.** capable of being perceived by the senses. **5.** perceptible to the mind. **6.** (sometimes foll. by *of*) aware: *sensible of your kindness.* —**'sensibly** *adv.*

sensitive ('sensɪtɪv) *adj.* **1.** easily hurt;

tender. **2.** responsive to external stimuli or impressions. **3.** easily offended or shocked. **4.** of the senses or sensation. **5.** (of an instrument) capable of registering small differences or changes in amounts. **6.** *Photog.* responding readily to light: *a sensitive emulsion.* **7.** *Chiefly U.S.* connected with matters affecting national security. **8.** (of a subject or issue) liable to arouse controversy or strong feelings. —**'sensitively** *adv.* —**,sensi'tivity** *n.*

sensitize *or* **-tise** ('sɛnsɪˌtaɪz) *vb.* to make sensitive. —**,sensiti'zation** *or* **-ti'sation** *n.*

sensor ('sɛnsə) *n.* a device that detects, measures, or records a physical property such as radiation.

sensory ('sɛnsərɪ) *adj.* of the senses or sensation.

sensual ('sɛnsjʊəl) *adj.* **1.** of the body and senses rather than the mind or soul. **2.** preoccupied with gratification of the senses. **3.** arousing the physical appetites, esp. the sexual appetite. —**'sensualist** *n.*

sensuality (ˌsɛnsjʊ'ælɪtɪ) *n.* **1.** the quality or state of being sensual. **2.** excessive indulgence in sensual pleasures.

sensuous ('sɛnsjʊəs) *adj.* **1.** aesthetically pleasing to the senses. **2.** appreciative of qualities perceived by the senses. **3.** of or derived from the senses. —**'sensuously** *adv.*

sent (sɛnt) *vb.* past of **send.**

sentence ('sɛntəns) *n.* **1.** a sequence of words capable of standing alone to make an assertion, ask a question, or give a command, usually consisting of a subject and a predicate. **2. a.** the decision of a lawcourt, esp. as to what punishment is to be imposed. **b.** the punishment imposed. ~*vb.* **3.** to pronounce sentence on (a convicted person) in a lawcourt. —**sentential** (sɛn-'tɛnʃəl) *adj.*

sententious (sɛn'tɛnʃəs) *adj.* **1.** full of or fond of using proverbs. **2.** given to pompous moralizing. —**sen'tentiousness** *n.*

sentient ('sɛntɪənt) *adj.* capable of perception and feeling. —**sentience** ('sɛnʃəns) *n.*

sentiment ('sɛntɪmənt) *n.* **1.** susceptibility to tender or romantic emotion: *she has too much sentiment to be successful in business.* **2.** (*often pl.*) a thought, opinion, or attitude. **3.** exaggerated or mawkish emotion. **4.** a mental attitude based on a mixture of thoughts and feelings: *there is a strong revolutionary sentiment in this country.* **5.** a feeling conveyed or intended to be conveyed in words.

sentimental (ˌsɛntɪ'mɛntˀl) *adj.* **1.** tending to indulge the emotions excessively. **2.** making a direct appeal to the emotions, esp. to romantic feelings. —**,senti'menta,lism** *n.* —**,senti'mentalist** *n.* —**sentimentality** (ˌsɛntɪmɛn'tælɪtɪ) *n.* —**,senti'mentally** *adv.*

sentimentalize *or* **-lise** (ˌsɛntɪ'mɛntˀ,laɪz) *vb.* to make sentimental or behave sentimentally.

sentimental value *n.* the value of an article to a particular person because of its sentimental associations.

sentinel ('sɛntɪnˀl) *n.* a sentry.

sentry ('sɛntrɪ) *n., pl.* **-tries.** a soldier who guards or prevents unauthorized access to a place.

sentry box *n.* a small shelter with an open front in which a sentry may stand during bad weather.

sepal ('sɛpˀl) *n.* any of the separate parts of the calyx of a flower.

separable ('sɛpərəbˀl) *adj.* able to be separated. —**,separa'bility** *n.*

separate *vb.* ('sɛpəˌreɪt). **1.** to act as a barrier between: *a range of mountains separates the two countries.* **2.** to part or be parted from a mass or group. **3.** to discriminate between: *to separate the men from the boys.* **4.** to divide or be divided into component parts. **5.** to sever or be severed. **6.** (of a married couple) to stop living together. ~*adj.* ('sɛprɪt, 'sɛpərɪt). **7.** existing or considered independently: *a separate problem.* **8.** set apart from the main body or mass. **9.** distinct or individual. —**'separately** *adv.* —**'separateness** *n.* —**'sepaˌrator** *n.*

separates ('sɛprɪts, 'sɛpərɪts) *pl. n.* garments, such as skirts, blouses, and trousers, that only cover part of the body and are designed to be worn together or separately.

separate school *n.* (in certain Canadian provinces) a school for a large religious minority financed by provincial grants in addition to the education tax.

separation (ˌsɛpə'reɪʃən) *n.* **1.** a separating or being separated. **2.** the place or line where a separation is made. **3.** a gap that separates. **4.** *Family law.* an arrangement by which a husband and wife cease to live together.

separatist ('sɛpərətɪst) *n.* a person who advocates secession from an organization or country for his own political, religious, or racial group. —**'separa,tism** *n.*

sepia ('siːpɪə) *n.* **1.** a dark reddish-brown pigment obtained from the inky secretion of the cuttlefish. ~*adj.* **2.** dark reddish-brown.

sepoy ('siːpɔɪ) *n.* (formerly) an Indian soldier in the service of the British.

sepsis ('sɛpsɪs) *n.* poisoning caused by the presence of pus-forming bacteria in the body.

sept (sɛpt) *n.* a clan, esp. in Ireland or Scotland.

Sept. September.

September (sɛp'tɛmbə) *n.* the ninth month of the year.

septennial (sɛp'tɛnɪəl) *adj.* **1.** occurring every seven years. **2.** lasting seven years.

septet (sɛp'tɛt) *n.* **1.** *Music.* a group of seven performers or a piece of music composed for such a group. **2.** a group of seven people or things.

septic ('sɛptɪk) *adj.* of or caused by bacteria. —**septicity** (sɛp'tɪsɪtɪ) *n.*

septicaemia *or* **septicemia** (ˌsɛptɪ-'siːmɪə) *n.* a disease caused by certain microorganisms and their poisonous products in the blood. —ˌ**septi'caemic** *or* ˌ**septi'cemic** *adj.*

septic tank *n.* a tank, usually below ground, in which sewage is decomposed by the action of bacteria.

septuagenarian (ˌsɛptjʊədʒɪ'nɛərɪən) *n.* **1.** a person who is from 70 to 79 years old. ~*adj.* **2.** between 70 and 79 years old.

Septuagint ('sɛptjʊəˌdʒɪnt) *n.* the ancient Greek version of the Old Testament, including the Apocrypha.

septum ('sɛptəm) *n., pl.* **-ta** (-tə). *Biol., anat.* a dividing partition between two tissues or cavities, as in the nose.

septuple ('sɛptjʊpˀl) *adj.* **1.** seven times as much or as many. **2.** consisting of seven parts or members. ~*vb.* **3.** to multiply by seven.

sepulchral (sɪ'pʌlkrəl) *adj.* **1.** suggestive of a tomb; gloomy. **2.** of a sepulchre.

sepulchre *or U.S.* **sepulcher** ('sɛpəlkə) *n.* **1.** a burial vault, tomb, or grave. ~*vb.* **2.** to bury in a sepulchre.

sepulture ('sɛpəltʃə) *n.* the act of placing in a sepulchre.

sequel ('siːkwəl) *n.* **1.** anything that follows from something else. **2.** a consequence. **3.** a novel, play, or film that continues a previously related story.

sequence ('siːkwəns) *n.* **1.** an arrangement of two or more things in a successive order. **2.** the successive order of two or more things: *chronological sequence.* **3.** an action or event that follows another or others. **4.** *Maths.* an ordered set of numbers or other quantities in one-to-one correspondence with the integers 1 to *n.* **5.** a section of a film forming a single uninterrupted episode.

sequential (sɪ'kwɛnʃəl) *adj.* characterized by or having a regular sequence.

sequester (sɪ'kwɛstə) *vb.* **1.** to remove or separate. **2.** to seclude. **3.** *Law.* to confiscate (property) temporarily until creditors are satisfied or a court order is complied with.

sequestrate (sɪ'kwɛstreɪt) *vb. Law.* same as **sequester** (sense 3). —**sequestration** (ˌsiːkwɛ'streɪʃən) *n.* —**sequestrator** ('siːkwɛsˌtreɪtə) *n.*

sequin ('siːkwɪn) *n.* a small usually round piece of shiny metal foil, used to decorate garments. —'**sequined** *adj.*

sequoia (sɪ'kwɔɪə) *n.* a giant Californian coniferous tree.

seraglio (sɛ'rɑːlɪˌəʊ) *n., pl.* **-raglios.** **1.** the harem of a Muslim house or palace. **2.** a Turkish sultan's palace.

seraph ('sɛrəf) *n., pl.* **-aphs** *or* **-aphim** (-əfɪm). *Theol.* a member of the highest order of angels in the celestial hierarchy. —**seraphic** (sɪ'ræfɪk) *adj.*

Serb (sɜːb) *n., adj.* same as **Serbian.**

Serbian ('sɜːbɪən) *adj.* **1.** of Serbia, in Yugoslavia, its people, or their dialect of Serbo-Croatian. ~*n.* **2.** the dialect of Serbo-Croatian spoken in Serbia. **3.** a person from Serbia.

Serbo-Croatian (ˌsɜːbəʊkrəʊ'eɪʃən) *or* **Serbo-Croat** (ˌsɜːbəʊ'krəʊæt) *n.* **1.** the chief official language of Yugoslavia. ~*adj.* **2.** of this language.

serenade (ˌsɛrɪ'neɪd) *n.* **1.** a piece of music played outside a woman's window by a lover. **2.** a piece of music suitable for this. **3.** an orchestral suite for a small ensemble. ~*vb.* **4.** to play a serenade (to).

serendipity (ˌsɛrən'dɪpɪtɪ) *n.* the natural talent for making fortunate discoveries by accident.

serene (sɪ'riːn) *adj.* **1.** peaceful or tranquil; calm. **2.** (of the sky) clear or bright. —**se'renely** *adv.* —**serenity** (sɪ'rɛnɪtɪ) *n.*

serf (sɜːf) *n.* (esp. in medieval Europe) a labourer bound to the land on which he worked. —'**serfdom** *n.*

serge (sɜːdʒ) *n.* a strong twill-weave fabric made of wool, cotton, silk, or rayon, used for clothing.

sergeant ('sɑːdʒənt) *n.* **1.** a noncommissioned officer in the armed forces. **2.** (in Britain) a police officer ranking between constable and inspector.

sergeant at arms *n.* an officer of a legislative body or court responsible for keeping order.

sergeant major *n.* a noncommissioned officer of the highest rank in a military headquarters.

serial ('sɪərɪəl) *n.* **1.** a story published or broadcast in instalments at regular intervals. **2.** a publication that is regularly issued and consecutively numbered. ~*adj.* **3.** of, in, or forming a series. **4.** published or presented as a serial.

serialize *or* **-lise** ('sɪərɪəˌlaɪz) *vb.* to publish or present in the form of a serial. —ˌ**seriali'zation** *or* **-li'sation** *n.*

serial number *n.* any of the consecutive numbers assigned to objects in a series for identification.

series ('sɪəriːz) *n., pl.* **-ries.** **1.** a group or succession of related things, usually arranged in order. **2.** a set of radio or television programmes dealing with the same subject, esp. one having the same characters but different stories. **3.** *Maths.* the sum of a finite or infinite sequence of numbers or quantities. **4.** *Electronics.* an arrangement of two or more components connected in a circuit so that the same current flows in turn through each of them: *a number of resistors in series.* **5.** a set of geological strata that represents the rocks formed during an epoch.

serif ('sɛrɪf) *n. Printing.* a small line projecting from a main stroke in a character.

seriocomic (ˌsɪərɪəʊ'kɒmɪk) *adj.* mixing serious and comic elements.

serious ('sɪərɪəs) *adj.* **1.** grave in nature or disposition: *a serious person.* **2.** in earnest; sincere: *is he serious or joking?* **3.** concerned with important matters: *a serious conversation.* **4.** requiring concentration: *a serious book.* **5.** giving cause for concern: *a serious illness.* —'**seriously** *adv.* —'**seriousness** *n.*

serjeant ('sɑːdʒənt) *n.* same as **sergeant.**

sermon ('sɜːmən) *n.* **1.** a speech on a religious or moral subject given by a clergyman as part of a church service. **2.** a serious talk on behaviour, morals, or duty, esp. a long and tedious one.

seropositive (ˌsɪərəʊ'pɒzɪtɪv) *adj.* (of a person whose blood has been tested for a specific disease, such as AIDS) showing a significant level of serum antibodies, indicating the presence of the disease.

serous ('sɪərəs) *adj.* of, containing, or like serum.

serpent ('sɜːpənt) *n.* **1.** *Literary.* a snake. **2.** a sly or treacherous person.

serpentine[1] ('sɜːpənˌtaɪn) *adj.* **1.** of or like a serpent. **2.** twisting; winding.

serpentine[2] ('sɜːpənˌtaɪn) *n.* a soft green or brownish-red mineral.

serrate *adj.* ('sɛrɪt, -eɪt). **1.** having a notched or sawlike edge. ~*vb.* (sɛ'reɪt). **2.** to make serrate. —**ser'rated** *adj.* —**ser'ration** *n.*

serried ('sɛrɪd) *adj.* in close or compact formation: *serried ranks of troops.*

serum ('sɪərəm) *n.* **1.** the yellowish watery fluid left after the clotting factors have been removed from blood. **2.** antitoxin obtained from the blood serum of immunized animals. **3.** *Physiol., zool.* any clear watery animal fluid.

servant ('sɜːv°nt) *n.* a person employed to work for another, esp. one who does household duties.

serve (sɜːv) *vb.* **1.** to work as a servant for (a person). **2.** to be of service to (a person, community, or cause); help. **3.** to perform an official duty or duties: *he served on the committee for three years.* **4.** to attend to (customers) in a shop. **5.** to provide (guests) with food or drink: *she served her guests with cocktails.* **6.** to provide (food or drink) for customers: *do you serve coffee?* **7.** to provide with something needed

by the public: *the area served by London Transport.* **8.** to meet the needs of: *this will serve my purpose.* **9.** to perform a function: *this wood will serve to build a fire.* **10.** to go through (a due period of service, apprenticeship, or imprisonment). **11.** (of a male animal) to copulate with (a female animal). **12.** *Tennis, squash, etc.* to put (the ball) into play. **13.** to deliver (a legal document) to (a person). **14. serve someone right.** *Informal.* to be what someone deserves, esp. for doing something stupid or wrong. ~*n.* **15.** *Tennis, squash, etc.* short for **service.** —'**server** *n.*

service ('sɜːvɪs) *n.* **1.** an act of help or assistance. **2.** an organization or system that provides something needed by the public: *telephone service.* **3.** the installation or maintenance of goods provided by a dealer after a sale. **4.** availability for use by the public: *the trams are no longer in service.* **5.** a periodic overhaul made on a machine or vehicle. **6.** the serving of guests or customers: *service is included in the price.* **7.** a department of public employment and its employees: *civil service.* **8.** one of the branches of the armed forces. **9.** the serving of food. **10.** a set of dishes, cups, and plates for use at table. **11.** a formal religious ceremony. **12.** *Tennis, squash, etc.* **a.** the act, manner, or right of serving a ball. **b.** the game in which a particular player serves: *he has lost his service.* **13.** (*modifier*) of or for the use of servants or employees: *service door.* **14.** (*modifier*) serving the public rather than producing goods: *service industry.* ~*vb.* **15.** to provide service or services to. **16.** to overhaul (a vehicle or machine). **17.** (of a male animal) to mate with (a female animal). ~See also **services.**

serviceable ('sɜːvɪsəb°l) *adj.* **1.** useful or ready for service. **2.** capable of giving good service. —ˌ**servicea'bility** *n.*

service area *n.* a place on a motorway providing garage services, restaurants, and toilet facilities.

service car *n. N.Z.* a bus operating on a long-distance route.

service charge *n.* a percentage added to a bill in a hotel or restaurant to pay for service.

service flat *n.* a flat where domestic services are provided by the management.

serviceman ('sɜːvɪsmən) *n., pl.* -**men.** **1.** a person in the armed services. **2.** a man employed to service and maintain equipment. —'**service,woman** *fem. n.*

service road *n. Brit.* a narrow road running parallel to a main road that provides access to houses and shops situated along its length.

services ('sɜːvɪsɪz) *pl. n.* **1.** work performed in a job: *your services are no longer required.* **2.** (usually preceded by *the*) the armed forces. **3.** a system of providing the public with something it needs, such as gas or water.

service station *n.* **1.** a place that sells fuel and oil for motor vehicles and often carries out repairs and servicing. **2.** same as **service area.**

serviette (ˌsɜːvɪˈɛt) *n. Chiefly Brit.* a table napkin.

servile (ˈsɜːvaɪl) *adj.* **1.** obsequious or fawning in attitude or behaviour. **2.** of or suitable for a slave. —**servility** (sɜːˈvɪlɪtɪ) *n.*

serving (ˈsɜːvɪŋ) *n.* a portion of food.

servitor (ˈsɜːvɪtə) *n. Archaic.* a servant or attendant.

servitude (ˈsɜːvɪˌtjuːd) *n.* **1.** slavery or bondage. **2.** the state or condition of being completely dominated.

servomechanism (ˈsɜːvəʊˌmɛkəˌnɪzəm) *n.* an automatic system in which feedback is used to compare output to input and any deviations in control are corrected.

sesame (ˈsɛsəmɪ) *n.* a plant of the East Indies, cultivated for its seeds and oil, which are used in cooking.

sessile (ˈsɛsaɪl) *adj.* **1.** (of flowers or leaves) having no stalk. **2.** (of animals) fixed in one position.

session (ˈsɛʃən) *n.* **1.** a meeting of a court, parliament, or council. **2.** a series or period of such meetings. **3.** a school or university term or year. **4.** any period devoted to a particular activity. —**ˈsessional** *adj.*

sestet (sɛˈstɛt) *n.* **1.** *Prosody.* the last six lines of a sonnet. **2.** same as **sextet** (sense 1).

set¹ (sɛt) *vb.* **setting, set. 1.** to put in a certain position or into a specified condition: *to set someone free.* **2.** (foll. by *to* or *on*) to bring (something) into contact with (something else): *he set fire to the house.* **3.** to put into order or readiness for use: *to set the table for dinner.* **4.** to form or be formed into a firm or rigid state: *the jelly set in three hours.* **5.** to put (a broken bone) or (of a broken bone) to be put into a normal position. **6.** to adjust (a clock or other instrument) to a particular position. **7.** to establish: *we have set the date for our wedding; set a bad example.* **8.** to prescribe or assign (a task or material for study): *the examiners have set "Paradise Lost".* **9.** to arrange in a decorative fashion: *she set her hair; a brooch set with rubies.* **10.** to provide music for (a poem or other text to be sung). **11.** *Printing.* **a.** to arrange (type) for printing. **b.** to put (text) into type. **12.** to arrange (a stage or television studio) with scenery and props. **13.** to represent (a scene or story) as happening at a certain time or place: *his novel is set in Russia.* **14.** (foll. by *on* or *by*) to value (something) at a specified price or worth: *he set a high price on his services.* **15.** (of the sun or moon) to

disappear beneath the horizon. **16.** (of plants) to produce (fruits or seeds) or (of fruits or seeds) to develop. **17.** to place (a hen) on (eggs) for the purpose of incubation. **18.** (of a gun dog) to turn in the direction of game. ~*n.* **19.** a setting or being set. **20.** a condition of firmness or hardness. **21.** bearing, carriage, or posture: *the set of a gun dog when pointing.* **22.** the scenery and other props used in a play or film. **23.** same as **sett.** ~*adj.* **24.** fixed or established by authority or agreement: *set hours of work.* **25.** rigid or inflexible: *she is set in her ways.* **26.** unmoving; fixed: *a set expression on his face.* **27.** conventional or stereotyped: *she made her apology in set phrases.* **28.** (foll. by *on* or *upon*) determined to (do or achieve something): *he is set upon marrying.* **29.** ready: *all set to go.* **30.** (of material for study) prescribed for students' preparation for an examination. ~See also **set about, set against,** etc.

set² (sɛt) *n.* **1.** a number of objects or people grouped or belonging together: *a set of coins.* **2.** a group of people who associate with each other or have similar interests: *the tennis set.* **3.** *Maths.* a collection of numbers or objects that satisfy a given condition or share a property. **4.** a television or piece of radio equipment. **5.** *Tennis, squash, etc.* a group of games in a match, of which the winner must win a certain number. **6.** a series of songs or tunes performed by a musician or group on a given occasion: *the set included no new songs.*

set about *vb.* **1.** to start or begin. **2.** to attack.

set against *vb.* **1.** to balance or compare. **2.** to cause to be unfriendly to.

set aside *vb.* **1.** to reserve for a special purpose. **2.** to discard or reject.

set back *vb.* **1.** to hinder; impede. **2.** *Informal.* to cost (a person) a specified amount. ~*n.* **setback. 3.** anything that hinders or impedes.

set down *vb.* **1.** to record in writing. **2.** to judge or regard: *he set him down as an idiot.* **3.** *Brit.* to allow (passengers) to alight from a bus, etc.

set forth *vb. Formal or archaic.* **1.** to state, express, or utter. **2.** to start out on a journey.

set in *vb.* **1.** to become established: *the winter has set in.* **2.** to insert.

set off *vb.* **1.** to embark on a journey. **2.** to cause (a person) to act or do something, such as laugh. **3.** to cause to explode. **4.** to act as a contrast to: *that brooch sets your dress off well.*

set on *or* **upon** *vb.* to attack or cause to attack: *they set the dogs on him.*

set out *vb.* **1.** to present, arrange, or display. **2.** to give a full account of: *he set out the matter in full.* **3.** to begin or embark on an undertaking, esp. a journey.

set piece *n.* **1.** a work of literature, music, or art, intended to create an impressive effect. **2.** a display of fireworks.

set square *n.* a thin flat piece of plastic or metal in the shape of a right-angled triangle, used in technical drawing.

sett *or* **set** (sɛt) *n.* **1.** a small rectangular paving block made of stone. **2.** a badger's burrow.

settee (sɛ'tiː) *n.* a seat, for two or more people, with a back and usually with arms.

setter ('sɛtə) *n.* a large long-haired gun dog trained to point out game by standing rigid.

set theory *n. Maths.* the branch of mathematics concerned with the properties and interrelationships of sets.

setting ('sɛtɪŋ) *n.* **1.** the surroundings in which something is set. **2.** the scenery, properties, or background used to create the location for a stage play or film. **3.** *Music.* a composition consisting of a certain text and music arranged for it. **4.** the metal mounting in which a gem is set. **5.** the tableware and cutlery for a single place at table. **6.** one of the positions or levels to which the controls of a machine can be adjusted.

settle¹ ('sɛt²l) *vb.* **1.** to put in order: *he settled his affairs before he died.* **2.** to arrange or be arranged firmly or comfortably: *he settled himself by the fire.* **3.** to come down to rest: *a bird settled on the hedge.* **4.** to establish or become established as resident: *the family settled in the country.* **5.** to establish or become established in a way of life or job. **6.** to migrate to (a country) and form a community; colonize. **7.** to make or become quiet, calm, or stable. **8.** to cause (sediment) to sink to the bottom in a liquid or (of sediment) to sink thus. **9.** to subside: *the dust settled.* **10.** (sometimes foll. by *up*) to pay off (a bill or debt). **11.** to decide or dispose of: *to settle an argument.* **12.** (often foll. by *on* or *upon*) to agree or fix: *to settle upon a plan.* **13.** (usually foll. by *on* or *upon*) to bestow (a title or property) on a person by gift or legal deed: *he settled his property on his wife.* **14.** to decide (a legal dispute) by agreement without court action: *they settled out of court.*

settle² ('sɛt²l) *n.* a long wooden bench with a high back and arms, sometimes having a storage space under the seat.

settle down *vb.* **1.** to make or become quiet and orderly. **2.** (often foll. by *to*) to apply oneself diligently: *please settle down to work.* **3.** to adopt an orderly and routine way of life, esp. after marriage.

settle for *vb.* to accept or agree to in spite of dissatisfaction.

settlement ('sɛt²lmənt) *n.* **1.** a settling or being settled. **2.** a place newly settled; colony. **3.** subsidence of all or part of a building. **4.** an official agreement ending a dispute. **5.** *Law.* **a.** an arrangement by which property is transferred to a person's possession. **b.** the deed transferring such property.

settler ('sɛtlə) *n.* a person who settles in a new country or a colony.

set to *vb.* **1.** to begin working. **2.** to start fighting. ~*n.* **set-to. 3.** *Informal.* a brief disagreement or fight.

set up *vb.* **1.** to put into a position of power or wealth. **2.** to begin or enable (someone) to begin (a new venture). **3.** to build or construct: *to set up a shed.* **4.** to begin or produce: *to set up a wail.* **5.** to restore the health of: *the sea air will set you up again.* **6.** to establish: *set up a theory.* **7.** *Informal.* to cause (a person) to be blamed or accused. ~*n.* **setup. 8.** *Informal.* the way in which anything is organized or arranged. **9.** *Slang, chiefly U.S. & Canad.* an event the result of which is prearranged.

seven ('sɛv²n) *n.* **1.** the cardinal number that is the sum of one and six. **2.** a numeral, 7, VII, representing this number. **3.** something representing or consisting of seven units. ~*det.* **4.** amounting to seven. —'**seventh** *adj., n.*

sevenfold ('sɛv²n,fəʊld) *adj.* **1.** having seven times as many. **2.** composed of seven parts. ~*adv.* **3.** by seven times as much.

seven seas *pl. n.* all the oceans of the world.

seventeen ('sɛv²n'tiːn) *n.* **1.** the cardinal number that is the sum of ten and seven. **2.** a numeral, 17, XVII, representing this number. **3.** something representing or consisting of seventeen units. ~*det.* **4.** amounting to seventeen. —'**seven'teenth** *adj., n.*

seventh heaven *n.* a state of supreme happiness.

seventy ('sɛv²ntɪ) *n., pl.* -**ties. 1.** the cardinal number that is the product of ten and seven. **2.** a numeral, 70, LXX, representing this number. **3.** (*pl.*) the numbers 70–79, esp. the 70th to the 79th year of a person's life or of a century. **4.** something represented by or consisting of seventy units. ~*det.* **5.** amounting to seventy. —'**seventi-eth** *adj., n.*

sever ('sɛvə) *vb.* **1.** to put or be put apart. **2.** to divide or be divided into parts. **3.** to break off or dissolve (a tie or relationship). —'**severable** *adj.* —'**severance** *n.*

several ('sɛvrəl) *det.* **1.** more than a few: *several people objected.* ~*adj.* **2.** respective; separate: *the members with their several occupations.* **3.** distinct; different: *three several times.*

severance pay *n.* compensation paid by a firm to an employee for loss of employment.

severe (sɪ'vɪə) *adj.* **1.** strict or harsh in the treatment of others: *a severe parent.* **2.**

serious in appearance or manner: *a severe expression; a severe hairstyle.* **3.** serious or dangerous: *a severe illness; a severe shortage.* **4.** causing discomfort by its harshness: *severe weather.* **5.** hard to perform or accomplish: *a severe test.* —**se'verely** *adv.* —**severity** (sɪ'vɛrɪtɪ) *n.*

Seville orange (sə'vɪl) *n.* a bitter orange used to make marmalade.

Sèvres ('sɛvrə) *n.* a kind of fine French porcelain.

sew (səʊ) *vb.* **sewing, sewed; sewn** *or* **sewed. 1.** to join or decorate (pieces of fabric) by means of a thread repeatedly passed through with a needle. **2.** (often foll. by *on* or *up*) to attach, fasten, or close by sewing. ~See also **sew up.**

sewage ('suːɪdʒ) *n.* waste matter that is carried away in sewers or drains.

sewage farm *n.* a place where sewage is treated so that it can be used as manure or disposed of safely.

sewer (suːə) *n.* a drain or pipe, usually underground, used to carry away surface water or sewage.

sewerage ('suːərɪdʒ) *n.* **1.** a system of sewers. **2.** the removal of surface water or sewage by means of sewers.

sewing ('səʊɪŋ) *n.* a piece of fabric or an article, that is sewn or to be sewn.

sewing machine *n.* a machine designed to sew material, with a needle driven by an electric motor, by a foot treadle, or by hand.

sewn (səʊn) *vb.* a past participle of **sew.**

sew up *vb.* **1.** to fasten or mend completely by sewing. **2.** *Informal.* to complete or negotiate successfully: *to sew up a deal.*

sex (sɛks) *n.* **1.** the characteristic of being either male or female. **2.** either of the two categories, male or female, into which organisms are placed. **3.** short for **sexual intercourse. 4.** feelings or behaviour connected with having sex or the desire to have sex. **5.** sexual matters in general. ~*modifier.* **6.** of sexual matters: *sex education.* **7.** based on or arising from the difference between the sexes: *sex discrimination.* ~*vb.* **8.** to ascertain the sex of.

sexagenarian (ˌsɛksədʒɪ'nɛərɪən) *n.* **1.** a person from 60 to 69 years old. ~*adj.* **2.** being from 60 to 69 years old.

sex appeal *n.* sexual attractiveness.

sex chromosome *n.* either of the chromosomes that determine the sex of an animal.

sexism ('sɛksɪzəm) *n.* discrimination on the basis of sex, esp. the oppression of women by men. —**'sexist** *n., adj.*

sexless ('sɛkslɪs) *adj.* **1.** neither male nor female. **2.** having no sexual desires. **3.** sexually unattractive.

sex object *n.* someone, esp. a woman, regarded only in terms of physical attractiveness and not as a person.

sexology (sɛk'sɒlədʒɪ) *n.* the study of sexual behaviour in human beings. —**sex'olo-gist** *n.*

sextant ('sɛkstənt) *n.* an instrument used in navigation for measuring angular distance, as between the sun and the horizon, to enable the position of a ship or aeroplane to be calculated.

sextet (sɛks'tɛt) *n.* **1.** *Music.* a group of six performers or a piece of music composed for such a group. **2.** a group of six people or things.

sexton ('sɛkstən) *n.* a man employed to look after a church and its churchyard.

sextuple ('sɛkstjʊpᵊl) *n.* **1.** a sixfold quantity or number. ~*adj.* **2.** six times as many. **3.** composed of six parts.

sextuplet ('sɛkstjʊplɪt) *n.* one of six children born at one birth.

sexual ('sɛksjʊəl) *adj.* **1.** of or characterized by sex. **2.** (of reproduction) characterized by the union of male and female gametes. —**sexuality** (ˌsɛksjʊ'ælɪtɪ) *n.* —**'sexually** *adv.*

sexual harassment *n.* the persistent unwelcome directing of sexual remarks, looks, or advances, at a woman, esp. in the workplace.

sexual intercourse *n.* the sexual act in which the male's erect penis is inserted into the female's vagina, usually followed by the ejaculation of semen.

sexy ('sɛksɪ) *adj.* **sexier, sexiest.** *Informal.* **1.** provoking or intended to provoke sexual interest: *a sexy dress.* **2.** interesting, exciting, or trendy: *a sexy project; a sexy new car.* —**'sexiness** *n.*

sf *or* **sfz** *Music.* sforzando.

SF *or* **sf** science fiction.

SFA Scottish Football Association.

sforzando (sfɔː'tsændəʊ) *adv. Music.* to be played with sudden emphasis.

Sgt. Sergeant.

sh (*spelling pron.* ʃ) *interj.* be quiet!

shabby ('ʃæbɪ) *adj.* **-bier, -biest. 1.** threadbare or dilapidated in appearance. **2.** wearing worn and dirty clothes. **3.** mean or unworthy: *shabby treatment.* —**'shabbily** *adv.* —**'shabbiness** *n.*

shack (ʃæk) *n.* **1.** a roughly built hut. ~*vb.* **2.** See **shack up.**

shackle ('ʃækᵊl) *n.* **1.** (*often pl.*) a metal ring or fastening, usually in pairs, used to secure a person's wrists or ankles. **2.** (*often pl.*) anything that confines or restricts freedom. **3.** a metal loop or link closed by a bolt, used for securing ropes or chains. ~*vb.* **4.** to confine or fasten with or as if with shackles.

shack up *vb.* (foll. by *with*) *Slang.* to live with (a lover).

shad (ʃæd) *n., pl.* **shad** *or* **shads.** a herring-like food fish.

shade (ʃeɪd) n. 1. relative darkness produced by blocking out sunlight. 2. a place made relatively darker or cooler than other areas by blocking out sunlight. 3. a position of relative obscurity: *his present puts mine in the shade.* 4. something used to provide a shield or protection from a direct source of light, such as a lampshade. 5. a shaded area in a painting or drawing. 6. a colour that varies slightly from a standard colour: *a darker shade of green.* 7. a slight amount: *a shade of difference.* 8. *Literary.* a ghost. ~*vb.* 9. to screen or protect from heat or light. 10. to make darker or dimmer. 11. to represent (a darker area) in (a painting or drawing), by graded areas of tone, lines, or dots. 12. to change slightly or by degrees.

shades (ʃeɪdz) *pl. n.* 1. gathering darkness at nightfall. 2. *Slang.* sunglasses. 3. (foll. by *of*) a reminder: *shades of Robin Hood!*

shading (ˈʃeɪdɪŋ) n. the graded areas of tone, lines, or dots, indicating light and dark in a painting or drawing.

shadow (ˈʃædəʊ) n. 1. a dark image or shape cast on a surface when something stands between a light and the surface. 2. an area of relative darkness. 3. the dark portions of a picture. 4. a hint or faint trace: *beyond a shadow of a doubt.* 5. a weakened remnant: *a shadow of one's past self.* 6. a threatening influence: *a shadow over one's happiness.* 7. an inseparable companion. 8. a person who trails another in secret, such as a detective. 9. (*modifier*) *Brit.* designating a member or members of the main opposition party in Parliament who would hold ministerial office if their party were in power: *shadow cabinet.* ~*vb.* 10. to cast a shade or shadow over. 11. to make dark or gloomy. 12. to follow or trail secretly.

shadow-box *vb. Boxing.* to box against an imaginary opponent for practice. —ˈshadow-ˌboxing n.

shadowy (ˈʃædəʊɪ) adj. 1. dark; shady. 2. resembling a shadow in faintness: *a shadowy figure.* 3. illusory or imaginary.

shady (ˈʃeɪdɪ) adj. **shadier, shadiest.** 1. full of shade; shaded. 2. giving or casting shade. 3. *Informal.* questionable as to honesty or legality. —ˈshadiness n.

shaft (ʃɑːft) n. 1. **a.** a spear or arrow. **b.** its long narrow stem. 2. something directed at a person in the manner of a missile: *shafts of wit.* 3. a ray or streak of light. 4. the handle of a tool. 5. a revolving rod in a machine that transmits motion or power. 6. one of the two wooden poles by which an animal is harnessed to a vehicle. 7. the middle part of a column or pier, between the base and the capital. 8. a vertical passageway through a building, as for a lift. 9. a vertical passageway into a mine.

shag¹ (ʃæg) n. 1. a matted tangle of hair or wool. 2. a napped fabric, usually a rough wool. 3. shredded coarse tobacco.

shag² (ʃæg) n. same as **cormorant.**

shaggy (ˈʃægɪ) adj. **-gier, -giest.** 1. having or covered with rough unkempt fur, hair, or wool: *a shaggy dog.* 2. rough or unkempt. —ˈshagginess n.

shagreen (ʃæˈɡriːn) n. 1. the skin of a shark, used as an abrasive. 2. a rough grainy leather made from certain animal hides.

shah (ʃɑː) n. a ruler of certain Middle Eastern countries, esp. (formerly) Iran.

shake (ʃeɪk) *vb.* **shaking, shook, shaken.** 1. to move up and down or back and forth with short quick movements. 2. to sway or totter or cause to sway or totter. 3. to clasp or grasp (the hand) of (a person) in greeting or agreement: *he shook John's hand.* 4. **shake on it.** *Informal.* to shake hands in agreement or reconciliation. 5. to wave or brandish: *he shook his sword.* 6. (often foll. by *up*) to rouse or agitate. 7. to shock, disturb, or upset: *he was shaken by the news.* 8. to undermine or weaken: *the crisis shook his faith.* 9. *U.S. & Canad. informal.* to get rid of. 10. *Music.* to perform a trill on (a note). 11. **shake one's head.** to indicate disagreement or disapproval by moving the head from side to side. ~*n.* 12. the act or an instance of shaking. 13. a tremor or vibration. 14. **the shakes.** *Informal.* a state of uncontrollable trembling. 15. *Informal.* a very short period of time: *in half a shake.* 16. *Music.* same as **trill¹** (sense 1). 17. short for **milk shake.** ~See also **shake down, shake off, shake up.**

shake down *vb.* 1. to fall or settle or cause to fall or settle by shaking. 2. to go to bed, esp. in a makeshift bed. ~*n.* **shakedown.** 3. a makeshift bed.

shake off *vb.* 1. to remove or be removed with or as if with a quick movement: *she shook off her depression.* 2. to escape from; elude: *they shook off the police.*

shaker (ˈʃeɪkə) n. 1. a container from which a powdered substance is shaken. 2. a container in which the ingredients of alcoholic drinks are shaken together.

Shakespearean *or* **Shakespearian** (ʃeɪkˈspɪərɪən) adj. 1. of William Shakespeare, English dramatist and poet, or his works. ~*n.* 2. a student of or specialist in Shakespeare's works.

shake up *vb.* 1. to shake in order to mix. 2. to reorganize drastically. 3. *Informal.* to shock mentally or physically. ~*n.* **shake-up.** 4. *Informal.* a radical reorganization, such as the reorganization of employees in a company.

shako (ˈʃækəʊ) n., pl. **shakos** *or* **shakoes.** a tall cylindrical peaked military hat with a plume.

shaky (ˈʃeɪkɪ) adj. **shakier, shakiest.** 1.

tending to shake or tremble. **2.** unsound or infirm. **3.** uncertain or questionable: *your arguments are very shaky.* —'**shakily** *adv.*

shale (ʃeɪl) *n.* a soft fine-grained sedimentary rock formed by compression of successive layers of clay.

shall (ʃæl; *unstressed* ʃəl) *vb. past* **should.** used as an auxiliary: **1.** (esp. with *I* or *we* as subject) to make the future tense: *we shall see you tomorrow.* **2.** (with *you, he, she, it, they,* or a noun as subject) **a.** to indicate determination on the part of the speaker: *you shall pay for this!* **b.** to indicate compulsion or obligation, now esp. in official documents. **c.** to indicate certainty or inevitability: *our day shall come.* **3.** (with *I* or *we* as subject) in questions asking for advice or agreement: *what shall we do now? shall I shut the door?*
Usage. The usual rule given for the use of *shall* and *will* is that where the meaning is one of simple futurity, *shall* is used for the first person of the verb and *will* for the second and third: *I shall go tomorrow; they will be there now.* Where the meaning involves command, obligation, or determination, the positions are reversed: *it shall be done; I will definitely do it.* However, *shall* has come to be largely neglected in favour of *will.*

shallot (ʃə'lɒt) *n.* a small, onion-like plant with clusters of round bulbs which are used in cooking for flavouring.

shallow ('ʃæləʊ) *adj.* **1.** having little depth. **2.** lacking depth of intellect or character; superficial. ~*n.* **3.** (*often pl.*) a shallow place in a body of water. —'**shallowness** *n.*

sham (ʃæm) *n.* **1.** anything that is not genuine or is not what it appears to be. **2.** a person who pretends to be something other than he is. ~*adj.* **3.** counterfeit or false. ~*vb.* **shamming, shammed. 4.** to fake or feign (something); pretend: *to sham illness.*

shaman ('ʃæmən) *n.* **1.** a priest of shamanism. **2.** a medicine man or witch doctor of a similar religion.

shamanism ('ʃæmə,nɪzəm) *n.* a religion of northern Asia, based on a belief in good and evil spirits who can be influenced or controlled only by the shamans. —'**shamanist** *n., adj.*

shamble ('ʃæmbºl) *vb.* **1.** to walk or move along in an awkward or unsteady way. ~*n.* **2.** an awkward or unsteady walk. —'**shambling** *adj., n.*

shambles ('ʃæmbºlz) *n.* (*functioning as sing. or pl.*) **1.** a place of great disorder: *the room was a shambles after the party.* **2.** a slaughterhouse. **3.** any scene of great slaughter.

shambolic (ʃæm'bɒlɪk) *adj. Informal.* completely disorganized; chaotic.

shame (ʃeɪm) *n.* **1.** a painful emotion resulting from an awareness of having done something dishonourable, unworthy, or foolish. **2.** capacity to feel such an emotion: *have you no shame?* **3.** ignominy or disgrace. **4.** a person or thing that causes this. **5.** a cause for regret or disappointment: *it's a shame you can't come with us.* **6. put to shame. a.** to disgrace. **b.** to surpass totally. ~*vb.* **7.** to cause to feel shame. **8.** to bring shame on. **9.** (often foll. by *into*) to compel through a sense of shame: *I shamed him into apologizing.*

shamefaced ('ʃeɪm,feɪst) *adj.* **1.** bashful or modest. **2.** showing shame. —**shamefacedly** (ʃeɪm'feɪsɪdlɪ) *adv.*

shameful ('ʃeɪmfʊl) *adj.* causing or deserving shame. —'**shamefully** *adv.*

shameless ('ʃeɪmlɪs) *adj.* **1.** having no sense of shame. **2.** without decency or modesty. —'**shamelessly** *adv.*

shammy ('ʃæmɪ) *n., pl.* -**mies.** *Informal.* same as **chamois** (sense 3).

shampoo (ʃæm'puː) *n.* **1.** a soapy liquid used to wash the hair. **2.** a similar liquid for washing carpets or upholstery. **3.** the process of shampooing. ~*vb.* -**pooing, -pooed. 4.** to wash (the hair, carpets, or upholstery) with shampoo.

shamrock ('ʃæm,rɒk) *n.* a small clover-like plant with three round leaves on each stem: the national emblem of Ireland.

shandy ('ʃændɪ) *n., pl.* -**dies.** a drink made of beer and ginger beer or lemonade.

shanghai ('ʃæŋhaɪ, ʃæŋ'haɪ) *Slang.* ~*vb.* -**haiing, -haied. 1.** to kidnap (a man) for enforced service at sea. **2.** to force or trick (someone) into doing something. **3.** *Austral. & N.Z.* to shoot with a catapult. ~*n.* **4.** *Austral. & N.Z.* a catapult.

shank (ʃæŋk) *n.* **1.** the part of the leg between the knee and the ankle. **2.** a cut of meat from the top part of an animal's shank. **3.** the long narrow part of a tool, key, spoon, or other object.

shanks's pony *or U.S.* **shanks's mare** ('ʃæŋksɪz) *n. Informal.* one's own legs as a means of transportation.

shan't (ʃɑːnt) shall not.

shantung (,ʃæn'tʌŋ) *n.* a heavy silk fabric with a knobbly surface.

shanty[1] ('ʃæntɪ) *n., pl.* -**ties.** a ramshackle hut; crude dwelling.

shanty[2] ('ʃæntɪ) *or* **chanty** *n., pl.* -**ties.** a rhythmical song originally sung by sailors as an accompaniment to work.

shantytown ('ʃæntɪ,taʊn) *n.* a town inhabited by poor people living in shanties.

shape (ʃeɪp) *n.* **1.** the outward form of an object, produced by its outline. **2.** the figure or outline of the body of a person. **3.** organized or definite form: *my plans are taking shape.* **4.** the specific form or guise that anything assumes. **5.** pattern; mould. **6.** condition or state of efficiency: *to be in* *good shape.* **7. take shape.** to assume a definite form. ~*vb.* **8.** (often foll. by *into* or *up*) to receive or cause to receive shape or form. **9.** to mould into a particular pattern or form. **10.** to plan, devise, or prepare: *to shape a plan of action.* ~See also **shape up.**

shapeless (ˈʃeɪplɪs) *adj.* **1.** having no definite shape or form: *a shapeless mass.* **2.** lacking a pleasing shape: *a shapeless figure.* —ˈ**shapelessness** *n.*

shapely (ˈʃeɪplɪ) *adj.* **-lier, -liest.** (esp. of a woman's body or legs) pleasing or attractive in shape. —ˈ**shapeliness** *n.*

shape up *vb. Informal.* **1.** to proceed or develop satisfactorily. **2.** to develop a definite or proper form.

shard (ʃɑːd) *or* **sherd** *n.* a broken piece or fragment of pottery, glass, or metal.

share¹ (ʃɛə) *n.* **1.** a part or portion of something that belongs to or is contributed by a person or group. **2.** (*often pl.*) any of the equal parts into which the capital stock of a company is divided. ~*vb.* **3.** (often foll. by *out*) to divide and distribute. **4.** (often foll. by *in*) to receive or contribute a portion of: *we can share the cost of the petrol.* **5.** to join with another or others in the use of (something): *can I share your umbrella?*

share² (ʃɛə) *n.* short for **ploughshare.**

shareholder (ˈʃɛəˌhəʊldə) *n.* the owner of one or more shares in a company.

shark (ʃɑːk) *n.* **1.** a large, usually ferocious fish with a long body, two dorsal fins, and rows of sharp teeth. **2.** a person who swindles or extorts money from other people.

sharkskin (ˈʃɑːkˌskɪn) *n.* a smooth glossy fabric used for sportswear and petticoats.

sharp (ʃɑːp) *adj.* **1.** having a keen edge suitable for cutting. **2.** tapering to an edge or point. **3.** involving a sudden change in direction: *a sharp bend; a sharp rise in prices.* **4.** moving, acting, or reacting quickly: *sharp reflexes.* **5.** clearly defined: *a sharp contrast.* **6.** mentally acute; keen-witted; attentive. **7.** sly; clever in an underhand way: *sharp practice.* **8.** bitter or harsh: *sharp words.* **9.** shrill or penetrating: *a sharp cry.* **10.** having a bitter or sour taste. **11.** keen; biting: *a sharp wind.* **12.** *Music.* **a.** (of a note) raised in pitch by one semitone: *F sharp.* **b.** (of an instrument or voice) out of tune by being too high in pitch. **13.** *Informal.* stylish: *a sharp dresser.* ~*adv.* **14.** in a sharp manner. **15.** exactly: *six o'clock sharp.* **16.** *Music.* **a.** higher than a standard pitch. **b.** out of tune by being too high in pitch: *she sings sharp.* ~*n.* **17.** *Music.* **a.** an accidental that raises the pitch of a note by one semitone. **b.** a note affected by this accidental. **18.** *Informal.* a cheat; sharper. —ˈ**sharpish** *adj.* —ˈ**sharply** *adv.* —ˈ**sharpness** *n.*

sharpen (ˈʃɑːpˀn) *vb.* to make or become sharp or sharper. —ˈ**sharpener** *n.*

sharper (ˈʃɑːpə) *n.* a person who cheats or swindles; fraud.

sharpshooter (ˈʃɑːpˌʃuːtə) *n.* a skilled marksman.

sharp-tongued *adj.* bitter or critical in speech; sarcastic.

sharp-witted *adj.* having or showing a keen intelligence; perceptive.

shatter (ˈʃætə) *vb.* **1.** to break suddenly into many small pieces. **2.** to impair or destroy: *his nerves were shattered by the torture.* **3.** to dumbfound or thoroughly upset: *she was shattered by the news.* **4.** *Informal.* to cause (someone) to be tired out or exhausted. —ˈ**shattered** *adj.* —ˈ**shattering** *adj.*

shave (ʃeɪv) *vb.* **shaving, shaved; shaved** *or* **shaven** (ˈʃeɪvˀn). **1.** to remove (the beard or hair) from (the face, head, or body) by using a razor or shaver. **2.** to remove thin slices from (wood or other material) with a sharp cutting tool. **3.** to touch (someone or something) lightly in passing. ~*n.* **4.** the act or an instance of shaving. **5.** a tool for cutting off thin slices. **6. close shave.** *Informal.* a narrow escape.

shaver (ˈʃeɪvə) *n.* **1.** an electrically powered razor. **2.** *Informal.* a young boy.

Shavian (ˈʃeɪvɪən) *adj.* **1.** of or like George Bernard Shaw, Irish dramatist, or his works. ~*n.* **2.** an admirer of Shaw or his works.

shaving (ˈʃeɪvɪŋ) *n.* **1.** a thin slice of something such as wood, which has been shaved off. ~*modifier.* **2.** used when shaving: *shaving cream.*

shawl (ʃɔːl) *n.* a piece of woollen cloth worn over the head or shoulders by a woman or wrapped around a baby.

she (ʃiː) *pron.* refers to: **1.** the female person or animal previously mentioned or in question: *she is an actress.* **2.** something regarded as female, such as a car, ship, or nation. ~*n.* **3.** a female person or animal.

sheaf (ʃiːf) *n., pl.* **sheaves.** **1.** a bundle of reaped corn tied together. **2.** a bundle of objects tied together. ~*vb.* **3.** to bind or tie into a sheaf.

shear (ʃɪə) *vb.* **shearing, sheared** *or archaic,* **Austral.,** *&* **N.Z.** *sometimes* **shore; sheared** *or* **shorn. 1.** to remove (the fleece) of (a sheep) by cutting or clipping. **2.** to cut or cut through (something) with shears or a sharp instrument. **3.** *Engineering.* to cause (a part) to deform or fracture or (of a part) to deform or fracture through strain, fatigue, or twisting. **4.** (often foll. by *of*) to strip or divest: *to shear someone of his power.* ~*n.* **5.** deformation or fracture caused through strain, fatigue, or twisting. ~See also **shears.** —ˈ**shearer** *n.*

shears (ʃɪəz) *pl. n.* **a.** large scissors. **b.** a

large scissor-like cutting tool with flat blades, used for cutting hedges.

sheath (ʃiːθ) *n., pl.* **sheaths** (ʃiːðz). **1.** a case or covering for the blade of a knife or sword. **2.** *Biol.* an enclosing or protective structure. **3.** same as **condom**. **4.** a close-fitting dress.

sheathe (ʃiːð) *vb.* **1.** to insert (a knife or sword) into a sheath. **2.** to enclose or encase in a sheath or sheathing.

sheathing (ˈʃiːðɪŋ) *n.* any material used as an outer layer.

sheave (ʃiːv) *vb.* to gather or bind into sheaves.

sheaves (ʃiːvz) *n.* the plural of **sheaf**.

shebeen *or* **shebean** (ʃəˈbiːn) *n. Irish, Scot., & S. African.* a place where alcoholic drink is sold illegally.

shed¹ (ʃɛd) *n.* **1.** a small, roughly made building used for storage or shelter. **2.** a large barnlike structure used for storage, repairing locomotives, or other purposes.

shed² (ʃɛd) *vb.* **shedding, shed. 1.** to pour forth or cause to pour forth: *to shed tears.* **2. shed light on** *or* **upon.** to clarify (a problem or situation). **3.** to cast off or lose: *the snake shed its skin.* **4.** to cause to flow off: *this coat sheds water.* **5.** to separate or divide (a group of sheep).

sheen (ʃiːn) *n.* a gleaming or glistening brightness; lustre.

sheep (ʃiːp) *n., pl.* **sheep. 1.** a cud-chewing mammal with a thick woolly coat, kept for its wool or meat. **2.** a meek or timid person. **3. separate the sheep from the goats.** to pick out the members of a group who are superior in some respects. —ˈsheep-ˌlike *adj.*

sheep-dip *n.* **1.** a liquid disinfectant and insecticide in which sheep are immersed. **2.** a deep trough containing such a liquid.

sheepdog (ˈʃiːpˌdɒg) *n.* **1.** a dog used for herding sheep. **2.** a breed of dog reared originally for herding sheep.

sheepfold (ˈʃiːpˌfəʊld) *n.* a pen or enclosure for sheep.

sheepish (ˈʃiːpɪʃ) *adj.* abashed or embarrassed, esp. through looking foolish. —ˈsheepishly *adv.*

sheepshank (ˈʃiːpˌʃæŋk) *n.* a knot made in a rope to shorten it temporarily.

sheepskin (ˈʃiːpˌskɪn) *n.* the skin of a sheep with the wool still attached, used to make clothing and rugs.

sheer¹ (ʃɪə) *adj.* **1.** perpendicular; very steep: *a sheer cliff.* **2.** (of textiles) so fine as to be transparent. **3.** absolute: *sheer folly.* ~*adv.* **4.** steeply. **5.** completely or absolutely.

sheer² (ʃɪə) *vb.* (foll. by *off* or *away* (*from*)). **1.** to change or cause to change course suddenly. **2.** to avoid an unpleasant person, thing, or topic.

sheet¹ (ʃiːt) *n.* **1.** a large rectangular piece

of cloth, generally one of a pair used as inner bedclothes. **2.** a thin piece of material such as paper or glass, usually rectangular. **3.** a broad continuous surface or layer: *a sheet of water.* **4.** a newspaper. ~*vb.* **5.** to provide with, cover, or wrap in a sheet.

sheet² (ʃiːt) *n. Naut.* a line or rope for controlling the position of a sail.

sheet anchor *n. Naut.* a large strong anchor for use in an emergency.

sheeting (ˈʃiːtɪŋ) *n.* any material from which sheets are made.

sheet metal *n.* metal formed into a thin sheet by rolling or hammering.

sheet music *n.* music printed on unbound sheets of paper.

sheikh (ʃeɪk) *n.* (in Muslim countries) **a.** the head of an Arab tribe, village, or family. **b.** a religious leader. —ˈsheikhdom *n.*

sheila (ˈʃiːlə) *n. Austral. & N.Z. informal.* a girl or woman.

shekel (ˈʃɛkˀl) *n.* **1.** a former coin and unit of weight of the Near East. **2.** (*often pl.*) *Informal.* money.

shelduck (ˈʃɛlˌdʌk) *or* (*masc.*) **sheldrake** (ˈʃɛlˌdreɪk) *n., pl.* **-ducks, -duck** *or* **-drakes, -drake.** a large brightly coloured wild duck of the Old World.

shelf (ʃɛlf) *n., pl.* **shelves. 1.** a thin flat plank of wood or other hard material, fixed horizontally against a wall or in a cupboard, for the purpose of holding objects. **2.** a projecting layer of ice or rock on land or in the sea. **3. on the shelf.** put aside or abandoned; used esp. of unmarried women considered to be past the age of marriage.

shelf life *n.* the length of time a packaged product will last without deteriorating.

shell (ʃɛl) *n.* **1.** the protective outer layer of an egg, fruit, or nut. **2.** the hard outer covering of an animal such as a crab or tortoise. **3.** any hard outer case. **4.** the external structure of a building, car, or ship, esp. one that is unfinished or gutted by fire. **5.** an explosive artillery projectile that can be fired from a large gun. **6.** a small-arms cartridge. **7.** *Rowing.* a very light narrow racing boat. **8. come** (*or* **bring**) **out of one's shell.** to become (*or* help to become) less shy and reserved. ~*vb.* **9.** to remove the shell or husk from. **10.** to bombard with artillery shells. ~See also **shell out.** —ˈshell-ˌlike *adj.*

she'll (ʃiːl; *unstressed* ʃɪl) she will *or* she shall.

shellac (ʃəˈlæk, ˈʃɛlæk) *n.* **1.** a yellowish resin used in varnishes and polishes. **2.** a varnish made by dissolving shellac in alcohol. ~*vb.* **-lacking, -lacked. 3.** to coat with shellac.

shellfish (ˈʃɛlˌfɪʃ) *n., pl.* **-fish** *or* **-fishes.** an aquatic animal, esp. an edible one, having a shell or shell-like covering.

shell out vb. Informal. to pay out or hand over (money).

shell shock n. a neurotic condition characterized by anxiety, depression, and irritability, that occurs as a result of prolonged exposure to battle conditions. —'shell-,shocked adj.

Shelta ('ʃɛltə) n. a cant or jargon, based on Gaelic, used by some tinkers.

shelter ('ʃɛltə) n. **1.** something that provides cover or protection, as from weather or danger. **2.** the protection afforded by such a cover. ~vb. **3.** to provide with shelter; protect. **4.** to take cover, as from rain.

sheltered ('ʃɛltəd) adj. **1.** protected from wind and rain. **2.** protected from outside influences: a sheltered upbringing. **3.** specially designed to provide a safe environment for the elderly, handicapped, or disabled: sheltered housing.

shelve[1] (ʃɛlv) vb. **1.** to place (something, such as a book) on a shelf. **2.** to provide with shelves: to shelve a cupboard. **3.** to put aside or postpone from consideration: to shelve a project. **4.** to dismiss (someone) from active service.

shelve[2] (ʃɛlv) vb. to slope away gradually.

shelves (ʃɛlvz) n. the plural of **shelf.**

shelving ('ʃɛlvɪŋ) n. **1.** material for shelves. **2.** shelves collectively.

shenanigan (ʃɪ'nænɪgən) n. Informal. **1.** (usually pl.) nonsense; mischief. **2.** trickery.

shepherd ('ʃɛpəd) n. **1.** a person employed to tend sheep. **2.** a person, such as a clergyman, who watches over a group of people. ~vb. **3.** to guide or watch over in the manner of a shepherd. —'shepherd-ess fem. n.

shepherd's pie n. Chiefly Brit. a baked dish of minced meat covered with mashed potato.

Sheraton ('ʃɛrətən) adj. denoting furniture made by or in the style of Thomas Sheraton, English furniture maker, characterized by lightness and elegance.

sherbet ('ʃɜːbət) n. **1.** a fruit-flavoured slightly effervescent powder, eaten as a sweet or used to make a drink. **2.** U.S. & Canad. same as **sorbet.**

sherd (ʃɜːd) n. same as **shard.**

sheriff ('ʃɛrɪf) n. **1.** (in the U.S.) the chief elected law-enforcement officer in a county. **2.** (in Canada) a municipal officer who enforces court orders and escorts convicted criminals to prison. **3.** (in England and Wales) the chief executive officer of the Crown in a county, having chiefly ceremonial duties. **4.** (in Scotland) a judge in a sheriff court.

sheriff court n. (in Scotland) a court having jurisdiction to try all but the most serious crimes and to deal with most civil actions.

Sherpa ('ʃɜːpə) n., pl. **-pas** or **-pa.** a member of a Tibetan people living on the southern slopes of the Himalayas.

sherry ('ʃɛrɪ) n., pl. **-ries.** a pale or dark brown fortified wine, originally from southern Spain.

Shetland pony ('ʃɛtlənd) n. a very small sturdy breed of pony with a long shaggy mane and tail.

shibboleth ('ʃɪbə,lɛθ) n. **1.** a slogan or catch phrase, usually considered outworn, characteristic of a particular party or sect. **2.** a custom, phrase, or use of language that reliably distinguishes a member of one group or class from another.

shickered ('ʃɪkəd) adj. Austral. & N.Z. slang. drunk.

shied (ʃaɪd) vb. past of **shy.**

shield (ʃiːld) n. **1.** a piece of defensive armour carried in the hand or on the arm to intercept blows or missiles. **2.** any person or thing that protects, hides, or defends. **3.** Heraldry. a representation of a shield used for displaying a coat of arms. **4.** anything that resembles a shield in shape, such as a trophy in a sports competition. ~vb. **5.** to protect, hide, or defend (someone or something) from danger or harm.

shift (ʃɪft) vb. **1.** to move from one place or position to another. **2.** U.S. to change for another or others. **3.** to pass (blame or responsibility) onto someone else: don't try to shift the blame onto me. **4.** to change (gear) in a motor vehicle. **5.** to remove or be removed: no detergent can shift these stains. **6.** Slang. to move quickly. ~n. **7.** the act or an instance of shifting. **8. a.** a group of workers who work during a specific period. **b.** the period of time worked by such a group. **9.** an expedient, contrivance, or stratagem. **10.** a loose-fitting straight underskirt or dress.

shiftless ('ʃɪftlɪs) adj. lacking in ambition or initiative.

shifty ('ʃɪftɪ) adj. **shiftier, shiftiest.** untrustworthy, furtive, or evasive. —'shifti-ness n.

shillelagh or **shillala** (ʃə'leɪlə, -lɪ) n. (in Ireland) a stout club or cudgel.

shilling ('ʃɪlɪŋ) n. **1.** a former British coin worth one twentieth of a pound, replaced by the 5p piece in 1970. **2.** the standard monetary unit in several E African countries.

shillyshally ('ʃɪlɪ,ʃælɪ) vb. Informal. **-lying, -lied.** to be indecisive; vacillate.

shim (ʃɪm) n. **1.** a thin strip of wood, metal, or plastic, placed between two close surfaces to fill a gap. ~vb. **shimming, shimmed. 2.** to fit or fill up with a shim.

shimmer ('ʃɪmə) vb. **1.** to shine with a faint unsteady light. ~n. **2.** a faint unsteady light. —**'shimmering** or **'shimmery** adj.

shin (ʃɪn) n. **1.** the front part of the lower leg. **2.** Chiefly Brit. a cut of beef including the lower foreleg. ~vb. **shinning, shinned.** **3.** (often foll. by up) to climb (something, such as a rope or pole) by gripping with the hands or arms and the legs and hauling oneself up.

shinbone (ʃɪnˌbəʊn) n. the nontechnical name for **tibia.**

shindig (ʃɪnˌdɪg) or **shindy** (ʃɪndɪ) n., pl. **-digs** or **-dies.** Slang. **1.** a noisy party or dance. **2.** a quarrel or commotion.

shine (ʃaɪn) vb. **shining, shone. 1.** to give off or reflect light. **2.** to direct the light of (a lamp or torch): he shone the torch in my eyes. **3.** (p.t. & p.p. **shined**) to cause to gleam by polishing: to shine shoes. **4.** to excel: she shines at tennis. **5.** to appear clearly. ~n. **6.** the state or quality of shining; sheen; lustre. **7. take a shine to someone.** Informal. to take a liking to someone.

shiner (ʃaɪnə) n. Informal. a black eye.

shingle[1] (ʃɪŋgʰl) n. **1.** a thin rectangular tile laid with others in overlapping rows to cover a roof or a wall. **2.** a woman's short-cropped hairstyle. ~vb. **3.** to cover (a roof or a wall) with shingles. **4.** to cut (the hair) in a short-cropped style.

shingle[2] (ʃɪŋgʰl) n. coarse gravel found on beaches.

shingles (ʃɪŋgʰlz) n. (functioning as sing.) an acute viral disease characterized by painful blisters, often around the waist.

Shinto (ʃɪntəʊ) n. a Japanese religion emphasizing the worship of ancestors and nature spirits. —**'Shintoism** n. —**'Shintoist** n., adj.

shinty (ʃɪntɪ) n. **1.** a game like hockey but with taller goals. **2.** (pl. **-ties**) the stick used in this game.

shiny (ʃaɪnɪ) adj. **shinier, shiniest. 1.** glossy or polished; bright. **2.** (of clothes or material) worn to a smooth and glossy state by continual rubbing.

ship (ʃɪp) n. **1.** a large, seagoing vessel propelled by engines or sails. **2.** short for **airship** or **spaceship. 3. when one's ship comes in.** when one has become successful. ~vb. **shipping, shipped. 4.** to send or transport by any carrier, esp. a ship. **5.** Naut. to take in (water) over the side. **6.** to bring or go aboard a vessel: to ship oars. **7.** (often foll. by off) Informal. to send away: they shipped the children off to boarding school. **8.** to be hired to serve aboard a ship: I shipped aboard a Liverpool liner.

shipboard (ʃɪpˌbɔːd) n. (modifier) taking place on or used aboard a ship: a shipboard computer.

shipbuilder (ʃɪpˌbɪldə) n. a person or company that builds ships. —**'ship,building** n.

shipmate (ʃɪpˌmeɪt) n. a sailor who serves on the same ship as another.

shipment (ʃɪpmənt) n. **1.** goods shipped together as part of the same lot: a shipment of grain. **2.** the act of shipping cargo.

shipper (ʃɪpə) n. a person or company that ships.

shipping (ʃɪpɪŋ) n. **1.** the business of transporting freight, esp. by ship. **2.** ships collectively: there is a lot of shipping in the Channel.

shipshape (ʃɪpˌʃeɪp) adj. **1.** neat; orderly. ~adv. **2.** in a neat and orderly manner.

shipwreck (ʃɪpˌrɛk) n. **1.** the destruction of a ship at sea. **2.** the remains of a wrecked ship. **3.** ruin or destruction: the shipwreck of all my hopes. ~vb. **4.** to wreck or destroy (a ship). **5.** to bring to ruin or destruction.

shipwright (ʃɪpˌraɪt) n. someone, esp. a carpenter, who builds or repairs ships.

shipyard (ʃɪpˌjɑːd) n. a place where ships are built and repaired.

shire (ʃaɪə) n. **1.** a county. **2. the Shires.** the Midland counties of England.

shire horse n. a large powerful cart-horse.

shirk (ʃɜːk) vb. to avoid doing (work or a duty). —**'shirker** n.

shirt (ʃɜːt) n. **1.** a garment worn on the upper part of the body, esp. by men, usually having a collar and sleeves and buttoning up the front. **2. keep your shirt on.** Informal. keep your temper. **3. put one's shirt on something.** Informal. to bet all one has on something.

shirtsleeve (ʃɜːtˌsliːv) n. **1.** the sleeve of a shirt. **2. in one's shirtsleeves.** not wearing a jacket.

shirt-tail n. the part of a shirt that extends below the waist.

shirtwaister (ʃɜːtˌweɪstə) or U.S. **shirtwaist** n. a woman's dress with a tailored bodice resembling a shirt.

shirty (ʃɜːtɪ) adj. **shirtier, shirtiest.** Slang, chiefly Brit. bad-tempered or annoyed.

shish kebab (ʃiːʃ kəˈbæb) n. a dish consisting of small pieces of meat and vegetables threaded onto skewers and grilled.

shit (ʃɪt) Taboo. ~vb. **shitting; shitted** or **shit. 1.** to defecate. ~n. **2.** faeces; excrement. **3.** Slang. rubbish; nonsense. **4.** Slang. an obnoxious or worthless person. ~interj. **5.** Slang. an exclamation expressing anger or disgust. —**'shitty** adj.

shiver[1] (ʃɪvə) vb. **1.** to tremble, as from cold or fear. ~n. **2.** a shivering. **3. the shivers.** a fit of shivering through fear or illness. —**'shivering** n., adj. —**'shivery** adj.

shiver[2] (ʃɪvə) vb. **1.** to break into fragments. ~n. **2.** a splintered piece.

shoal[1] (ʃəʊl) n. **1.** a large group of fish swimming together. **2.** a large group of people or things. ~vb. **3.** to gather or move in such a group.

shoal[2] (ʃəʊl) n. **1.** a stretch of shallow water. **2.** a sandbank or rocky area, esp. one that is visible at low water. ~vb. **3.** to make or become shallow.

shock[1] (ʃɒk) vb. **1.** to cause (someone) to experience extreme horror, disgust, or astonishment: *the atrocities shocked us.* **2.** to cause a state of shock in (a person). ~n. **3.** a sudden and violent jarring blow or impact. **4. a.** sudden and violent emotional disturbance. **b.** something causing this. **5.** *Pathol.* a state of bodily collapse, as from severe injury, burns, or fright. **6.** pain and muscular spasm as the physical reaction to the passage of an electric current through a person's body. —'**shocker** n.

shock[2] (ʃɒk) n. **1.** a number of grain sheaves set on end in a field to dry. ~vb. **2.** to set up (sheaves) in shocks.

shock[3] (ʃɒk) n. a thick bushy mass of hair.

shock absorber n. any device designed to absorb mechanical shock, esp. one fitted to a motor vehicle to reduce the effects of travelling over bumpy surfaces.

shocking ('ʃɒkɪŋ) adj. **1.** causing shock, horror, or disgust. **2. shocking pink.** of a garish shade of pink. **3.** *Informal.* very bad or terrible: *shocking weather.*

shockproof ('ʃɒk,pruːf) adj. capable of absorbing shock without damage.

shock therapy or **treatment** n. the treatment of certain psychotic conditions by injecting drugs or by passing an electric current through the brain.

shod (ʃɒd) vb. past of **shoe.**

shoddy ('ʃɒdɪ) adj. **-dier, -diest. 1.** imitating something of better quality. **2.** of poor quality; shabby: *shoddy treatment.* —'**shoddily** adv. —'**shoddiness** n.

shoe (ʃuː) n. **1.** one of a matching pair of coverings shaped to fit the foot, made of leather or other strong material and usually ending below the ankle. **2.** anything resembling a shoe in shape, function, or position. **3.** short for **horse shoe. 4. be in a person's shoes.** *Informal.* to be in another person's situation. ~vb. **shoeing, shod. 5.** to furnish with shoes. **6.** to fit (a horse) with horseshoes.

shoehorn ('ʃuː,hɔːn) n. a smooth curved implement inserted at the heel of a shoe to ease the foot into it.

shoelace ('ʃuː,leɪs) n. a cord or lace for fastening shoes.

shoemaker ('ʃuː,meɪkə) n. a person who makes or repairs shoes or boots. —'**shoe-,making** n.

shoestring ('ʃuː,strɪŋ) n. **1.** same as **shoe-lace. 2.** *Informal.* a very small amount of money: *the film was made on a shoestring.*

shoetree ('ʃuː,triː) n. a long piece of metal, plastic, or wood, inserted into a shoe or boot to stretch it or preserve its shape.

shone (ʃɒn; *U.S.* ʃəʊn) vb. past of **shine.**

shoo (ʃuː) interj. **1.** go away!: used to drive away unwanted or annoying people or animals. ~vb. **shooing, shooed. 2.** to drive away by or as if by crying "shoo".

shook (ʃʊk) vb. the past tense of **shake.**

shoot (ʃuːt) vb. **shooting, shot. 1.** to hit, wound, or kill with a missile discharged from a weapon. **2.** to discharge (a missile or missiles) from a weapon. **3.** to fire (a weapon). **4.** to send out or be sent out as if from a weapon: *he shot questions at her.* **5.** to move very rapidly. **6.** to slide or push into or out of a fastening: *to shoot a bolt.* **7.** to go or pass quickly over or through: *to shoot rapids.* **8.** to hunt game with a gun for sport. **9.** (of a plant) to put forth (a new growth or sprout). **10.** to photograph or film. **11.** to variegate or streak, as with colour: *his dark hair was shot with streaks of grey.* **12.** *Sport.* to take a shot at the goal. ~n. **13.** the act of shooting. **14.** a new growth or sprout of a plant. **15.** *Chiefly Brit.* a meeting or party organized for hunting game with guns. **16.** an area where game can be hunted with guns. **17.** a steep descent in a stream; rapid. —'**shooter** n.

shooting star n. *Informal.* a meteor.

shooting stick n. a device that resembles a walking stick, having a spike at one end and a folding seat at the other.

shoot up vb. **a.** to grow or increase rapidly: *prices have shot up in the last year; your children have shot up since I last saw them.* **b.** to inject oneself with heroin or another strong drug.

shop (ʃɒp) n. **1.** a place for the retail sale of goods and services. **2.** a place where a specified type of work is done; workshop: *printing shop.* **3. all over the shop.** *Informal.* scattered everywhere: *his papers were all over the shop.* **4. shut up shop.** to close business at the end of the day or permanently. **5. talk shop.** *Informal.* to discuss one's business or work, esp. on a social occasion. ~vb. **shopping, shopped. 6.** (often foll. by *for*) to visit a shop or shops in order to buy (goods). **7.** *Slang, chiefly Brit.* to inform on (someone), esp. to the police. —'**shopper** n.

shop around vb. *Informal.* **1.** to visit a number of shops or stores to compare goods and prices. **2.** to consider a number of possibilities before making a choice.

shop assistant n. a person who serves in a shop.

shop floor n. **1.** the production area of a factory. **2.** workers, esp. factory workers, as opposed to management.

shopkeeper ('ʃɒp,kiːpə) n. a person who

owns or manages a shop. —'shop-
,keeping n.

shoplifter ('ʃɒpˌlɪftə) n. a customer who
steals goods from a shop. —'shop,lifting n.

shopping ('ʃɒpɪŋ) n. 1. the act of going to
shops and buying things. 2. things that
have been bought in shops.

shopping centre n. 1. the area of a
town where most of the shops are situated.
2. a complex of stores, restaurants, and
sometimes banks, usually under the same
roof.

shopping mall n. Chiefly U.S., Canad., &
Austral. a large enclosed shopping centre.

shopping plaza n. Chiefly U.S. & Canad.
a shopping centre, usually a small group of
stores built as a strip.

shopsoiled ('ʃɒpˌsɔɪld) adj. soiled or faded,
from being displayed in a shop.

shop steward n. a trade-union official
elected by his fellow workers to be their
representative in dealing with their employer.

shoptalk ('ʃɒpˌtɔːk) n. conversation concerning one's work, carried on outside
working hours.

shopwalker ('ʃɒpˌwɔːkə) n. Brit. a person
employed by a department store to supervise sales personnel and assist customers.

shore[1] (ʃɔː) n. 1. the land along the edge of
a sea, lake, or wide river. 2. land, as opposed to water: fifty yards from shore. 3.
(pl.) a country: his native shores.

shore[2] (ʃɔː) n. 1. a prop placed under or
against something as a support. ~vb. 2.
(foll. by up) to make (something) safe with
or as if with a shore.

shoreline ('ʃɔːˌlaɪn) n. the edge of a sea,
lake, or wide river.

shorn (ʃɔːn) vb. a past participle of **shear**.

short (ʃɔːt) adj. 1. of little length; not long.
2. of little height; not tall. 3. of limited
duration. 4. deficient: the number of places
laid at the table was short by four. 5. (foll.
by of or on) lacking in: short of money;
short on talent. 6. concise; succinct: the
short answer is no. 7. (of drinks) consisting chiefly of a spirit, such as whisky. 8.
(of someone's memory) lacking the ability
to retain a lot of facts. 9. abrupt to the
point of rudeness: the salesman was very
short with me. 10. (of betting odds) almost
even. 11. Finance. a. not possessing at the
time of sale the stocks or commodities one
sells. b. relating to such sales, which depend on falling prices for profit. 12. Phonetics. (of a vowel) of relatively brief duration. 13. (of pastry) crumbly in texture.
14. in short supply. scarce. 15. short and
sweet. brief and to the point; pertinent.
16. short for. a shortened form of. ~adv.
17. abruptly: to stop short. 18. be caught
short. to have a sudden need to go to the
toilet. 19. go short. not to have enough.

20. short of. except: nothing short of a
miracle can save him now. ~n. 21. a drink
of spirits. 22. a short film shown before
the main feature in a cinema. 23. same as
short circuit. 24. for short. Informal. as a
shortened form: he is called J.R. for short.
25. in short. briefly. ~vb. 26. to short-
circuit. ~See also **shorts**. —'**shortness** n.

shortage ('ʃɔːtɪdʒ) n. a deficiency of something needed.

shortbread ('ʃɔːtˌbrɛd) n. a rich crumbly
biscuit made with a large proportion of
butter.

shortcake ('ʃɔːtˌkeɪk) n. 1. shortbread. 2.
a dessert made of layers of biscuit or cake
filled with fruit and cream.

short-change vb. 1. to give (someone)
less than the correct change. 2. Slang. to
cheat or swindle (someone).

short circuit n. 1. a faulty or accidental
connection between two points of different
potential in an electric circuit, creating a
path of low resistance through which the
current is deflected, usually causing failure
of the circuit. ~vb. **short-circuit**. 2. to
develop a short circuit. 3. to bypass (a
procedure). 4. to hinder or frustrate (a
plan).

shortcoming ('ʃɔːtˌkʌmɪŋ) n. a failing or
defect.

shortcrust pastry ('ʃɔːtˌkrʌst) n. a type of
pastry with a crisp but crumbly texture.

short cut n. 1. a route that is shorter
than the usual one. 2. a means of saving
time or effort.

shorten ('ʃɔːt²n) vb. to make or become
short or shorter.

shortening ('ʃɔːt²nɪŋ) n. butter or other fat,
used in pastry to make it crumbly.

shortfall ('ʃɔːtˌfɔːl) n. 1. failure to meet a
requirement. 2. the amount of such a failure.

shorthand ('ʃɔːtˌhænd) n. a system of rapid
writing using simple strokes and other symbols to represent words or phrases.

shorthand typist n. Brit. a person skilled
in the use of shorthand and in typing.

shorthorn ('ʃɔːtˌhɔːn) n. a member of a
breed of cattle with short horns.

short list Chiefly Brit. ~n. 1. Also
called (Scot.): **short leet**. a list of suitable
candidates for a job or prize, from which
the successful candidate will be selected.
~vb. **short-list**. 2. to put (someone) on a
short list.

short-lived adj. lasting only for a short
time: his success was short-lived.

shortly ('ʃɔːtlɪ) adv. 1. in a short time;
soon. 2. in a curt or rude manner.

shorts (ʃɔːts) pl. n. 1. trousers reaching the
top of the thigh or partway to the knee. 2.
Chiefly U.S. & Canad. men's underpants.

short shrift n. brief and unsympathetic
treatment.

short-sighted *adj.* **1.** unable to see far-away things clearly. **2.** lacking foresight: *a short-sighted plan.* **—,short-'sighted-ness** *n.*

short-tempered *adj.* easily angered.

short-term *adj.* of, for, or lasting a short time.

short wave *n.* a radio wave with a wavelength in the range 10–100 metres.

short-winded *adj.* tending to run out of breath easily.

shot¹ (ʃɒt) *n.* **1.** the act or an instance of firing a gun or rifle. **2.** small round pellets of lead collectively, as used in shotguns. **3.** a person who shoots, with regard to his ability: *he is a good shot.* **4.** *Informal.* an attempt: *I had a shot at changing the wheel.* **5.** *Informal.* a guess. **6.** *Sport.* the act or an instance of hitting, kicking, or throwing the ball. **7.** the launching of a rocket or spacecraft to a specified destination: *a moon shot.* **8. a.** a single photograph. **b.** an uninterrupted sequence of film taken by a single camera. **9.** *Informal.* an injection of a vaccine or narcotic drug. **10.** *Informal.* a drink of spirits. **11.** *Sport.* a heavy metal ball used in the shot put. **12. like a shot.** without hesitating. **13. shot in the arm.** *Informal.* something that brings back energy or confidence. **14. shot in the dark.** a wild guess.

shot² (ʃɒt) *vb.* **1.** past of **shoot.** *~adj.* **2.** (of textiles) woven to give a changing colour effect. **3.** streaked with colour.

shotgun (ˈʃɒtˌgʌn) *n.* a gun for firing a charge of shot at short range, used for hunting small game.

shot put *n.* an athletic event in which contestants hurl a heavy metal ball called a shot as far as possible. **—'shot-,putter** *n.*

should (ʃʊd) *vb.* the past tense of **shall:** used to indicate that an action is considered by the speaker to be obligatory (*you should go*) or to form the subjunctive mood (*I should like to see you; if I should die; should I be late, start without me.*).
Usage. **Should** has, as its most common meaning in modern English, the sense *ought to* as in *I should go to the party, but I don't see how I can.* However, the older sense of the subjunctive of *shall* is often used with *I* or *we* to indicate a more polite form than *would: I should like to go, but I can't.*

shoulder (ˈʃəʊldə) *n.* **1.** the part of the body where the arm, wing, or foreleg joins the trunk. **2.** a cut of meat including the upper part of the foreleg. **3.** the part of a garment that covers the shoulder. **4.** the strip of unpaved land that borders a road. **5. a shoulder to cry on.** a person one turns to for sympathy with one's troubles. **6. put one's shoulder to the wheel.** *Informal.* to work very hard. **7. rub shoulders with someone.** *Informal.* to mix with someone socially. **8. shoulder to shoulder. a.** side

by side. **b.** working together. *~vb.* **9.** to bear (a burden or responsibility). **10.** to push with one's shoulder: *he shouldered his way through the crowd.* **11.** to lift or carry on one's shoulders. **12. shoulder arms.** *Mil.* to bring one's rifle vertically close to one's right side with the muzzle uppermost.

shoulder blade *n.* either of two large flat triangular bones one on each side of the back part of the shoulder.

shoulder strap *n.* a strap worn over the shoulder to hold up a garment or to support a bag.

shouldn't (ˈʃʊdᵊnt) should not.

shout (ʃaʊt) *n.* **1.** a loud cry, often to convey emotion or a command. **2.** *Informal.* one's turn to buy a round of drinks. *~vb.* **3.** to cry out loudly. **4.** *Austral. & N.Z. informal.* to treat (someone) to (something, such as a round of drinks).

shout down *vb.* to silence (someone) by talking loudly.

shove (ʃʌv) *vb.* **1.** to give a violent push to. **2.** to push (one's way) roughly. **3.** *Informal.* to put (something) somewhere quickly and carelessly: *shove it in the bin.* *~n.* **4.** an instance of shoving.

shovel (ˈʃʌvᵊl) *n.* **1.** a tool for lifting or moving loose material, consisting of a broad blade attached to a large handle. **2.** a machine or part of a machine resembling a shovel in function. *~vb.* **-elling, -elled** *or U.S.* **-eling, -eled.** **3.** to lift or move (loose material) with a shovel. **4.** to put away large quantities of (something) in a hurried manner: *he shovelled food into his mouth.*

shove off *vb.* *Informal.* to go away; depart.

show (ʃəʊ) *vb.* **showing, showed; shown** *or* **showed.** **1.** to make, be, or become visible or noticeable: *to show one's dislike; his anger showed.* **2.** to present for inspection: *he showed me a picture.* **3.** to demonstrate or prove: *to show that the earth moves round the sun.* **4.** to instruct by demonstration: *show me how to swim.* **5.** to indicate: *a barometer shows changes in the weather.* **6.** to grant or bestow: *to show favour to someone.* **7.** to exhibit or display (works of art): *three artists are showing at the gallery.* **8.** to present (a film or play) or (of a film or play) to be presented. **9.** to guide or escort: *please show me to my room.* **10.** *Informal.* to arrive. *~n.* **11.** a display or exhibition. **12.** a public spectacle. **13.** pretence; mere display. **14.** a theatrical or other entertainment. **15.** *Slang, chiefly Brit.* a thing or affair: *a poor show.* *~See also* **show off, show up.**

show business *n.* the entertainment industry. Also (informal): **show biz.**

showcase (ˈʃəʊˌkeɪs) *n.* **1.** a glass case used to display objects in a museum or shop. **2.** a setting in which anything may be displayed to best advantage.

showdown ('ʃəʊˌdaʊn) *n. Informal.* a confrontation that settles a dispute.

shower ('ʃaʊə) *n.* **1.** a brief period of rain, hail, sleet, or snow. **2.** a sudden abundant fall of objects: *a shower of sparks.* **3. a.** a kind of bath in which a person stands upright and is sprayed with water from a nozzle. **b.** a device, room, or booth for such a bath. **4.** *Brit. slang.* a contemptible group of people. **5.** *U.S., Canad., Austral., & N.Z.* a party held to honour and present gifts to a prospective bride or prospective mother. ~*vb.* **6.** to sprinkle with or as if with a shower. **7.** to give (things) in abundance or present (a person) with things in abundance. **8.** to take a shower. —'**showery** *adj.*

showing ('ʃəʊɪŋ) *n.* **1.** a presentation, exhibition, or display. **2.** manner of presentation.

showjumping ('ʃəʊˌdʒʌmpɪŋ) *n.* the sport of riding horses in competitions to demonstrate skill in jumping. —'**show,jumper** *n.*

showman ('ʃəʊmən) *n., pl.* -**men. 1.** a person who presents or produces a show. **2.** a person skilled at presenting anything in an effective manner. —'**showmanship** *n.*

shown (ʃəʊn) *vb.* a past participle of **show.**

show off *vb.* **1.** to exhibit or display (something) so as to invite admiration. **2.** *Informal.* to behave flamboyantly in an attempt to attract attention. ~*n.* **show-off. 3.** *Informal.* a person who behaves flamboyantly in an attempt to attract attention.

showpiece ('ʃəʊˌpiːs) *n.* **1.** anything displayed or exhibited. **2.** anything prized as a fine example of its type.

showplace ('ʃəʊˌpleɪs) *n.* a place visited for its beauty or interest.

showroom ('ʃəʊˌruːm) *n.* a room in which goods for sale are on display.

show up *vb.* **1.** to reveal or be revealed clearly. **2.** to expose the faults or defects of (someone or something) by comparison. **3.** *Informal.* to put (someone) to shame; embarrass. **4.** *Informal.* to arrive.

showy ('ʃəʊɪ) *adj.* **showier, showiest. 1.** gaudy or ostentatious. **2.** making an imposing display. —'**showily** *adv.* —'**showiness** *n.*

shrank (ʃræŋk) *vb.* a past tense of **shrink.**

shrapnel ('ʃræpn'l) *n.* **1.** an artillery shell containing a number of small pellets or bullets which it is designed to scatter on explosion. **2.** fragments from this type of shell.

shred (ʃrɛd) *n.* **1.** a long narrow piece torn off something. **2.** a very small amount: *not a shred of evidence.* ~*vb.* **shredding, shredded** *or* **shred. 3.** to tear into shreds. —'**shredder** *n.*

shrew (ʃruː) *n.* **1.** a small mouselike animal with a long snout. **2.** a bad-tempered woman. —'**shrewish** *adj.*

shrewd (ʃruːd) *adj.* clever and perceptive. —'**shrewdly** *adv.* —'**shrewdness** *n.*

shriek (ʃriːk) *n.* **1.** a shrill and piercing cry. ~*vb.* **2.** to utter (words or sounds) in a shrill piercing tone.

shrift (ʃrɪft) *n.* See **short shrift.**

shrike (ʃraɪk) *n.* a bird with a heavy hooked bill, which impales small animals on thorns.

shrill (ʃrɪl) *adj.* **1.** (of a sound) sharp and high-pitched. ~*vb.* **2.** to utter (words or sounds) in a shrill tone. —'**shrillness** *n.* —'**shrilly** *adv.*

shrimp (ʃrɪmp) *n.* **1.** a small edible shellfish with a long tail and a pair of pincers. **2.** *Informal.* a small person. ~*vb.* **3.** to fish for shrimps.

shrine (ʃraɪn) *n.* **1.** a place of worship associated with a sacred person or object. **2.** a container for sacred relics. **3.** the tomb of a saint or other holy person. **4.** a place that is visited and honoured because of its association with a famous person or event.

shrink (ʃrɪŋk) *vb.* **shrinking; shrank** *or* **shrunk; shrunk** *or* **shrunken. 1.** to become or cause to become smaller, sometimes because of wetness, heat, or cold. **2.** (foll. by *from*) **a.** to recoil or withdraw: *to shrink from the sight of blood.* **b.** to feel great reluctance (to perform a task or duty). ~*n.* **3.** *Slang.* a psychiatrist.

shrinkage ('ʃrɪŋkɪdʒ) *n.* **1.** the fact of shrinking. **2.** the amount by which anything decreases in size, value, or weight.

shrink-wrap *vb.* **-wrapping, -wrapped.** to package (a product) in a flexible plastic wrapping which shrinks about its contours to seal it.

shrivel ('ʃrɪv'l) *vb.* **-elling, -elled** *or* *U.S.* **-eling, -eled.** to make or become shrunken and withered.

shroud (ʃraʊd) *n.* **1.** a piece of cloth used to wrap a dead body in. **2.** anything that hides things: *a shroud of mist.* ~*vb.* **3.** to hide (something): *shrouded in mist; shrouded in secrecy.*

Shrove Tuesday (ʃrəʊv) *n.* the day before Ash Wednesday.

shrub (ʃrʌb) *n.* a woody plant, smaller than a tree, with several stems instead of a trunk. —'**shrubby** *adj.*

shrubbery ('ʃrʌbərɪ) *n., pl.* -**beries. 1.** an area planted with shrubs. **2.** shrubs collectively.

shrug (ʃrʌg) *vb.* **shrugging, shrugged. 1.** to draw up and drop (the shoulders) abruptly in a gesture expressing indifference or doubt. ~*n.* **2.** the gesture so made.

shrug off *vb.* **1.** to dismiss (a matter) as unimportant. **2.** to get rid of (someone).

shrunk (ʃrʌŋk) *vb.* a past tense and past participle of **shrink.**

shrunken ('ʃrʌŋk'n) *vb.* **1.** a past participle of **shrink.** ~*adj.* **2.** reduced in size.

shudder ('ʃʌdə) *vb.* **1.** to shake or tremble

suddenly and violently, sometimes from horror or fear. ~n. 2. a convulsive shaking or trembling.

shuffle (ˈʃʌfᵊl) vb. 1. to walk or move (the feet) with a slow dragging motion. 2. to mix together in a jumbled mass: *he shuffled the papers nervously*. 3. to mix up (playing cards) so as to change their order. ~n. 4. an instance of shuffling. 5. a rearrangement: *a Cabinet shuffle*. 6. a dance with short dragging movements of the feet.

shufti (ˈʃʌftɪ) n. *Brit. slang.* a look; peep.

shun (ʃʌn) vb. **shunning, shunned.** to avoid deliberately.

shunt (ʃʌnt) vb. 1. to move (objects or people) to a different position. 2. *Railways.* to transfer (engines or carriages) from track to track. 3. to evade (work) by putting it off onto someone else. ~n. 4. the act of shunting. 5. a railway point. 6. *Electronics.* a conductor connected in parallel across a part of a circuit to divert a known fraction of the current.

shush (ʃʊʃ) *interj.* 1. be quiet! hush! ~vb. 2. to quiet (someone) by saying "shush".

shut (ʃʌt) vb. **shutting, shut.** 1. to move (something) so as to cover an opening: *to shut a door.* 2. to close (something) by bringing together the parts: *to shut a book.* 3. (foll. by *up*) to close or lock the doors of: *to shut up a house.* 4. (foll. by *in*) to confine or enclose. 5. (foll. by *out*) to exclude. 6. (of a shop or other establishment) to stop operating for the day: *the pubs shut at eleven.* ~adj. 7. closed or fastened. ~See also **shutdown, shut off,** etc.

shutdown (ˈʃʌtˌdaʊn) n. 1. the closing of a factory, shop, or other business. ~vb. **shut down.** 2. to cease or cause to cease operation.

shuteye (ˈʃʌtˌaɪ) n. *Slang.* sleep.

shut off vb. 1. to cut off the flow or supply of. 2. to isolate or separate.

shut out vb. 1. to keep out or exclude. 2. to conceal from sight: *we planted trees to shut out the view of the road.*

shutter (ˈʃʌtə) n. 1. a hinged doorlike cover, usually one of a pair, for closing off a window. 2. **put up the shutters.** to close business at the end of the day or permanently. 3. *Photog.* a device in a camera that opens to allow light through the lens so as to expose the film when a photograph is taken. ~vb. 4. to close with a shutter or shutters. 5. to equip with a shutter or shutters.

shuttle (ˈʃʌtᵊl) n. 1. a bobbin-like device used in weaving to pass the weft thread between the warp threads. 2. a small bobbin-like device used to hold the thread in a sewing machine. 3. a bus, train, or aircraft that makes frequent journeys between two places which are fairly near to each other. ~vb. 4. to travel by shuttle.

shuttlecock (ˈʃʌtᵊlˌkɒk) n. a rounded piece of cork or plastic having a flat end stuck with feathers, which is struck to and fro in badminton.

shut up vb. 1. *Informal.* to stop talking or cause (someone) to stop talking: often used in commands. 2. to confine or imprison (someone).

shy¹ (ʃaɪ) adj. 1. not at ease in the company of others. 2. easily frightened; timid. 3. (foll. by *of*) cautious or wary of. 4. showing disinclination: *workshy.* ~vb. **shying, shied.** 5. to move back or aside suddenly, as from fear: *the horse shied at the snake in the road.* 6. (foll. by *away from*) to draw back from (doing something), through lack of confidence. ~n., pl. **shies.** 7. a sudden movement back or aside, as from fear. —ˈshyly adv. —ˈshyness n.

shy² (ʃaɪ) vb. **shying, shied.** 1. to throw (something). ~n., pl. **shies.** 2. a quick throw.

Shylock (ˈʃaɪˌlɒk) n. a heartless or demanding creditor.

si (siː) n. *Music.* same as **te.**

Si *Chem.* silicon.

SI See **SI unit.**

Siamese (ˌsaɪəˈmiːz) n., pl. **-mese.** 1. same as **Siamese cat.** ~adj., n., pl. **-mese.** 2. same as **Thai.**

Siamese cat n. a short-haired cream-coloured cat with a tapering tail, blue eyes, and dark ears, tail, and paws.

Siamese twins pl. n. twins born joined together at some point, such as at the hip.

sibilant (ˈsɪbɪlənt) adj. 1. having a hissing sound. ~n. 2. *Phonetics.* a consonant, such as *s* or *z*, that is pronounced with a hissing sound.

sibling (ˈsɪblɪŋ) n. a brother or sister.

sibyl (ˈsɪbɪl) n. (in ancient Greece and Rome) a prophetess. —**sibylline** (ˈsɪbɪˌlaɪn) adj.

sic¹ (sɪk) adv. thus: inserted in brackets in a text to indicate that an odd reading is in fact accurate.

sic² (sɪk) vb. **sicking, sicked.** 1. to attack: used only in commands to a dog. 2. to urge (a dog) to attack (someone).

sick (sɪk) adj. 1. vomiting or likely to vomit. 2. suffering from ill health. 3. of or for ill people: *sick benefits.* 4. deeply affected with mental or spiritual distress: *sick at heart.* 5. mentally or spiritually disturbed. 6. *Informal.* making fun of death, illness, or misfortune: *sick humour.* 7. Also: **sick and tired.** (foll. by *of*) *Informal.* disgusted by or weary of: *I am sick of his everlasting laughter.* ~n., vb. 8. *Informal.* same as **vomit.**

sickbay (ˈsɪkˌbeɪ) n. a room for the treatment of sick people, for example on a ship.

sicken (ˈsɪkən) vb. 1. to make (someone) feel nauseated or disgusted. 2. (foll. by *for*) to show symptoms of (an illness).

sickening (ˈsɪkənɪŋ) adj. 1. causing sickness or revulsion. **2.** *Informal.* extremely annoying. —**'sickeningly** *adv.*

sickie ('sɪkɪ) *n. Austral. & N.Z. informal.* a day of sick leave from work.

sickle ('sɪk²l) *n.* a tool for cutting grass and grain crops, with a curved blade and a short handle.

sick leave *n.* leave of absence from work through illness.

sickly ('sɪklɪ) *adj.* **-lier, -liest. 1.** not healthy; weak. **2.** suggesting sickness: *a sickly pallor.* **3.** (of a smell or taste) causing revulsion or nausea. **4.** insipid: *a sickly smile.* ~*adv.* **5.** suggesting sickness: *sickly pale.* —**'sickliness** *n.*

sickness ('sɪknɪs) *n.* **1.** an illness or disease. **2.** nausea or queasiness. **3.** vomiting.

side (saɪd) *n.* **1.** a line or surface that borders anything. **2.** *Geom.* a line forming part of the perimeter of a plane figure: *a hexagon has six sides.* **3.** either of two parts into which an object, surface, or area can be divided: *the right side and the left side.* **4.** either of the two surfaces of a flat object: *write on both sides of the page.* **5.** the sloping part of a hill or bank. **6.** either the left or the right half of the body, esp. the area around the waist: *I have a pain in my side.* **7.** the area immediately next to a person or thing: *he stood at her side.* **8.** a location within an area identified by reference to a central point: *the south side of the city.* **9.** the area at the edge of something, as opposed to the centre: *the side of the road.* **10.** aspect or part: *look on the bright side.* **11.** one of two or more contesting groups or teams. **12.** a position held in opposition to another in a dispute. **13.** line of descent: *he gets his brains from his mother's side.* **14.** *Informal.* a television channel. **15.** *Brit. slang.* insolence or pretentiousness: *to put on side.* **16. on one side.** apart from the rest. **17. on the side.** apart from or in addition to the main thing or part. **18. side by side. a.** close together. **b.** (foll. by *with*) beside or near to. **19. take sides.** to support one party in a dispute against another. ~*adj.* **20.** situated at the side: *the side door.* **21.** subordinate: *a side road.* ~*vb.* **22.** (foll. by *with*) to support (one party in a dispute).

sideboard ('saɪd,bɔːd) *n.* a piece of furniture for a dining room, with drawers, cupboards, and shelves to hold tableware.

sideboards ('saɪd,bɔːdz) *or esp. U.S. & Canad.* **sideburns** ('saɪd,bɜːnz) *pl. n.* a man's whiskers grown down either side of the face in front of the ears.

sidecar ('saɪd,kɑː) *n.* a small passenger car attached to the side of a motorcycle.

side effect *n.* **1.** a usually unwanted effect caused by a drug in addition to its intended one. **2.** any additional effect, usually an undesirable one.

sidekick ('saɪd,kɪk) *n. Informal.* a close friend or associate.

sidelight ('saɪd,laɪt) *n.* **1.** *Brit.* either of two small lights at the front of a motor vehicle. **2.** light coming from the side. **3.** either of the two navigational lights used by ships at night.

sideline ('saɪd,laɪn) *n.* a subsidiary interest or source of income.

sidelines ('saɪd,laɪnz) *pl. n.* **1.** *Sport.* **a.** the lines that mark the side boundaries of a playing area. **b.** the area just outside the playing area, where substitute players sit. **2. on the sidelines.** only passively involved.

sidelong ('saɪd,lɒŋ) *adj.* **1.** directed to the side; oblique. ~*adv.* **2.** from the side; obliquely.

sidereal (saɪ'dɪərɪəl) *adj.* of or determined with reference to the stars: *the sidereal day.*

side-saddle *n.* **1.** a riding saddle originally designed for women in skirts, allowing the rider to sit with both legs on the same side of the horse. ~*adv.* **2.** on or as if on a side-saddle.

sideshow ('saɪd,ʃəʊ) *n.* **1.** a small show or entertainment offered along with the main show at a circus or fair. **2.** a subordinate event or incident.

side-splitting *adj.* causing a great deal of laughter.

sidestep ('saɪd,stɛp) *vb.* **-stepping, -stepped. 1.** to step out of the way of (something). **2.** to dodge (an issue). ~*n.* **side step. 3.** a movement to one side, as in dancing or boxing.

sideswipe ('saɪd,swaɪp) *n.* **1.** a glancing blow along or from the side. ~*vb.* **2.** to strike (someone) with such a blow.

sidetrack ('saɪd,træk) *vb.* to distract (someone) from a main subject.

sidewalk ('saɪd,wɔːk) *n. U.S. & Canad.* a pavement.

sideways ('saɪd,weɪz) *adv.* **1.** moving, facing, or inclining towards one side. **2.** from one side; obliquely. **3.** with one side forward. ~*adj.* **4.** moving or directed to or from one side.

side whiskers *pl. n.* same as **sideboards**.

siding ('saɪdɪŋ) *n.* a short stretch of railway track connected to a main line, used for loading and unloading freight and storing engines and carriages.

sidle ('saɪd²l) *vb.* to move in a furtive manner.

SIDS sudden infant death syndrome; cot death.

siege (siːdʒ) *n.* **1.** a military operation carried out to capture a place by surrounding and blockading it. **2.** a similar operation carried out by police, for example to force people out of a place. **3. lay siege to.** to subject (a place) to a siege.

siemens ('si:mənz) *n., pl.* **siemens.** the SI unit of electrical conductance.

sienna (sɪ'ɛnə) *n.* **1.** a natural earth used as a reddish-brown or yellowish-brown pigment. ~*adj.* **2. burnt sienna.** reddish-brown. **3. raw sienna.** yellowish-brown.

sierra (sɪ'ɛərə) *n.* a range of mountains with jagged peaks in Spain or America.

siesta (sɪ'ɛstə) *n.* an afternoon nap, taken in hot countries.

sieve (sɪv) *n.* **1.** a device for sifting or straining, consisting of a mesh container through which the material is shaken or poured. ~*vb.* **2.** to pass (material) through a sieve.

sift (sɪft) *vb.* **1.** to sieve (a powdery substance) in order to remove the coarser particles. **2.** to separate (pieces of information) as if with a sieve. **3.** to examine minutely: *to sift evidence.*

sigh (saɪ) *vb.* **1.** to draw in and audibly let out a deep breath as an expression of sadness, weariness, longing, or relief. **2.** to make a sound resembling this. **3.** (foll. by *for*) to long for. **4.** to utter (something) with a sigh. ~*n.* **5.** the act or sound of sighing.

sight (saɪt) *n.* **1.** the power or faculty of seeing; vision. **2.** an instance of seeing. **3.** the range of vision: *within sight of land.* **4.** point of view; judgment: *in his sight she could do no wrong.* **5.** anything that is seen. **6.** anything worth seeing: *the sights of London.* **7.** *Informal.* anything unpleasant to see: *his room was a sight!* **8.** a device used to assist the eye in aiming a gun or making an observation with an optical instrument. **9.** an aim or observation made with such a device. **10. a sight.** *Informal.* a great deal: *she's a sight too good for him.* **11. a sight for sore eyes.** a welcome sight. **12. catch sight of.** to glimpse. **13. know someone by sight.** to be able to recognize someone without having personal acquaintance with him. **14. lose sight of. a.** to be unable to see (something) any longer. **b.** to forget: *don't lose sight of your original intention.* **15. on sight.** as soon as someone or something is seen. **16. set one's sights on.** to have (a specified goal) in mind. **17. sight unseen.** without having seen the object at issue: *to buy a car sight unseen.* ~*vb.* **18.** to see, view, or glimpse. **19.** to aim (a firearm) using the sight.

sighted ('saɪtɪd) *adj.* not blind.

sightless ('saɪtlɪs) *adj.* blind.

sight-read ('saɪt,ri:d) *vb.* **-reading, -read** (-,rɛd). to sing or play (music in a printed form) without previous preparation. —'**sight-,reading** *n.*

sightscreen ('saɪt,skri:n) *n. Cricket.* a large white screen placed near the boundary behind the bowler, which helps the batsman see the ball.

sightseeing ('saɪt,si:ɪŋ) *n. Informal.* the act or practice of visiting the famous or interesting sights of a place. —'**sight-,seer** *n.*

sigma ('sɪgmə) *n.* **1.** the 18th letter in the Greek alphabet (Σ, σ). **2.** *Maths.* the symbol Σ, indicating summation.

sign (saɪn) *n.* **1.** something that indicates a fact or condition that is not immediately or outwardly observable: *a sign of weakness.* **2.** an action or gesture intended to convey an idea or information. **3.** a board or placard displayed in public and intended to advertise, inform, or warn. **4.** a conventional mark or symbol that has a specific meaning, for example £ for pounds. **5.** *Maths.* **a.** any symbol used to indicate an operation: *a plus sign.* **b.** a symbol used to indicate positivity or negativity of a number or expression. **6.** a visible indication: *the house showed no signs of being occupied.* **7.** an omen. **8.** *Med.* any objective evidence of the presence of a disease or disorder. **9.** *Astrol.* short for **sign of the zodiac.** ~*vb.* **10.** to write (one's name) on (a document or letter) to show its authenticity or one's agreement. **11.** to make a sign to someone so as to convey an idea or information. **12.** to engage or be engaged by signing a contract: *the team have signed a new player.* ~See also **sign away, sign in,** etc.

signal ('sɪgn²l) *n.* **1.** any sign, gesture, sound, or action used to communicate information. **2.** anything that causes immediate action: *the rise in prices was a signal for rebellion.* **3. a.** a variable voltage, current, or electromagnetic wave, by which information is conveyed through an electronic circuit. **b.** the information so conveyed. ~*adj.* **4.** remarkable or notable. ~*vb.* **-nalling, -nalled** or *U.S.* **-naling, -naled.** **5.** to communicate (information) by signal. —'**signally** *adv.*

signal box *n.* a building from which railway signals are operated.

signalize *or* **-lise** ('sɪgnə,laɪz) *vb.* to make noteworthy.

signalman ('sɪgn²lmən) *n., pl.* **-men.** a railwayman in charge of the signals and points within a section.

signatory ('sɪgnətrɪ) *n., pl.* **-ries.** **1.** a person, organization, or state that has signed a document such as a treaty. ~*adj.* **2.** having signed a document or treaty.

signature ('sɪgnɪtʃə) *n.* **1.** a person's name written by himself, used in signing. **2.** a distinctive characteristic that identifies a person or animal. **3.** *Music.* a sign at the beginning of a piece to show key or time. **4.** *Printing.* a sheet of paper printed with several pages, which when folded becomes a section of a book.

signature tune *n. Brit.* a melody used to

introduce or identify a television or radio programme or performer.

sign away *vb.* to dispose of (something) by or as if by signing a document.

signboard ('saɪn,bɔːd) *n.* a board carrying a sign or notice, often to advertise a business or product.

signet ('sɪgnɪt) *n.* a small seal, used to stamp or authenticate documents.

signet ring *n.* a finger ring bearing a signet.

significance (sɪg'nɪfɪkəns) *n.* **1.** consequence or importance. **2.** meaning: *what is the significance of the name?*

significant (sɪg'nɪfɪkənt) *adj.* **1.** having or expressing a meaning. **2.** very important. —**sig'nificantly** *adv.*

significant figures *pl. n. Maths.* **1.** the figures of a number that express a magnitude to a specified degree of accuracy: *3.141 59 to four significant figures is 3.142.* **2.** the number of such figures: *3.142 has four significant figures.*

signify ('sɪgnɪ,faɪ) *vb.* **-fying, -fied.** **1.** to indicate or suggest. **2.** to stand as a symbol or sign for. **3.** to be important.

sign in *vb.* **1.** to sign a register on arrival at a place. **2.** to admit (a nonmember) to a club or institution as a guest by signing a register on his behalf.

sign language *n.* a system of communication by manual signs or gestures, such as one used by deaf people.

sign off *vb.* to announce the end of a radio or television programme.

sign of the zodiac *n. Astrol.* any of the 12 areas into which the zodiac is divided.

sign on *vb.* **1.** *Brit.* to register and report regularly at an unemployment-benefit office. **2.** to commit oneself to a job or activity by signing a form or contract.

signor ('siːnjɔː) *n., pl.* **signors** *or* **signori** (siːˈnjɔːriː). an Italian term of address equivalent to *sir* or *Mr.*

signora (siːnˈjɔːrə) *n., pl.* **-ras** *or* **-re** (-reɪ). an Italian term of address equivalent to *madam* or *Mrs.*

signorina (,siːnjɔːˈriːnə) *n., pl.* **-nas** *or* **-ne** (-neɪ). an Italian term of address equivalent to *madam* or *Miss.*

sign out *vb.* to sign a register to indicate that one is leaving a place.

signpost ('saɪn,pəʊst) *n.* **1.** a post bearing a sign that shows the way. **2.** a clue or indication. ~*vb.* **3.** to mark (the way) with signposts.

sign up *vb.* to enlist for military service.

Sikh (siːk) *n.* **1.** a member of an Indian religion that teaches that there is only one God. ~*adj.* **2.** of the Sikhs or their religious beliefs or customs. —**'Sikh,ism** *n.*

silage ('saɪlɪdʒ) *n.* any crop harvested while

green for fodder and kept succulent by partial fermentation in a silo.

silence ('saɪləns) *n.* **1.** the state or quality of being silent. **2.** the absence of sound. **3.** refusal or failure to speak or communicate when expected: *his silence on their promotion was alarming.* ~*vb.* **4.** to cause (someone or something) to become silent. **5.** to put a stop to: *to silence all opposition.*

silencer ('saɪlənsə) *n.* any device designed to reduce noise, for example one fitted to the exhaust system of a motor vehicle or one fitted to the muzzle of a gun.

silent ('saɪlənt) *adj.* **1.** characterized by an absence or near absence of sound: *a silent house.* **2.** tending to speak very little. **3.** failing to speak or communicate when expected: *the witness chose to remain silent.* **4.** not spoken: *silent disapproval.* **5.** (of a letter) used in the spelling of a word but not pronounced, such as the *k* in *know.* **6.** denoting a film that has no soundtrack. —**'silently** *adv.*

silhouette (,sɪluːˈet) *n.* **1.** the outline of a dark figure seen against a light background. **2.** an outline drawing, often a profile portrait, filled in with black. ~*vb.* **3.** to show (something) in silhouette.

silica ('sɪlɪkə) *n.* a hard glossy mineral, silicon dioxide, which occurs naturally as quartz and is used in the manufacture of glass.

silicate ('sɪlɪkɪt) *n. Mineral.* a compound of silicon, oxygen, and a metal.

silicon ('sɪlɪkən) *n.* **1.** a brittle non-metallic element: used in transistors, solar cells, and alloys. Symbol: Si **2.** (*modifier*) denoting an area of a country that contains much high-technology industry: *Silicon Valley.*

silicon chip *n.* same as **chip** (sense 6).

silicone ('sɪlɪ,kəʊn) *n. Chem.* a tough synthetic material made from silicon and used in lubricants, paints, and resins.

silicosis (,sɪlɪˈkəʊsɪs) *n. Pathol.* a chronic lung disease caused by breathing in silica dust.

silk (sɪlk) *n.* **1.** the fine soft fibre produced by a silkworm. **2.** thread or fabric made from this fibre. **3.** (*pl.*) garments made of this. **4.** *Brit.* **a.** the gown worn by a Queen's (or King's) Counsel. **b.** *Informal.* a Queen's (or King's) Counsel. **c. take silk.** to become a Queen's (or King's) Counsel.

silken ('sɪlkən) *adj.* **1.** made of silk. **2.** resembling silk in smoothness or softness.

silk hat *n.* a top hat covered with silk.

silk-screen printing *n.* same as **screen process.**

silkworm ('sɪlk,wɜːm) *n.* a caterpillar that spins a cocoon of silk.

silky ('sɪlkɪ) *adj.* **silkier, silkiest.** **1.** resembling silk in texture; glossy. **2.** made of silk. **3.** (of a voice or manner) suave; smooth. —**'silkiness** *n.*

sill (sɪl) n. 1. a shelf at the bottom of a window, either inside or outside a room. 2. the lower horizontal part of a window or door frame.

silly ('sɪlɪ) adj. -lier, -liest. 1. lacking in good sense; foolish. 2. dazed, as from a blow. 3. Cricket. (of a fielding position) near the batsman's wicket: silly mid-on. ~n., pl. -lies. 4. Informal. a foolish person. —'silliness n.

silo ('saɪləʊ) n., pl. -los. 1. an airtight pit or tower in which silage is made and stored. 2. an underground structure in which missile systems are sited for protection.

silt (sɪlt) n. 1. a fine sediment of mud or clay deposited by moving water. ~vb. 2. (foll. by up) to fill or choke up with silt.

Silurian (saɪ'lʊərɪən) adj. Geol. of a period of geological time about 425 million years ago, during which fishes first appeared.

silvan ('sɪlvən) adj. same as **sylvan**.

silver ('sɪlvə) n. 1. a precious greyish-white metallic element: used in jewellery, tableware, and coins. Symbol: Ag 2. a coin or coins made of silver. 3. any household articles made of silver. 4. short for **silver medal**. ~adj. 5. greyish-white. 6. (of anniversaries) the 25th in a series: Silver Jubilee; silver wedding. ~vb. 7. to coat with silver or a silvery substance: to silver a spoon. 8. to cause (something) to become silvery in colour.

silver beet n. a beet of Australia and New Zealand with edible spinach-like leaves.

silver birch n. a tree with silvery-white peeling bark.

silverfish ('sɪlvə,fɪʃ) n., pl. -fish or -fishes. 1. a silver-coloured fish. 2. a small wingless silver-coloured insect.

silver lining n. a hopeful aspect of an otherwise desperate or unhappy situation.

silver medal n. a medal of silver awarded to a competitor who comes second in a contest or race.

silver plate n. 1. a thin layer of silver deposited on a base metal. 2. articles, such as tableware, made of silver plate. —,silver-'plate vb.

silver screen n. the. Informal. 1. films collectively or the film industry. 2. the screen onto which films are projected in a cinema.

silverside ('sɪlvə,saɪd) n. Brit. & N.Z. a cut of beef from below the rump and above the leg.

silversmith ('sɪlvə,smɪθ) n. a craftsman who makes or repairs articles of silver.

silver thaw n. Canad. 1. a freezing rainstorm. 2. same as **glitter** (sense 7).

silverware ('sɪlvə,wɛə) n. articles, such as tableware, made of or plated with silver.

silvery ('sɪlvərɪ) adj. 1. having the appearance of silver: the silvery moon. 2. having a clear ringing sound.

silviculture ('sɪlvɪ,kʌltʃə) n. the cultivation of forest trees.

simian ('sɪmɪən) adj. 1. of or resembling a monkey or ape. ~n. 2. a monkey or ape.

similar ('sɪmɪlə) adj. 1. showing resemblance in qualities, characteristics, or appearance. 2. Geom. (of two or more figures) different in size or position, but with exactly the same shape. —**similarity** (,sɪmɪ'lærɪtɪ) n. —**similarly** adv.

simile ('sɪmɪlɪ) n. a figure of speech that likens one thing to another of a different category, usually introduced by as or like.

similitude (sɪ'mɪlɪ,tjuːd) n. likeness; similarity.

simmer ('sɪmə) vb. 1. to cook (food) gently at just below boiling point. 2. to be in a state of suppressed rage. ~n. 3. the state of simmering.

simmer down vb. Informal. to grow calmer after intense rage.

simnel cake ('sɪmn°l) n. Brit. a fruit cake covered with a layer of marzipan, traditionally eaten during Lent or at Easter.

simony ('saɪmənɪ) n. Christianity. the practice of buying or selling Church benefits such as pardons.

simoom (sɪ'muːm) n. a hot suffocating sand-laden desert wind.

simper ('sɪmpə) vb. 1. to smile in a silly or affected way. 2. to utter (something) with a simper. ~n. 3. a simpering smile. —'simpering adj.

simple ('sɪmp°l) adj. 1. easy to understand or do: a simple problem. 2. plain; unadorned: a simple dress; the simple truth. 3. not combined or complex: a simple mechanism. 4. unaffected or unpretentious: although he became famous, he remained a simple man. 5. sincere; frank: her simple explanation was readily accepted. 6. of humble condition or rank: a simple peasant. 7. feeble-minded. 8. straightforward: a simple case of mumps. 9. Music. denoting a time where the number of beats per bar may be two, three, or four. —**simplicity** (sɪm'plɪsɪtɪ) n.

simple fraction n. Maths. a fraction in which the numerator and denominator are both whole numbers.

simple fracture n. a fracture in which the broken bone does not pierce the skin.

simple interest n. Finance. interest paid only on the original amount of a debt.

simple-minded adj. 1. stupid; foolish. 2. mentally defective. 3. unsophisticated; artless. —,simple-'mindedness n.

simple sentence n. a sentence consisting of a single main clause.

simpleton ('sɪmp°ltən) n. a foolish or very unintelligent person.

simplify ('sɪmplɪ,faɪ) vb. -fying, -fied. 1. to make (something) less complicated. 2. Maths. to reduce (an equation or fraction) to its simplest form. **—simplification** (ˌsɪmplɪfɪ'keɪʃən) n.

simplistic (sɪm'plɪstɪk) adj. over-simplified or oversimplifying.

simply ('sɪmplɪ) adv. **1.** in a simple manner. **2.** merely. **3.** absolutely; altogether: a simply wonderful holiday.

simulate ('sɪmjʊˌleɪt) vb. **1.** to make a pretence of: to simulate anxiety. **2.** to imitate the conditions of (a situation), as in carrying out an experiment: to simulate weightlessness. **3.** to have the appearance of: simulated leather. **—simulation** (ˌsɪmjʊ-'leɪʃən) n.

simulator ('sɪmjʊˌleɪtə) n. a device that simulates specific conditions for the purposes of research or training: a flight simulator.

simultaneous (ˌsɪməl'teɪnɪəs) adj. occurring or existing at the same time. **—ˌsimul'taneously** adv. **—simultaneity** (ˌsɪməltə'niːɪtɪ) n.
Usage. see **unique.**

simultaneous equations pl. n. Maths. a set of equations that are all satisfied by the same values of the variables, the number of variables being equal to the number of equations.

sin[1] (sɪn) n. **1.** the breaking of a religious or moral law. **2.** any offence against a principle or standard. **3. live in sin.** Old-fashioned, informal. (of an unmarried couple) to live together. ~vb. **sinning, sinned. 4.** to commit a sin. **—'sinner** n.

sin[2] (saɪn) Maths. sine.

SIN (in Canada) Social Insurance Number.

sin bin n. Slang. the penalty box in ice hockey.

since (sɪns) prep. **1.** during the period of time after: since May it has only rained once. ~conj. **2.** (sometimes preceded by ever) continuously from the time given when: I've been busy since we last spoke. **3.** for the reason that; because. ~adv. **4.** from that time: I haven't seen him since.
Usage. see **ago.**

sincere (sɪn'sɪə) adj. without pretence or deceit; genuine: sincere regret. **—sin'cerely** adv. **—sincerity** (sɪn'sɛrɪtɪ) n.

sine (saɪn) n. (in trigonometry) the ratio of the length of the opposite side to that of the hypotenuse in a right-angled triangle.

sinecure ('saɪnɪˌkjʊə) n. a paid job involving minimal duties.

sine die ('saɪnɪ 'daɪɪ) adv. without fixing a day for future action or meeting.

sine qua non ('sɪnɪ kwɑː 'nəʊn) n. an essential requirement.

sinew ('sɪnjuː) n. **1.** Anat. same as **tendon. 2. a.** a source of strength or power. **b.** Literary. muscular strength.

sinewy ('sɪnjuɪ) adj. lean and muscular.

sinful ('sɪnfʊl) adj. **1.** having committed or tending to commit sin: a sinful person. **2.** being a sin; wicked: a sinful act.

sing (sɪŋ) vb. **singing, sang, sung. 1.** to produce musical sounds with the voice. **2.** to perform (a song). **3.** (foll. by of) to tell a story in song about. **4.** (of certain birds and insects) to utter musical calls. **5.** to make a humming, ringing, or whistling sound: the arrow sang past his ear. **6.** (of one's ears) to be filled with a continuous ringing sound. **7.** to bring (someone) to a given state by singing: to sing a child to sleep. **8.** Slang, chiefly U.S. to act as an informer. ~See also **sing out. —'singer** n. **—'singing** adj., n.
Usage. see **ring**[2].

sing. singular.

singe (sɪndʒ) vb. **1.** to burn superficially; scorch: to singe one's clothes. ~n. **2.** a superficial burn.

Singhalese (ˌsɪŋə'liːz) n., pl. **-leses** or **-lese,** adj. same as **Sinhalese.**

singing telegram n. a service by which a person is employed to present greetings to someone by singing.

single ('sɪŋg'l) adj. **1.** existing alone; solitary: at the top of the hill stood a single tower. **2.** distinct from others of the same kind: every single day. **3.** designed for one user: a single bed. **4.** unmarried. **5.** involving two individuals: single combat. **6.** even one: there wasn't a single person on the beach. **7.** (of a flower) having only one circle of petals. ~n. **8.** a hotel bedroom for one person. **9.** a gramophone record with one short piece of music on each side. **10.** Cricket. a hit from which one run is scored. **11. a.** Brit. a pound note or coin. **b.** U.S. & Canad. a dollar bill. **12.** short for **single ticket.** ~vb. **13.** (foll. by out) to select from a group of people or things: he singled him out for special mention. ~See also **singles.**

single-breasted adj. (of a jacket or coat) having the fronts overlapping only slightly and with one row of fastenings.

single-decker n. Brit. informal. a bus with only one passenger deck.

single entry n. a book-keeping system in which all transactions are entered in one account only.

single file n. a line of people, one behind the other.

single-handed adj., adv. unaided or working alone: a single-handed Atlantic crossing; he crossed the Atlantic single-handed. **—ˌsingle-'handedly** adv.

single-minded adj. having one aim only; dedicated. **—ˌsingle-'mindedly** adv. **—ˌsingle-'mindedness** n.

single-parent family n. a family consisting of one parent and his or her child or children living together, the other parent being dead or permanently absent.

singles ('sɪŋˀlz) *pl. n. Sport.* a match played with one person on each side.

singles bar *n.* a bar that is a social meeting place for single people.

singlet ('sɪŋglɪt) *n. Chiefly Brit.* a man's sleeveless vest.

single ticket *n. Brit.* a ticket valid for a one-way journey only.

singleton ('sɪŋgˀltən) *n. Cards.* the only card of a particular suit held by a player.

singly ('sɪŋglɪ) *adv.* one at a time; one by one.

sing out *vb.* to call out loudly; shout.

singsong ('sɪŋˌsɒŋ) *n.* **1.** *Brit.* an informal group singing session. ~*adj.* **2.** having a monotonous rise and fall in tone: *a singsong accent.*

singular ('sɪŋgjʊlə) *adj.* **1.** *Grammar.* (of a word or form) denoting only one person or thing: *a singular noun.* **2.** remarkable; extraordinary: *a singular feat.* **3.** unusual; odd: *a singular character.* ~*n.* **4.** *Grammar.* the singular form of a word. —**singularity** (ˌsɪŋgjʊ'lærɪtɪ) *n.* —'**singularly** *adv.*

Sinhalese (ˌsɪnhə'liːz) *or* **Singhalese** *n.* **1.** (*pl.* **-leses** *or* **-lese**) a member of a people living mainly in Sri Lanka. **2.** the language of this people. ~*adj.* **3.** of this people or their language. ~See also **Sri Lankan.**

sinister ('sɪnɪstə) *adj.* **1.** threatening or suggesting evil or harm: *a sinister glance.* **2.** *Heraldry.* of, on, or starting from the bearer's left side.

sink (sɪŋk) *vb.* **sinking, sank** *or* **sunk; sunk** *or* **sunken.** **1.** to descend or cause to descend, esp. beneath the surface of a liquid. **2.** to appear to descend towards or below the horizon. **3.** (foll. by *into*) to pass into a specified lower state or condition: *to sink into apathy.* **4.** (of a voice) to become quieter. **5.** to make or become lower in amount or value. **6.** to become weaker in health. **7.** to seep or penetrate. **8.** to dig, drill, or excavate (a hole or shaft). **9.** to drive (a stake) into the ground. **10.** (foll. by *in* or *into*) to invest (money). **11.** *Golf, snooker.* to hit (the ball) into the hole or pocket: *he sank a 15-foot putt.* ~*n.* **12.** a fixed basin in a kitchen or bathroom, with a water supply and drainpipe.

sinker ('sɪŋkə) *n.* a weight attached to a fishing line or net to cause it to sink in water.

sink in *vb.* to penetrate the mind: *eventually the news sank in.*

sinking fund *n.* a fund set aside to repay a long-term debt.

Sinn Féin ('ʃɪn 'feɪn) *n.* an Irish Republican political movement linked to the revolutionary Irish Republican Army.

Sino- ('saɪnəʊ) *combining form.* Chinese: *Sino-Tibetan; Sinology.*

Sinology (saɪ'nɒlədʒɪ) *n.* the study of Chinese history, language, and culture. —**Si'nologist** *n.*

sinuous ('sɪnjʊəs) *adj.* **1.** full of curves. **2.** having smooth twisting movements. —**sinuosity** (ˌsɪnjʊ'ɒsɪtɪ) *n.*

sinus ('saɪnəs) *n. Anat.* a hollow space in bone, such as one in the skull opening into a nasal cavity.

sinusitis (ˌsaɪnə'saɪtɪs) *n.* inflammation of the membrane lining a sinus.

sip (sɪp) *vb.* **sipping, sipped.** **1.** to drink (a liquid) in small mouthfuls. ~*n.* **2.** a quantity that is sipped. **3.** an instance of sipping.

siphon *or* **syphon** ('saɪfˀn) *n.* **1.** a tube placed with one end at a certain level in a container of liquid and the other end outside the container below this level, so that atmospheric pressure forces the liquid through the tube and out of the container. **2.** same as **soda siphon.** ~*vb.* **3.** (foll. by *off*) to draw (liquid) off through a siphon.

sir (sɜː) *n.* a polite term of address for a man.

Sir (sɜː) *n.* a title placed before the name of a knight or baronet: *Sir Walter Raleigh.*

sire ('saɪə) *n.* **1.** a male parent of a horse or other domestic animal. **2.** *Archaic.* a respectful term of address used to a king. ~*vb.* **3.** to father.

siren ('saɪərən) *n.* **1.** a device that gives out a loud wailing sound as a warning or signal. **2.** *Gk myth.* one of several sea nymphs whose singing lured sailors to destruction on the rocks. **3.** a dangerously alluring woman.

sirloin ('sɜːˌlɔɪn) *n.* a prime cut of beef from the upper part of the loin.

sirocco (sɪ'rɒkəʊ) *n., pl.* **-cos.** a hot oppressive wind blowing from N Africa into S Europe.

sis (sɪs) *n. Informal.* short for **sister.**

sisal ('saɪsˀl) *n.* a stiff fibre obtained from a Mexican plant and used for making rope.

siskin ('sɪskɪn) *n.* a yellow-and-black finch.

sissy *or* **cissy** ('sɪsɪ) *n., pl.* **-sies.** **1.** an effeminate, weak, or cowardly person. ~*adj.* **2.** effeminate, weak, or cowardly.

sister ('sɪstə) *n.* **1.** a woman or girl having the same parents as another person. **2.** a female fellow member of a group, race, or profession. **3.** a female nurse in charge of a ward. **4.** *Chiefly R.C. Church.* a nun. **5.** (*modifier*) of the same class, origin, or design, as another: *a sister ship.*

sisterhood ('sɪstəˌhʊd) *n.* **1.** the state of being sisters or like sisters. **2.** a religious group of sisters. **3.** a group of women united by common interests, aims, or beliefs.

sister-in-law *n., pl.* **sisters-in-law.** **1.** the sister of one's husband or wife. **2.** one's brother's wife.

sisterly ('sɪstəlɪ) *adj.* of or like a sister; affectionate.

sit (sɪt) *vb.* **sitting, sat.** 1. to rest one's body on one's buttocks with one's torso upright: *to sit on a chair.* 2. to cause (someone) to adopt such a posture. 3. (of an animal) to rest with its hindquarters lowered to the ground. 4. (of a bird) to perch or roost. 5. (foll. by *on*) (of a bird) to cover its eggs so as to hatch them. 6. to be located. 7. to pose for a painting or photograph. 8. to occupy a seat in some official capacity: *she sits on a number of committees.* 9. (of an official body) to be in session. 10. to remain unused: *his car sat in the garage.* 11. (of a garment) to fit or hang as specified: *that dress sits well on you.* 12. *Chiefly Brit.* to take (an examination): *he's sitting his bar finals.* 13. (foll. by *for*) *Chiefly Brit.* to be a candidate for (a qualification): *he's sitting for a BA.* 14. **sit tight.** *Informal.* **a.** to wait patiently. **b.** to maintain one's position firmly. ~See also **sit back, sit down,** etc.

sitar (sɪ'tɑː) *n.* an Indian stringed musical instrument with a long neck and a rounded body.

sit back *vb.* to relax or be passive when action should be taken: *many people just sit back and ignore the problems of today.*

sitcom ('sɪtˌkɒm) *n. Informal.* short for **situation comedy.**

sit down *vb.* 1. to adopt or cause (someone) to adopt a sitting posture. 2. (foll. by *under*) to suffer (insults or humiliations) without resistance. ~*n.* **sit-down.** 3. a short rest sitting down. ~*adj.* **sit-down.** 4. (of a meal) eaten while sitting down at a table.

sit-down strike *n.* a strike in which workers refuse to leave their place of employment until a settlement is reached.

site (saɪt) *n.* 1. the piece of ground where something was, is, or is intended to be located: *a building site.* ~*vb.* 2. to locate (something) on a specific site.

sit-in *n.* 1. a protest in which the demonstrators occupy seats in a public place and refuse to move. ~*vb.* **sit in.** 2. (foll. by *for*) to deputize for. 3. (foll. by *on*) to be present at (a meeting) as an observer.

sitkamer ('sɪtˌkɑːmə) *n. S. African.* a sitting room.

sitka spruce ('sɪtkə) *n.* a tall North American spruce tree, now often grown in Britain.

sit on *vb. Informal.* 1. to delay action on: *he's been sitting on that report for weeks.* 2. to check or rebuke (someone).

sit out *vb.* 1. to endure to the end: *although the play was terrible, I sat it out.* 2. to take no part in (a dance or game).

sitter ('sɪtə) *n.* 1. a person posing for his portrait or photograph. 2. same as **baby-sitter.**

sitting ('sɪtɪŋ) *n.* 1. a continuous period of being seated at some activity: *I read his novel at one sitting.* 2. one of the times when a meal is served, when there is not enough space for everyone to eat at the same time: *dinner will be served in two sittings.* 3. a period of posing for a painting or photograph. 4. a meeting of an official body to conduct business. ~*adj.* 5. current: *the sitting member for Hillhead.* 6. seated: *in a sitting position.*

sitting duck *n. Informal.* a person or thing in a defenceless or vulnerable position.

sitting room *n.* a room in a house or flat where people sit and relax.

sitting tenant *n.* a tenant occupying a house or flat.

situate ('sɪtjʊˌeɪt) *vb.* to place.

situation (ˌsɪtjʊ'eɪʃən) *n.* 1. location, with regard to the surroundings. 2. **a.** state of affairs. **b.** a complex or critical state of affairs. 3. social or financial circumstances. 4. a position of employment.

situation comedy *n.* (on television or radio) a comedy series involving the same characters in various everyday situations.

sit up *vb.* 1. to raise oneself from a lying position into a sitting one. 2. to remain out of bed until a late hour. 3. *Informal.* to become suddenly interested: *devaluation of the dollar made the money market sit up.* ~*n.* **sit-up.** 4. a physical exercise in which the body is brought into a sitting position from one of lying on the back.

SI unit *n.* any of the units (metre, kilogram, second, ampere, kelvin, candela, and mole) adopted for international use under the Système International d'Unités, now employed for all scientific and most technical purposes.

six (sɪks) *n.* 1. the cardinal number that is the sum of one and five. 2. a numeral, 6, VI, representing this number. 3. something representing or consisting of six units. 4. *Cricket.* a score of six runs, obtained by hitting the ball so that it crosses the boundary without bouncing. 5. **at sixes and sevens.** in a state of confusion. 6. **knock someone for six.** *Informal.* to upset or overwhelm someone completely. 7. **six of one and half a dozen of the other.** a situation in which there is no real difference between the alternatives. ~*det.* 8. amounting to six. —**sixth** *adj., n.*

sixfold ('sɪksˌfəʊld) *adj.* 1. having six times as many. 2. composed of six parts. ~*adv.* 3. by six times as much.

sixpence ('sɪkspəns) *n.* (formerly) a small British coin worth six old pennies, or 2½ pence.

six-shooter *n. U.S. informal.* a revolver that fires six shots without reloading.

sixteen ('sɪks'tiːn) *n.* 1. the cardinal number that is the sum of ten and six. **2.** a numeral, 16, XVI, representing this number. **3.** something representing or consisting of sixteen units. ~*det.* **4.** amounting to sixteen. —'**six'teenth** *adj., n.*

sixth form *n.* (in England and Wales) the most senior form in a secondary school, in which pupils over sixteen may take A levels or retake O levels. —'**sixth-,former** *n.*

sixth sense *n.* intuition or perception beyond the five senses of sight, hearing, touch, taste, and smell.

sixty ('sıkstı) *n., pl.* -**ties.** **1.** the cardinal number that is the product of ten and six. **2.** a numeral, 60, LX, representing this number. **3.** (*pl.*) the numbers 60-69, esp. the 60th to the 69th year of a person's life or of a century. **4.** something representing or consisting of sixty units. ~*det.* **5.** amounting to sixty. —'**sixtieth** *adj., n.*

sizable *or* **sizeable** ('saɪzəb'l) *adj.* quite large.

size[1] (saɪz) *n.* **1.** the dimensions, amount, or extent of something. **2.** large dimensions, amount, or extent. **3.** one of a series of graduated measurements for goods: *she takes size 4 shoes.* **4.** *Informal.* state of affairs as summarized: *he's bankrupt, that's about the size of it.* ~*vb.* **5.** to sort (things) according to size.

size[2] (saɪz) *n.* **1.** a thin gluey substance that is used as a glaze or sealer on paper or plaster surfaces. ~*vb.* **2.** to treat (a surface) with size.

sized (saɪzd) *adj.* of a specified size: *medium-sized.*

size up *vb. Informal.* to make an assessment of (a person or situation).

sizzle ('sız'l) *vb.* **1.** to make a hissing sound like the sound of frying fat. **2.** *Informal.* to be very hot. **3.** *Informal.* to be very angry. ~*n.* **4.** a hissing sound. —'**sizzling** *adj.*

skate[1] (skeɪt) *n.* **1.** same as **ice skate** *or* **roller skate**. **2. get one's skates on.** *Informal.* to hurry. ~*vb.* **3.** to glide swiftly on skates. **4. skate on thin ice.** to place oneself in a dangerous situation. —'**skater** *n.* —'**skating** *n.*

skate[2] (skeɪt) *n., pl.* **skate** *or* **skates.** a large fish with a broad flat body, a short spineless tail, and a pointed snout.

skateboard ('skeɪt,bɔːd) *n.* **1.** a narrow board mounted on roller-skate wheels, usually ridden while standing up. ~*vb.* **2.** to ride on a skateboard. —'**skate-,boarding** *n.*

skate round *or* **over** *vb.* to avoid discussing or dealing with (a matter) fully.

skedaddle (skı'dæd'l) *vb. Informal.* to run off hastily.

skein (skeın) *n.* a length of yarn or thread wound in a long coil.

skeleton ('skɛlıtən) *n.* **1.** the hard frame-

work of bones that supports and protects the organs and muscles of the body. **2.** *Informal.* an extremely thin person or animal. **3.** the essential framework of any structure. **4.** an outline consisting of bare essentials: *the skeleton of a novel.* **5.** (*modifier*) reduced to a minimum: *a skeleton staff.* **6. skeleton in the cupboard** *or* **closet.** a discreditable fact from one's past that one keeps secret. —'**skeletal** *adj.*

skeleton key *n.* a key designed so that it can open many different locks.

skeptic ('skɛptık) *n. Archaic & U.S.* same as **sceptic.**

sketch (skɛtʃ) *n.* **1.** a quick rough drawing. **2.** a brief descriptive piece of writing. **3.** a short humorous piece of acting forming part of a show. **4.** any brief outline. ~*vb.* **5.** to make a quick rough drawing (of). **6.** (foll. by *out*) to make a brief description of.

sketchbook ('skɛtʃ,bʊk) *n.* a book of blank pages for sketching on.

sketchy ('skɛtʃı) *adj.* **sketchier, sketchiest.** superficial or incomplete. —'**sketchily** *adv.*

skew (skjuː) *adj.* **1.** having a slanting position. ~*n.* **2.** a slanting position. ~*vb.* **3.** to take or cause to take an oblique or slanting position. **4.** to distort.

skewbald ('skjuː,bɔːld) *adj.* **1.** marked or spotted in white and another colour. ~*n.* **2.** a horse with this marking.

skewer (skjʊə) *n.* **1.** a long pin for holding meat together during cooking. ~*vb.* **2.** to fasten or pierce with or as if with a skewer.

skewwhiff ('skjuː'wıf) *adj. Brit. informal.* not straight.

ski (skiː) *n., pl.* **skis** *or* **ski.** **1.** one of a pair of wooden, metal, or plastic runners that are used, fastened to boots, for gliding over snow. ~*vb.* **skiing; skied** *or* **ski'd.** **2.** to travel on skis. —'**skier** *n.* —'**skiing** *n.*

skid (skıd) *vb.* **skidding, skidded.** **1.** (of a vehicle or person) to slide sideways while in motion. ~*n.* **2.** an instance of skidding.

skidoo (skı'duː) *Canad.* ~*n., pl.* -**doos.** **1.** a snowmobile. ~*vb.* -**dooing, -dooed.** **2.** to travel using a snowmobile.

skid row (rəʊ) *n. Slang, chiefly U.S. & Canad.* a dilapidated section of a city, frequented by down-and-outs.

skiff (skıf) *n.* a small boat propelled by oars, sail, or motor.

ski jump *n.* a steep snow-covered slope ending in a horizontal ramp from which skiers compete to make the longest jump.

skilful *or U.S.* **skillful** ('skılful) *adj.* having or showing skill. —'**skilfully** *or U.S.* '**skillfully** *adv.*

ski lift *n.* any device, such as a chair lift, for carrying skiers up a slope.

skill (skıl) *n.* **1.** special ability or expertise, often acquired by training. **2.** something, such as a trade, requiring special training or expertise. —**skilled** *adj.*

skillet ('skɪlɪt) *n.* **1.** a small frying pan. **2.** *Chiefly Brit.* a long-handled cooking pot.

skim (skɪm) *vb.* **skimming, skimmed.** **1.** to remove floating material from the surface of (a liquid): *to skim milk.* **2.** to glide smoothly over (a surface). **3.** to throw (something) across a surface, so as to bounce it: *to skim stones over water.* **4.** (foll. by *through*) to read (a piece of writing) quickly and superficially.

skimmed *or* **skim milk** *n.* milk from which the cream has been removed.

skimp (skɪmp) *vb.* **1.** to be extremely sparing or supply (someone) sparingly. **2.** to do (something) carelessly or with inadequate materials.

skimpy ('skɪmpɪ) *adj.* **skimpier, skimpiest.** meagre, insufficient, or scanty.

skin (skɪn) *n.* **1.** the tissue forming the outer covering of the body. **2.** a person's complexion: *a fair skin.* **3.** any outer layer or covering: *a banana skin.* **4.** a film on the surface of a liquid. **5.** the outer covering of a fur-bearing animal, removed and prepared for use. **6.** a container for liquids, made from animal skin. **7. by the skin of one's teeth.** by a narrow margin. **8. get under one's skin.** *Informal.* to annoy one. **9. no skin off one's nose.** *Informal.* not a matter that concerns one. **10. save one's skin.** to save one from death or harm. **11. skin and bone.** extremely thin. **12. thick** (*or* **thin**) **skin.** an insensitive (*or* sensitive) nature. ~*vb.* **skinning, skinned.** **13.** to remove the outer covering from. **14.** to injure (a part of the body) by scraping some of the skin off: *he skinned his knee.* **15.** *Slang.* to swindle. —'**skinless** *adj.*

skin-deep *adj.* superficial; shallow.

skin diving *n.* the sport or activity of underwater swimming using only light breathing apparatus and without a special diving suit. —'**skin-,diver** *n.*

skin flick *n. Slang.* a pornographic film.

skinflint ('skɪn,flɪnt) *n.* a miserly person.

skin graft *n.* a piece of skin removed from one part of the body and surgically grafted at the site of a severe burn or other injury.

skinhead ('skɪn,hɛd) *n. Brit.* a White boy who has closely cropped hair and wears heavy boots and braces.

skinny ('skɪnɪ) *adj.* **-nier, -niest.** extremely thin.

skint (skɪnt) *adj. Brit. slang.* without money.

skintight ('skɪn'taɪt) *adj.* (of garments) fitting tightly over the body; clinging.

skip[1] (skɪp) *vb.* **skipping, skipped.** **1.** to spring or move lightly by hopping from one foot to the other. **2.** to jump over a skipping-rope. **3.** to cause (a stone) to skim over a surface or (of a stone) to move in this way. **4.** to omit (intervening matter): *he skipped a chapter of the book.* **5.** (foll. by *through*) *Informal.* to read or deal with (something) quickly or superficially. **6. skip it!** *Informal.* it doesn't matter! **7.** *Informal.* to miss deliberately: *to skip school.* **8.** *Informal, chiefly U.S. & Canad.* to leave (a place) in haste: *to skip town.* ~*n.* **9.** a skipping movement or action.

skip[2] (skɪp) *n.* **1.** a large open container for transporting building materials or rubbish. **2.** a cage used as a lift in mines.

ski pants *pl. n.* stretch trousers, worn for skiing or as a fashion garment, which are kept taut by straps under the feet.

skipper ('skɪpə) *n.* **1.** the captain of a ship or aircraft. **2.** the captain of a sporting team. ~*vb.* **3.** to be the captain of.

skipping ('skɪpɪŋ) *n.* the act of jumping over a rope held either by the person jumping or by two other people, as a game or for exercise.

skipping-rope *n. Brit.* a rope, sometimes with handles, that is held in the hands and swung round and down so that the holder or others can jump over it.

skirl (skɜːl) *Scot. & N English dialect.* ~*vb.* **1.** (of bagpipes) to give out a shrill sound. ~*n.* **2.** the sound of bagpipes.

skirmish ('skɜːmɪʃ) *n.* **1.** a minor short-lived battle. **2.** any brief or unimportant clash. ~*vb.* **3.** to engage in a skirmish.

skirt (skɜːt) *n.* **1.** a woman's or girl's garment hanging from the waist. **2.** the part of a dress or coat below the waist. **3.** a circular hanging flap, for example round the base of a hovercraft. **4.** *Brit.* a cut of beef from the flank. **5. bit of skirt.** *Offensive slang.* a girl or woman. ~*vb.* **6.** to lie along or form the edge of (something). **7.** (foll. by *around*) to go around the outer edge of (something). **8.** to avoid dealing with (an issue).

skirting board *n.* a moulding or board round the bottom of an interior wall where it joins the floor.

ski stick *or* **pole** *n.* one of a pair of sharp pointed sticks used by skiers to gain speed and maintain balance.

skit (skɪt) *n.* a brief satirical sketch.

ski tow *n.* a device for pulling skiers uphill, usually a motor-driven rope grasped by the skier while riding on his skis.

skittish ('skɪtɪʃ) *adj.* **1.** playful or lively. **2.** (of a horse) excitable and easily frightened.

skittle ('skɪt'l) *n.* **1.** (*pl.; functioning as sing.*) a bowling game in which players knock over as many wooden or plastic pins as possible by rolling a wooden ball at them. **2.** a pin used in this game.

skive (skaɪv) *vb.* (often foll. by *off*) *Brit. informal.* to evade (work or responsibility). —'**skiver** *n.*

skivvy (ˈskɪvɪ) *Chiefly Brit., often disparaging.* ~*n., pl.* -**vies.** 1. a female domestic servant; drudge. ~*vb.* -**vying, -vied.** 2. to work as a skivvy.

skookum (ˈskuːkəm) *adj. W Canad.* large.

skua (ˈskjuːə) *n.* a predatory aquatic gull-like bird having a dark plumage and long tail.

skulduggery *or U.S.* **skullduggery** (skʌlˈdʌgərɪ) *n. Informal.* underhand dealing; trickery.

skulk (skʌlk) *vb.* 1. to move stealthily, so as to avoid notice. 2. to lie in hiding; lurk.

skull (skʌl) *n.* 1. the bony framework of the head. 2. *Informal.* the head or mind: *can't you get it into your thick skull?*

skull and crossbones *n.* a picture of the human skull above two crossed thigh-bones, formerly on the pirate flag, now used as a warning of danger or death.

skullcap (ˈskʌlˌkæp) *n.* a rounded brimless hat fitting the crown of the head.

skunk (skʌŋk) *n., pl.* **skunk** *or* **skunks.** 1. a mammal with a black-and-white coat and bushy tail, which gives out a foul-smelling fluid when attacked. 2. *Informal.* a despicable person.

sky (skaɪ) *n., pl.* **skies.** 1. the upper atmosphere as seen from earth. 2. **to the skies.** extravagantly. ~*vb.* **skying, skied.** 3. *Informal.* to hit (a ball) high in the air.

sky-blue *adj.* bright clear blue.

skydiving (ˈskaɪˌdaɪvɪŋ) *n.* the sport of jumping from an aircraft and performing manoeuvres before opening the parachute. —ˈsky**ˌdiver** *n.*

Skye terrier (skaɪ) *n.* a short-legged terrier with long wiry hair and erect ears.

sky-high *adj., adv.* 1. very high. 2. **blow sky-high.** to destroy.

skyjack (ˈskaɪˌdʒæk) *vb.* to hijack (an aircraft).

skylark (ˈskaɪˌlɑːk) *n.* 1. a lark that sings while hovering at a great height. ~*vb.* 2. *Informal.* to romp or play jokes.

skylight (ˈskaɪˌlaɪt) *n.* a window placed in a roof or ceiling to admit daylight.

skyline (ˈskaɪˌlaɪn) *n.* 1. the line at which the earth and sky appear to meet. 2. the outline of buildings, trees, or hills, seen against the sky.

skyrocket (ˈskaɪˌrɒkɪt) *n.* 1. same as **rocket** (sense 1). ~*vb.* 2. *Informal.* to rise rapidly.

skyscraper (ˈskaɪˌskreɪpə) *n.* a very tall building.

skyward (ˈskaɪwəd) *adj.* 1. towards the sky. ~*adv. also* **skywards.** 2. towards the sky.

slab (slæb) *n.* a broad flat thick piece of wood, stone, or other material.

slack¹ (slæk) *adj.* 1. not tight, tense, or taut. 2. negligent or careless. 3. (esp. of water) moving slowly. 4. (of trade) not busy. ~*n.* 5. a part that is slack or hangs loose: *take in the slack.* 6. a period of decreased activity. ~*vb.* 7. to neglect (one's work or duty). 8. (often foll. by *off*) to loosen or slacken. ~See also **slacks.** —ˈslackness *n.*

slack² (slæk) *n.* small pieces of coal with a high ash content.

slacken (ˈslækən) *vb.* (often foll. by *off*) 1. to make or become looser. 2. to make or become slower or less intense.

slacker (ˈslækə) *n.* a person who evades work or duty; shirker.

slacks (slæks) *pl. n.* informal trousers.

slag (slæg) *n.* 1. the waste material left after metal has been smelted. ~*vb.* **slagging, slagged.** 2. to form into slag. 3. (sometimes foll. by *off*) *Slang.* to make disparaging comments about; slander. —ˈslagging *n.* —ˈslaggy *adj.*

slag heap *n.* a pile of waste matter from metal smelting or coal mining.

slain (sleɪn) *vb.* the past participle of **slay.**

slake (sleɪk) *vb.* 1. *Literary.* to satisfy (thirst or desire). 2. to add water to (lime) to produce calcium hydroxide.

slalom (ˈslɑːləm) *n. Skiing, canoeing.* a race over a winding course marked by artificial obstacles.

slam¹ (slæm) *vb.* **slamming, slammed.** 1. to close violently and noisily. 2. to throw (something) down violently. 3. *Slang.* to criticize harshly. 4. to strike with violent force. ~*n.* 5. the act or noise of slamming.

slam² (slæm) *n.* the winning of all (**grand slam**) or all but one (**little slam**) of the 13 tricks at bridge.

slander (ˈslɑːndə) *n.* 1. *Law.* the utterance of a false and damaging statement about a person. 2. such a statement. ~*vb.* 3. to utter or circulate slander (about). —ˈslanderous *adj.*

slang (slæŋ) *n.* 1. informal words, expressions, and meanings avoided in formal speech or writing and often restricted to a particular social group or profession. ~*vb.* 2. to use abusive language to (someone). —ˈslangy *adj.*

slant (slɑːnt) *vb.* 1. to slope or cause to slope at an oblique angle. 2. to write or present (information) in a biased way. ~*n.* 3. a sloping line or position. 4. a point of view, esp. a biased one. 5. **on a** (*or* **the**) **slant.** sloping. ~*adj.* 6. oblique; sloping. —ˈslanting *adj.*

slap (slæp) *n.* 1. a sharp blow or smack with something flat, such as the open hand. 2. the sound made by or as if by such a blow. 3. **slap and tickle.** *Brit. informal.* sexual play. 4. **a slap in the face.** an insult or rebuff. 5. **a slap on the back.** congratulations. ~*vb.* **slapping, slapped.** 6. to strike sharply with something flat, such as the open hand. **7.** to bring (something) down forcefully: *he slapped the papers on the table.* **8.** (usually foll. by *against*) to strike (something) with a slapping sound. **9.** *Informal, chiefly Brit.* to apply in large quantities, quickly or carelessly: *she slapped butter on the bread.* **10. slap on the back.** to congratulate. ~*adv. Informal.* **11.** exactly: *slap on time.* **12.** forcibly or abruptly: *to fall slap on the floor.*

slapdash ('slæp,dæʃ) *adv.* **1.** carelessly or hastily. ~*adj.* **2.** careless or hasty.

slaphappy ('slæp,hæpɪ) *adj.* **-pier, -piest.** *Informal.* cheerfully irresponsible or careless.

slapstick ('slæp,stɪk) *n.* comedy characterized by horseplay and boisterous action.

slap-up *adj. Brit. informal.* (esp. of meals) large and luxurious; lavish.

slash (slæʃ) *vb.* **1.** to cut (a person or thing) with sharp sweeping strokes. **2.** to make large gashes in: *to slash tyres.* **3.** to reduce drastically: *prices are being slashed.* **4.** to criticize harshly. ~*n.* **5.** a sharp sweeping stroke. **6.** a cut made by such a stroke. **7.** same as **solidus. 8.** *Brit. slang.* the act of urinating.

slasher ('slæʃə) *n. N.Z.* a tool used for cutting scrub or undergrowth in the bush.

slat (slæt) *n.* a narrow thin strip of wood or metal, as used in a Venetian blind.

slate[1] (sleɪt) *n.* **1.** a fine-grained rock that can be easily split into thin layers and is used as a roofing material. **2.** a roofing tile of slate. **3.** (formerly) a writing tablet of slate. **4.** a dark grey colour. **5.** *Chiefly U.S. & Canad.* a list of candidates in an election. **6. clean slate.** a record without dishonour. **7. on the slate.** *Brit. informal.* on credit. ~*vb.* **8.** to cover (a roof) with slates. **9.** *Chiefly U.S.* to plan or schedule: *the visit is slated for October 16th.* ~*adj.* **10.** of the colour slate. —'**slaty** *adj.*

slate[2] (sleɪt) *vb. Informal, chiefly Brit.* to criticize harshly. —'**slating** *n.*

slattern ('slætən) *n.* a slovenly woman or girl. —'**slatternliness** *n.* —'**slatternly** *adj.*

slaughter ('slɔːtə) *n.* **1.** the killing of animals for food. **2.** the savage killing of a person. **3.** the indiscriminate or brutal killing of large numbers of people. ~*vb.* **4.** to kill (animals) for food. **5.** to kill in a brutal manner. **6.** to kill indiscriminately or in large numbers.

slaughterhouse ('slɔːtə,haʊs) *n.* a place where animals are killed for food.

Slav (slɑːv) *n.* a member of any of the peoples of E Europe or Soviet Asia who speak a Slavonic language.

slave (sleɪv) *n.* **1.** a person legally owned by another for whom he has to work without freedom, pay, or rights. **2.** a person under the domination of another or of some

habit or influence: *a slave to money.* **3.** a drudge. ~*vb.* **4.** (often foll. by *away*) to work like a slave.

slave-driver *n.* **1.** (esp. formerly) a person forcing slaves to work. **2.** a person who makes people work very hard.

slaver[1] ('sleɪvə) *n.* **1.** a dealer in slaves. **2.** a ship used in the slave trade.

slaver[2] ('slævə) *vb.* **1.** to dribble saliva. **2.** (often foll. by *over*) to fawn or drool (over someone). ~*n.* **3.** saliva dribbling from the mouth. **4.** *Informal.* drivel.

slavery ('sleɪvərɪ) *n.* **1.** the state or condition of being a slave. **2.** the practice or institution of owning slaves. **3.** toil or drudgery.

slave trade *n.* the buying and selling of slaves, esp. the transportation of Black Africans to America and the Caribbean from the 16th to the 19th centuries.

slavish ('sleɪvɪʃ) *adj.* **1.** of or like a slave. **2.** unoriginal; imitative. —'**slavishly** *adv.*

Slavonic (slə'vɒnɪk) *or esp. U.S.* **Slavic** *n.* **1.** a group of languages including Bulgarian, Russian, Polish, and Czech. ~*adj.* **2.** of this group of languages. **3.** of the people who speak these languages.

slay (sleɪ) *vb.* **slaying, slew, slain.** *Archaic or literary.* to kill, esp. violently. —'**slayer** *n.*

SLD Social and Liberal Democratic Party.

sleazy ('sliːzɪ) *adj.* **-zier, -ziest.** dirty, squalid, or disreputable: *a sleazy nightclub.* —'**sleaziness** *n.*

sledge[1] (slɛdʒ) *or esp. U.S. & Canad.* **sled** (slɛd) *n.* **1.** a vehicle mounted on runners, drawn by horses or dogs, for transporting people or goods over snow. **2.** a light wooden frame used, esp. by children, for sliding over snow. ~*vb.* **3.** to convey or travel by sledge.

sledge[2] (slɛdʒ) *n.* short for **sledgehammer.**

sledgehammer ('slɛdʒ,hæmə) *n.* **1.** a large heavy hammer with a long handle, used for breaking rocks and concrete. **2.** (*modifier*) crushingly powerful: *a sledgehammer blow.*

sleek (sliːk) *adj.* **1.** smooth, shiny, and glossy: *sleek black hair.* **2.** (of a person) having a well-fed or well-groomed appearance. ~*vb.* **3.** to make sleek.

sleep (sliːp) *n.* **1.** a periodic state of rest during which the eyes are closed, the muscles and nerves are relaxed, and the mind is unconscious. **2.** a period spent sleeping. **3.** a state of inactivity, like sleep. **4.** *Poetic.* death. ~*vb.* **sleeping, slept.** **5.** to be in or as in the state of sleep. **6.** to be inactive or dormant. **7.** to have sleeping accommodation for (a certain number): *the boat sleeps six.* **8.** *Poetic.* to be dead. **9. sleep on it.** to delay making a decision about (something) until the next day, in order to think about it. ~See also **sleep around, sleep in,** etc.

sleep around *vb. Informal.* to be sexually promiscuous.

sleeper ('sliːpə) *n.* **1.** a railway sleeping car or compartment. **2.** *Brit.* one of the blocks supporting the rails on a railway track. **3.** *Chiefly Brit.* a small plain gold ring worn in a pierced ear lobe to prevent the hole from closing up.

sleep in *vb. Brit.* to sleep longer than usual.

sleeping bag *n.* a large well-padded bag for sleeping in, esp. outdoors.

sleeping car *n.* a railway carriage with berths for people to sleep in.

sleeping partner *n.* a partner in a business who shares in the financing but does not play an active role.

sleeping pill *n.* a pill or tablet containing a sedative drug, used to induce sleep.

sleeping policeman *n.* a bump built across a road to deter motorists from speeding.

sleeping sickness *n.* an infectious, usually fatal, African disease transmitted by the bite of the tsetse fly, characterized by fever and sluggishness.

sleepless ('sliːplɪs) *adj.* **1.** without sleep or rest: *a sleepless journey.* **2.** unable to sleep. **3.** always alert. **4.** *Chiefly poetic.* always active. —**'sleeplessness** *n.*

sleep off *vb. Informal.* to get rid of by sleeping: *to sleep off a hangover.*

sleep out *vb.* to sleep in the open air.

sleepwalk ('sliːpˌwɔːk) *vb.* to walk while asleep. —**'sleep,walker** *n.* —**'sleep,walking** *n.*

sleep with *vb.* to have sexual intercourse and, usually, spend the night with.

sleepy ('sliːpɪ) *adj.* **sleepier, sleepiest.** **1.** ready for sleep; about to fall asleep. **2.** inducing sleep. **3.** without activity or bustle: *a sleepy town.* —**'sleepily** *adv.*

sleet (sliːt) *n.* **1.** partly melted falling snow or hail or (esp. U.S.) partly frozen rain. ~*vb.* **2.** to fall as sleet.

sleeve (sliːv) *n.* **1.** the part of a garment covering the arm. **2.** a tubelike part which fits over or completely encloses another part. **3.** a flat cardboard container to protect a gramophone record. **4. up one's sleeve.** secretly ready: *he has a few tricks up his sleeve.* —**'sleeveless** *adj.*

sleigh (sleɪ) *n.* **1.** same as **sledge¹** (sense 1). ~*vb.* **2.** to travel by sleigh.

sleight (slaɪt) *n. Archaic.* **1.** skill; dexterity. **2.** cunning.

sleight of hand *n.* **1.** manual dexterity used in performing conjuring tricks. **2.** the performance of such tricks.

slender ('slɛndə) *adj.* **1.** of small width relative to length or height. **2.** (esp. of a person's figure) slim and graceful. **3.** small or inadequate in amount or size: *slender resources.*

slept (slɛpt) *vb.* past of **sleep.**

sleuth (sluːθ) *n. Informal.* a detective.

slew¹ (sluː) *vb.* the past tense of **slay.**

slew² *or esp. U.S.* **slue** (sluː) *vb.* **1.** to twist or swing sideways, esp. awkwardly. ~*n.* **2.** the act of slewing.

slice (slaɪs) *n.* **1.** a thin flat piece or wedge cut from something: *a slice of pork.* **2.** a share or portion: *a slice of the company's revenue.* **3.** a utensil having a broad flat blade. **4.** *Sport.* the hitting of a ball so that it travels obliquely. ~*vb.* **5.** to cut (something) into slices. **6.** (usually foll. by *through*) to cut through in a clean and effortless manner, with or as if with a knife. **7.** (usually foll. by *off, from, away*) to cut or be cut (from) a larger piece. **8.** to hit (a ball) with a slice.

slick (slɪk) *adj.* **1.** persuasive and glib: *a slick salesman.* **2.** skilfully devised or executed: *a slick show.* **3.** *Informal, chiefly U.S. & Canad.* shrewd; sly. **4.** *Informal.* well-made and attractive, but superficial: *a slick publication.* **5.** *Chiefly U.S. & Canad.* slippery. ~*n.* **6.** a slippery area, esp. a patch of oil floating on water. ~*vb.* **7.** to make smooth or sleek.

slide (slaɪd) *vb.* **sliding, slid** (slɪd), **slid.** **1.** to move smoothly along a surface in continual contact with it: *doors that slide open.* **2.** to slip: *he slid on his back.* **3.** (usually foll. by *into, out of, away from*) to pass or move unobtrusively: *she slid into the room.* **4.** (usually foll. by *into*) to go (into a specified condition) by degrees: *he slid into loose living.* **5. let slide.** to allow to deteriorate by neglect: *to let things slide.* ~*n.* **6.** the act or an instance of sliding. **7.** a smooth surface, as of ice, for sliding on. **8.** a structure with a steep smooth slope for sliding down in playgrounds. **9.** a small glass plate on which specimens are mounted for study under a microscope. **10.** a photograph on a transparent base, mounted in a frame, that can be viewed by means of a projector. **11.** *Chiefly Brit.* an ornamental clip to hold hair in place. **12.** the sliding curved tube of a trombone that is moved in and out to allow different notes to be played.

slide rule *n.* a calculating device consisting of two strips, one sliding along a central groove in the other, each strip graduated in two or more logarithmic scales of numbers.

sliding scale *n.* a variable scale according to which things such as wages or prices fluctuate in response to changes in other factors.

slight (slaɪt) *adj.* **1.** small in quantity or extent: *a slight accent.* **2.** of small importance. **3.** slim and delicate. **4.** lacking in strength or substance. ~*vb.* **5.** to show disregard for (someone); snub. ~*n.* **6.** an act of snubbing (someone). —**'slightly** *adv.*

slim (slɪm) *adj.* **slimmer, slimmest.** **1.** small in width relative to height or length. **2.** poor; meagre: *slim chances of success.* ~*vb.* **3.** to make or become slim, esp. by diets and exercise. **4.** to reduce in size: *the workforce was slimmed.* —**'slimmer** *n.* —**'slimming** *n.*

Slim (slɪm) *n.* the E African name for **AIDS.**

slime (slaɪm) *n.* **1.** soft runny mud or any sticky substance. esp. when disgusting or unpleasant. **2.** a thick, sticky substance produced by various fish, slugs, and fungi.

slimy ('slaɪmɪ) *adj.* **slimier, slimiest.** **1.** of, like, or covered with slime. **2.** *Chiefly Brit.* offensively ingratiating.

sling[1] (slɪŋ) *n.* **1.** a rope or strap by which something may be lifted. **2.** *Med.* a wide piece of cloth suspended from the neck for supporting an injured hand or arm. **3.** a simple weapon consisting of a strap tied to cords, in which a stone is whirled and then released. ~*vb.* **slinging, slung.** **4.** *Informal.* to throw. **5.** to carry or hang loosely from or as if from a sling: *to sling washing from the line.* **6.** to hurl with or as if with a sling.

sling[2] (slɪŋ) *n.* a sweetened mixed drink with a spirit base: *gin sling.*

slingback ('slɪŋˌbæk) *n.* a shoe with a strap instead of a complete covering for the heel.

sling off *vb.* (often foll. by *at*) *Austral. & N.Z. informal.* to mock; deride; jeer.

slink (slɪŋk) *vb.* **slinking, slunk.** to move or act in a furtive manner from or as if from fear or guilt.

slinky ('slɪŋkɪ) *adj.* **slinkier, slinkiest.** *Informal.* **1.** moving in a sinuously graceful or provocative way. **2.** (of clothes) figure-hugging.

slip[1] (slɪp) *vb.* **slipping, slipped.** **1.** to move smoothly and easily: *the catch slips into place.* **2.** to place quickly or stealthily: *he slipped a coin into her hand.* **3.** to put on or take off easily or quickly: *to slip on a sweater.* **4.** to lose balance and slide unexpectedly: *he slipped on the ice.* **5.** to let loose or be let loose. **6.** to pass out of (the mind or memory). **7.** to move or pass swiftly or unperceived: *to slip quietly out of the room.* **8.** (sometimes foll. by *up*) to make a mistake. **9.** to become worse; weaken. **10.** to dislocate (a bone). **11.** to pass (a stitch) from one needle to another without knitting it. **12. let slip. a.** to allow to escape. **b.** to say unintentionally. ~*n.* **13.** a slipping. **14.** a mistake or oversight: *a slip of the pen.* **15.** a woman's sleeveless undergarment, worn under a dress. **16.** same as **slipway.** **17.** *Cricket.* **a.** the fielder who stands a little behind and to the offside of the wicket-keeper. **b.** this position. **18. give someone the slip.** to escape from someone. ~See also **slip up.**

slip[2] (slɪp) *n.* **1.** a small piece of paper: *a receipt slip.* **2.** a cutting taken from a plant. **3.** a young slender person: *a slip of a child.*

slip[3] (slɪp) *n.* clay mixed with water to a thin paste, used for decorating or patching a ceramic piece.

slipe (slaɪp) *n. N.Z.* wool removed from the pelt of a slaughtered sheep by immersion in a chemical bath.

slipknot ('slɪpˌnɒt) *n.* a nooselike knot tied so that it will slip along the rope round which it is made.

slip-on *adj.* **1.** (of a garment or shoe) made so as to be easily and quickly put on. ~*n.* **2.** a slip-on garment or shoe.

slipped disc *n. Pathol.* a painful condition in which one of the discs which connects the bones of the spine becomes displaced and presses on the adjacent nerves.

slipper ('slɪpə) *n.* a light soft shoe for indoor wear. —**'slippered** *adj.*

slippery ('slɪpərɪ, -prɪ) *adj.* **1.** liable or tending to cause objects to slip: *a slippery road.* **2.** liable to slip from one's grasp. **3.** not to be trusted: *a slippery character.* —**'slipperiness** *n.*

slippy ('slɪpɪ) *adj.* **-pier, -piest.** **1.** *Informal or dialect.* same as **slippery** (senses 1, 2). **2.** *Brit. informal.* alert; quick: *look slippy!* —**'slippiness** *n.*

slip road *n. Brit.* a short road connecting a motorway to another road.

slipshod ('slɪpˌʃɒd) *adj.* **1.** (of an action) negligent; careless. **2.** (of a person's appearance) slovenly; down-at-heel.

slip-slop *n. S. African.* same as **flip-flop** (sense 5).

slipstream ('slɪpˌstriːm) *n.* the stream of air forced backwards by an aircraft propeller or other moving object.

slip up *Informal.* ~*vb.* **1.** to make a mistake. ~*n.* **slip-up. 2.** a mistake.

slipway ('slɪpˌweɪ) *n.* a large ramp that slopes down from the shore into the water, on which a ship is built or repaired and from which it is launched.

slit (slɪt) *vb.* **slitting, slit.** **1.** to make a straight long incision in. **2.** to cut into strips lengthwise. ~*n.* **3.** a long narrow cut or opening.

slither ('slɪðə) *vb.* **1.** to move or slide unsteadily, as on a slippery surface. ~*n.* **2.** a slithering motion. —**'slithery** *adj.*

sliver ('slɪvə) *n.* **1.** a thin piece that is cut or broken off lengthwise. ~*vb.* **2.** to cut or break off in slivers.

Sloane Ranger (sləʊn) *n.* (in Britain) *Informal.* a young upper-class person having a home in London and in the country, characterized as wearing expensive informal clothes.

slob (slɒb) *n. Informal.* a stupid or coarse person.

slobber ('slɒbə) vb. **1.** to dribble (liquid or saliva) from the mouth. **2.** to behave in a gushy or maudlin way. **3.** to smear with liquid dribbling from the mouth. ~n. **4.** liquid or saliva spilt from the mouth. —'**slobbery** adj.

slob ice n. Canad. sludgy masses of floating ice.

sloe (sləʊ) n. **1.** the small sour blue-black fruit of the blackthorn. **2.** same as **blackthorn.**

sloe-eyed adj. having dark almond-shaped eyes.

slog (slɒg) vb. **slogging, slogged. 1.** to hit hard. **2.** to work hard; toil. **3.** to make one's way with difficulty. ~n. **4.** a long and difficult walk. **5.** long exhausting work. **6.** a heavy blow.

slogan ('sləʊgən) n. a catchword or phrase used in politics or advertising.

sloop (sluːp) n. a single-masted sailing vessel, rigged fore-and-aft.

sloot (sluːt) n. S. African. a ditch for irrigation or drainage.

slop (slɒp) vb. **slopping, slopped. 1.** (often foll. by about) to splash or spill (liquid) or (of liquid) to splash or spill. **2.** (foll. by over) Informal, chiefly U.S. & Canad. to be gushingly sentimental. ~n. **3.** a puddle of spilt liquid. **4.** (pl.) kitchen swill used to feed animals, esp. pigs. **5.** (pl.) waste food or liquid refuse. **6.** (often pl.) Informal. liquid food.

slope (sləʊp) vb. **1.** to slant or cause to slant. **2.** (esp. of natural features) to follow an inclined course: many paths sloped down the hillside. **3.** (foll. by off or away) Informal. to go furtively. **4.** Mil. **slope arms.** (formerly) to hold (a rifle) in a sloping position against the shoulder. ~n. **5.** an inclined portion of ground. **6.** (pl.) hills or foothills. **7.** any inclined surface. **8.** the degree of such inclination.

slop out vb. (of prisoners) to empty chamber pots and collect water.

sloppy ('slɒpɪ) adj. **-pier, -piest. 1.** wet; slushy. **2.** Informal. careless; untidy. **3.** Informal. gushingly sentimental. —'**sloppily** adv. —'**sloppiness** n.

slosh (slɒʃ) n. **1.** slush. **2.** Brit. slang. a heavy blow. **3.** the sound of splashing liquid. ~vb. **4.** Informal. to throw or pour (liquid) carelessly. **5.** (often foll. by about or around) Informal. **a.** to shake or stir (something) in a liquid. **b.** (of a person) to splash (around) in water or mud. **6.** Brit. slang. to deal a heavy blow to. **7.** (usually foll. by about or around) Informal. to shake (a container of liquid) or (of liquid in a container) to be shaken. —'**sloshy** adj.

sloshed (slɒʃt) adj. Slang, chiefly Brit. drunk.

slot (slɒt) n. **1.** a narrow opening or groove, such as one in a vending machine

for inserting a coin. **2.** Informal. a place in a series or scheme. ~vb. **slotting, slotted. 3.** to provide with a slot or slots. **4.** (usually foll. by in or into) to fit or be fitted into a slot.

sloth (sləʊθ) n. **1.** a slow-moving shaggy-coated animal of Central and South America, which hangs upside down in trees by its long arms and feeds on vegetation. **2.** laziness; indolence.

slothful ('sləʊθfʊl) adj. lazy; indolent.

slot machine n. a machine, esp. for gambling, worked by placing a coin in a slot.

slouch (slaʊtʃ) vb. **1.** to sit, stand, or move with a drooping posture. ~n. **2.** a drooping posture. **3.** (usually used in negative constructions) Informal. an incompetent or slovenly person: he's no slouch at football.

slouch hat n. a soft hat with a brim that can be pulled down over the ears.

slough¹ (slaʊ) n. **1.** a swamp or marshy area. **2.** (sluː). U.S. & Canad. a large hole where water collects. **3.** despair or hopeless depression.

slough² (slʌf) n. **1.** any outer covering that is shed, such as the dead outer layer of the skin of a snake. ~vb. **2.** (often foll. by off) to shed (an outer covering) or (of an outer covering) to be shed.

slough off (slʌf) vb. to cast off (something unwanted or unneccessary).

sloven ('slʌv³n) n. a person who is habitually untidy, lazy, or careless in appearance or manner.

slovenly ('slʌvənlɪ) adj. **1.** habitually unclean or untidy. **2.** negligent and careless: slovenly manners. ~adv. **3.** in a slovenly manner. —'**slovenliness** n.

slow (sləʊ) adj. **1.** taking a longer time than is usual or expected. **2.** characterized by lack of speed: a slow walker. **3.** adapted to or producing slow movement: the slow lane of a motorway. **4.** (of a clock or watch) indicating a time earlier than the correct time. **5.** not quick to understand: a slow mind. **6.** dull or uninteresting: the play was very slow. **7.** not easily aroused: slow to anger. **8.** (of business) unproductive; slack. **9.** (of a fire or oven) giving off low heat. **10.** Photog. requiring a relatively long time of exposure: a slow film. ~adv. **11.** in a slow manner. ~vb. **12.** (often foll. by up or down) to decrease or cause to decrease in speed or activity. —'**slowly** adv.

slowcoach ('sləʊˌkəʊtʃ) n. Brit. informal. a person who moves or works slowly.

slow motion n. **1.** Films & television. action that is made to appear slower than normal by filming at a faster rate or by replaying a video recording more slowly. ~adj. **slow-motion. 2.** of or relating to such action. **3.** moving at considerably less than usual speed.

slow virus n. a type of virus that is present

in the body for a long time before it becomes active or infectious.

slowworm ('sləʊ,wɜːm) n. a legless lizard with a brownish-grey snakelike body.

sludge (slʌdʒ) n. **1.** soft mud or snow. **2.** any muddy or slushy sediment. **3.** sewage. —'**sludgy** adj.

slug¹ (slʌg) n. a mollusc like a snail but without a shell.

slug² (slʌg) n. **1.** a bullet. **2.** Printing. a line of type produced by a Linotype machine. **3.** a mouthful of alcoholic drink, esp. spirits.

slug³ (slʌg) vb. **slugging, slugged. 1.** Chiefly U.S. & Canad. to hit very hard. ~n. **2.** U.S. & Canad. a heavy blow.

sluggard ('slʌgəd) n. a person who is habitually lazy.

sluggish ('slʌgɪʃ) adj. **1.** lacking energy. **2.** functioning at below the normal rate.

sluice (sluːs) n. **1.** a channel that carries a rapid current of water, with a sluicegate to control the flow. **2.** the water controlled by a sluicegate. **3.** same as **sluicegate. 4.** Mining. a sloping trough for washing ore. ~vb. **5.** to draw off or drain by means of a sluice. **6.** to wash with a stream of water. **7.** (often foll. by away or out) (of water) to run or flow from or as if from a sluice.

sluicegate ('sluːs,geɪt) n. a valve or gate fitted to a sluice to control the rate of flow of water.

slum (slʌm) n. **1.** a squalid overcrowded house. **2.** (often pl.) a squalid overpopulated section of a city. ~vb. **slumming, slummed. 3.** to visit slums, esp. for curiosity. **4.** Also: **slum it.** to experience poorer than usual conditions. —'**slummy** adj.

slumber ('slʌmbə) vb. **1.** to sleep. ~n. **2.** (sometimes pl.) sleep. —'**slumbering** adj.

slump (slʌmp) vb. **1.** (of commercial activity or prices) to decline suddenly. **2.** to sink or fall heavily and suddenly. ~n. **3.** a decline in commercial activity or prices; depression. **4.** a sudden or marked decline or failure.

slung (slʌŋ) vb. past of **sling**¹.

slunk (slʌŋk) vb. past of **slink**.

slur (slɜː) vb. **slurring, slurred. 1.** to pronounce or utter (words) indistinctly. **2.** to speak disparagingly of. **3.** Music. to sing or play (successive notes) smoothly by moving from one to the other without a break. **4.** (often foll. by over) to treat superficially, hastily, or carelessly. ~n. **5.** a slighting remark intended to damage one's reputation. **6.** a slurring of words. **7.** Music. **a.** a slurring of successive notes. **b.** the curved line (⌢ or ⌣) indicating this.

slurp (slɜːp) Informal. ~vb. **1.** to eat or drink (something) noisily. ~n. **2.** a slurping sound.

slurry ('slʌrɪ) n., pl. -ries. a thin watery mixture of cement, mud, or other substance.

slush (slʌʃ) n. **1.** any watery muddy substance, esp. melting snow. **2.** Informal. sloppily sentimental language or writing. —'**slushy** adj.

slush fund n. a fund for financing political or commercial corruption.

slut (slʌt) n. **1.** a dirty slovenly woman. **2.** a promiscuous woman. —'**sluttish** adj.

sly (slaɪ) adj. **slyer, slyest** or **slier, sliest. 1.** crafty; artful: a sly dodge. **2.** secretive and cunning: a sly manner. **3.** roguish: sly humour. **4. on the sly.** secretively. —'**slyly** adv.

Sm Chem. samarium.

smack¹ (smæk) vb. **1.** to slap sharply. **2.** to strike loudly or to be struck loudly. **3.** to open and close (the lips) loudly to show pleasure or anticipation. ~n. **4.** a sharp resounding slap, or the sound of such a slap. **5.** a loud kiss. **6.** a sharp sound made by the lips in enjoyment. **7. smack in the eye.** Informal, chiefly Brit. a snub or rebuff. ~adv. Informal. **8.** directly; squarely: smack in the middle. **9.** sharply and unexpectedly: he drove smack into the back of our car.

smack² (smæk) n. **1.** a slight flavour, suggestion, or trace (of something): the smack of corruption. **2.** Slang. heroin. ~vb. (foll. by of) **3.** to have a slight smell or flavour (of something): to smack of the sea. **4.** to have a suggestion (of something): his speeches smacked of bigotry.

smack³ (smæk) n. a small single-masted fishing vessel.

smacker ('smækə) n. Slang. **1.** a loud kiss. **2.** a pound note or dollar bill.

small (smɔːl) adj. **1.** not large in size or amount. **2.** of little importance or on a minor scale: a small business. **3.** mean, ungenerous, or petty: a small mind. **4.** modest or humble: small beginnings. **5. feel small.** to be humiliated. **6.** (of a child or animal) young; not mature. **7.** unimportant; trivial: a small matter. **8.** (of a letter) written or printed in lower case rather as a capital. ~adv. **9.** into small pieces: cut it small. ~n. **10.** a small narrow part, esp. of the back. **11.** (pl.) Informal, chiefly Brit. underwear. —'**smallish** adj. —'**smallness** n.

small beer n. Informal, chiefly Brit. people or things of no importance.

small change n. coins of low value.

small fry pl. n. **1.** people regarded as unimportant. **2.** young children.

small goods pl. n. Austral. & N.Z. meats bought from a delicatessen, such as sausages.

smallholding ('smɔːl,həʊldɪŋ) n. a piece of agricultural land smaller than a farm. —'**small,holder** n.

small hours pl. n. **the.** the early hours of

the morning, after midnight and before dawn.

small intestine *n.* the narrow, longer part of the alimentary canal, in which digestion is completed.

small-minded *adj.* narrow-minded; intolerant.

smallpox ('smɔːl,pɒks) *n.* a highly contagious viral disease causing fever, a rash, and blisters which usually leave permanent scars on the skin.

small print *n.* matter in a contract or document printed in small type, esp. when considered to be a trap for the unwary.

small-scale *adj.* of limited size or scope.

small talk *n.* light conversation for social occasions.

small-time *adj. Informal.* insignificant; minor: *a small-time criminal.*

smarm (smɑːm) *vb. Brit. informal.* **1.** (often foll. by *down*) to flatten (the hair) with grease. **2.** to ingratiate oneself (with).

smarmy ('smɑːmɪ) *adj.* **smarmier, smarmiest.** obsequiously flattering or unpleasantly suave.

smart (smɑːt) *adj.* **1.** astute or shrewd. **2.** quick, witty, and often impertinent in speech: *a smart talker.* **3.** fashionable; chic: *a smart hotel.* **4.** well-kept; neat. **5.** causing a sharp stinging pain. **6.** vigorous or brisk: *a smart pace.* ~*vb.* **7.** to feel or cause a sharp stinging physical pain or keen mental distress: *he smarted under their abuse.* **8.** (often foll. by *for*) to suffer a harsh penalty. ~*n.* **9.** a stinging pain or feeling. ~*adv.* **10.** in a smart manner. ~See also **smarts.** —'**smartly** *adv.* —'**smartness** *n.*

smart aleck ('ælɪk) *n. Informal.* a conceited know-all.

smarten ('smɑːtᵊn) *vb.* (usually foll. by *up*) to make or become smart.

smarts (smɑːts) *pl. n. Slang, chiefly U.S.* know-how, intelligence, or wits: *street smarts.*

smash (smæʃ) *vb.* **1.** to break into pieces violently and noisily. **2.** (often foll. by *against, through* or *into*) to throw or crash (against) vigorously, causing shattering: *the sea smashed the boat against the rocks.* **3.** to hit or collide forcefully and suddenly. **4.** *Sport.* to hit (the ball) fast and powerfully with an overhead stroke. **5.** to defeat or destroy: *police smashed a drug ring.* ~*n.* **6.** an act or sound of smashing. **7.** a violent collision, esp. of vehicles. **8.** a total failure or collapse, as of a business. **9.** *Sport.* a fast and powerful overhead stroke. **10.** *Informal.* a popular success. ~*adv.* **11.** with a smash.

smash-and-grab *adj. Informal.* of a robbery in which a shop window is broken and the contents removed.

smasher ('smæʃə) *n. Informal, chiefly Brit.*

a person or thing that is very attractive or outstanding.

smashing ('smæʃɪŋ) *adj. Informal, chiefly Brit.* excellent or first-rate.

smash-up *Informal.* ~*n.* **1.** a bad collision, esp of cars. ~*vb.* **smash up.** **2.** to damage to the point of complete destruction: *they smashed the place up.*

smattering ('smætərɪŋ) *n.* a slight or superficial knowledge.

smear (smɪə) *vb.* **1.** to daub or cover with a greasy or sticky substance. **2.** to apply (a greasy or sticky substance) thickly. **3.** to rub so as to produce a smudge. **4.** to slander. ~*n.* **5.** a dirty mark or smudge. **6.** a slanderous attack. **7.** a small amount of a substance smeared onto a glass slide for examination under a microscope. —'**smeary** *adj.*

smear test *n. Med.* same as **Pap test.**

smell (smɛl) *vb.* **smelling, smelt** *or* **smelled.** **1.** to perceive the scent of (a substance) by means of the nose. **2.** (foll. by an adj.) to have a specified smell: *the curry smells spicy.* **3.** (often foll. by *of*) to emit an odour (of): *the park smells of flowers.* **4.** (sometimes foll. by an adv.) to emit an unpleasant odour. **5.** (often foll. by *out*) to detect through shrewdness or instinct: *I smell danger.* **6.** to use the sense of smell; sniff. **7.** (foll. by *of*) to give indications of: *this action smells of treachery.* ~*n.* **8.** the sense by which scents or odours are perceived. **9.** an odour or scent. **10.** the act of smelling.

Usage. *Smell* in its neutral sense of giving out an odour is followed by an adjective rather than by an adverb: *the soup smells good* (rather than *well*). *Smell* in the sense of giving out an unpleasant odour is followed by an adverb.

smelling salts *pl. n.* a pungent preparation containing crystals of ammonium carbonate, sniffed to relieve faintness.

smelly ('smɛlɪ) *adj.* **smellier, smelliest.** having a nasty smell. —'**smelliness** *n.*

smelt[1] (smɛlt) *vb.* to extract (a metal) from (an ore) by heating.

smelt[2] (smɛlt) *n., pl.* **smelt** *or* **smelts.** a small silvery food fish.

smelt[3] (smɛlt) *vb.* a past tense and past participle of **smell.**

smelter ('smɛltə) *n.* an industrial plant in which smelting is carried out.

smile (smaɪl) *n.* **1.** a facial expression in which the corners of the mouth are turned up, showing amusement or friendliness. ~*vb.* **2.** to wear or assume a smile. **3.** (foll. by *at*) **a.** to look at with a kindly expression. **b.** to look with amusement at. **4.** (foll. by *on* or *upon*) to regard favourably. **5.** to express by a smile: *she smiled a welcome.*

smirch (smɜːtʃ) *vb.* **1.** to dirty; soil. ~*n.*

2. a smirching or being smirched. **3.** a smear or stain.

smirk (smɜːk) *n.* **1.** a smile expressing smugness rather than pleasure. ~*vb.* **2.** to give such a smile.

smite (smaɪt) *vb.* **smiting, smote; smitten** *or* **smit** (smɪt). *Archaic.* **1.** to strike with a heavy blow. **2.** to affect severely: *smitten with flu.* **3.** to afflict in order to punish. **4.** (foll. by *on*) to strike forcibly or abruptly: *the sun smote down on him.*

smith (smɪθ) *n.* **1.** a person who works in metal: *silversmith.* **2.** See **blacksmith.**

smithereens (ˌsmɪðəˈriːnz) *pl. n.* shattered fragments.

smithy (ˈsmɪðɪ) *n., pl.* **smithies.** the workshop of a blacksmith; forge.

smitten (ˈsmɪtən) *vb.* **1.** a past participle of **smite.** ~*adj.* **2.** affected by love (for).

smock (smɒk) *n.* **1.** a loose outer garment, worn to protect the clothes. **2.** a loose blouselike garment worn by women. **3.** a loose protective overgarment decorated with smocking, worn formerly by farm workers. ~*vb.* **4.** to decorate with smocking.

smocking (ˈsmɒkɪŋ) *n.* ornamental needlework used to gather material.

smog (smɒg) *n.* a mixture of smoke and fog. —ˈsmoggy *adj.*

smoke (sməʊk) *n.* **1.** the visible vapour arising from something burning. **2.** the act of smoking tobacco. **3.** *Informal.* a cigarette or cigar. **4. go up in smoke. a.** to come to nothing. **b.** to burn up vigorously. ~*vb.* **5.** to give off smoke, sometimes excessively or in the wrong place. **6. a.** to draw the smoke of (burning tobacco) into the mouth and exhale it again. **b.** to do this habitually. **7.** to cure (meat or fish) by treating with smoke.

Smoke (sməʊk) *n.* **the.** *Brit. & Austral.* *slang.* a big city, esp. (in Britain) London.

smokeless (ˈsməʊklɪs) *adj.* having or producing little or no smoke: *smokeless fuel.*

smokeless zone *n.* an area where only smokeless fuels are permitted to be used.

smoke out *vb.* **1.** to drive out of hiding by means of smoke. **2.** to bring into the open: *they smoked out the plot.*

smoker (ˈsməʊkə) *n.* **1.** a person who habitually smokes tobacco. **2.** a train compartment where smoking is permitted.

smoke screen *n.* **1.** *Mil.* a cloud of smoke produced to obscure movements. **2.** something said or done to hide the truth.

smokestack (ˈsməʊkˌstæk) *n.* a tall chimney that carries smoke away from a factory.

smoko *or* **smokeho** (ˈsməʊkəʊ) *n., pl.* **-kos** *or* **-hos.** *Austral. & N.Z. informal.* **1.** a short break from work for tea or a cigarette. **2.** refreshment taken during this break.

smoky (ˈsməʊkɪ) *adj.* **smokier, smokiest.** **1.** filled with or giving off smoke, sometimes excessively: *a smoky fire.* **2.** having the colour of smoke. **3.** having a smoky flavour. **4.** made dirty or hazy by smoke. —ˈsmokiness *n.*

smolt (sməʊlt) *n.* a young salmon at the stage when it migrates from fresh water to the sea.

smooch (smuːtʃ) *Slang.* ~*vb.* **1.** (of two people) to kiss and cuddle. **2.** *Brit.* to dance very slowly and amorously with one's arms around another person or (of two people) to dance together in such a way. ~*n.* **3.** the act of smooching.

smoodge *or* **smooge** (smuːdʒ) *vb. Austral. & N.Z.* **1.** same as **smooch** (sense 1). **2.** to seek to ingratiate oneself.

smooth (smuːð) *adj.* **1.** having an even surface with no roughness, bumps, or holes. **2.** lacking obstructions or difficulties. **3.** charming or persuasive, often in an insincere way. **4.** without lumps: *smooth batter.* **5.** free from jolts: *smooth driving.* **6.** not harsh in taste: *a smooth wine.* ~*adv.* **7.** in a smooth manner. ~*vb.* **8.** (often foll. by *down*) to make or become even or without roughness. **9.** (often foll. by *out* or *away*) to remove in order to make smooth: *she smoothed out the creases in her dress.* **10.** to make calm; soothe. **11.** to make easier: *smooth his path.* ~*n.* **12.** the smooth part of something. **13.** the act of smoothing. —ˈsmoothly *adv.*

smoothie *or* **smoothy** (ˈsmuːðɪ) *n., pl.* **smoothies.** *Slang.* a man who is smooth or slick in speech, dress, or manner.

smooth over *vb.* to ease or gloss over: *to smooth over a difficulty.*

smooth-talking *or* **smooth-tongued** *adj.* speaking persuasively but not necessarily sincerely.

smorgasbord (ˈsmɔːgəsˌbɔːd) *n.* a variety of savoury dishes served as hors d'oeuvres or as a buffet meal.

smote (sməʊt) *vb.* the past tense of **smite.**

smother (ˈsmʌðə) *vb.* **1.** to suffocate or stifle. **2.** to surround or overwhelm (with): *he smothered her with love.* **3.** to extinguish (a fire) by covering so as to cut it off from the air. **4.** to suppress or stifle: *smother a giggle.* **5.** to cover over thickly.

smoulder *or U.S.* **smolder** (ˈsməʊldə) *vb.* **1.** to burn slowly without flame, usually giving off smoke. **2.** (of anger or hatred) to exist in a suppressed state. ~*n.* **3.** a smouldering.

smudge (smʌdʒ) *vb.* **1.** to make or become smeared or soiled. ~*n.* **2.** a smear or dirty mark. **3.** a blurred form or area: *that smudge in the distance is a quarry.* —ˈsmudgy *adj.*

smug (smʌg) *adj.* **smugger, smuggest.** excessively self-satisfied. —ˈsmugly *adv.* —ˈsmugness *n.*

smuggle ('smʌgᵊl) vb. 1. to import or export (prohibited or dutiable goods) secretly. 2. (often foll. by *into* or *out of*) to bring or take secretly. —'**smuggler** n. —'**smuggling** n.

smut (smʌt) n. 1. a speck of soot or a dark mark left by soot. 2. something obscene or indecent. 3. a fungal disease of cereals, in which black sooty masses cover the affected parts. ~vb. **smutting, smutted.** 4. to mark or become marked with smuts. —'**smutty** adj.

Sn Chem. tin.

snack (snæk) n. a light quick meal eaten between or in place of main meals.

snack bar n. a place where light meals or snacks are sold.

snaffle ('snæfᵊl) n. 1. a simple jointed bit for a horse. ~vb. 2. Brit. informal. to steal or take. 3. to equip or control (a horse) with a snaffle.

snafu (snæ'fuː) Slang, chiefly mil. ~n. 1. confusion or chaos regarded as the normal state. ~adj. 2. confused or muddled up, as usual.

snag (snæg) n. 1. a difficulty or disadvantage: *the snag is that I have nothing to wear.* 2. a sharp projecting point that may catch on things. 3. a small hole in a fabric caused by a sharp object. 4. a tree stump in a riverbed that is dangerous to navigation. ~vb. **snagging, snagged.** 5. to tear or catch on a snag.

snail (sneɪl) n. a slow-moving mollusc with a spirally coiled shell.

snail's pace n. a very slow speed.

snake (sneɪk) n. 1. a reptile with a long scaly limbless body, lidless eyes, a tapering tail, and a jaw modified for swallowing large prey. 2. Also: **snake in the grass.** a deceitful or treacherous person. ~vb. 3. to glide or move in a winding course, like a snake.

snakebite ('sneɪk,baɪt) n. 1. the bite of a snake. 2. a drink of cider and lager.

snake charmer n. an entertainer who appears to hypnotize snakes by playing music.

snakes and ladders n. (functioning as sing.) a board game in which players move counters along a series of squares by means of dice, going up the ladders to squares nearer the finish and down the snakes to squares nearer the start.

snaky ('sneɪkɪ) adj. **snakier, snakiest.** 1. twisting; winding. 2. treacherous.

snap (snæp) vb. **snapping, snapped.** 1. to break suddenly, esp. with a sharp sound. 2. to make or cause to make a sudden sharp cracking sound: *snap one's fingers.* 3. to give way or collapse suddenly under strain. 4. to move or close with a sudden sharp sound. 5. to move in a sudden or abrupt way. 6. (often foll. by *at* or *up*) to seize

suddenly or quickly. 7. (often foll. by *at*) to bite at (something) suddenly. 8. to speak (words) sharply or abruptly. 9. to take a snapshot of. 10. **snap one's fingers at.** Informal. **a.** to dismiss contemptuously. **b.** to defy. 11. **snap out of it.** Informal. to recover quickly, esp. from depression or anger. ~n. 12. the act of breaking suddenly or the sound of a sudden breakage. 13. a sudden sharp sound. 14. a catch, clasp, or fastener that closes with a snapping sound. 15. a sudden grab or bite. 16. a thin crisp biscuit: *ginger snaps.* 17. Informal. same as **snapshot.** 18. a sudden brief spell of cold weather. 19. Brit. a card game in which the word *snap* is called when two similar cards are turned up. 20. (modifier) done on the spur of the moment: *a snap decision.* ~adv. 21. with a snap. ~interj. 22. **a.** Cards. the word called while playing snap. **b.** an exclamation used to draw attention to the similarity of two things. ~See also **snap up.**

snapdragon ('snæp,drægən) n. a plant with spikes of colourful flowers that can open and shut like a mouth; antirrhinum.

snap fastener n. same as **press stud.**

snappy ('snæpɪ) adj. **-pier, -piest.** 1. Also: **snappish.** irritable or cross. 2. brisk or lively: *a snappy pace.* 3. chilly: *snappy weather.* 4. smart and fashionable: *a snappy dresser.* 5. **make it snappy.** Slang. hurry up! —'**snappiness** n.

snapshot ('snæp,ʃɒt) n. an informal photograph taken with a simple camera.

snap up vb. to take advantage of eagerly and quickly: *to snap up bargains.*

snare¹ (snɛə) n. 1. a trap for birds or small animals, usually a flexible loop that is drawn tight around the prey. 2. anything that entangles someone or something unawares. ~vb. 3. to catch in or as if in a snare.

snare² (snɛə) n. Music. a set of strings fitted against the lower head of a snare drum, which produces a rattling sound when the drum is beaten.

snare drum n. Music. a small drum fitted with a snare.

snarl¹ (snɑːl) vb. 1. (of an animal) to growl viciously, baring the teeth. 2. to speak or say (something) viciously. ~n. 3. a vicious growl or facial expression. 4. the act of snarling.

snarl² (snɑːl) n. 1. a tangled mass. 2. a complicated or confused state. ~vb. 3. (often foll. by *up*) to be, become, or make tangled or complicated.

snarl-up n. Informal, chiefly Brit. a confused, disorganized situation such as a traffic jam.

snatch (snætʃ) vb. 1. to seize or grasp (something) suddenly: *he snatched the chocolate.* 2. (usually foll. by *at*) to attempt to seize suddenly. 3. to take hurriedly: *to snatch some sleep.* **4.** to remove suddenly: *she snatched her hand away.* ~*n.* **5.** an act of snatching. **6.** a fragment or incomplete part: *snatches of conversation.* **7.** a brief spell: *snatches of time off.* **8.** *Slang, chiefly U.S.* an act of kidnapping. **9.** *Brit. slang.* a robbery: *a diamond snatch.*

snazzy ('snæzɪ) *adj.* **-zier, -ziest.** *Informal.* (esp. of clothes) stylishly and often flashily attractive.

sneak (sni:k) *vb.* **1.** to move furtively. **2.** to behave in a cowardly or underhand manner. **3.** to bring, take, or put stealthily. **4.** *Informal, chiefly Brit.* to tell tales (esp. in schools). ~*n.* **5.** a person who acts in an underhand or cowardly manner, esp. as an informer. ~*adj.* **6.** without warning: *a sneak attack.* —'**sneaky** *adj.*

sneakers ('sni:kəz) *pl. n. Chiefly U.S. & Canad.* canvas shoes with rubber soles.

sneaking ('sni:kɪŋ) *adj.* **1.** acting in a furtive or cowardly way. **2.** secret: *a sneaking desire to marry a millionaire.* **3.** slight but nagging: *a sneaking suspicion.*

sneak thief *n.* a burglar who sneaks into premises through open doors and windows.

sneer (snɪə) *n.* **1.** a facial expression of scorn or contempt, typically with the upper lip curled. **2.** a scornful or contemptuous remark. ~*vb.* **3.** to assume a facial expression of scorn or contempt. **4.** to say (something) in a scornful manner. —'**sneering** *adj., n.*

sneeze (sni:z) *vb.* **1.** to expel air from the nose suddenly and involuntarily, esp. as the result of irritation in the nostrils. ~*n.* **2.** the act or sound of sneezing.

sneeze at *vb.* (usually with a negative) *Informal.* to dismiss lightly: *his offer is not to be sneezed at.*

sneezewood ('sni:z,wʊd) *n.* **1.** a South African tree. **2.** its exceptionally hard wood, used for furniture, gateposts, and railway sleepers.

snick (snɪk) *n.* **1.** a small cut; notch. **2.** *Cricket.* a glancing blow off the edge of the bat. ~*vb.* **3.** to make a small cut or notch in (something). **4.** *Cricket.* to hit (the ball) with a snick.

snicker ('snɪkə) *n., vb.* (esp. U.S. and Canad.) same as **snigger.**

snide (snaɪd) *adj.* maliciously derogatory: *snide comments.*

sniff (snɪf) *vb.* **1.** to inhale through the nose in short audible breaths. **2.** (often foll. by *at*) to perceive or attempt to perceive (a smell) by sniffing. ~*n.* **3.** the act or sound of sniffing. —'**sniffer** *n.*

sniff at *vb.* to express contempt or dislike for.

sniffle ('snɪf°l) *vb.* **1.** to sniff repeatedly, as when the nasal passages are congested. ~*n.* **2.** the act or sound of sniffling.

sniffles ('snɪf°lz) *or* **snuffles** *pl. n.* **the.** *Informal.* a cold in the head.

sniff out *vb.* to detect through shrewdness or instinct.

sniffy ('snɪfɪ) *adj.* **-fier, -fiest.** *Informal.* contemptuous or disdainful.

snifter ('snɪftə) *n.* **1.** a pear-shaped brandy glass. **2.** *Informal.* a small quantity of alcoholic drink.

snig (snɪg) *vb.* **snigging, snigged.** *N.Z.* to drag (a felled log) by a chain or cable.

snigger ('snɪgə) *n.* **1.** a sly or disrespectful laugh, esp. one partly stifled. ~*vb.* **2.** to utter such a laugh.

snip (snɪp) *vb.* **snipping, snipped. 1.** to cut with small quick strokes with scissors or shears. ~*n.* **2.** the act or sound of snipping. **3.** a small piece snipped off. **4.** a small cut made by snipping. **5.** *Informal, chiefly Brit.* a bargain.

snipe (snaɪp) *n., pl.* **snipe** *or* **snipes. 1.** a wading bird with a long straight bill. ~*vb.* **2.** (often foll. by *at*) to shoot (a person or persons) from a place of hiding. **3.** (often foll. by *at*) to criticize a person or persons from a position of security. —'**sniper** *n.*

snippet ('snɪpɪt) *n.* a small scrap or fragment: *snippets of information.*

snitch (snɪtʃ) *Slang.* ~*vb.* **1.** to steal or pilfer. **2.** to act as an informer. ~*n.* **3.** an informer.

snitchy ('snɪtʃɪ) *adj.* **snitchier, snitchiest.** *N.Z. informal.* bad-tempered or irritable.

snivel ('snɪv°l) *vb.* **-elling, -elled** *or U.S.* **-eling, -eled. 1.** to cry and sniffle. **2.** to utter (something) tearfully; whine. **3.** to have a runny nose. ~*n.* **4.** the act of snivelling.

snob (snɒb) *n.* **1.** a person who tries to associate with those of higher social status and who despises those of a lower social status. **2.** a person who feels smugly superior with regard to his tastes or interests: *an intellectual snob.* —'**snobbery** *n.* —'**snobbish** *adj.*

snoek (snʊk) *n.* a South African edible marine fish.

snog (snɒg) *Brit. slang.* ~*vb.* **snogging, snogged. 1.** to kiss and cuddle. ~*n.* **2.** the act of kissing and cuddling.

snood (snu:d) *n.* a pouchlike hat, often of net, loosely holding a woman's hair at the back.

snook (snu:k) *n.* **cock a snook at.** *Brit.* **a.** to make a rude gesture at by putting one thumb to the nose with the fingers of the hand outstretched. **b.** to show contempt for.

snooker ('snu:kə) *n.* **1.** a game played on a billiard table with 15 red balls, six balls of other colours, and a white cue ball. **2.** a shot in which the cue ball is left in a position such that another ball blocks the target ball. ~*vb.* **3.** to leave (an opponent) in an unfavourable position by playing a snooker. **4.** (*often passive*) to thwart; defeat.

snoop (snuːp) *Informal.* ~*vb.* **1.** (often foll. by *about* or *around*) to pry into the private business of other people. ~*n.* **2.** the act of snooping. —**'snooper** *n.* —**'snoopy** *adj.*

snooty (ˈsnuːtɪ) *adj.* **snootier, snootiest.** *Informal.* supercilious or snobbish.

snooze (snuːz) *Informal.* ~*vb.* **1.** to take a brief light sleep. ~*n.* **2.** a nap.

snore (snɔː) *vb.* **1.** to breathe with snorting sounds while asleep. ~*n.* **2.** the act or sound of snoring.

snorkel (ˈsnɔːkˀl) *n.* **1.** a tube allowing a swimmer to breathe while face down on the surface of the water. **2.** (on a submarine) a retractable device for air intake when submerged. ~*vb.* **-kelling, -kelled** *or U.S.* **-keling, -keled. 3.** to swim with a snorkel.

snort (snɔːt) *vb.* **1.** to exhale forcibly and noisily through the nostrils. **2.** to express contempt or annoyance by snorting. **3.** to utter with a snort. ~*n.* **4.** a forcible exhalation of air through the nostrils, esp. to express contempt or annoyance.

snot (snɒt) *n.* (*usually considered vulgar*) **1.** nasal mucus or discharge. **2.** *Slang.* a contemptible person.

snotty (ˈsnɒtɪ) *adj.* **-tier, -tiest.** (*considered vulgar*) **1.** dirty with nasal discharge. **2.** *Slang.* contemptible; nasty. **3.** snobbish; conceited. —**'snottiness** *n.*

snout (snaʊt) *n.* **1.** the projecting nose and jaws of an animal. **2.** anything projecting like a snout. **3.** *Slang.* a person's nose.

snow (snəʊ) *n.* **1.** frozen vapour falling from the sky in flakes. **2.** a layer of snow on the ground. **3.** a falling of snow. **4.** *Slang.* cocaine. ~*vb.* **5.** (with *it* as subject) to be the case that snow is falling: *it's snowing outside.* **6.** (usually passive, foll. by *over, under, in,* or *up*) to cover or confine with a heavy fall of snow. **7.** to fall as or like snow. **8. be snowed under.** to be overwhelmed, esp. with paperwork. —**'snowy** *adj.*

snowball (ˈsnəʊˌbɔːl) *n.* **1.** snow pressed into a ball for throwing. ~*vb.* **2.** to increase rapidly in size or importance. **3.** to throw snowballs at.

snowberry (ˈsnəʊbərɪ) *n., pl.* **-ries.** a shrub cultivated for its white berries.

snow-blind *adj.* temporarily blinded by the intense reflection of sunlight from snow. —**snow blindness** *n.*

snowbound (ˈsnəʊˌbaʊnd) *adj.* shut in or blocked off by snow.

snowcap (ˈsnəʊˌkæp) *n.* a cap of snow, as on top of a mountain. —**'snow,capped** *adj.*

snowdrift (ˈsnəʊˌdrɪft) *n.* a bank of deep snow driven together by the wind.

snowdrop (ˈsnəʊˌdrɒp) *n.* a plant with small drooping white bell-shaped flowers.

snowfall (ˈsnəʊˌfɔːl) *n.* **1.** a fall of snow. **2.** *Meteorol.* the amount of snow that falls in a specified place and time.

snowflake (ˈsnəʊˌfleɪk) *n.* a single crystal of snow.

snow goose *n.* a North American goose having a white plumage with black wing tips.

snow lily *n. Canad.* same as **dogtooth violet.**

snow line *n.* (on a mountain) the altitude above which there is permanent snow.

snowman (ˈsnəʊˌmæn) *n., pl.* **-men.** a figure like a man, made of packed snow.

snowmobile (ˈsnəʊməˌbiːl) *n.* a motor vehicle for travelling on snow, esp. one with caterpillar tracks and front skis.

snowplough *or esp. U.S.* **snowplow** (ˈsnəʊˌplaʊ) *n.* a vehicle for clearing away snow.

snowshoe (ˈsnəʊˌʃuː) *n.* a racket-shaped frame with a network of thongs stretched across it, worn on the feet to facilitate walking on snow.

snowstorm (ˈsnəʊˌstɔːm) *n.* a storm with heavy snow.

SNP Scottish National Party.

Snr *or* **snr** senior.

snub (snʌb) *vb.* **snubbing, snubbed. 1.** to insult (someone) deliberately. ~*n.* **2.** a deliberately insulting act or remark. ~*adj.* **3.** (of a nose) short and turned up.

snub-nosed *adj.* having a short turned-up nose.

snuff[1] (snʌf) *vb.* **1.** to inhale through the nose. **2.** (esp. of an animal) to examine by sniffing. ~*n.* **3.** a sniff.

snuff[2] (snʌf) *n.* **1.** finely powdered tobacco for sniffing up the nostrils. ~*vb.* **2.** to take snuff.

snuff[3] (snʌf) *vb.* **1.** (often foll. by *out*) to put out (a candle). **2.** to cut off the charred part of (a candle wick). **3.** (usually foll. by *out*) *Informal.* to put an end to. **4. snuff it.** *Brit. informal.* to die. ~*n.* **5.** the burned portion of the wick of a candle.

snuffbox (ˈsnʌfˌbɒks) *n.* a small container for holding snuff.

snuffle (ˈsnʌfˀl) *vb.* **1.** to breathe noisily or with difficulty. **2.** to say or speak in a nasal tone. **3.** to snivel. ~*n.* **4.** an act or the sound of snuffling. —**'snuffly** *adj.*

snug (snʌg) *adj.* **snugger, snuggest. 1.** comfortably warm and well protected; cosy: *the children were snug in bed.* **2.** small but comfortable: *a snug cottage.* **3.** fitting closely and comfortably. ~*n.* **4.** (in Britain and Ireland) a small room in a pub. —**'snugly** *adv.*

snuggery (ˈsnʌgərɪ) *n., pl.* **-geries.** a cosy and comfortable place or room.

snuggle (ˈsnʌgˀl) *vb.* to nestle into or draw

close to (somebody or something) for warmth or from affection.

so[1] (səʊ) *adv.* **1.** to such an extent: *the river is so dirty that it smells.* **2.** (*used with a negative;* it replaces the first *as* in a comparison) to the same extent as: *she is not so old as you.* **3.** extremely: *it's so lovely.* **4.** in the state or manner expressed or implied: *they're happy and will remain so.* **5.** also: *I can speak Spanish and so can you.* **6.** thereupon: *and so we ended up in France.* **7. and so on** *or* **forth.** and continuing similarly. **8. or so.** approximately: *fifty or so people came to see me.* **9. so be it.** an expression of agreement or resignation. **10. so much. a.** a certain degree or amount (of). **b.** a lot (of): *it's just so much nonsense.* **11. so much for. a.** no more need be said about. **b.** used to express contempt for something that has failed: *so much for all our plans.* ~*conj.* (often foll. by *that*) **12.** in order (that): *to die so that you might live.* **13.** with the consequence (that): *he was late home, so that there was trouble.* **14. so as.** in order (to): *to diet so as to lose weight.* **15.** *Not universally accepted.* in consequence: *she wasn't needed, so she left.* **16. so what!** *Informal.* that is unimportant. ~*pron.* **17.** used to substitute for a clause or sentence, which may be understood: *you'll stop because I said so.* ~*adj.* **18.** true: *it can't be so.* ~*interj.* **19.** an exclamation of surprise, triumph, or realization.

Usage. So should not be used as a conjunction to indicate either purpose (*he did it so he could feel happier*) or result (*he could not do it so he did not try*). In the former case *in order to* should be used instead and in the latter case *and so* or *and therefore* would be more acceptable.

so[2] (səʊ) *n. Music.* same as **soh.**

soak (səʊk) *vb.* **1.** to make, become, or be thoroughly wet or saturated. **2.** (usually foll. by *in* or *into*) (of a liquid) to penetrate or permeate. **3.** (usually foll. by *in* or *up*) to take in; absorb: *the earth soaks up rainwater.* ~*n.* **4.** a soaking or being soaked. **5.** *Slang.* a person who drinks to excess. —'**soaking** *n., adj.*

so-and-so *n., pl.* **so-and-sos.** *Informal.* **1.** a person whose name is not specified. **2.** *Euphemistic.* a person or thing regarded as unpleasant: *which so-and-so broke my razor?*

soap (səʊp) *n.* **1.** a cleaning agent used with water to produce suds, made from an alkali and fats. **2.** *Informal.* short for **soap opera.** ~*vb.* **3.** to apply soap to.

soapbox ('səʊp,bɒks) *n.* a crate used as a platform for speech-making.

soap opera *n.* a serialized radio or television drama, usually dealing with domestic themes.

soapstone ('səʊp,stəʊn) *n.* a compact soft variety of talc, used for making table tops, hearths, and ornaments.

soapsuds ('səʊp,sʌdz) *pl. n.* foam or lather made from soap.

soapy ('səʊpɪ) *adj.* **soapier, soapiest.** **1.** containing or covered with soap: *soapy water.* **2.** like soap. **3.** *Slang.* flattering. —'**soapiness** *n.*

soar (sɔː) *vb.* **1.** to rise or fly upwards into the air. **2.** (of a bird or aircraft) to glide while maintaining altitude. **3.** to rise or increase suddenly above the usual level: *soaring prices.*

sob (sɒb) *vb.* **sobbing, sobbed.** **1.** to weep with convulsive gasps. **2.** to utter with sobs. ~*n.* **3.** the act or sound of sobbing.

sober ('səʊbə) *adj.* **1.** not drunk. **2.** temperate, esp. with regard to alcohol. **3.** serious and thoughtful: *a sober attitude to a problem.* **4.** (of colours) plain and dull or subdued. **5.** free from exaggeration: *he told us the sober truth.* ~*vb.* **6.** (usually foll. by *up*) to make or become less drunk. —'**sobering** *adj.*

sobriety (səʊ'braɪətɪ) *n.* the state or quality of being sober.

sobriquet *or* **soubriquet** ('səʊbrɪ,keɪ) *n.* a nickname.

sob story *n.* a tale of personal distress intended to arouse sympathy.

Soc. *or* **soc.** **1.** socialist. **2.** society.

soca ('səʊkə) *n.* a mixture of soul and calypso music typical of the E Caribbean.

so-called *adj.* called or named thus, esp. (in the speaker's opinion) incorrectly: *a so-called genius.*

soccer ('sɒkə) *n.* a game in which two teams of eleven players try to kick or head a ball into their opponents' goal, only the goalkeeper on either side being allowed to touch the ball with his hands.

sociable ('səʊʃəb'l) *adj.* **1.** friendly or companionable. **2.** (of an occasion) providing the opportunity for friendliness and conviviality. —,**socia'bility** *n.* —'**sociably** *adv.*

social ('səʊʃəl) *adj.* **1.** living or preferring to live in a community rather than alone. **2.** of or relating to human society or organization. **3.** of the behaviour and interaction of persons living together in groups. **4.** of or for companionship or communal activities: *a social club.* **5.** of or engaged in social services: *a social worker.* **6.** relating to a certain class of society. **7.** (of certain species of insects) living together in organized colonies: *social bees.* ~*n.* **8.** an informal gathering, esp. of an organized group. —'**socially** *adv.*

social contract *or* **compact** *n.* an agreement among individuals to cooperate for greater security, which entails the surrender of some personal liberties.

social democrat *n.* **1.** a socialist who

believes in the gradual transformation of capitalism into democratic socialism. **2.** (*usually cap.*) a member of a Social Democratic Party. —**social democracy** *n*.

social fund *n*. (in Britain) a social security fund from which loans or payments may be made to people in cases of extreme need.

socialism ('səʊʃə,lɪzəm) *n*. a political and economic theory or system in which the means of production, distribution, and exchange are owned by the community collectively, usually through the state. —**'socialist** *n*., *adj*.

socialite ('səʊʃə,laɪt) *n*. a person who is prominent in fashionable society.

socialize *or* **-lise** ('səʊʃə,laɪz) *vb*. **1.** to behave in a sociable manner. **2.** to prepare for life in society. **3.** *Chiefly U.S.* to organize in accordance with socialist principles. —**,sociali'zation** *or* **-li'sation** *n*.

social science *n*. the scientific study of society and of human relationships within society. —**social scientist** *n*.

social security *n*. public provision for the economic welfare of the aged, unemployed, or sick, through pensions and other financial aid.

social services *pl. n*. welfare activities organized by the state or a local authority.

social studies *n*. (*functioning as sing.*) the study of how people live and organize themselves in society.

social welfare *n*. **1.** social services provided by a state for the benefit of its citizens. **2.** (*caps.*) (in New Zealand) a government department concerned with pensions and benefits for the elderly, the sick, etc.

social work *n*. any of various social services designed to help the poor and aged and to increase the welfare of children. —**social worker** *n*.

society (sə'saɪətɪ) *n*., *pl*. **-ties. 1.** mankind, considered as a community. **2.** a group of people forming a single community with its own distinctive cultural patterns and institutions. **3.** the structure, cultural patterns, and institutions of such a group. **4.** an organized group of people sharing a common aim or interest: *a learned society*. **5.** the privileged class of people in a community, esp. as considered superior or fashionable. **6.** companionship: *I enjoy her society*.

Society of Friends *n*. the Quakers.

Society of Jesus *n*. the religious order of the Jesuits.

socioeconomic (,səʊsɪəʊ,iːkə'nɒmɪk, -,ɛkə-) *adj*. of or involving economic and social factors.

sociology (,səʊsɪ'ɒlədʒɪ) *n*. the study of the development, organization, functioning, and classification of human societies. —**sociological** (,səʊsɪə'lɒdʒɪkəl) *adj*. —**,soci'ologist** *n*.

sociopolitical (,səʊsɪəʊpə'lɪtɪkəl) *adj*. of or involving political and social factors.

sock[1] (sɒk) *n*. **1.** a cloth covering for the foot, reaching to between the ankle and knee and worn inside a shoe. **2. pull one's socks up.** *Brit. informal*. to make a determined effort to improve. **3. put a sock in it.** *Brit. slang*. be quiet!

sock[2] (sɒk) *Slang*. ~*vb*. **1.** to hit with force. ~*n*. **2.** a forceful blow.

socket ('sɒkɪt) *n*. **1.** a device into which an electric plug can be inserted in order to make a connection in a circuit. **2.** *Anat*. a bony hollow into which a part or structure fits: *an eye socket*.

Socratic (sɒ'krætɪk) *adj*. of the Greek philosopher Socrates, or his teachings.

Socratic method *n*. *Philosophy*. the method of instruction used by Socrates, in which a series of questions and answers lead to a logical conclusion.

sod[1] (sɒd) *n*. **1.** a piece of grass-covered surface soil; turf. **2.** *Poetic*. the ground.

sod[2] (sɒd) *Slang, chiefly Brit*. ~*n*. **1.** an obnoxious person. **2.** *Jocular*. a person. **3. sod all.** *Slang*. nothing. ~*interj*. **4.** a strong exclamation of annoyance. —**'sodding** *adj*.

soda ('səʊdə) *n*. **1.** a simple inorganic compound of sodium, such as sodium carbonate or sodium bicarbonate. **2.** same as **soda water. 3.** *U.S. & Canad*. a sweet fizzy drink.

soda bread *n*. a type of bread leavened with sodium bicarbonate.

soda fountain *n*. *U.S. & Canad*. **1.** a counter that serves soft drinks and snacks. **2.** an apparatus dispensing soda water.

soda siphon *n*. a sealed bottle containing soda water under pressure, which is forced up a tube when a lever is pressed.

soda water *n*. a fizzy drink made by charging water with carbon dioxide under pressure.

sodden ('sɒdən) *adj*. **1.** completely saturated. **2.** dulled, esp. by excessive drinking.

sodium ('səʊdɪəm) *n*. a very reactive soft silvery-white metallic element. Symbol: Na

sodium bicarbonate *n*. a white crystalline soluble compound used in fizzy drinks, baking powder, and in medicine as an antacid.

sodium carbonate *n*. a colourless or white soluble crystalline compound used in the manufacture of glass, ceramics, soap, and paper, and as a cleansing agent.

sodium chlorate *n*. a colourless crystalline compound used as a bleaching agent, antiseptic, and weedkiller.

sodium chloride *n*. common table salt; a soluble colourless crystalline compound widely used as a seasoning and preservative for food and in the manufacture of chemicals, glass, and soap.

sodium hydroxide n. a white strongly alkaline solid used in making rayon, paper, and soap.

sodomite ('sɒdə,maɪt) n. a person who practises sodomy.

sodomy ('sɒdəmɪ) n. anal intercourse committed by a man with another man or a woman.

Sod's Law (sɒdz) n. Informal. a jocular maxim stating that if something can go wrong or turn out inconveniently it will.

sofa ('səʊfə) n. an upholstered seat with back and arms for two or more people.

soft (sɒft) adj. **1.** easy to dent, shape, or cut: soft material. **2.** not hard; giving way easily under pressure: a soft bed. **3.** fine, smooth, or fluffy to the touch: soft fur. **4.** (of music or sounds) low and pleasing. **5.** (of light or colour) not excessively bright or harsh. **6.** (of a breeze or climate) temperate, mild, or pleasant. **7.** slightly blurred; not sharply outlined: soft focus. **8.** kind or lenient, often excessively so. **9.** easy to influence or impose upon. **10.** Informal. feeble or silly; simple: soft in the head. **11.** not strong or robust; unable to endure hardship. **12.** loving; tender: soft words. **13.** Informal. requiring little exertion; easy: a soft job. **14.** Chem. (of water) relatively free of mineral salts and therefore easily able to make soap lather. **15.** (of a drug) nonaddictive. **16.** Phonetics. denoting the consonants c and g when they are pronounced sibilantly, as in cent and germ. **17. soft on. a.** lenient towards. **b.** feeling infatuation for. ~adv. **18.** softly: to speak soft. ~interj. **19.** Archaic. quiet! —'**softly** adv.

softball ('sɒft,bɔːl) n. a variation of baseball using a larger softer ball.

soft-boiled adj. (of an egg) boiled for a short time so that the yolk is still soft.

soft coal n. same as **bituminous coal.**

soft drink n. a nonalcoholic drink.

soften ('sɒfˀn) vb. **1.** to make or become soft or softer. **2.** to make or become more gentle. —'**softener** n.

soft furnishings pl. n. Brit. curtains, hangings, rugs, and covers.

softhearted (,sɒft'hɑːtɪd) adj. easily moved to pity.

soft option n. in a number of choices, the one involving the least exertion.

soft palate n. the fleshy portion at the back of the roof of the mouth.

soft-pedal vb. **-alling, -alled** or U.S. **-aling, -aled. 1.** to deliberately avoid emphasizing (something). ~n. **soft pedal. 2.** a pedal on a piano that softens the tone.

soft sell n. a method of selling based on indirect suggestion or inducement.

soft-soap vb. Informal. to flatter (a person).

soft-spoken adj. speaking or said with a soft gentle voice.

soft touch n. Informal. a person easily imposed on, esp. to lend money.

software ('sɒft,wɛə) n. Computers. the programs used with a computer.

softwood ('sɒft,wʊd) n. the open-grained wood of coniferous trees.

softy or **softie** ('sɒftɪ) n., pl. **softies.** Informal. a person who is easily upset.

soggy ('sɒgɪ) adj. **-gier, -giest. 1.** soaked with liquid. **2.** moist and heavy: a soggy cake. —'**sogginess** n.

soh or **so** (səʊ) n. Music. the name used for the fifth note of a scale.

soigné or (fem.) **soignée** ('swɑːnjeɪ) adj. well-groomed; elegant.

soil[1] (sɔɪl) n. **1.** the top layer of the land surface of the earth. **2.** a specific type of this material: loamy soil. **3.** land, country, or region: one's native soil.

soil[2] (sɔɪl) vb. **1.** to make or become dirty or stained. **2.** to bring disgrace upon. ~n. **3.** a soiled spot. **4.** refuse, manure, or excrement.

soiree ('swɑːreɪ) n. an evening party or gathering.

sojourn ('sɒdʒɜːn, 'sʌdʒ-) n. **1.** a temporary stay. ~vb. **2.** to stay or reside temporarily.

sol[1] (sɒl) n. Music. same as **soh.**

sol[2] (sɒl) n. a liquid colloidal solution.

solace ('sɒlɪs) n. **1.** comfort in misery or disappointment. **2.** something that gives comfort or consolation. ~vb. **3.** to give comfort or cheer to (a person) in time of sorrow or distress.

solan or **solan goose** ('səʊlən) n. Archaic. same as **gannet.**

solar ('səʊlə) adj. **1.** of the sun. **2.** operating by or using the energy of the sun: solar cell.

solarium (səʊ'lɛərɪəm) n., pl. **-laria** (-'lɛərɪə) or **-lariums.** an establishment with beds equipped with ultraviolet lights used for acquiring an artificial suntan.

solar plexus n. **1.** Anat. a network of nerves behind the stomach. **2.** (not in technical usage) the vulnerable part of the stomach beneath the diaphragm.

solar system n. the system containing the sun and the planets, comets, and asteroids that go round it.

sold (səʊld) vb. **1.** past of **sell.** ~adj. **2. sold on.** Slang. uncritically attached to or enthusiastic about.

solder ('səʊldə; U.S. 'sɒdər) n. **1.** an alloy used for joining two metal surfaces by melting the alloy so that it forms a thin layer between the surfaces. ~vb. **2.** to join or mend or be joined or mended with solder.

soldering iron *n.* a hand tool with an iron or copper tip that is heated and used to melt and apply solder.

soldier ('səʊldʒə) *n.* **1. a.** a person who serves or has served in an army. **b.** a noncommissioned member of an army. ~*vb.* **2.** to serve as a soldier. —'**soldierly** *adj.*

soldier of fortune *n.* a man who seeks money or adventure as a soldier; mercenary.

soldier on *vb.* to persist in one's efforts in spite of difficulties or pressure.

sole[1] (səʊl) *adj.* **1.** being the only one; only. **2.** not shared; exclusive: *sole rights.*

sole[2] (səʊl) *n.* **1.** the underside of the foot. **2.** the underside of a shoe. **3.** the lower surface of an object. ~*vb.* **4.** to provide (a shoe) with a sole.

sole[3] (səʊl) *n., pl.* **sole** *or* **soles.** a flatfish highly valued as food.

solecism ('sɒlɪˌsɪzəm) *n.* **1.** a violation of the grammar or idiom of a language. **2.** a violation of good manners. —ˌsole'**cistic** *adj.*

solely ('səʊllɪ) *adv.* **1.** only; completely. **2.** without others; singly.

solemn ('sɒləm) *adj.* **1.** serious; deeply sincere: *a solemn vow.* **2.** characterized by pomp, ceremony, or formality. **3.** serious or glum. **4.** inspiring awe: *a solemn occasion.*

solemnity (sə'lɛmnɪtɪ) *n., pl.* **-ties. 1.** the state or quality of being solemn. **2.** (*often pl.*) a solemn ceremony or ritual.

solemnize *or* **-ise** ('sɒləmˌnaɪz) *vb.* **1.** to celebrate or perform (a ceremony, esp. of marriage). **2.** to make solemn or serious. —ˌsolemni'**zation** *or* **-i'sation** *n.*

solenoid ('səʊlɪˌnɔɪd) *n.* a coil of wire, usually cylindrical, in which a magnetic field is set up by passing a current through it. —ˌsole'**noidal** *adj.*

sol-fa ('sɒl'fɑ) *n.* short for **tonic sol-fa.**

solicit (sə'lɪsɪt) *vb.* **1.** (foll. by *for*) to seek or request, esp. in a formal or persistent manner. **2.** to approach (a person) with an offer of sexual relations in return for money. —soˌlici'**tation** *n.*

solicitor (sə'lɪsɪtə) *n.* (in Britain) a lawyer who advises clients on matters of law, draws up legal documents, and prepares cases for barristers.

Solicitor General *n., pl.* **Solicitors General.** (in Britain) the law officer of the Crown ranking next to the Attorney General (in Scotland to the Lord Advocate) and acting as his assistant.

solicitous (sə'lɪsɪtəs) *adj.* **1.** showing consideration, concern, or attention. **2.** keenly anxious or willing; eager. —so'**licitousness** *n.*

solicitude (sə'lɪsɪˌtjuːd) *n.* **1.** the state or quality of being solicitous. **2.** anxiety or concern.

solid ('sɒlɪd) *adj.* **1.** (of a substance) in a physical state in which it resists changes in size and shape; not liquid or gaseous. **2.** consisting of matter all through; not hollow. **3.** of the same substance all through: *solid rock.* **4.** sound; proved or provable: *solid facts.* **5.** reliable or sensible; upstanding: *a solid citizen.* **6.** firm, strong, or substantial: *a solid table.* **7.** (of a meal or food) substantial. **8.** without interruption; continuous or unbroken: *solid bombardment.* **9.** financially sound: *a solid institution.* **10.** strongly united or consolidated: *a solid relationship.* **11.** *Geom.* having or relating to three dimensions. **12.** adequate; sound, but not brilliant: *a solid piece of work.* **13.** of a single uniform colour or tone. ~*n.* **14.** *Geom.* a three-dimensional shape. **15.** a solid substance. —**solidity** (sə'lɪdɪtɪ) *n.* —'**solidly** *adv.*

solidarity (ˌsɒlɪ'dærɪtɪ) *n., pl.* **-ties.** agreement in interests or sympathies among members of a group; total unity.

solid geometry *n.* the branch of geometry concerned with three-dimensional figures.

solidify (sə'lɪdɪˌfaɪ) *vb.* **-fying, -fied. 1.** to make or become solid or hard. **2.** to make or become strong, united, or determined. —soˌlidifi'**cation** *n.*

solid-state *n.* (*modifier*) (of an electronic device) using a semiconductor component, such as a transistor or silicon chip, in which current flow is through solid material, rather than a valve or mechanical part, in which current flow is through a vacuum.

solidus ('sɒlɪdəs) *n., pl.* **-di** (-ˌdaɪ). a short oblique stroke used in text to separate items, such as *and/or.*

soliloquize *or* **-ise** (sə'lɪləˌkwaɪz) *vb.* to utter a soliloquy.

soliloquy (sə'lɪləkwɪ) *n., pl.* **-quies. 1.** the act of speaking alone or to oneself, esp. as a theatrical device. **2.** a speech in a play that is spoken in soliloquy.

solipsism ('sɒlɪpˌsɪzəm) *n. Philosophy.* the denial of the possibility of any knowledge other than of one's own existence. —'**solipsist** *n.*

solitaire (ˌsɒlɪ'tɛə) *n.* **1.** a game played by one person, involving moving and taking pegs in a pegboard with the object of being left with only one. **2.** *U.S.* patience (the card game). **3.** a gem, esp. a diamond, set alone in a ring.

solitary ('sɒlɪtrɪ) *adj.* **1.** following or enjoying a life of solitude: *a solitary disposition.* **2.** experienced or performed alone: *a solitary walk.* **3.** (of a place) unfrequented. **4.** single; sole: *a solitary cloud.* **5.** having few companions; lonely. ~*n., pl.* **-taries. 6.** a person who lives in seclusion; hermit. **7.** *Informal.* short for **solitary confine-**

ment: *ten days in solitary.* —**'solitariness** *n.*

solitary confinement *n.* isolation imposed on a prisoner by confinement in a special cell.

solitude ('sɒlɪˌtjuːd) *n.* the state of being solitary or secluded.

solo ('səʊləʊ) *n., pl.* **-los. 1.** a musical composition for one performer. **2. a.** any performance by an individual without assistance. **b.** (*as modifier*): *a solo flight.* **3.** Also: **solo whist.** a card game in which each person plays on his own. ~*adv.* **4.** by oneself; alone: *to fly solo.* —**soloist** ('səʊləʊɪst) *n.*

Solomon ('sɒləmən) *n.* any person credited with great wisdom.

Solomon's seal *n.* a plant with greenish flowers and long waxy leaves.

so long *interj.* **1.** *Informal.* farewell; goodbye. ~*adv.* **2.** *S. African slang.* for the time being; meanwhile.

solstice ('sɒlstɪs) *n.* either the shortest day of the year (**winter solstice**) or the longest day of the year (**summer solstice**).

soluble ('sɒljʊb°l) *adj.* **1.** (of a substance) capable of being dissolved. **2.** (of a mystery or problem) capable of being solved. —ˌsolu'bility *n.*

solute ('sɒljuːt) *n.* the substance in a solution that is dissolved.

solution (sə'luːʃən) *n.* **1.** a specific answer to or way of answering a problem. **2.** the act or process of solving a problem. **3.** a mixture of two or more substances in which the molecules or atoms of the substances are completely dispersed. **4.** the act or process of forming a solution. **5.** the state of being dissolved: *the sugar is held in solution.*

solve (sɒlv) *vb.* to find the explanation for or solution to (a mystery or problem). —**'solvable** *adj.*

solvent ('sɒlvənt) *adj.* **1.** capable of meeting financial obligations. **2.** (of a liquid) capable of dissolving other substances. ~*n.* **3.** a liquid capable of dissolving other substances. —**'solvency** *n.*

solvent abuse *n.* the deliberate inhaling of intoxicating fumes given off by certain solvents.

Som. Somerset.

somatic (səʊ'mætɪk) *adj.* of or relating to the body as distinct from the mind: *a somatic disease.*

sombre *or U.S.* **somber** ('sɒmbə) *adj.* **1.** dismal; melancholy: *a sombre mood.* **2.** (of a place) dim, gloomy, or shadowy. **3.** (of colour or clothes) sober, dull, or dark. —**'sombrely** *or U.S.* **'somberly** *adv.*

sombrero (sɒm'brɛərəʊ) *n., pl.* **-ros.** a hat with a very wide brim, as worn in Mexico.

some (sʌm; *unstressed* səm) *det.* **1.** (a) certain unknown or unspecified: *some man*

called for you. **2.** an unknown or unspecified quantity or number of: *there's some rice left.* **3. a.** a considerable number or amount of: *he lived some years afterwards.* **b.** a little: *show some respect.* **4.** *Informal.* an impressive or remarkable: *that was some game!* ~*pron.* **5.** certain unknown or unspecified persons or things: *some can teach and others can't.* **6.** an unknown or unspecified quantity of something or number of persons or things: *I've got some at home.* ~*adv.* **7.** approximately: *some thirty pounds.*

somebody ('sʌmbədɪ) *pron.* **1.** some person; someone. ~*n., pl.* **-bodies. 2.** a person of great importance: *she was determined to be somebody.*
Usage. see **everyone.**

someday ('sʌmˌdeɪ) *adv.* at some unspecified time in the future.

somehow ('sʌmˌhaʊ) *adv.* **1.** in some unspecified way. **2.** for some unknown reason: *somehow it didn't seem to matter.*

someone ('sʌmˌwʌn, -wən) *pron.* some person; somebody.
Usage. see **everyone.**

someplace ('sʌmˌpleɪs) *adv. U.S. & Canad. informal.* same as **somewhere.**

somersault ('sʌməˌsɔːlt) *n.* **1.** a rolling movement in which the head is placed on the ground and the trunk and legs are turned over it. **2.** such a rolling movement performed in midair, as in diving or gymnastics. ~*vb.* **3.** to perform a somersault.

something ('sʌmθɪŋ) *pron.* **1.** an unspecified or unknown thing; some thing: *take something warm with you.* **2.** an unspecified or unknown amount: *something less than a hundred.* **3.** an impressive or important person, thing, or event: *isn't that something?* **4. something else.** *Slang, chiefly U.S.* a remarkable person or thing. ~*adv.* **5.** to some degree; somewhat: *he looks something like me.*

sometime ('sʌmˌtaɪm) *adv.* **1.** at some unspecified point of time. ~*adj.* **2.** former: *the sometime President.*

sometimes ('sʌmˌtaɪmz) *adv.* now and then; from time to time.

someway ('sʌmˌweɪ) *adv.* in some unspecified manner.

somewhat ('sʌmˌwɒt) *adv.* rather; a bit: *she found it somewhat odd.*

somewhere ('sʌmˌwɛə) *adv.* **1.** in, to, or at some unknown or unspecified place or point: *somewhere in England; somewhere between 3 and 4 o'clock.* **2. getting somewhere.** *Informal.* making progress.

somnambulism (sɒm'næmbjʊˌlɪzəm) *n.* walking while asleep or in a hypnotic trance. —**som'nambulist** *n.*

somnolent ('sɒmnələnt) *adj.* drowsy; sleepy. —**'somnolence** *n.*

son (sʌn) *n.* **1.** a male offspring. **2.** a

familiar term of address for a boy or man.
3. a male who comes from a certain place or one closely connected with a certain environment, etc.: *a son of the circus.*

Son (sʌn) *n. Christianity.* the second person of the Trinity, Jesus Christ.

sonar ('səʊnɑː) *n.* a communication and position-finding device used in underwater navigation and target detection using sound waves.

sonata (sə'nɑːtə) *n.* an instrumental composition, usually in three or more movements, for piano or for another instrument with or without piano.

son et lumière ('sɒn eɪ 'luːmɪˌɛə) *n.* an entertainment staged at night at a famous building or historical site, at which its history is presented by means of lighting effects, sound effects, and narration.

song (sɒŋ) *n.* **1.** a piece of music with words, composed for the voice. **2.** the tuneful call or sound made by certain birds or insects. **3.** the act or process of singing: *they raised their voices in song.* **4. for a song.** at a bargain price. **5. make a song and dance.** *Brit. informal.* to make an unnecessary fuss.

songbird ('sɒŋˌbɜːd) *n.* any bird that has a musical call.

songololo (ˌsɒŋgʊ'lɒlɒ) *n., pl.* **-los.** *S. African.* a kind of millipede.

songstress ('sɒŋstrɪs) *n.* a female singer, esp. of popular songs.

song thrush *n.* a common thrush noted for its song.

sonic ('sɒnɪk) *adj.* of, involving, or producing sound.

sonic barrier *n.* same as **sound barrier.**

sonic boom *n.* a loud explosive sound caused by the shock wave of an aircraft travelling at supersonic speed.

son-in-law *n., pl.* **sons-in-law.** the husband of one's daughter.

sonnet ('sɒnɪt) *n. Prosody.* a verse form consisting of 14 lines with a fixed rhyme scheme and rhythm pattern.

sonny ('sʌnɪ) *n. Often patronizing.* a familiar term of address to a boy or man.

sonorous (sə'nɔːrəs, 'sɒnərəs) *adj.* **1.** (of a sound) deep or resonant. **2.** (of speech) consciously grand; pompous. **—sonority** (sə'nɒrɪtɪ) *n.*

soon (suːn) *adv.* **1.** in or after a short time; before long. **2. as soon as.** at the very moment that: *as soon as she saw him.* **3. as soon ... as.** used to indicate that the first alternative is slightly preferable to the second: *I'd just as soon go by train as drive.*

sooner ('suːnə) *adv.* **1.** the comparative of **soon:** *he came sooner than I thought.* **2.** rather; in preference: *I'd sooner die than give up.* **3. no sooner ... than.** immediately after or when: *no sooner had he got home*

than the rain stopped. **4. sooner or later.** eventually; inevitably.

soot (sʊt) *n.* a black powder deposited during the incomplete combustion of organic substances such as coal. **—'sooty** *adj.*

sooth (suːθ) *n.* **in sooth.** *Archaic or poetic.* in truth.

soothe (suːð) *vb.* **1.** to make (someone) calm or tranquil. **2.** to relieve or assuage (pain, longing, etc.). **—'soothing** *adj.*

soothsayer ('suːθˌseɪə) *n.* a seer or prophet.

sop (sɒp) *n.* **1.** a concession or bribe given to placate or mollify someone: *a sop to one's feelings.* **2.** (*pl.*) food soaked in a liquid before being eaten. **3.** *Informal.* a stupid or weak person. **~vb. sopping, sopped. 4.** (often foll. by *up*) to mop or absorb (liquid) as with a sponge.

sophism ('sɒfɪzəm) *n.* an argument that seems plausible though actually invalid and misleading.

sophist ('sɒfɪst) *n.* a person who uses clever or quibbling but unsound arguments. **—sophistic** (sə'fɪstɪk) *adj.*

sophisticate *vb.* (sə'fɪstɪˌkeɪt). **1.** to make (someone) less natural or innocent, as by education. **2.** to make (a machine or method) more complex or refined. **~n.** (sə'fɪstɪˌkeɪt, -kɪt). **3.** a sophisticated person. **—soˌphistiˈcation** *n.*

sophisticated (sə'fɪstɪˌkeɪtɪd) *adj.* **1.** having refined or cultured tastes and habits. **2.** appealing to sophisticated people: *a sophisticated restaurant.* **3.** (of machines or methods) complex and refined.

sophistry ('sɒfɪstrɪ) *n.* **1.** the practice of using arguments which seem plausible though actually invalid and misleading. **2.** (*pl.* **-ries**) an instance of this.

sophomore ('sɒfəˌmɔː) *n. Chiefly U.S. & Canad.* a second-year student.

soporific (ˌsɒpə'rɪfɪk) *adj.* **1.** inducing sleep. **~n. 2.** a drug that induces sleep.

sopping ('sɒpɪŋ) *adj.* completely soaked; wet through. Also: **sopping wet.**

soppy ('sɒpɪ) *adj.* **-pier, -piest.** *Brit. informal.* silly or sentimental. **—'soppily** *adv.*

soprano (sə'prɑːnəʊ) *n., pl.* **-pranos. 1.** the highest adult female voice. **2.** the voice of a young boy before puberty. **3.** a singer with such a voice. **4.** the highest part of a piece of harmony. **5.** the highest or second highest instrument in a family of instruments.

sorbet ('sɔːbeɪ) *n.* a water ice made from fruit juice, egg whites, etc.

sorcerer ('sɔːsərə) *or* (*fem.*) **sorceress** ('sɔːsərɪs) *n.* a person who uses magic powers; a wizard.

sorcery ('sɔːsərɪ) *n., pl.* **-ceries.** the practice of magic, esp. black magic.

sordid ('sɔːdɪd) *adj.* **1.** dirty or squalid. **2.**

degraded; vile; base. **3.** selfish and grasping: *sordid avarice.*

sore (sɔː) *adj.* **1.** (of a wound, injury, etc.) painfully sensitive; tender. **2.** causing annoyance: *a sore point.* **3.** resentful; annoyed. **4.** urgent; pressing: *in sore need.* ~*n.* **5.** a painful or sensitive wound or injury. ~*adv.* **6. sore afraid.** *Archaic.* greatly frightened.

sorely (ˈsɔːlı) *adv.* **1.** painfully or grievously: *sorely wounded.* **2.** pressingly or greatly: *to be sorely tempted.*

sorghum (ˈsɔːgəm) *n.* a grass cultivated for grain, hay, and as a source of syrup.

sorority (səˈrɒrɪtɪ) *n., pl.* **-ties.** *Chiefly U.S.* a society of female students.

sorrel[1] (ˈsɒrəl) *adj.* **1.** light brown to brownish-orange. ~*n.* **2.** a horse of this colour.

sorrel[2] (ˈsɒrəl) *n.* a plant with acid-tasting leaves which are used in salads and sauces.

sorrow (ˈsɒrəʊ) *n.* **1.** the feeling of sadness, grief, or regret associated with loss, bereavement, or sympathy for another's suffering. **2.** a particular cause of this. ~*vb.* **3.** to mourn or grieve. —ˈsorrowful *adj.* —ˈsorrowfully *adv.*

sorry (ˈsɒrɪ) *adj.* **-rier, -riest. 1.** (often foll. by *for*) feeling or expressing pity, sympathy, grief, or regret: *I feel sorry for him.* **2.** pitiful, wretched, or deplorable: *a sorry sight.* **3.** poor; paltry: *a sorry excuse.* ~*interj.* **4.** an exclamation expressing apology or requesting someone to repeat what he has said.

sort (sɔːt) *n.* **1.** a class, group, or kind, as distinguished by some common quality or characteristic. **2.** *Informal.* a type of character: *he's a good sort.* **3.** a more or less adequate example: *it's a sort of review.* **4. of sorts** *or* **of a sort. a.** of an inferior kind. **b.** of an indefinite kind. **5. out of sorts.** not in normal good health or temper. **6. sort of.** as it were; rather: *I sort of fell; sort of frightening.* ~*vb.* **7.** to arrange (things or people) according to class, type, etc. **8.** to put (something) into working order. **9.** to arrange (computer information) by machine in an order convenient to the user. **Usage.** see **kind**[2].

sortie (ˈsɔːtɪ) *n.* **1.** a short trip to an unfamiliar place. **2.** (of troops) the act of attacking from a besieged position. **3.** an operational flight made by one aircraft. ~*vb.* **-tieing, -tied. 4.** to make a sortie.

sort out *vb.* **1.** to find a solution to (a problem): *to sort out the mess.* **2.** to take or separate (things or people) from a larger group: *to sort out the likely ones.* **3.** to organize (things or people) into an orderly and disciplined group. **4.** *Informal.* to scold or punish (someone).

SOS *n.* **1.** an internationally recognized distress signal in which the letters SOS are

repeatedly spelt out in Morse code. **2.** *Informal.* any call for help.

so-so *Informal.* ~*adj.* **1.** neither good nor bad. ~*adv.* **2.** in an average or indifferent manner.

sostenuto (ˌsɒstəˈnuːtəʊ) *adv.* *Music.* in a smooth sustained manner.

sot (sɒt) *n.* a habitual drunkard. —ˈsottish *adj.*

sotto voce (ˈsɒtəʊ ˈvəʊtʃɪ) *adv.* in an undertone.

sou (suː) *n.* **1.** a former French coin of low value. **2.** a very small amount of money: *I haven't a sou.*

soubrette (suːˈbrɛt) *n.* a minor female role in comedy, often that of a pert lady's maid.

soubriquet (ˈsuːbrɪˌkeɪ) *n.* same as **sobriquet.**

soufflé (ˈsuːfleɪ) *n.* a light fluffy dish made with beaten egg whites combined with other ingredients such as cheese or fish or chocolate and gelatin.

sough (saʊ) *vb.* (of the wind) to make a sighing sound.

sought (sɔːt) *vb.* past of **seek.**

souk (suːk) *n.* an open-air marketplace in Muslim countries.

soul (səʊl) *n.* **1.** the spirit or immaterial part of man, regarded as the centre of human personality, intellect, will, and emotions: believed by many to survive the body after death. **2.** the essential part or fundamental nature of anything: *the soul of the American people.* **3.** deep and sincere feelings: *you've got no soul.* **4.** Also called: **soul music.** a type of Black music resulting from the addition of jazz, gospel, and pop elements to blues. **5.** (*modifier*) of or relating to Black Americans and their culture: *soul food.* **6. the life and soul.** *Informal.* a person regarded as the main source of gaiety or merriment: *the life and soul of the party.* **7.** a person regarded as typifying some characteristic or quality: *the soul of discretion.* **8.** a person: *a decent soul.*

soul-destroying *adj.* (of an occupation or situation) extremely monotonous.

soul food *n.* *Informal.* food, such as chitterlings and yams, which is traditionally eaten by U.S. Blacks.

soulful (ˈsəʊlfʊl) *adj.* expressing profound feelings.

soulless (ˈsəʊllɪs) *adj.* **1.** lacking human qualities or influences; mechanical: *soulless work.* **2.** (of a person) lacking in sensitivity.

soul mate *n.* a person whom one finds instinctively compatible.

soul-searching *n.* deep examination of one's motives, actions, and beliefs.

sound[1] (saʊnd) *n.* **1.** *Physics.* mechanical vibrations that travel in waves through the air, water, etc. **2.** the sensation produced by such vibrations in the organs of hearing.

3. anything that can be heard. **4.** impression or implication: *I don't like the sound of that.* **5.** (*often pl.*) *Slang.* music, esp. rock, jazz, or pop. ~*vb.* **6.** to cause (an instrument, etc.) to make a sound or (of an instrument, etc.) to emit a sound. **7.** to announce (something) by a sound: *to sound the alarm.* **8.** to resonate with a certain quality or intensity: *to sound loud.* **9.** to give the impression of being as specified: *to sound reasonable.* **10.** to pronounce (something) distinctly or audibly: *to sound one's r's.*

sound² (saʊnd) *adj.* **1.** free from damage, injury, or decay. **2.** firm; substantial: *a sound basis.* **3.** financially safe or stable: *a sound investment.* **4.** showing good judgment or reasoning; wise: *sound advice.* **5.** holding approved beliefs; ethically correct; honest. **6.** (of sleep) deep; peaceful; unbroken. **7.** thorough: *a sound defeat.* ~*adv.* **8.** **sound asleep.** in a deep sleep. —'**soundly** *adv.*

sound³ (saʊnd) *vb.* **1.** to measure the depth of (a well, the sea, etc.). **2.** *Med.* to examine (a part of the body) by tapping or with a stethoscope. ~See also **sound out.**

sound⁴ (saʊnd) *n.* a channel between two larger areas of sea or between an island and the mainland.

sound barrier *n.* a sudden increase in the force of air against an aircraft flying at or above the speed of sound.

sound effects *pl. n.* sounds artificially produced, as from a recording, to create certain theatrical effects in a play or film.

sounding board *n.* a person or group used to test a new idea or opinion.

soundings ('saʊndɪŋz) *pl. n.* measurements of the depth of a river, lake, etc.

sound out *vb.* to question (someone) in order to discover his opinion: *I intend to sound him out before the meeting.*

soundproof ('saʊnd,pruːf) *adj.* **1.** not penetrable by sound. ~*vb.* **2.** to make (a room) soundproof.

soundtrack ('saʊnd,træk) *n.* the recorded sound accompaniment to a film.

sound wave *n.* a wave that carries sound.

soup (suːp) *n.* **1.** a liquid food made by simmering meat, fish, or vegetables. **2. in the soup.** *Slang.* in trouble or difficulties. —'**soupy** *adj.*

soupçon ('suːpsɒn) *n.* a slight amount; dash.

soup kitchen *n.* a place where food and drink is served to needy people.

soup up *vb. Slang.* to modify the engine of (a car or motorcycle) in order to increase its power.

sour ('saʊə) *adj.* **1.** having a sharp biting taste like the taste of lemon juice or vinegar. **2.** made acid or bad, as in the case of milk, by fermentation. **3.** (of a person's temperament) sullen or disagreeable. **4. go** *or* **turn sour.** to become unfavourable or inharmonious: *his marriage went sour.* ~*vb.* **5.** to make or become unfavourable or inharmonious. —'**sourly** *adv.*

source (sɔːs) *n.* **1.** the point, person, or place from which something originates. **2.** the area or spring where a river or stream begins. **3.** any person, book, or organization from which information or evidence is obtained.

sour cream *n.* cream soured by bacteria for use in salad dressings, dips, etc.

sour grapes *n.* (*functioning as sing.*) the attitude of pretending to despise something because one cannot have it oneself.

sourpuss ('saʊə,pʊs) *n. Informal.* a person who is habitually gloomy or sullen.

souse (saʊs) *vb.* **1.** to plunge (something) into water or other liquid. **2.** to drench. **3.** to steep or cook (food) in a marinade. ~*n.* **4.** the liquid used in pickling. **5.** the act or process of sousing.

soused (saʊst) *adj. Slang.* drunk.

soutane (suːˈtæn) *n. R.C. Church.* a priest's robe.

south (saʊθ) *n.* **1.** one of the four cardinal points of the compass, at 180° from north and 90° clockwise from east and anticlockwise from west. **2.** the direction along a meridian towards the South Pole. **3. the south.** (*often cap.*) any area lying in or towards the south. ~*adj.* **4.** situated in, moving towards, or facing the south. **5.** (esp. of the wind) from the south. ~*adv.* **6.** in, to, or towards the south.

South (saʊθ) *n.* **the. 1.** the southern part of England. **2.** (in the U.S.) the Southern states that formed the Confederacy during the Civil War. ~*adj.* **3.** of or denoting the southern part of a country, area, etc.

South African *adj.* **1.** of or relating to the Republic of South Africa. ~*n.* **2.** a person from the Republic of South Africa.

southeast (,saʊθˈiːst; *Naut.* ,saʊˈiːst) *n.* **1.** the direction midway between south and east. ~*adj.* also **southeastern. 2.** of or denoting that part of a country, area, etc. which lies in the southeast. **3.** situated in, moving towards, or facing the southeast. **4.** (esp. of the wind) from the southeast. ~*adv.* **5.** in, to, or towards the southeast. —,**south'easterly** *adj., adv., n.*

Southeast (,saʊθˈiːst) *n.* **the.** the southeast of Britain, esp. the London area.

southeaster (,saʊθˈiːstə; *Naut.* ,saʊˈiːstə) *n.* a strong wind or storm from the southeast.

southerly ('sʌðəlɪ) *adj.* **1.** of or in the south. ~*adv., adj.* **2.** towards the south. **3.** from the south: *a southerly wind.*

southern ('sʌðən) *adj.* **1.** situated in or towards the south. **2.** facing or moving towards the south. **3.** (*sometimes cap.*) of or characteristic of the south or South. —'**southern,most** adj.

Southerner ('sʌðənə) n. a person from the south of a country or area, esp. England or the U.S.

southern hemisphere n. that half of the globe lying south of the equator.

southern lights pl. n. same as **aurora australis**.

southpaw ('sauθ,pɔː) Informal. ~n. **1.** any left-handed person, esp. a boxer. ~adj. **2.** left-handed.

South Pole n. the southernmost point on the earth's axis, at a latitude of 90°S.

South Seas pl. n. the seas south of the equator.

southward ('sauθwəd; Naut. 'sʌðəd) adj., adv. also **southwards**. **1.** towards the south. ~n. **2.** the southward part, direction, etc.

southwest (,sauθ'wɛst; Naut. ,sau'wɛst) n. **1.** the direction midway between west and south. ~adj. also **southwestern**. **2.** of or denoting that part of a country, area, etc. which lies in the southwest. **3.** situated in, moving towards, or facing the southwest. **4.** (esp. of the wind) from the southwest. ~adv. **5.** in, to, or towards the southwest. —,south'westerly adj., adv., n.

Southwest (,sauθ'wɛst) n. **the.** the southwestern part of Britain, esp. Cornwall, Devon, and Somerset.

southwester (,sauθ'wɛstə; Naut. ,sau'wɛstə) n. a strong wind or storm from the southwest.

souvenir (,suːvə'nɪə) n. an object that reminds one of a certain place, occasion, or person; memento.

sou'wester (sau'wɛstə) n. a waterproof hat with a very broad rim at the back worn by seamen.

sovereign ('sɒvrɪn) n. **1.** a person who has supreme authority, esp. a monarch. **2.** a former British gold coin worth one pound sterling. ~adj. **3.** independent of outside authority: a sovereign state. **4.** supreme in rank or authority: a sovereign lord. **5.** excellent or outstanding: a sovereign remedy.

sovereignty ('sɒvrəntɪ) n., pl. **-ties. 1.** supreme and unrestricted power, as of a state. **2.** the position or authority of a sovereign.

soviet ('səuvɪət, 'sɒv-) n. (in the Soviet Union) an elected government council at the local, regional, and national levels.

Soviet ('səuvɪət, 'sɒv-) adj. **1.** of or relating to the Soviet Union, its people, or its government. ~n. **2.** a person from the Soviet Union.

sow¹ (səu) vb. **sowing, sowed; sown** or **sowed. 1.** to scatter or place (seed) in or on (a piece of ground) so that it may grow: to sow wheat; to sow a strip of land. **2.** to

implant or introduce: to sow a doubt in someone's mind.

sow² (sau) n. a female adult pig.

soya bean ('sɔɪə) or U.S. & Canad. **soybean** ('sɔɪ,biːn) n. a bean which is used as food, forage, and as the source of an oil.

soy sauce (sɔɪ) n. a salty dark brown sauce made from fermented soya beans, used esp. in Chinese cookery.

sozzled ('sɒz²ld) adj. Informal. drunk.

spa (spɑː) n. a mineral-water spring or a place where such a spring is found.

space (speɪs) n. **1.** the unlimited three-dimensional expanse in which all material objects are located. **2.** an interval of distance or time between two points, objects, or events. **3.** a blank portion or area. **4.** unoccupied area or room: there is no space for a table. **5.** the region beyond the earth's atmosphere containing other planets, stars, and galaxies; the universe. ~vb. **6.** to place or arrange (things) at intervals or with spaces between them.

space age n. **1.** the period in which the exploration of space has become possible. ~adj. **space-age. 2.** futuristic or ultramodern: a space-age car.

space-bar n. a bar on a typewriter that is pressed in order to leave a space between words or letters.

space capsule n. a vehicle, sometimes carrying people or animals, designed to obtain scientific information from space and to be recovered on returning to earth.

spacecraft ('speɪs,krɑːft) n. a vehicle designed to orbit the earth or to travel to the Moon or to other planets.

Space Invaders n. Trademark. a video game in which players try to obliterate a series of symbols moving down the screen by operating levers or buttons.

spaceman ('speɪs,mæn) or (fem.) **spacewoman** n., pl. **-men** or (fem.) **-women.** a person who travels in space.

space probe n. a vehicle equipped to obtain scientific information, normally transmitted back to earth by radio, about a planet or conditions in space.

spaceship ('speɪs,ʃɪp) n. a manned spacecraft.

space shuttle n. a manned reusable spacecraft designed for making regular flights.

space station n. a large manned artificial satellite designed to orbit the earth during a long period of time thus providing a base for scientific research in space and for people travelling in space.

spacesuit ('speɪs,suːt) n. a sealed protective suit worn by astronauts.

space-time or **space-time continuum** n. Physics. the four-dimensional continuum having three space coordinates and one time coordinate that together completely specify the location of a particle or an event.

spacious ('speɪʃəs) *adj.* having a large capacity or area. —'**spaciousness** *n.*

spade[1] (speɪd) *n.* **1.** a tool for digging, with a flat steel blade and a long wooden handle. **2. call a spade a spade.** to speak plainly and frankly.

spade[2] (speɪd) *n.* **1. a.** (*pl.*) the suit of playing cards marked with a black symbol resembling a heart-shaped leaf with a stem. **b.** a card with one or more of these symbols on it. **2.** *Offensive.* a Black person. **3. in spades.** *Informal.* in the extreme; emphatically: *Hamburg's got nightlife, in spades.*

spadework ('speɪd,wɜːk) *n.* dull or routine preparatory work.

spadix ('speɪdɪks) *n.,* *pl.* **spadices** (speɪ-'daɪsiːz). a spike of small flowers on a fleshy stem.

spaghetti (spə'gɛtɪ) *n.* pasta in the form of long strings.

spaghetti junction *n.* a junction between motorways with a large number of intersecting roads.

spaghetti western *n.* a cowboy film made in Europe by an Italian director.

spake (speɪk) *vb. Archaic.* past of **speak.**

Spam (spæm) *n. Trademark.* tinned luncheon meat made largely from pork.

span (spæn) *n.* **1.** the interval, space, or distance between two points, such as the ends of a bridge. **2.** the complete extent: *the span of his life.* **3.** short for **wingspan. 4.** a unit of length based on the width of an expanded hand, usually taken as nine inches. ~*vb.* **spanning, spanned. 5.** to stretch or extend across, over, or around: *his career in Hollywood spanned three decades; three bridges span the East River.*

spangle ('spæŋg'l) *n.* **1.** a small piece of metal or other shiny material used as a decoration, esp. on clothes; sequin. ~*vb.* **2.** to make (something) glitter as if with spangles. **3.** to cover (something) with spangles.

Spaniard ('spænjəd) *n.* a person from Spain.

spaniel ('spænjəl) *n.* a dog with long drooping ears and a silky coat.

Spanish ('spænɪʃ) *n.* **1.** the official language of Spain, Mexico, and most countries of South and Central America. **2. the Spanish.** (*functioning as pl.*) the people of Spain. ~*adj.* **3.** relating to Spain, Spaniards, or the Spanish language.

Spanish fly *n.* a beetle, the dried body of which is used medicinally.

Spanish Main *n.* **1.** the N coast of South America. **2.** the Caribbean Sea, the S part of which in colonial times was the haunt of pirates.

spank (spæŋk) *vb.* **1.** to slap (someone)

with the open hand, esp. on the buttocks. ~*n.* **2.** such a slap.

spanking[1] ('spæŋkɪŋ) *n.* a series of spanks, usually as a punishment for children.

spanking[2] ('spæŋkɪŋ) *adj.* **1.** *Informal.* outstandingly fine, smart, or large: *in spanking condition.* **2.** quick and energetic: *a spanking pace.*

spanner ('spænə) *n.* **1.** a steel tool with jaws or a hole, designed to grip a nut or bolt. **2. throw a spanner in the works.** *Brit. informal.* to create an impediment or annoyance.

spanspek ('spæn,spɛk) *n. S. African.* a cantaloupe melon.

spar[1] (spɑː) *n.* a piece of nautical gear resembling a pole and used as a mast, boom, or gaff.

spar[2] (spɑː) *vb.* **sparring, sparred. 1.** *Boxing.* to box using light blows, as in training. **2.** to argue with someone.

spar[3] (spɑː) *n.* a light-coloured, crystalline, easily split mineral.

spare (spɛə) *vb.* **1.** to refrain from killing, punishing, or injuring (someone). **2.** to shield (someone) from (something unpleasant): *spare me the indignity.* **3.** to be able to afford or give: *I can't spare the time.* **4. not spare oneself.** to exert oneself to the full. **5. to spare.** more than is required: *two minutes to spare.* ~*adj.* **6.** in excess of what is needed; additional. **7.** able to be used when needed: *a spare part.* **8.** (of a person) thin. **9.** (of a style) very plain or simple. **10.** *Brit. slang.* upset, angry, or distracted: *Mum will go spare when she finds out.* ~*n.* **11.** a duplicate kept as a replacement in case of damage or loss.

spareribs (,spɛə'rɪbz) *pl. n.* a cut of pork ribs with most of the meat trimmed off.

spare tyre *n.* **1.** an additional tyre kept in a motor vehicle in case of puncture. **2.** *Brit. slang.* a roll of fat just above the waist.

sparing ('spɛərɪŋ) *adj.* (sometimes foll. by *of*) economical or frugal (with).

spark (spɑːk) *n.* **1.** a fiery particle thrown out or left by burning material or caused by the friction of two hard surfaces. **2.** a momentary flash of light accompanied by a sharp crackling noise, produced by a sudden electrical discharge through the air. **3.** a trace or hint: *a spark of interest.* **4.** vivacity, enthusiasm, or humour: *there is no spark about him.* ~*vb.* **5.** to give off sparks. **6.** (often foll. by *off*) to initiate: *this discovery sparked off the investigation.*

sparkle ('spɑːk'l) *vb.* **1.** to issue or reflect bright points of light. **2.** (of wine or mineral water) to be slightly fizzy. **3.** to be vivacious or witty. ~*n.* **4.** a point of light, spark, or gleam. **5.** vivacity or wit.

sparkler ('spɑːklə) *n.* **1.** a type of hand-held firework that throws out sparks. **2.** *Informal.* a sparkling gem; esp. a diamond.

spark plug *n.* a device in an internal-combustion engine which ignites the explosive mixture by means of an electric spark. Also called: **sparking plug.**

sparring partner ('spɑːrɪŋ) *n.* **1.** a person who practises with a boxer during training. **2.** a person with whom one has friendly arguments.

sparrow ('spærəʊ) *n.* a very common small brown or grey bird which feeds on seeds and insects.

sparrowhawk ('spærəʊˌhɔːk) *n.* a small hawk which preys on smaller birds.

sparse (spɑːs) *adj.* scattered or scanty. —**'sparsely** *adv.*

Spartan ('spɑːt²n) *adj.* **1.** of or relating to the ancient Greek city of Sparta. **2.** very strict or austere: *a Spartan upbringing.* ~*n.* **3.** a citizen of Sparta. **4.** a very strict or austere person.

spasm ('spæzəm) *n.* **1.** an involuntary muscular contraction. **2.** a sudden burst of activity or feeling: *to work in spasms; a spasm of anger.*

spasmodic (spæz'mɒdɪk) *adj.* taking place in sudden brief spells. —**spas'modically** *adv.*

spastic ('spæstɪk) *n.* **1.** a person who has cerebral palsy. ~*adj.* **2.** affected by spasms: *a spastic colon.* **3.** suffering from cerebral palsy.

spat[1] (spæt) *n.* a slight quarrel.

spat[2] (spæt) *vb.* a past of **spit**[1].

spate (speɪt) *n.* **1.** a fast flow, rush, or outpouring: *a spate of words.* **2. in spate.** *Chiefly Brit.* (of a river) flooded.

spathe (speɪð) *n.* a large bract that encloses a flower cluster.

spatial ('speɪʃəl) *adj.* of or relating to space: *spatial distance.* —**'spatially** *adv.*

spats (spæts) *pl. n.* cloth or leather coverings formerly worn by men over the ankle and instep.

spatter ('spætə) *vb.* **1.** to scatter or splash (a substance, esp. a liquid) in scattered drops: *to spatter mud on the car.* **2.** to sprinkle, cover, or spot (an object or a surface) with a liquid. ~*n.* **3.** the sound of spattering. **4.** something spattered, such as a spot or splash.

spatula ('spætjʊlə) *n.* a utensil with a broad flat blade, used for lifting, spreading, or stirring foods or paint.

spawn (spɔːn) *n.* **1.** the jelly-like mass of eggs laid by fish, amphibians, or molluscs. ~*vb.* **2.** (of fish, amphibians, or molluscs) to lay eggs. **3.** to cause (something) to be created: *the film spawned a successful TV series.*

spay (speɪ) *vb.* to remove the ovaries from (a female animal).

speak (spiːk) *vb.* **speaking, spoke, spoken.**

1. to make verbal utterances; utter (words). **2.** to communicate or express (something) in words. **3.** to deliver a speech or lecture. **4.** to know how to talk in (a specified language): *he does not speak German.* **5. on speaking terms.** on good terms; friendly. **6. so to speak.** as it were. **7. speak one's mind.** to express one's opinions frankly and plainly. **8. to speak of.** of a significant or worthwhile nature: *no support to speak of.*

speakeasy ('spiːkˌiːzɪ) *n., pl.* **-easies.** *U.S.* a place where alcoholic drink was sold illicitly during Prohibition.

speaker ('spiːkə) *n.* **1.** a person who speaks, esp. at a formal occasion. **2.** same as **loudspeaker.**

Speaker ('spiːkə) *n.* the presiding officer in any of numerous law-making bodies.

speak for *vb.* **1.** to speak as a representative of (other people). **2. speak for itself.** to be so evident that no further comment is necessary: *his talent speaks for itself.* **3. speak for yourself!** *Informal.* do not presume that other people agree with you!

speak up *or* **out** *vb.* **1.** to state one's beliefs bravely and firmly. **2.** to speak more loudly and clearly.

spear[1] (spɪə) *n.* **1.** a weapon consisting of a long shaft with a sharp point, which may be thrown or thrust. ~*vb.* **2.** to pierce (someone or something) with or as if with a spear.

spear[2] (spɪə) *n.* a shoot, stalk, or blade, as of grass.

spearhead ('spɪəˌhɛd) *vb.* **1.** to lead or initiate (an attack or a campaign). ~*n.* **2.** the leading force in a military attack.

spearmint ('spɪəmɪnt) *n.* a minty flavouring used for sweets and toothpaste, which comes from a purple-flowered plant.

spec (spɛk) *n.* **on spec.** *Informal.* as a speculation or gamble: *all the tickets were sold so I went to the theatre on spec.*

special ('spɛʃəl) *adj.* **1.** distinguished from or better than others of its kind. **2.** designed or reserved for a particular purpose: *special boots for hill walking.* **3.** not usual or commonplace: *a special case.* **4.** particular or primary: *his special interest was music.* **5.** relating to the education of handicapped children: *a special school.* ~*n.* **6.** something that is special in some way, such as an extra edition of a newspaper. **7.** a dish or meal given prominence, usually at a low price, in a café, pub, or restaurant. **8.** short for **special constable.** —**'specially** *adv.*

Usage. see **especial.**

Special Branch *n.* (in Britain) the department of the police force that is concerned with political security.

special constable *n.* a person recruited for occasional police duties, as in time of emergency.

special delivery *n.* the delivery of a piece of mail outside the time of a scheduled delivery, for an extra fee.

specialist ('spɛʃəlɪst) *n.* a person who specializes in a particular activity or field of knowledge.

speciality (,spɛʃɪ'ælɪtɪ) *or esp. U.S. & Canad.* **specialty** *n., pl.* **-ties.** **1.** a special interest or skill. **2.** a service or product specialized in.

specialize *or* **-ise** ('spɛʃə,laɪz) *vb.* **1.** to train in or devote oneself to a particular area of study, occupation, or activity: *she specializes in criminal law.* **2.** to modify (something) for a special use or purpose: *specialized television systems.* —,**speciali-** '**zation** *or* **-i**'**sation** *n.*

special licence *n. Brit.* a licence permitting a marriage to take place without following all the usual legal procedures.

specialty ('spɛʃəltɪ) *n., pl.* **-ties.** *Chiefly U.S. & Canad.* same as **speciality.**

specie ('spiːʃiː) *n.* coin money, as distinguished from paper money.

species ('spiːʃiːz) *n., pl.* **-cies.** *Biol.* any of the groups into which a genus is divided, the members of which are able to interbreed.

specific (spɪ'sɪfɪk) *adj.* **1.** explicit, particular, or definite. **2.** relating to a particular thing: *a specific treatment for arthritis.* ~*n.* **3.** (*pl.*) particular qualities or aspects of something: *let's get down to specifics.* **4.** *Med.* any drug used to treat a particular disease. —**spe**'**cifically** *adv.*

specification (,spɛsɪfɪ'keɪʃən) *n.* **1.** a detailed description of the required constituents, construction, or performance of a material or apparatus. **2.** an item or a detail specified. **3.** a specifying.

specific gravity *n. Physics.* the ratio of the density of a substance to the density of water.

specify ('spɛsɪ,faɪ) *vb.* **-fying, -fied.** **1.** to refer to or state (something) specifically. **2.** to state (something) as a condition.

specimen ('spɛsɪmɪn) *n.* **1.** an individual or part regarded as typical of its group or class. **2.** *Med.* a sample of tissue, blood, or urine taken for analysis. **3.** *Informal.* a person: *a fine healthy specimen.*

specious ('spiːʃəs) *adj.* apparently correct or true, but actually wrong or false.

speck (spɛk) *n.* **1.** a very small mark or spot. **2.** a small or tiny piece of something: *a speck of dust.* ·

speckle ('spɛkᵊl) *n.* **1.** a small mark usually of a contrasting colour, as on the skin or on an egg. ~*vb.* **2.** to mark (something) with speckles. —'**speckled** *adj.*

specs (spɛks) *pl. n. Informal.* **1.** short for **spectacles.** **2.** short for **specifications** (see **specification**).

spectacle ('spɛktəkᵊl) *n.* **1.** a strange or interesting scene. **2.** an impressive, grand, or dramatic public show. **3. make a spectacle of oneself.** to draw attention to oneself by behaving outrageously.

spectacles ('spɛktəkᵊlz) *pl. n.* a pair of glasses for correcting faulty vision.

spectacular (spɛk'tækjʊlə) *adj.* **1.** impressive, grand, or dramatic. ~*n.* **2.** a spectacular show. —**spec**'**tacularly** *adv.*

spectate (spɛk'teɪt) *vb.* to be a spectator; watch.

spectator (spɛk'teɪtə) *n.* a person viewing anything; onlooker; observer.

spectator ion *n. Chem.* an ion which is present in a mixture but plays no part in a reaction.

spectre *or U.S.* **specter** ('spɛktə) *n.* **1.** a ghost; phantom. **2.** an unpleasant or menacing mental image: *the spectre of redundancy.* —'**spectral** *adj.*

spectrometer (spɛk'trɒmɪtə) *n. Physics.* an instrument for producing a spectrum, usually one in which wavelength, energy, or intensity can be measured.

spectroscope ('spɛktrə,skəʊp) *n. Physics.* an instrument for forming or recording a spectrum by passing a light ray through a prism or grating.

spectrum ('spɛktrəm) *n., pl.* **-tra** (-trə). **1.** *Physics.* the distribution of colours produced when white light is dispersed by a prism or grating: violet, indigo, blue, green, yellow, orange, and red. **2.** *Physics.* the whole range of electromagnetic radiation with respect to its wavelength or frequency. **3.** a range or scale of anything such as opinions or emotions.

speculate ('spɛkjʊ,leɪt) *vb.* **1.** to conjecture about something without knowing all the facts. **2.** to buy securities or property in the hope of selling them at a profit. —,**specu**'**lation** *n.* —'**speculative** *adj.* —'**specu,lator** *n.*

sped (spɛd) *vb.* a past of **speed.**

speech (spiːtʃ) *n.* **1.** the ability to speak: *he lost the power of speech.* **2.** that which is spoken; utterance: *in everyday speech.* **3.** a talk given to an audience: *the best man gives his speech.* **4.** a person's manner of speaking: *his speech was slurred.* **5.** a national or regional language or dialect: *cockney speech.*

speech day *n. Brit.* (in schools) an annual day on which prizes are presented and speeches are made by guest speakers.

speechify ('spiːtʃɪ,faɪ) *vb.* **-fying, -fied.** to make a speech, usually one that is pompous and boring.

speechless ('spiːtʃlɪs) *adj.* **1.** temporarily unable to speak, owing to strong emotion, amazement, or shock. **2.** unable to be expressed in words: *speechless fear.*

speed (spiːd) *n.* **1.** the quality of acting or moving fast; rapidity. **2.** the rate at which something moves, is done, or acts. **3.** a gear ratio in a motor vehicle or bicycle: *a three-speed gear.* **4.** *Photog.* a measure of the sensitivity to light of a particular type of film. **5.** *Slang.* amphetamine. **6. at speed.** quickly. ~*vb.* **speeding; sped** *or* **speeded. 7.** to move or go somewhere quickly. **8.** to drive a motor vehicle faster than the legal limit. ~See also **speed up.**

speedboat ('spiːdˌbəʊt) *n.* a high-speed motorboat.

speed limit *n.* the maximum speed at which a vehicle may legally travel on a particular road.

speedo ('spiːdəʊ) *n., pl.* **speedos.** *Informal.* a speedometer.

speedometer (spɪ'dɒmɪtə) *n.* a device in a vehicle which shows the speed of travel.

speed up *vb.* to increase or cause to increase in speed or rate; accelerate.

speedway ('spiːdˌweɪ) *n.* **1.** the sport of racing on light powerful motorcycles round cinder tracks. **2.** the track or stadium where such races are held.

speedwell ('spiːdˌwɛl) *n.* a small blue or pinkish-white flower.

speedy ('spiːdɪ) *adj.* **speedier, speediest. 1.** done without delay. **2.** (of a vehicle) able to travel fast. —'**speedily** *adv.*

spek (spɛk) *n. S. African.* bacon.

speleology *or* **spelaeology** (ˌspiːlɪ-'ɒlədʒɪ) *n.* the scientific study of caves.

spell[1] (spɛl) *vb.* **spelling; spelt** *or* **spelled. 1.** to write or name in correct order the letters that make up (a word): *how do you spell 'coyote'?* **2.** (of letters) to make up (a word): *d-o-g spells dog.* **3.** to indicate or signify: *this flood spells ruin.* ~See also **spell out.**

spell[2] (spɛl) *n.* **1.** a verbal formula considered to have magical force. **2.** an irresistible influence; fascination. **3.** a state induced as by a spell; trance: *to break the spell.* **4. under someone's spell.** fascinated by someone.

spell[3] (spɛl) *n.* **1.** a period of time: *a spell of rain.* **2.** a period of duty after which one person or group relieves another. **3.** *Scot., Austral., & N.Z.* a period of rest. ~*vb.* **spelling, spelled. 4.** to take over from (a person) for an interval of time.

spellbinding ('spɛlˌbaɪndɪŋ) *adj.* entrancing or enthralling.

spellbound ('spɛlˌbaʊnd) *adj.* completely fascinated; as if in a trance.

spelling ('spɛlɪŋ) *n.* **1.** the way a word is spelt: *'center' is the U.S. spelling.* **2.** a person's ability to spell: *his spelling is atrocious.*

spell out *vb.* **1.** to make (something) clear or explicit: *let me spell out the problem.* **2.** to read with difficulty, working out each word letter by letter.

spelt (spɛlt) *vb.* the past of **spell**[1].

spend (spɛnd) *vb.* **spending, spent. 1.** to pay out (money). **2.** to pass (time) in a specific way or place: *we spent the night in London.* **3.** to concentrate (effort) on an activity. **4.** to use up completely: *the hurricane spent its force.* —'**spending** *n.*

spendthrift ('spɛndˌθrɪft) *n.* **1.** a person who spends money extravagantly. ~*adj.* **2.** of or like a spendthrift: *his spendthrift ways.*

spent (spɛnt) *vb.* **1.** past of **spend.** ~*adj.* **2.** used up or exhausted.

sperm (spɜːm) *n.* **1.** (*pl.* **sperm** *or* **sperms**) one of the male reproductive cells released in the semen during ejaculation. **2.** same as **semen.**

spermaceti (ˌspɜːmə'sɛtɪ, -'siːtɪ) *n.* a white waxy substance obtained from the sperm whale.

spermatozoon (ˌspɜːmətəʊ'zəʊɒn) *n., pl.* **-zoa** (-'zəʊə). same as **sperm** (sense 1).

spermicide ('spɜːmɪˌsaɪd) *n.* a substance that kills sperm.

sperm oil *n.* an oil obtained from the head of the sperm whale, used as a lubricant.

sperm whale *n.* a large whale which is hunted for spermaceti and ambergris.

spew (spjuː) *vb.* **1.** to vomit. **2.** (usually foll. by *out*) to send or be sent out in or as if in a stream: *flames spewed out.*

sphagnum ('sfægnəm) *n.* a moss which is found in bogs and which decays to form peat.

sphere (sfɪə) *n.* **1.** *Geom.* a round solid figure in which every point on the surface is equally distant from the centre. **2.** an object having this shape, such as a planet. **3.** a particular field of activity. **4.** a social class.

spherical ('sfɛrɪkəl) *adj.* shaped like a sphere.

spheroid ('sfɪərɔɪd) *n. Geom.* a solid figure that is almost but not exactly a sphere.

sphincter ('sfɪŋktə) *n. Anat.* a ring of muscle surrounding the opening of a hollow organ and contracting to close it.

sphinx (sfɪŋks) *n.* **1.** one of the huge statues built by the ancient Egyptians, having the body of a lion and the head of a man. **2.** a mysterious person.

Sphinx (sfɪŋks) *n.* **the. 1.** *Greek myth.* a monster with a woman's head and a lion's body, who set a riddle for travellers, killing them when they failed to answer it. Oedipus answered the riddle and the Sphinx then killed herself. **2.** the huge statue of a sphinx near the pyramids at El Gîza in Egypt.

spice (spaɪs) *n.* **1. a.** an aromatic substance, such as ginger or cinnamon, used as flavouring. **b.** such substances collectively. **2.** something that adds zest or interest. ~*vb.* **3.** to flavour (food) with spices. **4.** to add zest or interest to (something): *his speech was spiced up with a few jokes.*

spick-and-span *or* **spic-and-span** ('spıkən'spæn) *adj.* very neat and clean.

spicy ('spaısı) *adj.* **spicier, spiciest.** **1.** flavoured with spice. **2.** *Informal.* suggestive of scandal: *a spicy piece of gossip.*

spider ('spaıdə) *n.* a small eight-legged creature, many species of which weave webs in which to trap insects for food. —'**spidery** *adj.*

spider monkey *n.* a tree-living monkey with very long legs, a long prehensile tail, and a small head.

spiel (ʃpiːl) *n.* glib plausible talk, associated mainly with salesmen.

spigot ('spıgət) *n.* **1.** a stopper for the vent hole of a cask. **2.** a wooden tap fitted to a cask.

spike[1] (spaık) *n.* **1.** a sharp point. **2.** a sharp-pointed metal object. **3.** a long metal nail. **4.** (*pl.*) sports shoes with metal spikes on the soles for greater grip. ~*vb.* **5.** to secure or supply (something) with spikes: *spiked shoes.* **6.** to impale on or injure with a spike or spikes. **7.** to add alcohol to (a drink). —'**spiky** *adj.*

spike[2] (spaık) *n. Bot.* **1.** an arrangement of flowers attached at the base to a long stem. **2.** an ear of grain.

spikenard ('spaıknɑːd, 'spaıkə,nɑːd) *n.* **1.** a fragrant Indian plant with rose-purple flowers. **2.** an ointment obtained from this plant.

spill[1] (spıl) *vb.* **spilling; spilt** *or* **spilled.** **1.** to fall or cause to fall from or as from a container by accident. **2.** (of large numbers of people) to come out of a place: *the crowds spilled out on the street.* **3.** to shed (blood). **4. spill the beans.** *Informal.* to give away a secret. ~*n.* **5.** *Informal.* a fall or tumble. **6.** an amount of liquid spilt. —'**spillage** *n.*

spill[2] (spıl) *n.* a splinter of wood or strip of paper for lighting pipes or fires.

spillikin ('spılıkın) *n.* a thin strip of wood, cardboard, or plastic used in spillikins.

spillikins ('spılıkınz) *n.* (*functioning as sing.*) *Brit.* a game in which players try to pick each spillikin from a heap without moving the others.

spin (spın) *vb.* **spinning, spun.** **1.** to rotate or cause to rotate rapidly. **2.** to draw out and twist (natural fibres, such as silk or cotton) into a long continuous thread. **3.** (of a spider or silkworm) to form (a web or cocoon) from a silky fibre that comes out of the body. **4. spin a yarn.** to tell an improbable story. **5.** *Sport.* to throw, hit, or kick (a ball) so that it spins and changes direction or changes speed on bouncing. **6.** same as **spin-dry.** **7.** to reel or grow dizzy: *my head is spinning.* ~*n.* **8.** a rapid rotating motion. **9.** a flight manoeuvre in which an

aircraft performs a continuous spiral descent. **10.** *Sport.* a spinning motion given to a ball. **11.** *Informal.* a short car drive taken for pleasure. ~See also **spin out.** —'**spinning** *n.*

spina bifida ('spaınə 'bıfıdə) *n.* a congenital condition in which part of the spinal cord protrudes through a gap in the backbone, sometimes causing paralysis.

spinach ('spınıdʒ, -ıtʃ) *n.* a dark green leafy vegetable.

spinal column *n.* same as **spine** (sense 1).

spinal cord *n.* the thick cord of nerve tissue within the spine, which connects the brain to the nerves of the body.

spin bowler *n. Cricket.* same as **spinner** (sense 1b).

spindle ('spınd³l) *n.* **1.** a rod with a notch in the top for drawing out, twisting and winding the thread in spinning. **2.** a rotating rod that acts as an axle.

spindlelegs ('spınd³l,lɛgz) *or* **spindle-shanks** *n.* (*functioning as sing.*) a person with long thin legs.

spindly ('spındlı) *adj.* **-dlier, -dliest.** tall, slender, and frail.

spindrift ('spın,drıft) *n.* spray blown up from the sea.

spin-dry *vb.* **-drying, -dried.** to dry (clothes) in a spin-dryer.

spin-dryer *n.* a device that extracts water from clothes by spinning them in a perforated drum.

spine (spaın) *n.* **1.** the row of bony segments that surround and protect the spinal column. **2.** the back of a book, record sleeve, or video-tape box. **3.** a sharp point on the body of an animal or on a plant. —'**spinal** *adj.*

spine-chiller *n.* a film or story that arouses terror. —'**spine-,chilling** *adj.*

spineless ('spaınlıs) *adj.* **1.** lacking character, willpower, or courage. **2.** having no spine.

spinet (spı'nɛt, 'spınıt) *n.* a small harpsichord.

spinnaker ('spınəkə; *Naut.* 'spæŋkə) *n.* a large triangular sail set from the foremast of a racing yacht.

spinner ('spınə) *n.* **1.** *Cricket.* **a.** a ball that is bowled with a spinning motion. **b.** a bowler who specializes in bowling such balls. **2.** a fishing lure that revolves in the water. **3.** a person or thing that spins.

spinneret ('spınə,rɛt) *n.* an organ through which silk threads come out of the body of a spider or insect.

spinney ('spını) *n. Chiefly Brit.* a small wood.

spinning jenny *n.* an early type of spinning frame with several spindles.

spinning wheel *n.* a wheel-like machine

for spinning at home, having one hand- or foot-operated spindle.

spin-off *n.* **1.** a product or development derived incidentally as a result of activities designed to achieve something else. **2.** a television series derived from an earlier successful series.

spin out *vb.* **1.** to take longer than necessary to do (something). **2.** to make (money) last as long as possible.

spinster ('spɪnstə) *n.* an unmarried woman. —'**spinsterish** *adj.*

spiny ('spaɪnɪ) *adj.* **spinier, spiniest.** (of animals or plants) covered with spines.

spiracle ('spaɪərək²l, 'spaɪrə-) *n. Zool.* a small blowhole for breathing through, such as that of a whale.

spiraea *or esp. U.S.* **spirea** (spaɪ'rɪə) *n.* a plant with small white or pink flowers.

spiral ('spaɪərəl) *n.* **1.** *Geom.* a plane curve formed by a point winding about a fixed point at an ever-increasing distance from it. **2.** something that follows a winding course or that has a twisting form. **3.** *Econ.* a continuous upward or downward movement in economic activity or prices. ~*adj.* **4.** having the shape of a spiral. ~*vb.* **-ralling, -ralled** *or U.S.* **-raling, -raled. 5.** to follow a spiral course or be in the shape of a spiral. **6.** to increase or decrease with steady acceleration: *prices continue to spiral.* —'**spirally** *adv.*

spire ('spaɪə) *n.* a tall structure that tapers upwards to a point, as on the roof of a church.

spirit¹ ('spɪrɪt) *n.* **1.** the force that gives life to the body of living things. **2.** temperament or disposition: *noble in spirit.* **3.** liveliness: *they set to it with spirit.* **4.** the fundamental, emotional, and activating principle of a person; will: *the experience broke his spirit.* **5.** the prevailing feeling: *a spirit of joy pervaded the atmosphere.* **6.** mood or attitude: *he did it in the wrong spirit.* **7.** (*pl.*) an emotional state: *in high spirits.* **8.** the deeper more significant meaning as opposed to a literal interpretation: *the spirit of the law.* **9.** the nonphysical aspect of a person: *I shall be with you in spirit.* **10.** a ghostly being, usually the soul of a dead person. ~*vb.* **11.** (foll. by *away* or *off*) to carry (someone or something) off mysteriously or secretly.

spirit² ('spɪrɪt) *n.* **1.** distilled alcoholic liquor, such as whisky or gin. **2.** *Chem.* **a.** a solution of ethanol obtained by distillation. **b.** the essence of a substance, extracted as a liquid by distillation. **3.** *Pharmacol.* a solution of a volatile oil in alcohol.

spirited ('spɪrɪtɪd) *adj.* **1.** showing animation, vigour, or liveliness. **2.** characterized by mood or disposition as specified: *high-spirited; public-spirited.*

spirit gum *n.* a solution of gum in ether, used to stick on false hair.

spirit lamp *n.* a lamp that burns methylated or other spirits instead of oil.

spirit level *n.* a device for checking whether a surface is level, which consists of a block of wood or metal containing a tube partially filled with liquid set so that the air bubble when the block rests between two marks on the tube when the block is level.

spiritual ('spɪrɪtjʊəl) *adj.* **1.** relating to the spirit or soul and not to physical things. **2.** relating to sacred things. ~*n.* **3.** Also called: **Negro spiritual.** a type of religious song originating among Black slaves in the American South. —**spirituality** (,spɪrɪtjʊ-'ælɪtɪ) *n.* —'**spiritually** *adv.*

spiritualism ('spɪrɪtjʊə,lɪzəm) *n.* the belief that the spirits of the dead can communicate with the living. —'**spiritualist** *n.*

spirituous ('spɪrɪtjʊəs) *adj.* containing alcohol.

spirogyra (,spaɪrə'dʒaɪrə) *n.* a multicellular green freshwater plant that floats on the surface of ponds and ditches.

spit¹ (spɪt) *vb.* **spitting, spat** *or* **spit. 1.** to force saliva out of one's mouth. **2.** *Informal.* to show scorn or hatred by spitting. **3.** (often foll. by *out*) to force (something) out of one's mouth: *he spat the food out.* **4.** (of a fire or hot fat) to throw out sparks or particles violently and explosively. **5.** to rain very lightly. **6.** (often foll. by *out*) to utter (short sharp words) in a violent manner. **7. spit it out!** *Brit. informal.* a command given to someone to say what is on his mind. ~*n.* **8.** same as **spittle. 9.** *Informal, chiefly Brit.* same as **spitting image.**

spit² (spɪt) *n.* **1.** a pointed rod on which meat is skewered and roasted over a fire or in an oven. **2.** a long strip of land projecting from a shore.

spit and polish *n. Informal.* strict attention to neatness and cleanliness, as in the armed forces.

spite (spaɪt) *n.* **1.** maliciousness; deliberate nastiness. **2. in spite of.** regardless of: *he went in spite of my warning.* ~*vb.* **3.** to annoy (someone) deliberately, out of spite: *she went out with Tom just to spite John.* —'**spiteful** *adj.* —'**spitefully** *adv.*

spitfire ('spɪt,faɪə) *n.* a woman or girl who often has outbursts of spiteful temper.

spitting image *n. Informal.* a person who bears a strong physical resemblance to another.

spittle ('spɪt²l) *n.* the fluid that is produced in the mouth; saliva.

spittoon (spɪ'tuːn) *n.* a bowl for spittle.

spitz (spɪts) *n.* a dog with a stocky build, a pointed face, erect ears, and a tightly curled tail.

spiv (spɪv) *n. Brit. slang.* a person who makes a living by underhand dealings; black marketeer.

splake (spleɪk) *n.* the hybrid offspring of a speckled trout and a lake trout.

splash (splæʃ) *vb.* **1.** to scatter (liquid) about in blobs; spatter. **2.** to cause (liquid) to fall or (of liquid) to fall upon (something) in scattered blobs. **3.** to print (a story or photograph) prominently in a newspaper. ~*n.* **4.** a splashing sound. **5.** an amount splashed. **6.** a mark created by or as if by splashing. **7. make a splash.** *Informal.* to attract a lot of attention. **8.** a small amount of liquid added to a drink.

splashdown ('splæʃ,daʊn) *n.* **1.** the landing of a spacecraft on water at the end of a flight. ~*vb.* **splash down. 2.** (of a spacecraft) to make a splashdown.

splatter ('splætə) *vb.* **1.** to splash (something or someone) with small blobs. ~*n.* **2.** a splash of liquid.

splay (spleɪ) *vb.* to spread out; turn out or expand: *splayed fingers.*

splayfooted ('spleɪ,fʊtɪd) *adj.* same as **flat-footed.**

spleen (spliːn) *n.* **1.** a spongy organ near the stomach, which filters bacteria from the blood. **2.** spitefulness or ill humour: *to vent one's spleen.*

spleenwort ('spliːn,wɜːt) *n.* a kind of fern that grows on walls.

splendid ('splendɪd) *adj.* **1.** very good: *a splendid idea.* **2.** brilliant or fine in appearance. —**'splendidly** *adv.*

splendiferous (splen'dɪfərəs) *adj.* *Facetious.* grand; splendid.

splendour *or U.S.* **splendor** ('splendə) *n.* the state or quality of being splendid.

splenetic (splɪ'netɪk) *adj.* spiteful or irritable.

splice (splaɪs) *vb.* **1.** to join up the trimmed ends of (two pieces of wire, film, or tape) with an adhesive material. **2.** to join (two ropes) by intertwining the strands. **3. get spliced.** *Informal.* to get married.

splint (splɪnt) *n.* a piece of wood used to support and restrict movement of a broken bone.

splinter ('splɪntə) *n.* **1.** a small thin sharp piece of wood or other material, broken off from something. ~*vb.* **2.** to break or be broken into small sharp fragments.

splinter group *n.* a number of members of an organization, who split from the main body and form an independent group of their own.

split (splɪt) *vb.* **splitting, split. 1.** to break or cause (something) to break into separate pieces. **2.** to separate (a piece) or (of a piece) to be separated from (something). **3.** to separate (a group) or (of a group) to be separated into smaller groups, through disagreement. **4.** (of a couple or group) to separate or to cause (a couple or group) to separate through disagreement. **5.** (often foll. by *up*) to divide (something) among two or more persons. **6.** *Slang.* to depart; leave. **7.** (foll. by *on*) *Slang.* to betray; inform: *he split on me to the cops.* **8. split one's sides.** to laugh heartily. ~*n.* **9.** a gap or rift caused by splitting. **10.** a division in a group or the smaller group resulting from such a division. **11.** a dessert of sliced fruit and ice cream, covered with whipped cream and nuts: *banana split.* ~*adj.* **12.** having a split or splits: *split ends.* ~See also **splits, split up.**

split infinitive *n.* (in English grammar) an infinitive used with another word between *to* and the verb, as in *to really finish it.* This practice is not universally accepted.

Usage. The traditional rule against placing an adverb between *to* and its verb is gradually disappearing. Although it is true that a split infinitive may result in a clumsy sentence, very often the most natural position of the adverb is between *to* and the verb (*he decided to really try*) and to change it would result in an artificial and awkward construction (*he really decided to try*). The current view is therefore that the split infinitive is not a grammatical error. Nevertheless, many writers prefer to avoid splitting infinitives in formal English, since readers with a more traditional point of view are likely to interpret this as incorrect.

split-level *adj.* (of a house or room) having the floor level of one part about half a storey above that of the other.

split pea *n.* a pea dried and split and used in soups or as a vegetable.

split personality *n.* **1.** the tendency to change mood rapidly. **2.** a mental disorder in which a person's mind appears to have separated into two or more personalities.

splits (splɪts) *n.* (*functioning as sing.*) (in gymnastics and dancing) the act of sinking to the floor into a sitting position, with both legs straight, pointing in opposite directions, and at right angles to the body.

split second *n.* **1.** an extremely short period of time; instant. ~*adj.* **split-second. 2.** made in an extremely short time: *a split-second decision.*

splitting ('splɪtɪŋ) *adj.* (of a headache) extremely painful.

split up *vb.* **1.** to separate (something) into parts; divide. **2.** to become parted through disagreement. ~*n.* **split-up. 3.** a separating.

splodge (splɒdʒ) *or U.S.* **splotch** (splɒtʃ) *n.* **1.** a large irregular spot. ~*vb.* **2.** to mark (something) with a splodge or splodges.

splurge (splɜːdʒ) *n.* **1.** a bout of extravagance. ~*vb.* **2.** (foll. by *on*) to spend (money) extravagantly: *he splurged his wages on a new suit.*

splutter ('splʌtə) *vb.* **1.** to spit out (something) from the mouth in an explosive manner, as through choking or laughing. **2.** to utter (words) with spitting sounds, as through rage or choking. **3.** to throw out or to be thrown out in an explosive manner: *sparks spluttered from the fire.* ~*n.* **4.** the act or noise of spluttering.

Spode (spəud) *n.* china or porcelain manufactured by the English potter Josiah Spode or his company.

spoil (spɔil) *vb.* **spoiling, spoilt** *or* **spoiled. 1.** to damage (something), with regard to its value, beauty, or usefulness. **2.** to weaken the character of (a child) by giving it all it wants. **3.** (of perishable substances) to become unfit for consumption or use. **4. be spoiling for.** to have an aggressive desire for: *they are spoiling for a fight.* ~See also **spoils.**

spoilage ('spɔilidʒ) *n.* an amount of material that has been spoilt.

spoiler ('spɔilə) *n.* **1.** a device fitted to an aircraft wing to increase drag and reduce lift. **2.** a similar device fitted to a car.

spoils (spɔilz) *pl. n.* **1.** valuables seized by violence: *the spoils of war.* **2.** the rewards and benefits of public office.

spoilsport ('spɔil,spɔːt) *n. Informal.* a person who spoils the pleasure of other people.

spoke¹ (spəuk) *vb.* the past tense of **speak.**

spoke² (spəuk) *n.* **1.** a bar joining the centre of a wheel to the rim. **2. put a spoke in someone's wheel.** *Brit.* to hinder someone's plans.

spoken ('spəukən) *vb.* **1.** the past participle of **speak.** ~*adj.* **2.** uttered in speech: *the spoken word.* **3.** having speech as specified: *soft-spoken.* **4. spoken for.** engaged or reserved.

spokesman ('spəuksmən), **spokesperson** ('spəuks,pɜːsⁿn), *or* **spokeswoman** ('spəuks,wumən) *n., pl.* **-men, -persons** *or* **-people,** *or* **-women.** a person authorized to speak on behalf of another person or group.

spoliation (,spəuli'eiʃən) *n.* a plundering.

spondee ('spɒndiː) *n. Prosody.* a metrical foot consisting of two long syllables (ˉ ˉ). —**spondaic** (spɒn'deiik) *adj.*

sponge (spʌndʒ) *n.* **1.** a sea animal with a porous absorbent elastic skeleton. **2.** the skeleton of a sponge, or a piece of artificial sponge, used for bathing or cleaning. **3.** a soft absorbent material like a sponge. **4.** same as **sponge cake. 5.** Also called: **sponge pudding.** *Brit.* a light steamed or baked spongy pudding. **6.** a rub with a wet sponge. **7. throw in the sponge.** See **throw in** (sense 3). ~*vb.* **8.** (often foll. by *down*) to clean (something) by rubbing it with a wet sponge. **9.** (usually foll. by *off, away,* or *out*) to remove (marks) by rubbing them with a wet sponge. **10.** to get (something) from someone by taking advantage of his

generosity: *he sponges money off her; he sponges off his wife.* —'**spongy** *adj.*

sponge bag *n.* a small waterproof bag for holding toilet articles when travelling.

sponge cake *n.* a light cake made of eggs, sugar, and flour.

sponger ('spʌndʒə) *n. Informal.* a person who lives off other people by continually taking advantage of their generosity.

sponsor ('spɒnsə) *n.* **1.** a person or group that promotes another person or group in an activity or the activity itself, either for profit or for charity. **2.** *Chiefly U.S. & Canad.* a person or firm that pays the costs of a radio or television programme in return for advertising time. **3.** a person who presents and supports a proposal or suggestion. **4.** a person who makes certain promises on behalf of a person being baptized and takes responsibility for his Christian upbringing. ~*vb.* **5.** to act as a sponsor for (someone or something). —'**sponsored** *adj.* —'**spon-sor,ship** *n.*

spontaneous (spɒn'teiniəs) *adj.* **1.** arising from a natural impulse; voluntary; unpremeditated: *spontaneous applause.* **2.** occurring or produced through natural processes without outside influence. —**spon'taneously** *adv.* —**spontaneity** (,spɒntə'niːiti, -'nei-) *n.*

spontaneous combustion *n. Chem.* the bursting into flame of a substance as a result of internal oxidation processes, without heat from an outside source.

spoof (spuːf) *Informal.* ~*n.* **1.** a mildly satirical parody. **2.** a good-humoured deception or trick. ~*vb.* **3.** to indulge in a spoof of (a person or thing).

spook (spuːk) *Informal.* ~*n.* **1.** a ghost. **2.** a strange and frightening person. ~*vb.* *U.S. & Canad.* **3.** to frighten: *to spook a person.* —'**spooky** *adj.*

spool (spuːl) *n.* a cylinder around which film, thread, tape, or wire can be wound.

spoon (spuːn) *n.* **1.** a small shallow bowl attached to a handle, used for eating, stirring, or serving food. **2. be born with a silver spoon in one's mouth.** to inherit wealth or social standing. ~*vb.* **3.** to scoop up (food or liquid) with or as if with a spoon. **4.** *Old-fashioned slang.* to kiss and cuddle.

spoonbill ('spuːn,bil) *n.* a wading bird with a long flat bill.

spoonerism ('spuːnə,rizəm) *n.* the accidental changing over of the first sounds of a pair of words, often with an amusing result, such as *hush my brat* for *brush my hat.*

spoon-feed *vb.* **-feeding, -fed. 1.** to feed (someone, usually a baby) using a spoon. **2.** to overindulge or spoil (someone).

spoor (spuə, spɔː) *n.* the trail of an animal.

sporadic (spə'rædik) *adj.* occurring at irregular points in time; intermittent: *sporadic firing.* —**spo'radically** *adv.*

spore (spɔː) *n.* a reproductive body, produced by many plants, that develops into a new individual.

sporran ('spɒrən) *n.* a large pouch worn hanging from a belt in front of the kilt in Scottish Highland dress.

sport (spɔːt) *n.* **1.** an individual or group activity pursued for exercise or pleasure, often taking a competitive form: *football is my favourite sport.* **2.** such activities collectively: *do you like sport?* **3.** the pleasure derived from a pastime: *they hunt for sport rather than for food.* **4.** playful or good-humoured joking: *I only did it in sport.* **5. make sport of someone.** to mock someone. **6.** *Informal.* a person who reacts cheerfully even in trying circumstances; a good loser. **7.** an animal or plant that differs markedly from others of the same species, usually because of a mutation. **8.** *Austral. & N.Z. informal.* a term of address between males. ~*vb.* **9.** *Informal.* to wear proudly: *she was sporting a new hat.* ~See also **sports.**

sporting ('spɔːtɪŋ) *adj.* **1.** of sport. **2.** conforming to the ideas of sportsmanship; fair. **3. a sporting chance.** likelihood of a favourable outcome: *she's got a sporting chance of getting the job.*

sportive ('spɔːtɪv) *adj.* playful or joyous.

sports (spɔːts) *n.* **1.** (*modifier*) of or used in sports: *sports equipment.* **2.** Also called: **sports day.** *Brit.* a meeting held at a school or college for competitions in various athletic events.

sports car *n.* a fast car having a low body and usually seating only two persons.

sportscast ('spɔːts‚kɑːst) *n.* *U.S.* a broadcast consisting of sports news. —**'sports‚caster** *n.*

sports jacket *n.* a man's informal jacket, usually made of tweed. Also called (U.S., Austral., & N.Z.): **sports coat.**

sportsman ('spɔːtsmən) *n., pl.* -**men. 1.** a man who plays sports. **2.** a person who shows fairness, observance of the rules, and good humour when losing. —**'sportsman‚like** *adj.* —**'sportsman‚ship** *n.*

sportsperson ('spɔːts‚pɜːs*ə*n) *n.* a person who plays sports.

sportswear ('spɔːts‚wɛə) *n.* clothes worn for sport or outdoor leisure wear.

sportswoman ('spɔːts‚wumən) *n., pl.* -**women.** a woman who plays sports.

sporty ('spɔːtɪ) *adj.* **sportier, sportiest. 1.** (of a person) interested in sport. **2.** (of clothes) suitable for sport. **3.** (of a car) small and fast.

spot (spɒt) *n.* **1.** a small mark on a surface, which has a different colour or texture from its surroundings. **2.** a location: *this is the exact spot.* **3.** a blemish or pimple on the skin. **4.** a flaw in a person's character. **5.** *Informal, chiefly Brit.* a small amount: *a spot of lunch.* **6.** *Informal.* an awkward situation: *I'm in a spot.* **7.** a short period between regular television or radio programmes that is used for advertising. **8.** a part of a show assigned to a specific performer. **9.** short for **spotlight** (sense 1). **10. high spot.** an outstanding event: *the high spot of the holiday.* **11. in a tight spot.** in a difficult situation. **12. knock spots off someone.** to be much better than someone. **13. on the spot. a.** immediately: *he died on the spot.* **b.** at the place in question: *the police were on the spot within minutes.* **c.** in an awkward predicament: *you've really put me on the spot.* **14. soft spot.** a special affection for someone: *I've always had a soft spot for Paul.* ~*vb.* **spotting, spotted. 15.** to see (something or someone) suddenly. **16.** to put stains or spots on (something). **17.** (of some fabrics) to be susceptible to spotting by or as if by water: *silk spots easily.* **18.** to look out for and note (trains, planes, or talent). **19.** to rain lightly. —**'spotless** *adj.* —**'spotlessly** *adv.* —**'spotlessness** *n.*

spot check *n.* a quick random examination.

spotlight ('spɒt‚laɪt) *n.* **1.** a powerful light focused so as to light up a small area. **2. the.** the centre of attention: *he's tired of being in the spotlight.* ~*vb.* -**lighting,** -**lit** or -**lighted. 3.** to direct a spotlight on (something). **4.** to focus attention on (something).

spot-on *adj.* *Brit. informal.* absolutely correct; very accurate: *her impression of the Prime Minister was spot-on.*

spotted ('spɒtɪd) *adj.* **1.** having a pattern of spots. **2.** stained or blemished.

spotted dick *n.* *Brit.* suet pudding containing dried fruit.

spotter ('spɒtə) *n.* a person whose hobby is watching for and noting numbers or types of trains or planes.

spotty ('spɒtɪ) *adj.* -**tier,** -**tiest. 1.** having spots or marks. **2.** not consistent; irregular or uneven. —**'spottiness** *n.*

spouse (spaʊs, spaʊz) *n.* a person's partner in marriage.

spout (spaʊt) *vb.* **1.** to discharge (a liquid) in a stream or jet or (of a liquid) to gush thus. **2.** *Informal.* to utter (a stream of words), often in a boring manner. ~*n.* **3.** a projecting tube or lip allowing the pouring of liquids. **4.** a stream or jet of liquid. **5. up the spout.** *Slang.* **a.** ruined or lost: *our plans are up the spout.* **b.** pregnant.

spouting ('spaʊtɪŋ) *n.* *N.Z.* **a.** a rainwater downpipe on the outside of a building. **b.** such pipes collectively.

sprain (spreɪn) *vb.* **1.** to injure (a joint) by a sudden twist. ~*n.* **2.** this injury, which causes swelling and temporary disability.

sprang (spræŋ) *vb.* a past tense of **spring**.

sprat (spræt) *n.* a small food fish of the herring family.

sprawl (sprɔːl) *vb.* **1.** to sit or lie in an ungainly manner with one's limbs spread out. **2.** to spread out in a straggling fashion: *his handwriting sprawled all over the paper.* ~*n.* **3.** a sprawling arrangement: *urban sprawl.* —'**sprawling** *adj.*

spray[1] (spreɪ) *n.* **1.** fine particles of a liquid. **2. a.** a liquid designed to be discharged from an aerosol or atomizer: *hair spray.* **b.** the aerosol or atomizer itself. **3.** a number of small objects flying through the air: *a spray of bullets.* ~*vb.* **4.** to scatter (liquid) in fine particles. **5.** to squirt (a liquid) from an aerosol or atomizer. **6.** to cover with a spray: *to spray the lawn.*

spray[2] (spreɪ) *n.* **1.** a sprig or branch with buds, leaves, flowers, or berries. **2.** an ornament or design like this.

spray gun *n.* a device that sprays fine particles of a fluid such as paint.

spread (sprɛd) *vb.* **spreading, spread.** **1.** to extend or unfold to the fullest width: *she spread the map.* **2.** to extend over a larger expanse: *the political unrest spread over several years.* **3.** to apply or be applied in a coating: *spread jam on the bread.* **4.** to be displayed to its fullest extent: *the landscape spread before us.* **5.** to send or be sent out in all directions; distribute or be distributed: *someone is spreading rumours; the disease spread quickly.* ~*n.* **6.** a spreading; distribution, dispersion, or expansion. **7.** *Informal.* the wingspan of an aircraft or bird. **8.** *Informal, chiefly U.S. & Canad.* a ranch or other large area of land. **9.** *Informal.* a large meal. **10.** a soft food which can be spread: *salmon spread.* **11.** two facing pages in a book or magazine. **12.** a widening of the hips and waist: *middle-age spread.*

spread-eagled *adj.* with arms and legs outstretched.

spree (spriː) *n.* a bout of overindulgence, usually in drinking or in spending money.

sprig (sprɪg) *n.* **1.** a shoot, twig, or sprout. **2.** an ornamental device like this. ~*vb.* **sprigging, sprigged.** **3.** to ornament (fabric) with a design of sprigs.

sprightly ('spraɪtlɪ) *adj.* **-lier, -liest.** full of vitality; lively and brisk. —'**sprightliness** *n.*

spring (sprɪŋ) *vb.* **springing, sprang** *or* **sprung; sprung.** **1.** to jump suddenly upwards or forwards. **2.** to release or be released from a forced position by elasticity: *the bolt sprang back.* **3.** to cause (something) to happen unexpectedly: *to spring a surprise.*| **4.** (usually foll. by *from*) to originate; be descended: *the idea sprang from a chance meeting; he sprang from peasant stock.* **5.** (often foll. by *up*) to come into being or appear suddenly: *factories spring-*

ing up. **6.** to provide (something, such as a mattress) with springs. **7.** *Informal.* to arrange the escape of (someone) from prison. ~*n.* **8.** a leap or jump. **9.** the quality of resilience; elasticity. **10.** a natural pool forming the source of a stream. **11.** a coil which can be compressed, stretched, or bent and then return to its original shape when released. **12.** the season between winter and summer. —'**spring,like** *adj.*

spring balance *or esp. U.S.* **spring scale** *n.* a device that indicates the weight of an object by the extension of a spring to which the object is attached.

springboard ('sprɪŋ,bɔːd) *n.* **1.** a flexible board used to gain height or momentum in diving or gymnastics. **2.** anything that serves as a beginning or impetus.

springbok ('sprɪŋ,bɒk) *n., pl.* **-bok** *or* **-boks.** a S African antelope which moves in leaps.

spring chicken *n.* **1.** *Chiefly U.S.* a young chicken, which is tender for cooking. **2. he** *or* **she is no spring chicken.** *Informal.* he *or* she is no longer young.

spring-clean *vb.* **1.** to clean (a house) thoroughly, traditionally at the end of winter. ~*n.* **2.** an instance of this. —,**spring-'cleaning** *n.*

springer spaniel *or* **springer** ('sprɪŋə) *n.* a spaniel with a slightly domed head and ears of medium length.

spring onion *n.* an immature onion with a tiny bulb and long green leaves, eaten in salads.

spring tide *n.* either of the two tides at or just after new moon and full moon: the greatest rise and fall in tidal level.

springtime ('sprɪŋ,taɪm) *n.* the season of spring.

springy ('sprɪŋɪ) *adj.* **springier, springiest.** having resilience or elasticity. —'**springiness** *n.*

sprinkle ('sprɪŋkᵊl) *vb.* **1.** to scatter (liquid or powder) in tiny drops or particles over (something). **2.** to distribute over (something): *the field was sprinkled with flowers.* —'**sprinkler** *n.*

sprinkling ('sprɪŋklɪŋ) *n.* a small quantity or amount: *a sprinkling of snow.*

sprint (sprɪnt) *n.* **1.** *Athletics.* **a.** a short race run at top speed. **b.** a fast run at the end of a longer race. **2.** any quick run. ~*vb.* **3.** to go at top speed, as in running or cycling. —'**sprinter** *n.*

sprit (sprɪt) *n.* *Naut.* a light spar crossing a sail diagonally from the mast to the peak.

sprite (spraɪt) *n.* (in folklore) an elf.

spritsail ('sprɪt,seɪl; *Naut.* 'sprɪtsəl) *n.* *Naut.* a sail mounted on a sprit.

spritzer ('sprɪtsə) *n.* a tall drink of wine and soda water.

sprocket ('sprɒkɪt) *n.* **1.** Also called: **sprocket wheel.** a wheel with teeth on the rim, that drives or is driven by a chain. **2.**

a cylindrical wheel with teeth on one or both rims for pulling film through a camera or projector.

sprout (spraʊt) *vb.* **1.** (of a plant or seed) to produce (new leaves or shoots). **2.** (often foll. by *up*) to begin to grow or develop. ~*n.* **3.** a new shoot or bud. **4.** same as **Brussels sprout.**

spruce[1] (spruːs) *n.* **1.** an evergreen pyramid-shaped tree with needle-like leaves and light-coloured wood. **2.** the wood of this tree.

spruce[2] (spruːs) *adj.* neat and smart.

spruce up *vb.* to make neat and smart.

spruit (spreɪt) *n. S. African.* a small tributary stream or watercourse.

sprung (sprʌŋ) *vb.* a past tense and the past participle of **spring.**

spry (spraɪ) *adj.* **spryer, spryest** or **sprier, spriest.** active and brisk; nimble.

spud (spʌd) *n. Informal.* a potato.

spume (spjuːm) *n.* **1.** foam or froth. ~*vb.* **2.** to foam or froth.

spun (spʌn) *vb.* **1.** past of **spin.** ~*adj.* **2.** made by spinning: *spun gold; spun glass.*

spunk (spʌŋk) *n. Informal.* courage or spirit. —'**spunky** *adj.*

spur (spɜː) *n.* **1.** a sharp spiked wheel fixed to the heel of a rider's boot and used to urge his horse on. **2.** a stimulus or incentive. **3.** a sharp horny part sticking out from a cock's leg. **4.** a ridge sticking out from a mountain side. **5. on the spur of the moment.** on impulse. **6. win one's spurs.** to prove one's ability; gain distinction. ~*vb.* **spurring, spurred. 7.** (often foll. by *on*) to encourage (someone).

spurge (spɜːdʒ) *n.* a plant with milky sap and small flowers.

spurious ('spjʊərɪəs) *adj.* not genuine or real.

spurn (spɜːn) *vb.* to reject (a person or thing) with contempt.

spurt (spɜːt) *vb.* **1.** to gush or cause (something) to gush out in a sudden stream or jet. **2.** to make a sudden effort. ~*n.* **3.** a short burst of activity, speed, or energy. **4.** a sudden stream or jet.

sputnik ('spʊtnɪk) *n.* a Soviet artificial satellite.

sputter ('spʌtə) *vb., n.* same as **splutter.**

sputum ('spjuːtəm) *n., pl.* **-ta** (-tə). saliva, usually mixed with mucus.

spy (spaɪ) *n., pl.* **spies. 1.** a person employed to obtain secret information about other countries or organizations. **2.** a person who secretly keeps watch on others. ~*vb.* **spying, spied. 3.** (foll. by *on*) to keep a secret watch on someone. **4.** to work as a spy. **5.** to catch sight of (someone or something).

spyglass ('spaɪˌɡlɑːs) *n.* a small telescope.

spy out *vb.* to discover (something) secretly.

sq. square.

Sq. Square.

squab (skwɒb) *n., pl.* **squabs** or **squab.** a young unfledged bird.

squabble ('skwɒbəl) *vb.* **1.** to quarrel over a small matter. ~*n.* **2.** a petty quarrel.

squad (skwɒd) *n.* **1.** the smallest military formation, usually a dozen soldiers. **2.** any small group of people working together: *antiriot squads.* **3.** *Sport.* a number of players from which a team is to be selected.

squadron ('skwɒdrən) *n.* the basic unit of an air force.

squadron leader *n.* a fairly senior commissioned officer in the air force.

squalid ('skwɒlɪd) *adj.* **1.** dirty and unattractive. **2.** morally sordid.

squall[1] (skwɔːl) *n.* a sudden strong wind or brief violent storm.

squall[2] (skwɔːl) *vb.* **1.** to cry noisily; yell. ~*n.* **2.** a noisy cry or yell.

squalor ('skwɒlə) *n.* the condition of being squalid; disgusting filth.

squander ('skwɒndə) *vb.* to spend (money) wastefully.

square (skwɛə) *n.* **1.** a plane figure with four equal sides and four right angles. **2.** anything of this shape. **3.** an open area in a town, sometimes including the surrounding buildings, which may form a square. **4.** *Maths.* the number produced when a number is multiplied by itself: *9 is the square of 3, written 3*^{2}. **5.** *Informal.* an old-fashioned person. **6. go back to square one.** to return to the start because of failure or lack of progress. ~*adj.* **7.** being a square in shape. **8. a.** having the same area as that of a square with sides of a specified length: *a circle of four square feet.* **b.** denoting a square having a specified length on each side: *a board four feet square.* **9.** fair and honest: *a square deal.* **10.** *Informal.* old-fashioned. **11.** having all debts or accounts settled: *if I give you 50 pence, then we'll be square.* **12. all square.** on equal terms; even in score. **13. square peg in a round hole.** *Informal.* a misfit. ~*vb.* **14.** *Maths.* to multiply (a number or quantity) by itself. **15.** to position so as to be straight or level: *to square the shoulders.* **16.** to settle (a debt or account). **17.** to level the score in (a game). **18.** to agree or cause to agree: *your ideas don't square with mine.* ~*adv.* **19.** *Informal.* same as **squarely.** ~See also **square off, square up.**

square-bashing *n. Brit. mil. slang.* drill on a barracks square.

square bracket *n.* either of a pair of characters [ ], used to separate a section of writing or printing from the main text.

square dance *n.* a formation dance in which the couples form squares.

square leg *n. Cricket.* a fielding position on the batsman's left.

squarely ('skwεəlı) *adv.* **1.** directly; straight: *he hit me squarely on the nose.* **2.** in an honest, frank, and just manner: *he faced the problem squarely.*

square off *vb.* to assume a posture of opposition, as in boxing.

square-rigged *adj. Naut.* having sails set at right angles to the keel.

square root *n.* a number that when multiplied by itself gives a given number: *the square roots of 4 are 2 and −2.*

square up *vb.* **1.** to settle bills or debts. **2.** (foll. by *to*) to prepare to confront (a problem or a person).

squash[1] (skwɒʃ) *vb.* **1.** to press or squeeze (something) so as to crush or flatten it. **2.** to suppress or overcome (a person or thing). **3.** to humiliate (someone) with a crushing retort. **4.** (foll. by *in* or *into*) to push or force (oneself or a thing) into a confined space. ~*n.* **5.** *Brit.* a drink made from fruit juice or fruit syrup diluted with water. **6.** a crush, usually of people in a confined space. **7.** Also called: **squash rackets.** a game for two players played in an enclosed court with a small rubber ball and long-handled rackets.

squash[2] (skwɒʃ) *n., pl.* **squashes** or **squash.** *U.S. & Canad.* a marrow-like vegetable.

squashy ('skwɒʃı) *adj.* **squashier, squashiest.** easily squashed; pulpy.

squat (skwɒt) *vb.* **squatting, squatted.** **1.** to crouch with the knees bent and the weight on the feet. **2.** *Law.* to occupy an unused building to which one has no legal title. ~*adj.* **3.** short and broad. ~*n.* **4.** a building occupied by squatters.

squatter ('skwɒtə) *n.* a person who occupies an unused building to which he has no legal title.

squaw (skwɔ:) *n. Offensive.* a North American Indian woman.

squawk (skwɔ:k) *n.* **1.** a loud harsh cry; screech. **2.** *Informal.* a loud complaint. ~*vb.* **3.** to make a squawk.

squeak (skwi:k) *n.* **1.** a short shrill cry or sound. **2. a narrow squeak.** *Informal.* a narrow escape or success. ~*vb.* **3.** to make a squeak. **4.** (foll. by *through* or *by*) to pass (an examination) with only a narrow margin. —'**squeaky** *adj.* —'**squeakiness** *n.*

squeal (skwi:l) *n.* **1.** a high shrill yelp. ~*vb.* **2.** to make a squeal. **3.** *Slang.* to inform on someone to the police. **4.** *Informal, chiefly Brit.* to complain loudly. —'**squealer** *n.*

squeamish ('skwi:mıʃ) *adj.* easily sickened, shocked, or frightened.

squeegee ('skwi:dʒi:) *n.* an implement with a rubber blade used for wiping away surplus water from a surface.

squeeze (skwi:z) *vb.* **1.** to grip or press (something) firmly. **2.** to crush or press (something) so as to extract (a liquid): *to squeeze an orange; freshly squeezed orange juice.* **3.** to push or force (oneself or a thing) into a confined space. **4.** to hug (someone) closely. **5.** to put pressure on (someone) in order to obtain (something): *to squeeze money out of a victim by blackmail.* ~*n.* **6.** a squeezing. **7.** a hug. **8.** a crush of people in a confined space. **9.** *Chiefly Brit.* a restriction on borrowing imposed by a government to counteract price inflation. **10.** an amount extracted by squeezing: *a squeeze of lemon juice.* **11. put the squeeze on someone.** *Informal.* to put pressure on someone in order to obtain something.

squelch (skwɛltʃ) *vb.* **1.** to make a sucking noise, as by walking through mud. **2.** *Informal.* to silence (someone) with a crushing retort. ~*n.* **3.** a squelching sound. —'**squelchy** *adj.*

squib (skwıb) *n.* **1.** a firework that burns with a hissing noise before exploding. **2. damp squib.** something intended to impress but failing to do so.

squid (skwıd) *n., pl.* **squid** or **squids.** a ten-limbed sea creature with a torpedo-shaped body.

squiffy ('skwıfı) *adj.* **-fier, -fiest.** *Brit. informal.* slightly drunk.

squiggle ('skwıg'l) *n.* a wavy line. —'**squiggly** *adj.*

squill (skwıl) *n.* a Mediterranean plant of the lily family.

squint (skwınt) *vb.* **1.** to cross one's eyes partly. **2.** to have a squint. ~*n.* **3.** an eye disorder in which one or both eyes turn inwards or outwards from the nose. **4.** *Informal.* a quick look; glance: *have a squint at this.* ~*adj.* **5.** *Informal.* not straight; crooked.

squire ('skwaıə) *n.* **1.** a country gentleman in England, usually the main landowner in a country community. **2.** *Informal, chiefly Brit.* a term of address used by one man to another. ~*vb.* **3.** (of a man) to escort (a woman).

squirm (skwɜ:m) *vb.* **1.** to wriggle. **2.** to feel deep discomfort, guilt, or embarrassment. ~*n.* **3.** a wriggling movement.

squirrel ('skwırəl) *n.* a small bushy-tailed tree-living rodent which feeds on nuts.

squirt (skwɜ:t) *vb.* **1.** to force (a liquid) or (of a liquid) to be forced out of a narrow opening. **2.** to cover or spatter (a person or thing) with liquid in this manner. ~*n.* **3.** a jet of liquid. **4.** a squirting. **5.** *Informal.* an insignificant or contemptible short person.

squish (skwıʃ) *vb.* **1.** to crush (something) with a soft splashing noise. **2.** to make a splashing noise. ~*n.* **3.** a soft splashing sound. —'**squishy** *adj.*

Sr 1. (after a name) senior. 2. Señor. 3. *Chem.* strontium.

Sri Lankan (srı ˈlæŋkən) *adj.* 1. of Sri Lanka, a republic in S Asia, or its inhabitants. ~*n.* 2. a person from Sri Lanka.

SRN (in Britain) State Registered Nurse.

SS 1. an organization in the Nazi party that provided Hitler's bodyguard, security forces, and concentration-camp guards. 2. steamship.

St 1. Saint. 2. Street.

st. stone.

stab (stæb) *vb.* **stabbing, stabbed.** 1. to pierce (something) or injure (someone) with a sharp pointed instrument. 2. (often foll. by *at*) to make a thrust (at); jab. 3. **stab someone in the back.** to do harm to someone in a treacherous manner. ~*n.* 4. a stabbing. 5. a sudden, usually unpleasant, sensation: *a stab of pity.* 6. *Informal.* an attempt: *I'll have a stab at it.* 7. **stab in the back.** an action of betrayal that harms a person. —ˈstabbing *n.*

stability (stəˈbɪlɪtɪ) *n.* the quality of being stable.

stabilize *or* **-ise** (ˈsteɪbɪˌlaɪz) *vb.* to make or become more stable or more stable. —ˌstabiliˈzation *or* -iˈsation *n.*

stabilizer *or* **-iser** (ˈsteɪbɪˌlaɪzə) *n.* 1. a device for stabilizing a child's bicycle, an aircraft, or a ship. 2. a substance added to food to preserve its texture.

stable¹ (ˈsteɪbºl) *n.* 1. a building where horses are kept. 2. an establishment that breeds and trains racehorses. 3. *Informal.* a source of training: *the two athletes were out of the same stable.* ~*vb.* 4. to put or keep (a horse) in a stable.

stable² (ˈsteɪbºl) *adj.* 1. steady in position or balance; firm. 2. lasting: *a stable relationship.* 3. firm in character. 4. (of an elementary particle) not subject to decay. 5. (of a chemical compound) not easily decomposed.

staccato (stəˈkɑːtəʊ) *adj.* 1. *Music.* (of notes) short and separate. 2. consisting of short abrupt sounds: *staccato cries.* ~*adv.* 3. in a staccato manner.

stack (stæk) *n.* 1. an ordered pile. 2. a large orderly pile of hay or straw. 3. (*often pl.*) a large amount. 4. same as **chimney stack, smokestack.** 5. an area in a computer memory for temporary storage. ~*vb.* 6. to place (things) in a stack. 7. to load or fill (something) up with piles of objects: *to stack a lorry with bricks.* 8. to control (a number of aircraft) waiting to land at an airport so that each flies at a different altitude.

stadium (ˈsteɪdɪəm) *n., pl.* **-diums** *or* **-dia** (-dɪə). a sports arena with tiered seats for spectators.

staff (stɑːf) *n., pl.* **staffs** *for senses 1 & 2;* **staffs** *or* **staves** *for senses 3 & 4.* 1. the

people employed in a company, school, or organization. 2. *Mil.* the officers appointed to assist a commander. 3. a stick with some special use, such as a walking stick or an emblem of authority. 4. *Music.* a set of five horizontal lines on which music is written and which, along with a clef, indicates pitch. ~*vb.* 5. to provide (a company, school, or organization) with a staff.

staff nurse *n.* a qualified nurse ranking just below a sister or charge nurse.

Staffs. (stæfs) Staffordshire.

staff sergeant *n. Mil.* a noncommissioned officer in an army or in the U.S. Air Force or Marine Corps.

stag (stæg) *n.* 1. the adult male of a deer. 2. (*modifier*) (of a social gathering) attended by men only.

stag beetle *n.* a beetle with large branched jaws.

stage (steɪdʒ) *n.* 1. a distinct step or period of development, growth, or progress. 2. the platform in a theatre where actors perform. 3. **the.** the theatre as a profession. 4. the scene of an event or action. 5. a portion of a journey. 6. short for **stagecoach.** 7. *Brit.* a division of a bus route for which there is a fixed fare. ~*vb.* 8. to present (a dramatic production) on stage: *to stage "Hamlet".* 9. to organize and carry out (an event).

stagecoach (ˈsteɪdʒˌkəʊtʃ) *n.* a large four-wheeled horse-drawn vehicle formerly used to carry passengers and mail on a regular route.

stage direction *n.* an instruction to an actor, written into the script of a play.

stage door *n.* a door at a theatre leading backstage.

stage fright *n.* nervousness or panic felt by a person about to appear in front of an audience.

stagehand (ˈsteɪdʒˌhænd) *n.* a person who sets the stage and moves props in a theatrical production.

stage-manage *vb.* to arrange (an event) from behind the scenes.

stage manager *n.* a person who supervises the stage arrangements of a theatrical production.

stage-struck *adj.* having an intense desire to act.

stage whisper *n.* 1. a loud whisper from an actor, intended to be heard by the audience. 2. any loud whisper that is intended to be overheard.

stagflation (stægˈfleɪʃən) *n.* inflation combined with stagnant or falling output and employment.

stagger (ˈstægə) *vb.* 1. to walk unsteadily. 2. to astound or overwhelm (someone), as with shock: *I was staggered by his death.* 3. to arrange in alternating or overlapping positions or periods: *staggered holidays.*

~*n.* **4.** a staggering. —'**staggering** *adj.*
—'**staggeringly** *adv.*

staggers ('stægəz) *n.* (*functioning as sing. or pl.*) a disease of horses and other domestic animals that causes staggering.

staging ('steɪdʒɪŋ) *n.* a temporary support used in building.

stagnant ('stægnənt) *adj.* **1.** (of water or air) standing still; without flow or current; smelling foul from standing still. **2.** stale or dull from inaction; not growing or developing.

stagnate (stæg'neɪt) *vb.* to be stagnant.
—**stag'nation** *n.*

stag party *n.* a party for men only, held for a man who is about to get married.

stagy *or U.S.* **stagey** ('steɪdʒɪ) *adj.* **stagier, stagiest.** too theatrical or dramatic.

staid (steɪd) *adj.* sedate, steady, and rather dull.

stain (steɪn) *vb.* **1.** to discolour (something) with marks that are not easily removed. **2.** to dye (something) with a penetrating pigment. ~*n.* **3.** a mark or discoloration that is not easily removed. **4.** a moral blemish or slur: *a stain on one's character.* **5.** a liquid used to penetrate the surface of a material, such as wood, and colour it without covering up the surface or grain.

stained glass *n.* glass that has been coloured for artistic purposes.

stainless steel ('steɪnlɪs) *n.* a type of steel that does not rust, as a result of the presence of large amounts of chromium.

stair (stɛə) *n.* **1.** one step in a flight of stairs. **2.** a series of steps: *a narrow stair.* ~See also **stairs**.

staircase ('stɛəˌkeɪs) *n.* a flight of stairs, usually with a handrail or banisters.

stairs (stɛəz) *pl. n.* a flight of steps going from one level to another, usually indoors.

stairway ('stɛəˌweɪ) *n.* a staircase.

stairwell ('stɛəˌwɛl) *n.* a vertical shaft that contains a staircase.

stake[1] (steɪk) *n.* **1.** a stick or metal bar driven into the ground as part of a fence or as a support or marker. **2. be burned at the stake.** to be executed by being tied to a stake in the centre of a pile of wood that is then set on fire. ~*vb.* **3.** to lay (a claim) to land or rights. **4.** to support (something, such as a plant) with a stake.

stake[2] (steɪk) *n.* **1.** the money that a player must risk in order to take part in a gambling game or make a bet. **2.** an interest, usually financial, held in something: *a stake in the company's future.* **3.** (*pl.*) the money that a player has available for gambling. **4.** (*pl.*) a prize in a race or contest. **5.** (*pl.*) a horse race in which all owners of competing horses contribute to the prize. **6. at stake.** at risk: *lives are at stake.* ~*vb.* **7.** to risk (something, such as money) on a result. **8.** to give financial support to (a business).

stakeout ('steɪkaʊt) *n.* **1.** *Slang, chiefly U.S. & Canad.* a police surveillance of an area or house. ~*vb.* **stake out.** **2.** *Slang, chiefly U.S. & Canad.* to keep an area or house under surveillance. **3.** to surround (a piece of land) with stakes.

stalactite ('stæləkˌtaɪt) *n.* a cylindrical mass of calcium carbonate hanging from the roof of a cave: formed by continually dripping water.

stalagmite ('stæləɡˌmaɪt) *n.* a cylindrical mass of calcium carbonate sticking up from the floor of a cave: formed by continually dripping water from a stalactite.

stale (steɪl) *adj.* **1.** (esp. of food) no longer fresh, having being kept too long. **2.** (of air) stagnant; foul. **3.** uninteresting from overuse: *stale clichés.* **4.** no longer new: *stale news.* **5.** lacking in energy or ideas through overwork or lack of variety. —'**staleness** *n.*

stalemate ('steɪlˌmeɪt) *n.* **1.** a chess position in which any of a player's moves would place his king in check: in this position the game ends in a draw. **2.** a situation in which further action by two opposing forces is impossible or futile; deadlock.

Stalinism ('stɑːlɪˌnɪzəm) *n.* the theory and form of government associated with Joseph Stalin (1879–1953), general secretary of the Communist Party of the Soviet Union 1922–53, which advocates only one political party and loyalty to the Soviet state. —'**Stalinist** *n., adj.*

stalk[1] (stɔːk) *n.* **1.** the main stem of a plant. **2.** a stem that joins a leaf or flower to the main stem of a plant.

stalk[2] (stɔːk) *vb.* **1.** to follow or approach (an animal or person) stealthily. **2.** to spread over (a place) in a menacing way: *fever stalked the camp.* **3.** to walk in a haughty or stiff way.

stalking-horse *n.* something used as a means of concealing plans; pretext.

stall[1] (stɔːl) *n.* **1.** a compartment in a stable or shed for a single animal. **2.** a small stand or booth for the sale of goods. **3.** (*pl.*) (in a church) a row of seats, divided by armrests or a small screen, for the choir or clergy. **4.** any small room or compartment: *a shower stall.* **5.** (*pl.*) *Brit.* the seats on the ground floor of a theatre or cinema. ~*vb.* **6.** to stop (a motor vehicle or its engine) or (of a motor vehicle or its engine) to stop, by incorrect use of the clutch or incorrect adjustment of the fuel mixture.

stall[2] (stɔːl) *vb.* to employ delaying tactics towards (someone); be evasive.

stallion ('stæljən) *n.* an uncastrated male horse, usually used for breeding.

stalwart ('stɔːlwət) *adj.* **1.** strong and sturdy. **2.** solid, dependable, and courageous. ~*n.* **3.** a stalwart supporter.

stamen ('steɪmɛn) n. the part of a flower that produces pollen.

stamina ('stæmɪnə) n. enduring energy and strength.

stammer ('stæmə) vb. 1. to speak or say (something) hesitantly, as a result of a speech disorder or through fear or other emotion. ~n. 2. a speech disorder characterized by involuntary repetitions and hesitations.

stamp (stæmp) vb. 1. (often foll. by on) to bring (the foot) down heavily on (something, such as the ground). 2. to walk with heavy or noisy footsteps. 3. (foll. by on) to suppress: he stamped on her enthusiasm. 4. to impress or mark (a pattern or sign) on (something). 5. to mark (something) with an official seal or device. 6. to impress permanently: the date was stamped on her memory. 7. to stick a postage stamp on (an envelope). 8. to characterize: that behaviour stamps him as a cheat. ~n. 9. a stamping. 10. same as **postage stamp**. 11. a piece of gummed paper like a postage stamp, used for commercial or trading purposes. 12. an instrument for stamping a design or device. 13. a design, device, or mark that has been stamped. 14. a characteristic feature: the stamp of truth. 15. Brit. informal. a national insurance contribution, formerly recorded by a stamp on an official card. 16. type or class: men of his stamp.

stampede (stæm'piːd) n. 1. an impulsive headlong rush of startled cattle or horses. 2. headlong rush of a crowd. ~vb. 3. to run away in a stampede.

stamping ground n. a favourite meeting place.

stamp out vb. 1. to suppress by force: to stamp out a rebellion. 2. to put out by stamping: to stamp out a fire.

stance (stæns, stɑːns) n. 1. the manner and position in which a person stands. 2. Sport. the position taken when about to play the ball. 3. a standpoint; attitude: a leftist stance.

stanch (stɑːntʃ) vb. same as **staunch**[2].

stanchion ('stɑːnʃən) n. a vertical pole or bar used as a support.

stand (stænd) vb. **standing, stood.** 1. to be upright. 2. to rise to an upright position. 3. to place (something) upright. 4. to have a specified height when standing: to stand six feet tall. 5. to be situated: the house stands in the square. 6. to be in a specified state or condition: to stand in awe of someone. 7. to be in a specified position: I stand to lose money in this venture. 8. to remain unchanged or valid: my orders stand. 9. (foll. by at) (of a score or an account) to be in the specified position: the score stands at 20 to 1. 10. (sometimes foll. by for) to tolerate or bear: I won't stand for laziness; I can't stand spiders. 11. to survive: to stand

the test of time. 12. (often foll. by for) Chiefly Brit. to be a candidate: stand for Parliament. 13. Informal. to buy: to stand someone a drink. 14. **stand a chance.** to have a chance of succeeding. 15. **stand one's ground.** to maintain a stance in the face of opposition. 16. **stand trial.** to be tried in a lawcourt. ~n. 17. a stall or counter from which goods may be sold: a hamburger stand. 18. a structure at a sports ground where people can sit or stand. 19. a standing. 20. a firmly held opinion: he took a stand on capital punishment. 21. U.S. a place in a lawcourt where a witness stands. 22. a rack on which such articles as coats and hats may be hung. 23. a small table or piece of furniture where articles may be placed or stored: a music stand. 24. a halt to counter-attack, usually during a retreat and having some duration or success: Custer's last stand. 25. Cricket. a long period at the wicket by two batsmen. 26. See **one-night stand.** ~See also **stand by, stand down,** etc.

standard ('stændəd) n. 1. an accepted example of something against which others are judged or measured. 2. a moral principle. 3. a level of excellence or quality. 4. a distinctive flag, as of a nation or cause. 5. an upright pole or beam used as a support: a lamp standard. 6. a song that has remained popular for many years. ~adj. 7. of a usual, medium, or accepted kind: a standard size. 8. of recognized authority: the standard work on Greece. 9. denoting pronunciations or grammar regarded as correct and acceptable by educated native speakers.

standard-bearer n. 1. a person who carries a flag. 2. a leader of a movement or party.

standard gauge n. 1. a railway track with a distance of 56½ inches (1.435 m) between the lines; used on most railways. ~adj. **standard-gauge.** 2. denoting a railway with a standard gauge.

standardize or **-ise** ('stændə,daɪz) vb. to make (things) standard: standardized tests. —,standardi'zation or -i'sation n.

standard lamp n. a lamp attached to an upright pole or beam on a base.

standard of living n. the level of comfort and wealth of a person or group.

standard time n. the official local time of a region or country determined by the distance from Greenwich of a line of longitude passing through the area.

stand by vb. 1. to be available and ready to act if needed: stand by with drinks for the runners. 2. to be present as an onlooker or without taking any action: he stood by at the accident. 3. to be faithful to: I'll stand by you. ~n. **stand-by.** 4. a person or thing that is ready for use or can be relied on in an emergency. 5. **on stand-**

by. ready for action or use. *~adj.* **stand-by. 6.** not booked in advance but subject to availability: *a stand-by ticket.*

stand down *vb.* to resign or withdraw, often in favour of another.

stand for *vb.* **1.** to represent: *UK stands for United Kingdom.* **2.** to support and symbolize (an idea or a belief): *I hate all that he stands for.* **3.** *Informal.* to tolerate or bear: *he won't stand for it.*

stand in *vb.* **1.** to act as a substitute: *she stood in for me while I was ill.* *~n.* **stand-in. 2.** a person who acts as a substitute for another.

standing ('stændɪŋ) *n.* **1.** social or financial status or reputation: *a man of some standing.* **2.** duration: *a friendship of some ten years' standing.* **3.** (*modifier*) used to stand in or on: *standing room.* *~adj.* **4.** *Athletics.* (of a jump or the start of a race) begun from a standing position. **5.** permanent, fixed, or lasting: *a standing joke.*

standing order *n.* **1.** an instruction to a bank by a depositor to pay a stated sum to a person or organization at regular intervals. **2.** a rule or order governing the procedure of an organization.

standoff ('stænd,ɒf) *n.* **1.** *U.S. & Canad.* the act or an instance of standing off or apart. **2.** a deadlock or stalemate. *~vb.* **stand off. 3.** to stay at a distance.

standoffish (,stænd'ɒfɪʃ) *adj.* reserved or haughty.

stand out *vb.* **1.** to be distinctive or conspicuous. **2.** to refuse to agree or comply: *they stood out for a better price.*

standpipe ('stænd,paɪp) *n.* a temporary freshwater outlet installed in a street when household water supplies are cut off.

standpoint ('stænd,pɔɪnt) *n.* a mental position from which things are viewed.

standstill ('stænd,stɪl) *n.* a complete stoppage or halt: *come to a standstill.*

stand to *vb.* **1.** *Mil.* to take up positions in order to resist attack. **2. stand to reason.** to be obvious or logical: *it stands to reason that he will be angry.*

stand up *vb.* **1.** to rise to one's feet. **2.** *Informal.* to fail to keep an appointment with (a boyfriend or girlfriend): *he stood her up.* **3.** to withstand examination: *his story won't stand up in court.* **4. stand up for.** to support or defend. **5. stand up to. a.** to confront or resist (someone) bravely. **b.** to withstand or endure (something, such as criticism). *~adj.* **stand-up. 6.** (of a comedian) telling jokes directly to an audience. **7.** being in an erect position: *a stand-up collar.* **8.** done while standing: *a stand-up meal.*

stank (stæŋk) *vb.* a past tense of **stink.**

stannary ('stænərɪ) *n., pl.* **-ries.** a tin-mine.

stanza ('stænzə) *n. Prosody.* a verse of a poem.

staple[1] ('steɪpᵊl) *n.* **1.** a short length of wire bent into a square U-shape, used to fasten papers or secure things. *~vb.* **2.** to secure (things) with staples. —'**stapler** *n.*

staple[2] ('steɪpᵊl) *adj.* **1.** of prime importance; principal: *staple foods.* *~n.* **2.** something that forms a main part of the product, consumption, or trade of a region. **3.** a main constituent of anything.

star (stɑː) *n.* **1.** a planet or meteor visible in the clear night sky as a point of light. **2.** a hot gaseous mass, such as the sun, that radiates energy as heat and light, or in some cases as radio waves and x-rays. **3.** (*pl.*) same as **horoscope** (sense 1). **4.** an emblem with five or more radiating points, often used as a symbol of rank or an award. **5.** same as **asterisk. 6.** a distinguished or glamorous celebrity, often from the entertainment world. **7. see stars.** to see flashes of light, as from a blow on the head. *~vb.* **starring, starred. 8.** to mark (something) with a star or stars. **9.** to feature (an actor or actress) or (of an actor or actress) to be featured as a star: *Olivier starred in "Hamlet".*

starboard ('stɑːbəd, -,bɔːd) *n.* **1.** the right side of an aeroplane or ship when facing forwards. *~adj.* **2.** of or on the starboard side.

starch (stɑːtʃ) *n.* **1.** a fine white powder obtained from potatoes and some grain which, in solution with water, is used to stiffen fabric. **2.** food containing a large amount of starch, such as rice and potatoes. *~vb.* **3.** to stiffen (cloth) with starch.

starchy ('stɑːtʃɪ) *adj.* **starchier, starchiest. 1.** of or containing starch. **2.** very formal or stiff in manner.

star-crossed *adj.* (of lovers) destined to misfortune.

stardom ('stɑːdəm) *n.* the status of a star in the entertainment or sport world.

stare (stɛə) *vb.* **1.** (often foll. by *at*) to look or gaze fixedly. **2. stare one in the face.** to be glaringly obvious. *~n.* **3.** a staring.

starfish ('stɑː,fɪʃ) *n., pl.* **-fish** *or* **-fishes.** a star-shaped sea creature with a flat body and five arms.

star fruit *n.* same as **carambola.**

stargazer ('stɑː,geɪzə) *n. Informal.* an astrologer. —'**star,gazing** *n.*

stark (stɑːk) *adj.* **1.** grim; desolate: *a stark landscape.* **2.** without elaboration; blunt: *the stark facts.* **3.** utter; absolute: *stark folly.* *~adv.* **4.** completely: *stark staring mad.* —'**starkly** *adv.* —'**starkness** *n.*

stark-naked *adj.* completely naked. Also (*informal*): **starkers.**

starlet ('stɑːlɪt) *n.* a young actress who is presented as a potential star.

starlight ('stɑː,laɪt) *n.* the light that comes from the stars.

starling ('stɑːlɪŋ) *n.* a common songbird

with shiny blackish feathers and a short tail.

starlit ('stɑːˌlɪt) *adj*. lit by starlight.

Star of David *n*. a symbol of Judaism, consisting of a star formed by two interlaced equilateral triangles.

starry ('stɑːrɪ) *adj*. **-rier, -riest.** **1.** (of a sky or night) full of or lit by stars. **2.** of or like a star or stars: *a starry reception*.

starry-eyed *adj*. full of naive optimism.

Stars and Stripes *n*. (*functioning as sing*.) **the.** the national flag of the United States of America.

Star-Spangled Banner *n*. **the.** **1.** the national anthem of the United States of America. **2.** same as **Stars and Stripes.**

star-studded *adj*. featuring many well-known performers: *a star-studded cast*.

start (stɑːt) *vb*. **1.** to begin (something or to do something); come or cause (something) to come into being or operation: *don't start a fight; work has started already*. **2.** (sometimes foll. by *up*) to set or be set in motion: *he started up the machine*. **3.** to make a sudden involuntary movement, as from fright; jump. **4.** to establish; set up: *to start a business*. **5.** to support (someone) in the first part of a venture or career. **6.** *Brit. informal*. to commence quarrelling or causing a disturbance: *don't start with me*. **7. to start with.** in the first place. ~*n*. **8.** the first part of something. **9.** the place or time of starting, as of a race or performance. **10.** a signal to begin, as in a race. **11.** a lead or advantage, either in time or distance, in a competitive activity: *he had an hour's start on me*. **12.** a slight involuntary movement, as from fright or surprise: *she gave a start as I entered*. **13.** an opportunity to enter a career or undertake a project. **14. for a start.** in the first place. ~See also **start off, start on,** etc.

starter ('stɑːtə) *n*. **1.** *Chiefly Brit*. the first course of a meal. **2. for starters.** *Slang*. in the first place. **3.** a device for starting an internal-combustion engine. **4.** a person who signals the start of a race. **5.** a competitor in a race or contest. **6. under starter's orders.** (of competitors in a race) awaiting the signal to start.

startle ('stɑːt²l) *vb*. to slightly surprise or frighten someone. —'**startling** *adj*.

start off *vb*. **1.** to set out on a journey. **2.** to be or make the first step in (an activity); initiate: *he started the show off with a song*. **3.** to cause (a person) to do something, such as laugh.

start on *vb. Brit. informal*. to pick a quarrel with: *don't start on me now*.

start out *vb*. **1.** to set out on a journey. **2.** to take the first steps, for example in one's career or on a course of action: *he started out as a salesman; they started out wanting a house, but finally got a flat*.

start up *vb*. **1.** to come or cause (something, such as a business) to come into being; originate. **2.** to set (something) in motion: *he started up the engine*.

starve (stɑːv) *vb*. **1.** to die from lack of food. **2.** to deprive of food. **3.** *Informal*. to be very hungry: *I'm starving*. **4.** (foll. by *of*) to deprive (someone) of something that he needs: *the child was starved of affection*. **5.** (foll. by *into*) to bring someone into a specified condition by starving: *to starve someone into submission*. —**star'vation** *n*.

Star Wars *n*. (*functioning as sing*.) (in the U.S.) a proposed system of artificial satellites armed with lasers to destroy enemy missiles in space.

stash (stæʃ) *vb*. **1.** (often foll. by *away*) *Informal*. to store (money or valuables) in a secret place for safekeeping. ~*n*. **2.** *Informal, chiefly U.S. & Canad*. a secret store, usually of drugs, or the place where this is hidden.

state (steɪt) *n*. **1.** the condition of a person or thing. **2.** ceremonious style, as befitting wealth or dignity: *to live in state*. **3.** a sovereign political power or community. **4.** the territory of such a community. **5.** the sphere of power in such a community: *affairs of state*. **6.** (*often cap*.) one of a number of areas or communities having their own governments and forming a federation under a sovereign government, as in the U.S. **7.** (*often cap*.) the government, civil service, and armed forces. **8. in a state.** *Informal*. in an emotional or agitated condition. **9. lie in state.** (of a body) to be placed on public view before burial. **10. state of affairs.** circumstances or condition: *the current state of affairs*. ~*modifier*. **11.** controlled or financed by a state: *state university*. **12.** of or concerning the State: *State trial*. **13.** of a ceremonious occasion: *state visit*. ~*vb*. **14.** to express (something) in words; utter.

State Enrolled Nurse *n*. a nurse who has completed a two-year training course.

state house *n. N.Z*. a rented house built by the government.

stateless ('steɪtlɪs) *adj*. without nationality: *stateless persons*.

stately ('steɪtlɪ) *adj*. **-lier, -liest.** having a graceful, dignified, and imposing appearance or manner. —'**stateliness** *n*.

stately home *n. Brit*. a large mansion, usually one open to the public.

statement ('steɪtmənt) *n*. **1.** something stated, usually a formal prepared announcement or reply. **2.** the act of stating. **3.** an account containing a summary of bills or invoices and showing the total amount due. **4.** an account prepared by a bank for a client, usually at regular intervals, to show all credits and debits and the balance at the end of the period.

state of the art *n*. **1.** the current level of

knowledge and development achieved in a technology, science, or art. ~*adj.* **state-of-the-art. 2.** the most recent and therefore considered the best; up-to-the-minute: *a state-of-the-art amplifier.*

State Registered Nurse *n.* a nurse who has completed an extensive three-year training course.

stateroom ('steɪt,ruːm) *n.* **1.** a private room on a ship. **2.** *Chiefly Brit.* a large room in a palace or other building for use on state occasions.

States (steɪts) *n.* (*functioning as sing. or pl.*) *Informal.* the United States of America.

state school *n.* a school maintained by the state, in which education is free.

statesman ('steɪtsmən) *n., pl.* **-men.** an experienced and respected political leader. —**'statesmanship** *n.*

static ('stætɪk) *adj.* **1.** not active or moving; stationary. **2.** *Physics.* (of a weight, force, or pressure) acting but causing no movement. **3.** *Physics.* of forces that do not produce movement. ~*n.* **4.** hissing or crackling or a speckled picture caused by interference in the reception of radio or television transmissions. **5.** electric sparks or crackling produced by friction.

static electricity *n.* same as **static** (sense 5).

statics ('stætɪks) *n.* (*functioning as sing.*) the branch of mechanics concerned with the forces producing a state of equilibrium.

station ('steɪʃən) *n.* **1.** a place along a route or line at which a bus or train stops to pick up passengers or goods. **2.** the headquarters of an organization such as the police or fire service. **3.** a building with special equipment for some particular purpose: *power station; petrol station.* **4.** *Mil.* a place of duty. **5.** a television or radio channel. **6.** position in society: *he's getting ideas above his station.* **7.** *Austral. & N.Z.* a large sheep or cattle farm. **8.** the place or position where a person is assigned to stand: *don't leave your station before lunchtime.* ~*vb.* **9.** to assign (someone) to a station.

stationary ('steɪʃənərɪ) *adj.* **1.** not moving. **2.** unchanging: *the doctors said his condition was stationary.*

stationer ('steɪʃənə) *n.* a person who sells stationery or a shop where this is sold.

stationery ('steɪʃənərɪ) *n.* writing materials, such as paper, envelopes, and pens.

stationmaster ('steɪʃən,mɑːstə) *n.* the senior official in charge of a railway station.

stations of the Cross *pl. n. R.C. Church.* **1.** a series of 14 crosses, often with pictures or carvings, arranged around the walls of a church, to commemorate 14 stages in Christ's journey to Calvary. **2.** a series of 14 prayers relating to each of these stages.

station wagon *n. U.S.* an estate car.

statistic (stə'tɪstɪk) *n.* a piece of numerical information which has been collected and classified systematically. —**sta'tistical** *adj.* —**sta'tistically** *adv.* —**statistician** (,stætɪ'stɪʃən) *n.*

statistics (stə'tɪstɪks) *n.* **1.** (*functioning as sing.*) the science dealing with the collection, classification, and interpretation of numerical information. **2.** (*functioning as pl.*) numerical information which has been collected, classified, and interpreted.

statuary ('stætjʊərɪ) *n.* statues collectively.

statue ('stætjuː) *n.* a sculpture of a human or animal figure, usually life-size or larger.

statuesque (,stætjʊ'ɛsk) *adj.* (of a woman) like a statue; tall and well-proportioned.

statuette (,stætjʊ'ɛt) *n.* a small statue.

stature ('stætʃə) *n.* **1.** height of a person. **2.** the degree of development of a person: *the stature of a champion.* **3.** intellectual or moral greatness: *a man of stature.*

status ('steɪtəs) *n.* **1.** social position. **2.** a high position or standing. **3.** the legal standing or condition of a person: *the status of a minor.* **4.** degree of importance, as of a topic for discussion.

status quo (kwəʊ) *n.* **the.** the existing state of affairs.

status symbol *n.* a possession regarded as a mark of social position or wealth.

statute ('stætjuːt) *n.* **1.** a law made by a government and expressed in a formal document. **2.** a permanent rule made by a company or other institution.

statute law *n.* **1.** a law made by a government. **2.** such laws collectively.

statutory ('stætjʊtrɪ) *adj.* **1.** prescribed or authorized by statute. **2.** (of an offence) declared by statute to be punishable.

staunch[1] (stɔːntʃ) *adj.* loyal and firm: *a staunch ally.*

staunch[2] (stɔːntʃ) *or* **stanch** (stɑːntʃ) *vb.* to stop the flow of (blood) from someone's body.

stave (steɪv) *n.* **1.** one of the long strips of wood joined together to form a barrel or bucket. **2.** a stick carried as a symbol of office. **3.** a verse of a poem. **4.** *Music.* same as **staff.** ~*vb.* **staving, staved** *or* **stove. 5.** (foll. by *in*) to burst a hole in something.

stave off *vb.* to avert (something) temporarily: *to stave off hunger.*

staves (steɪvz) *n.* a plural of **staff** or **stave.**

stay[1] (steɪ) *vb.* **1.** to continue or remain in a place, position, or condition: *to stay outside; to stay awake.* **2.** to reside temporarily: *to stay at a hotel.* **3.** *Scot. & S. African.* to reside permanently or habitually; live. **4.** to endure (something testing or difficult): *to stay the course.* ~*n.* **5.** the period during which one stays in a place. **6.** the suspension of a judicial proceeding: *stay of execution.*

stay² (steɪ) *n.* something that supports or steadies something, such as a prop or buttress.

stay³ (steɪ) *n.* a rope, cable, or chain, used for supporting uprights, such as masts or funnels.

stay-at-home *adj.* 1. (of a person) enjoying a quiet, settled, and unadventurous life. ~*n.* 2. a stay-at-home person.

staying power *n.* endurance; stamina.

stays (steɪz) *pl. n.* old-fashioned corsets with bones in them.

staysail ('steɪˌseɪl; *Naut.* 'steɪs°l) *n.* a sail fastened on a stay.

STD 1. sexually transmitted disease. 2. subscriber trunk dialling.

STD code *n. Brit.* a code preceding a local telephone number, which enables a caller to dial direct, without the operator's help.

stead (stɛd) *n.* 1. **stand someone in good stead.** to be useful to someone in the future. 2. *Rare.* the function or position that should be taken by another: *to come in someone's stead.*

steadfast ('stɛdfəst, -ˌfɑːst) *adj.* firm or determined. —'**steadfastly** *adv.* —'**steadfastness** *n.*

steady ('stɛdɪ) *adj.* **steadier, steadiest.** 1. not shaky. 2. without much change or variation: *a steady pace.* 3. not easily excited; sober. 4. regular; habitual: *a steady drinker.* 5. continuous: *a steady flow.* ~*vb.* **steadying, steadied.** 6. to make or become steady. ~*adv.* 7. in a steady manner. 8. **go steady.** *Informal.* to date one person regularly. ~*n., pl.* **steadies.** 9. *Informal.* one's regular boyfriend or girlfriend. ~*interj.* 10. a warning to keep calm or be careful. —'**steadily** *adv.* —'**steadiness** *n.*

steady state *n. Physics.* the condition of a system when all or most changes or disturbances have been eliminated from it.

steak (steɪk) *n.* 1. a lean piece of beef for grilling or frying. 2. a cut of beef for braising or stewing. 3. a thick slice of pork, veal, or fish.

steakhouse ('steɪkˌhaʊs) *n.* a restaurant that specializes in steaks.

steal (stiːl) *vb.* **stealing, stole, stolen.** 1. to take (something) from someone without permission or unlawfully. 2. to obtain (something) surreptitiously: *to steal a kiss.* 3. to use (someone else's ideas or work) without acknowledgment. 4. to move stealthily: *they stole along the corridor.* ~*n.* 5. *U.S. & Canad. informal.* something acquired easily or at little cost.

stealth (stɛlθ) *n.* 1. moving with great care and quietness, so as to avoid detection. 2. cunning or underhand behaviour. —'**stealthy** *adj.* —'**stealthily** *adv.*

steam (stiːm) *n.* 1. the gas or vapour into which water changes when boiled. 2. the

mist formed when such gas or vapour condenses in the atmosphere. 3. *Informal.* power, energy, or speed. 4. **let off steam.** *Informal.* to release pent-up energy or feelings. 5. (*modifier*) operated, heated, or powered by steam: *a steam radiator.* ~*vb.* 6. to give out steam. 7. (of a vehicle) to move by steam power. 8. *Informal.* to proceed quickly and often forcefully. 9. to cook (food) in steam. 10. to treat (something) with steam or apply steam to (something), as in cleaning or pressing clothes. ~See also **steam up.**

steam engine *n.* an engine that uses steam to produce mechanical work.

steamer ('stiːmə) *n.* 1. a boat or ship driven by steam engines. 2. a container with holes in the bottom, used to cook food by steam.

steam iron *n.* an electric iron that uses steam produced from water put into the iron to take creases out of clothes.

steamroller ('stiːmˌrəʊlə) *n.* 1. a steam-powered vehicle with heavy rollers used for flattening road surfaces during road-making. ~*vb.* 2. to make (someone) do what one wants by overpowering force.

steamship ('stiːmˌʃɪp) *n.* a ship powered by steam engines.

steam up *vb.* 1. to cover (windows or glasses) or (of windows or glasses) to become covered with steam. 2. **steamed up.** *Slang.* excited or angry.

steamy ('stiːmɪ) *adj.* **steamier, steamiest.** 1. full of steam. 2. *Informal.* lustful or erotic: *a steamy play.*

steatite ('stɪəˌtaɪt) *n.* same as **soapstone.**

steed (stiːd) *n. Archaic or literary.* a horse.

steel (stiːl) *n.* 1. an alloy of iron and carbon, often with small quantities of other elements. 2. a steel rod used for sharpening knives. 3. the quality of hardness, with regard to a person's character or attitude. ~*vb.* 4. to make hard and unfeeling: *he steeled his heart against her sorrow; he steeled himself for the blow.* —'**steely** *adj.*

steel band *n. Music.* a band, popular in the Caribbean Islands, consisting of percussion instruments made from oil drums, hammered or embossed to produce notes.

steel-blue *adj.* dark bluish-grey.

steel wool *n.* a mass of fine steel fibres, used for cleaning metal surfaces.

steelworks ('stiːlˌwɜːks) *n.* (*functioning as sing. or pl.*) a factory where steel is made. —'**steelˌworker** *n.*

steep¹ (stiːp) *adj.* 1. having a sharp slope. 2. *Informal.* (of a fee, price, or demand) unduly high; unreasonable. —'**steeply** *adv.* —'**steepness** *n.*

steep² (stiːp) *vb.* 1. to soak or be soaked in a liquid in order to soften or cleanse. 2. **steeped in.** filled with: *steeped in history.*

steepen ('stiːpᵊn) vb. to become or cause (something) to become steep or steeper.

steeple ('stiːpᵊl) n. a tall ornamental tower on a church roof.

steeplechase ('stiːpᵊl,tʃeɪs) n. 1. a horse race over a course with obstacles to be jumped. 2. a track race in which the runners have to leap hurdles and a water jump. ~vb. 3. to race in a steeplechase.

steeplejack ('stiːpᵊl,dʒæk) n. a person who repairs steeples and chimneys.

steer[1] (stɪə) vb. 1. to direct the course of (a vehicle or vessel) with a steering wheel or rudder. 2. to direct the movements or course of (a person or conversation). 3. to pursue (a specified course). 4. **steer clear of.** to avoid.

steer[2] (stɪə) n. a castrated male ox or bull.

steerage ('stɪərɪdʒ) n. 1. the cheapest accommodation on a passenger ship. 2. a steering.

steering committee n. a committee set up to prepare and arrange topics to be discussed, and the order of business, for a government or other group.

steering wheel n. a wheel turned by the driver of a vehicle in order to change direction.

steersman ('stɪəzmən) n., pl. **-men.** the person who steers a vessel.

stein (staɪn) n. an earthenware beer mug.

stele ('stiːlɪ, stiːl) or **stela** ('stiːlə) n., pl. **stelae** ('stiːliː) or **steles.** an upright stone slab or column decorated with figures or inscriptions, common in prehistoric times.

stellar ('stɛlə) adj. of or like a star or stars.

stem[1] (stɛm) n. 1. the long thin central part of a plant. 2. a stalk that bears a flower, fruit, or leaf. 3. the long slender part of anything, such as a goblet. 4. Linguistics. the form of a word that remains after removal of all inflectional endings. ~vb. **stemming, stemmed.** 5. (foll. by from) to be derived; originate.

stem[2] (stɛm) vb. **stemming, stemmed.** to stop (the flow of something): to stem the flow of illegal drugs.

stemmed (stɛmd) adj. having a stem: a long-stemmed glass.

stench (stɛntʃ) n. a strong and very unpleasant odour.

stencil ('stɛnsᵊl) n. 1. a device for marking a design or letters on a surface, consisting of a thin sheet of plastic, metal, or paper, in which the design or letters have been cut so that ink or paint can be applied through the cuts onto the surface. 2. a design or letters made in this way. ~vb. **-cilling, -cilled** or U.S. **-ciling, -ciled.** 3. to make (a design or letters) with a stencil.

Sten gun (stɛn) n. a light sub-machine-gun.

stenographer (stə'nɒgrəfə) n. U.S. & Canad. a shorthand typist.

stentorian (stɛn'tɔːrɪən) adj. (of the voice) very loud: stentorian tones.

step (stɛp) n. 1. the act of moving and setting down one's foot, as when walking. 2. the distance covered by such a movement. 3. the sound made by such a movement. 4. manner of walking; gait. 5. one of a sequence of foot movements that make up a dance. 6. one of a sequence of stages in the progression towards a goal. 7. a rank or grade in a series or scale. 8. a surface that offers support for the foot when ascending or descending. 9. (pl.) a flight of stairs, usually out of doors. 10. (pl.) same as **stepladder.** 11. a short easily walked distance: it is only a step. 12. **break step.** to stop marching in step. 13. **in step. a.** marching or dancing at a specified pace or at exactly the same time as other people. **b.** Informal. in agreement or harmony: in step with public opinion. 14. **out of step. a.** not marching or dancing at a specified pace or at exactly the same time as other people. **b.** Informal. not in agreement; out of harmony. 15. **step by step.** gradually. 16. **take steps.** to do what is necessary (to achieve something). 17. **watch one's step. a.** Informal. to behave with caution. **b.** to walk carefully. ~vb. **stepping, stepped.** 18. to move by executing a step, as in walking. 19. to walk a short distance: step this way. 20. (foll. by into) to enter (a situation) apparently with ease: she stepped into a life of luxury. ~See also **step down, step in,** etc.

stepbrother ('stɛp,brʌðə) n. a son of one's stepmother or stepfather.

stepchild ('stɛp,tʃaɪld) n., pl. **-children.** a stepson or stepdaughter.

stepdaughter ('stɛp,dɔːtə) n. a daughter of one's husband or wife by an earlier relationship.

step down vb. Informal. to resign from a position.

stepfather ('stɛp,fɑːðə) n. a man who has married one's mother after the death or divorce of one's father.

stephanotis (,stɛfə'nəʊtɪs) n. a tropical climbing shrub with sweet-smelling white flowers.

step in vb. Informal. to intervene (in a quarrel or difficult situation).

stepladder ('stɛp,lædə) n. a folding portable ladder made of broad flat steps fixed to a self-supporting frame.

stepmother ('stɛp,mʌðə) n. a woman who has married one's father after the death or divorce of one's mother.

step on vb. 1. to place or press the foot on (something): step on the accelerator. 2. Informal. to behave harshly or contemptuously towards (someone). 3. **step on it.** Informal. to go more quickly; hurry up.

step out *vb.* **1.** to leave a room briefly. **2.** to walk quickly, taking long strides.

step-parent ('stɛp,pɛərənt) *n.* a stepfather or stepmother.

steppe (stɛp) *n.* (*often pl.*) a wide grassy plain without trees.

stepping stone *n.* **1.** one of a series of stones acting as footrests for crossing a stream. **2.** something that helps progress towards some goal.

stepsister ('stɛp,sɪstə) *n.* a daughter of one's stepmother or stepfather.

stepson ('stɛp,sʌn) *n.* a son of one's husband or wife by an earlier relationship.

step up *vb. Informal.* to increase (something) by stages; accelerate.

stereo ('stɛrɪəʊ, 'stɪər-) *adj.* **1.** short for **stereophonic.** ~*n., pl.* **stereos. 2.** a stereophonic record player. **3.** stereophonic sound: *to broadcast in stereo.*

stereophonic (,stɛrɪə'fɒnɪk, ,stɪər-) *adj.* (of a sound system) using two or more separate microphones to feed two or more loudspeakers through separate channels.

stereotype ('stɛrɪə,taɪp, 'stɪər-) *n.* **1.** a standardized image or idea of a type of person. **2.** an idea that has grown stale through fixed usage. ~*vb.* **3.** to form a standard image or idea of (a type of person).

sterile ('stɛraɪl) *adj.* **1.** free from germs. **2.** unable to produce offspring. **3.** (of plants) not producing or bearing seeds. **4.** lacking inspiration or vitality. —**sterility** (stə'rɪlɪtɪ) *n.*

sterilize *or* **-ise** ('stɛrɪ,laɪz) *vb.* to make sterile. —,**sterili'zation** *or* **-i'sation** *n.*

sterling ('stɜːlɪŋ) *n.* **1.** British money: *pound sterling.* ~*adj.* **2.** genuine and reliable: first-class: *sterling quality.*

sterling silver *n.* **1.** an alloy containing at least 92.5 per cent of silver. **2.** articles made of sterling silver.

stern[1] (stɜːn) *adj.* **1.** strict. **2.** difficult and, often, unpleasant: *the stern demands of parenthood.* **3.** severe in appearance. —'**sternly** *adv.*

stern[2] (stɜːn) *n.* the rear part of a vessel.

sternum ('stɜːnəm) *n., pl.* **-na** (-nə) *or* **-nums.** a long flat bone in the front of the body, to which the collarbone and most of the ribs are attached.

steroid ('stɪərɔɪd) *n. Biochem.* an organic compound containing a carbon ring system, such as sterols and many hormones.

sterol ('stɛrɒl) *n. Biochem.* a natural insoluble alcohol such as cholesterol and ergosterol.

stertorous ('stɜːtərəs) *adj.* (of breathing) laboured and noisy.

stet (stɛt) *vb.* **setting, stetted. 1.** used as an instruction to indicate to a printer that certain deleted matter is to be retained. **2.** to mark (matter) in this way.

stethoscope ('stɛθə,skəʊp) *n. Med.* an instrument for listening to the sounds made inside the body, consisting of a hollow disc that transmits the sound through hollow tubes to earpieces.

stetson ('stɛts'n) *n.* a felt hat with a broad brim and high crown, worn mainly by cowboys.

stevedore ('stiːvɪ,dɔː) *n.* a person employed to load or unload ships.

stew (stjuː) *n.* **1.** a dish of meat, fish, or other food, cooked by stewing. **2. in a stew.** *Informal.* in a troubled or worried state. ~*vb.* **3.** to cook by long slow simmering. **4.** *Informal.* (of a person) to be too hot. **5.** to cause (tea) to become bitter or (of tea) to become bitter through infusing for too long. **6. stew in one's own juice.** to suffer unaided the consequences of one's actions.

steward (stjʊəd) *n.* **1.** a person who looks after passengers and serves meals on a ship or aircraft. **2.** an official who helps to supervise a public event, such as a race. **3.** a person who administers someone else's property. **4.** a person who manages the eating arrangements, staff, or service at a club or hotel. **5.** See **shop steward.** ~*vb.* **6.** to act as a steward (of).

stewardess ('stjʊədɪs, ,stjʊə'dɛs) *n.* a female steward on an aircraft or ship.

stewed (stjuːd) *adj.* **1.** (of food) cooked by stewing. **2.** *Brit.* (of tea) bitter through having been left to infuse for too long. **3.** *Slang.* drunk.

stick[1] (stɪk) *n.* **1.** a small thin branch of a tree. **2. a.** a long thin piece of wood. **b.** such a piece of wood shaped for a special purpose: *a walking stick; a hockey stick.* **3.** a piece of something shaped like a stick: *a stick of celery.* **4.** *Slang.* verbal abuse, criticism: *I got some stick for my mistake.* **5.** (*pl.*) pieces of furniture: *these few sticks are all I have.* **6.** (*pl.*) *Informal.* a country area considered remote or backward: *I live out in the sticks.* **7.** *Informal.* a person: *not a bad old stick.* **8. get hold of the wrong end of the stick.** to misunderstand a situation or an explanation completely.

stick[2] (stɪk) *vb.* **sticking, stuck. 1.** to push (a pointed object) or (of a pointed object) to be pushed into another object. **2.** to fasten (something) in position by or as if by pins or nails: *to stick a picture on the wall.* **3.** (foll. by *out, up, through,* etc.) to protrude or cause to protrude: *to stick one's hand up.* **4.** *Informal.* to place (something) in a specified position: *stick your coat on this chair.* **5.** to fasten or be fastened by or as if by an adhesive substance. **6.** to come or be brought to a standstill: *stuck in a traffic jam; the wheels stuck.* **7.** to remain for a long time: *the memory sticks in my mind.*

8. *Slang, chiefly Brit.* to tolerate; abide: *I can't stick him.* **9. be stuck.** *Informal.* to be at a loss; be baffled or puzzled: *I was totally stuck for an answer.* **10.** *Slang.* to impose something unpleasant. ~See also **stick around, stick by,** etc.

stick around *vb. Informal.* to remain in a place, often when waiting for something.

stick by *vb.* to remain faithful to: *she stuck by him through thick and thin.*

sticker ('stɪkə) *n.* **1.** an adhesive label or paper. **2.** a persevering or industrious person.

sticking plaster *n.* a piece of adhesive material used for covering slight wounds.

stick insect *n.* a tropical insect with a long thin body and legs, which resembles a twig.

stick-in-the-mud *n. Informal.* a conservative person who lacks initiative or imagination.

stickleback ('stɪk²l,bæk) *n.* a small fish with a series of spines along its back.

stickler ('stɪklə) *n.* a person who makes insistent demands: *a stickler for accuracy.*

stick out *vb.* **1.** to project or cause (something) to project: *the child stuck his tongue out.* **2.** *Informal.* to endure (something disagreeable): *I hate my job but I'll stick it out till May.* **3. stick out a mile** *or* **like a sore thumb.** *Informal.* to be very obvious. **4. stick out for.** to insist on (a demand), refusing to yield until it is met.

stick to *vb.* **1.** to adhere or cause (something) to adhere to: *toffee sticks to your teeth.* **2.** to remain faithful to (a person, promise, or rule). **3.** not to move away from: *stick to the subject.*

stick-up *n. Slang, chiefly U.S.* a robbery at gunpoint; hold-up.

stick up for *vb. Informal.* to support or defend (oneself, another person, or a principle).

sticky ('stɪkɪ) *adj.* **stickier, stickiest.** **1.** covered with an adhesive substance: *sticky hands.* **2.** intended to stick to a surface: *sticky tape.* **3.** (of weather) warm and humid. **4.** *Informal.* difficult or painful: *a sticky situation.* —'**stickiness** *n.*

sticky wicket *n.* **on a sticky wicket.** *Informal.* in a difficult situation.

stiff (stɪf) *adj.* **1.** not easily bent; inflexible. **2.** not moving easily: *a stiff handle.* **3.** difficult to accept in its severity: *a stiff punishment.* **4.** moving with pain or difficulty: *a stiff neck.* **5.** difficult: *a stiff exam.* **6.** unrelaxed or awkward; formal. **7.** fairly firm in consistency; thick. **8.** powerful; strong: *a stiff breeze; a stiff drink.* ~*n.* **9.** *Slang.* a corpse. ~*adv.* **10.** completely or utterly: *bored stiff.* —'**stiffly** *adv.* —'**stiffness** *n.*

stiffen ('stɪf²n) *vb.* to make or become stiff or stiffer.

stiff-necked *adj.* haughtily stubborn.

stifle ('staɪf²l) *vb.* **1.** to smother or suppress (something): *stifle a cough.* **2.** to feel discomfort and difficulty in breathing. **3.** to kill (someone) by preventing him from breathing.

stigma ('stɪgmə) *n., pl.* **stigmas** *or* **stigmata** ('stɪgmətə, stɪg'mɑːtə). **1.** a mark of social disgrace: *the stigma of having been in prison.* **2.** *Bot.* the part of a flower that receives pollen. **3.** (*pl.*) *Christianity.* marks resembling the wounds of the crucified Christ, believed to appear on the bodies of certain individuals.

stigmatize *or* **-ise** ('stɪgmə,taɪz) *vb.* to mark (something) out as being shameful.

stile (staɪl) *n.* a set of steps in a wall or fence to allow people, but not animals, to pass over.

stiletto (stɪ'letəʊ) *n., pl.* **-tos.** **1.** Also called: **spike heel, stiletto heel.** a high narrow heel on a woman's shoe or a shoe with such a heel. **2.** a small dagger with a slender tapered blade.

still¹ (stɪl) *adj.* **1.** motionless; stationary. **2.** undisturbed; silent and calm. **3.** (of a soft drink) not fizzy. **4.** gentle or quiet; subdued. ~*adv.* **5.** continuing now or in the future as in the past: *do you still love me?* **6.** up to this or that time; yet: *I still can't hear you.* **7.** even or yet: *still more insults.* **8.** even then; nevertheless: *the baby has been fed and still cries.* **9.** quietly or without movement: *sit still.* ~*n.* **10.** *Poetic.* silence or tranquillity: *the still of the night.* **11.** a still photograph from a film. ~*vb.* **12.** to make or become still, quiet, or calm. **13.** to relieve or end: *her fears were stilled.* —'**stillness** *n.*

still² (stɪl) *n.* an apparatus for distilling spirits.

stillborn ('stɪl,bɔːn) *adj.* **1.** (of a baby) dead at birth. **2.** (of an idea or plan) completely unsuccessful. —'**still,birth** *n.*

still life *n., pl.* **still lifes.** **1.** a painting or drawing of objects such as fruit or flowers. **2.** this kind of painting or drawing.

still room *n. Brit.* **1.** a room in which distilling is carried out. **2.** a pantry or storeroom in a large house.

stilt (stɪlt) *n.* **1.** either of a pair of long poles with footrests on which a person stands and walks, as used by circus clowns. **2.** a long post or column used with others to support a building above ground level.

stilted ('stɪltɪd) *adj.* (of speech, writing, or behaviour) formal or pompous; not flowing continuously or naturally.

Stilton ('stɪltən) *n. Trademark.* a strong-flavoured blue-veined cheese.

stimulant ('stɪmjʊlənt) *n.* **1.** a drug, food, or drink that increases the heart rate or other physical or mental activity. **2.** any stimulating thing. ~*adj.* **3.** stimulating.

stimulate ('stɪmjʊ,leɪt) vb. **1.** to arouse the senses of (a person). **2.** Physiol. to excite (a nerve or organ) with a stimulus. —'stimu,lating adj. —,stimu'lation n.

stimulus ('stɪmjʊləs) n., pl. **-li** (-,laɪ, -,liː). **1.** something that stimulates or acts as an incentive to (someone). **2.** something, such as a drug or electrical impulse, that is capable of causing a response in a person or an animal.

sting (stɪŋ) vb. **stinging, stung. 1.** (of certain animals and plants) to inflict a wound on (someone) by the injection of poison. **2.** to feel or cause (someone) to feel a sharp mental or physical pain. **3.** to goad or incite: they were stung into action. **4.** Informal. to cheat (someone) by overcharging. ~n. **5.** a skin wound caused by stinging. **6.** pain caused by or as if by a sting. **7.** a mental pain: a sting of conscience. **8.** the sharp pointed organ of certain animals or plants by which poison can be injected. **9.** Slang. a deceptive trick. —'stinging adj.

stinging nettle n. same as **nettle** (sense 1).

stingray ('stɪŋ,reɪ) n. a flat fish with a jagged whiplike tail which can inflict painful wounds.

stingy ('stɪndʒɪ) adj. **-gier, -giest.** mean or miserly. —'stinginess n.

stink (stɪŋk) n. **1.** a strong unpleasant smell. **2. make, create, or kick up a stink.** Slang. to make a fuss. ~vb. **stinking, stank or stunk; stunk. 3.** to give off a strong unpleasant smell. **4.** Slang. to be thoroughly unpleasant: this town stinks.

stink bomb n. a small glass globe used by practical jokers: it releases a liquid with a strong unpleasant smell when broken.

stinker ('stɪŋkə) n. Slang. a difficult or very unpleasant person or thing.

stinking ('stɪŋkɪŋ) adj. **1.** having a strong unpleasant smell. **2.** Informal. unpleasant or disgusting. ~adv. **3. stinking rich.** Informal. very wealthy.

stink out vb. **1.** to drive (people) away by a foul smell. **2.** Brit. to cause (a place) to stink: his cigars stink out the room.

stint (stɪnt) vb. **1.** to be miserly with (something): don't stint on the potatoes. ~n. **2.** an allotted amount of work.

stipend ('staɪpɛnd) n. a regular amount of money paid as a salary or allowance, as to a clergyman.

stipendiary (staɪ'pɛndɪərɪ) adj. **1.** receiving a stipend. ~n., pl. **-aries. 2.** a person who receives a stipend.

stipple ('stɪp³l) vb. to draw, engrave, or paint (something) using dots or flecks.

stipulate ('stɪpjʊ,leɪt) vb. to specify (something) as a condition of an agreement. —,stipu'lation n.

stir¹ (stɜː) vb. **stirring, stirred. 1.** to move an implement such as a spoon around in (a liquid) so as to mix it up. **2.** to change or cause to change position. **3.** (foll. by from) to depart (from one's usual or preferred place). **4.** to get up after sleeping. **5.** to excite or stimulate (someone) emotionally. **6.** to move (oneself) briskly or vigorously; exert (oneself). **7.** to awaken: to stir someone from sleep. ~n. **8.** a stirring. **9.** a strong reaction, usually of excitement: his publication caused a stir. ~See also **stir up.**

stir² (stɜː) n. Slang. prison: in stir.

stir-crazy adj. Slang, chiefly U.S. & Canad. mentally disturbed as a result of being in prison.

stir-fry vb. **-frying, -fried. 1.** to cook (food) rapidly by stirring it in a wok or frying pan over a high heat. ~n., pl. **-fries. 2.** a dish cooked in this way.

stirrer ('stɜːrə) n. Informal. a person who deliberately causes trouble.

stirring ('stɜːrɪŋ) adj. exciting the emotions; stimulating.

stirrup ('stɪrəp) n. a metal loop attached to a saddle, with a flat footpiece through which a rider puts his foot for support.

stirrup cup n. a cup containing an alcoholic drink offered to a horseman ready to ride away.

stirrup pump n. a hand-operated pump, the base of which is placed in a bucket of water: used in fighting fires.

stir up vb. to set (something) in motion; instigate: he stirred up trouble.

stitch (stɪtʃ) n. **1.** a link made by drawing a thread through material with a needle. **2.** a loop of yarn formed around a needle or hook in knitting or crocheting. **3.** a particular kind of stitch. **4.** Informal. a suture. **5.** a sharp pain in the side caused by running or exercising. **6. in stitches.** Informal. laughing uncontrollably. **7. not a stitch.** Informal. no clothes at all. ~vb. **8.** to sew or fasten (something) with stitches. **9.** to be engaged in sewing. —'stitching n.

stoat (stəʊt) n. a small brown N European mammal related to the weasels: in winter it has a white coat and is then known as an ermine.

stock (stɒk) n. **1.** the total amount of goods kept on the premises of a shop or business. **2.** a supply of something stored for future use. **3.** Finance. **a.** the money raised by a company through selling shares entitling their holders to dividends, partial ownership, and usually voting rights. **b.** the proportion of this money held by an individual shareholder. **c.** the shares of a specified company or industry. **4.** standing or status. **5.** farm animals bred and kept for their meat, skins, etc. **6.** the original type from which a particular race, family, or group is derived. **7.** the part of a rifle or air gun into which the barrel is set: held by the firer against the shoulder. **8.** a liquid or broth in which meat, fish, bones, or vegetables have been simmered for a long time. **9.** a kind of plant cultivated for its brightly coloured flowers. **10.** See **laughing stock. 11. in stock.** stored on the premises or available for sale or use. **12. out of stock.** not immediately available for sale or use. **13. take stock.** to make a general appraisal of a situation or resources. ~*adj.* **14.** staple; standard: *stock sizes in clothes.* **15.** being a cliché; hackneyed: *a stock phrase.* ~*vb.* **16.** to keep (goods) for sale. **17.** (usually foll. by *up* or *up on*) to obtain a store of (something) for future use or sale: *to stock up on beer.* **18.** to supply (a farm) with animals or (a lake or stream) with fish. ~See also **stocks.**

stockade (stɒˈkeɪd) *n.* an enclosure or barrier of stakes.

stockbreeder (ˈstɒkˌbriːdə) *n.* a person who breeds or rears livestock.

stockbroker (ˈstɒkˌbrəʊkə) *n.* a person who buys and sells stocks and shares on a commission basis for customers. —**ˈstockˌbroking** *n.*

stock car *n.* a car that has been strengthened and modified for a form of racing in which the cars often collide.

stock exchange *n.* **1. a.** a highly organized market for the purchase and sale of stocks and shares, operated by professional stockbrokers and market makers according to fixed rules. **b.** a place where stocks and shares are traded. **2.** the prices or trading activity of a stock exchange: *the stock exchange fell heavily today.*

stockholder (ˈstɒkˌhəʊldə) *n.* an owner of some of a company's stock.

stockinet (ˌstɒkɪˈnɛt) *n.* a machine-knitted elastic fabric.

stocking (ˈstɒkɪŋ) *n.* a close-fitting garment of nylon or knitted yarn to cover the foot and part or all of the leg.

stockinged (ˈstɒkɪŋd) *adj.* **in one's stockinged feet.** wearing stockings, tights, or socks but no shoes.

stock in trade *n.* anything constantly used by someone as a part of his profession or trade: *friendliness is the salesman's stock in trade.*

stockist (ˈstɒkɪst) *n. Commerce, Brit.* a dealer who stocks a particular product.

stock market *n.* same as **stock exchange.**

stockpile (ˈstɒkˌpaɪl) *vb.* **1.** to store a large quantity of (something) for future use. ~*n.* **2.** a large store accumulated for future use.

stockpot (ˈstɒkˌpɒt) *n. Chiefly Brit.* a pot in which stock for soup is made.

stockroom (ˈstɒkˌruːm) *n.* a room in which a stock of goods is kept, as in a shop or factory.

stock route *n. Austral. & N.Z.* a route

designated for droving farm animals, so as to avoid traffic.

stocks (stɒks) *pl. n. History.* an instrument of punishment consisting of a heavy wooden frame with holes in which the feet, hands, or head of an offender were locked.

stock-still *adv.* absolutely still; motionless.

stocktaking (ˈstɒkˌteɪkɪŋ) *n.* **1.** the examination, counting, and valuing of goods in a shop or business. **2.** a reassessment of one's current situation and prospects.

stocky (ˈstɒkɪ) *adj.* **stockier, stockiest.** (of a person) broad and sturdy. —**ˈstockily** *adv.* —**ˈstockiness** *n.*

stockyard (ˈstɒkˌjɑːd) *n.* a large yard with pens or covered buildings where farm animals are sold.

stodge (stɒdʒ) *n. Informal.* heavy filling starchy food.

stodgy (ˈstɒdʒɪ) *adj.* **stodgier, stodgiest. 1.** (of food) heavy or uninteresting. **2.** (of a person) excessively formal and conventional. —**ˈstodginess** *n.*

stoep (stuːp) *n.* (in South Africa) a veranda.

stoic (ˈstəʊɪk) *n.* **1.** a person who has stoical qualities. ~*adj.* **2.** same as **stoical.**

Stoic (ˈstəʊɪk) *n.* **1.** a member of the ancient Greek school of philosophy which believed that virtue and happiness could be achieved only by submission to destiny and the natural law. ~*adj.* **2.** of or relating to the Stoics. —**Stoicism** (ˈstəʊɪˌsɪzəm) *n.*

stoical (ˈstəʊɪkˀl) *adj.* suffering great difficulties without showing one's feelings. —**ˈstoically** *adv.* —**stoicism** (ˈstəʊɪˌsɪzəm) *n.*

stoke (stəʊk) *vb.* **1.** to feed, stir, and tend (a fire or furnace). **2.** to arouse or encourage (a strong emotion) in oneself or someone else. ~Also **stoke up.**

stokehold (ˈstəʊkˌhəʊld) *n. Naut.* the hold for a ship's boilers; fire room.

stokehole (ˈstəʊkˌhəʊl) *n.* a hole in a furnace through which it is stoked.

stoker (ˈstəʊkə) *n.* a person employed to tend a furnace, as on a steamship.

stole[1] (stəʊl) *vb.* the past tense of **steal.**

stole[2] (stəʊl) *n.* a long scarf or shawl, worn by women.

stolen (ˈstəʊlən) *vb.* the past participle of **steal.**

stolid (ˈstɒlɪd) *adj.* showing little or no emotion or interest. —**stoˈlidity** *n.* —**ˈstolidly** *adv.*

stoma (ˈstəʊmə) *n., pl.* **stomata** (ˈstəʊmətə, stəʊˈmɑːtə). **1.** *Bot.* a pore in a plant leaf that controls the passage of gases into and out of the plant. **2.** *Zool.* a mouth or mouth-like part.

stomach (ˈstʌmək) *n.* **1.** an organ inside the body in which food is stored until it has been partially digested. **2.** the abdominal region. **3.** desire, appetite, or inclination: *I have no stomach for arguments.* ~*vb.* **4.** to tolerate; bear: *I can't stomach his bragging.*

stomachache ('stʌmək,eɪk) *n.* pain in the stomach, as from indigestion. Also called: **stomach upset, upset stomach.**

stomacher ('stʌməkə) *n. Hist.* a decorative V-shaped panel of stiff material worn over the chest and stomach mainly by women.

stomach pump *n. Med.* a suction device for removing stomach contents through a tube inserted down the throat.

stomp (stɒmp) *vb.* to tread or stamp heavily.

stone (stəʊn) *n.* **1.** the hard nonmetallic material of which rocks are made. **2.** a small lump of rock; pebble. **3.** Also called: **gemstone.** a precious or semiprecious stone that has been cut and polished. **4.** a piece of rock used for some particular purpose: *gravestone; millstone.* **5.** something that resembles a stone: *hailstone.* **6.** the hard central part of such fruits as the peach or date. **7.** (*pl.* **stone**) *Brit.* a unit of weight equal to 14 pounds or 6.350 kilograms. **8.** *Pathol.* a stonelike mineral growth found in organs of the body. **9.** (*modifier*) made of stoneware: *a stone jar.* **10. heart of stone.** a hard or unemotional nature. **11. leave no stone unturned.** to do everything possible to achieve something. ~*vb.* **12.** to throw stones at (someone), esp. to kill him. **13.** to remove the stones from (a fruit).

Stone Age *n.* a period in human culture identified by the use of stone implements.

stonechat ('stəʊn,tʃæt) *n.* a songbird that has a black plumage with a reddish-brown breast.

stone-cold *adj.* **1.** completely cold. ~*adv.* **2. stone-cold sober.** completely sober.

stoned (stəʊnd) *adj. Slang.* under the influence of drugs or alcohol.

stone-deaf *adj.* completely deaf.

stone fruit *n.* same as **drupe.**

stonemason ('stəʊn,meɪs³n) *n.* a person who is skilled in preparing stone for building.

stone's throw *n.* a short distance.

stonewall (,stəʊn'wɔːl) *vb.* **1.** to obstruct or hinder discussion. **2.** *Cricket.* (of a batsman) to play defensively.

stoneware ('stəʊn,wɛə) *n.* a hard opaque pottery, fired at a very high temperature.

stonewashed ('stəʊn,wɒʃt) *adj.* (of clothes or fabric) given a worn faded look by being washed with many small pieces of stone.

stonework ('stəʊn,wɜːk) *n.* any structure or part of a building made of stone.

stony *or* **stoney** ('stəʊnɪ) *adj.* **stonier, stoniest. 1.** covered with stones: *a stony*

beach. **2.** (of a face, voice, or attitude) unfeeling or hard. —**'stonily** *adv.*

stony-broke *adj. Brit. slang.* completely without money; penniless.

stood (stʊd) *vb.* past of **stand.**

stooge (stuːdʒ) *n.* **1.** an actor who feeds lines to a comedian or acts as the butt of his jokes. **2.** *Slang.* someone who is taken advantage of by someone in a superior position.

stool (stuːl) *n.* **1.** a seat with legs but no back. **2.** waste matter from the bowels.

stool pigeon *n.* an informer for the police.

stoop¹ (stuːp) *vb.* **1.** to bend (the body) forward and downward. **2.** to carry oneself with head and shoulders habitually bent forward. **3.** (foll. by *to*) to degrade oneself: *I wouldn't stoop to his level.* ~*n.* **4.** the act, position, or habit of stooping. —**'stooping** *adj.*

stoop² (stuːp) *n. U.S.* an open porch or small platform with steps leading up to it at the entrance to a building.

stop (stɒp) *vb.* **stopping, stopped. 1.** to cease from doing (something); discontinue. **2.** to cause (something moving) to halt or (of something moving) to come to a halt. **3.** to prevent the continuance or completion of (something). **4.** (often foll. by *from*) to prevent or restrain: *he stopped George from fighting.* **5.** to keep back: *to stop supplies.* **6.** (foll. by *up*) to block or plug: *to stop up a pipe.* **7.** to instruct a bank not to honour (a cheque). **8.** to deduct (money) from pay. **9.** *Informal.* to receive (a blow or hit). **10.** to stay or rest: *we stopped at the Robinsons'.* **11.** *Music.* to alter the vibrating length of (a string on a violin, guitar, etc.) by pressing down on it at some point with the finger. **12. stop at nothing.** to be prepared to do anything; be unscrupulous or ruthless. ~*n.* **13.** prevention of movement or progress: *to put a stop to something.* **14.** the act of stopping or the state of being stopped: *to come to a stop.* **15.** a place where something halts or pauses: *a bus stop.* **16.** the act or an instance of blocking or obstructing. **17.** a device that prevents, limits, or ends the motion of a mechanism or moving part. **18.** *Brit.* a full stop. **19.** *Music.* a knob on an organ that is operated to allow sets of pipes to sound. **20. pull out all the stops.** to make a great effort.

stopbank ('stɒp,bæŋk) *n. N.Z.* an embankment to prevent flooding.

stopcock ('stɒp,kɒk) *n.* a valve used to control or stop the flow of a fluid in a pipe.

stopgap ('stɒp,gæp) *n.* a temporary substitute.

stop off *vb.* (often foll. by *at*) to halt and call somewhere on the way to another place.

stopover ('stɒp,əʊvə) n. 1. a break in a journey. ~vb. **stop over.** 2. to make a stopover.

stoppage ('stɒpɪdʒ) n. 1. the act of stopping something or the state of being stopped. 2. a deduction of money, as from pay. 3. an organized stopping of work, as during a strike.

stopper ('stɒpə) n. a plug or bung for closing a bottle, pipe, etc.

stop press n. Brit. news items inserted into a newspaper after the printing has been started.

stopwatch ('stɒp,wɒtʃ) n. a watch used for timing sporting events accurately, having a device for stopping the hands instantly.

storage ('stɔːrɪdʒ) n. 1. the act of storing or the state of being stored. 2. space for storing. 3. Computers. the process of storing information in a computer.

storage device n. a piece of computer equipment, such as a magnetic tape or a disk in or on which information can be stored.

storage heater n. an electric device capable of accumulating and radiating heat generated by off-peak electricity.

store (stɔː) vb. 1. to keep, set aside, or accumulate (things) for future use. 2. to place furniture or other possessions in a warehouse for safekeeping. 3. to supply or stock (certain goods). 4. Computers. to enter or retain (information) in a storage device. ~n. 5. a shop (in Britain usually a large one). 6. a large supply or stock kept for future use. 7. short for **department store.** 8. a storage place, such as a warehouse. 9. Computers, chiefly Brit. same as **memory** (sense 7). 10. **in store.** forthcoming or imminent: I wonder what's in store for us today. 11. **set great store by something.** to value something or regard something as important. ~See also **stores.**

storehouse ('stɔː,haʊs) n. a place where things are stored.

storeroom ('stɔː,ruːm) n. a room in which things are stored.

stores (stɔːz) pl. n. supply or stock of food and other essentials for a journey.

storey or esp. U.S. **story** ('stɔːrɪ) n., pl. -reys or -ries. a floor or level of a building.

stork (stɔːk) n. a large wading bird with very long legs, a long bill, and a white-and-black plumage.

storm (stɔːm) n. 1. a violent weather condition of strong winds, rain, hail, thunder, lightning, etc. 2. a violent disturbance or quarrel. 3. a heavy discharge of bullets or missiles. 4. **take a place by storm. a.** to capture or overrun a place by a violent assault. **b.** to overwhelm and enthral a place or the people in it. ~vb. 5. to attack or capture (a place) suddenly and violently. 6. to shout angrily. 7. to move or rush violently or angrily: he stormed out of the meeting.

storm centre n. 1. the centre of a storm, where pressure is lowest. 2. the centre of any disturbance or trouble.

storm door n. an additional door outside an ordinary door, providing extra protection against wind, cold, and rain.

storm trooper n. a member of the Nazi terrorist militia.

stormy ('stɔːmɪ) adj. **stormier, stormiest.** 1. characterized by storms: stormy weather. 2. involving violent disturbance or emotional outbursts: a stormy relationship.

stormy or **storm petrel** n. 1. a small petrel with dark plumage and paler underparts. 2. a person who brings trouble.

story[1] ('stɔːrɪ) n., pl. -ries. 1. a description of a chain of events told or written in prose or verse. 2. Also called: **short story.** a piece of fiction, briefer and usually less detailed than a novel. 3. Also called: **story line.** the plot of a book or film. 4. a newspaper report. 5. the event or material for such a report. 6. Informal. a lie.

story[2] ('stɔːrɪ) n., pl. -ries. Chiefly. U.S. same as **storey.**

storybook ('stɔːrɪ,bʊk) n. 1. a book containing stories for children. ~adj. 2. unreal or fantastic: a storybook world.

stoup or **stoop** (stuːp) n. a small basin for holy water.

stoush (staʊʃ) Austral. & N.Z. slang. ~vb. 1. to hit or punch (someone). ~n. 2. fighting or violence.

stout (staʊt) adj. 1. solidly built or fat. 2. resolute or brave: stout fellow. 3. strong and robust. ~n. 4. strong dark beer. —'**stoutly** adv.

stouthearted (,staʊt'hɑːtɪd) adj. resolute or brave.

stove[1] (stəʊv) n. 1. same as **cooker** (sense 1). 2. any heating apparatus, such as a kiln.

stove[2] (stəʊv) vb. a past tense and past participle of **stave.**

stovepipe ('stəʊv,paɪp) n. a pipe that serves as a flue to a stove.

stow (stəʊ) vb. (often foll. by away) to pack or store (something).

stowage ('stəʊɪdʒ) n. 1. space, room, or a charge for stowing goods. 2. a stowing.

stowaway ('stəʊə,weɪ) n. 1. a person who hides aboard a vehicle, ship, or aircraft in order to travel free. ~vb. **stow away.** 2. to travel in such a way.

strabismus (strə'bɪzməs) n. Pathol. same as **squint** (sense 3).

straddle ('stræd³l) vb. 1. to have one leg or part on each side of (something). 2. U.S. & Canad. informal. to be in favour of both sides of (an issue).

Stradivarius (,strædɪ'vɛərɪəs) n. a violin

manufactured in Italy by Antonio Stradivari (?1644–1737) or his family.

strafe (strɑːf) *vb.* to machine-gun (troops) from the air.

straggle ('stræg'l) *vb.* 1. to go or spread in a rambling or irregular way. 2. to linger behind or wander from a main line or part. —'**straggler** *n.* —'**straggly** *adj.*

straight (streɪt) *adj.* 1. not curved or crooked; continuing in the same direction without bending. 2. straightforward, outright, or candid: *a straight rejection.* 3. even, level, or upright. 4. in keeping with the facts; accurate. 5. honest, respectable, or reliable. 6. continuous; uninterrupted: *in straight succession.* 7. (of an alcoholic drink) undiluted; neat. 8. not wavy or curly: *straight hair.* 9. correctly arranged; orderly. 10. (of a play or acting style) straightforward or serious. 11. *Slang.* heterosexual. 12. *Informal.* no longer owing or being owed something: *if you buy the next round we'll be straight.* 13. *Slang.* conventional in views, customs, or appearance. ~*adv.* 14. in a straight line or direct course. 15. immediately; at once: *he came straight back.* 16. in an even, level, or upright position: *stand up straight.* 17. continuously; uninterruptedly. 18. (often foll. by *out*) frankly; candidly: *he told me straight out.* 19. **go straight.** *Informal.* to reform after having been a criminal. ~*n.* 20. a straight line, form, part, or position. 21. *Brit.* a straight part of a racetrack.

straightaway (,streɪtə'weɪ) *or* **straight away** *adv.* at once.

straighten ('streɪt'n) *vb.* (sometimes foll. by *up* or *out*) 1. to make or become straight. 2. to make (something) neat or tidy.

straighten out *vb.* to make (something) less complicated or confused.

straight face *n.* a serious facial expression which conceals a desire to laugh. —,**straight-'faced** *adj.*

straight fight *n.* a contest between two candidates only.

straightforward (,streɪt'fɔːwəd) *adj.* 1. (of a person) honest, frank, or simple. 2. *Chiefly Brit.* (of a task) simple; easy.

straight man *n.* an actor who acts as stooge to a comedian.

strain[1] (streɪn) *vb.* 1. to draw (something) taut or be drawn taut. 2. to exert or use (resources) to the utmost extent. 3. to injure or damage (oneself or a part of one's body) by overexertion: *he strained himself.* 4. to make intense or violent efforts: *he is straining to keep up with the other runners.* 5. to subject (someone) to mental tension or stress. 6. to pour (a substance) through a sieve or filter. 7. (foll. by *at*) to push, pull, or work with violent exertion (on something). ~*n.* 8. the damage resulting from excessive physical exertion. 9. an intense physical or mental effort. 10. (*pl.*) *Music.* a theme, melody, or tune. 11. a great demand on the emotions, resources, etc. 12. a way of speaking; tone of voice: *don't go on in that strain.* 13. tension or tiredness resulting from overwork or worry. 14. *Physics.* the change in dimension of a body caused by outside forces.

strain[2] (streɪn) *n.* 1. a group of animals or plants within a species or variety, distinguished by one or more minor characteristics. 2. a streak; trace.

strained (streɪnd) *adj.* 1. (of an action, expression, etc.) not natural or spontaneous. 2. (of an atmosphere, relationship, etc.) not relaxed; tense.

strainer ('streɪnə) *n.* a sieve used for straining sauces, vegetables, or tea.

strait (streɪt) *n.* 1. (*often pl.*) a narrow channel of the sea linking two larger areas of sea. 2. (*pl.*) a position of acute difficulty: *in dire straits.*

straitened ('streɪt'nd) *adj.* **in straitened circumstances.** not having much money.

straitjacket ('streɪt,dʒækɪt) *n.* 1. a strong canvas jacket with long sleeves for binding the arms of violent prisoners or mental patients. 2. a restriction or limitation.

strait-laced *or* **straight-laced** *adj.* prudish or puritanical.

strand[1] (strænd) *vb.* 1. to leave or drive (ships or fish) ashore. 2. to leave (someone) helpless, for example without transport or money. ~*n.* 3. *Chiefly poetic.* a shore or beach.

strand[2] (strænd) *n.* 1. one of the individual fibres or threads of string, wire, etc., that form a rope, cord, etc. 2. a single length of string, hair, wool, wire, etc. 3. a string of pearls or beads. 4. a constituent element of something.

strange (streɪndʒ) *adj.* 1. odd, unusual, or peculiar. 2. not known, seen, or experienced before; unfamiliar. 3. (foll. by *to*) inexperienced (in) or unaccustomed (to): *strange to a task.* —'**strangely** *adv.* —'**strangeness** *n.*

stranger ('streɪndʒə) *n.* 1. any person whom one does not know. 2. a person who is new to a particular locality or who comes from another region or town. 3. (foll. by *to*) a person who is unfamiliar with or new to something: *he is no stranger to computers.*

strangle ('stræŋg'l) *vb.* 1. to kill (someone) by pressing his windpipe; throttle. 2. to prevent the growth or development of: *to strangle originality.* 3. to suppress (an utterance) by or as if by swallowing suddenly: *a strangled cry.* —'**strangler** *n.*

stranglehold ('stræŋg'l,həʊld) *n.* 1. a wrestling hold in which a wrestler's arms are pressed against his opponent's windpipe. **2.** complete power or control over a person or situation.

strangulate (ˈstræŋɡjʊˌleɪt) *vb.* **1.** *Pathol.* to constrict (a hollow organ or vessel) so as to stop the flow of air or blood through it: *a strangulated hernia.* **2.** same as **strangle.** —ˌstranguˈlation *n.*

strap (stræp) *n.* **1.** a strip of leather or similar material used for carrying, lifting, fastening, or holding things in place. **2.** a loop of leather or rubber, hanging from the roof in a bus or train for standing passengers to hold on to. **3.** short for **shoulder strap. 4. the strap.** a beating with a strap as a punishment. ~*vb.* **strapping, strapped. 5.** to tie or bind (something) with a strap.

straphanger (ˈstræpˌhæŋə) *n. Informal.* a passenger in a bus or train who has to travel standing and holding on to a strap.

strapping (ˈstræpɪŋ) *adj.* tall and sturdy: *a strapping young man.*

strata (ˈstrɑːtə) *n.* a plural of **stratum.**

stratagem (ˈstrætɪdʒəm) *n.* a clever plan to deceive an enemy.

strategic (strəˈtiːdʒɪk) *adj.* **1.** of or characteristic of strategy. **2.** (of weapons, esp. missiles) directed against an enemy's homeland rather than used on a battlefield. —straˈtegically *adv.*

strategy (ˈstrætɪdʒɪ) *n., pl.* **-gies. 1.** the art of the planning and conduct of a war. **2.** a long-term plan for success, as in politics or business. —ˈstrategist *n.*

strath (stræθ) *n. Scot.* a flat river valley.

strathspey (ˌstræθˈspeɪ) *n.* **1.** a Scottish dance with gliding steps, slower than a reel. **2.** music for this dance.

stratified (ˈstrætɪˌfaɪd) *adj.* **1.** (of rocks) formed in layers or strata. **2.** *Sociol.* (of a society) divided into status groups. —ˌstratifiˈcation *n.*

stratocumulus (ˌstrætəʊˈkjuːmjʊləs) *n., pl.* **-li** (-ˌlaɪ). *Meteorol.* a uniform stretch of cloud containing dark grey masses.

stratosphere (ˈstrætəˌsfɪə) *n.* the atmospheric layer between about 15 and 50 km above the earth.

stratum (ˈstrɑːtəm) *n., pl.* **-ta** or **-tums. 1.** any of the distinct layers into which certain rocks are divided. **2.** a layer of ocean or atmosphere marked off either naturally or arbitrarily. **3.** a social class.

stratus (ˈstreɪtəs) *n., pl.* **-ti** (-taɪ). a grey layer cloud.

straw (strɔː) *n.* **1. a.** stalks of threshed grain, such as wheat or barley, used for plaiting or as fodder. **b.** (*as modifier*): *a straw hat.* **2.** a single stalk of straw. **3.** a long thin hollow paper or plastic tube, used for sucking up liquids into the mouth. **4. clutch at straws.** to turn in desperation to measures with little chance of success. **5. draw the short straw.** to be the person chosen to perform an unpleasant task. ~*adj.* **6.** pale yellow.

strawberry (ˈstrɔːbərɪ) *n., pl.* **-ries.** a sweet fleshy red fruit with small seedlike parts on the outside.

strawberry blonde *adj.* **1.** (of hair) reddish blonde. ~*n.* **2.** a woman with such hair.

strawberry mark *n.* a red birthmark.

straw poll *or* **vote** *n.* an unofficial poll or vote taken to determine the opinion of a group or the public on some issue.

stray (streɪ) *vb.* **1.** to wander away from the correct path or from a given area. **2.** to move away from the point or lose concentration. **3.** to deviate from certain moral standards: *he promised his wife that he would never stray again.* ~*n.* **4. a.** a domestic animal that has wandered away from its place of keeping and is lost. **b.** (*as modifier*): *stray dogs.* **5.** a lost or homeless person, esp. a child: *waifs and strays.* ~*adj.* **6.** scattered, random, or haphazard: *a stray bullet.*

streak (striːk) *n.* **1.** a long thin stripe or trace of some contrasting colour. **2.** (of lightning) a sudden flash. **3.** a quality or characteristic: *a jealous streak.* **4.** a short stretch of good or bad luck: *a winning streak.* **5.** *Informal.* an instance of running naked through a public place. ~*vb.* **6.** to mark (something) with a streak or streaks: *her face was streaked with tears.* **7.** to move rapidly in a straight line. **8.** *Informal.* to run naked through a public place. —**streaked** *or* **streaky** *adj.* —ˈstreaker *n.*

stream (striːm) *n.* **1.** a small river. **2.** any steady flow of water or other fluid. **3.** something that resembles a stream in moving continuously in a line or particular direction: *a steady stream of customers.* **4.** a rapid or unbroken flow of speech: *a stream of abuse.* **5.** *Brit.* a class of schoolchildren grouped together because of similar ability. ~*vb.* **6.** to pour in a continuous flow: *his nose streamed blood.* **7.** (of a crowd of people or vehicles) to move in unbroken succession. **8.** to float freely or with a waving motion: *bunting streamed in the wind.* **9.** *Brit.* to group (school children) in streams. —ˈstreaming *n.* —ˈstreamlet *n.*

streamer (ˈstriːmə) *n.* **1.** a long coiled ribbon of coloured paper that unrolls when tossed. **2.** a long narrow flag.

streamline (ˈstriːmˌlaɪn) *vb.* to make (something) streamlined.

streamlined (ˈstriːmˌlaɪnd) *adj.* **1.** offering or designed to offer the minimum resistance to the flow of a gas or liquid. **2.** made more efficient, esp. by simplifying.

street (striːt) *n.* **1.** a public road that is usually lined with buildings, esp. in a town: *Oxford Street.* **2.** the part of the road between the pavements, used by vehicles. **3.** the people living in a particular street.

4. on the streets. homeless. **5. right up one's street.** *Informal.* just what one knows or likes best. **6. streets ahead of.** *Informal.* superior to or more advanced than.

streetcar ('striːtˌkɑː) *n. U.S. & Canad.* a tram.

streetwalker ('striːtˌwɔːkə) *n.* a prostitute who tries to find customers in the streets.

streetwise ('striːtˌwaɪz) *adj.* knowing how to survive or succeed in poor and often criminal sections of big cities.

strength (strɛŋθ) *n.* **1.** the state or quality of being physically or mentally strong. **2.** the ability to withstand great force, stress, or pressure. **3.** something regarded as beneficial or a source of power: *their chief strength is technology.* **4.** potency, as of a drink or drug. **5.** power to convince: *the strength of an argument.* **6.** degree of intensity or concentration of colour, light, sound, or flavour. **7.** the total number of people in a group: *at full strength; below strength.* **8. go from strength to strength.** to have ever-increasing success. **9. on the strength of.** on the basis of or relying upon.

strengthen ('strɛŋθən) *vb.* to make (something) stronger or become stronger.

strenuous ('strɛnjʊəs) *adj.* requiring or involving the use of great energy or effort. —**'strenuously** *adv.*

streptococcus (ˌstrɛptəʊ'kɒkəs) *n., pl.* **-cocci** (-'kɒkaɪ). a bacterium occurring in chains and including many disease-causing species.

streptomycin (ˌstrɛptəʊ'maɪsɪn) *n.* an antibiotic used in the treatment of tuberculosis and other bacterial infections.

stress (strɛs) *n.* **1.** special emphasis or significance. **2.** mental, emotional, or physical strain or tension. **3.** emphasis placed upon a syllable by pronouncing it more loudly than those that surround it. **4.** *Physics.* force producing a change in shape or volume. ~*vb.* **5.** to give emphasis to (a point or subject): *she stressed the need for improved facilities for the disabled.* **6.** to pronounce (a word or syllable) more loudly than those surrounding it. **7.** to subject (someone or something) to stress. —**'stressful** *adj.*

stretch (strɛtʃ) *vb.* **1.** to draw out or extend (something) or to be drawn out or extended in length or area. **2.** to distort or lengthen (something) or to be distorted or lengthened permanently. **3.** to extend (the limbs or body), for example when one has just woken up. **4.** to reach or suspend (a rope, etc.) from one place to another. **5.** to draw (something) tight; tighten. **6.** (often foll. by *out, forward,* etc.) to reach or hold out (a part of one's body). **7.** (usually foll. by *over*) to extend in time: *the course stretched over three months.* **8.** (foll. by *for, over,* etc.) (of a region) to extend in

length or area. **9.** to put a great strain upon (one's money or resources). **10.** to make do with (limited resources): *to stretch one's budget.* **11.** to extend (someone) to the limit of his abilities. **12. stretch a point.** to make a concession or exception not usually made. ~*n.* **13.** the act of stretching. **14.** a large or continuous expanse or distance: *a stretch of water.* **15.** extent in time. **16. a.** ability to be stretched, as in some garments. **b.** (*as modifier*): *stretch pants.* **17.** *Slang.* a term of imprisonment. **18. at a stretch.** *Chiefly Brit.* **a.** with some difficulty; by making a special effort. **b.** at one time: *he sometimes read for hours at a stretch.* —**'stretchy** *adj.*

stretcher ('strɛtʃə) *n.* a device for transporting an ill or injured person consisting of a frame covered by canvas or other material.

stretcher-bearer *n.* a person who helps to carry a stretcher.

strew (struː) *vb.* **strewing, strewed; strewn.** to spread or scatter (things) or to be spread or scattered over a surface or area.

strewth (struːθ) *interj.* an expression of surprise or dismay.

stria ('straɪə) *n., pl.* **striae** ('straɪiː). *Geol.* a scratch or groove on the surface of a rock crystal.

striation (straɪ'eɪʃən) *n.* **1.** an arrangement or pattern of striae. **2.** same as **stria.** —**striated** (straɪ'eɪtɪd) *adj.*

stricken ('strɪkən) *adj.* badly affected by disease, pain, grief, etc.: *grief-stricken.*

strict (strɪkt) *adj.* **1.** adhering closely to specified rules. **2.** (of a rule or law) enforced stringently; rigorous: *a strict code of conduct.* **3.** severely correct in attention to conduct or morality: *a strict teacher.* **4.** (of a punishment, etc.) harsh; severe. **5.** complete; absolute: *strict secrecy.* —**'strictly** *adv.* —**'strictness** *n.*

stricture ('strɪktʃə) *n.* a severe criticism.

stride (straɪd) *n.* **1.** a long step or pace. **2.** the space measured by such a step. **3.** a striding walk. **4.** progress or development: *we have made rapid strides in computer technology.* **5.** a regular pace or rate of progress: *it put me off my stride.* **6. take something in one's stride.** to do something without difficulty or effort. ~*vb.* **striding, strode, stridden** ('strɪdən). **7.** to walk with long steps or paces, as in haste. **8.** (foll. by *over* or *across*) to cross (over a space or an obstacle) with a stride.

strident ('straɪdənt) *adj.* **1.** (of a voice or sound) loud or harsh. **2.** loudly persistent or forceful: *strident demands.* —**'stridency** *n.*

strife (straɪf) *n.* angry or violent struggle; conflict.

strike (straɪk) *vb.* **striking, struck. 1.** (of

workers) to cease work collectively as a protest against working conditions, low pay, etc. **2.** to hit (someone). **3.** to cause (something) to come into sudden or violent contact with something. **4.** (foll. by *at*) to attack (someone or something). **5.** to cause (a match) to light by friction. **6.** to sound (a specific note) on a musical instrument. **7.** (of a clock) to indicate (a specific time) by the sound of a bell. **8.** (of a poisonous snake) to cause injury by biting. **9.** to affect (someone) deeply in a particular way: *her appearance struck him as strange.* **10.** to enter the mind of: *it struck me that he had become very quiet.* **11.** (*past participle* **struck** *or* **stricken**) to render: *struck dumb.* **12.** to be noticed by; catch: *the glint of metal struck his eye.* **13.** to arrive at (something) suddenly or unexpectedly: *to strike on a solution.* **14.** to afflict (someone) with a disease: *he was struck with polio.* **15.** to discover or come upon a source of (gold, oil, etc.). **16.** to take apart or pack up: *to strike camp.* **17.** to form or impress (a coin or metal) by or as if by stamping it. **18.** to take up (an attitude or a posture). **19.** to reach (something) by agreement: *to strike a bargain.* **20. strike home.** to achieve the intended effect. **21. strike it rich.** *Informal.* to have an unexpected financial success. ~*n.* **22.** a stopping of work, as a protest against working conditions, low pay, etc.: *on strike.* **23.** an act or instance of striking. **24.** a military attack, esp. an air attack on a surface target: *an air strike.* **25.** *Baseball.* a pitched ball swung at and missed by the batter. **26.** *Tenpin bowling.* the knocking down of all the pins with one bowl. **27.** the discovery of a source of gold, oil, etc. ~See also **strike off, strike out, strike up.**

strikebreaker ('straɪkˌbreɪkə) *n.* a person who tries to make a strike fail by working or by taking the place of those on strike.

strike off *vb.* to remove the name of (a doctor or lawyer who has done something wrong) from an official register, preventing him from practising again.

strike out *vb.* **1.** to score out (something written). **2.** to start out or begin: *to strike out on one's own.*

strike pay *n.* money paid to strikers by a trade union.

striker ('straɪkə) *n.* **1.** a person who is on strike. **2.** *Soccer.* an attacking player.

strike up *vb.* **1.** (of a band or an orchestra) to begin to play. **2.** to bring about; start: *to strike up a friendship.*

striking ('straɪkɪŋ) *adj.* **1.** attracting attention; fine; impressive: *a striking beauty.* **2.** conspicuous; noticeable: *a striking difference.* —**'strikingly** *adv.*

Strine (straɪn) *n.* a humorous transliteration of Australian pronunciation, as in *Gloria Soame* for *glorious home.*

string (strɪŋ) *n.* **1.** thin cord or twine used for tying, hanging, or binding things: *a ball of string.* **2.** a group of objects threaded on a single strand: *a string of beads.* **3.** a series of things or events: *a string of girlfriends.* **4.** a tightly stretched wire or cord by means of which stringed instruments, such as the violin, guitar, and piano, are played. **5.** *Music.* (*pl.*; usually preceded by *the*) **a.** violins, violas, cellos, and double basses collectively. **b.** the section of an orchestra consisting of such instruments. **6.** a group of characters that can be treated as a unit by a computer program. **7.** (*pl.*) complications or conditions: *no strings attached.* **8.** (*modifier*) composed of stringlike strands woven in a large mesh: *a string vest.* **9. pull strings.** *Informal.* to exert power or influence, esp. secretly or unofficially. ~*vb.* **stringing, strung. 10.** to provide (something) with a string or strings. **11.** to hang or stretch (something) from one point to another. **12.** to thread (beads) on a string. **13.** to extend in a line or series: *signposts strung out along the road.* —**'string,like** *adj.*

string along *vb. Informal.* **1.** (foll. by *with*) to accompany: *I'll string along with you.* **2.** to deceive (someone) over a period of time: *she's just stringing him along till something better turns up.*

string course *n. Archit.* an ornamental projecting band along a wall.

stringed (strɪŋd) *adj.* (of musical instruments) having strings.

stringent ('strɪndʒənt) *adj.* requiring strict attention to rules or detail. —**'stringency** *n.*

stringer ('strɪŋə) *n.* **1.** *Archit.* a long horizontal timber beam that connects upright posts. **2.** a journalist employed by a newspaper on a part-time basis to cover a particular town or area.

string quartet *n. Music.* **1.** a group of musicians consisting of two violins, one viola, and one cello. **2.** a piece of music composed for such a group.

string up *vb. Informal.* to kill (a person) by hanging.

stringy ('strɪŋɪ) *adj.* **stringier, stringiest. 1.** resembling strings: *stringy hair.* **2.** (of meat or other food) fibrous.

strip¹ (strɪp) *vb.* **stripping, stripped. 1.** to take (the covering or clothes) off (oneself, another person, or thing). **2. a.** to undress completely. **b.** to perform a striptease. **3.** to empty (a building) of all furniture. **4.** to take something away from (someone): *stripped of possessions.* **5.** to remove (paint) from (a surface or furniture): *stripped pine.* **6.** to dismantle (an engine or a mechanism). ~*n.* **7.** the act or an instance of undressing or of performing a striptease.

strip² (strɪp) *n.* **1.** a long narrow piece of

something. **2.** short for **airstrip. 3.** the clothes worn by the members of a football team.

strip cartoon *n.* a sequence of drawings in a newspaper or magazine, telling a humorous story or an adventure.

strip club *n.* a club in which striptease performances take place.

stripe[1] (straɪp) *n.* **1.** a long band of colour that differs from the surrounding material. **2.** a strip, band, or chevron worn on a uniform to indicate rank. ~*vb.* **3.** to mark (something) with stripes. —**striped** *or* **'stripy** *adj.*

stripe[2] (straɪp) *n.* a stroke from a whip, rod or cane.

strip lighting *n.* electric lighting by means of long glass tubes that are fluorescent lamps.

stripling ('strɪplɪŋ) *n.* a lad.

stripper ('strɪpə) *n.* **1.** a striptease artiste. **2.** a device or substance for removing paint or varnish.

strip-searching *n.* the practice by police or customs officials of stripping a prisoner or suspect naked and searching him or her for drugs or smuggled goods.

striptease ('strɪpˌtiːz) *n.* a form of erotic entertainment in which a person gradually undresses to music.

strive (straɪv) *vb.* **striving, strove, striven** ('strɪv°n). to make a great effort: *to strive for freedom.*

strobe (strəʊb) *n.* short for **strobe lighting** or **stroboscope.**

strobe lighting *n.* a flashing beam of very bright light produced by a perforated disc rotating in front of a light source.

stroboscope ('strəʊbəˌskəʊp) *n.* an instrument producing a very bright flashing light which makes moving people appear stationary.

strode (strəʊd) *vb.* the past tense of **stride.**

stroganoff ('strɒgəˌnɒf) *n.* a dish of sliced beef cooked with onions and mushrooms, served in a sour-cream sauce. Also called: **beef stroganoff.**

stroke (strəʊk) *n.* **1.** *Pathol.* rupture of a blood vessel in the brain resulting in loss of consciousness, often followed by paralysis. **2.** a blow, knock, or hit. **3.** an action, movement, or occurrence of the kind specified: *a stroke of luck; a stroke of genius.* **4. a.** the striking of a clock. **b.** the hour registered by this: *on the stroke of three.* **5.** a mark made by a pen or paintbrush. **6.** same as **solidus**: used esp. when dictating or reading aloud. **7.** a light touch or caress with the fingers. **8.** the swinging at and hitting of the ball in sports such as golf or cricket. **9.** any one of the repeated movements used by a swimmer. **10.** a particular style of swimming, such as the crawl. **11.** a single pull on an oar or oars in rowing. **12.**

at a stroke. with one action. **13. not a stroke (of work).** no work at all. ~*vb.* **14.** to touch or brush (someone or something) lightly or gently.

stroll (strəʊl) *vb.* **1.** to walk about in a leisurely manner. ~*n.* **2.** a leisurely walk.

strong (strɒŋ) *adj.* **stronger** ('strɒŋgə), **strongest** ('strɒŋgɪst). **1.** possessing strength. **2.** solid or robust; not easily broken or injured. **3.** resolute or morally firm: *strong views.* **4.** intense in quality; not faint or feeble: *a strong voice; a strong smell.* **5.** easily defensible: *strong arguments.* **6.** concentrated; not weak or diluted. **7.** containing or having a specified number: *a navy 40 000 strong.* **8.** having a powerful taste or smell: *strong cheese.* **9.** having an extreme or drastic effect: *strong discipline.* **10.** emphatic or immoderate: *strong language.* **11.** (of a colour) having a high degree of purity; very intense. **12.** (of a wind, current, or earthquake) moving fast. **13.** (of a currency, an industry, etc.) characterized by firm or increasing prices. ~*adv.* **14. come on strong.** to make a forceful or exaggerated impression. **15. going strong.** *Informal.* thriving. —**'strongly** *adv.*

strong-arm *n.* (*modifier*) *Informal.* involving physical force or violence: *strong-arm tactics.*

strongbox ('strɒŋˌbɒks) *n.* a box in which valuables are locked for safety.

strong drink *n.* alcoholic drink.

stronghold ('strɒŋˌhəʊld) *n.* **1.** a defensible place; fortress. **2.** an area of predominance of a particular belief: *a Tory stronghold.*

strong-minded *adj.* firm, resolute, and determined.

strong point *n.* something at which one excels: *maths was never my strong point.*

strongroom ('strɒŋˌruːm) *n.* a specially designed room in which valuables are locked for safety.

strontium ('strɒntɪəm) *n.* *Chem.* a soft silvery-white metallic element. The radioactive isotope **strontium-90** is used in nuclear power sources and is a hazardous nuclear fallout product. Symbol: Sr

strop (strɒp) *n.* a leather strap or an abrasive strip for sharpening razors.

stroppy ('strɒpɪ) *adj.* **-pier, -piest.** *Brit. informal.* angry or awkward.

strove (strəʊv) *vb.* the past tense of **strive.**

struck (strʌk) *vb.* past of **strike.**

structural ('strʌktʃərəl) *adj.* **1.** of or having structure or a structure. **2.** of or forming part of the structure of a building. **3.** *Chem.* of or involving the arrangement of atoms in molecules: *a structural formula.* —**'structurally** *adv.*

structuralism ('strʌktʃərəˌlɪzəm) *n.* an approach to social sciences and to literature in terms of oppositions, contrasts, and structures, esp. as they might reflect universal mental characteristics or organizing principles. —**'structuralist** n., adj.

structure ('strʌktʃə) n. **1.** a complex construction. **2.** the arrangement and interrelationship of parts in a construction. **3.** the manner of construction or organization. **4.** *Chem.* the arrangement of atoms in a molecule of a chemical compound. **5.** *Geol.* the way in which a rock is made up of its component parts. ~vb. **6.** to give a structure to (something).

strudel ('struːdəl) n. a thin sheet of filled dough rolled up and baked: *apple strudel.*

struggle ('strʌgªl) vb. **1.** to work or strive: *they struggled for independence; we struggled to finish the work on time.* **2.** to move about strenuously so as to escape from something confining. **3.** to fight with someone, often for possession of something. **4.** to go or progress with difficulty. ~n. **5.** a laboured or strenuous exertion or effort. **6.** a fight or battle. —**'struggling** adj.

strum (strʌm) vb. **strumming, strummed. 1.** to play (a stringed instrument) with a downward or upward sweep of the thumb or of a plectrum. **2.** to play (a tune) in this way.

strumpet ('strʌmpɪt) n. *Archaic.* a prostitute or promiscuous woman.

strung (strʌŋ) vb. past of **string.**

strung up adj. *Informal.* tense or nervous: *I was too strung up to eat anything.*

strut (strʌt) vb. **strutting, strutted. 1.** to walk in a pompous manner; swagger. ~n. **2.** a piece of wood or metal that forms part of the framework of a structure.

strychnine ('strɪkniːn) n. a very poisonous drug used in small quantities as a stimulant.

Stuart ('stjʊət) adj. of or relating to the royal house that ruled Scotland from 1371 to 1714 and England from 1603 to 1714.

stub (stʌb) n. **1.** a short piece remaining after something has been used: *a cigar stub.* **2.** the section of a ticket or cheque which the purchaser keeps as a receipt. ~vb. **stubbing, stubbed. 3.** to strike (one's toe or foot) painfully against a hard surface. **4.** (foll. by *out*) to put out (a cigarette or cigar) by pressing the end against a surface.

stubble ('stʌbªl) n. **1.** the short stalks left in a field where a crop has been harvested. **2.** the short bristly hair on the chin of a man who has not shaved for a while. —**'stubbly** adj.

stubble-jumper n. *Canad. slang.* a prairie grain farmer.

stubborn ('stʌbªn) adj. **1.** refusing to agree or give in. **2.** persistent and determined. **3.** difficult to handle, treat, or overcome: *a stubborn stain.* —**'stubbornness** n.

stubby ('stʌbɪ) adj. **-bier, -biest.** short and broad.

stucco ('stʌkəʊ) n. **1.** any of various types of cement or plaster used for coating or decorating outside walls. ~vb. **-coing, -coed. 2.** to apply stucco to (a building).

stuck (stʌk) vb. **1.** past of **stick²**. ~adj. **2.** *Informal.* baffled. **3.** (foll. by *on*) *Slang.* infatuated (with). **4. get stuck in.** *Informal.* to perform a task with determination.

stuck-up adj. *Informal.* conceited, arrogant, or snobbish.

stud¹ (stʌd) n. **1.** a small piece of metal protruding from a surface, usually as decoration. **2.** a fastener consisting of two discs at either end of a short bar, usually used with clothes. **3.** one of a number of rounded objects attached to the sole of a football boot to give better grip. ~vb. **studding, studded. 4.** to decorate or cover (something) with or as if with studs: *the park was studded with daisies.*

stud² (stʌd) n. **1.** a male animal, esp. a stallion, kept principally for breeding purposes. **2.** Also: **stud farm.** a place where animals are bred. **3.** the state of being kept for breeding purposes. **4.** *Slang.* a virile or sexually active man.

student ('stjuːdªnt) n. **1.** a person following a course of study in a school, college, or university. **2.** a person who makes a thorough study of a subject: *a student of human nature.*

studied ('stʌdɪd) adj. carefully practised or planned: *with studied indifference.*

studio ('stjuːdɪəʊ) n., pl. **-dios. 1.** a room in which an artist, photographer, or musician works. **2.** a room used to record television or radio programmes or to make films or records. **3.** (pl.) the premises of a radio, television, record, or film company.

studio couch n. a backless couch that can be converted into a double bed.

studio flat n. a flat with one main room and, usually, a small kitchen and bathroom.

studious ('stjuːdɪəs) adj. **1.** of a serious, thoughtful, and hard-working character. **2.** precise, careful, or deliberate. —**'studiously** adv.

study ('stʌdɪ) vb. **studying, studied. 1.** to apply the mind to the learning or understanding of (a subject), esp. by reading. **2.** to investigate or examine (something), as by observation and research. **3.** to look at (something or someone) closely; scrutinize. ~n., pl. **studies. 4.** the act or process of studying. **5.** a room used for studying, reading, or writing. **6.** (often pl.) work relating to a particular area of learning: *environmental studies.* **7.** an investigation and analysis of a particular subject. **8.** a product of studying, such as a written paper or book. **9.** a drawing, sculpture, etc., done for practice or in preparation for another work. **10.** a musical composition intended to develop one aspect of performing technique.

stuff (stʌf) vb. **1.** to pack or fill (something) completely; cram. **2.** to force, shove, or squeeze (something somewhere): to stuff money into a pocket. **3.** to fill (food such as poultry or tomatoes) with a stuffing. **4.** to fill (a dead animal's skin) with material so as to restore the shape of the live animal. **5.** Taboo slang. to have sexual intercourse with (a woman). **6. get stuffed!** Brit. taboo slang. an exclamation of contemptuous anger or annoyance with someone. **7. stuff oneself** or **one's face.** to eat large quantities. ~n. **8.** any general or unspecified substance or accumulation of objects. **9.** the raw material of something. **10.** subject matter, skill, etc.: he knows his stuff. **11.** woollen fabric. **12. do one's stuff.** Informal. to do what is expected of one.

stuffed shirt n. Informal. a pompous person.

stuffed-up adj. having the passages of one's nose blocked with mucus.

stuffing ('stʌfɪŋ) n. **1.** the material with which something is stuffed. **2.** a mixture of ingredients with which poultry or meat is stuffed before cooking.

stuffy ('stʌfɪ) adj. **-ier, -iest. 1.** lacking fresh air. **2.** excessively dull, staid, or conventional. —'**stuffiness** n.

stultify ('stʌltɪˌfaɪ) vb. **-fying, -fied.** to dull (the brain) by boring routine. —'**stulti,fying** adj.

stumble ('stʌmb²l) vb. **1.** to trip or fall while walking or running. **2.** to walk in an awkward, unsteady, or unsure way. **3.** to make mistakes or hesitate in speech or actions. **4.** (foll. by across, on, or upon) to come across (someone or something) by accident. ~n. **5.** a false step, trip, or blunder.

stumbling block n. any impediment or obstacle.

stump (stʌmp) n. **1.** the base of a tree trunk left standing after the tree has been cut down or has fallen. **2.** the part of something, such as a tooth, limb, or blade, that remains after a larger part has been removed. **3.** Cricket. any of three upright wooden sticks that, with two bails laid across them, form a wicket. ~vb. **4.** to stop or confuse (someone). **5.** to plod or trudge heavily. **6.** Cricket. to dismiss (a batsman) by breaking his wicket with the ball. **7.** Chiefly U.S. & Canad. to campaign or canvass (an area), by political speech-making.

stump up vb. Brit. informal. to give (the money required).

stumpy ('stʌmpɪ) adj. **stumpier, stumpiest.** short and thick like a stump; stubby.

stun (stʌn) vb. **stunning, stunned. 1.** (of a heavy blow or fall) to make (someone) unconscious. **2.** to shock or overwhelm (someone).

stung (stʌŋ) vb. past of **sting.**

stunk (stʌŋk) vb. a past of **stink.**

stunner ('stʌnə) n. Informal. a person or thing of great beauty.

stunning ('stʌnɪŋ) adj. Informal. very attractive or impressive. —'**stunningly** adv.

stunt[1] (stʌnt) vb. to prevent or impede (the growth or development) of a plant, animal, or person. —'**stunted** adj.

stunt[2] (stʌnt) n. **1. a.** an acrobatic or dangerous piece of action in a film or television programme. **b.** (as modifier): a stunt man. **2.** anything spectacular or unusual done for attention: a publicity stunt.

stupefaction (ˌstjuːpɪˈfækʃən) n. the state of being stupefied.

stupefy ('stjuːpɪˌfaɪ) vb. **-fying, -fied. 1.** to make (someone) feel insensitive or lethargic. **2.** to confuse or astound (someone). —'**stupe,fying** adj.

stupendous (stjuːˈpɛndəs) adj. astounding, wonderful, or huge. —**stu'pendously** adv.

stupid ('stjuːpɪd) adj. **1.** lacking in common sense, perception, or intelligence. **2.** dazed or stupefied: stupid from lack of sleep. **3.** trivial or silly. —**stu'pidity** n. —'**stupidly** adv.

stupor ('stjuːpə) n. **1.** a state of unconsciousness. **2.** mental dullness.

sturdy ('stɜːdɪ) adj. **-dier, -diest. 1.** (of a person) healthy, strong, and vigorous. **2.** (of a piece of furniture, shoes, etc.) strongly built or made. —'**sturdily** adv.

sturgeon ('stɜːdʒən) n. a bony fish of the N hemisphere, from which caviar is obtained.

stutter ('stʌtə) vb. **1.** to speak (a word or phrase) with recurring repetition of initial consonants. ~n. **2.** the act or habit of stuttering. —'**stuttering** n.

sty[1] (staɪ) n., pl. **sties.** a pen in which pigs are kept.

sty[2] or **stye** (staɪ) n., pl. **sties** or **styes.** inflammation of a gland at the base of an eyelash.

Stygian ('stɪdʒɪən) adj. Chiefly literary. dark or gloomy.

style (staɪl) n. **1.** a form of appearance, design, or production; type or make. **2.** the way in which something is done: the modern style of education. **3.** a distinctive, formal, or characteristic manner of expression in words, music, painting, etc. **4.** elegance or refinement of manners, dress, etc.: he's got lots of style. **5.** prevailing fashion in dress, looks, etc.: that look has gone out of style. **6.** a fashionable or showy way of life: to live in style. **7.** the particular kind of spelling, punctuation, design, etc., followed in a book, journal, or publishing house. **8.** Bot. the stemlike part of a flower that bears the stigma. ~vb. **9.** to design, shape, or tailor: to style hair. **10.** to name or call: to style a man a fool.

styling mousse n. a light foamy substance

applied to the hair before styling in order to hold the style.

stylish (ˈstaɪlɪʃ) *adj.* smart; fashionable. —ˈ**stylishly** *adv.*

stylist (ˈstaɪlɪst) *n.* **1.** a hairdresser who styles hair. **2.** a person who performs, writes, or acts with attention to style.

stylistic (staɪˈlɪstɪk) *adj.* of artistic or literary style. —**styˈlistically** *adv.*

stylized *or* -**ised** (ˈstaɪlaɪzd) *adj.* conforming to an established stylistic form.

stylus (ˈstaɪləs) *n.* a needle-like device in the pick-up arm of a record player that rests in the groove in the record and picks up the sound signals.

stymie (ˈstaɪmɪ) *vb.* -**mieing**, -**mied**. **1.** to hinder or thwart (someone). ~*n.*, *pl.* -**mies**. **2.** *Golf.* (formerly) a situation in which an opponent's ball is blocking the line between the hole and the ball about to be played.

styptic (ˈstɪptɪk) *adj.* **1.** used to stop bleeding: *a styptic pencil.* ~*n.* **2.** a styptic drug.

suave (swɑːv) *adj.* (esp. of a man) smooth and sophisticated in manner. —ˈ**suavely** *adv.*

sub (sʌb) *n.* **1.** short for **subeditor, submarine, subscription,** or **substitute**. **2.** *Brit. informal.* an advance payment of wages or salary. Formal term: **subsistence allowance**. ~*vb.* **subbing, subbed**. **3.** to act as a substitute.

sub- *or before* r **sur-** *prefix*. used with many main words to mean: **1.** situated under or beneath: *subterranean*. **2.** secondary in rank; subordinate: *sublieutenant; surrogate*. **3.** falling short of; less than or imperfectly so: *subarctic; subhuman*. **4.** forming a subdivision or subordinate part: *subcommittee*.

subaltern (ˈsʌbᵊltən) *n.* any commissioned army officer below the rank of captain.

subaqua (ˌsʌbˈækwə) *adj.* of or relating to underwater sport: *subaqua swimming*.

subatomic (ˌsʌbəˈtɒmɪk) *adj. Physics.* of, relating to, or being one of the particles making up an atom.

subcommittee (ˈsʌbkəˌmɪtɪ) *n.* a small committee which consists of members of a larger committee and which is set up to look into a particular matter.

subconscious (sʌbˈkɒnʃəs) *adj.* **1.** acting or existing without one's awareness. ~*n.* **2.** *Psychol.* the part of the mind that contains memories and motives of which one is not aware but which can influence one's behaviour. —**subˈconsciously** *adv.*

subcontinent (sʌbˈkɒntɪnənt) *n.* a large land mass that is a distinct part of a continent, such as India is of Asia.

subcontract *n.* (sʌbˈkɒntrækt). **1.** a subordinate contract under which the supply of materials, labour, etc., is let out to someone other than a party to the main contract.

~*vb.* (ˌsʌbkənˈtrækt). **2.** to let out (work) on a subcontract. —ˌ**subconˈtractor** *n.*

subculture (ˈsʌbˌkʌltʃə) *n.* a subdivision of a national culture with a distinct pattern of behaviour, beliefs, and attitudes.

subcutaneous (ˌsʌbkjuːˈteɪnɪəs) *adj. Med.* beneath the skin.

subdivide (ˌsʌbdɪˈvaɪd, ˈsʌbdɪˌvaɪd) *vb.* to divide (a part of something) into smaller parts. —**subdivision** (ˈsʌbdɪˌvɪʒən) *n.*

subdue (səbˈdjuː) *vb.* -**duing**, -**dued**. **1.** to overcome and bring (a person or people) under control by persuasion or force. **2.** to make (feelings, colour, or lighting) less intense.

subeditor (sʌbˈɛdɪtə) *n.* a person who checks and edits text for a newspaper or other publication.

subgroup (ˈsʌbˌɡruːp) *n.* a small group that is part of a larger group.

subheading (ˈsʌbˌhedɪŋ) *n.* the heading of a subdivision of a piece of writing.

subhuman (sʌbˈhjuːmən) *adj.* less than human.

subject *n.* (ˈsʌbdʒɪkt). **1.** the main theme or topic, as of a book or discussion. **2.** any branch of learning considered as a course of study. **3.** *Grammar.* a word or phrase that represents the person or thing performing the action of the verb in a sentence; for example, *the cat* in the sentence *The cat catches mice*. **4.** a person or thing that undergoes an experiment or treatment. **5.** a person under the rule of a monarch or government: *British subjects*. **6.** a figure, scene, etc., as portrayed by an artist or photographer. ~*adj.* (ˈsʌbdʒɪkt). **7.** being under the rule or a monarch or government: *subject peoples*. **8. subject to. a.** showing a tendency towards: *a child subject to indiscipline.* **b.** exposed or vulnerable to: *subject to ribaldry.* **c.** conditional upon: *the results are subject to correction.* ~*adv.* (ˈsʌbdʒɪkt). **9. subject to.** under the condition that something takes place: *we accept, subject to her agreement.* ~*vb.* (səbˈdʒɛkt). **10.** (foll. by *to*) to cause (someone) to experience (something unpleasant): *they subjected him to torture.* **11.** (foll. by *to*) to bring under the control or authority (of): *to subject a soldier to discipline.* —**subˈjection** *n.*

subjective (səbˈdʒɛktɪv) *adj.* **1.** of or based on a person's emotions or prejudices. **2.** *Grammar.* denoting a case of nouns and pronouns that identifies the subject of a verb. ~*n.* **3.** *Grammar.* the subjective case. —**subˈjectively** *adv.*

sub judice (ˈdʒuːdɪsɪ) *adj.* before a court of law: *we cannot comment on this matter publicly because it is sub judice.*

subjugate (ˈsʌbdʒʊˌɡeɪt) *vb.* **1.** to bring a group of people) under one's control. **2.** to make (someone) subservient or submissive. —ˌ**subjuˈgation** *n.*

subjunctive (səb'dʒʌŋktɪv) *Grammar.* ~*adj.* **1.** denoting a mood of verbs used when the content of the clause is being doubted, supposed, or feared true, for example *were* in the sentence: *I'd think seriously about it if I were you.* ~*n.* **2.** the subjunctive mood.

sublet (sʌb'lɛt) *vb.* **-letting, -let.** to rent out property which one is renting from somebody else.

sublieutenant (ˌsʌblə'tɛnənt) *n.* a junior officer in a navy.

sublimate ('sʌblɪˌmeɪt) *vb. Psychol.* to direct the energy of (a primitive impulse) into activities that are socially more acceptable. —ˌsubli'mation *n.*

sublime (sə'blaɪm) *adj.* **1.** of high moral, intellectual, or spiritual value; noble. **2.** unparalleled; supreme. ~*n.* **3. the sublime.** something that is sublime. ~*vb.* **4.** *Chem., physics.* to change directly from a solid to a vapour without first melting. —sub'limely *adv.*

subliminal (sʌb'lɪmɪn³l) *adj.* resulting from or relating to mental processes of which the individual is not aware: *subliminal advertising.*

sub-machine-gun *n.* a portable automatic or semiautomatic light gun.

submarine ('sʌbməˌriːn, ˌsʌbmə'riːn) *n.* **1.** a vessel, esp. a warship, capable of operating below the surface of the sea. ~*adj.* **2.** existing or located below the surface of the sea: *a submarine cable.* —**submariner** (sʌb'mærɪnə) *n.*

submerge (səb'mɜːdʒ) *vb.* **1.** to plunge, sink, or dive or cause (something) to plunge, sink, or dive below the surface of water or other liquid. **2.** to overwhelm (someone), as with work. —**sub'mersion** *n.*

submersible (səb'mɜːsɪb³l) *adj.* **1.** capable of operating under water. ~*n.* **2.** a vessel designed to operate under water.

submission (səb'mɪʃən) *n.* **1.** an act or instance of submitting. **2.** something submitted, such as a proposal. **3.** the quality or condition of being submissive.

submissive (səb'mɪsɪv) *adj.* showing quiet obedience, humility, or servility. —**sub'missively** *adv.* —**sub'missiveness** *n.*

submit (səb'mɪt) *vb.* **-mitting, -mitted. 1.** to yield to the will of another person or a superior force. **2.** to be voluntarily subjected (to analysis or treatment). **3.** to refer (something) to someone for judgment or consideration.

subnormal (sʌb'nɔːməl) *adj.* **1.** less than the normal. **2.** having a low intelligence. ~*n.* **3.** a subnormal person.

subordinate *adj.* (sə'bɔːdɪnɪt). **1.** of lesser rank or importance. ~*n.* (sə'bɔːdɪnɪt). **2.** a person or thing that is subordinate. ~*vb.* (sə'bɔːdɪˌneɪt) **3.** (usually foll. by *to*) to regard (something) as less important than another. —**sub₍ordi'nation** *n.*

subordinate clause *n. Grammar.* a clause that functions as an adjective, an adverb, or a noun rather than one that functions as a sentence in its own right.

suborn (sə'bɔːn) *vb.* to bribe or incite (a person) to commit a wrongful act.

subplot ('sʌbˌplɒt) *n.* a secondary plot in a novel, play, film, etc.

subpoena (səb'piːnə) *n.* **1.** a legal document issued by a court of law requiring a person to appear before the court at a specified time. ~*vb.* **-naing, -naed. 2.** to serve (someone) with a subpoena.

sub-post office *n.* (in Britain) a post office which is run by a sub-postmaster or sub-postmistress as a self-employed agent for the Post Office.

sub rosa ('rəʊzə) *adv.* in secret.

subroutine ('sʌbruːˌtiːn) *n.* a section of a computer program that is stored only once but can be used at several different points in the program.

subscribe (səb'skraɪb) *vb.* **1.** (usually foll. by *to*) to pay (money) as a contribution (to a fund, for a magazine, etc.), esp. at regular intervals. **2.** (foll. by *to*) to give support or approval: *to subscribe to the theory of reincarnation.* —**sub'scriber** *n.*

subscriber trunk dialling *n. Brit.* a system by which telephone users can obtain trunk calls by dialling direct without the help of an operator.

subscript ('sʌbskrɪpt) *Printing.* ~*adj.* **1.** (of a character) written or printed below the line. ~*n.* **2.** a subscript character.

subscription (səb'skrɪpʃən) *n.* **1.** a payment for consecutive issues of a publication over a specified period of time. **2.** money paid or promised, as to a charity, or the fund raised in this way. **3.** *Chiefly Brit.* the membership fees paid to a society. **4.** an advance order for a new product.

subsection ('sʌbˌsɛkʃən) *n.* any of the smaller parts into which a section may be divided.

subsequent ('sʌbsɪkwənt) *adj.* occurring after; succeeding. —**'subsequently** *adv.*

subservient (səb'sɜːvɪənt) *adj.* overeager to comply with someone else's wishes. —**sub'servience** *n.*

subset ('sʌbˌsɛt) *n.* a mathematical set contained within a larger set.

subside (səb'saɪd) *vb.* **1.** to become less loud, excited, or violent; abate. **2.** to sink to a lower level. **3.** (of the surface of the earth) to cave in; collapse. —**subsidence** (səb'saɪd³ns, 'sʌbsɪd³ns) *n.*

subsidiary (səb'sɪdɪərɪ) *adj.* **1.** of lesser importance; subordinate. ~*n., pl.* **-aries. 2.** a subsidiary person or thing. **3.** Also called: **subsidiary company.** a company which is at least half owned by another company.

subsidize *or* **-ise** ('sʌbsɪ,daɪz) *vb.* to aid or support (an industry, a person, a public service, or a venture) with a subsidy.

subsidy ('sʌbsɪdɪ) *n., pl.* **-dies.** 1. financial aid supplied by a government, for example to industry, or for public welfare. 2. any financial aid, grant, or contribution.

subsist (səb'sɪst) *vb.* (foll. by *on*) to be sustained; manage to live: *to subsist on milk.* —**sub'sistence** *n.*

subsistence farming *n.* a type of farming in which most of the produce is consumed by the farmer and his family.

subsoil ('sʌb,sɔɪl) *n.* the layer of soil beneath the surface soil.

subsonic (sʌb'sɒnɪk) *adj.* being or moving at a speed below that of sound.

substance ('sʌbstəns) *n.* 1. the basic matter of which a thing consists. 2. a specific type of matter with definite or fairly definite chemical composition: *an oily substance.* 3. the essential meaning of a speech, thought, or written article. 4. solid or meaningful quality: *an education of substance.* 5. material possessions or wealth: *a man of substance.* 6. **in substance.** with regard to the most important points.

substandard (sʌb'stændəd) *adj.* below an established or required standard.

substantial (səb'stænʃəl) *adj.* 1. of a considerable size or value: *substantial funds; a substantial reform.* 2. (of food or a meal) sufficient and nourishing. 3. solid or strong: *a substantial door.* 4. real; actual; true: *substantial evidence.* 5. of or relating to the basic material substance or aspects of a thing. —**sub'stantially** *adv.*

substantiate (səb'stænʃɪ,eɪt) *vb.* to establish (a story) as genuine. —**sub,stanti'ation** *n.*

substantive ('sʌbstəntɪv) *n.* 1. *Grammar.* a noun or pronoun used in place of a noun. ~*adj.* 2. of, relating to, containing, or being the essential element of a thing.

substitute ('sʌbstɪ,tjuːt) *vb.* 1. (often foll. by *for*) to take the place of or put (someone or something) in place of another person or thing. 2. *Chem.* to replace (an atom or group in a molecule) with (another atom or group). ~*n.* 3. a person or thing that takes the place of another, such as a player who takes the place of a team-mate. —**,substi'tution** *n.*

substitution reaction *n. Chem.* the replacing of an atom or group in a molecule by another atom or group.

substructure ('sʌb,strʌktʃə) *n.* 1. a structure that forms the basis of anything. 2. a structure that forms a foundation or framework for a building.

subsume (səb'sjuːm) *vb.* to incorporate (an idea, case, etc.) under a comprehensive or inclusive classification.

subtenant (sʌb'tɛnənt) *n.* a person who rents property from a tenant. —**sub'tenancy** *n.*

subtend (səb'tɛnd) *vb. Geom.* to be opposite (an angle or side).

subterfuge ('sʌbtə,fjuːdʒ) *n.* a trick used to conceal something, avoid an argument, etc.

subterranean (,sʌbtə'reɪnɪən) *adj.* 1. found or operating below the surface of the earth. 2. existing or operating in concealment.

subtitle ('sʌb,taɪtᵊl) *n.* 1. (*pl.*) *Films.* a written translation at the bottom of the picture in a film with foreign dialogue. 2. a secondary title given to a book or play. ~*vb.* 3. to provide a subtitle for (a book or play) or subtitles for (a film).

subtle ('sʌtᵊl) *adj.* 1. not immediately obvious. 2. delicate or highly refined: *a subtle scent.* 3. marked by or requiring mental ingenuity; discriminating. —**'subtly** *adv.*

subtlety ('sʌtᵊltɪ) *n.* 1. (*pl.* **-ties**) a fine distinction. 2. the state or quality of being subtle; delicacy.

subtract (səb'trækt) *vb.* 1. *Maths.* to take (one number or quantity) away from another. 2. to remove (a part of something) from the whole. —**subtraction** (səb'trækʃən) *n.*

subtropical (sʌb'trɒpɪkᵊl) *adj.* of the region lying between the tropics and temperate lands.

suburb ('sʌbɜːb) *n.* a residential district on the outskirts of a city or town.

suburban (sə'bɜːbᵊn) *adj.* 1. of, in, or inhabiting a suburb. 2. *Mildly disparaging.* narrow or unadventurous in outlook.

suburbanite (sə'bɜːbə,naɪt) *n.* a person who lives in a suburb.

suburbia (sə'bɜːbɪə) *n.* suburbs or the people living in them considered as an identifiable community or class in society.

subvention (səb'vɛnʃən) *n.* a grant or subsidy, for example one from a government.

subversion (səb'vɜːʃən) *n.* the act or an instance of attempting to weaken or overthrow a government or an institution.

subversive (səb'vɜːsɪv) *adj.* 1. intended or intending to weaken or overthrow a government or an institution. ~*n.* 2. a person engaged in subversive activities.

subvert (səb'vɜːt) *vb.* to bring about the downfall or ruin of (something existing by a system of law, such as a government).

subway ('sʌb,weɪ) *n.* 1. *Brit.* an underground tunnel enabling pedestrians to cross a road or railway. 2. an underground railway.

subzero (sʌb'zɪərəʊ) *adj.* lower than zero: *subzero temperatures.*

succeed (sək'siːd) *vb.* 1. to accomplish an aim. 2. to happen in the manner desired: *the plan succeeded.* 3. to do well in a specified field: *one must be ruthless to suc-ceed in business.* **4.** to come next in order after (someone or something): *three weeks of frantic activity were succeeded by a week of calm.* **5.** (often foll. by *to*) to take over (a position) from (someone): *to suc-ceed to the throne; Bush succeeded Reagan as President.* —**suc'ceeding** *adj.*

success (sək'sɛs) *n.* **1.** the favourable out-come of something attempted. **2.** the at-tainment of wealth, fame, or position. **3.** a person or thing that is successful: *her last novel was a huge success.*

successful (sək'sɛsful) *adj.* **1.** having a favourable outcome. **2.** having attained fame, wealth, or position. —**suc'cessfully** *adv.*

succession (sək'sɛʃən) *n.* **1.** a number of people or things following one another in order. **2.** the act, process, or right by which one person succeeds to the position of an-other. **3. in succession.** one after another: *three years in succession.*

successive (sək'sɛsɪv) *adj.* following an-other or others without interruption: *six successive months.* —**suc'cessively** *adv.*

successor (sək'sɛsə) *n.* a person or thing that follows another, esp. a person who takes over another's job or position.

succinct (sək'sɪŋkt) *adj.* brief and clear: *a succinct account of the events.* —**suc-'cinctly** *adv.*

succour *or U.S.* **succor** ('sʌkə) *n.* **1.** help in time of difficulty. ~*vb.* **2.** to give aid to (someone in time of difficulty).

succubus ('sʌkjubəs) *n., pl.* -**bi** (-ˌbaɪ). a female demon fabled to have sexual inter-course with sleeping men.

succulent ('sʌkjulənt) *adj.* **1.** juicy. **2.** (of plants) having thick fleshy leaves or stems. ~*n.* **3.** a plant that can exist in very dry conditions by using water stored in its fleshy tissues. —**'succulence** *n.*

succumb (sə'kʌm) *vb.* (foll. by *to*) **1.** to give way to the force of or desire for (some-thing). **2.** to die of (a disease).

such (sʌtʃ) *det.* **1.** of the sort specified or understood: *such books; such is life; rob-bers, rapists, and such.* **2.** so great; so much: *such a help.* **3. as such.** in itself or themselves: *intelligence as such can't guar-antee success.* **4. such and such.** specific, but not known or named: *at such and such a time.* **5. such as.** for example: *animals, such as tigers.* ~*adv.* **6.** extremely: *such a nice person.*

suck (sʌk) *vb.* **1.** to draw (a liquid) into the mouth throught pursed lips. **2.** to extract liquid from (a solid food): *to suck a lemon.* **3.** to draw in (fluid) as if by sucking: *plants suck moisture from the soil.* **4.** to drink milk from (a mother's breast); suckle. **5.** to take (something) into the mouth and mois-ten, dissolve, or roll it around with the tongue: *to suck one's thumb.* **6.** (often foll.

by *down, in,* etc.) to draw (a thing or person somewhere) by using irresistible force. ~*n.* **7.** a sucking.

sucker ('sʌkə) *n.* **1.** *Slang.* a person who is easily deceived or swindled. **2.** *Slang.* a person who cannot resist something: *he's a sucker for blondes.* **3.** *Zool.* a part of the body of certain animals that is used for sucking or adhering. **4.** a cup-shaped de-vice, generally made of rubber, that may be attached to articles allowing them to adhere to a surface by suction. **5.** *Bot.* a strong shoot that arises in a mature plant from a root or the base of the main stem.

suck into *vb.* to draw (someone) into (a situation) by using strong inducement or force: *he was sucked into a life of crime.*

suckle ('sʌkᵊl) *vb.* to give (a baby or young animal) milk from the breast or udder or (of a baby or young animal) to suck milk from its mother's breast or udder.

suckling ('sʌklɪŋ) *n.* a baby or young ani-mal that is still sucking milk from its moth-er's breast or udder.

suck up to *vb. Informal.* to flatter (some-one) for one's own profit.

sucrose ('suːkrəʊz, -krəʊs) *n. Chem.* sugar.

suction ('sʌkʃən) *n.* **1.** the act or process of sucking. **2.** the force produced by drawing air out of a space to make a vacuum that will suck in a substance from another space.

Sudanese (ˌsuːdᵊ'niːz) *adj.* **1.** of or relat-ing to the Sudan, in NE Africa. ~*n., pl.* -**nese.** **2.** a person from the Sudan.

sudden ('sʌdᵊn) *adj.* **1.** occurring or per-formed quickly and without warning. ~*n.* **2. all of a sudden.** without warning; unex-pectedly. —**'suddenly** *adv.* —**'sudden-ness** *n.*

sudden death *n. Sport.* an extra period of play to decide the winner of a tied competi-tion: *the first player or team to go into the lead is the winner.*

sudden infant death syndrome *n.* same as **cot death.**

sudorific (ˌsjuːdə'rɪfɪk) *adj.* **1.** causing sweating. ~*n.* **2.** a drug that causes sweating.

suds (sʌdz) *pl. n.* the bubbles on the surface of water in which soap or detergent has been dissolved; lather.

sue (suː) *vb.* **suing, sued.** to start legal proceedings (against): *they sued the sur-geon for negligence; she's going to sue for divorce.*

suede (sweɪd) *n.* a leather with a fine velvet-like surface on one side.

suet ('suːɪt) *n.* a hard fat obtained from sheep and cattle and used for making pas-try and puddings.

suffer ('sʌfə) *vb.* **1.** to undergo or be sub-jected to (pain). **2.** to be set at a disadvant-age: *this author suffers in translation.* **3.** to tolerate: *he does not suffer fools gladly.* **4. suffer from.** to be afflicted with: *he suffers from bronchitis.* —**'sufferer** *n.* —**'suffering** *n.*

sufferance (ˈsʌfərəns, ˈsʌfrəns) *n.* **on sufferance.** tolerated with reluctance: *she knew she was there on sufferance.*

suffice (səˈfaɪs) *vb.* **1.** to be adequate or satisfactory for a purpose. **2. suffice it to say** ... it is enough to say...: *suffice it to say that I missed the bus.*

sufficiency (səˈfɪʃənsɪ) *n., pl.* **-cies.** an adequate amount.

sufficient (səˈfɪʃənt) *adj.* enough to meet a need or purpose; adequate. —**sufˈficiently** *adv.*

suffix (ˈsʌfɪks) *Grammar.* ~*n.* **1.** a letter or letters added to the end of a word to form another word, such as *-s* and *-ness* in *dogs* and *softness*. ~*vb.* **2.** to add (a letter or letters) to the end of a word to form another word.

suffocate (ˈsʌfəˌkeɪt) *vb.* **1.** to kill or die through lack of oxygen, as by blockage of the air passage. **2.** to feel discomfort from heat and lack of air. —**'suffoˌcating** *adj.* —**ˌsuffoˈcation** *n.*

suffragan (ˈsʌfrəgən) *n.* a bishop subordinate to and assisting his superior archbishop.

suffrage (ˈsʌfrɪdʒ) *n.* the right to vote in public elections.

suffragette (ˌsʌfrəˈdʒɛt) *n.* (in Britain at the beginning of the 20th century) a woman who campaigned militantly for women to be given the right to vote in public elections.

suffragist (ˈsʌfrədʒɪst) *n.* (in Britain at the beginning of the 20th century) a person who campaigned for women to be given the right to vote in public elections.

suffuse (səˈfjuːz) *vb.* to spread through or over (something): *a room suffused with light.* —**suffusion** (səˈfjuːʒən) *n.*

sugar (ˈʃʊgə) *n.* **1.** a sweet-tasting carbohydrate, usually in the form of white or brown crystals, which is found in many plants and is used to sweeten food and drinks. **2.** *Informal, chiefly U.S. & Canad.* a term of affection. ~*vb.* **3.** to add sugar to (food or drink) to make it sweet. **4.** to cover with sugar: *sugared almonds.* **5. sugar the pill.** to make something unpleasant more agreeable by adding something pleasant. —**'sugared** *adj.*

sugar beet *n.* a beet cultivated for its white roots from which sugar is obtained.

sugar cane *n.* a tropical grass cultivated for its tall stout canes from which sugar is obtained.

sugaring off *n. Canad.* the boiling down of maple sap to produce sugar, traditionally a social event in early spring.

sugar loaf *n.* a large cone-shaped mass of hard refined sugar.

sugar maple *n.* a North American maple tree, grown as a source of sugar, which is extracted from the sap.

sugary (ˈʃʊgərɪ) *adj.* **1.** of, like, or containing sugar. **2.** deceptively pleasant; insincere: *a sugary smile.* —**'sugariness** *n.*

suggest (səˈdʒɛst) *vb.* **1.** to put forward (a plan or an idea) for consideration: *I suggest that we wait for Mother.* **2.** to bring (a person or thing) to the mind by the association of ideas: *that painting suggests home to me.* **3.** to give an indirect hint of: *his face always suggests his peace of mind.*

suggestible (səˈdʒɛstɪb²l) *adj.* easily influenced by ideas provided by other persons.

suggestion (səˈdʒɛstʃən) *n.* **1.** something that is suggested. **2.** a hint or indication: *a suggestion of the odour of violets.* **3.** *Psychol.* the process whereby the presentation of an idea to a receptive individual leads to the acceptance of that idea.

suggestive (səˈdʒɛstɪv) *adj.* **1.** improper or indecent: *suggestive remarks.* **2. suggestive of.** conveying a hint of.

suicidal (ˌsuːɪˈsaɪd²l) *adj.* **1.** tending towards suicide. **2.** liable to result in suicide: *a suicidal attempt.* **3.** liable to destroy one's own interests or prospects; dangerously rash.

suicide (ˈsuːɪˌsaɪd) *n.* **1.** the act or an instance of killing oneself intentionally: *she committed suicide.* **2.** a person who killed himself intentionally. **3.** the self-inflicted ruin of one's own prospects or interests: *a merger would be financial suicide.*

suit (suːt) *n.* **1.** a set of clothes of the same material designed to be worn together, usually a jacket with matching trousers or skirt. **2.** an outfit worn for a specific purpose: *a bathing suit.* **3.** any of the four types of card in a pack of playing cards: spades, hearts, diamonds, or clubs. **4.** a civil proceeding; lawsuit. **5. follow suit.** to act in the same way as someone else. ~*vb.* **6.** to be fit or appropriate for: *that dress suits your figure.* **7.** to be agreeable or acceptable to (someone). **8. suit oneself.** to do what one wants without considering other people. —**'suited** *adj.*

suitable (ˈsuːtəb²l) *adj.* appropriate; proper; fit. —**ˌsuitaˈbility** *n.* —**'suitably** *adv.*

suitcase (ˈsuːtˌkeɪs) *n.* a portable travelling case for clothing.

suite (swiːt) *n.* **1.** a set of connected rooms in a hotel. **2.** a matching set of furniture, for example two armchairs and a settee. **3.** a group of attendants or followers. **4.** *Music.* an instrumental composition consisting of several movements in the same key.

suitor (ˈsuːtə) *n.* **1.** *Old-fashioned.* a man who wants to marry a woman; wooer. **2.** *Law.* a person who starts legal proceedings against someone; plaintiff.

sulk (sʌlk) *vb.* **1.** to be silent and resentful

because of a wrong done to one: *the child sulked after being slapped.* ~*n.* **2.** (*often pl.*) a resentful or sullen mood: *he's in a sulk; he's got the sulks.*

sulky ('sʌlkı) *adj.* **sulkier, sulkiest.** moody or withdrawn through or as if through resentment. —'**sulkily** *adv.* —'**sulkiness** *n.*

sullen ('sʌlən) *adj.* unwilling to talk or be sociable; sulky; morose. —'**sullenly** *adv.* —'**sullenness** *n.*

sully ('sʌlı) *vb.* **-lying, -lied.** to ruin (someone's reputation).

sulpha *or U.S.* **sulfa drug** ('sʌlfə) *n. Pharmacol.* any of a group of sulphonamides that prevent the growth of bacteria: used to treat bacterial infections.

sulphate *or U.S.* **sulfate** ('sʌlfeɪt) *n. Chem.* a salt or ester of sulphuric acid.

sulphide *or U.S.* **sulfide** ('sʌlfaɪd) *n. Chem.* a compound of sulphur with another element.

sulphite *or U.S.* **sulfite** ('sʌlfaɪt) *n.* any salt or ester of sulphurous acid.

sulphonamide *or U.S.* **sulfonamide** (sʌl-'fɒnə,maɪd) *n. Pharmacol.* any of a class of organic compounds that prevent the growth of bacteria. An important class of sulphonamides are the sulpha drugs.

sulphur *or U.S.* **sulfur** ('sʌlfə) *n. Chem.* a light yellow, highly inflammable, nonmetallic element used in the production of sulphuric acid, in the vulcanization of rubber, and in medicine. Symbol: S —**sulphuric** *or U.S.* **sulfuric** (sʌl'fjʊərɪk) *adj.*

sulphur dioxide *n. Chem.* a strong-smelling colourless soluble gas, used in the manufacture of sulphuric acid and in the preservation of foodstuffs.

sulphureous *or U.S.* **sulfureous** (sʌl-'fjʊərɪəs) *adj.* same as **sulphurous** (sense 1).

sulphuric acid *n. Chem.* a colourless dense oily corrosive liquid used in the manufacture of fertilizers and explosives.

sulphurize, -ise, *or U.S.* **sulfurize** ('sʌlfjʊ,raɪz) *vb. Chem.* to combine with or treat (something) with sulphur or a sulphur compound.

sulphurous *or U.S.* **sulfurous** ('sʌlfərəs) *adj. Chem.* **1.** of or resembling sulphur: *a sulphurous colour.* **2.** containing sulphur, esp. with a valence of four.

sultan ('sʌltən) *n.* the sovereign of a Muslim country.

sultana (sʌl'tɑːnə) *n.* **1.** the dried fruit of a small white seedless grape. **2.** a wife, concubine, or female relative of a sultan.

sultanate ('sʌltə,neɪt) *n.* **1.** the territory ruled by a sultan. **2.** the office or rank of a sultan.

sultry ('sʌltrı) *adj.* **-trier, -triest.** **1.** (of weather or climate) very hot and humid. **2.** displaying or suggesting passion; sensual: *sultry eyes.*

sum (sʌm) *n.* **1.** the result of the addition

of numbers or quantities. **2.** one or more columns or rows of numbers to be added, subtracted, multiplied, or divided. **3.** a quantity of money: *he borrows enormous sums.* **4.** the essence or gist of a matter: *in sum.* **5.** (*modifier*) complete or final: *the sum total.* ~*vb.* **summing, summed.** **6.** See **sum up.**

summarize *or* **-ise** ('sʌmə,raɪz) *vb.* to make a summary of (something).

summary ('sʌmərı) *n., pl.* **-maries.** **1.** a brief account giving the main points of something. ~*adj.* **2.** performed quickly, without formality or attention to details: *a summary execution.* —'**summarily** *adv.*

summation (sʌ'meɪʃən) *n.* **1.** the process of working out a sum; addition. **2.** the result of such a process. **3.** a summary.

summer ('sʌmə) *n.* **1.** the warmest season of the year, between spring and autumn. **2.** a time of blossoming or of greatest happiness. —'**summery** *adj.*

summerhouse ('sʌmə,haʊs) *n.* a small building in a garden, used for shade in the summer.

summer school *n.* an academic course held during the summer.

summer solstice *n.* the time, about June 21, at which the sun is at its northernmost point in the sky.

summertime ('sʌmə,taɪm) *n.* the period or season of summer.

summing-up *n.* **1.** a review or summary of the main points of an argument, speech, or piece of writing. **2.** concluding statements made by a judge to the jury before they retire to consider their verdict.

summit ('sʌmɪt) *n.* **1.** the highest point or part of a mountain or hill. **2.** the highest possible degree or state; peak or climax: *the summit of ambition.* **3.** a meeting of chiefs of governments or other high officials.

summon ('sʌmən) *vb.* **1.** to order (someone) to come; send for (someone), esp. to attend court, by issuing a summons. **2.** to order or instruct (someone) to do something or call (someone) to something: *the bell summoned them to their work.* **3.** to convene (a meeting). **4.** (often foll. by *up*) to gather (one's strength, courage, or other quality).

summons ('sʌmənz) *n., pl.* **-monses.** **1.** a call or an order to attend a specified place at a specified time. **2.** an official order requiring a person to attend court, either to answer a charge or to give evidence. ~*vb.* **3.** to take out a summons against (a person).

sumo ('suːməʊ) *n.* the national style of wrestling of Japan, in which two contestants of great height and weight attempt to force each other out of the ring.

sump (sʌmp) *n.* **1.** a receptacle in an internal-combustion engine into which oil can drain. **2.** same as **cesspool.** **3.** *Mining.*

a hollow at the bottom of a shaft where water collects.

sumptuary ('sʌmptjʊərɪ) *adj.* controlling expenditure or extravagance.

sumptuous ('sʌmptjʊəs) *adj.* expensive or extravagant; splendid: *sumptuous costumes.*

sum up *vb.* **1.** to summarize (the main points of an argument, speech, or piece of writing). **2.** to form a quick opinion of: *I summed him up in five minutes.*

sun (sʌn) *n.* **1.** the star that is the source of heat and light for the planets in the solar system. **2.** any star around which a system of planets revolves. **3.** the heat and light received from the sun; sunshine. **4. catch the sun.** to become slightly sun-tanned. **5. under the sun.** on earth; at all: *nobody under the sun eats more than you.* ~*vb.* **sunning, sunned. 6.** to expose (oneself) to the sunshine. —'**sunless** *adj.*

Sun. Sunday.

sunbathe ('sʌnˌbeɪð) *vb.* to lie or sit in the sunshine, in order to get a suntan. —'**sunˌbather** *n.* —'**sunˌbathing** *n.*

sunbeam ('sʌnˌbiːm) *n.* a ray of sunlight.

sunburn ('sʌnˌbɜːn) *n.* painful reddening of the skin caused by overexposure to the sun. —'**sunˌburnt** *or* '**sunˌburned** *adj.*

sundae ('sʌndɪ, -deɪ) *n.* ice cream topped with a sweet sauce, nuts, whipped cream, and fruit.

Sunday ('sʌndɪ) *n.* the first day of the week and the Christian day of worship.

Sunday best *n.* one's best clothes, sometimes regarded as those most suitable for churchgoing.

Sunday school *n.* a school for the religious instruction of children on Sundays, usually held in a church.

sundial ('sʌnˌdaɪəl) *n.* a device indicating the time during the hours of sunlight by means of a pointer that casts a shadow onto a surface marked in hours.

sundown ('sʌnˌdaʊn) *n.* same as **sunset.**

sundry ('sʌndrɪ) *det.* **1.** several or various; miscellaneous. ~*pron.* **2. all and sundry.** everybody. ~*n., pl.* **-dries. 3.** (*pl.*) miscellaneous unspecified items.

sunfish ('sʌnˌfɪʃ) *n., pl.* **-fish** *or* **-fishes.** a large sea fish with a rounded body.

sunflower ('sʌnˌflaʊə) *n.* **1.** a very tall plant which has large flower heads with yellow rays. **2. sunflower seed oil.** the oil extracted from sunflower seeds, used as a salad oil and in margarine.

sung (sʌŋ) *vb.* the past participle of **sing.**

sunglasses ('sʌnˌglɑːsɪz) *pl. n.* glasses with darkened lenses that protect the eyes from the sun's glare.

sun-god *n.* the sun considered as a god.

sunk (sʌŋk) *vb.* a past tense and past participle of **sink.**

sunken ('sʌŋkən) *vb.* **1.** a past participle of **sink.** ~*adj.* **2.** unhealthily hollow: *sunken cheeks.* **3.** situated at a lower level than the surrounding or usual one: *a sunken bath.* **4.** situated under water; submerged: *sunken treasure.*

sun lamp *n.* a lamp that gives off ultra-violet rays, used for obtaining an artificial suntan or for muscular therapy.

sunlight ('sʌnlaɪt) *n.* the light that comes from the sun. —'**sunlit** *adj.*

sun lounge *or U.S.* **sun parlor** *n.* a room with large windows designed to receive as much sunlight as possible.

sunny ('sʌnɪ) *adj.* **-nier, -niest. 1.** full of or exposed to sunlight. **2.** full of good humour: *a sunny disposition.*

sunroof ('sʌnˌruːf) *n.* a panel in the roof of a car that may be opened to allow air or sunshine into the car.

sunrise ('sʌnˌraɪz) *n.* **1.** the daily appearance of the sun above the horizon. **2.** the time at which the sun rises.

sunrise industry *n.* any of the fast-developing high-technology industries, such as electronics.

sunset ('sʌnˌsɛt) *n.* **1.** the daily disappearance of the sun below the horizon. **2.** the time at which the sun sets.

sunshade ('sʌnˌʃeɪd) *n.* a device, such as a parasol or awning, used to shade people from the sun.

sunshine ('sʌnˌʃaɪn) *n.* **1.** the light and warmth from the sun. **2.** a light-hearted or ironic term of address.

sunspot ('sʌnˌspɒt) *n.* **1.** *Informal.* a sunny holiday resort. **2.** a dark cool patch on the surface of the sun.

sunstroke ('sʌnˌstrəʊk) *n.* a condition resulting from prolonged exposure to intensely hot sunlight and causing high fever and sometimes loss of consciousness.

suntan ('sʌnˌtæn) *n.* a brownish colouring of the skin caused by exposure to the sun or a sun lamp. —'**sunˌtanned** *adj.*

sup[1] (sʌp) *vb.* **supping, supped. 1.** to consume (liquid) by swallowing a little at a time. ~*n.* **2.** a sip.

sup[2] (sʌp) *vb.* **supping, supped.** *Archaic.* to have supper.

super ('suːpə) *Informal.* **1.** ~*adj.* outstanding; exceptional. ~*n.* **2.** *Austral. & N.Z. informal.* superannuation. **3.** *Austral. & N.Z. informal.* superphosphate.

super- *prefix.* used with many main words to mean: **1.** above or over: *superscript.* **2.** outstanding: *superstar.* **3.** of greater size, extent, or quality: *supermarket.*

superabundant (ˌsuːpərə'bʌndənt) *adj.* existing in very large numbers or amount. —ˌ**supera'bundance** *n.*

superannuated (ˌsuːpər'ænjʊˌeɪtɪd) *adj.* **1.** discharged with a pension, owing to age or illness. **2.** too old to be useful; obsolete.

superannuation (ˌsuːpərˌænjuˈeɪʃən) n. **a.** the amount deducted regularly from employees' incomes in a contributory pension scheme. **b.** the pension finally paid.

superb (suˈpɜːb) adj. **1.** extremely good. **2.** majestic or imposing. —**suˈperbly** adv.

Super Bowl n. American football. the championship game held annually between the best team of the American Football Conference and that of the National Football Conference.

supercharge (ˈsuːpəˌtʃɑːdʒ) vb. **1.** to increase the power of (an internal-combustion engine) with a supercharger. **2.** to charge (the atmosphere, a remark, etc.) with an excess amount of (tension, emotion, etc.). **3.** to apply pressure to (a fluid); pressurize.

supercharger (ˈsuːpəˌtʃɑːdʒə) n. a device that increases the power of an internal-combustion engine by forcing extra air into it.

supercilious (ˌsuːpəˈsɪlɪəs) adj. showing arrogant pride or scorn. —ˌsuperˈciliously adv. —ˌsuperˈciliousness n.

superconductivity (ˌsuːpəˌkɒndʌkˈtɪvɪtɪ) n. Physics. the ability of certain substances to conduct electric current with almost no resistance at very low temperatures. —ˌsuperconˈductive adj. —ˌsuperconˈductor n.

superego (ˌsuːpərˈiːgəʊ, -ˈɛgəʊ) n., pl. -gos. Psychoanal. that part of the unconscious mind that acts as a conscience.

supererogation (ˌsuːpərˌɛrəˈgeɪʃən) n. the act of doing more work than is required.

superficial (ˌsuːpəˈfɪʃəl) adj. **1.** of, near, or forming the surface: superficial bruising. **2.** without thoroughness or care: a superficial inspection. **3.** only outwardly apparent rather than genuine or actual: the similarity was merely superficial. **4.** (of a person) having no depth of character or feeling. —**superficiality** (ˌsuːpəˌfɪʃɪˈælɪtɪ) n. —ˌsuperˈficially adv.

superfluous (suːˈpɜːfluəs) adj. more than is sufficient or required. —**superˈfluity** n.

superglue (ˈsuːpəˌgluː) n. an extremely strong and quick-drying glue.

superhuman (ˌsuːpəˈhjuːmən) adj. beyond normal human ability or experience: a superhuman strength.

superimpose (ˌsuːpərɪmˈpəʊz) vb. to set or place (something) on or over something else.

superintend (ˌsuːpərɪnˈtɛnd) vb. to supervise (a person or an activity).

superintendent (ˌsuːpərɪnˈtɛndənt) n. **1.** a senior police officer. **2.** a person who directs and manages an organization or office.

superior (suːˈpɪərɪə) adj. **1.** greater in quality, usefulness, quantity, etc. **2.** of

high or extraordinary worth or merit. **3.** higher in rank or status. **4.** believing oneself to be better than others. **5.** placed higher up. **6.** Printing. (of a character) written or printed above the line. ~n. **7.** a person of greater rank or status. **8.** See **mother superior.** —**superiority** (suːˌpɪərɪˈɒrɪtɪ) n.

superlative (suːˈpɜːlətɪv) adj. **1.** of outstanding quality; supreme. **2.** Grammar. denoting the form of an adjective or adverb that expresses the highest degree of quality. ~n. **3.** the highest quality. **4.** Grammar. the superlative form of an adjective or adverb.

superman (ˈsuːpəˌmæn) n., pl. -men. any man of apparently superhuman powers.

supermarket (ˈsuːpəˌmɑːkɪt) n. a large self-service store selling food and household goods.

supernatural (ˌsuːpəˈnætʃərəl) adj. **1.** of or relating to things that cannot be explained according to natural laws. ~n. **2. the supernatural.** supernatural forces, occurrences, and beings collectively.

supernova (ˌsuːpəˈnəʊvə) n., pl. -vae (-viː) or -vas. a star that explodes, and for a few days, becomes one hundred million times brighter than the sun.

supernumerary (ˌsuːpəˈnjuːmərərɪ) adj. **1.** exceeding a regular or proper number; extra. **2.** employed as a substitute or assistant. ~n., pl. -aries. **3.** a person or thing that exceeds the required or regular number. **4.** a substitute or assistant. **5.** an actor who has no lines.

superphosphate (ˌsuːpəˈfɒsfeɪt) n. a chemical fertilizer, esp. one made by treating rock phosphate with sulphuric acid.

superpower (ˈsuːpəˌpaʊə) n. an extremely powerful state, such as the U.S.

superscript (ˈsuːpəˌskrɪpt) Printing. ~adj. **1.** (of a character) written or printed above the line. ~n. **2.** a superscript character.

supersede (ˌsuːpəˈsiːd) vb. **1.** to take the place of (something old-fashioned or less appropriate); supplant. **2.** to replace (someone) in function or office.

supersonic (ˌsuːpəˈsɒnɪk) adj. being, having, or capable of a speed greater than the speed of sound.

superstar (ˈsuːpəˌstɑː) n. an extremely popular and famous entertainer or sportsperson.

superstition (ˌsuːpəˈstɪʃən) n. **1.** irrational belief in the significance of particular omens, charms, etc. **2.** a notion, act, or ritual that derives from such belief. —ˌsuperˈstitious adj.

superstore (ˈsuːpəˌstɔː) n. a large supermarket.

superstructure (ˈsuːpəˌstrʌktʃə) n. **1.** any structure or concept erected on something else. **2.** *Naut.* any structure above the main deck of a ship.

supertanker (ˈsuːpəˌtæŋkə) *n.* a very large fast tanker.

supertax (ˈsuːpəˌtæks) *n.* an extra tax on incomes above a certain level.

supervene (ˌsuːpəˈviːn) *vb.* to occur as an unexpected development. —**supervention** (ˌsuːpəˈvɛnʃən) *n.*

supervise (ˈsuːpəˌvaɪz) *vb.* **1.** to direct or oversee the performance or operation of (an activity or a process). **2.** to watch over (people) so as to maintain order. —**supervision** (ˌsuːpəˈvɪʒən) *n.* —ˈsuper,visor *n.* —ˈsuper,visory *adj.*

supine (ˈsuːpaɪn) *adj.* lying on one's back.

supper (ˈsʌpə) *n.* a light evening meal.

supplant (səˈplɑːnt) *vb.* to take the place of (someone or something).

supple (ˈsʌpˀl) *adj.* **1.** (of a person) capable of or showing easy or graceful movement. **2.** bending easily without damage. —ˈsuppleness *n.*

supplement *n.* (ˈsʌplɪmənt). **1.** an addition designed to complete something or make up for a lack. **2.** a magazine that is inserted into a weekly newspaper. **3.** a section added to a publication to supply further information or correct errors. ~*vb.* (ˈsʌplɪˌment). **4.** to provide a supplement to (something), esp. in order make up for a lack. —ˌsuppleˈmentary *adj.*

supplementary benefit *n.* (in Britain) an earlier form of income support.

supplicant (ˈsʌplɪkənt) *n.* a person who makes a supplication.

supplication (ˌsʌplɪˈkeɪʃən) *n.* a humble request for help.

supply (səˈplaɪ) *vb.* **-plying, -plied. 1.** to provide (a person or an institution) with something required: *can you supply me with the appropriate forms?* **2.** to make available or provide (something desired or lacking): *to supply books to the library.* ~*n., pl.* **-plies. 3.** the act of providing something. **4.** an amount available for use; stock: *food supply.* **5.** (*pl.*) food and equipment needed for a campaign or trip. **6.** *Econ.* the amount of a commodity that producers are willing and able to offer for sale at a specified price: *supply and demand.* **7. a.** a person who acts as a temporary substitute. **b.** (*as modifier*): *a supply teacher.* —ˈsupplier *n.*

support (səˈpɔːt) *vb.* **1.** to carry the weight of (a thing or person). **2.** to provide the necessities of life for (a family or person). **3.** to tend to establish (a theory or statement) by providing new facts. **4.** to speak in favour of (a motion). **5.** to give practical or emotional help to (someone). **6.** to give approval to (a cause or principle). **7.** to take an active interest in and be loyal to (a particular football or other sport team). **8.**

(in a concert) to perform earlier than (the main attraction). **9.** *Films, theatre.* to play a subordinate role (to the leading actor or actress). ~*n.* **10.** the act of supporting or the condition of being supported. **11.** a thing that bears the weight of a construction. **12.** a person who gives someone practical or emotional help. **13.** the means of maintenance of a family or person. **14.** a band or entertainer not topping the bill. —supˈportive *adj.*

supporter (səˈpɔːtə) *n.* a person who supports a sports team, politician, etc.

suppose (səˈpəʊz) *vb.* **1.** to presume (something) to be true without certain knowledge: *I suppose he meant to kill her.* **2.** to consider (something) as a possible suggestion for the sake of discussion: *suppose that he wins.* **3.** (of a theory) to depend on the truth or existence of: *your policy supposes full employment.*

supposed (səˈpəʊzd, -ˈpəʊzɪd) *adj.* **1. supposed to.** expected or obliged to: *I'm supposed to be there.* **2.** presumed to be true without certain knowledge; doubtful: *the supposed advantages.* —**supposedly** (səˈpəʊzɪdlɪ) *adv.*

supposition (ˌsʌpəˈzɪʃən) *n.* **1.** an idea or a statement that is supposed. **2.** the act of supposing: *that statement is based on supposition.*

supposititous (ˌsʌpəˈzɪʃəs) *or* **supposititious** (səˌpɒzɪˈtɪʃəs) *adj.* **1.** deduced from supposition; hypothetical. **2.** substituted with intent to mislead or deceive.

suppository (səˈpɒzɪtrɪ) *n., pl.* **-ries.** *Med.* a solid medication for insertion into the vagina or rectum.

suppress (səˈprɛs) *vb.* **1.** to put an end to (something). **2.** to hold (an emotion or a response) in check; restrain: *I was obliged to suppress a smile.* **3.** to prevent circulation or publication of: *to suppress seditious pamphlets.* **4.** *Electronics.* to reduce or eliminate (interference) in a circuit. —**suppression** (səˈprɛʃən) *n.*

suppurate (ˈsʌpjʊˌreɪt) *vb. Pathol.* (of a wound or sore) to produce or leak pus.

supremacy (sʊˈprɛməsɪ) *n.* **1.** supreme power; authority. **2.** the quality or condition of being supreme.

supreme (sʊˈpriːm) *adj.* **1.** of highest status or power: *the Supreme Court.* **2.** of highest quality, importance, etc.: *supreme artistry.* **3.** greatest in degree; extreme: *supreme folly.* —suˈpremely *adv.*

supremo (sʊˈpriːməʊ) *n., pl.* **-mos.** *Brit. informal.* a person in overall authority.

sur-¹ *prefix.* over; above; beyond: *surcharge; surrealism.*

sur-² *prefix.* See **sub-**.

surcharge *n.* (ˈsɜːˌtʃɑːdʒ). **1.** a charge in addition to the usual payment or tax. **2.** an excessive sum charged, often unlawfully.

~*vb.* (sɜːˈtʃɑːdʒ, ˈsɜːˌtʃɑːdʒ). **3.** to charge (someone) an additional sum or tax. **4.** to overcharge (someone) for something.

surd (sɜːd) *Maths.* ~*n.* **1.** an irrational number. ~*adj.* **2.** of or relating to a surd.

sure (ʃʊə, ʃɔː) *adj.* **1.** free from hesitancy or uncertainty (in regard to a belief or conviction): *we are sure of the accuracy of the data; I am sure that he is lying.* **2.** (foll. by *of*) having no doubt, as of the occurrence of a future state or event: *sure of success.* **3.** reliable in indication or accuracy: *a sure sign.* **4.** not open to doubt: *sure proof.* **5.** bound to be or occur; inevitable: *victory is sure.* **6.** bound inevitably (to be or do something); certain: *she is sure to be there.* **7.** physically secure: *a sure footing.* **8. be sure.** to be careful or certain: *be sure to shut the door.* **9. for sure.** without a doubt. **10. make sure.** to make certain; ensure: *make sure the gas is turned off.* **11. sure enough.** *Informal.* in fact: *I thought I might see him and sure enough, there he was.* **12. to be sure.** it has to be acknowledged; admittedly. ~*adv.* **13.** *U.S. & Canad. informal.* without question; certainly: *it sure is hot.* ~*interj.* **14.** *U.S. & Canad. informal.* willingly; yes. —ˈsureness *n.*

sure-fire *adj. Informal.* certain to succeed; assured: *a sure-fire scheme.*

sure-footed *adj.* **1.** unlikely to fall, slip, or stumble. **2.** unlikely to make a mistake.

surely (ˈʃʊəlɪ, ˈʃɔː-) *adv.* **1.** am I not right in thinking that?; I am sure that: *surely you don't mean it?* **2.** without doubt; assuredly. **3. slowly but surely.** gradually but noticeably. ~*interj.* **4.** *Chiefly U.S. & Canad.* willingly; yes.

surety (ˈʃʊətɪ, ˈʃʊərɪtɪ) *n., pl.* **-ties. 1.** a person who takes legal responsibility for the fulfilment of another's debt or obligation. **2.** security given as a guarantee that an obligation will be met.

surf (sɜːf) *n.* **1.** foam caused by waves breaking on the shore or on a reef. ~*vb.* **2.** to take part in surfing. —ˈsurfer *n.*

surface (ˈsɜːfɪs) *n.* **1.** the outside or top of an object. **2.** the size of such an area. **3.** material covering the surface of an object. **4.** the superficial appearance as opposed to the real nature of something. **5.** *Geom.* **a.** the complete boundary of a solid figure. **b.** something that has length and breadth but no thickness. **6.** the uppermost level of the land or sea. **7. come to the surface.** to become apparent. ~*vb.* **8.** to rise to the surface of water. **9.** to give (something) a particular kind of surface. **10.** to become apparent. **11.** *Informal.* to get up out of bed.

surface tension *n. Physics.* a property of liquids, caused by molecular forces, that leads to the apparent presence of a surface film and to rising and falling in contact with solids.

surfboard (ˈsɜːfˌbɔːd) *n.* a long narrow board used in surfing.

surfeit (ˈsɜːfɪt) *n.* **1.** an excessive amount. **2.** overindulgence in eating or drinking. **3.** disgust or nausea caused by such overindulgence.

surfing (ˈsɜːfɪŋ) *n.* the sport of riding towards shore on the crest of a wave by standing or lying on a surfboard.

surge (sɜːdʒ) *n.* **1.** a sudden increase: *a surge of anger.* **2.** a strong rolling movement of the sea. **3.** a heavy rolling motion or sound: *the surge of the crowd.* ~*vb.* **4.** (of the sea) to rise or roll with a heavy swelling motion. **5.** to move forward strongly and suddenly.

surgeon (ˈsɜːdʒən) *n.* a medical doctor who specializes in surgery.

surgery (ˈsɜːdʒərɪ) *n., pl.* **-geries. 1.** medical treatment in which a person's body is cut open by a surgeon in order to treat or remove the problem part. **2.** *Brit.* a place where, or time when, a doctor or dentist can be consulted. **3.** *Brit.* a time when an MP can be consulted.

surgical (ˈsɜːdʒɪkˀl) *adj.* involving or used in surgery. —ˈsurgically *adv.*

surgical spirit *n.* methylated spirit used medically for cleaning wounds and sterilizing equipment.

surly (ˈsɜːlɪ) *adj.* **-lier, -liest.** ill-tempered and rude.

surmise (sɜːˈmaɪz) *vb.* **1.** to guess (something) from incomplete or uncertain evidence. ~*n.* **2.** a conclusion reached on the basis of incomplete or uncertain evidence.

surmount (sɜːˈmaʊnt) *vb.* **1.** to overcome (a problem). **2.** to lie on top of (something): *a steeple surmounted by a cross.* —surˈmountable *adj.*

surname (ˈsɜːˌneɪm) *n.* a family name as opposed to a Christian name.

surpass (sɜːˈpɑːs) *vb.* **1.** to be greater than (something or someone) in degree or extent. **2.** to be superior to (someone or something) in achievement or excellence.

surplice (ˈsɜːplɪs) *n.* a loose wide-sleeved knee-length garment, worn by clergymen and choristers.

surplus (ˈsɜːpləs) *n.* **1.** a quantity or amount in excess of what is required. **2.** *Accounting.* an excess of income over spending. ~*adj.* **3.** being in excess; extra: *surplus to our requirements.*

surprise (səˈpraɪz) *vb.* **1.** to cause (someone) to feel amazement or wonder. **2.** to encounter or discover (someone) unexpectedly or suddenly. **3.** to capture or attack (someone) suddenly and without warning. **4.** (foll. by *into*) to provoke (someone) to unintended action by a trick, etc. ~*n.* **5.** the act of taking someone unawares: *an element of surprise.* **6.** a sudden or unexpected event, gift, etc.: *what a pleasant* *surprise.* **7.** the feeling of being surprised; astonishment: *much to my surprise.* **8.** (*modifier*) causing surprise: *a surprise move.* **9. take someone by surprise.** to capture someone unexpectedly or catch someone unprepared. —**sur'prised** *adj.* —**sur'prising** *adj.* —**sur'prisingly** *adv.*

surrealism (sə'rɪəˌlɪzəm) *n.* (*sometimes cap.*) a movement in art and literature in the 1920s, involving the combination of images that would not normally be found together, as if in a dream. —**sur'real** *adj.* —**sur'realist** *n., adj.* —**sur,real'istic** *adj.*

surrender (sə'rɛndə) *vb.* **1.** to give (something) up to another, under pressure or on demand: *to surrender a city.* **2.** to give (something) up voluntarily to another: *he surrendered his place to a lady.* **3.** to give oneself up physically to an enemy. **4.** to allow oneself to yield to a temptation or an influence. ~*n.* **5.** the act or instance of surrendering.

surreptitious (ˌsʌrəp'tɪʃəs) *adj.* done in secret or by improper means: *a surreptitious glance at the clock.* —**ˌsurrep'titiously** *adv.*

surrogate ('sʌrəgɪt) *n.* **a.** a person or thing acting as a substitute. **b.** (*as modifier*): *a surrogate uncle.*

surrogate mother *n.* a woman who gives birth to a child on behalf of a couple who cannot have a baby themselves, usually by artificial insemination. —**surrogate motherhood** *or* **surrogacy** ('sʌrəgəsɪ) *n.*

surround (sə'raʊnd) *vb.* **1.** to encircle or enclose (something or someone). **2.** to exist around (someone or something): *the people who surround her.* ~*n.* **3.** Chiefly Brit. a border, such as the area of uncovered floor between the walls of a room and the carpet. —**sur'rounding** *adj.*

surroundings (sə'raʊndɪŋz) *pl. n.* the conditions, scenery, etc., around a person, place, or thing.

surtax ('sɜːˌtæks) *n.* an extra tax on incomes above a certain level.

surveillance (sɜː'veɪləns) *n.* close observation of a person in custody or under suspicion.

survey *vb.* (sɜː'veɪ, 'sɜːveɪ). **1.** to view or consider (something) in a comprehensive or general way: *she surveyed his handiwork.* **2.** to make a detailed map of (an area of land) by measuring or calculating distances and height. **3.** Brit. to inspect (a building) to assess its condition and value. **4.** to run a statistical survey on the incomes, opinions, etc. (of a group of people). ~*n.* ('sɜːveɪ). **5.** a detailed investigation of the incomes, opinions, etc., of a group of people. **6.** the act of making a detailed map of an area of land by measuring or calculating distance and height. **7.** Brit. an inspection of a building to assess its condition and value. —**sur'veying** *n.* —**sur'veyor** *n.*

survival (sə'vaɪv°l) *n.* **1. a.** the condition of having survived something. **b.** (*as modifier*): *survival kit.* **2.** a person or thing that survives, such as a custom.

survive (sə'vaɪv) *vb.* **1.** to live after the death of (another). **2.** to continue in existence or use after (a passage of time or a difficult or dangerous experience). —**sur'vivor** *n.*

susceptibility (səˌsɛptə'bɪlɪtɪ) *n., pl.* **-ties.** **1.** the quality or condition of being susceptible to something. **2.** (*pl.*) emotional feelings.

susceptible (sə'sɛptəb°l) *adj.* **1. susceptible to. a.** yielding readily to: *susceptible to control.* **b.** liable to be afflicted by: *susceptible to colds.* **2.** easily impressed emotionally.

sushi ('suːʃɪ) *n.* a Japanese dish consisting of small cakes of cold rice with a topping, esp. of raw fish.

suspect *vb.* (sə'spɛkt). **1.** to believe (someone) guilty of a specified offence without proof. **2.** to think (something) false or questionable: *she suspected his sincerity.* **3.** to believe (something) to be the case; think probable: *I suspect they are planning a surprise party; the police suspect fraud.* ~*n.* ('sʌspɛkt). **4.** a person who is believed guilty of a specified offence. ~*adj.* ('sʌspɛkt). **5.** causing suspicion.

suspend (sə'spɛnd) *vb.* **1.** to hang (something) from a high place. **2.** to cause (something) to remain floating or hanging: *a cloud of smoke was suspended over the town.* **3.** to cause (something) to cease temporarily: *to suspend hostilities.* **4.** to remove (someone) temporarily from a job or position, usually as a punishment.

suspended animation *n.* a temporary stoppage of the vital functions, as by freezing an animal.

suspended sentence *n.* a sentence of imprisonment that is not served by an offender unless he commits a further offence during a specified time.

suspender belt *n.* a belt with suspenders hanging from it for holding up women's stockings.

suspenders (sə'spɛndəz) *pl. n.* **1.** Brit. **a.** elastic straps attached to a belt or corset, with fasteners for holding up women's stockings. **b.** similar fasteners attached to garters for holding up men's socks. **2.** U.S. & Canad. braces.

suspense (sə'spɛns) *n.* **1.** mental uncertainty; anxiety: *their father's illness kept them in a state of suspense.* **2.** excitement felt at the approach of the climax of a book, film, or play: *a play of terrifying suspense.* —**sus'penseful** *adj.*

suspension (sə'spɛnʃən) *n.* **1.** an interruption or temporary cancellation: *the suspen-*

sion of a law. **2.** temporary removal from a job or position, usually as a punishment. **3.** the act of suspending or the state of being suspended. **4.** a system of springs and shock absorbers that supports the body of a vehicle. **5.** a device or structure, usually a wire or spring, that suspends or supports something, such as the pendulum of a clock. **6.** *Chem.* a mixture in which fine solid or liquid particles are suspended in a fluid.

suspension bridge *n.* a bridge suspended from cables or chains that hang between two towers and are anchored at both ends.

suspicion (sə'spɪʃən) *n.* **1.** the act or an instance of suspecting; belief without sure proof that something is wrong. **2.** a feeling of mistrust. **3.** a slight trace: *the least suspicion of danger.* **4. above suspicion.** not suspected of any wrongdoing, through having an unblemished reputation. **5. under suspicion.** suspected of wrongdoing.

suspicious (sə'spɪʃəs) *adj.* **1.** arousing suspicion; questionable: *suspicious circumstances.* **2.** suspecting or inclined to suspect something wrong: *a suspicious nature.* —**sus'piciously** *adv.*

suss out (sʌs) *vb. Brit. & N.Z. slang.* to work out (a situation or a person's character), using one's intuition.

sustain (sə'steɪn) *vb.* **1.** to suffer (an injury or loss): *to sustain a broken arm.* **2.** to maintain or prolong: *to sustain a discussion.* **3.** to support (something) physically from below. **4.** to keep up the vitality or courage of (someone): *a cup of coffee to sustain you; her faith sustains her.* **5.** to affirm the justice or validity of: *to sustain a decision.* —**sus'tained** *adj.*

sustenance ('sʌstənəns) *n.* means of maintaining health or life; nourishment.

suture ('suːtʃə) *n. Surgery.* a stitch made with catgut or silk thread, to join the edges of a wound together.

suzerain ('suːzə,reɪn) *n.* **1.** a state or sovereign that has some degree of control over a dependent state. **2.** (formerly) a person who had power over many people. —**suzerainty** ('suːzərəntɪ) *n.*

svelte (svɛlt, sfɛlt) *adj.* attractively or gracefully slim; slender.

SW **1.** southwest(ern). **2.** short wave.

swab (swɒb) *n.* **1.** *Med.* a small piece of cotton wool used for applying medication or cleansing a wound. ~*vb.* **swabbing, swabbed.** **2.** to clean or medicate (a wound) with a swab. **3.** to clean (the deck of a ship) with a mop.

swaddle ('swɒd'l) *vb.* to wrap (a baby) in swaddling clothes.

swaddling clothes *pl. n.* long strips of cloth formerly wrapped round a newborn baby.

swag (swæg) *n.* **1.** *Slang.* stolen property.

2. *Austral. & N.Z. informal.* a swagman's pack containing personal belongings.

swagger ('swægə) *vb.* **1.** to walk or behave in an arrogant manner. ~*n.* **2.** an arrogant walk or manner.

swagger stick *n.* a short cane carried by army officers.

swagman ('swæg,mæn, -mən) *n., pl.* -**men.** *Austral. & N.Z. informal.* a tramp who carries his possessions on his back.

Swahili (swɑː'hiːlɪ) *n.* a language of E Africa that is an official language of Kenya and Tanzania.

swain (sweɪn) *n. Archaic or poetic.* **1.** a male lover or admirer. **2.** a country youth.

swallow[1] ('swɒləʊ) *vb.* **1.** to pass (food, drink, etc.) through the mouth and gullet to the stomach. **2.** *Informal.* to believe (something) trustingly: *he will never swallow such an excuse.* **3.** not to show: *to swallow one's disappointment.* **4.** to put up with (an insult) without retaliation. **5.** to make a gulping movement in the throat, as when nervous. **6. be swallowed up.** to be taken into and made a part of something: *he was swallowed up by the crowd.* ~*n.* **7.** the act of swallowing. **8.** the amount swallowed at any single time; mouthful.

swallow[2] ('swɒləʊ) *n.* a songbird with long pointed wings and a forked tail.

swallow dive *n.* a dive in which the diver keeps his legs straight and his arms outstretched while in the air, finally entering the water headfirst.

swallowtail ('swɒləʊ,teɪl) *n.* **1.** a butterfly with a long tail-like part on each hind wing. **2.** the forked tail of a swallow or similar bird.

swam (swæm) *vb.* the past tense of **swim.**

swami ('swɑːmɪ) *n., pl.* -**mies** *or* -**mis.** a Hindu religious teacher.

swamp (swɒmp) *n.* **1.** an area of permanently waterlogged ground. ~*vb.* **2.** *Naut.* to cause (a boat) to sink or fill with water. **3.** to overburden or overwhelm (a person or place), for example with excess work or great numbers of people. —**'swampy** *adj.*

swan (swɒn) *n.* **1.** a large, usually white, water bird with a long neck. ~*vb.* **swanning, swanned.** **2.** (foll. by *around* or *about*) *Informal.* to wander about idly.

swank (swæŋk) *Informal.* ~*vb.* **1.** to show off or boast. ~*n.* **2.** showing off or boasting. —**'swanky** *adj.*

swan song *n.* the last performance, publication, etc., of a person before retirement or death.

swap *or* **swop** (swɒp) *vb.* **swapping, swapped** *or* **swopping, swopped.** **1.** to exchange (something) for something else. ~*n.* **2.** an exchange.

SWAPO *or* **Swapo** ('swɑːpəʊ) South-West Africa People's Organization.

sward (swɔːd) *n.* a stretch of turf or grass.

swarm[1] (swɔːm) n. **1.** a group of bees, led by a queen, that has left the hive to make a new home. **2.** a large mass of insects or other small animals. **3.** a moving mass of people. ~vb. **4.** to move in a swarm. **5.** to be overrun: *swarming with rats.*

swarm[2] (swɔːm) vb. (foll. by *up*) to climb (a ladder or rope) by gripping it with the hands and feet: *the boys swarmed up the rigging.*

swarthy (ˈswɔːðɪ) adj. **swarthier, swarthiest.** dark-complexioned.

swash (swɒʃ) n. the rush of water up a beach following each break of the waves.

swashbuckler (ˈswɒʃˌbʌklə) n. a daredevil adventurer, esp. in period films. —ˈswash-ˌbuckling adj.

swastika (ˈswɒstɪkə) n. **1.** a primitive religious symbol in the shape of a Greek cross with the ends of the arms bent at right angles. **2.** this symbol with clockwise arms as the emblem of Nazi Germany.

swat (swɒt) vb. **swatting, swatted. 1.** to hit sharply: *to swat a fly.* ~n. **2.** a sharp blow.

swatch (swɒtʃ) n. **1.** a sample of cloth. **2.** a collection of such samples.

swath (swɔːθ) or **swathe** (sweɪð) n., pl. **swaths** (swɔːðz) or **swathes. 1.** the width of one sweep of a scythe or of the blade of a mowing machine. **2.** the strip cut in one such sweep. **3.** the quantity of cut crops left in one such sweep. **4.** a long narrow strip of land.

swathe (sweɪð) vb. **1.** to wrap a bandage, garment, or piece of cloth around (a person or part of the body). ~n. **2.** a bandage or wrapping. **3.** same as **swath.**

sway (sweɪ) vb. **1.** to swing to and fro: *the door swayed in the wind.* **2.** to lean to one side and then the other: *sway in time to the music.* **3.** waver between two or more opinions. **4.** to influence (someone) in his opinion or judgment. ~n. **5.** power or influence. **6.** a swinging or leaning movement. **7. hold sway.** to have power or influence.

swear (sweə) vb. **swearing, swore, sworn. 1.** to blaspheme or use swearwords. **2.** to promise solemnly on oath; vow: *he swore he would never be unfaithful again.* **3.** (foll. by *by*) to have complete confidence in (something). **4.** to state (something) with great earnestness: *I swear I saw a mouse.* **5.** to give evidence on oath in a lawcourt.

swear in vb. to make (someone) take an oath when taking up an official position or entering the witness box to give evidence in court: *to be sworn in as president.*

swear off vb. to promise to give up: *to swear off drink.*

swearword (ˈsweəˌwɜːd) n. a word considered obscene or blasphemous.

sweat (swɛt) n. **1.** the salty liquid that comes out of the pores of one's skin during strenuous activity in excessive heat or when nervous or afraid. **2.** the state or condition of sweating: *he broke into a sweat.* **3.** Slang. drudgery or hard labour: *mowing lawns is a real sweat!* **4. in a sweat.** Informal. in a state of worry. **5. no sweat.** Slang. no problem. ~vb. **sweating; sweat or sweated. 6.** to have sweat come through the pores of one's skin, as a result of strenuous activity, excessive heat, nervousness, or fear. **7.** Informal. to suffer anxiety or distress. **8. sweat blood.** Informal. **a.** to work very hard. **b.** to be filled with anxiety. ~See also **sweats.** —ˈsweaty adj.

sweatband (ˈswɛtˌbænd) n. a piece of cloth tied around the forehead or around the wrist to absorb sweat, for example in sports.

sweater (ˈswɛtə) n. a warm knitted garment covering the upper part of the body.

sweat off vb. Informal. to get rid of (weight) by strenuous exercise.

sweat out vb. **sweat it out.** Informal. to endure hardships for a time.

sweats (swɛts) pl. n. sweat shirts and sweat-suit trousers collectively.

sweat shirt n. a long-sleeved casual top made of knitted cotton or cotton mixture, brushed on the reverse side.

sweatshop (ˈswɛtˌʃɒp) n. a workshop where employees work long hours in poor conditions for low pay.

sweat suit n. a suit worn by athletes for training, comprising a sweat shirt and trousers made of the same material.

swede (swiːd) n. a round root vegetable with a purplish-brown skin and yellow flesh.

Swede (swiːd) n. a person from Sweden.

Swedish (ˈswiːdɪʃ) adj. **1.** relating to Sweden, its people, or their language. ~n. **2.** the official language of Sweden.

sweep (swiːp) vb. **sweeping, swept. 1.** to clean (a floor or chimney) with a brush. **2.** (often foll. by *up*) to remove or collect (dirt or rubbish) with a brush. **3.** to move smoothly and quickly: *cars swept along the road.* **4.** to move in a proud or dignified fashion: *she swept past.* **5.** to spread rapidly across or through (a place): *the news swept through the town.* **6.** to direct (one's gaze, line of fire, etc.) over (a place). **7.** (foll. by *away* or *off*) to overwhelm (someone) emotionally: *she was swept away by his charm.* **8.** to brush or lightly touch (a surface): *the dress swept along the ground.* **9.** (often foll. by *away*) to convey, clear, or abolish (something), esp. with strong or continuous movements: *the sea swept the sandcastle away; secondary modern schools were swept away.* **10.** to stretch out gracefully or majestically, esp. in a wide circle: *the plains sweep down to the sea.* **11.** to win overwhelmingly in an election: *Labour* *swept the country.* **12. sweep the board.** to win every event or prize in a contest. ~*n.* **13.** the act or an instance of sweeping. **14.** a swift or steady movement: *with a sweep of the hand.* **15.** a wide expanse: *the sweep of the plains.* **16.** any curving line or contour, such as a driveway. **17.** short for **sweepstake. 18.** *Chiefly Brit.* same as **chimney sweep. 19. make a clean sweep.** to win an overwhelming victory.

sweeper ('swiːpə) *n.* **1.** a device for sweeping carpets. **2.** *Informal, soccer.* a defensive player usually positioned in front of the goalkeeper.

sweeping ('swiːpɪŋ) *adj.* **1.** comprehensive and wide-ranging: *sweeping reforms.* **2.** indiscriminate or without reservations: *sweeping statements.* **3.** decisive or overwhelming: *a sweeping victory.* **4.** taking in a wide area: *a sweeping glance.*

sweepstake ('swiːpˌsteɪk) *or esp. U.S.* **sweepstakes** *n.* **1.** a lottery in which the stakes of the participants make up the prize. **2.** a horse race involving such a lottery.

sweet (swiːt) *adj.* **1.** having a taste like that of sugar. **2.** agreeable to the senses or the mind: *sweet music.* **3.** having pleasant manners; kind and gentle: *a sweet child.* **4.** (of wine) having a high sugar content; not dry. **5.** fresh, clear, and clean: *sweet water; sweet air.* **6. sweet on someone.** fond of or infatuated with someone. ~*n.* **7.** *Brit.* any of numerous kinds of confectionery consisting wholly or partly of sugar. **8.** *Brit.* a dessert. —'**sweetly** *adv.* —'**sweetness** *n.*

sweet-and-sour *adj.* (of food) cooked in a sauce made from sugar and vinegar and other ingredients.

sweetbread ('swiːtˌbrɛd) *n.* the pancreas of an animal, used for food.

sweetbrier ('swiːtˌbraɪə) *n.* a wild rose with sweet-smelling leaves and pink flowers.

sweet corn *n.* **1.** a kind of maize whose kernels are rich in sugar and eaten as a vegetable when young. **2.** the sweet kernels removed from the maize cob, cooked as a vegetable.

sweeten ('swiːtᵊn) *vb.* **1.** to make (food or drink) sweet or sweeter. **2.** to be nice to (someone) in order to ensure cooperation. **3.** to make (an offer or a proposal) more agreeable.

sweetener ('swiːtᵊnə) *n.* **1.** a sweetening agent that does not contain sugar. **2.** *Slang.* a bribe.

sweetheart ('swiːtˌhɑːt) *n.* **1.** one's boyfriend or girlfriend. **2.** *Informal.* a lovable, generous, or obliging person: *your father is an old sweetheart.* **3.** a term of endearment.

sweetie ('swiːtɪ) *n. Informal.* **1.** a term of endearment. **2.** *Brit.* same as **sweet** (sense

7). **3.** *Chiefly Brit.* a lovable, generous, or obliging person.

sweetmeat ('swiːtˌmiːt) *n.* a sweetened delicacy, such as a sweet, cake, or pastry.

sweet pea *n.* a climbing plant widely cultivated for its sweet-smelling pastel-coloured flowers.

sweet pepper *n.* the large bell-shaped fruits of the pepper plant, which is eaten unripe (**green pepper**) or ripe (**red pepper**) as a vegetable.

sweet potato *n.* a root vegetable, grown in the tropics, with pinkish-brown skin and yellow flesh.

sweet-talk *Informal.* ~*vb.* **1.** to coax (someone) by flattery: *he sweet-talked me into making dinner.* ~*n.* **sweet talk. 2.** flattery; coaxing.

sweet tooth *n.* a strong liking for sweet foods.

sweet william ('wɪljəm) *n.* a garden plant with clusters of white, pink, red, or purple flowers.

swell (swɛl) *vb.* **swelling, swelled; swollen** *or* **swelled. 1.** to grow or cause (something) to grow in size, as a result of injury or infection or by being filled with air or liquid: *her finger swelled up; rice swells when it is boiled.* **2.** to grow or cause (something) to grow in numbers, amount, intensity, or degree: *the party is swelling with new recruits.* **3.** to puff or be puffed up with pride or another emotion. **4.** (of the seas) to rise in waves. **5.** (of a sound) to become gradually louder and then die away. ~*n.* **6.** the waving movement of the surface of the open sea. **7.** an increase in size, numbers, amount, or degree. **8.** a bulge. **9.** *Informal.* a person who is very fashionably dressed or of high social standing. **10.** *Music.* an increase in sound followed by an immediate dying away. ~*adj.* **11.** *Slang, chiefly U.S.* excellent; first-class.

swelling ('swɛlɪŋ) *n.* an enlargement of a part of the body as the result of injury or infection.

swelter ('swɛltə) *vb.* **1.** to suffer under extreme heat. ~*n.* **2.** a sweltering condition: *I'm in a swelter.*

sweltering ('swɛltərɪŋ) *adj.* uncomfortably hot: *a sweltering day.*

swept (swɛpt) *vb.* past of **sweep.**

swerve (swɜːv) *vb.* **1.** to turn aside from a course sharply or suddenly. ~*n.* **2.** the act of swerving.

swift (swɪft) *adj.* **1.** moving or able to move quickly; fast. **2.** occurring or performed quickly or suddenly: *a swift exit.* **3. swift to.** prompt to (do something): *swift to take revenge.* ~*n.* **4.** a small fast-flying insect-eating bird with long wings. —'**swiftly** *adv.* —'**swiftness** *n.*

swig (swɪg) *Informal.* ~*n.* **1.** a large swallow or deep drink, esp. from a bottle. ~*vb.*

swigging, swigged. 2. to drink (some liquid) in large swallows, esp. from a bottle.

swill (swɪl) vb. **1.** to drink large quantities of (an alcoholic drink). **2.** (often foll. by *out*) *Chiefly Brit.* to rinse (something) in large amounts of water. ~n. **3.** wet food for pigs, consisting of kitchen waste, skim milk, etc. **4.** a deep drink, esp. of beer.

swim (swɪm) vb. **swimming, swam, swum. 1.** to move along in water by means of movements of the arms and legs, or (in the case of fish) tail and fins. **2.** to cover (a distance or stretch of water) in this way: *the youngest person to swim the Channel.* **3.** to float on a liquid: *flies swimming on the milk.* **4.** to reel or seem to reel: *my head swam; the room swam around me.* **5.** (often foll. by *in* or *with*) to be covered or flooded with water or other liquid. ~n. **6.** the act, an instance, or a period of swimming. **7. in the swim.** *Informal.* fashionable or active in social or political activities. —'**swimmer** n. —'**swimming** n.

swimming bath n. an indoor swimming pool.

swimming costume or **bathing costume** n. *Chiefly Brit.* same as **swimsuit.**

swimmingly ('swɪmɪŋlɪ) adv. successfully, effortlessly, or well: *the party went swimmingly.*

swimming pool n. an artificial pool for swimming in.

swimsuit ('swɪm,suːt) n. a woman's swimming garment that leaves the arms and legs bare.

swindle ('swɪndᵊl) vb. **1.** to cheat (someone) out of money. **2.** to obtain (money) from someone by fraud. ~n. **3.** an instance of cheating someone out of money. —'**swindler** n.

swine (swaɪn) n. **1.** a contemptible person. **2.** (pl. **swine**) same as **pig.** —'**swinish** adj.

swing (swɪŋ) vb. **swinging, swung. 1.** to move rhythmically to and fro; sway. **2.** to walk with a relaxed and swaying motion. **3.** to pivot or cause (something) to pivot, as on a hinge. **4.** to move in a curve: *the car swung around the bend.* **5.** to hang so as to be able to turn freely. **6.** *Slang.* to be hanged: *he'll swing for it.* **7.** to alter one's opinion, attitude, etc., in a sudden or extreme way. **8.** *Informal.* to manipulate successfully: *I hope he can swing the deal.* **9.** (often foll. by *at*) to hit out with a sweeping motion. **10.** to play (music) in the style of swing. **11.** *Slang.* to be lively and modern. ~n. **12.** the act of swinging. **13.** a sweeping stroke or punch. **14.** a suspended seat on which a person may swing back and forth. **15.** popular dance music played by big bands in the 1930s. **16.** *Informal.* the normal round or pace: *it's hard to get back into the swing of things after a holiday.* **17.** a sudden or extreme change, for example in some business activity or voting pat-

tern. **18. go with a swing.** to go well; be successful: *the party went with a swing.* **19. in full swing.** at the height of activity.

swingboat ('swɪŋ,bəʊt) n. a boat-shaped carriage for swinging in at a fairground.

swing bridge n. a bridge that can be swung open to let ships pass through.

swingeing ('swɪndʒɪŋ) adj. *Chiefly Brit.* punishing; severe: *a swingeing rent increase.*

swipe (swaɪp) vb. **1.** (usually foll. by *at*) *Informal.* to try to hit (someone or something) with a sweeping blow. **2.** *Slang.* to steal (something). ~n. **3.** *Informal.* a hard blow.

swirl (swɜːl) vb. **1.** to turn in a twisting spinning fashion. ~n. **2.** a whirling or spinning motion. **3.** a twisting shape. —'**swirling** adj.

swish (swɪʃ) vb. **1.** to move with or cause (something) to make a whistling or hissing sound. ~n. **2.** a hissing or rustling sound or movement. ~adj. **3.** *Informal, chiefly Brit.* fashionable; smart.

Swiss (swɪs) adj. **1.** relating to Switzerland or its people. ~n., pl. **Swiss. 2.** a person from Switzerland.

swiss roll n. a sponge cake spread with jam or cream and rolled up.

switch (swɪtʃ) n. **1.** a mechanical, electrical, or electronic device for opening or closing a circuit. **2.** a sudden swift change. **3.** an exchange or swap. **4.** a flexible rod or twig, used for punishment. **5.** *U.S. & Canad.* a pair of movable rails for diverting moving trains from one track to another. ~vb. **6.** to change swiftly and suddenly. **7.** to exchange (places); replace (something by something else). **8.** *Chiefly U.S. & Canad.* to transfer (rolling stock) from one railway track to another. **9.** See **switch off, switch on.**

switchback ('swɪtʃ,bæk) n. a steep mountain road, railway, or track with very sharp bends.

switchboard ('swɪtʃ,bɔːd) n. an installation in a telephone exchange or office building where telephone calls are connected.

switch off vb. **1.** to cause (a device) to stop operating by moving a switch, knob, or lever: *he switched the lamp off.* **2.** *Informal.* to become bored and stop paying attention: *when the conversation turned to football I switched off.*

switch on vb. **1.** to cause (a device) to operate by moving a switch, knob, or lever. **2.** *Informal.* to produce (charm, tears, or a smile) suddenly or automatically.

swither ('swɪðə) *Scot.* ~vb. **1.** to hesitate; be perplexed. ~n. **2.** hesitation; perplexity; agitation.

swivel ('swɪvᵊl) n. **1.** a coupling device which allows an attached object to turn freely. ~*vb*. **-elling, -elled** or U.S. **-eling, -eled. 2.** to turn or swing as if on a pivot.

swivel chair *n*. a chair, whose seat is joined to the legs by a swivel, enabling it to be spun round.

swizz (swɪz) *n. Brit. informal.* a swindle or disappointment.

swizzle stick ('swɪz²l) *n*. a small stick used to stir cocktails.

swollen ('swəʊlən) *vb*. **1.** a past participle of **swell.** ~*adj*. **2.** enlarged by swelling.

swoon (swuːn) *vb*. **1.** *Literary.* to faint. **2.** to become ecstatic: *all the girls were swooning over the new history teacher.* ~*n*. **3.** *Literary.* a faint. —'**swooning** *adj*.

swoop (swuːp) *vb*. **1.** (usually foll. by *down, on,* or *upon*) to sweep or pounce suddenly. ~*n*. **2.** the act of swooping.

swoosh (swʊʃ) *vb*. **1.** to make a swirling or rustling sound when moving or pouring out. ~*n*. **2.** a swirling or rustling sound or movement.

swop (swɒp) *vb*. **swopping, swopped,** *n*. same as **swap.**

sword (sɔːd) *n*. **1.** a weapon with a long blade. **2. the sword. a.** military power. **b.** death; destruction: *to be put to the sword.*

sword dance *n*. a dance in which the performer dances over swords on the ground.

swordfish ('sɔːd₁fɪʃ) *n., pl.* **-fish** or **-fishes.** a large fish with a very long upper jaw.

Sword of Damocles ('dæmə₁kliːz) *n*. a disaster that is about to take place.

swordplay ('sɔːd₁pleɪ) *n*. the action or art of fighting with a sword.

swordsman ('sɔːdzmən) *n., pl.* **-men.** a person who is skilled in the use of a sword. —'**swordsmanship** *n*.

swordstick ('sɔːd₁stɪk) *n*. a hollow walking stick that contains a short sword.

swore (swɔː) *vb*. the past tense of **swear.**

sworn (swɔːn) *vb*. **1.** the past participle of **swear.** ~*adj*. **2.** bound or pledged by or as if by an oath: *sworn enemies.*

swot[1] (swɒt) *Brit. informal.* ~*vb*. **swotting, swotted. 1.** (often foll. by *up*) to study (a subject) very hard, as for an examination; cram. ~*n*. **2.** a person who works or studies hard.

swot[2] (swɒt) *vb*. **swotting, swotted,** *n*. same as **swat.**

swum (swʌm) *vb*. the past participle of **swim.**

swung (swʌŋ) *vb*. past of **swing.**

sybarite ('sɪbə₁raɪt) *n*. **1.** a person devoted to luxury and pleasure. ~*adj*. **2.** luxurious; sensuous. —**sybaritic** (₁sɪbə'rɪtɪk) *adj*.

sycamore ('sɪkə₁mɔː) *n*. **1.** a tree with five-pointed leaves and two-winged fruits. **2.** U.S. & Canad. an American plane tree.

sycophant ('sɪkəfənt) *n*. a person who uses flattery to win favour from people with

power or influence. —'**sycophancy** *n*. —**sycophantic** (₁sɪkə'fæntɪk) *adj*.

syllabic (sɪ'læbɪk) *adj*. of or relating to syllables.

syllabify (sɪ'læbɪ₁faɪ) *vb*. **-fying, -fied.** to divide (a word) into syllables. —**syl₁labifi-'cation** *n*.

syllable ('sɪləb²l) *n*. **1.** a part of a word which is pronounced as a unit, which contains a single vowel sound, and which may or may not contain consonants: for example, "paper" has two syllables. **2.** the least mention: *don't breathe a syllable of it.* **3. in words of one syllable.** simply; bluntly.

syllabub ('sɪlə₁bʌb) *n. Brit.* a dessert made from milk or cream beaten with sugar, wine, and lemon juice.

syllabus ('sɪləbəs) *n., pl.* **-buses** or **-bi** (-₁baɪ). *Brit.* **a.** the subjects studied for a particular course. **b.** a list of these subjects.

syllogism ('sɪlə₁dʒɪzəm) *n*. a form of reasoning consisting of two premises and a conclusion, for example *some temples are in ruins; all ruins are fascinating; so some temples are fascinating.* —₁**syllo'gistic** *adj*.

sylph (sɪlf) *n*. **1.** a slender graceful girl or young woman. **2.** an imaginary being supposed to inhabit the air. —'**sylph₁like** *adj*.

sylvan or **silvan** ('sɪlvən) *adj. Chiefly poetic.* of or consisting of woods or forests.

symbiosis (₁sɪmbɪ'əʊsɪs) *n*. **1.** *Biol.* a close association of two animals or plants of different species. **2.** a similar relationship between persons or groups. —**symbiotic** (₁sɪmbɪ'ɒtɪk) *adj*.

symbol ('sɪmb²l) *n*. **1.** something that represents or stands for something else, usually a material object used to represent something abstract. **2.** a letter, figure, or sign used in mathematics, music, etc., to represent a quantity, operation, function, etc.

symbolic (sɪm'bɒlɪk) *adj*. **1.** of or relating to a symbol or symbols. **2.** being a symbol of something. —**sym'bolically** *adv*.

symbolism ('sɪmbə₁lɪzəm) *n*. **1.** the representation of something by the use of symbols. **2.** an art movement involving the use of symbols to express mystical or abstract ideas.

symbolize or **-ise** ('sɪmbə₁laɪz) *vb*. to be a symbol of (something). —₁**symboli'zation** or **-i'sation** *n*.

symmetry ('sɪmɪtrɪ) *n., pl.* **-tries. 1.** the state of having two halves that are mirror images of each other. **2.** beauty resulting from a proportionate arrangement of parts. —**symmetrical** (sɪ'mɛtrɪk²l) *adj*. —**sym'metrically** *adv*.

sympathetic (₁sɪmpə'θɛtɪk) *adj*. **1.** feeling or showing sympathy; understanding. **2.** likeable; appealing: *a sympathetic character.* **3. sympathetic to.** showing agreement with or favour towards: *sympathetic to the cause.* —ˌsympaˈthetically *adv.*

sympathize *or* **-ise** (ˈsɪmpəˌθaɪz) *vb.* (foll. by *with*) **1.** to feel or express sympathy for: *he sympathized with my troubles.* **2.** to agree with or support: *she sympathized with the miners' strike.* —ˈsympaˌthizer *or* **-iser** *n.*

sympathy (ˈsɪmpəθɪ) *n., pl.* **-thies. 1.** the sharing of someone's sorrow or anguish; compassion. **2.** agreement with someone's feelings or interests: *I found myself in sympathy with the hero's wife.* **3.** mutual affection or understanding arising from a sympathetic relationship. **4.** feelings of loyalty or support for an idea or a cause: *his sympathies lay with the Confederates.*

symphony (ˈsɪmfənɪ) *n., pl.* **-nies. 1.** a large-scale orchestral composition with several movements. **2.** an orchestral movement in a vocal work such as an oratorio. **3.** short for **symphony orchestra. 4.** anything that has a pleasing arrangement of colours or shapes: *she was a symphony in black and gold.* —**symphonic** (sɪmˈfɒnɪk) *adj.*

symphony orchestra *n. Music.* a large orchestra that performs symphonies.

symposium (sɪmˈpəʊzɪəm) *n., pl.* **-siums** *or* **-sia** (-zɪə). **1.** a conference for the discussion of an academic topic or social problem. **2.** a collection of essays on a particular subject.

symptom (ˈsɪmptəm) *n.* **1.** *Med.* an indication of a disease noticed by a patient. **2.** anything that is taken as an indication that something is wrong: *a symptom of a decline in moral standards.* —ˌsymptoˈmatic *adj.*

synagogue (ˈsɪnəˌɡɒɡ) *n.* a building for Jewish religious services and religious instruction.

sync *or* **synch** (sɪŋk) *Films, television, computers, informal.* ~*vb.* **1.** to synchronize. ~*n.* **2.** synchronization: *the film is out of sync.*

synchromesh (ˈsɪŋkrəʊˌmɛʃ) *adj.* **1.** (of a gearbox) having a system of clutches that synchronizes the speeds of the gearwheels before engagement. ~*n.* **2.** a gear system having these features.

synchronism (ˈsɪŋkrəˌnɪzəm) *n.* the quality or condition of being synchronous.

synchronize *or* **-ise** (ˈsɪŋkrəˌnaɪz) *vb.* **1.** (of two or more people) to perform (an action) at the same time: *synchronized swimming.* **2.** to cause (two or more clocks or watches) to indicate the same time. **3.** *Films.* to match (the soundtrack and the action of a film) precisely. —ˌsynchroniˈzation *or* **-iˈsation** *n.*

synchronous (ˈsɪŋkrənəs) *adj.* occurring at the same time and rate.

syncline (ˈsɪŋklaɪn) *n. Geol.* a downward fold of rock in which the strata slope towards a vertical axis.

syncopate (ˈsɪŋkəˌpeɪt) *vb. Music.* to stress the weak beats in (a rhythm or a piece of music) instead of the strong beats. —ˌsyncoˈpation *n.*

syncope (ˈsɪŋkəpɪ) *n.* **1.** *Med.* a faint. **2.** *Linguistics.* the omission of sounds or letters from the middle of a word, as in *ne'er* for *never.*

syndic (ˈsɪndɪk) *n. Brit.* a business agent of some universities or other bodies.

syndicalism (ˈsɪndɪkəˌlɪzəm) *n.* a movement advocating seizure of the means of production and distribution by workers' unions. —ˈsyndicalist *n.*

syndicate *n.* (ˈsɪndɪkɪt). **1.** an association of business enterprises or individuals organized to undertake a joint project. **2.** an association of individuals who control organized crime. **3.** a news agency that sells articles, photographs, etc., to a number of newspapers for simultaneous publication. ~*vb.* (ˈsɪndɪˌkeɪt). **4.** to sell (articles, photographs, etc.) to several newspapers for simultaneous publication. **5.** to form a syndicate of (people). —ˌsyndiˈcation *n.*

syndrome (ˈsɪndrəʊm) *n.* **1.** *Med.* a combination of signs and symptoms that indicate a particular disease. **2.** a set of symptoms or characteristics indicating the existence of a particular condition or problem.

synecdoche (sɪnˈɛkdəkɪ) *n.* a figure of speech in which a part is substituted for a whole or a whole for a part, as in *50 head of cattle* for *50 cows.*

synod (ˈsɪnəd, ˈsɪnɒd) *n.* a special church council, formally convened to discuss church affairs.

synonym (ˈsɪnənɪm) *n.* a word that means the same as another word, such as *bucket* and *pail.*

synonymous (sɪˈnɒnɪməs) *adj.* (foll. by *with*) **1.** having the same meaning. **2.** closely associated (with): *his name was synonymous with greed.*

synopsis (sɪˈnɒpsɪs) *n., pl.* **-ses** (-siːz). a brief review of a subject; summary.

synoptic (sɪˈnɒptɪk) *adj.* **1.** of or relating to a synopsis. **2.** *Bible.* of or relating to (the Gospels of Matthew, Mark, and Luke). —**synˈoptically** *adv.*

synovia (saɪˈnəʊvɪə, sɪ-) *n.* a clear thick fluid that lubricates the body joints. —**synˈovial** *adj.*

syntax (ˈsɪntæks) *n.* the grammatical arrangement of words in a language. —**synˈtactic** *or* **synˈtactical** *adj.*

synthesis (ˈsɪnθɪsɪs) *n., pl.* **-ses** (-ˌsiːz). **1.** the process of combining objects or ideas into a complex whole. **2.** the combination produced by such a process. **3.** the process of producing a compound by one or more chemical reactions, usually from simpler starting materials.

synthesize or **-sise** ('sɪnθɪˌsaɪz) vb. **1.** to combine (objects or ideas) into a complex whole. **2.** to produce (a compound) by synthesis.

synthesizer ('sɪnθɪˌsaɪzə) n. a keyboard instrument in which speech, music, or other sounds are produced electronically.

synthetic (sɪn'θɛtɪk) adj. **1.** (of a substance or material) made artificially by chemical reaction. **2.** not genuine; insincere: synthetic compassion. ~n. **3.** a synthetic substance or material. —**syn'thetically** adv.

syphilis ('sɪfɪlɪs) n. a sexually transmitted disease that causes sores on the genitals and eventually on other parts of the body. —**syphilitic** (ˌsɪfɪ'lɪtɪk) adj.

syphon ('saɪfᵊn) n., vb. same as **siphon.**

Syrian ('sɪrɪən) adj. **1.** of or relating to Syria, a republic in W Asia, its people, or their dialect of Arabic. ~n. **2.** a person from Syria.

syringa (sɪ'rɪŋgə) n. same as **mock orange** (sense 1) or **lilac.**

syringe ('sɪrɪndʒ, sɪ'rɪndʒ) n. **1.** Med. a device consisting of a hollow cylinder of glass or plastic, a tightly fitting piston, and a hollow needle, used for withdrawing or injecting fluids, cleaning wounds, etc. ~vb. **2.** to cleanse, inject, or spray with a syringe: I'm going to have my ears syringed.

syrup ('sɪrəp) n. **1.** a solution of sugar dissolved in water and often flavoured with fruit juice: used for sweetening fruit, etc. **2.** a thick sweet liquid prepared for cooking or table use from molasses, sugars, etc.: maple syrup. **3.** Informal. excessive sentimentality. **4.** a liquid medicine containing a sugar solution: syrup of figs. —**'syrupy** adj.

system ('sɪstəm) n. **1.** a method or set of methods: he has a perfect system at roulette. **2.** orderliness; an ordered manner. **3. the system.** society or the government regarded as exploiting, restricting, and repressing individuals. **4.** any scheme of classification or arrangement. **5.** a network of communications, transportation, or distribution. **6** Biol. an animal considered as a whole. **7.** Biol. any of various bodily parts or structures that together perform some function: the digestive system. **8.** one's physiological or psychological constitution: get it out of your system. **9.** an assembly of electronic or mechanical parts forming a self-contained unit: a brake system.

systematic (ˌsɪstɪ'mætɪk) adj. using or showing order and planning; methodical: a systematic administrator. —**ˌsystem'atically** adv.

systematize or **-tise** ('sɪstɪməˌtaɪz) vb. to arrange (information) in a system. —**ˌsystemati'zation** or **-i'sation** n.

systemic (sɪ'stɛmɪk, -'stiː-) adj. Biol. (of a poison, disease, etc.) affecting the entire animal or body. —**sys'temically** adv.

systems analysis n. the analysis of the requirements of a task and the expression of these in a form that enables a computer to perform the task. —**systems analyst** n.

systole ('sɪstəlɪ) n. Physiol. contraction of the heart, during which blood is pumped into the arteries. —**systolic** (sɪ'stɒlɪk) adj.

T

t *or* **T** (tiː) *n., pl.* **t's, T's,** *or* **Ts.** **1.** the 20th letter of the English alphabet. **2.** something shaped like a T. **3. to a T.** in every detail; perfectly.

t **1.** tonne(s). **2.** troy (weight).

T *Chem.* tritium.

t. **1.** temperature. **2.** ton(s).

ta (tɑː) *interj. Brit. informal.* thank you.

Ta *Chem.* tantalum.

TA (in Britain) Territorial Army (now superseded by **TAVR**).

tab[1] (tæb) *n.* **1.** a small flap of material, esp. one on a garment for decoration or for fastening to a button. **2.** any similar flap, such as a piece of paper attached to a file for identification. **3.** *Chiefly U.S. & Canad.* a bill, esp. for a meal or drinks. **4. keep tabs on.** *Informal.* to keep a watchful eye on. ~*vb.* **tabbing, tabbed.** **5.** to supply (something) with a tab or tabs.

tab[2] (tæb) *n.* short for **tabulator.**

tabard (ˈtæbəd) *n.* **1.** a sleeveless jacket, esp. (in the Middle Ages) one worn by a knight over his armour. **2.** a short coat bearing the coat of arms of the sovereign, worn by a herald.

Tabasco (təˈbæskəʊ) *n. Trademark.* a very hot red sauce made from peppers.

tabby (ˈtæbɪ) *adj.* **1.** (esp. of cats) having dark stripes or wavy markings on a lighter background. ~*n., pl.* **-bies. 2.** a tabby cat.

tabernacle (ˈtæbəˌnækˀl) *n.* **1.** (*often cap.*) *Bible.* the portable sanctuary in which the ancient Israelites carried the Ark of the Covenant. **2.** any place of worship that is not called a church. **3.** *R.C. Church.* a receptacle in which the Blessed Sacrament is kept.

tabla (ˈtæblə) *n., pl.* **-bla** *or* **-blas.** one of a pair of drums used in Indian music, played with the hands.

table (ˈteɪbˀl) *n.* **1.** a flat horizontal slab or board supported by one or more legs. **2.** an arrangement of words, numbers, or signs, in parallel columns. **3.** any flat or level area, such as a plateau. **4.** a tablet on which laws were inscribed by the ancient Romans, Hebrews, and others. **5. turn the tables.** to cause a complete reversal of circumstances. ~*vb.* **6.** *Brit.* to submit (a bill) for consideration by a legislative body. **7.** *U.S.* to suspend discussion of (a proposal) indefinitely.

tableau (ˈtæbləʊ) *n., pl.* **-leaux** (-ləʊ, -ləʊz) *or* **-leaus.** a group of people arranged motionlessly on a stage to represent a scene from history, legend, or literature.

tablecloth (ˈteɪbˀlˌklɒθ) *n.* a cloth for covering the top of a table, esp. during meals.

table d'hôte (ˈtɑːbˀl ˈdəʊt) *adj.* **1.** (of a meal) consisting of a set number of courses with a limited choice of dishes offered at a fixed price. ~*n., pl.* **tables d'hôte** (ˈtɑːbˀlz ˈdəʊt). **2.** a table d'hôte meal or menu.

tableland (ˈteɪbˀlˌlænd) *n.* a flat area of high ground.

table licence *n.* a licence authorizing the sale of alcoholic drinks with meals only.

tablespoon (ˈteɪbˀlˌspuːn) *n.* **1.** a spoon, larger than a dessertspoon, used for serving food. **2.** Also called: **tablespoonful.** the amount contained in such a spoon. **3.** a unit of capacity used in cooking, equal to half a fluid ounce.

tablet (ˈtæblɪt) *n.* **1.** a pill consisting of a compressed medicinal substance. **2.** a flattish cake of some substance, such as soap. **3.** a slab of stone, wood, etc., used for inscriptions. **4.** a pad of writing paper.

table tennis *n.* a miniature form of tennis played on a table with bats and a small light ball.

tabloid (ˈtæblɔɪd) *n.* a small-sized newspaper, usually with many photographs and a concise and often sensational style.

taboo *or* **tabu** (təˈbuː) *adj.* **1.** forbidden or disapproved of: *taboo words.* ~*n., pl.* **-boos** *or* **-bus. 2.** a restriction or prohibition resulting from social or other conventions. **3.** ritual prohibition, esp. of something that is considered holy or unclean.

tabor (ˈteɪbə) *n.* a small drum used esp. in the Middle Ages, struck with one hand while the other held a pipe.

tabular (ˈtæbjʊlə) *adj.* arranged in parallel columns so as to form a table.

tabulate (ˈtæbjʊˌleɪt) *vb.* to arrange (information) in tabular form. —ˌtabuˈlation *n.*

tabulator (ˈtæbjʊˌleɪtə) *n.* a key on a typewriter or word processor that sets stops so that data can be arranged in columns.

tachograph (ˈtækəˌgrɑːf) *n.* a tachometer that produces a record (**tachogram**) of its readings, esp. a device for recording the speed of a vehicle and the distance that it covers.

tachometer (tæˈkɒmɪtə) *n.* any device for measuring speed, esp. the rate of revolution of a shaft.

tacit (ˈtæsɪt) *adj.* implied or inferred without direct expression; understood: *a tacit agreement.*

taciturn (ˈtæsɪˌtɜːn) *adj.* habitually silent, reserved, or uncommunicative. —ˌtaciˈturnity *n.*

tack¹ (tæk) *n.* **1.** a short sharp-pointed nail with a large flat head. **2.** *Brit.* a long loose temporary stitch used in dressmaking. **3.** a temporary fastening. ~*vb.* **4.** to secure (something) by a tack or tacks. **5.** *Brit.* to sew (something) with long loose temporary stitches. **6.** to attach or append: *tack this letter onto the other pages.*

tack² (tæk) *n.* **1.** *Naut.* the heading of a vessel that is sailing to windward, stated in terms of the side of the sail against which the wind is pressing: *on the port tack.* **2.** a course of action or a policy: *they didn't seem convinced, so I tried another tack.* ~*vb.* **3.** *Naut.* to steer a sailing vessel on a zigzag course, so as to make progress against the wind. **4.** *Naut.* to change the heading of a sailing vessel to the opposite tack.

tack³ (tæk) *n.* riding harness for horses, including saddles and bridles.

tackies (ˈtækɪz) *pl. n., sing.* **tacky.** *S. African informal.* tennis shoes or plimsolls.

tackle (ˈtækᵊl) *n.* **1.** an arrangement of ropes and pulleys designed to lift heavy weights. **2.** the equipment required for a particular sport or occupation: *fishing tackle.* **3.** *Sport.* an attempt to get the ball away from an opposing player. **4.** *Naut.* the halyards and other running rigging aboard a vessel. ~*vb.* **5.** to undertake (a task). **6.** to confront (esp. an opponent) with a difficult proposition. **7.** *Sport.* to attempt to get the ball away from (an opposing player).

tacky¹ (ˈtækɪ) *adj.* **tackier, tackiest.** slightly sticky. —ˈtackiness *n.*

tacky² (ˈtækɪ) *adj.* **tackier, tackiest.** *Informal.* **1.** shabby or shoddy: *a row of tacky shops.* **2.** ostentatious and vulgar: *tacky jewellery.* —ˈtackiness *n.*

tact (tækt) *n.* **1.** a sense of what is fitting and considerate in dealing with others, so as to avoid giving offence. **2.** skill in handling difficult situations; diplomacy. —ˈtactful *adj.* —ˈtactfully *adv.* —ˈtactless *adj.* —ˈtactlessly *adv.* —ˈtactlessness *n.*

tactic (ˈtæktɪk) *n.* a tactical move. See also **tactics.**

tactical (ˈtæktɪkᵊl) *adj.* **1.** of or employing tactics: *a tactical error.* **2.** (of missiles, bombing, etc.) for use in limited military operations. —ˈtactically *adv.*

tactics (ˈtæktɪks) *pl. n.* **1.** (*functioning as sing.*) *Mil.* the science of the detailed direction of forces in battle to achieve an aim or task. **2.** the manoeuvres used to achieve an aim or task. **3.** plans followed to achieve a particular short-term aim. —**tactician** (tækˈtɪʃən) *n.*

tactile (ˈtæktaɪl) *adj.* of or having a sense of touch: *a tactile organ.*

tadpole (ˈtædˌpəʊl) *n.* the aquatic larva of frogs and toads, which develops from a limbless tailed form with external gills into a form with internal gills, limbs, and a reduced tail.

taffeta (ˈtæfɪtə) *n.* a thin plain-weave fabric of silk or rayon used esp. for women's clothes.

taffrail (ˈtæfˌreɪl) *n.* *Naut.* a rail at the stern of a vessel.

Taffy (ˈtæfɪ) *n., pl.* **-fies.** *Slang.* a Welshman.

tag¹ (tæg) *n.* **1.** a piece of paper, leather, etc., for attaching to something as a mark or label: *a price tag.* **2.** a point of metal or plastic at the end of a cord or lace. **3.** a verbal appendage such as the refrain of a song or the moral of a fable. **4.** a brief quotation. **5.** an electronic device worn by a prisoner under house arrest so that his movements can be monitored. ~*vb.* **tagging, tagged. 6.** to mark with a tag. **7. tag along.** to accompany someone, esp. when uninvited: *would you mind if I just tagged along?*

tag² (tæg) *n.* **1.** a children's game in which one player chases the others in an attempt to catch one of them, who will then become the chaser. ~*vb.* **tagging, tagged. 2.** to catch (another child) in the game of tag. ~Also called: **tig.**

Tagalog (təˈɡɑːlɒɡ) *n.* **1.** (*pl.* **-logs** *or* **-log**) a member of a people of the Philippines. **2.** the language of this people. ~*adj.* **3.** of this people or their language.

tag end *n.* **1.** *Chiefly U.S. & Canad.* the last part of something. **2.** a loose end of cloth, thread, etc.

tagetes (tæˈdʒiːtiːz) *n., pl.* **-tes.** any of a genus of plants with yellow or orange flowers, including the French and African marigolds.

tagliatelle (ˌtæljəˈtɛlɪ) *n.* a form of pasta made in narrow strips.

tail¹ (teɪl) *n.* **1.** the rear part of an animal's body, usually forming a flexible appendage to the trunk. **2.** anything resembling such an appendage: *the tail of a shirt.* **3.** the last part or parts: *the tail of the storm.* **4.** the rear part of an aircraft. **5.** *Astron.* the luminous stream of gas and dust particles driven from the head of a comet when it is close to the sun. **6.** *Informal.* a person employed to follow and spy upon another. **7.** (*modifier*) coming from or situated in the rear: *a tail wind.* **8. turn tail.** to run away; escape. **9. with one's tail between one's legs.** completely defeated and demoralized. ~*vb.* **10.** *Informal.* to follow (someone) stealthily. ~See also **tail off, tails.** —ˈtailless *adj.*

tail² (teɪl) *n.* *Law.* the limitation of an estate

or interest to a person and his descendants. —'**tailless** *adj.*

tailback ('teɪlˌbæk) *n.* a queue of traffic stretching back from an obstruction.

tailboard ('teɪlˌbɔːd) *n.* a board at the rear of a lorry, etc., that can be removed or let down.

tail coat *n.* a man's black coat having a horizontal cut over the hips and a tapering tail with a vertical slit up to the waist.

tailgate ('teɪlˌgeɪt) *n.* **1.** same as **tailboard**. **2.** a door at the rear of a hatchback vehicle.

tail-light ('teɪlˌlaɪt) *or* **tail-lamp** *n.* U.S. & Canad. same as **rear light**.

tail off *or* **away** *vb.* to decrease gradually: *her interest in stamp collecting tailed off over the years.*

tailor ('teɪlə) *n.* **1.** a person who makes, repairs, or alters outer garments, esp. menswear. ~*vb.* **2.** to cut or style (material) to satisfy certain requirements. **3.** to adapt so as to make suitable: *he tailored his speech to suit a younger audience.* —'**tailored** *adj.*

tailorbird ('teɪləˌbɜːd) *n.* any of several tropical Asian warblers that build nests by sewing together large leaves using plant fibres.

tailor-made *adj.* **1.** (of clothing) made by a tailor to fit exactly. **2.** perfect for a particular purpose: *a girl tailor-made for him.* ~*n.* **3.** a tailor-made garment.

tailpiece ('teɪlˌpiːs) *n.* **1.** an appendage. **2.** a decorative design at the end of a chapter.

tailpipe ('teɪlˌpaɪp) *n.* a pipe from which exhaust gases are discharged, esp. the pipe at the end of the exhaust system of a motor vehicle.

tailplane ('teɪlˌpleɪn) *n.* a small horizontal wing at the tail of an aircraft to provide longitudinal stability.

tails (teɪlz) *pl. n.* **1.** *Informal.* same as **tail coat**. ~*interj., adv.* **2.** with the side of a coin uppermost that does not have a portrait of a head on it.

tailspin ('teɪlˌspɪn) *n.* **1.** *Aeronautics.* same as **spin** (sense 9). **2.** *Informal.* a state of confusion or panic.

tailwind ('teɪlˌwɪnd) *n.* a wind blowing in the same direction as the course of an aircraft or vehicle.

taint (teɪnt) *vb.* **1.** to affect by pollution or contamination. **2.** to tarnish (someone's reputation, etc.). ~*n.* **3.** a defect or flaw. **4.** a trace of contamination or infection.

take (teɪk) *vb.* **taking, took, taken. 1.** to remove from a place, usually by grasping with the hand: *he took a book from the shelf.* **2.** to accompany, escort, or convey: *we took the children to Spain.* **3.** to use as a means of transport: *I shall take the bus.* **4.** to conduct or lead: *this road takes you to*

the station. **5.** to obtain possession of (something), often dishonestly: *someone has taken my watch.* **6.** to win or capture (a trick, piece, etc.). **7.** to put an end to: *she took her own life.* **8.** to require (time, resources, or ability): *the job took two days.* **9.** to use as a particular case: *take hotels for example.* **10.** to proceed to occupy: *to take a seat.* **11.** to assume the obligations of: *to take office.* **12.** to receive in a specified way: *she took the news very well.* **13.** to receive and make use of: *to take advice; take an opportunity.* **14.** to receive into the body; swallow: *to take a pill.* **15.** to perform (an action, esp. one that brings some benefit to the person who does it): *to take a look; take a deep breath; take a chance; take a bath.* **16.** to put into effect: *to take steps to ascertain the answer.* **17.** to make (a photograph). **18.** to write down or copy: *to take notes.* **19.** to work at or study: *to take economics at college.* **20.** to begin to experience or feel: *to take an interest; take offence.* **21.** to consider or regard: *I take him to be honest.* **22.** to accept (responsibility, etc.): *to take the blame for an accident.* **23.** to accept as valid: *I take your point.* **24.** to stand up to or endure: *I can't take his arrogance.* **25.** to adopt as one's own: *to take someone's part in a quarrel.* **26.** to ascertain by measuring: *to take a pulse.* **27.** to subtract or deduct. **28.** to aim or direct: *he took a swipe at Jim.* **29.** to have or produce the intended effect: *her vaccination took.* **30.** (of seedlings) to start growing successfully. **31. take account of** *or* **take into account.** to consider and make plans or allowances for: *to take account of two years of overspending.* **32. take advantage of.** to make use of (someone or something) for one's own benefit, esp. unfairly. **33. take care.** to watch out or look after oneself. **34. take care of.** to look after; tend. **35. take it.** to assume or believe: *I take it you'll be back later.* **36. take part.** to participate or join in. **37. take place.** to happen. **38. take upon oneself.** to assume the right or duty (to do something). **39. take your time.** use as much time as you need. ~*n.* **40.** *Films, music.* one of a series of recordings from which the best will be selected. ~See also **take after, take apart,** etc. —'**taker** *n.*

take after *vb.* to resemble in appearance, character, or behaviour.

take apart *vb.* **1.** to separate (something) into component parts. **2.** to criticize severely.

take away *vb.* **1.** to subtract: *take away four from nine to leave five.* ~*prep.* **2.** minus: *nine take away four is five.* ~*adj.* **takeaway. 3.** *Brit., Austral., & N.Z.* sold for consumption away from the premises: *a takeaway meal.* ~*n.* **takeaway.** *Brit., Austral., & N.Z.* **4.** a shop or restaurant that sells such food. **5.** a meal sold for consumption away from the premises.

take back *vb.* **1.** to retract or withdraw (something said or promised). **2.** to regain possession of. **3.** to return for exchange: *to take back an unsatisfactory garment.* **4.** to accept (someone) back (into one's home, affections, etc.). **5.** to remind one of the past: *that tune takes me back.*

take down *vb.* **1.** to record in writing. **2.** to dismantle or remove. **3.** to reduce (someone) in power, arrogance, etc.: *we'll take him down a peg or two.*

take for *vb. Informal.* to consider or suppose to be, esp. mistakenly: *the fake coins were taken for genuine; what do you take me for?*

take-home pay *n.* the remainder of one's pay after income tax and other compulsory deductions have been made.

take in *vb.* **1.** to understand. **2.** to include: *her thesis takes in that point.* **3.** to receive into one's house: *to take in lodgers.* **4.** to make (clothing) smaller by altering seams. **5.** *Informal.* to cheat or deceive. **6.** *U.S.* to go to: *let's take in a movie tonight.*

taken ('teɪkən) *vb.* **1.** the past participle of **take.** ~*adj.* **2.** (foll. by *with*) enthusiastically impressed by.

take off *vb.* **1.** to remove (a garment). **2.** (of an aircraft) to become airborne. **3.** *Informal.* to set out or cause to set out on a journey: *they took off for Spain.* **4.** *Informal.* to become successful or popular. **5.** to deduct: *the shop took off ten per cent.* **6.** *Informal.* to mimic (someone). ~*n.* **take-off.** **7.** the act or process of making an aircraft airborne. **8.** *Informal.* an act of mimicry.

take on *vb.* **1.** to employ or hire. **2.** to assume or acquire: *his voice took on a plaintive note.* **3.** to agree to do; undertake. **4.** to compete against; fight.

take out *vb.* **1.** to extract or remove. **2.** to obtain or secure: *I want to take out an insurance policy.* **3.** to go out with; escort. **4. take it** *or* **take it out of.** *Informal.* to sap the energy or vitality of. **5. take it out on.** *Informal.* to vent (anger) on: *just because she let you down you don't have to take it out on me.* ~*adj., n.* **takeout.** **6.** *U.S. & Canad.* See **takeaway** (senses 3, 4, 5).

take over *vb.* **1.** to obtain control or management of. ~*n.* **takeover.** **2.** the act of obtaining control of something, esp. of another company by buying its shares.

take to *vb.* **1.** to form a liking for. **2.** to have recourse to: *to take to the bottle.*

take up *vb.* **1.** to occupy or fill (space or time). **2.** to adopt the study, practice, or activity of: *to take up gardening.* **3.** to shorten (a garment). **4.** to accept (an offer). **5. take up on. a.** to discuss (something) further with (someone): *can I take you up on two points in your talk?* **b.** to

accept what is offered by (someone): *let me take you up on your invitation.* **6. take up with. a.** to discuss (an issue) with (someone). **b.** to begin to keep company or associate with.

taking ('teɪkɪŋ) *adj.* charming, fascinating, or intriguing.

takings ('teɪkɪŋz) *pl. n.* receipts; earnings.

talc (tælk) *n. also* **talcum. 1.** See **talcum powder. 2.** a soft mineral, consisting of magnesium silicate, used in the manufacture of ceramics, paints, and talcum powder.

talcum powder ('tælkəm) *n.* a powder made of purified talc, usually scented, used for perfuming the body.

tale (teɪl) *n.* **1.** a report, narrative, or story. **2. a.** a malicious piece of gossip. **b.** a false statement. **3. tell tales. a.** to tell fanciful lies. **b.** to report malicious stories or trivial complaints, esp. to someone in authority. **4. tell a tale.** to reveal something important. **5. tell its own tale.** to be self-evident.

talent ('tælənt) *n.* **1.** innate ability, aptitude, or faculty: *a talent for cooking; a child with talent.* **2.** a person or persons with such ability. **3.** any of various units of weight and money used by the ancient Babylonians, Greeks, Romans, and others. **4.** *Informal.* members of the opposite sex collectively: *the local talent.* —'**talented** *adj.*

talent scout *n.* a person whose occupation is the search for talented people, such as sportsmen or performers, for engagements as professionals.

talisman ('tælɪzmən) *n., pl.* -**mans.** a stone or other small object, usually inscribed or carved, believed to protect the wearer from evil influences. —**talismanic** (,tælɪz-'mænɪk) *adj.*

talk (tɔːk) *vb.* **1.** (often foll. by *to* or *with*) to express one's thoughts, feelings, or desires by means of words. **2.** (usually foll. by *about*) to exchange ideas or opinions about (a subject). **3.** to give voice to; utter: *to talk rubbish.* **4.** to discuss: *to talk business.* **5.** to reveal information: *the prisoner talked after torture.* **6.** to know how to communicate in (a language or idiom): *he talks English.* **7.** to spread rumours or gossip. **8.** to be effective or persuasive: *money talks.* **9. now you're talking.** *Informal.* at last you're saying something agreeable. **10. you can** *or* **can't talk.** *Informal.* you are in no position to comment or criticize. ~*n.* **11.** a speech or lecture. **12.** an exchange of ideas or thoughts. **13.** idle chatter, gossip, or rumour. **14.** (*often pl.*) a conference, discussion, or negotiation. ~See also **talk back, talk down,** etc. —'**talker** *n.*

talkative ('tɔːkətɪv) *adj.* given to talking a great deal.

talk back *vb.* **1.** to answer (someone)

boldly or impudently. ~n. **talkback.** 2. *Television, radio.* a system of telephone links enabling spoken directions to be given during the production of a programme.

talk down *vb.* 1. (foll. by *to*) to speak to someone in a patronizing manner. 2. to give instructions to (an aircraft) by radio to enable it to land.

talkie ('tɔːkɪ) *n. Informal.* an early film with a soundtrack.

talking book *n.* a recording of a book, designed to be used by the blind.

talking-to *n. Informal.* a session of criticism: *I got a severe talking-to when I got home.*

talk into *vb.* to persuade (someone) to do something by talking to him: *I talked her into buying the house.*

talk out *vb.* 1. to resolve (a problem) by talking. 2. *Brit.* to block (a bill) in a legislative body by lengthy discussion. 3. **talk out of.** to dissuade (someone) from doing something by talking to him.

talk round *vb.* 1. to persuade (someone) to agree with one's opinion or suggestion. 2. to discuss (a subject), esp. without coming to a conclusion.

tall (tɔːl) *adj.* 1. of more than average height. 2. having a specified height: *five feet tall.*

tallboy ('tɔːl,bɔɪ) *n.* a high chest of drawers made in two sections placed one on top of the other.

tall order *n. Informal.* a difficult or unreasonable request.

tallow ('tæləʊ) *n.* a fatty substance extracted from the suet of sheep and cattle: used for making soap, candles, and food.

tall story *n. Informal.* an exaggerated or unlikely account of something.

tally ('tælɪ) *vb.* **-lying, -lied.** 1. to correspond one with the other: *the two stories don't tally.* 2. to keep score. ~n., *pl.* **-lies.** 3. any record of debit, credit, the score in a game, etc. 4. an identifying label or mark. 5. a stick used (esp. formerly) as a record of the amount of a debt according to the notches cut in it.

tally clerk *n. Austral. & N.Z.* a person, esp. on a wharf, who checks the count of goods being loaded or unloaded.

tally-ho (,tælɪ'həʊ) *interj.* the cry of a participant at a hunt when the quarry is sighted.

Talmud ('tælmʊd) *n. Judaism.* the primary source of Jewish religious law. —**Tal-**'**mudic** *adj.* —'**Talmudist** *n.*

talon ('tælən) *n.* a sharply hooked claw, esp. of a bird of prey.

tamarind ('tæmərɪnd) *n.* a tropical evergreen tree with fruit whose acid pulp is used as a food and to make beverages and medicines.

tamarisk ('tæmərɪsk) *n.* a tree or shrub of the Mediterranean region and S Asia, with scalelike leaves, slender branches, and feathery flower clusters.

tambour ('tæmbʊə) *n.* 1. a small embroidery frame, consisting of two hoops over which the fabric is stretched while being worked. 2. a drum.

tambourine (,tæmbə'riːn) *n. Music.* a percussion instrument consisting of a single piece of skin stretched over a circular wooden frame, which is hung with pairs of metal discs that jingle when it is struck or shaken.

tame (teɪm) *adj.* 1. changed by man from a wild state into a domesticated state. 2. (of animals) not fearful of human contact. 3. meek or submissive: *a tame personality.* 4. flat, insipid, or uninspiring: *a tame ending to a book.* ~vb. 5. to make (an animal) tame; domesticate. 6. to break the spirit of, subdue.

Tamil ('tæmɪl) *n.* 1. (*pl.* **-ils** *or* **-il**) a member of a people of S India and Sri Lanka. 2. the language of this people. ~adj. 3. of this people or their language.

tam-o'-shanter (,tæmə'ʃæntə) *n.* a Scottish brimless wool or cloth cap with a bobble in the centre.

tamp (tæmp) *vb.* to force or pack down firmly by repeated blows: *to tamp down concrete.*

tamper ('tæmpə) *vb.* (foll. by *with*) 1. to interfere. 2. to attempt to influence someone, esp. by bribery.

tampon ('tæmpɒn) *n.* a plug of lint, cotton wool, etc., inserted into a wound or body cavity to stop the flow of blood or absorb secretions.

tan[1] (tæn) *n.* 1. the brown colour produced on the skin after exposure to ultraviolet rays, esp. those of the sun. ~vb. **tanning, tanned.** 2. to go brown after exposure to ultraviolet rays. 3. to convert (a skin or hide) into leather by treating it with a tanning agent. 4. *Slang.* to beat or flog. ~adj. 5. yellowish-brown. —'**tanner** *n.*

tan[2] (tæn) *Maths.* tangent.

tandem ('tændəm) *n.* 1. a bicycle with two sets of pedals and two saddles, arranged one behind the other for two riders. 2. a two-wheeled carriage drawn by two horses harnessed one behind the other. ~adv. 3. one behind the other.

tandoori (tæn'dʊərɪ) *n.* an Indian method of cooking spiced meat or vegetables on a spit in a clay oven.

tang (tæŋ) *n.* 1. a strong taste or smell. 2. a trace or hint of something. 3. the pointed end of a tool, such as a chisel, which is fitted into a handle or shaft. —'**tangy** *adj.*

tangent ('tændʒənt) *n.* 1. a geometric line, curve, or plane that touches another curve or surface at one point but does not intersect it. 2. a trigonometric function that in a right-angled triangle is the ratio of the length of the opposite side to that of the adjacent side. **3. at a tangent.** on a completely different or divergent course, esp. of thought. ~*adj.* **4.** of or involving a tangent. **5.** touching at a single point.

tangential (tæn'dʒɛnʃəl) *adj.* **1.** of or in the direction of a tangent. **2.** of superficial relevance only; digressive. —**tan'gentially** *adv.*

tangerine (ˌtændʒə'riːn) *n.* **1.** an Asian citrus tree cultivated for its small orange-like fruits which have a sweet juicy flesh. ~*adj.* **2.** reddish-orange.

tangi ('tæŋiː) *n.* *N.Z.* **1.** a Maori funeral ceremony. **2.** *Informal.* a lamentation.

tangible ('tændʒɪbʰl) *adj.* **1.** capable of being touched or felt. **2.** capable of being clearly grasped by the mind. **3.** having a physical existence: *tangible property.* —ˌtangi'bility *n.* —'tangibly *adv.*

tangle ('tæŋgʰl) *n.* **1.** a confused or complicated mass of things, such as hair or fibres, knotted or coiled together. **2.** a complicated problem or situation. ~*vb.* **3.** to twist (things, such as hair or fibres) together in a confused mass. **4.** (often foll. by *with*) to come into conflict: *to tangle with the police.* **5.** to ensnare or trap, as in a net. —'tangled *adj.*

tango ('tæŋgəʊ) *n., pl.* **-gos. 1.** a Latin-American dance characterized by long gliding steps and sudden pauses. **2.** music for this dance. ~*vb.* **-going, -goed. 3.** to perform this dance.

tank (tæŋk) *n.* **1.** a large container for the mass storage of liquids or gases. **2.** an armoured combat vehicle moving on tracks and armed with guns. **3.** Also called: **tankful.** the quantity contained in a tank.

tankard ('tæŋkəd) *n.* a large one-handled drinking vessel sometimes fitted with a hinged lid.

tanked up *adj.* *Slang, chiefly Brit.* very drunk.

tanker ('tæŋkə) *n.* a ship or lorry designed to carry liquid in bulk, such as oil.

tank farming *n.* same as **hydroponics.** —**tank farmer** *n.*

tannery ('tænərɪ) *n., pl.* **-neries.** a place or building where skins and hides are tanned.

tannic ('tænɪk) *adj.* of, containing, or produced from tan, tannin, or tannic acid.

tannin ('tænɪn) *n.* a yellowish compound found in many plants and used as a tanning agent, mordant, medical astringent, etc. Also called: **tannic acid.**

Tannoy ('tænɔɪ) *n. Trademark.* a type of public-address system.

tansy ('tænzɪ) *n., pl.* **-sies.** a plant with yellow flowers in flat-topped clusters.

tantalize *or* **-lise** ('tæntəˌlaɪz) *vb.* to tease or make frustrated, for example by tormenting (someone) with the sight of some-

thing that he wants but cannot have. —'tanta,lizing *or* -,lising *adj.* —'tanta,lizingly *or* -,lisingly *adv.*

tantalum ('tæntələm) *n.* a hard greyish-white metallic element that resists corrosion. Symbol: Ta

tantalus ('tæntələs) *n. Brit.* a case in which bottles may be locked with their contents tantalizingly visible.

tantamount ('tæntəˌmaʊnt) *adj.* (foll. by *to*) as good as; equivalent in effect to.

tantrum ('tæntrəm) *n.* (*often pl.*) an outburst of bad temper.

Taoism ('taʊɪzəm) *n.* a system of religion and philosophy advocating a simple honest life and noninterference with the course of natural events. —'**Taoist** *n., adj.*

tap¹ (tæp) *vb.* **tapping, tapped. 1.** to strike (something) lightly and usually repeatedly. **2.** to strike lightly with (something): *to tap one's finger on the desk.* ~*n.* **3.** a light blow or knock, or the sound made by it. **4.** the metal piece attached to the toe or heel of a shoe used for tap-dancing. ~See also **taps.**

tap² (tæp) *n.* **1.** *Chiefly Brit.* a valve by which the flow of a liquid or gas from a pipe can be controlled. Usual U.S. word: **faucet. 2.** a stopper to plug a cask or barrel. **3.** *Med.* the withdrawal of fluid from a bodily cavity. **4.** *Electronics, chiefly U.S. & Canad.* a connection made at some point between the terminals of an inductor, resistor, etc. Usual Brit. word: **tapping. 5.** a concealed listening or recording device connected to a telephone. **6. on tap. a.** *Informal.* ready for use. **b.** (of drinks) on draught. ~*vb.* **tapping, tapped. 7.** to connect a tap to (a telephone). **8.** to make a connection to (a pipe, drain, etc.). **9.** to draw off with or as if with a tap. **10.** to cut into (a tree) and draw off sap from it. **11.** *Brit. informal.* to ask (someone) for money: *he tapped me for a fiver.*

tap dance *n.* a dance in which the performer wears shoes with taps that make a rhythmic sound on the stage as he dances. —'tap-,dancer *n.* —'tap-,dancing *n.*

tape (teɪp) *n.* **1.** a long thin strip of cotton or linen used for binding or fastening. **2.** a long narrow strip of paper, metal, etc. **3.** a string stretched across the track at the end of a race course. **4.** See **magnetic tape, ticker tape, tape recording.** ~*vb.* **5.** to bind or fasten with tape. **6. have (a person** or **situation) taped.** *Brit. informal.* to have full understanding and control of (a person or situation). **7.** Also: **tape-record.** to record (speech, music, etc.) on magnetic tape.

tape deck *n.* the platform supporting the spools, cassettes, or cartridges of a tape recorder, incorporating the motor and the playback, recording, and erasing heads.

tape measure *n.* a tape or length of

metal marked off in centimetres or inches, used for measuring.

taper ('teɪpə) vb. 1. to become narrower towards one end. 2. **taper off.** to become gradually less. ~n. 3. a thin candle. 4. a thin wooden or waxed strip for transferring a flame; spill. 5. a narrowing.

tape recorder n. an electrical device used for recording and reproducing sounds on magnetic tape.

tape recording n. 1. the act of recording sounds on magnetic tape. 2. the magnetic tape used for this. 3. the sounds so recorded.

tapestry ('tæpɪstrɪ) n., pl. -**tries.** 1. a heavy woven fabric, often in the form of a picture, used for wall hangings or furnishings. 2. same as **needlepoint** (sense 1). —'**tapestried** adj.

tapeworm ('teɪp‚wɜːm) n. a long flat parasitic worm that inhabits the intestines of vertebrates, including man.

tapioca (‚tæpɪ'əʊkə) n. a beadlike starch obtained from cassava root, used in puddings.

tapir ('teɪpə) n., pl. -**pirs** or -**pir.** a piglike mammal of South and Central America and SE Asia, having a long snout, three-toed hind legs, and four-toed forelegs.

tappet ('tæpɪt) n. a short steel rod in an engine which moves up and down transferring movement from one part of the machine to another.

taproom ('tæp‚ruːm) n. Old-fashioned. the public bar in a hotel or pub.

taproot ('tæp‚ruːt) n. the main root of plants such as the dandelion, which grows vertically downwards and bears smaller lateral roots.

taps (tæps) n. (functioning as sing.) (in the Guide movement) a closing song sung at an evening camp fire or at the end of a meeting.

tapster ('tæpstə) n. 1. Old-fashioned. a barman. 2. (in W Africa) a man who taps palm trees for their sap.

tar[1] (tɑː) n. 1. a dark sticky substance obtained by distillation of organic matter such as coal, wood, or peat. 2. same as **coal tar.** ~vb. **tarring, tarred.** 3. to coat with tar. 4. **tar and feather.** to cover (someone) with tar and feathers as a punishment. 5. **tarred with the same brush.** having the same faults.

tar[2] (tɑː) n. Informal. a seaman.

tarakihi ('tærə‚kiːhiː) or **terakihi** ('tɛrə‚kiːhiː) n., pl. -**kihis.** a common edible sea fish of New Zealand waters.

taramasalata (‚tærəmɑsə'lɑːtə) n. a creamy pale pink pâté, made from the eggs of fish, esp. smoked cod, and served as an hors d'oeuvre.

tarantella (‚tærən'tɛlə) n. 1. a peasant dance from S Italy. 2. a piece of music for this dance.

tarantula (tə'ræntjʊlə) n., pl. -**las** or -**lae** (-‚liː). any of various large hairy spiders of tropical America with a poisonous bite.

tarboosh (tɑː'buːʃ) n. a felt or cloth brimless cap, usually red and often with a silk tassel, formerly worn by Muslim men.

tardy ('tɑːdɪ) adj. -**dier, -diest.** 1. occurring later than expected. 2. slow in progress, growth, etc. —'**tardily** adv. —'**tardiness** n.

tare[1] (tɛə) n. 1. any of various vetch plants of Eurasia and N Africa. 2. Bible. a weed, thought to be the darnel.

tare[2] (tɛə) n. 1. the weight of the wrapping or container in which goods are packed. 2. the weight of an unladen vehicle.

target ('tɑːgɪt) n. 1. an object at which an archer or marksman aims, usually a round flat surface marked with circles. 2. any point or area aimed at. 3. a fixed goal or objective. 4. a person or thing at which criticism or ridicule is directed. ~vb. 5. to direct or aim: to target benefits at those most in need.

tariff ('tærɪf) n. 1. a. a tax levied by a government on imports or occasionally exports. b. a list of such taxes. 2. a list of fixed prices: a hotel tariff. 3. Chiefly Brit. a method of charging for services such as gas and electricity by setting a price per unit.

tarlatan ('tɑːlətən) n. an open-weave cotton fabric, used for stiffening garments.

Tarmac ('tɑːmæk) n. 1. Trademark. (often not cap.) a paving material made of crushed stone bound with a mixture of tar and bitumen, used for a road or airport runway. ~vb. -**macking, -macked.** 2. (usually not cap.) to apply Tarmac to (a surface).

tarn (tɑːn) n. a small mountain lake.

tarnish ('tɑːnɪʃ) vb. 1. (of a metal) to lose its shine, esp. by exposure to air or moisture. 2. to damage; taint: a fraud that tarnished his reputation. ~n. 3. a tarnished condition, surface, or film on a surface.

taro ('tɑːrəʊ) n., pl. -**ros.** an Asian plant with a large edible rootstock.

tarot ('tærəʊ) n. 1. one of a special pack of cards, now used mainly for fortune-telling. 2. a card in a tarot pack with distinctive symbolic design.

tarpaulin (tɑː'pɔːlɪn) n. 1. a heavy waterproof fabric made of canvas or similar material coated with tar, wax, or paint. 2. a sheet of this fabric.

tarragon ('tærəgən) n. a European herb with narrow leaves, which are used as seasoning in cooking.

tarry ('tærɪ) vb. -**rying, -ried.** Old-fashioned. 1. to delay; linger. 2. to stay briefly.

tarsal ('tɑːsᵊl) *adj.* **1.** of the tarsus or tarsi. ~*n.* **2.** a tarsal bone.

tarseal ('tɑː,siːl) *n. N.Z.* **1.** the bitumen surface of a road. **2. the tarseal.** the main highway.

tarsus ('tɑːsəs) *n., pl.* **-si** (-saɪ). **1.** the bones of the ankle and heel collectively. **2.** the corresponding part in other mammals and in amphibians and reptiles.

tart[1] (tɑːt) *n.* **1.** *Chiefly Brit.* a pastry case, often having no top crust, with a sweet filling, such as jam or custard. **2.** *Chiefly U.S.* a small open pie with a fruit filling.

tart[2] (tɑːt) *adj.* **1.** (of a flavour) sour; acid. **2.** cutting; sharp: *a tart remark.* —**'tartly** *adv.* —**'tartness** *n.*

tart[3] (tɑːt) *n. Informal.* a sexually provocative or promiscuous woman.

tartan ('tɑːtᵊn) *n.* **1.** a design of straight lines, crossing at right angles to give a chequered appearance, esp. one of the distinctive designs each of which is associated with a Scottish clan. **2.** a fabric or garment with this design.

tartar[1] ('tɑːtə) *n.* **1.** a hard deposit on the teeth. **2.** a brownish-red substance deposited in a cask during the fermentation of wine.

tartar[2] ('tɑːtə) *n.* a fearsome or formidable person.

Tartar ('tɑːtə) *n., adj.* same as **Tatar.**

tartaric (tɑː'tærɪk) *adj.* of or derived from tartar or tartaric acid.

tartaric acid *n.* a colourless crystalline acid which is found in many fruits.

tartar sauce *n.* a mayonnaise sauce mixed with hard-boiled egg yolks, chopped herbs, and capers.

tartrazine ('tɑːtrə,ziːn) *n.* a dye that produces a yellow colour: used as a food additive, in drugs, and to dye textiles.

tart up *vb. Brit. informal.* **1.** to dress and make (oneself) up in a sexually provocative way. **2.** to decorate in a cheap and flashy way: *to tart up a bar.*

Tarzan ('tɑːzən) *n.* (*sometimes not cap.*) *Informal, often ironical.* a man with great physical strength, agility, and virility.

task (tɑːsk) *n.* **1.** a specific piece of work required to be done. **2.** an unpleasant or difficult job or duty. **3. take to task.** to criticize or rebuke. ~*vb.* **4.** to subject to severe strain; tax.

task force *n.* **1.** a temporary grouping of military units formed to undertake a specific mission. **2.** any organization set up to carry out a continuing task.

taskmaster ('tɑːsk,mɑːstə) *n.* a person who enforces hard or continuous work. —**'task-,mistress** *fem. n.*

Tasmanian devil (tæz'meɪnɪən) *n.* a small ferocious flesh-eating marsupial of Tasmania.

Tass (tæs) *n.* the principal news agency of the Soviet Union.

tassel ('tæsᵊl) *n.* a tuft of loose threads secured by a knot or knob, used to decorate something, such as a lampshade or piece of clothing.

taste (teɪst) *n.* **1.** the sense by which the flavour of a substance is distinguished by the taste buds. **2.** the sensation experienced by means of the taste buds. **3.** a small amount eaten, sipped, or tried on the tongue. **4.** a brief experience of something: *a taste of the whip.* **5.** a liking for something: *to have a taste for danger.* **6.** the ability to appreciate what is beautiful and excellent. ~*vb.* **7.** to distinguish the taste of (a substance) by means of the taste buds. **8.** to take a small amount of (a food or liquid) into the mouth, esp. in order to test the flavour. **9.** (often foll. by *of*) to have a specific flavour or taste: *the tea tastes of soap.* **10.** to have an experience of (something): *to taste success.*

taste bud *n.* any of the cells on the surface of the tongue, by means of which the sensation of taste is experienced.

tasteful ('teɪstful) *adj.* having or showing good taste: *a tasteful design.* —**'tastefully** *adv.*

tasteless ('teɪstlɪs) *adj.* **1.** lacking in flavour; insipid. **2.** lacking social or aesthetic taste. —**'tastelessly** *adv.* —**'tasteless-ness** *n.*

taster ('teɪstə) *n.* a person who tastes, esp. one employed to test the quality of food or drink by tasting it.

tasty ('teɪstɪ) *adj.* **tastier, tastiest.** having a pleasant flavour.

tat[1] (tæt) *vb.* **tatting, tatted.** to make (lace) by looping a thread of cotton or linen with a hand shuttle.

tat[2] (tæt) *n.* tatty or tasteless articles.

ta-ta (tæ'tɑː) *interj. Brit. informal.* goodbye.

Tatar *or* **Tartar** ('tɑːtə) *n.* **1.** a member of a Mongoloid people who established a powerful state in central Asia in the 13th century. They are now scattered throughout the Soviet Union. ~*adj.* **2.** of the Tatars.

tater ('teɪtə) *n. Dialect.* a potato.

tattered ('tætəd) *adj.* **1.** ragged or torn: *a tattered coat.* **2.** wearing ragged or torn clothing: *a tattered old man.*

tatters ('tætəz) *pl. n.* **1.** torn ragged clothing. **2. in tatters. a.** (of clothing) torn in several places. **b.** (of an argument, plan, etc.) completely destroyed.

tatting ('tætɪŋ) *n.* **1.** an intricate type of lace made by looping a thread of cotton or linen with a hand shuttle. **2.** the work of producing this.

tattle ('tætᵊl) *vb.* **1.** to gossip about someone else's personal matters or secrets. **2.** to talk idly; chat. ~*n.* **3.** the act or an instance of tattling. —**'tattler** *n.*

tattletale (ˈtætᵊlˌteɪl) *n. Chiefly U.S. & Canad.* a scandalmonger or gossip.

tattoo[1] (tæˈtuː) *n., pl.* **-toos. 1.** (formerly) a signal by drum or bugle ordering soldiers to return to their quarters. **2.** a military display or pageant. **3.** any drumming or tapping.

tattoo[2] (tæˈtuː) *vb.* **-tooing, -tooed. 1.** to make (pictures or designs) on (a person's skin) by pricking and staining it with indelible colours. **~n., pl.** **-toos. 2.** a design made by this process. **—tatˈtooer** *or* **tatˈtooist** *n.*

tatty (ˈtætɪ) *adj.* **-tier, -tiest.** *Chiefly Brit.* worn out, shabby, or unkempt.

taught (tɔːt) *vb.* past of **teach.**

taunt (tɔːnt) *vb.* **1.** to tease or provoke (someone) with jeering remarks. **~n. 2.** a jeering remark. **—ˈtaunting** *adj.*

taupe (təʊp) *adj.* brownish-grey.

Taurus (ˈtɔːrəs) *n.* the second sign of the zodiac; the bull.

taut (tɔːt) *adj.* **1.** tightly stretched: *a taut rope.* **2.** showing nervous strain. **3.** *Naut.* in good order; neat.

tauten (ˈtɔːtᵊn) *vb.* to make or become taut.

tautology (tɔːˈtɒlədʒɪ) *n., pl.* **-gies.** the use of words that merely repeat elements of the meaning already conveyed, as in "adequate enough". **—tautological** (ˌtɔːtəˈlɒdʒɪkᵊl) *or* **tautologous** (tɔːˈtɒləgəs) *adj.*

tavern (ˈtævən) *n.* **1.** a pub. **2.** *U.S., Canad., & N.Z.* a place licensed for the sale and consumption of alcoholic drink.

tawdry (ˈtɔːdrɪ) *adj.* **-drier, -driest.** cheap, showy, and of poor quality: *tawdry jewellery.*

tawny (ˈtɔːnɪ) *adj.* brown to brownish-orange.

tawny owl *n.* a European owl having a reddish-brown plumage and a round head.

tawse *or* **taws** (tɔːz) *n. Scot.* a leather strap having one end cut into thongs, formerly used as an instrument of punishment by schoolteachers.

tax (tæks) *n.* **1.** a compulsory financial contribution imposed by a government to raise revenue, levied on income, property, or goods and services. **2.** a heavy demand on something; strain: *a tax on our resources.* **~vb. 3.** to levy a tax on (persons, companies, etc.). **4.** to make heavy demands on; strain. **5.** to accuse: *he was taxed with the crime.* **—ˈtaxable** *adj.*

taxation (tækˈseɪʃən) *n.* the act or principle of levying taxes or the condition of being taxed.

tax avoidance *n.* reduction of tax liability by lawful methods.

tax-deductible *adj.* legally deductible from income or wealth before tax assessment.

tax evasion *n.* reduction of tax liability by illegal methods.

tax haven *n.* a country or state having a lower rate of taxation than elsewhere.

taxi (ˈtæksɪ) *n., pl.* **taxis** *or* **taxies. 1.** Also called: **cab, taxicab.** a car, usually fitted with a taximeter, that may be hired to carry passengers to any specified destination. **~vb. taxiing, taxied. 2.** (of an aircraft) to move along the ground, esp. before takeoff and after landing. **3.** to travel in a taxi.

taxidermy (ˈtæksɪˌdɜːmɪ) *n.* the art or process of preparing, stuffing, and mounting animal skins so that they have a lifelike appearance. **—ˈtaxiˌdermist** *n.*

taximeter (ˈtæksɪˌmiːtə) *n.* a meter fitted to a taxi to register the fare, based on the length of the journey.

taxi rank *n.* a place where taxis wait to be hired.

taxonomy (tækˈsɒnəmɪ) *n.* **1.** the branch of biology concerned with the classification of plants and animals into groups based on their similarities and differences. **2.** the science or practice of classification. **—taxonomic** (ˌtæksəˈnɒmɪk) *adj.* **—taxˈonomist** *n.*

taxpayer (ˈtæksˌpeɪə) *n.* a person or organization that pays taxes.

tax return *n.* a declaration of personal income used as a basis for assessing an individual's liability for taxation.

Tb *Chem.* terbium.

TB tuberculosis.

T-bone steak *n.* a large choice steak cut from the sirloin of beef, containing a T-shaped bone.

tbs. *or* **tbsp.** tablespoon(ful).

Tc *Chem.* technetium.

te *or* **ti** (tiː) *n. Music.* (in tonic sol-fa) the syllable used for the seventh note or subtonic of any scale.

Te *Chem.* tellurium.

tea (tiː) *n.* **1.** an evergreen shrub of tropical and subtropical Asia with white fragrant flowers. **2. a.** the dried and shredded leaves of this shrub, used to make a drink by infusion in boiling water. **b.** such a drink, served hot or iced. **3.** *Chiefly Brit.* a light meal eaten in midafternoon, usually consisting of tea and cakes, sometimes with sandwiches. **4.** *Brit., Austral., & N.Z.* the main evening meal.

tea bag *n.* a small bag containing tea leaves, infused in boiling water to make tea.

tea ball *n. Chiefly U.S.* a perforated metal ball filled with tea leaves, used to make tea.

teacake (ˈtiːˌkeɪk) *n. Brit.* a flat bun, usually eaten toasted and buttered.

teach (tiːtʃ) *vb.* **teaching, taught. 1.** to help to learn; tell or show (someone) how to do something. **2.** to give instruction or lessons in (a subject) to (students). **3.** to cause to learn or understand: *experience taught him that he could not be a journalist.* —'**teachable** *adj.*

teacher ('tiːtʃə) *n.* a person whose occupation is teaching others, esp. children.

tea chest *n.* a large light wooden box used for exporting tea or storing things in.

teaching ('tiːtʃɪŋ) *n.* **1.** the art or profession of a teacher. **2.** (*sometimes pl.*) something taught; precept.

tea cloth *n.* same as **tea towel.**

tea cosy *n.* a covering for a teapot to keep the contents hot.

teacup ('tiː,kʌp) *n.* **1.** a cup out of which tea may be drunk. **2.** Also called: **teacupful.** the amount a teacup will hold.

teahouse ('tiː,haʊs) *n.* a restaurant, esp. in Japan or China, where tea and light refreshments are served.

teak (tiːk) *n.* the hard yellowish-brown wood of an East Indian tree, used for furniture making.

teal (tiːl) *n., pl.* **teals** or **teal.** a small freshwater duck related to the mallard.

tea leaves *pl. n., sing.* **tea leaf.** the dried and shredded leaves of the tea shrub, esp. those left behind in a cup or teapot after tea has been made and drunk.

team (tiːm) *n.* (*sometimes functioning as pl.*) **1.** a group of players forming one of the sides in a sporting contest. **2.** a group of people organized to work together. **3.** two or more animals working together. ~*vb.* **4.** (often foll. by *up with*) to make or join a team.

team-mate *n.* a fellow member of a team.

team spirit *n.* willingness to cooperate as part of a team.

teamster ('tiːmstə) *n.* **1.** (formerly) a driver of a team of horses. **2.** *U.S. & Canad.* a truck driver.

teamwork ('tiːm,wɜːk) *n.* the cooperative work done by a team.

teapot ('tiː,pɒt) *n.* a container with a lid, spout, and handle, in which tea is made and from which it is served.

tear[1] (tɪə) *n.* **1.** Also called: **teardrop.** a drop of salty fluid appearing in and falling from the eye. **2. in tears.** weeping.

tear[2] (tɛə) *vb.* **tearing, tore, torn. 1.** to come apart or cause to come apart; rip. **2.** to make (a hole or split) in (something). **3.** (often foll. by *along*) to hurry or rush. **4.** (usually foll. by *away* or *from*) to remove or take by force: *the boat was torn from its moorings by the storm.* **5.** (foll. by *at*) to cause distress or anguish to: *it tore at her heartstrings to see the starving children.* ~*n.* **6.** a hole, cut, or split. **7.** the act of tearing. ~See also **tear away, tear down, tear into.**

tear away (tɛə) *vb.* **1.** to persuade (oneself or someone else) to leave: *I couldn't tear myself away from the television.* ~*n.* **tear-**

away. **2.** *Brit.* a reckless, impetuous, or unruly person.

tear down (tɛə) *vb.* to destroy or demolish: *to tear down an argument.*

tear duct (tɪə) *n.* a short tube in the inner corner of the eyelid, through which tears drain into the nose.

tearful ('tɪəfʊl) *adj.* crying or about to cry. —'**tearfully** *adv.*

tear gas (tɪə) *n.* a gas that makes the eyes sore and causes temporary blindness; used in warfare and to control riots.

tearing ('tɛərɪŋ) *adj.* violent or furious: *I'm in a tearing hurry this morning.*

tear into (tɛə) *vb. Informal.* to attack vigorously and damagingly.

tear-jerker ('tɪə,dʒɜːkə) *n. Informal.* an excessively sentimental film or book.

tearoom ('tiː,ruːm) *n. Brit.* a restaurant where tea and light refreshments are served.

tease (tiːz) *vb.* **1.** to make fun of (someone) in a provocative and often playful manner. **2.** to comb (flax, wool, or hair) so as to get the tangles out. **3.** to raise the nap of (a fabric) with a teasel. ~*n.* **4.** a person or thing that teases. **5.** the act of teasing. —'**teaser** *n.* —'**teasing** *adj.*

teasel, teazel, or **teazle** ('tiːzəl) *n.* **1.** a plant of Eurasia and N Africa, with prickly heads of yellow or purple flowers. **2.** the dried flower head of a teasel, used for teasing.

teaspoon ('tiː,spuːn) *n.* **1.** a small spoon used for stirring tea or coffee. **2.** Also called: **teaspoonful.** the amount contained in such a spoon.

teat (tiːt) *n.* **1.** the nipple of a breast or udder. **2.** something resembling a teat such as the rubber mouthpiece of a feeding bottle.

tea towel or **tea cloth** *n.* a towel for drying dishes.

tech (tɛk) *n. Informal.* a technical college.

tech. **1.** technical. **2.** technology.

technetium (tɛk'niːʃɪəm) *n.* a silvery-grey metallic element, produced artificially, esp. by the fission of uranium. Symbol: Tc

technical ('tɛknɪk°l) *adj.* **1.** of or specializing in industrial, practical, or mechanical arts and applied sciences: *a technical institute.* **2.** skilled in practical activities rather than abstract thinking. **3.** relating to a particular field of activity: *the technical jargon of linguistics.* **4.** existing by virtue of a strict application of rules or a strict interpretation of wording: *a technical loophole in the law.* **5.** showing technique: *technical brilliance.* —'**technically** *adv.*

technical college *n. Brit.* an institution for further education that provides courses in art and technical subjects.

technical drawing *n.* drawing done by a

draughtsman with compasses, T-squares, etc.

technicality (ˌtɛknɪˈkælɪtɪ) n., pl. **-ties. 1.** a petty formal point arising from a strict interpretation of the law or a set of rules. **2.** the state or quality of being technical.

technical knockout n. Boxing. a judgment of a knockout given when a boxer is, in the referee's opinion, too badly beaten to continue without risk of serious injury.

technician (tɛkˈnɪʃən) n. a person skilled in a particular technical field: a laboratory technician.

Technicolor (ˈtɛknɪˌkʌlə) n. Trademark. a process of producing colour film by superimposing synchronized films of the same scene, each having a different colour filter.

technique (tɛkˈniːk) n. **1.** a practical method, skill, or art applied to a particular task. **2.** proficiency in a practical or mechanical skill. **3.** special facility; knack.

technocracy (tɛkˈnɒkrəsɪ) n., pl. **-cies.** government by scientists, engineers, and other experts. —**technocrat** (ˈtɛknəˌkræt) n. —ˌtechnoˈcratic adj.

technology (tɛkˈnɒlədʒɪ) n., pl. **-gies. 1.** the application of practical or mechanical sciences to industry or commerce. **2.** the methods governing such application. —**technological** (ˌtɛknəˈlɒdʒɪk²l) adj. —techˈnologist n.

tectonics (tɛkˈtɒnɪks) n. (functioning as sing.) Geol. the study of the earth's crust and the forces that produce changes in it.

ted[1] (tɛd) vb. **tedding, tedded.** to shake out (hay), so as to dry it.

ted[2] (tɛd) n. Informal. short for **teddy boy.**

teddy[1] (ˈtɛdɪ) n., pl. **-dies.** short for **teddy bear.**

teddy[2] (ˈtɛdɪ) n., pl. **-dies.** a woman's one-piece undergarment incorporating a camisole top and French knickers.

teddy bear n. a stuffed toy bear.

teddy boy n. (in Britain, esp. in the mid-1950s) a youth who wore mock Edwardian fashions.

Te Deum (ˌtiː ˈdiːəm) n. Christianity. an ancient Latin hymn beginning Te Deum Laudamus (we praise thee, O God).

tedious (ˈtiːdɪəs) adj. causing fatigue or tedium; monotonous. —ˈtediously adv. —ˈtediousness n.

tedium (ˈtiːdɪəm) n. the state of being bored or the quality of being boring; monotony.

tee[1] (tiː) n. a pipe fitting in the form of a letter T, used to join three pipes.

tee[2] (tiː) n. **1.** a support for a golf ball, usually a small wooden or plastic peg, used when teeing off. **2.** an area on a golf course from which the first stroke of a hole is made. **3.** a mark used as a target in certain games such as curling and quoits. ~See also **tee off.**

tee-hee or **te-hee** (ˈtiːˈhiː) interj. an exclamation of mocking laughter.

teem[1] (tiːm) vb. (usually foll. by with) to be abundant (in): the town was teeming with sightseers.

teem[2] (tiːm) vb. (of rain) to pour down in torrents.

teen (tiːn) adj. Informal. same as **teenage.**

teenage (ˈtiːnˌeɪdʒ) adj. of the time in a person's life between the ages of 13 and 19.

teenager (ˈtiːnˌeɪdʒə) n. a person between the ages of 13 and 19.

teens (tiːnz) pl. n. **1.** the years of a person's life between the ages of 13 and 19. **2.** all the numbers that end in -teen.

teeny (ˈtiːnɪ) adj. **-nier, -niest.** extremely small; tiny.

teenybopper (ˈtiːnɪˌbɒpə) n. Old-fashioned slang. a young teenager, usually a girl, who avidly follows fashions in clothes and pop music.

tee off vb. Golf. to strike (the ball) from a tee, as when starting a hole.

teepee (ˈtiːpiː) n. same as **tepee.**

teeter (ˈtiːtə) vb. to move or cause to move unsteadily; wobble.

teeth (tiːθ) n. **1.** the plural of **tooth. 2.** the power to produce a desired effect: a law with no teeth. **3. armed to the teeth.** very heavily armed. **4. get one's teeth into.** to become engrossed in. **5. in the teeth of.** in direct opposition to; against.

teethe (tiːð) vb. to cut one's baby (deciduous) teeth.

teething ring n. a hard ring on which babies may bite while teething.

teething troubles pl. n. problems arising during the early stages of a project.

teetotal (tiːˈtəʊt²l) adj. practising total abstinence from alcoholic drink. —ˈtee-ˈtotaller n.

te-hee (ˈtiːˈhiː) interj. same as **tee-hee.**

tel. telephone.

tele- combining form. **1.** at or over a distance: telescope. **2.** television: telecast. **3.** via telephone or television: teleshopping.

telecast (ˈtɛləˌkɑːst) vb. **-casting, -cast** or **-casted. 1.** to broadcast by television. ~n. **2.** a television broadcast. —ˈteleˌcaster n.

telecommunications (ˌtɛlɪkəˌmjuːnɪˈkeɪʃənz) n. (functioning as sing.) communications using electronic equipment, such as telephony, radio, and television.

telegram (ˈtɛlɪˌgræm) n. (formerly) a communication transmitted by telegraph.

telegraph (ˈtɛlɪˌgrɑːf) n. **1.** (formerly) a system by which information could be transmitted over a distance, using electrical signals sent along a transmission line. ~vb. **2.** (formerly) to send (a message) to (a person or place) by telegraph. **3.** Canad. informal. to cast (a vote) illegally by impersonating a registered voter. —**telegrapher**

(tɪˈlɛgrəfə) *or* **teˈlegraphist** *n.* —ˌtele-
ˈgraphic *adj.*

telegraphy (tɪˈlɛgrəfɪ) *n.* (formerly) a system of telecommunications providing reproduction at a distance of written, printed, or
pictorial matter.

telekinesis (ˌtɛlɪkɪˈniːsɪs) *n.* movement of a
body by thought or willpower, without the
application of a physical force. —**teleki-
netic** (ˌtɛlɪkɪˈnɛtɪk) *adj.*

telemeter (tɪˈlɛmɪtə) *n.* any device for recording or measuring a distant event and
transmitting the data to a receiver. —**tele-
metric** (ˌtɛlɪˈmɛtrɪk) *adj.*

teleology (ˌtiːlɪˈɒlədʒɪ) *n.* **1.** *Philosophy.*
the doctrine that there is evidence of purpose or design in the universe. **2.** *Biol.* the
belief that natural phenomena have a predetermined purpose and are not determined
by mechanical laws. —**teleological** (ˌtiːlɪə-
ˈlɒdʒɪkᵊl) *adj.* —ˌtele**ologist** *n.*

telepathy (tɪˈlɛpəθɪ) *n.* the communication
between people of thoughts and feelings
involving mechanisms that cannot be
understood in terms of known scientific
laws. —**telepathic** (ˌtɛlɪˈpæθɪk) *adj.* —te-
ˈlepathist *n.*

telephone (ˈtɛlɪˌfəʊn) *n.* **1.** an electrical
device for transmitting speech, consisting
of a microphone and receiver mounted on a
handset and connected to a telecommunications network. ~*vb.* **2.** to call or talk to (a
person) by telephone. —**telephonic** (ˌtɛlɪ-
ˈfɒnɪk) *adj.*

telephone box *n.* a soundproof enclosure
from which a paid telephone call can be
made.

telephone directory *n.* a book listing
the names, addresses, and telephone numbers of subscribers in a particular area.

telephonist (tɪˈlɛfənɪst) *n.* *Brit.* a person
who operates a telephone switchboard.

telephony (tɪˈlɛfənɪ) *n.* a system of telecommunications for the transmission of
speech or other sounds.

telephotography (ˌtɛlɪfəˈtɒgrəfɪ) *n.* the
process or technique of photographing distant objects using a telephoto lens.

telephoto lens (ˈtɛlɪˌfəʊtəʊ) *n.* a lens fitted
to a camera to produce a magnified image of
a distant object.

teleprinter (ˈtɛlɪˌprɪntə) *n.* an apparatus,
similar to a typewriter, by which typed
messages are sent and received by wire.

Teleprompter (ˈtɛlɪˌprɒmptə) *n.* *Trademark.* a device for displaying a script under
a television camera, so that a speaker can
read it while appearing to look at the camera.

telesales (ˈtɛlɪˌseɪlz) *pl. n.* the selling of a
commodity or service by telephone.

telescope (ˈtɛlɪˌskəʊp) *n.* **1.** an optical
instrument for making distant objects appear closer by use of a combination of

lenses. **2.** See **radio telescope.** ~*vb.* **3.** to
fit together as a set of cylinders that slide
into one another, thus allowing extension
and shortening. **4.** to crush so as to foreshorten: *the car was telescoped by the impact.* —**telescopic** (ˌtɛlɪˈskɒpɪk) *adj.*

telescopic sight *n.* a sight on a rifle, etc.,
consisting of a telescope, used for aiming at
distant objects.

teletext (ˈtɛlɪˌtɛkst) *n.* a videotext service
in which the consumer is not able to interact with the computer. Cf. **viewdata.**

Teletype (ˈtɛlɪˌtaɪp) *n.* *Trademark.* a type
of teleprinter.

televangelist (ˌtɛlɪˈvændʒəlɪst) *n.* *U.S.* an
evangelical preacher who appears regularly
on television, preaching the gospel and appealing for donations from viewers.

televise (ˈtɛlɪˌvaɪz) *vb.* to transmit (a programme) by television.

television (ˈtɛlɪˌvɪʒən) *n.* **1.** the system or
process of producing on a distant screen a
moving image with accompanying sound.
2. Also called: **television set.** a device designed to receive and convert incoming electrical signals into a series of visible images
on a screen together with accompanying
sound. **3.** the content of television programmes. **4.** (*modifier*) of or used in television: *a television transmitter.* ~Abbrev.:
TV —**televisual** (ˌtɛlɪˈvɪʒʊəl) *adj.*

telex (ˈtɛlɛks) *n.* **1.** an international text-
transmission service in which teleprinters
are rented out to subscribers. **2.** a teleprinter used in such a service. **3.** a message
transmitted or received by telex. ~*vb.* **4.**
to transmit (a message) by telex.

Telidon (ˈtɛlɪˌdɒn) *n.* *Trademark.* a Canadian interactive viewdata service.

tell (tɛl) *vb.* **telling, told.** **1.** to say to
(someone); assure or notify: *he told me he
would go.* **2.** to order or instruct (someone
to do something): *I told her to send the
letter airmail.* **3.** (usually foll. by *of*) to
give an account of (an event or situation).
4. to communicate by words: *to tell the
truth.* **5.** (used with *can* or *could*) to discover, distinguish, or discern: *I can tell
what is wrong; he couldn't tell chalk from
cheese.* **6.** to have or produce an impact or
effect: *every step told on his bruised feet.*
7. *Informal.* to reveal secrets or gossip. **8.**
tell the time. to read the time from a clock.
9. you're telling me. *Slang.* I know that
very well. ~See also **tell apart, tell off.**

tell apart *vb.* to distinguish between: *can
you tell the twins apart?*

teller (ˈtɛlə) *n.* **1.** a bank cashier. **2.** a
person appointed to count votes.

telling (ˈtɛlɪŋ) *adj.* having a marked effect
or impact: *a telling blow.*

tell off *vb.* *Informal.* to reprimand (someone).

telltale (ˈtɛlˌteɪl) *n.* **1.** a person who tells

tales about others. **2.** (*modifier*) indicating something concealed: *telltale signs of movement.*

tellurian (tɛˈlʊərɪən) *adj.* of the earth.

tellurium (tɛˈlʊərɪəm) *n.* a brittle silvery-white nonmetallic element. Symbol: Te

telly (ˈtɛlɪ) *n., pl.* **-lies.** *Informal, chiefly Brit.* short for **television.**

temerity (tɪˈmɛrɪtɪ) *n.* rashness or boldness.

temp (tɛmp) *Informal.* ~*n.* **1.** a person, esp. a typist or other office worker, employed on a temporary basis. ~*vb.* **2.** to work as a temp.

temp. 1. temperature. **2.** temporary.

temper (ˈtɛmpə) *n.* **1.** a sudden outburst of anger: *to get into a temper.* **2.** a tendency to have sudden outbursts of anger: *she has a nasty temper.* **3.** a mental condition of moderation and calm: *he lost his temper; keep your temper.* **4.** a person's frame of mind; mood or humour: *what sort of temper is he in?* ~*vb.* **5.** to modify so as to make less extreme or more acceptable: *he tempered his criticism with sympathy.* **6.** to strengthen or toughen (a metal) by heating and quenching. **7.** *Music.* to adjust the frequency differences between the notes of a scale on (a keyboard instrument).

tempera (ˈtɛmpərə) *n.* a painting medium for powdered pigments, consisting usually of egg yolk and water.

temperament (ˈtɛmpərəmənt) *n.* a person's character or disposition.

temperamental (ˌtɛmpərəˈmɛntˀl) *adj.* **1.** tending to be moody and have sudden outbursts of anger. **2.** of or caused by temperament. **3.** *Informal.* working erratically and inconsistently; unreliable: *a temperamental sewing machine.* —ˌtemperaˈmentally *adv.*

temperance (ˈtɛmpərəns) *n.* **1.** restraint or moderation, esp. in yielding to one's appetites or desires. **2.** abstinence from alcoholic drink.

temperate (ˈtɛmpərɪt) *adj.* **1.** having a climate intermediate between tropical and polar. **2.** mild in quality or character; exhibiting temperance.

Temperate Zone *n.* those parts of the earth's surface lying between the Arctic Circle and the tropic of Cancer and between the Antarctic Circle and the tropic of Capricorn.

temperature (ˈtɛmprɪtʃə) *n.* **1.** the degree of hotness of a body, substance, or medium, esp. as measured on a scale that has one or more fixed reference points. **2.** *Informal.* a body temperature in excess of the normal.

tempest (ˈtɛmpɪst) *n.* *Literary.* a violent wind or storm.

tempestuous (tɛmˈpɛstjʊəs) *adj.* **1.** of or relating to a tempest. **2.** violent or stormy. —temˈpestuously *adv.*

template (ˈtɛmplɪt) *n.* a wood or metal pattern, used to help cut out shapes accurately.

temple¹ (ˈtɛmpˀl) *n.* a building or place dedicated to the worship of a deity or deities.

temple² (ˈtɛmpˀl) *n.* the region on each side of the head in front of the ear and above the cheek bone.

tempo (ˈtɛmpəʊ) *n., pl.* **-pos** *or* **-pi** (-piː). **1.** the speed at which a piece of music is played or meant to be played. **2.** rate or pace.

temporal¹ (ˈtɛmpərəl) *adj.* **1.** of or relating to time. **2.** of secular as opposed to spiritual or religious affairs. **3.** lasting for a relatively short time.

temporal² (ˈtɛmpərəl) *adj.* *Anat.* of or near the temple or temples.

temporal bone *n.* either of two compound bones forming the sides of the skull.

temporary (ˈtɛmpərərɪ) *adj.* not permanent; lasting only a short time: *temporary accommodation; temporary relief from pain.* —ˈtemporarily *adv.*

temporize *or* **-ise** (ˈtɛmpəˌraɪz) *vb.* **1.** to delay, act evasively, or protract a negotiation in order to gain time or effect a compromise. **2.** to adapt oneself to circumstances, as by temporary or apparent agreement.

tempt (tɛmpt) *vb.* **1.** to entice (someone) to do something, esp. something morally wrong or unwise. **2.** to allure or attract. **3.** to risk provoking: *she was tempting fate.* —ˈtempter *n.* —ˈtemptress *fem. n.*

temptation (tɛmpˈteɪʃən) *n.* **1.** the act of tempting or the state of being tempted. **2.** a person or thing that tempts.

tempting (ˈtɛmptɪŋ) *adj.* attractive or inviting: *a tempting meal.* —ˈtemptingly *adv.*

ten (tɛn) *n.* **1.** the cardinal number that is the sum of nine and one. **2.** a numeral, 10, X, representing this number. **3.** something representing or consisting of ten units. ~*det.* **4.** amounting to ten. —**tenth** *adj., n.*

ten. *Music.* **1.** tenor. **2.** tenuto.

tenable (ˈtɛnəbˀl) *adj.* able to be upheld, believed, maintained, or defended: *a tenable proposition.* —ˌtenaˈbility *n.* —ˈtenably *adv.*

tenacious (tɪˈneɪʃəs) *adj.* **1.** holding firmly: *a tenacious grip.* **2.** exceptionally good at remembering: *a tenacious memory.* **3.** stubborn or persistent: *a tenacious character.* —teˈnaciously *adv.* —**tenacity** (tɪˈnæsɪtɪ) *n.*

tenancy (ˈtɛnənsɪ) *n., pl.* **-cies. 1.** the temporary possession by a tenant of lands or property owned by another. **2.** the period of holding or occupying such property.

tenant (ˈtɛnənt) *n.* **1.** a person who pays rent for the use of land or property. **2.** any holder or occupant.

tenant farmer   *n.* a person who farms land rented from another.

tenantry ('tɛnəntrɪ) *n. Old-fashioned.* tenants collectively.

tench (tɛntʃ) *n.* a European freshwater game fish of the carp family.

Ten Commandments *pl. n.* **the.** *Bible.* the commandments given by God to Moses on Mount Sinai, summarizing the basic obligations of man towards God and his fellow men.

tend¹ (tɛnd) *vb.* (usually foll. by *to* or *towards*) **1.** to have a general disposition to take a particular kind of action or to be in a particular condition; be inclined: *children tend to prefer sweets to meat.* **2.** to go or move (in a particular direction): *to tend to the south.*

tend² (tɛnd) *vb.* **1.** to care for; look after: *to tend a sick mother.* **2.** (foll. by *to*) to attend to: *to tend to someone's wishes.* **3.** to handle or control: *to tend a fire.*

tendency ('tɛndənsɪ) *n., pl.* **-cies. 1.** (often foll. by *to*) an inclination to act in a particular way. **2.** the general course, purport, or drift of something, esp. a written work.

tendentious (tɛn'dɛnʃəs) *adj.* having or showing a particular tendency or bias, esp. a controversial one. **—ten'dentiously** *adv.*

tender¹ ('tɛndə) *adj.* **1.** having or expressing gentle and sympathetic feelings: *a tender smile; a tender heart.* **2.** easily damaged; vulnerable or sensitive: *at a tender age.* **3.** easily hurt when touched: *a tender spot on one's hand.* **—'tenderly** *adv.* **—'tenderness** *n.*

tender² ('tɛndə) *vb.* **1.** to present or offer: *to tender one's resignation.* **2.** (foll. by *for*) to make a formal offer or estimate (for a job or contract). *~n.* **3.** a formal offer to supply specified goods or services at a stated cost or rate. **—'tenderer** *n.*

tender³ ('tɛndə) *n.* **1.** a small boat that brings supplies to larger vessels in a port. **2.** a vehicle drawn behind a steam locomotive to carry the fuel and water.

tenderfoot ('tɛndə,fʊt) *n., pl.* **-foots** *or* **-feet. 1.** a newcomer, esp. to the mines or ranches of the southwestern U.S. **2.** (formerly) a beginner in the Scouts or Guides.

tenderize *or* **-ise** ('tɛndə,raɪz) *vb.* to make (meat) tender, as by pounding it or adding a substance to break down the fibres. **—'tender,izer** *or* **-,iser** *n.*

tenderloin ('tɛndə,lɔɪn) *n.* a tender cut of pork or other meat from between the sirloin and ribs.

tendon ('tɛndən) *n.* a band of tough tissue that attaches a muscle to a bone or some other part.

tendril ('tɛndrɪl) *n.* a threadlike leaf or stem of a climbing plant that attaches itself to a support by twining.

tenement ('tɛnəmənt) *n.* a large building divided into several different apartments or flats.

tenet ('tɛnɪt, 'tiːnɪt) *n.* a belief, opinion, or dogma.

tenfold ('tɛn,fəʊld) *adj.* **1.** having ten times as many or as much. **2.** composed of ten parts. *~adv.* **3.** ten times as many or as much.

ten-gallon hat   *n.* (in the U.S.) a cowboy's broad-brimmed felt hat with a very high crown.

Tenn. Tennessee.

tenner ('tɛnə) *n. Informal.* **1.** *Brit.* a ten-pound note. **2.** *U.S.* a ten-dollar bill.

tennis ('tɛnɪs) *n.* a game played between two players or pairs of players who use a racket to hit a ball to and fro over a net on a rectangular court. See also **lawn tennis, real tennis, table tennis.**

tennis elbow   *n.* inflammation of the elbow, typically caused by exertion in playing tennis.

tenon ('tɛnən) *n.* a projecting end of a piece of timber, formed to fit into a corresponding slot in another piece.

tenor ('tɛnə) *n.* **1.** *Music.* **a.** the male voice between alto and baritone. **b.** a singer with such a voice. **c.** a saxophone, horn, or other musical instrument between the alto and baritone or bass. **2.** general drift of thought; purpose. **3.** a settled course of progress.

tenpin bowling ('tɛn,pɪn) *n.* a bowling game in which bowls are rolled down a lane to knock over the ten target pins.

tense¹ (tɛns) *adj.* **1.** characterized by, causing, or suffering from mental or emotional strain: *a very tense person; a tense atmosphere.* **2.** stretched or stressed tightly; taut or rigid. *~vb.* **3.** (often foll. by *up*) to make or become tense. **—'tenseness** *n.*

tense² (tɛns) *n. Grammar.* a category of the verb or verbal inflections, typically present, past, and future, that expresses the temporal relations between what is reported in a sentence and the time of its utterance.

tensile ('tɛnsaɪl) *adj.* of or relating to tension or being stretched: *the tensile strength of steel.*

tensile strength   *n.* a measure of the ability of a material to withstand lengthwise stress, expressed as the greatest stress that the material can stand without breaking.

tension ('tɛnʃən) *n.* **1.** a force that stretches or the state or degree of being stretched tight. **2.** mental or emotional strain; stress. **3.** a situation or condition of hostility, suspense, or uneasiness. **4.** *Physics.* a force that tends to produce an elongation of a body or structure. **5.** *Physics.*

voltage, electromotive force, or potential difference.

tent (tɛnt) *n.* **1.** a portable shelter made of canvas or other fabric supported on poles, stretched out, and fastened to the ground by pegs and ropes. **2.** something resembling this in function or shape.

tentacle ('tɛntək'l) *n.* any of various flexible organs that grow near the mouth in many invertebrates and are used for feeding, grasping, etc. —'**tentacled** *adj.*

tentative ('tɛntətɪv) *adj.* **1.** provisional or experimental: *a tentative plan.* **2.** hesitant, uncertain, or cautious: *a tentative smile.* —'**tentatively** *adv.* —'**tentativeness** *n.*

tenter ('tɛntə) *n.* a frame on which cloth is stretched in order that it may retain its shape while drying.

tenterhook ('tɛntə,hʊk) *n.* **1.** one of a series of hooks used to hold cloth on a tenter. **2. on tenterhooks.** in a state of tension or suspense.

tenth (tɛnθ) *adj., n.* See **ten.**

tenuous ('tɛnjʊəs) *adj.* **1.** insignificant or flimsy: *a tenuous argument.* **2.** slim, fine, or delicate: *a tenuous thread.* —'**tenuously** *adv.*

tenure ('tɛnjʊə, 'tɛnjə) *n.* **1.** the possession or holding of an office or position. **2.** the length of time an office or position lasts. **3.** the holding of a teaching position on a permanent basis. **4.** the legal right to live in a place or to use land or buildings for a period of time.

tenuto (tɪ'njuːtəʊ) *adj., adv. Music.* (of a note) to be held for or beyond its full time value.

tepee *or* **teepee** ('tiːpiː) *n.* a cone-shaped tent of animal skins, formerly used by American Indians.

tepid ('tɛpɪd) *adj.* **1.** slightly warm; lukewarm. **2.** relatively unenthusiastic or apathetic: *the play had a tepid reception.* —**te'pidity** *n.* —'**tepidly** *adv.*

tequila (tɪ'kiːlə) *n.* a Mexican spirit that is distilled from the agave plant.

ter. **1.** terrace. **2.** territory.

tera- ('tɛrə) *prefix.* one million million.

terbium ('tɜːbɪəm) *n.* a soft silvery-grey element of the lanthanide series of metals. Symbol: Tb

tercel ('tɜːs'l) *n.* a male falcon or hawk.

tercentenary (,tɜːsɛn'tiːnərɪ) *or* **tercentennial** *adj.* **1.** of a 300th anniversary. ~*n., pl.* -**tenaries** *or* -**tennials.** **2.** an anniversary of 300 years.

tercet ('tɜːsɪt, tɜː'sɛt) *n.* a group of three lines of verse that rhyme with adjacent groups of three lines.

teredo (tɛ'riːdəʊ) *n., pl.* -**dos** *or* -**dines** (-dɪ-,niːz). a marine mollusc that bores into and destroys submerged timber.

tergiversate ('tɜːdʒɪvə,seɪt) *vb.* **1.** to change sides or loyalties. **2.** to be evasive or ambiguous. —,**tergiver'sation** *n.* —'**tergiver,sator** *n.*

term (tɜːm) *n.* **1.** a word or expression used for some particular thing, esp. in a specialized field of knowledge: *a medical term.* **2.** any word or expression. **3.** a limited period of time: *a prison term.* **4.** the end of a specific period of time: *the project had reached full term.* **5.** the period of pregnancy when childbirth is imminent. **6.** a division of the academic year during which a school, college, or university is in session. **7.** one of the periods of time during which sessions of courts of law are held. **8.** *Maths.* any distinct quantity making up a fraction or proportion, or contained in a sequence, series, etc. **9.** *Logic.* any of the three subjects or predicates occurring in a syllogism. ~*vb.* **10.** to designate; call: *a breakthrough in what is termed "birth technology".* ~See also **terms.**

termagant ('tɜːməgənt) *n. Literary.* an unpleasant shrewish woman; scold.

terminable ('tɜːmɪnəb'l) *adj.* capable of being terminated: *a terminable annuity.* —,**termina'bility** *n.*

terminal ('tɜːmɪn'l) *adj.* **1.** (of an illness) terminating in death. **2.** situated at an end, terminus, or boundary: *a terminal bud.* ~*n.* **3.** a terminating point, part, or place. **4.** a point at which current enters or leaves an electrical device. **5.** *Computers.* a device, usually a keyboard and a visual display unit, having input/output links with a computer. **6.** a place where vehicles, passengers, or goods begin or end a journey: *a bus terminal; an oil terminal.* —'**terminally** *adv.*

terminal velocity *n. Physics.* the maximum velocity reached by a body falling under gravity through a fluid, esp. in the atmosphere.

terminate ('tɜːmɪ,neɪt) *vb.* to come to an end or put an end to; conclude.

termination (,tɜːmɪ'neɪʃən) *n.* **1.** the act of terminating or the state of being terminated. **2.** something that terminates. **3.** a final result.

terminology (,tɜːmɪ'nɒlədʒɪ) *n., pl.* -**gies.** the body of specialized words and expressions relating to a particular subject. —**terminological** (,tɜːmɪnə'lɒdʒɪk'l) *adj.* —,**termin'ologist** *n.*

terminus ('tɜːmɪnəs) *n., pl.* -**ni** (-naɪ) *or* -**nuses.** **1.** the final point. **2.** either end of a railway, bus route, etc. **3.** a station or town at such a point.

termite ('tɜːmaɪt) *n.* a whitish antlike insect of warm and tropical regions.

terms (tɜːmz) *pl. n.* **1.** the actual language or mode of presentation used: *he described the project in loose terms.* **2.** the conditions of an agreement. **3.** (usually preceded by *on*) mutual relationship or standing: *they are on affectionate terms.* **4. come to**

terms. to reach acceptance or agreement. **5. in terms of.** as expressed by; regarding: *in terms of money he was no better off.*

tern (tɜːn) *n.* a sea bird with a forked tail, long narrow wings, and a typically black-and-white plumage.

ternary ('tɜːnərɪ) *adj.* **1.** consisting of three items or groups of three items. **2.** *Maths.* (of a number system) to the base three.

Terpsichore (tɜːp'sɪkərɪ) *n. Greek myth.* the Muse of the dance and of choral song.

Terpsichorean (,tɜːpsɪkə'rɪən, -'kɔːrɪən) *adj. Often used facetiously.* of or relating to dancing.

terrace ('tɛrəs) *n.* **1.** a row of houses, usually identical and joined together by common dividing walls, or the street onto which they face. **2.** a paved area alongside a building. **3.** a horizontal flat area of ground, often one of a series in a slope. **4.** (*usually pl.*) unroofed tiers around a football pitch on which the spectators stand. ~*vb.* **5.** to make into terraces.

terraced house *n. Brit.* a house that is part of a terrace.

terracotta (,tɛrə'kɒtə) *n.* **1.** a hard unglazed brownish-red earthenware used for pottery, sculpture, etc. ~*adj.* **2.** made of terracotta. **3.** brownish-orange.

terra firma ('fɜːmə) *n.* the solid earth; firm ground.

terrain (tə'reɪn) *n.* a piece of ground, esp. with reference to its physical character: *a rocky terrain.*

terra incognita ('tɛrə ɪn'kɒgnɪtə) *n.* an unexplored region.

terrapin ('tɛrəpɪn) *n.* a web-footed reptile of N America that lives in fresh water and on land and feeds on small aquatic animals.

terrarium (tɛ'rɛərɪəm) *n., pl.* **-riums** or **-ria** (-rɪə). **1.** an enclosure for small land animals. **2.** a glass container, often a globe, in which plants are grown.

terrazzo (tɛ'rætsəʊ) *n., pl.* **-zos.** a floor made by setting marble chips into a layer of mortar and polishing the surface.

terrestrial (tə'rɛstrɪəl) *adj.* **1.** of the planet earth. **2.** of the land as opposed to the sea or air. **3.** (of animals and plants) living or growing on the land. **4.** earthly, worldly, or mundane.

terrible ('tɛrəb'l) *adj.* **1.** very serious or extreme: *a terrible cough.* **2.** *Informal.* of poor quality; unpleasant or bad: *a terrible play.* **3.** causing terror. —**'terribly** *adv.*

terrier ('tɛrɪə) *n.* any of several small active breeds of dog, originally trained to hunt animals living underground.

terrific (tə'rɪfɪk) *adj.* **1.** very great or intense: *a terrific noise.* **2.** *Informal.* very good; excellent: *a terrific singer.* **3.** very frightening. —**ter'rifically** *adv.*

terrify ('tɛrɪ,faɪ) *vb.* **-fying, -fied.** to inspire fear or dread in; frighten greatly. —**'terri,fying** *adj.* —**'terri,fyingly** *adv.*

terrine (tɛ'riːn) *n.* **1.** an oval earthenware cooking dish with a tightly fitting lid. **2.** the food cooked or served in such a dish, esp. pâté.

territorial (,tɛrɪ'tɔːrɪəl) *adj.* **1.** of or relating to a territory or territories. **2.** restricted to or owned by a particular territory. **3.** local or regional. **4.** pertaining to a territorial army, providing a reserve of trained men for use in emergency. —**,terri'torially** *adv.* —**territoriality** (,tɛrɪ,tɔːrɪ'ælɪtɪ) *n.*

Territorial (,tɛrɪ'tɔːrɪəl) *n.* a member of a Territorial Army.

Territorial Army *n.* (in Britain) a standing reserve army.

territorial waters *pl. n.* the waters over which a nation exercises jurisdiction and control.

territory ('tɛrɪtrɪ) *n., pl.* **-ries. 1.** any tract of land; district. **2.** the geographical domain under the jurisdiction of a political unit, esp. a sovereign state. **3.** the district for which a travelling salesman is responsible. **4.** an area inhabited and defended by a particular animal or pair of animals. **5.** an area of knowledge. **6.** (*often cap.*) a region of a country, esp. of a federal state, that enjoys less autonomy and a lower status than most constituent parts of the state.

terror ('tɛrə) *n.* **1.** great fear, panic, or dread. **2.** a person or thing that inspires great dread. **3.** *Informal.* a troublesome person, esp. a child.

terrorism ('tɛrə,rɪzəm) *n.* the systematic use of violence and intimidation to achieve political ends. —**'terrorist** *n., adj.*

terrorize *or* **-ise** ('tɛrə,raɪz) *vb.* **1.** to coerce or control by violence, fear, threats, etc. **2.** to inspire with dread; terrify. —**,terrori'zation** *or* **-i'sation** *n.* —**'terror,izer** *or* **-,iser** *n.*

terry ('tɛrɪ) *n., pl.* **-ries. 1.** an uncut loop in the pile of towelling or a similar fabric. **2.** a fabric with such a pile.

terse (tɜːs) *adj.* **1.** neatly brief and concise. **2.** curt; abrupt. —**'tersely** *adv.* —**'terseness** *n.*

tertiary ('tɜːʃərɪ) *adj.* third in degree, order, etc.

Tertiary ('tɜːʃərɪ) *adj. Geol.* of the period of geological time lasting from about 65 million years ago to 600 000 years ago.

Terylene ('tɛrɪ,liːn) *n. Trademark.* a synthetic polyester fibre or fabric.

tessellated ('tɛsɪ,leɪtɪd) *adj.* paved or inlaid with a mosaic of small tiles.

tessera ('tɛsərə) *n., pl.* **-serae** (-sə,riː). a small square tile of stone, glass, etc., used in mosaics.

test¹ (tɛst) *vb.* **1.** to ascertain (the worth, capability, or endurance) of (a person or thing) by trying it out. **2.** (often foll. by *for*) to carry out an examination on (a substance, material, or system) in order to discover whether a particular substance, component, or feature is present: *to test food for arsenic.* ~*n.* **3.** a method, practice, or examination designed to test a person or thing. **4.** a series of questions or problems designed to test a specific skill or knowledge. **5.** a standard of judgment; criterion. **6.** a chemical reaction or physical procedure for testing the composition or other qualities of a substance. **7.** *Sport.* See **test match.** —**'testable** *adj.* —**'testing** *adj.*

test² (tɛst) *n.* the hard outer covering of certain invertebrates.

testa ('tɛstə) *n., pl.* **-tae** (-tiː). the hard outer layer of a seed.

testaceous (tɛ'steɪʃəs) *adj. Biol.* of or possessing a hard continuous shell.

testament ('tɛstəmənt) *n.* **1.** *Law.* a will: *last will and testament.* **2.** a proof or tribute: *his success was a testament to his skills.* —,testa'mentary *adj.*

Testament ('tɛstəmənt) *n.* either of the two main parts of the Bible; the Old Testament or the New Testament.

testate ('tɛsteɪt, 'tɛstɪt) *Law.* ~*adj.* **1.** having left a legally valid will at death. ~*n.* **2.** a person who dies testate. —**testacy** ('tɛstəsɪ) *n.*

testator (tɛ'steɪtə) *or* (*fem.*) **testatrix** (tɛ-'steɪtrɪks) *n. Law.* a person who has made a will, esp. one who has died testate.

test case *n.* a legal action that serves as a precedent in deciding similar succeeding cases.

testicle ('tɛstɪkᵊl) *n.* either of the two male reproductive glands, in most mammals enclosed within the scrotum, that produce spermatozoa.

testify ('tɛstɪˌfaɪ) *vb.* **-fying, -fied. 1.** *Law.* to declare or give (evidence) under oath, esp. in court. **2.** (often foll. by *to*) to be evidence of; serve as witness to: *the money testified to his good faith.*

testimonial (ˌtɛstɪ'məʊnɪəl) *n.* **1.** a recommendation of the character, ability, etc., of a person or of the quality of a product or service. **2.** a tribute given for services or achievements. ~*adj.* **3.** of a testimony or testimonial.

testimony ('tɛstɪmənɪ) *n., pl.* **-nies. 1.** a declaration of truth or fact. **2.** *Law.* evidence given by a witness, esp. in court under oath. **3.** evidence testifying to something: *her success was a testimony to her good luck.*

testis ('tɛstɪs) *n., pl.* **-tes.** same as **testicle.**

test match *n.* (in various sports, esp. cricket) any of a series of international matches.

testosterone (tɛ'stɒstəˌrəʊn) *n.* a steroid male sex hormone secreted by the testes.

test paper *n.* **1.** the question sheet of a test. **2.** *Chem.* paper impregnated with an indicator for use in chemical tests.

test pilot *n.* a pilot who flies aircraft of new design to test their performance in the air.

test tube *n.* a cylindrical round-bottomed glass tube open at one end: used in scientific experiments.

test-tube baby *n.* **1.** a fetus that has developed from an ovum fertilized in an artificial womb. **2.** a baby conceived by artificial insemination.

testy ('tɛstɪ) *adj.* **-tier, -tiest.** irritable or touchy. —**'testily** *adv.* —**'testiness** *n.*

tetanus ('tɛtənəs) *n.* an acute infectious disease in which sustained muscular spasm, contraction, and convulsion are caused by the release of toxins from a bacterium; lockjaw.

tetchy ('tɛtʃɪ) *adj.* **tetchier, tetchiest.** cross, irritable, or touchy. —**'tetchily** *adv.* —**'tetchiness** *n.*

tête-à-tête (ˌteɪtɑ'teɪt) *n., pl.* **-têtes** *or* **-tête. 1.** a private conversation between two people. ~*adv.* **2.** intimately; in private.

tether ('tɛðə) *n.* **1.** a rope or chain by which an animal is tied to a particular spot. **2. at the end of one's tether.** at the limit of one's patience or endurance. ~*vb.* **3.** to tie with or as if with a tether.

tetra- *combining form.* four: *tetrahedron.*

tetrad ('tɛtræd) *n.* a group or series of four.

tetraethyl lead (ˌtɛtrə'iːθaɪl lɛd) *n.* a colourless oily insoluble liquid used in petrol to prevent knocking.

tetragon ('tɛtrəˌgɒn) *n.* same as **quadrilateral** (sense 2).

tetrahedron (ˌtɛtrə'hiːdrən) *n., pl.* **-drons** *or* **-dra** (-drə). a solid figure having four plane faces. —,tetra'hedral *adj.*

tetralogy (tɛ'trælədʒɪ) *n., pl.* **-gies.** a series of four related works, as in drama or opera.

tetrameter (tɛ'træmɪtə) *n. Prosody.* a line of verse consisting of four metrical feet.

Teut. Teuton(ic).

Teuton ('tjuːtən) *n.* **1.** a member of an ancient Germanic people of N Europe. **2.** a member of any people speaking a Germanic language, esp. a German. ~*adj.* **3.** Teutonic.

Teutonic (tjuː'tɒnɪk) *adj.* **1.** characteristic of or relating to the German people. **2.** of the ancient Teutons.

Tex. Texas.

Tex-Mex ('tɛksˌmɛks) *adj.* **1.** combining elements of Texan and Mexican culture. ~*n.* **2.** Tex-Mex music or cooking.

text (tɛkst) *n.* **1.** the main body of a printed or written work as distinct from items such as notes or illustrations. **2.** words displayed on a visual display unit. **3.** a short passage of the Bible used as a starting point for a sermon. **4.** a novel or play prescribed as part of a course of study.

textbook ('tɛkst,bʊk) n. **1.** a book used as a standard source of information on a particular subject. **2.** perfect; exemplary: *she made a textbook landing.*

textile ('tɛkstaɪl) n. **1.** any fabric or cloth, esp. woven. **2.** raw material suitable to be made into cloth. ~adj. **3.** of or relating to fabrics.

textual ('tɛkstjʊəl) adj. of, based on, or relating to, a text or texts. —'**textually** adv.

texture ('tɛkstʃə) n. **1.** the surface of a material, esp. as perceived by the sense of touch. **2.** the structure, appearance, and feel of a woven fabric. ~vb. **3.** to give a distinctive texture to (something). —'**textural** adj.

Th Chem. thorium.

Thai (taɪ) adj. **1.** of Thailand, its people, or their language. ~n. **2.** (pl. **Thais** or **Thai**) a person from Thailand. **3.** the language of Thailand.

thalidomide (θə'lɪdə,maɪd) n. a drug formerly used as a sedative and hypnotic but withdrawn from use when found to cause abnormalities in developing fetuses.

thallium ('θælɪəm) n. a soft highly toxic white metallic element. Symbol: Tl

than (ðæn; unstressed ðən) conj., prep. **1.** used to introduce the second element of a comparison, the first element of which expresses difference: *shorter than you.* **2.** used after the adverbs *rather* and *sooner* to introduce a rejected alternative: *rather than be imprisoned, I shall die.*
Usage. In sentences such as *he does it far better than I,* than is usually regarded as a conjunction governing an unexpressed verb: *he does it far better than I (do it).* The case of any pronoun therefore depends on whether it is the subject or the object of the unexpressed verb: *she likes him more than I (like him); she likes him more than (she likes) me.* However, in informal usage *than* is often treated as a preposition and any pronoun is therefore used in its objective form, so that *she likes him more than me* is ambiguous.

thane or **thegn** (θeɪn) n. **1.** (in Anglo-Saxon England) a noble retainer who held land from the king or from a superior nobleman in return for certain services. **2.** (in medieval Scotland) a person of rank holding land from the king.

thank (θæŋk) vb. **1.** to convey feelings of gratitude to. **2.** to hold responsible: *he has his creditors to thank for his bankruptcy.* **3. thank you** or **thanks.** a polite response or expression of gratitude. **4. thank good-**ness, **thank heavens,** or **thank God.** an exclamation of relief.

thankful ('θæŋkfʊl) adj. grateful and appreciative. —'**thankfully** adv.

thankless ('θæŋklɪs) adj. **1.** receiving no thanks or appreciation. **2.** ungrateful. —'**thanklessly** adv. —'**thanklessness** n.

thanks (θæŋks) pl. n. **1.** an expression of appreciation or gratitude. **2. thanks to.** because of: *thanks to him we lost the match.* ~interj. **3.** Informal. an exclamation expressing gratitude.

thanksgiving (,θæŋks'gɪvɪŋ) n. a formal public expression of thanks to God.

Thanksgiving Day n. (in North America) an annual day of holiday celebrated on the fourth Thursday of November in the United States and on the second Monday of October in Canada.

that det. (ðæt). **1.** used preceding a noun that has been mentioned or is already familiar: *that idea of yours.* **2.** used preceding a noun that denotes something more remote: *that building over there.* **3. and (all) that.** Informal. and everything connected with the subject mentioned: *he knows a lot about building and that.* **4. at that.** additionally, all things considered, or nevertheless: *I might decide to go at that.* **5. that is. a.** to be precise. **b.** in other words. **6. that's that.** there is no more to be said or done. ~pron. (ðæt). **7.** used to denote something already mentioned or understood: *don't eat that.* **8.** used to denote a more remote person or thing: *that is John and this is his wife.* **9.** used to introduce a restrictive relative clause: *the book that we want.* ~conj. (ðæt; unstressed ðət). **10.** used to introduce a noun clause: *I believe that you'll come.* **11.** used, usually after *so,* to introduce a clause of purpose: *they fought so that others might have peace.* **12.** used to introduce a clause of result: *he laughed so hard that he cried.* **13.** Literary. used to introduce a clause expressing desire, indignation, or amazement: *oh, that I had never lived!* ~adv. (ðæt). **14.** Also: **all that.** Informal. (used for emphasis): *he wasn't that upset.*
Usage. *That* is used as a relative pronoun in restrictive clauses and *which* in nonrestrictive clauses. In *the book that is on the table is mine,* the clause *that is on the table* is used to distinguish one particular book (the one on the table) from another or others (which may be anywhere, but not on the table). In *the book, which is on the table, is mine,* the *which* clause is merely descriptive or incidental. The more formal the level of language, the more important it is to preserve the distinction between the two relative pronouns; but in informal or colloquial usage, the words are often used interchangeably.

thatch (θætʃ) n. **1.** Also called: **thatching.** a

roofing material that consists of straw or reeds. **2.** a roof made of such a material. **3.** anything resembling this, such as the hair of the head. ~*vb.* **4.** to cover with thatch. —'thatcher *n.*

thaw (θɔː) *vb.* **1.** to melt or cause to melt: *the snow thawed.* **2.** (of frozen food) to become or cause to become unfrozen; defrost. **3.** to be the case that the ice or snow is melting: *it's thawing fast.* **4.** to become more relaxed or friendly. ~*n.* **5.** the act or process of thawing. **6.** a spell of relatively warm weather, causing snow or ice to melt.

the[1] (*stressed or emphatic* ðiː; *unstressed before a consonant* ðə; *unstressed before a vowel* ðɪ) *det.* (*article*) **1.** used preceding a noun that has been previously specified or is a matter of common knowledge: *the pain should disappear soon.* **2.** used to indicate a particular person or object: *ask the man standing outside.* **3.** used preceding certain nouns associated with one's culture, society, or community: *to go to the doctor; to listen to the news.* **4.** used preceding an adjective that is functioning as a collective noun: *the deaf and the blind.* **5.** used preceding titles and certain proper nouns: *the United States; the Chairman.* **6.** used preceding a qualifying adjective or noun in certain names or titles: *Edward the First.* **7.** used preceding a noun to make it refer to its class generically: *the white seal is hunted for its fur.* **8.** used instead of *my, your, her,* etc., with parts of the body: *take me by the hand.* **9.** (*stressed*) the best or most remarkable: *Harry's is the club in this town.*

the[2] (ðə, ðɪ) *adv.* used correlatively before each of two comparative adjectives or adverbs to indicate equality: *the sooner you come, the better; the more I see you, the more I love you.*

theatre *or U.S.* **theater** ('θɪətə) *n.* **1.** a building designed for the performance of plays, operas, etc. **2.** a large room or hall with tiered seats for an audience. **3.** a room in a hospital equipped for surgical operations. **4. the theatre.** the world of actors and theatrical companies. **5.** *U.S., Austral., & N.Z.* same as **cinema** (sense 1).

theatrical (θɪ'ætrɪk°l) *adj.* **1.** of or relating to the theatre or dramatic performances. **2.** exaggerated and affected in manner or behaviour. —**the,atri'cality** *n.* —**the'atrically** *adv.*

theatricals (θɪ'ætrɪk°lz) *pl. n.* dramatic performances, esp. as given by amateurs.

thee (ðiː) *sing. pron. Archaic.* the objective form of **thou**[1].

theft (θɛft) *n.* the act or an instance of stealing.

thegn (θeɪn) *n.* same as **thane** (sense 1).

their (ðɛə) *det.* of or associated with them: *their own clothes; she tried to combat their mocking her.*

theirs (ðɛəz) *pron.* **1.** something or some-

one belonging to or associated with them: *ours is easy, theirs is difficult.* **2. of theirs.** belonging to them.

theism ('θiːɪzəm) *n.* **1.** belief in one God as the creator of everything in the universe. **2.** belief in the existence of a God or gods. —'theist *n., adj.* —the'istic *or* the'istical *adj.*

them (ðɛm; *unstressed* ðəm, əm) *pl. pron.* (*objective*) refers to things or people other than the speaker or people addressed.

theme (θiːm) *n.* **1.** the main idea or topic in a discussion or lecture. **2.** (in literature, music, or art) an idea, image, or motif, repeated or developed throughout a work. **3.** *Music.* a group of notes forming a recognizable melodic unit, used as the basis of part or all of a composition. **4.** a short essay, esp. one set as an exercise for a student. —**thematic** (θɪ'mætɪk) *adj.* —**the'matically** *adv.*

theme park *n.* an area planned as a leisure attraction in which all the displays and activities are based on a particular theme, story, or idea.

themselves (ðəm'sɛlvz) *pron.* **1. a.** the reflexive form of *they* or *them: they introduced themselves.* **b.** (used for emphasis): *the team themselves voted in favour of the proposal.* **2.** their normal or usual selves: *they don't seem themselves any more.*

then (ðɛn) *adv.* **1.** at that time; over that period of time: *there were no cars then; space travel will be commonplace then.* **2.** in that case; that being so: *then why don't you ask her? go on then, take it.* **3.** after that: *then John left the room.* **4. then and there.** immediately and in that place: *he signed the requisition then and there.* ~*pron.* **5.** that time: *from then on.* ~*adj.* **6.** existing or functioning at that time: *the then prime minister.*

thence (ðɛns) *adv. Formal.* **1.** from that place. **2.** from that time; thereafter. **3.** therefore.

thenceforth (ðɛns'fɔːθ) *or* **thenceforward** (ðɛns'fɔːwəd) *adv. Formal.* from that time on.

theocracy (θɪ'ɒkrəsɪ) *n., pl.* -cies. **1.** government by a deity or by a priesthood. **2.** a community under such government. —'theo,crat *n.* —,theo'cratic *adj.* —,theo'cratically *adv.*

theodolite (θɪ'ɒdə,laɪt) *n.* an instrument used in surveying for measuring horizontal and vertical angles.

theol. 1. theological. **2.** theology.

theologian (,θɪə'ləʊdʒɪən) *n.* a person versed in the study of theology.

theology (θɪ'ɒlədʒɪ) *n., pl.* -gies. **1.** the systematic study of religions and religious beliefs. **2.** a specific system, form, or branch of this study. —**theological** (,θɪə'lɒdʒɪk°l) *adj.* —,theo'logically *adv.*

theorem (ˈθɪərəm) *n.* a statement that can be deduced from the axioms of a formal system by means of its rules of inference.

theoretical (ˌθɪəˈrɛtɪkˀl) *or* **theoretic** *adj.* **1.** of or based on theory. **2.** lacking practical application or actual existence; hypothetical. **3.** using or dealing in theory; impractical. —ˌtheoˈretically *adv.*

theoretician (ˌθɪərɪˈtɪʃən) *n.* a student or user of the theory of a subject rather than its practical aspects.

theorize *or* **-ise** (ˈθɪəˌraɪz) *vb.* to produce or use theories; speculate. —ˈtheorist *n.*

theory (ˈθɪərɪ) *n., pl.* **-ries. 1.** a set of hypotheses related by logical arguments to explain a wide variety of connected phenomena in general terms: *the theory of relativity.* **2.** abstract knowledge or reasoning. **3.** a conjectural view or idea: *I have a theory about that.* **4.** an ideal or hypothetical situation: *in theory all British subjects are eligible.*

theosophy (θɪˈɒsəfɪ) *n.* a religious or philosophical system claiming to be based on an intuitive insight into the divine nature. —theosophical (ˌθɪəˈsɒfɪkˀl) *or* ˌtheoˈsophic *adj.* —theˈosophist *n.*

therapeutic (ˌθɛrəˈpjuːtɪk) *adj.* of or relating to the treatment and cure of disease. —ˌtheraˈpeutically *adv.*

therapeutics (ˌθɛrəˈpjuːtɪks) *n.* (*functioning as sing.*) the branch of medicine concerned with the treatment of disease.

therapy (ˈθɛrəpɪ) *n., pl.* **-pies.** the treatment of physical, mental, or social disorders or disease. —ˈtherapist *n.*

there (ðɛə) *adv.* **1.** in, at, or to that place or position: *we never go there.* **2.** in that respect: *I agree with you there.* ~*adj.* **3. not all there.** *Informal.* mentally defective or silly. ~*pron.* **4.** that place: *near there.* **5.** used as a grammatical subject when the true subject follows the verb, esp. the verb "to be": *there is a girl in that office.* **6. so there.** an exclamation that usually follows a declaration of refusal or defiance: *you can't have any more, so there.* **7. there you are. a.** an expression used when handing a person something requested or desired. **b.** an exclamation of satisfaction or vindication: *there you are, I knew that would happen.* ~*interj.* **8.** an expression of sympathy, as in consoling a child: *there, there, dear.*
Usage. The verb should agree with the number of the subject in such constructions as *there is a man waiting* and *there are several people waiting.* However, where the subject is compound it is acceptable to use the singular as in *there is a pen and a book on the table.*

thereabouts (ˈðɛərəˌbauts) *or U.S.* **thereabout** *adv.* near that place, time, amount, etc.: *meet at three o'clock or thereabouts.*

thereafter (ˌðɛərˈɑːftə) *adv. Formal.* from that time onwards.

thereby (ˌðɛəˈbaɪ, ˈðɛəˌbaɪ) *adv. Formal.* by that means.

therefore (ˈðɛəˌfɔː) *adv.* thus; hence; consequently: *those people have their umbrellas up, therefore it must be raining.*

therein (ˌðɛərˈɪn) *adv. Formal.* in or into that place or thing.

thereof (ˌðɛərˈɒv) *adv. Formal.* **1.** of or concerning that or it. **2.** from or because of that.

thereto (ˌðɛərˈtuː) *adv. Formal.* **1.** to that or it. **2.** Also: **thereunto.** in addition to that.

thereupon (ˌðɛərəˈpɒn) *adv.* **1.** immediately after that; at that point. **2.** *Formal.* concerning that subject.

therm (θɜːm) *n. Brit.* a unit of heat equal to 100 000 British thermal units. One therm is equal to $1.055\ 056 \times 10^8$ joules.

thermal (ˈθɜːməl) *adj.* **1.** of, caused by, or generating heat. **2.** hot or warm: *thermal baths.* **3.** (of garments) specially made so as to have exceptional heat-retaining qualities: *thermal underwear.* **4.** See **British thermal unit.** ~*n.* **5.** a column of rising air caused by uneven heating of the land surface, and used by gliders and birds to gain height.

thermionic valve *or esp. U.S. & Canad.* **thermionic tube** *n.* an electronic valve in which electrons are emitted from a heated rather than a cold cathode.

thermocouple (ˈθɜːməʊˌkʌpˀl) *n.* a device for measuring temperature, consisting of a pair of wires of different metals joined at both ends.

thermodynamics (ˌθɜːməʊdaɪˈnæmɪks) *n.* (*functioning as sing.*) the branch of physical science concerned with the relationship between heat and other forms of energy.

thermoelectric (ˌθɜːməʊɪˈlɛktrɪk) *or* **thermoelectrical** *adj.* of, relating to, or operated by the conversion of heat energy to electrical energy.

thermometer (θəˈmɒmɪtə) *n.* an instrument used to measure temperature, esp. one in which a thin column of liquid, such as mercury, expands and contracts within a graduated sealed tube.

thermonuclear (ˌθɜːməʊˈnjuːklɪə) *adj.* **1.** involving nuclear fusion. **2.** involving thermonuclear weapons.

thermoplastic (ˌθɜːməʊˈplæstɪk) *adj.* **1.** (of a material, esp. a synthetic plastic) becoming soft when heated and rehardening on cooling. ~*n.* **2.** a synthetic plastic or resin, such as polystyrene.

Thermos *or* **Thermos flask** (ˈθɜːməs) *n. Trademark.* a type of stoppered vacuum flask used to preserve the temperature of its contents.

thermosetting (ˌθɜːməʊˈsɛtɪŋ) *adj.* (of a material, esp. a synthetic plastic) hardening permanently after one application of heat and pressure.

thermostat (ˈθɜːməˌstæt) *n.* a device that is sensitive to temperature and that can operate a switch automatically when a certain temperature is reached. —ˌthermoˈstatic *adj.* —ˌthermoˈstatically *adv.*

thesaurus (θɪˈsɔːrəs) *n., pl.* **-ri** (-raɪ) *or* **-ruses.** a book containing systematized lists of synonyms and related words.

these (ðiːz) *det.* the form of **this** used before a plural noun: *these men.*

thesis (ˈθiːsɪs) *n., pl.* **-ses** (-siːz). **1.** a written work resulting from original research, esp. one submitted for a higher degree in a university. **2.** a doctrine maintained in argument. **3.** *Logic.* an unproved statement put forward as a premise in an argument.

Thespian (ˈθɛspɪən) *adj.* **1.** of or relating to drama and the theatre; dramatic. ~*n.* **2.** *Often facetious.* an actor or actress.

theta (ˈθiːtə) *n.* the eighth letter in the Greek alphabet (θ, Θ), used as a symbol in logic, linguistics, and the phonetic alphabet.

they (ðeɪ) *pl. pron.* (*subjective*) refers to: **1.** people or things other than the speaker or people addressed: *they fight among themselves.* **2.** people in general: *in Australia they have Christmas in the summer.*

they'd (ðeɪd) they would *or* they had.

they'll (ðeɪl) they will *or* they shall.

they're (ðɛə, ˈðeɪə) they are.

they've (ðeɪv) they have.

thiamine (ˈθaɪəˌmiːn) *or* **thiamin** (ˈθaɪəˌmɪn) *n.* vitamin B₁, a white crystalline compound that occurs in the outer coat of rice and other grains: deficiency of this vitamin leads to nervous disorders and to beriberi.

thick (θɪk) *adj.* **1.** of relatively great extent from one surface to the other: *a thick slice of bread.* **2.** of specific extent from one surface to the other: *ten centimetres thick.* **3.** having a dense consistency: *thick soup; a thick fog.* **4.** abundantly covered: *the furniture was thick with dust.* **5.** *Informal.* stupid, slow, or insensitive. **6.** throaty and badly articulated: *a voice thick with emotion.* **7.** (of an accent) pronounced: *a thick Irish accent.* **8. a bit thick.** *Brit. informal.* unfair or unreasonable: *only two pounds an hour, that's a bit thick!* **9. thick as thieves.** *Informal.* very friendly. ~*adv.* **10.** in order to produce something thick: *to slice bread thick.* **11.** profusely; in quick succession: *the replies came in thick and fast.* **12. lay it on thick.** *Informal.* **a.** to exaggerate a story. **b.** to flatter someone excessively. ~*n.* **13. the thick.** the most intense or active part: *in the thick of the battle.* **14. through thick and thin.** in good times and bad. —ˈthickish *adj.*

thicken (ˈθɪkən) *vb.* **1.** to make or become thick or thicker. **2.** to become more involved: *the plot thickened.* —ˈthickener *n.*

thickening (ˈθɪkənɪŋ) *n.* **1.** something added to a liquid to thicken it. **2.** a thickened part or piece.

thicket (ˈθɪkɪt) *n.* a dense growth of small trees, shrubs, and similar plants.

thickhead (ˈθɪkˌhed) *n. Slang.* a stupid or ignorant person; fool. —ˈthickˈheaded *adj.*

thickness (ˈθɪknɪs) *n.* **1.** the state or quality of being thick. **2.** the dimension through an object, as opposed to length or width. **3.** a layer: *three thicknesses of cloth.*

thickset (ˌθɪkˈset) *adj.* **1.** stocky in build; sturdy. **2.** densely planted or placed.

thick-skinned *adj.* insensitive to criticism or hints; not easily upset.

thief (θiːf) *n., pl.* **thieves** (θiːvz). a person who steals something from another. —ˈthievish *adj.*

thieve (θiːv) *vb.* to steal other people's possessions. —ˈthieving *adj.*

thigh (θaɪ) *n.* the part of the leg between the hip and the knee in man.

thighbone (ˈθaɪˌbəʊn) *n.* same as **femur.**

thimble (ˈθɪmbəl) *n.* a small metal or plastic cap used to protect the end of the finger from the needle when sewing.

thin (θɪn) *adj.* **thinner, thinnest. 1.** of relatively small extent from one side to the other. **2.** (of a person or animal) slim or lean. **3.** sparsely placed; meagre: *thin hair.* **4.** of low density: *a thin liquid.* **5.** weak; poor: *a thin disguise.* ~*adv.* **6.** in order to produce something thin: *to cut bread thin.* ~*vb.* **thinning, thinned. 7.** to make or become thin or sparse. —ˈthinness *n.*

thine (ðaɪn) *Archaic.* ~*det.* **1.** (*preceding a vowel*) of or associated with you (thou): *thine eyes.* ~*pron.* **2.** something belonging to you (thou): *thine is the greatest burden.*

thing (θɪŋ) *n.* **1.** an object, fact, circumstance, or concept considered as being a separate entity. **2.** any inanimate physical object. **3.** an object or entity that cannot or need not be precisely named. **4.** *Informal.* a person or animal: *you poor thing.* **5.** (*often pl.*) a possession, article of clothing, etc. **6.** *Informal.* a preoccupation or obsession: *she has a thing about dogs.* **7. do one's (own) thing.** to engage in an activity or mode of behaviour satisfying to one's personality. **8. make a thing of.** to exaggerate the importance of. **9. the thing.** the latest fashion.

thingumabob *or* **thingamabob** (ˈθɪŋəməˌbob) *n. Informal.* a person or thing the name of which is unknown, temporarily forgotten, or deliberately overlooked. Also: **thingumajig, thingamajig,** *or* **thingummy.**

think (θɪŋk) *vb.* **thinking, thought. 1.** to consider, judge, or believe: *he thinks my ideas are impractical.* **2.** (often foll. by *about*) to exercise the mind, for example in order to make a decision. **3.** to engage in conscious thought: *man is the only animal that thinks.* **4.** (usually foll. by *of*) to remember; recollect: *I can't think of his name.* **5.** (foll. by *of*) to make the mental choice (of): *think of a number.* **6.** to be considerate enough or remember to do something: *he did not think to thank them.* **7. think twice.** to consider something carefully before making a decision. ~*n.* **8.** *Informal.* a careful, open-minded assessment: *let's have a fresh think about this.* ~See also **think over, think up.** —'**thinker** *n.*

thinking ('θɪŋkɪŋ) *n.* **1.** opinion or judgment. **2.** the process of thought. ~*adj.* **3.** using intelligent thought: *thinking people.*

think over *vb.* to ponder or consider.

think-tank *n.* *Informal.* a group of specialists commissioned to undertake intensive study and research into specified problems.

think up *vb.* to invent or devise.

thinner ('θɪnə) *n.* (*often pl., functioning as sing.*) a solvent, such as turpentine, added to paint or varnish to dilute it.

thin-skinned *adj.* sensitive to criticism or hints; easily upset.

third (θɜːd) *adj.* **1.** coming after the second in order. **2.** rated, graded, or ranked below the second level. **3.** denoting the third from lowest forward ratio of a gearbox in a motor vehicle. ~*n.* **4.** one of three equal parts of an object or quantity. **5.** the fraction equal to one divided by three (⅓). **6.** the forward ratio above second of a gearbox in a motor vehicle. **7.** *Music.* the interval between one note and another three notes away from it counting inclusively along the diatonic scale. **8.** *Brit.* an honours degree of the third and usually the lowest class. ~*adv.* **9.** Also: **thirdly.** in the third place.

third class *n.* **1.** the class or grade next in value, quality, etc., to the second. ~*adj.* **2.** of the class or grade next in value, quality, etc., to the second.

third degree *n.* *Informal.* torture or bullying, esp. as used to extort confessions or information.

third-degree burn *n.* *Pathol.* the most severe type of burn, involving the destruction of both epidermis and dermis.

third dimension *n.* the dimension of depth, by which a solid object may be distinguished from a two-dimensional drawing or picture of it.

third man *n.* *Cricket.* a fielding position on the off side, near the boundary behind the batsman's wicket.

third party *n.* **1.** a person who is involved by chance or only incidentally in an event, legal proceeding, agreement, or other transaction. ~*adj.* **2.** *Insurance.* providing protection against liability caused by accidental injury or death of other persons.

third person *n.* a grammatical category of pronouns and verbs used when referring to objects or individuals other than the speaker or his addressee or addressees.

third-rate *adj.* mediocre or inferior.

Third World *n.* the countries of Africa, Asia, and Latin America collectively, esp. when viewed as underdeveloped.

thirst (θɜːst) *n.* **1.** a craving to drink, accompanied by a feeling of dryness in the mouth and throat. **2.** an eager longing, craving, or yearning. ~*vb.* **3.** to feel a thirst.

thirsty ('θɜːstɪ) *adj.* **thirstier, thirstiest. 1.** feeling a desire to drink. **2.** (foll. by *for*) feeling an eager desire for. **3.** causing thirst: *thirsty work.* —'**thirstily** *adv.*

thirteen ('θɜː'tiːn) *n.* **1.** the cardinal number that is the sum of ten and three. **2.** a numeral, 13, XIII, representing this number. **3.** something representing or consisting of thirteen units. ~*det.* **4.** amounting to thirteen. —'**thir'teenth** *adj., n.*

thirty ('θɜːtɪ) *n., pl.* **-ties. 1.** the cardinal number that is the product of ten and three. **2.** a numeral, 30, XXX, representing this number. **3.** something representing or consisting of thirty units. ~*det.* **4.** amounting to thirty. —'**thirtieth** *adj., n.*

Thirty-nine Articles *pl. n.* a set of formulas defining the doctrinal position of the Church of England.

this (ðɪs) *det.* **1.** used preceding a noun referring to something or someone that is closer: *look at this picture.* **2.** used preceding a noun that has just been mentioned or is understood: *this plan of yours won't work.* **3.** used to refer to something about to be mentioned: *consider this argument.* **4.** used to refer to the present time or occasion: *this time you'll know better.* **5.** *Informal.* an emphatic form of **a** or **the**¹: *I saw this big brown bear.* **6. this and that.** various unspecified and trivial events or facts. ~*pron.* **7.** used to denote a person or thing that is relatively close: *take this.* **8.** used to denote something already mentioned or understood: *I first saw this on Sunday.* **9.** used to denote something about to be mentioned: *listen to this.* **10.** the present time or occasion: *before this, I was mistaken.*

thistle ('θɪsᵊl) *n.* a plant with prickly-edged leaves, dense flower heads, and feathery hairs on the seeds. —'**thistly** *adj.*

thistledown ('θɪsᵊl,daʊn) *n.* the mass of feathery plumed seeds produced by a thistle.

thither ('ðɪðə) *adv.* *Formal.* to or towards that place; in that direction.

tho *or* **tho'** (ðəʊ) *conj., adv.* *U.S. or poetic.* same as **though.**

thole (θəʊl) *or* **tholepin** (ˈθəʊlˌpɪn) *n.* one of a pair of wooden pins set upright in the gunwale on either side of a rowing boat to serve as a fulcrum in rowing.

thong (θɒŋ) *n.* **1.** a thin strip of leather or other material. **2.** *U.S., Canad., Austral., & N.Z.* same as **flip-flop** (sense 5).

thorax (ˈθɔːræks) *n., pl.* **thoraxes** *or* **thoraces** (ˈθɔːrəˌsiːz, θɔːˈreɪsiːz). **1.** the part of the human body enclosed by the ribs. **2.** the part of an insect's body between the head and abdomen. —**thoracic** (θɔːˈræsɪk) *adj.*

thorium (ˈθɔːrɪəm) *n.* a silvery-white radioactive metallic element. It is used in electronic equipment and as a nuclear power source. Symbol: Th

thorn (θɔːn) *n.* **1.** a sharp pointed woody extension of a stem or leaf. **2.** any of various trees or shrubs having thorns, esp. the hawthorn. **3. a thorn in one's side** *or* **flesh.** a source of irritation: *she has been a thorn in the flesh since she arrived.* —**thornless** *adj.*

thorny (ˈθɔːnɪ) *adj.* **thornier, thorniest. 1.** bearing or covered with thorns. **2.** difficult or unpleasant: *a thorny problem.*

thorough (ˈθʌrə) *adj.* **1.** carried out completely and carefully. **2.** utter: *a thorough bore.* **3.** painstakingly careful. —**thoroughly** *adv.* —**thoroughness** *n.*

thoroughbred (ˈθʌrəˌbrɛd) *adj.* **1.** obtained through successive generations of selective breeding: *a thoroughbred stallion.* ~*n.* **2.** a pedigree animal, esp. a horse.

thoroughfare (ˈθʌrəˌfɛə) *n.* a way through from one place to another: *no thoroughfare.*

thoroughgoing (ˈθʌrəˌgəʊɪŋ) *adj.* **1.** extremely thorough. **2.** absolute; complete: *thoroughgoing incompetence.*

those (ðəʊz) *det.* the form of **that** used before a plural noun.

thou[1] (ðaʊ) *sing. pron.* (*subjective*) *Archaic.* refers to the person addressed: used mainly in familiar address.

thou[2] (θaʊ) *n., pl.* **thou.** *Informal.* **1.** one thousandth of an inch. **2.** a thousand.

though (ðəʊ) *conj.* **1.** (sometimes preceded by *even*) despite the fact that: *even though it was a hot day, she was wearing a fur coat.* ~*adv.* **2.** nevertheless; however: *he can't dance — he sings well, though.*

thought (θɔːt) *vb.* **1.** past of **think.** ~*n.* **2.** the act or process of thinking. **3.** a concept or idea. **4.** ideas typical of a particular time or place: *German thought in the 19th century.* **5.** application of mental attention; consideration: *I will give some thought to the problem.* **6.** purpose or intention: *I have no thought of giving up.* **7.** expectation: *no thought of reward.*

thoughtful (ˈθɔːtful) *adj.* **1.** considerate in the treatment of other people. **2.** showing careful thought: *a thoughtful essay.* **3.**

pensive; reflective. —**thoughtfully** *adv.* —**thoughtfulness** *n.*

thoughtless (ˈθɔːtlɪs) *adj.* inconsiderate; having no regard for the feelings of other people. —**thoughtlessly** *adv.* —**thoughtlessness** *n.*

thousand (ˈθaʊzənd) *n.* **1.** the cardinal number that is the product of one hundred tens. **2.** a numeral, 1000, 10^3, representing this number. **3.** (*often pl.*) a very large but unspecified number, amount, or quantity. **4.** something representing or consisting of 1000 units. ~*det.* **5.** amounting to a thousand. —**thousandth** *adj., n.*

thrall (θrɔːl) *n.* **1.** Also: **thralldom** *or U.S.* **thralldom** (ˈθrɔːldəm). the state or condition of being in the power of another person. **2.** a person who is in such a state.

thrash (θræʃ) *vb.* **1.** to beat (someone) with a whip or stick. **2.** to defeat totally: *the home team thrashed the visiting team.* **3.** to move about in a wild manner: *the boy was thrashing around, trying to get free.* **4.** same as **thresh.** ~*n.* **5.** the act of thrashing; beating. **6.** *Informal.* a party. ~See also **thrash out.**

thrashing (ˈθræʃɪŋ) *n.* a physical assault; flogging.

thrash out *vb.* to discuss (a problem or difficulty) fully in order to come to an agreement or decision about it.

thread (θrɛd) *n.* **1.** a fine strand, filament, or fibre of some material. **2.** a fine cord of twisted yarns, esp. of cotton, used in sewing or weaving. **3.** the spiral ridge on a screw, bolt, or nut. **4.** a very thin seam of coal or vein of ore. **5.** something acting as the continuous link or theme of a whole: *the thread of the story.* ~*vb.* **6.** to pass (thread) through (the eye of a needle) before sewing with it. **7.** to string together: *she threaded the beads onto a piece of string to make a necklace.* **8.** to make (one's way) through or over (a crowd of people or group of objects). —**thread-like** *adj.*

threadbare (ˈθrɛdˌbɛə) *adj.* **1.** (of cloth, clothing, or carpet) having the nap worn off so that the threads are exposed; worn out. **2.** hackneyed: *a threadbare argument.* **3.** wearing threadbare clothes; shabby.

threadworm (ˈθrɛdˌwɜːm) *n.* a small threadlike worm, esp. the pinworm.

threat (θrɛt) *n.* **1.** a declaration of an intention to inflict harm. **2.** an indication of imminent harm, danger, or pain. **3.** a person or thing that is regarded as dangerous and likely to inflict harm.

threaten (ˈθrɛtⁿn) *vb.* **1.** to express a threat to (a person or people). **2.** to be a threat to. **3.** to be a menacing indication of (something): *dark clouds threatened rain.* —**threatening** *adj.* —**threateningly** *adv.*

three (θriː) *n.* **1.** the cardinal number that is the sum of two and one. **2.** a numeral, 3,

III, representing this number. **3.** something representing or consisting of three units. ~*det.* **4.** amounting to three.

three-decker *n.* **1.** anything having three levels, layers, or tiers. **2.** a warship with guns on three decks.

three-dimensional *adj.* **1.** having three dimensions. **2.** lifelike: *the characters in the novel are three-dimensional.*

threefold ('θriː,fəʊld) *adj.* **1.** having three times as many or as much; triple. **2.** composed of three parts. ~*adv.* **3.** three times as many or as much.

three-legged race *n.* a race in which pairs of competitors run with their adjacent legs tied together.

three-ply *adj.* (of wool, wood, etc.) having three layers or strands.

three-point turn *n.* a complete turn of a motor vehicle using forward and reverse gears alternately, and completed after only three movements.

three-quarter *adj.* **1.** being three quarters of something. **2.** being three quarters of the normal length: *a three-quarter-length coat.* ~*n.* **3.** *Rugby.* one of the four players between the fullback and the scrum half, whose role is mainly to run with the ball when it is passed to them.

three Rs *pl. n.* **the.** reading, writing, and arithmetic regarded as the three fundamental skills to be taught in primary schools.

threescore ('θriː'skɔː) *det. Archaic.* sixty.

threesome ('θriːsəm) *n.* a group of three people.

threnody ('θrɛnədɪ) *n., pl.* **threnodies.** an ode, song, or speech of lamentation, esp. for the dead. —**threnodic** (θrɪ'nɒdɪk) *adj.* —'**threnodist** *n.*

thresh (θrɛʃ) *vb.* **1.** to beat stalks of ripe corn, rice, etc., either with a hand implement or a machine to separate the grain from the husks and straw. **2.** to beat or strike. **3.** (often foll. by *about*) to toss and turn; thrash.

thresher ('θrɛʃə) *n.* any of a genus of large sharks occurring in tropical and temperate seas. They have a very long whiplike tail.

threshold ('θrɛʃ,həʊld) *n.* **1.** the sill of an entrance or doorway, esp. one made of stone or hardwood. **2.** any doorway or entrance. **3.** the starting point of an experience, event, or venture. **4.** the strength at which a stimulus is just strong enough to produce a response: *the threshold of consciousness.*

threw (θruː) *vb.* the past tense of **throw.**

thrice (θraɪs) *adv.* **1.** three times. **2.** threefold. **3.** *Archaic.* greatly.

thrift (θrɪft) *n.* **1.** wisdom and caution in the management of money. **2.** a low-growing plant of Europe, W Asia, and North America, with narrow leaves and round heads of pink or white flowers. —'**thriftless** *adj.*

thrifty ('θrɪftɪ) *adj.* **thriftier, thriftiest.** showing thrift; economical or frugal. —'**thriftily** *adv.* —'**thriftiness** *n.*

thrill (θrɪl) *n.* **1.** a sudden sensation of excitement and pleasure. **2.** a situation producing such a sensation. **3.** a sudden trembling sensation caused by fear or emotional shock. ~*vb.* **4.** to feel or cause to feel a thrill. **5.** to tremble or cause to tremble; vibrate or quiver. —'**thrilling** *adj.*

thriller ('θrɪlə) *n.* a book, film, or play depicting crime, mystery, or espionage in an atmosphere of excitement and suspense.

thrips (θrɪps) *n., pl.* **thrips.** a small slender-bodied insect with piercing mouthparts which feeds on plant sap.

thrive (θraɪv) *vb.* **thriving; thrived** or **throve; thrived** or **thriven** ('θrɪv'n). **1.** to do well; prosper. **2.** to grow strongly and vigorously.

thro' or **thro** (θruː) *prep., adv. Informal.* same as **through.**

throat (θrəʊt) *n.* **1.** the top part of the alimentary and respiratory tract, running from the mouth and nose down towards the stomach and lungs. **2.** the front part of the neck. **3.** something resembling a throat, esp. in shape or function: *the throat of a chimney.* **4. cut someone's throat.** to kill someone. **5. cut one's (own) throat.** to bring about one's own ruin. **6. ram** or **force (something) down someone's throat.** to insist that someone listen to or accept (something).

throaty ('θrəʊtɪ) *adj.* **throatier, throatiest. 1.** indicating a sore throat; hoarse: *a throaty cough.* **2.** deep, husky, or guttural.

throb (θrɒb) *vb.* **throbbing, throbbed. 1.** to pulsate or beat repeatedly, esp. with abnormally strong force: *her head was throbbing.* **2.** (of engines, drums, etc.) to have a strong rhythmic vibration or beat. ~*n.* **3.** a throbbing, esp. a rapid pulsation as of the heart: *a throb of pleasure.*

throes (θrəʊz) *pl. n.* **1.** a condition of violent pangs, pain, or convulsions: *death throes.* **2. in the throes of.** struggling with great effort with: *a country in the throes of revolution.*

thrombosis (θrɒm'bəʊsɪs) *n., pl.* **-ses** (-siːz). coagulation of the blood in the heart or in a blood vessel, forming a blood clot.

throne (θrəʊn) *n.* **1.** the ceremonial seat occupied by a monarch or bishop on occasions of state. **2.** the office or rank of a royal person.

throng (θrɒŋ) *n.* **1.** a great number of people or things crowded together. ~*vb.* **2.** to gather in or fill (a place) in large numbers; crowd.

throstle ('θrɒs²l) *n. Poetic.* a song thrush.

throttle ('θrɒt²l) n. 1. a device that controls the fuel-and-air mixture entering an engine. ~vb. 2. to kill or injure (someone) by squeezing his throat. 3. to suppress or censor. 4. to control or restrict (a flow of fluid) by means of a throttle valve.

through (θru:) prep. 1. going in at one side and coming out at the other side of: *a path through the wood*. 2. occupying or visiting several points scattered around in (an area). 3. as a result of: *the thieves were captured through his vigilance*. 4. *Chiefly U.S.* up to and including: *Monday through Friday*. 5. during: *through the night*. ~adj. 6. at an end: *his days of acting were through*. 7. having successfully completed some specified activity. 8. (on a telephone line) connected. 9. no longer able to function successfully in some specified capacity: *as a journalist, you're through*. 10. continuous or unbroken: *a through train*. ~adv. 11. through some specified thing, place, or period of time: *all year through*. 12. **through and through.** completely: *the boards are rotten through and through*.

throughout (θru:'aut) prep. 1. through the whole of (a place or a period of time): *throughout the day*. ~adv. 2. throughout some specified period or area: *the children sat quietly throughout*.

throughput ('θru:,put) n. the amount of material processed in a given period, esp. by a computer.

throve (θrəuv) vb. a past tense of **thrive**.

throw (θrəu) vb. **throwing, threw, thrown.** 1. to hurl (something) through the air, esp. with a rapid motion of the arm. 2. (foll. by *in, on, onto*, etc.) to put or move suddenly, carelessly, or violently. 3. to bring to or cause to be in a specified state or condition, esp. suddenly: *the news threw them into a panic*. 4. to direct or cast (a shadow, light, etc.): *she threw him a nervous glance; the lamp threw a shadow on the ceiling*. 5. to project (the voice) so as to make it appear to come from some other source. 6. to give or hold (a party). 7. to cause to fall or be upset: *the horse threw his rider*. 8. **a.** to tip (dice) out onto a flat surface. **b.** to obtain (a specified number) in this way: *to throw two sixes*. 9. to shape (a pot or vessel) on a potter's wheel. 10. to move (a switch or lever) so as to engage or disengage a mechanism. 11. *Informal.* to confuse: *the question threw me*. 12. *Informal.* to lose (a contest) deliberately. 13. **throw oneself at.** to strive very hard to attract the attention or win the affection of. 14. **throw oneself into.** to involve oneself enthusiastically in. 15. **throw oneself on.** to rely entirely upon (someone's goodwill, etc.): *he threw himself on her mercy*. ~n. 16. the act or an instance of throwing. 17. *Chiefly U.S. & Canad.* a decorative blanket or cover. ~See also **throwaway, throwback,** etc.

throwaway ('θrəuə,wei) adj. 1. *Chiefly Brit.* said or done incidentally; casual: *a throwaway remark*. 2. designed to be discarded after use: *a throwaway carton*. ~n. 3. *Chiefly U.S. & Canad.* a handbill. ~vb. **throw away.** 4. to get rid of; discard. 5. to fail to make good use of; waste.

throwback ('θrəu,bæk) n. 1. a person, animal, or plant that has the characteristics of an earlier type. ~vb. **throw back.** 2. to revert to an earlier type. 3. (foll. by *on*) to force to depend (on): *the crisis threw her back on her faith in God*.

throw in vb. 1. to add at no additional cost: *the hotel throws in a cooked breakfast*. 2. to contribute (a remark) in a discussion. 3. **throw in the towel** or **sponge.** *Informal.* to give in; accept defeat. ~ n. **throw-in.** 4. *Soccer.* the method of putting the ball into play after it has gone out of play, by throwing it towards a team-mate.

throw off vb. 1. to free oneself of; discard: *to throw off the yoke of the oppressor*. 2. to utter in a casual manner: *to throw off a witty remark*.

throw out vb. 1. to discard or reject. 2. to expel or dismiss, esp. forcibly. 3. to utter in a casual or indirect manner: *to throw out a hint*.

throw over vb. to forsake or abandon; jilt.

throw together vb. 1. to assemble (something) hurriedly. 2. to cause to become casually acquainted.

throw up vb. 1. *Informal.* to vomit. 2. to give up; abandon: *he threw up his job*. 3. to construct (a building or structure) hastily. 4. to produce: *every generation throws up its own leaders*.

thru (θru:) prep., adv., adj. *Chiefly U.S.* same as **through.**

thrum¹ (θrʌm) vb. **thrumming, thrummed.** 1. to strum rhythmically but without expression on (a musical instrument). 2. to drum incessantly: *rain thrummed on the roof*. ~n. 3. a repetitive strumming.

thrum² (θrʌm) n. 1. any of the unwoven ends of warp thread remaining on the loom when the web has been removed. 2. such ends of thread collectively.

thrush¹ (θrʌʃ) n. any of a large group of songbirds, esp. one having a brown plumage with a spotted breast, such as the mistle thrush and song thrush.

thrush² (θrʌʃ) n. 1. a fungal disease, esp. of infants, in which whitish spots form on the mouth, throat, and lips. 2. a vaginal infection caused by the same fungus.

thrust (θrʌst) vb. **thrusting, thrust.** 1. to push (someone or something) with force. 2. to force upon (someone) or into (some condition or situation): *they thrust responsibilities upon her; they thrust her into a position of responsibility*. 3. (foll. by *through*) to pierce; stab. **4.** to make a stab or lunge at. ~*n.* **5.** a forceful drive, push, stab, or lunge. **6.** a force, esp. one that produces motion. **7.** a propulsive force produced by the fluid pressure in a jet engine or rocket engine. **8.** *Physics.* a continuous pressure exerted by one part of an object against another. **9.** *Informal.* intellectual or emotional drive; forcefulness: *a man with thrust and energy.* **10.** the essential or most forceful part: *the thrust of the argument.*

thud (θʌd) *n.* **1.** a dull heavy sound. **2.** a blow or fall that causes such a sound. ~*vb.* **thudding, thudded. 3.** to make or cause to make such a sound.

thug (θʌg) *n.* **1.** a tough and violent man, esp. a criminal. **2.** (*sometimes cap.*) (formerly) a member of an organization of robbers and assassins in India. —'**thuggery** *n.* —'**thuggish** *adj.*

thulium ('θjuːlɪəm) *n.* a silvery-grey element of the lanthanide series. Symbol: Tm

thumb (θʌm) *n.* **1.** the first and usually shortest and thickest finger of the hand. **2.** the part of a glove shaped to fit the thumb. **3. all thumbs.** very clumsy. **4. thumbs down.** an indication of refusal or disapproval. **5. thumbs up.** an indication of encouragement or approval. **6. under someone's thumb.** completely under someone else's control. ~*vb.* **7.** to touch, mark, or move with the thumb. **8.** (often foll. by *through*) to flip the pages of (a book or magazine) in order to glance at the contents. **9.** to attempt to obtain (a lift in a motor vehicle) by signalling with the thumb. **10. thumb one's nose at.** to deride or flout.

thumb index *n.* a series of notches cut into the fore-edge of a book to facilitate quick reference.

thumbnail ('θʌm,neɪl) *n.* **1.** the nail of the thumb. **2.** (*modifier*) concise and brief: *a thumbnail sketch.*

thumbscrew ('θʌm,skruː) *n.* (formerly) an instrument of torture that pinches or crushes the thumbs.

thump (θʌmp) *n.* **1.** the sound of something heavy hitting a comparatively soft surface. **2.** a heavy blow with the hand. ~*vb.* **3.** to strike or beat heavily; pound. **4.** to throb, beat, or pound violently: *my heart was thumping.*

thumping ('θʌmpɪŋ) *adj. Slang.* huge or excessive: *a thumping loss.*

thunder ('θʌndə) *n.* **1.** a loud cracking or deep rumbling noise caused by the rapid expansion of atmospheric gases that are suddenly heated by lightning. **2.** any loud booming sound. **3. steal someone's thunder.** to lessen the effect of someone's idea or action by anticipating it. ~*vb.* **4.** to make (a loud sound) or utter (words) in a manner suggesting thunder. **5.** to be the

case that thunder is being heard: *it is thundering.* **6.** to move fast, heavily, and noisily: *the bus thundered downhill.* —'**thundery** *adj.*

thunderbolt ('θʌndə,bəʊlt) *n.* **1.** a flash of lightning accompanying thunder. **2.** the imagined agency of destruction produced by a flash of lightning.

thunderclap ('θʌndə,klæp) *n.* **1.** a loud outburst of thunder. **2.** something as violent or unexpected as a clap of thunder.

thundercloud ('θʌndə,klaʊd) *n.* a towering electrically charged cloud associated with thunderstorms.

thundering ('θʌndərɪŋ) *adj. Slang.* very great or excessive: *a thundering idiot.*

thunderous ('θʌndərəs) *adj.* **1.** threatening; angry. **2.** resembling thunder in loudness.

thunderstorm ('θʌndə,stɔːm) *n.* a storm with thunder and lightning and usually heavy rain or hail.

thunderstruck ('θʌndə,strʌk) *or* **thunderstricken** ('θʌndə,strɪkən) *adj.* amazed or shocked.

thurible ('θjʊərɪbᵊl) *n.* same as **censer.**

Thurs. Thursday.

Thursday ('θɜːzdɪ) *n.* the fifth day of the week; fourth day of the working week.

thus (ðʌs) *adv.* **1.** in this manner: *do it thus.* **2.** to such a degree: *thus far and no further.* **3.** therefore: *We have failed. Thus we have to take the consequences.*

thwack (θwæk) *vb.* **1.** to beat with something flat. ~*n.* **2. a.** a blow with something flat. **b.** the sound made by it.

thwart (θwɔːt) *vb.* **1.** to prevent; frustrate: *they thwarted his plan.* ~*n.* **2.** an oarsman's seat lying across a boat.

thy (ðaɪ) *det. Archaic.* belonging to or associated in some way with you (thou): *thy goodness and mercy.*

thyme (taɪm) *n.* a small shrub with white, pink, or red flowers and scented leaves used for seasoning.

thymol ('θaɪmɒl) *n.* a white crystalline substance obtained from thyme, used as a fungicide, antiseptic, etc.

thymus ('θaɪməs) *n., pl.* **-muses** *or* **-mi** (-maɪ). a glandular organ situated near the base of the neck.

thyroid ('θaɪrɔɪd) *Anat.* ~*adj.* **1.** of or relating to the thyroid gland. **2.** of or relating to the largest cartilage of the larynx. ~*n.* **3.** the thyroid gland.

thyroid gland *n. Anat.* an endocrine gland that secretes hormones that control metabolism and body growth.

thyself (ðaɪ'sɛlf) *pron. Archaic.* the reflexive form of **thou¹.**

ti (tiː) *n. Music.* same as **te.**

Ti *Chem.* titanium.

tiara (tɪ'ɑːrə) *n.* **1.** a semicircular jewelled

headdress worn by women of high social rank for formal occasions. **2.** a headdress worn by the pope, consisting of a beehive-shaped diadem surrounded by three coronets.

tibia ('tɪbɪə) *n.*, *pl.* **tibiae** ('tɪbɪˌiː) *or* **tibias**. the inner and thicker of the two bones of the human leg below the knee; shinbone. —'**tibial** *adj.*

tic (tɪk) *n.* spasmodic twitching of a particular group of muscles.

tick[1] (tɪk) *n.* **1.** a mark (√) used to check off or indicate the correctness of something. **2.** a recurrent metallic tapping or clicking sound, such as that made by a clock. **3.** *Brit. informal.* a moment or instant: *I'll be back in a tick.* ~*vb.* **4.** (often foll. by *off*) to mark or check with a tick. **5.** to produce a recurrent tapping sound or indicate by such a sound: *the clock ticked the minutes away.* **6. what makes someone tick.** *Informal.* the basic motivation of a person. ~See also **tick off, tick over.**

tick[2] (tɪk) *n.* a small parasitic creature typically living on the skin of warm-blooded animals and feeding on the blood and tissues of their hosts.

tick[3] (tɪk) *n.* **1.** the strong covering of a pillow or mattress. **2.** *Informal.* short for **ticking.**

tick[4] (tɪk) *n. Brit. informal.* account or credit: *we bought the furniture on tick.*

ticker ('tɪkə) *n. Slang.* the heart.

ticker tape *n.* (formerly) a continuous paper tape on which current stock quotations were printed by machine.

ticket ('tɪkɪt) *n.* **1.** a printed piece of paper or cardboard showing that the holder is entitled to certain rights, such as travel on a train or bus or entry to a place of public entertainment. **2.** a label or tag attached to an article showing information such as its price and size. **3.** an official notification of a parking or traffic offence. **4.** *Chiefly U.S.* the declared policy of a political party. **5. that's (just) the ticket.** *Informal.* that's the right or appropriate thing. ~*vb.* **6.** to issue or attach a ticket or tickets to.

ticking ('tɪkɪŋ) *n.* a strong cotton fabric, often striped, used esp. for mattress and pillow covers.

tickle ('tɪk'l) *vb.* **1.** to touch or stroke (someone), so as to produce laughter or a twitching sensation. **2.** to delight or entertain: *to tickle someone's fancy.* **3.** to itch or tingle. **4. tickled pink** *or* **to death.** *Informal.* greatly pleased. ~*n.* **5.** a sensation of light stroking or itching. **6.** the act of tickling. **7.** *Canad.* (in the Atlantic Provinces) a narrow strait.

tickler ('tɪklə) *n. Informal, chiefly Brit.* a difficult problem.

ticklish ('tɪklɪʃ) *adj.* **1.** sensitive to being

tickled. **2.** delicate or difficult: *a ticklish situation.* **3.** easily upset or offended.

tick off *vb.* **1.** to mark with a tick. **2.** *Informal, chiefly Brit.* to reprimand (someone).

tick over *vb.* **1.** *Brit.* (of an engine) to run at low speed with the transmission disengaged. **2.** to run smoothly without any major changes: *the business is ticking over nicely.*

ticktack ('tɪkˌtæk) *n. Brit.* a system of sign language, mainly using the hands, by which bookmakers transmit their odds to each other at race courses.

ticktock ('tɪkˌtɒk) *n.* a ticking sound as made by a clock.

tidal ('taɪd'l) *adj.* **1.** relating to, characterized by, or affected by tides. **2.** dependent on the tide: *a tidal ferry.*

tidal wave *n.* **1.** a name (not in technical use) for **tsunami.** **2.** an unusually large incoming wave, often caused by high winds and spring tides. **3.** a forceful and widespread movement in public opinion, action, etc.

tiddler ('tɪdlə) *n. Brit. informal.* **1.** a very small fish, esp. a stickleback. **2.** a small child.

tiddly[1] ('tɪdlɪ) *adj.* **-dlier, -dliest.** *Brit.* small; tiny.

tiddly[2] ('tɪdlɪ) *adj. Slang, chiefly Brit.* slightly drunk.

tiddlywinks ('tɪdlɪˌwɪŋks) *n.* (*functioning as sing.*) a game in which players try to flick discs of plastic into a cup by pressing them with other larger discs.

tide (taɪd) *n.* **1.** the alternate rise and fall of sea level caused by the gravitational pull of the sun and moon. **2.** the current, ebb, or flow of water at a specified place resulting from these changes in level: *the tide is coming in.* **3.** a widespread tendency or movement: *the tide of resentment against the government.* **4.** *Archaic except in combination.* a season or time: *Christmastide.* ~*vb.* **5.** to be carried with or as if with the tide. **6.** to ebb and flow like the tide.

tidemark ('taɪdˌmɑːk) *n.* **1.** a mark left by the highest or lowest point of a tide. **2.** *Chiefly Brit.* a mark showing a level reached by a liquid: *a tidemark on the bath.* **3.** *Informal, chiefly Brit.* a dirty mark on the skin, indicating the extent to which someone has washed.

tide over *vb.* to help (someone) to get through (a period of difficulty or distress): *this will tide you over until you get paid.*

tidings ('taɪdɪŋz) *pl. n.* information or news.

tidy ('taɪdɪ) *adj.* **-dier, -diest.** **1.** characterized by neatness and order. **2.** *Informal.* considerable: *a tidy sum of money.* ~*vb.* **-dying, -died.** **3.** (usually foll. by *up*) to put (things) in order; neaten. ~*n.*, *pl.* **-dies.** **4.**

a small container for odds and ends. —**'tidily** adv. —**'tidiness** n.

tie (taɪ) vb. **tying, tied. 1.** (often foll. by up) to fasten or be fastened with string, rope, etc. **2.** to make (a knot or bow) in (something). **3.** to restrict or limit: her family commitments have always tied her down. **4.** to equal (the score) of a competitor or fellow candidate. ~n. **5.** a bond, link, or fastening. **6.** a restriction or restraint. **7.** a string, wire, etc., with which something is tied. **8.** a long narrow piece of material worn, esp. by men, under the collar of a shirt, tied in a knot close to the throat with the ends hanging down the front. **9. a.** an equality in score or attainment in a contest. **b.** the match or competition in which the scores or results are equal. **10.** a structural member such as a tie beam. **11.** Sport, Brit. a match in a knockout competition: a cup tie. **12.** U.S. & Canad. a sleeper on a railway track. **13.** Music. a curved line connecting two notes of the same pitch indicating that the sound is to be prolonged for their joint time value. ~See also **tie in, tie up.**

tie beam n. a horizontal beam that holds two parts of a structure together, such as one that connects two corresponding rafters in a roof.

tiebreaker ('taɪ,breɪkə) n. an extra game or question that decides the result of a contest that has ended in a draw.

tied (taɪd) adj. Brit. **1.** (of a public house) obliged to sell only the beer of a particular brewery. **2.** (of a house) rented out to the tenant for as long as he is employed by the owner.

tie-dyeing, tie-dye, or **tie and dye** n. a method of dyeing textiles to produce patterns by tying sections of the cloth together so that they will not absorb the dye. —**'tie-,dyed** adj.

tie in vb. **1.** to come or bring into a certain relationship; coordinate. ~n. **tie-in. 2.** a link, relationship, or coordination.

tiepin ('taɪ,pɪn) n. an ornamental pin used to pin the two ends of a tie to a shirt.

tier (tɪə) n. one of a set of rows placed one above and behind the other, such as theatre seats.

tiercel ('tɪəs²l) n. same as **tercel.**

tie up vb. **1.** to bind (someone or something) securely with string or rope. **2.** to moor (a vessel). **3.** to commit (funds, etc.) and so make unavailable for other uses. ~n. **tie-up. 4.** a link or connection.

tiff (tɪf) n. a petty quarrel.

tiffin ('tɪfɪn) n. (in India) a light meal, esp. at midday.

tiger ('taɪgə) n. **1.** a large Asian mammal of the cat family having a tawny yellow coat with black stripes. **2.** a dynamic, forceful,

or cruel person. —**'tigerish** or **'tigrish** adj.

tiger lily n. a lily of China and Japan with black-spotted orange flowers.

tiger moth n. a moth with conspicuously striped and spotted wings.

tight (taɪt) adj. **1.** stretched or drawn so as not to be loose; taut: a tight cord. **2.** fitting in a close manner. **3.** held, made, fixed, or closed firmly and securely: a tight knot. **4.** constructed so as to prevent the passage of water, air, etc. **5.** unyielding or stringent: to keep a tight hold on resources. **6.** cramped or constricted: a tight fit. **7.** mean or miserly. **8.** difficult and problematic: a tight situation. **9.** (of a match or game) very close or even: a tight race. **10.** Informal. drunk. ~adv. **11.** in a close, firm, or secure way. —**'tightly** adv. —**'tightness** n.

tighten ('taɪt²n) vb. to make (something) tight or tighter or become tight or tighter.

tightfisted (,taɪt'fɪstɪd) adj. mean; miserly.

tightknit (,taɪt'nɪt) adj. closely integrated: a tightknit community.

tight-lipped adj. **1.** unwilling to divulge information. **2.** with the lips pressed tightly together, as through anger.

tightrope ('taɪt,rəʊp) n. a rope stretched taut on which acrobats perform.

tights (taɪts) pl. n. a one-piece clinging garment covering the body from the waist to the feet, worn by women and also by acrobats, dancers, etc.

tigress ('taɪgrɪs) n. **1.** a female tiger. **2.** a fierce, cruel, or passionate woman.

tike (taɪk) n. same as **tyke.**

tiki ('tiːkiː) n. a Maori greenstone neck ornament in the form of a fetus.

tilde ('tɪldə) n. a mark (˜) placed over a letter to indicate a nasal sound, as in Spanish señor.

tile (taɪl) n. **1.** a flat thin slab of fired clay, linoleum, etc., used with others to cover a surface, such as a floor or wall. **2.** a short pipe used with others to form a drain. **3.** a rectangular block used as a playing piece in mahjong and other games. **4. on the tiles.** Informal. on a spree, esp. of drinking. ~vb. **5.** to cover (a surface) with tiles. —**'tiler** n.

tiling ('taɪlɪŋ) n. **1.** tiles collectively. **2.** something made of or surfaced with tiles.

till¹ (tɪl) conj., prep. short for **until.** **Usage.** Till is a variant of until that is acceptable at all levels of language. Until is, however, often preferred at the beginning of a sentence in formal writing.

till² (tɪl) vb. to cultivate and work (land) for the raising of crops. —**'tillable** adj. —**'tiller** n.

till³ (tɪl) n. a box or drawer into which money taken from customers is put, now usually part of a cash register.

tillage ('tɪlɪdʒ) n. **1.** the act, process, or art of tilling. **2.** tilled land.

tiller ('tɪlə) n. Naut. a handle used to turn the rudder when steering a boat.

tilt (tɪlt) vb. **1.** to incline at an angle. **2.** to attack or overthrow (a person) in a tilt or joust. **3.** (often foll. by at) to aim or thrust: to tilt a lance. ~n. **4.** a slope or angle: at a tilt. **5.** the act of tilting. **6.** (esp. in medieval Europe) **a.** a jousting contest. **b.** a thrust with a lance delivered during a tournament. **7.** any dispute or contest. **8.** (at) full tilt. at full speed or force.

tilth (tɪlθ) n. **1.** the tilling of land. **2.** the condition of land that has been tilled.

timber ('tɪmbə) n. **1.** wood, esp. when regarded as building material. **2.** trees collectively. **3.** a piece of wood used in a structure. **4.** Naut. a frame in a wooden vessel. —'timbered adj. —'timbering n.

timber limit n. Canad. **1.** the area to which rights of cutting timber, granted by a government licence, are limited. **2.** same as timber line.

timber line n. the geographical limit beyond which trees will not grow.

timbre ('tɪmbə, 'tæmbə) n. the distinctive quality of a sound produced by a particular voice or musical instrument.

timbrel ('tɪmbrəl) n. Chiefly biblical. a tambourine.

Timbuktu (,tɪmbʌk'tuː) n. any distant or outlandish place: from here to Timbuktu.

time (taɪm) n. **1.** the continuous passage of existence in which events pass from a state of potentiality in the future, through the present, to a state of finality in the past. **2.** Physics. a quantity measuring duration, with reference to the rotation of the earth or from the vibrations of certain atoms. **3.** a specific point in time expressed in hours and minutes: the time is four o'clock. **4.** a system of reckoning for expressing time: Greenwich Mean Time. **5.** an unspecified interval; a while: I was there for a time. **6.** (often pl.) a period or point marked by specific attributes or events: the Victorian times. **7.** a sufficient interval or period: have you got time to help me? **8.** an instance or occasion: I called you three times. **9.** an occasion or period of specified quality: have a good time. **10.** a suitable moment: it's time I told you. **11.** (pl.) indicating an amount calculated by multiplication with the number specified: ten times three is thirty. **12.** Brit. the time at which licensed premises are legally obliged to stop selling alcoholic drinks. **13. a.** a customary or full period of work. **b.** the rate of pay for this period. **14. a.** the system of combining beats in music into successive groupings by which the rhythm of the music is established. **b.** a specific system having a specific number of beats in each grouping or bar: duple time. **15. against time.** in an

effort to complete something in a limited period. **16. ahead of time.** before the deadline. **17. at one time. a.** once; formerly. **b.** simultaneously. **18. at the same time. a.** simultaneously. **b.** nevertheless; however. **19. at times.** sometimes. **20. beat time.** to indicate the tempo of a piece of music by waving a baton, hand, etc. **21. do time.** to serve a term in jail. **22. for the time being.** for the moment; temporarily. **23. from time to time.** at intervals; occasionally. **24. have no time for.** to have no patience with; not tolerate. **25. in no time.** very quickly. **26. in one's own time. a.** outside paid working hours. **b.** at one's own rate. **27. in time. a.** early or at the appointed time. **b.** eventually: in time he'll see sense. **c.** Music. at a correct metrical or rhythmical pulse. **28. make time.** to find an opportunity. **29. on time.** at the expected or scheduled time. **30. pass the time of day.** to exchange casual greetings (with an acquaintance). **31. time and again.** frequently. **32. time of one's life.** a memorably enjoyable time. **33. time out of mind.** from time immemorial. **34.** (modifier) operating automatically at or for a set time: time lock; time switch. ~vb. **35.** to measure the duration or speed of: to time a race. **36.** to set a time for. ~interj. **37.** the word called out by a publican signalling that it is closing time.

time and a half n. a rate of pay one and a half times the normal rate, often offered for overtime work.

time and motion study n. the analysis of work procedures to determine the most efficient methods of operation.

time bomb n. a bomb containing a timing mechanism that determines when it will explode.

time capsule n. a container holding articles representative of the current age, buried for discovery in the future.

time clock n. a clock with a device for recording the time of arrival or departure of an employee.

time exposure n. a photograph produced by exposing film for a relatively long period, usually a few seconds.

time-honoured adj. having been observed for a long time and sanctioned by custom.

timekeeper ('taɪm,kiːpə) n. **1.** a person or thing that keeps or records time. **2.** an employee who maintains a record of the hours worked by the other employees. **3.** an employee whose record of punctuality is of a specified nature: a bad timekeeper. —'time,keeping n.

timeless ('taɪmlɪs) adj. **1.** unaffected or unchanged by time; ageless. **2.** eternal. —'timelessness n.

timely ('taɪmlɪ) adj. -lier, -liest, adv. at the right or an appropriate time.

time-out *n.* **1.** *Sport, chiefly U.S. & Canad.* an interruption in play during which players rest, discuss tactics, etc. **2. take time out.** to take a break from a job or activity.

timepiece ('taɪmˌpiːs) *n.* a device, such as a clock or watch which measures and indicates time.

timer ('taɪmə) *n.* a device for measuring time, esp. a switch or regulator that causes a mechanism to operate at a specific time.

timeserver ('taɪmˌsɜːvə) *n.* a person who compromises and changes his opinions to gain support or favour.

time sharing *n.* **1.** a system of part ownership of a property for use as a holiday home whereby each participant owns the property for a particular period every year. **2.** a system by which users at different terminals of a computer can communicate with it at the same time.

time signature *n. Music.* a sign usually consisting of two figures placed after the key signature, that indicates the tempo.

timetable ('taɪmˌteɪbəl) *n.* **1.** a list of departure and arrival times of trains or buses. **2.** a chart of the period allotted to different subjects at a school or college. **3.** a plan of the times when a job or activity should be done.

time value *n. Music.* the duration of a note relative to other notes in a composition and considered in relation to the basic tempo.

timeworn ('taɪmˌwɔːn) *adj.* **1.** showing the adverse effects of overlong use or of old age. **2.** hackneyed; trite.

time zone *n.* a region throughout which the same standard time is used.

timid ('tɪmɪd) *adj.* **1.** easily frightened or upset; shy. **2.** indicating shyness or fear. —ti'midity *or* 'timidness *n.* —'timidly *adv.*

timing ('taɪmɪŋ) *n.* the regulation of actions or remarks in relation to others to produce the best effect, as in music or in the theatre.

timorous ('tɪmərəs) *adj.* **1.** fearful or timid. **2.** indicating fear or timidity. —'timorously *adv.*

timpani *or* **tympani** ('tɪmpənɪ) *pl. n.* (*sometimes functioning as sing.*) a set of kettledrums. —'timpanist *or* 'tympanist *n.*

tin (tɪn) *n.* **1.** a soft silvery-white metallic element. Symbol: Sn **2.** an airtight metal container used for preserving and storing food or drink. **3.** any container made of metallic tin. **4.** Also called: **tinful.** the contents of a tin. **5.** *Brit., Austral., & N.Z.* galvanized iron: *a tin roof.* ~*vb.* **tinning, tinned. 6.** to put (food) into a tin or tins.

tin can *n.* a metal food container, esp. when empty.

tincture ('tɪŋktʃə) *n.* **1.** a medicinal extract in a solution of alcohol. **2.** a tint or tinge. **3.** a slight trace. ~*vb.* **4.** to tint or colour.

tinder ('tɪndə) *n.* dry wood or other easily combustible material used for lighting a fire. —'tindery *adj.*

tinderbox ('tɪndəˌbɒks) *n.* a small box for tinder, esp. one fitted with a flint and steel.

tine (taɪn) *n.* a slender prong of a fork or a deer's antler. —**tined** *adj.*

tinfoil ('tɪnˌfɔɪl) *n.* a paper-thin sheet of metal, used for wrapping foodstuffs.

ting (tɪŋ) *n.* a high metallic sound such as that made by a small bell.

ting-a-ling ('tɪŋə'lɪŋ) *n.* the sound of a small bell.

tinge (tɪndʒ) *n.* **1.** a slight tint or colouring. **2.** a very small amount; hint. ~*vb.* **tingeing** *or* **tinging, tinged. 3.** to colour or tint faintly. **4.** to give a slight trace to: *her thoughts were tinged with nostalgia.*

tingle ('tɪŋgəl) *vb.* **1.** to feel or cause to feel a prickling or stinging sensation of the flesh, as from cold or excitement. ~*n.* **2.** a feeling of tingling. —'tingling *adj.* —'tingly *adj.*

tin god *n.* a self-important person.

tinker ('tɪŋkə) *n.* **1.** (esp. formerly) a travelling mender of pots and pans. **2.** *Scot. & Irish.* a Gypsy. **3.** a mischievous person, esp. a child. ~*vb.* **4.** (foll. by *with*) to meddle with something, such as a car engine, esp. while undertaking repairs. **5.** to mend (pots and pans) as a tinker.

tinker's damn *or* **cuss** *n. Slang.* the slightest heed: *I don't give a tinker's damn what she says, I'm going anyway.*

tinkle ('tɪŋkəl) *vb.* **1.** to ring with a high tinny sound like a small bell. **2.** to cause to tinkle. ~*n.* **3.** a high clear ringing sound. **4.** *Brit. informal.* a telephone call. —'tinkly *adj.*

tinny ('tɪnɪ) *adj.* **-nier, -niest. 1.** of or resembling tin. **2.** cheap or shoddy. **3.** (of a sound) high, thin, and metallic.

tin-opener *n.* a small tool for opening tins.

tin plate *n.* thin steel sheet coated with a layer of tin to protect it from corrosion.

tinpot ('tɪnˌpɒt) *adj. Brit. informal.* **1.** inferior, cheap, or worthless. **2.** petty; unimportant: *a tinpot little dictatorship.*

tinsel ('tɪnsəl) *n.* **1.** a decoration consisting of a piece of metallic thread with thin strips of metal foil attached along its length. **2.** anything cheap, showy, and gaudy. ~*adj.* **3.** made of or decorated with tinsel. **4.** showily but cheaply attractive; gaudy. —'tinselly *adj.*

tinsmith ('tɪnˌsmɪθ) *n.* a person who works with tin or tin plate.

tint (tɪnt) *n.* **1.** a shade of a colour, esp. a pale one. **2.** a colour that is softened by the addition of white. **3.** a dye for the hair. **4.** a trace or hint. ~*vb.* **5.** to give a tint to (something, such as hair).

tintinnabulation (ˌtɪntɪˌnæbjʊ'leɪʃən) n. the ringing or pealing of bells.

tiny ('taɪnɪ) adj. **tinier, tiniest.** very small.

tip[1] (tɪp) n. **1.** a narrow or pointed end of something. **2.** the top or summit. **3.** a small piece forming an end: *a metal tip on a cane.* ~vb. **tipping, tipped. 4.** to adorn or mark the tip of.

tip[2] (tɪp) vb. **tipping, tipped. 1.** to tilt. **2. tip over.** to tilt so as to overturn or fall. **3.** *Brit.* to dump (rubbish). ~n. **4.** a tipping or being tipped. **5.** *Brit.* a dump for rubbish.

tip[3] (tɪp) n. **1.** an amount of money given to someone, such as a waiter, in return for service. **2.** a helpful hint or warning. **3.** a piece of inside information, esp. in betting or investing. ~vb. **tipping, tipped. 4.** to give a tip to.

tip[4] (tɪp) vb. **tipping, tipped. 1.** to hit or strike lightly. ~n. **2.** a light blow.

tip-off n. **1.** a warning or hint, esp. given confidentially and based on inside information. ~vb. **tip off. 2.** to give a hint or warning to.

tippet ('tɪpɪt) n. a scarflike piece of fur, often made from the whole skin of a dead animal, worn around a woman's shoulders.

tipple ('tɪpᵊl) vb. **1.** to make a habit of taking (alcoholic drink), esp. in small quantities. ~n. **2.** alcoholic drink. —'**tippler** n.

tipstaff ('tɪpˌstɑːf) n. **1.** a court official. **2.** a metal-tipped staff formerly used as a symbol of office.

tipster ('tɪpstə) n. a person who sells tips as to people betting on horse races or speculating on the stock market.

tipsy ('tɪpsɪ) adj. **-sier, -siest.** slightly drunk. —'**tipsiness** n.

tiptoe ('tɪpˌtəʊ) vb. **-toeing, -toed. 1.** to walk quietly with the heels off the ground. ~n. **2. on tiptoe.** on the tips of the toes or on the ball of the foot and the toes. ~adv. **3.** on tiptoe.

tiptop (ˌtɪp'tɒp) adj., adv. **1.** at the highest point of health, excellence, etc. ~n. **2.** the best in quality.

tip-up adj. able to be turned upwards around a hinge or pivot: *a tip-up seat.*

TIR International Road Transport.

tirade (taɪ'reɪd) n. a long angry speech or denunciation.

tire[1] ('taɪə) vb. **1.** to reduce the energy of, as by exertion; weary. **2.** to become wearied or bored; flag. —'**tiring** adj.

tire[2] ('taɪə) n., vb. *U.S.* same as **tyre.**

tired ('taɪəd) adj. **1.** weary; fatigued. **2.** no longer fresh; hackneyed: *the same tired old jokes.*

tireless ('taɪəlɪs) adj. unable to be tired. —'**tirelessly** adv.

tiresome ('taɪəsəm) adj. boring and irritating.

tiro ('taɪrəʊ) n., pl. **-ros.** same as **tyro.**

'tis (tɪz) *Poetic or dialect.* it is.

tissue ('tɪsjuː, 'tɪʃuː) n. **1.** a group of cells in an animal or plant having a similar structure and function. **2.** a thin piece of soft absorbent paper used as a disposable handkerchief, towel, etc. **3.** See **tissue paper. 4.** an interwoven series: *a tissue of lies.* **5.** a woven cloth, esp. of a light gauzy nature.

tissue paper n. very thin soft delicate paper used esp. to wrap breakable goods.

tit[1] (tɪt) n. any of various small European songbirds, such as the bluetit, that feed on insects and seeds.

tit[2] (tɪt) n. **1.** *Slang.* a female breast. **2.** a teat or nipple.

titan ('taɪtᵊn) n. a person of great strength or size.

titanic (taɪ'tænɪk) adj. possessing or requiring colossal strength: *a titanic battle.*

titanium (taɪ'teɪnɪəm) n. a strong white metallic element used in the manufacture of strong lightweight alloys, esp. aircraft parts. Symbol: Ti

titbit ('tɪtˌbɪt) or esp. *U.S.* **tidbit** n. **1.** a tasty small piece of food. **2.** a pleasing scrap of scandal.

titfer ('tɪtfə) n. *Brit. slang.* a hat.

tit for tat n. an equivalent given in return or retaliation; blow for blow.

tithe (taɪð) n. **1.** (often pl.) a tenth part of the annual produce of one's land or of one's annual income paid to support the church or clergy. **2.** a tenth or very small part of anything. ~vb. **3.** to exact or demand a tithe from. **4.** to pay a tithe or tithes. —'**tithable** adj.

tithe barn n. a large barn where, formerly, the agricultural tithe of a parish was stored.

Titian ('tɪʃən) adj. reddish-yellow.

titillate ('tɪtɪˌleɪt) vb. **1.** to arouse or excite pleasurably. **2.** to tickle. —'**titilˌlating** adj. —ˌtitil'lation n.

titivate ('tɪtɪˌveɪt) vb. to smarten up; spruce up. —ˌtiti'vation n.

title ('taɪtᵊl) n. **1.** the distinctive name of a work of art, musical, or literary composition, etc. **2.** a descriptive name or heading of a section of a book, speech, etc. **3.** See **title page. 4.** a name or epithet signifying rank, office, or function. **5.** a formal designation, such as *Mr.* **6.** *Sport.* a championship. **7.** *Law.* the legal right to possession of property.

title deed n. a document containing evidence of a person's legal right or title to property, esp. a house or land.

titleholder ('taɪtᵊlˌhəʊldə) n. a person who holds a title, esp. a sporting championship.

title page *n.* the page in a book that gives the title, author, publisher, etc.

title role *n.* the role of the character after whom a play or film is named.

titmouse ('tɪt,maʊs) *n., pl.* **-mice.** same as **tit**[1].

titrate ('taɪtreɪt) *vb. Chem.* to measure the volume or concentration of (a solution) by titration.

titration (taɪ'treɪʃən) *n. Chem.* an operation in which a measured amount of one solution is added to a known quantity of another solution until the reaction between the two is complete. If the concentration of one solution is known, that of the other can be calculated.

titter ('tɪtə) *vb.* **1.** to snigger, esp. derisively or in a suppressed way. ~*n.* **2.** a suppressed laugh or snigger.

tittle ('tɪt²l) *n.* a jot; particle.

tittle-tattle *n.* **1.** idle chat or gossip. ~*vb.* **2.** to chatter or gossip.

tittup ('tɪtəp) *vb.* **-tupping, -tupped** or *U.S.* **-tuping, -tuped.** **1.** to prance or frolic. ~*n.* **2.** a caper.

titular ('tɪtjʊlə) *adj.* **1.** of a title. **2.** in name only: *a titular leader.* **3.** bearing a title.

tizzy ('tɪzɪ) *n., pl.* **-zies.** *Informal.* a state of confusion or excitement.

T-junction *n.* a road junction in which one road joins another at right angles but does not cross it.

Tl *Chem.* thallium.

Tm *Chem.* thulium.

TN Tennessee.

TNT *n.* 2,4,6-trinitrotoluene; a yellow solid: used chiefly as a high explosive.

to (tuː; *unstressed* tʊ, tə) *prep.* **1.** used to indicate the destination of the subject or object of an action: *he climbed to the top.* **2.** used to mark the indirect object of a verb: *telling stories to children.* **3.** used to mark the infinitive of a verb: *he wanted to go.* **4.** as far as; until: *working from Monday to Friday.* **5.** used to indicate equality: *16 ounces to the pound.* **6.** against; upon; onto: *put your ear to the wall.* **7.** before the hour of: *five to four.* **8.** accompanied by: *dancing to loud music.* **9.** as compared with, as against: *the score was eight to three.* **10.** used to indicate a resulting condition: *they starved to death.* ~*adv.* **11.** towards a fixed position, esp. (of a door) closed. **Usage.** In formal usage, *to* is always used with an infinitive and never omitted as in *come see the show.* The use of *and* instead of *to* (*try and come*) is very common in informal speech but is avoided in formal written English.

toad (təʊd) *n.* **1.** a tailless amphibian with a dry warty skin, that lives on moist land. **2.** a loathsome person.

toadflax ('təʊd,flæks) *n.* a perennial plant with yellow-orange flowers.

toad-in-the-hole *n. Brit.* a dish made of sausages baked in a batter.

toadstool ('təʊd,stuːl) *n.* a fungus with a caplike top that is poisonous. Cf. **mushroom.**

toady ('təʊdɪ) *n., pl.* **toadies. 1.** a person who flatters and ingratiates himself in a fawning way. ~*vb.* **toadying, toadied. 2.** to fawn on and flatter (someone). —'**toadyism** *n.*

to and fro *adv., adj.* also **to-and-fro. 1.** back and forth. **2.** here and there. —**toing and froing** *n.*

toast[1] (təʊst) *n.* **1.** sliced bread browned by exposure to heat. ~*vb.* **2.** to brown (bread) under a grill or over a fire. **3.** to warm or be warmed: *to toast one's hands by the fire.*

toast[2] (təʊst) *n.* **1.** a proposal of health or success given to a person or thing and marked by people raising glasses and drinking together. **2.** a person or thing so honoured. ~*vb.* **3.** to propose or drink a toast to (a person or thing).

toaster ('təʊstə) *n.* an electrical device for toasting bread.

toastmaster ('təʊst,mɑːstə) *n.* a person who introduces speakers and proposes toasts at public dinners. —'**toast,mistress** *fem. n.*

tobacco (tə'bækəʊ) *n., pl.* **-cos** or **-coes.** an American plant with large leaves which are dried and prepared for snuff, chewing, or smoking.

tobacconist (tə'bækənɪst) *n. Chiefly Brit.* a person or shop that sells tobacco, cigarettes, pipes, etc.

-to-be *adj.* about to be; future: *a mother-to-be; the bride-to-be.*

toboggan (tə'bɒgən) *n.* **1.** a long narrow sledge used for sliding over snow and ice. ~*vb.* **2.** to ride on a toboggan.

toby ('təʊbɪ) *n., pl.* **-bies.** *N.Z.* a water stopcock at the boundary of a street and house section.

toby jug *n.* a beer mug or jug in the form of a stout seated man wearing a three-cornered hat and smoking a pipe.

toccata (tə'kɑːtə) *n.* a composition for the organ, harpsichord, or piano, usually in a rhythmically free style.

Toc H ('tɒk 'eɪtʃ) *n.* a society formed after World War I to encourage Christian comradeship.

tocsin ('tɒksɪn) *n.* **1.** a warning signal. **2.** an alarm bell.

tod (tɒd) *n.* **on one's tod.** *Brit. slang.* alone.

today (tə'deɪ) *n.* **1.** this day, as distinct from yesterday or tomorrow. **2.** the present age: *women of today.* ~*adv.* **3.** during or on this day. **4.** nowadays.

toddle ('tɒdʲl) *vb.* **1.** to walk with short unsteady steps, as a child. **2.** (foll. by *off*) *Jocular*. to depart: *I'll toddle off now.* ~*n.* **3.** a toddling.

toddler ('tɒdlə) *n.* a young child, usually between the ages of one and two and a half.

toddy ('tɒdɪ) *n., pl.* **-dies.** a drink made from spirits, esp. whisky, hot water, sugar, and usually lemon juice.

to-do (tə'duː) *n., pl.* **-dos.** a commotion, fuss, or quarrel.

toe (təʊ) *n.* **1.** any one of the digits of the foot. **2.** the part of a shoe or sock covering the toes. **3. on one's toes.** alert. **4. tread on someone's toes.** to offend a person, esp. by trespassing on his field of responsibility. ~*vb.* **toeing, toed.** **5.** to touch or kick with the toe. **6. toe the line.** to conform to expected attitudes or standards.

toecap ('təʊˌkæp) *n.* a reinforced covering for the toe of a boot or shoe.

toehold ('təʊˌhəʊld) *n.* **1.** a small space on a rock, mountain, etc., for supporting the toe of the foot in climbing. **2.** any means of gaining access, support, etc.

toff (tɒf) *n. Brit. slang.* a well-dressed or upper-class person.

toffee ('tɒfɪ) *n.* **1.** a sweet made from sugar or treacle boiled with butter, nuts, etc. **2. for toffee.** (preceded by *can't*) *Informal*. to be incompetent at: *he can't sing for toffee.*

toffee-apple *n.* an apple fixed on a stick and coated with a thin layer of toffee.

toffee-nosed *adj. Slang, chiefly Brit.* pretentious or supercilious; used esp. of snobbish people.

tofu ('təʊˌfuː) *n.* unfermented soya-bean curd: a food with a soft cheeselike consistency.

tog (tɒg) *Informal.* ~*vb.* **togging, togged.** **1.** (often foll. by *up* or *out*) to dress oneself, esp. in smart clothes. ~*n.* **2.** (*pl.*) clothes.

toga ('təʊgə) *n.* a garment worn by citizens of ancient Rome, consisting of a piece of cloth draped around the body. —'**togaed** *adj.*

together (tə'gɛðə) *adv.* **1.** with cooperation between members, etc.: *we worked together.* **2.** in or into contact with each other: *to stick papers together.* **3.** in or into one place; with each other: *the people are gathered together.* **4.** at the same time: *we left school together.* **5.** considered collectively: *all our wages put together couldn't buy that car.* **6.** continuously: *working for eight hours together.* **7.** *Informal.* organized: *to get things together.* **8. together with.** in addition to. ~*adj.* **9.** *Slang.* self-possessed, competent, and well-organized. **Usage.** see **plus.**

togetherness (tə'gɛðənɪs) *n.* a feeling of closeness or affection from being united with other people.

toggle ('tɒgʲl) *n.* **1.** a peg or rod at the end of a rope or chain for fastening by insertion through an eye in another rope or chain. **2.** a bar-shaped button inserted through a loop for fastening.

toggle joint *n.* a device consisting of two arms pivoted at a common joint and at their outer ends and used to apply pressure by straightening the angle between the two arms.

toggle switch *n.* **1.** an electric switch with a projecting lever that is moved in a particular way to open or close a circuit. **2.** a computer device used to turn a feature on or off.

toheroa (ˌtəʊə'rəʊə) *n.* a large edible bivalve mollusc of New Zealand with a distinctive flavour.

tohunga ('tɒhuŋə) *n. N.Z.* a Maori priest.

toil (tɔɪl) *n.* **1.** hard or exhausting work. ~*vb.* **2.** to work hard; labour. **3.** to progress with slow painful movements.

toilet ('tɔɪlɪt) *n.* **1. a.** a bowl fitted with a water-flushing device and connected to a drain, for receiving and disposing of urine and faeces. **b.** a room with such a fitment. **2.** the act of dressing and preparing oneself.

toilet paper *n.* thin absorbent paper used for cleaning oneself after defecation or urination.

toiletry ('tɔɪlɪtrɪ) *n., pl.* **-ries.** an object or cosmetic used in making up, dressing, etc.

toilette (twɑː'lɛt) *n.* same as **toilet** (sense 2).

toilet water *n.* a form of liquid perfume lighter than cologne.

toilsome ('tɔɪlsəm) *adj.* requiring hard work; laborious.

token ('təʊkən) *n.* **1.** a symbol, sign, or indication of something: *as a token of affection.* **2.** a memento. **3.** a gift voucher that can be used as payment for goods of a specified value. **4.** a metal or plastic disc, such as a substitute for currency for use in a slot machine. **5.** (*modifier*) as a matter of form only; nominal: *a token increase in salary.*

tokenism ('təʊkəˌnɪzəm) *n.* the practice of making only a token effort or doing no more than the minimum, esp. in order to comply with a law. —'**tokenist** *adj.*

token strike *n.* a brief stoppage of work intended to convey strength of feeling on a disputed issue.

told (təʊld) *vb.* past of **tell**[1].

tolerable ('tɒlərəbʲl) *adj.* **1.** able to be tolerated; endurable. **2.** *Informal.* fairly good. —'**tolerably** *adv.*

tolerance ('tɒlərəns) *n.* **1.** the quality of accepting other people's rights to their own opinions, beliefs, or actions. **2.** capacity to endure something, esp. pain or hardship. **3.** the permitted variation in some characteristic of an object or workpiece. **4.** *Med.*

the capacity to endure the effects of a continued or increasing dose of a drug, poison, etc.

tolerant ('tɒlərənt) *adj.* **1.** able to tolerate the beliefs, actions, etc., of others. **2.** able to withstand extremes as of heat and cold.

tolerate ('tɒlə‚reɪt) *vb.* **1.** to treat (someone) with generous respect. **2.** to permit (something) to happen. **3.** to put up with (someone or something).

toleration (‚tɒlə'reɪʃən) *n.* **1.** the act or practice of tolerating. **2.** freedom to hold religious opinions that differ from the established religion of a country.

toll¹ (təʊl) *vb.* **1.** to ring (a bell) slowly and recurrently. **2.** to announce by tolling: *the bells tolled the Queen's death.* ~*n.* **3.** the act or sound of tolling.

toll² (təʊl, tɒl) *n.* **1.** a charge for the use of certain roads and bridges. **2.** loss or damage incurred through a disaster: *the war took its toll of the inhabitants.*

tollgate ('təʊl‚geɪt, 'tɒl-) *n.* a gate across a toll road or bridge at which travellers must pay.

tollie ('tɒlɪ) *n. S. African.* a castrated calf.

tolu (tɒ'luː) *n.* an aromatic balsam obtained from a South American tree, used in medicine and perfume.

toluene ('tɒljʊ‚iːn) *n.* a flammable liquid obtained from petroleum and coal tar and used as a solvent and in the manufacture of dyes, explosives, etc.

tom (tɒm) *n.* the male of various animals, esp. the cat.

tomahawk ('tɒmə‚hɔːk) *n.* a fighting axe used by the North American Indians.

tomato (tə'mɑːtəʊ) *n., pl.* **-toes.** a soft fruit that grows on a South American plant, eaten in salads, as a vegetable, etc.

tomb (tuːm) *n.* **1.** a place for the burial of a corpse. **2.** a monument to the dead. **3. the tomb.** *Poetic.* death.

tombola (tɒm'bəʊlə) *n. Brit.* a type of lottery, in which tickets are drawn from a revolving drum.

tomboy ('tɒm‚bɔɪ) *n.* a girl who behaves or plays like a boy.

tombstone ('tuːm‚stəʊn) *n.* a gravestone.

tome (təʊm) *n.* a large heavy book.

tomfoolery (‚tɒm'fuːlərɪ) *n.* foolish behaviour.

Tommy ('tɒmɪ) *n., pl.* **-mies.** *Brit. informal.* a private in the British Army.

Tommy gun *n.* a type of .45-calibre sub-machine-gun.

tommyrot ('tɒmɪ‚rɒt) *n.* utter nonsense.

tomorrow (tə'mɒrəʊ) *n.* **1.** the day after today. **2.** the future. ~*adv.* **3.** on the day after today. **4.** at some time in the future.

Tom Thumb *n.* a dwarf; midget.

tomtit ('tɒm‚tɪt) *n. Brit.* a small European bird that eats insects and seeds.

tom-tom *n.* a drum usually beaten with the hands as a signalling instrument.

ton¹ (tʌn) *n.* **1.** *Brit.* a unit of weight equal to 2240 pounds or 1016.046 909 kilograms. **2.** *U.S. & Canad.* a unit of weight equal to 2000 pounds or 907.184 kilograms. **3.** See **metric ton.** ~*adv.* **4. tons.** much: *the new flat is tons better than the old one.*

ton² (tʌn) *n. Slang, chiefly Brit.* a hundred miles per hour, as on a motorcycle.

tonal ('təʊn°l) *adj.* of or relating to tone or tonality.

tonality (təʊ'nælɪtɪ) *n., pl.* **-ties. 1.** *Music.* the presence of a musical key in a composition. **2.** the overall scheme of colours and tones in a painting.

tone (təʊn) *n.* **1.** sound with reference to quality, pitch, or volume. **2.** *U.S. & Canad.* same as **note** (sense 9). **3.** *Music.* an interval of a major second; whole tone. **4.** the quality or character of a sound: *a nervous tone of voice.* **5.** general aspect, quality, or style: *I didn't like the tone of her speech.* **6.** high quality or style: *to lower the tone of a place.* **7.** the quality of a given colour, as modified by mixture with white or black; shade; tint. **8.** *Physiol.* the natural firmness of the tissues and normal functioning of bodily organs in health. ~*vb.* **9.** (often foll. by *with*) to be of a matching or similar tone (to). **10.** to give a tone to or correct the tone of. —'**toneless** *adj.* —'**tonelessly** *adv.*

tone-deaf *adj.* unable to distinguish subtle differences in musical pitch.

tone down *vb.* to moderate or become moderated in tone: *to tone down an argument.*

tone poem *n. Music.* an extended orchestral composition based on nonmusical material, such as a work of literature or a fairy tale.

tone up *vb.* to make or become more vigorous, healthy, etc.: *exercise tones up the muscles.*

tong (tɒŋ) *n.* (formerly) a secret society of Chinese Americans.

tongs (tɒŋz) *pl. n.* a tool for grasping or lifting, consisting of a hinged or pivoted pair of arms.

tongue (tʌŋ) *n.* **1.** a movable mass of muscular tissue attached to the floor of the mouth. It is used in tasting, eating, and (in man) speaking. **2.** the tongue of certain animals used as food. **3.** a language, dialect, or idiom: *the English tongue.* **4.** the ability to speak: *to lose one's tongue.* **5.** a manner of speaking: *a glib tongue.* **6.** a narrow strip of land that extends into a body of water. **7.** a flap of leather on a shoe. **8.** the clapper of a bell. **9.** a projecting strip along an edge of a board that is made to fit a groove in another board. **10. hold one's tongue.** to keep quiet. **11. on**

the tip of one's tongue. about to come to mind. **12. with (one's) tongue in (one's) cheek.** with insincere or ironical intent.

tongue-tie *n.* a congenital condition in which movement of the tongue is limited as the result of an abnormally short fold of skin under the tongue.

tongue-tied *adj.* speechless, esp. with embarrassment or shyness.

tongue twister *n.* a sentence or phrase that is difficult to say clearly and quickly, such as *Peter Piper picked a peck of pickled pepper*.

tonguing ('tʌŋɪŋ) *n.* a technique of playing a wind instrument by obstructing and uncovering the air passage through the lips with the tongue.

tonic ('tɒnɪk) *n.* **1.** a medicine that improves the functioning of the body or increases the feeling of wellbeing. **2.** anything that enlivens or strengthens. **3.** Also called: **tonic water.** a carbonated beverage containing quinine and often mixed with alcoholic drinks. **4.** *Music.* the first degree of a major or minor scale and the tonal centre of a piece composed in a particular key. *~adj.* **5.** serving to enliven and invigorate: *a tonic wine.* **6.** *Music.* of the first degree of a major or minor scale.

tonic sol-fa *n.* a method of teaching music, by which syllables are used as names for the notes of the major scale in any key.

tonight (tə'naɪt) *n.* **1.** the night or evening of this present day. *~adv.* **2.** in or during the night or evening of this day.

tonnage ('tʌnɪdʒ) *n.* **1.** the capacity of a merchant ship expressed in tons. **2.** the weight of the cargo of a merchant ship. **3.** the total amount of shipping of a port or nation.

tonne (tʌn) *n.* a unit of mass equal to 1000 kg or 2204.6 pounds.

tonsil ('tɒnsəl) *n.* either of two small oval lumps of spongy tissue situated one on each side of the back of the mouth. —'**tonsillar** *adj.*

tonsillectomy (ˌtɒnsɪ'lɛktəmɪ) *n., pl.* **-mies.** surgical removal of the tonsils.

tonsillitis (ˌtɒnsɪ'laɪtɪs) *n.* inflammation of the tonsils.

tonsorial (tɒn'sɔːrɪəl) *adj. Often facetious.* of a barber or his trade.

tonsure ('tɒnʃə) *n.* **1.** (in certain religions and monastic orders) **a.** the shaving of the head or the crown of the head only. **b.** the part of the head left bare by shaving. *~vb.* **2.** to shave the head of. —'**tonsured** *adj.*

ton-up *adj. Brit. informal.* **1.** (esp. of a motorcycle) capable of speeds of a hundred miles per hour. **2.** liking to travel at such speeds: *a ton-up boy.*

too (tuː) *adv.* **1.** as well; also: *can I come too?* **2.** in or to an excessive degree: *I have too many things to do.* **3.** extremely: *you're*

too kind. **4.** *U.S. & Canad. informal.* used to reinforce a command: *you will too do it!*

took (tʊk) *vb.* the past tense of **take.**

tool (tuːl) *n.* **1. a.** an implement, such as a hammer, saw, or spade, that is used by hand. **b.** a power-driven instrument; machine tool. **2.** the cutting part of such an instrument. **3.** a person used to perform dishonourable or unpleasant tasks for another. **4.** a necessary medium for one's profession: *numbers are the tools of the mathematician's trade. ~vb.* **5.** to work, cut, or form (something) with a tool. **6.** (often foll. by *up*) to furnish with tools.

tool-maker *n.* a person who specializes in the production or reconditioning of machine tools. —'**tool-ˌmaking** *n.*

toot (tuːt) *vb.* **1.** to give or cause to give (a short blast, hoot, or whistle). *~n.* **2.** the sound made by or as if by a horn, whistle, etc. **3.** *U.S. & Canad. slang.* a drinking spree.

tooth (tuːθ) *n., pl.* **teeth** (tiːθ). **1.** any of various bonelike structures set in the jaws of most vertebrates and used for biting, tearing, or chewing. **2.** anything resembling a tooth in shape, prominence, or function: *the tooth of a comb.* **3.** taste or appetite: *a sweet tooth.* **4. long in the tooth.** old or ageing. **5. tooth and nail.** with ferocity and force: *we fought tooth and nail.* —'**toothless** *adj.*

toothache ('tuːθˌeɪk) *n.* a pain in or about a tooth.

toothbrush ('tuːθˌbrʌʃ) *n.* a small brush with a long handle, for cleaning the teeth.

toothpaste ('tuːθˌpeɪst) *n.* a paste used for cleaning the teeth, applied with a toothbrush.

toothpick ('tuːθˌpɪk) *n.* a small wooden or plastic stick used for extracting pieces of food from between the teeth.

tooth powder *n.* a powder used for cleaning the teeth, applied with a toothbrush.

toothsome ('tuːθsəm) *adj.* of delicious or appetizing appearance, flavour, or smell.

toothy ('tuːθɪ) *adj.* **toothier, toothiest.** having or showing numerous, large, or projecting teeth: *a toothy grin.*

tootle ('tuːtᵊl) *vb.* **1.** to hoot softly or repeatedly. *~n.* **2.** a soft hoot or series of hoots.

top[1] (tɒp) *n.* **1.** the highest point or part of anything: *the top of a hill.* **2.** the most important or successful position: *the top of the class.* **3.** a lid, cap, or other device that covers the uppermost part of anything. **4.** the highest degree or point: *at the top of his career.* **5.** the most important person: *he's the top of this organization.* **6.** the loudest or highest pitch: *she was shouting at the top of her voice.* **7.** a garment, esp. for a woman, that extends from the shoulders to the waist or hips. **8.** the part of a plant that is above ground: *carrot tops.* **9.** same as **top gear. 10. off the top of one's head.** without previous preparation or careful thought: *I'll give you the estimate off the top of my head.* **11. on top of. a.** in addition to: *on top of his accident, he lost his job.* **b.** *Informal.* in complete control of: *I'm on top of the problem now.* **12. over the top. a.** over the edge of a trench. **b.** lacking restraint or a sense of proportion. ~*adj.* **13.** of, relating to, serving as, or situated on the top. ~*vb.* **topping, topped. 14.** to form a top on (something): *to top a cake with cream.* **15.** to reach or pass the top of. **16.** to be at the top of: *he tops the team.* **17.** to exceed or surpass: *the fund topped five hundred pounds.* ~See also **top off, top out,** etc.

top² (tɒp) *n.* **1.** a toy that is spun on its pointed base. **2. sleep like a top.** to sleep very soundly.

topaz (ˈtəʊpæz) *n.* a hard glassy yellow, pink, or colourless mineral used in making jewellery.

top brass *n.* (*functioning as pl.*) the most important or high-ranking officials or leaders.

topcoat (ˈtɒpˌkəʊt) *n.* **1.** an overcoat. **2.** a final coat of paint applied to a surface.

top dog *n. Informal.* the leader or chief of a group.

top drawer *n.* people of the highest social standing.

top dressing *n.* a layer of fertilizer or manure spread on the surface of land. —ˈtop-ˌdress *vb.*

tope¹ (təʊp) *vb.* to drink (alcohol) usually in large quantities. —ˈtoper *n.*

tope² (təʊp) *n.* a small grey shark of European coastal waters.

topee *or* **topi** (ˈtəʊpiː, -pɪ) *n., pl.* **-pees** *or* **-pis.** same as **pith helmet.**

top-flight *adj.* of superior or excellent quality.

topgallant (ˌtɒpˈgælənt; *Naut.* təˈgælənt) *n.* **1.** a mast or sail above a topmast. **2.** (*modifier*) of or relating to a topgallant.

top gear *n.* the highest forward ratio of a gearbox in a motor vehicle.

top hat *n.* a man's hat with a tall cylindrical crown and narrow brim, now worn for some formal occasions.

top-heavy *adj.* unstable through being overloaded at the top.

topiary (ˈtəʊpɪərɪ) *adj.* **1.** of or relating to the trimming of trees or bushes into artificial decorative shapes. ~*n.* **2.** topiary work. **3.** the art of topiary. —ˈtopiarist *n.*

topic (ˈtɒpɪk) *n.* a subject of a speech, book, conversation, etc.

topical (ˈtɒpɪkʰl) *adj.* of or relating to cur-

rent affairs. —**topicality** (ˌtɒpɪˈkælɪtɪ) *n.* —ˈtopically *adv.*

topknot (ˈtɒpˌnɒt) *n.* a crest, tuft, decorative bow, chignon, etc., on the top of the head.

topless (ˈtɒplɪs) *adj.* **1.** having no top. **2.** denoting or wearing a costume which has no covering for the breasts.

top-level *n.* (*modifier*) of, involving, or by those on the highest level of influence or authority: *top-level talks.*

topmast (ˈtɒpˌmɑːst; *Naut.* ˈtɒpməst) *n.* the mast next above a lower mast on a sailing vessel.

topmost (ˈtɒpˌməʊst) *adj.* at or nearest the top.

topnotch (ˈtɒpˈnɒtʃ) *adj. Informal.* excellent; superb: *a topnotch actress.*

top off *vb.* to finish or complete, esp. with some decisive action.

topography (təˈpɒgrəfɪ) *n., pl.* **-phies. 1.** the study or description of the surface features of a region, such as its hills, valleys, or rivers. **2.** the representation of these features on a map. **3.** the surveying of a region's surface features. —**toˈpographer** *n.* —**topographical** (ˌtɒpəˈgræfɪkʰl) *adj.*

topology (təˈpɒlədʒɪ) *n.* a branch of geometry describing the properties of a figure that are unaffected by continuous distortion. —**topological** (ˌtɒpəˈlɒdʒɪkʰl) *adj.*

top out *vb.* to place the highest stone on (a building).

topper (ˈtɒpə) *n. Informal.* a top hat.

topping (ˈtɒpɪŋ) *n.* **1.** a sauce or garnish for food. ~*adj.* **2.** *Brit. slang.* excellent; splendid.

topple (ˈtɒpʰl) *vb.* **1.** to tip over or cause (something) to tip over, esp. from a height. **2.** to overthrow; oust: *to topple a government.*

tops (tɒps) *Slang.* ~*n.* **1. the tops.** a person or thing of top quality. ~*adj.* **2.** excellent.

topsail (ˈtɒpˌseɪl; *Naut.* ˈtɒpsəl) *n.* a square sail carried on a yard set on a topmast.

top-secret *adj.* (of military or government information) classified as needing the highest level of secrecy and security.

topside (ˈtɒpˌsaɪd) *n.* **1.** *Brit. & N.Z.* a lean cut of beef from the thigh containing no bone. **2.** (*often pl.*) the part of a ship's sides above the water line.

topsoil (ˈtɒpˌsɔɪl) *n.* the surface layer of soil.

topsy-turvy (ˈtɒpsɪˈtɜːvɪ) *adj.* **1.** upside down. **2.** in a state of confusion. ~*adv.* **3.** in a topsy-turvy manner.

top up *vb. Brit.* **1.** to refill (a container), usually to the brim: *he topped up the petrol tank before he left.* **2.** to provide extra money, provisions, etc. to make (the total amount) sufficient: *to top up students' grants with loans.*

toque (təʊk) *n.* **1.** a woman's small round brimless hat. **2.** *Canad.* a knitted cap with a round tassel on top.

tor (tɔː) *n.* a high hill, esp. a bare rocky one.

Torah (ˈtɔːrə) *n.* the whole body of traditional Jewish teaching, including the Oral Law.

torch (tɔːtʃ) *n.* **1.** a small portable electric lamp powered by batteries. **2.** a wooden shaft dipped in wax or tallow and set alight. **3.** anything regarded as a source of enlightenment, guidance, etc.: *the torch of learning*. **4. carry a torch for.** to be in love with someone, esp. unrequitedly.

tore (tɔː) *vb.* the past tense of **tear²**.

toreador (ˈtɒrɪəˌdɔː) *n.* a bullfighter, esp. on horseback.

torero (tɒˈrɛərəʊ) *n., pl.* **-ros.** a bullfighter, esp. on foot.

torment *vb.* (tɔːˈmɛnt). **1.** to cause (someone) great pain, suffering, or anguish; torture. **2.** to tease or pester (a person or animal) in an annoying or cruel way: *don't torment the dog.* ~*n.* (ˈtɔːmɛnt). **3.** physical or mental pain. **4.** a source of pain, worry, or annoyance. —**torˈmentor** *n.*

tormentil (ˈtɔːməntɪl) *n.* a perennial plant with yellow flowers.

torn (tɔːn) *vb.* **1.** the past participle of **tear²**. ~*adj.* **2.** split or cut. **3.** divided or undecided, as in preference: *torn between staying and leaving.*

tornado (tɔːˈneɪdəʊ) *n., pl.* **-does** or **-dos.** a rapidly whirling column of air, usually characterized by a dark funnel-shaped cloud causing damage along its path.

torpedo (tɔːˈpiːdəʊ) *n., pl.* **-does.** **1.** a cylindrical self-propelled weapon carrying explosives that is launched from aircraft, ships, or submarines and follows an underwater path to hit its target. ~*vb.* **-doing, -doed.** **2.** to attack or hit (a ship) with one or a number of torpedoes. **3.** to destroy or wreck: *to torpedo the administration's plan.*

torpedo boat *n.* (formerly) a small high-speed warship for torpedo attacks.

torpid (ˈtɔːpɪd) *adj.* **1.** sluggish or dull: *a torpid mind.* **2.** (of a hibernating animal) dormant. **3.** unable to move or feel. —**torˈpidity** *n.*

torpor (ˈtɔːpə) *n.* drowsiness and apathy.

torque (tɔːk) *n.* **1.** a force that causes rotation around a central point such as an axle. **2.** an ancient Celtic necklace or armband made of twisted metal.

torr (tɔː) *n., pl.* **torr.** a unit of pressure equal to one millimetre of mercury.

torrent (ˈtɒrənt) *n.* **1.** a fast or violent stream, esp. of water. **2.** a rapid flow of questions, abuse, etc. —**torrential** (tɒˈrɛnʃəl) *adj.*

torrid (ˈtɒrɪd) *adj.* **1.** so hot and dry as to parch or scorch. **2.** arid or parched. **3.**

highly charged emotionally: *a torrid love scene.*

torsion (ˈtɔːʃən) *n.* the twisting of a part by equal forces being applied at both ends but in opposite directions. —**torsional** *adj.*

torso (ˈtɔːsəʊ) *n., pl.* **-sos.** **1.** the trunk of the human body. **2.** a statue of a nude human trunk, esp. without the head or limbs.

tort (tɔːt) *n. Law.* a civil wrong or injury, independent of any contract, for which an action for damages may be brought.

tortilla (tɔːˈtiːə) *n. Mexican cookery.* a kind of thin pancake made from corn meal.

tortoise (ˈtɔːtəs) *n.* a toothless land reptile with a heavy dome-shaped shell and clawed limbs.

tortoiseshell (ˈtɔːtəsˌʃɛl) *n.* **1.** the horny yellow-and-brown mottled shell of a sea turtle: used for making ornaments and jewellery. **2.** a domestic cat with black, cream, and brownish markings. **3.** a butterfly which has orange-brown wings with black markings. **4.** (*modifier*) made of tortoiseshell.

tortuous (ˈtɔːtjʊəs) *adj.* **1.** twisted or winding: *a tortuous road.* **2.** devious or cunning: *a tortuous argument.*

torture (ˈtɔːtʃə) *vb.* **1.** to cause (someone) extreme physical pain, esp. to extract information, etc.: *to torture prisoners.* **2.** to cause (someone) mental anguish. ~*n.* **3.** physical or mental anguish. **4.** the practice of torturing a person. **5.** a cause of mental agony. —**torturer** *n.* —**torturous** *adj.*

Tory (ˈtɔːrɪ) *n., pl.* **-ries.** **1.** a member of the Conservative Party in Great Britain or Canada. **2.** *History.* a member of the English political party that supported the Church and Crown and traditional political structures and opposed the Whigs. ~*adj.* **3.** of or relating to Tories. **4.** (*sometimes not cap.*) ultraconservative or reactionary. —**Toryism** *n.*

toss (tɒs) *vb.* **1.** to throw (something) lightly. **2.** to fling or be flung about, esp. in an violent way: *a ship tosses in a storm.* **3.** to coat (food) with a dressing by gentle stirring or mixing: *to toss the salad.* **4.** (of a horse) to throw (its rider). **5.** (of an animal) to butt with the head or the horns and throw into the air. **6.** to move (one's head) suddenly backwards, as in impatience. **7.** to toss up a coin with (someone) in order to decide something. ~*n* **8.** the act or an instance of tossing. **9.** the act of tossing up a coin. See **toss up**. **10.** a fall from a horse.

toss off *vb.* **1.** to perform, write, etc., quickly and easily: *she tossed off a letter to Jim.* **2.** to finish (a drink) in one swallow.

toss up *vb.* **1.** to spin (a coin) in the air in order to decide between alternatives by guessing which side will fall uppermost. ~*n.* **toss-up.** **2.** an instance of tossing up a coin. **3.** *Informal.* an even chance or risk: *it was a toss-up who would get there first.*

tot[1] (tɒt) *n.* **1.** a young child; toddler. **2.** a small measure of spirits.

tot[2] (tɒt) *vb.* **totting, totted.** (usually foll. by *up*) *Chiefly Brit.* to add (numbers) together.

total ('təʊt°l) *n.* **1.** the whole, esp. regarded as the sum of a number of parts. ~*adj.* **2.** complete: *a total failure.* **3.** being or related to a total: *the total number of passengers.* ~*vb.* **-talling, -talled** *or U.S.* **-taling, -taled.** **4.** to amount: *to total six pounds.* **5.** to add up: *to total a list of prices.* —'**totally** *adv.*

totalitarian (təʊˌtælɪˈtɛərɪən) *adj.* of a dictatorial one-party government. —**to,tali'tarianism** *n.*

totality (təʊˈtælɪtɪ) *n., pl.* **-ties.** **1.** the whole amount. **2.** the state of being total.

totalizator ('təʊt°laɪˌzeɪtə), **totalizer** *or* **totalisator, totaliser** *n.* a machine to operate a system of betting on a racecourse in which money is paid out to the winners in proportion to their stakes.

tote[1] (təʊt) *vb. Informal.* **1.** to carry or wear (a gun). **2.** to carry, convey, or drag.

tote[2] (təʊt) *n.* (usually preceded by *the*) *Informal.* short for **totalizator.**

tote bag *n.* a large handbag or shopping bag.

totem ('təʊtəm) *n.* **1.** (esp. among North American Indians) an object or animal symbolizing a clan or family. **2.** a representation of such an object. —**totemic** (təʊˈtɛmɪk) *adj.* —'**totem,ism** *n.*

totem pole *n.* a pole carved or painted with totemic figures set up by certain North American Indians as a tribal symbol.

totter ('tɒtə) *vb.* **1.** to move in an unsteady manner. **2.** to sway or shake as if about to fall. **3.** to be failing, unstable, or precarious: *the wartime Liberal Government was tottering.* ~*n.* **4.** the act or an instance of tottering.

toucan ('tuːkən) *n.* a tropical American fruit-eating bird with a large brightly coloured bill.

touch (tʌtʃ) *n.* **1.** the sense by which the texture and other qualities of objects can be experienced when they come in contact with a part of the body surface, esp. the tips of the fingers. **2.** the quality of an object as perceived by this sense; feel. **3.** the act or an instance of something coming into contact with the body. **4.** a gentle push, tap, or caress. **5.** a small amount; hint: *a touch of sarcasm.* **6.** any slight stroke or mark. **7.** characteristic style: *the artist had a distinctive touch.* **8.** a detail of some work: *she added a few finishing touches to the book.* **9.** a slight attack: *a touch of the flu.* **10. in touch.** aware of a situation or in contact with someone. **11.**

the technique of fingering a keyboard instrument. **12.** *Slang.* **a.** the act of asking for money. **b.** a person asked for money: *she was an easy touch.* ~*vb.* **13.** to cause or permit a part of the body to come into contact with (someone or something). **14.** to tap, feel, or strike (someone or something). **15.** to come or cause (something) to come into contact with (something else). **16.** to be in contact with (someone). **17.** to move or disturb by handling: *someone's touched my desk.* **18.** to have an effect on: *the war scarcely touched our town.* **19.** to produce an emotional response in: *she was touched by his sad story.* **20.** to eat or drink: *she doesn't touch alcohol.* **21.** (foll. by *on*) to allude to briefly or in passing: *the speech touched on several subjects.* **22.** to compare to in quality or attainment; equal or match: *there's no-one to touch her.* **23.** *Slang.* to ask (someone) for a loan or gift of money. ~See also **touchdown, touch off, touch up.**

touch and go *adj.* risky or critical: *it was touch and go whether we would be in time; a touch-and-go situation.*

touchdown ('tʌtʃˌdaʊn) *n.* **1.** the moment at which a landing aircraft or spacecraft comes into contact with the landing surface. ~*vb.* **touch down.** **2.** (of an aircraft or spacecraft) to land.

touché (tuːˈʃeɪ) *interj.* **1.** an acknowledgment of a scoring hit in fencing. **2.** an acknowledgment of the striking home of a remark or witty reply.

touched (tʌtʃt) *adj.* **1.** moved to sympathy or emotion: *I was touched by their generosity.* **2.** showing slight insanity: *she's a bit touched.*

touching ('tʌtʃɪŋ) *adj.* **1.** arousing tender feelings. ~*prep.* **2.** on the subject of; relating to.

touch judge *n.* one of the two linesmen in rugby.

touchline ('tʌtʃˌlaɪn) *n.* either of the lines marking the side of the playing area in certain games, such as rugby.

touch off *vb.* **1.** to cause to explode, as by touching with a match. **2.** to cause (a disturbance, violence, etc.) to begin.

touchpaper ('tʌtʃˌpeɪpə) *n.* paper soaked in saltpetre for firing gunpowder.

touchstone ('tʌtʃˌstəʊn) *n.* **1.** a standard by which judgment is made. **2.** a hard dark stone that is used to test gold and silver from the streak they produce on it.

touch-type *vb.* to type without looking at the keyboard. —'**touch-,typist** *n.*

touch up *vb.* to enhance, renovate, or falsify by putting extra touches to: *touch up a photograph.*

touchwood ('tʌtʃˌwʊd) *n.* something, esp. dry wood or fungus material, used as tinder.

touchy ('tʌtʃɪ) adj. **touchier, touchiest. 1.** easily upset or irritated. **2.** requiring careful and tactful handling: a touchy subject. —'**touchiness** n.

tough (tʌf) adj. **1.** strong or resilient; durable: a tough material. **2.** not tender: a tough steak. **3.** hardy and fit. **4.** rough or pugnacious: a tough gangster. **5.** resolute or intractable: a tough employer. **6.** difficult or troublesome to do or deal with: a tough problem. **7.** Informal. unfortunate or unlucky: it's tough on him. ~n. **8.** a rough, vicious, or pugnacious person. —'**toughness** n.

toughen ('tʌfən) vb. to make or become tough or tougher.

toupee ('tuːpeɪ) n. a hairpiece worn by men to cover a bald place.

tour (tʊə) n. **1.** an extended journey visiting places of interest along the route. **2.** Mil. a period of service, esp. in one place. **3.** a trip, as by a theatre company, to perform in several places. **4.** an overseas trip made by a cricket team, rugby team, etc., to play in several places. ~vb. **5.** to make a tour of (a place).

tour de force (ˌtʊə də 'fɔːs) n., pl. **tours de force.** a masterly or brilliant stroke, creation, effect, or accomplishment.

tourism ('tʊərɪzəm) n. tourist travel, esp. when regarded as an industry.

tourist ('tʊərɪst) n. **1.** a person who travels for pleasure, usually sightseeing and staying in hotels. **2.** a person on an excursion or sightseeing tour. **3.** the lowest class of accommodation on a passenger ship. ~adj. **4.** of the lowest class of accommodation on a passenger ship.

touristy ('tʊərɪstɪ) adj. Informal, often disparaging. full of tourists or tourist attractions.

tourmaline ('tʊəməˌliːn) n. a hard crystalline mineral used in jewellery and electrical equipment.

tournament ('tʊənəmənt) n. **1.** a sporting competition in which contestants play a series of games to determine an overall winner. **2.** Medieval history. Also: **tourney.** a contest in which mounted knights fought for a prize.

tournedos ('tʊənəˌdəʊ) n., pl. **-dos** (-ˌdəʊz). a thick round steak of beef.

tourniquet ('tʊənɪˌkeɪ) n. Med. any device for constricting an artery of the arm or leg to control bleeding.

tousle ('taʊz'l) vb. to tangle, ruffle, or disarrange (hair or clothes).

tout (taʊt) vb. **1.** to solicit (business, customers, etc.) or try to sell (goods), esp. in a persistent manner. **2.** to spy on racehorses being trained in order to obtain information for betting purposes. ~n. **3.** a person who sells tickets for a heavily booked event at inflated prices.

tow¹ (təʊ) vb. **1.** to pull or drag (a vehicle), esp. by means of a rope or cable. ~n. **2.** the act or an instance of towing. **3. in tow. a.** (of a vehicle) being towed. **b.** in one's charge or under one's influence: he arrived with his children in tow. **4. on tow.** (of a vehicle) being towed.

tow² (təʊ) n. the coarse and broken fibres of hemp, flax, jute, etc., prepared for spinning. —'**towy** adj.

towards (tə'wɔːdz, tɔːdz) prep. **1.** in the direction of: towards London. **2.** with regard to: her feelings towards me. **3.** as a contribution to: money towards a new car. **4.** just before: towards noon. ~Also: **toward.**

towbar ('təʊˌbɑː) n. a rigid metal bar or frame used for towing vehicles.

towel ('taʊəl) n. **1.** a piece of absorbent cloth or paper used for drying things. **2. throw in the towel.** See **throw in** (sense 3). ~vb. **-elling, -elled** or U.S. **-eling, -eled. 3.** to dry or wipe with a towel.

towelling or U.S. **toweling** ('taʊəlɪŋ) n. an absorbent fabric used esp. for making towels.

tower ('taʊə) n. **1.** a tall, usually square or circular structure, sometimes part of a larger building and usually built for a specific purpose. **2.** a place of defence or retreat. **3. tower of strength.** a person who supports or comforts someone else at a time of difficulty. ~vb. **4.** to be or rise like a tower; loom.

towering ('taʊərɪŋ) adj. **1.** very tall; lofty. **2.** very intense: a towering rage.

towhead ('təʊˌhed) n. **1.** a person with blond or yellowish hair. **2.** a head of such hair. —ˌ**tow'headed** adj.

town (taʊn) n. **1.** a densely populated urban area, typically smaller than a city and larger than a village. **2.** a city, borough, or other urban area. **3.** the nearest town or commercial district. **4.** London or the chief city of an area. **5.** the people of a town. **6. go to town.** to make a supreme or unrestricted effort. **7. on the town.** seeking out entertainments and amusements.

town clerk n. (in Britain until 1974) the chief administrative officer of a town.

town crier n. (formerly) a person employed to make public announcements in the streets.

townee (taʊ'niː) or **townie** ('taʊnɪ) n. Informal, often disparaging. a resident in a town, esp. as distinct from country dwellers.

town gas n. coal gas manufactured for domestic and industrial use.

town hall n. a large building in a town often containing the council offices and a hall for public meetings.

town house n. **1.** a terraced house in an urban area, esp. a fashionable one. **2.** a person's town residence as distinct from his country residence.

town planning *n.* the comprehensive planning of the physical and social development of a town.

township ('taʊnʃɪp) *n.* **1.** a small town. **2.** (in the U.S. and Canada) a territorial area, esp. a subdivision of a county: often organized as a unit of local government. **3.** (in Canada) a land-survey area, usually 36 square miles (93 square kilometres). **4.** (in South Africa) a planned urban settlement of Black Africans or Coloureds. **5.** *English history.* any of the local districts of a large parish.

townsman ('taʊnzmən) *n., pl.* **-men.** an inhabitant of a town. —'**towns,woman** *fem. n.*

townspeople ('taʊnz,piːpᵊl) *or* **townsfolk** ('taʊnz,fəʊk) *pl. n.* the people of a town; citizens.

towpath ('təʊ,pɑːθ) *n.* a path beside a canal or river, used by people or animals towing boats.

towrope ('təʊ,rəʊp) *n.* a rope or cable used for towing a vehicle or vessel.

toxaemia *or U.S.* **toxemia** (tɒk'siːmɪə) *n.* **1.** a condition characterized by the presence of bacterial toxins in the blood. **2.** a condition in pregnant women characterized by high blood pressure. —**tox'aemic** *or U.S.* **tox'emic** *adj.*

toxic ('tɒksɪk) *adj.* **1.** of or caused by a toxin or poison. **2.** harmful or deadly. —**toxicity** (tɒk'sɪsɪtɪ) *n.*

toxicology (,tɒksɪ'kɒlədʒɪ) *n.* the branch of science concerned with poisons, their effects, antidotes, etc. —**toxicological** (,tɒksɪkə'lɒdʒɪkᵊl) *adj.* —,**toxi'cologist** *n.*

toxin ('tɒksɪn) *n.* **1.** any of various poisonous substances produced by microorganisms and causing certain diseases. **2.** any other poisonous substance of plant or animal origin.

toy (tɔɪ) *n.* **1.** an object designed to be played with, esp. by children. **2.** any small thing of little value; trifle. **3.** a miniature variety of a breed of dog. ~*vb.* **4.** (usually foll. by *with*) to play, fiddle, or flirt.

toy boy *n.* the much younger male lover of an older woman.

trace¹ (treɪs) *n.* **1.** a mark, footprint, or other sign that a person, animal, or thing has been in a place. **2.** a scarcely detectable amount or characteristic: *a trace of humour.* **3.** any line drawn by a recording instrument or a record consisting of a number of such lines. **4.** something drawn, such as a tracing. ~*vb.* **5.** to follow, discover, or ascertain the course or development of (something). **6.** to track down and find, as by following a trail. **7.** to copy (a design, map, etc.) by drawing over the lines visible through a superimposed sheet of transpar-

ent paper. **8.** to outline or sketch (an idea, etc.). **9.** (usually foll. by *back*) to date back: *his ancestors trace back to the 16th century.* —'**traceable** *adj.*

trace² (treɪs) *n.* **1.** either of the two side straps that connect a horse's harness to the vehicle being pulled. **2. kick over the traces.** to escape or defy control.

trace element *n.* a chemical element that occurs in very small amounts in soil, water, etc., and is essential for healthy growth.

tracer ('treɪsə) *n.* **1.** a projectile that can be observed when in flight by the burning of chemical substances in its base. **2.** *Med.* an element or other substance introduced into the body to study metabolic processes.

tracer bullet *n.* a round of small arms ammunition containing a tracer.

tracery ('treɪsərɪ) *n., pl.* **-eries. 1.** a pattern of interlacing lines, esp. as used in a stained glass window. **2.** any fine lacy pattern resembling this.

trachea (trə'kiːə) *n., pl.* **-cheae** (-'kiːiː). *Anat., zool.* the tube that carries inhaled air from the throat to the lungs; windpipe.

tracheotomy (,trækɪ'ɒtəmɪ) *n., pl.* **-mies.** surgical incision into the trachea, as performed when the air passage has been blocked.

trachoma (trə'kəʊmə) *n.* a chronic contagious disease of the eye characterized by inflammation of the inner surface of the lids and the formation of scar tissue.

tracing ('treɪsɪŋ) *n.* **1.** a copy of something, such as a map, made by tracing. **2.** a line traced by a recording instrument.

track (træk) *n.* **1.** the mark or trail left by something that has passed by. **2.** any road or path, esp. a rough one. **3.** a rail or pair of parallel rails on which a vehicle, such as a train, runs. **4.** a course of action, thought, etc.: *don't start on that track again!* **5.** an endless band on the wheels of a tank to enable it to move across rough ground. **6.** a course for running or racing. **7.** any of a number of separate sections on either side of a gramophone record. **8. keep** (*or* **lose**) **track of.** to follow (*or* fail to follow) the course or progress of someone or something. **9. off the track.** away from what is correct or true. ~*vb.* **10.** to follow the trail of (a person or animal). **11.** to follow the flight path of (a satellite, etc.) by picking up signals transmitted or reflected by it. **12.** *Film.* to follow (a moving object) while filming. —'**tracker** *n.*

track down *vb.* to find (someone or something) by tracking or pursuing.

tracker dog *n.* a dog specially trained to search for missing people.

track event *n.* a competition in athletics, such as sprinting, that takes place on a running track.

track record *n. Informal.* the past record

of the accomplishments and failures of a person or organization.

tracks (træks) pl. n. **1.** (sometimes sing.) a mark, such as a footprint, left by someone or something that has passed. **2. in one's tracks.** on the very spot where one is standing: the screams stopped him dead in his tracks. **3. make tracks.** to leave or depart: it's late, I'd better make tracks.

track shoe n. a light running shoe fitted with steel spikes for better grip.

tracksuit ('træk,suːt) n. a warm suit worn by athletes, etc., esp. during training.

tract[1] (trækt) n. **1.** an extended area, as of land. **2.** Anat. a system of organs or glands that has a particular function: the digestive tract.

tract[2] (trækt) n. a pamphlet, esp. a religious one.

tractable ('træktəb'l) adj. easily controlled, managed, or dealt with: a tractable child; tractable materials. —,tracta'bility n.

traction ('trækʃən) n. **1.** the act of pulling, esp. by engine power. **2.** Med. the application of a steady pull on a limb using a system of weights and pulleys or splints. **3.** adhesive friction, as between a wheel of a motor vehicle and the road.

traction engine n. a steam-powered locomotive used, esp. formerly, for drawing heavy loads along roads or over rough ground.

tractor ('træktə) n. a motor vehicle with large rear wheels, used to pull heavy loads, esp. farm machinery.

trade (treɪd) n. **1.** the buying and selling of goods and services. **2.** a personal occupation, esp. a craft requiring skill. **3.** the people and practices of an industry, craft, or business. **4.** exchange of one thing for something else. **5.** the regular customers of a firm: open for the breakfast trade. **6.** amount of custom or commercial dealings; business: brisk trade. **7.** a specified market or business: the tailoring trade. ~vb. **8.** to buy and sell (merchandise). **9.** to exchange (one thing) for another. **10.** to engage in trade. **11.** to deal or do business (with). —'tradable or 'tradeable adj.

trade-in n. **1.** a used article given in part payment for the purchase of a new article. ~vb. **trade in. 2.** to give (a used article) as part payment for a new article.

trademark ('treɪd,mɑːk) n. **1. a.** the name or other symbol used by a manufacturer to distinguish his products from those of competitors. **b. Registered Trademark.** one that is officially registered and legally protected. **2.** any distinctive sign or mark of a person or thing.

trade name n. **1.** the name used by a trade to refer to a product or range of products. **2.** the name under which a commercial enterprise operates in business.

trade-off n. an exchange, esp. as a compromise.

trade on vb. to exploit or take advantage of: he traded on her endless patience.

trader ('treɪdə) n. **1.** a person engaged in trade. **2.** a ship regularly employed in trade.

tradescantia (,trædɛs'kænʃɪə) n. a widely cultivated plant with striped variegated leaves.

trade secret n. a secret formula, technique, or process known and used to advantage by only one manufacturer.

tradesman ('treɪdzmən) n., pl. -men. a man engaged in trade, esp. a shopkeeper. —'trades,woman fem. n.

Trades Union Congress n. the major association of British trade unions, which includes all the larger unions.

trade union or **trades union** n. an association of employees formed to improve their incomes and working conditions by collective bargaining. —**trade unionist** or **trades unionist** n.

trade wind (wɪnd) n. a wind blowing steadily towards the equator either from the northeast in the N hemisphere or the southeast in the S hemisphere.

trading estate n. Chiefly Brit. a large area in which a number of commercial or industrial firms are situated.

tradition (trə'dɪʃən) n. **1.** the handing down from generation to generation of customs, beliefs, etc. **2.** the body of customs, thought, etc., belonging to a particular country, people, family, or institution over a long period.

traditional (trə'dɪʃən'l) adj. of, relating to, or being a tradition. —**tra'ditionally** adv.

traduce (trə'djuːs) vb. to speak badly of (someone). —**tra'ducement** n. —**tra'ducer** n.

traffic ('træfɪk) n. **1.** the vehicles coming and going on roads. **2.** the movement of vehicles or people in a particular place or for a particular purpose: sea traffic. **3.** (usually foll. by with) dealings or business. **4.** trade, esp. of an illicit kind: drug traffic. ~vb. **-ficking, -ficked. 5.** (often foll. by in) to carry on trade or business, esp. of an illicit kind. **6.** (usually foll. by with) to have dealings. —'**trafficker** n.

traffic island n. a raised area in the middle of a road designed as a guide for traffic flow and to provide a stopping place for pedestrians crossing.

traffic light n. one of a set of coloured lights placed at a junction to control the flow of traffic.

traffic warden n. Brit. a person employed to supervise road traffic and report traffic offences.

tragedian (trə'dʒiːdɪən) or (fem.) **tragedienne** (trə,dʒiːdɪ'ɛn) n. **1.** an actor who specializes in tragic roles. **2.** a writer of tragedy.

tragedy ('trædʒɪdɪ) *n., pl.* **-dies. 1.** a shocking or sad event; disaster. **2.** a serious play, film, or opera in which the main character falls to disaster through the combination of a personal failing and adverse circumstances.

tragic ('trædʒɪk) *adj.* **1.** of, relating to, or characteristic of tragedy. **2.** mournful or pitiable: *a tragic face.* —**'tragically** *adv.*

tragicomedy (ˌtrædʒɪ'kɒmɪdɪ) *n., pl.* **-dies.** play or other written work having both comic and tragic aspects. —ˌtragi'comic *adj.*

trail (treɪl) *vb.* **1.** to drag, stream, or permit (something) to drag or stream along a surface, esp. the ground. **2.** to follow or hunt (an animal or person) by following marks or tracks. **3.** to lag behind (a person or thing). **4.** (esp. of plants) to extend or droop over or along a surface. **5.** to be falling behind in a race. **6.** to move wearily or slowly: *we trailed through the city.* ~*n.* **7.** a print, mark, or scent made by a person, animal, or object. **8.** a path, track, or road. **9.** something that trails behind. **10.** a sequence of results from an event: *a trail of disasters.*

trail away *or* **off** *vb.* to become fainter, quieter, or weaker: *his voice trailed away.*

trailblazer ('treɪlˌbleɪzə) *n.* **1.** a pioneer in a particular field. **2.** a person who blazes a trail. —'trail,blazing *adj., n.*

trailer ('treɪlə) *n.* **1.** a road vehicle, usually two-wheeled, towed by a motor vehicle: used for transporting boats, etc. **2.** the rear section of an articulated lorry. **3.** a series of short extracts from a film, used to advertise it in a cinema or on television. **4.** *U.S. & Canad.* same as **caravan** (sense 1).

train (treɪn) *vb.* **1.** to teach someone (to do something), as by subjecting to various exercises or experiences. **2.** to discipline (an animal) to perform tricks or obey commands. **3.** to control or guide towards a specific goal: *to train a plant up a wall.* **4.** to do exercises and prepare for a specific purpose: *the athlete trained for the Olympics.* **5.** to focus or bring to bear (on something): *to train a telescope on the moon.* ~*n.* **6.** a line of coaches or trucks coupled together and drawn by a railway engine. **7.** a sequence or series: *a train of thought.* **8.** the long back section of a dress that trails along the floor. **9.** a group of followers or attendants; retinue.

trainbearer ('treɪnˌbeərə) *n.* an attendant who holds up the train of a dignitary's robe or bride's gown.

trainee (treɪ'niː) *n.* a person undergoing training.

trainer ('treɪnə) *n.* **1.** a person who coaches athletes. **2.** a person who trains racehorses. **3.** a piece of equipment employed in training, such as a simulated aircraft cockpit. **4.** a running shoe.

training ('treɪnɪŋ) *n.* the process of bringing a person to an agreed standard of proficiency by practice and instruction.

train spotter *n.* a person who collects the numbers of railway locomotives.

traipse (treɪps) *Informal.* ~*vb.* **1.** to walk heavily or tiredly. ~*n.* **2.** a long or tiring walk.

trait (treɪt, treɪ) *n.* a characteristic feature or quality distinguishing a particular person or thing.

traitor ('treɪtə) *n.* a person who is guilty of treason or treachery, in betraying friends, country, a cause, etc. —'traitorous *adj.* —'traitress *fem. n.*

trajectory (trə'dʒɛktərɪ) *n., pl.* **-ries.** the path described by an object moving in air or space, esp. the curved path of a projectile.

tram (træm) *n.* **1.** an electrically driven public transport vehicle that runs on rails laid into the road. **2.** a small vehicle on rails for carrying loads in a mine.

tramline ('træmˌlaɪn) *n.* **1.** (*often pl.*) the tracks on which a tram runs. **2.** (*often pl.*) the outer markings along the sides of a tennis or badminton court.

trammel ('træməl) *n.* **1.** (*often pl.*) something that impedes free action or movement. **2.** a fishing net in three sections, the two outer nets having a large mesh and the middle one a fine mesh. ~*vb.* **-elling, -elled** *or U.S.* **-eling, -eled. 3.** to hinder or restrain. **4.** to catch or ensnare.

tramp (træmp) *vb.* **1.** to walk long and far; hike. **2.** to walk heavily or firmly across or through (a place). **3.** to wander about as a tramp. **4.** to make (a journey) on foot, esp. laboriously or wearily. **5.** to tread or trample. ~*n.* **6.** a person who travels about on foot, living by begging or doing casual work. **7.** a long hard walk; hike. **8.** the sound of heavy treading. **9.** a merchant ship that does not run on a regular schedule. **10.** *Slang, chiefly U.S. & Canad.* a promiscuous woman.

tramping ('træmpɪŋ) *n. N.Z.* the leisure activity of walking in the bush. —'tramper *n.*

trample ('træmp^əl) *vb.* (sometimes foll. by *on, upon,* or *over*) **1.** to stamp or walk roughly (on). **2.** to treat (someone) inconsiderately so as to hurt: *to trample on someone's feelings.* ~*n.* **3.** the action or sound of trampling.

trampoline ('træmpəlɪn, -ˌliːn) *n.* **1.** a tough canvas sheet suspended by springs or cords from a frame, used by acrobats, gymnasts, etc. ~*vb.* **2.** to exercise on a trampoline.

trance (trɑːns) *n.* **1.** a hypnotic state resembling sleep in which a person is unable to move or act of his own will. **2.** a dazed or stunned state. **3.** a state of ecstasy or mystic absorption so intense as to cause a temporary loss of consciousness at the earthly level.

trannie *or* **tranny** ('trænɪ) *n., pl.* **-nies.** *Informal, chiefly Brit.* a transistor radio.

tranquil ('træŋkwɪl) *adj.* calm, peaceful, or quiet. —'**tranquilly** *adv.*

tranquillity *or U.S. (sometimes)* **tranquillity** (træŋ'kwɪlɪtɪ) *n.* a state of calmness or peacefulness.

tranquillize, -ise, *or U.S.* **tranquilize** ('træŋkwɪˌlaɪz) *vb.* to make or become calm or calmer. —ˌtranquilli'zation, -i'sation, *or U.S.* ˌtranquili'zation *n.*

tranquillizer, -iser *or U.S.* **tranquilizer** ('træŋkwɪˌlaɪzə) *n.* a drug that calms someone suffering from anxiety, tension, etc.

trans. **1.** transaction. **2.** transitive. **3.** translated. **4.** transport(ation).

trans- *prefix.* **1.** across, beyond, crossing, on the other side: *transatlantic.* **2.** changing thoroughly: *transliterate.*

transact (træn'zækt) *vb.* to do, conduct, or negotiate (a business deal).

transaction (træn'zækʃən) *n.* **1.** something that is transacted, esp. a business deal. **2.** (*pl.*) the records of the proceedings of a society, etc.

transalpine (trænz'ælpaɪn) *adj.* situated in or relating to places beyond the Alps, esp. from Italy.

transatlantic (ˌtrænzət'læntɪk) *adj.* **1.** on or from the other side of the Atlantic. **2.** crossing the Atlantic.

transceiver (træn'siːvə) *n.* a combined radio transmitter and receiver.

transcend (træn'sɛnd) *vb.* **1.** to go above or beyond (a limit, expectation, etc.), as in degree or excellence. **2.** to be superior to.

transcendent (træn'sɛndənt) *adj.* **1.** exceeding or surpassing in degree or excellence. **2.** *Theol.* (of God) having existence outside the created world. —**tran'scendence** *or* **tran'scendency** *n.*

transcendental (ˌtrænsɛn'dɛnt'l) *adj.* **1.** superior or surpassing. **2.** *Philosophy.* based on intuition or innate belief rather than experience. **3.** supernatural or mystical. —ˌtranscen'dentally *adv.*

transcendentalism (ˌtrænsɛn'dɛntəˌlɪzəm) *n.* any system of philosophy that seeks to discover the nature of reality by examining the processes of thought rather than the things thought about, or that emphasizes intuition as a means to knowledge. —ˌtranscen'dentalist *n., adj.*

transcendental meditation *n.* a technique, based on Hindu traditions, for relaxing and refreshing the mind and body through the silent repetition of a special formula of words.

transcribe (træn'skraɪb) *vb.* **1.** to write, type, or print out (a text) fully from a speech or notes. **2.** to make an electrical

recording of (a programme or speech) for a later broadcast. **3.** *Music.* to rewrite (a piece of music) for an instrument other than that originally intended; arrange. —**tran'scriber** *n.*

transcript ('trænskrɪpt) *n.* **1.** a written, typed, or printed copy made by transcribing. **2.** *Chiefly U.S. & Canad.* an official record of a student's school progress.

transcription (træn'skrɪpʃən) *n.* **1.** the act of transcribing. **2.** something transcribed.

transducer (trænz'djuːsə) *n.* any device, such as a microphone or electric motor, that converts one form of energy into another.

transept ('trænsɛpt) *n.* either of the two wings of a cross-shaped church at right angles to the nave.

transfer *vb.* (træns'fɜː), **-ferring, -ferred.** **1.** to change or move from one thing, person, point, etc., to another: *they transferred from the Park Hotel to the Imperial; she transferred her affections to her dog.* **2.** *Law.* to make over (property) to another; convey. **3.** to move (a drawing or design) from one surface to another. ~*n.* ('trænsfɜː). **4.** the act, process, or system of transferring, or the state of being transferred. **5.** a person or thing that transfers or is transferred. **6.** a design or drawing that is transferred from one surface to another. **7.** *Law.* the passing of title to property or other right from one person to another; conveyance. **8.** any document effecting a transfer. —**trans'ferable** *or* **trans'ferrable** *adj.*

transfiguration (ˌtrænsfɪgjʊ'reɪʃən) *n.* a transfiguring or being transfigured.

Transfiguration (ˌtrænsfɪgjʊ'reɪʃən) *n.* **1.** *New Testament.* the change in the appearance of Christ on the mountain. **2.** the Church festival held in commemoration of this on Aug. 6.

transfigure (træns'fɪgə) *vb.* **1.** to change or cause to change in appearance. **2.** to become or cause to become more exalted.

transfix (træns'fɪks) *vb.* **-fixing, -fixed** *or* **-fixt.** **1.** to make (someone) motionless, esp. with horror or shock. **2.** to pierce through (a person or animal) with a sharp weapon or other device.

transform (træns'fɔːm) *vb.* **1.** to alter or be altered in form, function, etc. **2.** to convert (one form of energy) to another. **3.** *Maths.* to change the form of (an equation, expression, etc.) without changing its value. **4.** to change (an alternating current or voltage) using a transformer. —ˌtrans-for'mation *n.*

transformer (træns'fɔːmə) *n.* a device that transfers an alternating current from one circuit to one or more other circuits, usually with a change of voltage.

transfuse (træns'fjuːz) *vb.* **1.** to permeate or infuse. **2.** to inject (blood or other fluid) into a blood vessel.

transfusion (træns'fjuːʒən) n. 1. a transfusing. 2. the injection of blood, blood plasma, etc., into the blood vessels of a patient.

transgress (trænz'grɛs) vb. 1. to break (a law, etc.). 2. to overstep (a limit). —**trans'gression** n. —**trans'gressor** n.

transient ('trænzɪənt) adj. 1. for a short time only; temporary. ~n. 2. a transient person or thing. —'**transience** n.

transistor (træn'zɪstə) n. 1. a semiconductor device used to amplify electric currents. 2. Informal. a small portable radio containing transistors.

transistorize or **-ise** (træn'zɪstə,raɪz) vb. to equip (a device) with transistors.

transit ('trænsɪt, 'trænz-) n. 1. the passage or conveyance of goods or people. 2. a route. 3. Astron. the apparent passage of a celestial body across the meridian. 4. **in transit.** while travelling or being taken from one place to another: the parcel has been lost in transit.

transit camp n. a camp in which refugees, soldiers, etc., live temporarily.

transition (træn'zɪʃən) n. 1. change or passage from one state or stage to another. 2. the period of time during which something changes. 3. Music. a movement from one key to another. 4. a gradual change in the style of architecture, in Britain, from Norman to Early English. —**tran'sitional** adj.

transitive ('trænsɪtɪv) adj. Grammar. denoting a verb that requires a direct object.

transitory ('trænsɪtrɪ) adj. lasting only for a short time.

translate (træns'leɪt, trænz-) vb. 1. to express or be capable of being expressed in another language. 2. to act as translator. 3. to express or explain (something) in simple or less technical language. 4. to interpret the significance of (a gesture, action, etc.). 5. to transform or convert: to translate hope into reality. 6. to transfer from one place or position to another. —**trans'latable** adj. —**trans'lator** n.

translation (træns'leɪʃən, trænz-) n. 1. a piece of writing or speech that is or has been translated into another language. 2. a translating or being translated. 3. Maths. a transformation in which the origin of a coordinate system is moved to another position so that each axis retains the same direction. —**trans'lational** adj.

transliterate (trænz'lɪtə,reɪt) vb. to write or spell (a word, etc.) into corresponding letters of another alphabet. —,**transliter'ation** n. —**trans'liter,ator** n.

translucent (trænz'luːsᵊnt) adj. allowing light to pass through; semitransparent. —**trans'lucence** or **trans'lucency** n.

transmigrate (,trænzmaɪ'greɪt) vb. (of souls) to pass from one body into another at death. —,**transmi'gration** n.

transmission (trænz'mɪʃən) n. 1. the act of transmitting. 2. something that is transmitted, esp. a radio or television broadcast. 3. a system of shafts and gears that transmits power from the engine to the driving wheels of a motor vehicle.

transmit (trænz'mɪt) vb. -mitting, -mitted. 1. to pass (something, such as a message or disease) from one place or person to another. 2. to allow the passage of (particles, energy, etc.): radio waves are transmitted through the atmosphere. 3. **a.** to send out (signals) by means of radio waves. **b.** to broadcast (a radio or television programme). 4. to transfer (a force, motion, etc.) from one part of a mechanical system to another. —**trans'mittable** adj.

transmitter (trænz'mɪtə) n. 1. a person or thing that transmits. 2. a piece of equipment used for broadcasting radio or television programmes.

transmogrify (trænz'mɒgrɪ,faɪ) vb. -fying, -fied. Jocular. to change or transform (someone or something) into a different shape or appearance, esp. a grotesque or bizarre one. —**trans,mogrifi'cation** n.

transmute (trænz'mjuːt) vb. to change the form, character, or substance of. —,**transmu'tation** n.

transom ('trænsəm) n. 1. a horizontal bar across a window. 2. a horizontal bar that separates a door from a window over it.

transparency (træns'pærənsɪ) n., pl. -cies. 1. the state of being transparent. 2. a positive photograph on a transparent base, usually mounted in a frame or between glass plates. It can be viewed by means of a slide projector.

transparent (træns'pærənt) adj. 1. permitting the uninterrupted passage of light; clear. 2. easy to see through, understand, or recognize; obvious: a transparent lie. 3. candid, open, or frank. —**trans'parently** adv.

transpire (træn'spaɪə) vb. 1. to come to light; be known. 2. Not universally accepted. to happen or occur. 3. Physiol. to give off (water or vapour) through the pores of the skin, etc. —**transpiration** (,trænspə'reɪʃən) n.

transplant vb. (træns'plɑːnt). 1. Surgery. to transfer (an organ or tissue) from one part of the body or from one person to another. 2. to remove or transfer (esp. a plant) from one place to another. ~n. ('træns,plɑːnt). 3. Surgery. **a.** the procedure involved in transferring an organ or tissue. **b.** the organ or tissue transplanted. —,**transplan'tation** n.

transponder (træn'spɒndə) n. a type of radio or radar transmitter-receiver that transmits signals automatically when it receives predetermined signals.

transport vb. (træns'pɔːt). 1. to carry or move (people or goods) from one place to another, esp. over some distance. **2.** to exile (a criminal) to a penal colony. **3.** to have a strong emotional effect on: *transported with joy.* ~*n.* (ˈtrænsˌpɔːt). **4.** the business or system of transporting goods or people. **5.** *Brit.* freight vehicles generally. **6.** a vehicle used to transport goods or people, esp. troops. **7.** a transporting or being transported. **8.** ecstasy, rapture, or any powerful emotion. —**transˈportable** *adj.* —**transˈporter** *n.*

transportation (ˌtrænspɔːˈteɪʃən) *n.* **1.** a means or system of transporting. **2.** the act of transporting or the state of being transported. **3.** (esp. formerly) deportation to a penal colony.

transport café (ˈtrænsˌpɔːt) *n. Brit.* an inexpensive eating place on a main route, used mainly by long-distance lorry drivers.

transpose (trænsˈpəʊz) *vb.* **1.** to alter the positions of; interchange, as words in a sentence. **2.** *Music.* to play (notes, music, etc.) in a different key. **3.** *Maths.* to move (a term) from one side of an equation to the other with a corresponding reversal in sign. —**transposition** (ˌtrænspəˈzɪʃən) *n.*

transsexual (trænzˈsɛksjʊəl) *n.* **1.** a person who is completely identified with the opposite sex. **2.** a person who has had medical treatment to alter sexual characteristics to those of the opposite sex.

transship (trænsˈʃɪp) *vb.* **-shipping, -shipped.** to transfer or be transferred from one ship or vehicle to another. —**transˈshipment** *n.*

transubstantiation (ˌtrænsəbˌstænʃɪˈeɪʃən) *n.* (esp. in Roman Catholic theology) the doctrine that the whole substance of the bread and wine changes into the substance of the body and blood of Christ when consecrated in the Eucharist.

transuranic (ˌtrænzjʊˈrænɪk) *adj.* (of an element) having an atomic number greater than that of uranium.

transverse (trænzˈvɜːs) *adj.* crossing from side to side; crossways.

transvestite (trænzˈvɛstaɪt) *n.* a person, esp. a man, who seeks sexual pleasure from wearing clothes of the opposite sex. —**transˈvestism** *n.*

trap¹ (træp) *n.* **1.** a device or hole in which something, esp. an animal, is caught. **2.** a plan for tricking a person into being caught unawares. **3.** a bend in a pipe that contains standing water to prevent the passage of gases. **4.** a device that hurls clay pigeons into the air to be fired at. **5.** a boxlike stall in which greyhounds are enclosed before the start of a race. **6.** See **trap door. 7.** a light two-wheeled carriage. **8.** *Slang.* the mouth. ~*vb.* **trapping, trapped. 9.** to catch (an animal) in a trap. **10.** to trick (someone). **11.** to set traps in (a place), esp. for animals.

trap² (træp) *vb.* **trapping, trapped.** (foll. by *out*) to dress or adorn.

trap³ (træp) *n.* any fine-grained dark igneous rock, esp. basalt, used in road making.

trap door *n.* a hinged door in a ceiling, floor, or stage.

trapeze (trəˈpiːz) *n.* a free-swinging bar attached to two ropes, used by circus acrobats.

trapezium (trəˈpiːzɪəm) *n., pl.* **-ziums** *or* **-zia** (-zɪə). **1.** *Chiefly Brit.* a quadrilateral having two parallel sides of unequal length. **2.** *Chiefly U.S. & Canad.* a quadrilateral having neither pair of sides parallel. —**traˈpezial** *adj.*

trapezoid (ˈtræpɪˌzɔɪd) *n.* **1.** a quadrilateral having neither pair of sides parallel. **2.** *U.S. & Canad.* same as **trapezium** (sense 1).

trapper (ˈtræpə) *n.* a person who traps animals, esp. for their furs or skins.

trappings (ˈtræpɪŋz) *pl. n.* **1.** the accessories that symbolize a condition, office, etc.: *the trappings of success.* **2.** ceremonial harness for a horse or other animal.

Trappist (ˈtræpɪst) *n.* a member of a branch of the Cistercian order of Christian monks, noted for their rule of silence.

trash (træʃ) *n.* **1.** foolish ideas or talk; nonsense. **2.** *Chiefly U.S. & Canad.* unwanted objects; rubbish. **3.** *Chiefly U.S. & Canad.* a worthless person or group of people. —**ˈtrashy** *adj.*

trattoria (ˌtrætəˈrɪə) *n.* an Italian restaurant.

trauma (ˈtrɔːmə) *n.* **1.** *Psychol.* an emotional shock that may have long-lasting effects. **2.** *Pathol.* any bodily injury or wound. —**traumatic** (trɔːˈmætɪk) *adj.* —**trauˈmatically** *adv.* —**ˈtrauma,tize** *or* **-ise** *vb.*

travail (ˈtræveɪl) *Literary.* ~*n.* **1.** painful or excessive work. **2.** the pangs of childbirth; labour. ~*vb.* **3.** to suffer or labour painfully, esp. in childbirth.

travel (ˈtrævˀl) *vb.* **-elling, -elled** *or U.S.* **-eling, -eled. 1.** to go, move, or journey from one place to another. **2.** to go, move, or journey through or across (an area, region, etc.). **3.** to go, move, or cover a distance. **4.** to go from place to place as a salesman. **5.** (esp. of perishable goods) to withstand a journey. **6.** (of a machine or part) to move in a fixed path. **7.** *Informal.* to move rapidly: *that car certainly travels.* ~*n.* **8.** the act of travelling. **9.** (*usually pl.*) a tour or journey: *Mary told us all about her travels.* **10.** the distance moved by a mechanical part, such as the stroke of a piston.

travel agency *n.* an agency that arranges flights, hotel accommodation, etc., for travellers. —**travel agent** *n.*

traveller (ˈtrævələ, ˈtrævlə) *n.* **1.** a person who travels, esp. habitually. **2.** a travelling salesman.

traveller's cheque *n.* a cheque sold by a bank, travel agency, etc., to the bearer, who signs it on purchase and can cash it abroad by signing it again.

travelling salesman *n.* a salesman who travels within an assigned territory in order to sell goods or get orders for the commercial enterprise he represents.

travelogue ('trævˌlɒg) *n.* a film, lecture, or brochure on travels and travelling.

traverse ('trævɜːs, trə'vɜːs) *vb.* **1.** to pass or go over or back and forth over (something); cross. **2.** to move sideways or crosswise. **3.** to extend or reach across. **4.** to look over or examine carefully. ∼*n.* **5.** something being or lying across, such as a crossbar. **6.** the act or an instance of traversing or crossing. **7.** a path or road across. ∼*adj.* **8.** being or lying across; transverse. —**tra'versal** *n.*

travesty ('trævɪstɪ) *n., pl.* **-ties. 1.** a grotesque imitation; mockery. ∼*vb.* **-tying, -tied. 2.** to make or be a travesty of.

travois (trə'vɔɪ) *n., pl.* **-vois** (-'vɔɪz). *Canad.* a sled used for dragging logs.

trawl (trɔːl) *n.* **1.** a large net, usually in the shape of a sock or bag, drawn at deep levels behind special boats (trawlers). ∼*vb.* **2.** to catch (fish) with a trawl net.

trawler ('trɔːlə) *n.* a ship used for trawling.

tray (treɪ) *n.* **1.** a thin flat piece of wood, plastic, or metal, usually with a raised edge on which things, such as food or drink, can be carried. **2.** a shallow receptacle for papers, sometimes forming a drawer in a cabinet or box.

treacherous ('trɛtʃərəs) *adj.* **1.** betraying or likely to betray faith or confidence. **2.** unstable, unreliable, or dangerous: *treacherous conditions.*

treachery ('trɛtʃərɪ) *n., pl.* **-eries.** the act or an instance of wilful betrayal.

treacle ('triːkᵊl) *n. Brit.* a thick dark syrup obtained during the refining of sugar. —**'treacly** *adj.*

tread (trɛd) *vb.* **treading, trod, trodden** or **trod. 1.** to walk or trample in, on, over, or across (something). **2.** (sometimes foll. by *on*) to crush or squash by or as if by treading: *to tread grapes; to tread on a spider.* **3.** to do by walking or dancing: *to tread a measure.* **4.** (of a male bird) to copulate with (a female bird). **5. tread lightly.** to proceed in a delicate or tactful manner. **6. tread water.** to stay afloat in an upright position by moving the legs in a walking motion. ∼*n.* **7.** a style of walking or dancing: *a light tread.* **8.** the act of treading. **9.** the top surface of a step in a staircase. **10.** the outer part of a tyre or wheel that touches the road. **11.** the part of a rail that wheels touch. **12.** the part of a shoe that is generally in contact with the ground.

treadle ('trɛdᵊl) *n.* a lever operated by the foot to drive a sewing machine, spinning wheel, etc.

treadmill ('trɛdˌmɪl) *n.* **1.** (formerly) an apparatus turned by the weight of men or animals climbing steps on a revolving cylinder or wheel. **2.** a dreary routine. **3.** an exercise machine that consists of a continuous moving belt on which to walk or jog.

treason ('triːzᵊn) *n.* **1.** betrayal of one's sovereign or country, esp. by attempting to overthrow the government. **2.** any treachery or betrayal. —**'treasonable** *adj.*

treasure ('trɛʒə) *n.* **1.** wealth and riches, usually hoarded, esp. in the form of money, precious metals, or gems. **2.** a thing or person that is highly prized or valued: *my cleaning lady's a little treasure.* ∼*vb.* **3.** to cherish (someone or something). **4.** to store up and save (money, etc.); hoard.

treasure hunt *n.* a game in which players act upon successive clues to find a hidden prize.

treasurer ('trɛʒərə) *n.* a person appointed to look after the funds of a society or other organization.

treasure-trove *n. Law.* any articles, such as coins or valuable objects found hidden and of unknown ownership.

treasury ('trɛʒərɪ) *n., pl.* **-uries. 1.** a storage place for treasure. **2.** the revenues or funds of a government or organization.

Treasury ('trɛʒərɪ) *n.* (in various countries) the government department in charge of finance.

Treasury Bench *n.* (in Britain) the row of seats to the right of the Speaker in the House of Commons, traditionally reserved for members of the Government.

treat (triːt) *n.* **1.** a celebration, entertainment, gift, or meal given for or to someone and paid for by someone else. **2.** any delightful surprise or specially pleasant occasion. ∼*vb.* **3.** to deal with or regard in a certain manner: *she treats school as a joke.* **4.** to apply treatment to (an illness, injury, or disease). **5.** to subject to a process or to the application of a substance: *to treat photographic film with developer.* **6.** (often foll. by *to*) to provide (someone) with as a treat. **7.** (usually foll. by *of*) to deal with, as in writing or speaking. —**'treatable** *adj.*

treatise ('triːtɪz) *n.* a formal piece of writing that deals systematically with a particular subject.

treatment ('triːtmənt) *n.* **1.** the medical or surgical care given to a patient. **2.** the manner or practice of handling a person or thing, as in a literary or artistic work.

treaty ('triːtɪ) *n., pl.* **-ties. 1.** a formal written agreement between two or more states, such as an alliance or trade arrangement. **2.** an agreement between two parties concerning the purchase of property.

treble ('trɛb'l) adj. 1. threefold; triple. 2. of or denoting a soprano voice or part or a high-pitched instrument. ~n. 3. treble the amount, size, etc. 4. a soprano voice or part or a high-pitched instrument. ~vb. 5. to make or become three times as much: *the population has nearly trebled in thirty years.* —'**trebly** adv., adj.

treble chance n. a method of betting in football pools in which the chances of winning are related to the number of draws and the number of home and away wins forecast by the competitor.

treble clef n. *Music.* the clef that establishes G a fifth above middle C as being on the second line of the staff.

tree (triː) n. 1. any large woody perennial plant with a distinct trunk and usually having leaves and branches. 2. See **family tree, shoetree, saddletree.** 3. **at the top of the tree.** in the highest position of a profession. 4. **up a tree.** *U.S. & Canad. informal.* in a difficult situation. ~vb. **treeing, treed.** 5. to chase (an animal or person) up a tree. —'**treeless** adj.

tree creeper n. a small songbird of the N hemisphere that creeps up trees to feed on insects.

tree fern n. any of numerous large tropical ferns with a trunklike stem.

tree line n. same as **timber line.**

tree surgery n. the treatment of damaged trees by filling cavities, applying braces, etc. —**tree surgeon** n.

trefoil ('trɛfɔɪl) n. 1. a plant, such as clover, with leaves divided into three smaller leaves. 2. *Archit.* a carved ornament like this. —'**trefoiled** adj.

trek (trɛk) n. 1. a long and often difficult journey. 2. *S. African.* a journey or stage of a journey, esp. a migration by ox wagon. ~vb. **trekking, trekked.** 3. to make a trek.

trellis ('trɛlɪs) n. a frame made of vertical and horizontal strips of wood, esp. one used to support climbing plants. —'**trellis-,work** n.

tremble ('trɛmb'l) vb. 1. to shake with short slight movements: *she was trembling with fear.* 2. to experience fear or anxiety: *we trembled for him.* ~n. 3. the act or an instance of trembling. —'**trembling** adj.

tremendous (trɪ'mɛndəs) adj. 1. vast; huge: *tremendous pillars.* 2. *Informal.* very exciting or unusual: *a tremendous play.* 3. *Informal.* great: *a tremendous help.* —tre'**mendously** adv.

tremolo ('trɛmə,ləʊ) n., pl. **-los.** *Music.* 1. (in playing the violin or other stringed instrument) the rapid repetition of a note or notes to produce a trembling effect. 2. (in singing) a fluctuation in pitch.

tremor ('trɛmə) n. 1. an involuntary shudder or vibration: *she spoke with a tremor in her voice.* 2. a trembling movement: *an earth tremor.*

tremulous ('trɛmjʊləs) adj. trembling, as from fear, anxiety, or excitement. —'**tremulously** adv.

trench (trɛntʃ) n. 1. a long narrow ditch in the ground, esp. one used by soldiers as a defensive position. ~vb. 2. to make a trench in (a place). 3. to fortify with a trench.

trenchant ('trɛntʃənt) adj. 1. keen or incisive: *trenchant criticism.* 2. vigorous and effective: *a trenchant foreign policy.* —'**trenchancy** n.

trench coat n. a belted raincoat similar in style to a military officer's coat.

trencher ('trɛntʃə) n. (esp. formerly) a wooden board on which food was served or cut.

trencherman ('trɛntʃəmən) n., pl. **-men.** a person who enjoys food; hearty eater.

trench warfare n. a type of warfare in which opposing armies face each other in entrenched positions.

trend (trɛnd) n. 1. general tendency or direction. 2. fashion; mode. ~vb. 3. to take a certain trend.

trendsetter ('trɛnd,sɛtə) n. a person or thing that creates, or may create, a new fashion. —'**trend,setting** adj.

trendy ('trɛndɪ) *Brit. informal.* ~adj. **trendier, trendiest.** 1. consciously fashionable. ~n., pl. **trendies.** 2. a trendy person. —'**trendily** adv.

trepidation (,trɛpɪ'deɪʃən) n. a state of fear or anxiety.

trespass ('trɛspəs) vb. 1. (often foll. by *on* or *upon*) to go or intrude (on the property, privacy, or preserves of another) with no right or permission. 2. *Law.* to commit a trespass. ~n. 3. an intrusion on another's privacy, property, or rights. —'**trespasser** n.

tress (trɛs) n. (*often pl.*) a lock of hair, esp. a long lock of woman's hair.

trestle ('trɛs'l) n. a framework of a horizontal beam supported at each end by a pair of spreading legs, used to form a table top, etc.

trews (truːz) pl. n. *Chiefly Brit.* close-fitting trousers of tartan cloth.

tri- prefix. 1. three or thrice: *trisect.* 2. occurring every three: *trimonthly.*

triad ('traɪæd) n. 1. a group of three; trio. 2. *Music.* a three-note chord consisting of a note and the third and fifth above it. —tri'**adic** adj.

Triad ('traɪæd) n. any of several Chinese secret societies, esp. one involved in criminal activities, such as drug trafficking.

trial ('traɪəl, traɪl) n. 1. the act or an instance of trying or proving; test or experiment. 2. *Law.* judicial examination to decide whether a person is innocent or guilty of a crime by questioning them and considering the evidence. **3.** an annoying or frustrating person or thing. **4.** (*often pl.*) a competition for individuals: *sheepdog trials*. **5. on trial. a.** undergoing trial, esp. before a court of law. **b.** being tested, as before a commitment to purchase: *I only have the car out on trial*.

trial and error *n.* a method of discovery based on practical experiment and experience rather than on theory: *he learnt to cook by trial and error*.

trial balance *n. Book-keeping.* a statement of all the debit and credit balances in the double-entry ledger.

triangle ('traɪˌæŋg³l) *n.* **1.** *Geom.* a plane figure with three sides and three angles. **2.** any object shaped like a triangle. **3.** any situation involving three people or points of view. **4.** *Music.* a percussion instrument that consists of a metal bar bent into a triangular shape, beaten with a metal stick. —**tri'angular** *adj.*

triangulate (traɪ'æŋgjʊˌleɪt) *vb.* to survey (an area) by dividing it into triangles.

triangulation (traɪˌæŋgjʊ'leɪʃən) *n.* a method of surveying in which an area is divided into triangles, one side (the base line) and all angles of which are measured and the lengths of the other lines calculated by trigonometry.

Triassic (traɪ'æsɪk) *adj. Geol.* of the period of geological time about 230 million years ago.

triathlon (traɪ'æθlɒn) *n.* an athletic contest in which each athlete competes in three different events: swimming, cycling, and horse riding.

tribalism ('traɪbəˌlɪzəm) *n.* loyalty to a tribe, esp. as opposed to a modern political entity such as a state.

tribe (traɪb) *n.* a group of families or clans believed to have a common ancestor. —**'tribal** *adj.*

tribesman ('traɪbzmən) *n.,* pl. **-men.** a member of a tribe.

tribulation (ˌtrɪbjʊ'leɪʃən) *n.* great distress.

tribunal (traɪ'bjuːn³l, trɪ-) *n.* **1.** a court of justice. **2.** (in Britain) a special court, convened by the government to inquire into a specific matter. **3.** the seat of a judge.

tribune ('trɪbjuːn) *n.* **1.** a person who upholds public rights. **2.** (in ancient Rome) an officer elected by the plebs to protect their interests.

tributary ('trɪbjʊtərɪ) *n.,* pl. **-taries. 1.** a stream or river that flows into a larger one. **2.** a person, nation, or people that pays tribute. ~*adj.* **3.** (of a stream or river) flowing into a larger stream. **4.** given or owed as a tribute. **5.** paying tribute.

tribute ('trɪbjuːt) *n.* **1.** something given, done, or said as a mark of respect or admiration. **2.** a payment by one ruler or state

to another, usually as an acknowledgment of submission.

trice (traɪs) *n.* **in a trice.** in a moment: *I'll be back in a trice.*

triceps ('traɪsɛps) *n.* any muscle having three heads, esp. the one at the back of the upper arm.

trichology (trɪ'kɒlədʒɪ) *n.* the branch of medicine concerned with the hair and its diseases. —**tri'chologist** *n.*

trichromatic (ˌtraɪkrəʊ'mætɪk) *adj.* **1.** having or involving three colours. **2.** of or having normal colour vision. —**tri'chroma-ˌtism** *n.*

trick (trɪk) *n.* **1.** a deceitful or cunning action or plan. **2.** a mischievous, malicious, or humorous action or plan; joke: *she's up to her tricks again.* **3.** an illusory or magical feat or device: *a conjuring trick.* **4.** a simple feat learned by an animal or person. **5.** an adroit or ingenious device; knack: *a trick of the trade.* **6.** a habit or mannerism: *she had a trick of saying "oh dear".* **7.** *Cards.* a batch of cards played in turn and won by the person playing the highest card. **8. do the trick.** *Informal.* to produce the desired result. **9. how's tricks?** *Slang.* how are you? ~*vb.* **10.** to defraud, deceive, or cheat (someone). —**'trickery** *n.*

trickle ('trɪk³l) *vb.* **1.** to flow or cause to flow in a thin stream or drops: *the tears were trickling down her cheeks.* **2.** to move gradually: *the crowd trickled away.* ~*n.* **3.** a thin, irregular, or slow flow of something.

trick out *or* **up** *vb.* to dress up; deck out: *tricked out in frilly dresses.*

trickster ('trɪkstə) *n.* a person who deceives or plays tricks.

tricky ('trɪkɪ) *adj.* **trickier, trickiest. 1.** involving snags or difficulties: *a tricky job.* **2.** needing careful handling: *a tricky situation.* **3.** sly; wily: *a tricky dealer.* —**'tricki-ly** *adv.* —**'trickiness** *n.*

tricolour *or U.S.* **tricolor** ('trɪkələ) *n.* a flag with three equal stripes in different colours, esp. the French or Irish national flags.

tricot ('trɪkəʊ, 'triː-) *n.* **1.** a thin rayon or nylon fabric knitted or resembling knitting, used for dresses, etc. **2.** a type of ribbed dress fabric.

tricycle ('traɪsɪk³l) *n.* a three-wheeled cycle, esp. driven by pedals. —**'tricyclist** *n.*

trident ('traɪd³nt) *n.* a three-pronged spear.

Tridentine (traɪ'dɛntaɪn) *adj.* in accord with Tridentine doctrine: *Tridentine mass.*

tried (traɪd) *vb.* past of **try.**

triennial (traɪ'ɛnɪəl) *adj.* occurring every three years. —**tri'ennially** *adv.*

trier ('traɪə) *n.* a person or thing that tries.

trifle ('traɪf³l) *n.* **1.** a thing of little or no value or significance. **2.** a small amount; bit: *a trifle more enthusiasm.* **3.** *Brit.* a cold dessert made of sponge cake spread with jam or fruit, soaked in sherry, covered with custard and cream. ~*vb.* **4.** (usually foll. by *with*) to deal with as if worthless; dally: *to trifle with a person's affections.*

trifling ('traɪflɪŋ) *adj.* insignificant, petty, or frivolous: *a trifling matter.*

trig. 1. trigonometrical. **2.** trigonometry.

trigger ('trɪgə) *n.* **1.** a small lever that releases a catch on a gun or machine. **2.** any event that sets a course of action in motion. ~*vb.* **3.** (usually foll. by *off*) to set (an action or process) in motion.

trigger-happy *adj. Informal.* quick to resort to the use of guns or violence.

trigonometry (ˌtrɪgə'nɒmɪtrɪ) *n.* the branch of mathematics concerned with the relations of sides and angles of triangles used in surveying, navigation, etc. —**trigonometric** (ˌtrɪgənə'mɛtrɪk) *or* ˌtrigono'metrical *adj.*

trig point *n.* a point on a hilltop, etc., used for triangulation by a surveyor.

trike (traɪk) *n. Informal.* a tricycle.

trilateral (traɪ'lætərəl) *adj.* having three sides.

trilby ('trɪlbɪ) *n., pl.* -**bies.** a man's soft felt hat with an indented crown.

trill (trɪl) *n.* **1.** *Music.* a rapid alternation between a principal note and the note above it. **2.** a shrill warbling sound made by some birds. **3.** the articulation of an (r) sound produced by the rapid vibration of the tongue. ~*vb.* **4.** to sound, sing, or play (a trill or with a trill).

trillion ('trɪljən) *n.* **1.** (in Britain, France, and Germany) the number represented as one followed by eighteen zeros (10^{18}); a million million million. **2.** (in the U.S. and Canada) the number represented as one followed by twelve zeros (10^{12}); a million million. ~*det.* **3.** amounting to a trillion. —'**trillionth** *n., adj.*

trillium ('trɪljəm) *n.* a plant of Asia and North America, having three leaves at the top of the stem with a single white, pink, or purple three-petalled flower.

trilobite ('traɪləˌbaɪt) *n.* an extinct marine arthropod, found as a fossil.

trilogy ('trɪlədʒɪ) *n., pl.* -**gies.** a series of three plays, novels, operas, etc., which form a related group but are each complete works in themselves.

trim (trɪm) *adj.* **trimmer, trimmest. 1.** neat and spruce in appearance. **2.** slim; slender. **3.** in good condition. ~*vb.* **trimming, trimmed. 4.** to put (something, such as a hedge) in good order, esp. by cutting or pruning. **5.** to adorn or decorate (something, such as a garment) with lace, ribbons, etc. **6.** (sometimes foll. by *off* or *away*) to cut so as to remove: *to trim off a branch.* **7. a.** to adjust the balance of (a ship or aircraft) by shifting cargo, etc. **b.** to adjust (a ship's sails) to take advantage

of the wind. **8.** *Informal.* to thrash or beat. **9.** *Informal.* to rebuke. ~*n.* **10.** a decoration or adornment. **11.** the upholstery and decorative facings of a car's interior. **12.** proper order or fitness; good shape. **13.** a haircut that neatens but does not alter the existing hairstyle.

trimaran ('traɪməˌræn) *n.* a boat usually with two hulls flanking the main hull.

trimming ('trɪmɪŋ) *n.* **1.** an extra piece added to a garment for decoration. **2.** (*pl.*) usual or traditional accompaniments: *roast turkey with all the trimmings.*

Trinitarian (ˌtrɪnɪ'tɛərɪən) *n.* **1.** a person who believes in the doctrine of the Trinity. ~*adj.* **2.** of or relating to the Trinity. —ˌTrini'tarianˌism *n.*

trinitrotoluene (traɪˌnaɪtrəʊ'tɒljuˌiːn) *or* **trinitrotoluol** *n.* the full name for **TNT.**

trinity ('trɪnɪtɪ) *n., pl.* -**ties.** a group of three people or things.

Trinity ('trɪnɪtɪ) *n. Christian theol.* the union of three persons, the Father, Son, and Holy Spirit, in one Godhead.

Trinity Sunday *n.* the Sunday after Whit Sunday.

trinket ('trɪŋkɪt) *n.* a small or worthless ornament or piece of jewellery.

trio ('triːəʊ) *n., pl.* **trios. 1.** a group of three people or things. **2.** *Music.* a group of three singers or musicians or a piece of music composed for such a group.

trip (trɪp) *n.* **1.** an outward and return journey, often for a specific purpose. **2.** a false step; stumble. **3.** a light step or tread. **4.** a catch on a mechanism that acts as a switch. **5.** *Informal.* a hallucinogenic drug experience. ~*vb.* **tripping, tripped. 6.** (often foll. by *up, on,* or *over*) to stumble or cause (someone) to stumble. **7.** (often foll. by *up*) to trap or catch (someone) in a mistake. **8.** to go on a short journey. **9.** to move or tread lightly. **10.** *Informal.* to experience the effects of a hallucinogenic drug.

tripartite (traɪ'pɑːtaɪt) *adj.* involving or composed of three people or parts. —**tri'partism** *n.*

tripe (traɪp) *n.* **1.** the stomach lining of an ox, cow, or pig prepared for cooking. **2.** *Informal.* nonsense; rubbish.

triple ('trɪp'l) *adj.* **1.** consisting of three parts; threefold. **2.** (of musical time or rhythm) having three beats in each bar. **3.** three times as great or as much. ~*n.* **4.** a threefold amount. **5.** a group of three. ~*vb.* **6.** to increase threefold; treble. —'**triply** *adv.*

triple jump *n.* an athletic event in which the competitor has to perform a hop, a step, and a jump in a continuous movement.

triple point *n. Chem.* the temperature and pressure at which the three phases of a substance are in equilibrium.

triplet ('trɪplɪt) n. **1.** one of three offspring born at one birth. **2.** a group or set of three similar things. **3.** a group of three musical notes.

triplicate adj. ('trɪplɪkɪt). **1.** triple. ~vb. ('trɪplɪˌkeɪt). **2.** to multiply or be multiplied by three. ~n. ('trɪplɪkɪt). **3.** a group of three things. **4. in triplicate.** written out three times. —**tripli'cation** n.

tripod ('traɪpɒd) n. **1.** a three-legged stand to which a camera, etc., can be attached to hold it steady. **2.** a three-legged stool, table, etc.

tripos ('traɪpɒs) n. Brit. the final honours degree examinations at Cambridge University.

tripper ('trɪpə) n. Chiefly Brit. a tourist.

triptych ('trɪptɪk) n. a set of three pictures or panels, usually hinged together: often used as an altarpiece.

trireme ('traɪriːm) n. an ancient Greek warship with three banks of oars on each side.

trisect (traɪ'sɛkt) vb. to divide into three parts, esp. three equal parts. —**trisection** (traɪ'sɛkʃən) n.

trismus ('trɪzməs) n. Pathol. the state of being unable to open the mouth because of sustained contractions of the jaw muscles, caused by tetanus. Nontechnical name: **lockjaw**.

triste (triːst) adj. Archaic. sad.

trite (traɪt) adj. hackneyed; dull: a trite comment.

tritium ('trɪtɪəm) n. a radioactive isotope of hydrogen. Symbol: T or ^{3}H

triumph ('traɪəmf) n. **1.** the feeling of great happiness resulting from a victory or major achievement. **2.** the act or condition of being victorious; victory. **3.** (in ancient Rome) a procession held in honour of a victorious general. ~vb. **4.** (often foll. by over) to win a victory or control: to triumph over one's weaknesses. **5.** to rejoice over a victory. **6.** to celebrate a Roman triumph. —**triumphal** (traɪ'ʌmfəl) adj.

triumphant (traɪ'ʌmfənt) adj. **1.** experiencing or displaying triumph. **2.** exultant through triumph. —**tri'umphantly** adv.

triumvir (traɪ'ʌmvə) n. (esp. in ancient Rome) a member of a triumvirate.

triumvirate (traɪ'ʌmvɪrɪt) n. **1.** joint rule by three men. **2.** (in ancient Rome) a board of three officials jointly responsible for some task.

trivalent (traɪ'veɪlənt, 'trɪvələnt) adj. Chem. **1.** having a valency of three. **2.** having three valencies. —**tri'valency** n.

trivet ('trɪvɪt) n. **1.** a three-legged stand for holding a pot, kettle, etc., over a fire. **2.** a short metal stand on which hot dishes are placed on a table.

trivia ('trɪvɪə) n. (functioning as sing. or pl.) petty details or considerations.

trivial ('trɪvɪəl) adj. **1.** of little importance;

petty or frivolous: trivial complaints. **2.** ordinary or commonplace; trite: trivial conversation. —ˌtrivi'ality n. —'trivially adv.

trochee ('trəʊkiː) n. Prosody. a metrical foot consisting of one long and one short syllable (–◡). — **trochaic** (trəʊ'keɪɪk) adj.

trod (trɒd) vb. the past tense and a past participle of **tread**.

trodden ('trɒdən) vb. a past participle of **tread**.

troglodyte ('trɒgləˌdaɪt) n. a cave dweller, esp. of prehistoric times.

troika ('trɔɪkə) n. **1.** a Russian vehicle drawn by three horses abreast. **2.** three horses harnessed abreast. **3.** a group of three people in authority.

Trojan ('trəʊdʒən) n. **1.** a person from ancient Troy. **2.** a hard-working person. ~adj. **3.** of ancient Troy or its people.

Trojan Horse n. **1.** Greek myth. the huge wooden hollow figure of a horse used by the Greeks to enter Troy. **2.** a trap intended to undermine an enemy.

troll[1] (trəʊl) vb. Angling. **a.** to draw (a baited line, etc.) through the water. **b.** to fish (a stretch of water) by trolling. **c.** to fish (for) by trolling.

troll[2] (trəʊl) n. (in Scandinavian folklore) any of certain supernatural creatures that dwell in caves or mountains and are depicted either as dwarfs or as giants.

trolley ('trɒlɪ) n. **1.** Brit. a small table on casters used for carrying food or drink. **2.** Brit. a wheeled cart or stand used for moving heavy items, such as shopping in a supermarket or luggage at a railway station. **3.** Brit. See **trolley bus**. **4.** U.S. & Canad. See **trolley car**. **5.** a device, such as a wheel that collects the current from an overhead wire, to drive the motor of an electric vehicle. **6.** Chiefly Brit. a low truck running on rails, used in factories, mines, etc.

trolley bus n. an electrically driven public-transport vehicle that does not run on rails but takes its power from an overhead wire.

trolley car n. U.S. & Canad. same as **tram**[1] (sense 1).

trollop ('trɒləp) n. a promiscuous or untidy woman.

trombone (trɒm'bəʊn) n. a brass musical instrument with a sliding tube. —**trom'bonist** n.

trompe l'oeil (ˌtrɒmp 'lɜːɪ) n., pl. **trompe l'oeils**. **1.** a painting, etc., giving a convincing illusion that the objects represented are real. **2.** an effect of this kind.

tronk (trɒŋk) n. S. African slang. a prison.

troop (truːp) n. **1.** a large group or assembly. **2.** a subdivision of a cavalry or armoured regiment. **3.** (pl.) armed forces; soldiers. **4.** a large group of Scouts patrols.

~*vb.* **5.** to gather, move, or march in or as if in a crowd. **6.** *Mil., chiefly Brit.* to parade (the colour or flag) ceremonially: *the trooping of the colour.*

trooper ('truːpə) *n.* **1.** a soldier in a cavalry regiment. **2.** *U.S. & Austral.* a mounted policeman. **3.** *U.S.* a state policeman. **4.** a cavalry horse. **5.** *Informal, chiefly Brit.* a troopship.

troopship ('truːpˌʃɪp) *n.* a ship used to transport military personnel.

trope (trəup) *n.* a word or expression used in a figurative sense.

trophy ('trəufɪ) *n., pl.* **-phies. 1.** an object such as a silver cup that is symbolic of victory in a contest, esp. a sporting contest; prize. **2.** a memento of success, esp. one taken in war or hunting. **3.** (in ancient Greece and Rome) captured arms displayed as a memorial of victory. **4.** an ornamental carving that represents a group of weapons, etc.

tropic ('trɒpɪk) *n.* **1.** (*sometimes cap.*) either of the parallel lines of latitude at about 23½°N (**tropic of Cancer**) and 23½°S (**tropic of Capricorn**) of the equator. **2. the tropics.** (*often cap.*) that part of the earth's surface between the tropics of Cancer and Capricorn. ~*adj.* **3.** tropical.

tropical ('trɒpɪkˀl) *adj.* situated in, used in, characteristic of, or relating to the tropics. —'**tropically** *adv.*

tropism ('trəupɪzəm) *n.* the tendency of a plant or animal to turn or curve in response to an external stimulus.

troposphere ('trɒpəˌsfɪə) *n.* the lowest atmospheric layer, about 18 kilometres (11 miles) thick at the equator to about 6 km (4 miles) at the Poles.

trot (trɒt) *vb.* **trotting, trotted. 1.** to move or cause (a person or animal) to move at a trot. ~*n.* **2.** a gait of a horse in which diagonally opposite legs come down together. **3.** a steady brisk pace. **4. on the trot.** *Informal.* **a.** one after the other: *to read two books on the trot.* **b.** busy, esp. on one's feet: *I've been on the trot all day.* **5. the trots.** *Informal.* diarrhoea.

Trot (trɒt) *n. Informal.* a follower of Trotsky; Trotskyite.

troth (trəuθ) *n. Archaic.* **1.** a pledge of fidelity, esp. a betrothal. **2. in troth.** truely. **3.** loyalty; fidelity.

trot out *vb. Informal.* to bring forward (old information or ideas), as for approval or admiration, esp. repeatedly.

Trotskyite ('trɒtskɪˌaɪt) *or* **Trotskyist** ('trɒtskɪɪst) *adj.* **1.** of the theories or Leon Trotsky (1879-1940), Russian revolutionary and writer. ~*n.* **2.** a supporter of Trotsky. —'**Trotsky,ism** *n.*

trotter ('trɒtə) *n.* **1.** a horse that is specially trained to trot fast. **2.** (*usually pl.*) the foot of certain animals, esp. of pigs.

troubadour ('truːbəˌduə) *n.* any of a class of lyric poets in S France and N Italy from the 11th to the 13th century who wrote chiefly on courtly love.

trouble ('trʌbˀl) *n.* **1.** a state of mental distress or anxiety. **2.** a state of disorder or unrest: *industrial trouble.* **3.** a condition of disease, pain, or malfunctioning: *liver trouble.* **4.** a cause of distress, disturbance, or pain: *what's the trouble?* **5.** effort or exertion taken to do something. **6.** a personal weakness or cause of annoyance: *his trouble is he's too soft.* **7. in trouble. a.** likely to suffer punishment: *he's in trouble with the police.* **b.** pregnant when not married. ~*vb.* **8.** to cause trouble to. **9.** (foll. by *about*) to put oneself to inconvenience; be concerned: *don't trouble about me.* **10.** to take pains; exert oneself. **11.** to cause inconvenience or discomfort to: *does this noise trouble you?*

troublemaker ('trʌbˀlˌmeɪkə) *n.* a person who makes trouble, esp. between people. —'**trouble,making** *adj., n.*

troubleshooter ('trʌbˀlˌʃuːtə) *n.* a person employed to locate and correct faults in machinery or problems in a company. —'**trouble,shooting** *n., adj.*

troublesome ('trʌbˀlsəm) *adj.* causing trouble.

troublous ('trʌbləs) *adj. Archaic or literary.* unsettled; agitated.

trough (trɒf) *n.* **1.** a narrow open container, esp. one in which food or water for animals is put. **2.** a narrow channel, gutter, or gulley. **3.** *Meteorol.* an elongated area of low pressure.

trounce (trauns) *vb.* to beat or defeat (someone) utterly.

troupe (truːp) *n.* a company of actors or other performers, esp. one that travels.

trouper ('truːpə) *n.* **1.** a member of a troupe. **2.** an experienced person.

trouser ('trauzə) *n.* (*modifier*) of or relating to trousers: *trouser buttons.*

trousers ('trauzəz) *pl. n.* a garment that covers the body from the waist to the ankles or knees with separate tube-shaped sections for both legs.

trousseau ('truːsəu) *n., pl.* **-seaux** *or* **-seaus** (-səuz). the clothes, linen, and other possessions collected by a bride for her marriage.

trout (traut) *n., pl.* **trout** *or* **trouts.** any of various game fishes related to the salmon and found chiefly in fresh water in northern regions.

trove (trəuv) *n.* See **treasure-trove.**

trow (trəu) *vb. Archaic.* to think, believe, or trust.

trowel ('trauəl) *n.* **1.** any of various small hand tools having a flat metal blade, used for spreading plaster or similar materials.

2. a similar tool with a curved blade used by gardeners for lifting plants, etc.

troy weight *or* **troy** (trɔɪ) *n.* a system of weights used for precious metals and gemstones in which one pound equals twelve ounces.

truant ('truːənt) *n.* **1.** a person who is absent without leave, esp. from school. **2. play truant.** to stay away, esp. from school, without permission. ~*adj.* **3.** being or relating to a truant. —'**truancy** *n.*

truce (truːs) *n.* **1.** an agreement to stop fighting, esp. temporarily. **2.** a temporary halt of something unpleasant.

truck[1] (trʌk) *n.* **1.** *Brit.* a vehicle for carrying freight on a railway; wagon. **2.** *Chiefly U.S. & Canad.* a lorry. **3.** a frame carrying two or more pairs of wheels attached under an end of a railway coach, etc. **4.** any wheeled vehicle used to move goods.

truck[2] (trʌk) *n.* **1.** commercial exchange. **2.** payment of wages in kind. **3. have no truck with someone.** to have no dealings with someone. ~*vb.* **4.** to exchange (goods); barter.

truckle ('trʌkəl) *vb.* (usually foll. by *to*) to yield weakly; give in: *I'm sick of having to truckle to you!*

truckle bed *n.* a low bed on wheels, stored under a larger bed.

truculent ('trʌkjʊlənt) *adj.* defiantly aggressive or bad-tempered. —'**truculence** *n.*

trudge (trʌdʒ) *vb.* **1.** to walk or plod (somewhere) heavily or wearily. **2.** to pass over (something) by trudging. ~*n.* **3.** a long tiring walk.

true (truː) *adj.* **truer, truest. 1.** not false, fictional, or illusory; factual. **2.** real; not synthetic: *true leather.* **3.** faithful and loyal. **4.** conforming to a required standard, law, or pattern: *a true aim.* **5.** (of a compass bearing) according to the earth's geographical rather than magnetic poles: *true north.* **6. in** (*or* **out of**) **true.** in (or not in) correct alignment. ~*adv.* **7.** truthfully; rightly. **8.** precisely or unswervingly: *he shot true.*

true-blue *adj.* **1.** staunchly loyal. ~*n.* **true blue. 2.** *Chiefly Brit.* a staunch royalist or Conservative.

true-life *adj.* directly comparable to reality: *a true-life story.*

truelove ('truːˌlʌv) *n.* someone truly loved; sweetheart.

true north *n.* the direction from any point along a meridian towards the North Pole.

truffle ('trʌfəl) *n.* **1.** a round mushroom-like fungus regarded as a delicacy. **2.** Also called: **rum truffle.** *Chiefly Brit.* a sweet flavoured with chocolate or rum.

trug (trʌg) *n.* a long shallow basket for carrying garden tools, flowers, etc.

truism ('truːɪzəm) *n.* a statement that is clearly true and well known.

truly ('truːlɪ) *adv.* **1.** in a true, just, or faithful manner. **2.** really: *a truly great man.*

trump[1] (trʌmp) *n.* **1.** Also called: **trump card. a.** any card from the suit that ranks higher than any other suit in one particular game. **b.** this suit itself. **2.** a decisive or advantageous move, resource, etc., held in reserve. **3.** *Informal.* a fine or reliable person. ~*vb.* **4.** to play a trump card on (a card of a suit that is not trumps). **5.** to outdo or surpass. ~See also **trumps.**

trump[2] (trʌmp) *n. Archaic or literary.* **1.** a trumpet or the sound produced by one. **2. the last trump.** the final trumpet call on the Day of Judgment.

trumped up *adj.* (of charges, excuses, etc.) made up in order to deceive.

trumpery ('trʌmpərɪ) *n., pl.* -**eries. 1.** foolish talk or actions. **2.** a useless or worthless article. ~*adj.* **3.** useless or worthless.

trumpet ('trʌmpɪt) *n.* **1.** a valved brass musical instrument consisting of a narrow tube ending in a flare. **2.** a loud sound such as that of a trumpet. **3.** short for **ear trumpet. 4. blow one's own trumpet.** to boast about one's own skills or good qualities. ~*vb.* **5.** to proclaim or sound loudly. —'**trumpeter** *n.*

trumps (trʌmps) *pl. n.* **1.** (*sometimes sing.*) *Cards.* any one of the four suits that outranks all the other suits for the duration of a deal or game. **2. turn up trumps.** (of a person) to bring about a happy or successful conclusion, esp. unexpectedly.

truncate (trʌŋ'keɪt) *vb.* to shorten by cutting. —**trun'cation** *n.*

truncated (trʌŋ'keɪtɪd) *adj.* shortened by or as if by cutting off.

truncheon ('trʌntʃən) *n.* **1.** *Chiefly Brit.* a short thick stick carried by a policeman. **2.** a staff or baton carried as a symbol of authority.

trundle ('trʌndəl) *vb.* to move heavily on or as if on wheels: *the bus trundled by.*

trundler ('trʌndlə) *n. N.Z.* **1.** a golf or shopping trolley. **2.** a child's pushchair.

trunk (trʌŋk) *n.* **1.** the main stem of a tree. **2.** a large strong case or box used to contain clothes when travelling and for storage. **3.** the body excluding the head, neck, and limbs; torso. **4.** the long nasal part of an elephant. **5.** *U.S.* same as **boot**[1] (sense 2). ~See also **trunks.**

trunk call *n. Chiefly Brit.* a long-distance telephone call.

trunk line *n.* **1.** a direct link between two distant telephone exchanges or switchboards. **2.** the main route or routes on a railway.

trunk road *n. Brit.* a main road, esp. one that is suitable for heavy vehicles.

trunks (trʌŋks) *pl. n.* a man's garment worn for swimming, boxing, etc., extending from the waist to the thigh.

truss (trʌs) *vb.* **1.** to tie or bind (someone) up. **2.** to bind the wings and legs of (a fowl) before cooking. **3.** to support or stiffen (a roof, bridge, etc.) with a structural framework. ~*n.* **4.** a structural framework of wood or metal used to support a roof, bridge, etc. **5.** *Med.* a device for holding a hernia in place. **6.** a cluster of flowers or fruit growing at the end of a single stalk. **7.** a bundle or pack.

trust (trʌst) *n.* **1.** reliance on and confidence in the truth, worth, reliability, etc., of a person or thing; faith. **2.** the obligation of someone in a responsible position: *a position of trust.* **3.** custody, charge, or care: *a child placed in my trust.* **4. a.** an arrangement between two people whereby property is kept, used, or administered by one person for the benefit of the other. **b.** property that is the subject of such an arrangement. **5.** *Chiefly U.S. & Canad.* a group of companies joined together to control the market for any commodity. **6.** (*modifier*) of or relating to a trust or trusts. ~*vb.* **7.** to expect, hope, or suppose: *I trust that you are well.* **8.** to place confidence in (someone to do something); rely (upon). **9.** to consign for care: *the child was trusted to my care.* **10.** to allow (someone to do something) with confidence in his or her good sense or honesty.

trustee (trʌˈstiː) *n.* **1.** a person to whom the legal title to property is entrusted. **2.** a member of a board that manages the affairs of an institution or organization.

trustful (ˈtrʌstfʊl) *or* **trusting** *adj.* characterized by a readiness to trust others. —ˈtrustfully *or* ˈtrustingly *adv.*

trust fund *n.* money, securities, etc., held in trust.

trustworthy (ˈtrʌstˌwɜːðɪ) *adj.* (of a person) honest, reliable, or dependable.

trusty (ˈtrʌstɪ) *adj.* **trustier, trustiest.** **1.** faithful or reliable: *a trusty old dog.* ~*n., pl.* **trusties.** **2.** a trustworthy convict to whom special privileges are granted.

truth (truːθ) *n.* **1.** the quality of being true, genuine, actual, or factual. **2.** something that is true. **3.** a proven or verified fact, principle, etc.: *the truths of astronomy.*

truthful (ˈtruːθfʊl) *adj.* **1.** telling the truth; honest. **2.** realistic: *a truthful portrayal of the king.* —ˈtruthfully *adv.* —ˈtruthfulness *n.*

try (traɪ) *vb.* **trying, tried.** **1.** to make an effort or attempt: *I don't know if I can, but I'll try; he tried to climb a cliff.* **2.** to sample, test, or give experimental use to (something). **3.** to put strain or stress on: *he tries my patience.* **4.** to give pain, affliction, or vexation to: *I have been sorely tried by those children.* **5. a.** to examine and

determine the issues involved in (a cause) in a court of law. **b.** to hear evidence in order to determine the guilt or innocence of (a person). ~*n., pl.* **tries.** **6.** an attempt or effort. **7.** *Rugby.* a score made by placing the ball down behind the opposing team's goal line.

trying (ˈtraɪɪŋ) *adj.* upsetting, difficult, or annoying.

try on *vb.* **1.** to put on (a garment) to find out whether it fits. **2. try it on.** *Informal.* to attempt to deceive or fool someone. ~*n.* **try-on. 3.** *Brit. informal.* something done to test out a person's tolerance, etc.

try out *vb.* **1.** to test (something) or put (something) to experimental use. ~*n.* **tryout. 2.** *Chiefly U.S. & Canad.* a trial or test, as of an athlete or actor.

trysail (ˈtraɪˌseɪl; *Naut.* ˈtraɪsˀl) *n.* a small fore-and-aft sail set on a sailing vessel to help keep her head to the wind in a storm.

tryst (trɪst, traɪst) *n. Archaic or literary.* **1.** an appointment to meet, esp. secretly. **2.** the place of such a meeting or the meeting itself.

tsar *or* **czar** (zɑː) *n.* (until 1917) the emperor of Russia. —ˈtsardom *or* ˈczardom *n.*

tsarevitch *or* **czarevitch** (ˈzɑːrəvɪtʃ) *n.* the eldest son of a Russian tsar.

tsarina *or* **czarina** (zɑːˈriːnə) *n.* the wife of a Russian tsar; Russian empress.

tsetse fly *or* **tzetze fly** (ˈtsɛtsɪ) *n.* a bloodsucking African fly which transmits disease, esp. sleeping sickness.

T-shirt *or* **tee-shirt** *n.* a lightweight, usually short-sleeved, casual garment for the upper body.

tsp. teaspoon.

T-square *n.* a T-shaped ruler used for drawing horizontal lines and to support set squares when drawing vertical and inclined lines.

tsunami (tsuˈnɑːmɪ) *n., pl.* **-mis** *or* **-mi.** a large, often destructive, sea wave, usually caused by an earthquake under the sea.

TT 1. teetotal. **2.** teetotaller. **3.** tuberculin-tested.

TU trade union.

Tu. Tuesday.

tub (tʌb) *n.* **1.** a low wide, usually round container. **2.** a small plastic or cardboard container for ice cream, etc. **3.** *Chiefly U.S.* same as **bath**[1] (sense 1). **4.** Also called: **tubful.** the amount a tub will hold. **5.** a slow and uncomfortable boat or ship.

tuba (ˈtjuːbə) *n.* a valved brass musical instrument of low pitch.

tubby (ˈtʌbɪ) *adj.* **-bier, -biest.** (of a person) fat and short. —ˈtubbiness *n.*

tube (tjuːb) *n.* **1.** a long hollow cylindrical object, used for the passage of fluids or as a container. **2.** a pliable cylindrical container of soft metal or plastic closed with a cap, used to hold semiliquids or pastes: *a tube of* *toothpaste*. **3.** *Anat.* any hollow cylindrical structure. **4.** (*sometimes cap.*) *Brit.* **the tube.** an underground railway system, esp. that in London. **5.** *Electronics.* **a.** same as **valve** (sense 3). **b.** See **electron tube, cathode-ray tube. 6.** *Slang, chiefly U.S.* a television set. —'**tubeless** *adj.*

tuber ('tju:bə) *n.* a fleshy underground root of a plant, such as a potato plant.

tubercle ('tju:bək³l) *n.* **1.** a small rounded lump, esp. on the skin, on a bone, or on a plant. **2.** any abnormal hard swelling, esp. one characteristic of tuberculosis.

tubercular (tjʊ'bɜːkjʊlə) *or* **tuberculous** *adj.* **1.** of or symptomatic of tuberculosis. **2.** of or relating to a tubercle.

tuberculin (tjʊ'bɜːkjʊlɪn) *n.* a sterile liquid prepared from cultures of the tubercle bacillus and used in the diagnosis of tuberculosis.

tuberculin-tested *adj.* (of milk) produced by cows that have been certified as free of tuberculosis.

tuberculosis (tjʊ,bɜːkjʊ'ləʊsɪs) *n.* an infectious disease characterized by the formation of tubercles, esp. in the lungs.

tuberous ('tju:bərəs) *adj.* (of plants) forming, bearing, or resembling a tuber or tubers.

tubing ('tju:bɪŋ) *n.* **1.** a length of tube. **2.** a system of tubes.

tubular ('tju:bjʊlə) *adj.* **1.** having the shape of a tube or tubes. **2.** of or relating to a tube or tubing.

tubule ('tju:bju:l) *n.* any small tubular structure in an animal or plant.

TUC (in Britain) Trades Union Congress.

tuck (tʌk) *vb.* **1.** to push or fold into a small confined space or concealed place or between two surfaces: *to tuck a letter into an envelope.* **2.** to thrust the loose ends or sides of (something) into a confining space, so as to make neat and secure. **3.** to make a tuck or tucks in (a garment). ~*n.* **4.** a tucked object or part. **5.** a pleat or fold in a part of a garment, usually stitched down. **6.** *Brit. informal.* food, esp. cakes and sweets.

tuck away *vb. Informal.* **1.** to eat (a large amount of food). **2.** to store (something), esp. in a place difficult to find.

tucker ('tʌkə) *n.* a detachable yoke of lace, linen, etc., formerly worn over the breast of a low-cut dress.

tuck in *vb.* **1.** Also: **tuck into.** to put (someone) to bed and make snug. **2.** to thrust the loose ends or sides of (something) into a confining space: *tuck the blankets in.* **3.** Also: **tuck into.** *Informal.* to eat, esp. heartily. ~*n.* **4.** *Brit. informal.* a meal, esp. a large one.

tuck shop *n. Chiefly Brit.* a shop in or near a school, where cakes and sweets are sold.

Tudor ('tju:də) *adj.* **1.** of or relating to the English royal house ruling from 1485 to 1603. **2.** denoting a style of architecture characterized by half-timbered houses.

Tues. Tuesday.

Tuesday ('tju:zdɪ) *n.* the third day of the week; second day of the working week.

tufa ('tju:fə) *n.* a porous rock formed of calcium carbonate deposited from springs.

tuff (tʌf) *n.* a porous rock formed from volcanic dust or ash.

tuffet ('tʌfɪt) *n.* a small mound or low seat.

tuft (tʌft) *n.* a bunch of feathers, grass, hair, threads, etc., held together at the base. —'**tufted** *adj.* —'**tufty** *adj.*

tug (tʌg) *vb.* **tugging, tugged. 1.** to pull or drag with sharp or powerful movements: *the boy tugged at the door handle.* **2.** to tow (a vessel) by means of a tug. ~*n.* **3.** a strong pull or jerk. **4.** Also called: **tugboat.** a boat with a powerful engine, used for towing barges, ships, etc.

tug of war *n.* **1.** a contest in which two people or teams pull opposite ends of a rope in an attempt to drag the opposition over a central line. **2.** any hard struggle between two people or two groups.

tuition (tju:'ɪʃən) *n.* **1.** instruction, esp. that received individually or in a small group. **2.** the payment for instruction, esp. in colleges or universities.

tulip ('tju:lɪp) *n.* **1.** a spring-blooming bulb plant with single showy bell-shaped flowers. **2.** the flower or bulb.

tulip tree *n.* a North American tree with tulip-shaped greenish-yellow flowers and long conelike fruits.

tulle (tju:l) *n.* a fine net fabric of silk, rayon, etc.

tumble ('tʌmb³l) *vb.* **1.** to fall, esp. awkwardly or violently: *I tumbled down the stairs.* **2.** to decrease in value suddenly: *share prices tumbled.* **3.** (usually foll. by *about*) to roll or twist, esp. in playing: *the kittens tumbled about on the floor.* **4.** to perform leaps or somersaults. **5.** to move in a heedless or hasty way: *they came tumbling into the room.* **6.** to disturb, rumple, or toss around: *to tumble the bed clothes.* ~*n.* **7.** a tumbling. **8.** a fall or toss. **9.** an acrobatic feat, esp. a somersault. **10.** a confused or untidy state.

tumbledown ('tʌmb³l,daʊn) *adj.* (of a building) falling to pieces; dilapidated.

tumble dryer *n.* an electrically-operated machine that dries wet laundry by rotating it in warmed air inside a metal drum.

tumbler ('tʌmblə) *n.* **1. a.** a flat-bottomed drinking glass with no handle or stem. **b.** the amount a tumbler will hold. **2.** a person who performs somersaults and other acrobatic feats. **3.** same as **tumble dryer. 4.** a part of the mechanism of a lock.

tumble to *vb.* to understand; become aware of: *she quickly tumbled to his plan.*

tumbrel *or* **tumbril** ('tʌmbrəl) *n.* a farm cart, esp. one that tilts backwards to empty its load. A cart of this type was used to take condemned prisoners to the guillotine during the French Revolution.

tumescent (tjuːˈmɛsᵊnt) *adj.* swollen or becoming swollen.

tumid ('tjuːmɪd) *adj.* **1.** (of an organ or part) enlarged or swollen. **2.** pompous or fulsome in style: *tumid prose.* —**tu-** '**midity** *n.*

tummy ('tʌmɪ) *n., pl.* **-mies.** an informal or childish word for **stomach.**

tumour *or U.S.* **tumor** ('tjuːmə) *n. Pathol.* **a.** any abnormal swelling. **b.** a mass of tissue formed by a new growth of cells. —'**tumorous** *adj.*

tumult ('tjuːmʌlt) *n.* **1.** a loud confused noise, as of a crowd; commotion. **2.** violent agitation or disturbance. **3.** great emotional disturbance.

tumultuous (tjuːˈmʌltjʊəs) *adj.* **1.** exciting, confused, or turbulent: *tumultuous feelings; a tumultuous decade.* **2.** unruly, noisy, or excited: *a tumultuous welcome.*

tumulus ('tjuːmjʊləs) *n., pl.* **-li** (-liː). *Archaeol.* (*no longer in technical usage*) same as **barrow**².

tun (tʌn) *n.* **1.** a large beer cask. **2.** a measure of capacity, usually equal to 252 wine gallons.

tuna ('tjuːnə) *n., pl.* **-na** *or* **-nas. 1.** a large marine spiny-finned fish. **2.** the flesh of this fish, often tinned for food.

tundra ('tʌndrə) *n.* a vast treeless Arctic region with permanently frozen subsoil.

tune (tjuːn) *n.* **1.** a melody, esp. one for which harmony is not essential. **2.** the correct musical pitch: *this piano's out of tune.* **3. call the tune.** to be in control of the proceedings. **4. change one's tune.** to alter one's attitude or tone of speech. **5. in** (*or* **out of**) **tune with.** in (*or* not in) agreement with. **6. to the tune of.** *Informal.* to the amount or extent of. ~*vb.* **7.** to adjust (a musical instrument) to a certain pitch. **8.** (often foll. by *up*) to make fine adjustments to (an engine, machine, etc.) to obtain the proper or desired performance. —'**tuner** *n.*

tuneful ('tjuːnfʊl) *adj.* having a pleasant tune; melodious. —'**tunefully** *adv.*

tune in *vb.* **1.** (often foll. by *to*) to adjust (a radio or television) to receive (a station or programme). **2. tuned in to.** *Slang.* aware of or knowledgeable about: *tuned in to what computers can do.*

tuneless ('tjuːnlɪs) *adj.* having no melody or tune.

tune up *vb.* **1.** to adjust (a musical instrument) to a particular pitch. **2.** to adjust

(an engine) in (a car, etc.) to improve performance.

tungsten ('tʌŋstən) *n.* a hard greyish-white element. Symbol: W

tunic ('tjuːnɪk) *n.* any of various hip-length or knee-length garments, such as the loose sleeveless garb worn in ancient Greece or Rome, the jacket of some soldiers, or a woman's hip-length garment, worn with a skirt or trousers.

tuning fork *n.* a two-pronged metal fork that when struck produces a pure note of constant specified pitch.

tunnel ('tʌnᵊl) *n.* **1.** an underground passageway, esp. one for trains or cars. **2.** any passage or channel through or under something. ~*vb.* **-nelling, -nelled** *or U.S.* **-neling, -neled. 3.** to make or force (a way) through or under (something). **4.** (foll. by *through, under,* etc.) to make or force a way (through or under something).

tunnel vision *n.* **1.** a condition in which a person is unable to see things that are not straight in front of them. **2.** narrowness of viewpoint resulting from concentration on a single idea, opinion, etc.

tunny ('tʌnɪ) *n., pl.* **-nies** *or* **-ny.** same as **tuna.**

tup (tʌp) *n. Chiefly Brit.* a male sheep; ram.

tuppence ('tʌpəns) *n. Brit.* same as **two-pence.** —'**tuppenny** *adj.*

turban ('tɜːbᵊn) *n.* **1.** a head-covering worn esp. by Muslims, Hindus, and Sikhs. **2.** any head-covering resembling this. —'**turbaned** *adj.*

turbid ('tɜːbɪd) *adj.* **1.** muddy or clouded, as from having the sediment stirred up. **2.** dense, thick, or cloudy: *turbid fog.* —tur'**bidity** *n.*

turbine ('tɜːbɪn, -baɪn) *n.* a machine in which power is produced by a stream of water, air, etc., that pushes the blades of a wheel and causes it to rotate.

turbofan (ˌtɜːbəʊˈfæn) *n.* a type of engine in which a large fan driven by a turbine forces air rearwards to increase the propulsive thrust.

turbojet (ˌtɜːbəʊˈdʒɛt) *n.* **1.** a gas turbine in which the exhaust gases provide the propulsive thrust to drive an aircraft. **2.** an aircraft powered by turbojet engines.

turboprop (ˌtɜːbəʊˈprɒp) *n.* a gas turbine for driving an aircraft propeller.

turbot ('tɜːbət) *n., pl.* **-bot** *or* **-bots.** a European flatfish, highly valued as a food fish.

turbulence ('tɜːbjʊləns) *n.* **1.** a state or condition of confusion, movement, or agitation. **2.** *Meteorol.* instability in the atmosphere causing gusty air currents.

turbulent ('tɜːbjʊlənt) *adj.* **1.** being in a state of turbulence. **2.** wild or disobedient; unruly.

turd (tɜːd) *n. Taboo.* **1.** a piece of excrement. **2.** *Slang.* a contemptible person.

tureen (təˈriːn) n. a large deep dish with a cover, used for serving soups.

turf (tɜːf) n., pl. **turfs** or **turves**. 1. a surface layer of earth containing a dense growth of grasses with their roots; sod. 2. a piece cut from this layer. 3. **the turf. a.** a track where horse races are run. **b.** horse racing as a sport or industry. 4. same as **peat.** ~vb. 5. to cover (an area of ground) with pieces of turf.

turf accountant n. Brit. same as **bookmaker.**

turf out vb. Brit. informal. to throw (someone or something) out.

turgescent (tɜːˈdʒɛsªnt) adj. becoming or being swollen. —**turˈgescence** n.

turgid (ˈtɜːdʒɪd) adj. 1. swollen and distended. 2. (of language) pompous; bombastic. —**turˈgidity** n.

Turk (tɜːk) n. 1. a person from Turkey. 2. a native speaker of any Turkic language.

turkey (ˈtɜːkɪ) n., pl. **-keys** or **-key.** 1. a large bird of North America bred for its flesh. 2. U.S. & Canad. informal. something, esp. a theatrical production, that fails. 3. **cold turkey.** Slang. a method of curing drug addiction by abrupt withdrawal of all doses. 4. **talk turkey.** Informal, chiefly U.S. & Canad. to discuss, esp. business, frankly and practically.

turkey cock n. 1. a male turkey. 2. an arrogant person.

Turkic (ˈtɜːkɪk) n. a family of Asian languages including Turkish and Tatar.

Turkish (ˈtɜːkɪʃ) adj. 1. of Turkey, its people, or their language. ~n. 2. the official language of Turkey.

Turkish bath n. 1. a type of bath in which the bather sweats freely in a steam room, is then washed, often massaged, and has a cold plunge or shower. 2. (sometimes pl.) an establishment for such baths.

Turkish coffee n. very strong black coffee.

Turkish delight n. a jelly-like sweet flavoured with flower essences, usually cut into cubes and covered in icing sugar.

turmeric (ˈtɜːmərɪk) n. 1. a tropical Asian plant with yellow flowers and an aromatic underground stem. 2. the powdered stem of this plant, used as a flavouring and as a yellow dye.

turmoil (ˈtɜːmɔɪl) n. a violent or confused state; agitation.

turn (tɜːn) vb. 1. to move around an axis: to turn a knob. 2. to change or cause to change position by moving: he turned the chair to face the light. 3. to change or cause to change in course, direction, etc.: turn right at the end of the road. 4. to go round (a corner, etc.). 5. to assume or cause to assume a curved or folded form: the road turns here. 6. to reverse or cause to reverse position: turn the page. 7. to

perform or do by a rotating movement: to turn a somersault. 8. to shape (wood, metal, etc.) on a lathe. 9. (foll. by into or to) to change or convert or be changed or converted: to turn base metals into gold. 10. (foll. by into) to change or cause to change in nature, character, etc.: the frog turned into a prince. 11. to change so as to become: he turned nasty. 12. to cause (foliage, etc.) to change colour or (of foliage, etc.) to change colour. 13. to cause (milk) to become sour or (of milk) to become sour. 14. to change or cause to change in subject, trend, etc.: the conversation turned to fishing. 15. to direct or apply or be directed or applied: he turned his attention to the problem. 16. (foll. by to) to appeal or apply to for help, advice, etc. 17. to reach, pass, or progress beyond in age, time, etc.: she has just turned twenty. 18. to cause or allow to go: to turn an animal loose. 19. to affect or be affected with nausea or giddiness: it made my stomach turn. 20. to translate into another language. 21. (usually foll. by against or from) to transfer or reverse (one's loyalties, affections, etc.). 22. **turn someone's head.** to affect someone mentally or emotionally. ~n. 23. a turning or being turned. 24. a movement of complete or partial rotation. 25. a change of direction or position. 26. direction or drift: his thoughts took a new turn. 27. same as **turning** (sense 1). 28. the right or opportunity to do something in an agreed order or succession: now it's George's turn. 29. a change in nature, condition, etc.: a turn for the worse. 30. a period of action, work, etc. 31. a short walk, ride, or excursion. 32. natural inclination: a speculative turn of mind. 33. distinctive form or style: a neat turn of phrase. 34. a deed that helps or hinders someone: a good turn. 35. a twist, bend, or distortion in shape. 36. Music. a melodic ornament that makes a turn around a note, beginning with the note above, in a variety of sequences. 37. a short theatrical act: a comedy turn. 38. Informal. a shock or surprise: the news gave her quite a turn. 39. **turn and turn about.** one after another; alternately. 40. **to a turn.** to the proper amount; perfectly: cooked to a turn. ~See also **turn down, turn in,** etc. —**ˈturner** n.

turnabout (ˈtɜːnəˌbaʊt) n. 1. the act of turning so as to face a different direction. 2. a reversal of opinion, attitude, etc.

turnbuckle (ˈtɜːnˌbʌkªl) n. an open mechanical sleeve usually having a swivel at one end and a thread at the other to enable a threaded wire or rope to be tightened.

turncoat (ˈtɜːnˌkəʊt) n. a person who deserts one cause or party to join an opposing one.

turn down vb. 1. to reduce (the volume or brightness) of (something). 2. to reject or refuse: *I turned down his invitation.* **3.** to fold down (sheets, etc.).

turn in *vb. Informal.* **1.** to go to bed for the night. **2.** to hand in: *to turn in an essay.* **3.** to give up: *we turned in the game when it started to rain.*

turning ('tɜːnɪŋ) *n.* **1.** a road, river, or path that turns off the main way. **2.** the point where such a way turns off. **3.** the process of turning objects on a lathe. **4.** (*pl.*) the waste produced in turning on a lathe.

turning circle *n.* the smallest circle in which a vehicle can turn.

turning point *n.* a moment when a decisive change occurs.

turnip ('tɜːnɪp) *n.* a vegetable with a large yellow or white edible root.

turnkey ('tɜːn,kiː) *n. Archaic.* a jailer.

turn off *vb.* **1.** to leave (a road or path). **2.** (of a road or path) to deviate from (another road or path). **3.** to cause (something) to stop operating by turning a knob, pushing a button, etc. **4.** *Informal.* to cause (a person) to feel dislike for (something): *this music turns me off.* ~*n.* **turn-off. 5.** a road or other way branching off from the main thoroughfare. **6.** *Informal.* a person or thing that causes dislike.

turn on *vb.* **1.** to cause (something) to operate by turning a knob, etc. **2.** to become hostile to; retaliate against: *the dog turned on the children.* **3.** *Informal.* to produce suddenly or automatically: *turn on the charm.* **4.** *Slang.* to arouse emotionally or sexually. **5.** to depend or hinge on: *the success of the party turns on you.* ~*n.* **turn-on. 6.** *Slang.* a person or thing that causes emotional or sexual arousal.

turn out *vb.* **1.** to cause (something, esp. a light) to stop operating by or as if by turning a knob, etc. **2.** to produce by an effort or process: *she turned out fifty units per hour.* **3.** to dismiss or expel: *he was turned out of his new home.* **4.** to empty the contents of (something). **5.** to end up; result: *it all turned out well.* **6.** to fit as with clothes: *that woman turns her children out well.* **7.** to assemble or gather: *the crowd turned out for the fair.* **8.** (of a soldier) to parade or to call (a soldier) to parade. ~*n.* **turnout. 9.** the body of people appearing together at a gathering. **10.** the quantity or amount produced. **11.** an array of clothing or equipment.

turn over *vb.* **1.** to change or cause (something) to change position, esp. so as to reverse top and bottom. **2.** to start (an engine), esp. with a starting handle, or (of an engine) to start or function correctly. **3.** to shift or cause to shift position, as by rolling from side to side. **4.** to consider carefully: *he turned over the problem for hours.* **5.** *Slang.* to rob: *this shop has been turned over.* ~*n.* **turnover. 6. a.** the amount of business transacted by a compa-

ny during a specified period. **b.** the rate at which stock in trade is sold and replenished. **7.** a small pastry case filled with fruit or jam. **8.** the number of workers employed by a firm in a given period to replace those who have left.

turnpike ('tɜːn,paɪk) *n.* **1.** *Hist.* a barrier across a road to prevent vehicles or pedestrian passing until a charge (toll) had been paid. **2.** *U.S.* a motorway for use of which a toll is charged.

turnstile ('tɜːn,staɪl) *n.* a mechanical barrier with metal arms that are turned to admit one person at a time.

turntable ('tɜːn,teɪbʰl) *n.* **1.** the circular platform that rotates a gramophone record while it is being played. **2.** a circular platform used for turning locomotives and cars.

turn to *vb.* to set about a task.

turn up *vb.* **1.** to arrive or appear: *she turned up late.* **2.** to find or be found, esp. by accident: *the letter turned up in the drawer.* **3.** to increase the flow, volume, etc., of: *turn up the radio.* ~*n.* **turn-up. 4.** (*often pl.*) *Brit.* the turned-up fold at the bottom of some trouser legs. **5. a turn-up for the book.** *Informal.* an unexpected happening.

turpentine ('tɜːpʰn,taɪn) *n.* **1.** a semisolid mixture of resin and oil obtained from various coniferous trees and used as the main source of commercial turpentine. **2.** a colourless volatile oil distilled from turpentine resin. It is used as a solvent for paints and in medicine. **3.** (*not in technical usage*) any one of a number of thinners for paints and varnishes, consisting of fractions of petroleum.

turpitude ('tɜːpɪ,tjuːd) *n.* depravity; wickedness.

turps (tɜːps) *n.* (*functioning as sing.*) *Brit.* short for **turpentine** (sense 2).

turquoise ('tɜːkwɔɪz, -kwɑːz) *n.* **1.** a greenish-blue gemstone. ~*adj.* **2.** greenish-blue.

turret ('tʌrɪt) *n.* **1.** a small tower that projects from the wall of a building, esp. a castle. **2.** (on a tank or warship) a rotating structure on which weapons are mounted. **3.** (on a machine tool) a turret-like steel structure with tools projecting radially that can be pivoted to bring each tool to bear on the work. —'**turreted** *adj.*

turtle ('tɜːtʰl) *n.* **1.** an aquatic reptile with a flattened shell enclosing the body and flipper-like limbs adapted for swimming. **2. turn turtle.** (of a boat) to capsize.

turtledove ('tɜːtʰl,dʌv) *n.* an Old World dove noted for its soft cooing and devotion to its mate.

turtleneck ('tɜːtʰl,nɛk) *n.* a round high close-fitting neck on a sweater or the sweater itself.

tusk (tʌsk) *n.* a long pointed usually paired

tooth in the elephant, walrus, and certain other mammals. —**tusked** *adj.*

tussle ('tʌs³l) *vb.* **1.** to fight or wrestle in a vigorous way. ~*n.* **2.** a vigorous fight; scuffle.

tussock ('tʌsək) *n.* a dense tuft of vegetation, esp. of grass. —**'tussocky** *adj.*

tut (tʌt) *interj., n., vb.* **tutting, tutted.** short for **tut-tut.**

tutelage ('tjuːtɪlɪdʒ) *n.* **1.** the act or office of a guardian or tutor. **2.** instruction or guidance, esp. by a tutor. **3.** the condition of being supervised by a guardian or tutor.

tutelary ('tjuːtɪlərɪ) *adj.* **1.** invested with the role of guardian or protector. **2.** of a guardian.

tutor ('tjuːtə) *n.* **1.** a teacher, usually instructing individual pupils. **2.** (at a college or university) a member of staff responsible for the teaching and supervision of a certain number of students. ~*vb.* **3.** to act as a tutor to (someone). —**'tutorship** *n.*

tutorial (tjuː'tɔːrɪəl) *n.* **1.** a period of intensive tuition given by a tutor to an individual student or to a small group of students. ~*adj.* **2.** of or relating to a tutor.

tutti ('tutɪ) *adj., adv. Music.* to be performed by the whole orchestra, choir, etc.

tutti-frutti ('tuːtɪ'fruːtɪ) *n., pl.* **-fruttis.** an ice cream or other sweet food containing small pieces of candied or fresh fruits.

tut-tut ('tʌt'tʌt) *interj.* **1.** an exclamation of mild reprimand, disapproval, or surprise. ~*vb.* **-tutting, -tutted. 2.** to express disapproval by the exclamation of "tut-tut". ~*n.* **3.** the act of tut-tutting.

tutu ('tuːtuː) *n.* a very short skirt worn by ballerinas, made of projecting layers of stiffened material.

tu-whit tu-whoo (tə'wɪt tə'wuː) *interj.* an imitation of the sound made by an owl.

tuxedo (tʌk'siːdəʊ) *n., pl.* **-dos.** *U.S. & Canad.* a dinner jacket.

TV television.

TVEI technical and vocational educational initiative: a national educational scheme in which pupils gain practical experience in technology and industry, often through work placement.

twaddle ('twɒd³l) *n.* **1.** silly, trivial, or pretentious talk or writing. ~*vb.* **2.** to talk or write in a silly or pretentious way.

twain (tweɪn) *det., n. Archaic.* two.

twang (twæŋ) *n.* **1.** a sharp ringing sound produced by or as if by the plucking of a taut string. **2.** the act of plucking a string to produce such a sound. **3.** a strongly nasal quality in a person's speech. ~*vb.* **4.** to make or cause to make a twang: *to twang a guitar.* —**'twangy** *adj.*

twat (twæt, twɒt) *n. Taboo slang.* **1.** the female genitals. **2.** a foolish person.

tweak (twiːk) *vb.* **1.** to twist or pinch with

a sharp or sudden movement: *to tweak someone's nose.* ~*n.* **2.** a tweaking.

twee (twiː) *adj. Brit. informal.* excessively sentimental, sweet, or pretty.

tweed (twiːd) *n.* **1.** a thick woollen cloth produced originally in Scotland. **2.** (*pl.*) clothes made of this.

tweedy ('twiːdɪ) *adj.* **tweedier, tweediest. 1.** of, made of, or resembling tweed. **2.** showing a fondness for a hearty outdoor life, usually associated with wearers of tweeds.

tweet (twiːt) *interj.* **1.** an imitation of the thin chirping sound made by small birds. ~*vb.* **2.** to make this sound.

tweeter ('twiːtə) *n.* a loudspeaker used in high-fidelity systems for the reproduction of high audio frequencies.

tweezers ('twiːzəz) *pl. n.* a small pincer-like instrument used for such tasks as handling small objects or plucking out hairs.

Twelfth Day *n.* Jan. 6, the twelfth day after Christmas and the feast of the Epiphany.

twelfth man *n.* a reserve player in a cricket team.

Twelfth Night *n.* **a.** the evening of Jan 5, the eve of the Twelfth Day. **b.** the evening of Twelfth Day itself.

twelve (twelv) *n.* **1.** the cardinal number that is the sum of ten and two. **2.** a numeral, 12, XII, representing this number. **3.** something representing or consisting of twelve units. ~*det.* **4.** amounting to twelve. —**twelfth** *adj., n.*

twelve-tone *adj.* of or denoting the type of serial music which uses as musical material a tone row formed by the 12 semitones of the chromatic scale.

twenty ('twentɪ) *n., pl.* **-ties. 1.** the cardinal number that is the product of ten and two. **2.** a numeral, 20, XX, representing this number. **3.** something representing or consisting of twenty units. ~*det.* **4.** amounting to twenty. —**'twentieth** *adj., n.*

twerp *or* **twirp** (twɜːp) *n. Informal.* a silly, weak-minded, or contemptible person.

twice (twaɪs) *adv.* **1.** two times; on two occasions or in two cases. **2.** double in degree or quantity: *twice as long.*

twiddle ('twɪd³l) *vb.* **1.** to turn, twirl, or fiddle (with), often in an idle way: *she twiddled with a pencil.* **2. twiddle one's thumbs.** to rotate one's thumbs around one another, when inactive, waiting, or bored. ~*n.* **3.** an act or instance of twiddling.

twig¹ (twɪg) *n.* a small branch or shoot of a tree. —**'twiggy** *adj.*

twig² (twɪg) *vb.* **twigging, twigged.** *Brit. informal.* to realize or understand (something): *he hasn't twigged yet.*

twilight ('twaɪˌlaɪt) *n.* **1.** the soft dim light that occurs when the sun is just below the horizon, esp. following sunset. **2.** the period in which this light occurs. **3.** any faint light. **4.** a period in which strength, importance, etc., is gradually declining. **5.** (*modifier*) of or relating to twilight; dim. —**twilit** ('twaɪˌlɪt) *adj.*

twill (twɪl) *adj.* **1.** (in textiles) of a weave in which the yarns are worked to produce an effect of parallel diagonal lines or ribs. ~*n.* **2.** any fabric so woven.

twin (twɪn) *n.* **1.** either of two persons or animals conceived at the same time. **2.** either of two persons or things that are identical or very similar. ~*vb.* **twinning, twinned. 3.** to pair or be paired together. **4.** to bear twins.

twin bed *n.* one of a pair of matching single beds.

twine (twaɪn) *n.* **1.** string made by twisting fibres of hemp, cotton, etc., together. **2.** a twist or coil. ~*vb.* **3.** to twist together; interweave: *she twined the wicker to make a basket.* **4.** to form by or as if by twining: *to twine a garland.* **5.** (often foll. by *around*) to wind or cause to wind, esp. in spirals: *the creeper twines around the tree.*

twin-engined *adj.* (of an aeroplane) having two engines.

twinge (twɪndʒ) *n.* **1.** a sudden brief darting or stabbing pain. **2.** a sharp emotional pang: *a twinge of guilt.*

twinkle ('twɪŋkᵊl) *vb.* **1.** to shine brightly and intermittently; sparkle. **2.** (of the eyes) to sparkle, esp. with amusement or delight. ~*n.* **3.** a flickering brightness; sparkle. **4.** an instant.

twinkling ('twɪŋklɪŋ) *n.* **in the twinkling of an eye.** in a very short time; moment.

twinset ('twɪnˌsɛt) *n. Brit.* a matching jumper and cardigan.

twirl (twɜːl) *vb.* **1.** to move around rapidly and repeatedly in a circle. **2.** to twist, wind, or twiddle, often idly: *she twirled her hair around her finger.* ~*n.* **3.** a whirl or twist. **4.** a written flourish.

twist (twɪst) *vb.* **1.** to cause (one end or part) to turn or (of one end or part) to turn in the opposite direction from another. **2.** to distort or be distorted: *a twisted smile.* **3.** to wind or twine: *to twist flowers into a wreath.* **4.** to force or be forced out of the natural form or position: *to twist one's ankle.* **5.** to change the meaning of; pervert: *she twisted the statement.* **6.** to revolve; rotate. **7.** to wrench with a turning action: *to twist the top off a bottle.* **8.** to follow a winding course. **9.** to dance the twist. **10. twist someone's arm.** to persuade or coerce someone. ~*n.* **11.** a twisting. **12.** something formed by or as if by twisting. **13.** a decisive change of direction, aim, meaning, or character. **14.** (in a story, play, or film) an unexpected event, revelation, etc. **15.** a bend: *a twist in the road.* **16.** a distortion of the original shape or form. **17.** a jerky pull, wrench, or turn.

18. the twist. a dance popular in the 1960s, in which dancers vigorously twist the hips. **19. round the twist.** *Brit. slang.* mad; eccentric.

twister ('twɪstə) *n. Brit.* a swindling or dishonest person.

twit[1] (twɪt) *vb.* **twitting, twitted.** to tease, taunt, or reproach (someone) often in jest.

twit[2] (twɪt) *n. Informal, chiefly Brit.* a foolish or stupid person; idiot.

twitch (twɪtʃ) *vb.* **1.** (of a person or part of a person's body) to move in a jerky spasmodic way. **2.** to pull (something) with a quick jerky movement. ~*n.* **3.** a sharp jerking movement, esp. one caused by a nervous condition.

twitter ('twɪtə) *vb.* **1.** (esp. of a bird) to utter a succession of chirping sounds. **2.** to talk rapidly and tremulously. **3.** to utter in a chirping way. ~*n.* **4.** the act or sound of twittering. **5. in a twitter.** in a state of nervous excitement. —'**twittery** *adj.*

two (tuː) *n.* **1.** the cardinal number that is the sum of one and one. **2.** a numeral, 2, II, representing this number. **3.** something representing or consisting of two units. **4. in two.** in or into two parts. **5. put two and two together.** to reach an obvious conclusion by considering the evidence available. **6. that makes two of us.** the same applies to me. ~*det.* **7.** amounting to two.

two-edged *adj.* **1.** (of a knife, saw, etc.) having two cutting edges. **2.** (esp. of a remark) having two interpretations, such as *she looks nice when she smiles.*

two-faced *adj.* deceitful; hypocritical.

twofold ('tuːˌfəʊld) *adj.* **1.** equal to twice as many or twice as much. **2.** composed of two parts. ~*adv.* **3.** doubly.

two-handed *adj.* **1.** requiring the use of both hands. **2.** requiring the participation of two people.

twopence *or* **tuppence** ('tʌpəns) *n. Brit.* **1.** the sum of two pennies. **2.** something of little value: *not care twopence.*

twopenny *or* **tuppenny** ('tʌpənɪ) *adj. Chiefly Brit.* **1.** cheap or tawdry. **2.** worth or costing two pence. **3. not care a twopenny damn.** to not care at all.

two-piece *adj.* **1.** consisting of two separate parts, usually matching, as of a garment. ~*n.* **2.** such an outfit.

two-ply *adj.* **1.** made of two thicknesses, layers, or strands. ~*n., pl.* **-plies. 2.** a two-ply wood, knitting yarn, etc.

two-sided *adj.* **1.** having two sides or aspects. **2.** controversial; debatable: *a two-sided argument.*

twosome ('tuːsəm) *n.* two together, esp. two people.

two-step *n.* **1.** an old-time dance in duple time. **2.** a piece of music for this dance.

two-stroke *adj.* of an internal-combustion engine whose piston makes two strokes for every explosion.

two-time vb. Informal. to deceive (someone, esp. a lover) by carrying on a relationship with someone else. —,**two-'timer** n.

two-way adj. **1.** moving, permitting movement, or operating in either of two opposite directions: two-way traffic. **2.** involving reciprocal obligation or mutual action: a two-way cultural exchange. **3.** (of a radio, telephone, etc.) allowing communications in two directions using both transmitting and receiving equipment.

TX Texas.

tycoon (tai'ku:n) n. a businessman of great wealth and power.

tyke or **tike** (taik) n. **1.** Informal. a small or cheeky child. **2.** Brit. dialect. a rough ill-mannered person.

tympani ('timpəni) pl. n. same as **timpani**.

tympanic membrane n. same as **eardrum**.

tympanum ('timpənəm) n., pl. -**nums** or -**na** (-nə). **1. a.** the cavity of the middle ear. **b.** same as **tympanic membrane**. **2.** Archit. **a.** the recessed, esp. triangular, space bounded by the cornices of a pediment. **b.** the recessed space bounded by an arch and the lintel of a doorway or window below it. **3.** Music. a drum or drumhead. —**tympanic** (tim'pænik) adj.

Tynwald ('tinwəld, 'tain-) n. **the.** the Parliament of the Isle of Man.

type (taip) n. **1.** a kind, class, or category, the constituents of which share similar characteristics. **2.** a subdivision of a particular class; sort: what type of shampoo do you use? **3.** the general form, plan, or design distinguishing a particular group. **4.** Informal. a person, esp. of a specified kind: he's a strange type. **5.** a small metal or sometimes wooden block, bearing a letter or character on its upper surface for use in printing. **6.** characters printed from type; print. ~vb. **7.** to write (copy) using a typewriter or word processor. **8.** to be a symbol of; typify. **9.** to decide the type of.

typecast ('taip,kɑːst) vb. -**casting**, -**cast**. to cast (an actor or actress) in the same kind of role continually.

typeface ('taip,feis) n. same as **face** (sense 10).

typescript ('taip,skript) n. any typewritten document.

typeset ('taip,set) vb. -**setting**, -**set**. Printing. to set (textual matter) in type.

typesetter ('taip,setə) n. a person who sets type; compositor.

typewriter ('taip,raitə) n. a keyboard machine for writing mechanically in characters resembling print.

typhoid ('taifɔid) Pathol. ~adj. **1.** resembling typhus. ~n. **2.** short for **typhoid fever**.

typhoid fever n. an acute infectious disease characterized by high fever, spots, abdominal pain, etc. It is spread by contaminated food or water.

typhoon (tai'fu:n) n. a violent tropical storm, esp. in the China Seas and W Pacific.

typhus ('taifəs) n. an acute infectious disease transmitted by lice or mites and characterized by high fever, skin rash, and severe headache.

typical ('tipik³l) adj. **1.** being or serving as a representative example of a particular type; characteristic. **2.** considered to be an example of some undesirable trait: that is typical of you! **3.** of or relating to a representative specimen or type. —'**typically** adv.

typify ('tipi,fai) vb. -**fying**, -**fied**. **1.** to be typical of; characterize. **2.** to symbolize or represent completely, by or as if by a type.

typist ('taipist) n. a person who types, esp. for a living.

typography (tai'pɒgrəfi) n. **1.** the art, craft, or process of composing type and printing from it. **2.** the planning, selection, and setting of type for a printed work. —**typographical** (,taipə'græfik³l) adj. —,**typo'graphically** adv.

tyrannical (ti'rænik³l) adj. characteristic of a tyrant; oppressive.

tyrannize or -**ise** ('tirə,naiz) vb. to rule or exercise power (over) in a cruel or oppressive manner.

tyrannosaur (ti'rænə,sɔː) n. a large two-footed dinosaur common in North America in Cretaceous times.

tyranny ('tirəni) n., pl. -**nies**. **1. a.** government by a tyrant. **b.** oppressive and unjust government by more than one person. **2.** arbitrary or unreasonable behaviour or use of authority. **3.** a tyrannical act. —'**tyrannous** adj.

tyrant ('tairənt) n. **1.** a person who governs oppressively, unjustly, and arbitrarily. **2.** any person who exercises authority in a tyrannical manner.

tyre or U.S. **tire** ('taiə) n. a usually inflated rubber ring placed over the rim of a wheel of a road vehicle to grip the road.

Tyrian ('tiriən) n. **1.** a person from ancient Tyre, a port in S Lebanon and centre of ancient Phoenician culture. ~adj. **2.** of or relating to ancient Tyre.

tyro or **tiro** ('tairəu) n., pl. -**ros**. a novice or beginner.

tzar (zɑː) n. same as **tsar**.

tzetze fly ('tsetsi) n. same as **tsetse fly**.

U

u or **U** (juː) *n., pl.* **u's, U's,** *or* **Us.** **1.** the 21st letter of the English alphabet. **2.** something shaped like a U.

U **1.** united. **2.** unionist. **3.** university. **4.** (in Britain) universal (used to describe a film certified as suitable for viewing by anyone). **5.** *Chem.* uranium. ~*adj.* **6.** *Brit. informal.* (of language or behaviour) characteristic of the upper class.

UB40 *n.* (in Britain) **1.** a registration card issued to an unemployed person. **2.** *Informal.* a person registered as unemployed.

ubiquitous (juːˈbɪkwɪtəs) *adj.* being or seeming to be everywhere at once.

U-boat *n.* a German submarine.

u.c. *Printing.* upper case.

UCCA (ˈʌkə) (in Britain) Universities Central Council on Admissions.

udder (ˈʌdə) *n.* the large baglike milk-producing gland of cows, sheep, or goats, with two or more teats.

UDI Unilateral Declaration of Independence.

UEFA (juːˈeɪfə, ˈjuːfə) Union of European Football Associations.

UFO (ˌjuː ɛf ˈəʊ, ˈjuːfəʊ) unidentified flying object.

ugh (ʊx, ʊh, ʌx) *interj.* an exclamation of disgust, annoyance, or dislike.

ugli (ˈʌglɪ) *n., pl.* **-lis** *or* **-lies.** a yellow citrus fruit: a cross between a tangerine, grapefruit, and orange.

ugly (ˈʌglɪ) *adj.* **uglier, ugliest. 1.** of unpleasant appearance. **2.** repulsive or displeasing: *war is ugly.* **3.** ominous or menacing: *an ugly situation.* **4.** bad-tempered or sullen: *an ugly mood.* —**ˈugliness** *n.*

ugly duckling *n.* a person or thing, initially ugly or unpromising, that becomes beautiful or admirable.

UHF *Radio.* ultrahigh frequency.

UHT ultra-heat-treated (milk or cream).

UK United Kingdom.

ukase (juːˈkeɪz) *n.* **1.** (in imperial Russia) an edict of the tsar. **2.** *Rare.* an edict.

Ukrainian (juːˈkreɪnɪən) *adj.* **1.** of the Ukraine, its people, or their language. ~*n.* **2.** the official language of the Ukrainian SSR. **3.** a person from the Ukraine.

ukulele (ˌjuːkəˈleɪlɪ) *n.* a small four-stringed guitar.

ulcer (ˈʌlsə) *n.* an open sore on the surface of the skin or a mucous membrane.

ulcerate (ˈʌlsəˌreɪt) *vb.* to make or become ulcerous. —ˌulceˈration *n.*

ulcerous (ˈʌlsərəs) *adj.* of, like, or characterized by ulcers.

ulna (ˈʌlnə) *n., pl.* **-nae** (-niː) *or* **-nas.** the inner and longer of the two bones of the human forearm or of the forelimb in other vertebrates. —**ˈulnar** *adj.*

ulster (ˈʌlstə) *n.* a man's heavy double-breasted overcoat.

Ulsterman (ˈʌlstəmən) *n., pl.* **-men.** a person from Ulster. —**ˈUlsterˌwoman** *fem. n.*

ult. **1.** ultimate(ly). **2.** ultimo.

ulterior (ʌlˈtɪərɪə) *adj.* lying beyond what is revealed or seen: *ulterior motives.*

ultimate (ˈʌltɪmɪt) *adj.* **1.** final in a series or process: *ultimate success.* **2.** the highest or most significant: *the ultimate goal.* **3.** fundamental or essential. ~*n.* **4.** the highest or most significant thing. —**ˈultimately** *adv.*

ultimatum (ˌʌltɪˈmeɪtəm) *n., pl.* **-tums** *or* **-ta** (-tə). a final communication by a party setting forth conditions on which it insists, as during negotiations.

ultimo (ˈʌltɪˌməʊ) *adv. Now rare except when abbreviated to ult. in formal correspondence.* in or during the previous month: *a letter of the 7th ultimo.*

ultra (ˈʌltrə) *adj.* extreme or immoderate in beliefs or opinions.

ultra- *prefix.* **1.** beyond a specified extent, range, or limit: *ultrasonic.* **2.** extremely: *ultramodern.*

ultraconservative (ˌʌltrəkənˈsɜːvətɪv) *adj.* **1.** highly reactionary. ~*n.* **2.** a reactionary person.

ultrahigh frequency (ˈʌltrəˌhaɪ) *n.* a radio frequency between 3000 and 300 megahertz.

ultramarine (ˌʌltrəməˈriːn) *n.* **1.** a blue pigment originally made from lapis lazuli. ~*adj.* **2.** vivid blue.

ultramodern (ˌʌltrəˈmɒdən) *adj.* extremely modern.

ultramontane (ˌʌltrəmɒnˈteɪn) *adj.* **1.** on the other side of the mountains, usually the Alps, from the speaker or writer. **2.** of a movement in the Roman Catholic Church which favours supreme papal authority. ~*n.* **3.** a person from beyond the Alps. **4.** a member of the ultramontane party of the Roman Catholic Church.

ultrasonic (ˌʌltrəˈsɒnɪk) *adj.* of or producing sound waves with higher frequencies than humans can hear. —ˌultraˈsonically *adv.*

ultrasonics (ˌʌltrəˈsɒnɪks) *n.* (*functioning as sing.*) the branch of physics concerned with ultrasonic waves.

ultrasound (ˌʌltrəˈsaʊnd) *n.* ultrasonic waves, used in echo sounding, medical diagnosis, and therapy.

ultrasound scan *n.* an examination of an internal bodily structure by the use of ultrasonic waves, esp. for diagnosing abnormality in a fetus.

ultraviolet (ˌʌltrəˈvaɪəlɪt) *n.* **1.** the part of the electromagnetic spectrum with wavelengths shorter than light but longer than x-rays. ~*adj.* **2.** of or consisting of radiation lying in the ultraviolet: *ultraviolet radiation.*

ululate (ˈjuːljʊˌleɪt) *vb.* to howl or wail. —ˌuluˈlation *n.*

umbel (ˈʌmbᵊl) *n.* a type of compound flower in which the flowers arise from the same point in the main stem and have stalks of the same length, to give a cluster with the youngest flowers at the centre. —**umbellate** (ˈʌmbɪlɪt, -ˌleɪt) *adj.*

umbelliferous (ˌʌmbɪˈlɪfərəs) *adj.* of or denoting a plant with flowers in umbels, such as fennel, parsley, carrot, or parsnip.

umber (ˈʌmbə) *n.* **1.** a natural brown earth containing ferric oxide together with lime and oxides of aluminium, manganese, and silicon. **2.** a dark brown to greenish-brown colour produced by this pigment. ~*adj.* **3.** of or stained with umber.

umbilical (ʌmˈbɪlɪkᵊl, ˌʌmbɪˈlaɪkᵊl) *adj.* of or like the umbilicus or the umbilical cord.

umbilical cord *n.* the long flexible cord-like structure that connects a fetus with the placenta.

umbilicus (ʌmˈbɪlɪkəs, ˌʌmbɪˈlaɪkəs) *n. Anat.* the navel.

umbra (ˈʌmbrə) *n., pl.* **-brae** (-briː) *or* **-bras.** a shadow, usually the shadow cast by the moon onto the earth during a solar eclipse.

umbrage (ˈʌmbrɪdʒ) *n.* displeasure or resentment; offence (in **give** *or* **take umbrage**).

umbrella (ʌmˈbrɛlə) *n.* **1.** a portable device used for protection against rain, consisting of a light canopy supported on a collapsible metal frame mounted on a central rod. **2.** a protective shield or screen. **3.** anything that has the effect of a protective screen, general cover, or organizing agency: *under the umbrella of the UK air defence.* —um·brella-ˌlike *adj.*

umfazi (ˌʊmˈfɑːʒɪ) *n. S. African.* a Black married woman.

umiak, oomiak, *or* **oomiac** (ˈuːmɪˌæk) *n.* a large open boat made of stretched skins, used by Eskimos.

umlaut (ˈʊmlaʊt) *n.* **1.** the mark (¨) placed over a vowel, esp. in German, indicating change in its sound. **2.** (esp. in Germanic languages) the change of a vowel brought about by the influence of a vowel in the next syllable.

umlungu (ˌʊmˈlʊŋgʊ) *n. S. African.* a White man: used esp. as a term of address.

umpire (ˈʌmpaɪə) *n.* **1.** an official who rules on the playing of a game, as in cricket. ~*vb.* **2.** to act as umpire in (a game).

umpteen (ˈʌmpˈtiːn) *det. Informal.* very many: *umpteen things to do.* —ˈumpˈteenth *n., adj.*

UN United Nations.

un-[1] *prefix.* (*freely used with adjectives, participles, and their derivative adverbs and nouns: less frequently used with certain other nouns*) not; contrary to; opposite of: *uncertain; untidiness; unbelief; untruth.*

un-[2] *prefix forming verbs.* **1.** denoting reversal of an action or state: *uncover; untie.* **2.** denoting removal from, release, or deprivation: *unharness; unthrone.* **3.** (intensifier): *unloose.*

unable (ʌnˈeɪbᵊl) *adj.* (foll. by *to*) lacking the necessary power, ability, or authority to (do something); not able.

unaccountable (ˌʌnəˈkaʊntəbᵊl) *adj.* **1.** that cannot be explained. **2.** extraordinary: *an unaccountable fear of heights.* **3.** (foll. by *to*) not answerable to. —ˌunac·ˈcountably *adv.*

unaccustomed (ˌʌnəˈkʌstəmd) *adj.* **1.** (foll. by *to*) not used to: *unaccustomed to pain.* **2.** not familiar: *his unaccustomed leisure.*

unadopted (ˌʌnəˈdɒptɪd) *adj. Brit.* (of a road) not maintained by a local authority.

unadvised (ˌʌnədˈvaɪzd) *adj.* **1.** rash or unwise. **2.** not having received advice. —**unadvisedly** (ˌʌnədˈvaɪzɪdlɪ) *adv.*

unaffected[1] (ˌʌnəˈfɛktɪd) *adj.* unpretentious, natural, or sincere.

unaffected[2] (ˌʌnəˈfɛktɪd) *adj.* not affected.

unalienable (ʌnˈeɪljənəbᵊl) *adj. Law.* same as **inalienable.**

un-American *adj.* **1.** not in accordance with the aims, ideals, or customs of the U.S. **2.** against the interests of the U.S. —ˌun-Aˈmericanism *n.*

unanimous (juːˈnænɪməs) *adj.* **1.** in complete agreement. **2.** characterized by complete agreement: *a unanimous decision.* —**unanimity** (ˌjuːnəˈnɪmɪtɪ) *n.*

unabashed	unacquainted	unalloyed
unabated	unadorned	unalterable
unabridged	unadulterated	unambiguous
unacceptable	unadventurous	unambitious
unaccompanied	unafraid	unannounced

unapproachable (ˌʌnəˈprəʊtʃəbᵊl) *adj*. discouraging friendliness; aloof.

unarmed (ʌnˈɑːmd) *adj*. without weapons.

unassailable (ˌʌnəˈseɪləbᵊl) *adj*. **1.** not able to be attacked. **2.** undeniable.

unassuming (ˌʌnəˈsjuːmɪŋ) *adj*. modest or unpretentious.

unattached (ˌʌnəˈtætʃt) *adj*. **1.** not connected with any specific body or group. **2.** not engaged or married.

unavailing (ˌʌnəˈveɪlɪŋ) *adj*. useless or futile.

unaware (ˌʌnəˈwɛə) *adj*. **1.** not aware or conscious: *unaware of the time*. ~*adv*. **2.** *Not universally accepted*. same as **unawares**.
Usage. The adjective *unaware* (ignorant) should be distinguished from the adverb *unawares* (by surprise): *they were unaware of the danger; the danger caught them unawares*.

unawares (ˌʌnəˈwɛəz) *adv*. **1.** by surprise: *she caught him unawares*. **2.** without knowing: *he lost it unawares*.
Usage. see **unaware**.

unbalanced (ʌnˈbælənst) *adj*. **1.** lacking balance. **2.** mentally deranged. **3.** biased; one-sided: *unbalanced reporting*.

unbearable (ʌnˈbɛərəbᵊl) *adj*. not able to be endured. —**un'bearably** *adv*.

unbecoming (ˌʌnbɪˈkʌmɪŋ) *adj*. **1.** unattractive or unsuitable: *an unbecoming hat*. **2.** not proper or appropriate to a person or position: *conduct unbecoming to an officer*.

unbeknown (ˌʌnbɪˈnəʊn) *adv*. (foll. by *to*) without the knowledge of (a person): *unbeknown to him she had left the country*. Also (esp. Brit.): **unbeknownst**.

unbelievable (ˌʌnbɪˈliːvəbᵊl) *adj*. unable to be believed. —**unbe'lievably** *adv*.

unbeliever (ˌʌnbɪˈliːvə) *n*. a person who does not believe in a religion.

unbend (ʌnˈbɛnd) *vb*. **-bending, -bent. 1.** to release or be released from the restraints of formality and ceremony: *he did his best to unbend and get to know her relatives*. **2.** *Informal*. to relax (the mind) or (of the mind) to become relaxed. **3.** to straighten out from a bent shape.

unbending (ʌnˈbɛndɪŋ) *adj*. rigid or inflexible: *an unbending rule*.

unbidden (ʌnˈbɪdᵊn) *adj*. not ordered or asked; voluntary or spontaneous: *her tears came unbidden*.

unbind (ʌnˈbaɪnd) *vb*. **-binding, -bound. 1.** to set free from bonds or chains. **2.** to unfasten or untie.

unblushing (ʌnˈblʌʃɪŋ) *adj*. immodest or shameless.

unbolt (ʌnˈbəʊlt) *vb*. to unfasten a bolt of (a door).

unborn (ʌnˈbɔːn) *adj*. **1.** not yet born. **2.** still to come; future: *the unborn world*.

unbosom (ʌnˈbuzəm) *vb*. to relieve (oneself) of (secrets or feelings) by telling someone.

unbounded (ʌnˈbaʊndɪd) *adj*. having no boundaries or limits.

unbowed (ʌnˈbaʊd) *adj*. **1.** not bowed or bent. **2.** unsubdued: *bloody but unbowed*.

unbridled (ʌnˈbraɪdᵊld) *adj*. unrestrained: *unbridled greed*.

unbroken (ʌnˈbrəʊkən) *adj*. **1.** complete or whole. **2.** continuous: *unbroken sunshine*. **3.** (of animals, esp. horses) not tamed. **4.** not disturbed or upset: *unbroken silence*. **5.** (of a record) not improved upon.

unburden (ʌnˈbɜːdᵊn) *vb*. **1.** to remove a burden from. **2.** to relieve (one's mind or oneself) of a worry or trouble by telling someone about it.

uncalled-for (ˌʌnˈkɔːldfɔː) *adj*. unnecessary or unwarranted: *an uncalled-for remark*.

uncanny (ʌnˈkænɪ) *adj*. **1.** weird; mysterious: *an uncanny silence*. **2.** beyond what is normal: *uncanny accuracy*. —**un'cannily** *adv*. —**un'canniness** *n*.

uncared-for (ˌʌnˈkɛədfɔː) *adj*. not cared for; neglected.

unceremonious (ˌʌnsɛrɪˈməʊnɪəs) *adj*. without ceremony; abrupt, rude, or undignified. —ˌuncere'moniously *adv*.

uncertain (ʌnˈsɜːtᵊn) *adj*. **1.** not able to be accurately known or predicted: *the outcome is uncertain*. **2.** not definitely decided: *uncertain plans*. **3.** not to be depended upon: *an uncertain vote*. **4.** changeable: *the weather is uncertain*. —**un'certainty** *n*.

unchristian (ʌnˈkrɪstʃən) *adj*. not in accordance with Christian principles.

uncial (ˈʌnsɪəl) *adj*. **1.** of or written in

unanswerable	unattractive	uncaring
unappealing	unauthorized *or* -ised	unceasing
unappetizing	unavailable	unchallenged
unappreciated	unavoidable	unchangeable
unarguable	unbeatable	unchanged
unashamed	unbiased	uncharacteristic
unasked	unblemished	uncharitable
unassisted	unblinking	uncharted
unattainable	unblock	unchecked
unattended	unbreakable	

letters that resemble modern capitals, as used in Greek and Latin manuscripts of the third to ninth centuries. ~*n*. **2.** an uncial letter or manuscript.

uncircumcised (ʌnˈsɜːkəmˌsaɪzd) *adj*. **1.** not circumcised. **2.** not Jewish; gentile.

uncivil (ʌnˈsɪvəl) *adj*. lacking civility or good manners. —**unˈcivilly** *adv*.

uncivilized *or* **-ised** (ʌnˈsɪvɪˌlaɪzd) *adj*. **1.** (of a tribe or people) not yet civilized. **2.** lacking culture or sophistication.

unclasp (ʌnˈklɑːsp) *vb*. **1.** to unfasten the clasp of (something). **2.** to release one's grip on (an object).

uncle (ˈʌŋkəl) *n*. **1.** a brother of one's father or mother. **2.** the husband of one's aunt. **3.** a child's term of address for a male friend of its parents. **4.** *Slang*. a pawnbroker.

unclean (ʌnˈkliːn) *adj*. lacking moral, spiritual, or physical cleanliness.

Uncle Sam (sæm) *n*. a personification of the government of the United States.

Uncle Tom (tɒm) *n*. *Informal, offensive*. a Black person whose behaviour towards White people is regarded as servile.

unclose (ʌnˈkləʊz) *vb*. **1.** to open or cause to open. **2.** to come or bring to light.

unclothe (ʌnˈkləʊð) *vb*. **-clothing, -clothed** *or* **-clad**. **1.** to take off garments from; strip. **2.** to uncover or lay bare.

uncoil (ʌnˈkɔɪl) *vb*. to unwind or become unwound; untwist.

uncomfortable (ʌnˈkʌmftəbəl) *adj*. **1.** not comfortable. **2.** feeling or causing discomfort. —**unˈcomfortably** *adv*.

uncommitted (ˌʌnkəˈmɪtɪd) *adj*. not bound to a specific opinion, course of action, or cause.

uncommon (ʌnˈkɒmən) *adj*. **1.** beyond normal experience. **2.** in excess of what is normal: *an uncommon liking for honey*.

uncommonly (ʌnˈkɒmənlɪ) *adv*. **1.** in an unusual manner or degree. **2.** extremely: *you're uncommonly friendly*.

uncommunicative (ˌʌnkəˈmjuːnɪkətɪv) *adj*. disinclined to talk or give information.

uncompromising (ʌnˈkɒmprəˌmaɪzɪŋ) *adj*. not prepared to compromise; inflexible.

unconcern (ˌʌnkənˈsɜːn) *n*. apathy or indifference.

unconcerned (ˌʌnkənˈsɜːnd) *adj*. **1.** lacking in concern or involvement. **2.** unworried. —**unconcernedly** (ˌʌnkənˈsɜːnɪdlɪ) *adv*.

unconditional (ˌʌnkənˈdɪʃənəl) *adj*. without conditions or limitations: *unconditional surrender*.

unconscionable (ʌnˈkɒnʃənəbəl) *adj*. **1.** unscrupulous or unprincipled: *an unconscionable liar*. **2.** immoderate or excessive: *unconscionable demands*.

unconscious (ʌnˈkɒnʃəs) *adj*. **1.** lacking normal awareness through the senses; insensible. **2.** not aware of one's actions or behaviour: *unconscious of his mistake*. **3.** not realized or intended: *an unconscious blunder*. **4.** coming from or produced by the unconscious: *unconscious resentment*. ~*n*. **5.** *Psychoanal*. the part of the mind containing instincts, impulses, and ideas that are not available for direct examination. —**unˈconsciously** *adv*.

unconstitutional (ˌʌnkɒnstɪˈtjuːʃənəl) *adj*. at variance with or not permitted by a constitution. —**unconstitutionality** (ˌʌnkɒnstɪˌtjuːʃəˈnælɪtɪ) *n*.

unconventional (ˌʌnkənˈvɛnʃənəl) *adj*. not conforming to accepted rules or standards. —**unconventionality** (ˌʌnkənˌvɛnʃəˈnælɪtɪ) *n*.

uncork (ʌnˈkɔːk) *vb*. **1.** to draw the cork from (a bottle). **2.** to release (emotions).

uncouple (ʌnˈkʌpəl) *vb*. to disconnect or become disconnected.

uncouth (ʌnˈkuːθ) *adj*. lacking in good manners, refinement, or grace.

uncover (ʌnˈkʌvə) *vb*. **1.** to remove the cover or top from. **2.** to reveal or disclose: *to uncover a plot*. **3.** to take off (one's hat or cap) as a mark of respect.

uncrowned (ʌnˈkraʊnd) *adj*. **1.** with powers of or like royalty, but without the title. **2.** not yet crowned.

unction (ˈʌŋkʃən) *n*. **1.** *Chiefly R.C. & Eastern Churches*. the act of anointing with oil in sacramental ceremonies. **2.** oily charm. **3.** an ointment or unguent. **4.** anything soothing.

unctuous (ˈʌŋktjʊəs) *adj*. **1.** affecting an oily charm. **2.** slippery or greasy.

unclaimed	unconnected	uncorroborated
unclassified	unconquered	uncountable
unclear	uncontaminated	uncritical
uncluttered	uncontrollable	uncultured
uncomplaining	uncontroversial	uncurl
uncomplicated	unconvinced	uncut
uncomplimentary	unconvincing	undamaged
uncomprehending	uncooked	undated
unconcealed	uncooperative	
unconfirmed	uncoordinated	

undaunted (ʌnˈdɔːntɪd) *adj.* not put off, discouraged, or beaten.

undeceive (ˌʌndɪˈsiːv) *vb.* to reveal the truth to (someone previously misled or deceived).

undecided (ˌʌndɪˈsaɪdɪd) *adj.* 1. not having made up one's mind. 2. (of an issue or problem) not agreed or decided upon.

undeniable (ˌʌndɪˈnaɪəbᵊl) *adj.* 1. unquestionably true. 2. of unquestionable excellence: *a man of undeniable character.* —ˌundeˈniably *adv.*

under (ˈʌndə) *prep.* 1. directly below; on, to, or beneath the underside or base of: *under one's feet.* 2. less than: *under forty years.* 3. lower in rank than: *under a corporal.* 4. subject to the supervision, control, or influence of: *under the last Government.* 5. subject to (conditions); in (certain circumstances): *under stress.* 6. in (a specified category): *a book under theology.* 7. known by: *under an assumed name.* 8. planted with: *a field under corn.* 9. powered by: *under sail.* ~*adv.* 10. below; to a position underneath.

under- *prefix.* 1. below or beneath: *underarm; underground.* 2. of lesser importance or lower rank: *undersecretary.* 3. insufficient or insufficiently: *underemployed.* 4. indicating secrecy or deception: *underhand.*

underachieve (ˌʌndərəˈtʃiːv) *vb.* to fail to achieve a performance appropriate to one's age or talents. —ˌunderaˈchiever *n.*

underage (ˌʌndərˈeɪdʒ) *adj.* below the required or standard age, usually below the legal age for voting or drinking.

underarm (ˈʌndərˌɑːm) *adj.* 1. *Sport.* denoting a style of throwing, bowling, or serving in which the hand is swung below shoulder level. 2. below the arm. ~*adv.* 3. in an underarm style.

underbelly (ˈʌndəˌbɛlɪ) *n., pl.* -lies. 1. the part of an animal's belly nearest the ground. 2. a vulnerable or unprotected part, aspect, or region.

underbid (ˌʌndəˈbɪd) *vb.* -bidding, -bid. 1. to make a bid lower than that of (others): *I underbid the other dealers.* 2. *Bridge.* to bid (one's hand) at a lower level than the strength of the hand warrants.

undercarriage (ˈʌndəˌkærɪdʒ) *n.* 1. the assembly of wheels, shock absorbers, and struts that supports an aircraft on the ground and enables it to take off and land. 2. the framework supporting the body of a vehicle.

undercharge (ˌʌndəˈtʃɑːdʒ) *vb.* 1. to charge too little for something. 2. to load (a gun or electric circuit) with an inadequate charge.

underclothes (ˈʌndəˌkləʊðz) *pl. n.* same as **underwear.** Also called: **underclothing.**

undercoat (ˈʌndəˌkəʊt) *n.* 1. a coat of paint applied before the top coat. 2. *Zool.* a layer of soft fur beneath the outer fur of animals such as the otter. ~*vb.* 3. to apply an undercoat to (a surface).

undercover (ˌʌndəˈkʌvə) *adj.* done or acting in secret: *undercover operations.*

undercurrent (ˈʌndəˌkʌrənt) *n.* 1. a current that is not apparent at the surface. 2. an underlying opinion or emotion.

undercut *vb.* (ˌʌndəˈkʌt), **-cutting, -cut.** 1. to charge less than (a competitor) in order to obtain trade. 2. to cut away the under part of (something). 3. *Sport.* to hit (a ball) in such a way as to impart backspin. ~*n.* (ˈʌndəˌkʌt). 4. a tenderloin of beef.

underdeveloped (ˌʌndədɪˈvɛləpt) *adj.* 1. immature or undersized. 2. relating to societies lacking the finance, industries, and organization necessary to advance.

underdog (ˈʌndəˌdɒg) *n.* 1. the losing competitor in a fight or contest. 2. a person in adversity or a position of inferiority.

underdone (ˌʌndəˈdʌn) *adj.* insufficiently or lightly cooked.

underemployed (ˌʌndərɪmˈplɔɪd) *adj.* not fully or adequately employed.

underestimate *vb.* (ˌʌndərˈɛstɪˌmeɪt). 1. to make too low an estimate of: *he underestimated the cost.* 2. to think insufficiently highly of: *to underestimate a person.* ~*n.* (ˌʌndərˈɛstɪmɪt). 3. too low an estimate. —ˌunderˌestiˈmation *n.*

underexpose (ˌʌndərɪkˈspəʊz) *vb. Photog.* to expose (a film, plate, or paper) for too short a period or with insufficient light. —ˌunderexˈposure *n.*

underfelt (ˈʌndəˌfɛlt) *n.* thick felt laid under a carpet to increase insulation.

underfoot (ˌʌndəˈfʊt) *adv.* 1. underneath the feet; on the ground. 2. in a position of subjugation. 3. in the way.

undergarment (ˈʌndəˌgɑːmənt) *n.* a garment worn under the outer clothes.

undergo (ˌʌndəˈgəʊ) *vb.* **-going, -went, -gone.** to experience, endure, or sustain: *to undergo a change of feelings.*

undergraduate (ˌʌndəˈgrædjʊɪt) *n.* a person studying in a university for a first degree.

underground *adj.* (ˈʌndəˌgraʊnd), *adv.* (ˌʌndəˈgraʊnd). 1. occurring, situated, used, or going below ground level. 2. secret; hidden: *underground activities.* ~*n.* (ˈʌndəˌgraʊnd). 3. a movement dedicated to

undeclared	undefiled	undemonstrative
undefeated	undemanding	undercook
undefended	undemocratic	underfed

overthrowing a government or occupation forces. **4.** (often preceded by *the*) an electric passenger railway operated in underground tunnels. **5.** (usually preceded by *the*) any avant-garde, experimental, or subversive movement in popular art, films, or music.

undergrowth (ˈʌndəˌɡrəʊθ) *n.* small trees and bushes growing beneath taller trees in a wood or forest.

underhand (ˈʌndəˌhænd) *adj. also* **underhanded. 1.** sly, deceitful, and secretive. **2.** *Sport.* underarm. ~*adv.* **3.** in an underhand manner or style.

underlay *vb.* (ˌʌndəˈleɪ), **-laying, -laid. 1.** to place (something) underneath in order to support or raise. ~*n.* (ˈʌndəˌleɪ). **2.** a lining or support laid underneath something. **3.** felt or rubber laid under a carpet to increase insulation and resilience.

underlie (ˌʌndəˈlaɪ) *vb.* **-lying, -lay, -lain. 1.** to lie or be placed under. **2.** to be the foundation, cause, or basis of: *careful planning underlies all our decisions.*

underline (ˌʌndəˈlaɪn) *vb.* **1.** to put a line under. **2.** to emphasize.

underling (ˈʌndəlɪŋ) *n.* a subordinate.

underlying (ˌʌndəˈlaɪɪŋ) *adj.* **1.** concealed but detectable: *underlying guilt.* **2.** fundamental; basic: *the underlying principle.* **3.** lying under: *the underlying soil.*

undermentioned (ˈʌndəˌmɛnʃənd) *adj.* mentioned below or later.

undermine (ˌʌndəˈmaɪn) *vb.* **1.** to weaken gradually or insidiously: *he undermined her confidence.* **2.** (of the sea or wind) to wear away the base of (cliffs).

underneath (ˌʌndəˈniːθ) *prep., adv.* **1.** under; beneath. ~*adj.* **2.** lower. ~*n.* **3.** a lower part or surface.

undernourished (ˌʌndəˈnʌrɪʃt) *adj.* lacking the food needed for health and growth. —ˌunder'nourishment *n.*

underpants (ˈʌndəˌpænts) *pl. n.* a man's undergarment covering the body from the waist or hips to the thighs.

underpass (ˈʌndəˌpɑːs) *n.* **1.** a section of a road that passes under another road or a railway line. **2.** a subway.

underpay (ˌʌndəˈpeɪ) *vb.* **-paying, -paid.** to pay (someone) insufficiently. —ˌunder'payment *n.*

underpin (ˌʌndəˈpɪn) *vb.* **-pinning, -pinned. 1.** to support from beneath by a prop: *to underpin a wall.* **2.** to give strength or support to: *informal relationships that underpin any community.*

underplay (ˌʌndəˈpleɪ) *vb.* **1.** to achieve (an effect) by deliberate lack of emphasis.

2. *Cards.* to play a lower card deliberately when holding a higher one.

underprivileged (ˌʌndəˈprɪvɪlɪdʒd) *adj.* lacking the rights and advantages of other members of society; deprived.

underproduction (ˌʌndəprəˈdʌkʃən) *n. Commerce.* production below full capacity or below demand.

underrate (ˌʌndəˈreɪt) *vb.* to underestimate. —ˌunder'rated *adj.*

undersea (ˈʌndəˌsiː) *adj., adv.* below the surface of the sea.

underseal (ˈʌndəˌsiːl) *Brit.* ~*n.* **1.** a special coating applied to the underside of a motor vehicle to prevent corrosion. ~*vb.* **2.** to apply such a coating to (a motor vehicle).

undersecretary (ˌʌndəˈsɛkrətrɪ) *n., pl.* **-taries.** a senior civil servant or junior minister in a government department.

undersell (ˌʌndəˈsɛl) *vb.* **-selling, -sold.** to sell at a price lower than that of (another seller).

undersexed (ˌʌndəˈsɛkst) *adj.* having weaker than normal sexual urges.

undershirt (ˈʌndəˌʃɜːt) *n. U.S. & Canad.* a vest.

undershoot (ˌʌndəˈʃuːt) *vb.* **-shooting, -shot.** to land (an aircraft) short of (a runway) or (of an aircraft) to land in this way.

underside (ˈʌndəˌsaɪd) *n.* the bottom or lower surface.

undersigned (ˈʌndəˌsaɪnd) *n.* **1. the.** the person or persons who have signed at the foot of a document, statement, or letter. ~*adj.* **2.** having signed at the foot of a document, statement, or letter.

undersized (ˌʌndəˈsaɪzd) *adj.* of less than usual size.

underskirt (ˈʌndəˌskɜːt) *n.* a skirtlike garment worn under a skirt or dress; petticoat.

understand (ˌʌndəˈstænd) *vb.* **-standing, -stood. 1.** to know and comprehend the nature or meaning of: *I understand you.* **2.** to realize or grasp (something): *he understands your position.* **3.** to assume, infer, or believe: *I understand you are thinking of marrying.* **4.** to know how to translate or read: *can you understand Spanish?* **5.** to be sympathetic to or compatible with: *we understand each other.* —ˌunder'standable *adj.* —ˌunder'standably *adv.*

understanding (ˌʌndəˈstændɪŋ) *n.* **1.** the ability to learn, judge, or make decisions. **2.** personal opinion or interpretation of a subject: *my understanding of your position.* **3.** a mutual agreement, usually an informal or private one. ~*adj.* **4.** sympathetic, tolerant, or wise towards people.

understate (ˌʌndəˈsteɪt) *vb.* **1.** to state

---

underinsured   underpaid   understaffed
undermanned   underpopulated

(something) in restrained terms, often to obtain an ironic effect. **2.** to state that (something, such as a number) is less than it is. —**under'statement** n.

understood (ˌʌndəˈstʊd) vb. **1.** past of **understand.** ~adj. **2.** implied or inferred. **3.** taken for granted.

understudy (ˈʌndəˌstʌdɪ) vb. **-studying, -studied. 1.** to study (a role) so as to be able to replace the usual actor if necessary. **2.** to act as understudy to (an actor). ~n., pl. **-studies. 3.** an actor who studies a part so as to be able to replace the usual actor if necessary. **4.** anyone who is trained to take the place of another if necessary.

undertake (ˌʌndəˈteɪk) vb. **-taking, -took, -taken. 1.** to agree to or commit oneself to (something) or (to do something): to undertake a job. **2.** to promise.

undertaker (ˈʌndəˌteɪkə) n. a person whose profession is the preparation of the dead and the management of funerals.

undertaking (ˈʌndəˌteɪkɪŋ) n. **1.** a task or enterprise. **2.** an agreement to do something. **3.** the business of an undertaker.

undertone (ˈʌndəˌtəʊn) n. **1.** a quiet tone of voice. **2.** an underlying quality or feeling: undertones of dishonesty.

undertow (ˈʌndəˌtəʊ) n. **1.** the seaward undercurrent following the breaking of a wave on the beach. **2.** any strong undercurrent flowing in a different direction from the surface current.

undervalue (ˌʌndəˈvæljuː) vb. **-valuing, -valued.** to value (a person or thing) at less than the true worth or importance.

underwater (ˈʌndəˈwɔːtə) adj. **1.** situated, occurring, or for use under the surface of the water. ~adv. **2.** beneath the surface of the water.

under way adj. **1.** in progress; in operation: the show was under way. **2.** Naut. in motion in the direction headed.

underwear (ˈʌndəˌwɛə) n. clothing worn under the outer garments, usually next to the skin.

underweight (ˌʌndəˈweɪt) adj. weighing less than is average, expected, or healthy.

underwent (ˌʌndəˈwɛnt) vb. the past tense of **undergo.**

underworld (ˈʌndəˌwɜːld) n. **1.** criminals and their associates. **2.** Greek & Roman myth. the regions below the earth's surface regarded as the abode of the dead.

underwrite (ˈʌndəˌraɪt, ˌʌndəˈraɪt) vb. **-writing, -wrote, -written. 1.** to accept financial responsibility for (a commercial project or enterprise). **2.** to sign and issue (an insurance policy) thus accepting liability. **3.** to support. —**under,writer** n.

undesirable (ˌʌndɪˈzaɪərəbʰl) adj. **1.** not desirable or pleasant; objectionable. ~n. **2.** a person considered undesirable.

undies (ˈʌndɪz) pl. n. Informal. women's underwear.

undine (ˈʌndiːn) n. a female water spirit.

undo (ʌnˈduː) vb. **-doing, -did, -done. 1.** to untie, unwrap, or open or become untied, unwrapped, or opened. **2.** to reverse the effects of: all our patient work has been undone. **3.** to cause the downfall of.

undoing (ʌnˈduːɪŋ) n. **1.** ruin; downfall. **2.** the cause of someone's downfall: drink was his undoing.

undone[1] (ʌnˈdʌn) adj. not done or completed; unfinished.

undone[2] (ʌnˈdʌn) adj. **1.** ruined; destroyed. **2.** unfastened; untied.

undoubted (ʌnˈdaʊtɪd) adj. beyond doubt; certain or indisputable. —**un'doubtedly** adv.

undreamed (ʌnˈdriːmd) or **undreamt** (ʌnˈdrɛmt) adj. (often foll. by of) not thought of or imagined.

undress (ʌnˈdrɛs) vb. **1.** to take off clothes from (oneself or another). ~n. **2.** partial or complete nakedness. **3.** informal or ordinary working clothes or uniform. —**un'dressed** adj.

undue (ʌnˈdjuː) adj. excessive or unwarranted: undue pressure.

undulate (ˈʌndjʊˌleɪt) vb. **1.** to move or cause to move in waves. **2.** to have or provide with a wavy form or appearance. —**undu'lation** n.

unduly (ʌnˈdjuːlɪ) adv. excessively.

undying (ʌnˈdaɪɪŋ) adj. unending; eternal.

unearned (ʌnˈɜːnd) adj. **1.** not deserved. **2.** not yet earned.

unearned income n. income from property or investments rather than work.

unearth (ʌnˈɜːθ) vb. **1.** to dig up out of the earth. **2.** to discover by searching.

unearthly (ʌnˈɜːθlɪ) adj. **1.** ghostly; eerie: unearthly screams. **2.** heavenly; sublime: unearthly music. **3.** ridiculous or unreasonable: an unearthly hour. —**un'earthliness** n.

uneasy (ʌnˈiːzɪ) adj. **1.** (of a person) anxious; apprehensive. **2.** (of a condition) precarious: an uneasy truce. **3.** (of a thought

underused	undiluted	undismayed
undeserved	undiminished	undisputed
undetected	undiplomatic	undistinguished
undeterred	undisciplined	undisturbed
undeveloped	undiscovered	undivided
undignified	undisguised	

or feeling) disquieting. **—un'ease** n. **—un-'easily** adv. **—un'easiness** n.

uneatable (ʌn'iːtəbʰl) adj. (of food) so rotten or unattractive as to be unfit to eat. **Usage.** see **inedible**.

uneconomic (ˌʌniːkə'nɒmɪk, ˌʌnɛkə-) adj. not economic; not profitable.

unemployed (ˌʌnɪm'plɔɪd) adj. **1. a.** without paid employment; out of work. **b.** (as collective n.; preceded by the): the unemployed. **2.** not being used; idle.

unemployment (ˌʌnɪm'plɔɪmənt) n. **1.** the condition of being unemployed. **2.** the number of unemployed workers.

unemployment benefit n. (in the British National Insurance scheme) a regular payment to an unemployed person.

unequal (ʌn'iːkwəl) adj. **1.** not equal in quantity, size, rank, or value. **2.** (foll. by to) inadequate for: unequal to the task. **3.** not evenly balanced. **4.** of varying quality; inconsistent. **5.** (of a contest) having competitors of different ability. **—un'equally** adv.

unequalled or U.S. **unequaled** (ʌn'iːkwəld) adj. not equalled; supreme.

unequivocal (ˌʌnɪ'kwɪvəkʰl) adj. not ambiguous; plain. **—ˌune'quivocally** adv.

unerring (ʌn'ɜːrɪŋ) adj. never mistaken; consistently accurate.

UNESCO (juː'nɛskəʊ) United Nations Educational, Scientific, and Cultural Organization.

uneven (ʌn'iːvən) adj. **1.** (of a surface) not level or flat. **2.** not uniform; variable: an uneven performance. **3.** not parallel, straight, or horizontal. **4.** not fairly matched: an uneven race.

uneventful (ˌʌnɪ'vɛntfʊl) adj. ordinary, routine, or quiet. **—ˌune'ventfully** adv.

unexampled (ˌʌnɪg'zɑːmpʰld) adj. without precedent.

unexceptionable (ˌʌnɪk'sɛpʃənəbʰl) adj. beyond criticism or objection.

unexceptional (ˌʌnɪk'sɛpʃənʰl) adj. **1.** usual, ordinary, or normal. **2.** subject to or allowing no exceptions.

unexpected (ˌʌnɪk'spɛktɪd) adj. surprising or unforeseen. **—ˌunex'pectedly** adv.

unfailing (ʌn'feɪlɪŋ) adj. continuous; reliable: unfailing support. **—un'failingly** adv.

unfair (ʌn'fɛə) adj. **1.** unequal or unjust.

2. dishonest or unethical. **—un'fairly** adv. **—un'fairness** n.

unfaithful (ʌn'feɪθfʊl) adj. **1.** not true to a promise or vow. **2.** guilty of adultery. **—un'faithfulness** n.

unfamiliar (ˌʌnfə'mɪljə) adj. **1.** not known; strange: unfamilar surroundings. **2.** (foll. by with) not acquainted: I am unfamiliar with the procedure. **—unfamiliarity** (ˌʌnfəˌmɪlɪ'ærɪtɪ) n.

unfasten (ʌn'fɑːsʰn) vb. to undo, untie, or open or become undone, untied, or opened.

unfathomable (ʌn'fæðəməbʰl) adj. incomprehensible.

unfavourable or U.S. **unfavorable** (ʌn-'feɪvərəbʰl) adj. not favourable; adverse or inauspicious. **—un'favourably** or U.S. **un-'favorably** adv.

unfeeling (ʌn'fiːlɪŋ) adj. without sympathy; callous.

unfettered (ʌn'fɛtəd) adj. not limited or controlled: unfettered monopolies.

unfinished (ʌn'fɪnɪʃt) adj. **1.** incomplete or imperfect. **2.** (of paint) without an applied finish.

unfit (ʌn'fɪt) adj. **1.** (foll. by for) unqualified for or incapable of: unfit for military service. **2.** (often foll. by for) unsuitable: the ground was unfit for football. **3.** in poor physical condition. ~vb. **-fitting, -fitted. 4.** Rare. to make unfit.

unflappable (ʌn'flæpəbʰl) adj. Informal. hard to upset; calm; composed. **—un,flappa'bility** n.

unfledged (ʌn'flɛdʒd) adj. **1.** (of a young bird) not having developed adult feathers. **2.** immature and inexperienced.

unflinching (ʌn'flɪntʃɪŋ) adj. not shrinking from danger or difficulty.

unfold (ʌn'fəʊld) vb. **1.** to open or spread out or be opened or spread out from a folded state. **2.** to reveal or be revealed: the truth unfolds. **3.** to develop or be developed: the story unfolded.

unforthcoming (ˌʌnfɔːθ'kʌmɪŋ) adj. not inclined to speak, explain, or communicate.

unfortunate (ʌn'fɔːtʃənɪt) adj. **1.** causing or attended by misfortune: an unfortunate accident. **2.** unlucky: an unfortunate man. **3.** regrettable or unsuitable: an unfortunate comment. ~n. **4.** an unlucky person. **—un'fortunately** adv.

unfounded (ʌn'faʊndɪd) adj. (of ideas,

uneaten	unenlightened	unfashionable
uneconomical	unenthusiastic	unfeigned
uneducated	unenviable	unforeseen
unelectable	unescorted	unforgettable
unemotional	unethical	unforgivable
unencumbered	unexciting	unforgiving
unending	unexplained	unformed
unendurable	unexpurgated	unfulfilled

fears, or allegations) without good reason; groundless.

unfreeze (ʌnˈfriːz) vb. **-freezing, -froze, -frozen.** **1.** to thaw or cause to thaw. **2.** to relax governmental restrictions on (wages, prices, or credit).

unfriendly (ʌnˈfrɛndlɪ) adj. **-lier, -liest.** not friendly; hostile.

unfrock (ʌnˈfrɒk) vb. to deprive (a person in holy orders) of ecclesiastical status.

unfurl (ʌnˈfɜːl) vb. to unroll or spread out (an umbrella, flag, or sail) or (of an umbrella, flag, or sail) to be unrolled or spread out.

ungainly (ʌnˈɡeɪnlɪ) adj. **-lier, -liest.** lacking grace when moving. **—unˈgainliness** n.

ungodly (ʌnˈɡɒdlɪ) adj. **-lier, -liest.** **1.** wicked; sinful. **2.** Informal. unreasonable; outrageous: an ungodly hour. **—unˈgodliness** n.

ungovernable (ʌnˈɡʌvənəbəl) adj. not able to be disciplined or restrained: an ungovernable temper.

unguarded (ʌnˈɡɑːdɪd) adj. **1.** unprotected. **2.** open; frank: unguarded conversation. **3.** incautious or careless: an unguarded movement.

unguent (ˈʌŋɡwənt) n. an ointment.

ungulate (ˈʌŋɡjʊlɪt, -ˌleɪt) n. a hoofed mammal.

unhallowed (ʌnˈhæləʊd) adj. **1.** not consecrated or holy: unhallowed ground. **2.** sinful.

unhand (ʌnˈhænd) vb. Archaic or literary. to release from one's grasp.

unhappy (ʌnˈhæpɪ) adj. **-pier, -piest.** **1.** sad or depressed. **2.** unfortunate or wretched. **—unˈhappily** adv. **—unˈhappiness** n.

unhealthy (ʌnˈhɛlθɪ) adj. **-healthier, -healthiest.** **1.** characterized by ill health; sick. **2.** of, causing, or due to ill health: an unhealthy pallor. **3.** morbid or unwholesome: an unhealthy interest in death. **4.** Informal. dangerous; risky. **—unˈhealthiness** n.

unheard-of (ʌnˈhɜːdɒv) adj. **1.** without precedent: an unheard-of treatment. **2.** highly offensive: unheard-of behaviour.

unhinge (ʌnˈhɪndʒ) vb. to derange or unbalance (a person or his mind).

unholy (ʌnˈhəʊlɪ) adj. **-lier, -liest.** **1.** immoral or wicked. **2.** Informal. outrageous or unnatural: an unholy alliance. **—unˈholiness** n.

unhook (ʌnˈhʊk) vb. **1.** to remove (something) from a hook. **2.** to unfasten the hooks of (a garment).

unhorse (ʌnˈhɔːs) vb. to knock or throw from a horse.

uni (ˈjuːnɪ) n. Informal. short for **university.**

uni- combining form. of, consisting of, or having only one: unilateral.

unicameral (ˌjuːnɪˈkæmərəl) adj. of or with a single legislative chamber.

UNICEF (ˈjuːnɪˌsɛf) United Nations Children's Fund.

unicellular (ˌjuːnɪˈsɛljʊlə) adj. (of organisms) consisting of a single cell.

unicorn (ˈjuːnɪˌkɔːn) n. an imaginary creature usually depicted as a white horse with one horn growing from its forehead.

unicycle (ˈjuːnɪˌsaɪkəl) n. a one-wheeled vehicle driven by pedals, used in a circus. **—ˈuniˌcyclist** n.

uniform (ˈjuːnɪˌfɔːm) n. **1.** a special identifying set of clothes for the members of an organization, such as soldiers. ~adj. **2.** unvarying: a uniform surface. **3.** alike or like: a line of uniform toys. **—ˌuniˈformity** n. **—ˈuniˌformly** adv.

unify (ˈjuːnɪˌfaɪ) vb. **-fying, -fied.** to make or become one; unite. **—ˌunifiˈcation** n.

unilateral (ˌjuːnɪˈlætərəl) adj. **1.** of, affecting, or occurring on only one side. **2.** involving or done by only one side: unilateral disarmament. **—ˌuniˈlateralism** n.

unimpeachable (ˌʌnɪmˈpiːtʃəbəl) adj. of unquestionable honesty and truth.

uninterested (ʌnˈɪntrɪstɪd) adj. indifferent. Usage. see **disinterested.**

union (ˈjuːnjən) n. **1.** a uniting or being united. **2.** an association or confederation of individuals or groups for a common purpose, usually political. **3.** agreement or harmony. **4.** short for **trade union. 5.** marriage or sexual intercourse. **6.** (often cap.) **a.** an association of students at a university or college formed to look after the students' interests. **b.** the buildings of such an organization. **7.** Maths. a set con-

---

unfurnished	unhurried	uninhibited
ungenerous	unhurt	uninspired
ungracious	unhygienic	uninspiring
ungrammatical	unidentified	unintelligent
ungrateful	unimaginable	unintelligible
unharmed	unimaginative	unintended
unheard	unimpeded	unintentional
unheeded	unimportant	uninteresting
unhelpful	unimpressed	uninterrupted
unheralded	uninformed	uninvited
unhindered	uninhabited	

taining all members of two given sets. **8.** (in 19th-century England) a workhouse maintained by a number of parishes. **9.** (*modifier*) of a trade union.

unionism ('juːnjə,nɪzəm) *n.* **1.** the principles of trade unions. **2.** adherence to the principles of trade unions. —'**unionist** *n.*, *adj.*

Unionist ('juːnjənɪst) *n.* a supporter of union between Britain and Northern Ireland.

unionize *or* **-nise** ('juːnjə,naɪz) *vb.* **1.** to organize (workers) into a trade union. **2.** to subject to the rules of a trade union. —,**unioni'zation** *or* **-ni'sation** *n.*

Union Jack *n.* the national flag of the United Kingdom, combining the crosses of Saint George, Saint Andrew, and Saint Patrick.

union shop *n.* an establishment where nonunion labour is employed only on the condition that such labour joins the union within a specified time period.

unique (juːˈniːk) *adj.* **1.** being the only one of a particular type. **2.** without equal or like. **3.** *Informal.* remarkable. —u'**niquely** *adv.*

Usage. Certain words in English, such as *unique, perfect,* and *simultaneous,* describe absolute states, that is to say, states that cannot be qualified; something is either *unique* or it is *not unique,* but it cannot be, for example, *rather unique.* It is therefore best to avoid the use of comparatives or intensifiers, like *very,* where absolute states are concerned: *that is very exceptional* (not *very unique*); *this one comes nearer to perfection* (not *is more perfect*).

unisex ('juːnɪ,sɛks) *adj.* (of clothing, a hairstyle, or hairdressers) for both sexes.

unisexual (,juːnɪˈsɛksjʊəl) *adj.* **1.** of one sex only. **2.** (of an organism) having either male or female reproductive organs but not both.

unison ('juːnɪsˀn) *n.* **1.** *Music.* identical pitch. **2.** complete agreement: *they acted in unison throughout.*

unit ('juːnɪt) *n.* **1.** a single undivided entity or whole. **2.** a group or individual regarded as a basic element of a larger whole. **3.** a mechanical part that performs a specific function: *a filter unit.* **4.** a complete system or establishment that performs a specific function: *a production unit.* **5.** a subdivision of a military formation. **6.** a standard amount of a physical quantity, such as length or energy, used to express magnitudes of that quantity: *the second is a unit of time.* **7.** the digit or position immediately to the left of the decimal point. **8.** a piece of furniture designed to be fitted with other similar pieces: *kitchen units.* **9.** *Austral. & N.Z.* short for **home unit.**

Unitarian (,juːnɪˈtɛərɪən) *n.* **1.** a person who believes that God is one being and rejects the Trinity. ~*adj.* **2.** of Unitarians or Unitarianism. —,**Uni'taria,nism** *n.*

unitary ('juːnɪtrɪ) *adj.* **1.** of a unit or units. **2.** based on or marked by unity.

unit cost *n.* the actual cost of producing one article.

unite (juːˈnaɪt) *vb.* **1.** to make or become an integrated whole. **2.** to unify or be unified in purpose, action, or beliefs. **3.** to enter or cause to enter into an association or alliance.

united (juːˈnaɪtɪd) *adj.* **1.** produced by two or more persons or things in combination: *a united effort.* **2.** in agreement. **3.** in association or alliance.

United Kingdom *n.* a kingdom of NW Europe, consisting of the island of Great Britain together with Northern Ireland.

United Nations *n.* (*functioning as sing. or pl.*) an international organization of independent states, formed to promote peace and international security.

unit price *n.* the price charged per unit.

unit trust *n. Brit.* an investment trust that issues units for public sale and invests the money in many different businesses.

unity ('juːnɪtɪ) *n., pl.* **-ties. 1.** a being one; oneness. **2.** something complete that is composed of separate parts. **3.** mutual agreement; harmony: *unity of purpose.* **4.** *Maths.* the number or numeral one.

Univ. University.

univalent (,juːnɪˈveɪlənt, juːˈnɪvələnt) *adj.* *Chem.* same as **monovalent.**

universal (,juːnɪˈvɜːsˀl) *adj.* **1.** of or typical of the whole of mankind or of nature. **2.** common to all in a particular group. **3.** applicable to or affecting many individuals, conditions, or cases. **4.** existing everywhere. —**universality** (,juːnɪvɜːˈsælɪtɪ) *n.* —,**uni'versally** *adv.*

universal joint *or* **coupling** *n.* a form of coupling between two rotating shafts allowing freedom of movement in all directions.

universe ('juːnɪ,vɜːs) *n.* **1.** the whole of all existing matter, energy, and space. **2.** the world.

university (,juːnɪˈvɜːsɪtɪ) *n., pl.* **-ties. 1.** an institution of higher education having authority to award degrees. **2.** the buildings, members, staff, or campus of a university.

unjust (ʌnˈdʒʌst) *adj.* not fair or just.

unkempt (ʌnˈkɛmpt) *adj.* **1.** (of the hair) uncombed; dishevelled. **2.** ungroomed; slovenly: *unkempt appearance.*

unkind (ʌnˈkaɪnd) *adj.* lacking kindness; unsympathetic or cruel. —**un'kindly** adv. —**un'kindness** n.

unknown (ʌn'nəʊn) adj. **1.** not known, understood, or recognized. **2.** not famous: an unknown artist. **3. unknown quantity.** a person or thing whose action or effect is unknown or unpredictable. ~n. **4.** an unknown person, quantity, or thing. ~adv. **5. unknown to someone.** without someone being aware: unknown to them he was nearby.

unleaded (ʌn'lɛdɪd) adj. (of petrol) containing less tetraethyl lead, in order to reduce environmental pollution.

unlearn (ʌn'lɜːn) vb. **-learning, -learnt** or **-learned** (-'lɜːnd). to try to forget (something learnt) or to discard (accumulated knowledge).

unlearned (ʌn'lɜːnɪd) adj. ignorant or uneducated.

unlearnt (ʌn'lɜːnt) or **unlearned** (ʌn'lɜːnd) adj. **1.** denoting knowledge or skills innately present rather than learnt. **2.** not learnt or taken notice of: unlearnt lessons.

unleash (ʌn'liːʃ) vb. to release from or as if from a leash.

unleavened (ʌn'lɛvənd) adj. (of bread) made without yeast or leavening.

unless (ʌn'lɛs) conj. except under the circumstances that; except on the condition that: I'll sell it unless you want it.

unlettered (ʌn'lɛtəd) adj. uneducated; illiterate.

unlike (ʌn'laɪk) adj. **1.** dissimilar; different. ~prep. **2.** not like; not typical of: unlike his father he is tall. —**un'likeness** n.

unlikely (ʌn'laɪklɪ) adj. not likely; improbable. —**un'likeliness** n.

unlimited (ʌn'lɪmɪtɪd) adj. **1.** very large in size or amount: unlimited supplies. **2.** not restricted or limited: unlimited power.

unlisted (ʌn'lɪstɪd) adj. **1.** not entered on a list. **2.** (of securities) not quoted on a stock exchange.

unload (ʌn'ləʊd) vb. **1.** to remove (cargo) from (a ship, lorry, or plane). **2.** to give vent to (anxiety or troubles). **3.** to get rid of or dispose of. **4.** to remove the ammunition from (a firearm).

unlock (ʌn'lɒk) vb. **1.** to unfasten (a lock or door). **2.** to release or let loose.

unlooked-for (ˌʌn'lʊktfɔː) adj. unexpected; unforeseen.

unloose (ʌn'luːs) or **unloosen** vb. to set free; release.

unlovely (ʌn'lʌvlɪ) adj. unpleasant in appearance or character.

unlucky (ʌn'lʌkɪ) adj. **1.** characterized by

misfortune: an unlucky chance. **2.** ill-omened; inauspicious: an unlucky date. —**un'luckily** adv.

unmade (ʌn'meɪd) adj. **1.** (of a bed) with the bedclothes not smoothed and tidied. **2.** (of a road) not surfaced with tarmac. **3.** not yet made.

unmake (ʌn'meɪk) vb. **-making, -made. 1.** to undo or destroy. **2.** to depose from office or authority.

unman (ʌn'mæn) vb. **-manning, -manned. 1.** to cause to lose courage or nerve. **2.** to make effeminate.

unmanly (ʌn'mænlɪ) adj. **1.** not masculine or virile. **2.** cowardly or dishonourable.

unmanned (ʌn'mænd) adj. **1.** lacking personnel or crew: an unmanned ship. **2.** (of an aircraft or spacecraft) operated by automatic or remote control.

unmannerly (ʌn'mænəlɪ) adj. lacking manners; discourteous. —**un'mannerliness** n.

unmask (ʌn'mɑːsk) vb. **1.** to remove the mask or disguise from. **2.** to appear or cause to appear in true character.

unmeaning (ʌn'miːnɪŋ) adj. **1.** having no meaning. **2.** showing no intelligence.

unmentionable (ʌn'mɛnʃənəb'l) adj. unsuitable as a topic of conversation.

unmerciful (ʌn'mɜːsɪfʊl) adj. **1.** showing no mercy; relentless. **2.** extreme or excessive. —**un'mercifully** adv.

unmistakable or **unmistakeable** (ˌʌnmɪs'teɪkəb'l) adj. not mistakable; clear or unambiguous. —**ˌunmis'takably** or **ˌunmis'takeably** adv.

unmitigated (ʌn'mɪtɪˌgeɪtɪd) adj. **1.** not diminished in intensity. **2.** total; complete: an unmitigated disaster.

unmoral (ʌn'mɒrəl) adj. outside morality; amoral. —**unmorality** (ˌʌnmɒ'rælɪtɪ) n.

unmuzzle (ʌn'mʌz'l) vb. **1.** to take the muzzle off (a dog). **2.** to free from control or censorship.

unnatural (ʌn'nætʃərəl) adj. **1.** contrary to nature; abnormal. **2.** not in accordance with accepted standards of behaviour: unnatural love. **3.** affected or forced: an unnatural manner. **4.** inhuman; monstrous: an unnatural crime. —**un'naturally** adv.

unnecessary (ʌn'nɛsɪsərɪ) adj. not essential. —**un'necessarily** adv.

unnerve (ʌn'nɜːv) vb. to cause to lose courage, confidence, or self-control.

unnumbered (ʌn'nʌmbəd) adj. **1.** countless; innumerable. **2.** not counted or given a number.

UNO United Nations Organization.

unoccupied (ʌnˈɒkjʊˌpaɪd) *adj.* **1.** (of a building) without occupants. **2.** unemployed or idle. **3.** (of an area or country) not overrun by foreign troops.

unorganized *or* **-nised** (ʌnˈɔːgəˌnaɪzd) *adj.* **1.** not arranged into an organized system. **2.** (of workers) not unionized.

unpack (ʌnˈpæk) *vb.* **1.** to remove the packed contents of (a case). **2.** to take (something) out of a packed container.

unparalleled (ʌnˈpærəˌlɛld) *adj.* not equalled; supreme.

unparliamentary (ˌʌnpɑːləˈmɛntrɪ) *adj.* not consistent with parliamentary procedure or practice.

unperson (ˈʌnpɜːsˀn) *n.* a person whose existence is officially denied or ignored.

unpick (ʌnˈpɪk) *vb.* to undo (the stitches) of (a piece of sewing).

unpin (ʌnˈpɪn) *vb.* **-pinning, -pinned. 1.** to remove a pin or pins from. **2.** to unfasten by removing pins.

unpleasant (ʌnˈplɛzˀnt) *adj.* not pleasant or agreeable. —**unˈpleasantly** *adv.* —**unˈpleasantness** *n.*

unplumbed (ʌnˈplʌmd) *adj.* **1.** not measured. **2.** not understood in depth.

unpopular (ʌnˈpɒpjʊlə) *adj.* not popular with a person or group. —**unpopularity** (ˌʌnpɒpjʊˈlærɪtɪ) *n.*

unpractised *or U.S.* **unpracticed** (ʌnˈpræktɪst) *adj.* without skill or experience.

unprecedented (ʌnˈprɛsɪˌdɛntɪd) *adj.* having no precedent; unparalleled.

unprincipled (ʌnˈprɪnsɪpˀld) *adj.* lacking moral principles; unscrupulous.

unprintable (ʌnˈprɪntəbˀl) *adj.* unsuitable for printing for reasons of obscenity, libel, or indecency.

unprofessional (ˌʌnprəˈfɛʃənˀl) *adj.* **1.** contrary to the accepted code of a profession. **2.** not belonging to a profession.

unputdownable (ˌʌnpʊtˈdaʊnəbˀl) *adj.* (of a book, usually a novel) so gripping as to be read at one sitting.

unqualified (ʌnˈkwɒlɪˌfaɪd) *adj.* **1.** lacking the necessary qualifications. **2.** not modi-

fied: *an unqualified criticism.* **3.** total or complete: *an unqualified success.*

unquestionable (ʌnˈkwɛstʃənəbˀl) *adj.* not to be doubted; indisputable.

unquiet (ʌnˈkwaɪət) *adj. Chiefly literary.* anxious; uneasy.

unquote (ʌnˈkwəʊt) *interj.* an expression used parenthetically to indicate that the preceding quotation is finished.

unravel (ʌnˈrævˀl) *vb.* **-elling, -elled** *or U.S.* **-eling, -eled. 1.** to reduce (something knitted or woven) to separate strands. **2.** to explain or solve: *the mystery was unravelled.* **3.** to become unravelled.

unread (ʌnˈrɛd) *adj.* **1.** (of a book or article) not yet read. **2.** (of a person) having read little.

unreadable (ʌnˈriːdəbˀl) *adj.* **1.** illegible. **2.** too difficult or dull to read.

unready (ʌnˈrɛdɪ) *adj.* **1.** not ready or prepared. **2.** slow to act.

unreal (ʌnˈrɪəl) *adj.* **1.** imaginary or seemingly so: *an unreal situation.* **2.** insincere or artificial. —**unreality** (ˌʌnrɪˈælɪtɪ) *n.*

unreasonable (ʌnˈriːznəbˀl) *adj.* **1.** immoderate: *unreasonable demands.* **2.** refusing to listen to reason. —**unˈreasonably** *adv.*

unreasoning (ʌnˈriːzənɪŋ) *adj.* not controlled by reason; irrational.

unregenerate (ˌʌnrɪˈdʒɛnərɪt) *adj.* **1.** unrepentant; unreformed. **2.** obstinately adhering to one's own views.

unrelenting (ˌʌnrɪˈlɛntɪŋ) *adj.* **1.** refusing to relent or take pity. **2.** not diminishing in determination, effort, or force.

unremitting (ˌʌnrɪˈmɪtɪŋ) *adj.* never slackening or stopping; constant.

unreserved (ˌʌnrɪˈzɜːvd) *adj.* **1.** without reserve; open in manner. **2.** without reservation. **3.** not booked or bookable. —**unreservedly** (ˌʌnrɪˈzɜːvɪdlɪ) *adv.*

unrest (ʌnˈrɛst) *n.* **1.** a rebellious state of discontent. **2.** an uneasy or troubled state.

unrighteous (ʌnˈraɪtʃəs) *adj.* **1.** sinful; wicked. **2.** unfair; unjust.

unripe (ʌnˈraɪp) *adj.* not fully matured.

unofficial	unprepossessing	unrecognizable
unopened	unpretentious	unrelated
unorthodox	unproductive	unreliable
unpaid	unprofitable	unrepentant
unpalatable	unpromising	unrepresentative
unpardonable	unprompted	unrequited
unplanned	unpronounceable	unresolved
unplug	unprotected	unresponsive
unpolished	unprovoked	unrestrained
unpolluted	unpublished	unrestricted
unpredictable	unpunished	unrewarding
unprejudiced	unquestioning	
unprepared	unrealistic	

unrivalled *or U.S.* **unrivaled** (ʌnˈraɪvˀld) *adj.* having no equal; matchless.

unroll (ʌnˈrəʊl) *vb.* **1.** to open out or unwind (something rolled or coiled) or (of something rolled or coiled) to become opened out or unwound. **2.** to make or become visible or apparent.

unruffled (ʌnˈrʌfˀld) *adj.* **1.** unmoved; calm. **2.** still: *the unruffled seas.*

unruly (ʌnˈruːlɪ) *adj.* **-lier, -liest.** given to disobedience or indiscipline. **—unˈruliness** *n.*

unsaddle (ʌnˈsædˀl) *vb.* **1.** to remove the saddle from (a horse). **2.** to unhorse.

unsaid (ʌnˈsɛd) *adj.* not said or expressed.

unsaturated (ʌnˈsætʃəˌreɪtɪd) *adj.* **1.** not saturated. **2.** *Chem.* (of an organic compound) capable of undergoing addition reactions.

unsavoury *or U.S.* **unsavory** (ʌnˈseɪvərɪ) *adj.* objectionable or distasteful.

unsay (ʌnˈseɪ) *vb.* **-saying, -said.** to retract or withdraw (something said).

unscathed (ʌnˈskeɪðd) *adj.* not harmed or injured.

unscramble (ʌnˈskræmbˀl) *vb.* **1.** to resolve from confusion or disorderliness. **2.** to restore (a scrambled message) to an intelligible form. **—unˈscrambler** *n.*

unscrew (ʌnˈskruː) *vb.* **1.** to remove a screw from (an object). **2.** to loosen (a screw or lid) by rotating.

unscrupulous (ʌnˈskruːpjʊləs) *adj.* without scruples; unprincipled.

unseasonable (ʌnˈsiːzənəbˀl) *adj.* **1.** (esp. of the weather) inappropriate for the season. **2.** untimely; inopportune.

unseat (ʌnˈsiːt) *vb.* **1.** to throw or displace from a seat or saddle. **2.** to depose from office or position.

unseeded (ʌnˈsiːdɪd) *adj.* (of a player in a sport) not given a top player's position in the opening rounds of a tournament.

unseemly (ʌnˈsiːmlɪ) *adj.* not in good style or taste. **—unˈseemliness** *n.*

unselfish (ʌnˈsɛlfɪʃ) *adj.* not selfish; generous. **—unˈselfishly** *adv.* **—unˈselfishness** *n.*

unsettle (ʌnˈsɛtˀl) *vb.* **1.** to change or become changed from a fixed or settled condition. **2.** to confuse or agitate (a person or the mind).

unsettled (ʌnˈsɛtˀld) *adj.* **1.** lacking order

or stability: *an unsettled era.* **2.** disturbed and restless: *feeling unsettled.* **3.** constantly changing or moving from place to place: *an unsettled life.* **4.** (of controversy) not resolved. **5.** (of debts or law cases) not disposed of.

unshakable *or* **unshakeable** (ʌnˈʃeɪkəbˀl) *adj.* (of beliefs) utterly firm and unwavering.

unshaken (ʌnˈʃeɪkən) *adj.* (of faith or feelings) not having been weakened.

unsheathe (ʌnˈʃiːð) *vb.* to pull (a weapon) from a sheath.

unsightly (ʌnˈsaɪtlɪ) *adj.* unpleasant to look at; ugly. **—unˈsightliness** *n.*

unskilful *or U.S.* **unskillful** (ʌnˈskɪlfʊl) *adj.* lacking dexterity or proficiency. **—unˈskilfully** *or U.S.* **unˈskillfully** *adv.*

unskilled (ʌnˈskɪld) *adj.* not having or requiring any special skill or training.

unsociable (ʌnˈsəʊʃəbˀl) *adj.* (of a person) disinclined to associate with others.

unsocial (ʌnˈsəʊʃəl) *adj.* **1.** antisocial. **2.** (of the hours of work of a job) falling outside the normal working day.

unsophisticated (ˌʌnsəˈfɪstɪˌkeɪtɪd) *adj.* **1.** lacking experience or worldly wisdom. **2.** lacking refinement or complexity: *an unsophisticated machine.*

unsound (ʌnˈsaʊnd) *adj.* **1.** unhealthy or unstable: *of unsound mind.* **2.** based on faulty ideas: *unsound advice.* **3.** not firm: *unsound foundations.* **4.** not financially reliable: *an unsound enterprise.*

unsparing (ʌnˈspɛərɪŋ) *adj.* **1.** not frugal; lavish. **2.** harsh or severe. **—unˈsparingly** *adv.*

unspeakable (ʌnˈspiːkəbˀl) *adj.* **1.** incapable of expression in words: *unspeakable ecstasy.* **2.** indescribably bad or evil. **3.** not to be uttered: *unspeakable thoughts.* **—unˈspeakably** *adv.*

unstable (ʌnˈsteɪbˀl) *adj.* **1.** lacking stability or firmness. **2.** having abrupt changes of mood or behaviour. **3.** *Chem., physics.* readily decomposing.

unsteady (ʌnˈstɛdɪ) *adj.* **1.** not securely fixed: *an unsteady foothold.* **2.** (of a manner of walking, standing, or holding) shaky or staggering. **—unˈsteadily** *adv.* **—unˈsteadiness** *n.*

unstring (ʌnˈstrɪŋ) *vb.* **-stringing, -strung.** **1.** to remove the strings of. **2.** to remove (beads) from a string.

unsafe	unseen	unsolved
unsaleable	unselfconscious	unspoiled
unsatisfactory	unsentimental	unspoken
unsatisfied	unshaven	unsporting
unsatisfying	unshockable	unstinting
unscheduled	unsigned	unstoppable
unscientific	unsold	
unseeing	unsolicited	

unstructured (ʌnˈstrʌktʃəd) adj. without formal or systematic organization.

unstrung (ʌnˈstrʌŋ) adj. 1. emotionally distressed; unnerved. 2. (of a stringed instrument) with the strings detached.

unstuck (ʌnˈstʌk) adj. 1. freed from being stuck, glued, or fastened. 2. **come unstuck.** to suffer failure or disaster.

unstudied (ʌnˈstʌdɪd) adj. natural; spontaneous: *unstudied grace.*

unsubstantial (ˌʌnsəbˈstænʃəl) adj. 1. lacking weight or firmness. 2. having no material existence.

unsung (ʌnˈsʌŋ) adj. not acclaimed or honoured: *unsung deeds.*

unsuspected (ˌʌnsəˈspɛktɪd) adj. 1. not under suspicion. 2. not known to exist: *unsuspected difficulties.*

unswerving (ʌnˈswɜːvɪŋ) adj. not turning aside; constant.

untangle (ʌnˈtæŋɡəl) vb. to free from tangles or confusion.

untaught (ʌnˈtɔːt) adj. 1. without training or education. 2. acquired without instruction.

unthinkable (ʌnˈθɪŋkəbəl) adj. 1. not to be contemplated; out of the question. 2. unimaginable; inconceivable.

unthinking (ʌnˈθɪŋkɪŋ) adj. 1. thoughtless; inconsiderate. 2. heedless; inadvertent: *it was done in an unthinking moment.* **—unˈthinkingly** adv.

unthrone (ʌnˈθrəʊn) vb. to dethrone.

untidy (ʌnˈtaɪdɪ) adj. **-dier, -diest.** not neat; slovenly. **—unˈtidily** adv. **—unˈtidiness** n.

untie (ʌnˈtaɪ) vb. **-tying, -tied.** 1. to unfasten or free (something that is tied). 2. to free from constraint.

until (ʌnˈtɪl) conj. 1. up to a time that: *I laughed until I cried.* 2. (used with a negative) before (a time or event): *until we change, we can't leave.* ~prep. 3. (often preceded by up) in or throughout the period before: *wait until six.* 4. (used with a negative) before: *he won't come until Friday.* Usage. see till[1].

untimely (ʌnˈtaɪmlɪ) adj. 1. occurring before the expected or normal time: *an untimely death.* 2. inappropriate to the occasion or time: *his joking at the funeral was most untimely.* **—unˈtimeliness** n.

unto (ˈʌntuː) prep. Archaic. to.

untold (ʌnˈtəʊld) adj. 1. incapable of description: *untold suffering.* 2. incalculably great in number or quantity: *untold thousands.* 3. not told.

untouchable (ʌnˈtʌtʃəbəl) adj. 1. above reproach or suspicion. 2. unable to be touched. ~n. 3. a member of the lowest class in India, whose touch was formerly regarded as defiling to the four main castes.

untoward (ˌʌntəˈwɔːd) adj. 1. causing misfortune or annoyance. 2. unfavourable: *untoward circumstances.* 3. out of the ordinary; out of the way: *nothing untoward happened.*

untrue (ʌnˈtruː) adj. 1. incorrect or false. 2. disloyal. 3. diverging from a rule or standard; inaccurate.

untruthful (ʌnˈtruːθfʊl) adj. 1. (of a person) given to lying. 2. diverging from the truth. **—unˈtruthfully** adv.

untutored (ʌnˈtjuːtəd) adj. 1. without formal education. 2. lacking sophistication or refinement.

unused adj. 1. (ʌnˈjuːzd). not being or never having been used. 2. (ʌnˈjuːst). (foll. by to) not accustomed to.

unusual (ʌnˈjuːʒʊəl) adj. uncommon; extraordinary. **—unˈusually** adv.

unutterable (ʌnˈʌtərəbəl) adj. incapable of being expressed in words. **—unˈutterably** adv.

unvarnished (ʌnˈvɑːnɪʃt) adj. not elaborated upon; plain: *the unvarnished truth.*

unveil (ʌnˈveɪl) vb. 1. to remove the cover from in the ceremonial unveiling of a monument. 2. to remove the veil from (one's own or another person's face). 3. to make (something concealed) known or public.

unveiling (ʌnˈveɪlɪŋ) n. 1. a ceremony involving the removal of a veil covering a statue. 2. the presentation of something for the first time.

unvoiced (ʌnˈvɔɪst) adj. 1. not expressed or spoken. 2. Phonetics. voiceless.

unwaged (ʌnˈweɪdʒd) adj. (of a person) not having a paid job.

unwary (ʌnˈwɛərɪ) adj. lacking caution or prudence. **—unˈwarily** adv. **—unˈwariness** n.

unwell (ʌnˈwɛl) adj. not well; ill.

unwept (ʌnˈwɛpt) adj. not wept for or lamented.

---

unsubstantiated	unsympathetic	untroubled
unsuccessful	untamed	untrustworthy
unsuitable	untaxed	unusable
unsure	untenable	unwanted
unsurpassed	untested	unwarranted
unsurprising	untrained	unwavering
unsuspecting	untreated	unwearied
unsweetened	untried	unwelcome

unwholesome (ʌn'həʊlsəm) adj. 1. harmful to the body or mind: an unwholesome climate. 2. morally harmful: unwholesome practices. 3. unhealthy-looking. 4. (of food) of inferior quality.

unwieldy (ʌn'wiːldɪ) adj. too heavy, large, or awkward to be easily handled.

unwilling (ʌn'wɪlɪŋ) adj. 1. reluctant. 2. done or said with reluctance. —**un'willingly** adv. —**un'willingness** n.

unwind (ʌn'waɪnd) vb. -winding, -wound. 1. to slacken, undo, or unravel or cause to slacken, undo, or unravel. 2. to make or become relaxed: he finds it hard to unwind.

unwise (ʌn'waɪz) adj. lacking wisdom or prudence. —**un'wisely** adv.

unwitting (ʌn'wɪtɪŋ) adj. 1. not knowing or conscious. 2. not intentional; inadvertent. —**un'wittingly** adv.

unwonted (ʌn'wəʊntɪd) adj. out of the ordinary; unusual.

unworldly (ʌn'wɜːldlɪ) adj. 1. not concerned with material values or pursuits. 2. lacking sophistication; naive.

unworthy (ʌn'wɜːðɪ) adj. 1. (often foll. by of) not deserving: unworthy of the honour. 2. (often foll. by of) beneath the level considered befitting (to): an unworthy thought. 3. lacking merit or value. 4. undeserved. —**un'worthiness** n.

unwrap (ʌn'ræp) vb. -wrapping, -wrapped. to remove the wrapping from (something) or (of something wrapped) to have the covering removed.

unwritten (ʌn'rɪtˀn) adj. 1. not printed or in writing. 2. operating only through custom: an unwritten law.

unzip (ʌn'zɪp) vb. -zipping, -zipped. to unfasten the zip of (a garment) or (of a zip or a garment with a zip) to become unfastened: her skirt unzipped as she sat down.

up (ʌp) prep. 1. indicating movement to a higher position: go up the stairs. 2. at a higher or further level or position in or on: a shop up the road. ~adv. 3. to an upward, higher, or erect position, usually indicating readiness for an activity: up and about. 4. indicating intensity or completion of an action: he tore up the cheque. 5. to the place referred to or where the speaker is: a man came up to me. 6. a. to a more important place: up to London. b. to a more northerly place: up to Scotland. c. to or at university. 7. above the horizon: the sun is up. 8. appearing for trial: up before the judge. 9. having gained: ten pounds up on the deal. 10. higher in price: tea is up again. 11. all up with someone. Informal. over for or hopeless for someone. 12. something's up. Informal. something strange is happening. 13. up against. a. touching. b. having to cope with: look

what we're up against now. 14. up for. being a candidate or applicant for: he's up for the job. 15. up to. a. occupied with; scheming: she's up to no good. b. dependent upon: the decision is up to you. c. equal to or capable of (something or doing something): are you up to playing in the final? d. as far as: up to his neck in mud. e. as many as: up to two years' credit. f. comparable with: not up to my usual standard. 16. what's up? Informal. a. what is the matter? b. what is happening? ~adj. 17. of a high or higher position. 18. out of bed: aren't you up yet? 19. of or relating to a train going to a more important place: the up platform. ~vb. upping, upped. 20. to increase or raise. 21. (foll. by and with a verb) Informal. to do something suddenly: she upped and married someone else. ~n. 22. a high point: we have our ups and downs. 23. on the up and up. a. trustworthy or honest. b. Brit. on an upward trend: our firm's on the up and up.

up-and-coming adj. promising future success; enterprising.

upbeat ('ʌp,biːt) n. 1. Music. a. an unaccented beat. b. the upward gesture of a conductor's baton indicating this. ~adj. 2. Informal. cheerful; optimistic.

upbraid (ʌp'breɪd) vb. to reproach; censure.

upbringing ('ʌp,brɪŋɪŋ) n. the education of a person during his formative years.

upcountry (ʌp'kʌntrɪ) adj. 1. of or from the interior of a country. ~adv. 2. towards or in the interior of a country.

update (ʌp'deɪt) vb. to bring up to date.

upend (ʌp'end) vb. to turn or set or become turned or set on end.

upfront ('ʌp'frʌnt) adj. 1. open and frank. ~adv., adj. 2. (of money) paid out at the beginning of a business arrangement.

upgrade (ʌp'greɪd) vb. 1. to promote (a person or job) to a higher rank. 2. to raise in value, importance, or esteem.

upheaval (ʌp'hiːvˀl) n. a strong, sudden, or violent disturbance.

uphill ('ʌp'hɪl) adj. 1. sloping or leading upwards. 2. requiring a great deal of effort: an uphill task. ~adv. 3. up a slope.

uphold (ʌp'həʊld) vb. -holding, -held. 1. to maintain or defend against opposition. 2. to give moral support to. —**up'holder** n.

upholster (ʌp'həʊlstə) vb. to fit (chairs or sofas) with padding, springs, and covering. —**up'holsterer** n. —**up'holstery** n.

upkeep ('ʌp,kiːp) n. 1. the act or process of keeping something in good repair. 2. the cost of maintenance.

upland ('ʌplənd) n. 1. an area of high or relatively high ground. ~adj. 2. of or in an upland.

uplift *vb.* (ʌpˈlɪft). **1.** to raise; lift up. **2.** to raise morally or spiritually. *~n.* (ˈʌp-ˌlɪft). **3.** the act, process, or result of lifting up. **4.** the act or process of bettering moral, social, or cultural conditions. **5.** (*modifier*) denoting a bra for lifting and supporting the breasts. —**upˈlifting** *adj.*

up-market *adj.* expensive and of superior quality.

upmost (ˈʌpˌməʊst) *adj.* same as **uppermost**.

upon (əˈpɒn) *prep.* **1.** on. **2.** up and on: *climb upon my knee.*

upper (ˈʌpə) *adj.* **1.** higher or highest in physical position, wealth, rank, or status. **2.** *Geol.* denoting the late part or division of a period or system: *Upper Palaeolithic.* *~n.* **3.** the part of a shoe above the sole. **4.** **on one's uppers.** destitute.

upper-case *adj.* denoting capital letters as used in printed or typed matter.

upper class *n.* **1.** the highest social class; aristocracy. *~adj.* **upper-class.** **2.** of the upper class.

upper crust *n. Informal.* the upper class.

uppercut (ˈʌpəˌkʌt) *n.* a short swinging upward punch delivered to the chin.

upper hand *n.* **the.** the position of control: *he has the upper hand.*

Upper House *n.* one of the two houses of a two-chamber legislature.

uppermost (ˈʌpəˌməʊst) *adj. also* **upmost. 1.** highest in position, power, or importance. *~adv.* **2.** in or into the highest place or position.

uppish (ˈʌpɪʃ) *adj. Brit. informal.* uppity.

uppity (ˈʌpɪtɪ) *adj. Informal.* snobbish, arrogant, or presumptuous.

upright (ˈʌpˌraɪt) *adj.* **1.** vertical or erect. **2.** honest or just. *~adv.* **3.** vertically. *~n.* **4.** a vertical support, such as a post. **5.** short for **upright piano. 6.** the state of being vertical. —ˈup,rightness *n.*

upright piano *n.* a piano which has a rectangular vertical case.

uprising (ˈʌpˌraɪzɪŋ, ʌpˈraɪzɪŋ) *n.* a revolt or rebellion.

uproar (ˈʌpˌrɔː) *n.* a commotion or disturbance characterized by loud noise and confusion.

uproarious (ʌpˈrɔːrɪəs) *adj.* **1.** very funny. **2.** (of laughter) loud and boisterous.

uproot (ʌpˈruːt) *vb.* **1.** to pull up by or as if by the roots. **2.** to displace (a person or people) from native or usual surroundings. **3.** to remove or destroy utterly.

ups and downs *pl. n.* alternating periods of good and bad luck or high and low spirits.

upset *vb.* (ʌpˈsɛt), **-setting, -set. 1.** to tip or be tipped over; overturn or spill. **2.** to disturb the normal state or stability of: *to upset the balance of nature.* **3.** to disturb

mentally or emotionally. **4.** to make physically ill: *alcohol upsets my stomach.* *~n.* (ˈʌpˌsɛt). **5.** an unexpected defeat or reversal, as in a contest or plans. **6.** a disturbance or disorder of the emotions, mind, or body. *~adj.* (ʌpˈsɛt). **7.** overturned. **8.** emotionally or physically disturbed or distressed. —**upˈsetting** *adj.*

upset price *n. Chiefly Scot., U.S., & Canad.* the lowest price acceptable for something that is for sale, usually a house.

upshot (ˈʌpˌʃɒt) *n.* the final result; conclusion; outcome.

upside down (ˌʌpsaɪd ˈdaʊn) *adj.* **1.** turned over completely; inverted. **2.** *Informal.* confused; topsy-turvy. *~adv.* **3.** in an inverted fashion. **4.** in a chaotic manner.

upsides (ˌʌpˈsaɪdz) *adv. Informal, chiefly Brit.* (foll. by *with*) equal or level with, as through revenge.

upstage (ˈʌpˈsteɪdʒ) *adv.* **1.** on, at, or to the rear of the stage. *~adj.* **2.** of the back half of the stage. **3.** *Informal.* haughty. *~vb.* **4.** to move upstage of (another actor), forcing him to turn away from the audience. **5.** *Informal.* to draw attention to oneself from (someone else).

upstairs (ˈʌpˈstɛəz) *adv.* **1.** up the stairs; to or on an upper floor. **2.** *Informal.* to or into a higher rank or office. *~n.* (*functioning as sing. or pl.*) **3.** an upper floor. *~adj.* **4.** situated on an upper floor: *an upstairs room.*

upstanding (ʌpˈstændɪŋ) *adj.* **1.** of good character. **2.** upright and vigorous in build.

upstart (ˈʌpˌstɑːt) *n.* a person who has risen suddenly to a position of power and behaves arrogantly.

upstream (ˈʌpˈstriːm) *adv., adj.* in or towards the higher part of a stream; against the current.

upsurge (ˈʌpˌsɜːdʒ) *n.* a rapid rise or swell.

upswing (ˈʌpˌswɪŋ) *n.* **1.** *Econ.* a recovery period in the trade cycle. **2.** any increase or improvement.

upsy-daisy (ˈʌpsɪˈdeɪzɪ) *or* **upsadaisy** *interj.* an expression of reassurance, when a child stumbles or is being lifted up.

uptake (ˈʌpˌteɪk) *n.* **quick** (*or* **slow**) **on the uptake.** *Informal.* quick (*or* slow) to understand or learn.

upthrust (ˈʌpˌθrʌst) *n.* **1.** an upward push. **2.** *Geol.* a violent upheaval of the earth's surface.

uptight (ʌpˈtaɪt) *adj. Informal.* **1.** nervously tense, irritable, or angry. **2.** unable to express one's feelings.

up-to-date *adj.* modern or fashionable: *an up-to-date magazine.*

upturn *n.* (ˈʌpˌtɜːn). **1.** an upward trend or improvement. **2.** an upheaval. *~vb.* (ʌpˈtɜːn). **3.** to turn or cause to turn over or upside down.

upward (ˈʌpwəd) *adj.* **1.** directed or moving towards a higher place or level. ~*adv. also* **upwards. 2.** from a lower to a higher place, level, or condition.

upward mobility *n.* movement from a lower to a higher economic and social status.

upwind (ˈʌpˈwɪnd) *adv.* **1.** into or against the wind. **2.** towards or on the side where the wind is blowing. ~*adj.* **3.** going against the wind. **4.** on the windward side.

uranium (jʊˈreɪnɪəm) *n. Chem.* a radioactive silvery-white metallic element of the actinide series. It is used chiefly as a source of nuclear energy by fission of the radioisotope **uranium-235.** Symbol: U

Uranus (jʊˈreɪnəs, ˈjʊərənəs) *n.* **1.** *Greek myth.* a god; the personification of the sky. **2.** the seventh planet from the sun.

urban (ˈɜːbⁿn) *adj.* of or living in a city or town.

urban district *n.* formerly, an urban division of an administrative county with an elected council.

urbane (ɜːˈbeɪn) *adj.* characterized by courtesy, elegance, and sophistication.

urban guerrilla *n.* a guerrilla who operates in a town or city, engaging in terrorism and kidnapping.

urbanity (ɜːˈbænɪtɪ) *n.* the quality of being urbane.

urbanize *or* **-nise** (ˈɜːbəˌnaɪz) *vb.* (*usually passive*) to make (a rural area) more industrialized and urban. —ˌurbaniˈzation *or* -niˈsation *n.*

urban renewal *n.* the process of redeveloping dilapidated or neglected urban areas.

urchin (ˈɜːtʃɪn) *n.* **1.** a mischievous child. **2.** See **sea urchin.**

Urdu (ˈʊəduː, ˈɜː-) *n.* an Indic language of the Indo-European family which is an official language of Pakistan and is also spoken in India. It is closely related to Hindi but the script is primarily Persian.

urea (ˈjʊərɪə) *n.* a white soluble crystalline compound found in urine.

ureter (jʊˈriːtə) *n.* the tube that carries urine from the kidney to the bladder.

urethra (jʊˈriːθrə) *n., pl.* **-thrae** (-θriː) *or* **-thras.** the canal that in most mammals carries urine from the bladder out of the body.

urethritis (ˌjʊərɪˈθraɪtɪs) *n.* inflammation of the urethra.

urge (ɜːdʒ) *n.* **1.** a strong impulse, inner drive, or yearning. ~*vb.* **2.** to plead with or press (someone to do something): *we urged him to go.* **3.** to advocate earnestly and persistently: *to urge the need for safety.* **4.** to force, drive, or hasten onwards: *he urged the horses on.*

urgent (ˈɜːdʒənt) *adj.* **1.** requiring speedy action or attention: *the matter is urgent.* **2.** earnest and persistent. —ˈurgency *n.* —ˈurgently *adv.*

uric (ˈjʊərɪk) *adj.* of or derived from urine.

uric acid *n.* a white odourless crystalline acid present in the blood and urine.

urinal (jʊˈraɪⁿl, ˈjʊərɪ-) *n.* **1.** a sanitary fitting, used by men for urination. **2.** a room containing urinals.

urinary (ˈjʊərɪnərɪ) *adj. Anat.* of urine or the organs that secrete and pass urine.

urinary bladder *n.* a membranous sac that can expand in which urine excreted from the kidneys is stored.

urinate (ˈjʊərɪˌneɪt) *vb.* to excrete urine. —ˌuriˈnation *n.*

urine (ˈjʊərɪn) *n.* the pale yellow fluid excreted by the kidneys, containing waste products from the blood. It is stored in the bladder and discharged through the urethra.

urinogenital (ˌjʊərɪnəʊˈdʒɛnɪtⁿl) *adj.* same as **urogenital.**

urn (ɜːn) *n.* **1.** a vaselike container, usually with a foot and a rounded body. **2.** a vase used as a container for the ashes of the dead. **3.** a large metal container, with a tap, used for making and holding tea or coffee.

urogenital (ˌjʊərəʊˈdʒɛnɪtⁿl) *or* **urinogenital** *adj.* of the urinary and genital organs and their functions. Also: **genitourinary.**

urology (jʊˈrɒlədʒɪ) *n.* the branch of medicine concerned with the urogenital tract and its diseases.

ursine (ˈɜːsaɪn) *adj.* of or like a bear.

us (ʌs) *pl. pron.* (*objective*) **1.** refers to the speaker or writer and another person or other people: *don't hurt us.* **2.** refers to all people or people in general: *this table shows us the tides.* **3.** *Informal.* me: *give us a kiss!* **4.** a formal word for **me,** used by monarchs.

U.S. *or* **US** United States.

USA United States Army.

U.S.A. *or* **USA** United States of America.

usable (ˈjuːzəbⁿl) *adj.* able to be used. —ˌusaˈbility *n.*

usage (ˈjuːsɪdʒ, -zɪdʒ) *n.* **1.** the act or a manner of using; use. **2.** constant use, custom, or habit. **3.** what is actually said in a language.

use *vb.* (juːz). **1.** to put into service or action; employ for a given purpose: *use a spoon to stir with.* **2.** to make a practice of employing: *he uses his brain.* **3.** to behave towards in a particular way, usually selfishly: *he uses people.* **4.** to consume or expend: *the engine uses very little oil.* ~*n.* (juːs). **5.** a using or being used: *worn out through constant use.* **6.** the ability or permission to use. **7.** need or opportunity to use: *I have no use for this paper.* **8.** an instance or manner of using. **9.** usefulness; advantage: *it is of no use to complain.* **10.** custom; habit: *long use has inured him to it.* **11.** the purpose for which something is used. **12. have no use for. a.** to have no need of. **b.** to have a contemptuous dislike for. **13. make use of. a.** to employ; use. **b.** to exploit (a person). ~See also **use up.** —**'user** n.

used (juːzd) adj. second-hand: *used cars.*

used to (juːst) adj. **1.** accustomed to: *I am used to the cold.* ~vb. **2.** (*takes an infinitive or implied infinitive*) used as an auxiliary to express habitual or accustomed actions or states taking place in the past but no longer doing so: *I used to be rich.*

useful ('juːsful) adj. **1.** able to be used advantageously or for several purposes. **2.** *Informal.* commendable or capable: *a useful day's work.* —**'usefully** adv.

useless ('juːslɪs) adj. **1.** having no practical use. **2.** *Informal.* ineffectual, weak, or stupid: *he's useless at history.* —**'uselessly** adv. —**'uselessness** n.

user-friendly adj. easy to familiarize oneself with, understand, and use.

use up vb. to finish (a supply); consume completely.

usher ('ʌʃə) n. **1.** an official who shows people to their seats, as in a church. **2.** a person who acts as doorkeeper in a court of law. **3.** an officer who precedes persons of rank in a procession. ~vb. **4.** to conduct or escort. **5.** (foll. by *in*) to be a precursor or herald of.

usherette (ˌʌʃəˈrɛt) n. a woman assistant in a cinema, who shows people to their seats.

USSR Union of Soviet Socialist Republics.

usual ('juːʒuəl) adj. **1.** of the most normal, frequent, or regular type: *it's the usual thing to do.* ~n. **2.** ordinary or commonplace events: *nothing out of the usual.* **3. as usual.** as happens normally. **4. the usual.** *Informal.* the habitual or usual drink. —**'usually** adv.

usurp (juːˈzɜːp) vb. to seize (a position or power) without authority. —**ˌusurˈpation** n. —**uˈsurper** n.

usury ('juːʒərɪ) n., pl. -ries. **1.** the practice of loaning money at an exorbitant rate of interest. **2.** an unlawfully high rate of interest. —**'usurer** n.

UT Utah.

utensil (juːˈtɛnsəl) n. a tool or container for practical use: *writing utensils.*

uterine ('juːtəˌraɪn) adj. of or affecting the uterus.

uterus ('juːtərəs) n., pl. **uteri** ('juːtəˌraɪ). *Anat.* a hollow muscular organ lying within the pelvic cavity of female mammals, which houses the developing fetus; womb.

utilidor (juːˈtɪlədə; *Canad.* -ˌdɒr) n. *Canad.* above-ground insulated casing for pipes carrying water in permafrost regions.

utilitarian (juːˌtɪlɪˈtɛərɪən) adj. **1.** of utilitarianism. **2.** designed for use rather than beauty. ~n. **3.** an advocate of utilitarianism.

utilitarianism (juːˌtɪlɪˈtɛərɪəˌnɪzəm) n. *Ethics.* the doctrine that right action is that which brings about the greatest good for the greatest number.

utility (juːˈtɪlɪtɪ) n., pl. -ties. **1.** usefulness. **2.** something useful. **3.** a public service, such as water or electricity. ~adj. **4.** designed for use rather than beauty: *utility goods.*

utility room n. a room used for large domestic appliances and equipment.

utility truck n. *Austral. & N.Z.* a small truck with an open body and low sides.

utilize or **-lise** ('juːtɪˌlaɪz) vb. to make practical or worthwhile use of. —**ˌutiliˈzation** or **-liˈsation** n.

utmost ('ʌtˌməʊst) adj. **1.** of the greatest possible degree or amount: *the utmost degree.* **2.** at the furthest limit: *the utmost town on the peninsula.* ~n. **3.** the greatest possible degree or amount: *he tried his utmost.*

Utopia (juːˈtəʊpɪə) n. (*sometimes not cap.*) any real or imaginary society, place, or state considered to be perfect or ideal. —**Uˈtopian** adj.

utricle ('juːtrɪkˀl) n. **1.** *Anat.* the larger of the two parts of the internal ear. **2.** *Bot.* the bladder-like fruit of certain plants.

utter[1] ('ʌtə) vb. **1.** to express (something) audibly: *to utter a growl.* **2.** *Criminal law.* to put (counterfeit money or forged cheques) into circulation.

utter[2] ('ʌtə) adj. total; absolute: *an utter fool.* —**'utterly** adv.

utterance ('ʌtərəns) n. **1.** something uttered. **2.** the act or power of uttering.

uttermost ('ʌtəˌməʊst) adj., n. same as **utmost.**

U-turn n. **1.** a turn, made by a vehicle, in the shape of a U, resulting in a reversal of direction. **2.** a complete change in policy.

UV ultraviolet.

uvula ('juːvjʊlə) n., pl. -las or -lae (-ˌliː). the small fleshy part of the soft palate that hangs in the back of the throat. —**'uvular** adj.

uxorious (ʌkˈsɔːrɪəs) adj. excessively fond of or dependent on one's wife.

V

v *or* **V** (viː) *n., pl.* **v's, V's,** *or* **Vs. 1.** the 22nd letter of the English alphabet. **2.** something shaped like a V.

V 1. *Chem.* vanadium. **2.** volt. **3.** the Roman numeral for five.

v. 1. verb. **2.** verse. **3.** versus. **4.** very. **5.** see. **6.** volume.

VA *or* **Va.** Virginia.

vac (væk) *n. Brit. informal.* short for **vacation.**

vacancy (ˈveɪkənsɪ) *n., pl.* **-cies. 1.** the state of being vacant; emptiness. **2.** an unoccupied job or position: *we have a vacancy in the accounts department.* **3.** an unoccupied room in a hotel or guesthouse: *put up the "No Vacancies" sign.*

vacant (ˈveɪkənt) *adj.* **1.** without any contents; empty. **2.** having no job holder: *a vacant post.* **3.** having no tenant or occupant: *a vacant house.* **4.** suggesting lack of thought or intelligent awareness: *a vacant expression.* **5.** (of time) not allocated to any activity: *a vacant hour in one's day.* —ˈvacantly *adv.*

vacate (vəˈkeɪt) *vb.* **1.** to cause (something) to be empty by departing from it: *to vacate a room.* **2.** to give up (a job or position).

vacation (vəˈkeɪʃən) *n.* **1.** *Chiefly Brit.* a period of the year when the lawcourts or universities are closed. **2.** *U.S. & Canad.* same as **holiday** (sense 1). ~*vb.* **3.** *U.S. & Canad.* to take a holiday.

vaccinate (ˈvæksɪˌneɪt) *vb.* to inoculate (a person) with vaccine so as to produce immunity against a specific disease. —**vaccination** (ˌvæksɪˈneɪʃən) *n.*

vaccine (ˈvæksiːn) *n. Med.* **1.** a suspension of dead or weakened microorganisms for inoculation to produce immunity to a disease. **2.** a preparation of the virus of cowpox inoculated in humans to produce immunity to smallpox.

vacillate (ˈvæsɪˌleɪt) *vb.* to waver in one's opinions; be indecisive. —**vacillation** (ˌvæsɪˈleɪʃən) *n.*

vacuity (vəˈkjuːɪtɪ) *n.* **1.** the state or quality of being vacuous. **2.** (*pl.* **-ties**) an empty space or void. **3.** lack of normal intelligence or awareness.

vacuous (ˈvækjʊəs) *adj.* **1.** empty. **2.** lacking in ideas or intelligence. **3.** suggesting vacancy of mind: *a vacuous gaze.* **4.** indulging in no useful mental or physical activity.

vacuum (ˈvækjʊəm) *n., pl.* **vacuums** *or* **vacua** (ˈvækjʊə). **1.** a region containing no free matter: in technical contexts now often called **free space. 2.** the degree of exhaustion of gas within an enclosed space: *a perfect vacuum.* **3.** a feeling of emptiness: *his death left a vacuum in her life.* **4.** short for **vacuum cleaner.** ~*vb.* **5.** to clean (something) with a vacuum cleaner.

vacuum cleaner *n.* an electrical household appliance used for cleaning carpets, furniture, etc., by suction. —**vacuum cleaning** *n.*

vacuum flask *n.* an insulating flask that has double walls with an evacuated space between them. It is used for keeping drinks at high or low temperatures.

vacuum-packed *adj.* packed in an airtight container in order to maintain freshness.

vacuum tube *or* **valve** *n.* same as **valve** (sense 3).

vade mecum (ˈvɑːdɪ ˈmeɪkʊm) *n.* a handbook carried for immediate use when needed.

vagabond (ˈvægəˌbɒnd) *n.* **1.** a person with no fixed home. **2.** an idle wandering beggar or thief.

vagary (ˈveɪgərɪ, vəˈgɛərɪ) *n., pl.* **-garies.** an erratic notion or action.

vagina (vəˈdʒaɪnə) *n., pl.* **-nas** *or* **-nae** (-niː). the passage in most female mammals that extends from the neck of the womb to an external opening in the vulva. —**vaˈginal** *adj.*

vagrant (ˈveɪgrənt) *n.* **1.** a person of no settled home, income, or job; tramp. ~*adj.* **2.** wandering about. —ˈvagrancy *n.*

vague (veɪg) *adj.* **1.** (of statements, meaning, etc.) imprecise: *vague promises.* **2.** not clearly perceptible or discernible: *a vague idea.* **3.** not clearly established or known: *a vague rumour.* **4.** (of a person or his expression) absent-minded. —ˈvaguely *adv.*

vain (veɪn) *adj.* **1.** excessively proud of one's appearance, possessions, or achievements. **2.** senseless or futile: *a vain attempt.* ~*n.* **3. in vain.** without success. —ˈvainly *adv.*

vainglory (ˌveɪnˈglɔːrɪ) *n.* boastfulness or vanity. —ˌvainˈglorious *adj.*

valance (ˈvæləns) *n.* a short piece of drapery hung round the edge of a bed or above a window.

vale (veɪl) *n. Literary.* a valley.

valediction (ˌvælɪˈdɪkʃən) *n.* **1.** the act or an instance of saying goodbye. **2.** any farewell statement or speech. —ˌvaleˈdictory *adj.*

valence ('veɪləns) n. Chem. the phenomenon of forming chemical bonds.

valency ('veɪlənsɪ) or esp. U.S. & Canad. **valence** n., pl. **-cies** or **-ces**. Chem. the number of atoms of hydrogen that an atom or group could combine with or displace in forming compounds.

valentine ('vælən,taɪn) n. **1.** a card or gift expressing love, sent, often anonymously, on Saint Valentine's Day. **2.** the person to whom one sends such a greeting.

valerian (və'lɪərɪən) n. a plant with small white or pinkish flowers and a medicinal root.

valet ('vælɪt, 'væleɪ) n. a manservant who acts as personal attendant to his employer, looking after his clothing and serving his meals.

valetudinarian (,vælɪ,tjuːdɪ'nɛərɪən) n. **1.** a person who is chronically sick. **2.** a hypochondriac. ~adj. **3.** relating to or resulting from poor health. **4.** being a valetudinarian. —,vale,tudi'narian,ism n.

Valhalla (væl'hælə) n. Norse myth. the great hall of Odin where warriors who die as heroes in battle dwell eternally.

valiant ('væljənt) adj. courageous or brave: a valiant deed. —'valiantly adv.

valid ('vælɪd) adj. **1.** having some foundation; based on truth. **2.** legally acceptable: a valid licence. **3.** effective or convincing: a valid point in a debate. —**validity** (və-'lɪdɪtɪ) n.

validate ('vælɪ,deɪt) vb. **1.** to confirm or corroborate. **2.** to give legal force or official confirmation to. —,vali'dation n.

valise (və'liːz) n. a small overnight travelling case.

Valium ('vælɪəm) n. Trademark. a drug used as a tranquillizer.

Valkyrie ('vælkɪrɪ) n. Norse myth. any of the beautiful maidens who take the dead heroes to Valhalla.

valley ('vælɪ) n. a long area of low land between hills, usually containing a river.

valour or U.S. **valor** ('vælə) n. courage or bravery, esp. in battle. —'valorous adj.

valuable ('væljuəb'l) adj. **1.** having considerable monetary worth. **2.** of considerable importance or quality: valuable information. ~n. **3.** (pl.) valuable articles of personal property, such as jewellery.

valuation (,vælju'eɪʃən) n. **1.** the act of making a formal assessment of the worth of something, such as a house. **2.** the price arrived at by the process of valuing.

value ('væljuː) n. **1.** the desirability of a thing, often in terms of its usefulness or exchangeability. **2.** an amount of money or goods considered to be a fair exchange for a thing: the value of the picture is £10 000. **3.** satisfaction: value for money. **4.** (pl.) the moral principles or accepted standards of a person or group. **5.** Maths. a particular number or quantity represented by a figure or symbol. **6.** Music. short for **time value**. ~vb. **-uing, -ued**. **7.** to assess the worth, merit, or desirability of (someone or something). **8.** to have a high regard for (someone or something) in respect of worth, usefulness, or merit. **9.** to fix the financial or material worth of (something, such as a unit of currency or a work of art). —'valued adj. —'valueless adj. —'valuer n.

value-added tax n. See **VAT**.

value judgment n. a subjective assessment based on one's own values.

valve (vælv) n. **1.** any device that shuts off, starts, regulates, or controls the flow of a fluid. **2.** Anat. a flaplike structure in a hollow organ, such as the heart, that controls the one-way passage of fluid through that organ. **3.** an evacuated electron tube containing a cathode, anode, and, usually, one or more additional control electrodes. When a positive potential is applied to the anode, it produces a one-way flow of current. **4.** Zool. one of the hinged shells of an oyster or clam. **5.** Music. a device on some brass instruments by which the effective length of the tube may be varied.

valvular ('vælvjulə) adj. **1.** of, operated by, or having a valve or valves. **2.** having the shape or function of a valve.

vamoose (və'muːs) vb. Slang, chiefly U.S. to leave a place hurriedly.

vamp[1] (væmp) Informal. ~n. **1.** a seductive woman who exploits men by use of her sexual charms. ~vb. **2.** (of a woman) to seduce (a man).

vamp[2] (væmp) n. **1.** the front part of the upper of a shoe. ~vb. **2.** (foll. by up) to make (something) seem new. **3.** to improvise an accompaniment to (a tune).

vampire ('væmpaɪə) n. **1.** (in European folklore) a corpse that rises nightly from its grave to drink the blood of living people. **2.** a person who preys mercilessly upon others.

vampire bat n. a bat of tropical regions of Central and South America that feeds on the blood of birds and mammals.

van[1] (væn) n. **1.** a motor vehicle for transporting goods by road. **2.** Brit. a closed railway wagon in which the guard travels, for transporting goods.

van[2] (væn) n. short for **vanguard**.

vanadium (və'neɪdɪəm) n. Chem. a silvery-white metallic element used in steel alloys. Symbol: V

Van Allen belt (væn 'ælən) n. either of two regions of charged particles several thousand kilometres above the earth.

vandal ('vænd'l) n. a person who deliberately causes damage to personal or public property. —'vandal,ism n.

vandalize or **-lise** ('vændə,laɪz) vb. to

cause damage to (personal or public property) deliberately.

Vandyke beard ('vændaɪk) *n.* a short pointed beard.

vane (veɪn) *n.* **1.** a flat blade of metal mounted on a vertical axis in an exposed position to indicate wind direction. **2.** any one of the flat blades forming part of the wheel of a windmill. **3.** any flat or shaped plate used to direct fluid flow, for example in a turbine.

vanguard ('væn,gɑːd) *n.* **1.** the leading division or units of a military force. **2.** the leading position in any movement or field of activity or the people who occupy this position.

vanilla (və'nɪlə) *n.* **1.** the pod or bean of a tropical climbing orchid, used to flavour food. **2.** a flavouring extract prepared from vanilla beans and used in cooking. ~*adj.* **3.** flavoured with vanilla: *vanilla ice cream.*

vanish ('vænɪʃ) *vb.* **1.** to disappear suddenly or mysteriously. **2.** to cease to exist.

vanishing cream *n.* a cosmetic cream that is colourless once applied.

vanishing point *n.* the point in the distance at which parallel lines appear to meet.

vanity ('vænɪtɪ) *n.* **1.** the state or quality of being vain. **2.** (*pl.* **-ties**) something about which one is vain.

vanity unit *n.* a hand basin built into a surface, usually with a cupboard below it.

vanquish ('væŋkwɪʃ) *vb.* **1.** to defeat or overcome (someone) in a battle, contest, or argument. **2.** to conquer (an emotion).

vantage ('vɑːntɪdʒ) *n.* **1.** a state, position, or opportunity offering advantage. **2.** *Tennis.* an advantage.

vantage point *n.* a position that gives one an overall view of a scene or situation.

vapid ('væpɪd) *adj.* **1.** weak, colourless, or flavourless. **2.** boring or dull: *vapid talk.* —**va'pidity** *n.*

vapor ('veɪpə) *n. U.S.* same as **vapour.**

vaporize *or* **-rise** ('veɪpə,raɪz) *vb.* to change into vapour. —,**vapori'zation** *or* **-ri'sation** *n.*

vaporous ('veɪpərəs) *adj.* resembling or full of vapour.

vapour *or U.S.* **vapor** ('veɪpə) *n.* **1.** particles of moisture suspended in air and visible as clouds, smoke, or mist. **2.** the gaseous form of a substance that is usually a liquid or a solid. **3. the vapours.** *Archaic.* a depressed mental condition.

var. variant.

variable ('veərɪəb'l) *adj.* **1.** liable to or capable of change: *variable weather.* **2.** (of behaviour or emotions) lacking constancy. **3.** *Maths.* having a range of possible values. ~*n.* **4.** something that is subject to variation. **5.** *Maths.* an expression that can be

assigned any of a set of values. —,**varia'bility** *n.* —'**variably** *adv.*

variance ('veərɪəns) *n.* **1.** a disagreement. **2. at variance.** not in agreement.

variant ('veərɪənt) *adj.* **1.** displaying variation. **2.** differing from a standard or type: *a variant spelling.* ~*n.* **3.** something that differs from a standard or type.

variation (,veərɪ'eɪʃən) *n.* **1.** the act, process, condition, or result of changing or varying. **2.** an instance of varying or the amount, rate, or degree of such change. **3.** something that differs from a standard or convention. **4.** *Music.* a repetition of a musical theme in which the rhythm, harmony, or melody is altered or embellished.

varicoloured *or U.S.* **varicolored** ('veərɪ,kʌləd) *adj.* having many colours.

varicose ('værɪ,kəʊs) *adj.* of or resulting from varicose veins: *a varicose ulcer.*

varicose veins *pl. n.* veins, usually in the legs, which have become knotted, swollen, and sometimes painful.

varied ('veərɪd) *adj.* displaying variety; diverse.

variegated ('veərɪ,geɪtɪd) *adj.* **1.** displaying different-coloured spots or streaks. **2.** (of foliage) having pale patches. —**variega-tion** (,veərɪ'geɪʃən) *n.*

variety (və'raɪətɪ) *n., pl.* **-ties. 1.** the quality or condition of being diversified or various. **2.** a collection of unlike things of the same general group. **3.** a different form or kind within a general category: *varieties of behaviour.* **4.** *Taxonomy.* a race whose distinct characters do not justify classification as a separate species. **5.** a type of entertainment consisting of a series of short unrelated acts, such as comedy turns, songs, and dances.

various ('veərɪəs) *adj.* **1.** several different: *he is an authority on various subjects.* **2.** of different kinds: *his disguises are many and various.* —'**variously** *adv.*

Usage. Various of, as in *he wrote to various of his friends,* is not current in good usage. It is preferable to use *various* or *several of: he wrote to various friends; he wrote to several of his friends.*

varlet ('vɑːlɪt) *n. Archaic.* **1.** a menial servant. **2.** a rascal.

varmint ('vɑːmɪnt) *n. Informal.* an irritating or obnoxious person or animal.

varnish ('vɑːnɪʃ) *n.* **1.** a preparation consisting of a solvent, oil, and resin or rubber, which gives a hard glossy transparent coating to a surface. **2.** a similar preparation consisting of shellac dissolved in alcohol. **3.** a smooth surface, coated with or as if with varnish. **4.** an artificial, superficial, or deceptively pleasing manner, covering, or appearance. **5.** *Chiefly Brit.* same as **nail polish.** ~*vb.* **6.** to cover with varnish. **7.** to impart a more attractive appearance to.

varsity (ˈvɑːsɪtɪ) *n., pl.* **-ties.** *Brit. & N.Z. informal.* short for **university.**

vary (ˈvɛərɪ) *vb.* **varying, varied. 1.** to undergo or cause to undergo change or modification in appearance, character, or form. **2.** to be different or cause to be different; be subject to change. **3.** to give variety to. **4.** to change in accordance with another variable: *her mood varies with the weather.* —ˈ**varying** *adj.*

vas (væs) *n., pl.* **vasa** (ˈveɪsə). *Anat., zool.* a vessel or tube that carries a fluid.

vascular (ˈvæskjʊlə) *adj. Biol., anat.* of or relating to the vessels that conduct and circulate body fluids such as blood or sap: *a vascular bundle.*

vas deferens (ˈdɛfə,rɛnz) *n., pl.* **vasa deferentia** (ˌdɛfəˈrɛnʃɪə). *Anat.* the duct within each testicle that conveys sperm to the penis.

vase (vɑːz) *n.* a glass or pottery jar used as an ornament or for holding cut flowers.

vasectomy (vəˈsɛktəmɪ) *n., pl.* **-mies.** surgical removal of all or part of the vas deferens as a method of contraception.

Vaseline (ˈvæsɪ,liːn) *n. Trademark.* petroleum jelly.

vassal (ˈvæsˀl) *n.* **1.** (in feudal society) a man who gave military service to a lord in return for protection and often land. **2.** a person, nation, or state in a subordinate position to another. —ˈ**vassalage** *n.*

vast (vɑːst) *adj.* unusually large in size, degree, or number. —ˈ**vastly** *adv.* —ˈ**vastness** *n.*

vat (væt) *n.* a large container for holding or storing liquids.

VAT (ˌviː eɪ ˈtiː, væt) (in Britain) value-added tax: a tax levied on the difference between the cost of materials and the selling price of a commodity or service.

Vatican (ˈvætɪkən) *n.* **the. 1.** the palace of the Pope, in Rome. **2.** the authority of the Pope.

vaudeville (ˈvəʊdəvɪl, ˈvɔː-) *n.* variety entertainment consisting of short acts such as song-and-dance routines and comic turns.

vault[1] (vɔːlt) *n.* **1.** an arched structure that forms a roof or ceiling. **2.** an underground burial chamber. **3.** a strongroom for the storage of valuables. **4.** a cellar for the storage of wine. **5.** the sky. ~*vb.* **6.** to furnish with or as if with an arched roof. **7.** to construct in the shape of a vault.

vault[2] (vɔːlt) *vb.* **1.** to spring over (an object), with the aid of a long pole or with one's hands resting on the object. ~*n.* **2.** the act of vaulting. —ˈ**vaulter** *n.*

vaulting[1] (ˈvɔːltɪŋ) *n.* one or more vaults in a building or such structures considered collectively.

vaulting[2] (ˈvɔːltɪŋ) *adj.* excessively confident: *vaulting arrogance.*

vaunt (vɔːnt) *vb.* **1.** to describe, praise, or display (one's success or possessions) boastfully. ~*n.* **2.** a boast. —ˈ**vaunted** *adj.*

VC 1. Vice Chancellor. **2.** Victoria Cross. **3.** Vietcong: the Communist-led guerrilla force of South Vietnam.

VCR video cassette recorder.

VD venereal disease.

VDU visual display unit.

veal (viːl) *n.* the flesh of a calf, used as food.

vector (ˈvɛktə) *n.* **1.** *Maths.* a variable quantity, such as force, that has magnitude and direction. **2.** *Pathol.* an animal, usually an insect, that carries a disease-producing microorganism from person to person.

Veda (ˈveɪdə) *n.* any or all of the most ancient sacred writings of Hinduism. —ˈ**Vedic** *adj.*

veer (vɪə) *vb.* **1.** to change direction. **2.** to change from one position or opinion to another. ~*n.* **3.** a change of course or direction.

veg (vɛdʒ) *n. Informal.* a vegetable or vegetables.

vegan (ˈviːgən) *n.* a person who uses no animal products.

vegetable (ˈvɛdʒtəbˀl) *n.* **1.** a plant with parts that are used as food, such as peas, potatoes, cauliflowers, and onions. **2.** *Informal.* a person who is unable to move or think, as a result of brain damage. **3.** (*modifier*) of, derived from, or consisting of plants or plant material: *the vegetable kingdom.*

vegetable marrow *n.* an oblong green striped vegetable which can be cooked and eaten.

vegetable oil *n.* any of a group of oils that are obtained from plants.

vegetal (ˈvɛdʒɪtˀl) *adj.* of or relating to plant life.

vegetarian (ˌvɛdʒɪˈtɛərɪən) *n.* **1.** a person who does not eat meat or fish. ~*adj.* **2.** excluding meat and fish: *a vegetarian diet.* —ˌ**vegeˈtarianism** *n.*

vegetate (ˈvɛdʒɪ,teɪt) *vb.* to lead a life characterized by monotony, passivity, or mental inactivity.

vegetation (ˌvɛdʒɪˈteɪʃən) *n.* plant life as a whole.

vegetative (ˈvɛdʒɪtətɪv) *adj.* **1.** of or concerned with plant life or plant growth. **2.** (of reproduction) characterized by asexual processes.

vehement (ˈviːɪmənt) *adj.* **1.** expressing intensity of feeling or conviction. **2.** (of actions or gestures) performed with great energy, vigour, or force. —ˈ**vehemence** *n.* —ˈ**vehemently** *adv.*

vehicle ('viːik'l) n. 1. any conveyance in or by which people or objects are transported. 2. a medium for the expression or communication of ideas. 3. *Pharmacol.* an inactive substance mixed with the active ingredient in a medicine. 4. a painting medium, such as oil, in which pigments are suspended. —**vehicular** (vɪ'hɪkjʊlə) adj.

veil (veɪl) n. 1. a piece of more or less transparent material, usually attached to a hat or headdress, used to conceal a woman's face. 2. the part of a nun's headdress that falls round her face onto her shoulders. 3. something that covers, conceals, or separates: *a veil of reticence.* 4. **take the veil.** to become a nun. ~vb. 5. to cover, conceal, or separate with or as if with a veil.

veiled (veɪld) adj. disguised: *a veiled insult.*

vein (veɪn) n. 1. any of the tubes that convey blood to the heart. 2. any of the ribs that form the supporting framework of an insect's wing or a leaf. 3. a clearly defined mass of ore or mineral in rock. 4. an irregular streak of colour in marble, wood, or cheese. 5. a distinctive trait or quality in speech, writing, or character: *a vein of humour.* 6. a temporary mood: *the debate entered a frivolous vein.* —**veined** *or* **veiny** adj.

Velcro ('vɛlkrəʊ) n. *Trademark.* a fastening consisting of two strips of nylon fabric, one having tiny hooked threads and the other a coarse surface, that form a strong bond when pressed together.

veld *or* **veldt** (fɛlt, vɛlt) n. high open grassland in Southern Africa.

veleta (və'liːtə) n. a ballroom dance in triple time.

vellum ('vɛləm) n. 1. a fine parchment prepared from the skin of a calf, kid, or lamb. 2. a work printed or written on vellum. 3. a heavy paper resembling vellum.

velocipede (vɪ'lɒsɪˌpiːd) n. an early form of bicycle.

velocity (vɪ'lɒsɪtɪ) n., *pl.* -ties. speed of motion; swiftness.

velours *or* **velour** (və'lʊə) n. a fabric with a velvet-like finish.

velvet ('vɛlvɪt) n. 1. a fabric of silk, cotton, or nylon, with a thick close soft pile. 2. the furry covering of the newly formed antlers of a deer. 3. **on velvet.** *Slang.* in a condition of ease, advantage, or wealth. ~adj. 4. made of velvet. 5. soft or smooth like velvet. 6. **an iron hand in a velvet glove.** determination concealed by gentleness. —**velvety** adj.

velveteen (ˌvɛlvɪ'tiːn) n. a cotton fabric resembling velvet with a short thick pile.

Ven. Venerable.

venal ('viːn'l) adj. 1. easily bribed or corrupted: *a venal magistrate.* 2. associated with corruption or bribery. —**venality** (viː'nælɪtɪ) n. —**venally** adv.

vend (vɛnd) vb. to sell (goods).

vendetta (vɛn'dɛtə) n. 1. a private feud, in which the relatives of a murdered person seek vengeance by killing the murderer or some member of his family. 2. any prolonged feud.

vending machine n. a machine that automatically dispenses food, drinks, or cigarettes when money is inserted.

vendor ('vɛndə) n. 1. a person who sells goods such as newspapers or hamburgers from a stall, tray, or cart: *street vendors.* 2. *Chiefly law.* a person who sells property.

veneer (vɪ'nɪə) n. 1. a thin layer of fine wood, plastic, etc., that is bonded to the surface of a less expensive material. 2. a superficial appearance: *a veneer of gentility.* ~vb. 3. to cover (a surface) with a veneer. 4. to conceal (something) under a superficially pleasant surface.

venerable ('vɛnərəb'l) adj. 1. (of a person) worthy of reverence on account of great age, religious associations, or character. 2. (of inanimate objects) revered on account of age or historical or religious association. 3. *R.C. Church.* a title given to a dead person who is going to be declared a saint. 4. *Church of England.* a title given to an archdeacon.

venerate ('vɛnəˌreɪt) vb. to hold (someone) in deep respect. —**venerˌator** n.

veneration (ˌvɛnə'reɪʃən) n. 1. a feeling or expression of awe or reverence. 2. the act of venerating or the state of being venerated.

venereal (vɪ'nɪərɪəl) adj. 1. for the treatment of venereal diseases: *a venereal clinic.* 2. transmitted by sexual intercourse: *a venereal infection.* 3. of the genitals: *venereal warts.*

venereal disease n. any of various diseases, such as syphilis or gonorrhoea, transmitted by sexual intercourse.

Venetian (vɪ'niːʃən) adj. 1. of or relating to Venice, a port in NE Italy, or its inhabitants. ~n. 2. a person from Venice.

Venetian blind n. a window blind consisting of a number of horizontal slats.

vengeance ('vɛndʒəns) n. 1. the act of or desire for taking revenge. 2. **with a vengeance.** to an excessive degree: *he's a coward with a vengeance.*

vengeful ('vɛndʒfʊl) adj. 1. desiring revenge. 2. taking revenge: *a vengeful act.*

venial ('viːnɪəl) adj. easily excused or forgiven: *a venial sin.* —**veniality** (ˌviːnɪ'ælɪtɪ) n. —**venially** adv.

venison ('vɛnɪs'n) n. the flesh of a deer, used as food.

Venn diagram (vɛn) n. *Maths.* a diagram in which mathematical sets are represented by overlapping circles.

venom ('vɛnəm) n. **1.** a poisonous fluid produced by certain snakes and scorpions when they bite or sting. **2.** malice; spite. —'**venomous** adj. —'**venomously** adv.

venous ('viːnəs) adj. of or relating to veins.

vent¹ (vɛnt) n. **1.** a small opening for the escape of fumes, liquids, etc. **2.** the shaft of a volcano through which lava and gases erupt. **3.** the excretory opening of lower vertebrates. **4. give vent to.** to release (an emotion) in an outburst. ~vb. **5.** to release or express freely (an emotion): he vents his anger on his wife. **6.** to make vents in.

vent² (vɛnt) n. a vertical slit in the lower hem of a jacket, either in the middle of the back, or one of a pair at either side of the back.

ventilate ('vɛntɪˌleɪt) vb. **1.** to let fresh air into (a room or building). **2.** to expose (a question, grievance, etc.) to public discussion. —**ventilation** (ˌvɛntɪˈleɪʃən) n.

ventilator ('vɛntɪˌleɪtə) n. an opening or device, such as a fan, used to let fresh air into a room or building.

ventral ('vɛntrəl) adj. relating to the front part of the body. —'**ventrally** adv.

ventricle ('vɛntrɪkᵊl) n. Anat. **1.** a chamber of the heart that pumps blood to the arteries. **2.** any one of the four main cavities of the brain. —**ven'tricular** adj.

ventriloquism (vɛnˈtrɪləˌkwɪzəm) n. the art of producing vocal sounds that appear to come from another source. —**ven'triloquist** n.

venture ('vɛntʃə) n. **1.** an undertaking that is risky or of uncertain outcome. **2.** a commercial undertaking in which there is the risk of loss as well as the opportunity for profit. ~vb. **3.** to expose to danger: he ventured his life. **4.** to brave the dangers of (something): I'll venture the seas. **5.** to dare (to do something): does he venture to object? **6.** to express in spite of possible criticism: if I may venture an opinion; I venture that he is not that honest. **7.** (foll. by out or forth) to embark on a possibly hazardous journey or undertaking: to venture forth upon the high seas. —'**venturer** n.

Venture Scout or **Venturer** n. Brit. a member of the senior branch of the Scouts.

venturesome ('vɛntʃəsəm) adj. willing to take risks; daring.

venue ('vɛnjuː) n. **1.** any place where an organized gathering, such as a concert or a sporting event, is held. **2.** Law. **a.** the place fixed for a trial. **b.** the locality from which the jurors must be summoned.

Venus ('viːnəs) n. **1.** the Roman goddess of love. **2.** the planet second nearest to the sun.

Venus's-flytrap or **Venus flytrap** n. a plant with hinged two-lobed leaves which snap closed, trapping insects which it then digests.

veracious (vəˈreɪʃəs) adj. habitually truthful.

veracity (vəˈræsɪtɪ) n. **1.** habitual truthfulness. **2.** accuracy.

veranda or **verandah** (vəˈrændə) n. **1.** a porch, sometimes partly enclosed, along the outside of a building. **2.** N.Z. a continuous overhead canopy that gives shelter to pedestrians.

verb (vɜːb) n. any of a large class of words that serve to indicate the occurrence or performance of an action or the existence of a state. Such words as run, make, and do are verbs.

verbal ('vɜːbᵊl) adj. **1.** of, relating to, or using words: merely verbal concessions. **2.** spoken rather than written: a verbal agreement. **3.** Grammar. of or relating to a verb. —'**verbally** adv.

verbalism ('vɜːbəˌlɪzəm) n. an exaggerated emphasis on the importance of words.

verbalize or **-lise** ('vɜːbəˌlaɪz) vb. **1.** to express (an idea or feeling) in words. **2.** to be long-winded.

verbal noun n. a noun derived from a verb, such as smoking in the sentence smoking is bad for you.

verbatim (vɜːˈbeɪtɪm) adv., adj. using exactly the same words; word for word.

verbena (vɜːˈbiːnə) n. a plant with red, white, or purple sweet-smelling flowers.

verbiage ('vɜːbɪɪdʒ) n. the excessive and often meaningless use of words.

verbose (vɜːˈbəʊs) adj. using an excess of words, so as to be annoying or boring. —**verbosity** (vɜːˈbɒsɪtɪ) n.

verdant ('vɜːdᵊnt) adj. covered with green vegetation.

verdict ('vɜːdɪkt) n. **1.** the findings of a jury on the issues of fact submitted to it for examination and trial. **2.** any decision or conclusion.

verdigris ('vɜːdɪgriːs) n. a green or bluish coating which forms on copper, brass, or bronze that has been exposed to damp.

verdure ('vɜːdʒə) n. flourishing green vegetation or its colour.

verge¹ (vɜːdʒ) n. **1.** an edge or rim; margin. **2.** a limit beyond which something occurs: on the verge of ecstasy. **3.** Brit. a grass border along a road. ~vb. **4.** (foll. by on) **a.** to be near to: to verge on chaos. **b.** to serve as the edge of (something).

verge² (vɜːdʒ) vb. (foll. by to or towards) to move in a specified direction.

verger ('vɜːdʒə) n. Chiefly Church of England. **1.** a church official who acts as caretaker and attendant. **2.** an official who carries the rod of office before a bishop or dean in ceremonies and processions.

verify ('vɛrɪˌfaɪ) vb. **-fying, -fied. 1.** to prove (something) to be true; confirm. **2.** to check the truth of (something) by investigation. —'**veri,fiable** adj. —,**verifi'cation** n.

verily ('vɛrɪlɪ) adv. Archaic. in truth; truly: verily, thou art a man of God.

verisimilitude (,vɛrɪsɪ'mɪlɪ,tjuːd) n. the appearance of truth or reality.

veritable ('vɛrɪtəb°l) adj. rightly called; real: he's a veritable swine! —'**veritably** adv.

verity ('vɛrɪtɪ) n., pl. -**ties.** a true statement, idea, or principle.

vermicelli (,vɜːmɪ'tʃɛlɪ) n. **1.** very fine strands of pasta. **2.** tiny chocolate strands used as a topping for cakes or ice cream.

vermicide ('vɜːmɪ,saɪd) n. a substance used to kill worms.

vermiform ('vɜːmɪ,fɔːm) adj. resembling a worm.

vermiform appendix n. Anat. same as **appendix.**

vermilion (və'mɪljən) adj. **1.** orange-red. ~n. **2.** mercuric sulphide, used as an orange-red pigment; cinnabar.

vermin ('vɜːmɪn) n. (functioning as pl.) **1.** small animals collectively, such as insects and rodents, that spread disease and damage crops. **2.** unpleasant people. —'**verminous** adj.

vermouth ('vɜːməθ) n. wine flavoured with herbs.

vernacular (və'nækjʊlə) n. **1. the.** the commonly spoken language or dialect of a particular people or place. ~adj. **2.** relating to or in the vernacular.

vernal ('vɜːn°l) adj. of or occurring in spring. —'**vernally** adv.

vernier ('vɜːnɪə) n. a small movable scale in certain measuring instruments such as theodolites, used to obtain a fractional reading of one of the divisions on the main scale.

veronica (və'rɒnɪkə) n. a plant with small blue, pink, or white flowers.

verruca (və'ruːkə) n., pl. -**cae** (-siː) or -**cas.** Pathol. a wart, usually on the sole of the foot.

versatile ('vɜːsə,taɪl) adj. capable of many different uses or skills; able to change or be changed quickly; flexible. —**versatility** (,vɜːsə'tɪlɪtɪ) n.

verse (vɜːs) n. **1.** a division of a poem or song. **2.** poetry as distinct from prose. **3.** one of the short sections into which chapters of the books of the Bible are divided. **4.** a poem.

versed (vɜːst) adj. **versed in.** knowledgeable about, acquainted with, or skilled in.

versify ('vɜːsɪ,faɪ) vb. -**fying, -fied. 1.** to put (something) into verse. **2.** to write in verse. —,**versifi'cation** n. —'**versi,fier** n.

version ('vɜːʃən) n. **1.** an account of an incident from a certain point of view: his version of the accident is different from the policeman's. **2.** a translation from one language into another. **3.** a variant form of something. **4.** an adaptation, for example of a book or play into a film.

verso ('vɜːsəʊ) n., pl. -**sos. 1.** the back of a sheet of printed paper. **2.** any of the left-hand pages of a book, bearing the even numbers.

versus ('vɜːsəs) prep. **1.** (in a sporting competition or lawsuit) against. **2.** in contrast with.

vertebra ('vɜːtɪbrə) n., pl. -**brae** (-briː) or -**bras.** one of the bony segments of the spinal column. —'**vertebral** adj.

vertebrate ('vɜːtɪbrɪt) n. **1.** any animal with a backbone, such as a fish, amphibian, reptile, bird, or mammal. ~adj. **2.** having a backbone.

vertex ('vɜːtɛks) n., pl. -**texes** or -**tices** (-tɪ,siːz). **1.** the highest point. **2.** Maths. **a.** the point opposite the base of a figure. **b.** the point of intersection of two sides of a plane figure or angle.

vertical ('vɜːtɪk°l) adj. **1.** at right angles to the horizon; upright: a vertical wall. **2.** straight up and down: vertical stripes. **3.** Econ. of or relating to associated or consecutive, though not identical, stages of industrial activity: vertical integration. **4.** of or relating to the vertex. ~n. **5.** a vertical plane, position, or line. —'**vertically** adv.

vertiginous (vɜː'tɪdʒɪnəs) adj. producing dizziness.

vertigo ('vɜːtɪgəʊ) n. Pathol. a sensation of dizziness resulting from a disorder of the sense of balance.

vervain ('vɜːveɪn) n. a plant with long slender spikes of purple, blue, or white flowers.

verve (vɜːv) n. great vitality and liveliness.

very ('vɛrɪ) adv. **1.** used to add emphasis to adjectives that are able to be graded: very good; very tall. ~adj. **2.** used with nouns to give emphasis to the significance or relevance of a noun in a particular context, or to give exaggerated intensity to certain nouns: the very man I want to see; the very back of the room.
Usage. In strict usage adverbs of degree such as very, too, quite, really, and extremely are used only to qualify adjectives: he is very happy; she is too sad. By this rule, these words should not be used to qualify past participles that follow the verb to be, since they would then be technically qualifying verbs. With the exception of certain participles, such as tired or disappointed, that have come to be regarded as adjectives, all other past participles are qualified by adverbs such as much, greatly, seriously, or excessively: he has been much (not very) inconvenienced.

very high frequency n. a radio-frequency band lying between 300 and 30 megahertz.

Very light (ˈvɛrɪ) *n.* a coloured flare for signalling at night.

vesicle (ˈvɛsɪkᵊl) *n. Biol.* **a.** any small sac or cavity, esp. one filled with fluid. **b.** a blister.

vespers (ˈvɛspəz) *n.* (*functioning as sing.*) an evening service in some Christian churches.

vessel (ˈvɛsᵊl) *n.* **1.** an object used as a container for liquid. **2.** a ship or large boat. **3.** a tubular structure that transports fluids such as blood in humans and water in plants.

vest (vɛst) *n.* **1.** an undergarment covering the top half of the body. **2.** *U.S., Canad., & Austral.* a waistcoat. ~*vb.* **3.** (foll. by *in*) to place or settle (power, rights, or property) on: *power was vested in the committee.* **4.** (foll. by *with*) to bestow on: *the company was vested with authority.*

vestal (ˈvɛstᵊl) *adj.* **1.** chaste or pure. ~*n.* **2.** a chaste woman.

vestal virgin *n.* (in ancient Rome) one of the virgin priestesses dedicated to the goddess Vesta and to maintaining the sacred fire in her temple.

vested (ˈvɛstɪd) *adj. Property law.* having an existing right to the immediate or future possession of property.

vested interest *n.* **1.** *Property law.* an existing right to the immediate or future possession of property. **2.** a strong personal concern in something, usually resulting in personal gain.

vestibule (ˈvɛstɪˌbjuːl) *n.* a small entrance hall.

vestige (ˈvɛstɪdʒ) *n.* **1.** a small trace; hint: *a vestige of truth.* **2.** *Biol.* an organ or part that is a small nonfunctioning remnant of a functional organ in an ancestor. —**ves'tigial** *adj.*

vestments (ˈvɛstmənts) *pl. n.* **1.** robes denoting office, authority, or rank. **2.** ceremonial garments worn by the clergy at religious services.

vestry (ˈvɛstrɪ) *n., pl.* **-tries.** a room in or attached to a church, in which vestments and sacred vessels are kept.

vet[1] (vɛt) *n.* **1.** short for **veterinary surgeon.** ~*vb.* **vetting, vetted.** **2.** *Chiefly Brit.* to make a careful check of (a person, document, etc.) for suitability: *the candidates were well vetted.*

vet[2] (vɛt) *n. U.S. & Canad.* short for **veteran.**

vetch (vɛtʃ) *n.* **1.** a climbing plant with blue or purple flowers. **2.** the beanlike fruit of the vetch, used as fodder.

veteran (ˈvɛtərən) *n.* **1.** a person who has given long service in some capacity. **2.** a soldier who has seen a lot of active service. **3.** *U.S. & Canad.* a person who has served in the military forces.

veteran car *n. Brit.* a car constructed before 1919, esp. before 1905.

veterinarian (ˌvɛtrɪˈnɛərɪən) *n. U.S. & Canad.* a veterinary surgeon.

veterinary (ˈvɛtrɪnərɪ) *adj.* of or relating to veterinary science.

veterinary science *or* **medicine** *n.* the branch of medicine concerned with the treatment of animals.

veterinary surgeon *n. Brit.* a person qualified to practise veterinary science.

veto (ˈviːtəʊ) *n., pl.* **-toes.** **1.** the power to prevent legislation or action proposed by others: *the presidential veto.* **2.** the exercise of this power. ~*vb.* **-toing, -toed.** **3.** to refuse consent to (a proposal, such as a government bill). **4.** to prohibit or forbid: *her parents vetoed her trip.*

vex (vɛks) *vb.* to anger or annoy. —ˈ**vexing** *adj.*

vexation (vɛkˈseɪʃən) *n.* **1.** a vexing or being vexed. **2.** something that vexes.

vexatious (vɛkˈseɪʃəs) *adj.* vexing or tending to vex.

vexed (vɛkst) *adj.* **1.** annoyed, confused, or agitated. **2.** much debated: *a vexed question.*

VHF *or* **vhf** *Radio.* very high frequency.

VHS Video Home System: a video cassette recorder system using ½in. magnetic tape.

via (ˈvaɪə) *prep.* by way of; by means of: *to London via Paris.*

viable (ˈvaɪəbᵊl) *adj.* **1.** practicable: *a viable proposition.* **2.** (of seeds or eggs) capable of growth. **3.** (of a fetus) sufficiently developed to survive outside the uterus. —ˌ**via'bility** *n.*

viaduct (ˈvaɪəˌdʌkt) *n.* a bridge for carrying a road or railway across a valley.

vial (ˈvaɪəl) *n.* same as **phial.**

viand (ˈviːənd) *n.* **1.** a type of food. **2.** (*pl.*) provisions.

viaticum (vaɪˈætɪkəm) *n., pl.* **-ca** (-kə) *or* **-cums.** *Christianity.* Holy Communion given to a person dying or in danger of death.

vibes (vaɪbz) *pl. n.* **1.** *Informal.* short for **vibraphone.** **2.** *Slang.* **a.** the emotional reactions between people. **b.** the atmosphere of a place.

vibrant (ˈvaɪbrənt) *adj.* **1.** characterized by or exhibiting vibration. **2.** full of life, energy, and enthusiasm: *a vibrant image.* **3.** resonant: *vibrant tones.* —ˈ**vibrancy** *n.*

vibraphone (ˈvaɪbrəˌfəʊn) *n.* a percussion instrument consisting of metal bars over tubular metal resonators, which are made to vibrate electronically.

vibrate (vaɪˈbreɪt) *vb.* **1.** to move or cause to move back and forth rapidly. **2.** to resonate or cause to resonate. **3.** *Physics.* to undergo or cause to undergo vibration. —**vibratory** (ˈvaɪbrətərɪ) *adj.*

vibration (vaɪˈbreɪʃən) *n.* **1.** a vibrating. **2.**

Physics. **a.** a periodic motion about an equilibrium position, such as in the production of sound. **b.** a single cycle of such a motion.

vibrato (vɪ'brɑːtəʊ) *n., pl.* **-tos.** *Music.* a slight rapid fluctuation in the pitch of a note.

vibrator (vaɪ'breɪtə) *n.* a device for producing a vibratory motion, as in massage.

vicar ('vɪkə) *n.* **1.** *Church of England.* (in Britain) a clergyman appointed to act as priest of a parish from which, formerly, he did not receive tithes but a stipend. **2.** *R.C. Church.* a church officer acting as deputy to a bishop. —**vicarial** (vɪ'kɛərɪəl) *adj.*

vicarage ('vɪkərɪdʒ) *n.* the residence or benefice of a vicar.

vicar apostolic *n. R.C. Church.* a titular bishop having jurisdiction in missionary countries.

vicar general *n., pl.* **vicars general.** an official appointed to assist the bishop in his administrative duties.

vicarious (vɪ'kɛərɪəs, vaɪ-) *adj.* **1.** undergone at second hand as if by taking part in another's experiences. **2.** undergone or done as the substitute for another: *vicarious punishment.* **3.** delegated: *vicarious authority.*

Vicar of Christ *n. R.C. Church.* the Pope as Christ's earthly representative.

vice[1] (vaɪs) *n.* **1.** an immoral or evil habit, action, or trait. **2.** frequent indulgence in immoral practices. **3.** a specific form of immoral conduct, such as sexual perversion. **4.** an imperfection in character or conduct: *smoking is his only vice.*

vice[2] *or U.S. (often)* **vise** (vaɪs) *n.* an appliance with a pair of jaws for holding an object while work is done on it.

vice[3] (vaɪs) *adj.* serving in the place of.

vice[4] ('vaɪsɪ) *prep.* instead of; as a substitute for.

vice admiral *n.* a senior commissioned officer in certain navies.

vice chancellor *n.* the chief executive or administrator at some British universities.

vicegerent (ˌvaɪs'dʒɛrənt) *n.* a person appointed to exercise all or some of the authority of another.

vice president *n.* an officer ranking immediately below a president and serving as his deputy.

viceregal (ˌvaɪs'riːgᵊl) *adj.* **1.** of a viceroy. **2.** *Chiefly Austral. & N.Z.* of a governor or governor general.

viceroy ('vaɪsrɔɪ) *n.* a governor of a colony, country, or province who acts for and rules in the name of his sovereign or government. —**viceroyship** *or* ˌ**vice'royalty** *n.*

vice squad *n.* a police division responsible for the enforcement of gaming and prostitution laws.

vice versa ('vaɪsɪ 'vɜːsə) *adv.* the other way around.

Vichy water ('viːʃɪ) *n.* a natural mineral water from springs at Vichy in France.

vicinity (vɪ'sɪnɪtɪ) *n., pl.* **-ties.** **1.** a surrounding area; neighbourhood. **2.** a being close.

vicious ('vɪʃəs) *adj.* **1.** wicked or cruel: *a vicious thug.* **2.** characterized by violence or ferocity: *a vicious blow.* **3.** *Informal.* unpleasantly severe; harsh: *a vicious wind.* **4.** malicious: *vicious lies.* **5.** (of animals) ferocious or hostile. **6.** invalidated by defects; unsound: *a vicious inference.* —**viciously** *adv.* —**viciousness** *n.*

vicious circle *n.* **1.** a situation in which an attempt to resolve one problem creates new problems that recreate the original one. **2.** *Logic.* a form of reasoning in which a conclusion is inferred from premises the truth of which cannot be established independently of that conclusion.

vicissitude (vɪ'sɪsɪˌtjuːd) *n.* a variation in circumstance or fortune.

victim ('vɪktɪm) *n.* **1.** a person or thing that suffers harm or death: *victims of tyranny.* **2.** a person who is tricked or swindled. **3.** a living person or animal sacrificed in a religious rite.

victimize *or* **-mise** ('vɪktɪˌmaɪz) *vb.* **1.** to punish or discriminate against selectively or unfairly. **2.** to make a victim of. —ˌ**victimi'zation** *or* **-mi'sation** *n.*

victor ('vɪktə) *n.* **1.** a person or nation that has defeated an adversary in war. **2.** the winner of any contest, conflict, or struggle.

victoria (vɪk'tɔːrɪə) *n.* **1.** a light four-wheeled horse-drawn carriage with a folding hood. **2.** Also called: **victoria plum.** *Brit.* a large sweet variety of plum, red and yellow in colour.

Victoria Cross *n.* the highest decoration for gallantry in battle awarded to the British and Commonwealth armed forces.

Victorian (vɪk'tɔːrɪən) *adj.* **1.** of or characteristic of Queen Victoria or her reign (1837–1901). **2.** exhibiting the characteristics popularly attributed to the Victorians, esp. prudery, bigotry, or hypocrisy. ~*n.* **3.** a person who lived during the reign of Queen Victoria.

Victoriana (vɪkˌtɔːrɪ'ɑːnə) *n.* objects of the Victorian period.

victorious (vɪk'tɔːrɪəs) *adj.* **1.** having defeated an adversary: *the victorious nations.* **2.** of, indicating, or characterized by victory: *a victorious conclusion.*

victory ('vɪktrɪ) *n., pl.* **-ries.** **1.** final superiority in a war or battle. **2.** success attained in any contest or struggle.

victual ('vɪtᵊl) *vb.* **-ualling, -ualled** *or U.S.* **-ualing, -ualed.** to supply with or obtain victuals. —**victualler** *or U.S.* **-ualer** *n.*

victuals ('vɪtᵊlz) *pl. n.* food provisions.

vicuña (vɪ'kjuːnə) *n.* **1.** a tawny Andean

mammal like the llama. **2.** the fine wool obtained from this animal.

vide ('vaɪdɪ) (used to direct a reader to a specified place in a text or another book) refer to, see.

videlicet (vɪ'diːlɪˌsɛt) *adv.* namely: used to specify items.

video ('vɪdɪəʊ) *adj.* **1.** of or used in the transmission or reception of a televised image. ~*n., pl.* **-os. 2.** the visual elements of a television broadcast. **3.** a film recorded on a video cassette. **4.** short for **video cassette** *or* **video cassette recorder.** ~*vb.* **videoing, videoed. 5.** to record (a television programme or an event) on a video cassette recorder.

video cassette *n.* a cassette containing video tape.

video cassette recorder *n.* a tape recorder for vision and sound signals using magnetic tape in closed plastic cassettes: used for recording and playing back television programmes and films.

video frequency *n.* the frequency of a signal conveying the image and synchronizing pulses in a television broadcasting system.

video nasty *n.* a film, usually specially made for video, that is explicitly horrific and pornographic.

videophone ('vɪdɪəˌfəʊn) *n.* a telephonic device in which there is both verbal and visual communication between parties.

video recorder *n.* short for **video cassette recorder.**

video tape *n.* **1.** magnetic tape used mainly for recording the video-frequency signals of a television programme or film for subsequent transmission. ~*vb.* **videotape. 2.** to record (a film or programme) on video tape.

video tape recorder *n.* a tape recorder for visual signals, using magnetic tape on open spools: used in television broadcasting.

videotex ('vɪdɪəʊˌtɛks) *n.* same as **viewdata.**

videotext ('vɪdɪəʊˌtɛkst) *n.* a means of providing a written or graphical representation of computerized information on a television screen.

vie (vaɪ) *vb.* **vying, vied.** (foll. by *with* or *for*) to attempt to do or have (something) before or better than (another person). —'**vying** *adj., n.*

vies (fɪs) *adj. S. African slang.* angry.

Vietnamese (ˌvjɛtnəˈmiːz) *adj.* **1.** of Vietnam, in SE Asia, its people, or their language. ~*n.* **2.** (*pl.* **-ese**) a person from Vietnam. **3.** the language of Vietnam.

view (vjuː) *n.* **1.** the act of seeing or observing. **2.** vision or sight, esp. range of vision: *the church is out of view.* **3.** everything that can be seen from a particular

place or in a particular direction: *the view from the top was superb.* **4.** a pictorial representation of a scene, such as a photograph. **5.** (*sometimes pl.*) opinion: *my own view on the matter differs from yours.* **6.** (foll. by *to*) an intention: *he has a view to securing further qualifications.* **7. in view of.** taking into consideration. **8. on view.** exhibited to the public gaze. **9. take a dim** *or* **poor view of.** to regard (something) with disfavour. ~*vb.* **10.** to look at. **11.** to consider in a specified manner: *they view the growth of Communism with horror.* **12.** to examine or inspect carefully: *to view the accounts.* **13.** to watch (television).

viewdata ('vjuːˌdeɪtə) *n.* an interactive videotext service in which the consumer is linked to a computer by telephone and is thus able to select the information required.

viewer ('vjuːə) *n.* **1.** a person who views something, esp. television. **2.** any optical device used for viewing something, esp. one for viewing photographic transparencies.

viewfinder ('vjuːˌfaɪndə) *n.* a device on a camera that lets the user see what will be included in the photograph.

viewpoint ('vjuːˌpɔɪnt) *n.* the mental attitude that determines a person's judgments.

vigil ('vɪdʒɪl) *n.* **1.** a purposeful watch maintained, esp. at night, to guard, observe, or pray. **2.** *R.C. Church, Church of England.* the eve of certain major festivals.

vigilance ('vɪdʒɪləns) *n.* the fact, quality, or condition of being vigilant.

vigilance committee *n.* (in the U.S.) a self-appointed body of citizens organized to maintain order.

vigilant ('vɪdʒɪlənt) *adj.* keenly alert to or on the watch for trouble or danger.

vigilante (ˌvɪdʒɪˈlæntɪ) *n.* a self-appointed protector of public order.

vignette (vɪˈnjɛt) *n.* **1.** a small illustration at the beginning or end of a book or chapter. **2.** a short graceful literary sketch. **3.** a photograph or drawing with edges that are shaded off.

vigorous ('vɪgərəs) *adj.* **1.** having, bodily or mental strength or vitality. **2.** having, displaying, or performed with vigour: *vigorous growth.* —'**vigorously** *adv.*

vigour *or U.S.* **vigor** ('vɪgə) *n.* **1.** exuberant and resilient strength of body or mind. **2.** forcefulness: *I was surprised by the vigour of her complaints.* **3.** strong healthy growth.

Viking ('vaɪkɪŋ) *n.* any of the Scandinavians who raided by sea most of N and W Europe from the 8th to the 11th centuries.

vile (vaɪl) *adj.* **1.** morally wicked; evil: *vile accusations.* **2.** disgusting; foul: *a vile smell.* **3.** tending to humiliate or degrade: *only slaves would perform such vile tasks.* **4.** unpleasant or bad: *vile weather.* —'**vilely** *adv.*

vilify ('vɪlɪˌfaɪ) vb. **-fying, -fied.** to speak very badly of (someone); malign. —**vilification** (ˌvɪlɪfɪ'keɪʃən) n.

villa ('vɪlə) n. **1.** a large country residence. **2.** Brit. a detached or semidetached suburban house. **3.** a house rented to holidaymakers.

village ('vɪlɪdʒ) n. **1.** a small group of houses in the country, larger than a hamlet. **2.** the inhabitants of such a community. —**'villager** n.

villain ('vɪlən) n. **1.** a wicked or evil person. **2.** (in a novel or play) the main evil character.

villainous ('vɪlənəs) adj. of, like, or appropriate to a villain.

villainy ('vɪlənɪ) n., pl. **-lainies.** evil or vicious behaviour or action.

villein ('vɪlən) n. (in medieval Europe) a peasant personally bound to his lord, to whom he paid dues and services in return for his land. —**'villeinage** n.

vim (vɪm) n. Slang. exuberant vigour and energy.

vinaigrette (ˌvɪneɪ'grɛt) n. salad dressing made from oil and vinegar with seasonings.

vindicate ('vɪndɪˌkeɪt) vb. **1.** to clear from guilt, blame, or suspicion. **2.** to provide justification for: his promotion vindicated his unconventional attitude. —**'vindiˌcator** n. —**'vindiˌcatory** adj.

vindication (ˌvɪndɪ'keɪʃən) n. **1.** the act of vindicating or the condition of being vindicated. **2.** a fact or piece of evidence that serves to vindicate.

vindictive (vɪn'dɪktɪv) adj. **1.** disposed to seek vengeance. **2.** characterized by spite or rancour. —**vin'dictively** adv. —**vin'dictiveness** n.

vine (vaɪn) n. **1.** any of various plants, esp. the grapevine, with long flexible stems that climb by clinging to a support. **2.** the stem of such a plant. —**'viny** adj.

vinegar ('vɪnɪgə) n. **1.** a sour-tasting liquid made by fermentation of beer, wine, or cider: used as a condiment or preservative. **2.** sourness or peevishness of temper, speech, or character. —**'vinegary** adj.

vineyard ('vɪnjəd) n. a plantation of grapevines, esp. where wine grapes are produced.

vingt-et-un (ˌvænteɪ'æn) n. same as **pontoon**².

viniculture ('vɪnɪˌkʌltʃə) n. the process or business of growing grapes and making wine. —**ˌvini'culturist** n.

vino ('viːnəʊ) n., pl. **-nos.** Informal. wine.

vinous ('vaɪnəs) adj. of or characteristic of wine.

vintage ('vɪntɪdʒ) n. **1.** the wine obtained from a particular harvest of grapes. **2.** the harvest from which such a wine is obtained. **3.** a time of origin: a car of Edwardian vintage. ~adj. **4.** (of wine) of an outstandingly good year. **5.** representative of the best and most typical: vintage Shakespeare.

vintage car n. Chiefly Brit. an old car, esp. one constructed between 1919 and 1930.

vintner ('vɪntnə) n. a wine merchant.

vinyl ('vaɪnɪl) n. **1.** (modifier) of or containing the monovalent group of atoms CH_2CH-: vinyl chloride. **2.** any of various strong plastics made by the polymerization of vinyl compounds, such as PVC. **3.** (modifier) of or made of vinyl: a vinyl raincoat. **4.** conventional records made of vinyl as opposed to compact discs.

viol ('vaɪəl) n. any of a family of stringed musical instruments that preceded the violin, consisting of a fretted fingerboard, a body with a flat back, and six strings.

viola¹ (vɪ'əʊlə) n. a bowed stringed instrument of the violin family, slightly larger and lower in pitch than the violin.

viola² ('vaɪələ, vaɪ'əʊ-) n. any of various plants, the flowers of which have showy irregular petals, white, yellow, blue, or mauve in colour.

viola da gamba (vɪ'əʊlə də 'gæmbə) n. the second largest and lowest member of the viol family.

violate ('vaɪəˌleɪt) vb. **1.** to break, disregard, or infringe (a law, agreement, or treaty). **2.** to rape. **3.** to disturb rudely or improperly: no-one violated his privacy. **4.** to treat disrespectfully: he violated a sanctuary. —**ˌvio'lation** n. —**'vioˌlator** n.

violence ('vaɪələns) n. **1.** the exercise or an instance of physical force, usually intended to cause injuries or destruction. **2.** great force or strength as in actions, feeling, or expression. **3.** an unjust or unlawful display of force. **4. do violence to. a.** to inflict harm upon: they did violence to the prisoners. **b.** to distort the meaning of: the reporters did violence to my speech.

violent ('vaɪələnt) adj. **1.** marked or caused by great physical force or violence: a violent stab. **2.** marked by intensity of any kind: a violent clash of colours; I took a violent dislike to her. **3.** characterized by an undue use of force. —**'violently** adv.

violet ('vaɪəlɪt) n. **1.** any of a genus of plants, such as the **sweet** (or **garden**) **violet**, having mauve or bluish flowers with irregular showy petals. **2.** a purplish-blue colour. **3.** a dye or pigment of or producing this colour. ~adj. **4.** purplish-blue.

violin (ˌvaɪə'lɪn) n. a musical instrument, the highest member of the violin family, with four strings played with a bow.

violinist (ˌvaɪə'lɪnɪst) n. a person who plays the violin.

violist (vɪ'əʊlɪst) n. a person who plays the viola.

violoncello (ˌvaɪələn'tʃɛləʊ) n., pl. **-los.** same as **cello.**

VIP very important person.

viper ('vaɪpə) n. **1.** any of a family of venomous snakes. **2.** a malicious or treacherous person.

virago (vɪ'rɑːgəʊ) n., pl. **-goes** or **-gos.** a loud, violent, and ill-tempered woman.

viral ('vaɪrəl) adj. of or caused by a virus.

virgin ('vɜːdʒɪn) n. **1.** a person, esp. a woman, who has never had sexual intercourse. ~adj. **2.** of or like a virgin or virgins. **3.** pure and natural, uncorrupted or untouched: virgin purity. **4.** not yet cultivated, explored, or exploited by man: the virgin forests.

Virgin ('vɜːdʒɪn) n. **1. the.** same as **Virgin Mary. 2.** a statue or picture of the Virgin Mary.

virginal[1] ('vɜːdʒɪn²l) adj. **1.** of or characterized by virginity; chaste. **2.** extremely pure or fresh.

virginal[2] ('vɜːdʒɪn²l) n. (often pl.) an early keyboard instrument, like a small harpsichord, but oblong in shape.

Virgin Birth n. Christianity. the doctrine that Jesus Christ was conceived solely by the direct intervention of the Holy Spirit so that Mary remained miraculously a virgin.

Virginia creeper (və'dʒɪnɪə) n. a climbing plant of North America, with leaves that turn red in autumn.

virginity (və'dʒɪnɪtɪ) n. the condition or fact of being a virgin.

Virgin Mary n. **the.** Christianity. Mary, the mother of Christ.

Virgo ('vɜːgəʊ) n. the sixth sign of the zodiac; the virgin.

virgule ('vɜːgjuːl) n. Printing. same as **solidus.**

virile ('vɪraɪl) adj. **1.** of or characteristic of an adult male. **2.** (of a male) having a high sexual drive and capacity for sexual intercourse. **3.** strong, forceful, or vigorous. —**virility** (vɪ'rɪlɪtɪ) n.

virology (vaɪ'rɒlədʒɪ) n. the branch of medicine concerned with the study of viruses. —**virological** (,vaɪrə'lɒdʒɪk²l) adj.

virtual ('vɜːtʃʊəl) adj. **1.** having the essence or effect but not the appearance or form of: a virtual revolution. **2.** Computers. designed so as to extend the potential of a finite system beyond its immediate limits. **Virtual memory** increases the potential of a computer by transferring programs or parts of programs between core and store.

virtually ('vɜːtʃʊəlɪ) adv. in effect though not in fact; practically; nearly.

virtue ('vɜːtjuː) n. **1.** moral excellence or righteousness. **2.** a particular moral excellence: the virtue of tolerance. **3.** any admirable quality or trait. **4.** chastity, esp. in women. **5. by or in virtue of.** by reason of.

virtuoso (,vɜːtjʊ'əʊzəʊ, -səʊ) n., pl. **-sos** or **-si** (-siː). **1.** a skilled master of musical technique and artistry. **2.** a person who has a masterly or dazzling skill in any field of activity. **3.** (modifier) showing masterly skill or brilliance: a virtuoso performance. —**virtuosity** (,vɜːtjʊ'ɒsɪtɪ) n.

virtuous ('vɜːtʃʊəs) adj. **1.** characterized by or possessing virtue. **2.** (of a woman) chaste. —**virtuously** adv.

virulent ('vɪrʊlənt) adj. **1. a.** (of a microorganism) extremely infective. **b.** (of a disease) having a violent effect. **2.** extremely poisonous or injurious: a virulent poison. **3.** extremely bitter or hostile: virulent criticism. —**virulence** n.

virus ('vaɪrəs) n. **1.** any of a group of very simple organisms that are smaller than bacteria and can cause disease in animals and plants. **2.** Informal. a disease caused by a virus. **3.** any corrupting influence. **4.** Computers. a short program inserted without authorization into a computer's main program, which, when activated, interferes with the operation of the computer and other computers with which it is linked.

visa ('viːzə) n. an endorsement in a passport permitting its bearer to travel into or through the country of the government issuing it.

visage ('vɪzɪdʒ) n. Chiefly literary. **1.** face or countenance. **2.** appearance.

vis-à-vis (,viːzɑː'viː) prep. **1.** in relation to. **2.** face to face with. ~adv., adj. **3.** face to face; opposite. ~n., pl. **vis-à-vis. 4.** a person or thing that is opposite another.

viscera ('vɪsərə) pl. n., sing. **viscus** ('vɪskəs). Anat. the large internal organs of the body collectively.

visceral ('vɪsərəl) adj. **1.** of or affecting the viscera. **2.** characterized by instinct rather than intellect.

viscid ('vɪsɪd) adj. sticky.

viscose ('vɪskəʊs) n. **1.** a sticky solution obtained by dissolving cellulose: used in the manufacture of rayon and cellophane. **2.** rayon made from this material.

viscosity (vɪs'kɒsɪtɪ) n., pl. **-ties. 1.** the state or property of being viscous. **2.** Physics. the extent to which a fluid resists a tendency to flow.

viscount ('vaɪkaʊnt) n. (in the British Isles) a nobleman ranking below an earl and above a baron. —**viscountcy** n. —**viscountess** fem. n.

viscous ('vɪskəs) adj. (of liquids) thick and sticky; not flowing easily.

vise (vaɪs) n. U.S. same as **vice**[2].

visibility (,vɪzɪ'bɪlɪtɪ) n. **1.** the condition or fact of being visible. **2.** the relative possibility of seeing. **3.** the range of vision: visibility is 500 yards.

visible ('vɪzɪb²l) adj. **1.** capable of being perceived by the eye. **2.** capable of being perceived by the mind: no visible dangers. —**visibly** adv.

vision ('vɪʒən) n. **1.** the act of perceiving or

the ability to perceive with the eye; sight.
2. the image on a television screen. 3. great
perception, esp. of future developments: *a
man of vision*. 4. a hallucination, esp. one
resulting from a mystical or religious experience: *the vision of St John of the Cross*.
5. (*sometimes pl.*) a vivid mental image
produced by the imagination: *he had visions
of becoming famous*. 6. a person or thing of
extraordinary beauty.

visionary ('vɪʒənərɪ) *adj.* 1. marked by
vision or foresight: *a visionary leader*. 2.
idealistic but impractical. 3. given to having visions. 4. of, like, or seen in visions.
~*n., pl.* **-aries.** 5. a visionary person.

visit ('vɪzɪt) *vb.* 1. to go or come to see (a
person or place). 2. to stay with (someone)
as a guest. 3. (of a disease or disaster) to
afflict. 4. (foll. by *upon* or *on*) to inflict
(punishment). 5. (foll. by *with*) *U.S. &
Canad. informal.* to chat with (someone).
~*n.* 6. the act or an instance of visiting. 7.
a stay as a guest. 8. a professional or
official call.

visitant ('vɪzɪtənt) *n.* 1. a ghost; apparition. 2. a migratory bird temporarily resting in a particular region.

visitation (,vɪzɪ'teɪʃən) *n.* 1. an official visit for the purpose of inspecting an institution. 2. a visiting of punishment or reward
from heaven. 3. any disaster or catastrophe: *a visitation of the plague*.

Visitation (,vɪzɪ'teɪʃən) *n.* **a.** the visit made
by the Virgin Mary to her cousin Elizabeth
(Luke 1: 39–56). **b.** the Church festival commemorating this, held on July 2.

visitor ('vɪzɪtə) *n.* a person who pays a visit;
caller, guest, or tourist.

visor ('vaɪzə) *n.* 1. a transparent flap on a
helmet that can be pulled down to protect
the face. 2. a small movable screen used as
protection against glare from the sun, esp.
one attached above the windscreen of a
motor vehicle.

vista ('vɪstə) *n.* 1. a view, esp. through a
long narrow avenue of trees or buildings.
2. a comprehensive mental view of a series
of future events.

visual ('vɪʒʊəl) *adj.* 1. of, done by, or used
in seeing. 2. capable of being seen; visible.
—'**visually** *adv.*

visual aids *pl. n.* devices, such as films or
models, that display in visual form material
to be understood or remembered.

visual display unit *n. Computers.* a device that displays characters or diagrams
representing data in a computer memory.

visualize *or* **-lise** ('vɪʒʊəˌlaɪz) *vb.* to form a
mental image of (something not at that
moment visible). —,**visuali'zation** *or*
-li'sation *n.*

vital ('vaɪt'l) *adj.* 1. essential to maintain
life: *the lungs perform a vital function*. 2.
forceful, energetic, or lively: *a vital person*.

3. of or having life: *a vital organism*. 4.
indispensable or essential: *books vital to
this study*. 5. of great importance: *a vital
game*. ~*n.* 6. (*pl.*) the bodily organs, such
as the brain, liver, heart, and lungs, that are
necessary to maintain life. —'**vitally** *adv.*

vitality (vaɪ'tælɪtɪ) *n., pl.* **-ties.** 1. physical
or mental energy. 2. the power to continue
in existence, live, or grow: *the vitality of a
movement.*

vitalize *or* **-lise** ('vaɪtəˌlaɪz) *vb.* to make
vital or alive. —,**vitali'zation** *or* **-li-
'sation** *n.*

vital statistics *pl. n.* 1. population statistics, such as the numbers of births, marriages, and deaths. 2. *Informal.* the measurements of a woman's bust, waist, and
hips.

vitamin ('vɪtəmɪn, 'vaɪ-) *n.* any of a group of
substances that occur naturally in certain
foods and are essential for the normal functioning of metabolism in the body.

vitamin A *n.* a vitamin occurring in green
and yellow vegetables, butter, egg yolk, and
fish-liver oil. It prevents night blindness.

vitamin B *n., pl.* **B vitamins.** any of the
vitamins in the vitamin B complex.

vitamin B complex *n.* a large group of
vitamins occurring esp. in liver and yeast:
includes thiamine (**vitamin B₁**), riboflavin
(**vitamin B₂**), **vitamin B₆**, and **vitamin B₁₂**.

vitamin C *n.* a vitamin occurring in citrus
fruits, tomatoes, and green vegetables. It
prevents and cures scurvy.

vitamin D *n., pl.* **D vitamins.** any of the
vitamins occurring in fish-liver oils, milk,
butter, and eggs, and used in the treatment
of rickets.

vitamin E *n.* a vitamin occuring in wheat-
germ oil, lettuce, egg yolk, and milk. It is
thought to be necessary for some aspects of
reproduction.

vitamin K *n., pl.* **K vitamins.** any of the
vitamins, occurring in green leafy vegetables, fish meal, egg yolks, and tomatoes,
which are essential for the normal clotting
of blood.

vitamin P *n., pl.* **P vitamins.** any of a
group of crystalline substances occurring
mainly in citrus fruits, blackcurrants, and
rosehips: they regulate the strength of the
blood capillaries.

vitiate ('vɪʃɪˌeɪt) *vb.* 1. to spoil or weaken
the effectiveness of (something). 2. to destroy the legal effect of (a contract).
—,**viti'ation** *n.*

viticulture ('vɪtɪˌkʌltʃə) *n.* the cultivation of
grapevines.

vitreous ('vɪtrɪəs) *adj.* 1. of or like glass.
2. of or relating to the vitreous humour.

vitreous humour *or* **body** *n.* a transparent gelatinous substance that fills the eyeball between the lens and the retina.

vitrify ('vɪtrɪˌfaɪ) *vb.* **-fying, -fied.** to convert or be converted into glass or a glassy substance. —**vitrification** (ˌvɪtrɪfɪˈkeɪ-ʃən) *n*.

vitriol (ˈvɪtrɪɒl) *n*. **1.** sulphuric acid. **2.** speech or criticism displaying hatred or bitterness.

vitriolic (ˌvɪtrɪˈɒlɪk) *adj*. (of speech or criticism) severely bitter or caustic.

vituperate (vɪˈtjuːpəˌreɪt) *vb*. to speak (against) abusively; revile. —**viˌtuperˈation** *n*. —**viˈtuperative** *adj*.

viva[1] (ˈviːvə) *interj*. long live; up with (a specified person or thing).

viva[2] (ˈvaɪvə) *Brit*. ~*n*. **1.** an oral examination. ~*vb*. -**vaing**, -**vaed**. **2.** to examine orally.

vivace (vɪˈvɑːtʃɪ) *adv*. *Music*. to be performed in a lively manner.

vivacious (vɪˈveɪʃəs) *adj*. full of high spirits and animation.

vivacity (vɪˈvæsɪtɪ) *n*. the quality or condition of being vivacious.

vivarium (vaɪˈvɛərɪəm) *n*., *pl*. -**iums** *or* -**ia** (-ɪə). a place where live animals are kept under natural conditions.

viva voce (ˈvaɪvə ˈvəʊtʃɪ) *adv*., *adj*. **1.** by word of mouth. ~*n*., *vb*. **2.** same as **viva**[2].

vivid (ˈvɪvɪd) *adj*. **1.** (of a colour) very bright; intense. **2.** conveying striking realism, freshness, or trueness to life: *a vivid account*. **3.** (of a memory) remaining distinct. **4.** (of the imagination) easily forming lifelike images. —**ˈvividly** *adv*. —**ˈvividness** *n*.

vivify (ˈvɪvɪˌfaɪ) *vb*. -**fying**, -**fied**. **1.** to bring to life; animate. **2.** to make more vivid or striking.

viviparous (vɪˈvɪpərəs) *adj*. (of most mammals) giving birth to living offspring.

vivisect (ˈvɪvɪˌsɛkt, ˌvɪvɪˈsɛkt) *vb*. to subject (an animal) to vivisection. —**ˈviviˌsector** *n*.

vivisection (ˌvɪvɪˈsɛkʃən) *n*. the performing of experiments on living animals, involving cutting into or dissecting the body. —ˌviviˈsectionist *n*.

vixen (ˈvɪksən) *n*. **1.** a female fox. **2.** a quarrelsome or spiteful woman.

viz (vɪz) *adv*. namely: used to specify items.

vizier (vɪˈzɪə) *n*. a high official in certain Muslim countries.

vizor (ˈvaɪzə) *n*. same as **visor**.

VL Vulgar Latin.

V neck *n*. **a.** a neck on a garment that comes down to a point, like the letter V. **b.** a sweater with such a neck. —**ˈV-ˌneck** *or* **ˈV-ˌnecked** *adj*.

voc. *or* **vocat.** vocative.

vocab (ˈvəʊkæb) *n*. short for **vocabulary**.

vocable (ˈvəʊkəbʳl) *n*. any word regarded simply as a sequence of letters or spoken sounds.

vocabulary (vəˈkæbjʊlərɪ) *n*., *pl*. -**laries**. **1.** a listing containing the words and phrases of a language, with meanings or translations into another language. **2.** all the words used by a particular person, class, or profession. **3.** all the words contained in a language. **4.** a range of symbols or techniques as used in any of the arts or crafts: *a wide vocabulary of textures and colours*.

vocal (ˈvəʊkʳl) *adj*. **1.** of, for, or produced by the voice: *vocal music*. **2.** connected with the production of the voice: *vocal organs*. **3.** inclined to express opinions or criticisms strongly and clearly in speech: *a vocal minority*. ~*n*. **4.** a piece of jazz or pop music that is sung. —**ˈvocally** *adv*.

vocal cords *pl. n*. either of two pairs of membranous folds in the larynx. The lower pair can be made to vibrate and produce sound by forcing air from the lungs over them.

vocalist (ˈvəʊkəlɪst) *n*. a singer with a pop group.

vocalize *or* -**ise** (ˈvəʊkəˌlaɪz) *vb*. **1.** to express with or use the voice. **2.** to make vocal or articulate. **3.** *Phonetics*. to articulate (a speech sound) with voice. **4.** to sing a melody on a vowel. —ˌvocaliˈzation *or* -iˈsation *n*.

vocation (vəʊˈkeɪʃən) *n*. **1.** a specified profession or trade. **2. a.** a special urge to a particular calling or career, esp. a religious one. **b.** such a calling or career. —**voˈcational** *adj*.

vocative (ˈvɒkətɪv) *Grammar*. ~*adj*. **1.** denoting a case of nouns, in some inflected languages, used when addressing a person or thing. ~*n*. **2.** the vocative case.

vociferate (vəʊˈsɪfəˌreɪt) *vb*. to exclaim or cry out about (something) noisily or vehemently. —**voˌciferˈation** *n*.

vociferous (vəʊˈsɪfərəs) *adj*. noisy or vehement: *vociferous protests*.

vodka (ˈvɒdkə) *n*. a clear alcoholic spirit originating in Russia, made from grain.

vogue (vəʊg) *n*. **1.** the popular style at a given time: *miniskirts are in vogue*. **2.** a period of general popularity: *the vogue for such dances is over*. ~*adj*. **3.** fashionable: *a vogue word*. —**ˈvoguish** *adj*.

voice (vɔɪs) *n*. **1.** the sound made by the vibration of the vocal cords, esp. when modified by the tongue and mouth. **2.** distinctive tone of the speech sounds characteristic of a particular person. **3.** the condition or quality of such sounds: *a hysterical voice*. **4.** the musical sound of a singing voice: *she has a lovely voice*. **5.** the ability to speak or sing: *he has lost his voice*. **6.** written or spoken expression of feeling or opinion: *she gave voice to her fears*. **7.** a stated choice, wish, or opinion: *I had no voice in the decision*. **8.** an agency through which is communicated another's purpose or policy: *such groups are the voice of our enemies*. **9.** *Phonetics*. the sound characterizing the articulation of several speech sounds, that is produced when the vocal cords are vibrated by the breath. **10.** *Grammar*. a category of the verb that expresses whether it is active or passive. **11. in voice.** in a condition to sing or speak well. **12. with one voice.** unanimously. ~*vb.* **13.** to express: *to voice a complaint.* **14.** to articulate (a speech sound) with voice.

voiced (vɔɪst) *adj.* **1.** expressed by the voice. **2.** *Phonetics.* articulated with accompanying vibration of the vocal cords: *in English* (b) *is a voiced consonant.*

voiceless ('vɔɪslɪs) *adj.* **1.** without a voice. **2.** *Phonetics.* articulated without accompanying vibration of the vocal cords: *in English* (p) *is a voiceless consonant.*

voice-over *n.* the voice of an unseen commentator heard during a film.

void (vɔɪd) *adj.* **1.** without contents. **2.** not legally binding: *null and void.* **3.** (foll. by *of*) destitute or devoid: *void of hope.* **4.** useless: *all his efforts were rendered void.* ~*n.* **5.** an empty space or area. **6.** a feeling or condition of loneliness or deprivation. ~*vb.* **7.** to make ineffective or invalid. **8.** to empty (contents) or make empty of contents. **9.** to discharge the contents of (the bowels or bladder).

voile (vɔɪl) *n.* a light semitransparent dress fabric of silk, rayon, or cotton.

vol. **1.** volcano. **2.** volume. **3.** volunteer.

volatile ('vɒləˌtaɪl) *adj.* **1.** (of a substance) changing readily from a solid or liquid form to a vapour. **2.** (of persons) liable to sudden and unexpected changes of mood and behaviour. **3.** (of circumstances) liable to sudden change. —**volatility** (ˌvɒlə'tɪlɪtɪ) *n.*

volatilize *or* **-lise** (vɒ'lætɪˌlaɪz) *vb.* to change or cause to change from a solid or liquid to a vapour. —**voˌlatiliˈzation** *or* **-liˈsation** *n.*

vol-au-vent ('vɒləʊˌvɒŋ) *n.* a very light puff pastry case filled with a savoury mixture.

volcanic (vɒl'kænɪk) *adj.* **1.** of, produced by, or characterized by volcanoes: *a volcanic region.* **2.** suggestive of or like an erupting volcano: *a volcanic temper.*

volcano (vɒl'keɪnəʊ) *n., pl.* **-noes** *or* **-nos.** **1.** an opening in the earth's crust from which molten lava, ashes, dust, and gases are ejected from below the earth's surface. **2.** a mountain formed from volcanic material ejected from a vent.

vole (vəʊl) *n.* a small rodent with a stocky body, short tail, and inconspicuous ears.

volition (və'lɪʃən) *n.* the act or faculty of using the will: *of one's own volition.* —**vo'litional** *adj.*

volley ('vɒlɪ) *n.* **1.** the simultaneous discharge of several weapons. **2.** the missiles so discharged. **3.** a burst of words occur-

ring simultaneously or in rapid succession. **4.** *Sport.* a stroke, shot, or kick at a moving ball before it hits the ground. ~*vb.* **5.** to discharge (weapons) in or as if in a volley or (of weapons) to be discharged. **6.** *Sport.* to strike or kick (a moving ball) before it hits the ground.

volleyball ('vɒlɪˌbɔːl) *n.* a game in which two teams hit a large ball back and forth over a high net with their hands.

volt (vəʊlt) *n.* the derived SI unit of electric potential; the potential difference between two points on a conductor carrying a current of 1 ampere, when the power dissipated between these points is 1 watt.

voltage ('vəʊltɪdʒ) *n.* an electromotive force or potential difference expressed in volts.

voltaic (vɒl'teɪɪk) *adj.* same as **galvanic** (sense 1).

volte-face ('vɒlt'fɑːs) *n., pl.* **volte-face.** a reversal, as in opinion.

voltmeter ('vəʊltˌmiːtə) *n.* an instrument for measuring voltage.

voluble ('vɒljʊbʲl) *adj.* talking easily and at length. —ˌ**volu'bility** *n.* —'**volubly** *adv.*

volume ('vɒljuːm) *n.* **1.** the magnitude of the three-dimensional space enclosed within or occupied by something. **2.** a large mass or quantity: *the volume of protest.* **3.** an amount or total: *the volume of exports.* **4.** fullness of sound. **5.** the control on a radio, television, or record player, for adjusting the intensity of sound. **6.** a bound collection of printed or written pages; book. **7.** any of several books forming part of a series. **8.** a set of issues of a periodical over a specified period.

volumetric (ˌvɒljʊ'mɛtrɪk) *adj.* of or using measurement by volume: *volumetric analysis.*

voluminous (və'luːmɪnəs) *adj.* **1.** (of clothes) large and roomy. **2.** (of writing) consisting of or sufficient to fill volumes.

voluntary ('vɒləntrɪ) *adj.* **1.** done or undertaken by free choice: *a voluntary donation.* **2.** (of persons) serving without pay: *a voluntary social worker.* **3.** done by or composed of volunteers: *a voluntary association.* **4.** exercising or having the faculty of willing: *a voluntary agent.* **5.** (of muscles) having their action controlled by the will. **6.** maintained by the voluntary actions or contributions of individuals and not by the state: *voluntary schools.* ~*n., pl.* **-taries. 7.** *Music.* a composition, usually for organ, played at the beginning or end of a church service. —'**voluntarily** *adv.*

volunteer (ˌvɒlən'tɪə) *n.* **1.** a person who performs or offers to perform voluntary service. **2.** a person who freely undertakes military service. ~*vb.* **3.** to offer (oneself or one's services) by choice and without being forced. **4.** to do, give, or communicate voluntarily: *to volunteer help.* **5.** to enlist voluntarily for military service.

voluptuary (vəˈlʌptjʊərɪ) *n., pl.* **-aries.** a person devoted to luxury and sensual pleasures.

voluptuous (vəˈlʌptjʊəs) *adj.* **1.** of, characterized by, or consisting of sensual pleasures. **2.** (of a woman) sexually alluring through shapeliness or fullness of body. —**voˈluptuously** *adv.* —**voˈluptuousness** *n.*

volute (vɒljuːt, vəˈluːt) *n.* **1.** a spiral or twisting turn, form, or object. **2.** a carved spiral scroll, esp. on an Ionic capital. **3.** any of the whorls of a snail's spiral shell.

vomit (ˈvɒmɪt) *vb.* **1.** to eject (the contents of the stomach) through the mouth. **2.** to eject or be ejected forcefully. ~*n.* **3.** the matter ejected in vomiting.

voodoo (ˈvuːduː) *n.* **1.** Also called: **voodooism.** a religious cult involving witchcraft, common among Blacks in the West Indies. ~*adj.* **2.** relating to or associated with voodoo. ~*vb.* **-dooing, -dooed. 3.** to affect by or as if by voodoo. —**ˈvoodooist** *n.*

voorkamer (ˈfʊəˌkɑːmə) *n. S. African.* the front room of a house.

voracious (vɒˈreɪʃəs) *adj.* **1.** devouring or craving food in great quantities. **2.** very eager or insatiable in some activity: *voracious reading.* —**voracity** (vɒˈræsɪtɪ) *n.*

vortex (ˈvɔːtɛks) *n., pl.* **-texes** *or* **-tices** (-tɪˌsiːz). **1.** a whirling mass or motion, such as a whirlpool. **2.** any situation viewed as irresistibly engulfing. —**vortical** (ˈvɔːtɪkəl) *adj.*

votary (ˈvəʊtərɪ) *n., pl.* **-ries. 1.** *R.C. Church, Eastern Churches.* a person, such as a monk, who has dedicated himself to religion by taking vows. **2.** a person devoted to a cause. ~Also: **votarist.** —**ˈvotaress** *fem. n.*

vote (vəʊt) *n.* **1.** an indication of choice, opinion, or will on a question, such as the choosing of a candidate: *10 votes for Jones.* **2.** the opinion of a group of people as determined by voting: *it was put to the vote.* **3.** a body of votes or voters collectively: *the Jewish vote.* **4.** the total number of votes cast. **5.** the right to vote. **6.** a means of voting, such as a ballot. ~*vb.* **7.** to express (one's preference or will) (for or against a question): *to vote by ballot.* **8.** to declare oneself as being (something or in favour of something) by voting: *to vote socialist.* **9.** to authorize or allow by voting: *vote us a rise.* **10.** *Informal.* to declare by common opinion: *the party was voted a failure.*

vote down *vb.* to decide against or defeat in a vote: *the bill was voted down.*

voter (ˈvəʊtə) *n.* a person who can or does vote.

votive (ˈvəʊtɪv) *adj.* given, done, or dedicated in fulfilment of a vow.

vouch (vaʊtʃ) *vb.* **1.** (foll. by *for*) to give personal assurance of: *I'll vouch for his safety.* **2.** (foll. by *for*) to give supporting evidence for or be proof of.

voucher (ˈvaʊtʃə) *n.* **1.** a document serving as evidence for a transaction, such as having received or spent money. **2.** *Brit.* a ticket or card serving as a substitute for cash: *a gift voucher.*

vouchsafe (ˌvaʊtʃˈseɪf) *vb.* **1.** to give or grant: *she vouchsafed no reply.* **2.** to condescend to agree, promise, or permit: *he vouchsafed to come yesterday.*

vow (vaʊ) *n.* **1.** a solemn and binding promise made esp. to a deity or saint. **2. take vows.** to enter a religious order and commit oneself to its rule of life by the vows of poverty, chastity, and obedience. ~*vb.* **3.** to pledge, promise, or undertake solemnly: *he vowed to return.* **4.** to assert or swear emphatically.

vowel (ˈvaʊəl) *n.* **1.** *Phonetics.* a voiced speech sound made with the mouth open and the stream of breath unobstructed by the tongue, teeth, or lips. **2.** a letter or character representing a vowel.

vox pop (vɒks) *n.* interviews with members of the public on a radio or television programme.

vox populi (vɒks ˈpɒpjʊˌlaɪ) *n.* the voice of the people; public opinion.

voyage (ˈvɔɪɪdʒ) *n.* **1.** a long journey, esp. one to a distant land or by sea or in space. ~*vb.* **2.** to travel: *we will voyage to Africa.* —**ˈvoyager** *n.*

voyageur (ˌvɔɪəˈdʒɜː) *n.* (in Canada) a woodsman, guide, trapper, boatman, or explorer, esp. in the North.

voyeur (vwaɪˈɜː) *n.* a person who obtains sexual pleasure from watching people undressing or having sexual intercourse. —**voˈyeurism** *n.* —ˌvoyeurˈistic *adj.*

vrou (frəʊ) *n. S. African.* an Afrikaner woman, esp. a married woman.

vs versus

V-sign *n.* **1.** (in Britain) an offensive gesture made by sticking up the index and middle fingers with the palm of the hand inwards. **2.** a similar gesture with the palm outwards meaning victory or peace.

VSO (in Britain) Voluntary Service Overseas.

VSOP very special (*or* superior) old pale: used of brandy or port.

VT *or* **Vt.** Vermont.

VTOL (ˈviːtɒl) vertical takeoff and landing.

VTR video tape recorder.

vulcanite (ˈvʌlkəˌnaɪt) *n.* a hard black rubber produced by vulcanizing natural rubber with sulphur. It is used for electrical insulators.

vulcanize _or_ **-nise** ('vʌlkə,naɪz) _vb._ to treat (rubber) with sulphur under heat and pressure to improve elasticity and strength. —,vulcani'zation _or_ -ni'sation _n._

Vulg. Vulgate.

vulgar ('vʌlgə) _adj._ **1.** marked by lack of taste, culture, delicacy, or manners: _vulgar language._ **2.** (_often cap._) denoting a form of a language, esp. of Latin, current among common people. —'vulgarly _adv._

vulgar fraction _n._ same as **simple fraction.**

vulgarian (vʌl'gɛərɪən) _n._ a vulgar person, usually one who is rich.

vulgarism ('vʌlgə,rɪzəm) _n._ a coarse, crude, or obscene expression.

vulgarity (vʌl'gærɪtɪ) _n., pl._ **-ties. 1.** the condition of being vulgar; lack of good manners. **2.** a vulgar action or phrase.

vulgarize _or_ **-rise** ('vʌlgə,raɪz) _vb._ **1.** to make vulgar. **2.** to make (something little known or difficult to understand) popular. —,vulgari'zation _or_ -ri'sation _n._

Vulgar Latin _n._ any of the dialects of Latin spoken in the Roman Empire other than classical Latin.

Vulgate ('vʌlgeɪt, -gɪt) _n._ the fourth-century Latin version of the Bible.

vulnerable ('vʌlnərəb²l) _adj._ **1.** able to be physically or emotionally hurt. **2.** open to temptation or censure. **3.** _Mil._ exposed to attack. **4.** _Bridge._ (of a side who have won one game towards rubber) subject to increased bonuses or penalties. —,vulnera'bility _n._

vulpine ('vʌlpaɪn) _adj._ **1.** of or like a fox. **2.** clever and cunning.

vulture ('vʌltʃə) _n._ **1.** a very large bird of prey that feeds on carrion. **2.** a person or thing that preys greedily and ruthlessly on others.

vulva ('vʌlvə) _n._ the external genitals of human females.

vv vice versa.

W

w *or* **W** ('dʌbᵊl‚juː) *n., pl.* **w's, W's,** *or* **Ws.**
the 23rd letter of the English alphabet.

W 1. *Chem.* tungsten. **2.** watt. **3.** West.
4. *Physics.* work.

w. 1. week. **2.** weight. **3.** *Cricket.* wicket.
4. wide. **5.** wife. **6.** with.

WA 1. Washington (state). **2.** Western
Australia.

wacky ('wækɪ) *adj.* **wackier, wackiest.**
Slang. eccentric, funny, or exciting: *a
wacky new comedy.*

wad (wɒd) *n.* **1.** a small mass or ball of soft
material, such as cotton wool, used for
packing or stuffing. **2.** a roll or bundle of
something, esp. of banknotes. ~*vb.* **wadding, wadded. 3.** to make (something) into
a wad. **4.** to pack or stuff (something) with
wadding.

wadding ('wɒdɪŋ) *n.* a soft material used
for padding or stuffing.

waddle ('wɒdᵊl) *vb.* **1.** to walk with short
steps, rocking slightly from side to side.
~*n.* **2.** a swaying gait or motion.

wade (weɪd) *vb.* **1.** to walk slowly and
with difficulty through something such as
water or mud. **2. wade through.** to proceed with difficulty: *to wade through a
book.* **3. wade in** *or* **into.** to begin doing
something in an energetic way. ~*n.* **4.** the
act or an instance of wading.

wader ('weɪdə) *n.* a long-legged bird, such
as the heron or stork, that lives near water
and feeds on fish. Also called: **wading bird.**

waders ('weɪdəz) *pl. n.* long waterproof
boots worn by anglers.

wadi *or* **wady** ('wɒdɪ) *n., pl.* **-dies.** a
watercourse in N Africa and Arabia, which
is dry except in the rainy season.

wafer ('weɪfə) *n.* **1.** a thin crisp sweetened
biscuit, often served with ice cream. **2.**
Christianity. a thin disc of unleavened
bread used at Communion. **3.** *Electronics.* a
small thin slice of semiconductor material,
such as silicon, that is separated into numerous individual components or circuits.
4. a small disc of sticky paper used as a seal
on letters or documents.

waffle¹ ('wɒfᵊl) *Informal, chiefly Brit.*
~*vb.* **1.** (often foll. by *on*) to speak or write
in a vague and wordy manner. ~*n.* **2.**
vague and wordy speech or writing.

waffle² ('wɒfᵊl) *n.* a square crisp pancake
with deep hollows on both sides, forming a
grid-like pattern.

waft (wɑːft, wɒft) *vb.* **1.** to carry or be
carried gently on or as if on the air or
water: *the smell of her perfume wafted*
across the room. ~*n.* **2.** something, such
as a scent, carried on the air.

wag¹ (wæg) *vb.* **wagging, wagged. 1.** to
move rapidly and repeatedly from side to
side or up and down. ~*n.* **2.** the act or an
instance of wagging.

wag² (wæg) *n.* a humorous or jocular person; wit.

wage (weɪdʒ) *n.* **1.** (*often pl.*) the money
paid in return for a person's work, esp.
when paid weekly or daily rather than as a
monthly salary: *I get my wages on Thursday; less than the legal minimum wage.* **2.**
(*pl., sometimes functioning as sing.*) recompense or return: *the wages of sin is death.*
~*vb.* **3.** to engage in (an activity).

wager ('weɪdʒə) *n.* **1.** a bet on the outcome
of an event or activity. ~*vb.* **2.** to bet
(something, esp. money) on the outcome of
an event or activity.

waggle ('wægᵊl) *vb.* to move with a rapid
shaking or wobbling motion. —'**wag-
gly** *adj.*

Wagnerian (vɑːgˈnɪərɪən) *adj.* of or suggestive of the operas of Richard Wagner, German composer.

wagon *or* **waggon** ('wægən) *n.* **1.** a four-
wheeled vehicle used for carrying heavy
loads, esp. a trailer drawn by a horse or
tractor. **2.** *Brit.* an open railway freight
truck. **3. on** (*or* **off**) **the wagon.** *Informal.*
abstaining (*or* no longer abstaining) from
alcoholic drinks. —'**wagoner** *or* '**waggon-
er** *n.*

wagtail ('wæg‚teɪl) *n.* a small songbird of
Eurasia and Africa with a very long tail
that wags up and down when the bird
walks.

wahine (wɑːˈhiːnɪ) *n. N.Z.* a Maori woman.

waif (weɪf) *n.* **1.** a person, esp. a child, who
is homeless, friendless, or neglected. **2.**
anything found and apparently without an
owner. —'**waif‚like** *adj.*

wail (weɪl) *vb.* **1.** to utter a prolonged high-
pitched cry, as of grief or misery. **2.** to
make a sound resembling such a cry: *the
wind wailed in the trees.* ~*n.* **3.** a prolonged high-pitched mournful cry or sound.

wain (weɪn) *n. Chiefly poetic.* a farm cart.

wainscot ('weɪnskət) *n.* a wooden covering
on the lower half of the walls of a room.
Also called: **wainscoting** *or* **wainscotting.**

waist (weɪst) *n.* **1.** *Anat.* the part of the
body between the ribs and hips. **2.** the part
of a garment covering the waist. **3.** the
middle part of something, such as a violin,

that resembles the waist in narrowness or position.

waistband ('weɪst,bænd) n. a band of material sewn on to the waist of a garment to strengthen it.

waistcoat ('weɪs,kəʊt) n. a sleeveless waistlength garment which buttons up the front and is usually worn by men over a shirt and under a jacket.

waistline ('weɪst,laɪn) n. 1. an imaginary line around the body at the narrowest part of the waist. 2. the place where the upper and lower part of a garment are joined together.

wait (weɪt) vb. 1. (often foll. by for, until, or to) to stay in one place or remain inactive in expectation (of something). 2. to delay temporarily or be temporarily delayed: that work can wait. 3. (usually foll. by for) (of things) to be ready; be in store (for a person): supper was waiting for them when they got home. 4. to act as a waiter or waitress. ~n. 5. the act or a period of waiting. 6. lie in wait. to prepare an ambush (for someone). ~See also **wait on**, **wait up**.

waiter ('weɪtə) n. a man who serves people with food and drink in a restaurant.

waiting game n. the postponement of action or decision in order to gain the advantage.

waiting list n. a list of people waiting for something that is not immediately available.

waiting room n. a room in which people may wait, as at a railway station or doctor's surgery.

wait on vb. 1. to serve at the table of. 2. to act as an attendant to. ~interj. 3. N.Z. stop! hold on! ~Also (for senses 1, 2): **wait upon**.

waitress ('weɪtrɪs) n. a woman who serves people with food and drink in a restaurant.

wait up vb. to delay going to bed in order to await some event.

waive (weɪv) vb. 1. to give up; relinquish: to waive one's right to something. 2. to refrain from enforcing or applying (a law or penalty).

waiver ('weɪvə) n. the voluntary giving up of some claim or right.

wake[1] (weɪk) vb. **waking, woke, woken.** 1. (often foll. by up) to rouse or become roused from sleep. 2. (often foll. by up) to rouse or become roused from inactivity. 3. (often foll. by to or up to) to become conscious or aware: at last he woke up to the situation. 4. **waking hours.** the time when a person is awake: she spends most of her waking hours working. ~n. 5. a watch or vigil held over the body of a dead person during the night before burial. 6. **Wakes.** an annual holiday in various towns in Northern England.

Usage. Where there is an object and the sense is the literal one wake (up) and waken are the commonest forms: I wakened him; I woke him (up). Both verbs are also commonly used without an object: I woke up. Awake and awaken are preferred to other forms of wake where the sense is a figurative one: he awoke to the danger.

wake[2] (weɪk) n. 1. the track left by a ship moving through water. 2. **in the wake of.** following close behind: wrecked houses in the wake of the hurricane.

wakeful ('weɪkful) adj. 1. unable or unwilling to sleep. 2. sleepless. 3. alert. —'**wakefully** adv. —'**wakefulness** n.

waken ('weɪkən) vb. to rouse or be roused from sleep or some other inactive state.

wale (weɪl) n. 1. same as **weal**[1]. 2. the weave or texture of a fabric, such as the ribs in corduroy. 3. Naut. a ridge of planking along the rail of a ship.

walk (wɔːk) vb. 1. to move on foot at a moderate rate with at least one foot always on the ground. 2. to pass through, on, or over on foot. 3. to escort or accompany (a person or animal) by walking: to walk someone home; I must walk the dog. 4. to follow a certain course or way of life: to walk in misery. 5. to bring into a certain condition by walking: I walked my shoes to shreds. 6. to disappear or be stolen: where's my pencil? it seems to have walked. 7. **walk it.** to win easily. 8. **walk on air.** to be delighted or exhilarated. 9. **walk the streets.** to wander about, esp. when looking for work or when homeless. ~n. 10. the act or an instance of walking. 11. the distance walked. 12. a manner of walking; gait. 13. a place or route for walking. 14. social position or profession: the committee come from many different walks of life. ~See also **walk into**, **walk out**, etc. —'**walkable** adj.

walkabout ('wɔːkə,baʊt) n. an occasion when celebrities, royalty, or politicians walk among and meet the public.

walker ('wɔːkə) n. 1. a person who walks. 2. Also called: **baby walker.** a tubular frame on wheels or casters to support a baby learning to walk. 3. a similar support used by disabled or infirm people for walking.

walkie-talkie (,wɔːkɪ'tɔːkɪ) n., pl. **-talkies.** a small combined radio transmitter and receiver that can be carried around by one person.

walking stick n. a stick or cane carried in the hand to assist walking.

walk into vb. to meet with unwittingly: he had walked into their trap.

Walkman ('wɔːkmən) n., pl. **-mans.** Trademark. a small portable cassette player with headphones.

walk-on n. a small part in a play or film, esp. one without any lines.

walk out *vb.* **1.** to leave without explanation, esp. in anger. **2.** (of workers) to go on strike. **3. walk out on.** *Informal.* to abandon or desert someone. ~*n.* **walkout. 4.** a strike by workers. **5.** the act of leaving a meeting as a protest.

walkover ('wɔːk,əʊvə) *n.* **1.** *Informal.* an easy or unopposed victory. ~*vb.* **walk over. 2.** to win easily or without being opposed.

walkway ('wɔːk,weɪ) *n.* **1.** a path designed for pedestrian use. **2.** a passage or pathway between two buildings.

wall (wɔːl) *n.* **1.** a vertical structure made of stone, brick, or wood with a length and height much greater than its thickness, used to enclose, divide, or support. **2.** (*often pl.*) a fortification built around a position or place for defensive purposes. **3.** anything that suggests a wall in function or effect: *a wall of fire.* **4.** *Anat.* any lining or membrane that encloses a bodily cavity or structure: *abdominal wall.* **5. go to the wall.** *Informal.* to be ruined, esp. financially. **6. go** (*or* **drive**) **up the wall.** *Slang.* to become (*or* cause to become) crazy or furious. **7. have one's back to the wall.** to be in a very difficult situation. ~*vb.* **8.** to protect, provide, or confine with or as if with a wall. **9.** (often foll. by *up*) to block (an opening) with a wall. **10.** (often foll. by *in* or *up*) to seal by or within a wall or walls. **—walled** *adj.*

wallaby ('wɒləbɪ) *n., pl.* **-bies** *or* **-by.** a plant-eating marsupial of Australia and New Guinea, similar to but smaller than a kangaroo.

wallah ('wɒlə) *n. Informal.* a person involved with or in charge of (a specified thing): *the book wallah.*

wall bars *pl. n.* a series of horizontal bars attached to a wall and used in gymnastics.

wallet ('wɒlɪt) *n.* a small folding case, usually of leather, for holding paper money or other things, such as credit cards.

walleyed ('wɔːl,aɪd) *adj.* having eyes with an abnormal amount of white showing because of a divergent squint.

wallflower ('wɔːl,flaʊə) *n.* **1.** a plant grown for its clusters of yellow, orange, brown, red, or purple fragrant flowers. **2.** *Informal.* a woman who stays on the fringes of a dance or party because she is shy or does not have a partner.

Walloon (wɒ'luːn) *n.* **1.** a member of a French-speaking people living chiefly in S Belgium and adjacent parts of France. **2.** the French dialect of Belgium. ~*adj.* **3.** of the Walloons or their dialect.

wallop ('wɒləp) *Informal.* ~*vb.* **1.** to hit (someone or something) hard. **2.** to defeat (a person or team) utterly. ~*n.* **3.** a hard blow.

walloping ('wɒləpɪŋ) *Informal.* ~*n.* **1.** a

thrashing. ~*adj.* **2.** large or great: *a walloping drop in sales.*

wallow ('wɒləʊ) *vb.* **1.** to indulge oneself in some emotion: *to wallow in self-pity.* **2.** (esp. of certain animals) to roll about in mud or water for pleasure. **3.** (of a ship) to roll from side to side and move forward with difficulty. ~*n.* **4.** the act or an instance of wallowing. **5.** a muddy place where animals wallow.

wallpaper ('wɔːl,peɪpə) *n.* **1.** a printed or embossed paper for covering walls and ceilings. ~*vb.* **2.** to cover (a surface) with wallpaper.

Wall Street *n.* a street in lower Manhattan, New York, where the Stock Exchange and major banks are situated: regarded as the place where the most important financial business is conducted.

wall-to-wall *adj.* (esp. of carpeting) completely covering a floor.

wally ('wɒlɪ) *n., pl.* **-lies.** *Slang.* a stupid person.

walnut ('wɔːl,nʌt) *n.* **1.** a two-lobed edible nut with a hard wrinkled shell. **2.** any of various trees on which this nut grows. **3.** the yellowish-brown wood of any of these trees, used for making furniture.

walrus ('wɔːlrəs, 'wɒl-) *n., pl.* **-ruses** *or* **-rus.** a mammal of northern seas, having two tusks that project from the upper jaw, tough thick skin, and coarse whiskers.

waltz (wɔːls) *n.* **1.** a ballroom dance in triple time in which couples spin around as they progress round the room. **2.** music for this dance. ~*vb.* **3.** to dance a waltz. **4.** to move in a relaxed and confident way. **5.** *Informal.* to succeed easily.

wampum ('wɒmpəm) *n.* (formerly) money used by North American Indians, made of shells strung or woven together.

wan (wɒn) *adj.* **wanner, wannest.** unnaturally pale as a result of sickness, grief, or unhappiness. **—'wanly** *adv.*

wand (wɒnd) *n.* **1.** a rod used by a magician when performing a trick or by a fairy when casting a spell. **2.** a thin rod carried as a symbol of authority. **3.** a conductor's baton.

wander ('wɒndə) *vb.* **1.** to move or travel about, in, or through (a place) without any definite purpose or destination. **2.** to proceed in an irregular course; meander. **3.** to go astray, as from a path or course. **4.** (of the mind) to lose concentration. ~*n.* **5.** the act or an instance of wandering. **—'wanderer** *n.* **—'wandering** *adj., n.*

wandering Jew *n.* any of several creeping or trailing houseplants.

wanderlust ('wɒndə,lʌst) *n.* a great desire to travel.

wane (weɪn) *vb.* **1.** to decrease gradually in size, strength, or power. **2.** (of the moon) to show a gradually decreasing portion of illuminated surface, between full moon and new moon. ~*n.* **3.** a decrease, as in size, strength, or power. **4.** the period during which the moon wanes. **5. on the wane.** in a state of decline. —'**waney** *or* '**wany** *adj.*

wangle ('wæŋg²l) *vb. Informal.* to use devious methods to get or achieve (something): *he wangled himself a salary increase.*

wanigan ('wɒnɪgən) *n. Canad.* **1.** a lumberjack's chest or box. **2.** a cabin or houseboat.

wank (wæŋk) *Taboo slang.* ~*vb.* **1.** (of a man) to masturbate. ~*n.* **2.** an act of masturbating.

want (wɒnt) *vb.* **1.** to feel a need or longing for: *I want a new hat.* **2.** to wish, need, or desire (something or to do something): *he wants to go home.* **3.** (often foll. by *for*) to be lacking or deficient in (something necessary or desirable): *the child wants for nothing.* **4.** *Chiefly Brit.* to have need of or require (doing or being something): *your shoes want cleaning.* **5.** to be destitute. **6.** to request the presence of: *you're wanted upstairs.* **7.** *Informal.* should or ought (to do something): *you don't want to go out so late.* ~*n.* **8.** the act or an instance of wanting. **9.** anything that is needed, desired, or lacked: *to supply someone's wants.* **10.** a lack, shortage, or absence: *for want of common sense.* **11.** the state of being in need: *the state should help those in want.*

wanting ('wɒntɪŋ) *adj.* **1.** lacking or absent. **2.** not meeting requirements or expectations: *you have been found wanting.*

wanton ('wɒntən) *adj.* **1.** licentious or immoral. **2.** without motive, provocation, or justification: *wanton destruction.* **3.** maliciously and unnecessarily cruel. **4.** unrestrained: *wanton spending.* **5.** *Archaic or poetic.* playful or capricious. ~*n.* **6.** a licentious person, esp. a woman. ~*vb.* **7.** to behave in a wanton manner.

wapiti ('wɒpɪtɪ) *n., pl.* -**tis.** a large North American deer, now also found in New Zealand.

war (wɔː) *n.* **1.** open armed conflict between two or more parties, nations, or states. **2.** a particular armed conflict: *the Vietnam war.* **3.** the techniques of armed conflict as a study, science, or profession. **4.** any conflict or contest: *the war against crime.* **5.** (*modifier*) of, like, or caused by war: *war damage; a war story.* **6. have been in the wars.** *Informal.* to look as if one has been in a fight. ~*vb.* **warring, warred. 7.** to conduct a war.

War. Warwickshire.

warble ('wɔːb²l) *vb.* **1.** to sing (words or songs) in a high-pitched voice, often with trills and vibrations. ~*n.* **2.** the act or an instance of warbling.

warbler ('wɔːblə) *n.* any of various small songbirds.

war crime *n.* a crime committed in war-

time in violation of the accepted customs, such as ill-treatment of prisoners. —**war criminal** *n.*

war cry *n.* **1.** a rallying cry used by combatants in battle. **2.** a cry or slogan used to rally support for a cause.

ward (wɔːd) *n.* **1.** a room in a hospital for patients requiring similar kinds of care: *a maternity ward.* **2.** one of the districts into which a town, parish, or other area is divided for administration or elections. **3.** *Law.* Also called: **ward of court.** a person, esp. a child or one legally incapable of managing his own affairs, placed under the control or protection of a guardian or of a court. **4.** an internal ridge or notch in a lock that prevents an incorrectly cut key from turning. ~*See also* **ward off.** —'**wardship** *n.*

-ward *suffix.* **1.** (*forming adjectives*) indicating direction towards: *a backward step.* **2.** (*forming adverbs*) a variant and the usual U.S. and Canad. form of **-wards.**

warden ('wɔːd²n) *n.* **1.** a person who is in charge of a building and its occupants: *a youth hostel warden.* **2.** a public official, esp. one responsible for the enforcement of certain regulations: *a traffic warden.* **3.** *Chiefly U.S. & Canad.* the chief officer in charge of a prison.

warder ('wɔːdə) *or* (*fem.*) **wardress** *n. Chiefly Brit.* a prison officer.

ward off *vb.* to avert (something, such as danger or illness): *to ward off a punch; to ward off evil.*

wardrobe ('wɔːdrəʊb) *n.* **1.** a tall cupboard, with a rail or hooks on which to hang clothes. **2.** the total collection of articles of clothing belonging to one person. **3.** the collection of costumes belonging to a theatre or theatrical company.

wardroom ('wɔːd,ruːm, -,rʊm) *n.* the quarters assigned to the officers (except the captain) of a warship.

-wards *or* **-ward** *suffix forming adverbs.* indicating direction towards: *a step backwards.*

ware (wɛə) *n.* articles of the same kind or material: *silverware.* See also **wares.**

warehouse *n.* ('wɛə,haʊs). **1.** a place where goods are stored prior to their sale or distribution. **2.** *Chiefly Brit.* a large commercial, esp. wholesale, establishment. ~*vb.* ('wɛə,haʊz, -,haʊs). **3.** to store or place in a warehouse.

wares (wɛəz) *pl. n.* **1.** articles of manufacture considered as being for sale. **2.** any talent or asset regarded as a saleable commodity.

warfare ('wɔː,fɛə) *n.* **1.** the act of waging war. **2.** a violent conflict of any kind.

war game *n.* **1.** a notional tactical exercise for training military commanders, in which no military units are actually deployed. **2.** a game in which model soldiers are used to create battles, esp. past battles, in order to study tactics.

warhead ('wɔːˌhɛd) n. the front section of a missile or projectile that contains explosives.

warhorse ('wɔːˌhɔːs) n. 1. a horse used in battle. 2. *Informal*. a veteran soldier or politician.

warlike ('wɔːˌlaɪk) adj. 1. of, relating to, or used in war. 2. hostile or belligerent.

warlock ('wɔːˌlɒk) n. a man who practises black magic.

warm (wɔːm) adj. 1. characterized by or having a moderate degree of heat. 2. maintaining or imparting heat: *a warm coat*. 3. kindly or affectionate: *a warm personality*. 4. lively or passionate: *a warm debate*. 5. cordial or enthusiastic: *warm support*. 6. (of colours) predominantly red or yellow in tone. 7. (of a scent trail) recently made. 8. near to finding a hidden object or guessing facts, as in children's games. 9. *Informal*. uncomfortable or disagreeable: *I'll make things warm for her*. ~vb. 10. (sometimes foll. by *up*) to make or become warm or warmer. 11. (often foll. by *to*) to make or become excited or enthusiastic (about): *he warmed to the idea of buying a new car*. 12. (often foll. by *to*) to feel affection or kindness (for someone): *I warmed to her from the start*. ~n. *Informal*. 13. a warm place or area: *come into the warm*. 14. the act or an instance of warming or being warmed. ~See also **warm up**. —'**warmly** adv. —'**warmness** n.

warm-blooded adj. 1. ardent, impetuous, or passionate. 2. *Zool*. (of mammals and birds) having a constant body temperature, usually higher than the surrounding temperature. —ˌ**warm-'bloodedness** n.

war memorial n. a monument to those who die in a war, esp. those from a particular locality.

warm front n. *Meteorol*. the boundary between a warm air mass and the cold air it is replacing.

warm-hearted adj. kind, affectionate, or sympathetic. —ˌ**warm-'heartedly** adv. —ˌ**warm-'heartedness** n.

warming pan n. a long-handled pan, filled with hot coals and formerly drawn over the sheets to warm a bed.

warmonger ('wɔːˌmʌŋɡə) n. a person who fosters warlike ideas or advocates war. —'**war-ˌmongering** n.

warmth (wɔːmθ) n. 1. the state, quality, or sensation of being warm. 2. intensity of emotion: *he denied the accusation with some warmth*. 3. affection or cordiality.

warm up vb. 1. to make or become warm or warmer. 2. to prepare for a race, sporting contest, or exercise routine by doing gentle exercises immediately beforehand. 3. to run (an engine or machine) until the working temperature is reached or (of an engine or machine) to undergo this process. 4. to make or become more lively: *the party warmed up when Tom came*. 5. to reheat (already cooked food) or (of such food) to be reheated. ~n. **warm-up**. 6. the act or an instance of warming up. 7. a preparatory exercise routine.

warn (wɔːn) vb. 1. to notify or make (someone) aware of danger or harm. 2. to advise or caution (someone) about his behaviour: *I'm warning you, don't do that again*. 3. to inform (someone) in advance: *he warned them that he would arrive late*. 4. (usually foll. by *away* or *off*) to tell to go away or be off.

warning ('wɔːnɪŋ) n. 1. a hint, threat, or advance notice of harm or danger. 2. advice not to do something. ~adj. 3. intended or serving to warn: *a warning look*.

warp (wɔːp) vb. 1. to twist out of shape, as from heat or damp. 2. to turn from a true, correct, or proper course. 3. *Naut*. to move (a vessel) by hauling on a rope fixed to a stationary object ashore or (of a vessel) to be moved thus. ~n. 4. the state of being twisted out of shape. 5. a twist, distortion, or bias. 6. a mental or moral deviation. 7. the yarns arranged lengthways on a loom through which the weft yarns are woven. 8. *Naut*. a rope used for warping a vessel. —**warped** adj.

war paint n. 1. paint applied to the face and body by certain North American Indians before battle. 2. *Informal*. cosmetics.

warpath ('wɔːˌpɑːθ) n. **on the warpath. a.** preparing to engage in battle. **b.** *Informal*. in a state of anger.

warrant ('wɒrənt) n. 1. an official authorization. 2. a document that certifies or guarantees, such as a receipt or licence. 3. *Law*. an official document issued by a magistrate that grants the police permission to search premises or arrest someone. 4. (in certain armed services) the official authority for the appointment of warrant officers. ~vb. 5. to guarantee the quality or condition of (something). 6. to give authority or power to. 7. to attest to the character or worthiness of. 8. to guarantee (a purchaser of merchandise) against loss of, damage to, or misrepresentation concerning the merchandise. 9. to declare confidently. —'**warrantable** adj.

warrant officer n. an officer in certain armed services with a rank between those of commissioned and noncommissioned officers.

Warrant of Fitness n. *N.Z.* a six-monthly certificate required for a motor vehicle certifying that it is mechanically sound.

warrantor ('wɒrənˌtɔː) n. an individual or company that provides a warranty.

warranty ('wɒrəntɪ) n., pl. -ties. a guarantee or assurance that goods meet a specified standard or that the facts in a legal document are as stated.

warren ('wɒrən) n. **1.** a series of interconnected underground tunnels in which rabbits live. **2.** an overcrowded building or area of a city.

warrior ('wɒrɪə) n. a person engaged in, experienced in, or devoted to war.

warship ('wɔː,ʃɪp) n. a ship designed for naval warfare.

wart (wɔːt) n. **1.** *Pathol.* a firm abnormal growth on the skin caused by a virus. **2.** *Bot.* a small rounded outgrowth. **3. warts and all.** with all blemishes evident. —'**warty** adj.

wart hog n. a wild African pig with heavy tusks, wartlike lumps on the face, and a mane of coarse hair.

wartime ('wɔː,taɪm) n. a time of war.

wary ('wɛərɪ) adj. **warier, wariest. 1.** watchful or cautious. **2.** characterized by caution or watchfulness. —'**warily** adv. —'**wariness** n.

was (wɒz; *unstressed* wəz) vb. (used with *I, he, she, it,* and with singular nouns) the past tense of **be.**

wash (wɒʃ) vb. **1.** to apply water, usually with soap, to (oneself, a person, or a thing) in order to cleanse. **2.** (often foll. by *away, from, off,* etc.) to remove by the application of water and usually soap: *she washed the dirt from her clothes.* **3.** (of dye or a fabric) to be capable of being washed without damage or loss of colour. **4.** (of an animal such as a cat) to cleanse (itself or another animal) by licking. **5.** to make pure. **6.** to make wet or moist. **7.** (often foll. by *away*) to move or be moved by water: *the flood washed away the bridge.* **8.** (esp. of waves) to flow or sweep against or over (a surface or object), often with a lapping sound. **9.** to form by erosion or be eroded: *the stream washed a ravine in the hill.* **10.** to apply a thin coating of paint or metal to (a surface). **11.** to separate (ore) from (gravel or earth) by immersion in water. **12.** *Informal, chiefly Brit.* to be believable or acceptable when tested or scrutinized: *your excuses won't wash with me.* ~n. **13.** the act or process of washing. **14.** a quantity of articles washed together. **15.** a preparation or thin liquid used as a coating or in washing: *a thin wash of paint.* **16.** land that is habitually washed by tidal or river waters. **17.** the disturbance in the air or water produced at the rear of an aircraft, boat, or other moving object. **18.** liquid refuse fed to pigs. **19. come out in the wash.** *Informal.* to become known or apparent in the course of time. ~See also **wash down, wash out, wash up.** —'**washable** adj.

washbasin ('wɒʃ,beɪsᵊn) n. **1.** a basin or bowl for washing the face and hands. **2.** Also called: **wash-hand basin.** a bathroom fixture with taps, used for washing the face and hands.

wash down vb. **1.** to wash from top to bottom. **2.** to take drink with or after (food or another drink).

washed out adj. **1.** faded or colourless. **2.** pale through exhaustion.

washed up adj. *Informal, chiefly U.S., Canad., & N.Z.* no longer hopeful; finished: *our hopes for the new deal are all washed up.*

washer ('wɒʃə) n. a flat ring of rubber, felt, or metal used to provide a seal under a nut or bolt or in a tap or valve.

washerwoman ('wɒʃə,wʊmən) n., pl. **-women.** a woman who washes clothes for a living.

washing ('wɒʃɪŋ) n. articles that have been or are to be washed together on a single occasion.

washing machine n. a machine, usually powered by electricity, for washing clothes or linen.

washing soda n. crystalline sodium carbonate, esp. when used as a cleansing agent.

washing-up n. *Brit.* **1.** the washing of dishes and cutlery after a meal. **2.** dishes and cutlery waiting to be washed up.

wash out vb. **1.** to wash (the inside of something) so as to remove (dirt). **2.** Also: **wash off.** to remove or be removed by washing: *grass stains don't wash out easily.* ~n. **washout. 3.** *Informal.* a total failure or disaster.

washroom ('wɒʃ,ruːm, -,rʊm) n. *U.S. & Canad.* a toilet.

washstand ('wɒʃ,stænd) n. a piece of furniture designed to hold a basin for washing the face and hands.

wash up vb. **1.** *Chiefly Brit.* to wash (dishes and cutlery) after a meal. **2.** *U.S. & Canad.* to wash one's face and hands.

washy ('wɒʃɪ) adj. **washier, washiest. 1.** over-diluted or weak. **2.** lacking intensity or strength.

wasn't ('wɒzᵊnt) was not.

wasp (wɒsp) n. a common stinging insect with a smooth slender black-and-yellow body.

Wasp or **WASP** (wɒsp) n. *U.S. & Canad., usually offensive.* a White Anglo-Saxon Protestant.

waspish ('wɒspɪʃ) adj. easily annoyed or angered.

wasp waist n. a very slender waist. —'**wasp-,waisted** adj.

wassail ('wɒseɪl) n. **1.** (formerly) a toast made to a person at festivities. **2.** a festivity when much drinking takes place. ~vb. **3.** to drink the health of (a person) at a wassail.

wastage ('weɪstɪdʒ) n. **1.** anything lost by wear or waste. **2.** the process of wasting.

3. natural wastage. reduction in size of a workforce by not filling vacancies.

waste (weɪst) *vb.* **1.** to use, consume, or expend thoughtlessly, carelessly, or to no avail. **2.** to fail to take advantage of: *to waste an opportunity.* **3.** (often foll. by *away*) to lose or cause to lose bodily strength or health. **4.** to exhaust or become exhausted. ~*n.* **5.** the act of wasting or state of being wasted. **6.** a failure to take advantage of something. **7.** anything unused or not used to full advantage. **8.** anything or anyone rejected as useless, worthless, or in excess of what is required. **9.** garbage, rubbish, or trash. **10.** (*pl.*) a land or region that is wild or uncultivated. **11.** *Physiol.* matter excreted from the body, as faeces or urine. ~*adj.* **12.** rejected as useless, unwanted, or worthless. **13.** produced in excess of what is required. **14.** not cultivated, inhabited, or productive: *waste land.* **15.** *Physiol.* excreted from the body as faeces or urine. **16. lay waste.** to devastate or destroy.

wasteful (ˈweɪstfʊl) *adj.* tending to waste or squander. —ˈ**wastefully** *adv.*

wasteland (ˈweɪstˌlænd) *n.* **1.** a barren or desolate area of land. **2.** a place or time that is considered spiritually, intellectually, or aesthetically barren.

wastepaper (ˈweɪstˌpeɪpə) *n.* paper discarded after use.

waster (ˈweɪstə) *n.* a ne'er-do-well or wastrel.

wasting (ˈweɪstɪŋ) *adj.* reducing the vitality and strength of the body: *a wasting disease.*

wastrel (ˈweɪstrəl) *n.* **1.** a wasteful person; spendthrift; prodigal. **2.** an idler or vagabond.

watap (wæˈtɑːp, wɑː-) *n.* a stringy thread made by North American Indians from the roots of conifers.

watch (wɒtʃ) *vb.* **1.** to look at or observe closely or attentively. **2.** (foll. by *for*) to wait attentively. **3.** to guard or tend (something) closely or carefully. **4.** to keep vigil. **5.** to maintain an interest in: *to watch the progress of a child at school.* **6. watch it!** be careful! ~*n.* **7.** a small portable timepiece, usually worn strapped to the wrist (a **wristwatch**) or in a waistcoat pocket. **8.** a watching. **9.** a period of vigil, esp. during the night. **10.** *Naut.* **a.** any of the periods, usually of four hours, during which part of a ship's crew are on duty. **b.** those officers and crew on duty during a specified watch. **11. on the watch.** on the lookout. ~See also **watch out.** —ˈ**watcher** *n.*

watchdog (ˈwɒtʃˌdɒg) *n.* **1.** a dog kept to guard property. **2.** a person or group that acts as a guard against inefficiency or illegality.

watchful (ˈwɒtʃfʊl) *adj.* vigilant or alert. —ˈ**watchfully** *adv.* —ˈ**watchfulness** *n.*

watchmaker (ˈwɒtʃˌmeɪkə) *n.* a person who makes or mends watches and clocks. —ˈ**watch**ˌ**making** *n.*

watchman (ˈwɒtʃmən) *n., pl.* **-men.** a person employed to guard buildings or property.

watch-night service *n.* (in Protestant churches) a service held on the night of December 31, to mark the passing of the old year.

watch out *vb.* to be careful or on one's guard.

watchstrap (ˈwɒtʃˌstræp) *n.* a strap attached to a watch for fastening it around the wrist. Also called (U.S. and Canad.): **watchband.**

watchtower (ˈwɒtʃˌtaʊə) *n.* a tower on which a sentry keeps watch.

watchword (ˈwɒtʃˌwɜːd) *n.* **1.** a password. **2.** a rallying cry or slogan.

water (ˈwɔːtə) *n.* **1.** a clear colourless tasteless liquid that is essential for plant and animal life that falls as rain and forms oceans, rivers, and lakes. **2. a.** any body or area of this liquid, such as a sea, lake, river, etc. **b.** (*as modifier*): *water sports; a water plant.* **3.** the surface of such a body or area: *fish swam below the water.* **4.** any form of this liquid, such as rain. **5.** the level of the tide: *high water.* **6.** a solution of a chemical substance in water: *ammonia water.* **7.** *Physiol.* **a.** any fluid secreted from the body, such as sweat, urine, or tears. **b.** (*usually pl.*) the fluid surrounding a fetus in the womb. **8.** *Archaic.* the degree of brilliance in a diamond. **9. hold water.** to prove credible, logical, or consistent: *his alibi did not hold water.* **10. make** *or* **pass water.** to urinate. **11. of the first water.** of the highest quality or the most extreme degree: *she's a fool of the first water.* **12. water under the bridge.** events that are past and done with. ~*vb.* **13.** to sprinkle, moisten, or soak with water. **14.** (often foll. by *down*) to dilute. **15.** (of the eyes) to fill with tears. **16.** (of the mouth) to fill with saliva in anticipation of food. **17.** to irrigate or provide with water: *to water the land.* **18.** (of an animal) to drink water. ~See also **water down.** —ˈ**waterless** *adj.*

water bed *n.* a waterproof mattress filled with water.

water biscuit *n.* a thin crisp unsweetened biscuit, usually served with butter or cheese.

water buffalo *n.* an ox-like draught animal of swampy regions of S Asia, with widely spreading back-curving horns.

water cannon *n.* a machine that pumps a jet of water through a nozzle at high pressure, used to disperse crowds.

water chestnut *n.* the edible tuber of a Chinese plant, used in Oriental cookery.

water closet *n.* **1.** a toilet flushed by

water. **2.** a small room that has a toilet. ~Usually abbreviated to **WC.**

watercolour *or U.S.* **watercolor** ('wɔːtə,kʌlə) *n.* **1.** paint or pigment thinned with water rather than oil. **2.** a painting done in watercolours.

water-cooled *adj.* (of an engine) kept from overheating by a flow of water circulating in an enclosed jacket.

watercourse ('wɔːtə,kɔːs) *n.* the channel, bed, or route of a stream, river, or canal.

watercress ('wɔːtə,krɛs) *n.* a plant that grows in clear ponds and streams, with pungent leaves that are used in salads and as a garnish.

water diviner *n. Brit.* a person able to locate the presence of water, esp. underground, with a divining rod.

water down *vb.* **1.** to dilute or weaken with water. **2.** to modify, esp. so as to omit anything unpleasant or offensive: *to water down the truth.* —,**watered-'down** *adj.*

waterfall ('wɔːtə,fɔːl) *n.* a cascade of falling water where there is a vertical or almost vertical step in a river.

waterfowl ('wɔːtə,faʊl) *n.* **1.** a bird that lives on or near the water, esp. one that swims, such as a duck or swan. **2.** such birds collectively.

waterfront ('wɔːtə,frʌnt) *n.* the area of a town or city alongside a body of water, such as a harbour or dockyard.

water gate *n.* a gate in a canal that can be opened or closed to control the flow of water.

Watergate ('wɔːtə,ɡeɪt) *n.* any public scandal involving politicians or a possible cover-up.

water glass *n.* a syrupy solution of sodium silicate in water: used as a protective coating for cement and a preservative, esp. for eggs.

water hole *n.* a pond or pool in a desert or other dry area, used by animals as a drinking place.

water ice *n.* an ice cream made from a frozen sugar syrup flavoured with fruit juice or purée.

watering can *n.* a container with a handle and a spout with a perforated nozzle, used to sprinkle water over plants.

watering hole *n.* **1.** a place where animals drink; water hole. **2.** *Facetious slang.* a pub.

watering place *n.* **1.** a place where drinking water for people or animals may be obtained. **2.** *Brit.* a spa or seaside resort.

water jump *n.* a ditch or brook over which athletes or horses must jump in a steeplechase or similar contest.

water level *n.* **1.** the level reached by the surface of a body of water. **2.** same as **water line.**

water lily *n.* an aquatic plant with large leaves and showy flowers that float on the surface of the water.

water line *n.* the level to which a ship's hull will be immersed when afloat.

waterlogged ('wɔːtə,lɒɡd) *adj.* **1.** saturated with water. **2.** (of a boat still afloat) having taken in so much water as to be unmanageable.

water main *n.* a principal supply pipe in an arrangement of pipes for distributing water.

watermark ('wɔːtə,mɑːk) *n.* **1.** a mark impressed on paper during manufacture, visible when the paper is held up to the light. **2.** a line marking the level reached by a body of water. ~*vb.* **3.** to mark (paper) with a watermark.

water meadow *n.* a meadow that remains fertile by being periodically flooded by a stream.

watermelon ('wɔːtə,mɛlən) *n.* an African melon with a hard green rind and sweet watery reddish flesh.

water pistol *n.* a toy pistol that squirts a stream of water.

water polo *n.* a game played in water by two teams of seven swimmers in which each side tries to throw or propel an inflated ball into the opponents' goal.

water power *n.* the power of flowing or falling water to drive machinery, esp. for generating electricity.

waterproof ('wɔːtə,pruːf) *adj.* **1.** not allowing water to pass through. ~*n.* **2.** *Chiefly Brit.* a waterproof garment, esp. a raincoat. ~*vb.* **3.** to make (a fabric or garment) waterproof.

water rat *n.* same as **water vole.**

water rate *n.* a charge made for the public supply of water.

water-resistant *adj.* (of fabrics or garments) having a finish that resists the absorption of water.

watershed ('wɔːtə,ʃɛd) *n.* **1.** the dividing line between two adjacent river systems, such as a ridge. **2.** an important period or factor that serves as a dividing line.

waterside ('wɔːtə,saɪd) *n.* the area of land beside a body of water.

water-ski *n.* **1.** a type of ski used for gliding over water. ~*vb.* **-skiing, -skied** *or* **-ski'd. 2.** to ride over water on water-skis while holding a rope towed by a speedboat. —'**water-,skier** *n.* —'**water,skiing** *n.*

water softener *n.* a device or substance which removes the minerals that make water hard.

waterspout ('wɔːtə,spaʊt) *n.* a tornado occurring over water that forms a column of water and mist.

water table *n.* the level below which the ground is saturated with water.

watertight ('wɔːtə,taɪt) *adj.* **1.** not permitting the passage of water either in or out: *a* *watertight boat.* **2.** without loopholes: *a watertight argument.*

water tower ('tauə) *n.* a storage tank mounted on a tower so that water can be distributed at a uniform pressure.

water vapour *n.* water in the gaseous state, esp. when due to evaporation at a temperature below the boiling point.

water vole *n.* a small rat-like animal that can swim and lives on the banks of streams and ponds.

waterway ('wɔːtə,weɪ) *n.* a river, canal, or other navigable channel used as a means of travel or transport.

water wheel *n.* a large wheel with vanes set across its rim, which is turned by flowing water to drive machinery.

water wings *pl. n.* an inflatable rubber device shaped like a pair of wings, which is placed under the arms of a person learning to swim.

waterworks ('wɔːtə,wɜːks) *n.* **1.** (*functioning as sing.*) an establishment for storing, purifying, and distributing water for community supply. **2.** (*functioning as pl.*) *Brit. informal, euphemistic.* the urinary system. **3. turn on the waterworks.** *Informal.* to begin to cry deliberately in order to attract attention or gain sympathy.

watery ('wɔːtərɪ) *adj.* **1.** of, like, or containing water. **2.** (of eyes) filled with tears. **3.** insipid, thin, or weak: *watery sunshine.*

watt (wɒt) *n.* the SI unit of power, equal to 1 joule per second.

wattage ('wɒtɪdʒ) *n.* the amount of electrical power, expressed in watts, that an appliance uses or generates.

wattle ('wɒtˀl) *n.* **1.** a frame of rods or stakes interwoven with twigs or branches used to make fences. **2.** a loose fold of skin, often brightly coloured, hanging from the neck or throat of certain birds and lizards. **3.** any of various Australian acacia trees with spikes of small brightly coloured flowers and flexible branches. *~adj.* **4.** made of, formed by, or covered with wattle. —'**wattled** *adj.*

wattle and daub *n.* a method of building walls using interwoven twigs plastered with a mixture of clay and water.

wave (weɪv) *vb.* **1.** to move the hand to and fro as a greeting. **2.** to hold (something) up and move it from side to side, for example to attract attention. **3.** to direct (someone) to move in a particular direction by waving. **4.** to move freely to and fro: *the banner waved in the wind.* *~n.* **5.** one of a sequence of ridges or undulations that moves across the surface of a body of water, esp. the sea. **6.** a curve or series of curves in the hair. **7.** a sudden rise in the frequency of something: *a crime wave.* **8.** a widespread movement that advances in a body: *a wave of settlers.* **9.** the act or an instance of waving. **10.** *Physics.* an energy-carrying disturbance travelling through a medium or space by a series of vibrations without any overall movement of matter. **11.** a prolonged spell of some particular type of weather: *a heat wave.* **12. make waves.** to cause trouble; disturb the status quo. —'**waveless** *adj.*

waveband ('weɪv,bænd) *n.* a range of wavelengths or frequencies used for a particular type of radio transmission.

wave down *vb.* to signal to (the driver of a vehicle) to stop.

wavelength ('weɪv,lɛŋθ) *n.* **1.** the distance between two points of the same phase in consecutive cycles of a wave. **2.** the wavelength of the carrier wave used by a particular broadcasting station. **3. on someone's** *or* **the same wavelength.** *Informal.* having similar views, feelings, or thoughts (as someone else).

waver ('weɪvə) *vb.* **1.** to hesitate between possibilities; be indecisive. **2.** to become unsteady. **3.** to tremble: *her voice wavered.* **4.** to move back and forth or one way and another. **5.** (of light) to flicker or flash.

wavey ('weɪvɪ) *n. Canad.* a snow goose or other wild goose.

wavy ('weɪvɪ) *adj.* **wavier, waviest.** **1.** forming or full of waves. **2.** (of hair) set in or having waves.

wax[1] (wæks) *n.* **1.** any of various viscous or solid materials which are typically slightly shiny, insoluble in water, and soften when heated. **2.** short for **beeswax** or **sealing wax.** **3.** *Physiol.* a brownish-yellow waxy substance secreted by glands in the ear. *~vb.* **4.** to coat or polish with wax. —'**waxy** *adj.*

wax[2] (wæks) *vb.* **1.** to become larger, more powerful, or more intense. **2.** (of the moon) to show a gradually increasing portion of illuminated surface, between new moon and full moon. **3.** to become: *to wax eloquent.*

waxen ('wæksən) *adj.* **1.** made of, treated with, or covered with wax. **2.** resembling wax in colour or texture.

waxeye ('wæks,aɪ) *n.* a small New Zealand bird with a white circle around its eye.

wax paper *n.* paper treated or coated with wax or paraffin to make it waterproof.

waxwing ('wæks,wɪŋ) *n.* a songbird with red wing tips, a yellow tip to its tail, and a crested head.

waxwork ('wæks,wɜːk) *n.* **1.** a life-size lifelike wax figure of a famous person. **2.** (*pl.; functioning as sing. or pl.*) a museum or exhibition of wax figures.

way (weɪ) *n.* **1.** a manner, method, or means: *a way of life; two ways of looking at the problem.* **2.** a route or direction: *the way home.* **3.** a means or line of passage, such as a path or track. **4.** space or room for movement or activity: *you're in the way; get out of my way!* **5.** distance: *you've come a long way.* **6.** a passage or journey: *on the way.* **7.** characteristic style or manner: *I did it my way.* **8.** (*often pl.*) habit: *he has some offensive ways.* **9.** an aspect of something; particular: *in many ways he was right.* **10.** a street or road: *Icknield Way.* **11.** something wished for: *that child always gets his own way.* **12.** *Informal.* a state or condition, usually financial or concerning health: *she's in a bad way.* **13.** *Informal.* the area or direction of one's home: *drop in if you're ever over my way.* **14. a.** a choice or option, as in a vote: *the vote could go either way.* **b.** a group supporting a particular viewpoint: *a three-way split.* **15. by the way.** incidentally. **16. by way of. a.** via. **b.** serving as: *by way of introduction.* **17. come one's way.** to be encountered in one's everyday life. **18. give way. a.** to collapse or break down. **b.** to yield. **19. give way to. a.** to step aside for or stop for. **b.** to give full rein to (emotions). **20. go out of one's way.** to take considerable trouble or inconvenience oneself. **21. have it both ways.** to enjoy two things that would normally be mutually exclusive. **22. in a way.** in some respects. **23. in no way.** not at all. **24. lead the way. a.** to go first. **b.** to set an example. **25. make one's way. a.** to proceed or advance. **b.** to achieve success in life. **26. on the way out.** *Informal.* becoming unfashionable. **27. out of the way. a.** removed or dealt with so as to be no longer a hindrance. **b.** remote. **28. see one's way (clear).** to find it possible and be willing (to do something). **29. under way.** having started moving or making progress. ~*adv.* **30.** *Informal.* very far: *way over yonder; they're way up the mountain.*

waybill (ˈweɪˌbɪl) *n.* a document stating the nature, origin, and destination of goods in transit.

wayfarer (ˈweɪˌfɛərə) *n.* a person who goes on a journey. —ˈway,faring *n., adj.*

waylay (weɪˈleɪ) *vb.* **-laying, -laid. 1.** to lie in wait for and attack. **2.** to intercept (someone) unexpectedly. —**wayˈlayer** *n.*

wayleave (ˈweɪˌliːv) *n.* access to property granted by a landowner for payment, for example to allow a contractor access to a building site.

way-out *adj. Informal.* extremely unconventional or experimental.

ways and means *pl. n.* **1.** the methods and resources for accomplishing something. **2.** the money and the methods of raising the money needed for the functioning of a political unit.

wayside (ˈweɪˌsaɪd) *n.* **1.** (*modifier*) situated by the side of a road: *a wayside inn.* **2. fall by the wayside.** to cease or fail to continue doing something: *of the nine starters, three fell by the wayside.*

wayward (ˈweɪwəd) *adj.* erratic, selfish, or stubborn.

Wb *Physics.* weber.

WC *or* **wc** *n.* a toilet.

we (wiː) *pl. pron.* (*used as the subject of a verb*) **1.** the speaker or writer and another person or other people: *we should go now.* **2.** all people or people in general: *the planet on which we live.* **3.** a formal word for I used by editors or other writers, and formerly by monarchs. **4.** *Informal.* used instead of *you* with a tone of condescension or sarcasm: *how are we today?*

WEA (in Britain) Workers' Educational Association.

weak (wiːk) *adj.* **1.** lacking in physical or mental strength. **2.** liable to give way: *a weak link in a chain.* **3.** lacking in resolution or firmness of character. **4.** lacking strength or power: *a weak voice.* **5. a.** not functioning as well as is normal: *weak eyes.* **b.** easily upset: *a weak stomach.* **6.** lacking in conviction or persuasiveness: *a weak argument.* **7.** lacking in political or strategic strength: *a weak administration.* **8.** lacking the usual, full, or desirable strength of flavour: *weak tea.* **9.** (of a currency or shares) falling in price or characterized by falling prices. —ˈweakish *adj.*

weaken (ˈwiːkən) *vb.* to become or make weak or weaker.

weak-kneed *adj. Informal.* lacking strength, courage, or resolution.

weakling (ˈwiːklɪŋ) *n.* a person or animal that is lacking in strength or weak in constitution or character.

weakly (ˈwiːklɪ) *adj.* **-lier, -liest. 1.** sickly; feeble. ~*adv.* **2.** in a weak or feeble manner.

weak-minded *adj.* **1.** lacking resolution or willpower. **2.** of very low intelligence; foolish.

weakness (ˈwiːknɪs) *n.* **1.** a being weak. **2.** a failing, as in a person's character. **3.** a self-indulgent liking: *a weakness for chocolates.*

weal[1] (wiːl) *n.* a raised mark on the skin produced by a blow.

weal[2] (wiːl) *n. Archaic.* prosperity or wellbeing: *the common weal.*

wealth (wɛlθ) *n.* **1.** a large amount of money and valuable material possessions. **2.** the state of being rich. **3.** a great amount; abundance: *a wealth of gifts.*

wealthy (ˈwɛlθɪ) *adj.* **wealthier, wealthiest. 1.** possessing wealth; rich. **2.** of or relating to wealth. **3.** abounding: *wealthy in friends.* —ˈwealthiness *n.*

wean[1] (wiːn) *vb.* **1.** to accustom (a child or young mammal) to take food other than its mother's milk. **2.** (usually foll. by *from*) to cause (someone) to give up former habits.

wean[2] (weɪn) *n. Scot. & N English dialect.* a child.

weapon ('wɛpən) n. **1.** an object, such as a knife or gun, used in fighting. **2.** anything that serves to get the better of an opponent: *his power of speech was his best weapon.*

weaponry ('wɛpənrɪ) n. weapons regarded collectively.

wear (wɛə) vb. **wearing, wore, worn. 1.** to carry or have (a garment or jewellery) on one's person as clothing or ornament. **2.** to have or display in one's expression: *to wear a smile.* **3.** to deteriorate or cause to deteriorate by constant use or action. **4.** to react to constant use or action in a specified way: *his suit wears well.* **5.** to harass or weaken. **6.** (often foll. by *on*) (of time) to pass or be passed slowly. **7.** *Brit. informal.* to accept: *Larry won't wear that argument.* **8. wear thin.** to become weaker or less acceptable through overuse or repetition: *my patience is wearing thin; her excuses were starting to wear thin.* ~n. **9.** the act of wearing or state of being worn. **10.** anything designed to be worn: *leisure wear.* **11.** deterioration from constant or normal use. **12.** the quality of resisting the effects of constant use. ~See also **wear down, wear off, wear out.**

wear and tear n. damage, depreciation, or loss resulting from ordinary use.

wear down vb. **1.** to impair or be impaired by long or constant wearing or rubbing: *to wear down the heels on shoes.* **2.** to overcome or be overcome gradually by persistent effort: *to wear down the management.*

wearing ('wɛərɪŋ) adj. causing fatigue or exhaustion; tiring.

wearisome ('wɪərɪsəm) adj. causing fatigue or annoyance; tedious.

wear off vb. to gradually decrease in intensity: *the pain will wear off soon.*

wear out vb. **1.** to make or become unfit or useless through wear. **2.** to exhaust or tire.

weary ('wɪərɪ) adj. **-rier, -riest. 1.** tired or exhausted. **2.** causing fatigue or exhaustion. **3.** caused by or suggestive of weariness: *a weary laugh.* **4.** (often foll. by *of* or *with*) discontented or bored. ~vb. **-rying, -ried. 5.** to make or become weary. **6.** to make or become discontented or impatient. —'**wearily** adv. —'**weariness** n. —'**wearying** adj.

weasel ('wiːz²l) n., pl. **-sel** or **-sels.** a small flesh-eating mammal with reddish-brown fur, a long body and neck, and short legs.

weather ('wɛðə) n. **1.** the day-to-day atmospheric conditions such as temperature, cloudiness, and rainfall, affecting a specific place. **2. make heavy weather of.** *Informal.* to carry out a task with great difficulty or needless effort. **3. under the weather.** *Informal.* not in good health. ~adj. **4.** on or at the side or part towards the wind: *the weather anchor.* ~vb. **5.** to expose or be exposed to the action of the weather. **6.** to undergo or cause to undergo changes, such as discoloration, due to the action of the weather. **7.** to come safely through (a storm, problem, or difficulty). **8.** to sail to the windward of (a place or thing): *to weather a point.*

weather-beaten adj. **1.** worn or damaged as a result of exposure to the weather. **2.** tanned by exposure to the weather: *a weather-beaten face.*

weatherboard ('wɛðə,bɔːd) n. a timber board that is fixed with others in overlapping horizontal rows to form an exterior cladding on a wall or roof. —'**weather-,boarding** n.

weathercock ('wɛðə,kɒk) n. **1.** a weather vane in the shape of a cock. **2.** a person who is fickle or changeable.

weather eye n. **keep one's weather eye open.** to stay on the alert.

weathering ('wɛðərɪŋ) n. the breakdown of rocks by the action of the weather.

weatherman ('wɛðə,mæn) n., pl. **-men.** *Informal.* a person who forecasts the weather on radio or television.

weatherproof ('wɛðə,pruːf) adj. designed or able to withstand exposure to weather without deterioration.

weather vane n. a vane designed to indicate the direction in which the wind is blowing.

weave (wiːv) vb. **weaving, wove** or **weaved; woven** or **weaved. 1.** to form (a fabric) by interlacing (yarn) on a loom. **2.** to make by such a process: *to weave a shawl.* **3.** to construct by interlacing (cane or twigs). **4.** to compose (a story or plan) by combining separate elements into a whole. **6.** (often foll. by *in, into,* or *through*) to introduce: *to weave factual details into a fiction.* **7.** to move from side to side while going forwards: *to weave through a crowd.* **8. get weaving.** *Informal.* to hurry. ~n. **9.** the structure or pattern of a woven fabric: *an open weave.* —'**weaver** n.

web (wɛb) n. **1.** a mesh of fine tough threads built by a spider to trap insects. **2.** anything formed by or as if by weaving or interweaving. **3.** a membrane connecting the toes of some aquatic birds or the digits of such aquatic mammals as the otter. **4.** a continuous strip of paper fed from a reel into some printing presses. **5.** anything that is intricately formed or complex: *a web of intrigue.* —**webbed** adj.

webbing ('wɛbɪŋ) n. a strong fabric of hemp, cotton, or jute woven in strips and used under springs in upholstery or for straps.

weber ('veɪbə) n. the SI unit of magnetic flux.

web-footed or **web-toed** adj. (of certain

animals or birds) having webbed feet that aid swimming.

wed (wɛd) vb. **wedding, wedded** or **wed**. **1.** to take (a person) as a husband or wife; marry. **2.** to join (two people) in marriage. **3.** to unite closely. —**'wedded** adj.

Wed. Wednesday.

wedding ('wɛdɪŋ) n. **1.** the act of marrying or a marriage ceremony. **2.** the anniversary of a marriage (in such combinations as **silver wedding** or **diamond wedding**).

wedding breakfast n. the meal usually served after a wedding ceremony or just before the bride and bridegroom leave for their honeymoon.

wedding cake n. a rich iced fruit cake, with one, two, or more tiers, which is served at a wedding reception.

wedding ring n. a ring, typically of precious metal, worn to indicate that one is married.

wedge (wɛdʒ) n. **1.** a block of solid material, esp. wood or metal, that is shaped like a narrow V in cross section and can be pushed or driven between two objects or parts of an object in order to split or secure them. **2.** anything in the shape of a wedge: a wedge of cheese. **3.** something, such as an idea or action, that tends to cause division. **4.** Golf. a club with a wedge-shaped face, used for bunker or pitch shots. **5. the thin end of the wedge.** anything unimportant in itself that implies the start of something much larger. ~vb. **6.** to secure with or as if with a wedge. **7.** to squeeze or be squeezed like a wedge into a narrow space. **8.** to force apart or divide with or as if with a wedge.

Wedgwood ('wɛdʒwʊd) n. Trademark. a type of fine pottery with applied decoration in white on a coloured ground.

wedlock ('wɛdlɒk) n. **1.** the state of being married. **2. born out of wedlock.** born when one's parents are not legally married.

Wednesday ('wɛnzdɪ) n. the fourth day of the week.

wee[1] (wiː) adj. small in size, amount, or extent.

wee[2] (wiː) Informal, chiefly Brit. ~n. **1. a.** an instance of urinating. **b.** urine. ~vb. **2.** to urinate. ~Also: **wee-wee.**

weed (wiːd) n. **1.** any plant that grows wild and profusely, esp. one that grows among cultivated plants. **2.** Slang. **a. the weed.** tobacco. **b.** marijuana. **3.** Informal. a thin scraggy ineffectual person. ~vb. **4.** to remove (useless or troublesome plants) from (a garden).

weedkiller ('wiːd,kɪlə) n. a substance, usually a chemical or hormone, used for killing weeds.

weed out vb. to separate out, remove, or eliminate (anything unwanted): to weed out troublesome students.

weeds (wiːdz) pl. n. a widow's black mourning clothes.

weedy ('wiːdɪ) adj. **weedier, weediest. 1.** full of weeds: weedy land. **2.** (of a plant) resembling a weed in straggling growth. **3.** Informal. thin or weakly in appearance.

week (wiːk) n. **1.** a period of seven consecutive days, esp. one beginning with Sunday. **2.** a period of seven consecutive days from a specified day: a week from Wednesday. **3.** the period of time within a week devoted to work. ~adv. **4.** Chiefly Brit. seven days before or after a specified day: I'll visit you Wednesday week.

weekday ('wiːk,deɪ) n. any day of the week other than Saturday or Sunday.

weekend (,wiːk'ɛnd) n. the period from Friday night until the end of Sunday.

weekly ('wiːklɪ) adj. **1.** happening once a week or every week. **2.** determined or calculated by the week: weekly sales figures. ~adv. **3.** once a week or every week. ~n., pl. **-lies. 4.** a newspaper or magazine issued every week.

weeny ('wiːnɪ) adj. **-nier, -niest.** Informal. very small; tiny.

weep (wiːp) vb. **weeping, wept. 1.** to shed tears. **2.** (foll. by for) to lament (for something). **3.** to ooze liquid: a weeping sore. ~n. **4.** a spell of weeping.

weeping willow ('wiːpɪŋ) n. a willow tree with graceful drooping branches.

weepy ('wiːpɪ) Informal. ~adj. **weepier, weepiest. 1.** liable or tending to weep. ~n., pl. **weepies. 2.** a sentimental film or book.

weevil ('wiːvɪl) n. a beetle with a long snout that feeds on plants and plant products.

wee-wee n., vb. same as **wee**[2].

weft (wɛft) n. the yarn woven across the width of the fabric through the lengthways warp yarn.

weigh (weɪ) vb. **1.** to measure the weight of. **2.** to have weight: she weighs more than her sister. **3.** (often foll. by out) to measure out by weight. **4.** to consider carefully: to weigh the facts of a case. **5.** to be influential: his words weighed little with the jury. **6.** (often foll. by on) to be oppressive or burdensome to. **7. weigh anchor.** to raise a vessel's anchor or (of a vessel) to have its anchor raised. ~See also **weigh down, weigh in,** etc.

weighbridge ('weɪ,brɪdʒ) n. a machine for weighing vehicles by means of a metal plate set into a road.

weigh down vb. to press (a person) down by or as if by weight: weighed down by troubles.

weigh in vb. **1.** (of a boxer, wrestler, or jockey) to be weighed to check that one is of the declared weight. **2.** Informal. to contribute to a discussion or conversation: he weighed in with a few sharp comments.

~*n.* **weigh-in. 3.** *Sport.* the act of checking a competitor's weight.

weight (weɪt) *n.* **1.** the heaviness of an object; the amount anything weighs. **2.** *Physics.* the vertical force experienced by a mass as a result of gravitation. **3.** a system of units used to express weight: *troy weight.* **4.** a unit used to measure weight: *the kilogram is the weight used in SI units.* **5.** any mass or object used for its heaviness: *a paperweight.* **6.** an oppressive force: *the weight of cares.* **7.** any heavy load: *the bag was such a weight.* **8.** the main force; preponderance: *the weight of evidence.* **9.** importance; influence: *his opinion carries weight.* **10. pull one's weight.** *Informal.* to do one's full share of a task. **11. throw one's weight about** *or* **around.** *Informal.* to act in an aggressive overauthoritarian manner. ~*vb.* **12.** to add weight to. **13.** to burden or oppress. **14.** to increase the value of (an item or group of items in a list or average), so as to reflect their relative importance.

weighting ('weɪtɪŋ) *n.* an allowance paid to compensate for higher living costs: *a London weighting.*

weightless ('weɪtlɪs) *adj.* **1.** seeming to have very little weight or no weight at all. **2.** seeming not to be affected by gravity, as in the case of astronauts in an orbiting spacecraft. —**'weightlessness** *n.*

weightlifting ('weɪt,lɪftɪŋ) *n.* the sport of lifting barbells of specified weights in a prescribed manner. —**'weight,lifter** *n.*

weight training *n.* physical exercise using light or heavy weights as a way of improving muscle performance.

weighty ('weɪtɪ) *adj.* **weightier, weightiest. 1.** having great weight. **2.** important: *weighty problems.* **3.** causing worry: *weighty responsibilities.* —**'weightiness** *n.*

weigh up *vb.* to make an assessment of (a person or situation); judge.

weir (wɪə) *n.* **1.** a low dam that is built across a river to raise the water level, divert the water, or control its flow. **2.** a fence-like trap built across a stream to catch fish.

weird (wɪəd) *adj.* **1.** suggestive of the supernatural; eerie. **2.** strange or bizarre. —**'weirdly** *adv.* —**'weirdness** *n.*

weirdo ('wɪədəʊ) *n., pl.* **-dos.** *Informal.* a person who behaves in a bizarre or eccentric manner.

welch (wɛlʃ) *vb.* same as **welsh.**

welcome ('wɛlkəm) *adj.* **1.** gladly received or admitted: *a welcome guest.* **2.** bringing pleasure: *a welcome gift.* **3.** freely permitted or invited: *you are welcome to call.* **4. you're welcome.** an expression used to acknowledge someone's thanks. ~*n.* **5.** the act of greeting or receiving a person or thing; reception: *the new theory had a cool welcome.* **6. overstay one's welcome.** to come more often or stay longer than is pleasing. ~*vb.* **7.** to greet the arrival of (guests) cordially. **8.** to receive or accept, esp. gladly. —**'welcoming** *adj.*

weld (wɛld) *vb.* **1.** to join (pieces of metal or plastic), as by softening with heat and hammering or by fusion. **2.** to unite closely: *the tragedy welded the family together.* ~*n.* **3.** a joint formed by welding. —**'welder** *n.*

welfare ('wɛl,fɛə) *n.* **1.** health, happiness, prosperity, and wellbeing in general. **2.** financial and other assistance given to people in need. **3. on welfare.** *Chiefly U.S. & Canad.* receiving financial aid from a government agency or other source.

welfare state *n.* a system in which the government undertakes responsibility for the wellbeing of its population, usually through unemployment insurance, old age pensions, and other social-security measures.

well¹ (wɛl) *adv.* **better, best. 1.** satisfactorily: *the party went very well; well-proportioned.* **2.** skilfully: *she plays the violin well; a well-chosen example.* **3.** carefully: *listen well to my words.* **4.** prosperously: *to live well.* **5.** suitably; fittingly: *you can't very well say that.* **6.** intimately: *I knew him well.* **7.** in a kind or favourable manner: *she speaks well of you.* **8.** fully: *to be well informed.* **9.** by a considerable margin: *let me know well in advance; well over fifty.* **10.** (preceded by *could, might,* or *may*) indeed: *you may well have to do it yourself.* **11. all very well.** used ironically to express discontent or dissent. **12. as well. a.** in addition; too. **b.** (preceded by *may* or *might*) with equal effect: *you might as well come.* **13. as well as.** in addition to. **14. (just) as well.** preferable or advisable: *it would be just as well if you paid me now.* **15. leave well (enough) alone.** to refrain from interfering with something that is satisfactory. **16. well and good.** used to indicate calm acceptance, as of a decision. ~*adj.* **17.** in good health: *I'm very well, thank you; he's not a well man.* **18.** satisfactory or pleasing. **19.** prudent; advisable: *it would be well to make no comment.* ~*interj.* **20. a.** an expression of surprise, indignation, or reproof. **b.** an expression of anticipation in waiting for an answer or remark.

well² (wɛl) *n.* **1.** a hole or shaft bored into the earth to tap a supply of water, oil, or gas. **2.** a natural pool where water comes to the surface. **3.** a cavity, space, or container for holding a liquid, such as an inkwell. **4.** an open shaft through the floors of a building, such as one used for a staircase. **5.** a deep enclosed space in a building or between buildings that is open to the sky. **6.** (in England) the open space in the centre of a law court. **7.** an abundant source: *he is a well of knowledge.* ~*vb.* **8.** to flow or cause to flow upwards or outwards: *tears welled from her eyes.*

we'll (wiːl) we will *or* we shall.

well-advised *adj.* prudent or sensible: *you'd be well-advised to forget about him.*

well-appointed *adj.* (of a room or building) well equipped or furnished to a high standard.

well-balanced *adj.* sane or sensible.

well-behaved *adj.* **1.** having good manners; not causing trouble or mischief. **2.** (of an animal) properly trained.

wellbeing ('wɛl'biːɪŋ) *n.* the condition of being contented or healthy.

well-bred *adj.* **1.** Also: **well-born.** of respected or noble ancestry. **2.** indicating good breeding: *well-bred manners.* **3.** of good thoroughbred stock: *a well-bred spaniel.*

well-built *adj.* strong and well-proportioned.

well-connected *adj.* having influential or important relatives or friends.

well-disposed *adj.* inclined to be sympathetic, kindly, or friendly.

well-done *adj.* **1.** (of food, esp. meat) cooked thoroughly. **2.** made or accomplished satisfactorily.

well-founded *adj.* having good grounds: *well-founded rumours.*

well-groomed *adj.* having a tidy pleasing appearance.

well-grounded *adj.* well instructed in the basic elements of a subject.

wellhead ('wɛl,hɛd) *n.* **1.** the source of a well or stream. **2.** a source, fountainhead, or origin.

well-heeled *adj. Informal.* rich; prosperous; wealthy.

wellies ('wɛlɪz) *pl. n. Brit. informal.* Wellington boots.

well-informed *adj.* **1.** having knowledge about a great variety of subjects: *he seems to be a well-informed person.* **2.** possessing reliable information on a particular subject.

Wellington boots ('wɛlɪŋtən) *or* **wellingtons** *pl. n. Brit.* knee-length or calf-length rubber boots, worn in wet or muddy conditions.

well-intentioned *adj.* having good or kindly intentions, usually with unfortunate results.

well-known *adj.* **1.** widely known; famous. **2.** known fully or clearly.

well-meaning *adj.* having or indicating good intentions, usually with unfortunate results.

well-nigh *adv. Archaic or poetic.* nearly; almost: *it's well-nigh three o'clock.*

well-off *adj.* **1.** financially well provided for; moderately rich. **2.** in a comfortable or favourable position or state.

well-preserved *adj.* **1.** kept in a good condition. **2.** continuing to appear youthful: *a well-preserved old lady.*

well-read ('wɛl'rɛd) *adj.* having read widely and intelligently.

well-rounded *adj.* **1.** rounded in shape or well developed: *a well-rounded figure.* **2.** full, varied, and satisfying: *a well-rounded life.*

well-spoken *adj.* **1.** having a clear, articulate, and socially acceptable accent and way of speaking. **2.** spoken satisfactorily or pleasingly.

wellspring ('wɛl,sprɪŋ) *n.* **1.** the source of a spring or stream. **2.** a source of abundant supply.

well-thought-of *adj.* respected.

well-to-do *adj.* moderately wealthy.

well-wisher *n.* a person who shows benevolence or sympathy towards a person or cause. —**'well-,wishing** *adj., n.*

well-worn *adj.* **1.** so much used as to be affected by wear: *a well-worn coat.* **2.** hackneyed: *a well-worn phrase.*

welsh *or* **welch** (wɛlʃ) *vb.* (often foll. by *on*) to fail to pay a debt or fulfil an obligation.

Welsh (wɛlʃ) *adj.* **1.** of or relating to Wales, its people, their language, or their dialect of English. ~*n.* **2.** a Celtic language of Wales. **3. the Welsh.** (*functioning as pl.*) the people of Wales.

Welshman ('wɛlʃmən) *or* (*fem.*) **Welshwoman** *n., pl.* **-men** *or* **-women.** a person from Wales.

Welsh rabbit *n.* melted cheese sometimes mixed with milk or seasonings, served on hot toast. Also called: **Welsh rarebit, rarebit.**

welt (wɛlt) *n.* **1.** a raised or strengthened seam in a garment. **2.** a raised mark on the skin produced by a blow. **3.** (in shoemaking) a strip of leather between the outer sole and the inner sole and upper. ~*vb.* **4.** to put a welt in (a garment or shoe). **5.** to beat soundly.

welter ('wɛltə) *vb.* **1.** to roll about, writhe, or wallow. **2.** to lie drenched in blood. ~*n.* **3.** a confused mass; jumble.

welterweight ('wɛltə,weɪt) *n.* **1.** a professional boxer weighing up to 147 pounds or an amateur boxer weighing up to 148 pounds. **2.** a professional wrestler weighing up to 75 kg or an amateur wrestler weighing up to 74 kg.

wen (wɛn) *n. Pathol.* a harmless cyst on the scalp.

wench (wɛntʃ) *n.* **1.** a girl or young woman: now used facetiously. **2.** *Archaic.* a prostitute or female servant.

wend (wɛnd) *vb.* to direct (one's course or way); travel.

wensleydale ('wɛnzlɪ,deɪl) *n.* a type of white cheese with a flaky texture.

went (wɛnt) *vb.* the past tense of **go.**

wept (wɛpt) *vb.* the past of **weep.**

were (wɜː; *unstressed* wə) *vb.* the form of the past tense of **be** used after *we, you, they,* or a plural noun. It is also used as a subjunctive, esp. in conditional sentences. **Usage.** *Were* is used in formal contexts to express hypotheses (*if he were to die, she would inherit everything*), suppositions contrary to fact (*if I were you, I would be careful*), and desire (*I wish he were there now*). In informal speech, however, *was* is often used instead.

we're (wɪə) we are.

weren't (wɜːnt) were not.

werewolf (ˈwɪəˌwʊlf, ˈwɛə-) *n., pl.* **-wolves.** (in folklore) a person who has been changed or is able to change into a wolf.

Wesleyan (ˈwɛzlɪən) *adj.* **1.** of or characterizing Methodism. ~*n.* **2.** a member of the Methodist Church. —**ˈWesleyanˌism** *n.*

west (wɛst) *n.* **1.** the direction along a parallel towards the point, at 270° clockwise from north. **2. the west.** (*often cap.*) any area lying in or towards the west. ~*adj.* **3.** situated in, moving towards, or facing the west. **4.** (of the wind) from the west. ~*adv.* **5.** in, to, or towards the west. **6. go west.** *Informal.* **a.** to be lost or destroyed. **b.** to die.

West (wɛst) *n.* **the. 1.** the western part of the world contrasted historically and culturally with the East or Orient. **2.** the non-Communist countries of Europe and America contrasted with the Communist states of the East. ~*adj.* **3.** of or denoting the western part of a specified country or area.

westbound (ˈwɛstˌbaʊnd) *adj.* going or leading towards the west.

West Country *n.* **the.** the southwest of England, esp. Cornwall, Devon, and Somerset.

West End *n.* **the.** a part of W central London containing the main shopping and entertainment areas.

westerly (ˈwɛstəlɪ) *adj.* **1.** of or situated in the west. ~*adv., adj.* **2.** towards the west. **3.** (of the wind) from the west. ~*n., pl.* **-lies. 4.** a wind blowing from the west.

western (ˈwɛstən) *adj.* **1.** in, towards, or facing the west. **2.** (of a wind) coming from the west. —**ˈwesternˌmost** *adj.*

Western (ˈwɛstən) *adj.* **1.** of or characteristic of the Americas and the parts of Europe not under Communist rule. **2.** of or characteristic of the West as opposed to the Orient. ~*n.* **3.** (*often not cap.*) a film or book about cowboys in the western states of the U.S. in the 19th century.

westerner (ˈwɛstənə) *n.* a person from the west of any specific region.

Western Hemisphere *n.* that half of the globe containing the Americas.

westernize *or* **-ise** (ˈwɛstəˌnaɪz) *vb.* to influence or make familiar with the customs or practices of the West. —ˌwesterniˈzation *or* -iˈsation *n.*

Westminster (ˈwɛstˌmɪnstə) *n.* the British Houses of Parliament.

westward (ˈwɛstwəd) *adj., adv.* also **westwards. 1.** towards the west. ~*n.* **2.** the westward part or direction. —**ˈwestwardly** *adj., adv.*

wet (wɛt) *adj.* **wetter, wettest. 1.** moistened, covered, or soaked with water or some other liquid. **2.** not yet dry or solid: *wet varnish.* **3.** rainy: *wet weather.* **4.** *Brit. informal.* feeble or foolish. **5. wet behind the ears.** *Informal.* immature or inexperienced. ~*n.* **6.** wetness or moisture. **7.** rainy weather. **8.** *Brit. informal.* a feeble or foolish person. **9.** (*often cap.*) *Brit. informal.* a Conservative politician who supports moderate policies. ~*vb.* **wetting, wet** *or* **wetted. 10.** to make or become wet. **11.** to urinate on (something). —**ˈwetly** *adv.* —**ˈwetness** *n.*

wet blanket *n. Informal.* a person whose low spirits or lack of enthusiasm have a depressing effect on others.

wet dream *n.* an erotic dream accompanied by an emission of semen.

wether (ˈwɛðə) *n.* a male sheep, esp. a castrated one.

wetland (ˈwɛtlənd) *n.* (*sometimes pl.*) an area of marshy land.

wet nurse *n.* (esp. formerly) a woman hired to breast-feed the child of another.

wet suit *n.* a close-fitting rubber suit used by skin-divers or yachtsmen to retain body heat.

W. Glam. West Glamorgan.

whack (wæk) *vb.* **1.** to strike with a sharp resounding blow. ~*n.* **2.** a sharp resounding blow or the noise made by such a blow. **3.** *Informal.* a share or portion. **4. have a whack at.** to attempt.

whacked (wækt) *adj. Brit. informal.* completely exhausted.

whacking (ˈwækɪŋ) *Informal, chiefly Brit.* ~*adj.* **1.** enormous. ~*adv.* **2.** very: *a whacking big lie.*

whale (weɪl) *n., pl.* **whales** *or* **whale. 1.** any of various large marine mammals which have flippers and a horizontally flattened tail and breathe through a blowhole on the top of the head. **2. a whale of a.** *Informal.* an exceptionally large or fine example of a (person or thing): *I had a whale of a time.*

whalebone (ˈweɪlˌbəʊn) *n.* **1.** a horny elastic material that hangs from the upper jaw in the toothless (whalebone) whales and strains plankton from water entering the mouth. **2.** a thin strip of this substance, used, esp. formerly, for stiffening corsets and bodices.

whalebone whale *n.* any whale with a

double blowhole and strips of whalebone between the jaws instead of teeth, including the right whale and the blue whale.

whaler ('weɪlə) n. **1.** a person employed in whaling. **2.** a vessel engaged in whaling.

whaling ('weɪlɪŋ) n. the hunting and killing of whales for food or oil.

wham (wæm) n. **1.** a forceful blow or impact or the sound produced by it. ~vb. **whamming, whammed. 2.** to strike with great force.

wharepuni ('fɒrɛˌpunɪ) n. N.Z. in a Maori community, a lofty carved building used as a guesthouse.

wharf (wɔːf) n., pl. **wharves** (wɔːvz) or **wharfs.** a platform along the side of a waterfront for docking, loading, and unloading ships.

wharfage ('wɔːfɪdʒ) n. **1.** accommodation for ships at wharves. **2.** a charge for use of a wharf.

wharfie ('wɔːfɪ) n. Austral. & N.Z. a dock labourer.

what (wɒt) det. **1. a.** used with a noun in requesting further information about the identity or categorization of something: *what job does he do?; tell me what she said.* **b.** (*as pron.*): *what is her address?* **2.** the person, thing, people, or things that: *we photographed what animals we could see; bring me what you've written.* **3.** used in exclamations to add emphasis: *what a good book!* ~adv. **4.** in what respect? to what degree?: *what do you care?* **5. what about.** what do you think or know concerning? **6. what for?** why? **7. what have you.** someone or something unspecified: *cars, motorcycles, or what have you.* **8. what's what.** *Informal.* the true state of affairs.
Usage. In good usage, *what* is never used for *which,* as in *he gave me the letter what he had written. What* is used, however, when it means "the things which": *he saw what he had done.*

whatever (wɒt'ɛvə) pron. **1.** everything or anything that: *do whatever he asks you to.* **2.** no matter what: *whatever he does, he is forgiven.* **3.** Informal. an unspecified thing: *take a hammer, chisel, or whatever.* **4.** an intensive form of *what,* used in questions: *whatever can he have said to upset her so much?* ~det. **5.** an intensive form of *what:* *use whatever tools you can get hold of.* ~adj. **6.** at all: *I saw no point whatever in continuing.*

whatnot ('wɒtˌnɒt) n. Informal. unspecified similar things: *we had eggs, bacon, and whatnot.*

whatsoever (ˌwɒtsəʊ'ɛvə) adj. at all: used for emphasis after a noun phrase that uses words such as *none* or *any: no doubt whatsoever; is there any evidence whatsoever?*

wheat (wiːt) n. the light brown grain of any of a variety of grasses, used in making flour and pasta.

wheatear ('wiːtˌɪə) n. a small northern songbird with a conspicuous white rump.

wheaten ('wiːtᵊn) adj. made of the grain or flour of wheat.

wheat germ n. the vitamin-rich embryo of the wheat kernel.

wheatmeal ('wiːtˌmiːl) n. a brown flour intermediate between white flour and wholemeal flour.

wheedle ('wiːdᵊl) vb. **1.** to persuade or try to persuade (someone) by coaxing or flattery. **2.** to obtain thus: *she wheedled some money out of her father.* —'**wheedling** adj.

wheel (wiːl) n. **1.** a solid disc or circular rim joined to a hub by spokes, that is mounted on a shaft about which it can turn, as in vehicles. **2.** anything like a wheel in shape or function: *a steering wheel; a water wheel.* **3.** a pivoting movement. **4. at the wheel. a.** driving or steering a vehicle. **b.** in charge. **5. big wheel.** Informal, chiefly U.S. & Canad. an important or influential person. ~vb. **6.** to push or pull (a vehicle or object with wheels). **7.** to turn on or as if on an axis. **8.** (often foll. by round) to change direction or turn round suddenly. **9. wheel and deal.** to operate shrewdly and sometimes unscrupulously in order to advance one's own interests. ~See also **wheels.**

wheelbarrow ('wiːlˌbærəʊ) n. a shallow open box for carrying small loads, with a wheel at the front and two shafts for pushing or pulling it.

wheelbase ('wiːlˌbeɪs) n. the distance between the front and back axles of a motor vehicle.

wheelchair ('wiːlˌtʃɛə) n. a special chair on large wheels, for use by people for whom walking is impossible or inadvisable.

wheel clamp n. a device fixed onto one wheel of an illegally parked car to prevent the car being driven off. The driver has to pay to have the clamp removed.

wheeler-dealer ('wiːlə'diːlə) n. a person who wheels and deals.

wheelhouse ('wiːlˌhaʊs) n. an enclosed structure on the bridge of a ship from which it is steered.

wheelie ('wiːlɪ) n. a manoeuvre on a bicycle or motorbike in which the front wheel is raised off the ground.

wheels (wiːlz) pl. n. **1.** the main force and mechanism of an organization: *the wheels of government.* **2.** Informal. a car. **3. wheels within wheels.** a series of intricately connected events or plots.

wheelwright ('wiːlˌraɪt) n. a person who makes or mends wheels as a trade.

wheeze (wiːz) vb. **1.** to breathe with a rasping or whistling sound. ~n. **2.** a wheezing breath. **3.** Brit. old-fashioned

slang. a trick or plan. —**'wheezy** *adj.*
—**'wheeziness** *n.*

whelk (wɛlk) *n.* an edible mollusc of coastal waters, with a strong snail-like shell.

whelp (wɛlp) *n.* **1.** a young offspring of a wolf or dog. **2.** *Disparaging.* a youth. ~*vb.* **3.** (of an animal) to give birth to (young).

when (wɛn) *adv.* **1.** at what time? over what period?: *when is he due?*; *when was the act in force?* **2. say when.** to state when an action is to be stopped, as when someone is pouring a drink. ~*conj.* **3.** at a time at which; just as; after: *I found it easy when I tried.* **4.** although: *he drives when he might walk.* **5.** considering the fact that: *how did you pass the exam when you hadn't worked for it?* ~*pron.* **6.** at which time: *an age when men were men.*
Usage. Care should be taken so that *when* and *where* refer explicitly to time or place, and are not used loosely to substitute for *in which* after the verb *to be: paralysis is a condition in which* (not *when* or *where*) *parts of the body cannot be moved.*

whence (wɛns) *Archaic or formal.* ~*adv.* **1.** from what place, cause, or origin? ~*conj.* **2.** to the place which: *return whence you came.*
Usage. It is unnecessary to use *from* before *whence,* because *whence* itself means "from which place": *the tradition whence* (not *from whence*) *such ideas flow.*

whenever (wɛn'ɛvə) *conj.* **1.** at every or any time that; when: *I laugh whenever I see that.* ~*adv.* **2.** no matter when: *it'll be here, whenever you decide to come for it.* **3.** *Informal.* at an unknown or unspecified time: *I'll take it if it comes today, tomorrow, or whenever.* **4.** an intensive form of *when,* used in questions: *whenever did he escape?*

where (wɛə) *adv.* **1.** in, at, or to what place, point, or position?: *where are you going?*; *I don't know where they are.* ~*pron.* **2.** in, at, or to which place: *the hotel where we spent our honeymoon.* ~*conj.* **3.** in the place at which: *where we live it's always raining.*
Usage. see **when.**

whereabouts ('wɛərə,baʊts) *adv.* **1.** at what approximate place; where: *whereabouts are you?* ~*n.* **2.** (*functioning as sing. or pl.*) the place, esp. the approximate place, where a person or thing is.

whereas (wɛər'æz) *conj.* **1.** but on the other hand: *I like to go swimming whereas Sheila likes to sail.* **2.** (in formal documents) it being the case that; since.

whereby (wɛə'baɪ) *pron.* by or because of which: *the means whereby he took his life.*

wherefore ('wɛə,fɔː) *n.* **1. the whys and wherefores.** the reasons or explanation. ~*conj.* **2.** *Archaic or formal.* for which reason: used in legal preambles.

wherein (wɛər'ɪn) *Archaic or formal.* ~*adv.* **1.** in what place or respect? ~*pron.*

2. in which place or thing: *the room wherein she lay.*

whereof (wɛər'ɒv) *Archaic or formal.* ~*adv.* **1.** of what or which person or thing? ~*pron.* **2.** of which person or thing: *the man whereof I speak is no longer alive.*

whereupon (,wɛərə'pɒn) *conj.* at which point; upon which.

wherever (wɛər'ɛvə) *pron.* **1.** at, in, or to every place or point which; where: *wherever she went, he would be there.* ~*conj.* **2.** in, to, or at whatever place: *wherever we go the weather is always bad.* ~*adv.* **3.** no matter where: *I'll find you, wherever you are.* **4.** *Informal.* at, in, or to an unknown or unspecified place: *I'll go anywhere to escape: London, Paris, or wherever.* **5.** an intensive form of *where,* used in questions: *wherever can they be?*

wherewithal ('wɛəwɪð,ɔːl) *n.* **the wherewithal.** necessary funds, resources, or equipment: *these people lack the wherewithal for a decent existence.*

wherry ('wɛrɪ) *n., pl.* **-ries. 1.** a light rowing boat. **2.** a large light barge.
—**'wherryman** *n.*

whet (wɛt) *vb.* **whetting, whetted. 1.** to increase (appetite or desire). **2.** *Old-fashioned.* to sharpen.

whether ('wɛðə) *conj.* **1.** used to introduce an indirect question or a clause expressing doubt or choice: *he doesn't know whether she's in Britain or France; anyone, whether liberal or conservative, would agree with me; you'll eat it whether you like it or whether you don't.* **2. whether or no.** in any case: *he will be here tomorrow, whether or no.*

whetstone ('wɛt,stəʊn) *n.* a stone used for sharpening edged tools or knives.

whew (hwjuː) *interj.* an exclamation expressing relief, surprise, or delight.

whey (weɪ) *n.* the watery liquid that separates from the curd when milk is clotted, as in making cheese.

which (wɪtʃ) *det.* **1. a.** used with a noun in requesting that the particular thing being referred to is further identified or distinguished: *which house did you want to buy?*; *I don't know which route is quickest.* **b.** (*as pron.*): *which did you find?* **2. a.** whichever: *bring which car you want.* **b.** (*as pron.*): *choose which of the cars suits you.* ~*pron.* **3.** used in relative clauses referring to an inanimate noun: *the house, which is old, is in poor repair.* **4.** as; and that: *he died of cancer, which is what I predicted.*
Usage. see **that.**

whichever (wɪtʃ'ɛvə) *det.* **1. a.** any out of several: *take whichever car you like.* **b.** (*as pron.*): *choose whichever appeals to you.* **2. a.** no matter which one or ones: *whichever card you pick you'll still be making a mistake.* **b.** (*as pron.*): *it won't make any difference, whichever comes first.*

whiff (wɪf) *n.* **1.** a passing odour. **2.** a brief gentle gust of air or smoke. **3.** a trace or hint: *a whiff of scandal.*

Whig (wɪg) *n.* **1.** a member of an English, and later British, political party that supported a limited monarchy, later represented the desires of industrialists and Dissenters for political and social reform, and provided the core of the Liberal Party. ~*adj.* **2.** of or relating to Whigs. —'**Whiggery** or '**Whiggism** *n.* —'**Whiggish** *adj.*

while (waɪl) *conj. also* **whilst. 1.** at the same time that: *please light the fire while I'm cooking.* **2.** all the time that: *I stay inside while it's raining.* **3.** in spite of the fact that: *while I agree about his brilliance I still think he's rude.* **4.** whereas; and in contrast: *houses are expensive, while flats are cheap.* ~*n.* **5.** a period of time: *once in a long while.* **6. worth one's while.** worthy of time or effort.
Usage. The main sense of *while* is *during the time that.* It also means *although*: *while he disliked working, he was obliged to do so.* It is important to avoid any ambiguity that may result from the possibility of two interpretations of *while* in context: *while (although* or *during the time that) his brother worked in the park, he refused to do any gardening at home.*

while away *vb.* to pass (time) idly and usually pleasantly.

whilst (waɪlst) *conj. Chiefly Brit.* same as **while.**

whim (wɪm) *n.* a sudden, passing, and often fanciful idea.

whimper ('wɪmpə) *vb.* **1.** to cry, complain, or say (something) in a whining plaintive way. ~*n.* **2.** a soft plaintive whine.

whimsical ('wɪmzɪk^əl) *adj.* **1.** fanciful or playful. **2.** (of a person) given to whims; capricious. **3.** unusual in a quaint or fantastic way. —**whimsicality** (ˌwɪmzɪ'kælɪtɪ) *n.* —'**whimsically** *adv.*

whimsy or **whimsey** ('wɪmzɪ) *n., pl.* **-sies** or **-seys. 1.** a capricious idea. **2.** light or fanciful humour.

whin (wɪn) *n.* same as **gorse.**

whine (waɪn) *n.* **1.** a long high-pitched plaintive cry or moan. **2.** a peevish complaint, esp. one repeated. ~*vb.* **3.** to whine or utter in a whine. —'**whining** *n., adj.*

whinge (wɪndʒ) *vb.* **1.** to complain in a moaning manner. ~*n.* **2.** a complaint.

whinny ('wɪnɪ) *vb.* **-nying, -nied. 1.** (of a horse) to neigh softly or gently. ~*n., pl.* **-nies. 2.** a gentle or low-pitched neigh.

whip (wɪp) *vb.* **whipping, whipped. 1.** to strike (a person or thing) with several strokes of a strap or cane. **2.** (foll. by *out* or *away*) to pull or remove (something) with sudden rapid motion: *to whip out a gun.* **3.** (foll. by *down, into, out of,* etc.) *Informal.* to move in a rapid sudden manner: *they whipped into the bar for a drink.* **4.** to strike as if by whipping: *the cold wind whipped her face.* **5.** to bring (someone) into a particular condition: *whipped into a frenzy.* **6.** (often foll. by *on, out,* or *off*) to drive or urge by or as if by whipping. **7.** *Informal.* to steal (something). **8.** to wind (cord) round (a rope or cable) to prevent fraying. **9.** to beat (eggs or cream) with a whisk or similar utensil to incorporate air. ~*n.* **10.** a device consisting of a lash or flexible rod attached at one end to a stiff handle and used for driving animals or beating people. **11.** (in a legislative body) **a.** a member of a party chosen to organize and discipline the people in his party. **b.** a call issued to members of a party, insisting with varying degrees of urgency upon their presence or loyal voting behaviour. In the British Parliament this is done in writing, with each item of the week's schedule underlined to indicate its importance: three lines means that the item is very important. **12.** a dessert made from egg whites or cream beaten stiff. ~See also **whip-round, whip up.** —'**whipping** *n.*

whipcord ('wɪpˌkɔːd) *n.* a strong worsted or cotton fabric with a diagonally ribbed surface.

whip hand *n.* **the whip hand.** an advantage or dominating position.

whiplash ('wɪpˌlæʃ) *n.* a quick lash or stroke of a whip or like that of a whip.

whiplash injury *n.* any injury to the neck resulting from a sudden thrusting forwards and snapping back of the head, as in a car crash.

whipper-in *n., pl.* **whippers-in.** a huntsman's assistant who manages the hounds.

whippersnapper ('wɪpəˌsnæpə) *n.* an insignificant but pretentious person.

whippet ('wɪpɪt) *n.* a small slender breed of dog similar to a greyhound.

whipping boy *n.* a scapegoat.

whippoorwill ('wɪpʊˌwɪl) *n.* an American nightjar.

whip-round *n. Informal, chiefly Brit.* an impromptu collection of money.

whipstock ('wɪpˌstɒk) *n.* a whip handle.

whip up *vb.* **1.** to excite; arouse: *to whip up a mob; to whip up discontent.* **2.** *Informal.* to prepare quickly: *to whip up a meal.*

whirl (wɜːl) *vb.* **1.** to spin, turn, or revolve. **2.** to seem to spin from dizziness or confusion: *my head's whirling.* **3.** to move or drive or be moved or driven at high speed. ~*n.* **4.** the act or an instance of whirling. **5.** a confused or giddy condition: *her accident left me in a whirl.* **6.** a round of intense activity: *the social whirl.* **7. give (something) a whirl.** *Informal.* to attempt or try (something).

whirligig ('wɜːlɪˌgɪg) *n.* **1.** a spinning toy,

such as a top. **2.** same as **merry-go-round. 3.** anything that whirls.

whirlpool ('wɜːl,puːl) n. a powerful circular current or vortex of water, into which objects floating nearby are drawn.

whirlwind ('wɜːl,wɪnd) n. **1.** a column of air whirling violently upwards in a spiral. ~adj. **2.** done or happening much more quickly than normal: *a whirlwind romance*.

whirlybird ('wɜːlɪ,bɜːd) n. *Informal.* a helicopter.

whirr or **whir** (wɜː) n. **1.** a prolonged soft whiz or buzz. ~vb. **whirring, whirred. 2.** to make or cause to make a whir.

whisk (wɪsk) vb. **1.** to brush or sweep away lightly. **2.** to move or carry with a rapid sweeping motion: *the taxi whisked us to the airport.* **3.** to whip (eggs or cream) to a froth. ~n. **4.** the act of whisking. **5.** a light rapid sweeping movement. **6.** a utensil for whipping eggs or cream. **7.** a small brush or broom.

whisker ('wɪskə) n. **1.** any of the long stiff hairs growing on the face of a cat or other mammal. **2.** any of the hairs growing on a man's face, esp. on the cheeks or chin. **3.** (pl.) a beard or that part of it growing on the sides of the face. **4. by a whisker.** by a very small distance or amount: *he escaped death by a whisker.*

whiskey ('wɪskɪ) n. *Irish & U.S.* same as **whisky.**

whisky ('wɪskɪ) n., pl. **-kies.** a spirit made by distilling fermented cereals.

whisky-jack n. *Canad.* same as **Canada jay.**

whisper ('wɪspə) vb. **1.** to speak or utter (something) very softly, using the breath instead of the vocal cords. **2.** to speak or utter (something) secretly or privately. **3.** to make a low soft rustling sound. ~n. **4.** a low soft voice: *to speak in a whisper.* **5.** something uttered in a whisper. **6.** a low soft rustling sound. **7.** *Informal.* a rumour.

whist (wɪst) n. a card game for two pairs of players.

whist drive n. a social gathering where whist is played.

whistle ('wɪsᵊl) vb. **1.** to produce (a shrill sound) by forcing breath between the pursed lips. **2.** to signal or command by whistling or blowing a whistle: *the referee whistled the end of the game.* **3.** (of a kettle or train) to produce (a shrill sound) caused by the forcing of steam through a small opening. **4.** to move with a whistling sound. **5.** (of animals, esp. birds) to give a shrill cry. **6. whistle in the dark.** to try to keep up one's confidence in spite of fear. ~n. **7.** an instrument for making a shrill sound by means of air or steam under pressure. **8.** the act or sound of whistling. **9. blow the whistle.** (usually foll. by *on*) *In-*

formal. to inform (on). **10. wet one's whistle.** *Informal.* to take a drink.

whistle for vb. *Informal.* to seek or expect in vain.

whistle stop n. **1.** *U.S. & Canad.* a small town at which trains stop only if signalled. **2.** a brief appearance in a town, esp. by a political candidate.

whit (wɪt) n. (usually used with a negative) the smallest particle; iota; jot: *he has changed not a whit.*

Whit (wɪt) n. **1.** See **Whitsuntide.** ~adj. **2.** of Whitsuntide.

white (waɪt) adj. **1.** having no hue, owing to the reflection of all or almost all light. **2.** of light or pale colour. **3.** (of an animal) albino. **4.** pale, as from pain, emotion, illness, or fear. **5.** (of hair) having lost its colour, usually from age. **6.** (of coffee or tea) with milk or cream. **7.** (of wine) made from pale grapes or from black grapes separated from their skins. **8.** denoting flour, or bread made from flour, that has had part of the grain removed. **9. bleed white.** to deprive slowly of resources. ~n. **10.** a white colour. **11.** the clear fluid that surrounds the yolk of a bird's egg; albumen. **12.** *Anat.* the white part of the eyeball. **13.** *Chess, draughts.* **a.** a white or light-coloured piece or square. **b.** the player playing with such pieces. **14.** anything white, such as a white paint or white clothing. **15.** *Archery.* the outer ring of the target, having the lowest score. ~See also **whites.** —'**whiteness** n. —'**whitish** adj.

White (waɪt) n. **1.** a member of the Caucasoid race. **2.** a person of European ancestry. ~adj. **3.** of or denoting a White or Whites.

white ant n. same as **termite.**

whitebait ('waɪt,beɪt) n. the young of herrings, sprats, or pilchards cooked and eaten whole as a delicacy.

white blood cell n. a nontechnical name for **leucocyte.**

whitecap ('waɪt,kæp) n. a wave with a white broken crest.

white-collar adj. of or designating nonmanual workers employed in professional and clerical occupations.

white dwarf n. a small, faint, very dense star.

white elephant n. a possession that is unwanted by its owner.

white feather n. **1.** a symbol of cowardice. **2. show the white feather.** to act in a cowardly manner.

white fish n. any of various sea fishes with white flesh used as food, such as cod or haddock.

white flag n. a signal of surrender or to request a truce.

whitefly ('waɪt,flaɪ) n., pl. **-flies.** a tiny whitish insect harmful to greenhouse crops.

white friar n. a Carmelite friar, so called from the white cloak worn by these friars.

white gold n. a white lustrous hard-wearing alloy containing gold together with platinum or other metals, used in jewellery.

white goods pl. n. large household appliances, such as refrigerators or cookers.

Whitehall (ˌwaɪtˈhɔːl) n. 1. a street in London which is the site of the main government offices. 2. the British Government.

white heat n. 1. intense heat characterized by emission of white light. 2. Informal. a state of intense excitement or activity.

white hope n. Informal. a person who is expected to accomplish much.

white horse n. (usually pl.) a wave with a white broken crest.

white-hot adj. 1. at such a high temperature that white light is emitted. 2. Informal. in a state of intense emotion.

White House n. the. 1. the official Washington residence of the president of the U.S. 2. the executive branch of the U.S. government.

white lead (lɛd) n. a white powder, usually a mixture of lead carbonate and lead hydroxide, used as a pigment and in making putty and ointments.

white lie n. a small lie, usually told to avoid hurting someone's feelings.

white light n. light that contains all the wavelengths of the visible spectrum, such as sunlight.

White man's burden n. the supposed duty of the White race to bring education and Western culture to the non-White inhabitants of their colonies.

white matter n. the whitish tissue of the brain and spinal cord, consisting mainly of nerve fibres.

white meat n. any meat that is light in colour, such as veal or the breast of turkey.

whiten (ˈwaɪtˀn) vb. to make or become white or whiter. —ˈwhitening n.

white noise n. noise that has a wide range of frequencies of uniform intensity.

whiteout (ˈwaɪtaʊt) n. an atmospheric condition, in which blizzards or low clouds make it very difficult to see.

white paper n. (often caps.) an official government report which sets out the government's policy on a specific matter.

white pepper n. a condiment made from the husked seeds of the pepper plant.

White Russian adj. 1. of Byelorussia, an administrative division of the W Soviet Union. 2. of Byelorussia, its people, or their language. ~n. 3. the official language of Byelorussia. 4. a person from Byelorussia.

whites (waɪts) pl. n. 1. household linen or cotton goods, such as sheets. 2. white

clothing, such as that worn for playing cricket.

white sauce n. a thick sauce made from flour, butter, seasonings, and milk or stock.

white slave n. a girl or woman forced or sold into prostitution.

white spirit n. a colourless liquid obtained from petroleum and used as a substitute for turpentine.

white tie n. 1. a white bow tie worn as part of a man's formal evening dress. 2. formal evening dress for men.

whitewash (ˈwaɪtˌwɒʃ) n. 1. a suspension of lime or whiting in water for whitening walls and other surfaces. 2. Informal. an attempt to conceal defects or gloss over failings. ~vb. 3. to cover with whitewash. 4. Informal. to conceal the defects or gloss over the failings of.

white whale n. a small white toothed whale of northern waters.

whitewood (ˈwaɪtˌwʊd) n. 1. a light-coloured wood. 2. a tree yielding such wood.

whither (ˈwɪðə) Archaic or poetic. ~adv. 1. to what place? 2. to what end or purpose? ~conj. 3. to whatever place or purpose.

whiting¹ (ˈwaɪtɪŋ) n. an important white-fleshed food fish of European seas.

whiting² (ˈwaɪtɪŋ) n. white powdered chalk, used in making whitewash and metal polish.

whitlow (ˈwɪtləʊ) n. an inflamed sore on the end of a finger or toe.

Whitsun (ˈwɪtsˀn) n. 1. short for **Whitsuntide**. ~adj. 2. of Whit Sunday or Whitsuntide.

Whit Sunday n. the seventh Sunday after Easter.

Whitsuntide (ˈwɪtsˀnˌtaɪd) n. the week that begins with Whit Sunday.

whittle (ˈwɪtˀl) vb. 1. to cut or shave strips or pieces from (wood) with a knife. 2. to make or shape in this way. 3. (often foll. by away or down) to reduce, destroy, or wear away gradually.

whizz or **whiz** (wɪz) vb. **whizzing, whizzed.** 1. to make or cause to make a loud humming or buzzing sound. 2. to move or cause to move with such a sound. 3. Informal. to move or go rapidly. ~n., pl. **whizzes.** 4. a whizzing sound. 5. Informal. a person who is extremely good at something.

whizz kid or **whiz kid** n. Informal. a person who is outstandingly able and successful for his or her age.

who (huː) pron. 1. which person? what person? used in direct and indirect questions: he can't remember who did it; who met you? 2. used at the beginning of a relative clause referring to a person or persons already mentioned: the people who lived here have left. 3. the one or ones

who; whoever: *bring who you want.*
Usage. see **whom.**

WHO World Health Organization.

whoa (wəʊ) *interj.* a command used esp. to horses to stop or slow down.

whodunit *or* **whodunnit** (huːˈdʌnɪt) *n. Informal.* a novel, play, or film concerned with the solving of a crime, esp. murder.

whoever (huːˈɛvə) *pron.* **1.** any person who: *whoever wants it can have it.* **2.** no matter who: *I'll come round tomorrow, whoever may be here.* **3.** an intensive form of *who,* used in questions: *whoever could have thought that?* **4.** *Informal.* an unspecified person: *give those to Cathy or whoever.*

whole (həʊl) *adj.* **1.** containing all the component parts; complete: *a whole apple.* **2.** constituting the full quantity or extent: *the whole day.* **3.** uninjured or undamaged. **4.** healthy. **5.** having no fractional or decimal part; integral: *10 is a whole number.* ~*adv.* **6.** in an undivided or unbroken piece: *to swallow a plum whole.* ~*n.* **7.** all there is of a thing; totality. **8.** an assemblage of parts viewed together as a unit. **9.** a thing complete in itself. **10. as a whole.** considered altogether; completely. **11. on the whole. a.** taking all things into consideration. **b.** in general. —ˈwholeness *n.*

wholefood (ˈhəʊlˌfuːd) *n.* (*sometimes pl.*) food that has been refined or processed as little as possible.

wholehearted (ˌhəʊlˈhɑːtɪd) *adj.* done with total sincerity, enthusiasm, or commitment. —ˌwholeˈheartedly *adv.*

wholemeal (ˈhəʊlˌmiːl) *adj. Brit.* **a.** (of flour) made from the entire wheat kernel. **b.** made from wholemeal flour: *wholemeal bread.*

whole note *n. U.S. & Canad.* same as **semibreve.**

whole number *n.* **1.** an integer. **2.** a natural number.

wholesale (ˈhəʊlˌseɪl) *n.* **1.** the business of selling goods in large quantities to retailers for resale. ~*adj., adv.* **2.** of or by such business. **3.** on a large scale or indiscriminately. ~*vb.* **4.** to sell (goods) at wholesale. —ˈwholeˌsaler *n.*

wholesome (ˈhəʊlsəm) *adj.* **1.** promoting health or wellbeing. **2.** promoting moral wellbeing.

whole-wheat *adj. U.S. & Canad.* same as **wholemeal.**

wholly (ˈhəʊlɪ) *adv.* completely.

whom (huːm) *pron.* the objective form of *who: whom did you say you had seen? he can't remember whom he saw.*
Usage. In formal English *whom* is used when the objective form of *who* is required. In informal contexts, however, many people consider *whom* to be unnatural, esp. at the beginning of a sentence: *who were you look-*

ing for? Whom is often preferred where it closely follows a preposition: *to whom did you give it?* as contrasted with *who did you give it to?*

whomever (huːmˈɛvə) *pron.* the objective form of *whoever: I'll hire whomever I can find.*

whoop (wuːp) *vb.* **1.** to utter (speech) with loud cries, esp. of excitement or joy. **2.** (huːp). *Med.* to cough convulsively with a crowing sound. **3.** (wʊp, wuːp). **whoop it up.** *Informal.* to indulge in a noisy celebration. ~*n.* **4.** a loud cry, esp. of excitement or joy. **5.** (huːp). *Med.* the convulsive crowing sound made during whooping cough.

whoopee *Informal.* ~*interj.* (wʊˈpiː). **1.** an exclamation of joy or excitement. ~*n.* (ˈwʊpiː). **2. make whoopee. a.** to engage in noisy merrymaking. **b.** to make love.

whooping cough (ˈhuːpɪŋ) *n.* an acute infectious disease characterized by coughing spasms that end with a shrill crowing sound on breathing in.

whoops (wʊps) *interj.* an exclamation of surprise or of apology.

whop (wɒp) *Informal.* ~*vb.* **whopping, whopped. 1.** to strike, beat, or thrash. **2.** to defeat utterly. ~*n.* **3.** a heavy blow or the sound of it.

whopper (ˈwɒpə) *n. Informal.* **1.** an unusually large example of its kind. **2.** a big lie.

whopping (ˈwɒpɪŋ) *adj. Informal.* unusually large.

whore (hɔː) *n.* **1.** a prostitute or promiscuous woman: often a term of abuse. ~*vb.* **2.** to be or act as a prostitute. **3.** (of a man) to have promiscuous sexual relations, esp. with prostitutes.

whorehouse (ˈhɔːˌhaʊs) *n.* a brothel.

whorl (wɜːl) *n.* **1.** *Bot.* a circular arrangement of parts around a stem. **2.** *Zool.* a single turn in a spiral shell. **3.** anything shaped like a coil.

whortleberry (ˈwɜːtˈlˌbɛrɪ) *n., pl.* **-ries. 1.** a small Eurasian shrub with edible sweet blackish berries. **2.** the fruit of this shrub.

who's (huːz) who is *or* who has.

whose (huːz) *det.* **1.** of who? belonging to who? used in direct and indirect questions: *I told him whose fault it was; whose car is this?* **2.** of who; of which: used as a relative pronoun: *a man whose reputation has suffered.*
Usage. Since *whose* is the possessive of both *who* and *which,* it is quite acceptable to use *whose* of things as well as of people: *these are the houses whose foundations are unsteady; this is the man whose leg was broken.*

whosoever (ˌhuːsəʊˈɛvə) *pron. Archaic or formal.* same as **whoever.**

who's who *n.* a book or list containing the

names and short biographies of famous people.

why (waɪ) *adv.* **1. a.** for what reason?: *why are you here?* **b.** (*used in indirect questions*): *tell me why you're here.* ~*pron.* **2.** for or because of which: *there is no reason why he shouldn't come.* ~*n., pl.* **whys. 3.** (*usually pl.*) the cause of something: *I want to know the whys and wherefores.* ~*interj.* **4.** an exclamation of surprise, indignation, or impatience: *why, don't be silly!*

WI 1. West Indies. **2.** Wisconsin. **3.** (in Britain) Women's Institute.

wick (wɪk) *n.* **1.** a cord or tape in a candle or lamp through which the fuel reaches the flame. **2. get on** (**someone's**) **wick.** *Brit. slang.* to annoy (someone).

wicked ('wɪkɪd) *adj.* **1.** morally bad. **2.** playfully mischievous or roguish: *a wicked grin.* **3.** troublesome or unpleasant. **4.** *Slang.* very good. —'**wickedly** *adv.* —'**wickedness** *n.*

wicker ('wɪkə) *n.* **1.** a slender flexible twig, esp. of willow. ~*adj.* **2.** made of wicker.

wickerwork ('wɪkə,wɜːk) *n.* a material consisting of woven wicker.

wicket ('wɪkɪt) *n.* **1.** *Cricket.* **a.** either of two sets of three stumps stuck in the ground with two wooden bails resting on top, at which the batsman stands. **b.** the playing space between these. **c.** the act or instance of a batsman being got out: *the bowler took six wickets.* **2.** a small door or gate, esp. one that is near to or part of a larger one.

wicketkeeper ('wɪkɪt,kiːpə) *n. Cricket.* the fielder positioned directly behind the wicket.

widdershins ('wɪdə,ʃɪnz) *adv. Chiefly Scot.* same as **withershins.**

wide (waɪd) *adj.* **1.** having a great extent from side to side. **2.** spacious or extensive. **3. a.** having a specified extent from side to side: *two yards wide.* **b.** (*in combination*): extending throughout: *nationwide.* **4.** remote from the desired point or mark: *your guess is wide of the mark.* **5.** (of eyes) opened fully. **6.** exhibiting a considerable spread: *a wide variation.* **7.** *Brit. slang.* unscrupulous and shrewd: *a wide boy.* ~*adv.* **8.** over an extensive area: *to travel far and wide.* **9.** to a large or full extent: *he opened the door wide.* **10.** far from the desired point or mark. ~*n.* **11.** (in cricket) a ball bowled outside the batsman's reach, which scores a run for the batting side. —'**widely** *adv.*

wide-angle lens *n.* a lens on a camera which can cover a wider angle of view than an ordinary lens.

wide-awake *adj.* **1.** fully awake. **2.** keen, alert, or observant.

wide-eyed *adj.* innocent or naive.

widen ('waɪd³n) *vb.* to make or become wide or wider.

wide-open *adj.* **1.** open to the full extent. **2.** exposed to attack; vulnerable.

widespread ('waɪd,sprɛd) *adj.* **1.** extending over a wide area. **2.** accepted by or occurring among many people.

widgeon ('wɪdʒən) *n.* same as **wigeon.**

widow ('wɪdəʊ) *n.* **1.** a woman who has lost her husband by death and has not remarried. **2.** (*with a modifier*) *Informal.* a woman whose husband frequently leaves her alone while he indulges in a specified hobby or sport: *a golf widow.* ~*vb.* (*usually passive*) **3.** to cause to become a widow. —'**widowhood** *n.*

widower ('wɪdəʊə) *n.* a man who has lost his wife by death and has not remarried.

width (wɪdθ) *n.* **1.** the extent or measurement of something from side to side. **2.** the state or fact of being wide. **3.** a piece of something of a particular width: *a width of cloth.* **4.** the distance across a rectangular swimming bath, as opposed to its length.

wield (wiːld) *vb.* **1.** to handle or use (a weapon or tool). **2.** to exert or maintain (power or authority).

wife (waɪf) *n., pl.* **wives. 1.** a man's partner in marriage; a married woman. **2.** *Archaic or dialect.* a woman. —'**wifely** *adj.*

wig (wɪg) *n.* an artificial head of hair. —**wigged** *adj.*

wigeon *or* **widgeon** ('wɪdʒən) *n.* a wild duck of marshland.

wigging ('wɪgɪŋ) *n. Brit. slang.* a reprimand.

wiggle ('wɪg³l) *vb.* **1.** to move or cause to move with jerky movements from side to side. ~*n.* **2.** the act of wiggling. —'**wiggly** *adj.*

wight (waɪt) *n. Archaic.* a human being.

wigwam ('wɪg,wæm) *n.* a dwelling of the North American Indians, made of bark, rushes, or skins spread over a set of arched poles lashed together.

wilco ('wɪlkəʊ) *interj.* an expression in signalling and telecommunications, indicating that a message just received will be complied with.

wild (waɪld) *adj.* **1.** (of animals) living independently of man; not domesticated or tame. **2.** (of plants) growing in a natural state; not cultivated. **3.** uninhabited; desolate: *a wild stretch of land.* **4.** living in a savage or uncivilized way: *wild tribes.* **5.** lacking restraint or control: *wild merriment.* **6.** of great violence: *a wild storm.* **7.** dishevelled; untidy: *wild hair.* **8.** in a state of extreme emotional intensity: *wild with grief.* **9.** random: *a wild guess.* **10.** (foll. by *about*) *Informal.* very enthusiastic: *I'm wild about my new boyfriend.* **11.** *Informal.* very angry: *Dad will be wild when he hears this.* ~*adv.* **12.** in a wild manner.

13. run wild. a. to grow without cultivation: *the garden has run wild.* **b.** to behave without restraint: *his children run wild.* ~*n.* **14.** (*often pl.*) a desolate or uninhabited region. **15. the wild.** a free natural state of living. —**'wildly** *adv.*

wildcat ('waɪld,kæt) *n., pl.* -**cats** *or* -**cat. 1.** a wild European cat that resembles the domestic tabby but is larger and has a bushy tail. **2.** *Informal.* a savage or aggressive person. **3.** *Chiefly U.S. & Canad.* an exploratory drilling for petroleum or natural gas. **4.** (*modifier*) *Chiefly U.S.* risky, esp. financially unsound: *a wildcat project.*

wildcat strike *n.* a strike begun by workers spontaneously or without union approval.

wildebeest ('wɪldɪ,biːst, 'vɪl-) *n., pl.* -**beests** *or* -**beest.** same as **gnu.**

wilderness ('wɪldənɪs) *n.* **1.** a wild uninhabited uncultivated region. **2.** a confused mass or tangle. **3. a voice (crying) in the wilderness.** a person or group making a suggestion or plea that is ignored.

wildfire ('waɪld,faɪə) *n.* **1.** a highly flammable material formerly used in warfare. **2. spread like wildfire.** to spread very quickly or uncontrollably.

wild flower *n.* any flowering plant that grows in an uncultivated state.

wildfowl ('waɪld,faʊl) *n.* **1.** any game bird. **2.** such birds collectively. —**'wild,fowling** *adj., n.*

wild-goose chase *n.* an absurd or hopeless search or undertaking.

wildlife ('waɪld,laɪf) *n.* wild animals and plants collectively.

wild rice *n.* an aquatic North American grass with dark-coloured edible grain.

Wild West *n.* the western U.S. during its settlement, esp. with reference to its lawlessness.

wile (waɪl) *n.* **1.** (*usually pl.*) an artful or seductive trick or ploy. ~*vb.* **2.** to lure or beguile.

wilful *or U.S.* **willful** ('wɪlfʊl) *adj.* **1.** intent on having one's own way; headstrong or obstinate. **2.** intentional: *wilful murder.* —**'wilfully** *adv.*

will¹ (wɪl) *vb. past* **would.** used as an auxiliary: **1.** (esp. with *you, he, she, it, they,* or a noun as subject) to make the future tense. **2.** to express resolution on the part of the speaker: *I will buy that radio if it's the last thing I do.* **3.** to indicate willingness: *will you help me with this problem?* **4.** to express commands: *you will report your findings to me.* **5.** to express ability: *this rope will support a load.* **6.** to express probability or expectation: *that will be Jim telephoning.* **7.** to express customary practice: *boys will be boys.* **8.** to express desire: *stay if you will.* **Usage.** see **shall.**

will² (wɪl) *n.* **1.** the faculty of conscious and deliberate choice of action. **2.** the act or an instance of asserting a choice. **3. a.** the declaration of a person's wishes regarding the disposal of his property after his death. **b.** the document containing this. **4.** desire; wish. **5.** determined intention: *where there's a will there's a way.* **6.** attitude towards others: *he bears you no ill will.* **7. at will.** at one's own desire or choice. **8. with a will.** heartily; energetically. ~*vb.* **9.** to exercise the will in an attempt to accomplish (something): *he willed himself to recover.* **10.** to bequeath (property) by a will: *he willed his art collection to the nation.* **11.** to wish or desire: *wander where you will.*

willie *or* **willy** ('wɪlɪ) *n. Brit. informal.* a childish or jocular name for **penis.**

willies ('wɪlɪz) *pl. n.* **the.** *Slang.* nervousness, jitters, or fright: *spiders give me the willies.*

willing ('wɪlɪŋ) *adj.* **1.** favourably disposed or inclined; ready: *are you willing to agree?* **2.** cheerfully compliant: *a willing worker.* **3.** done or given freely or voluntarily. —**'willingly** *adv.* —**'willingness** *n.*

will-o'-the-wisp (,wɪləðə'wɪsp) *n.* **1.** a pale light sometimes seen over marshy ground at night. **2.** a person or thing that is elusive or allures and misleads.

willow ('wɪləʊ) *n.* a tree or shrub with pliant wood used in weaving baskets and making cricket bats.

willowherb ('wɪləʊ,hɜːb) *n.* a plant with narrow leaves and purplish flowers.

willow pattern *n.* a pattern incorporating a willow tree, river, bridge, and figures, usually in blue on a white ground, used on china.

willowy ('wɪləʊɪ) *adj.* **1.** slender and graceful. **2.** shaded with willows.

willpower ('wɪl,paʊə) *n.* the ability to control oneself and determine one's actions.

willy-nilly ('wɪlɪ'nɪlɪ) *adv.* whether desired or not.

wilt¹ (wɪlt) *vb.* **1.** to become or cause to become limp or drooping: *insufficient water makes plants wilt.* **2.** to lose or cause to lose courage or strength. ~*n.* **3.** a plant disease characterized by wilting.

wilt² (wɪlt) *vb. Archaic or dialect.* (used with the pronoun *thou*) a singular form of the present tense of **will¹.**

Wilts. (wɪlts) Wiltshire.

wily ('waɪlɪ) *adj.* **wilier, wiliest.** sly or crafty. —**'wiliness** *n.*

wimp (wɪmp) *n. Informal.* a feeble ineffective person. —**'wimpish** *or* **'wimpy** *adj.*

wimple ('wɪmpʰl) *n.* a piece of cloth draped around the head to frame the face, worn by women in the Middle Ages and now by some nuns.

Wimpy ('wɪmpɪ) *n., pl.* **-pies**. *Trademark*. a hamburger served in a soft bread roll.

win (wɪn) *vb.* **winning, won**. **1.** to achieve first place in a competition. **2.** to gain (a prize or first place) in a competition. **3.** to succeed in or gain (something) with an effort: *we won recognition*. **4.** to gain victory or triumph in (a battle, argument, or struggle). **5.** to gain (the sympathy, favour, or support) of someone. **6. you can't win**. *Informal*. there is no way to succeed. ~*n.* **7.** *Informal*. a success, victory, or triumph. **8.** profit; winnings. ~See also **win over**. —'**winnable** *adj.*

wince (wɪns) *vb.* **1.** to draw back slightly, as with sudden pain; flinch. ~*n.* **2.** the act of wincing.

winceyette (ˌwɪnsɪ'ɛt) *n. Brit.* a soft cotton fabric with slightly raised nap.

winch (wɪntʃ) *n.* **1.** a lifting or hauling device consisting of a rope or chain wound round a barrel or drum. **2.** a hand- or power-operated crank by which a machine is driven. ~*vb.* **3.** (often foll. by *up* or *in*) to haul or lift using a winch.

Winchester rifle ('wɪntʃɪstə) *n. Trademark*. a slide-action repeating rifle.

wind¹ (wɪnd) *n.* **1.** a current of air moving across the earth's surface. **2.** air artificially moved, as by a fan. **3.** a trend, tendency, or force: *the winds of revolution*. **4.** *Informal*. a hint; suggestion: *we got wind that you were coming*. **5.** foolish or empty talk: *that's a lot of wind*. **6.** breath, as used in respiration or talk: *you're just wasting wind*. **7.** (often used in sports) the power to breathe normally: *his wind is weak*. **8.** *Music*. a wind instrument or wind instruments collectively. **9.** gas in the stomach or intestines; flatulence. **10.** the air on which the scent of an animal is carried to hounds or on which the scent of a hunter is carried to his quarry. **11. break wind**. to release intestinal gas through the anus. **12. get** *or* **have the wind up**. *Informal*. to become frightened. **13. in the wind**. about to happen. **14. put the wind up**. *Informal*. to frighten or alarm. **15. sail close to the wind**. to come near the limits of honesty or decency. **16. take the wind out of someone's sails**. to disconcert or deflate someone. **17. which way the wind blows**. what appears probable. ~*vb.* **18.** to cause (someone) to be short of breath: *the blow winded him*. **19.** to detect the scent of. **20.** to cause (a baby) to bring up wind after feeding. —'**windless** *adj.*

wind² (waɪnd) *vb.* **winding, wound**. **1.** to coil (something flexible) around some object or (of something flexible) to be coiled around some object: *he wound a scarf around his head*. **2.** (often foll. by *up*) to tighten the spring of (a clockwork mechanism). **3.** to move in a twisting, spiral, or circular course: *the river winds through the*

hills. ~*n.* **4.** a winding or being wound. **5.** a single turn or bend: *a wind in the river*. ~See also **wind down**, **wind up**. —'**winding** *n., adj.*

windbag ('wɪndˌbæg) *n. Slang*. a person who talks a lot but says little of interest.

windblown ('wɪndˌbləʊn) *adj.* **1.** blown by the wind. **2.** (of trees or shrubs) growing in a shape determined by the prevailing winds.

wind-borne ('wɪnd-) *adj.* (esp. of plant seeds or pollen) carried by wind.

windbreak ('wɪndˌbreɪk) *n.* a fence or line of trees serving as a protection from the wind by breaking its force.

windcheater ('wɪndˌtʃiːtə) *n.* a warm jacket, usually with a close-fitting knitted neck, cuffs, and waistband.

wind-chill ('wɪnd-) *n.* the serious chilling effect of wind and low temperature.

wind cone (wɪnd) *n.* same as **windsock**.

wind down (waɪnd) *vb.* **1.** to lower or move down by cranking. **2.** (of a clockwork mechanism) to slow down before stopping completely. **3.** to diminish gradually in force or power; relax.

winded ('wɪndɪd) *adj.* temporarily out of breath from strenuous exercise or a blow to the stomach.

windfall ('wɪndˌfɔːl) *n.* **1.** a piece of unexpected good fortune, esp. financial gain. **2.** a fruit blown down by the wind.

wind gauge (wɪnd) *n.* same as **anemometer**.

winding sheet *n.* a sheet in which a corpse is wrapped for burial; shroud.

wind instrument (wɪnd) *n.* a musical instrument sounded by blowing air through it, such as a flute.

windjammer ('wɪndˌdʒæmə) *n.* a large merchant sailing ship.

windlass ('wɪndləs) *n.* **1.** a machine for lifting objects by winding a rope or chain around a barrel or drum driven by a crank or motor. ~*vb.* **2.** to lift (an object) by means of a windlass.

windmill ('wɪndˌmɪl) *n.* **1.** a machine for grinding or pumping driven by sails that are turned by the wind. **2.** *Brit.* a toy consisting of a stick with plastic vanes attached, which revolve in the wind. **3. tilt at windmills**. to fight an imaginary opponent or evil.

window ('wɪndəʊ) *n.* **1.** an opening in a wall that is provided to let in light or air or to see through. **2.** a framework that contains a glass pane or panes and is placed in an opening in a wall. **3.** short for **window-pane**. **4.** the display area behind a glass window in a shop. **5.** a window-like opening or structure.

window box *n.* a long narrow box, placed on a windowsill, in which plants are grown.

window-dressing *n.* **1.** the art of arranging goods in shop windows to attract customers. **2.** an attempt to make something seem better than it is by stressing only its attractive features.

windowpane ('wɪndəʊˌpeɪn) n. a sheet of glass in a window.

window seat n. **1.** a seat below a window. **2.** a seat beside a window in a bus, train, or aeroplane.

window-shopping n. looking at goods in shop windows without intending to buy. —'**window-ˌshop** vb.

windowsill ('wɪndəʊˌsɪl) n. a sill below a window.

windpipe ('wɪndˌpaɪp) n. a nontechnical name for **trachea.**

windscreen ('wɪndˌskriːn) n. Brit. the sheet of glass that forms the front window of a motor vehicle.

windscreen wiper n. Brit. an electrically operated blade with a rubber edge that wipes a windscreen clear of rain.

windshield ('wɪndˌʃiːld) n. U.S. & Canad. same as **windscreen.**

windsock ('wɪndˌsɒk) n. a cloth cone mounted on a mast, used, esp. at airports, to indicate wind direction.

Windsor chair ('wɪnzə) n. a style of wooden chair with a shaped seat and a back made up of turned spokes.

Windsor knot n. a wide triangular knot, produced by making extra turns in tying a tie.

windsurfing ('wɪndˌsɜːfɪŋ) n. the sport of riding on water using a surfboard steered and propelled by an attached sail.

windswept ('wɪndˌswɛpt) adj. exposed to or swept by the wind.

wind tunnel (wɪnd) n. a chamber through which a stream of air is forced to test the effects of wind on aircraft.

wind up (waɪnd) vb. **1.** to bring to or reach a conclusion: he wound up the proceedings. **2.** to tighten the spring of (a clockwork mechanism). **3.** (usually passive) Informal. to make nervous or tense: he was all wound up before the big fight. **4.** to roll (something flexible) into a ball. **5.** Informal. same as **liquidate** (sense 2). **6.** Informal. to end up (in a specified state): you'll wind up dead. **7.** Brit. slang. to tease (someone). ~n. **wind-up. 8.** the act of concluding. **9.** the end.

windward ('wɪndwəd) Chiefly naut. ~adj. **1.** of or in the direction from which the wind blows. ~n. **2.** the windward direction. ~adv. **3.** towards the wind.

windy ('wɪndɪ) adj. **windier, windiest. 1.** of or characterized by wind; stormy. **2.** swept by or exposed to winds. **3.** long-winded or pompous: windy orations. **4.** Informal. flatulent. **5.** Slang. frightened. —'**windiness** n.

wine (waɪn) n. **1. a.** an alcoholic drink produced by the fermenting of grapes with water and sugar. **b.** an alcoholic drink produced in this way from other fruits or flowers: elderberry wine. **2.** a dark red colour with a purplish tinge. ~vb. **3. wine and dine.** to entertain or be entertained with wine and fine food.

wine bar n. a bar in a restaurant, or an establishment that specializes in serving wine and usually food.

winebibber ('waɪnˌbɪbə) n. a person who drinks a great deal of wine.

wine cellar n. **1.** a cellar where wine is stored. **2.** the stock of wines stored there.

wineglass ('waɪnˌglɑːs) n. a glass for wine, usually having a small bowl on a stem, with a flared base.

winepress ('waɪnˌprɛs) n. a machine used to squeeze the juice from grapes in order to make wine.

wineskin ('waɪnˌskɪn) n. the skin of a sheep or goat sewn up and used to hold wine.

wing (wɪŋ) n. **1.** one of the limbs or organs of a bird, bat, or insect that are specialized for flight. **2.** one of the two winglike supporting parts of an aircraft. **3.** a means or cause of flight or rapid motion: fear gave wings to his feet. **4.** Brit. the part of a car body surrounding the wheels. **5.** Sport. **a.** either of the two sides of the pitch near the touchline. **b.** a player stationed in such a position; winger. **6.** a faction or group within a political party or other organization. **7.** a projecting part of a building. **8.** (pl.) the space offstage to the right or left of the acting area in a theatre. **9. in the wings.** ready to step in when needed. **10.** a tactical formation in some air forces, consisting of two or more squadrons. **11. on the wing. a.** flying. **b.** travelling. **12. spread one's wings.** to make full use of one's abilities. **13. take wing.** to lift off or fly away. **14. under one's wing.** in one's care. ~vb. **15.** to make (one's way) swiftly on or as if on wings. **16.** to shoot or wound superficially in the wing or arm. **17.** to cause to fly or move swiftly: to wing an arrow. **18.** to provide with wings. —**winged** adj. —'**wingless** adj.

wing chair n. an easy chair with side pieces extending forward from a high back.

wing commander n. a middle-ranking commissioned Air Force officer.

winger ('wɪŋə) n. Sport. a player stationed on the wing.

wing nut n. a threaded nut with two flat projections which allow it to be turned by the thumb and forefinger.

wingspan ('wɪŋˌspæn) or **wingspread** ('wɪŋˌsprɛd) n. the distance between the wing tips of an aircraft, bird, insect, or bat.

wink (wɪŋk) vb. **1.** to close and open one eye quickly as a signal. **2.** to close and open (an eye or the eyes) momentarily. **3.** (of a light) to twinkle. ~n. **4.** a winking, esp. as a signal. **5.** a twinkling of light. **6.** a brief moment of time. **7.** *Informal.* the smallest amount of sleep: *I didn't sleep a wink.* **8. tip the wink.** *Brit. informal.* to give a hint.

wink at *vb.* to pretend not to notice: *the authorities winked at corruption.*

winker ('wɪŋkə) *n.* a flashing light on a motor vehicle that indicates turning.

winkle ('wɪŋk³l) *n.* **1.** same as **periwinkle**[1]. ~*vb.* **2.** (usually foll. by *out*) *Informal, chiefly Brit.* to extract or prise out.

winkle-pickers *pl. n.* shoes with very pointed narrow toes.

winner ('wɪnə) *n.* **1.** a person or thing that wins. **2.** *Informal.* a person or thing that seems sure to win or succeed.

winning ('wɪnɪŋ) *adj.* **1.** charming, engaging, or attractive: *a winning smile.* **2.** gaining victory: *the winning goal.* ~*n.* **3.** (*pl.*) something won, esp. in gambling.

winnow ('wɪnəʊ) *vb.* **1.** to separate (grain) from (chaff) by a current of air. **2.** to examine in order to select the desirable elements.

wino ('waɪnəʊ) *n., pl.* **winos.** *Informal.* a down-and-out who habitually drinks cheap wine.

win over *vb.* to gain the support or consent of (someone).

winsome ('wɪnsəm) *adj.* charming; winning; engaging: *a winsome smile.*

winter ('wɪntə) *n.* **1.** (*sometimes cap.*) the coldest season of the year, between autumn and spring. ~*vb.* **2.** to spend the winter in a specified place.

wintergreen ('wɪntə,griːn) *n.* **1.** an evergreen shrub from which a pleasant smelling oil is obtained. **2. oil of wintergreen.** an aromatic compound, formerly made from this plant but now synthesized: used medicinally and for flavouring.

winter solstice *n.* the time in the northern hemisphere, about December 22, at which the sun is at its southernmost point in the sky.

winter sports *pl. n.* open-air sports held on snow or ice.

wintertime ('wɪntə,taɪm) *n.* the winter season.

wintry ('wɪntrɪ) *adj.* **-trier, -triest. 1.** (esp. of weather) of or characteristic of winter. **2.** lacking cheer or warmth; bleak: *a wintry stare.* —'**wintriness** *n.*

winy ('waɪnɪ) *adj.* **winier, winiest.** having the taste of wine; heady.

wipe (waɪp) *vb.* **1.** to rub (a surface or object) lightly, esp. with a cloth or the hand, to remove dirt or liquid from it. **2.** (usually foll. by *off, away, from* or *up*) to remove by or as if by wiping: *he wiped the dirt from his hands.* **3.** to erase (a recording) from (a tape). **4.** to apply (a substance) by wiping. **5. wipe the floor with**

(someone). *Informal.* to defeat (someone) decisively. ~*n.* **6.** the act or an instance of wiping.

wipe out *vb.* **1.** to destroy completely. **2.** *Informal.* to kill.

wiper ('waɪpə) *n.* **1.** a piece of cloth used for wiping. **2.** same as **windscreen wiper.**

wire ('waɪə) *n.* **1.** a slender flexible strand of metal. **2.** a length of this used to carry electric current in a circuit. **3.** anything made of wire, such as wire netting. **4.** a long continuous wire or cable connecting points in a telephone or telegraph system. **5.** *Informal.* a telegram or telegraph. **6. get one's wires crossed.** *Informal.* to misunderstand. ~*vb.* **7.** to send a telegram to (a person or place). **8.** to send (something) by telegraph: *he wired her the money to fly home.* **9.** to equip (an electrical system, circuit, or component) with wires. **10.** to fasten with wire.

wire-haired *adj.* (of an animal) having a rough wiry coat.

wireless ('waɪəlɪs) *n. Chiefly Brit.* same as **radio.**

wire netting *n.* a net made of wire, used for fencing.

wirepuller ('waɪə,pʊlə) *n. Chiefly U.S. & Canad.* a person who uses private or secret influence for his own ends.

wire service *n. Chiefly U.S. & Canad.* an agency supplying news by telegraph to subscribing newspapers, radio, and television stations.

wiretap ('waɪə,tæp) *vb.* **-tapping, -tapped. 1.** to make a connection to a telegraph or telephone wire in order to obtain information secretly. **2.** to tap (a telephone) or the telephone of (a person).

wire wool *n.* a mass of fine wire, used esp. to clean kitchen articles.

wireworm ('waɪə,wɜːm) *n.* a destructive wormlike beetle larva.

wiring ('waɪərɪŋ) *n.* the network of wires used in an electrical system, device, or circuit.

wiry ('waɪərɪ) *adj.* **wirier, wiriest. 1.** (of people or animals) slender but strong. **2.** resembling wire, esp. in stiffness: *wiry hair.* —'**wiriness** *n.*

wisdom ('wɪzdəm) *n.* **1.** the ability to use one's experience and knowledge to make sensible decisions or judgments. **2.** accumulated knowledge or learning. **3.** *Archaic.* a wise saying or sayings.

wisdom tooth *n.* any of the four molar teeth, one at the back of each side of the jaw, that are the last of the permanent teeth to come through.

wise[1] (waɪz) *adj.* **1.** possessing or showing wisdom. **2.** prudent; sensible: *a wise plan.* **3.** learned; erudite. **4. none the wiser.** knowing no more than before. **5. be** *or* **get wise.** (often foll. by *to*) *Informal.* to be or

become aware or informed (of something).
6. put wise. (often foll. by *to*) *Slang.* to inform or warn (of). —'**wisely** *adv.*

wise² (waɪz) *n. Archaic.* way, manner, or respect: *in any wise; in no wise.*

-wise *adv. combining form.* **1.** indicating direction or manner: *clockwise; likewise.* **2.** with reference to: *businesswise.*

wiseacre ('waɪz,eɪkə) *n.* a person who wishes to seem wise.

wisecrack ('waɪz,kræk) *Informal.* ~*n.* **1.** a flippant or sardonic remark. ~*vb.* **2.** to make a wisecrack.

wise guy *n. Informal.* a person who is given to making conceited, sardonic, or insolent comments.

wise up *vb. Slang, chiefly U.S. & Canad.* (often foll. by *to*) to become or cause to become aware or informed (of).

wish (wɪʃ) *vb.* **1.** to want or desire (something, often that which cannot be or is not the case): *I wish I lived in Italy.* **2.** to feel or express a hope concerning the welfare, health or success of (a person): *I wish you well.* **3.** to desire or prefer to be as specified: *I wish to leave now.* **4.** to greet as specified: *he wished us good afternoon.* ~*n.* **5.** the expression of some desire: *to make a wish.* **6.** something desired or wished for: *he got his wish.* **7.** (*usually pl.*) expressed hopes for someone's welfare, health, or success: *give your mother our best wishes.*

wishbone ('wɪʃ,bəʊn) *n.* the V-shaped bone above the breastbone in most birds.

wishful ('wɪʃfʊl) *adj.* desirous or longing. —'**wishfulness** *n.*

wishful thinking *n.* an interpretation of the facts as one would like them to be, rather than as they are.

wish on *vb.* to hope that (someone or something) should be imposed (on someone): *I wouldn't wish my cold on anyone.*

wishy-washy ('wɪʃɪ,wɒʃɪ) *adj. Informal.* **1.** lacking in character, force, or colour. **2.** watery; thin.

wisp (wɪsp) *n.* **1.** a thin, delicate, or filmy piece or strand: *a wisp of smoke.* **2.** a small bundle or tuft: *a wisp of hay.* **3.** anything slender and delicate: *a wisp of a girl.* —'**wispy** *adj.*

wisteria (wɪ'stɪərɪə) *n.* a twining woody climbing plant with blue, purple, or white flowers in large drooping clusters.

wistful ('wɪstfʊl) *adj.* sadly wishing for something lost or unobtainable. —'**wistfully** *adv.* —'**wistfulness** *n.*

wit¹ (wɪt) *n.* **1.** the ability to use words or ideas in a clever, amusing, and imaginative way. **2.** speech or writing showing this ability. **3.** a person possessing, or noted for such an ability. **4.** practical intelligence: *nobody had the wit to bring a tin-opener.* ~See also **wits**.

wit² (wɪt) *vb.* **to wit.** that is to say; namely (used to introduce statements, as in legal documents).

witblits ('vɪt,blɪts) *n. S. African.* alcoholic drink illegally distilled.

witch (wɪtʃ) *n.* **1.** a person, usually female, who practises magic or sorcery, esp. black magic. **2.** an ugly or wicked old woman. **3.** a fascinating or enchanting woman.

witchcraft ('wɪtʃ,krɑːft) *n.* **1.** the use of magic; sorcery. **2.** bewitching influence or charm.

witch doctor *n.* a man in certain tribal societies, who appears to possess magical powers, used to cure sickness but also to harm people.

witch-elm *n.* same as **wych-elm.**

witchery ('wɪtʃərɪ) *n., pl.* **-eries.** **1.** the practice of witchcraft. **2.** bewitching influence or charm.

witch hazel *or* **wych-hazel** *n.* **1.** a shrub of North America, with ornamental yellow flowers. **2.** an astringent medicinal solution made from the bark and leaves of this shrub, applied to treat bruises and inflammation.

witch-hunt *n.* a rigorous campaign to expose and discredit people considered to hold unorthodox views on the pretext of safeguarding the public welfare.

with (wɪð, wɪθ) *prep.* **1.** using; by means of: *he killed her with an axe.* **2.** accompanying; in the company of: *the lady you were with.* **3.** possessing; having: *a man with a red moustache.* **4.** concerning or regarding: *be patient with her.* **5.** in a manner characterized by: *writing with abandon.* **6.** as a result of: *shaking with rage.* **7.** having the same opinions as; supporting. **8.** following the line of thought of (a person). **9. with it.** *Informal.* **a.** fashionable; in style. **b.** alert and understanding what is going on.

withal (wɪ'ðɔːl) *adv.* **1.** *Literary.* as well. **2.** *Archaic.* with that.

withdraw (wɪð'drɔː) *vb.* **-drawing, -drew, -drawn.** **1.** to take or draw back or away; remove. **2.** to remove (money) from a bank account or savings account. **3.** to retract or recall (something said). **4.** to retire or retreat: *the troops withdrew.* **5.** (often foll. by *from*) to depart (from): *he withdrew from public life.* **6.** to detach oneself socially, emotionally, or mentally.

withdrawal (wɪð'drɔːəl) *n.* **1.** an act or process of withdrawing. **2.** the period a drug addict goes through after ceasing to use narcotics, usually characterized by physical and mental symptoms (**withdrawal symptoms**).

withdrawn (wɪð'drɔːn) *vb.* **1.** the past participle of **withdraw.** ~*adj.* **2.** unusually reserved or shy.

withe (wɪθ, wɪð, waɪð) *n.* a strong flexible

twig, esp. of willow, used for binding things together.

wither ('wɪðə) *vb.* **1.** to make or become dried up or shrivelled. **2.** (often foll. by *away*) to fade or waste: *all hope withered away.* **3.** to humiliate (someone) with a scornful look or remark. —'**withering** *adj.*

withers ('wɪðəz) *pl. n.* the highest part of the back of a horse, between the shoulders.

withershins ('wɪðə,ʃɪnz) *adv. Chiefly Scot.* in the direction opposite to the apparent course of the sun; anticlockwise.

withhold (wɪð'həʊld) *vb.* **-holding, -held.** **1.** to keep back: *he withheld his permission.* **2.** to hold back; restrain.

within (wɪ'ðɪn) *prep.* **1.** in; inside; enclosed by. **2.** before (a period of time) has passed: *within a week.* **3.** not beyond: *live within your means; within reach.* ~*adv.* **4.** *Formal.* inside; internally.

without (wɪ'ðaʊt) *prep.* **1.** not having: *a traveller without much money.* **2.** not accompanied by: *he came without his wife.* **3.** not making use of: *to undo screws without a screwdriver.* **4.** (foll. by a present participle) while not or after not: *she can sing for two minutes without drawing breath.* **5.** *Archaic.* outside: *without the city walls.* ~*adv.* **6.** *Formal.* outside.

withstand (wɪð'stænd) *vb.* **-standing, -stood.** to resist, oppose, or endure successfully.

witless ('wɪtlɪs) *adj.* lacking wit, intelligence, or sense. —'**witlessness** *n.*

witness ('wɪtnɪs) *n.* **1.** a person who has seen or can give first-hand evidence of some event. **2.** evidence; testimony: *his smile was a witness to his happiness.* **3.** a person who testifies in court. **4.** a person who attests to the genuineness of a document or signature by adding his own signature. **5. bear witness to. a.** to give testimony to. **b.** to be evidence or proof of. ~*vb.* **6.** to see, be present at, or know at first hand. **7.** to give evidence of. **8.** to be the scene or setting of: *this field has witnessed a battle.* **9.** to testify in court. **10.** to attest to the genuineness of (a document or signature) by adding one's own signature.

witness box or esp. U.S. **witness stand** *n.* the place in a court of law in which witnesses stand to give evidence.

wits (wɪts) *pl. n.* **1.** (*sometimes sing.*) the ability to reason and act, esp. quickly: *have one's wits about one.* **2.** (*sometimes sing.*) right mind, sanity: *out of one's wits.* **3. at one's wits' end.** at a loss to know what to do. **4. live by one's wits.** to gain a livelihood by craftiness rather than by hard work.

witter ('wɪtə) *vb.* (often foll. by *on*) *Informal.* to chatter or babble pointlessly or at unnecessary length.

witticism ('wɪtɪ,sɪzəm) *n.* a clever or witty remark.

witty ('wɪtɪ) *adj.* **-tier, -tiest.** characterized by clever humour or wit. —'**wittily** *adv.* —'**wittiness** *n.*

wives (waɪvz) *n.* **1.** the plural of **wife. 2. old wives' tale.** a superstitious tradition.

wizard ('wɪzəd) *n.* **1.** a magician or sorcerer. **2.** a person who is outstandingly gifted in some specified field. ~*adj.* **3.** *Informal, chiefly Brit.* superb; outstanding.

wizardry ('wɪzədrɪ) *n.* magic; sorcery.

wizened ('wɪz²nd) *adj.* shrivelled, wrinkled, or dried up, esp. with age.

woad (wəʊd) *n.* **1.** a European plant with leaves which yield a blue dye. **2.** this dye, used esp. by the ancient Britons as a body dye.

wobble ('wɒb²l) *vb.* **1.** to move or sway unsteadily. **2.** to shake: *her voice wobbled with emotion.* **3.** to waver with indecision. **4.** to cause to wobble. ~*n.* **5.** a wobbling movement or sound. —'**wobbly** *adj.*

wodge (wɒdʒ) *n. Brit. informal.* a thick lump or chunk of something.

woe (wəʊ) *n.* **1.** *Literary.* intense grief. **2.** (often pl.) affliction or misfortune. **3. woe betide (someone).** misfortune will befall (someone): *woe betide you if you arrive late.* ~*interj.* **4.** Also: **woe is me.** *Archaic.* alas.

woebegone ('wəʊbɪ,gɒn) *adj.* sorrowful or sad in appearance.

woeful ('wəʊfʊl) *adj.* **1.** sad; mournful. **2.** bringing or causing woe. **3.** pitiful; deplorable: *a woeful standard of work.* —'**woefully** *adv.* —'**woefulness** *n.*

wog (wɒg) *n. Brit. slang, offensive.* a person who is not White.

wok (wɒk) *n.* a large bowl-shaped metal Chinese cooking pot: used esp. for stir-frying.

woke (wəʊk) *vb.* the past tense of **wake**[1].

woken ('wəʊkən) *vb.* the past participle of **wake**[1].

wold (wəʊld) *n.* a tract of high open rolling country.

wolf (wʊlf) *n., pl.* **wolves. 1.** a predatory canine mammal which hunts in packs. **2.** *Informal.* a man who habitually tries to seduce women. **3. cry wolf.** to give a false alarm. **4. keep the wolf from the door.** to keep away poverty or hunger. **5. lone wolf.** a person or animal who prefers to be alone. **6. wolf in sheep's clothing.** a malicious person in a harmless or benevolent disguise. ~*vb.* **7.** (often foll. by *down*) to gulp (down).

wolfhound ('wʊlf,haʊnd) *n.* a large dog, used formerly to hunt wolves.

wolfram ('wʊlfrəm) *n.* same as **tungsten.**

wolfsbane ('wʊlfs,beɪn) *n.* a poisonous plant with hoodlike flowers.

wolf whistle *n.* a whistle made by a man to express admiration of a woman's appearance.

wolverine ('wʊlvəˌriːn) *n.* a large carnivorous mammal of Eurasia and North America with dark very thick fur.

wolves (wʊlvz) *n.* the plural of **wolf.**

woman ('wʊmən) *n., pl.* **women.** **1.** an adult female human being. **2.** (*modifier*) female: *a woman politician.* **3.** women collectively. **4.** (usually preceded by *the*) feminine nature or feelings: *babies bring out the woman in him.* **5.** a female servant or domestic help. **6.** *Informal.* a wife or girlfriend.

womanhood ('wʊmənˌhʊd) *n.* **1.** the state or quality of being a woman or being womanly. **2.** women collectively.

womanish ('wʊmənɪʃ) *adj.* **1.** unmanly; effeminate. **2.** characteristic of or suitable for a woman.

womanize *or* **-ise** ('wʊməˌnaɪz) *vb.* (of a man) to indulge in casual affairs with women. —'**woman,izer** *or* -ˌ**iser** *n.*

womanly ('wʊmənlɪ) *adj.* possessing qualities generally regarded as typical of, or appropriate to, a woman.

womb (wuːm) *n.* the nontechnical name for **uterus.**

wombat ('wɒmbæt) *n.* a heavily-built burrowing herbivorous Australian marsupial.

women ('wɪmɪn) *n.* the plural of **woman.**

womenfolk ('wɪmɪnˌfəʊk) *pl. n.* **1.** women collectively. **2.** a group of women, esp. the female members of one's family.

Women's Institute *n.* (in Britain and Commonwealth countries) a society for women interested in engaging in craft and cultural activities.

Women's Liberation *n.* a movement for the removal of inequalities based upon the assumption that men are superior to women. Also called: **women's lib.**

won (wʌn) *vb.* the past of **win.**

wonder ('wʌndə) *n.* **1.** the feeling of surprise, amazement, and sometimes awe, caused by something strange. **2.** something that causes such a feeling. **3.** (*modifier*) causing wonder by virtue of spectacular results achieved: *a wonder drug; a wonder boy.* **4.** **do** *or* **work wonders.** to achieve spectacularly good results. **5. no wonder.** (I am) not surprised at all (that): *no wonder he couldn't come.* **6. small wonder.** (I am) hardly surprised (that): *small wonder he couldn't make it tonight.* ~*vb.* **7.** (often foll. by *about*) to have curiosity or doubt about: *I wondered about what she said.* **8.** (often foll. by *at*) to be amazed (at something): *I wonder at your impudence.* —'**wonderment** *n.*

wonderful ('wʌndəfʊl) *adj.* **1.** causing a feeling of wonder. **2.** extremely fine; excellent. —'**wonderfully** *adv.*

wonderland ('wʌndəˌlænd) *n.* **1.** an imaginary land of marvels or wonders. **2.** an actual place of great or strange beauty.

wondrous ('wʌndrəs) *Archaic or literary.* ~*adj.* **1.** causing wonder; marvellous. ~*adv.* **2.** extremely: *wondrous cold.*

wonky ('wɒŋkɪ) *adj.* **-kier, -kiest.** *Brit. slang.* **1.** unsteady. **2.** crooked. **3.** liable to break down.

wont (wəʊnt) *adj.* **1.** accustomed (to doing something): *he was wont to get up early.* ~*n.* **2.** usual practice: *I got up early, as is my wont.*

won't (wəʊnt) will not.

wonted ('wəʊntɪd) *adj.* accustomed; usual: *she is in her wonted place.*

woo (wuː) *vb.* **wooing, wooed.** **1.** to court (a woman) with a view to marriage. **2.** to seek zealously: *to woo fame.* **3.** to coax or urge (someone).

wood (wʊd) *n.* **1.** the hard fibrous substance that occurs beneath the bark in trees and shrubs. **2.** this substance cut and prepared for use in building or carpentry; timber. **3.** a thick growth of trees, usually smaller than a forest: *an oak wood.* **4.** fuel; firewood. **5.** *Golf.* a long-shafted club with a wooden head. **6.** one of the biased wooden bowls used in the game of bowls. **7. not out of the wood** *or* **woods.** still in a difficult or dangerous situation. **8. cannot see the wood for the trees.** to be so involved in the details of something that one loses sight of the main issue. **9.** (*modifier*) made of, employing, or for use with wood: *a wood fire.* ~*See also* **woods.**

wood alcohol *n.* same as **methanol.**

wood anemone *n.* a woodland anemone with white flowers.

woodbine ('wuːdˌbaɪn) *n.* a wild honeysuckle with fragrant yellow flowers.

woodcarving ('wʊdˌkɑːvɪŋ) *n.* **1.** the act or craft of carving wood. **2.** a work of art produced by carving wood.

woodchuck ('wʊdˌtʃʌk) *n.* a North American marmot with coarse reddish-brown fur.

woodcock ('wʊdˌkɒk) *n.* a game bird like a large snipe.

woodcraft ('wʊdˌkrɑːft) *n. Chiefly U.S. & Canad.* **1.** ability and experience in matters relating to the woods such as hunting or camping. **2.** ability or skill at woodwork or carving.

woodcut ('wʊdˌkʌt) *n.* **1.** a block of wood with a design from which prints are made. **2.** a print from a woodcut.

woodcutter ('wʊdˌkʌtə) *n.* a person who fells trees or chops wood.

wooded ('wʊdɪd) *adj.* covered with woods or trees.

wooden ('wʊdᵊn) *adj.* **1.** made from or consisting of wood. **2.** awkward or clumsy. **3.** lacking spirit or animation: *a wooden expression.*

wood engraving *n.* **1.** the art of engraving pictures or designs on wood by cutting across the grain. **2.** a block of wood so engraved or a print taken from it.

wooden spoon *n.* a booby prize, esp. in sporting contests.

woodland ('wʊdlənd) *n.* land that is mostly covered with woods or trees.

woodlouse ('wʊdˌlaʊs) *n.*, *pl.* **-lice** (-ˌlaɪs). a very small land creature with a grey plated body and many legs that lives in damp places.

woodpecker ('wʊdˌpɛkə) *n.* a bird with a strong bill with which it bores into trees for insects.

wood pigeon *n.* a large pigeon with white patches on the wings and neck.

woodpile ('wʊdˌpaɪl) *n.* a pile of firewood.

wood pulp *n.* pulp made from wood fibre, used in the manufacture of paper.

woodruff ('wʊdrʌf) *n.* a plant with small sweet-scented white flowers and fragrant leaves.

woods (wʊdz) *pl. n.* closely packed trees forming a forest or wood.

woodshed ('wʊdˌʃɛd) *n.* a small shed for storing firewood.

woodsman ('wʊdzmən) *n.*, *pl.* **-men.** a person who lives in a wood or who is skilled in woodcraft.

woodwind ('wʊdˌwɪnd) *Music.* ~*adj.* **1.** of or denoting a type of wind instrument, such as the oboe. ~*n.* **2.** (*functioning as pl.*) the woodwind instruments of an orchestra.

woodwork ('wʊdˌwɜːk) *n.* **1.** the art or craft of making things in wood. **2.** things made of wood, such as doors.

woodworm ('wʊdˌwɜːm) *n.* **1.** a beetle larva that bores into wooden furniture or beams. **2.** the condition caused in wood by these larvae.

woody ('wʊdɪ) *adj.* **woodier, woodiest. 1.** covered with forest or woods. **2.** consisting of or containing wood: *woody tissue; woody stems.*

woody nightshade *n.* a woody plant with purple flowers and poisonous red berry-like fruits.

woof[1] (wuːf) *n.* same as **weft.**

woof[2] (wʊf) *interj.* **1.** the bark or growl of a dog. ~*vb.* **2.** (of dogs) to bark.

woofer ('wuːfə) *n.* a loudspeaker used in high-fidelity systems for the reproduction of low audio frequencies.

wool (wʊl) *n.* **1.** the soft, curly hair of sheep and other animals. **2.** yarn spun from this, used in weaving and knitting. **3.** cloth or a garment made from this yarn. **4.** something that looks like wool: *steel wool.* **5. pull the wool over someone's eyes.** to deceive someone.

woolgathering ('wʊlˌgæðərɪŋ) *n.* idle or absent-minded daydreaming.

woolgrower ('wʊlˌgrəʊə) *n.* a person who keeps sheep for their wool.

woollen *or U.S.* **woolen** ('wʊlən) *adj.* **1.** relating to or consisting partly or wholly of wool. ~*n.* **2.** (*often pl.*) a woollen garment, esp. a knitted one.

woolly *or U.S.* (*often*) **wooly** ('wʊlɪ) *adj.* **-lier, -liest. 1.** consisting of or like wool. **2.** covered in wool. **3.** confused or indistinct: *woolly thinking.* ~*n.*, *pl.* **-lies. 4.** (*often pl.*) a woollen garment, such as a sweater. —'**woolliness** *n.*

woolpack ('wʊlˌpæk) *n.* **1.** the cloth wrapping used to pack a bale of wool. **2.** a bale of wool.

woolsack ('wʊlˌsæk) *n.* (in Britain) the seat of the Lord Chancellor in the House of Lords, formerly made of a large square sack of wool.

woolshed ('wʊlˌʃɛd) *n. Austral. & N.Z.* a large building in which sheepshearing takes place.

woozy ('wuːzɪ) *adj.* **woozier, wooziest.** *Informal.* **1.** dazed or confused. **2.** experiencing slight dizziness or nausea. —'**wooziness** *n.*

wop (wɒp) *n. Slang, offensive.* a member of a Latin race, esp. an Italian.

Worcester sauce ('wʊstə) *n.* a piquant sauce, made from soy sauce, vinegar, and spices.

Worcs. Worcestershire.

word (wɜːd) *n.* **1.** the smallest single meaningful unit of speech or writing. **2.** a chat, talk, or discussion: *to have a word with someone.* **3.** an utterance, esp. a brief one: *a word of greeting.* **4.** news or information: *he sent word that he would be late.* **5.** a verbal signal for action; command: *when I give the word, fire!* **6.** a promise: *he kept his word.* **7.** an order: *his word must be obeyed.* **8.** a watchword or slogan: *the word now is "freedom".* **9.** *Computers.* a set of bits used to store, transmit, or operate upon an item of information in a computer. **10. as good as one's word.** doing what one has promised to do. **11. by word of mouth.** orally rather than by written means. **12. in a word.** briefly or in short. **13. take someone at his** *or* **her word.** to assume that someone means what he or she says: *when he told her to go, she took him at his word and left.* **14. take someone's word for it.** to accept or believe what someone says. **15. the last word. a.** the closing remark of a conversation or argument, esp. that supposedly settles an issue. **b.** the latest or most fashionable design: *the last word in bikinis.* **c.** the finest example: *the last word in luxury.* **16. (upon) my word!** an exclamation of surprise or annoyance. **17. word for word.** using exactly the same words; verbatim: *he has copied my report* *word for word.* **18. word of honour.** a promise; oath. ~*vb.* **19.** to state in words; phrase. ~See also **words.**

Word (wɜːd) *n.* **the.** the message and teachings contained in the Bible. Also: **the Word of God.**

word blindness *n.* the nontechnical name for **dyslexia.** —'**word-,blind** *adj.*

word game *n.* any game involving the discovery, formation, or alteration of a word or words.

wording ('wɜːdɪŋ) *n.* **1.** the way in which words are used to express something. **2.** the words themselves.

word order *n.* the order of words in a phrase, clause, or sentence.

word-perfect *or* U.S. **letter-perfect** *adj.* able to repeat from memory the exact words of a text one has learned.

word processing *n.* the storage and organization of text by electronic means, esp. for business purposes.

word processor *n.* an electronic machine for word processing, typically consisting of a keyboard, a VDU incorporating a microprocessor, and a printer.

words (wɜːdz) *pl. n.* **1.** the text of an actor's part. **2.** the text of a song, as opposed to the music. **3.** a quarrel: *we had words about his behaviour.* **4. eat one's words.** to retract a statement. **5. in other words.** expressing the same idea but differently. **6. in so many words.** explicitly or bluntly: *she called him a liar, in so many words.* **7. of many** (*or* **few**) **words.** (not) talkative. **8. put into words.** to express in speech or writing.

wordy ('wɜːdɪ) *adj.* **wordier, wordiest.** using or containing too many words: *a wordy document.* —'**wordiness** *n.*

wore (wɔː) *vb.* the past tense of **wear.**

work (wɜːk) *n.* **1.** physical or mental effort directed to doing or making something. **2.** paid employment at a job, trade, or profession. **3.** a duty or task: *there's lots of work to be done.* **4.** something done or made as a result of effort: *a work of art.* **5.** the place where a person is employed. **6.** decoration, esp. of a specified kind: *needlework.* **7.** *Physics.* the transfer of energy occurring when a force is applied to move a body. **8.** a fortification. **9. at work.** in action; working. **10. make short work of.** *Informal.* to finish (something) quickly. **11.** (*modifier*) of or for work: *work clothes; a work permit.* ~*vb.* **12.** to do work; labour; toil. **13.** to be employed. **14.** to cause to labour or toil: *he works his men hard.* **15.** to operate or cause to operate, esp. effectively: *to work a lathe; that clock doesn't work.* **16.** to cultivate (land). **17.** to knead or manipulate: *to work dough.* **18.** to shape or process: *to work copper.* **19.** to reach or cause to reach a specific condition gradually: *the rope worked loose.* **20.** to move in agitation: *his*

face worked with anger. **21.** (often foll. by *up*) to provoke or arouse: *to work someone into a frenzy.* **22.** to effect or accomplish: *to work wonders.* **23.** to make (one's way) with effort: *he worked his way through the crowd.* **24.** to sew or embroider: *she was working a sampler.* **25.** *Informal.* to manipulate to one's own advantage. ~See also **work in, work off, works,** etc.

workable ('wɜːkəb⁰l) *adj.* **1.** practicable or feasible. **2.** able to be worked. —,**work a'bility** *n.*

workaday ('wɜːkə,deɪ) *adj.* **1.** commonplace; ordinary. **2.** suitable for working days; practical: *workaday clothes.*

workaholic (,wɜːkə'hɒlɪk) *n.* a person obsessively addicted to work.

workbench ('wɜːk,bentʃ) *n.* a heavy table at which a craftsman or mechanic works.

worker ('wɜːkə) *n.* **1.** a person that works, usually at a specific job: *a research worker.* **2.** an employee, as opposed to an employer. **3.** a manual labourer in a manufacturing industry. **4.** a sterile female bee, ant, or wasp that works for the colony.

work ethic *n.* a belief in the moral value of work.

workforce ('wɜːk,fɔːs) *n.* **1.** the total number of workers employed by a company. **2.** the total number of people available for work: *the country's workforce is growing.*

workhouse ('wɜːk,haʊs) *n.* (formerly in England) a public institution where the very poor did work in return for food and accommodation.

work in *vb.* **1.** to insert, merge, or blend: *work the fat into the flour with your fingers.* **2.** to find space for; fit in: *I'll work this job in during the day.* ~*n.* **work-in.** **3.** a form of industrial action in which a factory that is to be closed down is occupied and run by its workers.

working ('wɜːkɪŋ) *n.* **1.** the operation or mode of operation of something. **2.** (*often pl.*) a part of a mine or quarry that is being or has been worked. **3.** a record of the steps by which the solution of a problem or calculation is obtained: *all working is to be submitted to the examiners.* ~*adj.* **4.** (of a person or thing) that works: *a working man.* **5.** concerned with, used in, or suitable for work: *working clothes.* **6.** capable of being operated or used: *a working model; in working order.* **7.** adequate for normal purposes: *a working majority; a working knowledge of German.* **8.** providing a temporary basis, allowing action or progress: *a working title.*

working class *n.* **1.** the social stratum that consists of those who earn wages, esp. as manual workers. ~*adj.* **working-class.** **2.** of or characteristic of the working class.

working day *or esp.* U.S. & Canad. **workday** *n.* **1.** a day on which work is done: *working days lost as a result of backache.*

2. the part of the day allocated to work: *the unions demand a shorter working day.*

working party *n.* a committee established to investigate a problem.

workload ('wɜːkˌləʊd) *n.* the amount of work to be done, esp. in a specified period.

workman ('wɜːkmən) *n., pl.* **-men.** **1.** a man who is employed in manual labour or who works an industrial machine. **2.** a craftsman of skill as specified: *a bad workman.*

workmanlike ('wɜːkmənˌlaɪk) *adj.* characteristic of a good workman.

workmanship ('wɜːkmənʃɪp) *n.* **1.** the art or skill of a workman; craftsmanship. **2.** the degree of art or skill exhibited in the finished product.

workmate ('wɜːkˌmeɪt) *n.* a person who works with another; fellow worker.

work of art *n.* **1.** a piece of fine art, such as a painting or sculpture. **2.** something that may be likened to a piece of fine art, in beauty or intricacy: *this car is a work of art.*

work off *vb.* to get rid of, as by effort: *he worked off some of his energy by digging the garden.*

work on *vb.* to persuade or influence or try to persuade or influence someone.

work out *vb.* **1.** to accomplish by effort. **2.** to solve or find out by reasoning or calculation: *to work out an answer; to work out a sum.* **3.** to devise or formulate: *to work out a plan.* **4.** to prove satisfactory: *did your plan work out?* **5.** to happen as specified: *it all worked out well.* **6.** to take part in physical exercise. **7.** (often foll. by *to* or *at*) to reach a total: *your bill works out at a pound.* ~*n.* **workout.** **8.** a session of physical exercise for training or to keep fit.

work over *vb. Slang.* to beat (someone) up severely.

works (wɜːks) *pl. n.* **1.** (*often functioning as sing.*) a place where something is manufactured. **2.** the sum total of a writer's or artist's achievements, esp. when considered together: *the works of Shakespeare.* **3.** the deeds of a person: *works of charity.* **4.** the interior parts of the mechanism of a machine: *the works of a clock.* **5. the works.** *Slang.* **a.** full treatment; the whole lot: *he bought her dinner, champagne, flowers — the works.* **b.** a very violent physical beating: *to give someone the works.*

workshop ('wɜːkˌʃɒp) *n.* **1.** a room or building in which manufacturing or other manual work is carried on. **2.** a group of people engaged in intensive study or work in a creative or practical field: *a music workshop.*

workshy ('wɜːkˌʃaɪ) *adj.* not inclined to work.

work station *n.* an area in an office or seat at a computer terminal where one person works.

worktable ('wɜːkˌteɪbᵊl) *n.* a table at which writing, sewing, or other work may be done.

worktop ('wɜːkˌtɒp) *n.* a surface in a kitchen, often of heat-resistant plastic, used for food preparation.

work-to-rule *n.* a form of industrial action in which employees keep strictly to all the working rules laid down by their employers with the deliberate intention of reducing the work rate.

work up *vb.* **1.** to arouse the feelings of; excite. **2.** to cause to grow or develop: *to work up an appetite.* **3.** to gain skill at (a subject). **4.** (foll. by *to*) to develop gradually towards: *working up to a climax.*

world (wɜːld) *n.* **1.** the earth as a planet. **2.** mankind; the human race. **3.** people generally; the public: *in the eyes of the world.* **4.** social or public life: *to go out into the world.* **5.** any planet or moon, esp. one that might be inhabited. **6.** (*often cap.*) a particular group of countries or period of history, or its inhabitants: *the Ancient World; the Third World.* **7.** an area, sphere, or realm considered as a complete environment: *the animal world; the world of television.* **8.** a state of existence: *the next world.* **9.** the total circumstances and experience of an individual that make up his life: *his narrow little world.* **10.** a great deal: *worlds apart; a world of difference.* **11.** worldly or secular life, ways, or people. **12. bring into the world.** to deliver or give birth to (a baby). **13. come into the world.** to be born. **14. for all the world.** in every way; exactly. **15. not for the world.** not for any inducement, however great. **16. in the world.** used to emphasize a statement: *no-one in the world can help; what in the world do you mean?; all the time in the world.* **17. man** (*or* **woman**) **of the world.** a man (or woman) experienced in social or public life. **18. on top of the world.** *Informal.* elated or very happy. **19. out of this world.** *Informal.* wonderful; excellent. **20. think the world of.** to be extremely fond of or think very highly of. **21.** (*modifier*) of or concerning the entire world; worldwide: *world politics; a world record.* **22.** (*in combination*) throughout the world: *world-famous.*

World Bank *n.* an international cooperative organization established to assist developing nations by loans.

world-beater *n.* a person or thing that surpasses all others; champion.

World Cup *n.* an international football championship competition held every four years between national teams.

worldly ('wɜːldlɪ) *adj.* **-lier, -liest.** **1.** not spiritual; earthly or temporal. **2.** absorbed in or concerned with material things. **3.**

wise in the ways of the world; sophisticated. —'**worldliness** n.

world music n. popular music of various
ethnic origins and styles.

world-shaking adj. of enormous significance; momentous.

World War I n. the war (1914–18) be-
tween the Allies (principally France, Rus-
sia, Britain, and Italy, and the U.S.) and the
Central Powers (principally Germany,
Austria-Hungary, and Turkey). Also: **First
World War.**

World War II n. the war (1939–45) be-
tween the Allies (Britain and France, the
U.S., and the Soviet Union) and the Axis
(Germany, Italy, and Japan). Also: **Second
World War.**

world-weary adj. no longer finding pleasure in living.

worldwide ('wɜːld'waɪd) adj. applying or
extending throughout the world.

worm (wɜːm) n. **1.** an invertebrate with a
long slender body and no limbs. **2.** an
insect larva resembling a worm. **3.** a
wretched or spineless person. **4.** a shaft on
which a spiral thread has been cut, as in a
gear arrangement in which such a shaft
drives a toothed wheel. ~vb. **5.** to move or
act with the slow sinuous movement of a
worm. **6.** (foll. by in, into, out of) to make
(one's way) slowly and stealthily; insinuate
(oneself). **7.** (often foll. by out of or from)
to extract (information) from someone by
persistent questioning. **8.** to purge of
worms. ~See also **worms.**

WORM (wɜːm) n. Computers. write once
read many times: an optical disk which
enables users to store their own data.

wormcast ('wɜːm,kɑːst) n. a coil of earth
or sand that has been excreted by a burrowing worm.

worm-eaten adj. eaten into by worms: a
worm-eaten table.

worm gear n. **1.** a device consisting of a
threaded shaft that drives a toothed gearwheel. **2.** a gear-wheel driven by a threaded shaft or worm.

wormhole ('wɜːm,həʊl) n. a hole made by a
worm in timber, plants, or fruit.

worms (wɜːmz) n. (functioning as sing.) a
disease caused by parasitic worms living in
the intestines.

wormwood ('wɜːm,wʊd) n. **1.** a plant
yielding a bitter oil used in making absinthe. **2.** an unpleasant experience that
causes bitterness.

wormy ('wɜːmɪ) adj. **wormier, wormiest.**
worm-infested or worm-eaten.

worn (wɔːn) vb. **1.** the past participle of
wear. ~adj. **2.** showing signs of long use
or wear: a worn suit. **3.** haggard; drawn:
looking tired and worn.

worn-out adj. **1.** worn or used until

threadbare, valueless, or useless. **2.** exhausted; very weary.

worrisome ('wʌrɪsəm) adj. causing worry;
vexing.

worry ('wʌrɪ) vb. **-rying, -ried. 1.** to be or
cause to be anxious or uneasy. **2.** to annoy;
bother: don't worry me with trivialities. **3.**
(often foll. by away) to struggle or work: to
worry away at a problem. **4.** (of a dog) to
bite or tear (at) repeatedly with the teeth:
your dog has been worrying sheep. ~n., pl.
-ries. 5. a state or feeling of anxiety. **6.** a
person or thing that causes anxiety.
—'**worried** adj. —'**worriedly** adv.
—'**worrying** adj., n.

worry beads pl. n. a string of beads that
when fingered or played with supposedly
relieves nervous tension.

worse (wɜːs) adj. **1.** the comparative of
bad. 2. none the worse for. not harmed by
(adverse events or circumstances). **3. the
worse for wear.** shabby or worn. **4. worse
luck!** Informal. unhappily; unfortunately.
5. worse off. in a worse, esp. a worse
financial, condition. ~n. **6.** something
that is worse. **7. for the worse.** into a
worse condition: a change for the worse.
~adv. **8.** more severely or unpleasantly:
his nose bled worse than before. **9.** less
effectively or successfully: you write even
worse than I do.

worsen ('wɜːs³n) vb. to grow or cause to
grow worse.

worship ('wɜːʃɪp) vb. **-shipping, -shipped**
or U.S. **-shiping, -shiped. 1.** to show profound religious devotion to; adore or venerate (a deity). **2.** to have intense love and
admiration for. **3.** to attend services for
worship. ~n. **4.** religious adoration or
devotion. **5.** rites, prayers, or other formal
expression of religious adoration. **6.** ad-
miring love or devotion. —'**worshipper** n.

Worship ('wɜːʃɪp) n. Chiefly Brit. (preceded
by Your, His, or Her) a title for a mayor or
magistrate.

worshipful ('wɜːʃɪpfʊl) adj. **1.** feeling or
showing reverence or adoration. **2.** (often
cap.) Chiefly Brit. (in titles for various people or bodies of distinguished rank) honourable, respected.

worst (wɜːst) adj. **1.** the superlative of
bad. ~adv. **2.** most extremely or badly:
the worst affected areas. ~n. **3. the
worst.** the least good person, thing, or part.
4. (often preceded by at) the worst quality
or condition: television is at its worst these
days. **5.** the greatest amount of damage or
wickedness possible: the invaders came and
did their worst. **6. at worst.** in the worst
possible situation. **7. get the worst of it.**
to be defeated. **8. if the worst comes to
the worst.** if the situation develops in the
worst possible way. ~vb. **9.** to defeat or
beat.

worsted ('wʊstɪd) n. **1.** a closely twisted

woollen yarn or thread. **2.** a hard smooth close-textured fabric made from this.

wort (wɜːt) n. **1.** (in combination) a plant, esp. one formerly used to cure diseases: liverwort. **2.** an infusion of ground malt, fermented to make a malt liquor.

worth (wɜːθ) adj. **1.** worthy of; meriting or justifying: it's not worth discussing. **2.** having a value of: the book is worth £30. **3. for all one is worth.** to the utmost. **4. worth one's weight in gold.** extremely useful, helpful, or kind. ~n. **5.** high quality; excellence. **6.** value; price. **7.** the amount of something that can be bought for a specified price: five pounds' worth of petrol.

worthless ('wɜːθlɪs) adj. **1.** without value or usefulness. **2.** without merit.

worthwhile ('wɜːθ'waɪl) adj. sufficiently important, rewarding, or valuable to justify time or effort spent.

worthy ('wɜːðɪ) adj. **-thier, -thiest. 1.** having sufficient merit or value (for a specified person or thing); deserving: not worthy of the honour. **2.** having worth, value, or merit. ~n., pl. **-thies. 3.** Often facetious. an important person. —'**worthily** adv. —'**worthiness** n.

would (wʊd; unstressed wəd) vb. used as an auxiliary: **1.** to form the past tense or subjunctive mood of **will**[1]: you said you would come. **2.** (with you, he, she, it, they, or a noun as subject) to express a polite request: would you help me, please? **3.** to describe a habitual past action: every day we would go for walks. **4.** I wish: would that he were here.

would-be adj. Usually disparaging. wanting or pretending to be: a would-be politician.

wouldn't ('wʊdᵊnt) would not.

wound[1] (wuːnd) n. **1.** an injury done to living tissue as the result of violence. **2.** an injury to the feelings or reputation. ~vb. **3.** to inflict a wound or wounds upon. —'**wounding** adj.

wound[2] (waʊnd) vb. the past of **wind**[2].

wove (wəʊv) vb. a past tense of **weave**.

woven ('wəʊvᵊn) vb. a past participle of **weave**.

wow (waʊ) interj. **1.** an exclamation of admiration or amazement. ~n. **2.** Slang. a person or thing that is amazingly successful. ~vb. **3.** Slang. to be a great success with.

wowser ('waʊzə) n. Austral. & N.Z. slang. **1.** a fanatically puritanical person. **2.** a teetotaller.

wp word processor.

WPC (in Britain) woman police constable.

wpm words per minute.

WRAC (in Britain) Women's Royal Army Corps.

wrack[1] or **rack** (ræk) n. collapse or destruction: wrack and ruin.

wrack[2] (ræk) n. seaweed that is floating in the sea or has been cast ashore.

WRAF (in Britain) Women's Royal Air Force.

wraith (reɪθ) n. **1.** the apparition of a living person, supposed to appear just before his death. **2.** a ghost.

wrangle ('ræŋgᵊl) vb. **1.** to argue noisily or angrily. ~n. **2.** a noisy or angry argument.

wrap (ræp) vb. **wrapping, wrapped. 1.** to fold or wind (something) around (a person or thing) so as to cover. **2.** (often foll. by up) to fold a covering around and fasten securely. **3.** to enclose, immerse, or absorb: wrapped in sorrow. **4.** (often foll. by about, around, round) to fold, wind, or coil: he wrapped his arms around her. ~n. **5.** a garment worn wrapped around the body, esp. the shoulders. **6.** Chiefly U.S. wrapping or a wrapper. **7. keep under wraps.** to keep secret. **8. take the wraps off.** to reveal.

wrapper ('ræpə) n. **1.** the cover, usually of paper or cellophane, in which something is wrapped. **2.** a dust jacket of a book. **3.** a loose negligee or dressing gown.

wrapping ('ræpɪŋ) n. the material used to wrap something.

wrapround ('ræp,raʊnd) or **wraparound** adj. **1.** made so as to be wrapped round something: a wrapround skirt. **2.** extending in a curve from the front around to the sides.

wrap up vb. **1.** to fold paper around. **2.** to put warm clothes on. **3.** (usually imperative) Slang. to be silent. **4.** Informal. to finish or settle (a matter).

wrasse (ræs) n. a brightly-coloured marine fish.

wrath (rɒθ) n. intense anger. —'**wrathful** adj.

wreak (riːk) vb. **1.** to inflict (vengeance) or to cause (chaos): to wreak havoc on the enemy. **2.** to express or gratify (anger or hatred).

wreath (riːθ) n., pl. **wreaths** (riːðz, riːθs). **1.** a twisted band or ring of flowers or leaves, placed on a grave as a memorial or worn on the head as a garland or a mark of honour. **2.** anything circular or spiral: wreaths of smoke.

wreathe (riːð) vb. **1.** to form into or take the form of a wreath by intertwining or twisting together. **2.** to encircle or adorn with or as if with a wreath: his face was wreathed in smiles. **3.** to move or cause to move in a twisting way: smoke wreathed up to the ceiling.

wreck (rɛk) vb. **1.** to break, spoil, or destroy completely. **2.** to cause the wreck of (a ship). ~n. **3. a.** the accidental destruction of a ship at sea. **b.** the ship so destroyed. **4.** a person in a poor mental or physical state. **5.** the remains of something destroyed.

wreckage ('rɛkɪdʒ) *n.* **1.** the act of wrecking or the state of being wrecked. **2.** the remains of something destroyed.

wrecker ('rɛkə) *n.* **1.** *Chiefly U.S. & Canad.* a person whose job is to demolish buildings or dismantle cars. **2.** (formerly) a person who lures ships to destruction to plunder the wreckage. **3.** *U.S. & Canad.* a breakdown van.

wren (rɛn) *n.* a small brown songbird with a stubby, erect tail.

Wren (rɛn) *n. Informal.* a member of the Women's Royal Naval Service.

wrench (rɛntʃ) *vb.* **1.** to give (something) a forceful twist or pull, esp. so as to remove it from that to which it is attached: *to wrench a door off its hinges.* **2.** to injure (a limb or joint) by a sudden twist. ~*n.* **3.** a forceful twist or pull. **4.** an injury to a limb or joint, caused by twisting. **5.** a parting that is difficult or painful to make. **6.** a spanner with adjustable jaws.

wrest (rɛst) *vb.* **1.** to take or force away by violent pulling or twisting. **2.** to seize forcibly by violent or unlawful means.

wrestle ('rɛs²l) *vb.* **1.** to fight (another person) by grappling and trying to throw or pin him to the ground. **2.** to participate in wrestling. **3.** (foll. by *with* or *against*) to struggle hard with (a person, problem, or thing): *wrestle with one's conscience.* ~*n.* **4.** the act of wrestling. **5.** a struggle or tussle. —'**wrestler** *n.*

wrestling ('rɛslɪŋ) *n.* a sport in which each contestant tries to overcome the other either by throwing or pinning him to the ground or by causing him to submit.

wretch (rɛtʃ) *n.* **1.** a despicable person. **2.** a person pitied for his misfortune.

wretched ('rɛtʃɪd) *adj.* **1.** in poor or pitiful circumstances. **2.** feeling misery; very unhappy. **3.** poor or inferior. **4.** undesirable or displeasing: *a wretched nuisance.* —'**wretchedly** *adv.*

wrick (rɪk) *n.* **1.** a sprain or strain. ~*vb.* **2.** to sprain or strain.

wriggle ('rɪg²l) *vb.* **1.** to make or cause to make twisting movements. **2.** to move along by twisting and turning. **3.** (foll. by *into* or *out of*) to manoeuvre oneself by clever or devious means: *wriggle out of an embarrassing situation.* ~*n.* **4.** a wriggling movement or action. —'**wriggly** *adj.*

wright (raɪt) *n.* (*now chiefly in combination*) a person who creates or builds something specified: *a playwright; a shipwright.*

wring (rɪŋ) *vb.* **wringing, wrung. 1.** (often foll. by *out*) to twist and compress to squeeze (a liquid) from (cloth). **2.** to twist forcibly: *wring its neck.* **3.** to clasp and twist (one's hands), esp. in anguish. **4.** to distress: *wring one's heart.* **5.** to grip

(someone's hand) vigorously in greeting. **6.** to obtain by forceful means: *wring information out of.* **7. wringing wet.** soaking; drenched. ~*n.* **8.** an act or the process of wringing.

wringer ('rɪŋə) *n.* same as **mangle**[2] (sense 1).

wrinkle[1] ('rɪŋk²l) *n.* **1.** a slight ridge in the smoothness of a surface, such as a crease in the skin as a result of age. ~*vb.* **2.** to make or become wrinkled. —'**wrinkly** *adj.*

wrinkle[2] ('rɪŋk²l) *n. Informal.* a useful hint or dodge.

wrist (rɪst) *n.* **1.** *Anat.* the joint between the forearm and the hand. **2.** the part of a sleeve that covers the wrist.

wristwatch ('rɪst,wɒtʃ) *n.* a watch worn strapped around the wrist.

writ (rɪt) *n.* a formal legal document ordering a person to do or refrain from doing some specified act.

write (raɪt) *vb.* **writing, wrote, written. 1.** to draw or mark (symbols, letters, or words) on a surface, usually paper, with a pen, pencil, or other instrument. **2.** to describe or record (something) in writing. **3.** to write (a letter) to or correspond regularly with (a person or organization). **4.** to say or communicate by letter: *he wrote that he was on his way.* **5.** *Informal, chiefly U.S. & Canad.* to send a letter to (a person or organization). **6.** to be the author or composer of (literature or music). **7.** to fill in the details for (a document, form, or cheque). **8.** to produce by writing: *he wrote ten pages.* **9.** to show clearly: *envy was written all over his face.* **10.** to produce writing of a specified kind: *write neatly.* **11.** *Computers.* to record (data) in a storage device.
Usage. *To* should not be omitted after the verb *write* in clauses without a direct object: *I'll write to you* (not *I'll write you*). This omission of *to* is very common in informal English in the U.S., but is nevertheless not accepted as good formal usage.

write down *vb.* **1.** to set down in writing. **2.** to disparage or belittle (a person) in writing. **3.** (foll. by *to* or *for*) to write in a simplified way (for a supposedly less cultured readership).

write off *vb.* **1.** *Accounting.* to cancel (a bad debt) from the accounts. **2.** to acknowledge as a complete loss. **3.** to dismiss from consideration: *he wrote her off as a hysterical woman.* **4.** to send a written order (for something): *she wrote off for a brochure.* **5.** *Informal.* to damage (something, esp. a car) beyond repair. ~*n.* **write-off. 6.** *Informal.* something damaged beyond repair, esp. a car.

write out *vb.* to put into writing or reproduce in full form in writing.

writer ('raɪtə) *n.* **1.** a person who writes as

an occupation; author. **2.** the person who has written something specified.

write up vb. **1.** to describe fully, complete, or bring up to date in writing: *write up a diary.* **2.** to praise or bring to public notice in writing. ~n. **write-up. 3.** a published account of something, such as a review in a newspaper or magazine.

writhe (raɪð) vb. **1.** to twist or squirm in or as if in pain. **2.** to suffer acute emotional discomfort: *writhe in embarrassment.*

writing ('raɪtɪŋ) n. **1.** anything which is written. **2.** short for **handwriting. 3.** literary composition. **4.** the work of a writer. **5.** literary style, art, or practice. **6.** written form: *give it to me in writing.* **7. writing on the wall.** a sign or signs of approaching disaster.

writing desk n. a piece of furniture with a writing surface and compartments for papers and writing materials.

writing paper n. paper for writing letters.

written ('rɪt²n) vb. **1.** the past participle of **write.** ~adj. **2.** taken down in writing: *written evidence; the written word.*

WRNS Women's Royal Naval Service.

wrong (rɒŋ) adj. **1.** not correct or truthful: *the wrong answer.* **2.** acting or judging in error: *you are wrong to think that.* **3.** immoral; bad: *it is wrong to cheat.* **4.** not in accordance with correct or conventional rules or standards. **5.** not intended or appropriate: *the wrong road.* **6.** not working properly; amiss: *something is wrong with the engine.* **7.** (of a side of a fabric or knitting) intended to face the inside so as not to be seen. **8. get on the wrong side of.** *Informal.* to come into disfavour with. ~adv. **9.** in the wrong direction or manner. **10. get (someone** or **something) wrong. a.** to fail to understand (someone or something) properly. **b.** to fail to provide the correct answer to. **11. go wrong. a.** to turn out other than intended: *my plans have gone wrong.* **b.** to make a mistake. **c.** (of a machine) to cease to function properly. **d.** to go astray morally. ~n. **12.** something

bad, immoral, or unjust. **13.** *Law.* an infringement of another person's rights or a violation of public rights and duties. **14. in the wrong.** mistaken or guilty. ~vb. **15.** to treat unjustly. **16.** to discredit, malign, or misrepresent. —'**wrongly** adv.

wrongdoer ('rɒŋ¡duːə) n. a person who acts immorally or illegally. —'**wrong-¡doing** n.

wrongful ('rɒŋful) adj. unjust or illegal. —'**wrongfully** adv.

wrong-headed adj. **1.** constantly wrong in judgment. **2.** foolishly stubborn; obstinate.

wrote (rəʊt) vb. the past tense of **write.**

wroth (rəʊθ, rɒθ) adj. *Archaic* or *literary.* angry; wrathful.

wrought (rɔːt) vb. **1.** *Archaic.* a past of **work.** ~adj. **2.** *Metallurgy.* shaped by hammering or beating.

wrought iron n. a pure form of iron with a low carbon content: often used for decorative work.

wrought-up adj. agitated or excited.

wrung (rʌŋ) vb. the past of **wring.**

WRVS Women's Royal Voluntary Service.

wry (raɪ) adj. **wrier, wriest** or **wryer, wryiest. 1.** dryly humorous; sardonic. **2.** (of a facial expression) produced by contorting the features. **3.** twisted, contorted, or askew. —'**wryly** adv.

wrybill ('raɪ¡bɪl) n. a New Zealand plover whose bill is bent to one side enabling it to search for food beneath stones.

wryneck ('raɪ¡nɛk) n. an Old World woodpecker which has a habit of twisting its neck round.

wt. weight.

wych-elm or **witch-elm** ('wɪtʃ¡ɛlm) n. a Eurasian elm tree with longish pointed leaves, clusters of small flowers, and winged fruits.

WYSIWYG ('wɪzɪ¡wɪg) n., adj. *Computers.* what you see is what you get: referring to what is displayed on the screen being the same as what will be printed out.

XYZ

x *or* **X** (ɛks) *n., pl.* **x's, X's,** *or* **Xs.** the 24th letter of the English alphabet.

x *Maths.* **1.** (along with *y* and *z*) an unknown quantity. **2.** the multiplication symbol.

X **1.** (formerly) indicating a film that may not be publicly shown to anyone under 18. Since 1982 replaced by symbol 18. **2.** denoting an unknown, unspecified, or variable factor, number, person, or thing. **3.** (on letters or greetings cards) denoting a kiss. **4.** (on ballot papers) indicating choice. **5.** (on examination papers) indicating error. **6.** the Roman numeral for ten.

Xanthippe (zæn'θɪpɪ) *or* **Xantippe** (zæn'tɪpɪ) *n.* a nagging, peevish, or irritable woman.

X-chromosome *n.* the sex chromosome that occurs in pairs in the females of many animals, including humans, and as one of a pair with the Y-chromosome in males.

Xe *Chem.* xenon.

xenon ('zɛnɒn) *n. Chem.* a colourless odourless gaseous element occurring in minute quantities in the air. Symbol: Xe

xenophobia (ˌzɛnə'fəʊbɪə) *n.* hatred or fear of foreigners or strangers. —ˌxeno'phobic *adj.*

xerography (zɪə'rɒɡrəfɪ) *n.* a photocopying process in which an image of the written or printed material is electrically charged on a surface and attracts oppositely charged dry ink particles which are then fixed by heating. —xerographic (ˌzɪərə'ɡræfɪk) *adj.*

Xerox ('zɪərɒks) *n.* **1.** *Trademark.* **a.** a machine for copying printed material. **b.** a copy made by such a machine. ~*vb.* **2.** to produce a copy of (a document) using such a machine.

Xhosa ('kɔːsə) *n.* **1.** (*pl.* **-sa** *or* **-sas**) a member of a Negroid people living chiefly in Cape Province in the Republic of South Africa. **2.** the language of this people, which has several clicks in its sound system. —'Xhosan *adj.*

Xmas ('ɛksməs, 'krɪsməs) *n. Informal.* short for **Christmas.**

x-ray *or* **X-ray** *n.* **1.** a stream of electromagnetic radiation of short wavelength that can pass through some solid materials. **2.** a picture produced by exposing photographic film to x-rays: used in medicine as a diagnostic aid, since parts of the body, such as bones, absorb x-rays and so appear as opaque areas on the picture. ~*vb.* **3.** to photograph, treat, or examine (a person or part of his body) using x-rays.

x-ray diffraction *n. Physics.* the scattering of x-rays on contact with matter, resulting in changes in radiation intensity, which is used for studying atomic structure.

xylem ('zaɪlɛm) *n. Bot.* a plant tissue that conducts water and mineral salts from the roots to all other parts.

xylene ('zaɪliːn) *n. Chem.* a hydrocarbon existing in three isomeric forms, all three being colourless flammable volatile liquids used as solvents and in the manufacture of synthetic resins, dyes, and insecticides.

xylophone ('zaɪlə,fəʊn) *n. Music.* a percussion instrument consisting of a set of wooden bars of graduated length. It is played with hard-headed hammers. —xylophonist (zaɪ'lɒfənɪst) *n.*

y *or* **Y** (waɪ) *n., pl.* **y's, Y's,** *or* **Ys.** the 25th letter of the English alphabet.

y *Maths.* (along with *x* and *z*) an unknown quantity.

Y **1.** an unknown , unspecified, or variable factor, number, person, or thing. **2.** *Chem.* yttrium.

yacht (jɒt) *n.* **1.** a large boat propelled by sail or power, used for pleasure cruising or racing. ~*vb.* **2.** to sail or cruise in a yacht. —'yachting *n., adj.*

yachtsman ('jɒtsmən) *or* (*fem.*) **yachtswoman** *n., pl.* **-men** *or* **-women.** a person who sails a yacht.

yack (jæk) *n., vb.* same as **yak²**.

yah (jɑː) *interj.* **1.** *Informal.* same as **yes.** **2.** an exclamation of derision or disgust.

yahoo (jə'huː) *n., pl.* **-hoos.** a crude, brutish, or obscenely coarse person.

Yahweh ('jɑːweɪ) *or* **Yahveh** ('jɑːveɪ) *n. Bible.* a personal name of God.

yak¹ (jæk) *n.* an ox of Tibet with long shaggy hair.

yak² (jæk) *Slang.* ~*n.* **1.** noisy, continuous, and trivial talk. ~*vb.* **yakking, yakked.** **2.** to chatter or talk in this way.

Yale lock (jeɪl) *n. Trademark.* a type of cylinder lock using a flat serrated key.

yam (jæm) *n.* **1.** any of various twining plants of tropical and subtropical regions, cultivated for their starchy roots which are eaten as a vegetable. **2.** *Southern U.S.* the sweet potato.

yammer ('jæmə) *Informal.* ~*vb.* **1.** to whine in a complaining manner. ~*n.* **2.** a yammering sound. **3.** nonsense; jabber.

Yang (jæŋ) *n.* See **Yin and Yang.**

yank (jæŋk) *vb.* **1.** to pull (someone or

something) with a sharp movement; tug. ~n. **2.** a jerk.

Yank (jæŋk) n. Slang. a person from the U.S.; American.

Yankee ('jæŋkɪ) n. **1.** Slang. same as **Yank. 2.** a person from New England or from a Northern state of the U.S. ~adj. **3.** of or characteristic of Yankees.

yap (jæp) vb. **yapping, yapped. 1.** (of a dog) to bark in quick sharp bursts; yelp. **2.** Informal. to talk at length in an annoying or stupid way; jabber. ~n. **3.** a high-pitched bark; yelp. **4.** Slang. annoying or stupid speech; jabber. —'**yappy** adj.

yarborough ('jɑːbərə) n. Bridge, whist. a hand in which no card is higher than nine.

yard¹ (jɑːd) n. **1.** a unit of length equal to 3 feet, or 0.9144 metre. **2.** Naut. a spar slung from a mast of a ship and used for suspending a sail.

yard² (jɑːd) n. **1.** a piece of enclosed ground, often adjoining or surrounded by a building or buildings. **2.** an enclosed or open area where a particular type of work is done: a builder's yard. **3.** U.S. & Canad. same as **garden** (sense 1). **4.** U.S. & Canad. the winter pasture of deer, moose, and similar animals.

Yard (jɑːd) n. **the.** Brit. informal. short for **Scotland Yard**.

yardarm ('jɑːd,ɑːm) n. Naut. the outer end of a yard.

Yardie ('jɑːdɪ) n. a member of a Black criminal syndicate originally based in Jamaica.

yardstick ('jɑːd,stɪk) n. **1.** a measure or standard used for comparison: she is my yardstick for success. **2.** a graduated measuring stick one yard long.

yarmulke ('jɑːməlkə) n. Judaism. a skullcap worn during prayer by Jewish men and at all times by Orthodox Jewish men.

yarn (jɑːn) n. **1.** a continuous twisted strand of natural or synthetic fibres, used in weaving or knitting. **2.** Informal. a long and often involved story, usually of incredible or fantastic events. **3. spin a yarn.** Informal. to tell such a story.

yarrow ('jærəʊ) n. a plant with finely divided leaves and flat clusters of white flower heads.

yashmak ('jæʃmæk) n. a veil worn by Muslim women in public, to cover their faces, apart from their eyes.

yaw (jɔː) vb. **1.** (of an aircraft) to turn about its vertical axis. **2.** (of a ship) to turn aside temporarily from a straight course. ~n. **3.** the movement of an aircraft about its vertical axis. **4.** (of a ship) the act of turning aside from a straight course.

yawl (jɔːl) n. **1.** a two-masted sailing boat. **2.** a ship's small boat.

yawn (jɔːn) vb. **1.** to open one's mouth wide and take in air deeply, often when sleepy or bored. **2.** to be open wide as if

threatening to engulf someone or something: the mine shaft yawned below. ~n. **3.** the act or an instance of yawning. —'**yawning** adj.

yaws (jɔːz) n. (usually functioning as sing.) an infectious disease of tropical climates characterized by red skin eruptions.

Yb Chem. ytterbium.

Y-chromosome n. the sex chromosome that occurs as one of a pair with the X-chromosome in the males of many animals, including humans.

yd or **yd.** yard (measure).

YDT (in Canada) Yukon Daylight Time.

ye¹ (jiː, unstressed jɪ) pron. Archaic or dialect. refers to more than one person including the person addressed.

ye² (ðiː, spelling pron. jiː) det. a form of **the**¹, used as a supposed archaism: ye olde oake.

yea (jeɪ) interj. **1.** same as **aye** (yes). ~adv. **2.** Archaic or literary. indeed; truly: yea, though they spurn me, I shall prevail.

yeah (jɛə) interj. Informal. same as **yes.**

year (jɪə) n. **1.** the period of time, the **calendar year,** containing 365 days or in a **leap year** 366 days. It is divided into 12 months, and reckoned from January 1 to December 31. **2.** a period of twelve months from any specified date. **3.** a specific period of time, usually occupying a definite part or parts of a twelve-month period, used for some particular activity: a school year. **4.** the period of time during which the earth makes one revolution around the sun, approximately 365 days. **5.** the period of time taken by a specified planet to complete one revolution around the sun. **6.** (pl.) a long time: it's years since I've been there. **7.** (pl.) age, usually old age: a man of his years should be more careful. **8.** (pl.) time: in years to come. **9.** a group of pupils or students who have started a course in the same academic year. **10. year in, year out.** regularly or monotonously, over a long period.

Usage. In writing spans of years, it is important to choose a style that avoids ambiguity. The general practice is, in four-figure dates, to specify the last two digits of the second date if it falls within the same century as the first: 1801-08; 1850-51; 1899-1901. In writing three-figure B.C. dates, it is advisable to give both dates in full: 159-156 B.C., not 159-56 B.C., unless of course the span referred to consists of 103 years rather than three years. It is also advisable to specify B.C. or A.D. in years under 1000 unless the context makes this self-evident.

yearbook ('jɪə,bʊk) n. a reference book published once a year that contains details of events of the previous year.

yearling ('jɪəlɪŋ) n. **1.** an animal that is between one and two years old. ~adj. **2.** being a year old.

yearly (ˈjɪəlɪ) *adj.* **1.** occurring, done, or appearing once a year or every year; annual. **2.** lasting or valid for a year; annual: *a yearly subscription.* ~*adv.* **3.** once a year; annually.

yearn (jɜːn) *vb.* **1.** to have an intense desire or longing: *we yearned for home.* **2.** to feel tenderness or affection: *her heart yearned for the starving child.* —ˈ**yearning** *n.*, *adj.*

yeast (jiːst) *n.* a yellowish fungus an extract of which is used in fermenting alcoholic drinks, such as beer or whisky, and in raising dough for bread.

yeasty (ˈjiːstɪ) *adj.* **yeastier, yeastiest. 1.** of, resembling, or containing yeast. **2.** fermenting or causing fermentation. **3.** (of talk) frivolous. **4.** covered with or containing froth or foam.

yell (jɛl) *vb.* **1.** to shout, scream, cheer, or utter in a loud or piercing way. ~*n.* **2.** a loud piercing inarticulate cry of pain, anger, or fear.

yellow (ˈjɛləʊ) *n.* **1.** any of a group of colours such as that of a lemon or an egg yolk, which vary in strength but have the same hue. **2.** a yellow pigment or dye. **3.** yellow cloth or clothing: *dressed in yellow.* ~*adj.* **4.** of the colour yellow. **5.** yellowish in colour or having parts or marks that are yellowish. **6.** having a yellowish skin; Mongoloid. **7.** *Informal.* cowardly or afraid. ~*vb.* **8.** to make or become yellow. —ˈ**yellowish** *adj.* —ˈ**yellowness** *n.*

yellow-belly *n., pl.* **-lies.** *Slang.* a coward. —ˈ**yellow-ˌbellied** *adj.*

yellow card *n. Soccer.* a card of a yellow colour raised by a referee to indicate that a player has been booked for a serious violation of the rules.

yellow fever *n.* an acute infectious tropical disease which causes fever, haemorrhages, vomiting, and jaundice: caused by a virus transmitted to man by the bite of a certain mosquito.

yellowhammer (ˈjɛləʊˌhæmə) *n.* a European songbird with a yellowish head and body and brown-streaked wings and tail.

Yellow Pages *pl. n. Trademark.* a telephone directory that lists people and companies under the headings of the type of business or service they provide.

yellow streak *n. Informal.* a cowardly or weak trait.

yelp (jɛlp) *vb.* **1.** (of an animal or a person) to utter a sharp or high-pitched cry, often indicating pain. ~*n.* **2.** a sharp or high-pitched cry.

yen[1] (jɛn) *n., pl.* **yen.** the standard monetary unit of Japan.

yen[2] (jɛn) *Informal.* ~*n.* **1.** a longing or desire. ~*vb.* **yenning, yenned. 2.** to have a longing.

yeoman (ˈjəʊmən) *n., pl.* **-men.** *History.* a member of a class of small freeholders who cultivated their own land.

yeoman of the guard *n.* a member of the ceremonial bodyguard (**Yeomen of the Guard**) of the British monarch.

yeomanry (ˈjəʊmənrɪ) *n.* **1.** yeomen collectively. **2.** (in Britain) a volunteer cavalry force, organized in 1761 for home defence: merged into the Territorial Army in 1907.

yep (jɛp) *interj. Informal.* same as **yes.**

yes (jɛs) *interj.* **1.** used to express affirmation, consent, agreement, or approval, or to answer when one is addressed. **2.** used to signal someone to speak or keep speaking, enter a room, or do something. ~*n.* **3.** an answer or vote of *yes.* **4.** a person who votes in the affirmative.

yes man *n.* a person who agrees with every suggestion or opinion offered by his employer in order to gain favour.

yesterday (ˈjɛstədɪ) *n.* **1.** the day before today. **2.** the recent past. ~*adv.* **3.** on or during the day before today. **4.** in the recent past.

yesteryear (ˈjɛstəˌjɪə) *Formal or literary.* ~*n.* **1.** last year or the past in general. ~*adv.* **2.** during last year or the past in general.

yet (jɛt) *conj.* **1.** nevertheless; still: *I want to, yet I haven't the courage.* ~*adv.* **2.** so far; up until then or now: *they're not home yet; is it teatime yet?* **3.** now (as contrasted with later): *we can't stop yet.* **4.** even; still: *yet more potatoes for sale.* **5.** eventually in spite of everything: *we'll convince him yet.* **6. as yet.** so far; up until then or now.

yeti (ˈjɛtɪ) *n.* same as **abominable snowman.**

yew (juː) *n.* an evergreen tree with flattened needle-like leaves, red berry-like fruits, and fine-grained elastic wood.

Y-fronts *pl. n. Trademark.* boys' or men's underpants having a front opening within an inverted Y shape.

YHA (in Britain) Youth Hostels Association.

yid (jɪd) *n. Slang, offensive.* a Jew.

Yiddish (ˈjɪdɪʃ) *n.* **1.** a language derived from High German, spoken by Jews in Europe and elsewhere by Jewish emigrants, and usually written in the Hebrew alphabet. ~*adj.* **2.** in or relating to this language.

yield (jiːld) *vb.* **1.** to give forth or supply (a product or result), for example by cultivation or labour; produce or bear. **2.** to furnish as a return: *the shares yielded three per cent.* **3.** (foll. by *up*) to give up; surrender. **4.** to give way, submit, or surrender, through force or persuasion: *she yielded to his superior knowledge.* **5.** (foll. by *to*) to agree to; comply with: *he eventually yielded to their request for money.* **6.** to grant or allow; concede: *to yield right of way.*

~n. **7.** the result, product, or amount yielded.

yielding ('jiːldɪŋ) adj. **1.** compliant, submissive, or flexible. **2.** pliable or soft: a yielding material.

Yin and Yang (jɪn) n. two complementary principles of Chinese philosophy: Yin is negative, dark, and feminine, Yang is positive, bright, and masculine.

yippee (jɪ'piː) interj. an exclamation of joy, pleasure, or anticipation.

YMCA Young Men's Christian Association.

yob (jɒb) or **yobbo** ('jɒbəʊ) n., pl. **yobs** or **yobbos**. Brit. slang. a bad-mannered aggressive youth. —'**yobbish** adj.

yodel ('jəʊdˀl) vb. **-delling, -delled** or U.S. **-deling, -deled. 1.** to sing (a song) with abrupt changes back and forth between the normal chest voice and falsetto, as in folk songs of the Swiss Alps. ~n. **2.** the act or sound of yodelling. —'**yodeller** or U.S. '**yodeler** n.

yoga ('jəʊgə) n. **1.** a Hindu system of philosophy aiming at spiritual, mental, and physical wellbeing by means of deep meditation, prescribed postures, and controlled breathing. **2.** a system of exercising involving such meditation, postures, and breathing.

yoghurt, yogurt, or **yoghourt** ('jəʊgət, 'jɒg-) n. a slightly sour, thick, custard-like food prepared from milk curdled by bacteria, often sweetened and flavoured with fruit.

yogi ('jəʊgɪ) n. a person who practises or is a master of yoga.

yo-heave-ho (ˌjəʊhiːv'həʊ) interj. a cry formerly used by sailors while pulling or lifting together in rhythm.

yoicks (haɪk, jɔɪks) interj. a cry used by fox-hunters to urge on the hounds.

yoke (jəʊk) n., pl. **yokes** or **yoke. 1.** a wooden frame with a bar for attaching to the necks of a pair of animals, such as oxen, so that they can be worked as a team. **2.** a pair of animals joined by a yoke. **3.** something resembling a yoke, such as a frame fitting over a person's shoulders for carrying buckets. **4.** an oppressive force or burden: the yoke of a tyrant. **5.** a fitted part of a garment, for example around the neck, shoulders, and chest or around the hips, to which a gathered, pleated, flared, or unfitted part is attached. ~vb. **6.** to harness (two animals) to a plough by means of a yoke. **7.** to join or be joined by means of a yoke; couple, unite, or link.

yokel ('jəʊkˀl) n. Disparaging. a person who lives in the country, usually one who is simple and old-fashioned.

yolk (jəʊk) n. the yellow part in the middle of an egg that nourishes the developing embryo.

Yom Kippur (jɒm 'kɪpə; kɪ'pʊə) n. an annual Jewish holiday celebrated as a day of fasting, with prayers of penitence.

yon (jɒn) det. **1.** Chiefly Scot. & N English. an archaic or dialect word for that: yon man. **2.** same as **yonder.** ~pron. **3.** yonder person or thing: yon's a fool.

yonder ('jɒndə) adv. **1.** at, in, or to that relatively distant place; over there. ~det. **2.** being at a distance, either within view or as if within view: yonder valleys.

yonks (jɒŋks) pl. n. Informal. a very long time; ages: I haven't seen him in yonks.

yoo-hoo ('juː,huː) interj. a call to attract a person's attention.

yore (jɔː) n. **of yore.** a long time ago: in days of yore.

yorker ('jɔːkə) n. Cricket. a ball bowled so as to pitch just under or just beyond the bat.

Yorkist ('jɔːkɪst) English history. ~n. **1.** a supporter of the royal House of York, esp. during the Wars of the Roses. ~adj. **2.** of or relating to the supporters or members of the House of York.

Yorks. (jɔːks) Yorkshire.

Yorkshire pudding ('jɔːkʃɪə) n. Chiefly Brit. a baked pudding made from a batter of flour, eggs, and milk, often served with roast beef.

Yorkshire terrier n. a very small terrier with a long straight steel-blue and tan coat.

you (juː; unstressed jʊ) pron. (sing. or pl., subjective or objective) refers to: **1.** the person or persons addressed: you know better; the culprit is among you. **2.** an unspecified person or people in general: you can't tell the boys from the girls. ~n. **3.** Informal. the personality of the person being addressed: that hat isn't really you.

you'd (juːd; unstressed jʊd) you had or you would.

you'll (juːl; unstressed jʊl) you will or you shall.

young (jʌŋ) adj. **younger** ('jʌŋgə), **youngest** ('jʌŋgɪst). **1.** having lived or existed for a relatively short time: a young man; a young movement. **2.** having qualities associated with youth; vigorous or lively: she has a very young outlook. **3.** of or relating to youth: in my young days. **4.** of or relating to a group representing the younger members of a larger organization: Young Socialists. ~n. **5.** (functioning as pl.) offspring, esp. young animals: a rabbit with her young. —**youngish** ('jʌŋgɪʃ) adj.

youngster ('jʌŋstə) n. a young person; child or youth.

your (jɔː, jʊə; unstressed jə) det. **1.** of, belonging to, or associated with you: your nose. **2.** of, belonging to, or associated with an unspecified person or people in general: the path is on your left heading north. **3.** Informal. used to indicate all things or people of a certain type: *your part-time worker is a problem.*

you're (jɔː; *unstressed* jə) *pron.* you are.

yours (jɔːz, jʊəz) *pron.* **1.** something belonging to you: *yours is the first name on the list; I prefer yours.* **2.** your family: *greetings to you and yours.* **3.** used in closing phrases at the end of a letter: *yours sincerely; yours faithfully.* **4. of yours.** belonging to you.

yourself (jɔːˈsɛlf, jʊə-) *pron., pl.* **-selves. 1. a.** the reflexive form of *you*. **b.** (used for emphasis): *you yourself control your destiny.* **2.** your normal self: *you're not yourself.*

yours truly *pron. Informal.* I *or* me.

youth (juːθ) *n.* **1.** the quality or condition of being young, immature, or inexperienced: *his youth told against him in the contest.* **2.** the period between childhood and maturity. **3.** the freshness, vigour, or vitality associated with being young. **4.** (*pl.* **youths** (juːðz)) a young man or boy. **5.** young people collectively: *the youth of today.*

youth club *n.* a club that provides leisure activities for young people.

youthful (ˈjuːθfʊl) *adj.* **1.** of, relating to, possessing, or associated with youth: *youthful enthusiasm.* **2.** vigorous or active: *he's surprisingly youthful for his age.* —**ˈyouthfully** *adv.* —**ˈyouthfulness** *n.*

youth hostel *n.* an inexpensive lodging place for young people travelling cheaply.

you've (juːv; *unstressed* jʊv) you have.

yowl (jaʊl) *vb.* **1.** to produce a loud mournful wail or cry; howl. *~n.* **2.** a wail or howl.

yo-yo (ˈjəʊjəʊ) *n., pl.* **-yos. 1.** a toy consisting of a spool attached to a string, the end of which is held while it is repeatedly spun out and reeled in. *~vb.* **yo-yoing, yo-yoed. 2.** to change repeatedly from one position to another.

yrs 1. years. **2.** yours.

YST (in Canada) Yukon Standard Time.

YT Yukon Territory.

YTS (in Britain) Youth Training Scheme.

ytterbium (ɪˈtɜːbɪəm) *n. Chem.* a soft silvery element that is used to improve the mechanical properties of steel. Symbol: Yb

yttrium (ˈɪtrɪəm) *n. Chem.* a silvery metallic element used in various alloys and in lasers. Symbol: Y

yuan (ˈjuːˈæn) *n., pl.* **-an.** the standard monetary unit of the People's Republic of China.

yucca (ˈjʌkə) *n.* a tropical plant with spikes of white flowers.

yucky *or* **yukky** (ˈjʌkɪ) *adj.* **yuckier, yuckiest** *or* **yukkier, yukkiest.** *Slang.* disgusting; nasty.

Yugoslav (ˈjuːɡəʊˌslɑːv) *n.* **1.** a person from Yugoslavia. *~adj.* **2.** of, relating to,

or characteristic of Yugoslavia or its people.

Yule (juːl) *n. Literary, archaic, or dialect.* Christmas or the Christmas season: *Yuletide.*

yummy (ˈjʌmɪ) *Slang. ~interj.* **1.** Also: **yum-yum.** an exclamation indicating pleasure or delight, as in anticipation of delicious food. *~adj.* **-mier, -miest. 2.** delicious, delightful, or attractive: *yummy ice cream.*

Yuppie (ˈjʌpɪ) *n.* **1.** a young urban (*or* upwardly mobile) professional. *~adj.* **2.** designed for or appealing to Yuppies.

YWCA Young Women's Christian Association.

z *or* **Z** (zɛd; *U.S.* ziː) *n., pl.* **z's, Z's,** *or* **Zs.** the 26th and last letter of the English alphabet.

z *Maths.* (along with *x* and *y*) an unknown quantity.

Z *Chem.* atomic number.

zabaglione (ˌzæbəˈljəʊnɪ) *n.* a dessert made of egg yolks, sugar, and wine, whipped together.

zambuck (ˈzæmbʌk) *n. Austral. & N.Z. informal.* a first-aid attendant at a sports event.

zany (ˈzeɪnɪ) *adj.* **zanier, zaniest.** comical in an endearing way.

zap (zæp) *Slang. ~vb.* **zapping, zapped. 1.** to kill (someone), esp. by shooting him. **2.** to move quickly. **3.** to change television channels rapidly by remote control. *~n.* **4.** energy or vigour.

zeal (ziːl) *n.* fervent or enthusiastic devotion, for example to a religious movement.

zealot (ˈzɛlət) *n.* an extremely zealous adherent to a cause; fanatic. —**ˈzealotry** *n.*

zealous (ˈzɛləs) *adj.* extremely eager or enthusiastic; fervent. —**ˈzealously** *adv.*

zebra (ˈziːbrə, ˈzɛbrə) *n., pl.* **-ras** *or* **-ra.** an African animal of the horse family, with a distinctive black-and-white striped hide.

zebra crossing *n. Brit.* a pedestrian crossing marked by broad alternate black-and-white stripes. Once on the crossing the pedestrian has right of way.

zebu (ˈziːbuː) *n.* a domesticated ox of Africa and Asia, with a humped back and long horns.

zed (zɛd) *n.* the British spoken form of the letter *z.*

zee (ziː) *n.* the U.S. spoken form of the letter *z.*

Zeitgeist (ˈtsaɪtˌɡaɪst) *n.* the spirit or general outlook of a specific time or period.

Zen (zɛn) *n.* a Japanese school of Buddhism teaching that contemplation of one's essential nature to the exclusion of all else is the only way of achieving pure enlightenment.

Zend-Avesta (ˌzɛndəˈvɛstə) *n.* the Zoroastrian scriptures (the **Avesta**), together with the traditional interpretive commentary known as the **Zend.**

zenith ('zεnιθ) n. 1. the point in the sky directly above an observer. 2. the highest point; peak: *the zenith of someone's achievements.* —'**zenithal** adj.

zephyr ('zεfə) n. a soft gentle breeze.

Zeppelin ('zεpəlιn) n. a large cylindrical rigid German airship of the early 20th century.

zero ('zιərəυ) n., pl. **-ros** or **-roes.** 1. the ordinal number between +1 and –1. 2. the symbol, 0, representing this number. 3. nothing; nil. 4. the lowest point or degree: *his prospects were put at zero.* 5. the line or point on a scale of measurement from which the graduations commence. 6. the temperature, pressure, etc., that registers a reading of zero on a scale. ~adj. 7. having no measurable quantity or magnitude. 8. *Meteorol.* (of visibility) limited to a very short distance. ~vb. **-roing, -roed.** 9. to adjust (an instrument or scale) so as to read zero.

zero gravity n. the state of weightlessness.

zero hour n. 1. *Mil.* the time set for the start of an operation. 2. *Informal.* a critical time, usually at the beginning of an action.

zero in on vb. 1. to aim a weapon at (a target). 2. to concentrate one's attention on (something). 3. *Informal.* to converge upon: *the police zeroed in on the criminals' hideout.*

zero-rated adj. denoting goods on which the buyer pays no value-added tax.

zest (zεst) n. 1. invigorating or keen excitement or enjoyment: *a zest for living.* 2. added interest, flavour, or charm: *her presence gave zest to the occasion.* 3. the peel of an orange or lemon, used as flavouring. —'**zestful** adj.

ziggurat ('zιgυˌræt) n. (in ancient Mesopotamia) a temple in the shape of a pyramidal tower.

zigzag ('zιgˌzæg) n. 1. a line or course having sharp turns in alternating directions. 2. one of a series of such turns. 3. something having the form of a zigzag. ~adj. 4. formed in or proceeding in a zigzag. ~adv. 5. in a zigzag manner. ~vb. **-zagging, -zagged.** 6. to move in a zigzag.

zilch (zιltʃ) n. *Slang, chiefly U.S. & Canad.* nothing.

zillion ('zιljən) n., pl. **-lions** or **-lion.** (*often pl.*) *Informal.* an extremely large but unspecified number: *zillions of flies in this camp.*

Zimmer ('zιmə) n. *Trademark.* a tubular frame with rubber feet, used as a support to help disabled or infirm people walk. Also: **Zimmer aid.**

zinc (zιŋk) n. *Chem.* a brittle bluish-white metallic element that is used in alloys such as brass, to form a protective coating on

metals, and in battery electrodes. Symbol: Zn

zinc ointment n. a medicinal ointment consisting of zinc oxide, petroleum jelly, and paraffin.

zinc oxide n. *Chem., pharmacol.* a white insoluble powder used as a pigment and in making zinc ointment.

zing (zιŋ) *Informal.* ~n. 1. a short high-pitched buzzing sound, like the sound of a bullet or vibrating string. 2. vitality; zest. ~vb. 3. to make or move with or as if with a high-pitched buzzing sound.

zinnia ('zιnιə) n. a plant of tropical and subtropical America, with solitary heads of brightly coloured flowers.

Zion ('zaιən) n. 1. the hill on which the city of Jerusalem stands. 2. **a.** the modern Jewish nation. **b.** Israel as the national home of the Jewish people. 3. *Christianity.* heaven.

Zionism ('zaιəˌnιzəm) n. a political movement for the establishment and support of a national homeland for Jews in what is now Israel. —'**Zionist** n., adj.

zip (zιp) n. 1. Also called: **zip fastener.** a fastener with two parallel rows of metal or plastic teeth on either side of a closure, which are interlocked by a sliding tab. 2. a short sharp whizzing sound, like the sound of a passing bullet. 3. *Informal.* energy; vigour; vitality. ~vb. **zipping, zipped.** 4. (often foll. by *up*) to fasten (clothing or a bag) with a zip. 5. to move with a zip: *the bullet zipped past.* 6. (often foll. by *along* or *through*) to hurry; rush.

zip code n. the U.S. equivalent of **postcode.**

zipper ('zιpə) n. *U.S. & Canad.* same as **zip** (sense 1).

zippy ('zιpι) adj. **-pier, -piest.** *Informal.* full of energy; lively.

zircon ('zɜːkən) n. *Mineral.* a reddish-brown, grey, green, blue, or colourless hard mineral consisting of zirconium silicate, which is used as a gemstone.

zirconium (zɜː'kəυnιəm) n. *Chem.* a greyish-white metallic element, occurring chiefly in zircon, that is exceptionally corrosion-resistant. Symbol: Zr

zither ('zιðə) n. a plucked musical instrument consisting of numerous strings stretched over a box, a few of which may be stopped on a fretted fingerboard. —'**zitherist** n.

zloty ('zlɒtι) n., pl. **-tys** or **-ty.** the standard monetary unit of Poland.

Zn *Chem.* zinc.

zodiac ('zəυdιˌæk) n. 1. an imaginary belt in the sky within which the sun, moon, and planets appear to move. It is divided into 12 equal areas called **signs of the zodiac,** each named after the constellation which once lay in it. 2. *Astrol.* a diagram, usually circular, representing this belt. —**zodiacal** (zəʊˈdaɪək³l) *adj.*

zombie *or* **zombi** (ˈzɒmbɪ) *n., pl.* **-bies** *or* **-bis.** **1.** a person who appears to be lifeless, apathetic, or totally lacking in independent judgment. **2.** a corpse brought to life supernaturally.

zone (zəʊn) *n.* **1.** a region, area, or section characterized by some distinctive feature or quality: *a demilitarized zone; the erogenous zones.* **2.** *Geog.* one of the latitudinal divisions of the earth's surface according to temperature. **3.** *Archaic or literary.* a girdle or belt. **4.** *N.Z.* a section on a transport route; fare stage. **5.** *N.Z.* a catchment area for a specific school. ~*vb.* **6.** to divide (a place) into zones for different uses or activities. **7.** to designate (a place) as a zone. —ˈ**zonal** *adj.* —ˈ**zoning** *n.*

zonked (zɒŋkt) *adj. Slang.* **1.** highly intoxicated with drugs or alcohol. **2.** exhausted.

zoo (zuː) *n., pl.* **zoos.** a place where live animals are kept, studied, bred, and exhibited to the public.

zooid (ˈzəʊɔɪd) *n.* **1.** any independent animal body, such as an individual of a coral colony. **2.** a cell or body, produced by an organism and capable of independent motion, such as a gamete.

zool. **1.** zoological. **2.** zoology.

zoological garden *n.* the formal term for **zoo.**

zoology (zəʊˈɒlədʒɪ, zuː-) *n.* the study of animals, including their classification, structure, physiology, and history. —**zoological** (ˌzəʊəˈlɒdʒɪk³l, ˌzuːə-) *adj.* —**zoˈologist** *n.*

zoom (zuːm) *vb.* **1.** to move very rapidly; rush: *we zoomed through town.* **2.** to make or move with a continuous buzzing or humming sound. **3.** (of prices) to rise rapidly. ~*n.* **4.** the sound or act of zooming. **5.** a zoom lens.

zoom in *or* **out** *vb. Photog., films, television.* to increase or decrease rapidly the magnification of the image of a distant object by means of a zoom lens.

zoom lens *n.* a lens system that allows the focal length of a camera lens to be varied continuously without altering the sharpness of the image.

zoophyte (ˈzəʊəˌfaɪt) *n.* any animal resembling a plant, such as a sea anemone.

Zoroastrianism (ˌzɒrəʊˈæstrɪənˌɪzəm) *or* **Zoroastrism** *n.* the dualistic religion founded by the ancient Persian prophet Zoroaster, based on the concept of a continuous struggle between the god of creation, light, and goodness, and the spirit of evil and darkness. —ˌ**Zoroˈastrian** *adj., n.*

Zouave (zuːˈɑːv, zwɑːv) *n.* (formerly) a member of a body of French infantry composed of Algerian recruits, noted for their dash, hardiness, and colourful uniforms.

zounds (zaʊndz) *interj. Archaic.* a mild oath indicating surprise or indignation.

Zr *Chem.* zirconium.

zucchetto (tsuːˈkɛtəʊ, suː-, zuː-) *n., pl.* **-tos.** *R.C. Church.* a small round skullcap worn by clergymen and varying in colour according to the rank of the wearer.

zucchini (zuːˈkiːnɪ) *n., pl.* **-ni** *or* **-nis.** *Chiefly U.S., Canad., & Austral.* a courgette.

Zulu (ˈzuːluː, -luː) *n.* **1.** (*pl.* **-lus** *or* **-lu**) a member of a tall Negroid people of SE Africa. **2.** the language of this people.

zygote (ˈzaɪgəʊt, ˈzɪg-) *n.* the cell resulting from the union of an ovum and a spermatozoon; fertilized egg cell.

zymotic (zaɪˈmɒtɪk) *adj.* **1.** of or causing fermentation. **2.** of or caused by infection or infectious disease. —**zyˈmotically** *adv.*

zymurgy (ˈzaɪmɜːdʒɪ) *n.* the branch of chemistry concerned with fermentation processes in brewing.